COMICS VALUES ANNUAL

2007 EDITION
THE COMIC BOOK PRICE GUIDE

by Alex G. Malloy

edited by Stuart W. Wells III

Preface: Robert J. Sodaro

©2007 by Alex G. Malloy & Stuart W. Wells III

Published by

krause publications
An Imprint of F+W Publications

700 East State Street • Iola, WI 54990-0001
715-445-2214 • 888-457-2873
www.krausebooks.com

Library of Congress Catalog Number: 1062-4503

ISBN: 978-0-89689-463-1

Designed by Stuart W. Wells III
Edited by Karen O'Brien

Printed in the United States of America

CONTENTS

Editorial

By Alex G. Malloy with Robert J. Sodaro

As in recent years, the back issue market remains a very active and profitable field for savvy investors. Still very hot are many of the Golden Age titles; especially Wow Comics, Wonder Woman, Planet, and EC, among others.

These Golden Age books, along with the usual standbys Superman and Batman, are constantly in demand. In fact, even these comics' reprints are solid sellers. Of course the front-runners in the back issue markets are Golden Age titles and characters. This year moving back into the hot category are historical World War II comics as well as any comic with references to Nazis, Hitler, Mussolini, and Hirohito.

Perhaps this has to do with an ever-growing sense of national pride in the Greatest Generation, especially given films like the Iwo Jima memorial film, Flags of our Fathers, or even the high-adventure WWI aerial action flick, Flyboys. Perhaps it was the constant insider talk of a Sgt. Rock flick that convinced DC to publish a six-issue Sgt. Rock limited series in the early part of 2006; or perhaps it was the promise of Joe Kubert and his boys teaming up that kick-started the project. Who cares? Fans were treated to a rousing WWII epic—Easy Company style.

On the whole, the vast sea of Four Color series continue to soar in value. Cowboy—or as some say Western comics—are moving up. Books like Roy Rogers, Red Rider, Gene Autry, and Hopalong Cassidy are all showing strong sales and popularity. Interestingly enough, even as some fans are looking backwards to the Old West or to the two Great Wars, others are looking forward to classic Sci-Fi, which always holds its value—as does the Horror genre, which still titillates the collectors. Never long out of vogue, Horror seems to run in cycles as several recent films and comic book anthologies seem to prove (more on this later).

As to be expected, the Silver Age titles of both DC and Marvel are the solid sellers for the year. It seems that fans both new and old are always on the look out for top quality Marvel and DC Silvers. These include the big title DC

Gene Autry Comics #1
© Fawcett Publications, 1941

and Marvel titles of the 1970s, especially the period from 1970-1975. This time period has long been thought of as not collectible or as dealers would say blowouts, however, books from this time period in top condition grades are starting to see their prices climb.

Lets face it, these comics are now 30 years old, and the kids that grew up on them are just as nostalgic for their lost youth as we "older folks" are for ours, so it is only to be expected that they would seek out and purchase comics from that halcyon era. (And—for that matter—who are we to blame them?) Ultimately, to sell top comics in high grade the comics must be evaluated and encapsulated by CGC. This grading service has proven to be the grading service of choice for the industry at large.

Finally, as we wind down the opening comments for 2007, we here at CVA would like to offer up a special con-gratulations to our very own Features

Astonishing Tales #1
© *Marvel Comics, 1970*

Editor, Robert J. Sodaro who returned to his own comic book roots and had a short story of his published in a new horror anthology. Entitled Psychosis!, the anthology was published in October of 2006.

Bob, in case you didn't know, began his professional career writing about comics for Amazing Heroes, and other comic magazines, (including our own Comic Values Monthly, Triton, and Toy Values Monthly). If, however, you were ever to ask him, he would tell you that he was only working as a journalist in the field biding his time until he could leverage his position in the comics community into a chance to get into the show itself. To Bob, to actually get to write comics rather than write about them, was the Holy Grail.

Well, he got his first chance back in 1977 with the publication of Renegade Press' Agent Unknown. With the publication of his short story "Never Judge a Book..." in Psychosis! #1 he is beginning what one comic book insider described as his "...second life in comics." It is with this thought we wish Bob all the best on his new (old) path.

Marvel Masterpiece I: Wolverine
© Marvel Ent. Group

Marvel Masterpiece I: Rogue
© Marvel Ent. Group

Edgar Rice Burroughs I: Lord of the Jungle
© Edgar Rice Burroughs, Inc.

Edgar Rice Burroughs II: Captive Princess
© Edgar Rice Burroughs, Inc.

Interview with Joe Jusko
By Bob Sodaro for CVA

As a comic book and fantasy artist and painter, Joe Jusko is exceptionally well known, especially for his covers and trading card sets. Among the numerous sets of cards that he has lovingly rendered include the first series of Marvel Masterpiece (1992) cards and the immensely detailed Edgar Rice Burroughs Collection card sets (1994 & 1995), plus his work is featured in both Conan and Vampirella card sets.

Joe's work has also appeared on the covers of Wizard magazine, Vampirella, The Punisher, Conan, Shi, Nick Fury, Black Panther, Heavy Metal Magazine, Marvel Double Shot, Crimson, 21 Down, and various other publications. His work has also been featured in books including The Art of Marvel and Joe Jusko's Art of Edgar Rice Burroughs.

We were able to catch up with Joe (via e-mail) and secure the following interview. To learn more about what Joe is up to, to see some of his work, or to purchase artwork from him, check out his Web site, www.joejusko.com.

******

Bob Sodaro: Tell us a little bit about your background, Joe. Do you have any formal training? If so where did you go to school?

Joe Jusko: I attended the High School of Art & Design in NYC from 1973-77. I had a choice to continue my education at one of the many Art Colleges I had qualified for or test the waters out in the real world. I chose the latter, though in hindsight I think continuing my studies would have saved me a lot of subsequent trial and error in my work.

Bob: Did you apprentice under any artist? If so who?

Joe: I was lucky enough to meet Howard Chaykin in a Greenwich Village comic shop soon after graduation, and he took me on as his assistant after seeing some samples of my work. It would seem an odd choice of apprenticeship considering the differences in our styles, but I learned more about illustration in the five or six months I assisted Howard than I

Wonder Woman art by Joe Jusko

did in all four years of high school! He really opened my eyes to a world much grander than just comic art.

Bob: Do you think school and/or apprenticing are good ideas for up-and-coming artists

Joe: Instruction is something I wholeheartedly endorse, as it would have definitely made my life so much simpler. I'm totally self-taught as a painter, and having even basic instruction at the beginning would have saved me so much time in learning my craft. Many artists have gotten careers off the ground without having apprenticed for anyone, but getting some inroads to how the field works from someone who knows could only be of help. Then, of course, there's the professional assessment and refinement of your own work that will help speed you on your way.

Bob: Who are your major art influences?

Joe: John Buscema was the first major influence I can remember. He was a genius at figure drawing and formed the basis of the style I developed even to this day. It saddens me to know that I will never see a new John Buscema story or illustration. He was and always will be the one artist I would call an idol. When I began to paint, my influences were the same as anyone who joined the field at the same time I did would site Frazetta, Boris, Bob Larkin, and James Bama. Since then, I've been alternately influenced by paperback artists (Bob McGinnis, Robert Maquire, Ron Lesser, etc.), wildlife artists (John Seerey Lester, Guy Coheleach, Simon Combes), and way too many other Fine and Commercial artists to name.

Bob: You've been around for a while now; have you ever had an artist come up in the industry and cite you as one of their influences? What's that like?

Joe: I've had several mention that and have read that several more times from others. It always brings a smile to my face, as I know that every time I start a job, I feel like I have no idea what I'm doing! LOL It's flattering to know that I've affected someone else in the same way that so many artists have affected me.

"Kolchak," © *by Joe Jusko*

Bob: What project(s) are you working on these days?

Joe: Mostly cover jobs at the moment; The Oz/Wonderland Chronicles, Vampirella, Marvel paperbacks for Pocket Books, and a lot of private commissions. I'm also painting a bunch of Warcraft gaming cards.

Bob: You are perhaps best known for your amazing covers. Have you ever done any interior work? Would you like to do any (more)?

Joe: I pride myself on being a pretty good storyteller, and occasionally have delved in that arena (Vampirella/Bloodlust, several issues of Black Panther for Marvel, and most recently Top Cow's Tomb Raider; The Greatest Treasure of All, which is probably the best work I've ever produced). My style, however, is not really tailored for sequential work, which needs to be done in a timely fashion, so I think I'll be foregoing it in the foreseeable future.

Bob: You've done some trading cards, is this easier or tougher than painted covers?

Joe: Some? More like 500 or so! LOL. They were easier 10 years ago when my eyes were better, but they were a joy to do while they lasted. Most were only pinup shots, which got monotonous after a while, which is why I chose to paint the

Edgar Rice Burroughs set as narrative cards. Covers give you a lot more room for actual painting, since most card art is painted no larger than 8"x10". I prefer covers for that reason.

Bob: What is your preferred medium?

Joe: I work in acrylics because of their versatility and speed, but plan on going back to oils for some personal pieces I have in mind.

Bob: Do you find that you have to go looking for work or do people just line up outside your door like customers at a deli waiting for you to say, "Next!"?

Joe: Ha! One of the joys (and surprises) of my job is opening up my e-mail in the morning and finding new inquires as to my availability for work. I guess I've been around long enough and have a large enough body of work to warrant me getting more every now and then! Oddly enough, I don't get work

"Back Off," © *by Joe Jusko*

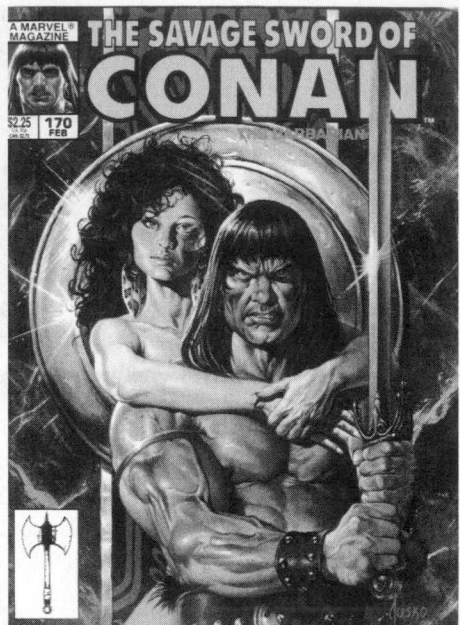

Bizarre Adventures # and The Savage Sword of Conan #170
Covers by Joe Jusko © Marvel Entertainment Group

from Marvel anymore, as I seem to have become one of the "Old Guys" in their eyes. I still don't get it, especially after all the years I put in up there. I've never had much success up at DC, either, maybe because I was perceived as a "Marvel Guy". How ironic, now that Marvel has no idea who I am.

Bob: Of all the characters you've rendered, which have you most enjoyed that you would like to draw/paint again? Who among the characters that you haven't yet done would you like to do?

Joe: That's easy! Vampirella and Lara Croft are by far my favorite female characters to paint and the Silver Surfer, Conan, and Tarzan are my favorite male characters. I'd love a crack at DC's stable as I've only had a couple of opportunities to play with them.

Bob: Is there one pantheon of heroes (or character(s)) that you prefer working on more than another (Marvel, DC, Image, etc.)

Joe: I grew up a Marvel kid, so I've always had an affinity for their characters. When you build that kind of attachment at an early age it's a hard thing to shake.

Bob: What is your favorite type of project to work on, superheroes, S&S, or does that matter?

Joe: Overall, I prefer the more reality-based characters to the cosmic or super heroic ones. I can do both, obviously, but over the years your tastes change, and I find myself more comfortable with the more "human" characters at this time.

Bob: What do you do to relax, and why?

Joe: I find lifting weights to be a great stress reliever, and I'm a BIG movie fan, as most people in our industry are. I love watching old 1940s "Film Noir."

Bob: Talk for a minute about your dream project.

Joe: Back at the time I did the Burroughs cards for FPG, we were planning to do all the Tarzan books in the same style as the Hildebrandt Fairy Tale books, but Disney bought the Tarzan rights and that project went "BOOM"! I'd love to get that back on track again.

Bob: Do you do the convention circuit, and if so, tell us where you are going to be in 2007.

Hulk #20 and Silver Surfer Vol. 4 #1, covers by Joe Jusko
© *Marvel Entertainment Group*

Joe: I've cut down my touring since getting married last year, but I will be in San Diego, as well as Vera Cruz, Mexico on May 19-20. I may be at the Belgium "Facts" Convention in October. I'm sure other dates will pop up.

The fearless creators of this book have also written others. Among them are:
Standard Guide to Golden Age Comics by Alex G. Malloy and Stuart W. Wells III
(KP Books, January 2006, ISBN 0-89689-181-X);
American Games by Alex G. Malloy (Krause, May 2000, ISBN 0-930615-60-9);
Kiddy Meal Collectibles by Robert J. Sodaro (Krause, ISBN 0-930625-16-1);
A Universe of Star Wars Collectibles, Identification and Price Guide, 2nd Edition,
by Stuart W. Wells III (Krause, July 2002, ISBN 0-87349-415-6);
See the copyright page for website and catalog information.

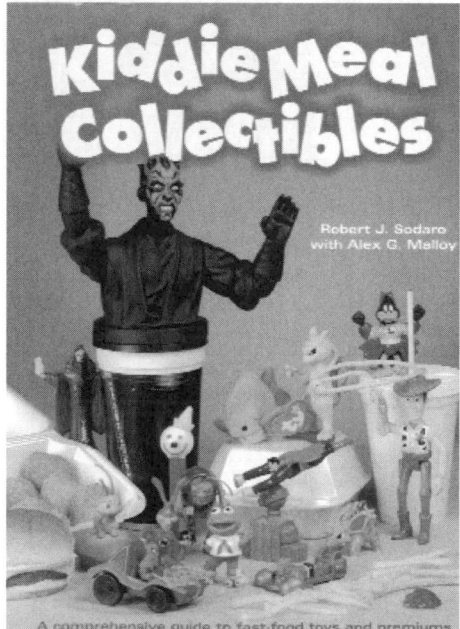

GRADING GUIDE

In David Brin's science fiction–fantasy novel, *The Practice Effect*, things improve with use. You start with a crudely made tool and keep using it until it becomes a fine instrument. If our world worked that way, you could read your Golden Age comics as often as you liked and they would just get better looking each time. Unfortunately, our world does not work that way, and reading your comics (along with just about everything else) causes comics to deteriorate.

Even if you could protect your comics from external light, heat, cold, moisture, pressure and everything else, you couldn't protect them from their own paper. Most comic books were printed on pulp paper, which has a high acid content. This means that the paper slowly turns brittle with age, no matter what you do to it, short of special museum-style preservation.

Very old, well-preserved comics are coveted collector's items. In most cases, people did not save their comic books for future generations. They read them and discarded them. Comic books were considered harmless ephemera for children. When these children outgrew their comics, their parents often threw them away. If everybody kept all of their comics, comics would not be valuable because everybody would have them scattered about the house!

The value of any comic depends on scarcity, popularity and condition. Scarcity increases with age and popularity depends on the whim of the public — only condition automatically decreases with age. Newer comics are generally available in near-mint condition, so newer comics in lesser condition have little collector potential. However, older comics are scarce, so they are still collectible in less than near-mint condition, but the value is obviously less. This is a basic tenet of all collectibles. A car is more valuable with its original paint. A baseball card is more valuable if it has not been marred by bicycle spokes. Coke bottles, stamps, coins, and toys in good condition are all more valuable than their abused counterparts. Comic books are no exception.

New comic book collectors should learn how to assess the prospective value of a comic in order to protect themselves from being fleeced by unscrupulous dealers or hucksters. Yet, a majority of dealers, especially store owners, can be considered reliable judges of comic grade. Because comic retail may be their primary source of income, certain dealers are particularly adept at noticing comic book imperfections, especially in issues they intend to purchase. As such, hobbyists and collectors must understand that dealers need to make a minimum profit on their investments. Buying collectible comics entails certain risks. Therefore, dealers must scrutinize a comic to determine if the particular book will stand a chance of resale. Well-preserved comics are invariably more desirable to dealers because they are more desirable to collectors.

There are eight standard comic grades: mint, near mint, very fine, fine, very good, good, fair, and poor. Clearly, these eight grades could be split into even finer categories when haggling over an exceptionally rare or coveted Golden Age comic. In most cases, however, comic books can be evaluated using these eight standard grades. The values listed in this book are all for comics in "Near Mint" condition. The grading/price chart given at the back of this book should be used to adjust this price for comics in different grades.

For many Golden Age comic issues, there are no known mint condition examples, but most issues have a few near mint copies in the hands of collectors. Many of these come from a few "pedigree" sources like the famous mile-high collection. There are, however, some

issues where no known example is in near mint condition. To be consistent, the value listed in this price guide is still for a "near mint" copy, even if no such copy exists. The grading/price chart in the back will still yield a price for the lesser grades that actually exist. And, who knows, maybe there is another treasure trove of old comics somewhere — maybe you'll even be the one who finds it!

Mint (CGC 9.5 or above)

Finding old comics in mint condition is almost impossible because of inferior storage techniques and materials. In the early days of collecting, few people anticipated that the very boxes and bags in which they stored their comics were contributing to decay. Acid from bags, backing boards, and boxes eat away at many comics.. Mint condition comics usually fetch prices higher than price guide listings. Mint comics can sell for 120% or more of the listed price.

Mint comics are perfect comics and allow no room for imperfections. Pages and covers must be free of discoloration, wear, and wrinkles. A mint comic is one that looks like it just rolled off the press. Staples and spine must meet perfectly without cover "rollover." The cover must be crisp, bright, and trimmed perfectly. The staples must not be rusted and the cover should not have any visible creases. The interior pages of a mint comic are equally crisp and new. A mint comic must not show any signs of age or decay. Because of the paper stock used on many older comics, acid and oxygen cause interior pages to yellow and flake.

Near Mint (CGC 9.4)

A near mint comic and a mint comic are close siblings, with their differences slight, even to an experienced eye. Most of the new comics on the shelf of the local comic shop are in near mint condition. These are comics that have been handled gingerly to preserve the original luster of the book. Near mint comics are bright, clean copies with no major or minor defects. Slight stress lines near the staples and perhaps a very minor printing defect are permissible. Corners must still be sharp and devoid of creases. Interior pages of newsprint stock should show almost no discernible yellowing. Near mint comics usually trade for 100% of the listed price, with just a small discount for slightly lower grades.

Very Fine (CGC 8.0)

A very fine comic is one that is routinely found on the shelves and back issue bins of most good direct market comic shops. This grade comic has few defects, none of them major. Stress around the staples of a very fine comic are visible but not yet radical enough to create wrinkles. Both the cover and interior pages should still be crisp and sharp, devoid of flaking and creases. Interior pages may be slightly yellowed from age.

Most high-quality older comics graded as very fine can obtain 80-90% of listed prices. More, if the comic is the highest-graded comic known to exist.

Fine (CGC 6.0)

Fine comics are often issues that may have been stored carefully under a bed or on a shelf by a meticulous collector. This grade of comic is also very desirable because it shows little wear and retains much of its original sharpness. The cover may be slightly off center from rollover. The cover retains less of its original gloss and may even possess a chip or wrinkle. The comers should be sharp but may also have a slight crease. Yellowing begins to creep into the interior pages of a comic graded as fine.

Fine comics are respectable additions to collections and sell for about 40-60% of the listed price.

Very Good (CGC 4.0)

A very good comic may have been an issue passed around or read frequently. This grade is the common condition of older books. Its cover will probably have lost some luster and may have two or three creases around the staples or edges. The corners of the book may begin to show the beginnings of minor rounding and chipping, but it is by no means a damaged or defaced comic. Comics in very good condition sell for about 30-40% of listed price.

Good (CGC 2.0)

A good comic is one that has been well read and is beginning to show its age. Although both front and back covers are still attached, a good grade comic may have a number of serious wrinkles and chips. The corners and edges of this grade comic may show clear signs of rounding and flaking. There should be no major tears in a good comic nor should any pages be clipped out or missing. Interior pages may be fairly yellowed and brittle. Good comics sell for about 15-25% of the listed price.

Fair (CGC 1.0)

A fair comic is one that has definitely seen better days and has considerably limited resale value for most collectors. This comic may be soiled and damaged on the cover and interior. Fair comics should be completely intact and may only be useful as a reading copy, or a comic to lend to friends. Fair comics sell for about 10-20% of the listed price.

Poor

Comics in poor condition are generally unsuitable for collecting or reading because they range from damaged to unrecognizable. Poor comics may have been water damaged, attacked by a small child, or worse, perhaps, gnawed on by the family pet! Interior and exterior pages may be cut apart or missing entirely. A poor comic sells for about 5-15% of the listed price.

Sniffing Out Grades

Despite everything that is mentioned about comic grading, the process remains relative to the situation. A comic that seems to be in very good condition may actually be a restored copy. A restored copy is generally considered to be in between the grade it was previous to restoration and the grade it has become. Many collectors avoid restored comics entirely.

Each collector builds his collection around what he believes is important. Some want every issue of a particular series or company. Others want every issue of a favorite artist or writer. Because of this, many collectors will purchase lower-grade comics to fill out a series or to try out a new series. Mint and near mint comics are usually much more desirable to hardcore collectors. Hobbyists and readers may find the effort and cost of collecting only high-grade comics financially prohibitive.

Getting artists or writers to autograph comics has also become a source of major dispute. Some collectors enjoy signed comics and others consider those very comics defaced! The current trends indicate that most collectors do enjoy signed comics. A signature does not usually change the grade of the comic.

As mentioned, comic grading is a subjective process that must be agreed upon by the buyer and seller. Buyers will often be quick to note minor defects in order to negotiate a better price. Sellers are sometimes selectively blind to their comic's defects.

Name	Abbr.	Name	Abbr.	Name	Abbr.	Name	Abbr.
Abel, Jack	JA	Bernstein, Robert	RbB	Capullo, Greg	GCa	Davis, Guy	GyD
Abell, Dusty	DAb	Bierbaum, Mary	MBm	Cardy, Nick	NC	Davis, Jack	JDa
Abnett, Dan	DAn	Bierbaum, Tom	TBm	Carey, Mike	MCy	Davis, Malcolm	MDa
Abrams, Paul	PIA	Biggs, Geoffrey	GB	Cariello, Sergio	SCi	Davison, Al	ADv
Adams, Art	AAd	Binder, Jack	JaB	Carlin, Mike	MCr	Day, Dan	Day
Adams, Neal	NA	Bingham, Jerry	JBi	Carpenter, Brent D.	BDC	Day, Gene	GD
Addeo, Stephen	StA	Birch, JJ	JJB	Carralero, Ricky	RCl	DeFalco, Tom	TDF
Adkins, Dan	DA	Biro, Charles	CBi	Carrasco, Dario	DoC	Deitch, Kim	KDe
Adlard, Charlie	CAd	Bisley, Simon	SBs	Carter, Joe	JCt	Delano, Jamie	JaD
Albano, John	JAo	Bissette, Stephen	SBi	Case, Richard	RCa	DeLaRosa, Sam	SDR
Albrecht, Jeff	JAl	Blair, Barry	BaB	Casey, Joe	JoC	Del Bourgo, Maurice	MDb
Alcala, Alfredo	AA	Blaisdell, Tex	TeB	Castellaneta, Dan	DaC	Delgado, Richard	RdD
Alcazar, Vincent	VAz	Blasco, Jesus	JBl	Castellini, Claudio	CCt	Dell, John	JhD
Alexander, Chris	CAx	Blevins, Bret	BBl	Castrillo, Anthony	ACa	DeMatteis, J. M.	JMD
Alibaster, Jo	JoA	Blum, Alex	AB	Chadwick, Paul	PC	DeMulder, Kim	KDM
Allred, Michael	MiA	Bode, Vaughn	VB	Chan, Ernie	ECh	Deodato, Jr., Mike	MD2
Alstaetter, Karl	KIA	Bogdanove, Jon	JBg	Chang, Bernard	BCh	Derenick, Tom	TDr
Althorp, Brian	BAp	Bolland, Brian	BB	Charest, Travis	TC	DeZago, Todd	TDz
Amaro, Gary	GyA	Bolle, Frank	FBe	Chase, Bobbie	BCe	DeZuniga, M.	MDb
Amendola, Sal	Sal	Boller, David	DdB	Chaykin, Howard	HC	DeZuniga, Tony	TD
Ammerman, David	DvA	Bolton, John	JBo	Check, Sid	SC	Diaz, Paco	PaD
Anderson, Bill	BAn	Bond, Philip	PBd	Chen, Mike	MCh	Dillin, Dick	DD
Anderson, Brent	BA	Booth, Brett	BBh	Chen, Sean	SCh	Dillon, Glyn	GlD
Anderson, Jeff	JAn	Boring, Wayne	WB	Chestney, Lillian	LCh	Dillon, Steve	SDi
Anderson, Murphy	MA	Bossart, William	WmB	Chiarello, Mark	MCo	Dini, Paul	PDi
Andriola, Alfred	AIA	Boxell, Tim	TB	Chichester, D.G.	DGC	Disbrow, Jay	JyD
Andru, Ross	RA	Bradstreet, Tim	TBd	Chiodo, Joe	JCh	Ditko, Steve	SD
Aparo, Jim	JAp	Braithwaite, Doug	DBw	Choi, Brandon	BCi	Dixon, Chuck	CDi
Aragones, Sergio	SA	Brasfield, Craig	CrB	Chriscross	Ccs	Dixon, John	JDx
Arcudi, John	JAr	Braun, Russell	RsB	Christopher, Tom	TmC	Dobbyn, Nigel	ND
Artis, Tom	TAr	Breeding, Brett	BBr	Chua, Ernie	Chu	Dodson, Terry	TyD
Ashe, Edd	EA	Brereton, Daniel	DlB	Chun, Anthony	ACh	Doherty, Peter	PD
Asamiya	KiA	Brewster, Ann	ABr	Churchhill, Ian	IaC	Dominguez, Luis	LDz
Augustyn, Brian	BAu	Breyfogle, Norm	NBy	Cirocco, Frank	FC	Doran, Colleen	CDo
Austin, Terry	TA	Bridwell, E. Nelson	ENB	Citron, Sam	SmC	Dorey, Mike	MDo
Avison, Al	AAv	Briefer, Dick	DBr	Claremont, Chris	CCl	Dorkin, Evan	EDo
Ayers, Dick	DAy	Bright, Mark	MBr	Clark, Mike	MCl	Dorman, Dave	DvD
Bachalo, Chris	CBa	Brigman, June	JBr	Clark, Scott	ScC	Doucet, Julie	JDo
Badger, Mark	MBg	Broderick, Pat	PB	Cockrum, Dave	DC	Dougherty, H.	HD
Bagley, Mark	MBa	Brodsky, Allyn	AyB	Cohn, Gary	GCh	Drake, Stan	SDr
Baikie, Jim	JBa	Broom, John	JBm	Coker, Tomm	TCk	Dresser, Larry	LDr
Bailey, Bernard	BBa	Broome, Matt	MtB	Colan, Gene	GC	Dringenberg, Mike	MDr
Bailey, M	MBi	Brothers, Hernandez	HB	Colby, Simon	SCy	Drucker, Mort	MD
Bair, Michael	MIB	Brown, Bob	BbB	Cole, Jack	JCo	DuBerkr, Randy	RDB
Baker, Kyle	KB	Browne, Dick	DkB	Cole, Leonard B.	LbC	Duffy, Jo.	JDy
Baker, Matt	MB	Brunner, Frank	FB	Colletta, Vince	ViC	Dumm, Gary	GDu
Balent, Jim	JBa	Bryant, Rick	RkB	Collins, Max Allan	MCn	Dunn, Ben	BDn
Banks, Darryl	DBk	Buckingham, Mark	MBu	Collins, Mike	MC	Duranona, Leo	LDu
Baron, Mike	MBn	Buckler, Rich	RB	Collins, Nancy	NyC	Duursema, Jan	JD
Barr, Mike	MiB	Budget, Greg	GBu	Colon, Ernie	EC	Dwyer, Kieron	KD
Barras, John	DBs	Bulanadi, Danny	DBl	Conner, Amanda	ACo	Eastman, Kevin	KEa
Barreiro, Mike	MkB	Burchett, Rick	RBr	Conway, Gerry	GyC	Eaton, Scott	SEa
Barreto, Ed	EB	Burgard, Tim	TmB	Cooper, Dave	DvC	Edginton, Ian	IEd
Barry, Dan	DBa	Burgos, Carl	CBu	Cooper, John	JCp	Edlund, Ben	BEd
Batista, Chris	CsB	Burke, Fred	FBk	Cooper, Sam.	SCp	Egeland, Marty	MEg
Battlefield, D.	DB	Burnley, Jack	JBu	Corben, Richard	RCo	Eisner, Will	WE
Battlefield, Ken	KBa	Burns, John	JBn	Costanza, Peter.	PrC	Elder, Bill	BE
Beatty, John	JhB	Burns, Robert	RBu	Cowan, Denys	DCw	Eldred, Tim	TEl
Beatty, Terry	TBe	Burroughs, W.	WBu	Cox, Jeromy	JCx	Elias, Lee	LEl
Beauvais, Denis	DB	Buscema, John	JB	Craig, Johnny	JCr	Elliot, D.	DE
Beck, C. C.	CCB	Buscema, Sal	SB	Crandall, Reed	RC	Ellis, Warren	WEl
Becker, Sam	SaB	Busiek, Kurt	KBk	Crespo, Steve	SCr	Ellison, Harlan	HaE
Beeston, John	JBe	Butler, Jeff	JBt	Crilley, Mark	MCi	Emberlin, Randy	RyE
Belardinelli, M.	MBe	Butler, Steve	SBt	Crumb, Robert	RCr	Englehart, Steve	SEt
Bell, Bob Boze	BBB	Buzz	Buzz	Cruz, E. R.	ERC	Ennis, Garth	GEn
Bell, George	GBl	Byrd, Mitch	MBy	Cruz, Jerry	JCz	Epting, Steve.	SEp
Bell, Julie	JuB	Byrne, John	JBy	Cruz, Roger	RCz	Erskine, Gary	GEr
Bendis, Brian Michael	BMB	Calafiore, Jim	JCf	Cuidera, Chuck	CCu	Erwin, Steve.	StE
Benefiel, Scott	ScB	Caldes, Charles	CCa	Cullins, Paris	PCu	Esposito, Mike	ME
Benes, Ed	EBe	Callahan, Jim	JiC	Currie, Andrew	ACe	Estes, John	JEs
Benitez, Joe	JBz	Calnan, John	JCa	Damaggio, Rodolfo	RDm	Estrada, Ric	RE
Benjamin, Ryan	RBn	Cameron, Don	DCn	Daniel, Tony	TnD	Evans, George	GE
Bennett, Joe	JoB	Cameron, Lou	LC	Danner, Paul	PuD	Evans, Ray	REv
Bennett, Richard	RiB	Campbell, Eddie	ECa	Darrow, Geof.	GfD	Everett, Bill	BEv
Benson, Scott	StB	Campbell, J. Scott	JSC	David, Peter	PDd	Ewins, Brett	BEw
Berger, Charles	ChB	Campbell, Stan	StC	Davis, Alan	AD	Ezquerra, Carlos	CE
Bernado, Ramon	RBe	Campenella, Robert	RbC	Davis, Bob	BD	Fabry, Glenn	GF
		Campos, Marc	MCa	Davis, Dan	DDv	Fago, Al	AFa

Name	Abbr.
Farmer, Mark	MFm
Fegredo, Duncan	DFg
Feldstein, Al	AF
Ferry, Pascual	PFe
Fine, Lou	LF
Fingeroth, Danny	DFr
Finnocchiaro, Sal	SF
Fleisher, Michael	MFl
Fleming, Robert	RFl
Flemming, Homer	HFl
Flessel, Creig	CF
Foreman, Dick	DiF
Forte, John	JF
Forton, Gerald	GFo
Fosco, Frank	FFo
Foster, Alan Dean	ADF
Fox, Gardner	GaF
Fox, Gill	GFx
Fox, Matt	MF
Fraga, Dan	DaF
Franchesco	Fso
Frank, Gary	GFr
Frazetta, Frank	FF
Freeman, John	JFr
Freeman, Simon	SFr
Frenz, Ron	RF
Frese, George	GFs
Friedman, Michael Jan	MFr
Friedrich, Mike	MkF
Frolechlich, August	AgF
Fry III, James	JFy
Fujitani(Fuje), Bob	BF
Furman, Simon	SFu
Gaiman, Neil	NGa
Galan, Manny	MaG
Gallant, Shannon	ShG
Gammill, Kerry	KGa
Garcia, Dave	DaG
Garner, Alex	AGo
Garney, Ron	RG
Garzon, Carlos	CG
Gascoine, Phil	PGa
Gaudino, Stefano	SGa
Gaughan, Jack	JGa
Gecko, Gabe	GG
Geggan	Ggn
Gerard, Ruben	RGd
Gerber, Steve	SvG
Giacoia, Frank	FrG
Giarrano, Vince	VGi
Gibbons, Dave	DGb
Gibson, Ian	IG
Giella, Joe	JoG
Giffen, Keith	KG
Gilbert, Michael T.	MGi
Giordano, Dick	DG
Glanzman, Sam	SG
Goldberg, Rube	RuG
Golden, Michael	MGo
Gonzalez, Jorge	JGz
Goodman, Till	TGo
Goodwin, Archie	AGw
Gordon, Al	AG
Gottfredson, Floyd	FG
Gould, Chester	ChG
Grandmetti, Jerry	JGr
Grant, Alan.	AlG
Grant, Steve	StG
Grau, Peter	PGr
Gray, Mick	MGy
Green, Alfonso	AGn
Green, Dan	DGr
Green, Justin	JsG
Green, Randy	RGr
Greene, Sid	SGe
Grell, Mike	MGr
Griffith, Bill	BG
Griffiths, Harley	HyG
Griffiths, Martin	MGs
Grindberg, Tom	TGb
Gross, Daerick	DkG
Gross, Peter	PrG
Grossman, R.	RGs
Gruenwald, Mark	MGu
Grummett, Tom	TG
Guardineer, Fred	FGu
Guay, Rebecca	RGu
Guice, Jackson	JG
Guichet, Yvel	YG
Guinan, Paul	PGn
Gulacy, Paul	PG
Gustavson, Paul	PGv
Gustovich, Mike	MG
Ha, Gene	GeH
Haley, Matt	MHy
Hall, Bob	BH
Halsted, Ted	TeH
Hama, Larry	LHa
Hamilton, Tim	TH
Hamner, Cully	CHm
Hampton, Bo.	BHa
Hampton, Scott	SHp
Hanna, Scott	SHa
Hannigan, Ed	EH
Hanson, Neil	NHa
Harmon, Jim	JHa
Harras, Bob	BHs
Harris, N. Steven	NSH
Harris, Tim	THa
Harris, Tony	TyH
Harrison, Lou	LuH
Harrison, Simon	SHn
Hart, Ernest	EhH
Hartsoe, Everette	EHr
Hathaway, Kurt	KtH
Hawkins, Matt	MHw
Hayes, Drew	DHa
Hayes, Rory	RHa
Haynes, Hugh.	HH
Hazlewood, Douglas.	DHz
Hearnes, David	DvH
Hearne, Jack	JH
Heath, Russ	RH
Hebbard, Robert	RtH
Heck, Don.	DH
Heisler, Mike.	MHs
Hempel, Mark.	MaH
Henry, Flint	FH
Herman, Jack	JH
Hernandez Brothers	HB
Hernandez, Gilbert	GHe
Hernandez, Jaime	JHr
Herrera,Ben	BHr
Hester, Phil	PhH
Hewlett, Jamie	JHw
Hibbard, E.E.	EHi
Hicklenton, John	JHk
Hicks, Arnold	AdH
Higgins, Graham	GHi
Higgins, John	JHi
Higgins, Michael	MHi
Hing, T. F.	TFH
Hitch, Bryan	BHi
Hobbs, Bill	BlH
Hoberg, Rick.	RHo
Hoffer, Mike	MkH
Hogarth, Burne	BHg
Holcomb, Art	AHo
Holdredge, John	JHo
Hoover, Dave	DHv
Hopgood, Kevin	KHd
Horie, Richard	RHe
Hotz, Kyle	KHt
Howarth, Matt.	MHo
Howell, Rich	RHo
Hudnall, James	JHl
Hughes, Adam	AH
Hultgren, Ken	KHu
Hund, Dave	DeH
Hunt, Chad	CH
Immonen, Stuart	SI
Infantino, Carmine	CI
Infantino, Jim	JI
Ingles, Graham	GrI
Iorio, Medio	MI
Isherwood, Geoff	GI
Ivie, Larry	LI
Ivy, Chris.	CIv
Jackson, Julius	JJn
Jaffee, Al	AJ
Janke, Dennis	DJa
Janson, Klaus	KJ
Javinen, Kirk	KJa
Jenkins, Paul	PJe
Jenney, Robert	RJ
Jensen, Dennis	DJ
Jimenez, Leonardo	LJi
Jimminiz, Phil	PJ
Johnson, Dave	DvJ
Johnson, Jeff	JJ
Johnson, Paul	PuJ
Johnson, Todd	TJn
Johnson, Walter	WJo
Jones, Casey	CJ
Jones, Gerard	GJ
Jones, J.B.	JJo
Jones, Jeff	JeJ
Jones, Kelley	KJo
Jones, Malcolm.	MJ
Jones, R.A.	RAJ
Jones, Robert	RJn
Jurgens, Dan.	DJu
Jusko, Joe	JJu
Kaluta, Mike	MK
Kamen, Jack	JKa
Kaminski, Len	LKa
Kane & Romita	K&R
Kane, Bob	BKa
Kane, Gil.	GK
Kanigher, Bob	BbK
Kaniuga, Trent	TKn
Karounos, Paris T.	PaK
Katz, Jack	JKz
Kavanagh, Terry	TKa
Kaye, Stan	StK
Kelly, Walt	WK
Kennedy, Cam	CK
Kennedy, Ian	IK
Keown, Dale	DK
Kerschl, Karl.	KlK
Kesel, Babara	BKs
Kesel, Karl	KK
Kiefer, Henry C.	HcK
Kieth, Sam	SK
Kihi, H. J.	HjK
Kildale, Malcolm	MKd
King, Hannibal	HbK
Kinsler, Everett R.	EK
Kirby, Jack	JK
Kirner	Kr
Kisniro, Yukito	YuK
Kitchen, Dennis	DKi
Kitson, Barry	BKi
Klein, George	GKl
Kobasic, Kevin	KoK
Kolins, Scott	ScK
Krause, Peter.	PKr
Krenkel, Roy.	RKu
Krigstein, Bernie	BK
Kristiansen, Teddy H..	TKr
Kruse, Brandon	BKr
Kubert, Adam	AKu
Kubert, Andy	NKu
Kubert, Joe	JKu
Kupperberg, Paul	PuK
Kurtzman, Harvey	HK
Kwitney, Alisa	AaK
LaBan, Terry	TLa
Lago, Ray	RyL
Laird, Peter	PLa
Lamme, Bob	BbL
Langridge, Roger	RLg
Lanning, Andy	ALa
Lansdale, Joe	JLd
Lapham, Dave	DL
Lark, Michael	MLr
Larkin, Bob.	BLr
LaRocque, Greg	GrL
Larroca, Salvador	SvL
Larsen, Erik	EL
Lash, Batton	BLs
Lashley, Ken	KeL
Lavery, Jim	JLv
Lawlis, Dan.	DLw
Lawrence, Terral	TLw
Lawson, Jim	JmL
Layton, Bob.	BL
Leach, Garry	GL
Leach, Rick	RkL
Lee, Elaine	ELe
Lee, Jae	JaL
Lee, Jim	JLe
Lee, Patrick	PtL
Lee, Scott	ScL
Lee, Stan	StL
Leeke, Mike	MLe
Leialoha, Steve	SL
Leon, John Paul	JPL
Leonard, Lank	LLe
Leonardi, Rick	RL
Levins, Rik	RLe
Lewis, Brian	BLw
Lieber, Larry	LLi
Liefeld, Rob.	RLd
Lightle, Steve	SLi
Lim, Ron.	RLm
Linsner, Joseph M.	JLi
Livingstone, Rolland	RLv
Lloyd, David	DvL
Lobdell, Scott	SLo
Locke, Vince	VcL
Loeb, Jeph	JLb
Lopez, Jose	JL
Lopresti, Aaron	AaL
Louapre, Dave	DLp
Lowe, John	Low
Lubbers, Bob.	BLb
Lustbader, Eric Van	ELu
Luzniak, Greg	GLz
Lyle, Tom	TL
Macchio, Ralph	RMc
Mack, David	DMk
Mackie, Howard	HMe
Madan, Dev	DeM
Madureira, Joe	JMd
Maggin, Elliot S.	ESM
Maguire, Kevin	KM
Magyar, Rick	RM
Mahlstedt, Larry	LMa
Mahnke, Doug	DoM
Mandrake, Tom.	TMd
Maneely, Joe.	JMn
Manley, Graham	GMy
Manley, Mike	MM
Mann, Roland.	RMn
Mann, Roland	Man
Manning, Russ	RsM
Marais, Raymond	RdM
Mariotte, Jeff	JMi
Maroto, Esteban	EM
Marrinan, Chris	ChM
Marrs, Lee	LMr

Name	Abbr.	Name	Abbr.	Name	Abbr.	Name	Abbr.
Martin, Gary	GyM	Morales, Rags	RgM	Pekar, Harvey	HP	Roach, David	DRo
Martin, Joe	JMt	Moreira, Ruben	RMo	Pelletier, Paul	PaP	Robbins, Frank	FR
Martinbrough, Shawn	SMa	Moretti, Mark	MMo	Peltz, George	GgP	Robbins, Trina	TrR
Martinez, Henry	HMz	Morgan, Tom.	TMo	Pence, Eric	ErP	Roberts, Mike	MRo
Martinez, Roy Allan	RMr	Morisi, Pete	PMo	Pennington, Mark	MPn	Robertson, Darrick	DaR
Marz, Ron	RMz	Moritz, Edward	EdM	Pensa, Shea Anton	SAP	Robinson, Cliff	CRb
Marzan, Jose	JMz	Morosco, Vincent	VMo	Perez, George	GP	Robinson, James	JeR
Mason, Tom	TMs	Morrison, Grant	GMo	Perham, James	JPh	Robinson, Jerry	JRo
Massengill, Nathan	NMa	Morrow, Gray	GM	Perlin, Don	DP	Rodier, Denis	DRo
Matsuda, Jeff.	JMs	Mortimer, Win	WMo	Perryman, Edmund	EP	Rodriguez, Spain	SRo
Mattsson, Steve	SMt	Moskowitz, Seymour	SMz	Peterson, Brandon	BPe	Roea, Doug	DgR
Maus, Bill	BMs	Motter, Dean	DMt	Peterson, Jonathan	JPe	Rogers, Boody	BRo
Maxwell, Stanley	StM	Moy, Jeffrey	JMy	Petrucha, Stefan	SPr	Rogers, Marshall	MR
Mayer, Sheldon	ShM	Murray, Brian	BrM	Peyer, Tom	TPe	Romita, John	JR
Mayerik, Val	VMk	Musial, Joe	JoM	Phillips, Joe	JoP	Romita, John Jr.	JR2
Mazzucchelli, David	DM	Muth, Jon J.	JMu	Phillips, Scott	SPl	Rosenberger, J.	JRo
McCann, Gerald	GMc	Mychaels, Marat	MMy	Phillips, Sean	SeP	Ross, Alex.	AxR
McCarthy, Brendon	BMy	Myers	Mys	Pike, Jay Scott.	JsP	Ross, David	DR
McCarthy, Jim	JMy	Naifeh, Ted	TNa	Pini, Richard	RPi	Ross, John	JRs
McCloud, Scott	SMl	Napolitano, Nick	NNa	Pini, Wendy	WP	Ross, Luke	LRs
McCorkindale, B	BMC	Napton, Bob	BNa	Pino, Carlos	CPi	Roth, Werner	WR
McCraw, Tom	TMw	Nauck, Todd	TNu	Platt, Stephen	SPa	Royle, Jim.	JRl
McCrea, John	JMC	Neary, Paul	PNe	Pleece, Warren	WaP	Royle, John	JRe
McDaniel, Scott	SMc	Nebres, Rudy	RN	Ploog, Mike	MP	Rozum, John	JRz
McDaniel, Walter	WMc	Nelson	Nel	Plunkett, Kilian	KPl	Rubano, Aldo	ARu
McDonnell, Luke	LMc	Netzer, Mike	MN	Poch	PcH	Rubi, Melvin	MvR
McDuffie, Dwayne	DMD	Newton, Don.	DN	Pollack, Rachel	RaP	Rubinstein, Joe	JRu
McFarlane, Todd	TM	Nguyen, Hoang	HNg	Pollard, Keith	KP	Rude, Steve	SR
McGregor, Don	DMG	Nichols, Art.	ANi	Pollina, Adam	AdP	Ruffner, Sean.	SRf
McKean, Dave	DMc	Nicieza, Fabian	FaN	Polseno, Jo	JP	Russell, P. Craig	CR
McKeever, Ted	TMK	Nino, Alex	AN	Pope, Paul	PPo	Russell, Vince	VRu
McKenna, Mike.	MkK	Nocenti, Ann	ANo	Porch, David	DPo	Ryan, Matt	MRy
McKie, Angus	AMK	Nocon, Cedric	CNn	Portacio, Whilce	WPo	Ryan, Paul	PR
McKone, Mike	MMK	Nodell, Martin	MnN	Porter, Howard	HPo	Ryder, Tom.	TmR
McLaughlin, Frank	FMc	Nodel, Norman	NN	Post, Howard	HwP	Sahle, Harry	HSa
McLaughlin, Sean	SML	Nolan, Graham	GN	Potts, Carl	CP	Sakakibara, Mizuki	MiS
McLeod, Bob	BMc	Nord, Cary	CNr	Powell, Bob	BP	Sakai, Stan	SS
McMahon, M.	MMc	Norem, Earl	EN	Power, Dermot	DPw	Sale, Tim	TSe
McManus, Shawn	SwM	Nostrand, Howard	HN	Pratt, George	GgP	Salmons, Tony.	TSa
McNeil, Colin	CMc	Novick, Irv	IN	Premaini, Bruno	BPr	Saltares, Javier	JS
McWilliams, Al	AMc	Nowlan, Kevin	KN	Prezio, Victor	VP	Sampson, Steve	SSm
Meagher, Fred	FMe	Nutman, Philip	PNu	Prichard, Pat	PPr	Sanders, Jim III	JS3
Medina, Angel	AMe	O'Barr, James	JOb	Priest, Christopher	CPr	Sasso, Mark	MSo
Medley, Linda	LiM	O'Neil, Denny	DON	Prosser, Jerry	JeP	Saunders, Norm	NS
Mercadoocasio, H.	HMo	O'Neill, Kevin	KON	Pugh, Steve	StP	Saviuk, Alex	AS
Meskin, Mort	MMe	Olbrich, Dave	DO	Pulido, Brian	BnP	Schaffenberger, Kurt	KS
Messmer, Otto	OM	Olivetti, Ariel	AOl	Queen, Randy	RQu	Schane, Tristan	TnS
Messner-Loebs, Bill	BML	Olliffe, Patrick	PO	Quesada, Joe	JQ	Schiller, Fred	FdS
Micale, Albert	AlM	One, Dark	DOe	Quinlan, Charles	CQ	Schmitz, Mark	MaS
Michelinie, David	DvM	Ordway, Jerry	JOy	Quinn, David	DQ	Schomburg, Alex.	ASh
Miehm, Grant	GtM	Orlando, Joe	JO	Quinones, Peter	PQ	Schrotter, Gustav	GS
Mighten, Duke	DMn	Ormston, Dean	DOr	Raab, Ben	BRa	Schultz, Mark	MSh
Mignola, Michael	MMi	Ortiz, Jose	JOt	Raboy, Mac	MRa	Scoffield, Sean	SSc
Miki, Danny	DaM	Oskner, Bob	BO	Ramos, Humberto	HuR	Scott, Jeffery	JSc
Milgrom, Al	AM	Ostrander, John	JOs	Ramos, Rodney	RyR	Scott, Trevor	TvS
Millar, Mark	MMr	Oughton, Thomas	TO	Ramsey, Ray	RR	Seagle, Steven T.	SSe
Miller, Frank	FM	Owen, James	JOn	Randall, Ron	RoR	Sears, Bart	BS
Miller, Mike S.	MsM	Ozkan, Tayyar	TOz	Randon, Arthur	ARn	Sekowsky, Mike	MSy
Miller, Sidney	SyM	Pace, Richard	RPc	Raney, Tom.	TR	Semeiks, Val	VS
Miller, Steve	SM	Pacella, Mark	MPa	Rankin, Rich	RRa	Senior, Geoff	GSr
Milligan, Peter	PrM	Pacheco, Carlos	CPa	Rapmund, Norm	NRd	Serpe, Jerry	JyS
Mills, Pat.	PMs	Palais, Rudy	RP	Rasmussen, H	HR	Severin, John	JSe
Minor, Jason	JnM	Palais, Walter	WlP	Raymond, Alex	AR	Severin, Marie	MSe
Mitchel, Barry	BM	Palmer, Tom	TP	Raymond, Kim	KR	Shamray, Gerry	GSh
Moder, Lee	LMd	Palmiotti, Jimmy	JP	Redondo, J.	JRd	Shanower, Eric.	EiS
Moe, C. S.	CSM	Pamai, Gene	GPi	Redondo, Nestor	NR	Sharp, Liam	LSh
Moebius	Moe	Panalign, Noly	NPl	Reed, David	DvR	Shaw, Sean.	SSh
Moeller, Chris	CsM	Paniccia, Mark	MPc	Reeves-Stevens, Judith	JRv	Shelton, Gilbert	GiS
Moench, Doug	DgM	Panosian, Dan	DPs	Reinhold, Bill.	BR	Sheridan, Dave	DSh
Moldoff, Sheldon	SMo	Parkhouse, Annie	APh	Richards, Ted	TR	Sherman, Jim	JSh
Montano, Steve	SeM	Parkhouse, Steve	SvP	Richardson, Mike	MRi	Shoemaker, Terry.	TSr
Mooney, Jim	JM	Parobeck, Mike	MeP	Richardson, J.	JRi	Shooter, Jim	JiS
Moore, Alan	AMo	Pascoe, James	JmP	Ricketts, Mark.	MRc	Shores, Syd	SSh
Moore, Jeff.	JMr	Pasko, Martin	MPk	Rico, Don	DRi	Shum, Howard	HSm
Moore, Jerome	JeM	Patterson, Bruce	BrP	Ridgeway, John.	JRy	Shuster, Joe	JoS
Moore, John Francis	JFM	Paul, Frank R.	FRP	Rieber, John Ney	JNR	Sibal, Jonathan	JSb
Moore, Terry	TMr	Payne, Pop	PP	Riley, John.	JnR	Siegel & Shuster	S&S
Morales, Lou	LM	Pearson, Jason	JPn	Riply	Rip	Sienkiewicz, Bill	BSz

Silvestri, Eric . . . . EcS	Straczynski, J.Michael MSz	Valentino, Jim . . . . JV	Wiesenfeld, Aron . . . . AWs
Silvestri, Mark . . . . MS	Stradley, Randy . . . . . RSd	Vallejo, Boris . . . . BV	Wildey, Doug . . . . DW
Sim, Dave . . . . DS	Strazewski, Len . . . . . . LeS	Van Buren, Raeburn . . RvB	Wildman, Andrew . . . . Wld
Simon & Kirby . . . . S&K	Streeter, Lin . . . . LnS	Van Fleet, John . . . . . . JVF	Williams, Anthony . . . . AWi
Simon, Allen . . . . ASm	Stroman, Larry . . . . LSn	Vancata, Brad . . . . BVa	Williams, David . . . . . DdW
Simon, Joe . . . . JSm	Sturgeon, Foolbert	Vance, Steve . . . . SVa	Williams, J H . . . . JWi
Simonson, Louise . . . . . LSi	(& Frank Stack) . . . FSt	VanHook, Kevin . . . . . KVH	Williams, Keith . . . . . . KWi
Simonson, Walt . . . . . . WS	Sullivan, Lee . . . . LS	Vargas, Vagner VV	Williams, Kent . . . . KW
Simpson, Don . . . . DSs	Sutton, Tom . . . . TS	Veitch, Rick . . . . RV	Williams, Robert . . . . . RW
Simpson, Howard . . . . HSn	Swan, Curt . . . . CS	Velez, Ivan, Jr. IV	Williams, Scott . . . . . . SW
Simpson, Will . . . . . . WSm	Sweetman, Dan . . . . . DSw	Velluto, Sal . . . . SaV	Williamson, Al . . . . AW
Sinnott, Joe . . . . JSt	Taggart, Tom . . . . TTg	Vess, Charles CV	Williamson, Skip . . . . SWi
Siryk . . . . Syk	Takenaga, Francis . . FTa	Vey, Al . . . . AV	Willingham, Bill . . . . . BWg
Skroce, Steve . . . . . . SSr	Takezaki, Tony . . . . . . ToT	Vigil, Tim . . . . TV	Willis, Damon . . . . . . DaW
Smith, Andy . . . . ASm	Talbot, Bryan . . . . BT	Vokes, Neil . . . . NV	Wilshire, Mary . . . . . . MW
Smith, Barry W . . . . . BWS	Tallarico, Tony . . . . . . TyT	Von Eeden, Trevor . . . TVE	Wilson, Colin . . . . CWi
Smith, Beau . . . . BSt	Tan, Billy . . . . BTn	Vosburg, Mike . . . . . . MV	Wilson, Gahan . . . . . . GW
Smith, Cam . . . . CaS	Tanaka, Masashi . . . . MTk	Wagner, Matt . . . . MWg	Wilson, Keith S . . . . . KSW
Smith, Jeff . . . . JSi	Tanghal, Romeo . . . . . RT	Wagner,Ron . . . . RoW	Wilson, S. Clay . . . . SCW
Smith, John . . . . JnS	Tappin, Steve . . . . . . SeT	Waid, Mark . . . . MWa	Woch, Stan . . . . SnW
Smith, Kevin . . . . KSm	Tartaglione, John . . . . JTg	Waldinger, Morris . . . MsW	Woggin, Bill . . . . BWo
Smith, Malcolm . . . . . MSt	Taylor, David . . . . DTy	Waldman, Ed . . . . EW	Wojtkiewicz, Chuck . . . Woj
Smith, Paul . . . . PS	Taylor, R.G. . . . . RGT	Walker, Kevin . . . . KeW	Wolf, Chance . . . . . . CWf
Smith, Robin . . . . RSm	Templeton, Ty . . . . . . TTn	Waller, Reed . . . . RWa	Wolfe, Joseph . . . . . . JWf
Smith, Ron . . . . RS	Teney, Tom . . . . TmT	Walsh, William . . . . . WmW	Wolfman, Marv . . . . . MWn
Snejbjerg, Peter . . . . . PSj	Tenney, Mark . . . . . . MaT	Waltrip, Jason . . . . . . JWp	Wolverton, Basil . . . . . BW
Sniegoski, Tom . . . . . TSg	Texeira, Mark . . . . MT	Waltrip, John . . . . JWt	Wood, Bob . . . . BoW
Spark . . . . Spk	Thibert, Art . . . . ATi	Ward, Bill . . . . BWa	Wood, Teri Sue . . . . . TWo
Sparling, Jack . . . . . . JkS	Thomas, Dann . . . . . . DTs	Warner, Chris . . . . CW	Wood, Wally . . . . WW
Spector, Irving . . . . IS	Thomas, Roy . . . . RTs	Warren, Adam . . . . . AWa	Woodbridge, George . GWb
Spiegelman, Art . . . . . ASp	Thomason, Derek . . . . DeT	Warren, Jack A . . . . . . JW	Woodring, Jim . . . . . . JWo
Spiegle, Dan . . . . DSp	Thompson, Jill . . . . JlT	Washington 3, Robert 3RW	Wormer, Kirk Van . . . . KWo
Spinks, Frank . . . . FrS	Thorne, Frank . . . . FT	Watkiss, John . . . . . . JWk	Wright, Greg . . . . GWt
Springer, Frank . . . . . . FS	Tinker, Ron . . . . RnT	Watson, Jim . . . . JWa	Wrightson, Berni . . . . BWr
Sprouse, Chris . . . . . . CSp	Todd, Fred . . . . FTd	Webb, Robert . . . . . . RWb	Wyman, M.C. . . . . . . MCW
St.Pierre, Joe . . . . JPi	Torres, Angelo . . . . AT	Weeks, Lee . . . . LW	Yaep, Chap . . . . CYp
Starlin, Jim . . . . JSn	Toth, Alex . . . . ATh	Wein, Len . . . . LWn	Yeates, Tom . . . . TY
Starr, Leonard . . . . . . LSt	Totleben, John . . . . . . JTo	Weinstein, Howard . . . HWe	Yeowell, Steve . . . . . . SY
Staton, Joe . . . . JSon	Trapain, Sal . . . . ST	Weiss, M . . . . MWs	Zabel, Joe . . . . JZe
Steacy, Ken . . . . KSy	Trimpe, Herb . . . . HT	Welch, Larry . . . . LyW	Zachary, Dean . . . . . . DZ
Steffan, Dan . . . . DnS	Truman, Timothy . . . . . TT	Welker, Gay . . . . GyW	Zaffino, Jorge . . . . JZ
Stein, Marvin . . . . MvS	Truog, Chas . . . . ChT	Wendel, Andrew . . . . . AdW	Zansky, Louis . . . . LZ
Steinberg, Irvin . . . . . . ISb	Tucci, Bill . . . . BiT	Wenzel, David . . . . . DWe	Zeck, Mike . . . . MZ
Stelfreeze, Brian . . . . . BSf	Tucker, James . . . . JT	Weringo, Mike . . . . . . MeW	Zick, Bruce . . . . BZ
Stephenson, Eric . . . . . ErS	Tukell, George . . . . . GTk	West, Kevin . . . . KWe	Zulli, Michael . . . . MZi
Steranko, Jim . . . . JSo	Turner, Dwayne . . . . . . DT	Weston, Chris . . . . . . CWn	Zyskowski, Joseph . . . JZy
Stern, Roger . . . . RSt	Turner, Ron . . . . RTu	Wheatley, Mark . . . . MkW	Zyskowski, Steven . . . . SZ
Stern, Steve . . . . SSt	Tuska, George . . . . . . GT	Whedon, Joss . . . . . . JoW	
Stevens, Dave . . . . . . DSt	Ulm, Chris . . . . CU	Whiteman, Ezra . . . . . EzW	
Stiles, Steve . . . . SvS	Ulmer, Al . . . . AU	Whitman, Bill . . . . . . BWh	
Story, Karl . . . . KlS	Vachss, Andrew . . . . . AVs	Whitney, Ogden . . . . . OW	
Stout, William . . . . . . WiS	Vado, Dan . . . . DVa	Wiacek, Bob . . . . BWi	

GENERAL ABBREVIATIONS FOR COMICS LISTINGS

Adaptation . . . . Adapt.	Giant Size . . . . G-Size	Prestige Format . . . . PF
Appearance of . . . . A:	Golden Age . . . . G.A.	Preview . . . . Prev.
Anniversary . . . . Anniv.	Graphic Album . . . . GAm	Reprinted issue . . . . rep.
Annual . . . . Ann.#	Graphic Novel . . . . . GN or GNv	Retold . . . . rtd.
Art & Cover . . . . (a&c)	Hardcover . . . . HC	Return/Revival of . . . . R:
Art & Plot . . . . (a&pl)	Identity Revealed . . . . IR:	Scripted/Written by . . . . (s)
Art & Script . . . . (a&s)	Inks by . . . . (i)	Scripts & inks . . . . (s&i)
Artist . . . . (a)	Introduction of . . . . I:	Silver Age . . . . S.A.
Back-Up Story . . . . BU:	Joins of . . . . J:	Softcover . . . . SC
Beginning of . . . . B:	King Size . . . . K-Size	Special . . . . Spec.
Birth of . . . . b:	Leaving of . . . . L:	Team-up . . . . T.U.
Cameo Appearance . . . . C:	New Costume . . . . N:	Trade Paperback . . . . TPB
Cover . . . . (c)	No Issue Number . . . . N#	Versus . . . . V: or vs.
Cover and Script . . . . (c&s)	Origin of . . . . O:	Wedding of . . . . W:
Crossover with . . . . x-over	Painted Cover . . . . P(c)	With . . . . w/
Death/Destruction of . . . . . . D:	Part . . . . pt. or Pt.	Without . . . . w/o
Edition . . . . Ed.	Pencils by . . . . (p)	
Ending of . . . . E:	Photographic cover . . . . Ph(c)	
Features . . . . F:	Plotted by . . . . (pl)	

Abbreviation	Name
3RW.	Robert Washington 3
AA	Alfredo Alcala
AAd	Art Adams
AaK	Alisa Kwitney
AaL	Aaron Lopresti
AAv	Al Avison
AB	Alex Blum
ABr	Ann Brewster
ACa	Anthony Castrillo
ACe	Andrew Currie
ACh	Anthony Chun
ACo	Amanda Conner
AD	Alan Davis
ADF	Alan Dean Foster
AdH	Arnold Hicks
AdP	Adam Pollina
ADv	Al Davison
AdW	Andrew Wendel
AF	Al Feldstein
AFa	Al Fago
AG	Al Gordon
AgF	A. Frolechlich
AGn	Alfonso Green
AGo	Alex Garner
AGw	Archie Goodwin
AH	Adam Hughes
AHo	Art Holcomb
AIA	Alfred Andriola
AJ	Al Jaffee
AKu	Adam Kubert
ALa	Andy Lanning
AlG	Alan Grant
AlM	Albert Micale
AM	Al Milgrom
AMc	Al McWilliams
AMe	Angel Medina
AMK	Angus McKie
AMo	Alan Moore
AN	Alex Nino
ANi	Art Nichols
ANo	Ann Nocenti
AOl	Ariel Olivetti
APh	Annie Parkhouse
AR	Alex Raymond
ARn	Arthur Randon
ARu	Aldo Rubano
AS	Alex Saviuk
ASh	Alex Schomburg
ASm	Andy Smith
ASm	Allen Simon
ASp	Art Spiegelman
AT	Angelo Torres
ATh	Alex Toth
ATi	Art Thibert
AU	Al Ulmer
AV	Al Vey
AVs	Andrew Vachss
AW	Al Williamson
AWa	Adam Warren
AWi	Anthony Williams
AWs	Aron Wiesenfeld
AxR	Alex Ross
AyB	Allyn Brodsky
BA	Brent Anderson
BaB	Barry Blair
BAn	Bill Anderson
BAp	Brian Althorp
BAu	Brian Augustyn
BB	Brian Bolland
BBa	Bernard Bailey
BbB	Bob Brown
BBB	Bob Boze Bell
BBh	Brett Booth
BbK	Bob Kanigher
BBl	Bret Blevins
BbL	Bob Lamme
BBr	Brett Breeding
BCe	Bobbie Chase
BCh	Bernard Chang
BCi	Brandon Choi
BD	Bob Davis
BDC	Brent D Carpenter
BDn	Ben Dunn
BE	Bill Elder
BEd	Ben Edlund
BEv	Bill Everett
BEw	Brett Ewins
BF	Bob Fujitani(Fuje)
BG	Bill Griffith
BH	Bob Hall
BHa	Bo Hampton
BHg	Burne Hogarth
BHi	Bryan Hitch
BHr	Ben Herrera
BHs	Bob Harras
BiT	Bill Tucci
BK	Bernie Krigstein
BKa	Bob Kane
BKi	Barry Kitson
BKr	Brandon Kruse
BKs	Babara Kesel
BL	Bob Layton
BLb	Bob Lubbers
BlH	Bill Hobbs
BLr	Bob Larkin
BLs	Batton Lash
BLw	Brian Lewis
BM	Barry Mitchel
BMB	Brian Michael Bendis
BMc	Bob McLeod
BMC	B. McCorkindale
BML	Bill Messner-Loebs
BMs	Bill Maus
BMy	Brendon McCarthy
BNa	Bob Napton
BnP	Brian Pulido
BO	Bob Oskner
BoW	Bob Wood
BP	Bob Powell
BPe	Brandon Peterson
BPr	Bruno Premaini
BR	Bill Reinhold
BRa	Ben Raab
BrM	Brian Murray
BRo	Boody Rogers
BrP	Bruce Patterson
BS	Bart Sears
BSf	Brian Stelfreeze
BSt	Beau Smith
BSz	Bill Sienkiewicz
BT	Bryan Talbot
BTn	Billy Tan
Buzz	Buzz
BV	Boris Vallejo
BVa	Brad Vancata
BW	Basil Wolverton
BWa	Bill Ward
BWg	Bill Willingham
BWh	Bill Whitman
BWi	Bob Wiacek
BWo	Bill Woggin
BWr	Berni Wrightson
BWS	Barry Windsor-Smith
BZ	Bruce Zick
CAd	Charlie Adlard
CaS	Cam Smith
CAx	Chris Alexander
CB	Carl Barks
CBa	Chris Bachalo
CBi	Charles Biro
CBu	Carl Burgos
CCa	Charles Caldes
CCB	C. C. Beck
CCl	Chris Claremont
Ccs	Chriscross
CCt	Claudio Castellini
CCu	Chuck Cuidera
CDi	Chuck Dixon
CDo	Colleen Doran
CE	Carlos Ezquerra
CF	Creig Flessel
CG	Carlos Garzon
CH	Chad Hunt
ChB	Charles Berger
ChG	Chester Gould
ChM	Chris Marrinan
CHm	Cully Hamner
ChT	Chas Truog
Chu	Ernie Chua
CI	Carmine Infantino
CIv	Chris Ivy
CJ	Casey Jones
CK	Cam Kennedy
CMc	Colin McNeil
CNn	Cedric Nocon
CNr	Cary Nord
CP	Carl Potts
CPa	Carlos Pacheco
CPi	Carlos Pino
CPr	Christopher Priest
CQ	Charles Quinlan
CR	P. Craig Russell
CRb	Cliff Robinson
CrB	Craig Brasfield
CS	Curt Swan
CsB	Chris Batista
CSM	C. S. Moe
CsM	Chris Moeller
CSp	Chris Sprouse
CU	Chris Ulm
CV	Charles Vess
CW	Chris Warner
CWf	Chance Wolf
CWi	Colin Wilson
CWn	Chris Weston
CYp	Chap Yaep
DA	Dan Adkins
DAb	Dusty Abell
DaC	Dan Castellaneta
DaF	Dan Fraga
DaG	Dave Garcia
DaM	Danny Miki
DAn	Dan Abnett
DaR	Darrick Robertson
DaW	Damon Willis
Day	Dan Day
DAy	Dick Ayers
DB	D. Battlefield
DBa	Dan Barry
DBk	Darryl Banks
DBl	Danny Bulanadi
DBr	Dick Briefer
DBs	John Barras
DBw	Doug Braithwaite
DC	Dave Cockrum
DCn	Don Cameron
DCw	Denys Cowan
DD	Dick Dillin
DdB	David Boller
DDv	Dan Davis
DdW	David Williams
DE	D. Elliot
DeH	Dave Hund
DeM	Dev Madan
DeT	Derek Thomason
DFg	Duncan Fegredo
DFr	Danny Fingeroth
DG	Dick Giordano
DGb	Dave Gibbons
DGC	D.G. Chichester
DgM	Doug Moench
DgR	Doug Roea
DGr	Dan Green
DH	Don Heck
DHa	Drew Hayes
DHv	Dave Hoover
DHz	Douglas Hazlewood
DiF	Dick Foreman
DJ	Dennis Jensen
DJa	Dennis Janke
DJu	Dan Jurgens
DK	Dale Keown
DkB	Dick Browne
DkG	Daerick Gross
DKi	Dennis Kitchen
DL	Dave Lapham
DIB	Daniel Brereton
DLp	Dave Louapre
DLw	Dan Lawlis
DM	David Mazzucchelli
DMc	Dave McKean
DMD	Dwayne McDuffie
DMG	Don McGregor
DMk	David Mack
DMn	Duke Mighten
DMt	Dean Motter
DN	Don Newton
DnS	Dan Steffan
DO	Dave Olbrich
DoC	Dario Carrasco
DOe	Dark One
DoM	Doug Mahnke
DON	O'Neil, Denny
DOr	Dean Ormston
DP	Don Perlin
DPo	Porch, David
DPs	Dan Panosian
DPw	Power, Dermot
DQ	David Quinn
DR	Ross, David
Rd	Richard Delgado
DRi	Don Rico
DRo	Denis Rodier
DRo	David Roach
DS	Dave Sim
DSh	Dave Sheridan
DSp	Dan Spiegle
DSs	Don Simpson
DSt	Dave Stevens
DSw	Dan Sweetman
DT	Dwayne Turner
DTs	Dann Thomas
DTy	David Taylor
DvA	David Ammerman
DVa	Dan Vado
DvC	Dave Cooper
DvD	Dave Dorman
DvH	David Hearnes
DvJ	Dave Johnson
DvL	David Lloyd
DvM	David Michelinie
DvR	David Reed
DW	Doug Wildey
DWe	David Wenzel
DZ	Dean Zachary
EA	Edd Ashe
EB	Ed Barreto
EBe	Ed Benes
EC	Ernie Colon
ECa	Eddie Campbell
ECh	Ernie Chan
EcS	Eric Silvestri
EdM	Edward Moritz
EDo	Evan Dorkin
EH	Ed Hannigan
EhH	Ernest Hart
EHi	E.E. Hibbard
EHr	Everette Hartsoe
EiS	Eric Shanower
EK	Everett R. Kinsler
EL	Erik Larsen

Abbr.	Name	Abbr.	Name	Abbr.	Name	Abbr.	Name
ELe	Elaine Lee	GS	Gustav Schrotter	JCt	Joe Carter	JOn	James Owen
ELu	Eric Van Lustbader	GSh	Gerry Shamray	JCx	Jeromy Cox	JoP	Joe Phillips
EM	Esteban Maroto	GSr	Geoff Senior	JCz	Jerry Cruz	JoS	Joe Shuster
EN	Earl Norem	GT	George Tuska	JD	Jan Duursema	JOs	John Ostrander
ENB	E. Nelson Bridwell	GTk	George Tukell	JDa	Jack Davis	JOt	Jose Ortiz
EP	Edmund Perryman	CtM	Grant Miehm	JDo	Julie Doucet	JoW	Joss Whedon
ERC	E.R. Cruz	GW	Gahan Wilson	JDx	John Dixon	JOy	Jerry Ordway
ErP	Eric Pence	GWb	George Woodbridge	JDy	Jo Duffy	JP	Jo Polseno
ErS	Eric Stephenson	GWt	Greg Wright	JeJ	Jeff Jones	JP	Jimmy Palmiotti
ESM	Elliot S. Maggin	GyA	Gary Amaro	JeM	Jerome Moore	JPe	Jonathan Peterson
EW	Ed Waldman	GyC	Gerry Conway	JeP	Jerry Prosser	JPh	James Perham
EzW	Ezra Whiteman	GyD	Guy Davis	JeR	James Robinson	JPi	Joe St.Pierre
FaN	Fabian Nicieza	GyM	Gary Martin	JEs	John Estes	JPL	John Paul Leon
FB	Frank Brunner	GyW	Gay Welker	JF	John Forte	JPn	Jason Pearson
FBe	Frank Bolle	HaE	Harlan Ellison	JFM	John Francis Moore	JQ	Joe Quesada
FBk	Fred Burke	HB	Hernandez Brothers	JFr	John Freeman	JR	John Romita
FC	Frank Cirocco	HbK	Hannibal King	JFy	James Fry III	JR2	John Romita, Jr.
FdS	Fred Schiller	HC	Howard Chaykin	JG	Jackson Guice	JRd	J. Redondo
FF	Frank Frazetta	HcK	Henry C. Kiefer	JGa	Jack Gaughan	JRe	John Royle
FFo	Frank Fosco	HD	H. Dougherty	JGr	Jerry Grandmetti	JRl	Jim Royle
FG	Floyd Gottfredson	HFl	Homer Flemming	JGz	Jorge Gonzalez	JRi	J Richardson
FGu	Fred Guardineer	HH	Hugh Haynes	JH	Jack Herman	JRo	J. Rosenberger
FH	Flint Henry	HjK	H. J. Kihi	JH	Jack Hearne	JRo	Jerry Robinson
FM	Frank Miller	HK	Harvey Kurtzman	JHa	Jim Harmon	JRs	John Ross
FMc	Frank McLaughlin	HMe	Howard Mackie	JhB	John Beatty	JRu	Joe Rubinstein
FMe	Fred Meagher	HMo	H. Mercadoocasio	JhD	John Dell	JRv	Judith Reeves-Stevens
FP	Frank R. Paul	HMz	Henry Martinez	JHi	John Higgins	JRy	John Ridgeway
FR	Frank Robbins	HN	Howard Nostrand	JHk	John Hicklenton	JRz	John Rozum
FrG	Frank Giacoia	HNg	Hoang Nguyen	JHl	James Hudnall	JS	Javier Saltares
FrS	Frank Spinks	HP	Harvey Pekar	JHo	John Holdredge	JS3	Jim Sanders III
FS	Frank Springer	HPo	Howard Porter	JHr	Jaime Hernandez	JSb	Jonathan Sibal
Fso	Franchesco	HR	H. Rasmussen	JHw	Jamie Hewlett	JSc	Jeffery Scott
FSt	Foolbert Sturgeon	HSa	Harry Sahle	JI	Jim Infantino	JSC	J. Scott Campbell
	(& Frank Stack)	HSm	Howard Shum	JiC	Jim Callahan	JSe	John Severin
FT	Frank Thorne	HSn	Howard Simpson	JiS	Jim Shooter	JsG	Justin Green
FTa	Francis Takenaga	HT	Herb Trimpe	JJ	Jeff Johnson	JSh	Jim Sherman
FTd	Fred Todd	HuR	Humberto Ramos	JJB	JJ Birch	JSi	Jeff Smith
GaF	Gardner Fox	HWe	Howard Weinstein	JJn	Julius Jackson	JSm	Joe Simon
GB	Geoffrey Biggs	HwP	Howard Post	JJo	J.B. Jones	JSn	Jim Starlin
GBl	George Bell	HyG	Harley Griffiths	JJu	Joe Jusko	JSo	Jim Steranko
GBu	Greg Budget	IaC	Ian Churchhill	JK	Jack Kirby	JSon	Joe Staton
GC	Gene Colan	IEd	Ian Edginton	JKa	Jack Kamen	JsP	Jay Scott Pike
GCa	Greg Capullo	IG	Ian Gibson	JkS	Jack Sparling	JSt	Joe Sinnott
GCh	Gary Cohn	IK	Ian Kennedy	JKu	Joe Kubert	JT	James Tucker
GD	Gene Day	IN	Irv Novick	JKz	Jack Katz	JTg	John Tartaglione
GDu	Gary Dumm	IS	Irving Spector	JL	Jose Lopez	JTo	John Totleben
GE	George Evans	ISb	Irvin Steinberg	JLb	Jeph Loeb	JuB	Julie Bell
GeH	Gene Ha	IV	Ivan Velez, Jr.	JLd	Joe Lansdale	JV	Jim Valentino
GEn	Garth Ennis	JA	Jack Abel	JLe	Jim Lee	JVF	John Van Fleet
GEr	Gary Erskine	JaB	Jack Binder	JLi	Joseph M. Linsner	JW	Jack A Warren
GF	Glenn Fabry	JaD	Jamie Delano	JIT	Jill Thompson	JWa	Jim Watson
GfD	Geof Darrow	JaL	Jae Lee	JLv	Jim Lavery	JWf	Joseph Wolfe
GFo	Gerald Forton	JAl	Jeff Albrecht	JM	Jim Mooney	JWi	J.H. Williams
GFr	Gary Frank	JAn	Jeff Anderson	JMC	John McCrea	JWk	John Watkiss
GFs	George Frese	JAo	John Albano	JMd	Joe Madureira	JWo	Jim Woodring
GFx	Gill Fox	JAp	Jim Aparo	JMD	J.M. DeMatteis	JWp	Jason Waltrip
GG	Gabe Gecko	JAr	John Arcudi	JMi	Jeff Mariotte	JWt	John Waltrip
Ggn	Geggan	JB	John Buscema	JmL	Jim Lawson	JyD	Jay Disbrow
GgP	George Pratt	JBa	Jim Baikie	JMn	Joe Maneely	JyS	Jerry Serpe
GHe	Gilbert Hernandez	JBa	Jim Balent	JmP	James Pascoe	JZ	Jorge Zaffino
GHi	Graham Higgins	JBe	John Beeston	JMr	Jeff Moore	JZe	Joe Zabel
GI	Geoff Isherwood	JBg	Jon Bogdanove	JMs	Jeff Matsuda	JZy	Joseph Zyskowski
GiS	Gilbert Shelton	JBi	Jerry Bingham	JMt	Joe Martin	K&R	Kane & Romita
GJ	Gerard Jones	JBl	Jesus Blasco	JMu	Jon J. Muth	KB	Kyle Baker
GK	Gil Kane	JBm	John Broom	JMy	Jeffrey Moy	KBa	Ken Battlefield
GKl	George Klein	JBn	John Burns	JMy	Jim McCarthy	KBk	Kurt Busiek
GL	Garry Leach	JBo	John Bolton	JMz	Jose Marzan	KD	Kieron Dwyer
GlD	Glyn Dillon	JBr	June Brigman	JnM	Jason Minor	KDe	Kim Deitch
GLz	Greg Luzniak	JBt	Jeff Butler	JnR	John Riley	KDM	Kim DeMulder
GM	Gray Morrow	JBu	Jack Burnley	JNR	John Ney Rieber	KEa	Kevin Eastman
GMc	Gerald McCann	JBy	John Byrne	JnS	John Smith	KeL	Ken Lashley
GMo	Grant Morrison	JBz	Joe Benitez	JO	Joe Orlando	KeW	Kevin Walker
GMy	Graham Manley	JCa	John Calnan	JoA	Jo Alibaster	KG	Keith Giffen
GN	Graham Nolan	JCf	Jim Calafiore	JoB	Joe Bennett	KGa	Kerry Gammill
GP	George Perez	JCh	Joe Chiodo	JoC	Joe Casey	KHd	Kevin Hopgood
GPi	Gene Pamai	JCo	Jack Cole	JOb	James O'Barr	KHt	Kyle Hotz
GrI	Graham Ingles	JCp	John Cooper	JoG	Joe Giella	KHu	Ken Hultgren
GrL	Greg LaRocque	JCr	Johnny Craig	JoM	Joe Musial	KiA	Kia Asamiya

Abbr	Name	Abbr	Name	Abbr	Name	Abbr	Name
KJ	Klaus Janson	MCi	Mark Crilley	MSy	Mike Sekowsky	RA	Ross Andru
KJa	Kirk Javinen	MCl	Mike Clark	MSz	J.Michael Straczynski	RAJ	R.A. Jones
KJo	Kelley Jones	MCn	Max Allan Collins	MT	Mark Texeira	RaP	Rachel Pollack
KK	Karl Kesel	MCo	Mark Chiarello	MtB	Matt Broome	RB	Rich Buckler
KlA	Karl Alstaetter	MCr	Mike Carlin	MTk	Masashi Tanaka	RbB	Robert Bernstein
KlK	Karl Kerschl	MCW	M.C. Wyman	MV	Mike Vosburg	RbC	Robert Campenella
KlS	Karl Story	MCy	Mike Carey	MvR	Melvin Rubi	RBe	Ramon Bernado
KM	Kevin Maguire	MD	Mort Drucker	MvS	Marvin Stein	RBn	Ryan Benjamin
KN	Kevin Nowlan	MD2	Mike Deodato, Jr.	MW	Mary Wilshire	RBr	Rick Burchett
KoK	Kevin Kobasic	MDa	Malcolm Davis	MWa	Mark Waid	RBu	Robert Burns
KON	Kevin O'Neill	MDb	M. DeZuniga	MWg	Matt Wagner	RC	Reed Crandall
KP	Keith Pollard	MDb	Maurice Del Bourgo	MWn	Marv Wolfman	RCa	Richard Case
KPl	Kilian Plunkett	MDo	Mike Dorey	MWs	M. Weiss	RCl	Ricky Carralero
KR	Kim Raymond	MDr	Mike Dringenberg	Mys	Myers	RCo	Richard Corben
Kr	Kirner	ME	Mike Esposito	MZ	Mike Zeck	RCr	Robert Crumb
KS	Kurt Schaffenberger	MEg	Marty Egeland	MZi	Michael Zulli	RCz	Roger Cruz
KSm	Kevin Smith	MeP	Mike Parobeck	NA	Neal Adams	RDB	Randy DuBerkr
KSW	Keith S. Wilson	MeW	Mike Weringo	NBy	Norm Breyfogle	RdM	Raymond Marais
KSy	Ken Steacy	MF	Matt Fox	NC	Nick Cardy	RDm	Rodolfo Damaggio
KtH	Kurt Hathaway	MFl	Michael Fleisher	ND	Nigel Dobbyn	RdD	Richard Delgado
KVH	Kevin VanHook	MFm	Mark Farmer	Nel	Nelson	RE	Ric Estrada
KW	Kent Williams	MFr.	Michael Jan Friedman	NGa	Neil Gaiman	REv	Ray Evans
KWe	Kevin West	MG	Mike Gustovich	NHa	Neil Hanson	RF	Ron Frenz
KWi	Keith Williams	MGi	Michael T. Gilbert	NKu	Andy Kubert	RFl	Robert Fleming
KWo	Kirk Van Wormer	MGo	Michael Golden	NMa	Nathan Massengill	RG	Ron Garney
LbC	Leonard B. Cole	MGr	Mike Grell	NN	Norman Nodel	RGd	Ruben Gerard
LC	Lou Cameron	MGs	Martin Griffiths	NNa	Nick Napolitano	RgM	Rags Morales
LCh	Lillian Chestney	MGu	Mark Gruenwald	NPl	Noly Panalign	RGr	Randy Green
LDr	Larry Dresser	MGy	Mick Gray	NR	Nestor Redondo	RGs	R. Grossman
LDu	Leo Duranona	MHi	Michael Higgins	NRd	Norm Rapmund	RGT	R.G. Taylor
LDz	Luis Dominguez	MHo	Matt Howarth	NS	Norm Saunders	RGu	Rebecca Guay
LEl	Lee Elias	MHs	Mike Heisler	NSH	N. Steven Harris	RH	Russ Heath
LeS	Len Strazewski	MHw	Matt Hawkins	NV	Neil Vokes	RHa	Rory Hayes
LF	Lou Fine	MHy	Matt Haley	NyC	Nancy Collins	RHe	Richard Horie
LHa	Larry Hama	MI	Medio Iorio	OM	Otto Messmer	RHo	Rick Hoberg
LI	Larry Ivie	MiA	Michael Allred	OW	Ogden Whitney	RHo	Rich Howell
LiM	Linda Medley	MiB	Mike Barr	PaD	Paco Diaz	RiB	Richard Bennett
LJi	Leonardo Jimenez	MiS	Mizuki Sakakibara	PaK	Paris T. Karounos	Rip	Riply
LKa	Len Kaminski	MJ	Malcolm Jones	PaP	Paul Pelletier	RJ	Robert Jenney
LLe	Lank Leonard	MK	Mike Kaluta	PB	Pat Broderick	RJn	Robert Jones
LLi	Larry Lieber	MkB	Mike Barreiro	PBd	Philip Bond	RkB	Rick Bryant
LM	Lou Morales	MKd	Malcolm Kildale	PC	Paul Chadwick	RkL	Rick Leach
LMa	Larry Mahlstedt	MkF	Mike Friedrich	PcH	Poch	RKu	Roy Krenkel
LMc	Luke McDonnell	MkH	Mike Hoffer	PCu	Paris Cullins	RL	Rick Leonardi
LMd	Lee Moder	MkK	Mike McKenna	PD	Peter Doherty	RLd	Rob Liefeld
LMr	Lee Marrs	MkW	Mark Wheatley	PDd	Peter David	RLe	Rik Levins
LnS	Lin Streeter	MlB	Michael Bair	PDi	Paul Dini	RLg	Roger Langridge
Low	John Lowe	MLe	Mike Leeke	PFe	Pascual Ferry	RLm	Ron Lim
LRs	Luke Ross	MLr	Michael Lark	PG	Paul Gulacy	RLv	R. Livingstone
LS	Lee Sullivan	MM	Mike Manley	PGa	Phil Gascoine	RM	Rick Magyar
LSh	Liam Sharp	MMc	M. McMahon	PGn	Paul Guinan	RMc	Ralph Macchio
LSi	Louise Simonson	MMe	Mort Meskin	PGr	Peter Grau	RMn	Roland Mann
LSn	Larry Stroman	MMi	Michael Mignola	PGv	Paul Gustavson	RMo	Ruben Moreira
LSt	Leonard Starr	MMK	Mike McKone	PhH	Phil Hester	RMr	Roy Allan Martinez
LuH	Lou Harrison	MMo	Mark Moretti	PJ	Phil Jimminiz	RMz	Ron Marz
LW	Lee Weeks	MMr	Mark Millar	PJe	Paul Jenkins	RN	Rudy Nebres
LWn	Len Wein	MMy	Marat Mychaels	PKr	Peter Krause	RnT	Ron Tinker
LyW	Larry Welch	MN	Mike Netzer	PlA	Paul Abrams	RoR	Ron Randall
LZ	Louis Zansky	MnN	Martin Nodell	PLa	Peter Laird	RoW	on Wagner
MA	Murphy Anderson	Moe	Moebius	PMo	Pete Morisi	RP	Rudy Palais
MaG	Manny Galan	MP	Mike Ploog	PMs	Pat Mills	RPc	Richard Pace
MaH	Mark Hempel	MPa	Mark Pacella	PNe	Paul Neary	RPi	Richard Pini
Man	Roland Mann	MPc	Mark Paniccia	PNu	Philip Nutman	RQu	Randy Queen
MaS	Mark Schmitz	MPk	Martin Pasko	PO	Patrick Olliffe	RR	Ray Ramsey
MaT	Mark Tenney	MPn	Mark Pennington	PP	Pop Payne	RRa	Rich Rankin
MB	Matt Baker	MR	Marshall Rogers	PPo	Paul Pope	RS	Ron Smith
MBa	Mark Bagley	MRa	Mac Raboy	PPr	Pat Prichard	RsB	Russell Braun
MBe	M. Belardinelli	MRc	Mark Ricketts	PQ	Peter Quinones	RSd	Randy Stradley
MBg	Mark Badger	MRi	Mike Richardson	PR	Paul Ryan	RsM	Russ Manning
MBi	M. Bailey	MRo	Mike Roberts	PrC	Peter Costanza	RSm	Robin Smith
MBm	Mary Bierbaum	MRy	Matt Ryan	PrG	Peter Gross	RSt	Roger Stern
MBn	Mike Baron	MS	Mark Silvestri	PrM	Peter Milligan	RT	Romeo Tanghal
MBr	Mark Bright	MSe	Marie Severin	PS	Paul Smith	RtH	Robert Hebbard
MBu	Mark Buckingham	MSh	Mark Schultz	PSj	Peter Snejbjerg	RTs	Roy Thomas
MBy	Mitch Byrd	MsM	Mike S. Miller	PtL	Patrick Lee	RtU	Ron Turner
MC	Mike Collins	MSo	Mark Sasso	PuD	Paul Danner	RuG	Rube Goldberg
MCa	Marc Campos	MSt	Malcolm Smith	PuJ	Paul Johnson	RV	Rick Veitch
MCh	Mike Chen	MsW	Morris Waldinger	PuK	Paul Kupperberg	RvB	Raeburn Van Buren

RW ..... Robert Williams	SLi .... Steve Lightle	TBd...... Tim Bradstreet	TSr ..... Terry Shoemaker
RWa .... Reed Waller	SLo .... Scott Lobdell	TBe........ Terry Beatty	TT ...... Timothy Truman
RWb ...... Robert Webb	SM........ Steve Miller	TBm ..... Tom Bierbaum	TTg....... Tom Taggart
RyE .... Randy Emberlin	SMa . Shawn Martinbrough	TC....... Travis Charest	TTn....... Ty Templeton
RyL........ Ray Lago	SmC........ Sam Citron	TCk ...... Tomm Coker	TV .... Tim Vigil
RyR..... Rodney Ramos	SMc ..... Scott McDaniel	TD ...... Tony DeZuniga	TVE.... Trevor Von Ecdon
S&K .... Simon & Kirby	SMl .... Scott McCloud	TDF ..... Tom DeFalco	TvS....... Trevor Scott
S&S .... Siegel & Shuster	SML .... Sean McLaughlin	TDr....... Tom Derenick	TWo ...... Teri Sue Wood
SA..... Sergio Aragones	SMo .... Sheldon Moldoff	TDz ..... Todd DeZago	TY .... Tom Yeates
SaB ..... Sam Becker	SMt ..... Steve Mattsson	TeB ..... Tex Blaisdell	TyD....... Terry Dodson
Sal....... Sal Amendola	SMz .. Seymour Moskowitz	TeH ...... Ted Halsted	TyH ...... Tony Harris
SAP .. Shea Anton Pensa	SnW ..... Stan Woch	TEl ...... Tim Eldred	TyT....... Tony Tallarico
SaV....... Sal Velluto	SPa ...... Stephen Platt	TFH.......... T. F. Hing	VAz ..... Vincent Alcazar
SB........ Sal Buscema	Spk .... Spark	TG ...... Tom Grummett	VB ...... Vaughn Bode
SBi .... Stephen Bissette	SPl...... Scott Phillips	TGb ..... Tom Grindberg	VcL....... Vince Locke
SBs ..... Simon Bisley	SPr..... Stefan Petrucha	TGo ..... Till Goodman	VGi....... Vince Giarrano
SBt .... Steve Butler	SR........ Steve Rude	TH........ Tim Hamilton	ViC....... Vince Colletta
SC........ Sid Check	SRf ..... Sean Ruffner	THa ...... Tim Harris	VMk....... Val Mayerik
ScB .... Scott Benefiel	SRo ..... Spain Rodriguez	TJn ...... Todd Johnson	VMo..... Vincent Morosco
ScC ..... Scott Clark	SS........ Stan Sakai	TKa ..... Terry Kavanagh	VP....... Victor Prezio
SCh ...... Sean Chen	SSc..... Sean Scoffield	TKn ..... Trent Kaniuga	VRu ..... Vince Russell
SCi ...... Sergio Cariello	SSe.... Steven T. Seagle	TKr .. Teddy H. Kristiansen	VS .... Val Semeiks
ScK ...... Scott Kolins	SSh ..... Sean Shaw	TL ...... Tom Lyle	VV .... Vagner Vargas
ScL........ Scott Lee	SSh ..... Syd Shores	TLa ...... Terry LaBan	WaP..... Warren Pleece
SCp ...... Sam Cooper	SSm ..... Steve Sampson	TLw ..... Terral Lawrence	WB ...... Wayne Boring
SCr....... Steve Crespo	SSr..... Steve Skroce	TM ...... Todd McFarlane	WBu..... W. Burroughs
SCW..... S. Clay Wilson	SSt....... Steve Stern	TmB ...... Tim Burgard	WE .... Will Eisner
SCy ...... Simon Colby	ST........ Sal Trapaln	TmC .... Tom Christopher	WEl....... Warren Ellis
SD .... Steve Ditko	StA...... Stephen Addeo	TMd ..... Tom Mandrake	WiS....... William Stout
SDi .... Steve Dillon	StB ..... Scott Benson	TMK ..... Ted McKeever	WJo..... Walter Johnson
SDr........ Stan Drake	StC ..... Stan Campbell	TMo ...... Tom Morgan	WK........ Walt Kelly
SDR .... Sam DeLaRosa	StE ..... Steve Erwin	TmR ...... Tom Ryder	Wld..... Andrew Wildman
SEa....... Scott Eaton	StG ..... Steve Grant	TMr....... Terry Moore	WlP....... Walter Palais
SeM ..... Steve Montano	StK....... Stan Kaye	TMs ...... Tom Mason	WmB..... William Bossart
SeP ...... Sean Phillips	StL....... Stan Lee	TmT ...... Tom Teney	WMc .... Walter McDaniel
SEp ...... Steve Epting	StM..... Stanley Maxwell	TMw ..... Tom McCraw	WMo .... Win Mortimer
SeT ...... Steve Tappin	StP....... Steve Pugh	TNa....... Ted Naifeh	WmW .... William Walsh
SEt ..... Steve Englehart	SVa ..... Steve Vance	TnD....... Tony Daniel	Woj.... Chuck Wojtkiewicz
SF ..... Sal Finnocchiaro	SvG ..... Steve Gerber	TnS ..... Tristan Schane	WP....... Wendy Pini
SFr..... Simon Freeman	SvL ..... Salvador Larroca	TNu....... Todd Nauck	WPo .... Whilce Portacio
SFu .... Simon Furman	SvP..... Steve Parkhouse	TO .... Thomas Oughton	WR ...... Werner Roth
SG...... Sam Glanzman	SvS ..... Steve Stiles	ToT ..... Tony Takezaki	WS....... Walt Simonson
SGa.... Stefano Gaudino	SW ..... Scott Williams	TOz ...... Tayyar Ozkan	WSm .... Will Simpson
SGe......... Sid Greene	SWi..... Skip Williamson	TP....... Tom Palmer	WW ...... Wally Wood
SHa ...... Scott Hanna	SwM.... Shawn McManus	TPe...... Tom Peyer	YG........ Yvel Guichet
ShG.... Shannon Gallant	SY ..... Steve Yeowell	TR........ Tom Raney	YuK ...... Yukito Kisniro
ShM..... Sheldon Mayer	Syk............ Siryk	TR......... Ted Richards	
SHn ..... Simon Harrison	SyM..... Sidney Miller	TrR....... Trina Robbins	
SHp ..... Scott Hampton	SZ .... Steven Zyskowski	TS......... Tom Sutton	
SI ...... Stuart Immonen	TA ...... Terry Austin	TSa ...... Tony Salmons	
SK ...... Sam Kieth	TAr .... Tom Artis	TSe .... Tim Sale	
SL....... Steve Leialoha	TB .... Tim Boxell	TSg...... Tom Sniegoski	

GENERAL ABBREVIATIONS FOR COMICS LISTINGS

A: .... Appearance of	GAm .... Graphic Album	pt. or Pt............... Part
(a)..................... Artist	GN or GNv...... Graphic Novel	rep. .... Reprinted issue
Adapt. .... Adaptation	G-Size .... Giant Size	R:........... Return/Revival of
Anniv........... Anniversary	HC .... Hardcover	rtd.............. Retold
Ann.#................. Annual	I:......... Introduction of	(s) .... Scripted/Written by
(a&c)........ Art & Cover	(i)............. Inks by	S.A. .... Silver Age
(a&pl)............ Art & Plot	IR:........ Identity Revealed	SC .... Softcover
(a&s)......... Art & Script	J:............ Joins of	(s&i)....... Scripts & inks
B:............. Beginning of	K-Size .... King Size	Spec............. Special
b:................ Birth of	L:.......... Leaving of	TPB ...... Trade Paperback
BU:...... Back-Up Story	N:......... New Costume	T.U. .... Team-up
C:........ Cameo Appearance	N#......... No Issue Number	V: or vs............. Versus
(c).................. Cover	O:.......... Origin of	W:.......... Wedding of
(c&s)...... Cover and Script	P(c) .... Painted Cover	w/................ With
D:...... Death/Destruction of	(p)............ Pencils by	w/o .... Without
Ed.................. Edition	PF .... Prestige Format	x-over .... Crossover with
E:............. Ending of	Ph(c) ...... Photographic cover	
F:.............. Features	(pl)........... Plotted by	
G.A............. Golden Age	Prev............. Preview	

BIBLIOGRAPHY

Daniels, Les. *Comix: A History of Comic Books in America*. New York, NY: Bonanza Books, 1971.

Gerber, Ernst. *The Photo Journal Guide to Comic Books*. Minden, NV: Gerber Publishing, 1989. Vols. 1 & 2.

Gerber, Ernst. *The Photo Journal Guide to Marvel Comics*. Minden, NV: Gerber Publishing, 1991. Vols. 3 & 4.

Goulart, Ron. *The Adventurous Decade*. New Rochelle, NY: Arlington House, 1975.

Goulart, Ron. *Comic Book Culture, An Illustrated History*. Portland, OR: Collectors Press, 2000

Goulart, Ron. *The Encyclopedia of American Comics*. New York, NY. Facts on File Publications, 1990.

Goulart, Ron. *Over 50 Years of American Comic Books*. Lincolnwood, IL: Mallard Press, 1991.

Hegenburger, John. *Collectors Guide to Comic Books*. Radnor, PA: Wallace Homestead Book Company, 1990.

Kennedy, Jay. *The Official Underground and Newave Price Guide*. Cambridge, MA: Boatner Norton Press, 1982.

Malan, Dan. *The Complete Guide to Classics Collectibles*. St. Louis, MO: Malan Classical Enterprises, 1991.

Miller, John Jackson et al. *The Standard Catalog of Comic Books*. Iola, WI: Krause Publications, 2002.

O'Neil, Dennis. *Secret Origins of DC Super Heroes*. New York, NY: Warner Books, 1976.

Overstreet, Robert. *The Overstreet Comic Book Price Guide (35th Edition)*. New York, NY. Random House, 2005

Rovin, Jeff. *The Encyclopedia of Super Heroes*. New York, NY: Facts on File Publications, 1985.

Rovin, Jeff. *The Encyclopedia of Super Villians*. New York, NY: Facts on File Publications, 1987.

Thompson, Don & Maggie. *The Golden Age of Comics, Summer 1982*. Tainpa, FL: New Media Publishing, 1982.

DC COMICS

A. BIZARRO
1999
1 (of 4) SvG,MBr,F:Al Bizarro 2.50
2 SvG,MBr,A:Superman 2.50
3 SvG,MBr, ... 2.50
4 SvG,MBr, Viva Bizarro 2.50

ACCELERATE
DC/Vertigo, June, 2000
1 (of 4) Great Escape 3.00
2 Great Escape,pt.2 . . . . 3.00
3 Great Escape,pt.3 . . . . 3.00
4 Great Escape,pt.4,concl. 3.00

Action Comics #17 © DC Comics, Inc.

ACTION
June, 1938
1 JoS,I&O:Superman;Rescues Evelyn
   Curry from electric chair . 575,000.00
2 JoS,V:Emil Norvell 60,000.00
3 JoS,V:Thorton Blakely 40,000.00
4 JoS,V:Coach Randall 25,000.00
5 JoS,Emergency of
   Vallegho Dam 25,000.00
6 JoS,I:Jimmy Olsen,
   V:Nick Williams 25,000.00
7 JoS,V:Derek Niles 50,000.00
8 JoS,V:Gimpy 15,000.00
9 JoS,A:Det.Captain Reilly . . 15,000.00
10 JoS,Superman fights
   for prison reform 30,000.00
11 JoS,Disguised as
   Homer Ramsey 7,500.00
12 JoS,Crusade against
   reckless drivers 8,000.00
13 JoS,I:Ultra Humanite 15,000.00
14 JoS,BKa,V:Ultra Humanite,
   B:Clip Carson 8,000.00
15 JoS,BKa,Superman in
   Kidtown 15,000.00
16 JoS,BKa,Crusade against
   Gambling 8,000.00
17 JoS,BKa,V:Ultra Humanite. 12,000.00
18 JoS,BKa,V:Mr.Hamilton
   O:Three Aces 8,000.00
19 JoS,BKa,V:Ultra Humanite
   B:Superman (c) 12,000.00
20 JoS,BKa,V:Ultra Humanite. 10,000.00
21 JoS,BKa,V:Ultra Humanite. 10,000.00

22 JoS,BKa,War between Toran
   and Galonia 10,000.00
23 JoS,BKa,SMo,I:Lex Luthor 16,000.00
24 JoS,BKa,BBa,SMo,FGu,Meets
   Peter Carnahan 10,000.00
25 JoS,BKa,BBa,SMo,
   V:Medini 10,000.00
26 JoS,BKa,V:ClarenceCobalt 10,000.00
27 JoS,BKa,V:Mr & Mrs.Tweed 6,000.00
28 JoS,BKa,JBu,V:Strongarm
   Bandit 6,000.00
29 JoS,BKa,V:Martin 7,000.00
30 JoS,BKa,V:Zolar 6,000.00
31 JoS,BKa,JBu,V:Baron
   Munsdorf 4,000.00
32 JoS,BKa,JBu,I:Krypto Ray Gun
   V:Mr.Preston 4,000.00
33 JoS,BKa,JBu,V:Brett Hall,
   O:Mr. America 4,000.00
34 JoS,BKa,V:Jim Laurg 4,000.00
35 JoS,BKa,V:Brock Walter . . 4,000.00
36 JoS,BKa,V:StuartPemberton 4,000.00
37 JoS,BKa,V:Commissioner
   Kennedy, O:Congo Bill . . . 3,900.00
38 JoS,BKa,V:Harold Morton . 3,900.00
39 JoS,BKa,Meets Britt Bryson 3,900.00
40 JoS,BKa,Meets Nancy
   Thorgenson 3,900.00
41 JoS,BKa,V:Ralph Cowan,
   E:Clip Carson 3,500.00
42 V:Lex Luthor,I&O:Vigilante . 5,000.00
43 V:Dutch O'Leary,Nazi(c) . . 3,500.00
44 V:Prof. Steffens,Nazi(c) . . . 3,500.00
45 V:Count Von Henzel,
   I:Stuff,Nazi(c) 3,500.00
46 V:The Domino 3,500.00
47 V:Lex Luthor—1st app. w/super
   powers,I:Powerstone 5,000.00
48 V:The Top 3,200.00
49 I:Puzzler 3,200.00
50 Meets Stan Doborak 3,200.00
51 I:Prankster 4,000.00
52 V:Emperor of America 4,500.00
53 JBu,V:Night-Owl. 3,500.00
54 JBu,Meets Stanley
   Finchcomb 3,500.00
55 JBu,V:Cartoonist Al Hatt . . 3,500.00
56 V:Emil Loring 3,500.00
57 V:Prankster 3,500.00
58 JBu,V:Adonis 3,500.00
59 I:Susie Thompkins,Lois
   Lane's niece 3,500.00
60 JBu,Lois Lane-Superwoman 3,500.00
61 JBu,Meets Craig Shaw 3,500.00
62 JBu,V:Admiral Von Storff . . 3,500.00
63 JBu,V:Professor Praline 3,500.00
64 I:Toyman 3,500.00
65 JBu,V:Truman Treadwell . . 3,500.00
66 JBu,V:Mr.Annister 3,500.00
67 JBu,Superman School for
   Officer's Training 3,500.00
68 A:Susie Thompkins 3,500.00
69 V:Prankster 3,500.00
70 JBu,V:Thinker 3,500.00
71 Superman Valentine's
   Day Special 3,000.00
72 V:Mr. Sniggle 3,000.00
73 V:Lucius Spruce 3,000.00
74 Meets Adelbert Dribble 3,000.00
75 V:Johnny Aesop 3,000.00
76 A Voyage with Destiny 3,000.00
77 V:Prankster 3,000.00
78 The Chef of Bohemia 3,000.00
79 JBu,A:J. Wilbur Wolfingham 3,000.00
80 A:Mr. Mxyzptlk (2nd App) . . . 3,500.00
81 Meets John Nicholas 3,000.00
82 JBu,V:Water Sprite 3,000.00

83 I:Hocus and Pocus 3,000.00
84 JBu,V:Dapper Gang 3,000.00
85 JBu,V:Toyman 3,000.00
86 JBu,V:Wizard of Wokit 3,000.00
87 V:Truck Hijackers 3,000.00
88 A:Hocus and Pocus 3,000.00
89 V:Slippery Andy 3,000.00
90 JBu,V:Horace Rikker and the
   Amphi-Bandits 3,000.00
91 JBu,V:Davey Jones 900.00
92 JBu,V:Nowmie Norman 900.00
93 Superman Christmas story . . . 900.00
94 JBu,V:Bullwer 'Bull' Rylie 900.00
95 V:Prankster 900.00
96 V:Mr. Twister 900.00
97 A:Hocus and Pocus 900.00
98 V:Mr. Mxyzptlk, A:Susie
   Thompkins 3,500.00
99 V:Keith Langwell 900.00
100 I:InspectorErskineHawkins. 1,300.00
101 V:Specs Dour,A-Bomb(c) . . 1,900.00
102 V:Mr. Mxyzptlk 1,400.00
103 V:Emperor Quexo 1,400.00
104 V:Prankster 1,400.00
105 Superman Christmas story 1,400.00
106 Clark Kent becomes Baron
   Edgestream 1,400.00
107 JBu,A:J.Wilbur Wolfingham 1,400.00
108 JBu,V:Vince Vincent 1,400.00
109 V:Prankster 1,400.00
110 A:Susie Thompkins 800.00
111 Cameras in the Clouds 800.00
112 V:Mr. Mxyzptlk 1,400.00
113 Just an Ordinary Guy 1,400.00
114 V:Mike Chesney 1,400.00
115 Meets Arthur Parrish 1,400.00
116 A:J. Wilbur Wolfingham . . . 1,400.00
117 Superman Christmas story 1,400.00
118 Execution of Clark Kent . . . 1,400.00
119 Meets Jim Banning 1,400.00
120 V:Mike Foss 1,400.00
121 V:William Sharp 1,400.00
122 V:Charley Carson 1,400.00
123 V:Skid Russell 1,400.00
124 Superman becomes
   radioactive 1,200.00
125 V:Lex Luthor 750.00
126 V:Chameleon 1,200.00
127 JKu,Superman on Truth or
   Consequences 2,100.00
128 V:'Aces' Deucey 2,000.00
129 Meets Gob-Gob 2,000.00

Action Comics #89 © DC Comics, Inc.

All comics prices listed are for *Near Mint* condition.   **CVA Page 25**

Action Comics #128 © DC Comics, Inc.

130 V:Captain Kidder 2,000.00
131 V:Lex Luthor. 2,000.00
132 Superman meets George
 Washington. 2,000.00
133 V:Emma Blotz 2,000.00
134 V:Paul Strong. 2,000.00
135 V:John Morton 2,000.00
136 Superman Show-Off! 2,000.00
137 Meets Percival Winter 2,000.00
138 Meets Herbert Hinkle. 2,000.00
139 Clark Kent...Daredevil! 2,000.00
140 Superman becomes Hermit 2,000.00
141 V:Lex Luthor. 2,000.00
142 V:Dan the Dip 2,000.00
143 Dates Nikki Larve. 2,000.00
144 O:Clark Kent reporting for
 Daily Planet 2,000.00
145 Meets Merton Gloop 2,000.00
146 V:Luthor 2,000.00
147 V:'Cheeks' Ross. 2,000.00
148 Superman, Indian Chief. . . 2,000.00
149 The Courtship on Krypton!. 2,000.00
150 V:Morko 2,000.00
151 V:Mr.Mxyzptlk,Lex Luthor
 and Prankster. 2,000.00
152 I:Metropolis Shutterbug
 Society 2,100.00
153 V:Kingpin 2,000.00
154 V:Harry Reed 2,000.00
155 V:Andrew Arvin 2,000.00
156 Lois Lane becomes Super-
 woman,V:Lex Luthor. 1,800.00
157 V:Joe Striker. 1,800.00
158 V:Kane Korrell
 O:Superman (retold). 2,500.00
159 Meets Oswald Whimple . . . 1,800.00
160 I:Minerva Kent 1,800.00
161 Meets Antara 1,800.00
162 V:'IT!' 1,800.00
163 Meets Susan Semple. 1,800.00
164 Meets Stefan Andriessen . . 1,800.00
165 V:Crime Czar 1,800.00
166 V:Lex Luthor. 1,800.00
167 V:Prof. Nero 1,800.00
168 O:Olaf. 1,800.00
169 Caveman Clark Kent!. 1,800.00
170 V:Mad Artist of Metropolis . 1,800.00
171 The Secrets of Superman . 1,800.00
172 Lois Lane..Witch! 1,800.00
173 V:Dragon Lang. 1,800.00
174 V:Miracle Twine Gang 1,800.00
175 V:John Vinden 1,800.00
176 V:Billion Dollar Gang 1,800.00
177 V:General. 1,800.00
178 V:Prof. Sands. 1,800.00
179 Superman in Mapleville . . . 1,800.00
180 V:Syndicate of Five 1,800.00

181 V:Diamond Dave Delaney . 1,200.00
182 Return from Planet Krypton 1,200.00
183 V:Lex Luthor. 1,200.00
184 Meets Donald Whitmore . . 1,200.00
185 V:Issah Pendleton 1,200.00
186 The Haunted Superman . . 1,200.00
187 V:Silver. 1,200.00
188 V:Cushions Raymond gang 1,200.00
189 Meets Mr.& Mrs. Vandeveir 1,200.00
190 V:Mr. Mxyzptlk 1,200.00
191 V:Vic Vordan 1,200.00
192 Meets Vic Vordan. 1,200.00
193 V:Beetles Brogan 1,200.00
194 V:Maln 1,200.00
195 V:Tiger Woman 1,200.00
196 Superman becomes Mental
 Man. 1,200.00
197 V:Stanley Stark. 1,200.00
198 The Six Lives of Lois Lane 1,200.00
199 V:Lex Luthor. 1,200.00
200 V:Morwatha 1,200.00
201 'V:Benny the Brute. 1,200.00
202 Lois Lane's X-Ray Vision. . 1,000.00
203 Meets Pietro Paresca 1,000.00
204 Meets Sam Spulby. 1,000.00
205 Sergeant Superman. 1,000.00
206 Imaginary story F:L.Lane. . 1,000.00
207 Four Superman Medals! . . 1,000.00
208 V:Mr. Mxyzptlk 1,000.00
209 V:'Doc' Winters 1,000.00
210 V:Lex,I:Superman Land . . . 1,000.00
211 Superman Spectaculars. . . 1,000.00
212 V:Thorne Varden 1,000.00
213 V:Paul Paxton 1,000.00
214 Superman,Sup.Destroyer! . 1,000.00
215 I:Superman of 2956 . . . . . . 1,000.00
216 A:Jor-El 1,000.00
217 Meets Mr&Mrs.Roger Bliss 1,000.00
218 I:Super-Ape from Krypton . 1,000.00
219 V:Art Shaler 1,000.00
220 Interplanetary Olympics . . . 1,000.00
221 V:Jay Vorrell 800.00
222 The Duplicate Superman . . 800.00
223 A:Jor-El 800.00
224 I:Superman Island. 800.00
225 The Death of Superman . . . 800.00
226 V:Lex Luthor 800.00
227 Man with Triple X-Ray Eyes 800.00
228 A:Superman Museum 800.00
229 V:Dr. John Haley. 800.00
230 V:Bart Wellins 800.00
231 Sir Jimmy Olsen, Knight of
 Metropolis 800.00
232 Meets Johnny Kirk 800.00
233 V:Torm. 800.00
234 Meets Golto 800.00
235 B:Congo Bill,
 B:Tommy Tomorrow. 800.00
236 A:Lex Luthor 800.00
237 V:Nebula Gang 800.00
238 I:King Krypton,the Gorilla . . 800.00
239 Superman's New Face 800.00
240 V:Superman Sphinx 800.00
241 WB,A:Batman,Fortress of
 Solitude (Fort Superman) . . 700.00
242 I&O:Brainiac. 5,000.00
243 Lady and the Lion 700.00
244 CS,A:Vul-Kor,Lya-La 700.00
245 WB,V:Kak-Kul 700.00
246 WB,A:Krypton Island. 700.00
247 WB,Superman Lost Parents 700.00
248 B&I:Congorilla. 700.00
249 A:Lex Luthor 700.00
250 WB,The Eye of Metropolis . 700.00
251 E:Tommy Tomorrow 700.00
252 I&O:Supergirl 5,000.00
253 B:Supergirl 1,300.00
254 I:Adult Bizarro 1,000.00
255 I:Bizarro Lois 800.00
256 Superman of the Future . . . 500.00
257 WB,JM,V:Lex Luthor. 500.00
258 A:Cosmic Man. 500.00

Action Comics #271 © DC Comics, Inc.

259 A:Lex Luthor,Superboy 500.00
260 A:Mighty Maid 500.00
261 I:Streaky,E:Congorilla 500.00
262 A:Bizarro 500.00
263 O:Bizarro World 600.00
264 V:Bizarro 500.00
265 A:Hyper-Man 500.00
266 A:Streaky,Krypto 500.00
267 JM,3rd A:Legion,I:Invisible
 Kid 1,200.00
268 WB,A:Hercules 400.00
269 A:Jerro. 400.00
270 CS,JM,A:Batman 500.00
271 A:Lex Luthor 400.00
272 A:Aquaman 400.00
273 A:Mr.Mxyzptlk 400.00
274 A:Superwoman 400.00
275 WB,JM,V:Brainiac 400.00
276 JM,6th A:Legion,I:Brainiac 5,
 Triplicate Girl,Bouncing Boy . 700.00
277 CS,JM,V:Lex Luthor 300.00
278 CS,Perry White Becomes
 Master Man 300.00
279 JM,V:Hercules,Samson 300.00
280 CS,JM,V:Braniac,
 A:Congorilla. 300.00
281 JM,A:Krypto 300.00
282 JM,V:Mxyzptlk. 300.00
283 CS,JM,A:Legion of Super
 Outlaws 400.00
284 A:Krypto,Jerro. 300.00
285 JM,Supergirl Existence Revealed,
 C:Legion (12th app.) 400.00
286 CS,JM,V:Lex Luthor 250.00
287 JM,A:Legion 250.00
288 JM,A:Mon-El 250.00
289 JM,A:Adult Legion. 250.00
290 JM,C:Phantom Girl 250.00
291 JM,V:Mxyzptlk. 250.00
292 JM,I:Superhorse 250.00
293 JM,O:Comet-Superhorse . . 300.00
294 JM,V:Lex Luthor 250.00
295 CS,JM,O:Lex Luthor 250.00
296 V:Super Ants 250.00
297 CS,JM,A:Mon-El 250.00
298 CS,JM,V:Lex Luthor 250.00
299 O:Superman Robots 250.00
300 JM,A:Mxyzptlk. 300.00
301 CS(c),JM,O:Superman 225.00
302 CS(c),JM,O:Superhorse . . . 200.00
303 CS(c),Red Kryptonite story . 225.00
304 CS,JM,I&O:Black Flame . . . 275.00
305 CS(c),O:Supergirl 225.00
306 JM,C:Mon-El,Brainiac 5 . . . 225.00
307 CS,JM,A:Saturn Girl 225.00
308 CS(c),V:Hercules 225.00
309 CS,A:Batman,JFK,Legion . . 275.00

310 CS,JM,I:Jewel Kryptonite . . . 200.00
311 CS,JM,O:Superhorse 200.00
312 CS,JM,V:Metallo-Superman . 200.00
313 JM,A:Supergirl,Lex,Batman . 200.00
314 JM,A:Justice League 200.00
315 JM,V:Zigi,Zag 200.00
316 JM,A:Zigi,Zag,Zyra 200.00
317 JM,V:Lex Luthor 200.00
318 CS,JM,A:Brainiac 200.00
319 CS,JM,A:Legion,V:L.Luthor . 200.00
320 CS,JM,V:Atlas,Hercules 200.00
321 CS,JM,A:Superhorse 200.00
322 JM,Coward of Steel 200.00
323 JM,A:Superhorse 200.00
324 JM,A:Abdul 200.00
325 CS,JM,SkyscraperSuperman 200.00
326 CS,JM,V:Legion of Super
   Creatures. 200.00
327 CS,JM,C:Brainiac 200.00
328 JM,Hands of Doom 200.00
329 JM,V:Drang 200.00
330 CS,JM,Krypto 200.00
331 CS,V:Dr.Supernatural 200.00
332 CS,A:Brainiac 200.00
333 CS(c),A:Lex Luthor 200.00
334 JM(c),A:Lex Luthor,80pgs. . . 300.00
335 CS,V:Lex Luthor 200.00
336 CS,O:Akvar. 200.00
337 CS,V:Tiger Gang. 200.00
338 CS,JM,V:Muto. 200.00
339 CS,V:Muto,Brainiac. 200.00
340 JM,I:Parasite. 200.00
341 CS,V:Vakox,A:Batman 175.00
342 WB,JM,V:Brainiac. 175.00
343 WB,V:Eterno 175.00
344 WB,JM,A:Batman 175.00
345 CS(c),A:Allen Funt 175.00
346 WB,JM 175.00
347 CS(c),A:Supergirl, 80pgs. . . . 250.00
348 WB,JM,V:Acid Master. 125.00
349 WB,JM,V:Dr.Kryptonite 125.00
350 A:JLA. 125.00
351 WB,I:Zha-Vam. 125.00
352 WB,V:Zha-Vam 125.00
353 WB,JM,V:Zha-Vam 125.00
354 JM,A:Captain Incredible 125.00
355 WB,JM,V:Lex Luthor. 125.00
356 WB,JM,V:Jr. Annihilitor 125.00
357 WB,JM,V:Annihilitor 125.00
358 NA(c),CS,JM,A:Superboy . . . 125.00
359 NA(c),CS,KS,C:Batman 125.00
360 CS(c),A:Supergirl, 80pgs. . . . 250.00
361 NA(c),A:Parasite 100.00
362 RA,KS,V:Lex Luthor 100.00
363 RA,KS,V:Lex Luthor 100.00
364 RA,KS,V:Lex Luthor 100.00
365 A:Legion & J.L.A. 100.00
366 RA,KS,A:J.L.A. 100.00
367 NA(c),CS,KS,A:Supergirl . . . 100.00
368 CS,KS,V:Mxyzptlk 100.00
369 CS,KS,Superman's Greatest
   Blunder 100.00
370 NA(c),CS,KS 100.00
371 NA(c),CS,KS 100.00
372 NA(c),CS,KS. 100.00
373 A:Supergirl,(giant size) 200.00
374 NA(c),CS,KS,V:Super Thief . . 75.00
375 KS,The Big Forget 75.00
376 CS,KS,E:Supergirl 75.00
377 CS,KS,B:Legion 75.00
378 CS,KS,V:Marauder 75.00
379 CS,JA,MA,V:Eliminator. 75.00
380 KS,Confessions of Superman. 75.00
381 CS,Dictators of Earth 75.00
382 CS,Clark Kent-Magician 60.00
383 CS,The Killer Costume 60.00
384 CS,The Forbidden Costume. . 60.00
385 CS,The Mortal Superman . . . 60.00
386 CS,Home For Old Superman . 60.00
387 CS,A:Legion,Even
   Supermen Die 60.00

388 CS,A:Legion,Puzzle of
   The Wild Word. 60.00
389 A:Legion,The Kid Who
   Struck Out Superman 60.00
390 CS,Self-Destruct Superman . . 60.00
391 CS,Punishment of
   Superman's Son 60.00
392 CS,E:Legion 60.00
393 CS,MA,RA,A:Super Houdini . . 60.00
394 CS,MA. 60.00
395 CS,MA,A:Althera. 60.00
396 CS,MA. 60.00
397 CS,MA,Imaginary Story 60.00
398 NA(c),CS,MA,I:Morgan Edge . 60.00
399 NA(c),CS,MA,A:Superbaby. . . 60.00
400 NA(c),CS,MA,Kandor Story . 100.00
401 CS,MA,V:Indians. 60.00
402 NA(c),CS,MA,V:Indians 75.00
403 CS,MA,Vigilante rep. 75.00
404 CS,MA,Aquaman rep. 75.00
405 CS,MA,Vigilante rep. 75.00
406 CS,MA,Atom & Flash rep. . . . 75.00
407 CS,MA,V:Lex Luthor 75.00
408 CS,MA,Atom rep. 75.00

Action Comics #423 © DC Comics Inc.

409 CS,MA,T.Tommorrow rep. . . . 75.00
410 CS,MA,T.Tommorrow rep. . . . 75.00
411 CS,MA,O:Eclipso rep. 75.00
412 CS,MA,Eclipso rep. 75.00
413 CS,MA,V:Brainiac 75.00
414 CS,MA,B:Metamorpho 40.00
415 CS,MA,V:Metroplis Monster . . 40.00
416 CS,MA. 40.00
417 CS,MA,V:Luthor 40.00
418 CS,MA,V:Luthor,
   E:Metamorpho. 40.00
419 CS,MA,CI,DG,I:HumanTarget . 45.00
420 CS,MA,DG,V:Towbee 35.00
421 CS,MA,B:Green Arrow 40.00
422 CS,DG,O:Human Target 35.00
423 CS,MA,DG,A:Lex Luthor. . . . 35.00
424 CS,MA,Green Arrow 40.00
425 CS,DD,NA,DG,B:Atom 75.00
426 CS,MA,Green Arrow 30.00
427 CS,MA,DD,DG,Atom. 30.00
428 CS,MA,DG,Luthor. 30.00
429 CS,BO,DG,C:JLA 30.00
430 CS,MA,DD,DG,Atom. 30.00
431 CS,MA,Green Arrow 30.00
432 CS,MA,DG,Toyman. 35.00
433 CS,BO,DD,DG,A:Atom 30.00
434 CS,DD,Green Arrow 30.00
435 FM(c),CS,DD,DG,Atom. 30.00
436 CS,DD,Green Arrow 30.00
437 CS,DG,Green Arrow,100-pg . . 60.00

438 CS,BO,DD,Atom. 30.00
439 CS,BO,DD,Atom. 30.00
440 1st MGr Green Arrow 45.00
441 CS,BO,MGr,A:Green Arrow,
   Flash,R:Krypto. 30.00
442 CS,MS,MGr,Atom 30.00
443 CS,A:JLA(100 pg.giant) 100.00
444 MGr,Green Arrow 30.00
445 MGr,Green Arrow 30.00
446 MGr,Green Arrow 30.00
447 CS,BO,RB,KJ,Atom 30.00
448 CS,BO,DD,JL,Atom 30.00
449 CS,BO,The Super-spy 40.00
450 MGr,Green Arrow 20.00
451 MGr,Green Arrow 15.00
452 CS,MGr,Green Arrow 15.00
453 CS,Atom 15.00
454 CS,E:Atom 15.00
455 CS,Green Arrow 15.00
456 CS,MGr,Green Arrow 15.00
457 CS,MGr,Green Arrow 15.00
458 CS,MGr,I:Black Rock 15.00
459 CS,BO,Blackrock 15.00
460 CS,I:Karb-Brak 15.00
461 CS,V:Karb-Brak 15.00
462 CS,V:Karb-Brak 15.00
463 CS,V:Karb-Brak 15.00
464 CS,KS,V:Pile-Driver 15.00
465 CS,FMc,Luthor 15.00
466 NA(c),CS,V:Luthor 15.00
467 CS,V:Mzyzptlk 15.00
468 NA(c),CS,FMc,V:Terra-Man. . 15.00
469 CS,TerraMan. 15.00
470 CS,Flash Green Lantern 15.00
471 CS,V:Phantom Zone Female . 15.00
472 CS,V:Faora Hu-Ul 15.00
473 NA(c),CS,Phantom Zone
   Villians. 15.00
474 KS,V:Doctor Light 15.00
475 KS,V:Karb-Brak,A:Vartox . . . 15.00
476 KS,V:Vartox. 15.00
477 CS,DD,Land Lords of Earth . . 15.00
478 CS,Earth's Last. 15.00
479 CS,Giant from Golden Atom . . 15.00
480 CS,A:JLA,V:Amazo 15.00
481 CS,A:JLA,V:Amazo 15.00
482 CS,Amazo. 15.00
483 CS,Amazo,JLA 15.00
484 CS,W:Earth 2 Superman
   & Lois Lane 25.00
485 NA(c),CS,rep.Superman#233. 20.00
486 GT,KS,V:Lex Luthor 15.00
487 CS,AS,O:Atom 15.00
488 CS,AS,A:Air Wave 15.00
489 CS,AS,A:JLA,Atom 15.00
490 CS,Brainiac. 15.00
491 CS,A:Hawkman. 15.00
492 CS,Superman's After Life 15.00
493 CS,A:UFO. 15.00
494 CS,Secret of the Super-S 15.00
495 CS,Attack of Ultimate Warrior 15.00
496 CS,A:Kandor. 15.00
497 CS,Command Performance . . 15.00
498 CS,Vartox 15.00
499 CS,Vartox 15.00
500 CS,Superman's Life Story
   A:Legion 28.00
501 KS,Mild-Mannered Superman . 7.00
502 CS,A:Supergirl,Gal.Golem 7.00
503 CS,A Save in Time 7.00
504 CS,The Power and Choice. . . . 7.00
505 CS,Creature that Charmed Kids 7.00
506 CS,V:Jorlan,Jor-El 7.00
507 CS,A:Jonathan Kent. 7.00
508 CS,A:Jonathan Kent 7.00
509 CS,JSn,DG 7.00
510 CS,Luthor 7.00
511 CS,AS,V:Terraman,
   A:Air Wave. 7.00
512 CS,RT,V:Luthor,A:Air Wave . . 7.00
513 CS,RT,V:Krell,A:Air Wave 7.00
514 CS,RT,V:Brainiac,A:Atom 7.00

Action Comics #606 © DC Comics, Inc.

515 CS,AS,A:Atom 7.00
516 CS,AS,V:Luthor,A:Atom 7.00
517 CS,DH,A:Aquaman 7.00
518 CS,DH,A:Aquaman 7.00
519 CS,DH,A:Aquaman 7.00
520 CS,DH,A:Aquaman 7.00
521 CS,AS,I:Vixen,A:Atom 7.00
522 CS,AS,A:Atom 7.00
523 CS,AS,A:Atom 7.00
524 CS,AS,A:Atom 7.00
525 JSon,FMc,AS,I:Neutron
    A:Air Wave 7.00
526 JSon,AS,V:Neutron 7.00
527 CS,AS,I:Satanis,A:Aquaman . . 9.00
528 CS,AS,V:Brainiac,A:Aquaman . 7.00
529 GP(c),CS,DA,AS,A:Aquaman,
    V:Brainiac 7.00
530 CS,DA,Brainiac 7.00
531 JSon,FMc,AS,A:Atom 7.00
532 CS,C:New Teen Titans 7.00
533 CS,V:H.I.V.E. 7.00
534 CS,AS,V:Satanis,A:Air Wave . . 7.00
535 GK(c),JSon,AS,
    A:Omega Men 7.00
536 JSon,AS,FMc,A:Omega Men . . 7.00
537 IN,CS,AS,V:Satanis
    A:Aquaman 7.00
538 IN,AS,FMc,V:Satanis,
    A:Aquaman 7.00
539 KG(c),GK,AS,DA,A:Flash,
    Atom,Aquaman 7.00
540 GK,AS,V:Satanis 7.00
541 GK,V:Satanis 7.00
542 AS,V:Vandal Savage 7.00
543 CS,V:Vandal Savage 7.00
544 CS,MA,GK,GP,45th Anniv.
    D:Ardora,Lexor 12.00
545 GK,Brainiac 7.00
546 GK,A:JLA,New Teen Titans . . . 7.00
547 GK(c),CS,V:Planeteer 7.00
548 GK(c),AS,Phantom Zone 7.00
549 GK(c),AS,Meets Zod Squad . . 7.00
550 AS(c),GT,Day Earth Exploded . 7.00
551 GK,Starfire becomes
    Red Star 7.00
552 GK,Forgotten Heroes
    (inc.Animal Man) 18.00
553 GK,Forgotten Heroes(inc.
    Animal Man) 18.00
554 GK(a&c) 7.00
555 CS,A:Parasite (X-over
    Supergirl #20) 7.00
556 CS,KS,C:Batman 7.00
557 CS,Terra-man 7.00
558 KS,All-Searing Eyes 7.00

559 KS,AS,Once & Future Peril . . . 7.00
560 AS,KG,BO,A:Ambush Bug . . 7.00
561 KS,WB,Toyman. 7.00
562 KS,Queen Bee 7.00
563 AS,KG,BO,A:Ambush Bug . . . 7.00
564 AS,V:Master Jailer 7.00
565 KG,KS,BO,A:Ambush Bug . . . 7.00
566 BO(i),MR. 7.00
567 KS,AS,PB 7.00
568 CS,AW,AN 7.00
569 IN,The Force of Revenge 7.00
570 KS, Jimmy Olsen's Alter-Ego . . 7.00
571 BB(c),AS,A:Thresh 222 . . . . . 7.00
572 WB,BO 7.00
573 KS,BO,AS 7.00
574 KS 7.00
575 KS,V:Intellax 7.00
576 KS,Earth's Sister Planet 7.00
577 KG,BO,V:Caitiff 7.00
578 KS,Parasite 7.00
579 KG,BO,Asterix Parody 7.00
580 GK(c),KS,Superman's Failure . 7.00
581 DCw(c),KS,Superman
    Requires Legal aid 7.00
582 AS,KS,Superman's Parents
    Alive. 7.00
583 CS,KS,AMo(s),Last Pre
    Crisis Superman 20.00
584 JBy,DG,A:NewTeenTitans,
    I:Modern Age Superman. 10.00
585 JBy,DG,Phantom Stranger 8.00
586 JBy,DG,Legends,V:New
    Gods,Darkseid. 8.00
587 JBy,DG,Demon 8.00
588 JBy,DG,Hawkman 8.00
589 JBy,DG,Gr.Lant.Corp. 8.00
590 JBy,DG,Metal Men 8.00
591 JBy,V:Superboy,A:Legion 8.00
592 JBy,Big Barda 8.00
593 JBy,Mr. Miracle 8.00
594 JBy,A:Booster Gold. 8.00
595 JBy,A:M.Manhunter,
    I:Silver Banshee 9.00
596 JBy,A:Spectre,Millenium 9.00
597 JBy,L.Starr(i),Lois V:Lana 9.00
598 JBy,TyT,I:Checkmate. 11.00
599 RA,JBy(i),A:MetalMen,
    Bonus Book 9.00
600 JBy,GP,KS,JOy,DG,CS,MA,
    MMi,A:Wonder Woman;
    Man-Bat,V:Darkseid 15.00
Becomes:

ACTION WEEKLY
1988–89

601 GK,DSp,CS,DJu,TD, B:Superman,
    Gr.Lantern,Blackhawk,Deadman,
    Secret Six,Wilddog 3.50
602 GP(c),GK,DSp,CS,DJu,TD . . . 3.50
603 GK,CS,DsP,DJu,TD 3.50
604 GK,DSp,CS,DJu,TD 3.50
605 NKu/AKu(c),GK,DSp,CS,
    DJu,TD 3.50
606 DSp,CS,DJu,TD 3.50
607 SLi(c),TD,DSp,CS,DJu 3.50
608 DSp,CS,DJu,TD,E:Blackhawk . 3.50
609 BB(c),DSp,DJu,TD,CS,
    E:Wild Dog,B:Black Canary. . . 3.50
610 KB,DJu,CS,DSp,TD,CS
    A:Phantom Stranger 3.50
611 AN(c),DJu,DSp,CS,BKi,TD,
    BKi,B:Catwoman 3.75
612 PG(c),DSp,CS,BKi,TD,
    E:Secret Six,Deadman 3.50
613 MK(c),BKi,CS,MA,TGr,
    Nightwing,B:Phantom Stranger . 3.50
614 TG,CS,Phantom Stranger
    E:Catwoman 3.50
615 MMi(c),CS,MA,BKi,TGr,
    Blackhawk,B:Wild Dog 3.50
616 ATh(c),CS,MA,E:Bl.Canary . . . 3.50
617 CS,MA,JO,A:Ph.Stranger 3.50

Action Comics #662 © DC Comics, Inc.

618 JBg(c),CS,MA,JKo,TD,
    B:Deadman,E:Nightwing 3.50
619 CS,MA,FS,FMc,KJo,TD,FMc,
    B:Sinister Six. 3.50
620 CS,MA,FS,FMc,KJo,TD 3.50
621 JO(c),CS,MA,FS,FMc,KJo,
    TD,MBr,E:Deadman 3.50
622 RF(c),MBr,TL,CS,MA,FS,
    FMc,A:Starman,E:Wild
    Dog,Blackhawk 3.50
623 MBr,TD,CS,MA,FS,FMc,JL,
    JKo,A:Ph.Stranger,
    B:Deadman,Shazam 3.50
624 AD(c),MBr,FS,FMc,CS,MA,
    TD,B:Black Canary 3.50
625 MBr,FS,FMc,CS,MA,
    TD,FMc 3.50
626 MBr,FS,FMc,CS,MA,JKo,TD,
    E:Shazam,Deadman 3.50
627 GK(c),MBr,RT,FS,FMc,CS,
    MA,TMd,B:Nightwing,Speedy . 3.50
628 TY(c),MBr,RT,TMd,CS,MA,
    FS,FMc,B:Blackhawk 3.50
629 CS,MA,MBr,RT,FS,FMc,TMd . 3.50
630 CS,MA,MBr,RT,FS,FMc,TMd,
    E:Secret Six. 3.50
631 JS(c),CS,MA,MBr,RT,TMd,
    B:Phantom Stranger 3.50
632 TGr(c),CS,MA,MBr,RT,TMd . . . 3.50
633 CS,MA,MBr,RT,TMd 3.50
634 CS,MA,MBr,RT,TMd,E:Ph.Strangr,
    Nightwing/Speedy,Bl.hawk 3.50
635 CS,MA,MBr,RT,EB,E:Black
    Canary,Green Lantern. 3.50
636 DG(c),CS,MA,NKu,MPa,FMc,
    B:Demon,Wild Dog,Ph.Lady,
    Speedy,A:Phantom Stranger . . . 3.50
637 CS,MA,KS,FMc,MPa,
    B:Hero Hotline 3.50
638 JK(c),CS,MA,KS,FMc,MPa. . . 3.50
639 CS,MA,KS,FMc,MPa 3.50
640 CS,KS,MA,FS,FMc,MPa,
    E:Speedy,Hero Hotline 3.50
641 CS,MA,JL,DG,MPa,E:Demon,
    Phant.Lady,Superman,Wild Dog,
    A:Ph.Stranger,Hum.Target. 3.50
642 GK,SD,ATi,CS,JAp,JM,CI,KN,
    Green Lantern,Superman 3.50

Becomes:

ACTION COMICS
1989–2005

643 B:RSt(s),GP,BBr,V:Intergang . . 4.50
644 GP,BBr,V:Matrix 3.50
645 GP,BBr,I:Maxima. 3.50

646 KG,V:Alien Creature,
A:Brainiac 4.00
647 GP,KGa,BBr,V:Brainiac. 3.50
648 GP,KGa,BBr,V:Brainiac. 3.50
649 GP,KGa,BBr,V:Brainiac. 3.50
650 JOy,BBr,CS,BMc,GP,KGa,
ATi,DJu,A:JLA,C:Lobo 5.50
651 JOy,BBr,D:Lex Luthor
Man #3,V:Maxima 3.50
652 GP,KGa,BBr,Day of Krypton
Man #6,V:Eradicator 5.00
653 BMc,BBr,D:Amanda 3.50
654 BMc,BBr,A:Batman Pt.3 . . . . . . 3.50
655 BMc,BBr,V:Morrisson,Ma
Kent's Photo Album 3.50
656 BMc,BBr,Soul Search #1,
V:Blaze 3.50
657 KGa,BBr,V:Toyman 3.50
658 CS,Sinbad Contract #3 . . . . . . 3.50
659 BMc,BBr,K.Krimson
Kryptonite #3 . . . . 5.00
660 BMc,BBr,D:Lex Luthor 4.50
661 BMc,BBr,A:Plastic Man 3.50
662 JOy,JM,TG,BMc,V:Silver
Banshee,Clark tells
Lois his identity 5.50
662a 2nd printing 5.00
663 BMc,Time & Time Again,pt.2,
A:JSA,Legion 3.50
664 BMc,Time & Time Again,pt.5 . 3.50
665 TG,V:Baron Sunday 3.50
666 EH,Red Glass Trilogy,pt.3 . . . . . 3.50
667 JOy,JM,TG,ATi,DJu,Revenge
of the Krypton Man,pt.4 . . . . . . 3.75
668 BMc,Luthor confirmed dead . . . 3.50
669 BMc,V:Intergang,A:Thorn 3.50
670 BMc,A:Waverider,JLA,JLE 3.50
671 KD,Blackout,pt.2 . . . . 3.50
672 BMc,Superman Meets Lex
Luthor II 3.50
673 BMc,V:Hellgramite 3.50
674 BMc,Panic in the Sky (Prologue)
R:Supergirl(Matrix) 6.00
675 BMc,Panic in the Sky #4,
V:Brainiac 3.50
676 B:KK(s),JG,A:Supergirl,Lex
Luthor II 3.50
677 JG,Supergirl V:Superman 3.50
678 JG,O:Lex Luthor II 3.50
679 JG,I:Shellshock 3.50
680 JG,Blaze/Satanus War,pt.2 . . . . 3.50
681 JG,V:Hellgramite 3.50
682 DAb,TA,V:Hi-Tech 3.50
683 JG,I:Jackal,C:Doomsday 3.50
683a 2nd printing 3.00
684 JG,Doomsday Pt.4 . . . . 4.00
684a 2nd printing 3.00
685 JG,Funeral for a Friend#2 . . . . 3.50
686 JG,Funeral for a Friend#6 . . . . 3.50
687 JG,Reign of Superman #1,Direct
Sales,Die-Cut(c),Mini-Poster,
F:Last Son of Krypton 3.00
687a newsstand Ed. 3.00
688 JG,V:Guy Gardner. 3.00
689 JG,V:Man of Steel,A:Superboy,
Supergirl,R:Real Superman . . . 3.50
690 JG,Cyborg Vs. Superboy 3.00
691 JG,A:All Supermen,V:Cyborg
Superman,Mongul 3.00
692 JG,A:Superboy,Man of Steel . . . 3.00
693 JG,A:Last Son of Krypton 3.00
694 JG,Spilled Blood#2,V:Hi-Tech . 3.00
695 JG,Foil(c),I:Cauldron,A:Lobo . . . 3.00
695a Newsstand Ed. 3.00
696 JG,V:Alien,C:Doomsday 3.00
697 JG,Bizarro's World #3,
V:Bizarro 3.00
698 JG,V:Lex Luthor 3.00
699 JG,A:Project Cadmus 3.00
700 JG,Fall of Metropolis#1 . . . . . . 4.00
700a Platinum Edition 15.00

701 JG,Fall of Metropolis#5,
V:Luthor 3.00
702 JG,DvM,B:DyM(s),R:Bloodsport 3.00
703 JG,DvM,Zero Hour 3.00
704 JG,DvM,Eradicator 3.00
705 JG,DvM,Supes real? 3.00
706 JG,DvM,A:Supergirl 3.00
707 JG,DvM,V:Shado Dragon 3.00
708 JG,DvM,R:Deathtrap 3.00
709 JG,DvM,A:Guy Gardner,
Warrior 3.00
710 JG,DvM,Death of Clark Kent,pt.3
[new Miraweb format begins] . . 3.00
711 JG,DvM,Death of Clark
Kent,pt.7 . . . . 3.00
712 Rescue Jimmy Olsen 3.00
713 Scarlet Salvation 3.00
714 R:The Joker 3.00
715 DvM,DaR,V:Parasite 3.00
716 DvM,DaR,Trial of Superman. . . 3.00
717 DvM,DaR,Trial of Superman. . . 3.00
718 DvM,DRo,mystery of Demolitia. 3.00
719 DvM,DRo 3.00
720 DvM,DRo,Lois ends
engagement. 3.50
721 DvM,DRo,lottery fever 3.00
722 DvM,DaR,Tornados in
Smallville 3.00
723 V:Brainiac 3.00
724 V:S.T.A.R.labs monster. 3.00
725 Tolos 3.00
726 DvM(s),TMo,DRo,Krisis of the
Krimson Kryptonite follow-up. . . 3.00
727 DvM(s),TMo,DRo,brutal weather
in Metropolis, Final Night tie-in . 3.00
728 DvM(s),TG,DRo, Some
Honeymoon! 3.00
729 DvM(s),TG,DRo, in Fortress of
Solitude 3.00
730 DvM(s),TG,Ro, ... 3.00
731 DvM(s),TG,DRo, R:Cauldron . 3.00
732 DvM(s),TG,DRo, Atomic Skull
rampages through Metropolis . . 3.00
733 DvM(s),TG,DRo, V:Matallo,
A:Ray. 3.00
734 DvM(s),TG,DRo, Superman &
Atom in Kandor 3.00
735 DvM(s),TG,DRo, V:Savior 3.00
736 DvM(s),TG,DRo. 3.00
737 MWa(s),TG,DRo, Luthor gets
day in court 3.00
738 SI,JMz,Lois sent to Australia . . 3.00
739 SI,JMz,Superman imprisoned. . 3.00
740 SI,JMz,Lucy Lane disappears. . 3.00
741 SI,JMz,V:C.O.M.P.U.T.O. 3.00

Action Comics #739 © DC Comics Inc.

742 SI,JMz 3.00
743 SI,JMz,F:Slam Bradley 3.00
744 SI,JMz,Millennium Giants
x-over 3.00
745 SI,JMz,The Prankster 3.00
746 SI,JMz,The Prankster,pt.2 . . . . 3.00
747 SI,JMz,The Prankster,pt.3 . . . . 3.00
748 SI,JMz,Dominus Theory 3.00
749 RMz(s),TGb,TP,City of the
Future, pt.1 x-over 3.00
750 SI,JMz,I:Crazytop, 48-page . . . 3.50
751 SI,JMz,A:Geo-Force 3.00
752 SI,JMz,Supermen of
America x-over 3.00
753 SI,JMz,A:JLA 3.00
754 SI,JMz,R:Dominus,
A:Wonder Woman 3.00
755 SI&MMr(s),King of the
World aftermath 3.00
756 VGi,old villain is back 3.00
757 TPe(s),TGb,Hawkworld,pt.3 . . . 3.00
758 SI,JMz,V:Boss Moxie 3.00
759 RF,SB,Strange Visitor,pt.3 . . . . 3.00
760 JRu,F:Encantadora 3.00
761 JRu 3.00
762 JRu,V:Demon Etrigan 3.00
763 JRu,V:Brainiac 13 . . . . 3.00
764 JRu,marital troubles 3.00
765 JRu,V:Joker & Harley Quinn . . . 3.00
766 F:Batman 3.00
767 CriticalCondition,pt.4,x-over . . . 3.00
768 F:Marvel Family 3.00
769 Superman:Arkham,concl. 3.00
770 Superman:Emperor,48-pg. 4.50
771 CDi(s),F:Nightwing 2.50
772 V:Ra's al Ghul,pt.1 . . . . 2.50
773 V:Ra's al Ghul,pt.2 . . . . 2.50
774 A:Martian Manhunter 2.50
775 48-page 15.00
775a 2nd printing (2004) 4.50
776 Return to Krypton,pt.4. . . . . 2.50
777 Kancer 2.50
778 MWm,Infestation x-over,pt.4 . . . 2.50
779 V:Killer,pt.1 . . . . 2.50
780 V:Killer,pt.2 . . . . 2.50
781 Our Worlds at War,All-OutWar . 2.50
782 Our Worlds at War,Casualties . 2.50
783 V:Ocean Master,Scorch 2.50
784 Joker:Last Laugh tie-in 2.50
785 R:Bizarro 2.50
786 PFe,kidnapped by aliens 2.50
787 PFe,Byakko, Gunshin, Sakki . . 2.50
788 PFe,Jikei Ketsuki,pt.1 . . . . 2.50
789 Evil from the Gorge. 2.50
790 Krypto vs. Kancer 2.50
791 Smallville, flash-back tale 2.50
792 Superman, detective. 2.50
793 PFe,Return to KryptonII,concl. . 2.50
794 F:Quintescence. 2.50
795 Ending Battle,pt.4 . . . . 2.50
796 Ending Battle,pt.8 . . . . 2.50
797 New General Zod 2.50
798 Lost Hearts, pt.4 x-over 2.50
799 TR,SHa,F:Girl 13 . . . . 2.50
800 64-page, life re-examined 4.50
801 metahumans 2.50
802 PFe,CaS,The Harvest,pt.1 . . . . 2.50
803 PFe,CaS,The Harvest,pt.2 . . . . 2.50
804 PFe,CaS,The Harvest,pt.3 . . . . 2.50
805 PFe,CaS,The Harvest,pt.4 . . . . 2.50
806 PFe,CaS,The Harvest,pt.5 . . . . 2.50
807 PFe,CaS,Supergirls 2.50
808 PFe,CaS,Supergirls 2.50
809 PFe,CaS,murder suspect 2.50
810 PFe,CaS,New Year's 2.25
811 KIK,Strange New Visitor 3.00
812 Godfall,pt.1 . . . . 7.00
812a 2nd printing 5.00
813 Godfall,pt.4 . . . . 4.00
814 MCa,Job in jeopardy 2.50
815 MCa,V:Gog 2.50
816 MCa,F:Teen Titans 2.50

Action Comics Annual #5
© DC Comics, Inc.

817 MCa,F:W.Woman & Superboy . 2.50
818 MCa,F:W.Woman & Superboy . 2.50
819 MCa,I:Sodom & Gomorrah 2.50
820 V:Silver Banshee 2.50
821 LRs,MCa,F:Preus 2.50
822 MCa,F:Superboy 2.50
823 MCa,F:Superboy, Krypto 2.50
824 MCa,V:Preus. 2.50
825 MCa,Villains unite,40-page 3.00
826 IaC,NRd,F:Captain Marvel 3.50
827 JBy,Nel,F:Dr.Polaris,V:Repulse. 3.00
828 JBy,Nel,V:Repulse 3.00
829 JBy,Nel,Sacrifice, x-over,pt.2 . . 4.00
830 JBy,Nel,Villains United tie-in . . 2.50
831 JBy,Nel,Villains United tie-in . . 2.50
832 JBy,Nel,F:Spectre, Satanus . . . 2.50
833 JBy,Nel,F:Queen of Fables 2.50
834 JBy,Nel,F:Queen of Fables 2.50
835 JBy,Nel,I:Livewire 2.50
836 EBe,DJu,This is your life,
     Superman 2.50
837 KBk,Up,Up & Away,pt.2,x-over . 2.50
838 KBk,Up,Up & Away,pt.4,x-over . 2.50
839 KBk,Up,Up & Away,pt.6,x-over . 3.00
840 KBk,Up,Up & Away,pt.8,x-over . 3.00
841 A:Teen Titans, Nightwing 3.00
842 A:Nightwing, Firestorm 3.00
843 A:Teen Titans 3.00
844 AKu, Last Son, pt.1 . . . . 3.00
845 AKu, Bizarro returns 3.00
Ann.#1 AAd,DG,A:Batman 8.00
Ann.#2 MMi,CS,GP,JOy,DJu,BBr,
     V:Mongul 4.00
Ann.#3 TG,Armageddon X-over. . . . 3.50
Ann.#4 Eclipso,A:Captain Marvel . . 3.50
Ann.#5 MZ(c),Bloodlines, I:Loose
     Cannon 3.50
Ann.#6 Elseworlds,JBy(a&S) 3.50
Ann.#7 Year One Annual 4.50
Ann.#8 DvM,Legends of the Dead
     Earth 3.50
Ann.#9 DvM,VGi,BBr,Pulp Heroes . 4.50
Gold.Ann.rep.#1 . . . . 2.50
#0 Peer Pressure,pt.4 (1994) 2.50
Spec.#1,000,000 MSh(s),RLm,JMz . 2.50

ADAM STRANGE
1990
1 NKu,A.Strange on Rann 5.00
2 NKu,Wanted:Adam Strange. 4.00
3 NKu,final issue. 4.00
TPB Man of Two Worlds (2003) . . 20.00

2nd Series, Sept. 2004
1 (of 8) PFe,R:Adam Strange 3.00
2 PFe 3.00
3 PFe 3.00
4 PFe, F:The Omega Man 3.00
5 PFe,V:L.E.G.I.O.N 3.00
6 PFe,Planet Rann 3.00
7 PFe,Planet Rann, Darkstars . . . 3.00
8 PFe,concl. 3.00
TPB Planet Heist 20.00

ADVANCED
DUNGEONS & DRAGONS
1988–91
1 JD,I:Onyx,Priam,Timoth,
     Cybriana,Vajra,Luna 5.00
2 JD,V:Imgig Zu,I:Conner 4.00
3 JD,V:Imgig Zu 4.00
4 JD,V:Imgig Zu,I:Kyriani 3.00
5 JD,Spirit of Myrrth I 3.00
6 JD,Spirit of Myrrth II. 3.00
7 thru 24 JD . . . . @2.50
25 thru 36 JD . . . . @2.25
Ann.#1 JD,RM,Tmd 4.00

ADVENTURE COMICS
Nov., 1938–83
[Prev: New Adventure Comics]
32 CF(c),S&S 7,000.00
33 CF(c),FGu,S&S,BKa 4,000.00
34 FGu(c),S&S,BKa 4,000.00
35 FGu(c),SMo,S&S,BKa 4,000.00
36 CF,Giant Snake(c),S&S . . . 4,000.00
37 CF,Rampaging Elephant(c) . 4,000.00
38 CF,Tiger(c),S&S 4,000.00
39 CF,Male Bondage(c),S&S . . 3,000.00
40 CF(c),1st app. Sandman . . 90,000.00
41 CF,Killer Shark(c),S&S. . . . 15,000.00
42 CF,Sandman(c) 30,000.00
43 CF&FGu(c),WB 9,000.00
44 CF,FGu,Sandman(c) 15,000.00
45 FGu(c),CF,BKa. 9,000.00
46 CF,Sandman(c) 14,000.00
47 CF,Sandman (c). 14,000.00
48 1st app.& B:Hourman 60,000.00
49 SMo(c),BKa,CF 6,000.00
50 BBa,Hourman(c) 6,000.00
51 BBa(c),Sandman(c) 9,000.00
52 BBa(c),Hourman(c) 5,500.00
53 BBa(c),1st app. Minuteman . 5,500.00
54 BBa(c),Hourman(c) 5,500.00
55 BBa(c),Hourman(c) 5,500.00
56 BBa(c),Hourman(c) 5,500.00
57 BBa(c),Hourman(c) 5,500.00
58 BBa(c),Hourman(c) 5,500.00
59 BBa(c),Hourman(c) 5,500.00
60 CF,Sandman(c) 4,800.00
61 CF(c),JBu,Starman(c) 25,000.00
62 JBu(c),JBu,Starman(c). . . . 7,000.00
63 JBu(c),JBu,Starman(c). . . . 5,000.00
64 JBu(c),JBu,Starman(c). . . . 5,000.00
65 JBu(c),JBu,Starman(c). . . . 5,000.00
66 JBu(c),JBu,O:Shining Knight,
     Starman(c) 5,500.00
67 JBu(c),JBu,O:Mist 5,000.00
68 JBu(c),JBu,same 5,000.00
69 JBu(c),JBu,1st app. Sandy,
     Starman(c) 5,000.00
70 JBu(c),JBu,Starman(c). . . . 5,000.00
71 JBu(c),JBu,same 5,000.00
72 JBu(c),S&K,JBu,Sandman. 30,000.00
73 S&K(c),S&K,I:Manhunter . . 31,000.00
74 S&K(c),S&K,You Can't Escape
     Your Fate-The Sandman . . 5,000.00
75 S&K(c),S&K,Sandman and
     Sandy Battle Thor. 5,000.00
76 S&K(c),Sandman(c),S&K. . 5,000.00
77 S&K,(c),S&K,same. 5,000.00
78 S&K(c),S&K,same 5,000.00
79 S&K(c),S&K,Manhunter . . . 12,000.00

80 S&K(c),Sandman(c),S&K. . . 5,000.00
81 S&K(c),MMe,S&K,same. . . . 3,000.00
82 S&K(c),S&K,Sandman
     X-Mas story 3,000.00
83 S&K(c),S&K,Sandman
     Boxing(c),E:Hourman 3,000.00
84 S&K(c),S&K 3,000.00
85 S&K(c),S&K,Sandman in
     The Amazing Dreams of
     Gentleman Jack 3,000.00
86 S&K(c),Sandman(c). 3,000.00
87 S&K(c),Sandman(c). 3,000.00
88 S&K(c),Sandman(c). 3,000.00
89 S&K(c),Sandman(c). 3,000.00
90 S&K(c),Sandman(c). 3,000.00
91 S&K(c),JK 3,000.00
92 S&K(c) 2,000.00
93 S&K(c),Sandman in Sleep
     for Sale 2,000.00
94 S&K(c),Sandman(c). 2,000.00
95 S&K(c),Sandman(c). 2,000.00
96 S&K(c),Sandman(c). 2,000.00
97 S&K(c),Sandman(c). 2,000.00
98 JK(c),Sandman in Hero
     of Dreams. 2,000.00
99 GK,Sandman(c) 2,000.00
100 JK(c&a) 2,000.00
101 S&K(c) 2,000.00
102 S&K(c) 2,000.00
103 B:Superboy stories,(c),BU:
     Johnny Quick,Aquaman,Shining
     Knight,Green Arrow 5,000.00
104 S&S,ToyTown USA 1,900.00
105 S&S,Palace of Fantasy . . . 1,500.00
106 S&S,Weather Hurricane . . 1,500.00
107 S&S,The Sky is the Limit. . 1,500.00
108 S&S,Proof of the Proverbs 1,500.00
109 S&S,You Can't Lose 1,500.00
110 S&S,The Farmer Takes
     it Easy. 1,500.00
111 S&S,The Whiz Quiz Club . . 1,500.00
112 S&S,Super Safety First . . . 1,500.00
113 S&S,The 33rd Christmas . . 1,400.00
114 S&S,Superboy Spells
     Danger 1,400.00
115 S&S,The Adventure of
     Jaguar Boy 1,400.00
116 S&S,JBu,Superboy Toy
     Tester 1,400.00
117 S&S,JBu,Miracle Plane . . . 1,400.00
118 S&S,JBu,The Quiz Biz
     Broadcast 1,400.00
119 WMo,JBu,Superboy
     Meets Girls 1,400.00
120 S&S,JBu,A:Perry White;
     I:Ringmaster 1,500.00

Adventure Comics #33
© DC Comics, Inc.

121 S&S,Great Hobby Contest. 1,600.00	179 World's Whackiest	224 Pa Kent Superman 500.00
122 S&S,Superboy-Super-	Inventors 900.00	225 Bird with Super-Powers 500.00
Magician 1,800.00	180 Grand Prize o/t Underworld . 900.00	226 Superboy's Super Rival! 500.00
123 S&S,Lesson For a Bully . . 1,600.00	181 Mask for a Hero 900.00	227 Good Samaritan of
124 S&S,Barbed Wire Boys	182 Super Hick from Smallville . . 800.00	Smallville 500.00
Town 1,200.00	183 Superboy and Cleopatra . . . 800.00	228 Clark Kent's Bodyguard 500.00
125 S&S,The Weight Before	184 Shutterbugs of Smallville . . . 800.00	229 End of the Kent Family 500.00
Christmas 1,200.00	185 The Mythical Monster 800.00	230 Secret o/t Flying Horse 450.00
126 S&S,Superboy:Crime	186 Smallville a Ghost Town 800.00	231 Super-Feats of Super-Baby . 450.00
Fighting Poet 1,200.00	187 25th Century Superboy 800.00	232 House where Superboy
127 MMe,O:Shining Knight;	188 Bull Fighter from	was Born 450.00
Super Bellboy 1,200.00	Smallville 800.00	233 Joe Smith, Man of Steel 450.00
128 WMo,How Clark Kent Met	189 Girl of Steel (Lana Lang) . . . 800.00	234 1,001 Rides of Superboy . . . 450.00
Lois Lane 1,200.00	190 The Terrible Truant 800.00	235 Confessions of Superboy . . . 450.00
129 WMo,Pupils of the Past . . . 1,200.00	191 The Two Clark Kents 800.00	236 Clark Kent's Super-Dad 450.00
130 WMo,Superboy Super	192 Coronation of Queen	237 Robot War of Smallville 450.00
Salesman 1,200.00	Lana Lang 800.00	238 Secret Past of
131 WMo,The Million Dollar	193 Superboy's Lost Costume. . . 800.00	Superboy's Father 450.00
Athlete 1,200.00	194 Super-Charged Superboy. . . 800.00	239 Super-Tricks of
132 WMo,Superboy Super	195 Lana Lang's Romance	the Dog of Steel. 450.00
Cowboy. 1,200.00	on Mars! 800.00	240 Super Teacher from Krypton. 450.00
133 WMo,Superboy's Report	196 Superboy vs. King Gorilla. . . 800.00	241 Super-Outlaw of Smallville . . 450.00
Card 1,200.00	197 V:Juvenile Gangs 800.00	242 The Kid From Krypton 450.00
134 WMo,Silver Gloves Sellout 1,200.00	198 Super-Carnival from Space. . 800.00	243 Super Toys from Krypton . . . 450.00
135 WMo,The Most Amazing	199 Superboy meets Superlad . . 800.00	244 Poorest Family in Smallville . 450.00
of All Boys 1,200.00	200 Superboy and the Apes! . . 1,000.00	245 The Mystery of Monster X . 450.00
136 WMo,My Pal Superboy . . . 1,200.00	201 Safari in Smallville! 750.00	246 Girl Who Trapped Superboy . 450.00
137 WMo,Treasure of Tondimo. 1,200.00	202 Superboy City, U.S.A. 750.00	247 I&O:Legion 10,000.00
138 WMo,Around the World in	203 Uncle Superboy! 750.00	248 Green Arrow 400.00
Eighty Minutes 1,200.00	204 Super-Brat of Smallville 750.00	249 CS,Green Arrow 400.00
139 WMo,Telegraph Boy 1,200.00	205 Journey of the Second	250 JK,Green Arrow 400.00
140 Journey to the Moon 1,200.00	Superboy! 750.00	251 JK,Green Arrow 400.00
141 WMo,When Superboy Lost	206 The Impossible Creatures. . . 750.00	252 JK,Green Arrow 400.00
His Powers 1,200.00	207 Smallville's Worst Athlete . . . 750.00	253 JK,1st Superboy &
142 WMo,The Man Who Walked	208 Rip Van Winkle of	Robin T.U. 600.00
With Trouble 1,200.00	Smallville! 750.00	254 JK,Green Arrow 400.00
143 WMo,Superboy Savings Bank,	209 Superboy Week! 750.00	255 JK,Green Arrow 400.00
A:Wooden Head Jones . . . 1,200.00	210 I:Krypto,The Superdog	256 JK,O:Green Arrow 1,200.00
144 WMo,The Way to Stop	from Krypton. 8,000.00	257 CS,LEI,A:Hercules,Samson . 350.00
Superboy 1,200.00	211 Superboy's Amazing Dream! 600.00	258 LEI,Aquaman,Superboy . . . 350.00
145 WMo,Holiday Hijackers . . . 1,200.00	212 Superboy's Robot Twin. 600.00	259 I:Crimson Archer. 350.00
146 The Substitute Superboy . . 1,200.00	213 Junior Jury of Smallville! . . . 600.00	260 1st S.A. O:Aquaman 1,400.00
147 Clark Kent,Orphan 1,200.00	214 A:Krypto 1,100.00	261 GA,A:Lois Lane. 300.00
148 Superboy Meets Mummies 1,200.00	215 Super-Hobby of Superboy . 500.00	262 O:Speedy 300.00
149 Fake Superboys. 1,200.00	216 The Wizard City 500.00	263 GA,Aquaman,Superboy . . . 300.00
150 FF,Superboy's Initiation . . . 1,100.00	217 Farewell to Smallville 500.00	264 GA,A:Robin Hood 300.00
151 FF,No Hunting(c). 850.00	218 Two World's of Superboy . . . 500.00	265 GA,Aquaman,Superboy . . . 300.00
152 Superboy Hunts For a Job. 1,000.00	219 Rip Van Wrinkle of	266 GA,I:Aquagirl. 300.00
153 FF,Clark Kent,Boy Hobo . . 1,100.00	Smallville 500.00	267 N:Legion(2nd app.) 1,800.00
154 The Carnival Boat Crimes . 1,000.00	220 Greatest Show on Earth	268 I:Aquaboy 300.00
155 FF,Superboy-Hollywood	A:Krypto. 600.00	269 I:Aqualad,E:Green Arrow . . . 450.00
Actor. 1,100.00	221 The Babe of Steel 500.00	270 2nd A:Aqualad,B.Congorilla . 300.00
156 The Flying Peril 1,000.00	222 Superboy's Repeat	271 O:Lex Luthor rtd 450.00
157 FF,The Worst Boy in	Performance 500.00	272 I:Human Flying Fish 300.00
Smallville 1,100.00	223 Hercules Junior. 500.00	273 Aquaman,Superboy 300.00
158 The Impossible Task 1,000.00		274 Aquaman,Superboy 300.00
159 FF,Superboy Millionaire? . . 1,100.00		275 O:Superman/Batman
160 Superboy's Phoney Father . . 950.00		T.U. rtd 400.00
161 FF. 1,100.00		276 Superboy,3rd A:Metallo. . . . 300.00
162 Super-Coach of		277 Aquaman,Superboy 300.00
Smallville High! 1,000.00		278 Aquaman,Superboy 300.00
163 FF,Superboy's Phoney		279 CS,Aquaman,Superboy . . . 300.00
Father. 1,100.00		280 CS,A:Lori Lemaris. 300.00
164 Discovers the Secret of		281 Aquaman,Superboy
a Lost Indian Tribe! 1,000.00		E:Congorilla. 300.00
165 Superboy's School for		282 5th A:Legion,I:Starboy. 400.00
Stunt Men! 1,000.00		283 I:Phantom Zone 400.00
166 Town That Stole Superboy. 1,000.00		284 CS,JM,Aquaman,Superboy . 250.00
167 Lana Lang, Super-Girl! . . . 1,100.00		285 WB,B:Bizarro World 350.00
168 The Boy Who Out Smarted		286 I:Bizarro World 350.00
Superboy 1,000.00		287 I:Dev-Em,Bizarro Perry White,
169 Clark Kent's Private Butler. 1,000.00		Jimmy Olsen 250.00
170 Lana Lang's Big Crush 900.00		288 A:Dev-Em 250.00
171 Superboy's Toughest Tasks . 900.00		289 Superboy. 250.00
172 Laws that Backfired 900.00		290 8th A:Legion,O&J:Sunboy,
173 Superboy's School of		I:Brainiac 5 . . . . 400.00
Hard Knocks 900.00		291 A:Lex Luthor 250.00
174 The New Lana Lang! 900.00		292 Superboy,I:Bizarro Lucy Lane,
175 Duel of the Superboys 900.00		Lana Lang 250.00
176 Superboy's New Parents! . . . 900.00		293 CS,O&I:Marv-El,I:Bizarro
177 Hot-Rod Chariot Race! 900.00		Luthor 350.00
178 Boy in the Lead Mask 900.00		294 I:Bizarro M.Monroe,JFK 300.00

Adventure Comics #230
© DC Comics Inc.

Adventure Comics #300
© DC Comics, Inc.

295 I:Bizarro Titano 250.00
296 A:Ben Franklin,George
    Washington 250.00
297 Lana Lang Superboy Sister . 250.00
298 The Fat Superboy 250.00
299 I:Gold Kryptonite 250.00
300 B:Legion,J:Mon-El,
    E:Bizarro World 1,000.00
301 CS,O:Bouncing Boy 300.00
302 CS,Legion 250.00
303 I:Matter Eater Lad 250.00
304 D:Lightning Lad 250.00
305 A:Chameleon Boy 250.00
306 I:Legion of Sub.Heroes 250.00
307 I:Element Lad 250.00
308 I:Light Lass 250.00
309 I:Legion of Super Monsters . 250.00
310 A:Mxyzptlk 250.00
311 CS,V:Legion of Substitue
    Heroes 250.00
312 CS&GKI(c),R:Lightning Lad . 250.00
313 CS,J:Supergirl 250.00
314 CS&GKI(c),A:Hitler 250.00
315 A:Legion of Substitute
    Heroes 250.00
316 CS&GKI(c),O:Legion 200.00
317 I&J:Dreamgirl 200.00
318 Mutiny of Legionnaires 200.00
319 Legion's Suicide Squad 200.00
320 CS&GKI(c),A:Dev-Em 200.00
321 I:Time Trapper 250.00
322 JF,A:Legion of Super Pets . . 175.00
323 JF,BU:Kypto 175.00
324 JF,I:Legion of Super Outlaws 175.00
325 JF,V:Lex Luthor 175.00
326 BU:Superboy 175.00
327 I&J:Timber Wolf 175.00
328 Lad who Wrecked Legion . . . 175.00
329 I:Legion of Super Bizarros . . 175.00
330 Mystery Legionnaire 175.00
331 Legion of Super-Villains 150.00
332 CS&GKI(c),Legion 150.00
333 CS&GKI(c),Legion 150.00
334 CS&GKI(c),Legion 150.00
335 CS&GKI(c),Legion 150.00
336 CS&GKI(c),Legion 150.00
337 CS&GKI(c),Legion 150.00
338 CS&GKI(c),Legion 150.00
339 CS&GKI(c),Legion 150.00
340 I:Computo 150.00
341 CS,D:Triplicate Girl (becomes
    Duo Damsel) 135.00
342 CS,Star Boy expelled 120.00
343 CS,V:Lords of Luck 120.00
344 CS,Super Stalag,pt.1 . . . . 120.00
345 CS,Super Stalag,pt.2 . . . . . . 120.00

346 CS,I&J:Karate Kid,Princess
    Projectra,I:Nemesis Kid 150.00
347 CS,Legion 120.00
348 I:Dr.Regulus 150.00
349 CS,I:Rond Vidar 120.00
350 CS,I:White Witch 150.00
351 CS,R:Star Boy 175.00
352 CS,I:Fatal Fire 175.00
353 CS,D:Ferro Lad 175.00
354 CS,Adult Legion 175.00
355 CS,J:Insect Queen 150.00
356 CS,Five Legion Orphans . . . 150.00
357 CS,I:Controller 150.00
358 I:Hunter 150.00
359 CS,Outlawed Legion,pt.1 . . . 150.00
360 CS,Outlawed Legion,pt.2 . . . 150.00
361 I:Dominators (30th century) . 150.00
362 I:Dr.Mantis Morto 150.00
363 V:Dr.Mantis Morlo 150.00
364 A:Legion of Super Pets 150.00
365 CS,I:Shadow Lass,
    V:Fatal Five 150.00
366 CS,J:Shadow Lass 150.00
367 N:Legion H.Q.,I:Dark Circle . 150.00
368 NA,Mutiny of Super-Heroines 150.00
369 CS,JAb,I:Mordru 150.00
370 CS,JAb,V:Mordru 150.00
371 CS,JAb,I:Chemical King 150.00
372 CS,JAb,J:Timber Wolf,
    Chemical King 150.00
373 I:Tornado Twins 65.00
374 WM,I:Black Mace 65.00
375 I:Wanderers 65.00
376 Execution of Cham.Boy 65.00
377 Heroes for Hire 65.00
378 Twelve Hours to Live 65.00
379 Burial In Space 65.00
380 The Amazing Space Odyssey
    of the Legion,E:Legion 65.00
381 The Supergirl Gang
    C:Batgirl,B:Supergirl 160.00
382 NA(c),The Superteams Split
    Up,A:Superman 75.00
383 NA(c),Please Stop my Funeral,
    A:Superman,Comet,Streaky . . 75.00
384 KS,The Heroine Haters,
    A:Superman 75.00
385 Supergirl's Big Sister 75.00
386 The Beast That Loved
    Supergirl 75.00
387 Wolfgirl of Stanhope;
    A:Superman;V:Lex Luthor . . . 75.00
388 Kindergarten Criminal;
    V:Luthor,Brainiac 75.00
389 A:Supergirl's Parents,
    V:Brainiac 75.00
390 Linda Danvers Superstar
    (80 page giant) 100.00
391 The Super Cheat;A:Comet . . . 50.00
392 Supergirls Lost Costume 50.00
393 KS,Unwanted Supergirl 50.00
394 KS,Heartbreak Prison 50.00
395 Heroine in Haunted House . . . 50.00
396 Mystery o/t Super Orphan . . . 50.00
397 Now Comes Zod,N:Supergirl,
    V:Luthor 50.00
398 Maid of Doom,A:Superman,
    Streaky,Krypto,Comet 50.00
399 CI,Johnny Dee,Hero Bum 60.00
400 MSy,35th Anniv.,Return of the
    Black Flame 40.00
401 MSy,JAb,The Frightened
    Supergirl,V:Lex Luthor 40.00
402 MSy,JAb,TD,I:Starfire,
    Dr.Kangle 50.00
403 68 page giant 90.00
404 MSy,JAb,V:Starfire 35.00
405 V:Starfire,Dr.Kangle 35.00
406 MSy,JAb,Suspicion 35.00
407 MSy,JAb,Suspicion Confirmed
    N:Supergirl 35.00
408 The Face at the Window 35.00

409 MSy,DG,Legion rep. 50.00
410 N:Supergirl 50.00
411 CI,N:Supergirl 50.00
412 rep.Strange Adventures #180
    (I:Animal Man). 55.00
413 GM,JKu,rep.Hawkman 50.00
414 Animal Man rep. 50.00
415 BO,GM,CI,Animal Man rep. . . 50.00
416 CI,All women issue,giantsize . 50.00
417 GM,inc.rep.Adventure #161,
    Frazetta art. 45.00
418 ATh,Black Canary 45.00
419 ATh,Black Canary 50.00
420 Animal Man rep. 45.00
421 MSy,Supergirl 30.00
422 MSy,Supergirl 30.00
423 MSy,Supergirl 30.00
424 MSy,E:Supergirl,A:JLA 30.00
425 AN,ATh,I:Captain Fear 45.00
426 MSy,DG,JAp,Vigilante 30.00
427 TD, The Voodoo Lizards 38.00
428 TD,I:Black Orchid 85.00
429 TD,AN,Black Orchid 45.00
430 A:Black Orchid 45.00
431 JAp,ATh,B:Spectre 85.00
432 JAp,AN,A:Spectre,Capt.Fear . 45.00
433 JAp,AN, The Swami 45.00
434 JAp, Nightmare Dummies . . . 45.00
435 MGr(1st work),JAp,Aquaman . 45.00
436 JAp,MGr,Aquaman 45.00
437 JAp,MGr,Aquaman 45.00
438 JAp,HC,DD,7 Soldiers 45.00
439 JAp, Voice that Doomed 45.00
440 JAp,O:New Spectre 60.00
441 JAp,B:Aquaman 20.00
442 JAp,A:Aquaman 20.00
443 JAp, The Dolphin Connection . 20.00
444 JAp, Death before Dishonor . 20.00
445 JAp,RE,JSon,Creeper. 22.00
446 JAp,RE,JSon,Creeper. 22.00
447 JAp,RE,JSon,Creeper. 22.00
448 JAp,Aquaman 20.00
449 JAp,MN,TA,J'onn J'onz. 20.00
450 JAp,MN,TA,Supergirl 20.00
451 JAp,MN,TA,Hawkman. 20.00
452 JAp,Aquaman 20.00
453 MA,CP,JRu,B:Superboy
    & Aqualad 20.00
454 CP,DG,A:Kryptonite Kid 20.00
455 CP,DG,A:Kryptonite Kid
    E:Aqualad 15.00
456 JSon,JA. 15.00
457 JSon,JA,JO,B:Eclipso 15.00
458 JSon,JAp,JO,BL,E:Superboy
    & Eclipso 15.00

Adventure Comics #426
© DC Comics, Inc.

DC COMICS

459 IN,FMc,JAp,JSon,DN,JA,A:Wond.
    Woman,New Gods,Green Lantern,
    Flash,Deadman,(giant size) . . 25.00
460 IN,FMc,JAp,DN,DA,JSon,JA,
    D:Darkseid. 25.00
461 IN,FMc,JAp,JSon,DN,JA,
    B:JSA & Aquaman. 25.00
462 IN,FMc,DH,JL,DG,JA,
    D:Earth 2,Batman. 25.00
463 DH,JL,JSon,FMc 20.00
464 DH,JAp,JSon,DN,DA,
    Deadman. 20.00
465 DN,JSon,DG,JL. 20.00
466 MN,JL,JSon,DN,DA 20.00
467 JSon,SD,RT,I:Starman
    B:Plastic Man 25.00
468 SD,JSon 8.00
469 SD,JSon,O:Starman 8.00
470 SD,JSon,O:Starman 8.00
471 SD,JSon,I:Brickface 8.00
472 SD,RT,JSon 8.00
473 SD,RT,JSon 8.00
474 SD,RT,JSon 8.00
475 BB(c),SD,RT,JSon,DG,
    B:Aquaman 8.00
476 SD,RT,JSon,DG 8.00
477 SD,RT,JSon,DG 8.00
478 SD,RT,JSon,DG 8.00
479 CI,DG,JSon,Dial H For Hero,
    E:Starman and Aquaman 8.00
480 CI,DJ,B:Dial H for Hero 8.00
481 CI,DJ. 8.00
482 CI,DJ,DH. 8.00
483 CI,DJ,DH. 8.00
484 GP(c),CI,DJ,DH 8.00
485 GP(c),CI,DJ. 8.00
486 GP(c),DH,RT,TVE 8.00
487 CI,DJ,DH. 8.00
488 CI,DJ,TVE 8.00
489 CI,FMc,TVE 8.00
490 GP(c),CI,E:Dial H for Hero . . . 8.00
491 KG(c),DigestSize,DN,
    Shazam,rep.other material . . . 20.00
492 KG(c),DN,E:Shazam. 20.00
493 KG(c),GT,B:Challengers of
    the Unknown,reprints 20.00
494 KG(c),GT,Challengers,
    reprints. 20.00
495 ATh,reprints,Challengers. . . . 20.00
496 GK(c),ATh,reprints,
    Challengers 20.00
497 ATh,DA,reps.,E:Challengers . . 20.00
498 GK(c),reprints,Rep.Legion . . 20.00
499 GK(c),reprints,Rep 20.00
500 KG(c),Legion reprints,Rep . . . 20.00
501 reprints,Rep 20.00
502 reprints,Rep 20.00
503 reprints,final issue 20.00
Giant #1, 80 page, 7 tales (1998) . 15.00

ADVENTURE COMICS
1999
1 JeR,PSj,F:Starman & The Atom . 2.25

ADVENTURES IN
THE DC UNIVERSE
1997–98
1 F:New JLA 6.00
2 F:The Flash,Catwoman 4.00
3 Wonder Woman vs. Cheetah;
    Poison Ivy vs. Batman. 4.00
4 F:Green Lantern vs. Glorious
    Godfrey; Mister Miracle. 4.00
5 F:Martian Manhunter, all alien
    issue 4.00
6 F:Ocean Master, Power Girl 4.00
7 SVa(s),F:Shazam Family 4.00
8 SVa(s),F:Blue Beetle &
    Booster Gold 4.00
9 SVa(s),F:Flash,V:Grodd,Cipher . . 4.00
10 SVa(s),Legion month 4.00

11 SVa(s),F:Gr.Lantern & W.Woman 4.00
12 SVa(s) 4.50
13 SVa(s),A:Martian Manhunter . . . 4.00
14 SVa(s),Flash races Superboy . . . 4.00
15 SVa(s),Shazam,Aquaman. 4.00
16 SVa(s),F:Green Lantern 4.00
17 SVa(s),F:Batman, Creeper 4.00
18 SVa(s),F:JLA. 4.50
19 F:Catwoman, Wonder Woman . . 4.00
Ann.#1 magic amulets,5 stories. . . 5.00

ADVENTURES IN THE
RIFLE BRIGADE
DC/Vertigo, Aug., 2000
1 (of 3) GEn, ... 2.50
2 F:Gerta Gash 2.50
3 GEn,Up Yours Fritz, concl. 2.50
TPB 15.00

ADVENTURES IN THE
RIFLE BRIGADE:
OPERATION BOLLOCK
DC/Vertigo, Aug., 2001
1 GEn,find Hitler's testicle! 2.50
2 GEn,still looking. 2.50
3 GEn,concl. 2.50

THE ADVENTURES OF
ALAN LADD
1949–51
1 Ph(c),Damascus Diamond . . 1,500.00
2 Ph(c),inc.Visit to Underworld . . 900.00
3 Ph(c),inc.Stuntman 550.00
4 Ph(c),inc.Hall of Hits 550.00
5 Ph(c),inc.Destination Danger. . 500.00
6 Ph(c),inc.Beautiful Bodyguard . 500.00
7 RMo(c&a),Hollywood Unknown 500.00
8 Grand Duchess takes over . . . 500.00
9 Deadlien in Rapula 500.00

THE ADVENTURES OF
BOB HOPE
1951
1 Ph(c). 3,000.00
2 Ph(c). 1,500.00
3 Ph(c). 1,000.00
4 Ph(c). 1,000.00
5 thru 10 . . . . @750.00
11 thru 20 . . . . @600.00
21 thru 40 . . . . @400.00
41 thru 60 . . . . @300.00
61 thru 90 . . . . @150.00
91 thru 93 . . . . @125.00
94 C:Aquaman. 150.00
95 1st Superhip 150.00
96 thru 105 . . . . @125.00
106 thru 109 NA. . . . . @200.00

ADVENTURES OF
DEAN MARTIN AND
JERRY LEWIS
1952–57
1 . . . . 2,700.00
2 . . . . 1,000.00
3 thru 5 . . . . @750.00
6 thru 10 . . . . @750.00
11 thru 20 . . . . @500.00
21 thru 40 . . . . @300.00
Becomes:

ADVENTURES OF
JERRY LEWIS
1957–71
41 thru 55 . . . . @250.00
56 thru 69 . . . . @200.00
70 thru 87 . . . . @150.00

88 A:Bob Hope. 150.00
89 thru 91 . . . . @50.00
92 C:Superman 70.00
93 Beatles 65.00
94 thru 96 . . . . @60.00
97 A:Batman & Joker. 125.00
98 thru 101. . . . . @55.00
102 NA,Beatles . . . . @125.00
103 and 104 NA . . . . @75.00
105 A:Superman 80.00
106 thru 111 . . . . @45.00
112 A:Flash 55.00
113 thru 116 . . . . @40.00
117 A:Wonder Woman. 80.00
118 thru 124 . . . . @35.00

ADVENTURES OF
FORD FAIRLANE
1990
1 thru 4 DH . . . . @3.00

ADVENTURES OF
THE OUTSIDERS
See: BATMAN &
THE OUTSIDERS

ADVENTURES OF
OZZIE AND HARRIET
1949–50
1 Ph(c). 1,500.00
2 . . . . 900.00
3 thru 5 . . . . @750.00

Adventures of Rex the Wonder
Dog #18 © DC Comics Inc.

ADVENTURES OF REX,
THE WONDER DOG
1952–59
1 ATh,Trail of Flower of Evil. . . 2,000.00
2 GK,ATh,Stunt Dog 1,000.00
3 GK,ATh,Circus Detective. 900.00
4 GK,CI,Terror Island 800.00
5 GK,Wanted, One P.O.W. 800.00
6 thru 10 . . . . @600.00
11 Atom Bomb 700.00
12 thru 20 . . . . @400.00
21 thru 46. . . . . @300.00

ADVENTURES
OF SUPERBOY
See: SUPERBOY

DC COMICS

ADVENTURES OF SUPERMAN
See: SUPERMAN

ALL-AMERICAN COMICS
1939–48
1 B:Hop Harrigan,Scribbly,Mutt&Jeff,
  Red,White&Blue,Bobby Thatcher,
  Skippy,Daiseybelle,Mystery Men
  of Mars,Toonerville 10,000.00
2 B:Ripley's Believe It or Not. . 5,000.00
3 Hop Harrigan (c). 3,500.00
4 Flag(c). 3,500.00
5 B:The American Way 3,500.00
6 ShM(c),Fredric Marchin in
  The American Way. 3,000.00
7 E:Bobby Thatcher,C.H.
  Claudy's A Thousand Years
  in a Minute 3,000.00
8 B:Ultra Man. 5,500.00
9 A:Ultra Man. 3,000.00
10 ShM(c),E:The American Way,
  Santa-X-Mas(c) 3,000.00
11 Ultra Man(c) 3,000.00
12 E:Toonerville Folks. 2,500.00
13 The Infra Red Des'Royers . . 2,500.00
14 Ultra Man 2,500.00
15 E:Tippie and Reg'lar Fellars 3,000.00
16 O&1st App:Green Lantern,
  B:Lantern(c) 220,000.00
17 SMo(c) 30,000.00
18 SMo(c) 25,000.00
19 SMo(c),O&I: Atom, E:Ultra
  Man. 30,000.00
20 I:Atom's Costume,Hunkle
  becomes Red Tornado . . . 10,000.00
21 E:Wiley of West Point
  & Skippy 6,000.00
22 SMo(c),F:Green Lantern . . 5,800.00
23 E:Daieybelle. 6,000.00
24 E:Ripley's Believe It or Not . 8,000.00
25 O&I:Dr. Mid-Nite. 20,000.00
26 O&I:Sargon the Sorcerer. . . 7,000.00
27 I:Doiby Dickles. 7,000.00
28 F:Green Lantern 3,000.00
29 ShM(c) 3,000.00
30 ShM(c) 3,000.00
31 Adventures of the Underfed
  Orphans 3,000.00
32 F:Green Lantern 2,500.00
33 Green Lantern(c) 2,500.00
34 Green Lantern(c) 2,500.00
35 Doiby discovers Lantern's ID2,500.00
36 Auto Racing (c) 2,500.00
37 Green Lantern(c) 2,500.00
38 ShM,V:A Modern Napoleon . 2,500.00
39 Green Lantern(c) 2,500.00
40 Doiby Dickles idol(c) 2,500.00
41 Gr.Lantern(c),Doiby Dickles. 2,000.00
42 ShM 2,000.00
43 Gr.Lantern(c),Doiby Dickles. 2,000.00
44 I Accuse the Green Lantern! 2,000.00
45 Gr.Lantern(c),Doiby Dickles. 2,000.00
46 Riddle of Dickles Manor. . . . 2,000.00
47 Hop Harrigan meets the
  Enemy,(c) 2,000.00
48 League of Three-Eyed Men. 2,000.00
49 Doiby Dickles Cab 2,000.00
50 E:Sargon 2,000.00
51 Murder Under the Stars 1,500.00
52 Spotlight on Crime 1,500.00
53 Green Lantern delivers
  the Mail. 1,500.00
54 Crime is an Art. 1,500.00
55 The Riddle of the
  Runaway Trolley. 1,500.00
56 V:Elegant Esmond. 1,500.00
57 V:The Melancholy Men 1,500.00
58 Marvelous Mervyn Mystery . 1,500.00
59 The Story of the Man Who
  Couldn't Tell The Truth 1,500.00

60 Desperate Dilemma. 1,500.00
61 O:Soloman Grundy,Fighters
  Never Quit 9,000.00
62 Da Distrik Attorney. 1,300.00
63 Garrulous Mr. Gabb 1,300.00
64 A Bag of Assorted Nuts!. . . . 1,300.00
65 The Man Who Lost
  Wednesday. 1,300.00
66 The Soles of Manhattan! . . . 1,300.00
67 V:King Shark 1,300.00
68 F:Napoleon & Joe Safeen . . 1,300.00
69 Backwards Man! 1,300.00
70 JKu,I:Maximillian O'Leary,
  V:Colley, the Leprechaun . . 1,300.00
71 E:Red,White&Blue,The
  Human Bomb 1,200.00
72 B:Black Pirate 1,200.00
73 B:Winkey,Blinky&Noddy,
  Mountain Music Mayhem . . 1,200.00
74 Slap-Happy Shoes. 1,200.00
75 Man Who Heard Too Much . 1,200.00
76 Spring Time for Doiby 1,200.00
77 Hop Harrigan(c). 1,200.00
78 The Giggling Gangsters. . . . 1,200.00
79 Mutt & Jeff 1,200.00
80 Long-Eared Larceny 1,200.00
81 Two Twisted Twerps. 1,200.00
82 The Beloved Bandit 1,200.00
83 Mutt & Jeff 1,200.00
84 The Adventure of the Man
  with Two Faces. 1,200.00
85 Rise & Fall of Crusher Crock1,200.00
86 V:Crime of the Month Club . 1,200.00
87 The Strange Case of
  Professor Nobody. 1,200.00
88 Canvas of Crime 1,200.00
89 O:Harlequin 1,700.00
90 O:Icicle. 1,700.00
91 Wedding of the Harlequin . . 1,700.00
92 The Icicle goes South 1,700.00
93 Double Crossing Decoy 1,700.00
94 A:Harlequin 1,700.00
95 The Unmasking of the
  Harlequin 1,700.00
96 ATh(c),Solve the Mystery
  of the Emerald Necklaces!. 1,700.00
97 ATh(c),The Country Fair
  Crimes 1,700.00
98 ATh,ATh(c),End of Sports!. . 1,700.00
99 ATh,ATh(c),E:Hop Harrigan . 1,700.00
100 ATh,I:Johnny Thunder 3,000.00
101 ATh,ATh(c),E:Mutt & Jeff . . 2,500.00
102 ATh,ATh(c),E:GrnLantern. . 7,000.00
Becomes:

ALL-AMERICAN WESTERN
1948–52
103 A:Johnny Thunder,The City
  Without Guns, All Johnny
  Thunder stories 1,400.00
104 ATh(c),Unseen Allies. 800.00
105 ATh(c),Hidden Guns 700.00
106 ATh(c),Snow Mountain
  Ambush 700.00
107 ATh(c),Cheyenne Justice . . 700.00
108 ATh(c),Vengeance of
  the Silver Bullet 400.00
109 ATh(c),Secret of
  Crazy River 400.00
110 ATh(c),Ambush at
  Scarecrow Hills 400.00
111 ATh(c),Gun-Shy Sheriff 400.00
112 ATh(c),Double Danger. 400.00
113 ATh(c),Johnny Thunder
  Indian Chief 400.00
114 ATh(c),The End of
  Johnny Thunder. 400.00
115 ATh(c),Cheyenne Mystery. . 400.00
116 ATh(c),Buffalo Raiders
  of the Mesa 400.00
117 ATh(c),V:Black Lightnin 300.00

All-American Western #115
© *DC Comics, Inc.*

118 ATh(c),Challenge of
  the Aztecs 300.00
119 GK(c),The Vanishing
  Gold Mine 300.00
120 GK(c),Ambush at
  Painted Mountain 300.00
121 ATh(c),The Unmasking of
  Johnny Thunder. 300.00
122 ATh(c),The Real
  Johnny Thunder. 300.00
123 GK(c),Johnny Thunder's
  Strange Rival. 300.00
124 ATh(c),The Iron Horse's
  Last Run 300.00
125 ATh(c),Johnny Thunder's
  Last Roundup 300.00
126 ATh(c),Phantoms of the
  Desert 300.00
Becomes:

ALL-AMERICAN MEN OF WAR
1952–66
127 (0) JGr(c),Unknown Marine 2,400.00
128 (1) IN, Bridgehead 1,500.00
2 JGr(c),Killer Bait 1,000.00
3 Pied Piper of Pyong-Yang . . . 900.00
4 JGr(c),The Hills of Hate. 900.00
5 One Second to Zero 900.00
6 IN(c),Jungle Killers. 800.00
7 IN(c),Beach to Hold 800.00
8 IN(c),Sgt. Storm Cloud. 800.00
9 IN(c),Death Mist. 800.00
10 JGr(c),Operation Avalance . . . 800.00
11 JGr(c),Dragon's Teeth 800.00
12 JGr(c),Bobsled Bombadier . . 700.00
13 JGr(c),Lost Patrol 700.00
14 IN(c),Pigeon Boss. 700.00
15 JGr(c),Flying Roadblock 700.00
16 JGr(c),The Flying Jeep 700.00
17 JGr(c),Booby Trap Ridge . . . 700.00
18 JKu(c),The Ballad of
  Battling Bells 700.00
19 JGr(c),IN,Torpedo Track 550.00
20 JGr(c),JKu,Lifenet to
  Beach Road. 550.00
21 JGr(c),IN,RH,The
  Coldest War. 550.00
22 JGr(c),IN,JKu,Snipers Nest . . 550.00
23 JGr(c),The Silent War 550.00
24 JGr(c),The Thin Line 550.00
25 JGr(c),IN,For Rent-One
  Foxhole 550.00
26 Dial W-A-R 550.00
27 JGr(c),RH,Fighting Pigeon . . 550.00

All-American Men of War #57
© DC Comics, Inc.

28 JGr(c),RA,JKu,Medal
  for A Dog 550.00
29 IN(c),JKu,Battle Bridges 550.00
30 JGr(c),RH,Frogman Hunt 550.00
31 JGr(c),Battle Seat 450.00
32 JGr(c),RH,Battle Station 450.00
33 JGr(c),IN,Sky Ambush 450.00
34 JGr(c),JKu,No Man's Alley . . . 450.00
35 JGr(c),IN, Battle Call 450.00
36 JGr(c),JKu,Battle Window 450.00
37 JGr(c),JKu,The Big Stretch . . . 450.00
38 JGr(c),RH,JKu,The
  Floating Sentinel 450.00
39 JGr(c),JKu,The Four Faces
  of Sgt. Fay 450.00
40 JGr(c),IN,Walking Helmet 450.00
41 JKu(c),RH,JKu,The 50-50 War 350.00
42 JGr(c),JKu,Battle Arm 350.00
43 JGr(c),JKu,Command Post . . . 350.00
44 JKu(c),The Flying Frogman . . . 350.00
45 JGr(c),RH,Combat Waterboy . . 350.00
46 JGr(c),IN,RH,Tank Busters . . . 350.00
47 JGr(c),JKu,MD,Battle Freight . 350.00
48 JGr(c),JKu,MD,Roadblock . . . 350.00
49 JGr(c),Walking Target 350.00
50 IN,RH,Bodyguard For A Sub. . 350.00
51 JGr(c),RH,Bomber's Moon . . . 300.00
52 JKu(c),RH,MD,Back
  Seat Driver 300.00
53 JKu(c),JKu,Night Attack 300.00
54 JKu(c),IN,Diary of a
  Fighter Pilot 300.00
55 JKu(c),RH,Split-Second Target 300.00
56 JKu,IN,RH,Frogman Jinx 300.00
57 Pick-Up for Easy Co. 300.00
58 JKu(c),RH,MD,A Piece of Sky 300.00
59 JGr(c),JKu,The Hand of War . 300.00
60 JGr(c),The Time Table 300.00
61 JGr(c),IN,MD,Blind Target. . . . 300.00
62 JGr(c),RH,RA,No(c) 300.00
63 JGr(c),JKu,Frogman Carrier . . 300.00
64 JKu(c),JKu,RH,The Other
  Man's War 300.00
65 JGr(c),JKu,MD,Same
  Old Sarge 300.00
66 JGr(c),The Walking Fort 300.00
67 JGr(c),RH,A:Gunner&Sarge,
  The Cover Man 800.00
68 JGr(c),Gunner&Sarge,
  The Man & The Gun 350.00
69 JKu(c),A:Tank Killer,
  Bazooka Hill 350.00
70 JKu(c),IN,Pigeon
  Without Wings 300.00
71 JGr(c),A:Tank Killer,Target
  For An Ammo Boy 250.00

72 JGr(c),A:Tank Killer,T.N.T.
  Broom 250.00
73 JGr(c),JKu,No Detour 250.00
74 The Minute Commandos 250.00
75 JKu(c),Sink That Flattop 250.00
76 JKu(c),A:Tank Killer,
  Just One More Tank 250.00
77 JKu(c),IN,MD,Big Fish-
  little Fish 250.00
78 JGr(c),Tin Hat for an
  Iron Man 250.00
79 JKu(c),RA,Showdown Soldier. 250.00
80 JGr(c),RA,The Medal Men . . . 250.00
81 JGr(c),IN,Ghost Ship of
  Two Wars. 200.00
82 IN(c),B:Johnny Cloud,
  The Flying Chief 350.00
83 IN(c),Fighting Blind 300.00
84 IN(c),Death Dive 200.00
85 RH(c),Battle Eagle 200.00
86 JGr(c),Top-Gun Ace 200.00
87 JGr(c),Broken Ace 200.00
88 JGr(c),The Ace of Vengeance 200.00
89 JGr(c),The Star Jockey 200.00
90 JGr(c),Wingmate of Doom . . . 175.00
91 RH(c),Two Missions To Doom 175.00
92 JGr(c),The Battle Hawk 175.00
93 RH(c),The Silent Rider 175.00
94 RH(c),Be Brave-Be Silent. . . . 175.00
95 RH(c),Second Sight
  For a Pilot 175.00
96 RH(c),The Last Flight
  of Lt. Moon 175.00
97 IN(c),A Target Called Johnny . 175.00
98 The Time-Bomb Ace 175.00
99 IN(c),The Empty Cockpit. 175.00
100 RH(c),Battle o/t Sky Chiefs. . 175.00
101 RH(c),Death Ship of
  Three Wars 150.00
102 JKu(c),Blind Eagle-Hungry
  Hawk 150.00
103 IN(c),Battle Ship-
  Battle Heart 150.00
104 JKu(c),The Last Target 150.00
105 IN(c),Killer Horse-Ship 150.00
106 IN(c),Death Song For
  A Battle Hawk 150.00
107 IN(c),Flame in the Sky 150.00
108 IN(c),Death-Dive of the Aces 150.00
109 IN(c),The Killer Slot. 150.00
110 RH(c),The Co-Pilot was
  Death. 150.00
111 RH(c),E:Johnny Cloud, Tag–
  You're Dead. 150.00
112 RH(c),B:Balloon Buster,Lt.
  Steve Savage-Balloon Buster 150.00
113 JKu(c),The Ace of
  Sudden Death 150.00
114 JKu(c),The Ace Who
  Died Twice 150.00
115 IN(c),A:Johnny Cloud,
  Deliver One Enemy Ace-
  Handle With Care 150.00
116 JKu(c),A:Baloon Buster,
  Circle of Death. 150.00
117 Sept.–Oct., 1966 . . . . 150.00

ALL-AMERICAN COMICS
1999
1 RMz(s),F:Green Lantern &
  Johnny Thunder. 2.25

ALL-FLASH
1941–47
1 EHi,O:Flash,I:The Monocle. 30,000.00
2 EHi,The Adventure of Roy
  Revenge 10,000.00
3 EHi,The Adventure of
  Misplaced Faces 4,000.00
4 EHi,Tale of the Time Capsule 4,000.00

All-Flash #25
© DC Comics Inc.

5 EHi,The Case of the Patsy
  Colt! Last Quarterly 3,000.00
6 EHi,The Ray that Changed
  Men's Souls 2,700.00
7 EHi,Adventures of a Writers
  Fantasy, House of Horrors . 2,700.00
8 EHi,Formula to Fairyland!. . . 2,700.00
9 EHi,Adventure of the Stolen
  Telescope 2,700.00
10 EHi,Case of the Curious Cat 2,700.00
11 EHi,Troubles Come
  in Doubles 2,500.00
12 EHi,Tumble INN to Trouble,
  Becomes Quarterly on orders
  from War Production Board
  O:The Thinker. 2,500.00
13 EHi,I:The King 2,500.00
14 EHi,I:Winky,Blinky & Noddy
  Green Lantern (c). 2,600.00
15 EHi,Secrets of a Stranger . . 2,500.00
16 EHi,A:The Sinister 2,500.00
17 Tales of the Three Wishes. . 2,500.00
18 A:Winky,Blinky&Noddy
  B:Mutt & Jeff reprints 2,500.00
19 No Rest at the Rest Home . 2,500.00
20 A:Winky, Blinky & Noddy . . . 2,500.00
21 I:Turtle 2,000.00
22 The Money Doubler, E:Mutt
  & Jeff reprints 2,000.00
23 The Bad Men of Bar Nothing 2,000.00
24 I:Worry Wart,3 Court
  Clowns Get Caught 2,000.00
25 I:Slapsy Simmons,
  Flash Jitterbugs 2,000.00
26 I:The Chef,The Boss,Shrimp
  Coogan,A:Winky, Blinky &
  Noddy 2,000.00
27 A:The Thinker, Gangplank
  Gus Story 2,000.00
28 A:Shrimp Coogan, Winky,
  Blinky & Noddy 2,000.00
29 The Thousand-Year Old Terror,
  A:Winky, Blinky & Noddy . . 2,500.00
30 The Vanishing Snowman . . . 2,000.00
31 A:Black Hat,Planet of Sport . 2,000.00
32 I:Fiddler,A:Thinker 2,500.00

ALL FUNNY COMICS
1943–48
1 Genius Jones 750.00
2 same 350.00
3 same 250.00
4 same 250.00
5 thru 10 . . . . @250.00
11 Genius Jones 250.00

DC COMICS

12 same	250.00
13 same	200.00
14	200.00
15	200.00
16 A:DC Superheroes	500.00
17 thru 23	@200.00

ALL-NEW ATOM, THE
July, 2006

1 JBy,TvS,F:Ryan Choi	3.00
2 JBy,TvS,V:M'ngalah	3.00
3 JBy,TvS,Ivytown mysteries	3.00
4 V:Giganta	3.00
5 V:Dwarfstar	3.00

ALL STAR BATMAN AND ROBIN, THE BOY WONDER
July, 2005

1 FM(s),JLe,SW	3.00
1a variant (c)	3.00
1b Special edition, 48-pg.	20.00
2 FM(s),JLe,SW	3.00
3 FM(s),JLe,SW	3.00
4 FM(s),JLe,SW, F:Black Canary	3.00
4a variant FM(c)	8.00
5 FM(s),JLe,SW,The Batcave	3.00
5a variant (c)	5.00
6 FM(s),JLe,SW,A:The Batgirl	3.00
6a variant FM (c)	5.00

ALL-STAR COMICS
1940–51

1 B:Flash,Hawkman,Hourman, Sandman,Spectre,Red White & Blue	26,000.00
2 B:Green Lantern and Johnny Thunder	10,000.00
3 First meeting of Justice Society with Flash as Chairman	65,000.00
4 First mission of JSA	10,000.00
5 V:Mr. X,I:Hawkgirl	8,000.00
6 Flash Leaves	5,500.00
7 Green Lantern Becomes Chairman, L:Hourman, C:Superman, Batman & Flash	6,000.00
8 I:Wonder Women;Starman and Dr. Mid-Nite Join,Hawkman Becomes Chairman	60,000.00
9 JSA in Latin America	6,000.00
10 C:Flash & Green Lantern, JSA Time Travel story	6,000.00

All-Star Comics #5
© DC Comics, Inc.

11 Wonder Women joins; I:Justice Battalion	8,000.00
12 V:Black Dragon society	5,000.00
13 V:Hitler	5,000.00
14 JSA in Occupied Europe	5,000.00
15 I:Brain Wave,A:JSA's Girl Friends	5,000.00
16 Propaganda/relevance issue	2,400.00
17 V:Brain Wave	2,400.00
18 I:King Bee	2,500.00
19 Hunt for Hawkman	2,400.00
20 I:Monster	2,400.00
21 Time Travel Story	2,500.00
22 Sandman and Dr. Fate Leave, I:Conscience, Good Fairy	2,500.00
23 I:Psycho-Pirate	2,500.00
24 Propaganda/relevance issue, A:Conscience&Wildcat,Mr.Terrific; L:Starman & Spectre; Flash & Green Lantern Return	2,500.00
25 JSA whodunit issue	3,000.00
26 V:Metal Men from Jupiter	4,000.00
27 Handicap issue,A:Wildcat	4,000.00
28 Ancient curse comes to life	4,000.00
29 I:Landor from 25th Century	4,000.00
30 V:Brain Wave	4,000.00
31 V:Zor	4,000.00
32 V:Psycho-Pirate	2,300.00
33 V:Soloman Grundy,A:Doiby Dickles, Last appearance Thunderbolt	5,600.00
34 I:Wizard	2,000.00
35 I:Per Degaton	2,000.00
36 A:Superman and Batman	6,000.00
37 I:Injustice Society of the World	3,000.00
38 V:Villians of History, A:Black Canary	4,000.00
39 JSA in Magic World, Johnny Thunder leaves	2,500.00
40 A:Black Canary,Junior Justice Society of America	2,500.00
41 Black Canary joins,A:Harlequin, V:Injustice Society of the World	2,500.00
42 I:Alchemist	2,400.00
43 V:Interdimensional gold men	2,400.00
44 I:Evil Star	2,400.00
45 Crooks develop stellar JSA powers	2,400.00
46 Comedy issue	2,400.00
47 V:Billy the Kid	2,400.00
48 Time Travel story	2,400.00
49 V:Comet-Being Invaders	2,400.00
50 V:Flash's Classmate	3,800.00
51 V:Diamond Men from Center of the Earth	2,400.00
52 JSA Disappears from Earth for Years	2,400.00
53 Time Travel issue	2,400.00
54 Circus issue	2,400.00
55 JSA Fly to Jupiter	2,400.00
56 V:Chameleons from 31st Century	2,400.00
57 I:Key	3,100.00

Becomes:

ALL STAR WESTERN
April-May, 1951

58 GK(c),Trigger Twins	800.00
59 GK(c),Trail of Double Decoys	500.00
60 CI(c),Raiders of Rocky City	500.00
61 thru 64 ATh	@400.00
65 CI,Green Bandanna Raiders	400.00
66 CI,Powderkeg Town	450.00
67 GK,B:Johnny Thunder	500.00
68 thru 81	@250.00
82 thru 98	@250.00
99 FF	250.00
100 CI,Sheriff for Hire	250.00
101 thru 104	@200.00
105 O:JSA, March, 1987	200.00
106 and 107	@200.00

108 O:Johnny Thunder	400.00
109 thru 116	@200.00
117 CI,O:Super-Chief	250.00
118 Eyes of Johnny Thunder	200.00
119 Ghost-Town Gunfight	200.00

ALL-STAR COMICS
1976–78

58 RE,WW,R:JSA,I:Power Girl	65.00
59 RE,WW,Brain Wave	40.00
60 KG,WW,I:Vulcan	40.00
61 KG,WW,V:Vulcan	40.00
62 KG,WW,A:E-2 Superman	40.00
63 KG,WW,A:E-2 Superman, Solomon Grundy	40.00
64 WW,Shining Knight	40.00
65 KG,WW,E-2 Superman, Vandal Savage	40.00
66 JSon,BL,Injustice Society	40.00
67 JSon,BL	40.00
68 JSon,BL	40.00
69 JSon,BL,A:E-2 Superman, Starman,Dr.Mid-Nite	60.00
70 JSon,BL,Huntress	40.00
71 JSon,BL	40.00
72 JSon,A:Golden.Age Huntress	40.00
73 JSon	40.00
74 JSon	40.00
TPB Justice Society, Vol. 1 (2006)	15.00

ALL STAR COMICS
1999

1 JeR(s),F:Justice Society of America, V:Stalker's Seven	3.00
2 JeR(s) conclusion	3.00
Giant #1 80-page	5.00

ALL STAR SQUADRON
1981–87

1 RB,JOy,JSa,I:Degaton	8.00
2 RB,JOy,Robotman	5.00
3 RB,JOy,Robotman	5.00
4 RB,JOy,Robotman	5.00
5 RB/JOy,I:Firebrand(Dannette)	5.00
6 JOy,Hawkgirl	5.00
7 JOy,Hawkgirl	5.00
8 DH/JOy,A:Steel	5.00
9 DH/JOy,A:Steel	5.00
10 JOy,V:Binary Brotherhood	5.00
11 JOy,V:Binary Brotherhood	5.00
12 JOy,R:Dr.Hastor O:Hawkman	5.00
13 JOy,photo(c)	5.00
14 JOy,JLA crossover	5.00
15 JOy,JLA crossover	5.00
16 I&D:Nuclear	5.00
17 Trial of Robotman	5.00
18 V:Thor	5.00
19 V:Brainwave	5.00
20 JOy,V:Brainwave	5.00
21 JOy,I:Cyclotron (1st JOy Superman)	7.00
22 JOy,V:Deathbolt,Cyclotron	5.00
23 JOy,I:Amazing-Man	5.00
24 JOy,I:Brainwave,Jr.	7.00
25 JOy,I:Infinity Inc.	7.00
26 JOy,Infinity Inc.	7.00
27 Spectre	5.00
28 JOy,Spectre	5.00
29 JOy,retold story	5.00
30 V:Black Dragons	5.00
31 All-Star gathering	5.00
32 O:Freedom Fighters	5.00
33 Freedom Fighters,I:Tsunami	5.00
34 Freedom Fighters	5.00
35 RB,Shazam family	5.00
36 Shazam family	5.00
37 A:Shazam Family	5.00
38 V:The Real American	5.00
39 V:The Real American	5.00
40 D:The Real American	5.00
41 O:Starman	5.00

All Star Squadron #29
© DC Comics Inc.

42 V:Tsunami,Kung 5.00
43 V:Tsunami,Kung 5.00
44 I:Night & Fog. 5.00
45 I:Zyklon 5.00
46 V:Baron Blitzkrieg 5.00
47 TM,O:Dr.Fate 10.00
48 A:Blackhawk 5.00
49 A:Dr.Occult 5.00
50 Crisis 7.00
51 AA,Crisis 5.00
52 Crisis 5.00
53 Crisis,A:The Dummy 5.00
54 Crisis,V:The Dummy 5.00
55 Crisis,V:Anti-Monitor 5.00
56 Crisis 5.00
57 A:Dr.Occult 5.00
58 I:Mekanique 5.00
59 A:Mekanique,Spectre 5.00
60 Crisis 1942, conclusion. 5.00
61 O:Liberty Belle 5.00
62 O:The Shining Knight 5.00
63 O:Robotman 5.00
64 WB/TD,V:Funny Face 5.00
65 DH/TD,O:Johnny Quick 5.00
66 TD,O:Tarantula 5.00
67 TD,Last Issue,O:JSA 5.00
Ann.#1 JOy,O:G.A.,Atom 5.00
Ann.#2 JOy,Infinity Inc. 5.00
Ann.#3 WB,JOy,KG,GP,DN 5.00

ALL STAR SUPERMAN
Nov., 2005
1 GMo(s) 4.00
2 GMo(s), Fortress of Solitude 3.00
3 GMo(s), Lois Lane, Superwoman 3.00
4 GMo(s), F:Jimmy Olsen 3.00
5 GMo(s),Clark Kent, convict 3.00
6 GMo(s),back to Smallville 3.00

ALL STAR WESTERN
See: WEIRD WESTERN TALES

AMBER:
THE GUNS OF AVALON
Aug., 1996
1 (of 3) adapt. of Roger Zelazny
 classic 7.00
2 and 3 conclusion . . . . @7.00

AMBUSH BUG
1985
1 KG,I:Cheeks 3.00

2 KG thru 4 . . . . @3.00
Spec.#1 Stocking Stuffer,
 KG,R:Cheeks (1986) 3.00
Spec.#1 Nothing Special
 KG,A:Sandman,Death (1992) . . 3.50

AMERICA VS.
JUSTICE SOCIETY
Jan.–April, 1985
1 AA,R,Thomas Script 10.00
2 AA 7.00
3 AA 7.00
4 AA, ... 7.00

AMERICAN CENTURY
DC/Vertigo, March, 2001
1 HC,vet hijacks plane 5.00
2 HC,Hell hotter for Harry 3.00
3 HC,Guatemalan Revolution 3.00
4 HC,Bananarama 3.00
5 HC,The Protector,pt.1 . . . . 3.00
6 HC,The Protector,pt.2 . . . . 3.00
7 HC,The Protector,pt.3 . . . . 3.00
8 HC,The Protector,pt.4 . . . . 3.00
9 HC,Route 66 . . . . 3.00
10 HC,White Lightning,pt.1 . . . . . . 3.00
11 HC,White Lightning,pt.2 . . . . . . 3.00
12 HC,White Lightning,pt.3 . . . . . . 3.00
13 HC,White Lightning,pt.4 . . . . . . 3.00
14 HC,An American in Paris,pt.1 . . 3.00
15 HC,An American in Paris,pt.2 . . 3.00
16 HC,An American in Paris,pt.3 . . 3.00
17 HC,Coming Home,pt.1 . . . . 3.00
18 HC,Coming Home,pt.2 . . . . 3.00
19 HC,Coming Home,pt.3 . . . . 3.00
20 HC,Coming Home,Pt.4 . . . . 3.00
21 HC,Coming Home,pt.5 . . . . 3.00
22 HC,Tramps,pt.1 . . . . 3.00
23 HC,Tramps,pt.2 . . . . 3.00
24 HC,one-shot 3.00
25 HC,Bite the Big Apple,pt.1 . . . . 3.00
26 HC,Bite the Big Apple,pt.2 . . . . 3.00
27 HC,Bite the Big Apple,pt.3 . . . . 3.00
TPB Scars and Stripes, HC 9.00
TPB Hollywood Babylon 13.00

AMERICAN FREAK: A
TALE OF THE UN-MEN
DC/Vertigo, 1994
1 B:DLp,(s),VcL,R:Un-Men 2.25
2 VcL,A:Crassus 2.25
3 VcL ,A:Scylla 2.25
4 VcL,A:Scylla 2.25
5 VcL,Final Issue 2.25

AMERICAN SPLENDOR
DC/Vertigo, Sept., 2006
1 (of 4) HP 3.00
2 HP 3.00
3 HP 3.00

AMERICAN VIRGIN
DC/Vertigo, March, 2006
1 You Always Remember Your
 First Time 3.00
2 Head, pt. 2 . . . . 3.00
3 Head, pt. 3 . . . . 3.00
4 Head, pt. 4 . . . . 3.00
5 Going Down, pt.1 . . . . 3.00
6 Going Down, pt.2 . . . . 3.00
7 Going Down, pt.3 . . . . 3.00
8 Going Down, pt.4 . . . . 3.00
9 Going Down, epilogue 3.00
TPB Head 10.00

AMETHYST
[Limited Series], 1983–84
[PRINCESS OF GEMWORLD]
1 Origin 2.50
2 thru 7 EC . . . . @2.50
8 EC,O:Gemworld 2.50
9 thru 12 EC . . . . @2.50
Spec.#1 KG 2.50

[Regular Series], 1985–86
1 thru 12 EC . . . . @2.50
13 EC,Crisis,A:Dr.Fate 2.50
14 EC 2.50
15 EC,Castle Amethyst Destroyed . 2.50
16 EC 2.50
Spec.#1 EM 2.50

[Mini-Series], 1987–88
1 EM 2.00
2 EM 2.00
3 EM 2.00
4 EM,O:Mordru 2.00

ANARKY
March, 1997
1 AIG(s),NBy,JRu,Anarky vs.
 Etrigan 4.00
2 AIG(s),NBy,JRu,V:Darkseid 2.50
3 AIG(s),NBy,JRu,A:Batman 2.50
4 AIG(s),NBy,JRu,A:Batman,concl . . 2.50

2nd Series,1999
1 AIG(s),NBy,JRu,F:JLA 2.50
2 AIG(s),NBy,JRu,F:GreenLantern . 2.50
3 AIG(s),NBy,JRu,F:GreenLantern . 2.50
4 AIG(s),NBy,JRu,V:Ra's al Ghul . . 2.50
5 AIG(s),NBy,JRu,V:Ra's
 al Ghul,pt.2 . . . . 2.50
6 AIG(s),NBy,JRu,F:Ra's
 al Ghul,pt.3 . . . . 2.50
7 AIG,NBy,JRu,Day of Judgment . 2.50
8 AIG(s),NBy,JRu, final issue 2.50

Angel and the Ape #2
© DC Comics, Inc.

ANGEL & THE APE
1991
1 Apes of Wrath,pt.1 . . . . 3.00
2 Wrath pt.2,A:G.Gardner 3.00
3 Wrath,pt.3,A:InferiorFive 3.00
4 Wrath,pt.4,A:InferiorFive 3.00

ANGEL AND THE APE
DC/Vertigo, Aug., 2001
1 (of 4) HC,F:Angel O'Day 3.00
2 thru 4 HC . . . . @3.00

DC COMICS

ANGELTOWN
DC/Vertigo, Nov., 2004
1 (of 5) SMa 3.00
2 thru 4 SMa . . . . @3.00
5 SMa 3.00

Anima #12 © DC Comics, Inc.

ANIMA
DC/Vertigo, 1994–95
1 R:Anima 2.50
2 V:Scarecrow. 2.50
3 V:Scarecrow. 2.50
4 A:Nameless one. 2.50
5 Cl,V:Arkana 2.50
6 Cl,V:Arkana 2.50
7 Zero Hour. 2.50
8 Nameless One. 2.50
9 Superboy & Nameless One. . . . 2.50
10 A:Superboy 2.50
11 V:Nameless One. 2.50
12 A:Hawkman,V:Shrike 2.50
13 A:Hawkman,Shrike 2.50
14 Return to Gotham City 2.50
15 V:Psychic Vampire, final issue . . 3.00

ANIMAL ANTICS
1946–49
1 B:Racoon Kids. 600.00
2 . . . . 300.00
3 thru 10 . . . . @200.00
11 thru 23 . . . . @125.00

ANIMAL-MAN
1988–95
1 BB(c),B:GMo(s),ChT,DHz,
  B:Animal Rights,I:Dr.Myers . . . 12.00
2 BB(c),ChT,DHz,A:Superman . . . 6.00
3 BB(c),ChT,DHz,A:B'wana Beast . 5.00
4 BB(c),ChT,DHz,V:B'wana Beast,
  E:Animal Rights. 5.00
5 BB(c),ChT,DHz,
  I&D:Crafty Coyote 5.00
6 BB(c),ChT,DHz,A:Hawkman . . . 5.00
7 BB(c),ChT,DHz,D:Red Mask . . . 5.00
8 BB(c),ChT,DHz,V:Mirror Master. . 5.00
9 BB(c),DHz,TG,A:Martian
  Manhunter. 5.00
10 BB(c),ChT,DHz,A:Vixen,
  B:O:Animal Man 5.00
11 BB(c),ChT,DHz,I:Hamed Ali,
  Tabu,A:Vixen. 3.00
12 BB(c),D:Hamed Ali,A:Vixen,
  B'wanaBeast 3.00

13 BB(c),I:Dominic Mndawe,R:B'wana
  Beast,Apartheid. 3.00
14 BB(c),TG,SeM,A:Future Animal
  Man,I:Lennox. 3.00
15 BB(c),ChT,DHz,A:Dolphin . . . 3.00
16 BB(c),ChT,DHz,A:JLA. 3.00
17 BB(c),ChT,DHz,A:Mirr.Master. . . 3.00
18 BB(c),ChT,DHz,A:Lennox 3.00
19 BB(c),ChT,DHz,D:Ellen,
  Cliff,Maxine 3.00
20 BB(c),ChT,DHz,I:Bug-Man 3.00
21 BB(c),ChT,DHz,N&V:Bug-Man . . 3.00
22 BB(c),PCu,SeM,A:Rip Hunter. . . 3.00
23 BB(c),A:Phantom Stranger 3.00
24 BB(c),V:Psycho Pirate 3.00
25 BB(c),ChT,MFm,I:Comic
  Book Limbo 3.00
26 BB(c),E:GMo(s),ChT,MFm,
  A:Grant Morrison 3.00
27 BB(c),B:PMi(s),ChT,MFm 3.00
28 BB(c),ChT,MFm,I:Nowhere Man,
  I&D:Front Page 3.00
29 ChT,SDi,V:National Man 3.00
30 BB(c),ChT,MFm,V:Angel Mob. . . 3.00
31 BB(c),ChT,MFm 3.00
32 BB(c),E:PMi(s),ChT,MFm 3.00
33 BB(c),B:TV(s),SDi,A:Travis
  Cody 3.00
34 BB(c),SDi,Requiem. 3.00
35 BB(c),SDi,V:Radioactive Dogs . . 3.00
36 BB(c),SDi,A:Mr.Rainbow 3.00
37 BB(c),SDi,Animal/Lizard Man . . . 3.00
38 BB(c),SDi,A:Mr.Rainbow 3.00
39 BB(c),TMd,SDi,Wolfpack in
  San Diego 3.00
40 BB(c),SDi,War of the Gods
  x-over. 3.00
41 BB(c),SDi,V:Star Labs
  Renegades,I:Winky 3.00
42 BB(c),SDi,V:Star Labs
  Renegades 3.00
43 BB(c),SDi,I:Tristess,A:Vixen 3.00
44 BB(c),SDi,A:Vixen. 3.00
45 BB(c),StP,SDi,I:L.Decker. 3.00
46 BB(c),SDi,I:Frank Baker. 3.00
47 BB(c),SDi,I:Shining Man,
  (B'wana Beast) 3.00
48 BB(c),SDi,V:Antagon. 3.00
49 BB(c),SDi,V:Antagon. 3.00
50 BB(c),E:TV(s),SDi,I:Metaman . . . 5.00
51 BB(c),B:JaD(s),StP,B:Flesh
  and Blood 3.00
52 BB(c),StP,Homecoming. 3.00
53 BB(c),StP,Flesh and Blood 3.00
54 BB(c),StP,Flesh and Blood 3.00
55 BB(c),StP,Flesh and Blood 3.00
56 BB(c),StP,E:Flesh and Blood,
  Double-sized 6.00

DC/Vertigo, 1993
57 BB(c),StP,B:Recreation,
  Ellen in NY. 3.00
58 BB(c),StP,Wild Side 3.00
59 BB(c),RsB,GHi(i),Wild Town 3.00
60 RsB,GHi(i),Wild life 3.00
61 BB(c),StP,Tooth and Claw#1. . . . 3.00
62 BB(c),StP,Tooth and Claw#2. . . . 3.00
63 BB(c),V:Leviathan 3.00
64 DlB(c),WSm,DnS(i),
  Breath of God 3.00
65 RDB(c),WSm,
  Perfumed Garden 3.00
66 A:Kindred Spirit 3.00
67 StP,Mysterious Ways #1 . . . . . . 3.00
68 StP,Mysterious Ways #2 . . . . . . 3.00
69 Animal Man's Family. 3.00
70 GgP(c),StP 3.00
71 GgP(c),StP,Maxine Alive? 3.00
72 StP 3.00
73 StP,Power Life Church 3.00
74 StP,Power Life Church 3.00
75 StP,Power Life Church 3.00
76 StP,Pilgrimage problems. 3.00

Animal Man #63
© DC Comics, Inc.

77 Cliff shot 3.00
78 StP,Animal Man poisoned. 3.00
79 New Direction 3.00
80 New Direction 3.00
81 Wild Type,pt.1 . . . . 3.00
82 Wild Type,pt.2 . . . . 3.00
83 Wild Type,pt.3 . . . . 3.00
84 F:Maxine,SupernaturalDreams. . 3.00
85 Animal Mundi,pt.1 . . . . 3.00
86 Animal Mundi,pt.2 . . . . 3.00
87 Animal Mundi,pt.3 . . . . 3.00
88 Morphogenetic Fields 3.00
89 final issue 3.00
Ann.#1 BB(c),JaD,TS(i),RIB(i),
  Children Crusade,F:Maxine. . . . 4.25
TPB Rep.#1 thru #10. . . . . 20.00
TPB Animal Man, 2nd pr. 20.00
TPB Origin of the Species 20.00
TPB Deus Ex Machina (2003) . . . 20.00

ANIMANIACS
Warner Bros./DC May, 1995
1 F:Yakko,Wakko,Dot 8.00
2 thru 20 . . . . @4.00
21 thru 59 . . . . @3.00
Christmas Spec.. . . . . 4.00

ANTHRO
1968–69
1 HwP. 150.00
2 HwP. 90.00
3 thru 5 HwP. . . . . @100.00
6 HwP,WW(c&a) 100.00

AQUAMAN
[1st Regular Series], 1962–78
1 NC,I:Quisp 2,000.00
2 NC,V:Captain Sykes. 1,000.00
3 NC,Aquaman from Atlantis . . . 750.00
4 NC,A:Quisp 500.00
5 NC,The Haunted Sea 500.00
6 NC,A:Quisp 400.00
7 NC,Sea Beasts of Atlantis 400.00
8 NC,Plot to Steal the Seas 400.00
9 NC,V:King Neptune 400.00
10 NC,A:Quisp. 400.00
11 I: Mera. 325.00
12 NC,The Cosmic Gladiators . . 325.00
13 NC,Invasion of the Giant
  Reptiles 325.00
14 NC,AquamanSecretPowers . . 325.00
15 NC,Menace of the Man-Fish. . 325.00

DC COMICS

16 NC,Duel of the Sea Queens . . 325.00
17 NC,Man Who Vanquished
    Aquaman 325.00
18 W:Aquaman & Mera 325.00
19 NC,Atlanteans for Sale 325.00
20 NC,Sea King's DoubleDoom . . 325.00
21 NC,I:Fisherman 150.00
22 NC,The Trap of the Sinister
    Sea Nymphs 150.00
23 NC,I:Aquababy 150.00
24 NC,O:Black Manta 150.00
25 NC,Revolt of Aquaboy 150.00
26 NC,I:O.G.R.E. 150.00
27 NC,Battle of the Rival
    Aquamen 150.00
28 NC,Hail Aquababy,King of
    Atlantis 150.00
29 I:Ocean Master 175.00
30 NC,C:JLA 175.00
31 NC,V:O.G.R.E. 175.00
32 NC,V:Tryton 175.00
33 NC,I:Aquagirl 200.00
34 NC,I:Aquabeast 125.00
35 I:Black Manta 125.00
36 NC,What Seeks the
    Awesome Threesome? 125.00
37 I:Scavenger 125.00
38 NC,I:Liquidator 125.00
39 NC,How to Kill a Sea King . . . 125.00
40 JAp,Sorcerers from the Sea . . 125.00
41 JAp,Quest for Mera,pt.1 . . . . . 100.00
42 JAp,Quest for Mera,pt.2 . . . . . 100.00
43 JAp,Quest for Mera,pt.3 . . . . . 100.00
44 JAp,Quest for Mera,pt.4 . . . . . 100.00
45 JAp,Quest for Mera,pt.5 . . . . . 100.00
46 JAp,Quest for Mera concl. 100.00
47 JAp,Revolution in Atlantis #1
    rep.Adventure #268 . . . . 100.00
48 JAp,Revolution in Atlantis #2
    rep.Adventure #260 . . . . 135.00
49 JAp,As the Seas Die 100.00
50 JAp,NA:Deadman 175.00
51 JAp,NA:Deadman 175.00
52 JAp,NA:Deadman 175.00
53 JAp,Is California Sinking? 40.00
54 JAp,Crime Wave 40.00
55 JAp,Return of the Alien 40.00
56 JAp,I&O:Crusader (1970) 40.00
57 JAp,V:Black Manta (1977) 40.00
58 JAp,O:Aquaman rtd 50.00
59 JAp,V:Scavenger 40.00
60 DN,V:Scavenger 40.00
61 DN,BMc,A:Batman 40.00
62 DN,A:Ocean Master 30.00
63 DN,V:Ocean Master,
    final issue 30.00

[1st Limited Series], 1986
1 V:Ocean Master 6.00
2 V:Ocean Master 4.00
3 V:Ocean Master 4.00
4 V:Ocean Master 4.00

[2nd Limited Series], 1989
1 CS,Atlantis Under Siege 3.50
2 CS,V:Invaders 3.00
3 CS,Mera turned Psychotic. 3.00
4 CS,Poseidonis Under Siege 3.00
5 CS,Last Stand,final issue. 3.00
Spec#1 MPa,Legend o/Aquaman . . 3.00

[2nd Regular Series], 1991–92
1 Poseidonis Under Attack,
    C:J'onn J'onzz,Blue Beetle 3.50
2 V:Oumland 2.50
3 I:Iqula 2.50
4 V:Iqula,A:Queequeg. 2.50
5 A:Aqualad,Titans,M.Manhunter,
    R:Manta 2.50
6 V: Manta. 2.50
7 R:Mera 2.50
8 A:Batman,V:NKV Demon 2.50
9 Eco-Wars#1,A:Sea Devils 2.50
10 Eco-Wars#2,A:Sea Devils. 2.50

11 V:Gigantic Dinosaur 2.50
12 A:Iaula. 2.50
13 V:The Scavenger 2.50
14 V:The Scavenger 2.50

[3rd Regular Series], 1994–2001
0 B:PDd(s),Paternal secret. 7.00
1 PDd(s),R:Aqualad,I:Charybdis. . . 6.00
2 V:Charybdis 7.00
3 B:PDd(s),Superboy 4.00
4 B:PDd(s),Lobo 4.00
5 New Costume 4.00
6 V:The Deep Six 4.00
7 Kako's Metamorphosis 4.00
8 V:Corona and Naiad 4.00
9 JPi(c&a),V:Deadline,A:Koryak . . . 3.00
10 A:Green Lantern,Koryak. 3.00
11 R:Mera 3.00
12 F:Mera. 3.00
13 V:Thanatos 3.00
14 PDd,V:Major Disaster,Underworld
    Unleashed tie-in 3.00
15 PDd,V:Tiamat 3.00
16 PDd,A:Justice League 3.00
17 PDd,V:underwater gargoyles . . . 3.00
18 PDd,Biblical Sense 3.00
19 PDd,V:Ocean Master 3.00
20 PDd,V:Ocean Master 3.00
21 PDd,JCf,A:Dolphin,
    V:ThiernaNaOge 3.00
22 PDd(s). 3.00
23 PDd(s),I:Deep Blue (Neptune
    Perkins) 3.00
24 PDd(s),A:Neptune Perkins 3.00
25 PDd(s),MEg,HSm,Atlantis united,
    Aquaman king? 3.00
26 PDd(s),MEg,HSm,Oceans
    threatened, Final Night tie-in . . . 3.00
27 PDd(s),MEg,HSm,V:Demon
    Gate, dolphin killer. 3.00
28 PDd(s),JCf,JP,A:J'onn J'onzz . . . 3.00
29 PDd(s),MEg,HSm, ... 3.00
30 PDd(s),MEg,HSm,The Pit. 3.00
31 PDd(s),V:The Shark, mind-
    controlled aquatic army 3.00
32 PDd(s),A:Swamp Thing 3.00
33 PDd(s),Aquaman's dark powers
    affect him physically 3.00
34 PDd(s),V:Triton 3.00
35 PDd(s),JCf,I:Gamesman,
    A:Animal Man 3.00
36 PDd(s),JCf,R:Poseidonis,
    Tempest,Vulko. 3.00
37 PDd,JCf,Genesis,V:Darkseid . . . 3.00
38 PDd,JCf,capitalism 3.00

Aquaman 3rd Series #51
© DC Comics Inc.

39 PDd,JCf,Perkins Family Reunion 3.00
40 PDd,JCf,Dr. Polaris. 3.00
41 PDd,JCf,BSf,F:Power Girl. 2.50
42 PDd,JCf. 2.50
43 PDd,JCf,Millennium Giants,
    pt.2 x-over, A:Superman Red . . 2.50
44 PDd,JCf,F:Golden Age Flash,
    Sentinel 2.50
45 PDd,JCf,V:Triton 2.50
46 PDd,JCf,news of Mera 2.50
47 DAn,Shadows on Water,pt.1. . . . 2.50
48 DAn,Shadows on Water,pt.2. . . . 2.50
49 DAn,ALa,JCf,V:Tempest 2.50
50 EL,NRd,New Costume 2.50
51 EL,NRd,V:King Noble 2.50
52 EL,V:Fire Trolls 2.50
53 EL,A:Superman. 2.50
54 EL,A:Landlovers 2.50
55 EL,wooing Mera 2.50
56 EL,V:Piranha Man,pt.1 . . . . 2.50
57 EL,V:Piranha Man,pt.2 . . . . 2.50
58 EL,V:DemonGate & BlackManta. 2.50
59 EL,drugs in Atlantis 2.50
60 NRd,W:Tempest & Dolphin 2.50
61 NRd,Day of Judgment x-over . . . 2.50
62 EL(s),NRd 2.50
63 NRd. 2.50
64 DJu,SEp,NRd 2.50
65 DJu,SEp,NRd 2.50
66 DJu,PR,NRd,F:JLA 2.50
67 DJu,SEp,NRd 2.50
68 DJu,SEp,NRd,V:Cerdia. 2.50
69 DJu,SEp,NRd,. 2.50
70 DJu,new alliance 3.00
71 DJu,SEp,NRd,A:Warlord. 3.00
72 DJu,SEp,NRd,V:Ch'Rinn 3.00
73 DJu,SEp,NRd,V:Valgos. 3.00
74 DJu,SEp,NRd,death of friend . . . 3.00
75 DJu,SEp,NRd,final issue 3.00
Ann.#1 Year One Annual, V:Triton,
    A:Superman,Mera 4.00
Ann.#2 Legends o/t Dead Earth . . 3.50
Ann.#3 Pulp Heroes (Hard Boiled) . 5.00
Ann.#4 PDa, Ghosts 3.50
Ann.#5 JOs(s),MBr,DG, JLApe
    Gorilla Warfare 3.50
Spec #1,000,000 DAn&ALa(s),TGb,
    BAn, King of Waterworld 3.00
Secret Files #1 EL 5.00
TPB Time and Tide 10.00

[4th Regular Series], Dec. 2002
1 Obsidian Age aftermath 3.00
2 F:Martian Manhunter 3.00
3 New look and costume 3.00
4 F:Tempest 3.00
5 V:The Thirst 3.00
6 V:The Thirst 3.00
7 undead pirates. 3.00
8 V:Black Manta 3.00
9 V:Black Mantra 3.00
10 V:The Thirst. 3.00
11 V:The Thirst. 3.00
12 V:The Thirst 3.00
13 Perfect storm 2.50
14 Octo-Man 2.50
15 American Tidal,pt.1 . . . . 2.50
16 American Tidal,pt.2 . . . . 2.50
17 American Tidal,pt.3 . . . . 2.50
18 American Tidal,pt.4 . . . . 2.50
19 F:Lorena 2.50
20 American Tidal,concl. 2.50
21 With the Fishes,pt.1 . . . . 2.50
22 With the Fishes,pt.2 . . . . 2.50
23 With the Fishes,pt.3 . . . . 2.50
24 JOs(s),CsB, Sharks 2.50
25 JAr(s),in San Diego. 2.50
26 JAr(s),I:Aquagirl 2.50
27 JAr(s),V:Ocean Master 2.50
28 JAr(s),V:Malrey 2.50
29 JAr(s),Malrey vs. Conger 2.50
30 JAr(s),Black Manta returns 2.50
31 JAr(s),V:Black Manta 2.50

32 JAr(s),V:Black Manta 2.50	
33 JAr(s),V:Black Manta 2.50	
34 JAr(s),reunited with Mera 2.50	
35 JAr(s),Omac project tie-in 2.50	
36 JAr(s),Koryak returns to Atlantis . 2.50	
37 JAr(s),V:Spectre 2.50	
38 JAr(s),New home in Sub Diego . 2.50	
39 JAr(s),V:Black Manta 2.50	
TPB Aquaman: The Water Bearer . 13.00	
Spec. Secret Files 2003. . . . . 5.00	

Becomes:

AQUAMAN:
SWORD OF ATLANTIS

40 KBk,Once and Future, pt.1 . . . . . 3.00	
41 KBk,Once and Future, pt.2 . . . . . 3.00	
42 KBk,Once and Future, pt.3 . . . . . 3.00	
43 KBk,Once and Future, pt.4 . . . . . 3.00	
44 KBk,Once and Future, pt.5 . . . . . 3.00	
45 KBk,Once and Future, pt.6 . . . . . 3.00	
46 KBk,A:King Shark 3.00	
47 KBk,A:Mera, Vulko 3.00	
TPB Once & Future 13.00	

AQUAMAN: TIME & TIDE
1993–94

1 PDd(s),O:Aquaman 3.00	
2 thru 4 PDd(s),O:Aquaman . . . @3.00	
TPB rep.#1–4 . . . . 10.00	

ARAK
1981–85

1 EC,O:Ara 3.00	
2 thru 12 EC . . . . @2.50	
13 thru 23 AA . . . . @2.50	
24 Double size 2.50	
25 thru 50 . . . . @2.50	
Ann.#1 . . . . 2.50	

ARCANA: THE BOOKS
OF MAGIC
DC/Vertigo, 1994

Ann.#1 JBo(c),JNR(s),PrG,Children's
Crusade,R:Tim Hunter,
A:Free Country 4.00

ARION,
LORD OF ATLANTIS
1982–85

1 JDu,Star Spawn Sun Death 3.00	
2 JDu,I:Mara 2.50	
3 JDu 2.50	
4 JDu,O:Arion 2.50	
5 JDu 2.50	
6 JDu 2.50	
7 thru 12 . . . . @2.50	
13 thru 15 JDu . . . . @2.50	
16 thru 35 . . . . @2.50	
Spec. 2.50	

ARION THE IMMORTAL
1992

1 RWi,R:Arion 3.00	
2 RWi,V:Garffon 2.25	
3 RWi,V:Garn Daanuth 2.25	
4 RWi,V:Garn Daanuth 2.25	
5 RWi,Darkworlet 2.25	
6 RWi,MG,A:Power Girl 2.25	

ARKHAM ASYLUM:
LIVING HELL
May 2003

1 (of 6) F:Warren White 3.00	
2 Food Fight 3.00	
3 Humphry Dumpler 3.00	
4 F:Killer Croc 3.00	
5 F:Jason Blood 3.00	
6 Concl.. 3.00	

TPB 13.00

ARMAGEDDON 2001
May, 1991

1 DJu,DG,I&O:Waverider 4.00	
1a 2nd printing 2.50	
1b 3rd printing (silver). 2.50	
2 DJu,ATi,Monarch revealed as Hawk,	
D:Dove,L:Capt Atom(JLE) 3.00	
Spec.#1 MR 3.00	

ARMAGEDDON 2001
ARMAGEDDON:
THE ALIEN AGENDA
1991–92

1 DJu,JOy,A:Monarch,Capt.Atom . . 2.50	
2 V:Ancient Romans 2.50	
3 JRu(i),The Old West 2.50	
4 DG,GP,V:Nazi's,last issue 2.50	

ARMAGEDDON:
INFERNO
1992

1 TMd,LMc,A:Creeper,Batman,	
Firestorm 2.50	
2 AAd,LMc,WS,I:Abraxis,A:Lobo . . 2.50	
3 AAd,WS,LMc,TMd,MN,R:Justice	
Society 2.50	
4 AAd,WS,LMc,TMd,MN,DG,	
V:Abraxis,A:Justice Society 2.50	

ARSENAL
Aug., 1998

1 (of 4) F:Black Canary 2.50	
2 F:Green Arrow 2.50	
3 F:Vandal Savage 2.50	
4 conclusion 2.50	

Artemis: Requiem #3
© DC Comics, Inc.

ARTEMIS: REQUIEM
1996

1 BML(s) (of 6). 3.00	
2 thru 6 BML(s),EBe, ... @3.00	

ATARI FORCE
1984–85

1 JL,I:TempestDart 5.00	
2 JL 3.00	
3 JL 3.00	
4 RA/JL/JO 3.00	

---

5 RA/JL/JO 3.00	
6 thru 12 JL . . . . @3.00	
13 KG. 3.00	
14 thru 21 EB . . . . @3.00	

ATLANTIS CHRONICLES
1990

1 EM,Atlantis 50,000 years ago . . . 3.50	
2 EM,Atlantis Sunk 3.25	
3 EM,Twin Cities of Poseidonis	
& Tritonis 3.25	
4 EM,King Orin's Daughter	
Cora Assumes Throne. 3.25	
5 EM,Orin vs. Shalako 3.25	
6 EM,Contact with Surface	
Dwellers. 3.25	
7 EM,Queen Atlanna gives Birth to	
son(Aquaman)48 pg.final issue . 3.25	

ATOM, THE
1962–68

1 MA,GK,I:Plant Master. 1,600.00	
2 MA,GK,V:Plant Master. 750.00	
3 MA,GK,I:Chronos. 650.00	
4 MA,GK,Snapper Carr. 500.00	
5 MA,GK. 500.00	
6 MA,GK. 500.00	
7 MA,GK,1st Atom & Hawkman	
team-up 600.00	
8 MA,GK,A:JLA,V:Doctor Light . . 400.00	
9 MA,GK 400.00	
10 MA,GK 400.00	
11 MA,GK 350.00	
12 MA,GK 350.00	
13 MA,GK 350.00	
14 MA,GK 350.00	
15 MA,GK 350.00	
16 MA,GK 250.00	
17 MA,GK 250.00	
18 MA,GK 250.00	
19 MA,GK,A:Zatanna 250.00	
20 MA,GK 250.00	
21 MA,GK 160.00	
22 MA,GK 160.00	
23 MA,GK 160.00	
24 MA,GK,V:Jason Woodrue 160.00	
25 MA,GK 160.00	
26 GK. 150.00	
27 GK. 150.00	
28 GK. 150.00	
29 GK,A:E-2 Atom,Thinker. 400.00	
30 GK. 150.00	
31 GK,A:Hawkman 140.00	
32 GK. 140.00	
33 GK. 140.00	
34 GK,V:Big Head 140.00	
35 GK. 140.00	
36 GK,A:Golden Age Atom 200.00	
37 GK,I:Major Mynah. 140.00	
38 Sinister stopover Earth 140.00	

Becomes:

ATOM & HAWKMAN
1968–69

39 MA, V:Tekla. 75.00	
40 DD,JKu,MA. 65.00	
41 DD,JKu,MA. 65.00	
42 MA,V:Brama 65.00	
43 MA,I:Gentleman Ghost 65.00	
44 DD. 65.00	
45 DD. 65.00	

AVATAR
1991

1 A:Midnight & Allies 7.00	
2 Search for Tablets 6.00	
3 V:Cyric, Myrkul, final issue 6.00	

AVENGERS/JLA
DC/Marvel 2003
2 (of 4) KBk,GP(c), 48-pg. 6.00
4 KBk,GP,48-pg. 6.00

AZRAEL
1994
1 I:New Azrael,Brian Bryan. 5.00
2 A:Batman,New Azreal 3.50
3 V:Order of St. Dumas 3.50
4 The System 3.00
5 BKi(c&a),R:Ra's al Ghul,Talia
  [new Miraweb format begins] . . 3.00
6 BKi(c&a),Ra's al Ghul,Talia 3.00
7 Sister Lily's Transformation 3.00
8 System Secret 2.50
9 Jean Paul Vanishes. 2.50
10 DON,BKi,JmP,F:Neron,
  Underworld Unleashed tie-in. . . 2.50
11 DON,BKi,JmP,A:Batman. 2.50
12 DON,BKi,JmP,Azrael looks
  for Shondra 2.50
13 DON,BKi,Demon Time,pt.1. . . . 2.50
14 DON,BKi,Demon Time,pt.2. . . . 2.50
15 DON,BKi,Contagion,pt.5. . . . . . 3.00
16 DON,BKi,Contagion,pt.10. . . . . 2.50
17 DON,BKi,JmP,A:Dr.Orchid 2.50
18 DON,BKi,JmP,A:Dr.Orchid 2.50
19 DON(s),BKi,Save the Innocents . 2.50
20 DON(s),BKi,A Prayer of Fire. . . 2.50
21 DON(s),BKi,Renunciation 2.50
22 DON(s),BKi,JmP,Angel in
  Hiding, pt.2 (of 3). 2.50
23 DON(s),BKi,JmP,Angel in
  Hiding, pt.3 . . . . 2.50
24 DON(s),BKi,JmP,The Order's
  return 2.50
25 DON(s),BKi,JmP,V:Brother
  Rollo 2.50
26 DON(s),BKi,Fall of St. Dumas . . 2.50
27 DON(s),BKi,JmP,Angel Insane,
  pt.1. 2.50
28 DON(s),BKi,JmP,Joker, Riddler
  & Two-Face escape from
  Arkham Asylum 2.50
29 DON(s),DBw,JmP, F:Ra's Al
  Ghul, pt.1. . . . . 2.50
30 DON(s),DBw,JmP, F:Ra's Al
  Ghul, pt.2. . . . . 2.50
31 DON(s),JmP Angel and the
  Monster Maker, pt.1 (of 3). 2.50
32 DON(s),JmP Angel and the
  Monster Maker, pt.2. . . . . 2.50

Azrael #20
© DC Comics Inc.

33 DON(s),JmP Angel and the
  Monster Maker, pt.3 concl. 2.50
34 DON(s),JmP,Genesis,
  a parademon 2.50
35 DON(s),JmP,F:Hitman 2.50
36 DON,JmP,Return of Bane,pt.1 . . 2.50
37 DON,JmP,Return of Bane,pt.2 . . 2.50
38 DON,JmP,Return of Bane,pt.3 . . 2.50
39 DON,JmP,Finally to Vanguish . . . 2.50
40 DON,JmP,Cataclysm,pt.4,x-over 4.50
41 DON,JmP,A:Devil Latour 2.50
42 DON,JmP,Madame Kalypso 2.50
43 DON,JmP,Lilhy,Brian Bryan 2.50
44 DON,JmP,Luc & Lilhy disappear 2.50
45 DON,JmP,V:Deathstroke,
  A:Calibax 2.50
46 DON(s),JmP,V:Calibax 2.50

Becomes:

AZRAEL,
AGENT OF THE BAT
1997
47 Road to No Man's Land, flip-book
  Batman:Shadow of the Bat 5.00
48 DON(s),JmP,No Man's Land. . . . 2.50
49 DON(s),JmP,New Costume 2.50
50 DON(s),JmP,New Costume 2.50
51 DON(s),JmP,V:Demonic Trio . . . 2.50
52 DON(s),JmP,No Man's Land. . . . 2.50
53 DON(s),JmP,V:Joker 2.50
54 DON(s),JmP,V:Death Dancer . . 2.50
55 DON(s),JmP,V:Death Dancer . . 2.50
56 DON(s),JmP,A:Batgirl 2.50
57 DON(s),JmP,No Man's Land. . . . 2.50
58 DON(s),JmP,Day of
  Judgment x-over 2.50
59 DON(s),JmP,F:Catwoman. 2.50
60 DON(s),JmP,Evacuation 2.50
61 DON(s),F:Batgirl,V:Joker 2.50
62 DON(s),JmP 2.50
63 DON(s),F:Huntress 2.50
64 DON(s),F:Huntress 2.50
65 DON(s),Nicholas Scratch 2.50
66 DON(s),F:Lilhi 2.50
67 DON(s),JmP,to Africa 2.50
68 DON(s),JmP,Mirage 2.50
69 DON(s),JmP,stranded 2.50
70 DON(s),SCi,JmP,Prophet,pt.1. . 2.50
71 DON(s),SCi,JmP,Prophet,pt.2. . 2.50
72 DON(s),SCi,JmP,Prophet,pt.3. . 2.50
73 DON(s),SCi,JmP,Batman,pt.1. . 2.50
74 DON(s),SCi,JmP,Batman,pt.2. . 2.50
75 DON(s),SCi,JmP,N:Azrael,
  F:Batman. 4.50
76 DON(s),SCi,JmP,A:Batman . . . 2.50
77 DON(s),SCi,V:Mr. Prymm 2.50
78 DON(s),SCi,Captain Death. 2.50
79 DON(s),SCi,F:Jean Paul. 2.50
80 DON(s),SCi,JmP,F:Jean Paul . . 2.50
81 DON(s),SCi,JmP,imprisoned. . . . 2.50
82 DON(s),SCi,JmP,escape. 2.50
83 DON(s),SCi,JmP,Jokerized. 2.50
84 DON(s),SCi,JmP,madman 2.50
85 DON(s),SCi,JmP,new villain 2.50
86 DON(s),SCi,JmP,Spartan 2.50
87 DON(s),SCi,new foe 2.50
88 DON(s),JmP,SCi,F:Nightwing . . 2.50
89 DON(s),F:Nightwing 2.50
90 DON(s),F:Nightwing 2.50
91 Bruce Wayne:Fugitive,pt.15 . . . 2.50
92 DON(s),SCi,F:Batman 2.50
93 DON(s),SCi,war on crime 3.00
94 DON(s),SCi,Demon Biis 3.00
95 DON(s),SCi,Biis,Two-face. 3.00
96 DON(s),SCi,A:Batman,
  V:Two-Face 3.00
97 DON(s),MZ,JOy,New costume . . 3.00
98 DON(s),MZ,JOy,on the brink . . . 3.00
99 DON(s),MZ,JOy, ... 3.00
100 DON(s),MZ,JOy,final issue 3.00
Ann.#1 Year One Annual 3.00

Ann.#2 Legends o/t Dead Earth . . . 4.00
Ann.#3 Pulp Heroes (Hard Boiled) . 5.00
Spec.#1,000,000 DON(s),VGi,JmP
  F:Green Arrow,Robin,Hawkman 3.00
GN Azrael/Ash 5.00

AZRAEL/ASH
March, 1997
1 one-shot DON(s),JlQ,V:Surtr,
  A:Batman, x-over. 5.00

AZRAEL PLUS
Oct., 1996
1 one-shot, DON(s),VGi,F:Vic
  Sage, The Question 3.00

AZTEK:
THE ULTIMATE MAN
1996–97
1 GMo&MMr(s),NSH,I:Aztek &
  Synth 6.00
2 GMo&MMr(s),NSH,A:Green
  Lantern 4.00
3 GMo&MMr(s),NSH,V:Doll-Face. . 4.00
4 GMo&MMr(s),NSH,I:Lizard King,
  Vanity 4.00
5 GMo&MMr(s),NSH,O:Aztek,
  V:Lizard King 4.00
6 GMo&MMr(s),NSH,V:Vanity,
  A: Joker 4.00
7 GMo&MMr(s),NSH,A:Batman . . . 4.00
8 GMo&MMr(s),NSH,return to Brotherhood of Zuetzatcoatl,A:Raptor. . 4.00
9 GMo&MMr(s),NSH,V:Parasite,
  A:Superman. 4.00
10 GMo&MMr(s),NSH,A:Justice
  League, final issue 12.00

BABYLON 5
1995
1 From TV series 15.00
2 From TV series 8.00
3 Mysterious Assassin 8.00
4 V:Mysterious Assassin 8.00
5 Shadows of the Present,pt.1 . . . . 8.00
6 Shadows of the Present,pt.2 . . . . 8.00
7 Shadows of the Present,pt.3 . . . . 7.00
8 Laser-Mirror Starweb,pt.1 . . . . . 7.00
9 Laser-Mirror Starweb,pt.2 . . . . . 7.00
10 Laser-Mirror-Starweb,pt.3 . . . . . 7.00
11 final issue 7.00
TPB The Price of Peace 10.00

Babylon 5: In Valen's Name #1
© DC Comics, Inc.

DC COMICS

BABYLON 5:
IN VALEN'S NAME
Jan., 1998
1 (of 3) PDd, from TV series..... 4.00
2 PDd 4.00
3 PDd 4.00

BATGIRL
Feb., 2000
1 No Man's Land follow-up...... 10.00
1a 2nd printing 2.50
2 saves dying man 7.00
3 A:Batman 4.00
4 A:Batman 4.00
5 V:Ezra 4.00
6 A:Batman 4.00
7 A:Batman 4.00
8 V:Lady Shiva 4.00
9 Batgirl questions her motives . 3.50
10 Too slow to stop a killer 3.50
11 This Issue: Batman Dies! ... 3.50
12 Officer Down tie-in 3.50
13 Government trained killers ... 3.50
14 A:Batman 3.50
15 RbC,ghastly murders 3.50
16 RbC,young boy's father 3.50
17 RbC,A:Oracle,Cassandra 3.50
18 RbC,A:Robin,V:Deadeye 3.50
19 RbC,Nobody dies tonight 3.50
20 CDi,F:The Spoiler 3.50
21 CDi,Joker:Last Laugh 3.50
22 RbC,F:Cain................. 3.50
23 RbC,F:Lady Shiva.......... 3.50
24 RbC,BruceWayne:Murderer,pt.2. 3.50
25 RbC,V:Lady Shiva,40-pg..... 4.00
26 VGi,Spoiler 3.00
27 RbC,Bruce Wayne:Fugitive,pt.4 . 3.00
28 RbC,I:Sensor 3.00
29 RbC,Bruce Wayne:Fugitive,pt.13 3.00
30 CDi,KJ,Roman military cult..... 3.00
31 CDi,F:Robin, Spoiler........ 3.00
32 CDi,all-star issue.......... 3.00
33 RbC,A:Batman,metahunt 3.00
34 RbC,A:Batman,detective skills . . 3.00
35 RbC,V:Alpha,A:Batman 3.00
36 RbC,V:Alpha............... 3.00
37 RbC,save the child 3.00
38 RbC,F:Spoiler 3.00
39 V:Black Wind.............. 3.00
40 V:Black Wind.............. 3.00
41 First date,A:Superboy....... 3.00
42 I:New Dr. Death 3.00
43 V:Dr. Death 3.00
44 V:Dr. Death 3.00
45 RL,drug Soul............... 3.00
46 RL,F:Oracle................ 3.00
47 RL,V:Doll Man.............. 2.50
48 missing girl 2.50
49 V:The Lost Girls 2.50
50 RL,V:Batman............... 3.25
51 RL,V:Poison Ivy 2.50
52 RL,V:Poison Ivy 2.50
53 F:Girl Wonder,V:Penguin 2.50
54 RL,vs. cyborg.............. 2.50
55 War Games,Act 1,pt.6 ...... 2.50
56 War Games,Act 2,pt.6 ...... 2.50
57 War Games,Act 3,pt.6 ...... 2.50
58 Fresh Blood, x-over,pt.2 .... 2.50
59 Fresh Blood, x-over,pt.4 .... 2.50
60 Bludhaven................. 2.50
61 Arms deal in Bludhaven 2.50
62 F:Spoiler 2.50
63 F:Deathstroke 2.50
64 V:Deathstroke 2.50
65 CaS,Father's Day 2.50
66 V:Verrraco, The Road Hog 2.50
67 F:Birds of Prey 2.50
68 V:Lady Shiva 2.50
69 Frozen.................... 2.50
70 Destruction's Daughter 2.50
71 V:Lady Shiva & team 2.50

72 V:Mad Dog, someone dies 2.50
73 End of Cassandra Cain 2.50
Ann.#1 Planet DC,A:Batman..... 3.50
Spec.#1 V: Cormorant,
        I:Slash (1988) 10.00
Spec. Secret Files #1, 48-pg. ... 5.00
TPB A Knight Alone, 160-page ... 13.00
TPB Silent Running, 144-page ... 13.00
TPB Death Wish 15.00
TPB Batgirl: Fists of Fury........ 15.00
TPB Year One 20.00
TPB Kicking Assassins 15.00
TPB Destruction's Daughter 20.00

BATGIRL ADVENTURES
Dec., 1997
1-shot RBr,V:Poison Ivy,A:Harley
        Quinn.................... 4.00

Batgirl Year One #6
© DC Comics, Inc.

BATGIRL: YEAR ONE
Dec. 2002
1 CDi(s),F:Barbara Gordon....... 3.00
2 CDi(s),meets JSA 3.00
3 CDi(s),Dynamic Duo 3.00
4 CDi(s),Dynamic Duo 3.00
5 CDi(s),Killer Moth.......... 3.00
6 CDi(s),F:Black Canary 3.00
7 CDi(s),A:Robin.............. 3.00
8 CDi(s),V:Blockbuster 3.00
9 CDi(s),Origin concl. 3.00
TPB O:Barbara Gordon 18.00

BATMAN
Spring, 1940
1 I:Joker,Cat (Catwoman),
        V:Hugo Strange 175,000.00
2 V:Joker/Catwoman team . . 30,000.00
3 V:Catwoman 20,000.00
4 V:Joker 15,000.00
5 V:Joker 9,000.00
6 V:Clock Maker 6,500.00
7 V:Joker 6,200.00
8 V:Joker 6,000.00
9 V:Joker 6,000.00
10 V:Catwoman 6,000.00
11 V:Joker,Penguin 11,000.00
12 V:Joker................. 5,000.00
13 V:Joker................. 5,000.00
14 V:Penguin;Propaganda sty . 5,000.00
15 V:Catwoman 5,000.00
16 I:Alfred,V:Joker 8,500.00
17 V:Penguin 4,000.00
18 V:Tweedledum &
        Tweedledee 4,500.00

19 V:Joker................. 5,000.00
20 V:Joker................. 4,000.00
21 V:Penguin 4,000.00
22 V:Catwoman,Cavalier 4,000.00
23 V:Joker................. 8,000.00
24 I:Carter Nichols, V:Tweedledum
        & Tweedledee........... 3,000.00
25 V:Joker/Penguin team 4,000.00
26 V:Cavalier 2,700.00
27 V:Penguin 4,500.00
28 V:Joker................. 2,500.00
29 V:Scuttler 2,500.00
30 V:Penguin,I:Ally Babble . . 2,500.00
31 I:Punch and Judy........ 2,000.00
32 O:Robin,V:Joker......... 2,000.00
33 V:Penguin,Jackall 2,300.00
34 A:Ally Babble 2,000.00
35 V:Catwoman 2,000.00
36 V:Penguin,A:King Arthur . . 1,700.00
37 V:Joker................. 2,400.00
38 V:Penguin 4,500.00
39 V:Catwoman,Xmas Story . . 1,700.00
40 V:Joker................. 2,500.00
41 V:Penguin 2,300.00
42 V:Catwoman 2,000.00
43 V:Penguin 2,000.00
44 V:Joker,A:Carter Nichols,Meets
        ancester Silas Wayne..... 2,500.00
45 V:Catwoman 1,300.00
46 V:Joker,A:Carter Nichols,
        Leonardo Da Vinci 1,300.00
47 O:Batman,V:Catwoman 5,500.00
48 V:Penguin, Bat-Cave story . 1,700.00
49 I:Mad Hatter & Vicki Vale . . 2,400.00
50 V:Two-Face,A:Vicki Vale . . . 1,400.00
51 V:Penguin 1,300.00
52 V:Joker................. 1,500.00
53 V:Joker................. 1,500.00
54 V:The Treasure Hunter ... 1,200.00
55 V:Joker................. 1,800.00
56 V:Penguin 1,400.00
57 V:Joker................. 1,200.00
58 V:Penguin 1,400.00
59 I:Deadshot 1,200.00
60 V:'Shark' Marlin 1,200.00
61 V:Penguin 1,300.00
62 O:Catwoman,I:Knight
        & Squire 2,000.00
63 V:Joker................. 1,200.00
64 V:Killer Moth........... 2,000.00
65 I:Wingman,V:Catwoman ... 1,200.00
66 V:Joker................. 1,000.00
67 V:Joker................. 1,000.00
68 V:Two-Face,Alfred story.... 1,000.00
69 I:King of the Cats,
        A:Catwoman............ 1,200.00
70 V:Penguin 850.00
71 V:Mr. Cipher 850.00
72 The Jungle Batman....... 850.00
73 V:Joker,A:Vicki Vale 1,200.00
74 V:Joker................. 850.00
75 I:The Gorilla Boss 850.00
76 V:Penguin 850.00
77 The Crime Predictor 850.00
78 The Manhunter from Mars . . 1,100.00
79 A:Vicki Vale 850.00
80 V:Joker................. 1,100.00
81 V:Two-Face............. 950.00
82 The Flying Batman 850.00
83 V:'Fish' Frye 850.00
84 V:Catwoman 1,100.00
85 V:Joker................. 850.00
86 V:Joker................. 850.00
87 V:Joker................. 850.00
88 V:Mr. Mystery 850.00
89 I:Aunt Agatha 850.00
90 I:Batboy................ 850.00
91 V:Blinky Grosset........ 850.00
92 I:Ace, the Bat-Hound 850.00
93 The Caveman Batman 700.00
94 Alfred Has Amnesia 675.00
95 The Bat-Train 675.00

Batman #97
© *DC Comics, Inc.*

96 Batman's College Days 675.00
97 V:Joker 675.00
98 A:Carter Nichols,Jules Verne . 675.00
99 V:Penguin,A:Carter Nichols,
    Bat Masterson 675.00
100 Great Batman Contest 3,500.00
101 The Great Bat-Cape Hunt . . . 700.00
102 V:Mayne Mallok 600.00
103 A:Ace, the Bat-Hound 600.00
104 V:Devoe 600.00
105 A:Batwoman 750.00
106 V:Keene Harper Gang 800.00
107 V:Daredevils 600.00
108 Bat-Cave Story 600.00
109 1,000 Inventions of Batman . 600.00
110 V:Joker 650.00
111 Gotham City Safari 500.00
112 I:Signalman 500.00
113 I:Fatman 500.00
114 I:Bat Ape 500.00
115 Million-Dollar Clues 500.00
116 City of Ancient Heroes 500.00
117 Mystery of Batman Bus 500.00
118 Battle of Police Island 500.00
119 Arch-Rivals of Gotham City . . 500.00
120 Curse of the Bat-Ring 500.00
121 I:Mr.Zero (Mr.Freeze) 650.00
122 Prisoners of Sargasso Sea . . 400.00
123 A:Joker 425.00
124 Mystery Seed from Space . . 400.00
125 Secret Life of Bat-Hound . . . 400.00
126 Mystery of the 49th Star 400.00
127 A:Superman & Joker 425.00
128 Interplanetary Batman 400.00
129 O:Robin (Retold) 450.00
130 Batman's Deadly Birthday . . 400.00
131 I:2nd Batman 375.00
132 Lair of the Sea-Fox 375.00
133 Crimes of the Kite-Man 375.00
134 The Rainbow Creature 375.00
135 Crimes of the Wheel 375.00
136 A:Joker, Bat-Mite 375.00
137 V:Mr. Marvel,The Brand 375.00
138 A:Bat-Mite 375.00
139 I:Old Batgirl 375.00
140 A:Joker 375.00
141 V:Clockmaster 375.00
142 Batman Robot Story 375.00
143 A:Bathound 375.00
144 A:Joker,Bat-Mite,Bat-Girl . . . 375.00
145 V:Mr.50,Joker 400.00
146 A:Bat-Mite,Joker 400.00
147 Batman becomes Bat-Baby . 300.00
148 A:Joker 350.00
149 V:Maestro 300.00

150 V:Biff Warner,Jack Pine 300.00
151 V:Harris Boys 250.00
152 A:Joker 260.00
153 Other Dimension story 250.00
154 V:Dr. Dorn 200.00
155 1st S.A. Penguin 550.00
156 V:Gorilla Gang 225.00
157 V:Mirror Man 225.00
158 A:Bathound,Bat-Mite 225.00
159 A:Joker,Clayface 250.00
160 V:Bart Cullen 225.00
161 A:Bat-Mite 225.00
162 F:Robin 225.00
163 A:Joker 225.00
164 CI,A:Mystery Analysts,new
    Batmobile 200.00
165 V:The Mutated Man 200.00
166 Escape story 200.00
167 V:Karabi & Hydra,
    the Crime Cartel 200.00
168 V:Mr. Mammoth 200.00
169 A:Penguin 225.00
170 V:Getaway Genius 200.00
171 CI,1st S.A. Riddler 700.00
172 V:Flower Gang 225.00
173 V:Elwood Pearson 225.00
174 V:Big Game Hunter 225.00
175 V:Eddie Repp 225.00
176 Giant rep.A:Joker,Catwom . . 225.00
177 BK,A:Elongated Man,Atom . . 225.00
178 CI 225.00
179 CI,2nd Riddler(Silver) 300.00
180 BK,A:Death-Man 175.00
181 CI,I:Poison Ivy 350.00
182 A:Joker,(giant size rep) 200.00
183 CI,A:Poison Ivy 200.00
184 CI,Mystery of the Missing
    Manhunters 175.00
185 Giant rep. 175.00
186 A:Joker 175.00
187 Giant rep.A:Joker 175.00
188 CI,A:Eraser 100.00
189 CI,A:Scarecrow 200.00
190 CI,A:Penguin 150.00
191 CI,The Day Batman Soldout . 100.00
192 CI,The Crystal ball that
    betrayed Batman 100.00
193 Giant rep. 150.00
194 MSy,BK,A:Blockbuster,Mystery
    Analysts of Gotham City 100.00
195 CI 100.00
196 BK,Psychic Super-Sleuth . . . 100.00
197 MSy,A:Bat Girl,Catwoman . . 200.00
198 A:Joker,Penguin,Catwoman,
    O:Batman rtd,(G-Size rep) . . 200.00
199 CI,Peril o/t Poison Rings 100.00
200 NA(c),O:rtd,A:Joker,Pengiun,
    Scarecrow 300.00
201 A:Batman Villians 150.00
202 BU:Robin 135.00
203 NA(c),(giant size) 200.00
204 FR(s),IN,JG 150.00
205 FR(s),IN,JG 150.00
206 FR(s),IN,JG 150.00
207 FR(s),IN,JG 150.00
208 GK,new O:Batman,
    A:Catwoman 175.00
209 FR(s),IN,JG 175.00
210 A:Catwoman 175.00
211 FR(s),IN,JG 150.00
212 FR(s),IN,JG 150.00
213 RA,30th Anniv.Batman,new O:
    Robin,rep.O:Alfred,Joker 125.00
214 IN,A:Batgirl 65.00
215 IN,DG 65.00
216 IN,DG,I:DaphnePennyworth . . 65.00
217 NA(c) 65.00
218 NA(c),giant 75.00
219 NA,IN,DG,Batman Xmas 75.00
220 NA(c),IN 50.00
221 IN,DG 50.00
222 IN,Rock'n Roll story 65.00

223 NA(c),giant 65.00
224 NA(c) 50.00
225 NA(c),IN,DG 50.00
226 IN,DG I:10-Eyed Man 50.00
227 IN,DG,A:Daphne
    Pennyworth 50.00
228 giant Deadly Traps rep. 75.00
229 IN 50.00
230 NA(c),Robin 50.00
231 F:Ten-Eyed Man 50.00
232 DON(s),NA,DG,
    I:Ras al Ghul 225.00
233 giant Bruce Wayne iss 75.00
234 NA,DG,IN,1stS.A.Two-Face . 250.00
235 CI,V:Spook 50.00
236 NA 50.00
237 NA,I:The Reaper 125.00
238 NA,JC,JKu,giant 125.00
239 NA,RB 50.00
240 NA(c),RB,giant,R-Ghul 50.00
241 IN,DG,RB,A:Kid Flash 50.00
242 RB,MK 50.00
243 NA,DG,Ras al Ghul 75.00
244 NA,Ras al Ghul 75.00
245 NA,IN,DG,FMc,Ras al Ghul . . 75.00
246 Many Ways Can a Robin Die . 40.00
247 Deadly New Year 40.00
248 Death-Knell for a Traitor 40.00
249 Citidel of Crime 40.00
250 IN,DG 40.00
251 NA,V:Joker 125.00
252 The Spook's Master Stroke . . 40.00
253 AN,DG,A:Shadow 40.00
254 NA,GK,B:100 page issues . . . 75.00
255 GK,CI,NA,DG,I:CrazyQuilt . . . 75.00
256 Catwoman 75.00
257 IN,DG,V:Penguin 75.00
258 IN,DG 75.00
259 GK,IN,DG,A:Shadow 75.00
260 IN,DG,Joker 100.00
261 CI,GK,E:100 page issues 75.00
262 A:Scarecrow 50.00
263 DG(i),A:Riddler 20.00
264 DON(s),DG,A:Devil Dayre . . . 20.00
265 RB,BWr 25.00
266 DG,Catwoman(old Costume) . 22.00
267 DG 20.00
268 DON(s),IN,TeB,V:Sheikh 20.00
269 A:Riddler 20.00
270 B:DvR(s) 20.00
271 IN,FMc 20.00
272 JLUnderworld Olympics '76 . . 20.00
273 V:Underworld Olympics '76 . . 20.00
274 Gotham City Treasure Hunt . . 20.00
275 Ferry Blows at Midnight 20.00

Batman #263
© *DC Comics Inc.*

Batman #289 © DC Comics, Inc.

Batman #433 © DC Comics, Inc.

323 IN,A:Catwoman 16.00
324 IN,A:Catwoman 16.00
325 IN,Death-20 Stories High 16.00
326 A:Catwoman 16.00
327 IN,A:Professor.Milo 16.00
328 A:Two-Face 16.00
329 IN,A:Two-Face 16.00
330 In,Target 16.00
331 DN,FMc,V:Electrocutioner 16.00
332 IN,DN,Ras al Ghul.1st solo
    Catwoman story 20.00
333 IN,DN,A:Catwoman,
    Ras al Ghul 15.00
334 FMc,Ras al Ghul,Catwoman . . 15.00
335 IN,FMc,Catwoman,Ras al
    Ghul 15.00
336 JL,FMc,Loser Villains 15.00
337 DN,V:Snow Man 15.00
338 DN,Deathsport 15.00
339 A:Poison Ivy 15.00
340 GC,A:Mole 15.00
341 A:Man Bat 15.00
342 V:Man Bat 15.00
343 GC,KJ,I:The Dagger 15.00
344 GC,KJ,Poison Ivy 15.00
345 I:New Dr.Death,A:Catwoman . 15.00
346 DN,V:Two Face 15.00
347 A:Alfred 15.00
348 GC,KJ,Man-Bat,A:Catwoman . 15.00
349 GC,AA,A:Catwoman 15.00
350 GC,TD,A:Catwoman 15.00
351 GC,TD,A:Catwoman 15.00
352 Col Blimp 15.00
353 JL,DN,DA,A:Joker 22.00
354 DN,AA,V:HugoStrange,A:
    Catwoman 15.00
355 DN,AA:A:Catwoman 15.00
356 DG,DN,Hugo Strange 15.00
357 DN,AA,I:Jason Todd 16.00
358 A:King Croc 15.00
359 DG,O:King Croc,Joker 20.00
360 I:Savage Skull 15.00
361 DN,Man-Bat,I:Harvey Bullock . 15.00
362 V:Riddler 15.00
363 V:Nocturna 15.00
364 DN,AA,J.Todd 1st full solo
    story (cont'd Detective #531) . 15.00
365 DN,AA,C:Joker 15.00
366 DN,AA,Joker,J.Todd in
    Robin Costume 20.00
367 DN,AA,PoisonIvy 14.00
368 DN,AA,I:2nd Robin
    (Jason Todd) 20.00
369 DN,AA,I:Dr.Fang,V:Deadshot . 12.00
370 DN,AA 12.00
371 DN,AA,V:Catman 10.00
372 DN,AA,A:Dr.Fang 7.00
373 DN,AA,V:Scarecrow 7.00
374 GC,AA,V:Penguin 8.00
375 GC,AA,V:Dr.Freeze 7.00
376 DN,Halloween issue 7.00
377 DN,AA,V:Nocturna 7.00
378 V:Mad Hatter 7.00
379 V:Mad Hatter 7.00
380 AA,V:Nocturna 7.00
381 V:Batman 7.00
382 A:Catwoman 8.00
383 GC,Night in the Life of Batman. 7.00
384 V:Calender Man 7.00
385 V:Calender Man 7.00
386 I:Black Mask 7.00
387 V:Black Mask 7.00
388 V:Capt.Boomerang & Mirror
    Master 7.00
389 V:Nocturna,Catwoman 7.00
390 V:Nocturna,Catwoman 7.00
391 V:Nocturna,Catwoman 7.00
392 A:Catwoman 7.00
393 PG,V:Cossack 6.00
394 PG,V:Cossack 6.00
395 V:Film Freak 6.00
396 V:Film Freak 6.00

276 The Haunting of the Spook . . . 20.00
277 Man Who Walked Backwards . 20.00
278 Stop Me Before I Kill Batman . 20.00
279 A:Riddler 22.00
280 The Only Crime in Town 20.00
281 Murder Comes in Black Boxes 20.00
282 Four Doorways to Danger . . . 20.00
283 V:Camouflage 20.00
284 JA,R:Dr.Tzin Tzin 20.00
285 Mystery of Christmas Lost . . . 20.00
286 V:Joker 30.00
287 BWi,MGr,Penguin 25.00
288 BWi,MGr,Penguin 25.00
289 MGr, V:Skull 20.00
290 MGr,V:Skull Dagger 20.00
291 B:Underworld Olympics #1,
    A:Catwoman 30.00
292 A:Riddler 20.00
293 A:Superman & Luthor 20.00
294 E:DvR(s),E:Underworld
    Olympics,A:Joker. 30.00
295 GyC(s),MGo,JyS,V:Hamton . . 20.00
296 B:DvR(s),V:Scarecrow 20.00
297 RB,Mad Hatter 20.00
298 JCA,DG,V:Baxter Bains 20.00
299 DG 20.00
300 WS,DG,A:Batman E-2,
    Robin E-2 . . . . 35.00
301 JCa,TeB 15.00
302 JCa,DG,V:Human Dynamo . . . 15.00
303 JCa,DG 15.00
304 E:DvR(s),V:Spook 15.00
305 GyC,JCa,DeH,V:Thanatos . . . 16.00
306 JCa,DeH,DN,V:Black Spider . . 20.00
307 B:LWn(s),JCa,DG,
    I:Limehouse Jack 20.00
308 JCa,DG,V:Mr.Freeze 16.00
309 E:LWn(s),JCa,FMc,
    V:Blockbuster 16.00
310 IN,DG,A:Gentleman Ghost . . . 16.00
311 SEt,FMc,IN,Batgirl,
    V:Dr.Phosphorus 16.00
312 WS,DG,Calenderman 16.00
313 IN,FMc,VTwo-Face 16.00
314 IN,FMc,V:Two-Face 16.00
315 IN,FMc,V:Kiteman 16.00
316 IN,FMc,F:Robin,
    V:Crazy Quilt 16.00
317 IN,FMc,V:Riddler 17.00
318 IN,I:Fire Bug 16.00
319 JKu(c),IN,DG,A:Gentleman
    Ghost,E:Catwoman 16.00
320 BWr(c). 17.00
321 DG,WS,A:Joker,Catwoman . . . 20.00
322 V:Cap.Boomerang,Catwoman 16.00

397 V:Two-Face,Catwoman 7.00
398 V:Two-Face,Catwoman 7.00
399 HaE(s),Two-Face 6.00
400 BSz,AAd,GP,BB,A:Joker. 25.00
401 JBy(c),TVE,Legends,
    A:Magpie 6.00
402 JSn,Fake Batman 6.00
403 DCw,Batcave discovered 6.00
404 DM,FM(s),B:Year 1,I:Modern
    Age Catwoman 25.00
405 FM,DM,Year 1. . . . . 16.00
406 FM,DM,Year 1. . . . . 16.00
407 FM,DM,E:Year 1 . . . . 16.00
408 CW,V:Joker,
    new O:Jason Todd 15.00
408a 2nd printing 3.00
409 DG,RA,V:Crime School 15.00
409a 2nd printing 3.00
410 DC,Jason Todd 15.00
411 DC,DH,V:Two Face 6.00
412 DC,DH,I:Mime. 6.00
413 DC,DH. 6.00
414 JAp,Slasher. 6.00
415 JAp,Millenium Week #2 . . . . . . 6.00
416 JAp,1st Batman/Nightwing
    T.U. 6.00
417 JAp,B:10 Nights,I:KGBeast . . . 12.00
418 JAp,V:KGBeast 12.00
419 JAp,V:KGBeast 12.00
420 JAp,E:10 Nights,D:KGBeast . . 12.00
421 DG 7.00
422 MBr,V:Dumpster Slayer 6.00
423 TM(c),DC,Who is Batman. 7.00
424 MBr,Robin 6.00
425 MBr,Gordon Kidnapped 6.00
426 JAp,B:Death in the Family,
    V:Joker 20.00
427 JAp,V:Joker. 18.00
428 JAp,D:2nd Robin. 18.00
429 JAp,A:Superman,
    E:Death in the Family 15.00
430 JAp,JSn,V:Madman 5.00
431 JAp,Murder Investigation 4.00
432 JAp 4.00
433 JBy,JAp,Many Deaths of the
    Batman #1. . . . . 5.00
434 JBy,JAp,Many Deaths #2 . . . . 4.50
435 JBy,Many Deaths #3. . . . . 4.50
436 PB,B:Year#3,A:Nightwing,I:Tim
    Drake as child 5.00
436a 2ndPrint(green DC logo). 3.00
437 PB,year#3. . . . . 4.00
438 PB,year#3. . . . . 3.50
439 PB,year#3. . . . . 3.50

440 JAp,Lonely Place of Dying #1,
A:Tim Drake (face not shown). . 4.00
441 JAp,Lonely Place Dying 4.00
442 JAp,I:3rd Robin(Tim Drake) . . . 7.00
443 JAp,I:Crimesmith. 3.00
444 JAp,V:Crimesmith. 3.00
445 JAp,I:K.G.Beast Demon 3.00
446 JAp,V:K.G.Beast Demon. 3.00
447 JAp,D:K.G.Beast Demon 3.00
448 JAp,A:Penguin#1 . . . . 3.50
449 MBr,A:Penguin#3 . . . . 3.50
450 JAp,I:Joker II. 3.00
451 JAp,V:Joker II 3.00
452 KD,Dark Knight Dark City#1 . . 3.00
453 KD,Dark Knight Dark City#2. . . 3.00
454 KD,Dark Knight Dark City#3. . . 3.00
455 Identity Crisis#1, A:Scarecrow . 3.00
456 IdentityCrisis#2 . . . . 4.00
457 V:Scarecrow,A:Robin,
New Costume 7.00
457a 2nd printing. 3.00
458 R:Sarah Essen 3.00
459 A:Sarah Essen 3.00
460 Sisters in Arms,pt.1
A:Catwoman 3.50
461 Sisters in Arms,pt.2
Catwoman V:Sarah.Essen 3.50
462 Batman in San Francisco 3.00
463 Death Valley 3.00
464 V:Two-Hearts 3.00
465 Batman/Robin T.U. 3.50
466 Robin Trapped 3.00
467 Shadowbox #1(sequel to
Robin Mini-Series). 3.50
468 Shadowbox #2 . . . . 3.00
469 Shadowbox #3 . . . . 3.00
470 War of the Gods x-over 3.00
471 V:Killer Croc 3.00
472 The Idiot Root,pt.1 . . . . 3.00
473 The Idiot Root,pt.3 . . . . 3.00
474 Destroyer,pt.1 (LOTDK#27) . . 3.50
475 R:Scarface,A:VickiVale 3.00
476 A:Scarface. 3.00
477 Ph(c),Gotham Tale,pt.1 . . . . . . 3.00
478 Ph(c),Gotham Tale,pt.2 . . . . . . 3.00
479 TMd,I:Pagan 3.00
480 JAp,To the father I never
knew 3.00
481 JAp,V:Maxie Zeus. 3.00
482 JAp,V:Maxie Zeus. 3.00
483 JAp,I:Crash & Burn. 3.00
484 JAp,R:Black Mask. 3.00
485 TGr,V:Black Mask. 3.00
486 JAp,I:Metalhead. 3.00
487 JAp,V:Headhunter. 3.00
488 JAp,N:Azrael 10.00
489 JAp,Bane vs Killer Croc,
I:Azrael as Batman 6.00
489a 2nd Printing. 3.00
490 JAp,Bane vs.Riddler 7.00
490a 2nd Printing. 2.50
490b 3rd Printing 2.00
491 JAp,V:Joker,A:Bane 4.50
491a 2nd Printing. 2.00
492 B:DgM(s),NB,Knightfall#1,
V:Mad Hatter,A:Bane 5.00
492a Platinum Ed. 10.00
492b 2nd Printing. 2.00
493 NB,Knightfall,#3,Mr.Zsasz. . . . 4.00
494 JAp,TMd,Knightfall #5,A:Bane,
V:Cornelius,Stirk,Joker 3.50
495 NB,Knightfall#7,V:Poison
Ivy,A:Bane 3.50
496 JAp,JRu,Knightfall#9,V:Joker,
Scarecrow,A:Bane 3.50
497 JAp,DG,Knightfall#11,V:Bane,
Batman gets back broken 7.00
497a 2nd printing. 2.50
498 JAp,JRu,Knightfall#15,A:Bane,
Catwoman,Azrael Becomes
Batman 3.00

499 JAp,SHa,Knightfall#17,
A:Bane,Catwoman. 3.00
500 JQ(c),JAp,MM,Die Cut(c),
Direct Market,Knightfall#19,
V:Bane,N:Batman 6.00
500a KJo(c),Newstand Ed. 3.50
501 MM,I:Mekros 3.00
502 MM,V:Mekros 3.00
503 MM,V:Catwoman 3.00
504 MM,V:Catwoman 3.00
505 MM,V:Canibal 3.00
506 KJo(c),MM,A:Ballistic 3.00
507 KJo(c),MM,A:Ballistic 3.00
508 KJo(c),MM,V:Abattior 3.00
509 KJo(c),MM,KnightsEnd#1,
A:Shiva 3.50
510 KJo(c),MM,Knights End #7,
V:Azrael. 3.00
511 Zero Hour, A:Batgirl. 3.00
512 Killer Croc sewer battles 3.00
513 Two-Face and convicts 3.00
514 Identity Crisis 3.00
515 KJo,Return of Bruce Wayne,
Troika,pt.1 . . . . 3.00
515 Collector's Edition 3.50
516 V:The Sleeper 3.00
517 V:The Sleeper. 3.00
518 V:The Black Spider 3.00
519 KJo,V:The Black Spider
[new Miraweb format begins] . . 3.00
520 EB,A:James Gordon. 3.00
521 R:Killer Croc 3.00
522 R:Scarecrow 3.00
523 V:Scarecrow 3.00
524 DgM,KJo,V:Scarecrow 3.00
525 DgM,KJo,Underworld
Unleashed tie-in 3.00
526 DgM,A:Alfred,Nightwing,Robin . 3.00
527 DgM,V:Two-Face,I:Schism 3.00
528 DgM,V:Two-Face,pt.2 . . . . 3.00
529 DgM,KJo,Contagion,pt.6 . . . . . 3.50
530 DgM,KJo,The Aztec
Connection,pt.1 . . . . 3.50
530a collector's edition 3.50
531 DgM,KJo,The Aztec
Connection,pt.2 . . . . 3.00
531a collectors edition 3.50
532 DgM(s),KJo,The Aztec Connec-
tion, pt.3, A:Deadman 3.00
532a card stock cover 3.50
533 DgM(s),KJo,Legacy prelude . . . 3.00
534 DgM(s),KJo,Legacy, pt.5 . . . . . 3.00
535 DgM(s),KJo,JhB,I:The Ogre,
double size 4.00
535a Collector's Edition,
gatefold cover 5.00

Batman #558 © DC Comics Inc.

536 DgM(s),KJo,JhB,V:Man-Bat,
Final Night tie-in 3.00
537 DgM(s),KJo,JhB,A:Man-Bat,
pt.2 . . . . 3.00
538 DgM(s),KJo,JhB,A:Man-Bat,
pt.3. 3.00
539 DgM(s),KJo,Boneyard Blues . . 3.00
540 DgM(s),KJo,JhB,Spectre,pt.1 . . 3.00
541 DgM(s),KJo,JhB,Spectre,pt.2 . . 3.00
542 DgM(s),KJo,JhB,V:Faceless,
pt. 1 . . . . 3.00
543 DgM(s),KJo,JhB,pt. 2 . . . . 3.00
544 DgM(s),KJo,JhB, F:Joker,pt.1 . . 3.00
545 DgM(s),KJo, F:Joker, Demon,
pt.2. 3.00
546 DgM(s),KJo,JhB,F:Joker,
Demon, pt.3 concl. 3.00
547 DgM,KJo,JhB,Genesis tie-in . . . 3.00
548 DgM,KJo,JhB,V:Penguin, pt.1 . 3.00
549 DgM,KJo,JhB,V:Penguin,pt.2 . . 3.00
550 DgM,KJo,JhB,I:Chase. 3.50
550a deluxe, with file card inserts . . 3.50
551 DgM,KJo,JhB,F:Ragman 2.50
552 DgM,. 2.50
553 DgM,KJo,SB,Cataclysm
x-over, pt.3. . . . . 4.50
554 DgM,KJo,SB,Cataclysm,. 3.00
555 DgM,JhB,SB,BSf,Aftershock . . 2.50
556 DGm,NBy,BSf,Aftershock 2.50
557 DGm,VGi,SB,BSf,F:Ballistic . . . 2.50
558 DGm,JAp,SB,doubts. 2.50
559 DgM(s),BH,SB,Aftershock 2.50
560 CDi,SB,A:Nightwing & Robin . . 2.50
561 CDi(s),JAp, No Man's Land. . . . 2.50
562 CDi(s),JAp, No Man's Land . . . 2.50
563 No Law and A New Order, pt.3 . 6.00
564 F:Batgirl, Mosaic,pt.1 . . . . 2.50
565 F:Batgirl, Mosaic,pt.3 . . . . 2.50
566 JBg,A:Superman. 2.50
567 SCi,F:Batgirl, pt.1,x-over. 2.50
568 DJu,BSz,Fruit of the
Earth, pt.2 . . . . 2.50
569 F:Batgirl. 2.50
570 MD2,No Man's Land, The
Code, pt.1 . . . . 2.50
571 CDi,MtB,Goin'Downtown,pt.1 . . 2.50
572 Jurisprudence,pt.1 . . . . 2.50
573 Shellgame,pt.1,A:Lex Luthor . . 2.50
574 Endgame, pt.2 x-over 2.50
575 LHa,SMc,KIS. 2.50
576 LHa,SMc,KIS,kidnapping 2.50
577 LHa,SMc,KIS,rodents 2.50
578 LHa,SMc,MPn,serial killer. 2.50
579 LHa,SMc,KIS,V:Orca,pt.1 . . . . 2.50
580 LHa,SMc,KIS,V:Orca,pt.2 . . . . 2.50
581 LHa,SMc,KIS,V:Orca,pt.3 . . . . 2.50
582 SMc,KIS,Fearless,pt.1 . . . . 2.50
583 SMc,KIs,Fearless,pt.2 . . . . 2.50
584 SMc,KIS,A:Penguin. 2.50
585 SMc,KIS,V:Penguin. 2.50
586 SMc,KIS,V:Penguin, This issue:
Batman Dies!. 2.50
587 RBr,RyR,Officer Down,pt.1 . . . . 2.50
588 SMc,KIS,Close Before Striking . 2.50
589 SMc,KIS,Close Before Striking . 2.50
590 SMc,KIS,Close Before Striking . 2.50
591 SMc,KIS,Shot thru the Heart . . 2.50
592 SMc,KIS,Shot thru the Heart . . 2.50
593 SMc,KIS,Worlds at War tie-in . . 2.50
594 SMc,KIS,Worlds at War tie-in . . 2.50
595 SMc,F:Lew Moxon 2.50
596 SMc,Joker:Last Laugh 2.50
597 SMc,V:Zeiss 2.50
598 SMc,Christmas in Gotham 2.50
599 Bruce Wayne:Murderer,pt.7 . . . 2.50
600 Bruce Wayne:Fugitive,pt.1 . . . . 6.00
600a 2nd printing. 4.00
601 Bruce Wayne:Fugitive,pt.3 . . . . 2.50
602 SMc,V:Nicodemus 2.50
603 Bruce Wayne:Fugitive,pt.11 . . . 2.50
604 SMc,Crime Alley 2.50
605 Bruce Wayne:Fugitive,concl. . . 3.50

Batman #612
© DC Comics, Inc.

606 SMc,F:Deadshot 2.50
607 SMc,F:Deadshot,pt.2 . . . . 2.50
608 JLb,JLe,SW,Hush,pt.1 . . . . . . 15.00
608a 2nd printing, new cover 40.00
609 JLb,JLe,SW,Hush,pt.2 . . . . . . 10.00
610 JLb,JLe,SW,Hush,pt.3 . . . . . . 6.00
611 JLb,JLe,SW,Hush,pt.4 . . . . . . 6.00
612 JLb,JLe,SW,Hush,pt.5 . . . . . . 20.00
612a 2nd printing, B&W(c) 25.00
613 JLb,JLe,SW,Hush,pt.6 . . . . . . 7.00
614 JLb,JLe,SW,Hush,pt.7 . . . . . . 5.00
615 JLb,JLe,SW,Hush,pt.8 . . . . . . 18.00
616 JLb,JLe,SW,Hush,pt.9 . . . . . . 5.00
617 JLb,JLe,SW,Hush,pt.10 . . . . . 4.00
618 JLb,JLe,SW,Hush,pt.11 . . . . . . 4.00
619 JLb,JLe,SW,Hush,pt.12 . . . . . 4.00
619a newsstand cover 3.00
620 Broken City, pt.1 . . . . 2.50
621 Broken City, pt.2 . . . . 2.50
622 Broken City, pt.3 . . . . 2.50
623 Broken City, pt.4 . . . . 2.50
624 Broken City, pt.5 . . . . 2.50
625 Broken City, pt.6 . . . . 2.50
626 As the Crow Flies,pt.1 . . . . 2.50
627 As the Crow Flies,pt.2 . . . . 2.50
628 As the Crow Flies,pt.3 . . . . 2.50
629 As the Crow Flies,pt.4 . . . . 2.50
630 As the Crow Flies,pt.5 . . . . 2.50
631 War Games,Act 1,pt.8 . . . . . . 2.50
632 War Games,Act 2,pt.8 . . . . . . 2.50
633 War Games, Act 3,pt.8,40-pg . . 3.00
634 War games epilogue 2.50
635 DoM,Under the Hood,pt.1 . . . . 10.00
636 DoM,Under the Hood,pt.2 . . . . . 6.00
637 DoM,Under the Hood,pt.3 . . . . . 6.00
638 DoM,Under the Hood,pt.4 . . . . . 6.00
639 DoM,Family Reunion,pt.1 . . . . . 4.00
640 DoM,Family Reunion,pt.2 . . . . . 4.00
641 DoM,Family Reunion,pt.3 . . . . . 3.00
642 V:Killer Croc 2.50
643 War Crimes,x-over, pt.2 . . . . . 2.50
644 War Crimes,x-over, pt.4 . . . . . 2.50
645 Gotham graveyard 2.50
646 DoM,Infinite Crisis tie-in 2.50
647 DoM,Infinite Crisis tie-in 2.50
648 DoM,F:Black Mask 2.50
649 DoM,Black Mask & Red Hood . 2.50
650 DoM,Jason Todd mystery 2.50
651 Face the Face, pt.2, x-over . . . 2.50
652 Face the Face, pt.4, x-over . . . 2.50
653 Face the Face, pt.6, x-over . . . 3.00
654 Face the Face, pt.8, x-over . . . 3.00
655 GMo,NKu, Batman and Son . . . 3.00
656 GMo,NKu, Batman and Son . . . 3.00
657 GMo,NKu, Batman and Son . . . 3.00

658 GMo,NKu, Batman and Son . . . 3.00
659 GMo,NKu, Joker's revenge . . . 3.00
Ann.#1 CS,O:Bat Cave 1,600.00
Ann.#2 . . . . 900.00
Ann.#3 A:Joker 900.00
Ann.#4 . . . . 500.00
Ann.#5 . . . . 500.00
Ann.#6 . . . . 400.00
Ann.#7 . . . . 300.00
Ann.#8 TVE,A:Ras al Ghul 10.00
Ann.#9 JOy,AN,PS 9.00
Ann.#10 DCw,DG,V:HugoStrange . . 9.00
Ann.#11 JBy(c),AMo(s),V:Penguin. 10.00
Ann.#12 RA,V:Killer 7.00
Ann.#13 A:Two-Face 8.00
Ann.#14 O:Two-Face 6.00
Ann.#15 Armageddon,pt.3 . . . . . . 8.00
Ann.#15a 2nd printing(silver) 4.00
Ann.#16 SK(c),Eclipso,V:Joker . . . 4.00
Ann.#17 EB,Bloodline#8,
　 I:Decimator 4.00
Ann.#18 Elseworld Story 5.00
Ann.#19 Year One, O:Scarecrow . . 6.00
Ann.#20 Legends o/t Dead Earth . . 5.00
Ann.#21 Pulp Heroes (Weird
　 Mystery) DgM(s) 6.00
Ann.#22 BWr(c) Ghosts 5.00
Ann.#23 CDi(s),GN,MPn, JLApe
　 Gorilla Warfare 5.00
Ann.#24 Planet DC 5.00
Ann.#25 Jason Todd's Secrets 5.00
Specials & 1-shots
Giant Ann.#1 Facsimile edition 6.00
Spec.#0 (1994) 4.00
Spec.#1 MGo,I:Wrath 5.00
Spec.#1,000,000 DgM(s),SB,
　 F:Toy Wonder 3.00
Spec.#1 Our Worlds at War (2001) . 4.00
Giant #1, 7 tales, 80-page (1998) . . 6.00
Giant #2, 80-page (1999) 6.00
Giant #3 CDi(s) 80-page (2000) . . . 7.00
Batman Allies Secret Files 2005 . . . 5.00
Batman: Arkham Asylum — Tales
　 of Madness, AIG, Cataclysm
　 tie-in (1998) 4.00
Batman: Batgirl, JBa,RBr,
　 Girlfrenzy (1998) 3.00
Batman: Blackgate, CDi(s), JSon,
　 in Blackgate prison (1996) 4.50
Batman: Blackgate — Isle of Men,
　 DgM, JAp,BSf,BSz,
　 Cataclysm (1998) 3.00
Batman Dark Knight Gallery (1995). 3.50
Batman: Day of Judgment 4.00
Batman: Death of Innocents, DON(s),
　 JSt, BSz, Land mine victims
　 (1996) 4.00
Batman Gallery,collection of past
　 (c),posters,pin-ups,JQ(c) (1992) 4.00
Batman: Gotham By Gaslight,MMi,
　 V:Jack the Ripper 6.00
Gotham City Secret Files #1 . . . . . . 5.00
Batman: The Hill (2000) 3.00
Batman: Joker's Apprentice 4.00
Batman: The Killing Joke,BB,AMo(s),
　 O:Joker,Batgirl paralyzed
　 (1988) 15.00
　 2nd thru 6th printings . . . . . . @5.00
Batman: Mitefall, V:Bane
　 Mite (1995) 5.00
Batman: Penguin Triumphant
　 (1992) 5.00
Batman: Plus (1997) 3.00
Batman Record Comic (1996) 2.00
Batman/Riddler: The Riddle
　 Factory (1995) 5.00
Secret Files #1 SMc(c) inc.
　 O:Batman (1997) 6.00
Batman: Seduction of the Gun,
　 V:Illegal Gun Control (1992) . . . 3.00
Spec. The 10-Cent Adventure 0.10
3-D Batman:Scarecrow 4.00

Batman 12-cent Adventure,
　 War Games,pt.1 . . . . 0.12
1-shot Batman/The Spirit (2006) . . . 5.00
Batman/Two-Face: Crime and
　 Punishment (1995) 5.00
　 2nd printing (1998) 5.00
Two-Face Strikes Twice #1 . . . . . . 5.25
Two-Face Strikes Twice #2 . . . . . . 5.25
Batman: Vengeance of Bane,
　 GN,I:Bane (1992) 30.00
　 2nd Printing 5.00
Batman: Vengeance of Bane II
　 (1995) 4.00
Batman Villains Secret Files,
　 AIG,CDi,RMz,BB,F:Greatest Foes
　 (1998) 5.00
Batman Villains Secret Files 2005 . 5.00
Elseworld 1-shots
Batman of Arkham (2000) 6.00
Batman: The Blue, The Grey, and
　 The Bat, JL (1992) 6.00
Batman: Brotherhood of the Bat
　 (1995) 6.00
Batman: Castle of the Bat 6.00
Batman: Dark Allegiances (1996) . . 6.00
Batman: Holy Terror (1991) 6.50
Batman: I, Joker, BH, in
　 2083 (1998) 5.00
Batman: In Darkest Knight
　 MiB(s),JBi (1994) 5.50
Batman Knightgallery (1995) 3.50
Batman: Masque, MGr, in turn of
　 the century Gotham 7.00
Batman: Master of the Future,EB,
　 Sequel to Goth.by Gaslight
　 (1991) 6.00
Batman: Scar of the Bat (1996) . . . 5.00
Batman: Two Faces (1998) 5.00
Batman: Master of the Future(1998) 6.00
Graphic Novels
The Abduction 6.00
Batman A Lonely Place of Dying
　 (1990) rep. Batman #440–442
　 & New Titans #60–61 . . . . 4.00
Batman: Blind Justice, rep. Detective
　 Comics #598–#600 (1992) 7.50
Batman: Bloodstorm 13.00
Batman: Bullock's Law 5.00
The Book of Shadows 6.00
Child of Dreams, manga 25.00
Crimson Mist, Elseworlds (2001) . . 15.00
Batman: Dark Joker, KJo 12.00
Many Deaths of the Batman;
　 rep. #433–#435 (1992) 4.00
Batman: Dreamland (2000) 6.00
Batman: Ego (2000) 7.00

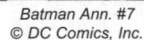

Batman Ann. #7
© DC Comics, Inc.

Batman: Full Circle AD,
  A:Reaper (1992) 7.00
Batman/Joker: Switch 7.00
Golden Steets of Gotham 7.00
Gotham Noir, 64-page (2001) 7.00
Batman: Harley Quinn (1998) 6.00
Batman: Man Who Laughs (2005). . 7.00
Batman: Mr. Freeze 5.00
Batman/Nightwing: Bloodborne
  48-pg. (2002). 6.00
No Man's Land, 48-page No Law
  and a New Order, pt.1 . . . . 3.00
No Man's Land, lenticular (c). 4.00
No Man's Land Gallery 4.00
Nosferatu 6.00
The Order of Beasts (2004). 6.00
Batman: Poison Ivy 5.00
Batman/Poison Ivy:
  Cast Shadows (2004) 7.00
Reign of Terror 5.00
Roomful of Strangers (2004) 6.00
Batman: Scar of the Bat 5.00
Scarface—A Psychodrama (2001) . 6.00
The Scottish Connection 6.00
Batman: Ten Knights of the Beast,
  rep. #417–#420 (1994) 6.00
Batman: Two Faces 5.00
Batman: The Ultimate Evil:
  1 Novel adaptation (of 2) 6.00
  2 Novel adaptation, finale 6.00
Trade Paperbacks
Batman: Absolution 18.00
The Batman Adventures 8.00
Batman: Anarky 13.00
Batman: Arkham Asylum,DMc . . . 15.00
As the Crow Flies (2004) 13.00
The Arrow, The Ring & The Bat. . . 20.00
Birth of the Demon, O:Ras al
  Ghul (1993) 13.00
Batman: Black and White 20.00
Black and White, Vol.2. . . . . 20.00
Batman: Bloodstorm,KJo,V:Joker,
  Vampires 13.00
Bride of the Demon, TGr, V:Ra's
  al Ghul 13.00
Broken City (2005). 15.00
Bruce Wayne-Fugitive, Vol. 1 . . . 13.00
Bruce Wayne-Fugitive, Vol. 2 . . . 13.00
Bruce Wayne-Fugitive, Vol. 3 . . . 13.00
Bruce Wayne-Murderer? 13.00
Batman: Cataclysm 18.00
Batman: The Chalice (2000) 15.00
Batman Chronicles (2005). 15.00
Batman Chronicles, Vol.2 (2006). . 15.00
Batman: Contagion 13.00
Contagion 20.00
Batman: The Cult. 20.00
The Dark Knight Adventures 8.00
Batman: Dark Knight Dynasty, three
  elseworlds stories (1999) 15.00
Dark Knight Strikes Again (2004). . 20.00
Batman: Dark Victory (2002) 20.00
Death and the Maidens (2004) . . . 20.00
Batman: A Death in the Family,
  rep. Batman #426-429 (1988)
  TPB 8.00
  2nd printing 5.00
  3rd printing 4.00
Batman/Deathblow: After the Fire . 13.00
Batman: Detective No. 27 (2004) . 13.00
Batman: Evolution (2001) 13.00
Batman: Faces (1995) 10.00
Batman: Face the Face (2006) . . . 15.00
Batman: Fortunate Son (1999) . . . 15.00
TPB Batman: Gotham by Gaslight 13.00
Batman: Gothic, rept. Legends of
  the Dark Knight #6–#10 (1992)13.00
Greatest Batman Stories 16.00
Greatest Batman Stories, Vol. 2 . . 17.00
Greatest Stories Ever Told (2005) . 20.00
Batman: Harvest Breed 18.00
Batman: Hong Kong (2004) 18.00

Batman/Huntress: Cry For Blood. . 13.00
Batman: Hush, Vol. 1 (2004) 13.00
Batman: Hush, Vol. 2 (2004) 13.00
Batman in the Forties. 20.00
Batman in the Fifties 20.00
Batman in the Sixties 20.00
Batman in the Seventies 20.00
Batman in the Eightics. 20.00
Greatest Joker Stories 15.00
Batman/Judge Dredd Files (2004). 15.00
Batman: Knight's End, rep. 15.00
Knightfall rep. #1–#11 . . . . 13.00
Knightfall rep. #12–#19 . . . . 13.00
Batman: The Last Angel, F:Catwoman
  V:Aztec bat-god (1994) 13.00
Batman: The Last Arkham 13.00
Legacy, seq.to Contagion 18.00
Batman: Night Cries,SHa. 13.00
Batman: Nine Lives 18.00
Batman: Officer Down (2001) 13.00
Batman: Prodigal, rep,. 15.00
Batman: Scarecrow Tales (2005). . 20.00
Batman: Son of the Demon,JBi . . . 25.00
  2nd thru 4th printings. . . . . . . @9.00
Batman: Strange Apparitions
  (1999) 13.00
Batman/Superman: World'sFinest. 20.00
Batman: Tales of the Demon (1991)
  TPB 20.00
  TPB (1999) 18.00
  TPB (2005) 18.00
Batman: Terror. 13.00
Batman: Thrillkiller 13.00
Under the Hood (2005) 10.00
Under the Hood, Vol.2 (2006) 10.00
Batman: War Drums (2004). 18.00
War Crimes (2006). 13.00
War Games Act One (2005) 15.00
War Games Act Two (2005). 15.00
War Games Act Three (2005) 15.00
Batman: Year One Rep. Batman
  #404-#407 (1998) 14.00
  Later Printings 10.00
Batman: Four of a Kind, from
  Year One annuals (1998) 15.00
Year Two (1990) rep. Detective
  Comics #575–#578 . . . . 10.00
Year Two: Fear the Reaper(2002). 18.00
Movies
TPB The Movies, (all 4) (1997) . . . 20.00
Batman, JOy, Movie adaptation 3.00
  Perfect Bound 6.00
Batman Returns, SE,JL Movie
  Adaption, ... 6.00
  Newsstand Format 4.00
Batman: Mask of the Phantasm,
  animated movie adapt. 6.00
  Newstand Ed. 3.50
Batman Forever, Movie Adaptation . 6.00
  Newsstand version 4.00
Batman and Robin, DON(s), Movie
  Adaptation (1997) 4.00
  Collector's edition, ... 6.00
Batman Begins movie adapt (2005) 7.00
Batman Begins: The Movie &
  Other Tales of the Dark Knight 13.00
GN Batman: Bane, BSz(c) movie
  tie-in (1997) 5.00
GN Batman: Batgirl, BSz(c) movie
  tie-in (1997) 5.00
GN Batman: Mr. Freeze, BSz(c)
  movie tie-in (1997). 5.00
GN Batman: Poison Ivy, BSz(c)
  movie tie-in (1997). 5.00
X-overs
Batman & Superman Adventures:
  World's Finest (1997) adaptation
  of animated adventures, 64pg. . 7.00
Batman/Captain America (DC/Marvel
  1996) Elseworlds. 6.00
Batman/Deadman, Death and
  Glory, JeR(s),JEs (1996) 13.00

Batman/Demon (1996) 5.00
Batman/Demon: A Tragedy (2000) . 6.00
Batman/Dracula: Red Rain KJo,MJ,
  Batman becomes Vampire,
  SC (1992) 12.00
  TPB Elseworlds (1999) 13.00
Batman/Green Arrow: The Poison
  Tomorrow,MN,JRu,V:Poison
  Ivy (1992) 6.25
  GN rep. (2000) 6.00
Batman/Houdini: The Devil's
  Workshop (1993) 6.50
Batman: Huntress/Spoiler—Blunt
  Trauma, CDi,Cataclysm (1988). 3.00
Batman/Judge Dredd: Judgement on
  Gotham,SBs,V:Scarecrow, Judge
  Death (1991) 9.00
Batman/Judge Dredd: Vendetta in
  Gotham, AIG(s),V:Ventriliquist
  (1993) 5.25
Batman/Judge Dredd: The Ultimate
  Riddle (1995). 5.00
Batman/Lobo, Elseworlds (2000). . 6.00
Batman/Phantom Stranger, AIG(s),
  Lemurian artifact (1997) 5.00
Batman/Punisher: Lake of Fire,
  DON(s),BKi,A:Punisher,V:Jigsaw
  (DC/Marvel 1994) 5.25
Batman/Spawn: War Devil, DgM,CDi,
  AIG(s), KJ,V:Croatoan (1994) . . 6.00
Batman/Spawn: War Devil (1999) . . 5.00
Batman/Spider-Man JMD,GN,KK,
  V:Kingpin&Ra's al Ghul(1997). . 5.00
Batman vs. The Incredible Hulk
  (DC/Marvel 1995) 4.00

Batman Adventures #3
© *DC Comics Inc.*

BATMAN ADVENTURES
1992–95
(Based on cartoon series)

1 MeP,V:Penguin 5.00
2 MeP,V:Catwoman 4.00
3 MeP,V:Joker. 3.00
4 MeP,V:Scarecrow. 3.00
5 MeP,V:Scarecrow. 3.00
6 MeP,A:Robin 3.00
7 MeP,V:Killer Croc,w/card 6.00
8 MeP,Larceny my Sweet. 3.00
9 MeP,V:Two Face 3.00
10 thru 24 MeP . . . . @3.00
25 MeP,dbl.size,Superman 3.50
26 thru 32. . . . . @3.00
33 thru 36 . . . . @2.50
Ann.#1 Roxy Rocket 3.00

Ann.#2 JBa,BBl,DG,TG,SHa,BKi,MM,
  GN,JRu,V:Demon,Ra's al
  Ghul,Etrigan.................3.50
Holiday Special 3.00
Spec. Mad Love...............4.00
TPB Collected Adventures #1 .....6.00
TPB Collected Adventures #2 .....6.00

BATMAN ADVENTURES:
THE LOST YEARS
Nov., 1997
1 (of 5) BHa,TBe,Batgirl 2.50
2 BHa,TBe,Dick Grayson quits....2.50
3 ....2.50
4 BHa,TBe,F:Tim Drake 2.50
5 BHa,TBe,Tim Drake new Robin .2.50

BATMAN ADVENTURES:
THE LOST YEARS
1999
1 (of 6) TBe...................2.50
2 thru 6 ....@2.50
TPB series rep................6.00

BATMAN ADVENTURES
May 2003
1 TTn 2.25
1a newsstand edition 2.25
2 TTn,F:Riddler...............2.25
3 F:Joker & Harley 2.25
4 TTn,RBr,V:Ra's Al Ghul 2.25
5 TTn,V:Deadshot..............2.25
6 TTn,TBe,V:Black Mask 2.25
7 RBr,TBe,V:Phantasm 2.25
8 RBr,TBe,V:Black Mask 2.25
9 death trap..................2.25
10 thru 14 RBr,TBe ....@2.25
15 TBe,Mr.Freeze 2.25
16 TBe,Joker & Harley wedding ...2.25
17 TBe,RBr 2.25
TPB Dangerous Dames & Demons 15.00
TPB Rogues' Gallery............7.00
TPB Shadows & Masks..........7.00

BATMAN/ALIENS II
DC/Dark Horse Dec. 2002
GN #1 (of 3) IEd(s) 6.00
GN #2 IEd(s) 6.00
GN #3 IEd(s) 6.00
TPB Batman/Aliens II...........15.00

Batman and the Outsiders #6
© DC Comics Inc.

BATMAN AND
THE OUTSIDERS
Aug., 1983
1 B:MiB(s),JAp,O:Outsiders,
  O:Geo Force 4.50
2 JAp,V:Baron Bedlam 3.00
3 JAp,V:Agent Orange 2.50
4 JAp,V:Fearsome Five 2.50
5 JAp,A:New Teen Titans 3.00
6 JAp,V:Cryonic Man 2.50
7 JAp,V:Cryonic Man 2.50
8 JAp,A:Phantom Stranger 2.50
9 JAp,I:Master of Disaster 2.50
10 JAp,A:Master of Disaster 2.50
11 JAp,V:Takeo 2.50
12 JAp,DG,O:Katana 2.50
13 JAp,Day,O:Batman 2.50
14 BWg,Olympics,V:Maxi Zeus 2.50
15 TVE,Olympics,V:Maxi Zeus 2.50
16 JAp,L:Halo 2.50
17 JAp,V:Ahk-Ton 2.50
18 JAp,V:Ahk-Ton 2.50
19 JAp,A:Superman.............2.50
20 JAp,V:Syonide,R:Halo 2.50
21 TVE,JeM,Solo Stories.........2.50
22 AD,O:Halo,I:Aurakles 2.50
23 AD,O:Halo,V:Aurakles.........2.50
24 AD,C:Kobra 2.50
25 AD,V:Kobra 2.50
26 AD 2.50
27 AD,V:Kobra 2.50
28 AD,I:Lia Briggs(Looker).......2.50
29 AD,V:Metamorpho...........2.50
30 AD,C:Looker 2.50
31 AD,I&J:Looker...............2.50
32 AD,L:Batman 2.50
Ann.#1 JA N:Geo-Force,
  I:Force of July 3.00
Ann.#2 V:Tremayne,W:Metamorpho
  & Sapphire Stagg 3.00
Becomes:

ADVENTURES OF
THE OUTSIDERS
May, 1986
33 AD,V:Baron Bedlam 2.25
34 AD,Masters of Disaster........2.25
35 AD,V:Adolph Hitler...........2.25
36 AD,A:Masters of Disaster 2.25
37 thru 38 ....@2.25
39 thru 47 JAp,reprints
  Outsiders #1-#9 ....@2.25

BATMAN AND ROBIN
ADVENTURES, THE
Nov., 1995
1 TTn 3.00
2 TTn,V:Two-Face 3.00
3 TTn,V:The Riddler 3.00
4 TTn,V:The Penguin 3.00
5 TTn 3.00
6 TTn,Robin Fired?.............2.50
7 TTn,V:Scarface 2.50
8 TTn(s) 2.50
9 TTn(s),F:Batgirl & Talia 2.50
10 TTn(s),F:Ra's Al Ghul 2.50
11 TTn(s),Alfred & Robin look
  for monster in Batcave 2.50
12 TTn(s),BKr,RBr, sequel to
  Bane TV episode............2.50
13 TTn(s),BKr,RBr,V:Scarecrow ...2.50
14 TTn(s),BKr,RBr,young criminal
  turns to Batman for help 2.50
15 TTn(s) 2.50
16 TTn(s),V:Catman,A:Catwoman..2.50
17 PDi&TTn(s),JSon,RBr,Mad
  Hatter dies in Arkham 2.50
18 TTn(s),BKr,TBe,A:Joker,
  Harley Quinn 2.50
19 TTn(s),BKr,TBe,The Huntress ..2.50

20 TTn(s),BKr,TBe, office pool 2.50
21 TTn(s),JSon,Riddler kidnaps
  Commissioner Gordon 2.50
22 TTn(s),BKr,TBe,V:Two-Face....2.50
23 TTn(s),TBe,V:Killer Croc.......2.50
24 TTn(c),F:Poison Ivy 2.50
25 TTn,TBe,final issue, 48pg......3.50
Ann.#1 PDi(s),TTn, sequel to
  Batman: Mask of the Phantasm 3.00
Ann.#2 JSon,TBe,V:Hypnotist 4.00
Sub-Zero one-shot, F:Mr. Freeze,
  Nora, 64pg.................4.00

BATMAN & SUPERMAN:
WORLD'S FINEST
1999
1 (of 10) KK(s),DTy,RbC,48-page..7.00
2 KK(s),DTy,RbC...............3.50
3 KK(s),DTy,RbC,Arkham Asylum .3.00
4 KK(s),DTy,RbC,Metropolis......3.00
5 KK(s),DTy,RbC,Batgirl 3.00
6 KK(s),DTy,RbC,trade identities ..3.00
7 KK(s),PD,RbC 3.00
8 KK(s),PD,RbC 3.00
9 KK(s),RbC,split issue..........3.00
10 concl.......................3.00
GN 7.00

BATMAN: THE ANKH
Nov., 2001
1 (of 2) CDi,JVF,ancient Egypt 6.00
2 CDi,JVF,V:Khatera, concl.......6.00

BATMAN:
BANE OF THE DEMON
Feb., 1998
1 (of 4) CDi,GN,TP, Bane &
  Ra's al Ghul................2.50
2 CDi,GN,TP,Talia..............2.50
3 CDi,GN,TP,the Lazarus Pit 2.50
4 CDi,GN,TP,Bane imprisoned....2.50

BATMAN BEYOND
Mini-series 1999
1 (of 6) RBr,TBe,Rebirth.........2.50
2 RBr,TBe,Rebirth,pt.2 ....2.50
3 RBr,TBe,V:Blight 2.50
4 JSon,TBe,F:Demon Etrigan.....2.50
5 JSon,TBe,V:Mummy 2.50
6 JSon,TBe,V:Inque 2.50
TPB rep. mini-series 10.00

Batman Beyond #1
© DC Comics, Inc.

BATMAN BEYOND
1999
1 Batman: Classic vs. Future 3.00
2 V:Inque. 2.50
3 . . . . 2.50
4 V:Royal Flush Gang. 2.50
5 V:Shriek 2.50
6 V:Stalker. 2.50
7 V:Jokerz 2.50
8 V:Vendetta 2.50
9 V:Curare. 2.50
10 V:Golem 2.50
11 nanotechnology. 2.50
12 F:Terminal. 2.50
13 Commissioner Barbara Gordon . 2.50
14 F:Etrigan the Demon. 2.50
15 thru 20 BSf(c) . . . . @2.50
21 I:Justice League Unlimited 2.50
22 In Blackest Day, concl. 2.50
23 New Royal Flush Gang. 2.50
24 final issue 2.50
Spec. Return of the Joker 3.00

BATMAN BLACK & WHITE
1996
1 JLe(c) numerous artists 9.00
2 thru 4 . . . . @7.00

BATMAN:
BOOK OF THE DEAD
1999
1 (of 2) DgM(s),BKi,Elseworlds . . . 5.00
2 DgM(s),BKi,Conclusion 5.00

BATMAN/CATWOMAN:
TRAIL OF THE GUN
Aug. 2004
1 & 2 48-pg. . . . . @6.00

BATMAN CHRONICLES
1995
1 CDi,LW,BSz, multiple stories 5.00
2 V:Feedback 4.00
3 All villains issue 4.00
4 F:Hitman 15.00
5 Oracle, Year One story 3.50
6 Ra's Al Ghul. 3.50
7 JOy,LW, woman on death row . . . 3.50
8 Talia goes to Gotham to
    eliminate Batman. 3.50
9 CDi(s),F:Batgirl, Mr. Freeze,
    Poison Ivy 3.50
10 BSn, anthology 3.50
11 CDi,JFM, Elseworlds stories 3.00
12 Cataclysm x-over 3.00
13 F:GCPD 3.00
14 SB(c),F:Alfred,Huntress 3.00
15 Road to No Man's Land 3.00
16 F:Batgirl,No Man's Land tie-in . . 3.00
17 V:Penguin,No Man's Land 3.00
18 No Man's Land 3.00
19 . . . . 3.00
20 SBe(s)&IEd(s),48-pg. 3.00
21 DG,JRu,3 Elseworlds tales 3.00
22 F:Lady Shiva,48-pg. 3.00
23 BSf(c) final issue 3.00
Gallery #1, Pin-ups 3.50
GN The Gauntlet 5.00

BATMAN: CITY OF LIGHT
Oct. 2003
1 (of 8) Gotham transformed 3.00
2 thru 8 . . . . @3.00

BATMAN: THE CULT
1988
1 JSn,BWr,V:Deacon Blackfire 8.00

---

2 thru 4 JSn,BWr . . . . @6.00
TPB Rep.#1-#4 . . . . 15.00

BATMAN:
CYBER REVOLUTION
May 2004
1 (of 5) Joker's robot army 3.00
2 thru 5 . . . . @3.00

BATMAN:
DARK DETECTIVE
May, 2005
1 (of 6) TA,MR 3.00
2 TA,MR 3.00
3 TA,MR 3.00
4 TA,MR 3.00
5 TA,MR 3.00
6 TA,MR 3.00
TPB Dark Detective 15.00

BATMAN:
DARK KNIGHT
OF THE ROUND TABLE
1998
1 (of 2) BL,DG,Elseworlds,48pg . . . 5.00
2 BL,DG, conclusion 5.00

BATMAN: THE DARK
KNIGHT RETURNS
1986
1 FM,KJ,V:Two-Face 30.00
1a 2nd printing 5.00
1b 3rd printing. 3.00
2 FM,KJ,V:Sons of the Batman . . 10.00
2a 2nd printing 3.00
2b 3rd printing. 2.50
3 FM,KJ,D:Joker 7.00
3a 2nd printing 3.00
4 FM,KJ,Batman vs.Superman,
    A:Green Arrow,D:Alfred 7.00
Paperback book 20.00
Warner paperback 17.00
    2nd-8th printing 13.00
TPB 10th Anniv. Spec, 224 pg. . . 15.00

BATMAN: THE DARK
KNIGHT STRIKES AGAIN
Dec., 2001
1 (of 3) FM,80-pg. 8.00
2 FM, 80-pg. 8.00
3 FM, 80-pg. concl. 8.00

BATMAN: DARK VICTORY
Oct., 1999
1 (of 13) JLb,TSe,48-pg. 6.00
2 JLb,TSe 5.00
3 JLb,TSe,V:Scarecrow 4.00
4 JLb,TSe,V:Two-Face 4.00
5 JLb,TSe,F:Catwoman 4.00
6 JLb,TSe,F:Penguin 4.00
7 JLb,TSe,V:Calendar Man 4.00
8 JLb,TSe,V:Hang Man 4.00
9 JLb,TSe,F:Bruce & Dick 4.00
10 JLb,TSe,V:Two-Face 4.00
11 JLb,TSe,V:Poison Ivy 4.00
12 JLb,TSe,Revenge 4.00
13 JLb,TSe, conclusion 5.00

BATMAN: DEATH
AND THE MAIDENS
Aug. 2003
1 (of 9) KJ,V:Ra's al Ghul 4.00
2 KJ,F:Nyssa 3.00
3 KJ,Ra's al Ghul, Nyssa 3.00
4 KJ,Ra's al Ghul 3.00

---

5 thru 8 KJ. . . . . @3.00
9 KJ 4.00

BATMAN/DEATHBLOW:
AFTER THE FIRE
DC/Wildstorm March, 2002
1 (of 3)TBd,x-over,48-pg. 6.00
2 TBd, 48-pg. 6.00
3 TBd, 48-pg., concl. 6.00

BATMAN: THE DOOM
THAT CAME TO GOTHAM
Sept., 2000
1 (of 3) Elseworlds 5.00
2 MMi,DJa, return from the Arctic. . 5.00
3 Elseworlds, concl. 5.00

Batman Family, 1st Series, #4
© DC Comics Inc.

BATMAN FAMILY
Sept.–Oct., 1975
1 MGr,NA(rep.) Batgirl &
    Robin begins,giant. 35.00
2 V:Clue Master 20.00
3 Batgirl & Robin reveal ID 20.00
4 I:Fatman. 20.00
5 I:Bat Hound 20.00
6 Joker Daughter 25.00
7 CS,A:Sportsmaster,
    G.A.Huntress 13.00
8 First solo Robin story,
    C:Joker's Daughter 13.00
9 Joker's Daughter 25.00
10 R:B'woman,1st solo Batgirl sty. 27.00
11 MR,Man-Bat begins 25.00
12 MR 25.00
13 MR,DN,BWi. 25.00
14 HC/JRu,Man-Bat. 22.00
15 MGo,Man-Bat 22.00
16 MGo,Man-Bat 22.00
17 JA,DH,MG,Batman, B:Huntress
    A:Demon,MK(c),A:Catwoman . 25.00
18 MGo,JSon,BL,Huntress,BM . . . 25.00
19 MGo,JSon,BL,Huntress,BM . . . 25.00
20 MGo,JSon,DH,A:Elongatedman,
    RagMan, Oct.–Nov.,1978 . . . . 25.00

BATMAN: FAMILY
Oct., 2002
1 (of 8) JFM,SFa,RHo,The Tracker 3.50
2 JFM,SFa,RHo,Athena 2.25
3 JFM,SFa,RHo,Bugg & Dr.Excess 2.25
4 JFM,SFa,RHo,Suicide King 2.25

All comics prices listed are for *Near Mint* condition.

5 JFM,SFa,RHo,Freeway 2.25
6 JFM,RHo,The Technician 2.25
7 JFM,Mr. Fun. 2.25
8 JFM,RHo,Blackout, 48-pg. 3.50

BATMAN: GCPD
Mini-Series Aug., 1996
1 thru 4 CDi(s),JAp,BSz . . . . @2.50

BATMAN: GORDON'S LAW
October, 1996
1 CDi(s),KJ,Gordon looks for
   bad cops 2.50
2 CDi(s),KJ,Gordon vs. corruption . 2.50
3 CDi(s),KJ, ... 2.50
4 (of 4) CDi(s),KJ, concl. 2.50

Batman: Gordon of Gotham #4
© DC Comics, Inc.

BATMAN: GORDON OF GOTHAM
April, 1998
1 (of 4) DON,DG,KJ,F:Jim Gordon . 2.50
2 DON,DG,KJ,Cuchulain. 2.50
3 DON,DG,KJ,break-in 2.50
4 DON,DG,KJ,past revealed 2.50

BATMAN: GOTHAM ADVENTURES
April, 1998
1 TTn,RBr,TBe,F:Joker. 3.50
2 TTn,RBr,TBe,F:Two-Face 2.50
3 TTn,RBr,TBe,V:Scarecrow. 2.50
4 TTn,RBr,TBe,A:Catwoman 2.50
5 RBr,TBe,TTn,A:Mr.Freeze 2.50
6 TTn,RBr,TBe,O:Deadman 2.50
7 TTn,RBe,TBe,V:Danger Dixon. . . 2.50
8 TTn,RBe,TBe,Batgirl 2.50
9 TTn,RBe,TBe,V:League
   of Assassins 2.50
10 TTn,RBe,TBe,F:Nightwing
   & Robin, A:Harley Quinn 2.50
11 TTn,RBe,TBe,V:Riddler. 2.50
12 TTn,RBe,TBe,V:Two-Face 2.50
13 RBe,TBe,V:Mastermind 2.50
14 TTn(s),TBe,V:Harley Quinn 2.50
15 V:Bane 2.50
16 TBe,Alfred Kidnapped. 2.50
17 TBe 2.50
18 TBe,R:Man-Bat. 2.50
19 TBe,Eden's Own,Poison Ivy 2.50

20 TBe, ... 2.50
21 TBe, ... 2.50
22 TBe,F:Comm.Gordon & Batgirl. . 2.50
23 TBe,V:Ra's al Ghul 2.50
24 TBe,F:Killer Croc 2.50
25 TBe,A:Flash 2.50
26 TBe,F:Kristov 2.50
27 TBe, ... 2.50
28 TBe,V:Riddler 2.50
29 CDi(s),TBe,Batman poisoned . . . 2.50
30 TBe,F:Clayface. 2.50
31 TTn,TBe,Blackout in Gotham . . . 2.50
32 TBe,V:Scarecrow 2.50
33 A:Phantom Stranger 2.50
34 V:Maxie Zeus 2.50
35 TBe,On the jury. 2.50
36 TBe,A:Superman 2.50
37 TBe,V:Joker, Penguin 2.50
38 TBe,F:Robin, Batgirl 2.50
39 TBe,V:Clayface 2.50
40 TBe,V:Mr. Freeze 2.50
41 TBe,The Man called Joe. 2.50
42 Tuesday Night. 2.50
43 TBe,F:Harley Quinn 2.50
44 TBe,F:Two-Face 2.50
45 TBe,Running the Asylum 2.50
46 TBe,Saving Face 2.50
47 TBe,Gotham's Underworld 2.50
48 TBe,RBr,F:Dick Grayson 2.50
49 TBe,Facade 2.50
50 TBe,Catwoman returns. 2.50
51 TA,Mr. Freeze 2.50
52 TBe,Bane 2.50
53 TBe,Poison Ivy superplant 2.50
54 TBe,crime spree 2.50
55 TBe,RBr,mobsters. 2.50
56 TBe,V:Riddler? 2.50
57 TBe,V:Riddler 2.50
58 TTn,V:Ventriloquist 2.50
59 TBe,financial scandal 2.50
60 TBe,final issue 2.50
TPB Batman: Gotham Adventures. 10.00

BATMAN: GOTHAM COUNTY LINE
Oct., 2005
1 (of 3) SHp, 48-page. 6.00
2 SHp, 48-page. 6.00
3 SHp, 48-page. 6.00
TPB 18.00

BATMAN: GOTHAM KNIGHTS
Feb., 2000
1 WEI,JLe 6.00
2 JBy,BB(c),F:Batgirl. 3.00
3 PPo,PR,BB(c),Samsara,pt.1 . . . . 3.00
4 PR,BB(c),Samsara,pt.2 . . . . 3.00
5 BB(c)V:The Key 3.00
6 WS,PR,JPL,F:Oracle 3.00
7 SD,PR, ... 3.00
8 Transference,pt.1 . . . . 3.00
9 Transference,pt.2 . . . . 3.00
10 Transference,pt.3, ... 3.00
11 BB(c),Transference,pt.4,48-pg. . . 3.50
12 This issue: Batman dies! 3.00
13 Officer Down,x-over,concl. 3.00
14 V:Double Dare 3.00
15 TPe,GC,V:Poison Ivy 3.00
16 Matatoa,pt.1 . . . . 3.00
17 Matatoa,pt.2 . . . . 3.00
18 Cavernous,F:Aquaman 3.00
19 CDi,MSh,DG,F:Titus 3.00
20 A:Superman 3.00
21 TA,Retribution, pt.2 . . . . 3.00
22 TA,Chemical attack. 3.00
23 BB(c),F:Scarecrow 3.00
24 TDz,Kls,F:Bruce Wayne 3.00
25 Bruce Wayne:Murderer,pt.4 . . . 4.00
26 Bruce Wayne:Murderer,pt.10 . . . 4.00

27 DCw,A:Man of Steel 3.00
28 Bruce Wayne:Fugitive,pt.7 . . . . 3.00
29 Mortician,pt.2 . . . . 3.00
30 Bruce Wayne:Fugitive,pt.14 . . . . 3.00
31 Bruce Wayne:Fugitive,pt.17 . . . . 3.00
32 MK,lives Batman impacts 3.00
33 SBe(s),BSz,F:Bane. 3.00
34 SBe(s),Tabula Rasa,pt.1. . . . . . 3.00
35 SBe(s),Tabula Rasa,pt.2 . . . . . . 3.50
36 SBe(s),F:Robin,Nightwing. 3.00
37 SBe(s),F:Spoiler 3.00
38 SBe(s),V:Checkmate 3.00
39 SBe(s),V:Checkmate 3.00
40 SBe(s),Knight Moves 3.00
41 SBe(s),V:Elongated Man 3.00
42 SBe(s),Alfred's illness 3.00
43 SBe(s),F:Batgirl,Robin 3.00
44 SBe(s),death of Jason Todd 3.00
45 SBe(s),Knights Passed 3.00
46 SBe(s),F:Nightwing,Robin. 3.00
47 WPo,F:Bane,Nightwing. 3.00
48 F:Bane,Nightwing 2.75
49 F:Bane 2.75
50 V:Hush 3.00
51 V:Hush,Riddler,Joker 3.00
52 F:Tailor,Hush,40-pg. 3.00
53 F:Hush,Green Arrow,40-pg. 3.00
54 F:Joker,40-pg. 3.00
55 Hush vs. Joker, 48-pg. 4.00
56 War Games,Act 1,pt.4 . . . . 2.50
57 War Games,Act 2,pt.4 . . . . 2.50
58 War Games,Act 3,pt.5 . . . . 2.50
59 CAd,JaL,F:Mr. Freeze 2.50
60 JaL(c),V:Hush 2.50
61 F:Hush, Ivy 2.50
62 F:Poison Ivy 2.50
63 F:Poison Ivy 2.50
64 F:Poison Ivy, Hush 2.50
65 F:Poison Ivy, conc. 3.00
66 F:Kobra & Prometheus 2.50
67 V:Hush,F:Poison Ivy 2.50
68 F:Alfred 2.50
69 F:Hush, Clayface 2.50
70 F:Clayfaces 2.50
71 Alfred arrested for Murder. 2.50
72 Dead Body, Parents Past 2.50
73 Joker returns. 2.50
74 V:Hush, Joker 2.50
TPB Hush Returns 13.00

(BATMAN:) GOTHAM NIGHTS
[Mini-Series] 1992
1 Gotham City 2.50
2 thru 4 Gotham Citizens Lives. . @2.50

BATMAN: GOTHAM NIGHTS II
1995
1 Sequel to Gotham Nights 2.50
2 F:Carmine Sansone. 2.50
3 Fire. 2.50
4 JQ(c) Decisions 2.50

BATMAN/GRENDEL
[First Series]
DC/Comico, 1993
1 MWg,Devil's Riddle 5.25
2 MWg,Devil's Masque. 5.25

[Second Series]
DC/Dark Horse, 1996
1 MWg,Devil's Bones 5.00
2 MWg,Devil's Dance 5.00

BATMAN: HARLEY & IVY
April 2004
1 (of 3) PDi 2.50
2 PDi,Zombie Root 2.50
3 PDi, finale 2.50

Batman/Grendel #1
© DC Comics, Inc.

BATMAN: HAUNTED GOTHAM
Dec., 1999
1 (of 4) DgM,KJo,JhB,Elseworlds . . 5.00
2 thru 4 DgM,KJo,JhB . . . . @5.00

BATMAN/HELLBOY/ STARMAN
DC/Dark Horse 1998
1 JeR(s),MMi, x-over 2.50
2 JeR(s),MMi, conclusion 2.50

BATMAN: HOLLYWOOD KNIGHT
Feb., 2001
1 (of 3) DG,Elseworlds 2.50
2 DG,F:Byron Wyatt 2.50
3 DG, concl. 2.50

BATMAN/HUNTRESS: CRY FOR BLOOD
April, 2000
1 (of 6) RBr,O:Huntress 2.50
2 thru 6 RBr. . . . . @2.50

BATMAN: IT'S JOKER TIME
May, 2000
1 (of 3) BH 5.00
2 BH 5.00
3 BH, concl. 5.00

BATMAN: JAZZ
Mini-Series 1995
1 I:Blue Byrd 2.50
2 V:Brotherhood of Bop 2.50
3 F:Blue Byrd 2.50

BATMAN: JEKYLL & HYDE
Apr., 2005
1 PJe(s),JaL,SeP(c),F:Two-Face . . 3.00
2 PJe(s),JaL,SeP(c) 3.00
3 PJe(s),JaL,SeP(c) 3.00
4 PJe(s),SeP. 3.00
5 PJe(s),SeP. 3.00
6 PJe(s),SeP, finale 3.00

BATMAN: JOURNEY INTO KNIGHT
Aug., 2005
1 (12) Batman's early years 2.50
2 Plague breaks out 2.50
3 Plague 2.50
4 Plague 2.50
5 V:Carrier. 2.50
6 Double-cross 2.50
7 Crossroads 2.50
8 Mysterious fires 2.50
9 Dangerous revelations. 2.50
10 Batman's early career. 3.00
11 Enter the Joker 3.00
12 V:Joker, finale 3.00

BATMAN/JUDGE DREDD: DIE LAUGHING
1998
1 (of 2) AlG(s),GF 48-pg. 5.00
2 AlG(s),GF conclusion 5.00

BATMAN: LEAGUE OF BATMEN
April, 2001
1 MBr,RT,48-page, Elseworlds 6.00
2 MBr,RT,48-page, concl. 6.00

BATMAN: LEGENDS OF THE DARK KNIGHT
1989
1 EH,Shaman of Gotham,pt.1,
  Yellow(c) 5.00
1a Blue,Orange or Pink(c) 4.00
2 EH,Shaman of Gotham,pt.2 . . . . 3.00
3 EH,Shaman of Gotham,pt.3 . . . . 3.00
4 EH,Shaman of Gotham,pt.4 . . . . 3.00
5 EH,Shaman of Gotham,pt.5 . . . . 3.00
6 KJ,Gothic,pt.1 . . . . 3.00
7 KJ,Gothic,pt.2 . . . . 3.00
8 KJ,Gothic,pt.3 . . . . 3.00
9 KJ,Gothic,pt.4 . . . . 3.00
10 KJ,Gothic,pt.5 . . . . 3.00
11 PG,TA,Prey,pt.1 . . . . 6.00
12 PG,TA,Prey,pt.2. . . . . 5.00
13 PG,TA,Prey,pt.3. . . . . 5.00
14 PG,TA,Prey,pt.4. . . . . 5.00
15 PG,TA,Prey,pt.5. . . . . 4.00
16 TVE,Venom,pt.1 . . . . 5.00
17 TVE,JL,Venom,pt.2 . . . . 5.00
18 TVE,JL,Venom,pt.3 . . . . 5.00
19 TVE,JL,Venom,pt.4 . . . . 5.00
20 TVE,JL,Venom,pt.5 . . . . 5.00
21 BS,Faith,pt.1 . . . . 3.00
22 BS,Faith,pt.2 . . . . 3.00
23 BS,Faith,pt.3 . . . . 3.00
24 GK,Flyer,pt.1 . . . . 3.00
25 GK,Flyer,pt.2 . . . . 3.00
26 GK,Flyer,pt.3 . . . . 3.00
27 Destroyer,pt.2 (Batman#474) . . . 3.50
28 MWg,Faces,pt.1,V:Two-Face . . . 4.00
29 MWg,Faces,pt.2,V:Two-Face . . . 4.00
30 MWg,Faces,pt.3,V:Two-Face . . . 4.00
31 BA,Family 3.00
32 Blades,pt.1 . . . . 3.00
33 Blades,pt.2 . . . . 3.00
34 Blades,pt.3 . . . . 3.00
35 BHa,Destiny Pt.1 . . . . 3.00
36 BHa,Destiny Pt.2 . . . . 3.00
37 I:Mercy,V:The Cossack 3.00
38 KON,R:Bat-Mite 3.00
39 BT,Mask#1 . . . . 3.00
40 BT,Mask#2 . . . . 3.00
41 Sunset. 3.00
42 CR,Hothouse #1 . . . . 3.00
43 CR,Hothouse #2,V:Poison Ivy . . 3.00
44 SMc,Turf #1 . . . . 3.00
45 Turf#2 . . . . 3.00

46 RH,A:Catwoman,V:Catman 3.00
47 RH,A:Catwoman,V:Catman 3.00
48 RH,A:Catwoman,V:Catman 3.00
49 RH,A:Catwoman,V:Catman 3.00
50 BBl,JLe,KN,KM,WS,MZ,BB,
  V:Joker 6.00
51 JKu,A:Ragman 3.00
52 Tao #1,V:Dragon. 3.00
53 Tao #2,V:Dragon. 3.00
54 MMi 3.50
55 B:Watchtower 3.00
56 CDi(s),V:Battle Guards 3.00
57 CDi(s),E:Watchtower 3.00
58 Storm. 3.00
59 DON(s),RoW,B:Qarry 3.00
60 RoW,V:Asp 3.00
61 RoW,V:Asp 3.00
62 RoW,KnightsEnd#4,A:Shiva,
  Nightwing. 4.50
63 Knights End #10,V:Azrael. 3.00
64 CBa. 3.00
65 Joker. 3.00
66 Joker 3.00
67 Going Sane,pt.3 . . . . 3.00
68 Going Sane,pt.4 . . . . 3.50
69 Criminals,pt.1 . . . . 3.50
70 Criminals,pt.2 . . . . 3.50
71 Werewolf,pt.1 . . . . 3.00
72 JWk(c&a),Werewolf,pt.2
  [new Miraweb format begins] . . 3.00
73 JWk(c&a),Werewolf,pt.3 . . . . . . 3.00
74 Engins,pt.1 . . . . 3.00
75 Engins,pt.2 . . . . 3.00
76 The Sleeping,pt.1 . . . . 3.00
77 The Sleeping,pt.2 . . . . 3.00
78 The Sleeping,pt.3 . . . . 3.00
79 Favorite Things. 3.00
80 Idols,pt.1 . . . . 3.00
81 Idols,pt.2 . . . . 3.00
82 Idols, climax 3.00
83 new villain 3.00
84 WEl(s) 3.00
85 JeR(s) 3.00
86 DgM,JWi,MGy,Conspiracy,pt.1 . . 3.00
87 DgM,JWi,MGy,Conspiracy,pt.2 . . 3.00
88 DgM,JWi,MGy,Conspiracy,pt.3 . . 3.00
89 AlG(s),Clay,pt. 1 . . . . 3.00
90 AlG(s),Clay,pt. 2 . . . . 3.00
91 Freakout, pt.1 . . . . 3.50
92 GEn(s),WSm,Freakout, pt.2 . . . . 3.50
93 GEn(s),WSm,Freakout, pt.3 . . . . 3.50
94 MGi(s),Saul Fisher's story 3.00
95 DAn&ALa(s),AWi,ALa,Dirty
  Tricks, pt.1. . . . . 3.00

Batman Legends of the Dark
Knight #6 © DC Comics, Inc.

96 DAn&ALa(s),AWi,ALa,Dirty
    Tricks, pt.2 . . . . 3.00
97 DAn&ALa(s),AWi,ALa,,Dirty
    Tricks, concl. 3.00
98 PJe(s),SeP,Steps, pt.1 . . . . 3.00
99 PJe(s),SeP,Steps, pt.2 . . . . 3.00
100 DON,JRo,F:Robin, 64pg. 6.00
101 CE,KN(c)100 years in future. . . 3.00
102 JRo,PuJ,Spook, pt.1 . . . . 3.00
103 JRo,PuJ,Spook, pt.2 . . . . 3.00
104 JRo,PuJ,Spook, pt.3 . . . . 3.00
105 TVE,JRu,Duty, pt.1 . . . . 3.00
106 TVE,JRu,Duty, pt.2 . . . . 3.00
107 LMr,Stalking, pt.1 . . . . 3.00
108 LMr,Stalking, pt.2 . . . . 3.00
109 SEt,DAb,Primal Riddle,pt.1. . . . 3.00
110 SEt,DAb,Primal Riddle,pt.2. . . 3.00
111 SEt,DAb,Primal Riddle,pt.3 . . . 3.00
112 DVa,FC,V:Lord Demise,pt.1 . . . 3.00
113 DVa,FC,V:Lord Demise,pt.2 . . . 3.00
114 JeR(s),DIB,TBd 3.00
115 LMc,DIB(c) 3.00
116 IEd,Bread and Circuses,pt.1 . . . 5.00
117 IEd,Bread and Circuses,pt.2 . . 2.50
118 JPn,Alfred in No Man's Land . . 2.50
119 MD2,Claim Jumping,pt.1. . . . . 2.50
120 MD2,Assembly 5.00
121 RBr,V:Mr.Freeze 3.50
122 LHa(s),PG, Low Road to Golden
    Mountain,pt.1. . . . . 3.50
123 PR,ALa,Underground
    Railroad,pt.1 . . . . 3.50
124 CDi(s),MkK,No Man's Land . . 3.50
125 No Man's Land 3.00
126 Endgame, pt.1 x-over 3.00
127 MRy,F:Green Arrow,pt.1 . . . . . 2.50
128 MRy,F:Green Arrow,pt.2 . . . . . 2.50
129 MRy,F:Green Arrow,pt.3 . . . . . 2.50
130 MRy,F:Green Arrow,pt.4 . . . . . 2.50
131 MRy,F:Green Arrow,pt.5 . . . . . 2.50
132 AGw,JeR,MR,BWi,Siege,pt.1 . 2.50
133 AGw,JeR,MR,BWi,Siege,pt.2 . 2.50
134 AGw,JeR,MR,BWi,Siege,pt.3 . 2.50
135 AGw,JeR,MR,BWi,Siege,pt.4 . 2.50
136 AGw,JeR,MR,BWi,Siege,pt.5 . 2.50
137 DgM,PG,JP,Terror,pt.1. . . . . . 2.50
138 DgM,PG,JP,Terror,pt.2. . . . . . 2.50
139 DgM,PG,JP,Terror,pt.3. . . . . . 2.50
140 DgM,PG,JP,Terror,pt.4. . . . . . 2.50
141 DgM,PG,JP,Terror,pt.5. . . . . . 2.50
142 CDi,JAp,Demon Laughs,pt.1 . 2.50
143 CDi,JAp,Demon Laughs,pt.2 . 2.50
144 CDi,JAp,Demon Laughs,pt.3 . 2.50
145 CDi,JaP,Demon Laughs,pt.4. . 2.50
146 DgM,BKi,Bad,pt.1 . . . . 2.50
147 DgM,BKi,Bad,pt.2 . . . . 2.50
148 DgM,BKi,Bad,pt.3 . . . . 2.50
149 JMD,TVE, Grimm, pt.1 . . . . . . 2.50
150 JMD,TVE, Grimm, pt.2 . . . . . . 2.50
151 JMD,TVE, Grimm, pt.3 . . . . . . 2.50
152 JMD,TVE, Grimm, pt.4 . . . . . . 2.50
153 JMD,TVE, Grimm, pt.5 . . . . . . 2.50
154 MBn,BR,Colossus,pt.1 . . . . . . 2.50
155 MBn,BR,Colossus,pt.2 . . . . . . 2.50
156 DGr,Blink,pt.1 . . . . 2.50
157 DGr,Blink,pt.2 . . . . 2.50
158 DGr,Blink,pt.3 . . . . 2.50
159 JOs,DGr,Loyalties,pt.1 . . . . . . 2.50
160 JOs,DGr,Loyalties,pt.2 . . . . . . 2.50
161 JOs,DGr,Loyalties,pt.3 . . . . . . 2.50
162 JAr(s),Auteurism,pt.1 . . . . 2.50
163 JAr(s),Auteurism,pt.2 . . . . 2.50
164 DMD,DGr,Don't Blink,pt.1. . . . 2.50
165 DMD,DGr,Don't Blink,pt.2. . . . 2.50
166 DMD,DGr,Don't Blink,pt.3. . . . 2.50
167 DMD,DGr,Don't Blink,pt.4. . . . 2.50
168 Urban Legend. 2.50
169 TyH,Irresistible,pt.1 . . . . 2.50
170 TyH,Irresistible,pt.2 . . . . 2.50
171 TyH,Irresistible,pt.3 . . . . 2.50
172 V:Rough Justice 2.50
173 V:Rough Justice 2.50

Batman: Legends of the Dark Knight
Ann. #7 © DC Comics, Inc.

174 O:Rough Justice 2.50
175 Testament,pt.6 . . . . 2.50
176 Testament,pt.5 . . . . 2.50
177 Lost Cargo,pt.1 . . . . 2.50
178 Lost Cargo,pt.2 . . . . 2.50
179 O:Fat Man & Little Boy 2.50
180 Virtual Gotham City. 2.50
181 Cyber-world. 2.50
182 War Games,Act 1,pt.2 . . . . . . 2.50
183 War Games,Act 2,pt.2 . . . . . . 2.50
184 War Games,Act 3,pt.2 . . . . . . 2.50
185 RyR,SeP,Riddle Me That, pt.1 . 2.50
186 RyR,SeP,Riddle Me That, pt.2 . 2.50
187 RyR,SeP,Riddle Me That, pt.3 . 2.50
188 RyR,SeP,Riddle Me That, pt.4 . 2.50
189 RyR,SeP,Riddle Me That, pt.5 . 2.50
190 V:Mr. Freeze 2.50
191 V:Mr. Freeze,pt.2 . . . . 2.50
192 Snow,pt.1,O: Mr. Freeze. 2.50
193 Snow,pt.2 . . . . 2.50
194 Snow,pt.3 . . . . 2.50
195 Snow,pt.4 . . . . 2.50
196 Snow,pt.5 . . . . 2.50
197 Blaze of Glory, pt.1 . . . . 2.50
198 Blaze of Glory, pt.2 . . . . 2.50
199 Blaze of Glory, pt.2 . . . . 2.50
200 ECa,F:Joker in E.R. 5.00
201 Cold Case, pt.1 . . . . 2.50
202 Cold Case, pt.2. . . . . 2.50
203 Cold Case, pt. 3 . . . . 2.50
204 Madmen of Gotham, pt.1 . . . . 3.00
205 Madmen of Gotham, pt.2 . . . . 3.00
206 Madmen of Gotham, pt.3 . . . . 3.00
207 Darker Than Death, pt.1 . . . . . 3.00
208 Darker Than Death, pt.2 . . . . . 3.00
209 Darker Than Death, pt.3 . . . . . 3.00
210 Darker Than Death, pt.4 . . . . . 3.00
211 Darker Than Death, pt.5 . . . . . 3.00
212 NMa,A cheap date 3.00
Ann.#1 JAp,KG,DSp,TL,JRu,
    MGo,JQ,`Duel',C:Joker 5.50
Ann.#2 MN,LMc,W:Gordn&Essen . 5.00
Ann.#3 MM,I:Cardinal Sin 5.00
Ann.#4 JSon(c),Elseworlds Story . 5.00
Ann.#5 CDi(s)Year One Annuals,
    O:Man-Bat 5.00
Ann.#6 Legends o/t Dead Earth . . . 4.00
Ann.#7 Pulp Heroes (War). 7.00
Halloween Spec.I. 8.00
Halloween Spec.II 5.00
Ghosts, Halloween Special 5.00
TPB Shaman rep.#1-#5 (1993) . . . 13.00
TPB Batman: Gothic, rep. #6-#10
    (1992) 13.00

TPB Prey, rep.Legends of the Dark
    Knight #11–#15 (1992) 13.00
TPB Batman: Venom, TVE, rep.
    #16–#20 (1993). 10.00
TPB Collected Legends of the Dark
    Knight,BB(c),rep.#32-#34,#38,
    #42-#43 (1994) 13.00
TPB Other Realms. 13.00

BATMAN:
THE LONG HALLOWEEN
Oct., 1996

1 (of 13) JLb,TSe,Who is Holiday?
    F: usual suspects. 11.00
2 JLb(s),TSe,V:Holiday,A:Solomon
    Grundy. 8.00
3 JLb,TSe, ... 9.00
4 JLb(s),TSe,New Year's Eve. . . . 9.00
5 JLb(s),TSe,F:Poison Ivy, Search
    for Holiday 6.00
6 JLb(s),TSe,F:Poison Ivy,
    Catwoman 6.00
7 JLb(s),TSe,V:The Riddler 5.00
8 JLb(s),TSe,V:Scarecrow 5.00
9 JLb(s),TSe,A:Holiday,Scarecrow. 5.00
10 JLb(s),TSe,V:Scarecrow,Mad
    Hatter. 5.00
11 JLb(s),TSe,V:Holiday 5.00
12 JLb(s),TSe,Harvey Dent. 5.00
13 JLb(s),TSe,concl.,48pg. 7.00
TPB Haunted Knight, rep. Fears,
    Madness & Ghosts 13.00
TPB The Long Halloween 20.00

BATMAN
AND THE MAD MONK
Aug., 2006

1 (of 6) MWg. 3.50
2 MWg 3.50
3 MWg 3.50
4 MWg 3.50

BATMAN: MAN-BAT
1995

1 R:Man-Bat, painted series 5.00
2 F:Marilyn Muno 5.00
3 JBo,Elseworlds story, concl. . . . 5.00
TPB rep. mini-series 15.00

BATMAN AND
THE MONSTER MEN
Nov., 2005

1 (of 6) MWg, Dark Moon Rising . . 3.00
2 MWg,V:Super-Villains 3.00
3 MWg,V:Professor Hugo 3.00
4 MWg,Genetic mutants 3.00
5 MWg,Mobsters & Mutants 3.00
6 MWg,concl. 40-pg. 3.50
TPB Batman and the Monster Men 15.00

BATMAN: NEVERMORE
April 2003

1 (of 5) Elseworlds,BWr(c) 2.50
2 GyD,BWr(c),Raven Murders 2.50
3 GyD,BWr(c),Raven Murders 2.50
4 GyD,BWr(c),Raven Murders 2.50
5 GyD,BWr(c),concl. 2.50

BATMAN:
NO MAN'S LAND
Sept., 1999

0 F:Huntress 5.00
Secret Files #1 . . . . 5.00
TPB Vol. 1 thru Vol. 5, x-over
    reps. . . . . @13.00

BATMAN: ORPHEUS RISING
Aug., 2001
1 (of 5) DT,DaM 2.50
2 DT,DaM,caught in cross-fire . . . 2.50
3 DT,DaM,who's behind it. 2.50
4 DT,DaM,The Deacons 2.50
5 DT,DaM,concl 2.50

BATMAN: OUTLAWS
July, 2000
1 (of 3) DgM,PG 5.00
2 DgM,PG,V:Bloodhawks 5.00
3 DgM,PG,concl. 5.00

Batman: Run, Riddler Run
© DC Comics Inc.

BATMAN: RUN, RIDDLER RUN
1992
1 MBg,Batman V:Riddler 5.50
2 MBg,Batman V:Riddler 5.25
3 MBg,V:Perfect Securities. 5.25

BATMAN: SECRETS
March, 2006
1 (of 5) SK, V:The Joker. 3.00
2 SK 3.00
3 SK, Toe to toe 3.00
4 SK, Mooley kidnapped. 3.00
5 SK, final battle V:Joker 3.00

BATMAN: SHADOW OF THE BAT
1992–97
1 NB,Last Arkham Pt.1 . . . . 5.00
1a Collector set,w/posters,pop-up . 6.00
2 NB,Last Arkham Pt.2. . . . . 4.00
3 NB,Last Arkham Pt.3 . . . . 4.00
4 NB,Last Arkham Pt.4 . . . . 4.00
5 NB,A:Black Spider 3.00
6 NB,I:Chancer 3.00
7 Misfits Pt.1 . . . . 3.00
8 Misfits Pt.2 . . . . 3.00
9 Misfits Pt.3 . . . . 3.00
10 MC,V:Mad Thane of Gotham . . . 3.00
11 V:Kadaver 2.50
12 V:Kadaver,A:Human Flea 2.50
13 NB,The Nobody 2.50
14 NB,Gotham Freaks#1 . . . . 2.50
15 NB,Gotham Freaks#2 . . . . 2.50

16 BBI,MM,A:Anarchy,Scarecrow . . 2.50
17 BBI,V:Scarecrow 2.50
18 BBI,A:Anarchy,Scarecrow 2.50
19 BBI,Knightquest:The Crusade,pt.2,
   V:Gotham criminals 2.50
20 VGi,Knightquest:The Crusade,
   V:Tally Man 2.50
21 BBI,Knightquest:The Search,
   V:Mr.Asp 2.50
22 BBI,Knightquest:The Search,
   In London 2.50
23 BBI,Knightquest:The Search. . . . 2.50
24 BBI,Knightquest:The Crusade . . 2.50
25 BSf(c),BBI,Knightquest: Crusade,
   A:Joe Public,V:Corrosive Man . . 2.50
26 BSf(c),BBI,Knightquest: Crusade,
   V:Clayface 2.50
27 BSf(c),BBI,Knightquest: Crusade,
   I:Clayface Baby 2.50
28 BSf(c),BBI 2.50
29 BSf(c),BBI,KnightsEnd#2,
   A:Nightwing 4.00
30 BSf(c),BBI,KnightsEnd#8,
   V:Azrael 2.50
31 Zero Hour, V:Butler 2.50
32 Ventriloquist,Two-Face 2.50
33 Two-Face 2.50
34 V:Tally Man 2.50
35 BKi,Return of Bruce Wayne,
   Troika,pt.2 . . . . 2.50
35a Collectors Edition 3.50
36 Black Canary 2.50
37 Joker Hunt 2.50
38 V:The Joker. 2.50
39 BSf(c),R:Solomon Grundy
   [new Miraweb format begins] . . 2.50
40 BSf(c), F:Anarky 2.50
41 Explosive Dirigible 2.50
42 BSz(c),Day the Music Died. 2.50
43 Secret of the Universe,pt1 . . . . . 2.50
44 AIG,BSz(c) Secret of the
   Universe,pt.3 . . . . 2.50
45 AIG,BSz(c) 100 year old corpse . 2.50
46 AIG,BSz(c) V:Cornelius Stirk 2.50
47 AIG, RSz(c) V:Cornelius Stirk 2.50
48 AIG 2.50
49 AIG,Contagion,pt.7 . . . . 2.50
50 AIG,Nightmare on Gotham,pt.1 . . 2.50
51 AIG,DTy, Nightmare on
   Gotham,pt.2 (of 3) 2.50
52 AIG(s),Nightmare on Gotham,
   pt.3. 2.50
53 AIG(s),Legacy, prelude 2.50
54 AIG(s),Legacy, pt. 4, x-over 2.50
55 AIG(s),RBr,KJ,Bruce Wayne a
   murderer? A:Nightwing 2.50
56 AIG(s),DTy,SnW,Leaves of
   Grass,pt.1,V:Poison Ivy. 2.50
57 AIG(s),DTy,SnW,Grass,pt.2. . . . . 2.50
58 AIG(s),DTy,SnW,Grass,pt.3. . . . . 2.50
59 AIG(s),DTy,SnW,Killer,
   Killer, pt.1. . . . . 2.50
60 AIG(s),DTy,SnW,Killer, pt.2 . . . . . 2.50
61 AIG(s),night of
   second chances 2.50
62 AIG(s),DTy,SnW,Two-Face,pt.1 . 2.50
63 AIG(s),DTy,SnW,Two-Face,pt.2 . 2.50
64 AIG(s),DTy,SnW,A:Jason Blood . 2.50
65 AIG(s),NBy,JRu, A:Oracle, pt.1 . . 2.50
66 AIG(s),NBy,JRu, V:Thinker,
   Cheat, pt.2. . . . . 2.50
67 AIG(s),NBy,SnW,CsM,V:Thinker,
   Cheat, pt.3, concl. 2.50
68 AIG(s),JAp,SnW,annual killer . . . 2.50
69 AIG(s),MBu,WF,CsM,
   The Spirit of 2000, pt. 1. . . . . . . 2.50
70 AIG(s),MBu,WF,CsM, pt.2. . . . . . 2.50
71 AIG(s),MBu,WF,CsM,detective . . 2.50
72 AIG(s),MBu,WF. 2.50
73 AIG(s),MBu,WF,Cataclysm
   x-over,pt.1 . . . . 3.50

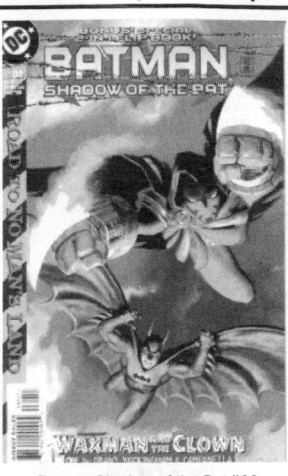

Batman Shadow of the Bat #80
© DC Comics Inc.

74 AIG(s),MBu,WF,Cataclysm
   cont. 2.50
75 AIG(s),MBu,WF,Aftershock 3.50
76 AIG(s),MBu,WF,Aftershock 2.50
77 AIG(s),MBu,WF,quake-torn 2.50
78 AIG(s),MBu,Aftershock 2.50
79 AIG(s),MBu,V:Mad Hatter,
   Narcosis. 2.50
80 Road to No Man's Land, flip-book
   Azrael:Agent of the Bat #47 . . . 5.00
81 AIG(s),MBu,No Man's Land 2.50
82 AIG(s),MBu,No Man's Land 2.50
83 No Law and a New Order, pt.3. 14.00
84 IEd,Bread and Circuses, pt.2 . . . 5.00
85 IEd(s),Bread & Circuses,concl. . . 5.00
86 GyD,No Man's Land 3.00
87 MD2, Claim Jumping, pt.2 . . . . . 3.00
88 D.Iu,BSz,Fruit of
   the Earth,pt.1. . . . . 3.00
89 IEd(s),SB,No Man's Land 3.00
90 LHa(s),PG,No Man's Land 3.00
91 PR,ALa,Underground
   Railroad,pt.2 . . . . 3.00
92 No Man's Land,A:Superman. . . . 3.00
93 No Man's Land 3.00
94 final issue 3.00
Ann.#1 TVE,DG,Bloodlines#3,
   I:Joe Public 4.00
Ann.#2 Elseworlds story 4.00
Ann.#3 Year One Annual 4.00
Ann.#4 Legends of the Dead
   Earth 3.00
Ann.#5 AIG(s), Pulp Heroes. 4.00
Spec.#1,000,000 AIG(s),MBu, Origin of
   853rd-century Dark Knight 2.00

BATMAN STRIKES, THE
Sept. 2004
1 thru 27 . . . . @2.25
TPB Vol. 1 Crime Time 7.00
TPB Vol. 2 In Darkest Knight. 7.00
TPB Vol. 3 Duty Calls 7.00
TPB Vol. 4 Behind the Shadows . . . 7.00
TPB Jam-Packed Action, from cartoon
   series. 8.00

BATMAN/SUPERMAN/ WONDER WOMAN: TRINITY
June 2003
1 (of 3) MWg, first meeting 7.00
2 MWg,V:Bizarro 7.00

3 MWg,concl. 7.00
TPB Trinity 18.00

BATMAN:
SWORD OF AZRAEL
1992–93
1 JQ,KN,I:Azrael 12.00
2 JQ,KN,A:Azrael 9.00
3 JQ,KN,V:Biis,A:Azrael 8.00
4 JQ,KN,V:Biis,A:Azrael 8.00
TPB rep.#1-#4 . . . . 11.00
TPB Platinum 25.00

BATMAN: TENSES
Aug. 2003
1 JoC(s) 7.00
2 JoC(s) 7.00

BATMAN: TOYMAN
1998
1 (of 4) LHa(s),AWi,KJ 2.50
2 thru 4 LHa(s),AWi,KJ . . . . @2.50

BATMAN:
TURNING POINTS
Nov., 2000
1 (of 5) F:Gordon & Batman 2.50
2 TTn(c),Robin arrives 2.50
3 DG,JKu(c),Batgirl dead 2.50
4 CDi,BA,HC(c),Azrael 2.50
5 No Man's Land 2.50

BATMAN vs. PREDATOR
DC/Dark Horse 1991–92
1 NKu,AKu,inc.8 trading cards
   bound in (Prestige) 5.00
1a Newsstand 4.00
2 NKu,AKu,Inc. pinups (prestige) . . 4.00
2a Newsstand 3.00
3 NKu,AKu,conclusion,inc.
   8 trading cards (Prestige) 4.00
3a Newsstand 3.00
TPB,rep.#1-#3 . . . . 6.00

BATMAN vs. PREDATOR II
BLOODMATCH
1994–95
1 R:Predators 3.00
2 A:Huntress 3.00

Batman vs. Predator II Bloodmatch
#2 © DC Comics, Inc.

3 Assassins 3.00
4 V:Head Hunters 3.00
TPB Rep.#1-#4 . . . . 7.00

BATMAN/PREDATOR III:
BLOOD TIES
DC/Dark Horse 1997
1 (of 4) CDi,RDm,RbC, vs. pair
   of Predators 2.50
2 CDi,RDm,RbC, pt.2 . . . . 2.50
3 CDi,RDm,RbC, pt.3 . . . . 2.50
4 CDi,RDm,RbC, concl. 2.50
TPB rep. 8.00

BATMAN/WILDCAT
Feb., 1997
1 (of 3) CDi&BSt(s),SCi,ATi,
   Batman and Robin discover
   Secret Ring of combat 2.50
2 CDi&BSt(s),SCi,V:KGBeast,
   Willis Danko 2.50
3 CDi&BSt(s),SCi, Batman vs.
   Wildcat, concl. 2.50

BATMAN:
YEAR ONE HUNDRED
Feb., 2006
1 (of 4) PPo,48-pg. 6.00
2 thru 4 PPo, Future Gotham . . . @6.00

BEAST BOY
Nov., 1999
1 (of 4)BRa,Clv 3.00
2 BRa,Clv,A:Nightwing 3.00
3 BRa,Clv,V:Nightwing 3.00
4 BRa,Clv,F:Flamebird 3.00

BATTLE CLASSICS
Sept.–Oct., 1978
1 JKu, reprints. 15.00

BEOWOLF
April-May, 1975
1 . . . . 25.00
2 thru 3 . . . . @10.00
4 Dracula 15.00
5 . . . . 10.00
6 Flying Saucer,Feb.–Mar.1976 . . 12.00

BEST OF THE
BRAVE & THE BOLD
1988
1 JL(c),NA,rep.B&B #85. . . . . 5.00
2 thru 6 JL(c),NA,rep.B&B . . . . . @5.00

BEWARE THE CREEPER
1968–69
1 SD,Where Lurks the Menace . 150.00
2 thru 6 SD . . . . @80.00

BEWARE THE CREEPER
DC/Vertigo, April 2003
1 thru 5 . . . . @3.00

BIG ALL-AMERICAN
COMIC BOOK
Dec., 1944
1 JKu,132-pages 20,000.00

BIG BOOK OF FUN
COMICS
Spring, 1936
1 . . . . 25,000.00

THE BIG BOOK OF ...:
DC/Paradox Press (B&W)
1994–2001
TPB Conspiracies (1995). 13.00
TPB Death (1994) 13.00
TPB Hoaxes (1996) 15.00
TPB Little Criminals (1996) 15.00
TPB Losers 15.00
TPB Martyrs (1997) 15.00
TPB Scandal (1997) 15.00
TPB Thugs (1996) 15.00
TPB Unexplained DgM(s) (1997). . 15.00
TPB Urban Legends (1994). 13.00
TPB Weirdos (1995) 13.00
TPB Weird Wild West (1998). 15.00
TPB Big Book of the '70s (2000). . 15.00
TPB Wild Women,192-pg.(2001) . 15.00

BIG TOWN
1951–58
1 TV, radio tie-in. 1,100.00
2 . . . . 500.00
3 thru 10 . . . . @350.00
11 thru 20 . . . . @300.00
21 thru 30 . . . . @250.00
31 thru 40 . . . . @150.00
41 thru 50 . . . . @125.00

BIRDS OF PREY:
MANHUNT
1996
1 CDi(s),MHy,F:Black Canary,
   Oracle 10.00
2 CDi(s),MHy,V,Archer Braun,
   A:Catwoman 7.00
3 CDi(s),MHy,V:Catwoman,
   Huntress 7.00
4 CDi(s),MHy,V:Lady Shiva 7.00
1-shot Birds of Prey: Batgirl CDi,
   Batgirl & Black Canary (1997). . 3.00
1-shot Birds of Prey: Revolution
   CDi(s),BMc 3.00
1-shot Birds of Prey: The Ravens,
   CDi, Girlfrenzy (1998) 3.00
1-shot Birds of Prey: Wolves
   CDi,DG (1997). 3.00

BIRDS OF PREY
1998
1 CDi(s),Black Canary & Oracle . 11.00
2 CDi(s),V:Jackie Pajamas 6.00
3 CDi(s),V:Hellbound 6.00
4 CDi(s),V:Ravens 6.00
5 CDi(s),V:Ravens,pt.2 . . . . 3.00
6 CDi(s),V:Ravens,pt.3 . . . . 3.00
7 CDi(s),PKr, ... 3.00
8 CDi(s),F:Nightwing. 30.00
9 CDi(s),V:Iron Brigade. 3.00
10 CDi(s),DG,V:Dr.Pop 3.00
11 CDi(s),DG 3.00
12 CDi(s),DG,F:Catwoman 3.00
13 CDi(s),DG 3.00
14 CDi(s),DG,V:Lashina. 3.00
15 CDi(s),JG 3.00
16 CDi(s),JG,V:maniac. 2.50
17 CDi(s),JG,V:Joker. 2.50
18 CDi(s),JG,Transbelvia 2.50
19 CDi(s),JG,A:Nightwing,Robin . . 2.50
20 CDi(s),Hunt for Oracle,pt.2 . . . 2.50
21 CDi(s),Hunt for Oracle,concl. . . 2.50
22 CDi(s),Gorilla City 2.50
23 CDi(s),Gorilla City 2.50
24 CDi,search for heart donor 3.00
25 CDi,Deathstroke,Blue Beetle . . 2.50
26 CDi,This issue Batman dies! . . 2.50
27 Officer Down x-over,pt.3 . . . . . . 2.50
28 CDi,History Lession,pt.1 . . . . . . 2.50
29 CDi,History Lession,pt.2 . . . . . . 2.50
30 CDi,History Lession,pt.3 . . . . . . 2.50
31 CDi,star-crossed love 2.50

32 CDi,love, and marriage?. 2.50
33 CDi,Black Canary,Ra's Al Ghul. . 2.50
34 CDi,A:Power Girl,Blue Beetle. . . 2.50
35 CDi,rescue Black Canary. 2.50
36 CDi,Joker: Last Laugh 2.50
37 CDi,Last Laugh aftermath. 2.50
38 CDi,F:Dinah 2.50
39 CDi,BruceWayne:Murderer,pt.5 . 6.00
40 CDi,BruceWayne:Murderer,pt.12 6.50
41 CDi,BruceWayne:Fugitive,pt.2 . . 6.50
42 CDi,GF,F:Power Girl 2.50
43 CDi,BruceWayne:Fugitive,pt.10 . 2.50
44 CDi,Deathstroke 2.50
45 CDi,Deathstroke, dinosaurs 2.50
46 CDi,Deathstroke 2.50
47 TMr(s),JP,Heartache,pt.1 . . . . . 2.50
48 TMr(s),JP,Heartache,pt.2 . . . . . 2.50
49 TMr(s),JP,Heartache,pt.3 . . . . . 2.50
50 GHe,CJ. 2.50
51 GHe,CJ. 2.50
52 GHe,CJ. 2.50
53 GHe,CJ. 2.50
54 GHe,CJ. 2.50
55 GHe,CJ. 2.50
56 EBe,V:Savant 6.00
57 EBe,V:Savant 5.00
58 EBe,V:Savant 5.00
59 EBe,V:Savant 4.00
60 EBe,R:Huntress 4.00
61 EBe,consequences. 3.00
62 EBe,F:Lady Shiva 3.00
63 EBe,F:Lady Shiva. 3.00
64 EBe,V:Cheshire. 2.50
65 EBe,F:Cheshire. 2.50
66 MGo,MM,ATh(c). 2.50
67 EBe,Sensei and Student. 2.50
68 Date for Huntress 2.50
69 Between Dark and Dawn,pt.1. . . 2.50
70 Between Dark and Dawn,pt.2. . . 2.50
71 Between Dark and Dawn,pt.3. . . 2.50
72 Between Dark and Dawn,pt.4. . . 2.50
73 Between Dark and Dawn,pt.5. . . 2.50
74 Between Dark and Dawn,pt.6. . . 2.50
75 EDe,40-pg. RU: EB. 3.00
76 EBe,Hero Hunters,pt.1 . . . . 3.00
77 EBe,Hero Hunters,pt.2 . . . . 2.50
78 Hero Hunters,pt.3 . . . . 2.50
79 EBe,Hero Hunters,pt.4 . . . . 2.50
80 EBe,Hero Hunters,pt.5, concl. . . 2.50
81 JoB,The Battle Within 2.50
82 JoB,F:Wildcat 2.50
83 JoB,Omac tie-in 2.50
84 JoB,mission to Singapore 2.50
85 JoB,The Battle Within, concl. . . . 2.50
86 Moving day-to Metropolis 2.50

87 JoB,Oracle, Calculator 2.50
88 JoB,V:Calculator 2.50
89 JoB,V:Calculator. 2.50
90 V:Deathstroke. 2.50
91 JP,Organ Donar 2.50
92 One Year Later. 2.50
93 Vengeance 2.50
94 V:Prometheus 3.00
95 Progeny. 3.00
96 Headhunting,pt.1. . . . . 3.00
97 Headhunting,pt.2. . . . . 3.00
98 A:Batgirl. 3.00
99 New outfits 3.00
100 DHz,New Team, 48-pg. 4.00
TPB Birds of Prey 18.00
   New edition (2002) 18.00
TPB Old Friends, New Enemies . . 18.00
TPB Of Like Minds. 15.00
TPB Sensei & Student. 18.00
TPB Between Dark and Dawn. . . . 17.00
TPB The Battle Within 18.00
Spec. Secret Files 2003. . . . . 5.00

BIRDS OF PREY:
Feb. 2003
Catwoman/Batgirl
1 JFM,JP,DaR. 6.00

Catwoman/Oracle
2 JFM,JP,DaR. 6.00

BITE CLUB
DC/Vertigo, April 2004
1 (of 6) HC(s),vampire,mafia 5.00
2 HC(s),Bikinis 4.00
3 HC(s),Leto Del Toro. 3.00
4 HC(s),plot for revenge 3.00
5 HC(s),Leto learns truth 3.00
6 HC(s),concl. 3.00
TPB 10.00

BITE CLUB:
VAMPIRE CRIME UNIT
DC/Vertigo, April, 2006
1 (of 5) HC, Breathe in, Bleed Out . 3.00
2 thru 5 HC . . . . @3.00

BLACK CANARY
[Limited Series], 1991–92
1 TVE/DG,New Wings,pt.1 . . . . 2.50
2 TVE/DG,New Wings,pt.2 . . . . 2.50
3 TVE/DG,New Wings,pt.3 . . . . . . 2.50
4 TVE/DG,New Wings,pt.4,Conc . . 2.50

[Regular Series], 1993
1 TVE,Hero Worship,pt.1 . . . . 3.00
2 TVE,Hero Worship,pt.2 . . . . 3.00
3 TVE,Hero Worship,pt.3 . . . . 3.00
4 TVE,V:Whorrsman. 3.00
5 TVE,Blynde Woman's Bluff 3.00
6 TVE,Caged Canary 3.00
7 TVE,V:Maniacal Killer 3.00
8 TVE,The Fish. 3.00
9 TVE,A:Huntress 3.00
10 TVE,A:Nightwing,Huntress 3.00
11 TVE,A:Nightwing. 3.00
12 Canary's Grave, final issue. 3.00

BLACK CANARY/ORACLE:
BIRDS OF PREY
1996
1-shot DDi, double size 10.00

BLACK CONDOR
1992–93
1 I&O:Black Condor 3.00
2 thru 11 . . . . @3.00

BLACKHAWK
Prev: Golden Age
1957–1984
108 DD,CCu,DD&CCu(c),The Threat
   from the Abyss A:Blaisie 750.00
109 DD,CCu,DD&CCu(c),The
   Avalance Kid 275.00
110 DD,CCu,DD&CCu(c),Mystery
   of Tigress Island 275.00
111 DD,CCu,DD&CCu(c),Menace
   of the Machines. 275.00
112 DD,CCu,DD(c),The Doomed
   Dog Fight. 275.00
113 DD,CCu,CCu(c),Volunteers
   of Doom. 275.00
114 DD,CCu,DD&CCu(c),Gladiators
   of Blackhawk Island. 275.00
115 DD,CCu,DD&CCu(c),The
   Tyrant's Return 275.00
116 DD,CCu,DD&CCu(c),Prisoners
   of the Black Island. 275.00
117 DD,CCu,DD&CCu(c),Menace
   of the Dragon Boat 275.00
118 DD,CCu,DD&SMo(c),FF,The
   Bandit With 1,000 Nets 300.00
119 DD,CCu,DD&SMo(c),
   V:Chief Blackhawk. 200.00
120 DD,CCu,DD&SMo(c),The
   Challenge of the Wizard 200.00
121 DD,CCu,DD&CCu(c),Secret
   Weapon of the Archer 200.00
122 DD,CCu,DD&CCu(c),The
   Movie That Backfired. 200.00
123 DD,CCu,DD&CCu(c),The
   Underseas Gold Fort. 200.00
124 DD,CCu,DD&CCu(c),Thieves
   With A Thousand Faces 200.00
125 DD,CCu,DD&CCu(c),Secrets
   o/t Blackhawk Time Capsule . 200.00
126 DD,CCu,DD&CCu(c),Secret
   of the Glass Fort 200.00
127 DD,CCu,DD&CCu(c),Blackie-
   The Winged Sky Fighter 200.00
128 DD,CCu,DD&CCu(c),The
   Vengeful Bowman 200.00
129 DD,CCu,DD&CCu(o),The
   Cavemen From 3,000 B.C. . . 200.00
130 DD,CCu,DD&SMo(c),The
   Mystery Missle From Space . 200.00
131 DD,CCu,DD&CCu(c),The
   Return of the Rocketeers . . . 150.00
132 DD,CCu,DD&CCu(c),Raid
   of the Rocketeers 150.00

Birds of Prey #55
© DC Comics Inc.

Blackhawk #109
© DC Comics, Inc.

133 DD,CCu,DD&CCu(c),Human
Dynamo 150.00
134 DD,CC,DD&CC(c),The
Sinister Snowman 150.00
135 DD,CCu,DD&CCu(c),The
Underworld Supermarket . . . 150.00
136 DD,CCu,DD&CCu(c),The
Menace of the Smoke-Master 150.00
137 DD,CCu,DD&CCu(c),The
Weapons That Backfired. . . . 150.00
138 DD,CCu,DD&SMo(c),The
Menace of the Blob 150.00
139 DD,CCu,DD&CCu(c),The
Secret Blackhawk 150.00
140 DD,CCu,DD&CCu(c),The
Space Age Marauders. 150.00
141 DD,CCu,DD&CCu(c),Crimes
of the Captive Masterminds . 125.00
142 DD,CCu,DD&CCu(c),Alien
Blackhawk Chief 125.00
143 DD,SMo,DD&CCu(c),Lady
Blackhawk's Rival 125.00
144 DD,CCu,DD&CCu(c),The
Underworld Sportsmen 125.00
145 DD,CCu,DD&CCu(c),The
Deadly Lensman 125.00
146 DD,CCu,DD&CCu(c),Black-
hawk's Fantastic Fables 125.00
147 DD,SMo,DD&CCu(c),The
Blackhawk Movie Queen. . . . 125.00
148 DD,CCu,DD&CCu(c),Four
Dooms For The Blackhawks . 125.00
149 DD,CCu,DD&CCu(c),Masks
of Doom. 125.00
150 DD,CCu,DD&SMo(c),Black-
hawk Mascot from Space . . . 125.00
151 DD,CCu,Lost City 135.00
152 DD,CCu,DD&SMo(c),Noah's
Ark From Space. 125.00
153 DD,CCu,DD&SMo(c),
Boomerang Master 125.00
154 DD,CCu,DD&SMo(c),The
Beast Time Forgot. 125.00
155 DD,CCu,DD&CCu(c),Killer
Shark's Land Armada 125.00
156 DD,CCu,DD&CCu(c),Peril of
the Plutonian Raider 125.00
157 DD,CCu,DD&SMo(c),Secret
of the Blackhawk Sphinx. . . . 125.00
158 DD,CCu,DD&SMo(c),Bandit
Birds From Space 125.00
159 DD,CCu,DD&CCu(c),Master
of the Puppet Men. 125.00
160 DD,CCu,DD&CCu(c),The
Phantom Spy. 125.00

161 DD,SMo,DD&SMo(c),Lady
Blackhawk's Crime Chief. . . . 125.00
162 DD,CCu,DD&CCu(c),The
Invisible Blackhawk 125.00
163 DD,CCu,DD&SMo(c),
Fisherman of Crime. 125.00
164 DD,O:Blackhawk retold. 135.00
165 DD,V:League of Anti
Blackhawks 125.00
166 DD,A:Lady Blackhawk 125.00
167 DD,The Blackhawk Bandits . . 90.00
168 DD,Blackhawk Time
Travelers 75.00
169 DD,Sinister Hunts of Mr.
Safari. 75.00
170 DD,A:Lady Blackhawk,V:Killer
Shark 75.00
171 DD,Secret of Alien Island . . . 75.00
172 DD,Challenge of the
GasMaster. 75.00
173 DD,The Super Jungle Man . . . 75.00
174 DD,Andre's Impossible
World. 75.00
175 DD,The Creature with
Blackhawk's Brain 75.00
176 DD,Stone Age Blackhawks . . 65.00
177 DD,Town that time Forgot. . . . 65.00
178 DD,Return of the Scorpions . . 65.00
179 DD,Invisible Dr.Dunbar 65.00
180 DD,Son of Blackhawk. 65.00
181 DD,I:Tom Thumb Blackhawk . 70.00
182 DD,A:Lady Blackhawk 100.00
183 DD,V:Killer Shark 100.00
184 DD,Island of Super
Monkeys 100.00
185 DD,Last 7 days of the
Blackhawks 100.00
186 DD,A:Lady Blackhawk 100.00
187 DD,V:Porcupine 100.00
188 DD,A:Lady Blackhawk 100.00
189 DD:O:rtd 100.00
190 DD,FantasticHumanStarfish . 100.00
191 DD,A:Lady Blackhawk 100.00
192 DD,V:King Condor 50.00
193 DD,The Jailer's Revenge 50.00
194 DD,The Outlaw Blackhawk. . . 50.00
195 DD,A:Tom Thumb Blackhawk. 50.00
196 DD,Blackhawk WWII Combat
Diary story. 50.00
197 DD:new look 50.00
198 DD:O:rtd 70.00
199 DD,Attack with the Mummy
Insects 70.00
200 DD,A:Lady Blackhawk,
I:Queen Killer Shark 90.00
201 DD,Blackhawk Detached Diary
Story,F:Hendrickson 70.00
202 DD,Combat Diary,F:Andre . . . 70.00
203 DD:O:Chop-Chop 70.00
204 DD,A:Queen Killer Shark 70.00
205 DD,Combat Diary story. 70.00
206 DD,Combat Diary, F:Olaf 70.00
207 DD,Blackhawk Devil Dolls . . . 70.00
208 DD,Detached service diary
F:Chuck. 70.00
209 DD,V:King Condor 70.00
210 DD,Danger..Blackhawk Bait
rep.Blackhawk #139. . . . . 50.00
211 DD,GC,Detached service
diary. 40.00
212 DD,Combat Diary,
F:Chop-Chop. 40.00
213 DD,Blackhawk goes
Hollywood 40.00
214 DD,Team of Traitors 40.00
215 DD,Detached service diary
F:Olaf. 40.00
216 DD,A:Queen Killer Shark 40.00
217 DD,Detached service diary
F:Stanislaus 40.00
218 DD,7 against Planet Peril 40.00
219 DD,El Blackhawk Peligroso . . 40.00

220 DD,The Revolt of the
Assembled Man. 40.00
221 DD,Detach service diary
F:Hendrickson 40.00
222 DD,The Man from E=MC2 . . . 40.00
223 DD,V:Mr.Quick CHange 40.00
224 DD,Combat Diary,
F:Stanislaus 40.00
225 DD,A:Queen Killer Shark 40.00
226 DD,Secret Monster of
Blackhawk Island. 40.00
227 DD,Detached Service diary
F:Chop-Chop. 40.00
228 DD (1st art on JLA characters)
Blackhawks become super-heroes,
Junk-Heap heroes #1(C:JLA) . 50.00
229 DD,Junk-Heap Heroes #2
(C:JLA) 40.00
230 DD,Junk-Heap Heroes concl.
(C:JLA) 40.00
231 DD,A:Lady Blackhawk 40.00
232 DD,A:Lady Blackhawk 40.00
233 DD,Too Late,The Leaper 40.00
234 DD,The Terrible Twins 40.00
235 DD,A Coffin for
a Blackhawk 40.00
236 DD,Melt,Mutant, Melt 40.00
237 DD,Magnificent 7 Assassins . . 40.00
238 DD,Walking Booby-Traps 40.00
239 DD,The Killer That Time
Forgot 40.00
240 DD,He Who Must Die 40.00
241 DD,A Blackhawk a Day. 40.00
242 Blackhawks back in blue &
black costumes 40.00
243 Mission Incredible (1968) 40.00

[Series Pause:] 1969–75
244 GE,new costumes,Blackhawks
become mercenaries (1976) . . 25.00
245 GE,Death's Double Deal. 25.00
246 RE,GE,Death's Deadly Dawn. 25.00
247 RE,AM,Operation:Over Kill. . . 25.00
248 JSh,Vengeance is Mine!..
Sayeth the Cyborg. 25.00
249 RE,GE,V:Sky-Skull 25.00
250 RE,GE,FS,D:Chuck (1977). . . 25.00

[Series Pause:] 1978–81
251 DSp,Back to WWII (1982). . . . 20.00
252 thru 258 DSp. . . . . @20.00
259 HC(c),DSp. 20.00
260 HC,ATh 20.00
261 thru 271 DSp. . . . . @20.00
272 DSp. 20.00

Blackhawk #148
© DC Comics, Inc.

Blackhawk #247
© DC Comics, Inc.

273 DSp 20.00
274 DSp 20.00

[2nd Series], 1988
1 HC Mini-series,Blackhawk accused
　of communism 5.00
2 HC,visits Soviet Union 4.00
3 HC,Atom Bomb threat to N.Y. . . . 4.00

[3rd Series], 1989
1 All in color for a Crime,pt.1
　I:The Real Lady Blackhawk 4.00
2 All in color for a Crime,pt.2 . . . . . 2.50
3 Agent Rescue Attempt in Rome . . 2.50
4 Blackhawk's girlfriend murdered . 2.50
5 I:Circus Organization 2.50
6 Blackhawks on false mission 2.50
7 V:Circus,A:Suicide Squad, rep.
　1st Blackhawk story 3.00
8 Project: Assimilation 2.50
9 V:Grundfest 2.50
10 Blackhawks Attacked 2.50
11 Master plan revealed 2.50
12 Raid on BlackhawkAirwaysHQ . . 2.50
13 Team Member Accused of 2.50
14 Blackhawk test pilots 2.50
15 Plans for independence 2.50
16 Independence, final issue 2.50
Ann.#1 Hawks in Albania 3.00
Spec.#1 Assassination of JFK
　to Saigon,1975 . . . . 3.50

BLACK HOOD
Impact, 1991–92
1 O:Black Hood 4.00
2 thru 12 . . . . @3.00
Ann#1 Earthquest,w/trading card . . 3.00

BLACK LAMB, THE
DC/Helix, Sept., 1996
1 TT,Vampire saga 2.50
2 thru 6 TT . . . . @2.50

BLACK LIGHTNING
1977–78
1 TVE/FS,I&O:Black Lightning . . . 15.00
2 TVE/FS,A.Talia 7.00
3 TVE,I:Tobias Whale 7.00
4 TVE,A:Jimmy Olsen 8.00
5 TVE,A:Superman 8.00
6 TVE,I:Syonide 7.00
7 TVE,V:Syonide 7.00
8 TVE,V:Tobias Whale 7.00
9 TVE,V:Annihilist 7.00
10 TVE,V:Trickster 7.00
11 TVE,BU:The Ray 10.00

[2nd Series], 1995–96
1 He's Back 3.00
2 V:Painkiller 3.00
3 V:Painkiller 3.00
4 V:Painkiller,Royal Family 3.00
5 Flashbacks of Past 3.00
6 V:Gangbuster 3.00
7 V:Gangbuster 3.00
8 V:Tobias Whale 3.00
9 I&V:Demolition 3.00
10 Jefferson Pierce becomes Black
　Lightning full time 3.00
11 Hunt for Sick Nick 3.00
12 V:Sick Nick's death squad 3.00
13 final issue 3.00

BLACK MASK
1993–94
1 I:Black Mask 5.00
2 V:Underworld 5.00
3 V:Valentine 5.00

BLACK ORCHID
1993–95
1 DMc,O:Black Orchid,
　A:Batman,Luthor,Poison Ivy . . . 6.00
2 DMc,O:cont,Arkham Asylum 7.00
3 DMc,A:SwampThing,conc. 6.00
TPB rep. #1 thru #3 . . . . 20.00

DC/Vertigo
1 DMc(c),B:DiF(s),JIT,SnW,I:Sherilyn
　Somers,I:Logos,F:Walt Brody . . 2.50
1a Platinum Ed. 12.00
2 JIT,SnW,Uprooting,V:Logos 2.50
3 JIT,SnW,Tainted Zone,
　V:Fungus 2.50
4 JIT,SnW,I:Nick & Orthia 2.50
5 DMc(c),JIT,SnW,
　A:Swamp Thing 2.50
6 JIT,BMc(i),God in the Cage 2.50
7 JIT,RGu,SnW,
　Upon the Threshold 2.50
8 DMc(c),RGu,A:Silent People 2.50
9 DMc(c),RGu 2.50
10 DMc(c),RGu 2.50
11 DMc(c),RGu,In Tennessee 2.50
12 DMc(c),RGu 2.50
13 DMc(c),RGu,F:Walt Brody 2.50
14 DMc(c),RGu,Black Annis 2.50
15 DMc(c),RGu,Kobolds 2.50
16 DMc(c),RGu,Suzy,Junkin 2.50
17 Twisted Season,pt.1 . . . . 2.50
18 Twisted Season,pt.2 . . . . 2.50
19 Twisted Season,pt.3 . . . . 2.50
20 Twisted Season,pt.4 . . . . 2.50
21 Twisted Season,pt.5 . . . . 2.50
22 Twisted Season,pt.6, final iss. . . 2.50
Ann.#1 DMc(c),DiF(s),GyA,JnM,F:Suzy,
　Childrens Crusade,BU:retells
　Adventure Comics#430 . . . . . . 4.25

BLASTERS SPECIAL
1989
1 A:Snapper Carr, Spider Guild . . . 2.00

BLOOD: A TALE
DC/Vertigo, Sept., 1996
[Mini-series,
re-release of Marvel Epic]
1 JMD(s),KW, quest for truth
　begins 3.00
2 JMD(s),KW, Blood falls in love . . 3.00
3 JMD(s),KW, companion dies 3.00
4 JMD(s),KW, finale 3.00
TPB (2004) 20.00

BLOOD & SHADOWS
DC/Vertigo, 1996
1 . . . . 6.00
2 Journal of Justice Jones 6.00
3 Chet Daley flung into
　21st century 6.00
4 V:God of the Razor, finale 6.00

BLOOD AND WATER
DC/Vertigo March 2003
1 (of 5) F:Adam Heller 3.00
2 vampire 3.00
3 sex for Adam 3.00
4 past, present, future 3.00
5 concl. 3.00

BLOODBATH
1993
1 A:Superman 4.00
2 A:New Heroes, Hitman 8.00

BLOODHOUND
July 2004
1 F:Travis Clevenger 3.00

2 thru 4 Concl. . . . . @3.00
5 Firestorm x-over 3.00
6 Return from prison 3.00
7 Psychic assault 3.00
8 V:Zeiss 3.00
9 V:Zeiss 3.00
10 V:Zeiss 3.00

BLOODPACK
[Mini-Series], 1995
1 I:Blood Pack, V:Demolition 2.25
2 A:Superboy 2.25
3 Loira's Corpse 2.25
4 Real Heroes Final Issue 2.25

BLOOD OF THE DEMON
March, 2005
1 JBy,F:Jason Blood 2.50
2 JBy,V:Etrigan 2.50
3 JBy,F:Batman & Zatanna 2.50
4 JBy,F:Morgain Le Fey 2.50
5 JBy,Jason Blood 2.50
6 JBy,F:Batman, Superman 2.50
7 JBy,Day of Vengeance tie-in 2.50
8 JBy,DGr 2.50
9 JBy,DGr 2.50
10 JBy,DGr 2.50
11 JBy,DGr, Joshua 2.50
12 JBy,DGr 2.50
13 JBy,DGr, One Year Later 2.50
14 JBy,DGr,Breaking of Etrigan . . . 2.50
15 JBy,V:Lord of the Damned 3.00
16 JBy,DGr, V:Lord of the Damned . . 3.00
17 JBy,DGr,final issue 3.00

Blood Syndicate #8
© DC Comics Inc.

BLOOD SYNDICATE
DC/Milestone, 1993–96
1 I:Blood Syndicate,Rob Chaplick,
　Dir.Mark.Ed.,w/B puzzle piece,
　Skybox card,Poster 3.50
1a Newstand Ed. 2.50
2 thru 9 . . . . @2.50
10 WS(c),Ccs,Shadow War,I:Iota,
　Sideshow,Rainsaw,Slag,Ash,
　Bad Betty,Oro 2.75
11 thru 34 . . . . @2.50
35 final issue 3.50

BLOODY MARY
DC/Helix, Aug., 1996
1 (of 4) GEn(s),CE, near-
　future war 3.00

2 thru 4 GEn(s),CE, near-future
    war, concl. . . . . @3.00
TPB 20.00

BLOODY MARY: LADY LIBERTY
DC/Helix, July, 1996
1 (of 4) GEn(s),CE, ... 4.00
2 GEn(s),CE,V:Achilles Seagal . . . 4.00
3 GEn(s),CE,V:Vatman 4.00
4 GEn(s),CE,V:Vatman, concl. 4.00

BLUE BEETLE
1986–88
1 O:Blue Beetle. 5.00
2 V:Fire Fist 2.50
3 V:Madmen 2.50
4 V:Doctor Alchemy 2.50
5 A:Question 2.50
6 V:Question 2.50
7 A:Question 2.50
8 A:Chronos 2.50
9 A:Chronos 2.50
10 Legends, V:Chronos 2.50
11 A:New Teen Titans 2.50
12 A:New Teen Titans 2.50
13 A:New Teen Titans 2.50
14 Pago Island,I:Catalyst 2.50
15 RA:V:Carapax 2.50
16 RA,Chicago Murders 2.50
17 R:Dan Garrett/Blue Beetle 2.50
18 D:Dan Garrett 2.50
19 RA,R:Dr. Cyber. 2.50
20 RA,Millennium,A:JLI 3.00
21 RA,A:Mr.Miracle,
    Millennium tie in. 2.25
22 RA,Prehistoric Chicago. 2.25
23 DH,V:The Madmen 2.25
24 DH,final issue 2.25

BLUE BEETLE
March, 2006
1 CHm,Who's Under the Mask?. . . 3.00
2 CHm,Totally changed world. 3.00
3 Trouble at 100 m.p.h.. . . . . 3.00
4 . . . . 3.00
5 Phantom Stranger 3.00
6 Secret of Beetle's armor 3.00
7 CHm, ... 3.00
8 Hits the road 3.00
9 Back in El Paso 3.00
TPB Shellshocked 13.00

BLUE DEVIL
1984–86
1 O:Blue Devil. 4.00
2 . . . . 2.50
3 . . . . 2.50
4 . . . . 2.50
5 . . . . 2.50
6 thru 16 . . . . @2.50
17 Crisis. 3.00
18 Crisis. 3.00
19 thru 31. . . . . @2.50
Ann.#1 . . . . 2.50

BOB, THE GALACTIC BUM
[Mini-Series], 1995
1 A:Lobo 2.50
2 Planet Gnulp,A:Lobo 2.50
3 V:Khunds 2.50
4 Rando's Coronation 2.50

BODY DOUBLES
Aug., 1999
1 (of 4) DAn,ALa,JoP 2.50
2 DAn,ALa,JoP 2.50
3 DAn,ALa,JoP 2.50

Body Doubles #1
© DC Comics, Inc.

BOMBA, THE JUNGLE BOY
1967–68
1 CI,MA,I:Bomba 300.00
2 The Phantom City of Death . . . 200.00
3 My Enemy...The Jungle 200.00
4 Deadly Sting of Ana Conda 200.00
5 Tampu Lives–Bombs Dies. . . . 200.00
6 Krag 200.00
7 Nightmare 200.00

BOOK OF FATE, THE
1997–98
1 KG(s),RoW,BR, ... 3.00
2 KG(s),RoW,BR,The Chaos-
    Order War, pt.1 (of 4) 3.00
3 KG(s),RoW,BR,The Chaos-
    Order War, pt.2 . . . . 3.00
4 KG(s),RoW,BR,The Chaos-
    Order War, pt.3, A:Two-Face. . . 3.00
5 KG(s),RoW,BR,The Chaos-
    Order War, pt.4 . . . . 3.00
6 KG(s),RoW,BR,Convergence,
    pt.1 x-over 3.00
7 KG(s),RoW,BR, Signs, pt.1 . . . . 3.00
8 KG(s),RoW,BR, Signs, pt.2 . . . . 3.00
9 KG,AIG,BR,Signs, pt.3 . . . . 3.00
10 KG,AIG,BR,Signs,pt.4 . . . . 3.00
11 KG,AIG, in a Swiss Jail 3.00
12 AIG,KG,F:Lobo, final issue 3.00

BOOKS OF FAERIE, THE
DC/Vertigo, Jan., 1997
1 PrG,F:Titania and Auberon 3.00
2 thru 3 PrG, ... @3.00
TPB 15.00

BOOKS OF FAERIE, THE: AUBERON'S TALE
DC/Vertigo, June, 1998
1 (of 3) PrG,VcL,F:Early life of
    King Auberon. 3.00
2 thru 3 PrG,VcL, early life . . . . . @3.00
TPB Books of Faerie 15.00

BOOKS OF FAERIE, THE: MOLLY'S STORY
DC/Vertigo, 1999
1 (of 4) JNR(s) 3.00
2 thru 4 CV(c) . . . . @3.00

BOOKS OF MAGIC
[Limited Series], 1990–91
1 B:NGa(s),JBo,F:Phantom Stranger,
    A:J.Constantine,Tim Hunter,
    Doctor Occult,Mister E. 11.00
2 SHp,F:J.Constantine,A:Spectre,
    Dr.Fate,Demon,Zatanna 11.00
3 CV,F:Doctor Occult,
    A:Sandman 8.00
4 E:NGa(s),PuJ,F:Mr.E,A:Death . . . 9.00
TPB rep.#1-#4 . . . . 20.00

[Regular Series]
DC/Vertigo, 1994–97
1 MkB,B:Bindings,R:Tim Hunter . . 13.00
1a Platinum Edition. 25.00
2 CV(c),MkB,V:Manticore 6.00
3 CV(c),MkB,E:Bindings 6.00
4 CV(c),MkB,A:Death 7.00
5 CV(c),I:Khara. 4.00
6 Sacrifices,pt.I 4.00
7 Sacrifices,pt.II 4.00
8 Tim vs. evil Tim 4.00
9 Artificial Heart,pt.1 . . . . 4.00
10 Artificial Heart,pt.2. . . . . 4.00
11 Artificial Heart,pt.3. . . . . 4.00
12 Small Glass Worlds,pt.1 . . . . . . 4.00
13 Small Glass Worlds,pt.2 . . . . . . 4.00
14 CV(c),A:The Wobbly 4.00
15 Hell and Back,pt.1. . . . . 4.00
16 Hall and Back,pt.2. . . . . 3.50
17 Playgrounds,pt.1 . . . . 3.50
18 JNR,PrG,Playgrounds,cont. . . . 3.50
19 JNR,PrG,Playgrounds,concl. . . . 3.50
20 Barabatos gives the orders. . . . 3.50
21 JNR,PrG,Molly seeks Mayra . . . 3.50
22 . . . . 3.50
23 JNR,V:Margraves Strafenkinder . 3.50
24 JNR,PrG,F:Molly vs. Amadan . . 3.50
25 JNR,PrG,Death and the Endless 3.50
26 JNR,PrG,Rites of Passage, pt.1 . 3.00
27 JNR,PrG,Rites of Passage, pt.2 . 3.00
28 JNR,PrG,Rites of Passage, pt.3,
    Cupid & Psyche. 3.00
29 JNR,PrG,Rite of Passage 3.00
30 JNR,PrG,Rite of Passage 3.00
31 JNR,PrG,Rite of Passage 3.00
32 JNR(s),PSj,Rites of Passage . . . 3.00
33 JNR(s),PSj,Rites of Passage . . . 3.00
34 JNR(s),PSj,Rites of Passage . . . 3.00
35 JNR(s),PrG,Rites of Passage . . . 3.00
36 JNR,Rites of Passage, cont 3.00
37 JNR,Rites of Passage, cont. . . . 3.00
38 JNR,Rites of Passage, concl. . . . 3.00
39 PrG, at Sphinx casino 3.00
40 JNR(s),F:Tim & Molly 3.00
41 JNR(s),V:Gargoyles 3.00
42 JNR(s),JIT,magical havok 3.00
43 JNR(s),PrG,F:The Wobbly 3.00
44 JNR(s),goodbye to Zatanna 3.00
45 JNR(s) Slave of Heavens, pt.1 . . 3.00
46 JNR(s) Slave of Heavens, pt.2 . . 3.00
47 JNR(s) Slave of Heavens, pt.3 . . 3.00
48 JNR(s) Slave of Heavens, pt.4 . . 3.00
49 JNR(s) Slave of Heavens, pt.5 . . 3.00
50 JNR(s) Slave of Heavens, pt.6 . . 3.00
51 PrG,MK,an Opener 2.50
52 PrG,MK,Homecoming 2.50
54 PrG,MK,V:Thomas 2.50
55 PrG,MK,Coming of the Other . . . 2.50
56 PrG,MK,Last Molly Story. 2.50
57 PrG,MK,after car crash 2.50
58 PrG,MK,The Other 2.50
59 PrG,MK,The Other 2.50
60 PrG,MK,The Other 2.50
61 PrG,MK(c),The Other, concl. . . . 2.50
62 PrG,MK(c),crossroads. 2.50
63 GyA,MK(c), ... 2.50
64 PrG,MK(c),Wild Hunt. 2.50
65 PrG,MK,new life cont. 2.50
66 PrG,A Day,A Night &
    A Dream,pt.1 . . . . 2.50

67 PrG,A Day, A Night & A Dream,concl.	2.50
68 PrG	2.50
69 PrG	2.50
70 PrG	2.50
71 PrG,MK(c)	2.50
72 PrG,MK(c),F:Timothy Hunter.	2.50
73 PrG,MK(c),V:Other self	2.50
74 PrG,MK(c),V:Other self	2.50
75 PrG,MK(c), final issue	2.50
Ann.#2 JNR(s) Minotaur	4.00
Ann.#3 PrG	4.00
TPB Rep. #5-#13 & Rave #1	13.00
TPB Reckonings, rep. #14–#20	13.00
TPB Reckonings, new printing.	15.00
TPB Bindings, GyA,PrG,WK	13.00
TPB Transformations PrG,MK	13.00
TPB The Books of Magic	20.00
TPB Girl in the Box	15.00
TPB The Burning Girl.	18.00
TPB Death After Death	20.00

BOOKS OF MAGICK, THE: LIFE DURING WARTIME
DC/Vertigo, July 2004

1 NGa(s),F:Timothy Hunter	2.50
2 thru 4 NGa(s)	@2.50
5 DOr	2.50
6 DFg	2.50
7 SeP, pt.1	2.50
8 DOr	2.50
9 Tumbling Dice,pt.1,DOr	2.50
10 Tumbling Dice,pt.2,DOr	2.50
11 DOr	2.50
12 DOr	2.50
13 Losing My Religion,pt.1,DOr.	2.75
14 Losing My Religion,pt.2,DOr.	2.75
15 series finale.	2.75
TPB Vol. 1	10.00

BOOSTER GOLD
1986–88

1 DJ,V:Blackguard	3.00
2 DJ,V:Minddancer	2.50
3 thru 25 DJ	@2.50

BOY COMMANDOS
Winter, 1942–43

1 S&K,O:Liberty Belle;Sandman & Newsboy Legion	13,000.00
2 S&K,Hitler(c)	4,000.00
3 S&K,WWII(c).	1,700.00
4 WWII(c).	1,400.00

Boy Commandos #11
© DC Comics, Inc.

5 WWII(c)	1,400.00
6 S&K,WWII(c).	1,400.00
7 S&K,WWII(c)	900.00
8 S&K,WWII(c)	900.00
9 WWII(c).	1,000.00
10 S&K,WWII(c).	900.00
11 WWII(c).	900.00
12 WWII(c).	900.00
13 WWII(c).	900.00
14	900.00
15 1st Crazy Quilt	800.00
16	700.00
17 Science Fiction(c)	800.00
18 S&K.	600.00
19 S&K.	600.00
20 Science Fiction (c)	800.00
21	500.00
22 Judy Canova.	500.00
23 S&K,S&K,(c)	600.00
24 Superhero	600.00
25 superhero(c)	550.00
26 Science Fiction(c)	550.00
27	600.00
28	650.00
29 S&K story	600.00
30 Baseball Story.	650.00
31	600.00
32 A:Dale Evans(c)	650.00
33	500.00
34 I:Wolf.	500.00
35	500.00
36 Sci-Fi(c),Nov.–Dec., 1949	600.00

BRAINBANX
DC/Helix, Jan., 1997

1 ELe(s),Down Upon the Darkness	2.50
2 ELe(s),Anna flees to the Sheol	2.50
3 Ele(s),Anna stranded	2.50
4 ELe(s),Anna & Logan	2.50
5 ELe(s),To Enter the Kingdom	2.50
6 (of 6)	2.50

BRAVE AND THE BOLD
Aug.–Sept., 1955

1 JKu,RH,IN,I:VikingPrince,Golden Gladiator,Silent Knight	7,000.00
2 F:Viking Prince	2,500.00
3 F:Viking Prince	1,500.00
4 F:Viking Prince	1,500.00
5 B:Robin Hood	1,300.00
6 JKu,F:Robin Hood,E:Golden Gladiator	900.00
7 JKu,F:Robin Hood	900.00
8 JKu,F:Robin Hood	900.00
9 JKu,F:Robin Hood	900.00
10 JKu,F:Robin Hood	900.00
11 JKu,F:Viking Prince.	700.00
12 JKu,F:Viking Prince.	700.00
13 JKu,F:Viking Prince.	700.00
14 JKu,F:Viking Prince	650.00
15 JKu,F:Viking Prince.	650.00
16 JKu,F:Viking Prince.	650.00
17 JKu,F:Viking Prince.	650.00
18 JKu,F:Viking Prince.	650.00
19 JKu,F:Viking Prince.	650.00
20 JKu,F:Viking Prince.	650.00
21 JKu,F:Viking Prince.	650.00
22 JKu,F:Viking Prince.	650.00
23 JKu,O:Viking Prince	900.00
24 JKu,E:Viking Prince,Silent Knight	700.00
25 RA,I&B:Suicide Squad	850.00
26 F:Suicide Squad	600.00
27 Creature of Ghost Lake	600.00
28 I:Justice League of America,O:Snapper Carr	10,000.00
29 F:Justice League	4,200.00
30 F:Justice League	3,000.00
31 F:Cave Carson	800.00
32 F:Cave Carson	500.00

The Brave and the Bold #28
© DC Comics Inc.

33 F:Cave Carson	500.00
34 JKu,I&O:S.A. Hawkman.	4,000.00
35 JKu:F:Hawkman.	1,000.00
36 JKu:F:Hawkman.	1,000.00
37 F:Suicide Squad	600.00
38 F:Suicide Squad	400.00
39 F:Suicide Squad	400.00
40 JKu,F:Cave Carson	300.00
41 F:Cave Carson	300.00
42 JKu,F:Hawkman.	600.00
43 JKu,O:Hawkman.	700.00
44 JKu,F:Hawkman.	600.00
45 CI,F:Strange Sports	200.00
46 CI,F:Strange Sports	200.00
47 CI,F:Strange Sports	200.00
48 CI,F:Strange Sports	200.00
49 CI,F:Strange Sports	200.00
50 F:GreenArrow & J'onnJ'onzz	400.00
51 JKu,F:Aquaman & Hawkman.	600.00
52 JKu,F:Sgt.Rock.	350.00
53 ATh,F:Atom & Flash	275.00
54 I&O:Teen Titans	600.00
55 F:Metal Man & Atom	250.00
56 F:Flash & J'onn J'onzz	250.00
57 I&O:Metamorpho.	550.00
58 F:Metamorpho.	275.00
59 F:Batman & Green Lantern	300.00
60 A:Teen Titans,I:Wonder Girl	300.00
61 MA,O:Starman,BlackCanary.	400.00
62 MA,O:Starman,BlackCanary.	400.00
63 F:Supergirl&WonderWoman .	200.00
64 F:Batman,V:Eclipso.	250.00
65 DG,FMc,F:Flash & Doom Patrol	200.00
66 F:Metamorpho & Metal Men	225.00
67 CI,F:Batman & Flash	200.00
68 F:Batman,Metamorpho,Joker, Riddler,Penguin	250.00
69 F:Batman & Green Lantern	175.00
70 F:Batman & Hawkman	175.00
71 F:Batman & Green Arrow	175.00
72 CI,F:Spectre & Flash	175.00
73 F:Aquaman & Atom.	175.00
74 B:Batman T.U.,A:Metal Men	175.00
75 F:Spectre	175.00
76 F:Plastic Man	175.00
77 F:Atom	175.00
78 F:Wonder Woman	175.00
79 NA,F:Deadman.	250.00
80 NA,DG,F:Creeper	200.00
81 NA,F:Flash	200.00
82 NA,F:Aquaman,O:Ocean Master	200.00
83 NA,F:Teen Titans	200.00

All comics prices listed are for *Near Mint* condition.

84 NA,F:Sgt.Rock 200.00
85 NA,F:Green Arrow 200.00
86 NA,F:Deadman 200.00
87 F:Wonder Woman 100.00
88 F:Wildcat 100.00
89 RA,F:Phantom Stranger 100.00
90 F:Adam Strange 100.00
91 F:Black Canary 100.00
92 F:Bat Squad 100.00
93 NA,House of Mystery 150.00
94 NC,F:Teen Titans 135.00
95 F:Plastic Man 135.00
96 F:Sgt.Rock 100.00
97 NC(i),F:Wildcat 100.00
98 JAp,F:Phantom Stranger 100.00
99 NC,F:Flash 100.00
100 NA,F:Green Arrow 150.00
101 JA,F:Metamorpho 75.00
102 NA,JA,F:Teen Titans 75.00
103 FMc,F:Metal Men 50.00
104 JAp,F:Deadman 50.00
105 JAp,F:Wonder Woman 50.00
106 JAp,F:Green Arrow 50.00
107 JAp,F:Black Canary 50.00
108 JAp,F:Sgt.Rock 50.00
109 JAp,F:Demon 50.00
110 JAp,F:Wildcat 50.00
111 JAp,F:Joker 60.00
112 JAp,F:Mr.Miracle. 100.00
113 JAp,F:Metal Men 100.00
114 JAp,F:Aquaman 100.00
115 JAp,O:Viking Prince 100.00
116 JAp,F:Spectre 100.00
117 JAp,F:Sgt.Rock 100.00
118 JAp,F:Wildcat,V:Joker 100.00
119 JAp,F:Man-Bat 30.00
120 JAp,F:Kamandi 30.00
121 JAp,F:Metal Men 30.00
122 JAp,F:Swamp Thing 30.00
123 JAp,F:Plastic Man 30.00
124 JAp,F:Sgt.Rock 30.00
125 JAp,F:Flash 30.00
126 JAp,F:Aquaman 30.00
127 JAp,F:Wildcat 30.00
128 JAp,F:Mr.Miracle 30.00
129 F:Green Arrow,V:Joker 35.00
130 F:Green Arrow,V:Joker 35.00
131 JAp,F:WonderWoman,
     A:Catwoman 30.00
132 JAp,F:King Fu Foom 25.00
133 JAp,F:Deadman 25.00
134 JAp,F:Green Lantern 25.00
135 JAp,F:Metal Men 25.00
136 JAp,F:Metal Men,Green Arr. . . 25.00
137 F:Demon 25.00
138 JAp,F:Mr.Miracle 25.00
139 JAp,F:Hawkman 25.00
140 JAp,F:Wonder Woman 25.00
141 JAp,F:Bl.Canary,A:Joker 40.00
142 JAp,F:Aquaman 15.00
143 O:Human Target 15.00
144 JAp,F:Green Arrow 15.00
145 JAp,F:Phantom Stranger 15.00
146 JAp,F:E-2 Batman 15.00
147 JAp,A:Supergirl 15.00
148 JSon,JAp,F:Plastic Man 15.00
149 JAp,F:Teen Titans 18.00
150 JAp,F:Superman 15.00
151 JAp,F:Flash 18.00
152 JAp,F:Atom 15.00
153 DN,F:Red Tornado 15.00
154 JAp,F:Metamorpho 15.00
155 JAp,F:Green Lantern 15.00
156 DN,F:Dr.Fate 15.00
157 JAp,F:Kamandi 15.00
158 JAp,F:Wonder Woman 15.00
159 JAp,A:Ras al Ghul 15.00
160 JAp,F:Supergirl 15.00
161 JAp,F:Adam Strange 15.00
162 JAp,F:Sgt.Rock 15.00
163 DGF,F:Black Lightning 15.00
164 JL,F:Hawkman 15.00

The Brave and the Bold #149
© DC Comics, Inc.

165 DN,F:Man-bat 15.00
166 DG,TA,DSp,F:Black Canary
     A:Penguin,I:Nemesis 15.00
167 DC,DA,F:Blackhawk 15.00
168 JAp,DSp,F:Green Arrow 9.00
169 JAp,DSp,F:Zatanna 9.00
170 JA,F:Nemesis 9.00
171 JL,DSp,V:Scalphunter 9.00
172 CI,F:Firestorm 9.00
173 JAp,F:Guardians 9.00
174 JAp,F:Green Lantern 9.00
175 JAp,A:Lois Lane 9.00
176 JAp,F:Swamp Thing 9.00
177 JAp,F:Elongated Man 9.00
178 JAp,F:Creeper 9.00
179 EC,F:Legion o/Superheroes . . 9.00
180 JAp,F:Spectre,Nemesis 9.00
181 JAp,F:Hawk & Dove 9.00
182 JAp,F:E-2 Robin 9.00
183 CI,V:Riddler 10.00
184 JAp,A:Catwoman 10.00
185 F:Green Arrow 9.00
186 JAp,F:Hawkman 9.00
187 JAp,F:Metal Men 9.00
188 JAp,F:Rose & Thorn 9.00
189 JAp,A:Thorn 9.00
190 JAp,F:Adam Strange 9.00
191 JAp,V:Joker,Penguin 15.00
192 JAp,F:Superboy 9.00
193 JAp,D:Nemesis 9.00
194 CI,F:Flash 9.00
195 JA,I:Vampire 9.00
196 JAp,F:Ragman 9.00
197 JSon,W:Earth II Batman &
     Catwoman 9.00
198 F:Karate Kid 9.00
199 RA,F:Spectre 9.00
200 DGb,JAp,A:Earth-2 Batman,I:
     Outsiders (GeoForce,Katana,Halo),
     E:Batman T.U.,final issue . . . 15.00
Ann. #1-1969 80-page giant (2001)10.00

[Limited Series]
1 SAP,Green Arrow/Butcher T.U. . . 2.50
2 SAP,A:Black Canary,Question . . . 2.50
3 SAP,Green Arrow/Butcher 2.50
4 SAP,GA on Trial;A:Black
     Canary 2.50
5 SAP,V:Native Canadians,I.R.A. . . 2.50

BRAVE OLD WORLD
DC/Vertigo, Dec., 1999
1 (of 4) BML,GyD,PhH,Y2K story . . 2.50
2 thru 4 BML,GyD,PhH . . . . @2.50

BREACH
Jan., 2005
1 F:Major Tim Porter,40-page 3.00
2 Long in the future, in Africa 2.50
3 South Africa 2.50
4 F:JLA 2.50
5 JLA fallout 2.50
6 Fallout continues 2.50
7 Rifter fallout 2.50
8 V:Talia's Kobra forces 2.50
9 F:Heardsman 2.50
10 F:Talia al Ghul 2.50
11 V:The Smoking Lady 2.50

BREATHTAKER
1990
1 I:Breathtaker(Chase Darrow) 6.00
2 Chase Darrow captured 6.00
3 O:Breathtaker 6.00
4 V:The Man, final issue 5.00
TPB Breathtaker 15.00

BROTHER POWER,
THE GEEK
Sept.–Oct., 1968
1 . . . . 75.00
2 Nov.–Dec., 1968 . . . . 50.00

BUGS BUNNY
1990
1 Search for Fudd Statues 3.50
2 V:WitchHazel 3.50
3 Bugs&Co.in outer space, final . . . 3.50
TPB Bugs & Friends Celebration
     Celebration (2000) 15.00

BUTCHER, THE
[Limited Series], 1990
1 MB,I:John Butcher 3.50
2 MB,in San Francisco 3.00
3 MB,V:Corporation 3.00
4 MB,A:Green Arrow 2.50
5 MB,A:Corvus,final issue 2.25

BUZZY
1944–58
1 . . . . 500.00
2 . . . . 300.00
3 thru 5 . . . . @250.00
6 thru 10 . . . . @150.00
11 thru 15 . . . . @150.00
16 thru 25 . . . . @150.00
26 thru 35 . . . . @125.00
36 thru 45 . . . . @100.00
46 thru 77 . . . . @100.00

CAMELOT 3000
Dec., 1982
1 BB,O:Arthur,Merlin 3.50
2 BB,A:Morgan LeFay 3.00
3 BB,J:New Knights 3.00
4 BB,V:McAllister 3.00
5 BB,O:Morgan Le Fay 3.00
6 BB,TA,W:Arthur 3.00
7 BB,TA,R:Isolde 3.00
8 BB,TA,D:Sir Kay 3.00
9 BB,TA,L:Sir Percival 3.00
10 BB,TA,V:Morgan Le Fay 3.00
11 BB,TA,V:Morgan Le Fay 3.00
12 BB,TA,D:Arthur 3.00

CAPER
Oct. 2003
1 (of 12) organized crime 3.00
2 . . . . 3.00
3 Jewish Mafia hitmen 3.00
4 Jacob & Isadore Weiss 3.00

5 thru 8 JSe	@3.00
9 thru 12	@3.00

CAPTAIN ACTION
[Based on toy] Oct.–Nov., 1968

1 WW,I:Captain Action,Action Boy,A:Superman	175.00
2 GK,WW, V:Krellik	125.00
3 GK,I:Dr.Evil	125.00
4 GK,A:Dr.Evil	125.00
5 GK,WW,A:Matthew Blackwell	75.00

CAPTAIN ATOM
March, 1987

1 PB,O:Captain Atom	4.50
2 PB,C:Batman	2.50
3 PB,O:Captain Atom	2.50
4 PB,A:Firestorm	2.50
5 PB,A:Firestorm	2.50
6 PB,Dr.Spectro	2.50
7 R:Plastique	2.50
8 PB,Capt.Atom/Plastique	2.50
9 V:Bolt	2.50
10 PB,A:JLI	2.50
11 PB,A:Firestorm	2.50
12 PB,I:Major Force	2.50
13 PB,Christmas issue	2.50
14 PB,A:Nightshade	2.50
15 PB,Dr.Spectro, Major Force	2.50
16 PB,A:JLI,V:Red Tornado	2.50
17 V:Red Tornado,A:Swamp Thing,JLI	2.50
18 PB,A:Major Force	2.50
19 PB,Drug War	2.50
20 FMc,BlueBeetle	2.50
21 PB,A:Plastique,Nightshade	2.50
22 PB,A:MaxLord,Nightshade, Plastique	2.50
23 PB,V:The Ghost	2.50
24 PB,Invasion X-over	2.50
25 PB,Invvasion X-over	2.50
26 A:JLA,Top Secret,pt.1	2.50
27 A:JLA,Top Secret,pt.2	2.50
28 V:Ghost, Top Secret,pt.3	2.50
29 RT,Captain Atom cleared (new direction)	2.50
30 Janus Directive #11,V:Black Manta	2.50
31 RT,Capt.Atom's Powers, A:Rocket Red	2.50
32 Loses Powers	2.50
33 A:Batman	3.00
34 C:JLE	2.50
35 RT,Secret o/t Silver Shield, A:Major Force	2.50
36 RT,Las Vegas Battle,A:Major Force	2.50
37 I:New Atomic Skull	2.50
38 RT,A:Red Tornado, Black Racer	2.50
39 RT,A:Red Tornado	2.50
40 RT,V:Kobra	2.50
41 RT,A:Black Racer, Red Tornado	2.50
42 RT,A:Phantom Stranger,Red Tornado,Black Racer, Death from Sandman	2.50
43 RT,V:Nekron	2.50
44 RT,V:Plastique	2.50
45 RT,A:The Ghost,I:Ironfire	2.50
46 RT,A:Superman	2.50
47 RT,A:SupermanV:Ghost	2.50
48 RT,R:Red Tornado	2.50
49 RT,Plastique on trial	2.50
50 RT,V:The Ghost,DoubleSize	3.00
51 RT	2.50
52 RT,Terror on RTE.91	2.50
53 RT,A:Aquaman	2.50
54 RT,A:Rasputin,Shadowstorm	2.50
55 RT,Inside Quantum Field	2.50
56 RT,Quantum Field cont.	2.50

57 RT,V:ShadowStorm, Quantum.Field	2.50
Ann.#1 I:Maj.Force	3.50
Ann.#2 A:RocketRed,Maj.Force	3.50

Captain Carrot #3 © DC Comics Inc.

CAPTAIN CARROT
1982–83

1 RA,A:Superman,Starro	2.50
2 AA	2.50
3 thru 20	@2.50

CAPTAIN STORM
May-June, 1964

1 IN(c),Killer Hunt	150.00
2 IN(c),First Shot-Last Shot	100.00
3 JKu,Death of a PT Boat	100.00
4 IN(c),First Command-Last Command	100.00
5 IN(c), Killer Torpedo	100.00
6 JKu,IN(c),Medals for an Ocean	100.00
7 IN(c),A Bullet For The General	100.00
8 IN(c),Death of A Sub	125.00
9 IN(c),Sink That Flattop	100.00
10 IN(c),Only The Last Man Lives	100.00
11 IN(c),Ride a Hot Torpedo	100.00
12 JKu(c),T.N.T. Tea Party Abroad PT 47	100.00
13 JKu,Yankee Banzai	100.00
14 RH(c),Sink Capt. Storm	100.00
15 IN(c),My Enemy-My Friend	100.00
16 IN(c),Battle of the Stinging Mosquito	100.00
17 IN(c),First Shot for a Dead Man	100.00
18 March-April, 1967	100.00

CARTOON CARTOONS
Jan., 2001

1 thru 33 From TV shows	@2.25
TPB Vol. 1 Name That Toon	7.00
TPB Vol. 2 The Gang's All Here	7.00

CARTOON NETWORK ACTION PACK
May, 2006

1	2.25
2	2.25
3	2.25
4	2.25
5	2.25
6	2.25

CARTOON NETWORK BLOCK PARTY
Sept. 2004

1 thru 2	@2.25
3 thru 26	@2.25
Spec. Jam-Packed Action	8.00
TPB Vol. 1 thru 4	@7.00

CARTOON NETWORK PRESENTS
Warner Bros./DC June, 1997

1 Dexter's Laboratory	4.50
2 thru 24 from TV shows	@2.50

CARTOON NETWORK STARRING
Warner Bros./DC, 1999

1 F:Powerpuff Girls	4.00
2 thru 18 From TV shows	@2.50

CATWOMAN
[Limited Series], 1989

1 O:Catwoman	11.00
2 Catwoman'sSister kidnapped	10.00
3 Battle	9.00
4 Final,V:Batman	9.00

[Regular Series], 1993

0 JBa,O:Catwoman	3.50
1 B:JDy(s),JBa,DG,A:Bane	5.00
2 JBa,DG,A:Bano	3.50
3 JBa,DG,at Santa Prisca	3.00
4 JBa,DG,Bane's Secret	3.00
5 JBa,V:Ninjas	3.00
6 JBa,A:Batman	3.00
7 JBa,A:Batman	3.00
8 JBa,V:Zephyr	3.00
9 JBa,V:Zephyr	3.00
10 JBa,V:Arms Dealer	3.00
11 JBa	3.00
12 JBa,Knights End #6,A:Batman	5.00
13 JBa,Knights End,Aftermath#2	3.00
14 JBa,Zero Hour	3.00
15 JBa,new path	3.00
16 JBa,Island forterss	3.00
17 JBa,Thief of Paris	3.00
18 JBa,Here Comes the Bride	3.00
19 Amazonia	3.00
20 Hollywood	3.00
21 JBa(c&a)V:Movie Monster [new Miraweb format begins]	2.50
22 JBa(c&a) Family Ties,pt.1	2.50
23 Family Ties,pt.2	2.50
24 JBa,Family Ties,pt.3	2.50
25 A:Robin,Psyba-Rats	3.00
26 AIG,JBa,The Secret of the Universe,pt.2 (of 3)	2.50
27 CDi,Underworld Unleashed tie-in	2.50
28 CDi,Catwoman enlists help.	2.50
29 CDi,A:Penguin	2.50
30 CDi,JBa,Great Plane Robbery	2.50
31 CDi,JBa,Flesh and Fire.	3.00
32 CDi,JBa,Contagion,pt.9	3.00
33 CDi,JBa,Hellhound,pt.1	2.50
34 CDi,JBa,Hellbound,pt.2 (of 3)	2.50
35 CDi,JBa	3.00
36 CDi,JBa, Legacy, pt.2 x-over	3.00
37 CDi,JBa, Panara, the Leopard Woman	2.50
38 DgM(s),JBa,MPn,Catwoman, Year One, pt.1 (of 3)	2.50
39 DgM(s),JBa,MPn,Catwoman, Year One, pt. 2	2.50
40 DgM(s),JBa,MPn,Catwoman, Year One, pt. 3	2.50
41 DgM(s),JBa,I:MorelandMcShane	2.50
42 DgM(s),JBa,RedFangClaw,pt.1	2.50
43 DgM(s),JBa,RedFangClaw,pt.2	2.50
44 DgM(s),JBa,Red FangClaw,pt.3	2.50

All comics prices listed are for *Near Mint* condition.

45 DgM(s),JBa,Nine Deaths of
   the Cat. 2.50
46 DgM(s),JBa,F:Two Face,pt.1 . . . 2.50
47 DgM(s),JBa,F:Two Face,pt.2 . . . 2.50
48 DgM(s),JBa,V:Morella,pt.1 . . . . 2.50
49 DgM(s),JBa,V:Morella,pt. 2. . . . 2.50
50 DgM(s),JBa,V:Cybercat 3.00
50a metallic cover, collectors ed.. . 3.00
51 DgM(s),JBa,F:Huntress,pt.1 . . . 2.50
52 DgM(s),JBa,F:Huntress,pt.2 . . . 2.50
53 DgM(s),JBa,F:identity learned . . 2.50
54 JBa,improving security 2.50
55 JBa,Shared Mentality 2.50
56 JBa,Cataclysm x-over,pt.6 . . . . 4.00
57 JBa,Cataclysm, V:Poison Ivy . . . 3.00
58 JBa,F:Scarecrow, pt.1. . . . . . . 2.50
59 JBa,F:Scarecrow, pt.2. . . . . . . 2.50
60 JBa,F:Scarecrow, pt.3. . . . . . . 2.50
61 JBa,Bank robbery 2.50
62 JBa,A:Nemesis 2.50
63 JBa,A:Batman & Joker, pt.1 . . . 2.50
64 JBa,A:Batman & Joker, pt.2 . . . 2.50
65 JBa,A:Batman & Joker, pt.3 . . . 2.50
66 JBa,I'll Take Manhattan,pt.1 . . . 2.50
67 JBa,I'll Take Manhattan,pt.2 . . . 2.50
68 JBa,I'll Take Manhattan,pt.3 . . . 2.50
69 JBa,I'll Take Manhattan,pt.4 . . . 2.50
70 JBa,I'll Take Manhattan,pt.5 . . . 2.50
71 JBa,I'll Take Manhattan,pt.6 . . . 2.50
72 JOs(s),JBa,A:Batman 2.50
73 JOs(s),JBa,No Man's Land. . . . 2.50
74 JOs(s),JBa,No Man's Land. . . . 2.50
75 JOs(s),JBa,No Man's Land. . . . 2.50
76 JOs(s),JBa,No Man's Land. . . . 2.50
77 JOs(s),JBa,No Man's Land. . . . 2.50
78 Plus Ca Change 2.50
79 A:Batman 2.50
80 going to jail 2.50
81 solitary confinement 2.50
82 payback time. 2.50
83 A:Batman, CommissionerGordon 2.25
84 F:Harley Quinn 2.25
85 anger & revenge. 2.25
86 V:Banner. 2.25
87 NSH, from Catwoman's past . . . 2.25
88 V:Banner. 2.25
89 This issue: Batman dies! 2.25
90 Officer Down x-over,pt.4 . . . . . . 2.25
91 Second Catwoman 2.25
92 JFM(s), V:Scarecrow,pt.1 . . . . . 2.25
93 JFM(s), V:Scarecrow,pt.2 . . . . . 2.25
94 JFM(s), final issue. 2.25
Ann.#1 Elseworlds Story,A:Ra's Al
   Ghul. 3.50
Ann.#2 JBa(c&a) Year One Annuals,
   Young Selina Kyle 4.50
Ann.#3 Legends of the Dead Earth . 4.00
Ann.#4 Pulp Heroes (Macabre). . . . 4.50
Spec. Catwoman Defiant,TGr,DG,
   V:Mr.Handsome. 6.00
Spec. Catwoman Plus, LKa,AWi,
   ALa, F:Screamqueen (1997). . . 3.00
Spec.#1,000,000 JBa, on prison
   planet of Pluto 2.00
TPB The Catfile, rep.#15–#19 . . . 10.00

CATWOMAN
Nov., 2001
1 MiA,R:Selina Kyle 7.00
2 MiA,serial murders. 4.00
3 MiA,Selina undercover. 3.00
4 MiA,V:Serial killer. 3.00
5 Selina & Holly 2.50
6 F:Holly 2.50
7 Holly in danger. 2.50
8 RBr,East End's Crooked Cops . . 2.50
9 RBr,Disguises 2.50
10 RBr,Death's Row killer 2.50
11 F:Slam Bradley 2.50
12 F:Slam Bradley, Bruce Wayne . . 2.50
13 F:Slam Bradley, Holly 2.50
14 Holly 2.50

15 V:Black Mask 2.50
16 V:Black Mask 2.50
17 No Easy Way Down,pt.1. . . . . . . 2.50
18 No Easy Way Down,pt.2. . . . . . . 2.50
19 No Easy Way Down,pt.3. . . . . . . 2.50
20 A: Wildcat 2.50
21 V:Captain Cold 2.50
22 V:Captain Cold 2.50
23 Opal City. 2.50
24 Wild Ride, concl. 2.50
25 JP,PG,back to Gotham 2.50
26 JP,PG,kidnapping 2.50
27 JP,PG,F:Batman 2.50
28 JP,PG,V:Penguin 2.50
29 JP,PG 2.50
30 JP,PG,V:Zeiss 2.50
31 JP,PG,Selina Kyle missing 2.50
32 SeP,East End 2.50
33 PG,JP,V:Galante 2.50
34 War Games,Act 1,pt.7,PG,JP . . . 2.50
35 War Games,Act 2,pt.7,PG,JP . . . 2.50
36 War Games,Act 3,pt.7,PG,JP . . . 2.50
37 JP,PG 2.50
38 JP,PG,I:Wooden Nickel 2.50
39 JP,PG,Wooden Nickel,pt.2 . . . . . 2.50
40 JP,PG,Wooden Nickel,pt.3 . . . . . 2.50
41 JP,PG,Immigrants from Brazil . . 2.50
42 JP,PG,Dog fights 2.50
43 RBr,V:Killer Croc. 2.50
44 V:Hush 2.50
45 Selina's new apartment 2.50
46 Deal with Hush 2.50
47 V:Hammer and Sickle 2.50
48 Heart of danger. 2.50
49 V:Black Mask 2.50
50 A:Zatanna 2.50
51 F:Batman 3.50
52 V:Black Mask 3.50
53 Selina Kyle not Catwoman 3.50
54 Holly 2.50
55 New Catwoman in training 3.00
56 A:Wildcat, Angle Man 3.00
57 The Replacements, concl. 3.00
58 F:Zatanna 3.00
59 Baby's Dad, V:Film Freak, ... 3.00
60 Black Mask dead, Holly in Jail . . 3.00
61 V:Film Freak 3.00
TPB The Dark End of the Street . . 13.00
TPB Crooked Little Town. 15.00
TPB Selina's Big Score 15.00
TPB Movie & Other Cat Tales 10.00
TPB 9 Lives of Feline Fatale 15.00
TPB The Dark End of the Street . . 15.00
TPB Relentless 20.00
TPB Wild Ride 15.00
GN Catwoman: The Movie 5.00
Spec. Secret Files #1. . . . . 5.00

CATWOMAN:
GUARDIAN OF GOTHAM
1999
1 (of 2) Elseworlds,V:Bat-Man 6.00
2 DgM,JBa 6.00

CATWOMAN:
WHEN IN ROME
Sept. 2004
1 (of 6) JLb(s),TSe 3.50
2 JLb(s),TSe 3.50
3 JLb,TSe 3.50
4 JLb,TSe,V:Cheetah 3.50
5 JLb,TSe 3.50
6 JLb,TSe,concl. 3.50

CATWOMAN/WILDCAT
June, 1998
1 (of 4) CDi,TP,SCi,BSf,
   V:Claw Hammer 3.00
2 CDi,BSt,TP,SCi,BSf 3.00
3 CDi,BSt,TP,SCi,BSf, ... 3.00

4 CDi,BSt,TP,SCi,BSf 3.00

CENTURIONS
June, 1987
1 DH,V:Doc Terror. 2.50
2 DH,O:Centurions 2.50
3 DH,V:Doc Terror. 2.50
4 DH,Sept., 1987 . . . . 2.50

Chain Gang War #1
© DC Comics, Inc.

CHAIN GANG WAR
1993–94
1 I:Chain Gang 3.00
2 V:8-Ball 2.50
3 C:Deathstroke 2.50
4 C:Deathstroke 2.50
5 Embossed(c),A:Deathstroke 3.00
6 A:Deathstroke,Batman. 2.50
7 V:Crooked Man 2.50
8 B:Crooked Man 2.50
9 V:Crooked Man 2.50
10 A:Deathstroke,C:Batman 2.50
11 A:Batman. 2.50
12 E:Crooked Man,D:Chain Gang,
   Final Issue. 2.50

CHALLENGERS OF
THE UNKNOWN
1958
1 JK&JK(c),The Man Who
   Tampered With Infinity 5,000.00
2 JK&JK(c),The Monster
   Maker 1,600.00
3 JK&JK(c),The Secret of the
   Sorcerer's Mirror. 1,500.00
4 JK,WW,JK(c),The Wizard of
   Time. 1,000.00
5 JK,WW&JK(c),The Riddle of
   the Star-Stone. 1,000.00
6 JK,WW,JK(c),Captives of
   the Space Circus 1,000.00
7 JK,WW,JK(c),The Isle of
   No Return 1,000.00
8 JK,WW,JK&WW(c),The
   Prisoners o/t Robot Planet . 1,000.00
9 The Plot To Destroy Earth 750.00
10 The Four Faces of Doom 750.00
11 The Creatures From The
   Forbidden World 600.00
12 The Three Clues To Sorcery. . 600.00
13 The Prisoner of the
   Tiny Space Ball 600.00
14 O: Multi Man. 600.00
15 Lady Giant and the Beast. . . . 600.00

Challengers of the Unknown #30
© DC Comics Inc.

16 Prisoners of the Mirage World 500.00
17 The Secret of the
     Space Capsules. 500.00
18 Menace of Mystery Island. . . . 500.00
19 The Alien Who Stole a Planet. 500.00
20 Multi-Man Strikes Back. 500.00
21 Weird World That Didn't Exist. 500.00
22 The Thing In
     Challenger Mountain 500.00
23 The Island In The Sky. 200.00
24 The Challengers Die At Dawn 200.00
25 Captives of the Alien Hunter. . 200.00
26 Death Crowns The
     Challenge King 200.00
27 Master of the Volcano Men. . . 200.00
28 The Riddle of the
     Faceless Man 200.00
29 Four Roads to Doomsday. . . . 200.00
30 Multi-Man...Villain Turned
     Hero 200.00
31 O:Challengers. 250.00
32 One Challenger Must Die 150.00
33 Challengers Meet
     Their Master 150.00
34 Beachhead, USA 150.00
35 War Against The Moon Beast. 150.00
36 Giant In Challenger Mountain . 150.00
37 Triple Terror of Mr. Dimension 150.00
38 Menace the Challengers Made 150.00
39 Phantom of the Fair 150.00
40 Super-Powers of the
     Challengers 150.00
41 The Challenger Who Quit. . . . 125.00
42 The League of
     Challenger-Haters 125.00
43 New look begins 125.00
44 The Curse of the Evil Eye. . . . 125.00
45 Queen of the
     Challenger-Haters 125.00
46 Strange Schemes of the
     Gargoyle 125.00
47 The Sinister Sponge 125.00
48 A:Doom Patrol. 125.00
49 Tyrant Who Owned the World 125.00
50 Final Hours for the
     Challengers 125.00
51 A:Sea Devil 125.00
52 Two Are Dead - Two To Go. . . 125.00
53 Who is the Traitor Among Us? 125.00
54 War of the Sub-Humans. 125.00
55 D:Red Ryan. 125.00
56 License To Kill. 125.00
57 Kook And The Kilowatt Killer . 125.00
58 Live Till Tomorrow 125.00
59 Seekeenakee - The Petrified
     Giant 125.00

60 R:Red Ryan 125.00
61 Robot Hounds of Chang. 125.00
62 Legion of the Weird 125.00
63 None Shall Escape the
     Walking Evil. 125.00
64 JKu(c),Invitation to a Hanging 125.00
65 The Devil's Circus. 50.00
66 JKu(c),Rendezvous With
     Revenge 50.00
67 NA(c),The Dream Killers. 50.00
68 NA(c),One of Us is a Madman . 50.00
69 JKu(c),I:Corinna 50.00
70 NA(c),Scream of Yesterdays. . . 50.00
71 NC(c),When Evil Calls 50.00
72 NA(c),A Plague of Darkness. . . 50.00
73 NC(c),Curse of the Killer
     Time Forgot 50.00
74 GT&NA(c),A:Deadman 125.00
75 JK(c),Ultivac Is Loose. 40.00
76 JKu(c),The Traitorous
     Challenger 40.00
77 JK(c),Menace of the
     Ancient Vials 40.00
78 JK(c),The Island of No Return . 40.00
79 JKu(c),The Monster Maker. . . . 40.00
80 NC(c),The Day The Earth
     Blew Up 40.00
81 MN&NA(c),Multi-Man's
     Master Plan 20.00
82 MN&NA(c),Swamp Thing 20.00
83 Seven Doorways to Destiny . . . 20.00
84 To Save A Monster 20.00
85 The Creature From The End
     Of Time 20.00
86 The War At Time's End. 20.00
87 final issue, July, 1978 . . . . 20.00

CHALLENGERS OF THE UNKNOWN
[Mini-Series], 1991
1 BB(c) In The Spotlight 3.00
2 thru 8 . . . . @2.50

CHALLENGERS OF THE UNKNOWN
1997
1 StG(s),JPL 3.00
2 StG(s),LKa,JPL,SMa,Zombies. . . 2.50
3 StG(s),JPL,death of Challenger. . 2.50
4 StG&LKa(s),JPL,SMa,
     O:Challengers 2.50
5 StG&LKa(s)JPL,SMa, V:The
     Fearslayer. 2.50
6 StG(s),JPL,SMa,Convergence
     pt. 3 x-over 2.50
7 StG(s),JPL,PastPerfect,pt.1 . . . . 2.50
8 StG(s),JPL,PastPerfect,pt.2. . . . 2.50
9 StG(s),JPL,PastPerfect,pt.3. . . . 2.50
10 StG(s),JIT,F:Brenda Ruskin . . . 2.50
11 StG(s),JPL,in Gothan, pt.1 . . . . 2.50
12 StG(s),JPL,in Gothan, pt.2 . . . . 2.50
13 StG(s),F:Marlon Corbett 2.50
14 StG(s),Dark Waters. 2.50
15 StG(s),JPL,Millennium Giants
     pt. 3, x-over 2.75
16 StG(s),JPL,MZ, original Chalis . . 2.75
17 StG(s),JPL,disappearances 2.75
18 StG(s),DRo,MZ, final issue. 2.75

CHALLENGERS OF THE UNKNOWN
June 2004
1 (of 6) HC 3.00
2 thru 5 HC . . . . @3.00
6 HC, concl. 3.00
TPB Challengers Must Die 20.00
TPB Stolen Moments, Borrowed
     Time. 17.00

CHASE
Dec., 1997
1 JWi,MGy,from Batman #550 . . . . 2.50
2 JWi,MGy 2.50
3 JWi,MGy,Rocket Reds. 2.50
4 JWi,MGy,F:Teen Titans 2.50
5 JWi,MGy,flashback story 2.50
6 JWi,MGy,Chase's past. 2.50
7 JWi,Shadowing the Bat,pt.1 . . . . 2.50
8 JWi,Shadowing the Bat,pt.2 . . . . 2.50
9 JWi,MBr,MGy,A:Green Lantern . . 2.50
Spec.#1,000,000 Final Issue 2.50

Checkmate #3
© DC Comics Inc.

CHECKMATE
April, 1988
1 From Vigilante & Action Comics . 4.00
2 Chicago Bombings cont. 2.50
3 V:Terrorist Right. 2.50
4 V:Crime Lords Abroad,B.U.Story
     `Training of a Knight' begins . . . 2.50
5 Renegade nation of Quarac 2.50
6 Secret Arms Deal. 2.50
7 Checkmate Invades Quarac 2.50
8 Consequences-Quarac Invasion . 2.50
9 Checkmate's security in doubt. . . 2.50
10 V:Counterfeiting Ring 2.50
11 Invasion X-over. 2.50
12 Invasion Aftermath extra 2.50
13 CommanderH.Stein's vacation . 2.50
14 R:Blackthorn 2.50
15 Janus Directive #1 . . . . 2.50
16 Janus Directive #3 . . . . 2.50
17 Janus Directive #6 . . . . 2.50
18 Janus Directive #9 . . . . 2.50
19 Reorganization of Group. 2.50
20 Shadow of Bishop
     A:Peacemaker,pt.1 . . . . 2.50
21 Peacemaker behind Iron
     Curtain,pt.2 . . . . 2.50
22 Mystery of Bishop Cont.,pt.3 . . . 2.50
23 European Scientists
     Suicides,pt.4 . . . . 2.50
24 Bishop Mystery cont.,pt.5 . . . . . 2.50
25 Bishop's Identity Revealed 2.50
26 Mazarin kidnaps H.Stein's kids . 2.50
27 Stein rescue attempt,I:Cypher . . 2.50
28 A:Cypher, Bishop-Robots 2.50
29 A:Cypher,Blackthorn 2.50
30 Irish Knight W.O'Donnell/British
     Knight L.Hawkins team-up 2.50
31 Patriotic Knights,pt.1. . . . . 2.50
32 Patriotic Knights,pt.2. . . . . 2.50
33 Patriotic Knights,pt.3. . . . . 2.50

CHECKMATE
April, 2006
1 Balance of power 3.00
2 Super-powered nations 3.00
3 F:White Bishop 3.00
4 The Game of Kings 3.00
5 Selection 3.00
6 Suicide Squad returns 3.00
7 Original Suicide Squad member . 3.00
8 Rival agency 3.00

CHILDREN'S CRUSADE
DC/Vertigo, 1993–94
1 NGa(s),CBa,MkB(i),F:Rowland,
　Payne (From Sandman) 4.75
2 NGa(s),AaK(s),JaD(s),PSj,A:Tim
　Hunter,Suzy,Maxine,final issue . 4.50

CHRISTMAS WITH
THE SUPER-HEROES
1988–89
1 JBy(c). 5.00
2 PC,GM,JBy,NKu,DG A:Batman
　Superman,Deadman,(last
　Supergirl appearance) 4.00

Chronos #1
© DC Comics, Inc.

CHRONOS
Jan., 1998
1 JFM,PGn,SL,Time Travel 2.50
2 JFM,PGn,SL 2.50
3 JFM,PGn,SL, in 1873 . . . . 2.50
4 JFM,PGn,SL,in Chronopolis . . . 2.50
5 JFM,PGn,DHz,SL,WalkerGabriel. 2.50
6 JFM,PGn,Tattooed man 2.50
7 JFM,PGn,DRo,SL,Star City 2.50
8 JFM,PGn,DRo,SL,
　V:Metrognomes 2.50
9 JFM(s),PGn,SL, The Man
　Who Chose Not to Exist 2.50
10 JFM(s),PGn,SL,Forever Engin . . 2.50
11 JFM(s),PGn,SL final issue 2.50
Spec.#1,000,000 JFM(s) Steals
　time gauntlets 2.50

CINDER & ASHE
March, 1988
1 JL,I:Cinder & Ashe 2.50
2 JL,Viet Nam Flashbacks 2.50
3 JL,Truth About Lacey revealed . . 2.50
4 JL,final issue, June, 1988 . . . . . . 2.50

CINNAMON: EL CICLO
Aug. 2003
1 (of 5) RbC, New West 2.50
2 thru 5 RbC,HC(c) . . . . @2.50

CLASH
1991
1 AKu,I:Joe McLash(b/w) 5.00
2 AKu,Panja-Rise to Power 5.00
3 AKu,V:Archons,conclusion 5.00

CLAW THE
UNCONQUERED
May-June, 1975
1 ECh,I&O:Claw 15.00
2 ECh 8.00
3 ECh,Bloodspear, nudity panel . . 10.00
4 thru 7 ECh . . . . @8.00
8 KG,Master of the Seventh Void . . 8.00
9 KG/BL,Origin 8.00
10 JKu(c),KG,Eater of Souls 8.00
11 JKu(c),KG,Death at Darkmorn . . 8.00
12 KG/BL,Aug.–Sept., 1978 . . . . . . 8.00

CODENAME: KNOCKOUT
DC/Vertigo, April, 2001
0 sexy spy thriller satire 3.00
1 MFm,JCh,Devil You Say,pt.1 . . . . 3.00
1a variant JCh(c) (1:2) 3.00
2 MFm,JCh,Devil You Say,pt.2 . . . 2.50
3 MFm,Little Orphan Angela 2.50
4 MFm,St. Grace Under Fire 2.50
5 MFm,Arms & Legs for Hostages. 2.50
6 MFm,Arms & Legs for Hostages. 2.50
7 MFm,Go-Go-A-Go-Go 2.50
8 MFm,A is for Anarchy 2.50
9 JP,ACo,Enigma Variations 2.50
10 Undressed to Kill,pt.1 . . . . 2.50
11 Undressed to Kill,pt.2 . . . . 2.50
12 Undressed to Kill,pt.3 . . . . 2.50
13 Fleshback 1932:Roma 2.50
14a JP,JLe(c) 2.50
14b variant JSC(c) 2.50
15 EBe,F:Whole cast 2.50
16 EBe,Amok in America,pt.1 . . . . . 2.75
17 EBe,Amok in America,pt.2 . . . . . 2.75
18 EBe,Amok in America,pt.3 . . . . . 2.75
19 Fleshback '69 . . . . 2.75
20 Rebel Yell 2.75
21 Secrets & Thighs,pt.1 . . . . 2.75
22 Secrets & Thighs,pt.2 . . . . 2.75
23 final issue 2.75

COMET, THE
Impact, 1991–92
1 TL,I&O:Comet 3.00
2 thru 9 TL . . . . @2.50
10 thru 18 . . . . @2.50
Ann.#1 Earthquest,w/trading card . . 2.50

COMIC CAVALCADE
1942–43
1 Green Lantern, Flash,
　Wildcat, Wonder Woman,
　Black Pirate 17,000.00
2 ShM,B:Mutt & Jeff 4,000.00
3 ShM,B:HotHarrigan,Sorcerer 2,700.00
4 Gay Ghost, A:Scribby,
　A:Red Tornado 2,500.00
5 Gr.Lantern,Flash,W.Woman . 2,400.00
6 Flash,W.Woman,Gr.Lantern . 2,000.00
7 A:Red Tornado, E:Scribby . . 2,000.00
8 Flash,W.Woman,Gr.Lantern . 2,000.00
9 Flash,W.Woman,Gr.Lantern . 2,000.00
10 Flash,W.Woman,Gr.Lantern. 2,000.00
11 Flash,W.Woman,Gr.Lantern. 1,500.00
12 E:Red, White & Blue 1,500.00
13 A:Solomon Grundy 2,500.00

14 Flash,W.Woman,Gr.Lantern. 1,500.00
15 B:Johnny Peril 1,500.00
16 Flash,W.Woman,Gr.Lantern. 1,800.00
17 Flash,W.Woman,Gr.Lantern. 1,500.00
18 Flash,W.Woman,Gr.Lantern. 1,500.00
19 Flash,W.Woman,Gr.Lantern. 1,500.00
20 Flash,W.Woman,Gr.Lantern. 1,500.00
21 Flash,W.Woman,Gr.Lantern. 1,500.00
22 A:Atom 1,500.00
23 A:Atom 1,500.00
24 A:Solomon Grundy 2,200.00
25 A:Black Canary 2,000.00
26 ATh, E:Mutt & Jeff 2,000.00
27 ATh,ATh(c) 2,000.00
28 ATh E:Flash, Wonder Woman
　Green Lantern 2,000.00
29 E:Johnny Peril 1,800.00
30 RG,B:Fox & Crow 700.00
31 thru 39 RG . . . . @500.00
40 RG,ShM 300.00
41 thru 49 RG,ShM . . . . @275.00
50 thru 62 RG,ShM . . . . @350.00
63 RG,ShM, July, 1954 . . . . 600.00

Congo Bill #6
© DC Comics, Inc.

CONGO BILL
1954–56
1 NC(c&a),Chota the Chimp . . 2,500.00
2 NC(c&a),Elephants' Grave . . 2,000.00
3 thru 6 NC(c&a) . . . . @1,500.00
7 NC(c&a) . . . . @2,000.00

CONGO BILL
DC/Vertigo, 1999
1 (of 4) RCo(c) 3.00
2 thru 4 . . . . @3.00

CONGORILLA
1992–93
1 R:Congo Bill 2.50
2 thru 4 BB(c),V:Congo Bill . . . . . @2.50

CONJURORS
1999
1 (of 3) CDi(s),EB, Elseworlds 3.00
2 CDi(s),EB 3.00
3 CDi(s),EB 3.00

CONNOR HAWKE:
DRAGON'S BLOOD
Nov., 2006
1 (of 6) CDi 3.00

CONQUEROR OF THE BARREN EARTH
1985
1 RoR,The Ravager 3.00
2 thru 4 RoR . . . . @3.00

COOL WORLD
1992
1 Prequel to Movie 2.25
2 Movie characters 2.25
3 Movie characters 2.25
4 Movie characters 2.25
1-shot Movie Adaptation 3.50

COPS
1988–89
1 PB,O:Cops,double-size 3.50
2 PB,V:Big Boss 2.50
3 PB,RT,V:Dr.Bad Vibes 2.50
4 BS,A:Sheriff Sundown 2.50
5 PB,Blitz the Robo-Dog 2.50
6 PB,A:Ms.Demeaner 2.50
7 PB,A:Tramplor 2.50
8 PB,V:BigBoss & Ally 2.50
9 PB,Cops Trapped 2.50
10 PB,Dr.Bad Vibes becomes
   Dr.Goodvibes 2.50
11 PB,V:Big Boss 2.50
12 PB,V:Dr.Badvibe's T.H.U.G.S . . . 2.50
13 Berserko/Ms.Demeanor
   marriage proposal 2.50
14 A:Buttons McBoom-Boom 2.50
15 Cops vs. Crooks, final issue 2.50

COSMIC BOY
Dec., 1986
1 KG,EC,Legends tie-In 2.50
2 KG,EC,Is History Destiny 2.50
3 KG,EC,Past,Present,Future 2.50
4 KG,EC,Legends 2.50

COSMIC ODYSSEY
1988
1 MMi,A:Superman,Batman,John
   Stewart,Starfire,J'onn J'onzz,
   NewGods,Demon,JSn story . . . 6.00
2 MMi,Disaster'(low dist) 6.00
3 MMi,Return to New Genesis 6.00
4 MMi,A:Dr.Fate, final 6.00
TPB Cosmic Odyssey (2003) 20.00

Creature Commandos #5
© DC Comics Inc.

CREATURE COMMANDOS
March, 2000
1 (of 8) TT,SEa, ... 2.50
2 TT,SEa,V:Saturna 2.50
3 TT,SEa, ... 2.50
4 TT,SEa, ... 2.50
5 TT,SEa,F:Claw 2.50
6 TT,SEa,V:Saturna 2.50
7 TT,SEa,V:Claw 2.50
8 TT,SEa,War Movie, concl. 2.50

CREEPER, THE
Oct., 1997
1 LKa,SMa,SB,R:Creeper 3.00
2 LKa,SMa,SB,A:Dr. Skolos 3.00
3 LKa,SMa,SB,V:Proteus 3.00
4 LKa,SMa,SB 3.00
5 LKa,SMa,SB, new job 3.00
6 LKa,SMa,SB, strange meals 3.00
7 LKa,SMa,SB,F:Joker, pt.1 . . . . . . 3.00
8 LKa,SMa,SB,F:Joker, pt.2 . . . . . . 3.00
9 DAn,ALa,All-star issue 3.00
10 LKa,SB,Jack Ryder 3.00
11 I.Ka,SB,SMa,Creeper splits
   again 3.00
Spec.#1,000,000 LKa,SB,final issue 3.00

CREEPER, THE
Aug., 2006
1 (of 6) F:Jack Ryder 3.00
2 Axeman 3.00
3 Dr. Katz's serum 3.00
4 A:Batman 3.00

CRIMSON AVENGER
1988
1 Mini-series 2.50
2 V:Black Cross 2.50
3 V:Killers of the Dark Cross 2.50
4 V:Dark Cross,final issue 2.50

CRISIS AFTERMATH: THE BATTLE FOR BLUDHAVEN
April, 2006
1 (of 6) JP,DJu 3.00
2 thru 6 JP,DJu . . . . @3.00

CRISIS AFTERMATH: THE SPECTRE
May, 2006
1 (of 3) Spectre has new host 3.00
2 F:Crispus Allen 3.00
3 Crispus Allen becomes Spectre . . 3.00

CRISIS ON INFINITE EARTHS
April, 1985
1 B:MWn(s),GP,DG,I:Pariah,I&O:Alex
   Luthor,D:Crime Syndicate 18.00
2 GP,DG,V:Psycho Pirate,
   A:Joker,Batman 12.00
3 GP,DG,D:Losers 10.00
4 GP,D:Monitor,I:2nd Dr.Light 10.00
5 GP,JOy,I:Anti-Monitor 10.00
6 GP,JOy,I:2nd Wildcat,A:Fawcett,
   Quality & Charlton heroes 10.00
7 GP,JOy,DG,D:Supergirl 25.00
8 GP,JOy,D:1st Flash 22.00
9 GP,JOy,D:Aquagirl 10.00
10 GP,JOy,D:Psimon,A:Spectre . . . 10.00
11 GP,JOy,D:Angle Man 12.00
12 E:MWn(s),GP,JOy,D:Huntress,Kole,
   Kid Flash becomes 2nd Flash,
   D:Earth 2 . . . . 15.00
TPB MWn,GP,DG,JOy,(2001) 30.00

CRISIS ON MULTIPLE EARTHS
July, 2002
TPB Justice League rep. 15.00
TPB Vol. 2 . . . . 15.00
TPB Vol. 3 . . . . 15.00
TPB The Team-Ups 15.00
TPB Vol. 4 . . . . 15.00

CROSSING MIDNIGHT
DC/Vertigo, Nov., 2006
1 . . . . 3.00

CRUCIBLE
Impact, 1993
1 JQ,F:The Comet 2.50
2 thru 6 JQ . . . . @2.50

CRUEL AND UNUSUAL
DC/Vertigo, 1999
1 (of 4) JaD&TPe(s),JMC,satire . . . 3.00
2 thru 4 JaD&TPe(s),JMC . . . . . . @3.00

CRUSADERS
Impact, May, 1992
1 DJu(c),I:Crusaders,inc Trading
   cards 2.50
2 thru 8 . . . . @2.50

CRUSADES, THE
DC/Vertigo, March, 2001
1 KJo,F:Venus 5.00
2 KJo,V:Dark Ages Knight 3.50
3 KJo,MBu,in San Francisco 3.50
4 KJo,MBu,Anton Marx 3.00
5 KJo,Marx eats crow 3.00
6 KJo,second Crusade 3.00
7 KJo,V:The Knight 3.00
8 KJo,Knight's lair 3.00
9 KJo,Godfrey 3.00
10 KJo,sex, sin, subjugation 3.00
11 KJo,origin of the Knight? 3.00
12 KJo,Knight's hidden enclave 3.00
13 KJo,Third Crusade begins 3.00
14 KJo,Ash Wednesday Killer 3.00
15 KJo,Ash Wednesday Killer 3.00
16 KJo,Ash Wednesday Killings . . . 3.00
17 KJo,Venus Kostopikas 3.00
18 KJo,Shockjock Anton 3.00
19 KJo,back to Medieval times 3.00
20 KJo,final issue 3.00
Spec. I:Urban Decree, KJo,48-page . 4.00

CYBERELLA
DC/Helix, Sept., 1996
1 HC(s),DCn, ... 2.25
2 thru 12 HC(s),DCn, ... @2.25

DALE EVANS COMICS
1948–52
1 Ph(c),ATh,B:Sierra Smith . . . 2,700.00
2 Ph(c),ATh 1,300.00
3 ATh 800.00
4 . . . . 425.00
5 . . . . 425.00
6 thru 11 . . . . @425.00
12 thru 20 . . . . @325.00
21 thru 24 . . . . @300.00

DAMAGE
1994–96
1 I:Damage,V:Metallo 4.00
2 Afterschool Special 3.00
3 The Damage Done 3.00
4 Troll's Day,A:Wyldheart 3.00
5 thru 20 . . . . @3.00
Spec. 0 Back Again 3.50

Danger Trail #2
© DC Comics Inc.

DANGER TRAIL
July-Aug., 1950
1 CI,ATh,I:King For A Day 1,700.00
2 ATh, King Faraday 1,200.00
3 ATh, King Faraday 1,800.00
4 ATh, King Faraday 1,200.00
5 March-April, 1951, John
    Pearl 1,200.00

DANGER TRAIL
[Mini-Series], 1993
1 thru 4 CI,FMc,F:King Faraday
    V:Cobra 2.25

DARK MANSION OF
FORBIDDEN LOVE, THE
Sept.–Oct., 1971
1 . . . . 300.00
2 NA(c) 150.00
3 and 4 March-April, 1972 . . . @125.00

DARKSEID VS.
GALACTUS THE HUNGER
1995
1-shot Orion vs. Silver Surfer 5.00
GN JBy,in Apokolips. 6.00

DARKSTARS
1992–96
0 History 2.00
1 TC(c),LSn,I:Darkstars 3.50
2 TC(c),LSn,F:Ferin Colos 2.50
3 LSn,J:Mo,Flint,V:Evil Star 2.50
4 TC,V:Evilstar 3.00
5 TC,A:Hawkman,Hawkwoman . . . 3.00
6 TC,A:Hawkman 2.50
7 TC,V:K'llash 2.50
8 F:Ferris Colos 2.50
9 Colos vs K'llash 2.50
10 V:Con Artists 2.50
11 TC,Trinity#4,A:Green Lantern,
    L.E.G.I.O.N. 2.50
12 TC(c),Trinity#7,A:Green Lantern,
    L.E.G.I.O.N. 2.50
13 thru 38 . . . . @2.50

A DATE WITH JUDY
1947
1 Teen-age 500.00
2 . . . . 350.00
3 . . . . 300.00

---

4 . . . . 300.00
5 . . . . 300.00
6 thru 10 . . . . @300.00
11 thru 20 . . . . @250.00
21 thru 30 . . . . @150.00
31 thru 50 . . . . @125.00
51 thru 78 . . . . @125.00
79 MD 150.00

DAY OF JUDGMENT
Sept., 1999
1 (of 5) Spectre x-over 6.00
2 F:Wonder Woman, Supergirl 5.00
3 F:Superman & Green Lantern . . . 5.00
4 F:Superman's team 5.00
5 conclusion 5.00
Spec. Secret Files #1 . . . . 6.00

DAY OF VENGEANCE
Apr., 2005
1 (of 6) F:Spectre, Enchantress . . . 8.00
1a 2nd printing 5.00
2 WS(c) Shadowpact 3.00
3 WS(c) 2.50
4 WS(c) 2.50
5 WS(c) 2.50
6 WS(c), The Death of Magic 2.50
TPB 13.00
Spec. Infinite Crisis, 48-pg. 4.00

DC CHALLENGE
Nov., 1985
1 GC,Batman 3.00
2 Superman 2.50
3 CI,Adam Strange 2.50
4 GK/KJ,Aquaman 2.50
5 DGb,Dr.Fate,Capt.Marvel 2.50
6 Dr. 13 . . . . 2.50
7 Gorilla Grodd 2.50
8 DG,Outsiders, New Gods 2.50
9 New Teen Titans,JLA 2.50
10 CS,New Teen Titans,JLA 2.50
11 KG,Outsiders 2.50
12 DCw,TMd,DSp,New Teen Titans,
    Oct., 1986 . . . . 2.50

DC COMICS PRESENTS
July-Aug., 1978
[all have Superman]
1 JL,DA,F:Flash 25.00
2 JL,DA,F:Flash 16.00
3 JL,F:Adam Strange 16.00
4 JL,F:Metal Men,A:Mr.IQ 16.00
5 MA,F:Aquaman 8.00
6 CS,F:Green Lantern 8.00
7 DD,F:Red Tornado 8.00
8 MA,F:Swamp Thing 8.00
9 JSon,JA,RH,F:Wonder Woman . . 8.00
10 JSon,JA,F:Sgt.Rock 8.00
11 JSon,F:Hawkman 7.00
12 RB,DG,F:Mr.Miracle 7.00
13 DD,DG,F:Legion 8.00
14 DD,DG,F:Superboy 7.00
15 JSon,F:Atom,C:Batman 7.00
16 JSon,F:Black Lightning 7.00
17 JL,F:Firestorm 7.00
18 DD,F:Zatanna 7.00
19 JSon,F:Batgirl 7.00
20 JL,F:Green Arrow 6.00
21 JSon,JSa,F:Elongated Man 6.00
22 DD,FMc,F:Captain Comet 6.00
23 JSon,F:Dr.Fate 6.00
24 JL,F:Deadman 6.00
25 DD,FMc,F:Phantom Stranger . . . 6.00
26 GP,DG,JSn,I:New Teen Titans,
    Cyborg,Raven,Starfire
    A:Green Lantern 30.00
27 JSn,RT,I:Mongul 7.00
28 JSn,RT,GK,F:Mongul 6.00
29 JSn,RT,AS,F:Spectre 6.00

---

30 CS,AS,F:Black Canary 6.00
31 JL,DG,AS,F:Robin 6.00
32 KS,AS,F:Wonder Woman 6.00
33 RB,DG,AS,F:Captain Marvel . . . 6.00
34 RB,DG,F:Marvel Family 6.00
35 CS,GK,F:Man-bat 6.00
36 JSn,F:Starman 7.00
37 JSn,AS,F:Hawkgirl 6.00
38 GP(c),DH,AS,DG,D:Crimson
    Avenger,F:Flash 6.00
39 JSon,AS,F:PlasticMan,Toyman. . 6.00
40 IN,FMc,AS,F:Metamorpho 6.00
41 JL,FMc,GC,RT,I:New Wonder
    Woman,A:Joker 8.00
42 IN,FMc,F:Unknown Soldier 6.00
43 BB(c),CS,F:Legion 6.00
44 IN,FMc,F:Dial H for Hero 7.00
45 RB,F:Firestorm 6.00
46 AS,I:Global Guardians 6.00
47 CS,I:Masters of Universe 15.00
48 GK(c),AA,IN,FMc,F:Aquaman . . . 5.00
49 RB,F:Shazam!,V:Black Adam . . . 5.00
50 KS,CS,F:Clark Kent 5.00
51 AS,FMc,CS,F:Atom,Masters
    of the Universe 7.00
52 KG,F:Doom Patrol,
    I:Ambush Bug 5.00
53 CS,TD,RA,DG,I:Atari Force 5.00
54 DN,DA,F:Gr.Arrow,Bl.Canary . . . 5.00
55 AS,F:Air Wave,A:Superboy 5.00
56 GK(c),F:Power Girl 5.00
57 AS,FMc,F:Atomic Knights 5.00
58 GK(c),AS,F:Robin,Elongated
    Man 5.00
59 KG,KS,F:Ambush Bug 5.00
60 GK(c),IN,TD,F:Guardians 5.00
61 GP,F:Omac 5.00
62 GK(c),IN,F:Freedom Fighters . . . 5.00
63 AS,EC,F:Amethyst 5.00
64 GK(c),AS,FMc,F:Kamandi 5.00
65 GM,F:Madame Xanadu 5.00
66 JKu,F:Demon 5.00
67 CS,MA,F:Santa Claus 5.00
68 GK(c),CS,MA,F:Vixen 5.00
69 IN,DJ,F:Blackhawk 5.00
70 AS,TD,F:Metal Men 5.00
71 CS,F:Bizarro 5.00
72 AS,DG,F:Phant.Stranger,Joker . . 6.00
73 CI,F:Flash 5.00
74 AS,RT,F:Hawkman 5.00
75 TMd,F:Arion 5.00
76 EB,F:Wonder Woman 5.00
77 CS,F:Forgotten Heroes 5.00
78 CS,F:Forgotten Villains 6.00
79 CS,AW,F:Legion 5.00
80 CS,F:Clark Kent 5.00
81 KG,BO,F:Ambush Bug 5.00
82 KJ,F:Adam Strange 5.00
83 IN,F:Batman/Outsiders 5.00
84 JK,ATh,MA,F:Challengers 7.00
85 RV,AW,AMo(s),
    F:Swamp Thing 7.00
86 Crisis,F:Supergirl 5.00
87 CS,AW,Crisis,I:Earth Prime
    Superboy 5.00
88 KG,Crisis,F:Creeper 5.00
89 MMi(c),AS,F:Omega Men 5.00
90 DCw,F:Firestorm,Capt.Atom 5.00
91 CS,F:Captain Comet. 5.00
92 CS,F:Vigilante 5.00
93 JSn(c),AS,KS,F:Elastic Four 5.00
94 GP(c),TMd,DH,Crisis,F:Lady
    Quark,Pariah,Harbinger 5.00
95 MA(i),F:Hawkman 5.00
96 JSon,KS,F:Blue Devil 5.00
97 RV,F:Phantom Zone Villians,
    final issue,double-sized 5.00
Ann.#1,RB,F:Earth 2 Superman . . . 5.00
Ann.#2 GK(c),KP,I:Superwoman . . . 5.00
Ann.#3 GK,F:Captain Marvel 5.00
Ann.#4 EB,JOy,F:Superwoman 5.00

DC Comics Presents #71
© DC Comics, Inc.

DC COMICS PRESENTS
July 2004
The Atom #1 . . . . 2.50
Batman #1 . . . . 2.50
The Flash #1 . . . . 2.50
Green Lantern #1. . . . . 2.50
Hawkman #1 . . . . 2.50
Justice League of America #1 . . . . . 2.50
Mystery in Space #1 . . . . 2.50
Superman #1 . . . . 2.50

DC COUNTDOWN
March, 2005
1 80-page 1.00

DC/MARVEL:
ALL ACCESS
October 1996
sequel to DC Versus Marvel
1 (of 4) RMz(s),JG,JRu, crossover
 crisis again, 48pg 4.00
2 RMz(s),JG,JRu,F:Jubilee,Robin,
 Daredevil,Two-Face. 3.00
3 RMz(s),JG,JRu,F:Doctor
 Strange, X-Men 3.00
4 RMz(s),JG,JRu,48pg 3.50

DC/MARVEL
CROSSOVER CLASSICS
TPB rep. all x-overs 18.00
TPB Vol. 2 (1998) 15.00
TPB Vol. 4 . . . . 15.00

DC FIRST
May, 2002
Superman/Lobo, 48-pg. 3.50
The Flash/Superman, 48-pg. 3.50
Batgirl/The Joker, 48-pg. 3.50
Green Lantern/Green Lantern 3.50

DC GRAPHIC NOVEL
Nov., 1983
1 JL,Star Raiders 16.00
2 Warlords 16.00
3 EC,Medusa Chain 16.00
4 JK,Hunger Dogs 50.00
5 Me and Joe Priest 16.00
6 Space Clusters. 16.00

DC MILLENNIUM
EDITIONS
Dec., 1999–2000
Action Comics #1. . . . . 4.00
Action Comics #252. . . . . 2.50
Adventure Comics #247 . . . . 2.50
Adventure Comics #761 . . . . 4.00
All-Star Comics #3 . . . . 4.00
All-Star Comics #3, chromium 5.00
All Star Comics #8 . . . . 4.00
All-Star Western #10 . . . . 3.00
Batman #1 . . . . 4.00
Batman #1 chromium. 5.00
Batman: Dark Knight Returns #1. . . 6.00
The Brave and the Bold #28 . . . . . 2.50
The Brave and the Bold #85 . . . . . 2.50
Crisis on Infinte Earths #1 . . . . 2.50
Detective Comics #27 . . . . 4.00
Detective Comics #38 . . . . 4.00
Detective Comics #327 . . . . 2.50
Detective Comics #359 . . . . 2.50
Detective Comics #395 . . . . 2.50
Flash Comics #1 . . . . 4.00
Flash #123 . . . . 2.50
Gen 13 #1 . . . . 2.50
Green Lantern/Green Arrow #76 . . . 2.50
Hellblazer #1 . . . . 3.00
House of Mystery #1 . . . . 2.50
House of Secrets #92 . . . . 2.50
JLA #1 . . . . 2.50
Justice League #1 . . . . 2.50
Justice League #1, chromium 5.00
Kingdom Come #1. . . . . 6.00
The Man of Steel #1 . . . . 2.50
Military Comics #1 . . . . 4.00
More Fun Comics #101 . . . . 3.00
Mysterious Suspense #1 . . . . 2.50
New Gods #1. . . . . 2.50
New Teen Titans #1. . . . . 2.50
Our Army at War #81 . . . . 2.50
Plop! #1 . . . . 2.50
Police Comics #1. . . . . 4.00
Preacher #1 . . . . 3.00
Saga of the Swamp Thing #21 . . . . 2.50
Sandman #1. . . . . 3.00
Sensation Comics #1. . . . . 4.00
The Shadow #1 . . . . 2.50
Showcase #22. . . . . 2.50
Showcase #4 . . . . 2.50
Spirit #1 . . . . 4.00
Superboy #1. . . . . 3.00
Superman #1 . . . . 4.00
Superman #1 Chromium edition . . . 5.00
Superman #76 . . . . 3.00
Superman #75 Death of Superman. 2.50
Superman's Pal Jimmy Olsen #1 . . 2.50
Watchmen #1. . . . . 2.50
Whiz Comics #2. . . . . 4.00
WildC.A.T.S #1. . . . . 2.50
Wonder Woman 1st.Series #1. . . . . 4.00
Wonder Woman #1 . . . . 2.50
World's Finest Comics #71 . . . . 2.50
Young Romance #1, JK, JSm 3.00

DC: THE NEW FRONTIER
Jan. 2004
1 (of 6) Silver age universe 8.00
2 thru 6 . . . . @7.00
TPB Vol. 1 . . . . 20.00
TPB Vol. 2 . . . . 20.00

DC 100-PAGE
SUPERSPECTACULAR
May 2004
Spec. Facsimile edition (2004) 7.00

DC ONE MILLION
1998
1 GMo(s),VS,in 853rd-century 3.00

2 GMo(s),VS,V:Hourman Virus. . . . 2.50
3 GMo(s),VS,V:Solaris 2.50
4 GMo(s),VS,finale 2.50
TPB series rep. 15.00

DC REPLICA EDITIONS
1999–2000
DC 100-Page Super-Spectacular:
 Love Stories 7.00
Justice Society of America
 100-page Super Spectacular #1 7.00
Teen Titans Annual #1 (1967) . . . 5.00
Sgt. Rock's Prize Battle Tales
 80-pg. Giant. 6.00

DC SCIENCE FICTION
GRAPHIC NOVEL
1985–87
1 KG,Hell on Earth 15.00
2 Nightwings 15.00
3 Frost and Fire 15.00
4 Merchants of Venus. 15.00
5 Metalzoic 15.00
6 MR,Demon-Glass Hand. 15.00
7 Sandkings 15.00

DC SPECIAL
Oct.–Dec., 1968
[All reprint]
1 CI,F:Flash,Batman,Adam Strange,
 (#1 thru #21 reps) 125.00
2 F:Teen Titans 150.00
3 GA,F:Black Canary 125.00
4 Mystery 65.00
5 JKu,F:Viking Prince/Sgt.Rock . . 65.00
6 Wild Frontier 65.00
7 F:Strangest Sports Stories. 65.00
8 Joker-Luthor, Incorporated. 65.00
9 F:Strangest Sports Stories. 65.00
10 Stop, You Can't Beat the Law. . 65.00
11 NA,BWr,F:Monsters 65.00
12 JKu,F:Viking Prince 65.00
13 F:Strangest Sports Stories 65.00
14 Wanted,F:Penguin/Joker 60.00
15 GA,F.Plastic Man (1971) 60.00
16 F:Super Heroes & Gorillas 30.00
17 F:Green Lantern 30.00
18 Earth Shaking Stories 30.00
19 F:War Against Gianta 30.00
20 Green Lantern. 30.00
21 F:War Against Monsters 30.00
22 Three Musketeers, Robin Hood 30.00
23 Three Musketeers, Robin Hood 30.00
24 Three Musketeers, Robin Hood 30.00
25 Three Musketeers, Robin Hood 30.00
26 F:Enemy Ace 30.00
27 RB,JR,F:Captain Comet 30.00
28 DN,DA,Earth disasters 30.00
29 JSon,BL,O:JSA. 50.00

DC SPECIAL SERIES
Sept., 1977
1 MN,DD,IN,FMc,JSon,JA,BMc,
 JRu,F:Batman,Flash,Green
 Lantern,Atom,Aquaman. 30.00
2 BWr(c),BWr,F:Swamp
 Thing rep. 15.00
3 JKu(c),F:Sgt.Rock 18.00
4 AN,RT,Unexpected Annual 18.00
5 CS,F:Superman 24.00
6 BMc(i),Secret Society Vs.JLA . . 18.00
7 AN,F:Ghosts 18.00
8 RE,DG,F:Brave&Bold,Deadman 18.00
9 SD,RH,DAy,F:Wonder Woman . 25.00
10 JSon,MN,DN,TA,Secret Origins,
 O:Dr.Fate. 18.00
11 JL,KS,MA,IN,WW,AS,F:Flash . 18.00
12 MK(c),RT,RH,TS,Secrets of
 Haunted House 20.00
13 JKu(c),RT,SBi,RE,F:Sgt.Rock. . 20.00

DC COMICS

14 BWr(c),F:Swamp Thing rep.... 18.00
15 MN,JRu,MR,DG,MGo,
   F:Batman................. 25.00
16 RH,D:Jonah Hex........... 75.00
17 F:Swamp Thing rep......... 12.00
18 JK(c),digest,F:Sgt.Rock rep.... 18.00
19 digest,Secret Origins
   O:Wonder Woman........... 18.00
20 BWr(c),F:Swamp Thing rep.... 12.00
21 FM,JL,DG,RT,DA,F:Batman,
   Legion................. 35.00
22 JKu(c),F:G.I.Combat......... 18.00
23 digest size,F:Flash.......... 18.00
24 F:Worlds Finest............ 18.00
25 F:Superman II,Photo Album ... 18.00
26 RA,F:Superman's Fortress.... 22.00
27 JL,DG,F:Batman vs.Hulk...... 35.00

DC SPECIAL: THE
RETURN OF DONNA TROY
June, 2005

1 (of 4) GP,PJ................. 3.00
2 thru 4 GP,PJ.............. @3.00

DC Super-Star #12
© DC Comics Inc.

DC SUPER-STARS
1976–78

1 F:Teen Titans rep........... 35.00
2 F:DC Super-Stars of Space.... 12.00
3 CS,F:Superman,Legion....... 12.00
4 DC,MA,F:Super-Stars of Space. 12.00
5 CI,F:Flash rep............... 12.00
6 MA,F:Super-Stars of Space.... 12.00
7 F:Aquaman rep............. 12.00
8 CI,MA,F:Adam Strange....... 15.00
9 F:Superman rep............. 12.00
10 DD,FMc,F:Superhero Baseball
   Special,A:Joker.......... 15.00
11 GM,Super-Stars of Magic..... 12.00
12 CS,MA,F:Superboy......... 12.00
13 SA..................... 25.00
14 RB,BL,JA,JRu,Secret Origins. 12.00
15 JKu(c),RB,RT(i),War Heroes .. 12.00
16 DN,BL,I:Star Hunters....... 12.00
17 JSon,MGr,BL,I&O:Huntress,O:Gr.
   Arrow,D:EarthII Catwoman ... 65.00
18 RT,DG,BL,F:Deadman,Phantom
   Stranger................ 20.00

DC TWO THOUSAND
July, 2000

1 (of 2) TPe,VS.............. 7.00
2 TPe,VS,JLA & Golden age JSA . 7.00

DC UNIVERSE
1997–2003

Heroes, Secret Files #1......... 5.00
Villains, Secret Files #1......... 5.00
TPB Christmas, Tyt(c) (2000) 20.00
GN Holiday Bash #1 (1997)...... 4.00
GN Holiday Bash #2 (1998)...... 4.00
GN Holiday Bash #3 (1999)...... 5.00
TPB The DC Universe Stories
   of Alan Moore (2003)........ 20.00

DCU:
BRAVE NEW WORLD
June, 2006

1-shot new projects preview, 80-pg. 1.00

DC UNIVERSE: TRINITY
1993

1 TC,GeH,BKi,F:Darkstars,Green
   Lantern,L.E.G.I.O.N.,V:Triarch . 4.00
2 BKi,SHa,F:Darkstars,Green Lantern,
   L.E.G.I.O.N.,V:Triarch........ 4.00

DC VS. MARVEL
1996

1 RMz..................... 5.50
1 2nd printing............... 4.00
2 & 3 see Marvel
4 PDa..................... 5.00

DEAD BOY DETECTIVES
DIGEST, THE
DC/Vertigo, July, 2005

1 JIT..................... 10.00

DEAD CORPS(E)
DC/Helix, July, 1998

1 StP, C.J.Rataan............. 2.50
2 StP, CJ becomes an expired 2.50
3 StP,Death is not the end....... 2.50
4 StP, conclusion.............. 2.50

DEADENDERS
DC/Vertigo, Jan., 2000

1 WaP,Stealing the Sun,pt.1...... 2.50
2 WaP,Stealing the Sun,pt.2...... 2.50
3 WaP,Stealing the Sun,pt.3...... 2.50
4 WaP,Stealing the Sun,pt.4...... 2.50
5 WaP,Now and Then,pt.1....... 2.50
6 WaP,Now and Then,pt.2....... 2.50
7 WaP,Now and Then,pt.3....... 2.50
8 WaP,scooter races........... 2.50
9 More Fun in New World,pt.1 .... 2.50
10 More Fun in New World,pt.2.... 2.50
11 Sector 9................. 2.50
12 V:Science Corp.............. 2.50
13 Scooter race.............. 2.50
14 Behind the Wheel, pt.1....... 2.50
15 Behind the Wheel, pt.2....... 2.50
16 Behind the Wheel, pt.3....... 2.50
TPB Stealing the Sun.......... 10.00

DEADMAN
May, 1985

1 CI,NA,rep................. 4.00
2 thru 7 NA,rep.............. @3.00

[Mini-Series], 1986

1 JL,A:Batman............... 3.00
2 JL,V:Sensei,A:Batman......... 3.00
3 JL,D:Sensei................ 3.00
4 JL,V:Jonah, final issue........ 3.00

DEADMAN
Dec., 2001

1 SVa(s) F:Boston Brand........ 2.50
2 SVa(s),Sirna................ 2.50

3 SVa(s),F:Duroc, drugs......... 2.50
4 SVa(s),nuclear submarine...... 2.50
5 SVa(s),Death & the Maiden,pt.1 . 2.50
6 SVa(s),Death & the Maiden,pt.2 . 2.50
7 SVa(s),children of Nanda Parbat . 2.50
8 SVa(s),Nanda Parbat,Onyx..... 2.50
9 SVa(s),final issue............ 2.50

DEADMAN
DC/Vertigo, Aug., 2006

1 JWk, F:Brandon Caycs........ 3.00
2 thru 4 JWk................ @3.00

DEADMAN: DEAD AGAIN
Aug., 2001

1 SVa,RBr,A:Flash............ 2.50
2 SVa,RBr,JAp,A:Robin......... 2.50
3 SVa,RBr,A:Superman,Doomsday 2.50
4 SVa,RBr,MBr,A:Green Lantern .. 2.50
5 SVa,RBr,concl.,............. 2.50

DEADMAN: EXORCISM
[Limited-Series], 1992

1 KJo,A:Phantom Stranger....... 5.25
2 KJo,A:Phantom Stranger....... 5.25

DEADMAN: LOST SOULS
TPB MBn, KJo, rep. Exorcism
   and Love After Death....... 20.00

DEADMAN: LOVE
AFTER DEATH
1989–90

1 KJo,Circus of Monsters........ 4.25
2 KJo,Circus of Monsters........ 4.25

DEADSHOT
1988–89

1 LMc,From Suicide Squad...... 2.50
2 LMc,Search for Son.......... 2.50
3 LMc,V:Pantha.............. 2.50
4 LMc,final issue.............. 2.50

DEADSHOT
Dec., 2004

1 (of 5) JP,MZ&JOy(c).......... 3.00
2 JP,A:Green Arrow............ 3.00
3 JP,V:Green Arrow............ 3.00
4 JP,Star City criminals......... 3.00
5 JP,conclusion............... 3.00

DEATH GALLERY
DC/Vertigo

1 DMc(c),NGa Death Sketch
   Various Pinups.............. 3.50

DEATH: THE HIGH
COST OF LIVING
DC/Vertigo, 1993

1 B:NGa(s),CBa,MBu(i),Death
   becomes Human,A:Hettie..... 6.00
1a Platinum Ed................ 50.00
2 CBa,MBu(i),V:Eremite,A:Hettie . 6.00
3 E:NGa(s),CBa,MBu(i),V:Eremite,
   A:Hettie.................. 6.00
3a Error Copy................ 7.00
TPB w/Tori Amos Intro.......... 20.00

DEATH: THE TIME
OF YOUR LIFE
DC/Vertigo, 1995

1 NGa,MBu,four-issue miniseries.. 3.00
2 NGa,MBu,F:Foxglove........ 3.00
3 NGa,MBu,conclusion......... 3.00
TPB NGa(s),rep.............. 13.00

Deathstroke: The Terminator #29
© DC Comics, Inc.

DEATHSTROKE:
THE TERMINATOR
1991–94
1 MZ(c),(from New Teen Titans)
  SE,I:2nd Ravager 4.00
1a Second Printing,Gold. 3.00
2 MZ(c),SE,Quraci Agents 4.00
3 SE,V:Ravager 4.00
4 SE,D:2ndRavager(Jackel) 3.00
5 Winter Green Rescue Attempt. . . 3.00
6 MZ(c),SE,B:City of Assassins,
  A:Batman. 3.00
7 MZ(c),SE,A:Batman. 2.50
8 MZ(c),SE,A:Batman. 2.50
9 MZ(c),SE,E:City of Assassins,
  A:Batman;I:2nd Vigilante 2.50
10 MZ(c),ANi,GP,A:2nd Vigilante. . 2.50
11 MZ(c),ANi,GP,A:2nd Vigilante . . 2.50
12 MGo,Short Stories re:Slade . . . 2.50
13 SE,V:Gr.Lant.,Flash,Aquaman . 2.50
14 ANi,Total Chaos#1,A:New Titans,
  Team Titans,V:Nightwing. 2.50
15 ANi,Total Chaos#4,A:New Titans,
  Team Titans,I:Sweet Lili. 2.50
16 ANi,Total Chaos#7 . . . . 2.50
17 SE,Titans Sell-Out #2
  A:Brotherhood of Evil 2.50
18 SE,V:Cheshire,R:Speedy 2.50
19 SE,V:Broth.of Evil,A:Speedy. . . 2.50
20 SE,MZ(c),V:Checkmate 2.50
21 SE,MZ(c),A:Checkmate 2.50
22 MZ(c),Quality of Mercy#1 . . . . . 2.50
23 MZ(c),Quality of Mercy#2 . . . . . 2.50
24 MZ(c),V:The Black Dome 2.50
25 MZ(c),V:The Black Dome 2.50
26 MZ(c),SE,in Kenya 2.50
27 MZ(c),SE,B:World Tour,
  in Germany 2.50
28 MZ(c),SE,in France. 2.50
29 KM(c),SE,in Hong Kong 2.50
30 SE,A:Vigilante. 2.50
31 SE,in Milwaukie 2.50
32 SE,in Africa. 2.50
33 SE,I:Fleur de Lis. 2.50
34 SE,E:World Tour 2.50
35 V:Mercenaries. 2.50
36 V:British General. 2.50
37 V:Assassin 2.50
38 A:Vigilante. 2.50
39 A:Vigilante. 2.50
40 Wedding in Red 2.50
Ann.#1 Eclipso,A:Vigilante. 4.00
Ann.#2 SE,I:Gunfire. 4.00
Ann.#3 Elseworlds Story 4.25

TPB Full Circle rep#1-#4,
  New Titans#70. . . . . 13.00
Becomes:

DEATHSTROKE:
THE HUNTED
1994–95
0 Slade 2.50
41 Bronze Tiger 2.50
42 Wounded. 2.50
43 . . . . 2.50
44 . . . . 2.50
45 A:New Titans. 2.50
Becomes:

DEATHSTROKE
1995–96
46 Checkmate,Wintergreen 2.50
47 I:New Vigilante 2.50
48 Crimelord/Syndicate War,pt.1 . . 2.50
49 Crimelord/Syndicate War,pt.4
  A:Supergirl, New Titans,
  Hawkman, Blood Pack 2.50
50 A:Titans,Outsiders,Steel 3.50
51 No Fate or Future,pt.1 . . . . 2.50
52 No Fate or Future,pt.2 . . . . 2.50
53 The Borgia Plague,pt.1 . . . . 2.50
54 The Borgia Plague,pt.2 . . . . 2.50
55 MWn,Rebirth?. 2.50
56 MWn,Night of the Karrion,pt.2 . . 2.50
57 . . . . 2.50
58 MWn,V:The Joker. 2.50
59 MWn,F:Hellriders 2.50
60 MWn,final issue 2.50

DEATHWISH
1994–95
1 New mini-series. 2.50
2 F:Rahme 2.50
3 . . . . 2.50
4 V:Boots 2.50

DEMOLITION MAN
1993–94
1 thru 4 Movie Adapt. 2.50

DEMON
[1st Regular Series], 1972–74
1 JK,I:Demon 90.00
2 JK. 45.00
3 JK. 30.00
4 JK. 30.00
5 JK. 30.00
6 thru 16 JK. . . . . @25.00

[Limited Series], 1987
1 MWg,B:Jason Blood's Case 3.00
2 MWg,Fight to Save Gotham 3.00
3 MWg,Fight to Save Gotham 3.00
4 MWg,final issue 3.00

[2nd Regular Series], 1990–95
0 Relationships 2.50
1 VS,A:Etrigan (32 pages) 4.00
2 VS,V:TheCrone 3.00
3 VS,A:Batman. 3.00
4 VS,A:Batman. 3.00
5 VS,ThePit. 3.00
6 VS,In Hell. 3.00
7 VS,Etrigan-King of Hell 3.00
8 VS,Klarion the Witch Boy 3.00
9 VS,Jason Leaves Gotham. 3.00
10 VS,A:PhantomStranger. 3.00
11 VS,A:Klarion,C:Lobo 3.00
12 VS,Etrigan Vs. Lobo 3.00
13 VS,Etrigan Vs. Lobo 3.00
14 VS,V:Odd Squad,A:Lobo 3.00
15 VS,Etrigan Vs.Lobo 3.00
16 VS,Etrigan & Jason Blood
  switch bodies. 3.00
17 VS, War of the Gods x-over 3.00
18 VS,V:Wotan,A:Scape Goat. . . . 3.00

The Demon #31
© DC Comics, Inc.

19 VS,O:Demon,Demon/Lobo
  pin-up. 3.50
20 VS,V:Golden Knight 2.50
21 VS,Etrigan/Jason,
  A:Lobo,Glenda. 2.50
22 MWg,V:Mojo & Hayden 2.50
23 VS,A:Robin 2.50
24 VS,A:Robin 2.50
25 VS,V:Gideon Ryme. 2.50
26 VS,B:America Rules 2.50
27 VS,A:Superman 2.50
28 VS,A:Superman 2.50
29 VS,E:America Rules 2.50
30 R:Asteroth 2.50
31 VS(c),A:Lobo. 2.50
32 VS(c),A:Lobo,W.Woman. 2.50
33 VS(c),A:Lobo,V:Asteroth. 2.50
34 A:Lobo. 2.50
35 A:Lobo,V:Belial 2.50
36 A:Lobo,V:Delial 2.50
37 A:Lobo,Morax 2.50
38 A:Lobo,Morax 2.50
39 A:Lobo. 2.50
40 New Direction,B:GEn(s) 3.50
41 V:Mad Bishop 3.00
42 V:Demons 3.00
43 A:Hitman 10.00
44 V:Gotho-Demon,A:Hitman 15.00
45 V:Gotho-Demon,A:Hitman 15.00
46 R:Haunted Tank 5.00
47 V:Zombie Nazis. 5.00
48 A:Haunted Tank,V:Zombie
  Nazis 5.00
49 b:Demon's Son,A:Joe Gun 2.50
50 GEn(s). 3.00
51 GEn(s),Son & Lovers 2.50
52 Etrigan & son—Hitman. 4.00
53 Glenda & child—Hitman. 4.00
54 Suffer the Children 4.00
55 Rebellion. 2.50
56 F:Etrigan 2.50
57 Last Stand 2.50
58 Last issue 2.50
Ann.#1 Eclipso,V:Klarion 3.25
Ann.#2 I:Hitman 15.00

DEMON, THE:
DRIVEN OUT
Sept. 2003
1 (of 6) ATi,F:Etrigan. 2.50
2 . . . . 2.50
3 . . . . 2.50
4 thru 6 ATi . . . . @2.50

DESPERADOES: QUIET OF THE GRAVE
Homage/DC May, 2001

1 (of 5) JMi,JSe	3.00
2 JMi,JSe	3.00
3 JMi,JSe	3.00
4 JMi,JSe	3.00
5 JMi,JSe, concl.	3.00
TPB JMi,JSe series rep.	15.00

DESTINY: A CHRONICLE OF DEATHS FORETOLD
DC/Vertigo, Sept., 1997

1 (of 3) F:Destiny of the Endless	6.00
2 Destiny of the Endless, pt.2	6.00
3 Destiny of the Endless, pt.3	6.00
TPB series rep.	15.00

DETECTIVE COMICS
March, 1937

1 I:Slam Bradley	100,000.00
2 JoS, Skyscraper Death	35,000.00
3 JoS,A Stowaway in Need	25,000.00
4 JoS,The Rajah's Ruby	12,000.00
5 JoS,Slam Bradley	10,000.00
6 JoS,Speed Saunders	8,000.00
7 JoS,In Atlantic City	7,500.00
8 JoS,Mr. Chang(c)	12,000.00
9 JoS,Case of the Hobo Hero	7,500.00
10 CF,Mystery at Oak Gables.	7,500.00
11 CF,Anarchist Sub Plot	6,500.00
12 CF,Indian Oil Well Mystery	6,500.00
13 CF,Little Tomm Murder Case	6,500.00
14 CF,Mystery of Hondoku Isle.	6,500.00
15 CF,Mystery of Darby Pearls.	6,500.00
16 CF,Case of Missing Corpse.	6,500.00
17 CF,I:Fu Manchu	6,500.00
18 S&S,Fu Manchu(c)	10,000.00
19 FGu,The Grogan Case	6,500.00
20 I:Crimson Avenger	9,000.00
21 FGu,The Glass of Poison	5,000.00
22 S&S,Return of Fui Onyui	6,500.00
23 FGu,The Ski Murder	5,000.00
24 FGu,Persian Jewel Mystery.	5,000.00
25 FGu,The Death Sled	5,000.00
26 FGu,Artists of Death	5,000.00
27 BK,I:Batman.	475,000.00
28 BK,V:Frenchy Blake	45,000.00
29 BK,I:Doctor Death	65,000.00
30 BK,V:Dr. Death.	15,000.00
31 BK,I:Monk	65,000.00
32 BK,V:Monk	13,000.00
33 O:Batman,V:Scarlet Horde	75,000.00
34 V:Due D'Orterre	9,000.00

35 V:Sheldon Lenox	22,000.00
36 I:Hugo Strange	16,000.00
37 V:Count Grutt, last Batman solo	15,000.00
38 I:Robin, the Boy Wonder	100,000.00
39 V:Green Dragon	14,000.00
40 I:Clayface (Basil Karlo)	15,000.00
41 V:Graves	8,000.00
42 V:Pierre Antal	6,500.00
43 V:Harliss Greer	6,500.00
44 Robin Dream Story	6,500.00
45 V:Joker	8,500.00
46 V:Hugo Strange	6,000.00
47 Meets Harvey Midas	6,000.00
48 Meets Henry Lewis	6,000.00
49 V:Clayface	6,000.00
50 V:Three Devils	6,000.00
51 V:Mindy Gang	5,000.00
52 V:Loo Chung	5,000.00
53 V:Toothy Hare Gang	5,000.00
54 V:Hook Morgan	5,000.00
55 V:Dr. Death	5,000.00
56 V:Mad Mack	5,000.00
57 Meet Richard Sneed	5,000.00
58 I:Penguin	9,000.00
59 V:Penguin	4,000.00
60 V:Joker,I:Air Wave	3,500.00
61 The Three Racketeers	3,000.00
62 V:Joker	5,000.00
63 I:Mr. Baffle	3,000.00
64 I:Boy Commandos,V:Joker	8,000.00
65 Meet Tom Bolton	6,000.00
66 I:Two-Face	8,000.00
67 V:Penguin	5,000.00
68 V:Two-Face	3,500.00
69 V:Joker	3,500.00
70 Meet the Amazing Carlo	2,500.00
71 V:Joker	2,700.00
72 V:Larry the Judge	2,200.00
73 V:Scarecrow	2,600.00
74 I:Tweedledum&Tweedledee.	2,500.00
75 V:Robber Baron	2,500.00
76 V:Joker	2,800.00
77 V:Dr. Matthew Thorne	2,600.00
78 V:Baron Von Luger	2,600.00
79 Destiny's Auction	2,600.00
80 V:Two-Face	2,700.00
81 I:Cavalier	1,700.00
82 V:Blackee Blondeen	1,700.00
83 V:Dr. Goodwin	1,800.00
84 V:Ivan Krafft	1,700.00
85 V:Joker	2,200.00
86 V:Gentleman Jim Jewell	1,700.00
87 V:Penguin	1,800.00
88 V:Big Hearted John	1,700.00
89 V:Cavalier	1,700.00
90 V:Capt. Ben	1,700.00
91 V:Joker	2,700.00
92 V:Braing Bulow	1,600.00
93 V:Tiger Ragland	1,600.00
94 V:Lefty Goran	1,600.00
95 V:The Blaze	1,600.00
96 F:Alfred	1,600.00
97 V:Nick Petri	1,600.00
98 Meets Casper Thurbridge	1,600.00
99 V:Penguin	1,600.00
100 V:Digger	1,600.00
101 V:Joe Bart	1,600.00
102 V:Joker	1,600.00
103 Meet Dean Gray	1,600.00
104 V:Fat Frank Gang	1,600.00
105 V:Simon Gurlan	1,600.00
106 V:Todd Torrey	1,600.00
107 V:Bugs Scarpis	1,600.00
108 Meet Ed Gregory	1,600.00
109 V:Joker	5,000.00
110 V:Prof. Moriarty	2,000.00
111 Coaltown, USA	2,000.00
112 Case Without A Crime	2,000.00
113 V:Blackhand	2,000.00
114 V:Joker	2,000.00
115 V:Basil Grimes	2,000.00

116 A:Carter Nichols, Robin Hood	2,000.00
117 Steeplejack's Slowdown.	2,000.00
118 V:Joker	2,500.00
119 V:Wiley Derek	1,500.00
120 V:Penguin	3,000.00
121 F:Commissioner Gordon	1,500.00
122 V:Catwoman	3,000.00
123 V:Shiner	1,300.00
124 V:Joker	1,600.00
125 V:Thinker	1,200.00
126 V:Penguin	1,200.00
127 V:Dr. Agar.	1,200.00
128 V:Joker.	1,600.00
129 V:Diamond Dan Mob	1,500.00
130 BK,V:Briggs Carson	1,500.00
131 V:Trigger Joe	1,500.00
132 V:Human Key.	1,500.00
133 Meets Arthur Loom	1,500.00
134 V:Penguin	1,500.00
135 A:Baron Frankenstein, Carter Nichols.	1,500.00
136 A:Carter Nichols.	1,500.00
137 V:Joker.	1,700.00
138 V:Joker,O:Robotman	1,900.00
139 V:Nick Bailey	1,400.00
140 I:Riddler	7,500.00
141 V:Blackie Nason.	1,400.00
142 V:Riddler	2,000.00
143 V:Pied Piper.	1,200.00
144 A:Kay Kyser (radio personality).	1,200.00
145 V:Yellow Mask Mob	1,200.00
146 V:J.J. Jason	1,200.00
147 V:Tiger Shark.	1,200.00
148 V:Prof. Zero	1,200.00
149 V:Joker.	1,500.00
150 V:Dr. Paul Visio	1,200.00
151 I&O:Pow Wow Smith	1,400.00
152 V:Goblin	1,200.00
153 V:Slits Danton	1,400.00
154 V:Hatch Marlin	1,200.00
155 A:Vicki Vale	1,200.00
156 The Batmobile of 1950	1,200.00
157 V:Bart Gillis	1,200.00
158 V:Dr. Doom	1,200.00
159 V:T. Worthington Chubb.	1,200.00
160 V:Globe-Trotter	1,200.00
161 V:Bill Waters	1,200.00
162 Batman on Railroad.	1,200.00
163 V:Slippery Jim Elgin.	1,200.00
164 Bat-signal story	1,200.00
165 The Strange Costumes of Batman.	1,200.00
166 Meets John Gillen	1,200.00
167 A:Carter Nichols, Cleopatra	1,200.00

168 O:Joker 7,000.00	236 SMo(c),V:Wallace Walby . . 1,000.00	290 SMo,Batman's robot story . . 350.00
169 V:Squint Tolmar 1,200.00	237 SMo(c),F:Robin. 750.00	291 Batman sci-fi story 350.00
170 Batman Teams with Navy	238 SMo(c),V:Checkmate(villain) 750.00	292 Last Roy Raymond 350.00
and Coast Guard 1,200.00	239 SMo(c),Batman robot story . 750.00	293 A:Aquaman,J'onn J'onzz . . . 350.00
171 V:Penguin 1,400.00	240 SMo(c),V:Burt Weaver 750.00	294 V:Elemental Men,
172 V:Paul Gregorian 1,100.00	241 SMo(c),The Rainbow Batman 750.00	A:Aquaman 350.00
173 V:Killer Moth. 1,100.00	242 SMo(c),Batcave story 600.00	295 A:Aquaman 350.00
174 V:Dagger 1,100.00	243 SMo(c),V:Jay Vanney 600.00	296 A:Aquaman 350.00
175 V:Kangaroo Kiloy 1,100.00	244 SMo(c),O:Batarang 600.00	297 SMo,A:Aquaman 350.00
176 V:Mr. Velvet 1,100.00	245 SMo(c),F:Comm.Gordon. . . . 600.00	298 I:Clayface(Matt Hagen). 600.00
177 Bat-Cave Story. 1,000.00	246 SMo(c), ... 600.00	299 Batman sci-fi stories 350.00
178 V:Baron Swane 1,000.00	247 SMo(c),I:Professor Milo 600.00	300 SMo,I:Mr.Polka-dot,
179 Mayor Bruce Wayne 1,000.00	248 Around the World in 8 Days . 600.00	E:Aquaman 300.00
180 V:Joker. 1,000.00	249 V:Collector 600.00	301 A:J'onn J'onzz. 250.00
181 V:Human Magnet. 1,000.00	250 V:John Stannor 600.00	302 A:J'onn J'onzz. 225.00
182 V:Maestro Dorn 1,000.00	251 V:Brand Ballard. 600.00	303 A:J'onn J'onzz. 225.00
183 V:John Cook 1,000.00	252 Batman in a movie 600.00	304 A:Clayface,J'onnJ'onz. 225.00
184 I:Firefly(Garfield Lynns) . . . 1,000.00	253 I:Terrible Trio 600.00	305 Batman sci-fi story 225.00
185 Secrets of Batman's	254 SMo(c),A:Bathound. 600.00	306 A:J'onn J'onzz. 225.00
Utility Belt 1,000.00	255 V:Fingers Nolan 600.00	307 A:J'onn J'onzz. 225.00
186 The Flying Bat-Cave 1,000.00	256 Batman outer-space story. . . 600.00	308 A:J'onn J'onzz. 225.00
187 V:Two-Face 1,000.00	257 Batman sci-fi story 600.00	309 A:J'onn J'onzz. 225.00
188 V:William Milden 1,000.00	258 Batman robot story 600.00	310 A:Bat-Mite,J'onn J'onzz 225.00
189 V:Styx. 1,000.00	259 SMo,I:Calendar Man. 600.00	311 I:Cat-Man,Zook 275.00
190 Meets Dr. Sampson,	260 Batman outer space story. . . 600.00	312 A:Clayface,J'onn J'onzz 200.00
O:Batman 1,200.00	261 I:Dr. Double X 450.00	313 A:J'onn J'onzz. 200.00
191 V:Executioner. 1,000.00	262 V:Jackal-Head. 450.00	314 A:J'onn J'onzz. 200.00
192 V: Nails Riley 1,000.00	263 V:The Professor 450.00	315 I:Jungle Man 200.00
193 V:Joker. 1,000.00	264 Peril at Playland Isle. 450.00	316 A:Dr.Double X,J'onn J'onzz . 200.00
194 V:Sammy Sabre. 1,000.00	265 O:Batman retold 600.00	317 A:J'onn J'onzz. 200.00
195 Meets Hugo Marmon. 1,000.00	266 SMo,V:Astro 450.00	318 A:Cat-Man,J'onn J'onzz 200.00
196 V:Frank Lumardi 1,000.00	267 SMo,I&O:Bat-Mite. 600.00	319 A:J'onn J'onzz. 200.00
197 V:Wrecker 1,000.00	268 V:'Big Joe' Foster 450.00	320 A:Vicki Vale 200.00
198 Batman in Scotland 1,000.00	269 V:Director 450.00	321 I:Terrible Trio 225.00
199 V:Jack Baker 1,000.00	270 Batman sci-fi story 450.00	322 A:J'onn J'onzz. 220.00
200 V:Brand Keldon 1,000.00	271 V:Crimson Knight,O:Martian	323 I:Zodiac Master,
201 Meet Human Target 1,000.00	Manhunter(retold) 450.00	A:J'onn J'onzz 220.00
202 V:Jolly Roger 1,000.00	272 V:Crystal Creature 450.00	324 A:Mad Hatter,J'onn J'onzz . . 220.00
203 V:Catwoman 1,000.00	273 A:Dragon Society 400.00	325 A:Cat-Man,J'onn J'onzz 220.00
204 V:Odo Neral 1,000.00	274 V:Nails Lewin 400.00	326 Batman sci-fi story 220.00
205 O:Bat-Cave 1,000.00	275 SMo,A:Zebra-Man. 400.00	327 CI,25th ann,symbol change . 250.00
206 V:Trapper. 1,000.00	276 A:Batmite. 400.00	328 D:Alfred,I:WayneFoundation. 250.00
207 Meets Merko the Great . . . 1,000.00	277 Batman Monster story. 400.00	329 A:Elongated Man 220.00
208 V:Groff 1,000.00	278 A:Professor Simms 400.00	330 "Fallen Idol of Gotham". 220.00
209 V:Inventor. 1,000.00	279 Batman robot story 400.00	331 A:Elongated Man 220.00
210 V:Brain Hobson 1,000.00	280 A:Atomic Man 400.00	332 A:Joker 150.00
211 V:Catwoman. 1,000.00	281 Batman robot story 350.00	333 CK(c),A:Gorla 150.00
212 Meets Jonathan Bard. 1,000.00	282 Batman sci-fi story 350.00	334 Man Who Stole from Batman 150.00
213 O:Mirror-Man 1,000.00	283 V:Phantom of Gotham City . . 350.00	335 CI,Trail of the Talking Mask . 150.00
214 The Batman Encyclopedia. 1,000.00	284 V:Hal Durgan 350.00	336 CI,V:Outsider. 150.00
215 I:Ranger, Legionairy, Gaucho &	285 V:Harbin 350.00	337 CI,Deep Freeze Menace. . . . 150.00
Musketeer,A:Knight & Squire	286 A:Batwoman 350.00	338 CI,Power-Packed Punch. . . . 150.00
(See: World's Finest 89) 900.00	287 SMo,A:Bathound. 350.00	339 CI,V:Living Beast-Bomb 150.00
216 A:Brane Taylor 900.00	288 V:Multicreature 350.00	340 CI,Outsider Strikes Again . . . 150.00
217 Meets Barney Barrows 900.00	289 SMo,A:Bat-Mite. 350.00	341 A:Joker 150.00
218 V:Dr. Richard Marston 900.00		342 CI,Raid of the Robin Gang . . 150.00
219 V:Marty Mantee. 900.00		343 BK,CI,Elongated Man 130.00
220 A:Roger Bacon, historical		344 CI,I&V:Johnny Witts 150.00
scientist/philosopher 900.00		345 CI,I:Blockbuster. 150.00
221 V:Paul King 900.00		346 Inescapable Doom-Trap 150.00
222 V:'Big Jim' Jarrell 900.00		347 CI,Elongated Man 150.00
223 V:'Blast' Varner 900.00		348 Elongated Man 150.00
224 The Batman Machine 900.00		349 BK(c),CI,Blockbuster. 150.00
225 I&O:Martian Manhunter		350 Elongated Man 150.00
(J'onn J'onzz) 10,000.00		351 CI,A:Elongated Man,
226 O:Robin's costume,		I:Cluemaster 150.00
A:J'onn J'onzz 2,500.00		352 BK,Elongated Man 150.00
227 A:Roy Raymond, J'onn		353 V:Weather Wizard. 150.00
J'onzz 1,000.00		354 BK,Elongated Man,I:Dr.
228 A:Roy Raymond, J'onn		Tzin-Tzin 150.00
J'onzz 1,000.00		355 CI,Elongated Man. 150.00
229 A:Roy Raymond, J'onn		356 BK,Outsider,Alfred 150.00
J'onzz 1,000.00		357 CI,Wayne Unmasks Batman. 150.00
230 A:Martian Manhunter,		358 BK,Elongated Man 150.00
I:Mad Hatter 1,100.00		359 CI,I:new Batgirl 250.00
231 A:Batman,Jr.,Roy Raymond		360 Case of Abbreviated Batman 135.00
J'onn J'onzz. 750.00		361 CI,Double-Deathtrap. 135.00
232 A:J'onn J'onzz. 1,000.00		362 CI,Elongated Man 135.00
233 SMo(c),I&O:Batwoman . . . 2,400.00		363 CI,Elongated Man 135.00
234 SMo(c),V:Jay Caird. 750.00		364 CI,BK,Elongated Man 135.00
235 SMo(c),O:Batman's	*Detective Comics #291*	365 CI,A:Joker 135.00
Costume. 1,100.00	*© DC Comics Inc.*	366 CI,Elongated Man 135.00

DC COMICS

367 CI,Elongated Man 135.00
368 CI,BK,Elongated Man 135.00
369 CA,Elongated Man,
   Catwoman 200.00
370 NA,BK,Elongated Man 175.00
371 CI,BK,Elongated Man 200.00
372 NA,BK,Elongated Man 125.00
373 BK,Elongated Man 125.00
374 BK,Elongated Man 125.00
375 CI,Elongated Man 125.00
376 Batman–Hunted or Haunted . 125.00
377 MA,Elongated Man,
   V:Riddler 125.00
378 Elongated Man 125.00
379 CI,Elongated Man 125.00
380 Elongated Man 125.00
381 GaF,Marital Bliss Miss 125.00
382 FR(s),BbB,JoG,GaF(s),SGe . 125.00
383 FR(s),BbB,JoG,GaF(s),SGe . 125.00
384 FR(s),BbB,JoG,GaF(s),SGe,
   BU:Batgirl 125.00
385 E:FR(s),BbB,JoG,NA(c&a),GK,
   MA,MkF,BU:Batgirl 125.00
386 BbK,MkF,BbB,JoG,
   BU:Batgirl 125.00
387 RA,rep.Detective #27 . . . . . 150.00
388 JBr(s),BbB,JoG,
   GK,MA,FR(s) 150.00
389 NA,FR(s),BbB,JoG,GK,MA . . 125.00
390 FR(s),BbB,JoG,GK,MA,
   A:Masquerader 125.00
391 FR(s),NA(c),BbB,
   JoG,GK,MA 100.00
392 FR(s),BbB,JoG,I:Jason Bard . 100.00
393 FR(s),BbB,JoG,GK,MA 100.00
394 FR(s),BbB,JoG,GK,MA 100.00
395 FR(s),NA,DG,GK,MA 125.00
396 FR(s),BbB,JoG,GK,MA 100.00
397 DON(s),NA,DG,GK,MA 125.00
398 FR(s),BbB,JoG,GK,ViC 100.00
399 NA(c),DON(s),BbB,JoG,
   GK,ViC,Robin 125.00
400 FR(s),NA,DG,GK,I:Man-Bat . 200.00
401 NA(c),FR(s),JoG,
   BbB,JoG,GK,ViC 75.00
402 FR(s),NA,DG,V:Man-Bat 100.00
403 FR(s),BbB,JoG,NA(c),GK,ViC,
   BU:Robin 100.00
404 NA,GC,GK,A:Enemy Ace . . . 110.00
405 IN,GK,I:League of Assassins . 100.00
406 DON(s),BbB,FrG 100.00
407 FR(s),NA,DG,V:Man-bat 110.00
408 MWn(s),LWn(s),NA,DG,
   V:DrTzin Tzin 110.00
409 B:FR(s),BbB,FrG,DH,DG 80.00
410 DON(s),FR(s),NA,DG,DH . . . 80.00
411 NA(c),DON(s),BbB,DG,DH . . . 70.00
412 NA(c),BbB,DG,DH 70.00
413 NA(c),BbB,DG,DH 70.00
414 DON(s),IN,DG,DH 75.00
415 BbB,DG,DH 75.00
416 DH 75.00
417 BbB,DG,DH,BU:Batgirl 75.00
418 DON(s),DH,IN,DG,A:Creeper . 75.00
419 DON(s),DH 75.00
420 DH 75.00
421 DON(s),BbB,DG,DH,A:Batgirl . 70.00
422 BbB,DG,DH,Batgirl 70.00
423 BbB,DG,DH 70.00
424 BbB,DG,DH,Batgirl 70.00
425 BWr(c),DON(s),IN,DG,DH . . . 70.00
426 LWn(s),DG,A:Elongated Man . 70.00
427 IN,DG,DH,BU:Batgirl 50.00
428 BbB,DG,ENB(s),DD,JoG,
   BU:Hawkman 50.00
429 DG,JoG,V:Man-Bat 50.00
430 BbB,NC,ENS(s),DG,
   A:Elongated Man 50.00
431 DON(s),IN,MA 50.00
432 MA,A:Atom 50.00
433 DD,DG,MA 50.00
434 IN,DG,ENB(s),RB,DG 50.00

435 E:FR(s),DG,IN 50.00
436 MA,(i),DG,A:Elongated Man . . 50.00
437 JA,WS,I:Manhunter 85.00
438 JA,WS,Manhunter 100.00
439 DG,WS,O:Manhunter,Kid
   Eternity rep. 100.00
440 JAp,WS 100.00
441 HC,WS 100.00
442 ATh,WS 100.00
443 WS,D:Manhunter 100.00
444 JAp,B:Bat-Murderer,
   A:Ra's Al Ghul 100.00
445 JAp,MGr,A:Talia 100.00
446 JAp,last giant 30.00
447 DG(i),A:Creeper 30.00
448 DG(i),E:Bat-Murderer,
   A:Creeper,Ra's Al Ghul 30.00

Detective Comics #422
© DC Comics, Inc.

449 Midnight Rustler in Gotham . . 30.00
450 TA,WS 30.00
451 TA 30.00
452 ECh,V:The Crime Exchange . . 30.00
453 ECh,V:The Crime Exchange . . 30.00
454 ECh,The Set-Up Caper 30.00
455 MGr,A:Hawkman,V:Vampire . . 30.00
456 V:Ulysses Vulcan 30.00
457 O:Batman rtd 30.00
458 A:Man Bat 30.00
459 A:Man Bat 30.00
460 I:Capt.Stingaree 30.00
461 V:Capt.Stingaree 25.00
462 V:Capt.Stingaree,A:Flash 25.00
463 TA,MGr,Atom,I:Calc.,Bl.Spider 25.00
464 MGr,BlackCanary 25.00
465 TA,Elongated Man 25.00
466 MR,TA,V:Signalman 35.00
467 MR,TA,RB 35.00
468 MR,TA,A:JLA 35.00
469 WS,I:Dr.Phosphorus 25.00
470 WS,AM,V:Dr.Phosphorus 25.00
471 MR,TA,A:Hugo Strange 35.00
472 MR,TA,A:Hugo Strange 35.00
473 MR,TA,R:Deadshot 35.00
474 MR,TA,A:Penguin,
   N:Deadshot 35.00
475 MR,TA,A:Joker 75.00
476 MR,TA,A:Joker 75.00
477 MR,DG,rep.NA 35.00
478 MR,DG,TA,I:3rd Clayface 35.00
479 MR,DG,A:3rd Clayface 35.00
480 DN,MA 25.00
481 JSt,CR,DN,DA,MR,
   A:ManBat 30.00
482 HC,MGo,DG,A:Demon 27.00

483 DN,DA,SD,A:Demon,
   40 Anniv. 25.00
484 DN,DA,Demon,O:1st Robin . . 25.00
485 DN,DA,D:Batwoman,A:Demon
   A:Ras al Ghul 25.00
486 DN,DA,DG,I:Odd Man,
   V:Scarecrow 25.00
487 DN,DA,A:Ras Al Ghul 25.00
488 DN,V:Spook,Catwoman 25.00
489 IN,DH,DN,DA,Ras Al Ghul . . . 25.00
490 DN,DA,PB,FMc,A:Black
   Lightning;A:Ras Al Ghul 25.00
491 DN,DA,PB,FMc,A:Black
   Lightning;V:Maxie Zeus 25.00
492 DN,DA,A:Penguin 25.00
493 DN,DA,A:Riddler 25.00
494 DN,DA,V:Crime Doctor 25.00
495 DN,DA,V:Crime Doctor 25.00
496 DN,DA,A:Clayface I 15.00
497 DN,DA. 15.00
498 DN,DA,V:Blockbuster 15.00
499 DN,DA,V:Blockbuster 15.00
500 DG,CI,WS,TY,JKu,Deadman,
   Hawkman,Robin 25.00
501 DN,DA. 15.00
502 DN,DA. 15.00
503 DN,DA,Batgirl,Robin,
   V:Scarecrow 15.00
504 DN,DA,Joker. 20.00
505 DN,DA,RB. 15.00
506 DN,DA,RB. 15.00
507 DN,DA,RB. 15.00
508 DN,DA,V:Catwoman 17.00
509 DN,DA,V:Catman,Catwoman . 17.00
510 DN,DA,V:Madhatter 15.00
511 DN,DA,RB,I:Mirage 15.00
512 GC,45th Anniv. 15.00
513 RB,V:Two-Face 17.00
514 RB. 15.00
515 RB. 15.00
516 RB. 15.00
517 The Monster in the Mirror 15.00
518 RB,V:Deadshot 15.00
519 Dreadnought in the Sky 15.00
520 A:Hugo Strange,
   Catwoman 17.00
521 IN,TVE,A:Catwoman,B:
   BU:Green Arrow 20.00
522 D:Snowman 15.00
523 V:Solomon Grundy 15.00
524 2nd A:J.Todd. 17.00
525 J.Todd 15.00
526 DN,AA,A:Joker,Catwoman
   500th A:Batman 30.00
527 V:Man Bat 7.00
528 Green Arrow,Ozone 7.00
529 I:Night Slayer,Nocturna 7.00
530 V:Nocturna 7.00
531 GC,AA,Chimera,J.Todd (see
   Batman #364) 7.00
532 GC,Joker. 9.00
533 Look to the Mountaintop 7.00
534 GC,A:Gr.Arrow,V:PoisonIvy . . . 7.00
535 GC,A:Gr.Arrow,V:Crazy Quitt
   2nd A:New Robin. 9.00
536 GC,A:Gr.Arrow,V:Deadshot . . . 7.00
537 GC,A:Gr.Arrow 7.00
538 GC,A:Gr.Arrow,V:Catman 7.00
539 GC,A:Gr.Arrow 7.00
540 GC,A:Gr.Arrow,V:Scarecrow . . . 7.00
541 GC,A:Gr.Arrow,V:Penguin. 7.00
542 GC,A:Gr.Arrow 9.00
543 GC,A:Gr.Arrow,V:Nightslayer . . 7.00
544 GC,A:Gr.Arrow,V:Nightslayer . . 7.00
545 By Darkness Masked 7.00
546 Hill's Descent 7.00
547 PB,KJ 7.00
548 PB,Beasts A-Prowl 7.00
549 PB,KJ,AMo(s),Gr.Arrow 9.00
550 KJ,AMo(s),Gr.Arrow 9.00
551 PB,V:Calendar Man 7.00
552 V:Black Mask 7.00

Detective Comics #468
© DC Comics, Inc.

553 V:Black Mask 7.00
554 KJ,N:Black Canary 7.00
555 GC,DD,GreenArrow 7.00
556 GC,Gr.Arrow,V:Nightslayer 7.00
557 V:Nightslayer 7.00
558 GC,Green Arrow 7.00
559 GC,Green Arrow 7.00
560 GC,A:Green Arrow 7.00
561 GC,Flying Hi 7.00
562 GC,V:Film Freak 7.00
563 V:Two Face 7.00
564 V:Two Face 7.00
565 GC,A:Catwoman 9.00
566 GC,Joker 10.00
567 GC,HarlanEllison 7.00
568 KJ,Legends tie-in,A:Penguin . . 9.00
569 AD,V:Joker 9.00
570 AD,EvilCatwoman,A:Joker 9.00
571 AD,V:Scarecrow 7.00
572 AD,CI,A:Elongated Man,Sherlock
    Holmes,SlamBradley,50thAnn. 10.00
573 AD,V:Mad Hatter 7.00
574 AD,End old J.Todd/Robin sty . . 7.00
575 AD,Year 2,pt.1,I:Reaper 25.00
576 TM,AA,Year 2,pt.2,
    R:Joe Chill 25.00
577 TM,AA,Year 2,pt.3,V:Reaper. . 25.00
578 TM,AA,Year 2,pt.4,
    D:Joe Chill 25.00
579 I:NewCrimeDoctor. 6.00
580 V:Two Face 6.00
581 V:Two Face 6.00
582 Millennium X-over 6.00
583 I:Ventriloquist 6.00
584 V:Ventriloquist 6.00
585 I:Rat Catcher 6.00
586 V:Rat Catcher 6.00
587 NB,V:Corrosive Man 6.00
588 NB,V:Corrosive Man 6.00
589 Bonus Book #5 . . . . 6.00
590 NB,V:Hassan 6.00
591 NB,V:Rollo 6.00
592 V:Psychic Vampire 6.00
593 NB,V:Stirh 6.00
594 NB,A:Mr.Potato 6.00
595 IN,bonus book #11 . . . . 6.00
596 V:Sladek 6.00
597 V:Sladek 6.00
598 DCw,BSz,Blind Justice #1 . . . . 7.00
599 DCw,BSz,Blind Justice #2 . . . . 7.00
600 DCw,BSz,Blind Justice #3,
    50th Anniv.(double size) 7.00
601 NB,I:Tulpa 4.00
602 NB,A:Jason Blood 3.00

603 NB,A:Demon 3.00
604 NB,MudPack #1,V:Clayface,
    poster insert. 3.00
605 NB,MudPack #2,V:Clayface . . . 3.00
606 NB,MudPack #3,V:Clayface . . . 3.00
607 NB,MudPack #4,V:Clayface,
    poster insert. 3.00
808 NB,I:Anarky 3.00
609 NB,V:Anarky 3.00
610 NB,V:Penguin 4.00
611 NB,V:Catwoman,Catman 4.00
612 NB,A:Vicki Vale 3.00
613 Search for Poisoner 3.00
614 V:Street Demons 3.00
615 NB,Return Penguin #2 (see
    Batman #448-#449). 3.50
616 NB 3.00
617 A:Joker 3.00
618 NB,DG,A:Tim Drake 3.00
619 NB,V:Moneyspider 3.00
620 NB,V:Obeah,Man 3.00
621 NB,SM,Obeah,Man. 3.00
622 Demon Within,pt.1 . . . . 3.00
623 Demon Within,pt.2 . . . . 3.00
624 Demon Within,pt.3 . . . . 3.00
625 JAp,I:Abattior 3.00
626 JAp,A:Electrocutioner 3.00
627 600th issue w/Batman,rep.
    Detective #27 . . . . 5.00
628 JAp,A:Abattoir 3.00
629 JAp,The Hungry Grass 3.00
630 JAp,I:Stiletto 3.00
631 JAp,V:Neo-Nazi Gangs 3.00
632 JAp,V:Creature 3.00
633 TMd,Fake Batman? 3.00
634 The Third Man 3.00
635 Video Game,pt.1 . . . . 3.00
636 Video Game,pt.2 . . . . 3.00
637 Video Game,pt.3. . . . . 3.00
638 JAp,Walking Time Bomb. 3.00
639 JAp,The Idiot Root,pt.2 . . . . 3.00
640 JAp,The Idiot Root,pt.4 . . . . 3.00
641 JAp,Destroyer,pt.3
    (see LOTDK#27) 3.00
642 JAp,Faces,pt.2 . . . . 3.00
643 JAp,Librarian of Souls 3.00
644 TL,Electric City,pt.1
    A:Electrocutioner 3.00
645 TL,Electric City,pt.2 . . . . 3.00
646 TL,Electric City,pt.3. . . . . 3.00
647 TL,V:Cluemaster,I:Spoiler 15.00
648 MWg(c),TL,V:Cluemaster 10.00
649 MWg(c),TL,V:Cluemaster 10.00
650 TL,A:Harold,Ace 3.00
651 TL,A Bullet for Bullock 3.00
652 GN,R:Huntress 3.00
653 GN,A:Huntress 3.00
654 MN,The General,pt.1 . . . . 3.00
655 MN,The General,pt.2 . . . . 3.00
656 MN,The General,pt.3,C:Bane . . 4.00
657 MN,A:Azrael,I:Cypher 5.00
658 MN,A:Azrael 3.50
659 MN,Knightfall#2,
    V:Ventriloquist,A:Bane 3.50
660 Knightfall#4,Bane Vs.
    Killer Croc 3.00
661 GN,Knightfall#6,V:Firefly,
    Joker,A:Bane 3.00
662 GN,Knightfall#8,V:Firefly,
    Joker,A:Huntress,Bane 3.00
663 GN,Knightfall#10,V:Trogg,
    Zombie,Bird,A:Bane 3.00
664 GN,Knightfall#12,A:Azrael 3.00
665 GN,Knightfall#16,A:Azrael 3.00
666 GN,SHa,A:Azrael,Trogg,
    Zombie,Bird 3.00
667 GN,SHa,Knightquest:Crusade,
    V:Trigger Twins 3.00
668 GN,SHa,Knightquest:Crusade,
    Robin locked out of Batcave . . . 3.00
669 GN,SHa,Knightquest:Crusade,
    V:Trigger Twins 3.00

Detective Comics #675
© DC Comics, Inc.

670 GN,SHa,Knightquest:Crusade,
    F:Rene Montoya 3.00
671 GN,SHa,V:Joker 3.00
672 KJ(c),GN,SHa,Knightquest:
    Crusade,V:Joker 3.00
673 KJ(c),GN,SHa,Knightquest:
    Crusade,V:Joker 3.00
674 KJ(c),GN,SHa,Knightquest:
    Crusade. 3.00
675 Foil(c),KJ(c),GN,SHa,Knightquest:
    Crusade,V:Gunhawk,foil(c) 4.00
675a Newsstand ed. 3.00
675b Platinum edition 5.00
676 KJ(c),GN,SHa,Knights End #3,
    A:Nightwing 4.00
677 KJ(c),GN,SHa,Knights End #9
    V:Azrael 3.00
678 GN,SHa,Zero Hour 3.00
679 Ratcatcher. 3.00
680 Batman,Two-Face. 3.00
681 CDi,GN,KJ,Jean-Paul Valley . . 3.00
682 CDi,GN,SHa,Return of Bruce
    Wayne,Troika,pt.3 . . . . 3.00
682a Collector's Edition 3.50
683 R:Penguin,I:Actuary 3.00
684 Daylight Heist 3.00
685 Chinatown War 3.00
686 V:King Snake,Lynx 3.00
687 CDi,SHa,V:River Pirate. 3.00
688 V:Captian Fear 3.00
689 F:Black Mask,Firefly 3.00
690 F:Black Mask,Firefly 3.00
691 V:Spellbinder 3.00
692 CDi,SHa,Underworld
    Unleashed tie-in 3.00
693 CDi,SHa,V:Poison Ivy
    & Agent Orange. 3.00
694 CDi,find plant-killer 3.00
695 CDi 3.00
696 CDi,GN,SHa,Contagion,pt.8 . . . 3.00
697 CDi,GN,SHa,pt.1 (of 3)
    V:Lock-up 3.00
698 CDi(s),A:Two-Face 3.00
699 CDi(s),. 3.00
700 double size, Legacy, pt.1
    x-over, R:Bane. 3.50
700a cardstock cover. 6.00
701 Legacy, pt. 6 x-over, V:Bane. . . 3.00
702 CDi(s),GN,SHa,Legacy
    aftermath 3.00
703 CDi(s),GN,SHa, riots in Gotham
    City, Final Night tie-in 3.00
704 CDi(s),GN,TP,V:Al Gabone. . . . 3.00

All comics prices listed are for *Near Mint* condition.

705 CDi(s),GN,Riddler & Cluemaster
    clash 3.00
706 CDi(s),GN 3.00
707 CDi(s),GN,Riddler/Cluemaster
    concl. 3.00
708 CDi(s),GN,BSz,F:Deathstroke,
    R:Gunhawk, pt.1 (of 3) 3.00
709 CDi(s),GN,BSz,F:Deathstroke,
    Gunhawk,pt.2 . . . . 3.00
710 CDi(s),GN,BSz,F:Deathstroke,
    Gunhawk,pt.3 . . . . 3.00
711 CDi(s),GN,CaS,Bruce Wayne
    fights crime 3.00
712 CDi(s),GN,I:Gearhead 3.00
713 CDi(s),GN,V:Gearhead,pt.2 . . . 3.00
714 CDi(s),GN,F:MartianManhunter 3.00
715 CDi(s),GN,F:MartianManhunter 3.00
716 CDi,JAp,SNw,BSf 3.00
717 CDi,GN,BSf,V:Gearhead,pt.1 . . 3.00
718 CDi,GN,BSf,V:Gearhead,pt.2 . . 3.00
719 CDi,JAp,BSz,Sound & Fury . . . 3.00
720 CDi,GN,KJ,Cataclysm
    x-over,pt.5 . . . . 4.00
721 CDi,GN,KJ,Cataclysm. 3.00
722 CDi,JAp,BSf,Aftershock 3.00
723 CDi,BSz,Brotherhood of
    the Fist x-over, pt.2 . . . . 3.00
724 CDi,JAp,BSf,F:Nightwing 3.00
725 CDi,TP,BSf,Aftershock 3.00
726 CDi(s),BSf,V:Joker 3.00
727 CDi,SB,Road to No Man's Land 3.00
728 CDi(s),BSf,SB,No Man's Land . 3.00
729 CDi(s),SB,No Man's Land. 3.00
730 No Law and a New Order,
    concl. 5.00
731 F:Batgirl, Mosaic, pt.2 . . . . 3.00
732 F:Batgirl, Mosaic, pt.4 . . . . 3.00
733 SB,Alfreds advice 3.00
734 F:Batgirl,pt.2 x-over 3.00
735 DJu,BSz,Fruit of
    the Earth,pt.3 . . . . 3.00
736 LHa(s),MD2,V:Bane 3.00
737 TMo, No Man's Land,
    The Code, concl. 3.00
738 CDi,MtB,Goin'Downtown,pt.2 . 3.00
739 Jurisprudence,concl. 3.00
740 Shellgame,pt.2 . . . . 3.00
741 Endgame, pt.3,40-pg.x-over . . 3.00
742 SMa,40-pg. 3.00
743 SMa,40-pg,new logo 3.00
744 SMa,40-pg. 3.00
745 SMa,V:Whisperer 3.00
746 SMa,B.U.:The Jacobian 3.00
747 JJ,F:Renee Montoya 3.00
748 JJ,Urban Renewal,pt.1 . . . . 3.00
749 JJ,PhH,Urban Renewal,pt.2 . . . 3.00
750 V:Ra's Al Ghul,64-pg. 6.00
751 SMa,JJ,DPS,F:Poison Ivy 4.00
752 SMa,JJ,DPs,F:Poison Ivy 3.00
753 SMa,JJ,DPs,This issue:
    Batman dies! 3.00
754 Officer Down x-over,pt.6 . . . . . 3.00
755 SMa,DPs,V:Two-Face. 3.00
756 Lord of the Ring x-over,pt.2 . . 3.00
757 RBr,RyR,DPs,Air Time 3.00
758 SMa,Crooked Cops in Gotham. 3.00
759 SMa,BU:Catwoman,pt.1 . . . . . . 3.00
760 SMa,V:Mad Hatter,BU:pt.2 . . . 3.00
761 SMa,BU:Catwoman,pt.3 . . . . . . 3.00
762 RBr,BU:Catwoman,concl. 3.00
763 SMa,F:Sasha,V:Cucilla 3.00
764 SMa,F:Vesper 3.00
765 RBr,James Gordon 3.00
766 Bruce Wayne:Murderer,pt.1 . . . 3.00
767 Bruce Wayne:Murderer,pt.8 . . . 5.00
768 MGy,shipment of heroin 3.00
769 Bruce Wayne:Fugitive,pt.5 . . . . 3.00
770 Bruce Wayne:Fugitive,pt.8 . . . . 3.00
771 BruceWayne:Fugitive,pt.12. . . . 3.00
772 BruceWayne:Fugitive,pt.16. . . . 2.75
773 F:Sasha Bordeaux in prison . . . 2.75
774 BSz(c),Checkmate 2.75

775 BSz(c),V:Checkmate 48-pg. . . . 3.50
776 BWi,A cop's vendetta 2.75
777 Dead Reckoning,pt.1 . . . . 2.75
778 Dead Reckoning,pt.2 . . . . 2.75
779 Dead Reckoning,pt.3 . . . . 2.75
780 Dead Reckoning,pt.4 . . . . 2.75
781 Dead Reckoning,pt.5 . . . . 2.75
782 Dead Reckoning,pt.6 . . . . 2.75
783 SMa,KJ,More Perfect 2.75
784 Made of Wood,pt.1 . . . . 2.75
785 Made of Wood,pt.2 . . . . 2.75
786 Made of Wood,pt.3 . . . . 2.75
787 RBr,Low,Mad Hatter,Man-Bat . 2.75
788 Randori Stone, pt.1 . . . . 2.75
789 Randori Stone, pt.2 . . . . 2.75
790 CaS,Scarification 2.75
791 CaS,The Surrogate,pt.1 . . . . . . 2.75
792 CaS,The Surrogate,pt.2 . . . . . . 2.75
793 CaS,The Surrogate,pt.3 . . . . . . 3.00
794 CaS,The Rotting,pt.1 . . . . 3.00
795 CaS,The Rotting,pt.2 . . . . 3.00
796 CaS,Mr.Zsasz 3.00
797 War Games,Act 1,pt.1,40-pg. . . 3.00
798 War Games,Act 2,pt.1,40-pg. . . 3.00
799 War Games,Act 3,pt.1,40-pg. . . 3.00
800 DL,CaS,48-page 3.50
801 DL,NMa,City of Crime,pt.1 . . . 3.00
802 DL,NMa,City of Crime,pt.2 . . . 3.00
803 DL,NMa,City of Crime,pt.3 . . . 3.00
804 DL,NMa,City of Crime,pt.4 . . . 3.00
805 DL,NMa,City of Crime,pt.5. . . .3.00
806 DL,NMa,City of Crime,pt.6 . . . 3.00
807 DL,NMa,City of Crime,pt.7 . . . 3.00
808 DL,NMa,City of Crime,pt.8 . . . 3.00
809 War Crimes, x-over, pt.1 . . . . . 3.00
810 War Crimes, x-over, pt.3 . . . . . 3.00
811 DL,NMa,City of Crime,pt.9 . . . 3.00
812 DL,NMa,City of Crime,pt.10 . . 3.00
813 DL,NMa,City of Crime, pt. 11 . . 2.50
814 DL,NMa,City of Crime,pt. 12. . . 2.50
815 Victims,pt.1 . . . . 2.50
816 Victims,pt.2 . . . . 2.50
817 Face the Face, pt.1, x-over. . . . 2.50
818 Face the Face, pt.3, x-over. . . . 2.50
819 Face the Face, pt.5, x-over. . . . 3.00
820 Face the Face, pt.7, x-over. . . . 3.00
821 PDi,JWi, V:Facade 3.00
822 PDi,JWi,F:The Riddler 3.00
823 PDi,F:Poison Ivy 3.00
824 PDi,Night of the Penguin 3.00
825 F:Doctor Phosphorous 3.00
Ann.#1 KJ,TD,A:Question,Talia,
    V:Penguin 6.00
Ann.#2 VS,A:Harvey Harris 6.00
Ann.#3 DJu,GB,Batman in Japan . . 2.50
Ann.#4 Armageddon,pt.10 . . . . 3.00
Ann.#5 SK(c),TMd,Eclipso,V:The
    Ventriloquist,Joker 3.00
Ann.#6 JBa,I:Geist. 2.75
Ann.#7 CDi,Elseworlds Story 3.25
Ann.#8 CDi,KD(c) Year One Annual
    O:The Riddler 4.00
Ann.#9 Legends o/t Dead Earth . . . 3.00
Ann.#10 Pulp Heroes (War) CDi(s),
    SB,KJ. 4.00
Spec.#1,000,000 CDi(s). 2.00
TPB Manhunter AGw,WS 10.00
TPB Batman: City of Crime 20.00

DETENTION COMICS
Aug., 1996
one-shot DON(s) 64pg, 3 stories. . . 3.50

DEVLIN WAUGH
Feb., 2005
TPB Red Tide, 2000 A.D. 20.00

DEXTER'S LABORATORY
Warner Bros./DC, 1999
1 Kirbytron 6000 . . . . 5.00
2 Let's Save the World, You Jerk . . 4.00

3 thru 10 . . . . @3.00
11 thru 24 . . . . @2.50
25 thru 34 . . . . @2.25

DISAVOWED
Homage/DC Jan., 2000
1 BCi. 2.50
2 thru 6 BCi(s). . . . . @2.50

DMZ
DC/Vertigo, Nov., 2005
1 by Brian Wood 3.00
2 Through War-torn Manhattan . . . 3.00
3 Matty captured by Gov. Army . . . 3.00
4 In Central Park. 3.00
5 Interview with tribal boss 3.00
6 Body of a Journalist, pt.1 . . . . . . 3.00
7 Body of a Journalist, pt.2 . . . . . . 3.00
8 Body of a Journalist, pt.3 . . . . . . 3.00
9 Body of a Journalist, pt.4 . . . . . . 3.00
10 Body of a Journalist, pt.5 . . . . . 3.00
11 Origin of Zee 3.00
12 A Guide to the DMZ 3.00
13 Public Works, pt.1 . . . . 3.00
TPB Vol. 1 On the Ground. 10.00

Doc Savage #1
© DC Comics Inc.

DOC SAVAGE
1987–88
1 AKu/NKu,D:Orig. Doc Savage . . . 3.00
2 AKu/NKu,V:Nazi's 3.00
3 AKu/NKu,V:Nazi's 3.00
4 AKu/NKu,V:Heinz. 3.00

[2nd Series], 1988–90
1 Five in the Sky'(painted cov.). . . . 3.00
2 Chip Lost in Himalayas 3.00
3 Doc declares war on USSR. 3.00
4 Doc Savage/Russian team-up. . . 3.00
5 V:The Erisians 3.00
6 U.S.,USSR,China Alliance
    vs. Erisians 3.00
7 Mind Molder,pt.1, I:Pat Savage . . 3.00
8 . . . . 3.00
9 In Hidalgo. 3.00
10 V:Forces of the Golden God. . . . 3.00
11 Sunlight Rising,pt.1. . . . . 3.00
12 Sunlight Rising,pt.2. . . . . 3.00
13 Sunlight Rising,pt.3. . . . . 3.00
14 Sunlight Rising,pt.4. . . . . 3.00
15 SeaBaron #1. . . . . 3.00
16 EB,Shadow & Doc Savage. 3.50
17 EB,Shadow & Doc Savage. 4.00
18 EB,Shadow/Doc Savage conc. . . 4.00
19 All new 1930's story 3.00

Doctor Fate #26 © DC Comics Inc.

20 V:Airlord & his Black Zepplin . . . 3.00
21 Airlord (30's story conc.) 3.00
22 Doc Savages Past,pt.1 . . . . 3.00
23 Doc Savages Past,pt.2 . . . . 3.00
24 Doc Savages Past,pt.3 (final) . . . 3.00
Ann.#1 1956 Olympic Games 4.50

DOCTOR FATE
July, 1987
1 KG,V:Lords of Chaos 3.00
2 KG,New Dr. Fate 3.00
3 KG,A:JLI 3.00
4 KG,V:Lords of Chaos Champion . 3.00

[2nd Series], 1988–92
1 New Dr.Fate,V:Demons 4.00
2 A:Andrew Bennett(I,Vampire) . . . 3.00
3 A:Andrew Bennett(I,Vampire) . . . 3.00
4 V:I,Vampire 3.00
5 Dr.Fate & I,Vampire in Europe . . . 3.00
6 A:Petey 3.00
7 Petey returns home dimension . . 3.00
8 Linda become Dr.Fate again 3.00
9 Eric's Mother's Ghost,
    A:Deadman 3.00
10 Death of Innocence,pt.1 . . . . . . 3.00
11 Return of Darkseid, Death of
    Innocence,pt.2 . . . . 3.00
12 Two Dr.Fates Vs.Darkseid,
    Death of Innocence,pt.3 . . . . . . 3.00
13 Linda in the Astral Realm,
    Death of Innocence,pt.4 . . . . . . 3.00
14 Kent & Petey vs. Wotan 3.00
15 V:Wotan,A:JLI 3.50
16 Flashback-novice Dr.Fate 2.50
17 Eric's Journey thru afterlife 2.50
18 Search for Eric 2.50
19 A:Dr.Benjamine Stoner, Lords of
    Chaos, Phantom Stranger,
    Search for Eric continued 2.50
20 V:Lords of Chaos,Dr.Stoner,
    A:Phantom Stranger 2.50
21 V:Chaos,A:PhantomStranger . . . 2.50
22 A:Chaos and Order 2.50
23 Spirits of Kent & Inza Nelson . . . 2.50
24 L:Dr.Fate Characters 2.50
25 I:New Dr. Fate 2.50
26 Dr.Fate vs. Orig.Dr.Fate 2.50
27 New York Crime 2.50
28 Diabolism 2.50
29 Kent Nelson 2.50
30 Resurrection 2.50
31 Resurrection' contd. 2.50
32 War of the Gods x-over 2.50
33 War of the Gods x-over 2.50

34 A:T'Gilian 2.50
35 Kent Nelson in N.Y. 2.50
36 Search For Inza,A:Shat-Ru 2.50
37 Fate Helmet Powers revealed . . 2.50
38 The Spirit Motor,'Flashback 2.50
39 U.S.Senate Hearing 2.50
40 A:Wonder Woman 2.50
41 O:Chaos and Order,last issue . . 2.50
Ann.#1 TS,R:Eric's dead mother . . . 3.00

DR. FATE
Aug. 2003
1 (of 5) Hector Hall 2.50
2 Salem mystics 2.50
3 Nabu disappeared 2.50
4 The Curse 2.50
5 Concl. 2.50

DOCTOR MID-NITE
1999
1 (of 3) MWg,F:Dr. Piter Cross 6.00
2 MWg 6.00
3 MWg, conclusion 6.00
TPB 20.00

DOOM FORCE
1992
Spec.#1 MMi(c),RCa,WS,PCu,KSy,
    I:Doom Force 3.00

DOOM PATROL
[1st series]
**See: MY GREATEST
ADVENTURE**

DOOM PATROL
[2nd Regular Series], 1987
1 SLi,R:Doom Patrol,plus Who's Who
    background of team, I:Kalki 5.00
2 SLi,V:Kalki 3.50
3 SLi,I:Lodestone 3.50
4 SLi,I:Karma 3.50
5 SLi,R:Chief 3.50
6 B:PuK(s),EL,GyM(i),
    I:Scott Fischer 4.50
7 EL,GyM(i),V:Shrapnel 3.50
8 EL,GyM(i),V:Shrapnel 3.50
9 E:PuK(s),EL,GyM(i),V:Garguax,
    & Bonus Book 3.50
10 EL,A:Superman 3.50
11 EL,R:Garguax 3.00
12 EL,A:Garguax 3.00
13 EL,A:Power Girl 3.00
14 EL,A:Power Girl 3.00
15 EL,Animal-Veg-.Mineral Man . . . 3.00
16 V:GenImmotus,Animal-Veg.-
    Mineral Man 3.00
17 D:Celsius,A:Aquaman & Sea
    Devils, Invasion tie-in 4.00
18 Invasion 3.00
19 B:GMo(s),New Direction,
    I:Crazy Jane 18.00
20 I:Rebis(new Negative-Being),
    A:CrazyJane,Scissormen 10.00
21 V:Scissormen 10.00
22 City of Bone,V:Scissormen 10.00
23 A:RedJack,Lodestone kidnap . . . 5.00
24 V:Red Jack 5.00
25 Secrets of New Doom Patrol . . . 5.00
26 I:Brotherhood of Dada 4.00
27 V:Brotherhood of Dada 4.00
28 Trapped in nightmare,V:Dada . . 4.00
29 Trapped in painting,
    A:Superman 4.00
30 SBs(c),V:Brotherhood of Dada . . 4.00
31 SBs(c),A:The Pale Police 4.00
32 SBs(c),V:Cult of
    Unwritten Book 4.00

33 SBs(c),V:Cult,A:Anti-God
    the DeCreator 4.00
34 SBs(c),Robotman vs. his brain,
    R:The Brain & Mr.Mallah 4.00
35 SBs(c),A:Men from
    N.O.W.H.E.R.E. 15.00
36 SBs(c),V:Men from
    N.O.W.H.E.R.E. 22.00
37 SBs(c),Rhea Jones Story 4.00
38 SBs(c),V:Aliens 4.00
39 SBs(c),V:Aliens 4.00
40 SBs(c),Aliens 4.00
41 SBS(c),Aliens 4.00
42 O:Flex Mentallo 25.00
43 SBs(c),V:N.O.W.H.E.R.E. 12.00
44 SBs(c),V:N.O.W.H.E.R.E. 12.00
45 SBs(c),The Beard Hunter 7.00
46 SBs(c),RCa,MkK,A:Crazy Jane,
    Dr.Silence 5.00
47 Scarlet Harlot (Crazy Jane) 4.00
48 V:Mr.Evans 4.00
49 TTg(c),RCa,MGb,I:Mr.Nobody . . 4.00
50 SBs(c),V:Brotherhood of Dada
    & bonus artists portfolio 4.00
51 SBs(c),Mr.Nobody Runs for
    President 4.00
52 SBs(c),Mr.Nobody saga conc . . . 4.00
53 SBs(c),Parody Issue,A:Phantom
    Stranger,Hellblazer,Mr.E 4.00
54 Rebis Transformation 4.00
55 SBs(c),V:Crazy Jane,
    Candle Maker 4.00
56 SBs(c),RCa,V:Candle Maker . . . 4.00
57 SBs(c),RCa,V:Candle Maker,
    O:Team,Double-sized 4.00
58 SBs(c),V:Candle Maker 4.00
59 TTg(c),RCa,SnW(i),A:Candlemaker
    D:Larry Trainor 4.00
60 JHw(c),RCa,SnW(i),
    V:Candlemaker,A:Magnus 4.00
61 TTg(c),RCa,SnW(i),A:Magnus
    D:Candlemaker 4.00
62 DFg(c),RCa,SnW(i),
    V:Nanomachines 4.00
63 E:GMo(s),RCa,R:Crazy Jane,
    V:Keysmiths,BU:Sliding from the
    Wreckage 4.00

DC/Vertigo, 1993
64 BB(c),B:RaP(s),RCa,SnW(i),
    B:Sliding from the Wreckage,
    R:Niles Caulder 3.00
65 TTg(c),RCa,SnW(l),Nannos 3.00
66 RCa,E:Sliding from the
    Wreckage 3.00

Doom Patrol #14 © DC Comics, Inc.

67 TTg(c),LiM,GHi(i),New HQ,I:Charlie,
   George,Marion,V:Wild Girl. . . . 3.00
68 TTg(c),LiM,GHi(i),I:Indentity
   Addict. 3.00
69 TTg(c),LiM,GHi(i),V:Identity
   Addict. 3.00
70 TTg(c),SEa,TS(i),I:Coagula,
   V:Codpiece 3.00
71 TTg(c),LiM,TS(i),Fox & Crow . . . 3.00
72 TTg(c),LiM,TS(i),Fox vs Crow. . . 3.00
73 LiM,GPi(i),Head's Nightmare . . . 3.00
74 LiM,TS(i),Bootleg Steele. 3.00
75 BB(c),TMK,Teiresias Wars#1,
   Double size 3.00
76 Teiresias Wars#2 . . . . 3.00
77 BB(c),TMK,N:Cliff 3.00
78 BB(c),V:Tower of Babel. 3.00
79 BB(c),E:Teiresias Wars. 3.00
80 V:Yapping Dogs 3.00
81 B:Masquerade. 3.00
82 E:Masquerade. 3.00
83 False Memory. 3.00
84 The Healers 3.00
85 Charlie the Doll 3.00
86 Imagine Ari's Friends 3.00
87 KB(c),final issue 3.00
Ann.#1 A:Lex Luthor 3.00
Ann.#2 RaP(s),MkW,Children's
   Crusade,F:Dorothy,A:Maxine . . 4.25
Doom Patrol/Suicide Squad #1 EL,
   D:Mr.104,Thinker,Psi,Weasel . . 2.50
TPB SBs(c),rep.#19-#25 . . . . 20.00

DOOM PATROL
Oct., 2001
1 JAr,R:Doom Patrol. 3.00
2 JAr,F:Robotman, Thayer 3.75
3 JAr,V:Gomz 2.50
4 JAr,new Doom Patrol?. 2.50
5 JAr,Doom Force. 2.50
6 JAr,Robotman gone. 2.50
7 JAr,search for Robotman. 2.50
8 JAr,new Robotman 2.50
9 JAr,Cliff Steele, Robotman. 2.50
10 JAr,Black Vulture,Amazo 2.50
11 JAr,in Hell 2.50
12 JAr,V:Demon Raum 2.50
13 JAr(s),Monsters,pt.1 . . . . 2.50
14 JAr(s),Monsters,pt.2 . . . . 2.50
15 JAr(s),F:Robotman 2.50
16 JAr(s),V:Purple Purposeless. . . 2.50
17 JAr(s),R:Tycho 2.50
18 JAr(s),ancient China 2.50
19 JAr(s),R:Tycho 2.50
20 television studios 2.50
21 O:Tycho. 2.50
22 final issue 2.50

DOOM PATROL
July 2004
1 JBy,DHz,V:Crucifer 2.50
2 JBy,DHz,escaped specimens . . . 2.50
3 JBy,DHz,Cold Night's Death 2.50
4 JBy,DHz,Waters Under World . . . 2.50
5 JBy,DHz 2.50
6 JBy,DHz,Robot Wars,pt.2 . . . . . . 2.50
7 JBy,DHz,V:Devolutionists,pt.1 . . 2.50
8 JBy,DHz,V:Devolutionists,pt.2 . . 2.50
9 JBy,DHz,V:Negative Man. 2.50
10 JBy,DHz,F:Metamorpho 2.50
11 JBy,DHz,F:Metamorpho 2.50
12 JBy,DHz,F:Metamorpho 2.50
13 JBy,DHz,time travel technology . 2.50
14 JBy,TA,alternate realities 2.50
15 JBy,DHz,hospital patients dead . 2.50
16 JBy,DHz,F:Nudge 2.50
17 JBy,DHz,Negative Man. 2.50
18 JBy,DHz,final issue. 2.50
TPB Crawling From the Wreckage 20.00
TPB Painting That Ate Paris 20.00
TPB Vol. 3 Down Paradise Way . . 20.00

TPB Musclebound 20.00

DOOMSDAY
1995
Ann.#1 Year One annuals 4.00

DOORWAY TO NIGHTMARE
1978
1 I:Madame Xanadu 20.00
2 thru 5 . . . . @15.00

DOUBLE ACTION COMICS
Jan., 1940
2 Pre-Hero DC. 27,000.00

DRAGONLANCE
1988–91
1 Krynn's Companion's advent. . . . 4.00
2 thru 7 . . . . @3.50
8 thru 34. . . . . @3.00
Ann.#1 Myrella of the Robed
   Wizards 3.00

DREAMING, THE
DC/Vertigo, June, 1996
1 TLa(s),PSj,GoldieFactor,pt.1 . . . . 4.50
2 TLa(s),PSj,GoldieFactor,pt.2 . . . . 4.00
3 TLa(s),PSj,GoldieFactor,pt.3 . . . . 4.00
4 SvP,The Lost Boy,pt.1 . . . . 3.50
5 SvP,The Lost Boy,pt.2 . . . . 2.50
6 SvP,The Lost Boy,pt.3 . . . . 2.50
7 SvP,The Lost Boy,pt.4 . . . . 2.50
8 AaK(s),MZi,visitor from past 2.50
9 BT(s),PD,TOz,Weird Romance,
   pt.1. . . . . 2.50
10 BT(s),PD,TOz,Romance,pt.2 . . . 2.50
11 BT(s),PD,TOz,Romance,pt.3 . . . 2.50
12 BT(s),PD,TOz,Romance,pt.4 . . . 2.50
13 TLa,JIT,Coyote's Kiss,pt.1. . . . . 2.50
14 TLa,JIT,Coyote's Kiss,pt.2. . . . . 2.50
15 . . . . 2.50
16 GyA,F:Nuala 2.50
17 PD,DMc,Souvenirs, pt.1 . . . . . . 2.50
18 PD,DMc,Souvenirs,pt.2 . . . . 2.50
19 PD,DMc,Souvenirs, pt.3 . . . . . . 2.50
20 ADv, The Dark Rose, pt.1 . . . . . 2.50
21 ADv, The Dark Rose, pt.2. . . . . . 2.50
22 The Unkindness of One, pt.1 . . . 2.50
23 The Unkindness of One, pt.2 . . . 2.50
24 The Unkindness of One, pt.3 . . . 2.50
25 My Life as a Man 2.50
26 Restitution 2.50
27 Caretaker Cain 2.50
28 Victims of famous fires 2.50
29 PSj,DMc,Abel'sHouse ofSecrets. 2.50
30 DMc(c),Lucien's mysteries 2.50
31 House of Secrets, 48-pg. 4.00
32 DG,SvP 2.50
33 The Little Mermaid 2.50
34 MaH, Cave of Nightmares 2.50
35 DMc(c),Kaleidoscope 2.50
36 DMc(c),The Gyres, pt.1 . . . . 2.50
37 DMc(c),The Gyres, pt.2 . . . . 2.50
38 DMc(c),The Gyres, pt.3 . . . . 2.50
39 DMc(c),Lost Language
   of Flowers 2.50
40 DMc(c),Foxes & Hounds,pt.1 . . 2.50
41 DMc(c),Foxes & Hounds,pt.2 . . 2.50
42 DMc(c),Foxes & Hounds,pt.3 . . 2.50
43 DMc(c),Foxes & Hounds,pt.4 . . 2.50
44 Trinket,pt.1 . . . . 2.50
45 Trinket,pt.2 . . . . 2.50
46 Trinket,pt.3 . . . . 2.50
47 CV,RoR 2.50
48 DMc(c),Scary Monsters 2.50
49 DMc(c),The Dawn Stone 2.50
50 DMc(c),rebuilding 2.50

Dreaming #44
© DC Comics, Inc.

51 DMc(c),in Manhattan 2.50
52 Exiles,pt.1 . . . . 2.50
53 Exiles,pt.2 . . . . 2.50
54 Exiles,pt.3 . . . . 2.50
55 F:Danny Nod. 2.50
56 1stAdventure of CatterinaPoe. . . 2.50
57 Rise,pt.1 . . . . 2.50
58 Rise,pt.2 . . . . 2.50
59 Rise,pt.3 . . . . 2.50
60 Rise,pt.4 . . . . 2.50
TPB Beyond the Shores of Night. . 20.00
TPB Through the Gates of
   Horn & Ivory 20.00
GN Trial and Error 6.00

DYNAMIC CLASSICS
Sept-Oct., 1978
1 NA,WS,rep.Detective 395&438 . 15.00

ECLIPSO
1992–94
1 BS,MPn,V:South American
   Drug Dealers. 2.50
2 BS,MPn,A:Bruce Gordon. 2.25
3 BS,MPn,R:Amanda Waller 2.25
4 BS,A:Creeper,Cave Carson. 2.25
5 A:Creeper,Cave Carson 2.25
6 LMc,V:Bruce Gordon 2.25
7 London,1891 . . . . 2.25
8 A:Sherlock Holmes 2.25
9 I:Johnny Peril. 2.25
10 CDo,V:Darkseid 2.25
11 A:Creeper,Peacemaker,Steel . . 2.25
12 V:Shadow Fighters 2.25
13 D:Manhunter,Commander Steel,
   Major Victory,Peacemaker,
   Wildcat,Dr.Midnight,Creeper . . 2.25
14 A:JLA. 2.25
15 A:Amanda Waller 2.25
16 V:US Army 2.25
17 A:Amanda Waller,Martian
   Manhunter,Wonder Woman,Flash,
   Bloodwynd,Booster Gold. 2.25
18 A:Spectre,JLA,final issue 2.25
Ann.#1 I:Prism. 2.50

ECLIPSO: THE DARKNESS WITHIN
1992
1 BS,Direct w/purple diamond,
   A:Superman,Creeper. 4.00
1a BS,Newstand w/out diamond . . 3.00

2 BS,MPn,DC heroes V:Eclipso,
D:Starman 3.00

EGYPT
1995–96
1 College Experiments 3.50
2 thru 7 . . . . @3.00

80 PAGE GIANTS
Aug., 1964
1 Superman 750.00
2 Jimmy Olsen 400.00
3 Lois Lane 300.00
4 Golden Age-Flash 300.00
5 Batman 300.00
6 Superman 400.00
7 JKu&JKu(c),Sgt. Rock's Prize
Battle Tales 250.00
8 Secret Origins,O:JLA,Aquaman,
Robin,Atom, Superman 600.00
9 Flash 300.00
10 Superboy. 600.00
11 Superman,A:Lex Luthor 400.00
12 Batman 350.00
13 Jimmy Olsen 250.00
14 Lois Lane 250.00
15 Superman & Batman 250.00
16 thru 89 in regular series runs

EL DIABLO
1989–91
1 I:El Diablo, double-size 3.00
2 thru 16 . . . . @2.50

DC/Vertigo, Jan., 2001
1 (of 4) Weird Western Tales 2.50
2 thru 4 . . . . @2.50

ELECTRIC WARRIOR
1986–87
1 SF series,I:Electric Warriors 2.50
2 thru 18 . . . . @2.25

ELFQUEST:
THE DISCOVERY
Jan., 2006
1 (of 4) RPi,WP, F:Sunbeam 4.00
2 RPi,WP 4.00
3 RPi,WP 4.00
4 RPi,WP, concl. 4.00
TPB 15.00

ELFQUEST:
THE GRAND QUEST
Jan. 2004
TPB Vol. 1 thru Vol. 14 WP . . . . @10.00
TPB The Searcher and the Sword. 15.00

ELFQUEST: 25th
ANNIVERSARY EDITION
DC 2003
Spec. WP,RPi, rep. Elfquest #1 . . . . 3.00

ELFQUEST: WOLFRIDER
Sept. 2003
TPB Vol. 1 . . . . 10.00
TPB Vol. 2 . . . . 10.00

ELONGATED MAN
1992
1 A:Copperhead 2.25
2 Modora,A:Flash,I:Sonar. 2.25
3 A:Flash,V:Wurst Gang 2.25

Elongated Man #1 © DC Comics, Inc.

ELRIC: THE MAKING
OF A SORCERER
Sept. 2004
1 (of 4) WS, from M.Moorcock 6.00
2 thru 4 WS . . . . @6.00

ELSEWORLD'S FINEST
DC/Elseworlds 1998
1 (of 2) JFM,KD,F:Bruce Wayne
and Clark Kent, ... 5.00
2 JFM,KD,concl.. . . . . 5.00
GN Supergirl & Batgirl 6.00

ELVIRA
1986–87
1 DSp,BB(c) 5.00
2 thru 10 . . . . @4.00
11 DSt(c)Find Cain. 5.00

EMPIRE
June 2003
0 JmP,from Gorilla Comics 5.00
1 thru 6 BKi,JmP . . . . @2.50
TPB 15.00

ENEMY ACE:
WAR IN HEAVEN
March, 2001
1 (of 2) GEn, 48-page. 6.00
2 GEn,48-page 6.00
TPB Enemy Ace:War in Heaven . . 15.00

ENGINEHEAD
April 2004
1 (of 8) TMK,six heroes in one 2.50
2 TMK,why am I here? 2.50
3 TMK,cosmic mechanic. 2.50
4 TMK,V:Metallo 2.50
5 TMK,band of terrorists 2.50
6 TMk,Metal Men 2.50

ENIGMA
DC/Vertigo, 1993
1 B:PrM(s),DFg,I:Enigma,Michael
Smith,V:The Head 3.00
2 DFg,I:The Truth 3.00
3 DFg,V:The Truth,I:Envelope Girl,
Titus Bird 3.00
4 DFg,D:The Truth,I:Interior
League. 3.00
5 DFg,I:Enigma's Mother 3.00

6 DFg,V:Envelope Girl 3.00
7 DFg,V:Enigma's Mother,D:Envelope
Girl,O:Enigma 3.00
8 E:PrM(s),DFg,final issue 3.00
TPB Rep. #1-#8 . . . . 20.00

ERADICATOR
1996
1 IV,Low, ... 2.50
2 IV,Low, ... 2.50
3 IV,Low,Reign of the Superman
concl.,A:Superboy 2.50

ESSENTIAL VERTIGO:
SWAMP THING
DC/Vertigo, Sept., 1996
B&W reprints
1 AMo(s), rep. Saga of
the Swamp Thing #21. . . . . 3.00
2 thru 11 AMo(s), rep. Saga of
the Swamp Thing #22–#31. . @3.00
12 AMo(s) rep. Saga Ann. #2 . . . . . 3.00
13 AMo(s) rep. Saga #32–#42. . . @3.00
24 AMo,Windfall, final issue. 3.00

ESSENTIAL VERTIGO:
THE SANDMAN
DC/Vertigo, 1996
3 NGa(s),SK,MDr,rep.. . . . . 3.00
4 NGa(s),SK,MDr,rep. F:Etrigan . . 3.00
5 NGa(s),SK,MJ,F:Morpheus,
John Dee 3.00
6 NGa(s),SK,MJ,V:Dr. Destiny 3.00
7 . . . . 3.00
8 NGa(s),MDr,MJ,The Sound
of Her Wings 3.00
9 NGa(s),MDr,MJ,The Doll's
House, F:Nada 3.00
10 NGa(s),MDr,MJ,Doll's House . . . 3.00
11 NGa(s),MDr,RT 3.00
12 NGa(s),CBa,MJ,Doll'sHouse . . . 3.00
13 NGa,rep.Doll's House,pt.4 . . . . . 3.00
14 NGa,rep.Doll's House,pt.5 . . . . . 3.50
15 NGa,rep.Doll's House,pt.6 . . . . . 3.00
16 NGa,rep.Lost Hearts. 3.00
17 NGa,rep.Dream Country. 3.00
18 NGa,Dream of Thousand Cats . . 3.00
19 NGa,rep.Sandman #19. . . . . 3.00
20 NGa,rep.Sandman #20. . . . . 3.00
21 NGa,rep.Sandman #21. . . . . 3.00
22 NGa,rep.Season of Mists pt.1 . . 3.00
23 NGa,rep.Season of Mists pt.2 . . 3.00
24 NGa,rep.Season of Mists pt.3 . . 3.00
25 NGa,rep.Season of Mists pt.4 . . 3.00
26 NGa,rep.Season of Mists pt.5 . . 3.00
27 NGa,rep.Season of Mists,pt.6. . . 3.00
28 NGa,rep.Season of Mists,epilog. 3.00
29 NGa,rep.Thermidor. 3.00
30 NGa,rep.August 3.00
31 NGa,rep.Three Septembers
and a January 3.00
32 NGa,rep. Sandman Special #1
final issue 4.50

EVERYTHING HAPPENS
TO HARVEY
1953–54
1 Teen-age humor. 325.00
2 . . . . 175.00
3 thru 7 . . . . @125.00

EXTERMINATORS, THE
DC/Vertigo, Jan., 2006
1 F:Henry James 3.00
2 Bug Brothers, pt.2 . . . . 3.00
3 Bug Brothers, pt.3 . . . . 3.00
4 Bug Brothers, pt.4 . . . . 3.00
5 Bug Brothers, pt.5 . . . . 3.00

DC COMICS

6 Insurgency, pt.1	3.00
7 Insurgency, pt.2	3.00
8 Two Girlfriends	3.00
9 Insurgency, pt.3	3.00
10 Insurgency,pt.4	3.00
11 Brother #38, pt.1	3.00
TPB Bug Brothers	10.00

EXTREME JUSTICE
1995–96

0 New Group	3.50
1 V:Captain Atom	3.00
2 V:War Cyborgs	3.00
3 V:Synge	3.00
4 R:Firestorm the Nuclear Man	3.00
5 Firestorm & Elementals	3.00
6 Monarch,Captain Atom, Booster Gold, Maxima	3.00
7 F:Monarch,Captain Atom	3.00
8 Look Before You Quantum Leap	3.00
9 F:Firestorm	3.00
10 Underworld Unleashed tie-in	3.00
11 Underworld Unleashed tie-in	3.00
12 Monarch's scheme revealed	3.00
13 Monarch vs. Captain Atom	3.00
14	3.00
15 TMo,V:The Slavemaster from the Stars	3.00
16 TMo,V:Legion of Doom	3.00
17 TMo,V:Legion of Doom	3.00

EXTREMIST
DC/Vertigo, 1993

1 B:PrM(s),TMK,I:The Order, Extremist(Judy Tanner)	2.50
1a Platinum Ed.	5.00
2 TMK,D:Extremist(Jack Tanner)	2.25
3 TMK,V:Patrick	2.25
4 E:PrM(s),TMK,D:Tony Murphy	2.25

FABLES
DC/Vertigo, May, 2002

1 SL, Legends in Exile,pt.1	20.00
1a variant (c).	20.00
2 SL, Legends in Exile,pt.2	15.00
3 SL, Legends in Exile,pt.3	8.00
4 BWg,Legends in Exile,pt.4	7.00
5 SL, Legends in Exile,pt.5	7.00
6 MBu,SL,Animal Farm,pt.1	7.00
7 MBu,SL,Animal Farm,pt.2	4.00
8 MBu,SL,Animal Farm,pt.3	4.00
9 MBu,SL,Animal Farm,pt.4	4.00
10 MBu,SL,Animal Farm,pt.5	4.00
11 Jack of the Tales	4.00
12 Fables caper,pt.1	4.00
13 Fables caper,pt.2	3.00
14 Storybook Love,pt.1	3.00
15 Storybook Love,pt.2	3.00
16 Storybook Love,pt.3	3.00
17 Storybook Love,pt.4	3.00
18 The Barley Corn Brides	2.50
19 MBu,SL	2.50
20 MBu,SL	2.50
21 MBu,SL	2.50
22 JP,Ex-wives Club	2.50
23 MBu,SL	2.50
24 MBu,SL,Boy Blue missing	2.50
25 MBu,SL,Wooden Soldiers	2.50
26 MBu,SL,Wooden Soldiers	2.50
27 MBu,SL,Wooden Soldiers	2.50
28 JP,War Stories,pt.1	2.50
29 JP,War Stories,pt.2	2.50
30 MBu,SL,The Year After,pt.1	2.50
31 MBu,SL,The Year After	2.50
32 MBu,SL,The Year After	2.50
33 MBu,SL,The Year After,concl.	2.50
34 Jack be Nimble, pt.1	2.50
35 Jack be Nimble, pt.2	2.50
36 Return to the Homelands,pt.1.	2.50
37 Return to the Homelands,pt.2.	2.50
38 Return to the Homelands,pt.3.	2.50

39 Fabletown	2.50
40 Return to the Homelands,pt.4.	3.00
41 Return to the Homelands,pt.5.	2.75
42 Arabian Nights & Days	2.75
43 Arabian Nights & Days	2.75
44 Arabian Nights & Days	2.75
45 Arabian Nights & Days	2.75
46 Ballad of Rodney and June	2.75
47 Ballad of Rodney and June	2.75
48 Wolves, pt.1	2.75
49 Wolves, pt.2	3.00
50 64-pg.	4.00
51 in Smalltown	3.00
52 Sons of the Empire,pt.1	3.00
53 Sons of the Empire,pt.2	3.00
54 Sons of the Empire,pt.3	3.00
55 Sons of the Empire,pt.4	3.00
TPB March of Wooden Soldiers	18.00
TPB Storybook Love	15.00
TPB Fables: Legends in Exile	15.00
TPB Fables: Animal Farm	13.00
TPB The Mean Seasons (2005)	15.00
TPB Black Flowers (2005)	15.00
TPB Vol. 6 Homelands	15.00
TPB Vol. 7 Arabian Nights (and Days) (2006)	15.00
TPB Vol. 8 Wolves (2006)	18.00
Spec. The Last Castle	6.00
Spec. Reprint of #1 (2006)	0.25

FALLEN ANGEL
July 2003

1 PDd(s),Bete Noire	2.50
2 PDd(s),Asia Minor	2.50
3 PDd(s),Little Better,pt.1	2.50
4 PDd(s),Little Better,pt.2	2.50
5 PDd(s),Little Better,pt.3	2.50
6 PDd(s),Little Better,pt.4	2.50
7 PDd(s),F:Black Mariah.	2.50
8 PDd(s),F:Black Mariah.	2.50
9 PDd(s),F:Black Mariah.	2.50
10 PDd(s),F:Black Mariah	3.00
11 PDd(s),F:Black Marian	2.50
12 PDd(s),Doctor Juris	2.50
13 PDd(s),V:Asia Minor	2.50
14 PDd(s),Bete Noire.	2.50
15 PDd(s).	2.50
16 PDd(s).	2.50
17 PDd(s),MK(c)	3.00
18 PDd(s),V:Hierachy	3.00
19 PDd(s),GP(c),A:Sachs & Violens	3.00
20 PDd(s),Sacred Cows, concl.	3.00
TPB	13.00

FAMILY MAN
Paradox 1995

1 I:Family Man	5.50
2 V:Brother Charles	5.50
3 Escape	5.50

FANBOY
1999

1 (of 6) SA, various artists	2.50
2 A:Hal Jordan	2.50
3 A:JLA	2.50
4 SA, A:Sgt. Rock	2.50
5 SA, A:Batman	2.50
6 SA, A:Wonder Woman, concl.	2.50
TPB F:Finster, 144-page(2001)	13.00

FATE
1994–96

1 Dr. Fate	2.50
2 Nabu,Astral plane	2.25
3 Bloodstain	2.25
4 Decisions	2.25
5 Judged by Enclave	2.25
6 V:Grimoire	2.25
7 V:Dark Agent	2.25
8 V:Dark Agent	2.25

Fanboy #2
© *DC Comics, Inc.*

9 Tries to change his destiny	2.25
10 A:Zatanna	2.25
11	2.25
12 A:Sentinel	2.25
13 V:Blaze	2.25
14 LKa,ALa,AWi,Underworld Unleashed tie-in	2.25
15 LKa,ALa,AWi,V:Charnelle	2.25
16 LKa,ALa,AWi,canibal drug-cult .	2.25
17 LKa,ALa,AWi.	2.25
18 LKa,ALa,AWi,V:Charnelle	2.25
19 LKa,ALa,AWi,V:men in black	2.25

FAULT LINES
DC/Vertigo, March, 1997
Mini-series

1 LMr(s),F:Tracey Farrand	2.50
2 LMr(s)	2.50
3 LMr(s)	2.50
4 LMr(s)	2.50
5 (of 6) LMr(s)	2.50
6 LMrs(s) concl.	2.50

FEATURE FILMS
1950

1 Captain China	1,200.00
2 Riding High, Bing Crosby	1,200.00
3 The Eagle and the Hawk	1,100.00
4 Fancy Pants, Bob Hope	1,400.00

52
May, 2006

1 52 Weeks without Superman, Batman & Wonder Woman	2.50
2 Looking Back at Tomorrow	2.50
3 New World Order	2.50
4 Dances with Monsters	2.50
5 Stars in Their Courses	2.50
6 F:China's super-hero team	2.50
7 F:Booster Gold.	2.50
8 F:John Henry Irons	2.50
9 New JLA	2.50
10 I:Supernova	2.50
11 New protector of Gotham	2.50
12 F:Black Adam	2.50
13 F:Sue Dibny	2.50
14 F:Steel and Montoya	2.50
15 O:Metamorpho	2.50
16 F:Black Adam and Isis	2.50
17 Lobo	2.50
18 Croatoans	2.50
19 Your own superhero identity	2.50
20 O:Adam Strange	2.50

21 Raven 2.50
22 Kon-El didn't die in Crisis 2.50
23 Isis. 2.50
24 Join New Justice League 2.50
25 Black Marvel Family 2.50
26 LexCorp 2.50
27 O:Power Girl 2.50
28 Red Tornado 2.50
29 O:Joker 2.50
30 Batman no more 2.50

FIGHT FOR TOMORROW
DC/Vertigo, Sept., 2002
1 (of 6) DCw,JLe(c) kung-fu 2.50
2 DCw,KW, more kung-fu 2.50
3 thru 6 DCw . . . . @2.50

Fighting American #6 © DC Comics Inc.

FIGHTING AMERICAN
1994
1 GrL,R:Fighting American 2.50
2 GrL,Media Circus 2.50
3 GrL,I&V:Gross Nation Product,
    Def Iffit 2.50
4 GrL,V:Gross Nation Product,
    Def Iffit 2.50
5 GrL,PhorOptor 2.50
6 Final Issue 2.50

FILTH, THE
DC/Vertigo, June, 2002
1 (of 13) GMo 3.00
2 GMo, Perfect Victim. 3.00
3 GMo, unexpected guest 3.00
4 GMo, Otto Von Vermun 3.00
5 GMo, Pornomancer 3.00
6 GMo,World of Anders Klimaaks. . 3.00
7 GMo,Libertania 3.00
8 GMo,Libertania 3.00
9 GMo,Answers 3.00
10 GMo,Mother Dirt 3.00
11 GMo,Greg Feely 3.00
12 GMo,Mother Dirt 3.00
13 GMo,concl. 3.00
TPB 20.00

FINAL NIGHT, THE
Sept., 1996
[Cross-Over Series]
1 KK(s),SI,JMz, Alien crash lands
    on Earth 7.00
2 KK(s),SI,JMz, Earth's sun
    extinguised 5.00

3 KK(s),SI,JMz, Attempts to stave
    off inevitable 5.00
4 KK(s),SI,JMz, Can they save the
    world, and at what price? 10.00
TPB rep. 13.00

FIREBRAND
1995
1 SaV,Alex Sanchez becomes
    Firebrand 2.25
2 SaV 2.25
3 SaV,Generation Prime case
    climax 2.25
4 SaV,Young gang member 2.25
5 SaV,V;serial killer(s). 2.25
6 thru 9 . . . . @2.25

FIRESTORM
March, 1978
1 AM,JRu,I&O:Firestorm 15.00
2 AM,BMc,A:Superman 7.00
3 AM,I:Killer Froat 7.00
4 AM,BMc,I:Hyena 7.00
5 AM,BMc,Hyena 7.00

FIRESTORM
May 2004
1 Ccs,F:Jason Rusch 2.50
2 Ccs,Eye Contact,pt.2 . . . . 2.50
3 Ccs,power's price 2.50
4 Ccs,Everybody Wants You 2.50
5 Ccs,Everybody Wants You 2.50
6 CsB,DGr,x-over 2.50
7 ALa,LSh,Bloodhound x-over 2.50
8 Heroes 2.50
9 Old foe 2.50
10 Return of Ronnie Raymond? . . . 2.50
11 V:Multiplex & Typhoon 2.50
12 V:Multiplex & Typhoon 2.50
13 Ronnie Raymond, conc. 2.50
14 Both Jason and Firestorm 2.50
15 Secret Origins, pt.1 . . . . 2.50
16 Secret Origins, pt.2 . . . . 2.50
17 Villains United tie-in 2.50
18 Omac project tie-in 2.50
19 Infinite Crisis 2.50
20 Infinite Crisis, A:Animal Man. . . . 2.50
21 Building a Better Firestorm 2.50
22 Building a Better Firestorm 2.50
Becomes:

FIRESTORM
THE NUCLEAR MAN
23 One Year Later 2.50
24 Firehawk vs. Killer Frost 2.50
25 V:Killer Frost & Mr. Freeze 3.00
26 F:The Pupil 3.00
27 Firehawk vs. Pupil. 3.00
28 In My Father's House,pt.1 . . . . . . 3.00
29 In My Father's House,pt.2 . . . . . 3.00
30 In My Father's House,pt.3 . . . . . 3.00
31 In My Father's House,pt.4 . . . . . 3.00

FIRESTORM, THE
NUCLEAR MAN
See: FURY OF FIRESTORM

FIRST ISSUE SPECIAL
April, 1975
1 JK,Atlas 20.00
2 Green Team 15.00
3 Metamorpho 15.00
4 Lady Cop 10.00
5 JK,Manhunter 20.00
6 JK,Dingbats 20.00
7 SD,Creeper 20.00
8 MGr,Warlord 30.00
9 WS,Dr.Fate 15.00
10 Outsiders(not Batman team). . . 12.00
11 NR,AM Code:Assassin 12.00

12 new Starman 12.00
13 return of New Gods 30.00

FLASH COMICS
Jan., 1940
1 SMo,SMo(c),O:Flash,Hawkman,The
    Whip & Johnny Thunder,B:Cliff
    Cornwall,Minute Movies . 150,000.00
2 B:Rod Rain 25,000.00
3 SMo,SMo(c),B:The King. . . 15,000.00
4 SMo,SMo(c),F:The Whip . . 12,000.00
5 SMo,SMo(c),F:The King . . 10,000.00
6 F:Flash 15,000.00
7 Hawkman(c) 12,000.00
8 Male bondage(c). 6,500.00
9 Hawkman(c) 7,000.00
10 SMo,SMo(c),Flash(c) 7,000.00
11 SMo,SMo(c) 5,500.00
12 SMo,SMo(c),B:Les Watts. . . 5,500.00
13 SMo,SMo(c) 5,500.00
14 SMo,SMo(c) 6,000.00
15 SMo,SMo(c) 6,000.00
16 SMo,SMo(c) 6,000.00
17 SMo,SMo(c),E:CliffCornwall 6,000.00
18 SMo,SMo(c) 6,000.00
19 SMo,SMo(c) 6,000.00
20 SMo,SMo(c) 6,000.00
21 SMo(c) 7,000.00
22 SMo,SMo(c) 6,000.00
23 SMo,SMo(c) 6,000.00
24 SMo,SMo(c),Flash V:Spider-
    Men of Mars,A:Hawkgirl . . . 7,000.00
25 SMo,SMo(c) 4,000.00
26 SMo,SMo(c) 4,000.00
27 SMo,SMo(c) 4,000.00
28 SMo,SMo(c),Flash goes
    to Hollywood 4,000.00
29 SMo,SMo(c),Flash inAdventure
    of the Curiosity Ray! 4,000.00
30 SMo,SMo(c),Flash inAdventure
    of the Curiosity Ray! 4,000.00
31 SMo,SMo(c),Hawkman(c) . . 4,000.00
32 SMo,SM(c),Flash inAdventure
    of the Fictious Villians. 4,000.00
33 SMo,SMo(c) 4,000.00
34 SMo,SMo(c),Flash in The Robbers
    of the Round Table 4,000.00
35 SMo,SMo(c) 4,000.00
36 SMo,SMo(c),F:Flash,Mystery of
    Doll Who Walks Like a Man 4,000.00
37 SMo,SMo(c). 3,500.00
38 SMo,SMo(c). 3,200.00
39 SMo,SMo(c). 3,200.00
40 SMo,SMo(c),F:Flash, Man Who
    Could Read Man's Souls!. . 4,000.00
41 SMo,SMo(c) 4,000.00

Flash Comics #31
© DC Comics, Inc.

Flash ##83 © DC Comics, Inc.

42 SMo,SMo(c),Flash V:The
  Gangsters Baby!......... 4,000.00
43 SMo,SMo(c)............. 4,000.00
44 SMo,SMo(c),Flash V:The
  Liars Club.............. 4,000.00
45 SMo,SMo(c),F:Hawkman,Big
  Butch Makes Hall of Fame. 4,000.00
46 SMo,SMo(c)............. 4,000.00
47 SMo,SMo(c),Hawkman in Crime
  Canned for the Duration... 2,500.00
48 SMo,SMo(c)............. 2,500.00
49 SMo,SMo(c)............. 2,500.00
50 SMo,SMo(c),Hawkman, Tale
  of the 1,000 Dollar Bill 2,500.00
51 SMo,SMo(c)............. 2,500.00
52 SMo,SMo(c),Flash, Machine
  that Thinks Like a Man.... 2,500.00
53 SMo,SMo(c),Hawkman, Simple
  Simon Met the Hawkman.. 2,500.00
54 SMo,SMo(c),Flash, Mysterious
  Bottle from the Sea 2,500.00
55 SMo,SMo(c),Hawkman, Riddle of
  the Stolen Statuette!...... 2,500.00
56 SMo,SMo(c)............. 2,500.00
57 SMo,SMo(c),Hawkman,
  Adventure of the Gangster
  & the Ghost 2,500.00
58 SMo,SMo(c),Merman meets
  the Flash............... 2,500.00
59 SMo,SMo(c),Hawkman
  V:Pied Piper 2,500.00
60 SMo,SMo(c),Flash
  V:The Wind Master....... 2,500.00
61 SMo,SMo(c),Hawkman
  V:The Beanstalk......... 2,500.00
62 JKu,Flash in High Jinks
  on the Rinks 3,000.00
63 JKu(c),Hawkman in The
  Tale of the Mystic Urn..... 2,400.00
64 The Fire Bandits 2,400.00
65 JKu(c),Hawkman in Return
  of the Simple Simon...... 2,400.00
66 Flash and the Black Widow. 2,400.00
67 JKu(c)................. 2,400.00
68 Flash in The Radio that
  Ran Wild............... 2,400.00
69 Adventure o/t Violent Violin . 2,400.00
70 JKu(c)................. 2,400.00
71 JKu(c),Hawkman in Battle
  of the Birdmen 2,400.00
72 JKu,Wizard o/t Wax Works . 2,400.00
73 JKu(c)................. 2,400.00
74 JKu(c)................. 2,400.00
75 JKu(c),Hawkman in Magic
  at the Mardi Gras........ 2,400.00
76 A:Worry Wart 2,400.00

77 Hawkman in The Case of
  the Curious Casket...... 2,400.00
78 Haunted Halloween 2,400.00
79 Hawkman in The Battle
  of the Birds............. 2,400.00
80 Flash in The Story of
  the Boy Genius......... 2,400.00
81 JKu(c),Hawkman's Voyage
  to Venus............... 2,400.00
82 A:Walter Jordan 2,400.00
83 JKu,JKu(c),Hawkman in
  Destined for Disaster 2,500.00
84 Flash V:The Changeling ... 2,500.00
85 JKu,JKu(c),Hawkman in
  Hollywood.............. 2,500.00
86 JKu,1st Black Canary,Flash
  V:Stone Age Menace 8,000.00
87 Hawkman meets the Foil... 3,200.00
88 JKu,Flash in The Case
  of the Vanished Year!..... 3,200.00
89 I:The Thorn 4,500.00
90 Flash in Nine Empty
  Uniforms.............. 3,200.00
91 Hawkman V:The Phantom
  Menace.............. 4,000.00
92 1st full-length Black
  Canary story.......... 10,000.00
93 Flash V:Violin of Villainy .. 4,000.00
94 JKu(c)................. 4,000.00
95 Cl(c),The Golden Flash 4,000.00
96 JKu,Return of the Centaurs . 4,000.00
97 Flash in The Dream
  that Didn't Vanish 4,000.00
98 JKu(c),Hawkman in
  Crime Costume! 4,000.00
99 Flash in The Star Prize
  of the Year 4,000.00
100 Hawkman in The Human
  -Fly Bandits! 6,500.00
101 Cl,A Switch in Time 5,500.00
102 Hawkman in The Flying
  Darkness 5,500.00
103 Cl,The Sword of Time 6,500.00
104 JKu,Hawkman in Flaming
  Darkness' Feb., 1949 .... 20,000.00
Revived as:

FLASH, THE
Feb.–March, 1959
105 Cl,O:Flash,I:Mirror
  Master................ 29,000.00
106 Cl,I&O:Gorilla Grodd,
  O:Pied Piper 7,000.00
107 Cl,A:Grodd............. 5,000.00
108 Cl,A:Grodd............. 4,500.00
109 Cl,A:Mirror Master 4,000.00
110 Cl,MA,I:Kid Flash,
  Weather Wizard 7,000.00
111 Cl,A:Kid Flash,The Invasion
  Of the Cloud Creatures ... 2,600.00
112 Cl,I&O:Elongated Man,
  A:Kid Flash............ 2,500.00
113 Cl,I&O:Trickster 1,500.00
114 Cl,A:Captain Cold 1,200.00
115 Cl,A:Grodd............. 900.00
116 Cl,A:Kid Flash,The Man
  Who Stole Central City ... 900.00
117 Cl,MA,I:Capt.Boomerang... 1,000.00
118 Cl,MA 800.00
119 Cl,W:Elongated Man....... 800.00
120 Cl,A:Kid Flash,Land of
  Golden Giants 800.00
121 Cl,A:Trickster 750.00
122 Cl,I&O:The Top........... 750.00
123 I:Earth 2,R:G.A.Flash..... 3,500.00
124 Cl,A:Capt.Boomerang...... 650.00
125 Cl,A:Kid Flash,The
  Conquerors of Time....... 650.00
126 Cl,A:Mirror Master 650.00
127 Cl,A:Grodd............. 650.00
128 Cl,O:Abra Kadabra 650.00
129 Cl,A:Capt.Cold,Trickster,A:Gold.
  Age Flash,C:JLA (flashback). 700.00

Flash #129
© DC Comics, Inc.

130 Cl,A:Mirror Master,
  Weather Wizard.......... 600.00
131 Cl,A:Green Lantern....... 400.00
132 Cl,A:Daphne Dean 400.00
133 Cl,A:Abra Kadabra 400.00
134 Cl,A:Captain Cold........ 400.00
135 Cl,N:Kid Flash.......... 400.00
136 Cl,A:Mirror Master 400.00
137 Cl,Vandal Savage,R:JSA,
  A:G.A.Flash.............. 900.00
138 Cl,A:Pied Piper 450.00
139 Cl,I&O:Prof.Zoom(Reverse
  Flash)................ 450.00
140 Cl,O:Heat Wave 450.00
141 Cl,A:Top 350.00
142 Cl,A:Trickster 350.00
143 Cl,A:Green Lantern....... 350.00
144 Cl,A:Man Missile,Kid Flash.. 350.00
145 Cl,A:Weather Wizard 350.00
146 Cl,A:Mirror Master 350.00
147 Cl,A:Mr.Element,A:Reverse
  Flash 350.00
148 Cl,A:Capt.Boomerang..... 350.00
149 Cl,A:Abra Kadabra 350.00
150 Cl,A:Captain Cold........ 350.00
151 Cl,A:Earth II Flash,
  The Shade.............. 400.00
152 Cl,V:Trickster 700.00
153 Cl,A:Mr.Element,Rev.Flash.. 700.00
154 Cl,The Day Flash Ran Away
  with Himself............. 700.00
155 Cl,A:MirrorMaster,Capt.Cold,Top
  Capt. Boomerang,Grodd 700.00
156 Cl,A:Kid Flash,The Super Hero
  who Betrayed the World 800.00
157 Cl,A:Doralla Kon,The Top... 700.00
158 Cl,V:The Breakaway Bandit
  A:The Justice League 500.00
159 Cl,A:Kid Flash........... 300.00
160 Cl,giant................ 500.00
161 Cl,A:Mirror Master 300.00
162 Cl,Who Haunts the Corridor
  of Chills 300.00
163 Cl,A:Abra kadabra 300.00
164 Cl,V:Pied Piper,A:Kid Flash . 300.00
165 Cl,W:Flash,Iris West....... 300.00
166 Cl,A:Captain Cold........ 300.00
167 Cl,O:Flash,I:Mopee....... 300.00
168 Cl,A:Green Lantern....... 300.00
169 Cl,O:Flash rtd,giant....... 325.00
170 Cl,A:Abra Kadabra,
  G.A.Flash............... 300.00
171 Cl,A:Dexter Myles,Justice
  League,Atom;V:Dr Light 300.00
172 Cl,A:Grodd............. 300.00

173 CI,A:Kid Flash,EarthII Flash
   V:Golden Man 700.00
174 CI,A:Mirror Master,Top
   Captain Cold 300.00
175 2nd Superman/Flash race,
   C:Justice League o/America . 500.00
176 giant-size. 300.00
177 RA,V:The Trickster 300.00
178 CI,(giant size) 350.00
179 RA,Fact or Fiction 300.00
180 RA,V:Baron Katana. 250.00
181 RA,V:Baron Katana. 200.00
182 A:Abra Kadabra 200.00
183 RA,V:The Frog 200.00
184 RA,V:Dr Yom. 200.00
185 RA,Threat of the High Rise
   Buildings 200.00
186 RA,A:Sargon. 200.00
187 CI,AbraKadabra,giant 175.00
188 A:Mirror Master 150.00
189 JKu(c),RA,A:Kid Flash 150.00
190 JKu(c),RA,A:Dexter Myles . . 150.00
191 JKu(c),RA,A:Green Lantern . 150.00
192 RA,V:Captain Vulcan 150.00
193 A:Captain Cold 150.00
194 NA(c). 150.00
195 GK,MA,NA 150.00
196 CI,giant 175.00
197 GK. 150.00
198 GK. 150.00
199 GK. 150.00
200 IN,MA 150.00
201 IN,MA,A:G.A. Flash. 75.00
202 IN,MA,A:Kid Flash 75.00
203 IN 75.00
204 NA 75.00
205 giant 150.00
206 NA,A:Mirror Master. 75.00
207 NA 75.00
208 NA. 75.00
209 A:Capt.Boomerang,Grodd
   Trickster. 75.00
210 CI 75.00
211 NA,O:Flash 75.00
212 A:Abra Kadabra 75.00
213 CI,NA 75.00
214 CI,rep.Showcase #37
   (O:Metal Men),giant size. . . . 80.00
215 IN,FMc,NA,rep.Showcase#14. 80.00
216 A:Mr.Element. 50.00
217 NA,A:Gr.Lant,Gr.Arrow 80.00
218 NA,A:Gr.Lant,Gr.Arrow 80.00
219 NA,L:Greeen Arrow. 80.00
220 IN,DG,A:KidFlash,Gr.Lantern . 60.00
221 IN 50.00
222 IN 50.00
223 DG,Green Lantern. 50.00
224 IN,DG,A:Green Lantern. 50.00
225 IN,DG,A:Gr.Lant,Rev.Flash . . 35.00
226 NA,A:Capt. Cold 55.00
227 IN,FMc,DG,Capt.Boomerang,
   Green Lantern 35.00
228 IN 35.00
229 IN,FMc,A:Green Arrow,
   V:Rag Doll (giant size). 80.00
230 A:VandalSavage,Dr.Alchemy . 30.00
231 FMc. 30.00
232 giant 75.00
233 giant 75.00
234 V:Reverse Flash 25.00
235 DG(c),V:Vandal Savage 20.00
236 MGr. 20.00
237 IN,FMc,MGr,A:Prof Zoom,
   Green Lantern 25.00
238 MGr. 20.00
239 Tailor Made Crimes. 20.00
240 MGr. 20.00
241 A:Mirror Master 20.00
242 MGr,D:Top. 20.00
243 IN,FMc,MGr,TA,O:Top,
   A:Green Lantern 20.00
244 IN,FMc,A:Rogue's Gallery . . 20.00

Flash #218
© *DC Comics Inc.*

245 IN,FMc,DD,TA,I:PlantMaster. . 20.00
246 IN,FMc,DD,TA,I:PlantMaster. . 20.00
247. . . . . 20.00
248 FMc,IN,I:Master 20.00
249 FMc,IN,V:Master. 20.00
250 IN,FMc,I:Golden Glider 20.00
251 FMc,IN,V:Golden Glider 15.00
252 FMc,IN,I:Molder 15.00
253 FMc,IN,V:Molder 15.00
254 FMc. 15.00
255 FMc,A:MirrorMaster 15.00
256 FMc,V:Top. 15.00
257 FMc,A:Green Glider 15.00
258 FMc,A:Black Hand 15.00
259 FMc,IN 15.00
260 FMc,IN 15.00
261 FMc,IN,V:Golden Glider 15.00
262 FMc,IN,V:Golden Glider 15.00
263 FMc,IN,V:Golden Glider 15.00
264 FMc,IN,V:Golden Glider 15.00
265 FMc,IN 15.00
266 FMc,IN,V:Heat Wave 15.00
267 FMc,IN,V:Heat Wave 15.00
268 FMc,IN,A:E2 Flash 15.00
269 FMc,IN,A:Kid Flash 15.00
270 FMc,IN,V:Clown 15.00
271 RB,V:Clown. 15.00
272 RB,V:Clown. 15.00
273 RB. 15.00
274 RB. 15.00
275 AS,D:Iris West,PCP story . . . 20.00
276 AS,A:JLA. 15.00
277 AS,FMc,A:JLA,
   V:MirrorMaster. 15.00
278 A:Captain.Boomerang
   & Heatwave 15.00
279 A:Captain.Boomerang
   & Heatwave 15.00
280 DH. 15.00
281 DH,V:Reverse Flash 20.00
282 DH,V:Reverse Flash 20.00
283 DH,V:Reverse Flash 20.00
284 DH,Flash's life story
   I:Limbo Lord 15.00
285 DH,V:Trickster. 15.00
286 DH,I:Rainbow Raider 15.00
287 DH,V:Dr.Alchemy 15.00
288 DH,V:Dr.Alchemy 15.00
289 DH,GP,1st GP DC art; V:Dr.
   Alchemy;B:B.U.Firestorm 20.00
290 GP. 10.00
291 GP,DH,V:Sabretooth 10.00
292 GP,DH,V:Mirror Master. 10.00
293 GP,DH,V:Pied Piper 10.00

294 GP,DH,V:Grodd. 10.00
295 CI,JSn,V:Grodd. 10.00
296 JSn,A:Elongated Man. 10.00
297 CI,A:Captain Cold 10.00
298 CI,V:Shade,Rainbowraider . . . 10.00
299 CI,V:Shade,Rainbowraider . . . 10.00
300 A:New Teen Titans 12.00
301 CI,A:Firestorm. 10.00
302 CI,V:Golden Glider 10.00
303 CI,V:Golden Glider 10.00
304 CI,PB,I:Col.Computron;E:B.U.
   Firestorm 10.00
305 KG,CI,A:G.A.Flash,B:Dr.Fate . 10.00
306 CI,KG,V:Mirror Master. 10.00
307 CI,KG,V:Pied Piper 10.00
308 CI,KG 10.00
309 CI,KG 10.00
310 CI,KG,V:Capt.Boomerang. . . . 6.00
311 CI,KG,V:Capt.Boomerang . . . 6.00
312 CI,A:Heatwave 6.00
313 KG,A:Psylon,E:Dr.Fate 6.00
314 CI,I:Eradicator. 6.00
315 CI,V:Gold Face 6.00
316 CI,V:Gold Face 6.00
317 CI,V:Gold Face 6.00
318 CI,DGb,V:Eradicator;B:
   B.U.Creeper. 6.00
319 CI,DGb,V:Eradicator 6.00
320 CI,V:Eradicator 6.00
321 CI,D:Eradicator 5.00
322 CI,V:Reverse Flash. 5.00
323 CI,V:Reverse Flash;E:
   B.U.Creeper 5.00
324 CI,D:Reverse Flash 5.50
325 CI,A:Rogues Gallery 5.00
326 CI,A:Weather Wizard 5.00
327 CI,A:JLA,G.Grodd 5.00
328 CI 5.00
329 CI,A:J.L.A.,G.Grodd 5.00
330 CI,FMc,V:G.Grodd. 5.00
331 CI,FMc,V:G.Grodd. 5.00
332 CI,FMc,V:Rainbow Raider . . . 5.00
333 CI,FMc,V:Pied Piper 5.00
334 CI,FMc,V:Pied Piper 5.00
335 CI,FMc,V:Pied Piper 5.00
336 CI,FMc,V:Pied Piper 5.00
337 CI,FMc,V:Pied Piper 5.00
338 CI,FMc,I:Big Sir. 5.00
339 CI,FMc,A.Big Sir. 5.00
340 CI,FMc,Trial,A:Big Sir 5.00
341 CI,FMc,Trial,A:Big Sir 5.00
342 CI,FMc,Trial,V:RogueGallery . . 5.00
343 CI,FMc,Trial,A:GoldFace 5.00
344 CI,O:Kid Flash,Trial. 5.00
345 CI,A:Kid Flash,Trial. 5.00
346 CI,FMc,Trial,V:AbraKadabra . . 5.00
347 CI,FMc,Trial,V:AbraKadabra . . 5.00
348 CI,FMc,Trial,V:AbraKadabra . . 5.00
349 CI,FMc,Trial,V:AbraKadabra . . 5.00
350 CI,FMc,Trial,V:AbraKadabra . . 7.00
Ann.#1 O:ElongatedMan,
   G.Grodd. 800.00

FLASH
[2nd Series] June, 1987
1 JG,Legends,C:Vandal Savage . . 12.00
2 JG,V:Vandal Savage 5.00
3 JG,I:Kilgore 5.00
4 JG,A:Cyborg. 4.00
5 JG,V:Speed Demon 4.00
6 JG,V:Speed Demon 4.00
7 JG,V:Red Trinity 4.00
8 JG,V:BlueTrinity,Millennium 4.00
9 JG,I:Chunk,Millennium 4.00
10 V:Chunk,Chunks World. 3.00
11 Return to Earth 3.00
12 Velocity 9 . . . . 3.00
13 Vandal Savage,V:Velocity 9
   Adicts. 3.00
14 V:Vandal Savage 3.00
15 A:Velocity 9 Junkies 3.00
16 C:V.Savage,SpeedMcGeePt.1 . 3.00

Flash 2nd Series #12
© DC Comics Inc.

Flash 2nd Series #21
© DC Comics, Inc.

17 GLa,Speed McGee,pt.2 . . . . 3.00
18 GLa,SpeedMcGeePt.3,
   V:V.Savage 3.00
19 JM:+bonus book,R:Rogue
   Gallery,O:Blue/Red Trinity 3.00
20 A:Durlan 3.00
21 A:Manhunter,Invasion x-over . . . 3.00
22 A:Manhunter,Invasion x-over . . . 3.00
23 V:Abrakadabra 3.00
24 GLa,FlashRegainsSpeed,
   A:L.Lane 3.00
25 GLa,Search for Flash 3.00
26 GLa,I:Porcupine Man 3.00
27 GLa,Porcupine Man as Flash . . . 3.00
28 GLa,A:Golden Glider,
   Capt.Cold. 3.00
29 A:New Phantom Lady 3.00
30 GLa,Turtle Saga,pt.1. . . . . 3.00
31 GLa,Turtle Saga,pt.2. . . . . 3.00
32 GLa,Turtle Saga,pt.3,
   R:G.A.Turtle 3.00
33 GLa,Turtle Saga,pt.4. . . . . 3.00
34 GLa,Turtle Saga,pt.5. . . . . 3.00
35 GLa,Turtle Saga,pt.6,
   D:G.A.Turtle 3.00
36 GLa,V:Cult 3.00
37 GLa,V:Cult 3.00
38 GLa,V:Cult 3.00
39 GLa,V:Cult 3.00
40 GLa,A:Dr.Alchemy 3.00
41 GLa,A:Dr.Alchemy 3.00
42 GLa,MechanicalTroubles 3.00
43 GLa,V:Kilgore 3.00
44 GLa,V:Velocity 3.00
45 V:Gorilla Grod 3.00
46 V:Gorilla Grod 3.00
47 V:Gorilla Grod 3.00
48 Persistence of Vision 3.00
49 A:Vandal Savage 3.00
50 N:Flash (double sz)V:Savage. . . 5.00
51 I:Proletariat 3.00
52 I.R.S. Mission 3.00
53 A:Superman,Race to Save
   Jimmy Olsen 3.00
54 Terrorist Airline Attack 3.00
55 War of the Gods x-over 3.00
56 The Way of a Will,pt.1. . . . . 3.00
57 The Way of a Will,pt.2. . . . . 3.00
58 Meta Gene-activated Homeless . 3.00
59 The Last Resort 3.00
60 Love Song of the Chunk 3.00
61 Wally's Mother's Wedding Day . . 3.00
62 GLa,Year 1,pt.1. . . . . 5.00
63 GLa,Year 1,pt.2. . . . . 4.00
64 GLa,Year 1,pt.3. . . . . 4.00

65 GLa,Year 1,pt.4. . . . . 4.00
66 A:Aq'man,V:Marine Marauder. . . 4.00
67 GLa,V:Abra Kadabra 4.00
68 GLa,V:Abra Kadabra 4.00
69 GLa,Gorilla Warfare#2 . . . . 4.00
70 Gorilla Warfare#4 . . . . 4.00
71 GLa,V:Dr.Alchemy 4.00
72 GLa,V:Dr.Alchemy,C:Barry
   Allen. 4.00
73 GLa,Xmas Issue,R:Barry Allen . . 6.00
74 GLa,A:Barry Allen? 5.00
75 GLa,A:Reverse Flash,V:Mob
   Violence 5.00
76 GLa,A:Reverse Flash 5.00
77 GLa,G.A.Flash vs
   Reverse Flash 5.00
78 GLa,V:Reverse Flash 5.00
79 GLa,V:Reverse Flash,48 pgs. . . 5.00
80 AD(c),V:Frances Kane 5.00
80a Newstand Ed 3.00
81 AD(c). 4.00
82 AD(c),A:Nightwing. 4.00
83 AD(c),A:Nightwing,Starfire 4.00
84 AD(c),I:Razer 4.00
85 AD(c),V:Razer 4.00
86 AD(c),A:Argus 4.00
86 V:Santa Claus 4.00
87 Christmas issue 4.00
88 Mean Streak 4.00
89 On Trial 4.00
90 On Trial#2 . . . . 4.00
91 Out of Time 5.00
92 I:3rd Flash 20.00
93 A:Impulse 5.00
94 Zero Hour 5.00
95 Terminal Velocity,pt.1 . . . . 4.00
96 Terminal Velocity,pt.2 . . . . 5.00
97 Terminal Velocity,pt.3 . . . . 4.00
98 Terminal Velocity,pt.4 . . . . 4.00
99 Terminal Velocity,pt.5 . . . . 4.00
100 I:New Flash. 5.00
100a Collector's Edition 4.00
101 Velocity Aftermath. 4.00
102 V:Mongul. 3.00
103 Supernatural threat from
   Linda's Past Secret 3.00
104 Exorcise Demons 3.00
105 Through a Glass Darkly 3.00
106 R:Magenta 3.00
107 MWa,Underworld Unleashed
   tie-in. 3.00
108 MWa,Dead Heat,pt.1 . . . . 3.00
109 MWa,Dead Heat,pt.2 . . . . 3.00
110 MWa,Dead Heat,pt.4. . . . . 3.00
111 MWa,Dead Heat,pt.6. . . . . 3.00
112 MWa,New Flash in town 3.00
113 MWa,F:Linda. 3.00
114 MWa,V:Chillblaine 3.00
115 thru 117 . . . . @3.00
118 MWa&BAu(s),Flash returns
   from the future. 3.00
119 MWa&BAu(s),PR,Final Night
   tie-in. 3.00
120 MWa&BAu(s),PR,Presidential
   Race,pt.1 . . . . 3.00
121 MWa&BAu(s),PR,Presidential
   Race,pt.2 . . . . 3.00
122 MWa&BAu(s),PR, ... 3.00
123 MWa&BAu(s),PR,Flash moves
   to Santa Marta 3.00
124 MWa&BAu(s),PR,Wally doesn't
   know reality from illusion 3.00
125 MWa&BAu(s),PR,California,
   V:Major Disaster 3.00
126 MWa&BAu(s),PR,V:Major
   Disaster 3.00
127 MWa&Bau(s),PR,Hell to Pay,
   pt.1 . . . . 3.00
128 MWa&BAu(s),PR,Hell to Pay
   pt.2, A:JLA 3.00
129 MWa&BAu(s),PR,HellPay,pt.3 . 3.00
130 GMo&MMr(s),PR,new menace . 3.00

131 GMo&MMr(s),PR,V:The Suit. . . 3.50
132 GMo&MMr(s),PR,V:The Suit. . . 3.50
133 GMo&MMr(s),PR,V:Mirror
   Master 3.00
134 GMo&MMr(s),PR,V:Weather
   Wizard & Captain Cold 3.00
135 GMo&MMr(s), ... 3.00
136 GMo&MMr(s),PR,Human
   Race,pt.1 . . . . 3.00
137 GMo&MMr(s),PR,Human
   Race,pt.2 . . . . 3.00
138 GMo&MMr(s),PR,Human
   Race,pt.3 . . . . 3.00
139 MMr(s),Clv,Black Flash,pt.1 . . 3.00
140 MMr(s),Clv,Black Flash,pt.2 . . 3.00
141 MMr(s),Clv,Black Flash,pt.3 . . 3.00
142 MWa&BAu(s),Clv,SLi,wedding of
   Wally West & Linda Park 3.00
143 MWa&BAu(s),Clv,V:CobaltBlue 3.00
144 MWa&BAu(s),Clv,O:CobaltBlue 3.00
145 MWa&BAu(s),PaP,VRu,
   Chain Lightning,pt.1 . . . . 3.00
146 MWa&BAu(s),PaP,VRu,
   Chain Lightning, pt.2 . . . . 3.00
147 MWa&BAu(s),PaP,VRu,
   Chain Lightning, pt.3 . . . . 3.00
148 MWa&BAu(s),PaP,VRu,
   Chain Lightning, pt.4 . . . . 3.00
149 MWa&BAu(s),PaP,VRu,
   Chain Lightning, pt.5 . . . . 3.00
150 MWa&BAu(s),PaP,VRu, Chain
   Lightning, pt.6, 48-page. 4.00
151 MWa&BAu(s),PaP,A:Robin
   & Aqualad, flashback issue 2.50
152 MWa&BAu(s),PaP,VRu,
   new costume 2.50
153 MWa&BAu(s),PaP,JMz,
   V:Folded Man 2.50
154 MWa&BAu(s),PaP,JMz, ... 2.50
155 MWa&BAu(s),PaP,JMz,
   V:Replicant 2.50
156 MWa&BAu(s),PaP,JMz 2.50
157 MWa&BAu(s),PaP,JMz,fate of
   Linda Park. 2.50
158 MWa&BAu(s),PaP,DHz. 2.50
159 MWa&BAu(s),PaP,Dark Flash . 3.00
160 BAu(s),Honeymoon on the Run 2.50
161 PaP,DHz,F:Original JSA 2.50
162 PaP,DHz,R:Felix Faust 2.50
163 RLm,DHz,A:JLA 2.50
164 DHz,BBo(c),Wonderland,pt.1 . 11.00
165 DHz,Wonderland,pt.2 . . . . 2.50
166 DHz,Wonderland,pt.3 . . . . 2.50
167 DHz,Wonderland,pt.4 . . . . 2.50

168 DHz,Wonderland,pt.5 . . . . 2.50
169 DHz,Wonderland,pt.6 . . . . 2.50
170 DHz,Blood Will Run,pt.1 . . . . . 2.50
171 DHz,Blood Will Run,pt.2 . . . . . 2.50
172 DHz,Blood Will Run,pt.3 . . . . . 2.50
173 DHz,Blood Will Run,pt.4 . . . . . 2.50
174 DHz,Moving Right Along 2.50
175 DHz,Deadly storm. 2.50
176 DHz,The Rainmaker 2.50
177 DHz,interdimensional menace . 2.50
178 DHz,Caged,V:Gorilla Grodd . . . 2.50
179 DHz,Joker:Last Laugh 2.50
180 DHz,V:Peekaboo 2.50
181 DHz,BB(c),V:Fallout 2.50
182 DPs,Absolute Zero 2.50
183 DHz,BB(c),new Trickster. 2.50
184 DHz,BB(c),Crossfire,pt.1 . . . . . 2.50
185 DHz,BB(c),Crossfire,pt.2 . . . . . 2.50
186 DHz,BB(c),Crossfire,pt.3 . . . . . 2.50
187 DHz,BB(c),Crossfire,pt.4 . . . . . 2.50
188 DHz,BB(c),Crossfire,pt.5 . . . . . 3.00
189 RBr,DPs,F:Cyborg, ... 2.50
190 Rogues spotlight,Pied Piper . . . 2.50
191 ScK,DHz,F:Hawkman 2.50
192 ScK,DHz,Run Riot,pt.1 . . . . . . 2.50
193 ScK,DHz,Run Riot,pt.2 . . . . . . 2.50
194 ScK,DHz,Run Riot,pt.3 . . . . . . 2.50
195 ScK,DHz,The Top 2.50
196 V:Peek-a-Boo 2.50
197 ScK,Blitz,pt.1 . . . . 10.00
198 ScK,Blitz,pt.2. . . . . 5.00
199 ScK,Blitz,pt.3. . . . . 3.00
200 ScK,DHz,Blitz,concl.48-pg. . . . 4.00
201 Ignition,pt.1 . . . . 2.25
202 Ignition,pt.2 . . . . 2.25
203 Ignition,pt.3 . . . . 2.25
204 Ignition,pt.4 . . . . 2.25
205 Ignition,pt.5 . . . . 2.25
206 Ignition,pt.6,concl. 2.25
207 Kid Flash & Jay Garrick 7.00
208 Kid Flash & Jay Garrick 4.00
209 Fastest Hero Alive. 3.00
210 F:New Teen Titans 3.00
211 F:Nightwing 3.00
212 F:Mirror Master 3.00
213 Sins of the Father,pro. 3.00
214 Sins of the Father,pt.1 . . . . . . 3.00
215 Sins of the Father,pt.2 . . . . . . 3.00
216 Sins of the Father, pt.3 . . . . . . 3.00
217 Identity Crisis aftermath 3.00
218 F:Heat Wave 3.00
219 Truth or Dare, x-over, pt.1. . . . 9.00
220 Rogue War,pt.1 . . . . 4.00
221 Rogue War,pt.2 . . . . 2.50
222 Rogue War,pt.3 . . . . 2.50
223 Rogue War,pt.4 . . . . 2.50
224 Rogue War,pt.5 . . . . 2.50
225 Rogue War,pt.6 . . . . 2.50
226 Wally climbs a mountain 2.50
227 ATi(c),Infinite Crisis approaches 2.50
228 ATi(c),Finish Line 2.50
229 ATi(c),Finish Line, pt.3 . . . . . . 2.50
230 ATi(c),V:Vandal Savage 2.50
Ann.#1 JG,The Deathtouch 4.00
Ann.#2 A:Wally's Father. 3.00
Ann.#3 Roots 3.00
Ann.#4 Armageddon,pt7 . . . . 3.00
Ann.#5 TC(1st Full Work),Eclipso,
    V:Rogue's Gallery 8.00
Ann.#6 Bloodlines#4,I:Argus 3.00
Ann.#7 Elseworlds story 3.50
Ann.#8 Year One story. 4.00
Ann.#9 Legends o/t Dead Earth . . . 3.50
Ann.#10 Pulp Heroes (Romance) . . 4.50
Ann.#11 BAu,BWr, Ghosts. 3.50
Ann.#12 DBw,AAd(c),JLApe: Gorilla
    Warfare 3.50
Ann.#13 Planet DC 4.00
Ann.#1 (1963) replica ed.(2001) . . . 7.50
Spec #1,IN,DG,CI,50th Anniv.,
    Three Flash's. 5.00

Spec.#1,000,000 MWa(s),JMz,
    A:Capt.Marvel of 853rd-cent. . . 2.50
Spec.#1 Our Worlds at War,48-pg . . 3.50
T.V. Spec.#1,JS,w/episode guide. . . 4.25
TPB Terminal Velocity 13.00
TPB The Life Story of the Flash . . 13.00
TPB The Return of Barry Allen . . . 13.00
TPB Born to Run 13.00
TPB Dead Heat 15.00
TPB Race Against Time, 168-pg. . 15.00
TPB Blood will Run (2002) 18.00
TPB Return of Barry Allen 13.00
TPB Rogues. 15.00
TPB Terminal Velocity 15.00
TPB Crossfire. 18.00
TPB Return of Barry Allen 13.00
TPB The Flash: Blitz 20.00
TPB Ignition (2005) 15.00
TPB Secret of Barry Allen (2005) . 20.00
TPB The Flash: Rogue War (2006) 18.00
GN Iron Heights, 48-page 6.00
GN Time Flies, 48-pg. (2002) 6.00
Secret Files #1 MWa,BAu,PRy,
    O:Flash family 6.00
Secret Files #2 (1999) 6.00
Secret Files #3, 48-page (2001) . . . 6.00
Giant #1 MWa,80-page (1998) 5.00
Giant #2 80-page 5.00

FLASH, THE:
FASTEST MAN ALIVE
June, 2006
1 KeL 3.00
1a variant NKu & JKu (c) 3.00
2 Betrayed by his family? 3.00
3 KIK, new hero of Keystone 3.00
4 Secret of the Speed Force. 3.00
5 After the Speed Force 3.00
6 Lightning in a Bottle. 3.00

FLASH & GREEN
LANTERN: THE BRAVE
& THE BOLD
1999
1 (of 6) MWa&TPe(s),BKi 2.50
2 MWa&TPe(s),BKi. 2.50
3 MWa&TPe(s),BKi. 2.50
4 MWa&TPe(s),BKi. 2.50
5 MWa&TPe(s),BKi. 2.50
6 MWa&TPe(s),BKi,concl. 2.50
TPB Flash & Green Lantern,
    Brave and the Bold, 144-page 13.00

THE FLASH PLUS
Nov., 1996
1 MWa(s),F:Wally West, Dick
    Grayson. 3.50

FLASH GORDON
1988
1 DJu,I:New Flash Gordon 3.00
2 DJu,A:Lion-Men,Shark-Men 3.00
3 DJu,V:Shark-Men. 3.00
4 DJu,Dale Kidnapped by Voltan . . 3.00
5 DJu,Alliance Against Ming 3.00
6 DJu,Arctic City 3.00
7 DJu,Alliance vs. Ming 3.00
8 DJu,Alliance vs. Ming 3.00
9 DJu,V:Ming, final issue 3.00

FLASHPOINT
Oct., 1999
1 (of 3) NBy,Elseworlds 3.00
2 NBy,Flash in wheelchair 3.00
3 NBy 3.00

FLINCH
DC/Vertigo, 1999
1 JLe,RCo,horror anthology 2.50
2 BSz,RCo(c),3 horror tales 2.50
3 KJo,3 horror tales 2.50
4 TTn,PGu,3 horror tales 2.50
5 JLd(s),RBr,3 horror tales 2.50
6 WML(s) 2.50
7 WML(s) 2.50
8 . . . . 2.50
9 3 Tales of horror. 2.50
10 . . . . 2.50
11 JLd(s) 2.50
12 . . . . 2.50
13 Hubris & dark whimsy 2.50
14 . . . . 2.50
15 3 grim tales 2.50
16 RCo(c) final issue 2.50

FLINTSTONES AND
THE JETSONS, THE
Warner Bros./DC, 1997
1 Ancestors & Descendents meet . 3.00
2 thru 21 . . . . @3.00

Flippity & Flop #19
© DC Comics, Inc.

FLIPPITY & FLOP
1952
1 Funny animal 325.00
2 . . . . 175.00
3 thru 5 . . . . @150.00
6 thru 10 . . . . @100.00
11 thru 20 . . . . @125.00
21 thru 47 . . . . @100.00

FLY, THE
Impact, 1991–92
1 I&O:Fly I:Arachnus,Chromium . . . 3.00
2 thru 17 . . . . @2.50
Ann.#1 Earthquest,pt.4,w/card. . . . 3.00

FORBIDDEN TALES
OF DARK MANSION
May-June, 1972
5 DH 75.00
6 JK 30.00
7 MK(c&a 25.00
8 MK(c&a). 25.00
9 NA(c),MK,AA 30.00
10 thru 15 Feb.–March, 1974 . . . . 25.00

All comics prices listed are for *Near Mint* condition.

DC COMICS

FOREVER MAELSTROM
Nov., 2002
1 (of 6) HC,EB,time-jumping 3.00
2 HC,EB,time past 3.00
3 HC,EB,V:Praetor 3.00
4 HC,EB,V:Ragnarok 3.00
5 HC,EB,robots 3.00
6 HC,EB,concl. 3.00

FOREVER PEOPLE, THE
1971–72
1 JK,I:Forever People,A:Superman,
   A:Darkseid 125.00
2 JK,A:Darkseid 75.00
3 JK,A:Darkseid 75.00
4 JK,A:Darkseid 75.00
5 JK 50.00
6 thru 11 JK . . . . @40.00

FOREVER PEOPLE
1988
1 Return of Forever People 3.00
2 Return of Earth of Yesterday 3.00
3 A:Mark Moonrider 3.00
4 The Dark controlls M.Moonrider . 3.00
5 R:MotherBox,Infinity Man 3.00
6 Donny's Fate, final issue 3.00

FORGOTTEN REALMS
1989–91
1 A:RealmsMaster, PriamAgrivar . . 4.00
2 Mystic Hand of Vaprak 3.00
3 thru 5 . . . . @2.75
6 thru 13 . . . . @2.50
14 thru 25 . . . . @2.25
Ann.#1 V:Advanced D&D crew . . . 3.50

FORMERLY KNOWN AS
THE JUSTICE LEAGUE
July 2003
1 (of 6) F:Maxwell Lord 2.50
2 JRu,KM 2.50
3 JRu,KM,V:Roulette 2.50
4 JRu,KM,F:Mary Marvel 2.50
5 JRu,R:G'nort 2.50
6 JRu,concl. 2.50
TPB 12.50

FOUR HORSEMEN
DC/Vertigo, Dec., 1999
1 (of 4) F:Famine 2.50
2 F:War 2.50
3 F:Pestilence 2.50
4 F:Death, concl. 2.50

FOUR STAR
BATTLE TALES
1973
1 MD 40.00
2 RH 25.00
3 MD 25.00
4 MD,JKo 25.00
5 MD,RH,BK 25.00

FOUR STAR
SPECTACULAR
March-April, 1976
1 . . . . 25.00
2 thru 6 . . . . @12.00

FOUR WOMEN
Homage/DC Oct., 2001
1 (of 5) SK 3.00
2 SK 3.00
3 thru 5 SK . . . . @3.00
TPB SK rep. #1-#5. . . . . 18.00

Fox and the Crow #4
© DC Comics, Inc.

FOX AND THE CROW
Dec.–Jan., 1951
1 . . . . 1,700.00
2 . . . . 800.00
3 . . . . 500.00
4 . . . . 500.00
5 . . . . 500.00
6 thru 10 . . . . @350.00
11 thru 20 . . . . @250.00
21 thru 40 . . . . @175.00
41 thru 60 . . . . @150.00
61 thru 80 . . . . @125.00
81 thru 94 . . . . @125.00
95 . . . . 125.00
96 thru 99 . . . . @75.00
100 . . . . 75.00
101 thru 108 . . . . @75.00
Becomes:

STANLEY & HIS
MONSTER
109 thru 112 Oct.Nov.,1968 . . . . @50.00

FREEDOM FIGHTERS
March-April, 1976
1 Freedom Fighters go to Earth-1 50.00
2 . . . . 20.00
3 . . . . 20.00
4 . . . . 20.00
5 A:Wonder Woman 25.00
6 . . . . 20.00
7 . . . . 20.00
8 . . . . 20.00
9 . . . . 20.00
10 O:Doll Man 20.00
11 O:Ray 20.00
12 O:Firebrand 25.00
13 O:Black Condor 25.00
14 A:Batgirl 25.00
15 O:Phantom Lady 25.00

FROM BEYOND THE
UNKNOWN
Oct.–Nov., 1969
1 JKu,CI 100.00
2 MA(c),CI,ATh 60.00
3 NA(c),CI 50.00
4 MA(c),CI 50.00
5 MA(c),CI 50.00
6 NA(c),I:Glen Merrit 60.00
7 CI,JKu(c) 60.00
8 NA(c),CI 60.00
9 NA(c),CI 60.00

10 MA(c),CI 60.00
11 MA(c),CI 60.00
12 JKu(c),CI 60.00
13 JKu(c),CI,WW 60.00
14 JKu(c),CI 60.00
15 MA(c),CI 60.00
16 MA(c),CI 60.00
17 MA(c),CI 60.00
18 MK(c),CI,Star Rovers 50.00
19 MK(c),CI,Star Rovers 50.00
20 . . . . 50.00
21 . . . . 50.00
22 MA(c) 55.00
23 CI,Space Museum 50.00
24 CI 50.00

FRONTIER FIGHTERS
1955–56
1 JKu,Davy Crocket, Buffalo Bill. 900.00
2 JKu. 500.00
3 thru 8 JKu. . . . . @475.00

FUNNY FOLKS
1946–1950
1 Nutsy Squirrel 500.00
2 . . . . 250.00
3 . . . . 175.00
4 1st Nutsy Squirrel(c) 175.00
5 HK 175.00
6 . . . . 125.00
7 . . . . 125.00
8 . . . . 125.00
9 . . . . 125.00
10 . . . . 125.00
11 thru 20 . . . . @125.00
21 thru 26 . . . . @125.00
Becomes:

HOLLYWOOD
FUNNY FOLKES
1950–54
27 . . . . 150.00
28 thru 40 . . . . @125.00
41 thru 60 . . . . @100.00

FUNNY STOCKING
STUFFER
March, 1985
1 . . . . 5.00

FUNNY STUFF
Summer, 1944
1 B:3 Mouseketeers Terrific
   Whatzit 1,800.00
2 . . . . 800.00
3 . . . . 500.00
4 . . . . 500.00
5 . . . . 500.00
6 thru 10 . . . . @300.00
11 thru 20 . . . . @250.00
21 . . . . 175.00
22 C:Superman 600.00
23 thru 30 . . . . @200.00
31 thru 78 . . . . @150.00
79 July-Aug., 1954 . . . . 150.00
Becomes:

DODO AND THE FROG
1954
80 F:Doodles Duck 250.00
81 thru 91 . . . . @150.00
92 scarce 200.00

FURY OF FIRESTORM
June, 1982
1 PB,I:Black Bison 7.00
2 PB,V:Black Bison 3.00
3 PB,V:Pied Piper, Killer Frost 2.50
4 PB,A:JLA,Killer Frost 2.50

5 PB,V:Pied Piper 2.50	58 I:Parasite II 2.50
6 V:Pied Piper 2.50	59 Glasshouse, V:Parasite 2.50
7 I:Plastique 2.50	60 Secret behind Hugo's accident. . 2.50
8 V:Typhoon 2.50	61 V:Typhoon 2.50
9 V:Typhoon 2.50	61a Superman Logo 40.00
10 V:Hyena 2.50	62 A:Russian Firestorm 2.50
11 V:Hyena. 2.50	63 A:Capt.Atom 2.50
12 PB,V:Hyena 2.50	64 A:Suicide Squad 2.50
13 PB,Split 2.50	Ann.#1 EC,A:Firehawk,
14 PB,I:Enforcer,A:Multiplex 2.50	V:Tokamak 2.50
15 V:Multiplex 2.50	Ann.#2 An Illustrated Novella. 2.50
16 V:Multiplex 2.50	Ann.#3 Spark 2.50
17 I:2000 Committee,Firehawk . . . 2.50	Ann.#4 KG,CS,GC,DG 2.50
18 I:Tokamak,A:Multiplex 2.50	**Becomes:**
19 GC,V:Goldenrod 2.50	
20 A:Killer Frost 2.50	

FIRESTORM, THE NUCLEAR MAN
Nov., 1987

21 D:Killer Frost 3.00	65 A:New Firestorm 2.00
22 O:Firestorm 3.00	66 A:Green Lantern 2.00
23 I:Bug & Byte 2.50	67 Millenium, Week 1 . . . . 2.00
24 I:Blue Devil,Bug & Byte 2.75	68 Millenium. 2.00
25 I:Silver Deer 2.50	69 V:Zuggernaut,Stalnivolk USA . . . 2.00
26 V:Black Bison 2.50	70 V:Flying Dutchman 2.00
27 V:Black Bison 2.50	71 Trapped In the Timestream. 2.00
28 I:Slipknot 2.50	72 V:Zuggernaut 2.00
29 I:2000 C'tee,I:Breathtaker. 2.50	73 V:Stalnivolk & Zuggernaut 2.00
30 V:2000 Committee 2.50	74 Quest for Martin Stein. 2.00
31 V:2000 Committee 2.50	75 Return of Martin Stein. 2.00
32 Phantom Stranger 2.50	76 Firestorm & Firehawk
33 A:Plastique 2.50	vs Brimstone 2.00
34 I:Killer Frost 2 . . . . 2.50	77 Firestorm & Firehawk in Africa . . 2.00
35 V:K.Frost/Plastique,I:Weasel . . 2.50	78 Exile From Eden,pt.1 . . . . 2.00
36 V:Killer Frost & Plastique 2.50	79 Exile From Eden,pt.2 . . . . 2.00
37 Not in our Stars but in Ourselves 2.50	80 A:Power Girl,Starman,Invasion
38 V:Weasel. 2.50	x-over. 2.00
39 V:Weasel. 2.50	81 A:Soyuz,Invasion aftermath 2.00
40 Graduation Day. 2.50	82 Invasion Aftermath 2.00
41 Crisis 2.50	83 V:Svarozhich 2.00
42 Crisis,A:Firehawk 2.50	84 Souls of Fire 2.00
43 V:Typhoon. 2.50	85 Soul of Fire,N:Firestorm 2.00
44 V:Typhoon 2.50	86 TMd,Janus Directive #7 . . . . . . 2.00
45 V:Multiplex 2.50	87 TMd. 2.00
46 A:Blue Devil 2.50	88 TMd,E:Air Wave B:Maser 2.00
47 A:Blue Devil 2.50	89 TMd,V:Firehawk,Vandermeer
48 I:Moonbow 2.50	Steel. 2.00
49 V:Moonbow 2.50	90 TMd,Elemental War #1 . . . . 2.00
50 W:Ed Raymond. 2.50	91 TMd,Elemental War #2 . . . . 2.00
51 A:King Crusher 2.50	92 TMd,Elemental War #3 . . . . 2.00
52 A:King Crusher 2.50	93 TMd,Elemental War concl. 2.00
53 V:Steel Shadow. 2.50	94 TMd,A:Killer Frost 2.00
54 I:Lava 2.50	95 TMd,V:Captains of Industry 2.00
55 Legends,V:World's	96 TMd,A:Shango,African God &
Luckiest Man 2.50	Obatala,Lord o/t White Cloth . . . 2.00
56 Legends,A:Hawk. 2.50	97 TMd,A:Obatala,V:Shango 2.00
57 Due Monday 2.50	98 TMd,A:Masar 2.00
	99 TMd,A:Brimstone,PlasmaGiant. . 2.00
	100 TMd,AM,V:Brimstone (Firestorm
	back-up story) final issue 3.00
	Ann.#5 JLI,Suicide Squad
	I:New Firestorm 2.50

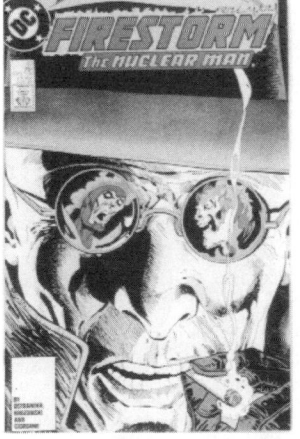

Fury of Firestorm #62
© DC Comics Inc.

GAMMARAUDERS
1989

1 I:Animal-Warrior Bioborgs 2.25	
2 thru 10 . . . . @2.25	

GANG BUSTERS
1947–58

1 DBa,Crime Agency 1,400.00	
2 DBa 600.00	
3 DBa,Fall Guy 400.00	
4 DBa,Jailbreak 400.00	
5 DBa 400.00	
6 DBa 400.00	
7 DBa 400.00	
8 DBa 400.00	
9 DBa,Ph(c) 300.00	
10 DBa,Ph(c) 300.00	
11 CS,Ph(c) 250.00	
12 DBa,CS,Ph(c) 250.00	

Gang Busters #35 © DC Comics Inc.

13 CS,Ph(c) 250.00	
14 FF,Ph(c) 500.00	
15 CS 200.00	
16 CS, Death on Wheels 200.00	
17 Dead Man's Beat 500.00	
18 CS, Black Ace Gang 175.00	
19 DBa,CS,Broadway Squad . . . 175.00	
20 CS 175.00	
21 thru 25 . . . . @150.00	
26 JK 150.00	
27 thru 40 . . . . @150.00	
41 thru 44 . . . . @125.00	
45 Comics Code 125.00	
46 thru 50 . . . . @125.00	
51 MD 125.00	
52 thru 67 . . . . @125.00	

GANGLAND
April, 1998

1 (of 4) crime anthology 3.00	
2 Platinum Nights 3.00	
3 Gang Buff. 3.00	
4 conclusion 3.00	
TPB series rep. 13.00	

GEMINI BLOOD
DC/Helix, 1996–97

1 Species: Paratwa, pt.1 . . . . 2.25	
2 Species: Paratwa, pt.2 . . . . 2.25	
3 Species: Paratwa, pt.3 . . . . 2.50	
4 Species: Paratwa, pt.4 . . . . 2.25	
5 WSi(c),Species: Paratwa,pt.5 . . . 2.25	
6 Species: Paratwa, pt.6 . . . . 2.50	
7 BSz, Gillian's secret revealed . . . 2.50	
8 Loothka BI-Modal,pt.1 . . . . 2.50	
9 Loothka BI-Modal,pt.2 . . . . 2.50	

GENESIS
Aug., 1997

1 (of 4) JBy,RoW,JRu,AD,MFm,	
Marvel x-over. 3.00	
2 JBy,RoW,JRu,AD,MFm,x-over. . . 3.00	
3 JBy,RoW,JRu,AD,MFm,x-over. . . 3.00	
4 JBy,RoW,JRu,AD,MFm,concl. . . . 3.00	

GHOSTDANCING
DC/Vertigo, 1995
[Mini-Series]

1 I:Snake,Ghost Dancing 2.50	
2 Secrets. 2.50	
3 I:Father Craft 2.50	
4 Coyote prisoner 2.50	
5 F:Snot Boy. 2.50	

DC COMICS

Ghosts #9 © DC Comics, Inc.

GHOSTS
Sept.–Oct., 1971

1 JAp,NC(c),Death's Bridegroom!................. 250.00
2 WW,NC(c),Mission
  Supernatural............ 125.00
3 TD,NC(c),Death is my Mother.. 90.00
4 GT,NC(c),The Crimson Claw... 90.00
5 NC(c),Death, The Pale
  Horseman............... 90.00
6 NC(c),A Specter Poured
  The Potion.............. 40.00
7 MK(c),Death's Finger Points ... 40.00
8 NC(c),The Cadaver In
  The Clock............... 40.00
9 AA,NC(c),The Last Ride
  Of Rosie The Wrecker...... 40.00
10 NC(c),A Specter Stalks Saigon. 40.00
11 NC(c),The Devils Lake....... 25.00
12 NC(c),The Macabre Mummy
  Of Takhem-Ahtem.......... 25.00
13 NC(c),Hell Is One Mile High.. 25.00
14 NC(c),The Bride Wore
  A Shroud................ 25.00
15 AA,NC(c),The Ghost That
  Wouldn't Die............ 25.00
16 NC(c),Death's Grinning Face.. 25.00
17 NC(c),Death Held the
  Lantern High............ 25.00
18 AA,NC(c),Graveyard of
  Vengeance............... 25.00
19 AA,NC(c),The Dead Live On.. 25.00
20 NC(c),The Haunting Hussar
  Of West Point........... 25.00
21 NC(c),The Ghost In The
  Devil's Chair........... 15.00
22 NC(c),The Haunted Horns
  Of Death................ 15.00
23 NC(c),Dead Is My Darling!... 15.00
24 AA,NC(c),You Too, Will Die... 15.00
25 AA,NC(c),Three Skulls On
  The Zambezi............. 15.00
26 DP,NC(c),The Freaky Phantom
  Of Watkins Glen.......... 15.00
27 NC(c),Conversation With
  A Corpse................ 15.00
28 DP,NC(c),Flight Of The
  Lost Phantom............ 15.00
29 NC(c),The Haunted Lady
  Of Death................ 15.00
30 NC(c),The Fangs of
  the Phantom............. 15.00
31 NC(c),Blood On The Moon.... 15.00
32 NC(c),Phantom Laughed Last. 15.00
33 NC(c),The Hangman of
  Haunted Island.......... 15.00

34 NC(c),Wrath of the Ghost Apes 15.00
35 NC(c),Feud with a Phantom... 15.00
36 NC(c),The Boy Who Returned
  From The Gave........... 15.00
37 LD(c),Fear On Ice........... 15.00
38 LD(c),Specter In The Surf..... 15.00
39 LD(c),The Haunting Hitchhiker 15.00
40 LD(c),The Nightmare That
  Haunted The World........ 30.00
41 LD(c),Ship of Specters....... 20.00
42 LD(c),The Spectral Sentries... 20.00
43 LD(c),3 Corpses On A Rope... 20.00
44 LD(c),The Case of the
  Murdering Specters....... 20.00
45 LD(c),Bray of the
  Phantom Beast........... 20.00
46 LD(c),The World's Most
  Famous Phantom.......... 20.00
47 LD(c),Wrath of the
  Restless Specters......... 20.00
48 DP,LD(c),The Phantom Head.. 20.00
49 The Ghost in the Cellar...... 20.00
50 Home Is Where The Grave Is.. 20.00
51 The Ghost Who Would Not Die 20.00
52 LD(c),Thunderhead Phantom.. 20.00
53 LD(c),Whose Spirit Invades Me 20.00
54 LD(c),The Deadly Dreams
  Of Ernie Caruso........... 20.00
55 LD(c),The House That Was
  Built For Haunting........ 20.00
56 LD(c),The Triumph Of The
  Teen-Age Phantom......... 20.00
57 LD(c),The Flaming Phantoms
  of Oradour.............. 20.00
58 LD(c),The Corpse in the Closet 20.00
59 LD(c),That Demon Within Me.. 20.00
60 LD(c),The Spectral Smile
  of Death................ 10.00
61 LD(c),When Will I Die Again... 10.00
62 LD(c),The Phantom Hoaxer!... 10.00
63 LD(c),The Burning Bride...... 10.00
64 LD(c),Dead Men Do Tell Tales. 10.00
65 LD(c),The Imprisoned Phantom 10.00
66 LD(c),Conversation With A
  Corpse................. 10.00
67 LD(c),The Spectral Sword.... 10.00
68 LD(c),The Phantom of the
  Class of '76............ 9.00
69 LD(c),The Haunted Gondola.... 9.00
70 LD(c),Haunted Honeymoon..... 9.00
71 LD(c),The Ghost Nobody Knew. 9.00
72 LD(c),The Ghost of
  Washington Monument...... 9.00
73 LD(c),The Specter Of The
  Haunted Highway.......... 9.00
74 LD(c),The Gem That Haunted
  the World!.............. 9.00
75 LD(c),The Legend Of The
  Lottie Lowry............ 9.00
76 LD(c),Two Ghosts of
  Death Row.............. 9.00
77 LD(c),Ghost, Where Do
  You Hide?............... 9.00
78 LD(c),The World's Most
  Famous Phantom.......... 9.00
79 LD(c),Lure of the Specter...... 9.00
80 JO(c),The Winged Specter..... 9.00
81 LD(c),Unburied Phantom...... 9.00
82 LD(c),The Ghost Who
  Wouldn't Die............ 9.00
83 LD(c),Escape From the Haunt
  of the Amazon Specter...... 9.00
84 LD(c),Torment of the
  Phantom Face............ 9.00
85 LD(c),The Fiery Phantom
  of Faracutin............. 9.00
86 LD(c),The Ghostly Garden..... 9.00
87 LD(c),The Phantom Freak..... 9.00
88 LD(c),Harem In Hell......... 9.00
89 JKu(c),Came The Specter
  Shrouded In Seaweed....... 9.00
90 The Ghost Galleon........... 9.00

91 LD(c),The Haunted Wheelchair. 9.00
92 DH(c),Double Vision......... 9.00
93 MK(c),The Flaming Phantoms
  of Nightmare Alley......... 9.00
94 LD(c),Great Caesar's Ghost.... 9.00
95 All The Stage Is A Haunt...... 9.00
96 DH(c),Dread of the
  Deadly Domestic.......... 9.00
97 JAp(c),A Very Special Spirit
  A:Spectre............... 15.00
98 JAp(c),The Death of a Ghost
  A:Spectre............... 15.00
99 EC(c),Till Death Do Us Join
  A:Spectre............... 15.00
100 EC&DG(c),The Phantom's
  Final Debt.............. 12.00
101 MK(c),The Haunted Hospital.. 5.00
102 RB&DG(c),The Fine Art
  Of Haunting............. 10.00
103 RB&DG(c),Visions and
  Vengeance............... 10.00
104 LD(c),The First Ghost....... 10.00
105 JKu(c)................. 10.00
106 JKu(c)................. 10.00
107 JKu(c)................. 10.00
108 JKu(c)................. 10.00
109 EC(c).................. 10.00
110 EC&DG(c)............... 10.00
111 JKu(c)................. 10.00
112 May, 1982.............. 10.00

GIANTKILLER
1999

1 (of 6)..................... 2.50
2 DIB....................... 2.50
3 DIB....................... 2.50
4 DIB,O:Jill.................. 2.50
5 DIB,V:Nox.................. 2.50
6 .... 2.50

G.I. COMBAT
Jan., 1957
Prev: Golden Age

44 RH,JKu,The Eagle and
  the Wolves............ 1,000.00
45 RH,JKu,Fireworks Hill....... 500.00
46 JKu,The Long Walk
  To Wansan.............. 400.00
47 RH, The Walking Weapon... 400.00
48 No Fence For A Jet......... 400.00
49 Frying Pan Seat........... 400.00
50 Foxhole Pilot.............. 400.00
51 RH,The Walking Weapon.... 400.00
52 JKu,JKu(c),Call For A Tank... 300.00
53 JKu,The Paper Trap........ 300.00
54 RH,JKu,Sky Tank.......... 300.00
55 Call For A Gunner.......... 300.00
56 JKu,JKu(c),The D.I.-And the
  Sand Fleas.............. 400.00
57 RH,Live Wire For Easy...... 350.00
58 JKu(c),Flying Saddle........ 350.00
59 JKu,Hot Corner........... 300.00
60 RH,Bazooka Crossroads.... 300.00
61 JKu(c),The Big Run........ 275.00
62 RH,JKu,Drop An Inch....... 275.00
63 MD,JKu(c),Last Stand....... 275.00
64 MD,RH,JKu,JKu(c),The
  Silent Jet.............. 275.00
65 JKu,Battle Parade.......... 275.00
66 MD,The Eagle of Easy
  Company................ 375.00
67 JKu(c),I:Tank Killer........ 375.00
68 JKu,RH,The Rock......... 1,200.00
69 JKu,RH,The Steel Ribbon.... 250.00
70 JKu,Bull's-Eye Bridge....... 250.00
71 MD,JKu(c),Last Stand....... 250.00
72 MD,JKu(c),Ground Fire...... 250.00
73 RH,JKu,Window War....... 250.00
74 RH,A Flag For Joey........ 250.00
75 RH,Dogtag Hill............ 300.00

76 MD,RH,JKu,Bazooka For
  A Mouse 300.00
77 RH,JKu,H-Hour For A Gunner 300.00
78 MD,RH,JKu(c),Who Cares
  About The Infantry. 300.00
79 JKu,RH,Big Gun-Little Gun. . 300.00
80 JKu,RH(c),Flying Horsemen. . 300.00
81 Jump For Glory. 250.00
82 IN,Get Off My Back. 250.00
83 Too Tired To Fight 250.00
84 JKu(c),Dog Company
  Is Holding 250.00
85 IN,JKu(c),The T.N.T. Trio 250.00
86 JKu,RH(c),Not Return 250.00
87 RH(c),I:Haunted Tank 1,200.00
88 RH,JKu(c),Haunted Tank Vs.
  Ghost Tank 400.00
89 JA,RH,IN,Tank With Wings. . . 250.00
90 JA,IN,RH,Tank Raiders. 250.00
91 IN,RH,Tank and the Turtle . . . 250.00
92 JA,IN,The Tank of Doom 250.00
93 RH(c),JA,No-Return Mission . 250.00
94 IN,RH(c),Haunted Tank Vs.
  The Killer Tank. 250.00
95 JA,RH(c),The Ghost of
  the Haunted Tank 250.00
96 JA,RH(c),The Lonesome Tank 250.00
97 IN,RH(c),The Decoy Tank . . . 250.00
98 JA,RH(c),Trap of Dragon's
  Teeth 250.00
99 JA,JKu,RH(c),Battle of the
  Thirsty Tanks 250.00
100 JA,JKu,Return of the
  Ghost Tank 250.00
101 JA,The Haunted Tank Vs.
  Attila's Battle Tiger. 175.00
102 JKu(c),Haunted Tank
  Battle Window 175.00
103 JKu,JA,RH(c),Rabbit Punch
  For A Tiger. 175.00
104 JA,JKu,RH(c),Blind
  Man's Radar 175.00
105 JA,JKu(c),Time Bomb Tank . 175.00
106 JA,JKu(c),Two-Sided War. . . 175.00
107 JKu(c),The Ghost Pipers . . . 175.00
108 JKu(c),The Wounded
  Won't Wait,I:Sgt.Rock 175.00
109 JKu(c),Battle of the Tank
  Graveyard 175.00
110 IN,JKu(c),Choose Your War . 175.00
111 JA,JKu(c),Death Trap 175.00
112 JA,JKu(c),Ghost Ace. 160.00
113 JKu,RH(c),Tank Fight In
  Death Town 160.00
114 JA,RH(c),O:Haunted Tank. . . 200.00
115 JA,RH(c),MedalsForMayhem 160.00
116 IN,JA,JKu(c),Battle Cry
  For A Dead Man 160.00
117 JA,RH,JKu(c),Tank In
  The Ice Box. 250.00
118 IN,JA,RH(c),My Buddy-
  My Enemy 160.00
119 IN,RH(c),Target For
  A Firing Squad. 160.00
120 IN,JA,RH(c),Pull a Tiger'sTail 160.00
121 RH(c),Battle of Two Wars . . . 125.00
122 JA,JKu(c),Who Dies Next?. . 125.00
123 IN,RH(c),The Target of Terro 125.00
124 IN,RH(c),Scratch That Tank . 125.00
125 RH(c),Stay Alive-Until Dark. . 125.00
126 JA,RH(c),Tank Umbrella 125.00
127 JA,JKu(c),Mission-Sudden
  Death. 125.00
128 RH(c),The Ghost of
  the Haunted Tank 125.00
129 JA,RH(c),Hold That Town
  For A Dead Man 125.00
130 RH(c),Battle of the Generals 125.00
131 JKu&RH(c),Devil For Dinner. 125.00
132 JA,JKu(c),The Executioner. . 125.00
133 JKu(c),Operation:Death Trap 125.00
134 MD,JKu(c),Desert Holocaust 125.00

G.I. Combat #190
© DC Comics, Inc.

135 GE,JKu(c),Death is the Joker 125.00
136 JKu(c),Kill Now-Pay Later. . . 125.00
137 JKu(c),We Can't See 125.00
138 JKu(c),I:The Losers 200.00
139 JKu(c),Corner of Hell 100.00
140 RH,MD,JKu(c),The LastTank 100.00
141 MD,JKu(c),Let Me Live..
  Let Me Die. 50.00
142 RH,JKu(c),Checkpoint-Death . 50.00
143 RH,JKu(c),Iron Horseman . . . 50.00
144 RH,MD,JKu(c),Every
  Man A Fort. 60.00
145 MD,JKu(c),Sand,Sun
  and Death 60.00
146 JKu(c),Move the World. 60.00
147 JKu(c),Rebel Tank 60.00
148 IN,JKu(c),The Gold-Plated
  General 60.00
149 JKu(c),Leave The
  Fighting To Us 50.00
150 JKu(c),The Death of the
  Haunted Tank 50.00
151 JKu(c),A Strong Right Arm . . 50.00
152 JKu(c),Decoy Tank 50.00
153 JKu(c),The Armored Ark 50.00
154 JKu(c),Battle Prize 50.00
155 JKu(c),The Long Journey . . . 26.00
156 JKu(c),Beyond Hell 25.00
157 JKu(c),The Fountain 25.00
158 What Price War. 25.00
159 JKu(c),Mission Dead End . . . 25.00
160 JKu(c),Battle Ghost. 25.00
161 JKu(c),The Day of the Goth . . 25.00
162 JKu(c),The Final Victor 25.00
163 A Crew Divided 25.00
164 Siren Song 25.00
165 JKu(c),Truce,Pathfinder 25.00
166 Enemy From Yesterday 25.00
167 JKu(c),The Finish Line 25.00
168 NA(c),The Breaking Point. . . 35.00
169 WS(c),The Death of the
  Haunted Tank 25.00
170 Chain of Vengeance 25.00
171 JKu(c),The Man Who
  Killed Jeb Stuart 25.00
172 RH(c),At The Mercy of
  My Foes. 25.00
173 JKu(c),The Final Crash. 25.00
174 JKu(c),Vow To A Dead Foe. . 25.00
175 JKu(c),The Captive Tank . . . 25.00
176 JKu(c),A Star Can Cry 25.00
177 JKu(c),The Tank That
  Missed D-Day 25.00
178 JKu(c),A Tank Is Born 25.00

179 JKu(c),One Last Charge. 25.00
180 JKu(c),The Saints Go
  Riding On 25.00
181 JKu(c),The Kidnapped Tank . . 25.00
182 JKu(c),Combat Clock 25.00
183 JKu(c),6 Stallions To
  Hell- And Back. 25.00
184 JKu(c),Battlefield Bundle . . . 25.00
185 JKu(c),No Taps For A Tank. . . 25.00
186 JKu(c),Souvenir
  From A Headhunter 25.00
187 JKu(c),The General
  Died Twice. 25.00
188 The Devil's Pipers 25.00
189 The Gunner is a Gorilla 25.00
190 The Tiger and The Terrier . . . 25.00
191 Decoy For Death. 25.00
192 The General Has Two Faces . 25.00
193 JKu(c),The War That
  Had To Wait. 25.00
194 GE(c),Blitzkrieg Brain 25.00
195 JKu(c),The War That
  Time Forgot. 25.00
196 JKu(c),Dead Men Patrol 25.00
197 JKu(c),Battle Ark. 25.00
198 JKu(c),The Devil
  Rides A Panzer 25.00
199 JKu(c),A Medal From A Ghost 25.00
200 JKu(c),The Tank That Died. . . 25.00
201 NA&RH(c),The Rocking
  Chair Soldiers 35.00
202 NA&RH(c),Walking Wounded
  Don't Cry 35.00
203 JKu(c),To Trap A Tiger 25.00
204 JKu(c),A Winter In Hell 25.00
205 JKu(c),A Gift From
  The Emperor 25.00
206 JKu(c),A Tomb For A Tank . . . 25.00
207 JKu(c),Foxhole for a Sherman 25.00
208 JKu(c),Sink That Tank. 25.00
209 JKu(c),Ring Of Blood 25.00
210 JKu(c),Tankers Also Bleed . . . 25.00
211 JKu(c),A Nice Day For Killing . 20.00
212 JKu(c),Clay Pigeon Crew 20.00
213 JKu(c),Back Door To War 20.00
214 JKu(c),The Tanker Who
  Couldn't Die. 20.00
215 JKu(c),Last Stand For Losers . 20.00
216 JKu(c),Ghost Squadron 20.00
217 JKu(c), The Pigeon Spies 20.00
218 JKu(c), 48 Hours to Die 20.00
219 thru 230 . . . . @20.00
231 thru 288 . . . . @20.00

GILGAMESH II
1989
1 JSn,O:Gilgamesh. 5.00
2 JSn,V:Nightshadow 4.50
3 JSn,V:Robotic Ninja. 4.50
4 JSn,final issue 4.00

GIRLS' LOVE STORIES
1949
1 ATh,EK,Romance 800.00
2 EK 400.00
3 thru 10 . . . . @275.00
11 thru 20 . . . . @200.00
21 EK 150.00
22 thru 83 . . . . @100.00

GIRLS' ROMANCES
1950
1 Ph(c) 800.00
2 ATh,Ph(c). 400.00
3 Ph(c) 275.00
4 thru 6 Ph(c) . . . . @250.00
7 thru 10 . . . . @250.00
11 . . . . 175.00
12 . . . . 175.00
13 ATh(c) 200.00
14 thru 20 . . . . @175.00

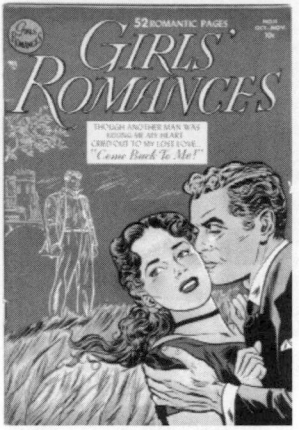

Girls' Romances #11
© DC Comics, Inc.

21 thru 31 . . . . @150.00
32 thru 50 . . . . @125.00
51 thru 80 . . . . @100.00

GIRL WHO WOULD BE DEATH, THE
DC/Vertigo, 1998
1 thru 4 F:Plath . . . . @2.50

GODDESS
DC/Vertigo, 1995–96
[Mini-Series]
1 I:Rosie Nolan 4.00
2 Rosie arrested 4.00
3 I:Jenny 4.00
4 CIA Chase 4.00
5 V:Agent Hooks 4.00
6 V:Harry Hooks 4.00
7 Mudhawks Past 4.00
8 finale 4.00
TPB Goddess, GEn, 256-page 20.00

GOLDEN AGE
Elseworld 1993–94
1 PS,F:JSA,All-Star Squadron 8.00
2 PS,I:Dynaman 7.00
3 PS,IR:Mr. Terrific is
    Ultra-Humanite 7.00
4 PS,D:Dynaman,Mr. Terrific 6.00
1 Secret Files,48-page(2000) 5.00

GOTHAM CENTRAL
Dec. 2002
1 MLr,F:Gotham Detectives 3.50
2 MLr,cop murdered 3.00
3 MLr,V:Firebug 3.00
4 MLr,V:Firebug 2.50
5 MLr,two cases 2.50
6 MLr,Half a Life,pt.1 . . . . 2.50
7 MLr,Half a Life,pt.2 . . . . 2.50
8 MLr,Half a Life,pt.3 . . . . 2.50
9 MLr,Half a Life,pt.4 . . . . 2.50
10 MLr,Half a Life,pt.5 . . . . 2.50
11 F:Stacy 2.50
12 A sniper strikes 2.50
13 shadow of the Joker 2.50
14 Joker's reign of terror 2.50
15 Joker sniper spree 2.50
16 Sarge and Crowe 2.50
17 Murder of businesswoman 2.50
18 Hot homicide case 2.50
19 Harvey Bullock 2.50

20 Mad Hatter, Penguin 2.50
21 Mad Hatter, Penguin, Harvey . . . 2.50
22 High School BB Massacre 2.50
23 War Games tie-in 2.50
24 War Games tie-in 2.50
25 MLr,SGa 2.50
26 MLr(c),F:Catwoman 2.50
27 MLr(c),F:Catwoman 2.50
28 MLr(c) 2.50
29 MLr(c),Keystone Ci ty 2.50
30 MLr(c) 2.50
31 Dr. Alchemy 2.50
32 Robin's body 2.50
33 Robin's body 2.50
34 F:Teen Titans 2.50
35 Batman's not talking 2.50
36 Dead Robin, concl. 2.50
37 A:Captain Marvel 2.50
38 The Spectre? 2.50
39 A Hero fallen 2.50
40 Another officer gone 2.50
TPB Batman: Gotham Central . . . 10.00
TPB Half a Life 15.00
TPB The Quick and the Dead 15.00
TPB Unresolved Targets 15.00

GOTHAM GIRLS
Aug., 2002
1 (of 5) F:Catwoman 2.25
2 Catwoman,Batgirl,P.Ivy,H.Quinn . 2.25
3 Poison Ivy, Harley Quinn 2.25
4 Batgirl 2.25
5 Renee Montoya, concl. 2.25

GREATEST STORIES EVER TOLD
TPB Superman (1989) 16.00
TPB Batman (1989) 16.00
TPB Vol.#2 Catwoman & Penguin . 17.00
TPB Joker (1989) BBo(c) 15.00
TPB Flash (1991) 15.00
TPB Golden Age (1990) 15.00
TPB Fifties 15.00
TPB Team-Up (1990) 15.00

GREEN ARROW
[Limited Series], 1983
1 TVE,DG,O:Green Arrow 5.00
2 TVE,DG,A:Vertigo 4.00
3 TVE,DG,A:Vertigo 4.00
4 TVE,DG,A:Black Canary 4.00

[Regular Series], 1988–97
1 EH,DG,V:Muncie 5.00
2 EH,DG,V:Muncie 4.00
3 EH,DG,FMc,V:Fyres 4.00
4 EH,DG,FMc,V:Fyres 4.00
5 EH,DG,FMc,Gauntlet 4.00
6 EH,DG,FMc,Gauntlet 4.00
7 EB,DG,A:Black Canary 4.00
8 DG,Alaska 3.50
9 EH,DG,FMc,R:Shado 3.50
10 EH,DG,FMc,A:Shado 3.50
11 EH,DG,FMc,A:Shado 3.50
12 EH,DG,FMc,A:Shado 3.00
13 DJu,DG,FMc,Moving Target 3.00
14 EH,DG,FMc. 3.00
15 EH,DG,FMc,Seattle And Die . . . 3.00
16 EH,DG,FMc,Seattle And Die . . . 3.00
17 DJu,DG,FMc,The Horse Man . . . 2.50
18 DJu,DG,FMc,The Horse Man . . . 2.50
19 EH,DG,A:Hal Jordan 2.50
20 EH,DG,FMc,A:Hal Jordan 2.50
21 DJu,DG,B:Blood of Dragon,
    A:Shado 4.00
22 DJu,DG,A:Shado 2.50
23 DJu,DG,A:Shado 2.50
24 DJu,DG,E:Blood of Dragon 2.50
25 TVE,Witch Hunt #1 . . . . 2.50
26 Witch Hunt #2 . . . . 2.50
27 DJu,DG,FMc,R:Warlord 2.50

Green Arrow #73
© DC Comics, Inc.

28 DJu,DG,FMc,A:Warlord 2.50
29 DJu,DG,FMc,Coyote Tears 2.50
30 DJu,DG,FMc,Coyote Tears 2.50
31 FMc,V:Drug Dealers 2.50
32 FMc,V:Drug Dealers 2.50
33 DJu,FMc,Psychology Issue 2.50
34 DJu,DG,A:Fryes,Arrested 2.50
35 B:Black Arrow Saga,A:Shade . . 2.50
36 Black Arrow Saga,A:Shade 2.50
37 Black Arrow Saga,A:Shade 2.50
38 E:Black Arrow Saga,A:Shade . . 2.50
39 DCw,Leaves Seattle 2.50
40 MGr,Spirit Quest,A:
    Indian Shaman 2.50
41 DCw,I.R.A. 2.50
42 DCw,I.R.A. 2.50
43 DCw,I.R.A. 2.50
44 DCw,Rock'n'Runes,pt.1 . . . . 2.50
45 Rock'n'Runes,pt.2. . . . . 2.50
46 DCw,Africa 2.50
47 DCw,V:Trappers 2.50
48 DCw,V:Trappers 2.50
49 V:Trappers 2.50
50 MGr(c),50th Anniv.,R:Seattle . . . 3.00
51 Tanetti's Murder,pt.1 . . . . 2.50
52 Tanetti's Murder,pt.2 . . . . 2.50
53 The List,pt.1,A:Fyres. 2.50
54 The List,pt.2,A:Fyres. 2.50
55 Longbow Hunters tie-in 2.50
56 A:Lt. Cameron. 2.50
57 And Not A Drop to Drink,pt.1 . . . 2.50
58 And Not A Drop to Drink,pt.2 . . . 2.50
59 Predator,pt.1 . . . . 2.50
60 Predator,pt.2. . . . . 2.50
61 FS,F:Draft Dodgers 2.50
62 FS 2.50
63 FS,B:Hunt for Red Dragon 2.50
64 FS,Hunt for Red Dragon 2.50
65 MGr(c),Hunt for Red Dragon . . . 2.50
66 MGr(c),E:Hunt for Red Dragon . . 2.50
67 MGr(c),FS,V:Rockband Killer . . . 2.50
68 MGr(c),FS,BumRap 2.50
69 MGr(c),Reunion Tour #1 . . . . . . 2.50
70 Reunion Tour #2 . . . . 2.50
71 Wild in the Streets #1 . . . . 2.50
72 MGr(c),Wild in the Streets#2 . . . 2.50
73 MGr(c),F:Vietnam Vet 2.50
74 SAP,MGr(c),V:Sniper 2.50
75 MGr(c),A:Speedy Shado,
    Black Canary 3.00
76 MGr(c),R:Eddie Fyers. 2.50
77 MGr(c),A:Eddie Fyers 2.50
78 MGr(c),V:CIA 2.50
79 MGr(c),V:CIA 2.50

80 MGr(c),F:MGr(s),V:CIA 2.50
81 B:CDi(s),JAp,V:Shrapnel,
   Nuklon 2.50
82 JAp,I:Rival 2.50
83 JAp,V:Yakuza 2.50
84 E:CDi(s),JAp,In Las Vegas 2.50
85 AlG(s),JAp,A:Deathstroke 2.50
86 DgM(s),JAp,A:Catwoman 2.50
87 JAp,V:Factory Owner 2.50
88 JAp,A:M.Manhunter,Bl.Beetle . . . 2.50
89 JAp,A:Anarky 2.50
90 Zero Hour 2.50
91 Hitman 2.50
92 Partner attacked 2.50
93 Secrets of Red File 2.50
94 I:Camo Rouge 2.50
95 V:Camo Rouge 2.50
96 I:Slyfox,A:Hal Jordan 3.00
97 Where Angels Fear to Tread 2.50
98 Where Angels Fear to
   Tread,pt.3, A:Arsenal 2.50
99 Where Angels Fear to Tread 2.50
100 JAp,Angels Fear to Tread 12.00
101 A:Superman,Black Canary . . . 35.00
102 CDi,RbC,Underworld
   Unleashed tie-in 3.00
103 CDi,RbC,Underworld
   Unleashed tie-in 3.00
104 CDi,RbC,A:Green Lantern 3.00
105 CDi,RbC,A:Robin 3.00
106 CDi,RbC 2.50
107 CDi,RbC,protects child-king . . . 2.50
108 CDi,A:Thorn 2.50
109 CDi,JAp,BSz,in Metropolis 2.50

Green Arrow #110
© DC Comics Inc.

110 CDi(s),RbC,I:Hatchet, Green
   Lantern x-over 3.50
111 CDi(s),RbC,I:Hatchet, Green
   Lantern x-over 3.50
112 CDi(s),RbC, ... 2.50
113 CDi(s),RbC,In the Mongolian
   wastes 2.50
114 CDi(s) RbC,airplane downed,
   Final Night tie-in 2.50
115 CDi(s),RbC,IronDeath,pt.1 . . . . 2.50
116 CDi(s),RbC,IronDeath,pt.2 . . . . 2.50
117 CDi(s),RbC,IronDeath,pt.3 . . . . 2.50
118 CDi(s),DBw,RbC,Endangered
   Species, pt.1 . . . . 2.50
119 CDi(s),DBw,RbC,Endangered
   Species, pt.2 . . . . 2.50
120 CDi(s),RbC,at grandfather's
   ranch 2.50

121 CDi(s),RbC,V:The Silver
   Monkey 2.50
122 CDi(s),RbC, at Idaho ranch . . . 2.50
123 CDi(s),JAp,KJ,The
   Stormbringers, concl 2.50
124 CDi(s),RbC,V:Milo Armitage . . . 2.50
125 CDi(s),DBw,Green Lantern
   x-over,pt.1, 48pg 3.50
126 CDi(s),DBw,x-over, pt.3 . . . . . . 3.00
127 CDi(s),DBw,to San Francisco . . 3.00
128 CDi(s),DWb,Russian Mob 3.00
129 CDi,DBw,Jansen prisoner,pt.2 . 3.00
130 CDi,DBw, ... 3.00
131 CDi,DBw,F:Crackshot 3.00
132 CDi,DBw,Eddie Fyers returns . . 3.00
133 CDi,DBw,Eddie Fyers pt.2 . . . . 3.00
134 CDi,DBw,Brotherhood of
   the Fist x-over,pt.1 . . . . 3.00
135 CDi,DBw,Brotherhood of the
   Fist x-over, concl. 3.00
136 CDi,DBw,Green Pastures,pt.1 . 3.00
137 CDi(s),A:Superman 15.00
Ann.#1 A:Question,FablesII 4.00
Ann.#2 EH,DG,FMc,A:Question . . . 3.50
Ann.#3 A:Question 3.50
Ann.#4 The Black Alchemist 3.50
Ann.#5 TVE,FS,Eclipso,Batman . . . 3.50
Ann.#6 JBa(c),I:Hook 3.50
Ann.#7 CDi, Year One 4.25
Spec. #0 Return 2.50
Spec.#1,000,000 CDi(s), A:Superman
   final issue 2.50

GREEN ARROW
Feb., 2001
1 PhH,Quiver,pt.1 . . . . 15.00
1a 2nd printing 3.00
2 PhH,Quiver,pt.2 . . . . 8.00
3 PhH,Quiver,pt.3 . . . . 6.00
4 PhH,Quiver,pt.4,A:JLA 6.00
5 PhH,Quiver,pt.5,A:Batman 6.00
6 PhH,Quiver,pt.6,F:Arsenal 4.00
7 PhH,Quiver,pt.7 . . . . 4.00
8 PhH,Quiver,pt.8 . . . . 4.00
9 PhH,Quiver,pt.9 . . . . 4.00
10 PhH,Quiver,concl. 4.00
11 KSm(s),PhH,rediscovery 3.50
12 KSm(s),PhH,Ollie,Connor 4.00
13 KSm(s),PhH,Oliver & Connor . . . 4.00
14 KSm(s),PhH,Onomatopoeia 4.00
15 KSm(s),PhH,last Smith issue . . . 4.00
16 PhH,Archers Quest,pt.1 . . . . 5.00
17 PhH,Archers Quest,pt.2 . . . . 3.50
18 PhH Archers Quest,pt.3 . . . . 3.50
19 PhH,Archers Quest,pt.4,F.JLA . . 0.00
20 PhH,Archers Quest,pt.5 . . . . 3.50
21 PhH,Archers Quest,pt.6 . . . . 3.50
22 PhH,V:Count Vertigo 3.00
23 CAd,Urban Knights,pt.1 x-over . . 3.00
24 CAd,Urban Knights,pt.3 x-over . . 3.00
25 CAd,Urban Knights,pt.5 x-over . . 3.00
26 PhH,Straight Shooter,pt.1 . . . . . 2.50
27 PhH,Straight Shooter,pt.2 . . . . . 2.50
28 PhH,Straight Shooter,pt.3 . . . . . 2.50
29 PhH,Straight Shooter,pt.4 . . . . . 2.50
30 PhH,Straight Shooter,pt.5 . . . . . 2.50
31 PhH,Straight Shooter,pt.6 . . . . . 2.50
32 F:Arsenal,Green Arrow II 2.50
33 SMa,F:Superman,Plastic Man . . 2.50
34 PhH,City Walls,pt.1 . . . . 2.50
35 PhH,City Walls,pt.2 . . . . 2.50
36 PhH,City Walls,pt.3 . . . . 2.50
37 PhH,City Walls,pt.4 . . . . 2.50
38 PhH,City Walls,pt.5 . . . . 2.50
39 PhH,City Walls,pt.6 . . . . 2.50
40 PhH,New Blood,pt.1 . . . . 2.50
41 PhH,New Blood,pt.2 . . . . 2.50
42 PhH,New Blood,pt.3 . . . . 2.50
43 PhH,New Blood, pt.4 . . . . 5.00
44 PhH,New Blood, pt.5 . . . . 3.00
45 PhH,New Blood, pt.6 . . . . 2.50
46 RyR,Team Green road trip 2.50

47 RyR,V:Brick, El Pasan Assassin . 2.50
48 RyR,V:Duke of Oil 2.50
49 RyR,V:Drakon 2.50
50 RyR,F:Batman, 40-page 3.50
51 Anarky returns 2.50
52 Heading into the Light 2.50
53 Heading into the Light 2.50
54 Heading into the Light 2.50
55 Heading Into the Light 2.50
56 Heading Into the Light, pt.3 . . . . 2.50
57 Heading into the Light, concl 2.50
58 Star City Under Attack 2.50
59 V:Merlyn 2.50
60 SMc,One Year Later 2.50
61 SMc,V:Deathstroke 3.00
62 SMc,V:Deathstroke 3.00
63 SMc,Flesh-eating monsters 3.00
64 SMc,Zombies attack 3.00
65 SMc,Away Game,pt.1 . . . . 3.00
66 SMc,Away Game,pt.2 . . . . 3.00
67 SMc,Deadly mercenaries 3.00
68 SMc,End of Ollie's training 3.00
Spec. Secret Files #1,64-pg. 5.00
GN Green Arrow by Jack Kirby 6.00
TPB Traitor, 144-page 13.00
TPB Quiver 18.00
TPB The Sounds of Violence 13.00
TPB Straight Shooter 13.00
TPB Archer's Quest 15.00
TPB City Walls (2005) 13.00
TPB Moving Targets (2006) 18.00
TPB Heading into the Light (2006) 13.00
GN Green Arrow, Legacy: Last WIll
   & Testament of Hal Jordan 18.00

GREEN ARROW
LONGBOW HUNTERS
Aug., 1987
1 MGr,N:GreenArrow,I:Shado 7.00
1a 2nd printing 3.00
2 MGr,Shadow Revealed 5.00
2a 2nd printing 3.00
3 MGr,Tracking Snow 5.00
TPB, rep. #1–#3 . . . . 13.00
TPB Longbow Hunters, new pr. . . . 15.00

GREEN ARROW:
THE WONDER YEARS
1993
1 MGr,GM,B:New O:Green Arrow . 2.50
2 MGr,GM,I:Brianna Stone 2.50
3 MGr,GM,A:Brianna Stone 2.50
4 MGr,GM,Conclusion 2.50

GREEN CANDLES
1995
1 Paradox Mystery,F:John Halting . 6.00
2 F:John Halting 6.00
3 finale 6.00
TPB B&W rep. #1–#3 . . . . 10.00

GREEN LANTERN
[Original Series], Autumn, 1941
1 O:Green Lantern, V:Master of
   Light, Arson in the Slums . 60,000.00
2 V:Baldy,Tycoon's Legacy . 12,000.00
3 War cover 8,500.00
4 Doiby and Green Lantern
   join the Army 6,500.00
5 V:Nazis and Black
   Prophet,A:General Prophet 4,400.00
6 V:Nordo & Hordes of War Hungry
   Henchmen,Exhile of Exiles,
   A:Shiloh 3,300.00
7 The Wizard of Odds 3,500.00
8 The Lady and Her Jewels,
   A:Hop Harrigan 3,300.00
9 V:The Whistler, The School
   for Vandals 3,000.00

DC COMICS

Green Lantern, Original Series #12
© DC Comics, Inc.

10 V:Vandal Savage,The Man Who
    Wanted the World,O:Vandal
    Savage 3,000.00
11 The Distardly Designs of
    Doiby Dickles' Pals. 2,200.00
12 O:The Gambler 2,200.00
13 A:Angela Van Enters 2,200.00
14 Case of the Crooked Cook . 2,200.00
15 V:Albert Zero, One...Two...
    Three...Stop Thinking 2,200.00
16 V:The Lizard. 2,200.00
17 V:Kid Triangle, Reward for
    Green Lantern 2,200.00
18 V:The Dandy,The Connoisseur
    of Crime, X-mas(c) 2,500.00
19 V:Harpies, Sing a Song of
    Disaster A:Fate. 2,100.00
20 A:Gambler 2,100.00
21 V:The Woodman,The Good
    Humor Man. 1,700.00
22 A:Dapper Dan Crocker. 1,700.00
23 Doiby Dickles Movie
    Ajax Pictures 1,700.00
24 A:Mike Mattson,OnceA Cop. 1,700.00
25 The Diamond Magnet 1,700.00
26 The Scourge of the Sea. . . . 1,700.00
27 V:Sky Pirate 1,700.00
28 The Tricks of the
    Sports Master 1,700.00
29 Meets the Challenge of
    the Harlequin 1,700.00
30 I:Streak the Wonder Dog . . . 1,700.00
31 The Terror of the Talismans . 1,500.00
32 The Case of the
    Astonishing Juggler 1,500.00
33 Crime Goes West 1,500.00
34 Streak meets the Princess . 1,500.00
35 V:Three-in-One Criminal . . . 1,500.00
36 The Mystery of the
    Missing Messenger 1,700.00
37 A:Sargon 1,700.00
38 DoublePlay,May-June,1949 . 1,700.00

GREEN LANTERN
[1st Regular Series],
1960–72, 1976–86

1 GK,O:Green Lantern. 8,000.00
2 GK,I:Qward,Pieface 1,700.00
3 GK,V:Qward. 1,000.00
4 GK,Secret of GL Mask. 900.00
5 GK,I:Hector Hammond 900.00
6 GK,I:Tomar-Re. 900.00
7 GK,I&O:Sinestro 700.00
8 GK,1st Story in 5700 A.D. . . . 600.00
9 GK,A:Sinestro 600.00

10 GK,O:Green Lantern's Oath 2,000.00
11 GK,V:Sinestro 550.00
12 GK,Sinestro,I:Dr.Polaris . . . 550.00
13 GK,A:Flash,Sinestro 750.00
14 GK,I&O:Sonar,1st Jordan
    Brothers story 500.00
15 GK,Zero Hour story. 500.00
16 GK,MA,I:Star Saphire,
    O:Abin Sur. 500.00
17 GK,V:Sinestro 500.00
18 GK. 500.00
19 GK,A:Sonar. 500.00
20 GK,A:Flash 500.00
21 GK,O:Dr.Polaris 400.00
22 GK,A:Hector Hammond,Jordan
    Brothers story 400.00
23 GK,I:Tattooed Man 400.00
24 GK,O:Shark. 400.00
25 GK,V:Sonar,HectorHammond. 400.00
26 GK,A:Star Sapphire 400.00
27 GK. 400.00
28 GK,I:Goldface. 400.00
29 GK,I:Black Hand 400.00
30 GK,I:Katma Tui 400.00
31 GK,Jordan brothers story . . . 350.00
32 GK. 350.00
33 GK,V:Dr. Light. 350.00
34 GK,V:Hector Hammond 350.00
35 GK,I:Aerialist. 350.00
36 GK. 350.00
37 GK,I:Evil Star 350.00
38 GK,A:Tomar-Re. 350.00
39 GK,V:Black Hand 350.00
40 GK,O:Guardians,A:Golden
    Age Green Lantern 900.00
41 GK,A:Star Sapphire 300.00
42 GK,A:Zatanna. 300.00
43 GK,A:Major Disaster 300.00
44 GK,A:Evil Star. 300.00
45 GK,I:Prince Peril,A:Golden
    Age Green Lantern 400.00
46 GK,V:Dr.Polaris. 300.00
47 GK,5700 A.D. V:Dr.Polaris . . . 300.00
48 GK,I:Goldface 300.00
49 GK,I:Dazzler 300.00
50 GK,V:Thraxon the Powerful . . 300.00
51 GK,Green Lantern's Evil
    Alter-ego 200.00
52 GK,A:Golden Age Green
    Lantern Sinestro 200.00
53 GK,CI:Jordon brothers story . . 200.00
54 GK,Menace in the Iron Lung. . 200.00
55 GK,Cosmic Enemy #1 . . . . . . 200.00
56 GK. 200.00
57 GK,V:Major Disaster 200.00
58 GK,Perils of the Powerless
    Green Lantern 200.00
59 GK,I:Guy Gardner(imaginary
    story) 375.00
60 GK,I:Lamplighter. 150.00
61 GK,A:Gold.Age Gr.Lantern . . . 150.00
62 Steel Small,Rob Big 150.00
63 NA(c),This is the Way the
    World Ends 150.00
64 MSy,We Vow Death to Green
    Lantern 150.00
65 MSy,Dry up and Die 150.00
66 MSy,5700 AD story 150.00
67 DD,The First Green Lantern . . 150.00
68 GK,I Wonder Where The
    Yellow Went?. 150.00
69 GK,WW,If Earth Fails the
    Test.. It Means War 150.00
70 GK,A Funny Thing Happened
    on the way to Earth 150.00
71 GK,DD,MA,Jordan brothers . . 125.00
72 GK,Phantom o/t SpaceOpera . 125.00
73 GK,MA,A:Star Saphire,
    Sinestro 125.00
74 GK,MA,A:Star Saphire,
    Sinestro 125.00
75 GK,Qward 125.00

Green Lantern, 1st Series #76
© DC Comics, Inc.

76 NA,Gr.Lantern & Gr.Arrow
    team-up begins 600.00
77 NA,Journey to Desolation. . . . 200.00
78 NA,A:Black Canary,A Kind of
    Loving..A Way to Death. 150.00
79 NA,DA,A:Black Canary,Ulysses
    Star is Still Alive 150.00
80 NA,DG,Even an Immortal
    can die. 150.00
81 NA,DG,A:Black Canary,Death
    be my Destiny 150.00
82 NA,DG,A:Black Canary,
    V:Sinestro,(BWr 1 page) 150.00
83 NA,DG,A:BlackCanary,Gr.Lantern
    reveals I.D. to Carol Ferris . . 150.00
84 NA,BWr,V:Black Hand 150.00
85 NA,Speedy on Drugs,pt.1,
    rep.Green Lantern #1 . . . . . . 175.00
86 NA,DG,Speedy on Drugs,pt.2,
    ATh(rep)Golden Age G.L. . . . 175.00
87 NA,DG,I:John Stewart,
    2nd Guy Gardner app. 150.00
88 all reprints. 75.00
89 NA,And Through Him Save
    the World 125.00
90 MGr,New Gr.Lantern rings . . . 50.00
91 MGr,V:Sinestro 30.00
92 MGr,V:Sinestro 30.00
93 MGr,TA,War Against the
    World Builders. 30.00
94 MGr,TA,DG,Green Arrow
    Assassin,pt.1 . . . . 30.00
95 MGr,Gr.Arrow Assassin,pt.2 . . 30.00
96 MGr,A:Katma Tui 30.00
97 MGr,V:Mocker. 30.00
98 MGr,V:Mocker. 30.00
99 MGr,V:Mocker. 30.00
100 MGr,AS,I:Air Wave 45.00
101 MGr,A:Green Arrow 30.00
102 AS,A:Green Arrow. 20.00
103 AS,Earth-Asylum for an Alien . 20.00
104 AS,A:Air Wave 20.00
105 AS,Thunder Doom 20.00
106 MGr,Panic..In High Places
    & Low 20.00
107 AS,Green Lantern Corp.story . 20.00
108 MGr,BU:G.A.Green Lantern,
    V:Replikon 25.00
109 MGr,Replicon#2,GA.GL.#2 . . . 20.00
110 MGr,GA.GL.#3 . . . . 20.00
111 AS,O:Green Lantern,
    A:G.A.Green Lantern. 25.00
112 AS,O&A:G.A. Green Lantern. . 35.00
113 AS,Christmas story 18.00
114 AS,I:Crumbler 18.00

115 AS,V:Crumbler. 18.00
116 Guy Gardner as Gr.Lantern . . 50.00
117 JSon,I:KariLimbo,V:Prof.Ojo . . 12.00
118 AS,V:Prof.Ojo 12.00
119 AS,G.L.& G.A.solo storys. 12.00
120 DH,A:Kari,V:El Espectro 6.00
121 DH,V:El Espectro 6.00
122 DH,A:Guy Gardner,Superman 10.00
123 JSon,DG,E:Green Lantern/Green
    Arrow T.U.,A:G.Gardner,
    V:Sinestro 12.00
124 JSon,V:Sinestro 6.00
125 JSon,FMc,V:Sinestro 6.00
126 JSon,FMc,V:Shark 6.00
127 JSon,FMc,V:Goldface. 6.00
128 JSon,V:Goldface 6.00
129 JSon,V:Star Sapphire 6.00
130 JSon,FMc,A:Sonar,B:Tales of the
    Green Lantern Corps. 6.00
131 JSon,AS,V:Evil Star 6.00
132 JSon,AS,E:Tales of GL Corps
    B:B.U.Adam Strange 6.00
133 JSon,V:Dr.Polaris 5.00
134 JSon,V:Dr.Polaris 5.00
135 JSon,V:Dr.Polaris 5.00
136 JSon,A:Space Ranger,
    Adam Strange 5.00
137 JSon,CI,MA,I:Citadel,A:Space
    Ranger,A.Strange 5.00
138 JSon,A&O:Eclipso. 6.00
139 JSon,V:Eclipso 5.00
140 JSon,I:Congressman Block
    Adam Strange 5.00
141 JSon,I:OmegaMen 7.00
142 JSon,A:OmegaMen. 6.00
143 JSon,A:OmegaMen. 6.00
144 JSon,D:Tattooed Man,Adam
    Strange 5.00
145 JSon,V:Goldface 5.00
146 JSon,CI,V:Goldface
    E:B.U.Adam Strange 5.00
147 JSon,CI,V:Goldface 5.00
148 JSon,DN,DA,V:Quadrians. 5.00
149 JSon,A:GL.Corps 5.00
150 JSon,anniversary 6.00
151 JSon,GL.Exiled in space. 5.00
152 JSon,CI,GL Exile #2 . . . . 5.00
153 JSon,CI,Gr.Lantern Exile #3 . . . 5.00
154 JSon,Gr.Lantern Exile #4 . . . . . 5.00
155 JSon,Gr.Lantern Exile #5 . . . . . 5.00
156 GK,Gr.Lantern Exile #6. . . . . . . 5.00
157 KP,IN,Gr.Lantern Exile #7 . . . . . 5.00
158 KP,IN,Gr.Lantern Exile #8. . . . . 5.00
159 KP,Gr.Lantern Exile #9 . . . . . . 5.00
160 KP,Gr.Lantern Exile #10 . . . . . 5.00
161 KP,A:Omega Men,Exile #11 . . 5.00
162 KP,Gr.Lantern Exile #12 . . . . . 6.00
163 KP,Gr.Lantern Exile #13 . . . . . 6.00
164 KP,A:Myrwhidden,Exile #14 . . . 5.00
165 KP,A:John Stewart & Gr.Arrow
    Green Lantern Exile #15 . . . . . . 5.00
166 GT,FMc,DGi,Exile #16 . . . . 5.00
167 GT,FMc,G.L.Exile #17 . . . . 5.00
168 GT,FMc,G.L. Exile #18 . . . . 5.00
169 Green Lantern Exile #19. . . . . . 5.00
170 GT,MSy,GreenLanternCorps. . . 5.00
171 ATh,TA,DGb,Green Lantern
    Exile #20 . . . . 5.00
172 DGb,E:Gr.Lant.Exile 5.00
173 DGb,I:Javelin,A:Congressman
    Bloch 5.00
174 DGb,V:Javelin. 4.50
175 DGb,A:Flash 4.50
176 DGb,V:The Shark 4.50
177 DGb,rep. Gr.Lant #128 . . . . . . 4.50
178 DGb,A:Monitor,V:Demolition
    Team 4.50
179 DGb,I:Predator 4.50
180 DGb,A:JLA 4.50
181 DGi,Hal Jordan quits as Green
    Lantern 4.50

182 DGi,John Stewart takes over
    V:Major Disaster 10.00
183 DGi,V:Major Disaster 3.50
184 DGb,Rep. Gr.Lant. #59 . . . . . . 4.00
185 DGi,DH,V:Eclipso 5.00
186 DGi,V:Eclipso 4.00
187 BWi,John Stewart meets
    Katma Tui 3.50
188 JSon,C:GrArrow,V:Sonar,John
    Stewart reveals I.D. to world . . . 7.00
189 JSon,V:Sonar 3.50
190 JSon,A:Green Arrow/Black
    Canary,Guy Gardner 3.50
191 JSon,IR:Predator is Star
    Sapphire 3.50
192 JSon,O:Star Sapphire 3.50
193 JSon,V:Replikon,A:G.Gardner . 3.50
194 JSon,Crisis,R:G.Gardner. 6.00
195 JSon,Guy Gardner as Green
    Lantern,develops attitude 12.00
196 JSon,V:Shark,Hal Jordan
    regains ring 4.00
197 JSon,V:Shark,Sonar,
    Goldface 4.00
198 JSon,D:Tomar-Re,Hal returns as
    Green Lantern,(double size) . . . 6.00
199 JSon,V:Star Sapphire 3.50
200 JSon,final Gr.Lantern issue. . . . 5.00
Becomes:

Green Lantern Corps #220
© DC Comics, Inc.

GREEN LANTERN
CORPS
1986–88

201 JSon,I:NewGr.LantCorps,V:Star
    Sapphire, Sonar, Dr.Polaris. . . . 3.50
202 JSon,set up headquarters. 3.50
203 JSon,tribute to Disney. 3.50
204 JSon,Arisia reaches puberty. . . 3.50
205 JSon,V:Black Hand 3.50
206 JSon,V:Black Hand. 3.50
207 JSon, Legends crossover. 3.00
208 JSon,I:Rocket Red Brigade,
    Green Lanterns in Russia#1 . . . 3.00
209 JSon,In Russia #2. . . . . 3.00
210 JSon,In Russia #3. . . . . 3.00
211 JSon,John Stewart proposes
    to Katma Tui 3.00
212 JSon,W:J.Stewart&KatmaTui . . 3.00
213 JSon,For Want of a Male 3.00
214 IG,5700 A.D. Story 3.00
215 IG,Salaak and Chip quit 3.00
216 IG,V:Carl 3.00
217 JSon,V:Sinestro 3.00

218 BWg,V:Sinestro. 3.00
219 BWg,V:Sinestro. 3.00
220 JSon,Millonnium,pt.3. . . . . 3.00
221 JSon,Millennium 3.00
222 JSon,V:Sinestro 3.00
223 GK,V:Sinestro 3.00
224 CK,V:Sinestro 3.00
Ann.#1 GK 3.00
Ann.#2 JSa,BWg,A:AnM 3.50
Ann.#3 JBy,JL,JR. 3.00
Spec.#1 A:Superman 3.00
Spec.#2 MBr,RT,V:Seeker 3.00
TPB rep.#84-#87,#89,Flash
    #217-#219 . . . . 13.00
TPB rep. reprints of #1-#7 . . . . . . 9.00

GREEN LANTERN
[2nd Regular Series], 1990
1 PB,A:Hal Jordan,John Stuart,
    Guy Gardner 5.00
2 PB,A:Tattooed Man 4.50
3 PB,Jordan vs.Gardner 4.50
4 PB,Vanishing Cities 4.00
5 PB Return to OA 4.00
6 PB 3GL'sCaptive 4.00
7 PB R:Guardians. 4.00
8 PB R:Guardians. 4.00
9 JSon,G.Gardner,pt.1 . . . . 4.00
10 JSon,G.Gardner,pt.2 . . . . 4.00
11 JSon,G.Gardner,pt.3 . . . . 4.00
12 JSon,G.Gardner,pt.4 . . . . 4.00
13 Jordan,Gardner,Stuart(giant) . . . 4.00
14 PB,Mosaic,pt.1 . . . . 4.00
15 RT,Mosaic,pt.2 . . . . 4.00
16 MBr,RT,Mosaic,pt.3. . . . . 4.00
17 MBr,RT,Mosaic,pt.4. . . . . 4.00
18 JSon,JRu,G.Gardner,
    A:Goldface. 4.00
19 MBr,PB,JSon,A:All Four G.L.'s,
    O:Alan Scott,A:Doiby Dickles
    (D.Size-50th Ann.Iss.) 5.00
20 PB,RT,Hal Jordan G.L. Corp
    story begins, A:Flicker 3.00
21 PB,RT,G.L. Corp.,pt.2,
    V:Flicker. 3.00
22 PB,RT,G.L. Corp.,pt.3,
    R:Star Sapphire 3.00
23 PB,RT,V:Star Sapphire,
    A:John Stuart. 3.00
24 PB,RT,V:Star Sapphire 3.00
25 MBr,JSon,RT,Hal Vs.Guy,
    A:JLA 3.00
26 MBr,V:Evil Star,Starlings 3.00
27 MBr,V:Evil Star,Starlings 3.00
28 MBr,V:Evil Star,Starlings 3.00
29 MBr,RT,R:Olivia Reynolds 3.00
30 MBr,RT,Gorilla Warfare#1 . . . . . 3.00
31 MBr,RT,Gorilla Warfare#3 . . . . . 3.00
32 RT(i),A:Floro,Arisia 3.00
33 MBr,RT,Third Law#1,
    A;New Guardians 3.00
34 MBr,RT,Third Law#2,I:Entropy . 3.00
35 MBr,RT,Third Law#3,V;Entropy. . 3.00
36 V:Dr.Light 3.00
37 MBg,RT,A:Guy Gardner 3.00
38 MBr,RT,A:Adam Strange. 3.00
39 MBr,RT,A:Adam Strange. 3.00
40 RT(i),A:Darkstar,
    V:Reverse Flash 3.00
41 MBr,RT,V:Predator,
    C:Deathstroke 3.00
42 MBr,RT,V:Predator,
    Deathstroke 3.00
43 RT(i),A:Itty 3.00
44 RT(i),Trinity#2,A:L.E.G.I.O.N. . . . 3.00
45 GeH,Trinity#5,A:L.E.G.I.O.N.,
    Darkstars 3.00
46 MBr,A:All Supermen,
    V:Mongul 8.00
47 A:Green Arrow 6.00
48 KM(c),B:Emerald Twilight,I:Kyle
    Rayner (Last Green Lantern) . 10.00

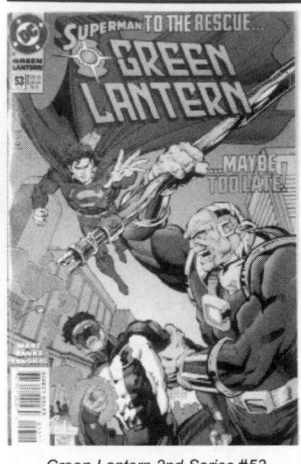

Green Lantern 2nd Series #53
© DC Comics, Inc.

49 KM(c),GJ(s),A:Sinestro 9.00
50 KM(c),GJ(s),D:Sinestro,Kiliwog,
   Guardians,I:Last Green
   Lantern (in Costume). 15.00
51 V:Ohm,A:Mongul. 6.00
52 V:Mongul. 4.00
53 A:Superman,V:Mongul 4.00
54 D:Alex, V:Major Force 4.00
55 Zero Hour,A:Alan Scott,
   V:Major Force 4.00
56 Green Lantern and ring 3.50
57 Psimon 3.50
58 Donna Troy,Felix Faust. 3.50
59 V:Dr. Polaris 3.50
60 Capital Punishment,pt.3 . . . . . . 3.50
61 V:Kalibak,A:Darkstar 3.50
62 V:Duality,R:Ganthet. 3.50
63 Parallax View: The Resurrection
   of Hal Jordan,pt.1 . . . . 3.00
64 Parallax View,pt.2,A:Superman,
   Flash,V:Parallax 3.00
65 Siege of ZiCharan,pt.2 . . . . 3.00
66 V:Sonar. 3.00
67 A:Flash,V:Sonar 3.00
68 RMz,RT,Underworld
   Unleashed tie-in 3.00
69 RMz,RT,Underworld
   Unleashed tie-in 3.00
70 RMz,RT,A:Supergirl 3.00
71 RMz,RT,Hero Quest,pt.1 . . . . . . 3.00
72 RMz,RT,Hero Quest,pt.2 . . . . . . 3.00
73 RMz,RT,Hero Quest,pt.3 . . . . . . 3.00
74 RMz,RT,A:Adam Strange,
   V:Grayven 3.00
75 A:Adam Strange 3.00
76 Green Arrow x-over. 3.00
77 Green Arrow x-over. 3.00
78 RMz(s),A Beginning 3.00
79 V:Sonar 3.00
80 RMz(s),JWi,MGy,V:Dr. Light,
   Final Night tie-in 3.00
81 RMz(s),DBk,RT,Memorial for
   Hal Jordan. 6.00
81a deluxe edition + extra stories,
   foil cover on cardstock 9.00
82 RMz(s),TGb,RT,F:Kyle Rayner,
   Alan Scott, Guy Gardner &
   John Stewart 3.00
83 RMz,Retribution,pt.1 . . . . 3.00
84 Retribution, pt.2 . . . . 3.00
85 Retribution, concl. 3.00
86 RMz,JJ,RT,A:Jade, V:Obsidian . . 3.00
87 RMz,TGb,RT,A:Martian
   Manhunter, vs. Alien Invasion . . 3.00

88 RMz(s),DBk,TA,A:Donna Troy,
   Visit Kyle's Mom 3.00
89 RM(s),TA,V:Machine Messiah . . 3.00
90 RM(s),Why did Kyle Rayner
   become Green Lantern 3.00
91 RMz(s),DBk,TA,V:Desaad. 3.00
92 RMz(s),DBk,TA,A:Green Arrow,
   x-over. 3.00
93 RMz(s),DBk,TA,F:Deadman 3.00
94 RMz(s),PaP,TA,F:Superboy 3.00
95 RMz(s),JSn,TA, deep space 3.00
96 RMz(s) 3.00
97 RMz(s),MMK,TA,V:Grayven. . . . 3.00
98 RMz,DBk, TA,Future Shock,pt.1 . 3.00
99 RMz,DBk,TA,Future Shock,pt.2 . 4.50
100 RMz,DBk,AT,Kyle Rayner and
   Hal Jordan,V:Sinestro, 48pg . . . 6.00
100a deluxe edition 4.00
101 RMz(s),JJ,BWi,Emerald
   Knights,pt.1, bi-weekly 4.00
102 RMz(s),PaP,TA,Emerald
   Knights,pt.2, bi-weekly 4.00
103 RMz(s),JJ,BWi,Emerald
   Knights,pt.3, bi-weekly 4.00
104 RMz(s),JJ,BWi,Greener Pastures
   x-over, concl., Emerald
   Knights,pt.4, bi-weekly 4.00
105 RMz(s),JJ,SEa,BWi,Emerald
   Knights,pt.5, bi-weekly 4.00
106 RMz(s),PaP,TA,Emerald
   Knights,concl. 4.00
107 RMz(s),TA,Emerald Knights
   aftermath 2.50
108 DBk,TA,A:Wonder Woman 2.50
109 RMz(s),PaP,TA 2.50
110 RMz(s),TA,A:Green Arrow. 2.50
111 RMz(s),TA,DBk,V:Fatality 2.50
112 RMz(s),TA,DBk,back to Earth. . 2.50
113 RMz(s),TA,DBk,Burning
   in Effigy,pt.1 . . . . 2.50
114 RMz(s),TA,DBk,Burning
   in Effigy,pt.2 . . . . 2.50
115 DJu(s),A:Plastic Man &
   Booster Gold, pt.1 . . . . 2.50
116 DJu(s),A:Plastic Man &
   Booster Gold, pt.1 . . . . 2.50
117 RMz(s),DBk,TA,R:Donna Troy . 2.50
118 RMz(s),DBk,TA,Day of
   Judgment x-over 2.50
119 RMz,DBk,CaS,Day of
   Judgment aftermath 9.00
120 RMz,DBk,CaS. 2.50
121 RMz,DBk,CaS. 2.50
122 RMz,DBk,CaS. 2.50
123 RMz,DBk,V:Controllers. 2.50
124 RMz,DBk,V:Controllers. 2.50
125 RMz,Unmooning secrets 2.50
126 Goes undercover 2.50
127 F:Effigy & Killer Frost 2.50
128 F:Arsenal. 2.50
129 DBk,ASm,V:Manhunters. 2.50
130 DBk,ASm,V:Manhunters. 2.50
131 DBk,ASm,V:Manhunters. 2.50
132 DBk,While Rome Burned,pt.1 . . 2.50
133 DBk,MBr,Rome Burned,pt.2 . . . 2.50
134 DBk,While Rome Burned,pt.3. . 2.50
135 DBk,While Rome Burned,pt.4. . 2.50
136 DBk,While Rome Burned,pt.5. . 2.50
137 DBk,Friends & Lovers. 2.50
138 DBk,Away From Home,pt.1 . . . 2.50
139 DBk,Away From Home,pt.2 . . . 2.50
140 DBk,A:Alan Scott 2.50
141 DBk,A:Jade,V:arsonist 2.50
142 V:Inferno 2.50
143 JLe,Joker:Last Laugh,tie-in. . . . 2.50
144 Battle to control his powers . . . 2.50
145 V:Nero. 7.00
146 incredible metamorphosis 6.00
147 F:John Stewart 2.50
148 A:Superman,R:Jade 2.50
149 F:JLA. 2.50
150 End of Ion,48-pg. 5.00

151 JLe(c) Hand of God,aftermath . 2.50
152 RbC,uncontrollable madness . . 2.50
153 JLe(c),high school reunion 2.50
154 JLe&SW(c),attacked 2.50
155 JLe&SW(c),A:Flash,JLA 2.50
156 John Stewart back,A:Sentinel. . 2.50
157 Girl Talk. 2.50
158 industrialist nomads 2.50
159 Boar Beasts 2.50
160 Child Guardians 2.50
161 V:Amazon 2.50
162 CAd,Urban Knights,pt.2 x-over. 2.50
163 CAd,Urban Knights,pt.4 x-over. 2.50
164 CAd,Urban Knights,pt.6 x-over. 2.50
165 RBr,A Tiny Spark. 2.50
166 RBr,The Blind,pt.1. . . . . 2.50
167 RBr,The Blind,pt.2. . . . . 2.50
168 RBr 2.50
169 RBr,Kilowog's soul 2.50
170 RBr 2.50
171 Wanted, pt.1 . . . . 2.50
172 kidnappers 2.50
173 V:Weaponers of Qward. 2.50
174 V:Black Circle 2.50
175 Qwardians,48-pg. 3.50
176 LRs,RyR,Homecoming,pt.1 . . . 4.00
177 LRs,RyR,Homecoming,pt.2 . . . 4.00
178 LRs,RyR,Homecoming,pt.3 . . . 4.00
179 LRs,RyR,Homecoming,pt.4 . . . 4.00
180 LRs,RyR,Homecoming,pt.5 . . . 4.00
181 LRs,RyR,Homecoming,pt.6 . . . 4.00
Ann.#1 Eclipso,V:Star Sapphire. . . . 4.00
Ann.#1 80pg, rep. 5.00
Ann.#2 Bloodlines#7,I:Nightblade . . 4.00
Ann.#3 Elseworlds Story 3.50
Ann.#4 Year One story. 4.00
Ann.#5 Legends o/t Dead Earth . . . 3.50
Ann.#6 RMz(s),JJ,Low,Pulp
   Heroes, 64pg. 4.50
Ann.#7 SV,RLm,Clv,BWr,Ghosts . . 3.50
Ann.#8 MCa,AAd(c),JLApe:Gorilla
   Warfare 3.50
Ann.#9 Planet DC 4.00
Spec.#1,000,000 RMz(s),BHi,PNe . 2.50
Spec. 3-D #1 V:Dr. Light 4.00
Spec.#1 Our Worlds at War(2001). . 3.00
Secret Files #1. . . . . 5.00
Secret Files Spec.#2 . . . . 5.00
Secret Files #3, 48-pg. 5.00
Green Lantern Plus, 1-shot RMz(s),
   F:The Ray,V:Dr. Polaris 3.00
Green Lantern/Silver Surfer, 1-shot
   DC/Marvel RMz,TA A:Thanos
   vs. Parallax 5.00

Green Lantern 2nd Series Ann. #2
© DC Comics, Inc.

DC COMICS

Green Lantern Gallery, 1 one-shot . 3.50
Green Lantern: Ganthet's Tale,
    1-shot, JBy,O:Guardians 7.00
Giant #1 80-page 5.50
Giant #2 80-page 5.50
Giant #3 80-page 6.00
GN Ganthet's Tale, JBy 6.00
GN Green Lantern/Superman:
    Legends of the Green Flame . . 6.00
GN 1001 Emerald Nights(2001) . . . 7.00
GN Brightest Day/Blackest Night . . 6.00
TPB A New Dawn 10.00
TPB Emerald Twilight 6.25
TPB Emerald Knights 13.00
TPB A New Dawn 10.00
TPB Baptism of Fire. 13.00
TPB Fear Itself. 15.00
TPB Emerald Allies, rep. 15.00
TPB New Journey, Old Path 15.00
TPB Circle of Fire 18.00
TPB Emerald Dawn (rep. 2003) . . 15.00
TPB The Power of Ion (2003) 15.00
TPB Emerald Dawn II (2003). 15.00
TPB Brother's Keeper 13.00
TPB The Road Back 15.00
TPB Emerald Twilight/New Dawn . 20.00
TPB Willworld. 18.00
TPB Gr.Lantern/Gr.Arrow,Vol.1 . . 13.00
TPB Gr.Lantern/Gr.Arrow,Vol.2 . . 13.00
TPB Passing the Torch 13.00

GREEN LANTERN
May, 2005
1 F:Hal Jordan, No Fear,40-page . . 3.50
2 No Fear, pt.2 . . . . 3.00
3 No Fear, pt.3 . . . . 3.00
4 F:Gilowog. 3.00
5 V:Shark 3.00
6 V:Black Hand 3.00
7 A:Green Arrow 3.00
8 A Perfect Life, pt.1 . . . . 3.00
9 A Perfect Life, pt.2, A:Batman . . 3.00
10 One Year Later 3.00
11 Revenge of the Green Lanterns . 3.00
12 Revenge of the Green Lanterns . 3.00
13 Wanted: Hal Jordan, pt.1 . . . . . 3.00
14 Wanted: Hal Jordan, pt.2 . . . . . 3.00
15 Wanted: Hal Jordan, pt.3 . . . . . 3.00
16 Wanted: Hal Jordan, pt.4 . . . . . 3.00
Secret Files 2005, 48-page 5.00
TPB Greatest Stories Ever Told . . . 20.00

GREEN LANTERN
& SENTINEL:
HEART OF DARKNESS
Feb., 1998
1 (of 3) RMz(s),PaP,DDv 3.00
2 RMz(s),PaP,DDv 3.00
3 RMz(s),PaP,DDv 3.00

GREEN LANTERN:
CIRCLE OF FIRE
Aug., 2000
1 (of 2) NBy,64-pg. x-over 5.00
2 48-pg.x-over concl. 5.00
Spec.Gr.Lant.: Adam Strange #1 . . 2.50
Spec.Gr.Lant.: The Atom #1. . . . . . 2.50
Spec.Gr.Lant.: Firestorm #1. . . . . . 2.50
Spec.Gr.Lant.: Green Lantern #1. . . 2.50
Spec.Gr.Lant.: Power Girl #1 . . . . . 2.50

GREEN LANTERN CORPS
June, 2006
1 DGb 3.00
2 thru 6 DGb . . . . @3.00

GREEN LANTERN
CORPS QUARTERLY
1992–94
1 DAb,JSon,FH,PG,MBr,F:Alan
    Scott G'nort 3.00
2 DAb,JSon,PG,AG,Alan Scott 2.75
3 DAb,RT,F:Alan Scott,G'Nort 2.75
4 TA,AG(i),F:H.Jordan,G'Nort. 2.75
5 F:Alan Scott,I:Adam. 2.75
6 JBa,TC,F:Alan Scott 3.25
7 Halloween Issue 3.25
8 GeH,SHa,final issue 3.25

GREEN LANTERN CORPS:
RECHARGE
Sept., 2005
1 (of 5) 40-page 3.50
2 thru 5 . . . . @3.00
TPB Recharge 13.00

GREEN LANTERN:
DRAGON LORD
April, 2001
1 (of 3) PG, 48-page 5.00
2 PG, 48-page. 5.00
3 PG, 48-page. 5.00

GREEN LANTERN:
EMERALD DAWN
[1st Limited Series], 1989–90
1 MBr,RT,I:Mod.Age.Gr.Lantern . . . 5.00
2 MBr,RT,I:Legion (not group) 4.00
3 MBr,RT,V:Legion 3.00
4 MBr,RT,A:Green Lantern Corps. . 3.00
5 MBr,RT,V:Legion 3.00
6 MBr,RT,V:Legion 3.00
TPB rep#1-#6. . . . . 5.50
[2nd Limited Series], 1991
1 MBr,A:Sinestro,Guy Gardner. . . . 2.00
2 MBr,RT,V:Alien Aliance 2.00
3 MBr,RT,Sincstro's Home Planet . 2.00
4 MBr,RT,Korugar Revolt 2.00
5 MBr,RT,A:G.Gardner 2.00
6 MBr,RT,Trial of Sinestro. 2.00

GREEN LANTERN:
EVIL'S MIGHT
Aug., 2002
1 (of 3) HC, Elseworlds, 48-pg. . . . 6.00
2 HC,F:Kyle Rayner 6.00
3 HC,concl. 6.00

GREEN LANTERN/
GREEN ARROW
1983–84
1 NA rep. 5.00
2 thru 7 NA,DG rep. . . . . @4.00
TPB Roadback. 9.00
TPB Traveling Heroes, Vol.1 . . . . 13.00
TPB Traveling Heroes, Vol.2 . . . . 13.00

GREEN LANTERN:
MOSAIC
1992–93
1 F:John Stewart. 2.25
2 D:Ch'p 2.25
3 V:Sinestro 2.25
4 F:The Children on Oa 2.25
5 V:Hal Jordan 2.25
6 A:Kilowog. 2.25
7 V:Alien Faction. 2.25
8 V:Ethereal Creatures 2.25
9 Christmas issue 2.25
10 V:Guardians 2.25
11 R:Ch'p 2.25

Green Lantern Mosaic #13
© DC Comics Inc.

12 V:KKK 2.25
13 V:KKK,Racism 2.25
14 A:Salaak,Ch'p 2.25
15 A:Katma Tui,Ch'p 2.25
16 LMc,A:JLA,Green Lantern 2.25
17 A:JLA. 2.25
18 final issue 2.25

GREEN LANTERN:
THE NEW CORPS
1999
1 (of 2) CDi(s),SEa 5.00
2 CDi(s),SEa, concl. 5.00

GREEN LANTERN:
REBIRTH
Oct. 2004
1 (of 6) 40-pg. 3.00
2 F:JLA 3.50
3 V:Spectre 3.50
4 A:JLA,JSA,&Teen Titans 3.00
5 To restore Hal Jordan 3.00
6 Hal Jordan's return 3.00

GREGORY
DC/Piranha
1 MaH, b&w 8.00
2 MaH 5.00
3 MaH Bookshelf Ed. 5.00
3a Platinum Ed. 8.00
4 MaH, b&w 5.00
TPB #1 Gregory Treasury,MaH . . . 10.00
TPB #2 Gregory Treasury,MaH . . . 10.00

GRIFFIN
1991–92
1 I:Matt Williams as Griffin 5.50
2 V:Carson 5.25
3 A:Mary Wayne 5.25
4 A:Mary Wayne 5.25
5 Face to Face with Himself. 5.25
6 Final Issue 5.25

GRIP: THE STRANGE
WORLD OF MEN
DC/Vertigo, Nov., 2001
1 (of 5) GHe 2.50
2 GHe 2.50
3 thru 5 GHe . . . . @2.50

GROSS POINT
July, 1997
1 MWa&BAu(s) parody	2.50
2 thru 14	@2.50

GUARDIANS OF METROPOLIS
Nov., 1994
1 Kirby characters	2.25
2 Donovan's creations	2.25
3	2.25
4 Female Furies	2.25

GUNFIRE
1994–95
1 B:LWn(s),StE,I:Ricochet	2.25
2 thru 13	@2.25

GUNS OF THE DRAGON
Aug., 1998
1 (of 4) TT, set in 1920s	2.50
2 TT	2.50
3 TT	2.50
4 TT conclusion	2.50

Guy Gardner #12 © DC Comics, Inc.

GUY GARDNER
1992–94
1 JSon,A:JLA,JLE	2.50
2 JSon,A:Kilowog	2.50
3 JSon,V:Big,Ugly Alien	2.50
4 JSon,G.Gardner vs Ice	2.50
5 JSon,A:Hal Jordan,V:Goldface	2.50
6 JSon,A:Hal Jordan,V:Goldface	2.50
7 JSon,V:Goldface	2.50
8 JSon,V:Lobo	2.50
9 JSon,Boodikka	2.50
10 JSon,V:Boodikka	2.50
11 JSon,B:Year One	2.50
12 JSon,V:Batman,Flash,Green Lantern	2.50
13 JSon,Year One#3	2.50
14 JSon,E:Year One	2.50
15 V:Bad Guy Gardner	2.50
16 B:CDi(s),MaT,V:Guy's Brother	2.50

Becomes:

GUY GARDNER: WARRIOR
1994–96
17 V:Militia	2.50
18 B:Emerald Fallout,N:Guy Gardner, V:Militia	4.00

19 A:G.A.Green Lantern,V:Militia	4.00
20 A:JLA,Darkstars	2.50
21 E:Emerald Fallout,V:H.Jordan	2.50
22 I:Dementor	2.50
23 A:Buck Wargo	2.50
24 Zero Hour	2.50
25 A:Buck Wargo	3.00
26 Zero Hour	2.50
27 Capital Punishment	2.50
28 Capital Punishment,pt.2	2.50
29 I:Warriors Bar	2.50
29a Collector's Edition	3.25
30 V:Superman,Supergirl	2.50
31 A:Sentinel,Supergirl, V:Dementor	2.50
32 Way of the Warrior,pt.1,A:JLA	2.50
33 Way of the Warrior,pt.4	2.50
34	2.50
35 Return of an Old Foe	2.50
36 Underworld Unleashed tie-in	2.50
37 Underworld Unleashed tie-in	2.50
38 A new woman	2.50
39 Guest stars galore	2.50
40	2.50
41 V:Dungeon	2.50
42 Martika revealed as Seductress	2.50
43 V:5 Foes	2.50
Ann.#1 Year One Annual, Leechun vs. Vuldarians	4.00
Ann.#2 Dead Earth	3.50

GUY GARDNER: COLLATERAL DAMAGE
Nov., 2006
1 (of 2) HC	6.00

GUY GARDNER: REBORN
1992
1 JSon,JRu,V:Goldface,C:Lobo	6.00
2 JSon,JRu,A:Lobo,V:Weaponers of Qward	5.50
3 JSon,JRu,A:Lobo,N:G.Gardner V:Qwardians	5.50

HACKER FILES
1992–93
1 TS,Soft Wars#1,I:Jack Marshall	2.25
2 TS,Soft Wars#2	2.25
3 TS,Soft Wars#3	2.25
4 TS,Soft Wars#4	2.25
5 TS,A:Oracle(Batgirl)	2.25
6 TS,A:Oracle,Green Lantern	2.25
7 TS,V:Digitronix	2.25
8 TS,V:Digitronix	2.25
9 TS,V:Digitronix	2.25
10 V:Digitronix	2.25
11 TS,A:JLE	2.25
12 TS,V:Digitronix,final issue	2.25

HAMMER LOCKE
1992–93
1 I:Hammerlocke	3.00
2 thru 8	@2.25

HARDCORE STATION
May, 1998
1 (of 6) JSn,JRu,F:Maximillian	2.50
2 JSn,JRu,V:Synnar	2.50
3 JSn,JRu,F:Kyle Rayner	2.50
4 JSn,JRu,V:Synnar	2.50
5 JSn,JRu,F:JLA	2.50
6 JSn,JRu,conclusion	2.50

HARD TIME
DC Focus Feb. 2004
1 F:Ethan Harrow	2.50
2 thru 12	@2.50
TPB rep, #1-#6	10.00
TPB 50 to Life	10.00

HARD TIME SEASON TWO
Dec., 2005
1	2.50
2	2.50
3 F:Cutter	2.50
4 F:Cindy	2.50
5	2.50
6	3.00
7 Finale	3.00

HARDWARE
DC/Milestone, 1993–96
1 DCw,I:Hardware,Edwin Alva,Reprise, Dir.Mark.Ed.,w/A puzzle piece, Skybox Card,Poster	4.00
1a NewsstandEd.	2.50
1b Platinum Ed.	6.00
2 thru 15	@2.50
16 Die-Cut(c),JBy(c),DCw, N:Hardware	4.25
16a Newsstand ED.	2.50
17 thru 24	@2.50
25 V:Death Row, Sanction	3.00
26 thru 49	@2.50
50 DGC(s), 48pg. anniversary issue	4.00
51 DMc(s) final issue	2.50

HARLEY QUINN
October, 2000
1 KK,TyD,A:Batman,48 pg.	3.00
2 KK,TyD,A:Two-Face,Poison Ivy	2.50
3 KK,TyD,A:Catwoman	2.50
4 KK,TyD,I:Quinntettes	2.50
5 KK,TyD,F:Quinntettes	2.50
6 KK,TyD,A:Oracle	2.50
7 KK,TyD,F:Big Barda	2.50
8 KK,TyD,Harley's Past	2.50
9 KK,TyD,V:Quinntettes	2.50
10 KK,TyD,F:Barbara Gordon	2.50
11 KK,TyD,F:Nightwing	2.50
12 KK,TyD,40-page	3.50
13 KK,Joker:Last Laugh	2.50
14 KK,TyD,to Metropolis	2.50
15 KK,TyD,Lovers advice	2.50
16 KK,TyD,City of Tomorrow	2.50
17 KK,TyD,F:Bizarro	2.50
18 KK,TyD,F:Bizarro	2.50
19 KK,TyD,A:Superman	2.50
20 KK,Harley pays price for evil	2.50
21 KK,ultimate prison	2.50
22 KK,TyD,Highwater	2.50
23 KK,TyD,World Without Harley	2.50
24 KK,DDv,back from Hell	2.50
25 KK,DDv,F:Batman,A:Joker	2.50
26 wanted for murder	2.50
27 Harley a psychiatrist	2.50
28 new patient	2.50
29 a stalker	2.50
30 Who framed Harley?	2.50
31 Harley and Doc	2.50
32 A:Joker	2.50
33 Behind Blue Eyes,pt.1	2.50
34 Behind Blue Eyes,pt.2	2.50
35 Behind Blue Eyes,pt.3	2.50
36 Behind Blue Eyes,pt.4	2.50
37 Behind Blue Eyes,pt.5	2.50
38 CAd,final issue	2.50
Spec.#1 Our Worlds at War,48-pg.	3.25
GN Harley & Ivy, Love on the Lam	6.50

HAVEN: THE BROKEN CITY
Dec., 2001
1 (of 9) AOI,F:JLA	2.50
2 AOI,A:JLA	2.50
3 AOI,A:Superman,I:HankVelveeda	2.50
4 AOI,F:Nia	2.50
5 AOI,Eater of Filth	2.50

6 AOI,search for crash survivors. . . 2.50
7 AOI,V:Ivas the ultra-powerful. . . 2.50
8 AOI,Anathema 2.50
9 AOI,Valadin 2.50

Hawk & Dove #7
© DC Comics, Inc.

HAWK & DOVE
[1st Regular Series], 1968–69
1 SD 150.00
2 SD 100.00
3 GK 75.00
4 GK 75.00
5 GK,C:Teen Titans. 75.00
6 GK 75.00

[Limited Series], 1988–89
1 RLd,I:New Dove. 4.00
2 RLd,V:Kestrel. 3.50
3 RLd,V:Kestrel. 3.50
4 RLd,V:Kestrel. 3.50
5 RLd,V:Kestrel,O:New Dove 3.50
TPB rep. #1-#5 . . . . 10.50

[2nd Regular Series], 1989–91
1 A:Superman,Green Lantern
   Hawkman. 2.50
2 V:Aztec Goddess. 2.50
3 V:Aztec Goddess. 2.50
4 I:The Untouchables 2.50
5 I:Sudden Death, A:1st Dove's
   Ghost. 2.50
6 A:Barter,Secrets o/Hawk&Dove. . 2.50
7 A:Barter,V:Count St.Germain . . . 2.50
8 V:Count St.Germain. 2.50
9 A:Copperhead 2.50
10 V:Gauntlet & Andromeda 2.50
11 A:New Titans,V:M.A.C.,
   Andromeda Gauntlet 2.50
12 A:New Titans,V:Scarab 2.50
13 1960's,I:Shellshock. 2.50
14 Prelue to O:Hawk & Dove,
   V:Kestrel. 2.50
15 O:Hawk & Dove begins 2.50
16 HawkV:Dove,V:Lord of Chaos . 2.50
17 V:Lords-Order & Chaos 2.50
18 The Creeper #1. . . . . 2.50
19 The Creeper #2. . . . . 2.50
20 KM,DG,Christmas Story 2.50
21 Dove 2.50
22 V:Sudden Death 2.50
23 A:Velv.Tiger,SuddenDeath 2.50
24 A:Velv.Tiger,SuddenDeath 2.50
25 Recap 1st 2 yrs.(48 pg) 2.50
26 Dove's past 2.50
27 The Hunt for Hawk 2.50

28 War of the Gods,A:Wildebeest
   A:Uncle Sam,final issue,
   double size 3.00
Ann.#1 In Hell 3.00
Ann.#2 CS,KGa,ArmageddonPt.5 . . 3.00
TPB RLd 10.00

HAWK & DOVE
Sept., 1997
1 (of 5) MBn,DZ,DG,Sasha Martens
   & Wiley Wolverman 2.50
2 MBn,DZ,DG,Vixen & Vigilante . . . 2.50
3 MBn,DZ,DG,grave desecrations . 2.50
4 MBn,DZ,DG,V:Suicide Squad . . . 2.50

HAWKMAN
[1st Regular Series], 1964–68
1 MA,V:Chac 1,500.00
2 MA,V:Tralls 600.00
3 MA,V:Sky Raiders 600.00
4 MA,I&O:Zatanna 550.00
5 MA 375.00
6 MA 375.00
7 MA,V:I.Q. 375.00
8 MA 375.00
9 MA,V:Matter Master. 375.00
10 MA,V:Caw 375.00
11 MA. 300.00
12 MA. 250.00
13 MA. 250.00
14 GaF,MA,V:Caw 250.00
15 GaF,MA,V:Makkar. 250.00
16 GaF,MA,V:Ruthvol. 250.00
17 GaF,MA,V:Raven 250.00
18 GaF,MA,A:Adam Strange 200.00
19 GaF,MA,A:Adam Strange 200.00
20 GaF,MA,V:Lionmane. 150.00
21 GaF,MA,V:Lionmane. 150.00
22 V:Falcon 150.00
23 V:Dr.Malevolo 150.00
24 Robot Raiders from
   Planet Midnight 150.00
25 DD,V:Medusa,G.A.Hawkman . 150.00
26 RdM,CCu,DD 150.00
27 DD,JKu(c),V:Yeti 150.00

[2nd Regular Series], 1986–87
1 DH,A:Shadow Thief 3.00
2 DH,V:Shadow Thief 2.50
3 DH,V:Shadow Thief 2.50
4 DH A:Zatanna 2.50
5 DH,V:Lionmane 2.50
6 DH,V:Gentleman Ghost,
   Lionmane 2.50
7 DH,Honor Wings 2.50
8 DH,Shadow War contd. 2.50
9 DH,Shadow War contd. 2.50
10 JBy(c),D:Hyatis Corp 2.50
11 End of Shadow War 2.50
12 Hawks on Thanagar 2.50
13 DH,Murder Case. 2.50
14 DH,Mystery o/Haunted Masks . . 2.50
15 DH,Murderer Revealed. 2.50
16 DH,Hawkwoman lost 2.50
17 EH,DH,final issue 2.50
TPB rep.Brave & Bold apps. 20.00

[3rd Regular Series], 1993–96
1 B:JOs(s),JD,R:Hawkman,
   V:Deadline. 5.00
2 JD,A:Gr.Lantern,V:Meta-Tech . . 3.00
3 JD,I:Airstryke 2.75
4 JD,RM 2.50
5 JD(c),V:Count Viper. 2.50
6 JD(c),A:Eradicator 2.50
7 JD(c),PuK(s),LMc,B:King of the
   Netherworld 2.50
8 LMc,E:King of the Netherworld . . 2.50
9 BML(s) 2.50
10 I:Badblood. 2.50
11 V:Badblood 2.50
12 V:Hawkgod 2.75
13 V:Hawkgod 2.75

14 New abilities,pt.1. . . . . 2.50
15 New abilities,pt.2. . . . . 2.50
16 Eyes of the Hawk,pt.3. . . . . 2.50
17 Eyes of the Hawk,pt.4. . . . . 2.50
18 Seagle,Ellis, Pepoy. 2.50
19 F:Hawkman. 2.50
21 RLm,V:Shadow Thief,
   Gentleman Ghost 2.75
22 Way of the Warrior,pt.3
   A:Warrior,JLA 2.75
23 Way of the Warrior,pt.6. . . . . . . 2.75
24 . . . . 2.75
25 V:Lionmane,painted(c) 2.75
26 WML,Underworld
   Unleashed tie-in 2.75
27 WML,Underworld
   Unleashed tie-in 2.75
28 WML,V:Doctor Polaris. 2.75
29 HC(c),V:Vandal Savage 2.75
30 . . . . 2.75
31 serial killer has Tangarian
   technology 2.75
32 MC,Search for serial killer 2.75
Ann.#1 JD,I:Mongrel 4.00
Ann.#2 Year One Annual 4.00

[4th Regular Series], 2002
1 RgM,MiB,Hawkman & Hawkgirl. . 2.50
2 RgM,MiB,F:Hawkgirl 2.50
3 RgM,MiB,inter-dimensional portal 2.50
4 RgM,MiB,trapped in Battlelands . 2.50
5 RgM,MiB,Slings and Arrows,pt.1. 2.50
6 RgM,MiB,Slings and Arrows,pt.2. 2.50
7 RgM,TT,Lives past 2.50
8 RgM,MiB,F:Atom 2.50
9 RgM,F:Dr.Fate 2.50
10 RgM,find Speed Saunders 2.50
11 RgM,V:Hath-Set 2.50
12 RgM,V:Darkraven 2.50
13 Hawk vs. Hawk 2.50
14 Hawkgirl's parents' murderer . . 2.50
15 Shayera Thai 2.50
16 RgM,The Thanagarian,pt.1 . . . . 2.50
17 RgM,The Thanagarian,pt.2. . . . 2.50
18 RgM,The Thanagarian,pt.3. . . . 2.50
19 F:Black Adam 2.50
20 RgM,MIB,V:Headhunter,pt.1 . . . 2.50
21 RgM,MIB,V:Headhunter,pt.2 . . . 2.50
22 RgM,MIB,V:Headhunter,pt.3 . . . 2.50
23 Black Reign,pt.2,x-over. 2.50
24 Black Reign,pt.4,x-over. 2.50
25 Black Reign,pt.6,x-over. 2.50
26 Rabid vampires. 2.50
27 SeP,Past Lives 2.50
28 Fate's Warning,pt.1. . . . . 2.50
29 Fate's Warning,pt.2. . . . . 2.50
30 Fate's Warning,pt.3. . . . . 2.50
31 Fate's Warning,pt.4. . . . . 2.50
32 JoB,F:The Atom 2.50
33 ASm,MGy,F:Monolith 2.50
34 V:Manticore. 2.50
35 JoB,V:Zombies 2.50
36 JoB,V:Zombies,A:Deadman . . . 2.50
37 JoB,V:Fadeaway Man. 2.50
38 previous incarnations visit. 4.00
39 JoB,Hawkman missing 3.00
40 JoB,F:Dr. Fate. 3.00
41 JoB,new Hawkman 5.00
42 JP(s),JoB,V:Pilgrim 2.50
43 JoB,Golden Eagle. 2.50
44 JoB,Golden Eagle. 2.50
45 JoB,F:JSA. 2.50
46 ATi,AKu(c),Rann/Thanagar War . 2.50
47 CsB,CaS,Coalition in Crisis 2.50
48 CsB,CaS,Coalition in Crisis 2.50
49 CsB,CaS,Coalition in Crisis 2.50
Spec. Secret Files #1, 48-pg. 5.00
TPB Endless Flight 13.00
TPB Enemies & Allies 15.00
TPB Wings of Fury. 18.00
TPB Golden Age Hawkman. 50.00
TPB Golden Eagle. 18.00
Becomes:

All comics prices listed are for *Near Mint* condition.

HAWKGIRL
March, 2006

50 WS,HC, One Year Later	2.50
51 WS,HC,St. Roch Museum	2.50
52 WS,HC,Lizard Kings voodoo	2.50
53 WS,HC,V:Khimaera	3.00
54 WS,HC,Friend from the pst	3.00
55 WS,HC,Hawkman returns	3.00
56 WS,HC,Truths and Evils	3.00
57 WS,JoB,HC(c)	3.00
58 WS,JoB,HC(c)	3.00

Hawkworld #19
© DC Comics, Inc.

HAWKWORLD
1989

1 TT,Hawkman, Origin retold	5.00
2 TT,Katar tried for treason	4.00
3 TT,Hawkgirl's debut	4.00

[1st Regular Series], 1990–93

1 GN,Byth on Earth,R:Kanjar Ro	3.00
2 GN,Katar & Shayera in Chicago	2.50
3 GN,V:Chicago Crime	2.50
4 GN,Byth's Control Tightens	2.50
5 GN,Return of Shadow Thief	2.50
6 GN,Stolen Thanagarian Ship	2.50
7 GN,V:Byth	2.50
8 GN,Hawkman vs. Hawkwoman	2.50
9 GN,Hawkwoman in Prison	2.50
10 Shayera returns to Thanagar	2.50
11 GN,Blackhawk,Express	2.50
12 GN,Princess Treska	2.50
13 TMd,A:Firehawk,V:Marauder	2.50
14 GN,Shayera's Father	2.50
15 GN,War of the Gods X-over	2.50
16 GN War of the Gods X-over	2.50
17 GN,Train Terrorists	2.50
18 GN,V:Atilla	2.50
19 GN,V:Atilla	2.50
20 V:Smir'Beau	2.50
21 GN,Thanagar Pt.1, A:J.S.A. Hawkman	2.50
22 GN,Thanagar Pt.2	2.50
23 GN,Thanagar Pt.3	2.50
24 GN,Thanagar Pt.4	2.50
25 GN,Thanagar Pt.5	2.50
26 GN,V:Attilla battle armor	2.50
27 JD,B:Flight's End	2.50
28 JD,Flight's End #2	2.50
29 TT(c),JDu,Flight's End #3	2.50
30 TT,Flight's End #4	2.50
31 TT,Flight's End #5	2.50
32 TT,V:Count Viper,final issue	3.00
Ann.#1 A:Flash	4.50

Ann.#2 Armageddon,pt.6	4.00
Ann.#2a reprint (Silver)	3.50
Ann.#3 Eclipso tie-in	3.25

HEAVY LIQUID
DC/Vertigo, 1999

1 PPo,pt 1 of 5	6.00
2 thru 5 PPo,pt.2 thru pt.5	@6.00
TPB PPo, 240-page	30.00

HECKLER, THE
1992–93

1 KG,MJ,I:The Heckler	2.25
2 KG,MJ,V:The Generic Man	2.25
3 KG,MJ,V:Cosmic Clown	2.25
4 KG,V:Bushwacker	2.25
5 KG,Theater Date	2.25
6 KG,I:Lex Concord	2.25
7 KG,V:Cuttin'Edge	2.25

HELLBLAZER
Jan., 1988

1 B:JaD(s),JRy,F:John Constantine	20.00
2 JRy,I:Papa Midnight	10.00
3 JRy,I:Blathoxi	8.00
4 JRy,I:Resurrection Crusade, Gemma	8.00
5 JRy,F:Pyramid of Fear	8.00
6 JRy,V:Resurrection Crusade, I:Nergal	6.00
7 JRy,V:Resurrection Crusade, I:Richie Simpson	6.00
8 JRy,AA,Constantine receives demon blood,V:Nergal	6.00
9 JRy,A:Swamp Thing	7.00
10 JRy,V:Nergal	6.00
11 MBu,Newcastle Incident,pt.1	5.00
12 JRy,D:Nergal	5.00
13 JRy,John has a Nightmare	5.00
14 JRy,B:The Fear Machine, I:Mercury,Marj,Eddie	5.00
15 JRy,Shepard's Warning	5.00
16 JRy,Rough Justice	5.00
17 MkH,I:Mr. Wester	5.00
18 JRy,R:Zed	5.00
19 JRy,I:Simon Hughes,Sandman	10.00
20 JRy,F:Mr.Webster	6.00
21 JRy,I:Jallakuntilliokan	6.00
22 JRy,E:The Fear Machine	6.00
23 I&D:Jerry O'Flynn	5.00
24 E:JaD(s),I:Sammy Morris	5.00
25 GMo(s),DvL,Early Warning	5.00
26 GMo(s)	5.00
27 NGa(s),DMc,Hold Me	22.00
28 B:JaD(s),RnT,KeW,F:S.Morris	5.00
29 RnT,KeW,V:Sammy Morris	5.00
30 RnT,KeW,D:Sammy Morris	5.00
31 E:JaD(s),SeP,Constantine's Father's Funeral	5.00
32 DiF(s),StP,I&D:Drummond	4.50
33 B:JaD(s),MPn,I:Pat McDonell	4.50
34 SeP,R:Mercury,Marj	4.50
35 SeP,Constantine's Past	4.50
36 Future Death,(preview of World Without End)	4.50
37 Journey to England's Secret Mystics	4.50
38 Constantine's Journey contd.	4.50
39 Journey to Discovery	4.50
40 DMc,I:2nd Kid Eternity	5.00
41 B:GEn(s),WSm,MPn,Dangerous Habits	10.00
42 Dangerous Habits	4.50
43 I:Chantinelle	4.50
44 Dangerous Habits	4.50
45 Dangerous Habits	4.50
46 Dangerous Habits epilogue, I:Kit(John's girlfriend)	4.50
47 SnW(i),Pub Where I Was Born	4.00
48 Love Kills	4.00

49 X-mas issue,Lord o/t Dance	4.00
50 WSm,Remarkable Lives,A:Lord of Vampires (48pgs)	6.00
51 JnS,SeP,Laundromat- Possession	5.00
52 GF(c),WSm, Royal Blood	5.00
53 GF(c),WSm, Royal Blood	5.00
54 GF(c),WSm, Royal Blood	5.00
55 GF(c),WSm, Royal Blood	5.00
56 GF(c),B:GEn(s),DvL, V:Danny Drake	5.00
57 GF(c),SDi,Mortal Clay#1, V:Dr. Amis	5.00
58 GF(c),SDi,Mortal Clay#2, V:Dr. Amis	5.00
59 GF(c),WSm,MkB(i),KDM,B:Guys & Dolls	5.00
60 GF(c),WSm,MkB(i),F:Tali, Chantinelle	5.00
61 GF(c),WSm,MkB(i),E:Guys & Dolls, V:First of the Fallen	5.00
62 GF(c),SDi,End of the Line,I:Gemma, AIDS storyline insert w/Death	6.00

DC/Vertigo, 1993

63 GF(c),SDi,C:Swamp Thing,Zatanna Phantom Stranger	5.00
64 GF(c),SDi,B:Fear & Loathing, A:Gabriel (Racism)	4.00
65 GF(c),SDi,D:Dez	4.00
66 GF(c),SDi,E:Fear and Loathing	4.00
67 GF(c),SDi,Kit leaves John	4.00
68 GF(c),SDi,F:Lord of Vampires, Darius,Mary	4.00
69 GF(c),SDi,D:Lord of Vampires	4.00
70 GF(c),SDi,Kit in Ireland	4.00
71 GF(c),SDi,A:WWII Fighter Pilot	4.00
72 GF(c),SDi,B:Damnation's Flame,A:Papa Midnight	4.00
73 GF(c),SDi,Nightmare NY, A:JFK	4.00
74 GF(c),SDi,I:Cedella,A:JFK	4.00
75 GF(c),SDi,E:Damnation'sFlame	4.00
76 GF(c),SDi,R:Brendan	4.00
77 Returns to England	4.00
78 GF(c),SDi,B:Rake at the Gates of Hell	4.00
79 GF(c),SDi,In Hell	4.00
80 GF(c),SDi,In London	4.00
81 GF(c),SDi	4.00
82 Kit	4.00
83 Rake,Gates of Hell	4.00
84 John's past	4.00
85 Warped Notions,pt.1	4.00
86 Warped Notions,pt.2	4.00
87 Warped Notions,pt.3	4.00
88 Warped Notions,pt.4	4.00
89 Dreamtime	4.00
90 Dreamtime,pt.2	4.00
91 Visits Battlefield	4.00
92 Critical Mass,pt.1	4.00
93 Critical Mass,pt.2	4.00
94 Critical Mass,pt.3	4.00
95 SeP,Critical Mass,pt.4	4.00
96 SeP,Critical Mass,pt.5	4.00
97 SeP,Critical Mass epilogue	4.00
98 SeP, helps neighbor	4.00
99 SeP	4.00
100 SeP, In a coma	5.00
101 SeP,deal with a demon	3.50
102 SeP,DifficultBeginnings,pt.1	3.50
103 SeP,DifficultBeginnings,pt.2	3.50
104 SeP,DifficultBeginnings,pt.3	3.50
105	3.50
106 PJe(s),SEp,In the Line of Fire, pt.1 (of 2)	3.50
107 PJe(s),SEp,Line of Fire,pt.2	3.50
108 PJe(s),SeP,a Bacchic celebration	3.50
109 PJe(s),SeP,cattle mutilations in Northern England	3.50
110 PJe(s),SeP,Last Man Standing,pt.1	3.50

111 PJe(s),SeP,Last Man,pt.2 . . . . 3.50
112 PJe(s),SeP,Last Man,pt.3 . . . . 3.50
113 PJe(s),SeP,Last Man,pt.4 . . . . 3.50
114 PJe(s),SeP,Last Man,pt.5 . . . . 3.50
115 PJe(s),SeP(s),Dani's ex-
    boyfriend 3.50
116 SeP,Widdershins,pt.1 (of 2) . . . 3.50
117 SeP,Widdershins,pt.2 . . . . 3.50
118 PJe(s),SeP,John's a Godfather. 4.00
119 PJe(s),SeP,disasters 3.50
120 PJe(s),SeP,10th anniv. 48pg. . . 3.00
121 PJe(s),SeP, Up the Down
    Staircase pt.1. . . . . 3.00
122 PJe(s),SeP, Up the Down
    Staircase pt.2. . . . . 3.00
123 PJe(s),SeP, Up the Down
    Staircase pt.3. . . . . 3.00
124 PJe(s),SeP, Up the Down
    Staircase pt.4. . . . . 3.00
125 PJe(s),SeP, How to Play
    with Fire, pt.1. . . . . 3.00
126 PJe(s),SeP,Play/Fire,pt.2 . . . . 3.00
127 PJe(s),SeP,Play/Fire,pt.3 . . . . 3.00
128 PJe(s),SeP,Play/Fire,pt.4 . . . . 3.00
129 . . . . 3.00
130 GEn,JHi,GF,Son of Man,pt.2 . . 3.00
131 GEn,JHi,GF,Son of Man,pt.3 . . 2.75
132 GEn,JHi,GF,Son of Man,pt.4 . . 2.75
133 GEn,JHi,GF,Son of Man,pt.5 . . 2.75
134 WEl(s),JHi,Haunted,pt.1 . . . . . . 2.75
135 WEl(s),JHi,Haunted,pt.2 . . . . . . 2.75
136 WEl(s),JHi,Haunted,pt.3 . . . . . . 2.75
137 WEl(s),JHi,Haunted,pt.4 . . . . . . 2.75
138 WEl(s),JHi,Haunted,pt.5 . . . . . . 2.75
139 WEl(s),JHi,Haunted,pt.6 . . . . . . 2.75
140 WEl(s),Locked. 2.75
141 WEl(s),ALa 2.75
142 WEl,TBd,Setting Sun 2.75
143 WEl,TBd,Telling Tales 2.75
144 GEr,ALa,Ashes & Honey,pt.1 . . 2.75
145 GEr,ALa,Ashes & Honey,pt.2 . . 2.75
146 RC,Hard Time. 2.75
147 RC,Hard Time,pt.2 . . . . 2.75
148 RC,Hard Time,pt.3 . . . . 2.75
149 RC,Hard Time,pt.4 . . . . 2.75
150 RC,Hard Time,concl. 2.75
151 Good Intentions,pt.1 . . . . 2.75
152 Good Intentions,pt.2 . . . . 2.75
153 Good Intentions,pt.3 . . . . 2.75
154 Good Intentions,pt.4 . . . . 2.75
155 Good Intentions,pt.5 . . . . 2.75
156 Good Intentions,pt.6 . . . . 2.75
157 SDi,"...and buried?". 2.75
158 Freezes Over,pl.1 . . . . 2.75
159 Freezes Over,pt.2 . . . . 2.75
160 Freezes Over,pt.3 . . . . 2.75
161 Freezes Over,pt.4 . . . . 2.75
162 Lapdogs and Englishmen 2.75
163 Lapdogs and Englishmen 2.75
164 Highwater, pt.1 . . . . 2.75
165 Highwater, pt.2 . . . . 2.75
166 Highwater, pt.3 . . . . 2.75
167 Highwater, pt.4 . . . . 2.75
168 A Fresh Coat of Red Paint 2.75
169 Constantine in LA 2.75
170 Ashes and Dust,pt.1 . . . . 2.75
171 Ashes and Dust,pt.2 . . . . 2.75
172 Ashes and Dust,pt.3 . . . . 2.75
173 Ashes and Dust,pt.4 . . . . 2.75
174 Ashes and Dust,pt.5 . . . . 2.75
175 SDi,JP,High on Life,pt.1 . . . . . . 2.75
176 SDi,JP,High on Life, pt.2 . . . . . . 2.75
177 Red Sepulchre,pt.1. . . . . 2.75
178 Red Sepulchre,pt.2. . . . . 2.75
179 Red Sepulchre,pt.3. . . . . 2.75
180 Red Sepulchre,pt.4. . . . . 2.75
181 Red Sepulchre,concl. 2.75
182 MCy(s),Black Flowers,pt.1 . . . . 2.75
183 MCy(s),Black Flowers,pt.2 . . . . 2.75
184 MCy(s),Wild Card 2.75
185 MCy(s),Ordeal 2.75
186 MCy(s),The Pit 2.75

Hellblazer #2
© DC Comics, Inc.

187 MCy(s),Bred in Bone,pt.1 . . . . 2.75
188 MCy(s),Bred in Bone,pt.2 . . . . 2.75
189 MCy(s),Staring at Wall,pt.1 . . . . 2.75
190 MCy(s),Staring at Wall,pt.2 . . . . 2.75
191 MCy(s),Staring at Wall,pt.3 . . . . 2.75
192 MCy(s),Staring at Wall,pt.4 . . . . 2.75
193 MCy(s),Staring at Wall,pt.5 . . . . 2.75
194 MCy(s) 2.75
195 MCy(s),Out of Season,pt.1 . . . . 2.75
196 MCy(s),Out of Season,pt.2 . . . . 2.75
197 Stations of the Cross,pt.1 . . . . . 2.75
198 Stations of the Cross,pt.2 . . . . . 2.75
199 Stations of the Cross,pt.3 . . . . . 2.75
200 Married life 4.50
201 Thieves 2.75
202 Reasons to be Cheerful,pt.1. . . 2.75
203 Reasons to be Cheerful,pt.2. . . 2.75
204 Reasons to be Cheerful,pt.3. . . 2.75
205 Reasons to be Cheerful,pt.4. . . 2.75
206 Chas' rampage 2.75
207 Down in the Ground,pt.1. . . . . . 2.75
208 Down in the Ground,pt.2. . . . . . 2.75
209 Down in the Ground,pt.3. . . . . . 2.75
210 Down in the Ground,pt.4. . . . . . 2.75
211 Down in the Ground,pt.5. . . . . . 2.75
212 Down in the Ground,pt.6. . . . . . 2.75
213 Back from Hell 2.75
214 MCy(s),R.S.V.P., pt.1 . . . . 2.75
215 MCy(s) 2.75
216 Empathy is the Enemy, pt.1 . . . 2.75
217 Empathy is the Enemy, pt.2 . . . 2.75
218 Empathy is the Enemy, pt.3 . . . 2.75
219 Empathy is the Enemy, pt.4 . . . 2.75
220 Empathy is the Enemy, pt.5 . . . 2.75
221 Empathy is the Enemy, pt.6 . . . 3.00
222 Empathy is the Enemy, pt.7 . . . 3.00
223 Empathy is the Enemy, concl . . 3.00
224 The Red Right Hand, pt.1 . . . . . 3.00
225 The Red Right Hand, pt.2. . . . . 3.00
226 The Red Right Hand, pt.3. . . . . 3.00
Ann.#1 JaD(s),BT,Raven Scar. . . . 7.00
Spec.#1 GF(c),GEn(s),SDi,John
    Constantine's teenage years. . . 4.50
Secret Files #1. . . . . 5.00
TPB Original Sins,rep.#1–#9 . . . . . 20.00
TPB Dangerous Habits 15.00
TPB Fear and Loathing 15.00
TPB Damnation's Flame 17.00
TPB Hard Time, 128-page. 10.00
TPB Good Intentions (2002) 13.00
TPB Haunted (2003) 13.00
TPB Hellblazer: Freezes Over. 15.00
TPB Rake at the Gates of Hell . . . 20.00
TPB Son of Man (2004). 13.00
TPB Highwater (2004). 20.00

TPB Setting Sun (2004). 13.00
TPB Freezes Over (2005) 15.00
TPB Tainted Love (2005). 17.00
TPB Red Sepulchre (2005) 13.00
TPB Staring at the Wall (2006) . . . 15.00
TPB Empathy is the Enemy (2006) 15.00
TPB Papa Midnite (2006) 13.00
TPB Lady Constantine (2006) 10.00
TPB All His Engines (2006). 15.00
TPB Stations of the Cross (2006) . 15.00

HELLBLAZER/
THE BOOKS OF MAGIC
Oct., 1997

1 (of 2) PJe,JNR. 2.50
2 PJe,JNR. 2.50

HELLBLAZER SPECIAL:
BAD BLOOD
DC/Vertigo, July, 2000

1 (of 4) JaD,PBd. 3.50
2 JaD,PBd. 3.50
3 JaD,PBd. 3.50
4 JaD,PBd,concl. 3.50

HELLBLAZER SPECIAL:
LADY CONSTANTINE
DC/Vertigo, Dec. 2002

1 (of 4) F:Johanna Constantine . . . 3.00
2 thru 4 . . . . @3.00

HERCULES UNBOUND
Oct.–Nov., 1975

1 WW 20.00
2 thru 8 . . . . @12.00
9 thru 12 WS,Aug.–Sept.,1977. . . 10.00

HERE'S HOWIE COMICS
1952–54

1 Teen-age humor. 350.00
2 . . . . 200.00
3 & 4 . . . . @150.00
5 Military humor 150.00
6 thru 10 . . . . @125.00
11 thru 18 . . . . @100.00

H-E-R-O
Feb. 2003

1 Jerry Feldon. 9.00
2 life-saving mission 5.00
3 F:Molly 5.00
4 Powers and Abilities 5.00
5 F:Matt Allen 3.00
6 F:Andrea Allen 3.00
7 Chaos, Inc. 3.00
8 Chaos, Inc.,pt.2 . . . . 3.00
9 World Made of Glass,pt.1 . . . . . . 3.00
10 World Made of Glass,pt.2 . . . . . 2.50
11 Prehistoric superhero? 2.50
12 Ch-Ch-Ch-Changes,pt.1 . . . . . . 2.50
13 Ch-Ch-Ch-Changes,pt.2 . . . . . . 2.50
14 Ch-Ch-Ch-Changes,pt.3 . . . . . . 2.50
15 Good Guys & Bad Guys,pt.1 . . . 2.50
16 Good Guys & Bad Guys,pt.2 . . . 2.50
17 Good Guys & Bad Guys,pt.3 . . . 2.50
18 Good Guys & Bad Guys,pt.4 . . . 2.50
19 Picking Up the Pieces,pt.1 . . . . 2.50
20 Picking Up the Pieces,pt.2 . . . . 2.50
21 Picking Up the Pieces,pt.3 . . . . 2.50
22 final battle over H-E-R-O device. 2.50
Spec. Double Feature,rep.#1&#2 . . 5.00
TPB Powers and Abilities. 10.00

HEROES
DC/Milestone, 1996

1 Six heroes join 3.50
2 thru 6 . . . . @2.50

HEROES AGAINST HUNGER
1986
1 NA,DG,JBy,CS,AA,BWr,BS,
   Superman,Batman 4.00

HERO HOTLINE
1989
1 thru 6, Mini-series . . . . @2.00

HEX
Sept., 1985
1 MT,I:Hex 7.00
2 MT 5.00
3 MT,V:Conglomerate 5.00
4 MT,V:Conglomerate 5.00
5 MT,A:Chainsaw Killer 5.00
6 MT,V:Conglomerate 5.00
7 MT,Tries to Return to own era . . . 5.00
8 MT,The Future 6.00
9 MT,Future Killer Cyborgs 5.00
10 MT,V:Death Cult 5.00
11 MT,V:The Batman 6.00
12 MT,A:Batman,V:Terminators 5.00
13 MT,I:New Supergroup 5.00
14 MT,A:The Dogs of War 5.00
15 KG,V:Chainsaw Killer 5.00
16 KG,V:Dogs of War 5.00
17 KG,Hex/Dogs of War T.U.
   V:XXGG 5.00
18 KGr,Confronting the Past,
   final issue 5.00

HI HI PUFFY AMIYUMI
Jan., 2006
Spec. Photo (c) 2.25
1 thru 3 . . . . @2.25

HISTORY OF DC UNIVERSE
Sept., 1986
1 GP, From start to WWII 5.00
2 GP, From WWII to present 5.00
TPB MWn(s),GP,KK,AxR(c)(2002) 10.00

HITCHHIKER'S GUIDE TO THE GALAXY
1993
1 Based on Douglas Adams book . 7.00
2 Based on the book 6.50
3 Based on the book 6.50
GN from Douglas Adams book . . . 15.00

HITMAN
1996–2001
1 GEn, F:Tommy Monaghan 10.00
2 GEn, Attempt to kill Joker 7.00
3 GEn(s),JMC, Mawzin & The
   Arkanonne 5.00
4 GEn(s),JMC, ... 4.00
5 GEn(s),JMC, ... 4.00
6 GEn(s),JMC,A:Johnny Navarone,
   Natt the Hatt 3.00
7 GEn(s),JMC, Pat's dead, Hitman
   wants revenge 3.00
8 GEn(s),JMC,barricaded in
   Noonan's Bar, Final Night tie-in. 3.00
9 GEn(s),JMC,A:Six-Pack 3.00
10 GEn(s),JMC,A:Green Lantern . . 3.00
11 . . . . 3.00
12 GEn(s),JMC,Local Heroes,
   A:Green Lantern 3.00
13 . . . . 3.00
14 GEn(s),JMC, Zombie Night at
   the Aquarium, concl. 3.00
15 GEn(s),JMC, Ace of
   Killers, pt.1, V:Mawzir 3.00

16 GEn(s),JMC,Ace of Killers,pt.2 . . 3.00
17 GEn(s),JMC,Ace of Killers,pt.3,
   A:Catwoman, Demon Etrigan . . 3.00
18 GEn(s),JMC,Ace of Killers,pt.4,
   A:Demon Etrigan, Baytor 3.00
19 GEn(s),JMC,Ace/Killers,pt.5, . . . 3.00
20 GEn(s),JMC,Ace/Killers,concl. . . 3.00
21 GEn(s),JMC,Romeo & Juliet 2.50
22 GEn(s),JMC,holiday special 2.50
23 GEn(s),JMC,Who Dares
   Wins,pt.1 . . . . 2.50
24 GEn(s),JMc,Dares/Wins,pt.2 . . . 2.50
25 GEn(s),JMc,Dares/Wins,pt.3 . . . 2.50
26 GEn(s),JMc,Dares/Wins,pt.4 . . . 2.50
27 GEn(s),JMc,Dares/Wins,pt.5 . . . 2.50
28 GEn(s),JMC, aftermath 2.50
29 GEn(s),JMC, Tommy's
   Heroes, pt.1 . . . . 2.50
30 GEn(s),JMC,Heroes, pt.2 . . . . . 2.50
31 GEn(s),JMC,Heroes, pt.3 . . . . . 2.50
32 GEn(s),JMC,Heroes, pt.4 . . . . . 2.50
33 GEn(s),JMC,Heroes, pt.5 . . . . . 2.50
34 GEn(s),A:Superman 2.50
35 GEn(s),Frances Monaghan 2.50
36 GEn(s), ... 2.50
37 GEn(s). 2.50
38 GEn(s),Dead Man's Land, concl. 2.50
39 GEn(s),JMC,A:RingoChen,pt.1 . . 2.50
40 GEn(s),JMC,A:RingoChen,pt.2 . . 2.50
41 GEn(s),JMC,A:RingoChen,pt.3 . . 2.50
42 GEn(s),JMC,A:RingoChen,pt.4 . . 2.50
43 GEn(s),JMC, ... 2.50
44 GEn(s),JMC 2.50
45 GEn(s),JMC 2.50
46 GEn(s),JMC 2.50
47 GEn(s),JMC,Old Dog 2.50
48 GEn(s),JMC,Old Dog,pt.2 . . . . . 2.50
49 GEn(s),JMC,Old Dog,pt.3 . . . . . 2.50
50 GEn(s),JMC,Hitman's future 2.50
51 GEn(s),JMc,Superguy,pt.1 . . . . 2.50
52 GEn(s),JMc,Superguy,pt.2 . . . . 2.50
53 GEn(s),JMc,ClosingTime,pt.1 . . . 2.50
54 GEn(s),JMc,ClosingTime,pt.2 . . . 2.50
55 GEn(s),JMc,ClosingTime,pt.3 . . . 2.50
56 GEn,JMC,GL,O:Tommy
   Monaghan 2.50
57 GEn,JMC,GL,O:Natt 2.50
58 GEn,JMC,GL,Closing time 2.50
59 GEn,JMC,GL,Closing time 2.50
60 GEn,JMC,GL,Closing time,final . 2.50
Ann.#1 Pulp Heroes (Western) 4.00
Spec.#1,000,000 GEn(s),JMC 2.50
Spec. Hitman/Lobo: That
   Stupid Bastich! 4.00
TPB rep. Demon Annual #2, Batman
   Chronicles #4, Hitman #1–#3 . 10.00
TPB Hitman,rep.#1-#3,+other 10.00
TPB Ten Thousand Bullets
   rep. #4–#8 . . . . 10.00
TPB Hitman: Ten Thousand Bullets 10.00
TPB Hitman: Local Heroes 18.00
TPB Hitman GEn(s),JMC 10.00
TPB Ace of Killers 18.00
TPB Who Dares Wins, GEn,JMC . 13.00

HOPALONG CASSIDY
Feb., 1954
86 GC,Ph(c):William Boyd & Topper,
   Secret o/t Tattooed Burro . . . 500.00
87 GC,Ph(c),Tenderfoot Outlaw. . 250.00
88 Ph(c),GC,15 Robbers of Rimfire
   Ridge 175.00
89 GC,Ph(c),One-Day Boom
   Town 175.00
90 GC,Ph(c),Cowboy Clown
   Robberies 175.00
91 GC,Ph(c),The Riddle of
   the Roaring R Ranch 175.00
92 GC,Ph(c),Sky-RidingOutlaws . 150.00
93 GC,Ph(c),Silver Badge
   of Courage 150.00

Hopalong Cassidy #100
© DC Comics, Inc.

94 GC,Ph(c),Mystery of the
   Masquerading Lion 150.00
95 GC,Ph(c),Showdown at the
   Post-Hole Bank 150.00
96 GC,Ph(c),Knights of
   the Range 150.00
97 GC,Ph(c),The Mystery of
   the Three-Eyed Cowboy 150.00
98 GC,Ph(c),Hopalong's
   Unlucky Day 150.00
99 GC,Ph(c),Partners in Peril . . . 150.00
100 GC,Ph(c),The Secrets
   of a Sheriff 175.00
101 GC,Ph(c),Way Out West
   Where The East Begins 125.00
102 GC,Ph(c),Secret of the
   Buffalo Hat. 125.00
103 GC,Ph(c),The Train-Rustlers
   of Avalance Valley 125.00
104 GC,Ph(c),Secret of the
   Surrendering Outlaws 125.00
105 GC,Ph(c),Three Signs
   to Danger. 125.00
106 GC,Ph(c),The Secret of
   the Stolen Signature 125.00
107 GC,Ph(c),The Mystery Trail
   to Stagecoach Town 125.00
108 GC,Ph(c),The Mystery
   Stage From Burro Bend 125.00
109 GC,The Big Gun on Saddletop
   Mountain 125.00
110 GC,The Dangerous Stunts
   of Hopalong Cassidy 100.00
111 GC,Sheriff Cassidy's
   Mystery Clue 100.00
112 GC,Treasure Trail to
   Thunderbolt Ridge 100.00
113 GC,The Shadow of the
   Toy Soldier. 100.00
114 GC,Ambush at Natural
   Bridge 100.00
115 GC,The Empty-Handed
   Robberies 100.00
116 GC,Mystery of the
   Vanishing Cabin. 100.00
117 GC,School for Sheriffs 100.00
118 GC,The Hero of
   Comanche Ridge. 100.00
119 GC,The Dream Sheriff of
   Twin Rivers 100.00
120 GC,Salute to a Star-Wearer . 100.00
121 GC,The Secret of the
   Golden Caravan 100.00
122 GC,The Rocking
   Horse Bandits 100.00

123 GK,Mystery of the
　　One-Dollar Bank Robbery . . . 100.00
124 GK,Mystery of the
　　Double-X Brand. 100.00
125 GK,Hopalong Cassidy's
　　Secret Brother 100.00
126 GK,Trail of the
　　Telltale Clues 100.00
127 GK,Hopalong Cassidy's
　　Golden Riddle 100.00
128 GK,The House That
　　Hated Outlaws. 100.00
129 GK,Hopalong Cassidy's
　　Indian Sign 100.00
130 GK,The Return of the
　　Canine Sheriff 100.00
131 GK&GK(c),The Amazing
　　Sheriff of Double Creek. 100.00
132 GK,Track of the
　　Invisible Indians. 100.00
133 GK,Golden Trail to Danger . . 100.00
134 GK,Case of the
　　Three Crack-Shots 100.00
135 GK,May-June, 1959 . . . . 100.00

HORRORIST
DC/Vertigo, 1995
1 I:Horrorist. 6.50
2 conclusion 6.50

HOT WHEELS
March-April, 1970
1 ATh. 200.00
2 ATh. 100.00
3 NA,ATh 125.00
4 ATh. 100.00
5 ATh. 100.00
6 NA(c) 125.00

HOURMAN
1999
1 TPe,RgM,A:JLA. 2.50
2 TPe(s),RgM,F:Tomorrow Woman 2.50
3 TPe(s),RgM,Timepoint,pt.1 . . . . 2.50
4 TPe(s),RgM,Timepoint,pt.2 . . . . 2.50
5 TPe(s),RgM,Rex Tyler's life. . . . 2.50
6 TPe,RgM,JLAndroids,pt.1 . . . . . 2.50
7 TPe,RgM,JLAndroids,pt.2 . . . . . 2.50
8 TPe,RgM,Day of Judgment
　　x-over. 2.50
9 TPe,RgM,F:Rick Tyler 2.50
10 TPe,RgM. 2.50
11 TPe,RgM,One Million,pt.1 . . . . 2.50
12 TPe,RgM,One Million,pt.2. . . . 2.50
13 TPe,RgM,One Million,pt.3. . . . 2.50
14 TPe,RgM,V:Undersoul 2.50
15 TPe,RgM,human secrets 2.50
16 TPe,RgM,F:Snapper. 2.50
17 TPe,100 Years of Solitude . . . 2.50
18 TPe,RgM,High Society,pt.1 . . . 2.50
19 TPe,RgM,High Society,pt.2 . . . 2.50
20 TPe,RgM,F:Snapper. 2.50
21 TPe,RgM,reduced to nothing . . 2.50
22 TPe,TyH 2.50
23 TPe,RgM,Unbelievable
　　Truth,pt.1 . . . . 2.50
24 TPE,RgM,Unbel.Truth,pt.2 . . . 2.50
25 TPE,RgM,final issue 2.50

HOUSE OF MYSTERY
Dec.–Jan., 1952
1 I Fell In Love With
　　a Monster 3,800.00
2 The Mark of X. 1,700.00
3 The Dummy of Death 1,300.00
4 The Man With the Evil Eye . . . 900.00
5 The Man With the Strangler
　　Hands!. 900.00
6 The Monster in Clay! 750.00
7 Nine Lives of Alger Denham! . . 750.00

House of Mystery #8
© DC Comics, Inc.

8 Tattoos of Doom 750.00
9 Secret of the Little Black Bag . 750.00
10 The Wishes of Doom 750.00
11 Deadly Game of G-H-O-S-T . . 650.00
12 The Devil's Chessboard 650.00
13 The Theater Of A
　　Thousand Thrills!. 650.00
14 The Deadly Dolls 650.00
15 The Man Who Could Change
　　the World 650.00
16 Dead Men Tell No Tales!. . . . 550.00
17 Man With the X-Ray Eyes . . . 475.00
18 Dance of Doom. 475.00
19 The Strange Faces of Death. . 475.00
20 The Beast Of Bristol 475.00
21 Man Who Could See Death . . 475.00
22 The Phantom's Return 475.00
23 Stamps of Doom. 475.00
24 Kill The Black Cat. 475.00
25 The Man With Three Eyes!. . . 475.00
26 The Man with Magic Ears. . . . 450.00
27 Fate Hold Four Aces! 450.00
28 The Wings Of Mr. Milo!. 450.00
29 CS,Hangman's House 450.00
30 The Demon Gun. 450.00
31 The Incredible Illusions! 450.00
32 Pied Piper of the Sea 450.00
33 Mr. Misfortune! 450.00
34 The Hundred Year Duel 450.00
35 The Fatal Superstition. 450.00
36 The Treasure of Montezuma! . 375.00
37 MD,The Statue That
　　Came to Life 375.00
38 The Voyage Of No Return . . . 375.00
39 Professor Smith's Magic Lamp 375.00
40 The Coins That Came To Life. 375.00
41 The Impossible Tricks! 375.00
42 The Stranger From Out There 375.00
43 Imp on the Flying Trapeze . . . 375.00
44 The Secret Of Hill 14 . . . . . . 375.00
45 The Magic Kite 375.00
46 The Bird of Fate 375.00
47 The Robot Named Think. 375.00
48 The Man Marooned On Earth. 375.00
49 The Mysterious Mr. Omen . . . 375.00
50 The Amazing Swami. 400.00
51 Man Who Stole Teardrops . . . 350.00
52 The Man With The Golden
　　Shoes 350.00
53 The Man Who Hated Mirrors . 350.00
54 The Woman Who Lived Twice 350.00
55 I Turned Back Time. 350.00
56 The Thing In The Black Box. . 350.00
57 The Untamed 350.00
58 Haunted Melody 350.00

59 The Tomb Of Ramfis. 350.00
60 The Prisoner On Canvas 350.00
61 JK,Superstition Day 350.00
62 The Haunting Scarecrow 325.00
63 JK,The Lady & The Creature . 350.00
64 The Golden Doom 325.00
65 JK,The Magic Lantern. 400.00
66 JK,Sinister Shadow. 400.00
67 The Wizard of Water. 325.00
68 The Book That Bewitched. . . . 325.00
69 The Miniature Disasters 325.00
70 JK,The Man With Nine Lives . 325.00
71 Menace of the Mole Man 325.00
72 JK,Dark Journey. 325.00
73 Museum That Came to Life . . 325.00
74 Museum That Came To Life . . 325.00
75 Assignment Unknown! 325.00
76 JK,Prisoners Of The Tiny
　　Universe 325.00
77 The Eyes That Went Berserk . 300.00
78 JK(c),The 13th Hour 325.00
79 JK(c),The Fantastic Sky
　　Puzzle 325.00
80 Man With Countless Faces! . . 300.00
81 The Man Who Made Utopia . . 300.00
82 The Riddle of the Earth's
　　Second Moon 300.00
83 The Mystery of the
　　Martian Eye 300.00
84 JK,BK,100-Century Doom . . . 375.00
85 JK(c),Earth's Strangest
　　Salesman. 350.00
86 The Baffling Bargains 325.00
87 The Human Diamond 325.00
88 Return of the Animal Man. . . . 325.00
89 The Cosmic Plant! 325.00
90 The Invasion Of the Energy
　　Creatures! 325.00
91 DD&SMo(c),The Riddle of the
　　Alien Satellite. 325.00
92 DD(c),Menace of the
　　Golden Globule 325.00
93 NC(c),I Fought The
　　Molten Monster 325.00
94 DD&SMo(c),The Creature
　　In Echo Lake. 325.00
95 The Wizard's Gift 325.00
96 The Amazing 70-Ton Man. . . . 325.00
97 The Alien Who Change
　　History 325.00
98 DD&SMo(c),The Midnight
　　Creature. 325.00
99 The Secret of the
　　Leopard God 325.00
100 The Beast Beneath Earth . . . 350.00

House of Mystery #53
© DC Comics Inc.

House of Mystery #113
© DC Comics, Inc.

101 The Magnificent Monster . . . 300.00
102 Cellmate to a Monster 300.00
103 Hail the Conquering Aliens . . 300.00
104 I was the Seeing-Eye Man . . . 300.00
105 Case of the Creature X-14 . . 300.00
106 Invaders from the Doomed
    Dimension 300.00
107 Captives o/t Alien
    Fisherman 300.00
108 RMo,Four Faces of Frank
    Forbes 300.00
109 ATh,JKu,Secret of the Hybrid
    Creatures 300.00
110 Beast Who Stalked Through
    Time 300.00
111 Operation Beast Slayer 300.00
112 Menace of Craven's
    Creatures 300.00
113 RMo,Prisoners of Beast
    Asteroid 300.00
114 The Movies from Nowhere . . 300.00
115 Prisoner o/t Golden Mask . . . 300.00
116 RMo,Return of the
    Barsfo Beast 300.00
117 Menace of the Fire Furies . . . 225.00
118 RMo,Secret o/SuperGorillas . 225.00
119 Deadly Gift from the Stars . . . 225.00
120 ATh,Catman of KarynPeale . 225.00
121 RMo,Beam that Transformed
    Men 225.00
122 Menace fo the Alien Hero . . . 225.00
123 RMo,Lure o/t Decoy
    Creature 225.00
124 Secret of Mr. Doom 225.00
125 Fantastic Camera Creature . 225.00
126 The Human Totem Poles . . . 225.00
127 RMo,Cosmic Game o/Doom . 225.00
128 NC,The Sorcerer's Snares . . 225.00
129 Man in the Nuclear Trap 225.00
130 The Alien Creature Hunt 225.00
131 Vengeance o/t GeyserGod . . 200.00
132 MMe,Beware My Invisible
    Master 200.00
133 MMe,Captive Queen of
    Beast Island 200.00
134 MMe,Secret Prisoner of
    Darkmore Dungeon 200.00
135 MMe,Alien Body Thief 200.00
136 MMe,Secret o/t StolenFace . 200.00
137 MMe,Tunnel to Disaster 200.00
138 MMe,Creature Must Die 200.00
139 MMe,Creatures of
    Vengeful Eye 200.00
140 I&Only app.:Astro 200.00
141 MMe,The Alien Gladiator . . . 200.00

142 MMe,The Wax Demons 200.00
143 J'onn J'onzz begins 450.00
144 J'onn J'onzz on Weird
    World of Gilgana 250.00
145 J'onn J'onzz app 200.00
146 BP,J'onn J'onzz 200.00
147 J'onn J'onzz 200.00
148 J'onn J'onzz 200.00
149 ATh,J'onn J'onzz 200.00
150 MMe,J'onn J'onzz 200.00
151 J'onn J'onzz 200.00
152 MMe,J'onn J'onzz 200.00
153 J'onn J'onzz 200.00
154 J'onn J'onzz 200.00
155 J'onn J'onzz 200.00
156 JM,I:Dial H for Hero (Giantboy
    Cometeer,Mole)J.J'onzz sty . 175.00
157 JM,Dial H for Hero (Human
    Bullet,Super Charge,Radar
    Sonar Man) J.J'onzz sty 175.00
158 JM,Dial H for Hero (Quake
    MasterSquid)J'onn J'onzz sty 125.00
159 JM,Dial H for Hero (Human
    Starfish,Hypno Man,Mighty
    Moppet) J'onn J'onzz sty 125.00
160 JM,Dial H for Hero (King Kandy
    A:Plastic Man,I:Marco Xavier (J'onn
    J'onzz new secret I.D.) 200.00
161 JM,Dial H for Hero (Magneto,
    Hornet Man,Shadow Man) . . 100.00
162 JM,Dial H for Hero (Mr.Echo,
    Future Man) J'onnJ'onzz sty . 100.00
163 JM,Dial H for Hero(Castor&Pollux,
    King Coil) J'onnJ'onzz sty . . . 100.00
164 JM,Dial H for Hero (Super Nova
    Zip Tide) J'onnJ'onzz sty 100.00
165 JM,Dial H for Hero (Whoozis,
    Whatsis,Howzis) J'onn J'onzz
    story 100.00
166 JM,Dial H for Hero (Yankee
    Doodle Kid,Chief Mighty Arrow)
    J'onn J'onzz sty 100.00
167 JM,Dial H for Hero (Balloon Boy,
    Muscle Man,Radar Sonar Man)
    J'onn J'onzz sty 100.00
168 JM,Dial H for Hero (Thunderbolt,
    Mole,Cometeer,Hoopster)
    J'onn J'onzz sty 100.00
169 JM,I:Gem Girl in Dial H for
    Hero,J'onn J'onzz sty 100.00
170 JM,Dial H for Hero (Baron
    BuzzSaw,Don Juan,Sphinx
    Man) J'onn J'onzz sty 100.00
171 JM,Dial H for Hero (King Viking
    Whirl-I-Gig)J'onn J'onzz sty . . 90.00
172 JM,Dial H for Hero 90.00
173 E:Dial H for Hero,F:J'onn
    J'onzz 90.00
174 New direction,SA pg.13 . . . . 650.00
175 I:Cain 350.00
176 SA,Cain's Game Room 300.00
177 Curse of the Car 300.00
178 NA,The Game 300.00
179 BWr,NA,JO,Widow'sWalk . . . 350.00
180 GK,WW,BWr,SA,Room 13 . . 200.00
181 BWr,The Siren on Satan . . . 200.00
182 ATh,The Devil's Doorway . . . 75.00
183 BWr,WW(i),DeadCanKill 200.00
184 ATh,GK,WW,Eye o/Basilisk . . 75.00
185 AW,The Beautiful Beast 75.00
186 BWr,NA,Nightmare 75.00
187 ATh,Mask of the Red Fox 60.00
188 TD,BWr,NA(c),House of
    Madness 75.00
189 WW(i),NA(c),Eyes of the Cat . 60.00
190 ATh,Fright 60.00
191 BWr,TD,NA(c),Christmas
    Story 85.00
192 JAp,GM,DH,NA(c),Garnener
    of Eden 60.00
193 BWr(c), Voodoo Vengeance . . 60.00

194 ATh,NR,RH(rep),JK(rep)
    Born Loser 85.00
195 NR,BWr,ThingsOld..Things
    Forgotten 100.00
196 GM,GK,ATh(rep)A Girl &
    Her Dog 60.00
197 DD,NR,NA(c),House of
    Horrors 65.00
198 MSy,NC,Day of the Demon . . 75.00
199 WW,RB,NA(c),Sno'Fun 85.00
200 MK,TD,The Beast's Revenge . 85.00
201 JAp,The Demon Within 60.00
202 MSy,GC(rep),SA,The Poster
    Plague,John Prentice? 60.00
203 NR,Tower of Prey 60.00
204 BWr,AN,All in the Family 75.00
205 The Coffin Creature 35.00
206 MSy,TP,The Burning 35.00
207 JSn,The Spell 40.00
208 Creator of Evil 35.00
209 AA,JAp,Tomorrow I Hang . . . 40.00
210 The Immortal 35.00
211 NR,Deliver Us From Evil 40.00
212 MA,AN,Ever After 35.00
213 AN,Back from the Realm of
    the Damned 40.00
214 NR,The Shaggy Dog 40.00
215 The Man Who Wanted Power
    over Women 35.00
216 TD,Look into My Eyes & Kill . . 35.00
217 NR,AA,Swamp God 40.00
218 FT,An Ice Place to Visit 35.00
219 AA,NR,BWr(c),Pledge to
    Satan 45.00
220 AA,AN,They Hunt Butterflies
    Don't They? 35.00
221 FT,BWr,MK,He Who Laughs
    Last 45.00
222 AA,Night of the Teddy Bear . . 30.00
223 Demon From the Deep 30.00
224 FR,AA,SheerFear,B:100pg . . . 90.00
225 AA,FT,AN,See No Evil 90.00
226 AA,FR,NR,SA,Monster in House
    Tour of House of Mystery 90.00
227 NR,AA,The Carriage Man 90.00
228 FR,NA(i),The Rebel 90.00
229 NR,Nightmare Castle,
    last 100 page 90.00
230 Experiment In Fear 25.00
231 Cold,Cold Heart 25.00
232 Last Tango in Hell 25.00
233 FR,Cake! 25.00
234 AM,Lafferty's Luck 25.00
235 NR,Wings of Black Death 25.00
236 SD,NA(i),BWr(c),Death
    Played a Sideshow 35.00
237 FT,Night of the Chameleon . . . 25.00
238 A Touch of Evil 25.00
239 Day of the Witch 25.00
240 The Murderer 25.00
241 FR,NR,DeathPulls theStrings . 25.00
242 FR,The Balloon Vendor 25.00
243 Brother Bear 25.00
244 FT,Kronos..Zagros-Eborak . . 25.00
245 AN,Check the J.C.Demon
    Catalogue Under...Death 25.00
246 DeathVault of Eskimo Kings . . 25.00
247 SD,Death Rides the Waves . . . 25.00
248 NightJamieGaveUp theGhost . 25.00
249 Hit Parade of Death 25.00
250 AN,Voyage to Hell 25.00
251 WW,AA,NA(c),The Collector,
    68-pages 35.00
252 DP,RT,AA,FR,AN,NA(c),
    ManKillers 35.00
253 TD,AN,GK,KJ,NA(c),Beware
    the Demon Child 35.00
254 SD,AN,MR,NA(c),The
    Devil's Place 35.00
255 RE,GM,BWr(c),Sometimes
    Leopards 35.00

256 DAy,AN,BWr(c),Museum of
   Murders 35.00
257 RE,MGo,TD(i),MBr,Xmas iss . . 35.00
258 SD,RB,BMc,DG(i),The Demon
   and His Boy 35.00
259 RE,RT,MGo,DN,BL,Hair Today,
   Gone Tomorrow, last giant 35.00
260 Go to Hades 15.00
261 The Husker 15.00
262 FreedFrom Infernos of Hell . . . 15.00
263 JCr,Is There Vengeance
   After Death? 15.00
264 Halloween Issue 15.00
265 The Perfect Host 15.00
266 The Demon Blade 15.00
267 A Strange Way to Die 15.00
269 Blood on the Grooves 15.00
270 JSh,JRu,JBi,Black Moss 15.00
271 TS,HellHound of
   Brackenmoor 15.00
272 DN,DA,theSorcerer's Castle . . 15.00
273 The Rites of Inheritance 15.00
274 MR,JBi,Hell Park 15.00
275 JCr,Final Installment 15.00
276 SD,MN,Epode 15.00
277 HC,AMi,Limited Engagement . 15.00
278 TV or Not TV 15.00
279 AS,Trial by Fury 15.00
280 VMK,DAy,Hungry Jaws
   of Death 15.00
281 Now Dying in this Corner 15.00
282 JSw,DG,Superman/Radio
   Shack ins 15.00
283 RT,AN,Kill Me Gently 15.00
284 KG,King and the Dragon 15.00
285 Cold Storage 15.00
286 Long Arm of the Law 15.00
287 NR,AS,BL,Legend o/t Lost . . . 15.00
288 DSp,Piper at Gates of Hell . . . 15.00
289 Brother Bobby's Home for
   Wayward Girls & Boys 15.00
290 TS,I:I..Vampire 27.00
291 TS,DAy,I..Vampire #2 . . . . 15.00
292 TS,MS,TD,RE,DSp,Wendigo . 15.00
293 GT,TS,A:I..Vampire #3 . . . . . . 15.00
294 CI,TY,GT,TD,The Darkness . . 15.00
295 TS,TVE,JCr,I..Vampire #4 . . . . 15.00
296 CI,BH,Night Women 15.00
297 TS,DCw,TD,I..Vampire #5 . . . . 15.00
298 TS,Stalker on a StarlessNight . 15.00
299 TS,DSp,I..Vampire #6 . . . . 15.00
300 GK,DA,JSon,JCr,DSp,Anniv. . . 20.00
301 JDu,TVE,KG,TY `...Virginia' . . 17.00
302 TS,NR,DSp,I..Vampire #7 . . . . 17.00

House of Mystery #269
© DC Comics, Inc.

303 TS,DSp,I..Vampire #8 . . . . 17.00
304 EC,RE,I..Vampire #9 . . . . 17.00
305 TVE,EC,I..Vampire #10 . . . . . . 17.00
306 TS,TD,I..Vampire #11,
   A:Jack the Ripper 17.00
307 TS,I..Vampire #12 . . . . 17.00
308 TS,MT,NR,I..Vampire #13 . . . . 17.00
309 TS,I..Vampire #14 . . . . 17.00
310 TS(i),I..Vampire #15 . . . . 17.00
311 I..Vampire #16 . . . . 17.00
312 TS(i),I..Vampire #17 . . . . 17.00
313 TS(i),CI,I..Vampire #18 . . . . . . 17.00
314 TS,I..Vampire #19 . . . . 17.00
315 TS(i),TY,I..Vampire #20 . . . . . . 17.00
316 TS(i),GT,TVE,I..Vampire #21 . 17.00
317 TS(i),I..Vampire #22 . . . . 17.00
318 TS(i),I..Vampire #23 . . . . 17.00
319 TS,JOy,I..Vampire conc. 25.00
320 GM,Project: Inferior. 25.00
321 final issue 25.00
Welcome Back to the House of Mystery
   GN BWr(c) horror stories rep . . 25.00

HOUSE OF SECRETS
Nov.–Dec., 1956
1 MD,JM,The Hand of Doom . . 2,400.00
2 MMe,RMo,NC,Mask of Fear . . 900.00
3 JM,JK,MMe,The Three
   Prophecies. 750.00
4 JM,JK,MMe,Master of
   Unknown 600.00
5 MMe,The Man Who
   Hated Fear 425.00
6 NC,MMe,Experiment 1000 . . . 425.00
7 RMo,Island o/t Enchantress . . 425.00
8 JK,RMo,The Electrified Man . . 450.00
9 JM,JSt,The Jigsaw Creatures . 375.00
10 JSt,NC,I was a Prisoner
   of the Sea 375.00
11 KJ(c),NC,The Man who
   Couldn't Stop Growing. 375.00
12 JK,The Hole in the Sky 400.00
13 The Face in the Mist. 325.00
14 MMe,The Man who Stole Air . 325.00
15 The Creature in the Camera . . 325.00
16 NC,We Matched Wits with a
   Gorilla Genius 300.00
17 DW,Lady in the Moon 300.00
18 MMe,The Fantastic
   Typewriter 300.00
19 MMe,NC,Lair of the
   Dragonfly 300.00
20 Incredible Fireball Creatures. . 300.00
21 Girl from 50,000 Fathoms . . . 300.00
22 MMe,Thing from Beyond 300.00
23 MMe,I&O:Mark Merlin. 325.00
24 NC,Mark Merlin story 300.00
25 MMe,Mark Merlin story 275.00
26 NC,MMe, Mark Merlin story . . 275.00
27 MMe,Mark Merlin 275.00
28 MMe,Mark Merlin 275.00
29 NC,MMe,Mark Merlin 275.00
30 JKu,MMe,Mark Merlin. 275.00
31 DD,MMe,RH,Mark Merlin 250.00
32 MMe,Mark Merlin 250.00
33 MMe,Mark Merlin 250.00
34 MMe,Mark Merlin 250.00
35 MMe,Mark Merlin 250.00
36 MMe,Mark Merlin 250.00
37 MMe,Mark Merlin 250.00
38 MMe,Mark Merlin 250.00
39 JKu,MMe,Mark Merlin. 250.00
40 NC,MMe,Mark Merlin 250.00
41 MMe,Mark Merlin 250.00
42 MMe,Mark Merlin 250.00
43 RMo,MMe,CI,Mark Merlin . . . 250.00
44 MMe,Mark Merlin 250.00
45 MMe,Mark Merlin 250.00
46 MMe,Mark Merlin 250.00
47 MMe,Mark Merlin 250.00
48 ATh,MMe,Mark Merlin 250.00
49 MMe,Mark Merlin 250.00

House of Secrets #13
© DC Comics Inc.

50 MMe,Mark Merlin 250.00
51 MMe,Mark Merlin 250.00
52 MMe,Mark Merlin 250.00
53 CI,Mark Merlin 250.00
54 RMo,MMe,Mark Merlin 250.00
55 MMe,Mark Merlin 250.00
56 MMe,Mark Merlin 250.00
57 MMe,Mark Merlin 250.00
58 MMe,O:Mark Merlin 250.00
59 MMe,Mark Merlin 250.00
60 MMe,Mark Merlin 250.00
61 I:Eclipso,A:Mark Merlin 300.00
62 MMe,Eclipso,Mark Merlin 250.00
63 GC,ATh,Eclipso,Mark Merlin . . 200.00
64 MMe,ATh,M Merlin,Eclipso. . . 200.00
65 MMe,ATh,M Merlin,Eclipso . . . 200.00
66 MMe,ATh,M Merlin,Eclipso . . . 225.00
67 MMe,ATh,M Merlin,Eclipso . . . 200.00
68 MMe,Mark Merlin,Eclipso 200.00
69 MMe,Mark Morlin,Eclipso 200.00
70 MMe,Mark Merlin,Eclipso 200.00
71 MMe,Mark Merlin,Eclipso 200.00
72 MMe,Mark Merlin,Eclipso 200.00
73 MMe,D:Mark Merlin,I:Prince
   Ra-Man, Eclipso 200.00
74 MMe,Prince Ra-Man,Eclipso . 200.00
75 MMe,Prince Ra-Man,Eclipso . 200.00
76 MMe,Prince Ra-Man,Eclipso . 200.00
77 MMe,Prince Ra-Man,Eclipso . 200.00
78 MMe,Prince Ra-Man,Eclipso . 200.00
79 MMe,Prince Ra-Man,Eclipso . 200.00
80 MMo,Prince Ra-Man,Eclipso . 200.00
81 I:Abel, new mystery format
   Don't Move It 500.00
82 DD,NA,One & only, fully guaran–
   teed super-permanent 100%. 125.00
83 ATh,The Stuff that Dreams
   are Made of 125.00
84 DD,If I had but world enough
   and time. 125.00
85 DH,GK,NA,Second Chance . . 150.00
86 GT,GM,Strain 150.00
87 DD,DG,RA,MK,BWr,The Coming
   of Ghaglan. 160.00
88 DD,The Morning Ghost. 150.00
89 GM,DH,Where Dead MenWalk 150.00
90 GT,RB,NA,GM,The Symbionts 160.00
91 WW,MA,The Eagle's Talon . . . 150.00
92 BWr,TD(i),I:Swamp Thing
   (Alex Olson) 1,000.00
93 JAp,TD,ATh(rep.)Lonely in
   Death. 125.00
94 TD,ATh(rep.)Hyde.and
   go Seek 125.00
95 DH,NR,The Bride of Death . . . 125.00

96 DD,JAb,WW,BWr,the Monster 125.00
97 JAp,Divide and Murder 125.00
98 MK,ATh(rep),Born Losers . . . 125.00
99 NR,TD(i),BWr,,Beyond His
   Imagination 100.00
100 TP,TD,AA,BWr,Rest in Peace 125.00
101 AN,MK,Small Invasion 50.00
102 NR,MK,A Lonely Monstrosity . 50.00
103 AN,BWr,Village on Edge
    of Forever 50.00
104 NR,AA,GT,Ghosts Don't
    Bother Me...But. 50.00
105 JAp,,AA,MK,An Axe to Grind . . 50.00
106 AN,AA,BWr,This Will Kill You . 50.00
107 AA,BWr(c),The Night of
    the Nebbish 50.00
108 A New Kid on the Block 50.00
109 AA,AN...And in Death, there
    is no Escape 50.00
110 Safes Have Secrets, Too 50.00
111 TD,Hair-I-Kari 50.00
112 Case of the Demon Spawn . . . 50.00
113 MSy,NC,NR,Spawns
    of Satan 50.00
114 FBe,Night Game 50.00
115 AA,AN,Nobody Hurts My
    Brother. 50.00
116 NR,Like Father,Like Son 50.00
117 AA,AN,Revenge for the Deadly
    Dummy 50.00
118 GE,Very Last Picture Show . . 50.00
119 A Carnival of Dwarves. 50.00
120 TD,AA,The Lion's Share 50.00
121 Ms.Vampire Killer 50.00
122 AA,Requiem for Igor 35.00
123 ATh,A Connecticut Ice Cream
    Man in King Arthur's Court . . . 35.00
124 Last of the Frankensteins . . . 35.00
125 AA,FR,Instant Re-Kill 35.00
126 AN,On Borrowed Time 35.00
127 MSy,A Test of Innocence . . . 35.00
128 AN,Freak Out!. 35.00
129 Almost Human 35.00
130 All Dolled Up! 35.00
131 AN,Point of No Return 35.00
132 Killer Instinct 35.00
133 Portraits of Death 35.00
134 NR,Inheritance of Blood 35.00
135 BWr,The Vegitable Garden . . . 35.00
136 BWr,NR,Last Voyage of
    Lady Luck 35.00
137 BWr,The Harder They Fall . . . 35.00
138 Where Dreams are Born. 40.00
139 SD,NR,A Real Crazy Kid 40.00
140 NR,O:Patchwork Man 50.00
141 You Can't Beat the Devil 20.00
142 Playmate. 20.00
143 The Evil Side. 20.00
144 The Vampire of Broadway . . . 20.00
145 Operation was Successful,But 20.00
146 GM,Snake's Alive 20.00
147 AN,GM,See-Through Thief . . . 20.00
148 GM,SD,Sorcerer's Apprentice . 20.00
149 MK,The Evil One. 20.00
150 JSN(c),A:Phantom Stranger
    and Dr.13. . . . . 20.00
151 MGo,MK,Nightmare 20.00
152 Sister Witch. 20.00
153 VM,AN,Don't Look Now 20.00
154 TS,MK,JL,Last issue. 20.00

HOUSE OF SECRETS
DC/Vertigo, Aug., 1996
1 SSe(s),TKr, judgments on your
  darkest secrets 4.00
2 SSe(s),TKr, F:Rain. 3.00
3 SSe(s),TKr,Seattle's citizens
  secrets 3.00
4 SSe(s),TKr,Eric's secrets
  exposed. 3.00
5 SSe(s),TKr,Foundation Epilogue . 3.00

6 SSe(s),DFg,Other rooms:
  Meeting 3.00
7 SSe(s),TKr,Blueprint:
  Elevation A 3.00
8 SSe(s),TKr,Road to You,pt.1 . . 3.00
9 SSe(s),TKr,Road to You,pt.2 . . 3.00
10 SSe(s),TKr,Road to You,pt.3. . 3.00
11 The Book of Law, pt.1 (of 5) . . 3.00
12 The Book of Law, pt.2. . . . . . . 3.00
13 SSe,The Book of Law, pt.3 . . . 3.00
14 SSe The Book of Law, pt.4 . . . 3.00
15 SSe,The Book of Law, pt.5 . . . 3.00
16 SSe,Book of Law, epilogue . . . 3.00
17 SSe,The Road to You, pt.1 . . . 3.00
18 SSe,The Road to You, pt.2 . . . 3.00
19 SSe,The Road to You, pt.3 . . . 3.00
20 SSe,Other Rooms story 3.00
21 SSe,Basement, pt.1 . . . . 3.00
22 SSe,Basement, pt.2 . . . . 3.00
23 SSe,Basement, pt.3 . . . . 3.00
24 SSe,TKr,Attic. 3.00
25 SSe,TKr, final issue 3.00
TPB Foundation, rep.#1–#5. . . . . . 15.00

HOUSE OF SECRETS: FACADE
DC/Vertigo, March, 2001
1 (of 2) TKr, 48-page 6.00
2 TKr,48-page 6.00

HUMAN DEFENSE CORPS
May 2003
1 (of 6) TTn. 2.50
2 TTn,Parasitic aliens 2.50
3 TTn,What dreams may come . . . 2.50
4 TTn,Seance 2.50
5 TTn,War is Hell 2.50
6 TTn,concl. 2.50

HUMAN RACE, THE
March, 2005
1 (of 7) F:Delta Chi Delta 3.00
2 F:Ulysses 3.00
3 V:Paracelsus 3.00
4 Extraterrestrial parasite 3.00
5 Ulysses, Nymph. 3.00
6 Ulysses, Nymph. 3.00
7 finale 3.00

HUMAN TARGET SPECIAL
1991
1 DG(i),Prequel to T.V. Series. 3.00

HUMAN TARGET
DC/Vertigo, 1999
1 (of 4) PrM(s) 3.50
2 PrM(s) 3.00
3 PrM(s) 3.00
4 PrM(s), concl.. . . . . 3.00
TPB 13.00

HUMAN TARGET
DC/Vertigo, Aug. 2003
1 PrM(s),40-pg. 3.00
2 PrM(s),Unshredded Man,pt.1 . . . 3.00
3 PrM(s),Unshredded Man,pt.2 . . . 3.00
4 PrM(s),Ball Game, pt.1 . . . . 3.00
5 PrM(s),Ball Game, pt.2 . . . . 3.00
6 PrM(s),For I Have Sinned 3.00
7 PrM(s),Wind Blows,pt.1 . . . . 3.00
8 PrM(s),Wind Blows,pt.2 . . . . 3.00
9 PrM(s),Wind Blows,pt.3 . . . . 3.00
10 PrM(s),Five Days Grace 3.00
11 PrM(s),F:Mary 3.00
12 PrM(s),Crossing the Border . . . 3.00
13 PrM(s),Crossing the Border . . . 3.00
14 PrM(s),Second Coming,pt.1 . . . 3.00

Human Target Special #1
© DC Comics, Inc.

15 The Second Coming,pt.2 . . . . . . 3.00
16 The Second Coming 3.00
17 You Made Me Love You 3.00
18 Letter From the Front Line 3.00
19 The Stealer, pt.1 . . . . 3.00
20 The Stealer, pt.2 . . . . 3.00
21 The Stealer, pt.3 . . . . 3.00
TPB Human Target: Final Cut 20.00
TPB Strike Zones. 10.00
TPB Living in Amerika (2005) 15.00

HUNTER: THE AGE OF MAGIC
DC/Vertigo, July, 2001
1 R:The Hunter. 3.50
10 thru 25. . . . . @3.00

HUNTER'S HEART
1995
1 Cops vs. Serial Killer 5.00
2 thru 3 . . . . @5.00

HUNTRESS, THE
1989–90
1 JSon/DG 2.50
2 JSon,Search for Family's
  Murderer 2.50
3 JSon,A:La Bruja. 2.50
4 JSon,Little Italy/Chinatown
  Gangs 2.50
5 JSon,V:Doctor Mandragora 2.50
6 JSon,Huntress'secrets revealed . 2.50
7 JSon,V:Serial Killer 2.50
8 JSon,V:Serial Killer 2.50
9 JSon,V:Serial Killer 2.50
10 JSon,Nuclear Terrorists in NY. . . 2.50
11 JSon,V:Wyvern,Nuclear
   Terrorists contd. 2.50
12 JSon,V:Nuclear Terrorists cont . . 2.50
13 JSon,Violence in NY. 2.50
14 JSon,Violence contd.,New
   Mob boss. 2.50
15 JSon,I:Waterfront Warrior 2.50
16 JSon,Secret of Waterfront
   Warrior revealed 2.50
17 JSon,Batman+Huntress#1 . . . . 2.50
18 JSon,Batman+Huntress#2 . . . . 2.50
19 JSon,Batman+Huntress#3,final
   issue 2.50

HUNTRESS
[Limited Series], 1994
1 CDi(s),MN,V:Redzone 2.25
2 MN,V:Redzone. 2.25
3 MN,V:Redzone. 2.25
4 MN,V:Spano,Redzone. 2.25

HUNTRESS
DARK KNIGHT DAUGHTER
Dec., 2006
TPB 20.00

iCANDY
Sept. 2003
1 DAn&ALa(s). 2.50
2 DAn&ALa(s) thru 6. . . . . @2.50

ICON
DC/Milestone, 1993–96
1 Direct Market Ed.,MBr,MG,I:Icon,
   Rocket,S.H.R.E.D.,w/poster,
   card,C puzzle piece. 3.50
1a Newsstand Ed.. . . . . 2.00
2 thru 24 . . . . @2.50
25 V:Oblivion 3.00
26 thru 45 . . . . @2.50
TPB A Hero's Welcome 13.00

IDENTITY CRISIS
June 2004
1 (of 7) RgM,MIB,48-pg. 7.50
2 thru 5 RgM,MIB,40-pg. . . . . . . @6.00
6 RgM,MIB,40-page 4.00
7 RgM,MIB,concl. 4.00
1a thru 7a reps. . . . . @4.00
TPB 15.00

IMMORTAL DR. FATE
1995
1 WS,KG,rep. 2.25
2 and 3 KG,rep. . . . . @2.25

IMPACT WINTER
SPECIAL
Impact, 1991
1 CI/MR/TL,A:All Impact Heros,
   President Kidnapped 2.50

IMPULSE
1995–2002
1 Young Flash Adventures 6.00
2 V:Terrorists. 3.50
3 thru 12 . . . . @3.00
13 thru 25 . . . . @2.50
26 thru 89. . . . . @2.50
Ann.#2 Pulp Heroes (Western) 4.00
Spec.#1,000,000 BML(s) 2.25
GN Bart Saves the Universe 6.00
TPB Reckless Youth MWa(s) rep.
   Flash #92–#94. . . . . 15.00
Spec. Impulse/Atom Double-Shot
   DJu, x-over concl. (1997) 3.00
Spec. Impulse Plus 48pg.
   with Grossout (1997) 3.00

INDUSTRIAL GOTHIC
DC/Vertigo, 1995
1 Jail Break Plans. 2.50
2 thru 5 Jail Break Plans. . . . . . . @2.50

INFERIOR FIVE
March-April, 1967
1 MSy,Super-hero Satire 100.00
2 MSy,A:Plastic Man. 45.00
3 MSy,Darwin of the Apes 40.00
4 MSy,Valhallaballoo. 40.00

5 MSy,I was a Guillotine-age Hero 40.00
6 MSy,DC Stars and office 25.00
7 WMo,Drainy Day 25.00
8 WMo,V:Dr. Gruesome 25.00
9 WMo,Mummy's the Word 25.00
10 WMo,A:Superman (1968) 35.00
11 JO(c&a) (1972) 25.00
12 JO(c&a). 25.00

INFERNO
Aug., 1997
1 (of 4) SI, from Legion. 4.00
2 SI,mall grrls 3.00
3 SI,Legion Month tie-in 3.00
4 SI, concl. 3.00

Infinity Inc. #47
© *DC Comics, Inc.*

INFINITY, INC.
March, 1984
1 JOy,O:Infinity Inc.. . . . . 5.00
2 JOy,End of Origin 4.00
3 JOy,O:Jade 3.00
4 JOy,V:JSA 3.00
5 JOy,V:JSA 3.00
6 JOy,V:JSA 3.00
7 JOy,V:JSA 3.00
8 JOy,V:Ultra Humanite 3.00
9 JOy,V:Ultra Humanite 3.00
10 JOy,V:Ultra Humanite 3.00
11 DN,GT,O:Infinity Inc. 3.00
12 Infinity Unmasks,I:Yolanda
   Montez (New Wildcat). 3.00
13 DN,V:Rose & Thorn 3.00
14 1st TM DC art,V:Chroma 10.00
15 TM,V:Chroma 4.00
16 TM,I:Helix (Mr. Bones) 4.00
17 TM,V:Helix. 4.00
18 TM,Crisis. 4.00
19 TM,JSA,JLA x-over,
   I:Mekanique 4.00
20 TM,Crisis. 4.00
21 TM,Crisis,I:HourmanII,
   Dr.Midnight 4.00
22 TM,Crisis. 4.00
23 TM,Crisis. 4.00
24 TM,Crisis. 4.00
25 TM,Crisis,JSA 4.00
26 TM,V:Carcharo 4.00
27 TM,V:Carcharo 4.00
28 TM,V:Carcharo 4.00
29 TM,V:Helix. 4.00
30 TM,Mourning of JSA 4.00
31 TM,V:Psycho Pirate 4.00
32 TM,V:Psycho Pirate 4.00

33 TM,O:Obsidian 4.00
34 TM,A: Global Guardians 4.00
35 TM,V:Infinitors 4.00
36 TM,V:Injustice Unl. 4.00
37 TM,TD,O:Northwind 4.00
38 Helix on Trial 3.00
39 O:Solomon Grundy 3.00
40 V:Thunderbolt 3.00
41 Jonni Thunder. 3.00
42 TD,V:Hastor,L:Fury 3.00
43 TD,V:Hastor,Silver Scarab 3.00
44 TD,D:Silver Scarab 3.00
45 MGu,A:New Teen Titans,
   V:Ultra-Humanite 3.00
46 TD,Millennium,V:Floronic Man . . 3.00
47 TD,Millennium,V:Harlequin 3.00
48 TD,O:Nuklon 3.00
49 Silver Scarab becomes
   Sandman 3.00
50 TD,V:The Wizard,O:Sandman . . 3.50
51 W:Fury & Sandman,D:Skyman . . 3.00
52 V:Helix. 3.00
53 V:Justice Unlimited,last issue . . . 3.00
Ann.#1 TM,V:Thorn 4.00
Ann.#2 V:Degaton,x-over Young
   All-Stars Annual #1 . . . . 3.00
Spec.#1 TD,A:Outsiders,V:Psycho
   Pirate 3.00

INFINITE CRISIS
Oct., 2005
1 (of 7) PJ,ALa 5.00
1a variant (c). 6.00
2 (of 7) PJ,ALa 4.00
2a variant (c). 4.00
3 PJ,ALa 4.00
3a variant GP (c) 4.00
4 PJ,ALa, Batman vs. Nightwing . . 4.00
4a variant GP (c) 4.00
5 PJ,ALa,Superman vs. Superman 4.00
5a variant (c). 4.00
6 PJ,ALa,One Year Later 4.00
6a variant (c). 4.00
7 Conclusion 4.00
7a variant (c). 4.00
Spec. Secret Files 64-pg. (2006) . . . 6.00
Spec. Villains United 5.00
TPB Infinite Crisis Companion. . . . 15.00

INVASION!
1988–89
1 TM,I:Vril Dox,Dominators
   (20th century) 4.00
2 TM,KG,DG,I:L.E.G.I.O.N. 3.00
3 BS,DG,I:Blasters 3.00
Daily Planet-Invasion! 16p. 2.00

INVISIBLES
DC/Vertigo, 1994–96
1 GMo(s). 7.00
2 GMo(s),Down & Out,pt.1 . . . . 4.00
3 GMo(s),Down & Out,pt.2 . . . . 4.00
4 GMo(s),Down & Out,pt.3 . . . . 4.00
5 Arcadia,pt.1 . . . . 4.00
6 Arcadia,pt.2 . . . . 4.00
7 Arcadia,pt.3 . . . . 4.00
8 Arcadia,pt.4 . . . . 4.00
9 SeP(c),L:Dane 3.00
10 SeP(c),CWn,Jim Crow v. 3
   Zombies. 3.00
11 V:New Breed of Hunter 3.00
12 GMo,Best Man Fall 3.00
13 GMo,Sheman,pt.1 . . . . 3.00
14 GMo,SeP,Sheman,pt.2 . . . . 3.00
15 GMo,Sheman,pt.3. . . . . 3.00
16 GMo,An offer from Sir Miles . . . 3.00
17 GMo,Entropy in the U.K.,pt.1 . . . 3.00
18 GMo,Entropy in the U.K.,pt.2 . . . 3.00
19 GMo,Entropy in the U.K.,pt.3 . . . 3.00
20 GMo,F:RaggedRobin,Dane,Boy . 4.00
21 GMo,PuJ,F:Dane 4.00

All comics prices listed are for *Near Mint* condition.

22 GMo(s),MBu,MPn 4.00
23 GMo(s),MBu,MPn 4.00
24 GMo(s),MBu,MPn 4.00
25 GMo(s),MBu,MPn,final issue
Aug., 1996 . . . . 5.00

[Volume 2] DC/Vertigo, 1996
1 GMo(s),PJ,Black Science,pt.1 . . 4.00
2 GMo(s),PJ,Black Science,pt.2 . . 3.00
3 GMo(s),PJ,Black Science,pt.3 . . 3.00
4 GMo(s),PJ,Black Science,pt.4 . . 3.00
5 GMo(s),PJ,In SanFrancisco,pt.1 . 3.00
6 GMo(s),PJ,In SanFrancisco,pt.2 . 3.00
7 GMo(s),PJ,BB(c),Time Machine
Go, concl. 3.00
8 GMo(s),PJ,BB(c),Sensitive
Criminals,pt.1 . . . . 3.00
9 GMo(s),PJ,BB(c),Criminals,pt.2. . 3.00
10 GMo(s),PJ,Criminals,pt.3, ... 3.00
11 GMo(s),PJ,BB(c),Hand of Glory
pt.1 . . . . 3.00
12 GMo(s),PJ,BB(c),Glory,pt.2 . . . 3.00
13 GMo(s),PJ,BB(c),Glory,concl. . . 3.00
14 GMo(s),BB(c),Archons aftermath 3.00
15 GMo(s),BB(c), The Philadelphia
Experiment, pt.1 . . . . 3.00
16 GMo(s),BB(c),Experiment,pt.2 . . 3.00
17 GMo,CWn,BB,Black Science II
pt.1 . . . . 3.00
18 GMo,CWn,BB,Science,pt.2 . . . . 3.00
19 GMo,CWn,BB,Science,pt.3 . . . . 3.00
20 GMo,CWn,BB(c),Science,pt.4 . . 2.50
21 GMo,CWn,BB(c),King Mob 2.50
22 GMo,CWn,BB(c) The Tower 2.50
TPB Counting to None. 20.00
TPB Say You Want a Revolution . . 20.00
TPB Bloody Hell in America. 13.00
TPB Kissing Mister 20.00
TPB Apocalipstick, 208-page. 20.00
TPB Entropy in the U.K. 20.00

[Volume 3] DC/Vertigo, 1999
12 GMo,Satanstorm,pt.1 . . . . 3.00
11 GMo,Satanstorm,pt.2 . . . . 3.00
10 GMo,Satanstorm,pt.3 . . . . 3.00
9 GMo,Satanstorm,pt.4. . . . . 3.00
8 GMo,Karmageddon,pt.1 . . . . 3.00
7 GMo,Karmageddon,pt.2 . . . . 3.00
6 GMo,Karmageddon,pt.3 . . . . 3.00
5 GMo 3.00
4 GMo,Invisible Kingdom,pt.1. . . . . 3.00
3 GMo,Invisible Kingdom,pt.2. . . . . 3.00
2 GMo,Invisible Kingdom,pt.3 . . . . 3.00
1 GMo,conclusion 3.00
GN The Mystery Play. 10.00
TPB The Invisible Kingdom 20.00
TPB Kissing Mister Quimper 20.00

Isis #1 © DC Comics, Inc.

ION
April, 2006
1 RMz, Kyle Rayner returns 3.00
2 RMz, Is Kyle going mad? 3.00
3 RMz, F:Mogo 3.00
4 RMz,F:Green Lantern 3.00
5 RMz,F:Green Lantern 3.00
6 RMz,Guardians of the Universe . 3.00
7 RMz,Return to earth 3.00
8 RMz,A remote world 3.00

IRONWOLF
1986
1 HC,rep. 2.25

ISIS
Oct.–Nov., 1976
1 RE/WW 25.00
2 thru 6 . . . . @15.00
7 O:Isis 18.00
8 Dec.–Jan., 1977–78. . . . . 15.00

IT'S GAMETIME
Sept.–Oct., 1955
1 . . . . 1,100.00
2 Dodo and the Frog. 900.00
3 . . . . 900.00
4 March-April, 1956 . . . . 950.00

JACK CROSS
Aug., 2005
1 (of 4) WEI,GEr 2.50
2 WEI,GEr 2.50
3 WEI,GEr. 2.50
4 WEI,GEr, conclusion 2.50

JACKIE GLEASON AND THE HONEYMOONERS
June-July, 1956
1 Based on TV show 1,300.00
2 . . . . 750.00
3 thru 11 . . . . @600.00
12 April-May, 1958. . . . . 850.00

JACK KIRBY'S FOURTH WORLD
Jan., 1997
1 JBy,Worlds of New Genesis &
Apokolips become one 2.25
2 JBy,F:Big Barda vs. Thor 2.25
3 JBy,at Wall of the Source 2.25
4 JBy,Can Highfather save his son 2.25
5 JBy,conflict between the gods . . . 2.25
6 JBy,Cause of Orion's
transformation 2.25
7 JBy,Orion taught lesson. 2.25
8 JBy,WS,Genesis tie-in 2.25
9 JBy,WS(c),Genesis aftermath . . . 2.25
10 JBy,WS, ... 2.25
11 JBy,WS,F:Orion. 2.25
12 JBy,WS,F:Mister Miracle. 2.25
13 JBy,WS 2.25
14 JBy,WS,Promethean Giant 2.25
15 JBy,WS,Armaghetto 2.25
16 JBy,WS,Kalibak vs. Darkseid . . . 2.25
17 JBy,WS,Darkseid 2.25
18 JBy,WS,Darkseid freed. 2.25
19 JBy,WS,two stories. 2.25
20 JBy,WS,A:Superman,final issue . 2.25
TPB JK. 13.00

JACK OF FABLES
DC/Vertigo, July, 2006
1 BWg. 3.00
2 BWg,Mr. Revise. 3.00
3 BWg,Mr. Revise's prisoner 3.00
4 Great Escape is on 3.00

5 . . . . 3.00

JAGUAR
Impact, 1991
1 I&O:Jaguar 2.25
2 thru 14 . . . . @2.25
Ann.#1 Earthquest,w/trading card . . 2.50

JEMM, SON OF SATURN
Sept., 1984
1 GC/KJ mini-series 2.50
2 GC 2.50
3 GC,Origin. 2.50
4 A:Superman. 2.50
5 Kin 2.50
6 thru 12 GC, Aug., 1985 . . . . . @2.50

JIMMY OLSEN: ADVENTURES
July 2003
TPB JK. 20.00
TPB Vol. 2 JK. 20.00

JIMMY WAKELY
Sept.–Oct., 1949
1 Ph(c),ATh,The Cowboy
Swordsman. 1,800.00
2 Ph(c),ATh,The Prize Pony 750.00
3 Ph(c),ATh,The Return of
Tulsa Tom 650.00
4 Ph(c),ATh,FF,HK,Where There's
Smoke There's Gunfire 625.00
5 ATh,The Return of the
Conquistadores 500.00
6 ATh,Two Lives of
Jimmy Wakely 500.00
7 The Secret of Hairpin Canyon . 500.00
8 ATh,The Lost City of
Blue Valley. 500.00
9 ATh,The Return of the
Western Firebrands. 500.00
10 ATh,Secret of Lantikin'sLight . 350.00
11 ATh,Trail o/a Thousand Hoofs. 350.00
12 ATh,JKU,The King of Sierra
Valley. 350.00
13 ATh,The Raiders of Treasure
Mountain 350.00
14 ATh(c),JKu,The Badmen
of Roaring Flame Valley 350.00
15 GK(c),Tommyguns on the
Range 350.00
16 GK(c),The Bad Luck Boots. . . 300.00
17 GK(c),Terror atThunderBasin . 300.00
18 July-Aug., 1952. . . . . 350.00

JLA
Nov., 1996
1 GMo(s),HPo,JhD,V:Hyperclan . . 16.00
2 GMo(s),HPo,JhD,V:Hyperclan . . 12.00
3 GMo(s),HPo,JhD,War of the
Worlds 10.00
4 GMo(s),HPo,JhD,battle of the
super-heroes, conc. 10.00
5 GMo(s),HPo,JhD Woman of
Tomorrow. 7.00
6 GMo(s),HPo,JhD,Fire in theSky . 6.00
7 GMo(s),HPo,JhD,Heaven on
Earth 6.00
8 GMo(s),HPo,JhD,Imaginary
Stories, F:Green Arrow 6.00
9 GMo(s),V:The Key. 6.00
10 GMo(s),HPo,JhD,R:Injustice
Gang, pt.1 (of 6) 6.00
11 GMo(s),HPo,JhD,Rock of Ages,
pt.2. 6.00
12 GMo(s),HPo,JhD,Rock of Ages,
pt.3, A:Hourman 6.00

JLA A#67 © DC Comics Inc.

13 GMo(s),HPo,JhD,Rock of Ages,
pt.4. . . . . 6.00
14 GMo(s),HPo,JhD,Rock of Ages,
pt.5. . . . . 6.00
15 GMo(s),HPo,JhD,Rock of Ages
pt.6, concl, 48 pg. 6.00
16 GMo(s),HPo,JhD, new member . 6.00
17 GMo(s),HPo,JhD,V:Prometheus . 6.00
18 MWa,Engine of Chance,pt.1 . . . 6.00
19 MWa,Engine of Chance, pt.2 . . . 6.00
20 MWa,F:Adam Strange,pt.1 . . . . 6.00
21 MWa,F:Adam Strange,pt.2 . . . . 6.00
22 GMo(s),The Star Conqueror 2.50
23 GMo,V:Star Conqueror,
A:Sandman 2.50
24 GMo,HPo,Ultra-Marines,pt.1 . . . 2.50
25 GMo,HPo,Ultra-Marines,pt.2 . . . 2.50
26 GMo,HPo,Ultra-Marines,pt.3 . . . 2.50
27 GMo,HPo,CrisisTimesFive,pt.1 . . 2.50
28 GMo,HPo,CrisisTimesFive,pt.2 . . 2.50
29 GMo,HPo,CrisisTimesFive,pt.3 . . 2.50
30 GMo,HPo,CrisisTimesFive,pt.4 . . 2.50
31 GMo,HPo,CrisisTimes
Five,concl. 2.50
32 MWa(s),No Man's Land 2.50
33 MWa(s),No Man's Land 2.50
34 GMo,Super-villains riot 2.50
35 JMD(s),F:New Spectre 2.50
36 GMo,HPo,World War 3,pt.1 . . . 2.50
37 GMo,HPo,World War 3,pt.2 . . . 2.50
38 GMo,HPo,World War 3,pt.3 . . . 2.50
39 GMo,HPo,World War 3,pt.4 . . . 2.50
40 GMo,HPo,World War 3,pt.5 . . . 2.50
41 GMo,HPo,World War 3,
concl.48-pg. 4.00
42 Miniscule civilization 2.50
43 MWa(s),HPo,V:Ra's al Ghul 2.50
44 HPo,Tower of Babel,pt.2 . . . . . . 2.50
45 HPo,Tower of Babel,pt.3 . . . . . . 2.50
46 HPo,Tower of Babel,concl. 2.50
47 MWa,BHi,PNe,Queen ofFables . 2.50
48 MWa,BHi,PNe,Queen ofFables . 2.50
49 MWa,BHi,PNe,Queen ofFables . 2.50
50 MWa,BHi,PNe,48-page. 5.00
51 MWa,MsM,Man and Superman . 2.50
52 MWa,BHi,PNe. 2.50
53 MWa,BHi,PNe. 2.50
54 MWa,BHi,PNe,Man & Superman 2.50
55 MWa,Terror Incognita,pt.1 . . . . . 2.50
56 MWa,Terror Incognita,pt.2 . . . . . 2.50
57 MWa,Terror Incognita,pt.3 . . . . . 2.50
58 MWa,Terror Incognita,pt.4 . . . . . 2.50
59 CDi,DBk,Joker:Last Laugh 2.50
60 MWa,F:Santa Claus 2.50
61 DoM,TG,+16-pg.PowerCompany 2.50
62 DoM,Golden Perfect,pt.1 . . . . . . 2.50
63 DoM,Golden Perfect,pt.2 . . . . . . 2.50
64 DoM,Golden Perfect,pt.3 . . . . . . 2.50
65 DoM,Batman & Plastic Man 2.50
66 DoM,warrior priests. 2.50
67 DoM,human sacrifice 2.50
68 DoM,Obsidian Age prologue . . . 2.50
69 Hunt for Aquaman,pt.1 . . . . 2.50
70 DoM,Hunt for Aquaman,pt.2 . . . 2.50
71 DoM,Hunt for Aquaman,pt.3 . . . 2.50
72 DoM,Hunt for Aquaman,pt.4 . . . 2.50
73 DoM,Hunt for Aquaman,pt.5 . . . 2.50
74 DoM,Hunt for Aquaman,pt.6 . . . 2.50
75 DoM,Hunt for Aquaman,64-pg. . 5.00
76 DoM,after Obsidian Age 2.25
77 RV(s),memories stolen 2.25
78 DoM, ... 2.25
79 DoM,F:Faith 2.25
80 White Rage,pt.1 . . . . 2.25
81 White Rage,pt.2 . . . . 2.25
82 White Rage,pt.3 . . . . 2.25
83 Qurac 2.25
84 Trial by Fire,pt.1 . . . . 2.25
85 Trial by Fire,pt.2 . . . . 2.25
86 Trial by Fire,pt.3 . . . . 2.25
87 Trial by Fire,pt.4 . . . . 2.25
88 Trial by Fire,pt.5 . . . . 2.25

89 Trial by Fire,pt.6 . . . . 2.25
90 F:Batman,Wonder Woman 2.25
91 DON(s),Extinction,pt.1 . . . . 2.25
92 DON(s),Extinction,pt.2 . . . . 2.25
93 DON(s),Extinction,pt.3 . . . . 2.25
94 JBy,JOy,10th Circle,pt.1 . . . . . . 2.25
95 JBy,JOy,10th Circle,pt.2 . . . . . . 2.25
96 JBy,JOy,10th Circle,pt.3 . . . . . . 2.25
97 JBy,JOy,10th Circle,pt.4 . . . . . . 2.25
98 JBy,JOy,10th Circle,pt.5 . . . . . . 2.25
99 JBy,JOy,10th Circle,pt.6 . . . . . . 2.25
100 R:The Elite,48-pg. 3.50
101 RG,Pain of the Gods,pt.1 . . . . 2.25
102 RG,Pain of the Gods,pt.2 . . . . . 2.25
103 RG,Pain of the Gods,pt.3 . . . . . 2.25
104 RG,Pain of the Gods,pt.4 . . . . . 2.25
105 RG,Pain of the Gods,pt.5 . . . . . 2.25
106 RG,Pain of the Gods,pt.6 . . . . . 2.25
107 KBk(s).RG,DGr,space egg 5.00
108 KBk,Syndicate Rules,pt.2 . . . . . 4.00
109 KBk,Syndicate Rules,pt.3 . . . . . 2.25
110 KBk,Syndicate Rules,pt.4 . . . . . 2.25
111 KBk,Syndicate Rules,pt.5 . . . . . 2.25
112 KBk,Syndicate Rules,pt.6 . . . . . 2.25
113 KBk,Syndicate Rules,pt.7 . . . . . 2.25
114 KBk,Syndicate Rules,pt.8 . . . . . 2.25
115 MFm,Crisis of Conscience,pt.1 . 5.00
116 MFm,Crisis of Conscience,pt.2 . 3.00
117 MFm,Crisis of Conscience,pt.3 . 3.00
118 MFm,Crisis of Conscience,pt.4 . 2.50
119 MFm,Crisis of Conscience,pt.5 . 2.50
120 World Without Justice League . 2.50
121 World Without Justice League . 2.50
122 World Without Justice League . 2.50
123 World Without Justice League . 2.50
124 World Without Justice League . 2.50
125 World Without Justice League . 2.50
Ann.#1 Pulp Heroes (Hard Boiled) . 4.50
Ann.#2 TTn,BWr,Ghosts 3.50
Ann.#3 JLApe Gorilla Warfare 3.50
Ann.#4 Planet DC 4.00
Spec.#1,000,000 GMo(s),HPo,
V:Justice Legion A 2.50
SuperSpec.#1 Justice League
of America 6.00
Spec.#1 Our Worlds at War,48-pg . . 3.00
Giant #1, 7 new stories, 80-pg. 5.00
Giant #2, 80-page. 5.00
Giant #3, 80-page 6.00
SC Secret Origins, oversize. 8.00
JLA: Tomorrow Woman, 1-shot
TPe,Girlfrenzy (1998) 2.00
GN New World Order GMo(s),HPo,
JhD, rep. #1–#4 . . . . 6.00
GN American Dreams rep.#5–#9. . . 8.00

GN Secret Files 4.00
GN Secret Files deluxe 5.00
GN Secret Files #2 . . . . 4.00
GN Secret Files #3 How Talia stole
Batman's Secret Files 5.00
GN Foreign Bodies 6.00
GN JLA/WildC.A.T.S, GMo(s),
VS,x-over. 8.00
GN JLA/Haven: Arrival (2001) 6.00
GN JLA: Earth 2,96-page,
F:Crime Syndicate (2000) 15.00
GN Gods and Monsters 7.00
GN Seven Caskets,DIB, 48-page . . 6.00
GN JLA: Superpower. 6.00
GN JLA Primeval 6.00
GN Shogun of Steel,Elseworlds . . . 7.00
GN JLA/Haven:Anathema (2002) . . 6.00
GN The Island of Dr. Moreau,GP
Elseworlds (2002) 7.00
GN JLA: Liberty and Justice 10.00
JLA/Witchblade, x-over 6.00
TPB Heaven's Ladder 10.00
TPB JLA:Rock of Ages 10.00
TPB Strength in Numbers 13.00
TPB Justice League of America:
The Nail, Elseworlds 13.00
TPB Secret Origins Featuring JLA 15.00
TPB JLA:World War III,208-page. . 13.00
TPB JLA vs. Predator x-over 6.00
TPB Tower of Babel, 160-page . . . 13.00
TPB Divided We Fall (2002) 18.00
TPB A League of One, CsM (2002) 15.00
TPB Terra Incognita (2002) 13.00
JLA Showcase 80-pg Giant #1 . . . . 5.00
TPB The Golden Perfect 13.00
TPB Riddle of the Beast 15.00
TPB The Obsidian Age, Vol.1 . . . . 13.00
TPB The Obsidian Age, Vol.2 . . . . 13.00
TPB Zatanna's Search. 13.00
TPB Rules of Engagement 13.00
TPB Vol.14 Trial by Fire 13.00
Spec. JLA: Workweek 7.00
Spec. Secret Files 2004 . . . . 5.00
TPB Vol. 15 The 10th Circle (2005) 13.00
TPB JLA: Another Nail (2005) 13.00
TPB Pain of the Gods (2005) 13.00
TPB Syndicate Rules (2005) 18.00
Spec. JLA/Cyberforce (2005). 6.00
TPB JLA: The 10th Circle (2005). . 15.00
TPB JLA: Crisis of Conscience . . . 13.00
TPB Greatest JLA Stories Ever . . . 20.00
Spec. Amazing Adventures of JLA. . 4.00
TPB World Without Justice League 13.00

JLA: ACT OF GOD
Nov., 2000
1 (of 3) Elseworlds,48-page 5.00
2 powers gone,48-page 5.00
3 concl.,48-page 5.00

JLA: AGE OF WONDER
April 2003
1 (of 2) Elseworlds 6.00
2 concl. 6.00

JLA: BLACK BAPTISM
March, 2001
1 (of 4) F:Faust. 2.50
2 F:Faust. 2.50
3 V:Daiblos 2.50
4 concl. 2.50

JLA: CLASSIFIED
Nov., 2004
1 GMo(s),V:Gorilla Grodd 3.00
2 GMo(s),V:Gorilla Grodd 3.00
3 GMo(s),V:Gorilla Grodd,concl. 3.00
4 KG&JMD(s),KM&JRu, I Can't Believe
it's Not the Justice League,pt.1 . 3.00
5 KG&JMD(s),KM&JRu, pt.2 . . . . . 3.00

DC COMICS

JLA Classified #8 © DC Comics, Inc.

6 KG&JMD(s),KM&JRu, pt.3 . . . . . 3.00
7 KG&JMD(s),KM&JRu, pt.4 . . . . . 3.00
8 KG&JMD(s),KM&JRu, pt.5 . . . . . 3.00
9 KG&JMD(s),KM&JRu, pt.6 . . . . . 3.00
10 WEI(s),New Maps of Hell,pt.1 . . . 3.00
11 WEI(s),New Maps of Hell,pt.2 . . . 3.00
12 WEI(s),New Maps of Hell,pt.3 . . . 3.00
13 WEI(s),New Maps of Hell,pt.4 . . . 3.00
14 WEI(s),New Maps of Helll,pt.5 . . 3.00
15 WEI(s),New Maps of Hell,concl. . . 3.00
16 KJ,Hypothetical Woman,pt.1 . . . 3.00
17 KJ,Hypothetical Woman,pt.2 . . . 3.00
18 KJ,Hypothetical Woman,pt.3 . . . 3.00
19 KJ,Hypothetical Woman,pt.4 . . . 3.00
20 KJ,Hypothetical Woman,pt.5 . . . 3.00
21 KJ,Hypothetical Woman,pt.6 . . . 3.00
22 MFm, A Game of Chance,pt.1 . . 3.00
23 MFm, A Game of Chance,pt.2 . . 3.00
24 MFm, A Game of Chance,pt.3 . . 3.00
25 MFm, A Game of Chance,pt.4 . . 3.00
26 HC,KPI,Secret Trust, pt.1 . . . . . 3.00
27 HC,KPI,Secret Trust, pt.2 . . . . . 3.00
28 HC,KPI,Secret Trust, pt.3 . . . . . 3.00
29 HC,KPI,Sacret Trust, pt.4 . . . . . 3.00
TPB I Can't Believe It's Not the
   Justice League 13.00
TPB New Maps of Hell 13.00

JLA CLASSIFIED: COLD STEEL
Dec., 2005
1 (0f 2) 48-pg. 6.00
2 48-pg. 6.00

JLA: CREATED EQUAL
Feb., 2000
1 FaN,KM,JRu,Elseworlds 6.00
2 FaN,KM,JRu 6.00

JLA: DESTINY
June, 2002
1 (of 4) TMd,48-pg 6.00
2 JAr(s),TMd, Elseworlds 6.00
3 JAr(s),TMd,Luthor,Mongul 6.00
4 JAr(s),TMc,concl. 6.00

JLA: GATEKEEPER
Oct., 2001
1 (of 3) TT, 48-page 5.00
2 TT, 48-page 5.00
3 TT,48-page, concl. 5.00

JLA: INCARNATIONS
May, 2001
1 (of 7) JOs,VS,V:Wotan 3.50
2 JOs,VS,Batman joins 3.50
3 JOs,VS,V:Lex Luthor, Kobra 3.50
4 JOs,VS,F:Aquaman 3.50
5 JOs,VS,F:Aquaman 3.50
6 JOs,VS,two tales 3.50
7 JOs,VS,concl. 3.50

JLA/JSA
Nov., 2002
1 Secret files, Team-up,
   prelude,64-pg. 5.00
TPB Virtue and Vice 18.00

JLA: PARADISE LOST
Nov., 1997
1 (of 3) MMr,AOI,F:Zauriel 2.25
2 MMr,AOI,F:Zauriel,Martian
   Manhunter. 2.25

JLA: SCARY MONSTERS
Mar. 2003
1 (of 6) CCI,V:Ancient spirits. 2.50
2 CCI. 2.50
3 CCI,ancient evil 2.50
4 CCI,Kishana secret 2.50
5 CCI,Kishana's origin 2.50
6 CCI,concl. 2.50

JLA/THE SPECTRE: SOUL WAR
Jan. 2003
1 (of 2) DBk,PNe 6.00
2 DBk,PNe 6.00

JLA/TITANS
1998
1 (of 3) JLA vs. Teen Titans 3.00
2 . . . . 3.00
3 conclusion, New Titans 3.00
TPB The Technis Imperative 13.00

JLA: WORLD WITHOUT GROWN-UPS
June, 1998
1 (of 2) I:Young Justice 48pg 5.00
2 Young Justice, concl. 5.00
TPB World Without Grown-Ups. . . 10.00

JLA: YEAR ONE
Nov., 1997
1 (of 12) MWa,BAu,BKi,48pg. 6.00
2 MWa,BAu,BKi,V:Vandal Savage . 4.00
3 MWa,BAu,BKi 4.00
4 MWa,BAu,BKi,V:Locus 4.00
5 MWa,BAu,BKi,F:Doom Patrol . . . 4.00
6 MWa,BAu,BKi,V:Doom Patrol . . . 4.00
7 MWa,BAu,BKi,V:Weapon Master 4.00
8 MWa,BAu,BKi,MIB,V:Locus 4.00
9 MWa,BAu,BKi,MIB,V:Locus 3.00
10 MWa,BAu,BKi,MIB,V:Locus . . . 3.00
11 MWa,BAu,BKi,MIB 3.00
12 MWa,BAu,BKi,MIB, concl. 3.50
TPB Year One 20.00

JLA-Z
Sept. 2003
1 (of 3) handbook 2.50
2 thru 3 . . . . @2.50

JOHN CONSTANTINE— HELLBLAZER SPECIAL: PAPA MIDNITE
DC/Vertigo, Feb., 2005
1 (of 5) 3.00
2 thru 5 . . . . @3.00

JOHNNY THUNDER
Feb.–March, 1973
1 ATh. 30.00
2 GK,MD 15.00
3 ATh,GK,MD,July-Aug., 1973 . . . 15.00

JOKER, THE
1975–76
1 IN,DG,A:TwoFace 90.00
2 IN,JL WillieTheWeeper 40.00
3 JL,A:Creeper 40.00
4 JL,A:GreenArrow 30.00
5 IN,Joker Goes "Wilde" 30.00
6 IN,V:Sherlock Holmes 30.00
7 IN,A:Luthor. 30.00
8 IN,A:Scarecrow 30.00
9 IN,A:Catwoman 40.00
The Devil's Advocate HC GN 30.00
GN 13.00

JOKER, THE: LAST LAUGH
Oct., 2001
1 (of 6) CDi,Oracle vs. villains 3.00
2 CDi,Batman,Riot in the Slab 3.00
3 CDi,F:JLA vs. Joker army 3.00
4 CDi,F:Mr. Mind, Lex Luthor 3.00
5 CDi,Harley Quinn is last hope . . . 3.00
6 CDi,Joker's final stand. 3.00
Secret Files #1 64-page. 6.00

JONAH HEX
1977–85
1 Vengeance For A Fallen
   Gladiator 200.00
2 The Lair of the Parrot 100.00
3 The Fugitive. 75.00
4 The Day of Chameleon 75.00
5 Welcome to Paradise 75.00
6 The Lawman 60.00
7 Son of the Apache 75.00
8 O:Jonah Hex 75.00
9 BWr(c) 50.00
10 GM(c),Violence at Vera Cruz . . 50.00
11 The Holdout. 40.00
12 JS(c),Search for 'Gator Hawes. 40.00
13 The Railroad Blaster. 40.00
14 The Sin Killer 40.00
15 Saw Dust and Slow Death 40.00
16 The Wyandott Verdict! 35.00
17 Voyage to Oblivion 35.00
18 Amazon Treasure, and Death. . 35.00
19 The Duke of Zarkania! 35.00
20 Phantom Stage to William
   Bend 35.00
21 The Buryin'!. 35.00
22 Requiem For A Pack Rat 35.00
23 Massacre of the Celestials 35.00
24 Minister of the Lord. 35.00
25 The Widow Maker. 35.00
26 Death Race to Cholera Bend!. . 20.00
27 The Wooden Six Gun! 20.00
28 Night of the Savage 20.00
29 The Innocent. 20.00
30 O:Jonah Hex. 20.00
31 A:Arbee Stoneham 20.00
32 A:Arbee Stoneham 20.00
33 The Crusador 20.00
34 Christmas in an Outlaw Town. . 20.00
35 The Fort Charlotte Brigade 20.00
36 Return to Fort Charlotte 20.00

37 DAy,A:Stonewall Jackson	20.00
38 DSp,Iron Dog's Gold	20.00
39 The Vow of a Samurai!	20.00
40 DAy,The Rainmaker	20.00
41 DAy,Two for the Hangman!	20.00
42 Wanted for Murder	20.00
43 JKu(c),Death by Fire	20.00
44 JKu(c),DAy	20.00
45 DAy,Jonah gets married	20.00
46 JKu(c),DAy,Showdown	20.00
47 DAy,Doom Rides the Sundown Town	20.00
48 DAy,A:El Diablo	20.00
49 DAy,Reap the Grim Harvest	20.00
50 DAy,The Hunter	20.00
51 DAy,The Comforter	8.00
52 DAy,Rescue!	8.00
53 DAy,The Haunting	8.00
54 TD,Trapped in the Parrot's Lair	8.00
55 Trail of Blood	8.00
56 DAy,The Asylum	8.00
57 B:El Diablo backup story	8.00
58 DAy,The Treasure of Catfish Pond	8.00
59 DAy,Night of the White Lotus	8.00
60 DAy,Domain of the Warlord	8.00
61 DAy,In the Lair of the Manchus	8.00
62 DAy,Belly of the Malay Tiger	8.00
63 DAy,Ship of Doom	8.00
64 DAy,The Pearl!	8.00
65 DAy,The Vendetta!	8.00
66 DAy,Requiem for a Coward	8.00
67 DAy,Deadman's Hand!	8.00
68 DAy,Gunfight at Gravesboro!	8.00
69 DAy,The Gauntlet!	8.00
70 DAy,Mountain of the Manitou	8.00
71 DAy,The Masquerades	8.00
72 DAy,Tarantula	8.00
73 DAy,Jonah in a wheel chair	8.00
74 DAy,A:Railroad Bill	8.00
75 DAy,JAp,A:Railroad Bill.	8.00
76 DAy,Jonah goes to Jail	7.00
77 DAy,Over the Wall	7.00
78 DAy,Me Ling returns	7.00
79 DAy,Duel in the Sand	7.00
80 DAy,I D,A:Turnbull	7.00
81 thru 89 DAy	@8.00
90 thru 91 GM	@8.00
92 GM,A Blaze of Glory	25.00

JONAH HEX
Nov., 2005

1 LRs,Cemetery Without Crosses	2.50
2 LRs,Cross of solid gold	2.50
3 LRs,F:Bat Lash	2.50
4 LRs,JP	2.50
5 LRs,Nuns with Guns	2.50
6 LRs,V:Nuns with Guns	3.00
7 LRs,Oil Baron	3.00
8 JP,An old acquaintance	3.00
9 JP,TD,Flowers on a grave	3.00
10 JP,Louisiana swamplands	3.00
11 JP,return of El Diablo	3.00
12 JP,Snowstorm	3.00
13 JP,Origin, pt.1	3.00
TPB A Face Full of Violence	15.00

JONAH HEX AND OTHER WESTERN TALES
Sept.–Oct., 1979

1 TD,The Hundred Dollar Deal	20.00
2 NA,ATh,SA,GK	25.00
3 Jan.–Feb., 1980	20.00

JONAH HEX: RIDERS OF THE WORM AND SUCH
[Mini-Series] DC/Vertigo, 1995

1 R:Ronah Hex	4.00
2 At Wildes West Ranch	4.00

3 History Lesson	4.00
4 I:Autumn Brothers	4.00
5 V:Big worm, final issue	4.00

JONAH HEX: SHADOWS WEST
DC/Vertigo, 1998

1 (of 3) JLd(s),TTn	4.00
2 JLd(s),TTn	4.00
3 JLd(s),TTn concl.	4.00

JONAH HEX: TWO-GUN MOJO
DC/Vertigo, 1993

1 B:JLd(s),TT,SG(i),R:Jonah Hex, I:Slow Go Smith	7.00
1a Platinum Ed.	17.00
2 TT,SG(i),D:Slow Go Smith,I:Doc Williams,Wild Bill Hickok	4.00
3 TT,SG(i),Jonah captured	4.00
4 TT,SG(i),O:Doc Williams	4.00
5 TT,SG(i),V::Doc Williams	4.00

JONNI THUNDER
Feb., 1985

1 DG,origin issue	2.25
2 DG	2.25
3 DG	2.25

JONNY DOUBLE
DC/Vertigo, July, 1998

1	3.00
2 MCo(c) detective	3.00
3	3.00
4	3.00
TPB series rep.	13.00

JSA
1999

1 JeR,V:Dark Lord	12.00
2 JeR,AD&Mfm(c),A:Hawkgirl	6.00
3 JeR,AD&MFm(c),V:Dark Lord	5.00
4 JoR,AD&MFm(c),V:Mordru	5.00
5 JeR,AD&MFm(c),	5.00
6 AD&MFm,Justice Like Lightning	4.00
7 Darkness Falls,pt.1	4.00
8 Darkness Falls, pt.2	4.00
9 Darkness Falls, pt.3	4.00
10 V:Injustice Society	4.00
11 V:Kobra	4.00
12 V:Kobra,Whitehorse project	4.00
13 Hunt for Extant,pt.1	4.00
14 Hunt for Extant,pt.2	4.00
15 Hunt for Extant,concl.	4.00
16 Injustice be Done, pt.1	4.00
17 Injustice be Done, pt.2	4.00
18 Injustice be Done, pt.3	4.00
19 Injustice be Done, pt.4	4.00
20 Injustice be Done, pt.5	4.00
21 Hawkman prologue	4.00
22 Hawkman prologue	7.00
23 Return of Hawkman,pt.1	8.00
24 Return of Hawkman,pt.2	6.00
25 Return of Hawkman,pt.3,48-pg.	6.50
26 Return of Hawkman,pt.4	4.00
27 F:Captain Marvel,V:Black Adam	3.00
28 V:Roulette	3.00
29 PSj,Joker:Last Laugh,tie-in	3.00
30 V:Roulette	3.00
31 RgM(c),MakingWaves,A:Batman	3.00
32 RgM(c),Stealing Thunder,prev.	3.00
33 RgM(c),Stealing Thunder,pt.1	3.00
34 RgM(c),Stealing Thunder,pt.2	3.00
35 RgM(c),Stealing Thunder,pt.3	3.00
36 RgM(c),Stealing Thunder,pt.4	3.00
37 RgM(c),Thunder,pt.5,40-pg.	4.00
38 RgM(c),F:Rick Tyler	3.00
39 RgM(c),F:Power Girl	3.00
40 RgM(c),Shadower's grandson	3.00

JSA #58
© DC Comics, Inc.

41 RgM(c),V:Black Barax	3.00
42 V:Black Barax	3.00
43 F:JSA B.C.	3.00
44 F:Vandal Savage	3.00
45 F:Doctor Fate	3.00
46 Princes of Darkness,pt.1	3.00
47 Princes of Darkness,pt.2	3.00
48 Princes of Darkness,pt.3	3.00
49 Princes of Darkness,pt.4	3.00
50 Princes of Darkness,concl.	4.50
51 Dr. Fate	3.00
52 F:Black Adam	3.00
53 V:Crimson Avenger	3.00
54 F:Superman,Batman	3.00
55 F:Original members	2.50
56 Black Reign,pt.1,x-over.	3.00
57 Black Reign,pt.3,x-over.	3.00
58 Black Reign,pt.5,x-over.	3.00
59 SeP,F:Degaton	2.50
60 Redemption Lost,pt.1	2.50
61 TMd,Redemption Lost,pt.2	2.50
62 TMc,Redemption Lost,pt.3	2.50
63 JOy,Wake of Sandman,pt.1	2.50
64 JOy,Wake of Sandman,pt.2	2.50
65 Out of Time,pt.1	2.50
66 Out of Time,pt.2	2.50
67 DGh,Identity Crisis, tie-in	3.00
68 AxR(c),JSA/JSA	2.50
69 AxR(c),JSA/JSA,pt.2	2.50
70 JSA/JSa,pt.3	2.50
71 JSA/JSA,pt.4	2.50
72 JSA/JSA,pt.5	2.50
73 Black Vengeance,pt.1	5.00
74 Black Vengeance,pt.2	4.00
75 Black Vengeance,pt.3, 40-page	3.50
76 F:Mr. Terrific, Roulette	2.50
77 Alan Scott and Hal Jordan	2.50
78 A Day of Vengeance, tie-in	2.50
79 A Day of Vengeance, tie-in	2.50
80 Mordru vs. Dr. Fate	2.50
81 Stargirl's Past	2.50
82 GP,BWi,Infinite Crisis	2.50
83 RgM,LRs,One Year Later	2.50
84 RGm,LRs	2.50
85 RGm,LRs,O:Gentleman Ghost	3.00
86 RGm,JOy,LRs, A trap	3.00
87 RGm,JOy,LRs,final issue	3.00
Ann.#1 Planet DC	4.00
Spec.#1 Our Worlds at War,48-pg	3.50
Secret Files #1	7.00
Secret Files #2, 64-page	7.00
TPB Darkness Falls, 232-page	20.00
TPB Justice be Done	15.00
TPB The Return of Hawkman	20.00

TPB Fair Play. 15.00
TPB Stealing Thunder 15.00
TPB Savage Times 15.00
TPB The Liberty Files 20.00
TPB Prince of Darkness (2005). . . 20.00
TPB The Golden Age (2005) 20.00
TPB Black Reign (2005) 13.00
TPB Lost (2005). 20.00
TPB JSA: Black Vengeance (2006)20.00
TPB Mixed Signals (2006). 15.00

JSA: ALL-STARS
May 2003
1 (of 8) SaV,past and present. . . . 2.50
2 JLb,TSe,F:Hawkgirl 2.50
3 Salem Mass. 2.50
4 F:Stargirl 2.50
5 F:Hourman. 2.50
6 F:Dr. Mid-Nite. 2.50
7 40 pg.,BU: Mr. Terrific 3.50
8 F:Spectre. 2.50
TPB 15.00

JSA Classified #1
© *DC Comics, Inc.*

JSA CLASSIFIED
July, 2005
1 JP,ACo,O:Power Girl 5.00
2 JP,ACo,O:Power Girl 3.00
3 JP,ACo,O:Power Girl 3.00
4 JP,ACo,O:Power Girl, concl. . . . 3.00
5 PO,Honor Among Thieves. 3.00
6 PO,Honor Among Thieves,pt.2 . . 2.50
7 PO,Honor Among Thieves,pt.3 . . 2.50
8 F:Wildcat & Flash 2.50
9 F:Wildcat & Flash 2.50
10 PG,JP, One Year Later 2.50
11 Fall & Rise of Vandal Savage . . . 2.50
12 Fall & Rise of Vandal Savage. . . 3.00
13 Fall & Rise of Vandal Savage. . . 3.00
14 Double Trouble,pt.1 . . . . 3.00
15 Double Trouble,pt.2 . . . . 3.00
16 Double Trouble,pt.3 . . . . 3.00
17 SMc,The Venom Connection . . . 3.00
18 SMc,Hourman & Bane 3.00
19 RgM,Skin Game, pt.1 . . . . 3.00

JSA: THE LIBERTY FILES
Dec., 1999
1 (of 2) Elseworlds 7.00
2 TyH, concl. 7.00

JSA: STRANGE ADVENTURES #3
Aug. 2004
1 (of 6) BKi,GEr,V:Dynamo. 3.50
2 thru 6 BKi,GEr . . . . @3.50

JSA: THE UNHOLY THREE
Feb. 2003
1 (of 2) Elseworlds 7.00
2 concl. 7.00

JUDGE ANDERSON
2005
TPB Vol. 1 Anderson, Psi-Division. 15.00

JUDGE DREDD
1994–96
1 R:Judge Dredd. 3.00
2 Silicon Dreams. 2.50
3 Terrorists 2.75
4 Mega-City One crisis 2.50
5 Solitary Dredd 2.50
6 V:Richard Magg. 2.50
7 48 Hours,Heaven is Hell 2.50
8 V:Ministry of Fear. 2.50
9 V:Mister Synn 2.50
10 D:Judge Dredd 2.50
11 Mega-City One Chaos 2.50
12 V:Wally Squad 2.50
13 Block Wars,pt.1. . . . . 2.50
14 Block Wars,pt.2. . . . . 2.50
15 Block Wars,pt.3. . . . . 2.50
16 R:Judge with a Grudge. 2.50
17 F:Judge Cadet Lewis,
   Nova Scotia 2.50
18 final issue 2.50
Movie Adaptation 6.00

JUDGE DREDD
2005
TPB Judgment Day 2000 A.D.. . . . 15.00
TPB Dredd vs. Death. 13.00

JUDGE DREDD: LEGENDS OF THE LAW
1994–95
1 Organ Donor,pt.1 . . . . 3.00
2 Organ Donor,pt.2 . . . . 2.50
3 Organ Donor,pt.3 . . . . 2.50
4 Organ Donor,pt.4 . . . . 2.50
5 Trial By Gunfire,pt.1 . . . . 2.50
6 Trial By Gunfire,pt.2 . . . . 2.50
7 JHi(c),Trial By Gunfire,pt.3 . . . . 2.50
8 JBy(s),Fall From Grace,pt.1 . . . . 2.50
9 Fall From Grace,pt.2 . . . . 2.50
10 Fall From Grace,pt.3. . . . . 2.50
11 Dredd of Night,pt.1 . . . . 2.50
12 Dredd of Night,pt.2 . . . . 2.50
13 Dredd of Night,pt.3,final issue . . 2.50

JUSTICE
2005
1 (of 12) DBw,AxR,JLA,40-page. . . 3.00
2 DBw,AxR,Batman, Riddler. 3.50
3 DBw,AxR,Martian Manhunter . . . 3.50
4 DBw,AxR,. 3.50
5 DBw,AxR,Superman. 3.50
6 DBw,AxR,. 3.50
7 DBw,AxR,A:Metamorpho 3.50
8 DBw,AxR,. 3.50

JUSTICE, INC.
May-June, 1975
1 AMc,JKu(c),O:Avenger 25.00
2 JK,The Skywalker 20.00
3 JK,The Monster Bug 20.00

4 JK,JKu(c),Slay Ride in the Sky
   Nov.–Dec., 1975 . . . . 20.00
[Mini-Series], 1989
1 PerfectBound 'Trust & Betrayal' . 4.00
2 PerfectBound. 4.00

JUSTICE LEAGUE ADVENTURES
Nov., 2001
1 TTn,based on Cartoon show 2.50
2 . . . . 2.25
3 . . . . 2.25
4 . . . . 2.25
5 . . . . 2.25
6 thru 10 . . . . @2.25
11 thru 34 . . . . @2.25
TPB Justice League Adventures . . 10.00
TPB Vol. 1 Magnificent Seven. 7.00
TPB Vol. 2 Friends and Foes. 7.00

JUSTICE LEAGUE AMERICA
See: JUSTICE LEAGUE INTERNATIONAL)

JUSTICE LEAGUE ELITE
July 2004
1 (of 12) DoM 2.50
2 thru 4 DoM . . . . @2.50
5 DoM,I:Aftermath. 2.50
6 DoM,F:JSA 2.50
7 DoM,V:Drug cartel 2.50
8 DoM,V:Drug cartel 2.50
9 DoM,V:Eve. 2.50
10 DoM,V:Aftermath. 2.50
11 DoM,F:Manchester Black 2.50
12 DoM, finale 2.50
TPB Vol. 1 . . . . 20.00

JUSTICE LEAGUE EUROPE
1989–93
1 BS,A:Wonder Woman 4.00
2 BS,Search for Nazi-Killer. 3.00
3 BS,A:Jack O'Lantern,
   Queen Bee 2.50
4 BS,V:Queen Bee 2.50
5 JRu,BS,Metamorpho's Baby,
   A:Sapphire Starr 2.50
6 BS,V:Injustice League 2.50
7 BS,Teasdale Imperative#2,
   A:JLA. 2.50
8 BS,Teasdale Imperative#4,
   A:JLA. 2.50
9 BS,ANi,A:Superman 2.50
10 BS,V:Crimson Fox 2.50
11 BS,C:DocMagnus&Metal Men . . 2.50
12 BS,A:Metal Men 2.50
13 BS,V:One-Eyed Cat, contd
   from JLA #37 . . . . 2.50
14 I:VCR 2.50
15 BS,B:Extremists Vector saga,
   V:One-Eyed Cat,A:BlueJay 2.50
16 BS,A:Rocket Reds, Blue Jay . . . 2.50
17 BS,JLI in Another Dimension . . . 2.50
18 BS,Extremists Homeworld 2.50
19 BS,E:Extremist Vector Saga. . . . 2.50
20 MR,I:Beefeater,V:Kilowog. 2.50
21 MR,JRu,New JLE embassy in
   London,A:Kilowog 2.50
22 MR,JLE's Cat stolen 2.50
23 BS,O:Crimson Fox 2.50
24 BS,Worms in London 2.50
25 BS,V:Worms 2.50
26 BS,V:Starro 2.50
27 BS,JLE V:JLA:JLA,V:Starro. . . . 2.50
28 BS, JLE V:JLE,A:J'onn J'onzz,
   V:Starro 2.50

DC

Justice League Europe #1
© DC Comics, Inc.

29 BS,Breakdowns #2,V:Global
   Guardians 2.50
30 Breakdowns#4,V:J.O'Lantern . . . 2.50
31 Breakdowns #6,War of the
   Gods tie-in 2.50
32 Breakdowns #8,A:Chief(Doom
   Patrol) 2.50
33 Breakdowns #10,Lobo vs.
   Despero 2.50
34 Breakdowns #12,Lobo
   vs.Despero 2.50
35 Breakdowns #14,V:Extremists,
   D:Silver Sorceress 2.50
36 Breakdowns #16,All Quit 2.50
37 B:New JLE,I:Deconstructo 2.50
38 V:Deconstructo,A:Batman 2.50
39 V:Deconstructo,A:Batman 2.50
40 J:Hal Jordan,A:Metamorpho 2.50
41 A:Metamorpho,Wond.Woman . . . 2.50
42 A:Wonder Woman,V:Echidna . . . 2.50
43 V:Amos Fortune 2.50
44 V:Amos Fortune 2.50
45 Red Winter#1,V:Rocket Reds . . . 2.50
46 Red Winter#2 . . . . 2.50
47 Red Winter#3,V:Sonar 2.50
48 Red Winter#4,V:Sonar 2.50
49 Red Winter #5,V:Sonar 2.50
50 Red Winter#6,Double-sized,
   V:Sonar,J:Metamorpho 3.50
Ann.#1 A:Global Guardians 2.50
Ann.#2 MR,CS,ArmageddonPt.7 . . . 3.00
Ann.#3 RT(i),Eclipso tie-in 2.75
Justice League Spectacular JLE(c)
   New Direction 2.50
Becomes:

JUSTICE LEAGUE
INTERNATIONAL
[2nd Series]

JUSTICE LEAGUE
[INTERNATIONAL]
[1st Series], 1987
1 KM,TA,New Team,I:Max. Lord . . 10.00
2 KM,AG,A:BlueJay & Silver
   Sorceress 6.00
3 KM,AG,J:Booster Gold, V:Rocket
   Lords 5.00
3a Superman Logo 60.00
4 KM,AG,V:Royal Flush 5.00
5 KM,AG,A:The Creeper 5.00
6 KM,AG,A:The Creeper 5.00
Becomes:

JUSTICE LEAGUE
INTERNATIONAL
1988–89
7 KM,AG,L:Dr.Fate,Capt.Marvel,
   J:Rocket Red,Capt.Atom
   (Double size) 4.00
8 KM,AG,KG,Move to Paris Embassy,
   I:C.Cobert,B.U.Glob.Guardians. 3.50
9 KM,AG,KG,Millennium,Rocket
   Red-Traitor 3.50
10 KG,KM,AG,A:G.L.Corps,
   Superman,I:G'Nort. 3.50
11 KM,AG,V:Construct,C:Metron . . . 3.50
12 KG,KM,AG,O:Max Lord 3.50
13 KG,AG,A:Suicide Squad 3.50
14 SL,AG,J:Fire&Ice,L:Ron,
   I:Manga Kahn 3.50
15 SL,AG,V:Magna Kahn 3.50
16 KM,AG,I:Queen Bee 3.50
17 KM,AG,V:Queen Bee 3.50
18 KM,AG,MPn,A:Lobo,Guy Gardner
   (bonus book) 3.50
19 KM,JRu,A:Lobo vs.Guy Gardner,
   J:Hawkman & Hawkwoman . . . 3.50
20 KM,JRu(i),A:Lobo,G.Gardner . . . 3.50
21 KM,JRu(i),A:Lobo vs.Guy
   Gardner 3.50
22 KM,JRu,Imskian Soldiers 3.50
23 KM,JRu,I:Injustice League 3.50
24 KM,JRu,DoubleSize + Bonus
   Bk#13,I:JusticeLeagueEurope. . 4.00
25 KM(c),JRu(i),Vampire story 2.50
Ann.#1 BWg,DG,CR. 2.50
Ann.#2 BWg,JRu,A:Joker 3.00
Ann.#3 KM(c),JRu,JLI Embassies . . 2.50
Spec.#1 Mr.Miracle 2.00
Spec.#2,The Huntress 3.00
TPB new beginning,rep.#1-#7 . . . . 13.00
TPB The Secret Gospel of Maxwell
   Lord Rep. #8-#12, Ann.#1 . . . . 13.00
Becomes:

JUSTICE LEAGUE
AMERICA
1989–96
26 KM(c),JRu(i),Possessed Blue
   Beetle 3.00
27 KM(c),JRu,DG(i),'Exorcist',
   (c)tribute 2.50
28 KM(c),JRu(i), A:Black Hand 2.50
29 KM(c),JRu(i),V:Mega-Death 2.50
30 KM(c),BWg,JRu,J:Huntress,
   D:Mega-Death 2.50
31 ANi,AH,JRu,Teasdale Imperative
   #1,N:Fire,Ice,A:JLE 3.00
32 ANi,AH,Teasdale Imperative
   #3, A:JLE 3.00
33 ANi,AH,GuyGardner vs.Kilowog . 2.50
34 ANi,AH,'Club JLI,'A:Aquaman . . 2.50
35 ANi,JRu,AH,A:Aquaman 2.50
36 Gnort vs. Scarlet Skier 2.50
37 ANi,AH,L:Booster Gold 2.50
38 JRu,AH,R:Desparo,D:Steel. 2.50
39 JRu,AH,V:Desparo,D:Mr.Miracle,
   Robot 2.50
40 AH,Mr.Miracle Funeral 2.50
41 MMc,MaxForce 2.50
42 MMc,J:L-Ron. 2.50
43 AH,KG,The Man Who Knew Too
   Much #1. . . . . 2.50
44 AH,Man Knew Too Much #2 . . . 2.50
45 AH,MJ,JRu,Guy & Ice's 2nd
   date 2.50
46 Glory Bound #1,I:Gen.Glory 2.50
47 Glory Bound #2,J:Gen.Glory. . . . 2.50
48 Glory Bound #3,V:DosUberbot . . 2.50
49 Glory Bound #4. . . . . 2.50
50 Glory Bound #5 (double size). . . 3.00
51 JRu,AH,V:BlackHand,
   R:Booster Gold 2.50

Justice League of America #42
© DC Comics Inc.

52 TVE,Blue Beetle Vs. Guy Gardner
   A:Batman 2.50
53 Breakdowns #1, A:JLE 2.50
54 Breakdowns #3, A:JLE 2.50
55 Breakdowns #5,V:Global
   Guardians 2.50
56 Breakdowns #7, U.N. revokes
   JLA charter 2.50
57 Breakdowns #9,A:Lobo,
   V:Despero 2.50
58 BS,Breakdowns #11,Lobo
   Vs.Despero 2.50
59 BS,Breakdowns #13,
   V:Extremists. 2.50
60 KM,TA,Breakdowns #15,
   End of J.L.A. 2.50
61 DJu,I:Weapons Master,B:New
   JLA Line-up,I:Bloodwynd 3.00
62 DJu,V:Weapons Master 2.50
63 DJu,V:Starbreaker. 2.50
64 DJu,V:Starbreaker. 2.50
65 DJu,V:Starbreaker. 2.50
66 DJu,Superman V:Guy Gardner. . 2.50
67 DJu,Bloodwynd mystery 2.50
68 DJu,V:Alien Land Baron 2.50
69 DJu, Doomsday Pt.1-A 10.00
69a 2nd printing 2.50
70 DJu,Funeral for a Friend#1. . . . . 6.00
70a 2nd printing 2.50
71 DJu,J:Agent Liberty,Black Condor,
   The Ray,Wonder Woman 5.00
71a Newsstand ed. 2.50
71b 2nd Printing. 2.50
72 DJu,A:Green Arrow,Black
   Canary,Atom,B:Destiny's Hand . 4.00
73 DJu,Destiny's Hand #2 . . . . 3.00
74 DJu,Destiny's Hand #3 . . . . 2.50
75 DJu,E:Destiny's Hand #4,Martian
   Manhunter as Bloodwynd 2.50
76 DJu,Blood Secrets#1,
   V:Weaponmaster. 2.50
77 DJu,Blood Secrets#2,
   V:Weaponmaster. 2.50
78 MC,V:The Extremists 2.50
79 MC,V:The Extremists 2.50
80 KWe,N:Booster Gold 2.50
81 KWe,A:Captain Atom 2.50
82 KWe,A:Captain Atom 2.50
83 KWe,V:Guy Gardner 2.50
84 KWe,A:Ice 2.50
85 KWe,V:Frost Giants 2.50
86 B:Cults of the Machine 2.50
87 N:Booster Gold 2.50
88 E:Cults of the Machine 2.50

All comics prices listed are for *Near Mint* condition.

89 Judgement Day#1,
V:Overmaster 2.50
90 Judgement Day#4. . . . . 2.50
91 Aftershocks #1 . . . . 2.50
92 Zero Hour,I:Triumph 2.50
93 Power Girl and child 2.50
94 Scarabus. 2.50
95 Where the Wild Things Are. 2.50
96 Funeral 2.50
97 I:Judgment 2.50
98 J:Blue Devil, Ice Maiden 2.50
99 V:New Metahumes. 2.50
100 GJ,Woj,V:Lord Havok,dbl.size . 4.50
100a Collector's Edition. 4.50
101 GJ,Woj,Way of the
Warrior,pt.2 . . . . 2.50
102 Way of the Warrior,pt.5 . . . . 2.50
103 Oh, To Be Nobody 2.50
104 F:Metamorpho. 2.50
105 GJ,Woj,Underworld
Unleashed tie-in 2.50
106 GJ,Woj,Underworld
Unleashed tie-in 2.50
107 GJ,Woj,secret of Power
Girl's son 2.50
108 GJ,Woj,The Arcana revealed . . 2.50
109 GJ,Woj,All That Yazz 2.50
110 GJ,Woj,V:El Diablo 2.50
111 GJ,Woj,The Purge,pt.1 (of 3) . . 2.50
112 GJ,Woj,The Purge,pt.2 (of 3) . . 2.50
113 GJ,Woj,The Purge,pt.3 (of 3) . . 2.50
Ann.#4 KM(c),I:JL Antartica 3.50
Ann.#5 MR,KM,DJu,Armageddon . 3.50
Ann.#5a 2nd Printing,silver 2.50
Ann.#6 DC,Eclipso. 3.00
Ann.#7 I:Terrorsmith. 3.00
Ann.#8 Elseworlds Story 3.50
Ann.#9 Year One Annual 4.00
Ann.#10 CPr(s),SCi,NNa,Legends
of the Dead Earth 3.50
Justice League Spectacular DJu,
JLA(c) New Direction. 2.50
Archives Vol. 4 . . . . 50.00

JUSTICE LEAGUE
INTERNATIONAL
[2nd Regular Series], 1993–94
Prev: Justice League Europe
51 Aztec Cult 2.25
52 V:Aztec Cult 2.25
53 R:Fox's Husband 2.25
54 RoR,I:Creator 2.25
55 RoR,A:Creator 2.25
56 RoR,V:Terrorists 2.25
57 RoR,V:Terrorists 2.25
58 RoR,V:Aliens. 2.25
59 RoR,A:Guy Gardner 2.25
60 GJ(s),RoR 2.25
61 GJ(s),V:Godfrey 2.25
62 GJ(s),N:Metamorpho,V:Godfrey . 2.25
63 GJ(s),In Africa 2.25
64 GJ(s),V:Cadre 2.25
65 JudgmentDay#3,V:Overmaster. . 2.25
66 JudgmentDay#6,V:Overmaster. . 2.25
67 Aftershock #3 . . . . 2.25
68 Zero Hour, Final Issue 2.25
Ann.#4 Bloodlines#9,I:Lionheart . . . 2.75
Ann.#5 . . . . 3.25
Ann.#6 Elseworlds Story 3.00

JUSTICE LEAGUE
[INTERNATIONAL]
QUARTERLY
1990–94
1 I:Conglomerate 4.00
2 MJ(i),R:Mr.Nebula 3.50
3 V:Extremists, C:Original JLA. . . . 3.50
4 KM(c),MR,CR,A:Injustice
League. 3.00

5 KM(c),Superhero Attacks. 3.00
6 EB,Elongated Man,B.U.Global
Guardians,Powergirl,B.Beetle . . 3.00
7 EB,DH,MR.Global Guardians . . . 3.00
8 . . . . 3.00
9 DC,F:Power Girl,Booster Gold . . 3.50
10 F:Flash,Fire & Ice 3.50
11 F:JL Women 3.50
12 F:Conglomerate 3.50
13 V:Ultraa 7.00
14 MMi(c),PuK(s),F:Captain Atom,Blue
Beetle,Nightshade,Thunderbolt . 3.75
15 F:Praxis. 3.50
16 F:Gen Glory 3.50
17 Final Issue 3.50

JUSTICE LEAGUE:
A MIDSUMMER'S
NIGHTMARE
1996
1 (of 3) MWa(s),FaN,JJ,DaR, ... 5.00
2 MWa(s),FaN,JJ,DaR,Batman &
Superman attempt to free
other heroes 4.00
3 MWa&FaN(s), Know-Man's plot
revealed, finale 4.00
TPB Rep. 3 issues. 9.00

Justice League of America #90
© DC Comics, Inc.

JUSTICE LEAGUE
OF AMERICA
Oct.–Nov., 1960
1 MSy,I&O:Despero 29,000.00
2 MSy,A:Merlin 2,500.00
3 MSy,I&O:Kanjar Ro. 1,700.00
4 MSy,J:Green Arrow. 1,100.00
5 MSy,I&O:Dr.Destiny 1,000.00
6 MSy,Prof. Fortune 900.00
7 MSy,Cosmic Fun-House 900.00
8 MSy,For Sale-Justice League . 900.00
9 MSy,O:JLA 1,100.00
10 MSy,I:Felix Faust 900.00
11 MSy,A:Felix Faust 700.00
12 MSy,I&O:Dr Light 700.00
13 MSy,A:Speedy. 700.00
14 MSy,J:Atom. 700.00
15 MSy,V:Untouchable Aliens . . . 700.00
16 MSy,I:Maestro 600.00
17 MSy,A:Tornado Tyrant. 600.00
18 MSy,V:Terrane,Ocana. 600.00
19 MSy,A:Dr.Destiny 600.00
20 MSy,V:Metal Being 600.00

21 MSy,R:JSA,1st S.A Hourman,
Dr.Fate. 800.00
22 MSy,R:JSA 800.00
23 MSy,I:Queen Bee 500.00
24 MSy,A:Adam Strange 500.00
25 MSy,I:Draad,the Conqueror . . 500.00
26 MSy,A:Despero 500.00
27 MSy,V:I,A:Amazo 500.00
28 MSy,I:Headmaster Mind,
A:Robin 500.00
29 MSy,I:Crime Syndicate,A:JSA,
1st S.A. Starman 600.00
30 MSy,V:Crime Syndicate,
A:JSA. 500.00
31 MSy,J:Hawkman 450.00
32 MSy,I&O:Brain Storm 350.00
33 MSy,I:Endless One 300.00
34 MSy,A:Dr.Destiny,Joker 325.00
35 MSy,A:Three Demons. 300.00
36 MSy,A:Brain Storm,
Handicap story 300.00
37 MSy,A:JSA,x-over,
1st S.A.Mr.Terrific 400.00
38 MSy,A:JSA,Mr.Terrific 400.00
39 Giant 400.00
40 MSy,A:Shark,Penguin 325.00
41 MSy,I:Key 325.00
42 MSy,A:Metamorpho 175.00
43 MSy,I:Royal Flush Gang 175.00
44 MSy,A:Unimaginable. 175.00
45 MSy,I:Shaggy Man 175.00
46 MSy,A:JSA,Blockbuster,Solomon
Grundy,1st S.A.Sandman . . . 250.00
47 MSy,A:JSA,Blockbuster,
Solomon Grundy 200.00
48 Giant 210.00
49 MSy,A:Felix Faust 175.00
50 MSy,A:Robin 175.00
51 MSy,A:Zatanna,Elong.Man . . . 175.00
52 MSy,A:Robin,Lord of Time . . . 175.00
53 MSy,A:Hawkgirl 175.00
54 MSy,A:Royal Flush Gang 175.00
55 MSy,A:JSA,E-2 Robin 200.00
56 MSy,A:JSA,E-2 Robin 175.00
57 MSy,Brotherhood 175.00
58 Reprint(giant size). 185.00
59 MSy,V:Impossibles 175.00
60 MSy,A:Queen Bee,Batgirl . . . 175.00
61 MSy,A:Lex Luthor,Penguin . . . 150.00
62 MSy,V:Bulleters. 150.00
63 MSy,A:Key 150.00
64 DD,I:Red Tornado,A:JSA 160.00
65 DD,A:JSA 160.00
66 DD,A:Demmy Gog 150.00
67 MSy,Giant reprints 160.00
68 DD,V:Chaos Maker 160.00
69 DD,L:Wonder Woman. 150.00
70 DD,A:Creeper 150.00
71 DD,L:J'onn J'onzz. 150.00
72 DD,A:Hawkgirl. 150.00
73 DD,A:JSA 150.00
74 DD,D:Larry Lance,A:JSA 150.00
75 DD,J:Black Canary 150.00
76 Giant,MA,two page pin-up . . . 150.00
77 DD,A:Joker,L:Snapper Carr . . 100.00
78 DD,R:Vigilante 100.00
79 DD,A:Vigilante. 100.00
80 DD,A:Tomar-Re,Guardians. . . 100.00
81 DD,V:Jest-Master 100.00
82 DD,A:JSA 90.00
83 DD,A:JSA,Spectre 120.00
84 DD,Devil in Paradise. 75.00
85 Giant reprint 125.00
86 DD,V:Zapper. 75.00
87 DD,A:Zatanna,I:Silver
Sorceress,Blue Jay 100.00
88 DD,A:Mera 100.00
89 DD,A:Harlequin Ellis,
(i.e. Harlan Ellison) 100.00
90 CI(c),MA(ci),DD,V:Pale People 100.00
91 DD,A:JSA,V:Solomon Grundy 100.00
92 DD,A:JSA,V:Solomon Grundy 100.00

Justice League of America #206
© DC Comics Inc.

93 DD,A:JSA,(giant size)....... 100.00
94 DD,NA,O:Sandman,rep.
   Adventure #40........... 225.00
95 DD,rep.More Fun Comics #67,
   All American Comics #25 ... 125.00
96 DD,I:Starbreaker........... 110.00
97 DD,MS,O:JLA 100.00
98 DD,A:Sargon,Gold.Age reps.. 100.00
99 DD,G.A. reps.............. 100.00
100 DD,A:JSA,Metamorpho,
    R:7 Soldiers of Victory...... 120.00
101 DD,A:JSA,7 Soldiers........ 75.00
102 DD,DG,A:JSA,7 Soldiers
    D:Red Tornado 75.00
103 DD,DG,Halloween issue,
    A:Phantom Stranger........ 50.00
104 DD,DG,A:Shaggy Man,
    Hector Hammond 50.00
105 DD,DG,J:ElongatedMan 50.00
106 DD,DG,J:RedTornado...... 50.00
107 DD,DG,I:Freedom Fighters,
    A:JSA.................. 60.00
108 DD,DG,A:JSA,
    Freedom Fighters......... 60.00
109 DD,DG,L:Hawkman......... 60.00
110 DD,DG,A:John Stewert,
    Phantom Stranger 110.00
111 DD,DG,I:Injustice Gang 110.00
112 DD,DG,A:Amazo 110.00
113 DD,DG,A:JSA 110.00
114 DD,DG,A:SnapperCarr 110.00
115 DD,FMc,A:J'onn J'onzz..... 110.00
116 DD,FMc,I:Golden Eagle 110.00
117 DD,FMc,R:Hawkman 35.00
118 DD,FMc................. 35.00
119 DD,FMc,A:Hawkgirl 35.00
120 DD,FMc,A:Adam Strange 35.00
121 DD,FMc,W:Adam Strange ... 35.00
122 DD,FMc,JLA casebook story
    V:Dr.Light................ 35.00
123 DD,FMc,A:JSA 40.00
124 DD,FMc,A: JSA........... 40.00
125 DD,FMc,A:Two-Face........ 35.00
126 DD,FMc,A:Two-Face........ 35.00
127 DD,FMc,V:Anarchist 35.00
128 DD,FMc,J:W.Woman....... 35.00
129 DD,FMC,D:RedTornado 35.00
130 DD,FMc,O:JLASatellite...... 35.00
131 DD,FMc,V:Queen Bee,Sonar . 35.00
132 DD,FMc,A:Supergirl 35.00
133 DD,FMc,A:Supergirl 35.00
134 DD,FMc,A:Supergirl 35.00
135 DD,FMc,A:Squad.of Justice .. 35.00
136 DD,FMc,A:E-2Joker 40.00

137 DD,FMc,Superman vs.
    Capt. Marvel 40.00
138 NA(c),DD,FMc,A:Adam
    Strange 35.00
139 NA(c),DD,FMc,A:AdamStrange,
    Phantom Stranger,doub.size .. 25.00
140 DD,FMc,Manhunters........ 25.00
141 DD,FMc,Manhunters........ 25.00
142 DD,FMc,F:Aquaman,Atom,
    Elongated Man 25.00
143 DD,FMc,V:Injustice Gang 25.00
144 DD,FMc,O:JLA............ 25.00
145 DD,FMc,A:Phant.Stranger ... 25.00
146 J:Red Tornado,Hawkgirl 25.00
147 DD,FMc,A:Legion 25.00
148 DD,FMc,A:Legion 25.00
149 DD,FMc,A:Dr.Light 25.00
150 DD,FMc,A:Dr.Light 25.00
151 DD,FMc,A:Amos Fortune 20.00
152 DD,FMc................. 20.00
153 GT,FMc,I:Ultraa........... 20.00
154 MK(c),DD,FMc 20.00
155 DD,FMc................. 20.00
156 DD,FMc................. 20.00
157 DD,FMc,W:Atom.......... 20.00
158 DD,FMc,A:Ultraa.......... 20.00
159 DD,FMc,A:JSA,Jonah Hex,
    Enemy Ace 18.00
160 DD,FMc,A:JSA,Jonah Hex,
    Enemy Ace 18.00
161 DD,FMc,J:Zatanna......... 18.00
162 DD,FMc................. 18.00
163 DD,FMc,V:Mad Maestro 18.00
164 DD,FMc,V:Mad Maestro 18.00
165 DD,FMc................. 18.00
166 DD,FMc,V:Secret Society 18.00
167 DD,FMc,V:Secret Society 18.00
168 DD,FMc,V:Secret Society 18.00
169 DD,FMc,A:Ultraa.......... 18.00
170 DD,FMc,A:Ultraa.......... 18.00
171 DD,FMc,A:JSA,D:Mr.Terrific . 18.00
172 DD,FMc,A:JSA,D:Mr.Terrific . 18.00
173 DD,FMc,A:Black Lightning .. 18.00
174 DD,FMc,A:Black Lightning .. 18.00
175 DD,FMc,V:Dr.Destiny 18.00
176 DD,FMc,V:Dr.Destiny 15.00
177 DD,FMc,V:Desparo 10.00
178 JSn(c),DD,FMc,V:Desparo .. 10.00
179 JSn(c),DD,FMc,J:Firestorm .. 10.00
180 JSn(c),DD,FMc,V:Satin Satan 10.00
181 DD,FMc,L:Gr.Arrow,V:Star ... 11.00
182 DD,FMc,A:Green Arrow,
    V:Felix Faust 11.00
183 JSn(c),DD,FMc,A:JSA,
    NewGods................ 11.00
184 GP,FMc,A:JSA,NewGods.... 11.00
185 JSn(c),GP,FMc,A:JSA,
    New Gods 10.00
186 FMc,GP,V:Shaggy Man....... 9.00
187 DH,FMc,N:Zatanna......... 9.00
188 DH,FMc,V:Proteus 9.00
189 BB(c),RB,FMc,V:Starro...... 9.00
190 BB(c),RB,LMa,V:Starro...... 9.00
191 RB,V:Amazo 9.00
192 GP,O:Red Tornado 9.00
193 GP,RB,JOy,I:AllStarSquad 9.00
194 GP,V:Amos Fortune 9.00
195 GP,A:JSA,V:Secret Society.... 9.00
196 GP,RT,A:JSA,V:Secret Soc. ... 9.00
197 GP,RT,KP,A:JSA,V:Secret
    Society.................. 9.00
198 DH,BBr,A:J.Hex,BatLash 9.00
199 GP(c),DH,BBr,A:Jonah Hex,
    BatLash 9.00
200 GP,DG,BB (1st Batman),PB,TA,
    BBr,GK,CI,JAp,JKu,Anniv.,A:Adam
    Strange,Phantom Stranger,
    J:Green Arrow 10.00
201 GP(c),DH,A:Ultraa 5.00
202 GP(c),DH,BBr,JLA in Space .. 5.00
203 GP(c),DH,RT,V:Royal
    Flush Gang 5.00

204 GP(c),DH,RT,V:R.FlushGang .. 5.00
205 GP(c),DH,RT,V:R.FlushGang .. 5.00
206 DH,RT,A:Demons 3 .... 5.00
207 GP(c),DH,RT,A:All Star
    Squadron,JSA 6.00
208 GP(c),DH,RT,A:All Star
    Squadron,JSA 6.00
209 GP(c),DH,RT,A:All Star
    Squadron,JSA 5.00
210 RB,RT,JLA casebook #1...... 5.00
211 RB,RT,JLA casebook #2...... 5.00
212 GP(c),RB,PCu,RT,c.book #3 .. 5.00
213 GP(c),DH,RT............. 5.00
214 GP(c),DH,RT,I:Siren Sist.h'd.. 5.00
215 GP(c),DH,RT............. 5.00
216 DH.................... 5.00
217 GP(c),RT(i) 5.00
218 RT(i),A:Prof.Ivo........... 5.00
219 GP(c),RT(i),A:JSA......... 5.00
220 GP(c),RT,O:Bl.Canary,A:JSA .. 4.00
221 Beasts #1 .... 3.00
222 RT(i),Beasts #2........... 3.00
223 RT(i),Beasts #3........... 3.00
224 DG(i),V:Paragon 3.00
225 V:Hellrazor 3.00
226 FMc(i),V:Hellrazor......... 3.00
227 V:Hellrazor,I:Lord Claw....... 3.00
228 GT,AN,R:J'onn J'onzz,War of
    the Worlds,pt.1 .... 3.00
229 War of the Worlds,pt.2 ...... 3.00
230 War of the Worlds conc....... 3.00
231 RB(i),A:JSA,Supergirl 3.00
232 A:JSA Supergirl........... 3.00
233 New JLA takes over book,
    B:Rebirth,F:Vibe 3.00
234 F:Vixen 3.00
235 F:Steel................. 3.00
236 E:Rebirth,F:Gypsy......... 3.00
237 A:Superman,Flash,WWoman . 3.00
238 A:Superman,Flash,WWoman . 3.00
239 V:Ox 3.00
240 MSy,TMd............... 3.00
241 GT,V:Amazo 3.00
242 GT,V:Amazo,Mask(Toy tie-in)
    insert 3.00
243 GT,L:Aquaman,V:Amazo 3.00
244 JSon,Crisis,A:InfinityInc,JSA... 4.00
245 LMc,Crisis,N:Steel.......... 4.00
246 LMc,JLA leaves Detroit....... 3.00
247 LMc,JLA returns to old HQ 3.00
248 LMc,F:J'onn J'onzz......... 3.00
249 LMc,Lead-in to Anniv......... 3.00
250 LMc,Anniv.,A:Superman,
    Green Lantern,Green Arrow,
    Black Canary,R:Batman 3.00
251 LMc,V:Despero 3.00
252 LMc,V:Despero,N:Elongated
    Man 3.00
253 LMc,V:Despero 3.00
254 LMc,V:Despero 3.00
255 LMc,O:Gypsy 3.00
256 LMc,Gypsy 3.00
257 LMc,A:Adam,L:Zatanna 3.00
258 LMc,Legends x-over,D:Vibe ... 3.00
259 LMc,Legends x-over 3.00
260 LMc,Legends x-over,D:Steel... 6.00
261 LMc,Legends,final issue 8.00
Ann.#1 DG(i),A:Sandman 3.50
Ann.#2 I:NewJLA.............. 3.00
Ann.#3 MG(i),Crisis 3.00

JUSTICE LEAGUE
OF AMERICA

July, 2006

0 Batman, Superman, W.Woman .. 3.00
0a variant JSC (c).............. 3.00
1 EBe,The Tornado's Path 3.00
2 EBe,................... 3.00
3 EBe, V:Dr. Impossible 3.00
4 EBe 3.00
1a thru 4a variant (c)......... @3.00

JUSTICE LEAGUE OF AMERICA: ANOTHER NAIL
May 2004
1 AD,MFm,F:Superman 6.00
2 AD,MFm,Darkseid's secrets 6.00
3 AD,MFm,concl. 6.00

JUSTICE LEAGUE OF AMERICA: THE NAIL
June, 1998
Elseworlds
1 World without a Superman 5.00
2 AID,MFm,Robin & Batgirl dead . . 5.00
3 AID,MFm,concl. 5.00

JUSTICE LEAGUES
Jan., 2001
Pt.1 Justice Leagues #1,GP(c) 2.50
Pt.2 Just.League of Amazons #1. . . 2.50
Pt.3 Just.League of Atlantis #1 . . . . 2.50
Pt.4 Just.League of Arkham #1 . . . . 2.50
Pt.5 Just.League of Aliens #1 . . . . 2.50
Pt.6 Just.League of America #1. . . . 2.50

JUSTICE LEAGUE TASK FORCE
1993–96
1 F:Mart.Manhunter,Nightwing,
 Aquaman,Flash,Gr.Lantern 2.25
2 V:Count Glass,Blitz 2.25
3 V:Blitz,Count Glass 2.25
4 DG,F:Gypsy,A:Lady Shiva 2.25
5 JAl,Knightquest:Crusade,F:Bronze
 Tiger,Green Arrow,Gypsy 2.25
6 JAl,Knightquest:Search,F:Bronze
 Tiger,Green Arrow,Gypsy 2.25
7 PDd(s),F:Maxima,Wonder Woman,
 Dolphin,Gypsy,Vixen,V:Luta . . . 2.25
8 PDd(s),SaV,V:Amazons 2.25
9 GrL,V:Wildman. 2.25
10 Purification Plague #1. . . . . 2.25
11 Purification Plague #2. . . . . 2.25
12 Purification Plague #3. . . . . 2.25
13 Judgement Day #2,. 2.25
14 Jugdement Day#5,
 V:Overmaster 2.25
15 Aftershocks #2 . . . . 2.25
16 Zero Hour,A:Triumph 2.25
17 Savage 2.25
18 Savage 2.25
19 Martian Manhunter 2.25
20 thru 35 . . . . @2.25

JUSTICE LEAGUE UNLIMITED
Sept. 2004
1 From animated series 2.25
2 thru 27 . . . . @2.25
TPB Vol. 1 United They Stand 7.00
TPB Vol. 2 Jam-Packed Action . . 8.00
TPB Vol. 2 World's Greatest Heroes 7.00
TPB Vol. 3 Champions of Justice . . 7.00

JUSTICE RIDERS
1999
1-shot, Elseworlds 7.00

JUSTICE SOCIETY OF AMERICA
[Limited Series]
April–Nov., 1991
1 B:Veng.From Stars,A:Flash 3.00
2 A:BlackCanary,V:Solomon Grundy,
 C:G.A.Green Lantern. 2.50

3 A:G.A.Green Lantern,Black Canary,
 V:Sol.Grundy 2.50
4 A:G.A.Hawkman,C:G.A.Flash. . . . 2.50
5 A:G.A.Hawkman,Flash 2.50
6 FMc(i),A:Bl.Canary,G.A.Gr.Lantern,
 V:Sol.Grundy,V.Savage 2.50
7 JSA united,V:Vandal Savage 2.50
8 E:Veng.FromStar,V:V.Savage,
 Solomon Grundy 2.50
Spec.#1 DR,MG,End of JSA 2.50

[Regular Series], 1992–93
1 V:The New Order. 2.50
2 V:Ultra Gen 2.50
3 R:Ultra-Humanite 2.50
4 V:Ultra-Humanite 2.50
5 V:Ultra-Humanite 2.50
6 F:Johnny Thunderbolt 2.50
7 ..Or give me Liberty 2.50
8 Pyramid Scheme 2.50
9 V:Kulak. 2.50
10 V:Kulak,final issue. 2.50
TPB Justice Society
 Returns (2003) 20.00

JUST IMAGINE...
July, 2001
GN Aquaman, by StL & SMc 6.00
GN Batman, by StL & JKu 6.00
GN Catwoman, by StL & CBa 6.00
GN Crisis, by StL 6.00
GN The Flash, by StL & KM 6.00
GN Green Lantern, by StL & DGb . . 6.00
GN The JLA, by StL & JOy 6.00
GN Robin, by StL & JBy 6.00
GN Sandman, by StL & WS. 6.00
GN Shazam!, by StL & GFr 6.00
GN Superman, by StL & JB 6.00
GN Wonder Woman, by StL & JLe . 6.00
GN Just Imagine Secret Files 5.00
TPB The DC Universe, by StL 20.00

KAMANDI, THE LAST BOY ON EARTH
Oct.–Nov., 1972
1 JK,O:Kamandi. 125.00
2 JK,Year of the Rat 75.00
3 JK,Thing tht Grew on the Moon. 75.00
4 JK,I:Prince Tuftan 60.00
5 JK,The One-Armed Bandit 60.00
6 JK,Flower. 50.00
7 JK,The Monster Fetish 50.00
8 JK,Beyond Reason 50.00
9 JK,Traking Site 50.00
10 JK,Killer Germ. 50.00
11 JK,The Devil 30.00
12 JK,Devil and Mister Sacker . . . 30.00
13 thru 24 JK . . . . @30.00
25 thru 28 JK . . . . @25.00
29 JK,A:Superman. 30.00
30 JK,U.F.O. Wildest Trip Ever . . . 25.00
31 JK,The Gulliver Effect 25.00
32 JK,Double size 30.00
33 thru 57. . . . . @25.00
58 DAy,A:Karate Kid 30.00
59 JSn,A:Omac, Sept.–Oct,1978. . 30.00

KAMANDI: AT EARTH'S END
[Mini-Series], 1993
1 R:Kamandi 2.50
2 V:Kingpin,Big Q 2.50
3 A:Sleeper Zom,Saphira 2.50
4 A:Superman. 2.50
5 A:Superman,V:Ben Boxer 2.50
6 final issue. 2.50

KARATE KID
March-April, 1976
1 I:Iris Jacobs,A:Legion 25.00

2 A:Major Disaster 12.00
3 thru 10 . . . . @12.00
11 A:Superboy/Legion 12.00
12 A:Superboy/Legion 12.00
13 A:Superboy/Legion 12.00
14 A:Robin 12.00
15 July-Aug., 1978 . . . . 12.00

The Kents #9
© *DC Comics, Inc.*

KENTS, THE
1997
1 (of 12) JOs(s),TT,MiB 3.00
2 JOs(s),TT,MiB, tragedy strikes . . 3.00
3 JOs,TT,MiB,Jed & Nate Kent. . . . 3.00
4 JOs,TT,MiB,Bleeding Kansas,
 concl. 3.00
5 JOs,TT,Brother vs.Brother pt.1 . . 3.00
6 JOs,TT,Brother vs.Brother pt.2 . . 3.00
7 JOs,TT,MiB,Quantrill, Wild
 Bill Hickcock 3.00
8 JOs, ... 3.00
9 JOs,TMd,To the Stars
 by Hard Ways,pt.1 . . . . 3.00
10 JOs,TMd,To the Stars,pt.2 . . . . 3.00
11 JOs,TMd,To the Stars,pt.3 . . . . 3.00
12 JOs,TMd,To the Stars,pt.4 . . . . 3.00
TPB The Kents, rep. 20.00

KID ETERNITY
1991
1 GMo(s),DFg,O:Kid Eternity 5.50
2 GMo(s),DFg,A:Mr.Keeper 5.50
3 GMo(s),DFg,True Origin revealed,
 final issue. 5.50

KID ETERNITY
DC/Vertigo, 1993–94
1 B:ANo(s),SeP,R:Kid Eternity,
 A:Mdm.Blavatsky,Hemlock 2.75
2 SeP,A:Sigmund Freud,Carl Jung,
 A:Malocchio 2.50
3 SeP,A:Malocchio,I:Dr.Pathos 2.25
4 SeP,A:Neal Cassady 2.25
5 SeP,In Cyberspace 2.25
6 SeP,A:Dr.Pathos,Marilyn
 Monroe 2.25
7 SeP,I:Infinity. 2.25
8 SeP,In Insane Asylum 2.25
9 SeP,Asylum,A:Dr.Pathos 2.25
10 SeP,Small Wages 2.25
11 ANi(s),I:Slap 2.25
12 SeP,A:Slap 2.25
13 SeP,Date in Hell,pt.1. . . . . 2.25
14 SeP,Date in Hell,pt.2. . . . . 2.25
15 SeP,Date in Hell,pt.3. . . . . 2.25

Kid Eternity #7
© *DC Comics, Inc.*

16 SeP,The Zone 2.25
TPB GMo,DFg (2006) 15.00

KILL YOUR BOYFRIEND
DC/Vertigo, 1995, 1999
GNv PBd(c) (1995) 5.00
1-shot GMo (1999). 6.00

KINETIC
DC Focus, March 2004
1 WaP,F:Tom Morell 2.50
2 WaP,newfound super-powers . . . 2.50
3 thru 9 WaP . . . . @2.50
TPB rep. 10.00

KINGDOM, THE
1998
1 (of 2) MWa,AOl 5.00
2 MWa,MZ,JhB,V:Gog 4.00
Spec.#1 Kid Flash 2.25
Spec.#1 Offspring 2.25
Spec.#1 Nightstar. 2.25
Spec.#1 Planet Krypton 2.25
Spec.#1 Son of the Bat 2.25
DirectCurrents Spec.. . . . . free
TPB 15.00

KINGDOM COME
Elseworlds 1996
1 MWa,AxR. 9.00
2 MWa,AxR,R:JLA 9.00
3 MWa,AxR,A:Capt. Marvel 8.00
4 MWa,AxR, final issue. 8.00
TPB MWa,AxR, rep.. . . . . 15.00

KOBALT
DC/Milestone, 1994–95
1 JBy(c),I:Kobalt,Richard Page. . . . 3.00
2 thru 13 . . . . @2.50
14 Long Hot Summer, V:Harvester . 3.00
15 Long Hot Summer. 3.00

KOBRA
1976–77
1 JK,I:Kobra & Jason Burr 20.00
2 I:Solaris 10.00
3 KG/DG,TA,V:Solaris 10.00
4 V:Servitor 10.00
5 RB/FMc,A:Jonny Double 10.00
6 MN/JRu,A:Jonny Double 10.00
7 MN/JRu,A:Jonny Double last iss 10.00

KONG THE UNTAMED
June-July, 1975
1 AA,BWr(c) 20.00
2 AA,BWr(c) 12.00
3 AA 10.00
4 . . . . 10.00
5 Feb.–March, 1976 . . . . 10.00

KORAK, SON OF TARZAN
1975
(Prev. published by Gold Key)
46 JKu(c),B:Carson of Venus 25.00
47 JKu(c) 10.00
48 JKu(c) 10.00
49 JKu(c),Origin of Korak 15.00
50 thru 59 JKu(c),1975 . . . . 10.00
Becomes:

TARZAN FAMILY

KRYPTON CHRONICLES
1981
1 CS,A:Superman. 5.00
2 CS,A:Black Flame 4.00
3 CS,O:Name of Kal-El 4.00

KRYPTO THE SUPERDOG
Aug., 2006
1 From TV cartoon 2.25
2 thru 3 . . . . @2.25

LAB RATS
April, 2002
1 by the one and only JBy 7.00
1a 2nd printing 4.50
2 JBy, amusement park 6.00
2a 2nd printing 4.50
3 JBy, ... 2.50
4 JBy,time travel,pt.1 . . . . 2.50
5 JBy,time travel,pt.2 . . . . 2.50
6 JBy,time travel,pt.3,A:Superman . 2.50
7 JBy,interplanetary adventure 2.50
8 JBy, final issue. 2.50

LAND OF THE BLINDFOLDED
2005
Vol. 2 thru Vol. 9. . . . . @10.00

LAST DAYS OF THE JUSTICE SOCIETY
1986
1 . . . . 5.00

LAST ONE
DC/Vertigo, 1993
1 B:JMD(s),DSw,I:Myrwann,Patrick
     Maguire's Story 3.25
2 DSw,Pat's Addiction to Drugs . . . 3.00
3 DSw,Pat goes into Coma. 3.00
4 DSw,In Victorian age 3.00
5 DSw,Myrwann Memories. 3.00
6 E:JMD(s),DSw,final Issue 3.00

L.A.W.
1999
1 (of 6) BL,DG,Living Assault
     Weapons 2.50
2 thru 6 BL,DG . . . . @2.50

LAZARUS FIVE
May, 2000
1 (of 5) THy,F:Inquisitors 2.50
2 thru 5 THy . . . . @2.50

Leading Comics #9
© *DC Comics Inc.*

LEADING COMICS
Winter, 1941–42
1 O:Seven Soldiers of Victory,
     B:Crimson Avenger,Green Arrow
     & Speedy,Shining Knight,
     A:The Dummy 9,000.00
2 MMe,V:Black Star 4,000.00
3 V:Dr. Doome 3,000.00
4 Seven Steps to Conquest,
     V:The Sixth Sense 2,500.00
5 The Miracles that Money
     Couldn't Buy. 2,500.00
6 Treasure that Time Forgot . . 2,000.00
7 The Wizard of Wisstark 2,000.00
8 Seven Soldiers Go back
     through the Centuries. 2,000.00
9 V:Mr. X,Chameleon of Crime 2,000.00
10 King of the Hundred Isles . . 2,000.00
11 The Hard Luck Hat! 1,400.00
12 The Million Dollar
     Challenge! 1,400.00
13 The Trophies of Crime. 1,400.00
14 Bandits from the Book 1,400.00
15 (fa) King Oscar's Court. 300.00
16 thru 22 (fa) . . . . @125.00
23 (fa),I:Peter Porkchops. 250.00
24 thru 30 (fa) . . . . @125.00
31 (fa). 100.00
32 (fa). 100.00
33 (fa). 100.00
34 thru 40 (fa) . . . . @100.00
41 (fa),Feb.–March, 1950 . . . . . . 100.00
Becomes:

LEADING SCREEN COMICS
1950
42 thru 50 Funny Animal . . . . . @125.00
51 thru 60 . . . . @100.00
61 thru 70 . . . . @100.00
71 thru 77 . . . . @100.00

LEAGUE OF JUSTICE
1996
1 (of 2) Elseworlds 6.00
2 (of 2) Elseworlds 6.00

LEAVE IT TO BINKY
1948
1ShM, teen-age 450.00
2 ShM 225.00
3 . . . . 135.00
4 . . . . 135.00
5 A:Superman. 200.00
6 . . . . 125.00

All comics prices listed are for *Near Mint* condition.

DC COMICS

7	125.00
8	125.00
9	125.00
10	125.00
11 thru 13	@100.00
14 ShM	125.00
15 thru 20	@90.00
21 thru 27	@100.00
28 MD	125.00
29	100.00
30 thru 60	@100.00
61 thru 71	@35.00

LEGEND OF
THE HAWKMAN
July, 2000
1 BRa,Hawkman & Hawkgirl	5.00
2 BRa,V:Thanagarian zealots	5.00
3 BRa,concl.	5.00

LEGEND OF
THE SHIELD
DC/Impact, 1991–92
1 I:Shield,	2.50
2 thru 16	@2.50
Ann.#1 Earthquest,w/trading card.	2.25

LEGEND OF
WONDER WOMAN
1986
1 Return of Atomia	4.00
2 A:Queens Solalia & Leila	3.50
3 Escape from Atomia	3.50
4 conclusion	3.50

LEGENDS
1986–87
1 JBy,V:Darkseid	5.00
2 JBy,A:Superman	4.00
3 JBy,I:Suicide Squad.	4.00
4 JBy,V:Darkseid	4.00
5 JBy,A:Dr. Fate	4.00
6 JBy,I:Justice League	5.00
TPB rep.#1-#6 JBy(c)	10.00

Legends of Daniel Boon #1
© DC Comics, Inc.

LEGENDS OF
DANIEL BOONE, THE
Oct., 1955–Jan., 1957
1	900.00
2	600.00
3 thru 8	500.00

LEGENDS OF
THE DARK KNIGHT
See: BATMAN

LEGENDS OF
THE DC UNIVERSE
Dec., 1997
1 JeR,VS,PNe,A:Superman, pt.1	3.50
2 JeR,VS,PNe,A:Superman, pt.2	4.00
3 JeR,VS,PNe,A:Superman, pt.3	2.50
4 BML,MD2,VRu,Moments, pt.1	2.50
5 BML,MD2,VRu,Moments, pt.2	2.50
6 DTy,KN,Robin meets Superman	2.50
7 DON,DG,Peacemakers, pt.1	2.50
8 DON,DG,Peacemakers, pt.2	2.50
9 DON,DG,Peacemakers, pt.3	2.50
10 TyD,KN,F:Batman & Batgirl,pt.1	2.50
11 KN,TyD,F:Batman & Batgirl,pt.2	2.50
12 CPr(s),Critical Mass,pt.1	2.50
13 CPr(s),Critical Mass,pt.2	2.50
14 JK,BR,SR,64-page	5.00
15 RCa,Dark Matters, pt.1	2.50
16 RCa,Dark Matters, pt.2	2.50
17 RCa,Dark Matters, pt.3	2.50
18 MWn(s),JG,F:New Teen Titans	2.50
19 RT,F:Impulse	2.50
20 StG(s),MZ,KJ,Trail of the Traitor, pt.1	2.50
21 StG(s),MZ,KJ,Trail of the Traitor, pt.2	2.50
22 Transilvane,pt.1.	2.50
23 Transilvane,pt.2.	2.50
24 StP,The Jump,pt.1.	2.50
25 StP,The Jump,pt.2.	2.50
26 TVE,JRu,Aquaman&Joker,pt.1	2.50
27 TVE,JRu,Aquaman&Joker,pt.2	2.50
28 GK,KJ,pt.1.	2.50
29 GK,KJ,pt.2,F:Traitor	2.50
30 CPr(s),Wonder Woman,pt.1	2.50
31 CPr(s),Wonder Woman,pt.2	2.50
32 CPr(s),Wonder Woman,pt.3	2.50
33 JMD,MZi,VcL,F:Spectre,pt.1	2.50
34 JMD,MZi,VcL,F:Spectre,pt.2	2.50
35 JMD,MZi,VcL,F:Spectre,pt.3	2.50
36 JMD,MZi,VcL,F:Spectre,pt.4	2.50
37 ScK,KJ,Traitor Trilogy,pt.1	2.50
38 ScK,KJ,V:Traitor,pt.2.	2.50
39 RGr,Sole Survivor of Earth	2.50
40 RGr,Lessons in Time,pt.1	2.50
41 RGr,Lessons in Time,pt.2	2.50
Giant #1 JKu(c), 80 pg.	5.00
Spec 3-D Gallery #1	3.00
GN Crisis on Infinite Earths	5.00

LEGENDS OF
THE LEGION
Dec., 1997
1 (of 4) BKi,TPe,TNu,O:Ultra Boy.	2.75
2 thru 4 BKi,TPe	@2.50

LEGENDS OF THE
WORLD FINEST
1994
1 WS(s),DIB,V:Silver Banshee, Blaze,Tullus,Foil(c)	6.00
2 WS(s),DIB,V:Silver Banshee, Blaze,Tullus,Foil(c)	6.00
3 WS(s),DIB,V:Silver Banshee, Blaze,Tullus,Foil(c)	6.00
TPB	15.00

L.E.G.I.O.N. '89-94
1989–94
1 BKi,V:Computer Tyrants	6.00
2 BKi,V:Computer Tyrants	3.50
3 BKi,V:Computer Tyrants, A:Lobo	3.50
4 BKi,V: Lobo	3.50

5 BKi,J:Lobo(in the rest of the series),V:Konis-Biz	3.50
6 BKi,V:Konis-Biz	3.50
7 BKi,Stealth vs. Dox	3.50
8 BKi,R:Dox	3.50
9 BKi,J:Phase (Phantom Girl).	3.00
10 BKi,Stealth vs Lobo	3.00
11 BKi,V:Mr.Stoorr	3.00
12 BKi,V:Emerald Eye	3.00
13 BKi,V:Emerald Eye	3.00
14 BKi,V:Pirates.	3.00
15 BKi,V:Emerald Eye	3.00
16 BKi,J:LarGand.	3.00
17 BKi,V:Dragon-Ro	3.00
18 BKi,V:Dragon-Ro	3.00
19 V:Lydea,L:Stealth	3.00
20 Aftermath.	3.00
21 D:Lyrissa Mallor,V:Mr.Starr	3.00
22 V:Mr.Starr	3.00
23 O:R.J.Brande(double sized)	3.50
24 BKi,V:Khunds	3.00
25 BKi,V:Khunds	3.00
26 BKi,V:Khunds	3.00
27 BKi,J:Lydea Mallor	3.00
28 KG,Birth of Stealth's Babies	3.00
29 BKi,J:Capt.Comet,Marij'n Bek	3.00
30 BKi,R:Stealth.	3.00
31 Lobo vs.Capt.Marvel.	4.00
32 V:Space Biker Gang	3.00
33 A:Ice-Man	3.00
34 MPn,V:Ice Man	3.00
35 Legion Disbanded.	3.00
36 Dox proposes to Ignea	3.00
37 V:Intergalactic Ninjas	3.00
38 BKi,Lobo V:Ice Man	3.00
39 BKi,D:G'odd,V:G'oddSquad	3.00
40 BKi,V:Kyaltic Space Station	3.00
41 BKi,A:Stealth'sBaby	3.00
42 BKi,V:Yeltsin-Beta	3.00
43 BKi,V:Yeltsin-Beta	3.00
44 V:Yeltsin-Beta,C:Gr.Lantern	3.00
45 BKi,New Perspectives	3.00
46 BKi,A:Hal Jordan	3.00
47 BKi,Lobo vs Hal Jordan	3.00
48 BKi,R:Ig'nea	3.00
49 BKi,V:Ig'nea	3.00
50 BKi,V:Ig'nea,A:Legion'67	4.00
51 F:Lobo,Telepath	3.00
52 BKi,V:Cyborg Skull of Darius	3.00
53 BKi,V:Shadow Creature	3.00
54 BKi,V:Shadow Creature	3.00
55 BKi,V:Shadow Beast.	3.00
56 BKi,A:Masked Avenger.	3.00
57 BKi,Trinity,V:Green Lantern	3.00

L.E.G.I.O.N. '92 #44
© DC Comics, Inc.

58 BKi,Trinity#6,A:Green Lantern,
     Darkstar 3.00
59 F:Phase 3.00
60 V:Phantom Riders 3.00
61 Little Party 3.00
62 A:R.E.C.R.U.I.T.S. 3.00
63 A:Superman 3.00
64 BKi(c),V:Mr.B 3.00
65 BKi(c),V:Brain Bandit 3.00
66 Stealth and Dox name child 3.00
67 F:Telepath 3.00
68 Our Porduct is Peace 3.00
69 F:Phase & Jo; Minutes to Go . . . 3.00
70 Zero Hour, last issue 3.50
Ann.#1 A:Superman, V:Brainiac . . 5.50
Ann.#2 Armageddon 2001 . . . . . . 3.50
Ann.#3 Eclipso tie-in 3.25
Ann.#4 SHa(i),I:Pax 3.75
Ann.#5 Elseworlds story 3.50

LEGION, THE
Oct., 2001
1 DAn,ALa, New era dawns 5.00
2 DAn,ALa,F:Oversight Watch 4.00
3 DAn,ALa,new headquarters 4.00
4 DAn,ALa,Footstep Drive Tech. . . 3.50
5 DAn,ALa,Return to Lost Galaxy . 3.00
6 DAn,ALa,Moon & Inhabitants . . . 3.00
7 DAn,ALa,V:Ra's Al Ghul 3.00
8 DAn,ALa,V:Ra's Al Ghul 3.00
9 DAn,ALa,Apparition,Ultra-Boy . . . 3.00
10 DAn,ALa,Robotica to Earth 3.00
11 DAn,ALa,F:Robotica 2.75
12 DAn,ALa,F:JLA 2.75
13 DAn,ALa,V:Robotica 2.75
14 DAn,ALa,V:Robotica 2.75
15 DAn,ALa,F:Timber Wolf 2.75
16 DAn,ALa,F:Lone Wolf 2.75
17 DAn,ALa,The Fittest,pt.1 . . . . . . 2.75
18 DAn,ALa,The Fittest,pt.2 . . . . . . 2.50
19 DAn,MFm,Dream Crime,pt.1 . . . 2.50
20 DAn,MFm,Dream Crime,pt.2 . . . 2.50
21 DAn,MFm,Dream Crime,pt.3 . . . 2.50
22 DAn,MFm,Dream Crime,pt.4 . . . 2.50
23 DAn,MFm,Dream Crime,pt.5 . . . 2.50
24 DAn,ALa,F:Umbra 2.50
25 Foundations,pt.1,48-pg. 4.00
26 DAn,ALa,Foundations,pt.2 . . . . . 2.50
27 DAn,ALa,Foundations,pt.3 . . . . . 2.50
28 DAn,ALa,Foundations,pt.4 . . . . . 2.50
29 DAn,ALa,Foundations,pt.5 . . . . . 2.50
30 DAn,ALa,Foundations,pt.6 . . . . . 2.50
31 KG,AM,deadly virus 2.50
32 DAn,ALa,V:Credo 2.50
33 DAn,ALa,F:Livewire 2.50
34 SLi,Wildfire,Qward 2.50
35 DJu,ASm,No Better Reason 2.50
36 DJu,ASm,No Better Reason 2.50
37 DJu,ASm,No Better Reason 2.50
38 DJu,ASm,No Better Reason 2.50
GN Legion Secret Files 3003 . . . . . 5.00
TPB The Legion: Foundations 20.00

LEGION LOST
March, 2000
1 (of 12) DAn,ALa 8.00
2 DAn,ALa,V:Progeny 4.00
3 DAn,ALa,V:Progeny 4.00
4 DAn,ALa, ... 4.00
5 DAn,ALa,Brainiac 5.1 . . . . 4.00
6 DAn,ALa,F:Umbra 3.00
7 DAn,ALa,F:Ultra Boy 3.00
8 DAn,ALa, ... 3.00
9 DAn,ALa 3.00
10 DAn,ALa 3.00
11 DAn,ALA 3.00
12 DAn,ALA conclusion 3.00

LEGIONNAIRES
1992
1 CSp,V:Mano and the Hand,Bagged
    w/SkyBox promo card 4.00
1a w/out card 3.00
2 CSp,V:Mano 3.00
3 CSp,I:2nd Emerald Empress 3.00
4 CSp,R:Fatal Five 3.00
5 CSp,V:Fatal Five 3.00
6 thru 17 . . . . @2.50
18 Zero Hour, LSH 3.00
19 thru 49 . . . . @2.50
450 RSt&TMw(s),JMy,The Bride of
    Mordru, 48pg, with poster 5.00
51 thru 81 . . . . @2.50
Ann.#1 Elseworlds Story 3.50
Ann.#2 Year One Story 3.50
Ann.#3 RSt&TMw(s) 4.00
Spec.#1,000,000 TPe(s),SeP, Justice
    Legion L 2.50

LEGIONNAIRES THREE
1986
1 EC,Saturn Girl,Cosmic Boy 4.00
2 EC,V:Time Trapper,pt.1 . . . . 3.00
3 EC,V:Time Trapper,pt.2 . . . . 3.00
4 EC,V:Time Trapper,pt.3 . . . . 3.00

LEGION OF SUBSTITUTE HEROES
1985
Spec.#1 KG 3.00

LEGION OF SUPER-HEROES
[Reprint Series], 1973
1 rep. Tommy Tomorrow 50.00
2 rep. Tommy Tomorrow 30.00
3 rep. Tommy Tomorrow 30.00
4 rep. Tommy Tomorrow 30.00

[1st Regular Series], 1980–84
Prev: SUPERBOY (& LEGION)
259 JSon,L:Superboy 20.00
260 RE,I:Circus of Death 10.00
261 RE,V:Circus of Death 10.00
262 JSh,V:Engineer 10.00
263 V:Dagon the Avenger 10.00
264 V:Dagon the Avenger 10.00
265 JSn,DG,Superman/Radio Shack
    insert 10.00
266 R:Bouncing Boy,Duo Damsel . 10.00

Legion of Super-Heroes #282
© DC Comics Inc.

267 SD,V:Kantuu 10.00
268 SD,BWi,V:Dr.Mayavale 10.00
269 V:Fatal Five 10.00
270 V:Fatal Five 10.00
271 V:Tharok (Dark Man) 6.00
272 CI,SD,O:J:Blok, I:New
    Dial 'H' for Hero 6.00
273 V:Stargrave 6.00
274 SD,V:Captain Frake 6.00
275 V:Captain Frake 6.00
276 SD,V:Mordru 6.00
277 A:Reflecto(Superboy) 6.00
278 A:Reflecto(Superboy) 6.00
279 A:Reflecto(Superboy) 6.00
280 R:Superboy 6.00
281 SD,V:Time Trapper 6.00
282 V:Time Trapper 6.00
283 O:Wildfire 6.00
284 PB,V:Organleggor 6.00
285 PB,KG(1st Legion)V:Khunds . . 8.00
286 PB,KG,V:Khunds 8.00
287 KG,V:Kharlak 8.00
288 KG,V:Kharlak 8.00
289 KG,Stranded 8.00
290 KG,B:Great Darkness Saga,
    J:Invisible Kid II 8.00
291 KG,V:Darkseid's Minions 6.00
292 KG,V:Darkseid's Minions 6.00
293 KG,Daxam destroyed 6.00
294 KG,E:Great Darkness Saga,
    V:Darkseid,A:Auron,Superboy . 8.00
295 KG,A:Green Lantern Corps . . . 3.50
296 KG,D:Cosmic Boys family 3.50
297 KG,O:Legion,A:Cosmic Boy . . 3.50
298 KG,EC,I:Amethyst 3.50
299 KG,R:Invisible Kid I 3.50
300 KG,CS, JSon,DC,KS,DG 6.00
301 KG,R:Chameleon Boy 3.50
302 KG,A:Chameleon Boy 3.50
303 KG,V:Fatal Five 3.50
304 KG,V:Fatal Five 3.50
305 KG,V:Micro Lad 3.50
306 KG,CS,RT,O:Star Boy 3.50
307 KG,GT,Omen 3.50
308 KG,V:Omen 3.50
309 KG,V:Omen 3.50
310 KG,V:Omen 3.50
311 KG,GC,New Headquarters 3.50
312 KG,V:Khunds 3.50
313 KG,V:Khunds 3.50
Ann.#1 IT,KG,I:Invisible Kid 4.00
Ann.#2 DGb,W:Karate Kid and
    Princess Projectra 3.00
Ann.#3 CS,RT,A:Darkseid 3.00
Ann.#4 reprint 3.00
Ann.#5 reprint 3.00
Becomes:

TALES OF LEGION OF SUPER HEROES

LEGION OF SUPER-HEROES
[3rd Regular Series], 1984–89
1 KG,V:Legion of Super-Villians . . . 5.00
2 KG,V:Legion of Super-Villians . . . 4.00
3 KG,V:Legion of Super-Villians . . . 4.00
4 KG,D:Karate Kid 4.00
5 KG,D:Nemesis Kid 4.00
6 JO,F:Lightning Lass 3.00
7 SLi,A:Controller 3.00
8 SLi,V:Controller 3.00
9 Sli,V:Sklarians 3.00
10 V:Khunds 3.00
11 EC,KG,L:Orig 3 members 3.00
12 SLi,EC,A:Superboy 3.00
13 SLi,V:Lythyls,F:TimberWolf 3.00
14 SLi,J:Sensor Girl (Princess
    Projectra),Quislet,Tellus,Polar
    Boy,Magnetic Kid 3.00
15 GLa,V:Dr. Regulus 3.00

Legion of Super-Heroes, 3rd Series #27
© DC Comics, Inc.

16 SLi,Crisis tie-in,F:Braniac5 . . . . . 3.00
17 GLa,O:Legion 3.00
18 GLa,Crisis tie-in,V:InfiniteMan . . 3.00
19 GLa,V:Controller 3.00
20 GLa,V:Tyr 3.00
21 GLa,V:Emerald Empress 4.00
22 GLa,V:Restorer,A:Universo 4.00
23 SLi,GLa,A:Superboy,
    Jonah Hex 4.00
24 GLa,NBi,A:Fatal Five 4.00
25 GLa,V:FatalFive 4.00
26 GLa,V:FatalFive,O:SensorGirl . . 3.00
27 GLa,GC,A:Mordru 3.00
28 GLa,L:StarBoy 3.00
29 GLa,V:Starfinger 3.00
30 GLa,A:Universo 3.00
31 GLa,A:Ferro Lad,Karate Kid 3.00
32 GLa,V:Universo,I:Atmos 3.00
33 GLa,V:Universo 3.00
34 GLa,V:Universo 3.00
35 GLa,V:Universo,R:Saturn Girl . . . 3.00
36 GLa,R:Cosmic Boy 3.00
37 GLa,V:Universo,I:Superboy
    (Earth Prime) 15.00
38 GLa,V:TimeTrapper,
    D:Superboy 14.00
39 CS,RT,O:Colossal Boy 3.00
40 GLa,I:New Starfinger 3.00
41 GLa,V:Starfinger 3.00
42 GLa,Millennium,V:Laurel Kent . . 3.00
43 GLa,Millennium,V:Laurel Kent . . 3.00
44 GLa,O:Quislet 3.00
45 GLa,CS,MGr,DC,30th Ann 4.00
46 GLa,Conspiracy 3.00
47 GLa,PB,V:Starfinger 3.00
48 GLa,Conspiracy,A:Starfinger 3.00
49 PB,Conspiracy,A:Starfinger 3.00
50 KG,V:Time Trapper,A:Infinite
    Man,E:Conspiracy 4.00
51 KG,V:Gorak,L:Brainiac5 . . . . 3.00
52 KG,V:Gil'Dishpan 3.00
53 KG,V:Gil'Dishpan 3.00
54 KG,V:Gorak 3.00
55 KG,EC,JL,EL,N:Legion 3.00
56 EB,V:Inquisitor 3.00
57 KG,V:Emerald Empress 3.00
58 KG,V:Emerald Empress 3.00
59 KG,MBr,F:Invisible Kid 3.00
60 KG,B:Magic Wars 3.00
61 KG,Magic Wars 3.00
62 KG,D:Magnetic Lad 3.00
63 KG,E:Magic Wars #4,final iss . . . 3.50
Ann.#1 KG,Murder Mystery 3.00

Ann.#2 KG,CS,O:Validus,
    A:Darkseid 3.50
Ann.#3 GLa,I:2nd Karate Kid 3.00
Ann.#4 BKi,V:Starfinger 3.00
Ann #5 I:2nd Legion Sub.Heroes . . 3.00

[4th Regular Series], 1989–97
1 KG,R:Cosmic Boy, Chameleon . . 5.00
2 KG,R:Ultra Boy,I:Kono 4.00
3 KG,D:Block,V:Roxxas 4.00
4 KG,V:Time Trapper 4.00
5 KG,V:Mordru,A:Glorith 4.00
6 KG,I:Laurel Gand 4.00
7 KG,V:Mordru 3.00
8 KG,O:Legion 3.00
9 KG,O:Laurel Gand 3.00
10 KG,V:Roxxas 3.00
11 KG,V:Roxxas 3.00
12 KG,I:Kent Shakespeare 3.00
13 KG,V:Dominators,posters 3.00
14 KG,J:Tenzil Kem 3.00
15 KG,Khund Invasion 3.00
16 KG,V:Khunds 3.00
17 KG,V:Khunds 3.00
18 KG,V:Khunds 3.00
19 KG,cont.from Adv.of Superman
    #478,A:Original Dr. Fate 3.00
20 KG,V:Dominators 3.00
21 KG,B:Quiet Darkness,
    A:Lobo,Darkseid 3.50
22 KG,A:Lobo,Darkseid 3.00
23 KG,A:Lobo,Darkseid 3.00
24 KG,E:Quiet Darkness,A:Lobo,
    Darkseid,C:Legionairres 4.00
25 DAb,I:Legionairres 3.00
26 JPn,B:Terra Mosaic,V:B.I.O.N. . . 2.50
27 JPn,V:B.I.O.N. 2.50
28 JPn,O:Sun Boy 2.50
29 JPn,I:Monica Sade 2.50
30 JPn,V:Dominators 2.50
31 CS,AG,F:Shvaughn as man 2.50
32 JPn,D:Karate Kid,Prin.Projectra,
    Chameleon Boy(Legionaires) . . 2.50
33 R:Kid Quantum 2.50
34 R:Sun Boy 2.50
35 JPN,V:Dominators 2.50
36 JPn,E:Terra Mosaic 2.50
37 JBr,R:Star Boy,Dream Girl 2.50
38 JPn,Earth is destroyed 5.00
39 SI,A:Legionnaires 2.50
40 SI,Legion meets Legionnaires . . 2.50
41 SI,F:The Legionnaires 2.50
42 SI,V:Glorith 2.50
43 SI,B:Mordru Arises 2.50
44 SI,R:Karate Kid 2.50
45 SI,R:Roxxas 2.50
46 SI,Battle with the Dead 2.50
47 SI,Last Rites 2.50
48 SI,E:Mordru Arises 2.50
49 F:Matter Eater Lad 2.50
50 W:Tenzil & Saturn Queen,
    R:Wildfire,V:B.I.O.N. 4.00
51 R:Kent,Celeste,Ivy,V:Grimbor . . . 2.50
52 F:Timber Wolf 2.50
53 SI,V:Glorith 2.50
54 SI,Foil,Die-Cut(c),
    N:L.E.G.I.O.N. 5.00
55 SI,On Rimbor 2.50
56 SI,R:Espionage Squad 2.50
57 SI,R:Khund Legionnaires 2.50
58 SI,D:Laurel Gand 2.50
59 SI,R:Valor,Dawnstar 2.50
60 SI,End of an Era#3 . . . . 2.50
61 SI,End of an Era#6 . . . . 2.50
62 I:New Team 2.50
63 Alien Attack 2.50
64 Sibling Rivalry 2.50
65 Breakout 2.50
66 I:New Team Members 2.50
67 F:Leviathan 2.50
68 F:Leviathan 2.50
69 V:Durlan 2.50
70 A:Andromeda, Brainiac 5 . . . . . . 2.50

Legion of Super-Heroes 4th Series #65
© DC Comics, Inc.

71 Planet Trom 2.50
72 Absent Friends 2.50
73 Sibling Rivalry,pt.1 . . . . 2.50
74 Future Tense,pt2 . . . . 2.50
75 Two Timer,pt.1 (of 2). 2.50
76 F:Valor & Triad 2.50
77 F:Brainiac 5 . . . . 2.50
78 The Gathering Doom 2.50
79 Fatal Five attacks 2.50
80 V:Fatal Five 2.50
81 R:Dirk Morgna 2.50
82 Lifestyles of the Dead 2.50
83 TPe&TMw(s),Big Tears 2.50
84 TPe&TMw(s),Emerald Legion. . . 2.50
85 TPe&TMw(s),LMd,A:Superman,
    back in 20th century 2.50
86 TPe&TMw(s),LMd,Final Night
    tie-in 2.50
87 TPe&TMw(s),LMd,F:Deadman . . 2.50
88 TPe&TMw(s),LMd,A:Impulse . . . 2.50
89 TPe&TMw(s),LMd, ... 2.50
90 TPe&TMw(s),LMd,V:Dr. Psycho . 2.50
91 TPe&TMw(s),LMd,Legion back
    together, but trapped in
    timestream 2.50
92 TPe&TMs(s),LMd,Displaced
    in Time 2.50
93 TPe&TMw(s),MC, All-tragedy
    issue 2.50
94 TPe&TMw(s),LMd,22 short
    pages about the Legion of
    Super-Heroes 2.50
95 MFm,F:Brainiac 5 . . . . 2.50
96 MFm,wedding 2.50
97 TPe,LMd,Genesis tie-in 2.50
98 TPe&TMC,LMd,C,O,M,P,U,T,O.
    the Conqueror, pt.1 . . . . 2.50
99 TPe&TMw,LMd,Computo, pt.2 . . 2.50
100 TPe&TMw,LMd,Computo, pt.3 . 7.50
101 TPe&TMw(s),AD&MFm(c),
    F:Sparks 2.50
102 TPe&TMw(s), ... 2.50
103 TPe&TMw,AD&MFm(c),Star
    Boy 2.50
104 TPe&TMw,AD&MFm(c),
    changes 2.50
105 TPe&TMw,AD&MFm(c),
    Adventures in Action x-over . . 2.50
106 TPe&TMw,AD&MFm(c),Dark
    Circle Rising, x-over pt.2 . . . . . . 2.50
107 TPe&TMw,AD&MFm(c),Dark
    Circle Rising, x-over pt.4 . . . . . . 2.50
108 TPe&TMw,AD&MFm(c),Dark
    Circle Rising, x-over pt.6 . . . . . . 2.50

109 DDv,AD,MFm,F:Violet. 2.50
110 TPe,V:Thunder 2.50
111 TPe&TMw(s),V:Daxamite 2.50
112 TPe&TMw(s),In Space 2.50
113 TPe&TMw(s),Kinetix 2.50
114 TPe&TMw(s),Bizarro
    Legion,pt.1. . . . . 2.50
115 TPe&TMw(s),Bizarro
    Legion, pt.2 . . . . 2.50
116 TPe&TMw(s),V:Pernisius,pt.1 . . 2.50
117 TPe&TMw(s),V:Pernisius,pt.2 . . 2.50
118 TPe&TMw(s),V:Pernisius,pt.3 . . 2.50
119 TPe&TMw(s),A:Valor & Phase . . 2.50
120 TPe,TMw,V:Fatal Four,pt.1 . . . . 2.50
121 TPe,TMw,V:Fatal Five,pt.2 . . . . 2.50
122 DAn,ALa,Legion of
    the Damned,pt.1 . . . . 2.50
123 DAn,ALa,Legion of
    the Damned,pt.3 . . . . 2.50
124 DAn,ALa,Legion of the Damned,
    aftermath 10.00
125 DAn,ALa,final issue 2.50
Ann.#1 O:Ultra Boy,V:Glorith 3.50
Ann.#2 O:Valor. 3.50
Ann.#3 N:Timberwolf 4.00
Ann.#4 I:Jamm. 3.50
Ann.#5 SI(c),CDo,MFm,TMc,
    Elseworlds Story 3.75
Ann.#6 Year One Annual + pin-ups 4.00
Ann.#7 TPe(s),MC,MFm,Legends
    of the Dead Earth 3.50
Spec.#1,000,000 TPe(s),KG,AG . . . 2.50
TPB Great Darkness Saga 18.00
TPB DarknessSaga,no poster 15.00
TPB Legion Archives, rep.#1-#3 . 40.00
TPB Legion Archives, rep.#4 . . . . . 50.00
TPB The Beginnings of Tomorrow. 18.00
GN Secret Files, inc.O:Legion 5.00
GN Secret Files #2 . . . . 5.00

LEGION OF
SUPER-HEROES
Dec., 2004

1 MWα(α),BKi,10-page 3.00
2 MWa(s),BKi,work with the law?. . 3.00
3 MWa(s),BKi,F:Triplicate Girl 3.00
4 MWa(s),DGb,F:Invisible Kid 3.00
5 MWa(s),BKi,ATi,Lightning Lad
    & Saturn Girl 3.00
6 MWa(s),BKi,ATi 3.00
7 MWa(s),BKi,ATi 3.00
8 MWa(s),BKi,ATi, team work 3.00
9 MWa(s),ATi,split widens. 3.00
10 MWa(s),BKi,ATi,V:Terror Firma. . 3.00
11 MWa(s),BKi,V:Terror Firma 3.00
12 MWa(s),BKi,Team in shambles. . 3.00
13 MWa(s),BKi,Fifth Dimension . . 3.00
14 MWa(s),BKi,I:Atom Girl. 3.00
15 MWa(s),BKi,31st century heroes 3.00
TPB Vol. 1 Teenage Revolution . . 15.00
TPB Vol. 2 Death of a Dream 15.00
Becomes:

SUPERGIRL
AND THE LEGION
OF SUPERHEROES
March, 2006

16 MWa,BKi. 3.00
17 MWa,BKi, newest member 3.00
18 MWa,BKi,Mysteries Unfold 3.00
19 MWa,BKi,F:Chameleon 3.00
20 MWa,BKi,Brainiac & Dream Girl. 3.00
21 MWa,BKi,Colossal Boy's home . 3.00
22 MWa,BKi,Supergirl's Boyfriend. . 3.00
23 MWa,BKi,Supergirl on Krypton. . 3.00
23a variant (c) 3.00
24 MWa,BKi,Super-powered Villains 3.00
TPB Strange Visitor from Another
    Century 15.00

LEGION:
SCIENCE POLICE
June, 1998

1 (of 4) DvM,PR,JRu,set in
    30th century. 2.50
2 DvM,PR,JRu,Jarik Shadder. . . . 2.50
3 DvM,PR,JRu, ... 2.50
4 DvM,PR,JRu 2.25

LEGION WORLDS
April, 2001

1 (of 6) DAn,ALa. 4.00
2 DAn,ALa 4.00
3 DAn,ALa, On Braal 4.00
4 DAn,ALa, heading for Xanthu . . 4.00
5 DAn,ALa, SDi, on Steele 4.00
6 DAn,ALa, concl 4.00

LEX LUTHOR:
MAN OF STEEL
March, 2005

1 (of 5) Superman, alien villain. . . . 3.00
2 . . . . 3.00
3 F:Batman. 3.00
4 and 5 . . . . @3.00
TPB Lex Luthor: Man of Steel 13.00

LIFE, THE UNIVERSE
AND EVERYTHING
1996

1 thru 3 Doug Adams adapt. . . . . @7.00

LIGHT BRIGADE, THE
Feb. 2004

1 thru 4 PSj . . . . @6.00
TPB The Light Brigade (2005). . . . 20.00

LIMITED COLLECTORS
EDITION
Summer, 1973

21 Shazam. 40.00
22 Tarzan. 35.00
23 House of Mystery 45.00
24 Rudolph, the Red-nosed
    Reindeer 125.00
25 NA,NA(c),Batman 60.00
27 Shazam. 35.00
29 Tarzan. 35.00
31 NA,O:Superman 35.00
32 Ghosts. 50.00
33 Rudolph. 100.00
34 X-Mas with Superheroes 35.00
35 Shazam. 30.00
36 The Bible. 30.00
37 Batman. 40.00
38 Superman 30.00
39 Secret Origins. 30.00
40 Dick Tracy. 30.00
41 ATh,Super Friends 30.00
42 Rudolph. 65.00
43 X-mas with Super-Heroes 30.00
44 NA,Batman 30.00
45 Secret Origins-Super Villians . . 30.00
46 ATh,JLA. 30.00
47 Superman 30.00
48 Superman-Flash Race 30.00
49 Superboy & Legion of
    Super-Heroes 30.00
50 Rudolph. 60.00
51 NA,NA(c),Batman 35.00
52 NA,NA(c),The Best of DC. 30.00
57 Welcome Back Kotter 30.00
59 NA,BWr,Batman,1978. . . . . 35.00

LITTLE SHOP
OF HORRORS
Feb., 1987

1 GC 2.50

LOBO
[1st Limited Series], 1990–91

1 SBs,Last Czarnian #1 . . . . 4.00
1a 2nd Printing 2.00

Lobo #4
© DC Comics Inc.

2 SBs,Last Czarnian #2 . . . . 3.00
3 SBs,Last Czarnian #3 . . . . 3.00
4 SBs,Last Czarnian #4 . . . . 3.00
Ann.#1 Bloodlines#1,I:Layla 3.75
Lobo Paramilitary X-Mas SBs 5.50
Lobo:Blazing Chain of Love,DCw . . 2.00
TPB Last Czarnian,rep.#1-#4 . . . . 10.00
TPB Lobo's Greatest Hits 13.00

[Regular Series], 1993–97

0 O:Lobo (1994, between #9&#10) 3.00
1 VS,Foil(c),V:Dead Boys. 3.25
2 VS,Quigly Affair 3.00
3 VS,Quigly Affair 2.75
4 VS,Quigly Affair 2.75
5 V:Bludhound 2.50
6 I:Bim Simms. 2.50
7 A:Losers. 2.50
8 A:Losers. 2.50
9 V:Lobo. 2.50
10 Preacher 2.50
11 Goldstar vs. Rev.Bo 2.50
12 AIG 2.50
13 AIG 2.50
14 Lobo, P.I.. . . . . 2.50
15 Lobo, P.I.,pt.2 . . . . 2.50
16 Lobo, P.I.,pt.3 . . . . 2.50
17 Lobo, P.I.,pt.4 . . . . 2.50
18 Lobo, P.I.,pt.5 . . . . 2.50
19 AIG 2.50
20 Toilot Fight 2.50
21 AIG,KON,R:Space Cabby 2.50
22 AIG,UnderworldUnleashed tie-in . 2.50
23 AIG,Stargaze Rally,pt.1 . . . . 2.50
24 AIG,Stargaze Rally,pt.2 . . . . 2.50
25 AIG 2.50
26 AIG,V:Erik the Khund 2.50
27 AIG,V:Billy Krono. 2.50
28 AIG,The Heiress,pt.1 . . . . 2.50
29 AIG,The Heiress,pt.2. . . . . 2.50
30 AIG,The Heiress,pt.3. . . . . 2.50
31 AIG,The Heiress,pt.4 . . . . 2.50

DC COMICS

32 AIG(s),Lobo attends a seance,
   frags himself 2.50
33 AIG(s),Lobo returns from spirit
   world 2.50
34 AIG(s),vs. Japan, whaling, ... 2.50
35 AIG(s), Deathtrek 2.50
36 AIG(s) 2.50
37 AIG(s),BKi,Lobo's Guide to Girls 2.50
38 AIG(s),Bomandi The Last Boy
   on Earth. 2.50
39 AIG(s),In the Belly of the
   Behemoth,pt. 1 . . . . 2.50
40 AIG(s),Belly of Behemoth,pt.2. . . 2.50
41 AIG(s),roommates. 2.50
42 AIG(s),A:Perfidia 2.50
43 AIG(s),A:Jonas 2.50
44 AIG(s),Genesis tie-in. 2.50
45 AIG(s),battle royale 2.50
46 AIG(s),Jackie Chin 2.50
47 AIG(s),V:Kiljoy Riggs. 2.50
48 AIG(s),F:the penguins 2.50
49 AIG(s) 2.50
50 AIG(s),war on DC universe 2.50
51 AIG(s),Slater and Candy. 2.50
52 AIG(s),Goldstar funeral 2.50
53 AIG(s),disrupted ceremony 2.50
54 AIG(s),Good Vibes machine . . . 2.50
55 AIG(s),Sheepworld 2.50
56 AIG(s),MPn,GLz,the wedding . . 2.50
57 AIG(s),MPn,GLz, Intergalactic
   Police convention 2.50
58 KG&AIG(s) 2.50
59 AIG(s),V:Bad Wee Bastards 2.50
60 AIG(s),All-New, Nonviolent
   Adventures of Superbo, pt.1 . . . 2.50
61 AIG(s),Superbo, pt.2 . . . . 2.50
62 AIG(s),Superbo, pt.3 . . . . 2.50
63 AIG(s),Soul Brothers,pt.1 . . . . . . 2.50
64 AIG(s),Soul Brothers,pt.2 . . . . . . 2.50
Ann.#1 Bloodlines 4.00
Ann.#2 Elseworlds Story 3.50
Ann.#3 AIG Year One. 5.00
Spec.#1,000,000 AIG(s),GLz 2.50
Spec. Lobo's Big Babe Spring Break,
   Miss Voluptuous Contest. 2.50
Spec. Blazing Chains of Love 2.00
Spec. Bounty Hunting for Fun
   and Profit, F:Fanboy 5.00
Spec. Lobo: Chained AIG(s),
   Lobo in prison 2.50
Spec. Lobo/Demon: Hellowe'en,
   AIG(s),VGi 2.25
Spec. Lobo In the Chair, AIG(s). . . . 2.25
Spec. Lobo:I Quit,AIG,
   nicotine withdrawal 2.25
Spec. Lobo/Judge Dredd: Psycho
   Bikers vs. Mutants From Hell . . 5.00
Spec. Lobo: Portrait of a Victim
   VS,I:John Doe 2.25
GN Fragtastic Voyage AGr,
   miniaturized 6.00
TPB Lobo's Back's Back 10.00
TPB Lobo's Greatest Hits 13.00
Convention Special, comic con 2.00

LOBO: A CONTRACT ON GAWD
1994
1 AIG(s),KD. 2.50
2 AIG(s),KD,A:Dave 2.50
3 AIG(s),KD. 2.50
4 AIG(s),KD,Final Issue 2.50

LOBO'S BACK
1992
1 SBs,w/3(c) inside,V:Loo. 2.50
1a 2nd printing 2.00
2 SBs,Lobo becomes a woman 2.50
3 SBs,V:Heaven 2.50
4 SBs,V:Heaven 2.50
TPB GF(c),rep.#1-#4 . . . . 10.00

LOBO: DEATH & TAXES
[Mini-Series], Aug., 1996
1 (of 4) KG&AIG(s) 2.25
2 KG&AIG(s),Interstellar Revenue
   learns Lobo doesn't pay taxes . 2.25
3 KG&AIG(s),Lobo walks into
   IRS trap 2.25
4 KG&AIG(s),Lobo destroys IRS . . 2.25

LOBO: INFANTICIDE
1992–93
1 KG,V:Su,Lobo Bastards 2.50
2 Lobo at Boot Camp 2.50
3 KG,Lobo Vs.his offspring 2.50
4 KG,V:Lobo Bastards. 2.50

LOBO/MASK
1 AIG&JAr(s),DoM,Kwi, humorous
   x-over. 6.00
2 AIG&JAr(s),DoM,Kwi, concl. 6.00

LOBO: UNAMERICAN GLADIATORS
1993
1 CK,V:Satan's Brothers 2.50
2 CK,V:Jonny Caesar 2.50
3 CK,MMi(c),V:Satan Brothers 2.50
4 CK,MMi(c),V:Jonny Caeser 2.50

LOBO UNBOUND
June 2003
1 (of 6) mass-murder 3.00
2 thru 6 . . . . @3.00

LOBOCOP
1 StG(s). 2.25

LOIS AND CLARK: THE NEW ADVENTURES OF SUPERMAN
TPB 10.00
TPB stories that became episodes 10.00

LOIS LANE
Aug., 1986
1 and 2 GM . . . . @3.00

LONG HOT SUMMER, THE
Milestone, 1995
1 Blood Syndicate v. G.R.I.N.D. . . . 3.00
2 A:Icon,Xombi,Hardware 2.50

Looney Tunes #33 © DC Comics, Inc.

LOONEY TUNES MAG.
1 thru 6 . . . . @2.00

LOONEY TUNES
1994
1 thru 6 Warner Bros. cartoons. . @3.00
7 thru 11 Warner Bros. . . . . @3.00
12 thru 25. . . . . @2.50
26 thru 144 . . . . @2.25
Spec. Back in Action: Movie 4.00
TPB Bugs Bunny: What's Up Doc . 7.00
TPB Daffy Duck: You're Despicable 7.00

Loose Cannon #1 © DC Comics, Inc.

LOOSE CANNON
[Mini-Series], 1995
1 AdP,V:Bounty Hunters 2.50
2 V:Bounty Hunters & Eradicator . . 2.25
3 A:Eradicator 2.25

LORDS OF THE ULTRAREALM
1986
1 PB 3.50
2 PB 2.25
3 thru 6 PB . . . . @2.25
Spec.#1 PB,DG,Oneshot 2.25

LOSERS
DC/Vertigo, June 2003
1 crime espionage 4.00
2 thru 6 Goliath,pt.1–pt.5 . . . . . . @3.50
7 SMa,Downtime,pt.1 . . . . 3.00
8 SMa,Downtime,pt.2 . . . . 3.00
9 Island Life,pt.1 . . . . 3.00
10 Island Life,pt.2 . . . . 3.00
11 Island Life,pt.3. . . . . 3.00
12 Island Life,pt.4 . . . . 3.00
13 Sheikdown,pt.1 . . . . 3.00
14 Sheikdown,pt.2 . . . . 3.00
15 F:Aisha 3.00
16 The Pass,pt.1 . . . . 3.00
17 The Pass,pt.2. . . . . 3.00
18 The Pass,pt.3. . . . . 3.00
19 The Pass, pt.4. . . . . 3.00
20 London Calling, pt.1 . . . . 3.00
21 London Calling, pt.2 . . . . 3.00
22 London Calling, pt.3 . . . . 3.00
23 Anti-Heist, pt.1 . . . . 3.00
24 Anti-Heist, pt.2 . . . . 3.00
25 Anti-Heist, pt.3 . . . . 3.00
26 CWi,Unamerica,pt.1 . . . . 3.00
27 CWi,Unamerica,pt.2 . . . . 3.00

28 CWi,Unamerica,pt.3 . . . . 3.00
29 Endgame, pt.1 . . . . 3.00
30 Endgame, pt.2 . . . . 3.00
31 Endgame, pt.3 . . . . 3.00
32 final issue 3.00
TPB Ante Up 10.00
TPB Double Down (2005) 13.00
TPB Trifecta (2005) 15.00
TPB Vol. 4 Close Quarters (2006). 15.00
TPB Vol. 5 Endgame (2006) 15.00

LOSERS SPECIAL
1985
1 Crisis,D:Losers 4.00

LOVELESS
DC/Vertigo, Oct. 2005
1 Western, A Kin of Homecoming. . 3.00
2 A Kin of Homecoming,pt.2 . . . . . 3.00
3 A Kin of Homecoming,pt.3 . . . . . 3.00
4 A Kin of Homecoming,pt.4 . . . . . 3.00
5 A Kin of Homecoming 3.00
6 A Peace of Iron 3.00
7 F.Ruth Cutter 3.00
8 Born bad? 3.00
9 Thicker Than Blackwater,pt.1 . . . 3.00
10 Thicker Than Blackwater,pt.2 . . . 3.00
11 Thicker Than Blackwater,pt.3 . . . 3.00
12 Thicker Than Blackwater,pt.4 . . . 3.00
13 F:Colonel Silas Redd 3.00
TPB Vol. 1 A Kin of Homecoming . 10.00

LUCIFER
DC/Vertigo, Apr., 2000
1 Lucifer strugles to regain power . 6.00
2 Living Tarot Deck 4.00
3 V:Jill Presto 4.00
4 WaP,F:Elaine Belloc 4.00
5 PrG,House of Windowless
    Rooms,pt.1 . . . . 3.00
6 PrG,Windowless Rooms,pt.2 . . . 3.00
7 PrG,Windowless Rooms,pt.3 . . . . 3.00
8 PrG,Windowless Rooms,pt.4 . . . 3.00
9 Immortality 3.00
10 Children & Monsters,pt.1 . . . . . . 3.00
11 Children & Monsters,pt.2 . . . . . . 2.50
12 Children & Monsters,pt.3 . . . . . . 2.50
13 Children & Monsters,pt.4 . . . . . . 2.50
14 Triptych 2.50
15 Triptych,Two Edge Sword 2.50
16 Triptych,Ancestral Deed 2.50
17 Dalliance with the Dead,pt.1 . . . 2.50
18 Dalliance with the Dead,pt.2 . . . 2.50
19 Dalliance with the Dead,pt.3 . . . 2.50
20 The Thunder Sermon 2.50
21 Paradiso,pt.1 . . . . 2.50
22 Paradiso,pt.2 . . . . 2.50
23 Paradiso,pt.3 . . . . 2.50
24 The Writing on the Wall 2.50
25 Purgatorio,pt.1 . . . . 2.50
26 Purgatorio,pt.2 . . . . 2.50
27 Purgatorio,pt.3 . . . . 2.50
28 F:Gaudium 2.50
29 MCy,Inferno,pt.1 . . . . 2.50
30 MCy,Inferno,pt.2 . . . . 2.50
31 MCy,Inferno,pt.3 . . . . 2.50
32 MCy,Inferno,pt.4 . . . . 2.50
33 MCy,robbery 2.50
34 MCy,Come to Judgment,pt.1 . . . 2.50
35 MCy,Come to Judgment,pt.2 . . . 2.50
36 MCy,Naglfar,pt.1 . . . . 2.50
37 MCy,Naglfar,pt.2 . . . . 2.50
38 MCy,Naglfar,pt.3 . . . . 2.50
39 MCy,Naglfar,pt.4 . . . . 2.50
40 MCy,Naglfar,pt.5 . . . . 2.50
41 MCy,Sisters of Mercy 2.50
42 MCy,Brothers in Arms,pt.1 . . . . 2.50
43 MCy,Brothers in Arms,pt.2 . . . . 2.50
44 MCy,Brothers in Arms,pt.3 . . . . 2.50
45 MCy(s)F:John Sewell 2.50
46 Stitchglass Slide,pt.1 . . . . 2.50

47 Stitchglass Slide,pt.2 . . . . 2.50
48 Stitchglass Slide,pt.3 . . . . 2.50
49 Stitchflass Slide,pt.4 . . . . 2.50
50 CR,48-pg. 3.50
51 Wolf Beneath the Tree,pt.1 . . . . 2.50
52 Wolf Beneath the Tree,pt.2 . . . . 2.50
53 Wolf Beneath the Tree,pt.3 . . . . 2.50
54 Wolf Beneath the Tree,pt.4 . . . . 2.50
55 MCy,MaH,new religion 2.50
56 PrG,Lilith, Elaine,pt.1 . . . . 2.50
57 PrG,Lilith, Elaine,pt.2 . . . . 2.50
58 Escape to new universe 2.50
59 Breach, pt.1 . . . . 2.50
60 Breach, pt.2 . . . . 2.50
61 Breach, pt.3 . . . . 2.50
62 MCy,CDo. 2.50
63 Moringstar,pt.1 . . . . 2.50
64 Moringstar,pt.2 . . . . 2.50
65 Moringstar,pt.3 . . . . 2.75
66 MK,Creation crumbles 2.75
67 Moringstar,pt.4 . . . . 2.75
68 Morningstar,pt.5 . . . . 2.75
69 Morningstar,pt.6 . . . . 2.75
70 MCy. 2.75
71 Evensong, pt.1 . . . . 2.75
72 Evensong, pt.2 . . . . 2.75
73 Someone expendable. 2.75
74 Elaine Belloc picks up Godhood. 3.00
75 finale, 48-pg. 4.00
TPB Devil in the Gateway 15.00
TPB Children and Monsters. 18.00
TPB A Dalliance with the Damned. 15.00
TPB The Divine Comedy 18.00
TPB Lucifer: Inferno 15.00
TPB Mansions of the Silence 15.00
TPB Exodus (2005) 15.00
TPB Vol. 8 The Wolf Beneath
    the Tree (2005) 15.00
TPB Vol. 9 Crux 15.00
TPB Vol. 10 Morningstar 15.00
GN Nirvana, 48-pg. 6.00

MADAME XANADU
1981
1 MR/BB 5.00

MADARA
2005
Vol. 1 thru 5 . . . . @10.00

MAJESTIC
Aug. 2004
1 (of 4) KIK,F:Mr.Majestic 3.00
2 KIK 3.00
3 KIK 3.00
4 KK,finale 3.00
TPB Strange New Visitor 15.00

MAJOR BUMMER
June, 1997
1 JAr(s),DoM,I:Major Bummer 2.50
2 thru 15 . . . . @2.50

MAN-BAT
1975–76
1 SD,AM,A:Batman. 40.00
2 V:The Ten-Eyed Man 30.00
Reprint NA(c) 20.00

MAN-BAT
1996
1 CDi,terrorizes city 2.25
2 thru 3 . . . . @2.25

MAN-BAT
April, 2006
1 (of 5) R:Man-Bat 2.50
2 Kirk Langstrom must flee 3.00
3 Only Man-Bat remains 3.00

4 Batman vs. Man-Bat 3.00
5 finale 3.00

MAN-BAT vs. BATMAN
1 NA,DG,reprint. 4.00

A MAN CALLED AX
Aug., 1997
1 MWn(s),SwM, part rep. 2.50
2 thru 8 MWn(s),SwM, ... @2.50

Manhunter #13
© DC Comics Inc.

MANHUNTER
1988–90
1 from Millennium-Suicide Squad. . 2.50
2 in Tokyo,A:Dumas 2.25
3 The Yakuza,V:Dumas 2.25
4 Secrets Revealed-Manhunter,
    Dumas & Olivia 2.25
5 A:Silvia Kandery. 2.25
6 A:Argent,contd.Suicide Squad
    Annual #1 . . . . 2.25
7 Vlatavia, V:Count Vertigo. 2.25
8 FS,A:Flash,Invasion x-over 2.25
9 FS,Invasion Aftermath extra
    (contd from Flash #22) 2.25
10 Finders Keepers 2.25
11 Losers Weepers 2.25
12 Losers Weepers 2.25
13 V:Catman 2.25
14 Janus Directive #5 . . . . 2.25
15 I:Mirage. 2.25
16 V:Outlaw 2.25
17 In Gotham,A:Batman 2.25
18 Saints & Sinners,pt.1,R:Dumas . 2.25
19 Saints & Sinners,pt.2,V:Dumas. . 2.25
20 Saints & Sinners,pt.3,V:Dumas. . 2.25
21 Saints & Sinners,pt.4,
    A:Manhunter Grandmaster 2.25
22 Saints & Sinners,pt.5,
    A:Manhunter Grandmaster 2.25
23 Saints & Sinners,pt.6,V:Dumas. . 2.25
24 DG,Showdown, final issue 2.25
[2nd Series], 1994–95
0 Here Comes the Night. 2.50
1 True Fiction 2.50
2 N:Wild Huntsman 2.50
3 V:Malig. 2.50
4 Necrodyne 2.50
5 V:Skin Walker 2.50
6 V:Barbarian,Incarnate 2.50
7 V:Incarnate,A:White Lotus
    & Capt. Atom 2.25

8 V:Butcher Boys	2.25
9 V:Butcher Boys	2.25
10 V:Necrodyne	2.25
11 Return of Old Enemy	2.25
12 Underworld Unleashed, finale. .	2.25

[3rd Series],Aug. 2004

1 JP,JLe(c),Identity Crisis	3.00
2 thru 3 JP,JLe(c)	@4.00
4 JP.	4.00
5 JP,A:JLA	6.00
6 JP,Supervillain Trial	3.00
7 JP,Supervillain Trial	3.00
8 JP,V:Shadow Thief.	3.00
9 JP,V:Phobia	3.00
10 Manhunted	3.00
11 JP,Two ex-manhunters	3.00
12 Masks Upon Masks	3.00
13 Kate Spencer & Cameron Chase	3.00
14 Secret of Project Manhunter. .	3.00
15 Suit's secret history.	3.00
16 Manhunted aftermath	2.50
17 About to be Unmasked	2.50
18 An Old Foe	2.50
19 V:Her father.	2.50
20 Psychobabble	2.50
21 JSA family connection.	2.50
22 Trial of Dr. Psycho	3.00
23 New villain.	3.00
24 V:Dr. Psycho	3.00
25 F:Kate Spencer, final issue. . . .	3.00
TPB Vol. 1 Street Justice	13.00

MAN OF STEEL
1986

1 JBy,DG,I:Modern Superman	7.00
1a 2nd edition	7.00
2 JBy,DG,R:Lois Lane.	5.00
3 JBy,DG,A:Batman	5.00
4 JBy,DG,V:Lex Luther	5.00
5 JBy,DG,I:Modern Bizarro	5.00
6 JBy,DG,A:Lana Lang	5.00
TPB rep. Man of Steel #1–#6	20.00
TPBa 2nd printing	8.00

MANY LOVES OF
DOBIE GILLIS
May-June, 1960

1 From TV show	500.00
2	250.00
3	150.00
4	150.00
5 thru 9	@125.00
10 thru 25	@125.00
26 Oct., 1964	125.00

MARTIAN MANHUNTER
1988

1 A:JLI.	3.00
2 A:JLI,V:Death God	2.50
3 V:Death God,A:Dr.Erdel.	2.50
4 A:JLI,final issue	2.50

[Mini-Series]

1 EB,American Secrets #1	5.25
2 EB,American Secrets #2	5.25
3 EB,American Secrets #3	5.25

MARTIAN MANHUNTER
Aug., 1998

0 JOs,TMd,A:Batman,Superman .	3.00
1 JOs,TMd,V:Headman	2.50
2 JOs,TMd,V:Antares	2.50
3 JOs,TMd,V:Bette Noir	2.50
4 JOs,TMd,J'emm, Son of Saturn	2.50
5 JAr,JD,A:Chase	2.50
6 JOs,TMd,A:JLA,pt.1.	2.50
7 JOs(s),TMd,A:JLA,pt.2	2.50
8 JOs(s),TMd,A:JLA,pt.3	2.50
9 JOs(s),TMd,A:JLA,pt.4	2.50
10 JOs(s),A:Fire.	2.50

11 JOs,PNe,BHi,	2.50
12 JOs,TMd,Day of Judgment x-over.	2.50
13 JOs,TMd,Rings of Saturn,pt.1 .	2.50
14 JOs,TMd,Rings of Saturn,pt.2 .	2.50
15 JOs,TMd,Rings of Saturn,pt.3 .	2.50
16 JOs,TMd,Rings of Saturn,pt.4 .	2.50
17 JOs,TMd,Rings of Saturn,pt.5 .	2.50
18 JOs,TMd,V:Kanto	2.50
19 JOs,TMd,defeated, captured . .	2.50
20 JOs,TMd,year one on earth . . .	2.50
21 JOs,TT,A:Abin Sur	2.50
22 JOs,TMd,A:Batman.	2.50
23 JOs,TMd,F:Spectre.	2.50
24 JOs,TMd,F:Just.Leag.Int.	2.50
25 JOs,TMd,F:Gypsy.	2.50
26 JOs,TMd,Renegades of Mars. .	2.50
27 JOs,TMd,Renegades of Mars. .	2.50
28 JOs,TMd,at Stonehenge.	2.50
29 JOs,TMd,telepath	2.50
30 JOs,TMd,Altered Egos,pt.1.	2.50
31 JOs,TMd,Altered Egos,pt.2.	2.50
32 TMd,V:Bloodworms of Mars . .	2.50
33 TMd,J'onn J'onzz hidden life . .	2.50
34 JOs,V:Darkseid.	2.50
35 JOs,V:Malefic	2.50
36 JOs,final issue	2.50
Ann.#1 TT,AOI,BWr,Ghosts x-over .	3.00
Ann.#2 AAd(c),JLApe:Gorilla Warfare	3.00
Spec.#1,000,000 JOs,TMd	2.00

MARTIAN MANHUNTER
Aug., 2006

1 Martian Manhunter's past	3.00
2 Martian artifact.	3.00
3 Truth behind the Lies	3.00
4 Under attack	3.00

Mask #6
© DC Comics, Inc.

MASK
Dec., 1985

1 HC(c),TV tie-in,I:Mask Team . . .	2.50
2 HC(c),In Egypt,V:Venom	2.50
3 HC(c),Anarchy in the U.K.	2.50
4 HC(c),V:Venom, final issue, March, 1986	2.50

[2nd Series], Feb.–Oct., 1987

1 CS/KS,reg.series	2.50
2 CS/KS,V:Venom.	2.50
3 CS/KS,V:Venom.	2.50
4 CS/KS,V:Venom.	2.50
5 CS/KS,Mask operatives hostage.	2.50

6 CS/KS,I:Jacana	2.50
7 CS/KS,Mask gone bad?	2.50
8 CS/KS,Matt Trakker,V:Venom . .	2.50
9 CS/KS,V:Venom, last issue	2.50

MASTERS OF
THE UNIVERSE
May, 1986

1 GT,AA,O:He-Man.	6.00
2 GT,AA,V:Skeletor.	5.00
3 GT,V:Skeletor.	5.00

'MAZING MAN
Jan., 1986

1 I:Maze	3.00
2 Easy Money.	2.50
3 Doing What Married People Do. .	2.50
4 The Male Machine.	2.50
5 Writer's Block.	2.50
6 Shea Stadium	2.50
7 Shea Stadium	2.50
8 Cat-Sitting	2.50
9 Bank Hold-up.	2.50
10 Big Brother's Watching .	2.50
11 Jones Beach	2.50
12 FM(c),last issue, Dec., 1986. .	3.00
Spec.#1	2.25
Spec.#2	2.25
Spec.#3 KB/TM	2.25

MEN OF WAR
Aug., 1977

1 I:Gravedigger,Code Name: Gravedigger,I:Enemy Ace	40.00
2 JKu(c),The Five-Walled War . . .	20.00
3 JKu(c),The Suicide Strategem. .	20.00
4 JKu(c),Trail by Fire	20.00
5 JKu(c),Valley of the Shadow . . .	20.00
6 JKu(c),A Choice of Deaths	20.00
7 JKu(c),Milkrun .	20.00
8 JKu(c),Death-Stroke .	20.00
9 JKu(c),Gravedigger-R.I.P.	20.00
10 JKu(c),Crossroads	20.00
11 JKu(c),Berkstaten	15.00
12 JKu(c),Where Is Gravedigger?.	15.00
13 JKu(c),Project Gravedigger - Plus One	15.00
14 JKu(c),The Swirling Sands of Death	15.00
15 JKu(c),The Man With the Opened Eye	15.00
16 JKu(c),Hide and Seek The Spy	15.00
17 JKu(c),The River of Death	15.00
18 JKu(c),The Amiens Assault. . . .	15.00
19 JKu(c),An Angel Named Marie .	15.00
20 JKu(c),Cry:Jerico	15.00
21 JKu(c),Home-Is Where The Hell Is	15.00
22 JKu(c),Blackout On The Boardwalk	15.00
23 JKu(c),Mission: Six Feet Under	15.00
24 JKu&DG(c),The Presidential Peril	15.00
25 GE(c),Save the President.	15.00
26 March, 1980	15.00

METAL MEN
1965–78

[1st Regular Series]

1 RA,I:Missile Men.	1,000.00
2 RA,Robot of Terror.	400.00
3 RA,Moon's Invisible Army	250.00
4 RA,Bracelet of Doomed Hero .	250.00
5 RA,Menace of the Mammoth Robots	250.00
6 RA,I:Gas Gang	175.00
7 RA,V:Solar Brain	150.00
8 RA,Playground of Terror	150.00
9 RA,A:Billy.	150.00

Metal Men #15
© DC Comics, Inc.

10 RA,A:Gas Gang 150.00
11 RA,The Floating Furies 150.00
12 RA,A:Missle Men 125.00
13 RA,I:Nameless 125.00
14 RA,A:Chemo 125.00
15 RA,V:B.O.L.T.S. 125.00
16 RA,Robots for Sale 125.00
17 JKu(c),RA,V:Bl.Widow Robot . 125.00
18 JKu(c),RA 125.00
19 RA,V:Man-Horse of Hades . . . 125.00
20 RA,V:Dr.Yes 125.00
21 RA,C:Batman & Robin,Flash
    Wonder Woman. 100.00
22 RA,A:Chemo 100.00
23 RA,A:Sizzler 100.00
24 RA,V:Balloonman 100.00
25 RA,V:Chemo 100.00
26 RA,V:Metal Mods 100.00
27 RA,O:Metal Men,rtd 125.00
28 RA,You Can't Trust a Robot . . 100.00
29 RA,V:Robot Eater 100.00
30 RA,GK,in the Forbidden Zone 100.00
31 RA,GK,School for Robots 75.00
32 RA,Robot Amazon Blues 75.00
33 MS,The Hunted Metal Men. . . . 75.00
34 MS,Death Comes Calling 75.00
35 MS,Danger–Doom Dummies . . 75.00
36 MS,The Cruel Clowns. 75.00
37 MS,To walk among Men 75.00
38 MS,Witch Hunt–1979 . . . . 75.00
39 MS,Beauty of the Beast 75.00
40 MS,Destroy Doc Magnus 75.00
41 MS,Requiem for a Robot(1970) 75.00

1973–78
42 RA,reprint 25.00
43 RA,reprint 25.00
44 RA,reprint,V:Missile Men 25.00
45 WS 25.00
46 WS,V:Chemo 25.00
47 WS,V:Plutonium Man 25.00
48 WS,A:Eclipso 30.00
49 WS,A:Eclipso 30.00
50 WS,JSa. 20.00
51 JSn,V:Vox 20.00
52 JSn,V:Brain Children. 20.00
53 JA(c),V:Brain Children 20.00
54 JSn,A:Green Lantern 20.00
55 JSn,A:Green Lantern 20.00
56 JSn,V:Inheritor 20.00

[Limited Series], 1993–94
1 DJu,BBr,Foil(c). 5.00
2 DJu,BBr,O:Metal Men 3.00
3 DJu,BBr,V:Missile Men 3.00
4 DJu,BBr,final issue. 3.00

METAMORPHO
July-Aug., 1965
[Regular Series]
1 A:Kurt Vornok. 400.00
2 Terror from the Telstar 200.00
3 Who stole the USA 200.00
4 V:Cha-Cha Chaves 150.00
5 V:Bulark 150.00
6 JO,SMo . . . . '. . 150.00
7 thru 9 . . . . @100.00
10 I:Element Girl 140.00
11 thru 17 March-April, 1968 . . . @90.00

[Mini-Series], 1993
1 GN,V:The Orb of Ra 2.50
2 GN,A:Metamorpho's Son. 2.50
3 GN,V:Elemental Man. 2.50
4 GN,final Issue 2.50

METROPOLIS S.C.U.
Nov., 1994
1 Special Police unit 2.25
2 Eco-terror in Metropolis. 2.25
3 Superman 2.25
4 final issue. 2.25

MICHAEL MOORCOCK'S
MULTIVERSE
DC/Helix, Sept., 1997
1 WS,three stories, inc. Eternal
    Champion adapt. 2.50
2 WS,Existential Price of Fish . . . 2.50
3 WS,Being and Nothingness. . . . 2.50
4 WS,Loser Wins 2.50
5 WS,Longitude of Meaning 2.50
6 WS,Duke Elric 2.50
7 WS,Metatemporal Detective . . . 2.50
8 WS,Castle Silverskin 2.50
9 WS,Duke Elric 2.50
10 WS,Eternal Champion 2.50
11 WS,Silverskin 2.50
12 WS,Harmonies of Chaos 2.50
TPB rep. #1–#12 . . . . 20.00

MIDNIGHT, MASS
DC/Vertigo, April, 2002
1 JRz,F:Adam & Julia 2.50
2 JRz,a lone farmhouse 2.50
3 JRz,JP 2.50
4 JRz,JP,The Four Sisters,pt.1 . . . 2.50
5 JRz,JP,The Four Sisters,pt.2. . . . 2.50
6 JRz,JP,The Four Sisters,pt.3 . . . . 2.50
7 JRz,JP,3 uninvited visitors 2.50
8 JRz,Secrets 2.50

MIDNIGHT, MASS:
HERE THERE BE
MONSTERS
DC/Vertigo, Jan. 2004
1 (of 6) 3.00
2 thru 6 . . . . @3.00

MILLENNIUM
Jan., 1988
1 JSa,SEt, The Plan 3.00
2 JSa,SEt, The Chosen 2.50
3 JSa,SEt, Reagen/Manhunters . . . 2.50
4 JSa,SEt, Mark Shaw/Batman . . . 2.50
5 JSa,SEt, The Chosen 2.50
6 JSa,SEt, Superman. 2.50
7 JSa,SEt, Boster Gold. 2.50
8 JSa,SEt,I:New Guardians 2.50

MILLENNIUM FEVER
1995–96
1 Young Love 2.50
2 Nightmares Worsen. 2.50

Millennium #4
© DC Comics Inc.

3 Worst Nightmare 2.50
4 . . . . 2.50

MINX, THE
DC/Vertigo, Aug., 1998
1 PrM,SeP,The Chosen, pt.1 . . . . . 3.00
2 PrM,SeP,The Chosen, pt.2 . . . . . 2.50
3 PrM,SeP,The Chosen, pt.3 . . . . . 2.50
4 PrM,SeP,Monkey Quartet,pt.1 . . . 2.50
5 PrM,SeP,Monkey Quartet,pt.2 . . . 2.50
6 PrM,SeP,Monkey Quartet,pt.3 . . . 2.50
7 PrM,SeP,Monkey Quartet,pt.4 . . . 2.50
8 PrM,SeP,final issue 2.50

MISS BEVERLY HILLS
OF HOLLYWOOD
1949–50
1 Alan Ladd. 900.00
2 William Holden. 600.00
3 . . . . 500.00
4 Betty Hutton. 500.00
5 Bob Hope. 500.00
6 Lucile Ball 425.00
7 . . . . 425.00
8 Ronald Reagan 550.00
9 Wendell Corey 425.00

MISS MELODY LANE
OF BROADWAY
1950
1 . . . . 900.00
2 Sid Caesar. 500.00
3 Ed Sullivan. 500.00

MISTER E
1991
1 (From Books of Magic) 2.50
2 A:The Shadower 2.50
3 A:The Shadower 2.50
4 A:Tim Hunter, Dr. Fate, Phantom
    Stranger, final issue. 2.50

MISTER MIRACLE
1971–78
1 JK,I:Mr.Miracle 150.00
2 JK,I:Granny Goodness 75.00
3 JK,Paraniod Pill 75.00
4 JK,I:Barda, 52-page. 80.00
5 JK,I:Vermin Vundabar, 52-page. 80.00
6 JK,I:Female Furies, 52-page . . . 80.00
7 JK,V:Kanto, 52-page 80.00

8 JK,V:Lump, 52-page 80.00	
9 JK,O:Mr.Miracle,C:Darkseid . . . 30.00	
10 JK,A:Female Furies 30.00	
11 JK,V:Doctor Bedlum 30.00	
12 JK,Mystivac. 30.00	
13 JK,The Dictator's Dungeon. . . . 30.00	
14 JK,I:Madame Evil Eye. 30.00	
15 JK,O:Shilo Norman 30.00	
16 JK,F:Shilo Norman 30.00	
17 JK,Murder Lodge 30.00	
18 JK,W:Mr.Miracle & Barda 30.00	
19 MR,NA,DG,TA,JRu,AM 30.00	
20 MR,Eclipse 15.00	
21 MR,Command Performance. . . 15.00	
22 MR, Midnight of the Gods. . . . 15.00	
23 MG, As Ethos is my Judge . . . 15.00	
24 MG,RH,Double-Bind 15.00	
25 MG,RH,Doom Unto Others. . . . 15.00	
Spec.#1 SR (1987) 3.50	

[2nd Series], 1989–91

1 IG,O:Mister Miracle 3.00
2 IG. 2.50
3 IG,A:Highfather,Forever People . . 2.50
4 IG,A:The Dark,Forever People . . 2.50
5 IG,V:TheDark,A:Forever People . 2.50
6 A:G.L. Gnort. 2.50
7 A:Blue Beetle,Booster Gold. 2.50
8 RM,A:Blue Beetle,Booster Gold . 2.50
9 I:Maxi-Man 2.50
10 V:Maxi-Man. 2.50
11 What? And Give up Show Biz?. . 2.50
12 Head of the Clash. 2.50
13 Manga Khan Saga begins,
　A:L-Ron,A:Lobo. 3.00
14 A:Lobo. 2.50
15 Manga Khan cont.. . . . . 2.50
16 MangaKhan cont.,JLA#39tie-in. . 2.50
17 On Apokolips,A:Darkseid 2.50
18 On Apokolips. 2.50
19 Return to Earth, contd
　from JLA#42 . . . . 2.50
20 IG,Oberon. 2.50
21 Return of Shilo 2.50
22 New Mr.Miracle revealed 2.50
23 Secrets of the 2 Mr. Miracles
　revealed, A:Mother Box. 2.50
24 Nightmare 2.50
25 Big Barda and Friends 2.50
26 Monster Party,pt.1. . . . . 2.50
27 Monster Party,pt.2,
　A:Justice League. 2.50
28 final issue 2.50

[3rd Series], 1996

1 JK, new mythology 2.25
2 V:Justice League. 2.25
2 How can Scott Free save
　Big Barda. 2.25
3 accepts his powers 2.25
4 corruption throughout
　the cosmos 2.25
5 SCr. 2.25
6 SCr. 2.25
7 SCr,final issue 2.25
TPB Jack Kirby's Mister Miracle . . 13.00

MR. DISTRICT ATTORNEY
Jan.–Feb., 1948

1 The Innocent Forger. 1,500.00
2 The Richest Man In Prison . . . 700.00
3 The Honest Convicts 500.00
4 The Merchant of Death 500.00
5 The Booby-Trap Killer 500.00
6 The D.A. Meets Scotland Yard 350.00
7 The People vs. Killer Kane . . . 350.00
8 The Rise and Fall of 'Lucky'
　Lynn. 350.00
9 The Case of the Living
　Counterfeit. 350.00
10 The D.A. Takes a Vacation . . . 250.00

11 The Game That Has
　No Winners 250.00
12 Fake Accident Racket. 250.00
13 The Execution of Caesar
　Larsen 250.00
14 The Innocent Man In
　Murderers' Row 250.00
15 Prison Train. 250.00
16 The Wire Tap Crimes 250.00
17 The Bachelor of Crime 250.00
18 The Case of the Twelve
　O'Clock Killer. 250.00
19 The Four King's Of Crime. . . . 250.00
20 You Catch a Killer. 250.00
21 I Was A Killer's Bodyguard . . 175.00
22 The Marksman of Crime 175.00
23 Diary of a Criminal 175.00
24 The Killer In The Iron Mask . . 175.00
25 I Hired My Killer 175.00
26 The Case of the Wanted
　Criminals 175.00
27 The Case of the Secret Six . . 175.00
28 Beware the Bogus Beggars . . 175.00
29 The Crimes of Mr. Jumbo 175.00
30 Man of a Thousand Faces . . . 175.00
31 The Hot Money Gang 175.00
32 The Case o/t Bad Luck Clues. 175.00
33 A Crime Is Born. 175.00
34 The Amazing Crimes of Mr. X. 175.00
35 This Crime For Hire 175.00
36 The Chameleon of Crime 175.00
37 Miss Miller's Big Case 175.00
38 The Puzzle Shop For Crime . . 175.00
39 Man Who Killed Daredevils . . 175.00
40 The Human Vultures. 175.00
41 The Great Token Take 175.00
42 Super-Market Sleuth. 175.00
43 Hotel Detective 175.00
44 S.S. Justice,B:Comics Code. . 150.00
45 Miss Miller, Widow 150.00
46 Mr. District Attorney,
　Public Defender. 150.00
47 The Missing Persons Racket . 150.00
48 Manhunt With the Mounties . . 150.00
49 The TV Dragnet 150.00
50 The Case of Frank Bragan,
　Little Shot 150.00
51 The Big Heist 150.00
52 Crooked Wheels of Fortune . . 150.00
53 The Courtroom Patrol 150.00
54 The Underworld Spy Squad . . 150.00
55 The Flying Saucer Mystery. . . 150.00
56 The Underworld Oracle. 150.00
57 The Underworld Employment
　Agency. 150.00
58 The Great Bomb Scare. 150.00

Mr. District Attorney #13
© DC Comics, Inc.

59 Great Underworld Spy Plot. . . 150.00
60 The D.A.'s TV Rival 150.00
61 SMo(c),Architect of Crime. . . . 150.00
62 A-Bombs For Sale. 150.00
63 The Flying Prison 150.00
64 SMo(c),The Underworld
　Treasure Hunt 150.00
65 SMo(c),World Wide Dragnet. . 150.00
66 SMo(c),The Secret of the
　D.A.'s Diary 150.00
67 Jan.–Feb., 1959 . . . . 150.00

MNEMOVORE
DC/Vertigo, Apr., 2005
1 (of 6) 3.00
2 thru 5 . . . . @3.00

MOBFIRE
1994–95
1 WaP,Gangsters in London. 2.50
2 WaP,. 2.50
3 WaP,The Bocor 2.50
4 WaP,V:Bocor 2.50
5 WaP,Voice in My Head 2.50
6 WaP,Genetic Babies, final issue . 2.50

MODESTY BLAISE
1 DG,V:Gabriel 5.00
2 DG,V:Gabriel 5.00
GN Spy Thriller 20.00

MONOLITH, THE
Feb. 2004
1 JP(s),56-pg. 3.50
2 JP(s) 3.00
3 JP(s),Heart of Stone 3.00
4 JP(s),Last Rites,pt.1 . . . . 3.00
5 JP(s),Last Rites,pt.2 . . . . 3.00
6 JP(s),Friendly Fire,pt.1 . . . . 3.00
7 JP(s),Friendly Fire,pt.2 . . . . 3.00
8 JP(s),Friendly Fire,pt.3 . . . . 3.00
9 JP(s),gangsters retaliate 3.00
10 JP(s) 3.00
11 JP(s),Slavers. 3.00
12 JP(s),finale 3.00

MOONSHADOW
DC/Vertigo, 1994–95
1 JMD(s),JMu,rep. 2.50
2 thru 4 JMD . . . . @2.50
5 fully painted 2.50
6 . . . . 2.50
7 F:Shady Lady. 2.50
8 Rep. Search for Ira 2.50
9 JMD,JMu,A:Tittletat Twins 2.50
10 JMD,JMu,Interplanetary
　Prostitutes 2.50
11 JMu,Ira's life story. 2.50
12 Rep. w/6pg new material 3.50

MORE FUN COMICS
See: NEW FUN COMICS

MOVIE COMICS
1939
1 Gunga Din. 5,500.00
2 Stagecoach. 3,500.00
3 East Side of Heaven. 2,500.00
4 Captain Fury,B:Oregon Trail . 2,000.00
5 Man in the Iron Mask 2,200.00
6 Phantom Creeps. 3,000.00

MS. TREE QUARTERLY
1990
1 MGr,A:Batman. 5.00
2 A:Butcher. 4.00
3 A:Butcher. 4.00
4 Paper Midnight. 4.50
5 Murder/Rape Investigation. 4.50

Ms. Tree Quarterly #2
© *DC Comics, Inc.*

6 Gothic House 4.50
7 The Family Way 4.50
8 CI,FMc,Ms Tree Pregnant(c),
   B.U. King Faraday 4.50
9 Child Kidnapped 4.50
10 V:International Mob 4.00

MUCHA LUCHA
April 2003
1 (of 3) 2.25
2 It's All Buena 2.25
3 Flea loses match 2.25

MUKTUK WOLFSBREATH:
HARD-BOILED SHAMAN
DC/Vertigo, June, 1998
1 (of 3) TLa,SvP,Lady Shaman 2.50
2 . . . . 2.50
3 TLa,SvP, concl. 2.50

MUTT AND JEFF
1939
1 . . . . 2,000.00
2 . . . . 1,000.00
3 Bucking Broncos 700.00
4 and 5 . . . . @600.00
6 thru 10 . . . . @350.00
11 thru 20 . . . . @250.00
21 thru 30 . . . . @225.00
31 thru 50 . . . . @200.00
51 thru 70 . . . . @150.00
71 thru 80 . . . . @125.00
81 thru 99 . . . . @100.00
100 . . . . 125.00
101 thru 103 . . . . @100.00
104 thru 148 . . . . @100.00

MY FAITH IN FRANKIE
DC/Vertigo, Jan. 2004
1 (of 4) MaH 3.00
2 thru 4 MaH . . . . @3.00
TPB 7.00

MY GREATEST
ADVENTURE
Jan.–Feb., 1955
1 LSt,I Was King Of
   Danger Island 2,500.00
2 My Million Dollar Dive 1,400.00
3 I Found Captain
   Kidd's Treasure 1,100.00

4 I Had A Date With Doom . . . 1,100.00
5 I Escaped From Castle Morte 1,000.00
6 I Had To Spend A Million. . . . 1,000.00
7 I Was A Prisoner On Island X . 900.00
8 The Day They Stole My Face . 900.00
9 I Walked Through The Doors
   of Destiny 900.00
10 We Found A World Of
   Tiny Cavemen 900.00
11 LSt(c),My Friend, Madcap
   Manning 750.00
12 MMe(c),I Hunted Big Game
   in Outer Space 750.00
13 LSt(c),I Hunted Goliath
   The Robot 750.00
14 LSt,I Had the Midas
   Touch of Gold 750.00
15 JK, I Hunted the Worlds
   Wildest Animals 750.00
16 JK,I Died a Thousand Times . 750.00
17 JK,I Doomed the World 750.00
18 JK(c),We Discovered The
   Edge of the World 900.00
19 I Caught Earth's
   Strangest Criminal 700.00
20 JK,I Was Big-Game
   on Neptune 700.00
21 JK,We Were Doomed By
   The Metal-Eating Monster . . . 700.00
22 I Was Trapped In The
   Magic Mountains 650.00
23 I Was A Captive In
   Space Prison 650.00
24 NC(c),I Was The Robinson
   Crusoe of Space 650.00
25 I Led Earth's Strangest
   Safari! 650.00
26 NC(c),We Battled The
   Sand Creature 650.00
27 I Was the Earth's First Exile . . 650.00
28 I Stalked the Camouflage
   Creatures 650.00
29 I Tracked the
   Forbidden Powers 400.00
30 We Cruised Into the
   Supernatural! 400.00
31 I Was A Modern Hercules . . . 300.00
32 We Were Trapped In A Freak
   Valley! 300.00
33 I Was Pursued by
   the Elements 300.00
34 DD,We Unleashed The Cloud
   Creatures 300.00
35 I Solved the Mystery of
   Volcano Valley 300.00
36 I Was Bewitched
   By Lady Doom 300.00
37 DD&SMo(c),I Hunted the
   Legendary Creatures! 300.00
38 DD&SMo(c),I Was the Slave
   of the Dream-Master 300.00
39 DD&SMo(c),We were Trapped
   in the Valley of no Return . . . 300.00
40 We Battled the StormCreature 300.00
41 DD&SMo(c),I Was Tried
   by a Robot Court 275.00
42 DD&SMo(c),My Brother
   Was a Robot 275.00
43 DD&SMo(c),I Fought the
   Sonar Creatures 275.00
44 DD&SMo(c),We Fought the
   Beasts of Petrified Island . . . 275.00
45 DD&SMo(c),We Battled the
   Black Narwahl 275.00
46 DD&SMo(c),We Were Prisoners
   of the Sundial of Doom 275.00
47 We Became Partners of the
   Beast Brigade 275.00
48 DD&SMo(c),I Was Marooned
   On Earth 275.00
49 DD&SMo(c),I Was An Ally
   Of A Criminal Creature 275.00

50 DD&SMo(c),I Fought the
   Idol King 275.00
51 DD&SMo(c),We Unleashed
   the Demon of the Dungeon . . 260.00
52 DD&SMo(c),I Was A
   Stand-In For an Alien 260.00
53 DD&SMo(c),I, Creature Slayer 260.00
54 I Was Cursed With
   an Alien Pal 260.00
55 DD&SMo(c),I Became The
   Wonder-Man of Space 260.00
56 DD&SMo(c),My Brother-The
   Alien 260.00
57 DD&SMo(c),Don't Touch Me
   Or You'll Die 260.00
58 DD&SMo(c),ATh,I was Trapped
   in the Land of L'Oz 275.00
59 DD&SMo(c),Listen Earth-I
   Am Still Alive 275.00
60 DD&SMo(c),ATh,I Lived in
   Two Worlds 275.00
61 DD&SMo(c),ATh,I Battled For
   the Doom-Stone 275.00
62 DD&SMo(c),I Fought For
   An Alien Enemy 250.00
63 DD&SMo(c),We Braved the
   Trail of the Ancient Warrior . . 250.00
64 DD&SMo(c),They Crowned My
   Fiance Their King! 250.00
65 DD&SMo(c),I Lost the Life
   or Death Secret 250.00
66 DD&SMo(c),I Dueled with
   the Super Spirits 250.00
67 I Protected the Idols
   of Idoro! 250.00
68 DD&SMo(c),My Deadly Island
   of Space 250.00
69 DD&SMo(c),I Was A Courier
   From the Past 250.00
70 DD&SMo(c),We Tracked the
   Fabled Fish-Man! 250.00
71 We Dared to open the Door
   of Danger Dungeon 250.00
72 The Haunted Beach 250.00
73 I Defeiller Mountain 250.00
74 GC(c),We Were Challenged
   By The River Spirit 250.00
75 GC(c),Castaway Cave Men
   of 1950 . . . . 250.00
76 MMe(c),We Battled the
   Micro-Monster 250.00
77 ATh,We Found the Super-
   Tribes of Tomorrow 250.00
78 Destination-'Dead Man's Alley' 250.00
79 Countdown in Dinosaur Valley 200.00

My Greatest Adventure #75
© *DC Comics Inc.*

80 BP,I:Doom Patrol 750.00
81 BP,ATh,I:Dr. Janus 250.00
82 BP,F:Doom Patrol 225.00
83 BP,F:Doom Patrol 225.00
84 BP,V:General Immortus 225.00
85 BP,ATh,F:Doom Patrol 225.00
Becomes:

DOOM PATROL
March, 1964
86 BP,I:Brogherhood of Evil 150.00
87 BP,O:Negative Man 125.00
88 BP,O:Chief 125.00
89 BP,I:Animal-Veg.-MineralMan . 125.00
90 BP,A:Brotherhood of Evil 125.00
91 BP,I:Manto, Gargvax 125.00
92 BP,I:Dr.Tyme, A:Mento 125.00
93 BP,A:Brotherhood of Evil 125.00
94 BP,I:Dr.Radich, The Claw 125.00
95 BP,A:Animal-Vegetable
   -Mineral Man 125.00
96 BP,A:General Immortus,
   Brotherhood of Evil 125.00
97 BP,A:General Immortus,
   Brotherhood of Evil 125.00
98 BP,I:Mr.103 . . . . 125.00
99 I:Beast Boy 120.00
100 BP,O:Beast Boy,Robotman . . 130.00
101 BP,A:Beast Boy 75.00
102 BP,A:Beast Boy,Challengers
   of the Unknown 70.00
103 BP,A:Beast Boy 70.00
104 BP,W:Elasti-Girl,Mento,
   C:JLA,Teen Titans 70.00
105 BP,A:Beast Boy 70.00
106 BP,O:Negative Man 70.00
107 BP,A:Beast Boy, I:Dr.Death. . . 70.00
108 BP,A:Brotherhood of Evil 70.00
109 BP,I:Mandred 70.00
110 BP,A:Garguax,Mandred,
   Brotherhood of Evil 50.00
111 BP,I:Zarox-13,A:Brotherhood
   of Evil. 50.00
112 BP,O:Beast Boy,Madame
   Rouge 50.00
113 BP,A:Beast Boy,Mento 50.00
114 BP,A:Beast Boy 50.00
115 BP,A:Beast Boy 50.00
116 BP,A:Madame Rouge 50.00
117 BP,I:Black Vulture 50.00
118 BP,A:Beast Boy 50.00
119 BP,A:Madam Rouge 50.00
120 I:Wrecker. 50.00
121 JO,D:Doom Patrol. 150.00
122 rep.Doom Patrol #89. . . . . . . 15.00

Doom Patrol #117
© DC Comics, Inc.

123 rep.Doom Patrol #95. . . . . . . 15.00
124 rep.Doom Patrol #90. . . . . . . 15.00
[2nd Series]
See: DOOM PATROL

MY NAME IS CHAOS
1992
1 JRy,Song Laid Waste to Earth. . . 5.00
2 JRy,Colonization of Mars 5.00
3 JRy,Search for Eternal Beings. . . 5.00
4 JRy,final issue 5.00

MY NAME IS HOLOCAUST
DC/Milestone, 1995
[Mini-Series]
1 F:Holocaust (Blood Syndicate) . . 2.50
2 V:Cantano 2.50
3 A:Blood Syndicate 2.50

MYSTERY IN SPACE
April-May, 1951
1 CI&FrG(c),FF,B:Knights of the
   Galaxy,Nine Worlds to
   Conquer 6,000.00
2 CI(c),MA,A:Knights of the
   Galaxy, Jesse James-
   Highwayman of Space 3,000.00
3 CI(c),A:Knights of the
   Galaxy, Duel of the Planets 2,000.00
4 CI(c),S&K,MA,A:Knights of the
   Galaxy, Master of Doom. . . 1,900.00
5 CI(c),A:Knights of the Galaxy,
   Outcast of the Lost World. . 1,900.00
6 CI(c),A:Knights of the Galaxy,
   The Day the World Melted . 1,500.00
7 GK(c),ATh,A:Knights of the Galaxy,
   Challenge o/t Robot Knight 1,500.00
8 MA,It's a Women's World . . . 1,500.00
9 MA(c),The Seven Wonders
   of Space 1,200.00
10 MA(c),The Last Time I
   Saw Earth. 1,200.00
11 GK(c),Unknown Spaceman . 1,000.00
12 MA,The Sword in the Sky . . 1,000.00
13 MA(c),MD,Signboard
   in Space 1,000.00
14 MA,GK(c),Hollywood
   in Space 1,000.00
15 MA(c),Doom from Station X. 1,000.00
16 MA(c),Honeymoon in Space 1,000.00
17 MA(c),The Last Mile of
   Space 1,000.00
18 MA(c),GK,Chain Gang
   of Space 1,000.00
19 MA(c),The Great
   Space-Train Robbery 1,000.00
20 MA(c),The Man in the
   Martian Mask. 900.00
21 MA(c),Interplanetary
   Merry- Go-Round 900.00
22 MA(c),The Square Earth. 900.00
23 MA(c),Monkey-Rocket
   to Mars 900.00
24 MA(c),A:Space Cabby,
   Hitchhiker of Space 900.00
25 MA(c),Station Mars on the Air. 800.00
26 GK(c),Earth is the Target 800.00
27 The Human Fishbowl 800.00
28 The Radio Planet 800.00
29 GK(c),Space-Enemy
   Number One 800.00
30 GK(c),The Impossible
   World Named Earth. 800.00
31 GK(c),The Day the Earth
   Split in Two 700.00
32 GK(c),Riddle of the
   Vanishing Earthmen 700.00
33 The Wooden World War 700.00
34 GK(c),The Man Who
   Moved the World 700.00

Mystery in Space #4
© DC Comics, Inc.

35 The Counterfeit Earth 700.00
36 GK(c),Secret of the
   Moon Sphinx 700.00
37 GK(c),Secret of the
   Masked Martians 700.00
38 GK(c),The Canals of Earth . . . 700.00
39 GK(c),Sorcerers of Space. . . . 700.00
40 GK(c),Riddle of the
   Runaway Earth 700.00
41 GK(c),The Miser of Space . . . 600.00
42 GK(c),The Secret of the
   Skyscraper Spaceship. 600.00
43 GK(c),Invaders From the
   Space Satellites. 600.00
44 GK(c),Amazing Space Flight
   of North America 600.00
45 GK(c),MA,Flying Saucers
   Over Mars 600.00
46 GK(c),MA,Mystery of the
   Moon Sniper 600.00
47 GK(c),MA,Interplanetary Tug
   of War 600.00
48 GK(c),MA,Secret of the
   Scarecrow World 600.00
49 GK(c),The Sky-High Man 600.00
50 GK(c),The Runaway
   Space-Train 600.00
51 GK(c),MA,Battle of the
   Moon Monsters 600.00
52 GK(c),MSy,Mirror Menace
   of Mars 600.00
53 GK(c),B:Adam Strange stories,
   Menace o/t Robot Raiders . 4,000.00
54 GK(c),Invaders of the
   Underground World 1,000.00
55 GK(c),The Beast From
   the Runaway World. 900.00
56 GK(c),The Menace of
   the Super-Atom 600.00
57 GK(c),Mystery of the
   Giant Footsteps 600.00
58 GK(c),Chariot in the Sky . . . 600.00
59 GK(c),The Duel of the
   Two Adam Stranges 600.00
60 GK(c),The Attack of the
   Tentacle World. 600.00
61 CI&MA(c),Threat of the
   Tornado Tyrant. 500.00
62 CI&MA(c),The Beast with
   the Sizzling Blue Eyes. 500.00
63 The Weapon that
   Swallowed Men 500.00
64 The Radioactive Menace 500.00
65 Mechanical Masters of
   Rann 500.00

66 Space-Island of Peril....... 500.00
67 Challenge of the
  Giant Fireflies 500.00
68 CI&MA(c),Fadeaway Doom .. 500.00
69 CI&MA(c),Menace of the
  Aqua-Ray Weapon 500.00
70 CI&MA(c),Vengeance of
  the Dust Devil 500.00
71 CI&MA(c),The Challenge of
  the Crystal Conquerors 500.00
72 The Multiple Menace Weapon 400.00
73 CI&MA(c),The Invisible
  Invaders of Rann......... 400.00
74 CI&MA(c),The Spaceman
  Who Fought Himself 400.00
75 CI&MA(c),The Planet That
  Came to a Standstill 700.00
76 CI&MA(c),Challenge of
  the Rival Starman 400.00
77 CI&MA(c),Ray-Gun in the Sky 400.00
78 CI&MA(c),Shadow People
  of the Eclipse............. 400.00
79 CI&MA(c),The Metal
  Conqueror of Rann 400.00
80 CI&MA(c),The Deadly
  Shadows of Adam Strange .. 400.00
81 CI&MA(c),The Cloud-Creature
  That Menaced Two Worlds .. 375.00
82 CI&MA(c),World War on
  Earth and Rann........... 375.00
83 CI&MA(c),The Emotion-Master
  of Space 375.00
84 CI&MA(c),The Powerless
  Weapons of Adam Strange .. 375.00
85 CI&MA(c),Riddle of the
  Runaway Rockets 375.00
86 CI&MA(c),Attack of the
  Underworld Giants........ 375.00
87 MA(c),The Super-Brain of
  Adam Strange,B:Hawkman .. 600.00
88 CI&MA(c),The Robot Wraith
  of Rann 550.00
89 MA(c),Siren o/t Space Ark ... 500.00
90 CI&MA(c),Planets and
  Peril, E:Hawkman 500.00
91 CI&MA(c),Puzzle ot
  the Perilous Prisons 300.00
92 DD&SMo(c),The Alien Invasion
  From Earth,B:Space Ranger . 300.00
93 DD&SMo(c),The Convict
  Twins of Space 300.00
94 DD&SMo(c),The Adam
  Strange Story............ 300.00
95 The Hydra-Head From
  Outer Space 300.00
96 The Coins That Doomed
  Two Planets 300.00
97 The Day Adam Strange
  Vanished 300.00
98 The Wizard of the Cosmos... 300.00
99 DD&SMo(c),The World-
  Destroyer From Space 300.00
100 DD&SMo(c),GK,The Death
  of Alanna 300.00
101 GK(c),The Valley of
  1,000 Dooms............. 300.00
102 GK,The Robot World of Rann 300.00
103 The Billion-Dollar Time-
  Capsule(Space Ranger),I:Ultra
  the Multi-Agent 300.00
104 thru 109................@250.00
110 Series ends, Sept., 1966 ... 250.00
[Series Revived], Sept., 1980
111 JAp,SD,MR,DSp,.......... 10.00
112 JAp,TS,JKu(c).............. 10.00
113 JKu(c),MGo................ 10.00
114 JKu(c),JCr,SD,DSp 10.00
115 JKu(c),SD,GT,BB 10.00
116 JSn(c),JCr,SD 10.00
117 DN,GT,March, 1981 .... 10.00

MYSTERY IN SPACE
Sept., 2006
1 JSn, 48-pg. 4.00
1a variant NA (c) 4.00
2 JSn, Captain Comet 3.00
3 JSn, Hardcore Station 4.00

MYTHOS:
THE FINAL TOUR
DC/Vertigo, Oct., 1996
1 JNR(s),GyA,PrG,F:Rock Star
  Adam Case 6.00
2 JNR(s),PSj,F:Rock Star Adam
  Case 6.00
3 JNR(s), finale.............. 6.00

NAMES OF MAGIC, THE
DC/Vertigo, Dec., 2000
1 (of 5) JBo(c),F:Tim Hunter..... 10.00
2 thru 5 JBo(c) ....@10.00
TPB rep................... 15.00

NATHANIEL DUSK
Feb., 1984
1 GC(p)..................... 2.25
2 thru 4 GC(p)..............@2.25

NATHANIEL DUSK II
Oct., 1985
1 thru 4 GC,Jan., 1986 ....@2.25

NATIONAL COMICS
1999
1 MWa(s),AAl,F:Flash &
  Mr. Terrific 2.25

NAZZ, THE
1990–91
1 Michael'sBook 5.50
2 Johnny'sBook 5.00
3 Search for Michael Nazareth.... 5.00
4 V:Retaliators,final issue 5.00

NEIL GAIMAN'S
NEVERWHERE
DC/Vertigo, June, 2005
1 (of 9) GF 3.00
2 thru 4 novel adaptation ......@3.00
5 novel adaptation 3.00
6 thru 9 GF ....@3.00
TPB 20.00

NEVADA
DC/Vertigo, March, 1998
1 (of 6) SvG,SL,show girl 2.50
2 thru 6 SvG,SL.............@2.50
TPB Nevada, rep. 15.00

NEW ADVENTURES
OF CHARLIE CHAN
1958
1 GK,SGe,Secret of the Phantom
  Bells 1,000.00
2 SGe,Riddle of the Runaway
  Mummy 700.00
3 SGe,Two Lives of Charlie
  Chan 550.00
4 SGe,Case o/t Vanishing Man . 550.00
5 SGe,Monarch of Menace..... 550.00
6 SGe,Trail Across the Sky..... 550.00

NEW ADVENTURES
OF SUPERBOY
See: SUPERBOY

New Adventures of Charlie Chan #3
© DC Comics Inc.

NEW BOOK OF COMICS
1937
1 Dr.Occult............... 30,000.00
2 Dr.Occult............... 15,000.00

NEW COMICS
1935
1 .... 35,000.00
2 .... 14,000.00
3 thru 6 ....@9,000.00
7 thru 11 ....@8,000.00
Becomes:

NEW ADVENTURE
COMICS
Jan., 1937
12 S&S 7,500.00
13 thru 20 ....@6,000.00
21 .... 5,000.00
22 thru 31 ....@4,000.00
Becomes:

ADVENTURE COMICS

NEW FUN COMICS
Feb., 1935
1 B:Oswald the Rabbit,
  Jack Woods 65,000.00
2 .... 35,000.00
3 .... 20,000.00
4 .... 20,000.00
5 .... 20,000.00
6 S&S,B:Dr.Occult,
  Henri Duval........... 35,000.00
Becomes:

MORE FUN COMICS
Jan., 1936
7 S&S,WK 17,000.00
8 S&S,WK 15,000.00
9 S&S,E:Henri Duval....... 18,000.00
10 S&S 10,000.00
11 S&S,B:Calling all Girls 10,000.00
12 S&S 10,000.00
13 S&S 10,000.00
14 S&S,Color,Dr.Occult.... 19,000.00
15 S&S 10,000.00
16 S&S,Christmas(c) 10,000.00
17 S&S,CF 9,000.00
18 S&S,CF 3,500.00
19 S&S,CF 3,500.00
20 HcK,S&S 3,500.00
21 S&S,CF 3,800.00
22 S&S,CF 3,800.00

More Fun #23 © DC Comics, Inc.

23 S&S,CF 3,800.00
24 S&S,CF 3,800.00
25 S&S,CF 3,500.00
26 S&S,CF 3,200.00
27 S&S,CF 3,200.00
28 S&S,CF 3,000.00
29 S&S,CF 3,000.00
30 S&S 3,000.00
31 S&S , CF 3,200.00
32 S&S,E:Dr. Occult 3,000.00
33 S&S,BKa 3,000.00
34 S&S,BKa 3,000.00
35 S&S,BKa,CF(c) 3,000.00
36 B:Masked Ranger 3,000.00
37 thru 40 . . . . @4,500.00
41 E:Masked Ranger 6,200.00
42 thru 50 . . . . @3,500.00
51 I:The Spectre 9,000.00
52 O:The Spectre,pt.1,
  E:Wing Brady 135,000.00
53 O:The Spectre,pt.2,
  B:Capt.Desmo 80,000.00
54 E:King Carter,Spectre(c) . . 25,000.00
55 I:Dr.Fate,E:Bulldog Martin,
  Spectre(c) 30,000.00
56 B:Congo Bill,Dr.Fate(c) . . . 12,000.00
57 Spectre(c) 10,000.00
58 Spectre(c) 10,000.00
59 A:Spectre 10,000.00
60 Spectre(c) 10,000.00
61 Spectre(c) 10,000.00
62 Spectre(c) 7,000.00
63 Spectre(c),E:St.Bob Neal . . . 7,000.00
64 Spectre(c),B:Lance Larkin . . 7,000.00
65 Spectre(c) 7,000.00
66 Spectre(c) 7,000.00
67 Spectre(c),O:Dr. Fate,
  E:Congo Bill,Biff Bronson . 12,000.00
68 Dr.Fate(c),B:Clip Carson . . . 7,000.00
69 Dr.Fate(c) 7,000.00
70 Dr.Fate(c),E:Lance Larkin . . 7,000.00
71 Dr.Fate(c),I:Johnny Quick . 10,000.00
72 Dr. Fate has Smaller Helmet,
  E:Sgt. Carey,Sgt.O'Malley . 7,000.00
73 Dr.Fate(c),I:Aquaman,Green
  Arrow,Speedy 27,000.00
74 Dr.Fate(c),A:Aquaman 7,500.00
75 Dr.Fate(c) 7,000.00
76 Dr.Fate(c),MMe,E:Clip Carson,
  B:Johnny Quick 7,000.00
77 MMe,Green Arrow(c) 7,000.00
78 MMe,Green Arrow(c) 7,000.00
79 MMe,Green Arrow(c) 7,000.00
80 MMe,Green Arrow(c) 4,500.00
81 MMe,Green Arrow(c) 5,000.00
82 MMe,Green Arrow(c) 5,000.00
83 MMe,Green Arrow(c) 5,000.00

84 MMe,Green Arrow(c) 6,000.00
85 MMe,Green Arrow(c) 3,500.00
86 MMe 3,500.00
87 MMe,E:Radio Squad 3,500.00
88 MMe,Green Arrow(c) 3,500.00
89 MMe,O:Gr.Arrow&Speedy . 3,600.00
90 MMe,Green Arrow(c) 5,000.00
91 MMe,Green Arrow(c) 3,000.00
92 MMe,Green Arrow(c) 3,000.00
93 MMe,B:Dover & Clover 4,000.00
94 MMe,Green Arrow(c) 2,500.00
95 MMe,Green Arrow(c) 2,500.00
96 MMe,Green Arrow(c) 2,500.00
97 MMe,JKu,E:Johnny Quick . . 3,200.00
98 E:Dr. Fate 3,700.00
99 Green Arrow(c) 3,500.00
100 Anniversary Issue 3,500.00
101 O&I:Superboy,
  E:The Spectre 17,000.00
102 A:Superboy 4,000.00
103 A:Superboy 3,500.00
104 Superboy(c) 3,000.00
105 Superboy(c) 3,000.00
106 Superboy(c) 3,000.00
107 E:Superboy 3,000.00
108 A:Genius Jones,Genius
  Meets Genius 800.00
109 A:Genius Jones, The
  Disappearing Deposits 800.00
110 A:Genius Jones, Birds,
  Brains and Burglary 800.00
111 A:Genius Jones, Jeepers
  Creepers 800.00
112 A:Genius Jones, The
  Tell-Tale Tornado 800.00
113 A:Genius Jones, Clocks
  and Shocks 800.00
114 A:Genius Jones, The
  Milky Way 800.00
115 A:Genius Jones,Foolish
  Questions 800.00
116 A:Genius Jones,Palette
  For Plunder 800.00
117 A:Genius Jones,Battle of
  the Pretzel Benders 800.00
118 A:Genius Jones,The
  Sinister Siren 800.00
119 A:Genius Jones,A
  Perpetual Jackpot 800.00
120 A:Genius Jones,The Man
  in the Moon 800.00
121 A:Genius Jones,The
  Mayor Goes Haywire 800.00
122 A:Genius Jones,When Thug-
  Hood Was In Floor 800.00
123 A:Genius Jones,Hi Diddle Diddle,
  the Cat and the Fiddle 800.00
124 A:Genius Jones,
  The Zany Zoo 800.00
125 Genius Jones,
  Impossible But True 1,500.00
126 A:Genius Jones,The Case
  of the Gravy Spots 500.00
127 Nov.–Dec., 1947 . . . . 1,000.00

NEW GODS, THE
Feb.–March, 1971

1 JK,I:Orion 150.00
2 JK,O'Deadly Darkseid 100.00
3 JK,Death is the Black Racer . . . 50.00
4 JK,O:Manhunter, rep 40.00
5 JK,I:Fastbak & Black Racer 40.00
6 JK,The Glory Boat 40.00
7 JK,O:Orion 40.00
8 JK,Death Wish of Terrible Turpin 40.00
9 JK,I:Forager 40.00
10 JK,Earth–The Domed Dominion 40.00
11 JK,Darkseid and Sons (1972) . . 40.00
12 DN,DA,R:New Gods (1977) . . . 10.00
13 DN,DA,AM(c) 10.00
14 DN,DA,RB&AM(c) 10.00
15 RB,BMc,Apocalypse Child . . . 10.00

16 DN,DA,Titan and the Hunter . . . 10.00
17 DN,DA, The Memory Machine . 10.00
18 DN,DA,Song of the Source 10.00
19 DN,DA,The Secret Within Us . . 10.00

NEW GODS
(Reprints) 1984

1 JK reprint 4.00
2 thru 5 JK reprint . . . . @3.50
6 JK rep.+New Material 3.50

NEW GODS
[2nd Series], 1989

1 From Cosmic Odyssey 3.00
2 A:Orion of New Genesis 2.50
3 A:Orion 2.50
4 Renegade Apokolyptian Insect
  Colony 2.50
5 Orion vs. Forager 2.50
6 A:Eve Donner, Darkseid 2.50
7 Bloodline #1 . . . . 2.50
8 Bloodline #2 . . . . 2.50
9 Bloodline #3 . . . . 2.50
10 Bloodline #4 . . . . 2.50
11 Bloodline #5 . . . . 2.50
12 Bloodlines #6 . . . . 2.50
13 Back on Earth 2.50
14 I:Reflektor 2.50
15 V:Serial Killer 2.50
16 A:Fastbak & Metron 2.50
17 A:Darkseid, Metron 2.50
18 A:YugaKhan,Darkseid,
  Moniters 2.50
19 V:Yuga Khan 2.50
20 Darkseid Dethroned,
  V:Yuga Khan 2.50
21 A:Orion 2.50
22 A:Metron 2.50
23 A:Forever People 2.50
24 A:Forever People 2.50
25 The Pact #1,R:Infinity Man 2.50
26 The Pact #2 . . . . 2.50
27 Asault on Apokolips,Pact#3 . . . 2.50
28 Pact #4, final issue 2.50

[3rd Series], 1995–97

1 F:Orion vs. Darkseid 2.50
2 RaP,UnderworldUnleashed tie-in . 2.50
3 RaP,Darkseid destroyed 2.50
4 RaP,F:Lightray 2.50
5 RaP,F:Orion 2.50
6 RaP,Destruction of the Beast 2.50
7 RaP,R:Darkseid 2.50
8 RaP,DZ,F:Highfather,Darkseid . . . 2.50
9 thru 11 . . . . @2.50
12 JBy,BWi,F:Metron 2.50
13 JBy, BWi,Orion reappears
  on Earth 2.50
14 JBy,BWi,A:Forever People,
  Lightray 2.50
TPB rep. #1–#11,b&w 12.00
Secret Files #1 KK,JBy 5.00

NEW GUARDIANS
1988–89

1 JSon,from Millennium series 3.00
2 JSon,Colombian Drug Cartel 2.25
3 JSon,in South Africa,
  V:Janwillem's Army 2.25
4 JSon,V:Neo-Nazi Skinheads
  in California 2.25
5 JSon,Tegra Kidnapped 2.25
6 JSon, In China, Invasion x-over . 2.25
7 JSon, Guardians Return Home . . 2.25
8 JSon, V:Janwillem 2.25
9 JSon, A:Tome Kalmaku,
  V:Janwillem 2.25
10 JSon, A:Tome Kalmaku 2.25
11 PB,Janwillem's secret 2.25
12 PB,New Guardians Future
  revealed, final issue 2.25

NEW TEEN TITANS
Nov., 1980

1 GP,RT,V:Gordanians (see DC
  Comics Presents #26 . . . . 20.00
2 GP,RT,I:Deathstroke the
  Terminator, I&D:Ravager. 50.00
3 GP,I:Fearsome Five. 7.00
4 GP,RT,A:JLA,O:Starfire 6.00
5 CS,RT,O:Raven,I:Trigon 6.00
6 GP,V:Trigon,O:Raven. 6.00
7 GP,RT,O:Cyborg 6.00
8 GP,RT,A Day in the Life 6.00
9 GP,RT,A:Terminator,
  V:Puppeteer. 6.00
10 GP,RT,A:Terminator 10.00
11 GP,RT,V:Hyperion 4.00
12 GP,RT,V:Titans of Myth. 4.00
13 GP,RT,R:Robotman. 4.00
14 GP,RT,I:New Brotherhood of
  Evil,V:Zahl and Rouge. 4.00
15 GP,RT,A:Madame Rouge 4.00
16 GP,RT,I:Captain Carrot 4.00
17 GP,RT,I:Frances Kane 3.50
18 GP,RT,A:Orig.Starfire 3.50
19 GP,RT,A:Hawkman 3.50
20 GP,RT,V:Disruptor. 3.50
21 GP,RT,GC,I:Brother Blood,
  Night Force 3.50
22 GP,RT,V:Brother Blood 3.50
23 GP,RT,I:Blackfire. 3.50
24 GP,RT,A:Omega Men,I:X-hal . . 3.50
25 GP,RT,A:Omega Men 3.50
26 GP,RT,I:Terra,Runaway #1 . . . . 5.00
27 GP,RT,A:Speedy,Runaway #2. . 3.00
28 GP,RT,V:Terra 4.00
29 GP,RT,V:Broth.of Evil 3.00
30 GP,RT,V:Broth.of Evil,J:Terra . . 3.00
31 GP,RT,V:Broth.of Evil 3.00
32 GP,RT,I:Thunder & Lightning . . . 3.00
33 GP,I:Trident 3.00
34 GP,V:The Terminator. 3.00
35 KP,RT,V:Mark Wright. 3.00
36 KP,RT,A:Thunder & Lightning . . 3.00
37 GP,RT,A:Batman/Outsiders(x-over
  BATO#5),V:Fearsome Five 3.00
38 GP,O:Wonder Girl 3.00
39 GP,Grayson quits as Robin. 5.00
40 GP,A:Brother Blood. 3.00
Ann.#1 GP,RT,Blackfire 3.50
Ann.#2 GP,I:Vigilante 3.00
Ann.#3 GP,DG,D:Terra,A:Deathstroke
  V:The H.I.V.E. 3.50
Ann.#4 rep.Direct Ann.#1. . . . . . . 2.50

New Teen Titans #10
© DC Comics Inc.

TPB Judas Contract rep.#39-#44,
  Ann.#3,new GP(c) 15.00
TPB The Terror of Trigon 18.00

[Special Issues]
Keebler:GP,DG,Drugs 2.50
Beverage:Drugs,RA 2.50
IBM:Drugs 3.00
Becomes:

TALES OF THE
TEEN TITANS
1984–88

41 GP,A:Brother Blood 3.00
42 GP,DG,V:Deathstroke 5.00
43 GP,DG,V:Deathstroke 5.00
44 GP,DG,I:Nightwing,O:Deathstroke
  Joe Wilson becomes Jericho . . 8.00
45 GP,A:Aqualad,V:The H.I.V.E. . . 3.00
46 GP,A:Aqualad,V:The H.I.V.E. . . 3.00
47 GP,A:Aqualad,V:The H.I.V.E. . . 3.00
48 SR,V:The Recombatants 3.00
49 GP,CI,V:Dr.Light,A:Flash. 3.00
50 GP/DG W:Wonder Girl &
  Terry Long,C:Batman,
  Wonder Woman. 4.00
51 RB,A:Cheshire 2.50
52 RB,A:Cheshire 2.50
53 RB,I:Ariel,A:Terminator 2.50
54 RB,A:Terminator 2.50
55 A:Terminator 2.50
56 A:Fearsome Five. 2.50
57 A:Fearsome Five. 2.50
58 thru 91 rep. . . . . @2.50

NEW TEEN TITANS
[Direct sales series]
Aug., 1984

1 B:MWn(s),GP,L:Raven. 6.00
2 GP,D:Azareth,A:Trigon. 4.00
3 GP,V:Raven 4.00
4 GP,V:Trigon,Raven 4.00
5 GP,D:Trigon,Raven disappears . . 4.00
6 GP,A:Superman,Batman 3.00
7 JL,V:Titans of Myth 3.00
8 JL,V:Titans of Myth 3.00
9 JL,V:Titans of Myth,I:Kole 3.00
10 JL,O:Kole 3.00
11 JL,O:Kole 2.50
12 JL,Ghost story. 2.50
13 EB,Crisis 2.50
14 EB,Crisis 2.50
15 EB,A:Raven 2.50
16 EB,A:OmegaMen 2.50
17 EB,V:Blackfire 2.50
18 E:MWn(s),EB,V:Blackfire 2.50
19 EB,V:Mento. 2.50
20 GP(c),EB,V:Cheshire,J.Todd . . 2.50
21 GP(c),EB,V:Cheshire,J.Todd . . 2.50
22 GP(c),EB,V:Blackfire,Mento,
  Brother Blood 2.50
23 GP(c),V:Blackfire 2.50
24 CB,V:Hybrid 2.50
25 EB,RT,V:Hybrid,Mento,A:Flash. . 2.50
26 KGa,V:Mento 2.50
27 KGa,Church of Br.Blood 2.50
28 EB,RT,V:BrotherBlood,A:Flash . . 2.50
29 EB,RT,V:Brother Blood,
  A:Flash,Robin 2.50
30 EB,Batman,Superman 2.50
31 EB,RT,V:Brother Blood,A:Flash
  Batman,Robin,Gr.Lantern Corps
  Superman 2.50
32 EB,RT,Murder Weekend 2.50
33 EB,V:Terrorists 2.50
34 EB,RT,V:Mento,Hybrid 2.50
35 PB,RT,V:Arthur & Eve 2.50
36 EB,RT,I:Wildebeest 2.50
37 EB,RT,V:Wildebeest 2.50
38 EB,RT,A:Infinity 2.50
39 EB,RT,F:Raven 2.50
40 EB,RT,V:Gentleman Ghost 2.50

41 EB,V:Wildebeest,A:Puppeteer,
  Trident,Wildebeest. 2.50
42 EB,RT,V:Puppeteer,Gizmo,
  Trident,Wildebeest. 2.50
43 CS,RT,V:Phobia 2.50
44 RT,V:Godiva 2.50
45 EB,RT,A:Dial H for Hero 2.50
46 EB,RT,A:Dial H for Hero 2.50
47 O:Titans,C:Wildebeest 2.50
48 EB,RT,A:Red Star 2.50
49 EB,RT,A:Red Star 2.50
Ann.#1 A:Superman,V:Brainiac . . . 2.50
Ann.#2 JBy,JL,O:Brother Blood . . . 3.00
Ann.#3 I:Danny Chase. 2.50
Ann.#4 V:Godiva 2.50
Becomes:

NEW TITANS
1988–96

50 B:MWn(s),GP,BMc,B:Who is
  Wonder Girl?. 7.00
51 GP,BMc. 3.00
52 GP,BMc. 3.00
53 GP,RT 3.00
54 GP,RT,E:Who is Wonder Girl? . . 3.00
55 GP,RT,I:Troia. 3.00
56 MBr,RT,Tale of Middle Titans . . 3.00
57 GP,BMc,V:Wildebeast. 3.00
58 GP,TG,BMc,V:Wildebeast 3.00
59 GP,TG,BMc,V:Wildebeast 3.00
60 GP,TG,BMc,3rd A:Tim Drake
  (Face Revealed),Batman 5.00
61 GP,TG,BMc,A:Tim Drake,
  Batman 5.00
62 TG,AV,A:Deathstroke 3.00
63 TG,AV,A:Deathstroke 3.00
64 TG,AV,A:Deathstroke 3.00
65 TG,AV,A:Deathstroke,Tim Drake,
  Batman 3.00
66 TG,AV,V:Eric Forrester 2.50
67 TG,AV,V:Eric Forrester 2.50
68 SE,V:Royal Flush Gang 2.50
69 SE,V:Royal Flush Gang 2.50
70 SE,A:Deathstroke 3.00
71 TG,AV,B:Deathstroke,
  B:Titans Hunt. 5.00
72 TG,AV,D:Golden Eagle 4.00
73 TG,AV,I:Phantasm 4.00
74 TG,AV,I:Pantha 3.00
75 TG,AV,IR:Jericho/Wildebeest . . 3.00
76 TG,AV,V:Wildebeests 2.50
77 TG,AV,A:Red Star,N:Cyborg . . . 2.50
78 TG,AV,V:Cyborg 2.50
79 TG,AV,I:Team Titans 3.00
80 KGa,PC,A:Team Titans 2.50

New Titans #97
© DC Comics, Inc.

81 CS,AV,War of the Gods 2.50
82 TG,AV,V:Wildebeests 2.50
83 TG,AV,D:Jericho 3.00
84 TG,AV,E:Titans Hunt 2.50
85 TG,AV,I:Baby Wildebeest 2.50
86 CS,AV,E:Deathstroke. 2.50
87 TG,AV,A:Team Titans 2.50
88 TG,AV,CS,V:Team Titans 2.50
89 JBr,I:Lord Chaos. 2.50
90 TG,AV,Total Chaos#2,A:Team
   Titans,D'stroke,V:Lord Chaos . . 2.50
91 TG,AV,Total Chaos#5,A:Team
   Titans,D'stroke,V:Lord Chaos . 2.50
92 E:MWn(s),TG,AV,Total Chaos#8,
   A:Team Titans,V:Lord Chaos. . . 2.50
93 TG,AV,Titans Sell-Out#3 . . . . . . 2.50
94 PJ,F:Red Star & Cyborg 2.50
95 PJ,Red Star gains new powers. . 2.50
96 PJ,I:Solar Flare,
   V:Konstantine 2.50
97 TG,AV,B:The Darkening,R:Speedy
   V:Brotherhood of Evil 2.50
98 TG,AV,V:Brotherhood of Evil . . . 2.50
99 TG,AV,I:Arsenal (Speedy) 2.50
100 TG,AV,W:Nightwing&Starfire,
   V:Deathwing,Raven,A:Flash,Team
   Titans,Hologram(c) 4.00
101 AV(i),L:Nightwing. 2.50
102 AV(i),A:Prester John 2.50
103 AV(i),V:Bro. of Evil. 2.50
104 Terminus #1 . . . . 2.50
105 Terminus #2 . . . . 2.50
106 Terminus #3 . . . . 2.50
107 Terminus #4 . . . . 2.50
108 A:Supergirl,Flash. 2.50
109 F:Starfire 2.50
110 A:Flash,Serg.Steele. 2.50
111 A:Checkmate. 2.50
112 A:Checkmate. 2.50
113 F:Nightwing 2.75
114 L:Starfire, Nightwing,Panthra,
   Wildebeest. 2.50
115 A:Trigon 2.50
116 Changling 2.50
117 V:Psimon 2.50
118 V:Raven + Brotherhood 2.50
119 Suffer the Children,pt.1 . . . . . . 2.50
120 Forever Evil,pt.2 . . . . 2.50
121 Forever Evil,pt.3 . . . . 2.50
122 Crimelord/Syndicate War,pt.2
   J:Supergirl. 2.50
123 MWn(s),RRa,O:Minion 2.50
124 The Siege of Zi Charan 2.50
125 The Siege of Zi Charan 3.00
126 Meltdown,pt.1 . . . . 2.50
127 MWn,Meltdown, cont. 2.50
128 MWn,Meltdown, cont. 2.50
129 MWn,Meltdown, cont. 2.50
130 MWn,Meltdown,final issue 2.50
Ann.#5 V:Children of the Sun 3.00
Ann.#6 CS,F:Starfire 3.00
Ann.#7 Armageddon 2001,I:Future
   Teen Titans 4.00
Ann.#8 PJ,Eclipso,V:Deathstroke . 3.75
Ann.#9 Bloodlines#5,I:Anima. 3.75
Ann.#10 Elseworlds story 3.75
Ann.#11 Year One Annual 4.00
#0 Spec. Zero Hour,new team 2.50
TPB Terra Incognito (2006) 20.00

NEW T.H.U.N.D.E.R.
AGENTS, THE
July, 2003
1 JP. 3.00

NEW YEAR'S EVIL:
Dec., 1997
Body Doubles #1 DAn,ALa,JoP,
   JPn(c) 2.00
Dark Nemesis #1 DJu,Ccs,JPn(c). . 2.00
Darkseid #1 JBy,SB,JPn(c) 2.00

Gog #1 MWa,JOy,DJa,JPn(c) 2.00
Mr. Mxyzptlk #1 AIG,TMo,JPn(c) . . . 2.00
Prometheus #1 GMo,JPn(c) 2.00
Scarecrow #1 PrM,DFg,JPn(c) 2.00
The Rogues #1 BAu,RoW,JPn(c) . . 2.00

NEW YORK
WORLD'S FAIR
1939–40
1 1939 . . . . 40,000.00
2 1940 . . . . 25,000.00

NEXT, THE
July, 2006
1 Cross-over from other dimension 3.00
2 A:Superman. 3.00
3 Trapped in a time anomaly 3.00
4 The Fist of the Iron Ring 3.00
5 Showdown 3.00

NIGHTFALL:
THE BLACK CHRONICLES
Homage/DC, Oct., 1999
1 monsters living among us 3.00
2. . . . . 3.00
3 . . . . 3.00

Night Force #2 © DC Comics, Inc.

NIGHT FORCE
Aug., 1982
1 GC,1:Night Force. 5.00
2 thru 13 GC . . . . @3.00
14 GC,Sept.,1983 . . . . 3.00

NIGHT FORCE
Oct., 1996
1 MWn(s),BA,Baron Winters leads. 2.50
2 MWn(s) 2.25
3 MWn(s) 2.25
4 MWn(s),EB,HellSeemsHeaven . . 2.25
5 MWn(s),Low,SMa,Dreamers of
   Dreams,pt.1 . . . . 2.25
6 MWn(s),Low,SMa,Dreamers,pt.2. 2.25
7 MWn(s),Low,SMa,Dreamers,pt.3. 2.25
8 MWn(s),Convergence, x-over . . . 2.25
9 MWn(s),Low,Sma,The Eleventh
   Man pt.1 (of 3). 2.25
10 MWn(s),Eleventh Man, pt.2 . . . 2.50
11 MWn(s),Eleventh Man, pt.3 . . . 2.50
12 MWn(s),Lady of the Leopard
   final issue,Sept., 1997 . . . . 2.50

NIGHTWING
1995
1 R:Nightwing 5.00
2 N:Nightwing 4.00
3 visit to Kravia 4.00
4 conclusion 4.00
1-shot Alfred's Return, DG. 5.00

NIGHTWING
Aug., 1996
1 CDi(s),SMc,KIS,Nightwing goes
   to Bluhaven 18.00
2 CDi(s),SMc,KIS,V:smugglers . . . 10.00
3 CDi(s),SMc,KIS,run-down bank
   iheld up 10.00
4 CDi(s),SMc,KIS,V:Lady Vick 8.00
5 CDi(s),SMc,KIS, ... 8.00
6 CDi(s),SMc,KIS,A:Tim Drake. . . . 8.00
7 CDi(s),SMc,KIS,Rough Justice . . 8.00
8 CDi(s),SMc,KIS,V: the kingpin
   of Bluhaven 8.00
9 CDi(s),SMc,KIS,kidnapping, pt.1 . 8.00
10 CDi(s),SMc,KIS,nightmare
   or dream? 8.00
11 CDi(s),SMc,V:Soames,
   Blockbuster 8.00
12 CDi(s),SMc,Mutt 5.00
13 CDi(s),SMc,KIS,A:Batman 5.00
14 CDi(s),SMc,KIS,A:Batman,pt.2 . . 5.00
15 CDi(s),SMc,KIS,A:Batman,pt.3 . . 5.00
16 CDi(s),SMc,KIS,Nightwingmobile 3.00
17 CDi(s),SMc,KIS,V:Man-Bat 3.00
18 CDi(s),SMc,KIS. 3.00
19 CDi(s),SMc,KIS,Cataclysm
   x-over, pt.2 . . . . 4.00
20 CDi(s),SMc,KIS,Cataclysm 3.00
21 CDi(s),SMc,KIS,post Cataclysm 3.00
22 CDi(s),SMc,KIS,V:Lady Vic. 3.00
23 Brotherhood of
   the Fist x-over, pt.4 . . . . 3.00
24 CDi(s),SMc,KIS,cop story 3.00
25 CDi(s),SMc,KIS,A:Robin 3.00
26 CDi(s),SMc,KIS,A;Huntress 3.00
27 CDi(s),SMc,KIS,V:Torque 3.00
28 CDi(s),SMc,KIS,V:Torque 3.00
29 CDi(s),SMc,KIS,A:Huntress 3.00
30 CDi(s),SMc,KIS,A:Superman . . . 3.00
31 CDi(s),SMc,KIS,A:Nite-Wing. . . . 3.00
32 CDi(s),SMc,KIS,V:DoubleDare . . 3.00
33 CDi(s),SMc,KIS,
   V:Electrocutioner 3.00
34 CDi(s),SMc,KIS,x-over 3.00
35 CDi(s),SMc,KIS,No
   Man's Land,pt.1. . . . . 3.00
36 CDi(s),SMc,No
   Man's Land,pt.2. . . . . 3.00
37 CDi(s),SMc,KIS,No Man's
   Land, concl. 3.00
38 CDi(s),SMc,KIS,F:Oracle 3.00
39 CDi(s),SMc,KIS. 3.00
40 CDi(s),SMc,KIS,R:Tarantula 3.00
41 CDi(s),Police Academy grad. . . . 2.50
42 CDi(s),V:Nite-wing 2.50
43 CDi(s),V:Torque 2.50
44 CDi(s),F:Nite-wing. 2.50
45 CDi(s),Hunt for Oracle,pt.1 . . . . 2.50
46 CDi(s),Hunt for Oracle,pt.3 . . . . 2.50
47 CDi(s),showdown 2.50
48 CDi(s),JMz,F:Slyph. 2.50
49 CDi(s),JMz,F:Torque. 2.50
50 CDi,JMz,at crossroads,48-pg. . . 4.00
51 CDi,KD,O:Nite-wing 2.50
52 CDi,This issue: Batman dies! . . . 2.50
53 Officer Down x-over,pt.5 . . . . . . 2.50
54 CDi,life-threatening accident. . . . 2.50
55 CDi,A:Blockbuster,Shrike 2.50
56 CDi,V:Blockbuster,Shrike 2.50
57 CDi,RL,MFm,V:Shrike. 2.50
58 CDi,V:Shrike 2.50
59 CDi,RL,Where's Freddy Minh . . . 2.50
60 CDi,Low,V:Transbelvan mob . . . 2.50

61 CDi,V:Bank Robbers	2.50
62 CDi,Joker:Last Laugh	2.50
63 CDi,Last Laugh, aftermath	2.50
64 CDi,On a Christmas Evening	2.50
65 CDi,BruceWayne:Murderer,pt.3	2.50
66 CDi,BruceWayne:Murderer,pt.9	2.50
67 CDi,V:Amygdala	2.50
68 CDi,BruceWayne:Fugitive,pt.6	2.50
69 CDi,BruceWayne:Fugitive,pt.9	2.50
70 CDi,in Arizona	2.50
71 RL,Something About Mary,pt.1	2.50
72 RL,Something About Mary,pt.2	2.50
73 RL,Something About Mary,pt.3	2.50
74 RL,Something About Mary,pt.4	2.50
75 RL,MGo,40-pg	3.50
76 MGo(c)	2.50
77 cops go bad	2.50
78 V:new Tarantula	2.50
79 Source of madness	2.50
80 Venn Diagram,pt.1	2.50
81 Venn Diagram,pt.2	4.00
82 Venn Diagram,pt.3	2.50
83 Murder of Chief Redhorn	2.50
84 RL,Chief Redhorn case	2.50
85 Tarantula or Nite-Wing	2.50
86 Cyber-punks	2.50
87 V:Blockbuster	2.50
88 V:Blockbuster	2.50
89 V:Blockbuster	2.50
90 V:Blockbuster	2.50
91 V:Shrike	2.50
92 V:Blockbuster	2.50
93 V:Blockbuster showdown	2.50
94 F:Tarantula	2.50
95 Tarantula vs. Copperhead	2.50
96 War Games,Act 1,pt.3	2.50
97 War Games,Act 2,pt.3	2.50
98 War Games,Act 3,pt.3	2.50
99 SMc,Back to the Life	2.50
100 V:Trantula, 40-page	3.00
101 SMc,Nightwing,Year One,pt.1	8.00
102 SMc,Nightwing,Year One,pt.2	5.00
103 SMc,Nightwing,Year One,pt.3	6.00
104 SMc,Nightwing,Year One,pt.4	5.00
105 SMc,Nightwing,Year One,pt.5	3.00
106 SMc,Nightwing,Year One,pt.6	3.00
107 PhH,Bludhaven left	3.00
108 PhH,in New York	3.00
109 PhH,V:Black Mask	3.00
110 PhH,F:Robin	3.00
111 Dick Grayson undercover	2.50
112 V:Deathstroke	2.50
113 Villains united	2.50
114 PHe, Nightwing gone	2.50
115 PHe,V:Deathstroke	2.50
116 PHe,V:Deathstroke	2.50
117 PHe,V:Deathstroke	2.50
118 Hiding in New York	2.50
119 Twin Nightwings	2.50
120 V:Pierce Bros.	3.00
121 Dick Grayson to the rescue	3.00
122 Only one Nightwing remaining	3.00
123 Fire-throwing killer	3.00
124 Heads of the underworld	3.00
125 MWn,DJu,NRd,V:Raptor	3.00
126 MWn,DJu,NRd	3.00
Ann.#1 Pulp Heroes (Romance)	4.50
Spec.#1,000,000 CDi(s),SMc,KIS	2.50
Secret Files #1 64-page	5.50
Spec.#1 Our Worlds at War,48-pg	3.00
Giant #1 80-pg.CDi,I:Hella	6.00
GN The Target,CDi,SMc,48-page	6.00
TPB A Knight in Bludhaven,CDi, SMc,KIS, rep. #1–#8	15.00
TPB Ties That Bind, DON,AIG, DG,KIS,rep.	13.00
TPB Rough Justice	18.00
TPB Love and Bullets,rep.	18.00
TPB A Darker Shade of Justice	20.00
TPB Love and Bullets	18.00
TPB The Hunt for Oracle	15.00
TPB Nightwing/Huntress	10.00

TPB Nightwing: Big Guns	15.00
TPB On the Razor's Edge (2005)	15.00
TPB Year One (2005)	15.00
TPB Nightwing: Renegade (2006)	15.00
TPB Mobbed Up (2006)	13.00

NIGHTWING AND HUNTRESS
March, 1998

1 (of 4) BSz,conflict	2.50
2 BSz,good cop, bad cop	2.50
3 BSz,Malfatti	2.50
4 BSz,concl.	2.50

NUTSY SQUIRREL
Sept.–Oct., 1954

61 SM.	150.00
62 thru 71	@125.00
72 Nov., 1957	125.00

OMAC
Sept.–Oct., 1974

1 JK,I&O:Omac	75.00
2 JK,I:Mr.Big	30.00
3 JK,100,000 foes	30.00
4 JK,V:Kafka	30.00
5 JK,New Bodies for Old	30.00
6 JK,The Body Bank	30.00
7 JK,The Ocean Stealers	30.00
8 JK,Last issue	30.00

[2nd Series], 1991

1 JBy,B&W prestige	5.00
2 JBy,The Great Depression era	4.50
3 JBy,To Kill Adolf Hitler	4.50
4 JBy,D:Mr.Big	4.50

OMAC
July, 2006

1 (of 8) Dawn of a new Omac	3.00
2 In Las Vegas	3.00
3 Brother Eye	3.00
4 Mike Costner	3.00
5 Return of Brother Eye	3.00

OMAC PROJECT, THE
Apr., 2005

1 (of 6) Checkmate	2.50
2 Brother Eye satellite	2.50
3 F:Sasha Bordeaux	2.50
4 Brother Eye breaks free.	2.50
5 Pawn No More	2.50
6 concl.	2.50
Spec. Infinite Crisis Special	5.00
TPB	15.00

OMEGA MEN
Dec., 1982

1 KG,V:Citadel	3.50
2 KG,O:Broot	3.00
3 KG,I:Lobo	8.00
4 KG,D:Demonia,I:Felicity	3.00
5 KG,V:Lobo	3.00
6 KG,V:Citadel,D:Gepsen	2.50
7 O:Citadel,L:Auron	2.50
8 R:Nimbus,I:H.Hokum	2.50
9 V:HarryHokum,A:Lobo	2.50
10 A:Lobo (First Full Story)	6.00
11 V:Blackfire	2.50
12 R:Broots Wife	2.50
13 A:Broots Wife	2.50
14 Karna	2.50
15 Primus Goes Mad	2.50
16 Spotlight Issue	2.50
17 V:Psions	2.50
18 V:Psions	2.50
19 V:Psions,C:Lobo	2.50
20 V:Psions,A:Lobo	2.50
21 Spotlight Issue	2.50

Omega Men #13 © DC Comics Inc.

22 Nimbus	2.50
23 Nimbus	2.50
24 Okaara	2.50
25 Kalista	2.50
26 V:Spiderguild	4.00
27 V:Psions	4.00
28 V:Psions	2.50
29 V:Psions	2.50
30 R:Primus,I:Artin	2.50
31 Crisis tie-in	2.50
32 Felicity	2.50
33 Regufe World	2.50
34 A:New Teen Titans	2.50
35 A:New Teen Titans	2.50
36 Last Days of Broot	2.50
37 V:Spiderguild,A:Lobo	5.00
38 A:Tweener Network	2.50
Ann.#1 KG,R:Harpis	2.50
Ann.#2 KG,O:Primus	2.50

OMEGA MEN, THE
Oct., 2006

1 (of 6) Crimes Agains the Galaxy	3.00
2	3.00

100 BULLETS
DC/Vertigo, 1999

1 F:Dizzy Cordova & AgentGraves	12.00
2 Dizzy,pt.2	7.00
3 F:Mr.Shepard	5.00
4 Shot, Water Back,pt.1	5.00
5 Shot, Water Back,pt.2	5.00
6 Short Con, Long Odds,pt.1	4.00
7 Short Con, Long Odds,pt.2	4.00
8 F:Agent Graves	4.00
9 Right Ear,Left in the Cold,pt.1	4.00
10 Right Ear,Left in the Cold,pt.2.	4.00
11 F:Lilly Roach	3.50
12 Parlez Kung Vous,pt.1	3.50
13 Parlez Kung Vous,pt.2	3.50
14 Parlez Kung Vous,concl.	3.50
15 Hang Up on Hang Low,pt.1	3.50
16 Hang Up on Hang Low,pt.2	3.50
17 Hang Up on Hang Low,pt.3	3.00
18 Hang Up on Hang Low,pt.4	3.00
19 Hang Up on Hang Low,pt.5	3.00
20 Hot House	3.00
21 Sell Fish & Out to Sea,pt.1	3.00
22 Sell Fish & Out to Sea,pt.2	3.00
23 Red Prince Blues,pt.1	3.00
24 Red Prince Blues,pt.2	3.50
25 Red Prince Blues,pt.3	2.50
26 Mr. Branch & the Family Tree	2.50
27 Idol Chatter	2.50

28 Contrabandolero,pt.1 . . . . 2.50
29 Contrabandolero,pt.2 . . . . 2.50
30 Contrabandolero,pt.3 . . . . 2.50
31 Counterfeit Detective,pt.1 . . . . . . 2.50
32 Counterfeit Detective,pt.2 . . . . . . 2.50
33 Counterfeit Detective,pt.3 . . . . . . 2.50
34 Counterfeit Detective,pt.4 . . . . . . 2.50
35 Counterfeit Detective,pt.5 . . . . . . 2.50
36 Counterfeit Detective,pt.6 . . . . . . 2.50
37 On Accidental Purpose 2.50
38 Cole Burns Slow Hand 2.50
39 Ambition's Audition 2.50
40 Night of the Payday 2.50
41 A Crash 2.50
42 V:Wylie Times 2.50
43 Chill in the Oven,pt.1 . . . . 2.50
44 Chill in the Oven,pt.2 . . . . 2.50
45 Chill in the Oven,pt.3 . . . . 2.50
46 Chill in the Oven,pt.4 . . . . 2.50
47 In Stinked,pt.1 . . . . 2.50
48 In Stinked,pt.2 . . . . 2.50
49 In Stinked,pt.3 . . . . 2.50
50 Agent Graves,40-pg. 3.50
51 Wylie Runs the Voodoo Down . . 2.50
52 Wylie Runs the Voodoo Down . . 2.50
53 Wylie Runs the Voodoo Down . . 2.50
54 Wylie Runs the Voodoo Down . . 2.50
55 Wylie Runs the Voodoo Down . . 2.50
56 Wylie Runs the Voodoo Down . . 2.50
57 Wylie Runs the Voodoo Down . . 2.50
58 Lono & Loop Hughes 2.50
59 F:Victor "The Saint". 2.50
60 Staring at the Son,pt.1 . . . . 2.50
61 Staring at the Son,pt.2 . . . . 2.50
62 Staring at the Son,pt.3 . . . . 2.50
63 The Trust. 2.75
64 Jack heads to Atlantic City 2.75
65 Loop, Lono & Victor 2.75
66 Loop, Lono & Victor 2.75
67 Dizzy & Wylie 2.75
68 More dead Trust members 2.75
69 F:Augustus Medici 2.75
70 Gambling with their lives. 2.75
71 A Wake, pt.1 . . . . 2.75
72 A Wake, pt.2 . . . . 3.00
73 A Wake, pt.3 . . . . 3.00
74 A Wake, pt.4 . . . . 3.00
75 The Briefcase 3.00
76 Secret Armies of the Trust 3.00
77 On to Mexico. 3.00
78 In Mexico 3.00
TPB First Shot,Last Call 10.00
TPB Split Second Chance 15.00
TPB Hang Up on the Hang Low . . 10.00
TPB A Foregone Tomorrow 18.00
TPB The Counterfifth Detective . . 13.00
TPB Six Feet Under The Gun 13.00
TPB Samurai 13.00
TPB Vol. 8 The Hard Way (2005) . 15.00
TPB Vol. 10 Decayed (2006) 15.00
TPB Strychnine Lives (2006) 15.00

100%
DC/Vertigo, June, 2002
1 (of 5) PPo, 48-pg. b&w 6.00
2 thru 5 PPo, Sci-fi, 48-pg. b&w . @6.00
TPB PPo 25.00

ORION
April, 2000
1 WS,Darkseid 2.50
2 WS,V:Darkseid. 2.50
3 WS,FM,V:Suicide Jockeys. 2.50
4 WS,DGb,V:Darkseid 2.50
5 WS,V:Darkseid. 2.50
6 WS,EL,AG,F:Mortalla. 2.50
7 WS,HC,V:Kalibak. 2.50
8 WS,RLe,JLb,V:Kalibak. 2.50
9 WS,V:Desaad 2.50
10 WS,AAd,V:Desaad 2.50
11 WS,New Genesis,Anti-Life 2.50

12 WS,JLe,return to Apokolips 2.50
13 WS,TA,JBy,F:Captain Marvel . . . 2.50
14 WS,TA,JBy,F:Captain Marvel . . . 2.50
15 WS,JPL,48-page. 4.50
16 WS,Abysmal Plane,V:Clockworx 2.50
17 WS,Abysmal Plane,V:Clockworx 2.50
18 WS,AM,F:Rakar. 2.50
19 WS,ECa,Joker-crazed Deep Six. 2.50
20 WS,fall from Grace 2.50
21 WS,V:Arnicus Wolfram 2.50
22 WS,young teen 2.50
23 WS,BWi,young teen 2.50
24 WS,BWi,Tactical nuke. 2.50
25 WS,BWi,48-pg.final issue 4.25
TPB The Gates of Apokolips 13.00

OTHER SIDE, THE
DC/Vertigo, Oct., 2006
1 (of 5) Vietnam 3.00
2 . . . . 3.00

OTHERWORLD
DC/Vertigo, March, 2005
1 (of 12) PJ,ALa 3.00
2 thru 7 PJ,ALa . . . . @3.00
TPB Book One. 20.00

Our Army at War #7 ©
DC Comics, Inc.

OUR ARMY AT WAR
Aug., 1952
1 Cl(c),Dig Your Foxhole Deep. 3,500.00
2 Cl(c),Champ 1,500.00
3 GK(c),No Exit 1,000.00
4 IN(c),Last Man 900.00
5 IN(c),T.N.T. Bouquet 750.00
6 IN(c),Battle Flag. 750.00
7 IN(c),Dive Bomber 750.00
8 IN(c),One Man Army 750.00
9 GC(c),Undersea Raider. 750.00
10 IN(c),Soldiers on the
    High Wire. 750.00
11 IN(c),Scratch One Meatball. . . 750.00
12 IN(c),The Big Drop 750.00
13 BK(c),Ghost Ace 750.00
14 BK(c),Drummer of Waterloo . . 750.00
15 IN(c),Thunder in the Skies . . . 650.00
16 IN(c),A Million To One Shot . . 650.00
17 IN(c),The White Death 650.00
18 IN(c),Frontier Fighter 650.00
19 IN(c),The Big Ditch 650.00
20 IN(c),Abandon Ship 650.00
21 IN(c),Dairy of a Flattop 500.00
22 JGr(c),Ranger Raid. 500.00
23 IN(c),Jungle Navy 500.00
24 IN(c),Suprise Landing 500.00

25 JGr(c),Take 'Er Down 500.00
26 JGr(c),Sky Duel 500.00
27 IN(c),MD,Diary of a Frogman . 500.00
28 JGr(c),Detour-War 500.00
29 IN(c),Grounded Fighter. 500.00
30 JGr(c),Torpedo Raft 500.00
31 IN(c),Howitzer Hill. 500.00
32 JGr(c),Battle Mirror 500.00
33 JGr(c),Fighting Gunner 500.00
34 JGr(c),Point-Blank War. 500.00
35 JGr(c),Frontline Tackle 500.00
36 JGr(c),Foxhole Mascot 500.00
37 JGr(c),Walking Battle Pin 500.00
38 JGr(c),Floating Pillbox 500.00
39 JGr(c),Trench Trap 500.00
40 RH(c),Tank Hunter 500.00
41 JGr(c),Jungle Target 500.00
42 IN(c),Shadow Targets 400.00
43 JGr(c),A Bridge For Billy 400.00
44 JGr(c),Thunder In The Desert 400.00
45 JGr(c),Diary of a Fighter Pilot. 400.00
46 JGr(c),Prize Package 400.00
47 JGr(c),Flying Jeep 400.00
48 JGr(c),Front Seat 400.00
49 JKu(c),Landing Postponed . . . 400.00
50 JGr(c),RH,Mop-Up Squad . . . 400.00
51 JGr(c),Battle Tag. 400.00
52 JGr(c),Pony Express Pilot. . . . 400.00
53 JGr(c),One Ringside-For War. 400.00
54 JKu(c),No-Man Secret 400.00
55 JGr(c),No Rest For A Raider. . 400.00
56 JKu(c),You're Next 400.00
57 JGr(c),Ten-Minute Break. 400.00
58 JKu(c),The Fighting SnowBird 400.00
59 JGr(c),The Mustang Had
    My Number 400.00
60 JGr(c),Ranger Raid. 400.00
61 JGr(c),A Pigeon For Easy Co. 300.00
62 JKu(c),Trigger Man 300.00
63 JGr(c),The Big Toss 300.00
64 JKu(c),Tank Rider 300.00
65 JGr(c),Scramble-War Upstairs 300.00
66 RH(c),Gunner Wanted 300.00
67 JKu(c),MD,Boiling Point 300.00
68 JKu(c),MD,End of the Line . . . 300.00
69 JGr(c),Combat Cage. 300.00
70 JGr(c),Torpedo Tank 300.00
71 JGr(c),Flying Mosquitoes 300.00
72 JGr(c),No. 1 Pigeon 300.00
73 JKu(c),Shooting Gallery 300.00
74 JGr(c),Ace Without Guns 300.00
75 JGr(c),Blind Night Fighter 300.00
76 JKu(c),Clipped Hellcat 300.00
77 JGr(c),Jets Don't Dream 300.00
78 IN(c),Battle Nurse 300.00
79 JGr(c),MD,What's the Price
    of a B-17? 300.00
80 JGr(c),The Sparrow And
    The...Hawk 300.00
81 JGr(c),Sgt. Rock in The
    Rock of Easy Co. 5,000.00
82 JGr(c),MD,Gun Jockey . . . 1,200.00
83 JGr(c),MD,B:Sgt.Rock Stories,
    The Rock and the Wall 3,800.00
84 JKu(c),Laughter On
    Snakehead Hill 650.00
85 JGr(c),Ice Cream Soldier 800.00
86 RH(c),Tank 711 . . . . 600.00
87 RH(c),Calling Easy Co. 600.00
88 JKu(c),The Hard Way 600.00
89 RH(c),No Shoot From Easy . . 600.00
90 JKu(c),3 Stripes Hill 600.00
91 JGr(c),No Answer from
    Sarge 1,500.00
92 JGr(c),Luck of Easy 500.00
93 JGr(c),Deliver One Airfield . . . 500.00
94 JKu(c),Target-Easy Company. 500.00
95 JKu(c),Battle of the Stripes . . . 500.00
96 JGr(c),MD,Last Stand
    For Easy 500.00
97 JKu(c),What Makes A
    Sergeant Run? 500.00

Our Army at War #125
© DC Comics Inc.

98 JKu(c),Soldiers Never Die . . . 500.00
99 JKu(c),Easy's Hardest Battle . 500.00
100 JKu(c),No Exit For Easy 500.00
101 JKu(c),End Of Easy 400.00
102 JKu(c),The Big Star. 400.00
103 RH(c),Easy's Had It 400.00
104 JKu(c),A New Kind Of War . . 400.00
105 JKu(c),T.N.T. Birthday 400.00
106 JKu(c),Meet Lt. Rock 400.00
107 JKu(c),Doom Over Easy 400.00
108 JGr(c),Unknown Sergeant . . 400.00
109 JKu(c),Roll Call For Heroes . 400.00
110 JKu(c),That's An Order 400.00
111 JKu(c),What's The Price
    Of A Dog Tag 400.00
112 JKu(c),Battle Shadow 400.00
113 JKu(c),Eyes Of A
    Blind Gunner 400.00
114 JKu(c),Killer Sergeant 400.00
115 JKu(c),Rock's Battle Family . 400.00
116 JKu(c),S.O.S. Sgt. Rock . . . 400.00
117 JKu(c),Snafu Squad 400.00
118 RH(c),The Tank Vs. The
    Tin Soldier 400.00
119 JKu(c),A Bazooka For
    Babyface 400.00
120 JGr(c),Battle Tags
    For Easy Co. 300.00
121 JKu(c),New Boy In Easy 250.00
122 JKu(c),Battle of the
    Pajama Commandoes 250.00
123 JGr(c),Battle Brass Ring 250.00
124 JKu(c),Target-Sgt. Rock 250.00
125 JKu(c),Hold-At All Costs 250.00
126 RH(c),The End Of
    Easy Company 250.00
127 JKu(c),4 Faces of Sgt. Rock. 250.00
128 JKu(c),O:Sgt. Rock. 350.00
129 JKu(c),Heroes Need
    Cowards 250.00
130 JKu(c),No Hill For Easy 250.00
131 JKu(c),One Pair of
    Dogtags For Sale 250.00
132 JKu(c),Young Soldiers
    Never Cry 250.00
133 JKu(c),Yesterday's Hero . . . 250.00
134 JKu(c),The T.N.T. Book. . . . 250.00
135 JKu(c),Battlefield Double . . . 250.00
136 JKu(c),Make Me A Hero . . . 250.00
137 JKu(c),Too Many Sergeants . 250.00
138 JKu(c),Easy's Lost Sparrow . 250.00
139 JKu(c),A Firing Squad
    For Easy 250.00
140 JKu(c),Brass Sergeant 250.00
141 JKu(c),Dead Man's Trigger . . 250.00

142 JKu(c),Easy's New Topkick. . 250.00
143 JKu(c),Easy's T.N.T. Crop . . . 250.00
144 JKu(c),The Sparrow And
    The Tiger 250.00
145 JKu(c),A Feather For
    Little Suro Shot 250.00
146 JKu(c),The Fighting Guns
    For Easy 250.00
147 JKu(c),Book One:Generals
    Don't Die 250.00
148 JKu(c),Book Two:Generals
    Don't Die:Generals Are
    Sergeants With Stars. 250.00
149 JKu(c),Surrender Ticket 250.00
150 JKu(c),Flytrap Hill 250.00
151 JKu(c),War Party,
    I:Enemy Ace 800.00
152 JKu(c),Last Man-Last Shot . . 250.00
153 JKu(c),Easy's Last Stand . . . 500.00
154 JKu(c),Boobytrap Mascot . . . 200.00
155 JKu(c),No Stripes For Me . . . 400.00
156 JKu(c),The Human Tank Trap 200.00
157 JKu(c),Nothin's Ever
    Lost In War 200.00
158 JKu(c),Iron Major Rock
    Sergeant 200.00
159 JKu(c),The Blind Gun 200.00
160 JKu(c),What's The Color
    Of Your Blood 200.00
161 JKu(c),Dead End
    For A Dogface 200.00
162 JKu(c),The Price and
    The Sergeant. 200.00
163 JKu(c),MD,RE,Kill Me-Kill Me 200.00
164 JKu(c),CE,No Exit For Easy,
    reprint from #100 . . . . 475.00
165 GE,JKu(c),The Return of the
    Iron Major 200.00
166 GE,JKu(c),Half A Sergeant . . 200.00
167 GE,JKu(c),Kill One-
    Save One 200.00
168 GE,JKu(c),I Knew The
    Unknown Soldier 400.00
169 GE,JKu(c),Nazi On My Back 175.00
170 GE,JKu(c),Buzzard Bait Hill . 175.00
171 GE,JKu(c),The Sergeant
    Must Die 175.00
172 GE,JKu(c),A Slug for a
    Sergeant 175.00
173 GE,JKu(c),Easy's Hardest
    Battle, reprint from #99 . . . . . 175.00
174 GE,JKu(c),One Kill Too
    Many 175.00
175 JKu(c),T.N.T. Letter 175.00
176 MD,JKu(c),Give Me Your
    Stripes 175.00
177 RH,JKu(c),Target-Easy Company,
    reprint from #94, giant-size . . 250.00
178 RH,JKu(c),Only One Medal
    For Easy 150.00
179 RH,JKu(c),A Penny Jackie
    Johnson 150.00
180 RH,JKu(c),You Can't
    Kill A General. 150.00
181 RH,Monday's Coward-
    Tuesday's Hero 150.00
182 NA,RH,The Desert Rats
    of Easy 175.00
183 RH,NA,JKu(c),Sergeants
    Don't Stay Dead 200.00
184 RH,JKu(c),Candidate For A
    Firing Squad 150.00
185 RH,JKu(c),Battle Flag For
    A G.I. 150.00
186 RH,NA,JKu(c),3 Stripes Hill
    reprint from #90, Origin 150.00
187 RH,JKu(c),Shadow of a
    Sergeant 130.00
188 RH,JKu(c),Death Comes for
    Easy. 130.00
189 RH,JKu(c),The Mission Was
    Murder 130.00

Our Army at War #182
© DC Comics Inc.

190 RH,JKu(c),What Make's A
    Sergeant Run?, reprint
    from #97, giant-size. 300.00
191 RH,JKu(c),Death Flies High,
    A:Johnny Cloud 250.00
192 RH,JKu(c),A Firing Squad
    For A Sergeant 200.00
193 RH,JKu(c),Blood In
    the Desert 200.00
194 RH,JKu(c),Time For
    Vengeance. 200.00
195 RH,JKu(c),Dead Town 200.00
196 RH,JKu(c),Stop The War-
    I Want To Get Off. 200.00
197 RH,JKu(c),Last Exit For Easy 200.00
198 RH,JKu(c),Plugged Nickel . 200.00
199 RH,JKu(c),Nazi Ghost Wolf . 200.00
200 RH,GE,JKu(c),The
    Troubadour 150.00
201 RH,JKu(c),The Graffiti Writer 100.00
202 RH,JKu(c),Sarge Is Dead . . 100.00
203 RH,MD,JKu(c),Easy's Had It,
    reprint from # 103, giant-size 175.00
204 RH,JKu(c) 100.00
205 RH,JKu(c) 90.00
206 RH,JKu(c),There's A War On . 90.00
207 RH,JKu(c),A Sparrow's
    Prayer 90.00
208 RH,JKu(c),A Piece of Rag...
    And A Hank of Hair 90.00
209 RH,JKu(c),I'm Still Alive 90.00
210 RH,JKu(c),I'm Kilroy 90.00
211 RH,JKu(c),The Treasure of
    St. Daniel. 90.00
212 RH,MD,JKu(c),The Quiet War 90.00
213 RH,JKu(c),A Letter For
    Bulldozer. 90.00
214 RH,JKu(c),Where Are You? . . 90.00
215 RH,JKu(c),Pied Piper of Peril . 90.00
216 RH,JKu(c),Doom Over Easy,
    reprint from # 107, Giant-size 150.00
217 RH,JKu(c),Surprise Party 75.00
218 RH,JKu(c),Medic! 75.00
219 RH,JKu(c),Yesterday's Hero . 75.00
220 RH,JKu(c),Stone-Age War . . . 75.00
221 RH,JKu(c),Hang-Up 75.00
222 RH,JKu(c),Dig In, Easy. 75.00
223 RH,JKu(c),On Time. 75.00
224 RH,JKu(c),One For The
    Money 75.00
225 RH,JKu(c),Face Front. 75.00
226 RH,JKu(c),Death Stop 75.00
227 RH,JKu(c),Traitor's Blood 75.00
228 RH,JKu(c),It's A Dirty War. . . . 75.00

229 RH,JKu(c),The Battle of the
   Sergeants, reprint #128,
   Giant-size 100.00
230 RH,JKu(c),Home Is The
   Hunter 50.00
231 RH,JKu(c),My Brother's
   Keeper. 50.00
232 RH,JKu(c),3 Men In A Tub . . 50.00
233 RH,JKu(c),Head Count. 50.00
234 RH,JKu(c),Summer In Salerno 50.00
235 RH,ATh,JKu(c),Pressure
   Point, giant-size. 70.00
236 RH,JKu(c),Face The Devil,
   giant-size 70.00
237 RH,JKu(c),Nobody Cares,
   giant-size 70.00
238 RH,JKu(c),I Kid You Not,
   giant-size 70.00
239 RH,JKu(c),The Soldier,
   giant-size 70.00
240 RH,JKu(c),NA, giant-size . . . 100.00
241 RH,ATh,JKu(c),War Story,
   giant-size 70.00
242 RH,JKu(c),Infantry 70.00
243 RH,MD,JKu(c),24 Hour Pass . 60.00
244 RH,MD,JKu(c),Easy's First
   Tiger 60.00
245 RH,JKu(c),The Prisoner . . . 60.00
246 RH,JKu(c),Naked Combat . . . 60.00
247 RH,JKu(c),The Vision 40.00
248 RH,JKu(c),The Firing Squad. . 40.00
249 RH,JKu(c),The Luck of
   Easy,WW 45.00
250 RH,JKu(c),90 Day Wonder. . 40.00
251 RH,JKu(c),The Iron Major. . . 40.00
252 RH,JKu(c),The Iron Hand. . . . 40.00
253 RH,JKu(c),Rock and Iron . . . 40.00
254 RH,ATh,JKu(c),The Town . . . 40.00
255 RH,JKu(c),What's It Like. . . . 40.00
256 RH,JKu(c),School For
   Sergeants 40.00
257 RH,JKu(c),The Castaway . . . 40.00
258 RH,JKu(c),The Survivors . . . 40.00
259 RH,JKu(c),Lost Paradise 40.00
260 RH,JKu(c),Hell's Island. 40.00
261 RH,JKu(c),The Medal That
   Nobody Wanted. 40.00
262 RH,JKu(c),The Return 40.00
263 RH,JKu(c),The Cage 40.00
264 RH,JKu(c),The Hunt 40.00
265 RH,JKu(c),The Brother 40.00
266 RH,GE,JKu(c),The Evacuees . 40.00
267 RH,JKu(c),A Bakers Dozen . 40.00
268 RH,JKu(c),The Elite 40.00
269 RH,MD,GE,JKu(c), giant-size 100.00
270 RH,JKu(c),Spawn of the
   Devil. 40.00
271 RH,JKu(c),Brittle Harvest . . . 35.00
272 RH,JKu(c),The Bloody Flag . 35.00
273 RH,JKu(c),The Arena 35.00
274 RH,GE,JKu(c),Home Is The
   Hero. 35.00
275 RH,MD,JKu(c),Graveyard
   Battlefield, giant-size 100.00
276 RH,GE,JKu(c),A Bullet For
   Rock 32.00
277 RH,JKu(c),Gashouse Gang . . 32.00
278 RH,GE,JKu(c),Rearguard
   Action. 32.00
279 JKu(c),Mined City 32.00
280 RH,GE,MD,JKu(c),Mercy
   Mission 60.00
281 RH,JKu(c),Dead Man's Eyes . 30.00
282 JKu(c),Pieces of Time. 30.00
283 JKu(c),Dropouts 30.00
284 JKu(c),Linkup 30.00
285 JKu(c),Bring Him Back 30.00
286 JKu(c),Firebird 25.00
287 MGr,JKu(c),The Fifth
   Dimension 25.00
288 JKu(c),Defend-Or Destroy . . 25.00
289 JKu(c),The Line 25.00

Our Army at War #282
© *DC Comics, Inc.*

290 JKu(c),Super-Soldiers. 25.00
291 JKu(c),Death Squad 25.00
292 JKu(c),A Lesson In Blood . . . 25.00
293 JKu(c),It Figures 25.00
294 JKu(c),Coffin For Easy 25.00
295 JKu(c),The Devil in Paradise . 25.00
296 JKu(c),Combat Soldier 25.00
297 JKu(c),Percentages 25.00
298 JKu(c),Return to Chartres. . . . 25.00
299 JKu(c),Three Soldiers. 25.00
300 JKu(c),300th Hill 30.00
301 JKu(c),The Farm 25.00
Becomes:

SGT. ROCK
1977–88
302 JKu(c),Anzio-The Bloodbath,
   part I 40.00
303 JKu(c),Anzio, part II 20.00
304 JKu(c),Anzio, part III 20.00
305 JKu(c),Dead Man's Trigger,
   reprint from #141. . . . . 20.00
306 JKu(c),The Last Soldier 20.00
307 JKu(c),I'm Easy. 20.00
308 JKu(c),One Short Step 20.00
309 JKu(c),Battle Clowns 20.00
310 JKu(c),Hitler's Wolf Children. . 20.00
311 JKu(c),The Sergeant and
   the Lady. 15.00
312 JKu(c),No Name Hill 15.00
313 JKu(c),A Jeep For Joey 15.00
314 JKu(c),Gimme Sky 15.00
315 JKu(c),Combat Antenna 15.00
316 JKu(c),Another Hill. 15.00
317 JKu(c),Hell's Oven 15.00
318 JKu(c),Stone-Age War 15.00
319 JKu(c),To Kill a Sergeant 15.00
320 JKu(c),Never Salute a
   Sergeant 15.00
321 JKu(c),It's Murder Out Here . . 10.00
322 JKu(c),The Killer. 10.00
323 JKu(c),Monday's Hero 10.00
324 JKu(c),Ghost of a Tank. 10.00
325 JKu(c),Future Kill, part I 10.00
326 JKu(c),Future Kill, part II. 10.00
327 JKu(c),Death Express. 10.00
328 JKu(c),Waiting For Rock. 10.00
329 JKu(c),Dead Heat 10.00
330 JKu(c),G.I. Trophy 10.00
331 JKu(c),The Sons of War 10.00
332 JKu(c),Pyramid of Death. 10.00
333 JKu(c),Ask The Dead 10.00
334 JKu(c),What's Holding Up
   The War. 10.00
335 JKu(c),Killer Compass 10.00

336 JKu(c),The Red Maple Leaf . . 10.00
337 JKu(c),A Bridge Called Charlie 10.00
338 JKu(c),No Escape From
   the Front 10.00
339 JKu(c),I Was Here Before. . . . 10.00
340 JKu(c),How To Win A War. . . . 10.00
341 JKu(c),High-Flyer 10.00
342 JKu(c),The 6 sides of
   Sgt. Rock. 10.00
343 thru 350. . . . . @10.00
351 thru 422. . . . . @7.00

OUR FIGHTING FORCES
Oct.–Nov., 1954
1 IN,JGr(c),Human Booby Trap 2,000.00
2 RH,IN,IN(c),Mile-Long Step . . . 800.00
3 RA,JKu(c),Winter Ambush. . . . 600.00
4 RA,JGr(c),The Hot Seat 500.00
5 IN,RA,JGr(c),The Iron Punch . 500.00
6 IN,RA,JKu(c),The Sitting Tank . 425.00
7 RA,JKu,JGr(c),Battle Fist. 425.00
8 IN,RA,JGr(c),No War
   For A Gunner. 425.00
9 JKu,RH,JGr(c),Crash-
   Landing At Dawn 425.00
10 WW,RA,JKu(c),Grenade
   Pitcher. 425.00
11 JKu,JGr(c),Diary of a Sub. . . . 350.00
12 IN,JKu,JGr(c),Jump Seat 350.00
13 RA,JGr(c),Beach Party 350.00
14 JA,RA,IN,JGr(c),Unseen War . 350.00
15 RH,JKu,JGr(c),Target For
   A Lame Duck. 350.00
16 RH,JGr(c),Night Fighter 350.00
17 RA,JGr(c),Anchored Frogman 350.00
18 RH,JKu,JGr(c),Cockpit Seat. . 350.00
19 RA,JKu(c),StraightenThatLine 350.00
20 RA,MD,JGr(c),The
   Floating Pilot 400.00
21 RA,JKu(c),The Bouncing
   Baby of Company B 250.00
22 JKu,RA,JGr(c),3 Doorways
   To War 250.00
23 RA,IN,JA,JGr(c),Tin Fish Pilot 250.00
24 RA,RH,JGr(c),Frogman Duel . 250.00
25 RA,JGr(c),Dead End 250.00
26 IN,RH,JKu(c),Tag Day 250.00
27 MD,RA,JKu(c),TNT Escort . . . 250.00
28 RH,MD,JKu(c),AllQuiet atC.P. 250.00
29 JKu,JKu(c),Listen To A Jet . . 250.00
30 IN,RA,JKu(c),Fort
   For A Gunner. 250.00
31 MD,RA,JKu(c),Silent Sub . . . 250.00
32 RH,MD,RH(c),PaperWorkWar 250.00
33 RH,JKu,JKu(c),Frogman
   In A Net 250.00
34 JA,JGr,JKu(c),Calling U-217. . 250.00
35 JA,JGr,JKu(c),Mask of
   a Frogman. 250.00
36 MD,JA,JKu(c),Steel Soldier . . 250.00
37 JA,JGr,JGr(c),Frogman
   In A Bottle 250.00
38 RH,RA,JA,JGr(c),Sub Sinker . 250.00
39 JA,RH,RH(c),Last Torpedo . . . 250.00
40 JGr,JA,JKu,JKu(c),The
   Silent Ones 250.00
41 JGr,RH,JA,JKu(c),Battle
   Mustang. 300.00
42 RH,MD,JGr(c),Sorry-
   Wrong Hill 225.00
43 MD,JKu(c),Inside Battle . . 225.00
44 MD,RH,RA,JGr(c),Big Job
   For Baker. 225.00
45 RH,RA,JGr(c),B:Gunner and
   Sarge, Mop-Up Squad. 700.00
46 RH,RA,JGr(c),Gunner's
   Squad 300.00
47 RH,JKu(c),TNT Birthday 225.00
48 JA,RH,JGr(c),A Statue
   For Sarge 225.00
49 MD,RH,JGr(c),Blind Gunner . . 275.00

Our Fighting Forces #45
© DC Comics, Inc.

50 JA,RH,JGr(c),I:Pooch,My
   Pal, The Pooch 225.00
51 RA,JA,RH(c),Underwater
   Gunner. 200.00
52 RA,JKu,JKu(c),The Biggest
   Target in the World 175.00
53 MD,JKu,JKu(c),The Gunner
   and the Nurse 175.00
54 JA,RA,An Egg for Sarge 175.00
55 MD,RH,JGr(c),The Last Patrol 175.00
56 RI I,RA,JGr(c),Bridge of
   Bullets 175.00
57 JA,IN,JGr(c),A Tank For Sarge 175.00
58 JA,JGr(c),Return of the Pooch 175.00
59 RH,JA,JGr(c),Pooch-Patrol
   Leader. 175.00
60 RH,JA,JGr(c),Tank Target   175.00
61 JA,JGr(c),Pass to Peril . . .   175.00
62 JA,JGr(c),The Flying Pooch . . 175.00
63 JA,RH,JGr(c),Pooch-Tank
   Hunter 175.00
64 JK,RH,JGr(c),A Lifeline
   For Sarge 175.00
65 IN,JA,JGr(c),Dogtag Patrol . . . 175.00
66 JKu,JA,JGr(c),Trail of the
   Ghost Bomber 175.00
67 IN,JA,JGr(c),Purple Heart
   For Pooch 175.00
68 JA,JGr(c),Col. Hakawa's
   Birthday Party 175.00
69 JA,JKu,JGr(c),
   Destination Doom 175.00
70 JA,JKu(c),The Last Holdout . . 175.00
71 JA,JGr(c),End of the Marines . 150.00
72 JA,JGr(c),Four-Footed Spy . . . 150.00
73 IN,JGr(c),The Hero Maker . . . 150.00
74 IN,JGr(c),Three On A T.N.T.
   Bull's-Eye. 150.00
75 JKu(c),Purple Heart Patrol . . 150.00
76 JKu(c),The T.N.T. Seat 150.00
77 JKu(c),No Foxhole-No Home . 150.00
78 JGr(c),The Last Medal 150.00
79 JA,JGr(c),Backs to the Sea . . 150.00
80 JA,JGr(c),Don't Come Back . . 150.00
81 JGr(c),Battle of
   the Mud Marines 150.00
82 JA,JGr(c),Battle of the
   Empty Helmets 150.00
83 RA,JKu(c),Any Marine
   Can Do It 150.00
84 JA,JKu(c),The Gun of Shame. 150.00
85 Ja,JKu(c),The TNT Pin-Points 150.00
86 JKu(c),3 Faces of Combat . . . 150.00
87 JKu(c),Battle of the
   Boobytraps 150.00
88 GC,JKu(c),Devil Dog Patrol . . 150.00

89 JKu(c),TNT Toothache 150.00
90 JKu(c),Stop the War 150.00
91 JKu(c),The Human Shooting
   Gallery. 75.00
92 JA,JKu(c),The Bomb That
   Stopped The War. 75.00
93 IN,JKu(c),The Human Sharks. . 75.00
94 RH(c),E:Gunner,Sarge & Pooch,
   The Human Blockbusters . . . 75.00
95 GC,RH(c),B:The Fighting Devil
   Dog, Lt. Rock, The
   Fighting Devil Dog. 75.00
96 JA,RH(c),Battle of Fire 75.00
97 IN(c),Invitation To A
   Firing Squad 75.00
98 IN(c),E:The Fighting Devil
   Dog, Death Wore A Grin 75.00
99 JA,JKu(c),B:Capt. Hunter,
   No Mercy in Vietnam. 75.00
100 GC,IN(c),Death Also
   Stalks the Hunter. 75.00
101 JA,RH(c),Killer of Vietnam . . . 50.00
102 RH,JKu(c),Cold Steel
   For A Hot War 50.00
103 JKu(c),Tho Tunnels of Death . 50.00
104 JKu(c),Night Raid In Vietnam . 50.00
105 JKu(c),Blood Loyality 50.00
106 IN(c),Trail By Fury. 50.00
107 IN(c),Raid Of The Hellcats . . . 50.00
108 IN(c),Kill The Wolf Pack 50.00
109 IN(c),Burn, Raiders, Burn 50.00
110 IN(c),Mountains Full of Death . 50.00
111 IN(c),Train of Terror. 50.00
112 IN(c),What's In It For
   The Hellcats? 50.00
113 IN(c),Operation-Survival 50.00
114 JKu(c),No Loot For The
   Hellcats 50.00
115 JKu(c),Death In The Desert . . . 50.00
116 JKu(c),Peril From the Casbah 50.00
117 JKu(c),Colder Than Death . . . 50.00
118 JKu(c),Hell Underwater. 50.00
119 JKu(c),Bedlam In Berlin 50.00
120 JKu(c),Devil In The Dark 50.00
121 JKu(c),Take My Place. 50.00
122 JKu(c),24 Hours To Die 50.00
123 JKu(c),B:Born Losers,No
   Medals No Graves. 100.00
124 JKu(c),Losers Take All 35.00
125 Daughters of Death. 35.00
126 JKu(c),Lost Town 35.00
127 JKu(c),Angels Over Hell's
   Corner 35.00
128 JKu(c),7 11 War 35.00
129 JKu(c),Ride The Nightmare . . 35.00
130 JKu(c),Nameless Target 35.00
131 JKu(c),Half A Man. 35.00
132 JKu(c),Pooch, The Winner . . . 35.00
133 JKu(c),Heads or Tails,
   giant-size. 50.00
134 JKu(c),The Real Losers,
   giant-size. 50.00
135 JKu(c),Death Picks A Loser,
   giant-size. 50.00
136 JKu(c),Decoy For Death,
   giant-size. 50.00
137 JKu(c),God Of The Losers,
   giant-size. 50.00
138 JKu(c),The Targets 30.00
139 JKu(c),The Pirate 30.00
140 JKu(c),Lost...One Loser 30.00
141 JKu(c),Bad Penny, The. 30.00
142 JKu(c), 1/2 A Man 30.00
143 JKu(c),Diamonds Are
   For Never 30.00
144 JKu(c),The Lost Mission 30.00
145 JKu(c),A Flag For Losers 30.00
146 JKu(c),The Forever Walk 30.00
147 NA(c),The Glory Road 40.00
148 JKu(c),The Last Charge 30.00
149 FT(c),A Bullet For
   A Traitor. 30.00

Our Fighting Forces #151
© DC Comics, Inc.

150 JKu(c),Mark Our Graves. 30.00
151 JKu(c),Kill Me With Wagner . . 32.00
152 JK(c),A Small Place In Hell. . . 32.00
153 JK(c),Big Max 32.00
154 JK(c),Bushido,Live By The
   Code, Die By The Code 32.00
155 JK(c),The Partisans 32.00
156 JK(c),Good-Bye Broadway . . . 32.00
157 JK(c),Panama Fattie. 32.00
158 JK(c),Bombing Out On
   The Panama Canal. 32.00
159 JK(c),Mile-A-Minute Jones . . . 32.00
160 JKu(c),Ivan 32.00
161 JKu(c),The Major's Dream . . . 32.00
162 Gung-Ho 32.00
163 JKu(c),The Unmarked Graves 25.00
164 JKu(c),A Town Full Of Losers . 25.00
165 LD(c),The Rowboat Fleet 25.00
166 LD(c),Sword of Flame. 25.00
167 LD(c),A Front Seat In Hell. . . 25.00
168 LD(c),A Cold Day To Die. . . . 25.00
169 JKu(c),Welcome Home-And
   Die 25.00
170 JKu(c),A Bullet For
   The General 25.00
171 JKu(c),A Long Day...
   A Long War 25.00
172 JKu(c),The Two-Headed Spy . 25.00
173 JKu(c),An Appointment
   With A Direct Hit 25.00
174 JKu(c),Winner Takes-Death . . 25.00
175 JKu(c),Death Warrant 25.00
176 JKu(c),The Loser Is A
   Teen-Ager 25.00
177 JKu(c),This Loser Must Die . . 25.00
178 JKu(c),Last Drop For Losers . 25.00
179 JKu(c),The Last Loser 25.00
180 JKu(c),Hot Seat In A
   Cold War 25.00
181 JKu(c),Sept.–Oct., 1978 . . . . . 30.00

OUTCASTS
Oct., 1987
1 thru 11 . . . . @2.25

OUTLAW NATION
DC/Vertigo, Aug., 2000
1 JaD(s),F:pulp-fiction writer. 2.50
2 JaD(s),Southern bayou 2.50
3 JaD,F:Devil Kid 2.50
4 JaD,F:Kid Gloves. 2.50
5 JaD,F:Kid Gloves. 2.50
6 JaD, ... 2.50
7 JaD, ... 2.50

DC COMICS

8 JaD,Women,tequila & guns 2.50
9 JaD,Hell Holes 2.50
10 JaD,V:Gloves 2.50
11 JaD,Hate, Murder and Revenge . 2.50
12 JaD,Temptation 2.50
13 JaD,Desperado 2.50
14 JaD,The Devil Kid 2.50
15 JaD,The Devil Kid 2.50
16 JaD,Under siege 2.50
17 JaD,Quicksand 2.50
18 JaD,Old Asa 2.50
19 JaD,final issue 2.50

OUTLAWS
1991
1 LMc,I:Hood 2.25
2 thru 7 LMc . . . . @2.25

Outsiders #18
© *DC Comics, Inc.*

OUTSIDERS, THE
Nov., 1985
[1st Regular Series]
1 JAp,I:Looker 3.00
2 JAp,V:Nuclear Family 2.50
3 JAp,V:Force of July 2.50
4 JAp,V:Force of July 2.50
5 JAp,Christmas Issue 2.50
6 JAp,V:Duke of Oil 2.50
7 JAp,V:Duke of Oil 2.50
8 JAp,Japan 2.50
9 JAp,SD/JOp,Bik Lightning 2.50
10 JAp,I:Peoples Heroes 2.50
11 JAp,Imprisoned in death camp . 2.50
12 JAp,Imprisoned in death camp . . 2.50
13 JAp,Desert island 2.50
14 JAp,Looker/murder story 2.50
15 DJu,V:Bio-hazard 2.50
16 Halo vs.Firefly 2.50
17 JAp,J:Batman 2.50
18 JAp,BB,V:Eclipso 2.50
19 JAp,V:Windfall 2.50
20 JAp,Masters of Disaster 2.50
21 JAp,V:Kobra,I:Clayface IV 2.50
22 JAp,V:Strike Force Kobra 2.50
23 Return of People's Heroes 2.50
24 TVE,JAp,V:Skull,A:Duke of Oil . . 2.50
25 JAp,V:Skull 2.50
26 JAp,in Markovia 2.50
27 EL,Millennium 2.50
28 EL,Millennium,final issue 2.50
Ann.#1,KN,V:Skull,A:Batman 2.50
Spec.#1,A:Infinity,Inc 2.50

[2nd Regular Series], 1993–95
1 Alpha,TC(c),B:MiB(s),PaP,
   I:Technocrat,Faust,Wylde 3.00
1a Omega,TC(c),PaP,V:Vampires . 3.00
2 PaP,V:Sanction 2.25
3 PaP,V:Eradicator 2.25
4 PaP,A:Eradicator 2.25
5 PaP,V:Atomic Knight,A:Jihad . . . 2.25
6 PaP,V:Jihad 2.25
7 PaP,C:Batman 2.25
8 PaP,V:Batman,I:Halo 2.25
9 PaP,V:Batman 2.25
10 PaP,B:Final Blood, R:Looker . . . 2.50
11 PaP,Zero Hour,E:Final Blood . . . 2.25
12 PaP 2.25
13 New base 2.25
14 Martial Arts Spectacular 2.25
15 V:New Year's Evil 2.25
16 R:Windfall 2.25
17 A:Green Lantern 2.25
18 Sins of the Father 2.25
19 Sins of the Father, pt.2 . . . . 2.25
20 DvA,V:Metamorpho 2.25
21 A:Apokolips 2.25
22 Alien Assassin 2.25
23 V:Defilers 2.25
24 finale 2.25

OUTSIDERS
June 2003
1 TR,SHa 15.00
1a 2nd printing 4.00
2 TR,SHa,F:Jade 6.00
3 TR,SHa,Gorilla Grodd 3.00
4 Ccs,V:Brother Blood 3.00
5 CCs,V:Brother Blood 3.00
6 CCs,V:Brother Blood 2.50
7 TR,SHa,two Metamorphos 2.50
8 TR,F:Huntress 2.50
9 TR,F:Black Lightning 2.50
10 TR,F:Captain Marvel Jr. 2.50
11 F:Arsenal 2.50
12 V:Psimon 2.50
13 TR,Five by Five,pt.1 . . . . 2.50
14 TR,Five by Five,pt.2 . . . . 2.50
15 TR,Five by Five,pt.3 . . . . 2.50
16 V:Arsenal 2.50
17 TR,Most Wanted 2.50
18 Most Wanted, pt.2 . . . . 2.50
19 Most Wanted, pt.3 . . . . 2.50
20 Shift & Indy on a date 2.50
21 F:Batman 2.50
22 Arsenal vs. Batman 2.50
23 Lockdown 2.50
24 The Insiders, x-over, pt.2 . . . . . . 2.50
25 The Insdiers, x-over, pt.4 . . . . . . 3.50
26 Tick Tock, pt.1, A:Batman 2.50
27 Tick Tock, pt.2,A:Batman,Katana 2.50
28 ATi,Insider aftermath 2.50
29 ATi,Day of Vengeance tie-in 2.50
30 ATi,Day of Vengeance tie-in 2.50
31 ATi,Infinite Crisis tie-in. 2.50
32 ATi,Infinite Crisis tie-in. 2.50
33 ATi,Infinite Crisis tie-in. 2.50
34 ATi,One Year Later 2.50
35 ATi,Vs brutal regime 3.00
36 ATi,Nightwing's African Mission . 3.00
37 ATi,Monsieur Mallah & Brain. . . . 3.00
38 ATi,Mallah & Brain. 3.00
39 ATi 3.00
40 ATi 3.00
41 ATi, Old foe 3.00
42 ATi 3.00
TPB Looking For Trouble 13.00
TPB The Sum of All Evil (2005) . . . 15.00
TPB Looking For Trouble (2005) . . 13.00
TPB Vol. 3 Wanted (2005) 15.00
TPB Crisis Intervention (2006) 13.00

PARALLAX:
EMERALD NIGHT
Nov., 1996
1 RMz(s),MMK,MkK, pivotal tie-in
   to Final Night 4.50

PAT BOONE
1959
1 Ph(c),Jimmy Rodgers 750.00
2 Edd "Kookie" Byrnes 500.00
3 Fabian, Connie Francis 500.00
4 Bobby Darin, Johnny Mathis . . . 500.00
5 Dick Clark, Frankie Avalon . . . 500.00

PEACEMAKER
Jan., 1988
1 A:Dr.Tzin-Tzin 2.50
2 The Wages of Tzin. 2.50
3 and 4 . . . . @2.50

PENGUIN
TRIUMPHANT
1 JSon,A:Batman,Wall Street 6.00

PETER CANNON:
THUNDERBOLT
1992–93
1 thru 6 MC . . . . @2.25
7 MC,Battleground 2.25
8 MC,Cairo Kidnapped 2.25
9 MC 2.25
10 MC,A:JLA 2.25
11 MC,V:Havoc,A:Checkmate 2.25
12 MC,final Issue 2.25

PETER PANDA
Aug.–Sept., 1953
1 The Magic Rainbow 600.00
2 The Stolen Wand 300.00
3 thru 30 . . . . @200.00
31 Aug.–Sept., 1958 . . . . 200.00

PETER PORKCHOPS
Nov.–Dec., 1949
1 . . . . 400.00
2 . . . . 200.00
3 thru 10 . . . . @150.00
11 thru 30 . . . . @100.00
31 thru 61 . . . . @100.00
62 Oct.–Dec., 1960 . . . . 100.00

PHANTOM, THE
Oct., 1987
1 JO,A:Modern Phantom,13th
   Phantom 3.00
2 JO,Murder Trial in Manhattan . . . 3.00
3 JO,A:Chessman 3.00
4 JO,V:Chessman,final issue 3.00

PHANTOM, THE
1989–90
1 LMc,V:Gun Runners 3.00
2 LMc,V:Gun Runners 2.50
3 LMc,V:Drug Smugglers 2.50
4 LMc,In America,A:Diana Palner. . . 2.50
5 LMc,Racial Riots 2.50
6 LMc,in Africa,Toxic Waste
   Problem 2.50
7 LMc,Gold Rush 2.50
8 LMc,Train Surfing 2.50
9 LMc,The Slave Trade 2.50
10 LMc,Famine in Khagana. 2.50
11 LMc,Phantom/Diana Wedding
   proposal 2.50
12 LMc,Phantom framed for
   murder 2.50

13 W:Phantom & Diana Palner
  C:Mandrake last issue........ 2.50

PHANTOM STRANGER
Aug.–Sept., 1952
1 .... 3,000.00
2 .... 1,700.00
3 thru 5................ @1,500.00
6, June-July, 1953 .... 1,500.00

Phantom Stranger #37
© DC Comics Inc.

PHANTOM STRANGER
May-June, 1969
1 CI rep.&new material....... 450.00
2 CI rep.&new material....... 200.00
3 CI rep.&new material 200.00
4 NA,I:Tala,1st All-new issue ... 225.00
5 MSy,MA,A:Dr.13 .... 125.00
6 MSy,MA,A:Dr.13............. 125.00
7 JAp,V:Tala 125.00
8 JAp,A:Dr.13 .... 125.00
9 JAp,A:Dr.13 .... 125.00
10 JAp,I:Tannarak 125.00
11 JAp,V:Tannarak............ 60.00
12 JAp,TD,Dr.13 solo story 60.00
13 JAp,TD,Dr.13 solo.......... 60.00
14 JAp,TD,Dr.13 solo.......... 60.00
15 JAp,ATh(rep),TD,Iron Messiah,
  giant-size................ 70.00
16 JAp,TD,MMes(rep)Dr.13 solo
  giant-size................ 70.00
17 JAp,I:Cassandra Craft,
  giant-size................ 70.00
18 TD,Dr.13 solo, giant-size 70.00
19 JAp,TD,Dr.13 solo, giant-size . . 70.00
20 JAp,Child Shall Lead Them ... 50.00
21 JAp,TD,Dr.13 solo.......... 40.00
22 JAp,TD,I:Dark Circle......... 40.00
23 JAp,MK,I:Spawn-Frankenstein . 40.00
24 JAp,MA,Spawn Frankenstein . . 60.00
25 JAp,MA,Spawn Frankenstein . . 60.00
26 JAp,A:Frankenstein.......... 75.00
27 V:Dr. Zorn 60.00
28 BU:Spawn of Frankenstein 60.00
29 V:Dr.Zorn,BU:Frankenstein 60.00
30 E:Spawn of Frankenstein 60.00
31 B:BU:Black Orchid 70.00
32 NR,BU:Black Orchid 40.00
33 MGr,A:Deadman 50.00
34 BU:Black Orchid 40.00
35 BU:Black Orchid 40.00
36 BU:Black Orchid 40.00
37 Crimson Gold,BU:BlackOrchid . 40.00
38 Images of the Dead 40.00

39 A:Deadman................. 50.00
40 A:Deadman................. 50.00
41 A:Deadman................. 50.00

PHANTOM STRANGER
Oct., 1987–Jan., 1988
1 MMi,CR,V:Eclipso 3.00
2 and 4 MMi,CR,V:Eclipso .... @3.00

PHANTOM ZONE, THE
Jan., 1982
1 GD/TD,A:Jax-Ur.............. 2.50
2 GC/TD,A:JLA................ 2.50
3 GC/TD,A:Mon-El 2.50
4 GC/TD 2.50

PICTURE STORIES FROM THE BIBLE
Autumn, 1942–43
1 thru 4 Old Testament ..... @300.00
1 thru 3 New Testament .... @300.00

PINKY AND THE BRAIN
Warner Bros./DC, 1996
1 from animated TV series 3.00
2 thru 27 .... @3.00

PLASTIC MAN
[1st Series]
Nov.–Dec., 1966
1 GK,I:Dr.Drome (1966 series
  begins)................. 150.00
2 V:The Spider 75.00
3 V:Whed 75.00
4 V:Dr.Dome 75.00
5 1,001 Plassassins 75.00
6 V:Dr.Dome 60.00
7 O:Plastic Man Jr.,A:Original
  Plastic Man,Woozy Winks.... 60.00
8 V:The Weasel 60.00
9 V:Joe the Killer Pro 60.00
10 V:Doll Maker(series ends) ... 60.00
11 (1976 series begins) 15.00
12 I:Carrot-Man 15.00
13 A:Robby Reed.............. 15.00
14 V:Meat By-Product & Sludge .. 15.00
15 I:Snuffer,V:Carrot-Man 15.00
16 V:Kolonel Kool 15.00
17 O:Plastic Man 15.00
18 V:Professor Klean........... 15.00
19 I&Only App.Marty Meeker.... 15.00
20 V:Snooping Sneetches
  Oct.–Nov., 1977. .... 15.00

PLASTIC MAN
1988–89
1 Mini-series,Origin retold........ 2.25
2 V:The Ooze Brothers.......... 2.25
3 In Los Angeles............... 2.25
4 End-series,A:Superman........ 2.25

PLASTIC MAN
1999
Spec.#1 TTn(s),ALo,RBr,48-page . . 4.00

PLASTIC MAN
DC Dec. 2003
1 KB,O:Plastic Man............ 2.50
2 KB,Eel O'Brien on the Lam 3.00
3 KB,Eel O'Brien on the Lam 3.00
4 KB,Eel O'Brien on the Lam 3.00
5 KB,ghosts of his past.......... 3.00
6 KB,Eel O'Brien,concl. 3.00
7 Love Makes a Fella Woozy 3.00
8 Continuity Bandit,pt.1.......... 3.00
9 Continuity Bandit,pt.2.......... 3.00
10 Halloween issue 3.00

11 Homeland Security 3.00
12 KB 3.00
13 KB 3.00
14 KB 3.00
15 thru 18 KB .... @3.00
19 Edwina Crisis, pt.2 .... 3.00
20 final issue 3.00
GN The Lost Annual, rep. 7.00
TPB On the Lam 15.00
TPB Rubber Bandits (2006)....... 15.00

PLOP!
Sept.–Oct., 1973
1 SA-AA,GE,ShM 50.00
2 AA,SA 25.00
3 AA,SA 25.00
4 BW,SA 30.00
5 MA,MSy,SA,BWr 22.00
6 MSy,SA 20.00
7 SA 20.00
8 SA 20.00
9 SA 20.00
10 SA 20.00
11 ATh,SA 20.00
12 SA..................... 20.00
13 WW(c),SA 22.00
14 WW,SA 22.00
15 WW(c),SA 22.00
16 SD,WW,SA 22.00
17 SA 22.00
18 SD,WW,SA 22.00
19 WW,SA 22.00
20 SA,WW 22.00
21 JO,WW 25.00
22 JO,WW,BW............... 25.00
23 BW,WW.................. 25.00
24 SA,WW,Nov.–Dec., 1976 ..... 25.00

POWER COMPANY, THE
Jan., 2002
1 KBk,TG,V:Doctor Cyber........ 2.50
2 KBk,TG,V:Dragoneer.......... 2.50
3 KBk,TG,V:Dragoneer, Godstone . 2.50
4 KBk,TG,offices under attack 2.50
5 KDk,TG,F:Manhunter 2.50
6 KBk,TG,F:Green Arrow 2.50
7 KBk,F:Striker Z.............. 2.75
8 KBk,TG,Power Loss,pt.1 ...... 2.75
9 KBk,TG,Power Loss,pt.2 ...... 2.75
10 KBk,TG,anger aside 2.75
11 KBk,new member 2.75
12 KBk,F:Witchfire............ 2.75
13 KBk,TG,V:Dr. Polaris.......... 2.75
14 KBk,TG,V:Dr.Polaris,Cadre 2.75
15 KBk,TG,V:Dark Knight........ 2.75
16 KBk,TG,Witchfire............ 2.75
17 KBk,TG,barbaric world 2.75
18 KBk,TG,final issue 2.75
Spec. Josiah Power,A:Superman . . 2.50
Spec. Striker Z,A:Superboy 2.50
Spec. Witchfire,A:Wonder Woman.. 2.50
Spec. Skyrocket, A:Hal Jordan 2.50
Spec. Bork, A:Batman & Flash 2.50
Spec. Sapphire,A:JLA 2.50
Spec. Manhunter,A:Nightwing 2.50

POWER GIRL
[Mini-Series], 1988
1 .... 3.00
2 A:The Weaver, mongo Krebs.... 3.00
3 V:The Weaver 3.00
4 V:Weaver, final issue 3.00
TPB Power Girl (2006) 15.00

POWER OF SHAZAM!
1995–98
1 R:Captain Marvel............. 4.00
2 V:Arson Fiend 3.00
3 V:Ibac.................... 3.00

DC

4 JOy,R:Mary Marvel,Tawky,
Tawny 3.00
5 JOy(c&a),F:Mary Marvel,
V:Black Adam 3.00
6 R:Captain Marvel 3.00
7 V:Captain Nazi 3.00
8 R:Captain Marvel,Jr. 3.00
9 JOy,MM,V:Black Adam 3.00
10 JOy,MM,V:Seven Deadly
Enemies of Man 3.00
11 JOy,MM,R:Ibis as Capt.Marvel . . 3.00
12 JOy,MM,How Billy Batson's
father met Shazam 3.00
13 JOy,MM 3.00
14 JOy,GK,MM,F:CaptainMarvelJr . 3.00
15 JOy,MM,V:Mr.Mind 3.00
16 thru 18 . . . . @3.00
19 JOy(s),GK,MM,Captain Marvel
Jr. V:Captain Nazi 3.00
20 JOy(s),PKr,MM,A:Superman. . . 3.00
21 JOy(s),PKr,MM,V:Liquidator . . . 2.50
22 JOy(s),PKr,MM,A:Batman 2.50
23 JOy(s),PKr,MM, ... 2.50
24 JOy(s),PKr,MM,V:Baron Blitz-
krieg, prelude to new family . . . 2.50
25 JOy(s),PKr,MM,The Marvel
Family '97 . . . . 2.50
26 JOy(s),PKr,MM,new Capt.
Marvel framed for murder 2.50
27 JOy(s),PKr,MM,D:Captain
Marvel 2.50
28 JOy(s),DG, V:Patty Patty
Bang Bang. 2.50
29 JOy(c),DG,F:Hoppy. 2.50
30 JOy(c),PKr,DG,V:Mr. Finish. . . . 2.50
31 JOy,PKr,DG,Genesis x-over 2.50
32 JOy,PKr,DG,Genesis aftermath. . 2.50
33 JOy,PKr,DG,Madam M, Sin. . . . 2.50
34 JOy,PKr,DG,F:Gangbuster 2.50
35 JOy,PKr,DG,Lightning &
Stars, pt.2 x-over 2.50
36 JOy 2.50
37 JOy,MM,DG,F:Capt.Marvel Jr. . 2.50
38 JOy,PKr,DG,Monster Society
of Evil, pt.1. . . . . 2.50
39 JOy,PKr,DG,Monster, pt.2 . . . . . 2.50
40 JOy,PKr,DG,Monster, pt.3 . . . . . 2.50
41 JOy,PKr,DG,Monster, pt.4 . . . . . 2.50
42 JOy,DG,new logo & design 2.50
43 JOy,DG,I:Bulletgirl. 2.50
44 JOy,DG,V:Chain Lightning 2.50
45 JOy,DG,A:JLA 2.50
46 JOy,DG,A:Superman. 2.50
47 JOy,V:Black Adam, final issue . . 2.50
Ann.#1 JOy(s),MM,Legends of
the Dead Earth 3.00
Spec.#1,000,000 JOy,DG 2.50
GN Power of Shazam 7.50
GNv JOy(a&s),O:Captain Marvel. . 10.00
TPB JOy, reoffer 7.50

POWER OF THE ATOM
1988–89
1 1st Issue, Origin retold. 2.25
2 Return of Powers. 2.25
3 I:Strobe 2.25
4 A:Hawkman+bonus book #8 . . . . 2.25
5 DT,A:Elongated Man 2.25
6 JBy,V:Chronos 2.25
7 GN,Invasion,V:Khunds,Chronos . 2.25
8 GN,Invasion,V:Chronos 2.25
9 GN,A:Justice League. 2.25
10 GN,I:Humbug 2.25
11 GN,V:Paul Hoben 2.25
12 GN,V:Edg the Destroyer. 2.25
13 GN,Blood Stream Journey 2.25
14 GN,V:Humbug. 2.25
15 GN,V:Humbug. 2.25
16 GN,V:The CIA. 2.25
17 GN,V:The Sting. 2.25
18 GN,V:The CIA, last issue 2.25

POWERPUFF GIRLS
Warner Bros./DC March, 2000
1 . . . . 3.50
2 thru 70 . . . . @2.25
Double Whammy, rep. #1 & #2 . . . . 4.00
Spec.Powerpuff Girls movie comic . 3.00
TPB Titans of Townsville 7.00
TPB Go, Girls, Go 7.00

PREACHER
DC/Vertigo, 1995
1 I:Jesse Custer, Genesis. 22.00
2 Saint of Killers 18.00
3 GF(c),I:Angels 15.00
4 GF(c),V:Saint of Killers 10.00
5 Naked City,pt.1 . . . . 10.00
6 Naked City,pt.2 . . . . 10.00
7 Naked City,pt.3 . . . . 8.00
8 GEn,SDi,All in the Family,pt.1 . . . 5.00
9 GEn,SDi,All in the Family,pt.2 . . . 5.00
10 GEn,SDi,All in the Family,pt.3 . . 5.00
11 GEn,SDi,All in the Family,pt.4. . 5.00
12 GEn,SDi,All in.the Family,pt.5 . . 6.00
13 GEn,SDi,Hunters,pt.1 . . . . 5.00
14 GEn,SDi,Hunters,pt.2 (of 4) . . . 4.00
15 and 16. . . . . @4.00
17 Star captures Cassidy. 3.00
18 GEn(s),SDi,secret of Jesse
Custer's cigarette lighter 3.00
19 GEn(s),SDi,Crusaders, pt.1 . . . 3.00
20 GEn(s),SDi,Crusaders, pt.2 . . . 3.00
21 GEn(s),SDi,Crusaders, pt.3 . . . 3.00
22 GEn(s),SDi,Crusaders, pt.4 . . . 3.00
23 GEn(s),SDi,Crusaders, pt.5 . . . 3.00
24 GEn(s),SDi,Crusaders, concl. . . 3.00
25 GEn(s),SDi,Cry Blood, Cry
Erin 3.00
26 GEn(s),SDi,To the Streets of
Manhattan I Wandered Away . . 2.50
27 GEn(s),SDi, Jessie & Tulip in
New York, pt.1 . . . . 2.50
28 GEn(s),SDi, Jessie & Tulip in
New York, pt.2 . . . . 2.50
29 GEn(s),SDi, south to New
Orleans 2.50
30 GEn,SDi,in New Orleans 2.50
31 GEn,SDi,in New Orleans 2.50
32 GEn,SDi,in New Orleans 2.50
33 GEn,SDi,in New Orleans,concl. . 2.50
34 GEn,SDi,War in the Sun,pt.1 . . 2.50
35 GEn,SDi,War in the Sun,pt.2 . . 2.50
36 GEn,SDi,War in the Sun,pt.3 . . 2.50
37 GEn,SDi,War in the Sun,pt.4 . . 2.50
38 GEn,SDi,GF,Utah radioactive . . 2.50
39 GEn,SDi,GF,out of the desert . . 2.50
40 GEn,SDi,GF,Arsefaced World. . . 2.50
41 . . . . 2.50
42 GEn(s),SDi,GF,V:Meatman 2.50
43 GEn(s),SDi,GF,V:Meat Man . . . 2.50
44 GEn(s),SDi,GF,Gunther Hahn . . 2.50
45 GEn(s),SDi,GF,V:Meat Man . . . 2.50
46 GEn(s),SDi,GF,Miss Oatlash . . . 2.50
47 GEn(s),SDi,GF,Salvation 2.50
48 GEn(s),SDi,GF,Salvation 2.50
49 GEn(s),SDi,GF,First Contact. . . . 2.50
50 GEn(s),SDi,GF,48-page
I:100 Bullets. 4.00
51 GEn(s),SDi,GF,Tulip's past,pt.1 . 4.00
52 GEn(s),SDi,GF,Tulip's past,pt.2 . 2.50
53 GEn(s),SDi,GF,road trip story . . 2.50
54 GEn(s),SDi,GF,Jesse & Tulip . . 2.50
55 GEn(s),SKi,GF 2.50
56 GEn(s),GF. 2.50
57 GEn(s), ... 2.50
58 GEn(s),SDi,. 2.50
59 thru 64 GEn(s),SDi,
Alamo,pt.1 thru pt.6 . . . . @2.50
65 GEn(s),SDi,Alamo,pt.7 . . . . 5.00
66 GEn(s),SDi,Alamo,pt.8,
final issue 5.00
TPB Gone to Texas, rep.#1–#7 . . 15.00

TPB Proud Americans GEn(s). . . . 15.00
TPB Until the End of the World . . . 15.00
TPB Ancient History. 15.00
TPB War in the Sun. 15.00
TPB All Hell's A-Coming 18.00
TPB Alamo, GEn,SDi. 18.00
TPB Dead or Alive 20.00
GN Preacher Spec. Cassidy: Blood
and Whisky, GEn(s) (1997) 6.00
GN Tall in the Saddle. 6.00
Spec. The Good Old Boys, parody . 5.50
Spec. The Story of You-Know-Who
GEn(s),RCa,O:Arseface (1996) 5.00
Spec. One Man's War 5.00

PREACHER SPECIAL:
SAINT OF KILLERS
DC/Vertigo, 1996
1 GEn(s),StP 5.00
2 GEn(s),StP 4.50
3 GEn(s),StP 3.50
4 GEn(s),StP 3.00

PREZ
Aug.–Sept., 1973
1 I:Prez (from Sandman #54) 40.00
2 thru 4 F:Prez 20.00

PRIDE & JOY
DC/Vertigo, May, 1997
[Mini-series]
1 (of 4) GEn(s),JHi. 2.50
2 GEn(s),JHi. 2.50
3 GEn(s),JHi 2.50
4 GEn(s),JHi,concl. 2.50
TPB (2004). 15.00

Primal Force #0 © DC Comics, Inc.

PRIMAL FORCE
1994–95
O New Team. 2.25
1 Claw 2.25
2 thru 14 . . . . @2.25

PRINCE
DC/Piranha Press 1991
1 DCw,KW,based on rock star . . . 10.00
1a Second printing 2.50
1b 3rd printing. 2.00

All comics prices listed are for *Near Mint* condition.

PRINCESS NATASHA
June, 2006
1 (0f 4)	2.25
2 Undercover cheerleader	2.25
3 Robot Hamsters	2.25
4 concl.	2.25

PRISONER, THE
1988–89
1 Based on TV series	4.00
2 By Hook or by Crook	4.00
3 Confrontation	4.00
4 Departure, final issue	4.00

PROPOSITION PLAYER
DC/Vertigo, Oct., 2000
1 (of 6) PGn,BWg,	2.50
2 thru 6 PGn,BWg,	@2.50
TPB	15.00

PSYBA-RATS, THE
[Mini-Series], 1995
1 CDi,A:Robin	2.50
2 CDi,A:Robin	2.00
3 CDi,F:Razorsharp,final issue	2.00

PSYCHO, THE
1991
1 I:Psycho	12.00
2 Sonya Rescue	10.00
3 Psycho against the World	7.00

PULP FANTASTIC
DC/Vertigo, Dec., 1999
1 (of 3) HC,RBr,detective	2.50
2 HC,RBr	2.50
3 HC,RBr,conclusion	2.50

QUEST FOR CAMELOT
June, 1998
1-shot movie adaptation	5.00

QUESTION, THE
Feb., 1987
1 DCw,R:Question,I:Myra,A:Shiva	3.00
2 thru 10	@2.50
11 thru 20	@2.50
21 thru 36	@2.50
Ann.#1 DCw,A:Batman,G.A	3.00
Ann.#2 A:Green Arrow	4.00

QUESTION, THE
Nov., 2004
1 (of 6) F:Vic Sage	3.00
2 in Metropolis	3.00
3 Luthor's Science Spire	3.00
4 F:Superman	3.00
5 Sceince Spire	3.00
6 finale	3.00

QUESTION QUARTERLY
1990–92
1 DCw	4.50
2 DCw	4.00
3 DCw(c) Film	3.00
4 DCw,MM,Waiting for Phil	3.00
5 DCw,MMi,MM,last issue	3.00

RAGMAN
[1st Limited Series], 1976–77
1 I&O.Ragman	30.00
2 I:Opal	15.00
3 V:Mr. Big	10.00
4 JKu(1st interior on character)	10.00
5 JKu,O:Ragman,final issue	10.00

[2nd Limited Series], 1991–92
1 PB,O:Ragman	3.00
2 PB,O:Ragman Powers	3.00
3 PB,Original Ragman	3.00
4 PB,Gang War	3.00
5 PB,V:Golem	3.00
6 PB,V:Golem,A:Batman	3.00
7 PB,V:Golem,A:Batman	3.00
8 PB,V:Golem,A:Batman	3.00

RAGMAN:
CRY OF THE DEAD
1993–94
1 JKu(c),R:Ragman	3.50
2 JKu(c),A:Marinette	3.00
3 JKu(c),V:Marinette	3.00
4 JKu(c),Exorcism	3.00
5 JKu(c),V:Marinette	3.00
6 JKu(c),final issue	3.00

RANN/THANAGAR
WAR, THE
May, 2005
1 MCa,F:Adam Strange	8.00
1a 2nd printing	4.00
2 MCa,V:Khund hordes	3.50
3 MCa	3.00
4 MCa	3.00
5 MCa	3.00
6 MCa, Infinite Crisis lead-in	3.00
TPB	13.00
Spec. Infinite Crisis	5.00

THE RAY
[Limited Series], 1992
1 JQ,ANi,I&O:Ray(Ray Torril)	5.00
2 JQ,ANi,I:G.A. Ray	3.00
3 JQ,ANi,A:G.A. Ray	3.00
4 JQ,ANi,V:Dr.Polaris	4.00
5 JQ,ANi,V:Dr.Polaris	3.00
6 JQ,ANi,C:Lobo,final issue	3.00
TPB In A Blaze of Power	10.00

[Regular Series], 1994–96
1 JQ(c),RPr,V:Brinestone, A:Superboy	3.00
1a Newsstand Ed.	2.25
2 RPr,V:Brinestone,A:Superboy	2.25
3 RPr,I:Death Masque	2.25
4 JQ(c),RPr,I:Death Masque, Dr. Polarus	2.25
5 JQ(c),RPr,V:G.A.Ray	2.25
6 thru 28	@2.25
Ann.#1 Year One Annual	4.00

REAL FACT COMICS
March-April, 1946
1 S&K,Harry Houdini story	1,000.00
2 S&K, Rin-Tin-Tin story	750.00
3 H.G. Wells story	600.00
4 Jimmy Stewart story,B:Just Imagine	650.00
5 Batman & Robin(c)	3,000.00
6 O:Tommy Tomorrow	2,400.00
7 The Flying White House	300.00
8 VF,A:Tommy Tomorrow	1,200.00
9 S&K,Glen Miller story	500.00
10 MMe(s),The Vigilante	500.00
11 EK,How the G-Men Capture Public Enemies!	300.00
12 How G-Men are Trained	300.00
13 Dale Evans story	650.00
14 Will Rogers Story,Diary of Death	400.00
15 A.The Master Magician-Thurston,A-Bomb	400.00
16 A:Four Reno Brothers, T.Tommorrow	900.00
17 I Guard an Armored Car	400.00

Real Fact #8 © DC Comics Inc.

18 The Mystery Man of Tombstone	400.00
19 Weapon that Won the West	400.00
20 JKu,Daniel Boone	450.00
21 JKu,KitCarson,July-Aug.,1949	400.00

REAL SCREEN COMICS
Spring, 1945
1 B:Fox & the Crow,Flippity & Flop	1,400.00
2 inc. Tito and His Burrito	650.00
3 (fa)	400.00
4 thru 7 (fa)	@250.00
8 thru 11 (fa)	@200.00
12 thru 20 (fa)	@175.00
21 thru 30 (fa)	@150.00
31 thru 40 (fa)	@125.00
41 thru 128 (fa)	@100.00
Becomes:	

TV SCREEN CARTOONS
129 thru 137	@100.00
138 Jan.–Feb., 1961	100.00

REALWORLDS
March, 2000
GN Batman, 48-pg.	6.00
GN Wonder Woman, 48-pg.	6.00
GN JLA, 48-pg.	6.00
GN Superman	6.00

R.E.B.E.L.S '94–'96
0 New team	2.50
1 L.E.G.I.O.N.,Green Lantern	2.50
2 Dissent	2.50
3 Brains	2.50
4 Ship goes Insane	2.50
5 F:Dox	2.25
6 Dox Defeated	2.25
7 John Sin	2.25
8 V:Galactic Bank	2.25
9 F:Dox,Ignea,Garv,Strata	2.25
10 V:World Bank	2.25
11 Comet's Tail	2.25
12 F:Iceman Assassin	2.25
13 Underworld Unleashed tie-in	2.25
14 F:Lyrl Dox	2.25
15 V:Lyrl Dox	2.25
16 V:Lyrl Dox's satellite	2.25

RED TORNADO
1985
1 Cl/FMc	3.00
2 Cl/FMc,A:Superman	3.00
3 & 4 Cl/FMc	@3.00

DC COMICS

REIGN OF THE ZODIAC
Aug. 2003
1 thru 8 BWi,CDo . . . . @2.75

REMARKABLE WORLDS OF PHINEAS B. FUDDLE
DC/Paradox, 1999
1 (of 4) F:Angus & McKee 6.00
2 . . . . 6.00
3 ancient India 6.00
4 concl. 6.00
TPB 192-page 20.00

RESTAURANT AT THE END OF THE UNIVERSE
1994
1 Adapt. 2nd book in Hitchhikers'
  Guide to the Galaxy,
  I:The Restaurant 7.00
2 V:The Meal 7.00
3 Final issue 7.00

RESURRECTION MAN
March, 1997
1 DAn(s),JG,lenticular death's
  head cover. 6.00
2 DAn(s),JG,V:Amazo 5.00
3 DAn(s),JG,Scorpion Memories
  pt.1 (of 3). 4.00
4 DAn(s),JG,Scorpion,pt.2 . . . . . . 4.00
5 DAn(s),JG,Scorpion,pt.3, ... 4.00
6 DAn&ALa(s),JoP,Genesis tie-in . 3.00
7 DAn&ALa(s),TGb,BG,A:Batman . 3.00
8 DAn&ALa(s),BG,Big Howler. . . . 3.00
9 DAn&ALa(s),F:Hitman, pt.1 . . . . 3.00
10 DAn&ALa(s),F:Hitman, pt.2 . . . 3.00
11 DAn&ALa(s), Origin of the
  Species, pt.1 . . . . 2.50
12 DAn&ALa(s), Origin of the
  Species, pt.2 . . . . 2.50
13 DAn&ALa(s),Candy Man 2.50
14 DAn&ALa(s),really dead? 2.50
15 DAn&ALa(s),JG,V:Rider 2.50
16 DAn&ALa(s),BG,Avenging
  Angels x-over pt.1 . . . . 2.50
17 DAn&ALa(s),BG,Avenging
  Angels x-over pt.3 . . . . 2.50
18 DAn&ALa(s),A:Phantom Stranger,
  Deadman. 2.50
19 DAn&ALa(s),Cape Fear, pt.1 . . 2.50
20 DAn&ALa(s),Cape Fear, pt.2 . . 2.50
21 DAn&ALa(s),Cape Fear, pt.3 . . 2.50
22 DAn&ALa(s) 2.50
23 DAn&ALa(s),Resurrection
  Woman 2.50
24 DAn&ALa(s) 2.50
25 DAn&ALa(s)Millennium
  Meteor,pt.1. . . . . 2.50
26 DAn&ALa(s)Millennium Meteor,
  pt.2,A:Superman, Titans 2.50
27 DAn&ALa(s)Millennium Meteor,
  pt.3,final issue 2.50
Spec.#1,000,000 DAn&ALa(s). . . . 2.50

RICHARD DRAGON, KUNG FU FIGHTER
April-May, 1975
1 O:Richard Dragon 20.00
2 JSn/AM 15.00
3 JK. 12.00
4 thru 8 RE/WW . . . . @10.00
9 thru 17 RE . . . . @8.00
18 Nov.–Dec., 1977 . . . . 8.00

RICHARD DRAGON
May 2004
1 thru 12 CDi(s),SMc . . . . @2.50

Rima the Jungle Girl #1
© *DC Comics, Inc.*

RIMA, THE JUNGLE GIRL
April-May, 1974
1 NR,I:Rima,O:Pt. 1 . . . . 30.00
2 NR,O:Pt.2 . . . . 15.00
3 NR,O:Pt.3 . . . . 15.00
4 NR,O:Pt.4 . . . . 15.00
5 NR 15.00
6 NR 15.00
7 April-May, 1975 . . . . 15.00

RING, THE [OF THE NIEBLUNG]
1989
1 GK,Opera Adaption 12.00
2 GK,Sigfried's Father's Sword . . 7.00
3 GK,to save Brunhilde. 6.00
4 GK, final issue 6.00
TPB rep.#1 thru #4 . . . . 20.00

RIP HUNTER, TIME MASTER
March-April, 1961
1 . . . . 1,100.00
2 . . . . 550.00
3 thru 5 . . . . @400.00
6 and 7 Ath . . . . @250.00
8 thru 15 . . . . @200.00
16 thru 20 . . . . @200.00
21 thru 28 . . . . @150.00
29 Nov.–Dec., 1965 . . . . 150.00

ROBIN
[1st Limited Series], 1991
1 TL,BB(c),Trial,pt.1(&Poster). 5.00
1a 2nd printing 2.50
1b 3rd printing 2.25
2 TL,BB(c) Trial,pt.2 . . . . 3.00
2a 2nd printing 2.25
3 TL,BB(c) Trial,pt.3 . . . . 3.00
4 TL,Trial,pt.4 . . . . 3.00
5 TL,Final issue,A:Batman 3.00
TPB BB(c),rep 8.00

[2nd Limited Series], 1991
[ROBIN II: THE JOKER'S WILD]
1 Direct,Hologram(c)Joker face . . 3.00
1a (c)Joker straightjacket 2.25
1b (c)Joker standing 2.25
1c (c)Batman 2.25
1d Newsstand(no hologram). 2.25

1e collectors set,extra holo. 10.00
2 Direct,Hologram(c) Robin/Joker
  Knife 2.50
2a (c)Joker/Robin-Dartboard 2.25
2b (c)Robin/Joker-Hammer 2.25
2c Newsstand(no hologram). 2.25
2d collectors set,extra holo. 9.00
3 Direct,Holo(c)Robin standing. . . 2.50
3a (c)Robin swinging 2.25
3b Newsstand(no hologram). 2.25
3c collectors set,extra holo. 7.00
4 Direct,Hologram. 2.50
4a Newsstand (no hologram) 2.25
4b collectors set,extra holo. 2.25
Collectors set (#1 thru #4) 30.00

[3rd Limited Series], 1992–93
[ROBIN III: CRY OF THE HUNTRESS]
1 TL,A:Huntress,Collector's Ed.
  movable(c),poster 3.00
1a MZ(c),Newsstand Ed. 2.25
2 TL,V:KGBeast,A:Huntress 2.75
2a MZ(c),Newsstand Ed 2.25
3 TL,V:KGBeast,A:Huntress 2.75
3a MZ(c),newsstand Ed. 2.25
4 TL,V:KGBeast,A:Huntress 2.75
4a MZ(c),newsstand Ed. 2.25
5 TL,V:KGBeast,A:Huntress 2.75
5a MZ(c),newsstand Ed. 2.25
6 TL,V:KGBeast,King Snake,
  A:Huntress. 2.75
6a MZ(c),Newsstand Ed. 2.25

[Regular Series], 1993–2002
1 B:CDi(s),TG,SHa,V:Speedboyz . . 4.00
1a Newsstand Ed. 2.25
2 TG,V:Speedboyz 2.50
3 TG,V:Cluemaster,
  Electrocutioner. 2.50
4 TG,V:Cluemaster,Czonk,
  Electrocutioner. 2.50
5 TG,V:Cluemaster,Czonk,
  Electrocutioner. 2.50
6 TG,A:Huntress 2.50
7 TG,R:Robin's Father 2.50
8 TG,KnightsEnd#5,A:Shiva 3.00
9 TG,Knights End:Aftermath 2.50
10 TG,Zero Hour,V:Weasel 2.50
11 New Batman 2.50
12 Robin vs. thugs. 2.50
13 V:Steeljacket. 2.50
14 CDi(s),TG,Return of Bruce
  Wayne,Troika,pt.4 . . . . 3.00
14a Collector's edition 3.00
15 Cluemaster Mystery 2.50
16 F:Spoiler 2.50
17 I:Silver Monkey,V:King Snake,Lynx
  [New Miraweb format begins] . . 2.50
18 Gotham City sabotaged 2.50
19 V:The General. 2.50
20 F:Robin 2.50
21 Ninja Camp,pt.1 . . . . 2.50
22 CDi,TG,Ninja Camp,pt.2 . . . . . 2.50
23 CDi,Underworld Unleashed tie-in 2.50
24 CDi,V:Charaxes 2.50
25 CDi,F:Green Arrow 2.50
26 CDi,The Hard Lessons 2.50
27 CDi,Contagion. 2.50
28 CDi,Contagion: conclusion . . . 2.50
29 CDi,FFo,SnW,A:Maxie Zeus. . . 2.50
30 CDi,FFo,SnW,A:Maxie Zeus. . . 2.50
31 CDi(s),A:Wildcat 2.50
32 CDi(s),Legacy, pt. 3 x-over . . . 2.50
33 CDi(s),Legacy, pt. 7 x-over. . . . 2.50
34 CDi(s),JhD,action at a
  Shakespear play 2.50
35 CDi(s),Robin & Spoiler, Final
  Night tie-in 2.50
36 CDi(s),V:Toyman, The General. . 2.50
37 CDi(s),V:The General, Toyman. . 2.50
38 CDi(s), ... 2.50
39 CDi(s), pt.2 . . . . 2.50

Robin #15
© DC Comics Inc.

40 CDi(s),............................ 2.50
41 CDi(s),F:Tim and Ariana......... 2.50
42 CDi(s),F:Crocky the Crocodile .. 2.50
43 CDi(s),A:Spoiler................. 2.50
44 CDi(s) Pt.2 (of 2)............... 2.50
45 CDi(s) Tim Drake grounded 2.50
46 CDi(s) Genesis tie-in........... 2.50
47 CDi,V:General, pt.1............. 2.50
48 CDi,V:General, pt.2............. 2.50
49 CDi,to Paris.................... 2.50
50 CDi(s),F:Lady Shiva & King
     Snake, 48pg 3.50
51 CDi(s) 2.50
52 CDi(s) Cataclysm x-over,pt.7 ... 3.00
53 CDi(s),SnW,Cataclysm concl.... 3.00
54 CDi(s),SnW,Aftershock 2.50
55 CDi(s),SnW, Brotherhood of
     the Fist x-over, pt.3 .... 2.50
56 CDi(s),SnW,tearful turning point . 2.50
57 CDi(s),SnW,A:Spoiler 2.50
58 CDi(s),SnW,A:Spoiler 2.50
59 CDi(s),SnW,V:Steeljacket 2.50
60 CDi(s),SnW,Alvin Draper 2.50
61 CDi(s),SnW,V:Phil Delinger 2.50
62 CDi(s),SnW,A:Flash, pt.1 ...... 2.50
63 CDi(s),SnW,A:Flash, pt.2 ...... 2.50
64 CDi(s),SnW,A:Flash, pt.3 ...... 2.50
65 CDi(s),SnW,A:Spoiler 2.50
66 CDi(s),SnW,V:demons 2.50
67 CDi(s),SnW,No Man's Land 2.50
68 CDi(s),No Man's Land 2.50
69 CDi(s),No Man's Land 2.50
70 CDi(s),No Man's Land 2.50
71 CDi(s),V:Killer Croc........... 2.50
72 CDi(s) 2.50
73 CDi(s),F:Batgirl 2.50
74 CDi(s),F:Batman & Nightwing... 2.50
75 CDi(s),48-pg................... 3.50
76 CDi(s),R:Man-Bat 2.50
77 CDi(s),I:Jaeger 2.50
78 CDi(s),V:Arrakhat 2.50
79 CDi(s),F:Green Arrow 2.50
80 CDi(s),A:Star.................. 2.50
81 CDi(s),MPn, ... 2.50
82 CDi(s),Spoiler,Star............ 2.50
83 CDi,Vacation time............. 2.50
84 CDi,A:Lagoon Boy 2.50
85 CDi,This issue: Batman dies! ... 2.50
86 Officer Down x-over,pt.2 .... 5.00
87 CDi,A:Spoiler 2.50
88 CDi,Road trip 2.50
89 CDi,to Himalayas 2.50
90 CDi,V:mini-yeti 2.50
91 CDi,F:Danny Temple......... 2.50

92 CDi,SBe,A:Batman,Spoiler 2.50
93 CDi,F:Spoiler.................. 2.50
94 CDi,F:Spoiler,Wesley 2.50
95 CDi,Joker:Last Laugh tie-in ... 2.50
96 CDi,Last Laugh aftermath...... 2.50
97 CDi,F:Normandy 2.50
98 Bruce Wayne:Murderer,pt.8 ... 5.00
99 Bruce Wayne:Murderer,pt.11 .. 5.00
100 CDi,Spoiler,48-pg............ 5.00
101 WorldWithoutYoungJustice,pt.3 2.50
102 Spoiler....................... 2.50
103 Nocturna's secret 2.50
104 Astrology Lady 2.50
105 riddle of Natalia............. 2.50
106 A:Batman 2.50
107 F:Charaxis................... 2.50
108 F:Charaxis................... 2.50
109 V:Charaxis 2.50
110 F:Nightwing 2.50
111 F:Spoiler 2.50
112 to Pennsylvania.............. 2.50
113 V:The Riddler 2.50
114 The Wrong Town 2.50
115 The Wrong Town 2.50
116 Identity compromised 2.50
117 Identity compromised 2.50
118 Traitor's identity............. 2.50
119 Traitor's identity............. 2.50
120 Hell in a handbasket......... 2.50
121 BWg(s),Johnny Got His Gun .. 4.00
122 BWg(s),Bad to the Bone...... 3.00
123 BWg(s),Nemesis 3.00
124 F:Spoiler 3.00
125 BWg(s),secret identity 3.00
126 BWg(s),search for new Robin. 4.00
127 BWg(s),Girl Wonder,Batman . 3.00
128 BWg(s),V:Scarab 2.50
129 War Games,Act 1,pt.5 ...... 2.50
130 War Games,Act 2,pt.5 ...... 2.50
131 War Games,Act 3,pt.4 ...... 2.50
132 Fresh Blood, x-over, pt.1 ..... 2.50
133 Fresh Blood, x-over, pt.3 ..... 2.50
134 Bludhaven.................... 2.50
135 Rising Sun Archer & Dark Rider 2.50
136 V:Dark Rider 2.50
137 Rising Sun Archer & Dark Rider 2.60
138 V:Penguin 2.50
139 SMc,V:Junkyard Dog 2.50
140 SMc,F:The Veteran 2.50
141 Black Ops opportunity........ 2.50
142 Old Flame 2.50
143 Omac tie-in 2.50
144 Omac tie-in 2.50
145 A:Shadowpact................ 2.50
146 F:Teen Titans 2.50
147 F:Teen Titans 2.50
148 Wanted for Murder 2.50
149 Robin: Buy Wanted........... 2.60
150 Who Framed Robin?......... 3.00
151 League of Assassins job offer.. 3.00
152 V:Captain Boomerang........ 3.00
153 V:Captain Boomerang........ 3.00
154 Kidnappings 3.00
155 Superhero wannabe 3.00
156 A Life to save 3.00
TPB Robin/Batgirl: Fresh Blood... 13.00
Ann.#1 TL,Eclipso tie-in,V:Anarky .. 3.00
Ann.#2 KD,JL,Bloodlines#10,
     I:Razorsharp 2.75
Ann.#3 Elseworlds Story 3.25
Ann.#4 Year One Annual 3.00
Ann.#5 CDi,Legends of the Dead
     Earth 3.00
Ann.#5 Legends o/t Dead Earth ... 3.00
Ann.#6 Pulp Heroes (Western),
     CDi(s) 4.00
Spec.#1,000,000 CDi(s),SnW 2.00
Spec. Robin/Argent Double Shot
     DJu,CDi,V:Spoiler x-over (1997) 2.00
TPB A Hero Reborn,JAp,TL........ 5.00
TPB Tragedy and Triumph,
     TL,NBy. 10.00

TPB Robin: Flying Solo 13.00
TPB Robin: Unmasked 13.00
80-page Giant #1 CDi 6.00
TPB Robin: To Kill A Bird........ 15.00
TPB Days of Fire and Madness... 13.00

ROBIN PLUS
1996
1 MWa&BAu(s), F:Bart Allen, skiing
     rips, V:Mystral 3.00
2 LKa,CDi,AWi,ALa,F:Fang 3.00

ROBIN 3000
1992
1 CR,Elseworlds,V:Skulpt........ 5.25
2 CR,Elseworlds,V:Skulpt........ 5.25

ROBIN: YEAR ONE
October, 2000
1 CDi,SBe,F:Dick Grayson....... 5.00
2 CDi,SBe,F:Dick Grayson....... 5.00
3 CDi,SBe,RbC,F:Dick Grayson... 5.00
4 CDi,SBe,concl................. 5.00
TPB series rep 15.00

ROBIN HOOD TALES
1957–58
7 .... 450.00
8 thru 14 .... @400.00

ROBO-HUNTER
2005
TPB Verdus, IG, 2000 A.D. 15.00
TPB Day of the Droids, 2000 A.D.. 15.00

ROBOTECH
DEFENDERS
1985
1 MA,mini-series................. 3.50
2 MA 3.00

ROGAN GOSH
DC/Vertigo, 1994
1 PF PrM(s) (From Revolver)..... 7.25

ROMANCE TRAIL
1949–50
1 EK,ATh....................... 900.00
2 EK 400.00
3 EK,ATh....................... 425.00
4 ATh 300.00
5 .... 275.00
6 EK 275.00

RONIN
July, 1983
1 FM,1:Billy..................... 6.00
2 FM,I:Casey 5.00
3 FM,V:Agat 5.00
4 FM,V:Agat 5.00
5 FM,V:Agat 6.00
6 FM,D:Billy 8.00
Paperback, FM inc. Gatefold..... 12.00

ROOTS OF THE
SWAMP THING
July, 1986
1 BWr,rep.SwampThing#1&#2 .... 3.50
2 BWr,rep.SwampThing#3&#4 .... 3.50
3 BWr,rep.SwampThing#5&#6 .... 3.50
4 BWr,rep.SwampThing#7&#8 .... 3.50
5 BWr,rep.SwampThing#9&#10,
     H.O.S. #92, final issue 3.50

All comics prices listed are for *Near Mint* condition.

ROSE & THORN
Dec. 2003
1 thru 6 DGr . . . . @3.00

*Rudolph the Red-Nosed Reindeer
1956–57 © DC Comics Inc.*

RUDOLPH THE RED–NOSED REINDEER
Dec., 1950
1950 . . . . 275.00
1951 thru 1954 . . . . @150.00
1955 thru 1962 Winter . . . . . . @125.00

RUSH CITY
Nov., 2006
1 CDi, Racing thru New York City. . 3.00
2 CDi, Under the streets 3.00
3 CDi, A:Black Canary 3.00
4 CDi, Missing twin doubles 3.00
5 CDi, Death race with the mob . . . 3.00

SACHS AND VIOLENS
2006
TPB PDd,GP 15.00

SAGA OF RAS AL GHUL
1988
1 NA,DG,reprints 6.00
2 rep. 5.00
3 rep.Batman #242&#243 . . . . 5.00
4 rep.Batman #244&#245 . . . . 5.00
TPB reps 18.00

SAGA OF THE SWAMP THING
1982–85
1 JmP(s),TY,DSp,O:Swamp Thing,
 BU:PhantomStranger 7.00
2 Ph(c),TY,DSp,I:Grasp 4.00
3 TY,DSp,V:Vampires 4.00
4 TY,TD,V:Demon 4.00
5 TY,Scream of Hungry Flesh 4.00
6 TY,I:General Sunderland 4.00
7 TYmHaunting of Amanda Dove . . 4.00
8 TY,Here's Lookin' at You, Kid 4.00
9 TY,Prelude to Holocaust 4.00
10 TY,Number of the Beast 4.00
11 TY,I:Golem 4.00
12 LWn(s),TY 4.00
13 TY,D:Grasp 4.00

14 A:Phantom Stranger 4.00
15 TY,BHa,Empires Made of Sand . 4.00
16 SBi,JTo,TY,Secret Truths 5.00
17 I:Matthew Cable 5.00
18 JmP(s),LWn(s),SBi,JTo,BWr,
 R:Arcane 5.00
19 JmP(s),SBi,JTo,V:Arcane 5.00
20 B:AMo(s),Day,JTo(i),D:Arcane
 (Original incarnation) 22.00
21 SBi,JTo,O:Swamp Thing,I:Floronic
 Man,D:General Sunderland . . . 20.00
22 SBi,JTo,O:Floronic Man 15.00
23 SBi,JTo,V:Floronic Man 15.00
24 SBi,JTo,V:Floronic Man,A:JLA,
 In Arkham 15.00
25 SBi,A:Jason Blood,I:Kamara . . 16.00
26 SBi,A:Demon,
 D:Matthew Cable 10.00
27 SBi,D:Kamara,A:Demon 10.00
28 SwM,Burial of Alec Holland . . . 10.00
29 SBi,JTo,R:Arcane 10.00
30 SBi,AA,D:Abby,C:Joker,
 V:Arcane 9.00
31 RV,JTo,D:Arcane 9.00
32 SwM,Tribute to WK Pogo strip . 9.00
33 rep.H.O.S.#92,A:Cain & Abel . . 9.00
34 SBi,JTo,Swamp Thing & Abby
 Fall in Love 9.00
35 SBi,JTo,Nukeface,pt.1 . . . . 9.00
36 SBi,JTo,Nukeface,pt.2 . . . . 9.00
37 RV,JTo,I:John Constantine,
 American Gothic,pt.1 . . . . 40.00
38 SnW,JTo,V:Water-Vampires
 (Pt.1) A:J.Constantine 9.00
39 SBi,JTo,V:Water-Vampires
 (Pt.2) A:J.Constantine 9.00
40 SBi,JTo,C:J.Constantine,
 The Curse 9.00
41 SBi,AA,Voodoo Zombies #1 . . . . 4.00
42 SBi,JTo,RoR,
 Voodoo Zombies #2 . . . . 4.00
43 SnW,RoR,Windfall,
 I:Chester Williams 4.00
44 SBi,JTo,RoR,V:Serial Killer,
 C:Batman,Constantine,Mento . . 5.00
45 SnW,AA,Ghost Dance 4.00
Ann.#1 MT,TD,Movie Adaption 4.00
Ann.#2 AMo(s),E:Arcane,A:Deadman,
 Phantom Stranger,Spectre,
 Demon,Resurrection of Abby . . 8.00
TPB rep.#21-#27 . . . . 13.00
TPB rep.#28-#34,Ann.#2 . . . . 15.00
TPB Love and Death 20.00
Becomes:

SWAMP THING

SAMURAI JACK
Warner Bros./DC July, 2002
Spec. #1 64-pg 4.00

SANDMAN
[1st Regular Series], 1974–75
1 JK,I&O:Sandman,I:General
 Electric 60.00
2 V:Dr.Spider 25.00
3 Brain that Blanked
 out the Bronx 25.00
4 JK,Panic in the Dream Stream . 25.00
5 JK,Invasion of the Frog Men . . . 25.00
6 JK,WW,V:Dr.Spider 32.00

[2nd Regular Series], 1989–93
1 B:NGa(s),SK,I:2nd Sandman . . . 35.00
2 SK,A:Cain,Abel 20.00
3 SK,A:John Constantine 15.00
4 SK,A:Demon 15.00
5 SK,A:Mr.Miracle,J'onn J'onzz . . 15.00
6 V:Doctor Destiny 10.00
7 V:Doctor Destiny 10.00
8 Sound of her wings,F:Death . . . 25.00
8a Guest Ed.Pin-Up Cover 65.00

9 Tales in the Sand,Doll's House
 prologue 10.00
10 B:Doll's House,A:Desire
 & Despair,I:Brut & Glob 10.00
11 MovingIn,A:2ndS-man 10.00
12 Play House,D;2ndS'man 10.00
13 Men of Good Fortune,A:Death,
 Lady Constantine 10.00
14 Collectors,D:Corinthian 10.00
15 Into' Night,DreamVortex 10.00
16 E:Doll's House,Lost Hearts 10.00
17 Calliope 10.00
18 Dream of a 1000 Cats 10.00
18a error pg.1 . . . . 25.00
19 Midsummer Nights Dream 6.00
19a error copy 22.00
20 Strange Death Element Girl,
 A:Death 7.00
21 Family Reunion,B:Season
 of Mists 8.00
22 Season of Mists,I:Daniel Hall . . 13.00
23 Season of Mists 7.00
24 Season of Mists 7.00
25 Season of Mists 7.00
26 Season of Mists 6.00
27 E:Season of Mists 6.00
28 Ownership of Hell 6.00
29 A:Lady J.Constantine 5.00
30 Ancient Rome;A:Death,Desire . 5.00
31 Ancient Rome,pt.2 . . . . 5.00
32 B:The Game of You 5.00
33 The Game of You 5.00
34 The Game of You 4.00
35 The Game of You 4.00
36 The Game of You,48pgs 5.00
37 The Game of You,Epilogue 4.00
38 Convergence 4.00
39 Convergence,A:Marco Polo 4.00
40 Convergence,A:Cain,Abel,Eve,
 Matthew the Raven 4.00
41 JIT,VcL,(i),B:Brief Lives,
 F:Endless 4.00
42 JIT,VcL,(i),F:Delirium,Dream 4.00
43 JIT,VcL,(i),A:Death,Etain 4.00
44 JIT,VcL,(i),R:Corinthian,
 Destruction 4.00
45 JIT,VcL,(i),F:Tiffany,
 Ishtar(Belli) 4.00
46 JIT,VcL,(i),F:Morpheus/Bast,
 A:Aids insert story,F:Death 4.00
DC/Vertigo, 1994–96
47 JIT,VcL,(i),A:Endless 4.00
48 JIT,VcL,(i),L:Destruction 4.00
49 JIT,VcL,(i),E:Brief Lives,
 F:Orpheus 4.00
50 DMc(c),CR,Tales of Baghdad,
 pin-upsby TM,DMc,MK 5.00
50a Gold Ed 22.00
51 BT,MBu(i),B:Inn at the end of
 the World,Gaheris' tale 4.00
52 BT,MBu(i),JWk,Cluracan's
 Story 4.00
53 BT,DG,MBu(i),MZi,Hob's
 Leviathan 4.00
54 BT,MiA,MBu(i),R:Prez 4.00
55 SAp,VcL,BT,MBu(i),F:Klaproth
 Cerements's Story 4.00
56 BT,MBu(i),DG(i),SLi(i),GyA,TyH(i),
 E:Inn at the end of the World,
 C:Endless 4.00
57 MaH,B:Kindly Ones,Inc.American
 Freak Preview 5.00
58 MaH,Kindly Ones,pt.2,
 A:Lucifer 5.00
59 MaH,Kindly Ones,pt.3,R:Fury . . 5.00
60 MaH,Kindly Ones,pt.4 . . . . 5.00
61 MaH,Kindly Ones,pt.5 . . . . 5.00
62 Kindly Ones,pt.6,Murder 5.00
63 MaH,Kindly Ones,pt.7,
 A:Rose Walker 5.00
64 Kindly Ones,pt.8 . . . . 5.00

65 MaH,Kindly Ones,pt.9,Dream
   Kingdom 5.00
66 MaH,Kindly Ones,pt.10 . . . . 5.00
67 MaH,Kindly Ones,pt.11 . . . . 5.00
68 MaH,Kindly Ones,pt.12 . . . . 5.00
69 MaH,Kindly Ones finale 6.00
70 The Wake,pt.1 . . . . 4.00
71 The Wake,pt.2 . . . . 4.00
72 NGa,DMc,The Wake,pt.3 . . . . . 4.00
73 NGa,Sunday Mourning 4.00
74 NGa,V:Lord of Dreams 4.00
75 NGa,last issue 5.00
TPB Preludes & Nocturnes,
   rep. #1–#8 . . . . 20.00
TPB Doll's House, rep #8–#16 . . . 18.00
TPB Dream Country,Rep.#17–#20 . 15.00
TPB Fables & Reflections,rep.. . . . 20.00
TPB Season of Mists,rep.#21–#28 . 20.00
TPB A Game of You,rep.#32–#37 . 20.00
TPB Brief Lives 20.00
TPB The Wake, rep. #70–#75 . . . . 20.00
TPB World's End DMc(c). 20.00
Sandman Covers, 1989–96 . . . . . . 40.00
Spec.BT,Glow in the Dark(c),The
   Legend of Orpheus,
   (inc. Portrait Gallery) 6.00
1 special edition, 48-pg.(2006) 0.50

SANDMAN MYSTERY THEATRE
DC/Vertigo, 1993–99
1 B:MWg(s),GyD,R:G.A.Sandman,
   B:Tarantula,I:Mr.Belmont,
   Dian Belmont 5.00
2 GyD,V:Tarantula. 3.00
3 GyD,V:Tarantula. 3.00
4 GyD,E:Tarantula 3.00
5 JWk,B:The Face 3.00
6 JWk,The Face #2 . . . . 3.00
7 JWk,The Face #3 . . . . 3.00
8 JWk,E:The Face 3.00
9 RGT,B:The Brute,I:Rocket
   Ramsey 3.00
10 RGT,The Brute#2 . . . . 3.00
11 RGT,The Brute#3 . . . . 3.00
12 RGT,E:The Brute 3.00
13 GyD,B:The Vamp 3.00
14 GyD,The Vamp#2 . . . . 3.00
15 GyD,The Vamp#3 . . . . 3.00
16 GyD,E:The Vamp 3.00
17 GyD,B:The Scorpion 3.00
18 GyD,The Scorpion,pt.2 . . . . 3.00
19 GyD,The Scorpion,pt.3 . . . . 3.00
20 GyD,The Scorpion,pt.4 . . . . 3.00
21 Dr. Death 3.00
22 Dr. Death,pt.2 . . . . 3.00
23 Dr. Death,pt.3 . . . . 3.00
24 Dr. Death,pt.4 . . . . 3.00
25 The Butcher,pt.1 . . . . 3.00
26 The Butcher,pt.2 . . . . 3.00
27 The Butcher,pt.3 . . . . 3.00
28 The Butcher,pt.4 . . . . 3.00
29 The Hourman,pt.1 . . . . 3.00
30 The Hourman,pt.2 . . . . 3.00
31 The Hourman,pt.3 . . . . 3.00
32 The Hourman,pt.4 . . . . 3.00
33 The Python,pt.1 . . . . 3.00
34 The Python,pt.2 . . . . 3.00
35 The Python,pt.3 . . . . 3.00
36 The Python,pt.4 . . . . 3.00
37 The Mist,pt.1 . . . . 3.00
38 The Mist,pt.2 . . . . 3.00
39 The Mist,pt.3 . . . . 3.00
40 The Mist,pt.4 . . . . 3.00
41 MWg&SSe(s),GyD,Phantom of
   the Fair,pt.1 . . . . 2.50
42 MWg&SSe(s),GyD,Phantom of
   the Fair,pt.2 . . . . 2.50
43 MWg&SSe(s),GyD,Phantom of
   the Fair pt. 3 . . . . 2.50

44 MWg&SSe(s),GyD,Phantom of
   the Fair pt. 4 . . . . 2.50
45 MWg&SSe(s),Blackhawk,pt.1 . . . 2.50
46 MWg&SSe(s),Blackhawk,pt.2 . . . 2.50
47 MWg&SSe(s),Blackhawk,pt.3 . . . 2.50
48 MWg&SSe(s),RCa,Blackhawk . . . 2.50
49 MWg&SSe(s),ScarletGhost,pt.1 . 2.50
50 MWg&SSe(s),The Scarlet
   Ghost, pt.2, 48pg. 4.50
51 MWg&SSe(s),ScarletGhost,pt.3 . 2.50
52 MWg&SSe(s),ScarletGhost,pt.4 . 2.50
53 MWg&SSe(s),The Crone,pt.1 . . . 2.50
53 MWg&SSe(s),The Crone,pt.2 . . . 2.50
54 SSe&MWg(s),The Crone,pt.3 . . . 2.50
55 SSe&MWg(s),The Crone,pt.4 . . . 2.50
56 SSe&MWg(s),The Crone, concl. . 2.50
57 SSe&MWg(s),The Cannon,pt.1 . . 2.50
58 SSe&MWg(s),The Cannon,pt.2 . . 2.50
59 SSe&MWg(s),The Cannon,pt.3 . . 2.50
60 SSe&MWg(s),The Cannon,pt.4 . . 2.50
61 SSe(s),GyD,The City, pt.1 . . . . . 2.50
62 SSe(s),GyD,The City, pt.2 . . . . . 2.50
63 SSe(s),GyD,The City, pt.3 . . . . . 2.50
64 SSe(s),GyD,The City, pt.4 . . . . . 2.50
65 SSe,GyD,The Goblin, pt.1 . . . . . 2.50
66 SSe,GyD,The Goblin, pt.2 . . . . . 2.50
67 SSe,GyD,The Goblin, pt.3 . . . . . 2.50
68 SSe,GyD,The Goblin, pt.4 . . . . . 2.50
69 SSe,GyD 2.50
70 SSe,GyD,final issue 2.50
Ann.#1 . . . . 4.00
TPB The Tarantula 15.00
TPB Vol 1 The Tarantula (2004) . . 10.00
TPB The Dream Hunters 20.00
TPB Season of the Mists 20.00
TPB Sandman Companion 15.00
TPB Vol 2 Face & the Brute (2004) 20.00
TPB Vol. 3 The Vamp (2005) 13.00
TPB Vol. 4 The Scorpion 13.00

SANDMAN PRESENTS:
LOVE STREET
DC/Vertigo, 1999
1 (of 3) MZi,VcL, ... 3.00
2 MZi,VcL,I":John Constantine 3.00
3 MZi,VcL,Concl. 3.00

LUCIFER
DC/Vertigo, 1999
1 (of 3) SHp, Morningstar Option . . 3.00
2 SHp 3.00
3 SHp, conclusion. 3.00

PETREFAX
DC/Vertigo, 2000
1 (of 4) SL 3.00
2 thru 4 SL . . . . @3.00

DEAD BOY DETECTIVES
DC/Vertigo, 2001
1 (of 4) 2.50
2 thru 4 SL . . . . @2.50

CORINTHIAN, THE
DC/Vertigo, 2001
1 (of 3) 2.50
2 thru 3 . . . . @2.50

THESSALIAD, THE
DC/Vertigo, 2002
1 (of 4) 2.50
2 thru 4 DMc(c). . . . . @2.50

BAST
DC/Vertigo, 2003
1 (of 3) F:Lady Bast 3.00
2 thru 3 . . . . @3.00
Spec.1-Shot, Merv Pumpkinhead
   Agent of Dream,MBu. 6.00
Spec. Everything You've Ever
   Wanted to Know About Dreams
   But Were Afraid to Ask 4.50
TPB The Furies (2003) 18.00

TPB Taller Tales (2003) 20.00

THESSALY
DC Vertigo, Feb. 2004
1 (of 4) Witch for Hire 3.00
2 thru 4 . . . . @3.00

SCARAB
DC/Vertigo, 1993–94
1 GF(c),B:JnS(s),SEa,MkB(i),
   R&O:Scarab,V:Halaku-umid . . . 2.25
2 thru 8 GF(c),SEa,MkB(i) . . . . . @2.25

SCARE TACTICS
Oct., 1996
1 LKa(s),AWi,ALa, ... 2.25
2 thru 11 . . . . @2.25

Scarlett #14 © DC Comics, Inc.

SCARLETT
1993–94
1 I:Scarlett,Blood of the Innocent . . 3.50
2 Blood of the Innocent cont. 2.25
3 Blood of the Innocent cont. 2.25
4 thru 14 . . . . @2.25

SCENE OF THE CRIME
DC/Vertigo, 1999
1 (of 4) 2.50
2 thru 4 . . . . @2.50
TPB A Little Piece of Goodnight . . 13.00

S.C.I.-SPY
DC/Vertigo, Feb., 2002
1 (of 6) DgM,PG,JP,F:Sebastian
   Starchild secret agent 2.50
2 thru 6 DgM,PG,JP . . . . @2.50

SCOOBY-DOO
Warner Bros./DC June, 1997
1 . . . . 5.00
2 thru 50 . . . . @2.50
51 thru 114 . . . . @2.25
Spooky Spectacular 2000 . . . . 4.00
Spooky Summer Special #1 . . . . . . 4.00
Spec. Super Scarefest #1 . . . . 4.00
Spec. Dollar Comic, rep.#1 . . . . . . 1.00
TPB Vol. 1 You Meddling Kids 7.00
TPB Vol. 2 Ruh Roh! 7.00
TPB Vol. 3 All Wrapped Up 7.00
TPB Vol. 4 The Big Squeeze 7.00
TPB Vol. 5 Surf's Up 7.00
TPB Vol. 6 Space Fright 7.00

All comics prices listed are for *Near Mint* condition.

SCRATCH
June 2004
1 (of 5) SK,werewolf v.Batman 2.50
2 thru 5 SK . . . . @2.50

SCRIBBLY
Aug., 1948–Dec.–Jan., 1951–52
1 SM 1,400.00
2 . . . . 900.00
3 thru 5 . . . . @750.00
6 thru 10 . . . . @500.00
11 thru 15 . . . . @450.00

Sea Devils #2 © DC Comics, Inc.

SEA DEVILS
Sept.–Oct., 1961
1 RH 1,000.00
2 RH 550.00
3 RH 400.00
4 RH 350.00
5 RH 350.00
6 thru 10 RH . . . . @275.00
11 . . . . 250.00
12 . . . . 250.00
13 JKu,GC,RA 250.00
14 thru 20 . . . . @250.00
21 I:Capt X,Man Fish 150.00
22 thru 35, May-June, 1967 . . . @150.00

SEAGUY
DC/Vertigo, May 2004
1 (of 3) GMo(s) 3.00
2 thru 3 GMo(s). . . . . @3.00
TPB GMo(s). 10.00

SEBASTIAN O
DC/Vertigo, 1993
1 GMo(s),SY,I:Sebastian O,A:Lord
    Lavender,Roaring Boys 2.50
2 GMo(s),SY,V:Roaring Boys,
    Assassins,A:Abbe 2.50
3 GMo(s),SY,D:Lord Lavender 2.50

SECRET FILES & ORIGINS
2000
TPB DAn,ALa,guide to DCU 7.00
GN Secret Files Guide to DCU
    2001-2002 . . . . 5.00

SECRET HEARTS
Sept.–Oct., 1949–July, 1971
1 Make Believe Sweetheart 800.00

2 ATh,Love Is Not A Dream 400.00
3 Sing Me A Love Song 300.00
4 ATh. 300.00
5 ATh. 300.00
6 . . . . 300.00
7 . . . . 500.00
8 thru 20 . . . . @225.00
21 thru 26 . . . . @175.00
27 B:Comics Code. 150.00
28 thru 30. . . . . @150.00
31 thru 70. . . . . @100.00
71 thru 110 . . . . @50.00
111 thru 120 . . . . @40.00
121 thru 150. . . . . @30.00
151 thru 153 . . . . @25.00

SECRET ORIGINS
Feb., 1973–Oct., 1974
1 O:Superman,Batman,Ghost,
    Flash 65.00
2 O:Green Lantern,Atom,
    Supergirl 35.00
3 O:Wonder Woman,Wildcat . . . 35.00
4 O:Vigilante by MMe 35.00
5 O:The Spectre 35.00
6 O:Blackhawk,Legion of Super
    Heroes 35.00
7 O:Robin, Aquaman 35.00

SECRET ORIGINS
April, 1986
1 JOy,WB,F:Superman 7.00
2 GK,F:Blue Beetle 4.00
3 JBi,F:Captain Marvel 4.00
4 GT,F:Firestorm 4.00
5 GC,F:Crimson Avenger 4.00
6 DG,MR,F:Batman. 5.00
7 F:Sandman,Guy Gardner 3.50
8 MA,F:Shadow Lass,Dollman . . . 2.50
9 GT,F:Skyman,Flash 2.50
10 JL,JO,JA,F:Phantom Stranger . . 2.50
11 LMc,TD,F:Hawkman,Powergirl . . 2.50
12 F:Challengers of the Unknown
    I:G.A. Fury 2.50
13 EL,F:Nightwing 3.00
14 F:Suicide Squad 2.50
15 KMo,DG,F:Deadman,Spectre . . 2.50
16 AKu,F:Hourman,Warlord 2.50
17 KGi,F:Green Lantern 2.75
18 KGi,F:Green Lantern, Creeper . . 2.50
19 JM(c),MA,Uncle Sam, Guardian . 2.50
20 RL,DG,F:Batgirl 3.00
21 GM,MA,F:Jonah Hex 2.50
22 F:Manhunter,Millennium tie-in. . 2.50
23 F:Manhunter,Millennium tie-in. . 2.50
24 F:Dr.Fate,Blue Devil 2.50
25 F:The Legion. 2.50
26 F:Black Lightning 2.50
27 F:Zatanna,Zatara 2.50
28 RLd,GK,F:Nightshade,Midnight . 2.50
29 F:Atom,Red Tornado. 2.50
30 F:Elongated Man 2.50
31 F:Justice Society of America. . . . 2.50
32 F:Justice League America. 3.00
33 F:Justice League Inter.. . . . . . . 2.50
34 F:Justice League Inter. 2.50
35 KSu,F:Justice League Inter. . . . 2.50
36 F:Green Lantern 3.00
37 F:Legion of Subst. Heroes 2.50
38 F:Green Arrow,Speedy 2.50
39 F:Batman,Animal Man 3.50
40 F:Gorilla City. 2.50
41 F:Flash Villains 2.75
42 DC,F:Phantom Girl 2.50
43 TVE,TT,F:Hawk & Dove 2.50
44 F:Batman,Clayface tie-in 3.00
45 F:Blackhawk,El Diablo 2.50
46 CS,F:All Headquarters 2.50
47 CS,F:The Legion. 2.50
48 KG,F:Ambush Bug 2.50
49 F: The Cadmus Project. 2.50

50 GP,CI,DG,F:Batman,Robin,
    Flash,Black Canary 4.00
Ann.#1 JBy,F:Doom Patrol 3.00
Ann.#2 CI,MA,F:Flash 2.50
Ann.#3 F:The Teen Titans 3.00
Spec.#1 SK,PB,DG,F:Batman's worst
    Villians,A:Penguin 4.00
TPB DG,New Origin Batman 4.50
GN rep of 1961 Annual 5.00
Replica Edition 80-page. 5.00
Vol.3 Even More Secret Origins . . . 7.00

SECRET ORIGINS OF
SUPER-VILLAINS
2000
1 80-pg. Giant. 5.00

SECRET SIX
May, 2006
1 (of 6) JP 3.00
2 thru 6 JP. . . . . @3.00

SECRET SOCIETY OF
SUPER-HEROES
Aug., 2000
1 (of 2) HC,MMK,JP,Elseworlds . . . 6.00
2 HC,MMK,JP,concl. 6.00

SECRET SOCIETY OF
SUPER-VILLAINS
May-June, 1976
1 A:Capt.Boomerang, Grodd,
    Sinestro 35.00
2 R:Capt.Comet,A:Green Lantern 20.00
3 A:Mantis, Darkseid. 15.00
4 A:Kalibak,Darkseid,Gr.Lantern . . 15.00
5 RB,D:Manhunter,A:JLA 15.00
6 RB,F:Green Lantern 15.00
7 RB/BL,A:Hawkgirl,Lex Luthor . . 15.00
8 RB/BL,A:Kid Flash 15.00
9 RB/BMc,A:Kid Flash, Creeper . . 15.00
10 DAy/JAb,A:Creeper. 15.00
11 JO,N:Wizard 15.00
12 BMc,A:Blockbuster 15.00
13 A:Crime Syndicate of America . 15.00
14 A:Crime Syndicate of America . 15.00
15 A:G.A.Atom, Dr. Mid Nite 15.00

SECRETS OF
HAUNTED HOUSE
April-May, 1975
1 LD(c),Dead Heat 75.00
2 ECh(c),A Dead Man. 30.00
3 ECh(c),Pathway To Purgatory . . 30.00
4 LD(c),The Face of Death. 30.00
5 BWr(c),Gunslinger! 35.00
6 JAp(c),Deadly Allegiance 25.00
7 JAp(c),It'll Grow On You 25.00
8 MK(c),Raising The Devil 25.00
9 LD(c),The Man Who Didn't
    Believe in Ghosts 25.00
10 MK(c),Ask Me No Questions . . 25.00
11 MK(c),Picasso Fever! 25.00
12 JO&DG(c),Yorick's Skull 25.00
13 JO&DG(c),The Cry of the
    Warewolf 25.00
14 MK(c),Selina 25.00
15 LD(c),Over Your Own Dead
    Body 20.00
16 MK(c),Water, Water Every Fear 20.00
17 LD(c),Papa Don 20.00
18 LD(c),No Sleep For The Dying . 20.00
19 LD(c),The Manner of Execution 20.00
20 JO(c),The Talisman of the
    Serpent 20.00
21 LD(c),The Death's Head
    Scorpion 20.00
22 LD(c),See How They Die 20.00

23 LD(c),The Creeping Red Death 20.00
24 LD(c),Second Chance To Die . . 20.00
25 LD(c),The Man Who Cheated
   Destiny. 20.00
26 MR(c),Elevator to Eternity. . . . 20.00
27 DH(c),Souls For the Master . . . 20.00
28 DH(c),Demon Rum 20.00
29 MK(c),Duel of Darkness 20.00
30 JO(c),For the Love of Arlo 20.00
31 I:Mister E. 25.00
32 The Legend of the Tiger's Paw. 15.00
33 In The Attic Dwells Dark Seth . . 15.00
34 Double Your Pleasure 15.00
35 Deathwing, Lord of Darkness . . 15.00
36 RB&DG(c),Sister Sinister 15.00
37 RB&DG(c),The Third Wish Is
   Death 15.00
38 RB&DG(c),Slaves of Satan. . . . 15.00
39 RB&DG(c),The Witch-Hounds
   of Salem 15.00
40 RB&DG(c),The Were-Witch
   of Boston 15.00
41 JKu(c),House at Devil's Tail . . . 15.00
42 JKu(c),Mystic Murder 15.00
43 JO(c),Mother of Invention 15.00
44 BWr(c),Halloween God 15.00
45 EC&JO(c),Star-Trakker 15.00
46 March, 1982 . . . . 15.00

SINISTER HOUSE OF SECRET LOVE

Oct.–Nov., 1971–April–May, 1972
1 Curse of the MacIntyres 250.00
2 TD,To Wed the Devil 100.00
3 ATh,Bride of the Falcon 125.00
4 TD,Kiss of the Serpent 100.00
Becomes:

SECRETS OF SINISTER HOUSE

June–July, 1972
5 NC(c),Death at Castle Dunbar . . 60.00
6 MK,JO,Brief Reunion 30.00
7 NR,MK,Panic. 30.00
8 NC,Man Who Cried Werewolf . . 30.00
9 JkS(c),Dance of the Damned . . 30.00
10 JkS(c),Castle Curse 35.00
11 thru 16 . . . . @20.00
17 DBa,NC,HC,WMo 20.00
18 NC,GK,June-July, 1974 . . . . . . 20.00

SECRETS OF THE LEGION OF SUPER-HEROES

Jan., 1981
1 O:Legion 3.50
2 O:Brainiac 5 . . . . 3.50
3 March, 1981,O:Karate Kid 3.50

SEEKERS INTO THE MYSTERY

1996
1 Pilgrimage of Lucas Hart,pt.1 . . 2.50
2 Pilgrimage of Lucas Hart,pt.2 . . 2.50
3 Pilgrimage of Lucas Hart,pt.3 . . 2.50
4 Pilgrimage of Lucas Hart,pt.4 . . 2.50
5 Pilgrimage of Lucas Hart,pt.5 . . 2.50
6 Falling Down to Heaven,pt.1 . . . 2.50
7 Falling Down to Heaven,pt.2 . . . 2.50
8 Falling Down to Heaven,pt.3 . . . 2.50
9 JMD(s),MZi,Falling Down from
   Heaven,pt.4 concl. 2.50
10 JMD(s),JMu,F:Charlie Limbo . . 2.50
11 JMD(s),JIT,God's Shadow,pt.1 . . 2.50
12 JMD(s),JIT,God's Shadow,pt.2 . . 2.50
13 JMD(s),JIT,God's Shadow,pt.3 . . 2.50
14 JMD(s),JIT,God's Shadow,pt.4 . . 2.50

15 JMD(s),JMu,Hart meets
   Magician, final issue 3.00

Sensation #22 © DC Comics Inc.

SENSATION COMICS

1942–52
1 I:Wonder Woman,Wildcat . . 60,000.00
2 I:Etta Candy & the Holiday
   Girls, Dr. Poison 10,000.00
3 Diana Price joins Military
   Intelligence 5,000.00
4 I:Baroness PaulaVonGunther 4,000.00
5 V:Axis Spies 3,500.00
6 Wonder Woman receives magic
   lasso,V:Baroness Gunther . 3,500.00
7 V:Baroness Gunther 2,500.00
8 Meets Gloria Bullfinch. 2,500.00
9 A:The Real Diana Prince . . . 2,500.00
10 V:Ishti. 2,500.00
11 I:Queen Desira. 2,500.00
12 V:Baroness Gunther 2,000.00
13 V:Olga,Hitler(c) 2,500.00
14 The Fir Tree's Story 2,000.00
15 V:Simon Slikery 2,000.00
16 V:Karl Schultz 2,000.00
17 V:Princess Yasmini 2,000.00
18 V:Quito 2,000.00
19 Wonder Woman Goes
   Berserk 2,000.00
20 V:Stoffer 2,000.00
21 V:American Adolf 1,800.00
22 V:Cheetah 1,800.00
23 'War Laugh Mania' 1,800.00
24 I:Wonder Woman's
   Mental Radio 1,800.00
25 Kidnapper o/t Astral Spirits . 1,800.00
26 A:Queen Hippolyte. 1,800.00
27 V:Ely Close 1,800.00
28 V:Mayor Prude. 1,800.00
29 V:Mimi Mendez 1,800.00
30 V:Anton Unreal. 1,800.00
31 Grow Down Land 1,400.00
32 V:Crime Chief. 1,400.00
33 Meets Percy Pringle. 1,400.00
34 I:Sargon 1,500.00
35 V:Sontag Henya in Atlantis . 1,200.00
36 V:Bedwin Footh 1,200.00
37 A:Mala((1st app. All-Star #8) 1,200.00
38 V:The Gyp 1,200.00
39 V:Nero 1,200.00
40 I:Countess Draska Nishki . . 1,200.00
41 V:Creeper Jackson 1,100.00
42 V:Countess Nishki 1,100.00
43 Meets Joel Heyday 1,100.00
44 V:Lt. Sturm 1,100.00
45 V:Jose Perez 1,100.00

46 V:Lawbreakers Protective
   League 1,100.00
47 V:Unknown. 1,100.00
48 V:Topso and Teena 1,100.00
49 V:Zavia. 1,100.00
50 V:'Ears' Fellock 1,100.00
51 V:Doss Brokol 1,000.00
52 Meets Prof. Toxino 1,000.00
53 V:Wanta Wynn 1,000.00
54 V:Dr. Fiendo. 1,000.00
55 V:Bughumans 1,000.00
56 V:Dr. Novel 1,000.00
57 V:Syonide. 1,000.00
58 Meets Olive Norton 1,000.00
59 V:Snow Man 750.00
60 V:Bifton Jones. 750.00
61 V:Bluff Robust 750.00
62 V:Black Robert of Dogwood . . 750.00
63 V:Prof. Vibrate. 750.00
64 V:Cloudmen 750.00
65 V:Lim Slait. 800.00
66 V:Slick Skeener. 800.00
67 V:Daredevil Dix 800.00
68 Secret of the Menacing
   Octopus 800.00
69 V:Darcy Wells 900.00
70 Unconquerable Woman of
   Cocha Bamba 900.00
71 V:Queen Flaming 900.00
72 V:Blue Seal Gang 900.00
73 Wonder Woman time
   travel story. 900.00
74 V:Spug Spangle 900.00
75 V:Shark 900.00
76 V:King Diamond 900.00
77 V:Boss Brekel 900.00
78 V:Furiosa. 900.00
79 Meets Leila and Solala 900.00
80 V:Don Enrago 900.00
81 V:Dr. Frenzi. 750.00
82 V:King Lunar. 600.00
83 V:Prowd 600.00
84 V:Duke Daxo. 600.00
85 Meets Leslie M. Gresham. . . . 600.00
86 Secret of the Amazing
   Bracelets 600.00
87 In Twin Peaks(in Old West) . . 600.00
88 Wonder Woman in Holywood . 600.00
89 V:Abacus Rackeett Gang 600.00
90 The Secret of the Modern
   Sphinx 600.00
91 Survivors of the Stone Age . . . 600.00
92 V:Duke of Deceptions 600.00
93 V:Talbot. 600.00
94 Girl Issue. 650.00
95 CI,Dr. Pat's First Love. 750.00
96 CI,W.Woman's RomanticRival 750.00
97 W.Woman Romance Editor . . 750.00
98 Strange Mission 750.00
99 I:Astra 750.00
100 W.Woman Hollywood Star . . 800.00
101 Battle for the Atom World . . . 750.00
102 Queen of the South Seas . . . 750.00
103 V:Robot Archers 750.00
104 The End of Paradise
   Island. 750.00
105 Secret of the Giant Forest . . 750.00
106 E:Wonder Woman. 750.00
107 ATh,Mystery issue 1,200.00
108 ATh,GK,I:Johnny Peril 750.00
109 Ath,GK,A:Johnny Peril 1,500.00
Becomes:

SENSATION MYSTERY

1952–53
110 MA(c),B:Johnny Peril 800.00
111 GK,Spectre in the Flame. . . . 750.00
112 GK,Death Has 5 Guesses . . 750.00
113 CI,The End of Death 750.00
114 GK,GC,The Haunted
   Diamond 750.00
115 GK,The Phantom Castle 750.00
116 The Toy Assassins 750.00

DC COMICS

SENSATION COMICS
1999
1 JeR(s),ScB, F:Wonder Woman &
Hawkgirl 2.25

Sergeant Bilko #5
© DC Comics, Inc.

SERGEANT BILKO
May-June, 1957
1 Based on TV show 1,000.00
2 . . . . 500.00
3 . . . . 400.00
4 . . . . 350.00
5 . . . . 350.00
6 thru 17 . . . . @300.00
18 March-April, 1960 . . . . 300.00

SERGEANT BILKO'S PVT. DOBERMAN
June-July, 1958
1 . . . . 600.00
2 . . . . 300.00
3 and 4 . . . . @225.00
5 photo (c). 225.00
6 thru 10 . . . . @150.00
11 Feb.–March, 1960 . . . . 150.00

SGT. ROCK
See: OUR ARMY AT WAR

SGT. ROCK
2005
GN Between Hell & A Hard
Place, JKu 18.00
TPB Combat Tales Vol. 1. . . . . . . 10.00

SGT. ROCK SPECIAL
Oct., 1988
#1 rep.Our Army at War#162-#63 . 12.00
#2 rep.Brave & Bold #52 . . . . 7.00
#3 rep.Showcase #45 . . . . 7.00
#4 rep.Our Army at War#147-#48 . . 7.00
#5 rep.Our Army at War#81&#103 . . 7.00
#6 rep.Our Army at War #160 . . . . . 7.00
#7 rep.Our Army at War #85 . . . . . . 7.00
#8 thru #20 reprints . . . . @7.00
Spec. #1 TT,MGo,JKu,CR,(new
stories) 5.00

SGT. ROCK'S PRIZE BATTLE TALES
Winter, 1964
1 . . . . 550.00

SEVEN SOLDIERS
Feb., 2005
0 GMo(s),JWi,48-page 3.00
1 48-pg. 4.00
1 GMo(s),JWi,culmination 3.00
TPB Seven Soldiers of Victory . . 15.00
TPB Seven Soldiers of Victory,#2 . 15.00
TPB Seven Soldiers of Victory,#3 . 15.00
TPB Seven Soldiers of Vistory,#4 . 15.00

SEVEN SOLDIERS: THE BULLETEER
Nov., 2005
1 (of 4) GMo(s) 3.00
2 thru 4 GMo(s). . . . . @3.00

SEVEN SOLDIERS: FRANKENSTEIN
Nov., 2005
1 (of 4) GMo(s),DoM. 3.00
2 GMo(s),DoM, on Mars 3.00
3 GMo(s),DoM,A:The Bride 3.00
4 GMo(s),DoM,V:Death Fairies . . . 3.00

SEVEN SOLDIERS: GUARDIAN
March, 2005
1 (of 4) GMo(s),masthead 3.00
2 GMo(s) . . . . , ... 3.00
3 GMo(s). 3.00
4 GMo(s). 3.00

SEVEN SOLDIERS: KLARION THE WITCH BOY
Apr., 2005
1 GMo(s),F:Klarion and Teek 3.00
2 GMo(s). 3.00
3 GMo(s). 3.00
4 GMo(s). 3.00

SEVEN SOLDIERS: MISTER MIRACLE
Sept., 2005
1 (of 4) GMo(s),PFe 3.00
2 GMo(s),PFe(c). 3.00
3 GMo(s),I:Baron Bedlam. 3.00
4 GMo(s),Forever-Flavored Man . . 3.00

SEVEN SOLDIERS: SHINING KNIGHT
March, 2005
1 (of 4) GMo(s),fantasy epic 3.00
2 GMo(s). 3.00
3 GMo(s). 3.00
4 GMo(s). 3.00

SEVEN SOLDIERS: ZATANNA
Apr., 2005
1 GMo(s),F:Zatanna 3.00
2 GMo(s). 3.00
3 & 4 GMo(s). . . . . @3.00

SGT. ROCK: THE PROPHECY
Jan., 2006
1 (of 6) JKu 3.00
1a & b variant (c)s. . . . . @3.00
2 JKu. 3.00
3 JKu. 3.00
4 JKu, Road to Riga 3.00
5 JKu, Farmer's Barn 3.00
6 JKu,concl. 3.00

SHADE
June-July, 1977
[1st Regular Series]
1 SD,I&O: Shade 25.00
2 SD,V:Form 20.00
3 SD,V:The Cloak 15.00
4 SD,Return to Meta-Zone 15.00
5 SD,V:Supreme Decider 15.00
6 SD,V:Khaos 15.00
7 SD,V:Dr.Z.Z. 15.00
8 SD,last issue 15.00

SHADE, THE
Feb., 1997
1 (of 4) JeR(s),GeH,A:Ludlows. . . . 3.00
2 JeR(s),JWi,MGy,poisoned by love
of his life 3.00
3 JeR(s),BBl,Golden Age Flash Jay
Garrick retiring 3.00
4 JeR(s),MZi,V:last of the Ludlows. 3.00

Shade the Changing Man #3
© DC Comics Inc.

SHADE, THE CHANGING MAN
July, 1990
1 B:PrM(s),CBa,MPn,I:Kathy George,
I&D:Troy Grezer 5.00
2 CBa,MPn,Who Shot JFK#1 . . . . . 4.00
3 CBa,MPn,Who Shot JFK#2 . . . . . 3.00
4 CBa,MPn,V:American Scream . . 3.00
5 CBa,MPn,V:Hollywood
Monsters 3.00
6 CBa,MPn,V:Ed Loot 3.00
7 CBa,MPn,I:Arnold Major 3.00
8 CBa,Mpn,I:Lenny 3.00
9 CBa,MPn,V:Arnold Major 3.00
10 CBa,MPn,Paranioa 2.75
11 CBa,MPn,R:Troy Grezer 2.50
12 CBa,MPn,V:Troy Grezer 2.50
13 CBa,MPn,I:Fish Priest 2.50
14 CBa,MPn,V:Godfather of Guilt . 2.50
15 CBa,MPn,I:Spirit 2.50
16 CBa,MPn,V:American Scream . . 2.50
17 RkB(i),V:Rohug. 2.50
18 MPn,E:American Scream 2.50
19 MPn,V:Dave Messiah Seeker. . . 2.50
20 JD,CBa,MPn,RkB,R:Roger. 2.50
21 MPn,The Road,A:Stringer. 2.25
22 The Road,Childhood. 2.25
23 The Road 2.25
24 The Road 2.25
25 The Road 2.25
26 MPn(i),F:Lenny 2.25
27 MPn(i),Shade becomes female . 2.25

All comics prices listed are for *Near Mint* condition.

28 MPn(i),Changing Woman #2 . . . 2.25
29 MPn(i),Changing Woman #3 . . . 2.25
30 Another Life. 2.25
31 Ernest & Jim #1 . . . . 2.25
32 Ernest & Jim #2 . . . . 2.25

DC/Vertigo, 1993
33 CBa,B:Birth Pains. 2.25
34 CBa,RkB(i),GID(i),A:Brian Juno,
Garden of Pain 2.25
35 CBa,RkB(i),E:Birth Pains,
V:Juno 2.25
36 CBa,PrG(i),RkB(i),B:Passion child,
I:Miles Laimling 2.25
37 CBa,RkB(i),Shade/Kathy 2.25
38 CBa,RkB(i),Great American
Novel 2.25
39 CBa,SEa,RkB(i),Pond Life 2.25
40 PBd,at Hotel Shade 2.25
41 GID,Pandora's Story,Kathy is
pregnant 2.25
42 CBa,RkB(i),SY,B:History Lesson,
A:John Constantine 2.50
43 CBa,RkB(i),PBd,Trial of William
Matthieson,A:J.Constantine. . . . 2.50
44 CBa,RkB(i),E:History Lesson,
D:William Matthieson,A:John
Constantine 2.50
45 CBa,B:A Season in Hell 2.25
46 CBa(c),GID,Season in Hell#2 . . . 2.25
47 CBa(c),GID,A:Lenny 2.25
48 CBa(c),GID 2.25
49 CBa(c),GID,Kathy's Past 2.25
50 GID,BBI,MiA,pin-up gallery 3.25
51 GID,BBI,MiA,Masks,pt.1 . . . . 2.00
52 GID,BBI,MiA,Masks,pt.2 . . . . 2.00
53 GID,BBI,MiA,Masks,pt.3 . . . . 2.00
54 MBu,RkB,Perpetual Motion 2.00
55 MBu,RkB,Life is Short,pt.1 . . . . . 2.00
56 MBu,RkB,Life is Short,pt.2 . . . . . 2.00
57 MBu,PrM,RkB,Life is Short,pt.3 . 2.00
58 PrM,Michael Lark 2.00
59 MBu,PrM,Nasty Infections,pt.1 . . 2.25
60 MBu,PrM,Nasty Infections,pt.2 . . 2.25
61 MBu,PrM,Nasty Infections,pt.3 . . 2.25
62 Nasty Infections,pt.4 . . . . 2.25
63 Nasty Infections,finale. 2.25
64 The Madness 2.25
65 The Roots of Madness,pt.1 . . . . . 2.25
66 The Roots of Madness,pt.2 . . . . . 2.25
67 The Roots of Madness,pt.3. . . . . 2.25
68 After Kathy,pt.1 . . . . 2.25
69 After Kathy,pt.2 . . . . 2.25
70 After Kathy,pt.3, final issue 2.25
TPB The American Scream 18.00

SHADO, SONG OF
THE DRAGON
1992
1 GM(i),From G.A. Longbow
Hunters 5.50
2 GM(i),V:Yakuza 5.00
3 GM(i),V:Yakuza 5.00
4 GM(i),V:Yakuza 5.00

SHADOW, THE
[1st Regular Series], 1973–75
1 MK,The Doom Puzzle 75.00
2 MK,V:Freak Show Killer. 35.00
3 MK,BWr. 40.00
4 MK,HC,BWr,Ninja Story. 35.00
5 FR 30.00
6 MK 32.00
7 FR 15.00
8 FR 15.00
9 FR 15.00
10 JCr 20.00
11 A:Avenger 15.00
12. . . . . 15.00

[Limited Series], 1986
1 HC,R:Shadow 5.00

2 HC,O:Shadow 4.00
3 HC,V:Preston Mayrock 3.00
4 HC,V:Preston Mayrock 3.00
TPB rep. #1 thru #4 . . . . 13.00

[2nd Regular Series], 1987–89
1 BSz,Shadows & Light,pt.1 . . . . . 3.50
2 BSz,Shadows & Light,pt.2 . . . . . 3.50
3 BSz,Shadows & Light,pt.3 . . . . . 3.50
4 BSz,Shadows & Light,pt.4 . . . . . 3.50
5 BSz,Shadows & Light,pt.5 . . . . . 3.50
6 BSz,Shadows & Light,pt.6 . . . . . 3.50
7 MR,KB,Harold Goes to
Washington 3.00
8 KB,Seven Deadly Finns,pt.1 . . . . 3.00
9 KB,Seven Deadly Finns,pt.2 . . . . 3.00
10 KB,Seven Deadly Finns,pt.3. . . . 3.00
11 KB,Seven Deadly Finns,pt.4 . . . . 3.00
12 KB,Seven Deadly Finns,pt.5. . . . 3.00
13 KB,Seven Deadly Finns,pt.6 . . . . 3.00
14 KB,Body And Soul,pt.1 . . . . 3.00
15 KB,Body And Soul,pt.2 . . . . 3.00
16 KB,Body And Soul,pt.3 . . . . 3.00
17 KB,Body And Soul,pt.4 . . . . 3.00
18 KB,Body And Soul,pt.5 . . . . 3.00
19 KB,Body And Soul,pt.6 . . . . 3.00
Ann.#1 JO,AA,Shadows & Light
prologue. 4.00
Ann.#2 KB,Agents 3.50

SHADOW CABINET
Milestone, 1994–95
0 WS(c),3RL,Shadow War,Foil(c),A:All
Milestone characters 3.00
1 JBy(c),3RW,I&D:Corpsickle 2.50
2 thru 17 . . . . @2.50

SHADOWDRAGON
ANNUAL
1995
Ann.#1 Year One Annual 3.50

SHADOW OF BATMAN
1 reprints of Detective Comics . . . 10.00
2 thru 4 . . . . @7.50

SHADOW OF
THE BATMAN
1985–86
1 WS,AM,MR,rep. 7.00
2 MR,TA,rep.A:Hugo Strange 5.00
3 MR,TA,rep.A:Penguin 5.00
4 MR,TA,rep.A:Joker 6.00
5 MR,DG,rep. 5.00

SHADOWPACT
2006
1 BWg,A:Superman 3.00
2 BWg. 3.00
3 BWg,V:Pentacle. 3.00
4 BWg,F:Blue Devil. 3.00
5 BWg,Killers assemble 3.00
6 Goodbye Ragman & Enchantress 3.00
7 BWg,V:The Congregation 3.00

SHADOW'S FALL
1994–95
1 JVF,Voyage of self-discovery. . . . 3.00
2 JVF,More of tale. 3.00
3 JVF,Shen confronts shadow 3.00
4 JVF,Gale wounded. 3.00
5 JVF,Shadow goes Berserk 3.00
6 JVF,F:Warren Gale,final issue . . . 3.00

SHADOW STRIKES!, THE
1989–92
1 EB,Death's Head 3.00
2 EB,EB,PoliticalKiller,V:Rasputin. . 2.50
3 EB,V:Mad Monk,V:Rasputin 2.50

4 EB,D:Mad Monk,V:Rasputin 4.00
5 EB,Shadow & Doc Savage#1 . . . 4.00
6 Shadow & Doc Savage #3 . . . . . 2.50
7 RM,A:Wunderkind,O:Shadow's
Radio Show. 2.50
8 EB,A:Shiwan Khan 2.50
9 Fireworks#2 . . . . 2.50
10 EB,Fireworks#3. . . . . 2.50
11 EB,O:Margo Lane 2.50
12 EB,V:Chicago Mob 2.50
13 EB,V:Chicago Mob 2.50
14 EB,V:Chicago Mob 2.50
15 EB,V:Chicago Mob 2.50
16 Assassins,pt.1. . . . . 2.50
17 Assassins,pt.2. . . . . 2.50
18 Shrevvie 2.50
19 NY,NJ Tunnel 2.50
20 Shadow+Margo Vs.Nazis 2.50
21 V:Shiwan Khan 2.50
22 V:Shiwan Khan 2.50
23 V:Shiwan Khan 2.50
24 Search for Margo Lane 2.50
25 In China 2.50
26 V:Shiwan Khan 2.50
27 V:Shiwan Khan,Margo
Rescued 2.50
28 SL,In Hawaii 2.50
29 DSp,Valhalla,V:Nazis 2.50
30 The Shadow Year One,pt.1 . . . . 2.50
31 The Shadow Year One,pt.2 . . . . 2.50
Ann.#1 DSp, Crimson Dreams 4.00

Shadow War of Hawkman #3
© DC Comics Inc.

SHADOW WAR
OF HAWKMAN
May, 1985
1 AA,V:Thangarians 2.50
2 AA,V:Thangarians 2.50
3 AA,V:Thangarians,A:Aquaman,
Elong.Man 2.50
4 AA,V:Thangarians 2.50
Spec.#1 V:Thangarians 2.50

SHAZAM!
1973–78
[1st Regular Series]
1 B:DON(s),CCB,O:Capt.Marvel . 75.00
2 CCB,A:Mr.Mind 25.00
3 CCB,V:Shagg Naste 25.00
4 E:DON(s),CCB,V:Ibac 25.00
5 B:ESM(s),CCB,A:Leprechaun . . 25.00
6 B:DON(s),CCB,Dr,Sivana 20.00
7 CCB,A:Capt Marvel Jr. 20.00
8 CCB,O:Marvel Family 90.00

Shazam #18 © DC Comics, Inc.

9 E:DON(S)DC,CCB,A:Mr.Mind,	
Captain Marvel Jr.	20.00
10 ESM(s)CCB,BO	20.00
11 ViCKS,BO,rep.	20.00
12 BO,DG	75.00
13 BO,KS,A:Luthor	75.00
14 KS,A:Monster Society	75.00
15 KS,BO,Luther	75.00
16 KS,BO	75.00
17 KS,BO	75.00
18 KS,BO	15.00
19 KS,BO,Mary Marvel	15.00
20 KS,A:Marvel Family	15.00
21 reprint	15.00
22 reprint	15.00
23 reprint	15.00
24 reprint	15.00
25 KS,DG,I&O:Isis	22.00
26 KS	15.00
27 KS,A:Kid Eternity	22.00
28 KS	15.00
29 KS	15.00
30 KS	15.00
31 KS,A:Minute Man	15.00
32 KS	15.00
33 KS	15.00
34 O:Capt.Marvel Jr.	15.00
35 DN,KS,A:Marvel Family	15.00
GN Power of Hope,64-page	15.00

SHAZAM! FAMILY
July, 2002

Annual #1 (1953, rep.) 80-pg. 6.00

SHAZAM, THE NEW BEGINNING
April, 1987

1 O:Shazam & Capt.Marvel	2.50
2 V:Black Adam	2.50
3 V:Black Adam	2.50
4 V:Black Adam	2.50

SHAZAM/SUPERMAN: FIRST THUNDER
Sept., 2005

1 (of 4) V:Cult, Giant Robots	3.50
2 A:Lex Luthor & Dr. Sivana	3.50
3 F:Eclipso	3.50
4 V:Dr. Sivana	3.50

SHERLOCK HOLMES
Sept.–Oct., 1975

1 ERc,WS 35.00

SHOWCASE
1956–70

1 F:Fire Fighters	6,000.00
2 JKu,F:Kings of Wild	1,800.00
3 F:Frogmen	1,700.00
4 CI,JKu,I&O:S.A. Flash	
(Barry Allen)	50,000.00
5 F:Manhunters	1,800.00
6 JK,I&O:Challengers of the	
Unknown	6,500.00
7 JK,F:Challengers	3,200.00
8 CI,F:Flash,I:Capt.Cold	18,000.00
9 F:Lois Lane	12,000.00
10 F:Lois Lane	5,500.00
11 JK(c),F:Challengers	3,000.00
12 JK(c),F:Challengers	3,000.00
13 CI,F:Flash,Mr.Element	7,500.00
14 CI,F:Flash,Mr.Element	8,000.00
15 I:Space Ranger	3,500.00
16 F:Space Ranger	2,000.00
17 GK(c),I:Adam Strange	4,500.00
18 GK(c),F:Adam Strange	2,500.00
19 GK(c),F:Adam Strange	2,700.00
20 I:Rip Hunter	1,800.00
21 F:Rip Hunter	1,000.00
22 GK,I&O:S.A. Green Lantern	
(Hal Jordan)	8,500.00
23 GK,F:Green Lantern	2,700.00
24 GK,F:Green Lantern	2,700.00
25 JKu,F:Rip Hunter	750.00
26 JKu,F:Rip Hunter	750.00
27 RH,I:Sea Devils	1,500.00
28 RH,F:Sea Devils	900.00
29 RH,F:Sea Devils	900.00
30 O:Aquaman	1,500.00
31 GK(c),F:Aquaman	1,200.00
32 F:Aquaman	1,200.00
33 F:Aquaman	1,300.00
34 GK,MA,I&O:S.A. Atom	3,000.00
35 GK,MA,F:Atom	1,500.00
36 GK,MA,F:Atom	1,200.00
37 RA,I:Metal Man	1,300.00
38 RA,F:Metal Man	900.00
39 RA,F:Metal Man	750.00
40 RA,F:Metal Man	700.00
41 F:Tommy Tomorrow	600.00
42 F:Tommy TOmorrow	600.00
43 F:Dr.No(James Bond 007)	750.00
44 F:Tommy Tomorrow	500.00
45 JKu,O:Sgt.Rock	500.00
46 F:Tommy Tomorrow	350.00
47 F:Tommy Tomorrow	350.00
48 F:Cave Carson	500.00
49 F:Cave Carson	400.00
50 MA,CI,F:I Spy	300.00
51 MA,CI,F:I Spy	300.00
52 F:Cave Carson	300.00
53 JKu(c),RH,F:G.I.Joe	500.00
54 JKu(c),RH,F:G.I.Joe	500.00
55 MA,F:Dr.Fate,Spectre,1st S.A.	
Gr. Lantern,Solomon Grundy	400.00
56 MA,F:Dr.Fate	300.00
57 JKu,F:Enemy Ace	1,000.00
58 JKu,F:Enemy Ace	800.00
59 F:Teen Titans	300.00
60 MA,F:Spectre	600.00
61 MA,F:Spectre	400.00
62 JO,I:Inferior 5	250.00
63 JO,F:Inferior 5	175.00
64 MA,F:Spectre	300.00
65 F:Inferior 5	150.00
66 I:B'wana Beast	175.00
67 F:B'wana Beast	150.00
68 I:Maniaks	200.00
69 F:Maniaks	200.00
70 I:Binky	180.00
71 F:Maniaks	150.00

72 JKu,ATh,F:Top Gun	150.00
73 SD,I&O:Creeper	250.00
74 I:Anthro	150.00
75 SD,I:Hawk & Dove	200.00
76 NC,I:Bat Lash	250.00
77 BO,I:Angel & Ape	100.00
78 I:Jonny Double	65.00
79 I:Dolphin	90.00
80 NA(c),F:Phantom Stranger	125.00
81 I:Windy & Willy	75.00
82 I:Nightmaster	400.00
83 BWr,MK,F:Nightmaster	300.00
84 BWr,MK,F:Nightmaster	300.00
85 JKu,F:Firehair	50.00
86 JKu,F:Firehair	50.00
87 JKu,F:Firehair	50.00
88 F:Jason's Quest	25.00
89 F:Jason's Quest	25.00
90 F:Manhunter	25.00
91 F:Manhunter	25.00
92 F:Manhunter	25.00
93 F:Manhunter (1970)	25.00

[Series Resumes], 1977

94 JA,JSon,I&O:2nd	
Doom Patrol	20.00
95 JA,JSon,F:2nd Doom Patrol	12.00
96 JA,JSon,F:2nd Doom Patrol	12.00
97 JO,JSon,O:Power Girl	12.00
98 JSon,DG,Power Girl	12.00
99 JSon,DG,Power Girl	12.00
100 JSon,all star issue	20.00
101 JKu(c),AM,MA,Hawkman	12.00
102 JKu(c),AM,MA,Hawkman	12.00
103 JKu(c),AM,MA,Hawkman	12.00
104 RE,OSS Spies	12.00
TPB Rep.1956–59	20.00

SHOWCASE '93

1 AAd(c),EH,AV,F:Catwoman,	
Blue Devil,Cyborg	4.00
2 KM(c),EH,AV,F:Catwoman,	
Blue Devil,Cyborg	3.50
3 KM(c),EH,TC,F:Catwoman,	
Blue Devil,Flash	3.00
4 F:Catwoman,Blue Devil,	
Geo-Force	3.00
5 F:KD,DG,BHi,F:Robin,Blue	
Devil,Geo-Force	3.00
6 MZ(c),KD,DG,F:Robin,Blue	
Devil,Deathstroke	3.00
7 BSz(c),KJ,Knightfall#13,F:Two-	
Face,Jade&Obsidian	5.00
8 KJ,Knightfall#14,F:Two-Face,	
Peacemaker,Fire and Ice	4.00

Showcase '93 #12
© DC Comics Inc.

9 F:Huntress,Peacemaker,Shining
Knight 3.00
10 BWg,SI,F:Huntress,Batman,
Dr.Light,Peacemaker,Deathstroke,
Katana,M.Manhunter 3.00
11 GP(c),F:Robin,Nightwing,
Peacemaker,Deathstroke,Deadshot,
Katana,Dr.Light,Won.Woman . . 3.00
12 AD(c),BMc,F:Robin,Nightwing,
Green Lantern,Creeper 3.00

SHOWCASE '94

1 KN,F:Joker,Gunfire,Orion,Metro . 3.00
2 KON(c),E:Joker,B:Blue Beetle . . 3.00
3 MMi(c),B:Razorsharpe 3.00
4 AIG(s),DG,F:Arkham Asylum inmates
E:Razorsharpe,Blue Bettle 3.00
5 WS(c),CDi(s),PJ,B:Robin&Huntress,
F:Bloodwynd,Loose Cannon . . . 3.00
6 PJ,KK(s),F:Robin & Huntress . . . 3.00
7 JaL(c),PDd(s),F:Comm. Gordon . 3.00
8 AIG(s),O:Scarface,Ventriloquist,
F:Monarch,1st Wildcat 3.25
9 AIG(s),DJ,O:Scarface,Ventriloquist,
F:Monarch,Waverider 3.00
10 JQ(c),AIG(s),F:Azrael,Zero Hour,
B:Black Condor 3.25
11 Black Condor, Man-Bat 3.00
12 Barbara Gordon 3.00

SHOWCASE '95

1 Supergirl 3.00
2 . . . . 3.00
3 F:Eradicator,Claw 3.00
4 A:Catwoman,Hawke 3.00
5 F:Thorne,Firehawk 3.00
6 thru 12 . . . . @3.00

SHOWCASE '96

1 F:Steel & Warrior 3.00
2 F:Steel and Warrior 3.00
3 thru 7 . . . . @3.00
8 F:Superman, Superboy &
Supergirl 5.00
9 F:Lady Shiva & Shadowdragon,
Martian Manhunter 3.00
10 F:Ultra Boy, Captain Comet 3.00
11 Legion of Super-Heroes 3.00
12 10,000 Brainiacs 3.00

SHOWCASE PRESENTS

2005–06

TPB Superman, Vol. 1 . . . . 17.00
TPB Green Lantern, Vol. 1 . . . . . . 17.00
TPB Metamorpho, Vol. 1 . . . . . . 17.00
TPB Jonah Hex 17.00
TPB Shazam, Jr. 1 . . . . 17.00
TPB Justice League of America . . 17.00
TPB Green Arrow, Vol. 1 . . . . 17.00
TPB The Unknown Soldier, Vol. 1 . 17.00
TPB House of Mystery, Vol. 1 . . . 17.00
TPB Superman Family, Vol. 1 . . . . 17.00
TPB Teen Titans, Vol. 1 . . . . 17.00
TPB Haunted Tank, Vol. 1 . . . . . . 17.00
TPB Superman, Vol. 2 . . . . 17.00
TPB The Elongated Man, Vol. 1 . . 17.00
TPB Batman, Vol. 1 . . . . 17.00
TPB Challengers of the Unknown . 17.00
TPB The Phantom Strangers 17.00

SILVER AGE
DC CLASSICS

Action #252(rep) 3.00
Adventure #247(rep) 3.00
Brave and Bold #28 (rep) 3.00
Detective #225 (rep) 3.00
Detective #327 (rep) 3.00
Green Lantern #76 (rep) 3.00
House of Secrets #92 (rep) 3.00
Showcase #4 (rep) 3.00

Showcase #22 (rep) 3.00
Sugar & Spike #99(1st printing) . . . 3.00

SILVER AGE
May, 2000

Secret Files #1 . . . . 5.00
Justice League of America #1 . . . . 2.50
Challengers of the Unknown #1 . . . 2.50
Teen Titans #1 . . . . 2.50
Doom Patrol #1 . . . . 2.50
Dial "H" For Hero #1 . . . . 2.50
The Flash #1 . . . . 2.50
Green Lantern #1 . . . . 2.50
The Brave and the Bold #1 . . . . . 2.50
Showcase #1 . . . . 2.50
80-Page Giant #1, 80-pg 6.50
Silver Age #1, 48-pg 4.00

Silverblade #2
© DC Comics Inc.

SILVERBLADE
Sept., 1987

1 KJ,GC,maxi-series 2.25
2 thru 12 GC . . . . @2.25

SINS OF YOUTH
March, 2000

Aquaboy/Lagoon Man #1 x-over . . . 2.50
Batboy & Robin #1 x-over 2.50
JLA/Jr. #1 x-over 2.50
Kid Flash/Impulse #1 x-over 2.50
Secret/Deadboy #1 x-over 2.50
Starwoman & JSA #1 x-over 2.50
Superman,Jr./Superboy,Sr.#1
x-over 2.50
Wonder Girls #1 x-over 2.50

SKIN GRAFT
DC/Vertigo, 1993

1 B:JeP(s),WaP,I:John Oakes,
A:Tattooed Man(Tarrant) 3.25
2 WaP,V:Assassins 3.00
3 WaP,In Kyoto,I:Mizoguchi Kenji . . 3.00
4 E:JeP(s),WaP,V:Tarrant,Kenji . . . 3.00

SKIZZ
(B&W) Feb., 2005

TPB AMo(s),JBa, 2000 A.D. 15.00

SKREEMER
May, 1989

1 thru 6 . . . . @2.25

TPB (2002) 20.00

SKULL AND BONES
1992

1 EH,I&O:Skull & Bones 5.00
2 EH,V:KGB 5.00
3 EH,V:KGB 5.00

SLASH MARAUD
Nov., 1987

1 PG 2.25
2 PG 2.25
3 thru 10 PG . . . . @2.25

SMALLVILLE
Sept., 2002

Spec. TV series 4.00

SMALLVILLE
March 2003

1 Camping trip, from TV show 5.00
2 Miss Smallville Pageant 4.00
3 F:Lex Luthor 4.00
4 F:Lex Luthor 4.00
5 Untold Tales 4.00
6 Lex & Clark,48-pg 4.00
7 TG,Television x-over,pt.1 . . . . . . 4.00
8 TG,Television x-over,pt.2 . . . . . . 4.00
9 Mysterious men 4.00
10 Who shot Lionel Luthor 4.00
11 48-page 4.00
TPB Rep 10.00

SMASH COMICS
1999

1 TPe(s),F:Doctor Mid-Nite
& Hourman 2.25

SMAX
DC/Vertigo, 2003

1 (of 5) AMo(s) 3.00
2 thru 4 AMo(s) 3.00

SOLO
2004

1 TSe,48-pg 4.00
2 RCo, 5 stories 5.00
3 PPo 5.00
4 HC 5.00
5 Darwyn Cooke 5.00
6 . . . . 5.00
7 MIA 5.00
8 NGa(s) 5.00
9 SHp 5.00
10 Five stories 5.00
11 SA 5.00
12 BMc,final issue 5.00

SONIC DISRUPTORS
1987–88

1 thru 10 . . . . @3.00

SON OF AMBUSH BUG
July, 1986

1 thru 6 KG . . . . @2.25

SON OF VULCAN
June, 2005

1 (of 6) Mikey Devante 3.00
2 . . . . 3.00
3 F:Green Lantern & JLA 3.00
4 Vulcan's superpowers 3.00
5 Coalition of Crime 3.00
6 Coalition of Crime, concl. 3.00

All comics prices listed are for *Near Mint* condition.

SOVEREIGN SEVEN
1995–98
1 CCl(s),DT,I:Sovereign Seven,
  V:Female Furies,A:Darkseid . . . 3.00
2 thru 11 CCl(s). . . . . @2.50
12 thru 36 CCl(s). . . . . @2.25
Ann.#1 CCl, Year One Annual 4.00
Ann.#2 CCl(s),RL,KJ,Legends of
  the Dead Earth 3.00
1-shot Sovereign Seven Plus
  (1977) 3.00
TPB CCl(s),DT, rep.#1–#5. . . . . . . 13.00

SPACE GHOST
Nov., 2004
1 AOl,O:Space Ghost 15.00
2 AOl. 6.00
3 thru 6 AOl,V:Zorak . . . . @3.00
TPB 15.00

Spanner's Galaxy #5 © DC Comics, Inc.

SPANNER'S GALAXY
Dec., 1984
1 mini-series 2.25
2 thru 6 . . . . @2.25

SPECIAL EDITION
1944–45
(Reprint giveaways
for U.S. Navy)
1 Action Comics #80,WB 750.00
2 Action Comics#81,WB 750.00
3 Superman #33 . . . . 750.00
4 Detective Comics#97 . . . . 750.00
5 Superman #34 . . . . 750.00
6 Action Comics #84,WB 750.00

SPECTRE, THE
1967–69
1 MA,V:Captain Skull 300.00
2 NA,V:Dirk Rawley 175.00
3 NA,A:Wildcat 175.00
4 NA 175.00
5 NA 175.00
6 MA 150.00
7 MA,BU:Hourman 150.00
8 MA,Parchment of Power
  Perilous 150.00
9 BWr(2nd BWr Art) 200.00
10 MA. 150.00

[2nd Regular Series], 1987–89
1 GC,O:Spectre 5.00
2 GC,Cult of BRM. 4.00

3 GC,Fashion Model Murders 3.00
4 GC 3.00
5 GC,Spectre's Murderer 3.00
6 GC,Spectre/Corrigan separated . 3.00
7 A:Zatanna,Wotan 3.00
8 A:Zatanna,Wotan 3.00
9 GM,Spectre's Revenge 3.00
10 GM,A:Batman,Millennium 3.00
11 GM,Millennium 3.00
12 GM,The Talisman,pt.1. . . . . 3.00
13 GM,The Talisman,pt.2. . . . . 3.00
14 GM,The Talisman,pt.3. . . . . 3.00
15 GM,The Talisman,pt.4. . . . . 3.00
16 Jim Corrigan Accused. 3.00
17 New Direction,Final Destiny . . . 3.00
18 Search for Host Body 3.00
19 Dead Again 3.00
20 Corrigan Detective Agency 3.00
21 A:Zoran 3.00
22 BS,Sea of Darkness,A:Zoran . . 3.00
23 A:Lords of Order,
  Invasion x-over 3.00
24 BWg,Ghosts i/t Machine#1 . . . . 3.00
25 Ghosts in the Machine #2. . . . . 3.00
26 Ghosts in the Machine #3. . . . . 3.00
27 Ghosts in the Machine #4. . . . . 3.00
28 Ghosts in the Machine #5. . . . . 3.00
29 Ghosts in the Machine #6. . . . . 3.00
30 Possession 3.00
31 Spectre possessed, final issue . . 3.00
Ann.#1, A:Deadman. 3.00

[3rd Regular Series], 1992–97
1 B:JOs(s),TMd,R:Spectre,
  Glow in the dark(c) 7.00
2 TMd,Murder Mystery 6.00
3 TMd,O:Spectre. 4.00
4 TMd,O:Spectre. 4.00
5 TMd,BB(c),V:Kidnappers 3.50
6 TMd,Spectre prevents evil 3.50
7 TMd 3.50
8 TMd,Glow in the dark(c) 5.00
9 TMd,MWg(c),V:The Reaver 3.00
10 TMd,V:Michael 3.00
11 TMd,V:Azmodeus 3.00
12 V:Reaver 3.00
13 TMd,V:Count Vertigo,
  Glow in the Dark(c) 4.00
14 JoP,A:Phantom Stranger. 2.50
15 TMd,A:Phantom Stranger,Demon,
  Doctor Fate,John Constantine. . 2.50
16 JAp,V:I.R.A. 2.50
17 TT(c),TMd,V:Eclipso 2.50
18 TMd,D:Eclipso. 2.50
19 TMd,V:Hate. 2.50
20 A:Lucien 2.50
21 V:Naiad,C:Superman 3.00
22 A:Superman 2.50
23 Book of Judgment, pt.1. . . . . . . 2.50
24 Book of Judgment, pt.2. . . . . . . 2.50
25 Book of Judgment, pt.3. . . . . . . 2.50
26 The Door of the Solstice. 2.50
27 R:Azmodus 2.50
28 V:Azmodus 2.50
29 V:Azmodus 2.50
30 V:Azmodus 2.50
31 Descent into Pandemonium 2.50
32 V:Killo 2.50
33 JOs 2.50
34 Power of the Undead 2.50
35 JOs,TMd,Underworld
  Unleashed tie-in 2.50
36 JOs,TMd,Underworld
  Unleashed tie-in 2.50
37 JOs,TMd,The Haunting of
  America,pt.1 . . . . 2.50
38 JOs,TMd,The Haunting of
  America,pt.2 . . . . 2.50
39 JOs,TMd,The Haunting of
  America,pt.3 . . . . 2.50
40 JOs,TMd,The Haunting of
  America,pt.4 . . . . 2.50

Spectre 3rd Series #6
© DC Comics, Inc.

41 JOs,TMd,The Haunting of
  America,pt.5 . . . . 2.50
42 JOs,TMd,The Haunting of
  America,pt.6 . . . . 2.50
43 Witchcraft 2.50
44 Madame Xanadu 2.50
45 JOs(s),Acts of God 2.50
46 JOs(s),TMd,discovery of the
  Spear of Destiny 2.50
47 JOs(s),TMd,The Haunting of
  America, Final Night tie-in 2.50
48 JOs(s),TMd,The Haunting of
  America 2.50
49 JOs(s),TMd,The Haunting of
  America 2.50
50 JOs(s),TMd, ... 2.50
51 JOs(s),TMd,A:Batman,Joker. . . . 2.50
52 JOs(s),TMd,Nate Kane discovers
  murder evidence 2.50
53 JOs(s),TMd,Haunting of Jim
  Corrigan, cont. 2.50
54 JOs(s),TMd,hunt for murderer of
  Mister Terrific. 2.50
55 JOs(s),TMd,Corrigan implicated
  in murder 2.50
56 JOs(s),TMd,JTo, Haunting of Jim
  Corrigan. 2.50
57 JOs(s),TMd,Spectre & Jim
  Corrigan in Heaven 2.50
58 JOs,TMd,Genesis tie-in 2.50
59 JOs,TMd,BWr(c), alien pod . . . 2.50
60 JOs,TMd,Quest for God, cont. . . 2.50
61 JOs,TMd,Quest for God, concl. . 2.50
62 JOs,TMd,final issue 2.50
Ann.#1 JOs,TMd,Year One 4.00
TPB Punishment and Crimes 10.00
TPB Crimes & Punishments 10.00

SPECTRE, THE
Jan., 2001
1 JMD,F:Hal Jordan 3.00
2 JMD,Redeeming the Demon,pt.1 2.50
3 JMD,Redeeming the Demon,pt.2 2.50
4 JMD,Redeeming the Demon,pt.3 2.50
5 JMD,F:Two-Face/Harvey Dent . . 2.50
6 JMD,The Redeemer,pt.1 . . . . 2.50
7 JMD,The Redeemer,pt.2 . . . . 2.50
8 JMD,The Redeemer,pt.3 . . . . 2.50
9 JMD,stolen soul 2.50
10 JMD,Joker:Last Laugh 2.50
11 JMD,F:Phantom Stranger 2.50
12 JMD,Spectre of Christmas 2.50
13 JMD,Eternity in an Hour 2.50
14 JMD,vampire-lord 2.50
15 JMD,NBy,Mystery in Space,pt.1 . 2.50
16 JMD,NBy,Mystery in Space,pt.2 . 2.50

17 JMD,NBy,Mystery in Space,pt.3 . 2.50
18 JMD,NBy,Abin Sur, Materna . . . 2.50
19 NBy,DJa,V:Darkseid 2.50
20 NBy,DJa,magazine publisher . . . 2.75
21 NBy,DJa,Stigmonus,C.Ferris . . . 2.75
22 NBy,DJa,A:G.Arrow,
    M.Manhunter 2.75
23 JMD,NBy,DJa,Return of
    Sinestro,pt.3 . . . . 2.75
24 JMD,DJa,F:DCU characters 2.75
25 JMD,DJa,F:Rabid 2.75
26 JMD,DJa,terrorist 2.75
27 JMD,DJa,final issue 2.75

SPEED FORCE
Sept., 1997
1 MWa,BAu,JBy,BML,JAp,BSn,
    Flash stories, 64pg. 4.00

SPELLJAMMER
Sept., 1990
1 RogueShip#1 . . . . 3.00
2 RogueShip#2 . . . . 2.50
3 thru 15 . . . . @2.25

SPIRIT, THE
TPB Best of the Spirit (2006) 15.00

STALKER
1975–1976
1 SD,WW,O&I:Stalker 25.00
2 thru 4 SD,WW . . . . @15.00

STANLEY & HIS MONSTER
See: FOX AND THE CROW

STANLEY & HIS MONSTER
1993
1 R:Stanley 2.25
2 I:Demon Hunter 2.25
3 A:Ambrose Biorce 2.25
4 final issue. 2.25

S.T.A.R. CORPS
1993
1 A:Superman 2.25
2 I:Fusion,A:Rampage 2.25
3 thru 6 . . . . @2.25

STAR CROSSED
DC/Helix, April, 1997
1 (of 3) MHo,Dyltah's romance
    with Saa. 2.50
2 MHo,Love During Wartime 2.50
3 concl. 2.50

[NEIL GAIMAN & CHARLES VESS']
STARDUST
DC/Vertigo, Oct., 1997
1 (of 4) NGa(s),CV 6.00
2 NGa(s),CV adult faerie tale 6.00
3 NGa(s),CV 6.00
4 NGa(s),CV 6.00

STARFIRE
1976–77
1 . . . . 20.00
2 thru 8 . . . . @12.00

STAR HUNTERS
Oct.–Nov., 1977
1 DN&BL. 20.00
2 LH&BL 12.00

3 MN&BL,D:Donovan Flint 12.00
4 thru 7 . . . . @12.00

STARMAN
1988–92
1 TL,I&O:New Starman 4.00
2 TL,V:Serial Killer,C:Bolt 3.00
3 TL,V:Bolt 3.00
4 TL,V:Power Elite 2.50
5 TL,Invasion,A:PowerGirl,
    Firestorm 2.50
6 TL,Invasion,A:G.L.,Atom 2.50
7 TL,Soul Searching Issue 2.50
8 TL,V:LadyQuark. 2.50
9 TL,A:Batman,V:Blockbuster 2.50
10 TL,A:Batman,V:Blockbuster . . . 2.50
11 TL,V:Power Elite 2.50
12 TL,V:Power Elite,A:Superman . . 2.50
13 TL,V:Rampage 2.50
14 TL,A:A:Superman,V:Parasite . . 2.50
15 TL,V:Deadline 2.50
16 TL,O:Starman 2.50
17 TL,V:Dr.Polaris,A:PowerGirl . . . 2.50
18 TL,V:Dr.Polaris,A:PowerGirl . . . 2.50
19 TL,V:Artillery 2.50
20 TL,FireFighting 2.50
21 TL,Starman Quits 2.50
22 TL,V:Khunds. 2.50
23 TL,A:Deadline 2.50
24 TL,A:Deadline 2.50
25 TL,V:Deadline 2.50
26 V:The Mist. 6.00
27 V:The Mist. 5.00
28 A:Superman 7.00
29 V:Plasmax 2.50
30 Seduction of Starman #1 . . . . . 2.50
31 Seduction of Starman #2 . . . . . 2.50
32 Seduction of Starman #3 . . . . . 2.50
33 Seduction of Starman #4 . . . . . 2.50
34 A:Batman 2.50
35 A:Valor,Mr.Nebula,ScarletSkier . 2.50
36 A:Les Mille Yeux 2.50
37 A:Les Mille Yeux 2.50
38 War of the Gods X-over 2.50
39 V:Plasmax 2.50
40 V:Las Vegas 2.50
41 V:Maaldor 2.50
42 Star Shadows,pt.1,A:Eclipso. . . . 3.00
43 Star Shadows,pt.2,A:Lobo,
    Eclipso. 2.50
44 Star Shadows,pt.3,A:Eclipso
    V:Lobo 2.50
45 Star Shadows,pt.4, V:Eclipso . . 2.50

[2nd Series], 1994
0 New Starman 8.00
1 Sins of the Father,pt.2 . . . . 8.00
2 Sins of the Father,pt.3 . . . . 7.00
3 Sins of the Father,pt.4 . . . . 6.00
4 A Day in the Opal. 6.00
5 V:Starman 6.00
6 Times Past Features 6.00
7 Sinister Circus 6.00
8 TyH(c),Sinister Circus 5.00
9 TyH(c),Mist's daughter breaks
    out of prison. 5.00
10 Sins of the Chile,prelude 5.00
11 JeR,TyH,13 Years Ago:5 Friends . 5.00
12 JeR,TyH,Sins of the Child,pt.1 . 5.00
13 JeR,TyH,Sins of the Child,pt.2 . 5.00
14 JeR,TyH,Sins of the Child,pt.3 . 5.00
15 JeR,TyH,Sins of the Child,pt.4 . 5.00
16 JeR,TyH,Sins of the Child,pt.5 . 5.00
17 JeR,TyH 5.00
18 JeR,TyH,Orig.Starman
    vs.The Mist 4.00
19 JeR,TyH,Talking with David 2 . . 4.00
20 JeR(s),TyH,GyD,Sand and
    Stars,pt.1 . . . . 4.00
21 JeR,TyH,GyD,Sand/Stars,pt.2 . . 3.00
22 JeR,TyH,GyD,Sand/Stars,pt.3 . . 3.00
23 JeR,TyH,GyD,Sand/Stars,pt.4 . . 3.00

24 JeR(s),TyH,Hell & Back,pt.1 . . . . 3.00
25 JeR(s),TyH,Hell & Back,pt.2 . . . . 3.00
26 JeR(s),TyH,Hell & Back,pt.3 . . . . 3.00
27 JeR(s),Christmas Knight. 3.00
28 JeR(s)Superfreaks and
    Backstabbers. 3.00
29 JeR(s),TyH,GyD,V:The Shade,
    Starman history 3.00
30 JeR(s),TyH,Infernal Devices
    pt.1 (of 6). 3.00
31 JeR(s),TyH,Devices,pt.2 . . . . 3.00
32 JeR(s),TyH,Devices,pt.3 . . . . 3.00
33 JeR(s),TyH,Infernal Devices
    pt.4,A:Batman, Sentinel. 3.00
34 JeR(s),TyH,A:Batman, Sentinel,
    Floronic Man 3.00
35 JeR(s),TyH,A:Batman, Floronic
    Man, Sentinel 3.00
36 JeR(s),TyH,F:Will Payton 3.00
37 JeR(s),TyH,F:GoldenAgeHeroes 3.00
38 JeR(s),TyH,new JLE 2.50
39 JeR(s),TyH,Lightning &
    Stars, pt.1 x-over 2.50
40 JeR(s),TyH 2.50
41 JeR(s),GEr,TyH. 2.50
42 JeR(s),MS,Nazis,Demon 2.50
43 JeR(s),TyH,help from JLA. 2.50
44 JeR(s),times past story 2.50
45 JeR(s),search for Will Payton . . . 2.50
46 JeR(s),TyH,Bobo. 2.50
47 JeR,SY,TyH, ... 2.50
48 JeR,SY,A:Swamp Thing 2.50
49 JeR,SY,Talking with David 2.50
50 JeR(s),PSj,48-page. 5.00
51 JeR(s),PSj,to Krypton 2.50
52 JeR(s),PSj,A:Adam Strange 2.50
53 JeR(s),PSj,A:Adam Strange 2.50
54 JeR(s),Times Past tale 2.50
55 JeR(s),PSj,A:Space Cabby. 2.50
56 JeR(s),PSj,A:ElongatedMan 2.50
57 JeR(s),PSj,TyH,AxR,A:Tigorr
    & Fastbak, pt.1 . . . . 2.50
58 JeR,TyH,AxR, pt.2 . . . . 2.50
59 JeR,TyH,AxR, pt.3 . . . . 2.50
60 JeR,TyH,AxR, concl. 2.50
61 JeR,TyH,AxR 2.50
62 JeR,PSj,Grand Guignol,pt.1 . . . ?.50
63 JeR,PSj,Grand Guignol,pt.2 . . . . 2.50
64 JeR,PSj,Grand Guignol,pt.3 . . . . 2.50
65 JeR,PSj,Grand Guignol,pt.4 . . . . 2.50
66 JeR,PSj,Grand Guignol,pt.5 . . . . 2.50
67 JeR,PSj,Grand Guignol,pt.6 . . . . 2.50
68 JeR,PSj,Grand Guignol,pt.7 . . . . 2.50
69 JeR,PSj,flashback. 2.50
70 JeR,PSj,Grand Guignol,pt.8 . . . . 2.50
71 JeR,PSj,Grand Guignol,pt.9 . . . . 2.50

Starman #25
© DC Comics Inc.

All comics prices listed are for *Near Mint* condition.

72 JeR,PSj,Grand Guignol, concl...	2.50
73 JeR,PSj,Grand Guignol,Eulogy	2.50
74 JeR,RH,Times Past	2.50
75 JeR,A:Superman............	2.50
76 JeR,Talking With David:2001 ...	2.50
77 JeR,1951,pt.1	2.50
78 JeR,1951,pt.2	2.50
79 JeR,1951,pt.3	2.50
80 JeR,48-page final issue	4.50
Ann.#1 Legends o/t Dead Earth ..	4.00
Ann.#2 Pulp Heroes (Romance) ...	4.50
Spec.#1,000,000 JeR(s),PSj	2.50
Secret Files #1,O:Starmen.......	5.00
Giant #1 80-page	5.00
Spec. Starman: The Mist, F:Mary	
Marvel, Girlfrenzy (1998).....	2.50
TPB Sins of the Father,rep.#0–#5 .	13.00
TPB Night and Day, rep. stories	
from #7–#16	15.00
TPB A Wicked Inclination, rep. ...	18.00
TPB Times Past..............	18.00
TPB Infernal Devices...........	18.00
TPB To Reach the Stars	18.00
TPB A Starry Knight (2002)	18.00
TPB Stars My Destination	15.00
TPB Grand Guignol	20.00
TPB Sons of the Father (2005) ...	15.00

STARS AND S.T.R.I.P.E.
1999

0 LMd,DDv,I:Courtney Whitman ...	3.00
1 LMd,DDv,O:Star-Spangled Kid .	2.50
2 LMd,DDv,V:Paintball	2.50
3 LMd,DDv,V:Skeeter	2.50
4 LMd,DDv,Day of Judgment	
x-over....................	2.50
5 LMd,DDv,F:Young Justice,pt.1..	2.50
6	2.50
7 LMd,DDv,F:Mike Dugan.......	2.50
8 LMd,DDv	2.50
9 LMd,DDv,R:Nebula Man	2.50
10 LMd,DDv,cheating..........	2.50
11 DDv,V:Dr. Graft.............	2.50
12 DDv,V:Dragon King.........	2.50
13 DDv,V:Dragon King.........	2.50
14 LMd,DDv,final issue	2.50

STAR SPANGLED
COMICS
Oct., 1941

1 O:Tarantula,B:Captain X of the	
R.A.F.,Star Spangled Kid,	
Armstrong of the Army	9,000.00
2 Star Spang.Kid V:Dr.Weerd .	3,000.00

Star Spangled Comics #1
© DC Comics, Inc.

3 Star Spang.Kid V:Dr.Weerd .	2,500.00
4 V:The Needle	2,500.00
5 V:Dr. Weerd, V:The Needle .	2,500.00
6 E:Armstrong	1,700.00
7 S&K,O&1st app:The Guardian,	
B:Robotman,The Newsboy	
Legion, TNT	11,000.00
8 O:TNT & Dan the Dyna-Mite	3,500.00
9 S&K(c&a),Newsboy Legion .	3,000.00
10 S&K(c&a),Newsboy Legion	3,000.00
11 S&K(c&a),Newsboy Legion .	2,700.00
12 S&K(c&a),Newsboy Legion,	
Prevue of Peril!........	2,700.00
13 S&K(c&a),Suicide Slum....	2,700.00
14 S&K,Meanest Man on Earth	2,700.00
15 S&K(c&a),Playmates ofPeril	2,700.00
16 S&K(c&a),Newsboy Legion .	2,700.00
17 S&K(c&a),V:Rafferty Mob ..	2,700.00
18 S&K,O:Star Spangled Kid .	3,000.00
19 S&K(c&a),E:Tarantula	2,700.00
20 S&K(c&a),B:Liberty Belle..	2,700.00
21 S&K,Newsboy Legion	2,500.00
22 S&K,Brains for Sale.......	2,500.00
23 S&K,Art for Scrapper'sSake	2,500.00
24 S&K,Death Strikes Bargain .	2,500.00
25 S&K,Victuals for Victory....	2,500.00
26 S&K,Newsboy Legion	2,500.00
27 S&K,Turn on the Heat	2,500.00
28 S&K,Poor Man's Rich Man .	2,500.00
29 JK,Cabbages and Comics ..	2,500.00
30 JK,Lady of Linden Lake....	1,500.00
31 S&K,Questions Please!	1,500.00
32 The Good Samaritan.......	1,500.00
33 Case of the Baleful Bride...	1,500.00
34 From Rags to Ruin	1,500.00
35 The Proud Poppa.........	1,500.00
36 Cowboy of Suicide Slum ...	1,500.00
37 Diamonds in the Rough....	1,500.00
38 Roll Out the Barrels.......	1,500.00
39 Two Guardians are a Crowd	1,500.00
40 Farewell to Crime.........	1,400.00
41 Time Out for the Guardian..	1,200.00
42 JK(c),Power of the Press...	1,200.00
43 CS(c),Trials of a Tenor.....	1,200.00
44 Etiquette in Suicide Slum...	1,200.00
45 Crime Gets Clipped.......	1,200.00
46 Clothes Make the Criminal .	1,200.00
47 Triumph of Tommy........	1,200.00
48 CS(c),Booty & the Blizzard .	1,200.00
49 CS(c),One Ounce to Victory	1,200.00
50 JKu,Guardian(c)...........	1,200.00
51 A:Robot Robber	1,200.00
52 Rehearsal for Crime.......	1,200.00
53 The Poet of Suicide Slum ..	1,200.00
54 Dead-Shot Dade's Revenge	1,200.00
55 Gabby Strikes a Gusher ...	1,200.00
56 The Treasuer of Araby.....	1,200.00
57 Recruit for the Legion	1,200.00
58 Matadors of Suicide Slum ..	1,200.00
59 JK,Answers Inc..........	1,200.00
60 CS(c),Steve Brodie Da 2nd .	1,200.00
61 CS,Great Ballroom Race...	1,200.00
62 Prevue of Tomorrow.......	1,200.00
63 CS,Code of the Newsstand .	1,200.00
64 Criminal Cruise	1,200.00
65 B:Robin,(c) & stories	2,700.00
66 V:No Face	1,600.00
67 The Castle of Doom.......	1,500.00
68 WMo(c&a),Octopus (c)	1,500.00
69 The Stolen Atom Bomb	2,000.00
70 V:The Clock	1,500.00
71 Perils of the Stone Age	1,500.00
72 Robin Crusoe	1,500.00
73 V:The Black Magician	1,500.00
74 V:The Clock	1,500.00
75 The State vs. Robin	1,500.00
76 V:The Fence	1,500.00
77 The Boy who Wanted Robin	
for Christmas	1,500.00
78 Rajah Robin.............	1,500.00
79 V:The Clock,The Tick-Tock	
Crimes	1,500.00

Star Spangled Comics #88
© DC Comics, Inc.

80 The Boy Disc Jockey......	1,400.00
81 The Seeing-Eye Dog Crimes	1,300.00
82 The Boy who Hated Robin . .	1,200.00
83 Who is Mr. Mystery,B:Captain	
Compass backup story....	1,200.00
84 How can we Fight Juvenile	
Delinquency?	1,400.00
85 Peril at the Pole..........	1,200.00
86 The Barton Brothers	1,200.00
87 V:Sinister Knight	1,500.00
88 Robin Declares War on	
Batman, B:Batman app....	1,400.00
89 Batman's Utility Belt?......	1,400.00
90 Rancho Fear!............	1,400.00
91 Cops 'n' Robbers?........	1,400.00
92 Movie Hero No. 1?........	1,400.00
93 Riddle of the Sphinx.......	1,400.00
94 Underworld Playhouse......	1,500.00
95 The Man with the Midas Touch,	
E:Robin(c),Batman story .	1,500.00
96 B:Tomahawk(c) & stories...	1,000.00
97 The 4 Bold Warriors	800.00
98 Robin's Rival.............	800.00
99 The Second Pocahontas ...	800.00
100 The Frontier Phantom	1,000.00
101 Peril on the High Seas	800.00
102 Riddle of Mohawk Valley ...	800.00
103 Tomahawk's Death Duel! ...	800.00
104 Race with Death!	800.00
105 The Unhappy Hunting	
Grounds.................	800.00
106 Traitor in the War Paint.....	800.00
107 The Brave who Hunted	
Tomahawk...............	800.00
108 'The Ghost called Moccasin	
Foot!'...................	800.00
109 The Land Pirates of	
Jolly Roger Hill!	800.00
110 Sally Raines Frontier Girl ...	800.00
111 The Death Map of Thunder	
Hill	800.00
112 Coin of Courage	800.00
113 FF,V:The Black Cougar ...	1,100.00
114 Return of the Black Cougar	1,100.00
115 Journey of a Thousand	
Deaths.................	800.00
116 The Battle of Junction Fort . .	800.00
117 Siege?.................	800.00
118 V:Outlaw Indians..........	750.00
119 The Doomed Stockade?	750.00
120 Revenge of Raven Heart!...	800.00
121 Adventure in New York!	750.00
122 I:Ghost Breaker,(c)& stories	1,000.00
123 The Dolls of Doom	700.00
124 Suicide Tower	700.00
125 The Hermit's Ghost Dog! ...	700.00

126 The Phantom of Paris! 700.00
127 The Supernatural Alibi! 700.00
128 C:Batman,The Girl who
     lived 5,000 Years! 700.00
129 The Human Orchids 750.00
130 The Haunted Town,
     July, 1952 . . . . 800.00
Becomes:

STAR SPANGLED
WAR STORIES
Aug., 1952

131 CS&StK(c),I Was A Jap
     Prisoner of War 2,000.00
132 CS&StK(c),The G.I. With
     The Million-Dollar Arm 1,600.00
133 CS&StK(c),Mission-San
     Marino. 1,400.00
3 CS&StK(c),Hundred-Mission
     Mitchell 900.00
4 CS&StK(c),The Hot Rod Tank . 900.00
5 LSt(c),Jet Pilot 900.00
6 CS(c),Operation Davy Jones . . 900.00
7 CS(c),Rookie Ranger,The 800.00
8 CS(c),I Was A
     Hollywood Soldier 800.00
9 CS&StK(c),Sad Sack Squad . . 800.00
10 CS,The G.I. & The Gambler . . 800.00
11 LSt(c),The Lucky Squad 800.00
12 CS(c),The Four Horseman of
     Barricade Hill 800.00
13 No Escape 800.00
14 LSt(c),Pitchfork Army 800.00
15 The Big Fish 800.00
16 The Yellow Ribbon 800.00
17 IN(c),Prize Target 800.00
18 IN(c),The Gladiator 800.00
19 IN(c),The Big Lift. 800.00
20 JGr(c),The Battle of
     the Frogmen 800.00
21 JGr(c),Dead Man's Bridge . . . 600.00
22 JGr(c),Death Hurdle 600.00
23 JGr(c),The Silent Frogman . . . 600.00
24 JGr(c),Death Slide 600.00
25 JGr(c),S.S. Liferaft 600.00
26 JGr(c),Bazooka Man. 600.00
27 JGr(c),Taps for a Tail Gunner . 600.00
28 JGr(c),Tank Duel. 700.00
29 JGr(c),A Gun Called Slugger . 600.00
30 JGr(c),The Thunderbolt Tank . 600.00
31 IN(c),Tank Block 400.00
32 JGr(c),Bridge to Battle 400.00
33 JGr(c),Pocket War 400.00
34 JGr(c),Fighting...Snowbirds . . 400.00
35 JGr(c),Zero Hour. 400.00
36 JGr(c),A G.I. Passed Here . . . 400.00
37 JGr(c),A Handful of T.N.T. . . . 400.00
38 RH(c),One-Man Army 400.00
39 JGr(c),Flying Cowboy 400.00
40 JGr(c),Desert Duel 400.00
41 IN(c),A Gunner's Hands 350.00
42 JGr(c),Sniper Alley 350.00
43 JGr(c),Top Kick Brother 350.00
44 JGr(c),Tank 711
     Doesn't Answer 350.00
45 JGr(c),Flying Heels 350.00
46 JGr(c),Gunner's Seat 350.00
47 JGr(c),Sidekick 350.00
48 JGr(c),Battle Hills 350.00
49 JGr(c),Payload 350.00
50 JGr(c),Combat Dust 350.00
51 JGr(c),Battle Pigeon 250.00
52 JGr(c),Cannon-Man 250.00
53 JGr(c),Combat Close-Ups . . . 250.00
54 JGr(c),Flying Exit 250.00
55 JKu(c),The Burning Desert . . . 250.00
56 JKu(c),The Walking Sub 250.00
57 JGr(c),Call For a Frogman . . . 250.00
58 JGr(c),MD,Waist Punch 250.00
59 JGr(c),Kick In The Door 250.00
60 JGr(c),Hotbox 250.00
61 JGr(c),MD,Tow Pilot 250.00

Star Spangled War Stories #43
© *DC Comics, Inc.*

62 JGr(c),The Three GIs 250.00
63 JGr(c),Flying Range Rider . . . 250.00
64 JGr(c),MD,Frogman Ambush . . 250.00
65 JGr(c),JSe,Frogman Block . . . 250.00
66 JGr(c),Flattop Pigeon 250.00
67 RH(c),MD,Ashcan Alley 250.00
68 JGr(c),The Long Step 250.00
69 JKu(c),Floating Tank, The 250.00
70 JKu(c),No Medal For
     Frogman 250.00
71 JKu(c),Shooting Star. 250.00
72 JGr(c),Silent Fish 250.00
73 JGr(c),MD,The Mouse &
     the Tiger 250.00
74 JGr(c),MD,Frogman Bait. 250.00
75 JGr(c),MD,Paratroop
     Mousketeers 250.00
76 MD,JKu(c),Odd Man 250.00
77 MD,JKu(c),Room to Fight 250.00
78 MD,JGr(c),Fighting Wingman . 250.00
79 MD,JKu(c),Zero Box 250.00
80 MD,JGr(c),Top Gunner 250.00
81 MD,RH(c),Khaki Mosquito . . . 250.00
82 MD,JKu(c),Ground Flier 250.00
83 MD,JGr(c),Jet On
     My Shoulder 250.00
84 MD,IN(c),O·Mademoiselle
     Marie 500.00
85 IN(c),A Medal For Marie 300.00
86 JGr(c),A Medal For Marie 300.00
87 JGr(c),T.N.T. Spotlight 300.00
88 JGr(c),The Steel Trap 300.00
89 IN(c),Trail of the Terror 300.00
90 RA(c),Island of
     Armored Giants 1,000.00
91 JGr(c),The Train of Terror. . . . 250.00
92 Last Battle of the
     Dinosaur Age. 400.00
93 Goliath of the Western Front . 250.00
94 JKu(c),The Frogman and
     the Dinosaur 550.00
95 Guinea Pig Patrol,Dinosaurs . 400.00
96 Mission X,Dinosaur. 400.00
97 The Sub-Crusher, Dinosaur . . 400.00
98 Island of Thunder, Dinosaur . . 400.00
99 The Circus of Monsters,
     Dinosaur 400.00
100 The Volcano of Monsters,
     Dinosaur 450.00
101 The Robot and the Dinosaur 300.00
102 Punchboard War,Dinosaur . . 300.00
103 Doom at Dinosaur Island,
     Dinosaur 300.00
104 The Tree of Terror,
     Dinosaurs 300.00
105 The War of Dinosaur Island . 300.00

106 The Nightmare War,
     Dinosaurs 300.00
107 Battle of the Dinosaur
     Aquarium 300.00
108 Dinosaur D-Day 300.00
109 The Last Soldiers 300.00
110 thru 133 . . . . @300.00
134 NA 300.00
135 . . . . 300.00
136 . . . . 300.00
137 Dinosaur 300.00
138 Enemy Ace 350.00
139 O:Enemy Ace 250.00
140 . . . . 200.00
141 . . . . 200.00
142 . . . . 200.00
143 . . . . 200.00
144 NA,JKu 250.00
145 . . . . 200.00
146 Enemy Ace(c) 150.00
147 New Enemy Ace 150.00
148 New Enemy Ace 150.00
149 . . . . 150.00
150 JKu,Viking Prince 150.00
151 I:Unknown Soldier. 300.00
152 Rep. New Enemy Ace. 150.00
153 . . . . 150.00
154 O:Unknown Soldier. 300.00
155 Rep. New Enemy Ace. 100.00
156 I:Battle Album 100.00
157 thru 160. . . . . 75.00
161 E:Enemy Ace 75.00
162 thru 170 . . . . @70.00
171 thru 200 . . . . @30.00
201 thru 204 . . . . @25.00
Becomes:

UNKNOWN SOLDIER
April-May, 1977

205 thru 247 . . . . @17.00
248 and 249 O:Unknown Soldier @12.00
250 . . . . 12.00
251 B:Enemy Ace 12.00
252 thru 268. . . . . @12.00

STAR SPANGLED COMICS
1999

1 CWn, F:Sandman & Star
     Spangled Kid 2.25

STAR TREK
1984–88
[1st Regular Series]

1 TS,The Wormhole Connection . 15.00
2 TS,The Only Good Klingon 8.00
3 TS,Errand of War. 7.00
4 TS,Deadly Allies. 7.00
5 TS,Mortal Gods 7.00
6 TS,Who is Enigma? 6.00
7 EB,O:Saavik 6.00
8 TS,Blood Fever 6.00
9 TS,Mirror Universe Saga #1 . . . 6.00
10 TS,Mirror Universe Saga #2 . . 6.00
11 TS,Mirror Universe Saga #3 . . . 6.00
12 TS,Mirror Universe Saga #4 . . . 6.00
13 TS,Mirror Universe Saga #5 . . . 5.00
14 TS,Mirror Universe Saga #6 . . . 5.00
15 TS,Mirror Universe Saga #7 . . . 5.00
16 TS,Mirror Universe Saga end . . . 5.00
17 TS,The D'Artagnan Three. 5.00
18 TS,Rest & Recreation 5.00
19 DSp,W.Koenig story 5.00
20 TS,Girl. 5.00
21 TS,Dreamworld. 5.00
22 TS,The Wolf #1. . . . . 5.00
23 TS,The Wolf #2. . . . . 4.00
24 TS,Double Blind #1. . . . . 4.00
25 TS,Double Blind #2. . . . . 4.00
26 TSV:Romulans 4.00
27 TS,Day in the Life. 4.00
28 GM,The Last Word 4.00

Star Trek #56
© DC Comics, Inc.

29 Trouble with Bearclaw 4.00
30 CI,F:Uhura 4.00
31 TS,Maggie's World 4.00
32 TS,Judgment Day 4.00
33 TS,20th Anniv. 5.00
34 V:Romulans 3.00
35 GM,Excelsior. 3.00
36 GM,StarTrek IV tie-in 3.00
37 StarTrek IV tie-in 3.00
38 AKu,The Argon Affair 3.00
39 TS,A:Harry Mudd 3.00
40 TS,A:Harry Mudd 3.00
41 TS,V:Orions. 3.00
42 TS,The Corbomite Effect 3.00
43 TS,Paradise Lost #1 . . . . 3.00
44 TS,Paradise Lost #2 . . . . 3.00
45 TS,Paradise Lost #3 . . . . 3.00
46 TS,Getaway 3.00
47 TS,Idol Threats 3.00
48 TS,The Stars in Secret
　　Influence 3.00
49 TS,Aspiring to be Angels 3.00
50 TS,Anniv. 4.00
51 TS,Haunted Honeymoon 3.00
52 TS,'Hell in a Hand Basket. 3.00
53 You're Dead,Jim 3.00
54 Old Loyalties 3.00
55 TS,Finnegan's Wake 3.00
56 GM,Took place during 5 year
　　Mission 3.00
Ann.#1 All Those Years Ago 4.00
Ann.#2 DJw,The Final Voyage. . . . 3.00
Ann.#3 CS,F:Scotty 3.00
Star Trek III Adapt.TS. 2.50
Star Trek IV Adapt. TS 2.50
StarTrek V Adapt. 2.50

[2nd Regular Series], 1989–96
1 The Return. 9.00
2 The Sentence 5.00
3 Death Before Dishonor 4.00
4 Reprocussions 4.00
5 Fast Friends. 4.00
6 Cure All 4.00
7 Not Sweeney! 4.00
8 Going,Going. 3.50
9 ...Gone. 3.50
10 Trial of James Kirk #1 . . . . 3.50
11 Trial of James Kirk #2 . . . . 3.50
12 Trial of James Kirk #3 . . . . 3.50
13 Return of Worthy #1 . . . . 3.50
14 Return of Worthy #2 . . . . 3.50
15 Return of Worthy #3 . . . . 3.50
16 Worldsinger 3.00
17 Partners? #1 . . . . 3.00
18 Partners? #2 . . . . 3.00
19 Once A Hero 3.00

20 . . . . 3.00
21 Kirk Trapped 3.00
22 A:Harry Mudd 3.00
23 The Nasgul,A:Harry Mudd 3.00
24 25th Anniv.,A:Harry Mudd 4.00
25 Starfleet Officers Reunion 3.00
26 Pilkor 3 . . . . 3.00
27 Kirk Betrayed 3.00
28 V:Romulans 3.00
29 Mediators 3.00
30 Veritas #1 . . . . 3.00
31 Veritas #2 . . . . 3.00
32 Veritas #3 . . . . 3.00
33 Veritas #4 . . . . 3.00
34 JD,F:Kirk,Spock,McCoy 3.00
35 Tabukan Syndrome#1 . . . . 3.00
36 Tabukan Syndrome#2 . . . . 3.00
37 Tabukan Syndrome#3 . . . . 3.00
38 Tabukan Syndrome#5 . . . . 3.00
39 Tabukan Syndrome#5 . . . . 3.00
40 Tabukan Syndrome#6 . . . . 3.00
41 Runaway 3.00
42 Helping Hand 3.00
43 V:Binzalans 3.00
44 Acceptable Risk 3.00
45 V:Trelane. 3.00
46 V:Captain Klaa 3.00
47 F:Spock & Saavik 3.00
48 The Neutral Zone 3.00
49 Weapon from Genesis 3.00
50 "The Peacemaker" 4.00
51 "The Price" 3.00
52 V:Klingons. 3.00
53 Timecrime #1 . . . . 3.00
54 Timecrime #2 . . . . 3.00
55 Timecrime #3 . . . . 3.00
56 Timecrime #4 . . . . 3.00
57 Timecrime #5 . . . . 3.00
58 F:Chekov. 3.00
59 Uprising. 3.00
60 Hostages 3.00
61 On Talos IV 3.00
62 Alone,pt.1, V:aliens 3.00
63 Alone,pt.2 . . . . 3.00
64 Kirk 3.00
65 Kirk in Space. 3.00
66 Spock 3.00
67 Ambassador Stonn 3.00
68 . . . . 3.00
69 Wolf in Cheap Clothing,pt.1 . . . . 3.00
70 Wolf in Cheap Clothing,pt.2 . . . . 3.00
71 Wolf in Cheap Clothing,pt.3 . . . . 2.75
72 Wolf in Cheap Clothing,pt.4 . . . . 2.75
73 Star-crossed,pt.1 . . . . 2.75
74 Star-crossed,pt.2 . . . . 2.50
75 Star-crossed,pt.3 . . . . 4.50
76 Tendar. 2.50
77 to the Romulan Neutral Zone . . . 2.50
78 The Chosen,pt.1 (of 3) 2.50
79 The Chosen,pt.2 . . . . 2.50
80 The Chosen,pt.3 . . . . 2.50
Ann.#1 GM,sty by G.Takei(Sulu) . . . 4.00
Ann.#2 Kirks 1st Yr At Star
　　Fleet Academy. 4.00
Ann #3 KD,F:Ambassador Sarek. . . 4.00
Ann.#4 F:Spock on Pike's ship 4.00
Ann.#6 Convergence,pt.1 . . . . 4.00
Spec.#1 PDd(s),BSz 4.00
Spec.#2 The Defiant 4.50
Spec.#3 V:Orion pirates 4.50
Debt of Honor,AH,CCl(s),HC 27.00
Debt of Honor SC 15.00
Spec. 25th Anniv.. . . . . 7.00
Star Trek VI,movie adapt(direct) . . . 6.00
Star Trek VI,movie(newsstand) 3.00
TPB Best of Star Trek reps. 20.00
TPB Star Trek: Revisitations
　　rep. #22–#24,F:Gary Seven,
　　#49–#50,F:Harry Mudd, 176pg 20.00
TPB Who Killed Captain Kirk?,
　　rep.Star Trek#49-#55. . . . . . . 17.00

TPB The Ashes of Eden, Shatner
　　novel adapt. 15.00

STAR TREK: THE
MODALA IMPERATIVE
1991

1 Planet Modula 6.00
2 Modula's Rebels 4.50
3 Spock/McCoy rescue Attempt . . . 4.00
4 Rebel Victory 4.00
TPB reprints both minis 20.00

STAR TREK: THE
NEXT GENERATION
Feb., 1988
[1st Regular Series]
1 based on TV series,Where No
　　Man Has Gone Before 10.00
2 Spirit in the Sky 8.00
3 Factor Q. 5.00
4 Q's Day 5.00
5 Q's Effects 5.00
6 Here Today 5.00

[2nd Regular Series], 1989–95
1 Return to Raimon 15.00
2 Murder Most Foul 9.00
3 Derelict 7.50
4 The Hero Factor 7.50
5 Serafin's Survivors 6.00
6 Shadows in the Garden 6.00
7 The Pilot 5.00
8 The Battle Within 5.00
9 The Pay Off 5.00
10 The Noise of Justice 5.00
11 The Imposter 4.00
12 Whoever Fights Monsters 4.00
13 The Hand of the Assassin 4.00
14 Holiday on Ice 4.00
15 Prisoners of the Ferengi 3.50
16 I Have Heard the Mermaids
　　Singing. 3.50
17 The Weapon 3.50
18 MM,Forbidden Fruit 3.50
19 The Lesson 3.50
20 Lost Shuttle 3.50
21 Lost Shuttle cont. 3.50
22 Lost Shuttle cont. 3.50
23 Lost Shuttle cont. 3.50
24 Lost Shuttle conc. 3.50
25 Okona S.O.S. 3.50
26 Search for Okona 3.50
27 Worf,Data,Troi,Okona trapped
　　on world. 3.50
28 Worf/K'Ehleyr story 3.50
29 Rift,pt.1 . . . . 3.50
30 Rift,pt.2 . . . . 3.50
31 Rift conclusion 3.50
32 . . . . 3.50
33 R:Mischievous Q. 3.50
34 V:Aliens,F:Mischievous Q 3.50
35 Way of the Warrior 3.50
36 Shore Leave in Shanzibar#1 . . . 3.25
37 Shore Leave in Shanzibar#2 . . . 3.25
38 Shore Leave in Shanzibar#3 . . . 3.25
39 Divergence #1. . . . . 3.25
40 Divergence #2. . . . . 3.25
41 V:Strazzan Warships 3.25
42 V:Strazzans 3.25
43 V:Strazzans 3.25
44 Disrupted Lives 3.25
45 F:Enterprise Surgical Team 3.25
46 Deadly Labyrinth 3.25
47 Worst of Both World's#1 . . . . . . 3.00
48 Worst of Both World's#2 . . . . . . 3.00
49 Worst of Both World's#3 . . . . . . 3.00
50 Double Sized,V:Borg. 4.00
51 V:Energy Beings 3.00
52 in the 1940's 3.00
53 F:Picard. 3.00

DC COMICS

54 F:Picard. 3.00
55 Data on Trial 3.00
56 Abduction 3.00
57 Body Switch 3.00
58 Body Switch 3.00
59 B:Children in Chaos 3.00
60 Children in Chaos#2 . . . . 3.00
61 E:Children in Chaos 3.00
62 V:Stalker 3.00
63 A:Romulans. 3.00
64 Geordie 3.00
65 Geordie 3.00
66 . . . . 3.00
67 Friends/Strangers 3.00
68 Friends/Strangers,pt.2 . . . . 3.00
69 Friends/Strangers,pt.3 . . . . 3.00
70 Friends/Strangers,pt.4 . . . . 3.00
71 War of Madness,pt.1 . . . . 3.00
72 War of Madness,pt.2. . . . . 3.00
73 War of Madness,pt.3. . . . . 3.00
74 War of Madness,pt.4. . . . . 3.00
75 War of Madness,pt.5. . . . . 4.50
76 F:Geordi 3.00
77 Gateway, pt.1 . . . . 3.00
78 Gateway, pt.2 . . . . 3.00
79 Crew transformed into androids . 3.00
80 Mysterious illness 3.00
Ann.#1 A:Mischievous Q 4.50
Ann.#2 BP,V:Parasitic Creatures . . . 4.00
Ann.#3 . . . . 4.00
Ann.#4 MiB(s),F:Dr.Crusher. 4.00
Ann.#6 Convergence,pt.2 . . . . 4.50
Series Finale 4.25
Spec.#1 . . . . 3.75
Spec.#2 CCI(s). 4.00
Star Trek N.G.:Sparticus. 5.00
TPB Beginnings, RSz(c) rep. 20.00

STAR TREK:
THE NEXT GENERATION
DEEP SPACE NINE
1994–95
1 Crossover with Malibu 2.50
2 . . . . 2.50

STAR TREK:
THE NEXT GENERATION
ILL WIND
1995–96
1 Solar-sailing race 2.50
2 Explosion Investigated. 2.50
3 A bomb aboard ship. 2.50
4 finale 2.50

STAR TREK
THE NEXT GENERATION
MODALA IMPERATIVE
1991
1 A:Spock,McCoy 6.00
2 Modula Overrun by Ferengi. 5.00
3 Picard,Spock,McCoy & Troi
   trapped 4.00
4 final issue. 4.00

STAR TREK
THE NEXT GENERATION
SHADOWHEART
1994–95
1 thru 3 . . . . @2.50
4 Worf Confront Nikolai 2.50

STATIC
Milestone, 1993–96
1 JPL,I:Static,Hotstreak,Frieda Goren,
   w/poster,card,D puzzle piece . . 4.00
1a Newstand Ed. 2.50
1b Platinum Ed. 8.00
2 thru 13 . . . . @2.50
14 Worlds Collide,V:Rift 3.00
15 thru 24 . . . . @2.50
25 V:Dusk, 48pgs. 4.00
26 thru 47 . . . . @2.50

STATIC SHOCK!:
REBIRTH OF THE COOL
DC/Milestone, Nov., 2001
1 (of 4) DMD 2.50
2 DMD,F:Hardware 2.50
3 DMD,A:Hardware,Iron Butterfly . . 2.50
4 DMD,V:Power Junkie. 2.50

STEEL
1994–98
1 JBg(c),B:LSi(s),CsB,N:Steel 3.00
2 JBg(c),CsB,V:Toastmaster. 2.50
3 JBg(c),CsB,V:Amertek. 2.50
4 JBg(c),CsB. 2.50
5 JBg(c),CsB,V:Sister's Attacker . . 2.50
6 JBg(c),CsB,Worlds Collide,pt.5 . . 2.50
7 Worlds Collide,pt.6. . . . . 2.50
8 Zero Hour,I:Hazard 2.50
9 F:Steel 2.50
10 F:Steel. 2.50
11 . . . . 2.50
12 . . . . 2.50
13 A:Maxima 2.50
14 A:Superman 2.50
15 R:White Rabbit 2.50
16 V:White Rabbit
   [new Miraweb format begins] . . 2.50
17 Steel controls armor powers. . . . 2.50
18 Abduction 2.50
19 . . . . 2.50
20 Body Rejects Armor 2.50
21 LSi,Underworld Unleashed tie-in 2.50
22 Steel separated from Superboy . 2.50
23 Steel attacked 2.50
24 V:Hazard's. 2.50
25 . . . . 2.50
26 Natasha gains superpowers. . . . 2.50
27 LSi,V:Hazard. 2.50
28 . . . . 2.50
29. . . . . 2.50
30. . . . . 2.50
31 LSi(s),V:Armorbeast 2.50
32 V:Blockbuster 2.50
33 JAp,DG,Natasha's drug abuse . . 2.50
34 CPr(s),DCw,TP,A:Natasha, in
   Jersey City. 2.50
35 CPr(s),DCw,TP,. 2.50
36 CPr(s),DCw,TP,Combing the
   sewers of Jersey City 2.50
37 CPr(s),DCw,TP,John Irons,
   Amanda Quick & Skorpio a
   romantic triangle 2.50
38 CPr(s),DCw,TP,A:The Question . 2.50
39 CPr(s),DCw,TP,V:Crash 2.50
40 CPr(s),VGi,Steel tries out
   new hammer 2.50
41 CPr(s),DCw,TMo, John Irons
   guilty of murder? 2.50
42 CPr(s),DCw,TP,Irons and
   Amanda assaulted. 2.50
43 CPr(s),DCw,TP,to Metropolis . . 2.50
44 CPr(s),DCw,TP,Genesis tie-in. . 2.50
45 CPr(s),DCw,TP,seek policeman . 2.50
46 CPr(s),DCw,TP,F:Superboy . . . 2.50
47 CPr(s),DCw,TP,F:Amanda 2.50
48 . . . . 2.50
49 CPr(s),DCw,TP,V:Deadline 2.50

50 CPr(s),DCw,TP,Millennium
   Giants 2.50
51 CPr(s),DCw,TP,bounty hunter. . . 2.50
52 CPr(s),final issue 2.50
1-shot, movie adaptation 5.00
Ann.#1 Elseworlds story 3.00
TPB The Forging of a Hero LSi(s) . 20.00

STEEL, THE
INDESTRUCTIBLE MAN
March, 1978
1 DH,I:Steel. 12.00
2 DH 8.00
3 DH 8.00
4 DH 8.00
5 Oct.–Nov., 1978. . . . . 12.00

Strange Adventures #9
© DC Comics Inc.

STRANGE ADVENTURES
1950–74
1 The Menace of the Green
   Nebula 6,000.00
2 S&K,JM(c),Doom From
   Planet X 3,000.00
3 The Metal World 1,800.00
4 BP,The Invaders From the
   Nth Dimension 1,800.00
5 The World Inside the Atom . . 1,800.00
6 Confessions of a Martian . . . 1,800.00
7 The World of Giant Ants 1,800.00
8 MA,ATh,Evolution Plus 1,800.00
9 MA,B:Captain Comet,The
   Origin of Captain Comet. . . 3,500.00
10 MA,CI,The Air Bandits
   From Space 1,800.00
11 MA,CI,Day the Past
   Came Back. 1,000.00
12 MA,CI,GK(c),The Girl From
   the Diamond Planet 1,000.00
13 MA,CI,GK(c),When the Earth
   was Kidnapped. 1,000.00
14 MA,CI,GK(c),Destination
   Doom 1,000.00
15 MA,CI,GK(c),Captain Comet-
   Enemy of Earth. 1,000.00
16 MA,CI,GK(c),The Ghost of
   Captain Comet 1,000.00
17 MA,CI,GK(c),Beware the
   Synthetic Men. 1,000.00
18 CI,MA(c),World of Flying
   Men. 1,000.00
19 CI,MA(c),Secret of the
   Twelve Eternals 1,500.00

Strange Adventures #21
© *DC Comics, Inc.*

20 CI,Slaves of the Sea Master 1,500.00
21 CI,MA(c),Eyes of the
  Other Worlds 800.00
22 CI,The Guardians of the
  Clockwork Universe. 800.00
23 CI,MA(c),The Brain Pirates
  of Planet X. 800.00
24 CI,MA(c),Doomsday on Earth. 800.00
25 CI,GK(c),The Day
  That Vanished 800.00
26 CI,Captain Vs. Miss Universe. 800.00
27 CI,MA(c),The Counterfeit
  Captain Comet 800.00
28 CI,Devil's Island in Space . . . 800.00
29 CI,The Time Capsule From
  1,000,000 B.C. 800.00
30 CI,MA(c),Menace From the
  World of Make-Believe 750.00
31 CI,Lights Camera Action. 750.00
32 CI,MA(c),The Challenge of
  Man-Ape the Mighty 750.00
33 CI,MA(c),The Human Beehive 750.00
34 CI,MA(c) 750.00
35 CI,MA(c),Cosmic Chessboard 750.00
36 CI,MA(c),The Grab-Bag
  Planet 750.00
37 CI,MA(c),The Invaders From
  the Golden Atom 750.00
38 CI,MA(c),Seeing-Eye Humans 750.00
39 CI,MA(c),The Guilty Gorilla. . . 750.00
40 CI,MA(c),The Mind Monster . . 750.00
41 CI,MA(c),The Beast From Out
  of Time. 750.00
42 CI,MD,MA(c),The Planet of
  Ancient Children 750.00
43 CI,MD,MA(c),The Phantom
  Prize Fighter 750.00
44 CI,MA(c),The Planet That
  Plotted Murder. 750.00
45 CI,MD,MA(c),Gorilla World . . . 750.00
46 CI,MA(c),E:Captain Comet
  Interplanetary War Base 750.00
47 CI,MA(c),The Man Who Sold
  the Earth 750.00
48 CI,MA(c),Human Phantom . . . 750.00
49 CI,MA(c),The Invasion
  from Indiana 750.00
50 CI,MA(c),The World Wrecker . 600.00
51 CI,MA(c),The Man Who
  Stole Air 600.00
52 CI,MA(c),Prisoner of the
  Parakeets 600.00
53 CI,MA(c),The Human Icicle. . . 600.00
54 CI,MA(c),The Electric Man . . . 500.00
55 CI,MA(c),The Gorilla Who
  Challanged the World,pt.I . . . 500.00

56 CI,The Jungle Emperor,pt.II . . 500.00
57 CI,The Spy from Saturn 500.00
58 CI,I Hunted the Radium Man . 500.00
59 CI,The Ark From Planet X. . . . 500.00
60 CI,Across the Ages 500.00
61 CI,The Mirages From Space. . 500.00
62 CI,The Fireproof Man 500.00
63 CI,I Was the Man in the Moon 500.00
64 CI,GK(c),Gorillas In Space . . . 500.00
65 CI,GK(c),Prisoner From Pluto. 500.00
66 CI,GK(c),The Human Battery . 500.00
67 CI,GK(c),Martian Masquerader500.00
68 CI,The Man Who Couldn't
  Drown 500.00
69 CI,Gorilla Conquest of Earth. . 500.00
70 CI,Triple Life of Dr. Pluto 500.00
71 CI,MSy,Zero Hour For Earth . . 400.00
72 CI,The Skyscraper That Came
  to Life. 400.00
73 CI,Amazing Rain of Gems . . . 400.00
74 CI,The Invisible Invader
  From Dimension X. 400.00
75 CI,Secret of the Man-Ape. . . . 400.00
76 CI,B:Darwin Jones,The Robot
  From Atlantis 400.00
77 CI,A:Darwin Jones,The World
  That Slipped Out of Space . . 400.00
78 CI,The Secret of the Tom
  Thumb Spaceman 400.00
79 CI,A:Darwin Jones,Invaders
  from the Ice World 400.00
80 CI,Mind Robbers of Venus . . . 400.00
81 CI,The Secret of the
  Shrinking Twins 400.00
82 CI,Giants of the Cosmic Ray . 300.00
83 CI,Assignment in Eternity 300.00
84 CI,Prisoners of the Atom
  Universe 300.00
85 CI,The Amazing Human Race 300.00
86 CI,The Dog That Saved the
  Earth 300.00
87 CI,New Faces For Old 300.00
88 CI,A:Darwin Jones,The Gorilla
  War Against Earth 300.00
89 CI,Earth For Sale 300.00
90 CI,The Day I Became a
  Martian 300.00
91 CI,Midget Earthmen of Jupiter 300.00
92 CI,GK(c),The Amazing Ray
  of Knowledge. 300.00
93 CI,GK(c),A:Darwin Jones,
  Space-Rescue By Proxy 300.00
94 MA,CI,GK(c),Fisherman of
  Space. 300.00
95 CI,The World at my Doorstep . 300.00
96 CI,MA(c),The Menace of
  Saturn's Rings 300.00
97 CI,MA(c),MSy,Secret of the
  Space-Giant 300.00
98 CI,GK(c),MSy,Attack on Fort
  Satellite 300.00
99 CI,MSy,GK(c),Big Jump Into
  Space. 300.00
100 CI,MSy,The Amazing Trial
  of John (Gorilla) Doe. 400.00
101 CI,MSy,GK(c),Giant From
  Beyond 250.00
102 MSy,GK(c),The Three Faces
  of Barry Morrell 250.00
103 GK(c),The Man Who
  Harpooned Worlds. 250.00
104 MSy,GK(c),World of Doomed
  Spacemen 250.00
105 MSy,GK(c),Fisherman From
  the Sea 250.00
106 MSy,CI,GK(c),Genie in the
  Flying Saucer 250.00
107 MSy,CI,GK(c),War of the
  Jovian Bubble-Men 250.00
108 MSy,CI,GK(c),The Human
  Pet of Gorilla Land 250.00

109 MSy,CI,GK(c),The Man Who
  Weighed 100 Tons. 250.00
110 MSy,CI,GK(c),Hand From
  Beyond 250.00
111 MSy,CI,GK(c),Secret of
  the Last Earth-Man 250.00
112 MSy,CI,GK(c),Menace of
  the Size-Changing Spaceman250.00
113 MSy,CI,GK(c),Deluge From
  Space. 250.00
114 MSy,CI,GK(c),Secret of the
  Flying Buzz Saw 250.00
115 MSy,CI,GK(c),The Great
  Space-Tiger Hunt. 250.00
116 MSy,CI,RH,GK(c),Invasion
  of the Water Warriors 250.00
117 MSy,CI,GK(c),I:Atomic
  Knights 1,000.00
118 MSy,CI,The Turtle-Men of
  Space. 275.00
119 MSy,CI,MA(c),Raiders
  From the Giant World 250.00
120 MSy,CI,MA,Attack of the Oil
  Demons 500.00
121 MSy,CI,MA(c),Invasion of the
  Flying Reptiles. 225.00
122 MSy,CI,MA(c),David and the
  Space-Goliath 225.00
123 MSy,CI,MA(c),Secret of the
  Rocket-Destroyer. 300.00
124 MSy,CI,MA(c),The Face-Hunter
  From Saturn 250.00
125 MSy,CI,The Flying Gorilla
  Menace 225.00
126 MSy,CI,MA(c),Return of the
  Neanderthal Man 400.00
127 MSy,CI,MA(c),Menace
  From the Earth-Globe 225.00
128 MSy,CI,MA(c),The Man
  With the Electronic Brain. . . . 225.00
129 MSy,CI,MA(c),The Giant
  Who Stole Mountains 250.00
130 MSy,CI,MA.War With the
  Giant Frogs 225.00
131 MSy,CI,MA(c),Emperor
  of the Earth 225.00
132 MSy,CI,MA(c),The Dreams
  of Doom. 250.00
133 MSy,CI,MA(c),The Invisible
  Dinosaur 225.00
134 MSy,CI,MA(c), The Aliens
  Who Raided New York 250.00
135 MSy,CI,MA(c),Fishing Hole
  in the Sky. 200.00
136 MSy,CI,MA(c),The Robot
  Who Lost Its Head. 175.00

Strange Adventures #80
© *DC Comics Inc.*

---

137 MSy,CI,MA(c),Parade of the
    Space-Toys 175.00
138 MSy,CI,MA(c),Secret of the
    Dinosaur Skeleton 200.00
139 MSy,CI,MA(c),Space-Roots
    of Evil. 175.00
140 MSy,CI,MA(c),Prisoner of
    the Space-Patch 175.00
141 MSy,CI,MA(c),Battle Between
    the Two Earths 200.00
142 MSy,CI,MA(c),The Return of
    the Faceless Creature. 175.00
143 MSy,CI,MA(c),The Face in
    the Atom-Bomb Cloud 175.00
144 MSy,CI,MA(c),A:Atomic
    Knights, When the Earth
    Blacked Out. 200.00
145 MSy,CI,MA,The Man Who
    Lived Forever 175.00
146 MSy,CI,MA(c),Perilous Pet
    of Space 175.00
147 MSy,CI,MA(c),The Dawn-
    World Menace 200.00
148 MSy,CI,MA(c),Earth Hero,
    Number One 175.00
149 MSy,CI,MA(c),Raid of
    the Rogue Star 175.00
150 MSy,CI,MA(c),When Earth
    Turned into a Comet 200.00
151 MSy,CI,MA(c),Invasion Via
    Radio-Telescope 175.00
152 MSy,MA(c),The Martian
    Emperor of Earth 175.00
153 MSy,MA(c),Threat of the
    Faceless Creature 175.00
154 CI,MSy,MA,GK(c),Earth's
    Friendly Invaders. 175.00
155 MSy,MA,GK(c),Prisoner
    of the Undersea World 175.00
156 MSy,CI,MA(c),The Man
    With the Head of Saturn 175.00
157 MSy,CI,MA(c),Plight of
    the Human Cocoons 175.00
158 MSy,CI,MA(c),The Mind
    Masters of Space. 175.00
159 MSy,CI,MA(c),The Maze
    of Time. 175.00
160 MSy,CI,MA(c),A:Atomic
    Knights, Here Comes the
    Wild Ones 175.00
161 MSy,CI,MA(c),Earth's Frozen
    Heat Wave,E:Space Museum 150.00
162 CI,MA(c),Mystery of the
    12 O'Clock Man. 150.00
163 MA(c),The Creature in
    the Black Light. 150.00
164 DD&SMo(c),I Became
    a Robot 150.00
165 DD&SMo(c),I Broke the
    Supernatural Barrier 150.00
166 DD&SMo(c),I Lived in
    Two Bodies 150.00
167 JkS(c),The Team That
    Conqured Time 150.00
168 JkS(c),I Hunted Toki
    the Terrible. 150.00
169 DD&SMo(c),The Prisoner
    of the Hour Glass 150.00
170 DD&SMo(c),The Creature
    From Strange Adventures . . . 150.00
171 The Diary of the
    9-Planet Man?. 150.00
172 DD&SMo(c),I Became
    the Juggernaut Man 150.00
173 The Secret of the
    Fantasy Films 150.00
174 JkS(c),The Ten Ton Man. . . . 150.00
175 Danger: This Town is
    Shrinking 150.00
176 DD&SMo(c),The Case of
    the Cosmonik Quartet 150.00

177 I Lived a Hundred Lives,
    O:Immortal Man. 150.00
178 JkS(c),The Runaway Comet. 150.00
179 JkS(c),I Buried Myself Alive . 150.00
180 CI,I:Animal Man,I Was the
    Man With Animal Powers . . . 300.00
181 The Man of Two Worlds 100.00
182 JkS(c),The Case of the
    Blonde Bombshell 100.00
183 JM(c),The Plot to Destroy
    the Earth 100.00
184 GK(c),A:Animal Man,The
    Return of the Man With
    Animal Powers 400.00
185 JkS(c),Ilda-Gangsters Inc. . . 100.00
186 Beware the Gorilla Witch . . . 100.00
187 JkS(c),O:The Enchantress . . 120.00
188 SD,JkS(c),I Was the
    Four Seasons 100.00
189 SD,JkS(c),The Way-Out
    Worlds of Bertram Tilley 100.00
190 CI,A:Animal Man,A-Man-the
    Hero with Animal Powers . . . 500.00
191 JkS(c),Beauty vs. the Beast . 100.00
192 Freak Island 100.00
193 The Villian Maker 100.00
194 JkS(c),The Menace of the
    Super- Gloves 100.00
195 JkS(c),Secret of the Three
    Earth Dooms,A:Animal Man . 250.00
196 JkS(c),Mystery of the
    Orbit Creatures 100.00
197 The Hostile Hamlet 75.00
198 JkS(c),Danger! Earth
    is Doomed 75.00
199 Robots of the Round Table . . . 75.00
200 The Guardian Eye. 75.00
201 JkS,Animal Man 125.00
202 Robinson Crusoe of the Sky. . 75.00
203 The Split Man 75.00
204 GK,Crazy Quilt Man 75.00
205 CI,I&O:Deadman. 300.00
206 NA,MSy,F:Deadman. 200.00
207 NA,F:Deadman 150.00
208 NA,F:Deadman 150.00
209 NA,F:Deadman 150.00
210 NA,F:Deadman 150.00
211 thru 216 NA,F:Deadman . . @150.00
217 MA,MSy,A:Adam Strange 25.00
218 MA,CI,MSy 50.00
219 CI,JKu 50.00
220 CI,JKu 50.00
221 CI,Two Adam Stranges 50.00
222 MA,New Adam Strange 75.00
223 MA,CI 50.00
224 MA,CI 50.00
225 MA,JKu 50.00
226 MA,JKu,New Adam Strange . . 75.00
227 JKu 50.00
228 NA(c). 70.00
229 MA,The Last Mile of Space. . . 60.00
230 GM(c) 50.00
231 E:Atomic Knights 50.00
232 JKu 50.00
233 JKu 50.00
234 JKu 50.00
235 NA(c). 60.00
236 CI,Human Fishbowl 40.00
237 Ray-Gun in the SKy 30.00
238 MK(c) 30.00
239 Metal Conqueror of Rann . . . 30.00
240 MK(c) 30.00
241 F:Adam Strange 30.00
242 MA. 30.00
243 F:Adam Strange 30.00
244 Oct.–Nov., 1974 . . . . 30.00

STRANGE ADVENTURES
DC/Vertigo, Sept., 1999
1 (of 4) BB,DGb 2.50
2 KJ,Expiration Date. 2.50
3 & 4 . . . . @2.50

STRANGE SPORTS
STORIES
Sept.–Oct., 1973
1 CS,DG 40.00
2 thru 6 . . . . @25.00

STREETS
1993
1 Tenderloin 5.00
2 Procurement 5.00
3 . . . . 5.00

Sugar and Spike #21
© DC Comics, Inc.

SUGAR & SPIKE
April-May, 1956
1 SM 4,000.00
2 SM 1,500.00
3 SM 1,000.00
4 SM 1,000.00
5 SM 1,000.00
6 thru 10 SM . . . . @600.00
11 thru 20 SM . . . . @500.00
21 thru 29 SM . . . . @350.00
30 SM,A:Scribbly 350.00
31 thru 50 SM . . . . @300.00
51 thru 70 SM . . . . @225.00
71 thru 79 SM . . . . @200.00
80 SM,I:Bernie the Brain 200.00
81 thru 97 SM . . . . @150.00
98 SM,Oct.–Nov., 1971 . . . . 150.00
1 Facsimile Edition,rep.(2002) . . . 3.00

SUICIDE SQUAD
1987–91
1 LMc,Legends,I:Jihad 4.00
2 LMc,V:The Jihad 2.50
3 LMc,V:Female Furies. 2.50
4 LMc,V:William Hell. 2.50
5 LM,A:Penguin 3.00
6 LM,A:Penguin 3.00
7 thru 12 LMc . . . . @2.50
13 LMc,X-over,JLI#13 . . . . 4.00
14 thru 22. . . . . @2.50
23 LMc,Invasion. 4.00
24 thru 47. . . . . @2.25
48 GI,New Thinker. 4.00
49 thru 63 . . . . @2.25
64 GI,A:Task Force X. 4.00
65 GI,Bronze Tiger. 2.25
66 GI,Final Iss.E:Suicide Squad . . . 2.25
Ann.#1 GN,V:Argent,A:Manhunter. . 2.25
[2nd Series] Sept., 2001
1 KG,R:Suicide Squad 2.50
2 thru 12 . . . . @2.50

Superboy #5
© DC Comics, Inc.

SUPERBOY
1949–76

1 WB&StK,Superman(c) 20,000.00
2 The Stunts of Superboy 5,000.00
3 Buperboy's Hall of Fame ... 3,700.00
4 The Oracle of Smallville 3,200.00
5 Superboy meets Supergirl,
Pre-Adventure #252...... 3,200.00
6 I:Humpty Dumpty,the Hobby
Robber 2,700.00
7 WB,V:Humpty Dumpty 2,700.00
8 CS,I:Superbaby,V:Humpty
Dumpty 2,500.00
9 V:Humpty Dumpty........ 2,500.00
10 CS,I:Lana Lang 2,500.00
11 CS,2nd Lang,V:Humpty
Dumpty 2,200.00
12 CS,The Heroes Club 2,000.00
13 CS,Scout of Smallville 2,000.00
14 CS,I:Marsboy........... 2,000.00
15 CS,A:Superman.......... 2,200.00
16 CS,A:Marsboy 2,000.00
17 CS,Superboy's Double 2,000.00
18 CS,Lana Lang-Hollywood
Star 2,000.00
19 CS,The Death of Young
Clark Kent............ 2,000.00
20 CS,The Ghost that Haunted
Smallville 2,000.00
21 CS,Lana Lang-Magician ... 1,000.00
22 CS,The New Clark Kent ... 1,000.00
23 CS,The Super Superboy ... 1,000.00
24 CS,The Super Fat Boy of
Steel 1,000.00
25 CS,Cinderella of Smallville . 1,000.00
26 CS,A:Superbaby 1,000.00
27 CS,Clark Kent-Runaway.... 1,000.00
28 CS,The Man Who Defeated
Superboy 1,000.00
29 CS,The Puppet Superboy .. 1,000.00
30 CS,I:Tommy Tuttle 800.00
31 CS,The Amazing Elephant
Boy From Smallville........ 800.00
32 CS,His Majesty King
Superboy 800.00
33 CS,The Crazy Costumes of
the Boy of Steel.......... 800.00
34 CS,Hep Cats o/Smallville 800.00
35 CS,The Five Superboys 800.00
36 CS,The Superboy Souvenirs . 800.00
37 CS,I:Thaddeus Lang........ 800.00
38 CS,Public Chimp #1 .... 800.00
39 CS,Boy w/Superboy Powers.. 800.00
40 CS,The Magic Necklace..... 700.00
41 CS,Superboy Meets
Superbrave 700.00

42 CS,Gaucho of Smallville..... 700.00
43 CS,Super-Farmer of
Smallville............... 700.00
44 The Amazing Adventure of
Superboy's Costume..... 700.00
45 A Trap For Superboy........ 700.00
46 The Battle of Fort Smallville .. 700.00
47 CS,A:Superman........... 700.00
48 CS,Boy Without Super-Suit .. 700.00
49 I:Metallo (Jor-El's Robot) 700.00
50 The Super-Giant of
Smallville............... 700.00
51 I:Krypto 500.00
52 CS,The Powerboy from
Earth 500.00
53 CS,A:Superman........... 500.00
54 CS,The Silent Superboy..... 500.00
55 CS,A:Jimmy Olson 500.00
56 CS,A:Krypto 500.00
57 CS,One-Man Baseball Team . 500.00
58 CS,The Great Kryptonite
Mystery 500.00
59 CS,A:Superbaby........... 500.00
60 The 100,000 Cowboy 500.00
61 The School For Superboys... 400.00
62 I:Gloria Kent 400.00
63 CS,The Two Boys of Steel ... 400.00
64 CS,A:Krypto 400.00
65 Superboy's Moonlight Spell .. 400.00
66 The Family with X-Ray Eyes . 400.00
67 I:Klax-Ar 400.00
68 O&I:Bizarro 1,400.00
69 How Superboy Learned
To Fly................. 300.00
70 O:Superboy's Glasses 300.00
71 A:Superbaby 300.00
72 The Flying Girl of Smallville .. 300.00
73 CS,A:Superbaby........... 300.00
74 A:Jor-El & Lara 300.00
75 A:Superbaby 300.00
76 I:Super Monkey........... 300.00
77 Superboy's Best Friend 300.00
78 O:Mr.Mzyzptik 500.00
79 A:Jar-El & Lara 300.00
80 Superboy meets Supergirl ... 400.00
81 The Weakling From Earth..... 275.00
82 A:Bizarro Krypto 275.00
83 I:Kryptonite Kid 275.00
84 A:William Tell............. 275.00
85 Secret of Mighty Boy 275.00
86 I:PeteRoss,A:Legion........ 500.00
87 I:Scarlet Jungle of Krypton .. 275.00
88 The Invader from Earth...... 275.00
89 I:Mon-El................. 275.00
90 A:Pete Ross 150.00
91 CS,Superboy in Civil War 150.00
92 CS,I:Destructo,A:Lex Luthor.. 150.00
93 A:Legion 150.00
94 I:Superboy Revenge Squad,
A:Pete Ross 150.00
95 Imaginary Story,The Super
Family From Krypton....... 150.00
96 A:Pete Ross,Lex Luther 150.00
97 Krypto Story 150.00
98 Legion,I&O:Ultraboy 150.00
99 O: The Kryptonite Kid 100.00
100 I:Phantom Zone.......... 275.00
101 The Handsome Hound
of Steel 125.00
102 O:Scarlet Jungle of Krypton . 125.00
103 CS,A:King Arthur,Jesse James
Red Kryptonite............ 125.00
104 O:Phantom Zone 125.00
105 CS,The Simpleton of Steel .. 125.00
106 CS,A:Brainiac 125.00
107 CS,I:Superboy Club of
Smallville.............. 150.00
108 The Kent's First Super Son . 125.00
109 The Super Youth of Bronze . 125.00
110 A:Jor-El 125.00
111 Red Kryptonite Story 90.00
112 CS,A:Superbaby 90.00

Superboy #114
© DC Comics, Inc.

113 The Boyhood of Dad Kent ... 90.00
114 A:Phantom Zone,
Mr.Mxyzptlk 90.00
115 A:Phantom Zone,Lex Luthor .. 90.00
116 The Wolfboy of Smallville 90.00
117 A:Legion 90.00
118 CS,The War Between
Superboy and Krypto........ 90.00
119 V:Android Double 90.00
120 A:Mr.Mxyzptlk 90.00
121 CS,A:Jor-El,Lex Luthor...... 90.00
122 Red Kryptonite Story 90.00
123 CS,The Curse of the
Superboy Mummy 90.00
124 I:Insect Queen 90.00
125 O:Kid Psycho 90.00
126 O:Krypto 90.00
127 A:Insect Queen 75.00
128 A:Phantom Zone,Kryptonite
Kid,Dev En 75.00
129 rep.A:Mon-El,SuperBaby ... 125.00
130 CS,Search for a Pet 75.00
131 A;Lex Luthor,Mr.Mxyzptlk,I:
Space Canine Patrol Agents .. 75.00
132, CS,A:Space Canine
Patrol Agents............. 75.00
133 A:Robin, repr. 75.00
134 The Scoundrel of Steel 75.00
135 A:Lex Luthor 75.00
136 A:Space Canine Agents 75.00
137 Mysterious Mighty Mites..... 75.00
138 giant, Superboy's Most
Terrific Battles 90.00
139 The Samson of Smallville.... 75.00
140 V:The Gambler 50.00
141 No Mercy for a Hero........ 50.00
142 A:Super Monkey.......... 50.00
143 NA(c),The Big Fall 50.00
144 Superboy's Stolen Identity .. 50.00
145 NA(c)Kents become young.... 50.00
146 NA(c),CS,The Runaway 50.00
147 giant O:Legion........... 55.00
148 NA(c),CS,C:PolarBoy....... 50.00
149 NA(c),A:Bonnie & Clyde 50.00
150 JAb,V:Mr.Cipher 50.00
151 NA(c),A:Kryptonite Kid 50.00
152 NA(c),WW................ 50.00
153 NA(c),WW,A:Prof Mesmer ... 50.00
154 WW(i),A:Jor-El & Lara
Blackout For Superboy 50.00
155 NA(c),WW,Revolt of the
Teenage Robots 50.00
156 Farewell to Smallville,giant.... 50.00
157 WW,NA(c),Get Lost Superboy 50.00
158 WW,A:Jor-El & Lara 50.00

DC COMICS

159 WW(i),A:Lex Luthor 50.00
160 WW,I Chose Eternal Exile . . . 50.00
161 WW,The Strange Death of
    Superboy 50.00
162 A:Phantom Zone 50.00
163 NA(c),Reform School Rebel . . 60.00
164 NA(c),Your Death Will
    Destroy Me 50.00
165 CS,Superdog,giant-size 50.00
166 NA(c),A:Lex Luthor 30.00
167 NA(c),MA,A:Superbaby 30.00
168 NA(c),MA,Hitler 30.00
169 MA,A:Lex Luthor 30.00
170 MA,A:Genghis Khan 30.00
171 MA,A:Aquaboy 30.00
172 MA(i),GT,A:Legion,
    O:Lightning Lad,Yango 35.00
173 NA(c),GT,DG,O:CosmicBoy . . 30.00
174 CS,Colossal Superdog,giant . . 50.00
175 NA(c),MA,Rejuvenation of
    Ma & Pa Kent 30.00
176 NA(c),MA,GT,WW,A:Legion . . 30.00
177 MA,A:Lex Luthor 40.00
178 NA(c),MA,Legion Reprint 40.00
179 MA,A:Lex Luthor 40.00
180 MA,O:Bouncing Boy 40.00
181 MA,CS,Insect Queen 40.00
182 MA,A:Bruce Wayne 40.00
183 MA,GT,CS(rep),A:Legion 40.00
184 MA,WW,O:Dial H rep 40.00
185 A:Legion 20.00
186 MA,Mutiny of the Damned . . . 20.00
187 MA,Iron Cage for a Hero 20.00
188 MA,DC,O:Karkan,A:Legn 20.00
189 MA,Runaway Superbaby 20.00
190 MA,WW,Murder the Leader . . 20.00
191 MA,DC,O:SunBoy retold 20.00
192 MA,The Deadly Dawn 20.00
193 MA,WW,N:Chameleon Boy,
    Shrinking Violet 20.00
194 MA,Super-Merman of the Sea 20.00
195 MA,WW,I:Wildfire,
    N:Phantom Girl 20.00
196 last Superboy solo 30.00
197 DC,Legion begins, New
    Costumes,I:Tyr 30.00
198 DC,N:Element Lad,
    Princess Projects 20.00
199 DC,A:Tyr, Otto Orion 20.00
200 DC,M:Bouncing Boy
    & Duo Damsel 25.00
201 DC,Wildfire returns 18.00
202 N:Light Lass 60.00
203 MGr,D:Invisible Kid 25.00

Superboy #212
© DC Comics Inc.

204 MGr,A:Supergirl 15.00
205 MGr,CG,100 pages 50.00
206 MGr,A:Ferro Lad 25.00
207 MGr,O:Lightning Lad 25.00
208 MGr,CS,68pp,Legion of
    Super Villains 28.00
209 MGr,N:Karate Kid 20.00
210 MGr,O:Karate Kid 25.00
211 MGr,The Ultimate Revenge . . 15.00
212 MGr,L:Matter Eater Lad 15.00
213 MGr,V:Benn Pares 15.00
214 MGr,V:Overseer 15.00
215 MGr,A:Emerald Empress 15.00
216 MGr,I:Tyroc 15.00
217 MGr,I:Laurel Kent 15.00
218 J:Tyroc,A:Fatal Five 15.00
219 MGr,A:Fatal Five 15.00
220 MGr,BWi 15.00
221 MGr,BWi,I:Grimbor 10.00
222 MGr,BWi,MN,BL,A:Tyroc 10.00
223 MGr,BWi 10.00
224 MGr,BWi,V:Pulsar Stargrave . . 10.00
225 MGr(c),BWi,JSh,MN 10.00
226 MGr(c),MN,JSh,JA,
    I:Dawnstar 10.00
227 MGr(c),JSon,JA,V:Stargrave . . 10.00
228 MGr(c),JSh,JA,
    D:Chemical King 10.00
229 MGr(c),JSh,JA,V:Deregon . . . 10.00
230 MGr(c),JSh,V:Sden 10.00
Spec. #147 facsimile (2003) 7.00
Becomes:

SUPERBOY & THE
LEGION OF
SUPER-HEROES
1976–79

231 MGr(c),JSh,MN,JA,doub.size
    begins,V:Fatal Five 18.00
232 MGr(c),JSh,RE,JA,V:
    Dr.Regulus 18.00
233 MGr(c),JSh,BWi,MN,BL,
    I:Infinite Man 18.00
234 MGr(c),RE,JA,V:Composite
    Creature 18.00
235 MGr,GT 18.00
236 MGr(c),BMc,JSh,MN,JRu,
    V:Khunds 18.00
237 MGr(c),WS,JA 18.00
238 JSn(c),reprint 18.00
239 MGR(c),JSn,JRu,Ultra Boy
    accused 18.00
240 MGr(c),HC,BWi,JSh,BMc,
    O:Dawnstar;V:Grimbor 18.00
241 JSh,BMc,A:Ontir 18.00
242 JSh,BMc,E:Double Size 18.00
243 MGr(c),JA,JSon 18.00
244 JSon,V:Dark Circle 18.00
245 MA,JSon,V:Mordu 18.00
246 MGr(c),JSon,DG,MA,
    V:Fatal Five 15.00
247 JSon,JA,anniv.issue 15.00
248 JSon 15.00
249 JSon,JA 15.00
250 JSn,V:Omega 15.00
251 JSn,Brainiac 5 goes insane . . 15.00
252 JSon,V:Starburst bandits 12.00
253 JSon,I:Blok,League of
    Super Assassins 12.00
254 JSon,V:League of Super
    Assassins 12.00
255 JSon,A:Jor-El 12.00
256 JSon 12.00
257 SD,JSon,DA,V:Psycho
    Warrior 12.00
258 JSon,V:Psycho Warrior 12.00
Becomes:

LEGION OF
SUPER HEROES
[2nd Series]

[NEW ADVENTURES OF]
SUPERBOY
Jan., 1980

1 KS 6.00
2 KS 3.00
3 KS 3.00
4 KS 3.00
5 KS 3.00
6 KS 3.00
7 KS,JSa 3.00
8 thru 33 KS . . . . @3.00
34 KS,I:Yellow Peri 3.00
35 thru 44 KS . . . . @3.00
45 KS,I:Sunburst 3.00
46 KS,A:Sunburst 3.00
47 KS,A:Sunburst 3.00
48 KS 3.00
49 KS,A:Zatara 3.00
50 KS,KG,A:Legion 3.00
51 KS,FM(c)In Between Years 3.00
52 KS 3.00
53 KS 3.00
54 KS 3.00

SUPERBOY
1990–91

1 TV Tie-in,JM,photo(c) 5.00
2 JM,T.J.White Abducted 3.00
3 JM,Fountain of Youth 3.00
4 JM,Big Man on Campus 3.00
5 JM,Legion Homage 3.00
6 JM,Luthor 3.00
7 JM,Super Boy Arrested 3.00
8 JM,AAd(i),Bizarro 3.00
9 JM/CS,PhantomZone#1 . . . . 3.00
10 JM/CS,PhantomZone#2 . . . . . . 3.00
11 CS 3.00
12 CS,X-Mas in Smallville 3.00
Becomes:

ADVENTURES OF
SUPERBOY
1991

13 A:Mr.Mxyzptlk 3.50
14 CS,A:Brimstone 3.00
15 CS,Legion Homage 3.00
16 CS,Into the Future 3.00
17 CS,A:Luthor 3.00
18 JM,At the Movies 3.00
19 JM,Blood Transfusion 3.00
20 JM,O:Nicknack,(G.Gottfried
    script) 3.00
21 V:Frost Monster 3.00
22 . . . . 3.00
Spec.#1 CS,A:Ma Kent 2.50

SUPERBOY
[2nd Series], 1994

1 B:KK(s),TG,DHz,V:Sidearm 4.00
2 TG,DHz,I:Knockout 2.50
3 TG,DHz,I:Scavenger 2.50
4 TG,DHz,MeP,I:Lock n' Load 2.50
5 TG,DHz,I:Silver Sword 2.50
6 TG,DHz,Worlds Collide,pt.3
    C:Rocket 2.50
7 Worlds Collide, pt.8,V:Rift 2.50
8 Zero Hour,A:Superboy 2.50
9 Silican Dragon 2.50
10 Monster 2.50
11 Techno 2.50
12 Copperhead 2.50
13 Watery Grave,pt.1 . . . . 2.50
14 Watery Grave,pt.2 . . . . 2.50
15 Watery Grave,pt.3 . . . . 2.50
16 TG,DHz,KK,V:Loose Cannon
    [New Miraweb format begins] . . 2.50
17 TG,DHz,KK Looking for
    Roxy Leech 2.50
18 V:Valor 2.50
19 TG,KK,DHz,T-K-O 2.50

Superboy 2nd Series #1
© DC Comics Inc.

20 R:Scavenger 2.50
21 KK,TG,DHz,Future Tense,Pt.1 . . 2.50
22 KK,TG,DHz,Underworld
   Unleashed x-over 2.50
23 KK,TG,DHz,V:Technician 2.50
24 KK,TG,DHz,V:Silversword. 2.50
25 New Gods 3.00
26 KK,DHz,Losin'it,pt.2 . . . . 2.25
27 KK,DHz,Losin'it,pt.3 . . . . 2.25
28 KK,DHz,Losin'it,pt.4 . . . . 2.25
29 KK,DHz,Losin'it,pt.5 . . . . 2.25
30 KK,DHz,Losin'it,pt.6 . . . . 2.25
31 KK,Summer Fun,V:Morpheriste . 2.25
32 RMz(s),RBe,DHz,V:King Shark . 2.25
33 RMz(s),RBe,DHz, survivors flee
   to Hawaii, Final Night tie-in . . . 2.25
34 RMz(s),RBe,DHz, V:Dubbilex. . . 2.25
35 RMz(s),RBe,DHz, Superboy
   abducted 2.25
36 RMz(s),RBe,DHz,V:King SHark . 2.25
37 RMz(s),SB,V:Sledge 2.25
38 RMz,RBe,DHz,Meltdown,pt.1 . . 2.25
39 RMz,RBe,DHz,Meltdown,pt.2 . . 2.25
40 RMz,RBe,DHz,Meltdown,pt.2,
   x-over. 2.25
41 RMz,RBe,DHz,Meltdown,pt.3 . . 2.25
42 SB,Ashes to Ashes 2.25
43 SB,Lanie & Ken 2.25
44 SB,island of teenagers 2.25
45 RMz,DHz,TGu,A:Legion 2.25
46 RMz,DHz,TGu,V:Silver Sword . . 2.25
47 RMz,DHz,TGu,F:Green Lantern . 2.25
48 BKs,DHz,TGu,theme park 2.25
49 DHz,Searching 2.25
50 KK,TGu,Last Boy on Earth pt.1 . 2.25
51 KK,TGu,Last Boy on Earth pt.2 . 2.25
52 KK,TGu,Last Boy on Earth pt.3 . 2.25
53 KK,TGu,Last Boy on Earth pt.4 . 2.25
54 KK,TGu,A:Wild Men 2.25
55 KK,TGu,V:Grokk, Hex. 2.25
56 KK,TGu,Project Cadmus 2.25
57 KK,TGu,Demolition Run,pt.1 . . 2.25
58 KK,TGu,Demolition Run,pt.2 . . 2.25
59 KK,DAb,A:Superman 2.25
60 KK,TGu,A:JLA,Hyper-Tension . . 2.25
61 KK,TGu,Hyper-Tension,pt.2 . . . 2.25
62 KK,TGu,Hyper-Tension,pt.3 . . . 2.25
63 KK,TGu,Hyper-Tension,pt.4 . . . 2.25
64 KK,TGu,Hyper-Tension,pt.5 . . . 2.25
65 KK,TGu,guest-star packed 2.25
66 KK,TGu,Wild Lands 2.25
67 KK,AaL, in Wild Lands 2.25
68 KK,TG,MM,Day of Judgment
   x-over, F:Demon 2.25
69 KK,TG,return to Hawaii 2.25

70 KK,TG,Evil Factory,pt.1 . . . . 2.25
71 KK,TG,Evil Factory,pt.2 . . . . 2.25
72 KK,TG,Evil Factory,pt.3 . . . . 2.25
73 KK,TG,Evil Factory,pt.4 . . . . 2.25
74 KK,TG,Sins of Youth 2.25
75 KK,TG,as normal teenager 2.25
76 KK,TG,still Superboy. 2.25
77 KK,TG,MBa,V:Kossak 2.25
78 KK,TG,prisoners 2.25
79 KK,TG,V:Kossak the Slaver 2.25
80 BHr,F:The Titans,pt.1 . . . . 2.25
81 BHr,F:The Titans,pt.2 . . . . 2.25
82 JMz,V:Negative G. 2.25
83 PFe,F:Young Justice 2.25
84 PFe,off to L.A.. . . . . 2.25
85 PFe,A:Batman,Batgirl 2.25
86 PFe,shotgun wedding 2.25
87 V:Shrapnel,Deadman 2.25
88 PFe,V:DNAngels. 2.25
89 PFe,Our Worlds at War, tie-in. . . 2.25
90 PFe,Our Worlds at War, tie-in. . . 2.25
91 PFe,Our Worlds at War, tie-in. . . 2.25
92 PFe,R:Doctor Sin 2.25
93 PFe,Joker:Last Laugh, tie-in. . . . 2.25
94 JMC,finding an apartment. 2.25
95 JP,JMC,Slaughterhouse Six 2.25
96 JP,Trixie & Wipeout. 2.25
97 JP,JMC,F:Wipeout 2.25
98 JP,JMC,F:Jimmy Olsen. 2.25
99 WorldWithoutYoungJustice,pt.4 . 2.25
100 JP,KK,TG,48-pg. 3.50
Ann.#1 Elseworlds Story 3.50
Ann.#2 KK,BKs, Year One 4.50
Ann.#3 Legends o/t Dead Earth . . . 3.50
Ann.#4 Pulp Heroes (High-
   Adventure). 4.50
Spec.#1,000,000 KK,TGu 2.50

SUPERBOY
& THE RAVERS
1996–98

1 KK&SMt(s),PaP,DDv,. 2.50
2 KK&SMt(s),PaP,DDv,InterC.E.P.T.
   pursues Superboy and Kaliber . 2.50
3 KK&SMT(s),PaP,DDv,teleported
   to Rann,V:Half-Life 2.50
4 KK&SMt(s),PaP,DDv,A:Adam
   Strange 2.50
5 KK&SMt(s),PaP,DDv,O:Hero 2.50
6 KK&SMt(s),PaP,DDv,. 2.50
7 KK&SMt(s),PaP,DDv, Road Trip,
   pt.1,A:Impulse 2.50
8 KK&SMt(s),PaP,DDv, Road Trip,
   pt.2,A:Guy Gardner 2.50
9 KK&SMt(s),PaP,DDv, Road Trip,
   pt.3,A:Aura. 2.50
10 KK&SMt(s),DDv,Meltdown,pt.4 . 2.50
11 KK&SMt(s),PaP,DDv, Superboy
   presumed dead 2.50
12 KK(s),AaL,. 2.50
13 KK(s),SMt,F:Hero,Sparx 2.50
14 KK&SMt(s),Genesis tie-in. 2.50
15 KK&SMt(s),new Rave 2.50
16 KK&SMt(s),Half-Life 2.50
17 KK&SMt(s),Kaliber 2.50
18 KK&SMt(s),V:Qward 2.50
19 . . . . 2.50

SUPERBOY PLUS
Nov., 1996

1 RMz(s),ASm,F:Captain
   Marvel Jr.. . . . . 3.50
2 LKa,AWi,ALa,F:Slither 3.00

SUPERBOY/RISK
DOUBLE-SHOT
Dec., 1997

1 DJu,JoP,x-over. 2.50

SUPERBOY'S LEGION
Feb., 2001

1 (of 2) Elseworlds, 48-page. 6.00
2 MFm,AD, concl. 6.00

Super DC Giant #14
© DC Comics, Inc.

SUPER DC GIANT
1970–71, 1976

S-13 Binky 175.00
S-14 JKu,GK,Top Guns of
   the West 75.00
S-15 JKu,GK,Western Comics . . . 65.00
S-16 JKu,Best of the Brave
   & the Bold 50.00
S-17 Love 1970 . . . . 450.00
S-18 Three Mouseketeers 150.00
S-19 NA,Jerry Lewis 175.00
S-20 NA,JK,House of Mystery . . . 100.00
S-21 Love 1971 . . . . 500.00
S-22 JKu,Top Guns of the West . . 40.00
S-23 The Unexpected 50.00
S-24 Supergirl 50.00
S-25 Challengers of the Unknown. 50.00
S-26 Aquaman 40.00
S-27 GK,Strange Flying Saucer
   Adventures (1976). 35.00

SUPER FRIENDS
Nov., 1976

1 ECh(c),JO,RE,Fury of the
   Superfoes,A:Penguin. 60.00
2 RE,A:Penguin 25.00
3 RF(c),RF,A:JLA 20.00
4 RF,V:Riddler,I:Skyrocket 20.00
5 RF(c),RF,V:Greenback. 20.00
6 RF(c),RF,A:Atom 15.00
7 RF(c),RF,I:Zan & Jana,
   A:Seraph 15.00
8 RF(c),RF,A:JLA 15.00
9 RF(c),RF,A:JLA,I:Iron Maiden . . 15.00
10 RF(c),RFTheMonkeyMenace . . 15.00
11 RF(c),RF 12.00
12 RF(c),RF,A:TNT 12.00
13 RF(c),RF 12.00
14 RF(c),RF 12.00
15 RF(c),RF, A:The Elementals . . . 12.00
16 RF(c),RF,V:The Cvags 12.00
17 RF(c),RF,A:Queen Hippolyte . . 12.00
18 KS(c),V:Tuantra,Time Trapper . 12.00
19 RF(c),RF,V:Menagerie Man . . . 12.00
20 KS(c),KS,V:Frownin' Fritz 12.00
21 RF(c),RF,V:Evil Superfriends
   Doubles 12.00
22 RF(c),RF,V:Matador Mob 12.00
23 FR(c),RF,V:Mirror Master 12.00

24 RF(c),RF,V:Exorians 12.00
25 RF(c),RF,V:Overlord,
  A:Green Lantern, Mera . . . 12.00
26 RF(c),RF,A:Johnny Jones. 12.00
27 RF(c),RF,The Spaceman Who
  Stole the Stars 12.00
28 RF(c),RF,A:Felix Faust 12.00
29 RF(c),RF,B.U.KS,Scholar From
  the Stars 12.00
30 RF(c),RF,V:Grodd & Giganta . . 12.00
31 RF(c),RF,A:Black Orchid. 15.00
32 KS(c),KS,A:Scarecrow 10.00
33 RF(c),RF,V:Menagerie Man . . . 10.00
34 RF(c)RF,The Creature That
  Slept a Million Years. 10.00
35 RT,Circus o/t Super Stars 10.00
36 RF(c),RF,A:Plastic Man
  & Woozy 10.00
37 RF(c),RF,A:Supergirl;
  B.U. A:Jack O'Lantern 10.00
38 RF(c),RF,V:Grax;
  B.U. A:Serpah 10.00
39 RF(c),RF,A:Overlord;
  B.U. A:Wonder Twins 10.00
40 RF(c),RF,V:The Monacle;
  B.U. Jack O'Lantern 10.00
41 RF(c),RF,V:Toyman;
  B.U. A:Seraph 10.00
42 RT,A:Flora,V:Flame; B.U.Wonder
  Twins' Christmas Special. 10.00
43 KS(c),RT,V:Futuro; B.U.JSon
  A:Plastic Man 10.00
44 KS(c),RT,Peril o/t Forgotten
  Identities'; B.U.Jack O'Lantern 10.00
45 KS(c),RT,A:Bushmaster,
  Godiva, Rising Sun, Olympian,
  Little Mermaid, Wild Huntsman;
  B.U. Plastic Man,V: Sinestro . . 10.00
46 RT,V:The Conqueror;
  B.U. BO,Seraph. 10.00
47 KS(c),RT,A:Green Fury
  Aug., 1981. . . . . 10.00
TPB Super Friends, 176-page. . . . 15.00
TPB Truth,Justice&Peace(2003) . . 15.00

SUPERGIRL
[1st Regular Series]
Nov., 1972—Sept., 1974
1 Trail of the Madman';
  Superfashions From Fans;
  B:B.U. DG,Zatanna 90.00
2 BO(c)A:Prof.Allan,Bottle
  City of Kandor 40.00
3 BO(c),The Garden of Death . . 35.00
4 V:Super Scavager 40.00
5 BO(c),A:Superman,V:Dax; B.U.
  MA:Rep.Hawkman #4 . . . . 50.00
6 BO(c),Love & War 40.00
7 BO(c),A:Zatanna 40.00
8 BO(c),A:Superman,Green
  Lantern, Hawkman 50.00
9 BO(c),V:Sharkman. 40.00
10 A:Prey,V:Master Killer 40.00

[DARING NEW
ADVENTURES OF]
SUPERGIRL
[2nd Regular Series]
Nov., 1982
1 CI,BO,I:Psi; B:B.U.Lois Lane. . . . 3.00
2 CI,BO,C:Decay 3.00
3 CI,BO,V:Decay,Decay Day 3.00
4 CI,BO,V:The Gang. 3.00
5 CI,BO,V:The Gang. 3.00
6 CI,BO,V:The Gang. 3.00
7 CI,BO,V:The Gang. 3.00
8 CI,BO,A:Doom Patrol. 3.00
9 CI,BO,V:Reactron
  A:Doom Patrol. 3.00

10 CI,BO,Radiation Fever 3.00
11 CI,BO,V:Chairman. 3.00
12 CI,BO,V:Chairman 3.00
13 CI,BO,N:Supergirl,A:Superman
  V:Blackstarr 3.00
Becomes:

SUPERGIRL
Dec., 1983–Sept., 1984
14 GK(c),CI,BO,V:Blackstarr
  A:Rabbi Nathan Zuber. 3.00
15 CI,BO,V:Blackstarr,
  A:Blackstarr's Mom 3.00
16 KG/BO(c),CI,BO,
  A:Ambush Bug 3.00
17 CI/DG(c),CI,BO,V:Matrix
  Prime 3.00
18 DG(c),CI,BO, V:Kraken 3.00
19 EB/BO(c),CI,BO,Who Stole
  Supergirl's Life. 3.00
20 CI,BO,C:JLA, Teen Titans:
  Teh Parasite 3.00
21 EB/BO(c),EB,Kryptonite Man . . 3.00
22 EB(c),CI,BO,I Have Seen the
  Future & it is Me 3.00
23 EB(c),CI,BO,The Future
  Begins Today. 3.00
Spec.#1 JL/DG(c),GM,MovieAdapt . 3.00
Spec.#1 AT,Honda give-away 3.00

[Limited Series], 1994
1 KGa(c),B:RSt(s),JBr,O:Supergirl . 5.00
2 KGa(c),JBr 4.00
3 KGa(c),JBr,D:Clones 3.00
4 KGa(c),RSt(s),JBr,final Issue. . . . 3.00

SUPERGIRL
Sept., 1996
1 PDd(s),GFr,CaS, ... 11.00
1a 2nd printing 3.00
2 PDd(s),GFr,CaS,V:Chakat. 5.00
3 PDd(s),GFr,CaS,V:Grodd, Final
  Night tie-in 5.00
4 PDd(s),GFr,CaS,transformed into
  savage 4.00
5 PDd(s),GFr,CaS,Supergirl visits
  the Kents,V:Chemo 4.00
6 PDd(s),GFr,CaS, ... 4.00
7 PDd(s),GFr,CaS,Supergirl learns
  about Linda Danvers 4.00
8 PDd(s),GFr,CaS,Buzz gets date
  with Supergirl. 4.00
9 PDd(s),GFr,CaS,V:Tempus 4.00
10 PDd(s),Linda tries to relax 4.00
11 PDd(s),CaS,V:Silver Banshee . 4.00

Supergirl #4
© *DC Comics, Inc.*

12 PDd(s),Mattie possessed by
  Silver Banshee 4.00
13 CaS, 3 girls dreams invaded by
  incubus 3.00
14 PDa,CaS,Genesis tie-in 3.00
15 PDa,CaS,V:Extremists 3.00
16 PDa,CaS,F:Power Girl 3.00
17 PDa,CaS,L-Ron, Despero 3.00
18 PDa,CaS,V:Despero. 3.00
19 . . . . 3.00
20 PDa,CaS,Millennium Giants 3.00
21 PDa,CaS,Comet 3.00
22 PDa, ... 3.00
23 PDa,A:Steel 3.00
24 PDa,Avenging Angels x-over . . . 3.00
25 PDa,truth about Comet 3.00
26 PDd,truth discovered 3.00
27 PDd(s),V:Female Furies,pt.1 . . . 3.00
28 PDd(s),V:Female Furies,pt.2 . . . 3.00
29 PDd(s),V:Female Furies,pt.3 . . . 3.00
30 PDd(s),V:Matrix. 3.00
31 PDd(s),A:Superman 3.00
32 PDd(s),SeP,V:Mr.Carnivean 3.00
33 PDd(s),V:Mr.Carnivean 3.00
34 PDd(s),V:Parasite 3.00
35 PDd(s),V:Parasite, conol. 3.00
36 PDd(s),Hell's Angel's,pt.2 . . . . . 2.50
37 PDd(s),Hell's Angels,pt.4 . . . . . 2.50
38 PDd(s),Day of Judgment x-over . 2.50
39 PDd(s),F:Comet 2.50
40 PDd(s). 2.50
41 PDd(s),F:Ember,V:Satan Girl . . . 2.50
42 PDd(s),dates Dick Malverne 2.50
43 PDd(s),date become nightmare . 2.50
44 PDd(s),F:Dick Malverne,dying . . 2.50
45 PDd(s),F:Comet,V:Carnivore . . . 2.50
46 PDd(s),V:Comet,Carnivore 2.50
47 PDd(s),V:Carnivore. 2.50
48 PDd(s), ... 2.50
49 PDd(s),V:Carnivore. 2.50
50 PDd(s),48-pg. 4.00
51 PDd(s),to Metropolis, minus
  powers 2.50
52 PDd(s),V:Riot & Prankster 2.50
53 PDd(s),F:Green Lantern 2.50
54 PDd(s),F:Green Lantern 2.50
55 PDd(s),A:Lex Luthor 2.50
56 PDd(s),Buzz's daughter 2.50
57 PDd(s),Daddy's Little Girl 2.50
58 PDd(s),Buzz close to death 2.50
59 PDd(s),Our Worlds at War,tie-in . 2.50
60 PDd(s),Our Worlds at War,tie-in . 2.50
61 PDd(s),Our Worlds at War,tie-in . 2.50
62 PDd(s),A:Two-Face. 2.50
63 PDd(s),Joker:Last Laugh,tie-in . . 5.00
64 PDd(s),A:Lagoon Boy 2.50
65 PDd(s),hearing-impaired kids . . . 2.50
66 PDd(s),F:Demon Etrigan 2.50
67 PDd(s),F:Demon Etrigan 2.50
68 PDd(s),F:Mary Marvel. 4.00
69 PDd(s),F:Capt.Marvel,Jr. 5.00
70 PDd(s),F:Mary Marvel. 2.50
71 PDd(s),V:Tara. 2.50
72 PDd(s),V:Quetzlcoatl 2.50
73 PDd(s),Garden of Eden 2.50
74 PDd(s),Linda,Supergirl re-merge 2.50
75 PDd(s),EBe,spacecraft crashes 12.00
76 PDd(s),F:Superboy,Kara Zor-El 20.00
77 PDd(s),V:Fatalist. 8.00
78 PDd(s),V:Fatalist. 5.00
79 PDd(s),S.A:Supergirl. 5.00
80 PDd(s),V:Kara & Xenon 5.00
Ann.#1 Legends o/t Dead Earth . . . 3.00
Ann.#2 TPe,CDi,ACa, Pulp Heroes. 4.00
Spec.#1,000,000 PDd(s),DAb 2.00
GN Wings, Elseworlds, 48-page . . . 6.00
TPB PDd(s),GFr,rep.#1–#9 . . . . . . 15.00
TPB Many Happy Returns. 15.00
Spec. Supergirl/Lex Luthor JBr,
  F:Lex Luthor (1993). 4.00
Spec. Supergirl/Prysm Double-Shot
  DJu,TGb,Clv, x-over (1997) . . . 2.00

SUPERGIRL
Aug., 2005
0 JLb(s),IaC,NRd,F:Kara Zor-el . . . 3.00
1 JLb(s),IaC,NRd,V:Power Girl. . . . 3.00
1a variant (c). 3.00
2 JLb(s),IaC,NRd,V:Superboy . . . 3.00
3 JLb(s),IaC,NRd,Spying on Kara . 3.00
4 JLb(s),IaC,NRd,F:JLA 3.00
4a variant (c). 3.00
5 JLb(s),IaC,NRd,Mistress of Might 3.00
6 JLb(s),IaC,NRd,A:Batman, Wonder
    Woman, F:Superman 3.00
7 IaC,New Flamebird & Nightwing . 3.00
8 EBe,V:Power Girl. 3.00
9 IaC,Supergirl's boyfriend 3.00
10 IaC,New secret identity. 3.00
11 IaC,NRd,A:Outsiders. 3.00
12 IaC,NRd,A:Batgirl, League of
    Assassins 3.00
TPB Supergirl: Power 15.00

SUPER HEROES
BATTLE SUPER GORILLA
Winter, 1976
1 Superman Flash rep. 20.00

SUPERMAN
1939–86
1 JoS,O:Superman,reprints Action
    Comics #1-#4 . . . . 350,000.00
2 JoS,I:George Taylor 24,000.00
3 JoS,V:Superintendent
    Lyman 14,000.00
4 JoS,V:Lex Luthor 14,000.00
5 JoS,V:Lex Luthor 10,000.00
6 JoS,V:Brute' Bashby. 5,000.00
7 JoS,I:Perry White 4,800.00
8 JoS,V:Jackal 4,500.00
9 JoS,V:Joe Gatson 4,500.00
10 JoS,V:Lex Luthor 3,800.00
11 JoS,V:Rolf Zimba 3,500.00
12 JoS,V:Lex Luthor 3,500.00
13 JoS,I:Jimmy Olsen,V:Lex
    Luthor,The Archer. 3,500.00
14 JoS,I:Lightning Master. 5,500.00
15 JoS,V:The Evolution King . 3,500.00
16 JoS,V:Mr. Sinus 2,700.00
17 JoS,V:Lex Luthor,Lois Lane
    first suspects Clark
    is Superman 2,700.00
18 JoS,V:Lex Luthor 2,700.00
19 JoS,V:Funnyface,
    1st Imaginary story 2,700.00
20 JoS,V:Puzzler,Leopard . . . 2,700.00
21 JoS,V:Sir Gauntlet 2,000.00
22 JoS,V:Prankster 2,000.00
23 JoS,Propaganda story 2,000.00
24 V:Cobra King 3,000.00
25 Propaganda story 3,000.00
26 I:J.Wilbur Wolfingham,
    A:Mercury 3,000.00
27 V:Toyman 3,000.00
28 V:J.Wilbur Wolfingham,
    A:Hercules 3,000.00
29 V:Prankster 3,000.00
30 I&O:Mr. Mxyztplk 3,500.00
31 V:Lex Luthor. 1,500.00
32 V:Toyman 1,500.00
33 V:Mr. Mxyztplk. 1,500.00
34 V:Lex Luthor. 1,500.00
35 V:J.Wilbur Wolfingham. . . . 1,500.00
36 V:Mr. Mxyztplk. 1,500.00
37 V:Prankster,A:Sinbad. 1,500.00
38 V:Lex Luthor. 1,500.00
39 V:J.Wilbur Wolfingham. . . . 1,500.00
40 V:Mr. Mxyzptlk,A:Susie
    Thompkins 1,500.00
41 V:Prankster 1,200.00
42 V:J.Wilbur Wolfingham. . . . 1,200.00
43 V:Lex Luthor. 1,200.00

Superman #5
© DC Comics, Inc.

44 V:Toyman,A:Shakespeare . . 1,200.00
45 A:Hocus & Pocus,Lois Lane
    as Superwoman 1,200.00
46 V:Mr. Mxyzptlk,Lex Luthor,
    Superboy flashback 1,200.00
47 V:Toyman 1,200.00
48 V:Lex Luthor. 1,200.00
49 V:Toyman 1,200.00
50 V:Prankster 1,200.00
51 V:Mr. Mxyzptlk. 1,000.00
52 V:Prankster 1,000.00
53 WB,O:Superman 4,400.00
54 V:Wrecker 1,000.00
55 V:Prankster 1,000.00
56 V:Prankster 1,000.00
57 V:Lex Luthor. 1,000.00
58 V:Tiny Trix 1,000.00
59 V:Mr.Mxyzptlk. 1,000.00
60 V:Toyman 1,000.00
61 I:Kryptonite,V:Prankster. . . . 2,000.00
62 V:Mr.Mxyzptlk,A:Orson
    Welles. 1,000.00
63 V:Toyman 1,000.00
64 V:Prankster 1,000.00
65 V:Mala,Kizo and U-Ban 1,000.00
66 V:Prankster 1,000.00
67 A:Perry Como,I:Brane
    Taylor 1,000.00
68 V:Lex Luthor. 1,000.00
69 V:Prankster,A:Inspector
    Erskine Hawkins. 1,000.00
70 V:Prankster 1,000.00
71 V:Lex Luthor 900.00
72 V:Prankster. 900.00
72a giveaway 1,100.00
73 Flashback story. 900.00
74 V:Lex Luthor 900.00
75 V:Prankster. 900.00
76 A:Batman, Superman &
    Batman reveal each other's
    identities 2,800.00
77 A:Pocahontas 900.00
78 V:Kryptonian snagriff,
    A:Lana Lang 900.00
79 V:Lex Luthor,A:Inspector
    Erskine Hawkins 900.00
80 A:Halk Kar. 900.00
81 V:Lex Luthor 900.00
82 V:Mr. Mxyzptlk. 800.00
83 V:The Brain 800.00
84 Time-travel story 800.00
85 V:Lex Luthor 800.00
86 V:Mr.Mxyzptlk 800.00
87 WB,V:The Thing from
    40,000 AD 800.00

88 WB,V:Lex Luthor,Toyman,
    Prankster team 900.00
89 V:Lex Luthor 800.00
90 V:Lex Luthor 900.00
91 The Superman Stamp. 800.00
92 Goes back to 12th Century
    England 800.00
93 V:The Thinker 800.00
94 Clark Kent's Hillbilly Bride. . . . 800.00
95 A:Susie Thompkins 800.00
96 V:Mr. Mxyzptlk. 600.00
97 Superboy's Last Day In
    Smallville 600.00
98 Clark Kent, Outlaw!. 600.00
99 V:Midnite gang 600.00
100 F:Superman-Substitute
    Schoolteacher. 3,000.00
101 A:Lex Luthor 550.00
102 I:Superman Stock
    Company 550.00
103 A:Mr.Mxyzptlk 550.00
104 F:Clark Kent,Jailbird 550.00
105 A:Mr.Mxyzptlk 550.00
106 A:Lex Luthor 575.00
107 F:Superman In 30th century
    (pre-Legion). 550.00
108 I:Perry White Jr. 550.00
109 I:Abner Hokum 550.00
110 A:Lex Luthor 550.00
111 Becomes Mysto the Great. . . 550.00
112 A:Lex Luthor 550.00
113 A:Jor-El 550.00
114 V:The Great Mento 550.00
115 V:The Organizer 550.00
116 Return to Smallville 550.00
117 A:Lex Luthor 550.00
118 F:Jimmy Olsen 550.00
119 A:Zoll Orr. 550.00
120 V:Gadget Grim 550.00
121 I:XL-49 (Futureman) 400.00
122 In the White House. 400.00
123 CS,pre-Supergirl tryout
    A:Jor-El & Lara 425.00
124 F:Lois Lane 400.00
125 F:Superman College Story . 400.00
126 F:Lois Lane 400.00
127 WB,I&O:Titano 425.00
128 V:Vard & Boka 400.00
129 WB,I&O:Lori Lemaris 425.00
130 A:Krypto,the Superdog 400.00
131 A:Mr. Mxyzptlk. 400.00
132 A:Batman & Robin 400.00
133 F:Superman Joins Army . . . 400.00
134 A:Supergirl & Krypto 400.00
135 A:Lori Lemaris,Mr.Mxyzptlk. . 400.00
136 O:Discovery Kryptonite 400.00
137 CS,I:Super-Menace 400.00

Superman #95 © DC Comics, Inc.

138 A:Titano,Lori Lemaris 400.00
139 CS,O:Red Kryptonite 400.00
140 WB,I:Bizarro Jr,Bizarro
    Supergirl,Blue Kryptonite. . . . 400.00
141 I:Lyla Lerrol,A:Jor-EL
    & Lara 350.00
142 WB,CS,A:Al Capone. 350.00
143 WB,F:Bizarro meets
    Frankenstein 350.00
144 O:Superboy's 1st Public
    Appearance 350.00
145 F:April Fool's Issue 350.00
146 F:Superman's life story 350.00
147 CS,I:Adult Legion 350.00
148 CS,V:Mxyzptlk. 300.00
149 CS:A:Luthor,C:JLA 300.00
150 CS,KS,V:Mxyzptlk 350.00
150 CS,KS,V:Mxyzptlk 350.00
151 CS 350.00
152 A:Legion 350.00
153 CS 350.00
154 CS,V:Mzyzptlk. 350.00
155 WB,CS,V:Cosmic Man 350.00
156 CS,A:Legion,Batman 350.00
157 CS,I:Gold kryptonite 350.00
158 CS,I:Nightwing&Flamebird . 350.00
159 CS,Imaginary Tale
    F:Lois Lane 350.00
160 CS,F:Perry White 350.00
161 D:Ma & Pa Kent 350.00
162 A:Legion 350.00
163 CS 350.00
164 CS,Luthor,I:Lexor 350.00
165 CS,A:Saturn Woman 350.00
166 CS 350.00
167 CS,I:Ardora,Brainiac 375.00
168 CS 300.00
169 Great DC Contest 300.00
170 CS,A:J.F.Kennedy,Luthor . . 300.00
171 CS,Mxyzptlk 300.00
172 CS,Luthor,Brainiac 300.00
173 CS,A:Batman 300.00
174 Mxyzptlk 300.00
175 CS,Luthor 300.00
176 CS,Green Kryptonite. 300.00
177 Fortress of Solitude. 300.00
178 CS, Red Kryptonite 300.00
179 CS,Clark Kent in Marines . . 300.00
180 CS 300.00
181 Superman 2965 . . . . 300.00
182 CS,Toyman 300.00
183 giant 300.00
184 Secrets of the Fortress 275.00
185 JM,Superman's Achilles
    Heel 275.00
186 CS,The Two Ghosts of
    Superman. 275.00
187 giant 275.00
188 V:Zunial,The Murder Man . . 275.00
189 WB,The Mystery of Krypton's
    Second Doom. 275.00
190 WB,I:Amalak. 275.00
191 The Prisoner of Demon 275.00
192 CS,Imaginary Story,
    I:Superman Jr. 275.00
193 giant 275.00
194 CS,Imaginary,A:Supes Jr. . . 275.00
195 CS,V:Amalak. 275.00
196 WB,reprint. 275.00
197 giant 275.00
198 CS,F:The Real Clark Kent . . 275.00
199 CS,F:Superman/Flash race,
    A:JLA. 500.00
200 WB,A:Brainiac 225.00
201 CS,F:Clark Kent Abandons
    Superman. 150.00
202 A:Bizarro,(giant size). 200.00
203 F:When Superman Killed His
    Friends 150.00
204 NA(c),RA,A:Lori Lemaras . . 150.00
205 NA(c),I:Black Zero 150.00

206 NA(c),F:The Day Superman
    Became An Assistant 150.00
207 CS,F:The Case Of the
    Collared Crimefighter 200.00
208 NA(c),CS. 150.00
209 CS,F:The Clark Kent
    Monster 150.00
210 CS,F:Clark Kent's Last Rites 150.00
211 CS,RA 150.00
212 giant 200.00
213 CS,JA,V:Luthor,C:Brainiac 5. 150.00
214 NA(c),CS,JA,F:The Ghosts
    That Haunted Superman . . . 150.00
215 NA(c),CS,JA,V:Luthor,
    Imaginary Story 150.00
216 JKu(c),RA,Superman in Nam 150.00
217 CS,A:Mr.Mxyzptlk 150.00
218 CS,JA,A:Mr.Mxyzptlk 150.00
219 CS,F:Clark Kent-Hero,
    Superman Public Enemy. . . . 150.00
220 CS,A:Flash 150.00
221 CS,F:The Two Ton
    Superman 150.00
222 giant 200.00
223 CS,A:Supergirl 100.00
224 CS,Imaginary Story. 100.00
225 CS,F:The Secret of the
    Super Imposter 100.00
226 CS,F:When Superman Became
    King Kong 100.00
227 Krypton,(giant) 150.00
228 CS,DA 100.00
229 WB,CS 100.00
230 CS,DA,Luthor 100.00
231 CS,DA,Luthor 100.00
232 F:Krypton,(giant) 150.00
233 CS,MA,I:Quarrum 100.00
234 NA(c),CS,MA 100.00
235 CS,MA. 100.00
236 CS,MA,DG,A:Green Arrow . . 100.00
237 NA(c),CS,MA 100.00
238 CS,MA,GM 100.00
239 giant 150.00
240 CS,DG,MK,A:I-Ching. 75.00
241 CS,MA,A:Wonder Woman . . . 75.00
242 CS,MA,A:Wonder Woman . . . 75.00
243 CS,MA. 75.00
244 CS,MA. 75.00
245 100 pg reprints 75.00
246 CS,MA,RB,I.S.T.A.R. Labs . . 75.00
247 CS,MA,Guardians o/Universe. 75.00
248 CS,MA,A:Luthor,I:Galactic
    Golem 75.00
249 CS,MA,DD,NA,I:Terra-Man. . 100.00
250 CS,MA,Terraman 75.00
251 CS,MA,RB. 75.00

Superman #289 © DC Comics Inc.

252 NA(c),rep.100pgs 75.00
253 CS,MA. 75.00
254 CS,MA,NA. 100.00
255 CS,MA,DG 50.00
256 CS,MA. 50.00
257 CS,MA,DD,DG,A:Tomar-Re . . 50.00
258 CS,MA,DC 50.00
259 CS,MA,A:Terra-Man 50.00
260 CS,DC,I:Valdemar. 50.00
261 CS,MA,V:Star Sapphire 50.00
262 CS,MA. 50.00
263 CS,MA,DD,FMc 50.00
264 DC,CS,I:Steve Lombard 50.00
265 CS,MA. 50.00
266 CS,MA,DD,V:Snowman 50.00
267 CS,MA,BO 50.00
268 CS,BO,DD,MA,A:Batgirl 50.00
269 CS,MA. 50.00
270 CS,MA,V:Valdemar. 50.00
271 CS,BO,DG,V:Brainiac 50.00
272 100pg.reprints 75.00
273 CS,DG. 50.00
274 CS 50.00
275 CS,DG,FMc 50.00
276 CS,BO,I&O:Captain Thunder . 50.00
277 CS 50.00
278 CS,BO,Terraman,100page . . 100.00
279 CS,Batgirl,Batman 35.00
280 CS,BO 35.00
281 CS,BO,I:Vartox 35.00
282 CS,KS,N:Luthor 35.00
283 CS,BO,Mxyzptlk 35.00
284 CS,BO,100p reprint 75.00
285 CS,BO. 35.00
286 CS,BO. 35.00
287 CS,BO,R:Krypto 35.00
288 CS,BO. 35.00
289 CS,BO,JL 35.00
290 CS,V:Mxyzptlk. 35.00
291 CS,BO. 35.00
292 CS,BO,AM,O:Luthor 35.00
293 CS,BO. 35.00
294 CS,JL,A:Brain Storm 35.00
295 CS,BO. 35.00
296 CS,BO,Identity Crisis #1. . . . . 35.00
297 CS,BO,Identity Crisis #2. . . . . 35.00
298 CS,BO,Identity Crisis #3. . . . . 35.00
299 CS,BO,Identity Crisis #4
    A:Luthor,Brainiac,Bizarro. . . . 35.00
300 CS,BO,2001,anniversary 65.00
301 BO,JL,V:Solomon Grundy. . . . 25.00
302 JL,BO,V:Luthor,A:Atom. 25.00
303 CS,BO,I:Thunder&Lightning . . 25.00
304 CS,BO,V:Parasite 25.00
305 CS,BO,V:Toyman 25.00
306 CS,BO,V:Bizarro 25.00
307 NA(c),JL,FS,A:Supergirl 25.00
308 NA(c),JL,FS,A:Supergirl 25.00
309 JL,FS,A:Supergirl 25.00
310 CS,V:Metallo 25.00
311 CS,FS,A:Flash 25.00
312 CS,FS,A:Supergirl. 25.00
313 NA(c),CS,DA,A:Supergirl 25.00
314 NA(c),CS,DA,A:Gr.Lantern . . . 25.00
315 CS,DA,V:Blackrock. 12.00
316 CS,DA,V:Metallo 12.00
317 NA(c),CS,DA,V:Metallo 12.00
318 CS 12.00
319 CS,V:Solomon Grundy 12.00
320 CS,V:Solomon Grundy 12.00
321 CS,V:Parasite 15.00
322 CS,V:Solomon Grundy 15.00
323 CS,DA,I:Atomic Skull 15.00
324 CS,A:Atomic Skull. 12.00
325 CS 12.00
326 CS,V:Blackrock. 12.00
327 CS,KS,V:Kobra,C:JLA 12.00
328 CS,KS,V:Kobra 12.00
329 KS,CS 12.00
330 CS,F:glasses explained 12.00
331 CS,I:Master Jailer 12.00
332 CS,V:Master Jailer 12.00

333 CS,V:Bizarro 12.00
334 CS 7.00
335 CS,W:Mxyzptlk 7.00
336 CS,V:Rose And Thorn 7.00
337 CS,A:Brainiac,Bizarro 7.00
338 CS,F:Kandor enlarged 7.00
339 CS,I:N.R.G.X 7.00
340 CS,V:N.R.G.X 7.00
341 CS,F:Major Disaster 7.00
342 CS,V:Chemo 7.00
343 CS 7.00
344 CS,A:Phantom Stranger 7.00
345 CS,When time ran backward . . 7.00
346 CS,Streak of Bad Luck 7.00
347 JL 7.00
348 CS 7.00
349 CS,V:Mxyzptlk 7.00
350 CS,Clark Kent's Vanishing
    Classmate 6.00
351 CS,JL,A:Mxyzptlk 6.00
352 CS,RB 6.00
353 CS,origin 6.00
354 CS,JSon,I:Superman 2020 . . . . 6.00
355 CS,JSon,F:Superman 2020 . . . 6.00
356 CS,V:Vartox 6.00
357 CS,DCw,F:Superman 2020 . . . 6.00
358 CS,DG,DCw 6.00
359 CS 6.00
360 CS,AS,F:World of Krypton 6.00
361 CS,AS 6.00
362 CS,KS,DA 6.00
363 CS,RB,C:Luthor 6.00
364 GP(c),RB,AS 6.00
365 CS,KS 6.00
366 CS,KS 6.00
367 CS,GK,F:World of Krypton 6.00
368 CS,AS 6.00
369 RB,FMc,V:Parasite 6.00
370 CS,KS,FMc,A:Chemo 6.00
371 CS 6.00
372 CS,GK,F:Superman 2021 . . . . 6.00
373 CS,V:Vartox 6.00
374 GK(c),CS,DA,KS,V:Vartox 6.00
375 CS,DA,GK,V:Vartox 6.00
376 CS,DA,CI,BO,SupergirlPrev . . . 5.00
377 GK(c),CS,V:Terra-Man 5.00
378 CS 5.00
379 CS,V:Bizarro 5.00
380 CS 5.00
381 GK(c),CS 5.00
382 GK(c),CS 5.00
383 CS 5.00
384 GK(c),CS 5.00
385 GK(c),CS,V:Luthor 5.00
386 GK(c),CS,V:Luthor 5.00

387 GK(c),CS 5.00
388 GK(c),CS 5.00
389 GK(c),CS 5.00
390 GK(c),CS,V:Vartox 5.00
391 GK(c),CS,V:Vartox 5.00
392 GK(c),CS,V:Vartox 5.00
393 IN,DG,V:Master Jailer 5.00
394 CS,V:Valdemar 5.00
395 CS,V:Valdemar 5.00
396 CS 5.00
397 EB,V:Kryptonite Man 5.00
398 CS,AS,DJ 5.00
399 CS,BO,EB 5.00
400 HC(c),FM,AW,JO,JSo,MR,
    TA,WP,MK,KJ,giant 8.00
401 CS,BO,V:Luthor 5.00
402 CS,BO,WB 5.00
403 CS,BO,AS 5.00
404 CI,BO,V:Luthor 5.00
405 KS,KK,AS,F:Super-Batman . . . 5.00
406 IN,AS,KK 5.00
407 IN,V:Mxyzptlk 5.00
408 CS,AW,JRu,F:Nuclear
    Holocaust 5.00
409 CS,AW,KS 5.00
410 CS,AW,V:Luthor 5.00
411 CS,MA,F:End Earth-Prime 5.00
412 CS,AW,V:Luthor 5.00
413 CS,AW,V:Luthor 5.00
414 CS,AW,Crisis tie-in 5.00
415 CS,AW,Crisis,W:Super Girl 6.00
416 CS,AW,Luthor 5.00
417 CS,V:Martians 5.00
418 CS,V:Metallo 5.00
419 CS,V:Iago 5.00
420 CS,F:Nightmares 5.00
421 CS,V:Mxyzptlk 5.00
422 BB(c),CS,TY,LMa,V:Werewolf. . 5.00
423 AMo(s),CS,GP,F:Last
    Superman 12.00
Ann.#1 I:Supergirl Rep 1,700.00
Ann.#2 I&O:Titano 650.00
Ann.#3 I:Legion 450.00
Ann.#4 O:Legion 350.00
Ann.#5 A:Krypton 275.00
Ann.#6 A:Legion 275.00
Ann.#7 O:Superman,Silver Anniv. 200.00
Ann.#8 F:Secret origins 175.00
Ann.#9 GK(c),ATh,TA,CS,
    A:Batman 7.00
Ann.#10 CS,MA,F:Sword of
    Superman 5.00
Ann.#11 AMo(s),DGb,A:Batman,
    Robin,Wonder Woman 6.00
Ann.#12 BB(c),AS,A:Lex Luthor,
    Last War Suit 4.00
Game Give-away 10.00
Giveaway CS,AT 2.25
Pizza Hut 1977 . . . . 6.00
Radio Shack 1980 JSw,DG 5.00
Radio Shack 1981 CS 5.00
Radio Shack 1982 CS 5.00
Spec.#1 GK 3.50
Spec.#2 GK,V:Brainiac 3.50
Spec.#3 IN,V:Amazo 3.50
Superman III Movie,CS 2.50
Superman IV Movie,DH,DG,FMc . . . 2.50
Becomes:

ADVENTURES OF
SUPERMAN
1987

424 JOy,I:Man O'War 6.00
425 JOy,Man O'War 3.00
426 JOy,Legends,V:Apokolips 3.00
427 JOy,V:Qurac 3.00
428 JOy,V:Qurac,I:JerryWhite 3.00
429 JOy,V:Concussion 3.00
430 JOy,V:Fearsome Five 3.00
431 JOy,A:Combattor 3.00
432 JOy,I:Jose Delgado 3.00
433 JOy,V:Lex Luthor 3.00

434 JOy,I:Gang Buster 3.00
435 JOy,A:Charger 3.00
436 JOy,Millennium x-over 5.00
437 JOy,Millennium X-over 3.50
438 JOy,N:Brainiac 3.00
439 JOy,R:Superman Robot 3.00
440 JOy,A:Batman,Wond.Woman . . 3.00
441 JOy,V:Mr.Mxyzptlk 3.00
442 JOy,V:Dreadnaught,A:JLI 3.00
443 JOy,DHz,I:Husque 3.00
444 JOy,Supergirl SagaPt.2 . . . . . . 3.00
445 JOy,V:Brainiac 3.00
446 JOy,A:Gangbuster,
    A:Luthor's Old Costume 3.00
447 JOy,A:Gangbuster 3.00
448 JOy,I:Dubbilex,A:Gangbuster . . 3.00
449 JOy,Invasion X-over 3.00
450 JOy,Invasion X-over 3.00
451 JOy,Superman in Space 3.00
452 DJu,V:Wordbringer 3.00
453 JOy,DJu,A:Gangbuster 3.00
454 JOy,DJu,I:New Mongul 4.00
455 DJu,ATb,A:Eradicator 3.50
456 DJu,ATb,V:Turmoil 3.50
457 DJu,V:Intergang 3.50
458 DJu,KJ,R:Elastic Lad
    (Jimmy Olsen) 3.50
459 DJu,V:Eradicator 3.50
460 DJu,NKu,V:Eradicator 3.50
461 DJu,GP,V:Eradicator 3.50
462 DJu,ATb,Homeless
    Christmas Story 3.50
463 DJu,ATb,Superman Races
    Flash 3.50
464 DJu,ATb,Day of Krypton
    Man #2,A:Lobo 6.00
465 DJu,ATb,Day of Krypton
    Man #5,V:Draaga 3.00
466 DJu,DG,V:Team Excalibur
    Astronauts,I:Hank Henshaw
    (becomes Cyborg Superman) . . 4.50
467 DJu,ATb,A:Batman 3.00
468 DJu,ATb,Man Of Steel's
    Journal,V:Hank Henshaw 3.00
469 DJu,ATb,V:Dreadnaught 3.00
470 DJu,ATb,Soul Search #3,
    D:Jerry White 3.00
471 CS,Sinbad Contract #2 . . . . 3.00
472 DJu,ATb,Krisis of Krimson
    Kryptonite #2 . . . . 3.00
473 DJu,ATb,A:Green Lantern,
    Guy Gardner 3.00
474 DJu,ATb,Drunk Driving issue . . 3.00
475 DJu,ATb,V:Kilgrave,Sleez 3.00

Superman #299
© DC Comics, Inc.

The Adventures of Superman #499
© DC Comics, Inc.

Adventures of Superman #516
© DC Comics Inc.

All comics prices listed are for *Near Mint* condition.

648 KIK,Infinite Crisis tie-in 2.50
649 KIK,This is your life, Superman 2.50
Becomes:

SUPERMAN
650 KBk,Up,Up & Away,pt.1,x-over . 2.50
651 KBk,Up,Up & Away,pt.3,x-over . 2.50
652 KBk,Up,Up & Away,pt.5,x-over . 3.00
653 KBk,Up,Up & Away,pt.7,x-over . 3.00
654 KBk,CPa,V:Intergang 3.00
655 KBk,CPa,Time-traveling magic . 3.00
656 KBk,CPa,V:Subjekt-17 . . . . 3.00
657 KBk,CPa, End of Civilization . . 3.00
658 KBk,CPa, End of Civilization . . 3.00
Ann.#1 JSn(c),DJu,I:Word Bringer . 3.00
Ann.#2 CS/JBy,KGa/DG,BMc,
    A:L.E.G.I.O.N.'90 (Lobo) 4.00
Ann.#3 BHi,JRu,DG,
    Armageddon 2001. . . . . 3.00
Ann.#4 BMc,A:Lobo,Guy Gardner,
    Eclipso tie-in 3.00
Ann.#5 TG,I:Sparx 2.75
Ann.#6 MMi(c),Elseworlds Story . . 3.00
Ann.#7 Year One Story 4.00
Ann.#8 Legends o/t Dead Earth . . . 3.00
Ann.#9 Pulp Heroes (Western) 4.00
Spec.#1,000,000 ALa&DAn(s)LMa,
    A:Teen Titans, V:Solaris 3.00
GN Vol. 1 Up, Up and Away 7.00
GN Vol. 2 Never-Ending Battle 7.00
TPB Ruin Revealed 15.00
TPB Up, Up and Away 15.00
TPB Infinite City 18.00

SUPERMAN'S BUDDY
1954
1 w/costume, giveaway 2,000.00
1 w/out costume, giveaway . . . 1,000.00

SUPERMAN'S
CHRISTMAS ADVENTURE
1 (1940) giveaway 6,000.00
2 (1944) giveaway 1,500.00

SUPERMAN AND THE
GREAT CLEVELAND FIRE
1948
1 for Hospital Fund, giveaway . . 800.00

SUPERMAN (miniature)
1942
1 Py-Co-Pay Tooth Powder
    Give- Away 1,000.00
2 CS,Superman Time Capsule . . 600.00
3 CS,Duel in Space 500.00
4 CS,Super Show in Metropolis . 500.00

SUPERMAN RECORD
COMIC
1966
1 w/record 250.00
1 w/out record 150.00

SUPERMAN
SPECTACULAR
1982
1 A:Luthor & Terra-Man 2.50

SUPERMAN-TIM
STORE PAMPHLETS
1942
Superman-Tim store Monthly Membership Pamphlets, stories, games
    (1942), each 1,500.00
    (1943), each 500.00
    (1944), each 475.00
    (1945), each 450.00

Superman Tim Stamp Album 1948
© DC Comics, Inc.

(1946), color(c) each 550.00
(1947), color(c) each 350.00
(1948), color(c) each 300.00
(1949), color(c) each 300.00
(1950), color(c) each 350.00
Superman-Tim stamp albums,
    (1946) 400.00
    (1947) Superman story 500.00
    (1948) 400.00

SUPERMAN WORKBOOK
1945
1 rep. Superman #14 . . . . 1,300.00

SUPERMAN
[2nd Regular Series], 1987
1 JBy,TA,I:Metallo 6.00
2 JBy,TA,V:Luthor 3.00
3 JBy,TA,Legends tie-in 3.00
4 JBy,KK,V:Bloodsport 3.00
5 JBy,KK,V:Host 3.00
6 JBy,KK,V:Host 3.00
7 JBy,KK,V:Rampage 3.00
8 JBy,KK,A:Superboy,Legion 3.00
9 JBy,KK,V:Joker 5.00
10 JBy,KK,V:Rampage. 3.00
11 JBy,KK,V:Mr.Mxyzptlk 3.00
12 JBy,KK,A:Lori Lemerias 3.00
13 JBy,KK,Millennium 3.00
14 JBy,KK,A:Green Lantern. 3.00
15 JBy,KK,I:New Prankster 3.00
16 JBy,KK,A:Prankster. 4.00
17 JBy,KK,O:Silver Banshee 3.00
18 MMi,KK,A:Hawkman 3.00
19 JBy,V:Skyhook 3.00
20 JBy,KK,A:Doom Patrol 3.00
21 JBy,A:Supergirl 4.00
22 JBy,A:Supergirl 3.00
23 MMi,CR,O:Silver Banshee 3.00
24 KGa,V:Rampage 3.00
25 KGa,V:Brainiac 3.00
26 KGa,BBr,V:Baron Sunday. 3.00
27 KGa,BBr,V:Guardian. 3.00
28 KGa,BBr,Supes Leaves Earth . . 3.00
29 DJu,BBr,V:Word Bringer 3.00
30 KGa,DJu,A:Lex Luthor 3.00
31 DJu,PCu,V:Mxyzptlk 3.00
32 KGa,V:Mongul. 3.00
33 KGa,A:Cleric 3.00
34 KGa,V:Skyhook. 3.00
35 CS,KGa,A:Brainiac 3.00
36 JOy,V:Prankster 3.00
37 JOy,A:Guardian. 3.00

38 JOy,Jimmy Olsen Vanished 3.00
39 JOy,KGa,V:Husque. 3.00
40 JOy,V:Four Armed Terror 3.00
41 JOy,Day of Krypton Man #1,
    A:Lobo 3.50
42 JOy,Day of Krypton Man #4,
    V:Draaga 3.50
43 JOy,V:Krypton Man 2.50
44 JOy,A:Batman. 2.50
45 JOy,F:Jimmy Olsen's Dairy. 2.50
46 DJu,JOy,A:Jade,Obsidian,
    I:New Terra-Man 2.50
47 JOy,Soul Search #2,V:Blaze. . . . 2.50
48 CS,Sinbad Contract #1. . . . . 2.50
49 JOy,Krisis of K.Kryptonite#1 . . . . 3.00
50 JBy,KGa,DJu,JOy,BBr,CS,Krisis
    of Krimson Kryptonite #4,
    Clark Proposes To Lois 6.00
50a 2nd printing 2.50
51 JOy,I:Mr.Z 2.50
52 KGa,V:Terra-Man 2.50
53 JOy,Superman reveals i.d. 3.50
53a 2nd Printing. 2.50
54 JOy,KK,Time & Time Again#3. . . 2.50
55 JOy,KK,Time & Time Again#6. . . 2.50
56 EH,KK,Red Glass Trilogy#1 . . . . 2.50
57 JOy,DJu,BBr,ATi,JBg,BMc,TG,
    Revenge o/t Krypton Man #2 . . 3.50
58 DJu,BBr,I:Bloodhounds. 2.50
59 DJu,BBr,A:Linear Men 2.50
60 DJu,EB,I:Agent Liberty,
    V:Intergang 2.50
61 DJu,BBr,A:Waverider,
    V:Linear Men 2.50
62 DJu,BBr,Blackout #4,A:Mr.Z . . . 2.50
63 DJu,A:Aquaman 2.50
64 JG,Christmas issue 2.50
65 DJu,Panic in the Sky#2,
    I:New Justice League 3.50
66 DJu,Panic in the Sky#6,
    V:Brainiac 8.00
67 DJu,Aftermath. 2.50
68 DJu,V:Deathstroke 2.50
69 WS(c),DJu,A:Agent Liberty 2.50
70 DJu,BBr,A:Robin,V:Vampires . . . 2.50
71 DJu,Blaze/Satanus War 2.50
72 DJu,Crisis at Hand#2 . . . . 2.50
73 DJu,A:Waverider,V:Linear
    Men,C:Doomsday 5.00
73a 2nd printing 2.50
74 DJu,V:Doomsday,A:JLA 8.00
74a 2nd printing. 2.00
75 DJu,V:Doomsday,D:Superman,
    Collectors Ed. 25.00
75a newstand Ed. 9.00

Superman 2nd Series #82
© DC Comics, Inc.

Superman, 2nd Series #85
© DC Comics Inc.

75b 2nd printing 4.00
75c 3rd printing 2.50
75d 4th Printing 2.50
75e Platinum Ed. 65.00
76 DJu,BBr,Funeral for Friend#4 . . . 3.00
77 DJu,BBr,Funeral for Friend#8 . . . 3.00
78 DJu,BBr,Reign of Supermen#3,
    Die-Cut(c),Mini poster,F:Cyborg
    Supes,A:Doomsday 3.00
78a Newsstand Ed. 2.50
79 DJu,BBr,Memorial Service for
    Clark 3.00
80 DJu,BBr,Coast City Blows up,
    V:Mongul 4.00
81 DJu,O:Cyborg Superman 3.50
82 DJu,Chromium(c),A:All Supermen,
    V:Cyborg Superman 15.00
82a Newstand Ed. 5.00
83 DJu,A:Batman. 3.00
84 DJu,V:Toyman. 3.00
85 DJu,V:Toyman. 3.00
86 DJu,A:Sun Devils 3.00
87 DJu(c&s),SI,JRu,Bizzaro's
    World#1, R:Bizarro 3.00
88 DJu(c&s),SI,JRu,Bizzaro's
    World#5, D:Bizarro 3.00
89 DJu(c&s),V:Cadmus Project 3.00
90 DJu(c&s),Battle for
    Metropolis#3 . . . . 3.00
91 DJu(c&s),Fall of Metropolis#3. . . 3.00
92 Massacre in Metropolis. 3.00
93 Zero Hour,A:Batman. 3.00
94 Conduit 3.00
95 Brainiac. 3.00
96 Virtual Reality 3.00
97 Shadow Dragon 3.00
98 R:Shadow Strike 3.00
99 R:Agent Liberty 3.00
100 BBr,DJu,Death of C.Kent,pt.1 . . 3.50
100a Collectors Edition 4.00
101 Death of Clark Kent,pt.5
    [New Miraweb format begins] . . 3.00
102 DJu,A:Captain Marvel. 3.00
103 O:Arclight 3.00
104 Revenge of Apokolips. 3.00
105 A:Green Lantern 3.00
106 DJu,RF,The Trial of Superman . 3.00
107 DJu,RF,The Trial of Superman . 3.00
108 DJu,RF,The Trial of Superman . 3.00
109 DJu,RF,V:Kill Fee 3.00
110 F:Plastic Man 3.00
111 DJu,RF,Cat Grant in charge . . . 3.00
112 DJu,RF,Lois & Clark 3.00
113 DJu(s),RF,JRu, ... 3.00

114 DJu(s),RF,JRu,A:Brainiac 3.00
115 DJu(s),RF,JRu,Lois leaves
    Metropolis 3.00
116 DJu(s),RF,JRu,battle city siga
    concl., V:Daxamite,B.U. Teen
    Titans preview 3.00
117 DJu(s),RF,JRu,V. his own
    robots, Final Night tie-in 3.00
118 DJu(s),RF,JRu,F:time-lost
    Legion of Super Heroes 3.00
119 DJu(s),RF,JRu,A:Legion of
    Super Heroes 3.00
120 DJu(s),RF,JRu, ... 3.00
121 DJu(s),RF,JRu,They Call it
    Suicide Slum 3.00
122 DJu(s),RF,JRu,Lois visits
    Fortress of Solitude 3.00
123 DJu(s),RF,Jru,Superman gets
    New Costume 4.00
123a collector's edition, glow-in-
    the-dark cover, ... 5.00
124 DJu(s),RF,JRu,A:Scorn, prince
    of Kandor 2.50
125 DJu(s),RF,JRu,Kandor and
    Metropolis,A:Atom 2.50
126 DJu(s),RF,JRu,A:Batman 2.50
127 DJu(s),RF,JRu,F:Jimmy Olsen . 2.50
128 DJu(s),RF,JRu, Genesis tie-in . 2.50
129 DJu(s),PR,JRu,A:Scorn 2.50
130 DJu(s),RF,JRu,dragon's tooth. . 2.50
131 DJu(s),RF,JRu,Luthor &
    Contessa's kid 2.50
132 DJu,RF,JRu,Red/Blue x-over . . 2.50
133 DJu,RF,JRu,Millennium Guard . 2.50
134 DJu,RF,JRu,Millennium Giants . 2.50
135 DJu,RF,JRu,aftermath. 3.50
136 DJu,PR,JRu,The Superman
    of 2999 A.D., pt.1 . . . . 2.50
137 DJu,PR,JRu,2000 AD,pt.2 . . . . . 2.50
138 DJu,PR,JRu,2999 AD,pt.3 . . . . . 2.50
139 DJu(s),JSn,JRu,V:Dominus . . . 2.50
140 RMz(s),TGb,TP,City of the
    Future, pt.3 x-over. 2.50
141 DJu(s),SEa,JRu,I:Outburst 2.50
142 DJu(s),JRu,F:Outburst 2.50
143 DJu(s),SEp,JRu,. 2.50
144 DJu(s),SEp,JRu,V:Lex Luthor . 2.50
145 DJu(s),SEp,JRu,hate mail 2.50
146 DJu(s),SEp,JRu,V:Toyman 2.50
147 RMz(s),TGb,BAn,A:JLA,pt.1 . . . 2.50
148 DJu(s),SEp,JRu, ... 2.50
149 RF,SB,Strange Visitor,pt.1 . . . . 2.50
150 DJu(s),SEp,JRu,48-pg. 3.50
150a foil cover 4.50
151 JLb,MMK,Faster than a
    speeding bullet 3.00
152 JLb,MMK,. 2.50
153 JLb,MMK,V:Imperiex. 3.00
154 JLb,CaS,V:Brainiac 13 . . . . . . 15.00
155 JLb,CaS,F:Superboy. 7.00
156 JLb,CaS,V:Parasite. 5.00
157 JLb,CaS,Lois vs. Superman? . . 5.00
158 JLb,CaS,CriticalCondition,pt.1 . . 3.00
159 JLb,CaS,F:Green Lantern. 3.00
160 JLb,CaS,Arkham,pt.1 . . . . 3.00
161 JLb,CaS,Superman:Emperor? . 3.50
162 JLb,CaS,A:Aquaman,pt.1 . . . . . 3.00
163 JLb,PaP,CaS,F:Aquaman,pt.2 . 2.50
164 JLb,CaS,V:Bizarro 2.50
165 JLb,AAd,A:Linear Man 2.50
166 JLb,CaS,O:Superman(new) . . . 4.00
166a holofoil(c) 7.00
167 JLb,CaS,Return toKrypton,pt.1 . 2.50
168 JLb,CaS,Lord of the Ring,pt.1 . 5.00
169 MWm,Infestation x-over,pt.1 . . . 2.50
170 JLb,CaS,DK,V:Mogul 2.50
171 JLb,OurWorlds atWar,prelude. . 2.50
172 JLb,All-Out War. 2.50
173 JLb,Casualties of War. 2.50
174 JLb,CaS,War aftermath 2.50
175 JLb,CaS,Last Laugh,48-pg 3.50
176 JLb,IaC,NRd,F:Dr. Foster 2.25

177 JLb,CaS,F:Toyman,Metallo. . . . 2.25
178 JLb,CaS,F:Uncle Sam 2.25
179 JLb,African-American hero 2.25
180 JLb,IaC,NRd,V:Dracula. 3.50
181 JLb,CaS,F:Bizarro. 3.50
182 JLb,CaS,F:Suicide Squad. 2.25
183 JLb,CaS,Clarke fired from job . 2.25
184 PFe,CaS,Return to Krypton II. . . 2.25
185 BA,PFe(c),baseball game. 2.25
186 PFe,CaS,Ending Battle,pt.1 . . . 2.25
187 PFe,CaS,Ending Battle,pt.5 . . . 2.25
188 F:Lois Lane. 2.25
189 PFe,Lost Hearts,pt.1 x-over . . . 2.25
190 SSe(c),SMc,rogue robot 2.25
190a spec.newsstand ed.,56-pg. . . 4.25
191 F:The Flash. 2.25
192 Supergirl vs. Radion 4.00
193 Supergirl vs. Radion 2.25
194 SMc,I:Ed 2.25
195 SMc,Futuresmiths. 2.25
196 SMc,new adversary 2.25
197 SMc,deaf Superman,Krypto . . . 2.25
198 SMc,V:Bizarro. 2.25
199 SMc,Supergirl origins 2.25
200 SMc,Futuresmiths, 48-pg. 3.50
201 KIK,Strange New Visitor 4.00
202 Godfall,pt.3 . . . . 5.00
203 Godfall,pt.6 . . . . 4.00
204 JLe,SW,I:FatherLeone,40-pg. . . 3.00
205 JLe,SW,For Tomorrow,pt.2 . . . . 3.50
206 JLe,SW,For Tomorrow,pt.3 . . . . 3.00
207 JLe,SW,For Tomorrow,pt.4 . . . . 3.00
208 JLe,SW,For Tomorrow,pt.5 . . . . 3.00
209 JLe,SW,For Tomorrow,pt.6 . . . . 3.00
210 JLe,SW,For Tomorrow,pt.7 . . . . 2.50
211 JLe,SW,For Tomorrow. 2.50
212 JLe,SW,Superman vanishes. . . 2.50
213 JLe,SW,For Tomorrow. 2.50
214 JLe,SW For Tomorrow 2.50
215 JLe,SW,For Tomorrow. 3.50
216 IaC,NRd,Lightning Strikes. 3.50
217 EBe,new Fortress of Solitude . . 5.00
218 EBe,I:Blackrock. 3.00
219 EBe,Sacrifice, x-over, pt.1 . . . . 5.00
220 EBe(c),Return of the Supermen 2.50
221 EBe,V:Bizarro 2.50
222 EBe,Crisis Begins 2.50
223 EBe,Infinite Crisis tie in. 2.50
224 EBe,Infinite Crisis tie-in. 2.50
225 Infinite Crisis tie-in 2.50
226 This is Your Life, Superman . . . 2.50
Ann.#1 RF,BBr,A:Titano 4.00
Ann.#2 RF,BBr,R:Newsboy Legion
    & Guardian 4.00

Superman 2nd Series Annual #2
© DC Comics Inc.

Superman Special #1 (1992)
© DC Comics, Inc.

Ann.#3 DAb(1st Work),TA,DG,
  Armageddon 2001. . . . . 9.00
Ann.#3a 2nd printing(silver). 3.00
Ann.#4 Eclipso. 3.00
Ann.#5 Bloodlines#6,DL,I:Myriad. . . 3.00
Ann.#6 Elseworlds Story 3.50
Ann.#7 WS(c),Year One Annual
  A:Dr. Occult 4.50
Ann.#8 Legends o/t Dead Earth . . . 3.00
Ann.#9 Pulp Heroes (High-
  Adventure) DJu 4.50
Ann.#10 DJu(s),PR,Clv,BWr,
  Ghosts 3.00
Ann.#11 JoP,AAd(c),JLApe:Gorilla
  Warfare 3.50
Ann.#12 Planet DC 3.50
Spec.#1,000,000 DAn&ALa(s),NBy . 2.50
Giant Ann.#1 Replica edition 5.00
Giant #1 80-page 5.00
Giant #2 80-page 5.00
Giant #3 80-page. 6.00
Spec.#0 PeerPressure,pt.3 (1994) . 2.00
Spec.King of the World, foil 5.00
Spec.King of the World, reg. 4.00
Spec. Superman: Lois Lane,
  Girlfrenzy (1998) 2.00
Spec.#1 WS,V:L.Luthor,
  Sandman (1992) 6.00
Spec. Superman Plus One (1997). . 3.00
Spec.#1 Superman: The Earth
  Stealers, JBy,CS,JOy (1988). . . 3.50
  2nd printing 3.00
Spec. Superman:Emperor?(2000). . 3.50
Spec. Superman Forever, KK,DJu,LSi,
  JBy,SI,DG, Luthor's kidnapped
  daughter (1998). 5.00
  Deluxe ed.,AxR(c), lenticular. . 6.00
Spec.#1 Superman: The Legacy of
  Superman,WS,JG,F:Guardian,
  Waverider,Sinbad (1993). 4.00
Spec. Superman & Savage Dragon:
  Metropolis, KK,JBg,x-over. 5.00
Spec. Superman/Toyman (1996). . . 2.00
Spec. Team Superman, MMr(s),
  DHz,48-page,F:Superboy,
  Supergirl & Steel 3.00
Spec. 3-D #1 LSi,V:Mainframe . . . 4.00
Spec. Whatever Happened to the
  Man of Tomorrow. 6.00
Spec. Superman Y2K,JBg (1999) . . 5.00
Newstime-The Life and Death of
  the Man of Steel-Magazine,
  DJu,BBr,JOy,JG,JBg 3.25
Spec.#1 Superman Gallery (1993) . 3.00

Superman Secret Files, DJu,JOy,
  etc.,inc. O:Superman (1997). . . 10.00
Secret Files #1 Superman Villains. . 10.00
Secret Files #2. . . . . 10.00
Secret Files #1 Our Worlds at War 10.00
Secret Files #1 President Luthor . . 10.00
Secret Files 2004. . . . . 10.00
Spec. Secret Files 2005. . . . . 5.00
Spec. Metropolis Secret Files #1. . . 5.00
Spec. Team Superman Secret Files 5.00
Spec. 1-shot,Superman:Lex 2000,
  JLb,TyH,DoM,Vote for Lex 3.50
Spec. 10-Cent Adventure,SMc. . . . 0.10
Spec. Superman vs. Darkseid:
  Apokolips Now, MSh(s),48-pg. . 3.00
Spec. Blood of my Ancestors. 7.00
GN Death of Superman rep.(1993) 6.00
  Later printings 6.00
  Platinum Edition 15.00
GN Superman At Earth's End
  (Elseworlds) 5.00
GN Superman: Distant Fires, HC,GK,
  nuclear winter (1997). 6.00
GN Superman: Earth Day 1991, KGa
  Metropolis Clean-Up 5.50
GN Superman For Earth (1991) . . . 5.00
GN Superman: Kal, Medieval
  Superman (Elseworlds 1995) . . 6.00
GN Superman: Last God of Krypton 5.00
GN Last Stand on Krypton (2003) . . 7.00
GN Superman's Metropolis, RLo &
  RTs(s),TMK, in Fritz Lang's
  Metropolis (Elseworlds 1996) . . 6.00
GN The Superman Monster. 7.00
GN A Nation Divided 5.00
GN Superman: The Odyssey. 5.00
GN Peace on Earth, oversized . . . 10.00
GN Superman Red/Superman Blue,
  V:Toyman, Cyborg, Superman
  split into two entities (1997). . . . 4.00
  Deluxe, 3-D cover 5.00
GN Superman: Silver Banshee, 48pg,
  prestige format (1998). 5.00
GN Superman: Speeding Bullets,
  EB (Elseworlds 1993) 6.00
GN Superman, Under a Yellow Sun
  by Clark Kent,KGa,EB (1994). . 6.00
GN Superman: The Wedding Album,
  collector's edition, 96 pg.,
  cardstock cover 5.00
GN War of the Worlds,Elseworlds . . 6.00
GN Superman, Inc. 7.00
GN Superman: Mann & Superman . 6.00
GN Superman:Where is thy Sting? . 7.00
GN Superman & Savage Dragon:
  Chicago, x-over, EL (2002) 6.00
  Metropolis, x-over,KK,JBg 5.00
TPB Superman: Bizarro's World . . 10.00
TPB Tales of the Bizarro World . . . 15.00
TPB Critical Condition (2003) 15.00
TPB Day of Doom (2003) 10.00
TPB Superman: The Death of Clark
  Kent, rep. (1997) 20.00
TPB End of the Century (2003). . . 18.00
TPB Eradication. 13.00
TPB Exile. 15.00
TPB Superman/Fantastic Four . . . 10.00
TPB Krisis of the Krimson Kryptonite
  rep. 13.00
TPB Panic in the Sky rep. 10.00
TPB President Lex (2003) 18.00
TPB Return of Superman rep. Reign
  of Superman 15.00
TPB The Revenge Squad (2000) . 13.00
TPB Son of Superman (2000) 15.00
TPB Superman Vs. Revenge
  Squad 13.00
TPB They Saved Luthor's Brain . . 15.00
TPB Time and Time Again (1994) . . 7.50
TPB The Wedding and
  Beyond rep. 15.00
TPB World Without Superman. 7.50

TPB Superman in the forties 20.00
TPB Superman in the fifties. 20.00
TPB Superman in the sixties 20.00
TPB Superman in the seventies . . 20.00
TPB Sunday Classics 1939–1943 . 20.00
TPB The Dailies,Vol.1 . . . . 15.00
TPB The Dailies,Vol.2 . . . . 15.00
TPB The Dailies,Vol.3 . . . . 15.00
TPB No Limits, 208-page. 15.00
TPB Endgame, 176-page 15.00
TPB Superman/Gen 13, 80-page . 10.00
TPB Superman Vs. Predator. 15.00
TPB Superman for All Seasons . . . 15.00
TPB Til Deat Do Us Part (2001) . . 18.00
TPB Our Worlds at War, Vol.1 . . . . 20.00
TPB Our Worlds at War, Vol.2 . . . . 20.00
TPB Greatest Superman Stories
  Ever Told 16.00
TPB Return to Krypton. 18.00
TPB Unconventional
  Warfare (2005) 15.00
TPB Public Enemies (2005). 13.00
TPB Superman vs. Flash (2005) . . 20.00
TPB The Wrath of Gog (2005). . . . 15.00
TPB Godfall (2005) 10.00
TPB That Healing Touch (2005) . . 15.00
TPB Birthright (2005). 20.00
TPB In the Name of Gog (2006) . . 18.00
TPB For Tomorrow, Vol. 2 (2006) . 15.00
Superman: The Greatest Stories
  Ever Told, Vol. 2 (2006) 20.00
TPB Superman: True Brit (2006) . . 18.00
TPB Sacrifice (2006) 15.00
TPB Superman Chronicles, Vol. 1. 15.00
TPB The Daily Planet (2006). 20.00
TPB Superman: The Journey 15.00
TPB Superman in the Eighties 20.00
TPB Superman: For Tomorrow . . . 15.00
TPB Superman vs. Lex Luthor . . . 20.00
TPB Superman/Shazam:
  First Thunder (2006) 13.00
TPB Superman: Strange Attractors 13.00
TPB Infinite Crisis (2006). 20.00
TPB Superman/Doomsday (2006) 20.00
TPB Our Worlds at War Complete. 25.00

SUPERMAN
ADVENTURES
Sept., 1996

1 PDi(s),RBr,TA, from animated
  TV show 3.00
2 thru 20 . . . . @2.50
21 Supergirl Adventures, 64pg. 5.50
22 thru 66 (c) . . . . @2.50
Ann.#1 JoS,DDv,V:Akamin 4.50
TPB rep.#1–#6. . . . . 8.00
Spec. #1 Superman vs. Lobo –
  Misery in Space, DvM,MM,
  A:Man of Tomorrow 4.00
Vol. 3 Last Son of Krypton (2006) . . 7.00
Vol. 4 The Man of Steel (2006) 7.00

SUPERMAN/BATMAN
Aug., 2003

1 JLb,V:Metallo 30.00
2 JLb,both injured 10.00
3 JLb,V:Gorilla Grodd 10.00
4 F:Captain Atom,Luthor. 6.00
5 JLb(s),V:Luthor 6.00
6 JLb(s),V:Luthor 13.00
7 JLb(s),F:Robin,Superboy. 8.00
8 Supergirl from Krypton,pt.1 . . . . . 6.00
9 Supergirl from Krypton,pt.2 . . . . . 4.00
10 Supergirl from Krypton,pt.3. . . . . 4.00
11 Supergirl from Krypton,pt.4 . . . . 3.50
12 Supergirl from Krypton,pt.5. . . . . 3.50
13 JLb(s) V:Darkseid 4.00
14 JLb(s),Absolute Power,pt.1 . . . . 3.50
15 JLb(s),Absolute Power,pt.2. . . . 3.25
16 JLb(s),Absolute Power,pt.3. . . . 3.25
17 JLb(s),Absolute Power,pt.4. . . . 3.25

18 JLb(s),Absolute Power,pt.5	3.25
19 JLb(s),IaC,NRd,F:Supergirl.	3.00
20 JLb(s),With a Vengeance,pt.1	6.00
21 JLb(s),With a Vengeance,pt.2	3.00
22 JLb(s),With a Vengeance,pt.3	3.00
23 JLb(s),With a Vengeance,pt.4	3.00
24 JLb(s),With a Vengeance,pt.5	3.00
25 JLb(s),With a Vengeance,concl	3.00
25a variant (c)	3.00
26 40-pg.	4.00
27 F:Power Girl & The Huntress	3.00
28 The Enemies Among Us,pt.1	3.00
29 The Enemies Among Us,pt.2	3.00
30 The Enemies Among Us,pt.3	3.00
31 V:Lex Luthor	3.00
Ann. #1 (2006)	4.00
Spec. Secret Files (2003)	10.00
TPB Superman: Greatest Stories	20.00
TPB Vol. 2 Supergirl	15.00
TPB Vol. 3 Absolute Power	13.00

SUPERMAN & BATMAN: GENERATIONS — AN IMAGINARY TALE
1998

1 (of 4) JBy, Elseworlds	5.00
2 JBy,V:Bat-Mite	5.00
3 JBy.	5.00
4 JBy, conclusion	5.00
TPB, rep.	15.00

SUPERMAN & BATMAN: GENERATIONS II
Aug., 2001

1 (of 4) JBy,Elseworlds,48-page	6.00
2 JBy,48-page	6.00
3 JBy,48-page	6.00
4 JBy,48-page, concl.	6.00
TPB JBy.	20.00

SUPERMAN & BATMAN: GENERATIONS III
Jan., 2003

1 (of 12) JBy,Elseworlds	3.00
2 JBy,Super Twins	3.00
3 JBy,22nd Century	3.00
4 JBy,23rd Century	3.00
5 JBy,24th Century	3.00
6 JBy,25th Century	3.00
7 JBy,26th Century	3.00
8 JBy,26th Century	3.00
9 JBy,27th Century	3.00
10 JBy,28th Century	3.00
11 JBy,29th century Superboy	3.00
12 JBy,earth destroyed	3.00

SUPERMAN & BATMAN: WORLD'S FUNNEST
Nov., 2000

1-shot, Elseworlds,	7.00

SUPERMAN & BUGS BUNNY
1999

1 (of 4) JSon,TP	2.50
2 thru 4 TP,JSon	@2.50

SUPERMAN: BIRTHRIGHT
July 2003

1 (of 12) F:Jor-El,40-pg.	4.00
2 South Africa,40-pg.	3.50
3 O:retold	3.50
4 Job interview	3.50
5 anti-terrorism weapons	3.50
6 Lex & Clark	3.00

7 Inhuman alien	3.00
8 Lex Luthor	3.00
9 Lex's Plans; Krypton	3.00
10 Threat to Krypton	3.00
11 Krypton Invades Earth	3.00
12 conclusion	3.00

SUPERMAN CONFIDENTIAL
Nov., 2006

1 TSe,Kryptonite	3.00

SUPERMAN: THE DARK SIDE
Elseworlds, Aug., 1998

1 JFM,KD,First Son of Apokolips	5.00
2	5.00
3 KD, conclusion.	5.00
TPB Superman: The Dark Side	13.00

SUPERMAN: DAY OF DOOM
Nov., 2002

1 (of 4) DJu,BSz,F:Ty Duffy	3.00
2 DJu,BSz.	3.00
3 DJu,BSz.	3.00
4 DJu,BSz,concl.	3.00

SUPERMAN/DOOMSDAY: HUNTER/PREY
1994

1 DJu(a&s),BBr,R:Doomsday,R:Cyborg Superman,A:Darkseid	5.50
2 DJu(a&s),BBr,V:Doomsday,Cyborg Superman,A:Darkseid	5.25
3 DJu(a&s),BBr,V:Doomsday	5.25
TPB Rep. #1-#3	15.00

SUPERMAN: THE DOOMSDAY WARS
1998

1 DJu,BBr,R:Doomsday	5.00
2 DJu,BBr,R:Doomsday	5.00
3 DJu,BBr,R:Doomsday	5.00

SUPERMAN FOR ALL SEASONS
June, 1998

1 (of 4) JLb,TSe, from farmboy to superhero	7.00
2 JLb,TSe,V:Lex Luthor	5.00
3 JLb,TSe,V:Lex Luthor	5.00
4 JLb,TSe, conclusion	5.00

SUPERMAN/GEN13
DC/Wildstorm April, 2000

1 (of 3) AH, x-over	2.50
1a variant cover (1:4)	2.50
2 AH,x-over	2.50
2a variant cover (1:4)	2.50
3 AH, 40-pg.	3.50

SUPERMAN: LAST SON OF EARTH
July, 2000

1 (of 2) Elseworlds	6.00
2 Green Lantern's powers	6.00

SUPERMAN: METROPOLIS
Feb. 2003

1 (of 12) F:Jimmy Olsen	3.00
2 Mystery of the Tech	3.00

3 Rebecca.	3.00
4 The Tech or the Devil.	3.00
5 Jimmy and Lena	3.00
6 Jimmy and Lena	3.00
7 thru 12	@3.00

Superman The Man of Steel #1
© DC Comics, Inc.

SUPERMAN: THE MAN OF STEEL
1991–2003

1 B:LSi(s),DJu,BMc,JOy,BBr,TG, Revenge o/t Krypton Man#1	5.00
2 JBg,V:Cerberus	4.00
3 JBg,War of the Gods X-over	3.00
4 JBg,V:Angstrom	3.00
5 JBg,CS,V:Atomic Skull	3.00
6 JBg,Blackout#3,A:Mr.Z	3.00
7 JBg,V:Cerberus	3.00
8 KD,V:Jolt,Blockhouse	3.00
9 JBg,Panic in the Sky#1, V:Brainiac.	3.50
10 JBg,Panic in the Sky#5, D:Draaga	3.00
11 JBg,V:Flashpoint	3.00
12 JBg,V:Warwolves	3.00
13 JBg,V:Cerberus.	3.00
14 JBg,A:Robin,V:Vampires	3.00
15 KG,KGa,Blaze/Satanus War	3.00
16 JBg,Crisis at Hand#1	3.00
17 JBg,V:Underworld, C:Doomsday	8.00
17a 2nd printing	2.50
18 JBg,I:Doomsday,V:Underworld	10.00
18a 2nd printing	4.00
18b 3rd printing	2.50
19 JBg,Doomsday,pt.5	7.00
19a 2nd printing	2.50
20 JBg,Funeral for a Friend#3	3.00
21 JBg,Funeral for a Friend#7	3.00
22 JBg,Reign of Supermen#4,Direct Sales,Die-Cut(c),mini-poster, F:Man of Steel	2.50
22a Newsstand Ed.	2.50
23 JBg,V:Superboy	2.50
24 JBg,V:White Rabbit,A:Mongul.	2.50
25 JBg,A:Real Superman	3.00
26 JBg,A:All Supermen,V:Mongul, Cyborg Superman	2.75
27 JBg,A:Superboy,Lex Luthor	2.50
28 JBg(c),A:Steel	2.50
29 LSi(s),JBg,Spilled Blood#3, V:Hi-Tech,Blood Thirst.	2.50
30 LSi(s),JBg,V:Lobo,Vinyl(c)	3.50
30a Newstand Ed.	2.50

31 MBr,A:Guardian 2.50
32 MBr,Bizarro's World#4,
     V:Bizarro 2.50
33 MBr,V:Parasite 2.50
34 JBg,A:Lex Men,Dubbile Men . . . 2.50
35 JBg,Worlds Collide#1,
     I:Fred Bentson 2.50
36 JBf,Worlds Collide,pt.10,V:Rift
     A:Icon 2.50
37 JBg,Zero Hour,A:Batman 2.50
38 Mystery 2.50
39 JBg,Luthor. 2.50
40 JBg,Mind Games 2.50
41 Locke 2.50
42 F:Locke 2.50
43 V:Deathtrap 2.50
44 Prologue to Death. 2.50
45 JGb,DJa,Death of Clark Kent,pt.4
     [New Miraweb format begins] . . 2.50
46 JBg,DJa,A:Shadowdragon 2.50
47 O:Bloodsport. 2.50
48 JBg,Here be Monsters 2.50
49 Skyhook 2.50
50 JBg,DJa,The Trial of
     Superman, 48pg 4.00
51 JBg,DJa,The Trial of Superman . 2.50
52 JBg,The Trial of Superman 2.50
53 JBg,DRo,A:Lex Luthor,Contessa 2.50
54 JBg 2.50
55 JBg,DJa, Clark dates Lori
     Lemaris 2.50
56 JBg,DJa, manipulator revealed. . 2.50
57 RSt,JBg,DJa, more twisters 2.50
58 LSi(s),JBg,DJa,A:Supergirl 2.50
59 LSi(s),JBg,DJa,Parasite, Steel . . 2.50
60 LSi(s),JBg,DJa,R:Bottled City
     of Kandor. 2.50
61 LSi(s),JBg,DJa,V:Riot 2.50
62 LSi(s),JBg,DJa, Superman
     looses powers, Final Night tie-in 2.50
63 LSi(s),JBg,DJa,Clark is
     kidnapped & revealed identity . . 2.50
64 LSi(s),JBg,DJa,Superman tries to
     restore his powers. 2.50
65 LSi(s),SB,DJa,V:Superman
     Revenge Squad. 2.50
66 LSi(s),JBg,DJa,V:Rajiv 2.50
67 LSi(s),JBg,DJa,New powers
     prequel. 3.00
68 LSi(s),JBg,DJa,V:Metallo 3.00
69 KK&LSi(s),SEa,DJa,A:Atom,
     in Kandor 2.50
70 LSi(s),SEa,DJa,V:Saviour 2.50
71 LSi(s),SEa,DJa,V:Mainframe,
     Superman Revenge Squad. . . . 2.50
72 LSi(s),SEa,JP,DJa,JBg,Genesis
     V:Mainframe 2.50
73 LSi&MWa(s),SEa,DJa,V:Revenge
     Squad 2.50
74 LSi(s),SEa,DJa,dragon's tooth . . 2.50
75 LSi(s),DJa,JBg,Mr.Mxyzptlk dies
     parody of Superman #75. . . . . . 2.50
76 LSi(s),JBb,DJa,V:Mokkari 2.50
77 JBg,Triangles 2.50
78 JBg, Millennium Giants, pt.1
     x-over. 2.50
79 JBg, Millennium Giants. 2.50
80 LSi,JBg,DJa,golden age?,pt.1 . . 2.50
81 LSi,JBg,DJa,golden age?,pt.2 . . 2.50
82 LSi,JBg,DJa,golden age?,pt.3 . . 2.50
83 LSi,SEa,DJa,Dominus 2.50
84 RMz(s),TGb,TP,City of the
     Future, pt.2 x-over. 2.50
85 JBg,DJa,V:Simyan & Mokkari . . . 2.50
86 LSi(s),SEa,DJa,dreams
     of disasters 2.50
87 MSh(s),DoM,DJa,A:Steel,
     Superboy, Supergirl. 2.50
88 MSh(s),DoM,DJa 2.50
89 MSh(s),DoM,V:Dominus 2.50
90 MSh(s),V:Superman's Robot . . . 2.50
91 MSh(s),DoM,paranoia. 2.50

92 TPe(s),TGb,TP,Secret
     origins,concl. 2.50
93 MSh,DoM 2.50
94 RF,SB,Strange Visitor,concl. . . . 2.50
95 MSh,DoM,Fortress of Solitude . . 2.50
96 MSh,DoM, ... 2.50
97 MSh,DoM,F:Eradicator 2.50
98 MSh,DoM,V:Brainiac 13 . . . . . . 2.50
99 MSh,DoM,new armor 2.50
100 MSh,DoM,new Fortress of
     Solitude, 48-pg. 4.00
100a Collectors edition 4.25
101 MSh,DoM,growing sicker 2.50
102 MSh,DoM,Crit.Condition,pt.3 . . 2.50
103 MSh,DoM,A:Supergirl 2.50
104 MSh,DoM,Arkham,pt.3 . . . . 2.50
105 MSh,DoM,Superman:Emperor . 2.50
106 MSh,HuR,V:Kosnor,Netkon . . . 2.50
107 MSh,DoM, to Phantom Zone . . 2.50
108 MSh,DoM, from Phantom Zone 2.50
109 MSh,A:Linear Man 2.50
110 MSh,DoM,A:Star-SpangledKid . 2.50
111 MSh,DoM,Return-Krypton,pt.3 . 2.50
112 MSh,A:Superdog. 2.50
113 MWm,Infestation x-over,pt.3 . . . 2.50
114 MSh,DoM,R:Eradicator 2.50
115 MSh,DoM,Metropolis abducted. 2.50
116 MSh,DoM,JMz,All-out War 2.50
117 MSh,DoM,Casualties of War. . . 2.50
118 MSh,DoM,F:Spectre 2.50
119 MSh,Joker:Last Laugh,tie-in . . . 8.00
120 MSh,V:LexCorp. 2.25
121 TNu,Royal Flush Gang 2.25
122 MSh(s),Entropy Aegis Armor . . 2.25
123 MSh(s),Metropolis Gangs,pt.1 . 2.25
124 MSh(s),Metropolis Gangs,pt.2 . 2.25
125 MSh(s),Metropolis Gangs,pt.3 . 2.25
126 MSh(s),The Pantheon,pt.1 . . . . 2.25
127 MSh(s),The Pantheon,pt.2 . . . . 2.25
128 MSh(s),ReturntoKryptonII,pt.3 . 2.25
129 Bloodsport. 2.25
130 MSh(s),Ending Battle,pt.3. . . . . 2.25
131 MSh(s),Ending Battle,pt.7. . . . . 2.25
132 MSh,Parade, A:Mr.Mxyzptlk . . . 2.25
133 Lost Hearts,pt.3 x-over 2.25
134 MSh,40-pg.,final issue 3.00
Ann.#1 Eclipso tie-in,A:Starman . . 3.00
Ann.#2 Bloodlines#2,I:Edge. 3.00
Ann.#3 MBr,Elseworlds Story 3.50
Ann.#4 Year One Annual 3.50
Ann.#5 Legends o/t Dead Earth . . . 3.50
Ann.#6 Pulp Heroes (Hard Boiled)
     LSi(s),DJa 4.50

Superman: The Man of Steel Ann. #6
© *DC Comics, Inc.*

Spec.#1,000,000 KK&JOy(s),
     AWi,DJa. 3.00
Gallery 1. 3.50
TPB 7.50
TPB The Man of Steel,Vol.1 . . . . 10.00
TPB The Man of Steel,Vol.2 . . . . 10.00
TPB The Man of Steel,Vol.3 . . . . 20.00
TPB The Man of Steel,Vol.4 . . . . 20.00
TPB The Man of Steel,Vol.5 . . . . 20.00

SUPERMAN:
THE MAN OF TOMORROW
1995–96

1 TGu,BBr,RSt(s),V:Lex Luthor. . . . 2.50
2 V:Parasite 2.50
3 TG,BBr, The Trial of Superman . . 2.50
4 RSt(s),PR,BBr,A:Shazam 2.50
5 RSt(s),PR,BBr,Wedding of Lex
     Luthor 2.50
6 RSt(s),PR,BBr,Superman V:
     Jackal again 2.50
7 RSt(s),PR,BBr, ... 2.50
8 RSt(s),PR,BBr,V:Carbide 2.50
9 RSt(s),PR,BBr,Ma and Pa Kent
     open their album 2.50
10 . . . . 2.50
11 LSi(s),PR,DJa,BBr 2.50
12 LSi(s),PR,DJa, ... 2.50
13 LSi(s),PR,DJa,A:JLA. 2.50
14 LSi(s),PR,DJa,V:Riot 2.50
15 Day of Judgment x-over,48-pg. . 3.00
Spec.#1,000,000 MSh(s),DRo 2.00

SUPERMAN: RED SON
April 2003

1 (of 3) Elseworlds,MMr(s) 6.00
2 MMr(s) 6.00
3 MMr(s),concl. 6.00
TPB series rep. 18.00

SUPERMAN RETURNS
July, 2006

GN The Movie Adaptation, 72-pg. . 7.00
TPB Movie & Other Tales, 168-pg. 13.00
Spec: Krypton to Earth, JBy. 4.00
Spec: Ma Kent, KIK 4.00
Spec: Lois Lane 4.00
Spec: Lex Luthor, RL 4.00
TPB The Prequels 13.00

SUPERMAN:
SECRET IDENTITY
Jan. 2004

1 (of 4) SI 6.00
2 SI Clark Kent gains powers. 6.00
3 SI 6.00
4 SI concl. 6.00
TPB Series rep. 20.00

SUPERMAN'S GIRL
FRIEND, LOIS LANE
1958–74

1 CS,KS,Witch of Metropolis . . 8,000.00
2 CS,KS,Secret Sweetheart . . 2,000.00
3 CS,KS,spanking panel 1,400.00
4 CS,KS,Super-Courtship 1,000.00
5 CS,KS,Greatest Sacrifice . . . 1,000.00
6 CS,KS,Superman Junior 850.00
7 CS,KS,Kiss of Death 850.00
8 CS,KS,Superwoman 750.00
9 CS,KS, A:Pat Boone 750.00
10 CS,KS,Cry-Baby of Metropolis 750.00
11 CS,KS,Leopard Girl of Jungle. 500.00
12 CS,KS,Mermaid of Metropolis 500.00
13 CS,KS,Lois Lane's Parents . . 500.00
14 KS,Three Nights in the
     Fortress of Solitude 500.00
15 KS,I:Van-Zee. 500.00

16 KS, Lois' Signal-Watch 500.00
17 KS,CS,A:Brainiac 500.00
18 KS,A:Astounding Man. 500.00
19 KS,Superman of the Past. . . . 500.00
20 KS,A:Superman 550.00
21 KS,A:Van-Zee 400.00
22 KS,A:Robin Hood 400.00
23 KS,A:Elastic Lass, Supergirl . . 400.00
24 KS,A:Van-Zee, Bizarro 400.00
25 KS,Lois' Darkest Secret 400.00
26 KS,A:Jor-El 400.00
27 KS,CS,A:Bizarro 400.00
28 KS,A:Luthor. 400.00
29 CS,A:Aquaman,Batman,Green
  Arrow. 400.00
30 KS,A:Krypto,Aquaman 250.00
31 KS,A:Lori Lemaris 250.00
32 KS,CS,A:Bizarro 250.00
33 KS,CS,A:Phantom Zone,Lori
  Lemaris, Mon-El 250.00
34 KS,A:Luthor,Supergirl 250.00
35 KS,CS,A:Supergirl 250.00
36 KS,CS,Red Kryptonite Story. . 250.00
37 KS,CS,The Forbidden Box . . . 250.00
38 KS,CS,A:Prof.Potter,
  Supergirl 250.00
39 KS,CS,A:Supergirl,Jor-El,
  Krypto, Lori Lemaris 250.00
40 KS,Lois Lane, Hag!. 250.00
41 KS,CS,The Devil and
  Lois Lane. 250.00
42 KS,A:Lori Lemaris 250.00
43 KS,A:Luthor. 250.00
44 KS,A:Lori Lemaris,Braniac,
  Prof. Potter 250.00
45 KS,CS,The Superman-Lois
  Hit Record 250.00
46 KS,A:Luthor. 250.00
47 KS,The Incredible Delusion . . 250.00
48 KS,A:Mr. Mxyzptlk. 250.00
49 KS,The Unknown Superman . 250.00
50 KS,A:Legion 275.00
51 KS,A:Van-Zee & Lori Lemaris. 200.00
52 KS,Truce Between Lois
  Lane and Lana Lang. 200.00
53 KS,A:Lydia Lawrence 200.00
54 KS,CS,The Monster That
  Loved Lois Lane 200.00
55 KS,A:Supergirl 200.00
56 KS,Lois Lane's
  Super-Gamble! 200.00
57 KS,The Camera From
  Outer Space 200.00
58 KS,The Captive Princess 200.00
59 KS,CS,A:Jor-El & Batman . . . 200.00

60 KS,Get Lost,Superman! 200.00
61 KS,A:Mxyzptlk. 200.00
62 KS,A:Mxyzptlk. 200.00
63 KS,The Satanic Schemes
  of S.K.U.L. 200.00
64 KS,A:Luthor. 200.00
65 KS,A:Luthor. 200.00
66 KS,They Call Me the Cat!. . . . 200.00
67 KS,The Bombshell of
  the Boulevards 200.00
68 giant size. 250.00
69 KS,Lois Lane's Last Chance . 200.00
70 KS,I:Silver Age Catwoman,
  A:Batman,Robin,Penguin . . . 600.00
71 KS,A:Catwoman,Batman,
  Robin,Penguin 350.00
72 KS,CS,A:Ina Lemaris 125.00
73 KS,The Dummy and
  the Damsel! 125.00
74 KS,A:Justice League & Bizarro
  World,I:Bizarro Flash. 150.00
75 KS,The Lady Dictator 125.00
76 KS,A:Hap-El 125.00
77 giant size. 200.00
78 KS,Courtship,Kryptonian Style 125.00
79 KS,B:NA(c) 125.00
80 KS,Get Out of My Life,
  Superman 125.00
81 KS,No Witnesses in
  Outerspace 125.00
82 GT,A:Brainiac&Justice League . 75.00
83 GT,Witch on Wheels 75.00
84 GT,KS,Who is Lois Lane?. . . . 75.00
85 GT,A:Kandorians. 75.00
86 giant size. 100.00
87 GT,KS,A:Cor-Lar. 75.00
88 GT,KS,Through a Murderer's
  Eyes. 75.00
89 CS,A:Batman & Batman Jr. . . 85.00
90 GT,A:Dahr-nel. 75.00
91 GT,A:Superlass. 75.00
92 GT,A:Superhorse 75.00
93 GT,A:Wonder Woman. 75.00
94 GT,KS,A:Jor 75.00
95 giant size. 125.00
96 GT,A:Jor 60.00
97 GT,KS,A:Lori Lemaris,
  Luma Lynai,Lyla Lerrol 60.00
98 GT,A:Phantom Zone 60.00
99 GT,KS,A:Batman. 60.00
100 GT,A:Batman. 60.00
101 GT,KS,The Super-Reckless
  Lois Lane 60.00
102 GT,KS,When You're Dead,
  You're Dead. 60.00
103 GT,KS,A:Supergirl. 60.00
104 giant size. 100.00
105 RA,I&O:Rose & Thorn 100.00
106 WR,I am Curious Black! 75.00
107 WR,The Snow-Woman Wept . 60.00
108 WR,The Spectre Suitor. 60.00
109 WR,I'll Never Fall
  in Love Again. 60.00
110 WR,Indian Death Charge!. . . 60.00
111 WR,A:Justice League 60.00
112 WR,KS,A:Lori Lemaris 75.00
113 giant size. 100.00
114 WR,KS,A:Rose & Thorn 60.00
115 WR,A:The Black Racer. 60.00
116 WR,A:Darkseid & Desaad. . . 60.00
117 WR,S.O.S From Tomorrow! . . 60.00
118 WR,A:Darkseid & Desaad. . . 60.00
119 WR,A:Darkseid & Lucy Lane . 60.00
120 WR,Who Killed Lucy Lane? . . 60.00
121 WR,A:The Thorn. 60.00
122 WR,A:The Thorn. 60.00
123 JRo,Ten Deadly Division
  of the 100 . . . . 60.00
124 JRo,The Hunters. 35.00
125 JRo,Death Rides Wheels!. . . 35.00
126 JRo,The Brain Busters 35.00
127 JRo,Curse of the Flame 35.00

128 JRo,A:Batman & Aquaman . . . 35.00
129 JRo,Serpent in Paradise. 35.00
130 JRo,The Mental Murster 35.00
131 JRo,Superman–Marry Me! . . . 35.00
132 JRo,Zatanna B.U. 35.00
133 JRo,The Lady is a Bomb 35.00
134 JRo,A:Kandor 35.00
135 JRo,Amazing After-Life
  of Lois Lane. 35.00
136 JRo,A:Wonder Woman 35.00
137 JRo,The Stolen Subway 50.00
Ann.#1 . . . . 500.00
Ann.#2 . . . . 300.00

SUPERMAN:
SILVER BANSHEE
1998
1 (of 2) DIB(s),ALa 2.25
2 DIB(s),ALa, conclusion 2.25

SUPERMAN'S NEMESIS,
LEX LUTHOR
1999
1 (of 4) VS,DJa, ... 2.50
2 VS,DJa. 2.50
3 VS,DJa. 2.50
4 VS,DJa, conclusion 2.50

SUPERMAN'S PAL,
JIMMY OLSEN
1954–74
1 CS,The Boy of 100 Faces! . 10,000.00
2 CS,The Flying Jimmy Olsen . 3,000.00
3 CS,The Man Who Collected
  Excitement 1,500.00
4 CS,King For A Day!. 1,000.00
5 CS,The Story of Superman's
  Souvenirs 1,000.00
6 CS,Kryptonite story 700.00
7 CS,The King of Marbles 700.00
8 CS,Jimmy Olsen, Crooner. . . 700.00
9 CS,The Missile of Steel 700.00
10 CS,Jungle Jimmy Olsen 700.00
11 CS,TNT Olsen,The Champ . . 450.00
12 CS,Invisible Jimmy Olsen. . . 450.00
13 CS,Jimmy Olsen's
  Super Issue 450.00
14 CS,The Boy Superman 450.00
15 CS,Jimmy Olsen,Speed
  Demon. 450.00
16 CS,The Boy Superman. 450.00
17 CS,J.Olsen as cartoonist . . . 450.00

Superman's Girl Friend Lois Lane #45
© DC Comics, Inc.

Superman's Pal Jimmy Olsen #5
© DC Comics Inc.

18 CS,A:Superboy 450.00
19 CS,Supermam's Kid Brother. . 450.00
20 CS,Merman of Metropolis. . . . 450.00
21 CS,The Wedding of Jimmy
   Olsen. 375.00
22 CS,The Super Brain of
   Jimmy Olsen 375.00
23 CS,The Adventure of
   Private Olsen. 375.00
24 CS,The Gorilla Reporter. 375.00
25 CS,The Day There Was
   No Jimmy Olsen 375.00
26 CS,Bird Boy of Metropolis . . . 375.00
27 CS,The Outlaw Jimmy Olsen . 375.00
28 CS,The Boy Who Killed
   Superman 375.00
29 CS,A:Krypto 375.00
30 CS,The Son of Superman . . . 375.00
31 CS,I:Elastic Lad 350.00
32 CS,A:Prof.Potter 350.00
33 CS,Human Flame Thrower . . . 350.00
34 CS,Superman's Pal of Steel . 350.00
35 CS,Superman's Enemy 350.00
36 CS,I:Lois Lane,O:Jimmy Olsen
   as Superman's Pal 350.00
37 CS,O:Jimmy Olsen's SignalWatch,
   A:Elastic Lad(Jimmy Olsen) . 350.00
38 CS,Olsen's Super-Supper . . . 350.00
39 CS,The Super-Lad of Space. . 350.00
40 CS,A:Supergirl,Hank White
   (Perry White's son) 350.00
41 CS,The Human Octopus. 300.00
42 CS,Jimmy The Genie 300.00
43 WB,CS,Jimmy Olsen's Private
   Monster 300.00
44 CS,Miss Jimmy Olsen. 300.00
45 CS,A:Kandor. 300.00
46 CS,A:Supergirl,Elastic Lad . . 300.00
47 CS,Monsters From Earth!. . . . 300.00
48 CS,I:Superman Emergency
   Squad 300.00
49 CS,A:Congorilla & Congo Bill . 300.00
50 CS,A:Supergirl,Krypto,Bizarro 300.00
51 CS,A:Supergirl 275.00
52 CS,A:Mr. Mxyzptlk,
   Miss Gzptlsnz 275.00
53 CS,A:Kandor,Lori Lemaris,
   Mr.Mxyztlk 275.00
54 CS,A:Elastic Lad. 275.00
55 CS,A:Aquaman,Thor. 275.00
56 KS,Imaginary story 275.00
57 KS,A:Supergirl,Imaginary story 250.00
58 CS,C:Batman 250.00
59 CS,A:Titano. 250.00
60 CS,The Fantastic Army of
   General Olsen 250.00

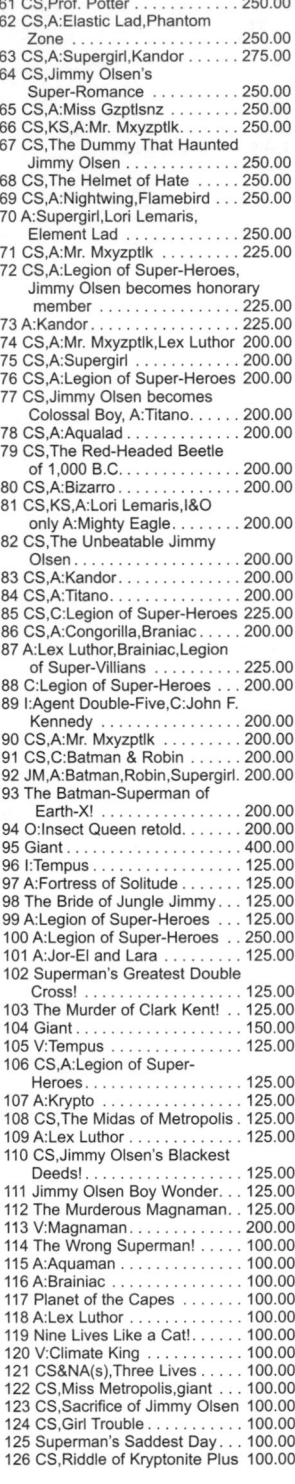

Superman's Pal Jimmy Olsen #55
© DC Comics, Inc.

61 CS,Prof. Potter 250.00
62 CS,A:Elastic Lad,Phantom
   Zone 250.00
63 CS,A:Supergirl,Kandor 275.00
64 CS,Jimmy Olsen's
   Super-Romance 250.00
65 CS,A:Miss Gzptlsnz 250.00
66 CS,KS,A:Mr. Mxyzptlk. 250.00
67 CS,The Dummy That Haunted
   Jimmy Olsen 250.00
68 CS,The Helmet of Hate 250.00
69 CS,A:Nightwing,Flamebird . . . 250.00
70 A:Supergirl,Lori Lemaris,
   Element Lad 250.00
71 CS,A:Mr. Mxyzptlk 225.00
72 CS,A:Legion of Super-Heroes,
   Jimmy Olsen becomes honorary
   member 225.00
73 A:Kandor. 225.00
74 CS,A:Mr. Mxyzptlk,Lex Luthor 200.00
75 CS,A:Supergirl 200.00
76 CS,A:Legion of Super-Heroes 200.00
77 CS,Jimmy Olsen becomes
   Colossal Boy, A:Titano. 200.00
78 CS,A:Aqualad 200.00
79 CS,The Red-Headed Beetle
   of 1,000 B.C. 200.00
80 CS,A:Bizarro. 200.00
81 CS,KS,A:Lori Lemaris,I&O
   only A:Mighty Eagle. 200.00
82 CS,The Unbeatable Jimmy
   Olsen. 200.00
83 CS,A:Kandor. 200.00
84 CS,A:Titano. 200.00
85 CS,C:Legion of Super-Heroes 225.00
86 CS,A:Congorilla,Braniac. 200.00
87 A:Lex Luthor,Brainiac,Legion
   of Super-Villians 225.00
88 C:Legion of Super-Heroes . . . 200.00
89 I:Agent Double-Five,C:John F.
   Kennedy 200.00
90 CS,A:Mr. Mxyzptlk 200.00
91 CS,C:Batman & Robin 200.00
92 JM,A:Batman,Robin,Supergirl. 200.00
93 The Batman-Superman of
   Earth-X! 200.00
94 O:Insect Queen retold. 200.00
95 Giant 400.00
96 I:Tempus 125.00
97 A:Fortress of Solitude 125.00
98 The Bride of Jungle Jimmy . . 125.00
99 A:Legion of Super-Heroes . . . 125.00
100 A:Legion of Super-Heroes . . 250.00
101 A:Jor-El and Lara 125.00
102 Superman's Greatest Double
   Cross! 125.00
103 The Murder of Clark Kent! . . 125.00
104 Giant 150.00
105 V:Tempus 125.00
106 CS,A:Legion of Super-
   Heroes. 125.00
107 A:Krypto 125.00
108 CS,The Midas of Metropolis . 125.00
109 A:Lex Luthor 125.00
110 CS,Jimmy Olsen's Blackest
   Deeds! 125.00
111 Jimmy Olsen Boy Wonder . . 125.00
112 The Murderous Magnaman. . 125.00
113 V:Magnaman. 200.00
114 The Wrong Superman! 100.00
115 A:Aquaman 100.00
116 A:Brainiac 100.00
117 Planet of the Capes 100.00
118 A:Lex Luthor 100.00
119 Nine Lives Like a Cat!. 100.00
120 V:Climate King 100.00
121 CS&NA(s),Three Lives 100.00
122 CS,Miss Metropolis,giant . . . 100.00
123 CS,Sacrifice of Jimmy Olsen 100.00
124 CS,Girl Trouble 100.00
125 Superman's Saddest Day . . . 100.00
126 CS,Riddle of Kryptonite Plus 100.00

Superman's Pal Jimmy Olsen #143
© DC Comics Inc.

127 CS,Jimmy in Revolutionary
   War 100.00
128 I:Mark Olsen(Jimmy'sFather) 100.00
129 MA,A:Mark Olsen 100.00
130 MA,A:Robin,Brainiac. 100.00
131 CS,Birdboy of Metropolis . . . 150.00
132 MA,When Olsen Sold out
   Superman 100.00
133 JK,B:New Newsboy Legion,
   I:Morgan Edge 200.00
134 JK,I:Darkseid. 250.00
135 JK,I:New Guardian 150.00
136 JK,O:New Guardian,
   I:Dubbilex. 125.00
137 JK,I:Four Armed Terror 100.00
138 JK,V:Four Armed Terror 100.00
139 JK,A:Don Rickles,I:Ugly
   Mannheim 100.00
140 Rep. Jimmy Olsen #69, #72
   and Superman #158 . . . . 100.00
141 JK,A:Don Rickles,Lightray
   B:Newsboy Legion rep 100.00
142 JK,I:Count Dragorian 100.00
143 JK,V:Count Dragorian 100.00
144 JK,A Big Thing in a Deep
   Scottish Lake. 100.00
145 JK,Brigadoon 100.00
146 JK,Homo Disastrous 100.00
147 JK,Superman on New
   Genesis,A:High Father,
   I:Victor Volcanium 100.00
148 JK,V:Victor Volcanium,
   E:Newsboy Legion rep 100.00
149 BO(i),The Unseen Enemy,
   B:Plastic Man rep. 100.00
150 BO(i) A Bad Act to Follow . . . 100.00
151 BO(i),A:Green Lantern 50.00
152 MSy,BO,I:Real Morgan Edge . 50.00
153 MSy,Murder in Metropolis. . . . 50.00
154 KS,The Girl Who Was Made
   of Money 50.00
155 KS,Downfall of Judas Olsen . . 50.00
156 KS,Last Jump for
   a Skyjacker 50.00
157 KS,Jimmy as Marco Polo 50.00
158 KS,A:Lena Lawrence
   (Lucy Lane). 50.00
159 KS,Jimmy as Spartacus 50.00
160 KS,A:Lena Lawrence
   (Lucy Lane). 50.00
161 KS,V:Lucy Lane 50.00
162 KS,A:Lex Luthor 50.00
163 KS,Jimmy as Marco Polo 50.00
Becomes:

SUPERMAN FAMILY
1974–82

164 KS,NC(c),Jimmy Olsen:Death
    Bites with Fangs of Stone 75.00
165 KS,NC(c),Supergirl:Princess
    of the Golden Sun 50.00
166 KS,NC(c),Lois Lane:The
    Murdering Arm of Metropolis .. 35.00
167 KS,NC(c),Jimmy Olsen:A
    Deep Death for Mr. Action 35.00
168 NC(c),Supergirl:The Girl
    with the See-Through Mind ... 35.00
169 NC(c),Lois Lane:Target of
    the Tarantula 35.00
170 KS(c),Jimmy Olsen:The Kid
    Who Adopted Jimmy Olsen ... 25.00
171 ECh(c),Supergirl:Cleopatra-
    Queen of America 25.00
172 KS(c),Lois Lane:The Cheat
    the Whole World Cheered 25.00
173 KS(c),Jimmy Olsen:Menace
    of the Micro-Monster 25.00
174 KS(c),Supergirl:Eyes of
    the Serpent 25.00
175 KS(c),Lois Lane:Fadeout
    For Lois 25.00
176 KS(c),Jimmy
    Olsen:Nashville, Super-Star .. 25.00
177 KS(c),Supergirl:Bride
    of the Stars 20.00
178 KS(c),Lois Lane:The Girl
    With the Heart of Steel 20.00
179 KS(c),Jimmy Olsen:I Scared
    Superman to Death 20.00
180 KS,Supergirl:The Secret of
    the Spell-Bound Supergirl 20.00
181 ECh(c),Lois Lane:The Secret
    Lois Lane Could Never Tell ... 20.00
182 CS&NA(c),Jimmy Olsen:
    Death on Ice 20.00
183 NA(c),Supergirl:Shadows
    of Phantoms 20.00
184 NA(c),Supergirl:The
    Visitors From The Void 20.00
185 NA(c),Jimmy Olsen: The
    Fantastic Fists and Fury
    Feet of Jimmy Olsen 20.00
186 JL&DG(c),Jimmy Olsen:
    The Bug Lady 20.00
187 JL(c),Jimmy Olsen:The
    Dealers of Death 20.00
188 JL&DG(c),Jimmy Olsen:
    Crisis in Kandor 20.00
189 JL(c),Jimmy Olsen:The
    Night of the Looter 20.00
190 Jimmy Olsen:Somebody
    Stole My Town 20.00
191 Superboy:The Incredible
    Shrinking Town 20.00
192 RA&DG(c),Superboy:This
    Town For Plunder 20.00
193 RA&DG(c),Superboy:Menace
    of the Mechanical Monster ... 20.00
194 MR,Superboy:When
    the Sorcerer Strikes 20.00
195 RA&DG(c),Superboy:The Curse
    of the Un-Secret Identity 20.00
196 JL&DG(c),Superboy:The
    Shadow of Jor-El. 20.00
197 JL(c),Superboy:Superboy's
    Split Personality 20.00
198 JL(c),Superboy:Challenge
    of the Green K-Tastrophe ... 20.00
199 RA&DG(c),Supergirl:The
    Case of Cape Caper 20.00
200 RA&DG(c),Lois Lane:
    Unhappy Anniversary 22.00
201 RA&DG(c),Supergirl:The
    Face on Cloud 9 .... 8.00
202 RA&DG(c),Supergirl:The
    Dynamic Duel 8.00

203 RA&DG(c),Supergirl:The
    Supergirl From Planet Earth ... 8.00
204 RA&DG(c),Supergirl:The
    Earth-quake Enchantment. 8.00
205 RA&DG(c),Supergirl:Magic
    Over Miami 8.00
206 RA&DG(c),Supergirl:Strangers
    at the Heart's Core 8.00
207 RA&DG(c),Supergirl:Look
    Homeward, Argonian. 8.00
208 RA&DG(c),Supergirl:The
    Super-Switch to New York. 8.00
209 Supergirl:Strike Three-
    You're Out 8.00
210 Supergirl:The Spoil Sport
    of New York. 8.00
211 RA&DG(c):Supergirl:The Man
    With the Explosive Mind 8.00
212 RA&DG(c):Supergirl:Payment
    on Demand 8.00
213   thru 222 .... @8.00

SUPERMAN:
SAVE THE PLANET
Aug., 1998

1 LSi,SEa,DRo,JP,KN, last
    front page 3.00
1 collector's edition 4.00

SUPERMAN: STRENGTH
Jan., 2005

1 (of 3) TA,48-page. 6.00
2 TA. 6.00
3 TA,ARo(c) 6.00

SUPERMAN:
THE KANSAS SIGHTING
Nov. 2003

GN #1 F:Jor-El. 7.00
GN #2 F:Jor-El. 7.00

SUPERMAN,
THE SECRET YEARS
Feb., 1985

1 CS,KS,FM(c) 3.00
2 CS,KS,FM(c) 2.50
3 CS,KS,FM(c) 2.50
4 CS,KS,FM(c), May, 1985. ...... 2.50

Superman, The Secret Years #4
© *DC Comics Inc.*

SUPERMAN VS.
AMAZING SPIDER-MAN
DC/Marvel April, 1976

1 RA/DG,oversized 125.00
1a 2nd printing, signed 225.00

SUPERMAN
VS. PREDATOR
DC/Dark Horse May, 2000

1 (of 3) weakened by virus 5.00
2 .... 5.00
3 conclusion 5.00

SUPERMAN/
WONDER WOMAN:
WHOM GODS DESTROY
Elseworlds Oct., 1996

1 CCl(s),DAb, Lois becomes the
    immortal Wonder Woman 5.00
2 CCl(s),DAb, search for Lana
    Lang. 5.00
3 .... 5.00
4 CCl(s),DAb, romance of the
    century, concl. 5.00

SUPERMEN OF AMERICA
1999

GN with membership kit. 5.00
GN standard edition. 4.00
1 (of 6) FaN,DBw, ... 2.50
2 FaN,DBw,V:Lex Luthor 2.50
3 FaN,DBw,F:Brahma 2.50
4 FaN,DBw,F:White Lotus 2.50
5 FaN,F:The Loser 2.50
6 FaN,A:Superman,concl.. ...... 2.50

SUPER POWERS
1984
[Kenner Action Figures]

1 A:Batman & Joker 5.50
2 A:Batman & Joker 5.50
3 A:Batman & Joker 5.50
4 A:Batman & Joker 5.50
5 JK(c),JK,A:Batman & Joker 5.50

[2nd Series], 1985–86

1 JK,Seeds of Doom. 4.00
2 JK,When Past & Present Meet .. 4.00
3 JK,Time Upon Time 4.00
4 JK,There's No Place Like Rome .. 4.00
5 JK,Once Upon a Tomorrow 4.00
6 JK,Darkseid o/t Moon 4.00

[3rd Series], 1986

1 CI,Threshold 3.50
2 CI,Escape 3.50
3 CI,Machinations. 3.50
4 CI,A World Divided 3.50

SUPER-TEAM FAMILY
1975–78

1 Reprints, giant-size 35.00
2 Creeper/Wildcat. 18.00
3 RE/WW,Flash & Hawkman 18.00
4 Revenge of Solomon Grundy .. 20.00
5 Batman vs. Eclipso 20.00
6 Return of Composite Superman 20.00
7 To Order is to Destroy 20.00
8 JSh,Challengers 22.00
9 JSh,Challengers 22.00
10 JSh,Challengers 22.00
11 Supergirl,Flash,Atom. 22.00
12 Green Lantern,Hawkman 22.00
13 Aquaman, Capt. Comet 22.00
14 Wonder Woman,Atom. 22.00
15 Flash & New Gods 25.00

SWAMP THING
[1st Regular Series]
Oct.–Nov., 1972

1 B:LWn(s),BWr,O:Swamp Thing	250.00
2 BWr,I:Arcane	90.00
3 BWr,I:Patchwork Man	60.00
4 BWr	50.00
5 BWr	50.00
6 BWr	50.00
7 BWr,A:Batman	55.00
8 BWr,Lurker in Tunnel 13	50.00
9 BWr	50.00
10 E:BWr,A;Arcane	50.00
11 thru 24 NR	@20.00
TPB rep.#1-#10,House of Secrets	
#92, Dark Genesis Saga	20.00

Swamp Thing #58 © DC Comics, Inc.

SWAMP THING
1986–96
Previously:
SAGA OF THE SWAMP THING

46 B:AMo(s) cont'd,SBi,JTo,Crisis, A:John Constantine,Phantom Stranger	5.00
47 SBi,Parliment of Trees,Full origin,A:Constantine	5.00
48 SBi,JTo,V:Brujeria, A:Constantine	4.00
49 SBi,AA,A:Constantine,Demon,Ph. Stranger,Spectre,Deadman	4.00
50 SBi,RV,JTo,concl.American Gothic,D:Zatara&Sargon, Double Size	6.00
51 RV,AA,L:Constantine	4.00
52 RV,AA,Arkham Asylum,A:Flor. Man,Lex Luthor,C:Joker, 2-Face,Batman	4.00
53 JTo,V:Batman,Swamp Thing Banished to Space	5.00
54 JTo script,RV,AA,C:Batman	4.00
55 RV,AA,JTo,A:Batman,	4.00
56 RV,AA,My Blue Heaven	4.00
57 RV,AA,A:Adam Strange	4.00
58 RV,AA,A:Adam Strange,GC, Spectre preview	4.00
59 JTo,RV,AA,D:Patchwork Man	4.00

Direct Sales Only

60 JTo,Loving the Alien	4.00
61 RV,AA,All Flesh is Grass G.L.Corps X-over	4.00
62 RV(&script),AA,Wavelength, A:Metron,Darkseid	4.00
63 RV,AA,Loose Ends(reprise)	4.00
64 E:AMo(s),SBi,TY,RV,AA, Return of the Good Gumbo	4.00
65 RV,JTo,A:Constantine	3.50
66 RV,Elemental Energy	3.00
67 RV,V:Solomon Grundy, Hellblazer preview	4.00
68 RV,O:Swamp Thing	3.00
69 RV,O:Swamp Thing	3.00
70 RV,AA,Quest for SwampThing	3.00
71 RV,AA,Fear of Flying	3.00
72 RV,AA,Creation	3.00
73 RV,AA,A:John Constantine	3.50
74 RV,AA,Abbys Secret	3.00
75 RV,AA,Plant Elementals	3.00
76 RV,AA,A:John Constantine	3.50
77 TMd,AA,A:John Constantine	3.50
78 TMd,AA,Phantom Pregnancy	3.00
79 RV,AA,A:Superman,Luthor	3.00
80 RV,AA,V:Aliends	3.00
81 RV,AA,Invasion x-over	3.00
82 RV,AA,A:Sgt.Rock & Easy Co.	3.00
83 RV,AA,A:Enemy Ace	3.00
84 RV,AA,A:Sandman	8.00
85 RV,TY,Time Travel contd.	3.00
86 RV,TY,A:Tomahawk	3.00
87 RV,TY,Camelot,A:Demon	3.00
88 RV,TY,A:Demon,Golden Gladiator	3.00
89 MM,AA,The Dinosaur Age	3.00
90 BP,AA,Birth of Abbys Child (Tefe)	3.25
91 PB,AA,Abbys Child (New Elemental)	3.00
92 PB,AA,Ghosts of the Bayou	3.00
93 PB,AA,New Power	3.00
94 PB,AA,Ax-Murderer	3.00
95 PB,AA,Toxic Waste Dumpers	3.00
96 PB,AA,Tefes Powers	3.00
97 PB,AA,Tefe,V:Nergal, A:Arcane	3.00
98 PB,AA,Tefe,in Hell	3.00
99 PB,AA,Tefe,A:Mantago, John Constantine	3.50
100 PB,AA,V:Angels of Eden, (48 pages)	4.00
101 AA,A:Tefe	3.00
102 V:Mantagos Zombies,inc. prev. of Worlds Without End.	3.00
103 Green vs. Grey	3.00
104 Quest for Elementals,pt.1	3.00
105 Quest for Elementals,pt.2	3.00
106 Quest for Elementals,pt.3	3.00
107 Quest for Elementals,pt.4	3.00
108 Quest for Elementals,pt.5	3.00
109 Quest for Elementals,pt.6	3.00
110 TMd,A:Father Tocsin	3.00
111 V:Ghostly Zydeco Musician	3.00
112 TMd,B:Swamp Thing for Governor	3.00
113 E:Swamp Thing for Governor	3.00
114 TMd,Hellblazer	3.25
115 TMd,A:Hellblazer,V:Dark Conrad	3.25
116 From Body of Swamp Thing	3.00
117 JD,The Lord of Misrule, Mardi Gras	3.00
118 A Childs Garden,A:Matthew the Raven	3.00
119 A:Les Perdu	3.00
120 F:Lady Jane	3.00
121 V:Sunderland Corporation	3.00
122 I:The Needleman	3.00
123 V:The Needleman	3.00
124 In Central America	3.00
125 V:Anton Arcane,20th Anniv.	4.00
126 Mescalito	3.00
127 Project Proteus #1	3.00
128 Project proteus #2	3.00

DC/Vertigo, 1993

129 CV(c),B:NyC(s),SEa,KDM(i), Sw.Thing's Deterioration	3.00

Swamp Thing #86
© DC Comics, Inc.

130 CV(c),SEa,KDM(i),A:John Constantine,V:Doctor Polygon	3.00
131 CV(c),SEa,KDM(i),I:Swamp Thing's,Doppleganger, F:The Folk	3.50
132 CV(c),SEa,KDM(i), V:Doppleganger	3.50
133 CV(c),SEa,KDM(i),R:General Sunderland,V:Thunder Petal	3.50
134 CV(c),SEa,KDM(i),Abby Leaves, C:John Constantine	3.50
135 CV(c),SEa,KDM(i),A:J.Constantine, Swamp Thing Lady Jane meld	3.50
136 CV(c),RsB,KDM(i),A:Lady Jane, Dr.Polygon,John Constantine	3.50
137 CV(c),E:NyC(s),RsB,KDM(i), IR:Sunderland is Anton Arcane, A:J.Constantine	3.50
138 CV(c),DiF(s),RGu,KDM,B:Mind Fields	3.50
139 CV(c),DiF(s),RGu,KDM,A:Black Orchid,In Swamp Thing's mind, cont'd fr.Black Orchid #5	3.50
140 B:Bad Gumbo	4.00
140a Platinum Ed.	12.00
141 A:Abigail Arcane	3.00
142 Bad Gumbo#3	3.00
143 E:Bad Gumbo	3.00
144 In New York City	3.00
145 In Amsterdam	3.00
146 V:Nelson Strong	3.00
147 Hunter	3.00
148 Sargon	3.00
149 Sargon	3.00
150 V:Sargon	3.50
151	3.00
152 River Run,pt.1	3.00
153 River Run	3.00
154 River Run	3.00
155 River Run	3.00
156 PJ,River Run	3.00
157	3.00
158	3.00
159 Swamp Dog	3.00
160 PhH,KDM,Atmospheres	3.00
161 Atmospheres	2.50
162 Atmospheres	2.50
163 Atmospheres	2.50
164	2.50
165 CS,KDM,F:Chester Williams	2.50
166 PhH,KDM,Trial by Fire,pt.1	2.50
167 PhH,KDM,Trial by Fire,pt.2	2.50
168 MMr(s),PhH,KDM,Trial,pt.3	2.50
169 MMr(s),PhH,KDM,Trial,pt.4	2.50
170 MMr(s),PhH,KDM,Trial,pt.5	2.50

171 MMr(s),PhH,KDM,Trial by Fire,
  pt.6, last issue 2.50
Ann.#3 AMo(s),Ape issue 4.00
Ann.#4 PB/AA,A:Batman 4.00
Ann.#5 A:BrotherPower Geek 4.00
Ann.#6 Houma 4.00
Ann.#7 CV(c),NyC(s),MBu(i),Childrens
  Crusade,F:Tefe,A:Maxine,BU:
  Beautyand the Beast 7.00

SWAMP THING
DC/Vertigo, March, 2000
1 JRu,F:Tefe Holland 4.00
2 JRu,new secrets 3.00
3 JRu, ... 3.00
4 Killing Time,pt.1 . . . . 3.00
5 Killing Time,pt.2 . . . . 3.00
6 Killing Time,pt.3 . . . . 3.00
7 RM 3.00
8 RM 3.00
9 RM 3.00
10 RM 3.00
11 RM,Red Harvest, pt.1 . . . . 3.00
12 RM,Red Harvest, pt.2 . . . . 3.00
13 RM,Red Harvest, pt.3 . . . . 3.00
14 RM,Red Harvest, pt.4 . . . . 3.00
15 RM,Red Harvest, pt.5 . . . . 3.00
16 RM,Red Harvest, pt.6 . . . . 3.00
17 Red Harvest, pt.7 . . . . 3.00
18 R:Original Swamp Thing 3.00
19 The Tree of Knowledge 3.00
20 final issue 3.00
Secret Files #1, 64-pg. 5.00
TPB The Curse, AMo(s). 20.00
TPB A Murder of Crows 20.00
TPB Earth to Earth. 18.00
TPB Dark Genesis (2003) 20.00
TPB Reunion (2003) 20.00

SWAMP THING
DC/Vertigo, March 2004
1 classic Swamp Thing 3.00
2 Bad Seed,pt.2 . . . . 3.00
3 Bad Seed,pt.3 . . . . 3.00
4 Bad Seed,pt.4 . . . . 3.00
5 Bad Seed,pt.5,40-pg. 3.00
6 Bad Seed,pt.6 . . . . 3.00
7 RCo,Missing Links,pt.1 . . . . 3.00
8 RCo,Missing Links,pt.2 . . . . 3.00
9 Love in Vain, pt.1 . . . . 3.00
10 Love in Vain, pt.2 . . . . 3.00
11 Love in Vain, pt.3 . . . . 3.00
12 Love in Vain, pt.4 . . . . 3.00
13 Measure of Faith, pt.1. . . . . 3.00
14 Measure of Faith, pt.2. . . . . 3.00
15 Healing the Breach,pt.1 . . . . . . 3.00
16 Healing the Breach,pt.2 . . . . . . 3.00
17 Healing the Breach,pt.3 . . . . . . 3.00
18 Healing the Breach,pt.4 . . . . . . 3.00
19 Alec's bizarre mentor 3.00
20 RCo, sub-atomic size 3.00
21 The Bleeding Raconteur 3.00
22 The Bleeding Raconteur 3.00
23 The Bleeding Raconteur 3.00
24 The Bleeding Raconteur 3.00
25 F:Abby. 3.00
26 Unforgivable actions 3.00
27 The Prison Tree, pt.1 . . . . 3.00
28 Floronic Man. 3.00
29 final issue 3.00
TPB Swamp Thing: Regenesis . . 18.00
TPB Secret of Swamp Thing 10.00
TPB Vol. 1 Bad Seed (2005) 10.00
TPB Vol. 2 Love in Vain (2005) . . . 15.00
TPB Spontaneous Generation 20.00
TPB Infernal Triangles 20.00
TPB Healing the Breach 18.00

SWORD OF SORCERY
Feb.–March, 1973
1 MK(c),HC 25.00

2 BWv,NA,Hc 30.00
3 BWv,HC,MK,WS 25.00
4 HC,WS 10.00
5 Nov.–Dec., 1973 . . . . 10.50

SWORD OF THE ATOM
Sept., 1983
1 GK 3.00
2 GK 3.00
3 GK 3.00
4 GK 3.00
Spec.#1 GK 2.50
Spec.#2 GK 2.50
Spec.#3 PB 2.50

TAILGUNNER JO
Sept., 1988
1 . . . . 2.50
2 thru 6 . . . . @2.50

TAKION
1996
1 PuK,AaL,Josh Sanders
  becomes Takion. 2.50
2 thru 4 . . . . @2.50
5 PuK,AaL,Adventures of Source
  Elemental, cont. 2.50
6 PuK,AaL,Final Night tie-in 2.50
7 PuK,AaL,Arzaz trains Takion,
  final issue 2.50

TALES OF THE GREEN LANTERN CORPS
May, 1981
1 JSon,FMc,O:Green Lantern. 2.50
2 JSon,FMc. 2.50
3 JSon,FMc. 2.50

TALES OF THE LEGION OF SUPER HEROES
Aug., 1984
Prev: Legion of Super Heroes
314 KG,V:Ontiir 2.50
315 KG(i),V:Dark Circle 2.50
316 KG(i),O:White Witch 2.50
317 KG(i),V:Dream Demon 2.50
318 KG(i),V:Persuader. 2.50
319 KG(i),V:Persuader,
  A:Superboy 2.50
320 DJu,V:Magpie 2.50
321 DJu,Exile,V:Kol 2.50
322 DJu,Exile,V:Kol 2.50
323 DJu,Exile,V:Kol 2.50
324 DJu,EC,V:Dev-Em 2.50
325 DJu,V:Dark Circle 2.50
326 thru 354 rep. of Legion of Super
  Heroes, 3rd Series #1–#29 . . . . 2.50
Ann.#4 rep. Baxter Ann.#1. . . . . . . 2.50
Ann.#5 rep. Baxter Ann.#2. . . . . . . 2.50

TALES OF THE NEW TEEN TITANS
June, 1982
1 GP, O:Cyborg. 3.50
2 GP, O:Raven. 3.50
3 GD, O:Changling 3.50
4 GP/EC,O:Starfire. 3.50

TALES OF THE TEEN TITANS
See: NEW TEEN TITANS

TALES OF THE UNEXPECTED
1956–68
1 The Out-Of-The-World Club . 2,500.00

2 Gorilla Who Saved the World 1,500.00
3 LSt,Man With 100 Wigs 1,000.00
4 Seven Steps to the Unknown 1,000.00
5 2nd Life of Geoffrey Hawkes 1,000.00
6 The Girl in the Bottle 800.00
7 NC(c),Pen That Never Lied . . . 800.00
8 LSt,Camera that Could Rob . . 800.00
9 LSt(c),The Amazing Cube 800.00
10 MMe(c),The Strangest Show
  On Earth 800.00
11 LSt(c),Who Am I? 500.00
12 JK,Four Threads of Doom . . . 700.00
13 JK(c),Weapons of Destiny . . . 700.00
14 SMo(c),The Forbidden Game . 500.00
15 JK,MMe,Three Wishes
  to Doom 800.00
16 JK,The Magic Hammer 800.00
17 JK,Who Is Mr. Ashtar? 800.00
18 JK(c),MMe,A Man Without A
  World 800.00
19 NC,Man From Two Worlds . . . 750.00
20 NC(c),The Earth Gladiator . . . 750.00
21 JK,The Living Phantoms 750.00
22 JK(c),The Man From Robot
  Island 750.00
23 JK,The Invitation From Mars! . 750.00
24 LC,The Secret Of Planetoid
  Zero! 750.00
25 The Sorcerer's Asteroid! 450.00
26 MMe,The Frozem City 450.00
27 MMe,The Prison In Space . . . 450.00
28 The Melting Planet 450.00
29 The Phantom Raider. 450.00
30 The Jinxed Planet. 450.00
31 RH,Keep Off Our Planet. 400.00
32 Great Space Cruise Mystery. . 400.00
33 The Man Of 1,000 Planets . . . 400.00
34 Ambush In Outer Space 400.00
35 MMe,I was a Space Refugee . 400.00
36 The Curse Of The
  Galactic Goodess 400.00
37 The Secret Prisoners
  Of Planet 13 . . . . 400.00
38 The Stunt Man Of Space 400.00
39 The Creatures From The
  Space Globe 400.00
40 B:Space Ranger,The Last
  Days Of Planet Mars! 2,000.00
41 SMo(c),The Destroyers From
  The Stars! 900.00
42 The Secret Of The
  Martian Helmet 900.00
43 The Riddle Of The Burning
  Treasures,I:Space Ranger . 2,000.00

Tales of the Unexpected #43
© DC Comics Inc.

Tales of the Unexpected #102
© DC Comics, Inc.

44 DD&SMo(c),The Menace Of
The Indian Aliens. 750.00
45 DD&SMo(c),The Sheriff
From Jupiter 750.00
46 DD&SMo(c),The
Duplicate Doom! 750.00
47 DD(c),The Man Who Stole
The Solar System 550.00
48 Bring 'Em Back Alive-
From Space. 550.00
49 RH,The Fantastic Lunar-Land 550.00
50 MA,King Barney The Ape 550.00
51 Planet Earth For Sale 550.00
52 Prisoner On Pluto 550.00
53 InterplanetaryTroubleShooter . 550.00
54 The Ugly Sleeper Of Klanth,
Dinosaur 550.00
55 The Interplanetary
Creature Trainer 550.00
56 B:Spaceman At Work,Invaders
From Earth 550.00
57 The Jungle Beasts Of Jupiter . 550.00
58 The Boss Of The
Saturnian Legion 550.00
59 The Man Who Won A World . . 550.00
60 School For Space Sleuths . . . 550.00
61 The Mystery Of The
Mythical Monsters 450.00
62 The Menace Of The Red
Snow Crystals 450.00
63 Death To Planet Earth 450.00
64 Boy Usurper Of Planet Zonn . 450.00
65 The Creature That
Couldn't Exist 450.00
66 MMe,Trap Of The Space
Convict. 450.00
67 The Giant That
Devoured A Village 450.00
68 Braggart From Planet Brax. . . 250.00
69 Doom On Holiday Asteroid . . . 250.00
70 The Hermit Of Planetoid X . . . 250.00
71 Manhunt In Galaxy G-2! 250.00
72 The Creature Of 1,000 Dooms 250.00
73 The Convict Defenders
Of Space!. 250.00
74 Prison Camp On Asteroid X-3! 250.00
75 The Hobo Jungle Of Space . . 250.00
76 The Warrior Of Two Worlds! . . 250.00
77 Dateline-Outer Space 250.00
78 The Siren Of Space 250.00
79 Big Show On Planet Earth!. . . 250.00
80 The Creature Tamer!. 250.00
81 His Alien Master!. 250.00
82 Give Us Back Our Earth!,
E:Space Ranger 250.00

83 DD&SMo(c),The Anti-Hex
Merchant!. 175.00
84 DD&SMo(c),The Menace Of
The 50-Fathom Men 175.00
85 JkS(c),The Man Who Stole My
Powers,B:Green Glob 175.00
86 DD&SMo(c),They'll Never
Take Me Alive! 150.00
87 JkS(c),The Manhunt Through
Two Worlds 150.00
88 DD&SMo(c),GK,The Fear
Master 150.00
89 DD,SMo(c),Nightmare on
Mars. 150.00
90 JkS(c),The Hero Of 5,000 BC. 150.00
91 JkS(c),The Prophetic Mirages,
I:Automan 175.00
92 The Man Who Dared To Die! . 150.00
93 JkS(c),Prisoners Of Hate
Island. 150.00
94 The Monster Mayor - USA . . . 150.00
95 The Secret Of Chameleo-Man 150.00
96 Wanted For Murder...1966...
6966. . . . . 150.00
97 One Month To Die. 150.00
98 Half-Man/Half Machine 150.00
99 JkS(c),Nuclear Super-Hero! . . 150.00
100 Judy Blonde, Secret Agent! . 175.00
101 The Man in The Liquid Mask! 125.00
102 Bang!Bang! You're Dead . . . 125.00
103 JA,ABC To Disaster 125.00
104 NA(c),Master Of The
Voodoo Machine 125.00

Becomes:

UNEXPECTED, THE
1968–82

105 The Night I Watched
Myself Die 150.00
106 B:Johnny Peril,The Doorway
Into Time 100.00
107 MD,JkS(c),The Whip Of
Fear! 100.00
108 JkS(c),Journey To
A Nightmare. 100.00
109 JkS(c),Baptism By Starfire!. . 100.00
110 NA(c),Death Town, U.S.A.! . . 100.00
111 NC(c),Mission Into Eternity . . 100.00
112 NA(c),The Brain Robbers!. . . 100.00
113 NA(c),The Shriek Of
Vengeance. 100.00
114 NA(c),My Self-My Enemy!. . . . 75.00
115 BWr,NA(c),Diary Of
A Madman 75.00
116 NC(c),Express Train
To Nowhere! 65.00
117 NC(c),Midnight Summons
The Executioner! 60.00
118 NA(c),A:Judge Gallows,Play
A Tune For Treachery 60.00
119 BWr,NC(c),Mirror,Mirror
On The Wall. 110.00
120 NC(c),Rambeau's Revenge . . 65.00
121 BWr,NA(c),Daddy's
Gone-A-Hunting. 65.00
122 WW,DG(c),The Phantom
Of The Woodstock Festival . . . 65.00
123 NC(c),Death Watch! 50.00
124 NA(c),These Walls Shall
Be Your Grave. 50.00
125 NC(c),Screech Of Guilt! 50.00
126 ATh,NC(c),You Are Cordially
Invited To Die! 50.00
127 GT,JK,ATh,NC(c),Follow The
Piper To Your Grave 50.00
128 DW,BWr,NC(c),Where Only
The Dead Are Free!. 60.00
129 NC(c),Farewell To A
Fading Star 50.00
130 NC(c),One False Step 50.00
131 NC(c),Run For Your Death! . . 50.00
132 MD,GT,NC(c),The Edge Of
Madness 55.00

133 WW,JkS(c),A:Judge Gallows,
Agnes Doesn't Haunt Here
Anymore!. 50.00
134 GT,NC(c),The Restless Dead . 50.00
135 NC(c),Death, Come
Walk With Me! 50.00
136 SMo,GT,NC(c),An Incident
of Violence 50.00
137 WW,NC(c),Dark Vengeance! . 25.00
138 WW,NC(c),Strange Secret of
the Huan Shan Idol 30.00
139 GT,NC(c),The 2 Brains of
Beast Bracken! 25.00
140 JkS(c),The Anatomy of Hate. . 25.00
141 NC(c),Just What Did Eric
See? 25.00
142 NC(c),Let The Dead Sleep! . . 25.00
143 NC(c),Fear is a Nameless
Voice 25.00
144 NC(c),The Dark Pit of
Dr. Hanley 25.00
145 NC(c),Grave of Glass 25.00
146 NC(c),The Monstrosity! 25.00
147 NC(c),The Daughter of
Dr. Jekyll 25.00
148 NC(c),Baby Wants Me Dead! . 25.00
149 NC(c),To Wake the Dead 25.00
150 NC(c),No One Escapes From
Gallows Island 25.00
151 NC(c),Sorry, I'm Not Ready
To Die! 25.00
152 GT,NC(c),Death Wears Many
Faces. 25.00
153 NC(c),Who's That Sleeping
In My Grave?. 25.00
154 NC(c),Murder By Madness . . . 25.00
155 NC(c),Non-Stop Journey
Into Fear 25.00
156 NC(c),A Lunatic Is Loose
Among Us!. 25.00
157 NC(c),The House of
the Executioner 60.00
158 NC(c),Reserved for Madmen
Only 60.00
159 NC(c),A Cry in the Night 60.00
160 NC(c),Death of an Exorcist. . . 60.00
161 BWr,NC(c),Has Anyone
Seen My Killer 60.00
162 JK,NC(c),I'll Bug You
To Your Grave 60.00
163 DD,LD(c),Room For Dying . . 20.00
164 House of the Sinister Sands . . 20.00
165 LD(c),Slayride in July 20.00
166 LD(c),The Evil Eyes of Night . 20.00
167 LD(c),Scared Stiff 20.00
168 LD(c),Freak Accident 20.00
169 LD(c),What Can Be Worse
Than Dying? 20.00
170 LD(c),Flee To Your Grave . . . 20.00
171 LD(c),I.O.U. One Corpse 20.00
172 LD(c),Strangler in Paradise . 20.00
173 LD(c),What Scared Sally? . . . 20.00
174 LD(c),Gauntlet of Fear 20.00
175 LD(c),The Haunted Mountain . 20.00
176 JkS(c),Having A
Wonderful Crime 20.00
177 ECh(c),Reward for the Wicked 20.00
178 LD(c),Fit To Kill! 20.00
179 LD(c),My Son, The Mortician . 20.00
180 GT,LD(c),The Loathsome
Lodger of Nightmare Inn 22.00
181 LD(c),Hum of the Haunted . . . 20.00
182 LD(c),Sorry, This Coffin
is Occupied 20.00
183 LD(c),The Dead Don't
Always Die. 20.00
184 LD(c),Wheel of Misfortune!. . . 20.00
185 LD(c),Monsters from a
Thousand Fathoms 20.00
186 LD(c),To Catch a Corpse 20.00
187 LD(c),Mangled in Madness . . 20.00
188 LD(c),Verdict From The Grave 20.00

189 SD,LD(c),Escape From The
   Grave. 20.00
190 LD(c),The Jigsaw Corpse 20.00
191 MR,JO(c),Night of the Voodoo
   Curse. 22.00
192 LD(c),A Killer Cold & Clammy. 18.00
193 DW,LD(c),Don't Monkey the
   Murder. 18.00
194 LD(c),Have I Got a Ghoul
   For You 18.00
195 JCr,LD(c),Whose Face is at
   My Window 18.00
196 LD(c),The Fear of Number 13 15.00
197 LD(c),Last Laugh of a Corpse 15.00
198 JSn(c),Rage of the
   Phantom Brain. 15.00
199 LD(c),Dracula's Daughter 15.00
200 GT,RA&DG(c),A:Johnny Peril,
   House on the Edge of Eternity 15.00
201 Do Unto Others. 15.00
202 JO,LD(c),Death Trap. 15.00
203 MK(c),Hang Down Your
   Head, Joe Mundy 15.00
204 DN,JKu(c),Twinkle, Twinkle
   Little Star 15.00
205 JkS,A:Johnny Peril,The Second
   Possession of Angela Lake. . . 15.00
206 JkS,A:Johnny Peril,The
   Ultimate Assassin 15.00
207 JkS,A:Johnny Peril,Secret of
   the Second Star. 15.00
208 JkS,A:Johnny Peril,Factory
   of Fear 15.00
209 JkS,Game for the Ghastly . . . 15.00
210 Vampire of the Apes,Time
   Warp 15.00
211 A:Johnny Peril,The Temple
   of the 7 Stars 15.00
212 JkS,MK(c),A:Johnny Peril,The
   Adventure of the Angel's Smile 15.00
213 A:Johnny Peril,The Woman
   Who Died Forever. 15.00
214 JKu(c),Slaughterhouse Arena. 15.00
215 JKu(c),Is Someone
   Stalking Sandra 15.00
216 GP,JKu(c),Samurai Nightmare 15.00
217 ShM,DSp,EC(c),Dear Senator 15.00
218 KG,ECh&DG(c),I'll Remember
   You Yesterday 15.00
219 JKu(c),A Wild Tale. 15.00
220 ShM,JKu(c),The Strange
   Guide. 15.00
221 SD,ShM,JKu(c),Em the
   Energy Monster. 15.00
222 KG,SD(c). 15.00

TALES OF THE UNEXPECTED
Oct., 2006
1 F:Spectre 4.00
2 . . . . 4.00

TANGENT COMICS
(All Oct., 1997)
The Atom #1 DJu,PR,V:Fatal Five. . 3.00
The Flash #1, TDz,GFr,CaS 3.00
Doom Patrol #1 DJu,SCh, ... 3.00
Green Lantern #1 JeR,JWi,MGy . . . 3.00
The Joker #1 KK,MHy,. 3.00
Metal Men #1 MRz,MkK 3.00
Nightwing #1 JOs,JD 3.00
Sea Devils #1 KBk,VGi,TP 3.00
The Secret Six #1 CDi,TG, ... 3.00

TANGENT '98
(All June, 1998)
The Batman #1 DJu,KJ 2.25
JLA #1 DJu,DBk,V:UltraHumanites . 2.25
Joker's Wild #1 KK 2.25
Nightwing: Night Force #1 JOs . . . 2.25

Tangent The Joker #1
© DC Comics, Inc.

Powergirl #1 RMz 2.25
The Superman #1 Harvey Dent. . . . 2.25
Tales of the Green Lantern #1. . . . . 2.25
The Trials of the Flash #1,
   V:Plastic Man. 2.25
Wonder Woman #1 PDa,. 2.25

TANK GIRL
1995
1 Movie Adaptation 6.00

TANK GIRL: APOCALYPSE
1995–96
1 AlG,BBo(c). 3.00
2 AlG,BBo(c)Tank Girl Pregnant . . 3.00
3 AlG,BBo(c). 3.00
4 AlG, finale. 3.00

TANK GIRL: THE ODYSSEY
DC/Vertigo, 1995
1 New Limited Series 3.00
2 BBo(c),Land of Milk & Honey . . 3.00
3 I:The Sirens 3.00

TARZAN
April, 1972
(Prev. published by Gold Key)
207 JKu,O:Tarzan,pt.1 . . . . 100.00
208 thru 210 JKu,O:Tarzan,pt.2–4. 40.00
211 thru 229 . . . . @30.00
230 RH. 50.00
231 thru 235 . . . . @45.00
236 and 237 . . . . @20.00
238 giant-size. 30.00
239 thru 258 Feb., 1977. . . . . . . @20.00

TARZAN FAMILY
Nov.–Dec., 1975
(Prev.: Korak, Son of Tarzan)
60 B:Korak 20.00
61 thru 66 Nov.–Dec.,1976 . . . . @15.00

TATTERED BANNERS
1998
1 (of 4) AlG(s),MMc 3.00
2 AlG&KG(s),MMc 3.00
3 AlG(s),MMc 3.00
4 AlG(s),MMc, conclusion 3.00

TEAM TITANS
1992–94
1 KM,Total Chaos#3,A:New Titans,
   Deathstroke,V:Lord Chaos,
   BU:KGa,Killowat 4.00
1a thru 1d variant (c)s. . . . . @2.50
2 thru 24 . . . . @2.50
Ann.#1 I:Chimera 3.50
Ann.#2 PJ,Elseworlds Story. 3.75

TEEN BEAT
Nov.–Dec., 1967
1 Monkees photo 125.00
Becomes:

TEEN BEAM
2 Monkees 125.00

TEEN TITANS
[1st Series]
Jan., 1966
1 NC,Titans join Peace Corps . . 500.00
2 NC,I:Garn Akaru 225.00
3 NC,I:Ding Dong Daddy 150.00
4 NC,A:Speedy. 150.00
5 NC,I:Ant. 150.00
6 NC,A:Beast Boy. 100.00
7 NC,I:Mad Mod 100.00
8 IN/JAb,I:Titans Copter 100.00
9 NC,A:Teen Titan Sweatshirts. . 100.00
10 NC,I:Bat-Bike 100.00
11 IN/NC A:Speedy 75.00
12 NC,in Spaceville 100.00
13 NC,Christmas story. 75.00
14 NC,I:Gargoyle. 75.00
15 NC,I:Capt. Rumble 75.00
16 NC,I:Dimension X 75.00
17 NC,A:Mad Mod 75.00
18 NC,1:Starfire (Russian). 75.00
19 GK,WW,J:Speedy. 75.00
20 NA,NC J:Joshua 100.00
21 NA,NC,A:Hawk,Dove 100.00
22 NA,NC,O:Wondergirl. 100.00
23 GK,NC,N:Wondergirl. 50.00
24 GK,NC. 50.00
25 NC,I:Lilith,A:J.L.A. 50.00
26 NC,I:Mal 50.00
27 NC,Nightmare in Space 50.00
28 NC,A:Ocean Master 50.00
29 NC,A:Ocean Master 50.00
30 NC,A:Aquagirl. 50.00
31 NC,GT,A:Hawk,Dove 50.00
32 NC,I:Gnarrk. 25.00
33 GT,NS,A:Gnarrk 25.00
34 GT,NC. 25.00

Teen Titans #9 © DC Comics, Inc.

35 GT,NC,O:Mal............... 25.00
36 GT,NC,JAp,V:Hunchback..... 25.00
37 GT,NC................... 25.00
38 GT,NC................... 25.00
39 GT,NC,Rep.Hawk & Dove..... 25.00
40 NC,A:Aqualad............. 25.00
41 NC,DC,Lilith Mystery....... 25.00
42 NC,Slaves o/t Emperor Bug .. 25.00
43 NC,Inherit the Howling Night .. 25.00
44 C:Flash (1976)............. 25.00
45 IN,V:Fiddler.............. 25.00
46 IN,A:Fiddler............. 25.00
47 C:Two-Face.............. 15.00
48 I:Bumblebee,Harlequin,
    A:Two-Face.............. 25.00
49 R:Mal As Guardian......... 15.00
50 DH,I:Teen Titans West....... 20.00
51 DH,A:Teen Titans West....... 15.00
52 DH,A:Teen Titans West....... 15.00
53 O:Teen Titans, A:JLA........ 15.00

TEEN TITANS, THE
Aug., 1996
1 DJu(s),GP,Titan's Children,
    pt.1 (of 3)................ 5.00
2 DJu(s),GP,Titan's Children,
    pt.2,V:Prysm.............. 4.00
3 DJu(s),GP,Titan's Children,
    pt.3.................... 4.00
4 DJu(s),GP,Coming Out,pt.1,
    A:Robin................. 3.00
5 DJu(s),GP,Coming Out,pt.2..... 3.00
6 DJu(s),DJu,GP,F:Risk....... 3.00
7 DJu(s),DJu,GP,The Atom quits
    team.................... 3.00
8 DJu(s),DJu,GP,J:Atom,V:Dark
    Nemesis................. 3.00
9 DJu(s),DJu,GP,Lost World of
    Skartaris, pt.1............. 3.00
10 DJu(s),DJu,GP,Lost World of
    Skartaris, pt.2............. 3.00
11 DJu(s),DJu,GP,Lost World of
    Skartaris, concl.,A:Warlord, ... 3.00
12 DJu(s),DJu,GP,Original Titans,
    pt.1 (of 4) 48pg........... 4.00
13 DJu,GP,Original Titans, pt.2
    Genesis tie-in............. 3.00
14 DJu,GP,Original Titans, pt.3 .. 3.00
15 DJu,GP,Original Titans, pt.4 ... 3.00
16 DJu,GP,aftermath........... 3.00
17 DJu,PJ,team reunites........ 3.00
18 DJu,PR.................. 3.00
19 DJu,PJ,Millennium Giants,
    A:Superman Red........... 3.00
20 DJu, night with the Titans...... 3.00
21 DJu,Titans Hunt,pt.1.......... 3.00
22 DJu,Titans Hunt,pt.2.......... 3.00
23 DJu,Titans Hunt,pt.3.......... 3.00
24 DJu,Titans Hunt,pt.4.......... 3.00
Ann.#1 Pulp Heroes (High-
    Adventure)................ 4.50
Ann.#1 (1967) 80-page, rep....... 5.00

TEEN TITANS
July 2003
1 MMK.................... 8.00
1a 2nd printing............. 3.50
2 MMK,Cyborg.............. 4.00
3 MMK,................... 7.00
4 MMK,disobey order.......... 4.00
5 MMk,Infighting............. 4.00
6 MMk,.................... 2.50
7 MMk,F:Superman........... 2.50
8 TG,F:Raven............... 2.50
9 Raven Rising,pt.1........... 2.50
10 Raven Rising,pt.2.......... 2.50
11 Raven Rising,pt.3.......... 2.50
12 Raven Rising,pt.4.......... 2.50
13 Raven Rising,pt.5.......... 2.50
14 Beast Boys and Girls,pt.1..... 2.50
15 Beast Boys and Girls,pt.2..... 2.50

16 MMk,Lost to the Legion,pt.1 .... 5.00
17 MMk,Titans Tomorrow,pt.1.... 5.00
18 MMK,Titans Tomorrow, pt.2 ... 10.00
19 MMK,Titans Tomorrow, pt.3 .... 5.00
20 TG,Nel,V:Warp,Electrocutioner .. 4.00
21 MMK,Lights Out,pt.1......... 8.00
22 MMK,Lights Out,pt. 2........ 5.00
23 MMK,Lights Out,pt. 3........ 5.00
24 MFm,The Insiders,x-over,pt.1 ... 4.00
25 MFm,The Insiders,x-over,pt.3 ... 3.50
26 TnD,F:Superboy,Raven....... 2.50
27 RLd,Cosmic chaos........... 2.50
28 RLd,Cosmic chaos, pt.2....... 2.50
29 V:Red Hood.............. 2.50
30 Brother Blood Returns, pt.1 ... 2.50
31 V:Brother Blood............ 2.50
32 Infinite Crisis tie-in......... 2.50
33 MWm(s),Infinite Crisis tie-in 2.50
34 One Year Later, New Teen
    Titans, pt.1.............. 2.50
34a variant (c)............... 2.50
35 New Teen Titans, pt.2........ 2.50
36 New Teen Titans, pt.3......... 3.00
37 New Teen Titans, pt.4......... 3.00
38 Titans Around the World,pt.1 ... 3.00
39 Titans Around the World,pt.2 ... 3.00
40 Titans Around the World,pt.3 ... 3.00
41 Titans Around the World, concl. ... 3.00
Ann. #1 MWm(s), 48-pg.(2006).... 5.00
TPB Family Lost.............. 10.00
TPB A Kid's Game............ 10.00
TPB Beast Boys and Girls (2005) . 10.00
Spec. Swingin' Elseworlds Spec.... 6.00
Spec. Teen Titans/Legion......... 4.00
Spec. Teen Titans Outsiders,
    Secret Files.............. 6.00
Spec. Teen Titans/Secret
    Files 2005............... 5.00
TPB The Future is Now (2006) ... 10.00
TPB Outsiders: Insiders (2006) ... 10.00
TPB Outsiders: Death and Return
    of Donna Troy (2006)....... 15.00
TPB Teen Titans: Life and Death.. 15.00

TEEN TITANS GO!
Nov. 2003
1 F:Robin,Cyborg,Beast Boy..... 2.50
2 thru 37.................. @2.25
TPB Digest No. 1.............. 7.00
TPB Digest No. 2.............. 7.00
TPB Digest No. 3 Bring it on..... 7.00
TPB Vol. 4 Ready for Action...... 7.00
TPB Vol. 5 On the Move......... 7.00
TPB Jam-Packed Action, Vol. 1.... 8.00

TEEN TITANS SPOTLIGHT
Aug., 1986
1 DCw,DG,Starfire Apartheid...... 4.00
2 DCw,DG,Starfire Apartheid#2.... 3.00
3 RA,Jericho............... 3.00
4 RA,Jericho............... 3.00
5 RA,Jericho............... 3.00
6 RA,Jericho............... 3.00
7 JG,Hawk................. 4.00
8 JG,Hawk................. 3.00
9 Changeling............... 3.00
10 EL,Aqualad And Mento........ 3.00
11 JO,Brotherhood of Evil........ 3.00
12 EC,Wondergirl............. 3.00
13 Cyborg................. 3.00
14 1st Nightwing/BatmanTeam-up. . 4.00
15 EL,Omega Men............ 3.00
16 Thunder And Lightning....... 3.00
17 DH,Magennta............. 3.00
18 ATi,Aqualad,A:Aquaman....... 3.00
19 Starfire,A:Harbinger,Millennium
    X-over................. 3.00
20 RT(i),Cyborg.............. 3.00
21 DSp,Flashback sty w/orig.Teen
    Titans.................. 3.00

*Teen Titans Spotlight #10 ©
DC Comics, Inc.*

TEMPEST
Mini-series Sept., 1996
1 (of 4) from Aquaman.......... 2.25
2 new costume............... 2.25
3 O:Tempest................ 2.25
4 finale................... 2.25

TEMPUS FUGITIVE
1990
1 KSy,Time Travel,I:Ray 27...... 6.00
2 KSy,Viet Nam.............. 6.00
3 KSy,World War I............ 6.00
4 KSy,final issue............. 6.00

TERMINAL CITY
DC/Vertigo, 1996–97
1 thru 3 DMt(s),MLr,.......... @2.50
4 DMt(s),MLr,I:Kid Gloves........ 2.50
5 DMt(s),MLr,Missing link on
    the loose............... 2.50
6 DMt(s),MLr,............... 2.50
7 DMt(s),MLr,A:Lady in Red...... 2.50
8 DMt(s),MLr,............... 2.50
9 (of 9) DMt(s),MLr,finale....... 2.50
TPB rep. mini-series........... 20.00

TERMINAL CITY: AERIAL GRAFFITI
DC/Vertigo, Sept., 1997
1 (of 5) DMt,MLr,MCo(c)......... 2.50
2 DMt,MLr,MCo(c),F:Cosmo Quinn 2.50
3 DMt,MLr,MCo(c).............. 2.50
4 DMt,MLr,MCo(c).............. 2.50

TESTAMENT
DC/Vertigo, Dec., 2005
1 LSh..................... 3.00
2 LSh, Rain of Fire............ 3.00
3 LSh, Reprogramming.......... 3.00
4 LSh,Gargantuan war machines.. 3.00
5 LSh,V:Demolition robots....... 3.00
6 LSh(c),West of Eden, pt.1...... 3.00
7 West of Eden, pt.2........... 3.00
8 Down to Egypt, pt.1.......... 3.00
9 Down to Egypt, pt.2.......... 3.00
10 Down to Egypt, pt.3.......... 3.00
11 F:Tyrone................. 3.00
12 .... 3.00
TPB Testament: Akedah......... 10.00

3-D Adventures of Superman #1
© DC Comics Inc.

3-D ADVENTURES OF SUPERMAN
1953
N# O:Superman 1,600.00

3-D BATMAN ADVENTURES
1953, 1966
1 with Bat-glasses 1,600.00
1a A:Tommy Tomorrow (1966) . . 500.00

THE THREE MOUSEKETEERS
1956–60
1 . . . . 300.00
2 . . . . 150.00
3 . . . . 125.00
4 . . . . 125.00
5 . . . . 125.00
6 thru 10 . . . . @125.00
11 thru 20 . . . . @100.00
21 thru 26 . . . . @100.00

THIRTEEN
Apr., 2005
TPR 2000 A.D., F:Mike Carey 13.00

THRILLER
Nov., 1983
1 TVE 2.25
2 TVE,O:Thriller 2.25
3 TVE 2.25
4 TVE 2.25
5 TVE,DG,Elvis satire 2.25
6 TVE,Elvis satire 2.25
7 thru 10 TVE . . . . @2.25
11 & 12 AN . . . . @2.25

THRILLING COMICS
1999
1 CDi(s),RH,F:Hawkman &
   Wildcat 2.25

THRILLKILLER
Elseworlds 1997
1 HC(s),DIB,F:Robin and Batgirl . . . 3.50
2 HC(s),DIB, ... 3.00
3 HC(s),DIB,conl. 3.00

THRILLKILLERS '62
Feb., 1998
GN HC,DIB 5.00

TIMBER WOLF
1992–93
1 AG(i),V:Thrust 2.25
2 V:Captain Flag 2.25
3 AG(i),V:Creeper 2.25
4 AG(i),V:Captain Flag 2.25
5 AG(i),V:Dominators,Capt.Flag . . . 2.25

TIME BREAKERS
DC/Helix, 1997
1 (of 5) RaP(s),CWn,time
   paradoxes created 2.50
2 RaP(s),CWn, ... 2.50
3 RaP(s),CWn,expedition to 20th
   century England 2.50
4 RaP(s),CWn,Angela travels back
   in time 2.50
5 RaP(s),CWn,final issue 2.50

TIME MASTERS
Feb., 1990
1 ATi,O:Rip Hunter,A:JLA 2.50
2 ATi,A:Superman 2.25
3 ATi,A:Jonah Hex, Cave Carson . . 2.25
4 thru 8 ATi, ... @2.25

TIME WARP
Oct.–Nov., 1979
1 JAp,RB,SD,MK(c),DN,TS 20.00
2 DN,JO,TS,HC,SD,MK(c),GK . . . 15.00
3 DN,SD,MK(c),TS 15.00
4 MN,SD,MK(c),DN 15.00
5 DN,MK(c),July, 1980 . . . . 12.00

TITANS
1999
1 MBu, new team, two covers 3.50
2 MBu,A:Superman 3.00
3 MBu 3.00
4 MBu,V:Goth 3.00
5 MBu,A:Siren. 3.00
6 MBu,A:Green Lantern 3.00
7 MBu,Velocity 10, pt.1 . . . . 3.00
8 MBu,Velocity 10, pt.2 . . . . 3.00
9 Day of Judgment x-over 3.00
10 MBu,F:Changeling
   & Deathstroke 3.00
11 MBu 3.00
12 MBu,This Immortal Coil,pt.3 . . . . 3.50
13 internal fight 3.00
14 to Scotland 3.00
15 MBu,pt.1 . . . . 3.00
16 MBu,V:Gargoyle 3.00
17 ALa,into space 3.00
18 ALa,into space,pt.2 . . . . 3.00
19 ALa,into space,pt.3 . . . . 3.00
20 ALa,end of Cyborg 3.00
21 PaP,Hangmen 3.00
22 PaP,Arsenal vs. Deathstroke . . . 3.00
23 PaP,Who's Troia?,pt.1 . . . . 3.00
24 PaP,Who's Troia?,pt.2. . . . . 3.00
25 MWn,GP,48-page 4.00
26 PaP,V:Shockwave 3.00
27 PaP,F:Cheshire,Epsilon 3.00
28 PaP,The All-Nighter 3.00
29 PaP,tower of troublemakers 3.00
30 JP,Sins of the Past 3.00
31 JP,V:Theta 3.00
32 V:Dakota Jameson 3.00
33 V:Theta 3.00
34 Cheshire Smile,Last Laugh 3.00
35 F:Beast Boy & Flamebird 3.00
36 V:Wildebeests 3.00
37 BKi,in the Orphanage 3.00
38 BKi,V:Epsilon,final stand 3.00

39 BKi,V:Dark Nemesis 3.00
40 BKi,F:The Favored 3.00
41 PGr,F:Nikki 3.00
42 BKi,Chemical World,pt.1 . . . . . . 3.00
43 BKi,Chemical World,pt.2 . . . . . . 3.00
44 BKi,JmP,Chemical World,pt.3 . . . 3.00
45 BKi,JmP,F:Damage 3.00
46 BKi,JmP,F:Damag,Jesse 3.00
47 TPe,BKi,PGr,JmP 3.00
48 TPe,BKi,JmP,Murder,pt.1 . . . . . . 3.00
49 TPe,BKi,JmP,Murder,pt.2 . . . . . . 3.00
50 TPe,BKi,JmP,final issue 3.00
Ann.#1 Planet DC 4.00
Spec. Secret Files #1. . . . . 5.50
Spec. Secret Files #2. . . . . 5.50
GN Scissors, Paper, Stone, manga
   style (1997) 5.50

TITANS SELL-OUT SPECIAL
1 SE,AV,I:Teeny Titans,
   w/Nightwing poster 3.75

TITANS, THE/LEGION OF SUPER-HEROES: UNIVERSE ABLAZE
Jan., 2000
1 (of 4) DJu,PJ 5.00
2 thru 4 DJu,PJ . . . . @5.00

TITANS, THE/ YOUNG JUSTICE: GRADUATION DAY
May 2003
1 (of 3) 20.00
2 Indigo 11.00
3 Concl. 13.00

TOE TAGS FEATURING GEORGE ROMERO
2004
1 . . . . 3.00
2 thru 6 . . . . @3.00

TOMAHAWK
1950
1 Prisoner Called Tomahawk . . 2,500.00
2 FF(4pgs),Four Boys
   Against the Frontier 1,000.00
3 Warpath 800.00
4 Tomahawk Wanted: Dead
   or Alive 800.00
5 The Girl Who Was Chief 800.00

Tomahawk #5
© DC Comics Inc.

6 Tomahawk-King of the Aztecs . 700.00
7 Punishment of Tomahawk 700.00
8 The King's Messenger. 700.00
9 The Five Doomed Men 700.00
10 Frontied Sabotage 700.00
11 Girl Who Hated Tomahawk. . . 500.00
12 Man From Magic Mountain. . . 500.00
13 Dan Hunter's Rival 500.00
14 The Frontier Tinker 500.00
15 The Wild Men of
    Wigwam Mountain 500.00
16 Treasure of the Angelique. . . . 500.00
17 Short-Cut to Danger 500.00
18 Bring In M'Sieur Pierre 500.00
19 The Lafayette Volunteers 500.00
20 NC(c),The Retreat of
    Tomahawk 500.00
21 NC(c),The Terror of the
    Wrathful Spirit 350.00
22 CS(c),Admiral Tomahawk 350.00
23 CS(c),The Indian Chief
    from Oxford 350.00
24 NC(c),Adventure In the
    Everglades. 350.00
25 NC(c),The Star-Gazer of
    Freemont 350.00
26 NC(c),Ten Wagons For
    Tomahawk 350.00
27 NC(c),Frontier Outcast 350.00
28 I:Lord Shilling 375.00
29 Conspiracy of Wounded Bear. 400.00
30 The King of the Thieves 350.00
31 NC(c),The Buffalo Brave
    From Misty Mountain. 350.00
32 NC(c),The Clocks That
    Went to War. 350.00
33 The Paleface Tribe 350.00
34 The Capture of General
    Washington 350.00
35 Frontier Feud 350.00
36 NC(c),A Cannon for Fort
    Reckless 350.00
37 NC(c),Feathered Warriors. . . . 350.00
38 The Frontier Zoo 350.00
39 The Redcoat Trickster. 350.00
40 Fearless Fettle-Daredevil 350.00
41 The Captured Chieftain. 350.00
42 The Prisoner Tribe 350.00
43 Tomahawk's Little Brother. . . . 350.00
44 The Brave Named Tomahawk 350.00
45 The Last Days of Chief Tory . . 350.00
46 The Chief With 1,000 Faces. . 200.00
47 The Frontier Rain-Maker. 200.00
48 Indian Twin Trouble. 200.00
49 The Unknown Warrior 200.00
50 The Brave Who Was Jinxed . . 200.00
51 General Tomahawk. 200.00
52 Tom Thumb of the Frontier . . . 200.00
53 The Four-Footed Renegade . . 200.00
54 Mystery of the 13th Arrows . . . 200.00
55 Prisoners of the Choctaw 200.00
56 The Riddle of the
    Five Little Indians 200.00
57 The Strange Fight
    at Fort Bravo 250.00
58 Track of the Mask 150.00
59 The Mystery Prisoner of
    Lost Island 150.00
60 The Amazing Walking Fort . . . 150.00
61 Tomahawk's Secret Weapons. 100.00
62 Strongest Man in the World . . 100.00
63 The Frontier Super Men 100.00
64 The Outcast Brave 100.00
65 Boy Who Wouldn't Be Chief . . 100.00
66 DD&SMo(c),A Trap For
    Tomahawk 100.00
67 DD&SMo(c),Frontier Sorcerer 100.00
68 DD&SMo(c),Tomahawk's
    Strange Ally 100.00
69 DD&SMo(c),Tracker-King
    of the Wolves. 100.00

Tomahawk #68
© DC Comics, Inc.

70 DD&SMo(c),Three Tasks
    for Tomahawk 100.00
71 DD&SMo(c),The Boy Who
    Betrayed His Country 100.00
72 DD&SMo(c),The Frontier Pupil 100.00
73 DD&SMo(c),The Secret of
    the Indian Sorceress 100.00
74 DD&SMo(c),The Great
    Paleface Masquerade 100.00
75 DD&SMo(c),The Ghost of
    Lord Shilling. 100.00
76 DD&SMo(c),The Totem-Pole
    Trail 100.00
77 DD&SMo(c),The Raids of
    the One-Man Tribe 100.00
78 DD&SMo(c),The Menace
    of the Mask 75.00
79 DD&SMo(c),Eagle Eye's
    Debt of Honor 75.00
80 DD&SMo(c),The Adventures
    of Tracker 60.00
81 The Strange Omens of
    the Indian Seer 60.00
82 The Son of the Tracker. 60.00
83 B:Tomahawk Rangers,
    Against the Tribe 60.00
84 There's a Coward Among
    the Rangers. 60.00
85 The Wispering War 60.00
86 Rangers vs. King Colossus . . . 40.00
87 The Secrets of Sgt.
    Witch Doctor 40.00
88 The Rangers Who Held
    Back the Earth. 40.00
89 The Terrible Tree-Man 40.00
90 The Prisoner In The Pit. 40.00
91 The Tribe Below the Earth . . . 40.00
92 The Petrified Sentry of
    Peaceful Valley 40.00
93 The Return of King Colosso . . 40.00
94 Rip Van Ranger 40.00
95 The Tribe Beneath the Sea. . . 40.00
96 The Ranger Killers 40.00
97 The Prisoner Behind the
    Bull's-Eye. 40.00
98 The Pied Piper Rangers 40.00
99 The Rangers vs.ChiefCobweb . 40.00
100 The Weird Water-Tomahawk . 50.00
101 Tomahawk, Enemy Spy 35.00
102 The Dragon Killers 35.00
103 The Frontier Frankenstein . . 35.00
104 The Fearful Freak of
    Dunham's Dungeon. 35.00
105 The Attack of the Gator God. . 35.00
106 The Ghost of Tomahawk. . . . 35.00

107 Double-Cross of the
    Gorilla Ranger 35.00
108 New Boss For the Rangers . . 35.00
109 The Caveman Ranger 35.00
110 Tomahawk Must Die 35.00
111 Vengeance of the Devil-Dogs . 35.00
112 The Rangers vs. Tomahawk . . 35.00
113 The Mad Miser of
    Carlisle Castle 35.00
114 The Terrible Power of
    Chief Iron Hands 35.00
115 The Deadly Flaming Ranger . . 35.00
116 NA(c),The Last Mile of
    Massacre Trail. 35.00
117 NA(c),Rangers'Last Stand. . . . 35.00
118 NA(c),Tomahawk, Guilty
    of Murder. 35.00
119 NA(c),Bait For a Buzzard 35.00
120 NC(c),The Coward Who
    Lived Forever 35.00
121 NA(c),To Kill a Ranger 35.00
122 IN(c),Must the Brave Die 35.00
123 NA(c),The Stallions of Death . 35.00
124 NA(c),The Valley of
    No Return 35.00
125 NA(c),A Chief's Feather
    For Little Bear 35.00
126 NA(c),The Baron of
    Gallows Hill 35.00
127 NA(c),The Devil is Waiting . . . 35.00
128 NA(c),Rangers-Your 9
    Lives For Mine. 35.00
129 NA(c),Treachery at
    Thunder Ridge. 35.00
130 NA(c),Deathwatch at
    Desolation Valley. 35.00
131 JKu(c),B:Son of Tomahawk,
    Hang Him High 35.00
132 JKu(c),Small Eagle...Brother
    Hawk 25.00
133 JKu(c),Scalp Hunter 25.00
134 JKu(c),The Rusty Ranger 25.00
135 JKu(c),Death on Ghost
    Mountain 25.00
136 JKu(c),A Piece of Sky. 30.00
137 JKu(c),Night of the Knife. 30.00
138 JKu(c),A Different Kind
    of Christmas 30.00
139 JKu(c),Death Council 35.00
140 Jku(c),The Rescue 30.00

TOR
May-June, 1975
1 JKu,O:Tor. 20.00
2 thru 6, Tor reprints . . . . @12.00

TOTAL JUSTICE
Sept., 1996
1 thru 3 CPr(s),RBe,DG, toy
    line tie-in . . . . @2.25

TOTAL RECALL
1990
1 Movie Adaption 3.00

TOUCH
DC Focus Apr. 2004
1 Rory Goodman, Las Vegas 2.50
2 thru 6 . . . . 2.50

TRANSMETROPOLITAN
DC/Helix, July, 1997
1 WEI,DaR,JeM, gonzo journalism
    in 21st century 10.00
2 WEI,DaR,Angels 8 district 6.00
3 WEI,DaR, riot in Angels 8 . . . . . . 5.00
4 WEI,DaR, Vs President of US . . . 4.00
5 WEI,DaR, Watches TV 4.00
6 WEI,DaR,evangelicals 4.00
7 WEI,DaR 4.00

Transmetropolitan #8
© *DC Comics Inc.*

8 WEI,DaR,AnotherColdMorning . . 4.00
9 WEI,DaR,Wild in the Country . . . 3.00
10 WEI,DaR,Freeze Me with
　Your Kiss, pt.1 . . . . 3.00
11 WEI,DaR,Freeze Me, pt.2 . . . . . 3.00
12 WEI,DaR,Freeze Me, pt.3 . . . . . 3.00
13 WEI,DaR,JaL(c),Year of the
　Bastard, pt.1 . . . . 3.00
14 WEI,DaR,JaL(c),Bastard,pt.2 . . 3.00
15 WEI,DaR,JaL(c),Bastard,pt.3 . . 3.00
16 WEI,DaR,Bastard,pt.4 . . . . 3.00
17 WEI,DaR,Bastard,pt.5 . . . . 3.00
18 WEI,DaR,Bastard, concl. 3.00
19 WEI,DaR,New Scum,pt.1 . . . . . 3.00
20 WEI,DaR,New Scum,pt.2 . . . . . 3.00
21 WEI,DaR,New Scum,pt.3 . . . . . 2.50
22 WEI,DaR,New Scum,pt.4 . . . . . 2.50
23 WEI,DaR,New Scum,pt.5 . . . . . 2.50
24 WEI,DaR,New Scum,pt.6 . . . . . 2.50
25 WEI,DaR,JLe(c),Days in
　the City #1 . . . . 2.50
26 WEI,DaR,RyR,JLe(c),Days in
　the City #2 . . . . 2.50
27 WEI,DaR,RyR,JLe(c) 2.50
28 WEI,DaR,RyR,LonelyCity,pt.1 . . 2.50
29 WEI,DaR,RyR,LonelyCity,pt.2 . . 2.50
30 WEI,DaR,RyR,LonelyCity,pt.3 . . 2.50
31 WEI,DaR,RyR,F:Spider. 2.50
32 WEI,DaR,RyR, ... 2.50
33 WEI,DaR,RyR 2.50
34 WEI,DaR,RyR,Gouge Away,pt.1 . 2.50
35 WEI,DaR,RyR,Gouge Away,pt.2 . 2.50
36 WEI,DaR,RyR,Gouge Away,pt.3 . 2.50
37 WEI,DaR,Back to Basics,pt.1 . . 2.50
38 WEI,DaR,Back to Basics,pt.2 . . 2.50
39 WEI,DaR,Back to Basics,pt.3 . . 2.50
40 WEI,DaR,Streets atNight,pt.1 . . 2.50
41 WEI,DaR,Streets atNight,pt.2 . . 2.50
42 WEI,DaR,Streets atNight,pt.3 . . 2.50
43 WEI,DaR,Dirge,pt.1 . . . . 2.50
44 WEI,DaR,Dirge,pt.2 . . . . 2.50
45 WEI,DaR,Dirge,pt.3 . . . . 2.50
46 WEI,DaR,Dirge aftermath 2.50
47 WEI,DaR,A Disaster Zone 2.50
48 WEI,DaR,Year Four begins. . . . 2.50
49 WEI,DaR,rebuild Spider's case. . 2.50
50 WEI,DaR,Filthy Assistants 2.50
51 WEI,DaR,F:Mitchell Royce 2.50
52 WEI,DaR,The Cure,pt.1 . . . . . . 2.50
53 WEI,DaR,The Cure,pt.2 . . . . . . 2.50
54 WEI,DaR,The Cure,pt.3 . . . . . . 2.50
55 WEI,DaR,Vita Severn Zone 2.50
56 WEI,DaR,Martial law. 2.50
57 WEI,DaR,White House siege . . . 2.50

58 WEI,DaR,martial law. 2.50
59 WEI,DaR,final meeting 2.50
60 WEI,DaR,final issue 2.50
GN I Hate it Here. 6.00
GN Filth of the City 6.00
TPB Lust For Life. 15.00
TPB Year of the Bastard 13.00
TPB Back on the Street 8.00
TPB New Scum, rep.#19–#24 . . . . 13.00
TPB Lonely City 15.00
TPB Gouge Away (2002). 15.00
TPB Spider's Thrash (2002) 15.00
TPB The Cure (2003) 15.00
TPB Dirge (2003). 15.00
TPB One More Time (2004) 15.00
TPB Tales of Human Waste (2004) 10.00

TRENCHCOAT BRIGADE
DC/Vertigo, 1999
1 (of 4) JNR(s),F:John Constantine,
　Mister E, Dr.Occult, Phantom
　Stranger 2.50
2 JNR 2.50
3 JNR 2.50
4 JNR, conclusion. 2.50

TRIALS OF SHAZAM
Aug., 2006
1 (of 12) HPo, The Boy & The Man 3.00
2 thru 4 HPo 3.00

TRIGGER
DC/Vertigo, Dec., 2004
1 JWk,F:Deirdre Myers 3.00
2 JWk 3.00
3 JWk 3.00
4 JWk 3.00
5 JWk 3.00
6 JWk, concl. 3.00
7 JWk, I:Leonard. 3.00
8 JWk 3.00

TRIUMPH
[Mini-Series], 1995
1 From Zero Hour 2.25
2 Teamates Peril 2.25
3 V:Mind Readers 2.25

TROUBLE MAGNET
Dec., 1999
1 (of 4) KPI, F:robot whose mind
　has been stolen. 2.50
2 KPI 2.50
3 KPI 2.50
4 KPI,concl. 2.50

TV SCREEN CARTOONS
See: REAL SCREEN COMICS

2020 VISIONS
DC/Vertigo, April, 1997
1 (of 12) the Disunited States
　of America 2.25
2 JaD(s), ... 2.25
3 JaD(s), ... 2.25
4 JaD(s),WaP,La Tormenta,pt.1 . . 2.25
5 JaD(s),WaP,La Tormenta,pt.2 . . 2.25
6 JaD(s),WaP,La Tormenta,pt.3 . . 2.25
7 JaD(s),Renegade,pt.1 . . . . 2.25
8 JaD(s),Renegade,pt.2 . . . . 2.25
9 JaD(s),Renegade,pt.3 . . . . 2.25
10 JaD(s),Repro-Man,pt.1 . . . . . . 2.25
11 JaD(s),Repro-Man,pt.2 . . . . . . 2.25
12 JaD(s),Repro-Man,pt.3 . . . . . . 2.25

TWILIGHT
1990–91
1 JL,Last Frontier 5.50

2 JL,K.SorensenVs.T.Tomorrow . . . 5.00
3 JL,K.SorensenVs.T.Tomorrow . . . 5.00

UNAUTHORIZED BIO
OF LEX LUTHOR
1989
1 EB 4.00

UNCLE SAM
DC/Vertigo, Nov, 1997
GN 1 (of 2) AxR 5.00
GN 2 AxR. 5.00
TPB 10.00

UNCLE SAM AND
THE FREEDOM FIGHTERS
July, 2006
1 (of 8) JP, Shade task force 3.00
2 JP, Wanted: Uncle Sam. 3.00
3 JP, Arizona Desert 3.00
4 JP. 3.00
5 JP. 3.00

UNDERWORLD
Dec., 1987
1 EC,New Yorks Finest. 2.50
2 EC,A:Black Racer 2.50
3 EC,V:Black Racer 2.50
4 EC,final issue. 2.50

UNDERWORLD
UNLEASHED
1995–96
1 PWa,F:Neron 5.00
2 PWa,Neron Vs.Green Lantern. . . 4.00
3 PWa,conclusion 4.00
Abyss—Hell's Sentinel 1-shot 3.00
Apokolips-Dark Uprising 1-shot . . . 3.00
Batman—Devil's Asylum 1-shot
　AIG,BSz 3.00
Patterns of Fear 1-shot 3.00

UNEXPECTED, THE
See: TALES OF
THE UNEXPECTED

UNKNOWN SOLDIER
See: STAR SPANGLED

UNKNOWN SOLDIER
April, 1988
1 True Origin revealed,Viet
　Nam 1970 . . . . 4.00
2 Origin contd.,Iran 1977 . . . . 3.00
3 Origin contd.Afghanistan1982 . . . 3.00
4 Nicaragua 3.00
5 Nicaragua contd. 3.00
6 . . . . 3.00
7 Libia 3.00
8 Siberia, U.S.S.R. 3.00
9 North Korea 1952 . . . . 3.00
10 C.I.A. 3.00
11 C.I.A., Army Intelligence 3.00
12 final issue,1989. . . . . 3.00

UNKNOWN SOLDIER
DC/Vertigo, Feb., 1997
1 (of 4) GEn(s),KPI,F:maverick
　CIA agent. 7.00
2 GEn(s),KPI,search for Unknown
　Soldier continues. 5.00
3 GEn(s),KPI,search for Unknown
　Soldier continues. 5.00
4 GEn(s),KPI,intrigue, finale 5.00
TPB series rep. 13.00

All comics prices listed are for *Near Mint* condition.

UNTOLD LEGEND OF BATMAN
July, 1980
1 JA,JBy,(1st DC work)O:Batman . 6.00
2 JA,O:Joker&Robin 4.50
3 JA,O:Batgirl 4.50

USER
DC/Vertigo, Jan., 2001
1 (of 3) 48-page 6.00
2 JBo,SeP,48-page 6.00
3 JBo,SeP,48-page 6.00

V
(TV Adaptation)
Feb., 1985
1 CI/TD 3.00
2 thru 5 CI/TD . . . . @2.25
6 thru 16 CI/TD . . . . @2.25
17 & 18 DG . . . . @2.25

Valor #22
© *DC Comics, Inc.*

VALOR
1992–94
1 N:Valor,A:Lex Luthor Jr 3.00
2 MBr,AG,V:Supergirl 2.50
3 MBr,AG,V:Lobo 2.50
4 MBr,AG,V:Lobo 2.50
5 MBr,A:Blasters 2.50
6 A:Blasters,V:Kanjar Ru 2.50
7 A:Blasters 2.50
8 AH(c),V:The Unimaginable 2.50
9 AH(c),PCu,A:Darkstar 2.50
10 AH(c),V:Unimaginable 2.50
11 A:Legionnaires 2.50
12 AH(c),B:D.O.A. 3.00
13 AH(c),D:Valor's Mom 3.00
14 AH(c),A:JLA,Legionnaires 2.50
15 SI(c),D.O.A #4. . . . . 2.50
16 CDo,D.O.A #5. . . . . 2.50
17 CDo,LMc,D:Valor 2.50
18 A:Legionnaires 2.50
19 CDo,A:Legionnaires,V:Glorith . . 2.50
20 CDo,A:Wave Rider 2.50
21 . . . . 2.50
22 End of an Era,pt.2. . . . . 2.50
23 Zero Hour 2.50

VAMPS
DC/Vertigo, 1994–95
1 BB(c) 3.00

2 thru 6 BB(c) . . . . @3.00
TPB 10.00

VAMPS: HOLLYWOOD & VEIN
DC/Vertigo, 1996
1 F:Mink 2.50
2 . . . . 2.50
3 I:Maggot. 2.50
4 F:Mink,Screech 2.50
5 off to rescue Hugh Evans (of 6) . 2.50
6 . . . . 2.50

VAMPS: PUMPKIN TIME
DC/Vertigo, 1998
1 (of 3) Halloween mini-series 2.50
2 thru 3 . . . . @2.50

VERMILLION
DC/Helix, Aug., 1996
1 ADv,MKu(c) Lucius Shepard
  story 2.50
2 ADv,MKu(c) Jonathan Cave's
  cover blown 2.50
3 ADv,riot aboard space ship,
  Ildiko's tale. 2.50
4 ADv,Starship's engines run wild. . 2.50
5 ADv 2.50
6 ADv,Creation of Vermillion 2.50
7 ADv,Jonathan Cave discovers
  hiding place of enemy 2.50
8 ADv,Joyland 2.50
9 GEr, the library in Kaia Mortai . . . 2.50
10 GEr, Lord Iron and Lady
  Manganese, pt.2 . . . . 2.50
11 GEr,Lord Iron and Lady
  Manganese, concl. 2.50
12 final issue 2.50

VERTICAL
DC/Vertigo, Dec. 2003
Spec. MiA,64-pg. 5.00

VERTIGO
DC/Vertigo, Oct., 2005
TPB First Taste,Six story sampler . . 5.00
TPB First Offenses, sampler 5.00

VERTIGO GALLERY: DREAMS AND NIGHTMARES
1995
1 Various artists 3.50

VERTIGO JAM
1993
1 GF(c),NGa(s),ANo(s),PrM(s),GEn(s),
  JaD(s),KN,SDi,SEa,NyC(s),EiS,PhH,
  KDM(i),SeP,MiA,RaP(s),MPn(i),
  Vertigo Short Stories 4.50

VERTIGO POP!
TOKYO
DC/Vertigo, July, 2002
1 (of 4) by Seth Fisher 3.00
2 thru 4 . . . . @3.00

LONDON
DC/Vertigo, Nov., 2002
1 (of 4) PrM,PBd 3.00
2 thru 4 PrM,PBd . . . . @3.00

BANGKOK
DC/Vertigo, May 2003
1 (of 4) 3.00
2 thru 4 . . . . @3.00

VERTIGO PREVIEW
1992
Preview of new Vertigo titles,
  new Sandman story. 2.25

VERTIGO SECRET FILES: HELLBLAZER
Jan., 2005
1 rep. 5.00

VERTIGO VERITE:
HELL ETERNAL
Feb., 1998
1-shot JaD,SeP 7.00
THE SYSTEM
1 thru 3 . . . . @3.00
GN Seven Miles a Second 8.00
THE UNSEEN HAND
DC/Vertigo, 1996
1 thru 3 TLa. . . . . @2.50
4 TLa, final issue 2.50
DR. OCCULT
1 F:Dr. Occult 4.00
DR. THIRTEEN
DC/Vertigo, July, 1998
GN evil artificial intelligence. 6.00

VERTIGO VISIONS:
THE GEEK
1993
1 RaP(s),MiA,V:Dr.Abuse 4.25
PHANTOM STRANGER
1993
1 AaK(s),GyD,The Infernal House . 3.75
THE EATERS
1995
1 I:The Quills. 5.00
TOMAHAWK
DC/Vertigo, May, 1998
GN RaP,TY 5.00

VERTIGO: WINTER'S EDGE
DC/Vertigo, 1998
TPB BB(c) rep. 8.00
GN Winter's Edge II. 7.00
GN Winter's Edge III 7.00

VEXT
1999
1 KG,MMK,MkM 2.50
2 th`ru 6 KG,MMK,MkM. . . . . . . @2.50

V FOR VENDETTA
Sept., 1988
1 Reps.Warrior Mag(U.K.),I:V,
  A:M.Storm (Moore scripts). 6.00
2 Murder Spree. 5.00
3 Govt. Investigators close in 4.00
4 T.V. Broadcast take-over 4.00
5 Govt.Corruption Expose 4.00
6 Evey in Prison 4.00
7 Evey released 4.00
8 Search for V,A:Finch 4.00
9 V:Finch 4.00
10 D:V 4.00
TPB 1990 . . . . 25.00

VIGILANTE
Oct., 1983
1 KP,DG,F:Adrian Chase 3.50
2 KP 3.00

Vigilante #33 © DC Comics, Inc.

3 KP,Cyborg 2.50
4 DN,V:Exterminator 2.50
5 KP 2.50
6 O:Vigilante 3.00
7 O:Vigilante 3.00
8 thru 16 . . . . @2.50
17 Moore 4.00
18 Moore 4.00
19 thru 49 . . . . @2.50
50 KSy(c)D:Vigilante 3.00
Ann.#1 . . . . 3.00
Ann.#2 V:Cannon 2.50

VIGILANTE
Sept., 2005
1 (of 6) 3.00
2 thru 6 . . . . @3.00

VIGILANTE: CITY LIGHTS, PRAIRIE JUSTICE
1995–96
1 JeR,MCo,(of 4) 2.50
2 JeR,V:Bugsy Siegel 2.50
3 JeR 2.50
4 finale 2.50

VILLAINS UNITED
May, 2005
1 (of 6) F:Mockingbird 12.00
1a 2nd printing 4.00
2 . . . . 3.50
2a 2nd printing 3.00
3 The Six 3.00
4 . . . . 3.00
5 Catman vs. Deadshot 3.00
6 F:Mockingbird, concl 3.00
TPB Villains United 13.00

VIMANARAMA!
DC/Vertigo, Feb., 2005
1 (of 3) GMo(s),PBd 3.00
2 GMo(s),PBd 3.00
3 GMo(s),PBd 3.00
TPB Vimanarama, GMo(s),PBd . . . 13.00

VIPER
1994
1 Based on the TV Show 2.25
2 . . . . 2.25
3 . . . . 2.25
4 final issue 2.25

WANDERERS
June, 1988
1 I:New Team 3.00
2 thru 13 . . . . @3.00

WANTED: THE WORLD'S MOST DANGEROUS VILLIANS
July-Aug., 1972
1 GK,rep. Batman,Green Lantern . 50.00
2 CI,Batman/Joker/Penguin 35.00
3 JK,MMe,Dr. Fate 30.00
4 Green Lantern 30.00
5 GK,Dollman/Green Lantern 30.00
6 JK,Starman 30.00
7 JK,MMe,Hawkman/Flash 30.00
8 Dr. Fate/Flash 30.00
9 Sandman/Superman 30.00

WARLORD
Jan., 1976
1 MGr,O:Warlord 40.00
2 MGr,I:Machiste 20.00
3 MGr,War Gods of Skartaris 15.00
4 MGr,Duel of the Titans 15.00
5 MGr,The Secret of Skartaris . . . 15.00
6 MGr,I:Mariah,Stryker 9.00
7 MGr,O:Machiste 9.00
8 MGr,A:Skyra 9.00
9 MGr,N:Warlord 9.00
10 MGr,I:Ashiya 9.00
11 MGr,rep.1st Issue special #8 . . 6.00
12 MGr,I:Aton 6.00
13 MGr,D:Stryker 6.00
14 MGr,V:Death 6.00
15 MGr,I:Joshua 6.00
16 MGr,I:Saaba 6.00
17 MGr,Citadel of Death 6.00
18 MGr,I:Shadow 6.00
19 MGr,Wolves of the Steppes 6.00
20 MGr,I:Joshua clone 7.00
21 MGr,D:Joshua clone,Shadow . . 5.00
22 MGr,Beast in the Tower 10.00
23 MGr,Children of Ba'al 5.00
24 MGr,I:Iligia 5.00
25 MGr,I:Ahir 5.00
26 MGr,The Challenge 5.00
27 MGr,Atlantis Dying 5.00
28 MGr,I:Wizard World 5.00
29 MGr,I:Mongo Ironhand 5.00
30 MGr,C:Joshua 5.00
31 MGr,Wing over Shamballah 5.00
32 MGr,I:Shakira 5.00
33 MGr,Birds of Prey,A:Shakira . . . 5.00
34 MGr,Sword of the Sorceror,
    I:Hellfire 5.00
35 MGr,C:Mike Grell 5.00
36 MGr,Interlude 5.00
37 MGr,JSn,I:Firewing,B:Omac . . . 6.00
38 MGr,I:Jennifer,A:Omac 5.00
39 MGr,JSn,Feast of Agravar 5.00
40 MGr,N:Warlord 5.00
41 MGr,A:Askir 5.00
42 MGr,JSn,A:Tara,Omac 5.00
43 MGr,JSn,Berserk'A:Omac 5.00
44 MGr,The Gamble 5.00
45 MGr,Nightmare in Vista
    Vision,A:Omac 5.00
46 MGr,D:Shakira 5.00
47 MGr,I:Mlkola,E:Omac 5.00
48 MGr,EC,TY,I:Arak,Claw(B) 5.00
49 MGr,TY,A:Shakira,E:Claw 3.00
50 MGr,By Fire and Ice 3.00
51 MGr,TY,rep.#1,
    I(B):Dragonsword 3.00
52 MGr,TY,Back in the U.S.S.R. . . . 3.00
53 MT,TY,Sorcerer's Apprentice . . . 3.00
54 MT,Sorceress Supreme,
    E:Dragonsword 3.00
55 MT,Have a Nice Day 3.00

56 MT,JD,I:Gregmore,(B:)Arion 3.00
57 MT,The Two Faces of
    Travis Morgan 3.00
58 MT,O:Greamore 3.00
59 MGr,A:Joshua 3.00
60 JD,Death Dual 3.00
61 JD,A:Greamore 3.00
62 JD,TMd,A:Mikola,E:Arion 3.00
63 JD,RR,I(B):Barren Earth 4.00
64 DJu,RRElsewhere 3.00
65 DJu,RR,A:Wizard World,
    No Barren Earth 3.00
66 DJuWizard World,
    No Barren Earth 3.00
67 DJu,RR,The Mark 3.00
68 DJu,RR 3.00
69 DJu,RR 3.00
70 DJu,Outback 3.00
71 DJu/DA,The Journey Back
    No Barren Earth 3.00
72 DJu,DA,I:Scarhart,No Barren
    Earth 3.00
73 DJ,DA,Cry Plague 3.00
74 DJu,No Barren Earth 3.00
75 DJu,All Dreams Must Pass
    No Barren Earth 3.00
76 DJu,DA,RR,A:Sarga 3.00
77 DJu,DA,RR,Let My People Go . . 3.00
78 DJu,RR,Doom's Mouth 3.00
79 PB,RM,Paradox,No Barren
    Earth 3.00
80 DJu,DA,RR,Future Trek 3.00
81 DJu,DA,RR,Thief's Magic 3.00
82 DJu,DA,RR,Revolution 3.00
83 DJu,RR,All the President's
    Men 3.00
84 DJu,DA,RR,Hail to the Chief . . . 3.00
85 DJu,RR,The Price of Change . . . 3.00
86 DJ,DA,No Barren Earth 3.00
87 DJu,RB,RR,I:Hawk 3.00
88 DJu,RB,RR,I:Patch,E:Barren
    Earth 3.00
89 RB,I:Sabertooth 3.00
90 RB,Demon's of the Past 3.00
91 DJu,DA,I:Maddox,O:Warlord
    O:Jennifer 3.00
92 NKu,Evil in Ebony 3.00
93 RR,A:Sabertooth 3.00
94 Assassin's Prey 3.00
95 AKu,Dragon's Doom 3.00
96 Nightmare Prelude 3.00
97 RB,A:Saaba,D:Scarhart 3.00
98 NKu,Crisis tie-in 3.00
99 NKuFire and Sword 3.00
100 AKu,D:Greamore,Sabertooth . . 4.00

Warlord #87 © DC Comics Inc.

DC COMICS

Warlord Ann. #6
© DC Comics, Inc.

101 MGr,Temple of Demi-god 3.00
102 I:Zuppara,Error-Machiste
with two hands. 3.00
103 JBi,Moon Beast. 3.00
104 RR,Dragon Skinner. 3.00
105 RR,Stalilers of Skinner 3.00
106 RR,I:Daimon 3.00
107 RR,Bride of Yano 3.00
108 RR,I:Mortella. 3.00
109 RR,A:Mortella. 3.00
110 RR,A:Skyra III 3.00
111 RR,Tearing o/t Island Sea 3.00
112 RR,Obsession 3.00
113 RR,Through Fiends
Destroy Me 3.00
114 RR,Phenalegeno Dies 3.00
115 RR,Citadel of Fear 3.00
116 RR,Revenge of the Warlord . . . 3.00
117 RR,A:Power Girl 3.00
118 RR,A:Power Girl 3.00
119 RR,A:Power Girl 3.00
120 ATb,A:Power Girl 3.00
121 ATb,A:Power Girl 3.00
122 ATb,A:Power Girl 3.00
123 JD,TMd,N:Warlord 3.00
124 JD,TMd,I:Scavenger 3.00
125 JD,TMd,A:Machiste. 3.00
126 JD,TMd,A:Machiste. 3.00
127 JD,The Last Dragon 3.00
128 JD,I:Agife 3.00
129 JD,Vision of Quest 3.00
130 JD,A:Maddox 3.00
131 JD,RLd,Vengeful Legacies 5.00
132 A New Beginning. 3.00
133 JD,final issue (44pg). 4.00
Ann.#1 MGr,A:Shakira 4.00
Ann.#2 I:Krystovar 3.00
Ann.#3 DJu,Full Circle 3.00
Ann.#4 A:New Gods,
Legends tie-in 3.00
Ann.#5 AKu,Hellfire 3.00
Ann.#6 F:New Gods 3.00
TPB Warlord:Savage Empire,
Rep.#1-#10,#12,Special #8 . . . 20.00

[Limited Series], 1992

1 Travis Morgan retrospective 2.25
2 Fate of T. Morgan revealed 2.25
3 Return of Deimos 2.25
4 V:Deimos 2.25
5 MGr(c),Skartaros at War 2.25
6 finale 2.25

WARLORD, THE
Feb., 2006

1 BS, F:Travis Morgan 3.00
2 BS, Return of the Warlord 3.00
3 BS, Travis Morgan. 3.00
4 BS, In Skartaris 3.00
5 BS, Sword of Truth 3.00
6 BS,Somewhere in Skartaris. 3.00
7 BS,F:Brovis 3.00
8 BS, Someone dies. 3.00
9 BS, Revenge 3.00
10 Final Issue 3.00

WAR OF THE GODS
1991

1 GP,A:Lobo,Misc.Heroes,Circe . . . 2.25
2 GP,A:Misc.Heroes,V:Circe,
w/poster 2.25
2a (Newsstand). 2.25
3 GP,A:Misc.Heroes,V:Circe,
w/poster 2.25
3a Newsstand 2.25
4 GP,A:Misc.Heroes,V:Circe,
w/poster 2.25
4a Newsstand 2.25

WAR STORY
DC/Vertigo, Sept., 2001

Spec. Johann's Tiger,GEn 5.00
Spec. D-Day Dodgers,GEn 5.00
Spec. Screaming Eagles,GEn 5.00
Spec. The Reivers 5.00
Spec. Nightingale,GEn 5.00
Spec. J for Jenny 5.00
Spec. Condors 5.00
Spec. Archangel. 5.00
Spec. Johann's Tiger 5.00
TPB 20.00
TPB Vol. 2 GEn (2006) 20.00

WASTELAND
Dec., 1987

1 Selection of Horror stories 2.25
2 thru 10 . . . . @2.25
11 thru 18 . . . . @2.25

WATCHMEN
Sept., 1986

1 B:AMo,DGb,D:Comedian 10.00
2 DGb,Funeral for Comedian 6.00
3 DGb,F:Dr.Manhattan 5.00
4 DGb,O:Dr.Manhattan 5.00
5 DGb,F:Rorschach 5.00
6 DGb,O:Rorschach 5.00
7 DGb,F:Nite Owl 5.00
8 DGb,F:Silk Spectre 5.00
9 DGb,O:Silk Spectre 5.00
10 DGb,A:Rorschach 5.00
11 DGb,O:Ozymandius 5.00
12 DGb,D:Rorsharch 5.00
TPB rep.#1-#12 . . . . 15.00
TPB 20.00

WEB, THE
DC/Impact, 1991–92

1 I:Gunny, Bill Grady, Templar 2.25
Ann.#1 Earthquest,w/trading card . . 2.50

WEIRD, THE
April, 1988

1 BWr,A:JLI. 4.00
2 BWr,A:JLI. 3.00
3 BWr,V:Jason 3.00
4 final issue. 3.00

WEIRD
DC/Paradox Press, 1997

1 B&W magazine 3.00

2 . . . . 3.00
3 . . . . 3.00

WEIRD SECRET ORIGINS
Aug. 2004

Spec. 80-page giant. 6.00

Weird War Tales #42
© DC Comics, Inc.

WEIRD WAR TALES
Sept.–Oct., 1971

1 JKu(c),JKu,RH,Fort which
Did Not Return. 400.00
2 JKu,MD,Military Madness 150.00
3 JKu(c),RA,The Pool 150.00
4 JKu(c),Ghost of Two Wars. . . . 125.00
5 JKu(c),RH,Slave 125.00
6 JKu(c),Pawns, The Sounds
of War 75.00
7 JKu(c),JKu,RH,Flying Blind . . . 75.00
8 NA(c),The Avenging Grave . . . 100.00
9 NC(c),The Promise 75.00
10 NC(c),Who is Haunting
the Haunted Chateau 75.00
11 NC(c),ShM,Oct. 30, 1918:
The German Trenches, WWI . 50.00
12 MK(c),God of Vengeance 50.00
13 LD(c),The Die-Hards. 50.00
14 LD(c),ShM,The Ghost of
McBride's Woman 50.00
15 LD(c),Ace King Just Flew
In From Hell. 50.00
16 LD(c),More Dead Than Alive . . 50.00
17 GE(c),Dead Man's Hands. 50.00
18 GE(c),Captain Dracula 50.00
19 LD(c),The Platoon That
Wouldn't Die 50.00
20 LD(c),Operation Voodoo 50.00
21 LD(c),One Hour To Kill 30.00
22 LD(c),Wings of Death 30.00
23 LD(c),The Bird of Death 30.00
24 LD(c),The Invisible Enemy 30.00
25 LD(c),Black Magic...White
Death 30.00
26 LD(c),Jump Into Hell. 30.00
27 LD(c),Survival of the
Fittest. 30.00
28 LD(c),Isle of Forgotten
Warriors 30.00
29 LD(c),Breaking Point. 30.00
30 LD(c),The Elements of Death . . 30.00
31 LD(c),Death Waits Twice 30.00
32 LD(c),The Enemy, The Stars . . 30.00
33 LD(c),Pride of the Master
Race 30.00

34 LD(c),The Common Enemy . . . 30.00
35 LD(c),The Invaders 30.00
36 JKu(c),Escape. 35.00
37 LD(c),The Three Wars of
   Don Q 15.00
38 JKu(c),Born To Die 15.00
39 JKu(c),The Spoils of War 15.00
40 ECh(c),Back From The Dead . . 15.00
41 JL(c), The Dead Draftees of
   Regiment Six 15.00
42 JKu(c),Old Soldiers Never
   Die 15.00
43 ECh(c),Bulletproof 15.00
44 JKu(c),ShM,The Emperor
   Weehawken 15.00
45 JKu(c),The Battle of Bloody
   Valley 15.00
46 Kill Or Be Killed 15.00
47 JKu(c),Bloodbath of the Toy
   Soldiers 15.00
48 JL(c),Ultimate Destiny 15.00
49 The Face Of The Enemy 15.00
50 ECh(c),-An Appointment With
   Destiny 15.00
51 JKu(c),Secret Weapon 15.00
52 JKu(c),The Devil Is A
   Souvenir Hunter 15.00
53 JAp(c), Deadly Dominoes 15.00
54 GM(c),Soldier of Satan 15.00
55 JKu(c),A Rebel Shall Rise
   From The Grave 15.00
56 AM(c),The Headless Courier . . 15.00
57 RT(c),Trial By Combat 15.00
58 JKu(c),Death Has A Hundred
   Eyes 15.00
59 The Old One 15.00
60 JKu(c),Night Flight 15.00
61 HC(c),Mind War 12.00
62 JKu(c),The Grubbers 12.00
63 JKu(c),Battleground 12.00
64 JKu(c),FM(1st DC),D-Day 40.00
65 JKu(c),The Last Cavalry
   Charge 12.00
66 JKu(c),The Iron Star 12.00
67 JKu(c),The Attack of the
   Undead 12.00
68 FM,JKu(c),The Life and Death of
   Charlie Golem 30.00
69 JKu(c),The Day After Doomsday 9.00
70 LD(c),The Blood Boat 9.00
71 LD(c),False Prophet 9.00
72 JKu(c),Death Camp 9.00
73 GF(c),The Curse of Zopyrus . . . 9.00
74 GE(c),March of the Mammoth . . 9.00
75 JKu(c),The Forgery 9.00
76 JKu(c),The Fire Bug 9.00
77 JKu(c),Triad 9.00
78 JKu(c),Indian War In Space . . . 9.00
79 JKu(c),The Gods Themselves . . 9.00
80 JKu(c),An Old Man's Profession. 9.00
81 JKu(c),It Takes Brains To
   Be A Killer 9.00
82 GE(c),Funeral Fire 9.00
83 GE(c),Prison of the Mind 9.00
84 JKu(c),Devil's Due 9.00
85 thru 124 June, 1983 . . . . @9.00

WEIRD WAR TALES
DC/Vertigo, April, 1997
1 (of 4) anthology 3.00
2 MK(c) 3.00
3 . . . . 3.00
4 final issue 3.00
Spec.#1 GEn (2000) 5.00

ALL-STAR WESTERN
Aug.–Sept., 1970
1 NA(c),CI 75.00
2 NA(c),GM,B:Outlaw 50.00
3 NA(c),GK,O:El Diablo 50.00
4 NA(c),GK,JKu,GM 50.00

All-Star Western #3
© DC Comics Inc.

5 NA(c),JAp,E:Outlaw 50.00
6 GK,B:Billy the Kid 50.00
7 JKu 40.00
8 E:Billy the Kid 40.00
9 FF 40.00
10 GM,I:Jonah Hex 550.00
11 GM,A:Jonah Hex 250.00
Becomes:

WEIRD WESTERN TALES
June-July, 1972
12 NA,BWr,JKu 225.00
13 . . . . 150.00
14 ATh 100.00
15 NA(c),GK 75.00
16 thru 28 . . . . @50.00
29 O:Jonah Hex 75.00
30 . . . . 35.00
31 thru 38 . . . . @\35.00
39 I&O:Scalphunter 35.00
40 thru 70 . . . . @20.00

WEIRD WESTERN TALES
DC/Vertigo, Feb., 2001
1 (of 4) 2.50
2 thru 4 . . . . @2.50

WEIRD WORLDS
Aug.–Sept., 1971
1 JO,MA,John Carter 50.00
2 NA,JO(c),MA,BWr 40.00
3 MA,NA 25.00
4 MK(c),MK 20.00
5 MK(c),MK 20.00
6 MK(c),MK 20.00
7 John Carter ends 20.00
8 HC,I:Iron Wolf 20.00
9 and 10 HC . . . . @20.00

WESTERN COMICS
Jan.–Feb., 1948
1 MMe,B:Vigilante,Rodeo Rick,
   Wyoming Kid, Cowboy
   Marshal 1,500.00
2 MMe,Vigilante vs. Dirk Bigger . 600.00
3 MMe,Vigilante vs. Pecos Kid . . 700.00
4 MMe,Vigilante as Pecos Kid . . 700.00
5 I:Nighthawk 500.00
6 Wyoming Kid vs. The
   Murder Mustang 300.00
7 Wyoming Kid in The Town
   That Was Never Robbed 300.00
8 O:Wyoming Kid 500.00

9 Wyoming Kid vs. Jack
   Slaughter 300.00
10 Nighthawk in Tunnel ofTerror . 300.00
11 Wyoming Kid vs. Mayor Brock 275.00
12 Wyoming Kid vs. Baldy Ryan . 275.00
13 I:Running Eagle 275.00
14 Wyoming Kid in The Siege
   of Prairie City 275.00
15 Nighthawk in Silver, Salt
   and Pepper 275.00
16 Wyoming Kid vs. Smilin' Jim . 275.00
17 BP,Wyoming Kid vs. Prof.
   Penny 275.00
18 LSt on Nighthawk,Wyoming Kid
   in Challenge of the Chiefs . . . 275.00
19 LSt,Nighthawk in The
   Invisible Rustlers 275.00
20 LSt,Nighthawk in The Mystery
   Mail From Defender Dip 250.00
21 LSt,Nighthawk in Rattlesnake
   Hollow 250.00
22 LSt,I:Jim Pegton 250.00
23 LSt,Nighthawk reveals
   ID to Jim 250.00
24 The $100,000 Impersonation . 250.00
25 V.Sioux Invaders 250.00
26 The Storming of the Sante
   Fe Trail 250.00
27 The Looters of Lost Valley . . . 250.00
28 The Thunder Creek Rebellion. 250.00
29 Six Guns of the Wyoming Kid. 250.00
30 V:Green Haired Killer 250.00
31 The Sky Riding Lawman. 250.00
32 Death Rides the Stage Coach 250.00
33 Wyoming Kid's Magic Finger . 250.00
34 Prescription For Killers 250.00
35 The River of Rogues. 250.00
36 Nighthawk(c),Duel in the Dark 200.00
37 The Death Dancer 200.00
38 Warpath in the Sky 200.00
39 Death to Fort Danger 200.00
40 Blind Man's Bluff. 200.00
41 thru 60. . . . . @175.00
61 thru 85. . . . . @150.00

WE3
DC/Vertigo, Aug. 2004
1 (of 3) GMo,Animal assassins. . . . 3.00
2 GMo 3.00
3 concl. 3.00
TPB 13.00

WHO'S WHO
1985–87
1 . . . . 5.00
2 thru 26 . . . . @4.00

WHO'S WHO IN THE DC UNIVERSE
1990–92
1 inc. Superman 6.00
1a 2nd printing 5.50
2 inc. Flash 5.50
2a 2nd printing 5.00
3 inc. Green Lantern. 5.50
4 inc. Wonder Woman 5.50
5 inc. Batman. 5.50
6 inc. Hawkman 5.50
7 inc. Shade 5.50
8 inc. Lobo 6.00
9 inc. Legion of Super-Heroes 5.50
10 inc. Robin 5.50
11 inc. L.E.G.I.O.N. '91 . . . . 5.50
12 inc. Aquaman 5.50
13 Villains issue, inc. Joker 6.00
14 inc. New Titans 5.50
15 inc. Doom Patrol 5.50
16 inc. Catwoman,final issue 5.00

DC COMICS

WHO'S WHO IN IMPACT
1991
1 Shield 5.00
2 Black Hood 5.00

WHO'S WHO IN THE LEGION
1987–88
1 History/Bio of Legionnaires 3.50
2 inc. Dream Girl 3.50
3 inc. Karate Kid 3.50
4 inc. Lightning Lad 3.50
5 inc. Phantom Girl 3.50
6 inc. Timber Wolf 3.50
7 wraparound(c) 3.50

WHO'S WHO IN STAR TREK
1987
1 HC(c) 6.00
2 HC(c) 6.00

WHO'S WHO UPDATE '87
1 inc. Blue Beetle 3.00
2 inc. Catwoman 3.00
3 inc. Justice League 3.00
4 . . . . 3.00
5 inc. Superboy 3.00

WHO'S WHO UPDATE '88
1 inc. Brainiac 3.00
2 inc. JusticeLeagueInternational . . 3.00
3 inc. Shado 3.00
4 inc. Zatanna 3.00

WHO'S WHO UPDATE '93
1 F:Eclipso,Azrael 5.25

WILD DOG
Sept., 1987
1 mini series DG(i),I:Wild Dog 3.00
2 DG(i),V:Terrorists 2.50
3 DG(i) 2.50
4 DG(i),O:Wild Dog, final issue 2.50
Spec.#1 . . . . 2.50

WILD WILD WEST
1999
1-shot movie adaptation 5.00

WILL EISNER COMPANION
Feb., 2006
TPB 13.00

WINDY & WILLY
May-June, 1969
1 . . . . 65.00
2 thru 4 . . . . @40.00

WISE SON: THE WHITE WOLF
DC/Milestone, Sept., 1996
1 by Ho Che Anderson 2.50
2 thru 4 . . . . @2.50

WITCHCRAFT
DC/Vertigo, 1994
1 CV(c),Three Witches from
  Sandman 4.00
2 F:Mildred 3.50
3 Final issue 3.25
TPB rep. mini-series 15.00

WITCHCRAFT: LA TERREUR
Feb., 1998
1 (of 3) JeR, sequel 2.50
2 & 3 JeR . . . . @2.50

WITCHING, THE
DC/Vertigo, June 2004
1 Triple Goddess 3.00
2 thru 4 . . . . @3.00
5 MBu 3.00
6 thru 9 . . . . @3.00
10 final issue 3.00

Witching Hour #47
© DC Comics, Inc.

WITCHING HOUR
1969–78
1 NA,ATh,Let the Judge Be You . 200.00
2 ATh, The Trip of Fools 100.00
3 ATh,BWr 100.00
4 ATh,A Matter of Conscience . . . 65.00
5 ATh,BWr 100.00
6 ATh,A Face in the Crowd 100.00
7 ATh 60.00
8 NA,ATh,3 Day Free Home Trial . 60.00
9 ATh,The Lonely Road Home . . . 60.00
10 ATh,Hold Softly, Hand of Death 60.00
11 ATh,The Mark of the Witch . . . 60.00
12 ATh,Double Edge 60.00
13 NA 75.00
14 AW,CG,NA(c) 90.00
15 thru 20 . . . . @30.00
21 thru 30 . . . . @25.00
31 thru 37 . . . . @25.00
38 100-pg. 90.00
39 thru 60 . . . . @20.00
61 thru 85 . . . . @15.00

THE WITCHING HOUR
DC/Vertigo, Dec., 1999
1 (of 3) JLb,CBa,ATi 6.00
2 JLb,CBa,ATi 6.00
3 JLb,CBa,ATi, concl. 6.00
TPB 20.00

WONDER WOMAN
1942–86
1 O:Wonder Woman,A:Paula
  Von Gunther 44,000.00
2 I:Earl of Greed,Duke of Deception
  and Lord Conquest 7,500.00
3 Paula Von Gunther reforms . 3,500.00
4 A:Paula Von Gunther 2,600.00
5 I:Dr. Psycho,A:Mars 2,600.00
6 I:Cheetah 2,000.00
7 Adventure of the Life Vitamin 2,000.00
8 I:Queen Clea 2,000.00
9 I:Giganto 2,000.00
10 I:Duke Mephisto Saturno . . 2,400.00
11 I:Hypnoto 1,700.00
12 I:Queen Desira 1,700.00
13 V:King Rigor & the Seal Men 1,700.00
14 I:Gentleman Killer 1,700.00
15 I:Solo 1,700.00
16 I:King Pluto 1,700.00
17 Wonder Woman goes to
  Ancient Rome 1,700.00
18 V:Dr. Psycho 1,700.00
19 V:Blitz 1,700.00
20 V:Nifty and the Air Pirates . . 1,700.00
21 I:Queen Atomia 1,500.00
22 V:Saturno 1,500.00
23 V:Odin and the Valkyries . . . 1,500.00
24 I:Mask 1,500.00
25 V:Purple Priestess 1,500.00
26 I:Queen Celerita 1,500.00
27 V:Pik Socket 1,500.00
28 V:Cheetah,Clea,Dr. Poison,
  Giganta,Hypnata,Snowman,
  Zara (Villainy,Inc.) 2,000.00
29 V:Paddy Gypso 2,000.00
30 The Secret of the
  Limestone Caves 2,000.00
31 V:Solo 1,000.00
32 V:Uvo 1,000.00
33 V:Inventa 1,000.00
34 V:Duke of Deception 1,000.00
35 Jaxo,Master of Thoughts . . . 1,000.00
36 V:Lord Cruello 1,000.00
37 A:Circe 1,000.00
38 V:Brutex 1,000.00
39 The Unmasking of Wonder
  Woman 1,000.00
40 Hollywood Goes To Paradise
  Island 1,000.00
41 Wonder Woman,Romance
  Editor 900.00
42 V:General Vertigo 900.00
43 The Amazing Spy Ring
  Mystery 900.00
44 V:Master Destroyer 900.00
45 The Amazon and the
  Leprachaun 1,500.00
46 V:Prof. Turgo 800.00
47 V:Duke of Deception 800.00
48 V:Robot Woman 800.00
49 V:Boss 800.00
50 V:Gen. Voro 800.00
51 V:Garo 600.00
52 V:Stroggo 600.00
53 V:Crime Master of Time 600.00
54 A:Merlin 600.00
55 The Chessmen of Doom 600.00
56 V:Plotter Gang 600.00
57 V:Mole Men 600.00
58 V:Brain 600.00
59 V:Duke Dozan 600.00
60 A:Paula Von Gunther 600.00
61 Earth's Last Hour 500.00
62 V:Angles Andrews 500.00
63 V:Duke of Deception 500.00
64 V:Thought Master 500.00
65 V:Duke of Deception 500.00
66 V:Duke of Deception 500.00
67 Confessions of a Spy 500.00
68 Landing of the Flying
  Saucers 500.00
69 A:Johann Gutenberg,Chris.
  Columbus, Paul Revere
  and the Wright Brothers 500.00
70 I:Angle Man 500.00
71 One-Woman Circus 500.00
72 V:Mole Goldings 500.00

Wonder Woman #76
© DC Comics, Inc.

73 V:Prairie Pirates 500.00
74 The Carnival of Peril 450.00
75 V:Angler 450.00
76 Bird Reveals Secret Identity . . 450.00
77 V:Smokescreen gang 450.00
78 V:Angle Man 450.00
79 V:Spider 450.00
80 V:Machino 450.00
81 V:Duke of Deception,
    Angle Man 450.00
82 A:Robin Hood 450.00
83 The Boy From Nowhere 450.00
84 V:Duke of Deception,
    Angle Man 450.00
85 V:Capt. Virago. 450.00
86 V:Snatcher 450.00
87 The Day the Clocks Stopped . 450.00
88 V:Duke of Deception 450.00
89 The Triple Heroine 450.00
90 Wonder Woman on Jupiter . . . 450.00
91 The Interplanetary Olympics . . 400.00
92 V:Angle Man 400.00
93 V:Duke of Deception 400.00
94 V:Duke of Deception,
    A:Robin Hood 400.00
95 O:Wonder Woman's Tiara 400.00
96 V:Angle Man 400.00
97 The Runaway Time Express. . 400.00
98 The Million Dollar Penny. 400.00
99 V:Silicons 400.00
100 Anniversary Issue 450.00
101 V:Time Master. 350.00
102 F:Steve Trevor 350.00
103 V:Gadget-Maker 350.00
104 A:Duke of Deception 350.00
105 O,I:Wonder Woman 1,500.00
106 W.Woman space adventure . 350.00
107 Battles space cowboys 400.00
108 Honored by U.S. Post Off. . . 350.00
109 V:Slicker 350.00
110 I:Princess 1003 . . . . 350.00
111 I:Prof. Menace. 350.00
112 V:Chest of Monsters 300.00
113 A:Queen Mikra 300.00
114 V:Flying Saucers 300.00
115 A:Angle Man 300.00
116 A:Professor Andro 300.00
117 A:Etta Candy 300.00
118 A:Merman 300.00
119 A:Mer Boy 300.00
120 A:Hot & Cold Alien 300.00
121 A:Wonder Woman Family . . . 250.00
122 I:Wonder Tot 250.00
123 A:Wonder Girl,Wonder Tot . . 250.00
124 A:Wonder Girl,Wonder Tot . . 250.00
125 WW-Battle Prize 250.00

126 I:Mr.Genie 250.00
127 Suprise Honeymoon 125.00
128 O:InvisiblePlane 125.00
129 A:WonderGirl,WonderTot . . . 125.00
130 A:Angle Man 125.00
131 Proving of Wonder Woman . . 400.00
132 V:Flying Saucer. 400.00
133 A:Miss X 450.00
134 V:Image-Maker 400.00
135 V:Multiple Man 400.00
136 V:Machine Men 750.00
137 V:Robot Wonder Woman . . . 500.00
138 V:Multiple Man 500.00
139 Amnesia revels Identity 500.00
140 A:Morpheus,Mr.Genie 600.00
141 A:Angle Man 400.00
142 A:Mirage Giants 500.00
143 A:Queen Hippolyte 400.00
144 I:Bird Boy 400.00
145 V:Phantom Sea Beast 400.00
146 $1,000 Dollar Stories 400.00
147 Wonder Girl becomes Bird Girl
    and Fish Girl 375.00
148 A:Duke of Deception. 400.00
149 Last Day of the Amazons . . . 500.00
150 V:Phantome Fish Bird 400.00
151 F:1st Full Wonder Girl story . 350.00
152 F:Wonder Girl 350.00
153 V:Duke of Deception 350.00
154 V:Boiling Man 350.00
155 I married a monster 350.00
156 V:Brain Pirate 300.00
157 A:Egg Fu,the First. 300.00
158 A:Egg Fu,the First. 300.00
159 Origin 400.00
160 A:Cheetah,Dr. Psycho. 250.00
161 A:Angle Man 250.00
162 O:Diana Prince 250.00
163 A:Giganta 250.00
164 A:Angle Man 250.00
165 A:Paper Man,Dr.Psycho 200.00
166 A:Egg Fu,The Fifth 200.00
167 A:Crimson Centipede 200.00
168 RA,ME,V:Giganta 200.00
169 RA,ME,Crimson Centipede. . 200.00
170 RA,ME,V:Dr.Pyscho 200.00
171 A:Mouse Man 200.00
172 IN,A:Android Wonder
    Woman 200.00
173 A:Tonia 200.00
174 A:Angle Man 200.00
175 V:Evil Twin 200.00
176 A:Star Brothers 200.00
177 A:Super Girl 250.00
178 MSy,DG,I:New Wonder
    Woman 250.00
179 D:Steve Trevor,I:Ching 150.00
180 MSy,DG,wears no costume
    I:Tim Trench. 150.00
181 MSy,DG,A:Dr.Cyber 150.00
182 MSy,DG. 150.00
183 MSy,DG,V:War 150.00
184 MSy,DG,A:Queen Hippolyte . 100.00
185 MSy,DG,V:Them 100.00
186 MSy,DG,I:Morgana 100.00
187 MSy,DG,A:Dr.Cyber 100.00
188 MSy,DG,A:Dr.Cyber 100.00
189 MSy,DG. 100.00
190 MSy,DG. 100.00
191 MSy,DG. 100.00
192 MSy,DG. 100.00
193 MSy,DG. 100.00
194 MSy,DG. 100.00
195 MSy,WW 100.00
196 MSy,DG,giant,Origin rep. . . . 110.00
197 MSy,DG. 110.00
198 MSy,DG. 110.00
199 JJ(c),DG 150.00
200 JJ(c),DG 175.00
201 DG,A:Catwoman 50.00
202 DG,A:Catwoman,I:Fafhrd
    & the Gray Mouser 50.00

Wonder Woman #236
© DC Comics Inc.

203 DG,Womens lib 35.00
204 DH,BO,rewears costume 90.00
205 DH,BO,Target WonderWoman 35.00
206 DH,O:Wonder Woman 35.00
207 RE,The Four Dooms. 35.00
208 RE,The Titanic Trials. 35.00
209 RE,Planet of Plunder 35.00
210 RE,The Shrinking Formula . . . 35.00
211 RE,giant 100.00
212 CS,A:Superman,tries to
    rejoin JLA 30.00
213 IN,A:Flash. 30.00
214 CS,giant,A:Green Lantern . . 100.00
215 A:Aquaman 25.00
216 A:Black Canary 25.00
217 DD,A:Green Arrow,giant 40.00
218 KS,Red Tornado 25.00
219 CS,A:Elongated Man 26.00
220 DG,NA,A:Atom 25.00
221 CS,A:Hawkman. 25.00
222 A:Batman 25.00
223 R:Steve Trevor 25.00
224 Wonder Woman vs. USA 25.00
225 Maximus, Emperor 25.00
226 A Life in Flames 25.00
227 My World in Ashes 25.00
228 B:War stories 25.00
229 Tomorrow Belongs to Me 25.00
230 V:Cheetah 25.00
231 This War has Been Cancelled 25.00
232 MN,A:JSA 25.00
233 GM,Seadeath 25.00
234 And Death my Destiny 25.00
235 The Biology Bomb 25.00
236 Armageddon Day 25.00
237 RB(c),O:Wonder Woman 30.00
238 RB(c),Assassin 20.00
239 RB(c),Duke named Deception 20.00
240 Wanted Dead or Alive 20.00
241 JSon,DG,A:Spectre 22.00
242 Tomorrow's Gods & Demons . 15.00
243 The Five-Sided Square 15.00
244 The Terrorist Dooms 15.00
245 Vengeance From Ice to Fire . 15.00
246 Darkness Everywhere. 15.00
247 The Inside-Out Man 15.00
248 D:Steve Trevor 20.00
249 A:Hawkgirl. 15.00
250 I:Orana 15.00
251 O:Orana 15.00
252 Empress of the Silver Snake . 20.00
253 Spirit of Silver Spirit of Gold . 15.00
254 The Angle in the Stars 15.00

All comics prices listed are for *Near Mint* condition.

Wonder Woman #307
© DC Comics, Inc.

255 V:Bushmaster 15.00
256 V:Royal Flush Gang 15.00
257 Case o/t Impossible Crimes . . 15.00
258 Long Grey Line of Death 15.00
259 A Power Gone Mad. 15.00
260 A Warrior in Chains 15.00
261 Palace at the Edge of Time . . 15.00
262 RE,A:Bushmaster 15.00
263 Power and the Pampas 15.00
264 A Bomb in the Bird 15.00
265 Land of the Scaled Gods 15.00
266 The Uninvited 15.00
267 R:Animal Man 20.00
268 A:Animal Man 20.00
269 WW(i),Rebirth of Wonder
    Woman,pt.1 . . . . 12.00
270 Rebirth,pt.2 . . . . 12.00
271 JSon,B:Huntress,Rebirth,pt.3 . 12.00
272 JSon 12.00
273 JSon,A:Angle Man 12.00
274 JSon,I:Cheetah II 12.00
275 JSon,V:Cheetah II 12.00
276 JSon,V:Kobra 12.00
277 JSon,V:Kobra 12.00
278 JSon,V:Kobra 12.00
279 JSon,A:Demon,Catwoman . . . 12.00
280 JSon,A:Demon,Catwoman . . . 12.00
281 JSon,Earth 2 Joker 10.00
282 JSon,Earth 2 Joker 10.00
283 Earth 2 Joker 10.00
284 Shadow of the Dragon 7.00
285 JSon,V:Red Dragon 7.00
286 Be Wonder Woman and Die. . . 7.00
287 DH,RT,JSon,Teen Titans. 8.00
288 GC,RT,New Wonder Woman . . 8.00
289 GC,RT,JSon,New W.Woman . . 7.00
290 GC,RT,JSon,New W.Woman . . 7.00
291 GC,FMc,A:Zatanna. 8.00
292 GC,FMc,RT,Supergirl 8.00
293 GC,FMc,Starfire,Raven. 8.00
294 GC,FMc,JSon,V:Blockbuster . . 7.00
295 GC,FMc,JSon,Huntress 7.00
296 GC,Fmc,JSon 7.00
297 MK(c),GC,FMc,JSon. 7.00
298 GC,FMc,JSon 7.00
299 GC,FMc,JSon 7.00
300 GC,FMc,RA,DG,KP,RB,KG
    C:New Teen Titans 9.00
301 GC,FMc. 7.00
302 GC,FMc,V:Artemis 7.00
303 GC,FMc,Huntress 7.00
304 GC,FMc,Huntress 7.00
305 GC,Huntress,I:Circe 8.00
306 DH,Huntress 7.00
307 DH,Huntress,Black Canary 7.00

308 DH,Huntress,Black Canary 7.00
309 DH,Huntress 7.00
310 DH,Huntress 7.00
311 DH,Huntress 7.00
312 DH,DSp,A:Gremlins 7.00
313 DH,V:Circe 7.00
314 DH,Huntress 7.00
315 DH,Huntress 7.00
316 DH,Huntress 7.00
317 DH,V:Cereberus 7.00
318 DH,V:Space Aliens 7.00
319 DH,V:Dr.Cyber 7.00
320 DH,Launch on Warning 7.00
321 DH,Huntress 7.00
322 IN,Bid Time Return 7.00
323 DH,A:Cheetah, Angle Man 7.00
324 DH,The Cassandra Complex . . 7.00
325 DH,Gremlin from the Kremlin . . 7.00
326 DH,Tropidor Heat 7.00
327 DH,Crisis. 7.00
328 DH,Crisis. 7.00
329 DH,Crisis, giant. 15.00

WONDER WOMAN
[2nd Regular Series], 1987

1 GP,O:Amazons,Wonder Woman . 8.00
2 GP,I:Steve Trevor. 6.00
3 GP,I:Julia Vanessa. 6.00
4 GP,V:Decay 6.00
5 GP,V:Deimos,Phobos 6.00
6 GP,V:Ares 5.00
7 GP,I:Myndi Mayer 5.00
8 GP,O:Legends,A:JLA,Flash 5.00
9 GP,I:New Cheetah 5.00
10 GP,V:Seven Headed Hydra,
    Challenge of the Gods,pt.1,
    gatefold(c) 4.00
10a regular(c). 3.00
11 GP,V:Echidna,Challenge
    of the Gods,pt.3. . . . . 4.00
12 GP,Millennium,V:Pan, Challenge
    of the Gods,pt.3,
    Millennium x-over 4.00
13 GP,Millennium,A:Ares,Challenge
    of the Gods,pt.4. . . . . 4.00
14 GP,A:Hercules. 4.00
15 GP,I:New Silver Swan 4.00
16 GP,V:Silver Swan 4.00
17 GP,DG,V:Circe. 4.00
18 GP,DG,V:Circe,+Bonus bk#4 . . 4.00
19 GP,FMc,V:Circe. 4.00
20 GP,BMc,D:Myndi Mayer 4.00
21 GP,BMc,L:Greek Gods,
    Destruction of Olympus 3.00
22 GP,BMc,F:Julia, Vanessa 3.00
23 GP,R:Hermes,V:Phobos,
    Prelude to New Titans #50 . . . . 3.00
24 GP,V:Ixion, Phobos. 3.00
25 CMa,Invasion,A:JLA 3.00
26 CMa,Invasion,V:Capt.Atom. 3.00
27 CMa,V:Khunds,A:Cheetah 3.00
28 CMa,V:Cheetah. 3.00
29 CMa,V:Cheetah. 3.00
30 CMa,V:Cheetah. 3.00
31 CMa,V:Cheetah. 3.00
32 TG,V:Amazons,A:Hermes 3.00
33 CMa,V:Amazons,Cheetah. 3.00
34 CMa,I:Shim'Tar 3.00
35 CMa,V:Shim'Tar 3.00
36 CMa,A:Hermes 3.00
37 CMa,V:Discord,A:Superman . . . 3.00
38 CMa,V:Eris 3.00
39 CMa,V:Eris,A:Lois Lane 3.00
40 CMa,V:Eris,A:Lois Lane 3.00
41 CMa,RT,F:Julia,Ties that Bind . . 3.00
42 CMa,RT,V:Silver Swan 3.00
43 CMA,RT,V:Silver Swan 3.00
44 CMa,RT,V:SilverSwan. 3.00
45 CM,RT,Pandora's Box. 3.00
46 RT,Suicide Issue,D:Lucy. 3.00
47 RT,A:Troia 3.00
48 RTP,A:Troia 3.00

Wonder Woman 2nd Series #43
© DC Comics, Inc.

49 recap of 1st four years 3.00
50 RT,SA,BB,AH,CM,KN,PCR,MW
    A:JLA,Superman 4.00
51 RT,V:Mercury 3.00
52 CM,KN,Shards,V:Dr.Psycho 3.00
53 RT,A:Pariah. 3.00
54 RT,V:Dr.Psycho. 3.00
55 RT,V:Dr.Psycho. 3.00
56 RT,A:Comm.Gordon 3.00
57 RT,A:Clark Kent,Bruce Wayne . 3.00
58 RT,War of the Gods,V:Atlas 3.50
59 RT,War of the Gods,
    A:Batman Robin 3.50
60 RT,War of the Gods,
    A:Batman, Lobo. 3.50
61 RT,War of the Gods,V:Circe 3.50
62 War o/t Gods,Epilogue. 3.00
63 BB(c)A:Deathstroke,Cheetah . . . 5.00
64 BB(c),Kidnapped Child 2.50
65 BB(c),PCu,V:Dr.Psycho 2.50
66 BB(c),PCu,Exodus In Space#1. . 2.50
67 BB(c),PCu,Exodus In Space#2. . 2.50
68 BB(c),PCu,Exodus In Space#3. . 2.50
69 PCu, Exodus In Space#4 . . . . . . 2.50
70 PCu,Exodus In Space#5. . . . . . . 2.50
71 BB(c),DC,RT,Return fr.space . . . 2.50
72 BB(c),O:retold 15.00
73 BB(c),Diana gets a job 3.00
74 BB(c),V:White Magician 2.50
75 BB(c),A:The White Magician. . . . 2.50
76 BB(c),A:Doctor Fate 2.50
77 BB(c) 2.50
78 BB(c),A:Flash 2.50
79 BB(c),V:Mayfly,A:Flash 2.50
80 BB(c),V:Ares Buchanan 2.50
81 BB(c),V:Ares Buchanan 2.50
82 BB(c),V:Ares Buchanan 2.50
83 BB(c),V:Ares Buchanan 2.50
84 BB(c),V:Ares Buchanan 2.50
85 BB(c). 13.00
86 BB(c),Turning Point. 6.00
87 BB(c),No Quarter,NoSanctuary . 6.00
88 BB(c),A:Superman 10.00
89 BB(c),A:Circle 10.00
90 New Direction 7.00
91 Choosing Wonder Woman 4.00
92 New Wonder Woman 4.00
93 New Wonder Woman 4.00
94 . . . . 5.00
95 V:Cheetah 5.00
96 V:The Joker. 5.00
97 V:The Joker. 5.00
98 BB(c),F:Artemis. 3.00
99 BB(c),A:White Magician 3.00

100 BB(c) White Magician defeats
   Artemis 6.00
100a Collector's ed., holo(c) 6.00
101 V:White Magician 3.00
102 V:Metron,Darkseid 2.50
103 JBy,A:Darkseid 2.50
104 JBy,Diana takes crown? 2.50
105 JBy,Grecian artifact comes
   to life 2.50
106 JBy,A:The Demon,Phantom
   Stranger. 2.50
107 . . . . 2.50
108 JBy,F:The Demon,Arion,The
   Phantom Stranger 2.50
109 JBy,V:The Flash,I:Champion . . 2.50
110 JBy,V:Sinestro 2.50
111 JBy,I:New Wonder Girl,
   V:Doomsday 2.50
112 JBy,V:Doomsday,A:Superman . 3.00
113 JBy,Wonder Girl vs. Decay 2.50
114 JBy,V:Doctor Psycho. 2.50
115 JBy,beneath the Arctic ice. 2.50
116 JBy,beneath the Arctic ice. 2.50
117 JBy,V:Earth Moovers. 2.50
118 JRy 2.50
119 JBy,fight to regain Cheetah's
   humanity, cont. 2.50
120 JBy,48pg., pin-ups 4.00
121 JBy,Wonder Woman reverting
   to clay 2.50
122 JBy,Gods of Olympus are back 2.50
123 JBy,R:Artemis 2.50
124 JBy,A:Demon 2.50
125 JBy,A:Donna Troy & JLA 2.50
126 JBy,JL,Genesis tie-in 2.50
127 JBy,JL(c),new era 2.50
128 JBy,JL,V:Egg Fu 2.50
129 JBy,JL,Hippolyta debuts as
   replacement Wonder Woman . . 2.50
130 JBy,JL,pt.1,A:Golden-age
   Flash 2.50
131 JBy,pt.2 . . . . 2.50
132 JBy,pt.3,A:Justice Society. 2.50
133 . . . . 2.50
134 JBy,Who is Donna Troy? 2.50
135 JBy,secret revealed 2.50
136 JBy,back to Earth 2.50
137 CPr,V:Circe, pt.1 . . . . 2.50
138 JBy,F:Hippolyta,V:Circe,pt.2 . . 2.50
139 MBr, ... 2.50
140 BMc,A:Superman & Batman. . . 2.50
141 BMc,A:Superman & Batman. . . 2.50
142 BMc,The Wonder Dome 2.50
143 BMc,Devastation,pt.1 . . . . 2.50
144 BMc,Devastation,pt.2 . . . . 2.50
145 BMc,Devastation,pt.3 . . . . 2.50
146 BMc,Devastation,pt.4 . . . . 2.50
147 BMc,GodWar begins. 2.50
148 BMc,GodWar, pt.2. . . . . 2.50
149 RBr,BMc,GodWar,pt.3. . . . . . . 2.50
150 GodWar, 48-pg 4.00
151 AH(c),V:Dr. Poison 2.50
152 . . . . 2.50
153 MMr,F:Wonder Girl 2.50
154 Three Hearts,pt.1 . . . . 2.50
155 Three Hearts,pt.2 . . . . 2.50
156 Devastation Returns,pt.1 . . . . . 2.50
157 Devastation Returns,pt.2 . . . . . 2.50
158 Devastation Returns,concl. 2.50
159 WonderDome comes to Earth . 2.50
160 A Piece of You,pt.1 . . . . 3.00
161 A Piece of You,pt.2 . . . . 3.00
162 GodComplex,pt.1,A:Aquaman . 2.50
163 GodComplex,pt.2,A:Aquaman . 2.50
164 Gods of Gotham,pt.1 . . . . 6.00
165 Gods of Gotham,pt.2 . . . . 3.00
166 Gods of Gotham,pt.3 . . . . 3.00
167 Gods of Gotham,pt.4 . . . . 3.00
168 GP,Paradise Island Lost,pt.1 . . 2.50
169 GP,Paradise Island Lost,pt.2 . . 2.50
170 PJ,ALa,Lois & Diana. 2.50
171 Our Worlds at War, tie-in 2.50

Wonder Woman 2nd Series #99
© *DC Comics Inc.*

172 Our Worlds at War, tie-in 3.00
173 Our Worlds at War, tie-in 2.50
174 PJ,ALa,Witch & Warrior,pt.1 . . 2.50
175 PJ,ALa,Witch & Warrior,pt.2 . . 8.00
176 PJ,ALa,Witch & Warrior,pt.3 . . 2.50
177 PJ,ALa,Our Worlds at War 2.50
178 PJ,ALa,date with Trevor 2.50
179 PJ,ALa,V:Villainy,Inc. 2.50
180 PJ,ALa,O:new Villainy, Inc.. . . 2.50
181 PJ,ALa,prisoners of Skartaris . . 2.50
182 PJ,ALa,Shamballa 2.50
183 PJ,ALa,Skartaris mastermind . . 2.50
184 PJ,ALa,Diana,pt.1 . . . . 2.50
185 PJ,ALa,Diana in '40s,pt.2 . . . . 2.25
186 PJ,ALa,V:Barbara Minerva . . . 2.25
187 PJ,ALa,Cat fight 2.25
188 PJ,ALa,Day in the Life 2.25
189 WS,JOy,CR,Game Gods,pt.1 . . 2.25
190 WS,JOy,CR,Game Gods,pt.2 . . 4.00
191 WS,JOy,CR,Game Gods,pt.3 . . 2.25
192 WS,JOy,CR,Game Gods,pt.4 . . 2.25
193 WS,JOy,CR,Game Gods,pt.5 . . 2.25
194 WS,JOy,CR,Game Gods,pt.6 . . 2.50
195 AH 3.00
196 Down to Earth,pt.1 . . . . 2.50
197 Down to Earth,pt.2 . . . . 2.50
198 Down to Earth,pt.3 . . . . 2.25
199 Down to Earth,pt.4 . . . . 2.25
200 Down to Earth, 64-pg. 4.00
201 Themyscira 2.25
202 V:Veronica Cale 2.25
203 Bitter Pills,pt.1. . . . . 2.25
204 Bitter Pills,pt.2. . . . . 2.25
205 Bitter Pills,pt.3. . . . . 2.25
206 Stoned,pt.1 . . . . 2.25
207 Stoned,pt.2 . . . . 2.25
208 Stoned,pt.3 . . . . 2.25
209 Stoned,pt.4 . . . . 2.25
210 Stoned, concl. 2.25
211 SeP 2.25
212 F:JLA 2.25
213 War on Olympus 2.25
214 Truth or Dare, F:Flash, x-over 15.00
215 RgM,MIB,Tartarus, pt.1 . . . . . 2.25
216 RgM,MIB,The Bronze Doors. . 2.25
217 RgM,MIB,The Bronze Doors. . 2.25
218 RgM,MIB, ... 2.25
219 Sacrifice,Superman,x-over,pt.4 10.00
220 A:Checkmate. 2.50
221 RgM,Power of Omac 2.50
222 RgM,F:Donna Troy, Cheetah . 2.50
223 RgM,V:Omacs. 2.50
224 RgM,Omacs attack 2.50
225 Uncertain Future 2.50
226 Final issue. 2.50

Ann.#1,GP,AAd,RA,BB,JBo,JL,CS
   Tales of Paradise Island 4.00
Ann.#2 CM,F:Mayer Agency 4.00
Ann.#3 Eclipso tie-in 3.00
Ann.#4 Year One Annual 4.00
Ann.#5 JBy,DC,NBy,Legends of the
   Dead Earth 3.50
Ann.#6 Pulp Heroes (Macabre). . . . 4.50
Ann.#7 Ghosts 3.50
Ann.#8 JLApe Gorilla Warfare 3.50
Annual #1 (1967) (rep.2003) 5.00
Spec.#1,000,000 CPr(s),MC,BMc . . 2.50
Spec #1 A:Deathstroke,Cheetah . . 2.25
Spec.#0 History of Amazons 7.00
Spec.#1 Our Worlds at War,48-pg. . 3.00
GN Amazonia, BML 8.00
GN The Once and Future Story. . . . 5.00
GN Amazonia, Elseworlds 8.00
GN The Gods of Gotham, rep. 6.00
Secret Files #2. . . . . 5.00
Secret Files #3, 48-pg 5.00
Spec. Wonder Woman: Donna Troy
   Girlfrenzy (1998) 2.00
Spec. Wonder Woman Plus CPr(s),
   MC, TP,Jesse Quick & Wonder
   Woman (1996), ... 3.00
Spec. The Blue Amazon (2003). . . . 7.00
TPB The Contest, rep. #90,#0
   #91-#93 . . . . 10.00
TPB The Challenge of Artemas. . . 10.00
TPB Second Genesis JBy, rep.
   #101–#105. . . . . 10.00
TPB Spirit of Truth, over-size. 10.00
TPB Paradise Lost, rep. 15.00
TPB Paradist Found (2003). 15.00
TPB The Hiketeia (2003) 18.00
TPB Gods and Mortals (2004). . . . 20.00
TPB Down to Earth (2004) 15.00
TPB Challenge of the Gods(2004) 20.00
TPB Bitter Rivals 13.00
TPB Vol. 3 Beauty and the Beasts 20.00
TPB Eyes of the Gorgon (2006) . . 20.00
TPB Land of the Dead (2006) 13.00
TPB Destiny Calling (2006) 20.00
TPB Mission's End (2006) 20.00

WONDER WOMAN
June, 2006
1 TyD, Who is Wonder Woman . . . 3.00
1a variant (c). 3.00
2 TyD,F:Wonder Girl. 3.00
3 TyD,Who is Wonder Woman 3.00
4 TyD,Cheetah, Giganta 3.00

WORLD OF KRYPTON
July, 1979
1 HC/MA.O:Jor-El. 10.00
2 HC/MA,A:Superman 6.00
3 HC 6.00

[2nd Series], 1987–88
1 MMi,John Byrne script. 3.00
2 MMi,John Byrne script. 3.00
3 MMi,John Byrne script. 3.00
4 MMi,A:Superman 3.00

WORLD OF METROPOLIS
1988
1 DG(i),O:Perry White. 2.50
2 DG(i),O:Lois Lane 2.50
3 DG(i),Clark Kent 2.50
4 DG(i),O:Jimmy Olsen. 2.50

WORLD OF SMALLVILLE
1988
1 KS/AA,Secrets of Ma&Pa Kent . . 3.00
2 KS/AA,Stolen Moments 3.00
3 KS/AA,Lana Lang/Manhunter . . . 3.00
4 KS/AA,final issue 3.00

WORLDS COLLIDE
1994
1 MBr(c),3RW,CsB,Ccs,DCw,
TG,A:Blood Syndicate,Icon,
Hardware,Static,Superboy,
Superman,Steel,Vinyl Cling(c). . 4.25
1a Newsstand Ed. 2.75

WORLD'S BEST COMICS
Oct. 2003
Spec. G.A. DC Archives Sampler. . . 1.00
Spec. S.A. DC Archives Sampler. . . 1.00

WORLD'S BEST COMICS
Spring, 1941
1 Superman vs. the Rainmaker,
Batman vs. Wright 27,000.00
Becomes:

WORLD'S FINEST
COMICS
1941–86
2 Superman V:The Unknown X,
Batman V:Ambrose Taylor 12,000.00
3 I&O:Scarecrow 9,000.00
4 Superman V:Dan Brandon,
Batman V:Ghost Gang 7,000.00
5 Superman V:Lemuel P.Potts,
Batman V:Brains Kelly 6,500.00
6 Superman V:Metalo,Batman
meets Scoop Scanlon 5,200.00
7 Superman V:Jenkins,Batman
V:Snow Man Bandits 5,200.00
8 Superman:Talent Unlimited
Batman V:Little Nap Boyd,
B:Boy Commandos 5,000.00
9 Superman:One Second to
Live,Batman V:Bramwell B.
Bramwell. 5,200.00
10 Superman V:The Insect Master,
Batman reforms OliverHunt 5,000.00
11 Superman V:Charlie Frost,
Batman V:Rob Calendar . . 4,200.00
12 Superman V:Lynx,Batman:
Alfred Gets His Man 4,200.00
13 Superman V:Dice Dimant,
Batman,V:Swami Pravhoz . 4,200.00
14 Superman V:Al Bandar,Batman
V:Jib Buckler. 4,200.00
15 Superman V:Derby Bowser,
Batman V:Mennekin 4,200.00
16 Superman:Music for the Masses,
Batman V:Nocky Johnson . 4,200.00
17 Superman:The Great Godini,
Batman V:Dr.Dreemo 4,200.00

World's Finest Comics #11
© DC Comics, Inc.

18 Superman:The Junior Reporters,
Batman V:Prof.Brane 4,000.00
19 A:The Joker 4,000.00
20 A:Toyman 4,000.00
21 Superman:Swindle in
Sweethearts!. 3,000.00
22 Batman V:Nails Finney 3,000.00
23 Superman:The Colossus
of Metropolis. 3,000.00
24 . . . . 3,000.00
25 Superman V:Ed Rook,Batman:
The Famous First Crimes. . 3,000.00
26 Confessions of Superman . . 3,000.00
27 The Man Who Out-Supered
Superman. 3,000.00
28 A:Lex Luther,Batman V:Glass
Man. 3,000.00
29 Superman:The Books that
Couldn't Be Bound 3,000.00
30 Superman:Sheriff Clark Kent,
Batman V:Joe Coyne 3,000.00
31 Superman's Super-Rival,Batman:
Man with the X-Ray Eyes. . 2,700.00
32 Superman Visits
Ancient Egypt. 2,700.00
33 Superman Press, Inc.,
Batman V:James Harmon . 2,700.00
34 The Un-Super Superman. . . 2,700.00
35 Daddy Superman,A:Penguin 2,700.00
36 Lois Lane,Sleeping Beauty . 2,700.00
37 The Superman Story,Batman
V:T-Gun Jones 2,700.00
38 If There were No Superman 2,700.00
39 Superman V:Big Jim Martin,
Batman V:J.J.Jason 2,700.00
40 Superman V:Check,Batman:4
Killers Against Fate! 2,700.00
41 I:Supermanium,
E:Boy Commandos 2,000.00
42 Superman goes to Uranus,
A:Marco Polo & Kubla Khan2,000.00
43 A:J.Wilbur Wolfingham. 2,000.00
44 Superman:The Revolt of the
Thought Machine 2,000.00
45 Superman:Lois Lane and Clark
Kent,Private Detectives . . . 2,000.00
46 Superman V:Mr. 7 . . . . 2,000.00
47 Superman:The Girl Who
Hated Reporters 2,000.00
48 A:Joker. 2,000.00
49 Superman Meets the
Metropolis Shutterbug
Society, A:Penguin 2,000.00
50 Superman Super Wrecker . . 2,000.00
51 Superman:The Amazing
Talents of Lois Lane 2,000.00
52 A:J.Wilbur Wolfingham. 2,000.00
53 Superman V:Elias Toomey. . 2,000.00
54 The Superman Who Avoided
Danger!. 2,000.00
55 A:Penguin. 2,000.00
56 Superman V:Dr.Vallin,Batman
V:Big Dan Hooker. 2,000.00
57 The Artificial Superman 2,000.00
58 Superman V:Mr.Fenton 2,000.00
59 A:Lex Luthor,Joker. 2,000.00
60 A:J.Wilbur Wolfingham. 2,000.00
61 A:Joker,Superman's
Blackout 1,500.00
62 A:Lex Luthor. 1,500.00
63 Superman:Clark Kent,
Gangster. 1,500.00
64 Superman:The Death of Lois
Lane,Batman:Bruce Wayne...
Amateur Detective 1,500.00
65 The Confessions of Superman,
Batman V:The Blaster 2,500.00
66 Superman,Ex-Crimebuster;
Batman V:Brass Haley 1,500.00
67 Superman:Metropolis-Crime
Center! 1,500.00
68 Batman V:The Crimesmith. . 1,500.00

World's Finest #60
© DC Comics, Inc.

69 A:Jor-El,Batman
V:Tom Becket 1,500.00
70 The Two Faces of Superman,
Batman:Crime Consultant . 1,500.00
71 B:Superman/Batman
team-ups. 3,000.00
72 V:Heavy Weapon gang 2,000.00
73 V:Fang 2,000.00
74 The Contest of Heroes 1,600.00
75 V:The Purple Mask Mob . . . 1,500.00
76 When Gotham City
Challenged Metropolis 1,200.00
77 V:Prof.Pender 1,200.00
78 V:Varrel mob 1,200.00
79 A:Aladdin 1,200.00
80 V:Mole 1,200.00
81 Meet Ka Thar from future . . . 900.00
82 A:Three Musketeers 900.00
83 The Case of the Mother
Goose Mystery 900.00
84 V:Thad Linnis Gang 900.00
85 Meet Princess Varina 900.00
86 V:Henry Bartle. 900.00
87 V:Elton Craig. 900.00
88 1st team-up Luthor & Joker . . 950.00
89 I:Club of Heroes 900.00
90 A:Batwoman 900.00
91 V:Rohtul,Descendent of Lex
Luthor 700.00
92 1st & only A:Skyboy 700.00
93 V:Victor Danning 700.00
94 O:Superman/Batman team,
A:Lex Luthor 1,200.00
95 Battle o/t Super Heroes 700.00
96 Super-Foes from Planet X . . . 700.00
97 V:Condor Gang. 700.00
98 I:Moonman 700.00
99 JK,V:Carl Verril 700.00
100 A:Kandor, Lex Luthor. 1,200.00
101 A:Atom Master 450.00
102 V:Jo-Jo Groff gang,
B:Tommy Tomorrow. 450.00
103 The Secrets of the
Sorcerer's Treasure. 450.00
104 A:Lex Luthor 450.00
105 V:Khalex 450.00
106 V:Duplicate Man 450.00
107 The Secret of the Time
Creature. 450.00
108 The Star Creatures 450.00
109 V:Fangan 450.00
110 The Alien Who Doomed
Robin! 450.00
111 V:Floyd Frisby 450.00
112 Menace of Superman's Pet. . 450.00

113 1st Bat-Mite/Mr.Mxyzptlk
team-up 450.00
114 Captives o/t Space Globes . . 450.00
115 The Curse That Doomed
Superman 350.00
116 V:Vance Collins 350.00
117 A:Batwoman,Lex Luthor 350.00
118 V:Vath-Gar. 350.00
119 V:General Grambly 350.00
120 V:Faceless Creature 350.00
121 I:Miss Arrowette 350.00
122 V:Klor 200.00
123 A:Bat-Mite & Mr. Mxyzptlk. . . 200.00
124 V:Hroguth,E:Tommy
Tomorrow. 200.00
125 V:Jundy,B:Aquaman 200.00
126 A:Lex Luthor 200.00
127 V:Zerno 200.00
128 V:Moose Morans. 200.00
129 Joker/Luthor T.U. 200.00
130 Riddle of the Four Planets . . 200.00
131 V:Octopus 200.00
132 V:Denny Kale,Shorty Biggs . 200.00
133 Beasts of the Supernatural . . 200.00
134 V:Band of Super-Villians. . . . 200.00
135 V:The Future Man. 200.00
136 The Batman Nobody
Remembered. 200.00
137 A:Lex Luthor 200.00
138 V:General Grote 200.00
139 V:Sphinx Gang,E:Aquaman . 200.00
140 CS,V:Clayface. 200.00
141 CS,A:Jimmy Olsen 200.00
142 CS,O:Composite Man. 200.00
143 CS,A:Kandor,I:Mailbag 150.00
144 CS,A:Clayface,Brainiac. 150.00
145 CS,Prison for Heroes 150.00
146 CS,Batman,Son of Krypton. . 150.00
147 CS,A:Jimmy Olsen 150.00
148 CS,A:Lex Luthor,Clayface. . . 150.00
149 CS,The Game of the
Secret Identities. 150.00
150 CS,V:Rokk and Sorban. 150.00
151 CS,A:Krypto,BU:Congorilla. . 150.00
152 CS,A:The Colossal Kids,Bat-
mite,V:Mr.Mxyzptlk 150.00
153 CS,V:Lex Luthor 150.00
154 CS,The Sons of Batman &
Superman(Imaginary) 150.00
155 CS,The 1000th Exploit of
Batman & Superman. 150.00
156 CS,I:BizarroBatman,V:Joker. 150.00
157 CS,The Abominable Brats
(Imaginary story) 135.00
158 CS,V:Brainiac 135.00
159 CS,A:Many Major villians,I:Jim
Gordon as Anti-Batman & Perry
White as Anti-Superman 135.00
160 V:Dr Zodiac. 135.00
161 CS,80 page giant 150.00
162 V:The Jousting Master 100.00
163 CS,The Court of No Hope . . 100.00
164 CS,I:Genia,V:Brainiac. 100.00
165 CS,The Crown of Crime 100.00
166 CS,V:Muto & Joker 125.00
167 CS,The New Superman &
Batman(Imaginary) V:Luthor . 100.00
168 CS,R:Composite Superman . 100.00
169 The Supergirl/Batgirl Plot;
V:Batmite,Mr.Mxyzptlk. 100.00
170 80 page giant,reprint. 150.00
171 CS,V:The Executioners. 100.00
172 CS,Superman & Batman
Brothers (Imaginary) 100.00
173 CS,The Jekyll-Hyde
Heroes. 175.00
174 CS,Secrets of the Double
Death Wish 125.00
175 NA(1st Batman),C:Flash. . . . 125.00
176 NA,A:Supergirl & Batgirl 125.00
177 V:Joker & Luthor 125.00
178 CS,The Has-Been Superman 100.00

World's Finest #210
© *DC Comics Inc.*

179 CS,giant 150.00
180 RA,ME,Supermans Perfect
Crime. 100.00
181 RA,ME. 100.00
182 RA,ME,The Mad Manhunter. 100.00
183 RA,ME,Superman's Crimes
of the Ages 100.00
184 RA,ME,A:JLA,Robin 100.00
185 CS,The Galactic Gamblers . 100.00
186 RA,ME,The Bat Witch. 100.00
187 RA,ME,Demon Superman . . 100.00
188 giant,reprint. 125.00
189 RA,ME,V:Lex Luthor 75.00
190 RA,V:Lex Luthor 60.00
191 RA,A:Jor-El,Lara. 60.00
192 RA,The Prison of No Escape . 60.00
193 The Breaking of Batman
and Superman. 60.00
194 RA,ME,Inside the Mafia 60.00
195 RA,ME,Dig Now-Die Later . . . 60.00
196 CS,The Kryptonite Express,
E:Batman. 60.00
197 giant 125.00
198 DD,B:Superman T.U.,
A:Flash 150.00
199 DD,Superman & Flash race . 150.00
200 NA(c),DD,Prisoners of the
Immortal World; A:Robin 75.00
201 NA(c),DD,A Prize of Peril,
A:Green Lantern,Dr. Fate. . . . 50.00
202 NA(c),DD,Vengeance of the
Tomb Thing,A:Batman. 50.00
203 NA(c),DD,Who's Minding the
Earth,A:Quamar. 50.00
204 NA(c),DD,Journey to the End
of Hope,A:Wonder Woman . . . 50.00
205 NA(c),DD,The Computer that
Captured a Town,Frazetta Ad,
A:Teen Titans. 55.00
206 DD,giant reprint. 95.00
207 DD,Superman,A:Batman,
V:Dr.Light. 50.00
208 NA(c),DD,A:Dr Fate 50.00
209 NA(c),DD,A:Green Arrow,
Hawkman,I&V:The Temper. . . 50.00
210 NA(c),DD,A:Batman 50.00
211 NA(c),DD,A:Batman 50.00
212 CS(c),And So My World
Begins,A:Martian Manhunter. . 50.00
213 DD,Peril in a Very Small
Place,A:The Atom 50.00
214 DD,A:Vigilante. 50.00
215 DD,Saga of the Super Sons
(Imaginary story) 75.00

216 DD,R:Super Sons,Little Town
with a Big Secret 25.00
217 DD,MA,Heroes with
Dirty Hands 25.00
218 DD,DC,A:Batman,
BU:Metamorpho 25.00
219 DD,Prisoner of Rogues Rock;
A:Batman. 25.00
220 DD,MA,Let No Man Write My
Epitaph,BU:Metamorpho 25.00
221 DD,Cry Not For My Forsaken
Son; R:Super Sons 25.00
222 DD,Evil In Paradise. 25.00
223 DD,giant,A:Deadman,Aquaman
Robotman 75.00
224 DD,giant,A:Super Sons,
Metamorpho,Johnny Quick . . . 75.00
225 giant,A:Rip Hunter,Vigilante,
Black Canary,Robin. 75.00
226 A:Sandman,Metamorpho,
Deadman,Martian Manhunter . 75.00
227 MGr,BWi,A:The Demonic Duo,
Vigilante,Rip Hunter,Deadman,
I:Stargrave. 75.00
228 ATh,A:Super Sons,Aquaman,
Robin,Vigilante 75.00
229 I:Powerman,A:Metamorpho . . 40.00
230 A:Super-Sons,Deadman,
Aquaman, giant-size 60.00
231 A:Green Arrow,Flash. 20.00
232 DD,The Dream Bomb 20.00
233 A:Super-Sons 20.00
234 CS,Family That Fled Earth . . 20.00
235 DD,V:Sagitaurus 20.00
236 DD,A:The Atom. 20.00
237 Intruder from a Dead World . . 20.00
238 DD,V:Luthor,A:Super-Sons. . 20.00
239 CS,A:Gold(from Metal Men) . 20.00
240 DD,A:Kandor. 18.00
241 Make Way For a New World. . 18.00
242 EC,A:Super-Sons 18.00
243 CS,AM,A:Robin. 18.00
244 NA(c),JL,MA,MN,TA,giant
B:Green Arrow. 25.00
245 NA(C),CS,MA,MN,TA,
GM,JSh,BWi,giant. 25.00
246 NA(c),KS,MA,MN,TA,GM,
DH,A:JLA. 25.00
247 KS,GM,giant 25.00
248 KS,GM,DG,TVE,A:Sgt.Rock . . 20.00
249 KS,SD,TVE,A:Phantom
Stranger,B:Creeper 20.00
250 GT,SD,Superman,Batman,
Wonder Woman,Green Arrow,
Black Canary,team-up 22.00
251 GT,SD,JBi,BL,TVE,RE,
JA,A:Poison Ivy,Speedy,
I:CountVertigo 22.00
252 GT,TVE,SD,JA,giant 22.00
253 KS,DN,TVE,SD,B:Shazam . . . 15.00
254 GT,DN,TVE,SD,giant 15.00
255 JL,DA,TVE,SD,DN,KS,
E:Creeper 15.00
256 MA,DN,KS,DD,Hawkman,Black
Lightning,giant. 15.00
257 DD,FMc,DN,KS,GT,RB,
RT,giant 15.00
258 NA(c),RB,JL,DG,DN,KS,RT,
giant. 17.00
259 RB,DG,MR,MN,DN,KS 15.00
260 RB,DG,MN,DN 15.00
261 RB,DG,AS,RT,EB,DN,
A:Penguin, Terra Man 15.00
262 DG,DN,DA,JSon,RT,
Aquaman. 15.00
263 RB,DG,DN,TVE,JSh,Aquaman,
Adam Strange 15.00
264 RB,DG,TVE,DN,Aquaman . . . 15.00
265 RB,DN,RE,TVE. 15.00
266 RB,TVE,DN. 15.00
267 RB,DG,TVE,AS,DN,
A:Challengers of the Unknown 15.00

World's Finest #269
© *DC Comics, Inc.*

268 DN,TVE,BBr,RT,AS 15.00
269 RB,FMc,TVE,BBr,AS,DN,DA . 15.00
270 NA(c),RB,RT,TVE,AS,
DN,LMa 15.00
271 GP(c),RB,FMc,O:Superman/
Batman T.U. 15.00
272 RB,DN,TVE,BBr,AS 14.00
273 TVE,LMa,JSon,AS,DN,DA,
A:Plastic Man 14.00
274 TVE,LMa,BBr,GC,AS,DN,
Green Arrow 14.00
275 RB,FMc,TVE,LMa,DSp,AS,
DN,DA,A:Mr.Freeze 14.00
276 GP(c),RB,TVE,LMa,DSp,CI,
DN,DA 14.00
277 GP(c),RT,TVE,DSp,AS,DN,
DH,V:Dr.Double X 14.00
278 GP(c),RB,TVE,LMa,DSp,DN . 14.00
279 KP,TVE,LMa,AS,DN,
B:Kid Eternity 14.00
280 RB,TVE,LMa,AS,DN 14.00
281 GK(c),IN,TVE,LMa,AS,DN . . . 14.00
282 IN,FMc,GK,CI,last giant
E:Kid Eternity 14.00
283 GT,FMc,GK 14.00
284 GT,DSp,A:Legion,E:G.Arrow . 14.00
285 FM(c),RB,A:Zatanna 14.00
286 RB,A:Flash 14.00
287 TVE,A:Flash 14.00
288 A:JLA 14.00
289 GK(c),Kryll way of Dying 14.00
290 TD(i),I:Stalagron 14.00
291 WS(c),TD(i),V:Stalagron 14.00
292 . . . . 14.00
293 . . . . 14.00
294 . . . . 14.00
295 FMc(i) 14.00
296 RA 14.00
297 GC,V:Pantheon 14.00
298 V:Pantheon 14.00
299 GC,V:Pantheon 14.00
300 RA,GP,KJ,MT,FMc,A:JLA . . . 14.00
301 Rampage 7.00
302 DM,NA(rep) 7.00
303 Plague 7.00
304 SLi,O:Null&Void 7.00
305 TVE,V:Null&Void 7.00
306 SLi,I:Swordfish & Barracuda . . . 7.00
307 TVE,V:Null&Void 7.00
308 GT,Night and Day 7.00
309 MT,AA,V:Quantum 7.00
310 I:Sonik 7.00
311 A:Monitor 7.00
312 AA,I:Network 7.00

313 AA(i),V:Network 7.00
314 AA(i),V:Executrix 7.00
315 V:Cathode 7.00
316 LSn,I:Cheapjack 7.00
317 LSn,V:Cheapjack 7.00
318 AA(i),A:Sonik 7.00
319 AA(i),I:REM 7.00
320 AA(i),V:REM 7.00
321 AA,V:Chronos 7.00
322 KG,The Search 7.00
323 AA(i),final issue 7.00
Spec.#1 Our Worlds at War,48-pg . . 6.00

WORLD'S FINEST
[Limited Series], 1990
1 SR,KK,Worlds Apart 8.00
2 SR,KK,Worlds Collide 6.00
3 SR,KK,Worlds At War 6.00
TPB rep.#1-#3 . . . . 20.00

WORLD'S FINEST: SUPERBOY/ROBIN
Oct., 1996
1 (of 2) CDi&KK(s),TG,SHa,
V:Poison Ivy, Metallo 5.00
2 CDi&KK(s),TG,SHa, V:Poison
Ivy, Metallo 5.00

WORLD'S GREATEST SUPER-HEROES
1977
1 A:Batman,Robin 35.00

WORLD WITHOUT END
1990
1 The Host, I:Brother Bones 5.00
2 A:Brother Bones 3.50
3 . . . . 3.50
4 House of Fams 2.50
5 Female Fury 2.50
6 conclusion 2.50

WRATH OF THE SPECTRE
May, 1988
1 JAp,rep.Adventure #431-#433 . . 4.00
2 JAp,rep.Adventure #434-#436 . . 4.00
3 JAp,rep.Adventure #437-#440 . . 4.00
4 JAp,reps.,final issue 5.00
TPB (2005) 20.00

XENOBROOD
1994–95
0 New team 2.25
1 Battles 2.25
2 Bestiary 2.25
3 A:Superman 2.25
4 V:Bestiary 2.25
5 V:Vimian 2.25
6 final issue 2.25

XERO
March, 1997
1 Cpr(s),Ccs,Trane Walker/Xero . . 3.00
2 CPr(s),Ccs,The Rookie 2.50
3 Cpr(s),Ccs,The Beast 2.50
4 CPr(s) 2.50
6 CPr, Genesis tie-in 2.50
7 CPr(s),O:Zero, pt.1 . . . . 2.50
8 CPr,O:Zero 2.25
9 CPr(s) 2.25
10 CPr,a matter of ethics 2.25
11 . . . . 2.25
12 CPr, final issue, Xero dead 2.25

XOMBI
Milestone, 1994–96
0 WS(c),DCw,Shadow War,Foil(c),
I:Xombi,Twilight 2.50
1 JBy(c),B:Silent Cathedrals 2.00
1a Platinum ed 7.00
2 I:Rabbi Simmowitz,Golms,Liam
Knight of the Spoken Fire 2.50
3 A:Liam 2.00
4 Silent Cathedrals 2.00
5 thru 20 . . . . @2.50
21 final issue 3.50

Y: THE LAST MAN
DC/Vertigo, July, 2002
1 JMz,UnManned,pt.1,40-pg 30.00
2 JMz,UnManned,pt.2 . . . . 25.00
3 JMz,UnManned,pt.3 . . . . 20.00
4 JMz,UnManned,pt.4 . . . . 15.00
5 JMz,UnManned,pt.5 . . . . 10.00
6 JMz,Cycles,pt.1 . . . . 7.00
7 JMz,Cycles,pt.2 . . . . 6.00
8 JMz,Cycles,pt.3 . . . . 6.00
9 JMz,Cycles,pt.4 . . . . 6.00
10 JMz,Cycles,pt.5 . . . . 4.00
11 JMz,One Small Step,pt.1 . . . . . . 4.00
12 JMz,One Small Step,pt.2 . . . . . . 4.00
13 JMz,One Small Step,pt.3 . . . . . . 4.00
14 JMz,One Small Step,pt.4 . . . . . . 3.50
15 JMz,One Small Step,pt.5 . . . . . . 3.50
16 JMz,Comedy&Tragedy,pt.1 . . . . 3.50
17 JMz,Comedy&Tragedy,pt.2 . . . . 3.00
18 JMz,Safeword,pt.1 . . . . 3.00
19 JMz,Safeword,pt.2 . . . . 3.00
20 JMz,Safeword,pt.3 . . . . 3.00
21 JMz,Widow's Pass,pt.1 . . . . 3.00
22 JMz,Widow's Pass,pt.2 . . . . 3.00
23 JMz,Widow's Pass,pt.3 . . . . 3.00
24 JMz,Tongues of Flame,pt.1 . . . . 3.00
25 JMz,Tongues of Flame,pt.2 . . . . 3.00
26 JMz,Hero's Journey 3.00
27 JMz,Ring of Truth,pt.1 . . . . 3.00
28 Ring of Truth, pt.2 . . . . 3.00
29 Ring of Truth, pt.3 . . . . 3.00
30 Ring of Truth, pt.4 . . . . 3.00
31 Ring of Truth, pt.5 . . . . 3.00
32 thru 35 Girl on Girl, pt.1–pt.4 . . @3.00
36 F:Beth Deville 3.00
37 Paper Dolls, pt.1 . . . . 3.00
38 Paper Dolls, pt.2 . . . . 3.00
39 Paper Dolls, pt.3 . . . . 3.00
40 The Women Left Behind 3.00
41 O:Agent 355 . . . . 3.00
42 F:Ampersand 3.00
43 A trip to Japan 3.00
44 Kimono Dragons 3.00
45 Kimono Dragons 3.00
46 Kimono Dragons, concl 3.00
47 Secret origin of Dr. Allison Mann 3.00
48 O:Alter Tse'elon 3.00
49 Motherland, pt.1 . . . . 3.00
50 Motherland, pt.2 . . . . 3.00
51 Motherland, pt.3 . . . . 3.00
TPB Unmanned 13.00
TPB Cycles 13.00
TPB One Small Step 13.00
TPB Safeword 13.00
TPB Vol. 5 Ring of Truth 15.00
TPB Girl on Girl (2006) 13.00
TPB Vol. 8 Kimono Dragons 15.00
TPB Paper Dolls 15.00

YEAR ONE: BATMAN/RA'S AL GHUL
June, 2005
1 (of 2) PG,JP48-page 6.00
2 PG,JP 6.00
TPB 10.00

YEAR ONE: BATMAN/SCARECROW
May, 2005
1 (of 2) 48-page 6.00
2 . . . . 6.00

YEAH!
Homage/DC, 1999
1 GHe 3.00
2 GHe 3.00
3 GHe 3.00
4 GHe,Origins of Yeah,pt.1 . . . . . . 3.00
5 GHe,Origins of Yeah,pt.2 . . . . . . 3.00
6 GHe, ... 3.00
7 GHe, ... 3.00
8 GHe, ... 3.00
9 GHe,final issue 3.00

YOUNG ALL STARS
June, 1987
1 I:IronMunro&FlyingFox,D:TNT . . . 4.50
2 V:Axis Amerika 2.50
3 V:Axis Amerika 2.25
4 I:The Tigress 2.25
5 I:Dyna-mite,O:Iron Munro 2.25
6 . . . . 2.25
7 Baseball Game,A:Tigress 2.25
8 Millennium 2.25
9 Millennium 2.25
10 Hugo Danner 2.25
11 Birth of Iron Munro 2.25
12 Secret of Hugo Danner 2.25
13 V:Deathbolt,Ultra-Humanite 2.25
14 Fury+Ultra Humanite 2.25
15 IronMunro At high school 2.25
16 Ozyan Inheritance 2.25
17 Ozyan Inheritance 2.25
18 Ozyan Inheritance 2.25
19 Ozyan 2.25
20 O:Flying Fox 2.25
21 Atom & Evil#1 . . . . 2.25
22 Atom & Evil#2 . . . . 2.25
23 Atom & Evil#3 . . . . 2.25
24 Atom & Evil#4 . . . . 2.25
25 . . . . 2.25
26 End of the All Stars? 2.25
27 Sons of Dawn' begins 2.25
28 Search for Hugo Danner 2.25
29 A:Hugo Danner 2.25
30 V:Sons of Dawn 2.25
31 V:Sons of Dawn,last issue 2.25
Ann.#1 MG,V:Mekanique 2.50

YOUNG HEROES IN LOVE
April, 1997
1 DeM,F:Hard Drive 3.00
2 DeM,sex, lies and superheroics . 2.50
3 A:Superman 2.50
4 F:Hard Drive 2.50
5 Genesis tie-in 2.50
6 The Rat Pack 2.50
7 Secret Identity Issue 2.50
8 V:Scarecrow 2.50
9 F:Frostbite & Bonfire 2.50
10 V:Grundo'mu 2.50
11 V:Grundo'mu 2.50
12 Hard Drive dead? 2.50
13 New leader picked 2.50
14 Man of Inches vs. Man
   of Candles 2.50
15 Junior vs. Birthday Boy 2.50
16 DeM,Zip-Kid 2.50
17 DeM,Monstergirl's Uncle 2.50
Spec.#1,000,000 DeM final issue . . 3.00

YOUNG JUSTICE
July, 1998
1 PDd,TNu,Robin,Superboy,
   Impulse 4.50
2 PDd,TNu,V:Super-Cycle 3.00
3 PDd(s),TNu,V:Mr.Mxyzptlk 3.00
4 PDd(s),TNu,Girls join team 3.00
5 PDd(s),TNu,V:Harm 3.00
6 PDd(s),TNu,F:JLA 3.00
7 PDd(s),TNu,A:Nightwing 3.00
8 CDi(s),TNu,A:Razorsharp 3.00
9 PDd(s),V:Huggathugees 3.00
10 PDd(s),V:The Acolyte 3.00
11 PDd(s),Rescue Red Tornado . . . 3.00
12 PDd(s),TNu,Supergirl x-over
   Hell's Angels,pt.1 . . . . 3.00
13 PDd(s), Hell's Angels,pt.3 . . . . . 3.00
14 PDd(s),Day of Judgment x-over . 3.00
15 PDd(s),F:Arrowette 3.00
16 PDd(s) 3.00
17 PDd(s),A.A.P.E.S. 3.00
18 PDd(s),Young Injustice 3.00
19 PDd(s),I:Empress 3.00
20 PDd(s),new team 3.00
21 PDd(s),all new? 2.75
22 Day in the life 2.75
23 PDd,TNu,AustraliaGames,pt.1 . . 2.75
24 PDd,TNu,AustraliaGames,pt.2 . . 2.75
25 PDd,TNu,Into space,pt.1 . . . . . . 2.75
26 PDd,TNu,Into space,pt.2 . . . . . . 2.75
27 PDd,TNu,Into space,pt.3 . . . . . . 2.75
28 PDd,TNu,New Genesis 2.75
29 PDd,TNu,F:Forever People 2.75
30 PDd,TNu,Secret vs. Spoiler . . . 2.75
31 PDd,TNu,F:Empress 2.75
32 PDd,TNu,F:Empress 2.75
33 PDd,TNu,WendyWerewolfHunter 2.75
34 PDd,TNu,wolf bites 2.75
35 PDd,TNu,Worlds at War,tie-in . . 2.75
36 PDd,TNu,Worlds at War,tie-in . . 2.75
37 PDd,TNu,stuck in Hell 2.75
38 PDd,TNu,jokerized Match 2.75
39 PDd,TNu,V:New Genesis 2.75
40 PDd(s),TNu,Christmas Past 2.75
41 PDd(s),TNu,F:Ray 2.75
42 PDd(s),TNu,F:Hal Jordan 2.75
43 PDd(s),TNu,F:Traya 2.75
44 PDd(s),TNu,WorldWithoutYJ,pt.1 2.75
45 PDd(s),TNu,WorldWithoutYJ,pt.5 2.75
46 PDd(s),TNu,election day at HQ . 2.75
47 PDd(s),TNu,Fighting MAAD,pt.1 . 2.75
48 PDd(s),TNu,Fighting MAAD,pt.2 . 2.75

Young Justice Secret Files #1
© DC Comics Inc.

49 PDd(s),TNu,Fighting MAAD,pt.3 . 2.75
50 PDd(s),TNu,F.MAAD,pg.4,48-pg. 4.00
51 PDd(s),TNu, on Zandia 2.75
52 PDd(s),TNu,Real World 2.75
53 PDd(s),TNu,V:Secret 2.75
54 PDd(s),TNu,V:Secret 2.75
55 PDd(s),TNu,final issue 2.75
Spec.#1,000,000 PDd(s),TNu 3.00
Giant#1 Secret Origins, 80-page . . . 5.00
Giant#1 80-page 5.00
Secret Files #1 . . . . 5.00
Spec.#1 Young Justice in
   No Man's Land, CDi(s) 4.00
Spec.#1 Young Justice: The Secret
   Impulse,Superboy,Robin (1998) 2.50
Spec.#1 Our Worlds at War 3.00
TPB A League of Their Own 15.00

YOUNG JUSTICE: SINS OF YOUTH
March, 2000
1 (of 2) PDd,x-over 4.00
2 PDd,x-over 4.00
Secret Files #1 . . . . 5.00
TPB Sins of Youth 20.00

YOUNG LOVE
Sept.–Oct., 1963
39 . . . . 75.00
40 thru 50 . . . . @50.00
51 thru 60 . . . . @40.00
61 thru 68 . . . . @40.00
69 giant size 75.00
70 thru 80 . . . . @40.00
81 thru 99 giants, 52-page . . . . . @30.00
100 . . . . 35.00
101 thru 106 . . . . @25.00
107 GC, Giant, 100-page 125.00
108 thru 114 Giant, 100-page . @100.00
115 thru 126 52-page . . . . @50.00

ZATANNA
1987
1 R:Zatanna 2.25
2 N:Zatanna 2.25
3 Come Together 2.25
4 V:Xaos 2.25

ZERO GIRL
DC/Homage Dec., 2000
1 (of 5) SK,F:Amy Snooster 3.00
2 SK, ... 3.00
3 SK,Vice Principal Hooly 3.00
4 SK,Mr. Foster 3.00
5 SK, concl. 3.00
TPB series rep. 144-page 13.00

ZERO GIRL: FULL CIRCLE
DC/Vertigo, Nov., 2002
1 (of 5) SK 3.00

ZERO HOUR: CRISIS IN TIME
1994
4 DJu(a&S),JOy,A:All DC Heroes,
   D;2nd Flash 4.50
3 DJu(a&S),JOy,D:G.A.Sandman,
   G:A.Atom,Dr.Fate,1st Wildcat
   IR:Time Trapper is Rokk Krinn,
   Hawkmen merged 2.50
2 DJu(a&s),JOy 2.50
1 DJu(a&s),JOy,b:Power Gir's
   Child 2.50
0 DJu(A&S),JOy,Gatefold(c),Extant
   vs. Spectre 2.50

All comics prices listed are for *Near Mint* condition.

DC COMICS

Bat-Thing #1
© *DC/Marvel*

Generation Hex #1
© *DC/Marvel*

Super-Soldier #1
© *DC/Marvel*

AMAZON
DC, 1996–97
1 JBy,TA 3.00
1 one-shot JBy,Princess Ororo
  is Wonder Woman 2.25

ASSASSINS
DC, 1996–97
1 DGC,SMc. 3.00
1 one-shot DGC(s),SMc,F:Dare
  and Catsai 2.25

BAT-THING
DC, 1997
1 one-shot LHa(s),RDm,BSz,
  V:motorcycle gang. 2.25

BRUCE WAYNE:
AGENT OF S.H.I.E.L.D.
Marvel, 1996
1 CDi, ... 3.00

BULLETS & BRACELETS
Marvel, 1996
1 JOs,GFr,CaS 3.00

CHALLENGERS OF
THE FANTASTIC
Marvel, 1997
1 KK,TGu,AV 2.25

DARK CLAW
ADVENTURES, THE
DC, 1997
1 one-shot TTy,RBr,V:Ladia Talia . . 2.25

DC VERSUS MARVEL
MARVEL VERSUS DC
1 (DC)DJu. 6.00
1a 2nd printing 4.00
2 (Marvel)PDd,DJu 5.00
2a 2nd printing 4.00
3 (Marvel)DJu. 4.00
4 (DC)PDd,DJu. 4.00
TPB rep. mini series #1–#4 . . . . . . 13.00

DOCTOR STRANGEFATE
DC, 1996–97
1 RMz,KN 3.00
1 one-shot RMz(s),JL,KN,Supreme
  Lord of Order 2.25

EXCITING X-PATROL
Marvel, 1997
1 BKs,BHi 2.25

GENERATION HEX
DC, 1997
1 one-shot,PrM(s),AdP,F:Jono Hex,
  Madam Banshee 2.25

IRON LANTERN
Marvel, 1997
1 KB,PSm,AW. 2.25

JLX
DC 1996–97
1 MWa,GJ, ... 3.00
1 one-shot,MWa(s),GJ,HPo,JhD . . 2.25

JLX UNLEASHED
DC, 1997
1 one-shot, CPr,The Inextinguish-
  able Flame. 2.25

LEGENDS OF
THE DARK CLAW
DC, 1996–97
1 LHa,JBa, ... 3.00
1 one-shot LHa(s),JBa, ... 2.25
1 2nd printing 2.25

LOBO THE DUCK
DC, 1997
1 one-shot, AlG,VS, ... 2.25

MAGNETO &
THE MAGNETIC MEN
Marvel, 1996
1 MWa,GJ,JMs,ATi 3.00

MAGNETIC MEN
FEATURING MAGNETO
Marvel, 1997
1 TPe,BKi,DPs 2.25

SPEED DEMON
Marvel, 1996
1 HMe,SvL,AM 3.00

SPIDER-BOY
Marvel, 1996
1 KK,MeW. 3.00

SPIDER-BOY TEAM-UP
Marvel, 1997
1 KK,RSt 2.25

SUPER-SOLDIER
DC, 1996–97
1 MWa,DGb 3.00
1-shot MWa(s),DGb,V:Ultra-
  Metallo, Green Skull, Hydra . . . 2.25

SUPER SOLDIER:
MAN OF WAR
DC, 1997
1 one-shot MWa(s),DGb,JP,
  V:Nazis 2.25

THORION OF
THE NEW ASGODS
Marvel, 1997
1 KG,JR2. 2.25

X-PATROL
Marvel, 1996
1 KK,BKs, ... 3.00
The Amalgam Age of Comics: The DC
  Comics Collection TPBs 13.00
The Amalgam Age of Comics: The
  Marvel Comics Collection TPBs . . 13.00
Return to the Amalgam Age of Comics:
  The DC Comics Collection TPB . . 13.00

MARVEL

ABOMINATIONS
1996
1 (of 3) IV,AMe, Future Imperfect
  spin-off. 2.25
2 IV,AMe, ... 2.25
3 IV,AMe, ... 2.25

ABRAHAM STONE
1995
1 JKu, Early 20th century 7.00
2 Wandering Man in the 20s. 7.00

ACTION FORCE
March, 1987
1 U.K. G.I. Joe Series 2.25
2 thru 40 . . . . @2.25

ACTUAL CONFESSIONS
See: LOVE ADVENTURES

ACTUAL ROMANCES
Oct., 1949
1 . . . . 150.00
2 Photo Cover. 100.00

ADVENTURE INTO FEAR
See: FEAR

ADVENTURE INTO MYSTERY
Marvel Atlas, 1956–57
1 BP,BEv(c),Future Tense 500.00
2 Man on the 13th Floor 300.00
3 Next Stop Eternity 300.00
4 BP,AW, The Hex 300.00
5 JO,BEv,The People Who
  Weren't 300.00
6 The Wax Man 300.00
7 AT,BEv(c) 300.00
8 AT,JWo,TSe 300.00

ADVENTURES INTO TERROR
See: JOKER COMICS

ADVENTURES INTO WEIRD WORLDS
Jan., 1952–June, 1954
1 RH,GT,The Walking Death . . 1,400.00
2 GT,JMn,Thing in the Bottle . . . 600.00
3 JMn,The Thing That Waited . . 500.00
4 BEv,RH,TheVillageGraveyard . 500.00
5 BEv,I Crawl Thru Graves. 500.00
6 The Ghost Still Walks 500.00
7 OW,Monsters In Disguise 500.00
8 DAy,Nightmares. 500.00
9 Do Not Feed 500.00
10 BEv,Down In The Cellar 500.00
11 JMn,Phantom 450.00
12 GT,Lost In the Graveyard 450.00
13 JeR,DRi,Where Dead Men
  Walk. 450.00
14 A Shriek In the Night. 450.00
15 GT,Terror In Our Town 450.00
16 The Kiss of Death 450.00
17 RH,He Walks With A Ghost . . 450.00
18 Ivan & Petroff 450.00
19 It Happened One Night. 450.00
20 JMn,The Doubting Thomas . . 450.00
21 JF,What Happened In
  the Cave,Hitler. 500.00

22 JMn,RH,Vampire's Partner . . . 450.00
23 JMn,The Kiss of Death 300.00
24 JF,Halfway Home 300.00
25 BEv,JSt,The Mad Mamba 300.00
26 DAy,Good-Bye Earth. 300.00
27 The Dwarf of Horror Moor. . . . 600.00
28 DW,Monsters From the Grave 500.00
29 Bone Dry. 250.00
30 JSt,The Impatient Ghost 250.00

Adventures of Captain America #2
© Marvel Entertainment Group

ADVENTURES OF CAPTAIN AMERICA
Sept., 1991
1 KM,JRu,O:Capt. America. 6.00
2 KM,KWe,TA,O:Capt.America. . . 5.50
3 KM,KWe,JRu,D:Lt.Col.Fletcher . 5.50
4 KWe,JRu,V:Red Skull 5.50

ADVENTURES OF CYCLOPS & PHOENIX
1994
1 SLo(s),GeH,AV,O:Cable 5.00
2 thru 4 SLo(s),GeH,AV,O:Cable @4.00
TPB rep. #1-#4 . . . . 15.00

ADVENTURES OF HOMER GHOST
Atlas, June–Aug., 1957
1 . . . . 250.00
2 . . . . 250.00

ADVENTURES OF PINKY LEE
Marvel Atlas, July, 1955
1 . . . . 400.00
2 . . . . 300.00
3 thru 5 . . . . @275.00

ADVENTURES OF SNAKE PLISSKIN
1997
1-shot LKa, *Escape From L.A.*
  movie adapt. 3.00

ADVENTURES OF SPIDER-MAN
1996
1 from animated TV show. 3.00
2 V:Hammerhead 3.00
3 thru 8 . . . . 3.00
8 AS,V:Kingpin 3.00
9 MHi,A:Dr. Strange, ... 3.00
10 AS,V:The Beetle 3.00
11 AS,V:Doctor Octopus, Venom . 3.00
12 AS,V:Doctor Octopus, Venom. . 3.00

THE ADVENTURES OF BIG BOY
Marvel Timely Comics, 1956
1 . . . . 1,500.00
2 . . . . 900.00
3 . . . . 500.00
Becomes:

ADVENTURES OF THE BIG BOY
Marvel Timely Comics, 1956
4 . . . . 450.00
5 . . . . 400.00
6 . . . . 300.00
7 . . . . 300.00
8 thru 10 . . . . @300.00
11 thru 20 . . . . @200.00
21 thru 30 . . . . @125.00
31 thru 40 . . . . @75.00
41 thru 50 . . . . @60.00
51 thru 60 . . . . @50.00
61 thru 70 . . . . @50.00

ADVENTURES OF THE THING
April–July, 1992
1 rep. Marvel 2 in 1 #50 . . . . 2.50
2 rep. Marvel 2 in 1 #80 . . . . 2.25
3 rep. Marvel 2 in 1 #51 . . . . 2.25
4 rep. Marvel 2 in 1 #77 . . . . 2.25

ADVENTURES OF THE UNCANNY X-MEN
1995
1 Rep. 2.50

ADVENTURES OF THE X-MEN
1996–97
1 from animated TV show. 3.00
2 X-Factor vs. X-Men 3.00
3 thru 12 . . . . @3.00

ADVENTURES ON THE PLANET OF THE APES
Oct., 1975
1 GT,Planet of the Apes Movie
  Adaptation 50.00
2 GT,Humans Captured 20.00
3 GT,Man Hunt 20.00
4 GT,Trial By Fear. 20.00
5 GT, Fury in the Forbidden Zone 20.00
6 GT,The Forbidden Zone,Cont'd . 35.00
7 AA,Man Hunt Cont'd 35.00
8 AA,Brent & Nova Enslaved 20.00
9 AA,Mankind's Demise 15.00
10 AA,When Falls the Lawgiver. . . 20.00
11 AA,Final Chapter,Dec.,1976 . . . 25.00

All comics prices listed are for *Near Mint* condition.   **CVA Page 193**

AGENT X
July, 2002–Oct., 2003
1 Taskmaster trainee,40-pg...... 3.50
2 thru 4 .... @3.00
5 thru 9 .... @2.50
10 thru 15 .... @2.50

AGENTS OF ATLAS
Aug., 2006
1 F:The Spaceman, The Goddess,
  The Robot, The Gorilla, The Spy3.00
2 A:Venus 3.00
3 A:Marvel Boy 3.00
4 A:Namora 3.00

AGE OF INNOCENCE
1995
1-shot Timeslid aftermath 2.50

AIRTIGHT GARAGE
Epic, July–Oct., 1993
1 thru 4 rep.Moebius GNv...... @3.50

AKIRA
Epic, Sept., 1988
1 The Highway,I:Kaneda,Tetsuo,
  Koy,Ryu,Colonel,Takaski..... 35.00
1a 2nd printing 4.00
2 Pursuit,I:Number27,(Masaru) .. 17.00
2a 2nd printing 3.50
3 Number 41,V:Clown Gang..... 12.00
4 King of Clowns,V:Colonel 12.00
5 Cycle Wars,V:Clown Gang 12.00
6 D:Yamagota................ 10.00
7 Prisoners and Players,I:Miyo... 10.00
8 Weapon of Vengeance 10.00
9 Stalkers 10.00
10 The Awakening 10.00
11 Akira Rising............... 7.00
12 Enter Sakaki............... 7.00
13 Desperation............... 7.00
14 Caught in the Middle........ 7.00
15 Psychic Duel.............. 7.00
16 Akira Unleashed 7.00
17 Emperor of Chaos......... 7.00
18 Amid the Ruins 6.00
19 To Save the Children 6.00
20 Revelations.............. 6.00
21 .... 6.00
22 .... 6.00
23 .... 6.00
24 Clown Gang 6.00

Alf #44
© *Marvel Entertainment Group*

25 Search For Kay.............. 6.00
26 Juvenile A Project 6.00
27 Kay and Kaneda............. 6.00
28 Tetsuo................... 6.00
29 Tetsuo 6.00
30 Tetsuo,Kay,Kaneda.......... 6.00
31 D:Kaori,Kaneda,Vs.Tetsuo 6.00
32 Tetsuo'sForces vs.U.S.Forces .. 6.00
33 Tetsuo V:Kaneda............ 6.00
34 64pt. R:Otomo 14.00
35 Leads toward final battle...... 14.00
36 Lady Miyako 14.00
37 ghost of Tetsuo 14.00
38 conclusion................ 14.00
TPB Akira:Reprints#1-#3 .... 14.00
TPB Akira:Reprints#4-#6 .... 14.00
TPB Akira:Reprints#7-#9 .... 14.00
TPB Akira:Reprints#10-#12 ...... 15.00
TPB Akira:Reprints#13-#15 ...... 15.00
TPB Akira:Reprints#16-#18 ...... 15.00
TPB Akira:Reprints#19-#21 ...... 17.00
TPB Akira:Reprints#22-#24 ...... 17.00
TPB Akira:Reprints#25-#27 ...... 17.00
TPB Akira:Reprints#28-#30 ...... 18.00

ALADDIN
1994
1 Aladdin's Quest 2.25
2 thru 12 .... @2.25

ALF
Star, March, 1988
1 Photo Cover................ 4.00
1a 2nd printing 2.50
2 thru 19 .... @2.50
20 thru 22 .... @3.00
23 thru 30 .... @2.50
31 thru 43 .... @3.00
44 thru 45................. @4.00
46 thru 49 .... @3.00
50 giant size................. 4.00
Ann.#1 Evol.War............. 3.00
Ann.#2 .... 3.00
Spring Spec.#1............... 3.00
Holiday Spec.#2.............. 3.00

ALIAS
Marvel Max, Sept., 2001
1 BMB(s)................... 10.00
2 BMB(s), F:Jessica Jones....... 6.00
3 BMB(s).................. 6.00
4 BMB(s),DMk(c) 6.00
5 BMB(s),DMk(c) 4.00
6 BMB(s),DMk(c),........... 4.00
7 BMB(s),BSz,.............. 4.00
8 BMB(s),BSz............... 4.00
9 BMB(s),2nd story, concl....... 4.00
10 BMB(s),J.J.Jameson,Jessica .. 3.50
11 BMB(s),to small town 3.50
12 BMB(s),in small town 3.50
13 BMB(s) 3.50
14 BMB(s),DMk(c),case concludes. 3.50
15 BMB(s),DMk(c),Cage again ... 3.50
16 BMB(s),DMk(c),Underneath ... 3.50
17 BMB(s),DMk(c),Underneath ... 3.50
18 BMB(s),DMk(c),Underneath ... 3.50
19 BMB(s),DMk(c),Underneath ... 3.50
20 BMB(s),DMk(c),Underneath ... 3.50
21 BMB(s),DMk(c),Underneath ... 3.50
22 BMB(s),DMk(c),Jessica Jones .. 3.25
23 BMB(s),DMk(c),Jessica Jones .. 3.25
24 BMB(s),DMk(c),Purple,pt.1.... 3.25
25 BMB(s),DMk(c),Purple,pt.2.... 3.25
26 BMB(s),DMk(c),Purple,pt.3.... 3.25
27 BMB(s),DMk(c),Purple,pt.4.... 3.25
28 BMB(s),DMk(c),Purple,pt.5.... 4.00
TPB Vol. 1 .... 20.00
TPB Vol. 2: Come Home 14.00
TPB Vol. 3: Underneath........ 17.00
TPB Vol. 4: Secret Origins....... 18.00

ALIEN LEGION
Epic, April, 1984
1 FC,TA,I:Sarigar,Montroc 4.00
2 FC,TA,CP,V:Harkilons 3.50
3 thru 20 .... @3.00

[2nd Series], Aug., 1987
1 LSn,I:Guy Montroc............ 3.00
2 thru 18 .... @2.50
GN Grimrod 6.00
1-shot Alien Legion: Binary Deep
  with trading card (1993) 3.50

ALIEN LEGION: JUGGER GRIMROD
Epic, Aug., 1992
Book One 6.00

ALIEN LEGION: ONE PLANET AT A TIME
Epic, Heavy Hitters May, 1993
1 HNg,CDi,One Planet at a Time .. 5.00
2 HNg,CDi................... 5.00
3 HNg,CDi................... 5.00

ALIEN LEGION: ON THE EDGE
Epic, Nov., 1990
1 LSn,V:B'Be No N'ngth 5.00
2 LSn,V:B'Be No N'ngth 5.00
3 LSn,V:B'Be No N'ngth 5.00
4 LSn,V:B'Be No N'ngth 5.00

ALIEN LEGION: TENANTS OF HELL
Epic, 1991
1 LSn,Nomad Squad On
  Combine IV 5.00
2 LSn,L:Torie Montroc,I:Stagg 5.00
TPB Alien Legion:Slaughterworld . 10.00

ALL-NEW OFFICIAL HANDBOOK OF THE MARVEL UNIVERSE A to Z
Jan., 2006
1 .... 4.00
2 thru 11 .... @4.00

ALL SELECT COMICS
Marvel Timely, (Daring Comics)
Fall, 1943
1 ASh(c),B:Capt.America,Sub-Mariner,
  Human Torch;WWII 25,000.00
2 ASh(c),A:Red Skull,V:Axis
  Powers 10,000.00
3 ASh(c),B:Whizzer,V:Axis.... 7,000.00
4 ASh(c),V: Axis 4,500.00
5 ASh(c),E:Sub-Mariner,V:Axis 4,500.00
6 ASh,A:The Destroyer,V:Axis . 3,200.00
7 ASh,MSu,E:Whizzer,V:Axis.. 3,200.00
8 ASh(c),MSu,V:Axis Powers . 3,200.00
9 ASh(c),V:Axis Powers....... 3,200.00
10 ASh(c),E:Capt.America,Human
  Torch;A:The Destroyer 3,200.00
11 SSh, I:Blonde Phantom,
  A:Miss America.......... 4,200.00
Becomes:

BLONDE PHANTOM
1946
12 SSh, B:Miss America;
  The Devil's Playground ... 2,500.00
13 SSh,B:Sub-Mariner;Horror
  In Hollywood........... 1,600.00

All-Select Comics #4
© *Marvel Entertainment Group*

14 SSh,E:Miss America;Horror
  At Haunted Castle 1,500.00
15 SSh,The Man Who Deserved
  To Die 1,500.00
16 SSh,A:Capt.America,Bucky;
  Modeled For Murder. 2,000.00
17 Torture & Rescue. 1,600.00
18 SSh,Jealously,Hate&Cruelty 1,600.00
19 SSh(c),Killer In the Hospital. 1,600.00
20 Blonde Phantom's Big Fall . 1,600.00
21 SSh,Murder At the Carnival . 1,600.00
22 V: Crime Bosses 1,600.00
Becomes:

LOVERS
1949
23 Love Stories 350.00
24 My Dearly Beloved 200.00
25 The Man I Love. 200.00
26 thru 29. . . . . @150.00
30 MK. 200.00
31 thru 36   . . . . @150.00
37 . . . . 300.00
38 BK. 300.00
39 . . . . 150.00
40 . . . . 150.00
41 BEv 200.00
42 thru 65 . . . . @150.00
66 . . . . 125.00
67 ATh 150.00
68 thru 86 Aug., 1957. . . . . . . @125.00

ALL SURPRISE
Marvel Timely, Fall, 1943
1 (fa),F:Super Rabbit,Gandy,
  Sourpuss 450.00
2 . . . . 200.00
3 . . . . 150.00
4 thru 10 . . . . @150.00
11 HK. 165.00
12 Winter, 1946 . . . . 150.00

ALL-TRUE CRIME
See: OFFICIAL TRUE
CRIME CASES

ALL WINNERS COMICS
Marvel Timely, Summer, 1941
1 S&K,BEv,B:Capt.America & Bucky,
  Human Torch & Toro,Sub-Mariner
  A:The Angel,Black Marvel 42,000.00
2 S&K,SSh, B:Destroyer,
  Whizzer. 10,000.00
3 BEv,Bucky & Toro Captured . 7,000.00

4 BEv,AAv,Battle For Victory
  For America 7,500.00
5 AAv,V:Nazl Invasion Fleet. . . 5,000.00
6 SSh,AAv,V:Axis Powers,A:
  Black Avenger. 6,000.00
7 V:Axis Powers. 4,500.00
8 V:Axis Powers. 4,200.00
9 V:Nazi Submarine Fleet. . . . 4,200.00
10 V:Nazi Submarine Fleet. . . . 4,500.00
11 V: Nazis 2,700.00
12 ASh(c),A:Red Skull,E:Destroyer;
  Jap P.O.W. Camp. 3,500.00
13 ASh(c),V:Japanese Fleet . . 3,000.00
14 ASh(c),V:Japanese Fleet . . 3,000.00
15 ASh(c),Jap Supply Train . . . 3,000.00
16 ASh(c),In Alaska
  V:Gangsters 3,000.00
17 V:Gansters;Atomic
  Research Department 3,000.00
18 ASh(c),V:Robbers;Internal
  Revenue Department 3,200.00
19 ASh(c),SSh,I:All Winners Squad,
  Fall, 1946 . . . . 10,000.00
21 SSh,AAv,A:All-Winners Squad;
  Riddle of Demented Dwarf . 7,500.00
Becomes:

ALL TEEN COMICS
1947
20 F:Georgie,Willie,
  Mitzi,Patsy Walker. 200.00
Becomes:

TEEN COMICS
1947
21 HK,A:George,Willie,Mitzi,
  Patsy Walker, Hey Look 200.00
22 A:George,Willie,Margie,
  Patsy Walker 125.00
23 SSh,A:P.Walker,Cindy,George 125.00
24 . . . . 150.00
25 thru 27. . . . . @125.00
28 . . . . 150.00
29 . . . . 125.00
30 HK,Hey Look 150.00
31 thru 34. . . . . @125.00
35 May, 1950 . . . . 125.00
Becomes:

JOURNEY INTO
UNKNOWN WORLDS
Marvel Atlas, Sept., 1950
36(1) RH,End of the Earth. . . . 4,000.00
37(2) BEv,GC,When Worlds
  Collide. 1,800.00
38(3) GT,Land of Missing Men 1,500.00
4 MSy,RH,Train to Nowhere . . 1,000.00
5 MSy,Trapped in Space 1,000.00
6 GC,RH,World Below
  the Atlantic 1,000.00
7 BW,RH,JMn,House That
  Wasn't. 1,500.00
8 RH,JMn,The Stone Thing . . . 1,000.00
9 MSy,JSt,The People Who
  Couldn't Exist 1,000.00
10 The Undertaker 1,000.00
11 BEv,Frankie Was Afraid 700.00
12 BK,Last Voice You Hear 700.00
13 The Witch Woman 600.00
14 BW,BEv,CondemnedBuilding1,200.00
15 JMn,They Crawl By Night . . 1,200.00
16 JMn,Scared to Death 600.00
17 BEv,GC,RH,The Ice
  Monster Cometh 700.00
18 The Broth Needs Somebody . 700.00
19 MF,GC,The Long Wait 700.00
20 GC,RH,The Race That
  Vanished 600.00
21 MF,JMn,JSt,Decapitation 450.00
22 thru 32. . . . . @450.00
33 SD,The Man in the Box 450.00
34 MK,AT,DAy 350.00

35 AT,MD 350.00
36 thru 44 . . . . @400.00
45 AW,SD. 400.00
46 & 47. . . . . @400.00
48 GW,GM 400.00
49 JF,JMn. 400.00
50 JDa,RC 400.00
51 WW,SD,JSe 400.00
52 . . . . 400.00
53 RC,BP 400.00
54 AT,BP 400.00
55 AW,RC,BEv. 400.00
56 BEv 400.00
57 JO 250.00
58 MD,JMn. 250.00
59 AW,Aug., 1957 . . . . 350.00

ALL WINNERS COMICS
[2nd Series], Aug., 1948
1 SSh,F:Blonde Phantom,A:Capt.Am.
Sub-Mariner,Human Torch 5,000.00
Becomes:

ALL WESTERN
WINNERS
1948–49
2 SSh,B,I&O:Black Rider,
  B:Two-Gun Kid, Kid-Colt . . 1,200.00
3 Black Rider V: Satan 600.00
4 Black Rider Unmasked 600.00
Becomes:

WESTERN WINNERS
1949
5 I Challenge the Army 600.00
6 The Mountain Mystery 500.00
7 Ph(c) Randolph Scott 500.00
Becomes:

BLACK RIDER
1950–55
8 Ph(c) of Stan Lee,B:Black Rider;
  Valley of Giants 800.00
9 SSh,JMn,Wrath of the Redskin 500.00
10 O:Black Rider 550.00
11 Redmen on the Warpath. 300.00
12 GT,The Town That Vanished. . 300.00
13 SSh,The Terrified Tribe 300.00
14 The Tyrant of Texas 300.00
15 Revolt of the Redskins 250.00
16 . . . . 250.00
17 . . . . 250.00
18. . . . . 250.00
19 SSh,GT,A:Two-Gun Kid 250.00
20 GT. 300.00

All Winners 2nd Series #1
© *Marvel Entertainment Group*

Black Rider #27
© *Marvel Entertainment Group*

21 SSh,GT,A:Two-Gun Kid 250.00
22 SSh,DAy(c),A:Two-Gun Kid . . 250.00
23 SSh,A:Two-Gun Kid 250.00
24 SSh,JSt 250.00
25 SSh,JSt,A:Arrowhead 250.00
26 SSh,A:Kid-Colt 250.00
27 SSh,JMn(c),A:Kid-Colt 300.00
Becomes:

WESTERN TALES OF
BLACK RIDER
1955

28 JSe,D:Spider 300.00
29 . . . . 200.00
30 . . . . 200.00
31 . . . . 200.00
Becomes:

GUNSMOKE WESTERN
1955–63

32 MD,MB,F:Kid Colt,Billy
    Buckskin 300.00
33 MD 200.00
34 MB 175.00
35 GC 200.00
36 AW,GC 200.00
37 JDa 175.00
38 . . . . 150.00
39 GC 150.00
40 AW 175.00
41 thru 43 . . . . @125.00
44 AT 125.00
45 & 46 . . . . @125.00
47 JK 150.00
48 & 49 . . . . @125.00
50 JK,RC 200.00
51 JK 150.00
52 thru 54 . . . . @125.00
55 & 56 MB . . . . @125.00
57 Two Gun Kid 100.00
58 & 59 . . . . @100.00
60 Sam Hawk (Kid Colt) 125.00
61 RC 150.00
62 thru 67 JK . . . . @100.00
68 . . . . 100.00
69 JK 100.00
70 . . . . 100.00
71 JK 125.00
72 O:Kid Colt 125.00
73 JK 135.00
74 thru 76 . . . . @100.00
77 JK,July, 1963 . . . . 150.00

(TIMELY PRESENTS:)
ALL-WINNERS
Oct., 1999
Spec. 48-pg 4.00

ALPHA FLIGHT
Aug., 1983

1 JBy,I:Puck,Marrina,Tundra 4.00
2 JBy,I:Master,Vindicator Becomes
   Guardian,B:O:Marrina 2.50
3 JBy,O:Master,A:Namor,Invisible
   Girl 2.50
4 JBy,A:Namor,Invisible Girl,
   E:O:Marrina,A:Master 2.50
5 JBy,B:O:Shaman,F:Puck 2.50
6 JBy,E:O:Shaman,I:Kolomag . . . 2.50
7 JBy,B:O:Snowbird,I:Delphine
   Courtney & Deadly Ernest. 2.50
8 JBy,E:O:Snowbird,O:Deadly
   Ernest,I:Nemesis 2.50
9 JBy,O:Aurora,A:Wolverine,
   Super Skrull 2.50
10 JBy,O:Northstar,V:SuperSkrull . . 2.50
11 JBy,I:Omega Flight,Wild Child
   O:Sasquatch 2.50
12 JBy,D:Guardian,V:Omega
   Flight 2.50
13 JBy,C:Wolverine,Nightmare 3.00
14 JBy,V:Genocide. 2.50
15 JBy,R:Master. 2.50
16 JBy,BWi,V:Master,C:Wolverine
   I:Madison Jeffries 2.75
17 JBy,BWi,A:Wolverine,X-Men . . . 3.00
18 JBy,BWi,J:Heather,I:Ranaq 2.50
19 JBy,I:Talisman,V:Ranaq 2.50
20 JBy,I:Gilded Lily,N:Aurora 2.50
21 JBy,BWi,O:Gilded Lily,Diablo . . . 2.50
22 JBy,BWi,I:Pink Pearl 2.50
23 JBy,BWi,D:Sasquatch,
   I:Tanaraq 2.50
24 JBy,BWi,V:Great Beasts,J:Box . . 2.50
25 JBy,BWi,V:Omega Flight
   I:Dark Guardian 2.50
26 JBy,BWi,A:Omega Flight,Dark
   Guardian 2.50
27 JBy,V:Omega Flight 2.50
28 JBy,Secret Wars II,V:Omega
   Flight,D:Dark Guardian 2.50
29 MMi,V:Hulk,A:Box 2.50
30 MMi,I&O:Scramble,R:Deadly
   Ernest 2.50
31 MMi,D:Deadly Ernest,
   O:Nemesis. 2.50
32 MMi(c),JBg,O:Puck,I:2nd
   Vindicator. 2.50
33 MMi(c),SB,X-Men,I:Deathstrike . 4.00
34 MMi(c),SB,Wolverine,V:
   Deathstrike 3.00
35 DR,R:Shaman. 2.50
36 MMi(c),DR,A:Dr.Strange 2.50
37 DR,O:Pestilence,N:Aurora 2.50
38 DR,A:Namor,V:Pestilence. 2.50
39 MMi(c),DR,WPo,A:Avengers 2.75
40 DR,WPo,W:Namor & Marrina . . . 2.75
41 DR,WPo,I:Purple Girl,
   J:Madison Jeffries 2.75
42 DR,WPo,I:Auctioneer,J:Purple
   Girl,A: Beta Flight 2.75
43 DR,WPo,V:Mesmero,Sentinels . . 2.75
44 DR,WPo,D:Snowbird,
   A:Pestilence. 2.75
45 JBr,WPo,R:Sasquatch,
   L:Shaman 2.75
46 JBr,WPo,I:2nd Box 2.75
47 MMi,WPo,TA,Vindicator solo . . . 2.75
48 SL(i),I:Omega 2.75
49 JBr,WPo,I:Manikin,D:Omega . . . 2.75
50 WS(c),JBr,WPo,L:Northstar,Puck,
   Aurora,A:Loki,Double size. 3.00
51 JLe(1st Marv),WPo(i),V:Cody . . . 7.00

52 JBr,WPo(i),I:Bedlam,
   A:Wolverine 3.00
53 JLe,WPo(i),I:Derangers,Goblyn
   D&V:Bedlam,A:Wolverine 4.00
54 WPo(i),O&J:Goblyn. 2.50
55 JLe,TD,V:Tundra. 3.50
56 JLe,TD,V:Bedlamites 3.50
57 JLe,TD,V:Crystals,
   C:Dreamqueen 3.50
58 JLe,AM,V:Dreamqueen. 3.50
59 JLe,AM,I:Jade Dragon,R:Puck . . 3.50
60 JLe,AM,V:J.Dragon,D.Queen . . . 3.50
61 JLe,AM,on Trial
   (1st JLe X-Men). 3.50
62 JLe,AM,V:Purple Man. 3.50
63 MG,V:U.S.Air Force. 2.50
64 JLe,AM,V:Great Beasts 3.50
65 JLe(c),AM(i),Dream Issue 3.00
66 JLe(c),I:China Force 3.00
67 JLe(c),O:Dream Queen 3.00
68 JLe(c),V:Dream Queen 3.00
69 JLe(c),V:Dream Queen 3.00
70 MM(i),V:Dream Queen 2.50
71 MM(i),I:Sorcerer 2.50
72 V:Sorcerer 2.50
73 MM(i),V:Sorcerer. 2.50
74 MM(i),Alternate Earth 3.00
75 JLe(c),MMi(i),Double Size 3.00
76 MM(i),V:Sorcerer. 2.25
77 MM(i),V:Kingpin 2.25
78 MM(i),A:Dr.Strange,Master 2.25
79 MM(i),AofV,V:Scorpion,Nekra . . . 2.25
80 MM(i),AofV,V:Scorpion,Nekra . . . 2.25
81 JBy(c),MM(i),B:R:Northstar. 2.25
82 JBy(c),MM(i),E:R:Northstar. 2.25
83 JSh 2.25
84 MM(i),Northstar 2.25
85 MM(i). 2.25
86 MBa,MM,V:Sorcerer 2.25
87 JLe(c),MM(i),A:Wolverine 3.00
88 JLe(c),MM(i),A:Wolverine 3.00
89 JLe(c),MM(i),R:Guardian,A:
   Wolverine. 3.00
90 JLe(c),MM(i),A:Wolverine 3.00
91 MM(i),A:Dr.Doom 2.25
92 Guardian vs.Vindicator 2.25
93 MM(i),A:Fant.Four,I:Headlok. . . . 2.25
94 MM(i),V:Fant.Four,Headlok. 2.25
95 MM(i),Lifelines. 2.25
96 MM(i),A:Master 2.25
97 B:Final Option,A:Her. 2.25
98 A:Avengers 2.25
99 A:Avengers 2.25
100 JBr,TMo,DR,LMa,E:Final Option
   A:Galactus,Avengers,D:
   Guardian,G-Size 2.50

Alpha Flight #5
© *Marvel Entertainment Group*

MARVEL

101 TMo,Final Option Epilogue,
    A:Dr.Strange,Avengers 2.25
102 TMo,I:Weapon Omega,. 2.25
103 TMo,V:Diablo,U.S.Agent. 2.25
104 TMo,N:Alpha Flight,Weapon
    Omega is Wild Child 2.25
105 TMo,V.Pink Pearl 2.25
106 MPa,Aids issue,Northstar
    acknowledges homosexuality . . 3.00
106a 2nd printing 2.50
107 A:X-Factor,V:Autopsy 2.25
108 A:Soviet Super Soldiers 2.25
109 V:Peoples Protectorate 2.25
110 PB,Infinity War,I:2nd Omega
    Flight,A:Wolverine 2.25
111 PB,Infinity War,V:Omega
    Flight,A:Wolverine 2.25
112 PB,Infinity War,V:Master 2.25
113 V:Mauler 2.25
114 A:Weapon X 2.25
115 PB,I:Wyre,A:Weapon X. 2.25
116 PB,I:Rok,V:Wyre 2.25
117 PB,V:Wyre 2.25
118 PB,V:Thunderball 2.25
119 PB,V:Wrecking Crew. 2.25
120 PB,10th Anniv.,V:Hardliners,
    w/poster. 3.00
121 PCu,V:Brass Bishop,A:Spider-
    Man,Wolverine,C:X-Men 2.50
122 PB,BKi,Inf.Crusade. 2.50
123 PB,BKi,Infinity Crusade 2.50
124 PB,BKi,Infinity Crusade 2.50
125 PB,V:Carcass 2.50
126 V:Carcass 2.50
127 SFu(s),Infinity Crusade. 2.50
128 B:No Future 2.50
129 C:Omega Flight. 2.50
130 E:No Future,last issue,
    Double Sized. 3.00
Ann.#1 LSn,V:Diablo,Gilded Lily . . . 3.00
Ann.#2 JBr,BMc. 2.50
Spec.#1 PB,A:Wolverine,
    O:First Team,V:Egghead 3.75
Spec.#1–#3 Newsstand versions
    of #97–#99. . . . . @2.50
Spec.#4 Newsstand ver.of #100 . . 2.50

[2nd Series] 1997
1 SSe,ScC, former team kidnapped,
    I:Murmur, Radius,Flex,Guardian 5.00
2 SSe,ScC 4.00
2 variant cover 3.50
3 SSe,ScC, ... 3.50
4 SSe,ScC,V:Mesmero 3.00
5 SSe,ScC,A:Mesmero 3.00
6 SSe,What's up with Sasquatch? . 3.00
7 SSe,Evils explode 3.00
8 SSe,ScC,North & South prelude . 3.00
9 SSe,ScC,North & South pt.1,
    X-Men x-over. 3.00
10 SSe,Flung into Prometheus Pit . 3.00
11 SSe,race to save 2 worlds 3.00
12 SSe,Alphan dies,48pg. 3.50
13 SSe,F:Basil Killbrew 2.50
14 SSe,I:Brass Bishop. 2.50
15 SSe 2.50
16 SSe,V:Brass Bishop 2.50
17 SSe,V:X the Unknown 2.50
18 SSe,Alpha:Omega,pt.1 . . . . 2.50
19 SSe,Alpha:Omega,pt.2 . . . . 2.50
20 SSe,Alpha:Omega,pt.3 . . . . 2.50
Spec. #1 SSe,In the Beginning,
    Flashback, A:Wolverine 2.50
Ann.1998 Alpha Flight/Inhumans. . 3.50

[3rd Series] March, 2004
1 SLo,You Gotta Be Kiddin,pt.1 . . . 3.00
2 SLo,You Gotta Be Kiddin,pt.2 . . . 3.00
3 SLo,You Gotta Be Kiddin,pt.3 . . . 3.00
4 SLo,You Gotta Be Kiddin,pt.4 . . . 3.00
5 SLo,You Gotta Be Kiddin,pt.5 . . . 3.00
6 SLo,You Gotta Be Kiddin,pt.6 . . . 3.00
7 Waxing Poetic,pt.1 . . . . 3.00
8 Waxing Poetic,pt.2 . . . . 3.00

9 Days of Future Present,pt.1 . . . . . 3.00
10 Days of Future Present,pt.2 . . . . 3.00
11 Days of Future Present,pt.3 . . . . 3.00
12 Days of Future Present,pt.4 . . . . 3.00
TPB Vol. 1:You Gotta be
    Kiddin' Me 15.00
TPB Vol. 2: Waxing Poetic. 15.00

ALPHA FLIGHT SPECIAL
1991
1 thru 4 reprints. . . . . @2.25

AMAZING ADVENTURES
June, 1961
1 JK,SD,O&B:Dr.Droom;Torr . 2,400.00
2 JK,SD,This is Manoo 900.00
3 JK,SD,Trapped in the
    Twilight World 850.00
4 JK,SD, I Am X 800.00
5 JK,SD, Monsteroso 800.00
6 JK,SD,E:Dr.Droom; Sserpo . . 800.00
Becomes:

Amazing Adult Fantasy #10
© Marvel Entertainment Group

AMAZING ADULT FANTASY
Dec., 1961
7 SD,Last Man on Earth 1,000.00
8 SD,The Coming of the Krills . . 900.00
9 SD,The Terror of Tim Boo Ba . 700.00
10 SD,Those Who Change 700.00
11 SD,In Human Form 700.00
12 SD,Living Statues 700.00
13 SD,At the Stroke of Midnight . 700.00
14 SD,Beware of the Giants 750.00
Becomes:

AMAZING FANTASY
Aug., 1962
15 JK(c),SD,I&O:Spider-Man,I:Aunt
    May, Flash Thompson, Burglar,
    I&D:Uncle Ben 50,000.00
Marvel Milestone rep.#15 (1992). . . 3.00

[Second Series], 1995
15a gold Rep. (1995). 25.00
16 KBk, O:Spider-Man,painted . . . 4.00
17 KBk, More early adventures 4.00
18 KBk,conclusion 4.00

AMAZING ADVENTURES
Aug., 1970
[1st Regular Series]
1 JK,JB,B:Inhumans,Bl.Widow . . . 90.00
2 JK,JB,A:Fantastic Four 45.00
3 JK,GC,BEv,V:Mandarin 45.00
4 JK,GC,BEv,V:Mandarin 45.00
5 NA,TP,DH,BEv,V:Astrologer . . . 60.00
6 NA,DH,SB,V:Maximus 60.00
7 NA,DH,BEv 60.00
8 NA,DH,BEv,E:Black Widow,
    A:Thor,(see Avengers #95) . . 60.00
9 MSy,BEv,V:Magneto 40.00
10 GK(c),MSy,V:Magneto,
    E:Inhumans 40.00
11 GK(c),TS,B:O:New Beast,
    A:X-Men. 250.00
12 GK(c),TS,MP,A:Iron Man 75.00
13 JR(c),TS,V:New Br'hood
    Evil Mutants,I:Buzz Baxter
    (Mad Dog) 75.00
14 GK(c),TS,JM,V:Quasimodo . . . 75.00
15 JSn(c),TS,A:X-Men,V:Griffin . . . 75.00
16 JSn(c),FMc(i),V:Juggernaut . . . 75.00
17 JSn,A:X-Men,E:Beast 75.00
18 HC,NA,B:Killraven. 75.00
19 HC,Sirens on 7th Avenues 12.00
20 Coming of the Warlords 12.00
21 Cry Killraven 12.00
22 Killraven 12.00
23 Killraven 12.00
24 New Year Nightmare-2019AD. . 12.00
25 RB,V:Skar 12.00
26 GC,V:Ptson-Rage Vigilante . . . 12.00
27 CR,JSn,V:Death Breeders 12.00
28 JSn,CR,V:Death Breeders 12.00
29 CR,Killraven 12.00
30 CR,Killraven 12.00
31 CR,Killraven 12.00
32 CR,Killraven 12.00
33 CR,Killraven 12.00
34 CR,D:Hawk 12.00
35 KG,Killraven Continued 12.00
36 CR,Killraven Continued 12.00
37 CR,O:Old Skull 12.00
38 CR,Killraven Continued. 12.00
39 CR,E:Killraven. 12.00
[2nd Regular Series], 1979
1 rep.X-Men#1,38,Professor X . . . 10.00
2 thru 14 reps. . . . . @8.00

AMAZING COMICS
Marvel Timely, 1944
1 ASh(c),F:Young Allies,Destroyer,
    Whizzer, Sergeant Dix 4,000.00
Becomes:

COMPLETE COMICS
2 ASh(c),F:Young Allies,Destroyer,
    Whizzer Sergeant Dix; 3,200.00

AMAZING DETECTIVE CASES
Marvel Atlas, Nov., 1950
3 Detective/Horror Stories 350.00
4 Death of a Big Shot 200.00
5 . . . . 200.00
6 Danger in the City 200.00
7 . . . . 175.00
8 . . . . 175.00
9 CC, The Man Who Wasn't 175.00
10 GT. 175.00
11 The Black Shadow 350.00
12 MSy,BK, Harrigan's Wake. . . . 350.00
13 BEv,JSt, ... 400.00
14 Hands Off; Sept., 1952. . . . . . 350.00

MARVEL

AMAZING FANTASY
June, 2004
1 (of 6) 4.00
2 thru 5 . . . . @4.00
6 . . . . 3.00
7 F:Scorpion,pt.1 . . . . 3.00
8 Motherless Country 3.00
9 Identity Politics. 3.00
10 F:all-new Scorpion 3.00
11 The New Pollution 3.00
12 Poison Tomorrow 3.00
13 KK,I:Vegas 3.00
14 KK,F:Vegas 3.00
15 48-pg. 4.00
16 Unnatural Selection,pt.1 . . . . . . 3.00
17 Unnatural Selection,pt.2 . . . . . . 3.00
18 Unnatural Selection,pt.3 . . . . . . 3.00
19 Unnatural Selection,pt.4 . . . . . . 3.00
20 Unnatural Selection,pt.5 . . . . . . 3.00
Digest Scorpion: Poison Tomorrow . 8.00

AMAZING HIGH ADVENTURE
Aug., 1984
1 BSz,JSo,JS 4.00
2 PS,AW,BSz,TA,MMi,BBI,CP,CW . 3.00
3 MMi,VM,JS 3.00
4 JBo,JS,SBi. 3.00
5 JBo; Oct., 1986 . . . . 3.00

AMAZING MYSTERIES
Marvel-Comics, 1949–50
32 The Isle of No Return 1,500.00
33 The Thing in the Vault. 750.00
34 Photo(c) 400.00
35 Photo(c) 400.00

AMAZING SCARLET SPIDER
1995
1 MBa,LMa,VirtualMortality,pt.2 . . . 2.50
2 TDF,MBa,CyberWar,pt.2 . . . . . . 2.50

AMAZING SPIDER-GIRL
Oct., 2006
0 RF,TDF,Spec., F:Mayday Parker. 2.00
1 RF,TDF, V:Black Tarantula 3.00
2 RF,TDF, V:Hobgoblin 3.00

AMAZING SPIDER-MAN
March, 1963
1 JK(c),SED,I:Chameleon,J.Jonah &
  John Jameson,A:F.Four . 45,000.00
2 SD,I:Vulture,Tinkerer
  C:Mysterio(disguised) 10,000.00
3 SD,I&O:Dr.Octopus. 8,000.00
4 SD,I&O:Sandman,I:Betty
  Brant,Liz Allen 7,500.00
5 SD,V:Dr.Doom,C:Fant.Four . 7,500.00
6 SD,I&O:Lizard,The Connors. 4,000.00
7 SD,V:Vulture 3,000.00
8 SD,JK,I:Big Brain,V:Human
  Torch,A:Fantastic Four 7,500.00
9 SD,I&O:Electro 3,500.00
10 SD,I:Enforcers,Big Man 3,500.00
11 SD,V:Dr.Octopus,
  D:Bennett Brant 1,500.00
12 SD,V:Dr.Octopus 1,500.00
13 SD,I:Mysterio 2,500.00
14 SD,I:Green Goblin,
  V:Enforcers, Hulk 4,700.00
15 SD,I:Kraven,A:Chameleon . 3,000.00
16 SD,A:Daredevil,
  V:Ringmaster 2,000.00
17 SD,2nd A:Green Goblin,
  A:Human Torch. 2,700.00
18 SD,V:Sandman,Enforcers,
  C:Avengers,F.F.,Daredevil . 1,800.00

Amazing Spider-Man #20
© Marvel Entertainment Group

19 SD,V:Sandman,I:Ned Leeds
  A:Human Torch. 1,500.00
20 SD,I&O:Scorpion 2,300.00
21 SD,A:Beetle,Human Torch . . 1,300.00
22 SD,V:The Clown,Masters of
  Menace. 1,200.00
23 SD,V:GreenGoblin(3rd App.) 2,700.00
24 SD,V:Mysterio 1,000.00
25 SD,I:Spider Slayer,Spencer
  Smythe,C:Mary Jane 1,100.00
26 SD,I:CrimeMaster,V:Green
  Goblin 1,200.00
27 SD,V:CrimeMaster,
  Green Goblin 1,300.00
28 SD,I:Molten Man,Peter Parker
  Graduates High School . . . 2,500.00
29 SD,V:Scorpion 1,000.00
30 SD,I:Cat Burglar. 1,000.00
31 SD,I:Gwen Stacy,Harry Osborn
  Prof.Warren,V:Dr.Octopus . 1,000.00
32 SD,V:Dr.Octopus. 500.00
33 SD,V:Dr.Octopus. 500.00
34 SD,V:Kraven 500.00
35 SD,V:Molten Man 500.00
36 SD,I:The Looter 500.00
37 SD,V:Professor Stromm,
  I:Norman Osborn 500.00
38 SD,V:Joe Smith(Boxer). 500.00
39 JR,IR:Green Goblin is Norman
  Osborn 1,500.00
40 JR,O:Green Goblin 1,600.00
41 JR,I:Rhino,C:Mary Jane 600.00
42 JR,V:John Jameson,I:Mary
  Jane (Face Revealed). 450.00
43 JR,O:Rhino 400.00
44 JR,V:Lizard(2nd App.) 400.00
45 JR,V:Lizard 400.00
46 JR,I&O:Shocker 425.00
47 JR,V:Kraven 400.00
48 JR,I:Fake Vulture,A:Vulture . . . 400.00
49 JR,V:Fake Vulture,Kraven 400.00
50 JR,I:Kingpin,Spidey Quits,
  C:Johnny Carson 2,500.00
51 JR,V:Kingpin 1,000.00
52 JR,V:Kingpin,I:Robbie
  Robertson,D:Fred Foswell. . . 350.00
53 JR,V:Dr.Octopus. 500.00
54 JR,V:Dr.Octopus. 500.00
55 JR,V:Dr.Octopus. 500.00
56 JR,V:Dr.Octopus,I:Capt.Stacy. 500.00
57 JR,DH,A:Ka-Zar 500.00
58 JR,DH,V:Spencer Smythe,
  Spider Slayer. 500.00
59 JR,DH,V:Kingpin 500.00
60 JR,DH,V:Kingpin 500.00

61 JR,DH,V:Kingpin 500.00
62 JR,DH,V:Medusa 400.00
63 JR,DH,V:1st & 2nd
  Vulture 400.00
64 JR,DH,V:Vulture 400.00
65 JR,JM,V:Prisoners 400.00
66 JR,DH,V:Mysterio 400.00
67 JR,JM,V:Mysterio,I:Randy
  Robertson 400.00
68 JR,JM,V:Kingpin 425.00
69 JR,JM,V:Kingpin 425.00
70 JR,JM,V:Kingpin 425.00
71 JR,JM,V:Quicksilver,C:Scarlet
  Witch,Toad,A:Kingpin 400.00
72 JR,JB,JM,V:Shocker 400.00
73 JR,JB,JM,I:Man Mountain Marko,
  Silvermane. 400.00
74 JR,JM,V:Silvermane 300.00
75 JR,JM,V:Silvermane,A:Lizard . 250.00
76 JR,JM,V:Lizard,A:H.Torch. . . . 250.00
77 JR,JM,V:Lizard,A:H.Torch. . . . 250.00
78 JR,JM,I&O:Prowler 200.00
79 JR,JM,V:Prowler 175.00
80 JR,JB,JM,V:Chameleon 175.00
81 JR,JB,JM,I:Kangaroo 175.00
82 JR,JM,V:Electro 175.00
83 JR,I:Richard Fisk(as Schemer),
  Vanessa(Kingpin's wife) 175.00
84 JR,JB,JM,V:Schemer,Kingpin . 175.00
85 JR,JB,JM,V:Schemer,Kingpin . 175.00
86 JR,JM,V:Black Widow, C:Iron
  Man, Hawkeye. 175.00
87 JR,JM,Reveals ID to his
  friends,changes mind 175.00
88 JR,JM,V:Dr.Octopus 175.00
89 GK,JR,V:Dr.Octopus 175.00
90 GK,JR,V:Dr.Octopus
  D:Capt.Stacy 250.00
91 GK,JR,I:Bullit. 200.00
92 GK,JR,V:Bullit,A:Iceman 200.00
93 JR,V:Prowler. 200.00
94 JR,SB,V:Beetle,O:Spider-Man 250.00
95 JR,SB,London,V:Terrorists . . . 175.00
96 GK,JR,A:Green Goblin,Drug
  Mention,No Comic Code 225.00
97 GK,V:Green Goblin,Drugs 225.00
98 GK,V:Green Goblin,Drugs 225.00
99 GK,Prison Riot,A:Carson 200.00
100 JR(c),GK,Spidey gets four
  arms from serum 325.00
101 JR(c),GK,I:Morbius,the
  Living Vampire,A:Lizard. 300.00
101a Reprint,Metallic ink 5.00
102 JR(c),GK,O:Morbius,
  V:Lizard 175.00
103 GK,V:Kraven,A:Ka-Zar 75.00
104 GK,V:Kraven,A:Ka-Zar 75.00
105 GK,V:Spenser Smythe,
  Spider Slayer. 75.00
106 JR,V:Spenser Smythe,
  Spider Slayer. 75.00
107 JR,V:Spenser Smythe,
  Spider Slayer. 75.00
108 JR,R:Flash Thompson,
  I:Sha-Shan,V:Vietnamese 75.00
109 JR,A:Dr.Strange,
  V:Vietnamese 75.00
110 JR,I:The Gibbon 75.00
111 JR,V:The Gibbon,Kraven 75.00
112 JR,Spidey gets an Ulcer 75.00
113 JSn,JR,I:Hammerhead
  V:Dr.Octopus 75.00
114 JSn,JR,V:Hammerhead,Dr.
  Octopus,I:Jonas Harrow 75.00
115 JR,V:Hammerhead,
  Dr.Octopus. 75.00
116 JR,JM,V:The Smasher 75.00
117 JR,JM,V:Smasher,Disruptor . 75.00
118 JR,JM,V:Smasher,Disruptor . 75.00
119 JR,A:Hulk 125.00
120 GK,JR,V:Hulk 125.00

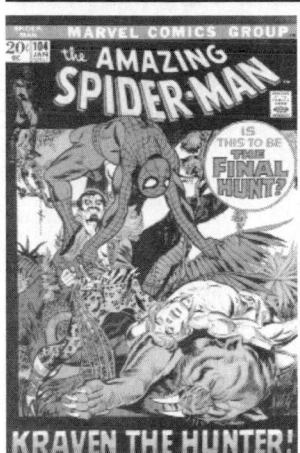

Amazing Spider-Man #104
© Marvel Entertainment Group

Amazing Spider-Man #252
© Marvel Entertainment Group

121 GK,JR,V:Green Goblin
   D:Gwen Stacy,Drugs 325.00
122 GK,JR,D:Green Goblin 350.00
123 GK,JR,A:Powerman 75.00
124 GK,JR,I:Man-Wolf 90.00
125 RA,JR,O:Man-Wolf 75.00
126 JM(c),RA,JM,V:Kangaroo,
   A: Human Torch 75.00
127 JR(c),RA,V:3rd Vulture,
   A:Human Torch 75.00
128 JR(c),RA,V:3rd Vulture 75.00
129 K&R(c),RA,I:Punisher,Jackal 600.00
130 JR(c),RA,V:Hammerhead,
   Dr.Octopus,I:Spider-Mobile . . . 50.00
131 GK(c),RA,V:Hammerhead,
   Dr.Octopus. 50.00
132 GK(c),JR,V:Molten Man 50.00
133 GK(c),RA,V:Molten Man 50.00
134 JR(c),RA,I:Tarantula,C:
   Punisher(2nd App.) 60.00
135 JR(c),RA,V:Tarantula,
   A.Punisher. 125.00
136 JR(c),RA,I:2nd GreenGoblin . 125.00
137 GK(c),RA,V:Green Goblin 90.00
138 K&R(c),RA,I:Mindworm 50.00
139 K&R(c),RA,I:Grizzly,V:Jackal . 50.00
140 GK(c),RA,I:Gloria Grant,
   V:Grizzly,Jackal 50.00
141 JR(c),RA,V:Mysterio 50.00
142 JR(c),RA,V:Mysterio 50.00
143 K&R(c),RA,I:Cyclone 50.00
144 K&R(c),RA,V:Cyclone 50.00
145 K&R(c),RA,V:Scorpion 50.00
146 RA,JR,V:Scorpion 50.00
147 JR(c),RA,V:Tarantula 50.00
148 GK(c),RA,V:Tarantula,IR:Jackal
   is Prof.Warren 60.00
149 K&R(c),RA,D:Jackal 100.00
150 GK(c),RA,V:Spenser Smythe . 60.00
151 RA,JR,V:Shocker 50.00
152 K&R(c),RA,V:Shocker. 30.00
153 K&R(c),RA,V:Paine. 30.00
154 JR(c),SB,V:Sandman 30.00
155 JR(c),SB,V:Computer 30.00
156 JR(c),RA,I:Mirage,W:Ned
   Leeds & Betty Brant 30.00
157 JR(c),RA,V:Dr.Octopus 30.00
158 JR(c),RA,V:Dr.Octopus 30.00
159 JR(c),RA,V:Dr.Octopus 30.00
160 K&R(c),RA,V:Tinkerer 30.00
161 K&R(c),RA,A:Nightcrawler,
   C:Punisher. 40.00
162 JR(c),RA,Nightcrawler,
   Punisher,I:Jigsaw. 40.00

163 JR(c),RA,Kingpin 25.00
164 JR(c),RA,Kingpin 25.00
165 JR(c),RA,Lizard. 25.00
166 JR(c),RA,Lizard. 25.00
167 JR(c),RA,V:Spiderslayer,
   I:Will-o-the Wisp 25.00
168 JR(c),KP,V:Will-o-the Wisp . . 27.00
169 RA,V:Dr.Faustas 25.00
170 RA,V:Dr.Faustas 25.00
171 RA,A:Nova 27.00
172 RA,V:Molten Man 25.00
173 JR(c),RA,JM,V:Molten Man . . 25.00
174 RA,TD,JM,A:Punisher. 30.00
175 RA,JM,A:Punisher,D:Hitman. . 30.00
176 RA,TD,V:Green Goblin 30.00
177 RA,V:Green Goblin 30.00
178 RA,JM,V:Green Goblin 30.00
179 RA,V:Green Goblin 30.00
180 RA,IR&V:Green Goblin is Bart
   Hamilton) 30.00
181 GK(c),SB,O:Spider-Man. 25.00
182 RA:Rocket Racer. 22.00
183 RA,BMc,V:Rocket Racer. 22.00
184 RA,V:White Tiger 22.00
185 RA,V:White Tiger 22.00
186 KP,A:Chameleon,Spidey
   cleared by police of charges . . 22.00
187 JSn,BMc,A:Captain
   America,V:Electro 22.00
188 KP,A:Jigsaw 22.00
189 JBy,JM,A:Man-Wolf. 25.00
190 JBy,JM,A:Man-Wolf 25.00
191 KP,V:Spiderslayer 25.00
192 KP,JM,V:The Fly 25.00
193 KP,JM,V:The Fly 25.00
194 KP,I:Black Cat. 50.00
195 KP,AM,JM,O:Black Cat 25.00
196 AM,JM,D:Aunt May,A:Kingpin. 20.00
197 KP,JM,V:Kingpin 20.00
198 SB,JM,V:Mysterio 20.00
199 SB,JM,V:Mysterio 20.00
200 JR(c),KP,JM,D:Burglar,Aunt May
   alive,O:Spider-Man 45.00
201 KP,JM,A:Punisher 20.00
202 KP,JM,A:Punisher 20.00
203 FM(c),KP,A:Dazzler. 16.00
204 JR2(c),KP,V:Black Cat 15.00
205 KP,JM,V:Black Cat 15.00
206 JBy,GD,V:Jonas Harrow 15.00
207 JM,V:Mesmero 15.00
208 JR2,AM,BBr,V:Fusion(1stJR2
   SpM art),I:Lance Bannon. 15.00
209 KJ,BMc,JRu,BWi,AM,
   I:Calypso, V:Kraven. 25.00
210 JR2,JSt,I:Madame Web 15.00
211 JR2,JM,A:Sub-mariner 15.00
212 JR2,JM,I:Hydro-Man 15.00
213 JR2,JM,V:Wizard 15.00
214 JR2,JM,V:Frightful Four,
   A: Namor,Llyra. 15.00
215 JR2,JM,V:Frightful Four,
   A: Namor,Llyra. 15.00
216 JR2,JM,A:Madame Web 15.00
217 JR2,JM,V:Sandman,
   Hydro-Man. 15.00
218 FM(c),JR2,JM,AM,V:Sandman
   Hydro-Man. 15.00
219 FM(c),LMc,JM,V:Grey
   Gargoyle,A:Matt Murdock 15.00
220 BMc,A:Moon Knight 12.00
221 JM(i),A:Ramrod. 12.00
222 WS(c),BH,JM,I:SpeedDemon. 12.00
223 JR2,AM,A:Red Ghost 12.00
224 JR2,V:Vulture 12.00
225 JR2,BWi,V:Foolkiller 12.00
226 JR2,JM,A:Black Cat 12.00
227 JR2,JM,A:Black Cat 12.00
228 RL,Murder Mystery 12.00
229 JR2,JM,V:Juggernaut 12.00
230 JR2,JM,V:Juggernaut 12.00
231 JR2,AM,V:Cobra 12.00
232 JR2,JM,V:Mr.Hyde 12.00

233 JR2,JM,V:Tarantula. 12.00
234 JR2,DGr,V:Tarantula 12.00
235 JR2,V:Tarantula,C:Deathlok
   O:Will-o-the Wisp 12.00
236 JR2,D:Tarantula 12.00
237 BH,A:Stilt Man. 12.00
238 JR2,JR,I:Hobgoblin (inc.
   Tattoo transfer) 100.00
238a w/out Tattoo 12.00
239 JR2,V:Hobgoblin 60.00
240 JR2,BL,Vulture 12.00
241 JR2,O:Vulture 12.00
242 JR2,Mad Thinker 12.00
243 JR2,Peter Quits School 12.00
244 JR2,KJ,V:Hobgoblin 18.00
245 JR2,V:Hobgoblin 20.00
246 JR2,DGr,Daydreams issue . . . 12.00
247 JR2,JR,V:Thunderball 12.00
248 JR2,BBr,RF,TA,V:Thunderball,
   Kid who Collects Spider-Man . 12.00
249 JR2,DGr,V:Hobgoblin,
   A:Kingpin 20.00
250 JR2,KJ,V:Hobgoblin 20.00
251 RF,KJ,V:Hobgoblin,Spidey
   Leaves for Secret Wars. 20.00
252 RF,BBr,returns from Secret
   Wars,N:Spider-Man 50.00
253 RL,I:Rose 12.00
254 RL,JRu,V:Jack O'Lantern 10.00
255 RF,JRu,Red Ghost 10.00
256 RF,JRu,I:Puma,A:Black Cat . . 10.00
257 RF,JRu,V:Puma,
   A:Hobgoblin 10.00
258 RF,JRu,A:Black Cat,Fant.Four,
   Hobgoblin,V:Black Costume . . 15.00
259 RF,JRu,A:Hobgoblin,O:
   Mary Jane 15.00
260 RF,JRu,BBr,V:Hobgoblin 12.00
261 CV(c),RF,JRu,V:Hobgoblin . . . 12.00
262 Ph(c),BL,Spidey Unmasked . . 13.00
263 RF,BBr,I:Spider-Kid 10.00
264 Paty,V:Red Nine 10.00
265 RF,JRu,V:Black Fox,
   I:Silver Sable 18.00
265a 2nd printing. 3.00
266 RF,JRu,I:Misfits,Toad 10.00
267 BMc,PDd(s),A:Human Torch . 10.00
268 JBy(c),RF,JRu,Secret WarsII . 10.00
269 RF,JRu,V:Firelord 10.00
270 RF,BMc,V:Firelord,
   A:Avengers,I:Kate Cushing . . . 10.00
271 RF,JRu,A:Crusher Hogan,
   V:Manslaughter 10.00
272 SB,KB,I&O:Slyde 10.00

All comics prices listed are for *Near Mint* condition.

Amazing Spider-Man #266
© Marvel Entertainment Group

273 RF,JRu,Secret Wars II,
A:Puma 10.00
274 TMo,JR,Secret Wars II,
Beyonder V:Mephisto,A:1st
Ghost Rider. 10.00
275 RF,JRu,V:Hobgoblin,O:Spidey
(From Amaz.Fantasy#15) 22.00
276 RF,BBr,V:Hobgoblin 15.00
277 RF,BL,CV,A:Daredevil,Kingpin 15.00
278 A:Hobgoblin,V:Scourge,
D:Wraith. 10.00
279 RL,A:Jack O'Lantern,
2nd A:Silver Sable. 10.00
280 RF,BBr,V:Sinister Syndicate,
A:Silver Sable,Hobgoblin,
Jack O'Lantern 10.00
281 RF,BBr,V:Sinister Syndicate,
A:Silver Sable,Hobgoblin,
Jack O'Lantern 15.00
282 RL,BL,A:X-Factor 10.00
283 RF,BL,V:Titania,Absorbing
Man,C:Mongoose 10.00
284 RF,BBr,JRu,B:Gang War,
A: Punisher,Hobgoblin. 15.00
285 MZ(c),A:Punisher,Hobgoblin. . 15.00
286 ANi(i),V:Hobgoblin,A:Rose . . 15.00
287 EL,ANi,A:Daredevl,Hobgoblin. 15.00
288 E:Gang War,A:Punisher,
Falcon,Hobgoblin,Daredevil,
Black Cat, Kingpin. 15.00
289 TMo,IR:Hobgoblin is Ned Leeds,
I:2nd Hobgoblin (Jack O'
Lantern). 25.00
290 JR2,Peter Proposes 10.00
291 JR2,V:Spiderslayer 10.00
292 AS,V:Spiderslayer,Mary
Jane Accepts proposal 10.00
293 MZ,BMc,V:Kraven. 12.00
294 MZ,BMc,D:Kraven. 12.00
295 BSz(c),KB(i),Mad Dog,pt.#2 . . 10.00
296 JBy(c),AS,V:Dr.Octopus 10.00
297 AS,V:Dr.Octopus. 10.00
298 TM,BMc,V:Chance,C:Venom
(not in costume). 60.00
299 TM,BMc,V:Chance,I:Venom . . 35.00
300 TM,O:Venom 110.00
301 TM,A:Silver Sable 20.00
302 TM,V:Nero,A:Silver Sable. . . . 20.00
303 TM,A:Silver Sable,Sandman. . 20.00
304 TM,JRu,V:Black Fox,Prowler
I:Jonathan Caesar 18.00
305 TM,JRu,V:BlackFox,Prowler. . 18.00
306 TM,V:Humbug,Chameleon . . . 15.00
307 TM,O:Chameleon 15.00

308 TM,V:Taskmaster,J.Caesar. . . 15.00
309 TM,I:Styx & Stone 15.00
310 TM,V:Killershrike 15.00
311 TM,Inferno,V:Mysterio 15.00
312 TM,Inferno,Hobgoblin V:
Green Goblin 22.00
313 TM,Inferno,V:Lizard. 15.00
314 TM,X-mas issue,V:J.Caesar. . 15.00
315 TM,V:Venom,Hydro-Man. 22.00
316 TM,V:Venom 22.00
317 TM,V:Venom,A:Thing 22.00
318 TM,V:Scorpion 22.00
319 TM,V:Scorpion,Rhino 15.00
320 TM,B:Assassin Nation Plot
A:Paladin,Silver Sable. 15.00
321 TM,A:Paladin,Silver Sable . . . 12.00
322 TM,A:Silver Sable,Paladin . . . 12.00
323 TM,A:Silver Sable,Paladin,
Captain America 12.00
324 TM(c),EL,AG,V:Sabretooth,A:
Capt.America,Silver Sable . . . 12.00
325 TM,E:Assassin Nation Plot,
V:Red Skull,Captain America,
Silver Sable 12.00
326 V:Graviton,A of V. 7.00
327 EL,AG,V:Magneto,A of V. 7.00
328 TM,V:Hulk,A of V. 12.00
329 EL,V:Tri-Sentinel 7.00
330 EL,A:Punisher,Black Cat. 7.00
331 EL,A:Punisher,C:Venom 6.00
332 EL,V:Venom,Styx & Stone 7.00
333 EL,V:Venom,Styx & Stone 7.00
334 EL,B:Sinister Six,A:Iron Man . . 5.00
335 EL,TA,A:Captain America 5.00
336 EL,D:Nathan Lubensky,
A:Dr.Strange,Chance. 5.00
337 WS(c),EL,TA,A:Nova 5.00
338 EL,A:Jonathan Caesar 5.00
339 EL,JR,E:Sinister Six,A:Thor
D:Jonathan Caesar 5.00
340 EL,V:Femme Fatales 5.00
341 EL,V:Tarantula,Powers Lost . . . 5.00
342 EL,A:Blackcat,V:Scorpion 5.00
343 EL,Powers Restored,
C:Cardiac,V:Chameleon 5.00
344 EL,V:Rhino,I:Cardiac,Cletus
Kassady(Carnage),A:Venom. . 15.00
345 MBa,V:Boomerang,C:Venom,
A:Cletus Kassady(infected
with Venom-Spawn). 15.00
346 EL,V:Venom 10.00
347 EL,V:Venom 10.00
348 EL,A:Avengers 4.00
349 EL,A:Black Fox 4.00
350 EL,V:Doctor Doom,Black Fox. . 6.00
351 MBa,A:Nova,V:Tri-Sentinal 6.00
352 MBa,A:Nova,V:Tri-Sentinal 4.00
353 MBa,B:Round Robin:The Side
Kick's Revenge,A:Punisher,
Nova,Moon Knight,Darkhawk . . 4.00
354 MBa,A:Nova,Punisher,
Darkhawk,Moon Knight. 4.00
355 MBa,A:Nova,Punisher,
Darkhawk,Moon Knight 4.00
356 MBa,A:Moon Knight,
Punisher,Nova 4.00
357 MBa,A:Moon Knight,
Punisher,Darkhawk,Nova 4.00
358 MBa,E:Round Robin:The Side
Kick's Revenge,A:Darkhawk,
Moon Knight,Punisher,Nova,
Gatefold(c). 4.00
359 CMa,A:Cardiac,C:Cletus
Kasady (Carnage) 5.00
360 CMa,V:Cardiac,C:Carnage 6.00
361 MBa,I:Carnage 9.00
361a 2nd printing 3.00
362 MBa,V:Carnage,Venom 6.00
362a 2nd printing 3.00
363 MBa,V:Carnage,Venom, ... 6.00
364 MBa,V:Shocker 3.00

365 MBa,JR,V:Lizard,30th Anniv.,
Hologram(c),w/poster,Prev.of
Spider-Man 2099 by RL 6.00
366 JBi,A:Red Skull,Taskmaster . . . 3.00
367 JBi,A:Red Skull,Taskmaster . . . 3.00
368 MBa,B:Invasion of the Spider
Slayers #1,BU:Jonah Jameson . 3.00
369 MBa,V:Electro,BU:Green
Goblin 3.00
370 MBa,V:Scorpion,BU:A.May. . . . 3.00
371 MBa,V:Spider-Slayer,
BU:Black Cat. 3.00
372 MBa,V:Spider-Slayer. 3.00
373 MBa,V:Sp.-Slayer,BU:Venom . . 4.00
374 MBa,V:Venom 5.00
375 MBa,V:Venom,30th Anniv.,Holo
graphx(c) 6.00
376 V:Styx&Stone,A:Cardiac 3.00
377 V:Cardiac,O:Styx&Stone 3.00
378 MBa,Total Carnage#3,V:Shriek,
Carnage,A:Venom,Cloak. 3.00
379 MBa,Total Carnage#7,
V:Carnage,A:Venom 3.00
380 MBa,Maximum Carnage#11 . . . 3.00
381 MBa,V:Dr.Samson,A:Hulk. 3.00
382 MBa,V:Hulk,A:Dr.Samson. 3.00
383 MBa,V:Jury 3.00
384 MBa,AM,V:Jury 3.00
385 B:DvM(s),MBa,RyE,V:Jury 3.00
386 MBa,RyE,B:Lifetheft,V:Vulture . 3.00
387 MBa,RyE,V:Vulture 3.00
388 Blue Foil(c),MBa,RyE,RLm,TP,
E:Lifetheft,D:Peter's Synthetic
Parents,BU:Venom,Cardiac,
Chance, ... 5.00
388a Newsstand Ed. 3.00
389 MBa,RyE,E:Pursuit,
V:Chameleon, ... 3.00
390 MBa,RyE,B:Shrieking,
A:Shriek,w/cel 4.00
390a Newsstand Ed. 3.00
391 MBa,RyE,V:Shriek,Carrion 3.00
392 MBa,RyE,V:Shriek,Carrion 3.00
393 MBa,RyE,E:Shrieking,
V:Shriek,Carrion 3.00
394 MBa,RyE,Power & Responsibility,
pt.2,V:Judas Traveller, ... 4.00
394a w/flip book,2 covers 3.00
395 MBa,RyE,R:Puma. 3.00
396 MBa,RyE,A:Daredevil,
V:Vulture, Owl 3.00
397 MBa,Web of Death,pt.1,
V:Stunner,Doc Ock 3.50
398 MBa,Web of Death,pt.3 . . . . . . 4.00

Amazing Spider-Man #400
© Marvel Entertainment Group

399 MBa,Smoke and Mirrors,pt.2 . . 2.50
400 MBa,Death of a Parker 6.00
400a die-cut cover 10.00
401 MBa,The Mark of Kaine,pt.2. . . 3.00
402 MBa,R:Judas Travellor 3.00
403 MBa,JMD,LMa The Trial of
    Peter Parker, pt.2 . . . . 3.00
404 Maximum Clonage 3.00
405 JMD,DaR,LMa,Exiled,pt.2, ... 3.00
406 I:New Doc Ock 3.00
407 TDF,MBa,LMa,Return of
    Spider-Man,pt.2 . . . . 3.00
408 TDF,MBa,LMa,Media
    Blizzard,pt.2 . . . . 3.00
409 . . . . 3.00
410 . . . . 3.00
411 TDF,MBa,LMa,Blood
    Brothers,pt.2 . . . . 3.00
412 . . . . 3.00
413 . . . . 3.00
414 A:The Rose 3.00
415 Onslaught saga,V:Sentinels . . . 3.00
416 Onslaught epilogue 3.00
417 TDF,RG,secrets of Scrier &
    Judas Traveler 3.00
418 Revelations,pt.3, R:Norman
    Osborn 3.00
419 TDF,SSr,V:Black Tarantula . . . 3.00
420 TDF,SSr,X-Man x-over,pt.1 . . . . 3.00
421 TDF,SSr,I:Dragonfly; Electro
    Kidnapped 3.00
422 TDF,SSr,V:Electro,Tarantula . . . 3.00
423 TDF,V:Electro 3.00
424 TDF,JoB,V:Black Tarantula, The
    Hand, Dragonfly, Delilah,
    The Rose, Elektra 3.00
425 TDF,SSr, V:Electro,double size. 4.00
426 TDF,SSr,V:Doctor Octopus 3.00
427 TDF,SSr,JR gatefold cover,
    V:Doctor Octopus 4.00
428 TDF,SSr,V:Doctor Octopus . . . 3.00
429 TDF,A:Daredevil, X-Man,
    Absorbing Man, Titania 3.00
430 TDF,SSr,V:Carnage,A:Silver
    Surfer 3.00
431 TDF,SSr,V:Carnage (with Silver
    Surfer's powers) 3.00
432 SSr,JR2,Spider-Hunt,pt.2
    x-over 4.00
432a variant cover 4.00
433 TDF,TL,Identity Crisis prelude,
    good-bye to Joe Robertson 3.00
434 TDF,JoB,Identity Crisis, as
    Ricochet vs. Black Tarantula . . . 3.00
435 TDF,MD2,Ricochet,A:Delilah . . 3.00
436 TDF,JoB,V:Black Tarantula . . . 3.00
437 TDF,JoB,V:Plant Man 3.00
Bi-weekly
438 TDF,V:Daredevil 3.00
439 TDF,future history chronicle . . . 3.00
440 JBy,The Gathering of the Five,
    Pt.2 (of 5) x-over 3.00
441 JBy,V:Green Goblin, The
    Final Chapter, pt.1 . . . . 5.00
Minus 1 Spec., TDF,JBe, flashback,
    early Kingpin 2.50
Ann.#1 SD,I:Sinister Six 1,700.00
Ann.#2 SD,A:Dr.Strange 600.00
Ann.#3 JR,DH,A:Avengers 250.00
Ann.#4 A:H.Torch,V:Mysterio,
    Wizard 225.00
Ann.#5 JR(c),A:Red Skull,I:Peter
    Parker's Parents 225.00
Ann.#6 JR(c),Rep.Ann.#1,Fant.
    Four Ann.#1,SpM #8 . . . . 75.00
Ann.#7 JR(c),Rep.#1,#2,#38 . . . . . 75.00
Ann.#8 Rep.#46,#50 . . . . 75.00
Ann.#9 JR(c),Rep.Spec.SpM #2 . 75.00
Ann.#10 JR(c),GK,V:Human Fly . . 30.00
Ann.#11 GK(c),DP,JM,JR2,AM, . . 20.00
Ann.#12 JBy(c),KP,Rep.#119,
    #120 . . . . 25.00

Ann.#13 JBy,TA,V:Dr.Octopus 25.00
Ann.#14 FM,TP,A:Dr.Strange,
    V:Dr.Doom,Dormammu 25.00
Ann.#15 FM,KJ,BL,Punisher 25.00
Ann.#16 JR2,JR,I:New Captain
    Marvel,A:Thing 10.00
Ann.#17 EH,JM,V:Kingpin 10.00
Ann.#18 RF,BL,JG,V:Scorpion 10.00
Ann.#19 JR(c),MW,V:Spiderslayer. 10.00
Ann.#20 BWi(i),V:Iron Man 2020 . . 10.00
Ann.#21 JR(c),PR,W:SpM,direct . . 20.00
Ann.#21a W:SpM,news stand 15.00
Ann.#22 JR(c),MBa(1stSpM),SD,
    JG,RLm,TD,Evolutionary War,
    I:Speedball,New Men 8.00
Ann.#23 JBy(c),RLd,MBa,RF,
    AtlantisAttacks#4,A:She-Hulk . . 7.00
Ann.#24 GK,SD,MZ,DGr,
    A:Ant Man 4.00
Ann.#25 EL(c),SB,PCu,SD,
    Vibranium Vendetta#1,Venom. . 6.00
Ann.#26 Hero Killers#1,A:New
    Warriors,BU:Venom,Solo. 6.00
Ann.#27 TL,I:Annex,w/card 4.00
Ann.#28 SDt(s),V:Carnage,BU:Cloak
    & Dagger,Rhino 4.00
Ann. '96 two new stories, 48pg,. . . 3.50
Ann. '97 RSt,TL,RJn, 48pg, ... 3.50
Ann. '98 TL,TDF,F:Spider-Man &
    Devil Dinosaur, 48pg 3.00
G-Size Superheroes #1 GK,
    A:Morbius,Man-Wolf 75.00
G-Size #1 JR(c),RA,DH,
    A:Dracula 40.00
G-Size #2 K&R(c),RA,AM,
    A:Master of Kung Fu 40.00
G-Size #3 GK(c),RA,DocSavage. . 40.00
G-Size #4 GK(c),RA,Punisher . . . 75.00
G-Size #5 GK(c),RA,V:Magnum . . 30.00
G-Size #6 Rep.Ann.#4 . . . . 30.00
G-Size Spec.#1 O:Symbiotes . . . 5.00
Marvel Milestone rep. #1 (1993) . . 3.00
Marvel Milestone rep. #3 (1995) . . 3.00
Marvel Milestone rep. #129 (1992) . 3.00
Marvel Milestone rep. #149 (1994) . 3.00
GN Fear Itself RA,A:S.Sable 13.00
GN Spirits of the Earth CV,Scotland,
    V:Hellfire Club 25.00
TPB Assassination Plot, rep. 15.00
TPB Carnage, rep 7.00
TPB Cosmic Adventures, rep. 20.00
TPB Kraven's Last Hunt, rep. 16.00
TPB Origin of the Hobgoblin, rep. . 15.00
TPB Saga of the Alien Costume . . 10.00
TPB Spider-Man Vs. Venom, rep. . 10.00
TPB Venom Returns rep. 13.00
TPB The Wedding, rep. 13.00
Nothing Can Stop the Juggernaut . . 4.00
Sensational Spider-Man,reps. 5.00
Skating on Thin Ice(Canadian) . . . 15.00
Skating on Thin Ice(US). 2.00
Soul of the Hunter MZ,BMc,
    R:Kraven 7.00
Unicef:Trial of Venom,
    A:Daredevil,V:Venom 50.00
See Also:
PETER PARKER;
SPECTACULAR SPIDER-MAN;
WEB OF SPIDER-MAN

AMAZING SPIDER-MAN

Jan., 1999
1 HMe,JBy,DHz,V:Scorpion,48-page
    prismatic etched (c) 7.00
1a Dynamic Forces JR2 . . . . 15.00
2 HMe,JBy,DHz,I:Shadrac 5.00
2a variant BiT cover 6.00
3 HMe,JBy,DHz,V:Shadrac,
    A:Iceman 3.00
4 HMe,JBy,SHa,A:Fantastic Four . . 3.00
5 HMe,JBy,SHa,I:new
    Spider-Woman. 3.00

Amazing Spider-Man Vol. 2 #1
© Marvel Entertainment Group

6 JBy,HMe,SHa,F:Spider-Woman. . 3.00
7 JBy,HMe,SHa,Reality Bent 3.00
8 JMy,HMe,SHa,JR2(c),
    Reality Bent x-over 3.00
9 JMy,HMe,SHa,JR2(c),V:Scorpion 3.00
10 JMy,HMe,SHa,JR2(c),MaryJane. 3.00
11 HMe,SHa,JBy,marital problems . 3.00
12 HMe,SHa,JBy,48-pg. 4.00
13 HMe,JBy 3.00
14 HMe,JBy,A:Sp.-Woman,x-over . . 3.00
15 HMe,JBy,DGr,x-over 3.00
16 HMe,JBy,DGr,Mary Jane gone . 3.00
17 HMe,JBy,DGr,A:Sandman 3.00
18 HMe,JBy,JR,V:Green Goblin . . . 3.00
19 HMe,EL,DGr,Eddie Brock 3.00
20 HMe,EL,JBy,100-pg 3.50
21 HMe,EL,JhB,AlistairSmythe . . . 3.00
22 HMe,JR2,SHa,Senator Ward . . . 3.00
23 HMe,JR2,SHa,Ranger 3.00
24 HMe,JR2,SHa,Max.Security . . . 3.00
25 I HMe,JR2,SHa,A:Green Goblin . . 3.00
25a holographic foil(c) 7.00
26 HMe,JR2,SHa,F:Spidey's dad . . 3.00
27 HMe,JR2,SHa,V:A.I.M. 3.00
28 HMe,JR2,SHa,Enforcers. 7.00
29 HMe,JR2,SHa,x-over 10.00
30 B:MSz(s),JR2,JSC(c) 15.00
31 MSz(s),JR2,JSC(c) 8.00
32 MSz(s),JR2,SHa,Ezekiel. 8.00
33 MSz(s),JR2,SHa,Morlun 8.00
34 MSz(s),JR2,SHa,V:Morlun. 8.00
35 MSz(s),JR2,SHa,pt.1 . . . . 8.00
36 MSz(s),JR2,SHa 20.00
37 MSz(s),JR2,SHa 5.00
38 MSz(s),JR2,SHa,'Nuff Said 3.00
39 MSz(s),JR2,SHa,Aunt May 3.00
40 MSz(s),JR2,SHa,Aunt May. 3.00
41 MSz(s),JR2,SHa 3.00
42 MSz(s),JR2,SHa 3.00
43 MSz(s),JR2,SHa 3.00
44 MSz(s),JR2,SHa 3.00
45 MSz(s),JR2,SHa 3.00
46 MSz(s),JR2,SHa 3.00
47 MSz(s),JR2,SHa 3.00
48 MSz(s),JR2,SHa 3.00
49 MSz(s),JR2,SHa 3.00
50 MSz(s),JR2,SHa,F:Mary Jane . . 4.50
51 MSz(s),JR2,SHa,F:Mary Jane . . 2.50
52 MSz(s),JR2,SHa,F:Mary Jane . . 2.50
53 MSz(s),JR2,SHa,F:Mary Jane . . 2.50
54 MSz(s),JR2,Digger 2.50
55 MSz(s),JR2,Consequences,pt.1 . 2.50
56 MSz(s),JR2,Consequences,pt.2 . 2.50
57 MSz(s),JR2,pt.1 . . . . 2.50

58 MSz(s),JR2,pt.2	2.50
500 MSz(s),JR2,48-pg.	4.00
501 MSz(s),JR2	2.50
502 MSz(s),JR2	2.50
503 JR2,A Dark Shadow,pt.1	2.50
504 JR2,A Dark Shadow,pt.2	2.50
505 MSz(s),JR2,Ezekiel,pt.1	2.50
506 MSz(s),JR2,Ezekiel,pt.2	2.50
507 MSz(s),JR2,Ezekiel,pt.3	2.50
508 MSz(s),JR2,Ezekiel,pt.4	2.50
509 MSz(s),MD2,Sins Past,pt.1	2.50
510 MSz(s),MD2,Sins Past,pt.2	2.50
511 MSz(s),MD2,Sins Past,pt.3	2.50
512 MSz(s),MD2,Sins Past,pt.4	2.50
513 MSz(s),MD2,Sins Past,pt.5	2.50
514 MSz(s),MD2	2.50
515 MSz(s),MD2,Skin Deep	2.50
516 MSz(s),MD2,Skin Deep	2.50
517 MSz(s),MD2,Skin Deep	2.50
518 MSz(s),MD2,JJu(c),Skin Deep	2.50
519 MSz(s),MD2,NewAvengers,pt.1	2.50
520 MSz(s),MD2,NewAvengers,pt.2	2.50
521 MSz(s),MD2,Moving Up	2.50
522 MSz(s),MD2,V:Hydra	2.50
523 MSz(s),MD2,Moving Up	2.50
524 MSz(s),MD2,Acts of Aggression	2.50
525 PDd(s),The Other,x-over,pt. 3.	4.00
526 MD2,The Other,x-over,pt.6	4.00
526a 2nd printing	5.00
527 MSz(s),The Other,x-over,pt.9	2.50
527a 2nd printing	5.00
528 MSz(s),The Other,x-over,pt.12	2.50
528a 2nd printing	5.00
529 MSz(s),RG, new outfit	12.00
529a 2nd printing	7.00
530 MSz(s),RG	2.50
531 Mr. Parker Goes to Washington	4.00
532 MSz(s),RG,War at Home,pt.1	4.00
533 MSz(s),RG,War at Home,pt.2	5.00
534 MSz(s),RG,War at Home,pt.3	4.00
535 MSz(s),RG,War at Home,pt.4	3.00
536 MSz(s),RG,War at Home,pt.5	3.00
537 MSz(s),RG,War at Home,pt.6	3.00
TPB Vol. 1:Coming Home	16.00
TPB Vol. 2:Revelations	9.00
TPB Vol. 3:Until the Stars Turn Cold.	13.00
TPB Vol. 4:Life & Death of Spiders	12.00
TPB Vol. 5:Unintended Consequences.	13.00
TPB Vol. 6:Happy Birthday	13.00
TPB Vol. 7:The Book of Ezekiel.	13.00
TPB Vol. 8:Sins Past	13.00
TPB Vol. 9:Skin Deep	10.00
TPB Vol. 10: New Avengers	15.00
Spec. Must Have,Rep. #30–#32	4.00
Ann.1999 JB,HMe, 48-page	4.00
Ann.2000 HMe,48-pg.	4.00
Ann.2001 48-page	4.00
Giant Sized 80-pg.	4.50
Spec.Spider-Man/Sentry,PJe,RL,TA	3.00
Spec.Spider-Man/Marrow,SLo	3.00
Spec.Coll. ed.,rep #30–#32	4.00
Coll.Classics rep. #300	2.50
Coll.Classics rep. #300 signed	30.00
Coll.Classics rep. Sp-M #1.	2.50
Coll.Classics rep. Sp-M #1 signed.	30.00
TPB Revelations, 96-pg.	9.00
TPB Spider-Man vs. Black Cat	15.00

AMAZING SPIDER-MAN INDEX
See: OFFICIAL MARVEL
INDEX TO THE AMAZING
SPIDER-MAN

AMAZING SPIDER-MAN COLLECTION

1 Mark Bagley card set	3.00
2 and 3 MBa, from card set	@3.00

AMAZING X-MEN, THE
March–June, 1995

1 X-Men after Xavier	4.00
2 Exodus,Dazzler,V:Abyss	3.00
3 F:Bishop	3.00
4 V:Apocalypse	2.50
TPB Rep. #1–#4	9.00

AMERICAN TAIL II
Dec., 1991

1 & 2 movie adaption	@2.25

A-NEXT
Aug., 1998

1 TDF,RF,BBr,Next Generation of Avengers	3.00
2 thru 12	@2.25
Digest Avengers Next Vol. 1 Second Coming	8.00

ANIMATED MOVIE-TUNES
Marvel-Margood Publ., 1945

1 Super Rabbit	350.00
2 Super Rabbit	350.00
Becomes:	

MOVIE TUNES
Marvel-Margood Publ., 1946

3	150.00
Becomes:	

FRANKIE
Marvel-Margood, 1946–48

4	200.00
5 thru 9	@125.00
10	100.00
11	100.00
Becomes:	

FRANKIE & LANA
Marvel-Margood, 1949

12	100.00
13	100.00
14	100.00
15	100.00
Becomes:	

FRANKIE FUDDLE
Marvel-Margood, 1949

16	100.00
17	100.00

ANIMAX
Star, 1986–87

1 Based on Toy Line	3.00
2 thru 4	@3.00

ANNEX
Aug.–Nov., 1994

1 WMc,I:Brace, Crucible of Power	2.25
2 WMc,V:Brace, Crucible, pt.2	2.25
3 Crucible of Power, pt.3	2.25
4 Crucible of Power, pt.4	2.25

ANNIE
(Treasury Edition)
Oct., 1982

1 Movie Adaptation	3.00
2 Nov., 1982	3.00

ANNIE OAKLEY
Marvel Timely, Spring, 1948

1 A:Hedy Devine	750.00
2 CCB,I:Lana,A:Hedy Devine	500.00
3	350.00
4	350.00
5	300.00
6	300.00

Annex #1
© *Marvel Entertainment Group*

7	300.00
8	300.00
9 AW,	300.00
10	250.00
11 June, 1956	250.00

ANNIHILATION
Sept., 2006

1 Silver Surfer, Super-Skrull, Ronan & Nova, V:Annihilus	3.00
2 F:Nova Ronan & Drax	3.00
3 F:Nova, Ronan.	3.00
4 F:Drax, Thanos, Nova	3.00

ANNIHILATION: NOVA
April, 2006

1 V:Annihilation Wave	3.00
2 thru 4	@3.00

ANNIHILATION: THE NOVA CORPS
Aug., 2006

1 Nova Corps files	4.00

ANNIHILATION: PROLOGUE
March, 2006

1 KG,V:Annihilation Wave	4.00

ANNIHILATION: RONAN
April, 2006

1 V:Annihilation Wave	3.00
2 thru 4	@3.00

ANNIHILATION: SILVER SURFER
April, 2006

1 V:Annihilation Wave	3.00
2 thru 4	@3.00

ANNIHILATION: SUPER-SKRULL
April, 2006

1 V:Annihilation Wave	3.00
2 thru 4	@3.00

ANT-MAN
Dec., 2003

1 (of 5) Size does matter	3.00
2 thru 5	@3.00

ANT-MAN
Oct., 2006

1 & 2 PhH	@3.00

ANT-MAN'S BIG CHRISTMAS
Dec., 1999
GN 48-pg. 6.00

A-1
1993
1 The Edge 8.00
2 Cheeky,Wee Budgie Boy 8.00
3 King Leon. 8.00
4 King Leon. 8.00

APACHE KID
Marvel-Comics, 1950–52
1 (53) 500.00
2 . . . . 300.00
3 . . . . 250.00
4 . . . . 250.00
5 . . . . 250.00
6 . . . . 150.00
7 RH 200.00
8 thru 10 . . . . @150.00
11 RH 125.00
12 . . . . 125.00
13 RH 125.00
14 thru 19 . . . . @100.00
Becomes:

WESTERN GUNFIGHTERS
Marvel Atlas, 1956–57
20 GC,JSe 150.00
21 RC. 150.00
22 WW,BP 250.00
23 AW 200.00
24 ATh 200.00
25 GM 100.00
26 GC. 100.00
27 GC,JSe 100.00

APACHE SKIES
July, 2002
1 (of 4) JOs,Apache Kid,wild west . 3.00
2 thru 4 JOs . . . . @3.00
TPB Rep. #1–#4 . . . . 13.00

APOCALYPSE STRIKEFILES
1 After Xavier special 2.50

ARANA: THE HEART OF THE SPIDER
Jan., 2005
1 Freshman Flu. 3.00
1a variant JQ(c) 3.00
2 A Tangled Web. 3.00
3 Ultimatum. 3.00
4 Between Life and Death,
  A:Spider-Man. 3.00
5 Heart of the Spider 3.00
6 Heart of the Spider,concl. 3.00
7 Unexpected Pasts,pt.1. . . . . 3.00
8 Unexpected Pasts,pt.2. . . . . 3.00
9 Unexpected Pasts,pt.3. . . . . 3.00
10 Unexpected Pasts,pt.4,V:Jade . . 3.00
11 V:Jade. 3.00
12 V:Wasps 3.00
Digest Vol.1: Heart of the Spider . . . 8.00
Digest Vol.2: In the Beginning 8.00
Digest Vol.3: Night of the Hunter . . . 8.00

ARCHANGEL
1996
1-shot B&W 2.50

ARES
Jan., 2006
1 F:Ares, God of War 3.00

2 thru 5 . . . . @3.00
TPB Ares: God of War 14.00

ARIZONA KID
Atlas, March, 1951
1 RH,Coming of the Arizons Kid. 300.00
2 RH,Code of the Gunman 150.00
3 RH(c) 125.00
4 PMo 125.00
5 PMo 125.00
6 PMo,JSt,Jan., 1952 . . . . 125.00

ARRGH!
Dec., 1974
Satire
1 MSy,TS,Vampire Rats 35.00
2 AA,TS. 25.00
3 TS,AA(c),Beauty and the
  Big Foot 25.00
4 The Night Gawker 25.00
5 Sept., 1975 . . . . 25.00

Arrowhead #4
© Marvel Entertainment Group

ARROWHEAD
April, 1954
1 JSt,Indian Warrior Stories 200.00
2 JSt 125.00
3 JSt 125.00
4 JSt,Nov., 1954 . . . . 125.00

MARVEL BOY
Dec., 1950
1 RH,O:Marvel Boy,Lost World 1,700.00
2 BEv,The Zero Hour 1,200.00
Becomes:

ASTONISHING
1951
3 BEv,Marvel Boy,V:Mr Death . 1,500.00
4 BEv,Stan Lee,The
  Screaming Tomb 1,100.00
5 BEv,Horror in the Caves of
  Doom 1,100.00
6 BEv,My Coffin is Waiting 1,100.00
7 JR,JMn,Nightmare 500.00
8 RH,Behind the Wall 500.00
9 RH(c),The Little Black Box . . . 500.00
10 BEv,Walking Dead 500.00
11 BF,JSt.Mr Mordeau 350.00
12 GC,BEv,Horror Show 350.00
13 BK,MSy,Ghouls Gold 500.00
14 BK,The Long Jump Down. . . . 500.00
15 BEv(c),Grounds for Death . . . 350.00

16 BEv(c),DAy,SSh,Don't Make
  a Ghoul of Yourself 350.00
17 Who Was the Wilmach
  Werewolf? 350.00
18 BEv(c),JR,Vampire at My
  Window 350.00
19 BK,Back From the Grave . . . 350.00
20 GC,Mystery at Midnight 350.00
21 Manhunter. 275.00
22 RH(c),Man Against Werewolf . 275.00
23 The Woman in Black. 300.00
24 JR,The Stone Face. 300.00
25 RC,I Married a Zombie 300.00
26 RH(c),I Died Too Often 275.00
27 . . . . 275.00
28 TLw,No Evidence 275.00
29 BEv(c),GC,Decapitation(c) . . . 275.00
30 Tentacled eyeball story 400.00
31 JMn 225.00
32 A Vampire Takes a Wife 225.00
33 SMo,JMn. 225.00
34 JMn,Transformation 225.00
35 . . . . 225.00
36 Pithecanthrope Giant 225.00
37 BEv,TLw,Poor Pierre. 225.00
38 The Man Who Didn't Belong. . 175.00
39 . . . . 175.00
40 . . . . 175.00
41 MD 175.00
42 TLw 175.00
43 BP,JR 175.00
44 RC,BP 190.00
45 BK 190.00
46 . . . . 190.00
47 BK,JO,BEv 190.00
48 BP 175.00
49 BEv 175.00
50 DCn 175.00
51 . . . . 175.00
52 GM 175.00
53 SD,JF,BEv. 190.00
54 BEv 190.00
55 BEv 200.00
56 JMn,JK 175.00
57 JR 200.00
58 JF,JO. 175.00
59 TSe,BEv 175.00
60 JF,BEv. 175.00
61 GM,JO,JR,BEv 175.00
62 MD,BEv. 200.00
63 BEv,August, 1957 . . . . 200.00

ASTONISHING TALES
Aug., 1970
1 BEv(c),JK,WW,Ka-Zar,Dr.Doom 90.00
2 JK,WW,Ka-Zar,Dr.Doom 40.00
3 BWS,WW,Ka-Zar,Dr.Doom . . . 50.00
4 BWS,WW,Ka-Zar,Dr.Doom . . . 50.00
5 BWS,GT,Ka-Zar,Dr.Doom 50.00
6 BWS,BEv,GT,I:Bobbi Morse . . . 50.00
7 HT,GC,Ka-Zar,Dr.Doom 25.00
8 HT,TS,GT,GC,TP,Ka-Zar 25.00
9 GK(c),JB,Ka-Zar,Dr.Doom 20.00
10 GK(c),BWS,SB,Ka-Zar 25.00
11 GK,O:Ka-Zar 25.00
12 JB,DA,NA,V:Man Thing 40.00
13 JB,RB,DA,V:Man Thing 30.00
14 GK(c),rep. Ka-Zar 15.00
15 GK,TS,Ka-Zar 15.00
16 RB,AM,A:Ka-Zar 15.00
17 DA,V:Gemini 15.00
18 JR(c),DA,A:Ka-Zar 15.00
19 JR(c),DA,JSn,JA,I:Victorious . . 15.00
20 JR(c),A:Ka-Zar 15.00
21 RTs(s),DAy,B:It 35.00
22 RTs(s),DAy,V:Granitor 25.00
23 RTs(s),DAy,A:Fin Fang Foom . . 25.00
24 RTs(s),DAy,E.It 25.00
25 RB(a&s),B:I&O:Deathlok,
  GP(1st art) 75.00
26 RB(a&s),I:Warwolf 20.00
27 RB(a&s),V:Warwolf. 20.00

Astonishing Tales #19
© Marvel Entertainment Group

28 RB(a&s),V:Warwolf 20.00
29 rep.Marv.Super Heroes #18 . . . 15.00
30 RB(a&s),KP, ... 15.00
31 RB(a&s),BW,KP,V:Ryker 18.00
32 RB(a&s),KP,V:Ryker 18.00
33 RB(a&s),KJ,I:Hellinger 18.00
34 RB(a&s),KJ,V:Ryker 18.00
35 RB(a&s),KJ,I:Doomsday-Mech. 18.00
36 RB(a&s),KP,E:Deathlok,
   I:Godwulf 25.00

ASTONISHING X-MEN
March–June, 1995
1 Uncanny X-Men 5.00
2 V:Holocaust 3.50
3 V:Abyss 3.00
4 V:Beast,Infinities 3.00
TPB Rep. #1–#4 . . . . 9.00

ASTONISHING X-MEN
July, 1999
1 (of 3) BPe,HMe,new X-Men team 2.50
2 BPe,HMe,The Shattering x-over . 2.50
3 BPe,HMe,Shattering,concl. 2.50
TPB 160-pg. 16.00

ASTONISHING X-MEN
May, 2004
1 Gifted,pt.1 . . . . 5.00
1a variant (c). 4.00
1b Director's Cut 5.00
2 thru 6 Gifted,pt.2 thru pt.6 . . . . @6.00
7 thru 12 JoW(s),Dangerous,pt.1
   thru pt. 6 . . . . @4.00
13 thru 18 JoW(s), Torn, pt.1
   thru pt. 6 . . . . @4.00
19 JoW(s) Unstoppable, pt.1 . . . . . 3.00
19a variant (c) 3.00
TPB Vol. 1: Gifted 15.00
TPB Vol. 2: Dangerous 15.00
1-shot Astonishing X-Men Saga
   48-pg. 4.00

A-TEAM
March, 1984
1 thru 3 . . . . @5.00

ATOMIC AGE
Epic, Nov., 1990
1 AW 4.50
2 AW 4.50
3 AW,Feb., 1991 . . . . 4.50

AVATAARS: COVENANT
OF THE SHIELD
July, 2000
1 (of 3) LKa,Capt.Avalon 3.00
2 LKa,Dreadlord 3.00

AVENGERS
Sept., 1963
1 JK,O:Avengers,V:Loki 6,500.00
2 JK,V:Space Phantom 2,000.00
3 JK,V:Hulk,Sub-Mariner 900.00
4 JK,R&J:Captain America . . . 3,500.00
5 JK,L:Hulk,V:Lava Men 850.00
6 JK,I:Masters of Evil 850.00
7 JK,V:BaronZemo,Enchantress. 850.00
8 JK,I:Kang 750.00
9 JK(c),DH,I&D:Wonder Man . . 750.00
10 JK(c),DH,I:Immortus 450.00
11 JK(c),DH,A:Spider-Man,
   V:Kang 1,000.00
12 JK(c),DH,V:Moleman,
   Red Ghost 500.00
13 JK(c),DH,I:Count Nefaria 500.00
14 JK,DH,V:Count Nefaria 500.00
15 JK,DH,D:Baron Zemo 450.00
16 JK,J:Hawkeye,Scarlet Witch,
   Quicksilver 450.00
17 JK(c),DH,V:Mole Man,A:Hulk . 325.00
18 JK(c),DH,V:The Commisar . . . 325.00
19 JK(c),DH,I&O:Swordsman,
   O:Hawkeye 325.00
20 JK(c),DH,WW,V:Swordsman,
   Mandarin 350.00
21 JK(c),DH,WW,V:Power Man
   (not L.Cage),Enchantress . . . 350.00
22 JK(c),DH,WW,V:Power Man . . 350.00
23 JK(c),DH,JR,V:Kang 200.00
24 JK(c),DH,JR,V:Kang 200.00
25 JK(c),DH,V:Dr.Doom 200.00
26 DH,V:Attuma 200.00
27 DH,V:Attuma,Beetle 200.00
28 JK(c),DH,I:1st Goliath,
   I:Collector 200.00
29 DH,V:Power Man,Swordsman 200.00
30 JK(c),DH,V:Swordsman 200.00
31 DH,V:Keeper of the Flame . . . 125.00
32 DH,I:Bill Foster 100.00
33 DH,V:Sons of the Serpent
   A:Bill Foster 100.00
34 DH,V:Living Laser 100.00
35 DH,V:Mandarin 100.00
36 DH,V:The Ultroids 100.00
37 GK(c),DH,V:Ultroids 150.00

Avengers #28
© Marvel Entertainment Group

38 GK(c),DH,V:Enchantress,
   Ares,J:Hercules 100.00
39 DH,V:Mad Thinker 100.00
40 DH,V:Sub-Mariner 100.00
41 JB,V:Dragon Man,Diablo 80.00
42 JB,V:Dragon Man,Diablo 80.00
43 JB,V:Red Guardian 80.00
44 JB,V:Red Guardian,
   O:Black.Widow 80.00
45 JB,V:Super Adoptoid 80.00
46 JB,V:Whirlwind 80.00
47 JB,GT,V:Magneto 150.00
48 GT,I&O:New Black Knight . . . 150.00
49 JB,V:Magneto 125.00
50 JB,V:Typhon 125.00
51 JB,GT,R:Iron Man,Thor,
   V:Collector 125.00
52 JB,J:Black Panther,
   I:Grim Reaper 125.00
53 JB,GT,A:X-Men; x-over
   X-Men #45 . . . . 180.00
54 JB,GT,V:Masters of Evil
   I:Crimson Cowl(Ultron) 150.00
55 JB,I:Ultron,V:Masters of Evil . . 150.00
56 JB,D:Bucky retold,
   V:Baron Zemo 150.00
57 JB,I:Vision,V:Ultron 300.00
58 JB,O&J:Vision 125.00
59 JB,I:Yellowjacket 125.00
60 JB,W:Yellowjacket & Wasp . . 125.00
61 JB,A:Dr.Strange,x-over
   Dr. Strange #178 . . . . 125.00
62 JB,I:Man-Ape,A:Dr.Strange. . . 125.00
63 GC,I&O:2nd Goliath(Hawkeye)
   V:Egghead 125.00
64 GC,V:Egghead,O:Hawkeye . . 125.00
65 GC,V:Swordsman,Egghead . . 125.00
66 BWS,I:Ultron 6,Adamantium . . 140.00
67 BWS,V:Ultron 6 . . . . 140.00
68 SB,V:Ultron 120.00
69 SB,I:Nighthawk,Grandmaster,
   Squadron Supreme, V:Kang . 120.00
70 SB,O:Squadron Supreme
   V:Kang 120.00
71 SB,I:Invaders,V:Kang 150.00
72 SB,A:Captain Marvel,
   I:Zodiac 100.00
73 HT(i),V:Sons of Serpent 100.00
74 JB,TP,V:Sons of Serpent,
   IR:Black Panther on TV 100.00
75 JB,TP,I:Arkon 100.00
76 JB,TP,V:Arkon 100.00
77 JB,TP,V:Split-Second Squad. . 100.00
78 SB,TP,V:Lethal Legion 100.00
79 JB,TP,V:Lethal Legion 100.00
80 JB,TP,I&O:Red Wolf 110.00
81 JB,TP,A:Red Wolf 100.00
82 JB,TP,V:Ares,A:Daredevil 100.00
83 JB,TP,I:Valkyrie,
   V:Masters of Evil 100.00
84 JB,TP,V:Enchantress,Arkon . . 100.00
85 JB,V:Squadron Supreme 100.00
86 JB,JM,A:Squad Supreme 100.00
87 SB(i),O:Black Panther,
   V: A.I.M. 125.00
88 SB,JM,V:Psyklop,A:Hulk,
   Professor.X 110.00
88a 2nd Printing 10.00
89 SB,B:Kree/Skrull War 45.00
90 SB,V:Sentry #459,Ronan,
   Skrulls 45.00
91 SB,V:Sentry #459,Ronan,
   Skrulls 45.00
92 SB,V:Super Skrull,Ronan, ... 55.00
93 NA,TP,V:Super-Skrull,G-Size . 125.00
94 NA,JB,TP,V:Super-Skrull,
   I:Mandroids 100.00
95 NA,TP,V:Maximus,Skrulls,
   A:Inhumans,O:Black Bolt 70.00
96 NA,TP,V:Skrulls,Ronan 70.00

MARVEL

Avengers #83
© Marvel Entertainment Group

97 GK&BEv(c),JB,TP,E:Kree-Skrull
    War,V:Annihilus,Ronan,Skrulls,
    A:Golden Age Heroes 60.00
98 BWS,SB,V:Ares,R:Hercules,
    R&N:Hawkeye 60.00
99 BWS,TS,V:Ares 60.00
100 BWS,JSr,V:Ares & Kratos . . . 150.00
101 RB,DA,A:Watcher 40.00
102 RB,JSt,V:Grim Reaper,
    Sentinels 40.00
103 RB,JSt,V:Sentinels 40.00
104 RB,JSt,V:Sentinels 40.00
105 JB,JM,V:Savage Land
    Mutates; A:Black Panther 40.00
106 GT,DC,RB,V:Space Phantom . 40.00
107 GT,DC,JSn,V:Space
    Phantom, Grim Reaper 36.00
108 DH,DC,JSt,V:Space
    Phantom,Grim Reaper 40.00
109 DH,FMc,V:Champion,
    L:Hawkeye 40.00
110 DH,V:Magneto,A:X-Men 50.00
111 DH,J:Bl.Widow,A:Daredevil,
    X-Men,V:Magneto 45.00
112 DH,I:Mantis,V:Lion-God,
    L:Black Widow 40.00
113 FBe(i),V:The Living Bombs . . . 25.00
114 JR(c),V:Lion-God,J:Mantis,
    Swordsman 25.00
115 JR(c),A:Defenders,V:Loki,
    Dormammu 25.00
116 JR(c),A:Defenders,S.Surfer
    V:Loki,Dormammu 25.00
117 JR(c),FMc(i),A:Defenders,Silv.
    Surfer,V:Loki,Dormammu 25.00
118 JR(c),A:Defenders,S.Surfer
    V:Loki,Dormammu 25.00
119 JR(c),DH(i),V:Collector 25.00
120 JSn(c),DH(i),V:Zodiac 25.00
121 JR&JSn(c),JB,DH,V:Zodiac . . 25.00
122 K&R(c),V:Zodiac 25.00
123 JR(c),DH(i),O:Mantis 25.00
124 JR(c),JB,DC,V:Kree,O:Mantis. 25.00
125 JR(c),JB,DC,V:Thanos 22.00
126 DC(i),V:Klaw,Solarr 22.00
127 GK(c),SB,JSon,A:Inhumans,
    V:Ultron,Maximus 22.00
128 K&R(c),SB,JSon,V:Kang. . . . 20.00
129 SB,JSon,V:Kang 20.00
130 GK(c),SB,JSon,V:Slasher,
    Titanic Three 20.00
131 GK(c),SB,JSon,V:Kang,
    Legion of the Unliving 20.00
132 SB,JSon,Kang,Legion
    of the Unliving 20.00

133 GK(c),SB,JSon,O:Vision 20.00
134 K&R(c),SB,JSon,O:Vision . . . 20.00
135 JSn&JR(c),GT,O:Mantis,
    Vision,C:Thanos 25.00
136 K&R(c),rep Amazing Adv#12 . 20.00
137 JR(c),GT,J:Beast,
    Moondragon 20.00
138 GK(c),GT,V:Toad 20.00
139 K&R(c),GT,V:Whirlwind 18.00
140 K&R(c),GT,V:Whirlwind 18.00
141 GK(c),GP,V:Squad.Sinister . . 12.00
142 K&R(c),GP,V:Squadron
    Sinister,Kang 12.00
143 GK(c),GP,V:Squadron
    Sinister,Kang 12.00
144 GP,GK(c),V:Squad.Sinister,
    O&J:Hellcat,O:Buzz Baxter . . 25.00
145 GK(c),DH,V:Assassin 12.00
146 GK(c),DH,KP,V:Assassin . . . 12.00
147 GP,V:Squadron Supreme . . . 12.00
148 JK(c),GP,V:Squad.Supreme . . 12.00
149 GP,V:Orka 15.00
150 GP,JK,rep.Avengers #16 . . . . 15.00
151 GP,new line-up,
    R:Wonder Man 15.00
152 JB,JSt,I:New Black Talon 15.00
153 JB,JSt,V:L.Laser,Whizzer 12.00
154 GP,V:Attuma 12.00
155 SB,V:Dr.Doom,Attuma 12.00
156 SB,I:Tyrak,V:Attuma 12.00
157 DH,V:Stone Black Knight 12.00
158 JK(c),SB,I&O:Graviton, ... 12.00
159 JK(c),SB,V:Graviton, ... 12.00
160 GP,V:Grim Reaper 14.00
161 GP,V:Ultron,A:Ant-Man 14.00
162 GP,V:Ultron,I:Jocasta 14.00
163 GT,A:Champions,V:Typhon. . . 15.00
164 JBy,V:Lethal Legion 15.00
165 JBy,V:Count Nefario 14.00
166 JBy,V:Count Nefario 14.00
167 GP,A:Guardians,A:Nighthawk,
    Korvac,V:Porcupine 8.00
168 GP,A:Guardians,V:Korvac,
    I:Gyrich 8.00
169 SB,I:Eternity Man 8.00
170 GP,R:Jocasta,C:Ultron,
    A:Guardians. 8.00
171 GP,V:Ultron,A:Guardians,
    Ms Marvel 8.00
172 SB,KJ,V:Tyrak. 8.00
173 SB,V:Collector 8.00
174 GP(c),V:Collector 8.00
175 V&O:Korvac,A:Guardians 8.00
176 V:Korvac,A:Guardians 8.00
177 DC(c),D:Korvac,A:Guardians . . 8.00
178 CI,V:Manipulator 8.00
179 JM,AG,V:Stinger,Bloodhawk . . 8.00
180 JM,V:Monolith,Stinger,
    D:Bloodhawk 8.00
181 JBy,GD,I:Scott Lang 10.00
182 JBy,KJ,V:Maximoff 10.00
183 JBy,KJ,J:Ms.Marvel. 10.00
184 JBy,KJ,J:Falcon,
    V:Absorbing Man 10.00
185 JBy,DGr,O:Quicksilver & Scarlet
    Witch,I:Bova,V:Modred 10.00
186 JBy,DGr,V:Modred,Chthon . . . 10.00
187 JBy,DGr,V:Chthon,Modred . . . 10.00
188 JBy,DGr,V:The Elements 10.00
189 JBy,DGr,V:Deathbird 10.00
190 JBy,DGr,V:Grey Gargoyle,
    A:Daredevil 10.00
191 JBy,DGr,V:Grey Gargoyle,
    A:Daredevil 10.00
192 I:Inferno 8.00
193 FM(c),SB,DGr,O:Inferno 10.00
194 GP,JRu,J:Wonder Man 10.00
195 GP,JRu,A:Antman,
    I&C:Taskmaster. 10.00
196 GP,JA,A:Antman,
    V:Taskmaster. 10.00
197 CI,JAb,V:Red Ronin 10.00

Avengers #250
© Marvel Entertainment Group

198 GP,DGr,V:Red Ronan 10.00
199 GP,DGr,V:Red Ronan 10.00
200 GP,DGr,V:Marcus,
    L:Ms.Marvel 11.00
201 GP,DGr,F:Jarvis 5.00
202 GP,V:Ultron 5.00
203 CI,V:Crawlers,F:Wonderman . . 5.00
204 DN,DGr,V:Yellow Claw 5.00
205 DGr,V:Yellow Claw 5.00
206 GC,DGr,V:Pyron 5.00
207 GC,DGr,V:Shadowlord 5.00
208 GC,DGr,V:Berserker 5.00
209 DGr,A:Mr.Fantastic,V:Skrull . . . 5.00
210 GC,DGr,V:Weathermen 5.00
211 GC,DGr,Moon Knight,J:Tigra . . 5.00
212 DGr,V:Elfqueen 5.00
213 BH,DGr,L:Yellowjacket 5.00
214 RH,DGr,V:Gh.Rider,A:Angel . . 7.00
215 DGr,A:Silver Surfer,
    V:Molecule Man 5.00
216 DGr,A:Silver Surfer,
    V:Molecule Man 5.00
217 BH,DGr,V:Egghead,
    R:Yellowjacket,Wasp3 . . . . 5.00
218 DP,V:M.Hardy 5.00
219 BH,A:Moondragon,Drax 5.00
220 BH,DGr,D:Drax,V:MnDragon . . 5.00
221 J:She Hulk 5.00
222 V:Masters of Evil. 5.00
223 A:Antman 5.00
224 AM,A:Antman 5.00
225 A:Black Knight. 5.00
226 A:Black Knight. 5.00
227 J:2nd Captain Marvel,
    O:Avengers 5.00
228 V:Masters of Evil. 5.00
229 JSt,V:Masters of Evil. 5.00
230 A:Cap.Marvel,L:Yellowjacke . . . 5.00
231 AM,JSi,J:2nd Captain Marvel,
    Starfox 5.00
232 AM,JSi. 5.00
233 JBy,V:Annihilus 5.00
234 AM,JSi,O:ScarletWitch 5.00
235 AM,JSi,V:Wizard 5.00
236 AM,JSi,A:SpM,V:Lava Men . . . 4.50
237 AM,JSi,A:SpM,V:Lava Men. . . . 4.50
238 AM,JSi,V:Moonstone,
    O:Blackout. 4.00
239 AM,JSi,A:David Letterman 4.00
240 AM,JSi,A:Dr.Strange 4.00
241 AM,JSi,V:Morgan LeFey 4.00
242 AM,JSi,Secret Wars 4.00
243 AM,JSi,Secret Wars 4.00
244 AM,JSi,V:Dire Wraiths 4.00
245 AM,JSi,V:Dire Wraiths. 4.00

246 AM,JSi,V:Eternals 4.00
247 AM,JSi,A:Eternals,V:Deviants . . 4.00
248 AM,JSi,A:Eternals,V:Deviants . . 4.00
249 AM,JSi,A:Maelstrom 4.00
250 AM,JSi,A:W.C.A.
    V:Maelstrom 5.00
251 BH,JSi,A:Paladin. 4.00
252 BH,JSi,J:Hercules
    V:Blood Brothers 4.00
253 BH,JSi,J:Black Knight. 4.00
254 BH,JSi,A:W.C.A. 4.00
255 TP,p(c),JB,Legacy of
    Thanos/Sanctuary II 4.00
256 JB,TP,A:Ka-Zar 4.00
257 JB,TP,D:Savage Land,
    I:Nebula 4.00
258 JB,TP,A:SpM,Firelord,Nebula . . 4.00
259 JB,TP,V:Nebula 4.00
260 JB,TP,SecretWarsII, IR:Nebula
    is Thanos' Granddaughter 4.00
261 JB,TP,Secret Wars II. 4.00
262 JB,TP,J:Submariner 4.00
263 JB,TP,X-Factor tie-in,
    Rebirth,Marvel Girl,pt.1 . . . . . . 6.00
264 JB,TP,I:2nd Yellow Jacket. 4.00
265 JB,TP,Secret Wars II. 3.50
266 JB,TP,Secret Wars II,A:
    Silver Surfer. 3.50
267 JB,TP,V:Kang 3.50
268 JB,TP,V:Kang 3.50
269 JB,TP,V:Kang,A:Immortus. 3.50
270 JB,TP,V:Moonstone. 3.50
271 JB,TP,V:Masters of Evil. 3.50
272 JB,TP,A:Alpha Flight. 3.50
273 JB,TP,V:Masters of Evil. 3.50
274 JB,TP,V:Masters of Evil. 3.50
275 JB,TP,V:Masters of Evil. 3.50
276 JB,TP,V:Masters of Evil. 3.50
277 JB,TP,V:Masters of Evil. 3.50
278 JB,TP,V:Tyrok,J:Dr.Druid. 3.50
279 JB,TP,new leader 3.50
280 BH,KB,O:Jarvis. 3.50
281 JB,TP,V:Olympian Gods 3.50
282 JB,TP,V:Cerberus 3.50
283 JB,TP,V:Olympian Gods 3.50
284 JB,TP,V:Olympian Gods 3.50
285 JB,TP,V:Zeus 3.50
286 JB,TP,V:Fixer 3.50
287 JB,TP,V:Fixer 3.50
288 JB,TP,V:Sentry 459. . . . . 3.50
289 JB,TP,J:Marrina. 3.50
290 JB,TP,V:Adaptoid. 3.50
291 JB,TP,V:Marrina 3.50
292 JB,TP,V:Leviathon. 3.50
293 JB,TP,V:Leviathon. 3.50
294 JB,TP,V:Nebula. 3.50
295 JB,TP,V:Nebula. 3.50
296 JB,TP,V:Nebula. 3.50
297 JB,TP,V:Nebula. 3.50
298 JB,TP,Inferno,Edwin Jarvis. . . . 3.50
299 JB,TP,Inferno,V:Orphan
    Maker,R:Gilgemesh. 3.50
300 JB,TP,WS,Inferno,V:Kang,
    O:Avengers,J:Gilgemesh,
    Mr.Fantastic,Invis.Woman 5.00
301 BH,DH,A:SuperNova 3.50
302 RB,TP,V:SuperNova,
    A:Quasar 3.50
303 RB,TP,V:SuperNova,A:FF. 3.50
304 RB,TP,V:U-Foes,Puma 3.50
305 PR,TP,V:Lava Men 5.00
306 PR,TP,O:Lava Men 3.50
307 PR,TP,V:Lava Men 3.50
308 PR,TP,A:Eternals,J:Sersi 3.50
309 PR,TP,V:Blastaar 3.50
310 PR,TP,V:Blastaar 3.50
311 PR,TP,Acts of Veng.,V:Loki. . . . 3.50
312 PR,TP,Acts of Vengeance,
    V:Freedom Force. 3.50
313 PR,TP,Acts of Vengeance,
    V:Mandarin,Wizard 3.50

Avengers #311
© Marvel Entertainment Group

314 PR,TP,J:Sersi,A:Spider-Man,
    V:Nebula 4.00
315 PR,TP,A:SpM,V:Nebula 4.00
316 PR,TP,J:Spider-Man 4.00
317 PR,TP,A:SpM,V:Nebula 4.00
318 PR,TP,A:SpM,V:Nebula 4.00
319 PR,B:Crossing Line 3.00
320 PR,TP,A:Alpha Flight 3.00
321 PR,Crossing Line#3 . . . . 3.00
322 PR,TP,Crossing Line#4. . . . . . . 3.00
323 PR,TP,Crossing Line#5. . . . . . . 3.00
324 PR,TP,E:Crossing Line 3.00
325 V:MotherSuperior,3
    Machinesmith 3.00
326 TP,I:Rage 5.00
327 TP,V:Monsters 3.00
328 TP,O:Rage 4.00
329 TP,J:Sandman,Rage 3.00
330 TP,V:Tetrarch of Entropy. 3.00
331 TP,J:Rage,Sandman 3.00
332 TP,V:Dr.Doom 3.00
333 HT,V:Dr.Doom 3.00
334 NKu,TP,B:Collector,
    A:Inhumans 3.00
335 RLm(c),SEp,TP,V:Thane
    Ector,A:Collector,. 3.00
336 RLm(c),SEp,TP. 3.00
337 RLm(c),SEp,TP,V:ThaneEctor . 3.00
338 RLm(c),SEp,TP,A:Beast,. 3.00
339 RLm(c),SEp,TP,E:Collector. . . . 3.00
340 RLm(c),F:Capt.Amer.,Wasp . . . 3.00
341 SEp,TP,A:New Warriors,V:Sons
    of Serpents 3.00
342 SEP,TP,A:New Warriors,
    V:Hatemonger 3.00
343 SEp,TP,J:Crystal,C&I:2nd
    Swordsman,Magdalene. 3.00
344 SEp,TP,I:Proctor 3.00
345 SEp,TP,Oper. Galactic Storm
    Pt.5,V:Kree,Shiar. 3.00
346 SEp,TP,Oper. Galactic Storm
    Pt.12,I:Star Force 3.00
347 SEp,TP,Oper. Galactic Storm
    Pt.19,D:Kree Race,Conclusion . 3.00
348 SEp,TP,F:Vision 3.00
349 SEp,TP,V:Ares 3.00
350 SEp,TP,rep.Avengers#53,A:Prof.
    X,Cyclops,V:StarJammers. 4.00
351 KWe,TP,V:Star Jammers 3.00
352 V:Grim Reaper 3.00
353 V:Grim Reaper 3.00
354 V:Grim Reaper 3.00
355 BHs(s),SEp,I:Gatherers,
    Coal Tiger 3.00

356 B:BHs(s),SEp,TP,A:Bl.Panther
    D:Coal Tiger 3.00
357 SEp,TP,A:Watcher 3.00
358 SEp,TP,V:Arkon 3.00
359 SEp,TP,A:Arkon 3.00
360 SEp,TP,V:Proctor,double-size,
    bronze foil(c) 4.50
361 SEp,I:Alternate Vision 2.50
362 SEp,TP,V:Proctor 3.00
363 SEp,TP,V:Proctor,D:Alternate
    Vision,C:Deathcry,Silver Foil(c),
    30th Anniv.. . . . . 4.00
364 SEp,TP,I:Deathcry,V:Kree 3.00
365 SEp,TP,V:Kree 3.00
366 SEp,TP,V:Kree,N:Dr.Pym,Gold
    Foil(c). 5.00
367 F:Vision 3.00
368 SEp,TP,Bloodties#1,
    A:X-Men. 4.00
369 SEp,TP,E:BHs(s),Bloodties#5,
    D:Cortez,V:Exodus,Platinum
    Foil(c). 4.00
370 SEp(c),TP(c),GI,V:Deviants,
    A:Kro,I:Delta Force 3.00
371 GM,TP,V:Deviants,A:Kro. 3.00
372 B:BHs(s),SEp,TP,I:2nd
    Gatherers,A:Proctor. 3.00
373 SEp,TP,I:Alternate Jocasta,
    V:Sersi 3.00
374 SEp,TP,O&IR:Proctor is Alternate
    Black Knight 3.00
375 SEp,TP,Double Sized,D:Proctor,
    L:Sersi,Black Knight 3.50
376 F:Crystal,I:Terrigen 3.00
377 F:Quicksilver 3.00
378 TP,I:Butcher 3.00
379 TP,Hercules,V:Hera. 3.00
379a Avengers Double Feature #1
    flip-book with Giant-Man #1 . . . 3.50
380 Hera 6.00
380a Avengers Double Feature #2
    flip-book with Giant Man #2.. . . 5.00
381 Quicksilvr, Scarlet Witch 4.00
381a Avengers Double Feature #3
    flip-book with Giant Man #3. . . . 3.00
382 Wundagore 2.50
382a Avengers Double Feature #4
    flip-book with Giant Man #4. . . . 3.00
383 A:Fantastic Force,V:Arides 3.00
384 Hercules Vs. Stepmom 4.00
385 V:Red Skull 3.00
386 F:Black Widow 3.00
387 Taking A.I.M.,pt.2 . . . . 3.00
388 Taking A.I.M.,pt.4 . . . . 3.00
389 B:Mike Deodato 3.00
390 BHs,TP,The Crossing, prelude . 3.00
391 BHs,Cont. From Avg. Crossing. 3.00
392 BHs,TP,The Crossing 3.00
393 BHs,TP,The Crossing 3.00
394 BHs,TP,The Crossing 3.00
395 BHs,TP,Timeslide concludes . . 3.00
396 . . . . 3.00
397 TP,Incred.Hulk #440 x-over . . . 3.00
398 TP,V:Unknown foe 3.00
399 . . . . 3.00
400 MeW,MWa,double size 4.50
401 MeW,MWa,Onslaught saga . . . 3.00
402 MWa,MD2,Onslaught, finale. . . 3.00
Ann.#1 DH,V:Mandarin,
    Masters of Evil. 250.00
Ann.#2 DH,JB,V:Scar.Centurion . 150.00
Ann.#3 rep.#4,T.ofSusp.#66-68 . 100.00
Ann.#4 rep.#5,#6 . . . . 50.00
Ann.#5 JK(c),rep.#8,#11 . . . . 25.00
Ann.#6 GP,HT,V:Laser,Nuklo,
    Whirlwind. 20.00
Ann.#7 JSn,JRu,V:Thanos,A:Captain
    Marvel,D:Warlock(2nd) 40.00
Ann.#8 GP,V:Dr.Spectrum 15.00
Ann.#9 DN,V:Arsenal 10.00
Ann.#10 MGo,A:X-Men,Spid.Woman,
    I:Rogue,V:Br.o/Evil Mutants. . . 40.00

Avengers Giant Size Special #1
© Marvel Entertainment Group

Ann.#11 DP,V:Defenders 6.00
Ann.#12 JG,V:Inhumans,Maximus . . 5.00
Ann.#13 JBy,V:Armin Zola 5.00
Ann.#14 JBy,KB,V:Skrulls 5.00
Ann.#15 SD,KJ,V:Freedom Force . . 5.00
Ann.#16 RF,BH,TP,JR2,BSz,KP,AW,
   MR,BL,BWi,JG,KN,A:Silver
   Surfer,Rebirth Grandmaster . . . 5.00
Ann.#17 MBr,MG,Evol.Wars,J:2nd
   Yellow Jacket 5.00
Ann.#18 MBa,MG,Atlan.Attack#8,
   J:Quasar 4.00
Ann.#19 HT,Terminus Factor 4.00
Ann.#20 Subterran.Odyssey#1 . . . 4.00
Ann.#21 Citizen Kang#4 . . . . 4.00
Ann.#22 I:Bloodwraith,w/card 4.00
Ann.#23 JB 4.00
G-Size#1 JR(c),RD,DA,I:Nuklo . . 35.00
G-Size#2 JR(c),DC,O:Kang,
   D:Swordsman,O:Rama-Tut . . . 20.00
G-Size#3 GK(c),DC,V:Kang,Legion
   of the Unliving 20.00
G-Size#4 K&R(c),DH,W:Scarlet Witch
   &Vision,O:Mantis,Moondragon 25.00
G-Size#5 rep,Annual #1. . . . . . . 15.00
GNv Death Trap.The Vault RLm,
   A:Venom 20.00
Marvel Milestone rep. #1 (1993) . . 3.00
Marvel Milestone rep. #4 (1995) . . 3.00
Marvel Milestone rep. #16 (1993) . . 3.00
TPB Greatest Battles of the
   Avengers 16.00
TPB Korvac Saga, rep. 13.00
TPB Yesterday Quest, rep. 7.00

[2nd Series] Nov., 1996
1 RLd,JV,CYp,JSb,Heroes Reborn,
   F:Thor, Captain America,
   V:Loki. 6.00
1A Variant cover 8.00
1 gold signature edition, bagged . 20.00
2 RLd,JV,CYp,JSb,V:Kang 4.00
3 RLd,JV,CYp,JSb,V:Kang,A:Nick
   Fury 4.00
4 RLd,JLb,CYp,JSb. 4.00
4A variant cover 4.00
5 RLd,CYp,JSb,V:Hulk,concl. 5.00
6 RLd,JLb,CYp,JSb,Industrial
   Revolution, pt.1 x-over 5.00
7 RLd,JLb,IaC,JSb,. 4.00
8 RLd,JLb,IaC,JSb,F:Simon
   Williams (Wonder Man),V:Ultron,
   Lethal Legion. 4.00
9 JLb,RLd,IaC,F:Vision, Wonder
   Man 5.00
10 WS,. 4.00

11 . . . . 4.00
12 WS,Galactus Saga, x-over 4.00
13 JeR, Wildstorm x-over 4.00
Minus 1 Spec., JLb,RLd,IaC,JSb,
   flashback 2.50

[3rd Series] Dec., 1997
1 GP,KBk,AV,F:Everyone,48 pg. . . 5.00
1a Variant (c) 10.00
2 KBk,GP,AV,A:Scarlet Witch 5.00
3 KBk,GP,AV,trapped in midieval
   present. 4.00
4 KBk,GP,AV,who makes the
   team?. 5.00
5 KBk,GP,AV,Squadron Supreme . . 5.00
6 KBk,GP,AV,V:SquadronSupreme 5.00
7 KBk,GP,AV,Live Kree or Die,pt.4 . 2.50
8 KBk,GP,AV,I:Triathlon 2.50
9 KBk,GP,AV,V:Moses Magnum . . 2.50
10 KBk,GP,AV,V:Grim Reaper 2.50
11 KBk,GP,AV,V:Grim Reaper 2.50
12 KBk,GP,AV,V:Thunderbolts,
   48-page 30.00
12a Variant, white background 3.00
13 KBk,GP,AV,R:New Warriors . . . 2.50
14 KBk,GP,AV,R:Beast. 2.50
15 KBk,GP,AV,A:Iron Man 2.50
16 JOy,AG,R:Photon 5.00
16a variant JOy,GP cover 2.50
17 JOy,AG,A:Warbird &
   Black Knight 2.50
18 JOy,AG,V:Wrecking Crew 2.50
19 KBk,GP,AV,Ultron,pt.1 . . . . 2.50
19a signed 30.00
20 KBk,GP,AV,Ultron,pt.2 . . . . 2.50
21 KBk,GP,AV,Ultron,pt.3 . . . . 2.50
22 KBk,GP,AV,Ultron,pt.4 . . . . 2.50
23 KBk,GP,AV,V:Wonder Man 2.50
24 KBk,GP,AV 2.50
25 KBk,GP,AV, 48-pg. 3.50
26 KBk,GP,AV,SI,V:Triune 2.50
27 KBk,GP,AV,100-pg. 3.50
28 KBk,GP,AV,Kulan Gath,pt.1 . . . 2.50
29 KBk,GP,AV,Kulan Gath,pt.2 . . . 2.50
30 KBk,GP,AV,Kulan Gath,pt.3 . . . 2.50
31 KBk,GP,AV,F:Vision 2.50
32 KBk,GP,AV,F:Black Widow 2.50
33 KBk,GP,AV,Thunderbolts 2.50
34 KBk,GP,AV,Thunderbolts 3.50
35 KBk,JR2,AV,MaximumSecurity . . 2.50
36 KBk,SEp,AV,A:Capt.Am.+poster. 2.50
37 KBk,SEp,AV,F:Capt.Am. 2.50
38 KBk,AD,MFm 2.50
39 KBk,AD,MFm,F:Silverclaw 2.50
40 KBk,AD,MFm,F:Hulk,Silverclaw . 2.50
41 KBk,AD,MFm,A:Kang 2.50
42 KBk,AD,MFm,A:Kang 2.50
43 KBk,AD,MFm,V:Kang 2.50
44 KBk,KK,V:Kang,Thor berserk . . . 2.50
45 KBk,KK,V:Conqueror 2.50
46 KBk,Kang Dynasty 2.50
47 KBk,Kang Dynasty 2.50
48 KBk,KD,100-page 4.00
49 KBk,KD,F:Kang,'Nuff Said 2.50
50 KBk,KD,V:Kang, 48-pg. 4.00
51 KBk,KD,F:Wonder Man,
   Scarlet Witch 2.25
52 KBk,KD,Kang War 2.25
53 KBk,KD,Avengers Avenge 2.25
54 KBk,KD,Kang War,concl. 2.25
55 KBk,KD,Kang War,aftermath . . . 2.25
56 KBk,F:Beast,She-Hulk,USAgent. 2.25
57 KD,World Trust, pt.1 . . . . 2.75
58 KD,World Trust, pt.2 . . . . 2.25
59 KD,World Trust, pt.3 . . . . 2.25
60 KD,World Trust, concl.,40-pg . . . 4.00
61 GFr,. 2.25
62 GFr 2.25
63 AD,MFm,Standoff,pt.3,x-over . . . 3.00
64 F:Falcon 2.25
65 ALa,Red Zone,pt.1 . . . . 2.25
66 ALa,Red Zone,pt.2 . . . . 2.25
67 ALa,Red Zone,pt.3 . . . . 2.25

68 ALa,Red Zone,pt.4 . . . . 2.25
69 Al.a,Red Zone,pt.5 . . . . 2.25
70 ALa,Red Zone,pt.6 . . . . 2.25
71 V:Wasp, Yellowjacket 3.00
72 ScK,Search for She-Hulk,pt.1 . . 2.25
73 ScK,Search for She-Hulk,pt.2 . . 2.25
74 ScK,Search for She-Hulk,pt.3 . . 2.25
75 ScK,Search for She-Hulk,pt.4 . . 2.25
76 JaL(c),an Avenger falls 2.25
77 Lionheart of Avalon,pt.1 . . . . . . 0.50
78 Lionheart of Avalon,pt.2 . . . . . . 2.25
79 Lionheart of Avalon,pt.3 . . . . . . 2.25
80 Lionheart of Avalon,pt.4 . . . . . . 2.25
81 Lionheart of Avalon, concl. 2.25
82 Once an Invader,pt.1 . . . . 2.25
83 Once an Invader,pt.2 . . . . 2.25
84 Once an Invader,pt.3 . . . . 2.25
500 BMB,Disassembled,pt.1,48-pg. 5.00
500a Director's Cut,64-pg. 8.00
501 BMB,Disassembled,pt.2,48-pg. 5.00
502 BMB,Disassembled,pt.3,48-pg. 5.00
503 BMB,Disassembled,pt.4,48-pg. 4.00
Ann. '98 Avengers/Squadron Supreme
   KBk,CPa,GP, 48pg 2.50
Ann 1999 KBk,JFM, Why Avengers
   disbanded, 48-page. 3.50
Ann.2000 KBk,NBy,48-pg 3.50
Ann.2001 KBk,IaC,NRd 3.00
Rough Cut Edition KBk,GP, 48pg,
   original pencils of #1, b&w 3.00
Spec. 1-1/2, 32-pg.RSt. 2.50
Spec. Avengers: Year in Review . . 3.00
GN Ultron Imperative,BWS(c) 6.00
TPB Avengers: Under Siege 17.00
TPB Avengers Visionaries:
   George Perez, 176-page. 17.00
TPB The Morgan Conquest. 15.00
TPB The Kree/Skrull War. 25.00
TPB Ultron Unlimited,112-page . . . 15.00
TPB Supreme Justice,304-page . . 18.00
TPB Clear & Present Danger 20.00
TPB Celestial Madonna (1999) . . . 20.00
TPB Avengers/Defenders War 18.00
TPB The Korvac Saga (2002) 20.00
TPB The Kang Dynasty (2002) . . . 30.00
TPB Vol.1: World Trust (2003). . . . 15.00
TPB Vol.2: Red Zone (2003) . . . 15.00
TPB Vol. 3: Search for She-Hulk . . 13.00
TPB Vol. 4: Lionheart of Avalon . . . 12.00
TPB Vol. 5: Once an Invader 15.00
TPB Living Legends (2004) 20.00
TPB Kang–Time and Time Again. . 20.00
TPB The Serpent Crown (2005) . . 16.00
TPB Vision and the Scarlet Witch . 16.00
TPB Galactic Storm Vol. 1 (2006) . 30.00
TPB Galactic Storm Vol. 2 (2006) . 30.00

**AVENGERS AND
POWER PACK ASSEMBLE**
Apr., 2006
1 thru 4 . . . . @3.00
TPB Rep., #1 thru #4. . . . . 7.00

**AVENGERS:
CELESTIAL QUEST**
Sept., 2001
1 (of 8) SEt,SHa 2.50
2 SEt,SHa,F:Mantis 3.00
3 SEt,SHa,F:Quoi,Mantis 3.00
4 SEt,SHa,F:Quoi,Thanos 2.50
5 SEt,SHa,F:Thanos 2.50
6 SEt,SHa,F:Mantis & Vision 2.50
7 SEt,SHa,F:Mantis,Quoi,Vision . . . 2.50
8 SEt,SHa,finale,48-pg. 3.50

**AVENGERS: EARTH'S
MIGHTIEST HEROES**
Nov., 2004
1 JoC,ScK, Avengers early days . . 3.50

2 thru 8 JoC,ScK. . . . . @3.50
TPB series rep. 25.00

AVENGERS: EARTH'S MIGHTIEST HEROES II
Nov., 2006
1 JoC, Avengers early days 4.00
2 JoC 4.00

AVENGERS FINALE
Nov., 2004
1-Shot 3.00

AVENGERS FOREVER
Oct., 1998
1 (of 12) GP,KBk,CPa,Rick Jones
　radiation poisoning 4.00
2 GP,KBk,CPa,new Avengers. 3.00
3 GP,KBk,CPa,Kang/Immortus. . . . 3.00
4 KBk,different eras 3.00
4a, b & c variant covers . . . . @3.00
5 KBk,RSt,A:1950s Avengers 3.00
6 KBk,RSt,V:Immortus 3.00
7 KBk,RSt,reunited 3.00
8 KBk,Immortus' plan 3.00
9 KBk,RSt,Kang the Conqueror . . . 3.00
10 KBk,RSt,V:Immortus 3.00
11 KBk,RSt,V:Avengers Battalion . . 3.00
12 KBk,RSt,concl. 3.00
TPB Avengers Forever,288-page. . 25.00

AVENGERS ICONS: TIGRA
March, 2002
1 (of 4) MD2,. 3.00
2 MD2,Brethren of the Blue Fist. . . 3.00
3 MD2,Brethren of the Blue Fist. . . 3.00
4 MD2,concl. 3.00

AVENGERS ICONS: THE VISION
Aug., 2002
1 (of 4) 3.00
2 thru 4 . . . . @3.00

AVENGERS INDEX
See: OFFICIAL MARVEL INDEX TO THE AVENGERS

AVENGERS INFINITY
July, 2000
1 (of 4) RSt,SCh,SHa 3.00
2 RSt,SCh,SHa,Servitors 3.00
3 RSt,SCh,SHa,Infinites 3.00
4 RSt,SCh,SHa,concl 3.00

AVENGERS LOG
1994
1 GP(c),History of the Avengers . . . 2.25

AVENGERS NEXT
Nov. 2006
1 RLm,V:Zombie Avengers,A:Nova 3.00
2 RLm. 3.00

AVENGERS SPOTLIGHT
Aug., 1989
Formerly: Solo Avengers
21 AM,DH,TMo,JRu,Hawkeye,
　Starfox 3.00
22 AM,DH,Hawkeye,O:Swordsman. 3.00
23 AM,DH,KD,Hawkeye,Vision . . . 2.50
24 AM,DH,Hawkeye,O:Espirita 2.50
25 AM,TMo,Hawkeye,Rick Jones . . 2.50
26 A of V,Hawkeye,Iron Man 2.50

27 A of V,AM,DH,DT,Hawkeye
　Avengers 2.50
28 A of V,AM,DH,DT,Hawkeye,
　Wonder Man,Wasp 2.50
29 A of V,DT,Hawkeye,Iron Man . . . 2.50
30 AM,DH,Hawkeye,New Costume . 2.50
31 AM,DH,KW,Hawkeye,US.Agent . 2.50
32 AM,KW,Hawkeye,U.S.Agent. . . . 2.50
33 AM,DH,KW,Hawkeye,US.Agent . 2.50
34 AM,DH,KW,SLi(c),Hawkeye
　U.S.Agent 2.50
35 JV,Gilgamesh 2.50
36 AM,DH,Hawkeye. 2.50
37 BH,Dr.Druid. 2.50
38 JBr,Tigra 2.50
39 GCo,Black Knight 2.50
40 Vision,Last Issue. 2.50

AVENGERS STRIKEFILE
1994
1 BHa(s),Avengers Pin-ups 2.25

AVENGERS: THE CROSSING
1995
1 BHs,Death of an Avenger,
　chromium cover,48pg. 6.00

AVENGERS: THE TERMINATRIX OBJECTIVE
1993
1 B:MGu(s),MG,Holografx(c),
　V:Terminatrix 2.75
2 MG,V:Terminatrix,A:Kangs. 2.25
3 MG,V:Terminatrix,A:Kangs. 2.25
4 MG,Last issue 2.25

AVENGERS/ THUNDERBOLTS
March, 2004
1 (of 6) FaN&KBk(s),BKi. 3.00
2 FaN&KBk(s),BKi 3.00
3 thru 6 FaN&KBk(s),TG. . . . . @3.00
TPB Vol. 1: Nefaria Protocols . . . 20.00
TPB Vol. 2: Best Intentions 15.00

AVENGERS: TIMESLIDE
1996
1 BHs,TKa,End of the Crossing
　Megallic chrome cover 5.00

AVENGERS TWO: WONDER MAN & THE BEAST
Mar., 2000
1 (of 3) RSt,MBa, ... 3.00
2 RSt,MBa, ... 3.00
3 RSt,MBa,concl. 3.00

AVENGERS/ULTRAFORCE
1995
1 V:Malibu's Ultraforce 4.00

AVENGERS: UNITED THEY STAND
Sept., 1999
1 TTn,RCa, Cartoon tie-in 3.00
2 TTn, ... 2.25
3 TTn, ... 2.25
4 TTn, ... 2.25
5 TTn,Hawkeye&Black Widow 2.25
6 TTn,A:Capt.America 2.25
7 TTn,F:Devil Dinosaur,Moonboy . . 3.25

AVENGERS UNIVERSE
June, 2000
1 rep. 3 stories, 80-pg. 5.00
2 rep. 3 stories, 80-pg. 5.00
3 rep. 3 stories, 80-pg. 5.00
4 rep. 3 stories, 80-pg. 4.25
5 rep. 3 stories, 80-pg. 4.25

AVENGERS UNLEASHED
1995
1 V:Count Nefarious 2.25
Becomes:

Avengers Unplugged #5
© Marvel Entertainment Group

AVENGERS UNPLUGGED
1996
2 Crushed by Graviton 2.25
3 x-over with FF Unplugged 2.25
4 The Old Ball and Chain 2.25
5 A:Captain Marvel 2.25
6 final issue. 2.25

AVENGERS WEST COAST
Sept., 1989
Prev: West Coast Avengers
47 JBy,V:J.Random 3.00
48 JBy,V:J.Random 3.00
49 JBy,V:J.Random,W.Man 3.00
50 JBy,R:G.A.Human Torch 4.00
51 JBy,R:Iron Man 2.50
52 JBy,V:MasterPandmonum. 2.50
53 JBy,Acts ofVeng.,V:U-Foes. . . . 2.50
54 JBy,Acts ofVeng.,V:MoleMan . . 2.50
55 JBy,Acts ofVeng.finale,V:Loki
　Magneto kidnaps Sc.Witch 4.00
56 JBy,V:Magneto 11.00
57 JBy,V:Magneto 5.00
58 V:Vibro, ... 2.50
59 TMo,V:Hydro-Man,A:Immortus . . 2.50
60 PR,V:Immortus,. 2.50
61 PR,V:Immortus 2.50
62 V:Immortus 2.50
63 PR,I:Living Lightning. 2.50
64 F:G.A.Human Torch 2.50
65 PR,V:Ultron,Grim Reaper 2.50
66 PR,V:Ultron,Grim Reaper 2.50
67 PR,V:Ultron,Grim Reaper 2.50
68 PR,V:Ultron. 2.50
69 PR,USAgent vs Hawkeye,
　I:Pacific Overlords 2.50
70 DR,V:Pacific Overlords 3.00
71 DR,V:Pacific Overlords 3.00
72 DR,V:Pacific Overlords 3.00

73 DR,V:Pacific Overlords 3.00
74 DR,J:Living Lightning,Spider
    Woman,V:Pacific Overlords. . . . 3.00
75 HT,A:F.F,V:Arkon,double 3.00
76 DR,Night Shift,I:Man-Demon . . 2.50
77 DR,A:Satannish & Nightshift 2.50
78 DR,V:Satannish & Nightshift 2.50
79 DR,A:Dr.Strange,V:Satannish . . . 2.50
80 DR,Galactic Storm,pt.2 . . . . 2.50
81 DR,Galactic Storm,pt.9 . . . . 2.50
82 DR,Galactic Storm,pt.16
    A:Lilandra 2.50
83 V:Hyena 2.50
84 DR,I:Deathweb,MBa,A:SpM,
    O:Spider-Woman 3.00
85 DR,A:SpM,V:Death Web. 2.50
86 DR,A:SpM,V:Death Web. 2.50
87 DR,A:Wolverine,V:Bogatyri 3.00
88 DR,A:Wolverine,V:Bogatyri 2.50
89 DR,V:Ultron 2.50
90 DR,A:Vision,V:Ultron 2.50
91 DR,V:Ultron,I:War Toy 2.50
92 DR,V:Goliath(Power Man) 2.50
93 DR,V:Doctor Demonicus 2.50
94 DR,J:War Machine 2.50
95 DR,A:Darkhawk,V:Doctor
    Demonicus. 2.50
96 DR,Inf.Crusade x-over 2.50
97 ACe,Inf.Crusade,V:Power
    Platoon 2.50
98 DR,I:4th Lethal Legion 2.50
99 DR,V:4th Lethal Legion 2.50
100 DR,D:Mockingbird,V:4th Lethal
    Legion,Red Foil(c) 4.50
101 DR,Bloodties#3,V:Exodus 4.00
102 DR,L:Iron Man,Spider-Woman,
    US Agent,Scarlet Witch,War
    Machine,last issue 4.00
Ann.#4 JBy,TA,MBa,Atlan.Attacks
    #12,V:Seven Brides of Set 4.00
Ann.#5 Terminus Factor. 3.50
Ann.#6 Subterranean Odyssey#5 . . 2.50
Ann.#7 Assault on Armor City#4 . . 2.25
Ann.#8 DR,I:Raptor w/card 3.25
TPB Vol. 1: Vision Quest, JBy 25.00

BACKPACK MARVELS:

Avengers (2001) 7.25
Spider-Man Vol. 1 (2001). 7.25
X-Men Vol.1 (2000) 7.25
X-Men Vol.2 (2000) 7.25

BALDER THE BRAVE

Nov., 1985
1 WS,SB,V:Frost Giants 3.00
2 WS,SB,V:Frost Giants 3.00
3 WS,SB,V:Frost Giants 3.00
4 WS,SB,V:Frost Giants;Feb,1986 . 3.00

BANNER

Startling Stories, July, 2001
1 (of 4) RCo, F:Hulk 3.00
2 RCo, ... 3.00
3 RCo, ... 3.00
4 RCo, concl. 3.00
TPB RCo(c) 96-page 13.00

BARBIE

Jan., 1991
1 polybagged with Credit Card . . . 15.00
2 . . . . 10.00
3 thru 49 . . . . @8.00
50 Anniv. issue, Disney World(c) . . 12.00
51 thru 66 . . . . @7.00

BARBIE FASHION

Jan., 1991
1 bagged with doorknob hanger . . 12.00
2 thru 63 . . . . @7.00

BATTLE

Marvel Atlas, March, 1951
1 They called Him a Coward . . . 375.00
2 The War Department Secrets . 200.00
3 The Beast of the Bataan 150.00
4 JMn,I:Buck Private O'Toole . . 150.00
5 Death Trap Of Gen. Wu. 150.00
6 RH, JMn. 150.00
7 Enemy Sniper 150.00
8 A Time to Die 150.00
9 RH 100.00
10 . . . . 100.00
11 SC 100.00
12 thru 21 . . . . @110.00
22 . . . . 100.00
23 BK 100.00
24 . . . . 100.00
25 . . . . 100.00
26 JR 100.00
27 . . . . 100.00
28 JSe 100.00
29 . . . . 100.00
30 . . . . 100.00
31 RH,JMn. 100.00
32 JSe,GT 100.00
33 GC,JSe,JSt 100.00
34 JSe 100.00
35 . . . . 100.00
36 BEv 100.00
37 RA,JSt. 125.00
38 thru 46 . . . . @100.00
47 JO 100.00
48 . . . . 100.00
49 JDa 100.00
50 BEv 100.00
51 . . . . 100.00
52 GWb 100.00
53 BP 100.00
54 . . . . 100.00
55 GC,AS,BP,AW,GWb 125.00
56 . . . . 100.00
57 . . . . 100.00
58 . . . . 100.00
59 AT 100.00
60 A:Combat Kelly 100.00
61 JMn,A:Combat Kelly 100.00
62 A:Combat Kelly 100.00
63 SD 150.00
64 JK 150.00
65 JK 150.00
66 JSe,JK,JDa 150.00
67 JSe,JK,AS,JDa 150.00
68 JSe,JK,AW,SD 150.00
69 RH,JSe,JK,SW 175.00
70 BEv,SD; June, 1960 . . . . 175.00

Battle #14
© Marvel Entertainment Group

Battlefront Action #1
© Marvel Entertainment Group

BATTLE ACTION

Marvel Atlas, Feb., 1952
1 . . . . 350.00
2 . . . . 200.00
3 JSt,RH 100.00
4 . . . . 100.00
5 . . . . 100.00
6 JeR 100.00
7 JeR 100.00
8 RH 125.00
9 thru 15 . . . . @100.00
16 thru 27 . . . . @100.00
28 GWb 100.00
29 . . . . 100.00
30 GWb,Aug., 1957 . . . . 100.00

BATTLEBOOKS

Nov., 1998
Captain America, BiT(c). 4.00
Citizen V, BiT(c). 4.00
Colossus, BiT(c). 4.00
Elektra, BiT(c) 4.00
Gambit, BiT(c) 4.00
Iron Man, BiT(c). 4.00
Rogue, BiT(c). 4.00
Spider-Girl, BiT(c) 4.00
Spider-Man, BiT(c). 4.00
Storm, BiT(c) 4.00
Thor, BiT(c) 4.00
Wolverine, BiT(c) 4.00

BATTLE BRADY

See: MEN IN ACTION

BATTLEFIELD

Marvel Atlas, April, 1952
1 RH, Slaughter on Suicide
    Ridge 250.00
2 RH 125.00
3 Ambush Patrol 125.00
4 . . . . 125.00
5 Into the Jaws of Death 125.00
6 thru 10 . . . . @100.00
11 GC,May, 1953 . . . . 100.00

BATTLEFRONT

Marvel Atlas, June, 1952
1 JeR,RH(c),Operation Killer . . . 350.00
2 JeR 200.00
3 JeR,Spearhead 150.00
4 JeR,Death Trap of General
    Chun 150.00
5 JeR,Terror of the Tank Men . . . 150.00

---

6 A:Combat Kelly 150.00
7 A:Combat Kelly 150.00
8 A:Combat Kelly 150.00
9 A:Combat Kelly 150.00
10 A:Combat Kelly 150.00
11 thru 20 . . . . @125.00
21 thru 39 . . . . @125.00
40 AW 125.00
41 . . . . 125.00
42 AW 125.00
43 thru 48 Aug.,1957 . . . . @135.00

BATTLEGROUND
Marvel Atlas, Sept., 1954
1 . . . . 250.00
2 JKz. 125.00
3 thru 8 . . . . @100.00
9 BK 100.00
10 . . . . 100.00
11 AW,GC,GT. 125.00
12 MD,JSe 100.00
13 AW 100.00
14 JD 125.00
15 thru 17 . . . . @100.00
18 AS 125.00
19 JMn,JSe 100.00
20 Aug., 1957. . . . . 100.00

BATTLESTAR GALACTICA
March, 1979
1 EC,B:TV Adaptation;
  Annihalation 12.00
2 EC,Exodus 8.00
3 EC,Deathtrap 8.00
4 WS,Dogfight 8.00
5 WS,E:TV Adaptation;Ambush . . 8.00
6 Nightmare 7.00
7 Commander Adama Trapped . . 7.00
8 Last Stand 7.00
9 Space Mimic 7.00
10 This Planet Hungers 7.00
11 WS,Starbuck's Dilemma 7.00
12 WS,Memory Ends. 7.00
13 WS,All Out Attack 7.00
14 Radiation Threat 7.00
15 Ship of Crawling Death. 7.00
16 . . . . 7.00
17 Animal on the Loose 7.00
18 Battle For the Forbidden Fruit. . . 7.00
19 Starbuck's Back 7.00
20 Duel to the Death 7.00
21 To Slay a Monster..To Deatroy
  a World 7.00
22 WS,A Love Story?. 7.00
23 Dec., 1981 . . . . 7.00

BATTLETIDE
1990
1 thru 4 F: Death's Head II and
  Killpower . . . . @2.25

BATTLETIDE II
1993
1 Foil embossed cover 3.25
2 thru 8 F: Death's Head II and
  Killpower . . . . @2.25

BEAST
March, 1997
1 (of 3) KG,CNn,F:Karma, Cannonball, V:Viper & Spiral 3.00
2 KG,CNn,V:Spiral. 3.00
3 KG,CNn, concl. 3.00

BEAUTY AND THE BEAST
Jan., 1985
1 DP,Beast & Dazzler,direct 3.00
1a DP,Beast & Dazzler,UPC 3.00

2 DP,Beast & Dazzler 3.00
3 & 4 DP,Beast & Dazzler . . . . . . @3.00

✳ BEAVIS & BUTT-HEAD
March, 1994
1 Based on the MTV Show. 5.00
1a 2nd Printing 2.50
2 Dead from the Neck up 3.50
3 Break out at Burger World. 3.00
4 thru 28 . . . . @2.50
TPB Greatest Hits, rep.#1–#4 . . . . 13.00
TPB Holidazed and Confused 13.00

BEFORE THE FANTASTIC 4:
GRIMM AND LOGAN
May, 2000
1 (of 3) LHa,Wolverine&Thing 3.25
2 LHa,A:Carol Danvers. 3.25
3 LHa,concl. 3.25

REED RICHARDS
July, 2000
1 (of 3) PDa,DFg,V:Dr.Doom 3.25
2 PDa,DFg. 3.25
3 PDa,DFg,concl. 3.25

THE STORMS
Oct., 2000
1 (of 3) TKa,CAd,F:Sue &
  Johnny Storm 3.25
2 V:St. Germaine 3.25
3 TKa,CaD,concl. 3.25

BEST LOVE
Marvel-Manvis Publ., 1949
(Formerly: Sub-Mariner #32)
33 JKu 150.00
34 . . . . 100.00
35 BEv 125.00
36 BEv 125.00

BEST OF MARVEL '96
TPB 224pg. 20.00

BEST WESTERN
June, 1949
58 A:KidColt,BlackRider,Two-Gun
  Kid; Million Dollar Train
  Robbery. 325.00
59 A:BlackRider,KidColt,Two-Gun
  Kid;The Black Rider Strikes. . 300.00
Becomes:

WESTERN OUTLAWS & SHERIFFS
1949
60 PH(c),Hawk Gaither 300.00
61 Ph(c),Pepper Lawson 250.00
62 Murder at Roaring
  House Bridge. 250.00
63 thru 65. . . . . @250.00
66 Hanging. 250.00
67 Cannibalism 250.00
68 thru 72. . . . . @225.00
73 June, 1952 . . . . 225.00

BEWARE
March, 1973
1 Reprints 25.00
2 thru 8 . . . . @20.00
Becomes:

TOMB OF DARKNESS
1974
9 Reprints 30.00
10 thru 22 . . . . @20.00
23 November, 1976 . . . . 25.00

Best Western #58
© Marvel Entertainment Group

BEYOND!
July, 2006
1 DMD,ScK, Nine heroes vs. Space
  Phantom 3.00
2 thru 5 . . . . @3.00

BIBLE TALES FOR YOUNG FOLK
Marvel/Atlas, 1953
1 . . . . 350.00
2 BEv,BK. 250.00
3 . . . . 200.00
4 JeR 225.00
5 . . . . 200.00

BIKER MICE FROM MARS
1993
1 I:Biker Mice 2.25
2 thru 3 . . . . 2.25

BILL & TED'S EXCELLENT COMICS
Dec., 1991
1 From Movie; Wedding Reception 2.25
2 thru 12 . . . . @2.25
1-shot Bill & Ted's Bogus Journey
  Movie Adaption (1991) 3.25

BILLY BUCKSKIN WESTERN
Marvel Atlas, Nov., 1955
1 MD,Tales of the Wild Frontier . 250.00
2 MD,Ambush 150.00
3 MD,AW, Thieves in the Night . 200.00
Becomes:

2-GUN KID
1956
4 SD,A: Apache Kid 200.00
Becomes:

TWO-GUN WESTERN
1956
5 B:Apache Kid,Doc Holiday,
  Kid Colt Outlaw 250.00
6 . . . . 225.00
7 . . . . 225.00
8 RC 200.00
9 AW 200.00
10 . . . . 200.00

11 AW. 225.00
12 Sept., 1957,RC 200.00

BISHOP
1994
1 Mountjoy, foil cover 4.00
2 foil stamped cover 4.00
3 JOs 3.50
4 V:Mountjoy. 3.50

BISHOP:
THE LAST X-MAN
Aug., 1999
1 R:Bishop, 48-page debut. 6.00
2A I:Nom,Link,Jinx & Scorch 2.50
2B variant (c) . . . . @2.50
3 thru 15 . . . . 2.50
16 NMa,Dream'sEnd,pt.3,x-over . . . 8.00

BISHOP: XAVIER'S
SECURITY ENFORCER
Nov., 1997
I (of 3) JOs,SEp. 3.00
2 JOs,SEp,hunted by X.S.E. 3.00
3 JOs,SEp,Bishop v. Rook, concl. . 3.00

BIZARRE ADVENTURES
See: MARVEL PREVIEW

BLACK AXE
1993
1 JR2(c),A:Death's Head II. 3.00
2 JR2(2),A:Sunfire,V:The Hand . . . 3.00
3 A:Death's Head II,V:Mesphisto . . 3.00
4 in ancient Egypt. 3.00
5 KJ(c),In Wakanda 3.00
6 KJ(c),A:Black Panther 3.00
7 KJ(c),A:Black Panther 3.00
8 thru 13 . . . . @3.00

BLACK CAT
[Limited Series]
1 Wld,A:Spider-Man,V:Cardiac,
   I:Faze. 2.25
2 Wld,V:Faze 2.25
3 Wld,Cardiac. 2.25
4 Wld,V:Scar. 2.25

BLACK DRAGON
Epic, May, 1985
1 JBo. 4.00

Black Dragon #3
© Marvel Entertainment Group

2 thru 6 JBo. . . . . @3.00

BLACK GOLIATH
Feb., 1976—Nov., 1976
1 GT,O:Black Goliath,Cont's
   From Powerman #24 . . . . 30.00
2 GT,V:Warhawk 15.00
3 GT,D:Atom-Smasher 15.00
4 KP,V:Stilt-Man 15.00
5 D:Mortag 15.00

BLACK KNIGHT, THE
Marvel Atlas, 1955–56
1 JMn,O: Crusader;The Black
   Knight Rides 1,500.00
2 JMn,Siege on Camelot 900.00
3 JMn,Black Knight Unmasked . 750.00
4 JMn,Betrayed 750.00
5 JMn,SSh,The Invincible Tartar. 750.00

BLACK KNIGHT
June, 1990—Sept., 1990
1 TD,R:Original Black Knight 2.00
2 TD,A:Dreadknight 2.00
3 RB,A:Dr.Strange 2.00
4 RB,TD,A:Dr Strange, Valkyrie . . . 2.00

BLACK KNIGHT: EXODUS
1996
1-shot R:Black Knight,A:Sersi,
   O:Exodus. 2.50

BLACK PANTHER
[1st Series]
Jan., 1977—May, 1979
1 JK,V:Collectors 40.00
2 JK,V:Six Million Year Man 20.00
3 JK,V:Ogar 20.00
4 JK,V:Collectors 20.00
5 JK,V:Yeti 20.00
6 JK,V:Ronin. 20.00
7 JK,V:Mister Little 20.00
8 JK,D:Black Panther 20.00
9 JK,V:Jakarra 20.00
10 JK,V:Jakarra 20.00
11 JK,V:Kilber the Cruel. 20.00
12 JK,V:Kilber the Cruel 20.00
13 JK,V:Kilber the Cruel 20.00
14 JK,A:Avengers,V:Klaw 25.00
15 JK,A:Avengers,V:Klaw 25.00
TPB Black Panther by JK (2005). . 20.00
TPB Vol. 2 Black Panther by JK . . 20.00

BLACK PANTHER
July, 1988—Oct., 1988
[1st Mini-Series]
1 I:Panther Spirit. 4.00
2 V:Supremacists 4.00
3 A:Malaika 4.00
4 V:Panther Spirit 4.00

[2nd Mini-Series]
PANTHER'S PREY
May, 1991
1 DT,A:W'Kabi,V:Solomon Prey . . . 5.00
2 thru 4 DT,V:Solomon Prey . . . . @5.00

BLACK PANTHER
[2nd Series] Sept., 1998
1 CPr,MT,A:T'Challa 6.00
2 CPr,MT,A:Mephisto 3.00
2a variant cover 3.00
3 CPr,MT,JQ,I:Achebe 3.00
4 CPr,MT,JQ,V:Mephisto. 3.00
5 CPr,V:Mephisto 3.00
6 thru 35 CPr. . . . . @2.50
36 CPr,SaV,100-page 4.00
37 thru 56 . . . . @2.50

Black Panther 1st Series #15
© Marvel Entertainment Group

57 thru 63. . . . . @3.00
TPB The Client, 128-page 15.00
TPB Enemy of the State, 224-pg. . 17.00

[3rd Series] Feb., 2005
1 JR2 . . . . 5.00
2 thru 6 JR2 . . . . @3.00
7 thru 17 . . . . @3.00
18 SEa,Bride of the Panther, 48-pg. 4.00
18a variant (c) 4.00
19 thru 22. . . . . @3.00
TPB Who is the Black Panther . . . 15.00
TPB Bad Mutha 11.00
TPB The Bride 15.00

BLACK RIDER
See: ALL WINNERS
COMICS

BLACK RIDER
RIDES AGAIN
Marvel Atlas, Sept., 1957
1 JK,Treachery at Hangman's
   Ridge 350.00

BLACKSTONE,
THE MAGICIAN
May, 1948—Sept., 1948
2 B:Blonde Phantom 1,000.00
3 BO(c),bondage (c). 650.00
4 Bondage(c) 650.00

BLACK WIDOW
Apr. 1999
1 (of 3) Black Widow replaced? . . . 6.00
1a variant cover (1:4) 7.00
2 A:Daredevil 4.00
3 conclusion 4.00
TPB Web of Intrigue, rep. 4.00

BLACK WIDOW
Nov., 2000
1 (of 3) SHp,Natasha vs.Yelena . . . 3.00
2 SHp. 3.00
3 SHp,concl. 3.00
TPB rep. 2 series, 144-page 16.00

BLACK WIDOW
Sept., 2004
1 (of 6) BSz,F:Natasha Romanova. 3.00
2 BSz 3.00

MARVEL

3 thru 6 BSz . . . . @3.00
TPB Homecoming 15.00

BLACK WIDOW: PALE LITTLE SPIDER
Marvel Max, April, 2002
1 (of 3) F:Belova 3.25
2 . . . . 3.25
3 concl. 3.25

BLACK WIDOW 2
Sept., 2005
1 (of 6) BSz,Things They Say 3.00
2 thru 6 BSz,Things They Say
   About Her. . . . . @3.00
TPB 16.00

BLACKWULF
1994–95
1 AMe,Embossied(c),I:Mammoth,
   Touchstone,Toxin,D:Pelops,
   V:Tantalus, ... 3.00
2 AMe,I:Sparrow,Wildwind 2.25
3 AMe,I:Scratch 2.25
4 AMe,I:Giant-man 2.25
5 AMe 2.25
6 AMe,Tantalus 2.25
7 AMe,V:Tantalus 2.25
8 AMe 2.25
9 Seven Worlds of Tantalus,pt.1
   A:Daredevil 2.25
10 Seven Worlds of Tantalus,pt.2,
   last issue 2.25

BLADE, THE VAMPIRE HUNTER
1994–95
1 Foil(c),Clv(i),R:Dracula 3.50
2 Clv(i),V:Dracula 2.50
3 Clv(i) 2.50
4 Clv(i) 2.50
5 Clv(i) 2.50
6 Clv(i) 2.50
7 Clv(i) 2.50
8 Bible John, Morbius 2.50
9 . . . . 2.50
10 R:Dracula 2.50
11 Dracula Untombed,pt.2 . . . . 2.50

BLADE
Sept., 1998
1 (of 6) DMG,40-page, photo(c) . . . 3.50
1a variant cover (1:4) 3.50
2 DMG,A:Morbius,Dominique 3.00
2a variant cover 3.00
3 DMG 3.00
4 DMG,F:Morbius 3.00
1-shot Blade: Crescent City Blues,
   MPe,V:Deacon Frost (1998) . . . 3.50
1-shot DMG, movie tie-in (1998) . . 3.00
1-shot movie adaptation,48 pg 6.00
TPB Duel with Dracula (2002) 18.00

BLADE: VAMPIRE HUNTER
Oct., 1999
1 (of 6) BS, 48-pg. 4.00
2 BS 3.00
3 BS,V:Reaper 3.00
4 BS,V:Hrolf 3.00
5 BS,V:Reaper 3.00
6 BS,V:Reaper, concl. 3.00

BLADE
Marvel Max, March, 2002
1 StP,V:Tryks. 3.25
2 StP,F:Tryks,Seven 3.25

3 StP,date with Susan. 3.25
4 StP,Fofo's missing fingers 3.25
5 StP,V:Rowks. 3.25
6 horror hits home 3.25
GN Bloodhunt, movie adapt. 6.00

BLADE
Sept., 2006
1 HC, A:Spider-Man 3.00
2 HC, V:Dr. Doom 3.00
3 HC 3.00

BLADE RUNNER
Oct., 1982
1 AW, Movie Adaption 4.00
2 AW, ... 4.00

BLAZE
[Limited Series], 1993–94
1 HMe(s),RoW,A:Clara Menninger . 2.50
2 HMe(s),RoW,I:Initiate. 2.50
3 HMe(s),RoW, ... 2.50
4 HMe(s),RoW,D:Initiate 2.50
[Regular Series], Aug., 1994
1 HMz,LHa,foil (c). 3.50
2 thru 5 HMz,LHa . . . . @2.50
6 thru 12 . . . . @2.50

Blaze Carson #4
© *Marvel Entertainment Group*

BLAZE CARSON
Sept., 1948
1 SSh(c),Fight,Lawman
   or Crawl 325.00
2 Guns Roar on Boot Hill 225.00
3 A:Tex Morgan 225.00
4 SSh,A:Two-Gun Kid 225.00
5 A:Tex Taylor 250.00
Becomes:

REX HART
1949
6 CCB,Ph(c),B:Rex Hart,
   A:Black Rider 300.00
7 Ph(c),Mystery at Bar-2 Ranch 200.00
8 Ph(c),The Hombre Who
   Killed His Friends 200.00
Becomes:

WHIP WILSON
1950
9 Ph(c),B:Whip Wilson,O:Bullet;
   Duel to the Death 800.00
10 Ph(c),Wanted for Murder 400.00
11 Ph(c) 400.00
Becomes:

GUNHAWK, THE
1950
12 The Redskin's Revenge 350.00
13 GT,The Man Who Murdered
   Gunhawk 300.00
14 . . . . 250.00
15 . . . . 250.00
16 EC 250.00
17 . . . . 250.00
18 JMn,Dec., 1951. . . . . 250.00

BLAZE OF GLORY
Dec., 1999
1 (of 4) JOs,F:John Woo 3.00
2 JOs 3.00
3 JOs 3.00
4 JOs,concl. 3.00
TPB westerns, 96-pg. (2002) 11.50

BLAZE, THE WONDER COLLIE
Oct., 1949
2 Ph(c),Blaze-Son of Fury 300.00
3 Ph(c), Lonely Boy;Feb.,1950 . . 300.00

BLINK
Dec., 2000
1 (of 4) SLo,AKu(c). 3.25
2 SLo,Age of Apocalypse story. . . . 3.25
3 SLo,AKu(c),in love. 3.25
4 SLo,AKu(c),V:Blastaar 3.25

BLONDE PHANTOM
See: ALL-SELECT COMICS

BLOOD
Feb., 1988—April, 1988
1 . . . . 6.00
2 thru 4 . . . . @5.00

BLOOD & GLORY
1993
1 KJ Cap & the Punisher 6.00
2 KJ Cap & the Punisher 6.00
3 KJ Cap & the Punisher 6.00

BLOODLINES
Epic, 1992
1 F:Kathy Grant-Peace Corps 6.00

BLOODSEED
1993
1 LSh,I:Bloodseed 2.25
2 LSh,V:Female Bloodseed 2.25

BLOODSTONE
Oct., 2001
1 DAn,ALa,SHa,F:Elsa Bloodstone 3.25
2 DAn,ALa,SHa,F:Dracula 3.25
3 DAn,ALa,SHa,Living Mummy . . . 3.25
4 DAn,ALa,SHa, concl. 3.25

BOOK OF LOST SOULS
Icon, Oct., 2005
1 thru 3 MSz,CDo,Dragons in the
   Dishwater. . . . . @3.00
4 thru 6 MSz,CDo . . . . @3.00
TPB 17.00

BOOK OF THE DEAD
1993–94
1 thru 5 Horror rep . . . . @4.00

BOOKS OF DOOM
Nov., 2005
1 F:Victor von Doom, early years . . 3.00
2 thru 6 . . . . @3.00

BORN
June, 2003
1 (of 4) GEn(s),O:Punisher 6.00
2 GEn(s),Capt. Frank Castle 4.00
3 GEn(s),attacked 4.00
4 GEn(s),concl. 4.00
TPB Punisher: Born (2004) 14.00

BOZZ CHRONICLES, THE
Epic, Dec., 1985
1 thru 5 . . . . @3.00
6 May, 1986 . . . . 3.00

BRATS BIZARRE
Epic, *Heavy Hitters* 1994
1 with trading card 3.25
2 thru 4 with trading card . . . . . @2.75

BREAK THE CHAIN
1 KB,KRS-One,w/audio tape 7.00

BROTHERHOOD, THE
May, 2001
1 BSz(c),F:Magneto 2.75
2A BSz(c), ... 2.50
2B variant cover 2.50
3 BSz(c) 2.50
4 JP,BWS(c) 2.50
5 JP,GF(c) 2.50
6 JP,GF(c) message to daddy 2.50
7 SeP,KW, X speaks out. 2.50
8 SeP,KW, ... 2.50
9 SeP,KW, final issue 2.50

Brute Force #1
© Marvel Entertainment Group

BRUTE FORCE
Aug., 1990
1 JD/JSt 2.50
2 . . . . 2.50
3 . . . . 2.50
4 November, 1990 . . . . 2.50

B-SIDES
Sept., 2002
1 SK, super-team from New Jersey 3.00
2 SK, F:Fantastic Four 3.00

3 SK, F:Fantastic Four 3.00

BUCK DUCK
Marvel Atlas, June, 1953
1 (fa) stories 200.00
2 and 3 . . . . @100.00
4 Dec., 1953 . . . . 100.00

BUCKAROO BANZAI
Dec., 1984
1 Movie Adaption 3.00
2 Conclusion, Feb., 1985 . . . . 2.50

BUG
1997
1-shot 48pg. 3.25

BULLET POINTS
Nov., 2006
1 . . . . 3.00

BULLSEYE: GREATEST HITS
Sept., 2004
1 (of 5) SDi,O:Bullseye 3.00
2 thru 5 SDi,F:Punisher. . . . . @3.00
TPB Bullseye: Greatest Hits 14.00

BULLWINKLE & ROCKY
Star, Nov., 1987
1 EC&AM,Based on 1960's TV
   Series 4.00
2 thru 9 EC&AM . . . . @3.00
TPB, Bullwinkle & Rocky Collection
   AM,early stories 5.00

CABLE
[Limited Series], 1992
1 JR2,DGr,V:Mutant Liberation
   Front,A:Weapon X. 4.00
2 JR2,DGr,V:Stryfe,O:Weapon X . . 3.00
[Regular Series], 1993
1 B:FaN(s),ATi, O:Cable,V:New
   Canaanites,A:Stryfe,foil(c). 5.00
2 ATi,V:Stryfe. 4.00
3 ATi,A:Six Pack 4.00
4 ATi,A:Six Pack 4.00
5 DaR,V:Sinsear 4.00
6 DT,A:Tyler,Zero,Askani,
   Mr.Sinister,C:X-Men. 4.00
7 V:Tyler,A:Askani,X-Men,Domino . 4.00
8 O:Cable,V:Tyler,A:X-Men,Cable is
   Nathan Summers 4.00
9 MCW,B:Killing Field,A:Excalibur,
   V:Omega Red 4.00
10 MCW,A:Acolytes,Omega Red. . . 4.00
11 MCW,E:Killing Field,D:Katu . . . 4.00
12 SLo(s),B:Fear & Loathing,
   V:Senyaka 4.00
13 V:D'Spayre 4.00
14 V:S'yM. 4.00
15 A:Thorn 4.00
16 Foil(c),Dbl-size,A:Jean,Scott
   Logan,V:Phalanx 9.00
16a Newsstand ed. 3.00
17 Deluxe ed. 3.00
17a Newsstand ed. 2.25
18 Deluxe ed. 3.00
18a Newsstand ed. 2.25
19 Deluxe ed. 3.00
19a Newsstand ed. 3.00
20 V:Legion, Deluxe ed. w/card. . . . 5.00
20a Newsstand ed. 2.25
21 Cable makes tough decisions,
   A:Domino. 3.00
22 V:Fortress 3.00
23 IaC,A:Domino 3.00
24 F:Blaquesmith. 3.00

25 IaC,SHa,F:Cable's Wife,foil(c) . . 5.00
26 Tries to return to X-Mansion 3.00
27 IaC, A:Domino. 3.00
28 IaC,SHa,concl. war in Genosha . 3.00
29 . . . . 3.00
30 . . . . 3.00
31 IaC, cont.X-Men/Cable war. 3.00
32 Onslaught saga. 3.50
33 Onslaught saga. 3.00
34 Onslaught saga. 3.00
35 Onslaught saga. 3.00
36 . . . . 3.00
37 JLb,IaC,SHa,V:Askani'son,Kane. 3.00
38 JLb,IaC,SHa,V:PSycho-Man,
   A:Kane. 3.00
39 JLb,IaC,SHa,V:Psycho-Man . . . 3.00
40 TDz,IaC,SHa,A:Renee Majcomb 3.00
41 TDz,SHa,F:Bishop 3.00
42 TDz,RGr,SHa,The Prophecy
   of the Twelve 3.00
43 TDz,RGr,Images of Nathan's
   past 3.00
44 TDz,RGr,SHa,A:Madelyne Pryor
   (Cable's mom). 3.00
45 JeR,RGr,Zero Tolerance,
   No Escape,pt.2 . . . . 3.00
46 JeR,RGr,SHa,Zero Tolerance,
   No Escape, pt.2 (of 3). 3.00
47 JeR,RGr,SHa, Operation Zero
   Tolerance, V:Batsion 3.00
48 JeR,SHa,V:Hellfire Club 3.00
49 JeR,SHa,V:Hellfire Club 3.00
50 JeR,SHa,A:Cyclops, Phoenix,
   Union Jack, 48pg. 4.00
51 JeR,Hellfire Hunt. 2.50
52 JeR,Hellfire Hunt, pt.5. . . . . 2.50
53 JoC,Hellfire Hunt, concl. 2.50
54 JoC,A:Black Panther,V:Klaw. . . 2.50
55 JoC,A:Irene Merryweather,
   Domino 2.50
56 JoC,V:Stilt-Man & Hydro-Man . . 2.50
57 JoC,Cable powers altered by
   EMP wave 2.50
58 JoC,Persecution, pt.1 . . . . 2.50
59 JoC,I:Agent 18,V:Zzaxx 2.50
60 JoC,Nemesis Contract,pt.2. . . . 2.50
61 JoC,Nemesis Contract,pt.3. . . . 2.50
62 JoC,Nemesis Contract,pt.4. . . . 2.50
63 JoC,Blood Brothers,pt.2,x-over. . 2.50
64 JoC,O:Cable 2.50
65 JoC,Millennium countdown. 2.50
66 JoC,Sign of the End Times,pt.1 . 2.50
67 JoC,Sign of the End Times,pt.2 . 2.50
68 JoC,Sign of the End Times,pt.3 . 2.50
69 JoC,A:Blaquesmith,Archangel . . 2.50

Cable #39
© Marvel Entertainment Group

70 JoC,A:Archangel............ 2.50
71 RLd,abandons his destiny,
with RLd poster........... 2.50
72 RLd,reunited with X-force...... 2.50
73 RLd,reunited 2.50
74 V:Caliban 2.50
75 RLd,Apocalypse........... 11.00
76 Apocalypse The 12:pt.6 ...... 8.00
77 Ages of Apocalypse,pt.2 ..... 15.00
78 mutant no more............. 3.00
79 X-Men: Revolution 3.00
79a variant (c) 3.50
80 Apocalypse gone 2.50
81 The Undying 2.50
82 Nathan Summers, murderer?... 2.50
83 R:Domino 2.50
84 Phoenix & Beast........... 2.50
85 Mother Askani, Gaunt....... 2.50
86 Gaunt 2.50
87 Dream'sEnd,pt.2,x-over 8.00
88 F:Nightcrawler.............. 2.50
89 in Washington DC.......... 2.50
90 Dark Sisterhood 2.50
91 Dark Sisterhood 2.50
92 Cable quits X-Men? 2.50
93 V:Dark Sisterhood.......... 2.50
94 V:Dark Sisterhood.......... 2.50
95 V:Dark Sisterhood,concl. 2.50
96 Old Man Coll.............. 2.50
97 Path of Most Resistance..... 2.50
98 Shining Path 2.50
99 V:Shining Path 2.50
100 V:Techno-OrganicVirus,64-pg. . 4.50
101 Macedonian Plot 2.50
102 Albanians' deadly plan 2.50
103 shot in the head 2.50
104 on the wrong side? 2.50
105 in Rio................... 2.50
106 In Kazakhstan 2.50
107 final issue 2.50
Ann. '98 AOI(c) F:Cable vs. Machine
Man, O:Bastion 3.00
Ann.1999 48-page 3.50
Minus 1 Spec., TDz,JeR, flashback. 2.00
GN Cable/Wolverine Guts 'N' Glory. 6.00
Cable: Second Genesis......... 4.00
TPB Cable,rep.New Mutants 16.00
TPB The Shining Path, 144-pg... 16.00
TPB Vol.2 The End (2002)...... 15.00

CABLE & DEADPOOL
Nov., 2003
1 RLd(c),Looks Could Kill,pt.1 .... 3.50
2 RLd(c),Looks Could Kill,pt.2 .... 3.50
3 RLd(c),Looks Could Kill,pt.3 .... 3.00
4 RLd(c),Looks Could Kill,pt.4 .... 3.00
5 RLd(c),Looks Could Kill,pt.5 .... 3.00
6 Looks Could Kill,pt.6 .... 3.00
7 Passion of the Cable,pt.1 ...... 3.00
8 Passion of the Cable,pt.2 ...... 3.00
9 Passion of the Cable,pt.3 ...... 3.00
10 Passion of the Cable,pt.4 ..... 3.00
11 FaN,Thirty Pieces,pt.1 .... 3.00
12 FaN,Thirty Pieces,pt.2 .... 3.00
13 A Murder in Paradise,pt.1 ..... 3.00
14 A Murder in Paradise,pt.2 ..... 3.00
15 Enema of the State,pt.1 ...... 3.00
16 Enema of the State,pt.2 ...... 3.00
17 Enema of the State,pt.3 ...... 3.00
18 Enema of the State,pt.4 ...... 3.00
19 FaN,Why, When I Was Your Age 3.00
20 FaN, Bosom Buddies 3.00
21 FaN, Bosom Buddies 3.00
22 FaN,Bosom Buddier 3.00
23 FaN,Bosom Buddies......... 3.00
24 FaN,V:Spider-Man 3.00
25 FaN,Living Legends 3.00
26 FaN,Born Again, pt.1 .... 3.00
27 FaN,Born Again, pt.2 .... 3.00
28 FaN, ... 3.00
29 FaN, ... 3.00
30 FaN,The Hero Hunter........ 3.00

31 FaN,For King and Country 3.00
32 FaN, ... 3.00
33 FaN,RLd(c) Domino Principle... 3.00
TPB Vol. 1: If Looks Could Kill.... 15.00
TPB Vol. 2: The Burnt Offering .. 15.00
TPB Vol. 3:The Human Race 15.00
TPB Vol. 4 Bosom Buddies 15.00

CABLE & X-FORCE
1995–97
Cable & X-Force '95 Spec. 4.00
Cable & X-Force '96 Spec.48pg.... 3.50
Cable & X-Force '97 Spec.#1
JFM,CJ,V:Malekith,48pg. 3.50

CADILLACS & DINOSAURS
Epic, Nov., 1990
1 Rep.Xenozoic Tales............ 5.00
2 thru 6 Rep.Xenozoic Tales.... @3.00

Cage #5
© Marvel Entertainment Group

CAGE
1992–93
1 DT,R:Luke Cage,I:Hardcore, ... 3.00
2 thru 20 .... @2.50

CAGE
Marvel Max, Feb., 2002
1 (of 5) RCo,Justice isn't cheap ... 5.00
2 RCo,teen-age girl murdered 4.00
3 RCo,..................... 4.00
4 RCo,secret shame............ 4.00
5 RCo,Hammerhead............. 4.00
TPB RCo 20.00
TPB 13.00

CALL, THE
April, 2003
1 PO, everyday heroes.......... 2.25
2 thru 4 PO .... @2.25
TPB Vol. 1, series rep............ 9.00

CALL OF DUTY, THE: THE BROTHER HOOD
June, 2002
1 (of 6) ATi,F:FDNY,48-pg. 4.00
2 thru 6 ATi,F:FDNY .... @2.50
The Call of Duty, Must Have ed. ... 3.00
TPB Vol. I................... 15.00
TPB Vol. II: Precinct & Wagon.... 15.00

THE CALL OF DUTY: THE PRECINCT
July, 2002
1 (of 5) TMd,F:NYPD 3.00
2 thru 5 TMd .... @2.50

THE CALL OF DUTY: THE WAGON
Marvel Aug., 2002
1 (of 4) F:NYC EMS 2.50
2 thru 4 .... @2.50

CAMP CANDY
May, 1990
1 thru 6, Oct., 1990 .... @4.00

CAPTAIN AMERICA COMICS
Timely/Atlas, 1941–54
1 S&K,SSh,JK(c),Hitler(c),I&O:Capt.
America & Bucky,A:Red Skull,
B:Hurricane, Tuk 165,000.00
2 S&K,RC,AAv,Hitler(c),
I:Circular Shield;Trapped
in the Nazi Stronghold ... 25,000.00
3 ASh(c),S&K,RC,AAv,Stan Lee's
1st Text,A:Red Skull,
Bondage(c) 20,000.00
4 ASh(c),S&K,AAv,Horror
Hospital 12,000.00
5 S&K,AAv,SSh,Ringmaster's
Wheel of Death 10,000.00
6 S&K,AAv,SSh,O:Father Time,
E:Tuk 10,000.00
7 S&K,SSh,A: Red Skull .. 12,000.00
8 S&K, The Tomb 8,000.00
9 S&K,RC,V:Black Talon 8,000.00
10 S&K,RC,Chamber
of Horrors............. 8,000.00
11 AAv,SSh,E:Hurricane;Feuding
Mountaneers........... 6,500.00
12 AAv,SSh,B:Imp,E:Father Time;
Pygmie's Terror......... 6,000.00
13 AAv,O:Secret Stamp;All Out
For America 6,500.00
14 AAv,V:Japs;Pearl Harbor
Symbol cover 6,500.00
15 AAv,Den of Doom 6,500.00
16 AAv,A:R.Skull;CapA
Unmasked 7,500.00
17 AAv,I:Fighting Fool;
Graveyard............. 5,500.00
18 AAv,SSh,V:Japanese 5,500.00
19 AAv,V:Ghouls,
B:Human Torch......... 5,000.00
20 AAv,A:Sub-Mariner,V:Nazis . 5,000.00
21 SSh(c),Bucky Captured 4,500.00
22 SSh(c),V:Japanese 4,500.00
23 SSh(c),V:Nazis.......... 4,500.00
24 SSh(c),V:Black
Dragon Society.......... 4,500.00
25 SSh(c),V:Japs;Drug Story .. 4,500.00
26 ASh(c),SSh,V:Nazi Fleet 4,300.00
27 ASh(c),SSh,AAv,CapAm&Russians
V:Nazis, E:Secret Stamp .. 4,300.00
28 ASh(c),SSh,Nazi Torture
Chamber.............. 4,300.00
29 ASh(c),SSh,V:Nazis;French
Underground.......... 4,300.00
30 SSh(c),Bucky Captured 4,300.00
31 ASh(c),Bondage(c)....... 4,000.00
32 SSh(c),V: Japanese Airforce 4,000.00
33 ASh(c),V:Nazis;BrennerPass 4,000.00
34 SSh(c),Bondage(c) 4,000.00
35 SSh(c),CapA in Japan 4,000.00
36 SSh(c),V:Nazis;Hitler(c).... 5,500.00
37 ASh(c),SSh,Captain America
in Berlin, A:Red Skull 5,000.00
38 ASh(c),V:Japs;Bondage(c).. 4,200.00

Captain America #7
© Marvel Entertainment Group

39 ASh(c),SSh,V:Japs;Boulder
   Dam 4,200.00
40 SSh(c),V:Japs;Ammo Depot 4,200.00
41 ASh(c),FinalJapaneseWar(c) 4,200.00
42 ASh(c),SSh,V:BankRobbers 4,000.00
43 ASh(c),V:Gangsters 4,000.00
44 ASh(c),V:Gangsters 4,000.00
45 ASh(c),V:Bank Robbers. . . . 4,000.00
46 ASh(c),Holocaust(c) 4,500.00
47 ASh(c),Final Nazi War(c) . . . 4,500.00
48 ASh(c),V:Robbers 3,500.00
49 ASh(c),V:Saboteurs 3,500.00
50 ASh(c),V:Gorilla Gang 3,600.00
51 ASh(c),V:Gangsters 3,500.00
52 ASh(c),V:AtomBombThieves 3,500.00
53 ASh(c),V:Burglars 3,500.00
54 ASh(c),TV Studio,
   V:Gangsters 3,500.00
55 SSh,V:Counterfeiters 3,500.00
56 SSh(c),V:Art Theives 3,500.00
57 SSh,AAv,Symbolic CapA(c) . 3,500.00
58 ASh(c),V:Bank Robbers. . . . 3,000.00
59 SSh(c)O:CapA Retold;Private
   Life of Captain America . . . 5,000.00
60 SSh,V:The Human Fly 3,000.00
61 SSh(c),V:Red Skull;
   Bondage(c). 6,000.00
62 SSh(c),Kingdom of Terror . . 3,000.00
63 SSh(c),AAv,I&O:Asbestos Lady;
   The Parrot Strikes. 3,100.00
64 SSh,Diamonds Spell Doom . 3,200.00
65 SSh,AAv,Friends Turn Foes 3,200.00
66 SSh,O:Golden Girl;Bucky
   Shot 3,300.00
67 SSh,E:Toro(in Human Torch);
   Golden Girl Team-Up 3,300.00
68 A:Golden Girl;Riddle of
   the Living Dolls. 3,200.00
69 Weird Tales of the Wee
   Males, A:Sun Girl 3,200.00
70 A:Golden Girl,Sub-Mariner,
   Namora;Worlds at War. . . . 3,200.00
71 A:Golden Girl; Trapped 3,200.00
72 AAv,Murder in the Mind 3,200.00
73 The Outcast of Time 3,200.00
74 A:Red Skull;Capt.America's
   Weird Tales. 10,000.00
75 Thing in the Chest 3,200.00
76 JR(c),Capt.America,Commie
   Smasher. 3,200.00
77 Capt.A,Commie Smasher . . 2,000.00
78 JR(c),V:Communists 2,000.00

CAPTAIN AMERICA
Prev: Tales of Suspense
April, 1968

100 JK,A:Avengers 600.00
101 JK,I:4th Sleeper 200.00
102 JK,V:Red Skull,4th Sleeper . 200.00
103 JK,V:Red Skull 200.00
104 JK,DA,JSo,V:Red Skull. . . . 200.00
105 JK,DA,A:Batroc. 150.00
106 JK,Cap.Goes Wild 150.00
107 JK,Red Skull 150.00
108 JK,Trapster 150.00
109 JK,O:Captain America 250.00
110 JSo,JSt,A:Hulk,Rick Jones
   in Bucky Costume 250.00
111 JSo,JSt,I:Man Killer 250.00
112 JK,GT,Album 125.00
113 JSo,TP,Avengers,
   D:Madame Hydra 200.00
114 JR,SB,C:Avengers 75.00
115 JB,SB,A:Red Skull 75.00
116 GC,JSt,A:Avengers 75.00
117 JR(c),GC,JSt,I:Falcon 100.00
118 JR(c),GC,JSt,A:Falcon 30.00
119 GC,JSt,O:Falcon 30.00
120 GC,JSt,A:Falcon 30.00
121 GC,JSt,V:Man Brute 25.00
122 GC,JSt,Scorpion 22.00
123 GC,JSt,A:NickFury,
   V:Suprema. 22.00
124 GC,JSt,I:Cyborg 22.00
125 GC,Mandarin. 22.00
126 JK&BEv(c),GC,A:Falcon. . . . 22.00
127 GC,WW,A:Nick Fury 22.00
128 GC,V:Satan's Angels 22.00
129 GC,Red Skull 22.00
130 GC,I:Batroc. 22.00
131 GC,V:Hood 22.00
132 GC,A:Bucky Barnes 22.00
133 GC,O:Modok,B:Capt.America/
   Falcon Partnership 22.00
134 GC,V:Stone Face 22.00
135 JR(c),GC,TP,A:Nick Fury . . . 22.00
136 CC,BEv,V:Tyrannus 22.00
137 GC,BEv,A:Spider Man 30.00
138 JR,A:Spider-Man. 28.00
139 JR,Falcon solo 22.00
140 JR,O:Grey Gargoyle 22.00
141 JR,JSt,V:Grey Gargoyle 20.00
142 JR,JSt,Nick Fury 20.00
143 JR,Red Skull 22.00
144 GM,JR,N:Falcon,V:Hydra . . . 20.00
145 GK,JR,V:Hydra 20.00
146 JR(c),SB,V:Hydra 18.00
147 GK(c),SB,V:Hydra. 18.00
148 SB,JR,Red Skull 18.00
149 GK(c),SB,JM,V:Batroc 18.00
150 K&R(c),SB,V:The Stranger . . . 18.00
151 SB,V:Mr.Hyde 18.00
152 SB,V:Scorpion,Mr.Hyde 18.00
153 SB,JM,V:50's Cap. 18.00
154 SB,V:50's Cap. 18.00
155 SB,FMc,O:50's Cap 18.00
156 SB,FMc,V:50's Cap. 18.00
157 SB,I:The Viper 18.00
158 SB,V:The Viper 18.00
159 SB,V:PlantMan,Porcupine . . . 18.00
160 SB,FMc,V:Solarr. 18.00
161 SB,V:Dr.Faustus 18.00
162 JSn(c),SB,V:Dr.Faustus 18.00
163 SB,I:Serpent Squad 18.00
164 JR(c),I:Nightshade 18.00
165 SB,FMc,V:Yellow Claw 18.00
166 SB,FMc,V:Yellow Claw 18.00
167 SB,V:Yellow Claw 18.00
168 SB,I&O:Phoenix
   (2nd Baron Zemo) 18.00
169 SB,FMc,C:Black Panther 18.00
170 K&R(c),SB,C:Black Panther . . 18.00
171 JR(c),SB,A:Black Panther. . . . 18.00
172 GK(c),SB,C:X-Men 22.00

Captain America #145
© Marvel Entertainment Group

173 GK(c),SB,A:X-Men 25.00
174 GK(c),SB,A:X-Men 25.00
175 SB,A:X-Men 25.00
176 JR(c),SB,O:Capt.America. . . . 18.00
177 JR(c),SB,A:Lucifer,Beast 15.00
178 SB,A:Lucifer 15.00
179 SB,A:Hawkeye 15.00
180 GK(c),SB,I:1st Nomad(Cap) . . 25.00
181 GK(c),SB,I&O:New Cap 20.00
182 FR,Madam Hydra 10.00
183 GK(c),FR,R:Cap,D:New Cap . 15.00
184 K&R(c),HT,A:Red Skull 10.00
185 GK(c),SB,FR,V:Red Skull 10.00
186 GK(c),FR,O:Falcon 15.00
187 K&R(c),FR,V:Druid 10.00
188 GK(c),SB,V:Druid 10.00
189 GK(c),FR,V:Nightshade 10.00
190 CK(o),FR,A:Nightshade 10.00
191 FR,A:Stilt Man,N.Fury 10.00
192 JR(c),FR,A:Dr.Faustus 10.00
193 JR(c),JK,`Mad Bomb' 20.00
194 JK,I:Gen.Heshin 22.00
195 JK,1984. . . . . 22.00
196 JK,Madbomb. 22.00
197 JK,Madbomb. 22.00
198 JK,Madbomb. 22.00
199 JK,Madbomb. 22.00
200 JK,Madbomb. 20.00
201 JK,Epilogue. 15.00
202 JK,Night People 15.00
203 JK,Night People 15.00
204 JK,I:Argon 15.00
205 JK,V:Argon 15.00
206 JK,I:Swine 15.00
207 JK,V:Swine 15.00
208 JK,I:Arnim Zola,D:Swine. 15.00
209 JK,O:Arnim Zola,I:Primus 15.00
210 JK,A:Red Skull 15.00
211 JK,A:Red Skull 15.00
212 JK,A:Red Skull 15.00
213 JK,I:Night Flyer 15.00
214 JK,D:Night Flyer 15.00
215 GT,Redwing 10.00
216 Reprint,JK 10.00
217 JB, I:Quasar(Marvel Boy)
   I:Vamp 10.00
218 SB,A:Iron Man 6.00
219 SB,JSt,V:TheCorporation 6.00
220 SB,D:L.Dekker 6.00
221 SB,Ameridroid. 6.00
222 SB,I:Animus(Vamp). 6.00
223 SB,Animus 6.00
224 MZ,V:Animus 6.00
225 SB,A:Nick Fury 6.00

MARVEL

#	Description	Price
226	SB,A:Nick Fury	6.00
227	SB,A:Nick Fury	6.00
228	SB,Constrictor.	6.00
229	SB,R:SuperAgents of Shield.	6.00
230	SB,A:Hulk	8.00
231	SB,DP,A:Grand Director	6.00
232	SB,DP,V:Grand Director	6.00
233	SB,DP,D:Sharon Carter	6.00
234	SB,DP,A:Daredevil	6.00
235	SB,FM,A:Daredevil	8.00
236	SB,V:Dr.Faustus	6.00
237	SB,'From the Ashes'.	6.00
238	SB,V:Hawk Riders	6.00
239	JBy(c),SB,V:Hawk Riders	6.00
240	SB,V:A Guy Named Joe	6.00
241	A:Punisher.	25.00
242	JSt,A:Avengers	6.00
243	GP(c),RB,V:Adonis	6.00
244	TS,'A Monster Berserk'.	6.00
245	CI,JRn,Nazi Hunter	6.00
246	GP(c),JBi,V:Joe	6.00
247	JBy,V:BaronStrucker	10.00
248	JBy,JRu,Dragon Man	10.00
249	JBy,O:Machinesmith, A:Air-Walker	10.00
250	JBy,Cap for Pres.	10.00
251	JBy,V:Mr.Hyde.	10.00
252	JBy,V:Batrok	10.00
253	JBy,V:Baron Blood	10.00
254	JBy,D:B.Blood,UnionJack,I:3rd Union Jack.	10.00
255	JBy,40th Anniv.,O:Cap	10.00
256	GC,V:Demon Druid	3.50
257	A:Hulk	3.50
258	MZ,V:Blockbuster	3.50
259	MZ,V:Dr. Octopus	3.50
260	AM,In Jail	3.50
261	MZ,A:Nomad.	4.00
262	MZ,V:Ameridroid	3.50
263	MZ,V:Red Skull	3.50
264	MZ,X-Men	4.00
265	MZ,A:Spider-Man,N.Fury	3.50
266	MZ,A:Spider-Man	3.50
267	MZ,V:Everyman	3.00
268	MZ,A:Defenders(x-over from Def.#106).	3.00
269	MZ,A:Team America	3.00
270	MZ,V:Tess-One	3.00
271	MZ,V:Mr.X	3.00
272	MZ,I:Vermin.	3.50
273	MZ,A:Nick Fury	3.00
274	MZ,D:SamSawyer.	3.00
275	MZ,V:Neo-Nazis	3.00
276	MZ,V:Baron Zemo.	3.00
277	MZ,V:Baron Zemo.	3.00
278	MZ,V:Baron Zemo.	3.00
279	MZ,V:Primus	3.00
280	MZ,V:Scarecrow	3.00
281	MZ,A:Spider Woman, R:'50's Bucky.	3.00
282	MZ,I:2nd Nomad.	6.00
282a	(second primting)	2.50
283	MZ,A:Viper	4.00
284	SB,Nomad.	3.00
285	MZ,V:Porcupine	3.00
286	MZ,V:Deathlok	5.00
287	MZ,V:Deathlok	5.00
288	MZ,V:Deathlok,D:Hellinger	5.00
289	MZ,A:Red Skull	3.00
290	JBy(c),RF,A:Falcon	3.00
291	JBy(c),HT,V:Tumbler	3.00
292	I&O:Black Crow	3.00
293	V:Mother Superior.	3.00
294	R:Nomad.	3.00
295	V:Sisters of Sin	3.00
296	V:Baron Zemo.	4.00
297	O:Red Skull.	4.00
298	V:Red Skull.	4.00
299	V:Red Skull.	3.00
300	D:Red Skull.	4.00
301	PNe,A:Avengers	3.00
302	PNe,I:Machete,V:Batroc	3.00
303	PNe,V:Batroc	3.00
304	PNe,V:Stane Armor.	3.00
305	PNe,A:Capt.Britain,V:Modred	3.00
306	PNe,A:Capt.Britain,V:Modred	3.00
307	PNe,I:Madcap	3.00
308	PNe,I:Armadillo, Secret WarsII.	3.00
309	PNe,V:Madcap	3.00
310	PNe,V:Serpent Society,I:Cotton Mouth,Diamondback	3.00
311	PNe,V:Awesome Android	3.00
312	PNe,I:Flag Smasher	3.00
313	PNe,D:Modok	3.00
314	PNe,A:Nighthawk	3.00
315	PNe,V:Serpent Society	3.00
316	PNe,A:Hawkeye	3.00
317	PNe,I:Death-Throws	3.00
318	PNe,V&D:Blue Streak	3.00
319	PNe,V:Scourge,D:Vamp	3.00
320	PNe,V:Scourge	3.00
321	PNe,V:Flagsmasher, I:Ultimatum	3.00
322	PNe,V:Flagsmasher	3.00
323	PNe,I:Super Patriot (US Agent)	5.00
324	PNe,V:Whirlwind,Trapster.	3.00
325	I:Slug,A:Nomad.	3.00
326	V:Dr.Faustus	3.00
327	MZ(c)V:SuperPatriot	4.00
328	MZ(c),I:Demolition Man	3.00
329	MZ(c),A:Demolition Man	3.00
330	A:Night Shift,Shroud	3.00
331	A:Night Shift,Shroud	3.00
332	BMc,Rogers resigns	7.00
333	B:John Walker Becomes 6th Captain America	5.00
334	I:4th Bucky	5.00
335	V:Watchdogs.	4.00
336	A:Falcon	3.00
337	TMo,I:The Captain	3.00
338	KD,AM,V:Professor Power	3.00
339	KD,TD,Fall of Mutants, V:Famine.	3.00
340	KD,AM,A:Iron Man,	3.00
341	KD,AM,I:Battlestar,A:Viper	3.00
342	KD,AM,A:D-Man,Falcon, Nomad,Viper	3.00
343	KD,AM,A:D-Man,Falcon, Nomad.	3.00
344	KD,AM,A:D-Man,Nomad.	4.00
345	KD,AM,V:Watchdogs	4.00
346	KD,AM,V:Resistants	4.00
347	KD,AM,V:RWinger&LWinger.	4.00
348	KD,AM,V:Flag Smasher	4.00
349	KD,AM,V:Flag Smasher	4.00
350	KD,AM,doub-size,Rogers Ret. as Captain Am,V:Red Skull, E:6th Cap	5.00
351	KD,AM,A:Nick Fury.	3.00
352	KD,AM,I:Supreme Soviets	3.00
353	KD,AM,V:Supreme Soviets.	3.00
354	KD,AM,I:USAgent, V:Machinesmith.	3.50
355	RB,AM,A:Falcon,Battlestar	3.00
356	AM,V:Sisters of Sin	3.00
357	KD,AM,V:Sisters of Sin Baron Zemo,Batroc	3.00
358	KD,B:Blood Stone Hunt	3.00
359	KD,V:Zemo,C:Crossbones	3.00
360	KD,I:Crossbones.	3.00
361	KD,V:Zemo,Batroc	3.00
362	KD,V:Zemo,Crossbones	3.00
363	KD,E:Blood Stone Hunt, V:Crossbones,C:Wolverine	3.00
364	KD,V:Crossbones	3.00
365	KD,Acts of Vengeance, V:SubMariner,Red Skull	3.00
366	1st RLm Capt.Amer.,Acts of Vengeance,V:Controller.	3.00
367	KD,Acts of Vengeance, Magneto Vs. Red Skull	3.00
368	RLm,V:Machinesmith	3.00
369	RLm,I:Skeleton Crew	3.00
370	RLm,V:Skeleton Crew.	3.00
371	RLm,V:Trump,Poundcakes.	3.00
372	RLm,B:Streets of Poison, Cap on Drugs,C:Bullseye	3.00
373	RLm,V:Bullseye,A:Bl.Widow	3.00
374	RLm,V:Bullseye,A:Daredevil.	3.00
375	RLm,A:Daredevil.	3.00
376	RLm,A:Daredevil.	3.00
377	RLm,V:Crossbones,Bullseye	3.00
378	RLm,E:Streets of Poison,Red Skull vs Kingpin,V:Crossbones	3.00
379	RLm(c),V:Serpent Society	3.00
380	RLm,V:Serpent Society.	3.00
381	RLm,V:Serpent Society.	3.00
382	RLm,V:Serpent Society.	3.00
383	RLm(c),RLm,50th Anniv. 64Pages.	5.00
384	RLm,A:Jack Frost	2.50
385	RLm,A:USAgent	2.50
386	RLm,Cap./USAgent T.U.	2.50
387	B:Superia Strategem	2.50
388	A:Paladin.	2.50
389	Superia Strategem #3	2.50
390	Superia Strategem #4.	2.50
391	Superia Strategem #5.	2.50
392	E:Superia Strategem.	2.50
393	V:Captain Germany	2.50
394	A:Red Skull,Diamondback	2.50
395	A:Red Skull,Crossbones.	2.50
396	I:2nd Jack O'Lantern.	2.50
397	V:Red Skull,X-Bones,Viper	2.50
398	Operation:Galactic Storm Pt.1,V:Warstar.	2.50
399	Operation Galactic Storm Pt.8,V:Kree Empire	2.50
400	Operation Galactic Storm Pt.15,BU:rep.Avengers #4.	4.00
401	R:D-Man,A:Avengers	2.50
402	RLe,B:Man & Wolf, A:Wolverine.	2.50
403	RLe,A:Wolverine.	2.50
404	RLe,A:Wolverine.	2.50
405	RLe,A:Wolverine.	2.50
406	RLe,A:Wolverine.	2.50
407	RLe,A:Wolverine,Cable.	2.50
408	RLe,E:Man & Wolf	2.50
409	RLe,V:Skeleton Crew	2.50
410	RLe,V:Crossbones,Skel.Crew	2.50
411	RLe,V:Snapdragon	2.50
412	RLe,V:Batroc,A:Shang-Chi	2.50
413	A:Shang-Chi,V:Superia	2.50
414	RLe,A:Ka-Zar,Black Panther.	2.50
415	Rle,A:Black Panther,Ka-Zar	2.50

Captain America #296
© *Marvel Entertainment Group*

Captain America #436
© Marvel Entertainment Group

416 RLe,Savage Land Mutates,
   A:Black.Panther,Ka-Zar 2.50
417 RLe,A:Black Panther,Ka-Zar,
   V:AIM 2.50
418 RLe,V:Night People 2.50
419 RLe,V:Viper 2.50
420 RLe,I:2nd Blazing Skull,
   A:Nightshift 3.00
421 RLe,V:Nomad 2.50
422 RLe,I:Blistik 2.50
423 RTs(s),MCW,V:Namor 2.50
424 MGv(s),A:Sidewinder 2.50
425 B:MGu(s),DHv,Embossed(c),
   I:2nd SuperPatriot,DeadRinger . 4.00
426 DHv,A:Super Patriot,Dead
   Ringer,V:Resistants 2.50
427 DHv,V:Super Patriot,Dead
   Ringer 2.50
428 DHv,I'Americop 2.50
429 DHv,V:Kono 2.50
430 Daemon Dran, Americop 2.50
431 DHv,I:Free Spirit 2.50
432 DHv,Fighting Chance 2.50
433 DHv,Baron Zemo 2.50
434 DHv,A:Fighting Spirit,
   V.King Cobra 2.50
435 DHv,Fighting Chance 2.50
436 V:King Cobra, Mister Hyde,
   Fighting Chance conclusion . . . 2.50
437 Cap in a Coma 2.50
438 I:New Body Armor 2.50
439 Dawn's Early Light,pt.2 . . . . . . 2.50
440 Taking A.I.M.,pt.1 . . . . 2.50
441 Taking A.I.M.,pt.3 . . . . 2.50
442 Batroc, Cap,V:Zeitgeist 2.50
443 MGu,24 hours to live 2.50
444 MWa,RG,President Kidnapped . 6.00
445 MWa,RG,R:Captain America . . . 4.00
446 MWa,RG,Operation
   Rebirth,pt.2 . . . . 4.00
447 MWa,RG,Op.Rebirth,pt.3 . . . . . 4.00
448 MWa,RG,Operation
   Rebirth,pt.4,double size 6.00
449 MWa,RG,A:Thor 4.00
450 MWa,RG,Man Without a
   Country, pt,1 . . . . 4.00
450a alternate cover 4.00
451 MWa,RG,DRo,Man Without
   A Country,pt.2,new costume . . . 3.50
452 MWa,RG,Man Without a
   Country, pt.2 . . . . 3.50
453 MWa,RG Man Without a
   Country, concl.,old costume . . . 3.50
454 MWa,RG,A:Avengers 3.50

Ann.#1 rep. 50.00
Ann.#2 rep. 35.00
Ann.#3 JK, ... 25.00
Ann.#4 JK,V:Magneto,I:Mutant
   Force 25.00
Ann.#5 'Deathwatcher' 6.00
Ann.#6 A:Contemplator 6.00
Ann.#7 O:Shaper of Worlds 6.00
Ann.#8 MZ,A:Wolverine 35.00
Ann.#9 MBa,SD,Terminus Factor
   #1,N:Nomad 4.50
Ann.#10 MM,Baron Strucker,pt.3
   (see Punisher Ann.#4) 4.00
Ann.#11 Citizen Kang#1 . . . . 4.00
Ann.#12 I:Bantam,w/card 4.00
Ann.#13 RTs(s),MCW, ... 4.00
Drug Wars PDd(s),SaV,A:New
   Warriors 3.00
G-Size#1 GK(c),rep.O:Cap.Amer. . . 7.00
Medusa Effect RTs(s),MCW,RB,
   V:Master Man 3.50
Movie Adapt. 3.00
Spec.#1 Rep.Cap.A #110,#111 . . . . 2.00
Spec.#2 Rep.Cap.A.#113
   & Strange Tales #169 . . . . 2.00
TPB Bloodstone Hunt, rep. 16.00
TPB Captain America: Man Without
   a Country, MWa,RG,SK, rep. . . 15.00
TPB Streets of Poison, rep. 13.00
TPB War and Remembrance, rep. 13.00
Collector's Preview 2.00
Ashcan 75

[2nd Series], Nov., 1996

1 RLd,CDi,JSb, Heroes Reborn,
   I:Nick Fury,48pg. 7.00
1A Stars and stripes background
   variant cover 7.50
1b gold signature edition,
   cardstock cover 18.00
1c San Diego Con edition 25.00
2 RLd,JLb,JSb,Falcon & Red Skull 3.00
3 RLd,JLb,JSb,A:Hulk,V:Red Skull
   & Master Man 3.00
4 RLd,JLb, JSb,F:Prince Namor, . . 3.00
5 RLd,JLb,JSb,V:Crossbones 3.00
6 RLd,JLb,JSb,Industrial
   Revolution, epilogue,A:Cable . . 3.00
7 RLd,JLb,DaF, ... 3.00
8 RLd,JLb,SPa,A:Nick Fury,
   WWII story 3.00
9 JLb,RLd,SPa,WWII story. 3.00
10 JLb,RLd,SPa,WWII story, concl. . 3.00
11 JeR,JoB,Odyssey across
   America, pt.4, concl. 3.00
12 JeR,JoB,Heroes Reborn, Galactus
   concl. 4.00
13 JeR,RLm,Wildstorm x-over 3.00
Ashcan, ComicCon 5.00

[3rd Series], Nov., 1997

1 MWa,RG,BWi,A:Lady Deathstrike,
   Red Skull, Sharon Carter, 48pg 4.00
1a variant cover 10.00
2 MWa,RG,BWi,A devastating loss. 5.00
2a variant cover 4.00
3 MWa,RG,BWi,V:Hydra 4.00
4 MWa,RG,BWi,F:Batroc 4.00
5 MWa,RG,BWi,V:Hordes of Hydra 3.00
6 MWa,RG,V:Skrulls 3.00
7 MWa,NKu,Power & Glory concl. . 3.00
8 MWa,Nku,Live Kree or Die, pt.2
   x-over. 3.50
9 MWa,NKu,American Nightmare,
   pt.1 . . . . 3.00
10 MWa,NKu,American Nightmare,
   pt.2 . . . . 3.00
11 MWa,NKu,American
   Nightmare, pt.3 . . . . 3.00
12 MWa,NKu,American Night-
   mare, pt.4, 48-page 4.00
13 MWa,MFm,R:Red Skull 2.50
14 MWa,MFm,R:Red Skull 2.50
15 MWa,NKu,V:Red Skull 2.50

Captain America, 2rd Series, #2
© Marvel Entertainment Group

16 MWa,NKu,V:Red Skull 2.50
17 MWa,NKu,V:Red Skull 2.50
18 MWa,LW,RbC,V:Cosmic Cube
   double-size 3.50
19 MWa,NKu,V:2 foes 2.50
20 MWa,NKu,Shield secrets 2.50
21 MWa,NKu,A:Black Panther. 2.50
22 MWa,NKu,A:Black Panther. 2.50
23 MWa,Capt.America convict?. . . . 2.50
24 TDF,RF,V:Hydra 2.50
25 DJu,NKu,DGr,Twisted
   Tomorrows,pt.1 . . . . 4.00
26 DJu,NKu,DGr,Twisted,pt.2 . . . . 2.50
27 DJu,NKu,DGr,Twisted,pt.3 . . . . 2.50
28 DJu,NKu,DGr,V:CountNefaria. . . 2.50
29 DJu,DGr,A:Ka-Zar. 2.50
30 DJu,DGr,NKu,Savage Land 2.50
31 DJu,NKu,DGr,F:Sharon Carter . . 2.50
32 DJu,JO,kidnapped 2.50
33 DJu,ATi,Protocide 2.50
34 DJu,ATi,Cache 2.50
35 DJu,ATi,Protocide 2.50
36 DJu,ATi,Maximum Security. 2.50
37 DJu,ATi,V:Protocide 2.50
38 DJu,NKu,Capt.Am. unleashed . . 2.50
39 DJu,V:A.I.M. 2.50
40 DJu,V:A.I.M. 2.50
41 DJu,Batroc the Leaper 2.50
42 DJu,BL,V:Crimson Dynamo 2.50
43 DJu,DR,BL,A:David Ferrari 2.50
44 DJu,BL,A:Taskmaster 2.50
45 DJu,BL,America Lost,pt.1 . . . . . 2.50
46 DJu,BL,America Lost,pt.2 . . . . . 2.50
47 DJu,BL,America Lost,pt.3 . . . . . 2.50
48 DJu,BL,America Lost,pt.4 . . . . . 2.50
49 DJu,BL,F:Sam Wilson 2.50
50 96-page, last issue 6.50
Ann.1998 Captain America/
   Citizen V,KBk,KK, 48-page 4.00
Ann. 1999 JoC,V:Flag Smasher . . . 4.00
Ann.2000 DJu,DGr,48-pg. 4.00
Ann.2001 DJu,48-page 3.50
Spec.#1 Captain America (2000). . . 2.50
Spec.Cap: A Universe X Special . . 4.00
GN Captain America/Nick Fury:
   The Otherworld War (2001). . . . 7.00
TPB The Classic Years,Vol.2 . . . . . 25.00
TPB To Serve and Protect 18.00

CAPTAIN AMERICA
April, 2002

1 JNR(s), terrorism, 48-pg. 4.00
2 JNR(s), terrorism,pt.2 . . . . 3.50
3 JNR(s), terrorism,pt.3 . . . . 3.50

MARVEL

4 JNR(s), terrorism,pt.4 . . . . 3.50	8 JoB,Brothers & Keepers,pt.1 . . . . 3.00
5 JNR(s), terrorism,pt.5 . . . . 3.50	9 . . . . 3.00
6 JNR(s), terrorism,concl. 3.50	10 . . . . 3.00
7 JNR(s) 3.50	11 CPr(s),JoB,Brothers & Keepers . 3.00
8 JNR(s),Extremists,pt.2 . . . . 3.50	12 CPr(s),JoB,Brothers & Keepers . 3.00
9 JNR(s),Extremists,pt.3 . . . . 3.50	13 CPr(s),DJu,American Psycho . . . 3.00
10 JNR(s),Extremists,pt.4 . . . . 3.50	14 CPr(s),DJu,finale. 3.00
11 JNR(s),Extremists,pt.5 . . . . 3.50	TPB Madbomb 17.00
12 JNR(s),JaL,Ice,pt.1 . . . . 3.50	TPB Vol. 1: Two Americas 10.00
13 JNR(s),JaL,Ice,pt.2 . . . . 3.50	TPB Vol. 2: Brothers and Keepers. 18.00
14 JNR(s),JaL,Ice,pt.3 . . . . 3.50	
15 JNR(s),JaL,Ice,pt.4 . . . . 3.50	**CAPTAIN AMERICA:**
16 JNR(s),JaL,Ice,pt.5 . . . . 3.50	**DEAD MAN RUNNING**
17 LW,Cap.Am Lives Again,pt.1 . . . 3.50	**Jan., 2002**
18 LW,Cap.Am Lives Again,pt.2 . . . 3.50	1 (of 3) distress call 3.25
19 LW,Cap.Am Lives Again,pt.3 . . . 3.50	2 . . . . 3.25
20 LW,Cap.Am Lives Again,pt.4 . . . 3.50	3 concl. 3.25
21 CBa,Homeland,pt.1. . . . . 3.00	
22 CBa,Homeland,pt.2. . . . . 3.00	**CAPTAIN AMERICA:**
23 CBa,Homeland,pt.3. . . . . 3.00	**SENTINEL OF LIBERTY**
24 CBa,Homeland,pt.4. . . . . 3.00	**July, 1998**
25 CBa,Homeland,pt.5. . . . . 3.00	1 MWa,RG,new foe, in future 2.50
26 CBa,F:Bucky Barnes 3.00	2A MWa,RG(c&a) F:Invaders,
27 ECa. 3.00	V:Nazis 2.25
28 ECa. 3.00	1 signed by MWa & RG 5.00
29 Avengers Disassembled tie-in . . 3.00	2B variant JSm(c). 2.25
30 Avengers Disassembled,pt.2 . . . 3.00	3 MWa,RG,DGr,A:Sub-Mariner . . . 2.25
31 Avengers Disassembled,pt.3 . . . 3.00	4 MWa,RG,DGr,A:Human Torch . . . 2.25
32 SEa,Disassembled,tie-in,pt.4 . . . 3.00	5 MWa,RG,MFm,Tales of
TPB The New Deal 17.00	Suspense pt.1 . . . . 2.25
TPB Vol. 2: Extremists. 14.00	6 MWa,RG,MFm,Tales of
TPB Vol. 3: Ice. 13.00	Suspense pt.2 . . . . 3.50
TPB Vol. 4: Lives Again 13.00	7 RSt,RF,civil war tale concl. 2.25
TPB Vol. 5: Homeland 20.00	8 MWa,R:Falcon 2.25
	9 MWa,A:Falcon 2.25
CAPTAIN AMERICA	10 psychedelic look back. 2.25
Nov., 2004	11 MWa,A:Human Torch 2.25
1 SEp,V:Red Skull 6.00	12 MWa,DGr,F:Bucky,48-page . . . 3.50
2 SEp,. 5.00	Spec.RoughCut #1,MWa,RG,48-pg . 3.00
3 SEp,F:Sharon Carter. 4.00	
4 SEp,home from Europe 4.00	**CAPTAIN AMERICA:**
5 SEp,flash-backs. 4.00	**WHAT PRICE GLORY**
6 SEp,Out of Time, finale 4.00	**March, 2003**
7 SEp,Winter Soldier,pt.1 . . . . 4.00	1 (of 4) SR 3.25
7a variant (c). 3.00	2 thru 4 SR . . . . @3.25
8 SEp,Winter Soldier,pt.1 . . . . 3.00	
8a variant (c). 3.00	**CAPTAIN BRITAIN**
9 SEp,Winter Soldier,pt.2 . . . . 3.00	**Jan., 2002**
10 SEp,Winter Soldier,pt.3. . . . . 3.00	TPB 208-pg. 20.00
11 SEp,Winter Soldier,pt.4. . . . . 3.00	
12 SEp,Winter Soldier,pt.5. . . . . 3.00	
13 SEp,Winter Soldier,pt. 3.00	
14 SEp,Winter Soldier,pt. 3.00	
15 A:Crossbones, Sin 3.00	
16 F:Crossbones, Sin 3.00	
17 F:Corssbones, Sin 3.00	
18 SEp,Twenty-First Century Blitz . 3.00	
19 SEp,Twenty-First Century Blitz . 3.00	
20 SEp,Twenty-First Century Blitz . 3.00	
21 SEp,Twenty-First Century Blitz . 3.00	
22 Civil War tie-in. 3.00	
23 Civil War tie-in. 3.00	
24 Civil War tie-in. 3.00	
TPB Vol. 1: Out of Time. 22.00	
TPB Bicentennial Battles, JK. . . . 20.00	
TPB Winter Soldier, Vol. 1 (2006) . 17.00	
TPB Winter Soldier, Vol. 2 (2006) . 15.00	
TPB Red Menace, Vol. 1 (2006) . . 12.00	
TPB Red Menace, Vol. 2 (2006) . . 11.00	
Spec. 65th Anniversary #1, 48-pg. . 5.00	
CAPTAIN AMERICA	
& THE FALCON	
March, 2004	
1 BS,Two Americas,pt.1 . . . . 3.00	
2 BS,Two Americas,pt.2 . . . . 3.00	
3 BS,Two Americas,pt.3 . . . . 3.00	
4 BS,Two Americas,pt.4 . . . . 3.00	
5 Avengers Disassembled tie-in . . 3.00	
6 Avengers Disassembled,pt.2 . . . . 3.00	
7 Avengers Disassembled,pt.3 . . . . 3.00	

CAPTAIN BRITAIN
CLASSICS

1 AD rep. 2.50

CAPTAIN CONFEDERACY
Epic, Nov., 1991

1 I:Capt.Confederacy,Kid Dixie. . . . 2.25
2 Meeting of Superhero Reps. 2.25
3 Framed for Murder. 2.25
4 Superhero conference,final iss. . . 2.25

CAPTAIN JUSTICE
March, 1988

1 Based on TV Series 2.25
2 April, 1988 . . . . 2.25

CAPTAIN MARVEL
May, 1968

1 GC,O:retold,V:Sentry#459. . . . 350.00
2 GC,V:Super Skrull 150.00
3 GC,V:Super Skrull 90.00
4 GC,Sub-Mariner. 90.00
5 DH,I:Metazoid 90.00
6 DH,I:Solam 75.00
7 JR(c),DH,V:Quasimodo 75.00
8 DH,I:Cuberex 75.00
9 DH,D:Cuberex 75.00
10 DH,V:Number 1. . . . . 75.00
11 BWS(c),I:Z0. . . . . 75.00
12 K&R(c),I:Man-Slayer. 50.00
13 FS,V:Man-Slayer. 50.00
14 FS,Iron Man 50.00
15 TS,DA,Z0 . . . . 40.00
16 DH,Ronan 40.00
17 GK,DA,O:R.Jones ret,N:Capt.
  Marvel 50.00
18 GK,JB,DA,I:Mandroid 40.00
19 GK,DA,Master.of.MM 40.00
20 GK,DA,I:Rat Pack. 40.00
21 GK,DA,Hulk. 40.00
22 GK(c),WB,V:Megaton 40.00
23 GK(c),WB,FMc,V:Megaton 40.00
24 GK(c),WB,ECh,I:L.Mynde. 40.00
25 1st JSn,Cap.Marvel,Cosmic
  Cube Saga Begins 35.00
26 JSn,DC,Thanos(2ndApp.)
  A:Thing 40.00
27 JSn,V:Thanos,A:Mentor,
  Starfox, I:Death 35.00
28 JSn,DGr,Thanos Vs.Drax,
  A:Avengers 35.00
29 JSn,AM,O:Zeus,C:Thanos
  I:Eon,O:Mentor 22.00
30 JSn,AM,Controller,C:Thanos . . 22.00
31 JSn,AM,Avengers,
  Thanos,Drax,Mentor 22.00
32 JSn,AM,DGr,O:Drax,
  Moondragon,A:Thanos 22.00
33 JSn,KJ,E:Cosmic Cube Saga
  1st D:Thanos 35.00
34 JSn,JA,V:Nitro(leads to
  his Death) 22.00
35 GK(c),AA,Ant Man 10.00
36 AM,Watcher,Rep.CM#1 . . . . . . 10.00
37 AM,KJ,Nimrod. 10.00
38 AM,KJ,Watcher 10.00
39 AM,KJ,Watcher 10.00
40 AM,AMc,Watcher 10.00
41 AM,BWr,CR,BMc,TA,Kree. 12.00
42 AM,V:Stranger,C:Drax. 8.00
43 AM,V:Drax. 8.00
44 GK(c),AM,V:Drax 12.00
45 AM,I:Rambu 12.00
46 AM,TA,D:Fawn 8.00
47 AM,TA,A:Human Torch 8.00
48 AM,TA,I:Chetah. 8.00
49 AM,V:Ronan,A:Cheetah 8.00
50 AM,TA,Avengers,
  V:Super Adaptiod. 9.00
51 AM,TA,V:Mercurio,4-D Man . . 12.00

Captain Justice #1
© Marvel Entertainment Group

Captain Marvel #30
© Marvel Entertainment Group

52 AM,TA,V:Phae-dor 12.00
53 AM,TA,A:Inhumans 8.00
54 PB,V:Nitro 8.00
55 PB,V:Death-grip 8.00
56 PB,V:Death-grip 8.00
57 PB,V:Thor,A;Thanos 12.00
58 PB,Drax/Titan 8.00
59 PB,Drax/Titan,I:Stellarax 8.00
60 PB,Drax/Titan 8.00
61 PB,V:Chaos 8.00
62 PB,V:Stellarax 8.00
G-Size #1 reprints 10.00

CAPTAIN MARVEL
1989
1 MBr,I:Powerkeg,V:Moonstone . . . 3.00
1 DyM(s),MBr,V:Skinhead(1993) . . 2.50
PF Death of Captain Marvel 8.00
TPB Life of Captain Marvel,JSn . . 15.00

CAPTAIN MARVEL
1995
1 FaN,R:Captain Marvel(son of) . . . 4.00
2 FaN,V:X-Treme,Erik the Red 3.00
3 FaN,V:X-treme 3.00
4 thru 6 FaN . . . . @3.00

CAPTAIN MARVEL
Jan., 2000
1A PDd,Ccs,A:Rick Jones 5.00
1B variant JOy (c) 5.50
2 PDd,Ccs 7.00
3 PDd,Ccs,V:Wendigo 3.00
4 PDd,Ccs,A:Moondragon 3.00
5 PDd,Ccs,V:Drax 3.00
6 PDd,Ccs,V:Marlo 3.00
7 PDd,Ccs,A:Comet Man 3.00
8 PDd,Ccs,V:Super-Skrull 3.00
9 PDd,Ccs,V:Hyssta 3.00
10 PDd,Ccs,V:Genis 3.00
11 PDd,JSn 3.00
12 PDd,Ccs,Maximum Security . . . 3.00
13 PDd,Ccs,V:kids of Yon-Rogg . . . 3.00
14 PDd,Ccs,F:Psycho-Man 3.00
15 PDd,Ccs,F:Psycho-Man 3.00
16 PDd,Ccs,V:Psycho-Man 3.00
17 PDd,JSn,AM,V:Thanos 3.00
18 PDd,JSn,AM,A:Thor,Thanos . . . 3.00
19 PDd,Ccs,A:Thor,Thanos 3.00
20 PDd,Ccs, ... 3.00
21 PDd,Ccs, ... 3.00
22 PDd,Ccs,Supreme Intelligence . . 3.00
23 PDd,Ccs, ... 3.00

24 PDd,Ccs,Negative Zone 3.00
25 PDd,Ccs,V:Quasar, ... 3.00
26 PDd,F:Rick Jones,'Nuff Said . . 3.00
27 PDd,CCs,Time Flies,pt.1 . . . . . 3.00
28 PDd,Time Flies, pt.2 . . . . 3.00
29 PDd,Time Flies, pt.3 . . . . 3.00
30 PDd,Time Flies, pt.4 . . . . 3.00
31 PDd,Ccs,F:Marlo,V:Mephisto . . 3.00
32 PDd,Ccs,V:Moondragon 3.00
33 PDd,Ccs,V:Magus 3.50
34 PDd,Ccs,V:Magus,Rick Jones . . 3.00
35 PDd, last issue 3.00
TPB The Life and Death of
    Captain Marvel, 304-pg. 25.00
TPB First Contact (2002) 17.00

CAPTAIN MARVEL
Sept., 2002
1 PDd,Ccs, U-Decide 3.00
1b Variant JJu(c) 2.25
1c Variant AxR(c) 2.25
2 PDd,Ccs,F:Punisher 2.25
3 PDd,Ccs,AxR 2.25
3a Director's Cut, AxR, 40-pg. . . . 3.50
4 PDd,CCs 2.25
5 PDd,CCs 2.25
6 PDd,CCs 2.25
7 PDd,A:Thor,pt.1 . . . . 2.25
8 PDd,A:Thor,pt.2 . . . . 3.00
9 PDd,Coven,pt.1 . . . . 3.00
10 PDd,Coven,pt.2 . . . . 3.00
11 PDd,Coven,pt.3 . . . . 3.00
12 PDd,Coven,pt.4 . . . . 3.00
13 PDd,Pop,V:Badoon 3.00
14 PDd,accidents do happen 3.00
15 PDd,NA(c),V:Kree 3.00
16 PDd,Crazy Like a Fox,pt.2 . . . . 3.00
17 PDd,Crazy Like a Fox,pt.3 . . . . 3.00
18 PDd,Crazy Like a Fox,pt.4 . . . . 3.00
19 PDd,Odyssey,pt.1 . . . . 3.00
20 PDd,Odyssey,pt.2 . . . . 3.00
21 PDd,Odyssey,pt.3 . . . . 3.00
22 PDd,AsL,Odyssey,pt.4 . . . . 3.00
23 PDd,AsL,Odyssey,pt.5 . . . . 3.00
24 PDd,Odyssey,pt.6 . . . . 3.00
25 PDd,Exit Strategy 3.00
TPB Vol. 1: Nothing to Lose 13.00
TPB Vol. 2: Coven 15.00
TPB Vol. 3: Crazy Like a Fox 15.00
TPB Vol. 4: Odyssey 17.00

CAPTAIN PLANET
Oct., 1991
1 I&O:Captain Planet 5.00
2 thru 12 . . . . @3.00

CAPT. SAVAGE & HIS
LEATHERNECK RAIDERS
Jan., 1968
1 SSh(c),C:Sgt Fury;The Last
    Bansai 80.00
2 SSh(c),O:Hydra;Return of Baron
    Strucker 40.00
3 SSh,Two Against Hydra 40.00
4 SSh,V:Hydra;The Fateful Finale 40.00
5 SSh,The Invincible Enemy 40.00
6 Mission;Save a Howler 40.00
7 SSh,Objective:Ben Grimm 40.00
8 Mission:Foul Ball 40.00
Becomes:

CAPT. SAVAGE & HIS
BATTLEFIELD RAIDERS
1968
9 . . . . 35.00
10 To the Last Man 35.00
11 A:Sergeant Fury 35.00
12 V:The Japanese 35.00
13 The Junk Heap Juggernauts . . . 35.00
14 Savage's First Mission 35.00

15 Within the Temple Waits Death. 30.00
16 V:The Axis Powers 30.00
17 V:The Axis Powers 30.00
18 V:The Axis Powers 30.00
19 March, 1970 . . . . 30.00

CAPTAIN UNIVERSE
Nov., 2005
1 F:Hulk 3.00
2 F:Daredevil 3.00
3 F:X-23 . . . . 3.00
4 F:Invisible Woman 3.00
5 F:Silver Surfer 3.00
TPB Power Unimaginable (2005) . 20.00
TPB Universal Heroes (2006) 14.00

CARE BEARS
Star, Nov., 1985
1 . . . . 3.00
2 thru 14 . . . . @3.00
Marvel 1988
15 thru 20 . . . . @3.00

CARNAGE
1-shot Carnage: Its a Wonderful
    Life (1996) 3.00
1-shot Carnage: Mindbomb
    foil cover (1996) 3.50

CARTOON KIDS
Marvel Atlas, 1957
1 JMn,A:Dexter the Demon, Little
    Zelda,Willie,Wise Guy 200.00

CAR WARRIORS
Epic, 1990
1 Based on Roll Playing Game . . . 2.50
2 Big Race Preparations 2.50
3 Ft.Delorean-Lansing Race begin . 2.50
4 Race End, Final issue 2.50

CASEY–CRIME
PHOTOGRAPHER
Aug., 1949
1 Ph(c),Girl on the Docks 300.00
2 Ph(c),Staats Cotsworth 250.00
3 Ph(c),He Walked With Danger 250.00
4 Ph(c),Lend Me Your Life 250.00
Becomes:

Cat #1
© Marvel Entertainment Group

TWO GUN WESTERN
[1st Series], 1950
5 JB,B,I&O:Apache Kid 300.00
6 JMn,The Outcast 225.00
7 Human Sacrifice 225.00
8 JR,DW,A:Kid Colt,Texas Kid,
  Doc Holiday 225.00
9 JMn,GM,A:Kid Colt,Marshall
  'Frosty' Bennet Texas Kid . . . 225.00
10 . . . . 225.00
11 thru 14 JMn,June, 1952 . . . @150.00

CASPER
1996
1 From Animated TV show 2.25
2 visit to Harvey Castle. 2.25
3 and 4 . . . . @2.25

CAT, THE
Nov., 1972—June, 1973
1 JM,I&O:The Cat 50.00
2 JM,V:The Owl 25.00
3 BEv,V:Kraken 25.00
4 JSn,V:Man-Bull 30.00

CAUGHT
Marvel-Vista Publications, 1956
1 JSe,Crime 350.00
2 MD,JSe 200.00
3 MMe,AI,JSe 200.00
4 MMe,JSe 200.00
5 RC,JSe,BK. 200.00

CENTURY:
DISTANT SONS
1996
1-shot DAn,48pg. 3.25

CHAMBER OF CHILLS
Nov., 1972
1 SSh,A Dragon Stalks By
  Night,(H.Ellison Adapt.) 40.00
2 FB,BEv,SD,Monster From the
  Mound,(RE Howard Adapt.) . . 20.00
3 FB,BEv,SD, Thing on the Roof . 20.00
4 FB,BEv,SD, Opener of the
  Crypt,(J.Jakes,E.A.Poe Adapt) 20.00
5 FB,BEv,SD, Devils Dowry 20.00
6 FB,BEv,SD, Mud Monster 20.00
7 thru 24 FB,BEv,SD . . . . @20.00
25 FB,BEv,SD Nov., 1976 . . . . 20.00

CHAMBER OF DARKNESS
Oct., 1969
1 JB, Tales of Maddening Magic 150.00
2 NA(script),Enter the Red Death 125.00
3 JK,BWS,JB, Something Lurks
  on Shadow Mountain. 100.00
4 JK Monster Man Came Walking,
  BU:BWS 125.00
5 JCr,JK,SD, And Fear Shall
  Follow, plus Lovecraft adapt. . 50.00
6 SD 50.00
7 SD,JK,BWr, Night of the
  Gargoyle 75.00
8 BWr(c),DA,BEv, Beast that Walks
  Like a Man Special, 5 Tales of
  Maddening Magic, Jan.,1972 125.00
Becomes:

MONSTERS ON
THE PROWL
1971
9 SAD,BWS,Monster Stories
  Inc,Gorgilla 45.00
10 JK,Roc 25.00
11 JK,A Titan Walks the Land 25.00

12 HT,JK,Gomdulla The Living
  Pharoah 25.00
13 HT,JK,Tragg 30.00
14 JK,SD,Return of the Titan 30.00
15 FrG,JK,The Thing Called It 25.00
16 JSe,SD,JK, Serpent God of
  Lost Swamp,A:King Kull 25.00
17 JK,SD,Coming of Colossus . . . 25.00
18 JK,SD,Bruttu 25.00
19 JK,SD,Creature From the
  Black Bog 25.00
20 JK,SD,Oog Lives Again 25.00
21 JK,SD,A Martian Stalks
  the City 25.00
22 JK,SD,Monster Runs Amok . . . 18.00
23 JK,The Return of Grogg 18.00
24 JK,SD, Magnetor 18.00
25 JK,Colossus Lives Again 18.00
26 JK,SD,The Two Headed Thing . 18.00
27 JK,Sserpo 18.00
28 JK,The Coming of Monsteroso . 18.00
29 JK,SD Monster at my Window . 18.00
30 JK,Diablo Demon from the 5th
  Dimension, Oct., 1974 . . . . . . 18.00

Champions #1
© Marvel Entertainment Group

CHAMPIONS
Oct., 1975
1 GK(c),DH,I&O:Champions 50.00
2 DH,O:Champions 15.00
3 GT,Assault on Olympus 13.00
4 GT,`Murder at Malibu' 12.00
5 DH,I:Rampage 15.00
6 JK(c),GT,V:Rampage 15.00
7 GT,O:Black Widow,I:Darkstar . . 15.00
8 BH,O:Black Widow 12.00
9 BH,BL,V:Crimson Dynamo 12.00
10 BH,BL,V:Crimson Dynamo 12.00
11 JBy,A:Black Goliath,Hawkeye . . 16.00
12 JBy,BL,V:Stranger. 16.00
13 JBy,BL,V:Kamo Tharn. 16.00
14 JBy,I:Swarm 16.00
15 JBy,V:Swarm. 16.00
16 BH,A:Magneto,Dr.Doom,
  Beast 12.00
17 GT,JBy,V:Sentinels,last issue . . 13.00

CHILI
May, 1969
1 Millie's Rival. 90.00
2 . . . . 50.00
3 . . . . 50.00
4 . . . . 50.00
5 . . . . 50.00

6 thru 15 . . . . @30.00
16 thru 20 . . . . @25.00
21 thru 25 . . . . @22.00
26 Dec., 1973 . . . . 22.00
Spec.#1, 1971. . . . . 45.00

CHUCK NORRIS
Star, Jan.–Sept., 1987
1 SD 4.00
2 thru 5 . . . . @5.00

CINDY COMICS
See: KRAZY COMICS

CITIZEN V
April, 2001
1 (of 3) FaN,F:V-Battalion 3.25
2 FaN, ... 3.25
3 FaN,F:Iron Cross 3.25

CITIZEN V
& THE V BATTALION:
THE EVERLASTING
Feb., 2002
1 (of 4) FaN, ... 3.25
2 FaN,Marduk 3.25
3 FaN, ... 3.25
4 FaN, concl. 3.25

CIVIL WAR
May, 2006
1 F: everybody, x-over-48-pg 5.00
1a variant (c) 22.00
1b director's cut, 64-pg. 6.00
2 . . . . 7.00
2a variant (c) 6.00
2b 2nd printing 6.00
3 . . . . 4.00
4 . . . . 3.50
5 . . . . 3.50
6 . . . . 3.00
7 . . . . 3.00
3a to 7a variant (c)s 5.00
Spec. Civil War Files #1. . . . . 4.00
Spec. Daily Bugle Civil War issue   0.50

CIVIL WAR: FRONT LINE
June, 2006
1 Embeded 4.00
2 thru 10 . . . . @3.00

CIVIL WAR: X-MEN
July, 2006
1 . . . . 3.50
2 thru 4 . . . . @3.00

CIVIL WAR: YOUNG
AVENGERS & RUNAWAYS
July, 2006
1 . . . . 3.50
2 thru 4 . . . . @3.00

CLANDESTINE
Oct., 1994–Sept., 1995
Preview issue, Intro (1994) 2.00
1 MFm,AD,foil(c). 3.25
2 Wraparound (c),A:Silver Surfer . . 2.75
3 I:Argent,Kimera,A:SilverSurfer. . 2.75
4 R:Adam 2.75
5 MFm,AD,O:Adam Destine 2.75
6 A:Spider-Man 2.75
7 A:Spider-Man 2.75
8 A:Dr.Strange. 2.75
9 thru 14 . . . . @2.75
TPB AD,MFm (1997) 12.00

MARVEL

CLASSIC CONAN
See: CONAN SAGA

CLASSIC X-MEN
See: X-MEN

CLAWS
Aug., 2006
1 JP,F:Wolverine & Black Cat..... 4.00
2 JP.......................... 4.00
3 JP.......................... 4.00

CLIVE BARKER'S BOOK OF THE DAMNED
Epic, Nov., 1991
1 JBo,Hellraiser companion 5.00
2 MPa,Hellraiser Companion 5.00

CLIVE BARKER'S HELLRAISER
Epic, 1989–93
1 BWr,DSp 7.00
2 .... 6.00
3 .... 6.50
4 .... 4.50
5 .... 4.50
6 .... 7.00
7 The Devil's Brigade #1 .... 7.00
8 The Devil's Brigade #2&3 ...... 7.00
9 The Devil's Brigade #4&5 ...... 7.00
10 The Devil's Brigade #6&7
    foil Cover.................. 5.00
11 The Devil's Brigade #8&9 ...... 4.50
12 The Devil's Brigade #10-12 .... 4.50
13 MMi,RH,Devil's Brigade #13.... 4.50
14 The Devil's Brigade #14 .... 5.00
15 The Devil's Brigade #15 .... 5.00
16 E:Devil's Brigade 5.00
17 BHa,DR,The Harrowing 10.00
18 O:Harrowers 5.00
19 A:Harrowers 5.00
20 NGa(s),DMc,Last Laugh....... 9.00
Dark Holiday Spec.#1 (1992)...... 5.00
Spring Slaughter Spec.#1 (1994)... 7.00
Summer Spec.#1 (1992.......... 6.00

CLOAK & DAGGER
(Limited Series) Oct., 1983
1 RL,TA,I:Det.O'Reilly,
    Father Delgado 3.00
2 RL,TA,V:Duane Hellman 3.00
3 RL,TA,V:Street Gang 3.00
4 RL,TA,O:Cloak & Dagger, ... 3.00

CLOAK & DAGGER
[1st Regular Series], July, 1985
1 RL,Pornography.............. 3.00
2 RL,Dagger's mother 2.50
3 RL,A:Spider-Man 2.50
4 RL,Secret Wars II 2.50
5 RL,I:Mayhem 2.50
6 RL,A:Mayhem 2.50
7 RL,A:Mayhem 2.50
8 TA, Drugs................... 2.50
9 AAd,TA,A:Mayhem 2.75
10 BBI,TA,V:Dr. Doom........... 2.50
11 BBI,TA,Last Issue 2.50

[Mutant Misadventures of] CLOAK & DAGGER
[2nd Regular Series] Oct., 1988
1 CR(i),A:X-Factor............. 3.00
2 CR(i),C:X-Factor,V:Gromitz..... 2.50
3 SW(i),JLe(c),A:Gromitz 2.50
4 TA(i),Inferno,R:Mayhem 2.50

Cloak & Dagger, Limited Series #4
© Marvel Entertainment Group

5 TA(i),R:Mayhem.............. 2.50
6 TA(i),A:Mayhem 2.50
7 A:Crimson Daffodil,V:Ecstacy .. 2.50
8 Acts of Vengeance prelude 2.50
9 Acts of Vengeance 2.50
10 Acts of Vengeance,X-Force
    name used,Dr.Doom 2.50
11 .... 2.50
12 A:Dr.Doom.................. 2.50
13 A:Dr.Doom.................. 2.50
14 & 15 RL................... @2.50
16 RL,A:Spider-Man 2.50
17 A:Spider-Man, ... 2.50
18 Inf.Gauntlet X-over,
    A:Spider-Man, Ghost Rider.... 2.50
19 O:Cloak & Dagger.final issue ... 2.50
GN Predator and Prey 15.00

A CLUELESS VALENTINE
1 characters from movie, 48pg 2.50

CODENAME: GENETIX
1993
1 PGa,A:Wolverine 3.00
2 PGa,V:Prime EvilA:Wolverine ... 3.00
3 .... 3.00
4 A:Wolverine,Ka-Zar 3.00

CODE OF HONOR
1996
1 (of 4) CDi,TnS,I:Jeff Piper,
    fully painted 6.00
2 thru 4 CDi, ... @6.00

CODE NAME: SPITFIRE
See: SPITFIRE AND THE TROUBLESHOOTERS

COLOSSUS
Aug., 1997
1-shot BRa,Colossus & Meggan
    V:Arcade, 48pg 3.50

COLOSSUS: GOD'S COUNTRY
PF V:Cold Warriors 7.00

COMBAT
Marvel Atlas, June, 1952
1 JMn,War Stories, Bare
    Bayonets 350.00

2 RH, Break Thru,(Dedicated to
    US Infantry)............. 250.00
3 JMn(c) 200.00
4 BK 225.00
5 thru 10 .... @200.00
11 April, 1953................ 250.00

COMBAT CASEY
See: WAR COMBAT

COMBAT KELLY AND THE DEADLY DOZEN
Marvel Atlas, Nov., 1951
1 RH,Korean War Stories 375.00
2 Big Push 200.00
3 The Volunteer 175.00
4 JMn,V:Communists 175.00
5 JMn,OW,V:Communists...... 175.00
6 V:Communists 175.00
7 JMn,V:Communists 175.00
8 JMn,Death to the Reds 175.00
9 .... 175.00
10 JMn(c)................... 175.00
11 .... 150.00
12 thru 16 .... @150.00
17 A:Combat Casey........... 175.00
18 A:Battle Brady............. 125.00
19 V:Communists............. 125.00
20 V:Communists 125.00
21 Transvestite Cover 75.00
22 thru 40 .... @100.00
41 thru 44 Aug., 1957 .... @100.00

COMBAT KELLY
June, 1972
1 JM, Stop the Luftwaffe........ 40.00
2 The Big Breakout............. 20.00
3 O:Combat Kelly 25.00
4 Mutiny,A:Sgt.Fury and the
    Howling Commandoes 25.00
5 Escape or Die 20.00
6 The Fortress of Doom 20.00
7 Nun Hostage,V:Nazis 20.00
8 V:Nazis.................... 20.00
9 Oct., 1973 .... 20.00

COMBAT ZONE
Jan., 2005
1 (of 5) DJu,G.I.s in Iraq 3.00
2 DJu 3.00
3 DJu,Hellfires to Avoid Damnation 3.00
4 and 5 .... @3.00
TPB Combat Zone............. 20.00

COMEDY COMICS
Marvel Timely, 1942
9 .... 4,400.00
10 .... 3,500.00
11 .... 750.00
12 .... 250.00
13 Funny animal 250.00
14 Super Rabbit.............. 700.00
15 .... 200.00
16 .... 200.00
17 .... 200.00
18 .... 200.00
19 .... 200.00
20 .... 200.00
21 thru 32 .... @150.00
33 HK 200.00
34 BW 300.00
Becomes:

MARGIE COMICS
Marvel Comics, 1946
35 thru 39 Glamour Girl ...... @250.00
40 .... 200.00
41 thru 49 .... @225.00
Becomes:

Comedy Comics #19
© Marvel Entertainment Group

RENO BROWNE
Marvel Comics, 1950
50 Photo(c); Western babe 400.00
51 Photo(c); 350.00
52 Photo(c); 350.00

COMEDY COMICS
Marvel Animirth 1948–49
1 HK, Romance,F:Hedy, Millie,
  Tessie 400.00
2 .... 200.00
3 .... 200.00
4 HK 225.00
5 .... 150.00
6 .... 150.00
7 .... 150.00
8 .... 150.00
9 .... 150.00
10 .... 150.00

COMET MAN
Feb., 1987
1 BSz(c),I:Comet Man 2.50
2 BSz(c),A:Mr.Fantastic 2.50
3 BSz(c),A:Hulk 2.50
4 BSz(c),A:Fantistic Four 2.50
5 BSz(c),A:Fantastic Four....... 2.50
6 BSz(c),Last issue, July,1987 .... 2.50

COMIC CAPERS
Marvel Comics, 1944
1 Funny animal, Super Rabbit .. 350.00
2 .... 200.00
3 .... 150.00
4 .... 150.00
5 .... 150.00
6 .... 150.00

COMICS FOR KIDS
Marvel Timely, 1945
1 Funny animal.............. 300.00
2 .... 300.00

COMIX BOOK
(black & white magazine) 1974
1 BW....................... 65.00
2 BW....................... 50.00
3 .... 35.00
4 & 5 ....@30.00

COMIX ZONE
1 video game tie-in............ 2.50
2 video game tie-in............ 2.50

COMMANDO ADVENTURES
Marvel Atlas, June, 1957
1 Seek, Find and Destroy...... 300.00
2 MD, Hit 'em and Hit 'em
  Hard, Aug.,1957 .... 150.00

COMPLETE COMICS
See: AMAZING COMICS

COMPLETE MYSTERY
Aug., 1948
1 Seven Dead Men 600.00
2 Jigsaw of Doom............ 500.00
3 Fear in the Night 500.00
4 A Squealer Dies Fast........ 500.00
Becomes:

TRUE COMPLETE MYSTERY
1949
5 Rice Mancini,
  The Deadly Dude 300.00
6 Ph(c),Frame-up that Failed ... 250.00
7 Ph(c),Caught 250.00
8 Ph(c),The Downfall of Mr.
  Anderson, Oct., 1949 ..... 250.00

CONAN
1995–96
1 Pit Fighter 3.00
2 LHa,Hyborean tortue factory 3.00
3 V:Cannibals 3.00
4 LHa,JP,Rune Conan Prelude.... 3.00
5 LHa,V:yeti 3.00
6 LHa, the plague 3.00
7 LHa,BBI,V:The Iron Man 3.00
8 thru 11 ....@3.00

CONAN: DEATH COVERED IN GOLD
July, 1999
1 (of 3) RTs................... 3.00
2 RTs...................... 3.00
3 RTs,JB,concl............... 3.00

CONAN THE ADVENTURER
1994–95
1 RT(s),RK,Red Foil(c) 3.00
2 RT(s),RK 2.50
3 RT(s),RK 2.50
4 thru 14 ....@2.50

CONAN THE BARBARIAN
Oct., 1970
1 BWS/DA,O:Conan,A:Kull..... 350.00
2 BWS/SB,Lair o/t Beast-Men .. 125.00
3 BWS,SB,Grey God Passes... 225.00
4 BWS,SB,Tower o/t Elephant .. 100.00
5 BWS,Zukala's Daughter 100.00
6 BWS,SB,Devil Wings Over
  Shadizar 75.00
7 BWS,SB,DA,C:Thoth-Amon,
  I:Set..................... 75.00
8 BWS,TS,TP,Keepers o/t Crypt.. 75.00
9 BWS,SB,Garden of Fear...... 75.00
10 BWS,SB,JSe,Beware Wrath of
  Anu;BU:Kull.............. 100.00
11 BWS,SB,Talons of Thak 100.00
12 BWS,GK,Dweller in the Dark,
  Blood of the Dragon B.U. 75.00
13 BWS,SB,Web o/t Spider-God . 75.00
14 BWS,SB,Green Empress of
  Melnibone 75.00
15 BWS,SB 75.00
16 BWS,Frost Giant's Daughter .. 60.00

17 GK,Gods of Bal-Sagoth,
  A:Fafnir 35.00
18 GK,DA,Thing in the Temple,
  A:Fafnir 35.00
19 BWS,DA,Hawks from
  the Sea................. 60.00
20 BWS,DA,Black Hound of
  Vengeance,A:Fafnir...... 60.00
21 BWS,CR,VM,DA,SB, Monster
  of the Monoliths........... 45.00
22 BWS,DA,rep.Conan #1....... 50.00
23 BWS,DA,Shadow of the
  Vulture,I:Red Sonja 75.00
24 BWS,Song of Red Sonja 75.00
25 JB,SB,JSe,Mirrors of Kharam
  Akkad,A:Kull 25.00
26 JB,Hour of the Griffin 20.00
27 JB,Blood of Bel-Hissar 20.00
28 JB,Moon of Zembabwei 20.00
29 JB,Two Against Turan........ 20.00
30 JB,The Hand of Nergal....... 20.00
31 JB,Shadow in the Tomb 12.00
32 JB,Flame Winds of Lost Khitai . 12.00
33 JB,Death & 7 Wizards 12.00
34 JB,Temptress in the Tower
  of Flame 12.00
35 JB,Hell-Spawn of Kara-Shehr.. 12.00
36 JB,Beware of Hyrkanians
  bearing Gifts 12.00
37 NA,Curse of the Golden Skull.. 25.00
38 JB,Warrior & Were-Woman ... 12.00
39 JB,Dragon from the
  Inland Sea 12.00
40 RB,Fiend from Forgotten City . 12.00
41 JB,Garden of Death & Life 15.00
42 JB,Night of the Gargoyle 15.00
43 JB,Tower o/Blood,A:RedSonja . 15.00
44 JB,Flame&Fiend,A:RedSonja .. 15.00
45 JB,NA,Last Ballad of
  Laza-Lanti 12.00
46 JB,NA,JSt,Curse of the
  Conjurer................. 12.00
47 JB,DA,Goblins in the
  Moonlight 12.00
48 JB,DG,DA,Rats Dance at Raven
  gard,BU:Red Sonja 12.00
49 JB,DG,Wolf-Woman 12.00
50 JB,DG,Dweller in the Pool 12.00
51 JB,DG,Man Born of Demon 8.00
52 JB,TP,Altar and the Scorpion ... 8.00
53 JB,FS,Brothers of the Blade 8.00
54 JB,TP,Oracle of Ophir......... 8.00
55 JB,TP,Shadow on the Land 8.00
56 JB,High Tower in the Mist..... 8.00

Conan The Barbarian #3
© Marvel Entertainment Group

Conan The Barbarian #39
© Marvel Entertainment Group

57 MP,Incident in Argos 8.00
58 JB,Queen o/tBlackCoast,
   2nd A:Belit 10.00
59 JB,Ballad of Belit,O:Belit. 7.00
60 JB,Riders o/t River Dragons 7.00
61 JB,She-Pirate,I:Amra 7.00
62 JB,Lord of the Lions,O:Amra . . . 7.00
63 JB,Death Among Ruins,
   V&D:Amra 7.00
64 JSon,AM,rep.Savage Tales#5 . . 7.00
65 JB,Fiend o/tFeatheredSerpent . . 7.00
66 JB,Daggers & Death Gods,
   C:Red Sonja 6.00
67 JB,Talons of the Man-Tiger,
   A:Red Sonja 6.00
68 JB,Of Once & Future Kings,
   V:KingKull,A:Belit,Red Sonja. . 6.00
69 VM,Demon Out of the Deep 6.00
70 JB,City in the Storm 6.00
71 JB,Secret of Ashtoreth 6.00
72 JB,Vengeance in Asgalun 6.00
73 JB,..In the Well of Skelos 6.00
74 JB,Battle at the Black Walls
   C:Thoth-Amon 6.00
75 JB,Hawk-Riders of Harakht 7.00
76 JB,Swordless in Stygia 7.00
77 JB,When Giants Walk
   the Earth 7.00
78 JB,rep.Savage Sword #1,
   A:Red Sonja 7.00
79 HC,Lost Valley of Iskander 7.00
80 HC,Trial By Combat 6.00
81 HC,The Eye of the Serpent 5.00
82 HC,The Sorceress o/t Swamp . . 5.00
83 HC,The Dance of the Skull 5.00
84 JB,Two Against the Hawk-City,
   I:Zula 5.00
85 JB,Of Swordsmen & Sorcerers,
   O:Zulu 5.00
86 JB,Devourer of the Dead 5.00
87 TD, rep. Savage Sword #3. . . . . 5.00
88 JB,Queen and the Corsairs 5.00
89 JB,Sword & the Serpent,
   A:Thoth-Amon 5.00
90 JB,Diadem of the Giant-Kings . . 5.00
91 JB,Savage Doings in Shem 5.00
92 JB,The Thing in the Crypt. 5.00
93 JB,Of Rage & Revenge 5.00
94 JB,BeastKing ofAbombi,L:Zulu . 5.00
95 JB,The Return of Amra 5.00
96 JB,Long Night of Fang
   & Talon,pt.1 . . . . 5.00
97 JB,Long Night of Fang
   & Talon,pt.2 . . . . 5.00

98 JB,Sea-Woman. 5.00
99 JB,Devil Crabs o/t Dark Cliffs . . 5.00
100 JB,Death on the Black Coast,
   D:Belit (double size) 7.00
101 JB,The Devil has many Legs . . 3.00
102 JB,The Men Who
   Drink Blood. 3.00
103 JB,Bride of the Vampire 3.00
104 JB,The Vale of Lost Women . . . 3.00
105 JB,Whispering Shadows. 3.00
106 JB,Chaos in Kush 3.00
107 JB,Demon of the Night 3.00
108 JB,Moon-Eaters of Darfar. 3.00
109 JB,Sons of the Bear God 3.00
110 JB,Beward the Bear of Heaven 3.00
111 JB,Cimmerian Against a City. . . 3.00
112 JB,Buryat Besieged 3.00
113 JB,A Devil in the Family 3.00
114 JB,The Shadow of the Beast . . 3.00
115 JB,A War of Wizards, A:Red
   Sonja Double size 10th Anniv.
   (L:Roy Thomas script). 4.00
116 JB,NA,Crawler in the Mist. 5.00
117 JB,Corridor of Mullah-Kajar. . . 3.00
118 JD,Valley of Forever Night 3.00
119 JB,Voice of One Long Gone . . 3.00
120 JB,The Hand of Erlik. 3.00
121 JB,BMc,Price of Perfection . . . 3.00
122 JB,BMc,The City Where Time
   Stood Still. 3.00
123 JB,BMc,Horror Beneath the
   Hills 3.00
124 JB,BMc,the Eternity War. 3.00
125 JB,BMc,the Witches ofNexxx . . 3.00
126 JB,BMc,Blood Red Eye
   of Truth 3.00
127 GK,Snow Haired Woman
   of the Wastes 3.00
128 GK,And Life Sprang Forth
   From These 3.00
129 GK,The Creation Quest 3.00
130 GK,The Quest Ends 3.00
131 GK,The Ring of Rhax 3.00
132 GK,Games of Gharn 3.00
133 GK,The Witch of Windsor 3.00
134 GK,A Hitch in Time 3.00
135 M3,JRu,Forest of the Night . . . 3.00
136 JB,The River of Death 3.00
137 AA,Titans Gambit 3.00
138 VM,Isle of the Dead 3.00
139 VM,In the Lair of
   the Damned. 3.00
140 JB,Spider Isle 3.00
141 JB,The Web Tightens 3.00
142 JB,The Maze,the Man,
   the Monster 3.00
143 JB,Life Among the Dead. 3.00
144 JB,The Blade & the Beast 3.00
145 Son of Cimmeria 3.00
146 JB,Night o/t Three Sisters. 3.00
147 JB,Tower of Mitra 3.00
148 JB,The Plague of Forlek. 3.00
149 JB,Deathmark 3.00
150 JB,Tower of Flame 3.00
151 JB,Vale of Death 3.00
152 JB,Dark Blade of
   Jergal Zadh 3.00
153 JB,Bird Men of Akah Ma'at . . . 3.00
154 JB,the Man-Bats of
   Ur-Xanarrh. 3.00
155 JB,SL,The Anger of Conan. . . 3.00
156 JB,The Curse 3.00
157 JB,The Wizard 3.00
158 JB,Night of the Wolf 3.00
159 JB,Cauldron of the Doomed . . 3.00
160 Veil of Darkness 3.00
161 JB,House of Skulls,A:Fafnir . . . 3.00
162 JB,Destroyer in the Flame,
   A:Fafnir 3.00
163 JB,Cavern of the Vines of
   Doom,A:Fafnir 3.00
164 The Jeweled Sword of Tem . . . 3.00

165 JB,V:Nadine 3.00
166 JB,Gl,Blood o/t Titan,A:Fafnir . . 3.00
167 JB,Creature From Time's
   Dawn,A:Fafnir 3.00
168 JB,Bird Woman & the Beast. . . 3.00
169 JB,Tomb of the Scarlet Mage . . 3.00
170 JB,Dominion of the Dead,
   A&D:Fafnir. 3.00
171 JB,Barbarian Death Song. 3.00
172 JB,Reavers in Borderland. 3.00
173 JB,Honor Among Thieves 3.00
174 JB,V:Tetra 3.00
175 JB,V:Spectre ofDeath 3.00
176 JB,Argos Rain. 2.50
177 JB,V:Nostume 2.50
178 JB,A:Tetra,Well of Souls 2.50
179 JB,End of all there is,A:Kiev . . . 2.50
180 JBV:AnitRenrut 2.50
181 JB,V:KingMaddoc II 2.50
182 JB,V:King of Shem 2.50
183 JB,V:Imhotep 2.50
184 JB,V:Madoc. 2.50
185 JB,R:Tetra 2.50
186 JB,The Crimson Brotherhood . . 2.50
187 JB,V:Council of Seven 2.50
188 JB,V:Devourer-Souls 2.50
189 JB,V:Devourer-Souls 2.50
190 JB,Devourer-Souls 2.50
191 Deliverance 2.50
192 JB,V:TheKeeper 2.50
193 Devourer-Souls 2.50
194 V:Devourer-Souls 2.50
195 Blood of Ages 2.50
196 V:Beast 2.50
197 A:Red Sonja 2.50
198 A:Red Sonja 2.50
199 O:Kaleb. 2.50
200 JB,D.sizeV:Dev-Souls 5.00
201 NKu,Gl,Thulsa Doom 2.50
202 . . . . 2.50
203 V:Thulsa Doom 2.50
204 VS,Gl,A:Red Sonja,I:Strakkus . 2.50
205 A:Red Sonja 2.50
206 VS,Gl,Heku trilogy,pt.1 . . . . 2.50
207 VS,Gl,Heku,pt.2,O:Kote 2.50
208 VS,Gl,Heku,pt.3 . . . . 2.50
209 VS,Gl,Heku epilogue 2.50
210 V3,Gl,V.Sevante 2.50
211 VS,Gl,V:Sevante 2.50
212 EC,Gl 2.50
213 V:Ghamud Assassins 2.50
214 AA 2.50
215 VS,AA,Conan Enslaved 2.50
216 V:Blade of Zed 2.50
217 JLe(c),V:Blade of Zed 2.50

Conan The Barbarian #169
© Marvel Entertainment Group

All comics prices listed are for *Near Mint* condition.

218 JLe(c),V:Picts 2.50	
219 JLe(c),V:Forgotten Beasts 2.50	
220 Conan the Pirate. 2.50	
221 Conan the Pirate. 2.50	
222 AA,DP,Revenge 2.50	
223 AA,Religious Cult 2.50	
224 AA,Cannibalism. 2.50	
225 AA,Conan Blinded. 2.50	
226 AA,Quest for Mystic Jewel 2.50	
227 AA,Mystic Jewel,pt.2 . . . . 2.50	
228 AA,Cannibalism,pt.1 . . . . 2.50	
229 AA,Cannibalism,pt.2 . . . . 2.50	
230 FS,SDr,Citadel,pt.1 . . . . 2.50	
231 FS,DP,Citadel,pt.2. . . . . 2.50	
232 RLm,Birth of Conan 3.00	
233 RLm,DA,B:Conan as youth . . . 2.50	
234 RLm,DA 2.50	
235 RLm,DA 2.50	
236 RLm,DA 2.50	
237 DA,V:Jormma 2.50	
238 DA,D:Conan 2.50	
239 Conan Possessed. 2.50	
240 Conan Possessed. 2.50	
241 TM(c),R:RoyThomasScript . . . 3.50	
242 JLe(c),A:Red Sonja. 2.50	
243 WPo(c),V:Zukala, ... 2.50	
244 A:Red Sonja,Zula 2.50	
245 A:Red Sonja,V:King	
of Vampires 2.50	
246 A:Red Sonja,V:MistMonster . . . 2.50	
247 A:Red Sonja,Zula 2.50	
248 V:Zulu 2.50	
249 A:Red Sonja,Zula 2.50	
250 A:RedSonja,Zula,V:Zug	
double size. 5.00	
251 Cimmeria,V:Shumu Gorath. . . . 3.00	
252 ECh. 3.00	
253 ECh,V:Kulan-Goth(X-Men	
Villain) 3.00	
254 ECh,V:Shuma-Gorath (Dr.	
Strange Villain) 3.00	
255 ECh,V:Shuma-Gorath 3.00	
256 ECh,D:Nemedia's King 3.00	
257 ECh,V:Queen Vammator 3.00	
258 AA(i),A:Kulan Gath 3.00	
259 V:Shuma-Gorath 3.00	
260 AA(i),V:Queen Vammatar 3.00	
261 V:Cult of the Death Goddess . . 3.00	
262 V:The Panther. 3.00	
263 V:Malaq. 3.00	
264 V:Kralic 3.00	
265 V:Karlik 3.00	
266 Conan the Renegade (adapt.) . 3.00	
267 adapt.,pt.2 . . . . 3.00	
268 adapt.,pt.3 . . . . 3.00	

Conan The Barbarian, Movie Spec. #2
© Marvel Entertainment Group

269 V:Agohoth,Prince Borin. 3.00
270 Devourer of the Dead 3.00
271 V:Devourer of Souls 3.00
272 V:Devourer 3.00
273 V:Purple Lotus 3.00
274 V:She-Bat 3.00
275 RTs(s),Last Issue cont. in
    Savage Sword of Conan 5.00
G-Size#1 GK,TS,Hour of the
    Dragon, inc.rep.Conan#3,
    I:Belit. 25.00
G-Size#2 GK,TS,Conan Bound,
    inc. rep Conan #5 . . . . 12.00
G-Size#3 GK,TS,To Tarantia
    & the Tower,inc.rep.Conan#6 . . 8.00
G-Size#4,GK,FS,Swords of the
    South,inc.rep.Conan #7. . . . . . . 8.00
G-Size#5 rep.Conan #14,#15
    & Back-up story #12 . . . . 8.00
KingSz.#1 rep.Conan #2,#4. . . . . . 13.00
Ann.#2 BWS,Phoenix on the Sword
    A:Thoth-Amon 10.00
Ann.#3 JB,HC,Mountain of
    the Moon God, B.U.Kull story . . 8.00
Ann.#4 JB,Return of the
    Conqueror,A:Zenobia 8.00
Ann.#5 JB,W:Conan/Zenobia 5.00
Ann.#6 GK,King of the
    Forgotten People. 5.00
Ann.#7 JB,Red Shadows
    & Black Kraken 4.00
Ann.#8 VM,Dark Night of the
    White Queen 4.00
Ann.#9 . . . . 4.00
Ann.#10 Scorched Earth
    (Conan #176 x-over) 4.00
Ann.#11 . . . . 4.00
Conan-Barbarian Movie Spec.#1 . . 3.00
Conan-Barbarian Movie Spec.#2 . . 3.00
Conan-Destroyer Movie Spec.#1 . . 3.00
Conan-Destroyer Movie Spec.#2 . . 3.00
Red Nails Special Ed.BWS 4.00
TPB Conan & Ravagers Out
    of Time. 10.00
TPB Conan the Reaver 10.00
TPB Conan the Rogue,JB 10.00
TPB Horn of Azroth 10.00
TPB Skull of Set. 10.00

CONAN: THE FLAME
AND THE FIEND
June, 2000

1 (of 3) RTs,GI,V:Kulan Gath 3.00
2 RTs,GI,Bone Dragon 3.00
3 RTs,GI,concl. 3.00

CLASSIC CONAN
June, 1987

1 BWS,rep. 7.00
2 BWS,rep. 5.00
3 BWS,rep. 5.00
Becomes:

CONAN SAGA
1987

4 thru 10 rep.. . . . . @3.50
11 thru 98 rep. . . . . @3.00

CONAN CLASSICS
1994–95

1 rep. Conan #1 . . . . 2.25
2 rep. Conan #2 . . . . 2.25
3 rep. Conan #3 . . . . 2.25
2 thru 11 rep.. . . . . @2.25

CONAN/RUNE
1995

1 BWS,Conan Vs. Rune. 3.50

CONAN
1997

1 CCt, ... 2.00
2 CCt,V:Sorcerer. 2.00
3 (of 3) CCt, ... 2.00

CONAN:
RIVER OF BLOOD
April, 1998

1 (of 3) Valeria, vs. giant crocs. . . . 2.50
2 Caught in the middle of a war . . . 2.50
3 Lord of the Crocodiles, concl. . . . 2.50

CONAN THE BARBARIAN
VS. THE LORD OF
THE SPIDERS
Jan., 1998

1 (of 3) RTs,V:Harpagus 2.50
2 RTs, ... 2.50
3 RTs,V:Harpagus. 2.50

CONAN:
THE RETURN OF STYRM
July, 1998

1 (of 3) V:Mecora 2.50
2 (of 3) V:Mecora 3.00
3 conclusion 3.00

Conan The Scarlet Sword #1
© Marvel Entertainment Group

CONAN:
THE SCARLET SWORD
Oct., 1998

1 (of 3) RTs,V:Thun'da 3.00
2 RTs,A:Helliana 3.00
3 RTs,conclusion. 3.00

CONAN: THE USURPER
Oct., 1997

1 (of 3) CDi,KJ,Conan attacks
    Cimmeria? 2.50
2 CDi,KJ, ... 2.50
3 CDi,KJ, concl. 2.50

KING CONAN
March, 1980

1 JB/ECh,I:Conn,V:Thoth-Amon . . . 7.00
2 thru 19 . . . . @4.00
Becomes:

CONAN THE KING
1984
20 MS,The Prince is Dead 4.00
21 thru 55 . . . . @3.00

CONAN THE SAVAGE
(B&W Magazine), 1995–96
1 New Series 3.00
2 thru 10 . . . . @3.00

CONEHEADS
1994
1 Based Saturday Night Live 2.25
2 There Goes the Neighborhood . . 2.25
3 In Paris. 2.25

CONSPIRACY
Dec., 1997
1 (of 2) DAn,Were the origins of
  Marvel's superheroes really a
  conspiracy, not an accident?. . . 3.00
2 DAn,concl. 3.00

CONTEST OF CHAMPIONS
June, 1982
1 JR2,Grandmaster vs. Mistress
  Death, A:Alpha Flight. 8.00
2 JR2,Grandmaster vs. Mistress
  Death, A:X-Men 7.00
3 JR2,D:Grandmaster, Rebirth
  Collector, A:X-Men. 7.00

CONTEST OF CHAMPIONS II
July, 1999
1 (of 5) CCI,Marvel vs. Marvel 3.00
2 CCI,Atlas vs. Storm 3.00
3 CCI,super hero slugfest. 3.00
4 CCI. 3.00
5 CCI, conclusion 3.00
TPB Contest of Champions,
  '70s rep. 18.00

COPS: THE JOB
1992
1 MGo(c),V:Serial killer. 2.25
2 MGo(c). 2.25
3 MGo(c),V:Eviscerator. 2.25
4 MGo(c),D:Eviscerator,Nick 2.25

COSMIC POWERS
1994
1 RMz(s),RLm,JP,F:Thanos 2.75
2 RMz(s),JMr,F:Terrax 2.75
3 RMz(s),F:Jack of Hearts 2.75
4 RMz(s),RLm,F:Legacy. 2.75
5 RMz(s),F&O:Morg 2.75
6 RMz(s),F&O:Tyrant 2.75

COSMIC POWERS UNLIMITED
1995–96
1 Surfer vs. Thanos 4.25
2 Jack of Hearts vs. Jakar 4.25
3 GWt,JB,F:Lunatik,64pg. 4.25
4 GWt,SEa,cont.StarMasters#3 . . 4.25
5 GWt,SEa,R:Captain Universe . . . 4.25

COUNT DUCKULA
Star, Nov., 1988
1 O:CountDuckula,B:DangerMouse 4.00
2 A:Danger Mouse 3.00
3 thru 15 . . . . @3.00

COWBOY ACTION
See: WESTERN THRILLERS

COWBOY ROMANCES
Oct., 1949
1 Ph(c),Outlaw and the Lady . . . 275.00
2 Ph(c),William Holden/Mona
  Freeman,Streets of Laredo . . 250.00
3 Phc,Romance in
  Roaring Valley 150.00
Becomes:

YOUNG MEN
1950
4 A Kid Names Shorty. 250.00
5 Jaws of Death 200.00
6 Man-Size 200.00
7 The Last Laugh 200.00
8 Adventure stories continued . . 200.00
9 Draft Dodging story 200.00
10 JMn,US Draft Story 200.00
11 Adventure stories continued . . 200.00
12 JMn,B:On the Battlefield,
  inc.Spearhead 200.00
13 RH,Break-through. 200.00
14 GC,RH,Fox Hole. 200.00
15 GC,JMn,Battlefield stories
  cont. 200.00
16 Sniper Patrol 200.00
17 Battlefield stories cont, ... 200.00
18 BEv,Warlord 200.00
19 BEv 200.00
20 BEv,E:On the Battlefield 200.00
21 B:Flash Foster and his High
  Gear Hot Shots 200.00
22 Screaming Tires 200.00
23 E:Flash Foster and his High
  Gear Hot Shots 200.00
24 BEv,B:Capt. America,Human
  Torch,Sub-Mariner,O:Capt.
  America,Red Skull 3,600.00
25 BEv,JR, Human Toroh,Capt.
  America,Sub-Mariner 1,500.00
26 BEv,Human Torch, Capt.
  America,Sub Mariner 1,500.00
27 Bev, Human Torch/Toro
  V:Hypnotist 1,400.00
28 E:Human Torch, Capt.America,
  Sub Mariner,June, 1954 . . . 1,400.00

Young Men #24
© Marvel Entertainment Group

COWGIRL ROMANCES
See: DARING MYSTERY

COYOTE
Epic, June, 1983
1 SL, ... 3.00
2 SL 2.50
3 BG 2.50
4 thru 6 SL . . . . @2.50
7 SL,SD 2.50
8 SL 2.50
9 SL,SD 2.50
10 SL 2.50
11 FS,1st TM art,O:Slash 7.00
12 TM. 4.00
13 TM. 4.00
14 FS,TM,A:Badger. 4.00
15 SL 3.00
16 SL,A:Reagan,Gorbachev 3.00

CRASH RYAN
Epic, Oct., 1984
1 War Story 2.25
2 thru 4 . . . . @2.25

CRAZY
Marvel Atlas, Dec., 1953
1 JMn,BEv,satire, Frank N.
  Steins Castle 450.00
2 JMn,BEv,Beast from 1000
  Fathoms. 300.00
3 JMn,BEv,RH,Madame Knock-
  wurst's Whacks Museum. . . . 250.00
4 JMn,BEv,DAv,I Love Lucy
  satire 250.00
5 JMn,BEv,Censorship satire . . . 250.00
6 JMn,BEv,MD,satire 300.00
7 JMn,BEv,RH,satire,July, 1954 250.00

CRAZY
Feb., 1973–June, 1973
1 Not Brand Echh reps,
  Forbushman 35.00
2 Big,Batty Love & Hisses issue . 25.00
3 Stupor-Man,A:FantasticalFour . . 25.00

CREATURES ON THE LOOSE
See: TOWER OF SHADOWS

CREW
May, 2003
1 JoB,DaM,Big Trouble,pt.1 . . . . . . 2.50
2 thru 7 JoB,Big Trouble,pt.2–7 . @2.50

CRIME CAN'T WIN
See: KRAZY COMICS

CRIME CASES COMICS
Marvel Atlas, 1950–52
(Formerly: WILLIE COMICS)
(See: IDEAL)
1 (24) Police 250.00
2 (25) 200.00
3 (26) 150.00
4 (27) 150.00
5 . . . . 150.00
6 . . . . 150.00
7 . . . . 150.00
8 . . . . 150.00
9 . . . . 150.00
10 . . . . 150.00
11 . . . . 150.00
12 . . . . 150.00

CRIME EXPOSED
Marvel Atlas Comics, 1948–52
1 . . . . 400.00
2 . . . . 250.00
3 GT 150.00

MARVEL

4 GT	150.00
5 thru 7	@150.00
8 MMe(c)	175.00
9	150.00
10	150.00
11 JeR	175.00
12 BK,JeR	200.00
13 BK	200.00
14	125.00

CRIMEFIGHTERS
April, 1948–Nov., 1949

1 Police Stories	350.00
2 Jewelry Robbery	200.00
3 The Nine Who Were Doomed, addiction	225.00
4 Human Beast at Bay	150.00
5 V:Gangsters	150.00
6 Pickpockets	150.00
7 True Cases, Crime Can't Win	150.00
8 True Cases, Crime Can't Win	150.00
9 Ph(c),It Happened at Night	150.00
10 Ph(c),Killer at Large	150.00

Becomes:

CRIME FIGHTERS ALWAYS WIN
Marvel Atlas, 1954–1955

11 JMn,V:Gangsters	175.00
12 V:Gangsters	150.00
13 Clay Pidgeon	150.00

CRIME MUST LOSE!
Marvel Atlas, 1950

4	300.00
5	200.00
6	200.00
7	200.00
8	200.00
9 JeR	225.00
10	200.00
11	200.00
12	200.00

CRIMINAL
Icon, Oct., 2006

1 SeP	3.00
2 SeP	3.00

CRIMSON DYNAMO
Marvel Epic, June, 2003

1 high tech weapon	3.00
2 thru 6	@2.50

CRITICAL MASS
Epic, Jan.–July, 1990

1 KS,GM,BSzF:ShadowlineSaga	5.00
2 thru 7	@5.00

CROSSOVER CLASSICS
TPB Marvel and D.C. GP(c),reprints both Spider-Man/Superman,the Batman/Hulk and the X-Men/New Teen Titans Battles 18.00
TPB Vol.1 320-pg. (2001) 25.00

CRYPT OF SHADOWS
Jan., 1973

1 BW,RH,GK,Midnight on Black Mountain	50.00
2 GT,BEv,JMn,Monster at the Door	35.00
3 Dead Man's Hand	25.00
4 CI,Secret in the Vault	25.00
5 JM,The Graveyard Ghoul	25.00
6 BEv,GK,Don't Bury Me Deep	35.00
7 JSt,The Haunting of Bluebeard	35.00
8 How Deep my Grave	25.00
9 Beyond Death	25.00

10 A Scream in the Dark	25.00
11 The Ghouls in my Grave	20.00
12 BP,Behind the Locked Door	25.00
13 BEv,SD,Back From the Dead	25.00
14 The Thing that Creeps	20.00
15 My Coffin is Crowded	20.00
16	20.00
17 In the Hands of Shandu	20.00
18 SD,Face of Fear	25.00
19 SD,Colossus that Challenged the World	25.00
20 A Monster walks Among Us	20.00
21 SD,Death Will Be Mine, Nov., 1975	25.00

CUPID
Dec., 1949–March, 1950

1 Ph(c),Cora Dod's Amazing Decision	350.00
2 Ph(c),BP,Bettie Page	500.00

CURSE OF THE WEIRD
1993–94

1 thru 4 SD,rep. 50's Sci-Fi	2.25

CUTTING EDGE
1995

1 WML,F:Hulk,Ghosts of the Future tie-in	3.25

CYBERSPACE 3000
1993

1 A:Dark Angel,Galactus,V:Badoon, Glow in the dark(c)	3.25
2 thru 11	@2.25

CYCLOPS
Aug., 2001

1 (of 4) MT,JP	2.75
2 MT,JP,I:Ulysses	2.75
3 MT,JP,in a savage land	2.75
4 MT,JP,V:Ulysses	2.75
TPB X-Men Icons: Cyclops	13.00

DAILY BUGLE
B&W 1996

1 (of 3) KlK,GA	2.75
2 KlK,GA	2.75
3 KlK,GA	2.75

DAKOTA NORTH
1986–87

1 (Now in Cage)	2.25
2 thru 5	@2.25

DAMAGE CONTROL
May, 1989

1 EC/BWi;A:Spider-Man	3.00
2 EC/BWi;A:Fant.Four	2.50
3 EC/BWi;A:Iron Man	2.50
4 EC/BWi;A:X-Men	2.50

[2nd Series], 1989–90

1 EC,A:Capt.America&Thor	3.00
2 EC,A:Punisher	2.50
3 EC	2.50
4 EC,Punisher	2.50

[3rd Series], 1991

1 Clean-up Crew Returns	2.50
2 A:Hulk,New Warriors	2.50
3 A:Avengers W.C.,Wonder Man, Silver Surfer	2.50
4 A:SilverSurfer & others	2.50

DANCES WITH DEMONS
Frontier 1993

1 CAd	3.50
2 CAd,V:Manitou	2.50

Damage Control #1
© *Marvel Entertainment Group*

3 CAd,V:Manitou	2.50
4 CAd,last issue	2.50
5 Okay, there's more!	2.50
6	2.50

DAREDEVIL
April, 1964

1 B:StL(s),JK(c),BEv,I&O:Daredevil, I:Karen Page,Foggy Nelson	6,000.00
2 JK(c),JO,V:Electro	1,500.00
3 JK(c),JO,I&O:The Owl	1,200.00
4 JK(c),JO,I&O:Killgrave	1,000.00
5 JK(c),WW,V:Masked Matador	800.00
6 WW,I&O Original Mr. Fear	500.00
7 WW,I:Red Costume,V:Namor	1,400.00
8 WW,I&O:Stiltman	350.00
9 WW(i),Killers Castle	350.00
10 WW(i),V:Catman	350.00
11 WW(i),R:Cat	250.00
12 JK,JR,2nd A:Ka-Zar	250.00
13 JK,JR,O:Ka-Zar	250.00
14 JR,If This Be Justice	250.00
15 JR,A:Ox	250.00
16 JR,A:Spider-Man, I:Masked Marauder	350.00
17 JR,A:Spider-Man	350.00
18 DON(s),JR,I:Gladiator	250.00
19 JR,V:Gladiator	200.00
20 JR(c),GC,V:Owl	200.00
21 GC,BEv,V:Owl	200.00
22 GC,V:Tri-man	200.00
23 GC,V:Tri-man	175.00
24 GC,A:Ka-Zar	225.00
25 GC,V:Leapfrog	200.00
26 GC,V:Stiltman	200.00
27 GC,Spider-Man	200.00
28 GC,V:Aliens	200.00
29 GC,V:The Boss	200.00
30 BEv(c),GC,A:Thor	200.00
31 GC,V:Cobra	150.00
32 GC,V:Cobra	150.00
33 GC,V:Beetle	150.00
34 BEv(c),GC,O:Beetle	150.00
35 BEv(c),GC,A:Susan Richards	150.00
36 GC,A:FF	150.00
37 GC,V:Dr.Doom	150.00
38 GC,A:FF	150.00
39 GC,GT,V:Unholy Three	150.00
40 GC,V:Unholy Three	150.00
41 GC,D:Mike Murdock	125.00
42 GC,DA,I:Jester	125.00
43 JK(c),GC,A:Capt.America	125.00
44 JSo(c),GC,V:Jester	100.00
45 GC,V:Jester	100.00

46 GC,V:Jester 100.00
47 GC,`Brother Take My Hand' . . 100.00
48 GC,V:Stiltman 100.00
49 GC,V:Robot,I:Starr Saxon. . . . 100.00
50 JR(c),BWS,JCr,V:Robot 125.00
51 B:RTs(s),BWS,V:Robot 125.00
52 BWS,JCr,A:Black Panther . . . 125.00
53 GC,O:Daredevil. 110.00
54 GC,V:Mr.Fear,A:Spidey. 100.00
55 GC,V:Mr.Fear 75.00
56 GC,V:Death Head. 75.00
57 GC,V:Death Head. 75.00
58 GC,V:Stunt Master 75.00
59 GC,V:Torpedo. 75.00
60 GC,V:Crime Wave 75.00
61 GC,V:Cobra 75.00
62 GC,O:Night Hawk 50.00
63 GC,V:Gladiator 50.00
64 GC,A:Stuntmaster. 50.00
65 GC,V:BrotherBrimstone 50.00
66 GC,V:BrotherBrimstone 50.00
67 BEv(c),GC,Stiltman. 50.00
68 AC,V:Kragg Blackmailer,
    a:Bl.Panther,DD'sID Rev. . . . 50.00
69 E:RTs(s),GC,V:Thunderbolts,
    A:Bl.Panther(DD's ID Rev) . . . 50.00
70 GC,V:Terrorists 50.00
71 RTs(s),GC,V:Terrorists 50.00
72 GyC(s),GC,Tagak,V:Quother . . 50.00
73 GC,V:Zodiac 50.00
74 B:GyC(s),GC,I:Smasher 50.00
75 GC,V:El Condor 50.00
76 GC,TP,V:El Condor. 50.00
77 GC,TP,V:Manbull. 50.00
78 GC,TP,V:Manbull. 50.00
79 GC,TP,V:Manbull. 50.00
80 GK(c),GC,TP,V:Owl. 50.00
81 GK(c),GC,JA,A:Black Widow . . 60.00
82 GK(c),GC,JA,V:Scorpion 35.00
83 JR(c),BWS,BEv,V:Mr.Hyde 40.00
84 GK(c),GC,Assassin. 35.00
85 GK(c),GC,A:Black Widow 35.00
86 GC,TP,V:Ox. 35.00
87 GC,TP,V:Electro 35.00
88 GK(c),GC,TP,O:Black Widow . . 35.00
89 GC,TP,A:Black Widow 35.00
90 E:StL(s),GK(c),GC,TP,V:Ox . . . 35.00
91 GK(c),GC,TP,I:Mr. Fear III 35.00
92 GK(c),GC,TP,A:BlackPanther . . 35.00
93 GK(c),GC,TP,A:Black Widow . . 35.00
94 GK(c),GC,TP,V:Damon Dran . . 35.00
95 GK(c),GC,TP,V:Manbull 35.00
96 GK(c),GC,ECh,V:Manbull 35.00
97 GK(c),V:Dark Messiah 35.00

Daredevil #28
© Marvel Entertainment Group

98 E:GyC(s),GC,ECh,V:Dark
    Messiah. 35.00
99 B:SvG(s),JR(c),V:Hawkeye. . . . 35.00
100 GC,V:Angar the Screamer . . . 40.00
101 RB,A:Angar the Screamer . . . 20.00
102 A:Black Widow 20.00
103 JR(c),DH,A:Spider-Man 20.00
104 GK(c),DH,V:Kraven. 20.00
105 DH,JSn,DP,C:Thanos. 25.00
106 JR(c),DH,A:Black Widow 18.00
107 JSn(c),JB(i),A:Capt.Marvel . . . 18.00
108 K&R(c),PG(i),V:Beetle 18.00
109 GK(c),DH(i),V:Beetle. 18.00
110 JR(c),GC,A:Thing,O:Nekra . . . 18.00
111 JM(i),I:Silver Samurai 20.00
112 GK(c),GC,V:Mandrill 18.00
113 JR(c),V:Gladiator. 18.00
114 GK(c),I:Death Stalker 18.00
115 V:Death Stalker 18.00
116 GK(c),GC,V:Owl 18.00
117 E:SvG(s),K&R(c),V:Owl. 18.00
118 JR(c),DH,I:Blackwing 18.00
119 GK(c),DH(i),V:Crusher 18.00
120 GK(c),V:Hydra,I:El Jaguar . . . 18.00
121 GK(c),A:Shield 15.00
122 GK(c),V:Blackwing 15.00
123 V:Silvermane,I:Jackhammer. . 15.00
124 B:MWn(s),GK(c),GC,KJ,
    I:Copperhead. 15.00
125 GK(c),KJ(i),V:Copperhead . . . 15.00
126 GK(c),KJ(i),D: 2nd Torpedo . . 15.00
127 GK(c),KJ(i),V:3rd Torpedo . . . 15.00
128 GK(c),KJ(i),V:Death Stalker . . 15.00
129 KJ(i),V:Man Bull 15.00
130 KJ(i),V:Brother Zed 15.00
131 KJ(i),I&O:2nd Bullseye 85.00
132 KJ(i),V:Bullseye. 60.00
133 JM(i),GK(c),V:Jester 15.00
134 JM(i),V:Chamelon 15.00
135 JM(i),V:Jester 15.00
136 JB,JM,V:Jester 15.00
137 JB,V:Jester 15.00
138 JBy,A:Ghost Rider 20.00
139 SB,V:A Bomber. 15.00
140 SB,V:Gladiator 15.00
141 GC,Bullseye. 30.00
142 GC,V:Cobra 15.00
143 E:MWn(s),GC,V:Cobra 15.00
144 CT,V:Manbull 15.00
145 GT,V:Owl 15.00
146 GC,V:Bullseye. 40.00
147 GC,V:Killgrave. 15.00
148 GC,V:Deathstalker 15.00
149 KI,V:Smasher 15.00
150 GC,KJ,I:Paladin 15.00
151 GC,Daredevil Unmasked 15.00
152 KJ,V:Paladin 15.00
153 GC,V:Cobra 15.00
154 GC,V:Mr. Hyde 15.00
155 V:Avengers 15.00
156 GC,V:Death Stalker. 15.00
157 GC,V:Death Stalker. 15.00
158 FM,V:Death Stalker 100.00
159 FM,V:Bullseye 50.00
160 FM,Bullseye 40.00
161 FM,V:Bullseye. 40.00
162 SD,JRu,`Requiem' 12.00
163 FM,V:Hulk,I:Ben Urich 25.00
164 FM,KJ,A:Avengers 25.00
165 FM,KJ,V:Dr.Octopus 25.00
166 FM,KJ,V:Gladiator 25.00
167 FM,KJ,V:Mauler 25.00
168 FM,KJ,I&O:Elektra 135.00
169 FM,KJ,V:Bullseye 50.00
170 FM,KJ,V:Bullseye 22.00
171 FM,KJ,V:Kingpin 20.00
172 FM,KJ,V:Bullseye 20.00
173 FM,KJ,V:Gliadator. 20.00
174 FM,KJ,A:Gladiator. 20.00
175 FM,KJ,A:Elektra,V:Hand 25.00
176 FM,KJ,A:Elektra 22.00
177 FM,KJ,A:Stick 25.00

Daredevil #100
© Marvel Entertainment Group

178 FM,KJ,A:PowerMan&I.Fist . . . 22.00
179 FM,KJ,V:Elektra 22.00
180 FM,KJ,V:Kingpin 22.00
181 FM,KJ,V:Bullseye,D:Elektra,
    A:Punisher. 42.00
182 FM,KJ,A:Punisher. 18.00
183 FM,KJ,V:PunisherDrug 18.00
184 FM,KJ,V:PunisherDrug 18.00
185 FM,KJ,V:King Pin 12.00
186 FM,KJ,V:Stiltman 12.00
187 FM,KJ,A:Stick 12.00
188 FM,KJ,A:Black Widow 12.00
189 FM,KJ,A:Stick,A:BlackWidow . 12.00
190 FM,KJ,R:Elektra 12.00
191 FM,TA,A:Bullseye 12.00
192 KJ,V:Kingpin 5.00
193 K,I,Betsy 5.00
194 KJ,V:Kingpin 5.00
195 KJ,Tarkington Brown. 5.00
196 KJ,A:Wolverine 16.00
197 V:Bullseye. 5.00
198 V:Dark Wind 5.00
199 V:Dark Wind 5.00
200 JBy(c),V:Bullseye 7.00
201 JBy(c),A:Black Widow. 5.00
202 I:Micah Synn. 5.00
203 JBy(c),I:Trump 5.00
204 BSz(c),V:Micah Synn 5.00
205 I:Gael 5.00
206 V:Micah Synn 5.00
207 BSz(c),A:Black Widow 5.00
208 Harlan Ellison 6.00
209 Harlan Ellison 6.00
210 DM,V:Micah Synn 5.00
211 DM,V:Micah Synn 5.00
212 DM,V:Micah Synn 5.00
213 DM,V:Micah Synn 5.00
214 DM,V:Micah Synn 5.00
215 DM,A:Two-Gun Kid 5.00
216 DM,V:Gael 5.00
217 BS(c),V:Gael. 5.00
218 KP,V:Jester 5.00
219 FM,JB 6.00
220 DM,D:Heather Glenn 5.00
221 DM,Venice. 5.00
222 DM,A:Black Widow 5.00
223 DM,Secret Wars II 5.00
224 DM,V:Sunturion. 5.00
225 DM,V:Vulture. 5.00
226 FM(plot),V:Gladiator 5.00
227 FM,Kingpin,Kar.Page 12.00
228 FM,DM,V:Kingpin 10.00
229 FM,Kingpin,Turk 10.00
230 R:Matt's Mother 10.00
231 FM,DM,V:Kingpin 10.00

232 FM,V:Kingpin,Nuke 10.00	303 V:The Owl. 5.00	339 Wages of Sin,pt.2 . . . . 3.00
233 FM,Kingpin,Nuke,Capt.Am. . . 10.00	304 AW,Non-action issue 5.00	340 R:Kingpin 3.00
234 SD,KJ,V:Madcap. 5.00	305 AW,A:Spider-Man 5.00	341 Kingpin 3.00
235 SD,KJ,V:Mr. Hyde. 5.00	306 AW,A:Spider-Man 5.00	342 DGc,KP,V:Kingpin 3.00
236 BWS,A:Black Widow. 6.00	307 1st SMc DD,Dead Man's	343 Without Costume 3.00
237 AW(i),V:Klaw 5.00	Hand #1,A:Nomad. 6.00	344 Identity Crisis,pt.1 . . . . 3.00
238 SB,SL,AAd(c)V:Sabretooth. . . 7.00	308 SMc,Dead Man's Hand #5,	345 Identity Crisis,pt.2 . . . . 3.00
239 AAd(c),AW,GI(i),V:Rotgut 5.00	A:Punisher,V:Silvermane. 5.00	346 V:Sir 3.00
240 AW,V:Rotgut 5.00	309 SMc,Dead Man's Hand#7,	347 V:mystery man 3.00
241 MZ(c),TM,V:Trixter 6.00	A:Nomad,Punisher 5.00	348 In NY City 3.50
242 KP,V:Caviar Killer 5.00	310 SMc,Inf.War,V:Calipso 5.00	349 Retreats to the Chaste 3.50
243 AW,V:Nameless One 5.00	311 SMc,V:Calypso 5.00	350 Double size 4.00
244 TD(i),V:Nameless One 5.00	312 Firefighting issue. 5.00	351 . . . . 3.00
245 TD(i),A:Black Panther 5.00	313 SMc,V:Pyromaniac 5.00	352 Return of Matt Murdock 3.00
246 TD(i),V:Chance 5.00	314 SMc,V:Mr.Fear,I:Shock 5.00	353 KK,CNr,A:Mr. Hyde 3.00
247 KG,A:Black Widow 5.00	315 SMc,V:Mr.Fear 5.00	354 KK,CNr,A:Spider-Man 3.00
248 RL,AW,A:Wolverine,	316 Goes Underground 5.00	355 KK,CNr,A:Pyro 3.00
V:Bushwhacker, ... 7.00	317 SMc,Comedy Issue. 5.00	356 KK,CNr, ... 3.00
249 RL,AW,V:Wolverine,	318 SMc,V:Taskmaster 5.00	357 KK,CNr, ... 3.00
Bushwhacker. 7.00	319 SMc,Fall from Grace Prologue,	358 KK,CNr,MRy,A:Mysterio 3.00
250 JR2,AW,I:Bullet 5.00	A:Silver Sable,Garrett,Hand . . . 7.00	359 KK,CNr,A:Absorbing Man . . . 3.00
251 JR2,AW,V:Bullet 5.00	319a 2nd Printing. 3.00	360 KK,CNr,MRy,V:Onslaught 3.00
252 JR2,AW,Fall o/Mutants 6.00		361 KK,CNr,MRy,A:Black Widow. . . 3.00
253 JR2,AW,V:Kingpin. 5.00		362 KK,CNr,Romance 3.00
254 JR2,AW,I:Typhoid Mary 13.00		363 KK,GC,CaS,V:Insomnia 3.00
255 JR2,AW,A:Kingpin,TMary 6.00		364 KK,CNr,MRy,V:Insomnia. 3.00
256 JR2,AW,A:Kingpin,TMary 6.00		365 CNr,MRy,V:Mr. Fear,
257 JR2,AW,A:Punisher 10.00		A:Molten Man 3.00
258 RLm,V:Bengal 6.00		366 GC,V:Gladiator 3.00
259 JR2,AW,V:TyphoidMary 5.00		367 GC,V:Gladiator, concl. 3.00
260 JR2,AW,V:T.Mary,K.pin 5.00		368 GC,A:Black Widow and Omega
261 JR2,AW,HumanTorch 5.00		Red 3.00
262 JR2,AW,Inferno 5.00		369 AOI,V:Soviet Super Soldiers . . . 3.00
263 JR2,AW,Inferno 5.00		370 GC,Black Widow, concl. 3.00
264 SD,AW,MM,V:The Owl 5.00		371 AOI,Matt Murdock & Karen
265 JR2,AW,Inferno 5.00		Page's relationship 3.00
266 JR2,AW,V:Mephisto 5.00		372 AOI,Killers after Karen Page. . . 3.00
267 JR2,AW,V:Bullet 5.00		373 AOI,V:The 3. . . . . 3.00
268 JR2,AW,V:TheMob 5.00		374 AOI,V:Mr. Fear 3.00
269 JR2,AW,V:Pyro&Bullet 5.00		375 AOI,RL,V:Mr. Fear,double size . 4.00
270 JR2,AW,A:Spider-Man,		376 SLo,CHm,Daredevil deep
I:Blackheart 5.00		undercover. 3.00
271 JR2,AW,I:Number9. . . . . 5.00		377 SLo,TMo,SHa,Flying Blind,pt.2 3.00
272 JR2,AW,I:Shotgun. 5.50		378 SLo,TMo,SHa,Flying Blind,pt.3. 3.00
273 JR2,AW,V:Shotgun. 5.00		379 SLo,CHm,Flying Blind,concl. . . 3.00
274 JR2,AW,V:Inhumans 5.00		380 DGC,LW,RbC, V:Bullseye,Bush-
275 JR2,AW,ActsOfVen.,V:Ultron . . 5.00		wacker,Kingpin, double size . . . 5.00
276 JR2,AW,ActsOfVen.,V:Ultron . . 5.00		Minus 1 Spec., GC, flashback 3.00
277 RL,AW,Vivian's Story 5.00	*Daredevil:#225*	Ann.#1 GC. 275.00
278 JR2,AW,V:Blackheart,	*© Marvel Entertainment Group*	Ann.#2 reprints. 200.00
A:Inhumans 5.00		Ann.#3 reprints. 150.00
279 JR2,AW,V:Mephisto,	320 SMc,B:Fall from Grace,	Ann.#4 (1976)GT,A:Black
A:Inhumans 5.00	V:Crippler,S.Sable,A:Stone 7.00	Panther,Namor 7.00
280 JR2,AW,V:Mephisto,	321 SMc,N:Daredevil,A:Venom,	Ann.#5 (1989)MBa,JLe,JR2,KJ,
A:Inhumans 5.00	Garret, V:Hellspawn,Glow	WPo,AM,Atlantis Attacks,
281 JR2,AW,V:Mephisto,	in the Dark(c). 6.00	A:Spider-Man. 5.00
A:Inhumans 5.00	321a Newsstand Ed. 5.00	Ann.#6 TS,Lifeform#2,A:Typhoid
282 JR2,AW,V:Mephisto,	322 SMc,A:Venom,Garret,Siege . . . 4.00	Mary. 5.00
A:Silver Surfer, Inhumans 5.00	323 SMc,V:Venom,A:Siege,Garret,	Ann.#7 JG,JBr,Von Strucker
283 MBa,AW,A:Captain America . . . 5.00	I:Erynys 4.00	Gambit,pt.1,A:Nick Fury 5.00
284 LW,AW,R:Bullseye 5.00	324 SMc,A:Garret,R:Elektra,	Ann.#8 Sys.Bytes#2,A:Deathlok . . . 5.00
285 LW,AW,B:Bullseye	A:Stone, Morbius 4.00	Ann.#9 MPa,I:Devourer,w/card,tie-in
become DD#1 . . . . 5.00	325 SMc,E:Fall from Grace, A:Garret,	to Fall From Grace 5.00
286 LW,AW,GCa,Fake	Siege,Elektra,Morbius,V:Hand,	Ann.#10 I:Ghostmaker,A:Shang
Daredevil #2 . . . . 5.00	D:Hellspawn,Double size 4.00	Chi, Elektra 4.00
287 LW,AW,Fake Daredevil #3 . . . . 5.00	326 SMc,B:Tree of Knowledge,	G-Size #1 GK(c),reprints 12.00
288 LW,AW,A:Kingpin 5.00	I:Killobyte,A:Capt.America. 3.00	TPB Born Again,rep.#227-#233 . . . 11.00
289 LW,AW,A:Kingpin 5.00	327 E:DGC(s),SMc,A:Capt.Amer. . . 3.00	TPB Fall of the Kingpin, rep. 16.00
290 LW,AW,E:Fake Daredevil 5.00	328 GtW(s),V:Wirehead,A:Captain	TPB Gangwar, rep. 13.00
291 LW,AW,V:Bullet 5.00	America,S.Sable,Wild Pack. . . . 3.00	TPB Marked for Death, rep. 10.00
292 LW,A:Punisher,V:Tombstone. . . 5.00	329 B:DGC(s),SMc,A:Captain	Daredevil/Punisher:Child's Play rep. 7.00
293 LW,A:Punisher,V:Tombstone. . . 5.00	America, S.Sable,Iron Fist. 3.00	TPB Daredevil: Man Without Fear. 16.00
294 LW,V:The Hand. 5.00	330 SMc,A:Gambit. 3.00	
295 LW,V:The Hand,A:GhostRider. . 5.00	331 SMc,A:Captain America,	**DAREDEVIL**
296 LW,AW,V:The Hand 5.00	VLHydra. 3.00	**Sept., 1998**
297 B:DGC(s),LW,AW,B:Last Rites,	332 A:Captain America,Gambit 3.00	1 JP,JQ,F:Matt Murdock 12.00
V:Typhoid Mary,A:Kingpin 5.00	333 TGb,GWt. 3.00	1a Deluxe edition 7.50
298 LW,AW,A:Nick Fury,Kingpin . . . 5.00	334 TGb,GWt. 3.00	2 JP,JQ,blind faith dilemma 10.00
299 LW,AW,A:Kingpin 5.00	335 . . . . 3.00	2a variant JSC cover 10.00
300 LW,AW,E:Last Rites, ... 8.00	336 . . . . 3.00	3 JP,JQ,Guardian Devil,pt.3 . . . . . . 6.00
301 V:The Owl 5.00	337 V:Kingpin,A:Blackwulf 3.00	4 JP,JQ,Guardian Devil,pt.4 . . . . . . 6.00
302 V:The Owl 5.00	338 Wages of Sin,pt.1 . . . . 3.00	5 JP,JQ,Guardian Devil,pt.5 . . . . . . 6.00

5a Variant (c)	7.00	58 BMB,King of Hell's Kitchen,pt.3	3.00
6 JP,JQ,Guardian Devil,pt.6	4.00	59 BMB,King of Hell's Kitchen,pt.4	3.00
7 JP,JQ,Guardian Devil,pt.7	4.00	60 BMB,King of Hell's Kitchen,pt.5	3.00
8 JP,JQ,Guardian Devil,concl.	4.00	61 BMB,The Widow,pt.1	3.00
8a signed	20.00	62 BMB,The Widow,pt.2	3.00
9 JP,JQ,DMk,V:Kingpin	4.00	63 BMB,The Widow,pt.3	3.00
9a signed	15.00	64 BMB,The Widow,pt.4	3.00
10 JP,JQ,DMk,I:Echo	4.00	65 BMB,Anniversary Spec.,48-pg.	4.00
11 JP,JQ,DMk,A:Kingpin	4.00	66 BMB,Golden Age,pt.1	3.00
12 JP,JQ,DMk,V:Kingpin	4.00	67 BMB,Golden Age,pt.2	3.00
13 JP,JQ,DMk,V:Kingpin	4.00	68 BMB,Golden Age,pt.3	3.00
14 JQ,DMk,V:Kingpin	5.00	69 BMB,Golden Age,pt.4	3.00
15 JQ,DMk,V:Echo	4.00	70 BMB,Golden Age,pt.5	3.00
16 BMB,DMk,	5.00	71 BMB,Decalogue,pt.1	3.00
17 BMB,DMk,F:Ben Urich	5.00	72 BMB,Decalogue,pt.2	3.00
18 BMB,DMk,F:Ben, Timmy	5.00	73 BMB,Decalogue,pt.3	3.00
19 BMB,DMk,F:Ben, Timmy	4.00	74 BMB,Decalogue,pt.4	3.00
20 40-page,BU:F:Spider-Man	5.00	75 BMB,Decalogue,pt.5, 48-pg.	4.00
21 A:Jester	4.00	76 BMB,The Murdock Papers,pt.1	3.00
22 Matt Murdock vs. Daredevil	4.00	77 BMB,The Murdock Papers,pt.2	3.00
23 Matt Murdock vs. Daredevil	4.00	78 BMB,The Murdock Papers,pt.3	3.00
24 MPn,the trial begins	4.00	79 BMB,The Murdock Papers,pt.4	3.00
25 Playing to the Camera	4.00	80 BMB, The Murdock Papers,pt.5	3.00
26 BMB,V:Nitro	12.00	81 BMB	3.00
27 BMB,V:Silke,Kingpin	5.00	82 MLr,Devil in Cell Block D,36-pg	3.50
28 BMB,Elektra x-over,'Nuff Said	5.00	83 MLr,Devil in Cell Block D	3.00
29 BMB,Kingpin's Empire	5.00	84 MLr,Devil in Cell Block D	3.00
30 BMB,Kingpin's Secrets	5.00	85 MLr,Devil in Cell Block D	3.00
31 BMB,plot twist	5.00	86 MLr,Devil in Cell Block D	3.00
32 BMB,Kingpin's Empire	7.00	87 MLr,Devil in Cell Block D	3.00
33 BMB,F:Matt Murdock	4.00	88 MLr,Secret Life of Foggy Nelson	3.00
34 BMB, anger's terms	3.00	89 MLr,Devil Takes A Ride, pt.1	3.00
35 BMB,V:Mr. Hyde	3.00	90 MLr,Devil Takes A Ride, pt.2	3.00
36 BMB,F:Luke Cage	3.00	91 MLr,Devil Takes A Ride, pt.3	3.00
37 BMB,F:Elektra	3.00	Spec.Daredevil vs. Punisher	3.50
38 BMB,Trial of White Tiger,pt.1	3.00	Spec. Daredevil/Deadpool, BCh, JHo,	
39 BMB,Trial of White Tiger,pt.2	3.00	Two annuals in one,48pg.(1997)	5.00
40 BMB,Trial of the Century	4.00	Spec. Daredevil/Batman, DGC,	
41 BMB,Lowlife,pt.1	4.00	SMc, 48pg. (1997)	6.00
42 BMB,Lowlife,pt.2	3.00	Spec.#1 Daredevil (2000)	2.25
43 BMB,Lowlife,pt.3	3.00	Spec. Daredevil Movie adapt.	3.50
44 BMB,Lowlife,pt.4	3.00	TPB rep. #1–#3	10.00
45 BMB,Lowlife,concl.	3.00	TPB Gang War,FM,KJ	16.00
46 BMB,Hardcore,pt.1	3.00	TPB Daredevil: Born Again	18.00
47 BMB,Hardcore,pt.2	3.00	TPB Visionaries: Frank Miller	25.00
48 BMB,Hardcore,pt.3	3.00	TPB Visionaries: Kevin Smith	20.00
49 BMB,Hardcore,pt.4	3.00	TPB Parts of a Hole, 160-pg.	17.00
50 BMB,Hardcore,pt.5	5.00	TPB Wake Up (2002)	10.00
51 DMk,R:Echo,pt.1	3.00	TPB Underboss, 144-pg. (2002)	15.00
52 DMk,V:Echo,pt.2	3.00	TPB Love's Labor Lost (2002)	20.00
53 DMk,V:Echo,pt.3	3.00	TPB Daredevil Movie adapt.	13.00
54 DMk,V:Echo,pt.4,F:Wolverine	3.00	TPB The Devil, Inside and Out	15.00
55 DMk,Echo's vision quest.	3.00	TPB Legends Vol.4.Typhoid Mary	20.00
56 BMB,New Kingpin	3.00	TPB Vol. 1:Guardian Devil	20.00
57 BMB,A:Spider-Man	3.00	TPB Vol. 2: Parts of a Hole	18.00
		TPB Vol. 3: Wake Up	10.00
		TPB Vol. 4: Underboss	15.00
		TPB Vol. 5: Out	20.00
		TPB Vol. 6: Lowlife	14.00
		TPB Vol. 7: Hardcore	14.00
		TPB Vol. 8: Echo – Vision Quest	14.00
		TPB Vol. 9: King of Hell's Kitchen	14.00
		TPB Vol. 10: The Widow	18.00
		TPB Vol. 11: Golden Age	14.00
		TPB Vol. 12: Decalogue	15.00
		TPB Vol. 13 The Murdock Papers	15.00

Daredevil The Man Without Fear #4
© Marvel Entertainment Group

5 JR2,AW,A:Mickey,Last Issue 6.00
TPB rep.#1#5. . . . . 16.00

DAREDEVIL: NINJA
Oct., 2000

1 (of 3) BMB,Stick 5.00
2 BMB,V:Hand 5.00
3 BMB,concl. 5.00
TPB rep. 80-page 9.00

DAREDEVIL: REDEMPTION
Feb., 2005

1 (of 6) Redemption Valley murder. 3.00
2 thru 6 BSz(c) . . . . @3.00
TPB Redemption, series rep. 15.00

DAREDEVIL/SHI SHI/DAREDEVIL
Marvel/Crusade 1996

1 (Daredevil/Shi) TSg,AW,
  x-over,pt.1 . . . . 5.00
1 (Shi/Daredevil) x-over, pt 2 . . . . . 5.00

DAREDEVIL/SPIDER-MAN
Nov., 2000

1 (of 4) AxR,PJe, ... 4.00
2 AxR,PJe,Gladiator,Stilt-Man. 4.00
3 AxR,PJe,Owl,Copperhead 4.00
4 AxR,PJe,TP,concl. 4.00

DAREDEVIL: THE TARGET
Nov., 2002

1 (of 4) KSm,GF,V:Bullseye 3.50

DAREDEVIL VS. PUNISHER
July, 2005

1(of 6) DL,Means and Ends 3.00
2 DL,Means and End 3.00
3 thru 6 DL, ... @3.00
TPB 16.00

DAREDEVIL: YELLOW
March, 2001

1 (of 6) JLb,TSe,O:Daredevil 10.00
2 JLb,TSe,Vengeance 7.00
3 JLb,TSe,F:Fantastic Four 7.00
4 JLb,TSe,V:Electro 7.00

Daredevil Vol. 2 #6
© Marvel Entertainment Group

DAREDEVIL: FATHER
April, 2004

1 (of 5) JQ,DaM 3.50
#1 Director's Cut. 3.00
2 thru 6 JQ . . . . @3.00

DAREDEVIL: THE MAN WITHOUT FEAR
1993–94

1 B:FM(s),JR2,AW,O:Daredevil,
  A:Stick,D:Daredevil's Father . . . 7.00
2 JR2,AW,A:Stick,Stone,Elektra . . . 6.00
3 JR2,AW,A:Elektra,Kingpin 6.00
4 JR2,AW,A:Kingpin,I:Mickey 6.00

MARVEL

MARVEL

5 JLb,TSe,V:Owl 7.00
6 JLb,TSe,last yellow costume 7.00
TPB series rep. 15.00

DARING MYSTERY COMICS
Marvel Timely, Jan., 1940
1 ASh(c),JSm,O:Fiery Mask,
  A:Monako John Steele,Doc Doyle,
  Flash FosterBarney Mullen,
  Sea Rover, Bondage (c) . . 50,000.00
2 ASh(c),JSm,O:Phantom Bullet
  A:Zephyr Jones & K4,Laughing
  Mask Mr.E,B:Trojak 30,000.00
3 ASh(c),JSm,A:Phantom
  Reporter,Marvex,Breeze
  Barton, B:Purple Mask . . 12,000.00
4 ASh(c),A:G-Man Ace,K4,
  Monako,Marvex,E:Purple
  Mask,B:Whirlwind Carter . . 8,000.00
5 ASh(c),JSm,B:Falcon,A:Fiery
  Mask,K4, Little Hercules,
  Bondage(c) 8,000.00
6 S&K,O:Marvel Boy,A:Fiery
  Mask, Flying Fame,Dynaman,
  Stuporman,E:Trojak 10,000.00
7 ASh(c),S&K,O:Blue Diamond,
  A:The Fin, Challenger,Captain
  Daring, Silver Scorpion,
  Thunderer 8,000.00
8 S&K,O:Citizen V,A:Thunderer,
  Fin Silver Scorpion,Captain
  Daring Blue Diamond 7,000.00
Becomes:

DARING COMICS
1944
9 ASh(c),B:Human Torch,Toro,
  Sub Mariner 3,000.00
10 ASh(c),A:The Angel 2,600.00
11 ASh(c),A:The Destroyer 2,600.00
12 E:Human Torch,Toro,Sub-
  Mariner, Fall, 1945 . . . . 2,600.00
Becomes:

JEANIE COMICS
1947
13 B:Jeanie,Queen of the
  Teens Mitzi,Willie 300.00
14 Baseball(c) 250.00
15 Schoolbus(c) 250.00
16 Swimsuit(c) 275.00
17 HK,Fancy Dress Party(c),
  Hey Look 225.00

Jeanie Comics #16
© Marvel Entertainment Group

18 HK,Jeanie's Date(c), Hey
  Look 200.00
19 Ice-Boat(c),Hey Look 225.00
20 Jukebox(c) 200.00
21 . . . . 200.00
22 HK, Hey Look 225.00
23 thru 25 . . . . @200.00
26 . . . . 200.00
27 E:Jeanie,Queen of Teens 200.00
Becomes:

COWGIRL ROMANCES
1950
28 Ph(c),Mona Freeman/MacDonald
  Carey,Copper Canyon 300.00

DARK ANGEL
See: HELL'S ANGEL

DARK CRYSTAL
April, 1983
1 movie adaption 3.00
2 movie adaption,May, 1983 . . . . . . 3.00

DARK GUARD
1993–94
1 A:All UK Heroes 3.00
2 A:All UK Heroes 2.25
3 V:Leader,MyS-Tech 2.25
4 V:MyS-Tech 2.25
5 . . . . 2.25
6 and 7 . . . . @2.25

DARKHAWK
March, 1991
1 MM,I&O:Darkhawk,
  A:Hobgoblin 5.00
2 MM,A:Spider-Man,V:Hobgoblin . . 3.00
3 MM,A:Spider-Man,V:Hobgoblin . . 3.00
4 MM,I:Savage Steel 3.00
5 MM,I:Portal 3.00
6 MM,A:Cap.Am,D.D.,Portal,
  V:U-Foes 3.00
7 MM,I:Lodestone 2.50
8 MM,V:Lodestone 2.50
9 MM,A:Punisher,V:Savage Steel . . 2.50
10 MM,A&N:Tombstone 2.50
11 MM,V:Tombstone 2.50
12 MM,V:Tombstone,R:Dark
  Hawks'Father 2.50
13 MM,V:Venom 3.00
14 MM,V:Venom,D:Dark
  Hawks Father 3.00
15 thru 24 . . . . @2.25
25 MM,O:Darkhawk,V:Evilhawk,
  Holo-graphx(c) 3.50
26 thru 49 . . . . @2.25
50 V:Overhawk 3.00
Ann.#1 MM,Assault on ArmorCity . . 3.00
Ann.#2 GC,AW,I:Dreamkiller,
  w/Trading card 3.00
Ann.#3 I:Damek 3.00

DARKHOLD
1992–94
1 RCa,I:Redeemers,Polybagged
  w/poster,A:Gh.Rider,Blaze 3.00
2 RCa,R:Modred 2.50
3 thru 16 . . . . @2.25

DARK MAN
MOVIE ADAPTION
Sept., 1990
1 BH/MT/TD 3.00
2 BH/TD 2.50
3 BH/TD,final issue 2.50

DARKMAN
Sept., 1990
1 JS,R:Darkman 4.50
2 JS,V:Witchfinder 3.00
3 JS,Witchfinder 3.00
4 JS,V:Dr.West 3.00
5 JS,Durant 3.00
6 JS,V:Durant 3.00

A DATE WITH MILLIE
Marvel Atlas, Oct., 1956
[1st Series]
1 . . . . 400.00
2 . . . . 250.00
3 thru 7 . . . . @200.00
[2nd Series], Oct., 1959
1 . . . . 250.00
2 thru 7 . . . . @200.00
Becomes:

LIFE WITH MILLIE
1960
8 . . . . 125.00
9 & 10 . . . . @75.00
11 thru 20 . . . . @65.00
Becomes:

MODELING WITH MILLIE
1963
21 . . . . 125.00
22 thru 54 June, 1967 . . . . @65.00

A DATE WITH PATSY
Sept., 1957
1 A:Patsy Walker 150.00

DAUGHTERS OF THE DRAGON
Jan., 2006
1 JP 3.00
2 thru 6 JP . . . . @3.00
TPB Samurai Bullets 16.00
Spec. #1 Deadly Hands, 80-pg. 4.00

DAYDREAMERS
Aug., 1997
1 (of 3) JMD,MEg,HSm 2.75
2 JMD,MEg,HSm 2.75
3 JMD,TDz,MEg,HSm,concl. 2.75

DAZZLER
March, 1981
1 AA,JR2,A:X-Men,Spm,
  O:Dazzler 5.00
2 WS,JR2,AA,X-Men,A:SpM 3.00
3 JR2,Dr.Doom 3.00
4 FS,Dr.Doom 3.00
5 FS,I:Blue Shield 3.00
6 FS,Hulk 3.00
7 FS,Hulk 3.00
8 FS,Quasar 3.00
9 FS,D:Klaw 3.00
10 FS,Galactus 3.00
11 FS,Galactus 3.00
12 FS,The Light That Failed 3.00
13 FS,V:Grapplers 3.00
14 FS,She Hulk 3.00
15 FS,BSz,Spider Women 3.00
16 FS,BSz,Enchantress. 3.00
17 FS,Angel,V:Doc Octopus 3.00
18 FS,BSz,A:Fantastic Four,Angel,
  V:Absorbing Man 3.00
19 FS,Blue Bolt,V:Absorbing Man . . 3.00
20 FS,V:Jazz and Horn 3.00
21 FS,A:Avengers,F.F.,C:X-Men,
  (double size) 3.00
22 FS,V:Rogue,Mystique 4.00

Dazzler #3
© Marvel Entertainment Group

23 FS,V:Rogue,A:Powerman,
  Iron Fist 3.00
24 FS,V:Rogue,A:Powerman,
  Iron Fist 4.00
25 FS,`The Jagged Edge' 3.00
26 FS,Lois London. 3.00
27 FS,Fugitive 3.50
28 FS,V:Rogue 4.00
29 FS,Roman Nekoboh 3.00
30 FS,Moves to California 3.00
31 FS,The Last Wave 3.00
32 FS,A:Inhumans 3.00
33 Chiller 3.50
34 FS,Disappearance 3.00
35 FS,V:Racine Ramjets 3.00
36 JBy(c),FS,V:Tatterdemalion 3.00
37 JDy(c),FS 3.00
38 PC,JG,X-Men 5.00
39 PC,JG,Caught in the grip of
  death 3.00
40 PC,JG,Secret Wars II 3.50
41 PC,JG,A:Beast 3.50
42 PC,JG,A:Beast,last issue 3.50

DEADLIEST HEROES
OF KUNG FU
Summer, 1975
1 Magazine size 30.00

DEADLINE
April, 2002
1 (of 4) GyD, F:Katherine Farrell
  Daily Bugle reporter. 3.25
2 GyD,The Judge 3.25
3 GyD,The Judge 3.25
4 GyD,finale 3.25
TPB series rep. 10.00

DEADLY FOES
OF SPIDER-MAN
May, 1991
1 AM,KGa,V:Sinister Syndicate . . . 4.00
2 AM,Boomerang on Trial 3.00
3 AM,Deadly Foes Split 3.00
4 AM,Conclusion. 3.00
TPB rep. #1–#4 . . . . 13.00

DEADLY HANDS
OF KUNG FU
April, 1974
1 NA(c),JSa,JSon,O:Sons of
  the Tiger, B:Shang-Chi,
  Bruce Lee Pin-up 50.00
2 NA(c),JSa 40.00
3 NA(c),JSon,A:Sons of the Tiger. 30.00
4 NA(Bruce Lee)(c),JSon,Bruce
  Lee biography 30.00
5 BWS,PG 25.00
6 GP,JSon,A:Sons of the Tiger . . 25.00
7 GP,JSon,A:Sons of the Tiger . . 30.00
8 GP,JSon,A:Sons of the Tiger. . . 22.00
9 GP,JSon,A:Sons of the Tiger. . . 22.00
10 GP,JSon,A:Sons of the Tiger . . 30.00
11 NA(c),GP,JSon,A:Sons
  of the Tiger 22.00
12 NA(c),GP,JSon,A:Sons
  of the Tiger 22.00
13 GP,JSon,A:Sons of the Tiger . . 22.00
14 NA(c),GP,HC,JSon,A:Sons
  of the Tiger 65.00
15 JS,PG,JSn,,Annual #1 . . . . . . 22.00
16 JSn,A:Sons of the Tiger 20.00
17 NA(c),JSn,KG,A:Sons
  of the Tiger 20.00
18 JSn,A:Sons of the Tiger 20.00
19 JSn,I:White Tiger 22.00
20 GP,O:White Tiger 20.00
21 . . . . 20.00
22 KG,C:Jack of Hearts 20.00
23 GK,Jack of Hearts. 25.00
24 KG,Ironfist 25.00
25 I:Shimaru. 25.00
26 . . . . 25.00
27 . . . . 20.00
28 Bruce Lee Special. 75.00
29 Ironfist vs. Shang Chi 25.00
30 Swordquest. 20.00
31 JSon, Jack of Hearts 20.00
32 MR,JSon,Daughters of the
  Dragon, ... 20.00
33 MR,Feb., 1977 . . . . 22.00
Spec. Album Ed.,NA, Sum.,1974. . 25.00

DEAD OF NIGHT
Dec., 1973–Aug., 1975
1 JSt,Horror reprints,A Haunted
  House is not a Home. 35.00
2 BEv(c),House that Fear Built . . 20.00
3 They Lurk Below 20.00
4 Warewolf Beware. 20.00
5 Deep Down 20.00
6 Jack the Ripper 20.00
7 SD,The Thirteenth Floor 20.00
8 Midnight Brings Dark Madness 20.00
9 Deathride 20.00
10 SD,I Dream of Doom 20.00
11 GK/BWr(c),I:Scarecrow, Fires
  of Rebirth,Fires of Death 40.00

DEADPOOL
1993
1 B:FaN(s),JMd,MFm(i),
  V:Slayback,Nyko 6.00
2 JMd,MFm(i),V:Black Tom
  Cassidy,Juggernaut. 5.00
3 JMd,MFm(i),I:Comcast,
  Makeshift,Rive,A:Slayback 5.00
4 E:FaN(s),JMd,MFm(i),
  A:Slayback,Kane 5.00

[2nd Limited Series], 1994
1 A:Banshee,Syrin,Juggernaut
  Black Tom 4.00
2 A:Banshee,Syrin,V:Juggernaut . . 4.00
3 A:Syrin,Juggernaut 4.00
4 Final issue 4.00

Deadpool, 2nd Limited Series, #2
© Marvel Entertainment Group

DEADPOOL
1996
1 NMa,V:Sasquatch,48pg, ... 15.00
2 NMa,A:Copycat 7.00
3 NMa,A:Siryn. 6.00
4 NMa,Will Hulk cure him? 6.00
5 NMa,A:Siryn,T-Ray 6.00
6 NMa,I: 6.00
7 AaL,A:Typhoid Mary. 5.00
8 NMa, cont. from Daredevil/
  Deadpool '97,A:Gerry 5.00
9 NMa, new villain 5.00
10 NMa,A:Great Lake Avengers . . . 5.00
11 NMa,Fall through time, A:Alfred . 7.00
12 NMa,Typhoid Mary, Zoe
  Culledon & Siryn return. 5.00
13 NMa,V:T-Rav 4.00
14 WMc,Deal of a Lifetime 4.00
15 WMc,A:Landau, Luckman
  & Lake 4.00
16 WMc, in middle east 4.00
17 WMc, Landau, Luckman
  & Lake's plan. 4.00
18 WMc,V:Ajax 4.00
19 WMc,more secrets of blind Al . . . 4.00
20 Cosmic Messiah 4.00
21 . . . . 4.00
22 WMc,A:Cable 4.00
23 WMc,Dead Reckoning,pt.1
  48-page 4.00
24 WMc,Dead Reckoning,pt.2 . . . . . 4.00
25 WMc,Dead Reckoning,pt.3 . . . . . 4.00
26 Dead Reckoning,aftermath 4.00
27 V:A.I.M. concl. 4.00
28 R:Weasel 4.00
29 V:Bullseye 4.00
30 A:Mercedes,T-Ray 4.00
31 V:T-Ray 4.00
32 V:T-Ray,A:Mercedes 4.00
33 V:T-Ray 6.00
34 CPr,Chapter Pt.1. . . . . 3.00
35 CPr 3.00
36 CPr 3.00
37 CPr,Chapter X,Addendum 3.00
38 CPr,F:Taskmaster 3.00
39 CPr,F:Taskmaster 3.00
40 CPr,space station 3.00
41 CPr,V:Dirty Wolf 2.50
42 V:Humbug 2.50
43 CPr,JCf,V:Rasputin 2.50
44 CPr,JCf,CatTrap,pt.1,x-over 2.50
45 CPr,JCf,Constrictor 2.50
46 JJu,JP,PC,CruelSummer,pt.1 . . . 2.50
47 JP,PC,CruelSummer,pt.2 . . . . . . 2.50

MARVEL

48 JP,PC,CruelSummer,pt.3 . . . . . . 2.50
49 JP,dating? 2.50
50 AAd,JP,DaR,I:Kid Deadpool 2.50
51 JP,DaR,F:Kid Deadpool 2.50
52 JP,AWi,ALa,V:Mercy Sisters 2.50
53 JP,AWi,ALa,V:Mercy Sisters 2.50
54 JP,V:Punisher 12.00
55 JP,V:Punisher, round two 10.00
56 F:Siryn. 2.50
57 JHo,BWS(c),Agent of Weapon X 3.00
58 JHo,BWS(c),Agent of Weapon X 3.00
59 JHo,BWS(c),Agent of Weapon X 3.00
60 JHo,BWS(s),Agent of Weapon X 3.00
61 Funeral For a Freak 1. . . . . 2.50
62 Funeral For a Freak 2. . . . . 2.50
63 Funeral For a Freak 3. . . . . 2.50
64 Funeral For a Freak 4. . . . . 2.50
65 Did Deadpool survive 3.50
66 steal from Rhino? 3.50
67 R:Dazzler 3.50
68 V:Black Swan, insanity 3.50
69 V:Black Swan 3.50
Ann. '98 BCh(c) F:Deadpool & Death,
    48pg. 3.00
Minus 1 Spec., ALo, flashback,
    O:Deadpool 2.00
Spec. Deadpool Team-Up,2
    Deadpools,F:Widdle Wade 3.00
Spec. Baby's First Deadpool Book . 3.00
Spec. Encyclopedia Deadpoolica . . 3.00
TPB Circle Chase,FaN,JMd,MFm, 13.00
TPB Mission Improbable 15.00
TPB MWa,IaC,Sins of the Past,rep. 6.00

DEATH3
1993
1 I:Death Metal,Death Wreck 3.00
2 V:Ghost Rider 2.50
3 A:Hulk,Cable,Storm,Thing 2.50
4 Last issue. 2.50

DEATHLOK
[Limited Series], July, 1990
1 JC,SW,I:Michael Colins
    (2nd Deathlok). 4.00
2 JC,SW,V:Wajler 3.50
3 DCw,SW,V:Cyberants 3.50
4 DCw,SW,V:Sunfire,final issue . . . 3.50

[Regular Series], 1991–94
1 DCw,MM,V:Warwolf 2.50
2 DCw,MM,A:Dr.Doom,Machine
    Man,Forge. 2.50

Deathlok #5
© *Marvel Entertainment Group*

3 DCw,MM,V:Dr.Doom,
    A:Mr.Fantastic 2.50
4 DCw,MM,A:X-Men,F.F.,Vision,
    O:Mechadoom 2.50
5 DCw,MM,V:Mechadoom,
    A:X-Men,Fantastic Four. 2.50
6 DCw,MM,A:Punisher,
    V:Silvermane 2.50
7 DCw,MM,A:Punisher,
    V:Silvermane 2.50
8 A:Main Frame,Ben Jacobs 2.00
9 DCw,MM,A:Ghost Rider,
    V:Nightmare. 2.50
10 DCw,MM,A:GhR,V:Nightmare. . . 2.50
11 DCw,MM,V:Moses Magnum . . . 2.50
12 DCw,MM,Biohazard Agenda. . . . 2.50
13 DCw,MM,Biohazard Agenda. . . . 2.50
14 DCw,MM,Biohazard Agenda. . . . 2.50
15 DCw,MM,Biohazard Agenda. . . . 2.50
16 DCw,MM,Inf.War,V:Evilok 2.50
17 WMc,MM,B:Cyberwar. 2.50
18 WMc,A:Silver Sable 2.50
18a Newstand Ed. 2.50
19 SMc,Cyberwar#3 . . . . 3.50
20 SMc,Cyberwar#4 . . . . 2.50
21 E:Cyberwar,A:Cold Blood
    Nick Fury. 2.50
22 V:MosesMagnum,A:Bl.Panther. . 2.50
23 A:Bl.Panther,V:Phreak,Stroke . . 2.50
24 V:MosesMagnum,A:Bl.Panther. . 2.50
25 WMc,V:MosesMagnum,A:Black
    Panther,holo-grafx(c). 3.50
26 V:Hobogoblin 2.50
27 R:Siege 2.50
28 Infinty Crusade 2.50
29 Inner Fears 2.50
30 KHd,V:Hydra 2.50
31 GWt(s),KoK,B:Cyberstrike,
    R:1st Deathlok. 2.50
32 GWt(s),KoK,A:Siege 2.50
33 GWt(s),KoK,V:Justice Peace . . . 2.50
34 GWt(s),KoK,E:Cyberstrike,V:Justice
    Peace,final issue 2.50
Ann.#1 JG,I:Timestream 3.00
Ann.#2 I:Tracer,w/card. 3.25

DEATHLOK
July, 1999
1 JoC,JQ&JaL(c),Marvel Tech 2.50
2 JoC,A:Nick Fury 2.25
2a variant cover 2.25
3 JoC,I:Billy Bailey 2.25
4 JoC,R:Clown 2.25
5 JoC,I:Jack Truman 2.25
6 JoC, ... 2.25
7 JoC,V:Serpent Society. 2.25
8 JoC,Nick Fury 2.50
9 JoC,V:Ringmaster 2.50
10 JoC,V:Clown 2.50
11 JoC,V:Clown 2.50

DEATHLOK: DETOUR
Jan., 2004
1 (of 4) DaR 3.00
2 thru 4 DaR . . . . @3.00

DEATHLOK SPECIAL
1991
1 Rep.Mini Series 2.50
2 Rep.Mini Series 2.50
3 Rep.Mini Series 2.50
4 Rep.Mini Series, final issue 2.50

DEATH METAL
Marvel UK, 1994
1 JRe,I:Argon,C:Alpha Flight 2.25
2 JRe,V:Alpha Flight. 2.25
3 JRe,I:Soulslug 2.25
4 Re,Last Issue. 2.25

DEATH METAL
VS. GENETIX
Marvel UK, 1993–94
1 PaD,w/card 3.00
2 PaD,w/card 3.00

DEATH'S HEAD
Marvel UK, Dec., 1988
1 V:Backbreaker 5.00
2 A:Dragons Claws 4.00
3 . . . . 4.00
4 V:Plague Dog. 3.00
5 V:Big Shot 3.00
6 V:Big Shot 3.00
7 & 8 . . . . @3.00
9 A:Fantastic Four. 3.50
10 A:Iron Man 3.50
TPB Reprints#1-#10 . . . . 13.00

DEATH'S HEAD
[Limited Series]
1 A:`Old' Death's Head 2.00

DEATH'S HEAD II
Marvel UK, March, 1992
[Limited Series]
1 LSh,I:2nd Death's Head,
    D:1st Death's Head 4.00
1a 2nd printing,Silver 2.50
2 LSh,A:Fantastic Four. 3.00
2a 2nd printing,Silver 3.00
3 LSh,I:Tuck 3.50
4 LSh,A:Wolverine,Spider-Man,
    Punisher 3.50

[Regular Series], 1992
1 LSh,A:X-Men,I:Wraithchilde. 3.00
2 LSh,A:X-Men 2.25
3 LSh,A:X-Men,V:Raptors. 2.25
4 LSh,A:X-Men,V:Wraithchilde 2.25
5 V:UnDeath's Head II,
    A:Warheads. 2.25
6 R:Tuck,V:Major Oak. 2.25
7 V:Major Oak. 2.25
8 V:Wizard Methinx. 2.25
9 BHi,V:Cybernetic Centaurs 2.25
10 DBw,A:Necker. 2.25
11 SCy,R:Charnel 2.25
12 DAn(s),SvL,V:Charnel. 2.25
13 SvL,A:Liger 2.25
14 SvL,Brain Dead Cold,Blue
    Foil(c). 3.25
15 SvL,V:Duplicates. 2.25
16 SvL,DAn 2.25
17 SvL,DAn 2.00
18 SvL,DAn 2.00
Spec. Gold Ed. LSh(a&s). 4.00

DEATH'S HEAD II/DIE CUT
Marvel UK, 1993
1 I:Die Cut. 3.25
2 O:Die Cut. 2.25

DEATH'S HEAD II/
KILLPOWER: BATTLETIDE
[1st Limited Series]
1 GSr,A:Wolverine 2.50
2 thru 4 GSr,A:Wolverine . . . . . @2.25
[2nd Limited Series]
1 A:Hulk 3.25
2 V:Hulk 2.25
3 A:Hulk 2.25
4 last issue 2.25

DEATH-WRECK
Marvel UK, 1994
1 A:Death's Head II. 2.25

2 V:Gangsters 2.25
3 A:Dr.Necker 2.25
4 last issue 2.25

DECIMATION:
HOUSE OF M
Nov., 2005
Spec. The Day After 4.00

DEEP, THE
Nov., 1977
1 CI,Movie Adaption 15.00

DEFENDERS
Aug., 1972
1 SB,I&D:Necrodames 175.00
2 SB,V:Calizuma 75.00
3 GK(c),SB,JM,V:UndyingOne . . . 50.00
4 SB,FMc,Bl.Knight,V:Valkyrie . . . 50.00
5 SB,FMc,D:Omegatron 50.00
6 SB,FMc,V:Cyrus Black 40.00
7 SB,FBe,A:Hawkeye 35.00
8 SB,FBe,Avengers,SilverSurfer . 45.00
9 SB,FMc,Avengers 45.00
10 SB,FBe,Thor vs. Hulk 100.00
11 SB,FBe,A:Avengers 40.00
12 SB,JA,Xemnu 20.00
13 GK(c),SB,KJ,J:Night Hawk 20.00
14 SB,DGr,O:Hyperion 20.00
15 SB,KJ,A:Professor X,V:Magneto,
   Savage Land Mutates 25.00
16 GK(c),SB,Professor X,V:Magneto,
   Savage Land Mutates 25.00
17 SB,DGr,Power Man 12.00
18 GK(c),SB,DGr,A:Power Man . . . 12.00
19 GK(c),SB,KJ,A:Power Man 12.00
20 K&R(c),SB,A:Thing 12.00
21 GK(c),SB,O:Valkyrie 7.00
22 GK(c),SB,V:Sons o/t Serpent . . . 7.00
23 GK(c),SB,A:Yellow Jacket. 7.00
24 GK(c),SB,BMc,A:Daredevil 7.00
25 GK(c),SB,JA,A:Daredevil 7.00
26 K&R(o),SB,A:Guardians 10.00
27 K&R(c),SB,A:Guardians
   C:Starhawk 10.00
28 K&R(c),SB,A:Guardians
   I:Starhawk 8.00
29 K&R(c),SB,A:Guardians 8.00
30 JA(i),A:Wong 6.00
31 GK(c),SB,JM,Nighthawk 6.00
32 CK(c),SB,JM,O:Nighthawk 6.00
33 GK(c),SB,JM,V:Headmen 6.00

Defenders #35
© Marvel Entertainment Group

34 SB,JM,V:Nebulon 6.00
35 GK(c),SB,KJ,I:Red Guardian . . 6.00
36 GK(c),SB,KJ,A:Red Guardian. . 12.00
37 GK(c),SB,KJ,J:Luke Cage 7.00
38 SB,KJ,V:Nebulon 12.00
39 SB,KJ,V:Felicia 5.00
40 SB,KJ,V:Assassin 5.00
41 KG,KJ,Nighthawk 5.00
42 KG,KJ,V:Rhino 5.00
43 KG,KJ,Cobalt Man,Egghead 5.00
44 KG,KJ,J:Hellcat,V:Red Rajah . . 5.00
45 KG,KJ,Valkyrie V:Hulk 5.00
46 KG,KJ,L:DrStrange,LukeCage . . 5.00
47 KG,KJ,Moon Knight. 5.00
48 KG,A:Wonder Man 5.00
49 KG,O:Scorpio 5.00
50 KG,Zodiac,D:Scorpio. 5.00
51 KG,Moon Knight 5.00
52 KG,Hulk,V:Sub Mariner 5.00
53 KG,DC,MG,TA,C&I:Lunatik 4.00
54 MG,Nigh Fury 4.00
55 CI,O:Red Guardian 4.00
56 CI,KJ,Hellcat,V:Lunatik 4.00
57 DC,Ms.Marvel 4.00
58 Return of Dr.Strange 4.00
59 I:Belathauzer 4.00
60 V:Vera Gemini 4.00
61 Spider-Man,A:Lunatik 5.00
62 Hercules,C:Polaris 3.00
63 Mutli Heroes 3.00
64 Mutli Heroes 3.00
65 Red Guardian 3.00
66 JB,Valkyrie I 3.00
67 Valkryie II 3.00
68 HT,When Falls the Mountain . . . 3.00
69 HT,A:The Anything Man 3.00
70 HT,A:Lunatik 3.00
71 HT,O:Lunatik 3.00
72 HT,V:Lunatik 3.00
73 HT,Foolkiller,V:WizardKing 3.00
74 HT,Foolkiller,L:Nighthawk 5.00
75 HT,Foolkiller 4.00
76 HT,O:Omega 2.50
77 HT,Moon Dragon. 2.50
78 HT,Yellow Jacket. 2.50
79 HT,Tunnel World 2.50
80 HT,DGr,Nighthawk 2.50
81 HT,Tunnel World 2.50
82 DP,JSt,Tunnel World 2.50
83 DP,JSt,Tunnel World 2.50
84 DP,JSt,Black Panther 2.50
85 DP,JSt,Black Panther 2.50
86 DP,JSt,Black Panther 2.50
87 DP,JSt,V:Mutant Force 2.50
88 DP,JSt,Matt Mardock 2.50
89 DP,JSt,D:Hellcat's
   Mother, O:Mad-Dog 2.50
90 DP,JSt,Daredevil 2.50
91 DP,JSt,Daredevil 2.50
92 DP,JSt,A:Eternity,
   Son of Satan 3.00
93 DP,JSt,Son of Satan 3.00
94 DP,JSt,I:Gargoyle 4.00
95 DP,JSt,V:Dracula,O:Gargoyle . . 2.50
96 DP,JSt,Ghost Rider 4.00
97 DP,JSt,False Messiah 2.50
98 DP,JSt,A:Man Thing 2.50
99 DP,JSt,Conflict 2.50
100 DP,JSt,DoubleSize,V:Satan . . . 6.00
101 DP,JSt,Silver Surfer 4.00
102 DP,JSt,Nighthawk 2.50
103 DP,JSt,I:Null 2.50
104 DP,JSt,Devilslayer,J:Beast . . . 2.50
105 DP,JSt,V:Satan 2.50
106 DP,Daredevil,D:Nighthawk 2.50
107 DP,JSt,Enchantress,A:D.D. . . . 2.50
108 DP,A:Enchantress 2.50
109 DP,A:Spider-Man. 3.00
110 DP,A:Devilslayer 2.50
111 DP,A:Hellcat. 2.50
112 DP,A:SquadronSupreme 2.50
113 DP,A:SquadronSupreme 2.50

Defenders #108
© Marvel Entertainment Group

114 DP,A:SquadronSupreme 2.50
115 DP,A:Submariner. 2.50
116 DP,Gargoyle 2.50
117 DP,Valkyrie 2.50
118 DP,V:Miracleman 2.50
119 DP,V:Miracleman 2.50
120 DP,V:Miracleman 4.00
121 DP,V:Miracleman 4.00
122 DP,A:Iceman 4.00
123 DP,I:Cloud,V:Secret Empire . . . 2.50
124 DP,V:Elf 2.50
125 DP,New Line-up:Gargoyle,Moon
   dragon,Valkyrie,Iceman,Beast,
   Angel,W:Son of Satan & Hellcat
   I:Mad Dog 5.00
126 DP,A:Nick Fury 2.50
127 DP,V:Professor Power 2.50
128 DP,V:Professor Power 2.50
129 DP,V:Professor Power,New
   Mutants X-over 2.50
130 DP,V:Professor Power 2.50
131 DP,V:Walrus,A:Frogman 2.50
132 DP,V:Spore Monster 2.50
133 DP,V:Spore Monster 2.50
134 DP,I:Manslaughter 2.50
135 DP,V:Blowtorch Brand. 2.50
136 DP,V:Gargoyle 2.50
137 DP,V:Gargoyle. 2.50
138 DP,O:Moondragon 2.50
139 DP,A:Red Wolf,V:Trolls 2.50
140 DP,V:Asgardian Trolls 2.50
141 DP,All Flesh is Grass 2.50
142 DP,V:M.O.N.S.T.E.R. 2.50
143 DP,I:Andromeda,Runner 2.50
144 DP,V:Moondragon 2.50
145 DP,V:Moondragon 2.50
146 DP,Cloud 2.50
147 DP,A:Andromeda,I:Interloper . . 2.50
148 DP,A:Nick Fury 2.50
149 DP,V:Manslaughter,O:Cloud . . . 2.50
150 DP,O:Cloud,double-size 5.00
151 DP,A:Interloper 2.50
152 DP,Secret Wars II,D:Moon-
   dragon,Valkyrie,Gargoyle 5.00
G-Size#1 GK(c),JSn,AM,O:Hulk . . 22.00
G-Size#2 GK,KJ,Son of Satan. . . . 15.00
G-Size#3 JSn,DA,JM,DN,A:D.D. . . 10.00
G-Size#4 GK(c),DH,A:YellowJack . 20.00
G-Size#5 K&R(c),DH,A:Guardians 25.00
Ann.#1 SB,KJ. 7.00

DEFENDERS
Jan., 2001
1 EL,KBk,KJ,48-page 6.00

2A EL,KBk,KJ, ... 3.00
2B variant AAd(c) 3.50
3 EL,KBk,KJ,V:Pluto 2.50
4 EL,KBk,KJ,V:Pluto 2.50
5 EL,KBk,KJ,A:Dr.Strange 2.50
6 EL,KBk,KJ,A:Red Raven 2.50
7 EL,KBk,KJ,A:Red Raven 2.50
8 EL,KBk,AG,V:Headmen 2.50
9 EL,KBk,RF,V:Headmen 2.50
10 EL,KBk,SB,V:Headmen 2.50
11 EL,KBk,SB,V:Attuma,DeepSix . . 2.50
12 EL,KBk,'Nuff Said,48-pg. 3.50
Spec.Day of the Defenders, mag. . 3.50

DEFENDERS
July, 2005
1(of 5) KG,JMD 3.00
2 KG,Hulk vs. Mindless Ones 3.00
3 KG,JMD 3.00
4 KG,JMD 3.00
5 KG 3.00

DEFENDERS OF
DYNATRON CITY
1992
1 FC,I:Defenders of Dynatron City
   (from video game & TV ser.) . . . 3.00
2 FC,O:Defender of D.City 3.00
3 FC,A:Dr Mayhem 3.00
4 FC 3.00
5 FC,V:Intelligent Fleas 3.00
6 FC,V:Dr.Mayhem 3.00

DEFENDERS OF
THE EARTH
Jan., 1987—Sept., 1984
1 AS,Flash Gordon & Mandrake . . . 5.00
2 AS,Flash Gordon & Mandrake . . . 4.00
3 AS,O:Phantom 4.00
4 AS,O:Mandrake 4.00

DELLA VISION
Marvel Atlas, April, 1955
1 The Television Queen 250.00
2 . . . . 200.00
3 . . . . 200.00
Becomes:

PATTY POWERS
1955
4 . . . . 200.00
5 & 6 . . . . @125.00
7 Oct., 1956 . . . . 100.00

DENNIS THE MENACE
Nov., 1981–Nov., 1982
1 . . . . 12.00
2 thru 13 . . . . @7.00

DESTROYER, THE
1989–90
1 Black & White Mag. 3.50
2 thru 10 . . . . @2.50
TPB rep. B/w mag(color) 10.00

THE DESTROYER:
TERROR
Dec., 1991
1 V:Nuihc 2.50
2 V:Nuihc 2.25
3 GM,V:Nuihc 2.25
4 DC,'The Last Dinosaur'. 2.25

DEVIL DINOSAUR
April, 1978—Dec., 1978
1 JK,I:Devil Dinosaur,Moon Boy . 25.00
2 JK,War With the Spider God . . . 15.00

3 JK,Giant 15.00
4 JK,Objects From the Sky 15.00
5 JK,The Kingdom of the Ants . . . 15.00
6 JK.The Fall 15.00
7 JK,Prisoner of the Demon Tree 15.00
8 JK,V:Dino Riders 15.00
9 JK,Lizards That Stand 15.00

DEVIL DINOSAUR
SPRING FLING
1997
Spec. F:Devil Dinosaur,Moon-Boy . . 3.00

DEVIL-DOG DUGAN
Marvel Atlas, July, 1956
1 War Stories 200.00
2 JSe(c) 200.00
3 . . . . 150.00
Becomes:

TALE OF THE MARINES
4 BP,War Stories 150.00
Becomes:

MARINES AT WAR
5 War Stories 150.00
6 . . . . 150.00
7 The Big Push, Aug., 1957 . . . . 150.00

DEXTER THE DEMON
See: MELVIN THE
MONSTER

DIE-CUT
Marvel UK, 1993–94
1 A:Beast 2.50
2 V:X-Beast. 2.25
3 A:Beast,Prof.X 2.25
4 V:Red Skull 2.25

DIE-CUT VS. G-FORCE
Marvel UK, 1993
1 SFr(s),LSh(c),I:G-Force 3.00
2 SFr(s),LSh(c),Last issue 3.00

DIGITEK
Marvel UK, 1992–93
1 DPw,I:Digitek,C:Deathlok. 2.25
2 DPw,A:Deathlok,V:Bacillicons . . . 2.25
3 DPw,A:Deathlok,V:Bacillicons . . . 2.25
4 DPw,V:Bacillicons 2.25

DINO RIDERS
Feb., 1989
1 Based on Toys 3.00
2 . . . . 3.00
3 May, 1989 . . . . 3.00

DINOSAURS: A
CELEBRATION
Epic, 1992
Horns and Heavy Armor 5.00
Bone-Heads and Duck-Bills. 5.00
Terrible Claws and Tyrants 5.00
Egg Stealers and Earth Shakers . . 5.00
TPB 192pg. 13.00

DIPPY DUCK
Marvel Atlas, 1957
1 Funny animal 100.00

DISNEY AFTERNOON
1994–95
1 DarkwingDuck vs.FearsomeFive. 3.50
2 thru 10 . . . . @3.00

Disney Comic Hits #6
© Marvel Entertainment Group

DISNEY COMIC HITS
1995
1 . . . . 5.00
2 thru 9 . . . . @4.00
10 Hunchback of Notre Dame 5.00
11 thru 17 . . . . @4.00

DISNEY PRESENTS
1 F:Aladdin 2.50
2 F:Timon & Pummba. 2.50
3 . . . . 2.50

DISTRICT X
May, 2004
1 Mr.M,pt.1,F:Bishop,Ismael 3.00
2 thru 6 Mr.M,pt.2 thru pt.6 . . . . @3.00
7 Underground,pt.1 . . . . 3.00
8 Underground,pt.2 . . . . 3.00
9 Underground,pt.3 . . . . 3.00
10 Underground,pt.4 . . . . 3.00
11 Underground,pt.5 . . . . 3.00
12 Underground, concl. 3.00
13 One of Us,pt.1. . . . . 3.00
14 One of Us,pt.2. . . . . 3.00
TPB Vol. 1: Mr. M. 15.00
TPB Vol. 2:Underground 20.00

DOC SAMSON
1996
1 From The Incredible Hulk 2.25
2 A:She-Hulk. 2.25
3 . . . . 2.25
4 . . . . 2.25

DOC SAMSON
Jan., 2006
1 . . . . 3.00
2 . . . . 3.00
3 A: New Scorpion 3.00
4 . . . . 3.00
5 . . . . 3.00

DOC SAVAGE
Oct., 1972
1 JM,Pulp Adapts,Death Eighty
   Stories High. 30.00
2 JSo(c),The Feathered Serpent
   Strikes 20.00
3 JSo(c),Silver Death's Head 20.00
4 JSo(c),The Hell Diver 15.00
5 GK(c),Night of the Monsters . . . 15.00

Doc Savage #2
© *Marvel Entertainment Group*

6 JSo(c),Where Giants Walk	15.00
7 JSo(c),Brand of the Werewolfs	15.00
8 In the Lair of the Werewolf	
Jan., 1974	15.00
G-Size#1 thru #2 Reprints	12.00

DOC SAVAGE
Aug., 1975
(black & white magazine)

1 JB,Ph(c),Ron Ely	20.00
2 JB	15.00
3 JB	15.00
4 thru 7	@15.00
8 Spring 1977	15.00

DOCTOR OCTOPUS:
NEGATIVE EXPOSURE
Oct., 2003

1 (of 5)	2.50
2 V:Vulture	2.50
3 thru 5	@3.00
TPB	14.00

DOCTOR SPECTRUM
Aug., 2004

1 (of 6) F:Corporal Joe Ledger	3.00
2 thru 6	@3.00
TPB Full Spectrum	17.00

DR. STRANGE
[1st Series], June, 1968
Prev: Strange Tales

169 DA,O:Dr.Strange	225.00
170 DA,A:Ancient One	75.00
171 TP,DA,V:Dormammu	65.00
172 GC,TP,V:Dormammu	65.00
173 GC,TP,V:Dormammu	65.00
174 GC,TP,I:Satannish	65.00
175 GC,TP,I:Asmodeus	65.00
176 GC,TP,V:Asmodeus	65.00
177 GC,TP,D:Asmodeus,	
N:Dr.Strange	65.00
178 GC,TP,A:Black Knight	65.00
179 BWS(c),rep.Amazing Spider-	
Man Ann.#2	65.00
180 GC,TP,V:Nightmare	65.00
181 FB(c),GC,TP,I:Demons of	
Despair	65.00
182 GC,TP,V:Juggernaut	60.00
183 BEv(c),GC,TP,	
I:Undying Ones	60.00

[2nd Regular Series], 1974–87

1 FB,DG,I:Silver Dagger	75.00
2 FB,DG,I:Soul Eater	35.00
3 FB,A:Dormammu	20.00
4 FB,DG,V:Death	20.00
5 FB,DG,A:Silver Dagger	20.00
6 FB(c),GC,KJ,A:Umar,I:Gaea	12.00
7 GC,JR,A:Dormammu	12.00
8 GK(c),GC,TP,O:Clea	12.00
9 GK(c),GC,A:Dormammu,O:Clea	12.00
10 B:MWn(s),GK(c),GC,A:Eternity.	12.00
11 JR(c),GC,TP,A:Eternity	7.00
12 GC,TP,A:Eternity	7.00
13 GC,TP,A:Eternity	7.00
14 GC,TP,A:Dracula	7.00
15 GC,TP,A:Devil	7.00
16 GC,TP,A:Devil	7.00
17 GC,TP,A:Styggro	7.00
18 GC,A:Styggro	7.00
19 GC,AA,I:Xander	7.00
20 A:Xander	7.00
21 DA,O:Dr.Strange	8.00
22 I:Apalla	8.00
23 F:MWn(s),JSn,A:Wormworld	8.00
24 JSn,A:Apalla,I:Visamajoris	8.00
25 AM,V:Dr.Strange Yet	8.00
26 JSn,A:The Ancient One	8.00
27 TS,A:Stygyro,Sphinx	8.00
28 TS,A:Ghost Rider,	
V:In-Betweener	5.00
29 TS,A:Nighthawk	4.00
30 I:Dweller	4.00
31 TS,A:Sub Mariner	4.00
32 A:Sub Mariner	4.00
33 TS,A:The Dreamweaver	4.00
34 TS,A:Nightmare,D:CyrusBlack	4.00
35 TS,V:Dweller,I:Ludi	4.00
36 Thunder of the Soul	4.00
37 Fear,the Final Victor	4.00
38 GC,DG,A:Baron Mordo	4.00
39 GC,DG,A:Baron Mordo	4.00
40 GC,A:Asrael	4.00
41 GC,A:Man Thing	3.50
42 GC,A:Black Mirror	3.50
43 V:Shadow Queen	3.50
44 GC,A:Princess Shialmar	3.50
45 GC,A:Demon in the Dark	3.50
46 FM,A:Sibylis	3.50
47 MR,TA,I:Ikonn	3.50
48 MR,TA,Brother Voodoo	3.50
49 MR,TA,A:Baron Mordo	3.50
50 MR,TA,A:Baron Mordo	3.50
51 MR,TA,A:Sgt. Fury,	
V:Baron Mordo	3.50
52 MR,TA,A:Nightmare	4.00
53 MR,TA,A:Nightmare,Fantastic	
Four,V:Rama-Tut	4.00
54 PS,V:Tiboro	4.00
55 MGo,TA,V:Madness	4.00
56 PS,TA,O:Dr.Strange	5.00
57 KN,TA,A:Dr.Doom	4.00
58 DGr,TA,V:Dracula	5.00
59 DGr,TA,V:Dracula	5.00
60 DGr,TA,V:Scarlet Witch	5.00
61 DGr,TA,V:Dracula	5.00
62 SL,V:Dracula	5.00
63 CP,V:Topaz	4.00
64 TSa,'Art Rage'	4.00
65 PS,Charlatan	4.00
66 PS,`The Cosen One'	4.00
67 SL,A:Jessica Drew,Shroud	4.00
68 PS,A:Black Knight	4.00
69 PS,A:Black Knight	4.00
70 BBl,V:Umar	4.00
71 DGr,O:Dormammu	4.00
72 PS,V:Umar	4.00
73 PS,V:Umar	4.00
74 MBg,Secret Wars II	4.00
75 A:Fantastic Four	4.00
76 A:Fantastic Four	4.00
77 A:Topaz	4.00
78 A:Cloak,I:Ecstasy	3.50

Doc Strange, 3rd Series, #78
© *Marvel Entertainment Group*

79 A:Morganna	3.00
80 A:Morganna,C:Rintah	3.00
81 V:Urthona,I:Rintah	3.00
Ann.#1 CR,'Doomworld'	15.00
GN Dr.Strange: What is it that	
Distrubs you, Stephen?, CR,	
revised from Dr.Strange Ann.#1,	
48pg bookshelf (Aug., 1997)	10.00
G-Size#1 K&R(c),reps Strange	
Tales#164-#168	10.00

[3rd Regular Series], 1988–96

1 V:Dorammu	4.00
2 V:Dorammu	3.00
3 I:Dragon Force	3.00
4 EL(c),A:Dragon Force	3.00
5 JG,V:Baron Mordo	3.50
6 JG,I:Mephista	3.00
7 JG,V:Agamotto,Mephisto	3.00
8 JG,V:Mephisto & Satanish	3.00
9 JG,O:Dr.Strange	3.00
10 JG,V:Morbius	3.50
11 JG,A of V,V:Hobgoblin,	
C:Morbius	4.00
12 JG,A of V,V:Enchantress	2.75
13 JG,A of V,V:Arkon	2.75
14 JG,B:Vampiric Verses,	
A:Morbius	3.50
15 JG,A:Morbius,Amy Grant(C)	5.00
16 JG,A:Morbius,Brother Voodoo	3.50
17 JV,TD,A:Morbius,Br.Voodoo	3.50
18 JG,E:Vampiric Verses,A:Morbius,	
Brother Voodoo,R:Varnae	3.50
19 GC,A:Azrael	2.50
20 JG,TD,A:Morbius,V:Zom	3.50
21 JG,TD,B:Dark Wars,	
R:Dormammu	2.50
22 JG,TD,LW,V:Dormammu	2.50
23 JG,LW,V:Dormammu	2.50
24 JG,E:Dark Wars,V:Dormammu	2.50
25 RLm,A:Red Wolf, Black Crow	2.50
26 GI,V:Werewolf By Night	2.50
27 GI,V:Werewolf By Night	2.50
28 X-over Ghost Rider #12,	
V:Zodiac	3.00
29 A:Baron Blood	2.50
30 Topaz' Fate	2.50
31 TD,Inf.Gauntlet,A:Silver Surfer	3.00
32 Inf.Gauntlet,A:Warlock,Silver	
Surfer,V:Silver Dagger	2.50
33 Inf.Gauntlet,V:Thanos,	
Zota,A:Pip	2.50
34 Inf.Gauntlet,V:Dr.Doom,	
A:Pip,Scarlet Witch	2.50
35 Inf.Gauntlet,A:Thor,Pip,	
Scarlet Witch	2.50

---

36 Inf.Gauntlet,A:Warlock(leads
  into Warlock&Inf.Watch#1) 3.00
37 GI,V:Frankensurfer 2.50
38 GI,Great Fear #1. . . . . 2.50
39 GI,Great Fear #2. . . . . 2.50
40 GI,Great Fear #3,A:Daredevil . . . 2.50
41 GI,A:Wolverine 3.00
42 GI,Infinity War,V:Galactus,A:
  Silver Surfer. 2.50
43 GI,Infinity War,Galactus Vs.
  Agamotto,A:Silver Surfer. 2.50
44 GI,Infinity War,V:Juggernaut 2.50
45 GI,Inf.War,O:Doctor Strange 2.50
46 GI,Inf.War,R:old costume 2.50
47 GI,Inf.War,V:doppleganger. 2.50
48 GI,V:The Vishanti 2.50
49 GI,R:Dormammu. 2.50
50 GI,A:Hulk,Ghost Rider,Silver
  Surfer,V:Dormammu(leads into
  Secret Defenders)holo-grafx(c). 3.50
51 GI,V:Religious Cult 2.50
52 GI,A:Morbius. 2.50
53 GI,Closes Mansion,L:Wong 2.50
54 GI,Infinity Crusade 2.50
55 GI,Inf.Crusade. 2.50
56 GI,Inf.Crusade. 2.50
57 A:Kyllian,Urthona 2.50
58 V:Urthona 2.50
59 GI,V:Iskelior 2.50
60 B:DQ(s),Siege of
  Darkness,pt.#7 . . . . 4.00
61 Siege of Darkness,pt.#15 . . . . . . 3.25
62 V:Dr.Doom 2.50
63 JJ(c),V:Morbius. 2.50
64 MvR,V:Namor 2.50
65 MvR,V:Namor,Vengeance. 2.75
66 A:Wong 2.75
67 R:Clea. 2.75
68 MvR. 2.50
69 MvR. 2.50
70 A:Hulk 2.50
71 V:Hulk 2.50
72 Metallic(c),Last Rites,pt.1 . . . . . 2.50
73 Last Rites,pt.2. . . . . 2.50
74 SY,DQ,Last Rites,pt.3 . . . . 2.50
75 Prismatic cover 4.00
76 I:New Costume 2.50
77 Mob Clean-up 2.50
78 R:Chton. 2.50
79 Doc's new Asylum. 2.50
80 Missing for four months? 2.50
81 A:Nick Fury 2.50
82 A:Hellstorm 2.50
83 V:Tempo Mob,Dormammu 2.50
84 The Homecoming,pt.1 . . . . 2.50
85 The Homecoming,pt.2 . . . . 2.50
86 The Homecoming,pt.3 . . . . 2.50
87 The Homecoming,pt.4 . . . . 2.50
88 The Fall of the Tempo,pt.1 . . . . . 2.50
89 The Fall of the Tempo,pt.2 . . . . . 2.50
90 final issue 2.50
Ann #2 Return of Defenders,Pt4 . . 5.00
Ann #3 GI,I:Killiam,w/card 3.50
Ann.#4 V:Salome 3.50
Spec. Dr. Strange/Ghost Rider#1
  Newsstand vers. of Dr.
  Strange #28 (1991) 6.00
Spec.#1 Dr. Strange vs. Dracula
  rep. MWn(s),GC (1994). 2.50
GNv Triumph and Torment MBg,
  F:Dr. Strange & Dr.Doom 10.00
HC 15.00
Ashcan 75
TPB A Separate Reality, 224-pg. . . 20.00

DOCTOR STRANGE
Dec., 1998
1 (of 4) TyH,killer pursued 3.00
2 TyH,secrets in Topaz 3.00
3 TyH,magic in Manhattan 3.00
4 TyH,PC,conclusion 3.00

DR. STRANGE CLASSICS
March, 1984
1 SD,Reprints 3.50
2 thru 4 . . . . @3.50

DOCTOR STRANGE: THE OATH
Oct., 2006
1 . . . . 3.00
2 . . . . 3.00

DOCTOR WHO
1984–86
1 BBC TV Series,UK reprints,
  Return of the Daleks 7.00
2 Star Beast 6.00
3 Transformation 5.00
4 A:K-9,Daleks 5.00
5 V:Time Witch,Colin Baker
  interview 5.00
6 B:Ancient Claw saga 5.00
7 . . . . 5.00
8 The Collector 5.00
9 The Life Bringer 5.00
10 This is your Life 5.00
11 The Deal 5.00
12 End of the Line 5.00
13 V:The Cybermen. 5.00
14 Clash of the Neutron Knight 5.00
15 B:Peter Davison-Dr. Who 5.00
16 Into the Realm of Satan. 5.00
17 Peter Davison Interview 5.00
18 A:Four Dr.Who's 5.00
19 A:The Sontarans 5.00
20 The Stockbridge Horror. 5.00
21 The Stockbridge Horror. 5.00
22 The Stockbridge Horror. 5.00
23 The Unearthly Child 5.00

DR. ZERO
Epic, April, 1988
1 BSz,DCw,I:Dr.Zero. 2.50
2 thru 8 . . . . @2.25

DOLLY DILL
1945
1 Newsstand 250.00

DOMINATION FACTOR
Sept., 1999
1.1 Fantastic Four (of 4) DJu,
  JOy,BMc,x-over 2.50
1.2 Avengers, DJu,JO,
  DJa, x-over 2.50
2.3 Fantastic Four, DJu,BMc 2.50
2.4 Avengers, DJu,JOy,DJa 2.50
3.5 Fantastic Four, DJu,BMc 2.50
3.6 Avengers, JOy,DJa 2.50
4.7 Fantastic Four, DJu,BMc 2.50
4.8 Avengers, DJa,JOy,concl. 2.50

DOMINO
1996
1 thru 3 . . . . @2.25

DOMINO
May, 2003
1 (of 4) BSf 2.50
2 thru 4 BSf. . . . . @2.50

DOOM 2099
1993–96
1 PB,I:Doom 2099,V:Tiger Wylde,
  foil(c) 3.00
2 I:Rook Seven 2.50
3 PB,V:Tiger Wylde. 2.50
4 PB,V:Tiger Wylde. 2.50

Doom 2099 #25
© *Marvel Entertainment Group*

5 PB,I:Fever 2.50
6 I:Duke Stratosphear. 2.50
7 PB,I:Paloma,V:Duke,Fever Haze 2.50
8 PB,C:Ravage. 2.50
9 EC,V:Jack the Ripper 2.50
10 PB,w/Poster 2.50
11 PB,I:Thandaza 2.50
12 PB,V:Thandaza. 2.50
13 PB(c),JFm(s),V:Necrotek 2.50
14 RLm(c),PB,Fall o/t Hammer#4 . 2.50
15 PB,I:Radian 2.50
16 EC(a&s). 2.50
17 PB,V:Radian,w/card 2.50
18 PB, ... 2.50
19 PB,C:Bloodhawk 2.50
20 PB,A:Bloodhawk 2.50
21 PB,Shadow King. 2.50
22 PB,R:Duke Stratosphere. 2.50
23 PB,R:Tyger Wylde 2.50
24 PB 2.50
25 PB 3.50
25a foil cover 4.00
26 . . . . 2.50
27 Revolution 2.50
28 Prologue to D-Day 2.50
Becomes:

DOOM 2099 A.D.
1995
29 Doom Invades America. 4.00
29a Chromium Cover. 4.00
30 D:Corporate Head. 2.50
31 PB,One Nation Under Doom . . . 2.50
32 Ravage Aftermath 2.50
33 . . . . 2.50
34 I:Anthony Herod 2.50
35 E:One Nation Under Doom. 2.50
36 thru 39. . . . . @2.50
40 Rage Against Time,pt.1. . . . . . . 2.50
41 Rage Against Time,pt.2. . . . . . . 2.50
TPB Villainy of Doctor Doom 18.00

DOOM
Aug., 2000
1 (of 3) CDi,F:Dr.Doom. 3.00
2 CDi,Al Khalad 3.00
3 CDi,concl. 3.00

DOOM: THE EMPEROR RETURNS
Nov., 2001
1 CDi,F:Dr. Doom 2.50
2 CDi,center of Counter-Earth 2.50
3 CDi, ... 2.50
TPB Doom, rep. 144-pg. 16.00

DOPEY DUCK COMICS
Marvel Timely, Fall, 1945
1 A:Casper Cat,Krazy Krow 250.00
2 A:Casper Cat,Krazy Krow 225.00
Becomes:

WACKY DUCK
1946
3 Paperchase(c) 225.00
4 Wacky Duck(c) 200.00
5 Duck & Devil(c) 175.00
6 Cliffhanger(c) 175.00
1 Baketball(c) 125.00
2 Traffic Light(c) 125.00
Becomes:
JUSTICE COMICS

DOUBLE DRAGON
July, 1991
1 I:Billy&Jimmy Lee 2.50
2 Dragon Statue Stolen,V:Stelth ... 2.50
3 Billy Vs. Jimmy 2.50
4 Dragon Force out of control..... 2.50
5 V:Stealth. 2.50
6 V:Nightfall, final issue 2.50

DOUBLE EDGE
1995
Alpha Punisher vs. Nick Fury 5.00
Omega D:Major Character........ 5.00

D.P. 7 #1
© Marvel Entertainment Group

D.P. 7
Nov., 1986
1 O:DP7 .... 2.50
2 thru 20 V:Headhunter........ @2.50
21 thru 32.................. @3.00
Ann.#1,I:Witness 3.00

DRACULA LIVES
B&W Magazine, 1973—75
1 GC...................... 100.00
2 NA,GC,JSn,O:Dracula........ 65.00
3 NA,JB,................... 60.00
4 MP...................... 35.00
5 GC...................... 35.00
6 JB,GC 35.00
7 GE...................... 35.00
8 GC...................... 35.00
9 AA,RG 35.00
10 .... 45.00
11 thru 13.................. @40.00

DRACULA:
LORD OF THE UNDEAD
Oct., 1998
1 (of 3) PO,TP,R:Dracula 3.00
2 PO,TP,V:Seward 3.00
3 PO,TP,conclusion 3.00

DRAFT, THE
1988
1 Sequel to The Pit............ 3.75

DRAGON LINES
Epic, *Heavy Hitters* 1993
[1st Limited Series]
1 RLm,V:Terrorist on Moon,
     Embossed(c) 3.00
2 RLm,V:Kuei Emperor.......... 2.25
3 RLm,V:Spirit Boxer 2.25
4 RLm,K:Kuei Emperor.......... 2.25
[Regular Series]
1 B:PQ(s),RLm,I:Tao............ 2.50
2 RLm, ... 2.50

DRAGONSLAYER
Oct.–Nov., 1981
1 Movie adapt. 3.00
2 Movie adapt. 3.00

DRAGON STRIKE
1994
1 Based on TSR Game 2.25

DRAGON'S TEETH/
DRAGON'S CLAWS
July, 1988
1 GSr,I:Mercy Dragon,
     Scavenger,Digit Steel 2.25
2 GSr,V:Evil Dead............. 2.25
3 GSr,Go Home 2.25
4 GSr 2.25
5 GSr,I:Death's Head 18.00
6 thru 10 GSr .... @2.00

DRAX THE DESTROYER
Sept., 2005
1 (of 4) KG(s) 4.00
2 thru 4 KG(s) .... @3.00
TPB Earth Fall 11.00

DREADLANDS
Epic, 1992
1 Post-Apocalyptic Mini-series 4.00
2 Trapped in Prehistoric Past..... 4.00
3 V:Alien Time Travelers......... 4.00
4 Final Issue................. 4.00

DREADSTAR
Epic, Nov., 1982
1 JSn,I:Lord Papal 5.00
2 thru 5 .... @3.50
6 thru 7 .... @4.00
8 thru 26 .... @3.00
Ann.#1 JSn,The Price 3.00
See COLOR COMICS section

DREADSTAR & COMPANY
July, 1985
1 JSo,reprint................. 2.25
2 thru 5 JSo,rep.............. @2.25

DREAM POLICE
June, 2005
1 MD2, 48-pg................. 4.00

DROIDS
Star, April, 1986
1 JR 25.00
2 AW 15.00
3 JR/AW 15.00
4 AW 15.00
5 AW 15.00
6 EC/AW,A:Luke Skywalker 15.00
7 EC/AW,A:Luke Skywalker 15.00
8 EC/AW,A:Luke Skywalker 15.00

DRUID
1995
1 R:Dr. Druid Surprise!!! 3.50
2 F:Nekra 3.00
3 deranged canibal wisemen 3.00
4 Why Must He Die?........... 3.00

Dune #1
© Marvel Entertainment Group

DUNE
April–June, 1985
1 Movie Adapt,Rep. Marvel
     Super Spec,BSz 3.50
2 Movie Adapt,BSz 3.50
3 Movie Adapt,BSz, ... 3.50

DYNOMUTT
Nov., 1977
1 Based on TV series 50.00
2 thru 5 .... @30.00
6 Sept., 1978 .... 30.00

EARTHWORM JIM
1995–96
1 I:Earthworm Jim............. 3.00
2 Cow tipping 3.00
3 V:Lawyers,conclusion 3.00

EARTH X
Jan., 1999
0 (of 14) AxR,JPL,Machine Man
     & Watcher 6.00
0a signed 25.00
1 AxR,JPL,V:Inhumans,32-page... 8.00
1a signed 30.00
2 AxR,JPL,fate of Fant.Four 4.00
3 AxR,JPL,World Super Powers... 4.00
4 JPL,AxR(c),A:new Hulk 4.00
5 JPL,AxR(c),V:Doombots 4.00
6 JPL,AxR(c),different X-Men 4.00
7 JPL,AxR(c),A:Hulk............ 4.00

8 JPL,AxR(c),A:Venom 4.00	
9 JPL,AxR(c),Revelations 4.00	
10 JPL,AxR(c) 4.00	
11 JPL,AxR(c),V:Skull 4.00	
12 JPL,AxR(c),concl 4.00	
Spec.X AxR(c) concl.,48-pg 6.00	
Sketchbook 6.00	
TPB 464-page, rep. 25.00	
TPB Earth X (2006) 30.00	

ECTOKID
Razorline 1993–94
1 I:Dex Mungo,BU:Hokum & Hex . 3.50
2 O:Dex 2.50
3 I:Ectosphere 2.50
4 I:Brothers Augustine 2.50
5 A:Saint Sinner 2.50
6 Highway 61 Revisited 2.50
7 . . . . 2.50
8 V:Ice Augustine 2.50
9 Love is like a Bullet 2.50
10 . . . . 2.50
Ectokid Unleashed 3.25

EDEN'S TRAIL
Nov., 2002
1 (of 6) western 3.00
2 thru 5 . . . . @3.00

ELECTRIC UNDERTOW
Dec., 1989
1 MBa,Strike Force 4.00
2 thru 5 MBa . . . . @4.00

ELEKTRA
Nov., 1996
1 PrM,MD2, ... 3.50
1A variant (c) 4.50
2 PrM,MD2,V:Bullseye, round two . 3.00
3 PrM,MD2, ... 3.00
4 PrM,MD2 . . . . 3.00
5 PrM,MD2, ... 3.00
6 PrM,MD2 . . . . 3.00
7 PrM,MD2,A:Konrad,The Architect 3.00
8 PrM,MD2,V:The Architect 3.00
9 PrM,MD2,V:The Four Winds . . . 3.00
10 PrM,MD2,V:Daredevil,American
    Samurai, pt.1 . . . . 3.00
11 PrM,MD2,F:Daredevil 3.00
12 PrM,MD2,F:Daredevil,V:American
    Samuri 3.00
13 PrM,MD2,F:Daredevil, concl. . . 3.00
14 LHa,MD2,A:Wolverine 3.00
15 LHa,MD2,A:Silver Samurai 3.00
16 LHa,MD2,A Hole in the Soul . . . 3.00
17 LHa,MD2,V:The Hand 3.00
18 LHa,MD2,A:Shang-Chi&Kingpin . 3.00
19 LHa,MD2,last issue 3.00
Minus 1 Spec.,PMg,MD2,flashback . 3.00

ELEKTRA
July, 2001
1 BMB,non-comics code series . . . 5.00
2A BMB,A:S.H.I.E.L.D. 3.00
2B variant BSz(c) 3.00
3 BMB,A:Hydra 3.50
4 BMB,A:Nick Fury 3.50
5 BMB,concl 3.50
6 BMB,F:Daredevil,'Nuff Said 3.50
7 Hubris, pt.1 . . . . 3.50
8 Hubris, pt.2 . . . . 3.50
9 Hubris, pt.3 . . . . 3.00
10 Hubris, concl. 3.00
11 Elektra between jobs 3.00
12 F:Mr. Locke 3.00
13 DaM 3.00
14 DaM,Elektra fights back 3.00
15 DaM 3.00
16 DaM 3.00
17 DaM 3.00

Elektra #1
© Marvel Entertainment Group

18 DaM 3.00
19 DaM 3.00
20 DaM,V:The Hand 3.00
21 V:The Hand 3.00
22 V:The Hand, concl. 3.00
23 BSz(c),pt.1 . . . . 3.00
24 BSz(c),pt.2 . . . . 3.00
25 BSz(c),How to,pt.1 . . . . 3.00
26 How to,pt.2 . . . . 3.00
27 How to,pt.3,concl. 3.00
28 Tables turned 3.00
29 Assassination 3.00
30 Prophet & Loss,pt.2 . . . . 3.00
31 Prophet & Loss,pt.3 . . . . 3.00
32 Fever,pt.1 . . . . 3.00
33 Fever,pt.2 . . . . 3.00
34 Fever,pt.3 . . . . 3.00
35 Visits grave 3.00
36 JoB,pt.1 . . . . 3.00
TPB Vol. 1: Introspect 17.00
TPB Vol. 2: Everything Old 17.00
TPB Vol. 3: Relentless 15.00
TPB Vol. 4: Frenzy 15.00
TPB Elektra Lives Again, FM 25.00
Spec., Elektra: The Movie 3.00

ELEKTRA: ASSASSIN
Aug., 1986
1 FM,BSz,V:Shield 8.00
2 FM,BSz,I:Garrett 5.00
3 FM,BSz,V:Shield,A:Garrett 5.00
4 FM,BSz,V:Shield,A:Garrett 5.00
5 FM,BSz,I:Chastity,A:Garrett 5.00
6 FM,BSz,A:Nick Fury,Garrett 5.00
7 FM,BSz,V:Ken Wind,A:Garrett . . 5.00
8 FM,BSz,V:Ken Wind,A:Garrett . . 6.00
TPB Rep #1-8 . . . . 13.00

ELEKTRA: GLIMPSE & ECHO
July, 2002
1 (of 4) F:The Hand 3.50
2 thru 4 . . . . @3.50

ELEKTRA: THE HAND
Sept., 2004
1 (of 5) The First Impression 3.00
2 thru 5 . . . . @3.00
TPB 14.00

ELEKTRA LIVES AGAIN
1991
Graphic Novel FM,R:Elektra,A:Matt
    Murdock,V:The Hand 30.00
TPB FM, rep. of HC, 80pg. 7.00

ELEKTRA: ROOT OF EVIL
1 V:Snakeroot 3.00
2 V:Snakeroot 3.00
3 Elektra's Brother 3.00
4 V:The Hand 3.00

ELEKTRA: SAGA
Feb., 1984
1 FM,rep.Daredevil 7.00
2 FM,rep.Daredevil 7.00
3 FM,rep.Daredevil 7.00
4 FM,rep.Daredevil 7.00
TPB Reprints#1-#4 . . . . 17.00
GN Book One FM,KJ, rep. from
    Daredevil, 96pg 4.00
GN Book Two FM,KJ, rep. from
    Daredevil, 96pg 4.00

ELEKTRA & WOLVERINE:
THE REDEEMER
Nov., 2001
GN#1 painted, 48-page 6.50
GN#2 48-page 6.50
GN#3 concl., 48-page 6.50

ELEKTRA/WITCHBLADE
1-shot Devil's Reign,
    pt.6, x-over 3.00

ELFQUEST
Star, Aug., 1985
1 WP,reprints 4.00
2 thru 31 WP . . . . @2.50
32 WP,Conclusion, March, 1988 . . 2.50

ELSEWHERE PRINCE
Epic, May–Oct., 1990
1 thru 6 . . . . @3.00

ELVIRA
Oct., 1988
Spec.B&W, Movie Adapt. 3.00

EMMA FROST
July, 2003
1 RGr,Higher Learning,pt.1 . . . . . . 7.00
2 RGr,Higher Learning,pt.2 . . . . . . 4.00
3 RGr,Higher Learning,pt.3 . . . . . . 4.00
4 RGr,Higher Learning,pt.4 . . . . . . 4.00
5 RGr,Higher Learning,pt.5 . . . . . . 4.00
6 RGr,White Queen 4.00
7 Mind Games,pt.1 . . . . 2.50
8 Mind Games,pt.2 . . . . 2.50
9 Mind Games,pt.3 . . . . 3.00
10 Mind Games,pt.4 . . . . 3.00
11 Mind Games,pt.5 . . . . 3.00
12 Mind Games,pt.6 . . . . 3.00
13 Bloom,pt.1 . . . . 3.00
14 Bloom,pt.2 . . . . 3.00
15 Bloom,pt.3 . . . . 3.00
16 Bloom,pt.4 . . . . 3.00
17 Bloom,pt.5 . . . . 3.00
18 Bloom,pt.6 . . . . 3.00
Digest Vol. 1: Higher Learning 8.00
Digest Vol. 2: Mind Games 8.00
Digest Vol. 3: Bloom 8.00

EPIC
1992
1 Wildcards,Hellraiser 6.00
2 Nightbreed,Wildcards 6.00

3 DBw,MFm,Alien Legion, ... 6.00
4 Stalkers,Metropol,Wildcards 6.00

EPIC ANTHOLOGY
April, 2004
1 . . . . 6.00

EPIC, GRAPHIC NOVEL
Moebius 1: Upon a Star 10.00
Moebius 2: Arzach 10.00
Moebius 3: Airtight Garage 10.00
Moebius 4: Long Tomorrow 10.00
Moebius 5: 10.00
Moebius 6: Pharadonesia 10.00
Last of Dragons 7.00
The Incal 1 Moebius 11.00
The Incal 2 Moebius. 11.00
The Incal 3 Moebius. 11.00
JBo,Someplace Strange 7.00
MZ,Punisher. 17.00

Epic Illustrated #34
© Marvel Entertainment Group

EPIC, ILLUSTRATED
Spring, 1980
1 Black and White/Color Mag. . . . 14.00
2 thru 10 . . . . @8.00
11 thru 20 . . . . @10.00
21 thru 25 . . . . @12.00
26 thru 34, March, 1986. . . . . . @14.00

EPIC, LITE
Epic, Nov., 1991
One-shot short stories 4.00

ESSENTIALS
1999–2006
(528 pages, B&W reprints)
TPB Ant-Man, 576-pg. (2002) 16.00
TPB Avengers, Vol.1 . . . . 16.00
TPB Avengers, Vol. 1 (2005) 17.00
TPB Avengers, Vol.2, ... 16.00
TPB Avengers, Vol.3,rep.#47–#68. 16.00
TPB Avengers, Vol.4 (2004) 17.00
TPB Avengers (2003) 17.00
TPB Captain America,Vol.1 . . . . . . 16.00
TPB Captain America,Vol.2 (2002) 16.00
TPB Classic X-Men, Vol. 2 (2006). 17.00
TPB Conan,Vol.1 . . . . 17.00
TPB Daredevil,Vol.1 (2002) 17.00
TPB Daredevil, Vol. 2 (2004) 17.00
TPB Daredevil, Vol. 1: (2005) 17.00
TPB Daredevil, Vol. 2: 17.00
TPB Daredevil, Vol. 3: (2005) 17.00
TPB Defenders, Vol. 1 (2005) 17.00

TPB Doctor Strange, Vol. 1 (2006) 17.00
TPB Doctor Strange, Vol. 2 (2005) 17.00
TPB Fantastic Four,Vol.1 . . . . 16.00
TPB Fantastic Four,Vol.2 (2000) . . 16.00
TPB Fantastic Four,Vol.3 (2001) . . 16.00
TPB Fantastic Four, Vol. 1: 17.00
TPB Fantastic Four, Vol. 2: 15.00
TPB Fantastic Four, Vol. 3:(2005) 15.00
TPB Fantastic Four, Vol. 4 (2005) . 17.00
TPB Ghost Rider, Vol. 1 . . . . 17.00
TPB Godzilla (2006) 20.00
TPB Howard the Duck (2002) 16.00
TPB Hulk, Vol. 1 (2002). 17.00
TPB Hulk, Vol. 2 (2003). 15.00
TPB Hulk, Vol. 3 (2005). 17.00
TPB Hulk, Vol. 4 (2006). 17.00
TPB Human Torch, Vol. 1 . . . . 17.00
TPB Incredible Hulk,Vol.1 . . . . 16.00
TPB Incredible Hulk,Vol.2 (2001). . 16.00
TPB Iron Fist, Vol. 1 (2004) 17.00
TPB Iron Man, Vol.1 (2002). 17.00
TPB Iron Man, Vol. 1 (2005) 17.00
TPB Iron Man, Vol. 2 (2004) 17.00
TPB Killraven, Vol. 1 (2005) 17.00
TPB Luke Cage, Vol. 1 (2005). . . . 17.00
TPB Luke Cage Power Man 17.00
TPB Man Thing, Vol. 1 (2006) 17.00
TPB Marvel Horror, Vol. 1 (2006) . 17.00
TPB Marvel Team-Up (2002) 16.00
TPB Marvel Team-Up, Vol.1 (2006) 17.00
TPB Marvel Team-Up, Vol.2 (2000) 17.00
TPB Marvel Two-In-One (2005) . . . 17.00
TPB Monster of Frankenstein 17.00
TPB Moon Knight, Vol. 1 (2006) . . 17.00
TPB Nova, Vol. 1 (2006) 17.00
TPB Official Handbook, Vol. 1 . . . . 17.00
TPB Official Handbook, Vol. 2 . . . . 17.00
TPB Official Handbook, Vol. 3 . . . . 17.00
TPB Official Handbook (2006). . . . 17.00
TPB Peter Parker, Spectacular
    Spider-Man (2005). 17.00
TPB Peter Parker, Spectacular
    Spider-Man, Vol. 2 (2006) 17.00
TPB Punisher,Vol.1 (2004) 15.00
TPB Punisher,Vol.1 (2006) 17.00
TPB Savage She-Hulk (2006) 17.00
TPB Silver Surfer,Vol.1 . . . . 16.00
TPB Spider-Man,Vol.1 (1997) 17.00
TPB Spider-Man,Vol.2 (1997) 17.00
TPB Spider-Man,Vol.3 . . . . 16.00
TPB Spider-Man,Vol.4 . . . . 16.00
TPB Spider-Man,Vol.5 (2002) 16.00
TPB Spider-Man,Vol.6 (2004) 17.00
TPB Spider-Man, Vol. 1: (2005). . . 15.00
TPB Spider-Man, Vol. 2: (2005). . . 17.00
TPB Spider-Man, Vol. 3: (2005). . . 17.00
TPB Spider-Man, Vol. 4: (2005). . . 17.00
TPB Spider-Man, Vol. 5: (2005). . . 15.00
TPB Spider-Man, Vol. 6: (2005). . . 17.00
TPB Spider-Man, Vol. 7: (2005). . . 17.00
TPB Spider-Woman,Vol.1 (2005). . 17.00
TPB Super-VillainTeam-up(2004) . 17.00
TPB Tales of the Zombie (2006) . . 17.00
TPB Thor,Vol.1. . . . . 16.00
TPB Thor, Vol. 1 (2005). 17.00
TPB Thor, Vol. 2 (2005). 17.00
TPB Thor, Vol. 3 (2006). 17.00
TPB Tomb of Dracula (2002) 17.00
TPB Tomb of Dracula,#2 (2004) . . 17.00
TPB Tomb of Dracula,#3 (2004 . . 17.00
TPB Tomb of Dracula,#4 (2005) . . 17.00
TPB Wolverine,Vol.1 . . . . 16.00
TPB Wolverine,Vol.2 . . . . 16.00
TPB Wolverine,Vol.3 (1998) 17.00
TPB Wolverine, Vol.1 (2005) 17.00
TPB Uncanny X-Men, Vol.1 (2002) 17.00
TPB Werewolf by Night (2005) . . . 17.00
TPB Wolverine, Vol. 1 (1999) 15.00
TPB Wolverine, Vol. 2 (1999) 15.00
TPB Wolverine, Vol. 3 (1999) 15.00
TPB Wolverine, Vol. 4 (1999) 15.00
TPB Wolverine, Vol. 4 (2006) 17.00

TPB X-Factor, Vol. 1 (2006). 17.00
TPB X-Men, Vol. 1 (1999) 16.00
TPB X-Men, Vol. 2 (1999) 16.00
TPB X-Men, Vol. 3 (1999) 16.00
TPB X-Men, Vol. 4 (1999) 16.00
TPB X-Men, Vol. 5 (2004) 17.00
TPB X-Men, Vol. 1 (2005) 15.00
TPB X-Men, Vol. 2 (2005) 15.00
TPB X-Men, Vol. 3 (2005) 15.00
TPB X-Men, Vol. 4 (2005) 15.00
TPB X-Men, Vol. 5 (2005) 17.00
TPB X-Men, Vol. 6 (2005) 17.00
TPB X-Men, Vol. 7 (2006) 17.00

ETERNAL
Marvel Max, June, 2003
1 Gift of the Gods,pt.1 . . . . 3.00
2 thru 6 Gift of the Gods,pt.2–6 . @3.00

ETERNALS
[1st Series], July, 1976
1 JK,I:Ikaris,25 cent edition 25.00
2 JK,I:Ajak,25 cent edition 15.00
3 JK,I:Sersi 10.00
4 JK,Night of the Demons. 10.00
5 JK,I:Makarri,Zuras Thena,Domo 10.00
6 JK,Gods & Men at City College. 10.00
7 JK,V:Celestials 10.00
8 JK,I:Karkas, Reject 10.00
9 JK,I:Sprite,Reject vs. Karkas . . . 10.00
10 JK,V:Celestials 10.00
11 JK,I:Kingo Sunen 10.00
12 JK,I:Uni-Mind 10.00
13 JK,I:ForgottenOne(Gilgamesh). 15.00
14 JK,V:Hulk 15.00
15 JK,V:Hulk 15.00
16 JK,I:Dromedan 15.00
17 JK,I:Sigmar 10.00
18 JK,I:Nerve Beast. 10.00
19 JK,Secret o/t Pyramid. 10.00
Ann.#1 JK,V:Timekillers. 12.00

Eternals #6
© Marvel Entertainment Group

[2nd Series], Oct., 1985
1 SB,I:Cybele 3.00
2 thru 7 SB,V:Deviants . . . . @2.50
8 thru 10 WS,SB,V:Deviants . . . . @2.50
11 &12 WS,KP,V:Deviants . . . . . @2.50

ETERNALS
June, 2006
1 NGa,JR2 . . . . 4.00
2 thru 6 NGa,JR2 . . . . @4.00
2a variant (c) 8.00

ETERNALS: HEROD FACTOR

Nov., 1991

1 MT/BMc,A:Sersi (giant size) 2.50

EVERYMAN

Epic, 1991

1-shot Supernatural Story 8.00

EWOKS

Star, June, 1985—Sept., 1987

1 Based on TV Series.	18.00
2	15.00
3	15.00
4 A:Foonars	15.00
5 Wicket vs. Ice Demon.	15.00
6 Mount Sorrow, A:Teebo	15.00
7 A:Logray,V:Morag	15.00
8	15.00
9 Lost in Time.	15.00
10 AW,Lost in Time	18.00
11 thru 15	@15.00

EXCALIBUR

April, 1988

1 AD,Special,O:Excalibur,	
V:Technet.	5.00
1a 2nd Printing	2.50
1b 3rd Printing	2.00
2 AAd,Mojo Mayhem,A:X-Babies . .	4.00
3 Air Apparent Spec.RLm,KJ,JG,TP,	
RL,EL,JRu,A:Coldblood.	4.00

[Regular Series]

1 B:CCl(s),AD,V:Warwolves,	
I:Widget	6.00
2 AD,V:Warwolves,I:Kylun	5.00
3 AD,V:Juggernaut	4.00
4 AD,V:Arcade,Crazy Gang	4.00
5 AD,V:Arcade	3.00
6 AD,Inferno,I:Alistaire Stuart	3.00
7 AD,Inferno	3.00
8 RLm,JRu,A:New Mutants	3.00
9 AD,I:Nazi-Excalibur	3.00
10 MR,V:Nazi-Excalibur	3.00
11 MR,V:Nazi-Excalibur	3.00
12 AD,Fairy Tale Dimension	3.00
13 AD,The Prince,N:Capt.Britian . . .	3.00
14 AD,Too Many Heroes	2.50
15 AD,I:US James Braddock	2.50
16 AD,V:Anjulie	2.50
17 AD,C:Prof.X,Starjammers	2.50
18 DJ,DA,V:Jamie Braddock	2.50
19 RL,TA,AM,V:Jamie Braddock . . .	2.50
20 RLm,JRu,V:Demon Druid	2.50
21 I:Crusader X	2.50
22 V:Crusader X	2.50
23 AD,V:Magik	2.50
24 AD,Return Home,C:Galactus . . .	2.50
25 E:CCl(s),AM,A:Galactus,Death,	
Watcher	2.50
26 RLm,JRu,V:Mastermind	2.50
27 BWS,BSz,A:Nth Man	3.00
28 BBI,Night at Bar	2.50
29 JRu,V:Nightmare,A:PowerPack .	2.50
30 DR,AM,A:Doctor Strange	2.50
31 DR,AM,V:Son of Krakoa	2.50
32 V:Mesmero	2.50
33 V:Mesmero	2.50
34 V:Mesmero	2.50
35 AM,Missing Child	2.50
36 AM,V:Silv.Sable,Sandman	2.50
37 A:Avengers W.C.,Dr.Doom	2.50
38 A:Avengers W.C.,Dr.Doom	2.50
39 A:Avengers W.C.,Dr.Doom	2.50
40 O:Excalibur,Trail-Lockheed	2.50
41 V:Warwolves,C:Cable	3.00
42 AD,Team Broken Up	3.50
43 AD,Nightcrawler,V:Capt.Brit	3.00
44 AD,Capt.Britain On Trial	3.00

45 AD,I:N-Men, ...	3.00
46 AD,Return of Kylun,C:Cerise . . .	3.00
47 AD,I:Cerise	3.00
48 AD,A:Anti-Phoenix	3.00
49 AD,MFm,V:Necrom,R:Merlyn . .	3.00
50 AD,Phoenix,V:Necrom,Merlyn . .	5.00
51 V:Giant Dinosaurs.	2.50
52 O:Phoenix,A:Prof X,MarvGirl . . .	2.50
53 A:Spider-Man,V:The Litter.	2.50
54 AD,MFm,V:Crazy Gang	2.50
55 AD,MFm,A:Psylocke	2.50
56 AD,MFm,A:Psylocke,	
V:Saturyne,Jamie Braddock . . .	3.00
57 A:X-Men,Alchemy,V:Trolls.	2.75
58 A:X-Men,Alchemy,V:Trolls.	2.75
59 A:Avengers	2.50
60 A:Avengers	2.50
61 AD,MFm,Phoenix Vs.Galactus .	2.50
62 AD,MFm,A:Galactus	2.50
63 AD,MFm,V:Warpies.	2.50
64 AD,MFm,V:RCX,R:Rachel	2.50
65 AD,MFm,R:Dark Phoenix	2.50
66 AD,MFm,V:Ahab,Sentinels,	
O:Widget	2.50
67 AD,MFm,V:Ahab,Sentinels	2.50
68 V:Starjammers	2.50
69 A:Starjammers.	2.50
70 A:Starjammers.	2.50
71 DaR,Hologram(c),N:Excalibur. .	5.00
72 KeL,V:Siena Blaze	2.50
73 TSr,V:Siena Blaze	2.50
74 InC,A:Mr.Sinster,Siena Blaze . .	2.50
75 SLo(s),KeL,I:Daytripper(Amanda	
Sefton),Britannic(Capt.Britain),	
BU:Nightcrawler.	4.00
75a Newstand Ed.	2.25
76 KeL,V:D'spayre	2.50
77 KeL,R:Doug Ramsey	2.50
78 A:Zero,Doug Ramsey	2.50
79 A:Zero,Doug Ramsey	2.50
80 A:Zero,Doug Ramsey	2.50
81 Doug Ramsey.	2.50
82	3.00
82a foil(c).	3.50
83 regular ed.	2.25
83a Deluxe ed. Kitty,Nightcrawler .	2.50
84 regular ed.	2.25
84a Deluxe ed.	2.50
85 regular ed.	2.25
85a Deluxe ed.	2.50
86 regular ed.	2.25
86a Deluxe ed.	2.50
87 KeL,Secrets of the Genoshan	
Mutate Technology	2.50
88 Dream Nails,pt.1	2.50
89 Dream Nails,pt.2	2.50
90 Between Uncreated,Phalanx . . .	4.00
91 F:Colossus	2.50
92 F:Colossus	2.50
93 F:Wolfsbane	2.50
94 A:Karma & Psylocke	2.50
95	2.50
96	2.50
97 BWi,B.Braddock's secrets told .	2.50
98	2.50
99 European Hellfire Club,	
Onslaught	2.50
100 Onslaught saga, double size . .	4.00
101	2.50
102	2.50
103 WEI,F:Colossus,Kitty &	
Nichtcrawler.	2.50
104 JAr,BHi,PNe,Douglock's	
dark side	2.50
105 JAr,BHi,PNe,V:Moonstar, ...	2.50
106	2.50
107 SvL,New direction.	2.50
108 Dragons of the Crimson Dawn .	2.50
109 V:Spiral,A:Captain Britain	2.50
110 V:The Dragons of the	
Crimson Dawn.	2.50

Excalibur #10
© Marvel Entertainment Group

111 F:Shadowcat,R:Rory Cambell	
(Ahab?)	2.50
112 Quicksilver tie-in	2.50
113 BRa,Colossus & Meggan	2.50
114 BRa,Vanisher	2.50
115 BRa,Quarantine,F:GenerationX	2.50
116 BRa,Legacy Virus, cont.	2.50
117 BRa,F:Kitty Pryde, Colossus &	
Nightcrawler.	2.50
118 BRa,V:Creatures from the	
Shadows	2.50
119 BRa,V:Nightmare	2.50
120 BRa,F:Kitty Pryde & Pete	
Wisdom	2.50
121 BRa,to Egypt.	2.50
122 BRa,V:Original X-Men?.	2.50
123 BRa,V:Mimic.	2.50
124 BBr,Captain Britain's bachelor	
party.	2.50
125 TvS,SHa, W:Captain Britain &	
Meggan, final issue	4.00
Minus 1 Spec., flashback,	
F:Nightcrawler	2.50
Ann.#1 I:Khaos,w/card.	3.25
Spec #1 The Possession	4.00
Spec #2 RLm,DT,JG,RL,	
A:Original X-Men.	3.00
PF Cold Blood	5.00
GN Weird War III	10.00
TPB Wild, Wild Life	6.00

EXCALIBUR

May, 2004

1 CCl,Forging the Sword,pt.1	3.00
2 CCl,Forging the Sword,pt.2	3.00
3 CCl,Forging the Sword,pt.3	3.00
4 CCl,Forging the Sword,pt.4	3.00
5 CCl,Food Fight,pt.1	3.00
6 CCl,Food Fight,pt.2	3.00
7 CCl,Food Fight,pt.3	3.00
8 ALo,Saturday Night Fever,pt.1. . .	3.00
9 ALo,Saturday Night Fever,pt.2. . .	7.00
10 CCl,ALo,Saturday Night Fever . .	3.00
11 CCl,ALo,Save My Child,pt.1 . . .	3.00
12 CCl,ALo,Save My Child,pt.2	3.00
13 CCl,ALo,House of M, prelude. . .	5.00
14 CCl,ALo,A:Dr. Strange	4.00
TPB Vol. 1: Forging the Sword . . .	10.00
TPB Vol. 2: Saturday Night Fever .	15.00
TPB House of M: Excalibur	12.00
TPB Classic Vol. 1 Sword is Drawn	20.00
TPB Classic Vol. 2 Two-Edged	
Sword	25.00

Excalibur #99
© Marvel Entertainment Group

EXCALIBUR:
SWORD OF POWER
Dec., 2000

1 (of 4) IaC,BRa,F:Capt.Britain....	3.00
2 BRa,	3.00
3 BRa,V:Roma	3.00
4 BRa, concl	3.00

EXILES
June, 2001

1 MkK,F:Blink, 48-page	10.00
2A MkK,	7.00
2B variant JWi(c)	6.00
3 MkK,trial of Phoenix	4.00
4 MkK,trial of Phoenix	4.00
5 MkK,JCf,F:Hulk	4.00
6 MkK,JCf,F:Alpha Flight	4.00
7 MkK,'Nuff Said (no words)	4.00
8 MkK,A World Apart,pt.1	4.00
9 MkK,A World Apart,pt.2	4.00
10 MkK,A World Apart,pt.3	4.00
11 MkK,F:Morph	3.50
12 MkK,New team	3.50
13 MkK,team must kill	3.50
14 MkK,V:Dr. Doom	3.50
15 MkK,Mimic vs. Namor	3.50
16 MkK,	3.50
17 world gone reptile	3.50
18 MkK,F:Morph	3.50
19 MkK,JHo	3.50
20 JCf,V:Legacy Virus,pt.1	3.00
21 JCf,V:Legacy Virus,pt.2	3.00
22 JCf,One goew down	3.00
23 With an Iron Fist,pt.1	3.00
24 With an Iron Fist,pt.2	3.00
25 With an Iron Fist,pt.3	3.50
26 Hard Choices,pt.1	3.00
27 Hard Choices,pt.2	3.00
28 Unnatural Selection,pt.1	3.00
29 Unnatural Selection,pt.2	3.00
30 Unnatural Selection,pt.3	3.00
31 Avengers Forever,pt.1	3.00
32 Avengers Forever,pt.2	3.00
33 A Second Farewell,pt.1	3.00
34 A Second Farewell,pt.2	3.00
35 Fantastic Voyage,pt.1	3.00
36 Fantastic Voyage,pt.2	3.00
37 Fantastic Voyage,pt.3	4.00
38 King Hyperion,pt.1	4.00
39 King Hyperion,pt.2	4.00
40 King Hyperion,pt.3	4.00
41 A Nocturne's Tale,pt.1	3.00
42 A Nocturne's Tale,pt.2	3.00

43 Blink in Time,pt.1	3.00
44 Blink in Time,pt.2	3.00
45 Blink in Time,pt.3	3.00
46 Earn Your Wings,pt.1	3.00
47 Earn Your Wings,pt.2	3.00
48 Earn Your Wings,pt.3	3.00
49 Capitol dome dump.	3.00
50 The Big M,pt.1	3.00
51 The Big M,pt.2	3.00
52 Living Planet,pt.1	3.00
53 Living Planet,pt.2	3.00
54 Chain Lightning	3.00
55 Bump in the Night, pt.1	3.00
56 Bump in the Night, pt.2	3.00
57 Bump in the Night, pt.3	3.00
58 F:Sasquatch, Tanaraq	3.00
59 F:Blink	3.00
60 Son of Apocalypse,pt.1	4.00
61 Son of Apocalypse,pt.2	4.00
62 Timebreakers,pt.1	4.00
63 Timebreakers,pt.2	4.00
64 Timebreakers,pt.3	3.00
65 Timebreakers,pt.4	3.00
66 Destroy All Monsters,pt.1	3.00
67 Destroy All Monsters,pt.2	3.00
68 Destroy All Monsters,pt.3	3.00
69 PaP,World Tour: Earth 616	3.00
70 PaP,World Tour: Earth 616	3.00
71 World Tour: House of M	3.00
72 World Tour: New Universe, pt. 1.	3.00
73 World Tour: New Universe, pt. 2.	3.00
74 World Tour: New Universe, pt. 3.	3.00
75 World Tour: 2099, pt. 1	3.00
76 World Tour: 2099, pt. 2	3.00
77 World Tour: Squadron Supreme	3.00
78 World Tour: Squadron Supreme	3.00
79 World Tour: Future Imperfect	3.00
80 World Tour: Future Imperfect	3.00
81 World Tour: Heroes Reborn	3.00
82 World Tour: Heroes Reborn	3.00
83 It's Your Funeral	3.00
84 Back in the Saddle	3.00
85 The New Exiles	3.00
86 Countdown to Infinite Wolverines	3.00
87 Superguardians,pt.1	3.00
88 Superguardians, pt.2	3.00
TPB Vol. 1: Down the Rabbit Hole	13.00
TPB Vol. 2: A World Apart	15.00
TPB Vol. 3: Out of Time	18.00
TPB Vol. 4: Legacy	13.00
TPB Vol. 5: Unnatural Instinct	15.00
TPB Vol. 6: Fantastic Voyage	18.00
TPB Vol. 7: A Blink in Time	20.00
TPB Vol. 8: Earn Your Wings	15.00
TPB Vol. 9: Bump in the Night	18.00
TPB Vol. 10: Age of Apocalypse	13.00
TPB Vol. 11: Time Breakers	18.00
TPB Vol. 12: World Tour	17.00
TPB Vol. 13: World Tour, Book 2	24.00

FACTOR X
1995

1 After Xavier	4.00
2 Scott vs. Alex Summers	3.00
3 Cyclops vs. Havok	3.00
4 Jean & Scott	3.00
TPB Rep. #1-#4	9.00

FAFHRD AND THE
GRAY MOUSER
Epic, Oct., 1990

1 MMi,Fritz Leiber adapt.	5.00
2 & 3 MMi	@5.00
4 MMi, Feb., 1991	5.00

FAITHFUL
Nov., 1949

1 Ph(c),I Take This Man	200.00
2 Ph(c),Love Thief,Feb.,1950	200.00

Falcon #4
© Marvel Entertainment Group

FALCON
Nov., 1983

1 PS,V:Nemesis	3.00
2 V:Sentinels	3.00
3 V:Electro	3.00
4 A:Capt.America, Feb., 1984	3.00

FALLEN ANGELS
April, 1987

1 KGa,TP,A:Sunspot,Warlock	3.00
2 KGa,TP,I:Gomi,Fallen Angels	2.50
3 KGa,TP,A:X-Factor	2.50
4 KGa,TP,A:Moon Boy, Devil	
Dinosaur	2.50
5 JSon,D:Angel,Don	2.50
6 JSon,Coconut Grove	2.50
7 KGa,Captured in CoconutGrove	2.50
8 KGa,L:Sunspot,Warlock	2.50

FANTASTIC FIRSTS
Marvel Dec., 2001

TPB Superhero origins, 428-pg.	30.00

FANTASTIC FIVE
Aug., 1999

1 TDF,PR,AM,New Team:Human Torch Thing,Ms.Fantastic,Psilord & Big Brain	2.25
2A TDF,PR,AM,Bloody Reunions x-over	2.25
2B variant MSh(c)	2.25
3 TDF,PR,AM,A:Spider-Girl	2.25
4 TDF,PR,AM	2.25
5 TDF,PR,AM,A:Kristoff	2.25
Digest In Search of Doom	8.00

FANTASTIC FORCE
1994–96

1 Foil stamped cover	3.00
2 thru 18	@2.25

FANTASTIC FOUR
Nov., 1961

1 JK,I&O:Mr.Fantastic,Thing Invisible Girl,Human Torch Mole Man	38,000.00
2 JK,I:Skrulls	9,000.00
3 JK,I:Miraceleman	6,000.00
4 JK,R:Submariner	7,500.00
5 JK,JSt,I&O:Doctor Doom	9,000.00

MARVEL

MARVEL

6 JK,V:Doctor Doom 5,000.00
7 JK,I:Kurrgo 4,000.00
8 JK,I:Alicia Masters,I&O:
  Puppet Master 4,000.00
9 JK,V:Submariner.......... 4,000.00
10 JK,V:Doctor Doom,I:Ovoids. 4,000.00
11 JK,I:Impossible Man....... 2,500.00
12 JK,V:Hulk............... 5,000.00
13 JK,SD,I&O:Red Ghost,
  I:Watcher 2,000.00
14 JK,SD,V:Submariner 1,500.00
15 JK,I:Mad Thinker 1,500.00
16 JK,V:Doctor Doom 1,500.00
17 JK,V:Doctor Doom......... 1,500.00
18 JK,I:Super Skrull 1,500.00
19 JK,I&O:Rama Tut......... 1,500.00
20 JK,I:Molecule Man 800.00
21 JK,I:Hate Monger 550.00
22 JK,V:Mole Man 500.00
23 JK,V:Doctor Doom 500.00
24 JK,I:Infant Terrible.......... 500.00
25 JK,Thing vs.Hulk 1,500.00
26 JK,V:Hulk,A:Avengers 1,500.00
27 JK,A:Doctor Strange 800.00
28 JK,1st X-Men x-over 650.00
29 JK,V:Red Ghost 500.00
30 JK,I&O:Diablo 500.00
31 JK,V:Mole Man 400.00
32 JK,V:Superskrull 400.00
33 JK,I:Attuma 400.00
34 JK,I:Gideon 400.00
35 JK,I:Dragon Man,A:Diablo ... 400.00
36 JK,I:Medusa,Frightful Four ... 400.00
37 JK,V:Skrulls.............. 375.00
38 JK,V:Frightful Four,I:Trapster . 375.00
39 JK,WW,A:Daredevil........ 375.00
40 JK,A:Daredevil,Dr.Doom..... 375.00
41 JK,V:Fright.Four,A:Medusa ... 400.00
42 JK,V:Frightful Four 400.00
43 JK,V:Frightful Four 400.00
44 JK,JSt,I:Gorgon,
  V:Dragon Man 300.00
45 JK,JSt,I:Inhumans(Black Bolt,
  Triton,Lockjaw,Crystal,
  Karnak) 500.00
46 JK,JSt,V:Seeker 350.00
47 JK,JSt,I:Maximus,Attilan,
  Alpha Primitives.......... 350.00
48 JK,JSt,I:Silver Surfer,
  C:Galactus 2,000.00
49 JK,JSt,A:Silver Surfer,
  V:Galactus.............. 750.00
50 JK,JSt,V:Galactus,Silver
  Surfer,I:Wyatt Wingfoot 900.00
51 JK,JSt,I:Negative Zone 500.00
52 JK,JSt,I:Black Panther 1,000.00
53 JK,JSt,I:Klaw,Vibranium 475.00
54 JK,JSt,I:Prester John 250.00
55 JK,JSt,A:Silver Surfer 700.00
56 JK,JSt,O:Klaw,A:Inhumans,
  C:Silver Surfer............ 300.00
57 JK,JSt,V:DocDoom,A:S.Surfer. 300.00
58 JK,JSt,V:DocDoom,A:S.Surfer. 300.00
59 JK,JSt,V:DocDoom,A:S.Surfer. 300.00
60 JK,JSt,V:DocDoom,A:S.Surfer. 300.00
61 JK,JSt,V:Sandman,A:S.Surfer 300.00
62 JK,JSt,I:Blastaar 250.00
63 JK,JSt,V:Blastaar 250.00
64 JK,JSt,I:The Kree,Sentry 250.00
65 JK,JSt,I:Ronan,Supreme
  Intelligence 250.00
66 JK,JSt,O:Him,A:Crystal...... 300.00
67 JK,JSt,I:Him 300.00
68 JK,JSt,V:Mad Thinker 250.00
69 JK,JSt,V:Mad Thinker 250.00
70 JK,JSt,V:Mad Thinker 250.00
71 JK,JSt,V:Mad Thinker 250.00
72 JK,JSt,A:Watcher,S.Surfer ... 350.00
73 JK,JSt,A:SpM,DD,Thor 350.00
74 JK,JSt,A:Silver Surfer 425.00
75 JK,JSt,A:Silver Surfer 300.00
76 JK,JSt,V:Psycho Man,S.Surf. . 235.00

77 JK,JSt,V:Galactus,S.Surfer... 235.00
78 JK,JSt,V:Wizard 235.00
79 JK,JSt,A:Crystall,V:Mad
  Thinker................ 235.00
80 JK,JSt,A:Crystal 235.00
81 JK,JSt,J:Crystal,V:Wizard 235.00
82 JK,JSt,V:Maximus......... 235.00
83 JK,JSt,V:Maximus......... 235.00
84 JK,JSt,V:Doctor Doom 235.00
85 JK,JSt,V:Doctor Doom 225.00
86 JK,JSt,V:Doctor Doom 225.00
87 JK,JSt,V:Doctor Doom 225.00
88 JK,JSt,V:Mole Man 225.00
89 JK,JSt,V:Mole Man 225.00
90 JK,JSt,V:Skrulls.......... 200.00
91 JK,JSt,V:Skrulls,I:Torgo..... 200.00
92 JK,JSt,V:Torgo,Skrulls. 200.00

Fantastic Four #12
© Marvel Entertainment Group

93 JK,V:Torgo,Skrulls.......... 200.00
94 JK,JSt,I:Agatha Harkness.... 200.00
95 JK,JSt,I:Monocle 200.00
96 JK,JSt,V:Mad Thinker 200.00
97 JK,JSt,V:Monster from
  Lost Lagoon............ 200.00
98 JK,JSt,V:Kree Sentry 200.00
99 JK,JSt,A:Inhumans 200.00
100 JK,JSt,V:Puppetmaster..... 350.00
101 JK,JSt,V:Maggia 200.00
102 JK,JSt,V:Magneto 200.00
103 JR,V:Magneto 200.00
104 JR,V:Magneto 200.00
105 JR,L:Crystal 200.00
106 JR,JSt,`Monster's Secret' ... 200.00
107 JB,JSt,V:Annihilus......... 200.00
108 JK,JB,JR,JSt, V:Annihilus ... 200.00
109 JB,JSt,V:Annihilus 200.00
110 JB,JSt,V:Annihilus 200.00
111 JB,JSt,A:Hulk............ 150.00
112 JB,JSt,Thing vs. Hulk 350.00
113 JB,JSt,I:Overmind 125.00
114 JR(c),JB,V:Overmind....... 125.00
115 JR(c),JB,JSt,I:Eternals 135.00
116 JB,JSt,O:Stranger 150.00
117 JB,JSt,V:Diablo 100.00
118 JR(c),JB,JM,V:Diablo 100.00
119 JB,JSt,V:Klaw 100.00
120 JB,JSt,I:Gabriel(Airwalker)
  (Robot)................ 100.00
121 JB,JSt,V:Silver Surfer,D:
  Gabriel Destroyer 125.00
122 JR(c),JB,JSt,V:Galactus,
  A:Silver Surfer 125.00
123 JB,JSt,V:Galactus,
  A:Silver Surfer 125.00

124 JB,JSt,V:Monster 75.00
125 E:StL(s),JB,JSt,V:Monster... 75.00
126 B:RTs(s),JB,JSt,
  O:FF,MoleMan........... 75.00
127 JB,JSt,V:Mole Man 75.00
128 JB,JSt,V:Mole Man 75.00
129 JB,JSt,I:Thundra,
  V:Frightful Four 75.00
130 JSo(c),JB,JSt,V:Frightful Four. 75.00
131 JSo(c),JB,JSt,V:QuickSilver .. 75.00
132 JB,JSt,J:Medusa 75.00
133 JSt(i),V:Thundra 75.00
134 JB,JSt,V:Dragon Man 75.00
135 JB,JSt,V:Gideon 75.00
136 JB,JSt,A:Shaper 75.00
137 JB,JSt,A:Shaper 75.00
138 JB,JSt,O:Miracle Man 75.00
139 JB,V:Miracle Man 75.00
140 JB,JSt,O:Annihilus 75.00
141 JR(c),JB,JSt,V:Annihilus 75.00
142 RB,JSt,A:Doc Doom 75.00
143 GK(c),RB,V:Doc Doom 75.00
144 RB,JSt,V:Doc Doom 75.00
145 JSt&GK(c),RA,I:Ternak 75.00
146 RA,JSt,V:Ternak 75.00
147 RB,JSt,V:Subby 75.00
148 RB,JSt,V:Frightful Four 75.00
149 RB,JSt,V:Sub-Mariner. 75.00
150 GK(c),RB,JSt,W:Crystal &
  Quicksilver,V:Ultron 80.00
151 RB,JSt,O:Thundra......... 30.00
152 JR(c),RB,JM,A:Thundra 30.00
153 GK(c),RB,JSt,A:Thundra 30.00
154 GK(c),rep.Str.Tales #127..... 30.00
155 RB,JSt,A:Surfer.......... 40.00
156 RB,JSt,A:Surfer,V:Doom 40.00
157 RB,JSt,A:Surfer.......... 40.00
158 RB,JSt,V:Xemu 30.00
159 RB,JSt,V:Xemu 30.00
160 K&R(c),JB,V:Arkon 30.00
161 RB,JSt,V:Arkon 20.00
162 RB,DA,JSt,V:Arkon........ 20.00
163 RB,JSt,V:Arkon 20.00
164 JK(c),GP,JSt,V:Crusader,R:
  Marvel Boy,I:Frankie Raye ... 20.00
165 GP,JSt,O:Crusader,
  O&D:Marvel Boy 20.00
166 GP,V:Hulk 35.00
167 GK(c),GP,JSt,V:Hulk 35.00
168 RB,JSt,J:Luke Cage 20.00
169 RB,JSt,V:Puppetmaster 20.00
170 GP,JSt,L:Luke Cage 20.00
171 JK(c),RB,GP,JSt,I:Gor....... 20.00
172 JK(c),GP,JSt,V:Destroyer 20.00
173 JB,JSt,V:Galactus,O:Heralds . 20.00
174 JB,V:Galactus............ 20.00
175 JB,A:High Evolutionary 20.00
176 GP,JSt,V:Impossible Man 20.00
177 JP,JS,A:Frightful Four
  I:Texas Twister,Capt.Ultra 20.00
178 GP,V:Frightful Four,Brute 20.00
179 JSt,V:Annihilus 20.00
180 reprint #101............. 20.00
181 E:RTs(s),JSt,V:Brute,
  Annihilus 20.00
182 SB,JSt,V:Brute,Annihilus.... 20.00
183 SB,JSt,V:Brute,Annihilus.... 20.00
184 GP,JSt,V:Eliminator........ 20.00
185 GP,JSt,V:Nich.Scratch 20.00
186 GP,JSi,I:Salem's Seven 20.00
187 GP,JSt,V:Klaw,Molecule Man . 20.00
188 GP,JSt,V:Molecule Man 20.00
189 reprint FF Annual #4........ 20.00
190 SB,O:Fantastic Four 22.00
191 GP,JSt,V:Plunderer,
  Team Breaks Up 20.00
192 GP,JSt,V:Texas Twister 20.00
193 KP,JSt,V:Darkoth,Diablo 20.00
194 KP,V:Darkoth,Diablo 20.00
195 KP,A:Sub-Mariner 20.00
196 KP,V:Invincible Man (Reed),
  A:Dr.Doom,Team Reunited ... 20.00

Fantastic Four #219
© Marvel Entertainment Group

Fantastic Four #285
© Marvel Entertainment Group

197 KP,JSt,Red Ghost 20.00
198 KP,JSt,V:Doc Doom 20.00
199 KP,JSt,V:Doc Doom 20.00
200 KP,JSt,V:Doc Doom 25.00
201 KP,JSt,FF's Machinery 10.00
202 KP,JSt,V:Quasimodo 10.00
203 KP,JSt,V:Mutant 10.00
204 KP,JSt,V:Skrulls 10.00
205 KP,JSt,V:Skrulls 10.00
206 KP,JSt,V:Skrulls,A:Nova 10.00
207 SB,JSt,V:Monocle,A:SpM 10.00
208 SB,V:Sphinx,A:Nova 10.00
209 JBy,JSt,I:Herbie,A:Nova 12.00
210 JBy,JS,A:Galactus 10.00
211 JBy,JS,I:Terrax,A:Galactus . . 12.00
212 JBy,JSt,V:Galactus,Sphinx . . 10.00
213 JBy,JSt,V:Terrax,Galactus
Sphinx 10.00
214 JBy,JSt,V:Skrull 10.00
215 JBy,JSt,V:Blastaar 10.00
216 JBy,V:Blastaar 10.00
217 JBy,JSt,A:Dazzler 10.00
218 JBy,JSt,V:FrightfulFour,
A:Spider-Man 10.00
219 BSz,JSt,A:Sub-Mariner 8.00
220 JBy,JSt,A:Vindicator 8.00
221 JBy,JSt,V:Vindicator 8.00
222 BSz,JSt,V:Nicholas Scratch . . 8.00
223 JBy,JSt,V:Salem's Seven 8.00
224 BSz,A:Thor 8.00
225 BSz,A:Thor 8.00
226 BSz,A:Shogun 8.00
227 BSz,JSt,V:Ego-Spawn 8.00
228 BSz,JSt,V:Ego-Spawn 8.00
229 BSz,JSt,I:Firefrost,Ebon
Seeker 8.00
230 BSz,JSt,A:Avengers,
O:Firefrost & Ebon Seeker 8.00
231 BSz,JSt,V:Stygorr 8.00
232 JBy,New Direction,V:Diablo . . 10.00
233 JBy,V:Hammerhead 8.00
234 JBy,V:Ego 8.00
235 JBy,O:Ego 8.00
236 JBy,V:Dr.Doom,A:Puppet
Master, 20th Anniv. 8.00
237 JBy,V:Solons 7.00
238 JBy,O:Frankie Raye,
new Torch 7.00
239 JBy,I:Aunt Petunia,
Uncle Jake. 7.00
240 JBy,A:Inhumans,b:Luna 7.00
241 JBy,A:Black Panther 7.00
242 JBy,A:Daredevil,Thor,Iron Man
Spider-Man,V:Terrax 7.00

243 JBy,A:Daredevil,Dr.Strange,
Spider-Man,Avengers,V:Galactus,
Terrax. 7.00
244 JBy,A:Avengers,Dr.Strange,
Galactus, Becomes Nova 7.00
245 JBy,V:Franklin Richards 7.00
246 JBy,V:Dr.Doom,
A:Puppet Master 7.00
247 JBy,A:Dr.Doom,I:Kristoff,
D:Zorba 7.00
248 JBy,A:Inhumans 7.00
249 JBy,V:Gladiator 7.00
250 JBy,A:Capt.Am.,SpM,
V:Gladiator. 7.00
251 JBy,A:Annihilus 7.00
252 JBy,1st sideways issue,V:
Ootah,A:Annihilus,w/tattoo 7.00
252a w/o tattoo 7.00
253 JBy,V:Kestorans,A:Annihilus. . . 7.00
254 JBy,V:Mantracora,
A:She-Hulk,Wasp 7.00
255 JBy,A:Daredevil,Annihilus,
V:Mantracora 7.00
256 JBy,A:Avengers,Galactus,
V:Annihilus,New Costumes 7.00
257 JBy,A:Galactus,Death,Nova,
Scarlet Witch 5.00
258 JBy,A:Dr.Doom,D:Hauptmann . 5.00
259 JBy,V:Terrax,Dr.Doom,
C:Silver Silver 5.00
260 JBy,V:Terrax, Dr.Doom,
A:Silver Surfer,Sub-Mariner. . . . 6.00
261 JBy,A:Sub-Mariner,Marrina,
Silver Surfer,Sc.Witch,Lilandra . 6.00
262 JBy,O:Galactus,A:Odin,
(J.Byrne in story) 5.00
263 JBy,V:Messiah,A:Mole Man . . . 5.00
264 JBy,V:Messiah,A:Mole Man . . . 5.00
265 JBy,A:Trapster,Avengers,
J:She-Hulk,Secret Wars 5.00
266 KGa,JBy,A:Hulk,Sasquatch,
V:Karisma 5.00
267 JBy,A:Hulk,Sasquatch,Morbius,
V:Dr.Octopus,Sue miscarries . . 5.00
268 JBy,V:Doom's Mask 5.00
269 JBy,R:Wyatt Wingfoot,
I:Terminus 5.00
270 JBy,V:Terminus 5.00
271 JBy,V:Gormuu 5.00
272 JBy,I:Warlord (Nathaniel
Richards) 5.00
273 JBy,V:Warlord 5.00
274 JBy,AG,cont.from Thing#19,
A:Spider-Man's Black Costume. 5.00
275 JBy,AG,V: I.J.Vance. 5.00
276 JBy,JOy,V:Mephisto,
A:Dr.Strange 5.00
277 JBy,JOy,V:Mephisto,
A:Dr.Strange,R:Thing. 5.00
278 JBy,JOy,O:Dr.Doom,A:Kristoff
(as Doom) 5.00
279 JBy,JOy,V:Dr.Doom(Kristoff),
I:New Hate-Monger 5.00
280 JBy,JOy,I:Malice,
V:Hate-Monger 5.00
281 JBy,JOy,A:Daredevil,V:Hate
Monger,Malice 5.00
282 JBy,JOy,A:Power Pack,Psycho
Man,Secret Wars II 5.00
283 JBy,JOy,V:Psycho-Man. 5.00
284 JBy,JOy,V:Psycho-Man. 5.00
285 JBy,JOy,Secret Wars II
A:Beyonder. 5.00
286 JBy,TA,R:Jean Grey,
A:Hercules Capt.America 6.00
287 JBy,JSt,A:Wasp,V:Dr.Doom . . . 5.00
288 JBy,JSt,V:Dr.Doom,Secret
Wars II 6.00
289 JBy,AG,D:Basilisk,V:Blastaar,
R:Annihilus 5.00
290 JBy,AG,V:Annihilus 5.00
291 JBy,CR,A:Nick Fury 5.00

292 JBy,AG,A:Nick Fury,V:Hitler . . . 5.00
293 JBy,AG,A:Avengers.W.C. 5.00
294 JOy,AG,V:FutureCentralCity . . . 3.00
295 JOy,AG,V:Fut.Central City. 3.00
296 BWS,KGa,RF,BWi,AM,KJ,JB,
SL,MS,JRu,JOy,JSt,25th
Anniv.,V:MoleMan 5.00
297 JB,SB,V:Umbra-Sprite 3.00
298 JB,SB,V:Umbra-Sprite 2.50
299 JB,SB,She-Hulk,V:Thing,
A:Spider-Man,L:She-Hulk 3.00
300 JB,SB,W:Torch & Fake Alicia
(Lyja),A:Puppet-Master,Wizard,
Mad Thinker,Dr.Doom 4.00
301 JB,SB,V:Wizard,MadThinker . . . 3.00
302 JB,SB,V:Project Survival. 3.00
303 JD,RT,A:Thundra,V:Machus . . . 3.00
304 JB,JSt,V:Quicksilver,
A:Kristoff 3.00
305 JB,JSt,V:Quicksilver,
J:Crystal,A:Dr.Doom 3.00
306 JB,JSt,A:Capt.America,
J:Ms.Marvel,V:Diablo 3.00
307 JB,JSt,L:Reed&Sue,V:Diablo . . 3.00
308 JB,JSt,I:Fasaud 3.00
309 JB,JSt,V:Fasaud 3.00
310 KP,JSt,V:Fasaud,N:Thing
& Ms.Marvel 3.00
311 KP,JSt,A:Black Panther,
Dr.Doom,V:THRob. 3.00
312 KP,JSt,A:Black Panther,
Dr.Doom,X-Factor 3.00
313 SB,JSt,V:Lava Men,
A:Moleman 3.00
314 KP,JSt,V:Belasco 3.00
315 KP,JSt,V:Mast.Pandem. 3.00
316 KP,JSt,A:CometMan 3.00
317 KP,JSt,L:Crystal 3.00
318 KP,JSt,V:Dr.Doom 3.00
319 KP,JSt,G-Size,O:Beyonder 3.00
320 KP,JSt,Hulk vs Thing. 3.00
321 RLm,RT,A:She-Hulk 3.00
322 KP,JSt,Inferno,V:Graviton 3.00
323 KP,JSt,RT,Inferno A.Mantis 3.00
324 KP,JSt,RT,A:Mantis 3.00
325 RB,RT,A:Silver Surfer,
D:Mantis 3.00
326 KP,RT,I:New Frightful Four 3.00
327 KP,RT,V:Frightful Four. 3.00
328 KP,RT,V:Frightful Four. 3.00
329 RB,RT,V:Mole Man 3.00
330 RB,RT,V:Dr.Doom 3.00
331 RB,RT,V:Ultron 3.00
332 RB,RT,V:Aron 3.00

333 RB,RT,V:Aron,Frightful Four . . . 3.00
334 RB,Acts of Vengeance 3.00
335 RB,RT,Acts of Vengeance 3.00
336 RLm,Acts of Vengeance, ... 3.00
337 WS,A:Thor,Iron Man,
   B:Timestream saga, ... 4.00
338 WS,V:Deathshead,A:Thor,
   Iron Man 3.00
339 WS,V:Gladiator 3.00
340 WS,V:Black Celestial 3.00
341 WS,A:Thor,Iron Man 3.00
342 A:Rusty,C:Spider-Man 3.00
343 WS,V:Stalin 3.00
344 WS,V:Stalin 3.00
345 WS,V:Dinosaurs 3.00
346 WS,V:Dinosaurs 3.00
347 AAd,ATi(i)A:Spider-Man,
   GhostRider,Wolverine,Hulk 4.00
347a 2nd printing 3.00
348 AAd,ATi(i)A:Spider-Man,
   GhostRider,Wolverine,Hulk 4.00
348a 2nd printing 3.00
349 AAd,ATi(i),AM(i)A:Spider-Man,
   Wolverine,GhostRider,Hulk,
   C:Punisher 3.50
350 WS,Am(i),R:Ben Grimm as
   Thing,(48p) 3.50
351 MBa,Kubic. 3.00
352 WS,Reed Vs.Dr.Doom 3.00
353 WS,E:Timestream Saga,
   A:Avengers, ... 3.00
354 WS,Secrets of the Time
   Variance Authority 3.00
355 AM,V:Wrecking Crew 3.00
356 B:TDF(s),PR,A:New Warriors,
   V:Puppet Master 3.00
357 PR,V:Mad Thinker,
   Puppetmaster, ... 3.00
358 PR,AAd,30th Anniv.,1st Marv.
   Die Cut(c),D:Lyja,V:Paibok,
   BU:Dr.Doom 3.50
359 PR,I:Devos the Devastator 3.00
360 PR,V:Dreadface 3.00
361 PR,V:Dr.Doom,X-masIssue . . . 3.00
362 PR,A:Spider-Man,
   I:WildBlood 3.00
363 PR,I:Occulus,A:Devos 3.00
364 PR,V:Occulus 3.00
365 PR,V:Occulus 3.00
366 PR,Infinity War,R:Lyja 3.00
367 PR,Inf.War,A:Wolverine 3.00
368 PR,V:Infinity War X-Men 3.00
369 PR,Inf.War,R:Malice,
   A:Thanos 3.00

370 PR,Inf.War,V:Mr.Fantastic
   Doppleganger 3.00
371 PR,V:Lyja,foil(c) 4.00
371a 2nd Printing 3.00
372 PR,A:Spider-Man,Silver
   Sable 3.00
373 PR,V:Aron,Silver sable 3.00
374 PR,V:Secret Defenders 3.00
375 V:Dr.Doom,A:Inhumans,Lyja,
   Holo-Grafix(c) 3.50
376 PR,A:Nathan Richards,V:Paibok,
   Devos,w/Dirt Magazine 3.50
376a w/out Dirt Magazine 2.50
377 PR,V:Paibok,Devos,Klaw,
   I:Huntara 2.50
378 PR,A:Sandman,SpM,DD 2.50
379 PR,V:Ms.Marvel 2.50
380 PR,A:Dr.Doom,V:Hunger 2.50
381 PR,D:Dr.Doom,Mr.Fantastic,
   V:Hunger 5.00
382 PR,V:Paibok,Devos,Huntara. . . 3.00
383 PR,V:Paibok,Devos,Huntara . . . 2.50
384 PR,A:Ant-Man,V:Franklin
   Richards 2.50
385 PR,A:Triton,Tiger Shark,
   Starblast#7. . . . . 2.50
386 PR,Starblast#11,A:Namor,Triton,
   b:Johnny & Lyja child 2.50
387 Die-Cut & Foil (c),PR,N:Invisible
   Woman,J:Ant-Man,A:Namor . . . 4.00
387a Newsstand Ed. 2.50
388 PR,I:Dark Raider,V:FF,
   Avengers,w/cards 2.50
389 PR,I:Raphael Suarez,A:Watcher,
   V:Collector 2.50
390 PR,A:Galactus 2.50
391 PR,I:Vibraxas 2.50
392 Dark Raider. 2.50
393 . . . . 2.50
394 Neon(c) w/insert print 3.00
394a Newsstand ed.,no bag/inserts 2.50
395 Thing V:Wolverine. 2.50
396 . . . . 2.50
397 Resurrection,pt.1. . . . . 2.50
398 regular edition. 2.50
398a Enhanced cover 3.00
399 Watcher's Lie 3.00
399a Foil stamped cover 3.00
400 Watcher's Lie,pt.3 . . . . 5.00
401 V:Tantalus 2.50
402 Atlantis Rising,Namor
   vs. Black Bolt. 2.50
403 TDF,PR,DBi,F:Thing,Medusa . . 2.50
404 R:Namor,I:New Villian 2.50
405 J:Namor 2.50
406 TDF,PR,DBi,R:Dr. Doom,
   I:Hyperstorm 2.50
407 TDF,PR,DBi,Return of
   Reed Richards. 2.50
408 TDF,PR,DBi,Original FF unite. . 2.50
409 TDF,PR,DBi,All new line-up . . . 2.50
410 . . . . 2.50
411 . . . . 2.50
412 TDF,PR,DBi,Mr.Fantastic
   vs. Sub-Mariner. 2.50
413 . . . . 2.50
414 Galactus vs. Hyperstorm 2.50
415 Onslaught saga, A:X-Men. 4.00
416 Onslaught saga, A:Dr. Doom,
   double size, finale 5.00
Ann.#1 JK,SD,I:Atlantis,Dorma,
   Krang,V:Namor,O:FF 1,500.00
Ann.#2 JK,JSt,O:Dr.Doom . . . 1,000.00
Ann.#3 JK,W:Reed and Sue 400.00
Ann.#4 JK,JSt,I:Quasimodo. 250.00
Ann.#5 JK,JSt,A:Inhumans,Silver
   Surfer,Black Panther,
   I:Psycho Man. 250.00
Ann.#6 JK,JSt,I:Annihilus,
   Franklin Richards 250.00
Ann.#7 JK(c),reprints 100.00
Ann.#8 JR(c),reprints. 50.00

Fantastic Four Ann. #24
© Marvel Entertainment Group

Ann.#9 JK(c),reprints. 50.00
Ann.#10 reprints Ann.#3 . . . . 50.00
Ann.#11 JK(c),JB,A:The Invaders . 12.00
Ann.#12 A:The Invaders 12.00
Ann.#13 V:The Mole Man 12.00
Ann.#14 GP,V:Salem's Seven 12.00
Ann.#15 GP,V:Dr.Doom,Skrulls . . . 10.00
Ann.#16 V:Dragonlord 10.00
Ann.#17 JBy,V:Skrulls 10.00
Ann.#18 KGa,V:Skrulls,W:Black
   Bolt and Medusa,A:Inhumans . 10.00
Ann.#19 JBy,V:Skrulls 10.00
Ann.#20 TD(i),V:Dr.Doom 4.00
Ann.#21 JG,JSt,Evol.Wars 4.00
Ann.#22 RB,Atlantis Attacks,
   A:Avengers 4.00
Ann.#23 JG,GCa,Days of Future
   Present #1. . . . . 5.00
Ann.#24 JG,AM,Korvac Quest #1,
   A:Guardians of the Galaxy 3.00
Ann.#25 Citizen Kang #3. . . . . 3.00
Ann.#26 HT,I:Wildstreak,
   V:Dreadface,w/card. 3.50
Ann.#27 MGu,V:Justice Peace 3.50
G-Size#1 RB,Thing/Hulk 17.00
G-Size#2 K&R(c),JB,Time to Kill . . 15.00
G-Size#3 RB,JSt,Four Horseman . 15.00
G-Size#4 JB,JSt,I:Madrox 15.00
G-Size#5 JK(c),V:Psycho Man,
   Molecule Man 12.00
G-Size#6 V:Annihilus. 12.00
Spec.#1 Rep.Ann.#1 JBy(c). 2.50
Rep.#347-349 . . . . 6.00
TPB Nobody Gets Out Alive, rep. . 16.00
TPB Trial of Galactus, rep. 10.00
Marvel Milestone rep. #1 (1991) . . . 3.00
Marvel Milestone rep. #5 (1992) . . . 3.00
Ashcan. 75
Spec. The Origin of Galactus. 2.50
Spec. Marvel's Greatest Comic:
   rep. #52: I:Black Panther (2006) 3.00
[2nd Series], Nov., 1996
1 JLe,BCi,SW, 48pg 5.00
1A Mole Man cover. 12.00
1B Gold signature, bagged,
   limited 25.00
2 JLe,BCi,V:Namor. 5.00
3 JLe,BCi,SW,A:Avengers 4.00
4 JLe,BCi,SW,I:Black Panther 4.00
4A x-mas cover. 5.00
5 JLe,BCi,SW,V:Dr. Doom 4.00
6 JLe,BCi,SW,Industrial Revolution
   prologue. 3.00
7 JLe,BCi,BBh,V:Blastaar 3.00

Fantastic Four #394
© Marvel Entertainment Group

8 JLe,BCi,BBh,V:Inhumans 3.00
9 JLe,BCi,BBh,V:Inhumans 3.00
10 JLe,BCi,BBh,A:Silver Surfer,
Tyrax 3.00
11 JLe,BCi,BBh,A:Silver Surfer,
Firelord, Terrax 3.00
12 JLe,BCi,BBh,GalactusSaga,pt.1,
reunited 5.00
13 JeR,Wildstorm x-over 3.00
Ashcan, signed, numbered 10.00

[3rd Series], Nov., 1997
1 SLo,AD,MFm, The Ruined, 48pg
debut 5.00
2 SLo,AD,MFm,A:Iconoclast. 4.00
3 SLo,AD,MFm,V:Red Ghost 4.00
4 SLo,SvL,ATi,A:Silver Surfer,
double size 4.00
4 signed by SLo, (500 copies) . . . 20.00
5 SLo,SvL,ATi,V:The Crucible 3.00
6 CCl,SvL, new villains 3.00
7 CCl,SvL,ATi,V:Technet. 3.00
8 CCl,SvL,V:Captain Britain corp. . . 3.00
9 CCl,SvL,A:Spider-Man. 3.00
10 CCl,SvL,ATi. 3.00
11 CCl,SvL,ATi,Crucible—unleashed
in Genosha 3.00
12 CCl,SvL,ATi,V:Fantastic Four
double-size 4.50
13 CCl,SvL,A:Ronan the Accuser . . 2.50
14 CCl,SvL,V:Ronan 2.50
15 CCl,SvL,ATi,Iron Man x-over . . . 2.50
16 CCl,SvL,ATi,V:Kree Avengers. . . 2.50
17 CCl,SvL,ATi,I:Lockdown 2.50
18 CCl,SvL,ATi,Jail Break 2.50
19 CCl,SvL,ATi,V:Annihilus 2.50
20 CCl,SvL,ATi,V:Ruined 2.50
21 CCl,SvL,ATi,V:Hades 2.50
22 CCl,SvL,ATi,V:Valeria
Von Doom 2.50
23 CCl,SvL,ATi,A:She-Hulk 2.50
24 CCl,SvL,ATI,F:FranklinRichards . 2.50
25 CCl,SvL,ATi,V:Dr.Doom 3.50
26 CCl,SvL,ATi,F:ValeriaVonDoom . 3.00
27 CCl,SvL,F:Invisible Woman 3.00
28 CCl,SvL,ATi,Planet Doom. 3.00
29 CCl,SvL,ATi,Frightful Four 2.50
30 CCl,SvL,ATi,Castle Doom. 2.25
31 CCl,SvL,ATi,InvisibleWoman . . . 2.25
32 CCl,SvL,ATi,InvisibleWoman . . . 2.25
33 JFM,SvL,ATi,Kid Colt 2.25
34 JFM,SvL,ATi,aliens 2.25
35A CPa,Diablo,foil (c). 5.00
35B painted (c) 2.25
36 CPa,Diablo triumphant 2.25
37 CPa,F:Johnny Storm. 2.25
38 CPa,JLb,V:Grey Gargoyle 2.25
39 CPa,JLb,V:Grey Gargoyle 2.25
40 CPa,JLb,Negative Zone 2.25
41 CPa,JLb,Hellscout 2.25
42 CPa,JLb,SI,V:Namor. 2.25
43 CPa,JLb,JoB,new Fant.Four. . . . 2.25
44 CPa,JLb,Negative Zone,concl. . . 2.25
45 CPa,JLb,one new costume. 2.25
46 CPa,JLb,Abraxas Saga 2.25
47 CPa,JLb,Abraxas,pt.3. . . . . 2.25
48 CPa,JLb,Abraxas,pt.4. . . . . 2.25
49 CPa,JLb,Abraxas,pt.5. . . . . 2.25
50 Four new stories,BWS(c),64-pg.. 5.00
51 MBa,KK,F:Inhumans. 3.50
52 MBa,KK,F:Dr. Doom 2.25
53 MBa,KK,Inhumans 2.25
54 MBa,KK,Inhumans, 100-pg. 4.00
55 KK,SI,Thing,Human Torch 2.25
56 F:Thing 2.25
57 AWa,F:Thing,pt.1 . . . . 2.25
58 AWa,F:Thing,pt.2 . . . . 2.25
59 AWa,F:Thing,pt.3 . . . . 2.25
60 MWa,KK 2.25
61 MWa,KK 3.00
62 MWa,KK,Sentient,pt.1, 48-pg . . 3.00
63 MWa,KK,Sentient,pt.2. . . . . 3.00
64 MWa,KK,Sentient,pt.3. . . . . 3.00

Fantastic Four 3rd Series #1
© Marvel Entertainment Group

65 MWa,MBu,Small Stuff/Big Stuff. . 3.00
66 MWa,MBu,Small Stuff/Big Stuff. . 3.00
67 MWa,KK,Unthinkable 5.00
68 MWa,KK,Unthinkable 3.50
69 MWa,KK,Unthinkable 3.50
70 MWa,Unthinkable 3.50
500 MWa,Unthinkable,48-pg. 5.00
500a Director's Cut, foil 6.00
501 MWa,CJ,Fifth Wheel,pt.1 . . . . . 2.25
502 MWa,CJ,Fifth Wheel,pt.2 . . . . . 2.25
503 MWa,Authoritative Action,pt.1. . 2.25
504 MWa,Authoritative Action,pt.2. . 2.25
505 MWa,Authoritative Action,pt.3. . 2.25
506 MWa,Authoritative Action,pt.4. . 2.25
507 MWa,Authoritative Action,pt.5. . 2.25
508 MWa,Authoritative Action,pt.6. . 2.25
509 MWa,Hereafter,pt.1 . . . . 2.25
510 MWa,Hereafter,pt.2 . . . . 2.25
511 MWa,Hereafter,pt.3 . . . . 2.25
512 MWa,Spider Sense,pt.1 . . . . . . 2.25
513 MWa,Spider Sense,pt.2 . . . . . . 2.25
514 MWa&KK(s),Dysfunctional,pt.1. 2.25
515 MWa&KK(s),Dysfunctional,pt.2. 2.25
516 MWa,KK(s),Dysfunctional,pt.3 . 2.25
517 MWa(s),Fourtitude,pt.1 . . . . . . 3.00
518 Fourtitude,pt.2. . . . . 3.00
519 Fourtitude,pt.3. . . . . 3.00
520 . . . . 3.00
521 . . . . 3.00
522 MWa,MeW,Galactus 3.00
523 MWa,MeW,Rising Storm, concl. 3.00
524 MWa,MeW, ... 3.00
525 KK,TGu,Dream Fever,pt.1 . . . . 3.00
526 KK,TGu,Dream Fever,pt.2 . . . . 3.00
527 MMK,Distant Music, Entity 5.00
528 MMK,Random Factors, Entity. . 3.00
529 MMK,Appointment Overdue . . . 3.00
530 MMK,Reunion with destiny 3.00
531 MSz(s),MMK,V:The Entity,pt.5 . 3.00
532 MSz(s),MMK,V:The Entity,pt.6 . 3.00
533 MSz(s),MMK,A:Hulk 3.00
534 MSz(s),MMK,A:Hulk 3.00
535 MSz(s),MMK,A:Hulk 3.00
536 MSz(s),MMK,Road to Civil War 5.00
537 MSz(s),MMK,Road to Civil War 4.00
538 MSz(s),MMK,Civil War tie-in . . 3.50
539 MSz(s),MMK,Civil War tie-in . . 3.50
540 MSz(s),MMK,Civil War tie-in . . 3.00
541 MSz(s),MMK,Civil War tie-in . . 3.00
542 MSz(s),MMK,Civil War tie-in . . 3.00
Ann.1998 Fant.Four & Fant.Four. . . 4.00
Ann.1999 CCl,I:Mechamage 4.00
Ann.2000 LSi,SvL,48-pg. 4.00
Ann.2001 Galactus,48-page 3.50

Spec.#1 KIK FantasticFour (2000). . 2.25
Spec. Fantastic Four/Sentry 3.00
Spec. Fantastic Fourth Voyage
of Sinbad, 48-page (2001) 6.00
Spec. The Movie,DJu (2005). 5.00
Spec. Franklin Richards, Son
Of a Genius, Rep. Power Pack . 3.00
Spec. The Wedding (2006) 5.00
TPB Heroes Return, 96-page 11.00
TPB Heroes Reborn, 176-pg. 18.00
TPB Into the Breach, 144-pg. 16.00
TPB (Vol.3) Flesh & Stone (2002). 13.00
TPB (Vol.1) Visionaries (2002) . . . 20.00
TPB Vol. 1: Imaginauts (2003). . . . 18.00
TPB Legends, Vol. 1 (2003) 14.00
TPB Vol. 2: Unthinkable (2003) . . . 18.00
TPB Vol. 3: Authoritative Action . . . 13.00
TPB Vol. 4: Hereafter. 12.00
TPB Vol. 5: Dissassembled 15.00
TPB Vol. 6: Rising Storm 14.00
TPB Unstable Molecules (2005) . . 14.00
TPB Visionaries: George Perez. . . 20.00
TPB Visionaries: George Perez#2. 20.00
TPB Visionaries #6: John Byrne . . 25.00
TPB The Movie 13.00
TPB Fantastic Four/Spider-Man
Classic. 17.00
TPB Fantastic Four by MSz. 15.00
TPB Resurrection of Nicholas
Scratch 15.00

FANTASTIC FOUR: ATLANTIS RISING
1995
1 B:Atlantis Rising. 5.00
2 TDF,MCW,finale, acetate(c). 5.00

FANTASTIC FOUR: A DEATH IN THE
May, 2006
1 64-pg. 4.00

FANTASTIC FOUR INDEX
See: OFFICIAL MARVEL INDEX TO THE FANTASTIC FOUR

FANTASTIC FOUR: FIRST FAMILY
Mar., 2006
1 CWn. 3.00
2 thru 6 CWn . . . . @3.00
TPB 16.00

FANTASTIC FOUR: FOES
Jan., 2005
1 (of 6) Puppet Master & Mad
Thinker. 3.00
2 Annihilus 3.00
3 Green Goblin 3.00
4 Mole Man. 3.00
5 Red Ghost 3.00
6 conclusion 3.00
TPB Fantastic Four: Foes 17.00

FANTASTIC FOUR: HOUSE OF M
July, 2005
1 (of 3) SEa, A:Magneto, Doom . . . 3.00
2 Sea 3.00
3 SEa, concl. 3.00

FANTASTIC FOUR/ IRON MAN: BIG IN JAPAN
Oct., 2005
1 . . . . 3.50

MARVEL

2 All-out Monster Riot 3.50
3 Do you know kung fu. 3.50
4 Chock Full'O Monsters 3.50
TPB 13.00

FANTASTIC FOUR: 1 2 3 4
June, 2001
1 (of 4) GMo,JaL,F:Thing 3.00
2 GMo,JaL,F:Invisible Woman 3.00
3 GMo,JaL,F:Human Torch. 3.00
4 GMo,JaL,F:Mr. Fantastic 3.00
TPB JaL,GMo 10.00

FANTASTIC FOUR ROAST
May, 1982
1 FH/MG/FM/JB/MA/TA 5.00

FANTASTIC FOUR'S BIG TOWN
Nov., 2000
1 (of 4) SEt,MMK,MkK,48-page . . . 3.50
2 SEt,MMK,MkK 3.00
3 SEt,MMK,MkK 3.00
4 SEt,MMK,MkK,48-page 3.50

FANTASTIC FOUR: THE END
Nov., 2006
1 AD 4.00
1a 3.00
2 AD 3.00

FANTASTIC FOUR: THE LIFE FANTASTIC
Sept., 2006
TPB 152-pg. 17.00

FANTASTIC FOUR 2099
1996
1 Cont. from 2099 Genesis. 4.00
2 thru 5 . . . . @2.25

FANTASTIC FOUR UNLIMITED
1993–96
1 HT,A:Bl.Panther,V:Klaw 4.50
2 HT,JQ(c),A:Inhumans 4.25
3 HT,V:Blastaar,Annihilus 4.25
4 RTs(s),HT,V:Mole Man,A:Hulk . . 4.25
5 RTs(s),HT,V:Frightful Four 4.25
6 RTs(s),HT,V:Namor 4.00
7 HT,V:Monsters 4.00
8 . . . . 4.00
9 A:Antman 4.00
10 RTs,HT,V:Maelstrom,A:Eternals . 4.00
11 RTs,HT,Atlantis Rising fallout . . . 4.00
12 RTs,TDF,V:Hyperstorm 4.00
13 . . . . 4.00

FANTASTIC FOUR UNPLUGGED
1995–96
1 comic for a buck 2.25
2 Reed Richard's Will 2.25
3 F:Mr. Fantastic. 2.25
4 . . . . 2.25
5 Back in NY,V:Blastaar 2.25

FANTASTIC FOUR: UNSTABLE MOLECULES
Jan., 2003
1 (of 4) GyD 3.00
2 GyD 3.00
3 GyD 3.00

FANTASTIC FOUR VS. X-MEN
Feb., 1987
1 JBg,TA,V:Dr.Doom. 5.00
2 JBg,TA,V:Dr.Doom. 4.00
3 JBg,TA,V:Dr.Doom. 4.00
4 JBg,TA,V:Dr.Doom, June, 1987. . 4.00
TPB Reprints Mini-series 13.00

FANTASTIC FOUR THE WORLD'S GREATEST COMIC MAGAZINE
Dec., 2000
1 (of 12) EL,ErS,V:Dr.Doom 3.00
2 F:Dr.Doom,Crystal 3.00
3 A:X-Men,Spider-Man 3.00
4 A:X-Men,Capt.America 3.00
5 EL(c),Hulk vs. Thing 3.00
6 MGo(c),A:Silver Surfer. 3.00
7 KG(c),A:Dr.Doom,Inhumans 3.00
8 KG(c),F:Avengers 3.00
9 EL,KG,A:Dr.Doom 3.00
10 EL,KG,Cosmic Cube 3.00
11 RF,Planet Doom 3.00
12 StL,EL,JSt, concl. 3.00

FANTASTIC WORLD OF HANNA-BARBERA
Dec., 1977
1 . . . . 30.00
2 . . . . 20.00
3 June, 1978 . . . . 20.00

FANTASY MASTERPIECES
Feb., 1966
1 JK/DH/SD,reprints 500.00
2 JK,SD,DH,Fin Fang Foom. . . . 250.00
3 GC,DH,JK,SD,Capt.A rep. . . . 250.00
4 JK,Capt.America rep. 250.00
5 JK,Capt.America rep. 250.00
6 JK,Capt.America rep. 250.00
7 SD,Sub Mariner rep. 250.00
8 H.Torch & Sub M.rep. 250.00
9 SD,MF,O:Human Torch Rep . 300.00
10 rep.All Winners #19 . . . . 250.00
11 JK,(rep),O:Toro 250.00
Becomes:

MARVEL SUPER-HEROES

FANTASY MASTERPIECES
[Volume 2], Dec., 1979
1 JB,JSt,Silver Surfer rep. 5.00
2 thru 7 JB,JSt,Silver Surfer rep. @5.00
8 thru 11 JB/JSn,.Strange Tales . @4.00
12 thru 14 JB,JSn,rep.Warlock . . @4.00

FAREWELL TO WEAPONS
1 DirtBag,W/Nirvana Tape 3.50

FEAR
Nov., 1970
1 JK,1950's Monster rep.B:I
  Found Monstrum,The Dweller
  in the Black Swamp. 75.00
2 JK,X The Thing That Lived 40.00
3 JK,Zzutak, The Thing That
  Shouldn't Exist. 40.00
4 JK,I Turned Into a Martian. 40.00
5 JK,I Am the Gorilla Man. 40.00
6 JK,SD,The Midnight Monster. . . 40.00
7 JK,SD,I Dream of Doom 25.00
8 JK,SD,It Crawls By Night! 25.00
9 JK,Dead Man's Escape 25.00
Becomes:

Adventure Into Fear #31
© Marvel Entertainment Group

ADVENTURE INTO FEAR
1972
10 HC,GM,B:Man-Thing 55.00
11 RB,I:Jennifer Kale,Thog 25.00
12 JSn,RB 25.00
13 VM,Where World's Collide 18.00
14 VM,Plague o/t Demon Cult. . . . 18.00
15 VM,Lord o/t Dark Domain 18.00
16 VM,ManThing in Everglades. . . 18.00
17 VM,I:Wundarr(Aquarian) 18.00
18 VM. 18.00
19 VM,FMc,I:Howard the Duck,
  E:Man-Thing 55.00
20 PG,GK,B:Morbius 55.00
21 GK,V:Uncanny Caretaker 20.00
22 RB,V:Cat-Demond 20.00
23 GC,GK,1st CR art,A World He
  Never Made. 20.00
24 CR,SMn,V:Blade, The Vampire
  Slayer 35.00
25 FR,GK,You Always Kill the
  One You Love 15.00
26 FR,GK,V:Uncanny Caretaker . . 15.00
27 FR,GK,V:Simon Stroud. 15.00
28 GK,Doorway Down into Hell. . . 15.00
29 Death has a Thousand Eyes . . 15.00
30 Bloody Sacrifice 15.00
31 FR,GK,last issue,Dec., 1975 . . 15.00

FEUD
Epic, 1993
1 I:Skids,Stokes,Kite 3.00
2 thru 4 . . . . @2.25

FIGHT MAN
1993
1 I:Fight Man. 2.25

FILM FUNNIES
Marvel Chipiden Publ., 1949–50
1 Funny animal 225.00
2 . . . . 150.00

FIRESTAR
March, 1986
1 MW,SL,O:Firestar,A:X-Men,
  New Mutants 5.00
2 MW,BWI,A:New Mutants 4.00
3 AAd&BSz(c),MW,SL,
  A:White Queen 4.00
4 MW,SL,V:White Queen 4.00
Digest X-Men: Firestar (2006) 8.00

FISH POLICE
1992–93
1 V:S.Q.U.I.D,Hook. 2.50
2 thru 6 . . . . @2.50

FLASH GORDON
1995
1 R:Flash Gordon 3.00
2 AW,V:Ming, final issue 3.00

FLINTSTONE KIDS
Star, Aug., 1987
1 thru 10 . . . . @5.00
11 April, 1989 . . . . 5.00

FLINTSTONES
Oct., 1977–Feb., 1979
1 From TV Series 75.00
2 . . . . 50.00
3 . . . . 30.00
4 A:Jetsons 30.00
5 thru 7 . . . . @35.00

FLYING HERO BARBIE
1 Super Hero Barbie 2.25

FOOFUR
Star, Aug., 1987
1 thru 6 . . . . @3.00

FOOLKILLER
Oct., 1990
1 I:Kurt Gerhardt
  (Foolkiller III) 3.50
2 O:Foolkiller I & II 3.00
3 Old Costume 3.00
4 N:Foolkiller. 2.50
5 Body Count 2.50
6 thru 10 . . . . @2.25

FORCE WORKS
1994–96
1 TmT,Pop-up(c),I:Century,V:Kree,
  N:US Agent 4.00
2 thru 11 . . . . @2.25
12 V:Recorder 3.00
13 thru 20. . . . . @2.25

Force Works #1
© *Marvel Entertainment Group*

411
April, 2003
1 thru 3 . . . . @3.50

FOR YOUR EYES ONLY
1 HC,James Bond rep. 3.00
2 HC,James Bond rep. 3.00

FRAGGLE ROCK
1985
1 thru 8 . . . . @5.00
[Volume 2], April, 1988
1 thru 5 rep. . . . . @2.50
6 Sept., 1988 . . . . 2.50

FRANCIS, BROTHER OF THE UNIVERSE
1980
1-shot SB. 5.00

FRANKENSTEIN
See: MONSTER OF FRANKENSTEIN

FRED HEMBECK
1-shot Destroys the Marvel
  Universe, parody (1989) 2.25
1-shot Sells the Marvel Universe
  parody (1990) 2.25

FRIENDLY NEIGHBORHOOD SPIDER-MAN
Oct., 2005
1 PDd(s),The Other, x-over,pt.1 . . . 6.00
1a 2nd printing 6.00
2 PDd(s),The Other, x-over,pt.4 . . . 3.00
2a 2nd printing 6.00
3 PDd(s),The Other, x-over,pt.7 . . . 3.00
3a 2nd printing 6.00
4 PDd(s),The Other, x-over,pt.10 . . 3.00
5 PDd(s),Weblog 3.00
6 PDd(s),Wrestling 3.00
7 PDd(s),Wrestling 3.00
8 PDd(s),MeW 3.00
9 PDd(s),Jumping the Tracks 3.00
10 PDd(s),Jumping the Tracks . . . 3.00
11 PDd(s),I Hate a Mystery,pt.1 . . . 3.00
12 PDd(s),I Hate a Mystery,pt.2 . . . 3.00
13 PDd(s),I Hate a Mystery,pt.3 . . . 3.00
14 PDd(s),A:Deb Whitman,V:Vulture 3.00
TPB Vol. 1 Derailed 15.00

FRIGHT
June, 1975
1 Son of Dracula. 15.00

FRONTIER WESTERN
Feb., 1956
1 RH,. 300.00
2 AW,GT,GC,JMn 200.00
3 MD 200.00
4 MD,Ringo Kid. 150.00
5 RC,DW,JDa 200.00
6 AW,GC. 175.00
7 JR,JMn. 150.00
8 RC,DW. 150.00
9 JMn 150.00
10 SC,Aug., 1957 . . . . 150.00

FUNNY FROLICS
Summer, 1945
1 Shardy Fox,KrazyKroid,(fa) . . . 300.00
2 . . . . 150.00
3 . . . . 100.00
4 . . . . 100.00
5 HK 125.00

Funny Frolics #1
© *Marvel Entertainment Group*

FUNNY TUNES
Marvel Timely, 1944–46
(KRAZY KOMICS spinoff)
16 Animated Funny
  Comic-Tunes 250.00
17 . . . . 200.00
18 . . . . 200.00
19 . . . . 200.00
20 . . . . 200.00
21 . . . . 200.00
22 . . . . 200.00
23 HK. 200.00
Becomes:

OSCAR

FURTHER ADVENTURES OF CYCLOPS AND PHOENIX
1996
1 thru 4 . . . . @3.00
TPB PrM,JPL, O:Mr. Sinister, ... 12.00

FURY
1994
1 MCW,O:Fury,A:S.A. Heroes 3.25

FURY
Marvel Max, Sept., 2001
1 (of 6) GEn,DaR,JP,F:Nick Fury . . 6.00
2 GEn,DaR,JP,F:Rudi Gagarin 4.00
3 GEn,DaR,JP, ... 4.00
4 GEn,DaR,JP 4.00
5 GEn,DaR,JP 4.00
6 GEn,DaR,JP 4.00
TPB GEn,DaR, 144-pg. 16.00

FURY/AGENT 13
March, 1998
1 (of 2) TKa,is Nick Fury alive? . . . 3.00
2 TKa,MZ(c),Sharon Carter's searches
  for Nick 3.00

FURY OF S.H.I.E.L.D.
1995
1 Foil etched cover 3.00
2 A:Iron Man 2.50
3 J:Hydra 2.50
4 w/decoder card 3.00

All comics prices listed are for *Near Mint* condition.

MARVEL

FURY: PEACEMAKER
Feb., 2006
1 GEn,DaR,JP, Kasserine Pass . . . 3.50
2 GEn,DaR,JP, War Without Army . 3.50
3 thru 6 GEn,DaR,JP . . . . @3.50
TPB Peacemaker. 18.00

GALACTIC GUARDIANS
1994
1 KWe,C:Woden 2.25
2 KWe,I:Hazmat,Savant,Ganglia . . 2.25
3 KWe 2.25
4 KWe,final issue 2.25

GALACTUS
THE DEVOURER
April, 1999
1 (of 6) JMu,LSi,A:Silver Surfer,
  Fant.Four & Avengers,48-page . 4.00
2 LSi,JB,BSz. 2.50
3 LSi,JB,BSz. 2.50
4 LSi,JB,BSz,A:Silver Surfer. 2.50
5 LSi,JB,BSz. 2.50
6 LSi,JB,BSz,concl 3.50

GAMBIT
1997
1 HMe(c),LW,KJ,V:Assassin'sGuild,
  D:Henri LeBeau,Embossed(c). . 5.00
1a Gold Ed. 15.00
2 LW,KJ,C:Gideon,A:Rogue 3.00
3 LW,KJ,A:Candra,Rogue,
  D:Gambit's Father 3.00
4 LW,KJ,A:Candra,Rogue,D:Tithe
  Collector 3.00
TPB Rep.#1-#4 . . . . 9.00

GAMBIT
1997
1 (of 4) HMe,KJ,In Miami 3.50
2 HMe,KJ, ... 3.00
3 HMe,KJ,in the Vatican 3.00
4 HMe V:Stoker, concl. 3.00

GAMBIT
Dec., 1998
1 FaN,SSr,O:Gambit,48-page. 4.00
1a signed 25.00
2 FaN,SSr,V:Storm 3.00
2a variant cover 3.00

Gambit #6
© Marvel Entertainment Group

---

3 FaN,SSr,V:Mengo Brothers 2.50
4 FaN,SSr,A:Blade 2.50
5 FaN,SSr,R:Rogue 2.50
6 FaN,SSr,I:The Pig 2.50
7 FaN,SSr, ... 2.50
8 FaN,A:Sinister,Sabretooth 2.50
9 FaN,The Shattering,x-over 2.50
10 FaN,V:Candra & Fenris 2.50
11 FaN,A:Daredevil 2.50
12 FaN 2.50
13 FaN,Black Womb 2.50
14 FaN,ALa,A:Mr. Sinister 2.50
15 FaN,F:Rogue 2.50
16 FaN,X-Men: Revolution 2.50
16a variant (c) 2.50
17 FaN,AssassinationGame,pt.1 . . 2.25
18 FaN,AssassinationGame,pt.2 . . 2.25
19 FaN,AssassinationGame,pt.3 . . 2.25
20 FaN,Fontanelle 2.25
21 FaN,Remy LeBeau 2.25
22 FaN,Neo,Remy LeBeau,Rax . . . 2.25
23 FaN,X-Cutioner 2.25
24 FaN,V:New Son 2.25
25 SLo, 48-page 3.50
Ann.1999 48-page 3.50
Ann.2000 FaN,F:X-Men 3.50
Giant Sized Gambit, 96-page, rep. . 4.00

GAMBIT
Sept., 2004
1 House of Cards,pt.1 . . . . 3.00
2 House of Cards,pt.2 . . . . 3.00
3 House of Cards,pt.3 . . . . 3.00
4 House of Cards,pt.4 . . . . 3.00
5 House of Cards,pt.5 . . . . 3.00
6 House of Cards, Concl. 3.00
7 Voodoo Economics,pt.1 . . . . 3.00
8 Voodoo Economics,pt.2 . . . . 3.00
9 Voodoo Economics,pt.3 . . . . 3.00
10 Hath No Fury,pt.1 . . . . 3.00
11 Hath No Fury,pt.2 . . . . 3.00
12 Hath No Fury,pt.3 . . . . 3.00
TPB Vol. 1:House of Cards 15.00
TPB Vol. 2:Hath No Fury 15.00

GAMBIT & BISHOP:
SONS OF THE ATOM
Jan., 2001
1 SLo,Bishop captured 2.25
2 SLo,on the run 2.25
3 SLo,common enemy 2.25
4 SLo, ... 2.25
5 SLo,Ultimate sacrifice 2.25
6 SLo,finale. 2.25
Spec. Alpha, SLo,CNr 2.25
Spec. Genesis,CCl 3.50

GAMBIT AND
THE X-TERNALS
1995
1 X-Force after Xavier 3.50
2 V:Deathbird,Starjammers. 2.50
3 V:Imperial Guard 2.50
4 Charles Kidnapped 2.50

GARGOYLE
June, 1985
1 BWr(c),from `Defenders' 4.00
2 thru 4 . . . . @3.00

GARGOYLES
1995–96
1 TV Series. 4.00
2 TV Series. 3.00
3 F:Broadway 3.00
4 V:Statues 3.00
5 Humanoid Gargoyles 3.00
6 Medusa Project concl. 3.00
7 Demona & Triad. 3.00

---

8 I:The Pack 3.00
9 V:Demonia,Triad 3.00
10 Demonia gains magical powers . 3.00
11 Elisa turns to Xanatos. 3.00
12 Sorceress traps Gargoyles 3.00
13 Behind Enemy Lines. 3.00
14 thru 16. . . . . @3.00

GAY COMICS
Marvel Timely, 1944
1 BW,Guys and gals humor 700.00
18 BW 400.00
19 BW 350.00
20 BW 350.00
21 BW 350.00
22 BW 350.00
23 BW 350.00
24 BW,HK,Hey Look 350.00
25 BW 350.00
26 BW 350.00
27 BW 350.00
28 BW 350.00
29 BW,HK,Hey Look 350.00
30 HK,Hey Look. 200.00
31 HK,Hey Look. 200.00
32 . . . . 125.00
33 HK,Hey Look. 200.00
34 HK,Hey Look. 200.00
35 thru 40 . . . . @125.00
Becomes:

HONEYMOON
Marvel Comics, 1950
41 Photo(c) 125.00

GENE DOGS
Marvel UK, 1993–94
1 I:Gene DOGS,w/cards. 3.00
2 V:Genetix 2.25
3 V:Hurricane 2.25
4 last issue 2.25

GENERATION M
Nov., 2005
1 Decimation. 3.00
2 thru 5 . . . . @3.00

GENERATION NEXT
1995
1 Generation X AX 3.50
2 Genetic Slave Pens 2.50
3 V:Sugar Man 2.50
4 V:Sugar Man 2.50

GENERATION X
Oct., 1994
1 CBa,Banshee & White Queen. . . 7.00
2 CBa,SLo 4.00
2a Deluxe edition 4.00
3 CBa 3.00
3a Deluxe edition 4.00
4 CBa,V:Nanny,Orphanmaker 3.00
4a Deluxe edition 4.00
5 SLo,CBa,MBu,two new young
  mutants at the Academy 3.50
6 A:Wolverine 3.50
7 SLo,F:Banshee,A:White Queen. . 3.50
8 F:Banshee 3.50
9 SLo,TG,Chamber in a kilt. 3.50
10 SLo,TG,MBu,Banshee vs.
  OmegaRed 3.50
11 SLo,TG,V:Omega Red 3.00
12 SLo,TG,V:Emplate 3.00
13 . . . . 3.00
14 . . . . 3.00
15 SLo,MBu,Synch goes psycho. . 3.00
16 . . . . 3.00
17 SLo,CBa,Onslaught saga,
  X-Cutioner vs. Skin 3.00
18 SLo,CBa,Onslaught saga 3.00

19 SLo,CBa,................... 3.00
20 SLo,CBa,................... 3.00
21 SLo,CBa,MBu,F:Skin & Chamber,
    A:Beverly Switzer, Howard
    the Duck 3.00
22 SLo,CBa,................... 3.00
23 SLo,CBa,V:Black Tom Cassidy . . 3.00
24 SLo,MBy,F:Monet,Emplate 3.00
25 SLo,CBa,double size 4.00
26 SLo,CBa,Shot down over the
    Atlantic. 3.00
27 SLo,CBa,on nuclear sub. 3.00
28 SLo,CBa,No Exit prelude 3.00
29 JeR,CBa, V:Sentinels 3.00
30 JeR,CBa, V:Zero Tolerance 3.00
31 JeR,CBa, ... 3.00
32 TDF,MBu,F:Banshee, Moira
    McTaggert 3.00
33 LHa,MBu,new direction........ 3.00
34 LHa,Truth behind M 3.00
35 LHa,Jubilee,V:Emplate 3.00
36 LHa,Final Fate of M 3.00
37 LHa,Final Fate of M 3.00
38 LHa,TyD,kids save universe 2.50
39 LHa,TyD, multi-dimensional trip . 2.50
40 LHa,TyD,Penance mystery
    revealed. 2.50
41 LHa,TyD,Jubilee,V:Bastion,
    Omega Red, Sabretooth 2.50
42 LHa,TyD,results of EMP wave . . 2.50
43 LHa,TyD,V:Bianca LaNiege 2.50
44 LHa,TyD,V:White Queen....... 2.50
45 LHa,TyD,F:Banshee 2.50
46 LHa,TyD,F:Forge 2.50
47 LHa,TyD,Danger Room 2.50
48 TyD,Jubilee vs. M 2.50
49 TyD,V:Maggott 2.50
50 TyD,War of the Mutants,pt.1 . . . . 3.50
50a signed 20.00
51 V:Hunter Brawn. 2.50
52 TyD,blackmail 2.50
53 TyD,V:Rising Sons,A:Paladin . . . 2.50
54 TyD,A:Paladin 2.50
55 TyD,in bodies of Hellions 2.50
56 TyD,A:X-Men of past. 2.50
57 TyD, double sized 3.50
58 TyD, new Penance 2.50
59 TyD,..................... 2.50
60 TyD,F:Siryn 2.50
61 TyD,ATi,R:Mondo 2.50
62 TyD,F:Monet St. Croix. 2.50
63 WEI,X-Men Revolution 2.50
63a variant (c) 2.50
64 WEI,Correction,pt.2. .... 2.25
65 WEI,Correction,pt.3. .... 2.25
66 WEI,Correction,pt.4. .... 2.25
67 WEI,Come On Die Young,pt.1 . 2.25
68 WEI,Come On Die Young,pt.2 . 2.25
69 WEI,Come On Die Young,pt.3 . 2.25
70 WEI,Come On Die Young,pt.4 . 2.25
71 WEI,Four Days,pt.1. .... 2.25
72 AAd(c),StP,Four Days,pt.2 ..... 2.25
73 AAd(c),StP,Four Days,pt.3 ..... 2.25
74 AAd(c),StP,Four Days,pt.4 ..... 2.25
75 AAd(c),StP,final issue 3.50
Minus 1 Spec., JeR,CBa, flashback,
    F:Banshee 2.50
Ann. '95 SLo,J:Mondo,
    V:Hellfire Club 4.50
Ann. '96 GN MGo,JJ,DPs,V:Fenris . 3.50
Ann. '97, Haunted by Ghosts
    of Hellions 3.50
Ann.1998 Generation X/Dracula . . 4.00
Ann.1999 48-pg. 4.00
Holliday Spec. 48-page 1-shot. . . . 4.00

GENERATION X/GEN 13
Dec., 1997
1-shot JeR,SvL,V:Mr. Pretorious . . . 4.00
1a variant cover CBa (1:4). 4.00

Generation X Gen 13
© Marvel Entertainment Group

GENERATION X: UNDERGROUND
March, 1998
1-shot by Jim Mahfood, b&w 2.50

GENERIC COMIC
1 .... 2.25

GENETIX
Marvel UK, 1993–94
1 B:ALa(s),w/cards 3.00
2 I:Tektos 2.25
3 V:Tektos 2.25
4 PGa,V:MyS-Tech 2.25
5 PGa,V:MyS-Tech 2.25
6 V:Tektos 2.25

GEORGIE COMICS
Spring, 1945
1 Georgie stories begin 350.00
2 Pet Shop (c) 175.00
3 Georgie/Judy(c) 135.00
4 Wedding Dress(c) 135.00
5 Monty/Policeman(c) 135.00
6 Classroom(c) 150.00
7 Fishing(c) 135.00
8 Soda Jerk(c) 135.00
9 Georgie/Judy(c),HK,Hey Look 135.00
10 Georgie/Girls(c),HK,Hey Look 135.00
11 Table Tennis(c),A:Margie,Millie 100.00
12 Camping(c) 100.00
13 Life Guard(c),HK,Hey Look. . 150.00
14 Classroom(c),HK,Hey Look . 150.00
15 Winter Sports(c) 100.00
16 .... 100.00
17 HK,Hey Look. 150.00
18 .... 100.00
19 Baseball(c) 100.00
Becomes:

GEORGIE & JUDY COMICS
20 .... 125.00
21 .... 100.00
Becomes:

GEORGIE COMICS
22 Georgie comics 100.00
23 & 24. ....@100.00
25 Driben painted (c)......... 125.00
26 thru 28. ....@100.00
29 .... 125.00
30 thru 38. ....@100.00
39 Oct., 1952. .... 100.00

GETALONG GANG
May, 1985—March, 1986
1 thru 6 .... @3.50

GHOST RIDER
1967
1 O&I:Ghost Rider (western) . . . 150.00
2 V:Tarantula. 75.00
3 Cougar's Circus of Fear 50.00
4 Sting Ray 50.00
5 Tarantula Strikes Back........ 50.00
6 Behold a Falling Star 50.00
7 Mystery of Massacre Mountain . 50.00

GHOST RIDER
**[1st Regular Series],
Sept., 1973**
1 GK,JSt,C:Son of Satan 150.00
2 GK,I:Son of Satan,A:Witch
    Woman 75.00
3 JR,D:Big Daddy Dawson,
    new Cycle 50.00
4 GK,A:Dude Jensen 50.00
5 GK,JR,I:Roulette 50.00
6 JR,O:Ghost Rider 35.00
7 JR,A:Stunt Master 35.00
8 GK,A:Satan,I:Inferno 35.00
9 GK,TP,O:Johnny Blaze 35.00
10 JSt,A:Hulk 35.00
11 GK,KJ,SB,A:Hulk 35.00
12 GK,KJ,FR,A:Phantom Eagle. . 20.00
13 GK,JS,GT,A:Trapster 20.00
14 GT,A:The Orb 20.00
15 SB,O:The Orb 20.00
16 DC,GT,Blood in the Water 20.00
17 RB,FR,I:Challenger. 20.00
18 RB,FR,A:Challenger,
    Spider-Man 20.00
19 GK,FR,A:Challenger. 20.00
20 GK,KJ,JBy,A:Daredevil 22.00
21 A:Gladiator,D:Eel. 10.00
22 AM,DH,KP,JR,A:Enforcer . . . 10.00
23 JK,DH,DN,I:Water Wiz. 10.00
24 GK,DC,DH,A:Enforcer 10.00
25 GK,DH,A:Stunt Master 10.00
26 GK,DP,A:Dr. Druid 10.00
27 SB,DP,A:Hawkeye 10.00
28 DP,A:The Orb 10.00
29 RB,DP,A:Dormammu 10.00
30 DP,A:Dr.Strange 10.00
31 FR,DP,BL,A:Bounty Hunt. . . . 10.00
32 KP,BL,DP,A:Bounty Hunt. 10.00
33 DP,I:Dark Riders 10.00

Ghost Rider #4
© Marvel Entertainment Group

MARVEL

34 DP,C:Cyclops	10.00
35 JSn,AM,A:Death	15.00
36 DP,Drug Mention	10.00
37 DP,I:Dick Varden	10.00
38 DP,A:Death Cult	10.00
39 DP,A:Death Cult	10.00
40 DP,I:Nuclear Man	10.00
41 DP,A:Jackal Gang	10.00
42 DP,A:Jackal Gang	10.00
43 CI:Crimson Mage	10.00
44 JAb,CI,A:Crimson Mage	10.00
45 DP,I:Flagg Fargo	10.00
46 DP,A:Flagg Fargo	10.00
47 AM,DP	10.00
48 BMc,DP	10.00
49 DP,I:The Manitou	10.00
50 DP,A:Night Rider	15.00
51 AM,PD,A:Cycle Gang	6.00
52 AM,DP	6.00
53 DP,I:Lord Asmodeus	6.00
54 DP,A:The Orb	6.00
55 DP,A:Werewolf By Night	6.00
56 DP,A:Moondark,I:Night Rider	6.00
57 AM,DP,I:The Apparition	6.00
58 DP,FM,A:Water Wizard	6.00
59 V:Water Wizard,Moon Dark	6.00
60 DP,HT,A:Black Juju	6.00
61 A:Arabian Knight	6.00
62 KJ,A:Arabian Knight	6.00
63 LMc,A:The Orb	6.00
64 BA,V:Azmodeus	6.00
65 A:Fowler	6.00
66 BL,A:Clothilde	6.00
67 DP,A:Sally Stantop	6.00
68 O:Ghost Rider	6.00
69	6.00
70 I:Jeremy	6.00
71 DP,I:Adam Henderson	6.00
72 A:Circus of Crime	6.00
73 A:Circus of Crime	6.00
74 A:Centurions	6.00
75 I:Steel Wind	6.00
76 DP,A:Mephisto,I:Saturnine	6.00
77 O:Ghost Rider's Dream	6.00
78 A:Nightmare	6.00
79 A:Man Cycles	6.00
80 A:Centurions	6.00
81 D:Ghost Rider	15.00

[2nd Regular Series], 1990–98

1 JS,MT,I:2nd Ghost Rider, Deathwatch	6.00
1a 2nd printing	3.00
2 JS,MT,I:Blackout	3.00
3 JS,MT,A:Kingpin,V:Blackout, Deathwatch	3.00
4 JS,MT,V:Mr.Hyde	3.00
5 JLe(c),JS,MT,A:Punisher	3.00
5a rep.Gold	2.50
6 JS,MT,A:Punisher	3.00
7 MT,V:Scarecrow	3.00
8 JS,MT,V:H.E.A.R.T	3.00
9 JS,MT,A:Morlocks,X-Factor	2.50
10 JS,MT,V:Zodiac	2.50
11 LSn,MT,V:Nightmare, A:Dr.Strange	2.50
12 JS,MT,A:Dr.Strange	2.50
13 MT,V:Snow Blind,R:J.Blaze	2.50
14 MT,Blaze Vs.Ghost Rider	2.50
15 MT,A:Blaze,V:Blackout Glow in Dark(c)	3.00
15a 2nd printing (gold)	2.50
16 MT,A:Blaze,Spider-Man, V:Hobgoblin	2.50
17 MT,A:Spider-Man,Blaze, V:Hobgoblin	2.50
18 MT,V:Reverend Styge	2.50
19 MT,A:Mephisto	2.50
20 MT(i),O:Zodiac	2.50
21 MT(i),V:Snowblind, A:Deathwatch	2.50
22 MT,A:Deathwatch,Ninjas	2.50
23 MT,I:Hag & Troll,A:Deathwatch	2.50

Ghost Rider 2nd Series Ann. #1
© Marvel Entertainment Group

24 MT,V:Deathwatch,D:Snowblind, C:Johnny Blaze	2.50
25 V:Blackout (w/Center spread pop-up)	3.00
26 A:X-Men,V:The Brood	3.00
27 A:X-Men,V:The Brood	3.00
28 NKu,JKu,Rise of the Midnight Sons#1,V:Lilith,w/poster	3.00
29 NKu,JKu,A:Wolverine,Beast	2.50
30 NKu,JKu,V:Nightmare	2.50
31 NKu,JKu,Rise o/t Midnight Sons#6, A:Dr.Strange,Morbius, Nightstalkers,Redeemers, V:Lilith,w/poster	3.00
32 BBi,A:Dr.Strange	2.50
33 BBi,AW,V:Madcap (inc.Superman tribute on letters page)	2.50
34 BBi,V:Deathwatchs' ninja	2.50
35 BBi,AW,A:Heart Attack	2.50
36 BBi,V:Mr.Hyde,A:Daredevil	2.50
37 BBi,A:Archangel,V:HeartAttack	2.50
38 MM,V:Scarecrow	2.50
39 V:Vengeance	2.50
40 Midnight Massacre#2, D:Demogblin	3.00
41 Road to Vengeance#1	2.50
42 Road to Vengeance#2	2.50
43 Road to Vengeance#3	2.50
44 Siege of Darkness,pt.#2	2.50
45 Siege of Darkness,pt.#10	2.50
46 HMe(s),New Beginning	2.50
47 HMe(s),RG	2.50
48 HMe(s),RG,A:Spider-Man	2.50
49 HMe(s),RG,A:Hulk,w/card	2.50
50 Red Foil(c),AKu,SMc,A:Blaze, R:2nd Ghost Rider	3.25
50a Newsstand Ed.	2.75
51 SvL	2.50
52 SvL	2.50
53 SvL,V:Blackout	2.50
54 SvL,V:Blackout	2.50
55 V:Mr. Hyde	2.50
56 The Next Wave	2.50
57 A:Wolverine	2.50
58 HMe,SvL,Betrayal,pt.1	2.50
59 Betrayal,pt.2	2.50
60 Betrayal,pt.3	2.50
61 Betrayal,pt.4	3.00
62 EventInChains,pt.1,A:Fury	2.50
63 EventInChains,pt.2	2.50
64 EventInChains,pt.3	2.50
65 EventInChains,pt.4,R:Blackout	2.50
66 V:Blackout	2.50
67 A:Gambit,V:Brood	2.50

68 A:Gambit,Wolverine,V:Brood	2.50
69 Domestic Violence	2.50
70 New Home in Bronx	2.50
71	2.50
72	2.50
73 John Blaze is back	2.50
74 A:Blaze, Vengeance	2.50
75	2.50
76 V:Vengeance	2.50
77 A:Dr. Strange	2.50
78 new costume, A:Dr. Strange	2.50
79 IV,New costume, A:Valkyrie,	2.50
80 IV,V:Furies,Valkyrie A:Black Rose	2.50
81 IV,A:Howard the Duck, Devil Dinosaur	2.25
82 IV,A:Devil Dinosaur	2.25
83 IV,A:Scarecrow,Lilith	2.25
84 IV,A:Scarecrow, Lilith	2.25
85 IV,V:Lilith, Scarecrow	2.25
86 IV,rampage through the Bronx	2.25
87 IV,KIK,AM,	2.25
88 IV, V:Pao Fu,Blackheart	2.25
89 IV,JS,	2.25
90 IV,JS,Last Temptation, pt.1	5.00
91 IV,JS,A:Blackheart	5.00
92 IV,JS,Journey into the past	5.00
93 IV,JS,MT,Last Temptation concl., double sized	10.00
94 IV,JS,MT,Becomes Lord of the Underworld, last issue	2.00
Ann.#1 I:Night Terror,w/card	3.25
Ann.#2 F:Scarecrow	3.00
GN Ghost Rider/Captain America: Fear, AW, V:Scarecrow (1992)	6.25
GN Ghost Rider/Wolverine/Punisher: Dark Design (1994)	6.00
GN Ghost Rider/Wolverine/Punisher: Hearts of Darkness, JR2/KJ,V: Blackheart, gatefold(c) (1991)	5.50
TPB Midnight Sons, rep.	20.00
TPB Resurrected rep.#1-#7	13.00
TPB Resurrected (2000)	13.00
Poster Book	5.00
Spec. Crossroads	4.00
Minus 1 Spec., IV,JS, flashback	2.00

GHOST RIDER

1 Director's Cut, GEn(s),48-pg.	4.00

GHOST RIDER

Sept., 2005

1 (of 6) GEn(s),Road to Damnation	3.00
2 thru 6 Gen(s),Road to Damnation	@3.00
TPB Essential Ghost Rider	17.00

GHOST RIDER

July., 2006

1 (of 6) MT,JS,Vicious Cycle.	3.00
1a variant (c).	3.00
2 thru 5 MT, JS,Vicious Cycle	@3.00

GHOST RIDER/ BALLISTIC/CYBLADE

Marvel/Top Cow 1996

1-shot IV,ACh,Devil's Reign, pt.2, x-over	3.25
1-shot WEI,BTn,Devil's Reign, pt.3, x-over	3.00

GHOST RIDER/BLAZE SPIRITS OF VENGEANCE

1992–94

1 AKu,polybagged w/poster,V:Lilith, Rise of the Midnight Sons#2	3.50
2 AKu,V:Steel Wind	3.00
3 AKu,CW,V:The Lilin	3.00
4 AKu,V:Hag & Troll,C:Venom	3.00

MARVEL

5 AKu,BR,Spirits of Venom#2,
  A:Venom,Spidey,Hobgoblin 5.00
6 AKu,Spirits of Venom#4,A:Venom,
  Spider-Man,Hobgoblin 3.50
7 AKu,V:Steel Vengeance. 2.25
8 V:Mephisto. 2.25
9 I:Brimstone. 2.25
10 AKu,V:Vengeance 2.25
11 V:Human Spider Creature 2.25
12 AKu,BR,Vengeance,glow in the
  dark(c) 3.25
13 AKu,Midnight Massacre#5 . . . . . 2.50
14 Missing Link#2 . . . . 2.25
15 Missing Link#3 . . . . 2.25
16 V:Zarathos,Lilith 2.25
17 HMe(s),Siege/Darkness,pt.8 . . . 2.25
18 HMe(s),Siege/Darkness,pt.13 . . . 2.25
19 HMe(s),HMz,V:Vampire 2.25
20 HMe(s),A:Steel Wind 2.25
21 HMe(s),HMz,V:Werewolves 2.25
22 HMe(s),HMz,V:Cardiac. 2.25
23 HMe(s),HMz,A:Steel Wind 2.25

GHOST RIDER:
THE HAMMER LANE
June, 2001
1 (of 6) TKn. 3.00
2 TKn,DaM 3.00
3 TKn,DaM,Gunmetal Gray 3.00
4 TKn,DaM,Gunmetal Gray 3.00
5 TKn,DaM,Gunmetal Gray 3.00
6 TKn,DaM,Gunmetal Gray 3.00
TPB series rep. 144-pg. 16.00

GHOST RIDER:
HIGHWAY TO HELL
June, 2001
Spec. 64-pages 3.50

GHOST RIDER 2099
1994–96
1 Holografx(c),LKa,CBa,MBu,I:Ghost
  Rider 2099,w/card 3.00
1a Newsstand Ed. 2.25
2 LKa,CBa,MBu 2.25
3 LKa,CBa,MBu,I:Warewolf 2.25
4 LKa,CBa,MBu,V:Warewolf. 2.25
5 LKa,CBa,MBu 2.25
6 LKa,CBa,MBu 2.25
7 LKa,CBa,MBu 2.25
8 LKa,CBa,MBu 2.25

Ghost Rider 2099 #13
© Marvel Entertainment Group

9 . . . . 2.25
10 . . . . 2.25
11 V:Bloodsport Society. 2.25
12 I:Coda 2.25
Becomes:

GHOST RIDER 2099 A.D.
1995
13 F:Doom 2.25
14 Deputized by Doom 2.25
15 One Nation Under Doom 2.25
16 V:Max Synergy 2.25
17 . . . . 2.25
18 V:L-Cipher 2.25
19 V:L-Cipher 2.25
20 . . . . 2.25
21 V:Vengeance 2099 . . . . 2.25
22 V:Vengeance 2099 . . . . 2.25
23 . . . . 2.25
24 . . . . 2.25
25 Double size final issue 3.50

GIANT-SIZE CHILLERS
1975
I AA, ... 75.00
2 . . . . 35.00
3 BWr,Night of the Gargoyle. 50.00

GIANT-SIZE CHILLERS
1974
1 I&O:Lilith,Γ:Curse of Dracula. . . 75.00
Becomes:
GIANT-SIZE DRACULA
2 Vengeance of the Elder Gods . . 40.00
3 rep. Uncanny Tales #6. . . . . 25.00
4 SD,Demon of Devil's Lake. 25.00
5 JBy, 1st Marvel art. 60.00

GIANT-SIZE
MINI-MARVELS:
STARRING SPIDEY
Dec., 2001
1 F:Hawkeye, 48-pg. 3.50

G.I. JOE:
A REAL AMERICAN HERO
June, 1982
1 HT,BMc,Baxter paper. 35.00
2 DP,JAb,North Pole. 25.00
3 HT,JAb,Trojan Robot 15.00
4 HT,JAb,Wingfield 15.00
5 DP,Central Park 15.00
6 HT,V:Cobra 15.00
7 HT,Walls of Death 15.00
8 HT,Sea Strike 15.00
9 The Diplomat 15.00
10 Springfield 15.00
11 thru 20 . . . . @12.00
21 SL(i),Silent Interlude 30.00
22 V:Destro 7.00
23 I:Duke 7.00
24 RH,I:Storm Shadow 7.00
25 FS,I:Zartan 7.00
26 SL(i),O:Snake Eyes 9.00
27 FS,O:Snake Eyes 9.00
28 Swampfire 7.00
29 FS,V:Destro 7.00
30 JBy(c),FS,V:Dreddnoks 7.00
31 thru 60 . . . . @3.00
2a to 36a 2nd printings . . . . @2.00
60 TM,I:Zanzibar 6.00
61 thru 90 . . . . @3.00
91 TSa,V:Red Ninjas,D:Blind
  Masters 4.00
92 MBr,V:Cobra Condor. 4.00
93 MBr,V:Baroness 15.00
94 MBr,A:Snake Eyes 6.00
95 MBr,A:Snake Eyes 6.00

G. I. Joe: A Real American Hero #38
© Marvel Entertainment Group

96 MBr,A:Snake Eyes 6.00
97 thru 109 . . . . @4.00
110 Mid-East Crisis 5.00
111 thru 119 . . . . @4.00
120 V:Red Ninjas,Slice & Dice 6.00
121 thru 134 . . . . @4.00
135 thru 143 . . . . @5.00
144 O: Snake Eyes 8.00
145 thru 147 . . . . @5.00
148 F:Star Brigade. 8.00
149. . . . . 5.00
150 Cobra Commander vs.
  Snake Eyes 15.00
151 V:Cobra. 15.00
152 First G.I. Joe 18.00
153 V:Cobra. 18.00
154 . . . . 22.00
155 final issue 35.00
SC GI Joe and the Transformers. . . 5.00
Spec. TM rep.#61 . . . . 4.00
Ann.#1 . . . . 4.00
Ann.#2 . . . . 4.00
Ann.#3 . . . . 4.00
Ann.#4 . . . . 4.00
Ann.#5 . . . . 4.00
Yearbook #1 (1985) 4.00
Yearbook #2 (1986) 4.00
Yearbook #3 (1987) 4.00
Yearbook #4 (1988) 4.00
TPB Vol.1, 240-pg. (2002). 25.00
TPB Vol.2, 240-pg. (2002). 25.00
TPB Vol.3, 240-pg. (2002). 25.00
TPB Vol.4 (2002) 26.00
TPB Vol 5 (2003). 25.00

G.I. JOE
EUROPEAN MISSIONS
June, 1988
1 British rep. 7.00
2 . . . . 5.00
3 . . . . 7.00
4 thru 15 . . . . @5.00

G.I. JOE
SPECIAL MISSIONS
Oct., 1986
1 HT,New G.I. Joe. 4.00
2 thru 9 HT . . . . @4.00
10 thru 20 HT . . . . @4.00
21 thru 28 . . . . @5.00

G.I. JOE AND THE TRANSFORMERS
1987
1 thru 4 HT,mini-series . . . . @3.00

G.I. JOE UNIVERSE
1 Biographies rep.#1. . . . . 3.50
2 thru 4 . . . . @2.50

G.I. TALES
See: SERGEANT BARNEY BARKER

GIRL COMICS
Marvel Atlas, Nov., 1949
1 Ph(c),True love stories,I Could
  Escape From Love 275.00
2 Ph(c),JKu,Blind Date 135.00
3 BEv,Ph(c),Liz Taylor 325.00
4 PH(c),Borrowed Love 125.00
5 Love stories 125.00
6 same 125.00
7 same 125.00
8 same 125.00
9 same 125.00
10 The Deadly Double-Cross . . . 125.00
11 Love stories. 125.00
12 BK,The Dark Hallway 150.00
Becomes:

GIRL CONFESSIONS
1952
13 . . . . 150.00
14 . . . . 125.00
15 . . . . 125.00
16 BEv 150.00
17 BEv 150.00
18 BEv 150.00
19 . . . . 110.00
20 . . . . 110.00
21 thru 34 . . . . @100.00
35 Aug., 1954. . . . . 100.00

GIRLS' LIFE
Marvel Atlas, Jan., 1954
1 . . . . 150.00
2 . . . . 125.00
3 . . . . 100.00
4 . . . . 100.00
5 . . . . 100.00
6 November, 1954 . . . . 100.00

G.L.A.
April, 2005
1 (of 4) F:Great Lakes Avengers . . 3.00
2 Dis-membership Drive 3.00
3 . . . . 3.00
4 Countdown to a Miscount 3.00

GLADIATOR/SUPREME
1997
1 KG,ASm,x-over 5.00

GLX-MAS
Dec., 2005
1-shot X-mas special 4.00

GODZILLA
Aug., 1977
1 HT,JM,Based on Movie Series . 30.00
2 HT,FrG,GT,Seattle Under Seige 12.00
3 HT,TD,A;Champions 20.00
4 TS,TD,V;Batragon 10.00
5 TS,KJ,Isle of the Living
  Demons. 10.00
6 HT,A Monster Enslaved 10.00
7 V:Red Ronin 10.00
8 V:Red Ronin 10.00

9 Las Gamble in Las Vegas 10.00
10 V:Yetrigar 10.00
11 V;Red Ronin,Yetrigar. 8.00
12 Star Sinister 8.00
13 V:Mega-Monster 8.00
14 V:Super-Beasts. 8.00
15 Stampede 8.00
16 Jaws of Fear 8.00
17 Godzilla Shrunk 8.00
18 Battle Beneath Eighth Avenue . . 8.00
19 Panic on the Pier 8.00
20 A;Fantastic Four 10.00
21 V;Devil Dinosaur 8.00
22 V:Devil Dinosaur 8.00
23 A;Avengers 10.00
24 July, 1979 . . . . 8.00

GOLDEN AGE OF MARVEL
TPB RyL. 10.00
Vol.1, 176-page 20.00
Vol.2, 176-page 20.00

GRAVITY
June, 2005
1(of 5) F:Greg Willis 3.00
2 . . . . 3.00
3 V:Black Death 3.00
4 . . . . 3.00
5 Finale 3.00
TPB Big-City Super Hero. 8.00

GREATEST SPIDER-MAN & DAREDEVIL TEAM-UPS
TPB 175pg. 10.00

GREEN GOBLIN
1995–96
1 I:New Green Goblin. 4.00
2 thru 13 . . . . @2.25

GROO CHRONICLES
Epic, 1989
1 SA 5.00
2 thru 6 SA . . . . @4.00

[SERGIO ARAGONE'S] GROO, THE WANDERER
(see Pacific, Eclipse)
Epic, 1985–95
1 SA,I:Minstrel 17.00
2 SA,A:Minstrel 9.00
3 SA,Medallions 8.00
4 SA,Airship 8.00
5 SA,Slavers 8.00
6 SA,The Eye of the Kabala 8.00
7 SA,A:Sage 8.00
8 SA,A:Taranto 8.00
9 SA,A:Sage 8.00
10 SA,I:Arcadio 8.00
11 thru 18 SA . . . . @6.00
19 thru 29 SA. . . . . @4.00
30 thru 49. . . . . @4.00
50 SA,double size 4.00
51 thru 87 SA. . . . . @3.00
88 SA,V:Cattlemen,B.U. Sage . . . 4.00
89 thru 99 SA . . . . @3.00
100 SA,Groo gets extra IQ points . . 8.00
101 thru 120 SA. . . . . @4.00
GNv Death of Groo 15.00
GNv 2nd print. 8.00
TPB Groo Adventures 9.00
TPB Groo Carnival. 9.00
TPB Groo Expose 9.00
TPB GRoo Festival 9.00
TPB Groo Garden 11.00

Groo, The Wanderer #18
© Marvel Entertainment Group

GROOVY
March, 1968—July, 1968
1 Monkeys,Ringo Starr,Photos . . 140.00
2 Cartoons,Gags,Jokes 125.00
3 . . . . 125.00

GUARDIANS
2004
1 (of 5) Reach for the Stars 3.00
2 thru 5 Reach for the Stars . . . . @3.00

GUARDIANS OF THE GALAXY
June, 1990
1 B:JV(a&s),I:Taserface,R:Aleta . . . 4.00
2 MZ(c),JV,V:Stark,C:Firelord 3.00
3 JV,V:Stark,I:Force,C:Firelord 3.00
4 JV,V:Stark,A:Force,Firelord 3.00
5 JV,TM(c),V:Force,I:Mainframe
  (Vision) 3.00
6 JV,V:Force,Vance Possesses
  Capt.America Shield 3.00
7 GP(c),JV,I:Malevolence,
  O:Starhawk 3.00
8 SLi(c),JV,V:Yondu,C:Rancor 3.00
9 RLd(c),JV,I:Replica,Rancor 3.00
10 JLe(c),JV,V:Rancor,The Nine
  I&C:Overkill(Taserface) 3.00
11 BWi(c),JV,V:Rancor,I:Phoenix . . . 3.00
12 ATb(c),JV,V:Overkill
  A:Firelord. 3.00
13 JV,A:Ghost Rider,Force,
  Malevolence 3.00
14 JS(c),JV,A:Ghost Rider,Force,
  Malevolence 3.00
15 JSn(c),JV,I:Protege,V:Force 3.00
16 JV,V:Force,A:Protege,
  Malevolence,L:Vance Astro 3.00
17 JV,V:Punishers(Street Army),
  L:Martinex,N:Charlie-27, ... 2.50
18 JV,V:Punishers,I&C:Talon,A:
  Crazy Nate 3.00
19 JV,V:Punishers,A:Talon. 2.50
20 JV,I:Major Victory (Vance Astro)
  J:Talon & Krugarr. 2.50
21 JV,V:Rancor 2.50
22 JV,V:Rancor 2.50
23 MT,V:Rancor,C:Silver Surfer. . . . 2.50
24 JV,A:Silver Surfer 3.00
25 JV, Prismatic Foil(c)
  V:Galactus,A:SilverSurfer 3.50
25a 2nd printing,Silver. 2.50

Guardians of the Galaxy #33
© Marvel Entertainment Group

26 JV,O:Guardians(retold) 2.25
27 JV,Infinity War,O:Talon,
    A:Inhumans 2.25
28 JV,Inf.War,V:Various Villians . . . 2.25
29 HT,Inf.War,V:Various Villians. . . 2.25
30 KWe,A:Captain America 2.25
31 KWe,V:Badoon,A:Capt.A. 2.25
32 KWe,V:Badoon Gladiator 2.25
33 KWe,A:Dr.Strange,R:Aleta 2.25
34 KWe,J:Yellowjacket II 2.25
35 KWe,A:Galatic Guardians,
    V:Bubonicus 2.25
36 KWe,A:Galatic Guardians,
    V:Dormammu 2.25
37 KWe,V:Dormammu,A:Galatic
    Guardians 2.25
38 KWe,N.Y.jacket,A:Beyonder 2.25
39 KWe,Rancor Vs. Dr.Doom,I:Iolo-
    grafx(c) 3.25
40 KWe,V:Loki,Composite 2.25
41 KWe,V:Loki,A:Thor 2.25
42 KWe,I:Woden 2.25
43 KWe,A:Woden,V:Loki 2.25
44 KWe,R:Yondu 2.25
45 KWe,O:Starhawk 2.25
46 KWe,N:Major Victory 2.25
47 KWe,A:Beyonder,Protoge,
    Overkill 2.25
48 KWe,V:Overkill 2.25
49 KWe,A:Celestial 2.25
50 Foil(c),R:Yondu,Starhawk sep-
    arated,BU:O:Guardians 3.25
51 KWe,A:Irish Wolfhound 2.25
52 KWe,A:Drax 2.25
53 KWe,V:Drax 2.25
54 KWe,V:Sentinels 2.25
55 KWe,Ripjack 2.25
56 Ripjack 2.25
57 R:Keeper 2.25
58 . . . . 2.25
59 A:Keeper 2.25
60 F:Starhawk 2.25
61 F:Starhawk 2.25
62 Guardians Stop War of the Worlds
    last issue 2.25
Ann.#1 Korvac Quest #4,I:Krugarr. . 3.25
Ann.#2 HT,I:Galactic Guardians,
    System Bytes #4 . . . . 3.25
Ann.#3 CDo,I:Irish Wolfhound,
    w/Trading card 3.25
Ann.#4 V:Nine 3.25
TPB rep #1 thru #6 . . . . 13.00

GUNHAWK, THE
See: BLAZE CARSON

GUNHAWKS
Oct., 1972
1 SSh,B:Reno Jones & Kid
    Cassidy Two Rode Together . . 35.00
2 Ride out for Revenge 30.00
3 Indian Massacre 30.00
4 Trial by Ordeal 30.00
5 The Reverend Mr. Graves 30.00
6 E:Reno Jones & Kid Cassidy
    D:Kid Cassidy 30.00
7 A Gunhawks Last Stand
    A;Reno Jones, Oct., 1973 . . . 30.00

GUNRUNNER
Marvel UK, 1993–94
1 I:Gunrunner,w/trading cards 3.00
2 A:Ghost Rider 2.25
3 V:Cynodd 2.25
4 . . . . 2.25
5 A:Enhanced 2.25
6 final issue 2.25

GUNSLINGERS
Dec., 1999
1-shot 64-pg. 3.00

GUNSLINGER
See: TEX DAWSON,
GUNSLINGER

GUNSMOKE WESTERN
See: ALL WINNERS
COMICS

GUN THEORY
Marvel Epic, Aug., 2003
1 (of 4) 2.50
2 thru 4 . . . . @2.50

HALO
July, 2006
GN from Microsoft game 25.00

HARROWERS
1993–94
1 MSt(s),GC,F:Pinhead 3.50
2 GC,AW(i) 3.00
3 GC,AW(i) 3.00
4 GC,AW(i) 3.00
5 GC,AW(i),Devil's Pawn#1 . . . . . . 3.00
6 GC,AW(I),Devil's Pawn#2 . . . . . . 3.00

HARVEY
Oct., 1970–Dec., 1972
1 . . . . 135.00
2 thru 6 . . . . @100.00

HARVEY PRESENTS:
CASPER
1 . . . . 2.25

HAUNT OF HORRORS:
EDGAR ALLAN POE
May, 2006
1 RCo, b&w, inc. The Raven 4.00
2 RCo, b&w, inc. Tell-Tale Heart . . . 4.00
3 RCo, b&w, three stories 4.00

HAVOK & WOLVERINE
Epic, March, 1988
1 JMu,KW,V:KGB,Dr.Neutron 5.00
2 JMu,KW,V:KGB,Dr.Neutron 4.00
3 JMu,KW,V:Meltdown 4.00
4 JMu,KW,V:Meltdown,Oct.1989 . . 4.00
TPB rep.#1-4 . . . . 17.00

Havok & Wolverine #1
© Marvel Entertainment Group

HAWKEYE
[1st Limited Series], Sept., 1983
1 A:Mockingbird 3.00
2 I:Silencer 3.00
3 I:Bombshell,Oddball 3.00
4 V:Crossfire,W:Hawkeye &
    Mockingbird, Dec., 1983 . . . . . 3.00
[2nd Limited Series], 1994
1 B:CDi(s),ScK,V:Trickshot,
    I:Javelynn,Rover 2.25
2 ScK,V:Viper 2.25
3 ScK,A:War Machine,N:Hawkeye,
    V:Secret Empire 2.25
4 E:CDi(s),ScK,V:Trickshot,Viper,
    Javelynn 2.25

HAWKEYE
Oct., 2003
1 FaN(s),High,Hard Shaft,pt.1 . . . . 3.00
2 FaN(s),High,Hard Shaft,pt.2 . . . . 3.00
3 FaN(s),High,Hard Shaft,pt.3 . . . . 3.00
4 FaN(s),High,Hard Shaft,pt.4 . . . . 3.00
5 FaN(s),High,Hard Shaft,pt.5 . . . . 3.00
6 FaN(s),High,Hard Shaft,pt.6 . . . . 3.00
7 FaN(s),A Little Murder,pt.1 . . . . . 3.00
8 FaN(s),A Little Murder,pt.2 . . . . . 3.00

HAWKEYE: EARTH'S
MIGHTIEST MARKSMAN
Aug., 1998
1-shot TDF,MBa,JJ,DR,AM 48pg. . . 3.00

HEADMASTERS
Star, July, 1987
1 FS,Transformers 2.25
2 and 3 . . . . @2.25
4 Jan., 1988 . . . . 2.25

HEATHCLIFF
Star, April, 1985
1 . . . . 7.00
2 thru 10 . . . . @4.00
11 thru 16 . . . . @3.00
17 Masked Moocher 5.00
18 thru 49 . . . . @3.00
50 Double-size 3.00
51 thru 55 . . . . @3.00

HEATHCLIFF'S FUNHOUSE
Star, May, 1987
1 thru 9 . . . . @3.00
10 1988 . . . . 3.00

HEAVY HITTERS
Ann.#1 (1993) 4.00

HEDY DEVINE COMICS
Aug., 1947—Sept., 1952
22 I:Hedy Devine 350.00
23 BW,Beauty and the Beach,
    HK,Hey Look 225.00
24 High Jinx in Hollywood,
    HK, Hey Look 225.00
25 Hedy/Bull(c),HK,Hey Look . . . 225.00
26 Skating(c),HK,Giggles&Grins . 250.00
27 Hedy at Show(c),HK,HeyLook 225.00
28 Hedy/Charlie(c),HK,HeyLook . 225.00
29 Tennis(c),HK,Hey Look 225.00
30 . . . . 175.00
31 thru 35 . . . . @175.00
Becomes:

Hedy Hollywood #40
© Marvel Entertainment Group

HEDY HOLLYWOOD
36 thru 50 . . . . @175.00

HEDY WOLFE
Marvel Atlas, Aug., 1957
1 Patsy Walker's Rival 125.00

HELLCAT
July, 2000
1 (of 3) SEt,NBy,F:PatsyWalker . . . 3.00
2 SEt,NBy, ... 3.00
3 SEt,NBy,Concl. 3.00

HELLHOUND
1993–94
1 Hellhound on my Trial 3.00
2 Love in Vain 3.00
3 Last Fair Deal Gone Down 3.00

HELLRAISER
See: CLIVE BARKER'S
HELLRAISER

HELLRAISER III
HELL ON EARTH
1 Movie Adaptation,(prestige) 5.00

1a Movie Adapt.(magazine) 3.00

HELLSTORM, PRINCE OF LIES
1993
1 R:Daimon Hellstrom,
    Parchment(c) 3.50
2 A:Dr.Strange,Gargoyle 3.00
3 O:Hellstorm 2.75
4 V:Ghost Rider 2.75
5 MB, ... 2.50
6 MB,V:Dead Daughter. 2.50
7 A:Armaziel 2.50
8 Hell is where the heart is 2.50
9 LKa(s),Highway to Heaven 2.50
10 LKa(s),Heaven's Gate 2.50
11 LKa(s),PrG,Life in Hell 2.50
12 Red Miracles 2.50
13 Red Miracles Sidewalking 2.50
14 Red Miracles Murder is Easy . . 2.50
15 Cigarette Dawn 3.00
16 Down Here 2.50
17 The Saint of the Pit 2.50
18 thru 21 . . . . @2.50

HELLSTORM: SON OF SATAN
Oct., 2006
1 Equinox, pt.1 . . . . 4.00
2 Equinox, pt.2 . . . . 4.00

HELL'S ANGEL
1992
1 GSr,A:X-Men,O:Hell's Angel 3.00
2 GSr,A:X-Men,V:Psycho Warriors . 2.50
3 GSr,A:X-Men,V:MyS-Tech 2.25
4 GSr,A:X-Men,V:MyS-Tech 2.25
5 GSr,A:X-Men,V:MyS-Tech 2.25
6 Gfr,A:X-Men,V:MyS-Tech 2.25
Becomes:

DARK ANGEL
1992
7 DMn,A:Psylocke,V:MyS-Tech . . . 2.25
8 DMn,A:Psylocke 2.25
9 A:Punisher 2.25
10 MyS-Tech Wars tie-in 2.25
11 A:X-Men,MyS-Tech wars tie-in . 2.25
12 A:X-Men 2.25
13 A:X-Men,Death's Head II 2.25
14 Aftermath#2 . . . . 2.25
15 Aftermath#3 . . . . 2.25
16 SvL,E:Aftermath,last issue 2.25

HERCULES
April, 2005
1 (of 5) MT 3.00
2 MT,v:king Eurytheses. 3.00
3 MT,12 Labors for Reality TV 3.00
4 MT,Final four labors 3.00
5 MT,final Four Labors 3.00
TPB New Labors of Hercules 14.00

HERCULES AND THE HEART OF CHAOS
Limited Series Aug., 1997
1 (of 3) TDF,RF,PO, ... 2.50
2 TDF,RF,PO, ... 2.50
3 TDF,RF,PO,V:Ares, concl. 2.50

HERCULES PRINCE OF POWER
Sept., 1982
1 BL,I:Recorder. 5.00
2 BL,I:Layana Sweetwater 3.00
3 BL,V:The Brothers,C:Galactus . . 3.00
4 BL,A:Galactus 3.00

[2nd Series], March, 1984
1 BL,I:Skyypi 3.00
2 BL,A:Red Wolf 2.50
3 BL,A:Starfox 2.50
4 BL,D:Zeus, June, 1984 . . . . 2.50
TPB BL rep. Vol.1 and Vol.2 . . . . . 6.00

HERO
May, 1990
1 . . . . 2.50
2 thru 6 . . . . @2.25

HERO FOR HIRE
June, 1972
1 GT,JR,I&O:Power Man 75.00
2 GT,A:Diamond Back 35.00
3 GT,I:Mace 25.00
4 V:Phantom of 42nd St. 25.00
5 GT,A:Black Mariah 25.00
6 V:Assassin 15.00
7 GT,Nuclear Bomb issue 15.00
8 GT,A:Dr.Doom 15.00
9 GT,A:Dr.Doom,Fant.Four 15.00
10 GT,A:Dr.Death,Fant.Four 15.00
11 GT,A:Dr.Death 12.00
12 GT,C:Spider-Man 12.00
13 A:Lion Fang. 12.00
14 V:Big Ben 12.00
15 Cage Goes Wild 12.00
16 O:Stilletto,D:Rackham. 12.00
Becomes:

POWER MAN

HEROES FOR HIRE
July, 1997
1 JOs,PFe,F:Iron Fist 5.00
2 JOs,PFe,V:Nitro 3.00
2A Variant PFe cover 3.00
3 JOs,PFe,V:Nitro. 3.00
4 JOs,Power Man vs. Iron Fist 3.00
5 JOs,V:Sersi, Diabolical Deviants . 3.00
6 JOs,PFe, Deviants. 3.00
7 JOs V:Thunderbolts 3.00
8 JOs,Iron Fist's agenda revealed . 3.00
9 JOs,Search for Punisher 3.00
10 JOs,Deadpool hired 3.00
11 JOs,PFe,A:Deadpool, V:Silver
    Sable and Wild Pack 3.00
12 JOs,PFe,Traitor revealed, 48pg . 3.50
13 JOs,PFe,V:Master. 3.00
14 JOs,F:Black Knight 3.00
15 JOs,PFe,Siege of Wundagore,
    pt.1 (of 5). 3.00
16 JOs,PFe,Siege of Wundagore,
    pt.3. . . . . 3.00
17 JOs,DBw,F:Luke Cage
    & She-Hulk 3.00
18 JOs,PFe,A:Wolverine 3.00
19 JOs,PFe,F:Wolverine 3.00
Ann.'98 JOs,BWi,PFe,Heroes For
    Hire/Quicksilver, The Siege of
    Wundagore, pt.5 (of 5) 48pg . . . 3.00

HEROES FOR HIRE
Aug., 2006
1 JP,BiT,Civil War tie-in 3.00
2 thru 4 JP,BiT. . . . . @3.00

HEROES FOR HOPE
1985
1 TA/JBy/HC/RCo/BWr,A:XMen . . . 7.00

HEROES REBORN: THE RETURN
Oct., 1997
? Heroes Reborn prequel, (Marvel/
    Wizard 1996) 7.50

---

1 (of 4) PDd,ATi,SvL,F:Franklin
  Richards 4.00
2 PDd,ATi,SvL, F:Spider-Man,
  Thunderbolts & Doctor Strange . 4.00
3 PDd,SvL,ATi,A UniverseMayDie . 4.00
4 PDd,SvL,ATi, crossover to Marvel
  Universe? 4.00
TPB Return of the Heroes 15.00

Hokum & Hex #4
© Marvel Entertainment Group

HOKUM & HEX
Razorline 1993–94
1 BU:Saint Sinner 3.00
2 thru 9 . . . . @2.25

HOLIDAY COMICS
Marvel Star, Jan., 1951
1 LbC(c),Christmas(c). 450.00
2 LbC(c),Easter Parade(c) 475.00
3 LbC(c),4th of July(c) 300.00
4 LbC(c),Summer Vacation. 275.00
5 LbC(c),Christmas(c). 275.00
6 LbC(c),Birthday(c) 275.00
7 LbC(c),Rodeo (c) 275.00
8 LbC(c),Xmas(c) Oct., 1952 . . 275.00
Becomes:

FUN COMICS
Marvel Star, 1953
9 LbC 275.00
10 LbC 250.00
11 LbC 250.00
12 LbC 250.00
Becomes:

MIGHTY BEAR
Marvel Star, 1954
13 LbC 100.00
14 LbC 100.00
Becomes:

UNSANE
Marvel Star, 1954
15 . . . . 475.00

HOLLYWOOD SUPERSTARS
Epic, Nov., 1990
1 DSp 3.00
2 thru 5 DSp, March, 1991 . . . . . @2.50

HOMER, THE HAPPY GHOST
March, 1955
1 . . . . 350.00
2 . . . . 250.00
3 . . . . 225.00
4 thru 15 . . . . @225.00
16 thru 22 . . . . @200.00
[2nd Series], Nov., 1969
1 . . . . 250.00
2 thru 5 . . . . @175.00

HOMER HOOPER
Marvel Atlas, 1953
1 Teen-age romance humor 150.00
2 . . . . 100.00
3 . . . . 100.00
4 . . . . 100.00

HONEYMOON
See: GAY COMICS

HOOD, THE
Marvel Max, May, 2002
1 (of 6) F:Parker Robbins,40-pg. . . 3.00
2 FBI attention 3.00
3 diamond heist 3.00
4 . . . . 3.00
5 . . . . 3.00
6 concl. 3.00
TPB Vol. 1: Blood From Stones. . . 15.00

HOOK
1992
1 JRy,GM,movie adaption. 2.25
2 JRy,Return to Never Land 2.25
3 Peter Pans Magic 2.25
4 conclusion 2.25
Hook Super Spec.#1 . . . . 3.00

HORRORS, THE
**Marvel Star Publications,
Jan., 1953–April, 1954**
11 LbC(c),JyD,Horrors of War . . . 360.00
12 LbC(c),Horrors of War 350.00
13 LbC(c),Horrors of Mystery . . . 300.00
14 LbC(c),Horrors of the
  Underworld 350.00
15 LbC(c),Horrors of the
  Underworld 350.00

HOT SHOTS
AVENGERS
1 Painted Pin-ups (1995) 3.00
SPIDER-MAN
1 Painted pin-ups 3.00
X-MEN
1 Painted pin-ups 3.00

HOUSE II
1 1987, Movie Adapt. 2.00

HOUSE OF M
June, 2005
1 (of 8) F:X-Men, New Avengers . 3.00
2 BMB,V:the Scarlet Witch 3.00
3 BMB,F:Wolverine. 3.00
4 BMB,F:Layla Miller. 3.00
5 BMB,F:Spider-man 3.00
6 BMB. 3.00
7 BMB 3.00
8 BMB 3.00
1a BMB var 8a variant (c). 3.00
Spec. Secrets of the House of M. . . 4.00
TPB House of M 25.00

Howard the Duck #27
© Marvel Entertainment Group

HOWARD THE DUCK
Jan., 1976
1 FB,SL,A:Spider-Man,I:Beverly. . 30.00
2 FB,V:TurnipMan&Kidney Lady. . 10.00
3 JB,Learns Quack Fu 10.00
4 GC,V:Winky Man 10.00
5 GC,Becomes Wrestler. 9.00
6 GC,V:Gingerbread Man. 6.00
7 GC,V:Gingerbread Man 6.00
8 GC,A:Dr.Strange,ran for Pres. . . . 6.00
9 GC,V:Le Beaver. 6.00
10 GC,A:Spider-Man 6.00
11 GC,V:Kidney Lady. 6.00
12 GC,I:Kiss. 25.00
13 GC,A:Kiss 30.00
14 thru 32 GC . . . . @4.00
33 BB(c),The Material Duck. 6.00
Ann.#1, V:Caliph of Bagmom 3.00
Holiday Spec. LHa,ATi,PFe (1996) . 3.50

HOWARD THE DUCK
Marvel Max, Jan., 2002
1 (of 6) SvG,Making the Band 4.00
2 SvG,Beverly's ex 3.00
3 SvG,GF,The former Duck. 3.00
4 SvG,GF,House of Mystery 3.00
5 SvG,GF,House of Mystery,pt.2. . . 3.00
6 SvG,GF,Duck or Mouse 3.00
TPB series rep. 15.00

HOWARD THE DUCK MAGAZINE
(B&W) Oct., 1979–March, 1981
1 . . . . 6.00
2 & 3 . . . . @5.00
4 Beatles,Elvis,Kiss 6.00
5 thru 9 . . . . @5.00

[NICK FURY'S] HOWLING COMMANDOS
Oct., 2005
1 KG,F:horror characters 3.00

HUGGA BUNCH
Star, Oct., 1986—Aug., 1987
1 . . . . 4.00
2 thru 6 . . . . @3.00

HULK, THE
Feb., 1999
1 JBy,RG,DGr,48-page 4.00
1a signed 20.00
1b gold foil cover 10.00
2 JBy,RG,DGr,Hulk unleashed 3.00
2a variant AdP cover 3.00
3 JBy,RG,DGr,Hulk berserk 3.00
4 JBy,RG,DGr,old foe 3.00
5 JBy,RG,DGr,V:Man-Thing 3.00
6 JBy,RG,DGr,V:Man-Thing 3.00
7 JBy,RG,DGr,A:Avengers 3.00
8 JBy,RG,DGr,V:Wolverine 20.00
9 RG,V:Thing. 3.00
10 RG. 3.00
11 PJe,RG,SB,A:DocSamson 3.00
Becomes:

INCREDIBLE HULK
2000
12 PJe,RG,SB,48-pg 3.00
13 PJe,RG,SB,new Hulk 2.50
14 PJe,RG,SB,V:Ryker 2.50
15 PJe,RG,SB,Dogs of War,pt.2 . . . 2.50
16 PJe,RG,SB,Dogs of War,pt.3 . . . 2.50
17 PJe,RG,SB,Dogs of War,pt.4 . . . 2.50
18 PJe,RG,SB,Dogs of War,pt.5 . . . 2.50
19 PJe,RG,SB,Dogs of War,pt.6 . . . 2.50
20 PJe,RG,SB,Dogs of War,pt.7 . . . 2.50
21 PJe,Maximum Security 2.50
22 PJe,Joe Fixit's Money 2.50
23 PJe,Nobby Stiles. 2.50
24 PJe,JR2,V:Abomination 2.50
25 PJe,JR2,V:Abomination 3.50
26 Psyche of child-like Hulk 2.50
27 PJe,JR2,TP. 2.50
28 PJe,JR2,TP,V:Devil Hulk. 2.50
29 FaN,A:Angela,Doc Samson 2.50
30 PJe,JoB,TP 2.50
31 PJe,JoB,TP,Banner gone 2.50
32 PJe,JoB,TP,Ant-Man inside 2.50
33 CPr,JBg,100-page. 4.00
34 JR2,TP,The beast within 5.00
35 JR2,TP,crosses the line? 3.00
36 JR2,TP,Gangs All Here,pt.1 . . . . 3.00
37 JR2,TP,Remember This,pt.2. . . . 3.00
38 JR2,TP, ... 3.00
39 JR2,TP,Tag-You're Dead. 3.00
40 LW,TP,madman with gun 3.00
41 JR2,TP,madman with gun 3.00
42 LW,TP,hostage crisis. 3.00
43 JR2,TP,hostage crisis,concl. . . . 3.00
44 SI. 3.00
45 SI,dream lover 3.00
46 SI. 3.00
47 SI. 3.00
48 SI. 3.00
49 SI. 3.00
50 MD2,R:Abomination,pt.1. . . . . . 4.00
51 MD2,R:Abomination,pt.2. . . . . . 3.00
52 MD2,R:Abomination,pt.3. . . . . . 3.00
53 MD2,R:Abomination,pt.4. . . . . . 3.00
54 MD2,R:Abomination,pt.5. . . . . . 3.00
55 Hide in Plain Sight,pt.1 . . . . 3.00
56 Hide in Plain Sight,pt.2 . . . . 3.00
57 Hide in Plain Sight,pt.3 . . . . 3.00
58 Hide in Plain Sight,pt.4 . . . . 3.00
59 Hide in Plain Sight,pt.5 . . . . 3.00
60 MD2,Split Decisions,pt.1 . . . . . . 3.00
61 MD2,Split Decisions,pt.2 . . . . . . 3.00
62 MD2,Split Decisions,pt.3. . . . . . 3.00
63 MD2,Split Decisions,pt.4. . . . . . 3.00
64 MD2,Split Decisions,pt.5. . . . . . 3.00
65 MD2,Split Decisions,concl. 3.00
66 MD2,Bury Me Not,pt.1 . . . . 3.00
67 DBw,MD2(c),Bury Me Not,pt.2 . . 3.00
68 DBw,MD2(c),Bury Me Not,pt.3 . . 3.00
69 DBw,MD2(c),Bury Me Not,pt.4 . . 3.00
70 MD2, Marvel Knights Hulk 3.00
71 MD2,Big Things,pt.1 . . . . 3.00
72 MD2,Big Things,pt.2 . . . . 3.00
73 MD2,Big Things,pt.3 . . . . 3.00

74 DBw,Big Things,pt.4 . . . . 3.00
75 DaR,Wake to Nightmare,48-pg. . 3.50
76 DBw,Shattered,48-pg. 3.50
77 PDd(s),LW,Tempest Fugit,pt.1 . . 4.00
78 PDd(s),LW,Tempest Fugit,pt.2 . . 3.00
79 PDd(s),LW,Tempest Fugit,pt.3 . . 3.00
80 PDd(s),LW,Tempest Fugit,pt.4 . . 3.00
81 PDd(s),LW,Tempest Fugit,pt.5 . . 3.00
82 PDd(s),JaL,vengeance 3.00
83 PDd(s),The Last Refuge,pt.1 . . . 3.00
84 PDd(s),The Last Refuge,pt.2 . . . 3.00
85 PDd(s),The Last Refuge,pt.3 . . . 3.00
86 PDd(s),The Last Refuge,pt.4 . . . 3.00
87 PDd(s),AKu,F:New Scorpion . . . 3.00
88 Peace in Our Time, pt.1 . . . . 3.50
89 Peace in Our Time, pt.2 . . . . 3.50
90 Peace in Our Time, pt.3 . . . . 3.50
91 Peace in Our Time, pt.4 . . . . 3.50
92 Planet Hulk: Exile, pt.1 . . . . 6.00
93 Planet Hulk: Exile, pt.2 . . . . 3.00
94 Planet Hulk: Exile, pt.3 . . . . 3.00
95 Planet Hulk: Exile, pt.4 . . . . 3.00
96 AaL,Planet Hulk: Anarchy, pt.1 . . 3.00
97 AaL,Planet Hulk: Anarchy, pt.2 . . 3.00
98 AaL,Planet Hulk: Anarchy, pt.3 . . 3.00
99 AaL,Planet Hulk: Anarchy, pt.4 . . 3.00
100 Hulk sized 104-pg. 4.00
100a variant (c) 4.00
Ann. 1999 JBy,DGr,48-page 4.00
Ann. 2001 EL,V:Thor 3.50
Spec. Hulk/Sentry 3.50
GN The End, DK, ... 6.00
TPB Transformations 18.00
TPB Ground Zero 18.00
TPB The Dogs of War,224-page . . 20.00
TPB Tempest Fugit 15.00
TPB Planet Hulk Prelude (2006) . . 14.00
TPB Vol. 1: Return of the Monster. 13.00
TPB Vol. 2: The Morning After 9.00
TPB Vol. 3: Transfer of Power 3.00
TPB Vol. 4: Abominable 12.00
TPB Vol. 5: Hide in Plain Sight . . . 12.00
TPB Vol. 6: Split Decisions 13.00
TPB Vol. 7: Dead Like Me 13.00
TPB Vol. 8: Big Things 18.00
Spec. Must Have, rep. #34–#36 . . 4.00
Spec. Planet Hulk: Gladiator
 Guidebook (2006) 4.00

HULK: DESTRUCTION
July, 2005
1 (of 4) PDd 3.00
2 PDd,v:Abomination 3.00
3 PDd 3.00
4 PDd 3.00

HULK: GRAY
Oct., 2003
1 JLb,TSe 3.50
2 thru 6 JLb,TSe . . . . @3.50
TPB Hulk: Gray 20.00

HULK: THE MOVIE
June, 2003
Spec. Movie adaptation, 48-pg. . . . 3.50
TPB Movie 13.00

HULK: NIGHTMERICA
June, 2003
1 (of 6) 3.00
2 thru 6 . . . . @3.00

HULK SMASH
Jan., 2001
1 (of 2) GEn,JMC 3.00
2 GEn,JMC 3.00

HULK & THING:
HARD KNOCKS
Sept., 2004
1 (of 4) JaL 3.50
2 JaL 3.50
3 . . . . 3.00
4 . . . . 3.00
TPB Hulk & Thing: Hard Knocks . . 15.00

HULK 2099
1994–95
1 GJ,Foil(c),V:Draco 3.00
2 GJ,V:Draco 2.25
3 I:Golden Boy 2.25
4 . . . . 2.25
5 Ultra Hulk 2.25
Becomes:

HULK 2099 A.D.
1995
6 Gamma Ray Scientist 2.25
7 A:Doom,Dr.Apollo 2.25
8 One Nation Under Doom 2.25
9 California Quake 2.25

HULK VISIONARIES
TPB Vol. 1: Peter David 20.00
TPB Vol. 2: Peter David 20.00
TPB Vol. 3: Peter David 20.00

HULK/WOLVERINE:
6 HOURS
Jan., 2003
1 (of 4) ScK,SBs(c),rescue 3.00
2 ScK,SBs(c) 3.00
3 ScK,SBs(c) 3.00
4 ScK,SBs(c),concl. 3.00
TPB Hulk Legends, Vol. 1, rep. . . . 14.00

HUMAN FLY
July, 1987
1 I&O:Human Fly,A:Spider-Man . 12.00
2 A:Ghost Rider 15.00
3 DC,JSt(c),DP,Fortress of Fear . . . 5.00
4 JB/TA(c),David Drier 5.00
5 V:Makik 5.00
6 Fear in Funland 5.00
7 ME,Fury in the Wind 5.00
8 V:White Tiger 5.00
9 JB/TA(c),ME,V:Copperhead,A:
 White Tiger,Daredevil 7.00

Human Fly #2
© *Marvel Entertainment Group*

All comics prices listed are for *Near Mint* condition.

10 ME,Dark as a Dungeon 5.00	
11 ME,A:Daredevil 5.00	
12 ME,Suicide Sky-Dive 5.00	
13 BLb/BMc(c),FS,V:Carl Braden . . 5.00	
14 BLb/BMc(c),SL,Fear Over	
Fifth Avenue. 5.00	
15 BLb/BMc(c),War in the	
Washington Monument 5.00	
16 BLb/BMc(c),V:Blaze Kendall. . . . 5.00	
17 BLb,DP,Murder on the Midway . . 5.00	
18 V:Harmony Whyte. 5.00	
19 BL(c),V:Jacopo Belbo	
March, 1979 . . . . 10.00	

RED RAVEN COMICS
Marvel Timely Comics Aug., 1940

1 JK,O:Red Raven,I:Magar,A:Comet
    Pierce & Mercury,Human Top,
    Eternal Brain 25,000.00
Becomes:

HUMAN TORCH
Marvel Comcis, 1940–49

2 (#1)ASh(c),BEv,B:Sub-Mariner
    A:Fiery Mask,Falcon,Mantor,
    Microman 60,000.00
3 (#2)Ash(c),BEv,V:Sub-
    Mariner,Bondage(c) 10,000.00
4 (#3)ASh(c),BEv,O:Patriot . . . 7,500.00
5 (#4)V:Nazis,A:Patriot,Angel
    crossover 6,000.00
5a(#5)ASh(c),V:Sub-Mariner . . 9,000.00
6 ASh(c),Doom Dungeon. 4,500.00
7 ASh(c),V:Japanese 4,700.00
8 ASh(c),BW,V:Sub-Mariner . . 6,000.00
9 ASh(c),V:General Rommel . . 5,000.00
10 ASh(c),BW,V:Sub-Mariner . . 5,000.00
11 ASh(c),Nazi Oil Refinery . . . 3,000.00
12 ASh(c),V:Japanese,
    Bondage(c). 5,000.00
13 ASh(c),V:Japanese,
    Bondage(c) 3,000.00
14 ASh(c),V:Nazis. 3,000.00
15 ASh(c),Toro Trapped 3,000.00
16 ASh(c),V:Japanese 2,500.00
17 ASh(c),V:Japanese 2,500.00
18 ASh(c),V:Japanese,
    MacArthurs HQ. 2,500.00
19 ASh(c),Bondage(c). 2,700.00
20 ASh(c),Last War Issue 2,500.00
21 ASh(c),V:Organized Crime . . 2,500.00
22 ASh(c),V:Smugglers. 2,500.00
23 ASh(c),V:Giant Robot. 2,800.00
24 SSh(c),V:Mobsters. 4,000.00

Human Torch #12
© Marvel Entertainment Group

25 The Masked Monster. 3,500.00	
26 SSh(c),Her Diary of Terror . . 3,500.00	
27 SSh(c),BEv,V:The Asbestos	
Lady. 3,500.00	
28 BEv,The Twins Who Weren't 3,500.00	
29 SSh(c),You'll Die Laughing . 3,500.00	
30 SSh(c),BEv,The Stranger,	
A:Namora 2,500.00	
31 A:Namora. 2,200.00	
32 SSh(c),A:Sungirl,Namora. . . 1,300.00	
33 Capt.America crossover . . . 2,500.00	
34 The Flat of the Land 2,200.00	
35 A;Captain America,Sungirl . . 2,500.00	

Becomes:

LOVE TALES
Revived As:

HUMAN TORCH
Marvel Comics, 1954

36 A:Submariner 2,000.00
37 BEv,A:Submariner 1,800.00
38 BEv,A:Submariner 1,800.00

HUMAN TORCH
Sept., 1974

1 JK,rep.StrangeTales #101 . . . . . 35.00
2 rep.Strange Tales #102 . . . . . . 25.00
3 rep.Strange Tales #103 . . . . . . 25.00
4 rep.Strange Tales #104 . . . . . . 25.00
5 rep.Strange Tales #105 . . . . . . 25.00
6 rep.Strange Tales #106 . . . . . . 25.00
7 rep.Strange Tales #107 . . . . . . 25.00
8 rep.Strange Tales #108 . . . . . . 25.00

HUMAN TORCH
April, 2003

1 KK(s),Burn,pt.1 . . . . 2.50
2 KK(s),Burn,pt.2 . . . . 2.50
3 KK(s),Burn,pt.3 . . . . 2.50
4 KK(s),Burn,pt.4 . . . . 2.50
5 KK(s),Burn,pt.5 . . . . 2.50
6 KK(s),Burn,concl. 2.50
7 KK(s),Plague of Locusts,pt.I . . . 2.50
8 KK(s),Plague of Locusts,pt.2 . . . 3.00
9 KK(s),Plague of Locusts,pt.3 . . . 3.00
10 KK(s),Plague of Locusts,pt.4 . . 3.00
11 KK(s),F:Namorita 3.00
12 KK(s),series finale. 3.00
TPB Human Torch: Burn, Vol.1 . . 15.00
Digest Vol. 1: Burn. 8.00

HUMAN TORCH COMICS
Feb., 1999

1-shot V:Sub-Mariner, 48-page 4.00

HYPERKIND
Marvel/Razorline 1993

1 I:Hyperkind,BU:EctoKid 3.00
2 thru 9 . . . . @2.25

HYPERKIND UNLEASHED
1994

1 BU,V:Thermakk 3.25

ICEMAN
Dec., 1984

1 DP,mini-series 3.00
2 DP,V:Kali 3.00
3 DP,A;Original X-Men,Defenders
    Champions 3.00
4 DP,Oblivion,June, 1985 . . . . 4.00

ICEMAN
Oct., 2001

1 (of 4) DAn,ALa,KIK 3.00
2 DAn,ALa,KIK,A:Augmen 3.00
3 DAn,ALa,KIK,F:Foe-Dog,Augmen 3.00
4 DAn,ALa, concl. 3.00

Ideal #4
© Marvel Entertainment Group

IDEAL
Marvel Timely, July, 1948

1 Antony and Cleopatra 450.00
2 The Corpses of Dr.Sacotti . . . 350.00
3 Joan of Arc 325.00
4 Richard the Lionhearted
    A:The Witness 500.00
5 Phc,Love and Romance 250.00
Becomes:

LOVE ROMANCES
6 Ph(c),I Loved a Scoundrel . . . 250.00
7 Ph(c) 175.00
8 Ph(c) 200.00
9 thru 12 Ph(c) . . . . @150.00
13 thru 20 . . . . @150.00
21 BK 125.00
22 . . . . 125.00
23 . . . . 125.00
24 BK 125.00
25 . . . . 125.00
26 thru 35 . . . . @125.00
36 BK 125.00
37 . . . . 150.00
38 BK 150.00
39 thru 44 . . . . @125.00
45 MB. 150.00
46 . . . . 150.00
47 . . . . 125.00
48 . . . . 125.00
49 ATh 150.00
50 . . . . 125.00
51 . . . . 125.00
52 . . . . 125.00
53 ATh 140.00
54 . . . . 125.00
55 . . . . 125.00
56 . . . . 125.00
57 MB. 135.00
58 thru 74 . . . . @135.00
75 MB. 135.00
76 . . . . 125.00
77 MB. 135.00
78 . . . . 125.00
79 . . . . 125.00
80 RH(c). 125.00
81 . . . . 125.00
82 MB,JK(c). 150.00
83 JSe,JK(c) 150.00
84 JK 150.00
85 JK 150.00
86 thru 95 . . . . @100.00
96 JK 150.00
97 . . . . 150.00
98 JK 160.00

MARVEL

99 JK 160.00
100 thru 104 . . . . @160.00
105 JK 160.00
106 JK,July, 1963 . . . . 160.00

IDEAL COMICS
Marvel Timely, Fall, 1944
1 B:Super Rabbit,Giant Super
   Rabbit V:Axis(c) 275.00
2 Super Rabbit at Fair(c) 200.00
3 Beach Party(c) 200.00
4 How to Catch Robbers 200.00
Becomes:

WILLIE COMICS
1946
5 B:Willie,George,Margie,Nellie
   Football(c) 250.00
6 Record Player(c) 175.00
7 Soda Fountain(c),HK 175.00
8 Fancy Dress(c) 150.00
9 . . . . 150.00
10 HK,Hey Look 175.00
11 HK,Hey Look 175.00
12 . . . . 150.00
13 . . . . 150.00
14 . . . . 150.00
15 . . . . 150.00
16 thru 18 . . . . @150.00
19 . . . . 175.00
20 Li'L Willie Comics 150.00
21 Li'L Willie Comics 150.00
22 . . . . 150.00
23 May, 1950 . . . . 150.00
Becomes:

CRIME CASES

IDENTITY DISK
June, 2004
1 (of 5) JP 3.00
2 thru 5 . . . . @3.00

IDOL
Epic, 1992
1 I:Idol 3.25
2 Phantom of the Set 3.25
3 Conclusion 3.25

I ♥ MARVEL
Feb., 2006
Marvel AI 3.00
Masked Intentions #1 . . . . 3.00
My Mutant Heart 3.00
Outlaw Love #1 . . . . 3.00
Web of Romance #1 . . . . 3.00

ILLUMINATOR
1993
1 . . . . 5.50
2 . . . . 5.50
3 . . . . 3.25
4 . . . . 3.25

IMMORTAL IRON FIST
Nov., 2006
1 . . . . 3.00

IMMORTALIS
1 A:Dr.Strange 2.25
2 A:Dr.Strange 2.25
3 A:Dr.Strange,V:Vampires 2.25
4 Mephisto, final issue 2.25

IMPERIAL GUARD
[Limited Series], 1997
1 (of 3) BAu,Woj, ... 2.25
2 and 3 BAu,Woj . . . . @2.25

IMPOSSIBLE MAN SUMMER VACATION
1990–91
1 GCa,DP 2.50
2 . . . . 2.50
Summer Fun Spec. TPe, Vacation
   on Earth 2.50

INCAL, THE
Epic, Nov., 1988
1 Moebius,Adult 12.00
2 Moebius,Adult 12.00
3 Moebius,Adult, Jan., 1989 . . . . 12.00

INCOMPLETE DEATH'S HEAD
1993
1 . . . . 3.50
2 thru 11 rep.Death's Head #1
   thru #11 . . . . @2.25

Incredible Hulk #4
© *Marvel Entertainment Group*

INCREDIBLE HULK
May, 1962
1 JK, I:Hulk(Grey Skin),Rick Jones,
   Thunderbolt Ross,Betty Ross,
   Gremlin,Gamma Base . . . 27,000.00
2 JK,SD,O:Hulk, (Green skin) . . 5,500.00
3 JK,O:rtd.,I:Ring Master,
   Circus of Crime 3,200.00
4 JK,V:Mongu 3,000.00
5 JK,I:General Fang 3,000.00
6 SD,I:Metal Master 3,800.00
See: Tales to Astonish #59–#101

April, 1968
102 MSe,GT,O:Retold 700.00
103 MSe,I:Space Parasite 250.00
104 MSe,O&N:Rhino 200.00
105 MSe,GT,I:Missing Link 150.00
106 MSe,HT,GT 150.00
107 HT,V:Mandarin 150.00
108 HT,JMe,A:Nick Fury 150.00
109 HT,JMe,A:Ka-Zar 125.00
110 HT,JMe,A:Ka-Zar 125.00
111 HT,DA,I:Galaxy Master 100.00
112 HT,DA,O:Galaxy Master 80.00
113 HT,DA,V:Sandman 80.00
114 HT,DA 80.00
115 HT,DA,A:Leader 80.00
116 HT,DA,V:Super Humanoid 80.00
117 HT,DA,A:Leader 80.00
118 HT,V:Sub-Mariner 80.00
119 HT,V:Maximus 75.00

120 HT,V:Maximus 75.00
121 HT,I:The Glob 75.00
122 HT,V:Thing 125.00
123 HT,V:Leader 75.00
124 HT,SB,V:Rhino,Leader 75.00
125 HT,V:Absorbing Man 75.00
126 HT,A:Dr.Strange 75.00
127 HT,Moleman vs.Tyrannus
   I:Mogol 50.00
128 HT,A:Avengers 50.00
129 HT,V:Glob 50.00
130 HT,Banner vs. Hulk 50.00
131 HT,A:Iron Man 50.00
132 HT,JSe,V:Hydra 50.00
133 HT,JSe,I:Draxon 50.00
134 HT,SB,I:Golem 50.00
135 HT,SB,V:Kang 50.00
136 HT,SB,I:Xeron 50.00
137 HT,V:Abomination 50.00
138 HT,V:Sandman 50.00
139 HT,V:Leader 50.00
140 HT,V:Psyklop 50.00
141 HT,JSe,I&O:Doc.Samson . . . 135.00
142 HT,JSe,V:Valkyrie,A:Doc
   Samson 60.00
143 DA,JSe,V:Dr.Doom 60.00
144 DA,JSe,V:Dr.Doom 60.00
145 HT,JSe,O:Retold 65.00
146 HT,JSe,Leader 30.00
147 HT,JSe,Doc.Samson loses
   Powers 30.00
148 HT,JSe,I:Fialan 30.00
149 HT,JSe,I:Inheritor 30.00
150 HT,JSe,I:Viking,A:Havoc 30.00
151 HT,JSe,C:Ant Man 30.00
152 HT,DA,Many Cameos 30.00
153 HT,JSe,C:Capt.America 30.00
154 HT,JSe,A:Ant Man,
   V:Chameleon 30.00
155 HT,JSe,I:Shaper of Worlds . . . 30.00
156 HT,V:Hulk 30.00
157 HT,I:Omnivac,Rhino 30.00
158 HT,C:Warlock,V:Rhino 30.00
159 HT,V:Abomination,Rhino 30.00
160 HT,V:Tiger Shark 30.00
161 HT,V:Beast 40.00
162 HT,I:Wendigo I 90.00
163 HT,I:Gremlin 25.00
164 HT,I:Capt.Omen 25.00
165 HT,I:Aquon 25.00
166 HT,I:Zzzax 25.00
167 HT,JAb,V:Modok 25.00
168 HT,JAb,I:Harpy 25.00
169 HT,JAb,I:Bi-Beast 25.00
170 HT,JAb,V:Volcano 25.00
171 HT,JAb,A:Abomination,Rhino . 25.00
172 HT,JAb,X:X-Men 50.00
173 HT,V:Cobolt Man 22.00
174 HT,V:Cobolt Man 22.00
175 JAb,V:Inhumans 22.00
176 HT,JAb,A:Man-Beast,C:Warlock
   Crisis on Counter-Earth 25.00
177 HT,JAb,D:Warlock 25.00
178 HT,JAb,Warlock Lives 25.00
179 HT,JAb 22.00
180 HT,JAb,I:Wolverine
   V:Wendigo I 400.00
181 HT,JAb,A:Wolverine (1st
   Full Story),V:Wendigo II . . 1,500.00
182 HT,JAb,I&D:Crackajack
   Jackson,C:Wolverine 175.00
183 HT,V:Zzzax 18.00
184 HT,V:Living Shadow 18.00
185 HT,V:General Ross 18.00
186 HT,I:Devastator 18.00
187 HT,JSt,V:Gremlin 18.00
188 HT,JSt,I:Droog 18.00
189 HT,JSt,I:Datrine 18.00
190 HT,MSe,Toadman 18.00
191 HT,JSt,Toadman,I:Glorian 18.00
192 HT,V:The Lurker 18.00

193 HT,JSt,Doc.Samson regains
    Powers. 18.00
194 SB,JSt,V:Locust 18.00
195 SB,JSt,V:Abomination. 18.00
196 SB,JSt,V:Army 18.00
197 BWr(c),SB,JSt,A:Man-Thing . . 18.00
198 SB,JSt,A:Man-Thing 18.00
199 SB,JSt,V:Shield,Doc.Samson . 18.00
200 SB,JSt,Multi,Hulk in Glenn
    Talbots Brain 40.00
201 SB,JSt,V:Fake Conan 7.00
202 SB,JSt,A:Jarella 7.00
203 SB,JSt,A:Jarella 7.00
204 SB,JStl:Kronus 7.00
205 SB,JSt,D:Jarella 7.00
206 SB,JSt,C:Dr.Strange 7.00
207 SB,JSt,A:Dr.Strange 7.00
208 SB,JSt,V:Absorbing Man. 7.00
209 SB,JSt,V:Absorbing Man. 7.00
210 SB,A:Dr.Druid,O:Merlin II 7.00
211 SB,A:Dr.Druid 7.00
212 SB,I:Constrictor. 8.00
213 SB,TP,I:Quintronic Man 7.00
214 SB,Jack of Hearts 7.00
215 SB,V:Bi-Beast 6.00
216 SB,Gen.Ross 6.00
217 SB,I:Stilts,A:Ringmaster 6.00
218 SB,KP,Doc.Samson versus
    Rhino 6.00
219 SB,V:Capt.Barravuda 6.00
220 SB,Robinson Crusoe 6.00
221 SB,AA,A:Sting Ray 6.00
222 JSn,AA,Cavern of Bones 6.00
223 SB,V:Leader 6.00
224 SB,V:The Leader 6.00
225 SB,V:Leader,A:Doc.Samson. . . 6.00
226 SB,JSt,A:Doc.Samson 6.00
227 SB,JK,A:Doc.Samson 6.00
228 SB,BMc,I:Moonstone,V:Doc
    Samson 8.00
229 SB,O:Moonstone,V:Doc
    Samson 6.00
230 JM,BL,A:Bug Thing 6.00
231 SB,I:Fred Sloan 6.00
232 SB,A:Capt America. 6.00
233 SB,A:Marvel Man 6.00
234 SB,Marvel Man Changes name
    to Quasar. 6.00
235 SB,A:Machine Man 6.00
236 SB,A:Machine Man 6.00
237 SB,A:Machine Man 6.00
238 SB,JAb,Jimmy Carter 6.00
239 SB,I:Gold Bug 6.00
240 SB,Eldorado 6.00
241 SB,A:Tyrannus 6.00

Incredible Hulk #255
© Marvel Entertainment Group

242 SB,Eldorado 6.00
243 SB,A:Gammernon. 6.00
244 SB,A:It. 6.00
245 SB,A:Super Mandroid 6.00
246 SB,V:Capt.Marvel 6.00
247 SB,A:Bat Dragon 6.00
248 SB,V:Gardener 6.00
249 SD,R:Jack Frost 6.00
250 SB,A:Silver Surfer. 15.00
251 MG,A:3-D Man 5.00
252 SB,A:Woodgod 5.00
253 SB,A:Woodgod 5.00
254 SB,I:U-Foes 5.00
255 SB,V:Thor 5.00
256 SB,I&O:Sabra 5.00
257 SB,I&O:Arabian Knight 5.00
258 I:Soviet Super Soldiers 5.00
259 SB,A:Soviet Super-Soldiers,
    O:Darkstar 5.00
260 SB,Sugata. 5.00
261 SB,V:Absorbing Man. 5.00
262 SB,I:Glazer 5.00
263 SB,Avalanche 5.00
264 SB,A:Corruptor 5.00
265 SB,I:Rangers. 5.00
266 SB,V:High Evolutionary 5.00
267 SB,V:Rainbow,O:Glorian. 5.00
268 SB,I:Pariah 5.00
269 SB,I:Bereet 5.00
270 SB,A:Abomination. 5.00
271 SB,I:Rocket Raccoon,
    20th Anniv. 5.00
272 SB,C:X-Men,I:Wendigo III. 6.00
273 SB,A:Alpha Flight 5.00
274 SB,Beroct 5.00
275 SB,JSt,I:Megalith 5.00
276 SB,JSt,V:U-Foes 5.00
277 SB,JSt,U-Foes 5.00
278 SB,JSt,C:X-Men,
    Avengers,Fantastic Four 6.00
279 SB,JSt,C:X-Men,
    Avengers,Fantastic Four 6.00
280 SB,JSt,Jack Daw 5.00
281 SB,JSt,Trapped in Space 5.00
282 SB,JSt,A:She Hulk 5.00
283 SB,JSt,A:Avengers 5.00
284 SB,JSt,A:Avengers 5.00
285 SB,JSt,Northwind,V:Zzzax 5.00
286 SB,JSt,V:Soldier 5.00
287 SB,JSt,V:Soldier 5.00
288 SB,JSt,V:Abomination. 5.00
289 SB,JSt,V:Modok 5.00
290 SB,JSt,V:Modok 5.00
291 SB,JSt,V:Thunderbolt Ross . . . 5.00
292 SB,JSt,V:Dragon Man 5.00
293 SB,V:Nightmare 5.00
294 SB,V:Boomerang 5.00
295 SB,V:Boomerang 5.00
296 SB,A:Rom 5.00
297 SB,V:Nightmare 5.00
298 KN(c),SB,V:Nightmare 5.00
299 SB,A:Shield. 5.00
300 SB,A:Spider-Man,Avengers
    Doctor Strange 8.00
301 SB,Crossroads 4.00
302 SB,Crossroads 4.00
303 SB,V:The Knights 4.00
304 SB,V:U-Foes 4.00
305 SB,V:U-Foes. 4.00
306 SB,V:Klaatu. 4.00
307 SB,V:Klaatu. 4.00
308 SB,V:Puffball Collective 4.00
309 SB,V:Goblin & Glow 4.00
310 Crossroads 4.00
311 Crossroads 4.00
312 Secret Wars II,O:Bruce. 4.50
313 A:Alpha Flight 4.00
314 JBy,V:Doc.Samson 6.00
315 JBy,A:Doc.Samson,Banner
    & Hulk Separated 4.00
316 JBy,A:Avengers,N:Doc
    Samson 4.00

Incredible Hulk #313
© Marvel Entertainment Group

317 JBy,I:Hulkbusters,A:Doc
    Samson 4.00
318 JBy,A:Doc.Samson 5.00
319 JBy,W:Bruce & Betty. 6.00
320 AM,A:Doc.Samson 3.00
321 AM,A:Avengers 3.00
322 AM,A:Avengers 3.00
323 AM,A:Avengers 3.00
324 AM,R:Grey Hulk(1st since #1),
    A:Doc.Samson. 15.00
325 AM,Rick Jones as Hulk. 6.00
326 A:Rick Jones,New Hulk. 7.00
327 AM,F:General Ross 3.00
328 AM,1st PDd(s),Outcasts 8.00
329 AM,V:Enigma 5.00
330 1st TM Hulk,D:T-bolt Ross . . . 28.00
331 TM,V:Leader 28.00
332 TM,V:Leader 20.00
333 TM,V:Leader 20.00
334 TM,I:Half-life 20.00
335 Horror Issue 6.00
336 TM,A:X-Factor. 20.00
337 TM,A:X-Factor, A:DocSamson 20.00
338 TM,I:Mercy,V:Shield 20.00
339 TM,A:RickJones 20.00
340 TM,Hulk vs Wolverine. 50.00
341 TM,V:Man Bull 9.00
342 TM,V:Leader 9.00
343 TM,V:Leader 9.00
344 TM,V:Leader 9.00
345 TM,V:Leader,Double-Size. . . . 10.00
346 TM,EL,L:Rick Jones 9.00
347 In Las Vegas,I:Marlo Chandler,
    V:Absorbing Man. 5.00
348 V:Absorbing Man 4.00
349 A:Spider-Man 4.00
350 Hulk vs Thing,A:Beast
    V:Dr.Doom. 5.00
351 R:Jarella's World. 3.00
352 V:Inquisitor 3.00
353 R:Bruce Banner 3.00
354 V:Maggia 3.00
355 V:Glorian. 3.00
356 V:Glorian,Cloot 3.00
357 V:Glorian,Cloot 3.00
358 V:Glorian,Cloot 3.00
359 JBy(c),C:Wolverine(illusion) . . . 4.00
360 V:Nightmare & Dyspare 3.00
361 A:Iron Man,V:Maggia 3.00
362 V:Werewolf By Night. 3.00
363 Acts of Vengeance 3.00
364 A:Abomination,B:Countdown . . 3.00
365 A:Fantastic Four 3.00
366 A:Leader,I:Riot Squad. 3.00

All comics prices listed are for *Near Mint* condition.

MARVEL

367 1st DK Hulk,I:Madman(Leader's
    brother),E:Countdown 13.00
368 SK,V:Mr.Hyde 5.00
369 DK,V:Freedom Force 3.00
370 DK,R:Original Defenders 3.00
371 DK,BMc,A:Orig.Defenders 3.00
372 DK,R:Green Hulk 10.00
373 DK,Green Hulk & Grey Hulk. . . 4.00
374 DK,BMc,Skrulls,
    R:Rick Jones 4.00
375 DK,BMc,V:Super Skrull. 4.00
376 DK,BMc,Green Hulk,Grey
    Hulk & Banner fight 5.00
377 DK,BMc,New Green Hulk,
    combination of green, grey, and
    Bruce Banner,A:Ringmaster . . 11.00
377a 2nd printing (gold). 5.00
378 V:Rhino,Christmas Issue 3.00
379 DK,MFm,I:Pantheon 4.00
380 A:Nick Fury,D:Crazy-8 . . . . 3.00
381 DK,MFm,Hulk,J:Pantheon 4.00
382 DK,MFm,A:Pantheon 4.00
383 DK,MFm,Infinity Gauntlet 4.00
384 DK,MFm,Infinity Gauntlet 4.00
385 DK,MFm,Infinity Gauntlet 4.00
386 DK,MFm,V:Sabra,A:Achilles . . . 4.00
387 DK,MFm,V:Sabra,A:Achilles . . . 4.00
388 DK,MFm,I:Speed Freak,Jim
    Wilson,revealed to have AIDS. . 5.00
389 1st Comic art By Gary Barker
    (Garfield),A:Man-Thing,Glob . . . 4.00
390 DK,MFm,B:War & Pieces,
    C:X-Factor 4.00
391 DK,MFm,V:X-Factor 4.00
392 DK,MFm,E:War & Pieces,
    A:X-Factor 4.00
393 DK,MFm,R:Igor,A:Soviet Super
    Soldiers,30th Ann.,Green foil(c) 6.00
393a 2nd printing,Silver 2.50
394 MFm(i),F:Atalanta,I:Trauma . . 3.00
395 DK,MFm,A:Punisher,
    I:Mr.Frost 3.00
396 DK,MFm,A:Punisher,
    V:Mr.Frost 3.00
397 DK,MFm,B:Ghost of the
    Past,V:U-Foes,A:Leader 3.00
398 DK,MFm,D:Marlo,V:Leader. . . . 3.00
399 JD,A:FF,Dr.Strange 3.00
400 JD,MFm,E:Ghost of the Past,
    V:Leader,1st Holo-grafx(c),1st
    GFr Hulk(pin-up) 3.50
400a 2nd Printing. 4.00
401 JDu,O:Agememnon 3.00
402 JDu,V:Juggernaut 3.00

Incredible Hulk #452
© Marvel Entertainment Group

403 GFr,V:Red Skull,A:Avengers. . . 3.00
404 GFr,V:Red Skull,Juggernaut,
    A:Avengers 3.50
405 GFr,Ajax vs. Achilles. 3.00
406 GFr,V:Captain America 3.00
407 GFr,I:Piecemeal,A:Madman,
    B:O:Ulysses. 3.00
408 GFr,V:Madman,Piecemeal,
    D:Perseus,A:Motormouth,
    Killpower 3.00
409 GFr,A:Motormouth,Killpower,
    V:Madman 3.00
410 GFr,A:Nick Fury,S.H.I.E.L.D.,
    Margo agrees to marry Rick . . . 3.00
411 GFr,V:Nick Fury,S.H.I.E.L.D. . . 3.00
412 PaP,V:Bi-Beast,A:She-Hulk. . . 3.00
413 GFr,CaS,B:Troyjan War,
    I:Cassiopea,Armageddon,
    V:Trauma 3.00
414 GFr,CaS,V:Trauma,C:S.Surfer . 3.00
415 GFr,CaS,V:Trauma,A:Silver
    Surfer,Starjammers 3.00
416 GFr,CaS,E:Troyjan War,D:Trauma,
    A:S.Surfer,Starjammers 3.00
417 GFr,CaS,Rick's/Marlo's Bachelor/
    Bachelorette Party. 5.00
418 GFr,CaS,W:Rick & Marlo,
    A:Various Marvel persons,
    Die Cut(c) 5.00
418a Newsstand ed. 4.00
419 CaS,V:Talos 3.00
420 GFr,CaS,AIDS Story,
    D:Jim Wilson 3.50
421 CaS,B:Myth Conceptions 3.00
422 GFr,Myth Conceptions,pt.2 . . . . 3.00
423 GFr,CaS,Myth Concept.,pt.3. . . 3.00
424 B:Fall of the Hammer 3.00
425 Regular edition 3.00
425a Enhanced cover 4.00
426 PDa,LSh,R:Mercy 3.00
426a Deluxe edition 3.00
427 A:Man-Thing 4.00
427a Deluxe edition 8.00
428 Suffer The Children. 3.00
429 Abortion Issue 3.00
430 A:Speed Freak 3.00
431 PDa,LSh R:Abomination. 3.00
432 V:Abomination. 3.00
433 PDd,V:Abomination. 3.00
434 Funeral of the Year 3.00
435 Hulk vs. Rhino baseball 4.00
436 PDd,AMe,Ghosts of the
    Future,pt.1 . . . . 3.00
437 PDd,AMe,Ghosts of the
    Future,pt.2 . . . . 3.00
438 PDd,AMe,Ghosts of the
    Future,pt.3 . . . . 3.00
439 PDd,AMe,Ghosts of the
    Future,pt.4 . . . . 3.00
440 PDd,AMe. 3.00
441 PDd,AMe,A:She-Hulk 3.00
442 A:Molecule Man, She-Hulk 3.00
443 Janis 3.00
444 Onslaught saga, V:Cable 4.50
445 Onslaught saga. 4.00
446 Blamed for loss of Fantastic
    Four and Avengers 3.50
447 PDd,MD2,F:Unleashed Hulk. . . 4.00
447a Variant Tank Smashing cover . 7.50
448 PDd,MD2,V:The Pantheon 3.00
449 PDd,MD2,I:Thunderbolts 10.00
450 PDd,MD2,F:Doctor Strange,
    56pg. 6.00
451 PDd,MD2, ... 3.00
452 PDd,MD2, ... 3.00
453 PDd,MD2,V:Future Hulk 3.00
454 PDd,AKu,MFm,A God,
    In Savage Land 3.00
455 PDd,AKu,MFm,in X-Mansion . . 3.00
456 PDd,AKu,MFm,A:Apocalypse . . 3.00
457 PDd,Hulk vs. Juggernaut 3.00
458 PDd,AKu,MFm,V:Mercy 3.00

459 PDd,AKu,MFm,V:Abomination . 3.00
460 PDa,AKu,MFm, Return of Bruce
    Banner. 4.00
461 PDa,V:Thunderbolt Ross 3.00
462 PDa,AKu,MFm,V:Thunderbolt
    Ross 3.00
463 PDa,AKu,MFm,V:Thunderbolt
    Ross 3.00
464 PDa,AKu,MFm,V:Troygens &
    Silver Surfer. 3.00
465 PDa,MFm,Poker game 3.00
466 PDa,AKu,MFm,tragic loss. 6.00
467 PDa,AKu,MFm,Hulk attempts
    suicide 6.00
468 JoC,new direction 2.50
469 JoC,LMa,F:Super-Adaptoid . . . 3.00
470 JoC,NMa,V:Ringmaster
    & Circus of Crime 2.50
471 JoC,NMa,Circus of
    Crime,concl.. . . . . 2.50
472 JoC,Great Astonishment,pt.1 . . 2.50
473 JoC,Great Astonishment,pt.2 . . 2.50
474 JoC,Great Astonishment,pt.3 . . 4.00
Spec.#1 A:Inhumans (1968) 125.00
Spec.#2 rep.O:Hulk,A:Leader
    (1969) 75.00
Spec.#3 rep.A:Leader (1971). 25.00
Spec.#4 IR:Hulk/Banner (1972). . 25.00
Ann.#5 V:Xemnu,Diablo (1976). . . 18.00
Ann.#6 HT,A:Dr.Strange,I:Paragon
    (Her) (1977). 12.00
Ann.#7 JBy,BL,A:Angel,Iceman
    A:Doc.Samson (1978). 12.00
Ann.#8 Alpha Flight (1979) 12.00
Ann.#9 Checkmate (1980). 6.00
Ann.#10 A:Captain Universe (1981) 6.00
Ann.#11 RB,JSt,A:Spider-Man,
    Avengers,V:Unis (1982) 5.00
Ann.#12 (1983) 4.00
Ann.#13 (1984) 4.00
Ann.#14 JBy,SB (1985) 4.00
Ann.#15 V:Abomitation (1986). . . . 4.00
Ann.#16 HT,Life Form #3,
    A:Mercy (1990) 4.00
Ann.#17 Subterran.Odyssey #2
    (1991) 4.00
Ann.#18 KM,TA,TC(1st Work),Return
    of the Defenders,Pt.1 (1992). . . 7.00
Ann.#19 I:Lazarus,w/card (1993). . 4.00
Ann.#20 SvL,SI (1994) 4.00
Ann.'98 F:Hulk&Sub-Mariner, 48pg . 3.00
Ann. Hulk 1999 . . . . 3.50
Marvel Milestone rep. #1 (1991) . . 3.00
G-Size#1 rep. Greatest Foes. . . . 10.00
Minus 1 Spec., PDd,AKu,MFm,
    flashback 3.00
Spec. '97 Onslaught aftermath . . . 3.00
Spec. Incredible Hulk
    vs. Superman, 48-pg. 6.00
Spec. Hulk vs. Superman, signed . 20.00
Milestone #181, F:Wolverine 3.00
Hulk vs. Thing, rep. 4.00
TPB Ground Zero rep.. . . . . 13.00
TPB Future Imperfect, PDd,GP . . . 12.00
TPB Ghosts of the Past, rep.. . . . . 12.00
TPB Transformations, 176pg. 12.00
TPB Beauty and the Beast 17.00

INCREDIBLE HULK: FUTURE IMPERFECT
1993

1 GP,V:Maestro. 10.00
2 GP,V:Maestro. 8.00
TPB Rep.. 13.00

INCREDIBLE HULK MEGAZINE

TPB six stories, 96pg. 4.00

Incredible Hulk Future Imperfect GN #1
© Marvel Entertainment Group

INCREDIBLE HULK/PITT
1997
Spec. PDd,DK,x-over. 6.00

INCREDIBLE HULK
VS. WOLVERINE
Oct., 1986
1 HT,rep. #181 B:,V:Wolverine. . . 12.00
1a 2nd printing 4.00

INDEPENDENCE DAY
1996
0 . . . . 5.00
1 and 2 . . . . @2.50
TPB rep. #0 #2, 96pg 7.00

[Further Adventures of]
INDIANA JONES
Jan., 1983–Mar., 1986
1 JBy/TA 3.00
2 JBy/TA 2.50
3 . . . . 2.50
4 KGa 2.50
5 KGa 2.50
6 HC/TA 2.50
7 thru 24 KGa . . . . @2.50
25 thru 34 SD. . . . . @2.50

INDIANA JONES AND
THE LAST CRUSADE
1 B&W,Mag.,movie adapt, 1989. . . 3.00
[Mini-Series], 1989
1 Rep., Movie adapt., 1989. . . . . . 3.50
2 Rep., Movie adapt. 3.50
3 Rep., Movie adapt. 3.50
4 Rep., Movie adapt. 3.50

INDIANA JONES AND
THE TEMPLE OF DOOM
1984
1 Movie adapt. 3.00
2 Movie adapt. 3.00
3 Movie adapt. 3.00

INFINITY ABYSS
June, 2002
1 (of 6) JSn,AM,V:Thanos 3.00
2 JSn,AM,F:Adam Warlock. 3.00

3 JSn,AM,Spider-Man,Capt.Marvel 3.00
4 JSn,AM,Eternity & Infinity 3.00
5 JSn,AM 3.00
6 48-pg.. 3.50
TPB JSn, rep. 18.00

INFINITY CRUSADE
1993
1 RLm,AM,I:Goddess,A:Marvel
   Heroes,foil(c). 4.00
2 RLm,AM,V:Goddess 3.00
3 RLm,AM,V:Goddess,Mephisto. . . 3.00
4 RLm,AM,V:Goddess,A:Magnus . . 3.00
5 RLm,AM,V:Goddess 3.00
6 RLm,AM,V:Goddess 3.00

INFINITY GAUNTLET
July, 1991
1 GP,O:Infinity Gauntlet 5.00
2 GP,JRu,2nd Rebirth:Warlock 4.00
3 GP,JRu,I:Terraxia. 4.00
4 GP,JRu,RLm,V:Thanos 4.00
5 JRu,RLm,V:Thanos,D:Terraxia . . 4.00
6 RLm,JRu,V:Nebula 4.00
TPB rep. #1 thru #6 . . . . 25.00
TPB GP,rep. #1–#6 (2002). 25.00

INFINITY WAR
1992
1 RLm,AM,R:Magus,Thanos 5.00
2 RLm,AM,V:Magus,A:Everyone . . 3.00
3 RLm,AM,V:Magus,A:Everyone . . 2.50
4 RLm,AM,Magus gets Gauntlet . . 2.50
5 RLm,AM,V:Magus 2.50
6 RLm,AM,V:Magus 2.50

INHUMANOIDS
Star, Jan.–July, 1987
1 Hasbro Toy. 3.00
2 O:Inhumanoids 3.00
3 V:D'Compose. 3.00
4 A:Sandra Shore 3.00

INHUMANS
Oct., 1975
1 GP,V:Blastaar. 30.00
2 GP,V:Blastaar. 15.00
3 GP,I:Kree S 20.00
4 GK,Maximus 20.00
5 CK,V:Maximus 20.00
6 GK,Maximus 20.00
7 GK,DP,I:Skorrn 20.00
8 GP,DP,Skorrn 20.00
9 rep., V:Mor-Tog 20.00
10 KP,D:Warkon.. . . . . 20.00
11 KP,JM,I:Pursuer 20.00
12 KP,Hulk. 20.00
Spec.#1(The Untold Saga),
   O:Inhumans. 4.00
Spec. Atlantis Rising story 3.00

INHUMANS
Sept., 1998
1 (of 12) PJe,JaL,F:Black Bolt,
   Medusa, Karnak, Triton, Gorgon,
   Crystal, Lockjaw 9.00
2 PJe,JaL,F:Tonaje 4.00
2a Variant cover 3.00
3 PJe,JaL,Attilan's dark side 3.00
4 PJe,JaL,War against Attilan. 3.00
5 PJe,JaL,Earth vs. Attilan 3.00
6 PJe,JaL,V:Maximus 3.00
7 PJe,JaL,F:Black Bolt 3.00
8 PJe,JaL,F:Lockjaw. 3.00
9 PJe,JaL,F:Triton. 3.00
10 PJe,JaL,F:Woz & Medusa 3.00
11 PJe,JaL,F:Black Bolt. 3.00
12 PJe,JaL,concl.. . . . . 3.00
TPB 264pg. 25.00

INHUMANS
Apr. 2000
1 (of 4) V:Ronan the Accuser 3.00
2 A:Kree 3.00
3 Maximus the Mad 3.00
4 concl.. . . . . 3.00

INHUMANS
May, 2003
1 Lunar,pt.1. . . . . 2.50
2 Lunar,pt.2. . . . . 2.50
3 Lunar,pt.3. . . . . 2.50
4 Culture Shock,pt.1 . . . . 2.50
5 Culture Shock,pt.2 . . . . 2.50
6 Culture Shock,pt.3 . . . . 2.50
7 San finds love 3.00
8 Alaris 3.00
9 No Matter the Cost,pt.1 . . . . 3.00
10 No Matter the Cost,pt.2 . . . . . . 3.00
11 No Matter the Cost,pt.3. . . . . . . 3.00
12 No Matter the Cost,pt.4 . . . . . . 3.00
TPB Vol. 1 Lunar 15.00

INTERFACE
Epic, Dec., 1989
1 ESP 2.50
2 thru 8 . . . . @2.25

Invaders #38
© Marvel Entertainment Group

INVADERS
Aug., 1975
1 FR,JR(c),A:Invaders,
   A:Mastermind 75.00
2 FR,JR(c),I:Brain Drain 25.00
3 FR,JR(c),I:U-Man. 25.00
4 FR,O&V:U-Man 25.00
5 RB,JM,V:Red Skull 25.00
6 FR,V:Liberty Legion 25.00
7 FR,I:Baron Blood,
   1st Union Jack. 25.00
8 FR,FS,J:Union Jack. 15.00
9 FR,FS,O:Baron Blood 15.00
10 FR,FS,rep.Captain
   America Comics #22 . . . . 15.00
11 FR,FS,I:Blue Bullet 10.00
12 FR,FS,I:Spitfire 10.00
13 FR,FS,GK(c),I:Golem,
   Half Face 10.00
14 FR,FS,JK(c),I:Crusaders. 10.00
15 FR,FS,JK(c),V:Crusaders 10.00
16 FR,JK(c),V:Master Man 10.00
17 FR,FS,GK(c),I:Warrior Woman . 10.00

MARVEL

MARVEL

18 FR,FS,GK(c),R:1st Destroyer . . 10.00
19 FR,FS,V:Adolph Hitler. 10.00
20 FR,FS,GK(c),I&J:2nd Union Jack,
    BU:rep.Marvel Comics #1 . . . . 15.00
21 FR,FS,GK(c),BU:rep.Marvel
    Mystery #10. . . . . 10.00
22 FR,FS,GK(c),O:Toro 8.00
23 FR,FS,GK(c),I:Scarlet Scarab . . 8.00
24 FR,FS,GK(c),rep.Marvel
    Mystery #17. . . . . 10.00
25 FR,FS,GK(c),V:Scarlet Scarab . . 8.00
26 FR,FS,GK(c),V:Axis Agent 8.00
27 FR,FS,GK(c),V:Axis Agent 8.00
28 FR,FS,I:2nd Human Top,
    Golden Girl,Kid Commandos. . . 8.00
29 FR,FS,I:Teutonic Knight 8.00
30 FR,FS,V:Teutonic Knight. 8.00
31 FR,FS,V:Frankenstein 8.00
32 FR,FS,JK(c),A:Thor 10.00
33 FR,FS,JK(c),A:Thor 10.00
34 FR,FS,V:Master Man 8.00
35 FR,FS,I:Iron Cross 8.00
36 FR,FS,O:Iron Cross 8.00
37 FR,FS,V:Iron Cross. 8.00
38 FR,FS,V:Lady Lotus 8.00
39 FR,FS,O:Lady Lotus 8.00
40 FR,FS,V:Baron Blood 8.00
41 E:RTs(s)FR,FS,V:Super Axis,
    double-size 18.00
Ann.#1 A:Avengers,R:Shark 50.00
G-Size#1 FR,rep.Submariner #1 . . 25.00

[Limited Series], 1993
1 R:Invaders 2.50
2 V:Battle Axis. 2.50
3 R:Original Vison (1950's). 2.50
4 V:The Axis 2.50

INVADERS
June, 2004
0 Once an Invader,pt.4 . . . . 3.00
1 To End All Wars,pt.1 . . . . 3.00
2 To End All Wars,pt.2 . . . . 3.00
3 To End All Wars,pt.3 . . . . 3.00
4 To End All Wars,pt.4 . . . . 3.00
5 To End All Wars,pt.5 . . . . 3.00
Becomes:

NEW INVADERS
6 Oil & Water,pt.1,A:Wolverine 3.00
7 Cruel and Unusual,pt.1 . . . . 3.00
8 Cruel and Unusual,pt.2 . . . . 3.00
9 Cruel and unusual, concl. 3.00
TPB To End All Wars 20.00

IRON FIST
Nov., 1975
1 JBy,A:Iron Man 90.00
2 JBy,V:H'rythl. 50.00
3 JBy,KP,KJ,V:Ravager. 30.00
4 JBy,V:Radion 30.00
5 JBy,V:Scimitar 30.00
6 JBy,O:Misty Knight. 30.00
7 JBy,V:Khimbala Bey. 30.00
8 JBy,V:Chaka 30.00
9 JBy,V:Chaka 30.00
10 JBy,DGr,A:Chaka 30.00
11 JBy,V:Wrecking Crew 30.00
12 JBy,DGr,V:Captain America . . . 30.00
13 JBy,A:Boomerang 25.00
14 JBy,I:Sabretooth 200.00
15 JBy,A&N:Wolverine,A:X-Men
    Sept., 1977 . . . . 90.00
Marvel Milestone rep. #14 (1992) . . 4.00

IRON FIST
May, 1998
1 (of 3) DJu,JG, from Heroes For
    Hire 3.00
2 DJu,JG,search for Scorpio Key,
    V:S.H.I.E.L.D. 3.00
3 DJu,JG,concl. 3.00

Iron Fist 1st Series #3
© Marvel Entertainment Group

IRON FIST
March, 2004
1 Breathless,pt.1. . . . . 3.00
2 thru 6 Breathless,pt.2–pt.6. . . . @3.00

IRON FIST/WOLVERINE
Sept., 2000
1 (of 4) F:DannyRand,Junzo Moto . 3.00
2 K'un L'un 3.00
3 A:Capt.America,Dragon Kings. . . 3.00
4 concl. 3.00

IRON MAN
May, 1968
1 B:StL,AGw(s),JCr,GC,
    I:Mordius. 1,200.00
2 JCr,I:Demolisher 300.00
3 JCr,V:The Freak. 400.00
4 JCr,A:Unicorn. 350.00
5 JCr,GT,I:Cerebos 300.00
6 JCr,GT,V:Crusher. 250.00
7 JCr,GT,V:Gladiator. 250.00
8 JCr,GT,O:Whitney Frost. 250.00
9 JCr,GT,A:Mandarin 250.00
10 JCr,GT,V:Mandarin 250.00
11 JCr,GT,V:Mandarin 200.00
12 JCr,GT,I:Controller 200.00
13 JCr,GT,A:Nick Fury 200.00
14 JCr,V:Night Phantom 200.00
15 JCr,GT,A:Red Ghost 200.00
16 JCr,GT,V:Unicorn 175.00
17 JCr,GT,I:Madam Masque,
    Midas. 175.00
18 JCr,GT,V:Madame Masque. . . 175.00
19 JCr,GT,V:Madame Masque. . . 175.00
20 JCr,I:Charlie Gray 175.00
21 JCr,I:Eddie 35.00
22 JCr,D:Janice Cord. 35.00
23 JCr,I:Mercenary. 38.00
24 JCr,GT,V:Madame Masque . . . 35.00
25 JCr,A:Sub-Mariner 38.00
26 JCr,DH,J:Val-Larr 35.00
27 JCr,DH,I:Firebrand 35.00
28 E:AGw(s),JCr,DH,
    V:Controller 35.00
29 B:StL,AyB(s),DH,V:Myrmidon . . 35.00
30 DH,I:Monster Master. 35.00
31 DH,I:Mastermind. 35.00
32 GT,I:Mechanoid. 35.00
33 DH,I:Spy Master 35.00
34 DH,A:Spy Master 35.00
35 DH,A:Daredevil,Spy Master . . . 35.00
36 E:AyB(s),DH,I:Ramrod 35.00

37 DH,A:Ramrod 35.00
38 GT,Jonah. 35.00
39 HT,I:White Dragon 30.00
40 GT,A:White Dragon. 30.00
41 GT,JM,I:Slasher 30.00
42 GT,I:Mikas. 30.00
43 GT,JM,A:Mikas,I:Guardsmen . . 50.00
44 GT,A:Capt.America 30.00
45 GT,A:Guardsman 30.00
46 GT,D:Guardsman 30.00
47 BS,JM,O:Iron Man 35.00
48 GT,V:Firebrand 22.00
49 GT,V:Adaptoid 22.00
50 B:RTs(s),GT,V:Prin.Python . . . 22.00
51 GT,C:Capt.America. 22.00
52 GT,I:Raga 22.00
53 GT,JSn,I:Black Lama 22.00
54 GT,BEv,Sub-Mariner,I:Madame
    MacEvil (Moondragon) 50.00
55 JSn,I:Destroyer,Thanos,Mentor
    Starfox(Eros),Blood Bros. . . . 225.00
56 JSn,I:Fangor. 45.00
57 GT,R:Mandarin 20.00
58 GT,V:Mandarin 20.00
59 GT,A:Firebrand 20.00
60 GT,C:Daredevil 20.00
61 GT,Marauder 20.00
62 whiplash 20.00
63 GT,A:Dr.Spectrum 20.00
64 GT,I:Rokk 20.00
65 GT,O:Dr.Spectrum. 20.00
66 GT,V:Thor 30.00
67 GT,V:Freak 20.00
68 GT,O:Iron Man 16.00
69 GT,V:Mandarin 15.00
70 GT,A:Sunfire 15.00
71 GT,V:Yellow Claw 15.00
72 E:RTs(s),GT,V:Black Lama . . . 15.00
73 B:LWn(s),KP,JM,V:Titanic
    Three 15.00
74 KP,V:Modok. 15.00
75 V:Black Lama 15.00
76 Rep., A:Hulk 15.00
77 V:Thinker. 15.00
78 GT,V:Viet Cong 15.00
79 GT,I:Quasar(not Current one). . 15.00
80 JK(c),O:Black Lama 15.00
81 A:Black Lama 15.00
82 MSe,A:Red Ghost 15.00
83 E:LWn(s),HT,MSe,Red Ghost. . 15.00
84 HT,A:Dr.Ritter 15.00
85 HT,MSe,A:Freak 15.00
86 B:MWn(s),GT,I:Blizzard. 15.00
87 GT,V:Blizzard 15.00
88 E:MWn(s),GT,
    V:Blood Brothers. 15.00
89 GT,A:D.D.,Blood Bros. 15.00
90 JK(c),GT,Controller,A:Thanos . . 14.00
91 GT,BL,A:Controller 12.00
92 JK(c),GT,V:Melter 12.00
93 JK(c),HT,V:Kraken 12.00
94 JK(c),HT,V:Kraken 12.00
95 JK(c),GT,PP,V:Ultimo 12.00
96 GT,DP,V:Ultimo 12.00
97 GT,DP,I:Guardsman II. 12.00
98 GT,DP,A:Sunfire 12.00
99 GT,V:Mandarin 12.00
100 JSn(c),GT,V:Mandarin. 35.00
101 GT,I:Dread Knight 14.00
102 GT,O:Dread Knight 14.00
103 GT,V:Jack of Hearts 14.00
104 GT,V:Midas 9.00
105 GT,V:Midas 9.00
106 GT,V:Midas 9.00
107 KP,V:Midas 9.00
108 CI,A:Growing Man 9.00
109 JBy(c),CI,V:Van Guard 9.00
110 KP,I:C.Arcturus 9.00
111 KP,O:Rigellians 9.00
112 AA,KP,V:Punisher from
    Beyond 9.00
113 KP,HT,V:Unicorn,Spy Master. . 10.00

Iron Man #129
© Marvel Entertainment Group

114 KG,I:Arsenal 9.00
115 JR2,O:Unicorn,V:Ani-men. 9.00
116 JR2,BL,V:Madame Masque . . . 9.00
117 BL,JR2,1st Romita Jr 11.00
118 JBy,BL,A:Nick Fury 12.00
119 BL,JR2,Alcoholic Plot 11.00
120 JR2,BL,A:Sub-Mariner,I:Rhodey
  (becomes War Machine),
  Justin Hammer. 11.00
121 BL,JR2,A:Submariner 10.00
122 DC,CI,BL,O:Iron Man 10.00
123 BL,JR2,V:Blizzard. 10.00
124 BL,JR2,A:Capt.America 8.00
125 BL,JR2,A:Ant-Man 8.00
126 BL,JR2,V:Hammer 8.00
127 BL,JR2,Rattlefield 8.00
128 BL,JR2,Alcohol 20.00
129 SB,A:Dread Night 7.00
130 BL,V:Digital Devil 7.00
131 BL,V:Hulk 10.00
132 BL,V:Hulk 10.00
133 BL,A:Hulk,Ant-Man 7.00
134 BL,V:Titanium Man 7.00
135 BL,V:Titanium Man 7.00
136 V:Endotherm 7.00
137 BL,Fights oil rig fire. 7.00
138 BL,Dreadnought,Spymaster . . . 7.00
139 BL,Dreadnought,Spymaster . . . 7.00
140 BL,V:Force 7.00
141 BL,JR2,V:Force. 7.00
142 BL,JR2,Space Armor 7.00
143 BL,JR2,V:Sunturion 7.00
144 BL,JR2,Sunturion,O:Rhodey. . . 7.00
145 BL,JR2,A:Raiders 7.00
146 BL,JR2,I:Black Lash 7.00
147 BL,JR2,V:Black Lash 7.00
148 BL,JR2,V:Terrorists 7.00
149 BL,JR2,V:Dr.Doom 7.00
150 BL,JR2,V:Dr.Doom,Dble 10.00
151 TA,BL,A:Ant-Man 5.00
152 BL,JR2,New Armor 5.00
153 BL,JR2,V:Living Laser 5.00
154 BL,JR2,V:Unicorn 5.00
155 JR2,V:Back-Getters 5.00
156 JR2,I:Mauler 5.00
157 V:Spores 5.00
158 CI,AM,Iron Man Drowning 5.00
159 PS,V:Diablo. 5.00
160 SD,V:Serpent'sSquad 5.00
161 A:Moon Knight 5.00
162 V:Space Ships. 5.00
163 V:Chessmen 5.00
164 LMc,A:Bishop 5.00
165 LMc,Meltdown. 5.00

166 LMc,V:Melter. 5.00
167 LMc,Alcoholic Issue 5.00
168 LMc,A:Machine Man. 5.00
169 LMc,B:Rhodey as 2nd
  Iron Man 10.00
170 LMc,2nd Iron Man. 8.00
171 LMc,2nd Iron Man. 5.00
172 LMc,V:Firebrand 3.00
173 LMc,Stane International 3.00
174 LMc,Alcoholism. 3.50
175 LMc,Alcoholism. 3.50
176 LMc,Alcoholism. 3.50
177 LMc,Alcoholism. 3.00
178 LMc,V:Wizard 3.00
179 LMc,V:Mandarin 3.00
180 LMc,V:Mandarin 3.00
181 LMc,V:Mandarin 3.00
182 LMc,Secret Wars 3.00
183 LMc,Turning Point. 3.00
184 LMc,Moves to California. 3.00
185 LMc,V:Zodiac Field. 3.00
186 LMc,I:Vibro 3.00
187 LMc,V:Vibro. 3.00
188 LMc,I:New Brother's Grimm . . . 3.00
189 LMc,I:Termite 3.00
190 LMc,O:Termite,A:Scar.Witch. . . 3.00
191 LMc,New Grey Armor 5.00
192 LMc,V:Iron Man(Tony Stark) . . . 5.00
193 LMc,V:Dr.Demonicus 3.00
194 LMc,I:Scourge,A:West Coast
  Avengers 3.00
195 LMc,A:Shaman 3.00
196 LMc,V:Dr.Demonicus 3.00
197 LMc,Secret Wars II 3.00
198 SB,V:Circuit Breaker. 3.00
199 LMc,E:Rhodey as 2nd Iron Man,
  V:Obadiah Stone. 3.00
200 LMc,D:Obadiah Stone. 6.00
201 MBr,V:Madam Masque 3.00
202 A:Ka-Zar 3.00
203 MBr,A:Hank Pym 3.00
204 MBr,V:Madame Masque 3.00
205 MBr,V:A.I.M. 3.00
206 MBr,V:Goliath 3.00
207 MBr,When the Sky Rains Fire . 3.00
208 MBr,V:A.I.M. 3.00
209 V:Living Laser 3.00
210 MBr,V:Morgan LeFey 3.00
211 AS,V:Living Laser 3.00
212 DT,V:Iron Monger 3.00
213 A:Dominic Fortune 3.00
214 A:Spider-Woman. 4.00
215 BL,A.I.M. 4.00
216 BL,MBr,D:Clymenstra. 3.00
217 BL,MRr,V:Hammer 3.00
218 BL,MBr,Titanic. 3.00
219 BL,V:The Ghost 3.00
220 BL,MBr,V:The Ghost,
  D:Spymaster 3.00
221 BL,MBr,V:The Ghost. 3.00
222 BL,MBr,R:Abrogast. 3.00
223 BL,MBr,V:Blizzard,Beetle 3.00
224 BL,V:Justin Hammer,Force. . . . 3.00
225 BL,MBr,B:Armor Wars. 5.00
226 BL,MBr,V:Stingray 4.50
227 BL,MBr,V:Mandroids, ... 4.00
228 BL,MBr,V:Guardsmen 4.00
229 BL,D:Titanium Man 4.00
230 V:Firepower, ... 4.00
231 V:Firepower,N:Iron Man 4.00
232 BWS,Nightmares,E:Armor
  Wars 4.50
233 JG,BL,A:Ant-Man 2.50
234 JG,BL,A:Spider-Man 4.00
235 JG,BL,V:Grey Gargoyle. 3.00
236 JG,BL,V:Grey Gargoyle. 3.00
237 JG,BL,V:SDI Monster 3.00
238 JG,BL,V:Rhino,D:M.Masque . . 2.50
239 JG,BL,R:Ghost 2.50
240 JG,BL,V:Ghost 2.50
241 BL,V:Mandarin 2.50
242 BL,BWS,V:Mandarin 3.00

243 BL,BWS,Stark Paralyzed 3.00
244 BL,V:Fixer,A:Force,double-size 5.00
245 BL(c),V:Dreadnaughts. 2.50
246 BL,HT,V:A.I.M.,Maggia 2.50
247 BL,A:Hulk 4.00
248 BL,Tony Stark Cured. 2.50
249 BL,V:Dr.Doom 2.50
250 BL,V:Dr.Doom,A of V 3.00
251 HT,AM,V:Wrecker,A of V 2.50
252 HT,AM,V:Chemistro,A of V . . . 2.50
253 BL,V:Slagmire 2.50
254 BL,V:Spymaster 2.50
255 HT,V:Devestator
  I:2nd Spymaster 2.50
256 JR2,V:Space Station 2.50
257 V:Samurai Steel 2.50
258 JR2,BWi,B:Armor Wars II,V:
  Titanium Man. 2.50
259 JR2,BWi,V:Titanium Man 2.50
260 JR2,BWi,V:Living Laser 2.50
261 JR2,BWi,A:Mandarin. 2.50
262 JR2,BWi,A:Mandarin. 2.50
263 JR2,BWi,A:Wonderman,
  V:Living Laser 2.50
264 JR2,BWi,A:Mandarin. 2.50
265 JR2,BWi,V:Dewitt. 2.50
266 JR2,BWi,E:Armor Wars II 2.50
267 PR,BWi,B:New O:Iron Man,
  Mandarin,V:Vibro. 2.50
268 PR,BWi,E:New O:Iron Man. . . . 2.50
269 PR,BWi,A:Black Widow 2.50
270 PR,BWi,V:Fin Fang Foom 2.50
271 PR,BWi,V:Fin Fang Foom 2.50
272 PR,BWi,O:Mandarin 2.50
273 PR,BWi,V:Mandarin 2.50
274 MBr,BWi,V:Mandarin. 2.50
275 PR,BWi,A:Mandarin,Fin Fang
  Foom, double-size. 4.00
276 PR,BWi,A:Black Widow 2.50
277 PR,BWi,A:Black Widow 2.50
278 BWi,Galactic Storm,pt.6
  A:Capt.America,V:Shatterax . . . 2.50
279 BWi,Galactic Storm,pt.13,
  V:Ronan,A:Avengers. 2.50
280 KHd,V:The Stark 2.50
281 KHd,I&V:Masters of Silence,
  C:War Machine Armor. 5.00
282 KHd,I:War Machine Armor,
  V:Masters of Silence 4.00
283 KHd,V:Masters of Silence. 2.50
284 KHd,Stark put under Cryogenic
  Freeze,B:Rhodey as Iron Man . 3.50
285 KHd,BWi(i),Tony's Funeral 2.50
286 KHd,V:Avengers West Coast . . 2.50
287 KHd,I:New Atom Smasher 2.50

Iron Man #267
© Marvel Entertainment Group

MARVEL

288 KHd,30th Anniv.,V:Atom
    Smasher,foil(c). 4.50
289 KHd,V:Living Laser,
    R:Tony Stark 2.50
290 KHd,30th Anniv.,N:Iron Man,
    Gold foil(c) 5.00
291 KHd,E:Rhodey as Iron Man,
    Becomes War Machine 2.50
292 KHd,Tony reveals he is alive . 2.50
293 KHd,V:Controller 2.50
294 KHd,Infinity Crusade 2.50
295 KHd,Infinity Crusade. 2.50
296 KHd,V:Modam,A:Omega Red . . 2.50
297 KHd,V:Modam,Omega Red . . . 2.50
298 KHd(c),I:Earth Mover 2.50
299 KHd(c),R:Ultimo 2.50
300 KHd,TMo,N:Iron Man,I:Iron
    Legion,A:War Machine,V:Ultimo
    Foil(c). 5.00
300a Newsstand ed. 2.75
301 KHd,B:Crash and Burn,
    A:Deathlok,C:Venom 2.50
302 KHd,V:Venom 2.50
303 KHd,V:New Warriors,
    C:Thundrstrike 2.50
304 KHd,C:Hulk,V:New Warriors,
    Thundrstrike,N:Iron Man 2.50
305 KHd,V:Hulk, ... 2.50
306 KHd,E:Stark Enterprise. 2.50
307 TMo,I:Vor/Tex,R:Mandarin . . . 2.50
308 TMo,Vor/Tex 2.50
309 TMo,Vor/Tex 2.50
310 regular. 3.00
310a Neon(c),with insert print 3.50
311 V:Mandarin 2.50
312 double-size 3.00
313 LKa,TMo,AA Meeting 2.50
314 LKa,TMo,new villain 2.50
315 A:Black Widow 2.50
316 I:Slag,A:Crimson Dynamo 2.50
317 In Dynamos Armor 3.00
318 LKa,TMo,V:Slag 2.50
319 LKa,TMo,New Space Armor . . . 2.50
320 F:Hawkeye 2.50
321 Cont. From Avg. Crossing 2.50
322 TKa,TheCrossing,V:JackFrost . 2.50
323 TKa,V:Avengers 2.50
324 TKa,The Crossing 2.50
325 TKa,Avengers:Timeslide after. . 3.50
326 First Sign,pt.3 . . . . 2.50
327 Frostbite 2.50
328 TKa,Tony Stark at ColumbiaU. . 2.50
329 Stark Enterprises taken over . . 2.50
330 & 331 . . . . @2.50
332 final issue 4.00
Ann.#1 rep.Iron Man #25 . . . . 45.00
Ann.#2 rep.Iron Man #6. . . . . 25.00
Ann.#3 SB,Manthing 15.00
Ann.#4 DP,GT,V:Modok,
    A:Champions. 10.00
Ann.#5 JBr,A:Black Panther 6.00
Ann.#6 A:Eternals,V:Brother
    Tode. 6.00
Ann.#7 LMc,A:West Coast
    Avengers, I:New Goliath 6.00
Ann.#8 A:X-Factor 6.00
Ann.#9 V:Stratosfire,A:Sunturion . . 5.00
Ann.#10 PS,BL,Atlantis Attacks #2
    A:Sub-Mariner 4.00
Ann.#11 SD,Terminus Factor #2 . . . 4.00
Ann.#12 Subterran.Odyssey #4. . . . 4.00
Ann.#13 GC,AW,Assault on Armor
    City,A:Darkhawk 4.00
Ann.#14 TMo,I:Face Theif,w/card,
    BU:War Machine 4.00
Ann.#15 GC,V:Controller 4.00
Spec.#1 rep.Sub-Mariner x-over . . 40.00
Spec.#2 rep.(1971) 20.00
Marvel Milestone rep. #55 (1992) . 3.00
G-Size#1 Reprints 15.00
1-shot Iron Manual, BSz(c),Guide
    to Iron Man's technology 2.50

1-shot Iron Man/Force Works Collec-
    tors' Preview, Neon wrap-around
    cover, double size, X-over. 2.50
GN Iron Man 2020 . . . . 6.00
TPB Armor Wars rep. 13.00
TPB Many Armors of Iron Man . . 16.00
TPB Power of Iron Man 10.00
TPB Iron Man vs. Dr. Doom, rep. . 13.00

Iron Man 2nd Series #7
© *Marvel Entertainment Group*

[2nd Series], Nov., 1996
1 JLe,SLo,WPo,SW,A:Bruce
    Banner, New O:Hulk,48pg. 4.00
1A variant Hulk showing cover 5.00
1 gold signature ed., bagged 18.00
2 JLe,SLo,WPo,SW 4.00
3 JLe,SLo,WPo,SW,Heroes brawl . 3.00
4 JLe,SLo,WPo,SW,V:Laser. 3.00
4A X-mas cover 5.00
5 JLe,SLo,WPo,SW, Whirlwind. . . . 3.00
6 JLe,SLo,WPo,SW,Industrial
    Revolution, pt.2 x-over 3.00
7 JLe,SLo,WPo,SW,A:Pepper
    Potts,Villain revealed. 3.00
8 JLe,SLo,RBn,fate of Rebel 3.00
9 JLe,SLo,RBn,V:Mandarin 3.00
10 JLe,SLo,RBn,F:The Hulk 3.00
11 JLb,RBn,V:Dr. Doom,A:Hydra. . . 3.00
12 WPo,JLe,JLb,F:Dr. Doom,
    Galactus 3.00
13 JeR,LSn,Wildstorm x-over 3.00

[3rd Series], 1997
1 SCh,KBk,V:Mastermind,48-pg. . . 5.00
2 KBk,SCh,in Switzerland. 3.50
3 KBk,SCh,V:Hydra Dreadnought
    Robot. 3.00
4 KBk,SCh,R:Firebrand 3.00
5 KBk,SCh,V:Firebrand. 3.00
6 KBk,F:Black Widow 3.00
7 KBk,SCh,Live Kree or Die,pt.1
    x-over. 3.00
8 KBk,SCh,secret identity out. 3.00
9 KBk,SCh,A:Black Widow 3.00
10 KBk,SCh,A:Avengers 3.00
11 KBk,SCh,A:Warbird &
    War Machine. 3.00
12 KBk,V:War Machine 3.00
13 KBk,SCh,V:Controller,48-pg. . . . 4.00
13a signed. 20.00
14 KBk,SCh,Fant.Four x-over 3.00
15 KBk,SCh,V:Nitro 3.00
16 KBk,RSt,V:Dragon Lord 3.00
17 KBk,RSt,SCh,V:Fin Fang Foom . 3.00
18 KBk,RSt,SCh,V:War Machine. . . 3.00
19 KBk,RSt,SCh,V:War Machine. . . 3.00

20 KBk,RSt,SCh,V:War Machine . . . 3.00
21 KBk,RSt,TGu,MBa,
    Eighth Day prologue 3.00
22 KBk,RSt,Eighth Day,pt.2,
    I:Carnivore 3.00
23 KBk,RSt,UltimateDanger,pt.1 . . 3.00
24 KBk,RSt,UltimateDanger,pt.2 . . 3.25
25 KBk,RSt,Ultimate
    Danger,pt.3, 48-pg. 3.50
26 JQ,Mask of Iron Man,pt.1 . . . . . 2.50
27 JQ,Mask of Iron Man,pt.2 . . . . . 2.50
28 JQ,Mask of Iron Man,pt.3 . . . . . 2.50
29 JQ,Mask of Iron Man,pt.4 . . . . . 2.50
30 JQ,Mask of Iron Man,pt.5 . . . . . 2.50
31 JQ,Sons of Yinsen,pt.1 . . . . 2.50
32 JQ,Sons of Yinsen,pt.2. . . . . . . 2.50
33 JQ,Sons of Yinsen,pt.3 . . . . 2.50
34 JQ,Dr. Power 2.50
35 JQ,Maximum Security. 2.50
36 CDi,PR 2.50
37 JQ,F:Tyberius Stone 2.50
38 R:classic foe 2.50
39 MPn,Remote Control 2.50
40 MPn,Remote Control 2.50
41 new art team 2.50
42 Big Bang Theory,pt.1 . . . . 2.50
43 Big Bang Theory,pt.2 . . . . 2.50
44 Big Bang,pt.3,new armor 2.50
45 Big Bang Theory,pt.4 . . . . 2.50
46 Frankenstein Syndrome,pt.1
    100-pages 4.00
47 IaC,Frankenstein Syndrome . . . 2.25
48 IaC,Frankenstein Syndrome . . . 2.25
49 CsB,V:Titanium Man 2.25
50 MGr,48-pg. 4.00
51 MGr,Jane Doe,pt.1 . . . . 2.25
52 MGr,Jane Doe,pt.2 . . . . 2.25
53 MGr,Book of Ten Rings. 2.25
54 MGr,Temugin. 2.25
55 MGr,would be #400 issue,54-pg. 4.00
56 MGr,fall-out begins 2.25
57 MGr,fight on, fight on 2.25
58 MGr 2.25
59 MGr,In Shining Armor 2.25
60 MGr,In Shining Armor,pt.2. . . . . 2.25
61 MGr,In Shining Armor,pt.3. . . . . 2.25
62 MGr,You Can't Always Get,pt.1 . 2.25
63 MGr,You Can't Always Get,pt.2 . 2.25
64 AD,MFm,MGr,Standoff,pt.1 . . . . 2.25
65 MGr,Manhunt,pt.1 . . . . 2.25
66 MGr,Manhunt,pt.2 . . . . 2.25
67 MGr,Manhunt,pt.3 . . . . 3.00
68 MGr,Manhunt,pt.4 . . . . 3.00
69 MGr,Manhunt,pt.5 . . . . 3.00
70 Vegal Bleeds Neon,pt.1. . . . . . . 3.00
71 Vegas Bleeds Neon,pt.2 . . . . . . 3.00
72 Vegas Bleeds Neon,pt.3 . . . . . . 3.00
73 The Best Defense,pt.1 . . . . 3.00
74 The Best Defense,pt.2 . . . . 3.00
75 Secretary of Defense? 3.00
76 The Best Defense,pt.4 . . . . 3.00
77 The Best Defense,pt.5 . . . . 3.00
78 The Best Defense,pt.6 . . . . 3.00
79 The Deep End,pt.1 . . . . 3.00
80 The Deep End,pt.2 . . . . 3.00
81 The Deep End,pt.3 . . . . 3.00
82 The Deep End,pt.4 . . . . 3.00
83 F:Titanium Man 3.00
84 Top-secret materials 5.00
85 Top-secret materials 5.00
86 Singularity,pt.1 . . . . 3.00
87 Singularity,pt.2 . . . . 3.00
88 Singularity,pt.3 . . . . 3.00
89 Singularity,pt.4 . . . . 3.00
Ann.1998 Iron Man/Captain
    America, KBk,MWa, 48-pg. 3.50
Ann.1999 KBk,JoC,48-pg. 3.50
Ann.2000 Sons of Yin-Sen,pt.3 . . . . 3.50
Ann.2001 CCI,48-pg. 3.00
Spec.#1 Age of Innocence, Avengers:
    Timeslide 2.50
TPB The Mask in the Iron Man . . . 15.00

IRON MAN
Nov., 2004

1 WEI,Extremis 3.00
2 WEI,Extremis 3.00
3 WEI,Extremis 3.00
4 WEI,Extremis 3.00
5 WEI,Extremis 3.00
6 WEI,Extremis 3.00
7 The List 3.00
7a variant (c) 7.00
8 The List 3.00
9 SHa,Execute Program 3.00
10 SHa,Execute Program 3.00
11 SHa,Execute Program 3.00
12 SHa,Execute Program 3.00
13 SHa,Civil War tie-in 3.00
14 SHa,Civil War tie-in 3.00

IRON MAN & SUBMARINER
April, 1968

1 GC, 2 stories 450.00

IRON MAN: BAD BLOOD
July, 2000

1 (of 4) BL,DvM,V:JustinHammer . . 3.00
2 BL,DvM,Spymaster 3.00
3 BL,DvM,James Rhodes 3.00
4 BL,DvM,Justin Hammer 3.00

IRON MAN: HOUSE OF M
July, 2005

1 (of 3) 3.00
2 . . . . 3.00
3 finale 3.00

IRON MAN: INEVITABLE
Dec., 2005

1 JoC 3.00
2 thru 6 . . . . @3.00
TPB Iron Man: Inevitable 15.00

IRON MAN: THE IRON AGE
June, 1998

1 (of 2) KBk,48pg bookshelf 6.00
2 KBk,48pg bookshelf, concl. 6.00

ISLAND OF DR. MOREAU
Oct., 1977

1 GK(c),movie adapt. 8.00

IT'S A DUCK'S LIFE
Feb., 1950

1 F;Buck Duck,Super Rabbit . . . 150.00
2 . . . . 100.00
3 thru 11 . . . . @100.00

JACK KIRBY'S GALACTIC BOUNTY HUNTERS
Icon, July, 2006

1 JK, 56-pg. 4.00
2 JK 3.00
3 JK 3.00
4 JK 3.00

JACK OF HEARTS
Jan., 1984

1 thru 4 . . . . @2.50

JAMES BOND JR.
1992

1 I&O:JamesBondJr.(TVseries) . . . 3.00
2 thru 12 . . . . @2.25

Jack of Hearts #2
© Marvel Entertainment Group

JANN OF THE JUNGLE
See: JUNGLE TALES

JEANIE COMICS
See: DARING MYSTERY

JIHAD
Epic

1 Cenobites vs. Nightbreed 4.50
2 E:Cenobites vs. Nightbreed 4.50

JLA/AVENGERS
Marvel/DC, Sept., 2003

1 KBk,GP(c),x-over,48-pg. 6.00
3 KBk,GP,x-over,48-pg. 6.00

JOHN CARTER, WARLORD OF MARS
June, 1977

1 GK,DC,O:John Carter,Created
    by Edgar Rice Burroughs 20.00
2 GK/DC(c),GK,RN, White Apes
    of Mars 7.00
3 GK,RN,Requiem for a Warlord . . 7.00
4 GK,RN, Raiding Party 7.00
5 GK,RN,Giant Battle Issue 7.00
6 GK/DC(c),GK,Alone Against a
    World 7.00
7 GK,TS,Showdown 7.00
8 GK,RN,Beast With Touch of
    Stone 7.00
9 GK,RN,Giant Battle Issue 7.00
10 GK,The Death of Barsoom? 7.00
11 RN,O:Dejah Thoris 7.00
12 RN,City of the Dead 7.00
13 RN,March of the Dead 7.00
14 RN,The Day Helium Died 7.00
15 RN,GK,Prince of Helium
    Returns 7.00
16 RN,John Carters Dilemna 7.00
17 BL,What Price Victory 10.00
18 FM,Tars Tarkas Battles Alone . . 7.00
19 RN(c),War With the Wing Men . . 7.00
20 RN(c),Battle at the Bottom
    of the World 7.00
21 RN(c),The Claws of the Banth . . 7.00
22 RN(c),The Canyon of Death 7.00
23 Murder on Mars 7.00
24 GP/TA(c),Betrayal 7.00
25 Inferno 7.00
26 Death Cries the Guild of
    Assassins 7.00

27 Death Marathon 7.00
28 Guardians of the Lost
    City Oct., 1979 . . . . 7.00
Ann.#1 RN(c),GK,Battle story 7.00
Ann.#2 RN(c),GK,Outnumbered . . . 7.00
Ann.#3 RN(c),GK,Battle story 7.00

JOKER COMICS
Marvel Timely, April, 1942

1 BW,I&B:Powerhouse Pepper,
    A:Stuporman 5,000.00
2 BW,I:Tessie the Typist 2,000.00
3 BW,A:Tessie the Typist,
    Squat Car Squad 1,500.00
4 BW,Squat Car (c) 1,400.00
5 BW,same 1,400.00
6 BW, ... 1,000.00
7 BW 1,000.00
8 BW 1,000.00
9 BW 1,000.00
10 BW,Shooting Gallery (c) . . . 1,000.00
11 BW 1,000.00
12 BW 1,000.00
13 BW 1,000.00
14 BW 1,000.00
15 BW 1,000.00
16 BW 1,000.00
17 BW 1,000.00
18 BW 1,000.00
19 BW 1,000.00
20 BW 1,000.00
21 BW 1,000.00
22 BW 1,000.00
23 BW,HK,Hey Look 1,000.00
24 BW,HK,Laff Favorites 800.00
25 BW,HK,same 1,100.00
26 BW,HK,same 1,100.00
27 BW 1,100.00
28 . . . . 250.00
29 BW 1,100.00
30 BW 1,100.00
31 BW 1,100.00
32 B:Millie,Hedy 250.00
33 HK 275.00
34 . . . . 250.00
35 HK 275.00
36 HK 250.00
37 . . . . 250.00
38 . . . . 250.00
39 . . . . 250.00
40 . . . . 250.00
41 A:Nellie the Nurse 250.00
42 I:Patty Pin-up 275.00
Becomes:

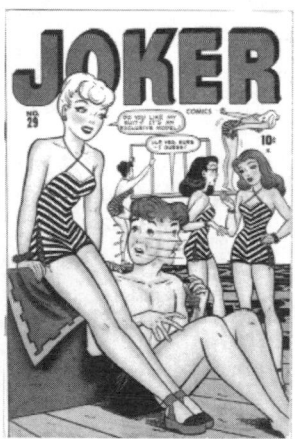

Joker #29
© Marvel Entertainment Group

Adventures Into Terror #3
© Marvel Entertainment Group

ADVENTURES INTO TERROR
1950

43(1)AH,B:Horror Stories 900.00
44(2)AH,Won't You Step Into
  My Palor 600.00
3 GC,I Stalk By Night 400.00
4 DR,The Torture Room 400.00
5 GC,DR,The Hitchhiker 375.00
6 RH,The Dark Room 325.00
7 GT(c),BW,JMn,Where Monsters
  Dwell 750.00
8 JSt,Enter... the Lizard 400.00
9 RH(c),JSt,The Dark
  Dungeon 375.00
10 JMn,When the Vampire Calls . 375.00
11 JMn,JSt,Dead Man's Escape . 325.00
12 BK,Man Who Cried Ghost . . . 350.00
13 BEv(c),The Hands of Death . . 350.00
14 GC,GT,The Hands 300.00
15 Trapped by the Tarantula . . . 300.00
16 RH(c),Her Name Is Death . . . 300.00
17 I Die Too Often,Bondage(c) . . 350.00
18 He's Trying To Kill Me 300.00
19 The Girl Who Couldn't Die . . . 275.00
20 . . . . 275.00
21 GC,JMn 250.00
22 JMn 250.00
23 . . . . 250.00
24 MF,GC 250.00
25 MF 300.00
26 GC 250.00
27 . . . . 250.00
28 GC 250.00
29 GC,JMn 250.00
30 . . . . 250.00
31 May, 1954 . . . . 250.00

JOURNEY INTO MYSTERY
June, 1952

1 RH(c),B:Mystery/Horror
  stories 6,000.00
2 Don't Look 2,500.00
3 I Didn't See Anything 2,200.00
4 RH,BEv(c),I'm Drowning,
  Severed Hand (c) 2,200.00
5 RH,BEv(c),Fright 1,500.00
6 BEv(c),Till Death Do
  Us Part 1,500.00
7 BEv(c),Ghost Guard 1,500.00
8 He Who Hesitates 1,500.00
9 BEv(c),I Made A Monster . . . 1,500.00
10 The Assassin of Paris 1,500.00
11 RH,GT,Meet the Dead 1,400.00

12 A Night At Dragmoor Castle. 1,200.00
13 The Living and the Dead . . . 1,200.00
14 DAy,RH,The Man Who
  Owned A World 1,200.00
15 RH(c),Till Death Do Us Part 1,200.00
16 DW,Vampire Tale 1,200.00
17 SC,Midnight On Black
  Mountain 1,200.00
18 He Wouldn't Stay Dead 1,200.00
19 JF,The Little Things 1,200.00
20 BEv,BP,After Man, What . . . 1,200.00
21 JKu,The Man With No Past . 1,200.00
22 Haunted House 1,200.00
23 GC,Gone, But Not Forgotten . 900.00
24 The Locked Drawer 900.00
25 The Man Who Lost Himself . . 900.00
26 The Man From Out There 900.00
27 BP,JSe,Masterpiece 900.00
28 The Survivor 900.00
29 Three Frightened People 900.00
30 JO,The Lady Who Vanished . . 900.00
31 The Man Who Had No Fear . . 900.00
32 Elevator In The Sky 900.00
33 SD,AW,There'll Be Some
  Changes Made 1,000.00
34 BP,BK,The Of The
  Mystic Ring 900.00
35 LC,JF,Turn Back The Clock . . 900.00
36 I, The Pharaoh 900.00
37 BEv(c),The Volcano 900.00
38 SD,Those Who Vanish 900.00
39 BEv(c),DAy,WW,The
  Forbidden Room 900.00
40 BEv(c),JF,The Strange
  Secret Of Henry Hill 900.00
41 BEv(c),GM,RC,I Switched
  Bodies 750.00
42 BEv(c),GM,What Was
  Farley's Other Face 750.00
43 AW,Ghost Ship 750.00
44 SD,JK,BEv 750.00
45 BEv,JO 700.00
46 . . . . 700.00
47 BEv 700.00
48 . . . . 700.00
49 . . . . 700.00
50 SD 700.00
51 SD,JK 750.00
52 JK 700.00
53 DH 700.00
54 AW 750.00
55 . . . . 750.00
56 thru 61 SD,JK . . . . @600.00
62 SD,JK,I:Xemnu 750.00
63 SD,JK 750.00
64 SD,JK 750.00
65 SD,JK 750.00
66 Hulk Type 800.00
67 SD,JK 650.00
68 SD,JK 650.00
69 SD,JK 650.00
70 Sandman Type 700.00
71 JK,SD 650.00
72 JK,SD 650.00
73 JK,DH,Spider-Man type 800.00
74 . . . . 650.00
75 JK,DH 650.00
76 JK,DH 600.00
77 DH,SD,JK 600.00
78 DH,Dr.Strange Type 750.00
79 JK,DH,SD 700.00
80 JK,DH,SD 600.00
81 JK,DH,SD 600.00
82 JK,DH,SD 600.00
83 JK,SD,I&O:Thor 12,000.00
84 JK,SD,DH,I:Executioner 3,200.00
85 JK,SD,I:Loki,Heimdall,Balder,
  Tyr,Odin,Asgard 2,000.00
86 JK,SD,DH,V:Tomorrow Man 1,300.00
87 JK,SD,V:Communists 1,000.00
88 JK,SD,V:Loki 1,000.00
89 JK,SD,O:Thor(rep) 1,000.00

90 SD,I:Carbon Copy 700.00
91 JSt,SD,I:Sandu 700.00
92 JSt,SD,V:Loki,I:Frigga 700.00
93 DAy,JK,SD,I:Radioactive Man 800.00
94 JSt,SD,V:Loki 625.00
95 JSt,SD,I:Duplicator 625.00
96 JSt,SD,I:Merlin II 625.00
97 JK,I:Lava Man,O:Odin 750.00
98 DH,JK,I&O:Cobra 600.00
99 DH,JK,I:Mr.Hyde,Surtur 600.00
100 DH,JK,V:Mr.Hyde 600.00
101 JK,V:Tomorrow Man 400.00
102 JK,I:Sif,Hela 400.00
103 JK,I:Enchantress,
  Executioner 400.00
104 JK,Giants 400.00
105 JK,V:Hyde,Cobra 400.00
106 JK,O:Balder 400.00
107 JK,I:Grey Gargoyle,Karnilla . 400.00
108 JK,A:Dr.Strange 400.00
109 JK,V:Magneto 750.00
110 JK,V:Hyde,Cobra,Loki 400.00
111 JK,V:Hyde,Cobra,Loki 400.00
112 JK,V:Hulk,O:Loki 850.00
113 JK,V:Grey Gargoyle 350.00
114 JK,I&O:Absorbing Man 350.00
115 JK,O:Loki,V:Absorbing Man . 400.00
116 JK,V:Loki,C:Daredevil 350.00
117 JK,V:Loki 350.00
118 JK,I:Destroyer 350.00
119 JK,V:Destroyer,I:Hogun,
  Fandrall,Volstagg 350.00
120 JK,A:Avengers,Absorbing
  Man 350.00
121 JK,V:Absorbing Man 350.00
122 JK,V:Absorbing Man 350.00
123 JK,V:Absorbing Man 350.00
124 JK,A:Hercules 375.00
125 JK,A:Hercules 375.00
Annual #1, JK,I:Hercules 450.00
Becomes:

THOR

JOURNEY INTO MYSTERY
[2nd series], Oct., 1972

1 GK,TP,MP,Dig Me No Grave . . 45.00
2 GK,Jack the Ripper 30.00
3 JSn,TP,Shambler From
  the Stars 30.00
4 GC,DA,Haunter of the Dark,
  H.P. Lovecraft adaptation 30.00
5 RB,FrG,Shadow From the
  Steeple,R. Bloch adaptation . . 30.00
6 Mystery Stories 25.00
7 thru 19 . . . . @25.00

JOURNEY INTO UNKNOWN WORLDS
See: ALL WINNERS COMICS

JUBILEE
Sept., 2004

1 In Los Angeles 3.00
2 F:Meg Devereaux 3.00
3 thru 6 . . . . @3.00

J-2
Aug., 1998

1 TDF,RLm,AM,F:J2 with the powers
  of Juggernaut 2.25
2 thru 12 TDF,RLm,AM . . . . @2.25

JUGGERNAUT
1997

1-shot 48pg 3.00

JUGGERNAUT: THE EIGHTH DAY
Sept., 1999
1-shot JoC,TSr,AKu(c),x-over,pt.4 . . 3.00

JUNGLE ACTION
Marvel Atlas, Oct., 1954
1 JMn,JMn(c),B:Leopard Girl . . . 450.00
2 JMn,JMn(c) 475.00
3 thru 6 JMn,JMn(c) . . . . @300.00

JUNGLE ACTION
Oct., 1972—Nov., 1976
1 JB(c),Lorna,Tharn,Jann
   reprints 25.00
2 GK(c),same 15.00
3 JSn(c),same 15.00
4 GK(c),same 15.00
5 JR(c),JB,B:Black Panther,
   V:Man-Ape 30.00
6 RB/FrG(c),RB,V:Kill-Monger . . 25.00
7 RB/KJ(c),RB,V:Venomn 15.00
8 RB/KJ(c),RB,GK,
   O:Black Panther 20.00
9 GK/KJ(c),RB,V:Baron Macabre 15.00
10 GK/FrG(c),V:King Cadaver . . . 15.00
11 GK(c),V:Baron Macabre,Lord
   Karnaj 15.00
12 RB/KJ(c),V:Kill Monger 10.00
13 GK/JK(c),V:White Gorilla,
   Sombre 10.00
14 GK(c),V:Prehistoric Monsters . . 10.00
15 GK(c),V:Prehistoric Monsters . . 10.00
16 GK(c),V:Venomm 10.00
17 GK(c),V:Kill Monger 10.00
18 JKu(c),V:Madame Slay 10.00
19 GK(c),V:KKK,Sacrifice of Blood 10.00
20 V:KKK,Slaughter In The
   Streets 10.00
21 V:KKK,Cross Of Fire, Cross
   Of Death 9.00
22 JB(c),V:KKK,Soul Stranger 9.00
23 JBy(c),V:KKK 9.00
24 GK(c),I:Wind Eagle 9.00

JUNGLE TALES
Marvel Atlas, Sept., 1954
1 B:Jann of the Jungle,Cliff
   Mason,Waku 500.00
2 GT,Jann Stories cont 350.00
3 Cliff Mason,White Hunter,
   Waku Unknown Jungle 350.00
4 Cliff Mason,Waku,Unknown
   Jungle 350.00
5 RH(c),SSh,Cliff Mason,Waku,
   Unknown Jungle 350.00
6 DH,SSh,Cliff Mason,Waku,
   Unknown Jungle 350.00
7 DH,SSh,Cliff Mason,Waku,
   Unknown Jungle 350.00
Becomes:

JANN OF THE JUNGLE
1955
8 SH,SSh,The Jungle Outlaw . . . 450.00
9 With Fang and Talons 250.00
10 AW,The Jackal's Lair 250.00
11 Bottomless Pit 250.00
12 The Lost Safari 250.00
13 When the Trap Closed 250.00
14 V:Hunters 250.00
15 BEv(c),DH,V:Hunters 250.00
16 BEv(c),AW,JungleVengeance . . 275.00
17 BEv(c),DH,AW,June, 1957 . . . 275.00

JUSTICE
Nov., 1986
1 I:Justice 2.25

2 . . . . 2.25
3 Yakuza Assassin 2.25
4 thru 31 . . . . @2.25
32 Last issue,A:Joker 2.25

JUSTICE COMICS
Marvel Atlas, Fall, 1947
7(1) B:FBI in Action,Mystery of
   White Death 350.00
8(2),HK,Crime is For Suckers . . 250.00
9(3),FBI Raid 225.00
4 Bank Robbery 225.00
5 Subway(c) 175.00
6 E:FBI In Action 175.00
7 Symbolic(c) 175.00
8 Funeral(c) 175.00
9 B:True Cases Proving Crime
   Can't Win 175.00
10 Ph(c),Bank Hold Up 175.00
11 Ph(c),Behind Bars 175.00
12 Ph(c),The Crime of
   Martin Blaine 135.00
13 Ph(c),The Cautious Crook . . . 135.00
14 Ph(c) 135.00
15 Ph(c) 135.00
16 F:"Ears"Karpik-Mobster 125.00
17 The Ragged Stranger 125.00
18 Criss-Cross 125.00
19 Death Of A Spy 125.00
20 Miami Mob 125.00
21 Trap 125.00
22 The Big Break 125.00
23 thru 40 . . . . @100.00
41 Electrocution cover 200.00
42 thru 51 . . . . @100.00
52 Flare Up 100.00
Becomes:

TALES OF JUSTICE
May, 1955—Aug., 1957
53 BEv,Keeper Of The Keys 200.00
54 thru 57 . . . . @175.00
58 BK 150.00
59 BK 150.00
60 thru 63 . . . . @100.00
64 RC,DW,JSe 125.00
65 RC 125.00
66 JO,AT 125.00
67 DW 125.00

JUSTICE: FOUR BALANCE
1994
1 A:Thing, Yancy Street Gang 2.25
2 V:Hate Monger 2.25
3 the story continues 2.25
4 ...to its conclusion 2.25

KABUKI
Icon, July, 2004
1 DMk,The Alchemy,pt.1 . . . . 3.00
2 thru 6 DMk,The Alchemy,pt.2–6 @3.00
7 DMk 3.00
8 DMk 3.00
GN Kabuki Reflections 5.00

KATHY
Marvel Atlas, Oct., 1959—Feb., 1964
1 Teenage Tornado 125.00
2 . . . . 100.00
3 thru 15 . . . . @75.00
16 thru 27 . . . . @60.00

KA-ZAR
[Reprint Series], Aug., 1970
1 X-Men ID 50.00
2 Daredevil 12, 13 . . . . 35.00
3 DDH,Spider-Man,March, 1971 . 35.00

Ka-Zar #7
© Marvel Entertainment Group

[1st Series], Jan., 1974
1 O:Savage Land 20.00
2 DH,JA,A:Shanna The She-Devil 10.00
3 DH,V:Man-God,A:El Tigre 10.00
4 DH,V:Man-God 10.00
5 DH,D:El-Tigre 8.00
6 JB/AA,V:Bahemoth 8.00
7 JB/BMcRevenge of the
   River-Gods 8.00
8 JB/AA,Volcano of
   Molten Death 8.00
9 JB,Man Who Hunted Dinosaur . . 8.00
10 JB,Dark City of Death 8.00
11 DH/FS,Devil-God of Sylitha 7.00
12 RH,Wizard of Forgotten
   Death 7.00
13 V:Lizard Men 7.00
14 JAb,V:Klaw 7.00
15 VM,V:Klaw,Hellbird 7.00
16 VM,V:Klaw 7.00
17 VM,V:Klaw 7.00
18 VM,V:Klaw,Makrum 7.00
19 VM,V:Klaw,Raknor the Slayer . . . 7.00
20 VM,V:Klaw,Fortress of Fear 7.00

[2nd Series], Apr. 1981
1 BA,O:Ka-Zar 4.00
2 thru 7 BA . . . . @3.00
8 BA,Ka-Zar Father 2.50
9 BA 2.50
10 BA,Direct D 2.50
11 BA/GK,Zabu 2.50
12 BA,Panel Missing 2.50
12a Scarce Reprint 2.50
13 BA 2.50
14 BA/GK,Zabu 2.50
15 BA 2.50
16 . . . . 2.50
17 Detective 2.50
18 & 19 . . . . @2.50
20 A:Spider-Man 3.00
21 . . . . 3.00
22 A:Spider-Man 3.00
23 A:Spider-Man 3.00
24 A:Spider-Man 3.00
25 A:Spider-Man 3.00
26 A:Spider-Man 3.00
27 A:Buth 3.00
28 Pangea 3.00
29 W:Ka-Zar & Shanna, Doub.Size . 3.00
30 V:Pterons 3.00
31 PangeaWarII 3.00
32 V:Plunderer 3.00
33 V:Plunderer 3.00
34 Last Issue Doub.Size 3.00

Kazar 3rd Series #2
© Marvel Entertainment Group

[3rd Series], 1997
1 MWa,NKu,Ka-Zar, Shanna, Zabu,
　V:Gregor, 40pg 5.00
1a 2nd printing 2.50
2 MWa,NKu,V:Gregor 4.00
2A NKu variant cover 3.00
3 MWa,NKu,Ka-Zar's son dead? . . 3.00
4 MWa,NKu,in New York City 3.00
5 MWa,NKu, ... 2.50
6 MWa,V:Rampaging Rhino 2.25
7 MWa,NKu,F:Shanna the
　She-Devil 2.25
8 MWa,NKu, Urban Jungle, pt.1 . . 2.25
9 MWa,NKu, Urban Jungle, pt.2 . . 2.25
10 MWa,NKu, Urban Jungle, pt.3 . . 2.25
11 MWa,NKu, Urban Jungle, pt.4,
　concl. 2.25
12 MWa,A:High Evolutionary 2.25
13 MWa,A:High Evolutionary 2.25
14 MWa,NKu,end old & begin new
　storyline, double size. 3.50
15 A:Punisher. 3.00
16 A:Punisher. 2.25
17 Ka-Zar clears his name,
　A:Jameka. 2.25
18 People of the Savage Land
　revolt 2.25
19 V:Gregor 2.25
20 A:Gregor,Zira, final issue 2.25
Ann. '97 V:Garrok, Petrified Man . . 2.50
Ann. '98 Ka-Zar/Daredevil heroes
　unite. 3.00
1-shot Ka-Zar of the Savage Land,
　CDi,V:Sauron, 48-pg., prelude to
　3rd series (1996) 3.00
1-shot Ka-Zar: Sibling Rivalry,
　MWa,TDz,Flashback (1997) . . . 2.00

KELLYS, THE
See: KID KOMICS

**KENT BLAKE OF THE
SECRET SERVICE**
May, 1951—July, 1953
1 U.S. Govt. Secret Agent
　stories,Bondage cover 250.00
2 JSt,Drug issue,Man with
　out A Face 175.00
3 JMn,Trapped By The Chinese
　Reds 125.00
4 Secret Service Stories 125.00
5 RH(c),Condemned To Death . . 125.00
6 Cases from Kent Blake files . . 125.00

7 RH(c),Behind Enemy Lines . . 125.00
8 GT,V:Communists 125.00
9 thru 14 . . . . @125.00

KICKERS INC.
Nov., 1986
1 SB,O:Kickers 2.50
2 SB 2.50
3 RF,Witches. 2.50
4 RF,FIST 2.50
5 RF,A:D.P.7 . . . . 2.50
6 thru 12 . . . . @2.50

KID & PLAY
1 Based on Rap Group 2.25
2 thru 9 . . . . @2.25

KID COLT OUTLAW
Marvel Atlas, Aug., 1948
1 B:Kid Colt,A:Two-Gun Kid . . 1,500.00
2 Gun-Fighter and the Girl 700.00
3 SSh,Colt-Quick Killers
　For Hire 550.00
4 Wanted,A:Tex Taylor 550.00
5 Mystery of the Misssing
　Mine,A:Blaze Carson. 550.00
6 A:Tex Taylor,Valley of
　the Werewolf 350.00
7 B:Nimo the Lion 350.00
8 . . . . 350.00
9 . . . . 350.00
10 The Whip Strikes,E:Nimo
　the Lion. 350.00
11 O:Kid Colt 400.00
12 . . . . 225.00
13 DRi 225.00
14 . . . . 225.00
15 Gun Whipped in ShotgunCity . 225.00
16 . . . . 225.00
17 . . . . 225.00
18 DRi 225.00
19 . . . . 200.00
20 The Outlaw 200.00
21 thru 30 . . . . @200.00
31 . . . . 200.00
32 . . . . 200.00
33 thru 45 A:Black Rider . . . . . @150.00
46 RH(c). 150.00
47 DW 150.00
48 RH(c),JKu 150.00
49 . . . . 150.00
50 . . . . 150.00
51 thru 56 . . . . @125.00
57 AW 125.00
58 AW 125.00
59 AW 125.00
60 AW 125.00
61 . . . . 100.00
62 . . . . 100.00
63 . . . . 100.00
64 RC 110.00
65 RC 110.00
66 AW 150.00
67 thru 78 . . . . @100.00
79 Origin Retold 110.00
80 thru 86. . . . . @100.00
87 JDa(reprint) 110.00
88 AW 120.00
89 AW,Matt Slade 120.00
90 thru 99 . . . . @100.00
100 JK 120.00
101 JK 60.00
102 JK 60.00
103 JK,The Great Train Robbery . . 60.00
104 JKu(c),DH,Trail of
　Kid Colt. 60.00
105 DH,V:Dakota Dixon 60.00
106 JKu(c),The Circus
　of Crime 60.00
107 JK,SciFi(c). 75.00
108 BEv 60.00

Kid Colt Outlaw #83
© Marvel Entertainment Group

109 DAy,V:The Barracuda 60.00
110 GC,V:Iron Mask 75.00
111 JKu(c),V:Sam Hawk, The
　Man Hunter 55.00
112 JKu(c),V:Mr. Brown 55.00
113 JKu(c),GC,V:Bull Barton 55.00
114 JKu(c),Return of Iron Mask. . . 55.00
115 JKu(c),V:The Scorpion 55.00
116 JKu(c),GC,V:Dr. Danger &
　Invisible Gunman. 55.00
117 JKu(c),GC,V:The Fatman &
　His Boomerang 55.00
118 V:Scorpion,Bull Barton,
　Dr. Danger 55.00
119 DAy(c),JK,V:Bassett The
　Badman 55.00
120 Cragsons Ride Again 55.00
121 A:Rawhide Kid,Iron Mask . . . 35.00
122 V:Rattler Ruxton 35.00
123 V:Ringo Barker 35.00
124 A:Phantom Raider. 35.00
125 A:Two-Gun Kid 35.00
126 V:Wes Hardin 35.00
127 thru 129. . . . . @35.00
130 O:Kid Colt 45.00
131 thru 150. . . . . @30.00
151 thru 200 reprints . . . . @25.00
201 thru 228 reprints . . . . @20.00
229 April, 1979. . . . . 20.00

KID FROM DODGE CITY
**Marvel Atlas, July, 1957—Sept.,
1957**
1 . . . . 150.00
2 . . . . 100.00

KID FROM TEXAS
**Marvel Atlas, June, 1957—Aug.,
1957**
1 . . . . 125.00
2 . . . . 100.00

KID KOMICS
Marvel Timely, Feb., 1943
1 SSh(c),BW,O:Captain Wonder
　& Tim Mulrooney I:Whitewash,
　Knuckles,Trixie Trouble,
　Pinto Pete Subbie. 7,500.00
2 AsH(c),F:Captain Wonder
　Subbie, B:Young Allies,
　B:Red Hawk,Tommy Tyme 3,500.00
3 AsH(c),AAv,SSh,A:The Vision
　& Daredevils 3,000.00

MARVEL

4 ASh(c),B:Destroyer,A:Sub-Mariner,
   E:Red Hawk,Tommy Tyme 2,200.00
5 ASh(c),V:Nazis 1,800.00
6 ASh(c),V:Japanese 1,800.00
7 ASh(c),B:Whizzer 1,600.00
8 ASh(c),V:Train Robbers . . . 1,600.00
9 ASh(c),V:Elves 1,600.00
10 ASh(c),E:Young Allies,
   The Destoyer,The Whizzer 1,600.00
Becomes:

KID MOVIE KOMICS
1946
11 F:Silly Seal,Ziggy Pig
   HK,Hey Look 300.00
Becomes:

RUSTY COMICS
1947
12 F:Rusty,A:Mitzi 225.00
13 Do not Disturb(c). 125.00
14 Beach(c),BW,HK,Hey Look. . 250.00
15 Picnic(c),HK,Hey Look 175.00
16 Juniors Grades,HK,HeyLook . 175.00
17 John in Trouble,HK,HeyLook . 175.00
18 John Fired. 125.00
19 Fridge raid(c),HK 125.00
20 And Her Family,HK 200.00
21 And Her Family,HK 250.00
22 HK. 250.00
Becomes:

KELLYS, THE
1950
23 F:The Kelly Family(Pop,
   Mom,Mike,Pat & Goliath) . . . 125.00
24 Mike's Date,A:Margie 75.00
25 Wrestling(c). 75.00
Becomes:

SPY CASES
1950
26(#1) Spy stories 350.00
27(#2) BEv,Bondage(c) 300.00
28(#3) Sabotage,A:Douglas
   Grant Secret Agent. 175.00
4 The Secret Invasion 150.00
5 The Vengeance of Comrade
   de Casto 150.00
6 A:Secret Agent Doug Grant . . 150.00
7 GT,A:Doug Grant 150.00
8 Atom Bomb(c),Frozen
   Horror 250.00
9 Undeclared War 125.00
10 Battlefield Adventures 125.00
11 Battlefield Adventures. 125.00
12 Battlefield Adventures 125.00
13 Battlefield Adventures 125.00
14 Battlefield Adventures 125.00
15 Doug Grant 125.00
16 Doug Grant 125.00
17 Doug Grant 125.00
18 Contact in Ankara 125.00
19 Final Issue,Oct., 1953. . . . . . 125.00

KID SLADE GUNFIGHTER
See: MATT SLADE

KILLFRENZY
1 . . . . 2.25
2 Castle Madspike 2.25

KILLPOWER:
THE EARLY YEARS
1993
1 B:MiB,Goes on Rampage 3.25
2 thru 3 O:Killpower . . . . @2.25
4 E:MiB,last issue 2.25

KILLRAVEN
Dec., 2000
Spec. JLi,R:Killraven 3.00

KILLRAVEN
Oct., 2002
1 (of 6) AD,MFm,V:Martians 3.00
2 AD,MFm. 3.00
3 AD,MFm. 3.00
4 AD,MFm. 3.00
5 AD,MFm. 3.00
6 AD,MFm. 3.00

KING ARTHUR & THE
KNIGHTS OF JUSTICE
1993–94
1 Based on Cartoon 2.25
2 Based on Cartoon 2.25
3 Based on Cartoon 2.25

KING CONAN:
See: CONAN THE KING

KINGPIN
Nov., 1997
1-shot StL,JR, bookshelf 48pg. . . . 6.00

KINGPIN
June, 2003
1 SeP,KJ,Wilson Fixk 2.50
2 thru 7 SeP,KJ . . . . @2.50

KISSNATION
1997
1 Rock & Roll, A:X-Men 10.00

KITTY PRYDE:
AGENT OF S.H.I.E.L.D.
Oct., 1997
1 (of 3) LHa,V:Ogun 2.50
2 LHa,V:Ogun. 2.50
3 LHa,Ogun's Slave? 2.50

KITTY PRYDE
& WOLVERINE
Nov., 1984
1 AM,V:Ogun. 6.00
2 AM,V:Ogun. 5.00
3 thru 5 AM,V:Ogun. . . . . @5.00
6 AM,D:Ogun, April, 1985. . . . . . . 5.00

KNIGHTS OF
PENDRAGON
[1st Regular Series], July, 1990
1 GEr 2.75
2 thru 18 . . . . @2.25

[2nd Regular Series], 1992
1 GEr,A:Iron Man,R:Knights of
   Pendragon. 2.25
2 thru 15 . . . . @2.25

KOMIC KARTOONS
Marvel Timely, 1945
1 Funny Animal. 225.00
2 . . . . 225.00

KRAZY KOMICS
Marvel Timely, July, 1942
1 B:Ziggy Pig,Silly Seal 750.00
2 Toughy Tomcat(c) 325.00
3 Toughy Tomcat/Bunny(c) 250.00
4 Toughy Tomcat/Ziggy(c) 250.00
5 Ziggy/Buzz Saw(c) 250.00
6 Toughy/Cannon(c) 250.00

7 Cigar Store Indian(c) 250.00
8 Toughy/Hammock(c) 250.00
9 Hitler(c) 275.00
10 Newspaper(c) 225.00
11 Canoe(c) 225.00
12 Circus(c) 300.00
13 Pirate Treasure(c) 200.00
14 Fishing(c) 200.00
15 Ski-Jump(c). 175.00
16 Airplane(c). 125.00
17 Street corner(c). 125.00
18 Mallet/Bell(c) 125.00
19 Bicycle(c). 125.00
20 Ziggy(c) 125.00
21 Toughy's date(c) 125.00
22 Crystal Ball(c) 125.00
23 Sharks in bathtub(c) 150.00
24 Baseball(c) 125.00
25 HK,Krazy Krow(c) 150.00
26 Super Rabbit(c) 125.00
Becomes:

CINDY COMICS
1947
27 HK,B:Margie,Oscar. 250.00
28 HK,Snow sled(c). 150.00
29 . . . . 150.00
30 . . . . 150.00
31 HK. 150.00
32 . . . . 100.00
33 A;Georgie 100.00
34 thru 40. . . . . @100.00
Becomes:

CRIME CAN'T WIN
1950
41 Crime stories. 300.00
42 . . . . 175.00
43 GT,Horror story 250.00
4 thru 11 . . . . @150.00
12 Sept., 1953. . . . . 125.00

KRAZY KOMICS
Marvel Timely
[2nd Series], 1948
1 BW,HK,R:Fustice Hayseed . . . 600.00
2 BW,O:Powerhouse Pepper . . . 400.00

KRAZY KROW
Summer, 1945
1 B:Krazy Krow 250.00
2 . . . . 150.00
3 Winter,, 1945-46 . . . . 150.00

Krazy Komics 2nd Series #1
© *Marvel Entertainment Group*

All comics prices listed are for *Near Mint* condition.

KREE-SKRULL WAR
Sept.–Oct., 1983
1 & 2 JB,NA,reprints . . . . @5.00

KRULL
Nov.–Dec., 1983
1 Ph(c),BBI,movie adapt. 2.50
2 BBI,rep.,Marvel Super Spec. . . . 2.50

Kull The Conqueror #5
© Marvel Entertainment Group

KULL THE CONQUEROR
[1st Series], June, 1971
1 MSe,RA,WW,A King Comes
  Riding,O:Kull 65.00
2 MSe,JSe,Shadow Kingdom. . . . 25.00
3 MSe,JSe,Death Dance of
  Thulsa Doom 25.00
4 MSe,JSe,Night o/t Red Slayers. 25.00
5 MSe,JSe,Kingdom By the Sea . . 25.00
6 MSe,JSe,Lurker Beneath
  the Sea 15.00
7 MSe,JSe,Delcardes'Cat,
  A:Thulsa Doom 15.00
8 MSe,JSe,Wolfshead 15.00
9 MSe,JSe,The Scorpion God . . . 15.00
10 MSe,Swords o/t White Queen . 15.00
11 MP,King Kull Must Die, O:Kull
  cont.,A:Thulsa Doom 10.00
12 MP,SB,Moon of Blood,V:Thulsa
  Doom,B:SD,B.U.stories 10.00
13 MP,AM,Torches From Hell,
  V:Thulsa Doom 10.00
14 MP,JA,The Black Belfry,
  A:Thulsa Doom 10.00
15 MP,Wings o/t Night-Beast,
  E:SD,B.U.stories 10.00
16 EH,Tiger in the Moon,
  A:Thulsa Doom 12.00
17 AA,EH,Thing from Emerald
  Darkness 6.00
18 EH,AA,Keeper of Flame
  & Frost. 6.00
19 EH,AA,The Crystal Menace 6.00
20 EH,AA,Hell Beneath Atlantis. . . . 6.00
21 City of the Crawling Dead. 10.00
22 Talons of the Devil-Birds. 10.00
23 Demon Shade. 10.00
24 Screams in the Dark. 9.00
25 A Lizard's Throne 9.00
26 Into Death's Dimension. 9.00
27 The World Within 9.00
28 Creature and the Crown,
  A:Thulsa Doom 9.00

29 To Sit the Topaz Throne,
  V:Thulsa Doom, final issue 9.00
[2nd Series], 1982
1 JB,Brule 4.00
2 Misareenia 3.00
[3rd Series], 1983–85
1 JB,BWi,DG,Iraina 3.50
2 JB,Battle to the Death 3.00
3 JB. 3.00
4 JB. 3.00
5 JB 3.00
6 JB 3.00
7 JB,Masquerade Death 3.00
8 JB 3.00
9 JB 3.00
10 JB 3.00

KULL AND THE BARBARIANS
May, 1975
1 NA,GK,reprint Kull #1 . . . . 27.00
2 BBI,reprint,Dec., 1983 . . . . 20.00
3 NA,HC,O:Red Sonja 20.00

LABRYNTH
1986–87
1 Movie adapt. 3.00
2 and 3 . . . . @3.00

LAFF-A-LYMPICS
1978–79
1 F;Hanna Barbera 45.00
2 thru 5 . . . . @30.00
6 thru 13 . . . . @35.00

LANA
Aug., 1948
1 F:Lana Lane The Show Girl,
  A:Rusty,B:Millie 250.00
2 HK,Hey Look,A:Rusty 200.00
3 Show(c),B:Nellie 100.00
4 Ship(c) 100.00
5 Audition(c) 100.00
6 Stop sign(c) 100.00
7 Beach(c) 100.00
Becomes:

LITTLE LANA
1949
8 Little Lana(c) 100.00
9 Final Issue,March, 1950 . . . . . 100.00

LANCE BARNES: POST NUKE DICK
Epic, 1993
1 I:Lance Barnes. 2.50
2 Cigarettes 2.50
3 Warring Mall Tribe 2.50
4 V:Ex-bankers,last issue 2.50

LAST AMERICAN
Epic, 1990–91
1 . . . . 3.50
2 . . . . 3.00
3 . . . . 2.50
4 Final issue.. . . . . 2.25

THE LAST AVENGERS STORY
1995
1 PDd, Alterverse,Future world. . . . 6.00
2 PDd, Final fate,fully painted. 6.00
TPB PDd,AOI, rep. Alterniverse
  story, 96pg. 13.00

LAST HERO STANDING
June, 2005
1 (of 5) PO 3.00
2 thru 5 Po . . . . @3.00
TPB series rep. 14.00

LAST PLANET STANDING
May, 2006
1 (of 5) PO 3.00
2 thru 5 Po . . . . @3.00
TPB series rep. 14.00

Last Starfighter #3
© Marvel Entertainment Group

LAST STARFIGHTER, THE
Oct.–Dec., 1984
1 JG(c),BBI,Movie adapt. 2.25
2 Movie adapt. 2.25
3 BBI 2.25

LAWBREAKERS ALWAYS LOSE
Marvel Crime Bureau Stories, 1948–49
1 HK; FBI Reward Poster Photo
  Adam and Eve, HK,Giggles
  and Grins. 500.00
2 FBI V:Fur Theives 250.00
3 . . . . 200.00
4 AyB(c),Vampire 200.00
5 AyB(c) 200.00
6 Anti Wertham Edition 225.00
7 Crime at Midnight 350.00
8 Prison Break 150.00
9 Ph(c),He Prowled at Night . . . 150.00
10 Phc(c),I Met My Murderer. . . . 150.00

LAWDOG
1993
1 B:CDi(s),FH,I:Lawdog 2.50
2 thru 10 FH . . . . @2.25
1-shot Lawdog & Grimrod: Terror
  at the Crossroads 3.50

LEGION OF MONSTERS
Sept., 1975
(black & white magazine)
1 NA(c),GM,I&O:Legion of
  Monsters,O:Manphibian 40.00

MARVEL

LEGION OF NIGHT
Oct., 1991

1 WPo/SW,A:Fin Fang Foom 5.50
2 WPo,V:Fin Fang Foom 5.50

LETHAL FOES OF SPIDER-MAN
1993

1 B:DFr(s),SMc,R:Stegron 3.00
2 SMc,A:Stegron 3.00
3 SMc,V:Spider-Man 3.00
4 E:DFr(s),SMc,Last Issue 3.00

LIFE OF CAPTAIN MARVEL
Aug., 1985

1 rep.Iron Man #55,
    Capt.Marvel #25,26 . . . . 9.00
2 rep.Capt.Marvel#26-28 . . . . 6.50
3 rep.Capt.Marvel#28-30
    Marvel Feature #12 . . . . 6.00
4 rep.Marvel Feature #12,Capt.
    Marvel #31,32,Daredevil#105 . . 6.00
5 rep.Capt.Marvel #32-#34 . . . . 6.00

LIFE OF CHRIST
1993

1 Birth of Christ 5.00
2 MW,The Easter Story 5.00

LIFE OF POPE JOHN-PAUL II
1983

1 JSt, Jan., 1983 . . . . 6.00
1a Special reprint 4.00

LIFE WITH MILLIE
See: DATE WITH MILLIE

LIGHT AND DARKNESS WAR
Epic, Oct., 1988

1 . . . . 4.00
2 . . . . 3.00
3 thru 6 Dec., 1989 . . . . @2.50

LINDA CARTER, STUDENT NURSE
Atlas, Sept., 1961

1 . . . . 90.00
2 thru 9, Jan., 1963 . . . . @60.00

LION KING

1 based on Movie 2.75

LI'L KIDS
Aug., 1970–June, 1973

1 . . . . 125.00
2 thru 12 . . . . @60.00

LI'L PALS
Sept., 1972

1 . . . . 90.00
2 thru 5, May, 1973 . . . . @50.00

LITTLE ASPIRIN
Marvel Comics, 1949

1 HK 200.00
2 HK 125.00
3 . . . . 100.00

LITTLE LANA
See: LANA

LITTLE LENNY
Marvel Classic Detective, 1949

1 . . . . 125.00
2 . . . . 100.00
3 . . . . 100.00

LITTLE LIZZIE
June, 1949

1 Roller Skating(c) 150.00
2 Soda(c) 100.00
3 Movies(c) 100.00
4 Lizzie(c) 100.00
5 Lizzie/Swing(c) April,1950 . . . 100.00

[2nd Series] Sept., 1953

1 . . . . 100.00
2 . . . . 75.00
3 Jan., 1954 . . . . 75.00

LITTLE MERMAID, THE
1993

1 . . . . 3.50
2 thru 13 . . . . @2.50

LIVEWIRES
Feb., 2005

1 (of 6) AWa(s), ... 3.00
2 Awa(s&c) 3.00
3 AWa(s&c) 3.00
4 AWa(s&c) 3.00
5 Awa(s&c) 3.00
6 AWa(s&c), finale 3.00
Digest Vol. 1: Clockwork Thugs, Yo. 8.00

LOGAN

1-shot HMe,48pg 6.00
1-shot Logan: Path of the
    Warrior (1996) 5.00
1-shot Logan: Shadow Society,
    HMe,TCk Early life of
    Wolverine (1996) 5.00

LOGAN'S RUN
Jan., 1977

1 GP,From Movie 20.00
2 GP,Cathedral KIII 10.00
3 GP,Lair of Laser Death 10.00
4 GP,Dread Sanctuary 10.00
5 GP,End Run 10.00
6 MZ,B.U.Thanos/Drax 25.00
7 TS,Cathedral Prime 10.00

LOKI
July, 2004

1 (of 4) 7.50
2 thru 4 . . . . @7.50
TPB 18.00

LONGSHOT
Sept., 1985

1 AAd,WPo(i),BA,I:Longshot 8.00
2 AAd,WPo(i),I:RicoshetRita 6.00
3 AAd,WPo(i),I:Mojo,Spiral 6.00
4 AAd,WPo(i),A:Spider-Man 6.00
5 AAd,WPo(i),A:Dr. Strange 6.00
6 AAd,WPo(i),A:Dr. Strange 6.00
TPB Reprints #1-#6 . . . . 17.00
1-shot, JMD,MZi,AW (1997) 4.00

LOOSE CANNONS

1 and 2 DAn . . . . @2.50
3 DAn 2.75

LORNA, THE JUNGLE GIRL
Marvel Atlas, 1953–57

1 Terrors of the Jungle,O:Lorna . 500.00

Lorna, The Jungle Girl #20
© Marvel Entertainment Group

2 Headhunter's Strike
    I:Greg Knight 225.00
3 . . . . 200.00
4 . . . . 200.00
5 . . . . 200.00
6 RH(c),GT 150.00
7 RH(c) 150.00
8 Jungle Queen Strikes Again . . 150.00
9 . . . . 150.00
10 White Fang 150.00
11 Death From the Skies 150.00
12 Day of Doom 125.00
13 thru 17 . . . . @125.00
18 AW(c) 150.00
19 thru 26 . . . . @100.00

LOVE ADVENTURES
Marvel Atlas, Oct., 1949

1 Ph(c) 250.00
2 BP,Ph(c),Tyrone Power/
    Gene Tierney 225.00
3 thru 12 . . . . @150.00
Becomes:

ACTUAL CONFESSIONS
1952

13 . . . . 100.00
14 Dec., 1952 . . . . 100.00

LOVE CLASSICS
Marvel Classic Detective, 1949

1 . . . . 200.00
2 . . . . 200.00

LOVE DRAMAS
Oct., 1949

1 Ph(c),JKa 225.00
2 Jan., 1950 . . . . 150.00

LOVELAND
1949

1 Ph(c) 150.00
2 Ph(c) 150.00

LOVE ROMANCES See: IDEAL

LOVERS
See: ALL-SELECT COMICS

LOVE SECRETS
Oct., 1949

1 . . . . 200.00
2 Jan., 1950 . . . . 150.00

MARVEL

All comics prices listed are for *Near Mint* condition.

LOVE TALES
Marvel Atlas, 1949–56
(Formerly: The Human Torch)
36 Ph(c) 250.00
37 . . . . 175.00
38 . . . . 150.00
39 thru 41 . . . . @150.00
42 thru 44 . . . . @125.00
45 BP 150.00
46 thru 51 . . . . @125.00
52 BK 150.00
53 thru 68 . . . . @125.00
69 BEv 150.00
70 thru 75 . . . . @100.00

LOVE TRAILS
Marvel Current Detective, 1949
1 western romance 175.00
2 . . . . 175.00

LUNATIK
1995
1 KG 2.25
2 V:The Avengers 2.25
3 conclusion 2.25

Machine Man #10
© Marvel Entertainment Group

MACHINE MAN
April, 1978
1 JK,From 2001 . . . . 25.00
2 JK 12.00
3 JK,V:Ten-For,The Mean
   Machine 12.00
4 JK,V;Ten-For,Battle on A
   Busy Street 12.00
5 JK,V;Ten-For,Day of the
   Non-Hero 12.00
6 JK,V;Ten-For 12.00
7 JK,With A Nation Against Him . . 12.00
8 JK,Escape:Impossible 12.00
9 JK,In Final Battle 12.00
10 SD,Birth of A Super-Hero 7.00
11 SD,V;Binary Bug 7.00
12 SD,Where walk the Gods 7.00
13 SD,Xanadu 7.00
14 SD,V:Machine Man 7.00
15 SD,A:Thing,Human Torch 7.00
16 SD,I:Baron Brimstone And the
   Satan Squad 7.00
17 SD,Madam Menace 7.00
18 A:Alpha Flight 25.00
19 I:Jack o'Lantern 25.00

MACHINE MAN
[Limited-Series]
Oct., 1984
1 HT,BWS,V:Baintronics 4.00
2 HT,BWS,C:Iron Man of 2020 . . . . 4.00
3 HT,BWS,I:Iron Man of 2020 . . . . 4.00
4 HT,BWS,V:Iron Man of 2020 . . . . 4.00
TPB rep.#1-4 . . . . 6.00

MACHINE MAN 2020
1994
1 rep. limited series #1–#2 . . . . . . 2.25
2 rep. limited series #3–#4 . . . . . . 2.25

MACHINE TEEN
May, 2005
1 (of 5) F:Adam Aaronson 3.00
2 History 101001 . . . . 3.00
3 History 101001 . . . . 3.00
4 Trust no one 3.00
5 Finale 3.00
TPB History 101001 . . . . 8.00

MAD ABOUT MILLIE
April, 1969
1 . . . . 125.00
2 thru 3 . . . . @100.00
4 thru 10 . . . . @50.00
11 thru 16 . . . . @45.00
17 Dec., 1970 . . . . 45.00
Ann.#1 . . . . 50.00

MADBALLS
Star, Sept., 1986
1 Based on Toys 4.00
2 thru 9 . . . . @4.00
10 June, 1988 . . . . 4.00

MAD DOG
1 from Bob TV Show 2.50
2 V:Trans World Trust Corp. 2.50
3 V:Cigarette Criminals 2.50
4 V:Dogs of War 2.50
5 thru 6 . . . . @2.50

MADE MEN
May, 1998
1-shot HMe gangster epic 6.00

MADROX
Sept., 2004
1 (of 5) PDd(s),F:Jamie Madrox . . 3.00
2 PDd(s) 3.00
3 . . . . 3.00
4 . . . . 3.00
5 PDd(c),V:Clay,concl. 3.00
TPB Multiple Choice 14.00

MAGIK
Dec., 1983
1 JB,TP,F:Storm and Illyana 4.00
2 JB,TP,A:Belasco,Sym 3.00
3 TP,A:New Mutants,Belasco 3.00
4 TP,V:Belasco,A:Sym 3.00

MAGNETO
1993
0 JD,JBo,rep. origin stories 6.00
0a Gold ed. 8.00
0b Platinum ed. 10.00

MAGNETO
1996
1 (of 4) PrM,KJo,JhB, Joseph. 2.50
2 PrM,KJo,JhB, Joseph's search
   for his past life 2.50
3 PrM,KJo,JhB 2.50
4 PrM,KJo,JhB, concl. 2.50
TPB 192-pg. 20.00

MAGNETO:
DARK SEDUCTION
April, 2000
1 (of 4) FaN,X-Men: Revolution . . . 3.00
2 FaN,Scarlet Witch 3.00
3 FaN,RCz,V:Scarlet Witch 3.00
4 FaN,RCz,concl. 3.00

MAGNETO REX
March, 1999
1 (of 3) BPe,takes over Genosha . . 2.50
1a signed 20.00
2 BPe,V:Rogue 2.50
3 BPe,A:Rogue,Quicksilver 2.50
GN Magneto Ascendant,
   96-page rep. 4.00

MAN COMICS
Marvel Atlas, 1949–53
1 GT 350.00
2 GT 250.00
3 . . . . 200.00
4 . . . . 200.00
5 . . . . 200.00
6 . . . . 200.00
7 JeR 200.00
8 BEv 200.00
9 EC,TSe,War format begins . . . 150.00
10 JeR,MMe(c) 150.00
11 RH,TSe,MMe 150.00
12 . . . . 150.00
13 . . . . 150.00
14 GT,JeR 175.00
15 . . . . 150.00
16 . . . . 150.00
17 RH 175.00
18 . . . . 150.00
19 . . . . 150.00
20 . . . . 150.00
21 EC-RH 175.00
22 BEv(c),BK 175.00
23 GT,JSt 175.00
24 . . . . 150.00
25 BEv(c) 175.00
26 . . . . 150.00
27 . . . . 150.00
28 Where Mummies Prowl 150.00

MANDRAKE
1995
1 fully painted series 3.25
2 V:Octon 3.25
3 final issue 3.25

MAN FROM ATLANTIS
Feb., 1978–Aug., 1978
1 TS,From TV Series,O:Mark
   Harris 20.00
2 FR,FS,The Bermuda Triangle
   Trap 12.00
3 FR,FS,Undersea Shadow 12.00
4 FR,FS,Beware the Killer
   Spores 12.00
5 FR,FS,The Ray of the
   Red Death 12.00
6 FR,FS,Bait for the Behemoth . . 12.00
7 FR,FS,Behold the Land
   Forgotten 12.00

MAN-THING
[1st Series] Jan., 1974
1 FB,JM,A:Howard the Duck . . . 75.00
2 VM,ST,Hell Hath No Fury 30.00
3 VM,JA,I:Original Foolkiller 25.00
4 VM,JA,O&D:Foolkiller 20.00

MARVEL

Man-Thing #3
© Marvel Entertainment Group

MAN-THING
July, 2004
1 (of 3) movie prequel 3.00
2 movie prequel,pt.2 . . . . 3.00
3 movie prequel,pt.3 . . . . 3.00
TPB Whatever Knows Fear 13.00

MARINES AT WAR
See: DEVIL-DOG DUGAN

MARINES IN ACTION
Marvel Atlas, June, 1955
1 B:Rock Murdock,Boot Camp
  Brady 125.00
2 thru 13 . . . . @100.00
14 Sept., 1957 . . . . 100.00

MARINES IN BATTLE
Marvel Atlas, Aug., 1954
1 RH,B:Iron Mike McGraw 250.00
2 . . . . 150.00
3 thru 6 . . . . @125.00
7 thru 1/ . . . . @125.00
18 thru 22 . . . . @100.00
23 . . . . 125.00
24 . . . . 100.00
25 Sept., 1958 . . . . 125.00

MARK HAZZARD: MERC
Nov., 1986–Oct., 1987
1 GM,O:Mark Hazard 2.25
2 GM 2.25
3 M,Arab Terrorists 2.25
4 thru 8 GM . . . . @2.25
9 NKu/AKu 2.25
10 thru 12 . . . . @2.25
Ann.#1 D:Merc 2.25

MARSHALL LAW
Epic, 1987–89
1 . . . . 4.50
2 . . . . 3.00
3 thru 6 . . . . @2.50

MARVEL ACTION HOUR:
FANTASTIC FOUR
1994–95
1 regular 2.25
1a bagged with insert print from
  animated series 3.00
2 thru 8 . . . . @2.25

Marvel Action Hour: Iron Man #5
© Marvel Entertainment Group

5 MP,Night o/t Laughing Dead . . . 20.00
6 MP,V:Soul-Slayers,Drug Issue . . 20.00
7 MP,A Monster Stalks Swamp . . . 20.00
8 MP,Man Into Monster 20.00
9 MP,Deathwatch 20.00
10 MP,Nobody Dies Forever 20.00
11 MP,Dance to the Murder 20.00
12 KJ,Death-Cry of a Dead Man . . 12.00
13 TS,V:Captain Fate 12.00
14 AA,V:Captain Fate 12.00
15 A Candle for Saint Cloud 12.00
16 JB,TP,Death of a Legend 12.00
17 JM,Book Burns in Citrusville . . . 12.00
18 JM,Chaos on the Campus 12.00
19 JM,FS,I:Scavenger 12.00
20 JM,A:Spider-Man,Daredevil,
  Shang-Chi,Thing 14.00
21 JM,O:Scavenger,Man Thing . . . 12.00
22 JM,C:Howard the Duck 12.00
G-Size #1 MP,SD,JK,rep.TheGlob. 10.00
G-Size #2 JB,KJ,The
  Monster Runs Wild 10.00
G-Size #3 AA,A World He
  Never Made 10.00
G-Size #4 FS,EH,inc.Howard the
  Duck vs.Gorko 10.00
G-Size #5 DA,EH,inc.Howard the
  Duck vs.Vampire 12.00

[2nd Series] 1979–1981
1 JM,BWi 11.00
2 BWi,JM,Himalayan Nightmare . . 10.00
3 BWi.JM,V:Snowman 10.00
4 BWi,DP,V:Mordo,A:Dr Strange . 10.00
5 DP,BWi,This Girl is Terrified 10.00
6 DP,BWi,Fraternity Rites 10.00
7 BWi,DP Return of Captain Fate . 10.00
8 BWi,DP,V:Captain Fate 10.00
9 BWi(c),Save the Life of My
  Own Child 10.00
10 BWi,DP,Swampfire 10.00
11 Final issue 10.00

[3rd Series] Oct., 1997
1 JMD,LSh, non-code 3.00
2 JMD,LSh, reunion with ex-wife,
  A:Dr. Strange 3.00
3 JMD,LSh, visit to Devil Slayer . . . 3.00
4 JMD,LSh, V:Devil-Slayer 3.00
5 JMD,LSh, new abilities revealed . 3.00
6 JMD,LSh, V:Cult of Entropy 3.00
7 JMD,LSh, Muck Monster, Namor . 3.00
8 JMD,LSh, Muck Monster turned
  back into Ted Sallis 3.00
Storyline continues in Strange Tales

MARVEL ACTION HOUR:
IRON MAN
1994–95
1 regular 2.25
1a bagged with insert print from
  animated series 3.25
2 thru 8 . . . . @2.25

MARVEL ACTION
UNIVERSE
TV Tie-in, Jan., 1989
1 Rep.Spider-Man & Friends 4.00

MARVEL ADVENTURES
STARRING DAREDEVIL
Dec., 1975–Oct., 1976
1 Rep,Daredevil #22 . . . . 20.00
2 thru 6, Rep.,Daredevil . . . . . . @10.00

MARVEL ADVENTURES
Feb., 1997
1 RMc,F:The Hulk 2.25
2 thru 20 RMc . . . . @2.25

MARVEL ADVENTURES
Flipbook, June, 2005
1 Marvel Adventures Spider-Man #1
  & Fantastic Four #1 . . . . 4.00
2 thru 13 . . . . @4.00
14 thru 17 . . . . @5.00

MARVEL ADVENTURES
FANTASTIC FOUR
May, 2005
0 SEa,Dr. Doom 2.00
1 . . . . 2.50
2 thru 10 . . . . @2.50
11 thru 18 . . . . @3.00
TPB Vol. 1 . . . . 7.00
TPB Vol. 2 Fantastic Voyages 7.00
TPB Vol. 3 World's Greatest 7.00
TPB Vol. 4 Cosmic Threats 7.00

MARVEL ADVENTURES
SPIDER-MAN
March, 2005
1 Birth of Spider-Man 2.25
2 thru 13 . . . . @2.50
14 thru 21 . . . . @3.00
Digest Vol. 1:The Sinister Six 7.00
Digest Vol. 2 Power Struggle 7.00
Digest Vol. 3 Doom with a View . . . 7.00
Digest Vol. 4 Concrete Jungle 7.00
TPB Vol. 1 . . . . 20.00

MARVEL ADVENTURES
THE AVENGERS
May, 2006
1 . . . . 3.00
2 thru 7 . . . . @3.00
Digest Vol. 1 Heroes Assembled . . 7.00

MARVEL ADVENTURES
THE THING
March, 2005
1 (of 4) Destiny's Song 2.25
2 Thing Vs. Hulk 2.25
3 Invisible Things 2.50

MARVEL AGE:
FANTASTIC FOUR
April, 2004
1 V:Mole Man 2.25

MARVEL

2 thru 12 . . . . @2.25
Digest #1 All for One 6.00
Digest #2 Doom. 6.00
Digest #3 Return of Doctor Doom . . 6.00

MARVEL AGE:
FANTASTIC FOUR TALES
Feb., 2005
1 V:Black Panther. 2.25
Digest Vol. 1: Fantastic Four Tales . 8.00

MARVEL AGE: HULK
Sept., 2004
1 . . . . 2.50
2 . . . . 2.50
3 . . . . 3.00
4 . . . . 3.00
Digest, rep. #1–#4 . . . . 6.00

MARVEL AGE RUNAWAYS
Digest #3 The Good Die Young. . . . 8.00

MARVEL AGE:
SENTINEL
2004
1 Salvage, digest 8.00
2 No Hero, digest 8.00

MARVEL AGE:
SPIDER-MAN
March, 2004
1 V:Vulture 2.25
2 thru 20 . . . . @2.25
Digest #1 thru #4 . . . . @6.00
Digest, rep. #17–#20 . . . . 6.00

MARVEL AGE
SPIDER-MAN TALES
Feb., 2005
1 O:Spider-Man. 2.25

MARVEL AGE:
SPIDER-MAN TEAM-UP
Sept., 2004
1 F:Fantastic Four. 2.50
2 F:Captain America 2.50
3 . . . . 2.25
4 . . . . 2.25
5 F:storm. 2.25
Digest, rep. #1–4 . . . . 6.00
Digest Vol. 1: A Little Helf From
   My Friends. 8.00

MARVEL &
DC PRESENTS
Nov., 1982
1 WS,TA,X-Men & Titans,A:Darkseid,
   Deathstroke(3rd App.), ... 25.00

MARVEL BOY
See: ASTONISHING

MARVEL BOY
June, 2000
1 (of 6) GMo,F:Noh-Varr. 4.00
2 GMo,V:Human Race 3.50
3 GMo,Hexus 3.50
4 GMo,Exterminatrix 3.50
5 GMo,Oubliette 3.50
6 GMo,V:Dr. Midas,concl. 3.50
TPB rep.,144-page. 16.00

MARVEL CHILLERS
Oct., 1975
1 GK(c),I:Mordred the Mystic 25.00
2 E:Mordred 12.00
3 HC/BWr(c),B:Tigra,The Were
   Woman 22.00
4 V:Kraven The Hunter 12.00
5 V:Rat Pack,A:Red Wolf 12.00
6 RB(c),JBy,V:Red Wolf 12.00
7 JK(c),GT,V:Super Skrull
   E:Tigra,Oct., 1976 . . . . 12.00
GN MGu(s),LSh,F:The Hulk 10.00
GN LHa(s) F:Wolverine 10.00

MARVEL CHRISTMAS
SPECIAL
1 DC/AAd/KJ/SB/RLm,A:Ghost Rider
   X-Men,Spider-Man. 2.25

Marvel Classics Comics #11
© Marvel Entertainment Group

MARVEL CLASSICS
COMICS
1976–78
1 GK/DA(c),B:Reprints from
   Pendulum Illustrated Comics
   Dr.Jekyll & Mr. Hyde 30.00
2 GK(c),AN,Time Machine 20.00
3 GK/KJ(c) The Hunchback of
   Notre Dame 20.00
4 GK/DA(c),20,000 Leagues–
   Beneath the Sea by Verne. . . 20.00
5 GK(c),RN,Black Beauty 20.00
6 GK(c),Gullivers Travels 20.00
7 GK(c),Tom Sawyer 20.00
8 GK(c),AN,Moby Dick 20.00
9 GK(c),NR,Dracula 20.00
10 GK(c),Red Badge of Courage . 20.00
11 GK(c),Mysterious Island 15.00
12 GK/DA(c),AN,3 Musketeers . . . 15.00
13 GK(c),Last of the Mohicans . . . 15.00
14 GK(c),War of the Worlds. 15.00
15 GK(c),Treasure Island. 15.00
16 GK(c),Ivanhoe. 12.00
17 JB/ECh(c),The Count of
   Monte Cristo. 12.00
18 ECh(c),The Odyssey. 12.00
19 JB(c),Robinson Crusoe. 12.00
20 Frankenstein. 12.00
21 GK(c),Master of the World . . . 12.00
22 GK(c),Food of the Gods 12.00
23 Moonstone by Wilkie Collins. . . 12.00
24 GK/RN(c),She. 12.00

25 The Invisible Man by H.G.Wells 12.00
26 JB(c),The Illiad by Homer. 12.00
27 Kidnapped. 12.00
28 MGo(1st art) The Pit and
   the Pendulum 15.00
29 The Prisoner of Zenda 12.00
30 The Arabian Nights 12.00
31 The First Men in the Moon 12.00
32 GK(c),White Fang. 12.00
33 The Prince and the Pauper. . . . 12.00
34 AA,Robin Hood 12.00
35 FBe,Alice in Wonderland 12.00
36 A Christmas Carol. 12.00

MARVEL COLLECTORS
ITEM CLASSICS
Feb., 1965
1 SD,JK,reprint FF #2. . . . . 375.00
2 SD,JK,reprint FF #3. . . . . 150.00
3 SD,JK,reprint FF #4. . . . . 135.00
4 SD,JK,reprint FF #7. . . . . 135.00
5 thru 10 SD,JK,rep.F.Four . . @100.00
11 thru 22 SD,JK,rep.F.Four . . @75.00
Becomes:

MARVEL'S GREATEST
COMICS
1969–81
23 thru 34 SD,JK,rep.F.Four . . @30.00
35 thru 37 JK,rep.F.Four . . . . . @20.00
38 thru 50 JK,rep.F.Four . . . . . @15.00
51 thru 75 JK,rep.F.Four . . . . . @10.00
76 thru 96 rep.F.Four . . . . @9.00

MARVEL COMICS
Oct.-Nov., 1939
1 FP(c),BEv,CBu,O:Sub-Mariner
   I&B:The Angel,A:Human Torch,
   Ka-Zar,Jungle Terror,
   B:The Masked Raider . . 400,000.00
Becomes:

MARVEL MYSTERY
COMICS
2 CSM(c),BEv,CBu,PGv,
   B:American, Ace,Human
   Torch,Sub-Mariner,Ka-Zar 50,000.00
3 ASh(c),BEv,CBu,PGv,
   E:American Ace 27,000.00
4 ASh(c),BEv,CBu,PGv,
   I&B:Electro,The Ferret,
   Mystery Detective. 25,000.00
5 ASh(c),BEv,CBu,PGv,
   Human Torch(c) 45,000.00
6 ASh(c),BEv,CBu,PGv,
   Anglel(c) 15,000.00
7 ASh(c),BEv,CBu,PGv,
   Bondage(c) 15,000.00
8 ASh(c),BEv,CBu,PGv,Human
   TorchV:Sub-Mariner 18,000.00
9 ASh(c),BEv,CBu,PGv,Human
   Torch V:Sub-Mariner(c) . . 45,000.00
10 ASh(c),BEv,CBu,PGv,B:Terry
   Vance Boy Detective 16,000.00
11 ASh(c),BEv,CBu,PGv,
   Human Torch V:Nazis(c). . . 6,500.00
12 ASh(c),BEv,CBu,
   PGv,Angel(c) 7,000.00
13 ASh(c),BEv,CBu,PGv,S&K,
   I&B:The Vision 9,000.00
14 ASh(c),BEv,CBu,PGv,S&K,
   Sub-Mariner V:Nazis 4,800.00
15 ASh(c),BEv,CBu,PGv,S&K,
   Sub-Mariner(c) 4,800.00
16 ASh(c),BEv,CBu,PGv,S&K,
   HumanTorch/NaziAirbase. . 4,800.00
17 ASh(c),BEv,CBu,PGv,S&K,
   Human Torch/Sub-Mariner 5,000.00
18 ASh(c),BEv,CBu,PGv,S&K,
   Human Torch & Toro(c) . . . 4,500.00

All comics prices listed are for *Near Mint* condition.

19 ASh(c),BEv,CBu,PGv,S&K,
  O:Toro,E:Electro 4,500.00
20 ASh(c),BEv,CBu,PGv,S&K,
  O:The Angel 4,500.00
21 ASh(c),BEv,CBu,PGv,S&K,
  I&B:The Patriot 4,500.00
22 ASh(c),BEv,CBu,PGv,S&K,
  AAv,Toro/Bomb(c). 4,000.00
23 ASh(c),BEv,CBu,PGv,S&K,
  O:Vision,E:The Angel 4,000.00
24 ASh(c),BEv,CBu,S&K,
  AAv,Human Torch(c). 4,000.00
25 BEv,CBu,S&K,ASh Nazi(c) . 4,000.00
26 ASh(c),BEv,CBu,S&K,
  Sub-Mariner(c) 3,500.00
27 ASh(c),BEv,CBu,
  S&K,E:Ka-Zar 3,500.00
28 ASh(c),BEv,CBu,S&K,Bondage
  (c),B:Jimmy Jupiter 3,500.00
29 ASh(c),BEv,CBu,SSh,
  Bondage(c). 3,500.00
30 BEv,CBu,SSh,Pearl
  Harbor(c) 3,500.00
31 BEv,CBu,Human Torch(c) . . 4,200.00
32 CBu,I:The Boboes 3,500.00
33 ASh(c),CBu,SSh,Jap(c) 3,000.00
34 ASh(c),CBu,SSh,V:Hitler . . . 3,500.00
35 ASh(c),SSh,BeachAssault(c) 3,000.00
36 ASh(c),Nazi Invasion of NY . 3,000.00
37 SSh(c),Nazi(c) 3,000.00
38 SSh(c),Battlefield(c). 3,000.00
39 ASh(c),Nazis/U.S(c). 3,000.00
40 ASh(c),SSh,Zeppelin(c) 3,000.00
41 ASh(c),Jap. Command(c) . . . 2,700.00
42 ASh(c),Japanese Sub(c) . . . 2,700.00
43 ASh(c),SSh,Destroyed
  Bridge(c). 2,700.00
44 ASh(c),Nazi Super Plane(c). 2,700.00
45 ASh(c),SSh,Nazi(c) 2,700.00
46 ASh(c),Hitler Bondage(c). . . 2,700.00
47 ASh(c),Ruhr Valley Dam(c) . 2,700.00
48 ASh(c),E:Jimmy Jupiter,
  Vision,Allied Invasion(c) . . . 2,700.00
49 SSh(c),O:Miss America,
  Bondage(c) 3,000.00
50 ASh(c),Bondage(c),Miss
  Patriot 2,700.00
51 ASh(c),Nazi Torture(c) 2,500.00
52 ASh(c),Bondage(c). 2,500.00
53 ASh(c),Bondage(c). 2,500.00
54 ASh(c),Bondage(c). 2,500.00
55 ASh(c),Bondage(c). 2,500.00
56 ASh(c),Bondage(c). 2,500.00
57 ASh(c),Torture/Bondage(c) . 2,500.00
58 ASh(c),Torture(c) 2,500.00
59 ASh(c),Testing Room(c). . . . 2,500.00
60 ASh(c),Japanese Gun(c) . . . 2,500.00
61 ASh(c),Torturer Chamber(c). 2,500.00
62 ASh(c),Violent(c) 2,500.00
63 ASh(c),Nazi High
  Command(c). 2,500.00
64 ASh(c),Last Nazi(c) 2,500.00
65 ASh(c),Bondage(c). 2,500.00
66 ASh(c),Last Japanese(c) . . . 2,500.00
67 ASh(c),Treasury raid(c) 2,500.00
68 ASh(c),Torture Chamber(c) . 3,600.00
69 ASh(c),Torture Chamber(c) . 2,500.00
70 Cops & Robbers(c) 2,500.00
71 ASh(c),Egyptian(c). 2,500.00
72 Police(c). 2,500.00
73 Werewolf Headlines(c). 2,500.00
74 ASh(c),Robbery(c),E:The
  Patriot. 2,500.00
75 SSh,Tavern(c),B:YoungAllies 2,500.00
76 ASh(c),Shoot-out(c),B:Miss
  America 2,500.00
77 SSh,Human Torch/Sub-
  Mariner(c) 2,500.00
78 SSh,Safe Robbery(c). 2,500.00
79 SSh,Super Villians(c),E:The
  Angel 2,500.00

80 SSh,I:Capt.America
  (In Marvel) 3,000.00
81 SSh,Mystery o/t Crimson
  Terror 2,200.00
82 SSh,I:Sub-Mariner/Namora
  Team-up, O:Namora,A:Capt.
  America 4,500.00
83 SSh,The Photo Phantom,
  E;Young Allies. 1,800.00
84 SSh,BEv,B:Blonde Phantom 3,000.00
85 SSh,BEv,A:Blonde Phantom,
  E;Miss America. 2,000.00
86 BEv,Blonde Phantom ID
  Revealed,E:Bucky 1,800.00
87 SSh,BEv,I:Capt.America/Golden
  Girl Team-up. 3,200.00
88 SSh,BEv,E:Toro 1,800.00
89 SSh,BEv,AAv,I:Human Torch/
  Sun Girl Team-up 1,800.00
90 BEv,Giant of the Mountains 1,800.00
91 BEv,I:Venus,E:Blonde
  Phantom,Sub-Mariner 1,800.00
92 BEv,How the Human Torch was
  Born,D:Professor Horton,I:The
  Witness,A.Capt.America. . . 5,500.00
92a Marvel #33(c)rare,reps. . . 40,000.00
Becomes:

MARVEL TALES
Aug., 1949

93 The Ghoul Strikes 2,200.00
94 BEv,The Haunted Love 1,400.00
95 The Living Death. 950.00
96 MSy,SSh(c),Monster Returns . 950.00
97 DRi,MSy,The Wooden
  Horror 1,200.00
98 BEv,BK,MSy,The Curse of
  the Black Cat 1,000.00
99 DRi,The Secret of the Wax
  Museum. 900.00
100 The Eyes of Doom. 1,000.00
101 The Man Who Died Twice . . 900.00
102 BW,A Witch Among Us . . . 1,300.00
103 RA,A Touch of Death 1,000.00
104 RH(c),BW,BEv,The Thing
  in the Mirror 1,300.00
105 RH(c),GC,JSt,The Spider. . 1,000.00
106 RH(c),BK,BEv,In The Dead of
  the Night 750.00
107 GC,OW,BK,The Thing in the
  Sewer 750.00
108 RH(c),BEv,JR,Horror in the
  Moonlight. 500.00
109 BEv(c),Sight for Sore Eyes. . 500.00
110 RH,SSh,A Coffin for Carlos . 500.00
111 BEv,Horror Under the Earth . 500.00
112 The House That Death Built . 500.00
113 RH,Terror Tale. 500.00
114 BEv(c),GT,JM,2 for Zombie. . 500.00
115 The Man With No Face. 500.00
116 JSt 500.00
117 BEv(c),GK,Terror in the
  North. 500.00
118 RH,DBr,GC,A World
  Goes Mad 500.00
119 RH,They Gave Him A Grave. 500.00
120 GC,Graveyard(c). 500.00
121 GC,Graveyard(c). 400.00
122 JKu,Missing One Body 400.00
123 No Way Out 400.00
124 He Waits at the Tombstone. . 400.00
125 JF,Horror House 400.00
126 DW,It Came From Nowhere . 375.00
127 BEv(c),GC,MD,Gone is the
  Gargoyle 375.00
128 Emily,Flying Saucer(c) 375.00
129 You Can't Touch Bottom . . . 375.00
130 RH(c),JF,The Giant Killer . . . 375.00
131 GC,BEv,Five Fingers 375.00
132 . . . . 250.00
133 . . . . 250.00
134 BK,JKu,Flying Saucer(c). . . . 250.00
135 thru 143. . . . . @250.00

144 AW 265.00
145 . . . . 250.00
146 MD 200.00
147 BEv 250.00
148 thru 151 BEv. . . . . @225.00
152 JMn 225.00
153 BEv 250.00
154 thru 158. . . . . @200.00
159 Aug., 1957. . . . . 225.00

Marvel Comics Presents #10
© Marvel Entertainment Group

MARVEL COMICS PRESENTS
Sept., 1988

1 WS(c),B:Wolverine(JB,KJ),Master
  of Kung Fu(TS),Man-Thing(TGr,DC)
  F:Silver Surfer(AM) 10.00
2 F:The Captain(AM) 5.00
3 JR2(c),F:The Thing(AM) 5.00
4 Γ:Thor(ΛM) 5.00
5 F:Daredevil(DT,MG). 5.00
6 F:Hulk 4.00
7 F:Submariner(SD) 4.00
8 CV(c),E:Master of Kung Fu,F:
  Iron Man(JS) 4.00
9 F:Cloak,El Aquila 4.00
10 E:Wolverine,B:Colossus(RL,CR),
  F:Machine Man(SD,DC) 4.00
11 F:Ant-Man(BL),Slag(RWi) 3.00
12 E:Man-Thing,F:Hercules(DH),
  Namorita(FS). 3.00
13 B:Black Panther(GC,TP),F:
  Shanna,Mr.Fantastic &
  Invisible Woman 3.00
14 F:Nomad(CP),Speedball(SD) . . 3.00
15 F:Marvel Girl(DT,MG),Red
  Wolf(JS). 3.00
16 F:Ka-Zar(JM),Longshot(AA) . . . 3.00
17 E:Colossus,B:Cyclops(RLm),
  F:Watcher(TS) 4.00
18 F:She-Hulk(JBy,BWi),Willie
  Lumpkin(JSt) 3.00
19 RLd(c)B:Dr.Strange(MBg),
  I:Damage Control(EC,AW) 3.00
20 E:Dr.Strange,F:Clea(RLm) 3.00
21 F:Thing,Paladin(RWi,DA) 3.00
22 F:Starfox(DC),Wolfsbane &
  Mirage 3.00
23 F:Falcon(DC),Wheels(RWi) . . . 3.00
24 E:Cyclops,B:Havok(RB,JRu),
  F:Shamrock(DJ,DA) 3.00
25 F:Ursa Major,I:Nth Man. 4.00
26 B&I:Coldblood(PG),F:Hulk . . . 2.50
27 F:American Eagle(RWi) 2.50

28 F:Triton(JS). 2.50
29 F:Quasar(PR). 2.50
30 F:Leir(TMo). 2.50
31 EL,E:Havok,B:Excalibur
   (EL,TA) 4.00
32 TM(c),F:Sunfire(DH,DC). 3.00
33 F:Namor(JLe 4.00
34 F:Captain America(JsP) 3.00
35 E:Coldblood,F:Her(EL,AG) 4.00
36 BSz(c),F:Hellcat(JBr) 4.00
37 E:Bl.Panther,F:Devil-Slayer 4.00
38 E:Excalibur,B:Wonderman(JS),
   Wolverine(JB),F:Hulk(MR,DA). . 4.00
39 F:Hercules(BL),Spider-Man 3.50
40 F:Hercules(BL),Overmind(DH) . . 3.50
41 F:Daughters of the Dragon(DA),
   Union Jack(KD) 3.50
42 F:Iron Man(MBa),Siryn(LSn). . . . 3.50
43 F:Iron Man(MBa),Siryn(LSn). . . . 3.50
44 F:Puma(BWi),Dr.Strange 3.50
45 E:Wonderman,F:Hulk(HT),
   Shooting Star. 3.50
46 RLd(c),B:Devil-Slayer,F:Namor,
   Aquarian 3.50
47 JBy(c),E:Wolverine,F:Captain
   America,Arabian Knight(DP) . . . 3.50
48 B:Wolverine&Spider-Man(EL),
   F:Wasp,Storm&Dr.Doom 5.00
49 E:Devil-Slayer,F:Daredevil(RWi),
   Gladiator(DH) 4.50
50 E:Wolverine&Spider-Man,B:Comet
   Man(KJo),F:Captain Ultra(DJ),
   Silver Surfer(JkS) 4.50
51 B:Wolverine(RLd),F:Iron Man
   (MBr,DH),Le Peregrine 4.00
52 F:Rick Jones,Hulk(RWi,TMo) . . . 4.00
53 E:Wolverine,Comet Man,F:
   Silver Sable&Black Widow
   (RLd,BWi),B:Stingray. 4.00
54 B:Wolverine&Hulk(DR),
   Werewolf,F:Shroud(SD,BWi) . . . 6.00
55 F:Collective Man(GLa) 6.00
56 E:Stingray,F:Speedball(SD) 6.00
57 DK(c),B:Submariner(MC,MFm),
   Black Cat(JRu) 6.00
58 F:Iron Man(SD). 6.00
59 E:Submariner,Werewolf,
   F:Punisher. 6.00
60 B:Poison,Scarlet Witch,
   F:Captain America(TL) 6.00
61 E:Wolverine&Hulk,
   F:Dr.Strange 6.00
62 F:Wolverine(PR),Deathlok(JG) . . 6.00
63 F:Wolverine(PR),E:Scarlet
   Witch,Thor(DH) 4.00
64 B:Wolverine&Ghost Rider(MT),
   Fantastic Four(TMo),F:Blade. . . 4.00
65 F:Starfox(ECh) 3.50
66 F:Volstagg. 3.50
67 E:Poison,F:Spider-Man(MG). . . . 3.50
68 B:Shanna(PG),E:Fantastic Four
   F:Lockjaw(JA,AM) 3.50
69 B:Daredevil(DT),F:Silver Surfer . 3.50
70 F:BlackWidow&Darkstar(AM) . . . 3.50
71 E:Wolverine&Ghost Rider,F:
   Warlock(New Mutants)(SMc). . . 3.50
72 B:Weapon X(BWS),E:Daredevil,
   F:Red Wolf(JS) 7.00
73 F:Black Knight(DC),
   Namor(JM). 5.00
74 F:Constrictor(SMc),Iceman &
   Human Torch(JSon,DA). 5.00
75 F:Meggan & Shadowcat,
   Dr.Doom(DC). 5.00
76 F:Death's Head(BHi,MFm),
   A:Woodgod(DC) 5.00
77 E:Shanna,B:Sgt.Fury&Dracula
   (TL,JRu),F:Namor 4.50
78 F:Iron Man(KSy),Hulk&Selene . . 4.50
79 E:Sgt.Fury&Dracula,F:Dr.Strange,
   Sunspot(JBy). 4.50

Marvel Comics Presents #149
© Marvel Entertainment Group

80 F:Daughters of the Dragon,Mister
   Fantastic(DJ),Captain America
   (SD,TA) 4.50
81 F:Captain America(SD,TA),
   Daredevil(MR,AW),Ant-Man . . . 4.00
82 B:Firestar(DT),F:Iron Man(SL),
   Power Man 4.00
83 F:Hawkeye,Hum.Torch(SD,EL) . 4.00
84 E:Weapon X 4.00
85 B:Wolverine(SK),Beast(RLd,JaL-
   1st Work),F:Speedball(RWi),
   I:Cyber. 7.00
86 F:PaladinE:RLd on Beast 5.00
87 E:Firestar,F:Shroud(RWi) 5.00
88 F:Solo,Volcana(BWi). 5.00
89 F:Spitfire(JSn),Mojo(JMa) 5.00
90 B:Ghost Rider & Cable,F:
   Nightmare 4.50
91 F:Impossible Man 3.50
92 E:Wolverine,Beast,
   F:Northstar(JMa) 3.50
93 SK(c),B:Wolverine,Nova,
   F:Daredevil 3.00
94 F:Gabriel 3.00
95 SK(c),E:Wolverine,F:Hulk 3.00
96 B:Wolverine(TT),E:Nova,
   F:Speedball 3.00
97 F:Chameleon,Two-Gun Kid,
   E:Ghost Rider/Cable 3.00
98 E:Wolverine,F:Ghost Rider,
   Werewolf by Night 2.50
99 F:Wolverine,Ghost Rider,
   Mary Jane,Captain America. . . . 2.50
100 SK,F:Ghost Rider,Wolverine,
   Dr.Doom,Nightmare. 3.00
101 SK(c),B:Ghost Rider&Doctor
   Strange,Young Gods,Wolverine
   &Nightcrawler,F:Bar With
   No Name 2.50
102 RL,GC,AW,F:Speedball 2.50
103 RL,GC,AW,F:Puck. 2.50
104 RL,GC,AW,F:Lockheed. 2.50
105 RL,GC,AW,F:Nightmare 2.50
106 RL,GC,AW,F:Gabriel,E:Ghost
   Rider&Dr.Strange. 2.50
107 GC,AW,TS,B:Ghost Rider&
   Werewolf 2.50
108 GC,AW,TS,SMc,E:Wolverine&
   Nightcrawler,B:Thanos 2.50
109 SLi,TS,SMc,B:Wolverine&
   Typhoid Mary,E:Young Gods . . . 2.50
110 SLi,SMc,F:Nightcrawler. 2.50
111 SK(c),SLi,RWi,F:Dr.Strange,
   E:Thanos 2.50

112 SK(c),SLi,F:Pip,Wonder Man,
   E:Ghost Rider&Werewolf. 2.50
113 SK(c),SLi,B:Giant Man,
   Ghost Rider&Iron Fist 2.50
114 SK(c),SLi,F:Arabian Knight. . . . 2.50
115 SK(c),SLi,F:Cloak&Dagger 2.50
116 SK(c),SLi,E:Wolverine &
   Typhoid Mary. 2.50
117 SK,PR,B:Wolverine&Venom,
   I:Ravage 2099. . . . . 4.00
118 SK,PB,RWi,E:Giant Man,
   I:Doom 2099 . . . . 3.00
119 SK,GC,B:Constrictor,E:Ghost
   Rider&Iron Fist,F:Wonder Man . 3.00
120 SK,GC,E:Constrictor,B:Ghost
   Rider/Cloak & Dagger,
   F:Spider-Man 2.50
121 SK,GC,F:Mirage,Andromeda . . 2.50
122 SK(c),GK,E:Wolverine&Venom,
   Ghost Rider&Cloak&Dagger,F:
   Speedball&Rage,Two-Gun Kid . 2.50
123 SK(c),DJ,SLi,B:Wolverine&Lynx,
   Ghost Rider&Typhoid Mary,
   She-Hulk,F:Master Man 2.50
124 SK(c),DJ,MBa,SLi,F:Solo 2.50
125 SLi,SMc,DJ,B:Iron Fist 2.50
126 SLi,DJ,E:She-Hulk 2.50
127 SLi,DJ,DP,F:Speedball 2.50
128 SLi,DJ,RWi,F:American Eagle . 2.50
129 SLi,DJ,F:Ant Man 2.50
130 DJ,SLi,RWi,E:Wolverine&Lynx,
   Ghost Rider&Typhoid Mary,Iron
   Fist,F:American Eagle. 2.50
131 MFm,B:Wolverine,Ghost Rider&
   Cage,Iron Fist&Sabretooth,
   F:Shadowcat 2.50
132 KM(c),F:Iron Man 2.50
133 F:Cloak & Dagger 2.50
134 SLi,F:Vance Astro 2.50
135 SLi,F:Daredevil 2.50
136 B:Gh.Rider&Masters of Silence,
   F:Iron Fist,Daredevil 2.50
137 F:Ant Man 2.50
138 B:Wolverine,Spellbound 2.50
139 F:Foreigner. 2.50
140 F:Captain Universe 2.50
141 BCe(s),F:Iron Fist 2.50
142 E:Gh.Rider&Masters of Silence,
   F:Mr.Fantastic 2.50
143 Siege of Darkness,pt.#3,
   B:Werewolf,Scarlet Witch,
   E:Spellbound 2.50
144 Siege of Darkness,pt.#6,
   B:Morbius 2.50
145 Siege of Darkness,pt.#11 . . . . . 2.50
146 Siege of Darkness,pt.#14 . . . . . 2.50
147 B:Vengeance,F:Falcon,Masters of
   Silence,American Eagle 2.50
148 E:Vengeance,F:Capt.Universe,
   Black Panther 2.50
149 F:Daughter o/t Dragon,Namor,
   Vengeance,Starjammers 2.50
150 ANo(s),SLi,F:Typhoid Mary,DD,
   Vengeance,Wolverine 2.50
151 ANo(s),F:Typhoid Mary,DD,
   Vengeance. 2.50
152 CDi(s),PR,B:Vengeance,Wolverine,
   War Machine,Moon Knight 2.50
153 CDi(s),A:Vengeance,Wolverine,
   War Machine,Moon Knight 2.50
154 CDi(s),E:Vengeance,Wolverine,
   War Machine,Moon Knight 2.50
155 CDi(s),B:Vengeance,Wolverine,
   War Machine,Kymaera 2.50
156 B:Shang Chi,F:Destroyer 2.50
157 F:Nick Fury 2.50
158 AD,I:Clan Destine,E:Kymaera,
   Shang Chi,Vengeance. 2.50
159 B:Hawkeye, New Warriors,
   F:Fun,E:Vengeance. 2.50
160 B:Vengeance,Mace. 2.50
161 E:Hawkeye 2.50

162 B:Tigra,E:Mace 2.50
163 E:New Warriors. 2.50
164 Tigra, Vengeance 2.50
165 Tigra, Vengeance 2.50
166 Turbo, Vengeance. 2.50
167 Turbo, Vengeance. 2.50
168 Thing, Vengeance 2.50
169 Mandarin, Vengeance 2.50
170 Force, Vengeance. 2.50
171 Nick Fury. 2.50
172 Lunatik 2.50
173 . . . . 2.50
174 . . . . 2.50
175 . . . . 2.50
TPB Ghost Rider & Cable,rep. 4.00
TPB Save the Tyger, rep. 4.00
TPB Vol. 1:Wolverine Classic 13.00
TPB Vol. 2 Wolverine. 13.00
TPB Vol. 3 Wolverine. 13.00

MARVEL COMICS SUPER SPECIAL
[Magazine, 1977]
1 JB,WS,Kiss,Features &Photos 200.00
2 JB,Conan(1978) 25.00
3 WS,Close Encounters 15.00
4 GP,KJ,Beatles story 65.00
Becomes:

MARVEL SUPER SPECIAL
5 Kiss 1978 . . . . 200.00
6 GC,Jaws II 15.00
7 Does Not Exist
8 Battlestar Galactica(Tabloid) . . . 20.00
9 Conan 15.00
10 GC,Starlord 11.00
11 JB,RN,Weirdworld. 11.00
12 JB,Weirdworld, ... 11.00
13 JB,Weirdworld. 11.00
14 GC,Meteor,adapt. 11.00
15 Star Trek 11.00
15a Star Trek 12.00
16 AW,B:Movie Adapts,Empire
    Strikes Back. 12.00
17 Xanadu 7.00
18 HC(c),JB,Raiders of the Lost
    Ark. 7.00
19 HC,For Your Eyes Only 9.00
20 Dragonslayer 7.00
21 JB,Conan 7.00
22 JSo(c),AW,Bladerunner 9.00
23 Annie 9.00
24 Dark Crystal 9.00
25 Rock and Rule 9.00
26 Octopussy. 8.00
27 AW,Return of the Jedi. 9.00
28 PH(c),Krull. 8.00
29 DSp,Tarzan of the Apes 8.00
30 Indiana Jones and the Temple
    of Doom 9.00
31 The Last Star Fighter 9.00
32 Muppets Take Manhattan 9.00
33 Buckaroo Banzai. 11.00
34 GM,Sheena. 9.00
35 JB,Conan The Destroyer 9.00
36 Dune 9.00
37 2010 . . . . 9.00
38 Red Sonja. 9.00
39 Santa Claus 9.00
40 JB,Labrynth 9.00
41 Howard the Duck,Nov.,1986 . . . 9.00

MARVEL DOUBLE FEATURE
Dec., 1973
1 JK,GC,B:Tales of Suspense
    Reprints,Capt.America,
    Iron-Man 25.00
2 JK,GC ,A:Nick Fury 15.00
3 JK,GC 15.00
4 JK,GC,Cosmic Cube 15.00

Marvel Double Feature #5
© Marvel Entertainment Group

5 JK,GC,V:Red Skull 15.00
6 JK,GC,V:Adaptoid. 15.00
7 JK,GC,V:Tumbler 15.00
8 JK,GC,V:Super Adaptoid 15.00
9 GC,V:Batroc 15.00
10 GC. 15.00
11 GC,Capt.America Wanted. 10.00
12 GC,V:Powerman,Swordsman. . 10.00
13 GC,A:Bucky 10.00
14 GC,V:Red Skull. 10.00
15 GK,GC,V:Red Skull. 10.00
16 GC,V:Assassin 10.00
17 JK,GC,V:Aim,Iron Man &
    Sub-Mariner #1 . . . . 10.00
18 JK,GC,V:Modok,Iron Man #1 . . 10.00
19 JK,GC,E:Capt.America 10.00
20 JK(c) 9.00
21 Capt.America,Black Panther
    March, 1977 . . . . 9.00

MARVEL DOUBLE-SHOT
Nov., 2002
1 JJu(c),Hulk, Thor 3.00
2 JJu(c),Doom & Avengers. 3.00
3 JJu(c),F:Mr. Fantastic 3.00
4 JJu(c),F:Iron Man. 3.00

MARVEL FANFARE
March, 1972
1 MG,TA,PS,F:Spider-Man,
    Daredevil,Angel 15.00
2 MG,SM,FF,TVe,F:SpM,Ka-Zar . 10.00
3 DC,F:X-Men 10.00
4 PS,TA,MG,F:X-Men,Deathlok . . 10.00
5 MR,F:Dr.Strange 8.00
6 F:Spider-Man,Scarlet Witch 9.00
7 F:Hulk/Daredevil 6.00
8 CI,TA,GK,F:Dr.Strange 6.00
9 GM,F:Man Thing 6.00
10 GP,B:Black Widow 7.00
11 GP,D:M.Corcoran 7.00
12 GP,V:Snapdragon. 7.00
13 GP,E:B.Widow,V:Snapdragon . . 7.00
14 F:Fantastic Four,Vision 3.00
15 BWS,F:Thing,Human Torch 3.00
16 DC,JSt,F:Skywolf 2.50
17 DC,JSt,F:Skywolf 2.50
18 FM,JRu,F:Captain America. . . . 3.00
19 RL,F:Cloak and Dagger 2.50
20 JSn,F:Thing&Dr.Strange 3.00
21 JSn,F:Thing And Hulk 3.00
22 KSy,F:Iron Man 2.50
23 KSy,F:Iron Man 2.50
24 F:Weird World 3.00

25 F:Weird World. 2.50
26 F:Weird World. 2.50
27 F:Daredevil 2.50
28 KSy,F:Alpha Flight 2.50
29 JBy,F:Hulk. 3.00
30 BA,AW,F:Moon Knight 2.50
31 KGa,F:Capt.America,
    Yellow Claw 2.50
32 KGa,PS,F:Capt.America,
    Yellow Claw 2.50
33 JBr,F:X-Men 5.00
34 CV,F:Warriors Three 2.50
35 CV,F:Warriors Three 2.50
36 CV,F:Warriors Three 2.50
37 CV,F:Warriors Three 2.50
38 F:Captain America 2.50
39 JSon,F:Hawkeye,Moon Knight . 2.50
40 DM,F:Angel,Storm,Mystique . . . 3.00
41 DGb,F:Dr.Strange 2.50
42 F:Spider-Man 3.00
43 F:Sub-Mariner,Human Torch . . . 2.50
44 KSy,F:Iron Man vs.Dr.Doom . . . 2.50
45 All Pin-up Issue,WS,AAd,MZ,
    JOy,BSz,KJ,HC,PS,JBy. 3.00
46 F:Fantastic Four 2.50
47 MG,F:Spider-Man,Hulk 3.00
48 KGa,F:She-Hulk 2.50
49 F:Dr.Strange 2.50
50 JSon,JRu,F:Angel 3.00
51 JB,JA,GC,AW,F:Silver Surfer . . 4.00
52 F:Fantastic Four 2.50
53 GC,AW,F:Bl.Knight,Dr.Strange . . 2.50
54 F:Black Knight,Wolverine 3.50
55 F:Powerpack,Wolverine 3.50
56 CI,DH,F:Shanna t/She-Devil . . . 2.50
57 BBI,AM,F:Shanna,Cap.Marvel . . 2.50
58 BBI,F:Shanna,Vision/Sc.Witch . . 2.50
59 BBI,F:Shanna,Hellcat 2.50
60 PS,F:Daredevil,Capt.Marvel . . . 2.50

MARVEL FANFARE
Second Series 1996
1 Captain America, Falcon 2.25
2 New Fantastic Four 2.25
3 BbB,F:Spider-Man, Ghost Rider, . 2.25
4 F:Longshot. 2.25
5 F:Longshot. 2.25
6 F:Power Man & Iron Fist V:
    Sabretooth 2.25

MARVEL FEATURE
[1st Regular Series]
Dec., 1971
1 RA,BE,NA,I&O:Defenders &
    Omegatron. 250.00
2 BEv,F:The Defenders 125.00
3 BEv,F:The Defenders 100.00
4 F:Ant-Man 45.00
5 F:Ant-Man 25.00
6 F:Ant-Man 20.00
7 CR,F:Ant-Man 20.00
8 JSc,CR,F:Ant-Man,O:Wasp . . . 20.00
9 CR,F:Ant-Man 20.00
10 CR,F:Ant-Man 20.00
11 JSn,JSt,F:Thing & Hulk 90.00
12 JSn,JSt,F:Thing,Iron Man,
    Thanos,Blood Brothers 50.00

[2nd Regular Series]
(All issues feature Red Sonja)
1 DG,The Temple of Abomination . 12.00
2 FT,Blood of the Hunter. 7.00
3 FT,Balek Lives 7.00
4 FT,Eyes of the Gorgon. 8.00
5 FT,The Bear God Walks 8.00
6 FT,C:Conan,Belit 8.00
7 FT,V:Conan,A:Belit,Conan#68 . . 12.00

MARVEL

MARVEL FRONTIER COMICS SPECIAL

1 All Frontier Characters........ 3.25
1994 .... 3.00

MARVEL GRAPHIC NOVEL
1982

1 JSn,D:Captain Marvel,A:Most
   Marvel Characters.......... 30.00
1a 2nd printing 10.00
1b 3rd-5th printing. 8.00
2 F:Elric,Dreaming City........ 12.00
2a 2nd printing 7.00
3 JSn,F:Dreadstar........... 15.00
3a 2nd-3rd printing 7.00
4 BMc,I:New Mutants,Cannonball
   Sunspot,Psyche,Wolfsbane. . . 22.00
4a 2nd printing 10.00
4b 3rd-4th printing. 8.00
5 BA,F:X-Men............. 22.00
5a 2nd printing 9.00
5b 3rd-5th printing 7.00
6 WS,F:Starslammers.......... 10.00
6a 2nd printing 7.00
7 CR,F:Killraven 10.00
8 RWi,AG,F:Super Boxers 10.00
8a 2nd printing 7.00
9 DC,F:Futurians 12.00
9a 2nd printing 7.00
10 RV,F:Heartburst 10.00
10a 2nd printing 6.00
11 VM,F:Void Indigo............ 12.00
12 F:Dazzler the Movie 10.00
12a 2nd printing 6.00
13 MK,F:Starstruck 10.00
14 JG,F:SwordsofSwashbucklers . 10.00
15 CV,F:Raven Banner 10.00
16 GLa,F:Alladin Effect 10.00
17 MS,F:Living Monolith 10.00
18 JBy,F:She-Hulk 15.00
18 later printings 14.00
19 F:Conan 15.00
20 F:Greenberg the Vampire..... 10.00
21 JBo,F:Marada the She-wolf 10.00
22 BWr,Hooky,F:Spider-Man 16.00
23 DGr,F:Dr.Strange 10.00
24 FM,BSz,F:Daredevil 15.00
25 F:Dracula 10.00
26 FC,TA,F:Alien Legion 15.00
27 BH,F:Avengers 15.00
28 JSe,F:Conan the Reaver 16.00
29 BWr,F:Thing & Hulk 10.00
30 F:A Sailor's Story 10.00
31 F:Wolf Pack 10.00
32 SA,F:Death of Groo 17.00
33 F:Thor 10.00
34 AW,F:Cloak & Dagger........ 10.00
35 MK/RH,F:The Shadow 18.00
36 F:Willow movie adaption...... 10.00
37 BL,F:Hercules.............. 15.00
38 JBf,F:Silver Surfer 20.00
39 F:Iron Man,Crash 14.50
40 JZ,F:The Punisher 12.00
41 F:Roger Rabbit 10.00
42 F:Conan of the Isles 15.00
43 EC,F:Ax. 12.00
44 BJ,F:Arena 10.00
45 JRy,F:Dr.Who 12.00
46 TD,F:Kull 10.00
47 GM,F:Dreamwalker......... 10.00
48 F:Sailor's Storm II........... 10.00
49 MBd,F:Dr.Strange&Dr.Doom... 25.00
50 F:Spider-Man,Parallel Lives ... 12.00
51 F:Punisher,Intruder 14.00
52 DSp,F:Roger Rabbit 12.00
53 PG,F:Conan 12.00
54 HC,F:Wolverine & Nick Fury... 20.00

MARVEL HALLOWEEN: THE SUPERNATURALS TOUR BOOK
Sept., 1999

1-shot, 16-page, cardstock cov 3.00

MARVEL HEROES

1 StL,FaN,Mega-Jam,48-pg. 3.00

MARVEL HEROES
Flipbook, June, 2005

1 New Avengers #1
   & Captain America #1 .... 4.00
2 New Aveng.#2 & Cap.Am.#2.... 4.00
3 New Aveng.#3 & Cap.Am.#3.... 4.00
4 New Aveng.#4 & Cap.am.#4 .... 4.00
5 New Aveng.#5 & Cap.Am.#5.... 4.00
6 thru 13 .... @4.00
14 thru 17 .... @5.00

MARVEL: HEROES AND LEGENDS 1997
Aug., 1997

1-shot, Stan Lee, JR(c) 6.00

Marvel Holiday Special 1994
© *Marvel Entertainment Group*

MARVEL HOLIDAY SPECIAL
1991–2006

1 AAd (1991)................ 4.00
n/n RLm,JSn,TA (1993) 3.50
n/n StG(s),PDd(s),RLm,PB (1994). . 3.25
1-shot MWa,KK (1996) 4.00
1-shot Marvel Holiday Special 2004 3.00
1-shot Marvel Holiday (2006)...... 8.00

MARVEL KIDS
1999

Fantastic Four: Franklin's
   Adventures 3.50
Incredible Hulk: Project Hide...... 3.50
Spider-Man Mysteries 3.50
X-Men: Mutant Search R.U.1...... 3.50

MARVEL KNIGHTS
May, 2000

1 JQ,JP,KJ 3.50
2A JQ,KJ,CDi,EB,V:Ulik 3.00
2B variant EB(c) 3.00

3 JQ,KJ,CDi,EB,V:Ulik 3.00
4 JQ,KJ,CDi,EB,Zaran 3.00
5 JQ,KJ,CDi,EB,DaddyWronglegs . 3.00
6 JQ,KJ,CDi,EB,MaximumSecurity. 3.00
7 JQ,KJ,CDi,EB,F:Dr.Strange..... 3.00
8 JQ,CDi,EB,V:Cloak........... 3.00
9 JQ,CDi,EB,Dagger vs. Cloak.... 3.00
10 JQ,CDi,EB,Punisher......... 3.00
11 CDi,EB,Luke Cage,Power Man.. 3.00
12 CDi,EB,A:Cloak.............. 3.00
13 CDi,EB,A:Black Widow,Dagger . 3.00
14 CDi,EB,one quits 3.00
15 CDi,EB,V:S.H.I.E.L.D......... 3.00
GN Millennial Visions,TyH,48-pg. .. 4.00

MARVEL KNIGHTS
March, 2002

1 Punisher,Daredevil,Black Widow . 3.00
2 thru 6 .... @3.00

MARVEL KNIGHTS: DOUBLE-SHOT
Oct., 2001

1 GEn,JQ,Daredevil & Punisher... 3.00
2 GEn,Nick Fury & Man-Thing 3.00
3 GF(c),Elektra & Cloak&Daggar .. 3.00
4 GeH,GF(c),Iron Fist.......... 3.00
5 GeH,GF(c),Daredevil.......... 3.00

MARVEL KNIGHTS 4
Feb., 2004

1 Wolf at the Door,pt.1 .... 3.00
2 thru 4 Wolf at the Door....... @3.00
5 thru 7 The Pine Barrens...... @3.00
8 Frozen,pt.1................ 3.00
9 Frozen,pt.2................ 3.00
10 Stuff of Dreams,pt.1 .... 3.00
11 Stuff of Dreams,pt.2 .... 3.00
12 Stuff of Dreams,pt.3 .... 3.00
13 Eyes Without a Face 3.00
14 Eyes Without a Face 3.00
15 Divine Time, prologue........ 3.00
16 Divine Time............... 3.00
17 Divine Time............... 3.00
18 Divine Time............... 3.00
19 Inhumane,pt.1............. 3.00
20 Inhumane,pt.2............. 3.00
21 Desperate Housewife 3.00
22 The Yancy Street Golem....... 3.00
23 F:Impossible Man 3.00
24 F:Impossible Man 3.00
25 Resurrection of Nicholas Scratch 3.00
26 Resurrection of Nicholas Scratch 3.00
27 Resurrection of Nicholas Scratch 3.00
28 Private Lives/Public Faces 3.00
29 Super Hero's Apprentice, pt.1... 3.00
30 Super Hero's Apprentice, pt.2. . . 3.00
TPB Vol. 1: Wolf at the Door 17.00
TPB Vol. 2: Stuff of Nightmares... 14.00
TPB Vol. 3: Divine Time......... 15.00
TPB Vol. 4: Impossible Things.... 15.00

MARVEL KNIGHTS MAGAZINE
May, 2001

2 thru 7, 80-page, rep. .... @4.00

MARVEL KNIGHTS SPIDER-MAN
April, 2004

1 TyD,Down Among the Dead,pt.1 . 3.00
2 TyD,Down Among the Dead,pt.2 . 3.00
3 TyD,Down Among the Dead,pt.3 . 3.00
4 TyD,Down Among the Dead,pt.4 . 3.00
5 Venomous,pt.1 .... 3.00
6 TyD,Venomous,pt.2 .... 3.00
7 TyD,Venomous,pt.3 .... 3.00
8 TyD,Venomous,pt.4 .... 3.00

9 TyD,The Last Stand,pt.1 . . . . . . 3.00
10 MMr,TyD,The Last Stand 3.00
11 MMr,TyD,V:Sinister Twelve 3.00
12 MMr,TyD,The Last Stand 3.00
13 BTn,Wild Blue Yonder. 3.00
14 BTn,Wild Blue Yonder. 3.00
15 BTn,Wild Blue Yonder. 3.00
16 BTn,Wild Blue Yonder. 3.00
17 BTn,Wild Blue Yonder. 3.00
18 BTn,Wild Blue Yonder. 3.00
19 PDd(s), The Other,x-over,pt.2. . . 3.00
20 PDd(s), The Other,x-over,pt.5. . . 3.00
21 PDd(s), The Other,x-over,pt.8. . . 3.00
22 PDd(s), The Other,x-over,pt.11 . . 3.00
TPB Vol. 1: Down Among the
    Dead Men 10.00
TPB Vol. 2: Venomous. 10.00
TPB Vol. 3: The Last Stand 10.00
TPB Vol. 4: Wild Blue Yonder 10.00
Digest Marvel Age, Vol. 1 . . . . 8.00
Becomes:

SENSATIONAL
SPIDER-MAN
Feb., 2006
23 AMe, Feral, pt.1 . . . . 3.00
24 AMe, Feral, pt.2 . . . . 3.00
25 AMe, Feral, pt.3 . . . . 3.00
26 AMe, Feral, pt.4 . . . . 3.00
27 AMe, Feral, pt.5 . . . . 3.00
28 AMe,War at Home tie-in 3.00
29 AMe,Deadly Foes of Spider-Man 3.00
30 AMe,Deadly Foes of Spider-Man 3.00
31 AMe,Deadly Foes of Spider-Man 3.00
32 The Husband or the Spider?. . . . 3.00

MARVEL KNIGHTS
TOUR BOOK
Aug., 1998
1-shot, cardstock cover 3.00

MARVEL KNIGHTS 2009
Sept., 2004
Spec. Daredevil #1. . . . . 3.00
Spec. Black Panther #1 . . . . 3.00
Spec. Inhumans #1 . . . . 3.00
Spec. Punisher #1 . . . . 3.00
Spec. Mutant #1. . . . . 3.00

MARVEL LEGACY
Feb., 2006
1 The 1960s Handbook 5.00
2 The 1970s Handbook 5.00
3 The 1980s Handbook 5.00

MARVEL:
THE LOST GENERATION
Jan., 2000
12 (of 12) JBy,AM,Fireball, Flatiron,
    Cassandra, Oxbow, etx. 3.00
11 JBy,AM,F:Justice. 3.00
10 JBy,AM,O:Walkabout 3.00
9 JBy,AM,Effigy,Black Fox 3.00
8 JBy,AM,Nocturne. 3.00
7 JBy,AM,Knight Templar 3.00
6 JBy,AM,First Line. 3.00
5 JBy,AM,F:Thor. 3.00
4 JBy,AM,Yankee Clipper 3.00
3 JBy,AM,Liberty Girl 3.00
2 JBy,AM,V:Yankee Clipper 3.00
1 JBy,AM,concl. 3.00

MARVEL MANGAVERSE
Jan., 2002
New Dawn #1 BDn 3.00
Avengers #1 . . . . 2.25
Fantastic Four #1 AWa 2.25
Ghost Rider #1 . . . . 2.25

Punisher #1 PDd(s) 2.25
Spider-Man #1 . . . . 2.25
X-Men #1 JMs 2.25
Eternal Twilight #1 BDn 3.00
TPB series rep. 224-pg.(2002) . . . 25.00
TPB Vol. 2 (2002) 13.00

MARVEL MANGAVERSE
April, 2002
1 BDn, F:Marvin Elwood. 3.00
2 BDn, Inhumans 2.25
3 BDn, V:Galactus 2.25
4 BDn, UN held hostage. 2.25
5 BDn 2.25
6 BDd, only Doom knows 2.25
TPB Vol. 3: Spider-Man 12.00
TPB Vol. 4: X-Men – Ronin 14.00

MARVEL MASTERPIECES
COLLECTION
1993
1 Joe Jusko Masterpiece Cards. . . 3.25
2 F:Wolverine,Thanos,Apocalypse . 3.00
3 F:Gambit,Venom,Hulk 3.00
4 F:Wolverine Vs. Sabretooth. 3.00

MARVEL MASTERPIECES
II COLLECTION
1994
1 thru 3 w/cards . . . . @3.00

MARVEL MILESTONES
March, 2005
1 Iron Man, silver-age reps. 4.00
2 Venom & Hercules, reps. 4.00
3 Wolverine, X-Men, Tuk
    The Cave Boy, Silver Age Reps. 4.00
4 Dr. Doom, Sub-Mariner
    & Red Skull, silver-age reps. . . . 4.00
5 Dr. Strange, Silver Surfer
    Sub-mariner & Hulk, Reps. 4.00
6 Captain Britain, Psylocke
    Golden Age Sub-Mariner, reps. . 4.00
7 Ghost Rider, Black Widow
    Iceman, Silver-age Reps. 4.00
8 Blade, Man-Thing, and
    Satanna, silver-age reps. 4.00
9 Ultimate Spider-Man, Ultimate
    X-Men, Microman 4.00
10 Bloodstone, X-51 & Captain
    Marvel II. 4.00
11 Dragon Lord, Speedball
    and The Man in the Sky 4.00
12 Star Brand & Quasar 4.00
13 Beast & Kitty. 4.00
14 Black Panther & Storm 4.00
15 Rawhid Kid & Two-Gun 4.00
16 Millie the Model & Patsy
    Walker 4.00
17 X-Men & The Starjammers 4.00
18 X-Men & The Starjammers 4.00
19 Legion of Monsters, Spider-
    Man and Brother Voodoo 4.00
20 Onslaught 4.00

MARVEL MINI-BOOKS
1966
(black & white)
1 F:Capt.America,Spider-Man,Hulk
    Thor,Sgt.Fury 75.00
2 F:Capt.America,Spider-Man,Hulk
    Thor,Sgt.Fury 75.00
3 F:Capt.America,Spider-Man,Hulk
    Thor,Sgt.Fury 75.00
4 thru 6 F:Capt.America,Spider-Man,
    Hulk,Thor,Sgt.Fury . . . . @75.00

MARVEL MONSTERS
Oct., 2005
1-shot Devil Dinosaur,rep. 4.00
1-shot Where Monsters Dwell, rep . 4.00
1-shot Fin Fang Four, rep. 4.00
1-shot Monsters on the Prowl, rep. . 4.00
1-shot Marvel Monsters 4.00
TPB Marvel Monsters 21.00

MARVEL MOVIE
PREMIERE
B&W Magazine, 1975
1 Land That Time Forgot 20.00

MARVEL MOVIE
SHOWCASE FEATURING
STAR WARS
Nov., 1982
1 Rep,Stars Wars #1-6 . . . . 5.00
2 Dec., 1982 . . . . 5.00

MARVEL MOVIE
SPOTLIGHT FEATURING
RAIDERS OF
THE LOST ARK
Nov., 1982
1 Rep,Raiders of Lost Ark#1-3 . . . 3.00

MARVEL
MYSTERY COMICS
See: MARVEL COMICS

MARVEL
MYSTERY COMICS
Oct., 1999
Spec. 80-pg. 4.00

MARVEL NEMESIS:
THE IMPERFECTS
May, 2005
1 (of 6) Rise of the Imperfects 3.00
2 Rise of the Imperfects 3.00
3 Birth of the Imperfects 3.00
4 JaL(c). 3.00
5 JaL(c) 3.00
6 Rise of the Imperfects, finale. . . . 3.00
TPB 8.00

Marvel Movie Raiders of the Lost Ark
© Marvel Entertainment Group

MARVEL NO-PRIZE BOOK
Jan., 1983
1 MGo(c),Stan Lee as
  Dr.Doom(c) 7.00

MARVEL: PORTRAITS OF A UNIVERSE
1 Fully painted moments. 3.00
2 Fully painted moments. 3.00
3 F:Death of Elektra 3.00
4 final issue................. 3.00

MARVEL POSTER BOOK
June, 2001
Summer 2001, 64-page 3.50
Winter 2001, 64-page 3.50

MARVEL PREMIERE
April, 1972
1 GK,O:Warlock,Receives Soul Gem,
  Creation of Counter Earth . . . 100.00
2 GK,JK,F:Warlock 50.00
3 BWS,F:Dr.Strange 90.00
4 FB,BWS,F:Dr.Strange 35.00
5 MP,CR,F:Dr.Strange,I:Sligguth . 30.00
6 MP,FB,F:Dr.Strange........... 20.00
7 MP,CR,F:Dr.Strange,I:Dagoth . . 20.00
8 JSn,F:Dr.Strange 20.00
9 NA,FB,F:Dr.Strange........... 20.00
10 FB,F:Dr.Strange,
  D:Ancient One............. 30.00
11 NA,FB,F:Dr.Strange,I:Shuma . 15.00
12 NA,FB,F:Dr.Strange 15.00
13 NA,FB,F:Dr.Strange 15.00
14 NA,FB,F:Dr.Strange 15.00
15 GK,DG,I&O:Iron Fist,pt.1 .... 125.00
16 DG,O:Iron Fist,pt.2,V:Scythe. . 50.00
17 DG,Citadel on the
  Edge of Vengeance........ 30.00
18 DG,V:Triple Irons............ 30.00
19 DG,A:Ninja 30.00
20 I:Misty Knight 30.00
21 V:Living Goddess 30.00
22 V:Ninja 30.00
23 PB,V:Warhawk 30.00
24 PB,V:Monstroid............. 30.00
25 1st JBy,AMc,E:Iron Fist. 35.00
26 JK,GT,F:Hercules 10.00
27 F:Satana 15.00
28 F:Legion Of Monsters,A:Ghost
  Rider,Morbius,Werewolf. 25.00
29 JK,I:Liberty Legion,
  O:Red Raven............... 6.00
30 JK,F:Liberty Legion........... 6.00
31 JK,I:Woodgod 6.00
32 HC,F:Monark............... 5.00
33 HC,F:Solomon Kane.......... 5.00
34 HC,F:Solomon Kane.......... 5.00
35 I&O:Silver Age 3-D Man 5.00
36 F:3-D Man................. 5.00
37 F:3-D Man................. 5.00
38 AN,MP,I:Weird World 5.00
39 AM,I:Torpedo(1st solo) 5.00
40 AM,F:Torpedo.............. 5.00
41 TS,F:Seeker 3000........... 5.00
42 F:Tigra................... 5.00
43 F:Paladin................. 5.00
44 KG,F:Jack of Hearts(1stSolo) . . . 5.00
45 GP,F:Manwolf 5.00
46 GP,F:Manwolf 5.00
47 JBy,I:2nd Antman(Scott Lang) . 10.00
48 JBy,F:2nd Antman........... 10.00
49 F:The Falcon............... 5.00
50 TS,TA,F:Alice Cooper......... 20.00
51 JBi,F:Black Panther,V:Klan ... 5.00
52 JBi,F:B.Panther,V:Klan 5.00
53 JBi,F:B.Panther,V:Klan 5.00
54 GD,TD,I:Hammer 5.00
55 JSt,F:Wonderman(1st solo) 6.00
56 HC,TA,F:Dominic Fortune...... 5.00

Marvel Premier #57
© *Marvel Entertainment Group*

57 WS(c),I:Dr.Who.............. 7.00
58 TA(c),FM,F:Dr.Who........... 5.00
59 F:Dr.Who.................. 5.00
60 WS(c),DGb,F:Dr.Who......... 5.00
61 TS,F:Starlord............... 5.00

MARVEL PRESENTS
Oct., 1975
1 BMc,F:Bloodstone 15.00
2 BMc,O:Bloodstone............ 9.00
3 AM,B:Guardians/Galaxy 20.00
4 AM,I:Nikki 12.00
5 AM,Planet o/t Absurd 12.00
6 AM,V:Karanada 12.00
7 AM,Embrace the Void 12.00
8 AM,JB,JSt,reprint.S.Surfer#2 . . 15.00
9 AM,O:Starhawk 12.00
10 AM,O:Starhawk 12.00
11 AM,D:Starhawk's Children ... 12.00
12 AM,E:Guardians o/t Galaxy ... 12.00

MARVEL PREVIEW
Feb., 1975
(black & white magazine)
1 NA,AN,Man Gods From
  Beyond the Stars 25.00
2 GM(c),O:Punisher 150.00
3 GM(c),Blade the VampireSlayer 30.00
4 GM(c),I&O:Starlord 20.00
5 Sherlock Holmes 20.00
6 Sherlock Holmes 20.00
7 KG,Satana In the Star . 20.00
8 GM,MP,Legion of Monsters 30.00
9 Man-God,O:Starhawk 15.00
10 JSn,Thor the Mighty 30.00
11 JBy,I:Starlord 15.00
12 MK,Haunt of Horror.......... 10.00
13 JSn(c),Starhawk 10.00
14 JSn(c),Starhawk 10.00
15 MK(c),Starhawk............ 10.00
16 GC,Detectives............. 10.00
17 GK,Black Mask 6.00
18 GC,Starlord............... 6.00
19 Kull 6.00
20 HC,NA,GP,Bizarre Adventures . . 7.00
21 SD,Moonlight 7.00
22 JB,King Arthur 6.00
23 JB,GC,FM,Bizarre Adventures . . 7.00
24 Debut Paradox 6.00
Becomes:

BIZARRE ADVENTURES
1981
25 MG,TA,MR,Lethal Ladies 12.00

26 JB(c),King Kull 12.00
27 JB,AA,GP,Phoenix,A:Ice-Man. . 15.00
28 MG,TA,FM,NA,The Unlikely
  Heroes,Elektra............. 15.00
29 JB,WS,Horror 10.00
30 JB,Tomorrow 10.00
31 JBy,After the Violence Stops. . . 12.00
32 Gods 12.00
33 Ph(c),Horror 12.00
34 PS,Christmas Spec,Son of Santa
  Howard the Duck,Feb.,1983 . . 10.00

MARVEL PREVIEW
1993
Preview of 1993............... 4.00

MARVEL REMIX
Nov., 1998
1 (of 3) Fantastic Four 3.00
1a signed 20.00
2 Fantastic Four:Fireworks....... 3.00
3 Fantastic Four:Fireworks....... 3.00

MARVEL ROMANCE
Feb., 2006
TPB Reps. 20.00

MARVEL ROMANCE REDUX
March., 2006
1 .... 3.00
2 Guys & Dolls 3.00
3 Restraining Orders for Other Girls 3.00
4 I Should Have Been A......... 3.00
5 Love is a Four Letter Word 3.00

MARVELS
1994
1 B:KBk(s),AxR,I:Phil Sheldon,
  A:G.A.Heroes,Human Torch Vs
  Namor 10.00
2 AxR,A:S.A.Avengers,FF,X-Men . . 8.00
3 AxR,FF vs Galactus.......... 8.00
4 AxR,Final issue 8.00

MARVEL SAGA
Dec., 1985
1 JBy,Fantastic Four,Wolv. 3.00
2 Hulk 2.50
3 Spider-Man 3.00
4 X-Men 3.00
5 thru 24 .... @2.50
25 O:Silver Surfer,Dec.,1987...... 2.75

MARVEL SELECT
Flipbook, June, 2005
1 Astonishing X-Men #1
  & New X-men: Academy X #1. . 4.00
2 Aston.X-Men#2 & Acad.X#2 .... 4.00
3 Aston.X-Men#3 & Acad.X#3 .... 4.00
4 Aston.x-men#4 & Acad.x#4 .... 4.00
5 Aston.X-Men#5 & Acad.X#5 .... 4.00
6 thru 18 .... @4.00

MARVEL SELECTS: FANTASTIC FOUR
Nov., 1999
1 (of 12) 2.75
2 rep. Vol. 1, #108, AD(c)........ 2.75
3 rep. Vol. 1, #109, AD(c)........ 2.75
4 rep. Vol. 1, #110, AD(c) 2.75
5 rep. Vol. 1, #111, AD(c) 2.75
6 rep. Vol. 1, #112, AD(c) 2.75

MARVEL SELECTS:
SPIDER-MAN
Nov., 1999
1 (of 12) 2.75
2 rep. Amaz.Sp-M #101 . . . . 2.75
3 rep. Amaz.Sp-M #102 . . . . 2.75
4 rep. Amaz.Sp-M #103 . . . . 2.75
5 rep. Amaz.Sp-M #104 . . . . 2.75
6 rep. Amaz.Sp-M #105 . . . . 2.75

MARVEL:
SHADOWS & LIGHT
B&W 1996
1-shot MGo,JPL,KJ,48-pg. 3.00

MARVEL 1602
Aug., 2003–March, 2004
1 thru 7 NGa(s),NKu . . . . @3.50
8 NGa(s),NKu,48-pg. 4.00
TPB 1602 (2005) 20.00

MARVEL 1602:
FANTASTICK FOUR
Sept., 2006
1 V:Count Otto von Doom 3.50
2 thru 3 . . . . @3.50

MARVEL 1602:
NEW WORLD
Aug., 2005
1 (of 5) Bruce David Banner 3.50
2 Peter Parquagh 3.50
3 Superpowers outlawed 3.50
4 Lord Iron vs. Hulk 3.50
5 War in Roanoke 3.50
TPB Marvel 1602 New World 15.00

MARVEL 65th
ANNIVERSARY
Sept., 2004
Spec. F:Sub-Mariner,Human
   Torch,48-pg. 5.00

MARVEL SPECTACULAR
Aug., 1973–Nov., 1975
1 JK,rep Thor #128 . . . . 15.00
2 thru 10 rep.Thor#129–#139 . . . @7.00
11 thru 19 rep Thor #140–#148 . . @6.00

Bizarre Adventures #27
© Marvel Entertainment Group

MARVEL SPOTLIGHT
[1st Regular Series] Nov., 1971
1 NA(c)WW,F:Red Wolf 55.00
2 MP,BEv,NA,I&O:Werewolf 225.00
3 MP,F:Werewolf 75.00
4 SD,MP,F:Werewolf 75.00
5 SD,MP,I&O:Ghost Rider 225.00
6 MP,TS,F:Ghost Rider 50.00
7 MP,TS,F:Ghost Rider 50.00
8 JM,MB,F:Ghost Rider 50.00
9 TA,F:Ghost Rider 45.00
10 SD,JM,F:Ghost Rider 45.00
11 SD,F:Ghost Rider 45.00
12 SD,2nd A:Son of Satan 45.00
13 F:Son of Satan 18.00
14 JM,F:Son of Satan,I:Ikthalon . . 18.00
15 JM, F:Son of Satan,
   I:Baphomet 15.00
16 JM,F:Son of Satan 15.00
17 JM,F:Son of Satan 15.00
18 F:Son of Satan, I:Allatou 15.00
19 F:Son of Satan 15.00
20 F:Son of Satan 15.00
21 F:Son of Satan 15.00
22 F:Son of Satan, Ghost Rider . . 18.00
23 F:Son of Satan 15.00
24 JM,F:Son of Satan 15.00
25 GT,F:Sinbad 15.00
26 F:The Scarecrow 12.00
27 F:The Sub-Mariner 22.00
28 F:Moon Knight (1st full solo) . . 35.00
29 F:Moon Knight 40.00
30 JSt,JB,F:Warriors Three 22.00
31 HC,JSn,F:Nick Fury 22.00
32 I:Spiderwoman, Jessica Drew . 22.00
33 F:Deathlok, I:Devilslayer 10.00

[2nd Regualar Series] 1979
1 PB,F:Captain Marvel 4.00
1a No`1' on Cover 12.00
2 FM(c),F:Captain Marvel,A:Eon . 3.00
3 PB,F:Captain Marvel 3.00
4 PB,F:Captain Marvel 3.00
5 FM(c),SD,F:Dragon Lord 3.00
6 F:Star Lord 3.00
7 FM(c),F:StarLord 3.00
8 FM,F:Captain Marvel 7.00
9 FM(c),SD,F:Captain Universe . . 3.00
10 SD,F:Captain Universe 3.00
11 SD,F:Captain Universe 3.00

MARVEL SPOTLIGHT
Dec., 2005
1 John Cassady & Saen McKeever 3.00
2 Warren Ellis, Jim Cheung 3.00
3 Joss Whedon & Michael Lark . . 3.00
4 David Finch & Roberto
   Aquirre-Sacasa 3.00
5 Daniel Way & Olivier Coipel . . . 3.00
6 Mark Millar & Steve McNiven . . 3.00
7 Neil Gaiman & Salvador Laroca . 3.00
8 Robert Kirkman & Greg Land . . 3.00
9 Ed Brubaker & Billy Tan 3.00
10 Stan Lee & Jack Kirby 3.00
11 Brian Michael Bendis &
   Mark Bagley 3.00

MARVEL SPOTLIGHT ON
CAPTAIN AMERICA
1 thru 4, Captain America rep. . . @3.00

MARVEL SPOTLIGHT ON
DR. STRANGE
1 thru 4, Dr. Strange, rep. . . . . . . @3.00

MARVEL SPOTLIGHT ON
SILVER SURFER
1 thru 4, Silver Surfer, rep. . . . . . @3.00

Marvel Super Action #1
© Marvel Entertainment Group

MARVEL SUPER ACTION
Jan., 1976
1-shot TD,GE,FS,MP,HC,F:Punisher,
   Weirdworld,Dominic Fortune,
   I:Huntress(Mockingbird) 100.00

MARVEL SUPER ACTION
May, 1977–Nov., 1981
1 JK,reprint,Capt.America #100 . . 15.00
2 JK,reprint,Capt.America #101 . . 10.00
3 JK,reprint,Capt.America #102 . . 10.00
4 BEv,RH,reprint,Marvel Boy #1 . . 10.00
5 JK,reprint,Capt.America #103 . . 10.00
6 JK,reprint,Capt.America #104 . . . 8.00
7 JK,reprint,Capt.America #105 . . . 8.00
8 JK,reprint,Capt.America #106 . . . 8.00
9 JK,reprint,Capt.America #107 . . . 8.00
10 JK,reprint,Capt.America #108 . . . 8.00
11 JK,reprint,Capt.America #109 . . . 8.00
12 JSo,reprint,Capt.America #110 . . 8.00
13 JSo,reprint,Capt.America #111 . . 8.00
14 JB,reprint,Avengers #55 . . . . . . 8.00
15 JB,reprint,Avengers #56 . . . . . . 8.00
16 Reprint,Avengers,annual #2 . . . 5.00
17 Reprint,Avengers # 5.00
18 JB(c),reprint,Avengers #57 . . . . 5.00
19 JB(c),reprint,Avengers #58 . . . . . 5.00
20 JB(c),reprint,Avengers #59 . . . . . 5.00
21 Reprint,Avengers #60 . . . . 4.00
22 JB(c),reprint,Avengers #61 . . . . . 4.00
23 Reprint,Avengers #63 . . . . 4.00
24 Reprint,Avengers #64 . . . . 4.00
25 Reprint,Avengers #65 . . . . 4.00
26 Reprint,Avengers #66 . . . . 4.00
27 BWS,Reprint,Avengers #67 . . . . 4.00
28 BWS,Reprint,Avengers #68 . . . . 4.00
29 Reprint,Avengers #69 . . . . 4.00
30 Reprint,Avengers #70 . . . . 4.00
31 Reprint,Avengers #71 . . . . 4.00
32 Reprint,Avengers #72 . . . . 4.00
33 Reprint,Avengers #73 . . . . 4.00
34 Reprint,Avengers #74 . . . . 4.00
35 JB(c),Reprint,Avengers #75 . . . . 4.00
36 JB(c),Reprint,Avengers #75 . . . . 4.00
37 JB(c),Reprint,Avengers #76 . . . . 4.00

MARVEL SUPERHEROES
Oct., 1966
1-shot Rep. D.D. #1, Avengers #2,
   Marvel Mystery #8 . . . . 200.00

MARVEL

MARVEL SUPER-HEROES

[1st Regular Series] 1967–71

(Prev.: Fantasy Masterpieces)

12 GC,I&O:Captain Marvel 225.00	
13 GC,2nd A:Captain Marvel 125.00	
14 F:Spider-Man 150.00	
15 GC,F:Medusa 75.00	
16 I:Phantom Eagle 75.00	
17 O:Black Knight 75.00	
18 GC,I:Guardians o/t Galaxy 90.00	
19 F:Ka-Zar 45.00	
20 F:Dr.Doom,Diablo 50.00	
21 thru 31 reprints . . . . @25.00	
32 thru 55 rep. Hulk/Submariner	
from Tales to Astonish . . . . . @10.00	
56 reprints Hulk #102. . . . . 7.00	
57 thru 105 reps.Hulk issues . . . . @7.00	

MARVEL SUPERHEROES

[2nd Regular Series] May, 1990

1 RLm,F:Hercules,Moon Knight,
   Magik,Bl.Panther,Speedball. . . . 7.00
2 . . . . 3.50
3 F:Captain America,Hulk,Wasp . . . 4.00
4 AD,F:SpM,N.Fury,D.D.,Speedball
   Wond.Man,Spitfire,Bl.Knight . . . 3.50
5 F:Thor,Thing,Speedball,
   Dr.Strange 3.50
6 RB,SD,F:X-Men,Power Pack,
   Speedball,Sabra 3.00
7 RB,F:X-Men,Cloak & Dagger . . 2.75
8 F:X-Men,Iron Man,Namor 2.75
9 F:Avengers W.C,Thor,Iron Man . . 3.00
10 DH,F:Namor,Fantastic Four,
   Ms.Marvel#24 . . . . 3.50
11 F:Namor,Ms.Marvel#25 . . . . 3.00
12 F:Dr.Strange,Falcon,Iron Man . . 3.00
13 F:Iron Man 3.00
14 BMc,RWi,F:Iron Man,
   Speedball, Dr.Strange 3.00
15 KP,DH,F:Thor,Iron Man,Hulk . . . 3.00
Holiday Spec.#1 AAd,DC,JRu,F:FF,
   X-Men,Spider-Man,Punisher . . . 3.25
Holiday Spec.#2 AAd(c),SK,MGo,
   RLm,SLi,F:Hulk,Wolverine,
   Thanos,Spider-Man 3.25
Fall Spec.RB,A:X-Men,Shroud,
   Marvel Boy,Cloak & Dagger . . . 3.00

MARVEL SUPERHEROES MEGAZINE

1 thru 6 rep.. . . . . @3.00

MARVEL SUPER SPECIAL
See: MARVEL COMICS

MARVEL SWIMSUIT
1992
1 Schwing Break. 10.00

MARVEL TAILS
Nov., 1983
1 ST,Peter Porker 5.00

MARVEL TALES
1964
1 All reprints,O:Spider-Man. 500.00
2 rep.Avengers #1,X-Men #1,
   Hulk #3 . . . . 300.00
3 rep.Amaz.SpM.#6 . . . . 150.00
4 rep.Amaz.SpM.#7 . . . . 100.00
5 rep.Amaz.SpM.#8 . . . . 100.00
6 rep.Amaz.SpM.#9 . . . . 100.00
7 rep.Amaz.SpM.#10 . . . . 100.00
8 rep.Amaz.SpM.#13 . . . . 75.00
9 rep.Amaz.SpM.#14 . . . . 75.00
10 rep.Amaz.SpM.#15 . . . . 75.00
11 rep.Amaz.SpM.#16 . . . . 75.00

---

12 rep.Amaz.SpM.#17 . . . . 75.00
13 rep.Amaz.SpM.#18
   rep.1950's Marvel Boy. 75.00
14 rep.Amaz.SpM.#19,
   reps.Marvel Boy. 50.00
15 rep.Amaz.SpM.#20,
   reps.Marvel Boy. 50.00
16 rep.Amaz.SpM.#21,
   reps.Marvel Boy. 50.00
17 thru 22 rep.Amaz.SpM.
   #22-#27 . . . . @50.00
23 thru 27 rep.Amaz.SpM.
   #30-#34 . . . . @50.00
28 rep.Amaz.SpM.#35&36. . . . . . 50.00
29 rep.Amaz.SpM.#39&40. . . . . . 50.00
30 rep.Amaz.SpM.#58&41. . . . . . 50.00
31 rep.Amaz.SpM.#42 . . . . 50.00
32 rep.Amaz.SpM.#43&44. . . . . . 50.00
33 rep.Amaz.SpM.#45&47. . . . . . 50.00
34 rep.Amaz.SpM.#48 . . . . 15.00
35 rep.Amaz.SpM.#49 . . . . 15.00
36 thru 41 rep.
   Amaz.SpM.#51-#56 . . . . . . @15.00
42 thru 53 rep.
   Amaz.SpM#59-#70 . . . . . . @15.00
54 thru 80 rep.
   Amaz.SpM.#73-#99 . . . . . . @15.00
81 rep.Amaz.SpM.#103 . . . . 15.00
82 rep.Amaz.SpM.#103-4 . . . . . . 15.00
83 thru 97 rep.
   Amaz.SpM.#104-#118. . . . . @15.00
98 rep.Amaz.SpM.#121 . . . . 15.00
99 rep.Amaz.SpM.#122 . . . . 15.00
100 rep.Amaz.SpM.#123,BU:Two
   Gun Kid,Giant-Size 4.00
101 thru 105 rep.Amaz.
   SpM.#124-#128 . . . . @4.00
106 rep.Amaz.SpM.#129,
   (I:Punisher) 4.00
107 thur 110 rep.Amaz.
   SpM.#130-133 . . . . @4.00
111 Amaz.SpM#134,A:Punisher. . . 4.00
112 Amaz.SpM#135,A:Punisher . . . 4.00
113 thru 125 rep.Amaz.Spider
   Man #136-#148 . . . . @4.00
126 rep.Amaz.Spider-Man#149 . . . . 4.00
127 rep.Amaz.Spider-Man#150 . . . . 4.00
128 rep.Amaz.Spider-Man#151 . . . . 4.00
129 thru 136 rep.Amaz.Spider
   Man #152-#159 . . . . @4.00
137 rep.Amaz.Fantasy#15. . . . . . . 7.00
138 rep.Amaz.SpM.#1 . . . . 7.00
139 thru 149 rep.
   AmazSpM#2-#12 . . . . @4.00

Marvel Tales #40
© *Marvel Entertainment Group*

---

150 rep.AmazSpM Ann#1 . . . . 4.00
151 rep.AmazSpM#13 . . . . 4.00
152 rep.AmazSpM#14 . . . . 4.00
153 thru 190
   rep.AmazSpM#15-52. . . . . . @2.50
191 rep. #96-98 . . . . 2.50
192 rep. #121-122 . . . . 2.50
193 thru 198 rep.Marv.Team
   Up#59-64 . . . . @2.50
199 . . . . 2.50
200 rep. SpM Annual 14 . . . . 2.50
201 thru 206 rep.Marv.
   Team Up#65-70. . . . . @2.50
207 thru 208 . . . . @2.50
209 MZ(c),rep.SpM#129,Punisher . . 3.00
210 MZ(c),rep.SpM#134 . . . . 4.00
211 MZ(c),rep.SpM#135 . . . . 4.00
212 MZ(c),rep.Giant-Size#4. . . . . . 4.00
213 MZ(c),rep.Giant-Size#4. . . . . . 4.00
214 MZ(c),rep.SpM#161 . . . . 4.00
215 MZ(c),rep.SpM#162 . . . . 3.00
216 MZ(c),rep.SpM#174 . . . . 3.00
217 MZ(c),rep.SpM#175 . . . . 3.00
218 MZ(c),rep.SpM#201 . . . . 3.00
219 MZ(c),rep.SpM#202 . . . . 3.00
220 MZ(c),rep.Spec.SpM #81 . . . . 3.00
221 MZ(c),rep.Spec.SpM #82 . . . . 3.00
222 MZ(c),rep.Spec.SpM #83 . . . . 2.25
223 thru 227 TM(c),rep.
   SpM #88-92 . . . . @2.50
228 TM(c),rep.Spec.SpM#17 . . . . 2.25
229 TM(c),rep.Spec.SpM#18 . . . . 2.25
230 TM(c),rep.SpM #203 . . . . 2.25
231 TM(c),rep.Team-Up#108 . . . . 2.25
232 TM(c),rep. 2.25
233 thru 236 TM(c),rep. X-Men . . @2.25
237 TM(c),rep. 2.25
238 TM(c),rep. 2.25
239 TM(c),rep.SpM,Beast 2.25
240 rep.SpM,Beast,MTU#90 . . . . . 2.25
241 rep.MTU#124 . . . . 2.25
242 rep.MTU#89,Nightcrawler. . . . 2.25
243 rep.MTU#117,SpM,Wolverine . . 2.25
244 MR(c),rep. 2.25
245 MR(c),rep. 2.25
246 MR(c),rep. 2.25
247 MR(c),rep.MTU Annual #6 . . . . 2.25
248 MR(c),rep. 2.25
249 MR(c),rep.MTU #14 . . . . 2.25
250 MR(c),rep.MTU #100 . . . . 2.25
251 rep.Amaz.SpM.#100 . . . . 2.25
252 rep.Amaz.SpM.#101 . . . . 3.50
253 rep.Amaz.SpM.#102 . . . . 3.00
254 rep.MTU #15,inc.2 Ghost
   Rider pin-ups by JaL 3.00
255 SK(c),rep.MTU #58,
   BU:Ghost Rider 2.25
256 rep. MTU. 2.25
257 rep.Amaz.SpM.#238 . . . . 2.25
258 rep.Amaz.SpM.#239 . . . . 2.25
259 thru 261 rep.Amaz.SpM.#249
   thru #251 . . . . @2.25
262 rep Marvel Team-Up #53 . . . . 2.25
263 rep Marvel Team-Up #54 . . . . 2.25
264 rep.B:Amaz.SpM.Ann.#5 . . . . 2.25
265 rep.E:Amaz.SpM.Ann.#5 . . . . 2.25
266 thru 275 rep.Amaz.SpM#252
   thru #261 . . . . @2.25
276 rep.Amaz.SpM#263 . . . . 2.25
277 rep.Amaz.SpM#265 . . . . 2.25
278 thru 282 rep.Amaz.SpM #268
   thru #272 . . . . @2.25
283 rep.Amaz.SpM#273 . . . . 2.25
284 thru 287 rep.Amaz.SpM#275
   thru #278 . . . . @2.25
288 rep.Amaz.SpM#280 . . . . 2.25
289 rep.Amaz.SpM#281 . . . . 2.25
290 & 291 rep.Amaz.SpM 2.25

MARVEL TALES
Flipbook, June, 2005
1 Amazing Spider-Man #34
  & Amazing Fantasy #1 . . . . 4.00
2 Amaz.Sp-M#35 & Amaz.Fant.#2 . 4.00
3 Amaz.Sp-M#33 & Amaz.Fant.#3 . 4.00
4 Amaz.sp-m#33 & Amaz.fant.#4 . . 4.00
5 thru 16 . . . . @4.00

MARVEL TALES
See: MARVEL COMICS

MARVEL TEAM-UP
March, 1972
(Spider-Man in all,unless *)
1 RA,F:Hum.Torch,V:Sandman. . 225.00
2 RA,F:Hum.Torch,V:Sandman. . . 75.00
3 F:Human Torch,V:Morbius 100.00
4 GK,F:X-Men,A:Morbius 100.00
5 GK,F:Vision 30.00
6 GK,F:Thing,O:Puppet Master,
  V:Mad Thinker 30.00
7 RA,F:Thor 30.00
8 JM,F:The Cat. 30.00
9 RA,F:Iron Man 30.00
10 JM,F:Human Torch 30.00
11 JM,F:The Inhumans 20.00
12 RA,F:Werewolf 35.00
13 GK,F:Captain America 30.00
14 GK,F:Sub-Mariner. 20.00
15 RA,F:Ghostrider 35.00
16 GK,JM,F:Captain Marvel 20.00
17 GK,F:Mr.Fantastic,
  A:Capt.Marvel 20.00
18 *F:Hulk,Human Torch 20.00
19 SB,F:Ka-Zar. 20.00
20 SB,F:Black Panther 17.00
21 SB,F:Dr.Strange 11.00
22 SB,F:Hawkeye 12.00
23 *F:Human Torch,Iceman,
  C:Spider-Man,X-Men 12.00
24 JM,F:Brother Voodoo 12.00
25 JM,F:Daredevil 12.00
26 *F:H.Torch,Thor,V:Lavamen. . . 12.00
27 JM,F:The Hulk 12.00
28 JM,F:Hercules 12.00
29 *F:Human Torch,Iron Man. . . . 12.00
30 JM,F:The Falcon 12.00
31 JM,F:Iron Fist 12.00
32 *F:Hum.Torch,Son of Satan . . 12.00
33 SB,F:Nighthawk 12.00
34 SB,F:Valkyrie 12.00

*Marvel Team-Up #36
Universe #10 © Marvel Ent. Group*

35 SB,*F:H.Torch,Dr.Strange 12.00
36 SB,F:Frankenstein 10.00
37 SB,F:Man-Wolf 10.00
38 SB,F:Beast 10.00
39 SB,F:H.Torch,I:Jean Dewolff. . . 10.00
40 SB,F:Sons of the Tiger 10.00
41 SB,F:Scarlet Witch 10.00
42 SB,F:Scarlet Witch,Vision. 10.00
43 SB,F:Dr.Doom. 10.00
44 SB,F:Moon Dragon 10.00
45 SB,F:Killraven 10.00
46 SB,F:Deathlok. 8.00
47 F:The Thing 7.00
48 SB,F:Iron Man,I:Wraith 7.00
49 SB,F:Iron Man. 7.00
50 SB,F:Dr.Strange 7.00
51 SB,F:Iron Man. 7.00
52 SB,F:Captain America 7.00
53 1st JBy New X-Men,F:Hulk. . . 35.00
54 JBy,F:Hulk,V:Woodgod 8.00
55 JBy,F:Warlock,I:Gardener 9.00
56 SB,F:Daredevil 8.00
57 SB,F:Black Widow 8.00
58 SB,F:Ghost Rider,V:Trapster . . 8.00
59 JBy,F:Yellowjacket,V:Equinox . . 8.00
60 JDy,F:Wasp,V:Equinox 8.00
61 JBy,F:Human Torch. 8.00
62 JBy,F:Ms.Marvel 8.00
63 JBy,F:Iron Fist. 8.00
64 JBy,F:Daughters o/t Dragon . . . 8.00
65 JBy,I:Captain Britain(U.S.)
  I:Arcade 7.50
66 JBy,F:Captain Britain 7.00
67 JBy,F:Tigra,V:Kraven 7.00
68 JBy,F:Man-Thing,I:D'Spayre . . . 7.00
69 JBy,F:Havok 7.00
70 JBy,F:Thor. 7.00
71 F:The Falcon,V:Plantman 6.00
72 F:Iron Man 6.00
73 F:Daredevil 6.00
74 BH,F:Not ready for prime time
  players(Saturday Night Live). . 6.00
75 JBy,F:Power Man 7.00
76 HC,F:Dr.Strange 6.00
77 HC,F:Ms Marvel 6.00
78 DP,F:Wonderman 6.00
79 JBy,TA,F:Red Sonja 6.00
80 SpM,F:Dr.Strange,Clea 5.00
81 F:Satana 5.00
82 SD,F:Black Widow 6.00
83 SB,F:Nick Fury 5.00
84 SB,F:Master of Kung Fu 5.00
85 SB,F:Bl.Widow,Nick Fury 5.00
86 BMc,F:Guardians o/t Galaxy. . . 4.00
87 GC,F:Black Panther 4.00
88 SB,F:Invisible Girl 4.00
89 RB,F:Nightcrawler. 4.50
90 BMc,F:The Beast 4.00
91 F:Ghost Rider 4.00
92 Cl,F:Hawkeye,I:Mr.Fear IV 3.50
93 Cl,F:Werewolf
  I:Tatterdemalion (named) 4.00
94 MZ,F:Shroud 3.50
95 I:Mockingbird(Huntress) 4.00
96 F:Howard the Duck. 3.50
97 *F:Hulk,Spider-Woman 3.50
98 F:Black Widow 3.50
99 F:Machine Man 3.50
100 FM,JBy,F:F.F.,I:Karma,
  BU:Storm & Bl.Panther 8.00
101 F:Nighthawk 3.00
102 F:Doc Samson,Rhino 3.00
103 F:Antman 3.00
104 *F:Hulk,Ka-zar. 3.00
105 *F:Powerman,Iron Fist,Hulk . . . 3.00
106 HT,F:Captain America. 3.00
107 HT,F:She-Hulk. 3.00
108 HT,F:Paladin 3.00
109 HT,F:Dazzler. 3.00
110 HT,F:Iron Man 3.00
111 HT,F:Devil Slayer. 3.00
112 HT,F:King Kull 3.00

*Marvel Team-Up #113
© Marvel Entertainment Group*

113 HT,F:Quasar,V:Lightmaster. . . . 3.00
114 HT,F:Falcon. 3.00
115 HT,F:Thor 3.00
116 HT,F:Valkyrie 3.00
117 HT,F:Wolv,V:Prof Power 12.00
118 HT,F:Professor X. 4.00
119 KGa,F:Gargoyle 3.00
120 KGa,F:Dominic Fortune 3.00
121 KGa,F:Human Torch,I:Leap
  Frog(Frog Man). 3.00
122 KGa,F:Man-Thing. 3.00
123 KGa,F:Daredevil 3.00
124 KGa,F:Beast 3.50
125 KGa,F:Tigra 3.00
126 BH,F:Hulk 3.00
127 KGa,F:Watcher,X-mass issue. . 3.00
128 Ph(c)KGa,F:Capt.America. 3.00
129 KGa,F:The Vision 3.00
130 KGa,F:The Scarlet Witch 3.00
131 KGa,F:Leap Frog 3.00
132 KGa,F:Mr.Fantastic. 3.00
133 KGa,F:Fantastic Four 3.00
134 F:Jack of Hearts 3.00
135 F:Kitty Pryde 3.00
136 F:Wonder Man 3.00
137 *F:Aunt May & F.Richards . . . 3.00
138 F:Sandman,I:New Enforcers. . . 3.00
139 F:Sandman,Nick Fury 3.00
140 F:Black Widow 3.00
141 SpM(2nd App Black Costume)
  F:Daredevil 12.00
142 F:Captain Marvel(2nd one). . . . 3.00
143 F:Starfox 3.00
144 F:M.Knight,V:WhiteDragon . . . 3.00
145 F:Iron Man 3.00
146 F:Nomad 3.50
147 F:Human Torch 3.00
148 F:Thor 3.00
149 F:Cannonball. 3.50
150 F:X-Men,V:Juggernaut 5.50
Ann.#1 SB,F:New X-Men. 30.00
Ann.#2 F:The Hulk. 10.00
Ann.#3 F:Hulk,PowerMan 6.00
Ann.#4 F:Daredevil,Moon Knight. . 5.00
Ann.#5 F:Thing,Scarlet Witch,
  Quasar,Dr.Strange. 5.00
Ann.#6 F:New Mutants,Cloak &
  Dagger(cont.New Mutants#22) . 5.00
Ann.#7 F:Alpha Flight 3.00

MARVEL TEAM-UP INDEX
See: OFFICIAL MARVEL
INDEX TO
MARVEL TEAM-UP

MARVEL

MARVEL TEAM-UP
1997
1 TPe,PO,AW, F:Spider-Man,
  Generation X 2.25
2 TPe,PO,AW, F:Spider-Man &
  Hercules 2.25
3 TPe,DaR,AW, F:Spider-Man &
  Sandman.................. 2.25
4 TPe,DaR,F:Spider-Man &
  Man-Thing 2.25
5 TPe,DaR,F:Spider-Man &
  Mystery guest 2.25
6 TPe,F:Spider-Man & Sub-Mariner 2.25
7 MWn,TPe,F:Spider-Man & Blade 2.25
8 TPe,F:Sub-Mariner & Doctor
  Strange 2.25
9 TPe,F:Sub-Mariner & Captain
  America 2.25
10 TPe,AW,F:Sub Mariner & Thing . 2.25
11 TPe,AW,PO,F:Sub-Mariner & Iron
  Man, final issue 2.25

MARVEL TEAM-UP
Nov., 2004
1 ScK, Golden Child, pt.1 .... 2.25
2 ScK, Golden Child, pt.2 .... 2.25
3 ScK, Fant. Four & Dr. Strange... 2.25
4 ScK, Iron Man, Hulk........... 2.25
5 Sck, Spider-man, X-23.......... 2.25
6 ScK,The Golden Child 2.25
7 ScK,Ring of the Master 2.25
8 Sck,Master of the Ring,pt.2 .... 3.00
9 ScK,Master of the Ring,pt.3..... 3.00
10 ScK,Master of the Ring,pt.4 .... 3.00
11 Titannus War,pt.1 .... 3.00
12 Titannus War,pt.2 .... 3.00
13 Titannus War,pt.3 .... 3.00
14 F:Spider-Man 3.00
15 League of Losers, pt.1 .... 3.00
16 League of Losers, pt.2 .... 3.00
17 League of Losers, pt.3 .... 3.00
18 League of Losers, pt.4 .... 3.00
19 Wolv. & Cable vs. Ringmaster .. 3.00
20 Freedom Ring................ 3.00
21 Freedom Ring................ 3.00
22 Freedom Ring................ 3.00
23 Freedom Ring................ 3.00
24 Freedom Ring................ 3.00
25 Final Issue 3.00
TPB Vol. 1: The Golden Child 15.00
TPB Vol. 2: Master of the Ring ... 18.00
TPB Vol. 3: League of Losers 14.00

MARVEL
Treasury Edition
Sept., 1974
1 SD,Spider-Man,I:Contemplator . 75.00
2 JK,F:Fant.Four,Silver Surfer ... 30.00
3 F:Thor 25.00
4 BWS,F:Conan 25.00
5 O:Hulk 25.00
6 GC,FB,SD,F:Dr.Strange....... 25.00
7 JB,JK,F:The Avengers 25.00
8 F:X-Mass stories 25.00
9 F:Super-Hero Team-Up 25.00
10 F:Thor 25.00
11 F:Fantastic Four 20.00
12 F:Howard the Duck.......... 20.00
13 F:X-Mas stories 20.00
14 F:Spider-Man 22.00
15 BWS,F:Conan,Red Sonja 22.00
16 F:Defenders 20.00
17 F:The Hulk 20.00
18 F:Spider Man,X-Men......... 25.00
19 F:Conan 22.00
20 F:Hulk 22.00
21 F:Fantastic Four 22.00
22 F:Spider-Man 25.00
23 F:Conan 22.00
24 F:The Hulk 22.00

25 F:Spider-Man,Hulk 22.00
26 GP,F:Hulk,Wolverine,Hercules . 25.00
27 HT,F:Hulk,Spider-Man........ 22.00
28 JB,JSt,F:SpM/Superman...... 50.00

MARVEL TREASURY OF OZ
(oversized) 1975
1 JB,movie adapt............. 30.00

MARVEL TREASURY SPECIAL
Vol. I Spider-Man, 1974 .... 30.00
Vol. II Capt. America, 1976 ..... 35.00

MARVEL TRIPLE ACTION
Feb., 1972
1 Rep..................... 30.00
2 thru 5 rep................ @20.00
6 thru 10 rep............... @15.00
11 thru 47 rep............... @8.00
G-Size#1 F:Avengers 10.00
G-Size#2 F:Avengers........... 10.00

MARVEL TWO-IN-ONE
Jan., 1974
(Thing in all, unless *)
1 GK,F:Man-Thing 85.00
2 GK,JSt,F:Namor,Namorita 30.00
3 F:Daredevil 30.00
4 F:Capt.America,Namorita 20.00
5 F:Guardians of the Galaxy..... 22.00
6 F:Dr.Strange............... 22.00
7 F:Valkyrie 14.00
8 F:Ghost Rider 20.00
9 F:Thor 14.00
10 KJ,F:Black Widow........... 14.00
11 F:Golem 10.00
12 F:Iron Man 10.00
13 F:Power Man 10.00
14 F:Son of Satan 11.00
15 F:Morbius 11.00
16 F:Ka-Zar 10.00
17 F:Spider-Man 10.00
18 F:Spider-Man 10.00
19 F:Tigra 10.00
20 F:The Liberty Legion 10.00
21 F:Doc Savage 7.00
22 F:Thor,Human Torch 7.00
23 F:Thor,Human Torch 7.00
24 SB,F:Black Goliath 7.00

Marvel Two-In-One #10
© *Marvel Entertainment Group*

25 F:Iron Fist 7.00
26 F:Nick Fury 7.00
27 F:Deathlok. 7.00
28 F:Sub-Mariner.............. 8.00
29 F:Master of Kung Fu......... 7.00
30 JB,F:Spiderwoman 15.00
31 F:Spiderwoman............. 7.00
32 F:Invisible girl 7.00
33 F:Modred the Mystic 7.00
34 F:Nighthawk,C:Deathlok...... 7.00
35 F:Skull the Slayer 7.00
36 F:Mr.Fantastic.............. 7.00
37 F:Matt Murdock............. 7.00
38 F:Daredevil 7.00
39 F:The Vision 7.00
40 F:Black Panther 7.00
41 F:Brother Voodoo 5.00
42 F:Captain America 5.00
43 JBy,F:Man-Thing............ 6.00
44 GD,F:Hercules 4.00
45 GD,F:Captain Marvel 5.00
46 F:The Hulk 12.00
47 GD,F:Yancy Street Gang,
  I:Machinesmith 4.00
48 F:Jack of Hearts 4.00
49 GD,F:Dr.Strange............ 4.00
50 JBy,JS,F:Thing & Thing 4.00
51 FM,BMc,F:Wonderman,Nick
  Fury, Ms.Marvel............ 8.00
52 F:Moon Knight,I:Crossfire 4.00
53 JBy,JS,F:Quasar,C:Deathlok ... 4.00
54 JBy,JS,D:Deathlok,
  I:Grapplers 11.00
55 JBy,JS,I:New Giant Man....... 4.00
56 GP,GD,F:Thundra 3.00
57 GP,GD,F:Wundarr........... 3.00
58 GP,GD,I:Aquarian,A:Quasar ... 3.00
59 F:Human Torch 3.00
60 GP,GD,F:Impossible Man,
  I:Impossible Woman 3.00
61 GD,F:Starhawk,I&O:Her 4.00
62 GD,F:Moondragon 4.00
63 GD,F:Warlock 4.00
64 DP,GD,F:Stingray,
  I:Serpent Squad 3.00
65 GP,GD,F:Triton 3.00
66 GD,F:Scarlet Witch,
  V:Arcade 3.00
67 F:Hyperion,Thundra 3.00
68 F:Angel,V:Arcade 3.00
69 GD,F:Guardians o/t Galaxy 3.00
70 F:The Inhumans 3.00
71 F:Mr.Fantastic,I:Deathurge,
  Maelstrom 3.00
72 F:Stingray 3.00
73 F:Quasar................. 3.00
74 F:Puppet Master,Modred 3.00
75 F:The Avengers,O:Blastaar.... 4.00
76 F:Iceman,O:Ringmaster 3.00
77 F:Man-Thing 3.00
78 F:Wonder Man 3.00
79 F:Blue Diamond,I:Star Dancer . 3.00
80 F:Ghost Rider 3.50
81 F:Sub-Mariner.............. 2.50
82 F:Captain America 2.50
83 F:Sasquatch 3.50
84 F:Alpha Flight 3.50
85 F:Giant-Man 3.00
86 O:Sandman................ 3.00
87 F:Ant-Man 3.00
88 F:She-Hulk 3.00
89 F:Human Torch 3.00
90 F:Spider-Man 4.00
91 V:Sphinx 3.00
92 F:Jocasta,V:Ultron........... 3.00
93 F:Machine Man,D:Jocasta..... 3.00
94 F:Power Man,Iron Fist 3.00
95 F:Living Mummy 3.00
96 F:Sandman,C:Marvel Heroes ... 3.00
97 F:Iron Man 3.00
98 F:Franklin Richards.......... 3.00
99 JBy(c),F:Rom 3.00

MARVEL

MARVEL

100 F:Ben Grimm 4.00
Ann.#1 SB,F:Liberty Legion 15.00
Ann.#2 JSn,2nd D:Thanos,A:Spider
  Man,Avengers,Capt.Marvel,
  I:Lord Chaos,Master Order . . . 50.00
Ann.#3 F:Nova. 7.00
Ann.#4 F:Black Bolt 7.00
Ann.#5 F:Hulk,V:Pluto 4.00
Ann.#6 I:American Eagle 4.00
Ann.#7 I:Champion,A:Hulk,Thor,
  DocSamson,Colossus,Sasquatch,
  Wonder Man 4.00

MARVEL UNIVERSE:
OFFICIAL HANDBOOK TO
Jan., 1983

1 Abomination-Avengers'
  Quintet. 7.50
2 BaronMordo-Collect.Man. 6.00
3 Collector-Dracula. 5.00
4 Dragon Man-Gypsy Moth 5.00
5 Hangman-Juggernaut 5.00
6 K-L. 4.00
7 Mandarin-Mystique 4.00
8 Na,oria-Pyro. 4.00
9 Quasar to She-Hulk. 4.00
10 Shiar-Sub-Mariner. 4.00
11 Subteraneans-Ursa Major. 4.00
12 Valkyrie-Zzzax. 4.00
13 Book of the Dead 4.00
14 Book of the Dead 4.00
15 Weaponry 4.00

[2nd Series] 1985

1 Abomination-Batroc 5.00
2 Beast-Clea. 4.00
3 Cloak & D.-Dr.Strange 4.00
4 Dr.Strange-Galactus 4.00
5 Gardener-Hulk 4.00
6 Human Torch-Ka-Zar 3.25
7 Kraven-Magneto 3.25
8 Magneto-Moleman. 3.25
9 Moleman-Owl. 3.25
10 . . . . 3.25
11 . . . . 3.00
12 S-T 3.00
13 . . . . 3.00
14 V-Z 3.00
15 . . . . 3.00
16 Book of the Dead 3.00
17 Handbook of the Dead,inc.
  JLe illus. 3.00
18 . . . . 3.00
19 . . . . 3.00
20 Inc.RLd illus. 3.00

Marvel Universe Update

1 thru 8 . . . . @3.00

Marvel Universe Packet

1 inc. Spider-Man 5.50
2 inc. Captain America 4.50
3 inc. Ghost Rider. 5.00
4 inc. Wolverine. 4.50
5 inc. Punisher 4.25
6 inc. She-Hulk 4.00
7 inc. Daredevil. 4.00
8 inc. Hulk. 4.00
9 inc. Moon Knight 4.00
10 inc. Captain Britain 4.00
11 inc. Storm 4.00
12 inc. Silver Surfer. 4.00
13 inc. Ice Man 4.50
14 inc. Thor 4.50
15 thru 22. . . . . @4.50
23 inc. Cage. 4.50
24 inc. Iron Fist 4.50
25 inc.Deadpool,Night Thrasher . . . 4.50
26 inc. Wonder Man. 5.00
27 inc.Beta Ray Bill,Pip 5.00
28 inc.X-Men 5.00
29 inc.Carnage. 5.00
30 thru 36. . . . . @5.00

MARVEL UNIVERSE
1996

1 Post Onslaught 3.25

MARVEL UNIVERSE
April, 1998

1 CPa(c),RSt,SEp,AW,F:Human
  Torch,Capt.Am.,Namor,48-pg. . . 3.00
2A JBy(c),RSt,SEp,AW,V:Hydra,
  Baron Strucker. 2.25
2B DGb(c). 2.25
3 RSt,SEp,AW,V:Hydra. 2.25
4 RSt,MM, all-star jam cover,
  F:Monster Hunters. 2.25
5 MM,RSt,F:The Monster Hunters . 2.25
6 MM,RSt,F:Monster Hunters,pt.3 . 2.25
7 MM,RSt,F:Monster Hunters,pt.4 . 2.25
TPB Vol. 1: Thanos 18.00

MARVEL UNIVERSE:
MILLENNIAL VISIONS
Dec., 2001

Spec.2001 48-page 4.00

MARVEL UNIVERSE:
THE END
March, 2003

1 (of 6) JSn,AM. 2.25
2 JSn,AM 2.25
3 JSn,AM 3.00
4 thru 6 JSn,AM . . . . @3.00

MARVEL
VALENTINE'S SPECIAL
1997

1-shot MWa,TDF, 48-pg. 3.00

MARVEL WEDDINGS
Feb., 2005

TPB Marvel Weddings 20.00

MARVEL WESTERNS
July., 2006

1 Three new tales. 4.00
2 Kid Colt & Arizona Annie 4.00
3 Two-Gun Kid 4.00
4 The Black. 4.00
Spec. Outlaw Files #1 . . . . 4.00
TPB Marvel Westerns 21.00

MARVEL X-MEN
COLLECTION
1994

1 thru 3 JL from the 1st series
  X-Men Cards . . . . @3.25

MARVEL YOUNG GUNS
SKETCH BOOK
Dec., 2004

2004 . . . . 3.00

MARVEL ZOMBIES
Dec., 2005

1 . . . . 2.50
2 thru 5 . . . . 3.00
TPB 20.00

MARVELOUS
ADVENTURES OF
GUS BEEZER
April, 2003

Spec. F:Spider-Man 3.00
Spec. F:X-Men 3.00

Spec. F:The Hulk. 3.00

MARVILLE
Sept., 2002

1 U-Decide 3.00
1b foil (c) 40-pg. 4.00
1c variant foil (c). 4.00
2 thru 6 . . . . @2.25
5a thru 6a MBr,variant (c). . . . . . @2.25
7 . . . . 3.00
TPB Vol. 1 . . . . 13.00

MARVIN MOUSE
Marvel Atlas, Sept., 1957

1 BEv,F:Marvin Mouse 150.00

MARY JANE
June, 2004

1 thru 4 . . . . 2.25
Digest Vol. 1 Circle of Friends. 6.00

Mary Jane: Homecoming #2
© Marvel Entertainment Group

MARY JANE:
HOMECOMING
March, 2005

1 (of 4) The Cheating Thing 3.00
2 the Friendship Thing 3.00
3 The Regret Thing. 3.00
4 The Homecoming Thing 3.00
Digest Vol. 2 Homecoming 7.00

MASTER OF KUNG FU,
SPECIAL MARVEL ED.
April, 1974
Prev: Special Marvel Edition

17 JSn,I:Black Jack Tarr 35.00
18 PG,1st Gulacy Art 20.00
19 PG,A:Man-Thing 22.00
20 GK(c),PG,AM,V:Samurai. 15.00
21 AM,Season of Vengeance..
  Moment of Death. 10.00
22 PG,DA,Death. 10.00
23 AM,KJ,River of Death 10.00
24 JSn,WS,AM,ST,Night of the
  Assassin 12.00
25 JSt(c),PG,ST,Fists Fury...
  Rites of Death 10.00
26 KP,ST,A:Daughter of
  Fu Manchu 10.00
27 SB,FS,A:Fu Manchu 10.00
28 EH,ST,Death of a Spirit. 10.00

29 PG,V:Razor-Fist 10.00
30 PG,DA,Pit of Lions 10.00
31 GK&DA(c),PG,DA,Snowbuster . 10.00
32 GK&ME(c),SB,ME,Assault on an
   Angry Sea 10.00
33 PG,Messenger of Madness,
   I:Leiko Wu 10.00
34 PG,Captive in A Madman's
   Crown 10.00
35 PG,V:Death Hand 10.00
36 The Night of the Ninja's 10.00
37 V:Darkstrider & Warlords of
   the Web 5.00
38 GK(c),PG,A:The Cat 5.00
39 GK(c),PG,A:The Cat 5.00
40 PG,The Murder Agency. 5.00
41 . . . . 5.00
42 GK(c),PG,TS,V:Shockwave 5.00
43 PG,V:Shockwave 5.00
44 SB(c),PG,V:Fu Manchu 5.00
45 GK(c),PG,Death Seed. 5.00
46 PG,V:Sumo 5.00
47 PG,The Cold White
   Mantle of Death 5.00
48 PG,Bridge of a 1,000 Dooms . . . 5.00
49 PG,V:Shaka Kharn,The
   Demon Warrior 5.00
50 PG,V:Fu Manchu 5.00
51 PG(c),To End...To Begin 5.00
52 Mayhem in Morocco 5.00
53 . . . . 5.00
54 JSn(c),Death Wears Three
   Faces. 5.00
55 PG(c),The Ages of Death 5.00
56 V:The Black Ninja 5.00
57 V:Red Baron 5.00
58 Behold the Final Mask 5.00
59 GK(c),B:Phoenix Gambit,
   Behold the Angel of Doom 5.00
60 A:Dr.Doom,Doom Came 5.00
61 V:Skull Crusher. 4.50
62 Coast of Death 4.50
63 GK&TA(c),Doom Wears
   Three Faces 4.50
64 PG(c),To Challenge a Dragon . . 4.50
65 V:Pavane 4.50
66 V:Kogar 4.50
67 PG(c),Dark Encounters. 4.50
68 Final Combats,V:The Cat 4.50
69 . . . . 4.50
70 A:Black Jack Tarr,Murder
   Mansion. 4.50
71 PG(c),Ying & Yang (c) 4.50
72 V:Shockwave 4.50
73 RN(c),V:Behemoths 4.50
74 TA(c),A:Shockwave. 4.50
75 Where Monsters Dwell 4.50
76 GD,Battle on the Waterfront 4.00
77 GD,I:Zaran 4.00
78 GD,Moving Targets 4.00
79 GD,This Side of Death 4.00
80 GD,V:Leopard Men 4.00
81 GD,V:Leopard Men 4.00
82 GD,Flight into Fear 4.00
83 GD, ... 4.00
84 GD,V:Fu Manchu 4.00
85 GD,V:Fu Manchu 4.00
86 GD,V:Fu Manchu 4.00
87 GD,V:Zaran, ... 4.00
88 GD,V:Fu Manchu 4.00
89 GD,D:Fu Manchu 4.00
90 MZ,Death in Chinatown 4.00
91 GD,Gang War,drugs 5.00
92 GD,Shadows of the Past 4.00
93 GD,Cult of Death 4.00
94 GD,V:Agent Synergon 4.00
95 GD,Raid 4.00
96 GD,I:Rufus Carter 4.00
97 GD,V:Kung Fu's Dark Side 4.00
98 GD,Fight to the Finish. 4.00
99 GD,Death Boat 4.00
100 GD,Doublesize 6.00

101 GD,Not Smoke,Nor Beads,
   Nor Blood 3.75
102 GD,Assassins,1st GD(p). 4.00
103 GD,V:Assassins 3.75
104 GD,Fight without Reason,
   C:Cerberus 3.75
105 GD,I:Razor Fist. 3.75
106 GD,C:Velcro 3.75
107 GD,A:Sata. 3.75
108 GD. 3.75
109 GD,Death is a Dark Agent 3.75
110 GD,Perilous Reign 3.75
111 GD. 3.75
112 GD(c),Commit and Destroy. . . . 3.75

Master of Kung Fu #84
© *Marvel Entertainment Group*

113 GD(c),V:Panthers 3.75
114 Fantasy o/t Autumn Moon. 3.75
115 GD. 3.75
116 GD. 3.75
117 GD,Devil Deeds Done
   in Darkness 3.75
118 GD,D:Fu Manchu,double 4.50
119 GD. 3.75
120 GD,Dweller o/t Dark Stream . . . 3.75
121 Death in the City of Lights 3.00
122 . . . . 3.00
123 V:Ninjas. 3.00
124 . . . . 3.00
125 double-size 6.00
G-Size#1,CR,PG 20.00
G-Size#2 PG,V:Yellow Claw 3.00
G-Size#3 . . . . 3.00
G-Size#4 JK,V:Yellow Claw 3.00
Spec.#1 Bleeding Black 3.00

MASTER OF KUNG FU: BLEEDING BLACK

1 V:ShadowHand, 1991 . . . . 3.00

MASTERS OF TERROR

July–Sept., 1975

1 GM(c),FB,BWS,JSn,NA 30.00
2 JSn(c),GK,VM, ... 25.00

MASTERS OF THE UNIVERSE

Star, May, 1986—March, 1988

1 I:Hordak. 7.00
2 thru 11 . . . . @4.00
12 D:Skeletor 8.00
Movie #1 GT 2.00

MATT SLADE, GUNFIGHTER

Atlas, May, 1956

1 AW,AT,F:Matt Slade,Crimson
   Avenger 250.00
2 AW,A:Crimson Avenger 175.00
3 A:Crimson Avenger 150.00
4 A:Crimson Avenger 125.00
Becomes:

KID SLADE GUNFIGHTER

5 F:Kid Slade 125.00
6 . . . . 100.00
7 AW,Duel in the Night 110.00
8 July, 1957 . . . . 100.00

MAVERICK

1997

1 JGz,F:Christopher Nord/David
   North/Maverick, 48-pg. 3.50
2 JGz,A:Victor Creed and Logan . . 3.00
2a variant cover 3.00
3 JGz,V:Puck & Vindicator 3.00
4 JGz,A:Wolverine 3.00
5 JGz,A:The Blob 3.00
6 JGz,V:Sabretooth. 3.00
7 JGz,V:Sabretooth. 3.00
8 JGz,V:The Confessor 3.00
9 JGz,Maverick's secrets 3.00
10 JGz,V:Ivan the Terrible, Chris
   Bradley becomes Bolt 3.00
11 JGz,A:Darkstar,Vanguard,
   Ursa Major. 3.00
12 JGz, double sized last issue. . . . 3.50
1-shot LHa, V:Sabretooth,48-pg. . . 3.00

MAXIMUM SECURITY

Oct., 2000

1 (of 3) KBk,JOy,x-over 3.00
2 KBk,JOy,x-over 3.00
3 KBk,JOy,x-over,concl. 3.00
Spec. Thor vs. Ego, 64-pg.,SL,JK . 3.00
Spec. Dangerous Planet 3.00

MEET MISS BLISS

Marvel Atlas, 1955

1 . . . . 150.00
2 . . . . 100.00
3 . . . . 100.00
4 . . . . 100.00

MEGA MORPHS

Aug., 2005

1 (of 4) Toy tie-in. 3.00
2 . . . . 3.00
3 Red Rampage 3.00
4 The Pawns and the Power 3.00
TPB 8.00

MEKANIX

Oct., 2002

1 (of 6) CCI,F:Kitty Pryde 3.00
2 CCI,back in school. 3.00
3 thru 6 CCI. . . . . @3.00

MELVIN THE MONSTER

Marvel Atlas, July, 1956

1 JMn 175.00
2 thru 6 . . . . @125.00
Becomes:

DEXTER THE DEMON

Sept., 1957

7 . . . . 100.00

MEMORIES

Epic

1 Space Adventures 2.50

Menace #2
© Marvel Entertainment Group

MENACE
Marvel Atlas, May, 1953
1 RH,BEv,GT,One Head Too
Many 1,000.00
2 RH,BEv,GT,JSt,Burton'sBlood . 650.00
3 BEv,RH,JR,The Werewolf 500.00
4 BEv,RH,The Four Armed Man . 500.00
5 BEv,RH,GC,GT,I&O:Zombie . . 750.00
6 BEv,RH,JR,The Graymoor
Ghost 450.00
7 JSt,RH,Fresh out of Flesh 400.00
8 RH,The Lizard Man 400.00
9 BEv,The Walking Dead 425.00
10 RH(c),Half Man,Half.... . . . . . 400.00
11 JKz,JR,Locked In,May, 1954 . 400.00

MEN IN ACTION
Marvel Atlas, April, 1952
1 Sweating it Out 200.00
2 US Infantry stories 150.00
3 RH 100.00
4 War stories 100.00
5 JMn,Squad Charge 100.00
6 War stories 100.00
7 RH(c),BK,No Risk Too Great . 150.00
8 JRo(c),They Strike By Night . 100.00
9 SSh(c),Rangers Strike Back . . 100.00
Becomes:

BATTLE BRADY
10 SSh(c),F:Battle Brady 150.00
11 SSh(c) 100.00
12 SSh(c),Death to the Reds 100.00
13 . . . . 100.00
14 Final Issue,June, 1953 . . . . . . 100.00

MEN IN BLACK
1 ANi, prequel to movie (1997) 4.00
Spec. Movie Adaptation (1997) 4.00

MEN IN BLACK: RETRIBUTION
Aug., 1997
1 continuation from movie 4.00

MEN'S ADVENTURES
See: TRUE WESTERN

MEPHISTO vs. FOUR HEROES
April–July, 1987
1 JB,BWi,A:Fantastic Four 3.50

---

2 JB,BWi,A:X-Factor 3.00
3 JB,AM,A:X-Men 3.00
4 JB,BWi,A:Avengers 3.00

METEOR MAN
1993–94
1 R:Meteor Man 2.25
2 V:GhostStrike,Malefactor,Simon . 2.25
3 A:Spider-Man 2.25
4 A:Night Thrasher 2.25
5 Exocet 2.25
6 final issue 2.25

[TED McKEEVER'S} METROPOL
Epic, 1991–92
1 Ted McKeever 3.00
2 thru 12 . . . . @3.00

METROPOL A.D.
Epic, 1992
1 R:The Angels 3.50
2 V:Demons 3.50
3 V:Nuclear Arsenal 3.50

MICRONAUTS
[1st Series] Jan., 1979
1 MGo,JRu,O:Micronauts 5.00
2 thru 36 MGo,JRu,Earth . . . . . . @3.00
37 KG,Nightcrawler 4.00
38 thru 59 GK,1st direct . . . . @2.50
Ann.#1,SD 2.50
#2 SD 2.50

[2nd Series] 1984
1 V:The Makers 2.50
2 thru 20 . . . . @2.50

MICRONAUTS
(Special Edition) Dec., 1983
1 MGo/JRu,rep. 3.00
2 MGo/JRu,rep. 3.00
3 & 4 Rep.MG/JRu . . . . @3.00
5 Rep.MG/JRu,April, 1984 . . . . . . 3.00

MIDNIGHT MEN
Epic *Heavy Hitters,* 1993
1 HC,I:Midnight Men 3.00
2 HC,J:Barnett 2.25
3 HC,Pasternak is Midnight Man . . 2.25
4 HC,Last issue 2.25

Midnight Sons Unlimited #3
© Marvel Entertainment Group

MIDNIGHT SONS UNLIMITED
1993–95
1 JQ,JBi,MT(c),A:Midnight Sons. . . 4.25
2 BSz(c),F:Midnight Sons 4.25
3 JR2(c),JS,A:Spider-Man 4.25
4 Siege of Darkness #17,
D:2nd Ghost Rider. 4.25
5 DQ(s),F:Mordred,Vengeance,
Morbius,Werewolf,Blaze,
I:Wildpride 4.25
6 DQ(s),F:Dr.Strange 4.00
7 DQ(s),F:Man-Thing 4.00
8 . . . . 4.00
9 J:Mighty Destroyer. 4.00

MIGHTY HEROES
Nov., 1997
1-shot SLo, Diaper Man, Rope Man,
Cuckoo Man, Tornado Man, Strong
Man, etc. 3.00

MIGHTY MARVEL WESTERN
Oct., 1968
1 JK,All reprints,B:Rawhide Kid
Kid Colt,Two-Gun Kids 150.00
2 JK,DAy,Beware of the Barker
Brothers 100.00
3 HT(c),JK,DAy,Walking Death. . 100.00
4 HT(c),DAy 100.00
5 HT(c),DAy,Ambush 100.00
6 HT(c),DAy Doom in the Desert 100.00
7 DAy,V:MurderousMasquerader 100.00
8 HT(c),DAy,Rustler's on the
Range 100.00
9 JSe(c),JK,DAy,V:Dr Danger . 100.00
10 OW,DH,Cougar. 100.00
11 V:The Enforcers 60.00
12 JK,V:Blackjack Bordon 75.00
13 V:Grizzly 75.00
14 JK.V:The Enforcers. 75.00
15 Massacre at Medicine Bend . . . 75.00
16 JK,Mine of Death 75.00
17 Ambush at Blacksnake Mesa . . 50.00
18 Six-Gun Thunderer 50.00
19 Reprints cont. 50.00
20 same 50.00
21 same 40.00
22 . . . . 40.00
23 same 40.00
24 JDa,E:Kid Colt 40.00
25 B:Matt Slade 40.00
26 thru 31 Reprints . . . . @40.00
32 JK,AW,Ringo Kid #23 . . . . 30.00
33 thru 36 Reprints . . . . @30.00
37 JK,AW Two-Gun #51 . . . . 30.00
38 thru 45 Reprints . . . . @30.00
46 same,Sept., 1976 . . . . 30.00

[SABAN'S] MIGHTY MORPHIN POWER RANGERS
1 SLo,FaN,New ongoing series . . . 2.25
2 thru 7 . . . . @2.25
Photo Adaptation 3.00

[SABAN'S] MIGHTY MORPHIN POWER RANGERS: NINJA RANGERS/ VR TROOPERS
1 FaN,RLm,JP,flip book 2.25
2 JP,flip book. 2.25
3 thru 6 . . . . @2.25

All comics prices listed are for *Near Mint* condition.

MARVEL

MIGHTY MOUSE
[1st Series] Fall, 1946
1 Terrytoons Presents	2,000.00
2	800.00
3	500.00
4 Summer, 1947	500.00

MIGHTY MOUSE
Oct., 1990
1 EC,Dark Mite Returns	3.00
2 EC,V:The Glove	2.25
3 EC/JBr(c)Prince Say More	2.25
4 EC/GP(c)Alt.Universe #1	2.25
5 EC,Alt.Universe #2	2.25
6 Ferment',A:MacFurline	2.25
7 EC,V:Viral Worm	2.25
8 EC,BAT-BAT:Year One, O:Bug Wonder	2.25
9 EC,BAT-BAT:Year One, V:Smoker	2.25
10 Night o/t Rating Lunatics	2.25

MILLIE THE MODEL
Winter, 1945
1 O:Millie the Model, Bowling(c)	1,500.00
2 Totem Pole(c)	750.00
3 Anti-Noise(c)	500.00
4 Bathing Suit(c)	500.00
5 Blame it on Fame	500.00
6 Beauty and the Beast	500.00
7 Bathing Suit(c)	500.00
8 Fancy Dress(c),HK,Hey Look	500.00
9 Paris(c),BW	600.00
10 Jewelry(c),HK,Hey Look	500.00
11 HK,Giggles and Grins	350.00
12 A;Rusty,Hedy Devine	250.00
13 A;Hedy Devine,HK,Hey Look	275.00
14 HK,Hey Look	275.00
15 HK,Hey Look	250.00
16 HK,Hey Look	250.00
17 thru 20	@275.00
21 thru 75	@225.00
76 thru 99	@150.00
100	200.00
101 thru 126	@150.00
127 Millie/Clicker	165.00
128 A:Scarlet Mayfair	125.00
129 The Truth about Agnes	125.00
130 thru 153	@125.00
154 B:New Millie	125.00
155 thru 206	@125.00

Millie The Model #6
© Marvel Entertainment Group

207 Dec., 1973	125.00
Ann.#1 How Millie Became a Model	450.00
Ann.#2 Millies Guide to the World of Modeling	300.00
Ann.#3 Many Lives of Millie	200.00
Ann.#4 Many Lives of Millie	175.00

MISS AMERICA COMICS
1944
1 Miss America(c),pin-ups	2,500.00

MISS AMERICA MAGAZINE
Nov., 1944—Nov., 1958
2 Ph(c),Miss America costume I;Patsy Walker,Buzz Baxter, Hedy Wolfe	1,900.00
3 Ph(c),A:Patsy Walker,Miss America	675.00
4 Ph(c),Betty Page,A:Patsy Walker,Miss America	675.00
5 Ph(c),A:Patsy Walker,Miss America	675.00
6 Ph(c),A:Patsy Walker	175.00
7 Patsy Walker stories	150.00
8 same	150.00
9 same	150.00
10 same	150.00
11 same	150.00
12 same	150.00
13 thru 18	@150.00
21	175.00
22 thru 93	@100.00

MISS FURY COMICS
Marvel Timely, Winter, 1942-43
1 Newspaper strip reprints, ASh(c) O:Miss Fury	6,000.00
2 V:Nazis(c)	3,000.00
3 Hitler/Nazi Flag(c)	2,500.00
4 ASh(c),Japanese(c)	2,000.00
5 ASh(c),Gangster(c)	1,500.00
6 ASh(c),Gangster(c)	1,500.00
7 Gangster(c)	1,200.00
8 Atom-Bomb Secrets(c) Winter, 1946	1,200.00

MISSION: IMPOSSIBLE
May, 1996
1 RLd,MWn(s),Movie adapt.	3.00

MISTY
Star, Dec., 1985
1 F:Millie the Models Niece	3.50
2 thru 5	@3.50
6 May, 1986	3.50

MITZI COMICS
Marvel Timely, Spring, 1948
1 HK:Hey Look,Giggles and Grins	300.00
Becomes:	

MITZI'S BOYFRIEND
2 F:Chip,Mitzi/Chip(c)	150.00
3 Chips adventures	125.00
4 thru 7 same	@125.00
Becomes:	

MITZI'S ROMANCES
8 Mitzi/Chip(c)	125.00
9	100.00
10 Dec., 1949	100.00

MODELING WITH MILLIE
See: DATE WITH MILLIE

MOEBIUS
Epic, Oct., 1987
1	12.00
2	12.00
3	15.00
4	12.00
5	12.00
6 1988	12.00

MOEBIUS: FUSION
1 128-pg. Sketchbook	20.00

Molly Manton's Romances #1
© Marvel Entertainment Group

MOLLY MANTON'S ROMANCES
Sept., 1949
1 Ph(c),Dare Not Marry	200.00
2 Ph(c),Romances of	150.00
Becomes:	

ROMANTIC AFFAIRS
3 Ph(c)	125.00

MOMENT OF SILENCE
Dec., 2001
Spec. 9-11-01 tribute issue	3.50

THE MONKEY AND THE BEAR
Marvel Atlas, 1953
1	100.00
2	65.00

MONSTER MENACE
1 thru 4 SD,rep.	@3.00

MONSTER OF FRANKENSTEIN
Jan., 1973
1 MP,Frankenstein's Monster	75.00
2 MP,Bride of the Monster	50.00
3 MP,Revenge	50.00
4 MP,Monster's Death	50.00
5 MP,The Monster Walks Among Us	50.00
Becomes:	

FRANKENSTEIN
1973–75
6 MP,Last of the Frankensteins	30.00
7 JB,The Fiend and the Fury	30.00
8 JB,A:Dracula	45.00
9 JB,A:Dracula	45.00
10 JB,Death Strikes Frankenstein	25.00

11 Carnage at CastleFrankenstein 20.00
12 Frankenstein's Monster today. . 20.00
13 Undying Fiend. 20.00
14 Fury of the Night Creature 20.00
15 Trapped in a Nightmare 20.00
16 The Brute and the Berserker . . 20.00
17 Phoenix Aflame. 20.00
18 Children of the Damned 20.00

MONSTER OF FRANKENSTEIN

TPB Vol. 1: Essential Monster
of Frankenstein 17.00

MONSTERS ON THE PROWL
See: CHAMBER OF DARKNESS

MONSTERS UNLEASHED
July, 1973

1 GM(c),GC,DW,B&W Mag 65.00
2 JB,FB,BEv,B:Frankenstein 50.00
3 NA(c),GK,GM,GT,B:Man Thing 50.00
4 JB,GC,BK,I:Satana 50.00
5 JB 35.00
6 MP 25.00
7 AW 35.00
8 GP,NA 40.00
9 A:Wendigo 40.00
10 O:Tigra 40.00
11 FB(C),April, 1975 . . . . 40.00
Ann.#1 GK 40.00

Moon Knight #1
© Marvel Entertainment Group

MOON KNIGHT
[1st Regular Series] Nov., 1980

1 BSz,O:Moon Knight 7.00
2 BSz,V:Slasher 3.50
3 BSz,V:Midnight Man 3.50
4 BSz,V:Committee of 5 . . . . 3.50
5 BSz,V:Red Hunter 3.50
6 BSz,V:White Angels 3.50
7 BSz,V:Moon Kings. 3.50
8 BSz,V:Moon Kings, Drug. 3.00
9 BSz,V:Midnight Man 3.00
10 BSz,V:Midnight Man 3.00
11 BSz,V:Creed (Angel Dust) 3.00
12 BSz,V:Morpheus 3.00
13 BSz,A:Daredevil & Jester 3.00
14 BSz,V:Stained Glass Scarlet . . 3.00
15 FM(c),BSz,1st Direct. 4.00

16 V:Blacksmith 3.00
17 BSz,V:Master Sniper. 3.00
18 BSz,V:Slayers Elite 3.00
19 BSz,V:Arsenal 3.00
20 BSz,V:Arsenal 3.00
21 A:Bother Voodoo 2.50
22 BSz,V:Morpheus 2.50
23 BSz,V:Morpheus 2.50
24 BSz,V:Stained Glass Scarlet . . 2.50
25 BSz,Black Specter 2.50
26 KP,V:Cabbie Killer 2.50
27 A:Kingpin. 2.50
28 BSz,Spirits in the Sands 2.50
29 BSz,V:Werewolf 2.50
30 BSz,V:Werewolf 2.50
31 TA,V:Savage Studs 2.50
32 KN,Druid Walsh 2.50
33 KN,V:Druid Walsh 2.50
34 KN,Marc Spector. 2.50
35 KN,X-Men,FF,V:The Fly
DoubleSized 3.00
36 A:Dr.Strange 2.50
37 V:Zohar 2.50
38 V:Zohar 2.50

[2nd Regular Series] 1985

1 O:Moon Knight,DoubleSize 2.50
2 Yucatan 2.50
3 V:Morpheus 2.50
4 A:Countess 2.50
5 V:Lt.Flint. 2.50
6 GI,LastIssue. 2.50

[3rd Regular Series] 1989–94

1 V:Bushmaster 4.00
2 A:Spider-Man 3.00
3 V:Bushmaster 2.50
4 RH,A:Midnight,Black Cat 2.50
5 V:Midnight,BlackCat. 2.50
6 A:BrotherVoodoo 2.50
7 A:BrotherVoodoo 2.50
8 TP,A:Punisher,A of V 3.00
9 TP,A:Punisher,A of V 3.00
10 V:Killer Shrike,A of V. 2.00
11 TP,V:Arsenal 2.00
12 TP,V:Bushman,A:Arsenal 2.50
13 TP,V:Bushman 2.50
14 TP,V:Bushman 2.50
15 TP,Trial o/Marc Spector #1,A:
Silv.Sable,Sandman,Paladin . . . 3.00
16 TP,Trial o/Marc Spector #2,A:
Silv.Sable,Sandman,Paladin . . . 3.00
17 TP,Trial o/Marc Spector #3 . . . . 3.00
18 TP,Trial o/Marc Spector #4 . . . . 3.00
19 RLd(c),TP,SpM,Punisher. 3.00
20 TP,A:Spider-Man,Punisher 3.00
21 TP,Spider-Man,Punisher 3.00
22 I:Harbinger 2.50
23 Confrontation 2.50
24 A:Midnight. 2.50
25 MBa,TP,A:Ghost Rider 3.00
26 BSz(c),TP,B:Scarlet Redemption
V:Stained Glass Scarlet. 2.50
27 TP,V:Stained Glass Scarlet 2.50
28 TP,V:Stained Glass Scarlet 2.50
29 TP,V:Stained Glass Scarlet 2.50
30 TP,V:Stained Glass Scarlet 2.50
31 TP,E:Scarlet Redemption,
A:Hobgoblin 2.75
32 TP,V:Hobgoblin,SpM(in Black) . 3.00
33 TP,V:Hobgoblin,A:Spider-Man. . 3.00
34 V:Killer Shrike 2.50
35 TP,Return of Randall Spector
Pt.1,A:Punisher 2.50
36 TP,A:Punisher,Randall 2.50
37 TP,A:Punisher,Randall 2.50
38 TP,A:Punisher,Randall 2.50
39 TP,N:Moon Knight,A:Dr.Doom . . 2.50
40 TP,V:Dr.Doom 2.50
41 TP,Infinity War,I:Moonshade . . . 2.50
42 TP,Infinity War,V:Moonshade . . 2.50
43 TP(i),Infinity War 2.50
44 Inf.War,A:Dr.Strange.FF 2.50
45 V:Demogoblin 2.50

46 V:Demogoblin 2.50
47 Legacy Quest Scenario 2.50
48 I:Deadzone 2.50
49 V:Deadzone 2.50
50 A:Avengers,I:Hellbent,
Die-cut(c). 3.50
51 A:Gambit,V:Hellbent 2.50
52 A:Gambit,Werewolf 2.50
53 Pang 2.50
54 . . . . 2.50
55 SPa,V:Sunstreak. 6.00
56 SPa,V:Seth 6.00
57 SPa,Inf.Crusade 4.00
58 SPa(c),A:Hellbent 3.00
59 SPa(c), ... 3.50
60 E:TKa(s),SPa,D:Moonknight. . . 5.00
Spec.#1 ANi,A:Shang-Chi 2.50
1-shot Moon Knight: Divided We Fall
DCw,V:Bushman (1992) 5.00

MOON KNIGHT
(Special Edition) Nov., 1983

1 BSz,reprints 2.50
2 BSz,reprints 2.50
3 BSz,reprints,Jan., 1984 . . . . 2.50

MOON KNIGHT
Nov., 1997–Feb., 1998

1 (of 4) DgM, Moon Knight returns. 2.50
1A signed by Tommy Lee Edwards
(250 copies). 20.00
2 DgM,A:Scarlet 2.50
3 DgM,Resurrection War,V:Black
Spectre 2.50
4 DgM,Resurrecton War, concl. . . . 2.50

MOON KNIGHT
Dec., 1998

1 (of 4) DgM,MT,A:Marlene 3.00
2 DgM,MT 3.00
3 DgM,MT 3.00
4 DgM,MT,concl. 3.00

MOON KNIGHT
April, 2006

1 The Bottom, pt.1 . . . . 3.00
2 thru 6 The Bottom, pt.2 – pt.6 . @3.00
7 Midnight Sun, pt.1 . . . . 3.00

MOONSHADOW
Epic, May, 1985

1 JMu,O:Moonshadow 6.00
2 thru 12 . . . . @4.00

MORBIUS
1992–95

1 V:Lilith,Lilin,A:Blaze,Gh.Rider,
Rise o/t Midnight Sons #3,
polybagged w/poster 3.00
2 V:Simon Stroud 2.50
3 A:Spider-Man 2.25
4 I:Dr.Paine,C:Spider-Man 2.25
5 V:Basilisk,(inc Superman tribute
on letters page) 2.25
6 V:Basilisk 2.25
7 V:Vic Slaughter 2.25
8 V:Nightmare 2.25
9 V:Nightmare. 2.25
10 Two Tales 2.25
11 A:Nightstalkers 2.25
12 Midnight Massacre#4 . . . . 2.50
13 R:Martine,A:Lilith. 2.25
14 RoW,V:Nightmare,A:Werewolf . . 2.25
15 A:Ghost Rider,Werewolf 2.25
16 GWt(s),Siege of Darkness#5 . . 2.25
17 GWt(s),Siege of Darkness#17 . 2.25
18 GWt(s),A:Deathlok 2.25
19 GWt(s),A:Deathlok 2.25
20 GWt(s),I:Bloodthirst. 2.25

21 B:Dance of the Hunter,A:SpM. . . 2.25
22 A:Spider-Man 2.25
23 E:Dance of the Hunter,A:SpM. . . 2.25
24 Return of the Dragon 2.25
25 RoW 2.50
26 . . . . 2.00
27 . . . . 2.00
28 A:Werewolf 2.00
29 . . . . 2.00
30 New Morbius 2.00
31 A:Mortine 2.00
32 Another Kill 2.00

MORBIUS REVISITED
1993
1 WMc,rep.Fear #20 . . . . 2.25
2 WMc,rep.Fear #28 . . . . 2.25
3 WMc,rep.Fear #29 . . . . 2.25
4 WMc,rep.Fear #30 . . . . 2.25
5 WMc,rep.Fear #31 . . . . 2.25

MORLOCKS
April, 2002
1 (of 4) SMa, outsiders 2.50
2 SMa,mutants stay hidden 2.50
3 SMa,where lurk the Morlocks . . . 2.50
4 SMa,concl 2.50

MORT THE DEAD TEENAGER
1993–94
1 LHa(s),I:Mort 2.25
2 thru 4 LHa(s), ... @2.25

MOTHER TERESA
1984
1 Mother Teresa Story 5.00

MOTOR MOUTH & KILLPOWER
Marvel UK, 1992–93
1 GFr,A:Nick Fury,I:Motor
   Mouth,Killpower 2.50
2 GFr,A:Nick Fury, ... 2.25
3 GFr,V:Killpower,A:Punisher 2.25
4 GFr,A:Nick Fury,Warheads,
   Hell's Angel,O:Killpower 2.25
5 GFr,A:Excalibur,Archangel 2.25
6 GFr,A:Cable,Punisher 2.25
7 EP,A:Cable,Nick Fury 2.25
8 JFr,A:Cable,Nick Fury 2.25
9 JFr,A:Cable,N.Fury,V:Harpies . . . 2.25
10 V:Red Sonja 2.25
11 V:Zachary Sorrow 2.25
12 A:Death's Head II 2.25
13 A:Death's Head II 2.25

MS. MARVEL
Jan., 1977
1 JB,O:Ms Marvel 20.00
2 JB,JSt,V:Scorpion 8.00
3 JB,JSt,V:Doomsday Man 8.00
4 JM,JSt,V:Destructor 8.00
5 JM,JSt,A:V:Vision 8.00
6 JM,JSt,V:Grotesk 8.00
7 JM,JSt,V:Modok 8.00
8 JM,JSt,GF(c),V:Grotesk 8.00
9 KP,JSt,I:Deathbird 9.00
10 JB,TP,V:Deathbird,Modok 7.00
11 V:Elementals 6.00
12 JSn(c),V:Hecate 6.00
13 Bedlam in Boston 6.00
14 CI,TA(c),V:Steeplejack 6.00
15 V:Tigershark 6.00
16 TA,V:Tigershark,A:Beast 15.00
17 TA,C:Mystique 12.00
18 I:Mystique,A;Avengers 22.00
19 A:Captain Marvel 6.00

MARVEL COMICS GROUP
30¢ 8
Ms. MARVEL
IN DEATH'S DARK WATERS!
GROTESK

Ms. Marvel #8
© *Marvel Entertainment Group*

20 V:Lethal Lizards,N:Ms.Marvel . . 6.00
21 V:Lethal Lizards 6.00
22 TA,V:Deathbirds 6.00
23 The Woman who Fell to Earth
   April, 1979 . . . . 6.00

MS. MARVEL
Mar., 2006
1 . . . . 3.00
2 thru 9 . . . . @3.00

MUPPET BABIES
Star, Aug., 1984
1 thru 10 . . . . @2.25
11 thru 25 July, 1989 . . . . @2.25

MUPPETS TAKE MANHATTAN
1 movie adapt,November, 1984 . . . 3.00
2 movie adapt 3.00
3 movie adapt,Jan., 1985 . . . . 3.00

MUTANTS: THE AMAZING X-MEN
1 X-Men After Xavier 3.50
2 Exodus, Dazzler,V:Abyss 2.25
3 F:Bishop 2.25
4 V:Apocalypse 2.25

MUTANTS: THE ASTONISHING X-MEN
1 Uncanny X-Men 3.50
2 V:Holocaust 2.25
3 V:Abyss 2.25
4 V:Beast,Infinities 2.25

MUTANTS: GENERATION NEXT
1 Generation X Ax 3.50
2 Genetic Slave Pens 2.25
3 V:Sugar Man 2.25
4 V:Sugar Man 2.25

MUTANT 2099
Sept., 2004
1 . . . . 3.00

MUTANT X
Aug., 1998
1 HMe,TR,F:Havok, 48-page 3.00

2 HMe,TR,F:Havok 2.50
2a variant cover 2.50
3 HMe,TR,V:Pack 2.50
4 HMe,TR,V:Goblin Queen 2.50
5 HMe,F:Brute, Fallen 2.50
6 HMe,A:Mutant-X Spider-Man . . . 2.50
7 HMe,Trial of the Brute 2.50
8 HMe,V:Goblin Queen 2.50
9 HMe,V:Sentinels 2.50
10 HMe,V:The Six 2.50
11 HMe,Bloodstorm vs. Havok . . . 2.50
12 HMe,O:Goblin Queen,Havok,
   48-page 3.50
13 O:Bloodstorm 2.50
14 HMe,CNr,I:Cyclops 2.50
15 HMe,F:Havok 2.50
16 HMe 2.50
17 HMe,CNr,V:Cyclops 2.50
18 HMe,CNr,A:Punisher 2.50
19 HMe,A:Professor X 2.50
20 HMe,A:Havok 2.50
21 HMe,BS,Prof.X & Apocalypse . . 2.50
22 HMe,BS,Galactus 2.50
23 HMe,TL,Apocalypse 2.50
24 HMe,TL,Master Planner 2.50
25 HMe,TL,The Six,48-pg 3.50
26 HMe,TL,The Six,Bloodstorm . . . 2.50
27 HMe,TL,Dagger,Outcasts 2.50
28 HMe,TL,F:Wolverine 2.50
29 HMe,TL,F:Wolverine 2.50
30 HMe,RLm,F:Capt.America 2.50
31 HMe,RLm,F:Capt.America 2.50
32 HMe,RLm,48-page, final 3.00
GN Mutant X, rep.#1 & #2 . . . . 6.00
Ann.1999, 48-page 3.50
Ann.2000 HMe,secrets 3.50
Ann.2001 HMe,48-page 3.00

MUTANT X
Oct., 2001
1 HC,JHo, TV show tie-in 3.00
2 HC,JHo, ... 2.50
Spec.#1 48-pg.,photo(c) (2002) . . . 3.50
Spec.Dangerous Discoveries (2002) 3.50

MUTANT X: FUTURE SHOCK
May, 2002
1 CCI,F:Shalimar,54-pg 3.50

MUTATIS
Epic
1 I:Mutatis 2.50
2 O:Mutatis 2.50
3 A:Mutatis 2.50

MUTIES
Feb., 2002
1 (of 6) F:Jared 2.50
2 in Japan, I:Seiji 2.50
3 F:Riek Bukenya 2.50
4 . . . . 2.50
5 . . . . 2.50
6 concl 2.50

MUTOPIA X
July, 2005
1 (of 5) House of M tie-in 3.00
2 House of M Tie-in 3.00
3 thru 5 . . . . @3.00

MY DIARY
Dec., 1949–March, 1950
1 Ph(c),The Man I Love 175.00
2 Ph(c),I Was Anybody's Girl . . . 150.00

All comics prices listed are for *Near Mint* condition.

WESTERN LIFE ROMANCES
Marvel Comics, 1949
1 .... 225.00
2 .... 200.00
Becomes:

MY FRIEND IRMA
Marvel Atlas, 1950
3 .... 225.00
4 HK 250.00
5 HK 175.00
6 .... 125.00
7 HK 125.00
8 .... 125.00
9 Paper dolls. 150.00
10 .... 125.00
11 .... 100.00
12 thru 22 .... @100.00
23 FF(one page) 125.00
24 thru 48 .... @100.00

MY GIRL PEARL
Marvel Atlas, 1955–61
1 .... 175.00
2 .... 150.00
3 .... 125.00
4 .... 125.00
5 .... 125.00
6 .... 125.00
7 .... 100.00
8 .... 100.00
9 .... 100.00
10 .... 100.00
11 .... 100.00

MY LOVE
July, 1949
1 Ph(c),One Heart to Give 175.00
2 Ph(c),Hate in My Heart 125.00
3 Ph(c), ... 125.00
4 Ph(c),Betty Page, April,1950 .. 400.00

MY LOVE
Sept., 1969
1 Love story reprints 80.00
2 thru 9 .... @40.00
10 .... 50.00
11 thru 38 .... @30.00
39 March, 1976 .... 30.00

MY ROMANCE
Sept., 1948
1 Romance Stories 175.00
2 .... 125.00
3 .... 125.00
Becomes:

MY OWN ROMANCE
4 Romance Stories Continue ... 250.00
5 thru 10 .... @150.00
11 thru 20 .... @150.00
21 thru 50 .... @125.00
51 thru 54 .... @100.00
55 ATh 125.00
56 thru 60 .... @100.00
61 thru 70 .... @100.00
71 AW 125.00
72 thru 76 .... @100.00
Becomes:

TEENAGE ROMANCE
77 Romance Stories Continue... 100.00
78 thru 85 .... @100.00
86 March, 1962 .... 100.00

MYS-TECH WARS
Marvel UK, 1993
1 BHi,A:FF,X-Men,Avengers...... 2.25
2 A:FF,X-Men,X-Force 2.25
3 BHi,A:X-Men,X-Force 2.25
4 A:Death's Head II............ 2.25

MYSTERY TALES
Marvel Atlas, March, 1952
1 GC,Horror Strikes at
    Midnight 1,400.00
2 BK,BEv,OW,The Corpse
    is Mine 700.00
3 RH,GC,JM, Vampire Strikes .. 550.00
4 Funeral of Horror 550.00
5 Blackout at Midnight 550.00
6 A-Bomb Picture 550.00
7 JRo,The Ghost Hunter 550.00
8 BEv 550.00
9 BEv(c),the Man in the Morgue 550.00
10 BEV(c),GT,What Happened
    to Harry 550.00
11 BEv(c) 450.00
12 GT,MF 475.00
13 .... 450.00
14 BEv(c),GT 450.00
15 RH(c),EK. 450.00
16 .... 450.00
17 RH(c). 450.00
18 AW,DAy,GC. 475.00
19 .... 450.00
20 Electric Chair 450.00
21 JF,MF,BP,Decapitation 450.00
22 JF,MF 450.00
23 thru 27. .... @400.00
28 .... 350.00
29 thru 32. .... @375.00
33 BEv 350.00
34 .... 350.00
35 BEv,GC. 350.00
36 .... 375.00
37 DW,BP,JR 350.00
38 BP,BEv 350.00
39 BK,BEv 375.00
40 JM 375.00
41 MD,BEv. 350.00
42 JeR 350.00
41 GC. 350.00
44 AW 350.00
45 SD. 325.00
46 RC,SD,JP 325.00
47 DAy,BP 325.00
48 BEv 350.00
49 GM,AT,DAy 350.00
50 JO,AW,GM 325.00
51 DAy,JO 325.00
52 DAy 325.00
53 BEv 325.00
54 RC,Aug., 1957 .... 350.00

MYSTICAL TALES
Marvel Atlas, June, 1956
1 BEv,BP,JO,Say the Magical
    Words 800.00
2 BEv(c),JO,Black Blob 550.00
3 BEv(c),RC,Four Doors To 600.00
4 BEv(c).The Condemned 600.00
5 AW,Meeting at Midnight 600.00
6 BK,AT,He Hides in the Tower . 500.00
7 BEv,JF,JO,AT,FBe,The
    Haunted Tower 500.00
8 BK,SC, Stone Walls Can't
    Stop Him,Aug., 1957 ..... 500.00

MYSTIC COMICS
Marvel Timely, March, 1940
[1st Series]
1 ASh(c),SSh,O;Blue Blaze,Dynamic,
    Man,Flexo,B:Dakor the Magician,
    A:Zephyr Jones,3X's, Deep Sea,
    Demon,bondage(c)...... 25,000.00
2 ASh(c),B:The Invisible Man
    Mastermind,Blue Blaze ... 7,500.00
3 ASh(c),O:Hercules 5,500.00
4 ASh(c),O:Thin Man,Black Widow
    E:Hercules,Blue Blazes,Dynamic
    Man,Flexo,Invisible Man... 5,700.00
5 ASh(c)O:The Black Marvel,
    Blazing Skull,Super Slave
    Terror,Sub-Earth Man 5,500.00
6 ASh(c),O:The Challenger,
    B:The Destroyer......... 6,500.00
7 S&K(c),B:The Witness,O:Davey
    and the Demon,E;The Black
    Widow,Hitler(c) 7,000.00
8 Bondage(c)............... 3,500.00
9 MSy,DRi,Hitler/Bondage(c) . 3,500.00
10 E:Challenger,Terror 3,600.00
[2nd Series] Oct., 1944
1 SSh,B:The Angel,Human Torch,
    Destroyer,Terry Vance,
    Tommy Tyme,Bondage(c) . 4,000.00
2 E:Human Torch,Terry
    Vance,Bondage(c) 2,000.00
3 E:The Angel,Tommy Tyme
    Bondage(c) 1,800.00
4 ASh(c),A:Young Allies
    Winter, 1944-45 .... 1,800.00

MYSTIC
[3rd Series] March, 1951
1 MSy,Strange Tree 2,000.00
2 MSy,Dark Dungeon 1,000.00
3 GC,Jaws of Creeping Death .. 900.00
4 BW,MSy,The Den of the
    Devil Bird 1,600.00
5 MSy,Face 750.00
6 BW,She Wouldn't Stay Dead 1,700.00
7 GC,Untold Horror waits
    in the Tomb 850.00
8 DAy(c),BEv,GK,A Monster
    Among Us 850.00
9 BEv 850.00
10 GC. 850.00
11 JR,The Black Gloves 800.00
12 GC. 800.00
13 In the Dark 800.00
14 The Corpse and I 800.00
15 GT,JR,House of Horror 700.00
16 A Scream in the Dark 700.00
17 BEv,Behold the Vampire..... 700.00
18 BEv(c),The Russian Devil.... 700.00
19 Swamp Girl................. 700.00
20 RH(c). 700.00
21 BEv(c),GC. 600.00
22 RH(c). 600.00
23 RH(c),RA,RMn,Chilling Tales . 600.00
24 GK,RMn,How Many Times Can
    You Die 600.00
25 RH(c),RA,E.C.Swipe....... 600.00

MARVEL

26 Severed Head(c). 600.00
27 Who Walks with a Zombie . . . 525.00
28 DW,RMn(c),Not Enough Dead 525.00
29 SMo,RMn(c),The Unseen. . . . 525.00
30 RH(c),DW 525.00
31 SC,JKz,RMn(c). 525.00
32 The Survivor 525.00
33 thru 36 . . . . @525.00
37 thru 51 . . . . @500.00
52 WW,RC 525.00
53 thru 57 . . . . @500.00
58 thru 60 . . . . @525.00
61 . . . . 475.00

MYSTIQUE
April, 2003
1 JLi(c),Drop Dead Gorgeous,pt.1 . 3.00
2 JLi(c),Drop Dead Gorgeous,pt.2 . 3.00
3 JLi(c),Drop Dead Gorgeous,pt.3 . 3.00
4 JLi(c),Drop Dead Gorgeous,pt.4 . 3.00
5 JLi(c),Drop Dead Gorgeous,pt.5 . 3.00
6 JLi(c),Drop Dead Gorgeous,pt.6 . 3.00
7 Tinker,Tailor,Mutant,Spy,pt.1 . . . . 3.00
8 Tinker,Tailor,Mutant,Spy,pt.2 . . . . 3.00
9 Tinker,Tailor,Mutant,Spy,pt.3 . . . . 3.00
10 Tinker,Tailor,Mutant,Spy,pt.4 . . . . 3.00
11 Maker's Mark,pt.1 . . . . 3.00
12 Maker's Mark,pt.2 . . . . 3.00
13 F:Shortpack. 3.00
14 Unnatural,pt.1 . . . . 3.00
15 Unnatural,pt.2 . . . . 3.00
16 Unnatural,pt.3 . . . . 3.00
17 Unnatural,pt.4 . . . . 3.00
18 Unnatural,pt.5 . . . . 3.00
19 Assassin's bullet 3.00
20 Quiet,pt.1 . . . . 3.00
21 Quiet,pt.2 . . . . 3.00
22 Quiet,pt.3 . . . . 3.00
23 Quiet,pt.4 . . . . 3.00
24 Quiet, concl. 3.00
TPB Vol. 1: Dead Drop Gorgeous . 15.00
TPB Vol. 2: Tinker Tailor 18.00
TPB Vol. 3: Unnatural 14.00
TPB Vol. 4: Quiet 15.00

MYTHOS
Jan., 2006
1 PJe,X-Men 4.00
2 PJe,Hulk 4.00

'NAM, THE
Dec., 1986
1 MGo,Vietnam War 3.00
1a 2nd printing 2.50
2 MGo,Dust Off. 2.50
3 thru 8 MGo. . . . . @2.25
9 MGo,Action Issue,Tunnel Rat . . . 3.50
10 thru 49 MGo . . . . @2.25
52 Frank Castle(Punisher)#1 . . . . 3.00
52a 2nd printing 2.25
53 Punisher #2. . . . . 2.50
54 thru 84 . . . . @2.25
TPB rep. #1–#4 (1999) 15.00

'NAM MAGAZINE, THE
(B&W) Aug., 1988–May, 1989
1 Reprints 3.00
2 thru 10 . . . . @2.50

NAMOR
April, 2003
1 MiS,manga. 2.25
2 MiS. 2.25
3 SvL. 2.25
4 SvL,F:Sandy 2.25
5 SvL,F:Sandy 2.25
6 SvL,Namor's choice. 2.25
7 PO, In Deep, pt.1. . . . . 2.25
8 PO, In Deep, pt.2. . . . . 2.25
9 PO, In Deep, pt.3. . . . . 3.00

---

10 PO,In Deep, pt.4 . . . . 3.00
11 JoB,In Deep,pt.5 . . . . 3.00
12 JoB,finale 3.00
TPB Vol. 1 Sea and Sand 13.00

NAMORA
Fall, 1948–Dec., 1948
1 BEv,DR 4,000.00
2 BEv,A:Sub-Mariner,Blonde
    Phantom 2,000.00
3 BEv,A:Sub-Mariner 2,300.00

Namor the Sub-Mariner #16
© Marvel Entertainment Group

NAMOR THE SUB-MARINER
April, 1990
1 JBy,BWi,I:Desmond
    & Phoebe Marrs 5.00
2 JBy,BWi,V:Griffin 3.00
3 JBy,BWi,V:Griffin 3.00
4 JBy,A:Reed & Sue Richards,
    Tony Stark 3.00
5 JBy,A:FF,IronMan,C:Speedball . 3.00
6 JBy,V:Sluj. 3.00
7 JBy,V:Sluj. 3.00
8 JBy,V:Headhunter,R:D.Rand . . . 3.00
9 JBy,V:Headhunter 3.00
10 JBy,V:Master Man,Warrior
    Woman 2.50
11 JBy,V:Mast.Man,War.Woman . . . 2.50
12 JBy,R:Invaders,Spitfire 2.50
13 JBy,Namor on Trial,A:Fantastic
    Four,Captain America,Thor 2.50
14 JBy,R:Lady Dorma,A:Ka-Zar
    Griffin 2.50
15 JBy,A:Iron Fist. 2.50
16 JBy,A:Punisher,V:Iron Fist 2.50
17 JBy,V:Super Skrull(Iron Fist). . . . 2.50
18 JBy,V:SuperSkrull,A:Punisher. . . 2.50
19 JBy,V:Super Skrull,D:D.Marrs. . . 2.50
20 JBy,Search for Iron Fist,
    O:Namorita 2.50
21 JBy,Visit to K'un Lun 2.50
22 JBy,Fate of Iron Fist,
    C:Wolverine 2.50
23 JBy,BWi,Iron Fist Contd.,
    C:Wolverine 2.50
24 JBy,BWi,V:Wolverine 3.00
25 JBy,BWi,V:Master Khan 2.50
26 JaL,BWi,Search For Namor 5.00
27 JaL,BWi,V:Namorita 4.00
28 JaL,BWi,A:Iron Fist. 3.00
29 JaL,BWi,After explosion 3.00

---

30 JaL,A:Doctor Doom 3.00
31 JaL,V:Doctor Doom. 3.00
32 JaL,V:Doctor Doom,
    Namor regains memory. 3.00
33 JaL,V:Master Khan 2.50
34 JaL,R:Atlantis 2.50
35 JaL,V:Tiger Shark 2.50
36 JaL,I:Suma-Ket,A:Tiger Shark . . 2.50
37 JaL,Blue Holo-Grafix,Altantean
    Civil War,N:Namor 2.75
38 JaL,O:Suma-Ket 2.50
39 A:Tigershark,V:Suma-Ket 2.50
40 V:Suma-Ket. 2.50
41 V:War Machine 2.50
42 MCW,A:Stingray,V:Dorcas 2.50
43 MCW,V:Orka,Dorcas. 2.50
44 I:Albatross 2.50
45 GI,A:Sunfire,V:Attuma. 2.50
46 GI, ... 2.50
47 GI,Starblast #2 . . . . 2.50
48 GI,Starblast #9,A:FF 2.50
49 GI,A:Ms. Marrs 2.50
50 GI,Holo-grafx(c),A:FF 4.00
50a Newsstand Ed. 2.50
51 AaL, ... 2.50
52 GI,I:Sea Leopard 2.50
53 GI,V:Sea Leopard 2.50
54 GI,I:Llyron 2.50
55 GI,V:Llyron 2.50
56 GI,V:Llyron 2.50
57 A:Capt. America, V:Llyron. 2.50
58 . . . . 2.50
59 GI,V:Abomination 2.50
60 A:Morgan Le Fay 2.50
61 Atlantis Rising 2.50
62 V:Triton 2.50
Ann.#1 Subterran.Odyssey #3. . . . 3.00
Ann.#2 Return o/Defenders,pt.3 . . 4.00
Ann.#3 I:Assassin,A:Iron Fist,
    w/Trading card. 3.25
Ann.#4 V:Hydra 3.25

NAVY ACTION
Aug., 1954
1 BP,US Navy War Stories 225.00
2 TLn,Navy(c) 125.00
3 BEv 100.00
4 and 5 . . . . @100.00
6 JH(c) 100.00
7 MD,JMn 100.00
8 JMn,GC. 100.00
9 thru 15 . . . . @100.00
16 BEv(c) 100.00
17 MD,BEv(c). 100.00
18 Aug., 1957. . . . . 100.00

NAVY COMBAT
Marvel Atlas, June, 1955
1 DH,JMn(c),B:Torpedo Taylor . . 225.00
2 DH 125.00
3 DH,BEv 100.00
4 DH 100.00
5 DH 100.00
6 JMn,A:Battleship Burke 100.00
7 thru 10 . . . . @100.00
11 MD,GC,JMn 100.00
12 RC. 125.00
13 GT 100.00
14 AT,GT 100.00
15 GT 100.00
16 . . . . 100.00
17 AW,AT,JMn 110.00
18 . . . . 100.00
19 . . . . 100.00
20 BEv,BP,AW,Oct., 1958 . . . . . 110.00

NAVY TALES
Marvel Atlas, Jan., 1957
1 BEv(c),BP,Torpedoes 200.00
2 AW,RC,JMn(c),One Hour
    to Live 175.00

3 JSe(c) 150.00
4 JSe(c),GC,JSt,RC,July, 1957 . 150.00

NELLIE THE NURSE
Marvel Atlas, 1945
1 Beach(c) 500.00
2 Nellie's Date(c) 250.00
3 Swimming Pool(c) 175.00
4 Roller Coaster(c) 175.00
5 Hospital(c),HK,Hey Look 175.00
6 Bedside Manner(c) 175.00
7 Comic book(c)A:Georgie 175.00
8 Hospital(c),A:Georgie 175.00
9 BW,Nellie/Swing(c)A:Millie ... 175.00
10 Bathing Suit(c),A:Millie 175.00
11 HK,Hey Look............... 200.00
12 HK,Giggles 'n' Grins 175.00
13 HK...................... 125.00
14 HK...................... 150.00
15 HK...................... 150.00
16 HK...................... 150.00
17 HK.A:Annie Oakley......... 150.00
18 HK...................... 150.00
19 .... 125.00
20 .... 125.00
21 .... 100.00
22 .... 100.00
23 .... 100.00
24 .... 100.00
25 .... 100.00
26 .... 100.00
27 .... 100.00
28 HK,Rusty Reprint 100.00
29 thru 35.................@100.00
36 Oct., 1952............... 100.00

NEW ADVENTURES OF CHOLLY & FLYTRAP
Epic
1 .... 5.00
2 .... 4.00
3 .... 4.00

NEW AVENGERS
Nov., 2004
1 BMB, The Breakout 4.00
1a variant (c)................. 4.00
2 BMB, The Breakout 3.00
2a variant (c)................. 3.00
3 BMB,The Breakout,pt.3 ..... 3.00
3a variant (c) 15.00
4 BMB,The Breakout,pt 4 ..... 3.00
5 BMB,The Breakout,pt.5 ..... 2.25
6 BMB,F:Captain America 2.25
7 BMB,the Sentry,pt.1......... 2.25
8 BMB,SB, The Sentry,pt.2..... 2.50
9 BMB,The Sentry,pt.3 .... 2.50
5a thru 9a Variant(c) ....@2.50
10 BMB,The Sentry,pt.4........ 2.50
11 BMB,Ronin,pt.1............ 2.50
12 BMB,Ronin,pt.2............ 2.50
13 BMB,Ronin,pt.3............ 2.50
14 BMB,F:Spider-Woman 2.50
15 BMB,V:J. Jonah Jameson 2.50
16 BMB,The Collective, prologue . 2.50
17 BMB, The Collective 3.50
18 BMB,The Collective 3.00
19 BMB,The Collective 3.00
20 BMB, The Collective 3.00
21 BMB,Civil War tie-in 3.00
22 BMB,Civil War tie-in 3.00
23 BMB,Civil War tie-in 3.00
24 BMB,Civil War tie-in 3.00
25 BMB,Civil War tie-in 3.00
26 BMB,A:Dr. Strange 3.00
Ann. #1 BMB 4.00
Spec.#1 Director's Cut (2004) 3.00
Spec. Handbook bios........... 4.00
Spec. Illuminati.............. 4.00
TPB Vol. 1: The Breakout (2006).. 15.00

TPB Vol. 2: The Sentry 15.00
TPB Vol. 3 Secrets and Lies 15.00
New Avengers: Must-Haves 4.00

NEW ETERNALS: APOCALYPSE NOW
Dec., 1999
1-shot JoB,SHa,64-pg........... 4.00

NEW EXCALIBUR
Nov., 2005
1 CCI...................... 3.00
2 CCI,Defenders of the Realm ... 3.00
3 CCI,V: Original X-Men 3.00
4 CCI,Choose Your Destiny 3.00
5 CCI,Choose Your Destiny 3.00
6 CCI,Black Monday 3.00
7 CCI,Black Monday........... 3.00
8 CCI,So Why is it I'm Not Dead .. 3.00
9 Chest Pains............... 3.00
10 The Last Days of Camelot ... 3.00
11 The Last Days of Camelot ... 3.00
12 The Last Days of Camelot ... 3.00
13 Unredoomod, pt.1.......... 3.00
TPB Defenders of the Realm..... 18.00

NEW MANGAVERSE
Jan., 2006
1 Rings of Fate.............. 3.00
2 thru 5 ....@5.00
TPB Rings of Fate 8.00

NEW MUTANTS, THE
March, 1983
1 BMc,MG,O:New Mutants 5.00
2 BMc,MG,V:Sentinels 4.00
3 BMc,MG,V:Brood Alien 3.50
4 SB,BMc,A:Peter Bristow 3.50
5 SB,BMc,A:Dark Rider 3.50
6 SB,AG,V:Viper 3.50
7 SB,BMc,V:Axe 3.50
8 SB,BMc,I:Amara Aquilla....... 3.50
9 SB,TMd.I:Selene 3.50
10 SB,BMc,C:Magma 3.50
11 SB,TMd,I:Magma 3.50
12 SB,TMd,J:Magma 3.50
13 SB,TMd,I:Cypher(Doug Ramsey)
  A:Kitty Pryde,Lilandra 4.00
14 SB,TMd,J:Magik,A:X-Men..... 3.00
15 SB,TMd,Mass.Academy 3.00
16 SB,TMd,V:Hellions,I:Warpath
  I:Jetstream................. 20.00
17 SB,TMd,V:Hellions,A:Warpath .. 4.00
18 BSz,V:Demon Bear,I:New
  Warlock,Magus 5.00
19 BSz,V:Demon Bear.......... 3.00
20 BSz,V:Demon Bear.......... 3.00
21 BSz,O&J:Warlock,doub.sz 5.00
22 BSz,A:X-Men 3.50
23 BSz,Sunspot,Cloak & Dagger... 3.00
24 BSz,A:Cloak & Dagger 3.00
25 BSz,A:Cloak & Dagger 6.00
26 BSz,I:Legion(Prof.X's son) 7.00
27 BSz,V:Legion 4.00
28 BSz,O:Legion 4.00
29 BSz,V:Gladiators,I:Guido
  (Strong Guy) 3.00
30 BSz,A:Dazzler............. 3.00
31 BSz,A:Shadowcat 3.00
32 SL,V:Karma 3.00
33 SL,V:Karma............... 3.00
34 SL,V:Amahl Farouk......... 3.00
35 BSz,J:Magneto 3.00
36 BSz,A:Beyonder 3.00
37 BSz,D:New Mutants 3.00
38 BSz,A:Hellions 3.00
39 BSz,A:White Queen 3.00
40 JG,KB,V:Avengers.......... 3.00
41 JG,TA,Mirage 3.00
42 JG,KB,A:Dazzler 3.00

New Mutants #2
© Marvel Entertainment Group

43 SP,V:Empath,A:Warpath 3.00
44 JG,V:Legion................ 5.00
45 JG,A:Larry Bodine........... 3.00
46 JG,KB,Mutant Massacre 3.50
47 JG,KB,V:Magnus............ 3.00
48 JG,CR,Future 3.00
49 VM,Future 3.00
50 JG,V:Magus,R:Prof.X 4.00
51 KN,A:Star Jammers 3.00
52 RL,DGr,Limbo.............. 3.00
53 RL,TA,V:Hellions 3.00
54 SB,TA,N:New Mutants 3.00
55 BBI,TA,V:Aliens 3.00
56 JBr,TA,V:Hellions,A:Warpath.... 3.00
57 BBI,TA,I&J:Bird-Boy 3.00
58 BBI,TA,Bird-Boy 3.00
59 BBI,TA,Fall of Mutants,
  V:Dr.Animus, ... 3.00
60 BBI,TA,F.of M.,D:Cypher...... 2.50
61 BBI,TA,Fall of Mutants 2.50
62 JMu,A:Magma,Hellions 2.50
63 BHa,JRu,Magik............. 2.50
64 BBI,TA,R:Cypher............ 2.50
65 BBI,TA,V:FreedomForce....... 2.50
66 BBI,TA,V:Forge............. 2.50
67 BBI,I:Gosamyr.............. 2.50
68 BBI,V:Gosamyr............. 2.50
69 BBI,AW,I:Spyder 2.50
70 TSh,AM,V:Spyder 2.50
71 BBI,AW,V:N'Astirh 2.50
72 BBI,A,Inferno.............. 2.50
73 BBI,W,A:Colossus 3.00
74 BBI,W,A:X-Terminators 2.50
75 JBy,Mc,Black King,V:Magneto .. 3.50
76 RB,TP,J:X-Terminators 2.50
77 RB,V:Mirage 2.50
78 RL,AW,V:FreedomForce....... 2.50
79 BBI,AW,V:Hela 2.50
80 BBI,AW,Asgard 2.50
81 LW,TSh,JRu,A:Hercules 2.50
82 BBI,AW,Asgard 2.50
83 BBI,Asgard 2.50
84 TSh,AM,A:QueenUla 2.50
85 RLd&TMc(c),BBI,V:Mirage 5.00
86 RLd,BWi,V:Vulture,C:Cable 6.00
87 RLd,BWi,I:Mutant Liberation
  Front,Cable 25.00
87a 2nd Printing................ 3.00
88 RLd,2nd Cable,V:Freedom
  Force.................... 7.50
89 RLd,V:Freedom Force 6.00
90 RLd,A:Caliban,V:Sabretooth.... 6.00
91 RLd,A:Caliban,Masque,
  V:Sabretooth 6.00
92 RLd(c),BH,V:Skrulls 4.00

All comics prices listed are for *Near Mint* condition.

93 RLd,A:Wolverine,Sunfire,
  V:Mutant Liberation Front 6.00
94 RLd,A:Wolverine,Sunfire,
  V:Mutant Liberation Front 5.00
95 RLd,Extinction Agenda,V:Hodge
  A:X-Men,X-Factor,D:Warlock . . 5.00
95a 2nd printing(gold) 5.00
96 RLd,ATb,JRu,Extinction Agenda
  V:Hodge,A:X-Men,X-Factor. . . . 5.00
97 E:LSi(s),RLd(c),JRu,Extinction
  Agenda,V:Hodge 5.00
98 FaN(s),RLd,I:Deadpool,Domino,
  Gideon,L:Rictor 25.00
99 FaN(s),RLd,I:Feral,Shatterstar,
  L:Sunspot,J:Warpath 5.00
100 FaN(s),RLd,J:Feral,Shatterstar,
  I:X-Force,V:Masque,Imperial
  Protectorate,A:MLF 6.00
100a 2nd Printing(Gold). 4.00
100b 3rd Printing(Silver) 3.50
Ann.#1 BMc,TP,L.Cheney 7.00
Ann.#2 AD,V:Mojo,I:Psylocke,Meggan
  (American App.). 10.00
Ann.#3 AD,PN,V:Impossible Man . . 4.00
Ann.#4 JBr,BMc,Evol.Wars 6.00
Ann.#5 RLd,JBg,MBa,KWi,Atlantis
  Attacks,A:Namorita,I:Surf 8.00
Ann.#6 RLd(c),Days o/Future Present
  V:FranklinRichards,(Pin-ups). . . 6.00
Ann.#7 JRu,RLd,Kings of Pain,
  I:Piecemeal & Harness,
  Pin-ups X-Force. 5.00
Spec #1,AAd,TA,Asgard War. 6.00
Summer Spec.#1 BBI,Megapolis . . . 3.50
TPB New Mutants: Demon Bear . . . 9.00

NEW MUTANTS
Sept., 1997
1 (of 3) BRa,BCh,F:Cannonball,
  Moonstar, Wolfsbane,Karma &
  Sunspot 2.50
2 BRa,BCh,meeting with mutants
  of the past 2.50
3 BRa, BCh, will Magik return
  for good? 2.50

NEW MUTANTS
May, 2003
1 R:Original New Mutants. 2.50
2 F:Dani Moonstar 2.50
3 new student 2.50
4 F:Karma. 2.50
5 mutant teens 2.50
6 V:Reavers 2.50
7 CBa(c),Ties That Bind,pt.1 . . . . . 2.50
8 CBa(c),Ties That Bind,pt.2 . . . . . 2.50
9 CBa(c),Ties That Bind,pt.3 . . . . . 2.50
10 CBa(c),Ties That Bind,pt.4 . . . . 3.00
11 CBa(c),Ties That Bind,pt.5 . . . . 3.00
12 CBa(c),Ties That Bind,pt.6 . . . . 3.00
13 The More Things Change 3.00
TPB Vol. 1 Back to School. 17.00

NEW THUNDERBOLTS
See: THUNDERBOLTS

NEW WARRIORS
July, 1990
1 B:FaN(s),MBa,AW,V:Terrax,
  O:New Warriors. 5.00
1a Gold rep. 2.50
2 thru 10 . . . . @3.50
11 thru 49 . . . . @2.50
50 reg. (c) 2.25
50a Glow-in-the-dark(c),V:Sphinx . 3.25
51 thru 59. . . . . @2.25
60 Nova Omega,pt.2 . . . . 2.50
61 thru 71. . . . . @2.25
Ann.#1 MBa,A:X-Force,V:Harness,
  Piecemeal,Kings of Pain #2 . . . 4.00
Ann.#2 Hero Killers #4,V:Sphinx . . . 2.75

New Warriors #10
© Marvel Entertainment Group

Ann.#3 LMa(i),E:Forces of Light,
  Forces of Darkness,I:Darkling
  w/card 3.25
Ann.#4 DaR(s),V:Psionex 3.25
TPB New Beginnings, rep.. . . . . . 13.00

NEW WARRIORS
Aug., 1999
1 F:Speedball,48-page 3.00
2 thru 10 . . . . @2.50

NEW WARRIORS
June, 2005
1 (of 6) 3.00
2 thru 6 . . . . @3.00

NEW X-MEN
See: X-MEN

NEW X-MEN
May, 2004
1 Choosing Sides,pt.1. . . . . 3.00
2 Choosing Sides,pt.2. . . . . 3.00
3 Choosing Sides,pt.3. . . . . 3.00
4 Choosing Sides,pt.4. . . . . 3.00
5 Choosing Sides,pt.5. . . . . 3.00
6 Choosing Sides,pt.6. . . . . 3.00
7 Haunted 3.00
8 Haunted 3.00
9 Haunted, Concl.. . . . . 3.00
10 Too Much Information,pt.1 . . . . . 3.00
11 Too Much Information 3.00
12 X-Posed 3.00
13 Campfire 3.00
14 Year's End,pt.1 . . . . 3.00
15 Year's End,pt.2 . . . . 3.00
16 AaL,House Divided,pt.1 . . . . 3.00
17 AaL,House Divided,pt.2 . . . . 3.00
18 AaL,House Divided,pt.3 . . . . 3.00
19 AaL,House Divided,pt.4 . . . . 3.00
20 Childhood's End,pt.1. . . . . 3.00
21 Childhood's End,pt.2. . . . . 3.00
22 Childhood's End,pt.3. . . . . 3.00
23 Childhood's End,pt.4. . . . . 3.00
24 Crusade,pt.1 . . . . 3.00
25 Crusade,pt.2 . . . . 3.00
26 Crusade,pt.3 . . . . 3.00
27 Crusade,pt.4 . . . . 3.00
28 Nimrod,pt.1 . . . . 3.00
29 Nimrod,pt.2 . . . . 3.00
30 Nimrod,pt.3 . . . . 3.00
31 Nimrod,pt.4 . . . . 3.00

32 Whatever Happened to Wither . . 3.00
Spec. Academy X Yearbook,AaL . . . 4.00
TPB Academy X Vol. 2: X-posed. . 15.00
TPB Academy X Vol. 3: Exposed. . 11.00
TPB Childhood's End, Vol. 1 . . . . . 11.00
TPB Childhood's End, Vol. 2 . . . . . 11.00

NEW X-MEN: HELLIONS
May, 2005
1 (of 4) 3.00
2 . . . . 3.00
3 Fortune and Glory 3.00
4 Fortune and Glory 3.00
TPB New X-Men: Hellions 10.00

NEXTWAVE
Jan., 2006
1 WEI,SI 3.00
2 thru 5 WEI,SI . . . . @3.00
Becomes:

NEXTWAVE:
AGENTS OF H.A.T.E.
6 thru 10 Agents of H.A.T.E. . . . . @3.00

NFL SUPERPRO
1 . . . . 7.00
Spec.#1 reprints. 2.50
  [Regular Series] Oct., 1991
1 A:Spider-Man,I:Sanzionaire 2.50
2 V:Quickkick 2.50
3 I:Instant Replay 2.50
4 V:Sanction 2.50
5 A:Real NFL Player. 2.50
6 Racism Iss.,recalled by Marvel . . 6.00
7 thru 11 . . . . @2.50
12 V:Nefarious forces of evil 2.50

NICK FURY, AGENT
OF S.H.I.E.L.D.
[1st Regular Series] June, 1968
1 JSo/JSt,I:Scorpio 250.00
2 JSo,A:Centaurius. 150.00
3 JSo,DA,V:Hell Hounds. 150.00
4 FS,O:Nick Fury 150.00
5 JSo,V:Scorpio 175.00
6 FS,Doom must Fall 125.00
7 FS,V:S.H.I.E.L.D. 125.00
8 FS,Hate Monger 100.00
9 FS,Hate Monger 100.00
10 FS,JCr,Hate Monger. 100.00
11 BS(c),FS,Hate Monger 100.00
12 BS 110.00
13 . . . . 110.00
14 . . . . 110.00
15 I:Bullseye 150.00
16 JK,rep. 50.00
17 JK,rep. 50.00
18 JK,rep. 50.00
  [Limited Series] 1983–94
1 JSo,rep. 4.00
2 JSo,rep. 3.50
  [2nd Regular Series] 1989–93
1 BH,I:New Shield,V:Death's
  Head(not British hero) 3.00
2 KP,V:Death's Head 2.25
3 KP,V:Death's Head 2.25
4 KP,V:Death's Head 2.25
5 KP,V:Death's Head 2.25
6 KP,V:Death's Head 2.25
7 KP,Chaos Serpent #1 . . . . 2.25
8 KP,Chaos Serpent #2 . . . . 2.25
9 KP,Chaos Serpent #3 . . . . 2.25
10 KP,Chaos Serpent ends,
  A:Capt.America. 2.25
11 D:Murdo MacKay 2.25
12 Hydra Affair #1 . . . . 2.25
13 Hydra Affair #2 . . . . 2.25
14 Hydra Affair #3 . . . . 2.25

Nick Fury Agent of Shield #5
© Marvel Entertainment Group

15 Apogee of Disaster #1 . . . . 2.25
16 Apogee of Disaster #2 . . . . 2.25
17 Apogee of Disaster #3 . . . . 2.25
18 Apogee of Disaster #4 . . . . 2.25
19 Apogee of Disaster #5 . . . . 2.25
20 JG,A:Red Skull 2.50
21 JG,R:Baron Strucker 2.25
22 JG,A:Baron Strucker,R:Hydra . . . 2.25
23 JG,V:Hydra 2.25
24 A:Capt.Am,Thing,V:Mandarin . . . 2.25
25 JG,Shield Vs. Hydra 2.25
26 JG,A:Baron Strucker,
   C:Wolverine 2.50
27 JG,V:Hydra,A:Wolverine 2.50
28 V:Hydra,A:Wolverine 2.50
29 V:Hydra,A:Wolverine 2.50
30 R:Leviathan,A:Deathlok 2.25
31 A:Deathlok,V:Leviathan 2.25
32 V:Leviathan 2.25
33 Super-Powered Agents 2.25
34 A:Bridge(X-Force),V:Balance
   of Terror 2.25
35 A:Cage,V:Constrictor 2.25
36 . . . . 2.25
37 . . . . 2.25
38 Cold War of Nick Fury #1 . . . . . 2.25
39 Cold War of Nick Fury #2 . . . . . 2.25
40 Cold War of Nick Fury #3 . . . . . 2.25
41 Cold War of Nick Fury #4 . . . . . 2.25
42 I:Strike Force Shield 2.25
43 R:Clay Quatermain 2.25
44 A:Captain America 2.25
45 A:Bridge 2.25
46 V:Gideon,Hydra 2.25
47 V:Baron Strucker,last issue 2.25
TPB Death Duty V:Night Raven . . . 6.00
TPB Captain America 6.00
TPB Scorpion Connection 8.00
TPB JSo, 248-pg 20.00
TPB Scorpio 15.00

NICK FURY, VERSUS S.H.I.E.L.D.
June, 1988
1 JSo(c),D:Quartermail 6.00
2 BSz(c),Into The Depths 5.00
3 Uneasy Allies 4.00
4 V:Hydra 4.00
5 V:Hydra 4.00
6 V:Hydra, Dec., 1988 . . . . 4.00
TPB Reprints #1-#6 . . . . 16.00

NICK FURY'S HOWLING COMMANDOS
Oct., 2005
1 KG 3.00
1a expanded edition 4.00
2 thru 6 KG . . . . @3.00

NIGHTBREED
Epic, April, 1990
1 . . . . 4.00
2 . . . . 3.00
3 thru 10 . . . . @2.50
11 thru 20 . . . . @2.25
21 thru 25 . . . . @2.50
Nightbreed:Genesis, Rep.#1-#4 . . 10.00

NIGHTCAT
1 DCw,I&O:Night Cat 4.50

NIGHTCRAWLER
Nov., 1985
1 DC,A;Bamfs 4.00
2 DC 3.50
3 DC,A:Other Dimensional X-Men . 3.50
4 DC,A:Lockheed,V:Dark Bamf . . . 3.50

NIGHTCRAWLER
Nov., 2001
1 (of 4) Passion Play 2.50
2 . . . . 2.50
3 . . . . 2.50
4 finale 2.50

NIGHTCRAWLER
Sept., 2004
1 DaR,Diabolique,pt.1 . . . . 3.00
2 DaR,Diabolique,pt.2 . . . . 3.00
3 DaR,The Devil Inside 3.00
4 DaR,The Devil Inside 3.00
5 DaR,Ghosts on the Rails,pt.1 . . . 3.00
6 DaR,Ghosts on the Rails 3.00
7 DaR,The Winding Way, pt.1 . . . . 3.00
8 DaR,The Winding Way, Pt.2 . . . . 3.00
9 DaR,The Winding Way,pt.3 . . . . 3.00
10 DaR,The Winding Way,pt.4 . . . . 3.00
11 DaR,The Winding Way,pt.5 . . . . 3.00
12 DaR,Loose Ends 3.00
TPB The Devil Inside 15.00
TPB The Winding Way 15.00

NIGHTHAWK
July, 1998
1 (of 3) RCa,BWi,Nighthawk shake
   off coma 3.00
2 (of 3) RCa,BWi,V:Mephisto 3.00
3 RCa,BWi,conclusion 3.00

NIGHTMARE
1994
1 ANo 2.25
2 & 3 ANo . . . . @2.25

NIGHTMARE CIRCUS
1 video-game tie-in 2.50
2 video-game tie-in 2.50

NIGHTMARE ON ELM STREET
Oct., 1989
1 RB/TD/AA.,Movie adapt 3.00
2 AA,Movie adapt,Dec., 1989 . . . . 2.25

NIGHTMASK
Nov., 1986
1 O:Night Mask 2.50
2 thru 12 . . . . @2.50

NIGHT NURSE
Nov., 1972
1 The Making of a Nurse 175.00
2 Moment of Truth 125.00
3 . . . . 125.00
4 Final Issue,May, 1973 . . . . 125.00

NIGHT RIDER
Oct., 1974–Aug., 1975
1 Reprint Ghost Rider #1 . . . . 22.00
2 Reprint Ghost Rider #2 . . . . 15.00
3 Reprint Ghost Rider #3 . . . . 15.00
4 Reprint Ghost Rider #4 . . . . 15.00
5 Reprint Ghost Rider #5 . . . . 15.00
6 Reprint Ghost Rider #6 . . . . 15.00

NIGHTSIDE
Oct., 2001
1 (of 4) TDr,The OThers 3.00
2 TDr,The Others 3.00
3 TDr,Sydney Taine 3.00
4 TDr,Black Dragons 3.00

NIGHTSTALKERS
1992–94
1 TP(i),Rise o/t Midnight Sons#5
   A:GR,J.Blaze,I:Meatmarket,
   polybagged w/poster 3.00
2 thru 18 . . . . @2.50

NIGHT THRASHER
[Limited Series] 1992–93
1 B:FaN(s),DHv,N:Night Thrasher,
   V:Bengal 2.50
2 thru 4 . . . . @2.25

[Regular Series] 1993–95
1 B:FaN(s),MBa,JS,V:Poison
   Memories 3.50
2 thru 21 . . . . @2.25

Nightwatch #10
© Marvel Entertainment Group

NIGHTWATCH
1994–95
1 RLm,I:Salvo,Warforce Holo(c) . . . 3.00
1a Newsstand ed 2.25
2 thru 12 . . . . @2.25

NOCTURNE
1995
1 DAn, in London 2.25
2 DAn,O:Nocturne 2.25

MARVEL

3 Interview with Amy 2.25
4 V:Dragon 2.25

NO ESCAPE
1994
1 & 2 Movie adaptation . . . . @2.25

NOMAD
[Limited Series] Nov., 1990
1 B:FaN(s),A:Capt.America 3.00
2 thru 4 . . . . @2.50

[Regular Series] 1992–94
1 B:FaN(s),R:Nomad,[Gatetfold(c),
　map] 3.00
2 V:Road Kill Club 2.50
3 thru 25 . . . . @2.25

NORTHSTAR
1994
1 SFr,DoC,V:Weapon:P.R.I.M.E. . . 2.25
2 SFr,DoC,V:Arcade 2.25
3 SFr,DoC,V:Arcade 2.25
4 SFr,DoC,final issue 2.25
N Presents James O'Barr 2.50

NOT BRAND ECHH
Aug., 1967
1 JK(c),BEv,Forbush Man(c) . . . 300.00
2 MSe,FrG,Spidey-Man,Gnat-Man
　& Rotten 150.00
3 MSe(C),TS,JK,FrG,O:Charlie
　America 150.00
4 GC,JTg,TS,Scaredevil,
　ECHHs-Men 150.00
5 JK,TS,GC,I&O:Forbush Man . 150.00
6 MSe(c),GC,TS,W:Human
　Torch 150.00
7 MSe(c),JK,GC,TS,O:Fantastical
　Four,Stupor Man 150.00
8 MSe(c),GC,TS,C:Beatles . . . 150.00
9 MSe,GC,TS,Bulk
　V:Sunk-Mariner 75.00
10 JK,TS,MSe,The Worst of... . . 200.00
11 King Konk 200.00
12 MSe,Frankenstein,
　A:Revengers 200.00
13 GC,MSe,Stamp Out Trading
　Cards(c). 200.00

NOTHING CAN STOP
THE JUGGERNAUT
1989
1 JR2,rep.SpM#229&#230 . . . . . . 4.00

NOVA
[1st Regular Series] Sept., 1976
1 B:MWn(s),JB,JSt,I&O:Nova . . . 25.00
2 JB,JSt,I:Condor,Powerhouse . . . 12.00
3 JB,JSt,I:Diamondhead 12.00
4 SB,TP,A:Thor,I:Corruptor 12.00
5 SB,V:Earthshaker 10.00
6 SB,V:Condor,Powerhouse,
　Diamondhead,I:Sphinx 10.00
7 SB,War in Space,O:Sphinx . . . 10.00
8 V:Megaman 10.00
9 V:Megaman 10.00
10 V:Condor,Powerhouse,
　Diamond-head Sphinx 10.00
11 V:Sphinx 11.00
12 A:Spider-Man 12.00
13 I:Crimebuster,A:Sandman 7.00
14 A:Sandman 7.00
15 CI,C:Spider-Man, Hulk 7.00
16 CI,A:Yellow Claw. 7.00
17 A:Yellow Claw 7.00
18 A:Yellow Claw, Nick Fury 7.00
19 CI,TP,I:Blackout 7.00
20 What is Project X? 7.00

Nova #9
© Marvel Entertainment Group

21 JB,BMc,JRu 7.00
22 CI,I:Comet. 7.00
23 CI,V:Dr.Sun 7.00
24 CI,I:New Champions,V:Sphinx . . 7.00
25 E:MWn(s),CI,A:Champions,
　V:Sphinx 7.00

[2nd Regular Series] 1994–95
1 B:FaN(s),ChM,V:Gladiator,Foil
　Embossed(c) 3.50
2 ChM,V:Tail Hook Rape 2.25
3 ChM,A:Spider-Man,Corruptor . . 2.25
4 ChM,I:NovaO:O 2.25
5 ChM,R:Condor,w/card 2.25
6 ChM,Time & Time Again,pt.3. . . 2.25
7 ChM,Time & Time Again,pt.6. . . 2.25
8 ChM,I:Shatterforce. 2.25
9 ChM,V:Shatterforce 2.25
10 ChM,V:Diamondhead 2.25
11 ChM,V:Diamondhead 2.25
12 ChM,A:Inhumans 2.25
13 ChM,A:Inhumans 2.25
14 A:Condor 2.25
15 V:Brethern of Zorr 2.25
16 Countdown Conclusion. 2.25
17 Nova Loses Powers 2.25
18 Nova Omega,pt.1 . . . . 2.25

NOVA
March, 1999
1 EL,JoB,F:Rich Rider,48-page . . . 3.00
2 EL,JoB,A:Capt.America 2.25
2a variant JoB cover. 2.25
3 EL,JoB,A:Capt.America & Hulk . . 2.25
4 EL,JoB,A:Mr.Fantastic 2.25
5 EL,JoB,A:Spider-Man 2.25
6 EL,JoB,V:Sphinx 2.25
7 EL,JoB, final issue. 2.25

Nth MAN
Aug., 1989
1 . . . . 2.25
2 thru 7 . . . . @2.25
8 DK 2.25
9 thru 16, finale, Sept., 1990. . . . @2.25

'NUFF SAID
Aug., 2002
TPB 240-pg., silent stories. 22.00

NYX
Oct., 2003
1 JQ,gutterpunks 14.00

2 JQ,self-preservation's price 10.00
3 JQ,Y-23 . . . . 50.00
4 JQ,F:Tatiana 10.00
5 JQ 5.00
6 JQ 3.00
7 JQ,finale. 3.00
NYX Must Have, rep.#1–#3 . . . . . . 5.00
NYX Must Have, rep.#4 & #5 . . . . . 4.00
TPB NYX: Wannabe 20.00

OBNOXIO THE CLOWN
April, 1983
1 X-Men 3.50

OFFCASTES
Epic *Heavy Hitters,* 1993
1 MV,I:Offcastes 2.50
2 MV,V:Kaoro 2.25
3 MV,Last Issue 2.25

OFFICIAL HANDBOOK OF
THE MARVEL UNIVERSE
Avengers 2004. . . . . 4.00
Daredevil 2004. . . . . 4.00
Hulk 2004. . . . . 4.00
Spider-Man 2004 . . . . 4.00
Wolverine 2004 . . . . 4.00
X-Men 2004 . . . . 4.00
Book of the Dear 2004. . . . . 4.00
Golden Age Marvel 2004 . . . . 4.00
Horror 2005. . . . . 4.00
Women of Marvel 2005 . . . . 4.00
Marvel Knights 2005 . . . . 4.00
Age of Apocalypse 2005 . . . . 4.00
Spider-Man 2005 . . . . 4.00
Teams 2005 . . . . 4.00
Fantastic Four 2005. . . . . 4.00
Avengers 2005. . . . . 4.00
Spider-Man & Fantastic Four (2005) 4.00
Alternate Universes (2005) 4.00
X-Men (2005) 4.00
Squadron Supreme (2005) 4.00
Ultimate Marvel Universe #2 . . . . . . 4.00

OFFICIAL MARVEL INDEX:
1985–88
TO THE AMAZING
SPIDER-MAN
Index 1 . . . . 3.00
Index 2 thru 9 . . . . @2.50
TO THE AVENGERS
Index 1 thru 7 . . . . @2.50
TO THE FANTASTIC FOUR
Index 1 thru 12 . . . . @2.25
TO MARVEL TEAM-UP
Index 1 thru 6 . . . . @2.25
TO THE X-MEN
Index 1 thru 7 . . . . @3.00
[Vol. 2] 1994
Index 1 thru 5 . . . . @2.25

OFFICIAL MARVEL
TIMELINE
1-shot, 48-pg. 6.00

OFFICIAL TRUE
CRIME CASES
Fall, 1947
24 (1)SSh(c),The Grinning Killer. 275.00
25 (2)She Made Me a Killer,HK . . 225.00
Becomes:

ALL-TRUE CRIME
1948
26 SSh(c),The True Story of Wilbur
   Underhill 400.00
27 Electric Chair(c),Robert Mais . 300.00
28 Cops V:Gangsters(c) 125.00
29 Cops V:Gangsters(c) 125.00
30 He Picked a Murderous Mind 125.00
31 Hitchiking Thugs(c) 125.00
32 Jewel Thieves(c) 125.00
33 The True Story of Dinton
   Phillips 125.00
34 Case of the Killers Revenge . . 125.00
35 Ph(c),Date with Danger 125.00
36 Ph(c) 125.00
37 Ph(c),Story of Robert Marone . 125.00
38 Murder Weapon,Nick Maxim . 125.00
39 Story of Vince Vanderee 125.00
40 . . . . 125.00
41 Lou 'Lucky' Raven 125.00
42 BK,Baby Face Nelson 150.00
43 Doc Channing Paulson 125.00
44 Murder in the Big House 125.00
45 While the City Sleeps 125.00
46 . . . . 125.00
47 Gangster Terry Craig 125.00
48 GT,They Vanish By Night 125.00
49 BK,Squeeze Play 150.00
50 Shoot to Kill 125.00
51 Panic in the Big House 125.00
52 Prison Break, Sept., 1952 . . . . 125.00

OLYMPIANS
Epic, July, 1991
1 Spoof Series 4.00
2 Conclusion 4.00

OMEGA THE UNKNOWN
March, 1976
1 JM,I:Omega 20.00
2 JM,A:Hulk 10.00
3 JM,A:Electro 10.00
4 JM,V:Yellow Claw 9.00
5 JM,V:The Wrench 9.00
6 JM,V:Blockbuster 9.00
7 JM,V:Blockbuster 9.00
8 JM,C:New Foolkiller,V:Nitro . . . 10.00
9 JM,A:New Foolkiller,
   D:Blockbuster 14.00
10 JM,D:Omega the Unknown . . . 8.00

ONE, THE
Epic, July, 1985
1 thru 5 . . . . @2.50
6 Feb., 1986 . . . . 2.50

100 GREATEST MARVELS
Sept., 2001
1 (of 5) weekly, 112-pages 8.00
2 thru 5 112-pages . . . . @8.00
5 Top 5 #5, 32-pages 4.00
4 Top 5 #4, 32-pages 4.00
3 Top 5 #3, 48-pages 4.00
2 Top 5 #2, 48-pages 4.00
1 Top 5 #1, 48-pages 4.00

101 WAYS TO END THE CLONE SAGA
1-shot (1997) 2.50

ONSLAUGHT
1996–97
Marvel Universe: AKu,SLo,MWd,
   Marvel Heroes vs. Onslaught . . 8.00
Marvel Universe: Gold edition 50.00
X-Men: AKu,SLo,MWd (1996) 7.00
X-Men: Gold editon 50.00
Onslaught: Epilogue (1997) 9.00

TPB Book 1 Awakening, rep. 30.00
TPB Book 2 To the Victor, rep. . . . 30.00
TPB Book 3 Comrades, rep. 30.00
TPB Book 4 Eve of Storm, rep. . . . 35.00
TPB Book 5 Front Line, rep. 35.00
TPB Book 6 Phyrric Victory, rep. . . 35.00

ONSLAUGHT REBORN
Nov., 2006
1 RLd 3.00
1a variant (c) 3.00

ONYX OVERLORD
Epic, 1992–93
1 JBi,Sequel to Airtight Garage . . . 3.00
2 JBi,The Joule 3.00
3 JBi,V:Overlord 3.00
4 V:Starbilliard 3.00

OPEN SPACE
Dec., 1989–Aug., 1990
1 . . . . 6.00
2 thru 4 . . . . @5.25

ORDER, THE
Feb., 2002
1 (of 6) KBk,JDy,MHy,F:Hulk, Namor,
   Dr. Strange, & Silver Surfer 2.25
2 KBk,JDy,MHy,A:Avengers 2.25
3 KBk,JDy,MHy,DPs,V:Avengers . . 2.25
4 KBk,JDy,DPs,Hulk,Nighthawk . . 2.25
5 KBk,JDy,DPs,F:Nighthawk 2.25
6 KBk,JDy,DPs,V:everybody 2.25

ORIGIN
Aug., 2001
1 (of 6) PJe,NKu,F:Wolverine 3.50
2 PJe,NKu,JQ(c) 3.50
3 PJe,NKu,JQ(c) 3.50
4 PJe,NKu,JQ(c) 3.50
5 PJe,NKu,JQ(c) 3.50
6 PJe,NKu,final part 3.50
TPB JQ(c) 15.00

ORIGINAL GHOST RIDER
1992–94
1 MT(c),rep. 2.25
2 thru 23 rep. . . . . @2.25

Original Ghost Rider #6
© Marvel Entertainment Group

ORIGINAL GHOST RIDER RIDES AGAIN
July, 1991
1 rep.GR#68+#69(O:JohnnyBlaze) 3.00
2 thru 7 rep.Ghost Rider. . . . . . . @2.25

ORIGINS OF MARVEL COMICS
TPB StL,JK,SD rep., 260-pg. 25.00

ORORO: BEFORE THE STORM
June, 2005
1 (of 4) Ororo Monroe in Cairo 3.00
2 thru 4 . . . . @3.00
TPB Before the Storm 7.00

OSBORN JOURNALS, THE
1997
1-shot KHt,F:Norman Osborn 3.00

OSCAR COMICS
Marvel USA Comics, 1947–49
(FUNNY TUNES spin-off)
1 (24) 225.00
2 (25) BW,HK,Hey Look 250.00
3 . . . . 135.00
4 . . . . 135.00
5 . . . . 135.00
6 . . . . 135.00
7 . . . . 135.00
8 . . . . 135.00
9 . . . . 135.00
10 HK 175.00
Becomes:

AWFUL OSCAR
Marvel USA Comics, 1949
11 . . . . 125.00
12 . . . . 125.00
Becomes:

OSCAR
13 . . . . 135.00

OUR LOVE
Sept., 1949
1 Ph(c),Guilt of Nancy Crane . . 175.00
2 Ph(c),My Kisses Were Cheap 125.00

OUR LOVE STORY
Oct., 1969
1 JB 100.00
2 JB 35.00
3 JB 35.00
4 . . . . 35.00
5 JSo,JB 125.00
6 thru 13 . . . . @50.00
14 Gary Friedrich &Tarpe Mills . . . 55.00
15 thru 37 . . . . @30.00
38 Feb., 1976. . . . . 30.00

OUTLAW FIGHTERS
Marvel Atlas, Aug., 1954
1 GT,Western Tales 150.00
2 GT ,JMn(c) 100.00
3 . . . . 100.00
4 A;Patch Hawk 100.00
5 RH, Final Issue,April, 1955 . . . 100.00

OUTLAW KID
Atlas, Sept., 1954
1 SSh,DW,JMn(c),B&O:Outlaw Kid,
   A;Black Rider 350.00
2 DW,JMn(c),A:Black Rider . . . 175.00
3 DW,AW,GWb,JMN(c) 175.00
4 DW(c),Death Rattle 150.00

5 JMn	150.00
6 JMn	150.00
7 JMn	150.00
8 AW,DW,JMn	150.00
9	125.00
10 JSe	125.00
11 thru 17	@100.00
18 AW,JMn	100.00
19 JSe,Sept., 1957	100.00

[2nd series] Aug., 1970

1 JSe(c),DW,Jo,Showdown,rep	40.00
2 DW,One Kid Too Many	25.00
3 HT(c),DW,Six Gun Double Cross	25.00
4 DW	20.00
5 DW	20.00
6 DW	20.00
7 HT(c),DW,Treachery on the Trail	20.00
8 HT(c),DW,RC,Six Gun Pay Off	30.00
9 JSe(c),DW,GWb,The Kids Last Stand	20.00
10 GK(c),DAy,NewO:Outlaw Kid	40.00
11 GK(c),Thunder Along the Big Iron	20.00
12 The Man Called Bounty Hawk	20.00
13 The Last Rebel	20.00
14 The Kid Gunslingers of Calibre City	20.00
15 GK(c),V:Madman of Monster Mountain	20.00
16 The End of the Trail	20.00
17 thru 29	@20.00
30 Oct., 1975	20.00

OVER THE EDGE AND UNDER A BUCK
1995–96

1 F:Daredevil vs. Mr. Fear	2.25
2 F:Doctor Strange	2.25
3 F:Hulk	2.25
4 in Cypress Hills	2.25
5	2.25
6 F:Daredevil	2.25
7 Doc & Nightmare	2.25

PARADISE X: THE HERALDS
Oct., 2001

1 (of 3) AxR, Earth X trilogy	3.50
2 AxR,	3.50
3 AxR,StP,concl.	3.50

PARADISE X
Feb., 2002

1 (of 13) AxR,Earth X trilogy	3.50
2 AxR,DBw,F:Captain Mar-Vell	3.50
3 AxR,DBw,King Britain,Medusa.	3.00
4 AxR,DBw,nature of new Paradise	3.00
5 AxR,DBw	3.00
6 AxR,DBw,the new Death	3.00
7 AxR,DBw	3.00
8 AxR,DBw	3.00
9 AxR,DBw,O:Ghost Rider	3.00
10 AxR, DBw,F:Matt Murcock	3.00
11 AxR, DBw,F:Harry Pym	3.00
12 AxR,DBw,concl.	3.00
Spec.#0, AxR, prologue to series	3.50
Special A DBw	3.00
Special 1-shot, Earth X	3.00
GN Paradise X:Xen, 56-pg.	4.50
GN Devils AxR, 48-pg.	4.50

PARADISE X/RAGNAROK
Jan., 2003

1 (of 2) AxR.	3.00
2 AxR	3.00

PARAGON

1 I:Paragon,Nightfire	5.00

PATSY & HEDY
Marvel Atlas, Feb., 1952

1 AJ(c),B:Patsy Walker & Hedy Wolfe	275.00
2 Skating(c)	175.00
3 Boyfriend Trouble	150.00
4 Swimsuit(c)	150.00
5 Patsy's Date(c)	150.00
6 Swimsuit/Picnic(c)	150.00
7 Double-Date(c)	150.00
8 AJ(c),The Dance	150.00
9	150.00
10	150.00
11 thru 25	@125.00
26 thru 50	@100.00
51 thru 60	@100.00
61 thru 109	@100.00
110 Feb., 1967	100.00

PATSY & HER PALS
May, 1953

1 MWs(c),F:Patsy Walker	225.00
2 MWs(c),Swimsuit(c)	125.00
3 MWs(c),Classroom(c)	100.00
4 MWs(c),Golfcourse(c)	100.00
5 MWs(c).Patsy/Buzz(c)	100.00
6 thru 10	@100.00
11 thru 28	@100.00
29 Aug., 1957.	100.00

PATSY WALKER
1945

1 F:Patsy Walker Adventures	700.00
2 Patsy/Car(c)	325.00
3 Skating(c)	250.00
4 Perfume(c)	250.00
5 Archery Lesson, Eye Injury(c)	300.00
6 Bus(c)	250.00
7 Charity Drive(c)	250.00
8 Organ Driver Monkey(c)	250.00
9 Date(c)	250.00
10 Skating(c),Wedding Bells, A:Millie	250.00
11 Date with a Dream,A:Mitzi	175.00
12 Love in Bloom,Artist(c), A:Rusty	175.00
13 Swimsuit(c),There Goes My Heart;HK,Hey Look	175.00

Patsy Walker #21
© Marvel Entertainment Group

14 An Affair of the Heart, HK,Hey Look	175.00
15 Dance(c)	175.00
16 Skating(c)	175.00
17 Patsy's Diary(c),HK,Hey Look	225.00
18 Autograph(c)	200.00
19 HK,Hey Look.	200.00
20 HK,Hey Look.	200.00
21 HK,Hey Look.	200.00
22 HK,Hey Look.	200.00
23	150.00
24	150.00
25 HK,Rusty.	200.00
26	150.00
27	150.00
28	150.00
29	150.00
30 HK,Egghead Double	150.00
31	125.00
32 thru 56.	@100.00
57 thru 58 AJ(c)	@125.00
59 thru 99	@100.00
100	100.00
Fashion Parade #1	150.00

PETER PARKER, THE SPECTACULAR SPIDER-MAN
Dec., 1976

1 SB,V:Tarantula	75.00
2 SB,V:Kraven,Tarantula.	25.00
3 SB,I:Lightmaster	20.00
4 SB,V:Vulture,Hitman	20.00
5 SB,V:Hitman,Vulture	20.00
6 SB,V:Morbius,rep.M.T.U.#3	22.00
7 SB,V:Morbius,A:Human Torch	23.00
8 SB,V:Morbius	23.00
9 SB,I:White Tiger	20.00
10 SB,A:White Tiger	15.00
11 JM,V:Medusa	15.00
12 SB,V:Brother Power	15.00
13 SB,V:Brother Power	15.00
14 SB,V:Brother Power	15.00
15 SB,V:Brother Power	15.00
16 SB,V:The Beetle	15.00
17 SB,A:Angel & Iceman Champions disbanded.	15.00
18 SB,A:Angel & Iceman	15.00
19 SB,V:The Enforcers	12.00
20 SB,V:Lightmaster	12.00
21 JM,V:Scorpion	10.00
22 MZ,A:Moon Knight,V:Cyclone	12.00
23 A:Moon Knight,V:Cyclone	12.00
24 FS,A:Hypno-Hustler	10.00
25 JM,FS,I:Carrion	11.00
26 JM,A:Daredevil,V:Carrion	10.00
27 DC,FM,I:Miller Daredevil, V:Carrion	50.00
28 FM,A:Daredevil,V:Carrion	40.00
29 JM,FS,V:Carrion	7.00
30 JM,FS,V:Carrion	7.00
31 JM,FS,D:Carrion	7.00
32 BL,JM,FS,V:Iguana	7.00
33 JM,FS,O:Iguana	7.00
34 JM,FS,V:Iguana,Lizard	7.00
35 V:Mutant Mindworm	7.00
36 JM,V:Swarm	7.00
37 DC,MN,V:Swarm	7.00
38 SB,V:Morbius	7.00
39 JM,JR2,V:Schizoid Man	8.00
40 FS,V:Schizoid Man	8.00
41 JM,V:Meteor Man,A:GiantMan	7.00
42 JM,A:Fant.Four,V:Frightful 4	7.00
43 JBy(c),MZ,V:The Ringer, V:Belladonna	7.00
44 JM,V:The Vulture	7.00
45 MSe,V:The Vulture	7.00
46 FM(c),MZ,V:Cobra	7.00
47 MSe,A:Prowler II.	7.00
48 MSe,A:Prowler II.	7.00
49 MSe,I:Smuggler	7.00

All comics prices listed are for *Near Mint* condition.

50 JR2,JM,V:Mysterio 7.00
51 MSe&FM(c),V:Mysterio 7.00
52 FM(c),D:White Tiger 7.00
53 JM,FS,V:Terrible Tinkerer 7.00
54 FM,WS,MSe,V:Silver Samurai . . 7.00
55 LMc,JM,V:Nitro 7.00
56 FM,JM,V:Jack-o-lantern 12.00
57 JM,V:Will-o-the Wisp. 6.00
58 JBy,V:Ringer,A:Beetle 7.00
59 JM,V:Beetle. 6.00
60 JM&FM(c),O:Spider-Man,
   V:Beetle 7.00
61 JM,V:Moonstone 5.00
62 JM,V:Goldbug 5.00
63 JM,V:Molten Man 5.00
64 JM,I:Cloak & Dagger. 15.00
65 BH,JM,V:Kraven,Calypso 5.00
66 JM,V:Electro 5.00
67 AMb,V:Boomerang 5.00
68 LMc,JM,V:Robot of Mendell
   Stromm 5.00
69 AM,A:Cloak & Dagger. 10.00
70 A:Cloak & Dagger. 10.00
71 JM,Gun Control issue 5.00
72 AM,V:Dr.Octopus 5.00
73 AM,.IM,V:Dr.Octopus,A:Owl 5.00
74 AM,JM,V:Dr.Octopus,R:Bl.Cat . . 5.00
75 AM,JM,V:Owl,Dr.Octopus 5.00
76 AM,Black Cat on deathbed 5.00
77 AM,V:Gladiator,Dr.Octopus 5.00
78 AM,V:Dr.Octopus,C:Punisher . . . 5.00
79 AM,V:Dr.Octopus,A:Punisher . . . 5.00
80 AM,F:J.Jonah Jameson 5.00
81 A:Punisher. 6.00
82 A:Punisher. 6.00
83 A:Punisher. 8.00
84 AM,F:Black Cat. 4.00
85 AM,O:Hobgoblin powers
   (Ned Leeds). 11.00
86 FH,V:Fly 4.00
87 AM,Reveals I.D.to Black Cat . . . 4.00
88 AM,V:Cobra,Mr.Hyde 4.00
89 AM,Secret Wars,A:Kingpin 5.00
90 AM,Secret Wars 6.00
91 AM,V:Blob 4.00
92 AM,I:Answer 4.00
93 AM,V:Answer 4.00
94 AM,A:Cloak & Dagger,V:
   Silver Mane 4.00
95 AM,A:Cloak & Dagger,V:
   Silvermane. 4.00
96 AM,A:Cloak & Dagger,V:
   Silvermane. 4.00
97 HT,JM,A:Black Cat 4.00

*Peter Parker The Spectacular
Spider-Man #12 © Marvel Ent.Group*

*Peter Parker The Spectacular Spider-
Man Ann. #2 © Marvel Ent.Group*

98 HT,JM,I:Spot 4.00
99 HT,JM,V:Spot 4.00
100 AM,V:Kingpin,C:Bl.Costume . . . 6.00
101 JBy(c),AM,V:Killer Shrike 3.00
102 JBy(c),AM,V:Backlash 3.00
103 AM,V:Blaze;Not John Blaze . . . 3.00
104 JBy(c),AM,V:Rocket Racer 3.00
105 AM,A:Wasp 3.00
106 AM,A:Wasp 3.00
107 RB,D:Jean DeWolf,I:SinEater . . 4.00
108 RB,A:Daredevil,V:Sin-Eater . . . 3.00
109 RB,A:Daredevil,V:Sin-Eater . . . 3.00
110 RB,A:Daredevil,V:Sin-Eater . . . 3.00
111 RB,Secret Wars II 3.00
112 RB,A:Santa Claus,Black Cat. . . 3.00
113 RB,Burglars,A:Black Cat 3.00
114 BMc,V:Lock Picker 3.00
115 BMc,A:Black Cat,Dr.Strange,
   I:Foreigner 4.00
116 A:Dr.Strange, Foreigner,
   Black Cat, Sabretooth 10.00
117 DT,C:Sabretooth,A:Foreigner,
   Black Cat,Dr.Strange 4.00
118 MZ,D:Alexander,V:SHIELD . . . 3.00
119 RB,BMc,V:Sabretooth,
   A:Foreigner,Black Cat 10.00
120 KG. 3.00
121 RB,BMc,V:Mauler 3.00
122 V:Mauler 3.00
123 V:Foreigner,Black Cat. 3.00
124 V:Dr.Octopus. 3.00
125 V:Wr.Crew,A:Spiderwoman 3.00
126 JM,A:Sp.woman,V:Wrecker . . . 3.00
127 AM,V:Lizard. 3.00
128 C:DDevil,A:Bl.Cat,Foreigner . . 3.50
129 A:Black Cat,V:Foreigner 3.00
130 A:Hobgoblin. 6.00
131 MZ,BMc,V:Kraven. 7.00
132 MZ,BMc,V:Kraven. 7.00
133 BSz(c),Mad Dog,pt.3 . . . . 5.00
Ann.#1 RB,JM,V:Dr.Octopus 10.00
Ann.#2 JM,I&O:Rapier. 7.00
Ann.#3 JM,V:Manwolf 5.00
Ann.#4 AM,O:Aunt May,A:Bl.Cat . . 5.00
Ann.#5 I:Ace,Joy Mercado. 5.00
Ann.#6 V:Ace 4.50
Ann.#7 Honeymoon iss,A:Puma . . 4.50
Becomes:

SPECTACULAR
SPIDER-MAN

PETER PARKER:
SPIDER-MAN
Nov., 1998
1 JR2,HMe,SHa,A:new Spider-Man,
   V:Ranger,48-page 3.00
1a signed 15.00
2 JR2,HMe,SHa,A:Thor 4.00
2a variant cover 4.00
3 HMe,JR2,SHa,A:Iceman,
   V:Shadrac 3.00
4 HMe,JR2,SHa,V:Marrow 3.00
5 HMe,SHa,BS,JBy(c),F:Spider-
   Woman,Aunt May, Black Cat. . . 3.00
6 HMe,SHa,RJ2,JBy(c),V:Kingpin . 3.00
7 JR2,HMe,SHa,Reality Bent 3.00
8 JR2,HMe,SHa,V:Bullseye 3.00
9 JR2,HMe,SHa,R:Venom 3.00
10 JR2,HMe,SHa,R:Carnage. 3.00
11 JR2,HMe,SHa,Eighth Day,pt.3
   x-over. 3.00
12 JR2,HMe,SHa, 48-pg. 3.50
13 JR2,HMe 3.00
14 JR2,HMe,A:Hulk 3.50
15 JR2,HMe,x-over 3.50
16 JR2,HMe,V:Sinister Six. 3.00
17 JR2,HMe,SHa,V:Kraven 2.50
18 HMe,JR2,SHa,V:Green Goblin . . 2.50
19 HMe,JR2,SHa,Mary Jane dies . . 2.50
20 PJe,MBu,DGr,Mary Jane dead . . 3.00
21 PJe,MBu,DGr,HumanTorch. 2.50
22 PJe,MBu,DGr,FlintMarko 2.50
23 PJe,MBu,DGr,Type Face 2.50
24 PJe,MBu,DGr,Max.Security 2.50
25 PJe,MBu,DGr,V:Green Goblin . 3.50
26 PJe,JoB,DGr,F:NYPD. 2.50
27 PJe,MBu,DGr,F:NYPD. 2.50
28 PJe,MBu,DGr, ... 2.50
29 PJe,CAd,DGr,x-over 7.00
30 PJe,MBu,HuR(c),I:Terminal 7.00
31 PJe,MBu,HuR(c),I:Fusion 3.50
32 PJe,MBu,HuR(c),V:Fusion 2.50
33 PJe,MBu,HuR(c),ballpark 2.50
34 PJe,MBu,cleanse the city 2.50
35 PJe,MBu,Jamal. 2.50
36 PJe,MBu,private-eye. 2.50
37 PJe,slice-of-life 2.50
38 PJe,MBu,V:Mimes,'Nuff Said . . . 2.50
39 PJe,MBu,return of Dr. Octopus . . 2.50
40 PJe,MBu,Doc Octopus,pt.2 . . . . 2.50
41 PJe,MBu,Doc Octopus,pt.3 . . . . 2.50
42 Spring Break,pt.1 . . . . 2.50
43 Spring Break,pt.2 . . . . 2.50
44 PJe,HuR,R:Green Goblin 6.00
45 PJe,HuR,R:Green Goblin,pt.2 . . 4.00
46 PJe,HuR,R:Green Goblin,pt.3 . . 2.50
47 PJe,HuR,R:Green Goblin,pt.4 . . 2.50
48 PJe,MBu 2.50
49 PJe,MBu 2.50
50 PJe,MBu 4.00
51 pt.1 . . . . 2.50
52 pt.2 . . . . 2.50
53 pt.1 . . . . 2.50
54 pt.2 . . . . 2.50
55 pt.3 . . . . 2.50
56 SK,Reborn,pt.1,F:Sandman 2.50
57 SK,Reborn,pt.2,F:Sandman 2.50
Ann.1999,CCs, 48-pg. 4.00
Ann.2000 CCl,JoB,80-pg. 4.00
Ann.2001 South America, 28-pg. . . 3.50
Spec. Peter Parker, Spider-
   Man 2000 . . . . 4.00
TPB Peter Parker:Spider-Man . . . 15.00
TPB One Small Break, 160-pg. . . . 17.00
TPB Return of the Goblin 9.00
TPB Trials & Tribulations 12.00
TPB Vol. 5: Senseless Violence . . 15.00

PETER PORKER
Star, May, 1985
1 Parody 4.50
2 thru 17 . . . . @3.00

PETER, THE LITTLE PEST
Nov., 1969–May, 1970
1 F:Peter 85.00
2 Rep,Dexter & Melvin 60.00
3 Rep,Dexter & Melvin 60.00
4 Rep,Dexter & Melvin 60.00

PHANTOM
1 Lee Falk's Phantom 4.00
2 V:General Babalar 4.00
3 final issue 4.00

Phanton 2040 33
© Marvel Entertainment Group

PHANTOM 2040
1 Based on cartoon 2.50
2 V:Alloy 2.50
3 MPa,V:Crime Syndicate 2.50
4 Vision Quest 2.50

PHOENIX
(UNTOLD STORY)
April, 1984
1 JBy,O:Phoenix (R.Summers) . . . 15.00

PILGRIM'S PROGRESS
1 adapts John Bunyans novel . . . 10.00

PINHEAD
1993–94
1 Red Foil(c),from Hellraiser 3.00
2 DGC(s),V:Cenobites 2.50
3 DGC(s),V:Cenobites 2.50
4 DGC(s),V:Cenobites 2.50
5 DGC(s),Devil in Disguise 2.50
6 DGC(s), ... 2.50

PINHEAD VS.
MARSHALL LAW
1993
1 KON,In Hell 3.00
2 KON 3.00

PINOCCHIO & THE
EMPEROR OF THE NIGHT
March, 1988
1 Movie adapt. 3.00

PINT-SIZED X-BABIES:
MURDERAMA
June, 1998
1-shot, Mojo, Arcade, 48-pg. 3.00

PIRATES OF
DARK WATERS
Nov., 1991
1 based on T.V. series 3.00
2 Search for 13 Treasures 3.00
3 V:Albino Warriors,Konk 3.00
4 A:Monkey Birds 3.00
5 Tula Steals 1st Treasuer 3.00
6 thru 9 . . . . @3.00

PITT, THE
March, 1988
1 SB,SDr,A:Spitfire 4.00

PLANET OF THE APES
Aug., 1974–Feb., 1977
(black & white magazine)
1 MP 45.00
2 MP 25.00
3 thru 10 . . . . @20.00
11 thru 20 . . . . @25.00
21 thru 29 . . . . @55.00

PLANET TERRY
Star, April, 1985
1 thru 11 . . . . @3.00
12 March, 1986 . . . . 3.00

PLASMER
Marvel UK, 1993–94
1 A:Captain America 3.50
2 A:Captain Britain,Black Knight . . . 2.25
3 A:Captain Britain 2.25
4 A:Captain Britain 2.25
5 thru 7 . . . . @2.00

PLASTIC FORKS
Epic, 1990
1 . . . . 6.00
2 thru 5 . . . . @5.50

POLICE ACADEMY
Nov., 1989
1 Based on TV Cartoon 2.25
2 thru 5 . . . . @2.25
6 Feb., 1990 . . . . 2.25

POLICE ACTION
Jan., 1954
1 JF,GC,JMn(c),Riot Squad 250.00
2 JF,Over the Wall 150.00
3 JMn 125.00
4 DAy 125.00
5 DAy,JMn 125.00
6 . . . . 125.00
7 BPNov., 1954 . . . . 125.00

POLICE BADGE #479
Marvel Atlas, 1955
5 . . . . 125.00

POLICE BADGE
See: SPY THRILLERS

POPPLES
Star, Dec., 1986
1 Based on Toys 3.00
2 thru 5 . . . . @3.00

POWDERED TOAST-MAN
Spec. F:Powder Toast-Man 3.25

Powerhouse Pepper Comics #1
© Marvel Entertainment Group

POWERHOUSE PEPPER
COMICS
1943—Nov., 1948
1 BW,Movie Auditions(c) 2,800.00
2 BW,Dinner(c) 1,200.00
3 BW,Boxing Ring(c) 1,100.00
4 BW,Subway(c) 1,100.00
5 BW,Bankrobbers(c) 1,300.00

POWERLESS
June, 2004
1 (of 6) 3.00
2 thru 6 . . . . @3.00

POWER LINE
Epic, May, 1988
1 BMc(i) 2.25
2 Aw(i) 2.25
3 A:Dr Zero 2.25
4 . . . . 2.25
5 thru 7 GM . . . . @2.25
8 GM Sept., 1989 . . . . 2.25

POWER MAN
Prev: Hero for Hire
Feb., 1974
17 GT,A:Iron Man 30.00
18 GT,V:Steeplejack 15.00
19 GT,V:Cottonmouth 15.00
20 GT,Heroin Story 15.00
21 GT:Original Power Man 10.00
22 V:Stiletto & Discus 10.00
23 V:Security City 10.00
24 GT,I:BlackGoliath(BillFoster) . . . 10.00
25 A:Circus of Crime 10.00
26 GT,V:Night Shocker 10.00
27 GP,AMc,V:Man Called X 10.00
28 V:Cockroach 10.00
29 V:Mr.Fish 10.00
30 RB,KJ,KP,I:Piranha 10.00
31 SB,NA(i),V:Piranha 10.00
32 JSt,FR,A:Wildfire 8.00
33 FR,A:Spear 8.00
34 FR,A:Spear,Mangler 8.00
35 DA,A:Spear,Mangler 8.00
36 V:Chemistro 8.00
37 V:Chemistro 8.00
38 V:Chemistro 8.00
39 KJ,V:Chemistro,Baron 8.00

MARVEL

40 V:Baron 8.00
41 TP,V:Thunderbolt,Goldbug 8.00
42 V:Thunderbolt,Goldbug 8.00
43 AN,V:Mace 8.00
44 TP,A:Mace 8.00
45 JSn,A:Mace 8.00
46 GT,I:Zzzax(recreated) 8.00
47 BS,A:Zzzax 10.00
48 JBy,A:Iron Fist 15.00
49 JBy,A:Iron Fist 15.00

Becomes:

POWER MAN & IRON FIST
1978

50 JBy,I:Team-up with Iron Fist . . . 15.00
51 MZ,Night on the Town 4.00
52 MZ,V:Death Machines 4.00
53 SB,O:Nightshade 4.00
54 TR,O:Iron Fist 4.00
55 Chaos at the Coliseum 4.00
56 Mayhem in the Museum 4.00
57 X-Men,V:Living Monolith 35.00
58 1st El Aguila(Drug) 4.00
59 BL(c),TVE,V:Big Apple
    Bomber 4.00
60 BL(c),V:Terrorists 4.00
61 BL(c),V:The Maggia 4.00
62 BL(c),KGa,V:Man Mountain
    D:Thunerbolt 4.00
63 BL(c),Cage Fights Fire 4.00
64 DGr&BL(c),V:Suetre,Muertre . . . 4.00
65 BL(c),A:El Aquila, ... 4.00
66 FM(c),Sabretooth(2nd App.) . . . 50.00
67 V:Bushmaster 4.00
68 FM(c),V:Athur Nagan 4.00
69 V:Soldier 4.00
70 FM(c)V:El Supremo 4.00
71 FM(c),I:Montenegro 4.00
72 FM(c),V:Chako 4.00
73 FM(c),V:Rom 4.00
74 FM(c),V:Ninja 4.00
75 KGa,O:IronFist 4.00
76 KGa,V:Warhawk 4.00
77 KGa,A:Daredevil 4.00
78 KGa,A:El Aguila,Sabretooth
    (Slasher)(3rd App.) 30.00
79 V:Dredlox 3.00
80 KJ(c),V:Montenegro 3.00
81 V:Black Tiger 3.00
82 V:Black Tiger 3.00
83 V:Warhawk 3.00
84 V:Constrictor,A:Sabretooth
    (4th App.) 30.00
85 KP,V:Mole Man 3.00
86 A:Moon Knight 3.00
87 A:Moon Kinght 3.00
88 V:Scimtar 3.00
89 V:Terrorists 3.00
90 V:Unus BS(c) 3.00
91 Paths and Angles 3.00
92 V:Hammeread,I:New Eel 3.00
93 A:Chemistro 3.00
94 V:Chemistro 3.00
95 Danny Rand 3.00
96 V,Chemistro 3.00
97 K'unlun,A:Fera 3.00
98 V:Shades & Commanche 3.00
99 R:Daught.of Dragon 3.00
100 O:K'unlun,DoubleSize 5.00
101 A:Karnak 3.00
102 V:Doombringer 3.00
103 O:Doombringer 3.00
104 V:Dr.Octopus,Lizard 3.00
105 F:Crime Buster 3.00
106 Luke Gets Shot 3.00
107 JBy(c),Terror issue 3.00
108 V:Inhuman Monster 3.00
109 V:The Reaper 3.00
110 V:Nightshade,Eel 3.00
111 I:Captain Hero 3.00
112 JBy(c),V:Control7 . . . . 3.00
113 JBy(c),A:Capt.Hero 3.00
114 JBy(c),V:Control7 . . . . 3.00

115 JBy(c),V:Stanley 3.00
116 JBy(c),V:Stanley 3.00
117 R:K'unlun 3.00
118 A:Colleen Wing 3.00
119 A:Daught.of Dragon 3.00
120 V:Chiantang 3.00
121 Secret Wars II 3.00
122 V:Dragonkin 3.00
123 V:Race Killer 3.00
124 V:Yellowclaw 3.00
125 MBr,LastIssue;D:Iron Fist 5.00
G-Size#1 reprints 4.00
Ann.#1 Earth Shock 20.00

POWER PACHYDERMS
Sept., 1989
1 Elephant Superheroes 2.50

Power Pack #1
© *Marvel Entertainment Group*

POWER PACK
Aug., 1984
1 JBr,BWi,I&O:Power Pack,
    I:Snarks 2.50
2 JBr,BWi,V:Snarks 2.25
3 JBr,BWi,V:Snarks 2.25
4 JBr,BWi,V:Snarks 2.25
5 JBr,BWi,V:Bogeyman 2.25
6 JBr,BWi,A:Spider-Man 2.25
7 JBr,BWi,A:Cloak & Dagger 2.25
8 JBr,BWi,A:Cloak & Dagger 2.25
9 BA,BWi,A:Marrina 2.25
10 BA,BWi,A:Marrina 2.25
11 JBr,BWi,V:Morlocks 2.25
12 JBr,BWi,A:X-Men,V:Morlocks . . . 3.00
13 BA,BWi,Baseball issue 2.25
14 JBr,BWi,V:Bogeyman 2.25
15 JBr,BWi,A:Beta Ray Bill 2.25
16 JBr,BWi,I&O:Kofi,J:Tattletale
    (Franklin Richards) 2.25
17 JBr,BWi,V:Snarks 2.25
18 BA,SW,Secret Wars II,V:Kurse . . 2.25
19 BA,SW,Doub.size,Wolverine . . . 4.00
20 BMc,A:NewMutants 2.25
21 BA,TA,C:Spider-Man 2.25
22 JBg,BWi,V:Snarks 2.25
23 JBg,BWi,V:Snarks,C:FF 2.25
24 JBg,BWi,V:Snarks,C:Cloak 2.25
25 JBg,BWi,A:FF,V:Snarks 2.25
26 JBg,BWi,A:Cloak & Dagger 2.25
27 JBg,AG,A:Wolverine,X-Factor,
    V:Sabretooth 5.00
28 A:Fantastic Four,Hercules 2.25
29 JBg,DGr,A:SpM,V:Hobgoblin . . 2.50
30 VM,Crack 2.25

31 JBg,I:Trash 2.25
32 JBg,V:Trash 2.25
33 JBg,A:Sunspot,Warlock,
    C:Spider-Man 2.25
34 TD,V:Madcap 2.25
35 JBg,A:X-Factor,D:Plague 2.25
36 JBg,V:Master Mold 2.25
37 SDr(i),I:Light-Tracker 2.25
38 SDr(i),V:Molecula 2.25
39 V:Bogeyman 2.25
40 A:New Mutants,V:Bogeyman . . . 2.25
41 SDr(i),V:The Gunrunners 2.25
42 JBg,SDr,Inferno,V:Bogeyman . . . 2.25
43 JBg,SDr,AW,Inferno,
    V:Bogeyman 2.25
44 JBr,Inferno,A:New Mutants 2.25
45 JBr,End battle w/Bogeyman 2.25
46 WPo,A:Punisher,Dakota North . . 2.50
47 JBg,I:Bossko 2.25
48 JBg,Toxic Waste #1 . . . . 2.25
49 JBg,JSh,Toxic Waste #2 . . . . 2.25
50 AW(i),V:Snarks 2.25
51 GM,I:Numinus 2.25
52 AW(i),V:Snarks,A:Numinus 2.25
53 EC,A of V,A:Typhoid Mary 2.25
54 JBg,V:Mad Thinker 2.25
55 DSp,V:Mysterio 2.25
56 TMo,A:Fant.Four,Nova 2.25
57 TMo,A:Nova,V:Star Stalker 2.25
58 TMo,A:Galactus,Mr.Fantastic . . . 2.25
59 TMo,V:Ringmaster 2.25
60 TMo,V:Puppetmaster 2.25
61 TMo,V:Red Ghost & Apes 2.25
62 V:Red Ghost & Apes
    (last issue) 2.25
Holiday Spec.JBr,Small Changes . . 2.25

POWER PACK
April, 2005
1 (of 4) I know what we did
    That Summer 3.00
2 Misadventures in Babysitting 3.00
3 F:Fantastic Four 3.00
4 End of the Rainbow 3.00
Digest Vol. 1 . . . . 7.00

POWER PACK:
PEER PRESSURE
June, 2000
1 (of 4) TA,CDo 3.00
2 TA,CDo,V:Snarks 3.00
3 TA,CDo, ... 3.00
4 Ta,CDo,concl 3.00

POWERS
Marvel Icon, July, 2004
1 BMB,F:Deena Pilgrim 3.00
2 thru 5 BMB . . . . @3.00
6 thru 12 . . . . @3.00
13 thru 18 Cosmic . . . . @3.00
19 thru 22 Secret Identity . . . . @3.00
TPB The Sellouts 20.00

PRINCE NAMOR,
THE SUB-MARINER
Sept., 1984
1 I:Dragonrider, Dara 3.00
2 I:Proteus 2.50
3 . . . . 2.50
4 Dec., 1984 . . . . 2.50

PRINCE VALIANT
1994–95
1 JRy,CV,Thule, Camelot
    and the Misty Isles 4.00
2 JRy,CV 4.00
3 JRy,CV 4.00
4 JRy, CV, final issue 4.00

PRIVATE EYE
Marvel Atlas, Jan., 1951
1 . . . . 250.00
2 . . . . 175.00
3 GT 175.00
4 . . . . 125.00
5 . . . . 125.00
6 JSt 125.00
7 . . . . 125.00
8 March, 1952. . . . . 125.00

PROFESSOR XAVIER AND THE X-MEN
1995
1 1st Year Together. 3.00
2 V:The Vanisher 2.50
3 FaN,F:The Blob 2.50
4 V:Magneto & Brotherhood 2.50
5 & 6 . . . . @2.50
7 FdS,Sub-Mariner 2.50
8 thru 12 . . . . @2.50
13 AHo,F:Juggernaut. 2.50
14 JGz,V:Juggernaut, ... 2.50
15 JGz,F:Quicksilver & Scarlet
    Witch 2.50
16 . . . . 2.50
17 JGz,V:Sentinels,F:Beast. 2.50
18 JGz,X-Men vs. Sentinels,
    final issue 2.50

PROWLER, THE
1994
1 Creatures of the Night, pt.1 . . . . 2.25
2 V:Nightcreeper, Creatures, pt.2 . 2.25
3 Creatures of the Night, pt.3 . . . . 2.25
4 V:Vulture, Creatures, pt.4 . . . . . 2.25

PSI FORCE
Nov., 1986
1 MT,O:PSI Force. 2.50
2 thru 9 MT . . . . @2.50
10 thru 32 . . . . @2.50
Ann.#1 . . . . 3.00

PSYCHONAUTS
Epic, 1993–94
1 thru 4 War in the Future. . . . . . @5.50

PSYLOCKE & ANGEL: CRIMSON DAWN
1997
1 SvL,ATi,V:Obsideon. 3.00
2 SvL,ATi, ... 3.00
3 BRa,SvL,ATi. 3.00
4 (of 4) BRa,SvL,ATi. 3.00

PULSE, THE
Feb., 2004
1 BMB,MBa,Thin Air,pt.1. . . . . 5.00
2 BMB,MBa,Thin Air,pt.2,F:Vulture. 3.50
3 BMB,MBa,Thin Air,pt.3. . . . . 3.00
4 BMB,MBa,Thin Air,pt.4. . . . . 3.00
5 BMB,MBa,Thin Air,pt.5. . . . . 3.00
6 BMB,BA,Secret War,pt.1) 3.00
7 BMB,BA,Secret War,pt.2 . . . . . . 3.00
8 BMB,Secret War,pt.3 . . . . 3.00
9 BMB,Secret War,pt.4, concl. . . . 3.00
10 BMB,House of M tie-in 4.00
11 BMB,Birth of Jessica Jones &
    Luke Cage's Baby. 3.00
12 BMB, A:D-Man 3.00
13 BMB,F:Jessica Jones, baby . . . 3.00
14 BMB,F:Luke Cage 3.00
Spec. BMB,House of M 0.50
TPB Vol. 1: Thin Air 14.00
TPB Vol. 2: Secret War 12.00
TPB Vol. 3: Fear 15.00

Punisher Mini-Series #2
© *Marvel Entertainment Group*

PUNISHER
[Limited Series] Jan., 1986
1 MZ,Circle of Blood,double size . 28.00
2 MZ,Back to the War. 18.00
3 MZ,V:The Right 15.00
4 MZ,V:The Right 15.00
5 V:Jigsaw,end Mini-Series. 15.00

[Regular Series] 1987–95
1 KJ,V:Wilfred Sobel,Drugs 12.00
2 KJ,V:General Trahn,Bolivia 6.00
3 KJ,V:Colonel Fryer. 5.00
4 KJ,I:The Rev,Microchip Jr. 5.00
5 KJ,V:The Rev. 5.00
6 DR,KN,V:The Rosettis. 5.00
7 DR,V:Ahmad,D:Rose. 5.00
8 WPo,SW(1st Punisher),
    V:Sigo & Roky. 4.00
9 WPo,SW,D:MicrochipJr,V:Sigo . 4.00
10 WPo,SW,A:Daredevil (x-over
    w/Daredevil #257). 7.00
11 WPo,SW,O:Punisher. 3.00
12 WPo,SW,V:Gary Saunders. . . . 3.00
13 WPo,SW,V:Lydia Spoto 3.00
14 WPo,SW,I:McDowell,Brooks. . . 3.00
15 WPo,SW,V:Kingpin 3.00
16 WPo,SW,V:Kingpin 3.00
17 WPo,SW,V:Kingpin 3.00
18 WPo,SW,V:Kingpin,C:X-Men . . 3.00
19 LSn,In Australia. 3.00
20 WPo(c),In Las Vegas 3.00
21 EL,SW,Boxing Issue 3.00
22 EL,SW,I:Saracen. 3.00
23 EL,SW,V:Scully. 3.00
24 EL,SW,A:Shadowmasters. 3.00
25 EL,AW,A:Shadowmasters. 3.00
26 RH,Oper.Whistle Blower#1. . . . 3.00
27 RH,Oper.Whistle Blower#2. . . . 3.00
28 BR,A:Dr.Doom,A of Veng. 3.00
29 BR,A:Dr.Doom,A of Veng. 3.00
30 BR,V:Geltrate 3.00
31 BR,V:Bikers #1 . . . . 2.50
32 BR,V:Bikers #2 . . . . 2.50
33 BR,V:The Reavers 2.50
34 BR,V:The Reavers 2.50
35 BR,MF,Jigsaw Puzzle #1 . . . . . 2.50
36 MT,MF,Jigsaw Puzzle #2 . . . . . 2.50
37 MT,Jigsaw Puzzle #3 . . . . 2.50
38 BR,MF,Jigsaw Puzzle #4 . . . . . 2.50
39 JSh,Jigsaw Puzzle #5. . . . . 2.50
40 BR,JSh,Jigsaw Puzzle #6. . . . . 2.50
41 BR,TD,V:Terrorists 2.50
42 MT,V:Corrupt Mili. School 2.50
43 BR,Border Run. 2.50

44 Flag Burner. 2.50
45 One Way Fare 2.50
46 HH,Cold Cache. 2.50
47 HH,Middle East #1 . . . . 2.50
48 HH,Mid.East #2,V:Saracen. . . . 2.50
49 HH,Punisher Hunted. 2.50
50 HH,MGo(c),I:Yo Yo Ng 2.50
51 Chinese Mafia. 2.50
52 Baby Snatchers 2.50
53 HH,in Prison 2.50
54 HH,in Prison 2.50
55 HH,in Prison 2.50
56 HH,in Prison 2.50
57 HH,in Prison 2.50
58 V:Kingpin's Gang,A:Micro. 2.50
59 MT(c),V:Kingpin 2.50
60 VM,AW,Black Punisher,
    A:Luke Cage 2.50
61 VM,A:Luke Cage. 2.50
62 VM,AW,A:Luke Cage 2.50
63 MT(c),VM,V:Thieves 2.50
64 Eurohit #1 . . . . 2.50
65 thru 70 Eurohit . . . . @2.50
71 AW(i). 2.50
72 AW(i). 2.50
73 AW(i),Police Action #1 . . . . 2.50
74 AW(i),Police Action #2 . . . . 2.50
75 AW(i),Police Action #3,foil(c),
    double size 3.00
76 LSn,in Hawaii 2.50
77 VM,Survive#1 . . . . 2.50
78 VM,Survive#2 . . . . 2.50
79 VM,Survive#3 . . . . 2.50
80 Goes to Church. 2.50
81 V:Crooked Cops 2.50
82 B:Firefight 2.50
83 Firefight#2. . . . . 2.50
84 E:Firefight 2.50
85 Suicide Run 2.25
86 Suicide Run#3,Foil(c), ... 3.00
87 Suicide Run#6 . . . . 2.25
88 LSh(c),Suicide Run#9. . . . . 2.25
89 . . . . 2.25
90 Hammered 2.25
91 Silk Noose. 2.25
92 Razor's Edge 2.25
93 Killing Streets 2.25
94 B:No Rules 2.25
95 No Rules. 2.25
96 . . . . 2.25
97 CDi 2.25
98 . . . . 2.25
99 . . . . 2.25
100 New Punisher 4.00

Punisher-Batman Spec.
© *Marvel Entertainment Group*

100a Enhanced ed. 5.00
101 CC,Raid's Franks Tomb 3.00
102 A:Bullseye 3.00
103 Countdown 4. . . . . 3.00
104 CDi,Countdown 1, V:Kingpin,
    final issue 4.00
Ann.#1 MT,A:Eliminators,
    Evolutionary War. 4.00
Ann.#2 JLe,Atlantis Attacks #5,
    A:Moon Knight. 3.50
Ann.#3 LS,MT,Lifeform #1 . . . . 3.50
Ann.#4 Baron Strucker,pt.2
    (see D.D.Annual #7) 3.50
Ann.#5 System Bytes #1 . . . . 3.50
Ann.#6 I:Eradikator,w/card. 3.50
GNv 5.00
Summer Spec.#1 VM,MT. 3.50
Summer Spec.#2 SBs(c) 2.50
Summer Spec.#3 V:Carjackers 2.50
Summer Spec.#4 . . . . 3.25
Spec. Punisher/Batman,CDi,JR2,
    48-pg. (1994). 5.00
Spec.#1 Punisher/Daredevil, rep.
    Daredevil 6.00
Punisher:No Escape A:USAgent,
    Paladin (1990). 5.50
Punisher Movie Spec.BA (1989) . . . 6.00
GNv Punisher: The Prize (1990) . . 5.50
Punisher:Bloodlines DC. 6.25
Punisher:Blood on the Moors 17.00
Punisher:G-Force. 5.25
Punisher:Origin of Mirco Chip #1,
    O:Mirco Chip 2.50
Punisher:Origin of Mirco Chip #2
    V:The Professor. 2.50
Classic Punisher rep early
    B&W magazines 7.00
Punisher:Back To School Spec.
    #1 JRy,short stories. 3.25
    #2 BSz. 3.00
Punisher:Die Hard in the Big
    Easy Mardi Gras 5.25
Holiday Spec.#1 V:Young
    Mob Capo 3.25
Holiday Spec #2. . . . . 3.00
Punisher:Ghosts of the Innocent#1
    TGr, V:Kingpin's Dead Men. . . . 6.00
Punisher:Ghosts of the Innocent#2
    TGr, V:Kingpin,Snake 6.00
TPB Punisher: Eye For An Eye . . . 10.00

[2nd Regular Series] 1995
1 JOs,TL,Clv,Punisher sent to
    the Electric Chair, foil(c) 3.00
2 JOs,TL,Clv,Crime family boss . . . 2.50
3 JOs,TL,Clv,V:Hatchetman 2.50
4 JOs,TL,Clv,A:Daredevil,Jigsaw . . 2.50
5 . . . . 2.50
6 . . . . 2.50
7 JOs,TL,Clv,V:Son of Nick Fury . . 2.50
8 . . . . 2.50
9 . . . . 2.50
10 . . . . 2.50
11 Onslaught saga. 2.50
12 A:X-Cutioner 3.00
13 JOs,TL, Working for S.H.I.E.L.D.?,
    A:X-Cutioner 2.50
14 . . . . 2.50
15 JOs,TL, X-Cutioner. 2.50
16 JOS,TL, concl.? 2.50
17 JOS,TL,A:Daredevil,Doc Samson,
    Spider-Man 2.50
18 JOS,TL,Frank Castle amnesia? . 2.50
19 JOS,TL,V:Taskmaster. 2.50
20 JOS,TL, fugitive Punisher. 2.50

PUNISHER
Sept., 1998
1 (of 4) BWr,JP,TSg,F:Frank
    Castle 3.00
2 BWr,JJu,JP,A:Hellstrom 3.00
3 BWr,JJu,TSg,JP,A:Gadriel 7.00

Punisher Vol. 2 #4
© *Marvel Entertainment Group*

4 BWr,JJu,TSg,JP,Hell on Earth . . . 3.00

PUNISHER
Jan., 2000
1 (of 12) JP,GEn,SDi,R:Punisher . . 3.00
2A JP,GEn,SDi,V:Ma Gnucci 3.00
2B variant SDi(c). 3.00
3 GEn,JP,SDi,polybaged 8.00
4 GEn,JP,SDi,Gnuccis 3.00
5 GEn,JP,SDi,Mr.Payback 3.00
6 GEn,JP,SDi,Elite 3.00
7 GEn,JP,SDi,Mr.Payback 3.00
8 GEn,JP,SDi,Gnuccis 3.00
9 GEn,JP,SDi,Russian 3.00
10 GEn,JP,SDi,Russian 3.00
11 GEn,JP,SDi,Russian 3.00
12 GEn,JP,SDi,concl. 3.00
Spec. Punisher/Painkiller Jane 3.50
GN Punisher Kills the Marvel
    Universe, 48-pg. GEn,DBw 6.00
TPB Welcome Back, Frank 25.00
TPB Circle of Blood 13.00

PUNISHER
June, 2001
1 GEn,JP,SDi,pt.1 . . . . 5.00
2A GEn,JP,SDi,pt.2 . . . . 3.00
2B variant SDi(c). 3.00
3 GEn,JP,SDi,Grand Nixon Island . 3.00
4 GEn,JP,SDi,Survivor 3.00
5 GEn,JP,SDi,V:Kriegkopf. 3.00
6 GEn,JP,Viet Nam 3.00
7 SDi,JP,'Nuff Said 3.00
8 TPe,Taxi Wars 3.00
9 TPe,Taxi Wars 3.00
10 TPe,Taxi Wars. 3.00
11 TPe,Taxi Wars, Medallion 3.00
12 TPE,Taxi Wars, concl. 3.00
13 GeN,SDi, to South America 3.00
14 GeN,SDi, in Columbia. 3.00
15 GeN,SDi,F:Wolverine 3.00
16 GeN,SDi,F:Wolverine 3.00
17 GeN,DaR,F:Wolverine 3.00
18 GeN,SDi,Northern Ireland. 3.00
19 GeN,SDi,. 3.00
20 GEn,SDi,Brotherhood,pt.1 . . . . . 3.00
21 GEn,SDi,Brotherhood,pt.2 . . . . . 3.00
22 GEn,SDi 3.00
23 GEn,SDi,Giant Squid 3.00
24 GEn,TMd,Hidden,pt.1 . . . . 3.00
25 GEn,TMd,Hidden,pt.2 . . . . 3.00
26 GEn,TMd,Hidden,pt.3 . . . . 3.00
27 GEn,SDi,F:Elektra. 3.00

---

28 GEn,CK,Streets of Loredo,pt.1 . . 3.00
29 GEn,CK,Streets of Loredo,pt.2 . . 3.00
30 GEn,CK,Streets of Loredo,pt.3 . . 3.00
31 GEn,CK,Streets of Loredo,pt.4 . . 3.00
32 GEn,CK,Streets of Loredo,pt.5 . . 3.00
33 GEn,JMC,Dunces,pt.1 . . . . 3.00
34 GEn,JMC,Dunces,pt.2 . . . . 3.00
35 GEn,JMC,Dunces,pt.3 . . . . 3.00
36 GEn,JMC,Dunces,pt.4 . . . . 3.00
37 GEn,JMC,Dunces,pt.5 . . . . 4.00
TPB Army of One, rep. 144-pg. . . . 16.00
TPB Vol. 3: Business as Usual . . . 15.00
TPB Vol. 4: Full Auto 18.00
TPB Vol. 5: Streets of Laredo 18.00
TPB Vol. 6: Confed. of Dunces . . . 15.00

PUNISHER
Max, 2004
1 GEn,In the Beginning,pt.1 . . . . . . 9.00
2 GEn,In the Beginning,pt.2 . . . . . . 5.00
3 GEn,In the Beginning,pt.3 . . . . . . 5.00
4 GEn,In the Beginning,pt.4 . . . . . . 5.00
5 GEn,In the Beginning,pt.5 . . . . . . 3.00
6 GEn,In the Beginning,pt.6 . . . . . . 3.00
7 GEn,Kitchen Irish,pt.1 . . . . 3.00
8 GEn,Kitchen Irish,pt.2 . . . . 3.00
9 GEn,Kitchen Irish,pt.3 . . . . 3.00
10 GEn,Kitchen Irish,pt.4. . . . . 3.00
11 GEn,Kitchen Irish,pt.5 . . . . 3.00
12 GEn,Kitchen Irish,pt.6. . . . . 3.00
13 GEn,DBw,Mother Russia, pt.1 . . 3.00
14 GEn,DBw,Mother Russia, pt.2 . . 3.00
15 GEn,DBw,Mother Russia, pt. 3. . 3.00
16 GEn,DBw,Mother Russia, pt.4 . . 3.00
17 GEn,DBw,Mother Russia 3.00
18 GEn,DBw,Mother Russia 3.00
19 GEn,DBw,Up is Down and
    Black Is White,pt.1. . . . . 3.00
20 GEn,Up is Down, Black is White 3.00
21 GEn,Up is Down, Black is White 3.00
22 GEn,Up is Down, Black is White 3.00
23 GEn,Up is Down, Black is White 3.00
24 GEn,Up is Down, Black is White 3.00
25 GEn,The Slavers,pt.1 . . . . 3.00
26 GEn,The Slavers,pt.2 . . . . 3.00
27 GEn,The Slavers,pt.3 . . . . 3.00
28 GEn,The Slavers,pt.4 . . . . 3.00
29 GEn,The Slavers,pt.5 . . . . 3.00
30 GEn,The Slavers,pt.6 . . . . 3.00
31 GEn,Barracuda,pt.1 . . . . 3.00
32 GEn,Barracuda,pt.2 . . . . 3.00
33 GEn,Barracuda,pt.3 . . . . 3.00
34 GEn,Barracuda,pt.4 . . . . 3.00
35 GEn,Barracuda,pt.5 . . . . 3.00
36 GEn,Barracuda,pt.6 . . . . 3.00
37 GEn,Man of Stone, pt.1 . . . . 3.00
38 GEn,Man of Stone, pt.2 . . . . 3.00
39 GEn,Man of Stone, pt.3 . . . . 3.00
40 GEn,Man of Stone, pt.4 . . . . 3.00
TPB Born 14.00
Spec. Punisher: Red X-Mas (2004) . 3.00
Spec. Punisher: The End,RCo. 5.00
Spec. X-Mas Special, The List 4.00
1-shot The Cell, GEn,56-pg. 5.00
1-shot Punisher Valentine's One . . . 4.00
1-shot Punisher Silent Night (2005). 4.00
1-shot Punisher: The Tyger (2006) . 5.00
TPB Vol. 1: In the Beginning 15.00
TPB Vol. 2: Kitchen Irish 15.00
TPB Vol. 3: Mother Russia 15.00
TPB Vol. 4: Up is Down, Blacks
\   is White 15.00
TPB Vol. 5: The Slavers 16.00
TPB Vol. 6: Barracuda 16.00
TPB Very Special Holidays 13.00

PUNISHER ARMORY
July, 1990
1 JLe(c). 3.00
2 JLe(c). 2.50
3 . . . . 2.50

MARVEL

4 thru 6 . . . . @2.50
7 thru 10 . . . . @2.50

PUNISHER/
CAPTAIN AMERICA:
BLOOD AND GLORY
1 thru 3 KJ,V:Drug Dealers . . . . . @6.25

CLASSIC PUNISHER
1 TDz 5.00

PUNISHER KILLS
THE MARVEL UNIVERSE
1995
1-shot Alterniverse 15.00

PUNISHER MAGAZINE
Oct., 1989
1 MZ,rep.,Punisher #1 . . . . 3.00
2 MZ,rep 2.50
3 thru 13 KJ,rep. . . . . @2.50
14 rep. PWJ #1&#2 . . . . 2.50
15 rep. PWJ 2.50
16 rep.,1990. . . . . 2.50

PUNISHER
MEETS ARCHIE
1994
1 JB. 4.25
1a newsstand ed. 3.25

PUNISHER MOVIE COMIC
Nov., 1989
1 Movie adapt. 2.25
2 Movie adapt. 2.25
3 Movie adapt,Dec., 1989 . . . . . . 2.25

PUNISHER: THE MOVIE
March, 2004
1 (of 3) PO 3.00
2 and 3 PO . . . . @3.00
TPB 13.00

PUNISHER P.O.V.
July, 1991
1 BWr,Punisher/Nick Fury. 5.50
2 BWr,A:Nick Fury,Kingpin 5.50
3 BWr,V:Mutant Monster,
   A:Vampire Slayer. 5.50
4 BWr,A:Nick Fury 5.25

PUNISHER 2099
1993–95
1 TMo,Jake Gallows family
   Killed, foil(c). 2.50
2 TMo,I:Fearmaster,Kron,Multi
   Factor 2.25
3 TMo,V:Frightening Cult 2.25
4 TMo,V:Cyber Nostra 2.25
5 TMo,V:Cyber Nostra,Fearmaster. 2.25
6 TMo,V:Multi-Factor 2.25
7 TMo,Love and Bullets#1 . . . . . . 2.25
8 TMo,Love and Bullets#2 . . . . . . 2.25
9 TMo,Love and Bullets#3 . . . . . . 2.25
10 TMo,I:Jigsaw. 2.25
11 TMo,V:Jigsaw. 2.25
12 TMo,A:Spider-Man 2099 . . . . . 2.25
13 TMo,Fall of the Hammer#5. . . . 2.25
14 WSm, ... 2.25
15 TMo,V:Fearmaster,
   I:Public Enemy 2.25
16 TMo,V:Fearmaster,
   Public Enemy 2.25
17 TMo,V:Public Enemy 2.25
18 TMo,I:Goldheart 2.25
19 TMo,I:Vendetta 2.25

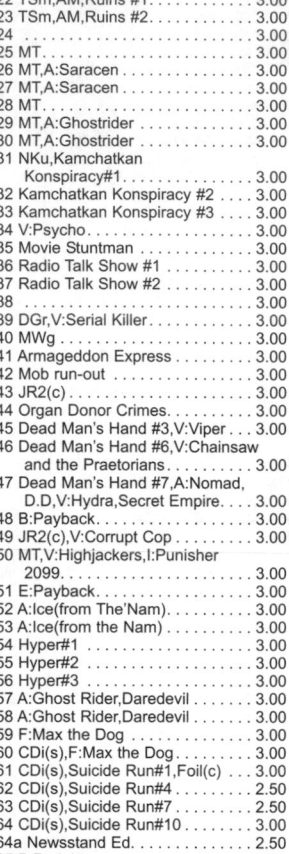

Punisher 2099 #25
© Marvel Entertainment Group

20 . . . . 2.25
21 . . . . 2.25
22 V:Hotwire 2.25
23 I:Synchron,V:Hotwire 2.25
24 V:Synchron 2.25
25 Enhanced cover 3.50
25a newsstand ed. 2.25
26 V:Techno-Shaman 2.25
27 R:Blue Max 2.25
Becomes:

PUNISHER 2099 A.D.
28 Minister of Punishment 2.25
29 Minister of Punishment 2.25
30 One Nation Under Doom 2.25
31 . . . . 2.25
32 Out of Ammo. 2.25
33 Counddown to final issue 2.25
34 final issue 2.25

PUNISHER VS. BULLSEYE
Nov., 2005
1 The Man's Got Style 3.00
2 The Drop 3.00
3 Massacre on 34th Street 3.00
4 Two of a Kind. 3.00
5 Profit and Loss. 3.00
TPB Punisher vs. Bullseye 14.00

PUNISHER
WAR JOURNAL
Nov., 1988
1 CP,JLe,O:Punisher 5.00
2 CP,JLe,A:Daredevil 4.00
3 CP,JLe,A:Daredevil 4.00
4 CP,JLeV:The Sniper. 4.00
5 CP,JLe,V:The Sniper 4.00
6 CP,JLe,A:Wolverine 4.00
7 CP,JLe,A:Wolverine 4.00
8 JLe,I:Shadowmasters 4.00
9 JLe,A:Black Widow 4.00
10 JLe,V:Sniper 4.00
11 JLe,Shock Treatment 3.50
12 JLe,AM,V:Bushwacker 3.50
13 JLe(c),V:Bushwacker 3.50
14 JLe(c),DR,RH,A:Spider-Man. . . 3.50
15 JLe(c),DR,RH,A:Spider-Man. . . 3.50
16 MT(i),Texas Massacre 3.50
17 JLe,AM,Hawaii 3.00
18 JLe,AM,Kahuna,Hawaii. 3.00
19 JLe,AM,Traume in Paradise . . . 3.00
20 AM. 3.00
21 TSm,AM 3.00

22 TSm,AM,Ruins #1. . . . . 3.00
23 TSm,AM,Ruins #2. . . . . 3.00
24 . . . . 3.00
25 MT. 3.00
26 MT,A:Saracen 3.00
27 MT,A:Saracen 3.00
28 MT. 3.00
29 MT,A:Ghostrider 3.00
30 MT,A:Ghostrider 3.00
31 NKu,Kamchatkan
   Konspiracy#1. . . . . 3.00
32 Kamchatkan Konspiracy #2 . . . 3.00
33 Kamchatkan Konspiracy #3 . . . 3.00
34 V:Psycho. 3.00
35 Movie Stuntman 3.00
36 Radio Talk Show #1 . . . . 3.00
37 Radio Talk Show #2 . . . . 3.00
38 . . . . 3.00
39 DGr,V:Serial Killer. 3.00
40 MWg 3.00
41 Armageddon Express 3.00
42 Mob run-out 3.00
43 JR2(c) 3.00
44 Organ Donor Crimes. 3.00
45 Dead Man's Hand #3,V:Viper . . 3.00
46 Dead Man's Hand #6,V:Chainsaw
   and the Praetorians. 3.00
47 Dead Man's Hand #7,A:Nomad,
   D.D,V:Hydra,Secret Empire. . . . 3.00
48 B:Payback. 3.00
49 JR2(c),V:Corrupt Cop 3.00
50 MT,V:Highjackers,I:Punisher
   2099. . . . . 3.00
51 E:Payback. 3.00
52 A:Ice(from The'Nam). 3.00
53 A:Ice(from the Nam) 3.00
54 Hyper#1 . . . . 3.00
55 Hyper#2 . . . . 3.00
56 Hyper#3 . . . . 3.00
57 A:Ghost Rider,Daredevil 3.00
58 A:Ghost Rider,Daredevil 3.00
59 F:Max the Dog 3.00
60 CDi(s),F:Max the Dog. 3.00
61 CDi(s),Suicide Run#1,Foil(c) . . 3.00
62 CDi(s),Suicide Run#4 . . . . 2.50
63 CDi(s),Suicide Run#7 . . . . 2.50
64 CDi(s),Suicide Run#10 . . . . 3.00
64a Newsstand Ed. 2.50
65 B:Pariah 2.50
66 A:Captain America 2.50
67 Pariah#3 . . . . 2.50
68 A:Spider-Man 2.50
69 E:Pariah 2.50
70 . . . . 2.50

Punisher War Journal #75
© Marvel Entertainment Group

MARVEL

71 . . . . 2.50
72 V:Fake Punisher 2.50
73 E:Frank Castle 2.50
74 . . . . 2.50
75 MT(c). 3.00
76 First Entry 2.50
77 R:Stone COld 2.50
78 V:Payback,Heathen 2.50
79 Countdown 3. . . . . 2.50
80 Countdown 0, A:Nick Fury,
    V:Bullseye, final issue 2.50
TPB reprints #6,7 . . . . 5.00

PUNISHER WAR JOURNAL
Nov., 2006
1 . . . . 3.00

PUNISHER WAR ZONE
1992
1 JR2,KJ,Punisher As Johnny Tower
   Die-Cut Bullet Hole(c) 3.00
2 JR2,KJ,Mafia Career 2.25
3 JR2,KJ,Punisher/Mafia,contd . . . 2.25
4 JR2,KJ,Cover gets Blown 2.25
5 JR2,KJ,A:Shotgun 2.25
6 JR2,KJ,A:Shotgun 2.25
7 JR2,V:Rapist in Central Park. . . . 2.25
8 JR2,V:Rapist in Central Park. . . . 2.25
9 JR2,V:Magnificent Seven 2.25
10 JR2,V:Magnificent Seven. 2.25
11 JR2,MM,V:Magnificent Seven. . . 2.25
12 Punisher Married 2.25
13 Self-Realization. 2.25
14 Psychoville#3 . . . . 2.25
15 Psychoville#4 . . . . 2.25
16 Psychoville#5 . . . . 2.25
17 Industrial Esponiage 2.25
18 Jerico Syndrome#2. . . . . 2.25
19 Jerico Syndrome#3. . . . . 2.25
20 B:2 Mean 2 Die. 2.25
21 2 Mean 2 Die#2 . . . . 2.25
22 A:Tyger Tyger 2.25
23 Suicide Run#2,Foil(c) 3.25
24 Suicide Run#5, ... 2.25
25 Suicide Run#8, ... 2.50
26 CDi(s),JB,Pirates 2.25
27 CDi(s),JB, ... 2.25
28 CDi(s),JB,Sweet Revenge 2.25
29 CDi(s),JB,The Swine 2.25
30 CDi(s),JB. 2.25
31 CDi(s),JB,River of Blood,pt.1 . . 2.25
32 CDi(s),JB,River of Blood,pt.2 . . 2.25
33 CDi(s),JB,River of Blood,pt.3 . . 2.25
34 CDi(s),JB,River of Blood,pt.4 . . 2.25
35 River of Blood,pt.5 . . . . 2.25
36 River of Blood,pt.6 . . . . 2.25
37 O:Max 2.25
38 Dark Judgment,pt.1 . . . . 2.25
39 Dark Judgment,pt.2 . . . . 2.25
40 In Court 2.25
41 CDi,Countdown 2, final issue . . 2.25
Ann.#1 Jb,MGo,(c),I:Phalanx,
   w/Trading card. 3.25
Ann.#2 CDi(s),DR 3.00
TPB CDi,JR2, rep. #1–#6. . . . . 16.00
TPB River of Blood (2005). 16.00

PUNISHER: YEAR ONE
1994
1 O:Punisher. 2.50
2 thru 4 . . . . @2.50

PUSSYCAT
(B&W Magazine) Oct., 1968
1 BEv,BWa,WW 300.00

QUASAR
Oct., 1989
1 O:Quasar. 3.00
2 V:Deathurge,A:Eon 2.50

3 A:Human Torch,V:The Angler . . . 2.50
4 Acts of Vengeance,A:Aquarian . . 2.50
5 A of Veng,V:Absorbing Man 2.50
6 V:Klaw,Living Laser,Venom,
   Red Ghost 3.00
7 MM,A:Cosmic SpM,V:Terminus . 2.50
8 MM,A:New Mutants,BlueShield . . 2.25
9 MM,A:Modam 2.25
10 MM,A:Dr.Minerva 2.25
11 MM,A:Excalibur,A:Modred. 2.25
12 MM,A:Makhari,Blood Bros. 2.25
13 JLe(c)MM,J.into Mystery #1 . . . 2.25
14 TM(c)MM,J.into Mystery #2 . . . 2.25
15 MM,Journey into Mystery #3 . . . 2.25
16 MM,Double sized 2.25
17 MM,Race,A:Makkari,Whizzer,
   Quicksilver,Capt.Marv,Super
   Sabre,Barry Allen Spoof 2.25
18 GCa,N:Quasar 2.25
19 GCa,B:Cosmos in Collision,
   C:Thanos. 2.25
20 GCa,A:Fantastic Four. 2.25
21 GCa,V:Jack of Hearts 2.25
22 GCa,D:Quasar,A:Ghost Rider. . 2.25
23 GCa,A:Ghost Rider. 2.25
24 GCa,A: I hanos,Galactus,
   D:Maelstrom 2.25

Quasar #52
© *Marvel Entertainment Group*

25 GCa,A:Eternity & Infinity,N:Quasar,
   E:Cosmos Collision 2.25
26 GCa,Inf.Gauntlet,A:Thanos. . . . 2.50
27 GCa,Infinity Gauntlet,I:Epoch . . 2.25
28 GCa,A:Moondragon,Her,
   X-Men 2.25
29 GCa,A:Moondragon,Her 2.25
30 GCa,What If? tie-in 2.25
31 GCa,R:New Universe 2.25
32 GCa,Op.GalacticStorm,pt.3 . . . 2.25
33 GCa,Op.GalacticStorm,pt.10 . . 2.25
34 GCa,Op.GalacticStorm,pt.17 . . 2.25
35 GCa,Binary V:Her 2.25
36 GCa,V:Soul Eater 2.25
37 GCa,V:Soul Eater 2.25
38 GCa,Inf.War,V:Warlock 2.25
39 SLi,Inf.War,V:Deathurge 2.25
40 SLi,Inf.War,V:Deathurge 2.25
41 R:Marvel Boy 2.25
42 V:Blue Marvel 2.25
43 V:Blue Marvel 2.25
44 V:Quagmire 2.25
45 V:Quagmire,Antibody 2.25
46 Neutron,Presence 2.25
47 1st Full Thunderstrike Story 2.25
48 A:Thunderstrike. 2.25

49 Kalya Vs. Kismet. 2.25
50 A:Man-Thing,Prism(c). 3.50
51 V:Angler,A:S.Supreme 2.25
52 V:Geometer. 2.25
53 . . . . 2.25
54 MGu(s),Starblast #2 . . . . 2.25
55 MGu(s),A:Stranger 2.25
56 MGu(s),Starblast #10 . . . . 2.25
57 MGu(s),A:Kismet. 2.25
58 . . . . 2.25
59 A:Thanos,Starfox. 2.25
60 final issue 2.25

QUEST
June, 2003
1 (of 6) Manga,F:Katherine West . . 2.50
2 Quest & Kaori 2.50

QUESTPROBE
Aug., 1984
1 JR,A:Hulk,I:Chief Examiner 3.00
2 AM,JM,A:Spider-Man 3.00
3 JSt,A:Thing & Torch. 3.00

QUICKSILVER
Sept., 1997
1 CJ,TPe, V:Exodus, cont. from
   Excalibur #113. . . . . 3.00
2 TPe,CJ,A:Knights of Wundagore. 2.25
3 TPe,CJ,V:Arkon 2.25
4 TPe, Crystal returns. 2.25
5 TPe,V:Inhumans 2.25
6 TPe,Inhumands trilogy concl. . . . 2.25
7 JOs,F:The Black Knight. 2.25
8 JOs,F:Pietro,V:Pyro 2.25
9 JOs,Savage Land concl.,A:High
   Evolutionary. 2.25
10 JOS,Live Kree or Die, pt.3,
    x-over. 2.25
11 JOs,The Seige of Wundagore,
    pt.2 (of 5). 2.25
12 JOs,The Seige of Wundagore,
    pt.4 (of 5) 48-pg. 3.00
13 JOc,Scige of Wundagore,pt.5,
    final issue 2.25

QUICK-TRIGGER
WESTERN
See: WESTERN
THRILLERS

RAIDERS OF
THE LOST ARK
Sept., 1981
1 JB/KJ,movie adaption 3.00
2 JB/KJ, ... 3.00
3 JB/KJ,Nov.,1981 . . . . 3.00

RAMPAGING HULK, THE
May, 1998
1 RL,double size, savage Hulk era. 3.00
2A RL,DGr,I:Ravage 2.25
2B JQ,JP,variant cover 2.25
3 RL,DGr,V:Ravage, concl. 2.25
4 DR,Trapped by an Avalanche . . . 2.25
5 RL,F:Fantastic Four. 2.25
6 RL,DGr,V:Puma. 2.25

RANGELAND LOVE
Marvel Comics, 1949
1 Robert Taylor 200.00
2 . . . . 150.00

RAVAGE 2099
1992–95
1 PR,I:Ravage 3.00
2 PR,V:Deathstryk 2.25

MARVEL

3 PR,V:Mutroids 2.25
4 PR,V:Mutroids 2.25
5 PR,Hellrock 2.25
6 PR,N:Ravage. 2.25
7 PR,New powers 2.25
8 V:Deathstryke. 2.25
9 PR,N:Ravage. 2.25
10 V:Alchemax. 2.25
11 A:Avatarr 2.25
12 Ravage Transforms 2.25
13 V:Fearmaster 2.25
14 V:Punisher 2099 . . . . 2.25
15 Fall of the Hammer #2 . . . . 2.25
16 I:Throwback 2.25
17 GtM,V:Throwback,O:X-11 . . . 2.25
18 GtM,w/card 2.25
19 GtM, ... 2.25
20 GtM,V:Hunter 2.25
21 Savage on the Loose 2.25
22 Exodus 2.25
23 Blind Justice 2.25
24 Unleashed. 2.25
25 Flame Bearer 2.25
25a Deluxe ed.. . . . . 3.00
26 V:Megastruck 2.25
27 V:Deathstryke. 2.25
28 R:Hela. 2.25
29 V:Deathstryke. 2.25
30 King Ravage 2.25
Becomes:

RAVAGE 2099 A.D.
31 V:Doom. 2.25
32 One Nation Under Doom 2.25
33 Final issue. 2.25

RAWHIDE KID
Atlas, March, 1955—May, 1979
1 JMn,B:Rawhide Kid & Randy,
  A:Wyatt Earp 1,400.00
2 JMn,Shoot-out(c) 650.00
3 V:Hustler 450.00
4 Rh(c) 450.00
5 GC,JMn 450.00
6 JMn,Six-Gun Lesson 375.00
7 AW 375.00
8 . . . . 375.00
9 . . . . 375.00
10 thru 16 Sept. 1957 . . . . @350.00
17 JK,O:Rawhide Kid; Aug. 1960 350.00
18 thru 20. . . . . @350.00
21 . . . . 350.00
22 . . . . 350.00
23 JK,O:Rawhide Kid Retold 400.00
24 thru 30 . . . . @275.00
31 JK,DAy,No Law in Mesa 275.00
32 JK,DAy,Beware of the
  Parker Brothers 275.00
33 JK(c),JDa,V:Jesse James. . . . 275.00
34 JDa,JK,V:Mister Lightning. . . . 275.00
35 JK(c),GC,JDa,
  I&D:The Raven 275.00
36 DAy,A Prisoner in
  Outlaw Town 175.00
37 JK(c),DAy,GC,V:The Rattler . . 175.00
38 DAy.V:The Red Raven 250.00
39 DAy. 175.00
40 JK(c),DAy,A:Two Gun Kid . . . 175.00
41 JK(c),The Tyrant of
  Tombstone Valley 175.00
42 JK 175.00
43 JK 250.00
44 JK(c),V:The Masked Maverick 175.00
45 JK(c),O:Rawhide Kid Retold. . 200.00
46 JK(c),ATh 175.00
47 JK(c),The Riverboat Raiders . 135.00
48 GC,V:Marko the Manhunter . . 125.00
49 The Masquerader 125.00
50 A;Kid Colt,V:Masquerader . . . 125.00
51 DAy,Trapped in the
  Valley of Doom 125.00

HE SHARES HIS SADDLE WITH DANGER

Rawhide Kid #1
© Marvel Entertainment Group

52 DAy,Revenge at
  Rustler's Roost 125.00
53 Guns of the Wild North 125.00
54 DH,BEv,The Last Showdown . 125.00
55 . . . . 125.00
56 DH,JTgV:The Peacemaker. . . 125.00
57 V:The Scorpion 125.00
58 DAy 125.00
59 V:Drako 125.00
60 DAy,HT,Massacre at Medicine
  Bend 125.00
61 DAy,TS,A:Wild Bill Hickok. . . 100.00
62 Gun Town,V:Drako 100.00
63 Shootout at Mesa City 100.00
64 HT,Duel of the Desparadoes . 100.00
65 JTg,HT,BE. 100.00
66 JTg,BEv,Death of a Gunfighter 100.00
67 Hostage of Hungry Hills 100.00
68 JB,V:The Cougar 100.00
69 JTg,The Executioner. 100.00
70 JTg,The Night of the Betrayers. 75.00
71 JTg,The Last Warrior 75.00
72 JTg,The Menace of Mystery
  Valley. 75.00
73 JTg,The Manhunt 75.00
74 JTg,The Apaches Attack 75.00
75 JTg,The Man Who Killed
  The Kid 75.00
76 JTg,V:The Lynx. 75.00
77 JTg,The Reckoning. 75.00
78 JTg 75.00
79 JTg,AW,The Legion of the Lost 75.00
80 Fall of a Hero 75.00
81 thru 85. . . . . @75.00
86 JK,O:Rawhide Kid retold. 80.00
87 thru 89 . . . . @100.00
90 Kid Colt 110.00
91 . . . . 35.00
92 & 93 giants . . . . @50.00
94 thru 99. . . . . @60.00
100 O:Rawhide Kid retold 50.00
101 thru 124. . . . . @35.00
125 JDa 40.00
126 thru 151 . . . . @35.00

RAWHIDE KID
Aug., 1985
1 JSe,mini-series 6.00
2 thru 4 . . . . @5.00

RAWHIDE KID
Marvel Max, Feb., 2003
1 (of 5) JSe. 3.00

2 thru 5 JSe. . . . . @3.00
3 JSe. 3.00
4 JSe. 3.00
5 JSe,concl. 3.00
TPB 13.00

RAZORLINE FIRST CUT
1993
1 Intro Razorline 2.25

REAL EXPERIENCES
See: TESSIE THE TYPIST

RED RAVEN
See: HUMAN TORCH

RED SONJA
[1st Series] Jan., 1977
1 FT,O:Red Sonja,Blood of the
  Unicorn 22.00
2 FT,Demon of the Maze 10.00
3 FT,The Games of Gita 10.00
4 FT,The Lake of the Unknown . . 10.00
5 FT,Master of the Bells 10.00
6 FT,The Singing Tower 10.00
7 FT,Throne of Blood 10.00
8 FT,Vengeance o/t Golden Circle 10.00
9 FT,Chariot o/t Fire-Stallions . . . 10.00
10 FT,Red Lace,pt.1 . . . . 10.00
11 FT,Red Lace,pt.2. . . . . 9.00
12 JB/JRu,Ashes & Emblems 9.00
13 JB/AM,Shall Skranos Fall 9.00
14 SB/AM,Evening on the Border . . 9.00
15 JB/TD,Tomb of 3 Dead Kings
  May, 1979 . . . . 9.00
[2nd Series] Feb., 1983
1 TD,GC, The Blood That Binds . . 4.00
2 GC, March,1983 . . . . 4.00
[3rd Series] Aug., 1983
1 . . . . 3.00
2 thru 13 . . . . @3.00
1 movie adaption, 1985 . . . . 2.50
2 movie adaption, 1985 . . . . 2.50

RED SONJA
1-shot Bros.Hildebrandt(c),48-pg. . . 3.00

RED WARRIOR
Atlas, Jan.–Dec., 1951
1 GT,Indian Tales 200.00
2 GT(c),The Trail of the Outcast 125.00
3 The Great Spirit Speaks 100.00
4 O:White Wing 100.00
5 . . . . 100.00
6 JMn(c) final issue. 100.00

RED WOLF
May, 1972–Sept., 1973
1 SSh(c),GK,JSe,F:Red Wolf
  & Lobo 35.00
2 GK(c),SSh,Day of the Dynamite
  Doom 20.00
3 SSh,War of the Wolf Brothers . 20.00
4 SSh,V:Man-Bear 20.00
5 GK(c),SSh 20.00
6 SSh,JA,V:Devil Rider 20.00
7 SSh,JA,Echoes from a Golden
  Grave 20.00
8 SSh,Hell on Wheels 20.00
9 DAy,To Die Again,O:Lobo 20.00

REN AND STIMPY SHOW
1992–96
1 Polybagged w/Air Fowlers,
  Ren(c) 5.00
1a Stimpy(c) 4.00
1b 2nd Printing 3.00
1c 3rd Printing. 2.00

MARVEL

2 Frankenstimpy	3.00
2a 2nd Printing	2.00
3 Christmas issue	3.00
3a 2nd Printing	2.00
4 thru 12	@3.00
13 Halloween issue	2.50
14 Mars needs Vecro	2.50
15 thru 24	@2.25
25 regular (c)	2.25
25a die-cut(c),A new addition	3.00
26 thru 42	@2.25
Spec.#1	3.25
Spec.#2	3.25
Spec.#3 Powder Toast Man	3.25
Spec.#4	3.25
Spec.#5 Virtual Stupidity	3.25
Spec.#6 History of Music	3.25
Holiday Special	3.00
Spec. Radio Dazed & Confused	2.50
Spec. Around the World in a Daze	3.00
TPB Running Joke,rep.	13.25
TPB Pick of the Litter	13.25
TPB Tastes Like Chicken	13.25
TPB Your Pals	13.00
TPB Seech Little Monkeys	13.00

RETURN OF THE JEDI

1 AW,movie adapt.	3.00
2 AW,movie adapt.	3.00
3 AW,movie adapt.	3.00
4 AW,movie adapt.	3.00

REX HART
See: BLAZE CARSON

RICHIE RICH

1 Movie Adaptation	3.00

RINGO KID

[2nd Series] Jan., 1970

1 AW,Reprints	35.00
2 JSe,Man Trap	22.00
3 JR,Man from the Panhandle	22.00
4 HT(c),The Golden Spur	22.00
5 JMn,Ambush	22.00
6 Capture or Death	22.00
7 HT(c),JSe,JA,Terrible Treasure of Vista Del Oro	22.00
8 The End of the Trail	22.00
9 JSe,Mystery of the Black Sunset	22.00
10 Bad day at Black Creek	22.00
11 Bullet for a Bandit	22.00
12 A Badge to Die For	30.00
13 DW,Hostage at Fort Cheyenne	15.00
14 Showdown in the Silver Cartwheel	15.00
15 Fang,Claw, and Six-Gun	15.00
16 Battle of Cattleman's Bank	15.00
17 Gundown at the Hacienda	15.00
18	15.00
19 Thunder From the West	15.00
20 AW	15.00
21 thru 29	@15.00
30 Nov., 1973	15.00

RINGO KID WESTERN

Atlas, Aug., 1954

1 JMn,JSt,O:Ringo Kid, B:Ringo Kid	350.00
2 JMn,I&O:Arab,A:Black Rider	200.00
3 JMn	125.00
4 JMn	125.00
5 JMn	125.00
6	125.00
7	125.00
8 JSe	125.00
9	100.00
10 JSe(c),AW	125.00
11 JSe(c)	100.00
12 JO	100.00

Ringo Kid #8
© Marvel Entertainment Group

13 AW	125.00
14 thru 20	@100.00
21 Sept., 1957	100.00

RIOT

Marvel Atlas, 1954–56

1 RH,MMe,GC,BEv	400.00
2 MMe,Li'l Abner	275.00
3 MMe(c)	250.00
4 JSe,MMe,BEv,Marilyn Monroe	300.00
5 JSe,MMe,BEv,Marilyn Monroe	325.00
6 MMe,JSe	250.00

ROBOCOP

March, 1990

1 LS,I:Nixcops	6.00
2 LS,V:Nixcops	4.00
3 LS	3.00
4 LS	3.00
5 LS,WarzonePt1	3.00
6 LS,WarzonePt2	3.00
7 thru 10 LS	@2.50
11 HT	2.50
12 thru 23	@2.50
Robocop Movie Adapt	5.00
Robocop II Movie Adapt	5.00

ROBOCOP II

Aug., 1990

1 MBa,rep.Movie Adapt	2.50
2 and 3 MBa,rep.Movie adapt.	@2.50

ROBOTIX

Feb., 1986

1 Based on toys	3.00

ROCKET RACCOON

May, 1985—Aug., 1985

1 thru 4 MM	@3.00

ROCKO'S MODERN LIFE

1994

1 and 2	@2.25
3 and 4	@2.25

ROGUE

1995

1 Enhanced cover	4.50
2 A:Gambit	4.00
3 Gamtit or Rogue?	3.00
4 final issue	3.00

ROGUE

Aug., 2001

1 (of 4) AaL,RyE,	2.50
2 AaL,RyE	2.50
3 AaL,RyE, leaves school	2.50
4 AaL,RyE,JuB(c)	2.50

ROGUE

July, 2004

1 Going Rogue,pt.1	3.00
2 Going Rogue,pt.2	3.00
3 Going Rogue,pt.3	3.00
4 Going Rogue,pt.4	3.00
5 Going Rogue,pt.5	3.00
6 Going Rogue,pt.6	3.00
7 Forget-Me-Not	3.00
8 Forget-Me-Not,A:Sunfire	3.00
9 Forget-Me-Not	3.00
10 Forget-Me-Not,V:Lady Deathstrike	3.00
11 Forget-Me-Not	3.00
12 Forget-Me-Not, concl.	3.00
TPB Going Rogue	15.00
TPB Forget-Me-Not	15.00

ROM

Dec., 1979

1 SB,I&O:Rom	15.00
2 thru 16	@5.00
17 SB,A:X-Men	10.00
18 SB,A:X-Men	10.00
19 thru 23	@5.00
24 thru 27	@7.00
28 thru 30	@4.00
31 thru 49	@3.00
50 SB,D:Torpedo,V:Skrulls	4.00
51 thru 55	@3.00
56 A:Alpha Flight	3.00
57 A:Alpha Flight	3.00
58 JG(c),A:Antman	3.00
59 SD,BL,V:Microbe Menace	3.00
60 SD,TP,V:Dire Wraiths	3.00
61thru 74	@2.50
75 SD,CR,Doublesize,last issue	7.00
Ann.#1 PB,A:Stardust	3.00
Ann.#2 I:Knights of Galador	3.00
Ann.#3 A:New Mutants	3.00
Ann.#4 V:Gladiator	3.00

ROMANCE DIARY

Dec., 1949

1	175.00
2 March, 1950	150.00

THE ROMANCES OF NURSE HELEN GRANT

Marvel Atlas, 1957

1	100.00

ROMANCES OF THE WEST

Nov., 1949

1 Ph(c),Calamity Jane, Sam Bass	300.00
2 March, 1950	175.00

ROMANCE TALES

Oct., 1949

(no #1 thru 6)

7	150.00
8	100.00
9 March, 1950	100.00

ROMANTIC AFFAIRS
See: MOLLY MANTON'S
ROMANCES

All comics prices listed are for *Near Mint* condition.

MARVEL

ROYAL ROY
Star, May, 1985
1 thru 5 . . . . @3.00
6 March, 1986 . . . . 3.00

Rugged Action #1
© Marvel Entertainment Group

RUGGED ACTION
Atlas, Dec., 1954
1 AyB,Man-Eater 150.00
2 JSe,DAy,JMn(c),Manta-Ray . . 100.00
3 DAy,JMn(c) 100.00
4 . . . . 100.00
Becomes:

STRANGE STORIES OF SUSPENSE
5 RH,JMn(c),Little Black Box . . . 500.00
6 BEv,The Illusion 300.00
7 JSe(c),BEv,Old John's House . 325.00
8 AW,BP,TYhumbs Down 325.00
9 BEv(c),Nightmare 350.00
10 RC,MME,AT 350.00
11 BEv(c) 225.00
12 AT 225.00
13 BEv,GM. 225.00
14 AW 250.00
15 BK 250.00
16 MF,BP, Aug., 1957 . . . . 250.00

RUINS
1995
1 Marvel's Alterverse 5.00
2 Fully painted, 32-pg. 5.00

RUNAWAYS
April, 2003
1 Pride & Joy, pt.1 . . . . 11.00
2 Pride & Joy, pt.2 . . . . 6.00
3 Pride & Joy, pt.3 . . . . 3.50
4 Pride & Joy, pt.4 . . . . 3.50
5 Pride & Joy, pt.5 . . . . 3.50
6 Pride & Joy, pt.6 . . . . 3.50
7 Teenage Wasteland,pt.1 . . . . . . 3.00
8 Teenage Wasteland,pt.2 . . . . . . 3.00
9 Teenage Wasteland,pt.3 . . . . . . 3.00
10 Teenage Wasteland,pt.4 . . . . . 3.00
11 Lost & Found,pt.1 . . . . 3.00
12 Lost & Found,pt.2 . . . . 3.00
13 thru 17 The Good Die Young . @3.00
18 Season Finale 3.00
TPB Vol. 1 Runaways: Pride & Joy 15.00
Spec Runaways/Sentinel flip book . 4.00

Digest Marvel Age, Vol. 1 . . . . 8.00
Digest Vol. 2:Teenage Wasteland . . 8.00
Digest Vol. 3: Good Die Young 8.00

RUNAWAYS
Feb., 2005
1 True Believers, pt.1 . . . . 5.00
2 True Believers, Pt.2 . . . . 5.00
3 True Believers, pt.3 . . . . 3.00
4 True Believers, pt.4 . . . . 3.00
5 True Believers, Pt.5 . . . . 3.00
6 True Believers, pt.6 . . . . 3.00
7 Sinister plan, Part 1 . . . . 3.00
8 Sinister Plan, Part 2. . . . . 3.00
9 East Coast/West Coast 3.00
10 East Coast/West Coast. 3.00
11 East Coast/West Coast. 3.00
12 East Coast/West Coast. 3.00
13 Molly Hayes alone 3.00
14 Parental Guidance,pt.1 . . . . 3.00
15 Parental Guidance,pt.2 . . . . 3.00
16 Parental Guidance,pt.3 . . . . 3.00
17 Parental Guidance,pt.4 . . . . 3.00
18 Parental Guidance,pt.5 . . . . 3.00
19 Dead Means Dead,pt.1 . . . . 3.00
20 Dead Means Dead,pt.2 . . . . 3.00
21 Dead Means Dead,pt.3 . . . . 3.00
22 Live Fast, pt.1 . . . . 3.00
Digest, Vol. 4 True Believers, rep. . . 8.00
Digest, Vol. 5 Escape to New York . 8.00
Digest, Vol. 6 Parental Guidance . . 8.00

RUSTY COMICS
See: KID KOMICS

SABLE & FORTUNE
Jan., 2006
1 F:Silver Sable & Dominic Fortune 3.00
2 thru 4 . . . . @3.00

SABRETOOTH
[Limited Series] 1993
1 B:LHa(s),MT,A:Wolverine 5.00
2 MT,A:Mystique,C:Wolverine. . . . 4.00
3 MT,A:Mystique,Wolverine 4.00
4 E:LHa(s),MT,D:Birdy 4.00
TPB rep. #1-#4 . . . . 13.00

SABRETOOTH
Oct., 2004
1 (of 5) BS,F:Sasquatch 3.00
2 thru 4 BS,F:Sasquatch . . . . . . @3.00
TPB Open Season. 10.00

SABRETOOTH CLASSICS
1994–95
1 rep. Power Man/Iron Fist #66 . . . 4.00
2 rep. Power Man/Iron Fist #78 . . . 3.00
3 rep. Power Man/Iron Fist #84 . . . 3.00
4 rep. Spider-Man #116 . . . . 3.00
5 rep. Spider-Man #119 . . . . 3.00
6 reprints 3.00
7 reprints 3.00
8 reprints 3.00
9 reprints 3.00
10 Morlock Massacre. 3.00
11 rep. Daredevil #238. . . . . 3.00
12 rep. V:Wolverine 3.00
13 rep. 3.00
14 A:Mauraders 3.00
15 Mutant Massacre, rep.
   Uncanny X-Men #221 . . . . 3.00

SABRETOOTH
Spec.#1 FaN, cont.from X-Men#48 . 5.00

SABRETOOTH
Oct., 1997
1-shot,F:Wildchild 2.50

Sabretooth Classics #1
© Marvel Entertainment Group

SABRETOOTH & MYSTIQUE
1 JGz,AOl, ... 2.50
2 thru 4 JGz,AOl . . . . @2.50

SABRETOOTH: MARY SHELLEY OVERDRIVE
June, 2002
1 (of 4) F:Creed 3.00
2 TyH 3.00
3 . . . . 3.00
4 TyH 3.00

SACHS & VIOLENS
Epic, 1993–94
1 GP,PDd(s) 3.00
2 GP,PDd(s),V:Killer 2.50
3 GP,PDd(s),V:White Slavers 2.50
4 GP,PDd(s),D:Moloch 2.50

SAGA OF CRYSTAR
May, 1983
1 O:Crystar 5.00
2 A:Ika 4.00
3 A:Dr.Strange. 4.00
4 . . . . 4.00
5 . . . . 4.00
6 A:Nightcrawler 4.00
7 I:Malachon 4.00
8 . . . . 4.00
9 . . . . 4.00
10 Chaos 4.00
11 Alpha Flight,Feb., 1985 . . . . . . 4.00

SAGA OF ORIGINAL HUMAN TORCH
1 RB,O:Original Human Torch 3.00
2 RB,A:Toro 2.50
3 RB,V:Adolph Hitler. 2.50
4 RB,Torch vs. Toro 2.50

ST. GEORGE
Epic, June, 1988
1 KJ,Shadow Line. 2.25
2 thru 8 . . . . @2.25

SAINT SINNER
Razorline 1993–94
1 I:Phillip Fetter. 2.75
2 thru 8 . . . . @2.25

SAM & MAX
GO TO THE MOON
1 Dirtbag Special,w/Nirvana Tape. . 4.00
[Regular Series]
1 MMi,AAd,F:Skull Boy 3.25
2 AAd,MMi 3.25
3 . . . . 3.25

SAMURAI CAT
Epic, 1991
1 I:MiaowaraTomokato 2.25
2 I:Con-Ed,V:Thpaghetti-Thoth 2.25
3 EmpireStateStrikesBack 2.25

SATANA
Nov., 1997
1 JaL,WEI,AOI,V:Doctor Strange,
   non-code series 3.00
2 WEI,AOI,to the gates of Hell 3.00

SAVAGE SWORD
OF CONAN
Aug., 1974
(black & white magazine)
1 BWS,JB,NA,GK,O:Blackmark,
   3rdA:Red Sonja,Boris(c) 150.00
2 NA(c),HC,GK,Black Colossus,
   B.U.King Kull;B.U.Blackmark . 65.00
3 JB,BWS,GK,At The Mountain
   of the Moon God;B.U.s:
   Kull;Blackmark 50.00
4 JB,RCo,GK,Iron Shadows in the
   Moon B.U.Blackmark,Boris(c) . 40.00
5 JB,Witch Shall be Born,Boris(c) 30.00
6 AN,Sleeper'Neath the Sands . . 30.00
7 JB,Citadel at the Center
   of Time Boris(c) 30.00
8 inc.GK,Corsairs against Stygia . 30.00
9 Curse of the Cat-Goddess,
   Boris(c),B.U.King Kull 30.00
10 JB,Sacred Serpent of Set
   Boris(c) 30.00
11 JB,The Abode of the Damned. . 20.00
12 JB,Haunters of Castle Crimson
   Boris(c) 20.00
13 GK,The Thing in the Temple,
   B.U. Solomon Kane 20.00
14 NA,Shadow of Zamboula,
   B.U.Solomon Kane 20.00
15 JB,Boris(c),Devil in Iron 20.00
16 JB,BWS,People of the Black
   Circle,B.U.Bran Mak Morn. . . . 20.00
17 JB,On to Yimsha!,
   B.U.Bran Mak Morn 20.00
18 JB,The Battle of the Towers
   B.U. Solomon Kane 20.00
19 JB,Vengeance in Vendhya
   B.U. Solomon Kane 20.00
20 JB,The Slithering Shadow
   B.U. Solomon Kane 18.00
21 JB,Horror in the Red Tower . . . 18.00
22 JB,Pool o/t Black One
   B.U. Solomon Kane 18.00
23 JB,FT,Torrent of Doom
   B.U. Solomon Kane 18.00
24 JB,BWS,Tower of the
   Elephant,B.U.Cimmeria 18.00
25 DG,SG,Jewels of Gwahlur,
   B.U.Solomon Kane 18.00
26 JB/TD,Beyond the Black River,
   B.U.Solomon Kane 18.00
27 JB/TD,Children of Jhebbal Sag 18.00
28 JB/AA,Blood of the Gods 18.00
29 ECh,FT,Child of Sorcery,
   B.U. Red Sonja 18.00
30 FB,The Scarlet Citadel 18.00
31 JB/TD,The Flaming Knife,pt.1 . . 15.00
32 JB/TD,Ghouls of Yanaldar,pt.2 . 15.00

Savage Sword of Conan #12
© Marvel Entertainment Group

33 GC,Curse of the Monolith,
   B.U.Solomon Kane 15.00
34 CI/AA,MP,Lair o/t Ice Worm;B.U.
   Solomon Kane,B.U.King Kull. . 15.00
35 ECh,Black Tears 15.00
36 JB,AA,Hawks over Shem 15.00
37 SB,Sons of the White Wolf
   B.U. Solomon Kane 15.00
38 JB/TD,The Road of the Eagles. 15.00
39 SB/TD,The Legions of the Dead,
   B.U.Solomon Kane concl. 15.00
40 JB/TD,A Dream of Blood 15.00
41 JB/TD,Quest for the Cobra Crown
   A:Thoth-Amon,B.U.Sol.Kane . . 15.00
42 JB/TD,Devil-Tree of Gamburu,
   A:Thoth-Amon,B.U.Sol.Kane. . 15.00
43 JB/TD,King Thoth-Amon,
   B.U.King Kull 15.00
44 SB/TD,The Star of Khorala 15.00
45 JB/TD,The Gem in the Tower,
   B.U. Red Sonja 15.00
46 EC/TD,Moon of Blood,
   B.U. Hyborian Tale 15.00
47 GK/JB/JRu,Treasure of Tranicos
   C:Thoth-Amon 15.00
48 JB/KJ,A Wind Blows from Stygia
   C:Thoth-Amon 15.00
49 JB/TD,When Madness Wears the
   Crown, B.U.Hyborian Tale. . . . 15.00
50 JB/TD,Swords Across the
   Alimane 18.00
51 JB/TD,Satyrs' Blood 10.00
52 JB/TD,Conan the Liberator. . . . 10.00
53 JB,The Sorcerer and the Soul,
   B.U. Solomon Kane 10.00
54 JB,The Stalker Amid the Sands,
   B.U. Solomon Kane 10.00
55 JB,Black Lotus & Yellow Death
   B.U. King Kull 10.00
56 JB/TD,The Sword of Skelos . . . 10.00
57 JB/TD,Zamboula. 10.00
58 JB/TD,KGa,For the Throne of
   Zamboula,B.U.OlgerdVladislav 10.00
59 AA,ECh,City ofSkulls,B.U.Gault 10.00
60 JB,The Ivory Goddess 10.00
61 JB,Wizard Fiend of Zingara . . . 10.00
62 JB/ECh,Temple of the Tiger,
   B.U. Solomon Kane 10.00
63 JB/ECh,TP/BMc,GK,Moat of Blood
   I:Chane of the Elder Earth. . . . 10.00
64 JB/ECh,GK,Children of Rhan,
   B.U. Chane 10.00
65 GK,JB,Fangs of the Serpent,
   B.U. Bront 10.00
66 thru 80 . . . . @10.00

81 JB/ECh,Palace of Pleasure,
   B.U. Bront 10.00
82 AA,BWS,Devil in the Dark.Pt.1
   B.U.repConan#24,Swamp Gas 10.00
83 AA,MW,NA,ECh,Devil in the Dark
   Pt.2,B.U. Red Sonja,Sol.Kane. 10.00
84 VM,Darksome Demon of
   Rabba Than 10.00
85 GK,Daughter of the God King. . 10.00
86 GK,Revenge of the Sorcerer . . 10.00
87 . . . . 10.00
88 JB,Isle of the Hunter 10.00
89 AA,MW,Gamesman of Asgalun,
   B.U. Rite of Blood 10.00
90 JB,Devourer of Souls 10.00
91 JB,VM,Forest of Friends,
   B.U. The Beast,The Chain . . . 10.00
92 JB,The Jeweled Bird. 10.00
93 JB/ECh,WorldBeyond the Mists 10.00
94 thru 101 . . . . @10.00
102 thru 161 . . . . @8.00
162 thru 175 . . . . @7.00
176 thru 235 . . . . @5.00
Ann.#1 SB,BWS,inc.Beware the
   Wrath of Anu,B.U. King
   Kull Vs.Thulsa Doom 5.00

SAVAGE TALES
May, 1971
(black & white magazine)
1 GM,BWS,JR,I&O:Man-Thing,
   B:Conan,Femizons,A:Ka-Zar 275.00
2 GM,FB,BWS,AW,BWr,A:King
   Kull rep,Creatures on
   the Loose #10 . . . . 90.00
3 FB,BWS,AW,JSo 60.00
4 NA(c),E:Conan 50.00
5 JSn,JB,B:Brak the Barbarian . . 50.00
6 NA(c),JB,AW,B:Ka-Zar 35.00
7 GM,NA 30.00
8 JB,A:Shanna,E:Brak 30.00
9 MK,A:Shanna 30.00
10 RH,NA,AW,A:Shanna 30.00
11 RH 30.00
12 Summer, 1975 . . . . 30.00
Ann.#1 GM,GK,BWS,O:Ka-Zar . . 30.00

SAVAGE TALES
Nov., 1985–March, 1987
(black & white magazine)
1 MGo,I:The `Nam 6.00
2 thru 9 MGo . . . . @4.00

SCARLET SPIDER
1995–96
1 HMe,GK,TP,VirtualMortality,pt.3 . 2.25
2 HMe,JR2,AW,CyberWar,pt.3 . . . 2.25
3 and 4 HMe . . . . @2.25

SCARLET SPIDER
UNLIMITED
1995
1 True Origin,64-pg. 4.50

SCARLET WITCH
1994
1 ALa(s),DAn(s),JH,I:Gargan,
   C:Master Pandemonium 2.25
2 C:Avengers West Coast. 2.25
3 A:Avengers West Coast. 2.25
4 V:Lore,last issue 2.25

SCOOBY-DOO
Oct., 1977
1 B:DynoMutt 40.00
2 thru 9 Feb., 1979 . . . . @30.00

All comics prices listed are for *Near Mint* condition.

SECRET DEFENDERS
1993–95

1 F:Dr.Strange(in all),Spider
  Woman,Nomad,Darkhawk,
  Wolverine,V:Macabre 3.25
2 F:Spider Woman,Nomad,Darkhawk,
  Wolverine,V:Macabre 2.50
3 F:Spider Woman,Nomad,Darkhawk,
  Wolverine,V:Macabre 2.25
4 F:Namorita,Punisher,
  Sleepwalker,V:Roadkill 2.25
5 F:Naromita,Punisher,
  Sleepwalker, V:Roadkill. 2.25
6 F:Spider-Man,Scarlet Witch,Captain
  America,V:Suicide Pack 2.25
7 F:Captain America,Scarlet Witch,
  Spider-Man 2.25
8 F:Captain America,Scarlet Witch,
  Spider-Man 2.25
9 F:War Machine,Thunderstrike,
  Silver Surfer. 2.25
10 F:War Machine,Thunderstrike,
  Silver Surfer. 2.25
11 TGb,F:Hulk,Nova,Northstar. . . 2.25
12 RMz(s),TGb,F:Thanos 2.75
13 RMz(s),TGb,F:Thanos,Super Skull,
  Rhino,Nitro,Titanium Man 2.25
14 RMz(s),TGb,F:Thanos,Super Skull,
  Rhino,Nitro,Titanium Man,
  A:Silver Surfer. 2.25
15 thru 17 F:Dr.Druid,Cage,
  Deadpool 2.25
18 F:Iron Fist,Giant Man 2.25
19 F:Dr.Druid,Cadaver,
  Shadowoman. 2.25
20 V:Venom 2.25
21 V:Slaymaker 2.25
22 thru 24 Final Defense,pt.1–pt.2@2.25
25 V:Dr.Druid 2.25

SECRET STORY ROMANCES
Marvel Atlas, 1953

1 BEv 175.00
2 . . . . 125.00
3 thru 9 . . . . @100.00
10 thru 21 ViC (in many) . . . . . @100.00

SECRET WAR
Feb., 2004

Book One BMB 10.00
Book One, Commemorative ed. . . . 6.00
Book Two BMB 5.00
Book Three BMB 4.00

SECRET WAR
2005

1 (of 5) BMB, 48-pg. 4.00
2 thru 5 BMB, 48-pg. 4.00
Spec. From the Files of Nick Fury . . 4.00

SECRET WARS
May, 1984

1 MZ,A:X-Men,Fant.Four,Avengers,
  Hulk,SpM in All,I:Beyonder 7.00
2 MZ,V:Magneto 6.00
3 MZ,I:Titania & Volcana. 6.00
4 BL,V:Molecule Man 6.00
5 BL,F:X-Men 6.00
6 MZ,V:Doctor Doom 6.00
7 MZ,I:New Spiderwoman. 7.00
8 MZ,I:Alien Black Costume
  (for Spider-Man) 25.00
9 MZ,V:Galactus 5.00
10 MZ,V:Dr.Doom 5.00
11 MZ,V:Dr.Doom. 5.00
12 MZ,Beyonder Vs. Dr.Doom. 7.00
TPB rep #1–#12 . . . . 20.00
TPB rep. 12 issues, 336-pg. 25.00

Secret Wars II #1
© Marvel Entertainment Group

SECRET WARS II
July, 1985

1 AM,SL,A:X-Men,New Mutants . . . 5.00
2 AM,SL,A:Fantastic Four. 3.00
3 AM,SL,A:Daredevil. 3.00
4 AM,I:Kurse 3.00
5 AM,SL,I:Boom Boom 3.50
6 AM,SL,A:Mephisto 3.00
7 AM,SL,A:Thing. 3.00
8 AM,SL,A:Hulk. 3.00
9 AM,SL,A:Everyone,double-size . . 5.00

SECTAURS
June, 1985

1 Based on toys 3.00
2 . . . . 3.00
3 . . . . 3.00
4 . . . . 3.00
5 thru 10 1986. . . . . @3.00

SEEKER 3000
April, 1998

1 (of 4) DAn,IEd,sci-fi adventure,
  48-pg. 3.00
2 DAn,IEd,encounter with aliens . . 3.00
3 DAn,IEd,V:Hkkkt. 3.00
4 DAn,IEd,V:Hkkkt, concl. 3.00

SEMPER FI
Dec., 1988

1 JSe. 2.50
2 JSe. 2.50
3 JSe. 2.50
4 JSe. 2.50
5 JSe. 2.50
6 and 8 . . . . @2.50
9 Aug., 1989,final issue 2.50

SENSATIONAL SPIDER-MAN

1 KM/TP/KJ,rep. (1989) 6.00

SENSATIONAL SPIDER-MAN
Jan., 1996

0 DJu,KJ,Return of Spider-Man,pt.1
  Lenticular cover. 6.00
1 DJu,KJ,Media Blizzard,pt.1,
  V:New Mysterio 5.00
2 DJu,KJ,Return of Kaine,pt.2 . . . . 4.00
3 DJu,KJ,Web of Carnage,pt.1 . . . . 4.00
4 DJu,KJ,Blood Brothers,pt.1 . . . . . 4.00

5 DJu 4.00
6 DJu 3.00
7 TDz,A:Onslaught 3.00
8 TDz,The Looter 3.00
9 TDz,Onslaught tie-in 3.00
10 TDz,RCa,V:Swarm 3.00
11 TDz,Revelations, pt.2 . . . . 3.00
11A bagged with card, etc. 5.00
12 TDz,SwM, V:Trapster 3.00
13 TDz,RCa,A:Ka-Zar, Shanna 3.00
14 TDz,RCa,Savage Land saga . . . 3.00
15 TDz,RCa,Savage Land saga . . . 3.00
16 TDz,RCa,R:Black Cat,
  V:Prowler,Vulture 3.00
17 TDz,RCa,V:Black Cat,
  Prowler,Vulture 3.00
18 TDz,RCa,V:Vulture 3.00
19 TDz,RCa,R:Living Monolith 2.50
20 TDz,RCa,Living Pharoah, concl.. 2.50
21 TDz,RCa,Techomancers. 2.50
22 TDz,RCa,A:Doctor Strange. 2.50
23 TDz,RCa,A:Doctor Strange. 2.50
24 TDz,RCa,A:S.H.I.E.L.D., Looter . 3.00
25 TDz,RCa,Spider-Hunt,pt1 x-over 4.00
26 TDz,RCa,JoB,Identity Crisis
  prelude. 2.50
27 TDz,RCa,MeW,Identity Crisis,
  as Hornet V:Phaeton 2.50
28 TDz,RCa,as Hornet, V:Vulture . . 2.50
29 TDz,RCa,V:Arcade, Black Cat . . 2.50
30 TDz,A:Black Cat,V:Arcade 2.50
31 TDz,MeW,RCa,V:Rhino 2.50
32 TDz,JoB,The Gathering of the
  Five, pt.1 (of 5) 2.50
33 TDz,JoB,Gathering of
  the Five,pt.5. . . . . 2.50
Minus 1 Spec.,TDz,RCa, flashback. 3.00
TPB In the Savage Land, rep. 6.00
TPB Sensational Spider-Man '96
  seq. to Kraven's Last Hunt . . . 3.00

SENSATIONAL SPIDER-MAN
See: MARVEL KNIGHTS SPIDER-MAN

SENTINEL
April, 2003

1 Salvage,pt.1. . . . . 3.00
2 Salvage,pt.2. . . . . 3.00
3 Salvage,pt.3. . . . . 3.00
4 Salvage,pt.4. . . . . 3.00
5 Salvage,pt.5. . . . . 2.50
6 Salvage,pt.6. . . . . 2.50
7 No Hero,pt.1 . . . . 2.50
8 No Hero,pt.2 . . . . 2.50
9 No Hero,pt.3 . . . . 2.50
10 Awakening,pt.1 . . . . 3.00
11 Awakening,pt.2 . . . . 3.00
12 Awakening,pt.3 . . . . 3.00
TPB Sentinel: Salvage, Vol. 1 . . . . 20.00
Digest Vol. 1 Marvel Age 8.00
Digest Vol. 2 No Hero 8.00

SENTINEL
Nov., 2005

1 V:Stealth Sentinel 3.00
2 thru 5 . . . . @3.00
Digest Past Imperfect 8.00

SENTINEL SQUAD O*N*E
Jan., 2006

1 Decimation tie-in 3.00
2 thru 5 . . . . @3.00

SENTRY
July, 2000

1 (of 5) PJe,JaL 20.00
2 PJe,JaL,Unicorn 10.00
3 PJe,JaL,Hulk,Spider-Man 10.00
4 PJe,JaL,Prof.X. 10.00

MARVEL

5 PJe,JaL.................. 10.00
TPB The Sentry, JaL........... 25.00
Spec.#1 Sentry vs. The Void,
  JaL,PJe (2001) 20.00

SENTRY, THE
Sept., 2005

1 JR2,V:Hords of Attuma 3.00
1a Rough Cut, Jr2 .... 4.00
2 thru 8 JR2 .... @3.00
TPB Sentry Reborn 22.00

SERGEANT BARNEY BARKER
Aug., 1956

1 JSe,Comedy 250.00
2 JSe,Army Inspection(c) 150.00
3 JSe,Tank(c) 150.00
Becomes:

G.I. TALES

4 JSe,At Grips with the Enemy . 125.00
5 .... 100.00
6 JO,BP,GWb, July, 1957 ..... 100.00

SGT. FURY & HIS HOWLING COMMANDOS
May, 1963–Dec., 1981

1 Seven Against the Nazis . . 3,000.00
2 JK,Seven Doomed Men 750.00
3 JK,Midnight on Massacre
  Mountain 400.00
4 JK,V:Lord Ha-Ha,D:Junior
  Juniper 400.00
5 JK,V:Baron Strucker 400.00
6 JK,The Fangs of the Fox 250.00
7 JK,Fury Court Martial 250.00
8 JK,V:Dr Zemo,I:Percival
  Pinkerton 250.00
9 DAy,V:Hitler 250.00
10 DAy,On to Okinawa,I:Capt.
  Savage 250.00
11 DAy,V:Capt.Flint 125.00
12 DAy,Howler deserts 125.00
13 DAy,JK,A:Capt.America 650.00
14 DAy,V:Baron Strucker 125.00
15 DAy,SD,Too Small to Fight
  Too Young to Die......... 125.00
16 DAy,In The Desert a Fortress
  Stands 125.00
17 DAy,While the Jungle Sleeps . 125.00
18 DAy,Killed in Action........ 125.00
19 DAy,An Eye for an Eye...... 125.00
20 DAy,V:the Blitz Squad 125.00

Sgt. Fury and His Howling Commandos
#26 © Marvel EntertainmEnt Group

21 DAy,To Free a Hostage...... 100.00
22 DAy,V:Bull McGiveney 100.00
23 DAy,The Man who Failed ... 100.00
24 DAy,When the Howlers Hit
  the Home Front........... 100.00
25 DAy,Every Man my Enemy... 100.00
26 DAy,Dum Dum Does it the
  Hard Way................ 100.00
27 DAy,O:Fury's Eyepatch...... 100.00
28 DAy,Not a Man Shall Remain
  Alive................... 100.00
29 DAy,V:Baron Strucker....... 100.00
30 DAy,Incident in Italy 100.00
31 DAy,Into the Jaws of Death . 100.00
32 DAy,A Traitor in Our Midst ... 100.00
33 DAy,The Grandeur That was
  Greece.................. 100.00
34 DAy,O:Howling Commandoes . 75.00
35 DAy,Berlin Breakout,J:Eric
  Koenig.................. 75.00
36 DAy,My Brother My Enemy.... 75.00
37 DAy,In the Desert to Die..... 75.00
38 This Ones For Dino 75.00
39 Into the Fortress of Fear..... 75.00
40 That France Might be Free ... 75.00
41 V:The Blitzers 75.00
42 Three Were AWOL 75.00
43 Scourge of the Sahara,A:Bob
  Hope,Glen Miller 75.00
44 JSe,The Howlers First Mission. 75.00
45 JSe,I:The War Lover 75.00
46 JSe,They Also Serve 75.00
47 Tea and Sabotage......... 75.00
48 A:Blitz Squad 75.00
49 On to Tarawa 75.00
50 The Invasion Begins 75.00
51 The Assassin 75.00
52 Triumph at Treblinka........ 75.00
53 To the Bastions of Bavaria ... 75.00
54 Izzy Shoots the Works 75.00
55 Cry of Battle, Kiss of Death .. 50.00
56 Gabriel Blow Your Horn 50.00
57 TS,The Informer 50.00
58 Second Front 50.00
59 D-Day for Dum Dum........ 50.00
60 Authorised Personnel Only ... 50.00
61 The Big Breakout 50.00
62 The Basic Training of Fury ... 50.00
63 V:Nazi Tanks............. 50.00
64 The Peacemonger,A:Capt
  Savage 50.00
65 Eric Koenig,Traitor 50.00
66 Liberty Rides the Underground. 50.00
67 With a Little Help From My
  Friends................. 75.00
68 Welcome Home Soldier 50.00
69 While the City Sleeps 50.00
70 The Missouri Marauders 50.00
71 Burn,Bridge,Burn 50.00
72 Battle in the Sahara 50.00
73 Rampage on the
  Russian Front 50.00
74 Each Man Alone 50.00
75 The Deserter............. 35.00
76 He Fought the Red Baron..... 35.00
77 A Traitor's Trap,A:Eric Koenig.. 35.00
78 Escape or Die........... 35.00
79 Death in the High Castle...... 35.00
80 To Free a Hostage 35.00
81 The All American........... 35.00
82 Howlers Hit The
  Home Front,rep 25.00
83 Dum DumV:Man-Mountain
  McCoy 25.00
84 The Devil's Disciple 25.00
85 Fury V:The Howlers 25.00
86 Germ Warfare.............. 25.00
87 Dum Dum does it...rep 25.00
88 Save General Patton 25.00
89 O:Fury's eyepatch,rep....... 25.00
90 The Chain That Binds 25.00
91 Not A Man...rep............. 25.00

92 Some Die Slowly, giant-sz..... 28.00
93 A Traitor...rep 20.00
94 GK(c),Who'll Stop the Bombs.. 20.00
95 7 Doomed Men, rep 20.00
96 GK(c),Dum-Dum Sees it
  Through.................. 20.00
97 Till the Last Man Shall Fail 20.00
98 A:Deadly Dozen 20.00
99 Guerillas in Greece.......... 20.00
100 When a Howler Falls 25.00
101 Pearl Harbor 18.00
102 Death For A Dollar 18.00
103 Berlin Breakout............ 18.00
104 The Tanks Are Coming 18.00
105 My Brother,My Enemy....... 18.00
106 Death on the Rhine......... 18.00
107 Death-Duel in the Desert 18.00
108 Slaughter From the Skies.... 18.00
109 This Ones For Dino,rep 18.00
110 JSe(c),The Reserve 18.00
111 V:Colonel Klaw 18.00
112 V:Baron Strucker 18.00
113 That France Might
  Be Free,rep............. 18.00
114 Jungle Bust Out 18.00
115 V:Baron Strucker.......... 18.00
116 End of the Road 18.00
117 Blitz Over Britain 18.00
118 War Machine............. 18.00
118 War Machine............. 18.00
119 They Strike by Machine...... 18.00
120 Trapped in the Compound of
  Death 18.00
121 An Eye for an Eye......... 12.00
122 A;The Blitz Squad.......... 12.00
123 To Free a Hostage 12.00
124 A:Bull McGiveney 12.00
125 The Man Who Failed 12.00
126 When the Howlers Hit Home.. 12.00
127 Everyman My Enemy,rep 12.00
128 Dum Dum does it...rep 12.00
129 O:Fury's Eyepatch......... 12.00
130 A:Baron Strucker 12.00
131 Armageddon 12.00
132 Incident in Italy 12.00
133 thru 140................ @12.00
141 thru 150................ @12.00
151 thru 167................ @12.00
Ann.#1 Korea #4,#5 .... 225.00
Ann.#2 This was D-Day........ 75.00
Ann.#3 Vietnam 45.00
Ann.#4 Battle of the Bulge....... 35.00
Ann.#5 Desert Fox........... 25.00
Ann.#6 Blaze of Battle.......... 25.00
Ann.#7 Armageddon 25.00

Sgt. Fury and His Howling Commandos
#126 © Marvel EntertainmEnt Group

SERGIO ARAGONES MASSACRES MARVEL
1996
1-shot Parody 5.00

SEVEN BLOCK
Epic, 1990
1 . . . . 2.50

SHADOWMASTERS
Oct., 1989–Jan., 1990
1 RH 7.00
2 . . . . 5.00
3 . . . . 4.00
4 . . . . 4.00

SHADOWRIDERS
1993
1 I:Shadowriders,A:Cable,
    Ghost Rider 3.00
2 A:Ghost Rider 2.50
3 A:Cable 2.50
4 A:Cable 2.50

SHADOWS & LIGHT
Dec., 1997
1 BSf,RMz,LWn,BWr,GeH,SD,B&W
    anthology series 3.00
2 JSn,LW,LSh,GK 3.00
3 BL,JSn 3.00
4 three new tales 3.00

SHANG-CHI: MASTER OF KUNG FU
Marvel Max, Sept., 2002
1 (of 6) DgM,PG 3.00
2 DgM,PG,JP 3.00
3 thru 6 PG,JP . . . . @3.00
TPB Vol. 1: Hellfire Apocalypse . . . 16.00

SHANNA, THE SHE-DEVIL
Dec., 1972–Aug., 1973
1 GT,F:Shanna 40.00
2 RA,The Dungeon of Doom 30.00
3 RA,The Hour of the Bull 20.00
4 RA,Mandrill 20.00
5 JR(c),RA,V:Nekra 20.00

SHANNA, THE SHE-DEVIL
Feb., 2005
1 (of 7) by Frank Cho 3.50
2 thru 7 . . . . @3.50
TPB Shanna, The She-Devil 17.00

SHEENA
Dec., 1984–Feb., 1985
1 and 2 Movie adapt . . . . @3.00

SHE-HULK
[1st Regular Series] Feb., 1980
1 JB,BWi,I&O:She-Hulk 15.00
2 BWi,D:She-Hulk's best friend . . . 7.00
3 BWi,Wanted for Murder 7.00
4 BWi,V:Her Father 7.00
5 BWi,V:Silver Serpent 7.00
6 A:Iron Man 5.00
7 BWi,A:Manthing 5.00
8 BWi,A:Manthing 5.00
9 BWi,Identity Crisis 5.00
10 V:The Word 5.00
11 BWi,V:Dr.Morbius 5.00
12 V:Gemini 5.00
13 V:Man-Wolf 5.00
14 V:Hellcat 5.00
15 V:Lady Kills 5.00
16 She Hulk Goes Berserk 5.00

She-Hulk #16
© Marvel Entertainment Group

17 V:Man-Elephant 5.00
18 V:Grappler 5.00
19 V:Her Father 5.00
20 A:Zapper 5.00
21 V:Seeker 5.00
22 V:Radius 5.00
23 V:Radius 5.00
24 V:Zapper 5.00
25 Double-sized,last issue 5.00

[2nd Regular Series] 1989–94
1 JBy,V:Ringmaster 4.00
2 JBy 2.50
3 JBy,A:Spider-Man 2.50
4 JBy,I:Blond Phantom 3.00
5 JBy 2.50
6 JBy,A:U.S.1,Razorback 2.50
7 JBy,A:U.S.1,Razorback 2.50
8 JBy,A:Saint Nicholas 2.50
9 AM(i) 2.50
10 AM(i) 2.50
11 . . . . 2.50
12 . . . . 2.50
13 SK(c) 2.50
14 MT(c),A:Howard the Duck 3.00
15 SK(c) 3.00
16 SK(c) 3.00
17 SK(c),V:Dr.Angst 3.00
18 SK(c) 2.50
19 SK(c),V:Nosferata 2.50
20 SK(c),Darkham Asylum 2.50
21 SK(c),V:Blonde Phantom 3.00
22 SK(c),V:Blonde Phantom,A:All
    Winners Squad 3.00
23 V:Blonde Phantom 3.00
24 V:Deaths'Head 4.00
25 A:Hercules,Thor 2.50
26 A:Excalibur 2.50
27 Cartoons in N.Y. 2.50
28 Game Hunter Stalks She-Hulk . . 2.50
29 A:Wolv.,Hulk,SpM,Venom 2.50
30 MZ(c),A:Silver Surfer,Thor
    Human Torch 2.25
31 JBy,V:Spragg the Living Hill . . . 2.50
32 JBy,A:Moleman,V:Spragg 2.50
33 JBy,A:Moleman,V:Spragg 2.50
34 JBy,Returns to New York 2.50
35 JBy,V:X-Humed Men 2.50
36 JBy,X-mas issue (#8 tie-in) 2.50
37 JBy,V:Living Eraser 2.50
38 JBy,V:Mahkizmo 2.50
39 JBy,V:Mahkizmo 2.50
40 JBy,V:Spraggs,Xemnu 2.50
41 JBy,V:Xemnu 2.50
42 JBy,V:USArcher 2.50

43 JBy,V:Xemnu 2.50
44 JBy,R:Rocket Raccoon 2.50
45 JBy,A:Razorback 2.50
46 JBy,A:Rocket Raccoon 2.50
47 V:D'Bari 2.50
48 JBy,A:Rocket Raccoon 2.50
49 V:Skrulls,D'Bari 2.50
50 JBy,WS,TA,DGb,AH,HC,
    D:She-Hulk 4.00
51 TMo,V:Savage She-Hulk 2.50
52 D:She-Hulk,A:Thing,Mr.Fantastic,
    I:Rumbler,V:Titania 2.50
53 AH(c),A:Zapper 2.50
54 MGo(c),A:Wonder Man 2.50
55 V:Rumbler 2.50
56 A:War Zone 2.50
57 A:Hulk 2.50
58 V:Electro 2.50
59 V:Various Villains 2.50
60 last issue 2.50
TPB rep. #1-#8 . . . . 13.00

SHE-HULK
March, 2004
1 F:Avengers 3.00
2 Class Action Comics 3.00
3 Dead Certain,F:The Thing 3.00
4 Web of Lies 3.00
5 The Big Picture,pt.1 . . . . 3.00
6 The Big Picture,pt.2 . . . . 3.00
7 Space Cases,pt.1 . . . . 3.00
8 Engagement Ring,pt.2 . . . . 3.00
9 A:Hercules 3.00
10 Titania 3.00
11 Balance of Power 3.00
12 Acceptable Losses 3.00
TPB Vol. 1: Single Green Female . 15.00
TPB Vol. 2: Superhuman Law . . . 15.00

SHE-HULK 2
Nov., 2005
1 A:New Avengers,Titan 3.00
2 Cause & Effect 3.00
3 104-pg. special 4.00
Becomes:

SHE-HULK
4 Return to Bone 3.00
5 New Kid in Town 3.00
6 I'm With Cupid 3.00
7 Beaus & Eros 3.00
8 Civil War tie-in 3.00
9 My Spoiler with Spoiler 3.00
10 V:Man-Wolf 3.00
11 Creature Comforts 3.00
12 F:Starfox, A:Thanos 3.00
13 Remember the Titans 3.00
TPB Time Trials (2006) 15.00

SHE HULK: CEREMONY
1989
1 JBr/SDr 4.00
2 JBr/FS 4.00

SHERRY THE SHOWGIRL
Marvel Atlas, 1956
1 . . . . 200.00
2 . . . . 135.00
3 . . . . 125.00
4 . . . . 125.00
5 thru 7 . . . . @125.00

SHIELD
Feb., 1973
1 JSo 25.00
2 JSo 20.00
3 JB,JSo,JK 20.00
4 JSo 20.00
5 JSo,Oct., 1973 . . . . 20.00

SHOGUN WARRIORS
Feb., 1979
1 HT,DGr,F:Raydeen, Combatra,
  Dangard Ace 15.00
2 HT,DGr,V:Elementals of Evil . . . 10.00
3 AM(c),HT,DGr,V:Elementals
  of Evil 10.00
4 HT,DGr,Menace of the
  Mech Monsters. 10.00
5 HT,DGr,Into The Lair
  of Demons 10.00
6 HT,ME 10.00
7 HT,ME 10.00
8 HT,ME 10.00
9 War Beneath The Waves. 10.00
10 Five Heads of Doom. 10.00
11 TA(c) 8.00
12 WS(c) 8.00
13 Demons on the Moon 8.00
14 V:Dr. Demonicus 8.00
15 . . . . 8.00
16 . . . . 8.00
17 . . . . 8.00
18 . . . . 8.00
19 A:Fantastic Four 8.00
20 Sept., 1980 . . . . 8.00

SHOWGIRLS
Marvel Atlas, 1957
1 . . . . 150.00
2 . . . . 125.00

SHROUD
Limited Series 1994
1 B:MiB(s),MCW,A:Spider-Man,
  V:Scorpion 2.25
2 MCW . . . . @2.25

Silly Tunes #4
© Marvel Entertainment Group

SILLY TUNES
Marvel Timely, 1945–47
1 Ziggy Pig 250.00
2 . . . . 125.00
3 . . . . 110.00
4 . . . . 110.00
5 . . . . 110.00
6 . . . . 110.00
7 . . . . 110.00

SILVERHAWKS
Aug., 1987
1 thru 5 . . . . @3.00
6 June, 1988 . . . . 3.00

SILVER SABLE
1992–95
1 Foil stamped(c),A:Sandman,
  Spider-Man 3.00
2 I:Gattling 2.50
3 V:Gattling,Foreigner. 2.50
4 Infinity War,V:Doctor Doom 2.50
5 Infinity War,V:Doctor Doom 2.50
6 A:Deathlok 2.50
7 A:Deathlok 2.50
8 V:Hydra 2.50
9 O:Silver Sable 2.50
10 A:Punisher,Leviathan 2.50
11 Cyber Warriors,Hydra 2.25
12 V:Cyberwarriorss,R:Sandman . . 2.25
13 For Love Nor Money#3,
  A:Cage,Terror 2.25
14 For Love Nor Money#6,
  A:Cage,Terror 2.25
15 V:Viper,A:Captain America 2.25
16 SBt,Infnty Crusade 2.25
17 Infinity Crusade. 2.25
18 A:Venom 2.25
19 Siege of Darkness x-over 2.25
20 GWt(s),StB,BU:Sandman,Fin . . 2.25
21 Gang War 2.25
22 . . . . 2.25
23 GWt(s),A:Deadpool,Daredevil,
  BU:Sandman 2.25
24 GWt(s),BU:Crippler,w/card 2.25
25 V:Hydra 2.50
26 F:Sandman 2.25
27 A:Code Blue 2.25
28 F:Chen 2.25
29 A:Wild Pack. 2.25
30 problems with law 2.25
31 V:terrorists. 2.25
32 A:The Foreigner 2.25
33 V:Hammerhead 2.25
34 . . . . 2.25
35 Li'l Silvie Tale 2.25

SILVER SURFER
[1st Series] Aug., 1968
1 B:SIL(s),JB,JSr,GC,O:Silver Surfer,
  O:Watcher,I:Shala Bal 2,500.00
2 JB,JSr,GC,A:Watcher 600.00
3 JB,JSr,GC,I:Mephisto 500.00
4 JB,A:Thor,low distribution
  scarce 950.00
5 JB,A:Fant.Four,V:Stranger . . . 700.00
6 JB,FB,A:Watcher 800.00
7 JB,A:Watcher,I:Frankenstein's
  Monster 750.00
8 JB,DA,A:Mephisto,I:Ghost . . . 700.00
9 JB,DA,A:Mephisto,A:Ghost . . . 700.00
10 JB,DA,South America 800.00
11 JB,DA 800.00
12 JB,DA,V:The Abomination . . . 700.00
13 JB,DA,V:Doomsday Man 700.00
14 JB,DA,A:Spider-Man 750.00
15 JB,DA,A:Human Torch 600.00
16 JB,V:Mephisto. 600.00
17 JB,V:Mephisto. 600.00
18 E:StL(s),JK,V:Inhumans 600.00

[2nd Regular Series] 1982
1 JBy,TP,Direct Only,V:Mephisto . 12.00

[3rd Regular Series] July, 1987
1 MR,JRu,A:Fantastic Four,
  Galactus,V:Champion 12.00
2 MR,A:Shalla Bal,V:Skrulls 6.00
3 MR,V:Collector & Runner 5.00
4 MR,JRu,A:Elders,I:Obliterator . . . 5.00
5 MR,JRu,V:Obliterator. 5.00
6 MR,JRu,O:Obliterator,A:Kree,
  Skrulls 5.00
7 MR,JRu,V:Supremor,Elders/
  Soul Gems. 5.00
8 MR,JRu,V:Supremor 5.00
9 MR,Elders Vs.Galactus 5.00

Silver Surfer #14
© Marvel Entertainment Group

10 MR,A:Galactus,Eternity. 5.00
11 JSon,JRu,V:Reptyl 4.50
12 MR,JRu,V:Reptyl,A:Nova 4.50
13 JSon,DC,V:Ronan 4.50
14 JSon,JRu,V:Skrull Surfer 4.50
15 RLm,JRu,A:Fantastic Four 6.00
16 RLm,Inbetweener possesses
  Soul Gem,A:Fantastic Four. . . . 4.00
17 RLm,A:Inbetweener,Galactus,
  Fantastic Four,D:Trader,
  Possessor,Astronomer 4.00
18 RLm,Galactus V:Inbetweener . . . 4.00
19 RLm,MR,V:Firelord 4.00
20 RLm,A:Superskrull,Galactus. . . . 4.00
21 MR,DC,V:Obliterator. 4.00
22 RLm,V:Ego 4.00
23 RLm,V:Dragon 4.00
24 RLm,V:G.I.G.O 4.00
25 RLm,V:Ronan,Kree Skrull War . . 4.00
26 RLm,V:Nenora 4.00
27 RLm,V:Stranger 4.00
28 RLm,D:Super Skrull,V:Reptyl . . . 4.00
29 RLm,V:Midnight Sun 4.00
30 RLm,V:Midnight Sun 4.00
31 RLm,O:Living Tribunal &
  Stranger (double size). 4.50
32 RF,JSt,A:Mephisto 4.00
33 RlLm,V:Impossible Man 4.00
34 RLm,(1stJSn),2nd R:Thanos . . . 5.00
35 RLm,A:Thanos,R:Drax 4.00
36 RLm,V:Impossible Man,A:Warlock
  Capt.Marvel,C:Thanos. 4.00
37 RLm,V:Drax,A:Mentor. 4.00
38 RLm,V:Thanos(continued in
  Thanos Quest). 4.00
39 JSh,V:Algol 3.00
40 RLm,V:Dynamo City 3.00
41 RLm,V:Dynamo City,A:Thanos . . 4.00
42 RLm,V:Dynamo City,A:Drax 3.00
43 RLm,V:DynamoCity 3.00
44 RLm,R:Thanos,Drax,
  O:Inf.Gems 4.00
45 RLm,Thanos vs. Mephisto 4.00
46 RLm,R:Warlock,A:Thanos 4.00
47 RLm,Warlock V:Drax,
  A:Thanos 4.00
48 RLm,A:Galactus,Thanos. 4.00
49 RLm,V:Thanos Monster 4.00
50 RLm,Silver Stamp(D.size),
  V:Thanos Monster 8.00
50a 2nd printing 3.00
50b 3rd printing 3.00
51 RLm,Infinity Gauntlet x-over 3.00
52 RLm,Infinity Gauntlet x-over 3.00

Silver Surfer 3rd Series #85
© Marvel Entertainment Group

53 RLm,Infinity Gauntlet x-over 3.00
54 RLm,I.Gauntlet x-over,V:Rhino . . 3.00
55 RLm,I.Gauntlet x-over,Universe
　According to Thanos,pt.1 . . . . . 3.00
56 RLm,I.Gauntlet x-over,Universe
　According to Thanos,pt.2 . . . . . 3.00
57 RLm,Infinity Gauntlet x-over 3.00
58 RLm(c),Infinity Gauntlet x-over,
　A:Hulk,Namor,Dr.Strange 3.00
59 RLm(c),TR,Infinity Gauntlet,
　Thanos V:Silver Surfer 3.00
60 RLm,V:Midnight Sun,
　A:Inhumans 2.50
61 RLm,I:Collection.Agency 2.50
62 RLm,O:Collection Agency 2.50
63 RLm,A:Captain Marvel 2.50
64 RLm,V:Dark Silver Surfer 2.50
65 RLm,R:Reptyl,I:Princess
　Alaisa 2.50
66 RLm,I:Avatar,Love & Hate 2.50
67 RLm(c),KWe,Inf.War,V:Galactus
　A:DrStrange 2.50
68 RLm(c),KWe,Inf.War,O:Nova . . . 2.50
69 RLm(c),KWe,Infinity War,
　A:Galactus 2.50
70 RLm(c),Herald War#1,I:Morg . . 2.50
71 RLm(c),Herald War#2,V:Morg . . 2.50
72 RLm(c),Herald War#3,R:Nova . . 2.50
73 RLm,R:Airwalker 2.50
74 RLm,V:Terrax 2.50
75 RLm,E:Herald Ordeal,V:Morg,
　D:Nova 3.00
76 RLm,A:Jack of Hearts 2.50
77 RLm,A:Jack of Hearts 2.50
78 RLm,R:Morg,V:Nebula 2.50
79 RLm,V:Captain Atlas 2.50
80 RLm,I:Ganymede,Terrax
　Vs.Morg 2.50
81 RLm,O:Ganymedel:Tyrant 2.50
82 RLm,V:Tyrant,double sized 2.50
83 Infinity Crusade 2.50
84 RLm(c),Infinity Crusade 2.50
85 RLm(c),Infinity Crusade 2.50
86 RLm(c), Blood & Thunder,pt.2
　V:Thor,A:Beta Ray Bill 2.50
87 RLm(c),Blood & Thunder,pt.7 . . 2.50
88 RLm(c),Blood & Thunder,pt.10 . . 2.50
89 RLm(c),CDo,C:Legacy 2.50
90 RLm(c),A:Legacy,C:Avatar 2.50
91 RLm 2.50
92 RLm,V:Avatar 2.50
93 V:Human Torch 2.50
94 A:Fantastic Four, Warlock 2.50
95 SEa,A:Fantastic Four 2.50

96 A:Fantastic Four,Hulk 2.50
97 A:Fantastic Four,R:Nova 2.50
98 R:Champion 2.50
99 A:Nova 2.50
100 V:Mephisto 2.50
100a enhanced ed. 5.00
101 RMz,JoP,A:Shalla Bal 2.25
102 V:Galactus 2.25
103 I:Death quad 2.25
104 Surfer Rampage 2.25
105 V:Super Skrull 2.25
106 A:Legacy,Morg 2.25
107 TGb,BAn,A:Galactus,Morg,
　Tyrant 2.25
108 Galactus Vs. Tyrant 2.25
109 Morg has Ultimate Nulifier 2.25
110 JB,F:Nebula 2.25
111 GP,TGb,BAn,to Other Side
　of Galaxy 2.25
112 GP,TGb,BAn, ... 2.25
113 GP,TGb,BAn,V:Blackbody 2.25
114 . . . . 2.25
115 GP,TGb,BAn,Surfer in pieces . . 2.25
116 GP,TGb,BAn,Pieces cause
　trouble 2.25
117 . . . . 2.25
118 . . . . 2.25
119 . . . . 2.25
120 . . . . 2.25
121 A:Quasar, Beta Ray Bill 2.25
122 GP,SEa, returns to Marvel
　Universe 2.25
123 GP,RG. 2.25
124 GP,RG. 2.25
125 RG,V:Hulk, double size 3.50
126 JMD,RG,BWi,A:Dr. Strange . . . 2.25
127 JMD,RG,BWi,A:Alicia Masters . . 2.25
128 JMD,RG,BWi,V:Puppet Master . 2.25
129 JMD,RG,BWi,back in time,
　late 1940s 2.25
130 JMD,CNr,BWi, trapped in past . 2.25
131 JMD,RG,BWi, ... 2.25
132 JMD,PaP,Puppet Master
　missing 2.25
133 JMD,MRy,PaP,V:PuppetMaster 2.25
134 JMD,TGm,MRy,Regains his
　memories, pt.1 (of 4). 2.25
135 JMD,TGm,MRy,Alicia summons
　Scrier 2.25
136 JMD,TGm,MRy, ... 2.25
137 JMD,TGm,MRy,Mephisto v.
　Scrier 2.25
138 JMD,RCz,MRy,A:The Thing,
　tie-in 2.25
139 JMD,RCz,MRy,V:Gargoyle 2.25
140 JMD,JMu,on Zenn-La untouched
　by Galactus 2.25
141 JMD,JMu,A:Sama-D,Alicia
　Masters 2.25
142 JMD,JMu,Tenebrae,The Union,
　Cipher 2.25
143 JMD,DCw,Tenebrae,V:Psycho
　Man 2.25
Bi-Weekly Issues
144 JMD,JMu,V:Psycho-Man,
　A:Tenebrae 2.25
145 JMD,JMu,A:Psycho-Man,
　Tenebrae,Cypphyrr 2.25
146 TDF,DCw,V:Firelord 2.25
Minus 1 Spec., JMD,RG,BWi,
　flashback, first human contact. . 2.25
Spec. Silver Surfer: Dangerous Arti-
　facts,RMz, Galactus,Thanos
　(1996) 4.00
Spec. Silver Surfer: Inner Demons,
　rep. JMD,RGa,BWi (1998) 3.00
Ann.#1 RLm,JSon,Evolution War . . 7.00
Ann.#2 RLm,Atlantis Attacks 5.00
Ann.#3 RLm,Lifeform #4 . . . . 4.00
Ann.#4 RLm,Korvac Quest #3,A:
　Guardians of Galaxy 3.00
Ann.#5 RLm,Ret.o/Defenders #3. . 3.00

Silver Surfer 3rd Series #122
© Marvel Entertainment Group

Ann.#6 RLm(c),I:Legacy,w/card. . . . 3.75
Ann.'97 1 JMD,VS,KJ,V:Scrier,
　48-pg. 3.00
Ann.'98 MPe,RBe,TDF,F:Thor. 3.00
TPB Silver Surger, The Enslavers . 17.00
TPB Homecoming,A:Moondragon . 13.00
TPB Silver Surfer: Parable, rep. . . . 6.00
TPB Rebirth of Thanos, rep. 13.00
TPB StL,JK, new origin 13.00
TPB Rebirth of Thanos (2006). . . . 25.00

SILVER SURFER
Epic, Dec., 1988
1 Moebius,V:Galactus. 5.00
2 Moebius,V:Galactus. 5.00
Graphic Novel 15.00

SILVER SURFER
July, 2003
1 JJu(c),children disappear. 2.50
2 JaL(c),Denise Waters 2.50
3 Denise Waters 2.50
4 Communion,pt.4 . . . . 2.25
5 Communion,pt.5 . . . . 2.25
6 Communion,pt.6 . . . . 2.25
7 Revelation,pt.1 . . . . 3.00
8 Revelation,pt.2 . . . . 3.00
9 Revelation,pt.3 . . . . 3.00
10 Revelation,pt.4 . . . . 3.00
11 Revelation,pt.5 . . . . 3.00
12 Revelation,pt.6 . . . . 3.00
13 Revelation,pt.7 . . . . 3.00
14 Revelation,pt.8 . . . . 3.00
TPB Vol. 1: Communion 15.00

SILVER SURFER:
LOFTIER THAN MORTALS
Aug., 1999
1 MFr,V:Dr. Doom 2.50
2 MFr,V:Dr. Doom, concl. 2.50

SILVER SURFER/
SUPERMAN
Marvel/DC 1996
Spec. GP,RLm,TA, x-over 6.00

SILVER SURFER VS.
DRACULA
1994
1 rep,MWn(s),GC,TP 2.50

MARVEL

SILVER SURFER/ WARLOCK: RESURRECTION
1993
1 JSn,V:Mephisto,Death 3.50
2 JSn,TA,V:Death 3.00
3 & 4 JSn,TA,V:Mephisto . . . . . @3.00

SILVER SURFER/ WEAPON ZERO
Marvel/Top Cow 1997
1-shot Devil's Reign, pt.8 . . . . 4.00

SISTERHOOD OF STEEL
Epic, Dec., 1984
1 I:Sisterhood 4.00
2 thru 8 . . . . @3.00

SIX FROM SIRIUS
Epic, July, 1984
1 PG,limited series 3.00
2 thru 4 PG . . . . @2.25

SIX FROM SIRIUS II
Epic, Feb., 1986
1 PG 2.25

SIX-GUN WESTERN
Marvel Atlas, Jan., 1957
1 JSe(c),RC,JR,Kid Yukon
Gunslinger 250.00
2 SSh,AW,DAy,JO,His Guns
Hang Low 175.00
3 AW,BP,DAy 175.00
4 JSe(c),JR,GWb 125.00

SKELETON WARRIORS
1995
1 based on cartoon 2.25
2 Legion of Light 2.25
3 V:Grimstar 2.25
4 Grimskull abandons Legion
of Light 2.25

SKRULL KILL CREW
1995
1 I:Kill Crew 3.00
2 V:Hydra 3.00
3 V:Captain America 3.00
4 V:Fantastic Four 3.00
5 Conclusion 3.00
TPB Skrull Kill Crew 17.00

SKULL, THE SLAYER
Aug., 1975
1 GK(c),O:Skull the Slayer 20.00
2 GK(c),Man Against Gods 15.00
3 Trapped in the Tower
of Time 15.00
4 Peril of the Pyramids,
A:Black Knight 15.00
5 A:Black Knight 15.00
6 The Savage Sea 15.00
7 Dungeon of Blood 15.00
8 JK(c),Nov., 1976 . . . . 15.00

SLAPSTICK
1992–93
1 TA(i),I:Slapstick 2.25
2 TA(i),A:Spider-Man,V:Overkill . . . 2.25
3 V:Dr.Denton 2.25
4 A:GR,DD,FF,Cap.America 2.25

SLEDGE HAMMER
Feb., 1988
1 . . . . 5.00
2 March, 1988 . . . . 3.00

Sleepwalker #31
© Marvel Entertainment Group

SLEEPWALKER
June, 1991
1 BBl,I:Rick Sheridan,C:8-Ball 3.00
2 BBl,V:8-Ball 2.25
3 BBl,A:Avengers,X-Men,X-Factor,
FF,I:Cobweb,O:Sleepwalker . . . 2.25
4 RL,I:Bookworm 2.25
5 BBl,A:SpM,K.Pin,V:Ringleader . . 2.25
6 BBl,A:SpM,Inf.Gauntlet x-over . . . 2.25
7 BBl,Infinity Gauntlet x over,
V:Chain Gang 2.25
8 BBl,A:Deathlok 2.25
9 BBl,I:Lullabye 2.25
10 BBl,MM,I:Dream-Team 2.25
11 BBl,V:Ghost Rider 2.25
12 JQ,A:Nightmare 3.00
13 BBl,MM,I:Spectra 2.25
14 BBl,MM,V:Spectra 2.25
15 BBl,MM,I:Thought Police 2.25
16 BBl,MM,A:Mr.Fantastic,Thing . . 2.25
17 BBl,A:Spider-Man,Darkhawk,
V:Brotherhood o/Evil Mutants . . 2.25
18 JQ(c),Inf.War,A:Prof.X 2.25
19 V:Cobweb,w/pop out Halloween
Mask 2.50
20 V:Chain Gang,Cobweb 2.25
21 V:Hobgoblin 2.25
22 V:Hobgoblin,8-Ball 2.25
23 V:Cobweb,Chain Gang 2.25
24 Mindfield#6 . . . . 2.25
25 O:Sleepwalker,Holo-grafx(c) . . . 3.50
26 V:Mindspawn 2.25
27 A:Avengers 2.25
28 I:Psyko 2.25
29 DG,V:Psyko 2.25
30 V:Psyko 2.25
31 DG(ci),A:Spectra 2.25
32 V:Psyko 2.25
33 V:Mindspawn,Last issue 2.25
Holiday Spec.#1 JQ(c) 2.50

SLEEZE BROTHERS
Aug., 1989
1 Private Eyes 2.25
2 . . . . 2.25
3 . . . . 2.25
4 thru 6 . . . . @2.25

SLINGERS
Oct., 1998
1 Ccs,F:Ricochet, Hornet,
Prodigy & Dusk, 48-page:
1a Ricochet edition 3.00
1b Hornet edition 3.00
1c Prodigy edition 3.00
1d Dusk edition 3.00
2 CCs,V:Maggia 2.50
2a variant cover 2.25
3 CCs,F:Prodigy 2.25
4 CCs,F:Prodigy 2.25
5 CCs,F:Black Marvel 2.25
6 CCs,Truth or Dare 2.25
7 CCs,V:The Griz 2.25
8 CCs,V:The Griz 2.25
9 CCs,A:Ricochet 2.25
10 CCs,Raising Hell'sChildren,pt.1 . 2.25
11 CCs,Raising Hell'sChildren,pt.2 . 2.25
12 CCs,Hell's Children,pt.3 final . . . 2.25

SMURFS
Dec., 1982
1 . . . . 10.00
2 . . . . 7.00
3 . . . . 7.00
Treasury Edition 30.00

SOLARMAN
Jan., 1989
1 JM 3.00
2 MZ/NR,A:Dr.Doom, May, 1990 . . 3.00

SOLDIER X
July, 2002
1 Cable's future, 40-pg. 3.00
2 . . . . 2.25
3 to Russia without love 2.25
4 Geo debuts 2.25
5 . . . . 2.25
6 . . . . 2.25
7 . . . . 2.25
8 Askani religion 2.25
9 V:Racist militia group 2.25
10 V:Racism 3.00
11 SEa,Dead Ends,pt.1 . . . . 3.00
12 SEa,Dead Ends,pt.2 . . . . 3.00

SOLO
[Limited Series] 1994
1 RoR,I:Cygnus 2.25
2 RoR,V.A.R.E.S. 2.25
3 RoR,V:Spidey 2.25
4 final issue 2.25

SOLO AVENGERS
Dec., 1987
1 MBr,JRu,JLe,AW,Hawkeye;
Mockingbird 4.00
2 MBr,JRu,KD,BMc,Hawkeye;
Capt.Marvel 2.50
3 MBr,JRu,BH,SDr,Hawkeye;
Moon Knight 2.50
4 RLm,JRu,PR,BL,Hawkeye;
Black Knight 2.50
5 MBr,JRu,JRy,Hawkeye;
Scarlet Witch 2.50
6 MBr,JRu,TGr,Hawkeye;Falcon . . 2.50
7 MBr,JG,BL,Hawkcyc;Bl.Widow . . 2.50
8 MBr,Hawkeye;Dr.Pym 2.50
9 MBr,JBr,SDr,Hawkeye;Hellcat . . 2.50
10 MBr,LW,Hawkeye;Dr.Druid 2.50
11 MBr,JG,BL,Hawkeye;Hercules . . 2.50
12 RLm,SDr,Hawkeye; New
Yellow Jacket 2.50
13 RLm,JG,Hawkeye;WonderMan . 2.50
14 AM,AD,JRu,Hawkeye;She-Hulk . 2.50
15 AM,Hawkeye;Wasp 2.50

MARVEL

16 AM,DP,JA,Hawkeye;
   Moondragon 2.50
17 AM,DH,DC,Hawkeye;
   Sub-Mariner. 2.50
18 RW,DH,Hawkeye;Moondragon . . 2.50
19 RW,DH,Hawkeye,BlackPanther . . 2.50
20 RW,DH,Hawkeye;Moondragon . . 2.50
Becomes:

AVENGERS SPOTLIGHT

SOLOMON KANE
Sept., 1985
1 F:Solomon Kane 3.00
2 . . . . 3.00
3 BBl,Blades of the Brotherhood . . 3.00
4 MMi 3.00
5 Hills of the Dead 3.00
6 . . . . 3.00

SON OF M
Dec., 2005
1 F:Quicksilver 3.00
2 thru 5 . . . . @3.00

SON OF SATAN
Dec., 1975–Feb., 1977
1 GK(c),JM,F:Daimon Hellstrom. . 32.00
2 Demon War,O:Possessor 20.00
3 . . . . 20.00
4 The Faces of Fear. 15.00
5 V:Mind Star 15.00
6 A World Gone Mad 15.00
7 Mirror of Judgement 15.00
8 RH,To End in Nightmare 15.00

SOVIET SUPER SOLDIERS
1 AMe,JS,I:Redmont 4 . . . . 2.25

SPACEKNIGHTS
Aug., 2000
1 (of 5) JSn,R:Spaceknights 3.00
2 JSn,Terminator. 3.00
3 JSn,Deathwings. 3.00
4 JSn,Wraith Knights 3.00
5 JSn,concl. 3.00

SPACEMAN
Marvel Atlas, Sept., 1953
1 BEv(c),F:Speed Carter and
   the Space Sentinals 1,000.00
2 JMn,Trapped in Space. 600.00

Space Squadron #5
© Marvel Entertainment Group

3 BEv(c),JMn,V:Ice Monster 475.00
4 JMn, A-Bomb 500.00
5 GT 475.00
6 JMn,Thing From Outer Space   475.00

SPACE SQUADRON
Atlas, June, 1951
1 AyB,F:Capt. Jet Dixon,Blast,
   Dawn,Revere,Rusty Blake   1,000.00
2 GT(c), ... 800.00
3 Planet of Madness,GT. 700.00
4 . . . . 700.00
5 AyB 700.00
Becomes:

SPACE WORLDS
April, 1952
6 Midnight Horror 650.00

SPECIAL COLLECTOR'S EDITION
Dec., 1975
1 Kung-Fu,Iron Fist 10.00

SPECIAL MARVEL EDITION
Jan., 1971
1 JK,B:Thor,B:Reprints 45.00
2 JK,V:Absorbing Man 25.00
3 JK,While a Universe
   Trembles 25.00
4 JK,Hammer and the Holocaust,
   E:Thor 25.00
5 JSe(c),JK,DAy,B:Sgt. Fury 25.00
6 HT(c),DAy,Death Ray of
   Dr. Zemo 12.00
7 DAy,V:Baron Strucker 12.00
8 JSe(c),DAy,On To Okinawa . . . 12.00
9 DAy,Crackdown-CaptainFlint . . 12.00
10 DAy 12.00
11 JK,DAy,A:Captain
   America & Bucky. 12.00
12 DAy,V:Baron Strucker 12.00
13 JK/DAy(c),DAy,SD,Too Small
   to Fight, Too Young To Die . . . 12.00
14 DAy,E:Reprints,Sgt. Fury 12.00
15 JSn,AM,I:Shang-Chi & Master of
   Kung Fu,I&O:Nayland Smith,
   Dr. Petrie 150.00
16 JSn,AM,I&O:Midnight 65.00
KingSz.Ann.#1 A:Iron Fist 18.00
Becomes:

MASTER OF KUNG FU

SPECTACULAR SCARLET SPIDER
1995
1 SB,BSz,Virtual Morality,pt.4 . . . . . 2.25
2 SB,BSz,CyberWar,pt.4. . . . . 2.25

SPECTACULAR SPIDER-MAN
(Magazine) July, 1968
1 JR,JM. 200.00
2 JR,JM,V:Green Goblin 175.00

SPECTACULAR SPIDER-MAN
Dec., 1976
Prev: Peter Parker
134 SB,A:Sin-Eater,V:Electro 4.00
135 SB,A:Sin-Eater,V:Electro 3.00
136 SB,D:Sin-Eater,V:Electro 3.00
137 SB,I:Tarantula II 3.00
138 SB,A:Capt.A.,V:TarantulaII 3.00
139 SB,O:Tombstone. 4.00

140 SB,A:Punisher,V:Tombstone . . . 3.50
141 SB,A:Punisher,V:Tombstone . . . 4.00
142 SB,A:Punisher,V:Tombstone. . . . 4.00
143 SB,A:Punisher,D:Persuader,
   I:Lobo Brothers. 4.00
144 SB,V:Boomerang 3.00
145 SB,A:Boomerang 3.00
146 SB,R:Green Goblin 5.00
147 SB,V:Hobgoblin (Demonic
   Power) 10.00
148 SB,Inferno. 3.00
149 SB,V:Carrion II 5.00
150 SB,A:Tombstone,Trial
   J.Robertson 3.00
151 SB,V:Tombstone 3.00
152 SB,O:Lobo Bros.,A:Punisher,
   Tombstone 4.00
153 SB,V:Hammerhead,A:
   Tombstone 3.00
154 SB,V:Lobo Bros.,Puma. 3.00
155 SB,V:Tombstone 3.00
156 SB,V:Banjo,A:Tombstone 3.00
157 SB,V:Shocker,Electro,
   A:Tombstone 3.00
158 SB,Super Spider Spec.,
   I:Cosmic Spider-Man 9.00
159 Cosmic Powers,V:Brothers
   Grimm 5.00
160 SB,A:Hydro Man,Shocker,
   Rhino,Dr.Doom 4.00
161 SB,V:Hobgoblin,Hammerhead,
   Tombstone 3.00
162 SB,V:Hobgoblin,Carrion II . . . 3.00
163 SB,V:Hobgoblin,D:Carrion II . . . 3.00
164 SB,V:Beetle. 3.00
165 SB,SDr,D:Arranger,I:Knight
   & Fogg. 3.00
166 SB,O:Knight & Fogg 3.00
167 SB,D:Knight & Fogg 3.00
168 SB,A:Kingpin,Puma,
   Avengers. 3.00
169 SB,I:Outlaws,A:R.Racer,
   Prowler,Puma,Sandman 3.00
170 SB,A:Avengers,Outlaws 3.00
171 SB,V:Puma 2.50
172 SB,V:Puma 2.50
173 SB,V:Puma 2.50
174 SB,A:Dr.Octopus. 2.50
175 SB,A:Dr.Octopus. 2.50
176 SB,I:Karona. 2.50
177 SB,V:Karona,A:Mr.Fantastic . . . 2.50
178 SB,B:Child Within,V:Green
   Goblin, A:Vermin 2.50
179 SB,V:Green Goblin,Vermin 2.50

Spectacular Spider-Man #198
© Marvel Entertainment Group

180 SB,V:Green Goblin,Vermin 2.50
181 SB,V:Green Goblin 2.50
182 SB,V:Green Goblin 2.50
183 SB,V:Green Goblin 2.50
184 SB,E:Child Within,V:Green
    Goblin 2.50
185 SB,A:Frogman,White Rabbit. . . 2.50
186 SB,B:FuneralArrangements
    V:Vulture 2.50
187 SB,V:Vulture 2.50
188 SB,E:Funeral Arrangements
    V:Vulture 2.50
189 SB,30th Ann.,Hologram(c),
    V:Green Goblin 6.00
189a Gold 2nd printing 3.00
190 SB,V:Rhino,Harry Osborn. . . . 2.50
191 SB,Eye of the Puma 2.50
192 SB,Eye of the Puma 2.50
193 SB,Eye of the Puma 2.50
194 SB,Death of Vermin#1 . . . . . . 2.50
195 SB,Death of Vermin#2 . . . . . . 4.00
195a Dirtbag Spec,w/Dirt#2 tape . . 2.50
196 SB,Death of Vermin#3 . . . . . . 2.50
197 SB,A:X-Men,V:Prof.Power . . . 2.50
198 SB,A:X-Men,V:Prof.Power . . . 2.50
199 SB,A:X-Men,Green Goblin . . . 2.50
200 SB,V:Green Goblin,D:Harry
    Osborn,Holografx(c) 5.00
201 SB,Total Carnage,V:Carnage,
    Shriek,A:Black Cat,Venom . . . 4.00
202 SB,Total Carnage#9,A:Venom,
    V:Carnage 4.00
203 SB,Maximum Carnage#13 . . . 4.00
204 SB,A:Tombstone 2.50
205 StG(s),SB,V:Tombstone,
    A:Black Cat 2.50
206 SB,V:Tombstone 2.50
207 SB,A:The Shroud 2.50
208 SB,A:The Shroud 2.50
209 StB,SB,I:Dead Aim,
    BU:Black Cat 2.50
210 StB,SB,V:Dead Aim,
    BU:Black Cat 2.50
211 Pursuit#2,V:Tracer 2.50
212 . . . . 2.50
213 ANo(s),V:Typhiod Mary,w/cel . . 3.50
213a Newsstand Ed. 2.50
214 V:Bloody Mary. 2.50
215 V:Scorpion 2.50
216 V:Scorpion 2.50
217 V:Judas Traveller,clone. 3.00
217a Foil(c),bonus stuff 5.00
218 V:Puma 2.50
219 Back from the Edge,pt.2 . . . . . 3.00
220 Web of Death,pt.3. . . . . 3.00
221 Web of Death,finale 3.00
222 The Price of Truth 2.50
223 Aftershocks,pt.4 . . . . 3.00
223a enhanced cover 3.00
224 The Mark of Kaine,pt.4 . . . . . . 2.50
225 SB,TDF,BSz,I:New Green
    Goblin, 48-pg. 3.00
225a 3-D HoloDisk Cover 5.00
226 SB,BSz,The Trial of Peter
    Parker,pt.4, identity revealed. . . 3.00
227 TDF,SB,BSz,Maximum
    Clonage,pt.5 . . . . 2.50
228 Timebomb,pt.1 . . . . 2.50
229 Greatest Responsibility,pt.3 . . 3.00
229a Special cover 5.00
230 SB,Return of Spider-Man,pt.4. . 2.50
231 SB,Return of Kaine,pt.1 . . . . . 2.50
232 . . . . 2.50
233 SB,JP,Web of Carnage,pt.4 . . . 2.50
234 SB,Blood Brothers,pt.4 . . . . . . 2.50
235 . . . . 2.50
236 . . . . 2.50
237 V:Lizard. 2.50
238 V:Lizard. 2.50
239 V:Lizard. 2.50
240 TDz,LRs,Book of Revelations,
    pt.1 (of 4). 3.00

241 Revelations epilogue 2.50
242 JMD,LRs,R:Chameleon,
    A:Kangaroo 2.50
243 JMD,LRs,R:Chameleon,
    A:Kangaroo 2.50
244 JMD,LRs,V:Chameleon 2.50
245 JMD,LRs,V:Chameleon,
    A:Kangaroo 2.50
246 JMD,LRs,V:Kangaroo,Grizzly . . 2.50
247 JMD,LRs,F:JackO'Lantern,pt.1. 2.50
248 JMD,LRs,DGr,F:Jack O'
    Lantern, pt.2 . . . . 2.50
249 JMD,LRs,DGr, Last Temptation
    of Flash Thompson 2.50
250 JR, V:Original Green Goblin,
    double gatefold cover 3.50
251 JMD,LRs,DGr,V:Kraven the
    Hunter 2.50
252 JMD,LRs,DGr,V:Norman
    Osborn. 2.50
253 JMD,LRs,DGr,V:Norman Osborn,
    Gibbon, Grizzly 2.50
254 JMD,LRs,DGr,V:Prof.Angst. . . 2.50
255 JMD,LRs,DGr,Spider-Hunt,pt.4
    x-over, double size 3.00
256 JMD,LRs,DGr,Identity Crisis
    prelude, A:Prodigy 2.50
257 JMD,LRs,DGr,Identity Crisis,
    as Prodigy, V:Conundrum 2.50
258 JMD,LRs,DGa,as Prodigy. . . . 2.50
259 RSt,LRs,DGa,V:Hobgoblin . . . 2.50
260 JR,RSt,LRs,DGa,Green Goblin
    vs. Hobgoblin. 2.50
261 RSt,LRs,AM,Goblins at the
    Gate,pt.3 . . . . 2.50
262 JBy, AM, LRs, The Gathering of
    the Five, pt.4 (of 5) x-over. 2.50
263 JBy,AM,LRs,The Final
    Chapter,pt.3 x-over 4.00
Ann.#8 MBa,RLm,TD,Evolutionary
    Wars,O:Gwen Stacy Clone 7.00
Ann.#9 DR,MG,DJu,MBa,Atlantis
    Attacks. 4.00
Ann.#10 SLi(c),RB,MM,TM,RA 6.00
Ann.#11 EL(c),RWi,Vib.Vendetta . . 3.00
Ann.#12 Hero Killers#2,A:New
    Warriors,BU:Venom. 4.50
Ann.#13 I:Noctune,w/Card. 3.25
Ann.#14 V:Green Goblin 3.00
Super-Size Spec.#1 Planet of the
    Symbiotes,pt.4,64-pg.flip-book . 4.00
Minus 1 Spec., JMD,LRs,DGr,
    flashback, F:Flash Thompson . . 2.00
TPB rep. 80-pg. (2002) 13.00

SPECTACULAR
SPIDER-MAN
June, 2003

1 HuR,V:Venom,pt.1 . . . . 2.25
2 HuR,V:Venom,pt.2 . . . . 2.25
3 HuR,V:Venom,pt.3 . . . . 2.25
4 HuR,V:Venom,pt.4 . . . . 2.25
5 HuR,V:Venom,pt.5 . . . . 2.25
6 HuR,Countdown,pt.1,V:Doc Ock . 2.25
7 HuR,Countdown,pt.2 . . . . 2.25
8 HuR,Countdown,pt.3 . . . . 2.25
9 HuR,Countdown,pt.4 . . . . 2.25
10 HuR,Countdown,concl. 2.25
11 The Lizard's Tale,pt.1 . . . . 2.25
12 The Lizard's Tale,pt.2 . . . . 2.25
13 The Lizard's Tale,pt.3 . . . . 2.25
14 F:Morbius 2.25
15 F:Captain America 2.25
16 F:Captain America 2.25
17 Changes,pt.1. . . . . 2.25
18 Changes,pt.2. . . . . 2.25
19 Changes,pt.3. . . . . 2.25
20 Disassembled, tie-in,pt.4 . . . . . . 2.25
21 . . . . 2.25
22 . . . . 2.25
23 SEa,Sins Remembered,pt.1 . . . 2.25
24 SEa,Sins Remembered,pt.2 . . . 2.25

Spectacular Spider-Man #263
© Marvel Entertainment Group

25 SEa,Sins Remembered,pt.3 . . . . 2.25
26 SEa,Sins Remembered,pt.4 . . . . 2.25
27 PJe,MBu,finale 3.00
TPB Vol. 1: The Hunger. 12.00
TPB Vol. 2: Countdown 12.00
TPB Vol. 3: Here There Be
    Monsters 10.00
TPB Vol. 4: Disassembled. 15.00
TPB Vol. 5: Sins Remembered . . . 10.00
TPB Vol. 6: The Final Curtain 15.00

SPEEDBALL
Sept., 1988

1 SD,JG,O:Speedball 2.50
2 SD,JG,V:Sticker,GraffitiGorillas . . 2.50
3 SD,V:Leaper Logan 2.50
4 SD,DA,Ghost Springdale High. . . 2.50
5 SD,V:Basher 2.50
6 SD,V:Bug-Eyed Voice 2.50
7 SD,V:Harlequin Hit Man. 2.50
8 SD,V:Bonehead Gang 2.50
9 SD,V:Nathan Boder. 2.50
10 SD,V:Mutated Pigs,Killer
    Chickens, last issue. 2.50

SPELLBINDERS
March, 2005

1 (of 6) F:Witches of Salem 3.00
2 Salem Ghosts 3.00
3 Pillar of Smoke 3.00
4 Pillar of Smoke 3.00
5 The Halls of the Dead 3.00
6 World of the Dead, finale 3.00
Digest Vol. 1: Signs and Wonders. . 8.00

SPELLBOUND
Marvel Atlas, March, 1952

1 AyB(c),Step into my Coffin . . 1,500.00
2 BEv,RH,Horror Story,
    A:Edgar A. Poe 800.00
3 RH(c),OW 700.00
4 RH,Decapitation story 700.00
5 AyB,BEv,JM,Its in the Bag . . . 700.00
6 AyB,BK,The Man Who Couldn't
    be Killed. 700.00
7 AyB,BEv,JMn,Don't Close
    the Door. 550.00
8 BEv(c),RH,JSt,DAy,
    The Operation 550.00
9 BEv(c),RH,The Death of
    Agatha Slurl. 550.00

10 AyB,BEv,RH,JMn(c),The Living
   Mummy 550.00
11 The Empty Coffin 450.00
12 RH,My Friend the Ghost. 450.00
13 JM,AyB,The Dead Men. 450.00
14 BEv(c),RH,JMn,Close Shave . 450.00
15 AyB,CI,Get Out of my
   Graveyard 450.00
16 RH,BEv,JF,JSt,Behind
   the Door. 450.00
17 BEv(c),GC,BK,Goodbye
   Forever 450.00
18 BEv(c),JM 400.00
19 BEv(c),BP,Witch Doctor 400.00
20 RH(c),BP 400.00
21 RH(c). 550.00
22 . . . . 550.00
23 . . . . 550.00
24 JMn(c),JR 500.00
25 JO,AyB,Look Into My Eyes. . . 500.00
26 JR,AyB,Things in the Box. . . . 500.00
27 JMn,JR,AyB,Trap in the
   Mirage 500.00
28 BEv 500.00
29 JSe(c),SD 550.00
30 BEv(c) 500.00
31 JMn. 500.00
32 BP,AyB,Almost Human 500.00
33 AT 500.00
34 June, 1957 . . . . 500.00

SPELLBOUND
Jan., 1988
1 thru 5 . . . . 2.50
6 double-size 3.00

SPIDER-GIRL
Aug., 1998
0 TDF,RF,BSz, cont. from What-If?
   #105, Peter & Mary Jane's
   daughter 5.00
1 TDF,PO,AW, F:Mayday Parker,
   V:Mr. Nobody. 7.00
2 TDF,PO,AW,V:Crazy Eight
   & Darkdevil 4.00
2a variant cover 4.00
3 TDF,PO,AW,A:Fantastic Five . . 2.50
4 TDF,PO,AW,turning points 2.50
5 TDF,PO,AW,Ghosts of the Past. . 2.50
6 TDF,PO,AW,Majority Rules 2.50
7 TDF,PO,AW,Last Days of
   Spider-Man 2.50
8 TDF,PO,AW,A:Spider-Man,
   Uneasy Allies. 2.50
8a autographed. 20.00
9 TDF,PO,AW,Critical Choices . . . 2.50
10 TDF,PO,AW,Incredible Journeys 2.50
11 TDF,PO,AW,V:Spider-Man 2.50
12 TDF,PO,AW,A:Darkdevil 2.50
13 TDF,Po,AW,Joins A-Next 2.50
14 TDF,PO,AW,Bloody Reunions
   x-over. 2.50
15 TDF,PO,AW,A:Speedball 2.50
16 TDF,PO,AW. 2.50
17 TDF,PO,AW,48-pg. 3.00
18 TDF,SB,RF,A:Buzz 2.50
19 TDF,AW,PO,V:A-Next foes 2.50
20 TDF,AW,PO,R:Green Goblin. . . 2.50
21 TDF,AW,PO,V:Earthshaker . . . 2.25
22 TDF,AW,PO,Darkdevil. 2.25
23 TDF,AW,PO,Basketball 2.25
24 TDF,AW,PO,Dragonfist 2.25
25 TDF,AW,PO,Savage Six 3.50
26 TDF,AW,PO,Phil Urich 2.25
27 TDF,AW,PO,Parker/Osborn
   war concl. 2.25
28 TDF,AW,PO,V:Raptor 2.25
29 TDF,AW,PO,A:Nova 2.25
30 TDF,AW,PO,V:Avengers 2.25
31 TDF,AW,PO,V:Avengers 2.25
32 TDF,PO,Steel Spider. 2.25

Spider-Girl #38
© Marvel Entertainment Group

33 TDF,AW,PO,A:Spider-Man 2.25
34 TDF,AW,PO,A:Fant.Five 2.25
35 TDF,AW,PO,V:Canis 2.25
36 TDF,AW,PO,V:Canis 2.25
37 TDF,AW,PO,V:Green Goblin . . . 2.25
38 TDF,AW,PO,V:Green Goblin . . . 2.25
39 TDF,AW,PO,Green Goblin 2.25
40 TDF,AW,PO,Death in the family . 2.25
41 TDF,AW,PO,V:Canis,'Nuff Said. . 2.25
42 TDF,RF,mothers 2.25
43 TDF,AW,PO,original Spider-Man. 2.25
44 TDF,AW,PO,F:Ben Reilly 2.25
45 TDF,AW,PO,A:Big Brain,H.Torch 2.25
46 TDF,AW,PO,F:Fantastic Five . . . 2.25
47 TDF,RF,V:Apox,+ Chapter 1 . . . 2.25
48 TDF,AW,PO,Spider-Man,Kaine . . 2.25
49 TDF,AW,PO,V:Green Goblin . . . 2.25
50 TDF,AW,PO,48-pg. 4.00
51 CJ,. 2.25
52 TDF,AW,RF 2.25
53 TDF,AW,PO. 2.25
54 TDF,AW,PO,Serpent,pt.1 . . . . . 2.25
55 TDF,AW,PO,Serpent,pt.2 . . . . . 2.25
56 TDF,AW,PO,Serpent,pt.3 . . . . . 2.25
57 TDF,AW,PO,Serpent,pt.4 . . . . . 2.25
58 TDF,AW,PO,Serpent,pt.5 . . . . . 2.25
59 TDF,RF,Serpent,pt.6 . . . . 3.00
60 TDF,RF,finale 3.00
61 TDF,RF,Marked for Death,pt.1 . . 3.00
62 TDF,RF,Marked for Death,pt.2 . . 3.00
63 TDF,RF,Marked for Death,pt.3 . . 3.00
64 TDF,RF,Marked for Death,pt.4 . . 3.00
65 TDF,RF,Marked for Death,pt.5 . . 3.00
66 TDF,RF,Marked for Death,pt.6 . . 3.00
67 TDF,RF,Monsters 3.00
68 TDF,RF,The Rules 3.00
69 TDF,RF,Truth,pt.1 . . . . 3.00
70 TDF,RF,Truth,pt.2 . . . . 3.00
71 TDF,RF,F:Doc Magus 3.00
72 TDF,RF,Whispers in the Night . . 3.00
73 TDF,RF,PO,F:Claw,the Cat 3.00
74 TDF,RF,PO,F:Claw,the Cat 3.00
75 TDF,RF,Team Spider. 3.00
76 TDF,RF,Spider-Girl Must Die. . . 3.00
77 TDF,RF,Betrayed. 3.00
78 TDF,RF,People Played
   by Games 3.00
79 RF,If this be my destiny 3.00
80 TDF(s),PO,V:Dragon King 3.00
81 TDF(s),PO F:Electro 3.00
82 TDF(s),RF,V:Venom 3.00
83 TDF(s),RF,Back in Black. 3.00
84 TDF(s),RF,V:New Venom 3.00
85 TDF(s),RF,V:Funny Face 3.00

86 TDF(s),RF,Family Business,pt.1 . 3.00
87 TDF(s),RF,Family Business,pt.2 . 3.00
88 TDF(s),RF,Family Business,pt.3 . 3.00
89 TDF(s),RF, ... 3.00
90 TDF(s),RF, spider-creature 3.00
91 TDF(s),RF,The Sinister Secret
   Of the Spider Shoppe 3.00
92 TDF(s),RF,In the Shadow of Evil 3.00
93 TDF(s),RF,Something Osborn This
   Way Comes. 3.00
94 TDF(s),RF,V:Avengers 3.00
95 TDF(s),RF,A:Green Goblin 3.00
96 TDF(s),RF,A:Kaine 3.00
97 TDF(s),RF,Here Comes
   Hobgoblin 3.00
98 TDF(s),RF,In black costume . . . 3.00
99 TDF(s),RF,A:Tarantula 3.00
100 TDF(s),RF,A:Spider-man,
   104-pg. 4.00
Ann.#1 TDF,PO,AW,A:Green Goblin 6.00
TPB rep. #1 & #2. . . . . 10.00
TPB Spider-Girl,208-page 20.00
Digest Marvel Age, Vol. 1 . . . . . . 8.00
Digest Vol. 1: Legacy. 8.00
Digest Vol. 2: Like Father, Like
   Daughter 8.00
Digest Vol. 3: Avenging Allies . . . 8.00
Digest Vol. 4: Turning Point. 8.00
Digest Vol. 5: Endgame. 8.00
Digest Vol. 6: Too Many Spiders . . 8.00
Digest Vol. 7: Betrayed. 8.00

SPIDER-GIRL PRESENTS: THE BUZZ
May, 2000
1 (of 3) TDF,RF,SB 3.00
2 TDF,RF,SB,A:Spider-Girl 3.00
3 TDF,RF,SB,Dr.Jade 3.00

SPIDER-GIRL PRESENTS: DARKDEVIL
Sept., 2000
1 (of 3) TDF,RF,AM,Kingpin 3.00
2 TDF,RF,AM,O:Darkdevil. 3.00
3 TDF,RF,AM, concl 3.00

SPIDER-MAN
Aug., 1990
1 TM Purple Web(c),V:Lizard,
   A:Calypso,B:Torment. 5.00
1a Silver Web(c). 6.00
1b Bag,Purple Web. 12.00
1c Bag,Silver Web 15.00
1d 2nd print,Gold(c) 5.00
1e 2nd print Gold UPC(rare). . . . 150.00
1f Platinum Ed. 125.00
2 TM,V:Lizard,A:Calypso 6.00
3 TM,V:Lizard,A:Calypso 6.00
4 TM,V:Lizard,A:Calypso 6.00
5 TM,V:Lizard,A:Calypso,
   E:Torment. 6.00
6 TM,A:Ghost Rider,V:Hobgoblin . . 6.00
7 TM,A:Ghost Rider,V:Hobgoblin . . 6.00
8 TM,B:Perceptions,A:Wolverine
   I:Wendigo IV 8.00
9 TM,A:Wolverine,Wendigo 8.00
10 TM,RLd,SW,JLe(i),A:Wolv. 8.00
11 TM,A:Wolverine,Wendigo. 8.00
12 TM,E:Perceptions,A:Wolv. 8.00
13 TM,V:Morbius,R:Black Cost. . . . 6.00
14 TM,V:Morbius,A:Black Cost. . . . 6.00
15 EL,A:Beast 6.00
16 TM,RLd,A:X-Force,V:Juggernaut,
   Black Tom,cont.in X-Force#4 . . 6.00
17 RL,AW,A:Thanos,Death 4.00
18 EL,B:Return of the Sinister Six,
   A:Hulk 4.00
19 EL,A:Hulk,Deathlok. 4.00
20 EL,A:Nova. 4.00
21 EL,A:Hulk,Deathlok,Solo. 4.00

Spider-Man #1
© *Marvel Entertainment Group*

22 EL,A:Ghost Rider,Hulk 4.00
23 EL,E:Return of the Sinister Six,
    A:Hulk,G.Rider,Deathlok,FF. . . . 4.00
24 Infinity War,V:Hobgoblin,
    Demogoblin 4.00
25 CMa,A:Excalibur,V:Arcade 4.00
26 RF,MBa,Hologram(c),30th Anniv.
    I:New Burglar. 5.00
27 MR,Handgun issue 3.00
28 MR,Handgun issue 3.00
29 CMa,Ret.to Mad Dog Ward#1 . . 3.00
30 CMa,Ret.to Mad Dog Ward#2 . . 3.00
31 CMa,Ret.to Mad Dog Ward#3 . . 3.00
32 BMc,A:Punisher,V:Master of
    Vengeance. 3.00
33 BMc,A:Punisher,V:Master of
    Vengeance. 3.00
34 BMc,A:Punisher,V:Master of
    Vengeance. 3.00
35 TL,Total Carnage#4,V:Carnage,
    Shriek,A:Venom,Black Cat 4.00
36 TL,Total Carnage#8,V:Carnage,
    A:Venom,Morblus 4.00
37 TL,Total Carnage#12,
    V:Carnage 4.00
38 thru 40 KJ,V:Electro 3.00
41 TKa(s),JaL,I:Platoon,
    A:Iron Fist 3.00
42 TKa(s),JaL,V:Platoon,
    A:Iron Fist 3.00
43 TKa(s),JaL,V:Platoon,
    A:Iron Fist 3.00
44 HMe(s),TL,V:Hobgoblin 3.00
45 HMe(s),TL,SHa,Pursuit#1,
    V:Chameleon. 2.50
46 HMe(s),TL,V:Hobgoblin,w/cel . . 3.25
46a Newsstand Ed. 2.25
47 TL,SHa,V:Demogoblin 2.50
48 TL,SHa,V:Hobgoblin,
    D:Demogoblin 2.50
49 TL,SHa,I:Coldheart 2.50
50 TL,SHa,I:Grim Hunter,foil(c) 5.00
50a newsstand ed. 2.50
51 TL,SHa,Power,pt.3,foil(c) 4.00
51a newsstand ed. 2.50
52 TL,SHa,Spide-clone,V:Venom . . 2.50
53 TL,SHa,Clone,V:Venom 2.50
54 Web of Life,pt.3 . . . . 3.00
55 Web of Life,finale 2.50
56 Smoke and Mirrors 2.50
57 Aftershocks,pt.1 . . . . 2.50
57a enhanced cover 3.00
58 The Mark of Kaine,pt.3 . . . . 2.50
59 F:Travellor,Host. 2.50
60 TL,SHa,HMa,The Trial of
    Peter Parker,pt.3 . . . . 2.50
61 TL,Maximum Clonage,pt.4 . . . . 2.50

62 HMe,TL,Exiled,pt.3 . . . . 2.50
63 HMe,TL,Greatest
    Responsibility,pt.2 . . . . 2.50
64 HMe,JR2,Return of
    Spider-Man,pt.3 . . . . 2.50
65 HMe,JR2,AW,Media
    Blizzard,pt.3 . . . . 2.50
66 HMe,JR2,Return of Kaine,pt.4 . . 2.50
67 HMe,JR2,Web of Carnage,pt.3. . 2.50
68 HMe,JR2,AW,Blood
    Brothers,pt.3 . . . . 2.50
69 HMe,JR2,Blood Brothers
    aftermath 2.50
70 HMe,JR2,A:Onslaught 3.00
71 HMe,JR2, ... 3.00
72 HMe,JR2,Onslaught saga. 3.00
73 HMe,JR2, ... 3.00
74 HMe,JR2,AW,A:Daredevil,
    V:Fortunato 3.00
75 HMe,JR2,Revelations, pt.4 . . . . 3.50
76 HMe,JR2,SHa,Post-Onslaught
    world,I:Shoc. 2.50
77 HMe,JR2,SHa,V:Morbius 2.50
Becomes:

PETER PARKER, SPIDER-MAN

78 HMe,JR2,SHa,F:Mary Jane
    Parker 2.50
79 HMe,JR2,SHa,V:Hydra,A:Captain
    Arthur Stacy 2.50
80 HMe,JR2,SHa,V:S.H.O.C. 2.50
81 HMe,JR2,SHa,V:Shang-Chi,pt.1. 2.50
82 HMe,JR2,SHa,Anti-Mutant
    Movement 2.50
83 HMe,JR2,SHa,V:Morbius 2.50
85 HMe,JR2,SHa,V:Friends of
    Humanity 2.50
86 HMe,JR2,SHa,F:Jimmy Six,
    Hammerhead. 2.50
87 HMe,JR2,SHa,A:Trapster &
    Shocker 2.50
88 HMe,JR2,SHa,Spider-Man is
    Public Enemy #1 . . . . 2.50
89 HMe,JR2,SHa,Spider-Hunt,pt.3
    x-over. 3.00
90 HMe,JR2,SHa,Identity Crisis
    prelude. 2.50
91 HMe,JR2,SHa,Identity Crisis,
    as Dusk 2.50
92 HMe,JR2,as Dusk, V:Trapster . 2.50
93 HMe,JS,R:Ghost Rider 2.50
94 HMe,JR2,SHa,Who wasJoeyZ?. 2.50
95 HMe,JR2,SHa,Trapped in
    elevator shaft 2.50
96 HMe,JR2,SHa,The Gathering of
    the Five (pt. 3 (of 5)x-over. . . . 2.50
97 HMe,JR2,SHa,JBy(c),The Final
    Chapter,pt.2 x-over 2.50
98 HMe,JR2,SHa,JBy(c),The Final
    Chapter,pt.4 x-over 2.50
98a alternate JBy(c) (1:2) 2.50
Minus 1 Spec., HMe,JR2,SHa,
    flashback, A:Stacys 2.50
Ann.'97 Simon Garth—Zombie 3.50
Ann.'98 HMe, Spider-Man/Elektra,
    V:The Silencer, 48-pg. 3.00
Spec. Chaos in Calgary 2.50
Spec. Double Trouble 2.50
Spec. Hit and Run, Canadian 2.50
Spec. Skating on Thin Ice 2.50
Spec. Trial of Venom,UNICEF 15.00
Spec.#1 Spider-Man (2000). 2.50
Spec. Spider-Man vs. Punisher 3.00
Spec. Year in Review(1999)48-pg. . 3.00
Holiday Spec.'95 . . . . 3.00
Sup.Sz.Spec#1 Planet of the
    Symbiotes, pt.2;
    flipbook F:Scarlet Spider 4.00
Giant-Sized CCI,JBy 4.00
1-shot Spider-Man Startling Stories:
    Megalomaniacal Spider-Man. . . 3.00

Peter Parker Spider-Man #96
© *Marvel Entertainment Group*

Spec.#1 Spider-Man/Daredevil 3.00
GN Fear Itself 13.00
GN Nothing Stops Juggernaut. 4.00
GN Parallel Lives 9.00
GN JMD,MZ,Soul of the Hunter. . . . 6.00
GN Spider-Man: Made Men
    HMe,gangster epic (1998). 6.00
GN Spider-Man ParallelLives(2002) 6.00
GN Sweet Charity,Scorpion,64-pg. . 5.00
TPB Assasination Plot 15.00
TPB Carnage 7.00
TPB Cosmic Adventures 20.00
TPB Death of Gwen Stacy. 15.00
TPB Hooky. 7.00
TPB Identity Crisis 20.00
TPB Maximum Carnage 25.00
TPB Origin of the Hobgoblin 15.00
TPB Return of the Sinister Six. . . . 16.00
TPB Spider-Man. Revelations,JR2,
    rep. +14 new pages (1997). . . 12.00
TPB Round Robin 16.00
TPB Saga of the Alien Costume . . 14.00
    2nd printing 13.00
TPB Spider-Man vs. Venom 10.00
TPB Torment Rep.#1-#5 . . . . 13.00
TPB Venom Returns 13.00
TPB Very Best of Spider-Man 16.00
TPB The Wedding 13.00
TPB Invasion Spider Slayers 16.00
TPB Clone Genesis 17.00
TPB V:Green Goblin 16.00
TPB Spider-Man'sGreatestVillains. 16.00
TPB Spider-Man vs. Doc Oc 18.00
TPB Kraven's Last Hunt (2001). . . 16.00
TPB Torment,128-page (2001) . . . 16.00
TPB Death of Gwen Stacy (2001). 15.00
TPB Visionaries: Todd McFarlane . 20.00
TPB Revenge of the Green Goblin 17.00
TPB Spider-Man: The Wedding . . 16.00
TPB Kraven's Last Hunt 16.00
TPB Death of Gwen Stacy, rep. . . 13.00
TPB Legends (2003) 20.00
TPB Legends, Vol.3 . . . . 25.00
TPB Legends, Vol.4 . . . . 14.00
TPB Death of Captain Stacy 13.00
TPB Son of the Goblin 16.00

SPIDER-MAN ADVENTURES
1994–96

1 From animated series 2.25
1a foil (c). 3.00
2 Animated Adventures. 2.25
3 V:Spider-Slayer 2.25
4 Animated Adventures. 2.25

MARVEL

Spider-Man Adventures #1
© Marvel Entertainment Group

5 V:Mysterio 2.25
6 V:Kraven 2.25
7 V:Doctor Octopus 2.25
8 O:Venom,pt.1 . . . . 2.25
9 O:Venom,pt.2 . . . . 2.25
10 V:Venom 2.25
11 V:Hobgoblin 2.25
12 V:Hobgoblin 2.25
13 V:Chameleon 2.25
14 V:Doc Octopus 2.25
15 Doc Conners 2.25
TPB Rep.#1–#5, 112-pg. 9.00

SPIDER-MAN
& AMAZING FRIENDS
Dec., 1981
1 DSp,A:Iceman,I:Firestar 10.00

SPIDER-MAN AND
POWER PACK
Nov., 2006
1 V: Sandman & Vulture 3.00

SPIDER-MAN
& WOLVERINE
June, 2003
1 (of 4) Stuff of Legends 3.00
2 . . . . 3.00
3 . . . . 3.00
4 concl. 3.00

SPIDER-MAN/BADROCK
Marvel/Maximum Press 1997
1 x-over, pt.1 . . . . 3.00
2 x-over, pt. 2 . . . . 3.00

SPIDER-MAN/BATMAN
1995
1 JMD,MBa,MFm,V:Carnage,Joker 6.00

SPIDER-MAN/BLACK CAT:
THE EVIL THAT MEN DO
June, 2002
1 (of 5) KSm,TyD 3.00
2 KSm,TyD 3.00
3 KSm,TyD 3.00
4 KSm,TyD,concl.(2005 . . . . 3.00
5 KSm,TyD,concl.,pt.2 (2005) 3.00
6 KSm,TyD,concl., pt.3 (2006) 3.00

SPIDER-MAN: BLUE
May, 2002
1 (of 6) JLb,TSe,Green Goblin 5.00
2 JLb,TSe,Gwen Stacy,Rhino 4.00
3 JLb,TSe,Gwen & Mary Jane 4.00
4 JLb,TSe,college years 4.00
5 thru 6 JLb,TSe, ... @4.00
TPB 15.00

SPIDER-MAN: BREAKOUT
April, 2005
1 (of 5) MD2(c) 3.00
2 MD2(c) 3.00
3 MD2(c) 3.00
4 . . . . 3.00
5 Finale 3.00
TPB Breakout. 14.00

SPIDER-MAN, CHAPTER 1
Oct., 1998
1 (of 13) JBy,formative years 2.50
1a signed 20.00
2 JBy,A:Fantastic Four 2.50
2a variant JBy cover 5.00
2b signed, both covers 30.00
3 JBy,V:J.Jonah Jameson 2.50
4 JBy,V:Dr.Octopus & Dr.Doom . . . 2.50
5 JBy,V:Lizard 2.50
6 JBy,V:Electro 2.50
7 JBy,V:Mysterio 2.50
8 JBy,V:Green Goblin 2.50
9 JBy,V:Circus of Crime 2.50
10 JBy,V:Green Goblin 2.50
11 JBy,V:Giant-Man 2.50
12 JBy,V:Sandman, double size
  final issue 4.00
Spec.#0 JBy,O:Sandman,Vulture
  & Lizard 2.50

SPIDER-MAN CLASSICS
1993–94
1 rep.Amazing Fantasy#15 . . . . . . 2.50
2 thru 14 rep.Amaz.SpM . . . . . . @2.50
15 rep.Amaz.SpM#14,w/cel 3.25
15a Newsstand Ed. 2.50

SPIDER-MAN
COMICS MAGAZINE
Jan., 1987
1 . . . . 7.00
2 thru 13 . . . . @6.00

SPIDER-MAN:
DEAD MAN'S HAND
1997
1-shot, RSt,DaR,JeM,V:Carrion . . . 3.00

SPIDER-MAN:
DEATH & DESTINY
June, 2000
1 (of 3) LW,RCa,F:Gwen Stacy 3.00
2 LW,RCa,Doctor Octopus 3.00
3 LW,RCa,concl. 3.00
Spec.Death of Gwen Stacy,64-pg.
  rep. of Amaz.Sp-M #88–#90 . . . 3.50

SPIDER-MAN/
DOCTOR OCTOPUS:
OUT OF REACH
2004
1 (of 5) 3.00
2 thru 5 concl. . . . . @3.00
Digest. 8.00

SPIDER-MAN/DOCTOR
OCTOPUS: YEAR ONE
June, 2004
1 (of 5) First battle 3.00
2 thru 5 concl. . . . . @3.00
TPB series rep. 14.00

SPIDER-MAN FAMILY
Oct., 2005
1-shot,TDF(s),RLm, Spider-Man
  Family 5.00
1-shot Featuring Spider-Clan 5.00
1-shot Featuring Amazing Friends . . 5.00

SPIDER-MAN:
THE FINAL ADVENTURE
1995–96
1 FaN,DaR,Clv,I:Tendril 3.00
2 FaN,DaR,JAl,V:Tendril 3.00
3 FaN,DaR,JAl,V:Tendril 3.00
4 FaN,DaR,JAl,V:Tendril,concl. 3.00

SPIDER-MAN:
FRIENDS AND ENEMIES
1995
1 V:Metahumes 2.00
2 A:Nova,Darkhawk,Speedball 2.00
3 V:Metahumes 2.00
4 F:Metahumes 2.00

SPIDER-MEN: FUNERAL
FOR AN OCTOPUS
1995
1 Doc Oc Dead 2.50
2 A:Sinister Six 2.00
3 Final Issue 2.00

SPIDER-MAN/GEN13
Marvel/Wildstorm 1996
1-shot PDd,SI,CaS x-over 5.00

SPIDER-MAN:
GET KRAVEN
June, 2002
1 (of 7) F:Alyosha Kravinoff 3.00
2 wants to make a movie 2.25
3 thru 6 JQ(c) . . . . @2.25

SPIDER-MAN:
HOBGOBLIN LIVES
1997
1 (of 3) RSt,RF,GP 2.50
2 RSt,RF,GP,Who was the original
  Hobgoblin? 2.50
3 RSt,RF,GP,Original identity
  revealed 2.50
TPB RF(c), series rep. 15.00

SPIDER-MAN:
HOUSE OF M
June, 2005
1 (of 5) MWa&TPe(s),SvL 3.00
2 MWa&tpe(s),Svl 3.00
3 MWa&TPe(s),SvL 3.00
4 MWa&TPe(s),SvL 3.00
5 MWa&TPe(s),Svl 3.00

SPIDER-MAN/
HUMAN TORCH
Jan., 2005
1 (of 5) TTn 3.00
2 TTn,catch You on the Flip-side . . 3.00
3 TTn 3.00

4 TTn,A:Black Cat 3.00
5 TTn,together Again 3.00
Digest I'm With Stupid 8.00

SPIDER-MAN & THE INCREDIBLE HULK
A.C.T.O.R./Marvel Epic, 2003
1-shot benefit issue 2.50

SPIDER-MAN: INDIA
Nov., 2004
1 (of 5) F:Pavitr Prabhakar 3.00
2 . . . . 3.00
3 V:Doc Ock 3.00
4 V:Green Goblin 3.00
5 . . . . 3.00
TPB 10.00

SPIDER-MAN: LEGEND OF THE SPIDER-CLAN
Marvel Mangaverse Oct., 2002
1 (of 3) 2.25
2 F:Manga Daredevil 2.25
3 F:Manga Green Govlin 2.25
4 . . . . 2.25
5 concl 2.25

SPIDER-MAN: LIFELINE
Feb., 2001
1 (of 3) FaN,SR,BWi, ... 3.00
2 FaN,SR,BWi,V:Hammerhead . . . 3.00
3 FaN,SR,BWi,concl. 3.00

SPIDER-MAN LOVES MARY JANE
Dec., 2005
1 The Boyfriend Thing 3.00
2 thru 12 . . . . @3.00
Digest Vol. 1: Super Crush 8.00

SPIDER-MAN: THE MANGA
Black & White, Oct., 1997
Bi-weekly
1 imported, translated 4.00
2 thru 14 . . . . @3.00
15 V:Mysterio, double size 4.00
16 thru 37 . . . . @3.00

Spider-Man The Manga #20
© Marvel Entertainment Group

SPIDER-MAN: MAXIMUM CLONAGE
1995
Alpha Maximum Clonage,pt.1 . . . . . 5.50
Omega TL,Maximum Clonage,pt.6 . 5.00

SPIDER-MAN MEGAZINE
1994–95
1 thru 4 rep . . . . @3.00
5 Vision rep. 3.00
6 V:Thing & Torch, rep. 3.00

SPIDER-MAN: THE MOVIE
April, 2002
GN StL,AD,photo(c), 48-pg. 6.00
TPB movie + stories, 112-pg. 13.00

SPIDER-MAN 2: THE MOVIE
June, 2004
1-shot 48-pg. 3.50
TPB The Movie 13.00

SPIDER-MAN: MUTANT AGENDA
0 thru 2 Paste in Book . . . . @2.25
3 Paste in Book 2.25

SPIDER-MAN: THE MYSTERIO MANIFESTO
Nov., 2000
1 (of 3) TDF,BMc,LW 3.00
2 TDF,BMc,LW 3.00
3 TDF,BMc,LW,concl. 3.00

SPIDER-MAN: POWER OF TERROR
1995
1 R:Silvermane,A:Deathlok. 2.25
2 V:Silvermane 2.25
3 New Scorpion 2.25
4 V:Silvermane 2.25

SPIDER-MAN/PUNISHER
Part 1 TL,A:Tombstone 3.00
Part 2 TL,A:Tombstone 3.00

SPIDER-MAN/PUNISHER/ SABERTOOTH: DESIGNER GENES
1 SMc,Foil(c). 9.50

SPIDER-MAN: QUALITY OF LIFE
May, 2002
1 (of 4) V:The Lizard, 40-pg 3.00
2 the Yith 3.00
3 V:The Lizard 3.00
4 concl 3.00
TPB series rep. 13.00

SPIDER-MAN: REDEMPTION
1996
1 thru 4 JMD,MZ,BMc, Mary Jane
   arrested for Murder . . . . @2.25

SPIDER-MAN: REVENGE OF THE GREEN GOBLIN
Aug., 2000
1 (of 3) RCa,LW,RSt,R:Norman
   Osborn 3.00

Spider-Man: Redemption #3
© Marvel Entertainment Group

2 LW,RSt,F:Norman Osborn 3.00
3 RSt,RF,PO, concl. 3.00

SPIDER-MAN SAGA
Nov., 1991
1 SLi(c),History from Amazing
   Fantasy #15-Amaz.SpM #100 . . 3.25
2 SLi(c),Amaz.SpM #101-#175 . . . . 3.25
3 Amaz.SpM #176-#238 . . . . 3.25
4 Amaz.SpM #239-#300 . . . . 3.25

SPIDER-MAN SPECIAL
Sept., 2006
1-shot Black and Blue and Read All 4.00

SPIDER-MAN SUPER SIZE SPECIAL
1 Planet of the Symbiotes,pt.2 . . . . 4.00

SPIDER-MAN TEAM-UP
1995–96
1 MWa,KeL,V:Hellfire Club 3.00
2 thru 4 . . . . @3.00
5 SvG,DaR,JFr,F:Gambit,
   Howard the Duck. 3.00
6 JMD,LHa,F:Hulk & Doctor
   Strange 3.00
7 KBk,SB,F:Thunderbolts 3.00

SPIDER-MAN TEAM-UP
March, 2005
1-shot Spider-Man & Fantastic Four
   Vs. Mole Man 3.00

SPIDER-MAN: THE ARACHNIS PROJECT
1984–95
1 Wld, beginnings 2.25
2 Wld,V:Diggers 2.25
3 Wld,V:Jury 2.25
4 Wld,V:Life Foundation 2.25
5 Wld,V:Jury 2.25

SPIDER-MAN: THE CLONE JOURNALS
1-shot (1995) 2.25

All comics prices listed are for *Near Mint* condition.   **CVA Page 321**

SPIDER-MAN: THE JACKAL FILES
1 Files of the Jackal (1995) 2.25

SPIDER-MAN: THE LOST YEARS
1995
0 JMD,JR2,LSh,64-pg.,rep. 4.00
1 History of Kaine,Ben 3.00
2 JMD,JR2,KJ,Kaine & Ben 3.00
3 Ben vs. Kaine 3.00

SPIDER-MAN: THE OTHER
Oct., 2005
Spec. Sketchbook 3.00

SPIDER-MAN: THE PARKER YEARS
1995
1 JR2,JPi,F:The Real Clone 2.50

SPIDER-MAN 2099
1992–96
1 RL,AW,I:Spider-Man 2099 . . . . . . 4.00
2 RL,AW,O:Spider-Man 2099 . . . . . 3.00
3 RL,AW,V:Venture 2.50
4 RL,AW,I:Specialist,
   A:Doom 2099 . . . . 2.25
5 RL,AW,V:Specialist 2.25
6 RL,AW,I:New Vulture 2.25
7 RL,AW,Vulture of 2099 . . . . 2.25
8 RL,AW,V:New Vulture 2.25
9 KJo,V:Alchemax. 2.25
10 RL,AW,O:Wellvale Home 2.25
11 RL,AW,V:S.I.E.G.E. 2.25
12 RL,AW,w/poster 2.25
13 RL,AW,V:Thanatos 2.25
14 PDd(s),RL(c),TGb,Downtown . . . 2.25
15 PDd(s),RL,I:Thor 2099,
   Heimdall 2099 . . . . 2.25
16 PDd(s),RL,Fall of the
   Hammer #1 . . . . 2.25
17 PDd(s),RL,V:Bloodsword 2.25
18 PDd(s),RLm,V:Lyla 2.25
19 PDd(s),RL,w/card 2.25
20 PDd(s),RL,Crash & Burn 2.25
21 V:Gangs 2.25
22 V:Gangs 2.25
23 RL,I:Risque 3.00
24 Kasey 2.25
25 A:Hulk 2099, dbl-size,foil(c) 4.00

Spiderman 2099 #42
© Marvel Entertainment Group

25a Newsstand ed. 2.50
26 V:Headhunter, Travesty 2.25
27 V:Travesty 2.25
28 V:Travesty 2.25
29 V:Foragers 2.25
30 V:Flipside 2.25
31 I:Dash 2.25
Becomes:

SPIDER-MAN 2099 A.D.
32 I:Morgue 2.25
33 One Nation Under Doom 2.25
34 V:Alchemex. 2.25
35 . . . . 2.25
36a Spider-Man 2099(c) 2.25
36b Venom 2099(c) 2.25
37a Venom 2099 . . . . 2.25
37b variant cover 2.25
38 . . . . 2.25
39 A:Venom 2099 . . . . 2.25
40 V:Goblin 2099 . . . . 2.25
41 and 42 . . . . @2.25
43 V:Sub-Mariner 2099 . . . . 2.25
Ann.#1 PDd(s),RL 3.00
Spec.#1 I:3 new villains 4.00

SPIDER-MAN UNLIMITED
1993
1 RLm,Maximun Carnage #1,
   I:Shriek,R:Carnage 6.00
2 RLm,Maximum Carnage #14. . . . 4.50
3 RLm,O:Doctor Octopus 4.50
4 RLm,V:Mystrerio,Rhino 4.25
5 RLm,A:Human Torch,
   I:Steel Spider 4.25
6 RLm,A:Thunderstrike 4.25
7 RLm,A:Clone 4.25
8 Tom Lyle. 4.25
9 The Mark of Kaine,pt.5 . . . . 4.25
10 SwM,Exiled,pt.4 . . . . 4.25
11 FaN,V:Black Cat 4.25
12 Blood Brother,tie-in 4.25
13 . . . . 3.25
14 JoB, an ally dies 3.25
15 TDF,JoB,F:Puma. 3.25
16 cont. from X-Force #64. . . . . 3.25
17 JoB, Revelations, sequel 3.25
18 TDF,JoB,F:Doctor Octopus. 3.25
19 JoB,F:Lizard 3.25
20 JoB,A:Hannibal King, V:Lilith . . . 3.25
21 MD2,Frankenstein Monster Lives 3.25
22 MD2,V:The Scorpion. 3.25

SPIDER-MAN UNLIMITED
Nov., 1999
1 cartoon, tie-in 3.50
2 thru 4 . . . . @2.25

SPIDER-MAN UNLIMITED
Jan., 2004
1 V:Slyde. 3.00
2 F:Mary Jane. 3.00
3 thru 10 . . . . @3.00
11 thru 15 . . . . @3.00

SPIDER-MAN UNIVERSE
Jan., 2000
1 rep. 3 stories, 80-pg. 5.00
2 thru 6 rep. 3 stories, 80-pg. . . . @5.00
7 thru 9 rep. 3 stories, 80-pg . . . . @4.00

SPIDER-MAN UNMASKED
1996
1-shot 64-pg. information source . . 6.00

SPIDER-MAN VS. DRACULA
1994
1 rep. 2.25

SPIDER-MAN VS. VENOM
1990
1 TM(c) 9.00

SPIDER-MAN: THE VENOM AGENDA
Nov., 1997
1-shot LHa,TL, J. Jonah Jameson,
   V:Venom 3.00

SPIDER-MAN VS. WOLVERINE
1990
1 MBr,AW,D:Ned Leeds(the original
   Hobgoblin),V:Charlie 25.00
1a reprint. 5.00

SPIDER-MAN: WEB OF DOOM
1994
1 3-part series. 2.25
2 Spidey falsely accused 2.25
3 conclusion 2.25

SPIDER-MAN & X-FACTOR: SHADOW GAMES
1 PB,I:Shadowforce 2.25
2 PB,V:Shadowforce 2.25
3 PB,V:Shadowforce, final issue. . . 2.25

SPIDER-WOMAN
April, 1978
1 CI,TD,O:Spider-Woman. 25.00
2 CI,TD,I:Morgan LeFey 6.00
3 CI,TD,I:Brothers Grimm 6.00
4 CI,TD,V:Hangman 6.00
5 CI,TD,Nightmares 6.00
6 CI,A:Werewolf By Night 7.00
7 CI,SL,AG,V:Magnus 6.00
8 CI,AG,Man Who Would Not Die . 6.00
9 CI,AG,A:Needle,Magnus 6.00
10 CI,AG,I:Gypsy Moth 6.00
11 CI,AG,V:Brothers Grimm 6.00
12 CI,AG,V:Brothers Grimm. 6.00
13 CI,AG,A:Shroud. 6.00
14 BSz(c),CI,AG,A:Shroud. 6.00
15 BSz(c),CI,AG,A:Shroud. 6.00
16 BSz(c),CI,AG,V:Nekra. 6.00
17 CI,Death Plunge 6.00
18 CI,A:Flesh 6.00
19 CI,A:Werewolf By Night,
   V:Enforcer 7.00
20 FS,A:Spider-Man 7.00
21 FS,A:Bounty Hunter 6.00
22 FS,A:Killer Clown 6.00
23 TVE,V:The Gamesmen. 6.00
24 TVE,V:The Gamesmen. 6.00
25 SL,Two Spider-Women 6.00
26 JBy(c),SL,V:White Gardenia. . . . 6.00
27 BSz(c),JBi,A:Enforcer. 6.00
28 BSz(c),SL,A:Enforcer,Spidey . . 7.00
29 JR2(c),ECh,FS,A:Enforcer,
   Spider-Man 7.00
30 FM(c),SL,JM,I:Dr.Karl Malus. . . 6.00
31 FM(c),SL,JM,A:Hornet 6.00
32 FM(c),SL,JM,A:Werewolf 6.00
33 SL,V:Yesterday's Villain 6.00
34 SL,AM,V:Hammer and Anvil . . . 6.00
35 SL,AG,V:Angar the Screamer . . 6.00
36 SL,Spider-Woman Shot 6.00
37 SL,TA,BWi,AM,FS,A:X-Men,I:
   Siryn,V:Black Tom 10.00
38 SL,BWi,A:X-Men,Siryn 10.00
39 SL,BWi,Shadows 5.00
40 SL,BWi,V:The Flying Tiger 5.00
41 SL,BWi,V:Morgan LeFay 5.00

MARVEL

42 SL,BWi,V:Silver Samurai 5.00
43 SL,V:Silver Samurai 5.00
44 SL,V:Morgan LeFay 5.00
45 SL,Spider-Man Thief cover 5.00
46 SL,V:Mandroids,A:Kingpin 5.00
47 V:Daddy Longlegs. 5.00
48 O:Gypsy Moth. 5.00
49 A:Tigra 5.00
50 PH(c),D:Spider-Woman 15.00

[Limited Series] 1993–94
1 V:Therak 2.25
2 O:Spider-Woman 2.25
3 V:Deathweb 2.25
4 V:Deathweb, last issue 2.25

SPIDER-WOMAN
May, 1999
1 JBy,BS,48-pg. 3.00
1a signed 20.00
2 BS,JBy,A:Dr. Octopus 2.25
2a variant JR2 cover. 2.25
3 BS,JBy,V:Flesh & Bones 2.25
4 BS,JBy,V:Flesh & Bones 2.25
5 BS,JBy,I:Shadowcaster 2.25
6 BS,JBy,V:Shadowcaster 2.25
7 BS,JBy. 2.25
8 BS,JBy,A:Cluster,x-over. 2.25
9 BS,JBy,A:Mattie 2.25
10 BS,JBy,A:Rhino. 2.25
11 BS,JBy,V:Exomorph 2.25
12 BS,JBy,F:J.Jonah Jameson . . . 2.25
13 BS,JBy,V:Werewolf 2.25
14 JBy,GN,BS(c),V:Nighteyes 2.25
15 JBy,BS,Itch & Scratch. 2.25
16 JBy,BS,Flesh. 2.25
17 JBy,BS,Flesh & Bones 2.25
18 JBy,BS,final issue 2.25

SPIDER-WOMAN
July, 2005
Giant Size #1 classic reprints 5.00

SPIDER-WOMAN: ORIGIN
Dec., 2005
1 BMB(s). 3.00
2 thru 5 BMB(s) 3.00

SPIDEY AND THE MINI MARVELS
April, 2003
Spec. Bullpen bits, 40-pg. 3.50

SPIDEY SUPER STORIES
Oct., 1974
1 Younger reader's series in
   association with the Electric
   Company,O:Spider-Man 55.00
2 A:Kraven 30.00
3 A:Ringleader 20.00
4 A:Medusa 20.00
5 A:Shocker 20.00
6 A:Iceman 20.00
7 A:Lizard, Vanisher 20.00
8 A:Dr. Octopus 20.00
9 A:Dr. Doom 20.00
10 A:Green Goblin 20.00
11 A:Dr. Octopus 18.00
12 A:The Cat,V:The Owl 18.00
13 A:Falcon 18.00
14 A:Shanna 20.00
15 A:Storm 18.00
16 . . . . 18.00
17 A:Captain America 18.00
18 A:Kingpin. 18.00
19 A:Silver Surfer,Dr. Doom. 18.00
20 A:Human Torch,Invisible Girl . 18.00
21 A:Dr. Octopus 16.00

Spidey Super Stories #26
© Marvel Entertainment Group

22 A:Ms. Marvel,The Beetle. 16.00
23 A:Green Goblin 16.00
24 A:Thundra 16.00
25 A:Dr. Doom. 16.00
26 A:Sandman 16.00
27 A:Thor,Loki 16.00
28 A:Medusa 16.00
29 A:Kingpin. 16.00
30 A:Kang 16.00
31 A:Moondragon,Dr. Doom 15.00
32 A:Spider-Woman,Dr. Octopus . . 15.00
33 . . . . 15.00
34 A:Sub-Mariner. 15.00
35 . . . . 15.00
36 A:Lizard. 15.00
37 A:White Tiger 15.00
38 A:Fantastic Four 15.00
39 A:Hellcat,Thanos. 18.00
40 A:Hawkeye 15.00
41 A:Nova,Dr. Octopus 15.00
42 A:Kingpin 15.00
43 A:Daredevil,Ringmaster 15.00
44 A:Vision 15.00
45 A:Silver Surfer,Dr. Doom. 18.00
46 A:Mysterio. 15.00
47 A:Spider-Woman,Stilt-Man 15.00
48 A:Green Goblin 15.00
49 Spidey for President 15.00
50 A:She-Hulk 15.00
51 and 52. . . . . @15.00
53 A:Dr. Doom 15.00
54 Attack of the Bird-Man 15.00
55 A:Kingpin. 15.00
56 A:Captain Britain,
   Jack O'Lantern 15.00
57 March, 1982 . . . . 15.00

SPITFIRE AND THE TROUBLESHOOTERS
Oct., 1986
1 HT/JSt 2.50
2 HT 2.50
3 HT,Macs Armor 2.50
4 TM/BMc(Early TM work) 3.50
5 HT/TD,A:Star Brand. 2.50
6 HT,Trial. 2.50
7 HT 2.50
8 HT,New Armor 2.50
9 . . . . 2.50
Becomes:
CODE NAME: SPITFIRE
10 MR/TD. 2.25
11 thru 13 . . . . @2.25

SPOOF
Oct., 1970
1 MSe 25.00
2 MSe,Brawl in the Family 15.00
3 MSe,Richard Nixon cover 15.00
4 MSe,Blechhula. 15.00
5 MSe,May, 1973 . . . . 20.00

SPORT STARS
Nov., 1949
1 The Life of Knute Rockne 600.00
Becomes:
SPORTS ACTION
2 BP(c),Life of George Gipp 600.00
3 BEv,Hack Wilson 300.00
4 Art Houtteman 250.00
5 Nile Kinnick 250.00
6 Warren Gun 250.00
7 Jim Konstanty 250.00
8 Ralph Kiner 275.00
9 Ed 'Strangler' Lewis 250.00
10 JMn,The Yella-Belly 250.00
11 The Killers. 250.00
12 BEv,Man Behind the Mask . . . 250.00
13 BEv,Lew Andrews. 260.00
14 MWs,Ken Roper,Sept.,1952 . . 260.00

SPOTLIGHT
Sept., 1978
1 F:Huckleberry Hound,Yogi Bear 50.00
2 Quick Draw McGraw 35.00
3 The Jetsons 35.00
4 Magilla Gorilla, March, 1979 . . . 30.00

SPUMCO COMIC BOOK
1 I:Jimmy the Hapless Boy 7.00
2 . . . . 7.00
3 64-pgs. of sick humor 7.00
4 More sick humor 7.00
TPB 25.00

SPY CASES
See: KID KOMICS

SPY FIGHTERS
March, 1951
1 GT 300.00
2 GT 150.00
3 . . . . 125.00
4 thru 13 . . . . @125.00
14 thru 15 July, 1953 . . . . . . @135.00

SPYKE
Epic *Heavy Hitters,* 1993
1 MBn,BR,I:Spyke. 2.75
2 MBn,BR,V:Conita. 2.75
3 thru 4 MBn,BR . . . . @2.00

SPY THRILLERS
Atlas, Nov., 1954
1 AyB(c),The Tickling Death 250.00
2 V:Communists 150.00
3 . . . . 100.00
4 . . . . 100.00
Becomes:
POLICE BADGE
5 Sept., 1955 . . . . 125.00

SQUADRON SUPREME
Sept., 1985
1 BH,L:Nighthawk. 5.00
2 BH,F:Nuke,A:Scarlet Centurion . 4.00
3 BH,D:Nuke. 4.00
4 BH,L:Archer. 4.00
5 BH,L:Amphibian. 4.00
6 PR,J:Institute of Evil 4.00
7 JB,JG,V:Hyperion. 4.00

8 BH,V:Hyperion	4.00
9 BSz(c),PR,D:Tom Thumb	4.00
10 PR,V:Quagmire	4.00
11 PR,V:Redeemers	4.00
12 PR,D:Nighthawk,Foxfire, Black Archer	4.00
GN Death of a Universe	12.00
TPB 352 pages	15.00

SQUADRON SUPREME
March, 2006

1 MSz(s)	3.00
2 thru 7 MSz(s)	@3.00
8 MSz(s),MD2	3.00
9 MSz(s),MD2	3.00
Spec.#1 Saga of the Squadron Supreme (Feb., 2006)	4.00

STALKERS
Epic, 1990–91

1 MT	2.25
2 thru 12 MT	@2.25

STAN LEE MEETS...
Sept., 2006

Spider-Man #1	4.00
Dr. Strange #1	4.00
The Thing #1	4.00
Silver Surfer #1	4.00
Dr. Doom #1	4.00

STARBLAST
1994

1 MGu(s),HT,After the Starbrand	2.25
2 MGu(s),HT,After the Starbrand	2.25
3 MGu(s),HT,After the Starbrand	2.25
4 MGu(s),HT,final issue	2.25

STARBRAND
Oct., 1986

1 JR2,O:Starbrand	2.50
2 thru 8 JR2/AW	@2.50
9 thru 15	@2.50
16 thru 19	@3.00
Ann.#1	3.00

STAR COMICS MAGAZINE
Dec., 1986 (digest size)

1 F:Heathcliff,Muppet Babies, Ewoks	2.25
2 thru 13 1988	@2.25

STARJAMMERS
1995–96

1 I:The Uncreated	3.00
2 thru 4	@3.00

STARJAMMERS
July, 2004

1 (of 6) Cadet & Corsairs,pt.1	3.00
2 thru 6 Cadet and the Corsairs, pt.2 thru pt.6	@3.00

STAR-LORD, SPECIAL EDITION
Feb., 1982

1 JBy reprints	6.00

STARLORD
Mini-Series 1996

1 (of 3) DLw	2.50
2 DLw	2.50
3 DLw,V:Damyish	2.50

STARLORD MEGAZINE

TPB CCI,JBy,TA, rep., 64-pg.	3.00

STAR MASTER

1 MGu,Cosmic Avengers assemble	2.25
2 MGu,World Engine saga	2.25
3 MGu,Cauldron of Conversion	2.25

STARRIORS
Aug., 1984

1	4.00
2	3.00
3	3.00
4	3.00

STARSTRUCK
March, 1985

1 MK	3.00
2 thru 8 MK, Feb., 1986	@3.00

STARTLING STORIES: THE THING–NIGHT FALLS ON YANCY ST.
May, 2003

1 (of 4) EDo(s),40-pg	3.50
2 EDo(s),40-pg.	3.50
3 EDo(s),40-pg.	3.50
4 EDo(s),concl.	3.50
Spec. Last Line of Defense	3.50

STARTLING STORIES: THE INCORRIGIBLE HULK
Jan., 2004

1-shot	3.00

STAR TREK
April, 1980

1 DC,KJ,rep.1st movie adapt.	15.00
2 DC,KJ,rep.1st movie adapt.	8.00
3 DC,KJ,rep.1st movie adapt.	8.00
4 thru 16	@8.00
17 EH,TP,The Long Nights Dawn	15.00
18 A Thousand Deaths,last issue	20.00

STAR TREK: DEEP SPACE NINE
1996

1 HWe(s),TGb,AM,DS9 in the Gamma Quadrant,pt.1 (of 2)	3.00
2 thru 15	@2.50

STAR TREK: EARLY VOYAGES
Dec., 1996

1 DAn,IEd,Captain Pike's crew, double size premier	4.00
2 thru 17	@2.50

STAR TREK

GN Star Trek, First Contact Movie adapt.	6.00
1-shot Mirror, Mirror (1996).	4.00
1-shot Operation Assimilation	3.00
1-shot Telepathy War, pt.4 x-over, 48-pg.(1997)	3.00

STAR TREK: THE NEXT GENERATION RIKER SPECIAL
May, 1998

1-shot, DAn,IEd,Riker photo cover	3.50

Star Trek Deep Space Nine #9
© Marvel Entertainment Group

STAR TREK: THE NEXT GENERATION/X-MEN: SECOND CONTACT
March, 1998

1-shot, DAn,IEd,64-pg.	5.00
1-shot, variant CNr cover (1:5)	5.00

STAR TREK: STARFLEET ACADEMY
1996

1 Cadets vs. Gorns	2.50
2 thru 19	@2.50

STAR TREK: UNLIMITED
1996

1 DAn,IEd,MBu,JeM,AW, Classic series & TNG	5.00
2 thru 10	@4.00

STAR TREK: THE UNTOLD VOYAGES
Jan., 1998

1	3.00
2	3.00
3	3.00
4	3.00
5 48-pg. finale	3.50

STAR TREK: VOYAGER
1996

1	3.00
2 thru 15	@3.00

STAR TREK: VOYAGER: SPLASHDOWN
Jan., 1998

1 thru 4 AM	@3.00

STAR TREK/X-MEN

1-shot SLo,MS, 64-pg.	5.00
1a rep. of STAR TREK/X-MEN	5.00

STAR WARS
July, 1977

1 HC,30 Cent,movie adaption.	65.00
1a HC,35 Cent(square Box).	725.00
1b "Reprint".	7.50
2 HC,movie adaptation	30.00

2b "Reprint". 4.00
3 HC,movie adaptation 25.00
3b "Reprint". 4.00
4 HC,SL,movie adapt.(low dist.) . . 22.00
4b "Reprint". 4.00
5 HC,SL,movie adaptation 22.00
5b "Reprint". 3.00
6 HC,DSt,E:movie adaption 22.00
6b "Reprint". 3.00
7 HC,FS,F:Luke & Chewbacca. . . 20.00
8 HC,TD,Eight against a World . . 20.00
9 HC,TP,V:Cloud Riders 20.00
7b thru 9b "Reprint". . . . . @2.50
10 HC,TP,Behemoth From Below . 22.00
11 CI,TP,Fate of Luke Skywalker. . 20.00

Star Wars #12
© *Marvel Entertainment Group*

12 TA,CI,Doomworld 20.00
13 TA,JBy,CI,Deadly Reunion 20.00
14 TA,CI. 20.00
15 CI,V:Crimson Jack 20.00
16 WS,V:The Hunter 20.00
17 Crucible, low dist. 20.00
18 CI,Empire Strikes,low dist. 20.00
19 CI,Ultimate Gamble,low dist . . . 20.00
20 CI,Death Game, scarce 20.00
21 TA,CI,Shadow of a Dark
    Lord(Scarce) 20.00
22 CI,Han Solo vs.Chewbacca . . . 15.00
23 CI,Flight Into Fury. 15.00
24 CI,Ben Kenobi Story 15.00
25 CI,Siege at Yavin 15.00
26 CI,Doom Mission 15.00
27 CI,V:The Hunter 15.00
28 CI,Cavern o/t Crawling Death. . 15.00
29 CI,Dark Encounter 15.00
30 CI,A Princess Alone 15.00
31 CI,Return to Tatooine 15.00
32 CI,The Jawa Express 15.00
33 CI,GD,V:Baron Tagge 15.00
34 CI,Thunder in the Stars. 15.00
35 CI,V:Darth Vader. 15.00
36 CI,V:Darth Vader. 15.00
37 CI,V:Darth Vader. 15.00
38 TA,MG,Riders in the Void 15.00
39 AW,B:Empire Strikes Back 25.00
40 AW,Battleground Hoth. 25.00
41 AW,Imperial Pursuit. 25.00
42 AW,Bounty Hunters. 25.00
43 AW,Betrayal at Bespin 25.00
44 AW,E:Empire Strikes Back 25.00
45 CI,GD,Death Probe. 15.00
46 DI,TP,V:Dreamnaut Devourer . . 15.00
47 CI,GD,Droid World 15.00
48 CI,Leia vs.Darth Vader 15.00
49 SW,TP,The Last Jedi 15.00
50 WS,AW,TP,G-Size issue 15.00

51 WS,TP,Resurrection of Evil. . . . 12.00
52 WS,TP,D:Death Star II 12.00
53 CI,WS,Gift of Alderaan 12.00
54 CI,WS,Starfire Rising 12.00
55 thru 66 WS,TP . . . . @12.00
67 TP, The Darker 12.00
68 GD,TP,O:Boba Fett. 20.00
69 GD,TP,Death in City of Bone . . 20.00
70 A:Han Solo 20.00
71 A:Han Solo 20.00
72 Fool's Boontu 20.00
73 Secret of Planet Lansbane 20.00
74 thru 91 . . . . @20.00
92 BSz(c),The Dream 22.00
93 thru 97 . . . . @20.00
98 AW,Supply & Demand 20.00
99 Touch of Goddess. 20.00
100 Painted(c),double-size 22.00
101 BSz, Far,Far Away 22.00
102 KRo's Back 15.00
103 thru 106. . . . . @15.00
107 WPo(i),last issue 90.00
Ann.#1 WS(c),V:Winged Warlords 100.00
Ann.#2 RN 15.00
Ann.#3 RN,Darth Vader(c) 15.00

STEELGRIP STARKEY
Epic, July, 1986
1 . . . . 2.50
2 thru 5 . . . . @2.50
6 June, 1987 . . . . 2.50

STEELTOWN ROCKERS
April, 1990—Sept., 1990
1 SL 2.25
2 thru 6 SL . . . . @2.25

STOKER'S DRACULA
Oct., 2004
1 (of 4) RTs,DG. 4.00
2 . . . . 4.00
3 RTs(s),DG 4.00
4 Rts(s),Dg 4.00

STORIES OF ROMANCE
Marvel Atlas, 1956
5 MB,ViC(c) 150.00
6 . . . . 100.00
7 . . . . 100.00
8 . . . . 100.00
9 ViC 125.00
10 . . . . 100.00
11 MB,ViC,JR. 150.00
12 . . . . 120.00
13 ABr 150.00

STORM
1 TyD,KIS,V:Candra 4.00
2 . . . . 4.00
3 . . . . 4.00
4 TyD,KIS, conclusion,foil cover . . . 4.00

STORM
Feb., 2006
1 Storm & Black Panther 3.00
2 thru 6 . . . . @3.00

STORMBREAKER: THE SAGA OF BETA RAY BILL
Jan., 2005
1 (of 6) 3.00
2 I:stardust 3.00
3 V:Stardust 3.00
4 . . . . 3.00
5 Return to Asgard 3.00
6 Vs. Spider-Man 3.00
TPB The Saga of Beta Ray Bill . . . 17.00

STRANGE
Sept., 2004
1 MSz,BPe,O:Dr.Strange 3.50
2 MSz,BPe,. 3.50
3 . . . . 3.50
4 MSz(s),BPe 3.50
5 MSz(s),Bpe,new Costume. 3.50
6 MSz(s),BPe, finale. 3.50
TPB Beginnings and Endings 18.00

STRANGE COMBAT TALES
1 and 2 . . . . @2.75
3 Tiger by the Tail 2.50
4 Midnight Crusade. 2.50

STRANGE STORIES OF SUS-PENSE See: RUGGED ACTION

STRANGE TALES
[1st Regular Series] June, 1951
1 The Room. 4,800.00
2 Trapped In A Tomb 1,500.00
3 JMn,Man Who Never Was . . 1,200.00
4 BEv,Terror in the Morgue . . . 1,300.00
5 A Room Without A Door 1,200.00
6 RH(c),The Ugly Man 800.00
7 Who Stands Alone 800.00
8 BEv(c),Something in the Fog. . 800.00
9 Drink Deep Vampire 800.00
10 BK,Hidden Head 900.00
11 BEv(c),GC,'O'Malley's Friend . 600.00
12 Graveyard At Midnight 600.00
13 BEv(c),Death Makes A Deal . . 600.00
14 GT,Horrible Herman 600.00
15 BK,Don't Look Down. 600.00
16 Decapitation cover 600.00
17 DBr,JRo,Death Feud. 600.00
18 Witch Hunt 600.00
19 RH(c),The Rag Doll 600.00
20 RH(c),GC,SMo,Lost World . . . 600.00
21 BEv 500.00
22 BK,JF 500.00
23 Strangest Tale in the World. . . 500.00
24 The Thing in the Coffin 500.00
25 . . . . 500.00
26 . . . . 500.00
27 JF,The Garden of Death 500.00
28 Come into my Coffin 500.00
29 Witch-Craft 500.00
30 The Thing in the Box 500.00
31 Man Who Played with Blocks . 500.00
32 . . . . 500.00
33 JMn(c),Step Lively Please . . . 500.00

Strange Tales #72
© *Marvel Entertainment Group*

MARVEL

34 Flesh and Blood 475.00
35 The Man in the Bottle 400.00
36 . . . . 400.00
37 Out of the Storm 400.00
38 . . . . 400.00
39 Karnoff's Plan 400.00
40 BEv,Man Who Caught
   a Mermaid 400.00
41 BEv,Riddle of the Skull 425.00
42 DW,BEv,JMn,Faceless One . . 425.00
43 JF,The Mysterious Machine . . 400.00
44 . . . . 400.00
45 JKa,Land of Vanishing Men . . 425.00
46 thru 57 . . . . @400.00
58 AW 400.00
59 BK 400.00
60 . . . . 375.00
61 BK 400.00
62 . . . . 375.00
63 . . . . 400.00
64 AW 400.00
65 . . . . 375.00
66 . . . . 375.00
67 thru 78 . . . . @450.00
79 SD,JK,Dr.Strange Prototype . 450.00
80 thru 83 SD,JK . . . . @350.00
84 SD,JK,Magneto Prototype . . . 350.00
85 SD,JK 350.00
86 SD,JK,I Created Mechano . . . 350.00
87 SD,JK,Return of Grogg 350.00
88 SD,JK,Zzutak 350.00
89 SD,JK,Fin Fang Foom 900.00
90 SD,JK,Orrgo Unconquerable . 350.00
91 SD,JK,The Sacrifice 350.00
92 SD,JK,Thing That Waits 350.00
93 SD,JK,The Wax People 350.00
94 SD,JK,Pildorr the Plunderer . 350.00
95 SD,JK,Two-Headed Thing . . . 350.00
96 SD,JK,I Dream of Doom 350.00
97 SD,JK,When A Planet Dies . . 700.00
98 SD,JK,No Human Can
   Beat Me 350.00
99 SD,JK,Mister Morgan's
   Monster 350.00
100 SD,JK,I Was Trapped
    in the Crazy Maze 350.00
101 B:StL(s),SD,JK,
    B:Human Torch 2,500.00
102 SD,JK,I:Wizard 1,000.00
103 SD,JK,I:Zemu 900.00
104 SD,JK,I:The Trapster 900.00
105 SD,JK,V:Wizard 900.00
106 SD,A:Fantastic Four 600.00
107 SD,V:Sub-Mariner 750.00
108 SD,JK,A:FF,I:The Painter . . . 600.00
109 SD,JK,I:Sorcerer 600.00
110 SD,I&B:Dr.Strange,
    Nightmare 3,000.00
111 SD,I:Asbestos,BaronMordo 1,100.00
112 SD,I:The Eel 325.00
113 SD,I:Plant Man 325.00
114 SD,JK,A:Captain America . 1,500.00
115 SD,O:Dr.Strange 1,500.00
116 SD,V:Thing 400.00
117 SD,V:The Eel 300.00
118 SD,V:The Wizard 400.00
119 SD,C:Spider-Man 400.00
120 SD,1st Iceman/Torch T.U. . . . 450.00
121 SD,V:Plant Man 200.00
122 SD,V:Dr.Doom 175.00
123 SD,A:Thor,I:Beetle 200.00
124 SD,I:Zota 175.00
125 SD,V:Sub-Mariner 200.00
126 SD,I:Dormammu,Clea 175.00
127 SD,V:Dormammu 175.00
128 SD,I:Demon 175.00
129 SD,I:Tiboro 175.00
130 SD,C:Beatles 175.00
131 SD,I:Dr.Vega 175.00
132 SD,I:Orini 175.00
133 SD,I:Shazana 175.00
134 SD,E:Torch,I:Merlin 175.00

135 SD,JK:I:Shield & Hydra
    B:Nick Fury 350.00
136 SD,JK,V:Dormammu 135.00
137 SD,JK,A:Ancient One 175.00
138 SD,JK,I:Eternity 175.00
139 SD,JK,V:Dormammu 175.00
140 SD,JK,V:Dormammu 175.00
141 SD,JK,I:Fixer,Mentallo 175.00
142 SD,JK,I:THEM,V:Hydra 175.00
143 SD,JK,V:Hydra 175.00
144 SD,JK,V:Druid,I:Jasper
    Sitwell 175.00
145 SD,JK,I:Mr.Rasputin 175.00
146 SD,JK,V:Dormammu,I:A.I.M. . 175.00
147 BEv,JK,F:Wong 175.00
148 BEv,JK,O:Ancient One 160.00
149 BEv,JK,V:Kaluu 135.00
150 BEv,JK,JB(1st Marvel Art)
    I:Baron Strucker,Umar 135.00
151 JK,JSo(1st Marvel Art),
    I:Umar 200.00
152 BEv,JK,JSo,V:Umar 135.00
153 JK,JSo,MSe,V:Hydra 135.00
154 JSo,MSe,I:Dreadnought 135.00
155 JSo,MSe,A:L.B.Johnson 135.00
156 JSo,MSe,I:Zom 135.00
157 JSo,MSe,A:Zom,C:Living
    Tribunal 135.00
158 JSo,MSe,A:Zom,I:Living
    Tribunal(full story) 135.00
159 JSo,MSe,O:Nick Fury,A:Capt.
    America,I:Val Fontaine 150.00
160 JSo,MSe,A:Captain America,
    I:Jimmy Woo 135.00
161 JSo,I:Yellow Claw 135.00
162 JSo,DA,A:Captain America . . 135.00
163 JSo,DA,V:Yellow Claw 125.00
164 JSo,DA,V:Yellow Claw 125.00
165 JSo,DA,V:Yellow Claw 125.00
166 DA,GT,JSo,A:AncientOne . . . 125.00
167 JSo,DA,V:Doctor Doom 150.00
168 JSo,DA,E:Doctor Strange,Nick
    Fury,V:Yandroth 125.00
169 JSo,I&O:Brother Voodoo 30.00
170 JSo,O:Brother Voodoo 25.00
171 GC,V:Baron Samed 25.00
172 GC,DG,V:Dark Lord 25.00
173 GC,DG,I:Black Talon 25.00
174 JB,JM,O:Golem 20.00
175 SD,R:Torr 20.00
176 F:Golem 20.00
177 FB,F:Golem 20.00
178 JSn,B&O:Warlock,I:Magus . . 60.00
179 JSn,I:Pip,I&D:Capt.Autolycus . 55.00
180 JSn,I:Gamora,Kray-tor 55.00

Strange Tales #163
© *Marvel Entertainment Group*

181 JSn,E:Warlock 55.00
182 SD,GK,rep. Str.Tales
    #123,124 . . . . 20.00
183 SD,rep.Str.Tales #130,131 . . 20.00
184 SD,rep.Str.Tales #132,133 . . 20.00
185 SD,rep.Str.Tales #134,135 . . 20.00
186 SD,rep.Str.Tales #136,137 . . 20.00
187 SD,rep.Str.Tales #138,139 . . 20.00
188 SD,rep.Str.Tales #140,141 . . 20.00
Ann.#1 V:Grottu,Diablo 900.00
Ann.#2 A:Spider-Man 1,300.00
Marvel Milestone rep. stories from
    #110–#111, #114–#115 (1995) . 3.00

[2nd Regular Series] 1987–88
1 BBI,CW,B:Cloak&Dagger,Dr.
  Strange,V:Lord of Light 3.00
2 BBI,CW,V:Lord of Light,Demon . . 2.50
3 BBI,AW,CW,A:Nightmare,Khat. . . 2.50
4 BBI,CW,V:Nightmare 2.50
5 BBI,V:Rodent,A:Defenders 2.50
6 BBI,BWi,V:Erlik Khan,
  A:Defenders 2.50
7 V:Nightmare,A:Defenders 2.50
8 BBI,BWi,V:Kaluu 2.50
9 BBI,BWi,A:Dazzler,I:Mr.Jip,
  V:Kaluu 2.50
10 BBI,BWi,RCa,A:Black Cat,
   V:Mr.Jip,Kaluu 2.50
11 RCa,BWi,V:Mr.Jip,Kaluu 2.50
12 WPo,BWi,A:Punisher,V:Mr.Jip . . 2.50
13 JBr,BWi,RCa,Punisher,
   Power Pack 2.50
14 JBr,BWi,RCa,Punisher,P.Pack . . 2.50
15 RCa,BMc,A:Mayhem 2.50
16 RCa,BWi,V:Mr.Jip 2.50
17 RCa,BWi,V:Night 2.50
18 RCa,KN,A:X-Factor,V:Night 2.50
19 MMi(c),EL,TA,RCa,A:Thing 2.50
TPB Fully painted 7.00

STRANGE TALES
June, 1998
1 JMD,PJe,LSh,Man-Thing, 64-pg. 5.00
2A JMD,PJe,LSh,Man-Thing,
   Werewolf, 64-pg 5.00
2B variant cover 5.00
3 JMD,PJe,NA(c),Man-Thing,
  Werewolf, 64-pg 5.00
4 JMD,PJe,LSh,F:Man-Thing
  final issue 5.00

STRANGE TALES:
DARK CORNERS
March, 1998
1-shot JEs, three stories, 48-pg 4.00

STRANGE TALES
OF THE UNUSUAL
Dec., 1955—Aug., 1957
1 JMn(c),BP,DH,JR,Man Lost . . . 600.00
2 BEv,Man Afraid 350.00
3 AW,The Invaders 350.00
4 The Long Wait 250.00
5 RC,SD,The Threat 300.00
6 BEv 250.00
7 JK,JO 250.00
8 . . . . 250.00
9 BEv(c),BK 275.00
10 GM,AT 250.00
11 BEv(c),Aug., 1957 . . . . 250.00

STRANGE WORLDS
Dec., 1958
1 JK,SD,Flying Saucer 1,200.00
2 SD 700.00
3 JK 550.00
4 AW 500.00
5 SD 400.00

STRAWBERRY SHORTCAKE
Star, June, 1985—April, 1986
1 . . . . 3.00
2 thru 7 . . . . @3.00

STRAY TOASTERS
Epic, Jan., 1988
1 BSz 5.00
2 BSz 4.50
3 and 4 BSz . . . . @4.00

STRIKEFORCE MORITURI
Dec., 1986
1 BA,SW,WPo(1st pencils-
  3 pages),I:Blackwatch 3.00
2 BA,SW,V:The Horde 2.50
3 BA,SW,V:The Horde 2.50
4 BA,SW,WPo,V:The Horde 2.50
5 BA,SW,V:The Horde 2.50
6 BA,SW,V:The Horde 2.50
7 BA,SW,V:The Horde 2.50
8 BA,SW,V:The Horde 2.50
9 BA,SW,V:THe Horde 2.50
10 WPo(1st pencils-full story),
  SW,R:Black Watch,O:Horde . . . 3.00
11 BA,SW,V:The Horde 2.50
12 BA,SW,D:Jelene 2.50
13 BA,SW,Old vs. NewTeam 2.50
14 BA,AW,V:The Horde 2.50
15 BA,AW,V:The Horde 2.50
16 WPo,SW,V:The Horde 2.50
17 WPo(c),SW,V:The Horde 2.50
18 BA,SW,V:Hammersmith 2.50
19 BA,SW,V:THe Horde,D:Pilar. . . 2.50
20 BA,SW,V:The Horde 2.50
21 MMi(c),TD(i),V:The Horde. 2.50
22 TD(i),V:The Horde. 2.50
23 MBa,VM,V:The Horde. 2.50
24 VM(i),I:Vax,V:The Horde 2.50
25 TD(i),V:The Horde. 3.00
26 MBa,VM,V:The Horde. 3.00
27 MBa,VM,O:Morituri Master 3.00
28 MBa,V:The Tiger. 3.00
29 MBa,V:Zakir Shastri 3.00
30 MBa,V:Andre Lamont,The Wind . 3.00
31 MBa(c),V:The Wind,last issue . . 3.00

STRONG GUY REBORN
Spec. TDz,ASm,ATi (1997) 3.00

STRYFE'S STRIKE FILE
1 LSn,NKu,GCa,BP,C:Siena
  Blaze,Holocaust (1993). 4.00
1a 2nd printing 2.25

SUB-MARINER
May, 1968
1 JB,O:Sub-Mariner 500.00
2 JB,A:Triton 200.00
3 JB,A:Triton 150.00
4 JB,V:Attuma 150.00
5 JB,I&O:Tiger Shark 150.00
6 JB,DA,V:Tiger Shark 175.00
7 JB,I:Ikthon 150.00
8 JB,V:Thing 150.00
9 MSe,DA,A:Lady Dorma 150.00
10 GC,DA,O:Lemuria. 150.00
11 GC,V:Capt.Barracuda 75.00
12 MSe,I:Lyna 75.00
13 MSe,JS,A:Lady Dorma 75.00
14 MSe,V:Fake Human Torch 80.00
15 MSe,V:Dragon Man 75.00
16 MSe,I:Nekaret,Thakos 80.00
17 MSe,I:Stalker,Kormok 75.00
18 MSe,A:Triton 50.00
19 MSe,I:Stingray 50.00
20 JB,V:Dr.Doom 50.00
21 MSe,D:Lord Seth 50.00

Sub-Mariner #7
© Marvel Entertainment Group

22 MSe,A:Dr.Strange 50.00
23 MSe,I:Orka 50.00
24 JB,JM,V:Tiger Shark 50.00
25 SB,JM,O:Atlantis. 40.00
26 SB,A:Red Raven. 40.00
27 SB,I:Commander Kraken 40.00
28 SB,V:Brutivae 40.00
29 SB,V:Hercules. 30.00
30 SB,A:Captain Marvel 35.00
31 SB,A:Triton 30.00
32 SB,JM,I&O:Llyra 35.00
33 SB,JM,I:Namora 40.00
34 SB,JM,AK,1st Defenders 125.00
35 SB,JM,A:Silver Surfer 125.00
36 BWr,SB,W:Lady Dorma 35.00
37 RA,D:Lady Dorma. 35.00
38 RA,JSe,O:Rec,I:Thakorr,Fon . . 36.00
39 RA,JM,V:Llyra 35.00
40 GC,I:Turalla,A:Spidey 25.00
41 GT,V:Rock. 22.00
42 GT,JM,V:House Named Death . 22.00
43 GC,V:Tunal,king-sz. 30.00
44 M3e,JM,V:Human Torch 25.00
45 MSe,JM,V:Tiger Shark 25.00
46 GC,D:Namor's Father. 20.00
47 GC,A:Stingray,V:Dr.Doom 20.00
48 GC,V:Dr.Doom 20.00
49 GC,V:Dr.Doom 20.00
50 BEv,I:Namorita 22.00
51 BEv,O:Namorita,C:Namora . . . 20.00
52 GK,V:Sunfire 20.00
53 BEv,V:Sunfire 18.00
54 BEv,AW,V:Sunfire,I:Lorvex . . . 18.00
55 BEv,V:Torg 18.00
56 DA,I:Coral 18.00
57 BEv,I:Venus. 18.00
58 BEv,I:Tamara. 18.00
59 BEv,V:Tamara,A:Thor 25.00
60 BEv,V:Tamara 15.00
61 BEv,JM,V:Dr.Hydro 15.00
62 HC,JSt,I:Tales of Atlantis. 15.00
63 HC,JSt,V:Dr.Hydro,I:Arkus . . . 15.00
64 HC,JSe,I:Maddox 15.00
65 DH,DP,V:She-Devil,inc.BEv
  Eulogy pin-up 15.00
66 DH,V:Orka,I:Raman 15.00
67 DH,A:FF,V:Triton,N:Namor
  I&O:Force 15.00
68 DH,O:Force. 15.00
69 GT,V:Spider-Man. 18.00
70 GT,I:Piranha 15.00
71 GT,V:Piranha. 15.00
72 DA,V:Slime/Thing 15.00
Spec.#1 rep. Tales to Astonish
  #70-#73 . . . . 30.00

Spec.#2 rep. Tales to Astonish
  #74-#76 . . . . 25.00
[Limited Series]
1 RB,BMc,Namor's Birth. 2.50
2 RB,BMc,Namor Kills Humans . . . 2.25
3 RB,BMc,V:Surface Dwellers 2.25
4 RB,BMc,V:Human Torch 2.25
5 RB,BMc,A:Invaders 2.25
6 RB,BMc,V:Destiny 2.25
7 RB,BMc,A:Fantastic Four 2.25
8 RB,BMc,A:Hulk,Avengers 2.25
9 RB,BMc,A:X-Men,Magneto 2.25
10 RB,BMc,V:Thing 2.25
11 RB,BMc,A:Namorita,Defenders . 2.25
12 RB,BMc,A:Dr.Doom,
  Alpha Flight 2.25

(SAGA OF THE) SUB-MARINER
[Mini-Series] Nov., 1988
1 RB,BMc,Namor's Birth. 3.00
2 RB,BMc,Namor Kills Humans . . . 3.00
3 RB,BMc,V:Surface Dwellers 3.00
4 RB,BMc,V:Human Torch 3.00
5 RB,BMc,A:Invaders 3.00
6 RB,BMc,V:Destiny 3.00
7 RB,BMc,A:Fantastic Four 3.00
8 RB,BMc,A:Hulk,Avengers 3.00
9 RB,BMc,A:X-Men,Magneto 3.50
10 RB,BMc,V:Thing 3.00
11 RB,BMc,A:Namorita,Defenders . 3.00
12 RB,BMc,A:Dr.Doom,Alp.Flight . 3.00

SUB-MARINER COMICS
Marvel Timely, Spring, 1941
1 ASh(c),BEv,PGv,B:Sub-
  Mariner, The Angel 65,000.00
2 ASh(c),BEv,Nazi
  Submarine (c) 10,000.00
3 ASh(c),BEv,Churchill. 9,500.00
4 ASh(c),BEv,BW 6,000.00
5 V:Axis Powers. 5,000.00
6 ASh(c),Panama Canal 4,500.00
7 ASm&FrG(c) 4,500.00
8 ASh(c),PGv 4,500.00
9 ASh(c),BW,Flag(c) 4,500.00
10 ASh(c),GS 4,500.00
11 ASh(c),Dragon(c) 4,500.00
12 ASh(c) 3,500.00
13 ASh(c),Bondage(c). 3,500.00
14 ASh(c) 3,500.00
15 ASh(c),V:Japs 3,500.00
16 ASh(c),CI,ASm,GS. 2,500.00
17 ASh(c),V:Japs 2,500.00

Sub-Mariner Comics #7
© Marvel Entertainment Group

18 ASh(c),ASm	2,500.00
19	2,500.00
20 ASh(c),V:Crooks	2,500.00
21 SSh(c),BEv,Last Angel	2,200.00
22 SSh(c),BEv,A:Young Allies	2,200.00
23 SSh(c),BEv,Human Torch	2,200.00
24 MSy(c),BEv,A:Namora, bondage cover	2,200.00
25 MSy(c),HK,B:The Blonde Phantom, A:Namora, bondage(c)	2,400.00
26 BEv,SSh,A:Namora	2,000.00
27 DRi(c),BEv,A:Namora	2,000.00
28 DRi(c),BEv,A:Namora	2,000.00
29 BEv,SSh,A:Namora,Human Torch	2,000.00
30 DRi(c),BEv,Slaves Under the Sea	2,000.00
31 BEv,The Man Who Grew, A:Capt. America,E:Blonde Phantom	2,000.00
32 BEv,O:Sub-Mariner	2,500.00
33 BEv,O:Sub-Mariner,A:Human Torch,B:Namora	2,200.00
34 BEv,A:Human Torch,bondage cover	2,000.00
35 BEv,A:Human Torch	2,000.00
36 BEv,Hidden World	2,000.00
37 JMn(c),BEv	2,000.00
38 SSh(c),BEv,JMn, O:Sub-Mariner	2,300.00
39 JMn(c),BEv,Commie Frogman	2,000.00
40 JMn(c),BEv,Secret Tunnel	2,000.00
41 JMn(c),BEv,A:Namora	2,000.00
42 BEv,Oct., 1955	2,400.00

SUBURBAN JERSEY NINJA SHE-DEVILS
1 I:Ninja She-Devils	2.25

SUNFIRE & BIG HERO 6
July, 1998
1 (of 3) SLo,from Alpha Flight	2.50
2 SLo,V:Everwraith	2.50
3 SLO,conclusion	2.50

SUN GIRL
Marvel Comics, 1948
1 Miss America	2,400.00
2 Blonde Phantom	1,700.00
3	1,700.00

SUPERNATURALS
Oct., 1998
1 (of 4) BnP,JBa(c),F:Brother Voodoo, V:Jack O'Lantern, with mask	4.00
1a signed	30.00
2 BnP,JBa(c), with mask	4.00
3 BnP,JBa(c), with mask	4.00
4 BnP,JBa(c), with mask, concl	4.00

SUPERNATURAL THRILLERS
Dec., 1972
1 JSo(c),JSe,FrG,I:IT!	50.00
2 VM,DA,The Invisible Man	30.00
3 GK,The Valley of the Worm	30.00
4 Dr. Jekyll and Mr. Hyde	30.00
5 RB,The Living Mummy	75.00
6 GT,JA,The Headless Horseman	40.00
7 VM,B:The Living Mummy, Back From The Tomb	40.00
8 VM,He Stalks Two Worlds	40.00
9 GK/AM(c),VM,DA,Pyramid of the Watery Doom	40.00
10 VM,A Choice of Dooms	40.00
11 VM,When Strikes the ASP	40.00

Supernatural Thrillers #6
© *Marvel Entertainment Group*

12 VM,KJ,The War That Shook the World	40.00
13 VM,DGr,The Tomb of the Stalking Dead	40.00
14 VM,AMc,All These Deadly Pawns	40.00
15 TS, E:The Living Mummy,Night of Armageddon, Oct.,1975	40.00

SUPER RABBIT
Marvel Timely, 1943
1 Hitler	1,200.00
2	500.00
3	350.00
4	350.00
5	350.00
6 Origin of Super Rabbit	325.00
7	225.00
8	225.00
9	225.00
10	225.00
11 HK,Hey Look	250.00
12	250.00
13	250.00
14	250.00

SUPER SOLDIERS
Marvel UK, 1993
1 I:Super Soldier,A:USAgent	2.75
2 A:USAgent	2.25
3 A:USAgent	2.25
4 A:USAgent,Avengers	2.25
5 A:Captain America,AWC	2.25
6 O:Super Soldiers	2.25
7 in Savage Land	2.25

SUPER-VILLAIN CLASSICS
May, 1983
1 O:Galactus	6.00

SUPER-VILLAIN TEAM-UP
Aug., 1975
1 GT/BEv(c),B:Dr.Doom/Sub-Mariner,A:Attuma,Tiger Shark	50.00
2 SB,A:Tiger Shark, Attuma	20.00
3 EH(c),JA,V:Attuma	20.00
4 HT,JM,Dr.Doom vs. Namor	20.00
5 RB/JSt(c),HT,DP,A:Fantastic Four,I:Shroud	20.00
6 HT,JA,A:Shroud,Fantastic Four	18.00

7 RB/KJ(c),HT,O:Shroud	18.00
8 KG,V:Ringmaster	18.00
9 ST,A:Avengers,Iron Man	18.00
10 BH,DP,A:Capt.America, V:Attuma,Red Skull	18.00
11 DC/JSt(c),BH,DP,B:Dr. Doom, Red Skull,A:Capt. America	18.00
12 DC/AM(c),BH,DP,Dr.Doom vs. Red Skull	18.00
13 KG,DP,Namor vs. Krang	18.00
14 JBy/TA(c),BH,DP,V:Magneto, x-over with Champions #15	18.00
15 GT,ME,A:Red Skull	18.00
16 CI,A:Dr. Doom	18.00
17 KP(c),Red Skull Vs.Hatemonger June, 1976	18.00
G-Size#1 F:Namor, Dr.Doom	18.00
G-Size#2 F:Namor, Dr.Doom	18.00

SUPREME POWER
Marvel Max, July, 2003
1 MSz(s),GFr	7.00
1a special edition, JQ(c)	10.00
2 MSz(s),GFr	4.00
3 MSz(s),GFr	4.00
4 thru 10 MSz(s),GFr	@3.00
11 thru 18 MSz(s),GFr	@3.00
TPB Vol. 1 Hyperion Project	15.00
TPB Vol. 1: Contact	15.00
TPB Vol. 2: Powers & Principalities	15.00
TPB Vol. 3: High Command	15.00

SUPREME POWER: HYPERION
Sept., 2005
1 (of 5) MSz(s),DJu	3.00
2 DJu,MD2,Hunting the Alien	3.00
3 thru 5	@3.00
TPB Supreme Power: Hyperion	15.00

SUPREME POWER: NIGHTHAWK
Sept., 2005
1 SDi,F:Kyle Richmond	3.00
2 SDi,put on a Happy Face	3.00
3 thru 6	@3.00
TPB Supreme Power: Nighthawk	17.00

SUSPENSE
Marvel Atlas, Dec., 1949
1 BP,Ph(c),Sidney Greenstreet/ Peter Lorne (Maltese Falcon)	900.00
2 Ph(c),Dennis O'Keefe/Gale Storm (Abandoned)	450.00
3 B:Horror stories,The Black Pit	500.00
4 Thing In Black	350.00
5 BEv,GT,RH,BK,DBr, Hangman's House	400.00
6 BEv,GT,PMo,RH,Madness of Scott Mannion	400.00
7 DBr,GT,DR,Murder	350.00
8 GC,DRi,RH,Don't Open the Door	350.00
9 GC,DRi,Back From The Dead	350.00
10 JMn(c),WIP,RH,Trapped In Time	350.00
11 MSy,The Suitcase	300.00
12 GT,Dark Road	300.00
13 JMn(c),Strange Man, bondage cover	300.00
14 RH,Death And Doctor Parker	450.00
15 JMn(c),OW,The Machine	300.00
16 OW,Horror Backstage	300.00
17 Night Of Terror	300.00
18 BK,The Cozy Coffin	350.00
19 BEv,RH	300.00
20	300.00
21 BEv(c)	300.00

All comics prices listed are for *Near Mint* condition.

22 BEv(c),BK,OW 300.00
23 BEv 300.00
24 RH,GT 350.00
25 I Died At Midnight 400.00
26 BEv(c) 250.00
27 DBr 275.00
28 BEv 275.00
29 JMn,BF,JRo,April, 1953 . . . . . 275.00

Swords of the Swashbucklers #10
© Marvel Entertainment Group

SWORDS OF THE SWASHBUCKLERS
Epic, 1985–87
1 JG,Adult theme 3.00
2 thru 7 JG . . . . @2.50
8 thru 12, June, 1987 . . . . @2.50

TALE OF THE MARINES
See: DEVIL-DOG DUGAN

TALES OF ASGARD
Oct., 1968
1 . . . . 75.00
Vol.2 #1 Feb,1984 . . . . 6.00

TALES OF G.I. JOE
Jan., 1988
1 reprints,#1 . . . . 3.00
2 thru 7 reprints . . . . @2.50

TALES OF JUSTICE
See: JUSTICE COMICS

TALES OF THE AGE OF APOCALYPSE
1996
1-shot SLo,JoB,Age of Apocalypse
stories 5.00
GN, rep 6.00

TALES OF THE AGE OF APOCALYPSE: SINISTER BLOODLINE
Dec., 1997
GN JFM,SEp, 48-pg. bookshelf 6.00

TALES OF THE MARVELS: BLOCKBUSTER
Fully painted (1995) 6.00

TALES OF THE MARVELS: INNER DEMONS
Fully painted, 48-pg. (1996) 6.00

TALES OF THE MARVELS: WONDER YEARS
1 & 2 DAb (1995) . . . . @5.00

TALES OF SUSPENSE
Jan., 1959
1 AW,DH,JB,SD,JK 3,000.00
2 SD,JK,RH,Robot 1,100.00
3 SD,JK,JB(c),Flying Saucer . . 1,100.00
4 AW,JK,BEv,SD 900.00
5 JK,SD,JF 600.00
6 SD,JK 600.00
7 SD,JK 650.00
8 SD,BEv,JK,Lava Man 550.00
9 SD,JK,TF,Iron man type 700.00
10 SD,RH,JK 550.00
11 SD,JK 450.00
12 RC,SD,JK 450.00
13 SK,JK,Elektro 450.00
14 SD,JK,Colossus (1) 600.00
15 SD,JK 450.00
16 JK,Metallo (1) 600.00
17 JK 450.00
18 JK 450.00
19 JK 450.00
20 JK,Colossus (2) 500.00
21 JK/DAy(c),SD,This Is Klagg . . 350.00
22 JK/DAy(c),SD,Beware
Of Bruttu 350.00
23 JK,DAy,SD,The Creature
in the Black Bog 350.00
24 JK,DAy,SD,Insect Man 350.00
25 JK,DAy,SD,The Death of
Monstrollo 350.00
26 JK,DAy,SD,The Thing That
Crawled By Night 300.00
27 JK,DAy,SD,When Oog Lives
Again 300.00
28 JK,DAy,SD,Back From
the Dead 300.00
29 JK,DAy,SD,DH,The Martian
Who Stole A City 275.00
30 JK,DAy,SD,DH,The Haunted
Roller Coaster 300.00
31 JK,DAy,SD,DH,The Monster
in the Iron Mask 325.00
32 JK,DAy,SD,DH,The Man in
the Bee-Hive 550.00
33 JK,DAy,SD,DH,Chamber of
Fear 275.00
34 JK,DAy,SD,DH,Inside The
Blue Glass Bottle 275.00
35 JK,DAy,SD,DH,The Challenge
of Zarkorr 350.00
36 SD,Meet Mr. Meek 275.00
37 DH,SD,Hagg 275.00
38 JDa,The Teenager Who Ruled
the World 275.00
39 JK,O&I:Iron Man 10,000.00
40 JK,C:Iron Man 3,000.00
41 JK,A:Iron Man,V:Dr.Strange . 1,700.00
42 DH,SD,I:Red Pharoah 1,000.00
43 DH,DH,I:Kala,A:Iron Man . . . 1,000.00
44 DH,SD,V:Mad Pharoah 1,000.00
45 DH,V:Jack Frost 1,000.00
46 DH,CR,I:Crimson Dynamo . . . 700.00
47 SD,V:Melter 700.00
48 SD,N:Iron Man 800.00
49 SD,A:Angel 1,000.00
50 DH,I:Mandarin 450.00
51 DH,I:Scarecrow 375.00
52 DH,I:Black Widow 550.00
53 DH,O:Watcher 350.00
54 DH,V:Mandarin 250.00
55 DH,V:Mandarin 250.00
56 DH,I:Unicorn 250.00

Tales of Suspense #58
© Marvel Entertainment Group

57 DH,I&O:Hawkeye 550.00
58 DH,GT,B:Captain America . . . 650.00
59 DH,1st S.A. Solo Captain
America,I:Jarvis 650.00
60 DH,JK,V:Assassins 325.00
61 DH,JK,V:Mandarin 200.00
62 DH,JK,O:Mandarin 200.00
63 JK,O:Captain America 450.00
64 DH,JK,A:Black Widow,
Hawkeye 200.00
65 DH,JK,I:Red Skull 350.00
66 DH,JK,O:Red Skull 350.00
67 DH,JK,V:Adolph Hitler 175.00
68 DH,JK,V:Red Skull 175.00
69 DH,JK,I:Titanium Man 175.00
70 DH,JK,GT,V:Titanium Man . . . 175.00
71 DH,JK,WW,GT,V:TitaniumMan 150.00
72 DH,JK,GT,V:The Sleeper 150.00
73 JA,JK,GT,A:Black Knight 150.00
74 JA,JK,GT,V:The Sleeper 150.00
75 JA,JK,I:Batroc,Sharon Carter . 150.00
76 JA,JR,V:Mandarin 150.00
77 JA,JK,JR,V:Ultimo,I:Peggy
Carter 150.00
78 JA,GC,JK,V:Ultimo 150.00
79 JA,GC,JK,V:Red Skull,
I:Cosmic Cube 175.00
80 JA,GC,JK,V:Red Skull 185.00
81 JA,GC,JK,V:Red Skull 150.00
82 GC,JK,V:The Adaptoid 150.00
83 GC,JK,V:The Adaptoid 150.00
84 GC,JK,V:Mandarin 150.00
85 GC,JK,V:Batroc 150.00
86 GC,JK,V:Mandarin 150.00
87 GC,V:Mole Man 150.00
88 GK,JK,GC,V:Power Man 150.00
89 GK,JK,GC,V:Red Skull 150.00
90 GK,JK,GC,V:Red Skull 150.00
91 GK,GC,JK,V:Crusher 150.00
92 GC,JK,A:Nick Fury 150.00
93 GC,JK,V:Titanium Man 150.00
94 GC,JK,I:Modok 150.00
95 GC,JK,V:Grey Gargoyle,
IR:Captain America 150.00
96 GC,JK,V:Grey Gargoyle 150.00
97 GC,JK,I:Whiplash,
A:Black Panther 150.00
98 GC,JK,I:Whitney Frost
A:Black Panther 175.00
99 GC,JK,A:Black Panther 200.00
Marvel Milestone rep. #39 (1993) . . 3.00
Becomes:

CAPTAIN AMERICA

TALES OF SUSPENSE: CAPTAIN AMERICA/ IRON MAN
Dec., 2004
1 Commemorative Edition 3.00

TALES OF THE ZOMBIE
Aug., 1973
(Black & White Magazine)
1 Reprint Menace #5,O:Zombie . 60.00
2 GC,GT 50.00
3 . . . . 50.00
4 Live and Let Die. 50.00
5 BH 50.00
6 . . . . 50.00
7 thru 9 AA . . . . @50.00
10 March, 1975 . . . . 50.00

TALES TO ASTONISH
Marvel Atlas, Jan., 1959
1 JDa,Ninth Wonder of the
  World 3,000.00
2 SD,Capture A Martian 1,300.00
3 SD,JK,The Giant From
  Outer Space 900.00
4 SD,JK,The Day The
  Martians Struck 900.00
5 SD,AW,The Things on
  Easter Island 900.00
6 SD,JK,Invasion of the
  Stone Men 700.00
7 SD,JK,The Thing on Bald
  Mountain 700.00
8 DAy,SD,JK,Mmmex, King of
  the Mummies. 700.00
9 DAy,JK(c),SD,Droom, the
  Living Lizard 700.00
10 DAy,JK,SD,Titano 700.00
11 DAy,JK,SD,Monstrom, the Dweller
  in the Black Swamp. 450.00
12 JK/DAy(c),SD,Gorgilla 450.00
13 JK,SD,Groot, the Monster
  From Planet X 450.00
14 JK,SD,Krang. 450.00
15 JK/DAy,The Blip 650.00
16 DAy,JK,SD,Thorr. 550.00
17 JK,SD,Vandoom 450.00
18 DAy,JK,SD,Gorgilla Strikes
  Again 450.00
19 DAy,JK,SD,Rommbu. 450.00
20 JK,SD,X, The Thing
  That Lived 450.00
21 JK,SD,Trull the Inhuman. 450.00
22 JK,SD,The Crawling
  Creature. 400.00
23 JK,SD,Moomba is Here!. 400.00
24 JK,SD,The Abominable
  Snowman. 400.00
25 JK,SD,The Creature From
  Krogarr. 400.00
26 JK,SD,Four-Armed Things . . . 400.00
27 StL(s),SD,JK,I:Ant-Man 8,000.00
28 JK,SD,I Am the Gorilla Man . . 350.00
29 JK,SD,When the Space
  Beasts Attack. 350.00
30 JK,SD,Thing From the
  Hidden Swamp 350.00
31 JK,SD,The Mummy's Secret. . 350.00
32 JK,SD,Quicksand 350.00
33 JK,SD,Dead Storage. 350.00
34 JK,SD,Monster at Window . . . 350.00
35 StL(s),JK,SD, B:Ant-Man
  (2nd App.). 3,500.00
36 JK,SD,V:Comrade X 1,500.00
37 JK,SD,V:The Protector 800.00
38 JK,SD,Betrayed By the Ants. . 800.00
39 JK,DH,V:Scarlet Beetle. 800.00
40 JK,SD,DH,The Day Ant-Man
  Failed. 800.00

Tales to Astonish #31
© Marvel Entertainment Group

41 DH,St,SD,V:Kulla 600.00
42 DH,JSe,SD,Voice of Doom. . . . 600.00
43 DH,SD,Master of Time 600.00
44 JK,SD,I&O:Wasp 800.00
45 DH,SD,V:Egghead 350.00
46 DH,SD,I:Cyclops(robot) 350.00
47 DH,SD,V:Trago 350.00
48 DH,SD,I:Porcupine 350.00
49 JK,DH,AM,Ant-Man Becomes
  Giant-Man 425.00
50 JK,SD,I&O:Human Top. 250.00
51 JK,V:Human Top. 250.00
52 I&O:Black Knight. 250.00
53 DH,V:Porcupine 250.00
54 DH,I:El Toro 225.00
55 V:Human Top 225.00
56 V:The Magician 225.00
57 A:Spider-Man 500.00
58 V:Colossus(not X-Men one) . . 225.00
59 V:Hulk,Black Knight 550.00
60 SD,B:Hulk,Giant Man 550.00
61 SD,I:Glenn Talbot,
  V:Egghead. 300.00
62 I:Leader,N:Wasp 300.00
63 SD,O:Leader(1st full story) . . 300.00
64 SD,V:Leader 350.00
65 BP,DH,SD,N:Giant-Man,. 300.00
66 BP,JK,SD,V:Leader,
  Chameleon 300.00
67 BP,JK,SD,I:Kanga Khan 300.00
68 BP,JK,N:Human Top,V:Leader 300.00
69 BP,JK,V:Human Top,Leader,
  E:Giant-Man 300.00
70 GC,JK,B:Sub-Mariner/Hulk,I:
  Neptune. 325.00
71 GC,JK,V:Leader,I:Vashti 140.00
72 GC,JK,V:Leader 140.00
73 GC,JK,V:Leader,A:Watcher . . 140.00
74 GC,JK,V:Leader,A:Watcher . . 140.00
75 GC,JK,A:Watcher 140.00
76 GC,GK,JK,Atlantis 140.00
77 JK,V:Executioner 140.00
78 BEv,GC,JK,Prince and
  the Puppet. 140.00
79 BEv,GC,JK,Hulk vs.Hercules . 140.00
80 BEv,GC,JK,Moleman vs.
  Tyrannus 140.00
81 BEv,GC,JK,I:Boomerang,Secret
  Empire,Moleman vs.Tyrannus 140.00
82 BEv,GC,JK,V:Iron Man 150.00
83 BEv,JK,V:Boomerang 140.00
84 BEv,GC,JK,Like a Beast
  at Bay 140.00
85 BEv,GC,JB,Missile &
  the Monster 140.00

86 BEv,JB,V:Warlord Krang 140.00
87 BEv,JB,IR:Hulk 140.00
88 BEv,GK,V:Boomerang. 140.00
89 BEv,GK,V:Stranger 140.00
90 JK,GK,BEv,I:Abomination 140.00
91 GK,BEv,DA,V:Abomination . . . 140.00
92 MSe,C:Silver Surfer x-over . . 150.00
93 MSe,Silver Surfer x-over. 175.00
94 BEv,MSe,V:Dragorr,High
  Evolutionary. 140.00
95 BEv,MSe,V:High Evolutionary. 140.00
96 MSe,Skull Island,High Evol. . . 140.00
97 MSe,C:Ka-Zar,X-Men 150.00
98 DA,MSe,I:Legion of the Living
  Lightning,I:Seth 140.00
99 DA,MSe,V:Legion of the Living
  Lighting 140.00
100 MSe,DA,Hulk vs.Sub-Mariner 175.00
101 MSe,GC,V:Loki 175.00
Becomes:

INCREDIBLE HULK

TALES TO ASTONISH
[2nd Series] Dec., 1979
1 JB,rep.Sub-Mariner#1 . . . . 5.00
2 thru 14 JB,rep.Sub-Mariner . . . @3.00

TANGLED WEB
April, 2001
1 GEn,JMC,The Thousand 3.00
2 GEn,JMC,The Thousand 3.00
3 GEn,JMC,V:The Thousand 3.00
4 Severance Package. 3.00
5 PrM,DFg,Flowers for Rhino. 3.00
6 PrM,DFg,Flowers/Rhino,pt.2 . . . 3.00
7 Gentlemen's Agreement 3.00
8 Gentlemen's Agreement 3.00
9 LW,Gentlemen's Agreement,pt.3 . 3.00
10 Impact on Kids 3.00
11 Open All Night, 48-pg. 3.50
12 I Was A Teenaged Frog-Man . . . 3.00
13 SeP,Double Shots. 3.00
14 The Last Shoot 3.00
15 The Collaborator 3.00
16 F:Tombstone, Kangaroo 3.00
17 Tombstone in jail 3.00
18 TMK 3.00
19 F:Grizzly & Rhino 3.00
20 J.Jonah Jameson 3.00
21 . . . . 3.00
22 The System. 3.00
TPB Spider-Man: Tangled Web . . . 16.00
TPB Spider-Man: Tangled Web 2 . 15.00
TPB Spider-Man: Tangled Web 3 . 16.00

TARZAN
June, 1977
1 JB,Edgar Rice Burroughs Adapt.25.00
2 JB,O:Tarzan 18.00
3 JB,The Alter of the Flaming
  God,I:LA 18.00
4 JB,TD,V:Leopards 18.00
5 JB,TD,Vengeance,A:LA 10.00
6 JB,TD,Rage of Tantor,A:LA 10.00
7 JB,TD,Tarzan Rescues The
  Moon 10.00
8 JB,Battle For The Jewel Of
  Opar. 10.00
9 JB,Histah, the Serpent. 10.00
10 JB,The Deadly Peril of
  Jane Clayton 10.00
11 JB 10.00
12 JB,Fangs of Death 10.00
13 JB,Lion-God 10.00
14 JB,The Fury of Fang and Claw. 10.00
15 JB,Sword of the Slaver. 10.00
16 JB,Death Rides the Jungle
  Winds. 10.00
17 JB,The Entrance to the
  Earths Core 10.00

18 JB,Corsairs of the Earth's Core 10.00
19 Pursuit. 10.00
20 Blood Bond 10.00
21 Dark and Bloody Sky 8.00
22 JM,RN,War In Pellucidar 8.00
23 To the Death 8.00
24 The Jungle Lord Returns 8.00
25 RB(c),V:Poachers 8.00
26 RB(c),Caged 8.00
27 RB(c),Chaos in the Caberet 8.00
28 A Savage Against A City 8.00
29 Oct., 1979 . . . . 8.00
Ann.#1 JB 7.00
Ann.#2 Drums of the
   Death-Dancers 7.00
Ann.#3 Ant-Men and the
   She-Devils 7.00

TARZAN OF THE APES
July, 1984
1 (movie adapt.) 4.00
2 . . . . 4.00

TASKMASTER
Feb., 2002
1 (of 4) F:Iron Man 3.00
2 crime syndicates 3.00
3 syndicates catch on 3.00
4 concl. 3.00

TEAM AMERICA
June, 1982
1 O:Team America 2.50
2 V:Marauder 2.50
3 LMc,V:Mr.Mayhem 2.50
4 LMc,V:Arcade Assassins 2.50
5 A:Marauder 2.50
6 A:R.U. Ready 2.50
7 LMc,V:Emperor of Texas 2.50
8 DP,V:Hydra 2.50
9 A:Iron Man 2.50
10 V:Minister Ashe 2.50
11 A:Marauder,V:Ghost Rider 3.00
12 DP,Marauder unmasked,
   May, 1083 . . . . 2.50

TEAM HELIX
1993
1 A:Wolverine 2.25
2 A:Wolverine 2.25

TEAM X/TEAM 7
1996
1-shot LHa,SEp,MRy 5.00

TEAM X 2000
Dec., 1998
1-shot, 48-page 3.50

TEEN COMICS
See: ALL WINNERS COMICS

TEENAGE ROMANCE
See: MY ROMANCE

TEK WORLD
See: WILLIAM SHATNER'S TEK
WORLD

TERMINATOR 2
Sept., 1991
1 KJ,movie adaption 3.00
2 KJ,movie adaption 3.00
3 KJ,movie adaption 3.00
Terminator II (bookshelf format) 5.00
Terminator II (B&W mag. size) 2.25

TERRARISTS
Epic, 1993–94
1 thru 4 w/card . . . . @2.50
5 thru 7 . . . . @2.50

TERROR INC.
1992–93
1 JZ,I:Hellfire 3.00
2 JZ,I:Bezeel,Hellfire 2.50
3 JZ,A:Hellfire 2.25
4 JZ,A:Hellfire,V:Barbados 2.25
5 JZ,V:Hellfire,A:Dr. Strange 2.25
6 JZ,MT,A:Punisher 2.25
7 JZ,V:Punisher 2.25
8 Christmas issue 2.25
9 JZ,V:Wolverine 2.25
10 V:Wolverine 2.25
11 A:Silver Sable,Cage 2.25
12 For Love Nor Money#4,A:Cage,
   Silver Sable 2.25
13 Inf.Crusade,A:Gh.Rider 2.25

TESSIE THE TYPIST
Marvel Timely, Summer, 1944
1 BW,Doc Rockblock 1,000.00
2 BW,Powerhouse Pepper 500.00
3 Football cover 200.00
4 BW 350.00
5 BW 350.00
6 BW,HK,Hey Look 350.00
7 BW 350.00
8 BW 350.00
9 BW,HK,Powerhouse Pepper . . 375.00
10 BW,A:Rusty 375.00
11 BW,A:Rusty 375.00
12 BW,HK 375.00
13 BW,A:Millie The Model,Rusty . 375.00
14 BW 375.00
15 HK,A:Millie,Rusty 375.00
16 HK 225.00
17 HK,A:Millie, Rusty 225.00
18 HK 225.00
19 Annie Oakley story 150.00
20 . . . . 150.00
21 A:Lana, Millie 150.00
22 . . . . 150.00
23 . . . . 150.00
Becomes:

TINY TESSIE
24 . . . . 100.00
Becomes:

REAL EXPERIENCES
25 Ph(c),Jan., 1950 . . . . 100.00

TEXAS KID
Marvel Atlas, Jan., 1951
1 GT,JMn,O:Texas Kid 300.00
2 JMn 200.00
3 JMn,Man Who Didn't Exist . . . 150.00
4 thru 9 JMn . . . . @150.00
10 JMn,July, 1952 . . . . 150.00

TEX DAWSON, GUN-SLINGER
Jan., 1973
1 JSo(c) 35.00
Becomes:

GUNSLINGER
2 . . . . 25.00
3 June, 1973 . . . . 25.00

TEX MORGAN
Aug., 1948
1 Tex Morgan & Lobo 350.00
2 Boot Hill Welcome For A
   Bad Man 225.00
3 A:Arizona Annie 150.00

Tex Morgan 38
© Marvel Entertainment Group

4 SSh,Trapped in the Outlaw's
   Den, A:Arizona Annie 125.00
5 Valley of Missing Cowboys . . . 125.00
6 Never Say Murder,
   A:Tex Taylor 150.00
7 CCB,Ph(c),Captain Tootsie,
   A:Tex Taylor 200.00
8 Ph(c),Terror Of Rimrock
   Valley, A:Diablo 200.00
9 Ph(c),Death to Tex Taylor,
   Feb., 1950 . . . . 200.00

TEX TAYLOR
Sept., 1948
1 SSh,Boot Hill Showdown 350.00
2 When Two-Gun Terror Rides
   the Range 200.00
3 SSh,Thundering Hooves and
   Blazing Guns 150.00
4 Ph(c),Draw or Die Cowpoke . . 200.00
5 Ph(c),The Juggler of Yellow
   Valley,A:Blaze Carson 200.00
6 Ph(c),Mystery of Howling Gap. 200.00
7 Ph(c),Trapped in Time's Lost
   Land,A:Diablo 225.00
8 Ph(c),The Mystery of Devil-
   Tree Plateau,A:Diablo 225.00
9 Ph(c),Guns Along the Border,
   A:Nimo,March, 1950 . . . . 225.00

THANOS
Oct., 2003
1 JSn 3.00
2 JSn,Galactus,Adam Warlock 3.00
3 JSn,F:Moondragon 3.00
4 JSn,Epiphany,pt.4 . . . . 3.00
5 JSn,Epiphany,pt.5 . . . . 3.00
6 JSn,concl. 3.00
7 KG,RLm 3.00
8 KG,RLm 3.00
9 KG,RLm 3.00
10 KG,RLm,V:The Maker 3.00
11 KG,RLm 3.00
12 KG,RLm 3.00
TPB The End, Vol.3 . . . . 20.00
TPB Vol. 4: Epiphany 15.00
TPB Vol. 5: Samaritan 15.00

THANOS QUEST
1990
1 JSn,RLm,V:Elders,
   for Soul Gems 8.00
1a 2nd printing 4.00

All comics prices listed are for *Near Mint* condition.

2 JSn,RLm,O:SoulGems,I:
Infinity Gauntlet (story
cont.in Silver Surfer #44)...... 8.00
2a 2nd printing 4.00

THANOS QUEST
Jan., 2000
GN JSn,RLm,96-pg.............. 4.00

THING, THE
July, 1983
1 JBy,O:Thing 3.50
2 JBy,Woman from past 2.50
3 JBy,A:Inhumans 2.50
4 JBy,A:Lockjaw 2.50
5 JBy,A:Spider-Man,She-Hulk ... 2.50
6 JBy,V:Puppet Master 2.50
7 JBy,V:Goody Two Shoes 2.50
8 JBy,V:Egyptian Curse 2.50
9 JBy,F:Alicia Masters 2.50
10 JBy,Secret Wars 2.50
11 JBy,B:Rocky Grimm 2.50
12 JBy,F:Rocky Grimm 2.50
13 JBy,F:Rocky Grimm 2.50
14 F:Rocky Grimm............. 2.50
15 F:Rocky Grimm 2.50
16 F:Rocky Grimm 2.50
17 F:Rocky Grimm 2.50
18 F:Rocky Grimm 2.50
19 F:Rocky Grimm 2.50
20 F:Rocky Grimm 2.50
21 V:Ultron 2.50
22 V:Ultron 2.50
23 R:Thing to Earth,A:Fant. Four .. 2.50
24 V:Rhino,A:Miracle Man 2.50
25 V:Shamrock 2.50
26 A:Vance Astro 2.50
27 I:Sharon Ventura 2.50
28 A:Vance Astro 2.50
29 A:Vance Astro 2.50
30 Secret Wars II,A:Vance Astro ... 2.50
31 A:Vance Astro 2.50
32 A:Vance Astro 2.50
33 A:Vance Astro,I:New Grapplers . 2.50
34 V:Titania,Sphinx 2.50
35 I:New Ms.Marvel,Power Broker . 2.50
36 Last Issue,A:She-Hulk 2.50

[Mini-Series]
1 rep.Marvel Two-in-One #50..... 2.50
2 rep Marvel Two-in-One,V:GR ... 2.50
3 rep Marvel Two-in-One #51..... 2.00
4 rep Marvel Two-in-One #43..... 2.00

THING, THE
Nov., 2005
1 Money Changes Every Thing ... 3.00
2 Fun 'N Games 3.00
3 Fun 'N Games 3.00
4 Paws ...and Fast Forward..... 3.00
5 Give Till It Hurts 3.00
6 Friendly Neighborhood Brouhaha 3.00
7 On the Way to the Forum 3.00
8 Poker game 3.00
TPB Idol of Millions 16.00

THING/SHE-HULK
March, 1998
1-shot TDz,V:Dragon Man, 48-pg . 3.00
1-shot The Long Night, 48-pg...... 3.00

THING, THE: FREAKSHOW
June, 2002
1 (of 4) ALa,grumpiest super-hero . 3.00
2 ALa,people are enthralled 3.00
3 ALa,ScK 3.00
4 ALa,ScK,concl............... 3.00
TPB Freakshow 18.00

THOR, THE MIGHTY
Prev: Journey Into Mystery
March, 1966
126 JK,V:Hercules 400.00
127 JK,I:Pluto,Volla 275.00
128 JK,V:Pluto,A:Hercules...... 275.00
129 JK,V:Pluto,I:Ares.......... 275.00
130 JK,V:Pluto,A:Hercules...... 275.00
131 JK,I:Colonizers.......... 275.00
132 JK,A:Colonizers,I:Ego 275.00
133 JK,A:Colonizers,A:Ego 275.00
134 JK,I:High Evolutionary,
Man-Beast............. 300.00
135 JK,O:High Evolutionary..... 200.00
136 JK,F:Odin 200.00
137 JK,I:Ulik 200.00
138 JK,V:Ulik,A:Sif........... 200.00
139 JK,V:Ulik 200.00
140 JK,V:Growing Man 200.00
141 JK,V:Replicus 150.00
142 JK,V:Super Skrull 150.00
143 JK,BEv,V:Talisman 150.00
144 JK,V:Talisman 150.00
145 JK,V:Ringmaster......... 150.00
146 JK,O:Inhumans Part 1 ..... 200.00
147 JK,O:Inhumans Part 2 ..... 200.00
148 JK,I:Wrecker,O:Black Bolt.. 200.00
149 JK,O:Black Bolt,Medusa ... 200.00
150 JK,A:Triton 200.00
151 JK,V:Destroyer 175.00
152 JK,V:Destroyer 175.00
153 JK,F:Dr.Blake 175.00
154 JK,I:Mangog 175.00
155 JK,V:Mangog 175.00
156 JK,V:Mangog 175.00
157 JK,D:Mangog 175.00
158 JK,O:Don Blake Part 1 .... 300.00
159 JK,O:Don Blake Part 2 ..... 175.00
160 JK,I:Travrians 135.00
161 JK,Shall a God Prevail 135.00
162 JK,O:Galactus........... 150.00
163 JK,I:Mutates,A:Pluto 100.00
164 JK,A:Pluto,V:Greek Gods ... 100.00
165 JK,V:Him/Warlock........ 250.00
166 JK,V:Him/Warlock........ 225.00
167 JK,F:Sif 100.00
168 JK,O:Galactus........... 150.00
169 JK,O:Galactus........... 150.00
170 JK,BEv,V:Thermal Man..... 100.00
171 JK,BEv,V:Wrecker........ 100.00
172 JK,BEv,V:Ulik 100.00
173 JK,BEv,V:Ulik,Ringmaster... 100.00
174 JK,BEv,V:Crypto-Man 100.00
175 JK,Fall of Asgard,V:Surtur .. 100.00
176 JK,V:Surtur 100.00
177 JK,I:Igon,V:Surtur 100.00
178 JK,C:Silver Surfer 125.00
179 JK,MSe,C:Galactus........ 100.00
180 NA,JSi,V:Loki 125.00
181 NA,JSi,V:Loki 125.00
182 JB,V:Dr.Doom 80.00
183 JB,V:Dr.Doom 80.00
184 JB,I:The Guardian........ 80.00
185 JB,JSt,V:Silent One....... 80.00
186 JB,JSt,V:Hela 80.00
187 JB,JSt,V:Odin 80.00
188 JB,JM,F:Odin 80.00
189 JB,JSt,V:Hela 80.00
190 JB,I:Durok 80.00
191 JB,JSt,V:Loki........... 80.00
192 JB 80.00
193 JB,SB,V:Silver Surfer 150.00
194 JB,SB,V:Loki............ 75.00
195 JB,JR,V:Mangog 75.00
196 JB,NR,V:Kartag......... 75.00
197 JB,V:Mangog 75.00
198 JB,V:Pluto 75.00
199 JB,V:Pluto,Hela......... 75.00
200 JB,Ragnarok........... 100.00
201 JB,JM,Odin resurrected...... 60.00
202 JB,V:Ego-Prime 60.00

203 JB,V:Ego-Prime 60.00
204 JB,JM,Demon from t/Depths.. 60.00
205 JB,V:Mephisto.......... 60.00
206 JB,V:Absorbing Man........ 50.00
207 JB,V:Absorbing Man 50.00
208 JB,V:Mercurio 50.00
209 JB,I:Druid 50.00
210 JB,DP,I:Ulla,V:Ulik........ 50.00
211 JB,DP,V:Ulik 50.00
212 JB,JSt,V:Sssthgar........ 50.00
213 JB,DP,I:Gregor 50.00
214 SB,JM,V:Dark Nebula 50.00
215 JB,JM,J:Xorr 50.00
216 JB,JM,V:4D-Man......... 50.00
217 JB,SB,I:Krista,V:Odin 50.00
218 JB,JM,A:Colonizers....... 50.00
219 JB,I:Protector 50.00
220 JB,V:Avalon............ 50.00
221 JB,V:Olympus 50.00
222 JB,JSe,A:Hercules,V:Pluto .. 50.00
223 JB,A:Hercules,V:Pluto..... 50.00
224 JB,V:Destroyer 50.00
225 JB,JSi,I:Fire Lord 55.00
226 JB,A:Watcher,Galactus 35.00
227 JB,JSi,V:Ego 35.00
228 JB,JSi,A:Galactus,D:Ego 35.00
229 JB,JSi,A:Hercules,I:Dweller . 35.00
230 JB,A:Hercules........... 35.00
231 JB,DG,V:Armak.......... 35.00
232 JB,JSi,A:Firelord 35.00

Thor, The Mighty #233
© Marvel Entertainment Group

233 JB,Asgard Invades Earth 35.00
234 JB,V:Loki................ 35.00
235 JB,JSi,I:Possessor
(Kamo Tharnn) 35.00
236 JB,JSi,V:Absorbing Man 35.00
237 JB,JSi,V:Ulik 35.00
238 JB,JSi,V:Ulik 35.00
239 JB,JSi,V:Ulik 35.00
240 SB,KJ,V:Seth 35.00
241 JB,JGi,I:Geb 35.00
242 JB,JSi,V:Servitor 35.00
243 JB,JSt,V:Servitor 35.00
244 JB,JSt,V:Servitor 35.00
245 JB,JSt,V:Servitor 35.00
246 JB,JSt,A:Firelord 35.00
247 JB,JSt,A:Firelord 35.00
248 JB,V:Storm Giant 35.00
249 JB,V:Odin 35.00
250 JB,D:Igron,V:Mangog 35.00
251 JB,A:Sif 25.00
252 JB,V:Ulik 25.00
253 JB,I:Trogg 25.00
254 JK,O:Dr.Blake rep........ 25.00
255 Stone Men of Saturn rep..... 25.00

Thor, The Mighty #292
© Marvel Entertainment Group

256 JB,I:Sporr 25.00
257 JK,JB,I:Fee-Lon 25.00
258 JK,JB,V:Grey Gargoyle 25.00
259 JB,A:Spider-Man 25.00
260 WS,I:Doomsday Star 25.00
261 WS,I:Soul Survivors 25.00
262 WS,Odin Found,I:Odin Force . 25.00
263 WS,V:Loki 25.00
264 WS,V:Loki 25.00
265 WS,V:Destroyer 25.00
266 WS,Odin Quest 25.00
267 WS,F:Odin 25.00
268 WS,V:Damocles 25.00
269 WS,V:Stilt-Man 25.00
270 WS,V:Blastaar 25.00
271 Avengers,Iron Man x-over. . . . 25.00
272 JB,Day the Thunder Failed . . . 25.00
273 JB,V:Midgard Serpent 25.00
274 JB,D.Balder,I.Hermod,Hoder . 25.00
275 JB,V:Loki,I:Sigyn 25.00
276 JB,Trial of Loki 25.00
277 JB,V:Fake Thor 25.00
278 JB,V:Fake Thor 25.00
279 A:Pluto,V:Ulik 25.00
280 V:Hyperion 25.00
281 O:Space Phantom 20.00
282 V:Immortus,I:Tempus 20.00
283 JB,V:Celestials 20.00
284 JB,V:Gammenon 20.00
285 JB,R:Karkas 20.00
286 KP,KRo,D:Kro,I:Dragona 20.00
287 KP,2nd App. & O:Forgotten
    One(Hero) 20.00
288 KP,V:Forgotten One 20.00
289 KP,V:Destroyer 20.00
290 I:Red Bull(Toro Rojo) 20.00
291 KP,A:Eternals,Zeus 20.00
292 KP,V:Odin 20.00
293 KP,Door to Mind's Eye 20.00
294 KP,O:Odin & Asgard,I:Frey . . . 20.00
295 KP,I:Fafnir,V:Storm Giants . . . 20.00
296 KP,D:Siegmund 20.00
297 KP,V:Sword of Siegfried 20.00
298 KP,V:Dragon(Fafnir) 20.00
299 KP,A:Valkyrie,I:Hagen 20.00
300 KP,giant,O:Odin & Destroyer,
    Ringgold Ring Quest ends,D:Uni-
    Mind,I:Mother Earth 30.00
301 KP,O:Mother Earth,V:Apollo . . 20.00
302 KP,V:Locus 20.00
303 Whatever Gods There Be 20.00
304 KP,V:Wrecker 20.00
305 KP,R:Gabriel(Air Walker) 20.00
306 KP,O&V:Firelord,O:Air Walker. 20.00
307 KP,I:Dream Demon 20.00

308 KP,V:Snow Giants 20.00
309 V:Bomnardiers 20.00
310 KP,V:Mephisto 20.00
311 KP,GD,A:Valkyrie 20.00
312 KP,V:Tyr 20.00
313 KP,Thor Trial 15.00
314 KP,A:Drax,Moondragon 15.00
315 KP,O:Bi-Beast 15.00
316 KP,A:Iron Man,Man Thing,
    V:Man-Beast 15.00
317 KP,V:Man-Beast 15.00
318 GK,V:Fafnir 15.00
319 KP,I&D:Zaniac 15.00
320 KP,V:Rimthursar 15.00
321 I:Menagerie 15.00
322 V:Heimdall 15.00
323 V:Death 15.00
324 V:Graviton 15.00
325 JM,O:Darkoth,V:Mephisto . . . 15.00
326 I:New Scarlet Scarab 15.00
327 V:Loki & Tyr 15.00
328 I:Megatak 15.00
329 HT,V:Hrungnir 15.00
330 BH,I:Crusader 15.00
331 Threshold of Death 15.00
332 V:Dracula 15.00
333 BH,V:Dracula 15.00
334 Quest For Rune Staff 15.00
335 V:Possessor 15.00
336 A:Captain Ultra 15.00
337 WS,I:Beta Ray Bill,A:Surtur . . 20.00
338 WS,O:Beta Ray Bill,I:Lorelei . . 18.00
339 WS,V:Beta Ray Bill 12.00
340 WS,A:Beta Ray Bill 12.00
341 WS,V:Fafnir 12.00
342 WS,V:Fafnir,I:Eilif 12.00
343 WS,V:Fafnir 12.00
344 WS,Balder vs. Loki,I:Malekith . 12.00
345 WS,V:Malekith 12.00
346 WS,V:Malekith 12.00
347 WS,V:Malekith,I:Algrim
    (Kurse) 12.00
348 WS,V:Malekith 12.00
349 WS,R:Beta Ray Bill,O:Odin,
    I&O:Vili & Ve(Odin's brothers). 12.00
350 WS,V:Surtur 12.00
351 WS,V:Surtur 12.00
352 WS,V:Surtur 12.00
353 WS,V:Surtur,D:Odin 10.00
354 WS,V:Hela 10.00
355 WS,SB,A:Thor's Great
    Grandfather 10.00
356 BL,BG,V:Hercules 10.00
357 WS,A:Beta Ray Bill 10.00
358 WS,A:Beta Ray Bill 10.00
359 WS,V:Loki 10.00
360 WS,V:Hela 10.00
361 WS,V:Hela 10.00
362 WS,V:Hela 10.00
363 WS,Secret Wars II,V:Kurse . . . 10.00
364 WS,I:Thunder Frog 10.00
365 WS,A:Thunder Frog 10.00
366 WS,A:Thunder Frog 10.00
367 WS,D:Malekith,A:Kurse 10.00
368 WS,F:Balder t/Brave,Kurse. . . 10.00
369 WS,F:Balder the Brave 10.00
370 JB,V:Loki 10.00
371 SB,I:Justice Peace,V:Zaniac . . 10.00
372 SB,V:Justice Peace 10.00
373 SB,A:X-Factor,(Mut.Mass) . . . 10.00
374 WS,SB,A:X-Factor,(Mut.Mass)
    A:Sabretooth 12.00
375 WS,SB,N:Thor(Exoskeleton) . . 8.00
376 WS,SB,V:Absorbing Man 8.00
377 WS,SB,N:Thor,A:Ice Man 8.00
378 WS,SB,V:Frost Giants 8.00
379 WS,V:Midgard Serpent 8.00
380 WS,V:Midgard Serpent 8.00
381 WE,SB,A:Avengers 8.00
382 WS,SB,V:Frost Giants,Loki . . . 10.00
383 BBr,Secret Wars story 8.00
384 RF,BBr,I:Future Thor(Dargo). . 12.00

Thor, The Mighty #338
© Marvel Entertainment Group

385 EL,V:Hulk 8.00
386 RF,BBr,I:Leir 8.00
387 RF,BBr,V:Celestials 8.00
388 RF,BBr,V:Celestials 8.00
389 RF,BBr,V:Celestials 8.00
390 RF,BBr,A:Avengers,V:Seth 8.00
391 RF,BBr,I:Mongoose,Eric
    Masterson,A:Spider-Man 12.00
392 RF,I:Quicksand 10.00
393 RF,BBr,V:Quicksand,A:DD . . . 10.00
394 RF,BBr,V:Earth Force 10.00
395 RF,V:Earth Force 10.00
396 RF,A:Black Knight 10.00
397 RF,A:Loki 10.00
398 RF,DH,R:Odin,V:Seth 10.00
399 RF,RT,R:Surtur,V:Seth 10.00
400 RF,JSt,CV,V:Surtur,Seth 12.00
401 V:Loki 7.00
402 RF,J3t,V.Quicksand 7.00
403 RF,JSt,V:Executioner 7.00
404 RF,JSt,TD,V:Annihilus 7.00
405 RF,JSt,TD,V:Annihilus 7.00
406 RF,JSt,TD,V:Wundagore 7.00
407 RF,JSt,R:Hercules,High Evol. . . 7.00
408 RF,JSt,I:Eric Masterson/Thor,
    V:Mongoose 8.00
409 RF,JSt,V:Dr.Doom 7.00
410 RF,JSt,V:Dr.Doom,She-Hulk . . . 7.00
411 RF,JSt,C:New Warriors
    V:Juggernaut,A of V 5.00
412 RF,JSt,I:New Warriors
    V:Juggernaut,A of V 6.00
413 RF,JSt,A:Dr.Strange 4.00
414 RF,JSt,V:Ulik 4.00
415 HT,O:Thor 4.00
416 RF,JSt,A:Hercules 4.00
417 RF,JSt,A:High Evolutionary 4.00
418 RF,JSt,V:Wrecking Crew 4.00
419 RF,JSt,B:Black Galaxy
    Saga,I:Stellaris 4.00
420 RF,JSt,A:Avengers,V:Stellaris . . 4.00
421 RF,JSt,V:Stellaris 4.00
422 RF,JSt,V:High Evol.,Nobilus . . . 4.00
423 RF,JSt,A:High Evol.,Celestials
    Count Tagar 4.00
424 RF,JSt,V:Celestials,E:Black
    Galaxy Saga 4.00
425 RF,AM,V:Surtur,Ymir 4.00
426 RF,JSt,HT,O:Earth Force 4.00
427 RF,JSt,A:Excalibur 4.00
428 RF,JSt,A:Excalibur 4.00
429 RF,JSt,A:Ghost Rider 4.00
430 RF,AM,A:Mephisto,Gh.Rider . . . 4.00
431 HT,AM,V:Ulik,Loki 4.00

Thor King-Size Annual #7
© Marvel Entertainment Group

432 RF,D:Loki,Thor Banished,Eric
    Masterson becomes 2nd Thor. . 6.00
433 RF,V:Ulik 7.00
434 RF,AM,V:Warriors Three 5.00
435 RF,AM,V:Annihilus 5.00
436 RF,AM,V:Titania,Absorbing
    Man,A:Hercules 5.00
437 RF,AM,V:Quasar 5.00
438 RF,JSt,A:Future Thor(Drago) . . 5.00
439 RF,JSt,A:Drago 5.00
440 RF,AM,I:Thor Corps 6.00
441 RF,AM,Celestials vs.Ego 6.00
442 RF,AM,Don Blake,Beta Ray
    Bill,Mephisto 4.00
443 RF,AM,A:Dr.Strange,Silver
    Surfer,V:Mephisto 4.00
444 RF,AM,Special X-mas tale 4.00
445 AM,Galactic Storm,pt.7,
    V:Gladiator 4.00
446 AM,Galactic Storm,pt.14,
    A:Avengers 4.00
447 RF,AM,V:Absorbing Man,
    A:Spider-Man. 4.00
448 RF,AM,V:Titania,A:SpM. 4.00
449 RF,AM,V:Ulik. 4.00
450 RF,AM,V:Heimdall,A:Code Blue
    Double-Sized,Gatefold(c),rep.
    Journey Into Mystery#87 . . . . . . 4.00
451 RF,AM,I:Bloodaxe 4.00
452 RF,AM,V:Bloodaxe 4.00
453 RF,AM,V:Mephisto 4.00
454 RF,AM,V:Mephisto,Loki,
    Karnilla. 4.00
455 AM(i),V:Loki,Karnilla,R:Odin,
    A:Dr.Strange 4.00
456 RF,AM,V:Bloodaxe 4.00
457 RF,AM,R:1st Thor 4.00
458 RF,AM,Thor vs. Eric 4.00
459 RF,AM,C&I:Thunderstrike(Eric
    Masterson). 3.00
460 I:New Valkyrie 3.00
461 V:Beta Ray Bill 3.00
462 A:New Valkyrie 3.00
463 Infinity Crusade. 3.00
464 Infinity Crusade,V:Loki 3.00
465 Infinity Crusade. 3.00
466 Infinity Crusade. 3.00
467 Infinity Crusade. 3.00
468 RMz(s),Blood & Thunder#1 . . 3.00
469 RMz(s),Blood & Thunder#5 . . 3.00
470 MCW,Blood & Thunder#9 . . . 3.00
471 MCW,E:Blood & Thunder 3.00
472 B:RTs(s),MCW,I:Godling,C:High
    Evolutionary. 3.00

473 MCW,V:Godling,High Evolutionary,
    I&C:Karnivore(Man-Beast) 3.00
474 MCW,C:High Evolutionary 3.00
475 MCW,Foil(c),A:Donald Blake,
    N:Thor 3.50
475a Newsstand ed. 3.00
476 V:Destroyer. 3.00
477 V:Destroyer,A:Thunderstrike . . 3.00
478 V:Norvell Thor. 3.00
479 V:Norvell Thor. 3.00
480 V:High Evolutionary 3.00
481 V:Grotesk 3.00
482 Don Blake construct 3.00
483 RTs,MCW,V:Loki 3.00
484 Badoy and Soul 3.00
485 V:The Thing 3.00
486 High Evolutionary,Godpack. . . . 3.00
487 V:Kurse 3.00
488 RTs,MCW,Kurse Saga concl. . . 3.00
489 RTs,V:Kurse,A:Hulk. 3.00
490 TDF,after Thunderstrike 3.00
491 N:Thor. 7.50
492 Worldengine's Secrets 5.00
493 Worldengine trigers Ragnarok . 3.00
494 Worldengine saga conclusion. . 3.00
495 BML,Avengers:Timeslide 3.00
496 MD2,BML,A:Capt.America 3.00
497 MD2,BML,Thor Must Die 3.00
498 BML,V:Absorbing Man 3.00
499 MD2,BML 3.00
500 MD2,BML,double size,A:Dr.
    Strange 3.50
501 MD2,BML,I:Red Norvell 3.00
502 MD2,BML,Onslaught tie-in, A:Red
    Norvell, Jane Foster, Hela. 3.00
Becomes:

JOURNEY INTO MYSTERY

[Third Series] Nov., 1996
503 TDF,MD2, The Lost Gods, New
    Norse gods? 2.50
504 TDF,Golden Realm in ruins,
    V:Ulik the Troll 2.50
505 TDF,MD2, V:Wrecker,
    A:Spider-Man. 2.50
506 TDF,MD2, R:Heimdall 2.50
507 TDF,Odin kidnapped 2.50
508 TDF 2.50
509 TDF,Battle for the Future
    of Asgard 2.50
510 TDF,Return of Loki,A:Seth 2.50
511 TDF,EBe,Lost Gods reunited
    with Odin 2.50
512 EBe, Odin vs. Seth 2.50
513 TDF,SB,AM, Odin vs.
    Seth, concl. 2.50
514 BRa,VRu,F:Shang Chi, Master
    of Kung Fu. 2.50
515 BRa,VRu,F:Shang Chi, Master
    of Kung Fu, pt.2. . . . . 2.50
516 BRa,VRu,F:Shang Chi, Master
    of Kung Fu, pt.3. . . . . 2.50
517 SLo,RGr,F:Black Widow 2.50
518 SLo,RGr,F:Black Widow 2.50
519 SLo,RGr,F:Black Widow, concl. 2.50
520 MWn,F:Hannibal King, pt.1 . . . 2.50
521 MWn,F:Hannibal King, pt.2. . . . 2.50
Ann.#2 JK,V:Destroyer 75.00
Ann.#3 JK,rep,Grey Gargoyle. 30.00
Ann.#4 JK,rep,TheLivingPlanet. . . 25.00
Ann.#5 JK,JB,Hercules,O:Odin . . . 25.00
Ann.#6 JK,JB,A:Guardians of the
    Galaxy,V:Korvac 25.00
Ann.#7 WS,Eternals. 20.00
Ann.#8 JB,V:Zeus 20.00
Ann.#9 LMc,Dormammu 20.00
Ann.#10 O:Chthon,Gaea,A:Pluto. . 15.00
Ann.#11 O:Odin 15.00
Ann.#12 BH,I:Vidar(Odin's son). . . 15.00
Ann.#13 JB,V:Mephisto 15.00
Ann.#14 AM,DH,Atlantis Attacks . . 7.00
Ann.#15 HT,Terminus Factor #3 . . . 5.00

Journey Into Mystery #510
© Marvel Entertainment Group

Ann.#16 Korvac Quest,pt.2,
    Guardians of Galaxy 3.00
Ann.#17 Citizen Kang#2 . . . . 3.00
Ann.#18 TGr,I:The Flame,w/card. . . 3.50
Ann.#19 V:Flame 3.50
G-Size.#1 Battles,A:Hercules 14.00
TPB Alone Against the Celestials . . 6.00
TPB Ballad of Beta Ray Bill, rep. . . 9.00
TPB The Eternals Saga (2006) . . . 25.00
Minus 1 Spec., TDF,EBe,flashback . 2.00
1-shot, Rough Cut, DJu,JR,original
    pencils, b&w 48-pg. 3.00

THOR

May, 1998
1 JR2,KJ,DJu,The hero returns,
    48-pg. 6.00
2A JR2,KJ,DJu,V:Destroyer,A:Hela,
    Marnot 3.50
2B JR2,KJ variant cover 3.50
3 DJu,JR2,KJ,A:Marnot,V:Sedna . . 3.00
4 DJu,JR2,KJ,A:Namor,Sedna 3.00
5 DJu,JR2,KJ,V:Charles Diamond . 3.00
6 DJu,JR2,KJ,V:Hercules 3.00
7 DJu,JR2,KJ,V:Zeus 3.00
8 DJu,JR2,KJ,PeterParker x-over. . 3.00
9 DJu,JB,JOy,War on
    Asgard,prelude 3.00
10 DJu,JR2,KJ,War on Asgard,pt.1 . 3.00
11 DJu,JR2,KJ,War on Asgard,pt.2 . 3.00
12 DJu,JR2,KJ,War on
    Asgard,concl. 48-page 3.50
12a signed 20.00
13 DJu,JR2,KJ,A:Marnot 2.50
14 DJu,Hammer secret 2.50
15 DJu,KJ,JR2(c),A:Warriors 3 . . . 2.50
16 DJu,KJ,JR2,A:Warriors 3 . . . . . 2.50
17 DJu,KJ,JR2,Eighth
    Day,pt.1, x-over 2.50
18 DJu,KJ,JR2,V:Enrakt 2.50
19 DJu 2.50
20 DJu,V:Loki. 2.50
21 DJu,JR2,KJ,R:Thanos 2.50
22 DJu,JR2,KJ,V:Thanos. 2.50
23 DJu,JR2,DG,V:Thanos 2.50
24 DJu,JR2,DG,V:Thanos 2.50
25A DJu,JR2,DG,48-pg.,foil(c) 6.00
25B variant (c). 3.00
26 DJu,EL,KJ,V:AbsorbingMan . . . 2.25
27 DJu,EL,KJ,Dr.Jane Foster 2.25
28 DJu,EL,KJ,WarriorsThree 2.25
29 DJu,NKu,SHa,Jagrfelm 2.25
30 DJu,NKu,SHa,MaxSecurity. 2.25
31 DJu,NKu,SHa,V:Malekith 2.25

MARVEL

32 DJu,NKu,SHa,100-page 4.00
33 DJu,SI,I:new 2.25
34 DJu,NKu,SHa 2.25
35 DJu,NKu,SHa,V:Gladiator,
  48-page 3.50
36 DJu,R:Loki,A:Destroyer 2.25
37 DJu,JSn,AM,A:Watcher 2.25
38 DJu,SI,BWS(c),V:Destroyer 2.25
39 DJu,SI,BWS(c),V:Surtur 2.25
40 DJu,SI,V:Surtur 3.00
41 DJu,SI,V:Surtur,concl. 2.25
42 DJu,SI,Asgard,Midgard 2.25
43 DJu,JoB,Thor:King of Asgard . . . 2.25
44 DJu,SI,Odin funeral,'Nuff Said . . 2.25
45 TR,new King in Asgard 2.25
46 DJu,SHa,TR,F:Thor-Girl 2.25
47 DJu,SHa,TR,Enchantress. 2.25
48 DJu,JoB,TP,V:Desak. 2.25
49 DJu,TR,SHa,V:Desak 2.25
50 DJu,TR,SHa,64-pg. 6.00
51 DJu,TR,SHa,F:Spider-Man 2.25
52 DJu,TP 2.25
53 DJu 2.25
54 DJu,TR,SHa 2.25
55 DJu,TR,SHa 2.25
56 DJu,TR, ... 2.25
57 DJu,JoB 2.25
58 DJu,AD,Standoff,pt.1,x-over . . . 2.50
59 CPr(s) 2.50
60 DJu,JoB,Spiral,pt.1 . . . . 2.25
61 DJu,Spiral,pt.2 . . . . 2.25
62 DJu,Spiral,pt.3 . . . . 3.00
63 DJu,Spiral,pt.4 . . . . 3.00
64 DJu,Spiral,pt.5 . . . . 3.00
65 DJu,Spiral,pt.6 . . . . 3.00
66 DJu,Spiral,pt.7 . . . . 3.00
67 DJu,Spiral,concl. 3.00
68 DJu,SEa,The Reigning,prologue 3.00
69 DJu,SEa,The Reigning,pt.1 . . . . 3.00
70 DJu,SEa,The Reigning,pt.2 . . . . 3.00
71 DKi,SEa,The Reigning,pt.3 . . . . 3.00
72 DJu,SEa,The Reigning,pt.4 . . . . 3.00
73 DJu,SEa,The Reigning,pt.5 . . . . 3.00
74 DJu,SEa,The Reigning,concl. . . . 3.00
75 DJu,SEa,Gods & Men,pt.1 . . . . . 3.00
76 DJu,SEa,Gods & Men,pt.2 . . . . . 3.00
77 DJu,SEa,Gods & Men,pt.3 . . . . . 3.00
78 DJu,SEa,Gods & Men,pt.4 . . . . . 3.00
79 DJu,SEa,Gods & Men,pt.5 . . . . . 3.00
80 F:The Avengers 15.00
81 F:The Avengers 10.00
82 Avengers Disassembled tie-in . . 7.00
83 Ragnarok,pt.3 . . . . 7.00
84 Ragnarok,pt.4 . . . . 6.00
85 Ragnarok,pt.5 . . . . 9.00
Ann.1999 DJu,KJ, 48-page 3.50
Ann.1999 signed 20.00
Ann.2000, 48-pg. 3.50
Ann.2001 TG,DJu,48-page 3.50
Spec.#1 Thor (2000) 2.25
Spec. rep.#1 & #2 . . . . 6.00
TPB The Dark Gods, 128-pg. 16.00
TPB Across All Worlds 17.00
TPB Thor Visionaries: Walt
  Simonson, 288-page 25.00
TPB The Death of Odin 13.00
TPB Lord of Asgard 16.00
TPB Vol. 2: Legends (2003) 25.00
TPB Vol. 3: Gods on Earth 22.00
TPB Vol. 4: Spiral (2003) 20.00
TPB Vol. 5: The Reigning 18.00
TPB Vol. 6: Gods & Men 14.00
TPB Visionaries MD2 . . . . 20.00

THOR: BLOOD OATH
Sept., 2005
1 (of 6) Classic Thor 3.00
2 Thor & Warriors 3.00
3 V:Hercules 3.00
4 thru 6 . . . . @3.00

THOR CORPS
[Limited Series]
1 TDF(s),PO,V:Demonstaff 2.25
2 TDF(s),PO,A:Invaders 2.25
3 TDF(s),PO,A:Spider-Man 2099 . . 2.25
4 TDF(s),PO,last issue 2.25

THOR: GODSTORM
Sept., 2001
1 (of 3) KBk,SR. 3.50
2 KBk,SR,V:Loki 3.50
3 KBk,SR,V:Loki,concl. 3.50

THOR: SON OF ASGARD
March, 2004
1 (of 6) The Warriors Teen,pt.1 . . . . 3.00
2 The Warriors Teen,pt.2 . . . . 3.00
3 The Warriors Teen,pt.3 . . . . 3.00
4 The Warriors Teen,pt.4 . . . . 3.00
5 The Warriors Teen,pt.5 . . . . 3.00
6 The Warriors Teen,pt.6 . . . . 3.00
7 Enchanted,pt.1 . . . . 3.00
8 Enchanted,pt.2 . . . . 3.00
9 Enchanted,pt.3 . . . . 3.00
10 . . . . 3.00
11 . . . . 3.00
12 Worthy, finale 3.00
Digest,Vol. 1 Warriors Teen 8.00
Digest,Vol. 2 Worthy 8.00

THOR: VIKINGS
Marvel Max, July, 2003
1 GEn(s),GF,Zombie Vikings 5.00
2 GEn(s),GF,F:Doctor Strange 4.00
3 GEn(s),GF 4.00
4 GEn(s),GF,back in time 4.00
5 GEn(s),GF,Zombie Vikings 4.00
TPB 14.00

3-D ACTION
Marvel Atlas 1954
1 Battle Brady 450.00

3-D TALES OF THE WEST
Marvel Atlas, 1954
1 . . . . 500.00

THREE MUSKETEERS
1 thru 2 movie adapt. 2.25

THUNDERBOLTS
Feb., 1997
1 KBk,MBa,VRu,Post-onslaught new
  team:Citizen V, Meteorite, Techno,
  Songbird, Atlas & Mach-1 . . . . 10.00
1 rep. 3.00
2 KBk,MBa,VRu,V:Mad Thinker . . . 6.00
2a variant cover by MBa&VRu 6.00
2 rep. 4.50
3 KBk,MBa,VRu,Freedom's Plaza . 4.50
4 KBk,MBa,VRu,I:Jolt 4.50
5 KBk,MBa,VRu,V:Elements-Doom 4.50
6 KBk,MBa,VRu,V:Elements-Doom 4.50
7 KBk,MBa,VRu,F:Citizen V 4.00
8 KBk,MBa,VRu,Songbird alone. . . 4.00
9 KBk,MBa,VRu,Black Widow 4.00
10 KBk,MBa,VRu,Identy discovered 4.00
11 KBk,MBa,VRu,V:Citizen V 4.00
12 KBk,MBa,VRu,A:FF,Avengers . 10.00
13 KBk,MBa,SHa,on trial 3.00
14 KBk,MBa,VRu,V:Citizen V 3.00
15 KBk,MBa,VRu,V:S.H.I.E.L.D. . . . 3.00
16 KBk,MBa,SHa,V:Lightningrods . . 3.00
17 KBk,MBa,SHa,V:Graviton 3.00
18 KBk,MBa,SHa,villains again? . . . 3.00
19 KBk,MBa,SHa 3.00
20 KBk,MBa,SHa,V:Masters-Evil . . . 3.00
21 KBk,MBa,SHa,F:Songbird 3.00

Thunderbolts #28
© Marvel Entertainment Group

22 KBk,MBa,SHa,A:Hercules 3.00
23 KBk,MBa,SHa,V:U.S.Agent 3.00
24 KBk,MBa,SHa,R:Citizen V 3.00
25 KBk,MBa,SHa,48-page. 3.50
25a signed 20.00
26 KBk,MBa,SHa,JoC,A:Mach-1 . . . 2.50
27 KBk,MBa,SHa,A:Archangel 2.50
28 KBk,MBa,SHa,V:Graviton 2.50
29 KBk,MBa,SHa,V:Graviton 2.50
30 KBk,MBa,SHa,V:Graviton 2.50
31 KBk,MBa,SHa,R:Citizen V 2.50
32 KBk,MBa,SHa,V:Citizen V 2.50
33 KBk,MBa,SHa,F:Jolt 2.50
34 MBa,SHa. 2.50
35 FaN,MBa,SHa. 2.50
36 FaN,MBa,SHa,V:Beetle 2.50
37 FaN,MBa,SHa,A:Hawkeye 2.50
38 FaN,MBa,SHa,V:Citizen V 2.50
39 FaN,MBa,SHa,100-pg. 3.00
40 FaN,MBa,SHa,V:Citizen V 2.25
41 FaN,MBa,Sandman 2.25
42 FaN,MBa,Avengers x-over 2.25
43 FaN,MBa,Avengers x-over 2.25
44 FaN,MBa,Avengers x-over 2.25
45 FaN,MBa,Maximum Security . . . 2.25
46 FaN,MBa,V:Scourge 2.25
47 FaN,MBa,A:Songbird 2.25
48 FaN,MBa,V:Scourge,pt.1 . . . . . . 2.25
49 FaN,V:Scourge,face shown 2.25
50 FaN,MBa,48-page. 4.00
51 FaN,AV,rescue mission. 2.25
52 FaN,AV,V:Dr.Doom 2.25
53 FaN,AV,F:Charcoal 2.25
54 FaN,AV,F:Fixer 2.25
55 FaN,AV,V:Redeemers 2.25
56 FaN,AV,V:Graviton 2.25
57 FaN,AV,V:Graviton 2.25
58 FaN,AV,V:Graviton 2.25
59 FaN,MBa,AV,Songbird,'NuffSaid. 2.25
60 FaN,MBa,AV,Chain Gang. 2.25
61 FaN,Heroes Return,pt.2 . . . . 2.25
62 FaN,Heroes Return,pt.3 . . . . 2.25
63 FaN,Hawkeye,Screaming Mimi . 2.25
64 FaN,F:Zemo 2.25
65 FaN,V:Masters of Evil 2.25
66 FaN,F:Baron Zemo,Jolt 2.25
67 FaN,F:Harrier, Hawkeye 2.25
68 FaN,F:Moonstone,PhantomEagle2.25
69 FaN,AV 2.25
70 FaN, ... 2.25
71 FaN 2.25
72 FaN 2.25
73 Fan,AV 2.25
74 FaN 2.25

MARVEL

75 FaN,48-pg.	3.50
76 Fight club	2.25
77 JAr(s)	2.25
78 JAr(s)	3.00
79 JAr(s)	3.00
80 JAr(s),F:Spider-Man,pt.1	2.25
81 JAr(s),F:Spider-Man,pt.2	2.25

Continued As:

NEW THUNDERBOLTS
Nov., 2004

1 FaN,TG,Zeroes to Heroes,pt.1	3.00
2 FaN,TG,Zeroes to Heroes,pt.2	3.00
3 FaN,TG,Zeroes to Heroes,pt.3	3.00
4 FaN,TG,Enemy of the State, Wolverine X-over	3.00
5 FaN,TG,V:Fathom 5.	3.00
6 FaN,TG,V:Hydra.	3.00
7 FaN,TG,modern Marvels	3.00
8 FaN,TG,F:Speed Demon,Blizzard	3.00
9 FaN,TG,F:Photon.	3.00
10 FaN,TG,Purple Reign,pt.1.	3.00
11 FaN,TG,Purple Reign,pt.2.	3.00
12 FaN,TG,Purple Reign,pt.3.	3.00
13 FaN,TG,A:New Avengers	3.00
14 FaN,TG,A:New Avengers	3.00
15 FaN,TG,F:Songbird.	3.00
16 FaN,TG,New Squadron Sinister	3.00
17 FaN,TG,V:Baron Zemo	3.00
18 FaN,TG,R:Moonstone	3.00
TPB Vol. 1: One Step Forward	15.00
TPB Vol. 2: Modern Marvels	15.00
TPB Vol. 3: Right to Power	15.00

Becomes:

THUNDERBOLTS
March, 2006

100 FaN,TG, V:Photon, 104-pg.	4.00
101 FaN,TG, Zemo & Songbird	3.00
102 FaN,TG, V:Speed Demon	3.00
103 FaN,TG, Civil War tie-in	6.00
103a 2nd printing	3.50
104 FaN,TG, Civil War tie-in	4.00
105 FaN,TG, Civil War tie-in	3.00
106 FaN,TG, Supervillain Army	3.00
107 FaN,TG, Supervillain Army	3.00
108 FaN,TG, V:Grandmaster	3.00
Ann. '97 KBk,MBa,TGu,GP, O:Thunderbolts, 48-pg.	3.00
Ann.2000 FaN,NBy, 48-pg.	3.50
Spec.#0 Wizard Nov., 1998	5.00
Spec.First Strikes, rep.#1 & #2	5.00
Spec #1 Distant Rumblings KBk, SEp,Flashback,F:Citizen V	2.50
Spec.Life Sentences (2001).	3.50
TPB 176-pg., secret history	12.00
TPB Vol. 1: How to Lose	15.00

THUNDERCATS
Star, Dec., 1985

1 JM,TV tie-in	10.00
1a 2nd printing	7.00
2 thru 10	@7.00
11 thru 24	@7.00

THUNDERSTRIKE
1993–95

1 B:TDF(s),RF,Holografx(c), V:Bloodaxe,I:Car Jack.	3.25
2 RF,V:Juggernaut	2.25
3 RF,I:Sangre	2.25
4 RF,A:Spider-Man,I:Pandora	2.25
5 RF,A:Spider-Man,V:Pandora	2.25
6 RF,I:Blackwulf,Bristle,Schizo,Lord Lucian,A:SpM,Code:Blue,Stellaris, V:SHIELD,Pandora,C:Tantalus	2.25
7 KP,V:Tantalus,D:Jackson.	2.25
8 RF,I&V:Officer ZERO	2.25
9 RF,V:Bloodaxe	2.25
10 RF,A:Thor	2.25
11 RF,A:Wildstreak.	2.25
12 RF,A:Whyte Out	2.25

13 RF,Inferno 42	2.25
13a Double Feature flip book with Code Blue #1	2.50
14 RF, Inferno 42.	2.25
14a Double Feature flip book	2.50
15 RF,V:Methisto	2.25
15a Double Feature flip book with Code Blue #3	2.50
16	2.25
17 V:Bloodaxe	2.25
18 V:New Villain.	2.25
19 Shopping Network	2.25
20 A:Black Panther	2.25
21 A:War Machine,V:Loki	2.25
22 TDF,AM,RF,Mystery of Bloodaxe blows open	2.25
23 TDF,A:Avengers	2.25
24 TDF,V:Bloodaxe, final issue	2.25

TIMELY PRESENTS: HUMAN TORCH COMICS
Aug., 1998

1-shot GN.	6.00

TIMESLIP COLLECTION
Sept., 1998

1-shot, 48-page	3.00

TIMESLIP: THE COMING OF THE AVENGERS
Aug., 1998

1-shot GN.	6.00

TIMESPIRITS
Epic, Jan., 1985

1 TY	3.00
2 thru 8	@2.25

TIMESTRYKE

1	2.25
2	2.25

TINY TESSIE
See: TESSIE THE TYPIST

TOMB OF DARKNESS
See: BEWARE

TOMB OF DRACULA
April, 1972

1 GC,Night of the Vampire	300.00
2 GC,Who Stole My Coffin?	100.00
3 GC,TP,I:Rachel Van Helsing	75.00
4 GC,TP,Bride of Dracula!	75.00
5 GC,TP,To Slay A Vampire	75.00
6 GC,TP,Monster of the Moors	60.00
7 GC,TP,Child is Slayer of the Man	60.00
8 GC(p),The Hell-Crawlers	60.00
9 The Fire Cross	60.00
10 GC,I:Blade Vampire Slayer	200.00
11 GC,TP,Master of the Undead Strikes Again!	50.00
12 GC,TP,House that Screams	75.00
13 GC,TP,O:Blade	100.00
14 GC,TP,Vampire has Risen from the Grave	50.00
15 GC,TP,Stay Dead	50.00
16 GC,TP,Back from the Grave	50.00
17 GC,TP,A Vampire Rides This Train!	50.00
18 GC,TP,A:Werewolf By Night	60.00
19 GC,TP,Snowbound in Hell	50.00
20 GC,TP,Manhunt For A Vampire	50.00
21 GC,TP,A:Blade	40.00
22 GC,TP,V:Gorna	25.00
23 GC,TP,Shadow over Haunted Castle	25.00

24 GC,TP,I am your Death	30.00
25 GC,TP,Blood Stalkers of Count Dracula	30.00
26 GC,TP,A Vampire Stalks the Night.	25.00
27 GC,TP,..And the Moon Spews Death!.	25.00
28 GC,TP,Five came to Kill a Vampire	30.00
29 GC,TP,Vampire goes Mad?	25.00
30 GC,TP,A:Blade	25.00
31 GC,TP,Child of Blood	25.00
32 GC,TP,The Vampire Walks Among Us.	25.00
33 GC,TP,Blood on My Hands.	25.00
34 GC,TP,Bloody Showdown.	25.00
35 GC,TP,A:Brother Voodoo	25.00
36 GC,TP,Dracula in America	25.00
37 GC,TP,The Vampire Walks Among Us.	25.00
38 GC,TP,Bloodlust for a Dying Vampire	25.00
39 GC,TP,Final Death of Dracula	25.00
40 GC,TP,Triumph of Dr.Sun	25.00
41 GC,TP,A:Blade	25.00
42 GC,TP,V:Dr.Sun	25.00
43 GC,TP,A:NewYear'sNightmare	25.00
44 GC,TP,A:Dr.Strange	25.00
45 GC,TP,A:Hannibal King	25.00
46 GC,TP,W:Dracula & Domini	20.00
47 GC,TP,Death-Bites	20.00
48 GC,TP,A:Hannibal King	20.00
49 GC,TP,A:Robin Hood, Frankenstein's Monster	20.00
50 GC,TP,A:Silver Surfer	30.00
51 GC,TP,A:Blade	15.00
52 GC,TP,V:Demon	15.00
53 GC,TP,A:Hannibal King,Blade	15.00
54 GC,TP,Twas the Night Before Christmas	15.00
55 GC,TP,Requiem for a Vampire	15.00
56 GC,TP,A:Harold H. Harold	15.00
57 GC,TP,The Forever Man.	15.00
58 GC,TP,A:Blade	35.00
59 GC,TP,The Last Traitor.	15.00
60 GC,TP,The Wrath of Dracula	15.00
61 GC,TP,Resurrection	15.00
62 GC,TP,What Lurks Beneath	15.00
63 GC,TP,A:Janus	15.00
64 GC,TP,A:Satan	15.00
65 GC,TP,Where No Vampire Has Gone Before.	15.00
66 GC,TP,Marked for Death	15.00
67 GC,TP,A:Lilith	15.00
68 GC,TP,Dracula Turns Human	15.00

Tomb of Dracula #25
© *Marvel Entertainment Group*

69 GC,TP,Cross of Fire 15.00
70 GC,TP,double size,last issue . . 30.00
Savage Return of Dracula. rep.
   Tomb of Dracula #1,#2 . . . . 2.50
Wedding of Dracula. rep.Tomb
   of Dracula #30,#45,#46 . . . . . . 2.50
Requiem for Dracula. rep.Tomb
   of Dracula #69,#70 . . . . 2.50

TOMB OF DRACULA
(B&W Mag.) Nov., 1979
1 . . . . 25.00
2 SD 18.00
3 FM 18.00
4 . . . . 15.00
5 . . . . 15.00
6 Sept., 1980 . . . . 15.00

TOMB OF DRACULA
[Mini-Series] Nov., 1991
1 GC,AW,Day of Blood 6.00
2 GC,AW,Dracula in D.C. 5.50
3 GC,AW,A:Blade 5.50
4 GC,AW,D:Dracula 5.50

TOMB OF DRACULA
2004
1 BSz(c) F:Blade. 3.00
2 . . . . 3.00
3 . . . . 3.00
4 Bsz(c). 3.00
TPB Essential Tomb of Dracula, #1 15.00
TPB Essential Tomb of Dracula, #2 17.00
TPB Essential Tomb of Dracula, #3 17.00
TPB Essential Tomb of Dracula, #4 17.00

TOMB OF DRACULA MEGAZINE
TPB Halloween, MWn,GC,TP 4.00

TOMORROW KNIGHTS
Eplc, June, 1990
I 2.25
2 thru 6 . . . . @2.25

TOP DOG
Star, April, 1985
1 . . . . 3.00
2 thru 14, June, 1987 . . . . @3.00

Top Dog #9
© *Marvel Entertainment Group*

TOR
Epic *Heavy Hitters*, 1993
1 JKu,R:Tor,magazine format 6.25
2 JKu. 6.25
3 JKu,V:The Iduard Ring 6.25

Tough Kid Squad Comics #1
© *Marvel Entertainment Group*

TOUGH KID SQUAD COMICS
Marvel Timely, March, 1942
1 AAv,SSh,O:The Human Top,
   Tough Kid Squad,A:The Flying
   Flame, V:Doctor Klutch . . 18,000.00

TOWER OF SHADOWS
Sept., 1969
1 JR(c),JSo,JCr,At The Stroke
   of Midnight. 275.00
2 JR(c),DH,DA,NA,The Hungry
   One 200.00
3 GC,BWs,GT,Midnight in the
   Wax Museum. 200.00
4 DH,Within The Witching Circle 150.00
5 DA,BWS,WW,Demon That
   Stalks Hollywood 150.00
6 WW,SD,Pray For the Man in
   the Rat-Hole 150.00
7 BWS,WW,Titano 150.00
8 WW,SD,Demons of
   Dragon-Henge. 150.00
9 BWr(c),TP,Lovecraft story 150.00
Becomes:

CREATURES ON THE LOOSE
March, 1971
10 BWr,A:King Kull 100.00
11 DAy,rep. Moomba is Here 30.00
12 JK,I Was Captured By Korilla . . 30.00
13 RC,The Creature
   From Krogarr. 30.00
14 MSe,Dead Storage 30.00
15 SD,Spragg the Living Mountain 30.00
16 GK,BEv,GK,B&O:Gullivar Jones,
   Warrior of Mars. 25.00
17 GK,Slaves o/t Spider Swarm . . 25.00
18 RA,The Fury of Phra. 25.00
19 WB,JM,GK,Red Barbarian
   of Mars 25.00
20 GK(c),GM,SD,The Monster...
   And the Maiden 25.00
21 JSo(c),GM,Two Worlds To
   Win,E:Guilliver. 25.00

22 JSo(c),SD,VM,B:Thongor,
   Warrior of Lost Lemuria. 28.00
23 VM,The Man-Monster Strikes . . 12.00
24 VM,Attack of the Lizard-Hawks 12.00
25 VM,GK(c),Wizard of Lemuria . . 12.00
26 VM,Doom of the Serpent Gods 12.00
27 VM,SD,Demons Dwell in the
   Crypts of Yamath 12.00
28 SD,The Hordes of Hell 12.00
29 GK(c),Day of the Dragon Wings,
   E:Thongor,Warrior of Lemuria . 12.00
30 B:Man-Wolf,Full Moon, Dark
   Fear. 30.00
31 GT,The Beast Within. 15.00
32 GT,V:Kraven the Hunter 15.00
33 GK(c),GP,The Name of the
   Game is Death 15.00
34 GP,Nightflight to Fear 12.00
35 GK(c),GP 12.00
36 GK(c),GP,Murder by Moonlight. 12.00
37 GP,Sept., 1975 . . . . 12.00

TOXIC AVENGER
March, 1991
1 VM(i),I&O:Toxic Avenger 2.25
2 VM(i) 2.25
3 VM(i),Night of Living H.bodies . . . 2.25
4 Legend of Sludgeface 2.25
5 I:Biohazard. 2.25
6 V:Biohazard 2.25
7 Sewer of Souviaki 2.25
8 Sewer of Souviaki' conc. 2.25
9 Abducted by Aliens 2.25
10 Die,Yuppie Scum,pt.1 . . . . 2.25

TOXIC CRUSADERS
1992
1 F:Toxic Avengers & Crusaders . . 2.25
2 SK(c),V:Custard-Thing. 2.25
3 SK(c),V:Custard-Thing. 2.25
4 V:Giant Mutant Rats 2.25
5 V:Dr.Killemoff 2.25
6 V:Dr.Killemoff 2.25
7 F:Yvonne 2.25
8 V:Psycho 2.25

[2nd Series]
1 . . . . 2.25
2 . . . . 2.25

TOXIN
April, 2005
1 (of 6) DaR 3.00
2 Dar,cut to the Chase 3.00
3 The Answer, My Friend 3.00
4 Zero Hour. 3.00
5 Razor Fist 3.00
6 DaR,V:Razor-Fist,concl. 3.00
TPB The Devil You Know 18.00

TRANSFORMERS
[1st Regular Series] Sept., 1984
1 FS,Toy Comic 20.00
2 FS,OptimusPrime V:Megatron . . 11.00
3 FS.A:Spider-Man 11.00
4 MT(c),FS 10.00
5 Transformers Dead? 10.00
6 Autobots vs.Decepticons 10.00
7 KB,V:Megatron. 10.00
8 KB,A:Dinobots. 10.00
9 MM,A:Circuit Breaker. 10.00
10 Dawn of the Devastator 10.00
11 HT 9.00
12 HT,V:Shockwave 9.00
13 DP,Return of Megatron 9.00
14 DP,V:Decepticons 9.00
15 DP 9.00
16 KN,A:Bumblebee 9.00
17 DP,I:New Transformers,pt.1 . . . . 9.00
18 DP,I:New Transformers,pt.2 . . . . 9.00
19 DP,I:Omega Supreme. 9.00

Transformers #9
© *Marvel Entertainment Group*

20 HT,Skid vs.Ravage 9.00
21 DP,I:Aerialbots 9.00
22 DP,I:Stuntacons(Menasor) 9.00
23 DP,Return of Circuit Breaker . . . 9.00
24 DP,D:Optimus Prime. 9.00
25 DP,Decpticons (full story) 9.00
26 DP. 9.00
27 DP,V:Head Hunter. 9.00
28 DP 9.00
29 DP,I:Scraplets, Triplechangers . . 9.00
30 DP,V:Scraplets 9.00
31 DP,Humans vs. Decepticons . . . 9.00
32 DP,Autobots for Sale. 9.00
33 DP,Autobots vs.Decepticons. . . . 9.00
34 V:Sky Lynx 9.00
35 JRy,I:U.K.version Transformers . 9.00
36 . . . . 9.00
37 . . . . 9.00
38 . . . . 9.00
39 . . . . 9.00
40 Autobots' New Leader. 9.00
41 . . . . 9.00
42 Return of Optimus Prime 9.00
43 Optimus Prime,Goldbug 9.00
44 FF,Return of Circuit Breaker. . . . 9.00
45 V:The Jammers. 9.00
46 I:New Transformers 9.00
47 B:Underbase saga,I:Seacons . . . 9.00
48 Optimus Prime/Megatron
   (past story). 9.00
49 Underbase saga cont. 9.00
50 E:Underbase saga,I:new
   characters 10.00
51 I:Pretender Decepticon Beasts . 10.00
52 I:Mecannibles,pt.1. . . . . 10.00
53 Mecannibles,pt.2. . . . . 10.00
54 I:Micromasters 10.00
55 MG 10.00
56 Return of Megatron. 10.00
57 Optimus Prime vs.Scraponok . . 10.00
58 V:Megatron 10.00
59 A:Megatron,D:Ratchet. 10.00
60 Battle on Cybertron 11.00
61 O:Transformers 11.00
62 B:Matrix Quest,pt.1 . . . . 11.00
63 . . . . 11.00
64 I:The Klud 11.00
65 GSr 17.00
66 E:Matrix Quest,pt.5 . . . . 17.00
67 V:Unicorn,also Alternative
   World. 17.00
68 I:Neoknights 17.00
69 Fate of Ratchet & Megatron
   revealed. 17.00

70 Megatron/Ratchet fused
   together 17.00
71 Autobots Surrender to
   Decepticons. 20.00
72 Decepticon Civil War,
   I:Gravitron 20.00
73 I:Unicron,A:Neoknights 20.00
74 A:Unicron & Brothers of Chaos. 20.00
75 V:Thunderwing & Dark Matrix. . 20.00
76 Aftermath of War 20.00
77 Unholy Alliance 20.00
78 Galvatron vs.Megatron 28.00
79 Decepticons Invade Earth. 28.00
80 Return of Optimus Prime,final . 40.00

[2nd Regular Series]
1 Split Foil(c),A:Dinobots 3.00
2 A:G.I.Joe,Cobra 2.25
3 . . . . 2.25
4 MaG,V:Jhiaxus. 2.25
5 . . . . 2.25
6 V:Megatron 2.25
7 V:Darkwing. 2.25
8 V:Darkwing. 2.25
9 . . . . 2.25
10 Total War. 2.25
11 . . . . 2.25

TRANSFORMERS COMICS MAGAZINE
1986–88
1 Digest-size 2.25
2 thru 11 . . . . @2.25

TRANSFORMERS, THE MOVIE
Dec., 1986–Feb., 1987
1 thru 3 Animated movie adapt. . @2.25

TRANSFORMERS UNIVERSE
Dec., 1986
1 . . . . 3.00
2 . . . . 3.00
3 . . . . 3.00
4 March, 1987 . . . . 3.00

TRANSMUTATION OF IKE GARUDA
Epic, 1991
1 JSh,I:Ike Garuda 4.00
2 JSh,conclusion. 4.00

TROUBLE
Marvel Epic, June, 2003
1 MMr(s),Tyd,Teenage Romance . . 3.50
2 MMr(s),Tyd,photo (c) 3.00
3 MMr(s),Tyd,consequences 3.00
4 MMr(s),TyD,consequences 3.00
5 MMr(s),TyD,concl. 3.00
TPB 15.00

TROUBLE WITH GIRLS: NIGHT OF THE LIZARD
Epic *Heavy Hitters,* 1993
1 BBI,AW,R:Lester Girls 2.75
2 BBI,AW,V:Lizard Lady 2.25
3 BBI,AW,V:Lizard Lady 2.25
4 BBI,AW,last issue. 2.25

TRUE COMPLETE MYSTERY
See: COMPLETE MYSTERY

TRUE LIFE TALES
Marvel Comics, 1949
1 (8) Ph(c). 125.00
2 Ph(c) 125.00

TRUE SECRETS
Marvel Atlas, 1950–56
Previously LOVE DIARY or OUR LOVE, depending on who you believe.
3 . . . . 150.00
4 . . . . 125.00
5 . . . . 125.00
6 BEv 135.00
7 . . . . 125.00
8 . . . . 125.00
9 . . . . 125.00
10 . . . . 125.00
11 thru 21 . . . . @110.00
22 BEv 125.00
23 . . . . 110.00
24 ViC 125.00
25 thru 28 . . . . @110.00
29 thru 39 . . . . @100.00
40 Sept., 1956 . . . . 100.00

TRUE WESTERN
Dec., 1949
1 Ph(c),Billy the Kid 200.00
2 Ph(c),Alan Ladd,Badmen vs.
   Lawmen 250.00
Becomes:

TRUE ADVENTURES
3 BP,MSy,Boss of Black Devil . . 200.00
Becomes:

MEN'S ADVENTURES
4 AvB,He Called me a Coward . 400.00
5 AvB,Brother Act 250.00
6 AvB,Heat of Battle 225.00
7 AvB,The Walking Death 225.00
8 AvB,RH,Journey Into Death . . 225.00
9 AvB,Bullets,Blades and Death 150.00
10 BEv,The Education of Thomas
   Dillon 150.00
11 Death of A Soldier. 150.00
12 Firing Squad. 150.00
13 RH(c),The Three Stripes. 150.00
14 GC,BEv,Steel Coffin 150.00
15 JMn(c). 150.00
16 AyB 150.00
17 AyB 150.00
18 AyB 150.00
19 JRo 125.00
20 GC,RH(c) 125.00
21 BEv(c),JSt,The Eye of Man . . 250.00
22 BEv,JR,Mark of the Witch. . . . 250.00
23 BEv(c),RC,The Wrong Body . . 275.00
24 RH,JMn,GT,Torture Master . . . 250.00
25 SSh(c),Who Shrinks My Head 450.00
26 Midnight in the Morgue 250.00
27 BP,CBu(c),A:Capt.America,
   Human Torch,Sub-Mariner . 1,500.00
28 BEv,A:Capt.America,Human Torch,
   Sub-Mariner,July, 1954. . . . 1,400.00

TRUTH: RED WHITE BLACK
Nov., 2002
1 (of 7) untold Capt. America 3.50
2 thru 7 KB . . . . @3.50
GN Truth, Red White & Black 4.00
TPB Truth, Red, White & Black . . . 15.00

TRY-OUT WINNER BOOK
March, 1988
1 Spider-Man vs. Doc Octopus . . 15.00

TV STARS
Aug., 1978
1 A:Great Grape Ape 40.00
2 . . . . 35.00
3 ATh,DSt 35.00
4 A:Top Cat,Feb., 1979 . . . . 30.00

2-GUN KID
See: BILLY BUCKSKIN

Two-Gun Kid #11
© *Marvel Entertainment Group*

TWO-GUN KID
Atlas, March, 1948—April, 1977
1 SSh,B:Two-Gun Kid,The
  Sheriff 1,800.00
2 Killers of Outlaw City 900.00
3 RH,SSh,A:Annie Oakley 700.00
4 RH,A:Black Rider 700.00
5 RH 800.00
6 .... 700.00
7 RH,Brand of a Killer 700.00
8 Secret of the Castle of Slaves 700.00
9 JSe,SSh,Trapped in Hidden
  Valley, A:Black Rider 700.00
10 JK(c),The Horrible Hermit
  of Hidden Mesa.......... 700.00
11 JMn(c),GT,A:Black Rider.... 450.00
12 JMn(c),GT,A:Black Rider ... 450.00
13 .... 400.00
14 .... 400.00
15 thru 24................. @400.00
25 AW,JMn.................. 400.00
26 DAy,JMn 300.00
27 DAy,JMn 300.00
28 JMn..................... 300.00
29 .... 300.00
30 AW 300.00
31 thru 44................. @250.00
45 JDa 200.00
46 JDa 200.00
47 JDa 200.00
48 .... 200.00
49 JMn..................... 200.00
50 .... 200.00
51 AW 200.00
52 thru 59................. @200.00
60 DAy,New O:Two-Gun Kid ... 250.00
61 JK,DAy,The Killer and The Kid 175.00
62 JK,DAy,At the Mercy of Moose
  Morgan 175.00
63 DAy,The Guns of Wild Bill
  Taggert................. 100.00
64 DAy,Trapped by Grizzly
  Gordon................. 100.00
65 DAy,Nothing Can Save Fort
  Henry................... 100.00
66 DAy,Ringo's Raiders........ 100.00
67 DAy,The Fangs of the Fox .. 100.00
68 DAy,The Purple Phantom.... 100.00
69 DAy,Badman Called Goliath.. 100.00
70 DAy,Hurricane 100.00
71 DAy,V:Jesse James 100.00

72 DAy,V:Geronimo.......... 100.00
73 Guns of the Galloway Gang.. 100.00
74 Dakota Thompson.......... 100.00
75 JK,Remember the Alamo 125.00
76 JK,Trapped on the Doom 125.00
77 JK,V:The Panther 125.00
78 V:Jesse James 90.00
79 The River Rats 90.00
80 V:The Billy Kid 90.00
81 The Hidden Gun 90.00
82 BEv,Here Comes the Conchos. 90.00
83 Durango,Two-Gun
  Kid Unmasked.............. 90.00
84 Gunslammer 90.00
85 Fury at Falcon Flats,
  A:Rawhide Kids............ 90.00
86 V:Cole Younger............ 90.00
87 OW,The Sidewinder and the
  Stallion................... 90.00
88 thru 101................ @80.00
102 thru 136............... @60.00

TWO-GUN KID: SUNSET RIDERS
1995
1 FaN,R:Two-Gun Kid,64-pg...... 7.00
2 FaN,concl. 64-pg. 7.00

TWO GUN WESTERN
See: CASEY–CRIME PHOTOGRAPHER

2001: A SPACE ODYSSEY
Oct., 1976
1 JK,FRg,Based on Movie 10.00

2001: A SPACE ODYSSEY
Dec., 1976—Sept., 1977
1 JK,Based on Movie 25.00
2 JK,Vira the She-Demon 15.00
3 JK,Marak the Merciless 15.00
4 JK,Wheels of Death......... 15.00
5 JK,Norton of New York 15.00
6 JK,Immortality ...Death 15.00
7 JK,The New Seed 15.00
8 JK,Capture of X-51,I&O:Mr.
  Machine(Machine-Man) 20.00
9 JK,A:Mr Machine 15.00
10 Hotline to Hades,A:Mr Machine 15.00

2010
April, 1985
1 TP,movie adapt 2.25
2 TP,movie adapt,May, 1985 ..... 2.25

2099 A.D.
1995
1 Chromium cover 4.00

2099 APOCALYPSE
1995
1 .... 5.00

2099 GENESIS
1996
1 Chromium Cover 4.00

2099: MANIFEST DESTINY
March, 1998
GN LKa,MMK,F:Miguel
  O'Hara, 48-pg.............. 6.00

2099 SPECIAL: THE WORLD OF DOOM
1995
1 The World of Doom 2.25

2099 Unlimited #2
© *Marvel Entertainment Group*

2099 UNLIMITED
1993–96
1 DT,I:Hulk 2099,A:Spider-Man 2099,
  I:Mutagen................. 4.50
2 DT,F:Hulk 2099,Spider-Man 2099,
  I:R-Gang 4.25
3 GJ(s),JJB,F:Hulk & SpM 2099.. 4.25
4 PR(c),GJ(s),JJB,I:Metalscream
  2099,Lachryma 2099........ 4.25
5 GJ(s),I:Vulx,F:Hazarrd 2099 ... 4.25
6 .... 4.25
Becomes:

2099 A.D. UNLIMITED
7 .... 4.25
8 F:Public Enemy 4.25
9 One Nation Under Doom...... 4.25
10 V:Chameleon 2099.......... 4.25
Spec. #1 The World of Doom ... 2.25

2099: WORLD OF TOMORROW
1996–97
1 .... 2.50
2 .... 2.50
3 MMk,MsM,ATi,F:Spider-Man,
  X-Men 2.50
4 ATi,X-Men 2099 discover secret . 2.50
5 ATi 2.50
6 PFe&ATi(c),Phalanx's final
  assault................... 2.50
7 Spider-Man 2099 searches for his
  brother: Green Goblin 2.50
8 Phalanx invasion aftermath 2.50
9 Humanity vs. Lunatika 2.50

TYPHOID
1995–96
1 ANo,JVF,Painted series........ 4.00
2 ANo,JVF,Hunt for serial killer.... 4.00
3 ANo,JVF,sex,blood & videotapes. 4.00
4 ANo,JVF,conclusion........... 4.00

ULTIMATE ADVENTURES (OF HAWK-OWL & ZIPPY)
Sept., 2002
1 JQ designs,U-Decide.......... 2.25
2 DFg 2.25
3 DFg 2.25
4 DFg,Hawk-Owl & Zippy 2.25
5 DFg 3.00

All comics prices listed are for *Near Mint* condition.

MARVEL

6 DFg	3.00
TPB	13.00

ULTIMATE ADVENTURES
TPB One Tin Soldier (2005) 13.00

ULTIMATE AGE
OF APOCALYPSE
Rep. #1-#4 Age of Apocalypse stories:

Ultimate Amazing X-Men	9.00
Ultimate Astonishing X-Men	9.00
Ultimate Factor X	9.00
Ultimate Gambit and the X-Ternals	9.00
Ultimate Generation Next	9.00
Ultimate Weapon X	9.00
Ultimate X-Calibre	9.00
Ultimate X-Man	9.00

ULTIMATE ANNUALS
TPB Annuals, rep. (2006) 14.00

ULTIMATE DAREDEVIL
& ELEKTRA
Nov., 2002

1 (of 4) DaM, at Columbia U.	5.00
2 SvL,DaM	3.50
3 SvL,DaM	3.50
4 SvL,concl.	3.50
TPB Series rep.	12.00

ULTIMATE ELEKTRA
Aug., 2004

1 (of 5) SvL,Devil's Due,pt.1	2.25
2 SvL,Devil's Due,pt.2	2.25
3 SvL,Devil's Due,pt.3	2.25
4 SvL,Devil's Due,pt.4	3.00
5 SvL,Devil's Due,pt.5	3.00
TPB Devil's Due	12.00

ULTIMATE EXTINCTION
Jan., 2006

1 WEl,BPe	3.00
2 thru 5	@3.00
TPB Ultimate Galactus Extinction	13.00

ULTIMATE
FANTASTIC FOUR
Dec., 2003

1 BMB,AKu,The Fantastic,pt.1	5.00
2 BMB,AKu,The Fantastic,pt.2	5.00
3 BMB,AKu,The Fantastic,pt.3	4.00
4 BMB,AKu,The Fantastic,pt.4	4.00
5 BMB,AKu,The Fantastic,pt.5	4.00
6 BMB,AKu,The Fantastic,pt.6	4.00
7 WEl(s),SI,Doom,pt.1	4.00
8 WEl(s),SI,Doom,pt.2	2.50
9 WEl(s),SI,Doom,pt.3	2.50
10 WEl(s),SI,Doom,pt.4	2.50
11 WEl(s),SI,Doom,pt.5	2.50
12 WEl(s),SI,Doom,pt.6	2.50
13 WEI,AKu,N-Zone,pt.1	2.25
14 WEI,AKu,N-Zone,pt.2	2.25
15 WEI,AKu,N-Zone,pt.3	2.25
16 WEI,AKu,N-Zone,pt.4	2.25
17 WEI,AKu,N-Zone,pt.5	2.25
18 WEI,AKu,N-Zone,pt.6	2.25
19 JaL,Think Tank,pt.1.	2.25
20 JaL,Think Tank,pt.2.	2.50
21 MMr(s),Crossover,pt.1	2.50
22 MMr(s),Crossover,pt.2	2.50
23 MMr(s),Crossover,pt.3	2.50
24 MMr(s),,Tomb of Namor,pt.1	2.50
25 MMr(s),Tomb of Namor.	2.50
26 MMr(s),Tomb of Namor.	2.50
27 MMr(s),President Thor,pt.1	2.50
28 MMr(s),President Thor, pt.2	2.50
29 MMr(s),President Thor,pt.3	3.00
30 MMr(s),Frightful, pt.1	3.00

31 MMr(s),Frightful, pt.2	3.00
32 MMr(s),Frightful, pt.3	3.00
33 PFe,God War, pt.1	3.00
34 PFe,God War, pt.2	3.00
35 PFe,God War, pt.3	3.00
36 PFe,God War, pt.4	3.00
Ann. #1 Enter the Inhumans	4.00
Ann. #2 Nursery Two	4.00
TPB Vol. 1: The Fantastic	13.00
TPB Vol. 2: Doom	13.00
TPB Vol. 3: N-Zone	13.00
TPB Vol. 4: Inhuman	13.00
TPB Vol. 5 Crossover	13.00

ULTIMATE IRON MAN
March, 2005

1 (of 5) AKu, Orson Scott Card(s)	6.00
1a Variant Foil (C).	6.00
2 AKu,O:Ultimate Iron Man.	3.00
3 AKu,F:Rhodey Rhodes	3.00
4 AKu	3.00
5 AKu	3.00
TPB Ultimate Iron Man	15.00

ULTIMATE MARVEL
Flipbook, June, 2005

1 Ultimate X-Men #1 & Ultimate Fantastic Four #1.	4.00
2 Ult.X-Men#2 & Ult. F.Four#2	4.00
3 Ult.X-Men#3 & Ult. F.Four#3	4.00
4 Ult.x-men#4 & Ult. F.four#4	4.00
5 Ult.X-Men#5 & Ult. F.Four#5	4.00
6 thru 11	@4.00
12 thru 18	5.00

Ultimate Marvel Team-Up #11
© Marvel Entertainment Group

ULTIMATE
MARVEL TEAM-UP
Feb., 2001

1 Spider-Man & Wolverine	5.00
2 Spider-Man & The Hulk	4.00
3 Spider-Man & The Hulk	4.00
4 Spider-Man & Iron Man	4.00
5 Spider-Man & Iron Man,MiA	4.00
6 Spider-Man & Punisher,BSz	3.50
7 Spider-Man & Daredevil,BSz	3.50
8 Spider-Man,Daredevil,Punisher	3.50
9 Spider-Man & Fantastic Four.	3.50
10 Spider-Man & Man-Thing	3.50
11 BMB(s),Spider-Man & X-Men	3.50
12 Spider-Man & Dr. Strange.	3.50
13 Spider-Man & Dr. Strange.	3.50
14 Spider-Man & Black Widow	3.50

15 Spider-Man & Shang-Chi	3.50
16 Spider-Man & Shang-Chi	3.50
TPB Vol. 1	15.00
TPB Vol. 2	12.00
TPB Vol. 3	13.00

ULTIMATE MARVEL
MAGAZINE
May, 2001

5 thru 11, 80-page, rep.	@4.00

ULTIMATE NIGHTMARE
Aug., 2004

1 (of 5) Tunguska	2.25
2 WEl(s)	2.25
3 WEl(s)	2.25
4 WEl(s)	3.00
5 WEl(s)	3.00
TPB Ultimate Nightmare	12.00

ULTIMATE POWER
Oct., 2006

1 BMB(s),V:Squadron Supreme	3.00
2 BMB(s),V:Squadron Supreme	3.00

ULTIMATES, THE
Jan., 2002

1 MMr,BHi,Nick Fury, heroes	6.00
2 MMr,BHi,Search for Cap.Am.	10.00
3 MMr,BHi,Cap.America lives	8.00
4 MMr,BHi,no one to fight.	8.00
5 MMr,BHi,	8.00
6 MMr,BHi,celebrities	5.00
7 MMr,BHi,new additions	5.00
8 MMr,Quicksilver&ScarletWitch.	3.00
9 MMr,BHi.	3.00
10 MMr,BHi,F:Hawkeye.	3.00
11 BHi,PNe	3.00
12 BHi,PNe	3.00
13 BHi,Chitauri,concl.48-pg.	3.50
Spec. Must Have rep. #1–#3	4.00
TPB Vol.1, 160-pg.	13.00
TPB Vol.2: Homeland Security	18.00

Vol. 2

1 BHi.	3.00

ULTIMATE SECRET
Dec., 2004

1 (of 4) WEl(s)	3.00
2 Wel(s), Mahr Vehl	3.00
3 WEl(s),V:Kree	3.00
4 WEl(s), conc.	3.00

ULTIMATE SIX
Sept., 2003

1 BMB,JQ,F:Villains	3.00
2 BMB,Sinister Six	3.00
3 BMB,Ultimate Spidey.	3.00
4 BMB,F:The Ultimates.	3.00
5 BMB,Spidey kidnapped	3.00
6 BMB,V:Sinister Six.	3.00
7 BMB,Green Goblin.	3.00

ULTIMATE SPIDER-MAN
Sept., 2000

1 BMB,JQ,MBa,ATi,A:Mary Jane 48-pg.red card(c).	125.00
1A variant white (c).	200.00
1B Dynamic Forces (c).	65.00
2A BMB,MBa,ATi,Dr.Otto Octopus, car.	50.00
2B Dynamic Forces JaL(c), Spider-Man swinging.	35.00
3 BMB,ATi,MBa,A:Mary Jane	40.00
4 BMB,ATi,MBa,D:Uncle Ben.	40.00
5 BMB,ATi,MBa,hand of fate, scarce	100.00
6 BMB,ATi,MBa,V:Green Goblin.	50.00

7 BMB,ATi,MBa,V:Green Goblin . . 35.00	
8 BMB,ATi,MBa,V:Shocker 20.00	
9 BMB,ATi,MBa,V:Kingpin 15.00	
10 BMB,ATi,MBa,V:Kingpin 10.00	
11 BMB,ATi,MBa,V:Kingpin 10.00	
12 BMB,ATi,MBa,V:Kingpin 10.00	
13 BMB,ATi,MBa,Mary Jane 15.00	
14 BMB,MBa,ATi,Doctor Octopus . 12.00	
15 BMB,MBa,ATi,Doctor Octopus . . 9.00	
16 BMB,MBa,ATi,F:Ock,Kraven. . . . 9.00	
17 BMB,MBa,ATi,F:Justin Hammer . 8.00	
18 BMB,MBa,ATi,Doc Oc kicks butt 8.00	
19 BMB,MBa,ATi,Justin Hammer . . 8.00	
20 BMB,MBa,ATi,Doc Oc,Kraven . . 8.00	
21 BMB,MBa,ATi,vs. the press 8.00	
22 BMB,MBa,ATi,R:Green Goblin	
+ Chapter 1, 54-pg. 8.00	
23 BMB,MBa,ATi,G.Goblin,G.Stacy . 8.00	
24 BMB,MBa,ATi,Green Goblin deal 4.00	
25 BMB,MBa,ATi 4.00	
26 BMB,MBa,ATi,S.H.I.E.L.D. 3.00	
27 BMB,MBa,ATi 3.00	
28 BMB,MBa,ATi 3.00	
29 BMB,MBa,ATi 3.00	
30 BMB,MBa,ATi 3.00	
31 BMB,MBa,ATi 3.00	
32 BMB,MBa,ATi 3.00	
33 BMB,MBa,ATi,V:Venom 10.00	
34 BMB,MBa,ATi,V:Venom 8.00	
35 BMB,MBa,ATi,V:Venom 8.00	
36 BMB,MBa,ATi,V:Venom 5.00	
37 BMB,MBa,ATi,V:Venom 5.00	
38 BMB,MBa,ATi,V:Venom,concl. . . 5.00	
39 BMB,MBa,ATi,F:Nick Fury 2.50	
40 BMB,MBa,Irresponsible,pt.1 . . . 2.50	
41 BMB,MBa,Irresponsible,pt.2 . . . 2.50	
42 BMB,MBa,Irresponsible,pt.3 . . . 2.50	
43 BMB,MBa,Irresponsible,pt.4 . . . 2.50	
44 BMB,MBa,Irresponsible,pt.5 . . . 2.50	
45 BMB,MBa,Irresponsible,pt.6 . . . 2.50	
46 BMB,MBa,F:S.H.I.E.L.D.,40-pg . 3.00	
47 BMB,MBa,Unfair,pt.1 . . . . 2.50	
48 BMB,MBa,Unfair,pt.2 . . . . 2.25	
49 BMB,MBa,Unfair,pt.3 . . . . 2.25	
50 BMB,MBa,Claws,pt.1 . . . . 3.00	
51 BMB,MBa,Claws,pt.2 . . . . 2.50	
52 BMB,MBa,Claws,pt.3 . . . . 2.50	
53 BMB,MBa,Claws,concl. 2.25	
54 BMB,MBa,Goes Hollywood,pt.1 . 3.00	
54a Arachnoman variant 12.00	
55 BMB,MBa,Goes Hollywood,pt.2 . 2.25	
56 BMB,MBa,Goes Hollywood,pt.3 . 2.25	
57 BMB,MBa,Goes Hollywood,pt.4 . 2.25	
58 BMB,MBa,Goes Hollywood,pt.5 . 2.25	
59 BMB,MBa,Goes Hollywood,pt.6 . 2.25	

60 BMB,MBa,Carnage,pt.1 . . . . . . 6.00	
61 BMB,MBa,Carnage,pt.2 . . . . . . 3.50	
62 BMB,MBa,Carnage,pt.3 . . . . . . 5.00	
63 BMB,MBa,Carnage,pt.4 . . . . . . 2.25	
64 BMB,MBa,Carnage,pt.5 . . . . . . 2.25	
65 BMB,MBa,Carnage,pt.6 . . . . . . 2.25	
66 BMB,MBa,Switcheroo,pt.1 . . . . 2.25	
67 BMB,MBa,Switcheroo,pt.2 . . . . 2.25	
68 BMB,MBa,F:Johnny Storm 2.25	
69 BMB,MBa,F:Johnny Storm 2.25	
70 BMB,MBa,Sorcerer Supreme . . 2.25	
71 BMB,MBa,Sorcerer Supreme . . 2.25	
72 BMB,MBa,Hobgoblin,pt.1 . . . . 2.25	
73 BMB,MBa,Hobgoblin,pt.2 . . . . 2.25	
74 BMB,MBa,Hobgoblin,pt.3 . . . . 2.25	
75 BMB,MBa,Hobgoblin,pt.4 . . . . 2.25	
76 BMB,MBa,Hobgoblin,pt.5 . . . . 2.25	
77 BMB,MBa,Hobgoblin,pt.6 . . . . 2.25	
78 BMB,MBa,I:Mark Raxton 2.50	
79 BMB,MBa,Warriors,pt.1 . . . . . . 3.00	
80 BMB,MBa,Warriors,pt.2 . . . . . . 2.50	
81 BMB,MBa,Warriors,pt.3 . . . . . . 2.50	
82 MBa,Warriors,pt.4, Gang War. . 2.50	
83 MBa,Warriors,pt.5, Gang War. . 2.50	
84 BMB,MBa,Warriors,pt.6 . . . . . . 2.50	
85 BMB,MBa,Warriors,pt.7 . . . . . . 2.50	
86 BMB,MBa,Silver Sable,pt.1 . . . 2.50	
87 BMB,MBa,Silver Sable,pt.2 . . . 2.50	
88 BMB,MBa,Silver Sable,pt.3 . . . 2.50	
89 BMB,MBa,Silver Sable,pt.4 . . . 2.50	
90 BMB,MBa,Silver Sable,pt.5 . . . 2.50	
91 BMB,MBa,Deadpool,pt.1 . . . . . 2.50	
92 BMB,MBa,Deadpool,pt.2 . . . . . 2.50	
93 BMB,MBa,Deadpool,pt.3 . . . . . 3.00	
94 BMB,MBa,Deadpool,pt.4 . . . . . 3.00	
95 BMB,MBa,Morbius 3.00	
96 BMB,MBa,Morbius V:Blade . . . 3.00	
97 BMB,MBa,Clone Saga,pt.1. . . . 3.00	
98 BMB,MBa,Clone Saga,pt.2 . . . . 3.00	
99 BMB,MBa,Clone Saga,pt.3 . . . . 4.00	
100 MBa,Clone Saga,pt.4, 64-pg. . 4.00	
100a variant (c) 4.00	
101 BMB,MBa,Clone Saga,pt.5. . . 3.00	
102 BMB,MBa,Clone Saga,pt.6. . . 3.00	
Ann #1 More than you	
Bargained for (2005) 4.00	
Ann.#2 (2006) 3.00	
Spec.1 Collected, rep.#1–#3 . . . . 4.00	
Spec.#1-#2-#3, 96-pg. 4.00	
Spec.#1 all-star artists, 54-pg. . . . 3.50	
TPB Vol. 1: Power & Responsibility 15.00	
TPB Vol. 2: Learning Curve 13.00	
TPB Vol. 3: Double Trouble 18.00	
TPB Vol. 4: Legacy 15.00	
TPB Vol. 5: Public Scutiny 12.00	
TPB Vol. 6: Venom 16.00	
TPB Vol. 7: Irresponsible 13.00	
TPB Vol. 8: Cats and Kings 18.00	
TPB Vol. 9:Ultimate Six 18.00	
TPB Vol.10:Hollywood 13.00	
TPB Vol. 11: Carnage 13.00	
TPB Vol. 12: Superstars 13.00	
TPB Vol. 13: Hobgoblin 16.00	
TPB Vol. 14 Warriors 16.00	
TPB Vol. 15 Silver Sable 16.00	
TPB Vol. 16 Deadpool 16.00	
Spec. Must Have, rep. 4.00	

ULTIMATE TALES
Flipbook, June, 2005

1 Ultimate Spider-Man #0
   & Ultimate Spider-Man #1 . . . . . 4.00
2 Ultimate Spider-Man #2 & #3 . . . 4.00
3 Ultimate Spider-Man #4 & #5 . . . 4.00
4 Ultimate Spider-Man #6 & #7 . . . 4.00
5 Ultimate Spider-Man #7 & #8 . . . 4.00
6 thru 13 . . . . @4.00
14 thru 18 . . . . @5.00

Ultimate Spider-Man #18
© *Marvel Entertainment Group*

ULTIMATES 2
Dec., 2004

1 MMr,BHi 3.00
2 MMr,BHi,Gods & Monsters 3.00
3 MMr,BHi,Trial of Incredible Hulk . 3.00
4 MMr,BHi,Nick Fury vs. Thor. 3.00
5 MMr,BHi,v:Thor 3.00
6 MMr,BHi,F:Hank Pym 3.00
7 MMr,BHi,Wolf in the Fold. 3.00
8 MMr,BHi,Grand Theft America . . . 3.00
9 MMr,BHi,Grand Theft America . . . 3.00
10 MMr,BHi,Grand Theft America . . 3.00
11 MMr,BHi,Grand Theft America . . 3.00
12 MMr,BHi,Grand Theft America . . 4.00
Ann.#1 The Reserves (2005). 4.00
Ann.#2 F:Arnim Zola (2006) 4.00
Spec. Must Have, rep. #1–#3 . . . . . 5.00
TPB Vol. 1: Gods and Monsters . . 16.00

ULTIMATE VISION
Nov., 2006

1-shot Visions 3.00

ULTIMATE WAR
Marvel Dec. 2002

1 (of 4) CBa,X-Men vs. Ultimates. . 5.00
2 CBa 4.00
3 CBa 4.00
4 CBa,concl. 4.00

ULTIMATE WOLVERINE VS. HULK
Dec., 2005

1 . . . . 3.00
2 . . . . 3.00
3 . . . . 3.00

ULTIMATE X-MEN
Dec., 2000

1 AKu,ATi,MMr,48-page, card (c) . 25.00
1A Dynamic Forces (c) 30.00
1B Preview 30.00
2 AKu,ATi,MMr,F:Wolverine 22.00
3 AKu,ATi,MMr,V:Magneto 15.00
4 AKu,ATi,MMr,V:Magneto 15.00
5 AKu,ATi,MMr,One traitor? 15.00
6 AKu,ATi,MMr,V:Magneto 15.00
7 AKu,ATi,MMr,Weapon X,pt.1 . . . 18.00
8 AKu,ATi,MMr,Weapon X,pt.2 . . . . 7.00
9 MMr,TR,SHa,Weapon X,pt.3 . . . . 7.00
10 MMr,TR,SHa,Weapon X,pt.4 . . . 7.00
11 MMr,AKu,ATi,Weapon X,pt.5 . . . 4.00
12 MMr,AKu,Weapon X,pt.6 . . . . . 4.00
13 AKu(c),F:Gambit 5.00
14 AKu(c),F:Gambit,pt.2 . . . . 4.00
15 AKu,MMr,Xavier's teachings . . . 4.00
16 AKu,MMr,to Scotland 4.00
17 AKu,MMr,Proteus Saga,pt.2 . . . 4.00
18 AKu,MMr,World Tour 4.00
19 AKu,MMr,World Tour,concl. 4.00
20 AKu,MMr,World Tour,epilogue . . 3.75
21 MMr,DaM,Hellfire & Brimstone . 3.75
22 MMr,DaM,Hellfire & Brimstone . . 3.75
23 MMr,DaM,Hellfire & Brimstone . . 3.75
24 MMr,DaM,Hellfire&Brimstone . . . 3.75
25 MMr,DaM,AKu(c), Hellfire &
   Brimstone, 48-pg. 5.00
26 MMr,AKu,Professor-X 5.00
27 MMr,AKu,V:Brotherhood 5.00
28 MMr,AKu,V:Brotherhood 5.00
29 MMr,AKu,Missing X-Man 5.00
30 MMr,AKu,Storm's gang 5.00
31 MMr,AKu,V:Magneto 5.00
32 MMr,AKu,Ultimate fate 4.50
33 MMr,AKu,Return of the King. . . . 3.50
34 BMB,Blockbuster,pt.1 . . . . 6.00
35 BMB,Blockbuster,pt.2 . . . . 3.25
36 BMB,Blockbuster,pt.3 . . . . 3.25
37 BMB,Blockbuster,pt.4 . . . . 3.25

MARVEL

38 BMB,Blockbuster,pt.5	3.25
39 BMB,Blockbuster,pt.6	2.75
40 BMB,New Mutants,pt.1	3.00
41 BMB,New Mutants,pt.2	2.75
42 BMB,New Mutants,pt.3	3.50
43 BMB,New Mutants,pt.4	2.25
44 BMB,New Mutants,pt.5	3.00
45 BMB,New Mutants,pt.6	2.25
46 BPe,The Tempest,pt.1	2.25
47 BPe,The Tempest,pt.2	2.25
48 BPe,The Tempest,pt.3	2.25
49 BPe,The Tempest,pt.4	2.25
50 NKu,Cry Wolf,pt.1	2.25
51 NKu,Cry Wolf,pt.2	2.25
52 NKu,Cry Wolf,pt.3	2.25
53 NKu,Cry Wolf,pt.4	2.25
54 SI,Longshot, pt.1	2.25
55 SI,Longshot, pt.2	2.25
56 SI,Longshot, pt.3	2.25
57 SI,The Most Dangerous Game	2.25
58 SI, A Hard Lesson	2.25
59 SI,F:Wolverine,pt.1	2.25
60 SI,F:Wolverine & Storm,pt.2	2.50
61 SI,Magnetic North,pt.1	15.00
62 SI,Magnetic North,pt.2	2.50
63 SI,Magnetic North,pt.3	2.50
64 SI,Magnetic North,pt.4	2.50
65 SI,Magnetic North,pt.5	2.50
66 TR,Date Night,pt.1	2.50
67 TR,Date Night,pt.2	2.50
68 TR,Date Night,pt.3	2.50
69 Phoenix, pt.1	3.00
70 Phoenix, pt.2	3.00
71 Phoenix, pt.3	3.00
72 TR,Magical,pt.1	3.00
73 TR,Magical,pt.2	3.00
74 TR,Magical,pt.3	3.00
Ann.#1 Ultimate Sacrifice (2005)	4.00
Ann.#2 F:Dazzler (2006)	4.00
Spec. #1-#2-#3, 96-pg.	4.00
TPB rep.#1–#6, 160-pg.	15.00
TPB Ultimate X-Men, Weapon X	15.00
TPB Ultimate Collection Book 1	25.00
TPB Vol.1: The Tomorrow People	16.00
TPB Vol.2: Return to Weapon X	15.00
TPB Vol.3, World Tour	18.00
TPB Vol.4, Hellfire & Brimstone	13.00
TPB Vol.5: Ultimate War	11.00
TPB Vol.6: Return of the King	17.00
TPB Vol.7: Blockbuster	13.00
TPB Vol.8: New Mutants	13.00
TPB Vol.9: The Tempest	11.00
TPB Vol. 10: Cry Wolf	9.00
TPB Vol. 11: The Most Dangerous Game	10.00
TPB Vol. 12 Hard Lessons	13.00
TPB Vol. 13 Magnetic North	13.00
TPB Vol. 14 Phoenix?	15.00
Spec. rep. Must Have #1–#3	4.00

ULTIMATE X-MEN/ FANTASTIC FOUR
Dec., 2005

1 x-over	3.00
1 Ultimate F.Four/X-Men x-over	3.00
TPB inc. Handbook	13.00

ULTRAFORCE/AVENGERS

1 V:Loki,A:Malibu's Ultraforce	4.00

ULTRA GIRL
[Mini-series] 1996

1 BKs,I&O:Ultra Girl	2.25
2 and 3 BKs	@2.25

ULTRA X-MEN COLLECTION

1 Metallic(c), art from cards	3.00
2 thru 5 art from cards	@3.00

ULTRA X-MEN III

Preview	3.00

ULTRON
June, 1999

1-shot Ultron Unleashed, rep.	3.50

Uncanny Origins #2
© Marvel Entertainment Group

UNCANNY ORIGINS
Sept., 1996

1 F:Cyclops	2.25
2 F:Quicksilver	2.25
3 DHv,BAn,F:Archangel	2.25
4 F:Firelord	2.25
5 MHi,F:Hulk	2.25
6 F:Beast	2.25
7 F:Venom	2.25
8 F:Nightcrawler	2.25
9 F:Storm	2.25
10 F:Black Cat	2.25
11 F:Luke Cage	2.25
12 F:Black Knight	2.25
13 LWn,MCa,F:Doctor Strange	2.25
14 LWn,MCW,F:Iron Fist	2.25

UNCANNY TALES
Marvel Atlas, June, 1952

1 RH,While the City Sleeps	1,300.00
2 JMn,BEv	650.00
3 Escape to What	550.00
4 JMn,Nobody's Fool	550.00
5 Fear	550.00
6 He Lurks in the Shadows	600.00
7 BEv,Kill,Clown,Kill	600.00
8 JMn,Bring Back My Face	500.00
9 BEv,RC,The Executioner	500.00
10 JMn,RH(c),JR,The Man Who Came Back To Life	500.00
11 GC,The Man Who Changed	350.00
12 BP,BEv,Bertha Gets Buried	350.00
13 RH,Scared Out of His Skin	350.00
14 RH,TLw,Victims of Vonntor	350.00
15 RA,JSt,The Man Who Saw Death	350.00
16 JMn,GC,Zombie at Large	350.00
17 GC,TLw,I Live With Corpses	350.00
18 JF,BP,Clock Face(c)	350.00
19 DBr,RKr,TLw,The Man Who Died Again	350.00
20 DBr,Ted's Head	350.00
21	300.00
22 DAy	300.00
23 TLw	300.00

24	300.00
25 MSy	300.00
26 Spider-Man prototype story	450.00
27 RA,TLw	300.00
28 TLw	325.00
29 JMn	250.00
30	250.00
31	250.00
32 BEv	250.00
33	250.00
34 BP	250.00
35 TLw,JMn	250.00
36 BP,BEv	250.00
37 MD	250.00
38 BP	250.00
39 BEv	250.00
40	250.00
41	250.00
42 MD	250.00
43	225.00
44	225.00
45 MD	225.00
46 GM	225.00
47 TSe	225.00
48 BEv	225.00
49 JO	225.00
50 JO	225.00
51 GM	250.00
52 GC	225.00
53 JO,AT	225.00
54	225.00
55	225.00
56 Sept., 1957	250.00

UNCANNY TALES FROM THE GRAVE
Dec., 1973—Oct., 1975

1 RC,Room of no Return	35.00
2 DAy,Out of the Swamp	25.00
3 No Way Out	25.00
4 JR,SD,Vampire	25.00
5 GK,GT,Don't Go in the Cellar	25.00
6 JR,SD,The Last Kkrul	25.00
7 RH,SD,Never Dance With a Vampire	25.00
8 SD,Escape Into Hell	25.00
9 JA,The Nightmare Men	25.00
10 SD,DH,Beware the Power of Khan	25.00
11 SD,JF,RH,Dead Don't Sleep	25.00
12 SD,Final Issue	25.00

UNCANNY X-MEN
See: X-MEN

UNDERWORLD
Feb., 2006

1 F:Jackie Dio	3.00
2 thru 5	@3.00

UNION JACK
Oct., 1998

1 (of 3) BRa,F:Joey Chapman	3.00
2 BRa,V:Baroness	3.00
3 BRa,conclusion	3.00
TPB 96-pg. (2002)	11.50

UNION JACK
Sept., 2006

1	3.00
2 thru 3	@3.00

UNIVERSE X
July, 2000

0 AxR,DBw,48-pg.	4.00
1 (of 12) AxR,DBw,Capt.MarVell	3.50
2 AxR,DBw,	3.50
3 AxR,DBw,	3.50
4 AxR,DBw,Cap.Am vs. Hydra	3.50

5 AxR,DBw,Mar-Vell vs.Death	3.50
6 AxR,DBw,Moonknight	3.50
7 AxR,DBw,Supreme Intelligence	3.50
8 AxR,DBw,Monster Generation	3.50
9 AxR,DBw,Supreme Intelligence	3.50
10 AxR,DBw,V:Mephisto	3.50
11 AxR,DBw,A:Belasco	3.50
12 AxR,DBw,V:Absorbing Man	3.50
Spec."4",F:Fantastic Four	4.00
Spec. Spidey,AxR,JG,JR,48-page	4.00
Spec. Beasts,AxR,48-page	4.00
Spec. Omnibus,AxR.	4.00
Spec. Iron Men, 48-page	4.00
Spec. Universe X:X 48-page	4.00
TPB Vol.1 384-pg.	25.00
TPB Vol.2 336-pg.	30.00

UNKNOWN WORLDS OF SCIENCE FICTION
Jan., 1975
(Black & White Magazine)

1 AW,RKr,AT,FF,GC	30.00
2 FB,GP	25.00
3 GM,AN,GP,GC	25.00
4	25.00
5 GM,NC,GC	25.00
6 FB,AN,GC,Nov., 1975	25.00
Spec.#1 AN,NR,JB.	30.00

UNTAMED
Epic *Heavy Hitters*, 1993

1 I:Griffen Palmer	2.75
2 V:Kosansui.	2.25
3 V:Kosansui.	2.25

UNTOLD LEGEND OF CAPTAIN MARVEL, THE
1997

1 (of 3) Early days of Captain Marvel	2.50
2 Early days of Captain Marvel	2.50
3 V:Kree	2.50

UNTOLD TALES OF SPIDER-MAN
Sept., 1995 – Sept., 1997

1 F:Young Spider-Man	3.00
2 V:Batwing.	2.25
3 V:Sandman	2.25
4 V:J.Jonah Jameson	2.25

Untold Legend of Captain Marvel #1
© Marvel Entertainment Group

5 V:Vulture	2.25
6 A:Human Torch	2.25
7	2.25
8	2.25
9 A:Batwing,Lizard	2.25
10 KBk,PO,I:Commanda	2.25
11 KBk,PO,	2.25
12 KBk,PO,	2.25
13 KBk,PO,	2.25
14 KBk,PO,	2.25
15 KBk,PO,AV,Gordon's plan to control the Bugle	2.25
16 Re-I:Mary Jane Watson	2.25
17 KBk,PO,AV,V:Hawkeye.	2.25
18 KBk,PO,AV,A:Green Goblin, Headsman.	2.25
19 KBk,PO,AW,F:Doctor Octopus	2.25
20 KBk,PO,AW,V:Vulture	2.25
21 KBk,PO,AW,V:Menace,A:Original X-Men	2.25
22 KBk,PO,AW,V:Scarecrow,	2.25
23 KBk,PO,AW,V:Crime Master, A:Green Goblin	2.25
24 KBk,PO,BMc, Fate of Batwing	2.25
25 LBl,PO,BMc, V:Green Goblin, final issue	2.25
Minus 1 Spec., RSt,JR, flashback, Peter's parents	2.25
Ann.'96 1 KBk,MiA,JSt,A date with Invisible Girl?	2.25
Ann.'97 KBk,TL,A:everyone, 48-pg.	3.00
TPB rep. #1–#8	17.00
one-shot GN KBk,SL,Encounter, A:Dr. Strange 48-pg.	6.00
TPB Spider-Man Visionaries: Kurt Busiek rep. #1–#8 (2006)	20.00

UNTOLD TALES OF THE NEW UNIVERSE
March, 2006

D.P. 7 #1	3.00
Justice #1.	3.00
Nightmask #1.	3.00
Starbrand #1	3.00
PSI-Force #1	3.00
TPB	16.00

U.S.A. COMICS
Marvel Timely, Aug., 1941

1 S&K(c),BW,AAv,SSh,Bondage(c), The Defender(c)	24,000.00
2 S&K(c),BW,SSh, Capt. Terror(c)	6,500.00
3 S&K(c),SSh,Capt.Terror(c)	4,800.00
4 SSh,Major Liberty	4,000.00
5 Hitler(c),O:AmericanAvenger	4,200.00
6 ASh(c),Capt.America(c)	5,000.00
7 BW,O:Marvel Boy	5,000.00
8 ASh(c),Capt.America (c)	3,500.00
9 ASh(c),Bondage(c), Captain America	3,500.00
10 ASh(c),Bondage(c), Captain America	3,500.00
11 SSh(c),Bondage(c), Captain America	2,500.00
12 ASh(c),Capt.America	2,500.00
13 ASh(c),Capt.America	2,500.00
14 AyB(c),Capt.America	2,000.00
15 Capt.America	2,000.00
16 ASh(c),Bondage(c), Capt.America	2,000.00
17 Bondage(c),Capt.America	2,000.00

U.S. 1
May, 1983–Oct., 1984

1 AM(c),HT,Trucking Down the Highway	3.00
2 HT,Midnight	3.00
3 FS,ME,Rhyme of the Ancient Highwayman	3.00

U.S. 1 #2
© Marvel Entertainment Group

4 FS,ME	3.00
5 FS,ME,Facing The Maze	3.00
6 FS,ME	3.00
7 FS,ME	3.00
8 FS,ME	3.00
9 FS,ME,Iron Mike-King of the Bike	3.00
10 thru 12 FS,ME	@3.00

U.S. AGENT
June–Dec., 1993

1 V:Scourge,O:U.S.Agent	2.25
2 V:Scourge	2.25
3 V:Scourge	2.25
4 last issue	2.25

U.S. AGENT
May, 2001

1 (of 3) JOy,KK,Maximum Security.	3.00
2 JOy,KK,	3.00
3 JOy,KK,A:Capt.America.	3.00

U.S. WAR MACHINE
Marvel Max, Sept., 2001

1 (of 12) Weekly series,24-page	2.25
2 thru 12	@2.25
TPB rep., 288-page	15.00

U.S. WAR MACHINE 2.0
June, 2003

1 (of 3) V:Iron Man	3.00
2	3.00
3 concl.	3.00

VALKYRIE
1996

1-shot JMD	2.50

VAMPIRE TALES
Aug., 1973
(black & white magazine)

1 BEv,B:Morbius the Living Vampire	90.00
2 JSo,I:Satana	60.00
3 A:Satana	50.00
4 GK	50.00
5 GK,O:Morbius The Living Vampire	60.00
6 AA,I:Lilith	50.00
7 HC,PG	50.00

All comics prices listed are for *Near Mint* condition.   **CVA Page 343**

8 AA,A:Blade The Vampire
   Slayer 65.00
9 RH,AA 50.00
10 . . . . 50.00
11 June, 1975 . . . . 50.00
Ann.#1 . . . . 50.00

Vault of Evil #14
© Marvel Entertainment Group

VAULT OF EVIL
Feb., 1973—Nov., 1975
1 GK,B:1950's reps,Come
  Midnight,Come Monster 35.00
2 The Hour of the Witch 25.00
3 The Woman Who Wasn't 25.00
4 Face that Follows 25.00
5 Ghost 25.00
6 GT,The Thing at the Window . . . 25.00
7 Monsters 25.00
8 The Vampire is my Brother 25.00
9 Giant Killer 25.00
10 MD,The Lurkers in the Caves. . 25.00
11 JK,BEv,Two Feasts For
  a Vampire 25.00
12 Midnight in the
  Haunted Mansion 25.00
13 Hot as the Devil 25.00
14 SD,Midnight in the Haunted
  Manor 25.00
15 SD,Don't Shake Hands with
  the Devil 25.00
16 A Grave Honeymoon. 25.00
17 Grave Undertaking 25.00
18 The Deadly Edge 25.00
19 Vengeance of Ahman Ra 25.00
20 SD. 25.00
21 Victim of Valotorr. 25.00
22 SD. 25.00
23 Black Magician Lives Again . . . 25.00

VENOM
April, 2003
1 SK(c),Shiver,pt.1 . . . . 3.00
2 Shiver,pt.2 . . . . 2.50
3 SK(c),Shiver,pt.3 . . . . 2.50
4 SK(c),Shiver,pt.4 . . . . 2.50
5 SK(c),Shiver,pt.5 . . . . 2.50
6 . . . . 2.50
7 SK(c) 2.50
8 SK(c) Run,pt.3,F:Wolverine 3.00
9 SK(c) Run,pt.4 . . . . 3.00
10 Run,pt.5 . . . . 3.00
11 Patterns,pt.1 . . . . 3.00
12 Patterns,pt.2 . . . . 3.00
13 Patterns,pt.3 . . . . 3.00

14 Twist,pt.1. . . . . 3.00
15 Twist,pt.2. . . . . 3.00
16 Twist,pt.3. . . . . 3.00
17 Twist,pt.4. . . . . 3.00
18 Twist,pt.5. . . . . 3.00
TPB Vol. 1: Shiver 14.00
TPB Vol. 2: Run. 20.00
TPB Vol. 3: Twist 14.00

VENOM: ALONG CAME A SPIDER
1996
1 LHA,GLz,V:New Spider-Man 3.00
2 LHa,JPi,V:New Spider-Man 3.00
3 . . . . 3.00
4 conclusion, 48-pg. 3.00

VENOM: CARNAGE UNLEASHED
1995
1 Venom vs. Carnage. 3.00
2 Venom vs. Carnage. 3.00
3 No Spider-Help 3.00
4 JRu,Wld,LHa,cardstock(c). 3.00

VENOM: THE ENEMY WITHIN
1994
1 BMc,Glow-in-the-dark(C),
  A:Demogoblin,Morbius 3.25
2 BMc,A:Demogoblin,Morbius 3.25
3 BMc,V:Demogoblin,A:Morbius . . . 3.25

VENOM: FINALE
1997–98
1 (of 3) LHa, ... 3.00
2 LJa, ... 3.00
3 LJa. 3.00

VENOM: FUNERAL PYRE
1993
1 TL,JRu,A:Punisher. 3.50
2 TL,JRu,AM,V:Gangs 3.50
3 TL,JRu,Last issue 3.50

VENOM: THE HUNGER
1996
1 thru 4 LKa,TeH,V:Dr. Paine . . . @2.25

VENOM: THE HUNTED
1996
1 LHa,3 part mini-series 3.00

VENOM: LETHAL PROTECTOR
1993
1 MBa,A:Spider-Man.holo-grafx(c) . 7.00
1a Gold Ed.. . . . . 25.00
2 MBa,A:Spider-Man. 3.50
3 MBa,Families of Venom's
  victims 3.50
4 RLm,A:Spider-Man,V:Life
  Foundation. 3.50
5 RLm,V:Five Symbiotes,A:SpM. . . 3.50
6 RLm,V:Spider-Man. 3.50
Super Size Spec.#1 Planet of
  the Symbiotes,pt.3. . . . . 4.00
Venom:Deathtrap:The Vault,RLm,
  A:Avengers,Freedom Force . . . 7.00
TPB Lethal Protector RLm,DvM . . 16.00

VENOM: LICENSE TO KILL
1997
1 (of 3) LHa,KHt, sequel to Venom
  on trial 2.25

2 LHa,V:Dr. Yes 2.25
3 LHa,V:Dr. Yes 2.25

VENOM: THE MACE
1994
1 Embossed(c),CP(s),LSh,I:Mace . 3.25
2 CP(s),LSh,V:Mace. 3.25
3 CP(s),LSh,V:Mace,final issue . . . 3.25

VENOM: THE MADNESS
1993–94
1 B:ANi(s),KJo,V:Juggernaut 3.50
2 KJo,V:Juggernaut 3.25
3 E:ANi(s),KJo,V:Juggernaut 3.25

VENOM: NIGHTS OF VENGEANCE
1994
1 RLm,I:Stalkers,A:Vengeance. . . . 3.25
2 RLm,A:Vengeance,V:Stalkers . . . 3.25
3 RLm,V:Stalkers 3.25
4 RLm,final issue 3.25

VENOM: ON TRIAL
Jan.–May, 1997
1 LHa,Tries to break out 2.25
2 LHa,Defended by Matt Murdock
  (Daredevil),A:Spider-Man 2.25
3 LHa,A:Spider-Man, Carnage,
  Daredevil. 2.25

VENOM: SEED OF DARKNESS
1997
1 LKa,JFy,Flashback, early Eddie
  Brock 2.25

VENOM: SEPARATION ANXIETY
1994–95
1 Embossed(c) 3.00
2 V:Symbiotes. 3.00
3 . . . . 3.00
4 . . . . 3.00
TPB Rep.#1-#4 HMe,RoR,SDR. . . 10.00

VENOM: SIGN OF THE BOSS
1997
1 (of 2) IV,TDr,V:Ghost Rider 2.25
2 (of 2) IV,TDr,conclusion 2.25

VENOM: SINNER TAKES ALL
1995
1 LHa,GLz,I:New Sin-Eater 3.00
2 V:Sineater 3.00
3 Wrong Man 3.00
4 LHa,GLz,V:Sin-Eater 3.00
5 LHa, finale 3.00

VENOM: TOOTH AND CLAW
1996–97
1 (of 3) LHa,JPi,AM, Dirtnap usurps
  Venom's body 2.25
2 LHa,JPi,AM,V:Wolverine 2.25
3 LHa,JPi,AM,V:Wolverine,
  Chimera. 2.25

VENOM VS. CARNAGE
June, 2004
1 (of 4) 3.00
2 F:Black Cat 3.00

MARVEL

3 . . . . 3.00
4 F:Toxin 3.00
TPB Venom vs. Carnage 10.00

Venus #10
© *Marvel Entertainment Group*

VENUS
Marvel Atlas, Aug., 1948
1 B:Venus,Hedy Devine,HK,Hey
　Look 2,000.00
2 Venus(c) 1,300.00
3 Carnival(c) 1,400.00
4 Cupid(c).HK,Hey Look 1,400.00
5 Serenade(c) 1,400.00
6 SSh(c),Wrath of a Goddess,
　A:Loki 1,000.00
7 Romance that Could Not Be. 1,000.00
8 The Love Trap 1,000.00
9 Whom the Gods Destroy . . . 1,000.00
10 JMn,B:Science Fiction/Horror,
　Trapped On the Moon 1,300.00
11 RH,The End of the World . . 1,500.00
12 GC,The Lost World 1,300.00
13 BEv,King o/t Living Dead . . . 1,300.00
14 BEv,The Fountain of Death . 1,300.00
15 BEv,The Empty Grave 1,500.00
16 BEv,Where Gargoyles Dwell 1,500.00
17 BEv,Tower of Death,
　Bondage(c) 1,300.00
18 BEv,Terror in the Tunnel . . . 1,300.00
19 BEv,PMo, Kiss Of Death . . . 1,300.00

VERY BEST OF MARVEL COMICS
1-shot reps Marvel Artists
　Favorite Stories 13.00

VIDEO JACK
Nov., 1987
1 KGi,O:Video Jack 3.00
2 KGi 2.50
3 KGi 2.50
4 KGi 2.50
5 KGi 2.50
6 KGi,NA,BWr,AW 2.50

VISION, THE
1994–95
1 BHs,mini-series 2.25
2 BHs 2.25
3 BHs 2.25
4 BHs 2.25

VISION & SCARLET WITCH
[1st Series] Nov., 1982
1 RL,V:Halloween 3.00
2 RL,V:Isbisa,D:Whizzer 3.00
3 RL,A:Wonderman,V:GrimReaper 3.00
4 RL,A:Magneto,Inhumans 3.00

[2nd Series] 1985–86
1 V:Grim Reaper 2.50
2 V:Lethal Legion,D:Grim Reaper . 2.50
3 V:Salem's Seven 2.50
4 I:Glamor & Illusion 2.50
5 A:Glamor & Illusion 2.50
6 A:Magneto 2.50
7 V:Toad 2.50
8 A:Powerman 2.50
9 V:Enchantress 2.50
10 A:Inhumans 2.50
11 A:Spider-Man. 2.50
12 Birth of V&S's Child 8.00

VISION: YESTERDAY AND TOMORROW
TPB Yesterday and Tomorrow 15.00

VISIONARIES
Star, Nov., 1987
1 thru 5 . . . . @2.50
6 Sept., 1988 . . . . 2.50

VOID INDIGO
Epic, Nov., 1984
1 VM,Epic Comics 2.50
2 VM,Epic Comics,March, 1985 . . 2.50

WACKY DUCK
See: DOPEY DUCK

WALLY THE WIZARD
Star, April, 1985
1 . . . . 4.00
2 thru 11 . . . . @4.00
12 March, 1986 . . . . 4.00

WAR, THE
1989
1 Sequel to The Draft & The Pit . . 4.00
2 . . . . 4.00
3 . . . . 4.00
4 1990 . . . . 4.00

WAR ACTION
Marvel Atlas, April, 1952
1 JMn,RH,War Stories, Six Dead
　Men 250.00
2 GT 125.00
3 Invasion in Korea 100.00
4 thru 10 . . . . @100.00
11 and 12 . . . . @125.00
13 BK 125.00
14 Rangers Strike,June, 1953 . . . 100.00

WAR ADVENTURES
Marvel Atlas, Jan., 1952
1 GT,Battle Fatigue 200.00
2 The Story of a Slaughter 125.00
3 JRo 100.00
4 RH(c) 100.00
5 RH,Violent(c) 100.00
6 Stand or Die 100.00
7 JMn(c) 100.00
8 BK 125.00
9 RH(c) 100.00
10 JRo(c),Attack at Dawn 100.00
11 Red Trap 100.00
12 . . . . 100.00

13 RH(c),The Commies Strike
　Feb., 1953 . . . . 100.00

WAR COMBAT
Marvel Atlas, March, 1952
1 JMn,Death of Platoon Leader . 175.00
2 . . . . 125.00
3 JMn(c) 100.00
4 JMn(c) 100.00
5 The Red Hordes 100.00
Becomes:

COMBAT CASEY
6 BEv,Combat Casey cont 175.00
7 . . . . 125.00
8 JMn(c) 100.00
9 . . . . 100.00
10 RH(c) 125.00
11 . . . . 100.00
12 . . . . 100.00
13 thru 19 . . . . @125.00
20 . . . . 100.00
21 thru 33 . . . . @100.00
34 July, 1957 . . . . 100.00

War Comics #2
© *Marvel Entertainment Group*

WAR COMICS
Marvel Atlas, Dec., 1950
1 You Only Die Twice 300.00
2 Infantry's War 150.00
3 . . . . 125.00
4 GC,The General Said Nuts . . 125.00
5 . . . . 125.00
6 The Deadly Decision of
　General Kwang 125.00
7 RH,JMn 125.00
8 RH,No Survivors 125.00
9 RH,JMn 125.00
10 . . . . 125.00
11 Flame thrower 150.00
12 thru 21 . . . . @100.00
22 . . . . 125.00
23 thru 37 . . . . @100.00
38 JKu 125.00
39 . . . . 100.00
40 . . . . 100.00
41 . . . . 100.00
42 JO 100.00
43 AT,MD 125.00
44 . . . . 100.00
45 . . . . 100.00
46 RC 125.00
47 . . . . 100.00
48 MD,JO 125.00
49 Sept., 1957 . . . . 125.00

All comics prices listed are for *Near Mint* condition.

WARHEADS
Marvel UK, 1992–93
1 GEr,I:Warheads,A:Wolverine, . . . 2.25
2 GEr,V:Nick Fury. 2.25
3 DTy,A:Iron Man 2.25
4 SCy,A:X-Force 2.25
5 A:X-Force,C:Deaths'Head II 2.25
6 SCy,A:Death's Head II. 2.25
7 SCy,A:Death's Head II,S.Surfer. . 2.25
8 SCy,V:Mephisto. 2.25
9 SCy,V:Mephisto 2.25
10 JCz,V:Mephisto. 2.25
11 A:Death's Head II 2.25
12 V:Mechanix 2.25
13 Xenophiles Reptiles 2.25
14 last issue. 2.25

WARHEADS: BLACK DAWN
1 A:Gh.Rider,Morbius 3.25
2 V:Dracula. 2.25

WAR IS HELL
Jan., 1973—Oct., 1975
1 BP,B:reps.,Decision at Dawn . . 35.00
2 Anytime,Anyplace,War is Hell . . 20.00
3 Retreat or Die 20.00
4 Live Grenade 20.00
5 Trapped Platoon 20.00
6 We Die at Dawn 20.00
7 While the Jungle Sleeps,A:Sgt
  Fury 20.00
8 Killed in Action,A;Sgt Fury 20.00
9 B:Supernatural,War Stories . . . 60.00
10 Death is a 30 Ton Tank. 20.00
11 thru 15 . . . . @20.00

WARLOCK
[1st Regular Series] Aug., 1972
1 MGr,GK,I:Counter Earth,
  A:High Evolutionary. 100.00
2 MGr,JB,TS,V:Man Beast 50.00
3 MGr,GK,TS,V:Apollo 50.00
4 MGr,JK,TS,V:Triax. 25.00
5 MGr,GK,TS,V:Dr.Doom 25.00
6 MGr,TS(i),O:Brute 25.00
7 MGr,TS(i),V:Brute,D:Dr.Doom . . 25.00
8 MGr,TS(i),R:Man-Beast(cont.
  in Hulk #176). 25.00
9 MGr,JSn,1st`Rebirth'Thanos,
  O:Magnus,N:Warlock,
  I:In-Betweener. 40.00

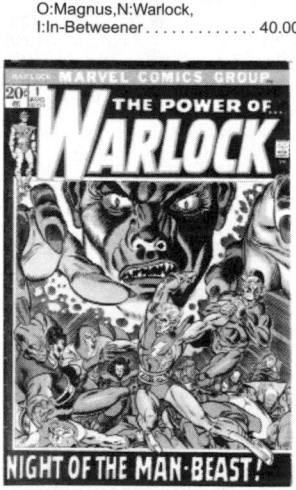

Warlock #1
© Marvel Entertainment Group

10 MGr,JSn,SL,O:Thanos,V:Magus,
  A:In-Betweener 50.00
11 MGr,JSn,SL,D:Magus,A:Thanos,
  In-Betweener. 40.00
12 MGr,JSn,SL,O:Pip,V:Pro-Boscis
  A:Starfox 25.00
13 MGr,JSn,SL,I&O:Star-Thief. . . . 25.00
14 MGr,JSn,SL,V:Star-Thief. 25.00
15 MGr,JSn,A:Thanos,V:Soul-Gem 40.00

[2nd Regular Series] 1992
1 JSn,rep.Strange Tales #178-180
  Baxter Paper 5.00
2 JSn,rep.Strange Tales #180
  & Warlock #9 . . . . 4.00
3 JSn,rep.Warlock #10-#12 . . . . . . 4.00
4 JSn,rep.Warlock #13-#15 . . . . . . 4.00
5 JSn,rep.Warlock #15 . . . . 4.00
6 JSn,rep. 4.00

WARLOCK
[Limited Series]
1 Rep.Warlock Series 3.50
2 thru 6 Rep.Warlock Series . . . @3.00

WARLOCK
Sept., 1998
1 (of 4) TL,RJn,R:Adam Warlock . . 3.00
2 TL,murderer revealed 3.00
3 TL,V:Drax. 3.00
4 TL,Concl. 3.00

WARLOCK
Aug., 1999
1 LSi,PFe,Marvel Tech 3.00
2 LSi,PFe,A:Iron Man 2.50
2a variant PFe cover 2.50
3 LSi,PFe,MMo,F:Psiren. 2.50
4 LSi,PFe,MMo,V:Mole Man. 2.50
5 LSi,PFe,MMo. 2.50
6 LSi,PFe,MMo,A:Kitty Pryde 2.50
7 LSi,PFe,MMo,R:Wolfsbane,
  Magus 2.50
8 LSi,PFe,MMo,V:Bastion. 2.50
9 LSi,PFe,MMo,F:Bastion. 2.50

WARLOCK
Sept., 2004
1 CAd,F:Adam Warlock 3.00
2 CAd 3.00
3 CAd 3.00
4 CAd 3.00

WARLOCK AND THE INFINITY WATCH
1992–95
1 AMe,Trial of the Gods(from
  Infinity Gauntlet) 3.00
2 AMe,I:Infinity Watch(Gamora,Pip,
  Moondragon,Drax & 1 other). . . 2.75
3 RL,TA,A:High Evolutionary,
  Nobilus,I:Omega 2.75
4 RL,TA,V:Omega. 2.50
5 AMe,TA,V:Omega 2.50
6 AMe,V:Omega(Man-Beast) 2.50
7 TR,TA,V:Mole Man,A:Thanos . . . 2.50
8 TR,TA,Infinity War,A:Thanos . . . 2.25
9 AMe,TA,Inf.War,O:Gamora 2.25
10 AMe,Inf.War,Thanos vs
  Doppleganger 2.50
11 O:Pip,Gamora,Drax,M'dragon. . . 2.25
12 TR,Drax Vs.Hulk 2.25
13 TR,Drax vs Hulk 2.25
14 AMe,V:United Nations. 2.25
15 AMe,Magnus,Him 2.25
16 TGr,I:Count Abyss 2.25
17 TGr,I:Maxam 2.25
18 AMe,Inf.Crusade,N:Pip 2.25
19 TGr,A:Hulk,Wolverine,Infinity
  Crusade. 2.25

20 AMe,Inf.Crusade 2.25
21 V:Thor. 2.25
22 AMe,Infinity Crusade. 2.25
23 JSn(s),TGb,Blood &
  Thunder#4 . . . . 2.25
24 JSn(s),TGb,V:Geirrodur 2.25
25 JSn(s),AMe,Die-Cut(c),Blood &
  Thunder #12 . . . . 3.50
26 A:Avengers 2.25
27 TGb,V:Avengers 2.25
28 TGb,V:Man-Beast. 2.25
29 A:Maya 2.25
30 PO. 2.25
31 . . . . 2.25
32 Heart & Soul 2.25
33 V:Count Abyss 2.25
34 V:Count Abyss 2.25
35 V:Tyrannus 2.25
36 . . . . 2.25
37 A:Zaharius. 2.25
38 . . . . 2.25
39 V:Domitron 2.25
40 A:Thanos. 2.25
41 Monster Island 2.25
42 Warlock vs. Maxam, Atlantis
  Rising, final issue 2.25

WARLOCK CHRONICLES
1993–94
1 TR,F:Adam Warlock,holo-grafx(c),
  I:Darklore,Meer'lyn 2.25
2 TR,Infinity Crusade,Thanos revealed
  to have the Reality Gem 2.25
3 TR,A:Mephisto. 2.25
4 TR,A:Magnus 2.25
5 TR(c),Inf.Crusade 2.25
6 TR,Blood & Thunder,pt.#3 . . . . . . 2.25
7 TR,Blood & Thunder,pt.#7 . . . . . . 2.25
8 TR,Blood & Thunder,pt.#11 . . . . . 2.25
9 TR 2.25
10 TR 2.25
11 TR 2.25

WAR MACHINE
1994–96
1 GG,Foil Embossed(c),B:LKa&StB,
  O:War Machine,V:Cable,
  C:Deathlok. 3.25
1a Newstand Ed. 2.25
2 GG,V:Cable,Deathlok,w/card . . . 3.25
3 GG,V:Cable,Deathlok. 3.25
4 GG,C:Force Works. 3.25
5 GG,I:Deachtoll 3.25
6 GG,V:Deathtoll. 3.25

War Machine #8
© Marvel Entertainment Group

7 GG,A:Hawkeye 3.25
8 reg ed. 3.25
8a neon(c),w/insert print. 3.00
9 Hands of Mandarin,pt.2 . . . . 2.25
10 Hands of Mandarin,pt.5 . . . . 2.25
11 X-Mas Party 2.25
12 V:Terror Device 2.25
13 V:The Rush Team 2.25
14 A:Force Works 2.25
15 In The Past of WWII 2.25
16 DAn,A:Rick Fury,Cap.America . . 2.25
17 The Man Who Won WWII 2.25
18 DAn,N:War Machine 2.25
19 DAn,A:Hawkeye 2.25
20 DAn,The Crossing 2.25
21 DAn,The Crossing 2.25
22 DAn,V:Iron Man 2.25
23 DAn,Avengers:Timeslide. 2.25

WAR MAN
Epic, 1993
1 thru 2 CDi(s) 2.50

WEAPON X
1995
1 Wolverine After Xavier 4.00
2 Full Scale War 2.25
3 Jean Leaves 2.25
4 F:Gateway 2.25
TPB Rep.#1-#4 . . . . 9.00

WEAPON X
Aug., 2002
1-shot Wild Child #1, JWi 2.50
1-shot Sauron #1, JWi,KIK. 2.50
1-shot Kane #1, JWi 2.50
1-shot Marrow #1, JWi, ... 2.50
1-shot Agent Zero #1, JWi 2.50
1 . . . . 2.25
2 F:Marrow 2.25
3 . . . . 2.25
4 Hunt for Sabretooth 2.25
5 Evil plans,D.Maggot. 3.00
6 NRd,special mission 2.25
7 The Underground,pt.1 . . . . 2.25
8 The Underground,pt.2 . . . . 3.00
9 The Underground,pt.3 . . . . 3.00
10 The Underground,pt.4. . . . . 3.00
11 The Underground,pt.5. . . . . 3.00
12 The Underground,pt.6. . . . . 3.00
13 The Underground,concl. 3.00
14 R:Mr. Sinister 3.00
15 Defection,pt.1,F:X-Man. 3.00
16 Defection,pt.2 . . . . 3.00
17 Defection,pt.3 . . . . 3.00
18 Defection,pt.4 . . . . 3.00
19 Countdown to Zero,pt.1 . . . . . . 3.00
20 Countdown to Zero,pt.2 . . . . . . 3.00
21 Countdown to Zero,pt.3 . . . . . . 3.00
22 Mutant feared 3.00
23 TMd,War of the Programs,pt.1 . . 3.00
24 TMd,War of the Programs,pt.2 . . 3.00
25 TMd,War of the Programs,pt.3 . . 3.00
26 TMd,Man and Superman,pt.1 . . . 3.00
27 TMd,Man and Superman,pt.2. . . 3.00
28 TMd,Man and Superman,pt.3. . . 3.00
TPB Vol. 1 . . . . 22.00
TPB The Underground. 20.00

WEAPON X:
DAYS OF FUTURE NOW
July, 2005
1 (of 5) BS 3.00
2 Bs. 3.00
3 BS(c). 3.00
4 BS,Lord Magnus 3.00
5 BS 3.00
TPB Days of Future Now. 14.00

WEAVEWORLD
Epic, 1991–92
1 MM, Clive Barker adaptation 5.00
2 MM,Into the Weave 5.00
3 MM 5.00

WEB OF
SCARLET SPIDER
1995–96
1 TDF,Virtual Mortality,pt.1 . . . . . . 2.00
2 TDF,CyberWar,pt.2 . . . . 2.00
3 Nightmare in Scarlet,pt.1 . . . . . . 2.00
4 Nightmare in Scarlet,pt.3 . . . . . . 2.00

WEB OF SPIDER-MAN
April, 1985
1 JM,V:New Costume 25.00
2 JM,V:Vulture 15.00
3 JM,V:Vulture 15.00
4 JM,JBy,V:Dr.Octopus 10.00
5 JM,JBy,V:Dr.Octopus 10.00
6 MZ,BL,JM,Secret Wars II. 10.00
7 SB,A:Hulk.V:Nightmare,
    C:Wolverine 10.00
8 V:Smithville Thunder 10.00
9 V:Smithville Thunder 10.00
10 JM,A:Dominic Fortune,
    V:Shocker 10.00
11 BMc,V:Thugs. 10.00
12 BMc,SB,V:Thugs. 10.00
13 BMc,V:J.JonahJameson 10.00
14 KB,V:Black Fox. 10.00
15 V:Black Fox,I:Chance 7.00
16 MS,KB,V:Magma 7.00
17 MS,V:Magma 8.00
18 MS,KB,Where is Spider-Man? . 10.00
19 MS,BMc,I:Solo,Humbug 7.00
20 MS,V:Terrorists 7.00
21 V:Fake Spider-Man 7.00
22 MS,V:Terrorists 7.00
23 V:Slyde 7.00
24 SB,V:Vulture,Hobgoblin 7.00
25 V:Aliens 7.00
26 V:Thugs. 7.00
27 V:Headhunter 7.00
28 BL,V:Thugs 7.00
29 A:Wolverine,2nd App:New
    Hobgoblin 10.00
30 KB,O:Rose,C:Daredevil,Capt.
    America,Wolverine,Punisher . . 10.00
31 MZ,BMc,V:Kraven 9.00
32 MZ,BMc,V:Kraven 9.00
33 BSz(c),SI,.V:Kingpin,Mad
    Dog Ward,pt.#1 . . . . 6.00
34 SB,A:Watcher 6.00
35 AS,V:Living Brain 6.00
36 AS,V:Phreak Out,I:Tombstone . . 7.00
37 V:Slasher 7.00
38 AS,A:Tombstone,V:Hobgoblin. . . 7.00
39 AS,V:Looter(Meteor Man) 6.00
40 AS,V:Cult of Love 6.00
41 AS,V:Cult of Love 6.00
42 AS,V:Cult of Love 6.00
43 AS,V:Cult of Love 6.00
44 AS,V:Warzone,A:Hulk 5.00
45 AS,V:Vulture 5.00
46 A:Dr.Pym,V:Nekra 5.00
47 AS,V:Hobgoblin. 6.00
48 AS,O:New Hobgoblin's Demonic
    Power 12.00
49 VM,V:Drugs. 5.00
50 AS,V:Chameleon(double size) . . 7.00
51 MBa,V:Chameleon,Lobo Bros. . . 5.00
52 FS,JR,O:J.Jonah Jameson
    V:Chameleon. 5.00
53 MBa,V:Lobo Bros.,C:Punisher
    A:Chameleon. 5.00
54 AS,V:Chameleon,V:Lobo Bros. . . 5.00
55 AS,V:Chameleon,Hammerhead,
    V:Lobo Bros. 5.00

Web of Spider-Man #24
© *Marvel Entertainment Group*

56 AS,I&O:Skin Head,
    A:Rocket Racer. 5.00
57 AS,D:SkinHead,
    A:Rocket Racer. 5.00
58 AS,V:Grizzly 5.00
59 AS,Acts of Vengeance,V:Titania
    A:Puma,Cosmic Spider-Man . . . 7.00
60 AS,A of V,V:Goliath 5.00
61 AS,A of V,V:Dragon Man. 5.00
62 AS,V:Molten Man 3.00
63 AS,V:Mister Fear. 3.00
64 AS,V:Graviton,Titania,Trapster . . 3.00
65 AS,V:Goliath,Trapster,Graviton . . 3.00
66 AS,V:Tombstone,A:G.Goblin 3.00
67 AS,A:GreenGoblin,
    V:Tombstone 3.00
68 AS,A:GreenGoblin,
    V:Tombstone 3.00
69 AS,V:Hulk 4.00
70 AS,I:The Spider/Hulk. 4.00
71 A:Silver Sable 3.00
72 AM,A:Silver Sable 3.00
73 AS,A:Human Torch,
    Colossus,Namor 3.00
74 AS,I:Spark,V:Bora 3.00
75 AS,C:New Warriors 3.00
76 AS,Spidey in Ice 3.00
77 AS,V:Firebrand,Inheritor 3.00
78 AS,A:Firebrand,Cloak&Dagger . . 3.00
79 AS,V:Silvermane 3.00
80 AS,V:Silvermane 3.00
81 I:Bloodshed 3.00
82 V:Man Mountain Marko. 3.00
83 V:A.I.M. Supersuit. 3.00
84 AS,B:Name of the Rose 3.00
85 AS,Name of the Rose 3.00
86 AS,I:Demogoblin 3.00
87 AS,I:Praetorian Guard. 3.00
88 AS,Name of the Rose 3.00
89 AS,E:Name of the Rose,
    I:Bloodrose 3.00
90 AS,30th Ann.,w/hologram,
    polybagged,V:Mysterio 3.50
90a Gold 2nd printing 3.00
91 AS,V:Whisper And Pulse 3.00
92 AS,V:Foreigner 3.00
93 AS,BMc,V:Hobgoblin,A:Moon
    Knight,Foreigner 3.00
94 AS,V:Hobgoblin,A:MoonKnight . . 3.00
95 AS,Spirits of Venom#1,A:Venom,
    J.Blaze,GR,V:Hag & Troll 3.00
96 AS,Spirits of Venom#3, A:G.R,
    J.Blaze,Venom,Hobgoblin 3.00
97 AS,I:Dr.Trench,V:Bloodrose 3.00

98 AS,V:Bloodrose,Foreigner 3.00
99 I:Night Watch,V:New Enforcer . . 3.00
100 AS,JRu,V:Enforcers,Bloodrose,
    Kingpin(Alfredo),I:Spider Armor,
    O:Night Watch,Holografx(c). . . . 4.00
101 AS,Total Carnage,V:Carnage,
    Shriek,A:Cloak and Dagger,
    Venom 3.00
102 Total Carnage#6,V:Carnage,
    A:Venom,Morbius 3.00
103 AS,Maximum Carnage#10,
    V:Carnage 3.00
104 AS,Infinity Crusade 2.50
105 AS,Infinity Crusade 2.50
106 AS,Infinity Crusade 2.75
107 AS,A:Sandman,Quicksand 2.50
108 B:TKa(s),AS,I:Sandstorm,
    BU:Cardiac 2.50
109 AS,V:Shocker,A:Night Thrasher,
    BU:D:Calypso 2.50
110 AS,I:Warrant,A:Lizard 2.50
111 AS,V:Warrant,Lizard 2.50
112 AS,Pursuit#3,V:Chameleon,
    w/card 2.50
113 AS,A:Gambit,Black Cat,w/cel . . 3.50
113a Newsstand Ed. 2.50
114 AS 2.50
115 AS,V:Facade 2.50
116 AS,V:Facade 2.50
117 Foil(c), flip book with
    Power & Responsibility #1 . . . . 5.00
117a Newsstand ed. 2.50
118 Spider-clone,V:Venom 3.00
119 Clone,V:Venom 3.00
119a bagged with Milestone rep.
    Amazing Sp-Man #150,checklist 8.00
120 Web of Life,pt.1. . . . . 2.50
121 Web of Life,pt.3. . . . . 2.50
122 Smoke and Mirrors,pt.1 . . . . . . 2.50
123 The Price of Truth,pt.2 . . . . 2.25
124 The Mark of Kaine,pt.1. . . . . . . 2.00
125 R:Gwen Stacy. 3.00
125a 3-D Holodisk cover 4.25
126 The Trial of Peter Parker,pt.1 . . 2.25
127 Maximum Clonage,pt.2. . . . . . . 2.25
128 TDF,Exiled,pt.1 . . . . 2.50
129 Timebomb,pt.2 . . . . 3.00
Ann.#1 V:Future Max. 7.00
Ann.#2 AAd,MMi,A:Warlock. 10.00
Ann.#3 AS,DP,JRu,JM,BL 4.50
Ann.#4 AS,TM,RLm,Evolutionary
    Wars,A:Man Thing,V:Slug 5.00
Ann.#5 AS,SD,JS,Atlantis
    Attacks,A:Fantastic Four 4.00
Ann.#6 SD,JBr,SB,A:Punisher. 4.50
Ann.#7 Vibranium Vendetta #3 . . . . 3.50
Ann.#8 Hero Killers#3,A:New
    Warriors,BU:Venom,Black Cat . 3.50
Ann.#9 CMa,I:Cadre,w/card. 3.50
Ann.#10 V:Shriek 4.00
Super Size Spec.#1 Planet of
    the Symbiotes,pt.5. . . . . 4.00

WEBSPINNERS: TALES
OF SPIDER-MAN
Nov., 1998
1 JMD,JR,MZi,A:Mysterio,seq.to
    Amaz.Sp-M#38, 48-page. 3.00
1a signed 7.00
2 JMD,JR,V:J.Jonah Jameson 2.50
2a variant SR cover 2.50
3 JMD,V:Mysterio, concl. 2.50
4 KG,ErS,seq.to Silver Surfer#18 . . 2.50
5 KG,ErS,A:Silver Surfer. 2.50
6 KG,ErS,F:Silver Surfer,
    Psycho-Man & Annihilus 2.50
7 BS,MPn,V:Sandman 2.50
8 BS,MPn,V:Sandman 2.50
9 V:Sandman 2.50
10 V:Chameleon, pt.1 . . . . 2.50
11 V:Chameleon, pt.2 . . . . 2.50

12 conclusion, 48-pg. 3.50
13 . . . . 2.50
14 HMe,BS,A:Carnage 2.50
15 V:Vulture 2.50
16 V:Vulture 2.50
17 TDF, black costume 2.50
18 TDF, Silversable 2.50

Weird Wondertales #20
© *Marvel Entertainment Group*

WEIRD WONDERTALES
Dec., 1973
1 B:Reprints 45.00
2 I Was Kidnapped by a Flying
    Saucer 25.00
3 BP,The Thing in the Bog 25.00
4 SD,SK,It Lurks Behind
    the Wall 25.00
5 SD 25.00
6 The Man Who Owned a Ghost . 25.00
7 BP,The Apes That Walked
    like Men 25.00
8 JMn,Reap A Deadly Harvest . 25.00
9 The Murder Mirror 25.00
10 SD,SK,Mister Morgan's
    Monster 25.00
11 SD,SK,Slaughter in
    Shrangri-La 20.00
12 SD,MD,The Stars Scream
    Murder. 20.00
13 SD,The Totem Strikes 20.00
14 Witching Circle 20.00
15 . . . . 20.00
16 GC,The Shark. 20.00
17 Creature From Krogarr 20.00
18 Krang 20.00
19 SD,A:Dr Druid 20.00
20 SD,MD,The Madness 20.00
21 SD,A:Dr Druid 20.00
22 The World Below,May, 1975 . . . 20.00

WENDY PARKER COMICS
Marvel Atlas, 1953
1 . . . . 150.00
2 . . . . 100.00
3 . . . . 125.00
4 . . . . 125.00
5 . . . . 125.00
6 . . . . 125.00
7 . . . . 125.00
8 . . . . 125.00

WEREWOLF BY NIGHT
Sept., 1972
1 MP(cont from Marvel Spotlight)
    FullMoonRise..WerewolfKill. . 200.00
2 MP,Like a Wild Beast at Bay . . . 75.00
3 MP,Mystery of the Mad Monk . . 50.00
4 MP,The Danger Game. 50.00
5 MP,A Life for a Death. 50.00
6 MP,Carnival of Fear. 40.00
7 MP,JM,Ritual of Blood 40.00
8 MP,Krogg,Lurker from Beyond . 40.00
9 TS,V:Tatterdemalion 40.00
10 TS,bondage cover 40.00
11 GK,TS,Full Moon..Fear Moon . . 30.00
12 GK,Cry Monster 30.00
13 MP,ManMonsterCalledTaboo . 25.00
14 MP,Lo,the Monster Strikes 25.00
15 MP,(new)O:Werewolf,
    V:Dracula. 50.00
16 MP,TS,A:Hunchback of Notre
    Dame. 35.00
17 Behold the Behemoth 35.00
18 War of the Werewolves. 35.00
19 V:Dracula. 32.00
20 The Monster Breaks Free. 30.00
21 GK(c),To Cure a Werewolf 15.00
22 GK(c),Face of a Friend. 15.00
23 Silver Bullet for a Werewolf . . . 15.00
24 GK(c),V:The Brute 15.00
25 GK(c),Eclipse of Evil. 15.00
26 GK(c),A Crusade of Murder . . . 15.00
27 GK(c),Scourge o/t Soul-Beast . 15.00
28 GK(c),V:Dr.Glitternight 15.00
29 GK(c),V:Dr.Glitternight 15.00
30 GK(c),Red Slash across
    Midnight. 15.00
31 Death in White 15.00
32 I&O:Moon Knight 160.00
33 Were-Beast..Moon Knight
    A:Moon Knight(2nd App) 160.00
34 GK(c),TS,House of Evil..House
    of Death. 15.00
35 TS,JS,BWi,Jack Russell vs.
    Werewolf 15.00
36 Images of Death 15.00
37 BWr(c),BW,A:Moon Knight,
    Hangman,Dr.Glitternight 20.00
38 . . . . 22.00
39 V:Brother Voodoo 22.00
40 A:Brother Voodoo,V:Dr.
    Glitternight. 15.00
41 V:Fire Eyes 15.00
42 A:IronMan,Birth of a Monster . . 15.00
43 Tri-Animal Lives,A:Iron Man . . . 15.00
G-Size#2,SD,A:Frankenstein
    Monster (reprint) 15.00
G-Size#3 GK(c),Transylvania 15.00
G-Size#4 GK(c),A:Morbius 15.00
G-Size#5 GK(c),Peril of
    Paingloss. 10.00

WEREWOLF BY NIGHT
Dec., 1997
1 PJe,F:Jack Russell returns 3.00
2 PJe,Search for wolf Amulet 3.00
3 PJe,Stuck between man & wolf . . 3.00
4 PJe,to the depths of hell 3.00
5 PJe, confronts demon 3.00
6 PJe, visit Underworld nightclub . . 3.00
Storyline continues in Strange Tales

WEST COAST AVENGERS
[Limited Series] Sept., 1984
1 BH,A:Shroud,J:Hawkeye,IronMan,
    WonderMan,Mockingbird,Tigra . 4.00
2 BH,V:Blank. 3.00
3 BH,V:Graviton 3.00
4 BH,V:Graviton 3.00

[Regular Series] 1985–89
1 AM,JSt,V:Lethal Legion 4.00

MARVEL

West Coast Avengers #1
© Marvel Entertainment Group

2 AM,JSt,V:Lethal Legion 3.00
3 AM,JSt,V:Kraven 3.00
4 AM,JSt,A:Firebird,Thing,I:Master
   Pandemonium 3.00
5 AM,JSt,A:Werewolf,Thing 3.00
6 AM,KB,A:Thing 3.00
7 AM,JSt,V:Ultron 3.00
8 AM,JSt,V:Rangers,A:Thing 3.00
9 AM,JSt,V:Master Pandemonium . 3.00
10 AM,JSt,V:Headlok,Griffen 3.00
11 AM,JSt,A:Nick Fury 3.00
12 AM,JSt,V:Graviton 3.00
13 AM,JSt,V:Graviton 3.00
14 AM,JSt,V:Pandemonium 3.00
15 AM,JSt,A:Hellcat 3.00
16 AM,JSt,V:Tiger Shark,
   Whirlwind 3.00
17 AM,JSt,V:Dominus' Minions 3.00
18 AM,JSt,V:The Wild West 3.00
19 AM,JSt,A:Two Gun Kid 3.00
20 AM,JSt,A:Rawhide Kid 3.00
21 AM,JSt,A:Dr.Pym,Moon Knight . . 3.00
22 AM,JSt,A:Fant.Four,Dr.Strange,
   Night Rider 3.00
23 AM,RT,A:Phantom Rider 3.00
24 AM,V:Dominus 3.00
25 AM,V:Abomination 3.00
26 AM,V:Zodiac 3.00
27 AM,V:Zodiac 3.00
28 AM,V:Zodiac 3.00
29 AM,V:Taurus,A:Shroud 3.00
30 AM,C:Composite Avenger 3.00
31 AM,V:Arkon 3.00
32 AM,TD,V:Yetrigar,J:Wasp 3.00
33 AM,O:Ant-Man,Wasp;
   V:Madam X,El Toro 3.00
34 AM,V:Quicksilver,J:Vision &
   Scarlet Witch 3.00
35 AM,V:Dr.Doom,Quicksilver 3.00
36 AM,V:The Voice 3.00
37 V:The Voice,A:Mantis 3.00
38 AM,TMo,V:Defiler 3.00
39 AM,V:Swordsman 3.00
40 AM,MGu,V:NightShift,
   A:Shroud 3.00
41 TMo,I:New Phantom Rider,
   L:Moon Knight 3.00
42 JBy,Visionquest#1,V:Ultron 3.50
43 JBy,Visionquest#2, ... 3.00
44 JBy,Visionquest#3,J:USAgent . . 3.00
45 JBy,Visionquest#4,
   I:New Vision 3.50
46 JBy,I:Great Lakes Avengers 3.00
Ann. #1 MBr,GI,V:Zodiak 3.25

Ann. #2 AM,A:SilverSurfer,V:Death,
   Collector,R:Grandmaster 3.00
Ann. #3 AM,RLm,TD,Evolutionary
   Wars,R:Giant Man 3.50
Becomes:

AVENGERS WEST COAST

WESTERN GUNFIGHTERS
[2nd series] Aug., 1970
1 JK,JB,DAy,B:Ghost Rider
   A:Fort Rango,The Renegades
   Gunhawk 75.00
2 HT(c),DAy,JMn,O:Nightwind,
   V:Tarantula 35.00
3 DAy,MD,V:Hurricane, rep. 35.00
4 HT(c),DAy,TS,B:Gunhawk,
   Apache Kid,A;Renegades . . . 45.00
5 DAy,FrG,A:Renegades 35.00
6 HT(c),DAy,SSh,Death of
   Ghost Rider 30.00
7 HT(c),DAy,SSh,O:Ghost Rider
   retold,E:Ghost Rider,Gunhawk 30.00
8 DAy,SSh,B:Black Rider,Outlaw
   Kid(rep) 25.00
9 DW,Revenge rides the Range . . 25.00
10 JK,JMn,O:Black Rider,B:Matt
   Slade,A:Outlaw Kid 25.00
11 JK,Duel at Dawn 25.00
12 JMn,O:Matt Slade 30.00
13 Save the Gold Coast Expires . . 25.00
14 JSo(c),Outlaw Town 25.00
15 E:Matt Slade,Showdown in
   Outlaw Canyon 25.00
16 B:Kid Colt,Shoot-out in Silver
   City 25.00
17 thru 20 . . . . @25.00
21 thru 24 . . . . @15.00
25 . . . . 15.00
26 F:Kid Colt,Gun-Slinger,
   Apache Kid 15.00
27 thru 32 . . . . @15.00
33 Nov., 1975 . . . . 15.00

WESTERN KID
[1st Series] Dec., 1954
1 JR,B:Western Kid,O:Western Kid
   (Tex Dawson) 250.00
2 JMn,JR,Western Adventure . . 125.00
3 JMn(c),JR,Gunfight(c) 100.00
4 JMn(c),JR,The Badlands 100.00
5 JR 100.00
6 JR 100.00

Western Kid #3
© Marvel Entertainment Group

7 JR 100.00
8 JR 100.00
9 JR,AW 125.00
10 JR,AW,Man in the Middle 125.00
11 thru 16 . . . . @100.00
17 Aug., 1957 . . . . 100.00
[2nd Series]
Dec., 1971–Aug., 1972
1 Reprints 35.00
2 . . . . 20.00
3 AW 25.00
4 . . . . 20.00
5 . . . . 20.00

WESTERN OUTLAWS
Marvel Atlas,
Feb., 1954—Aug., 1957
1 JMn(c),RH,BP,The Greenville
   Gallows,Hanging(c) 300.00
2 . . . . 150.00
3 thru 10 . . . . @125.00
11 AW,MD 150.00
12 JMn 100.00
13 MB,JMn 125.00
14 AW 125.00
15 AT,GT 100.00
16 BP,JMn,JSe,AW 100.00
17 JMn,AW 100.00
18 JSe 100.00
19 JMn,JSe,RC 100.00
20 and 21 JSe . . . . @100.00

WESTERN OUTLAWS
& SHERIFFS
See: BEST WESTERN

WESTERN TALES
OF BLACK RIDER
See: ALL WINNERS COMICS

WESTERN TEAM-UP
Nov., 1973
1 Rawhide Kid/Dakota Kid 50.00

WESTERN THRILLERS
Nov., 1954
1 JMn,Western tales 200.00
2 . . . . 100.00
3 . . . . 100.00
4 . . . . 100.00
Becomes:

COWBOY ACTION
March, 1955–March, 1956
5 JMn(c),The Prairie Kid 150.00
6 . . . . 100.00
7 . . . . 100.00
9 . . . . 100.00
10 . . . . 100.00
11 MN,AW,The Manhunter 125.00
Becomes:

QUICK-TRIGGER
WESTERN
May, 1956–Sept., 1957
12 Bill Larson Strikes 175.00
13 AW,The Man From Cheyenne 175.00
14 BEv,RH(c) 175.00
15 AT,RC 150.00
16 JK,JD 125.00
17 GT 125.00
18 GM 125.00
19 JSe 100.00

WESTERN TRAILS
Marvel Atlas, 1957
1 MMe,FBe,JSe(c),Ringo Kid . . . 165.00
2 MMe,FBe,JSe(c) 100.00

MARVEL

WESTERN WINNERS
See: ALL WINNERS COMICS

WHAT IF?

[1st Regular Series] Feb., 1977

1 Spider-Man joined Fant.Four . . . 35.00
2 GK(c),Hulk had Banner brain . . 15.00
3 GK,KJ,F:Avengers 12.00
4 GK(c),F:Invaders 12.00
5 F:Captain America 12.00
6 F:Fantastic Four. 12.00
7 GK(c),F:Spider-Man. 10.00
8 GK(c),F:Daredevil 10.00
9 JK(c),F:Avengers of the '50s . . . 10.00
10 JB,F:Thor 10.00
11 JK,F:FantasticFour 8.00
12 F:Hulk 8.00
13 JB,Conan Alive Today. 8.00
14 F:Sgt. Fury 6.00
15 CI,F:Nova 6.00
16 F:Master of Kung Fu. 6.00
17 CI,F:Ghost Rider. 6.00
18 TS,F:Dr.Strange 5.00
19 PB,F:Spider-Man 6.00
20 F:Avengers 5.00
21 GC,F:Sub-Mariner. 5.00
22 F:Dr.Doom. 5.00
23 JB,F:Hulk 5.00
24 GK,RB,Gwen Stacy had lived . . . 6.00
25 F:Thor,Avengers,O:Mentor 5.00
26 JBy(c),F:Captain America. 5.00
27 FM(c),Phoenix hadn't died 22.00
28 FM,F:Daredevil,Ghost Rider. . . . 15.00
29 MG(c),F:Avengers. 6.00
30 RB,F:Spider-Man 10.00
31 Wolverine killed the Hulk 25.00
32 Avengers lost to Korvac 5.00
33 BL,Dazzler herald of Galactus . . 5.00
34 FH,FM,JBy,BSz:Humor issue . . . 5.00
35 FM,Elektra had lived. 6.00
36 JBy,Fant.Four had no powers. . . 5.00
37 F:Thing,Beast,Silver Surfer. 5.00
38 F:Daredevil,Captain America . . . 5.00
39 Thor had fought Conan. 5.00
40 F:Dr.Strange 5.00
41 F:Sub-Mariner. 5.00
42 F:Fantastic Four 5.00
43 F:Conan 5.00
44 F:Captain America 5.00
45 F:Hulk,Berserk 5.00
46 Uncle Ben had lived 7.00
47 F:Thor,Loki 5.00
Spec.#1 F:Iron Man,Avengers 6.00
Best of What If? rep.#1,#24,
    #27,#28 . . . . 13.00
TPB Classic Vol. 1, rep. #1–#6 . . . 25.00
TPB Classic Vol. 2, rep. #7–#12 . . 25.00

[2nd Regular Series]

1 RWi,MG,The Avengers had lost
    the Evolutionary War. 5.00
2 GCa,Daredevil Killed Kingpin,
    A:Hobgoblin, The Rose 4.00
3 Capt.America Hadn't Given Up
    Costume,A:Avengers. 3.50
4 MBa,Spider-Man kept Black
    Costume,A:Avengers,Hulk 4.50
5 Vision Destroyed Avengers,
    A:Wonder Man. 3.50
6 RLm,X-Men Lost Inferno,
    A:Dr.Strange 6.00
7 RLd,Wolverine Joined Shield,
    A:Nick Fury,Black Widow 7.00
8 Iron Man Lost The Armor Wars,
    A:Ant Man 3.50
9 RB,New X-Men Died 6.00
10 MZ(c),BMc,Punisher's Family
    Didn't Die,A:Kingpin 3.00
11 TM(c),JV,SM,Fant.Four had the
    Same Powers,A:Nick Fury . . . 3.50
12 JV,X-Men Stayed in Asgard,
    A:Thor,Hela 5.00

What If 2nd Series #1
© Marvel Entertainment Group

13 JLe(c),Prof.X Became
    Juggernaut,A:X-Men 3.50
14 RLm(c),Capt.Marvel didn't die
    A:Silver Surfer. 3.50
15 GCa,Fant.Four Lost Trial of
    Galactus,A:Gladiator 3.00
16 Wolverine Battled Conan,
    A:X-Men,Red Sonja. 5.00
17 Kraven Killed Spider-Man,
    A:Daredevil,Captain America . . 3.00
18 LMc,Fant.Four fought Dr.Doom
    before they gained powers 3.00
19 RW,Vision took over Earth,
    A:Avengers,Dr.Doom. 3.00
20 Spider-Man didn't marry Mary
    Jane,A:Venom,Kraven. 3.00
21 Spider-Man married Black Cat,
    A:Vulture,Silver Sable 3.00
22 RLm,Silver Surfer didn't escape
    Earth,A:F.F,Mephisto,Thanos . . 4.00
23 New X-Men never existed,
    A:Eric the Red,Lilandra 3.00
24 Wolverine Became Lord of
    Vampires,A:Punisher. 3.00
25 Marvel Heroes lost Atlantis
    Attacks,double size 3.50
26 LMc,Punisher Killed Daredevil,
    A:Spider-Man. 3.00
27 Submariner Joined Fantastic
    Four,A:Dr. Doom 3.00
28 RW,Capt.America led Army of
    Super-Soldiers,A:Submariner . . 3.00
29 RW,Capt.America formed the
    Avengers 3.00
30 Inv.Woman's 2nd Child had
    lived,A:Fantastic Four 3.00
31 Spider-Man/Captain Universe
    Powers. 3.00
32 Phoenix Rose Again,pt.1 . . . . . . 3.00
33 Phoenix Rose Again,pt.2 . . . . . . 3.00
34 Humor Issue 3.00
35 B:Time Quake,F.F. vs.Dr. Doom
    & Annihilus. 3.00
36 Cosmic Avengers,V:Guardians
    of the Galaxy. 3.00
37 X-Vampires,V:Dormammu 3.00
38 Thor was prisoner of Set 3.00
39 E:Time Quake,Watcher saved the
    Universe 3.00
40 Storm remained A thief? 3.00
41 JV,Avengers fought Galactus . . . 3.00
42 KWe,Spidey kept extra arms . . . 3.00
43 Wolverine married Mariko. 3.50
44 Punisher possessed by Venom . 3.00

45 Barbara Ketch became G.R. 3.00
46 Cable Killed Prof.X,Cyclops &
    Jean Grey 3.00
47 Magneto took over USA 3.00
48 Daredevil Saved Nuke 3.00
49 Silver Surfer had Inf.Gauntlet? . . 3.50
50 Hulk killed Wolverine 7.00
51 PCu,Punisher is Capt.America . . 3.00
52 BHi,Wolverine led Alpha Flight . . 3.50
53 F:Iron Man,Hulk 3.00
54 F:Death's Head. 3.00
55 LKa(s),Avengers lose G.Storm . . 3.00
56 Avengers lose G.Storm#2 . . . . . . 3.00
57 Punisher a member of SHIELD . . 3.00
58 Punisher kills SpM 3.00
59 Wolverine lead Alpha Flight 3.50
60 RoR,Scott & Jean's Wedding . . . 3.00
61 Spider-Man's Parents 3.00
62 Woverine vs Weapon X 3.50
63 F:War Machine,Iron Man 3.00
64 Iron Man sold out 3.00
65 Archangel fell from Grace. 3.00
66 Rogue and Thor 3.00
67 Cap.America returns. 3.00
68 Captain America story. 3.00
69 Stryfe Killed X-Men 3.00
70 Silver Surfer 3.50
71 The Hulk 3.00
72 Parker Killed Burglar. 3.00
73 Daredevil,Kingpin 3.00
74 Sinister Formed X-Men. 8.00
75 Gen-X's Blink had lived 3.00
76 Flash Thompson Spider-Man . . . 3.00
77 Legion had killed Magneto 10.00
78 FF had stayed together 3.00
79 Storm had Phoenix's Power 3.00
80 KGa,Hulk was Cured 3.00
81 Age of Apocalypse didn't end . . 11.00
82 WML,J.JonahJameson
    adopted Spider-Man 3.00
83 Daredevil. 3.00
84 Shard 3.00
85 Magneto Ruled all mutants. 3.00
86 Scarlet Spider vs. Spider-Man . . 3.00
87 Sabretooth 3.00
88 Spider-Man. 3.00
89 Fantastic Four. 3.00
90 Cyclops & Havok 3.00
91 F:Hulk, nice guy, Banner violent. 3.00
92 F:Cannonball,Husk 3.00
93 F:Wolverine. 3.50
94 JGz,F:Juggernaut 3.00
95 IV,F:Ghost Rider. 3.00
96 CWo,F:Quicksilver, ... 3.00

What If? Minus 1 Spec.
© Marvel Entertainment Group

97 F:Black Knight. 3.00
98 F:Nightcrawler & Rogue 3.00
99 F:Black Cat. 3.00
100 IV,KJ,F:Gambit &
   Rogue, 48-pg. 7.00
101 ATi,F:Archangel. 3.00
102 F:Daredevil's Dad 3.00
103 DaF,F:Captain America. 3.00
104 F:Silver Surver,ImpossibleMan . 3.00
105 TDF,RF,F:Spider-Man and
   Mary Jane's Daughter. 25.00
106 TDF,F:X-Men,Gambit
   sentenced to death 3.00
107 TDF,RF,BSz,F:Thor. 3.00
108 TDF,F:The Avengers. 3.00
109 TA,F:Fantastic Four 3.00
110 TDF,F:Wolverine 3.00
111 TDF,F:Wolverine 3.00
112 F:Ka-Zar 3.00
113 F:Iron Man, Dr. Strange, ... 3.00
114 F:Secret Wars, 32-page,
   final issue 7.00
Minus 1 Spec., AOI, flashback,
   F:Bishop 3.00
TPB Best of What If?. 13.00

WHAT IF
Dec., 2004
1-shot Aunt May Had Died Instead
   Of Uncle Ben. 3.00
1-shot Karen Page Had Lived 3.00
1-shot Jessica Jones Had Joined
   The Avengers 3.00
1-shot Magneto Had Formed the
   X-Men with Professor X 3.00
1-shot Dr. Doom Had Become
   The Thing 3.00
1-shot General Ross Had Become
   The Hulk 3.00
1-shot Wha...Huh? (2005) 4.00
TPB Vol. 1 . . . . 20.00

WHAT IF?
Dec., 2005
1 Fantastic Four were cosmonauts 3.00
2 Stephen Rogers/Captain America 3.00
3 Thor transformed into Herald
   of Galactus 3.00
4 Public Enemy Number One. 3.00
5 Namor grew up on land. 3.00
6 Samurai Devil Who Dares 3.00
TPB Mirror Mirror 17.00

WHAT IF?
Nov., 2006
Avengers Disassembled #1 . . . . 4.00
Spider-Man #1 . . . . 3.00
Wolverine Enemy of the State #1 . . 3.00

WHAT THE -?!
[Parodies]
Aug., 1988
1 . . . . 5.00
2 JBy,JOy,AW,. 4.00
3 TM,. 5.00
4 . . . . 3.00
5 EL,JLe,WPo,Wolverine 5.00
6 Wolverine,Punisher 3.00
7 . . . . 2.50
8 DK 2.50
9 . . . . 2.50
10 JBy,X-Men,Dr.Doom, Cap.
   America 2.50
11 DK,RLd(part). 2.50
12 Conan, F.F.,Wolverine. 2.50
13 Silver Burper,F.F.,Wolverine. . . . 2.50
14 Spittle-Man 2.50
15 Capt.Ultra,Wolverina 2.50
16 Ant Man,Watcher 2.50

17 Wulverean/Pulverizer,Hoagl/
   Spider-Ham,Sleep Gawker,F.F. . 2.50
18. . . . . 2.50
19. . . . . 2.50
20 Infinity Wart Crossover 2.50
21 Weapon XX,Toast Rider 2.50
22 F:Echs Farce 2.50
23. . . . . 2.50
24 Halloween issue 2.50
25 . . . . 2.50
26 Spider-Man 2099 . . . . 2.50
Summer Spec. 2.50
Fall Spec. 2.50

WHERE CREATURES ROAM
July, 1970—Sept., 1971
1 JK,SD,DAy,B:Reprints
   The Brute That Walks 40.00
2 JK,SD,Midnight/Monster 25.00
3 JK,SD,DAy,Thorg 25.00
4 JK,SD,Vandoom 25.00
5 JK,SD,Gorgilla 25.00
6 JK,SD,Zog 25.00
7 SD 25.00
8 The Mummy's Secret,E:Reprints 25.00

WHERE MONSTERS DWELL
Jan., 1970
1 JK,SD,B:Reprints,Cyclops 50.00
2 JK,Sporr 35.00
3 JK,Grottu 35.00
4 . . . . 35.00
5 JK,Taboo 35.00
6 JK,Groot 35.00
7 JK,Rommbu 35.00
8 JK,SD,The Four-Armed Men . 35.00
9 JK,Bumbu 35.00
10 JK,SD,Monster That Walks
   Like A Man. 35.00
11 JK,Gruto 25.00
12 JK,GC,SD,Orogo,giant-size . . . 40.00
13 JK,The Thing That Crawl 25.00
14 JK,The Green Thing 25.00
15 JK,JSe,Kraa- The Inhuman 25.00
16 JK,Beware the Son Of Goom . . 25.00
17 SD,The Hidden Vampires 25.00
18 SD,The Mask of Morghum 25.00
19 SD,The Insect Man. 25.00
20 Klagg 25.00
21 Fln Fang Foom 25.00
22 Elektro. 25.00
23 SD,The Monster Waits For Me . 25.00
24 SD,The Things on
   Easter Island 25.00
25 SD,The Ruler of the Earth 25.00
26 . . . . 25.00
27 . . . . 25.00
28 Droom,The Living Lizard. 25.00
29 thru 37 Reprints . . . . @25.00
38 AW,reprints, Oct., 1975. . . . . . . 25.00

WHIP WILSON
See: BLAZE CARSON

WHITE TIGER
Nov., 2006
1 A Hero's compulsion 3.00

WILD
Marvel Atlas, Feb., 1954
1 BEv,JMn,Charlie Chan
   Parody. 350.00
2 BEv,RH,JMn,Witches(c). 200.00
3 CBu(c),BEv,RH,JMn, ... 175.00
4 GC,Didja Ever See a Cannon
   Brawl 175.00
5 RH,JMn,Aug., 1954 . . . . 175.00

WILD CARDS
Epic, Sept., 1990
1 JG 5.50
2 JG,V:Jokers 4.50
3 A:Turtle. 4.50

WILDC.A.T.S/X-MEN: THE DARK AGE
Dec., 1997
1-shot MtB,WEI,V:Daemonites
   & Sentinels, 48-pg. 4.50
1a variant cover MGo 4.50

WILD THING
Marvel UK, 1993
1 A:Virtual Reality Venom and
   Carnage. 3.00
2 A:VR Venom and Carnage 2.25
3 A:Shield 2.25
4 . . . . 2.25
5 Virtual Reality Gangs. 2.25
6 Virtual Reality Villians 2.25
7 V:Track. 2.26
8 . . . . 2.25
9 . . . . 2.25
10 . . . . 2.25
11 . . . . 2.25
12 . . . . 2.25
13 . . . . 2.25

WILD THING
Aug., 1999
1 RLm,AM,LHa,F:Wolverine's
   daughter Rina 2.25
2A RLm,AM,LHa,Bloody
   Reunions 2.25
2B variant AW (c) 2.25
3 RLm,AM,LHa,A:Rina 2.25
4 RLm,AM,LHa 2.25
5 RLm,AM,LHa,V:Robot monster . . 2.25

WILD WEST
Spring, 1948
1 SSh(c),B:Two Gun Kids,Tex
   Taylor,Arizona Annie. 450.00
2 SSh(c),CCb, Captain Tootsie. . 300.00
Becomes:

WILD WESTERN
1948
3 SSh(c),B:Tex Morgan,Two Gun
   Kid,Tex Taylor,Arizona Annie 350.00

Wild Western #3
© Marvel Entertainment Group

MARVEL

MARVEL

4 Rh,SSh,CCB,Capt. Tootsie.
  A:Kid Colt,E:Arizona Annie . . 250.00
5 RH,CCB,SSh,Captain Tootsie
  A;Black Rider,Blaze Carson . 300.00
6 A:Blaze Carson,Kid Colt 200.00
7 Two-Gun Kid 200.00
  Kid,Tex Taylor,Arizona Annie 350.00
8 RH 200.00
9 Ph(c),B:Black Rider,
  Tex Morgan 225.00
10 Ph(c), Black Rider. 250.00
11 Black Rider 200.00
12 Black Rider 200.00
13 Black Rider 200.00
14 Prairie Kid,Black Rider 175.00
15 Black Rider 175.00
16 thru 18 Black Rider . . . . . . @175.00
19 Black Rider 185.00
20 thru 29 Kid Colt . . . . @150.00
30 JKa, Kid Colt. 150.00
31 thru 40. . . . . @100.00
41 thru 47. . . . . @100.00
48 AW 125.00
49 thru 53 . . . . @100.00
54 AW 125.00
55 AW 125.00
56 and 57 Sept., 1957 . . . . . . @100.00

WILLIAM SHATNER'S TEK WORLD
1992–94
1 LS,Novel adapt. 2.25
2 LS,Novel adapt.cont. 2.25
3 LS,Novel adapt.cont. 2.25
4 LS,Novel adapt.cont. 2.25
5 LS,Novel adapt.concludes. 2.25
6 LS,V:TekLords 2.25
7 E:The Angel 2.25
8 . . . . 2.25
9 . . . . 2.25
10 . . . . 2.25
11 thru 17 . . . . @2.25
18 . . . . 2.25
19 Sims of the Father#1 . . . . 2.25
20 Sims of the Father#2 . . . . 2.25
21 Who aren't in Heaven 2.25
22 Father and Guns 2.25
23 We'll be Right Back 2.25
24 . . . . 2.25

WILLIE COMICS
See: IDEAL COMICS

WILLIE THE WISE-GUY
Marvel Atlas, 1957
1 MMe. 125.00

WILLOW
Aug., 1988
1 Movie adapt. 3.00
2 Movie adapt. 3.00
3 Movie adapt,Oct., 1988. . . . . . . 3.00

WISDOM
Nov., 2006
1 F:Pete Wisdom 4.00

WITCHES
June, 2004
1 MD2,F:Kale,Topaz,Satana 3.00
2 MD2,F:Kale,Topaz,Satana 3.00
3 MD2 . . . . 3.00
4 MD2 . . . . 3.00
TPB Vol. 1 . . . . 10.00

WITNESS, THE
Sept., 1948
1 . . . . 3,000.00

WOLFPACK
Aug., 1988
1 I:Wolfpack 10.00
2 thru 11 . . . . @2.50
12 July, 1988 . . . . 2.50

WOLVERINE
[Limited Series] Sept., 1982
1 B:CCl(s),FM,JRu,A:Mariko,
  I:Shingen 75.00
2 FM,JRu,A:Mariko,I:Yukio . . . 50.00
3 FM,JRu,A:Mariko,Yukio 50.00
4 B:CCl(s),FM,JRu,A:Mariko,
  D:Shingen 55.00

[Regular Series] 1988
1 JB,AW,V:Banipur 50.00
2 JB,KJ,V:Silver Samurai 25.00
3 JB,AW,V:Silver Samurai 17.00
4 JB,AW,I:Roughouse,
  Bloodsport 17.00
5 JB,AW,V:Roughouse,
  Bloodsport 17.00
6 JB,AW,V:Roughouse,
  Bloodsport 17.00
7 JB,A:Hulk 17.00
8 JB,A:Hulk 17.00
9 GC,Old Wolverine Story 17.00
10 JB,BSz,V:Sabretooth
  (1st battle) 35.00
11 JB,BSz,B:Gehenna Stone . . . 10.00
12 JB,BSz,Gehenna Stone 10.00
13 JB,BSz,Gehenna Stone 10.00
14 JB,BSz,Gehenna Stone 10.00
15 JB,BSz,Gehenna Stone 10.00
16 JB,BSz,E:Gehenna Stone. . . . 10.00
17 JBy,KJ,V:Roughouse 10.00
18 JBy,KJ,V:Roughouse 10.00
19 JBy,KJ,A of V,I:La Bandera . . . 10.00
20 JBy,KJ,A of V,V:Tigershark . . . 7.00
21 JBy,KJ,V:Geist 7.00
22 JBy,KJ,V:Geist,Spore 7.00
23 JBy,KJ,V:Geist,Spore 7.00
24 GC,Snow Blind 6.00
25 JB,O:Wolverine(part) 6.00
26 KJ,Return to Japan 6.00
27 thru 30 Lazarus Project 6.00
31 MS,DGr,A:Prince o'Mandripoor . 6.00
32 MS,DGr,V:Ninjas. 6.00
33 MS,Wolverine in Japan. 6.00
34 MS,DGr,Wolverine in Canada. . . 6.00
35 MS,DGr,A:Puck. 6.00
36 MS,DGr,A:Puck,Lady D'strike. . . 6.00
37 MS,DGr,V:Lady Deathstrike . . . 6.00
38 MS,DGr,A:Storm,I:Elsie Dee . . . 6.00
39 MS,DGr,Wolverine Vs. Clone . . . 6.00
40 MS,DGr,Wolverine Vs. Clone . . . 6.00
41 MS,DGr,R:Sabretooth,
  A:Cable 8.00
41a 2nd printing 2.25
42 MS,DGr,A:Sabretooth,Cable. . . 9.00
42a 2nd printing 2.50
43 MS,DGr,A:Sabretooth,C:Cable . . 7.00
44 LSn,DGr 6.00
45 MS,DGr,A:Sabretooth 7.00
46 MS,DGr,A:Sabretooth 7.00
47 V:Tracy 6.00
48 LHa(s),MS,DGr,B:Shiva
  Scenario 6.00
49 LHa(s),MS,DGr, ... 6.00
50 LHa(s),MS,DGr,A:X-Men,Nick Fury,
  I:Shiva,Slash-Die Cut(c) 8.00
51 MS,DGr,A:Mystique,X-Men. . . . 5.00
52 MS,DGr,A:Mystique,V:Spiral . . . 5.00
53 MS,A:Mystique,V:Spiral,Mojo . . 5.00
54 A:Shatterstar 5.00
55 MS,V:Cylla,A:Gambit,Sunfire . . . 5.00
56 MS,A:Gambit,Sunfire,V:Hand,
  Hydra 5.00
57 MS,D:Lady Mariko,A:Gambit . . . 5.50
58 A:Terror 5.00
59 A:Terror 5.00

Wolverine #75
© *Marvel Entertainment Group*

60 Sabretooth vs.Shiva,
  I:John Wraith 5.00
61 MT,History of Wolverine and
  Sabretooth,A:John Wraith 5.00
62 MT,A:Sabretooth,Silver Fox 5.00
63 MT,V:Ferro,D:Silver Fox 5.00
64 MPa,V:Ferro,Sabretooth 5.00
65 MT,A:Professor X 5.00
66 MT,A:X-Men 5.00
67 MT,A:X-Men 5.00
68 MT,V:Epsilon Red 5.00
69 DT,A:Rogue,V:Sauron,tie-in to
  X-Men#300 . . . . 5.00
70 DT,Sauron,A:Rogue,Jubilee 5.00
71 DT,V:Sauron,Brain Child,
  A:Rogue, Jubilee 5.00
72 DT,Sentinels 5.00
73 DT,V:Sentinels 5.00
74 ANi,V:Sentinels 5.00
75 AKu,Hologram(c),Wolv.has
  Bone Claws,leaves X-Men . . . 10.00
76 DT(c),B:LHa(s),A:Deathstrike,
  Vindicator,C:Puck 5.00
77 AKu,A:Vindicator,Puck,V:Lady
  Deathstrike 5.00
78 AKu,V:Cylla,Bloodscream 5.00
79 AKu,V:Cyber,I:Zoe Culloden 5.00
80 IaC,V:Cyber, ... 5.00
81 IaC,V:Cyber,A:Excalibur 5.00
82 AKu,BMc,A:Yukio,Silver
  Samurai 5.00
83 AKu,A:Alpha Flight 5.00
84 A:Alpha Flight 5.00
85 Phalanx Covenant, Final Sanction,
  V:Phalanx,holografx(c) 5.50
85a newsstand ed. 5.00
86 AKu,V:Bloodscream 3.00
87 AKu,deluxe,V:Juggernaut 3.00
87a newsstand ed. 3.00
88 AKu,deluxe ed. 3.00
88a newsstand ed. 3.00
89 deluxe ed. 3.00
89a newsstand ed. 2.00
90 V:Sabretooth, deluxe ed. 4.00
90a newsstand ed. 2.00
91 LHa,Logan's future unravels. . . . 3.00
92 LHa,AKu,DGr,A:Sabretooth 3.00
93 R:Cyber. 3.00
94 Feral Wolverine. 3.00
95 LHa,AKu,DGr,V:Dark Riders . . . 3.00
96 LHa,Aku,DGr,Death of Cyber . . . 3.00
97 LHa,AKu,DGr,A:Genesis. 3.00
98 LHa,AKu,F:Genesis 3.00
99 . . . . 3.00

All comics prices listed are for *Near Mint* condition.

Wolverine #125
© Marvel Entertainment Group

100 LHa,AKu,DGA:Elektra;double-
   size, Foil Hologram cover 12.00
100a regular edition 4.00
101 LHa,AKu,A:Elektra 3.00
102 LHa 3.00
103 LHa,Elektra,A:Onslaught 3.00
104 LHa,Gateway, Onslaught 3.00
105 LHa,Gateway, Elektra 3.00
106 LHa 3.00
107 LHa,VS,prologue to Elektra#1 . 3.00
108 LHa,back to Tokyo,A:Yukio 3.00
109 LHa,DG, ... 3.00
110 LHa,DG,Who's spying on
   Logan 3.00
111 LHa,DG,Logan moves to NYC . 3.00
112 LHa,DG,Logan in NYC 3.00
113 LHa,R:Ogun,A:Lady Deathstrike
   & Spiral 3.00
114 LHa,back in costume,V:Cyborg
   Donald Pierce 3.00
115 LHa,Zero Tolerance,V:Bastion . 3.00
116 LHa,Zero Tolerance, ... 3.00
117 LHa,Zero Tolerance, V:Prime
   Sentinels 3.00
118 LHa,Zero Tolerance aftermath . 3.00
119 WEI,Pt.1 (of 4) 3.00
120 WEI,The White Ghost 3.00
121 WEI,Not Yet Dead, pt.3 . . . . . . 3.00
122 WEI,Not Yet Dead, pt.4 . . . . . . 3.00
123 TDF,DCw,R:Roughouse,
   Bloodscream 3.00
124 TDF,DCw,A:Captain America,
   V:Rascal 3.00
125 CCl,V:Viper,48-pg. 7.50
125a Dynamic Forces (c). 6.50
126 CCl,V:Sabretooth 3.50
127 CCl,Sabretooth takes over 3.00
128 CCl,V:Hydra, The Hand 3.00
129 TDz,A:Wendigo 3.00
130 TDz,V:Viper 3.00
131 TDz,V:Viper 3.00
131a Uncensored 12.00
132 TDz,Halloween in SalemCenter 3.00
133 EL,JMs,F:Warbird 3.00
133a variant EL cover (1:4) 6.00
134 EL,JMs,V:Big Apple heroes . . . 3.00
135 EL,JMs,Joins Starjammers 3.00
136 EL,JMs,on prison planet 3.00
137 EL,JMs,V:The Collector 3.00
138 EL,JMs,Great Escape concl. . . 3.00
139 EL,A:Cable 3.00
140 EL,Xavier paranoid 3.00
141 EL,Wolverine paranoid 3.00
142 EL,R:Alpha Flight 3.00
143 EL,A:Alpha Flight 3.00

144 EL,A:Hercules,V:Leader 3.00
145 EL,25th Anniv. 48-pg. 8.00
145A Foil Stamped (c) 25.00
146 EL 25.00
147 FaN 15.00
148 EL,Ages of Apocalypse,pt.3 . . 10.00
149 EL,mutant no more? 3.00
150 X-Men: Revolution 5.00
150a variant (c) 8.00
151 SSr,V:Lord Haan 3.00
152 SSr,Lord Haan, Gom 3.00
153 SSr,Kia 3.00
154 RLd,ErS,Deadpool 3.00
155 RLd,Watchtower,Siryn 3.00
156 RLd,IaC,F:Spider-Man 3.00
157 RLd,IaC,F:Spider-Man 3.00
158 RLd,IaC,V:Administrator 3.00
159 SCh,V:Mr.X 3.00
160 SCh,V:Lady Killers,Mr.X 3.00
161 SCh,V:Mr.X 3.00
162 SCh,A:Sabretooth 3.00
163 SCh,F:Beast 3.00
164 SCh,F:Beast 3.00
165 SCh,NRd,trapped 3.50
166 SCh,NRd,BWS,48-page 10.00
167 DaF,NRd,BWS(c),V:Viper 2.50
168 DaF,NRd,F:Patch 2.50
169 DaF,NRd,Bloodsport,concl. . . . 2.50
170 SCh,NRd,Stay Alive,pt.1 . . . . . . 2.50
171 SCh,NRd,V:Wendigo,'Nuff Said 2.50
172 SCh,NRd,Stay Alive,pt.3 . . . . . . 2.50
173 SCh,NRd,in Las Vegas 2.50
174 SCh,NRd,Amiko & Yukio 2.50
175 SCh,NRd,Omega Red,48-pg. . . 4.00
176 SCh,NRd, ... 2.25
177 SCh,DaF,Shadow Pulpit,pt.1 . . 2.25
178 SCh,DaF,Shadow Pulpit,pt.2 . . 2.25
179 SCh&MRd(c),R:Alpha Flight . . . 2.25
180 AKu(c) 2.25
181 SCh, new direction 2.25
182 SCh,TP 2.25
183 SCh,, 48-pg. 3.50
184 SCh,When Animals Attack 2.25
185 SCh,When Animals Attack 2.25
186 SCh,V:Punisher, Round 2 . . . . . 3.00
187 JMC 2.25
188 pt.1 . . . . 2.25
189 pt.2 . . . . 2.25
Ann. '97 JOs,V:Volk 4.00
Ann.1999 F:Deadpool, 48-pg. 4.00
Ann.2000 48-page 4.00
Ann.2001 48-page 3.50
Spec. '95 LHa,F:Nightcrawler 4.00
Spec.Minus 1, LHa,CNn, flashback,
   F:Weapon X 2.25

Wolverine #140
© Marvel Entertainment Group

Spec.Global Jeapordy,PDd(s) 3.00
Spec.Save the Tiger,rep. 3.00
Spec.Winter Spec. MWa B&W 3.00
Spec.JungleAdventure,MMi,deluxe . 5.50
1-shot Bloodlust,AD,V:Siberian
   Were-Creatures 6.00
GN Acts of Vengeance, rep. 7.00
GN Black Rio, 48-page 6.00
GN Bloody ChoicesJB,A:N.Fury . . 13.00
GN Inner Fury,BSz,V:Nanotech
   Machines 6.25
GN Killing, KSW,JNR 6.00
GN Rahne of Terror, C:Cable 8.00
GN Scorpio Rising, T.U.Fury 6.00
GN Typhoid's Kiss,rep. 7.00
GN Bloodhungry SK 7.00
TPB Wolverine rep. Marvel Comics
   Presents #1–#10 . . . . 13.00
TPB Triumphs & Tragedies 17.00
TPB Not Dead Yet 15.00
TPB Wolverine:Weapon X,BWS . . 16.00
TPB Blood Debt, 112-page 13.00
TPB Wolverine/Gambit: Victims. . . 13.00
TPB Wolverine/Deadpool:
   WeaponX 22.00
TPB The Best There Is 13.00
TPB Legends, Vol. 3 . . . . 13.00
TPB Legends, Vol. 4:Xisle 14.00
TPB Snikt, Vol. 5 . . . . 14.00

WOLVERINE
May, 2003

1 DaR,Brothers,pt.1, relaunch 3.50
2 DaR,Brothers,pt.2 . . . . 2.25
3 DaR,Brothers,pt.3 . . . . 2.25
4 DaR,Brothers,pt.4 . . . . 2.25
5 DaR,Brothers,pt.5 . . . . 2.25
6 DaR,F:Nightcrawler 2.25
7 Coyote Crossing,pt.1 . . . . 2.25
8 Coyote Crossing,pt.2 . . . . 2.25
9 Coyote Crossing,pt.3 . . . . 2.25
10 Coyote Crossing,pt.4 . . . . 2.25
11 Coyote Crossing,concl. 2.25
12 Dreams 2.25
13 DaR,Feral,pt.1 . . . . 2.25
14 DaR,Feral,pt 2 . . . . 2.25
15 DaR,Return of the Native,pt.3 . . 2.25
16 DaR,Return of the Native,pt.4 . . 2.25
17 DaR,Return of the Native,pt.5 . . 2.25
18 DaR,Return of the Native,pt.6 . . 2.25
19 DaR,Return of the Native,pt.7 . . 2.25
20 JR2,Enemy of the State,pt.1 . . . 3.00
21 JR2,Enemy of the State,pt.2 . . . 3.00
22 MMr,JR2,Enemy of the State . . . 3.00
23 MMr,JR2,Enemy of the State . . . 2.25
24 MMr,JR2,Enemy of the State . . . 2.25
25 MMr,JR2,Enemy of the State . . . 2.25
26 MMr,JR2,Agent of S.H.I.E.L.D. . . 2.25
26a variant MS(c) 10.00
27 MMr,JR2,Agent of S.H.I.E.L.D. . . 2.25
28 MMr,JR2,Agent of S.H.I.E.L.D. . . 2.25
29 MMr,JR2,Agent of S.H.I.E.L.D. . . 2.50
30 MMr,JR2,Agent of S.H.I.E.L.D. . . 2.50
31 MMr,JR2,Agent of S.H.I.E.L.D. . . 2.50
32 MMr,Prisoner Number Zero 2.50
33 Chasing Ghosts,pt.1 . . . . 2.50
34 Chasing Ghosts,pt.2 . . . . 2.50
35 Chasing Ghosts,pt.3 . . . . 2.50
36 Origins and Endings,pt.1 . . . . . . 2.50
37 Origins and Endings,pt.2 . . . . . . 2.50
38 Origins and Endings,pt.3 . . . . . . 2.50
39 Origins and Endings,pt.4 . . . . . . 2.50
40 Origins and Endings,pt.5 . . . . . . 3.00
41 The Package, 48-pg. 4.00
42 Vendetta,pt.1, Civil War tie-in . . . 5.00
43 Vendetta,pt.2, Civil War tie-in . . . 3.50
44 Vendetta,pt.3, Civil War tie-in . . . 3.50
45 Vendetta,pt.4, Civil War tie-in . . . 3.00
46 Vendetta,pt.5, Civil War tie-in . . . 3.00
47 Vendetta,pt.6, Civil War tie-in . . . 3.00
48 Vendetta epilogue 3.00
TPB Vol. 1 The Brotherhood 13.00

All comics prices listed are for *Near Mint* condition.

TPB Vol. 2 Coyote Crossing 12.00
TPB Vol. 3 Return of the Native . . 18.00
TPB Legends,Vol. 6 . . . . 20.00
Spec. Marvel Must Have, rep.
 #20–#22 Enemy of the State 4.00
TPB Vol. 1: Enemy of the State . . . 15.00

*Wolverine & Punisher: Damaging
Evidence #2 © Marvel Ent. Group*

WOLVERINE & PUNISHER: DAMAGING EVIDENCE
1993
1 B:CP(s),GEr,A:Kingpin 3.00
2 GEr,A:Kingpin,Sniper 3.00
3 GEr,Last issue 3.00

WOLVERINE/ CAPTAIN AMERICA
March, 2004
1 Alien technology stolen 3.00
2 thru 4 . . . . 3.00

WOLVERINE CLASSIC
2005
TPB Wolverine Classic Vol. 1 . . . . 13.00
TPB Wolverine Classic Vol. 2 . . . . 13.00
TPB Wolverine Classic Vol. 3 . . . . 15.00
TPB Wolverine Classic Vol. 4 . . . . 15.00

WOLVERINE: DAYS OF FUTURE PAST
Oct., 1997
1 (of 3) JFM,JoB,JHo, Logan &
 Magneto in far future 2.50
2 JFM,JoB,JHo,with Jubilee 2.50
3 JFM,JoB,JHo,V:Council of the
 Chosen, concl 2.50

WOLVERINE: DOOMBRINGER
Nov., 1997
1-shot DgM,JP,F:Silver Samurai . . . 3.00

WOLVERINE/DOOP
May, 2003
1 (of 2) 3.00
2 . . . . 3.00

WOLVERINE ENCYCLOPEDIA
Vol. 1 AKu(c) 48-pg 8.50
Vol. 2 48-pg 6.50
Vol. 3 48-pg 6.50

WOLVERINE: THE END
Nov., 2003
1 (of 6) CCt 10.00
2 thru 3 CCt . . . . @5.00
4 thru 6 CCt . . . . @3.50

WOLVERINE/GAMBIT: VICTIMS
1995
1 Takes Place in London 3.00
2 Is Wolverine the Killer? 3.00
3 V:Mastermind 3.00
4 conclusion 3.00

WOLVERINE/HULK
Feb., 2002
1 (of 4) SK, and a girl named Po . . 3.50
2 SK,snowy wasteland 3.50
3 SK,ghostly little girl 3.50
4 SK,concl 3.50
TPB series rep 10.00

WOLVERINE/NETSUKE
Sept., 2002
1 (of 4) GgP, Wolverine Samurai . . 3.00
2 GgP 4.00
3 GgP 4.00
4 GgP, concl 4.00

WOLVERINE ORIGINS
Apr., 2006
1 SDi 30.00
2 SDi 12.00
3 SDi,Born in Blood 9.00
4 SDi,Born in Blood 5.00
5 SDi,Born in Blood 5.00
6 SDi,Savior, pt.1 . . . . 5.00
7 SDi,Savior, pt.2 . . . . 4.00
8 SDi,Savior, pt.3 . . . . 4.00

WOLVERINE/PUNISHER
March 2004
1 (of 5) LW 3.00
2 thru 5 LW . . . . @3.00
TPB Vol. 1 . . . . 14.00

WOLVERINE/PUNISHER: REVELATION
Apr. 1999
1 (of 4) TSg,PtL,Revelation 3.00
1a signed 30.00
2 TSg,PtL,V:Revelation 3.00
3 TSg,PtL,V:Revelation 3.00
4 TsG,PtL,V:Revelation,concl 3.00
TPB rep 15.00

WOLVERINE SAGA
Sept., 1989
1 RLd(c), ... 6.50
2 . . . . 5.50
3 . . . . 5.50
4 Dec., 1989 . . . . 5.50

WOLVERINE: SNIKT!
May, 2003
1 (of 5) 3.00
2 alien landscape 3.00
3 . . . . 3.00
4 V:Mandate aliens 3.00
5 Concl 3.00

WOLVERINE: SOULTAKER
March, 2005
1 (of 5) Mark of Mana 3.00
2 Mark of Mana 3.00
3 V:demon-lord Ryuki 3.00
4 V:Hana,Ryuki 3.00
5 Finale 3.00
TPB Soultaker 14.00

WOLVERINE: X-ISLE
April, 2003
1 (of 5) A:Amiko 2.50
2 thru 5 . . . . @2.50

WOMEN OF MARVEL
Aug., 2006
TPB 25.00

WONDER DUCK
Sept., 1949
1 Whale(c) 175.00
2 . . . . 125.00
3 March, 1950 . . . . 125.00

WONDERMAN
March, 1986
1 KGa,one-shot special 3.00

WONDER MAN
Sept., 1991
1 B:GJ(s),JJ,V:Goliath 2.50
2 JJ,A:West Coast Avengers 2.25
3 JJ,V:Abominatrix,I:Spider 2.25
4 JJ,I:Splice,A:Spider 2.25
5 JJ,A:Beast,V:Rampage 2.25
6 JJ,A:Beast,V:Rampage 2.25
7 JJ,Galactic Storm,pt.4,
 A:Hulk & Rich Jones 2.25
8 JJ,GalacticStorm,pt.11,A:Vision . . 2.25
9 JJ,GalacticStorm,pt.18,A:Vision . . 2.25
10 JJ,V:Khmer Rouge 2.25
11 V:Angkor 2.25
12 V:Angkor 2.25
13 Infinity War 2.25
14 Infinity War,V:Warlock 2.25
15 Inf.War,V:Doppleganger 2.25
16 JJ,I:Armed Response,
 A:Avengers West Coast 2.25
17 JJ,A:Avengers West Coast 2.25
18 V:Avengers West Coast 2.25
19 . . . . 2.25
20 V:Splice,Rampage 2.25
21 V:Splice,Rampage 2.25
22 JJ,V:Realm of Death 2.25
23 JJ,A:Grim Reaper,Mephisto 2.25
24 JJ,V:Grim Reaper,Goliath 2.25
25 JJ,N:Wonder Man,D:Grim Reaper,
 V:Mephisto 3.25
26 A:Hulk,C:Furor,Plan Master 2.25
27 A:Hulk 2.25
28 RoR,A:Spider-Man 2.25
29 RoR,A:Spider-Man 2.25
30 V:Hate Monger 2.25
31 . . . . 2.25
32 . . . . 2.25
33 . . . . 2.25
Spec.#1 (1985),KGa 3.00
Ann.#1 System Bytes #3 . . . . 2.25
Ann.#2 I:Hit-Maker,w/card 3.00

WORLD CHAMPIONSHIP WRESTLING
1 F:Lex Luger,Sting 2.25
2 . . . . 2.25
3 . . . . 2.25
4 Luger Vs El Gigante 2.25
5 Rick Rude Vs. Sting 2.25
6 F:Dangerous Alliance,R.Rude . . . 2.25

7 F:Steiner Brothers 2.25
8 F:Sting,Dangerous Alliance 2.25
9 Bunkhouse Brawl. 2.25
10 Halloween Havoc 2.25
11 Sting vs Grapplers. 2.25
12 F:Ron Simmons 2.25

World of Fantasy #2
© Marvel Entertainment Group

WORLD OF FANTASY
Marvel Atlas, May, 1956
1 The Secret of the Mountain . . . 750.00
2 JMn,AW,Inside the Tunnel. . . . 400.00
3 DAy,SC, The Man in the Cave. 350.00
4 BEv(c),BP,JF,Back to the
    Lost City 275.00
5 BEv(c),BP,In the Swamp 275.00
6 BEv(c),RP,The Strange Wife
    of Henry Johnson 275.00
7 BEv(c),GM,Man in Grey 275.00
8 GM,JO,MF,The Secret of the
    Black Cloud 300.00
9 BEv,BK. 275.00
10 . . . . 275.00
11 AT 200.00
12 BEv(c). 200.00
13 BEv,JO 200.00
14 JMn(c),GM,JO,CI,JM 200.00
15 JK(c) 200.00
16 AW,SD,JK 275.00
17 JK(c),SD 275.00
18 JK(c) 275.00
19 JK(c),SD,Aug., 1959. . . . . 275.00

WORLD OF MYSTERY
Marvel Atlas, 1956–57
1 BEv(c),AT,JO,The Long Wait . 650.00
2 BEv(c),The Man From
    Nowhere 250.00
3 SD,AT,JDa, The Bugs 300.00
4 SD(c),BP,What Happened in
    the Basement 300.00
5 JO,She Stands in Shadows . . 250.00
6 AW,SD,GC,Sinking Man 300.00
7 GC,JSe,Pick A Door 250.00

WORLD OF SUSPENSE
Marvel Atlas, April, 1956
1 JO,BEv,JMn,A Stranger
    Among Us 500.00
2 SD,LC,JMN(c),When Walks
    the Scarecrow 300.00
3 AW,JMN(c),The Man Who
    Couldn't Be Touched 300.00

4 Something is in This House . . 225.00
5 BEv,DH,JO. 225.00
6 BEv(c),BP 225.00
7 AW,The Face 300.00
8 Prisoner of the Ghost Ship . . . 225.00

WORLD'S GREATEST SONGS
Marvel Atlas, 1954
1 Eddie Fisher, Frank Sinatra. . . 500.00

WORLDS UNKNOWN
May, 1973
1 GK,AT,The Coming of the
    Martians,Reprints 30.00
2 GK,TS,A Gun For A Dinosaur . . 20.00
3 The Day the Earth Stood
    Still. 20.00
4 JB,Arena 20.00
5 DA,JM,Black Destroyer 20.00
6 GK(c),The Thing Called It 20.00
7 GT,The Golden Voyage of
    Sinbad,Part 1 . . . . 20.00
8 The Golden Voyage of
    Sinbad,Part 2, Aug., 1974 . . . 20.00

WYATT EARP
Marvel Atlas, Nov., 1955
1 JMn,F:Wyatt Earp 250.00
2 AW,Saloon(c). 150.00
3 JMn(c),The Showdown,
    A:Black Bart 125.00
4 Ph(c),Hugh O'Brian,JSe,
    India Sundown 125.00
5 Ph(c),Hugh O'Brian,DW,
    Gun Wild Fever 125.00
6 BEv(c) 125.00
7 AW 125.00
8 JMn,Wild Bill Hickok 125.00
9 and 10 . . . . @125.00
11 . . . . 125.00
12 AW,JMn 125.00
13 . . . . 100.00
14 . . . . 100.00
15 thru 20 . . . . @100.00
21 JDa(c). 100.00
22 thru 29. . . . . @100.00
30 AW,Reprints 35.00
31 thru 33 Reprints . . . . @30.00
34 June, 1973 . . . . 30.00

XAVIER INSTITUTE ALUMNI YEARBOOK
GN 48-pg. (1996). 6.00

X-CALIBRE
1995
1 Excaliber After Xavier 4.00
2 V:Callisto & Morlock Crew. 3.00
3 D:Juggernaut. 3.00
4 Secret Weapon 3.00
TPB Rep.#1-#4 . . . . 9.00

X-FACTOR
Feb., 1986
1 WS(c),JG,BL,JRu,I:X-Factor,
    Rusty 10.00
2 JG,BL,I:Tower. 5.00
3 JG,BL,V:Tower 5.00
4 KP,JRu,V:Frenzy 5.00
5 JG,JRu,I:Alliance of Evil,
    C:Apocalypse 7.00
6 JG,BMc,I:Apocalypse. 15.00
7 JG,JRu,V:Morlocks,I:Skids. . . . 5.00
8 MS,JRu,V:Freedom Force. 5.00
9 JRu(i),V:Freedom Force
    (Mutant Massacre). 5.00

X-Factor #9
© Marvel Entertainment Group

10 WS,BWi,V:Marauders(Mut.Mass),
    A:Sabretooth 6.00
11 WS,BWi,A:Thor(Mutant Mass) . . 5.00
12 MS,BWi,V:Vanisher. 4.00
13 WS,DGr,V:Mastermold 4.00
14 WS,BWi,V:Mastermold 4.00
15 WS,BWi,D:Angel. 5.00
16 DM,JRu,V:Masque 4.00
17 WS,BWi,I:Rictor. 5.00
18 WS,BWi,V:Apocalypse 4.00
19 WS,BWi,V:Horsemen of
    Apocalypse 3.50
20 JBr,A:X-Terminators 3.50
21 WS,BWi,V:The Right. 3.50
22 SB,BWi,V:The Right 3.50
23 WS,BWi,C:Archangel 8.00
24 WS,BWi,Fall of Mutants,
    I:Archangel 14.00
25 WS,BWi,Fall of Mutants 3.50
26 WS,BWi,Fall of Mutants,
    N:X-Factor. 3.50
27 WS,BWi,Christmas Issue 3.50
28 WS,BWi,V:Ship. 3.50
29 WS,BWi,V:Infectia. 3.50
30 WS,BWi,V:Infectia,Free.Force . . 3.50
31 WS,BWi,V:Infectia,Free.Force . . 3.50
32 SLi,A:Avengers 3.50
33 WS,BWi,V:Tower & Frenzy,
    R:Furry Beast 3.50
34 WS,BWi,I:Nanny,
    Orphan Maker 3.50
35 JRu(i),WS(c),V:Nanny,
    Orphan Maker 3.50
36 WS,BWi,Inferno,V:Nastirh. 3.50
37 WS,BWi,Inferno,V:Gob.Queen . . 3.50
38 WS,AM,Inferno,A:X-Men,D:
    MadelynePryor(GoblinQueen). . 3.50
39 WS,AM,Inferno,A:X-Men,
    V:Mr.Sinister. 3.50
40 RLd,AM,O:Nanny,Orphan Maker
    1st Liefeld Marvel work 6.00
41 AAd,AM,I:Alchemy 3.50
42 AAd,AM,A:Alchemy 3.50
43 PS,AM,V:Celestials. 3.50
44 PS,AM,V:Rejects. 3.50
45 PS,AM,V:Rask 3.50
46 PS,AM,V:Rejects. 3.50
47 KD,AM,V:Father 3.50
48 thru 49 PS,AM,V:Rejects 3.50
50 RLd&TM(c),RB,AM,A:Prof.X
    (double sized),BU:Apocalypse . 5.00
51 AM,V:Sabretooth,Caliban 4.00
52 RLd(c),AM,V:Sabretooth,
    Caliban 3.00

MARVEL

X-Factor #103
© Marvel Entertainment Group

53 AM,V:Sabretooth,Caliban 3.00
54 MS,AM,A:Colossus,I:Crimson . . . 3.00
55 MMi(c),CDo,AM,V:Mesmero . . . 3.00
56 AM,V:Crimson 3.00
57 NKu,V:Crimson 3.00
58 JBg,AM,V:Crimson 3.00
59 AM,V:Press Gang 3.00
60 JBg,AM,X-Tinction Agenda#3 . . . 4.00
60a 2nd printing(gold) 2.50
61 JBg,AM,X-Tinction Agenda#6 . . . 3.50
62 JBg,AM,JLe(c),E:X-Agenda 3.50
63 WPo,I:Cyberpunks 3.50
64 WPo,ATb,V:Cyberpunks 3.00
65 WPo,ATb,V:Apocalypse 3.00
66 WPo,ATb,I:Askani,
    V:Apocalypse. 3.00
67 WPo,ATb,V:Apocalypse,I:Shinobi
    Shaw,D:Sebastian Shaw 3.00
68 WPo,ATb,JLe(c),V:Apocalypse,
    L:Nathan,(taken from future). . . . 3.00
69 WPo,V:Shadow King. 3.00
70 MMi(c),JRu,Last old team. 3.00
71 LSn,AM,New Team 4.00
71a 2nd printing 2.50
72 LSn,AM,Who shot Madrox
    revealed 3.00
73 LSn,AM,Mob Chaos in D.C.. . . . 3.00
74 LSn,AM,I:Slab 3.00
75 LSn,AM,I:Nasty Boys(doub.sz) . . 3.50
76 LSn,AM,A:Hulk,Pantheon 3.25
77 LSn,AM,V:Mutant Lib. Front 3.25
78 LSn,AM,V:Mutant Lib. Front 3.25
79 LSn,AM,V:Helle's Belles 3.25
80 LSn,AM,V:Helle's Belles,
    C:Cyber 3.25
81 LSn,AM,V:Helle's Belles,Cyber. . 3.25
82 JQ(c),LSn,V:Brotherhood of Evil
    Mutants,I:X-iles 3.25
83 MPa,A:X-Force,X-iles 3.25
84 JaL,X-Cutioners Song #2,
    V:X-Force,A:X-Men 3.25
85 JaL,X-Cutioners Song #6,
    Wolv.& Bishop,V:Cable 3.25
86 JaL,AM,X-Cutioner's Song#10,
    A:X-Men,X-Force,V:Stryfe 3.25
87 JQ,X-Cutioners Song
    Aftermath 3.00
88 JQ,AM,V:2nd Genegineer,
    I:Random 4.00
89 JQ,V:Mutates,Genosha. 3.00
90 JQ,AM,Genosha vs. Aznia 3.00
91 AM,V:Armageddon 3.00
92 JQ,AM,V:Fabian Cortez,
    Acolytes,hologram(c). 6.00
93 Magneto Protocols 3.00

94 PR,J:Forge 3.00
95 B:JMD(s),AM,Polaris
    Vs. Random. 3.00
96 A:Random. 3.00
97 JD,I:Haven,A:Random 3.00
98 GLz,A:Haven,A:Random. 3.00
99 JD,A:Haven,Wolfsbane returns
    to human 3.00
100 JD,Red Foil(c),V:Haven,
    D:Madrox. 6.00
100a Newstand Ed. 3.00
101 JD,AM,Aftermath. 2.50
102 JD,AM,V:Crimson Commando,
    Avalanche 2.50
103 JD,AM,A:Malice 2.50
104 JD,AM,V:Malice,
    C:Mr. Sinister. 2.50
105 JD,AM,V:Malice 2.50
106 Phalanx Covenant,Life Signs
    Holografx(c). 3.50
106a newsstand ed 2.50
107 A:Strong Guy. 2.50
108 A:Mystique, deluxe ed. 2.50
108a newsstand ed.. . . . . 2.00
109 A:Mystique,V:Legion, deluxe. . 2.50
109a newsstand ed.. . . . . 2.25
110 Invasion. 2.50
110a deluxe ed. 2.25
111 Invasion. 2.50
111a deluxe ed. 2.25
112 AM,JFM,SEp,F:Guido,Havok . . 2.50
113 A:Mystique. 2.50
114 AM,Wild Child & Mystique. . . . 2.50
115 F:Wild Child,Havok 2.50
116 F:Wild Child. 2.50
117 HMe,AM,F:Cyclops. 2.50
118 HMe,AM,A:Random,Shard . . . 2.50
119 HMe,AM,F:Sabretooth 2.50
120 A:Sabretooth 2.50
121 A:Sabretooth 2.50
122 HMe,SEp,AM,J:Sabretooth. . . 2.50
123 A:Hound 2.50
124 A:Onslaught 3.50
125 Onslaught saga, double size . . 4.00
126 Beast vs. Dark Beast 2.50
127 Mystique 2.50
128 HMe,JMs,AM,Hound Program . 2.50
129 HMe,JMs,AM,Graydon Creed's
    campaign. 2.50
130 HMe,JMs,AM,Assassination of
    Graydon Creed 2.50
131 HMe,JMs,ATi,Havok strikes
    back. 2.50
132 HMe,JMs,ATi,Break away from
    government 2.50
133 HMe,JMs,ATi,A:Multiple Man &
    Strong Guy 2.50
134 HMe,JMs,Ati,Operation X-Factor
    Underground, cont. 2.50
135 HMe,JMs,Strong Guy awakes . 2.50
136 HMe,JMs,ATi, A:Sabretooth . . . 2.50
137 HMe,JMs,ATi, Final fate of
    Shard and Polaris 2.50
138 HMe,JMs,ATi,Sabertooth,
    V:Maberick. 2.50
139 HMe,ATi,Who killed Graydon
    Creed. 2.50
140 HMe,ATi,Who killed Graydon
    Creed, A:Mystique. 2.50
141 HMe,ATi,Shard's Plan. 2.50
142 ATi,F:Wild Child. 2.50
143 HMe,ATi,Havok vs.DarkBeast. . 2.50
144 HMe,ATi,V:Brotherhood,
    Dark Beast. 2.50
145 HMe,ATi,Havok vs. X.U.E. 2.50
146 HMe,ATi,Havok, Multiple
    Man,V:Polaris 2.50
147 HMe,Havok v. Mandroids 2.50
148 F:Shard 2.50
149 HMe,Polaris & Madrox rejoin . . 3.50
Spec #1 JG,Prisoner of Love 5.00
Ann.#1 BL,BBr,V:CrimsonDynamo . 5.00

Ann.#2 TGr,JRu,A:Inhumans 4.00
Ann.#3 WS(c),AM,JRu,PC,TD,
    Evolutionary War 3.50
Ann.#4 JBy,WS,JRu,MBa,Atlantis
    Attacks,BU:Doom & Magneto . . 3.50
Ann.#5 JBg,AM,DR,GI,Days of Future
    Present,A:Fant.Four,V:Ahab. . . . 4.00
Ann.#6 Flesh Tears Saga,pt.4,
    A:X-Force, New Warriors 4.00
Ann #7 JQ,JRu,Shattershot,pt.3 . . . 4.00
Ann.#8 I:Charon,w/card 3.25
Ann.#9 JMD(s),MtB,V:Prof.Power,
    A:Prof.X,O:Haven 3.25
Minus 1 Spec., HMe,JMs,ATi,
    flashback,F:Havok. 2.50
GN X-Men: Wrath of Apocalypse,
    rep.X-Factor#65-#68 . . . . 5.00
TPB X-Factor Visionaries, PDd . . . 16.00

X-FACTOR
April, 2002
1 (of 4) When will it stop. 2.50
2 FBI agents 2.50
3 in San Francisco 2.50
4 Concl.. . . . . 2.50
TPB Vol. 1 . . . . 10.00

X-FACTOR
Dec., 2005
1 PDd(s) 4.00
2 PDd(s), Decimation tie-in. 3.00
3 PDd(s), Decimation tie-in. 3.00
4 PDd(s), Strong Guy & Wolfsbane . 3.00
5 PDd(s) 3.00
6 PDd(s), The Butterfly Defect 3.00
7 PDd(s), Two Meetings 3.00
8 PDd(s), Civil War tie-in 4.00
9 PDd(s), Civil War tie-in 4.00
10 PDd(s). 3.00
11 PDd(s). 3.00
12 PDd(s), V:Mr. Tryp & Singularity . 3.00
13 PDd(s), Re-X-Aminations 3.00

X-51
July, 1999
1 JQ&JP(c) Marvel Tech. 2.50
2 JoB,V:Brotherhood of Mutants. . . 2.50
2a variant cover 2.50
3 JoB,A:X.E.R.O. 2.50
4 JoB,A:Avengers 2.50
5 JoB,V:Vision. 2.50
6 JoB. 2.50
7 JoB,A:Sebastian Shaw 2.50
8 JoB,F:X-Men 2.50
9 JoB, ... 2.50
10 JoB,F:Machine Man 2.50
11 JoB,F:Celestial 2.50
12 JoB,final issue. 2.50

X-FORCE
Aug., 1991
1 RLd,V:Stryfe,Mutant Liberation
    Front,bagged, white on black
    graphics with X-Force Card. . . . 4.00
1a with Shatterstar Card. 4.00
1b with Deadpool Card. 4.00
1c with Sunspot & Gideon Card . . . 4.00
1d with Cable Card. 5.00
1e Unbagged Copy. 2.75
1f 2nd Printing. 2.50
2 RLd,I:New Weapon X,V:
    Deadpool 3.50
3 RLd,C:Spider-Man,
    V:Juggernaut,Black Tom 3.00
4 RLd,SpM/X-Force team-up,
    V:Juggernaut(cont.from SpM#16)
    Sideways format 3.00
5 RLd,A:Brotherhood Evil Mutants . 3.00
6 RLd,V:Bro'hood Evil Mutants. . . . 3.00
7 RLd,V:Bro'hood Evil Mutants. . . . 3.00

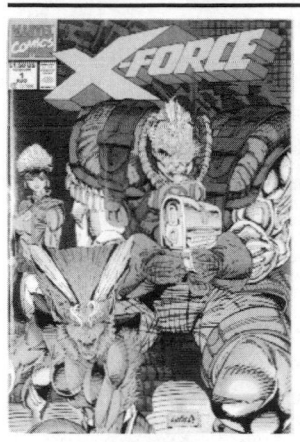

X-Force #1
© Marvel Entertainment Group

8 MMi,O:Cable(Part)............. 3.50
9 RLd,D:Sauron,Masque 3.00
10 MPa,V:Mutant Liberation Front.. 3.00
11 MPa,Deadpool Vs Domino 3.00
12 MPa,A:Weapon Prime,Gideon .. 2.50
13 MPa,V:Weapon Prime 2.50
14 TSr,V:Weapon Prime,Krule..... 2.50
15 GCa,V:Krule,Deadpool 2.50
16 GCa,X-Cutioners Song #4,
    X-Factor V:X-Force 3.00
17 GCa,X-Cutioners Song#8,
    Apocalypse V:Stryfe 3.00
18 GCa,X-Cutioners Song#12,
    Cable vs Stryfe 3.00
19 GCa,X-Cutioners Song
    Aftermath,N:X-Force 2.50
20 GCa,O:Graymalkin 2.50
21 GCa,V:War Machine,SHIELD .. 2.50
22 GCa,V:Externals 2.50
23 GCa,V:Saul,Gigeon,A:Six Pack . 2.50
24 GCa,A:Six Pack,A:Deadpool ... 2.50
25 GCa,A:Mageneto,Exodus,
    R:Cable 5.00
26 GCa(c),MtB,I:Reignfire 2.50
27 GCa(c),MtB,V:Reignfire,MLF,
    I:Moonstar,Locus 2.50
28 MtB,V:Reignfire,MLF.......... 2.50
29 MtB,V:Arcade,C:X-Treme 2.50
30 TnD,V:Arcade,A:X-Treme 2.50
31 F:Siryn..................... 2.50
32 Child's Play#1,A:New Warriors . 2.50
33 Child's Play#3,A:New Warriors,
    V:Upstarts 2.50
34 F:Rictor,Domino,Cable 3.00
35 TnD,R:Nimrod 2.50
36 TnD,V:Nimrod 2.50
37 PaP,I&D:Absalom 2.50
38 TaD,Life Signs,pt.2,
    I:Generation X, foil(c) 5.00
38a newsstand ed.............. 2.50
39 TaD 2.50
40 TaD, deluxe................ 2.50
40a newsstand ed.............. 2.50
41 TaD,O:feral,deluxe 2.50
41a newsstand ed.............. 2.25
42 Emma Frost, deluxe 2.50
42a newsstand ed.............. 2.25
43 Home is Where Heart........ 2.50
43a deluxe ed................. 2.50
44 AdP,Prof.X,X-Mansion........ 2.50
45 AdP,Caliban vs. Sabretooth ... 2.50
46 R:The Mimic 2.50
47 A:Deadpool 2.50
48 AdP,Siryn Takes Charge...... 2.50
49 ADp,MBu,Holocaust is here ... 2.50
50 AdP,MPn,F:Sebastian Shaw ... 3.00

50a prismatic foil cover 4.50
50b variant RLd(c)............. 6.00
51 AdP,MPn,V:Risque 2.50
52 A:Onslaught................ 3.50
53 .... 2.50
54 AdP, Can X-Force
    protect X-Ternals? 2.50
55 V:S.H.I.E.L.D. 2.50
56 Deadpool, A:Onslaught....... 4.00
57 Onslaught saga............. 2.50
58 Onslaught saga............. 2.50
59 Longshot, with card.......... 2.50
60 JLb,,F:Shatterstar,A:Long Shot.. 2.50
61 JLb,R:Longshot,O:Shatterstar .. 2.50
62 JLb,F:Sunspot 2.50
63 JFM,AdP,F:Risque,Cannonball.. 2.50
64 JFM,AdP,In Latveria, searching
    for Doctor Doom's weapons ... 2.50
65 JFM,AdP,Warpath follows Risque
    to Florida 2.50
66 JFM,AdP,A:Risque,James
    Proudstar.................. 2.50
67 JFM,AdP,F:Warpath, Risque.... 2.50
68 JFM,AdP,Zero Tolerance...... 2.50
69 JFM,AdP,Zero Tolerance
    aftermath 2.50
70 JFM,AdP,new direction starts ... 2.50
71 JFM,AdP,new direction 2.50
72 JFM,AdP,on the road 2.50
73 JFM,AdP,in New Orleans 2.50
74 JFM,ASm,Skids is back 2.50
75 JFM,AdP,A:Reignfire,
    double size 3.00
76 JFM,AdP,F:Shatterstar........ 2.50
77 JFM,AdP,F:Sunfire & Meltdown . 2.50
78 JFM,AdP,Reignfire makes his
    move 2.50
79 JFM,AdP,O:Reignfire 2.50
80 JFM,AdP,V:Reignfire 2.50
81 JFM,AdP,trip to Hawaii,
    V:Lava Men, AdP Poster...... 2.50
82 JFM,V:Griffin, Damocles
    Foundation................. 2.50
83 JFM,F:Cannonball............ 2.50
84 JFM,V:Deviants............. 2.50
85 JFM,Return of Skids......... 2.50
86 JFM,A:Hulk................. 2.50
87 JFM,V:new Hellions 2.50
88 JFM,V:new Hellions 2.50
89 JFM,prisoners of the Hellions .. 2.50
90 JFM,Hellion War,concl........ 2.50
91 JFM,home to San Francisco.... 2.50
92 JFM,F:Domino 2.50
93 JFM,Domino returns 2.50
94 JFM,destination Genosha..... 2.50
95 JFM,F:Magneto.............. 2.50
96 JFM,A:Selene 2.50
97 JFM,V:Reignfire 2.50
98 .... 2.50
99 JFM,F:Dani Moonstar 2.50
100 JFM,Four Personas,48-pg..... 3.00
101 new members,some gone 2.50
102 WPo,X-Men: Revolution 2.50
102a variant (c)................ 5.00
103 WPo,WEI,Games Without
    Frontiers,pt.2 .... 2.50
104 WPo,WEI,Games,pt.3........ 2.50
105 WPo,WEI,Games,pt.4........ 2.50
106 WEI,IEd,WPo,Murder
    Ballads,pt.1 .... 2.50
107 WEI,IEd,MurderBallads,pt.2 ... 2.50
108 WEI,IEd,Ballads,pt.3......... 2.50
109 WEI,IEd,Ballads,pt.4......... 2.50
110 WEI,IEd,Rage War,pt.1 ...... 2.50
111 WEI,IEd,Rage War,pt.2 ...... 2.50
112 WEI,IEd,Rage War,pt.3 ...... 2.50
113 WEI,IEd,Rage War,pt.4 ...... 2.50
114 .... 2.50
115 IEd,final issue? 2.50
116 PrM,MiA,new team 5.00
117 PrM,MiA,new members....... 5.00
118 PrM,MiA,F:U-Go Girl......... 2.50

X-Force #62
© Marvel Entertainment Group

119 PrM,MiA,F:U-Go Girl......... 2.50
120 PrM,MiA,A:Wolverine 2.50
121 PrM,MiA,I:Lacuna 2.50
122 PrM,MiA,F:Lacuna 2.50
123 PrM,MiA,'Nuff Said 2.50
124 PrM,Orphan & U-Go Girl 2.50
125 PrM,Anarchist, Doop......... 2.50
126 PrM,MiA,one won't come home 2.50
127 PrM,MiA,who won't come home 2.50
128 PrM,MiA,body bag time 2.50
129 PrM,DFg,something
    even worse 2.50
Ann.#1 Shattershot,pt1 .... 3.00
Ann.#2 JaL,LSn,I:X-Treme,w/card.. 3.25
Ann.#3...................... 3.50
Ann.1998 X-Force/Champions..... 6.00
Ann.1999 R:Shatterstar & Rictor ... 3.50
Spec.#102 Rough cut edition...... 3.00
Minus 1 Spec., JFM,AdP, flashback,
    F:John Proudstar........... 2.50
TPB X-Force & Spider-Man:
    Sabotage, rep............... 7.00
TPB New Beginnings.......... 13.00
TPB Vol.2 (2002) 20.00

X-FORCE
Aug., 2004
1 RLd,X-Men: Reload Wave...... 3.00
2 RLd,Cable completes team 3.00
3 RLd,Cable vs. Cannonball...... 3.00
4 RLd,F:Wolverine & Deadpool ... 3.00
5 RLd,F:Fantastic Four.......... 3.00
6 Fan,rld, V:skornn,concl......... 3.00
TPB Big Guns 16.00

X-FORCE MEGAZINE
TPB LSi,RLd, rep. New Mutants ... 4.00

X-FORCE: SHATTERSTAR
Feb., 2005
1 (of 4) RLd(c),MMy 3.00
2 Rld(c),Mmy 3.00
3 RLd(c),MMy 3.00
4 RLd(c),MMy,finale 3.00
TPB X-Force Shatterstar, rep..... 16.00

X-MAN
March, 1995
1 Cable after Xavier 5.00
2 Sinister's Plan 4.00
3 V:Domino................... 3.00
4 V:Sinister................... 3.00

5 Into this World 3.00	52 TKa,LRs,V:Psi-Ops 2.50	40 DH,GT,V:Frankenstein,
6 V:X-Men 2.50	53 TKa,Strange Relations,pt.1 . . . . . 2.50	O:Cyclops 250.00
7 Evil from Age of Apocalypse 2.50	54 TKa,Strange Relations,pt.2 . . . . . 2.50	41 DH,GT,I:Grotesk,O:Cyclops . . 250.00
8 Crossover Adventure 2.50	55 TKa,M'Kraan Crystal. 2.50	42 DH,GT,JB,V:Grotesk,
9 F:Nate's Past 2.50	56 TKa,Nate in Greyville 2.50	O:Cyclops,D:Prof.X 150.00
10 Nate's Past 2.50	57 TKa,V:Mysterio 2.50	43 GT,JB,V:Magneto,Quicksilver,
11 Young Nate seeks out X-Men . . . 2.50	58 TKa,V:Threnody 2.50	Scarlet Witch,C:Avengers . . . 200.00
12 F:Excalibur 2.50	59 TKa 2.50	44 V:Magneto,Quicksilver,Sc.Witch,
13 . . . . 2.50	60 TKa, ... 2.50	R:Red Raven,O:Iceman 200.00
14 . . . . 2.50	61 TKa, ... 2.50	45 PH,JB,V:Magneto,Quicksilver,
15 JOs,X-Men/Cable war aftermath 3.00	62 TKa,trapped 2.50	Scarlet Witch,O:Iceman 200.00
16 Holocaust,A:Onslaught 2.50	63 WEI,X-Men: Revolution 2.25	46 DH,V:Juggernaut,O:Iceman . . 275.00
17 Holocaust,Quicksilver,Scarlet	63a variant(c). 2.25	47 DH,I:Maha Yogi. 225.00
Witch, A:Onslaught 2.50	64 WEI,No Direction Home,pt.2. . . . 2.25	48 DH,JR,V:Quasimodo. 225.00
18 Onslaught saga. 2.50	65 WEI,No Direction Home,pt.3. . . . 2.25	49 JSo,DH,C:Magneto,I:Polaris,
19 Onslaught saga. 2.50	66 WEI,No Direction Home,pt.4. . . . 2.25	Mesmero,O:Beast 225.00
20 . . . . 2.50	67 WEI,Down the Spiral,pt.1 . . . . . . 2.25	50 JSo,V:Magneto,O:Beast 250.00
21 TKa,RCz,F:Nate 2.50	68 WEI,Down the Spiral,pt.2 . . . . . . 2.25	51 JSo,V:Magneto,Polaris,
22 TKa,RCz,F:Threnody,A:Madelyne	69 WEI,Down the Spiral,pt.3 . . . . . . 2.25	Erik the Red,O:Beast. 250.00
Pryor 2.50	70 WEI,Down the Spiral,pt.4 . . . . . . 2.25	52 DH,MSe,JSt,O:Lorna Dane
23 TKa,RCz,F:Bishop 2.50	71 AOI,StG,Fearful	V:Magneto,O:Beast 225.00
24 TKa,RCz,Spider-Man vs. Nate . . 2.50	Symmetries,pt.1. . . . . 2.25	53 1st BWS,O:Beast 225.00
25 TKa,RCz,Madelyne Pryor,	72 AOI,StG,Symmetries,pt.2 . . . . . . 2.25	54 BWS,DH,I:Havok,O:Angel . . . 225.00
double size 4.00	73 AOI,StG,Symmetries,pt.3 . . . . . . 2.25	55 BWS,DH,O:Havok,Angel 200.00
26 TKa,RCz,Nate limps to Muir	74 AOI,StG,Symmetries,pt.4 . . . . . . 2.25	56 NA,V:LivingMonolith,O:Angel . 225.00
Isle,A:Moira Mactaggert 2.50	75 Anti-Man, final issue 3.00	57 NA,V:Sentinels,A:Havok 225.00
27 TKa,RCz,Hellfire Club, concl. . . . 2.50	Minus 1 Spec., TKa,RCz,	58 NA,A:Havoc,V:Sentinels 275.00
28 TKa,RCz,Dark Beast's offer 2.50	flashback,O:Nate Grey 2.00	59 NA,V:Sentinels,A:Havoc. 300.00
29 TKa,RCz,Back in New York, ... 2.50	Spec.#1 X-Man '96 . . . . 3.50	60 NA,I:Sauron 225.00
30 TKa,RCz,F:Nate Grey. 2.50	Ann. '97 RBe, Nate, Sugar Man,	61 NA,V:Sauron 225.00
31 RL,DGr,F:Nate Grey 2.50	Dark Beast, Holocaust. 3.00	62 NA,A:Ka-Zar,Sauron,Magneto 225.00
32 TKa,V:Jacknife 2.50	Ann. '98 X-Man, The Hulk, Thanos,	63 A:Ka-Zar,V:Magneto 220.00
33 TKa,V:Jacknife 2.50	48-pg. 3.00	64 DH,A:Havok,I:Sunfire 225.00
34 TKa,Secret of Nate's popularity . 2.50	GNv X-Man,BRa,TyD, 48-pg. 6.00	65 NA,MSe,A:Havok,Shield,
35 TKa,Terrorists Strike 2.50		Return of Prof.X. 225.00
36 TKa,V:Purple Man. 2.50		66 SB,MSe,V:Hulk,A:Havok. 225.00
37 TKa,Nate leaves N.Y.,	**X-MEN**	67 rep.X-Men #12,#13 . . . . 150.00
A:Spider-Man. 2.50	**Sept., 1963**	68 rep.X-Men #14,#15 . . . . 150.00
38 TKa,A:Spider-Man, Gwen Stacy . 2.50	1 JK,O:X-Men,I:Professor X,Beast	69 rep.X-Men #16,#19 . . . . 150.00
39 TKa,AOI,Nate & Madeline Pryor . 2.50	Cyclops,Marvel Girl,Iceman	70 rep.X-Men #17,#18 . . . . 150.00
40 TKa,RPc,V:Great Beasts 2.50	Angel,Magneto 16,000.00	71 rep.X-Men #20 . . . . 150.00
41 TKa,RCz,Madelyne Pryor 2.50	2 JK,I:Vanisher. 5,000.00	72 rep.X-Men #21,#24 . . . . 150.00
42 TKa,RCz,hunted by leprechauns 2.50	3 JK,I:Blob 2,000.00	73 thru 93 rep.X-Men #25-45. . @125.00
43 TKa,RCz,Nate Grey–murderer?! 2.50	4 JK,I:Quicksilver,Scarlet Witch	94 GK(c),B:CCl(s),DC,BMc,B:2nd
44 TKa,RCz,F:Nate Grey,Gauntlet . . 2.50	Mastermind,Toad 3,000.00	X-Men,V:Count Nefaria . . 1,500.00
45 TKa,prelude to X-Man/Cable	5 JK,V:Broth. of Evil Mutants . 2,000.00	95 GK(c),DC,V:Count Nefaria,
x-over. 2.50	6 JK,V:Sub-Mariner 1,000.00	Ani-Men,D:Thunderbird 300.00
46 TKa,Cable x-over 2.50	7 JK,V:Broth. of Evil Mutants,	96 DC,I:Moira McTaggert,
47 TKa,Blood Brothers,pt.3 . . . . . . 2.50	Blob 1,000.00	Kierrok. 200.00
48 LRs,V:Crusader 2.50	8 JK,I:Unus,1st Ice covered	97 DC,V:Havok,Polaris,Eric
49 LRs,TKa,F:Nate 2.50	Iceman 1,000.00	the Red,I:Lilandra 200.00
50 TKa,LRs,War of the	9 JK,A:Avengers,V:Lucifer 1,400.00	98 DC,V:Sentinels,Stephen Lang 165.00
Mutants,pt.2, 48-page 3.50	10 JK,I:Modern Ka-Zar 1,400.00	99 DC,V:Sentinels,S.Lang 150.00
51 TKa,LRs,V:Psi-Ops 2.50	11 JK,I:Stranger 900.00	100 DC,V:Stephen Lang 250.00
	12 JK,O:Prof.X,I:Juggernaut . . . 1,500.00	
	13 JK,JSt,V:Juggernaut 750.00	
	14 JK,I:Sentinels 750.00	
	15 JK,O:Beast,V:Sentinels. 750.00	
	16 JK,V:Mastermold,Sentinels. . . 750.00	
	17 JK,V:Magneto 500.00	
	18 V:Magneto. 500.00	
	19 I:Mimic. 500.00	
	20 V:Lucifer. 500.00	
	21 V:Lucifer,Dominus. 350.00	
	22 V:Maggia 350.00	
	23 V:Maggia 350.00	
	24 I:Locust(Prof.Hopper) 350.00	
	25 JK,I:El Tigre 350.00	
	26 V:El Tigre 275.00	
	27 C:Fant.Four,V:Puppet Master . 275.00	
	28 I:Banshee 450.00	
	29 V:Super-Apaptoid 300.00	
	30 JK,I:The Warlock. 175.00	
	31 JK,I:Cobalt Man 225.00	
	32 V:Juggernaut. 225.00	
	33 GK,A:Dr.Strange,Juggernaut . 225.00	
	34 V:Tyrannus,Mole Man 225.00	
	35 JK,A:Spider-Man,Banshee . . . 225.00	
	36 V:Mekano 225.00	
	37 DH,V:Blob,Unus 225.00	
	38 DH,A:Banshee,O:Cyclops. . . . 250.00	
	39 DH,GT,A:Banshee,V:Mutant	
	Master,O:Cyclops 350.00	

X-Man #53
© Marvel Entertainment Group

X-Men #91
© Marvel Entertainment Group

101 DC,I:Phoenix,Black Tom,
A:Juggernaut 250.00
102 DC,O:Storm,V:Juggernaut,
Black Tom 125.00
103 DC,V:Juggernaut,Bl.Tom . . . 125.00
104 DC,V:Magneto,I:Star
Jammers,A:Lilandra 100.00
105 DC,BL,V:Firelord 90.00
106 DC,TS,V:Firelord 90.00
107 DC,DGr,I:Imperial Guard,Star
Jammers,Gladiator,Corsair . . 100.00
108 JBy,TA,A:Star Jammers,
C:Fantastic Four,Avengers . . . 125.00
109 JBy,TA,I:Vindicator 110.00
110 TD,DC,V:Warhawk 75.00
111 JBy,TA,V:Mesmero,A:Beast,
Magneto 75.00
112 GP(c),JBy,TA,V:Magneto,
A:Beast 75.00
113 JBy,TA,V:Magneto,A:Beast . . 75.00
114 JBy,TA,A:Beast,R:Sauron 90.00
115 JBy,TA,V:Sauron,Garokk,
A:Ka-Zar,I:Zaladane 75.00
116 JBy,TA,V:Sauron,Garokk,
A:Ka-Zar 75.00
117 JBy,TA,O:Prof.X,I:Amahl
Farouk (Shadow King) 70.00
118 JBy,I:Moses Magnum,A:Sunfire
C:Iron Fist,I:Mariko 70.00
119 JBy,TA,V:Moses Magnum,
A:Sunfire 70.00
120 JBy,TA,I:AlphaFlight (Shaman,
Sasquatch,Northstar,Snowbird,
Aurora) 125.00
121 JBy,TA,V:Alpha Flight 100.00
122 JBy,TA,A:Juggernaut,Black
Tom,Arcade,Power Man 70.00
123 JBy,TA,V:Arcade,A:SpM 60.00
124 JBy,TA,V:Arcade 60.00
125 JBy,TA,A:Beast,Madrox the
Multiple Man,Havok,Polaris . . . 70.00
126 JBy,TA,I:Proteus,
A:Havok,Madrox 70.00
127 JBy,TA,V:Proteus,A:Havok,
Madrox 70.00
128 GP(c),JBy,TA,V:Proteus,
A:Havok,Madrox 70.00
129 JBy,TA,I:Shadow Cat,White
Queen,C:Hellfire Club 110.00
130 JR2(c),JBy,TA,I:Dazzler
V:White Queen 70.00
131 JBy,TA,V:White Queen,
A:Dazzler 70.00
132 JBy,TA,I:Hellfire Club,
V:Mastermind 70.00
133 JBy,TA,V:Hellfire Club,
Mastermind,F:Wolverine 70.00
134 JBy,TA,V:Hellfire Club,Master
mind,I:Dark Phoenix,A:Beast 100.00
135 JBy,TA,V:Dark Phoenix,C:SpM,
Fant.Four,Silver Surfer 70.00
136 JBy,TA,V:Dark Phoenix,
A:Beast 70.00
137 JBy,TA,D:Phoenix,V:Imperial
Guard,A:Beast 80.00
138 JBy,TA,History of X-Men,
L:Cyclops,C:Shadow Cat 60.00
139 JBy,TA,A:Alpha Flight,R:Wendigo,
N:Wolverine,J:Shadowcat 65.00
140 JBy,TA,V:Wendigo,A:Alpha
Flight 60.00
141 JBy,TA,I:2nd Brotherhood of Evil
Mutants,I:Rachel (Phoenix II) . 75.00
Becomes:

UNCANNY X-MEN

142 JBy,TA,V:Evil Mutants,
A:Rachel (Phoenix II) 75.00
143 JBy,TA,V:N'Garai,I:Lee
Forrester 50.00
144 BA,JRu,A:Man-Thing,
O:Havok, V:D'Spayre 20.00
145 DC,JRu,V:Arcade,A:DrDoom . 20.00

Uncanny X-Men #195
© Marvel Entertainment Group

146 DC,JRu,V:Dr.Doom,Arcade . . 20.00
147 DC,JRu,V:Dr.Doom,Arcade . . 20.00
148 DC,JRu,I:Caliban,A:Dazzler
Spiderwoman 20.00
149 DC,JRu,A:Magneto 20.00
150 DC,JRu,BWi,V:Magneto 22.00
151 JSh,BMc,JRu,V:Sentinels 20.00
152 BMc,JRu,V:White Queen 20.00
153 DC,JRu,I:Bamf 20.00
154 DC,JRu,BWi,I:Sidrian Hunters
A:Corsair,O:Cyclops(part) . . . 20.00
155 DC,BWi,V:Deathbird,I:Brood . . 20.00
156 DC,BWi,V:Death Bird,
A:Tigra, Star Jammers 20.00
157 DC,BWi,V:Deathbird 20.00
158 DC,BWi,2nd A:Rogue,
Mystique 25.00
159 BSz,BWi,V:Dracula 20.00
160 BA,BWi,V:Belasco,I:Magik . . . 20.00
161 DC,BWi,I:Gabrielle Haller,
O:Magneto,Professor X 20.00
162 DC,BWi,V:Brood 25.00
163 DC,BWi,V:Brood 20.00
164 DC,BWi,V:Brood,I:Binary 18.00
165 PS,BWi,V:Brood 20.00
166 PS,BWi,V:Brood,A:Binary,
I:Lockheed 18.00
167 PS,BWi,V:Brood,A:N.Mutants . 22.00
168 PS,BWi,I:Madelyne Pryor 20.00
169 PS,BWi,I:Morlocks 18.00
170 PS,BWi,A:Angel,V:Morlocks . . 18.00
171 WS,BWi,J:Rogue,V:Binary . . . 28.00
172 PS,BWi,V:Viper,Silver
Samurai, ... 20.00
173 PS,BWi,V:Viper,Silver
Samurai. 18.00
174 PS,BWi,A:Mastermind 18.00
175 PS,JR2,BWi,W:Cyclops and
Madelyne,V:Mastermind 20.00
176 JR2,BWi,I:Val Cooper 12.00
177 JR2,JR,V:Brotherhood of
Evil Mutants 12.00
178 JR2,BWi,BBr,V:Brotherhood
of Evil Mutants 12.00
179 JR2,DGr,V:Morlocks 12.00
180 JR2,DGr,BWi,Secret Wars . . . 15.00
181 JR2,DGr,A:Sunfire 12.00
182 JR2,DGr,V:S.H.I.E.L.D. 12.00
183 JR2,DGr,V:Juggernaut 12.00
184 JR2,DGr,V:Selene,I:Forge . . . 16.00
185 JR2,DGr,V:Shield,U.S.
Govt.,Storm loses powers 12.00
186 BWS,TA,Lifedeath,
V:Dire Wraiths 14.00

187 JR2,DGr,V:Dire Wraiths 12.00
188 JR2,DGr,V:Dire Wraiths 12.00
189 JR2,SL,V:Selene,A:Magma . . 12.00
190 JR2,DGr,V:Kulan Gath,A:SpM,
Avengers,New Mutants 12.00
191 JR2,DGr,A:Avengers,Spider-Man,
New Mutants,I:Nimrod 12.00
192 JR2,DGr,V:Magus 12.00
193 JR2,DGr,V:Hellions,I:Firestar
Warpath,20th Anniv. 20.00
194 JR2,DGr,SL,V:Nimrod 12.00
195 BSz(c),JR2,DGr,A:Power
Pack,V:Morlocks 12.00
196 JR2,DGr,J:Magneto 15.00
197 JR2,DGr,V:Arcade 12.00
198 BWS,F:Storm,Lifedeath II 12.00
199 JR2,DGr,I:Freedom Force,
Rachel becomes 2nd Phoenix 12.00
200 JR2,DGr,A:Magneto,I:Fenris . . 20.00
201 RL,WPo(i),I:Nathan
Christopher (Cyclops son) 22.00
202 JR2,AW,Secret Wars II 12.00
203 JR2,AW,Secret Wars II 12.00
204 JBr,WPo,V:Arcade 12.00
205 BWS,A:Lady Deathstrike . . 22.00
206 JR2,DGr,V:Freedom Force . . . 12.00
207 JR2,DGr,V:Selene 12.00
208 JR2,DGr,V:Nimrod,
A:Hellfire Club 12.00
209 JR2,CR,V:Nimrod,A:Spiral . . . 12.00
210 JR2,DGr,I:Marauders,
(Mutant Massacre) 25.00
211 JR2,BBl,AW,V:Marauders,
(Mutant Massacre) 25.00
212 RL,DGr,V:Sabretooth,
(Mutant Massacre) 35.00
213 AD,V:Sabretooth (Mut.Mass) . 35.00
214 BWS,BWi,V:Malice,A:Dazzler . 12.00
215 AD,DGr,I:Stonewall,Super
Sabre,Crimson Commando . . . 12.00
216 BWS(c),JG,DGr,V:Stonewall . . 12.00
217 WS(c),JG,SL,V:Juggernaut . . . 12.00
218 AAD(c),MS,DGr,V:Juggernaut 12.00
219 BBl,DGr,V:Marauders,Polaris
becomes Malice,A:Sabertooth 12.00
220 MS,DGr,A:Naze 12.00
221 MS,DGr,I:Mr.Sinister,
V:Marauders 24.00
222 MS,DGr,V:Marauders,Eye
Killers,A:Sabertooth 25.00
223 KGa,DGr,A:Freedom Force . . 12.00
224 MS,DGr,V:Adversary 15.00
225 MS,DGr,Fall of Mutants
I:1st US App Roma 16.00
226 MS,DGr,Fall of Mutants 16.00
227 MS,DGr,Fall of Mutants 16.00
228 RL,TA,A:OZ Chase 14.00
229 MS,DGr,I:Reavers,Gateway . . 14.00
230 RL,DGr,Xmas Issue 14.00
231 RL,DGr,V:Limbo 12.00
232 MS,DGr,V:Brood 12.00
233 MS,DGr,V:Brood 12.00
234 MS,JRu,V:Brood 15.00
235 RL,CR,V:Magistrates 12.00
236 MS,DGr,V:Magistrates 12.00
237 RL,TA,V:Magistrates 12.00
238 MS,DGr,V:Magistrates 12.00
239 MS,DGr,Inferno,A:Mr.Sinister . 12.00
240 MS,DGr,Inferno,V:Marauders . 15.00
241 MS,DGr,Inferno,O:Madeline
Pryor,V:Marauders 12.00
242 MS,DGr,Inferno,D:N'Astirh,
A:X-Factor,Double-sized 12.00
243 MS,Inferno,A:X-Factor 12.00
244 MS,DGr,I:Jubilee 25.00
245 RLd,DGr,Invasion Parody 12.00
246 MS,DGr,V:Mastermold,
A:Nimrod 12.00
247 MS,DGr,V:Mastermold 12.00
248 JLe(1st X-Men Art),DGr,
V:Nanny & Orphan Maker 35.00
248a 2nd printing 3.00

Uncanny X-Men #296
© *Marvel Entertainment Group*

249 MS,DGr,C:Zaladane,
   V:Savage Land Mutates...... 10.00
250 MS,SL,I:Zaladane. 10.00
251 MS,DGr,V:Reavers 14.00
252 JLe,BSz(c),RL,SW,V:Reavers 10.00
253 MS,SL,V:Amahl Farouk 10.00
254 JLe(c),MS,DGr,V:Reavers ... 10.00
255 MS,DGr,V:Reavers,D:Destiny. 10.00
256 JLe,SW,Acts of Vengeance,
   V:Manderin,A:Psylocke 20.00
257 JLe,JRu,AofV,V:Manderin.... 15.00
258 JLe,SW,AofV,V:Manderin 15.00
259 MS,DGr,V:Magistrates, ... 8.00
260 JLe(c),MS,DGr,A:Dazzler 8.00
261 JLe(c),MS,DGr,V:Hardcase &
   Harriers 8.00
262 KD,JRu,V:Masque,Morlocks .. 8.00
263 JRu(i),O:Forge,V:Morlocks ... 8.00
264 JLe(c),MC,JRu,V:Magistrate .. 8.00
265 JRu(i),V:Shadowking 8.00
266 NKu(c),MC,JRu,I:Gambit 50.00
267 JLe,WPo,SW,V:Shadowking.. 25.00
268 JLe,SW,A:Captain America,
   Black Widow,V:The Hand,
   Baron Strucker............. 25.00
269 JLe,ATi,Rogue V:Ms.Marvel .. 10.00
270 JLe,ATi,SW,X-Tinction Agenda
   #1, A:Cable,New Mutants 12.00
270a 2nd printing(Gold).......... 4.00
271 JLe,SW,X-Tinction Agenda
   #4,A:Cable,New Mutants..... 10.00
272 JLe,SW,X-Tinction Agenda
   #7,A:Cable,New Mutants..... 10.00
273 JLe,WPo,JBy,KJ,RL,MS,MGo,
   LSn,SW,A:Cable,N.Mutants .. 10.00
274 JLe,SW,V:Zaladane,A:Magneto,
   Nick Fury,Ka-Zar 10.00
275 JLe,SW,R:Professor X,A:Star
   Jammers,Imperial Guard..... 12.00
275a 2nd Printing (Gold) 3.00
276 JLe,SW,V:Skrulls,Shi'ar 10.00
277 JLe,SW,V:Skrulls,Shi'ar 10.00
278 PS,Professor X Returns to
   Earth,V:Shadowking 8.00
279 NKu,SW,V:Shadowking 7.00
280 E:CCl(s),NKu,A:X-Factor,
   D:Shadowking,Prof.X Crippled . 7.00
281 WPo,ATi,new team (From X-Men
   #1),D:Pierce,Hellions,V:Sentinels,
   I:Trevor Fitzroy,Upstarts 10.00
281a 2nd printing,red(c)......... 3.00
282 WPo,ATi,V:Fitzroy,C:Bishop . 15.00
282a 2nd printing,gold(c) of #281
   inside.................... 3.00

283 WPo,ATi,I:Bishop,Malcolm,
   Randall 17.00
284 WPo,ATi,SOS from USSR..... 5.00
285 WPo,I:Mikhail(Colossus'
   brother from Russia) 5.00
286 JLe,WPo,ATi,A:Mikhail 5.00
287 JR2,O:Bishop,
   D:Malcolm,Randall 6.00
288 NKu,BSz,A:Bishop 5.00
289 WPo,ATi,Forge proposes
   to Storm................. 5.00
290 WPo,SW,V:Cyberpunks,
   L:Forge 5.00
291 TR,V:Morlocks.............. 5.00
292 TR,V:Morlocks.............. 5.00
293 TR,D:Morlocks,Mikhail 5.00
294 BP,TA,X-Cutioner's Song#1,
   Stryfe shoots Prof X,A:X-Force,
   X-Factor,polybag.w/ProfX card . 5.00
295 BP,TA,X-Cutioners Song #5,
   V:Apocalypse............... 5.00
296 BP,TA,X-Cutioners Song #9,
   A:X-Force,X-Factor,V:Stryfe ... 5.00
297 BP,X-Cutioners Song
   Aftermath.................. 5.00
298 BP,TA,V:Acolytes 5.00
299 BP,A:Forge,Acolytes,I:Graydon
   Creed (Sabretooth's son) 5.00
300 JR2,DGr,BP,V:Acolytes,A:Forge,
   Nightcrawler,Holografx(c) 12.00
301 JR2,DGr,I:Sienna Blaze,
   V:Fitzroy.................. 5.00
302 JR2,V:Fitzroy 5.00
303 JR2,V:Upstarts,D:Illyana...... 6.00
304 JR2,JaL,PS,L:Colossus,
   V:Magneto,Holo-grafx(c) 8.00
305 JD,F:Rogue,Bishop.......... 5.00
306 JR2,V:Hodge............... 5.00
307 JR2,Bloodties#4,A:Avengers,
   V:Exodus,Cortez 6.00
308 JR2,Scott & Jean announce
   impending marriage.......... 5.00
309 JR2,O:Professor X & Amelia .. 5.00
310 JR2,DG,A:Cable,V:X-Cutioner,
   w/card 5.00
311 JR2,DG,AV,V:Sabretooth,
   C:Phalanx................. 5.00
312 JMd,DG,A:Yukio,I:Phalanx,
   w/card 5.00
313 JMd,DG,V:Phalanx 5.00
314 LW,BSz,R:White Quen 5.00
315 F:Acolytes................. 5.00
316 V:Phalanx,I:M,Phalanx Covenant
   Generation Next,pt.1, holo(c) .. 5.00
316a newsstand ed............... 3.00
317 JMd,V:Phalanx,prism(c) 5.00
317a newsstand ed............... 3.00
318 JMd,L:Jubilee, deluxe........ 5.00
318a newsstand ed............... 3.00
319 R:Legion, deluxe............ 5.00
319a newsstand ed............... 3.00
320 deluxe ed.................. 5.00
320 newsstand ed.............. 3.00
321 R:Lilandra, deluxe ed........ 5.00
321 newsstand ed.............. 3.00
322 SLo,TGu,Rogue,Iceman run from
   Gambit's Secret............. 8.00
323 I:Onslaught................ 5.00
324 SLo,F:Cannonball............ 5.00
325 R:Colossus 7.00
326 SLo,JMd,F:Gambit,Sabretooth . 4.00
327 SLo,JMd,Magneto's Fate 4.00
328 SLo,JMd,Sabretooth freed 4.00
329 SLo,JMd,A:Doctor Strange ... 4.00
330 Dr.Strange................. 4.00
331 White Queen 4.00
332 SLo,JMd, cont from
   Wolverine #100............. 4.00
333 SLo,JMd, Operation: Zero
   Tolerance, Onslaught saga ... 4.00
334 SLo,JMd, Onslaught saga 4.00
335 SLo,JMd, Onslaught saga 4.00

336 Apocalypse vs. Onslaught 4.00
337 Operation: Zero Tolerance 4.00
338 SLo,JMd,R:Angel 4.00
339 SLo,JMd,F:Cyclops, J.J.
   Jameson, Havok............ 4.00
340 SLo,JMd,F:Iceman 4.00
341 SLo,JMd,Rogue gets gift 4.00
342 SLo,JMd, Shi'ar Empire, pt.1 .. 5.00
342a Rogue cover............. 15.00
343 SLo,JMd, Shi'ar Empire, pt.2 .. 4.00
344 SLo,JMd, Shi'ar Empire, pt.3 .. 4.00
345 SLo,JMd, trip home, A:Akron .. 5.00
346 SLo,JMd,Zero Tolerance,
   A:Spider-Man.............. 4.00
347 SLo,JMd,Zero Tolerance..... 4.00
348 SLo,JMd,at Magneto's base... 4.00
349 SLo,JMd,Maggot vs. Psylocke
   & Archangel............... 4.00
350 SSe,JMd,Trial of Gambit,
   double-sized 5.00
350a Gambit (c).............. 15.00
351 SSe,JMd,Dr. Cecilia Reyes.... 3.00
352 SSe,EBe,Cyclops & Phoenix
   leave, Facade arrives 3.00
353 SSe,CBa,Rogues Anguish 3.00
354 SSe,CBa,F:Rogue 10.00
354a Jean Gray (c) 12.00
355 SSe,CBa, North & South
   pt.2 x-over 5.00
356 SSe,CBa, originals V:Phoenix . 3.00
357 SSe,Cyclops & Phoenix 3.00
358 SSe,CBa,Phoenix collapses .. 3.00
359 SSe,CBa,Rogue............ 3.00
360A SSe,CBa, I:New X-Men, foil
   etched cover 5.00
360B regular cover 4.00
361 SSe,SSr,R:Gambit 3.50
362 SSe,CBa,Hunt for Xavier,pt.1 . 3.50
363 SSe,CBa,Hunt for Xavier,pt.3 . 3.50
364 SSe,Hunt for Xavier,pt.5 ...... 3.00
365 SSe,CBa,A:Professor X 3.00
366 AD,BPe,Magneto War,pt.1 .... 3.00
367 AD,Magneto War,pt.3 .... 3.00
368 AD,AKu,Requiem for an X-Man 3.00
368a signed 20.00
369 AD,AKu,V:Juggernaut........ 3.00
370 AD,AKu,in the past 3.00
371 AD,AKu(c),Rage Against
   the Machine,pt.1 x-over 3.00
371a signed 20.00
372 AKu,AD,The Shattering,pt.1 .. 3.00
373 AKu,AD,The Shattering,pt.2 .. 3.00
374 AKu,AD,The Shattering...... 3.00
375 AKu,AD,48-pg. 5.00

Uncanny X-Men #374
© *Marvel Entertainment Group*

376 AKu,AD 10.00
377 AKu,AD,Apocalypse12,pt.5 . . . 10.00
378 AKu,AD,TTn,Ages of
   Apocalypse,pt.1,x-over 3.00
379 AKu,AD,TTn,mutants no more . 3.00
380 AD,TR,poly-bagged w/Genesis. 4.00
381 CCl,AKu,TTn,X-Men:
   Revolution 10.00
381a foil (c) 15.00
382 CCl,TTn,Shockwave Riders . . . 3.00
383 CCl,AKu,TTn,48-pg. 3.50
384 CCl,AKu,TTn,I:Killion 3.00
385 CCl,TR,Red Pirates 3.00
386 CCl,TR,Phoenix 3.00
387 CCl,TTn,Maximum Security . . . 3.00
388 CCl,SvL,Dream's End,pt.1 . . . . 5.00
389 CCl,SvL,F:Cecilia Reyes 3.00
390 CCl,SvL,Legacy Virus,
   D:Colossus 12.00
391 SLo,SvL,return 3.00
392 SLo,SvL,Eve of Destruction . . . 3.00
393 SLo,SvL,Eve of Destruction . . . 5.00
394 JoC,IaC,F:Warp Savant 5.00
395A JoC,IaC,Poptopia,pt.1 . . . . 3.00
395B variant BWS(c) 3.00
396 JoC,IaC,Poptopia,pt.2 . . . . 3.00
397 JoC,IaC,Poptopia,pt.3 . . . . 3.00
398 JoC,IaC,Poptopia,pt.4 . . . . 3.00
399 JoC,SHa,X-Ranch 3.00
400 F:XStacy,48-page 5.00
401 JoC,RG,F:Banshee,'Nuff Said . 3.50
402 JoC,RG,vs.X-Corp. 2.50
403 JoC,AaL,DaM,X-Corp's secret . 2.50
404 JoC,RG,V:Multiple Men 2.50
405 JoC,SeP,V:Banshee 2.50
406 JoC,AaL,X-Corps,concl. 2.50
407 JoC,SeP,Nightcrawler 2.50
408 JoC,SeP,V:Vanisher 2.50
409 JoC,SeP,V:Vanisher 2.50
410 RG,Hope 2.50
411 RG,Hope,pt.2 . . . . 2.50
412 RG,Hope,pt.3 . . . . 2.50
413 RG,Annie's Moving 2.50
414 Northstar Joins team. 2.50
415 SeP,F:Nightcrawler 2.50
416 KIA,F:Juggernaut 4.00
417 KiA,Dominant Species 3.00
418 KiA,Dominant Species 3.00
419 KiA,Archangel and Husk. 2.25
420 KiA,Dominant Species,concl. . . 2.25
421 RG,V:Alpha Flight,pt.1. . . . . . . 2.25
422 RG,V:Alpha Flight,pt.2,48-pg. . . 3.50
423 RG,Holy War,pt.1 . . . . 1.00
424 RG,Holy War,pt.2 . . . . 2.25
425 Sacred Vows,pt.1 . . . . 2.25
426 Sacred Vows,pt.2 . . . . 2.25
427 F:Jubilee, Angel, Husk 2.25
428 O:Nightcrawler,F:Mystique 2.25
429 Draco,pt.1 . . . . 2.25
430 Draco,pt.2 . . . . 2.25
431 Draco,pt.3 . . . . 2.25
432 Draco,pt.4 . . . . 2.25
433 Draco,pt.5 . . . . 2.25
434 Draco,pt.6 . . . . 2.25
435 Trial of the Juggernaut,pt.1 . . . 2.25
436 Trial of the Juggernaut,pt.2 . . . 2.25
437 She Lies With Angels,pt.1 . . . . 2.50
438 She Lies With Angels,pt.2 . . . . 2.25
439 She Lies With Angels,pt.3 . . . . 2.25
440 She Lies With Angels,pt.4 . . . . 2.25
441 She Lies With Angels,pt.5 . . . . 2.25
442 Of Darkest Nights,pt.1 . . . . . . 2.25
443 Of Darkest Nights,pt.2 . . . . . . 2.25
444 The End of History,pt.1 . . . . . . 2.25
445 The End of History,pt.2 . . . . . . 2.25
446 The End of History,pt.3 . . . . . . 2.25
447 The End of History,pt.4 . . . . . . 2.25
448 CCl,Guess Who's Back,pt.1 . . 2.25
449 CCl,Guess Who's Back,pt.2 . . 2.25
450 CCl,AD,Cruelest Cut,pt.1 . . . . 3.00
451 CCl,AD,Cruelest Cut,pt.2 . . . . 2.25
452 CCl(s),Chasing Hellfire 2.25

453 CCl(s),Chasing Hellfire 2.25
454 CCl(s),Chasing Hellfire, concl. . 2.25
455 CCl(s),On Ice,pt.1 . . . . 2.25
456 CCl(s),On Ice,pt.2 . . . . 2.25
457 CCl(s),AD,On Ice 2.25
458 CCl(s),AD,On Ice,A:Ka-Zar. . . 2.25
459 CCl(s),AD,On Ice 2.50
460 CCl(s),TR,Mojo Rising,pt.1 . . . 2.50
461 CCl(s),TR,Mojo Rising,pt.2 . . . 5.00
462 CCl(s),AD,Season of the Witch 2.50
463 CCl(s),AD,Season of the Witch 2.50
464 CCl,CBa,Season of the Witch . 2.50
465 CCl,CBa,Season of the Witch . 2.50
466 Grey's End, Decimation tie-in . 2.50
467 Grey's End, Decimation tie-in . 2.50
468 Grey's End, Decimation tie-in . 2.50
469 CCl,Wand'ring Star,pt.1 . . . . . . 2.50
470 CCl,Wand'ring Star,pt.2 . . . . . . 2.50
471 CCl,Wand'ring Star,pt.3 . . . . . . 2.50
472 CCl,CBa,First Foursaken, pt.1 . 3.00
473 CCl,CBa,First Foursaken, pt.2 . 3.00
474 CCl,CBa,First Foursaken, pt.3 . 3.00
475 Rise and Fall of Shi'ar Empire . 3.00
476 Rise and Fall of Shi'ar Empire . 3.00
477 Rise and Fall of Shi'ar Empire . 3.00
478 Rise and Fall of Shi'ar Empire . 3.00
479 Rise and Fall of Shi'ar Empire . 3.00
480 Rise and Fall of Shi'ar Empire . 3.00
Ann.#1 rep.#9,#11 . . . . 200.00
Ann.#2 rep.#22,#23 . . . . 100.00
Ann.#3 GK(c),GP,TA,A:Arkon . . . 40.00
Ann.#4 JR2,BMc,A:Dr.Strange . . . 25.00

X-Men King-Size Annual #5
© Marvel Entertainment Group

Ann.#5 BA,BMc,A:F.F. 20.00
Ann.#6 BSz,BWi,Dracula. 20.00
Ann.#7 MGo,TMd,BWi,TA,BBr,
   BA,JRu,BBl,SL,AM,
   V:Impossible Man 15.00
Ann.#8 SL,Kitty's story. 15.00
Ann.#9 AAd,AG,MMi,Asgard,V:Loki,
   Enchantress,A:New Mutants . . 20.00
Ann.#10 AAd,TA,V:Mojo,
   J:Longshot,A:New Mutants . . . 18.00
Ann.#11 AD,V:Horde,A:CaptBrit. . . . 7.00
Ann.#12 AAd,BWi,RLm,TD,Evol.
   War,V:Terminus,Savage Land . . 7.00
Ann.#13 MBa,JRu,Atlantis Attacks . 6.00
Ann.#14 AAd,DGr,BWi,AM,ATi,
   V:Ahab,A:X-Factor. 15.00
Ann.#15,TR,JRu,MMi(c),Flesh Tears,
   Pt.3,A:X-Force,New Warriors . . 6.00
Ann.#16 JaL,JRu,Shattershot
   Part.2 . . . . 5.00

Ann.#17 JPe,MFm,I:X-Cutioner,
   D:Mastermind,w/card. 5.00
Ann.#18 JR2,V:Caliban,
   BU:Bishop 4.00
Ann.1999 AD 3.50
Ann.2000 SLo,F:Professor X 3.50
Ann.2001 JoC,48-pg. 3.50
Ann. #1 (2006). 4.00
Marvel Milestone rep. #1 (1991) . . 3.00
Marvel Milestone rep. #9 (1993) . . 3.00
Marvel Milestone rep. #28 (1994) . . 3.00
G-Size #1,GK,DC,I:New X-Men
   (Colossus,Storm,Nightcrawler,
   Thunderbird,3rd A:Wolv.) . . 1,500.00
G-Size #2,rep.#57-59. . . . . 150.00
Marvel Milestone rep. Giant
   Size #1 (1991). 4.00
Spec.#1 X-Men: Earth Fall,
   rep. #232–#234 (1996) 3.00
Spec.#1 X-Men vs. Dracula, rep.
   X-Men Ann.#6 (1993) 2.00
GN X-Men: Days of Future Past
   rep. X-Men #141-142 . . . . 5.00
GN Pryde of the X-Men 11.00
GN God Loves,Man Kills,
   (1994) prestige 7.00
GN X-Men Firsts, I:Wolverine,Rogue,
   Gambit & Mr. Sinister, rep.
   Avengers Ann.#10, Uncanny
   X-Men 221,#266 & Incredible
   Hulk #181 (1996). 5.00
GN X-Men Rarities,F:Classic
   Stories (1995) 6.00
TPB Asgardian Wars 16.00
TPB Bloodties V:Exodus 16.00
TPB Coming of Bishop, rep.(1995) 13.00
TPB Dark Phoenix Saga 13.00
TPB Dark Phoenix, 192-pg.(2001) 20.00
TPB X-Men: Days of Future Present,
   MMi(c), rep. 15.00
TPB Fall of the Mutants, 272-pg. . . 25.00
TPB Fatal Attractions (1994) 18.00
TPB From the Ashes 17.00
TPB Greatest Battles. 16.00
TPB X-Men: Poptopia (2001). 17.00
TPB X-Men: Inferno, 352-pg. 20.00
TPB X-Men Megazine,CCl,JLe,rep.. 4.00
TPB X-Men: Mutant Massacre,rep. 25.00
TPB Savage Land 10.00
TPB X-Cutioner's Song 25.00
TPB X-Tinction Agenda, rep. 20.00
X-Men Survival Guide to the
   Mansion, NKu(c) (1993) 7.00
TPB Vol. 1: Hope 13.00
TPB Vol. 2: Dominant Species. . . . 12.00
TPB Vol. 3: Holy War. 18.00
TPB Vol. 4: The Draco (2004) 16.00
TPB Vol. 5: She Lies With Angels . 12.00
TPB Vol. 6: Bright New Mourning . 15.00
TPB New Age Vol. 1 The End
   Of History 13.00
TPB New Age Vol. 2: The
   Cruelest Cut 12.00
TPB New Age Vol. 3: On Ice 16.00
TPB New Age Vol. 4 End of Greys 15.00
TPB New Age Vol. 5 First
   Foursaken 12.00

X-MEN

[2nd Regular Series] Oct., 1991
1A(c);Storm,Beast,B:CCl(s),JLe,SW
   I:Fabian Cortez,Acolytes,
   V:Magneto 5.00
1B(c);Colossus,Psylocke 8.00
1C(c);Cyclops,Wolverine 8.00
1D(c);Magneto 8.00
1E(c);Gatefold w/pin-ups 9.00
2 JLe,SW,V:Magneto Contd. 5.00
3 E:CCl(s),JLe,SW,V:Magneto . . . 6.00
4 JBy(s),JLe,SW,I:Omega Red,
   V:Hand. 8.00

5 B:SLo(s),JLe,SW,V:Hand,
  Omega Red,I:Maverick 6.00
6 JLe,SW,V:Omega Red, Hand,
  Sabretooth 6.00
7 JLe,SW,V:Omega Red,Hand,
  Sabretooth 6.00
8 JLe,SW,Bishop vs. Gambit 6.00
9 JLe,SW,A:Ghost Rider,V:Brood . . 5.00
10 JLe,SW,MT,Longshot Vs. Mojo,
  BU:Maverick 5.00
11 E:SLo(s)JLe,MT,V:Mojo,
  BU:Maverick 5.00
12 B:FaN(s),ATb,BWi,I:Hazard 4.00
13 ATb,BWi,V:Hazard 4.00
14 NKu,X-Cutioners Song#3,A:X-Fact.
  X-Force,V:Four Horsemen 4.00
15 NKu,X-Cutioners Song #7,
  V:Mutant Liberation Front 4.00
16 NKu,MPn,X-Cutioners Song #11,
  A:X-Force,X-Factor,V:Dark Riders,
  Apocalypse Vs.Archangel,IR:Stryfe
  is Nathan Summers. 4.00
17 NKu,MPn,R:Illyana,A:Darkstar . . 4.00
18 NKu,MPn,R:Omega Red,V:Soul
  Skinner 4.00
19 NKu,MPn,V:Soul Skinner,
  Omega Red. 4.00
20 NKu,MPn,J.Grey vs Psylocke. . 4.00
21 NKu,V:Silver Samurai,Shinobi . . 4.00
22 BPe,V:Silver Samurai,Shinobi . . 4.00
23 NKu,MPn,V:Dark Riders,
  Mr.Sinister 4.00
24 NKu,BSz,A Day in the Life 4.00
25 NKu,Hologram(c),V:Magneto,
  Wolverine's Adamantium skeleton
  pulled out. 15.00
25a Gold Edition 25.00
25b B&W cover 35.00
26 NKu,Bloodties#2,A:Avengers,
  I:Unforgiven 4.00
27 RiB,I:Threnody 4.00
28 NKu,MRy,F:Sabretooth 4.00
29 NKu,MRy,V:Shinobi 4.00
30 NKu,MRy,W:Cyclops&Jean Grey,
  w/card 6.00
31 NKu,MRy,A:Spiral,Matsuo,
  D:Kwannon 4.00
32 NKu,MRy,A:Spiral,Matsuo. 3.50
33 NKu,MRy,F:Gambit &
  Sabretooth 3.50
34 NKu,MRy,A:Riptide 3.50
35 LSh,A:Nick Fury 3.50
36 NKu,MRy,I:Synch,PhalanxCovenant
  Generation Next,pt.2, deluxe. . 5.00
36a Newsstand ed. 2.25
37 NKu,MRy,Generation Next,pt.3
  foil(c) 5.00
37a newsstand ed. 2.50
38 NKu,MRy,F:Psylocke 3.50
38a newsstand ed. 3.00
39 X-Treme, deluxe 3.50
39a newsstand ed. 3.00
40 deluxe 3.50
40a newsstand ed. 3.00
41 V:Legion, deluxe 3.50
41a newsstand ed. 3.00
42 PS,PaN,Mysterious Visitor 3.00
43 Rogue and Iceman 3.00
44 FaN,Mystery of Magneto 3.00
45 20th Anniv.pt.2 . . . . 5.00
46 FaN,Aku,V:Comcast 3.00
47 SLo,AKu,CaS,F:Dazzler 3.00
48 SLo,AKu,CaS,F:Sabretooth . . . 3.00
49 SLo,AKu,Bishop wanted 3.00
50 Onslaught(c). 7.00
50a regular edition 12.00
51 MWa,Onslaught 6.00
52 MWa,AKu,CaS,V:Sinister 6.00
53 Onslaught saga. 10.00
54 Onslaught saga. 5.00
54a Foil cover 25.00
55 Onslaught saga. 3.50

56 Onslaught saga. 3.50
57 Operation: Zero Tolerence 3.50
58 SLo,NKu 3.50
59 . . . . 3.50
60 SLo,NKu,F:Ororo, V:Candra. . . 3.50
61 SLo,CNn,F:Storm, V:Candra. . . 3.50
62 SLo,CPa,F:Sebastian Shaw,
  Shang Chi 3.50
62A variant Storm/Wolverine(c) . . 15.00
63 SLo,CPa,ATi,A:Sebastian Shaw,
  Inner Circle 3.00
64 SLo,CPa,ATi,V:Hellfire Club . . . 3.00
65 SLo,CPa,ATi, No Exit prelude. . . 3.00
66 SLo,CPa,ATi, Zero Tolerance,
  A:Bastion 3.00
67 SLo,CPa,ATi, Zero Tolerance,
  F:Iceman, Cecilia Reyes 3.00
68 SLo,CPa,ATi, Operation: Zero
  Tolerance 3.00
69 SLo,CPa, Operation: Zero
  Tolerance, concl. 3.50
70 ATi,Who will join X-Men?,
  double-sized 5.00
71 ATi,Cyclops banished 4.00
72 ATi,Professor Logan's School of
  Hard Knocks 3.00
73 ATi,Marrow visits Callisto 3.00
74 ATi,Terror in Morlock Tunnels . . . 3.00
75 ATi,V:N'Garai, double size 4.00
76 CCI,V:Sabretooth, 35th anniv
  kickoff 3.00
77 ATi,A:Black Panther,Maggott . . . 3.00
78 Return of Professor X 3.00
79 ATi,Cannonball must leave team 3.00
80A BPe, ATi, cont. from Uncanny
  X-Men #360, etched foil (c). . . . 7.50
80B regular cover 6.00
81 AKu,MFm,Search for Prof.X 3.00
82 AKu,MFm,Hunt for Xavier 3.00
83 AKu,MFm,Hunt for Xavier,pt.4 . . . 3.00
84 AJu,Hunt for Xavier,concl. 3.50
85 AD,MFm,R:Magneto 3.00
85a signed 30.00
86 AD,MFm,Magneto War,pt.2,
  O:Joseph 3.50
87 AD,MFm,Magneto War,pt.4. . . . . 3.50
88 AD,MFm,F:Juggernaut 3.00
89 AD,MFm,In the past 3.00
90 AD,MFm,In the past,concl. 3.00
91 AD,AKu,Rage Against
  the Machine, pt.2 x-over 3.00
91a signed 30.00
92 AD,MFm,The Shattering x-over . 3.00
93 AD,MFm,The Shattering x-over . 3.00

X-Men 2nd Series #24
© Marvel Entertainment Group

94 AD,MFm,Shattering,x-over 4.00
95 AD,TR,A:Death, ... 3.00
96 AD 12.00
97 AD,MFm,Apocalypse12,pt.7 . . . 10.00
97a variant (c) 20.00
98 AD,MFm,Ages of Apocalypse . . 10.00
99 AD,BBh,mutants no more? 3.00
100 CCI,X-Men:Revolution,48-pg. . . 6.00
100a variant covers 7.00
101 CCI,X-Men:Revolution 3.00
102 CCI,R:Wolverine 3.00
103 CCI,Wolverine v. Rogue 3.00
104 CCI,V:Killion 3.00
105 CCI,Archangel,Psylocke 3.00
106 CCI,Neo,Cecelia Reyes 3.50
107 CCI,Cadre K 4.00
108 CCI,Dream'sEnd,pt.4,x-over . . . 5.00
109 CCI,at X-Mansion, 100-page . . . 4.00
110 SLo,F:Kitty Pryde 4.00
111 SLo,F:Trish Tilby 3.25
112 SLo,Eve of Destruction,pt.2 . . . 3.25
113 SLo,Eve of Destruction,pt.4 . . . 3.25
Becomes:

NEW X-MEN
114 GMo,E is for Extinction,pt.1 . . . 8.00
115A GMo,E for Extinction,pt.2 . . . . 6.00
115B variant BWS(c) 4.00
116 GMo,E for Extinction,pt.3 . . . . . 3.50
117 GMo,F:Beast. 3.50
118 GMo,GermFreeGeneration,pt.1 3.50
119 GMo,Germ Free Gen.,pt.2 . . . . 3.50
120 GMo,Germ Free Gen.,concl. . . . 3.00
121 GMo,Xavier's mind,'Nuff Said. . 3.00
122 GMo,Imperial,pt.1 . . . . 3.00
123 GMo,Imperial,pt.2 . . . . 2.50
124 GMo,Imperial,pt.3 . . . . 2.50
125 GMo,Imperial,pt.4 . . . . 2.50
126 GMo,Imperial,pt.5 . . . . 3.50
127 GMo,F:Xorn 3.00
128 GMo,Jean Grey, Emma Frost. . 3.00
129 GMo,Weapon XII 2.50
130 GMo 2.50
131 GMo,JPL,BSz 2.50
132 GMo,PJ,F:Storm 2.25
133 . . . . 2.25
134 GMo,NRd,no Magneto 2.25
135 GMo,Riot At Xavier's 2.25
136 GMo,Riot At Xavier's 2.25
137 GMo,Riot At Xavier's 2.25
138 GMo,Riot At Xavier's,concl. . . . 2.25
139 GMo,PJ,Murder at Mansion . . . 2.25
140 GMo,PJ,Murder at Mansion . . . 2.25
141 GMo,PJ,Murder at Mansion . . . 2.25
142 GMo,CBa,Weapon Plus,pt.1. . . 2.25
143 GMo,CBa,Weapon Plus,pt.2. . . 2.25
144 GMo,CBa,Weapon Plus,pt.3. . . 2.25
145 GMo,CBa,Weapon Plus,pt.4. . . 2.25
146 PJ,Planet X,pt.1 . . . . 2.25
147 PJ,Planet X,pt.2 . . . . 2.25
148 PJ,Planet X,pt.3 . . . . 2.25
149 PJ,Planet X,pt.4 . . . . 2.25
150 PJ,Planet X,finale,48-pg. 3.50
151 MS,Here Comes Tomorrow . . . 2.25
152 MS,Here Comes Tomorrow . . . 2.25
153 MS,Here Comes Tomorrow . . . 2.25
154 MS,Here Comes Tomorrow . . . 2.25
155 SvL,Bright New Mourning,pt.1 . 2.25
156 SvL,Bright New Mourning,pt.2 . 2.25
becomes:

X-MEN
157 SvL,Day of the Atom,pt.1 . . . . . 2.25
158 SvL,Day of the Atom,pt.2 . . . . . 2.25
159 SvL,Day of the Atom,pt.3 . . . . . 2.25
160 SvL,Day of the Atom,pt.4 . . . . . 2.25
161 SvL,Heroes & Villains,pt.1 . . . . 2.25
162 SvL,Heroes & Villains,pt.2 . . . . 2.25
163 SvL,Heroes & Villains,pt.3 . . . . 2.25
164 SvL,Heroes & Villains,pt.4 . . . . 2.25
165 . . . . 2.25
166 SvL,Golgotha,pt.1 . . . . 2.25
167 SvL,Golgotha,pt.2 . . . . 2.25

168 SvL,Golgotha,pt.3 . . . . 2.25
169 SvL,Golgotha,pt.4 . . . . 2.50
170 SvL,Golgotha,pt.5, concl. 2.50
171 SvL,Bizarre Love Triangle,pt.1 . 2.50
172 SvL,Bizarre Love Triangle,pt.2 . 2.50
173 SvL,Bizarre Love Triangle,pt.3 . 2.50
174 SvL,Bizarre Love Triangle,pt.4 . 2.50
175 SvL,Wild Kingdom,x-over,pt.1 . . 2.50
176 SvL,Wild Kingdom,x-over,pt.3 . . 2.50
177 SvL,House Arrest, pt.1 . . . . 2.50
178 SvL,House Arrest, pt.2 . . . . 2.50
179 SvL,House Arrest, pt.3 . . . . 2.50
180 SvL,What Lorna Saw,pt.1 . . . . . 2.50
181 SvL,What Lorna Saw,pt.2 . . . . . 2.50
182 SvL,Blood of Apocalypse, pt.1 . 2.50
183 SvL,Blood of Apocalypse, pt.2 . 2.50
184 SvL,Blood of Apocalypse, pt.3 . 2.50
185 SvL,Blood of Apocalypse, pt.4 . 3.00
186 SvL,Blood of Apocalypse, pt.5 . 3.00
187 SvL,Blood of Apocalypse, after. 3.00
188 CBo,Supernovas,pt.1 . . . . 3.00
189 CBo,Supernovas,pt.2 . . . . 3.00
190 CBo,Supernovas,pt.3 . . . . 3.00
191 CBo,Supernovas,pt.4 . . . . 3.00
192 CBo,Supernovas,pt.5 . . . . 3.00
193 CBo,Supernovas,pt.6 . . . . 3.00
Ann.#1 JLe,Shattershot,pt.1,
  I:Mojo II 4.00
Ann.#2 I:Empyrean,w/card. 4.00
Ann.#3 F:Storm 4.00
Ann. Uncanny X-Men '97, V:Brother-
  hood, 48-pg. 3.50
Ann. '98 RMz, F:X-Men & Doctor
  Doom 3.50
Ann. '98 X-Men/Fantastic Four, JoC,
  PaP, 48-pg. 3.50
Ann.1999 Rage Against the
  Machine, pt.3 x-over, 48-pg. . . . 3.50
Ann.2000 CCl,SHa,SEa,48-pg. . . . 4.00
Ann. 2001 GMo,Marvelscope 7.50
Uncanny X-Men'95 Spec. F:Husk . 4.00
Giant Size X-Men #3 (2005) 5.00
Giant Size X-Men #4 (2005) 5.00
Spec.X-Men'95, F:Mr.Sinister 4.00
Spec.X-Men'96 LHa, 64-pg., F:Gambit,
  Rogue, Magneto, Jubilee
  & Wolverine 4.00
Spec. X-Men'97,JFM,SEp,F:Gambit,
  Joesph & Phoenix 4.00
Minus 1 Spec., SLo,JMd,, flashback,
  discovery of mutants 2.00
Spec.#1 X-Men: Road to Onslaught
  (1996) 2.50

X-Men Ann. #2
© *Marvel Entertainment Group*

Spec. X-Men Universe: Past,
  Present and Future 3.00
Spec. X-Men.Year In Review 3.00
Spec.#1 X-Men (2000). 3.50
Spec. Millennial Visions 4.00
Spec.2001, Millennial Vision
  48-page 3.50
Spec. X-Men:Declassified,48-pg . . 3.50
Spec. Unearthed Archives
  Sketchbook 3.00
Spec. X-Men/Sentry, PJe,MT. 3.00
Spec. God Loves, Man Kills. 5.00
Spec. rep. Must Have #114–#116 . . 4.00
Chrom.Classics GN,TKa,AD,MFm,
  Age of Apocalypse. 3.00
TPB Dark Phoenix Saga 16.00
TPB Dawn of the Age of
  Apocalypse, gold foil cover 9.00
TPB Twilight of the Age of
  Apocalypse, gold foil cover 9.00
TPB Legion Quest 9.00
TPB Magneto Returns 16.00
TPB Rise of Apocalypse 9.00
TPB Crossroads. 16.00
TPB Phoenix Rising. 15.00
TPB Road Trippin 20.00
TPB Zero Tolerance, 336-pg. 25.00
TPB The Origin of Generation X . . 25.00
TPB X-Men: Vignettes 17.00
TPB Visionaries Joe Madureira . . . 18.00
TPB Visionaries Neal Adams. 25.00
TPB Jim Lee, 288-pg. (2002) 23.00
TPB Jim Lee (2002). 30.00
TPB Mutant Genesis (2002) 18.00
TPB Mutant Genesis (2006) 20.00
TPB Vol. 2, Imperial (2002) 20.00
TPB X-Men/Spider-Man: The Savage
  Land, rep. #1–#4, 80-pg. 10.00
TPB Vol. 3: New Worlds 15.00
TPB Vol. 4: Riot at Xaviers 12.00
TPB Vol. 5: Weapon Plus 15.00
TPB Evolution Vol. 2 . . . . 12.00
TPB X-Men Legends,Vol.1 . . . . . . 18.00
TPB X-Men Legends,Vol.2 . . . . . . 20.00
TPB X-Men Legends,Vol.3 . . . . . . 25.00
TPB Vol. 1: Day of the Atom 9.00
TPB Vol. 4: Legends 20.00
TPB Vol. 6: Planet X 13.00
TPB Vol. 7: Here Comes Tomorrow 11.00
TPB Days of Future Past. 20.00
TPB Eye of Destruction (2005) . . . 15.00
TPB Bizarre Love Triangle (2005). 10.00
TPB Golgotha (2005). 13.00
TPB Day of the Atom (2005) 20.00
TPB X-Men: Blood of Apocalypse . 25.00

X-MEN ADVENTURES
[1st Season] 1992–94
1 V:Sentinals, Based on TV
  Cartoon 6.00
2 V:Sentinals,D:Morph 5.00
3 V:Magneto,A:Sabretooth 4.00
4 V:Magneto 4.00
5 V:Morlocks 4.00
6 V:Sabretooth 3.50
7 V:Cable,Genosha,Sentinels 3.00
8 A:Colossus,A:Juggernaut 3.00
9 I:Colussus(on cartoon),
  V:Juggernaut 3.00
10 A:Angel,V:Mystique 3.00
11 I:Archangel(on cartoon) 3.00
12 V:Horsemen of Apocalypse. 2.50
13 RMc(s),I:Bishop(on cartoon). . . . 2.50
14 V:Brotherhood of Evil Mutants . . 2.50
15 . . . . 2.50
TPB Vol.1 . . . . 5.00
TPB Vol.2 . . . . 5.00
TPB Vol.3 . . . . 6.00
TPB Vol.4 rep. Days of Future Past
  and Final Conflict. 7.00

X-Men Adventures #5
© *Marvel Entertainment Group*

[2nd Season] 1994–95
1 R:Morph,I:Mr. Sinister
  (on cartoon) 3.00
2 I:Nasty Boys (on cartoon) 2.50
3 I:Shadow King (on cartoon) 2.50
4 I:Omega Red (on cartoon) 2.50
5 I:Alpha Flight (on cartoon) 2.50
6 F:Gambit 2.50
7 A:Cable,Bishop,Apocalypse 2.50
8 A:Cable,Biship,Apocalypse 2.50
9 O:Rogue 2.50
10 . . . . 2.50
11 F:Mojo,Longshot 2.50
12 Reunions,pt.1 . . . . 2.50
13 Reunions,pt.1 . . . . 2.50

[3rd Season] 1995–96
1 Out of the Past,pt.1 . . . . 3.00
2 V:Spirit Drinker. 2.50
3 Phoenix Saga,pt.1 . . . . 2.50
4 Phoenix Saga,pt.2 . . . . 2.50
5 Phoenix Saga,pt.3 . . . . 2.50
6 Phoenix Saga,pt.4 . . . . 2.50
7 Phoenix Saga,pt.5 . . . . 2.50
8 War in The Savage Land. 2.50
9 F:Ka-Zar. 2.50
10 Dark Phoenix,Saga,pt.1 . . . . 2.50
11 Dark Phoenix Saga,pt.2 . . . . 2.50
12 Dark Phoenix Saga,pt.3 . . . . 2.50
13 Dark Phoenix Saga,pt.4 . . . . 2.50

X-MEN:
AGE OF APOCALYPSE
March, 2005
1-shot Age of Apocalypse, 48-pg. . . 4.00
1 (Of 6) CBa 3.00
2 CBa 3.00
3 thru 5 CBa . . . . @3.00
6 CBa,finale 3.00
TPB Vol.1:Age of Apocalypse Epic 30.00
TPB Vol.2:Age of Apocalypse Epic 30.00
TPB New Age of Apocalypse. 21.00
TPB Complete Age of Apocalypse. 30.00

X-MEN: ALPHA
1994
1 Age of Apocalypse, double size. . 9.00
1a gold edition, 48pp 50.00

X-MEN/ALPHA FLIGHT
Jan., 1986
1 PS,BWi,V:Loki 5.00
2 PS,BWi,V:Loki 5.00

All comics prices listed are for *Near Mint* condition.

X-MEN/ALPHA FLIGHT: THE GIFT
Jan., 1998
1-shot CCI,PS, rep. of limited series 6.00

X-MEN AND POWER PACK
Oct., 2005
1 (of 4) 3.00
2 thru 4 . . . . @3.00
Digest The Power of X. 8.00

X-MEN/ ANIMATION SPECIAL
TV Screenplay Adapt 11.00

X-MEN: APOCALYPSE/ DRACULA
Feb., 2006
1 . . . . 3.00
2 thru 4 . . . . 3.00
TPB X-Men: Apocalypse/Dracula . . 11.00

X-Men Archives #3
© *Marvel Entertainment Group*

X-MEN ARCHIVES: CAPTAIN BRITAIN
1995
1 AMo,AD,Secret History 3.00
2 AMo,AD,F:Captain Britain 3.00
3 AMo,AD,Trial of Captain Britain . . 3.00
4 AMo,AD,Trial cont. 3.00
5 AD,AMo,F:Captain Britain 3.00
6 AMo,AD,Final Apocalypse? 3.00
7 AMo,AD,conclusion 3.00

X-MEN: ASKANI'SON
1 SLo,GeH,sequel to Adventures of
  Cyclops & Phoenix 3.00
2 SLo,GeH,A:Stryfe 3.00
3 SLo,GeH 3.00
4 SLo,GeH,conclusion 3.00
Books of Askani, portraits (1995). . . 3.00

X-MEN AT STATE FAIR
1 KGa,Dallas Times Herald 65.00

X-MEN/BLACK PANTHER
Jan., 2006
TPB SaL. 12.00

X-MEN: BLACK SUN
Sept., 2000
1 (of 5) CCI,New X-Men 3.00
2 CCI,Storm 3.00
3 CCI,RT,Banshee & Sunfire 3.00
4 CCI,LSi,Colossus&Nightcrawler . 3.00
5 CCI,Wolverine & Thunderbird . . . 3.00

X-MEN: CHILDREN OF THE ATOM
Jan., 2000
1 (of 6) JoC,SR,O:X-Men 5.00
2 JoC,SR,F:Professor X 3.00
3 JoC,SR 3.00
4 JoC,SR 3.00
5 JoC,SR, ... 3.00
6 JoC,SR,concl. 3.00

X-MEN CHRONICLES
1995
1 X-Men Unlimited AX 5.00
2 V:Abbatoir 5.00

X-MEN/CLANDESTINE
1996
1 & 2 AD,MFm,48-pg. . . . . @3.00

X-MEN CLASSICS
Dec., 1983
1 NA,rep. 7.00
2 NA,rep. 7.00
3 NA,rep. 7.00

CLASSIC X-MEN
Sept., 1986
1 AAd(c),JBo,New stories, rep.
  giant size X-Men 1 . . . . 9.00
2 rep.#94,JBo/AAd(c) 6.00
3 thru 9 rep#95-101,JBo/AAd(c) . @4.00
10 rep.#102,JBo/AAd(c),BU:Wolv. . . 8.00
11 rep.#103,JBo/BL(c), ... 3.00
12 rep.#104,JBo/AAd(c),BU:
  O:Magneto. 7.00
13 thru 16 rep.,JBo/AAd(c) . . . . . @3.00
17 rep.#111,JBo/TA(c) 5.00
18 rep.#112,JBo/AAd(c). 4.00
19 rep.#113,JBo/AAd(c). 4.00
20 thru 22 rep.,JBo/AAd(c) . . . . . @3.00
23 thru 25 rep.,JBo/KGa(c) . . . . . @3.00
26 rep.#120,JBo/KGa(c). 4.00
27 thru 29 rep.,JBo/KD(c) . . . . . . @3.00
30 thru 35 rep.,JBo/SLi(c) . . . . . . @3.00
36 rep.#130,MBr/SLi(c) 3.00
37 rep.#131,RL/SLi(c) 3.00
38 rep.#132,KB/SLi(c) 3.00
39 rep.#133,2nd JLe X-Men/SLi(c) 11.00
40 thru 42 rep.,SLi(c) . . . . @3.00
43 rep.#137,JBy(c). 3.00
Becomes:

X-MEN CLASSICS
1990
44 rep.#138,KD/SLi(c) 3.00
45 thru 49 rep.#139-#145,SLi(c) . @3.00
50 thru 69 rep.#146-#165 . . . . . @3.00
70 thru 105 rep.#166-#201 . . . . . @2.50
106 Phoenix vs. Beyonder. 2.50
107 F:Rogue 2.50
108 F:Nightcrawler. 2.50
109 Rep. Uncanny X-Men #205 . . . 2.50
110 Rep. Uncanny X-Men #206 . . . 2.50

X-MEN: COLOSSUS–BLOODLINE
Sept., 2005
1 (of 5) Colossus 3.00
2 Russia 3.00
3 thru 5 . . . . @3.00

TPB X-Men: Colossus Bloodline . . 14.00

X-MEN: DEADLY GENESIS
Nov., 2005
1 . . . . 4.00
2 Decimation tie-in 3.50
3 thru 5 . . . . @3.50

X-MEN: EARLY YEARS
1 rep. X-Men (first series) #1 . . . . 2.50
2 rep. X-Men (first series) #2 . . . . 2.50
3 rep. X-Men (first series) #3 . . . . 2.50
4 thru 16 rep. X-Men (first series)
  #4 to #16 . . . . @2.50
17 Rep. X-Men #17 & #18 . . . . 2.50

X-MEN: THE END
Aug., 2004
1 Dreamers and Demons,pt.1 . . . . 3.00
2 thru 6 Dreamers and Demons . @3.00
TPB X-Men: The End–Dreamers
  and Demons 15.00

X-MEN: THE END– HEROES AND MARTYRS
March, 2005
1 (of 6) CCI(s). 3.00
2 CCI(s). 3.00
3 CCI(s). 3.00
4 CCI(s). 3.00
5 & 6 CCI(s) . . . . @3.00
TPB The End–Heroes & Martyrs . . 15.00

X-MEN: THE END– MEN AND X-MEN
Jan., 2006
1 CCI. 3.00
2 thru 6 CCI. . . . . @3.00
TPB X-Men: End: Men & X-Men . . 15.00

X-MEN EVOLUTION
Nov., 2001
1 cartoon series tie-in 2.25
2 F:Cyclops. 2.25
3 F:Jean Grey 2.25
4 F:Nigntcrawler, Shadowcat,
  Spyke, Rogue 2.25
5 F:Mystique, Rogue. 2.25
6 I:Mimic 2.25
7 new recruits, Beast 2.25
8 F:Angel, Storm. 2.25
9 F:Professor X, Brotherhood. 2.25
10 . . . . 2.25
TPB Vol.1, 96-pg. 9.00
Digest. 6.00

X-MEN FAIRY TALES
May, 2006
1 Kitty's Fairy Tale. 3.00
2 Professor X and Magneto 3.00
3 Rogue and Gambit 3.00
4 Logan. 3.00
TPB X-Men Fairy Tales 11.00

X-MEN/FANTASTIC FOUR
Dec., 2004
1 (of 5) PtL 3.50
2 PtL 3.50
3 PtL 3.50
4 PtL,Brood attack 3.50
5 PtL,Finale. 3.50

X-MEN FIRST CLASS
Sept., 2006
1 . . . . 3.00
2 V:The Lizard 3.00
3 . . . . 3.00

X-MEN FOREVER
Nov., 2000
1 (of 6) FaN,KM, ... 5.00
2 FaN,KM,displaced in time 4.00
3 FaN,KM, crucial points 4.00
4 FaN,KM,Toad. 3.50
5 FaN,KM,Prosh 3.50
6 FaN,KM, concl. 3.50

X-MEN: HELLFIRE CLUB
Nov., 1999
1 (of 4) AKu,BRa,CAd. 3.00
2 AKu,BRa,CAd,O:Inner Circle. . . . 3.00
3 AKu,BRa,CAd,O:cont. 3.00
4 AKu,BRa,O:Concl. 3.00

X-MEN: THE HIDDEN YEARS
Oct., 1999
1 JBy,TP,Original team,48-pg. 4.00
2 JBy,TP 3.00
3 JBy,TP, ... 3.00
4 JBy,TP,Savage Land concl. 3.00
5 JBy,TP,A:Candy Southern 3.00
6 JBy,TP,F:Storm 3.00
7 JBy,TP,V:Deluge 3.00
8 JBy,TP,Fant.Four 3.00
9 JBy,TP,Phoenix 3.00
10 JBy,TP,Candy Southern 3.00
11 JBy,TP,Beast 3.00
12 JBy,TP,48-pg. 4.00
13 JBy,TP,Beast. 3.00
14 JBy,TP,Beast,Angel. 3.00
15 JBy,X-Mansion 3.00
16 JBy,return, to new conflicts 3.00
17 JBy,Kraven,Beast 3.00
18 JBy,Tad Carter,Lorna Dane. . . . 3.00
19 JBy,TP,Lorna,Angel,Promise . . . 3.00
20 JBy,TP,Sub-Mariner,Magneto . . . 3.00
21 JBy,TP,Namor,Magneto 3.00
22 JBy,TP,X-Men & Fant.Four 3.00

X-MEN ICONS: CHAMBER
Aug., 2002
1 (of 4) NRd 3.50
2 thru 4 NRd . . . . @3.00

X-MEN INDEX
See: OFFICIAL MARVEL INDEX TO THE X-MEN

X-MEN: KITTY PRYDE– SHADOW & FLAME
June, 2005
1 (of 5),Kitty Pryde & Lockhead . . . 3.00
2 thru 5 Finale. . . . . @3.00

X-MEN: LIBERATORS
Sept., 1999
1 (of 4) PJ,F:Wolverine,Nightcrawler
& Colossus 3.00
2 PJ,V:Russian army 3.00
3 PJ,V:Nikolas. 3.00
4 PJ,V:Omega Red. 3.00

X-MEN: LOST TALES
1997
1 CCI,JBo,rep. from Classic X-Men 3.00
2 CCI,JBo,rep. from Classic X-Men 3.00

X-MEN: MAGIK
Oct., 2000
1 (of 4) DAn,ALa,LSh 3.00
2 DAn,ALa,LSh,V:Mephisto 3.00
3 DAn,ALa,LSh,F:Limbo 3.00
4 DAn,ALa,LSh,concl. 3.00

X-MEN/MICRONAUTS
Jan., 1984
1 JG,BWi,Limited Series 4.00
2 JG,BWi,KJo,V:Baron Karza 3.00
3 JG,BWi,V:Baron Karza. 3.00
4 JG,BWi,V:Baron Karza,Apr.1984 . 3.00

X-MEN: THE MAGNETO WAR
Jan., 1999
1-shot AD, Joseph vs. Magneto. . . . 3.00
1a signed 20.00

X-Man The Manga#15
© Marvel Entertainment Group

X-MEN: THE MANGA
Jan., 1998
1 b&w,translated,F:Jubilee 4.00
2 Jubilee joins, V:Sentinels. 3.00
3 Agent Gyrich strikes. 3.00
4 Beast captured, morph dead 3.00
5 Magneto attempts to rescue
Beast 3.00
6 Beast on trial, A:Sabretooth. 3.00
7 V:Magneto 3.00
8 V:Magneto 3.00
9 V:Morlocks. 3.00
10 V:Morlocks, 40-pg. finale 3.00
11 Wolverine vs. Sabretooth 3.00
12 Wolverine vs. Sabretooth 3.00
13 F:Storm, Jubilee & Gambit 3.00
14 . . . . 3.00
15 . . . . 3.00
16 A:Colossus,V:Juggernaut,
double-size 4.00
17 F:Cable & Angel 3.00
18 Angel becomes Archangel 3.00
19 Angel becomes Death. 3.00
20 Rogue vs. Apocalypse 3.00
21 V:Four Horsemen 3.00
22 V:Sentinels 3.00
23 RGr(c),F:Bishop 3.00
24 RGr(c),V:Nimrod 3.00
25 Bishop vs. Gambit. 3.00
26 V:Brotherhood of Evil Mutants . . 3.00
27 Magneto Returns 3.00
28 V:Master Mold,A:Magneto 3.00
29 thru 32 . . . . @3.00

X-MEN: THE MOVIE
June, 2000
Magneto, photo(c) 6.00
Rogue, photo(c). 6.00

Wolverine, photo(c) 6.00
X-Men The Movie, photo(c). 6.00
TPB Beginnings, 144-pg. 15.00
TPB X-Men The Movie, 4 diff.
photo(c)s . . . . @15.00

X-MEN OMEGA
1995
1 FaN,Slo,After Xavier, concl. 10.00
1a Gold ed. Chromium(c) 48-pg. . 50.00

X-MEN: PHOENIX
Oct., 1999
1 (of 3) JFM,F:Rachel Summers . . 3.00
2 JFM 3.00
3 JFM,concl. 3.00

X-MEN: PHOENIX
May, 2003
1 (of 3) Legacy of Fire 3.00
2 Sword of Limbo 3.00
3 Concl.. . . . . 3.00

X-MEN: PHOENIX – ENDSONG
Jan., 2005
1 (of 5) Phoenix Force 5.00
2 thru 5 . . . . @5.00

X-MEN: PHOENIX – WARSONG
Sept., 2006
1 (of 5) 5.00
2 thru 3 . . . . @5.00

X-MEN PRIME
1995
1 SLo,FaN,BHi,major plotlines for
all X books begin, chromium(c)10.00

X-MEN: PRYDE & WISDOM
1 WEI,TyD,KIS 3.00
2 & 3 Wei,TyD,KIS3.00

X-MEN: RONIN
March, 2003
1 (of 5) manga mania 3.00
2 . . . . 3.00
3 . . . . 3.00
4 . . . . 3.00
5 . . . . 3.00

X-MEN: THE 198
Jan., 2006
1 Decimation tie-in 3.00
2 thru 5 . . . . @3.00

X-MEN: THE RISE OF APOCALYPSE
1 TKa,AdP, ancient history of
X-Men 3.50
2 thru 4 TKa,AdP, ... @3.00
TPB 10.00

X-MEN: THE SEARCH FOR CYCLOPS
Oct., 2000
1A (of 4) TR,SHa, ... 5.00
1B variant AdP 5.00
2A TR,SHa,Scott alive? 3.00
2B variant AdP(c) 3.00
3A TR,SHa, ... 3.00
3B variant AdP(c) 3.00
4A TR,SHa, concl. 5.00

MARVEL

X-MEN SPOTLIGHT ON STARJAMMERS
1990
1 DC,F:Starjammers,A:Prof.X 5.00
2 DC,F:Starjammers,A:Prof.X 5.00

X-MEN: TRUE FRIENDS
July, 1999
1 (of 3) CCI,RL,JP,F:Shadowcat . . . 3.00
2 CCI,RL,JP,A:Kitty Pryde 3.00
3 CCI,RL,JP,A:Wolverine,concl. . . . 3.00

X-MEN 2099
1993–96
1 B:JFM(s),RLm,JP,I:X-Men 2099 . 4.00
1a Gold Ed 5.00
2 RLm,JP,V:Rat Pack 3.00
3 RLm,JP,D:Serpentina 3.00
4 RLm,JP,I:Theatre of Pain 3.00
5 RLm,JP,Fall of the Hammer#3. . . 3.00
6 RLm,JP,I:Freakshow 3.00
7 RLm,JP,V:Freakshow 3.00
8 RLm(c),JS3,JP,N:Metalhead,
    I:2nd X-Men 2099 . . . . 3.00
9 RLm,JP,V:2nd X-Men 2099 . . . . . 3.00
10 RLm,JP,A:La Lunatica 3.00
11 RLm,JP,V:2nd X-Men 2099 . . . . 3.00
12 RLm,JP,A:Junkpile 3.00
13 RLm,JP 3.00
14 RLm,JP,R:Loki 3.00
15 RLm,JP,F:Loki,I:Haloween Jack . 3.00
16 . . . . 3.00
17 X'ian 3.00
18 Haloween Jack 3.00
19 Conclusion Halloween Jack 3.00
Becomes:

X-MEN 2099 A.D.
20 F:Bloodhawk 3.00
21 Doom Factor 3.00
22 One Nation Under Doom 3.00
23 V:Junkpile 3.00
24 . . . . 3.00
25 X-Men Reunited 3.00
25a variant cover 4.25
26 V:Graverobber 3.00
27 . . . . 3.00
28 X-Nation x-over 3.00
29 X-Nation x-over 3.00
30 & 31 . . . . @3.00
32 V:Foolkiller 3.00
Spec.#1 Bros.Hildebrandt(c) 4.50

X-Men 2099 #5
© Marvel Entertainment Group

GN X-Men 2099: Oasis, rep., Greg
    Hildebrandt(c) 64-pg., (1998) . . 6.00

X-MEN 2: THE MOVIE
March, 2003
Prequel Wolverine, TMd 3.50
Prequel Nightcrawler 3.50
Spec. Movie Adapt., 48-pg. 3.50
TPB The Movie 13.00

X-MEN UNIVERSE
Oct., 1999
1 rep. July 99 stories, 80-pg. 5.00
2 thru 11 rep., 80-pg. . . . . @5.00
12 thru 17,rep., 80-pg. . . . . @4.00

X-MEN UNLIMITED
1993
1 CBa,BP,O:Siena Blaze 7.00
2 JD,O:Magneto 6.00
3 FaN(s),BSz(c),MMK,Sabretooth
    joins X-Men,A:Maverick. 7.00
4 SLo(s),RiB,O:Nightcrawler,Rogue,
    Mystique,IR:Mystique is
    Nightcrawler's mother 5.00
5 JFM(s),LSh,After Shi'ar/
    Kree War 4.50
6 JFM(s),PS,Sauron 4.50
7 JR2,HMe,O:Storm 4.50
8 Legacy Virus Victim 4.50
9 LHa,Wolverine & Psylocke 4.50
10 MWa,Dark Beast,Beast,
    double-size 8.00
11 Rogue & Magneto, double-size . 8.00
12 Onslaught x-over,A:Juggernaut . 3.00
13 GP,Binary gone berserk 3.00
14 TKa, Onslaught fallout 3.00
15 HMe,F:Wolverine, Iceman &
    Maverick 3.00
16 MvR,F:Banshee, White Queen,
    I:Primal 3.00
17 TKa,Wolverine vs. Sabretooth,
    minds are switched 4.00
18 TDF,V:Hydro Man 3.00
19 BRa,Nightcrawler v. Belasco . . . 3.00
20 F:Generation X 3.00
21 TDz,Strong Guy returns 3.00
22 into Marrow's World 4.00
23 F:Professor X 3.00
24 F:Wolverine & Cecilia Reyes . . . 3.00
25 BBh,48-pg. 3.00
26 BBh,Ages of Apocalypse,pt.4 . . 7.00
27 BBh,X-Men: Revolution 3.00
28 BBh,Russia 3.00
29 BBh,Maximum Security 3.00
30 BBh, ... 3.00
31 MGo(c) three stories 3.00
32 JIT(c) 3.00
33 MK(c),Sabretooth,Blob 3.00
34 Marvel Girl vs. Sabretooth 3.50
35 F:Emma Frost, Jubilee 3.50
36 three stories 3.50
37 multiple dimensions, 48-pg. 3.50
38 DaR,F:Colossus 2.50
39 KIS,48-pg. 3.50
40 All evil issue, 48-pg. 3.50
41 I:MC Mystik,48-pg. 3.50
42 F:Prof. X, Jean Grey,48-pg. 3.50
43 CCI,BSz 2.50
44 animal cruelty 2.50
45 V:Alpha Flight 2.50
46 SB,F:Wolverine 2.50
47 Return of Psylocke 2.50
48 Mystique returns 2.50
49 F:Nightcrawler 2.50
50 PS,Japan connections 3.00

X-MEN UNLIMITED
March, 2004
1 TMd 3.00

2 F:Bishop 3.00
3 F:Gambit 3.00
4 F:Juggernaut 3.00
5 F:Wolverine 3.00
6 Ladies of X 3.00
7 F:nightcrawler, Kitty Pryde 3.00
8 F:Angel, Beast 3.00
9 F:Wolverine, Iceman 3.00
10 F:The Beast 3.00
11 MD2(c),Rachel & Havok 3.00
12 F:Wolverine 3.00
13 Decimation tie-in 3.00
14 F:Colossus 3.00

X-MEN VS. AVENGERS
April, 1987
1 MS,JRu,V:Soviet SuperSoldiers . 5.00
2 MS,JRu,V:Sov.Super Soldiers . . 3.50
3 MS,JRu,V:Sov.Super Soldiers . . 3.50
4 KP,JRu,BMc,AW,AM,V:Magneto
    July, 1987 . . . . 3.50
TPB 13.00

X-MEN VS. THE BROOD
1996
1 and 2 Day of Wrath . . . . @3.00
TPB rep. 17.00

X-NATION 2099
1996
1 . . . . 4.00
2 . . . . 2.50
3 At Herod's Themepark 2.50

X.S.E.
Mini-Series 1996
1 (of 4) JOs,Bishop & Shard's
    secrets 2.25
2 JOs, How did Shard die 2.25
3 JOs, How Shard died. 2.25
4 JOs, conclusion 2.25

X-STATIX
July, 2002
1 PrM,MiA,super-team, 40-pg. 3.00
2 PrM,MiA, ... 2.50
3 PrM,MiA 2.50
4 PrM,MiA, sex = death? 2.50
5 PrM,PPo 2.50
6 PrM,MiA,pt.1 . . . . 2.50
7 PrM,MiA 2.50
8 PrM,MiA,Orphan's New Love . . . 2.50
9 PrM,MiA, ... 2.50
10 PrM,Diaries of Edie Sawyer . . . 3.00
11 PrM,F:Latino 3.00
12 PrM,If You Think I'm Sexy 3.00
13 PrM,MiA,Di Another Day,pt.1 . . 3.00
14 PrM,MiA,Di Another Day,pt.2 . . 3.00
15 PrM,MiA,Di Another Day,pt.3 . . 3.00
16 PrM,MiA,Di Another Day,pt.4 . . 3.00
17 PrM,MiA,Back from Dead,pt.4 . . 3.00
18 PrM,MiA,Back from Dead,pt.5 . . 3.00
19 PrM,MiA,Back from Dead,pt.6 . . 3.00
19 PrM,MiA,The Cure,pt.1 . . . . 3.00
20 PrM,MiA,The Cure,pt.2 . . . . 3.00
21 PrM,MiA,V:Avengers,pt.1 . . . . . 3.00
22 PrM,MiA,V:Avengers,pt.2 . . . . . 3.00
23 PrM,MiA,V:Avengers,pt.3 . . . . . 3.00
24 PrM,MiA,V:Avengers,pt.4 . . . . . 3.00
25 PrM,MiA,V:Avengers,pt.5 . . . . . 3.00
26 PrM,MiA,finale 3.00
TPB Vol.1 . . . . 12.00
TPB Vol.2:GoodGuys & BadGuys . 16.00
TPB Vol.3:Back From the Dead. . . 20.00
TPB Vol.4: X-Statix vs. Avengers . . 20.00

X-TERMINATORS
Oct., 1988—Jan., 1989
1 JBg,AW,AM,I:N'astirh 4.00

X Terminators #4
© Marvel Entertainment Group

2 JBg,AM,V:N'astirh 3.50
3 JBg,AM,V:N'astirh 3.00
4 JBg,AM,A:New Mutants. 3.00

X-TREME X-MEN
June, 2001
1 CCI,SvL,Destiny,48-page. 4.50
2A CCI,SvL,Guardia,Vargas 3.50
2B variant CPa(c) 3.50
3 CCI,SvL,V:Vargas 3.00
4 CCI,SvL,V:Vargas 3.00
5 CCI,SvL,F:Gambit 3.00
6 CCI,SvL,F:Gambit,Rogue 3.00
7 CCI,SvL 3.00
8 CCI,SvL,concl.'Nuff Said 3.00
9 CCI,SvL,V:Lady Mastermind 3.00
10 CCI,SvL,Dimension X,pt.1 . . . . . 3.00
11 CCI,SvL,Dimension X,pt.2 . . . . . 3.00
12 CCI,SvL,V:Shaltan,Khan 3.00
13 CCI,SvL,F:Gambit,Lifeguard 3.00
14 CCI,SvL,F:Storm, Sage. 3.00
15 CCI,SvL,F:Storm,Rogue 3.00
16 CCI,SvL,F:Rogue, Gambit 3.00
17 CCI,SvL 3.00
18 CCI,SvL,F:Jean Grey,Beast,
   Nightcrawler. 3.00
19 CCI,F:Jean Grey 3.00
20 CCI,SvL,Scism,pt.1 . . . . 3.00
21 CCI,SvL,Scism,pt.2 . . . . 3.00
22 CCI,SvL,Scism,pt.3 . . . . 3.00
23 CCI,SvL,Scism,pt.4 . . . . 3.00
24 CCI,SvL,R:Cannonball 3.00
25 CCI,SvL,God Loves,Man Kills2. . 3.00
26 CCI,SvL,God Loves,Man Kills2. . 3.00
27 CCI,SvL,God Loves,Man Kills2. . 3.00
28 CCI,SvL,God Loves,Man Kills2. . 3.00
29 CCI,SvL,God Loves,Man Kills2. . 3.00
30 CCI,SvL,God Loves,Man Kills2. . 3.00
31 CCI,SHa,Intifada,pt.1 . . . . 3.00
32 CCI,SHa,Intifada,pt.2 . . . . 3.00
33 CCI,SHa,Intifada,pt.3 . . . . 3.00
34 CCI,SHa,Intifada,pt.4 . . . . 3.00
35 CCI,SHa,Intifada,pt.5 . . . . 3.00
36 Storm: The Arena,pt.1. . . . . 3.00
37 Storm: The Arena,pt.2. . . . . 3.00
38 Storm: The Arena,pt.3. . . . . 3.00
39 Storm: The Arena,pt.4. . . . . 3.00
40 CCI,Bogan,pt.1,Prisoner of Fire . 3.00
41 CCI,Bogan,pt.2,Prisoner of Fire . 3.00
42 CCI,Bogan,pt.3,Prisoner of Fire . 3.00
43 CCI,Bogan,pt.4,Prisoner of Fire . 3.00
44 CCI,Prisoner of Fire,pt.5 . . . . . . 3.00
45 CCI,Prisoner of Fire,pt.6 . . . . . . 3.00
46 CCI,finale 3.50
Ann.2001 CCI,SvL,64-pg. 5.00
TPB rep.#1-#4, 192-pg. (2002) . . . 19.00
TPB Vol. 2: Invasion 20.00

TPB Vol. 3: Schism 17.00
TPB Vol. 4: Mekanix 17.00
TPB Vol. 5: God Loves, Man Kills . 20.00
TPB Vol. 6: Intifada 17.00
TPB Vol. 7: Storm–The Arena 17.00
TPB Vol. 8: Prisoner of Fire. 20.00

X-TREME X-MEN:
SAVAGE LAND
July, 2001
1 (of 4) CCI,F:Rogue 3.50
2 CCI,Velociraptors & T-Rexes 3.00
3 CCI 3.00
4 CCI,concl. 3.00
TPB 96-pg. 13.00

X-TREME X-MEN:
X-POSE
Nov., 2002
1 (of 2) Ccl, two reporters 3.00
2 CCI,Forbidden Mutant Love 3.00

X-23
Jan., 2005
1 (of 6) BTn,Innocence Lost,pt.1 . . 6.00
2 Btn,o:x-23 . . . . 4.00
3 BTn,Innocence Lost 3.00
4 BTn,Innocence Lost. 3.00
5 BTn,Innocence Lost. 3.00
6 BTn,Innocence Lost,concl. 3.00

X-UNIVERSE
1995
1 The Other Heroes 5.00
2 F:Ben Grimm,Tony Stark 5.00

YELLOW CLAW
Marvel Atlas, 1956
1 MMe 1,400.00
2 JK,JSe 1,100.00
3 BEv 1,100.00
4 JK,JSe 1,100.00

YOGI BEAR
Nov., 1977
1 A:Flintstones 40.00
2 thru 9 March, 1979 . . . . @25.00

YOUNG ALLIES COMICS
Timely,
Summer, 1941—Oct., 1946
1 S&K,SSh,Hitler(c),I&O:Young Allies
   1st meeting Capt. America &
   Human Torch,A:Red Skull 45,000.00
2 S&K,A;Capt.America,Human
   Torch. 9,000.00
3 Remember Pearl Harbor(c) . 8,000.00
4 A;Capt. America,Torch,Red Skull
   ASh(c),Horror In Hollywood
   A:Capt.America,Torch. 9,000.00
5 ASh(c),AAv,Capt.America . . . 3,500.00
6 ASh(c) 2,800.00
7 ASh(c),SSh 2,800.00
8 ASh(c),WW2,Bondage 2,800.00
9 ASh(c),Axis leaders(c),
   B:Tommy Type,Hitler 3,000.00
10 ASh(c),O:Tommy Type. 2,800.00
11 ASh(c) 2,000.00
12 ASh(c),Decapitation 2,000.00
13 ASh(c) 2,000.00
14 ASh(c) 2,000.00
15 ASh(c),AAv 2,000.00
16 ASh(c) 2,000.00
17 ASh(c),SSh 2,000.00
18 ASh(c) 1,800.00
19 ASh(c),E:Tommy Type 1,800.00
20 SSh 1,800.00

Young Allies #8
© Marvel Entertainment Group

YOUNG AVENGERS
Feb., 2005
1 Sidekicks 5.00
2 Sidekicks 3.00
3 Sidekicks 3.00
4 Sidekicks 3.00
5 Sidekicks 3.00
6 Sidekicks,concl. 3.00
7 Secret Identities,pt.1 . . . . 3.00
8 Secret Identities,pt.2 . . . . 3.00
9 New team member 3.00
10 Family Matters 3.00
11 Kree-Skrull War II 3.00
12 Family Matters 3.00
Spec. #1 Secret History (2005) 3.00
TPB Vol. 1 Sidekicks 15.00

YOUNG HEARTS
Nov., 1949—Feb., 1950
1 . . . . 150.00
2 Feb., 1950 . . . . 100.00

YOUNG MEN
See: COWBOY ROMANCES

YUPPIES FROM HELL
1989
1 Satire 3.00
2 . . . . 3.00
3 . . . . 3.00

ZIGGY PIG,
SILLY SEAL
Marvel Timely, 1944
1 Funny Animals vs. Japs. 350.00
2 . . . . 150.00
3 . . . . 125.00
4 . . . . 125.00
5 . . . . 125.00
6 . . . . 150.00

ZOMBIE
Sept., 2006
1 . . . . 4.00
2 . . . . 4.00
3 . . . . 4.00

ZORRO
Marvel UK, 1990
1 Don Diego 3.00
2 thru 12 . . . . @3.00

MARVEL

A-1 COMICS
Magazine Enterprises, 1944
N# F:Kerry Drake,BU:Johnny
  Devildog & Streamer Kelly . . 300.00
1 A:Dotty Driple,Mr. EX,Bush
  Berry and Lew Loyal 150.00
2 A:Texas Slim & Dirty Dalton,
  The Corsair,Teddy Rich, Dotty
  Dripple,Inca Dinca,Tommy Tinker
  Little Mexico and Tugboat . . . 100.00
3 same 100.00
4 same 100.00
5 same 100.00
6 same 100.00
7 same 100.00
8 same 100.00
9 Texas Slim Issue 125.00
10 Same characters as
  issues #2–#8 . . . . 100.00
11 Teena 150.00
12 Teena 100.00
13 JCr,Guns of Fact and Fiction,
  narcotics & junkies featured . 400.00
14 Tim Holt #1. . . . . 1,100.00
15 Teena 100.00
16 Vacation Comics. 75.00
17 Tim Holt #2, E:"A-1" on cover . 600.00
18 Jimmy Durante, Ph(c). 700.00
19 Tim Holt #3 . . . . 400.00
20 Jimmy Durante Ph(c) 600.00
21 OW,Joan of Arc movie adapt.. 400.00
22 Dick Powell (1949) 350.00
23 Cowboys N' Indians #6. . . . . 175.00
24 FF(c),LbC,Trail Colt #1 . . . . . 600.00
25 Fibber McGee & Molly (1949). 125.00
26 LbC, Trail Colt #2 . . . . 500.00
27 GhostRider#1,O:GhostRider 1,700.00
28 Christmas (Koko & Kola #6). . . 75.00
29 FF(c), Ghost Rider #2 . . . . 1,200.00
30 BP, Jet Powers #1 . . . . 600.00
31 FF,Ghost Rider #3,O:Ghost
  Rider 1, 200.00
32 AW,GE,Jet Powers #2 . . . . . 550.00
33 Muggsy Mouse #1 . . . . 100.00
34 FF(c),Ghost Rider #4 . . . . . 1,100.00
35 AW,Jet Powers#3 . . . . 550.00
36 Muggsy Mouse #2 . . . . 125.00
37 FF(c),Ghost Rider #5. . . . . 1,100.00
38 AW,WW,Jet Powers#4, Drugs 900.00
39 Muggsy Mouse #3 . . . . 100.00
40 Dogface Dooley #1 . . . . 100.00
41 Cowboys 'N' Indians #7 . . . . . 100.00
42 BP,Best of the West #1. . . . . 700.00
43 Dogface Dooley#2 . . . . 75.00
44 Ghost Rider #6 . . . . 500.00
45 American Air Forces #5 . . . . . 200.00
46 Best of the West #4 . . . . 650.00
47 FF,Thunda #1. . . . . 2,200.00
48 Cowboys N' Indians #8. . . . . 150.00
49 Dogface Dooley #3 . . . . 75.00
50 BP,Danger is Their
  Business #11. . . . . 200.00
51 Ghost Rider #7 . . . . 500.00
52 Best of the West #3 . . . . 400.00
53 Dogface Dooley #4 . . . . 75.00
54 BP,American Air Forces #6. . . 100.00
55 BP,U.S. Marines #5. . . . . 100.00
56 BP,Thunda #2. . . . . 350.00
57 Ghost Rider #8, Drugs 600.00
58 American Air Forces #7 . . . . . 100.00
59 Best of the West #4 . . . . 350.00
60 The U.S. Marines #6. . . . . . . 100.00
61 Space Ace #5 . . . . 900.00
62 Starr Flagg #5. . . . . 600.00
63 FF,Manhunt #13 . . . . 550.00

64 Dogface Dooley #5 . . . . 75.00
65 BP,American Air Forces #8 . . . 100.00
66 Best of the West #5 . . . . 350.00
67 American Air Forces #9 . . . . . 100.00
68 U.S. Marines #7 . . . . 100.00
69 Ghost Rider #9, Drugs 600.00
70 Best of the West #6 . . . . 300.00
71 Ghost Rider #10 . . . . 500.00
72 U.S. Marines #8 . . . . 100.00
73 BP,Thunda #3 . . . . 300.00
74 BP,American Air Forces #10 . . 100.00
75 Ghost Rider #11 . . . . 400.00
76 Best of the West #7 . . . . 250.00
77 LbC,Grl,Manhunt #14 . . . . 450.00
78 BP,Thunda #4 . . . . 300.00
79 American Air Forces #11. . . . . 100.00
80 Ghost Rider #12, Bondage(c). 500.00
81 Best of the West #8 . . . . 200.00
82 BP,Cave Girl #11. . . . . 700.00
83 BP,Thunda #5 . . . . 250.00
84 Ghost Rider #13 . . . . 400.00
85 Best of the West #9 . . . . 200.00
86 BP,Thunda #6 . . . . 250.00
87 Best of the West #10 . . . . 200.00
88 Bobby Benson's B-Bar-B #29. 150.00
89 BP,Home Run #3,Stan Musial. 275.00
90 Red Hawk #11 . . . . 100.00
91 BP,American Air Forces #12. . 100.00
92 Dream Book of Romance #5 . 175.00
93 BP,Great Western #8 . . . . 300.00
94 FF,White Indian #11 . . . . 350.00
95 BP,Muggsy Mouse #4. . . . . 75.00
96 BP,Cave Girl #12 . . . . 500.00
97 Best of the West #11 . . . . 200.00
98 Undercover Girl #6 . . . . 600.00
99 Muggsy Mouse #5 . . . . 75.00
100 Badmen of the West #1 . . . . 325.00
101 FF,White Indian #12 . . . . 325.00
101(a) BP(c),FGu, Dream Book of
  Romance #6, Marlon Brando 300.00
103 BP,Best of the West #12. . . . 200.00
104 FF,White Indian #13 . . . . 325.00
105 Great Western #9 . . . . 200.00
106 BP,Dream Book of Love #1 . 200.00
107 Hot Dog #1 . . . . 125.00
108 BP,LbC,Red Fox #15 . . . . . . 350.00
109 BP,Dream Book of Romance 150.00
110 Dream Book of Romance #8 150.00

111 BP,I'm a Cop #1 . . . . 200.00
112 Ghost Rider #14 . . . . 400.00
113 BP,Great Western #10 . . . . . 175.00
114 Dream Book of Love #2 . . . . 150.00
115 Hot Dog #2 . . . . 100.00
116 BP,Cave Girl #13. . . . . 500.00
117 White Indian #14. . . . . 175.00
118 BP(c),Starr Flagg–
  Undercover Girl #7 . . . . 550.00
119 Straight Arrow's Fury #1 . . . . 225.00
120 Badmen of the West #2 . . . . 250.00
121 Mysteries of the
  Scotland Yard #1. . . . . 250.00
122 Black Phantom #1. . . . . 550.00
123 Dream Book of Love #3 . . . . 125.00
124 Hot Dog #3 . . . . 100.00
125 BP,Cave Girl #14 . . . . 500.00
126 BP,I'm a Cop #2. . . . . 150.00
127 BP,Great Western 200.00
128 BP,I'm a Cop #3 . . . . 150.00
129 The Avenger #1 . . . . 600.00
130 BP,Strongman #1 . . . . 325.00
131 BP,The Avenger #2. . . . . 450.00
132 Strongman #2 . . . . 300.00
133 BP,The Avenger #3. . . . . 450.00
134 Strongman #3 . . . . 300.00
135 White Indian #15. . . . . 175.00
136 Hot Dog #4 . . . . 100.00
137 BP,Africa #1 . . . . 350.00
138 BP,Avenger #4 . . . . 450.00
139 BP,Strongman #4, 1955 . . . . 300.00

ABBIE AN' SLATS
United Features Syndicate, March–Aug., 1948
1 RvB(c) 250.00
2 RvB(c) 175.00
3 RvB(c) 150.00
4 Aug., 1948 . . . . 150.00
N# 1940,Earlier Issue 600.00
N#. 500.00

ABBOTT AND COSTELLO
St. John Publishing Co., Feb., 1948
1 PP(c), Waltz Time 800.00
2 Jungle Girl and Snake(c). 450.00
3 Outer Space (c) 300.00
4 MD, Circus (c) 250.00
5 MD,Bull Fighting (c) 250.00
6 MD,Harem (c) 250.00
7 MD,Opera (c). 250.00
8 MD,Pirates (c) 250.00
9 MD,Polar Bear (c) 250.00
10 MD,PP(c),Son of Sinbad tale . 300.00
11 MD. 200.00
12 PP(c), Movie issue 250.00
13 Fire fighters (c) 200.00
14 Bomb (c) 200.00
15 Bubble Bath (c). 200.00
16 thru 29 MD . . . . @175.00
30 thru 39 MD . . . . @150.00
40 MD,Sept., 1956. . . . . 150.00
3-D #1, Nov., 1953. . . . . 500.00

ACE COMICS
David McKay Publications, April, 1937
1 JM, F:Katzenjammer Kids . . 5,500.00
2 JM, A:Blondie 1,500.00
3 JM, A:Believe It Or Not. 1,000.00
4 JM, F:Katzenjammer Kids . . 1,000.00
5 JM, A:Believe It Or Not. 1,000.00
6 JM, A:Blondie. 750.00

A-1 Comics #61
© *Magazine Enterprises*

7 JM, A:Believe It Or Not 750.00
8 JM, A:Jungle Jim 750.00
9 JM, A:Blondie. 750.00
10 JM, F:Katzenjammer Kids. . . . 700.00
11 I:The Phantom series. 1,200.00
12 A:Blondie, Jungle Jim 600.00
13 A:Ripley's Believe It Or Not . . 500.00
14 A:Blondie, Jungle Jim 500.00
15 A:Blondie. 475.00
16 F:Katzenjammer Kids 475.00
17 A:Blondie. 475.00
18 A:Ripley's Believe It Or Not . . 475.00
19 F:Katzenjammer Kids 475.00
20 A:Jungle Jim 475.00
21 A:Blondie. 450.00
22 A:Jungle Jim 450.00
23 F:Katzenjammer Kids 450.00
24 A:Blondie. 450.00
25 . . . . 450.00
26 O:Prince Valiant 1,500.00
27 thru 36. . . . . @450.00
37 Krazy Kat Ends. 350.00
38 thru 40 . . . . @350.00
41 thru 59. . . . . @300.00
60 thru 69 . . . . @250.00
70 thru 89 . . . . @150.00
90 thru 99. . . . . @125.00
100 F:The Phantom. 150.00
101 thru 109. . . . . @125.00
110 thru 119 . . . . @100.00
120 thru 143. . . . . @100.00
144 Phantom covers begin 125.00
145 thru 150. . . . . @100.00
151 Oct.–Nov., 1949 . . . . 125.00

ACES HIGH
E.C. Comics, March–April, 1955
1 GE(a&c),JDa,WW,BK 500.00
2 GE(a&c),JDa,WW,BK 300.00
3 GE(a&c),JDa,WW,BK 250.00
4 GE(a&c),JDa,WW,BK 250.00
5 GE(c),JDa,WW,BK. 250.00

ADVENTURE IS MY CAREER
Street & Smith Publ., 1944
n# U.S.Coast Guard Academy. . . 300.00

ADVENTURES
St. John Publishing Co., Nov. 1949–Feb. 1950
1 Adventures in Romance 350.00
2 Spectacular Adventures 500.00

ADVENTURES IN 3-D
Harvey Publications, Nov. 1953–Jan 1954
1 with glasses 350.00
1a rep. O'Dells Adventures
  in 3-D 300.00
2 with glasses 300.00

ADVENTURES INTO DARKNESS
Standard Publications, Aug., 1952
5 JK(c), ATh 700.00
6 GT, JK 500.00
7 JK(c) 500.00
8 ATh. 500.00
9 JK,ATh. 500.00
10 JK,ATh,MSy 450.00
11 JK,ATh,MSy 450.00
12 JK,ATh,MSy 450.00
13 Cannibalism feature 600.00
14 Frozen Death 350.00

Adventures Into the Unknown #19
© American Comics Group

ADVENTURES INTO THE UNKNOWN!
American Comics Group, Fall 1948
1 FGu, Haunted House (c) . . . 5,000.00
2 Haunted Island (c) 2,000.00
3 AF, Sarcophagus (c) 2,000.00
4 Monsters (c). 950.00
5 Monsters (c). 950.00
6 Giant Hands (c) 900.00
7 Skeleton Pirate (c) 900.00
8 Horror. 900.00
9 Snow Monster 900.00
10 Red Bats 900.00
11 Death Shadow 900.00
12 OW(c) 900.00
13 OW(c),Dinosaur 500.00
14 OW(c),Cave 500.00
15 Red Demons 500.00
16 OW(c) 400.00
17 OW(c),The Thing Type 600.00
18 OW(c),Wolves. 500.00
19 OW(c),Graveyard 500.00
20 OW(c),Graveyard 500.00
21 OW(c),Bats and Dracula. . . . 400.00
22 Witches' Wrath 400.00
23 OW(c),Bats 400.00
24 Swamp Monster 400.00
25 The Were-Tiger of Assam. . . . 400.00
26 DW(s) 400.00
27 AW,RKu,OW(c). 400.00
28 thru 37. . . . . @400.00
38 A-Bomb 600.00
39 thru 49. . . . . @500.00
50 Giant fly (c) 500.00
51 H. Lazarus 500.00
52 H. Lazarus, 3-D-ish. 500.00
53 thru 55. . . . . @500.00
56 H. Lazarus 500.00
57 SMo,OW(c). 500.00
58 H. Lazarus 500.00
59 3-D-ish 400.00
60 Hospitality; Tomb for Titus. . . 300.00
61 OW,Rocket ship (c). 300.00
62 thru 69. . . . . @250.00
70 thru 79. . . . . @250.00
80 thru 90 . . . . @200.00
91 AW 250.00
92 thru 95. . . . . @150.00
96 AW 225.00
97 thru 99 . . . . @150.00
100 JB 200.00
101 thru 106. . . . . @150.00
107 AW 225.00

108 thru 115 . . . . @150.00
116 AW,AT 225.00
117 thru 127 . . . . @150.00
128 AW,Forbidden Worlds 150.00
129 thru 151. . . . . @150.00
152 JCr 150.00
153 A:Magic Agent. 150.00
154 O:Nemesis 200.00
155 Nemesis 125.00
156 A:Magic Agent. 125.00
157 thru 167 . . . . @125.00
168 JB,SD, Nemesis. 125.00
169 Nemesis vs. Hitler. 150.00
170 thru 174, Aug., 1967 . . . . . @125.00

ADVENTURES IN WONDERLAND
Lev Gleason Publications, April, 1955
1 . . . . 200.00
2 . . . . 150.00
3 and 4 . . . . @125.00
5 Christmas. 150.00

ADVENTURES OF ALICE
Civil Service Publ., 1945–46
1 In Wonderland 300.00
2 Through the Looking Glass . . . 200.00
3 Monkey Island 200.00

THE ADVENTURES OF HOMER COBB
Say/Bart Prod., Sept. 1947
1 . . . . 500.00

ADVENTURES OF LITTLE ORPHAN ANNIE COMICS
Giveaway 1940–42
N#(1) 600.00
N#(2) 500.00
N#(3) 500.00

MIGHTY MOUSE ADVENTURES
St. John Publishing Co., Nov., 1951
1 Mighty Mouse Adventures 400.00
Becomes:

ADVENTURES OF MIGHTY MOUSE
St. John Publishing Co., Nov., 1951
2 Menace of the Deep 400.00
3 Storm Clouds of Mystery 300.00
4 Thought Control Machine 300.00
5 Jungle Peril 300.00
6 'The Vine of Destruction' 250.00
7 Space Ship(c) 250.00
8 Charging Alien(c). 250.00
9 Meteor(c) 200.00
10 'Revolt at the Zoo'. 200.00
11 Jungle(c). 200.00
12 A:Freezing Terror 200.00
13 A:Visitor from Outer Space . . . 200.00
14 V:Cat. 200.00
15 . . . . 200.00
16 . . . . 200.00
17 . . . . 200.00
18 May, 1955 . . . . 200.00

ADVENTURES OF MIGHTY MOUSE
See: TERRY-TUNES COMICS

GOLDEN AGE

AGGIE MACK
Four Star Comics/
Superior Comics, Jan., 1948
1 AF,HR(c),Johnny Prep 600.00
2 JK(c) 300.00
3 AF,JK(c) 300.00
4 AF, Johnny Prep 400.00
5 AF,JK(c) 300.00
6 AF,JK(c) 275.00
7 AF,Burt Lancaster on cover . . . 325.00
8 AF,JK(c), Aug., 1949 . . . . 275.00

BILL BARNES
Street & Smith Publ.,July, 1940
1 (Bill Barnes Comics) 1,500.00
Becomes:

Bill Barnes, America's Air Ace #2
© Street & Smith

BILL BARNES,
AMERICA'S AIR ACE
Street & Smith Publ., 1940
2 Second Battle Valley Forge . . . 750.00
3 A:Aviation Cadets 500.00
4 Shotdown(c). 500.00
5 A:Air Warden, Danny Hawk . . . 500.00
6 A:Danny Hawk,RocketRodney. 400.00
7 How to defeat the Japanese . . 400.00
8 Ghost Ship 400.00
9 Flying Tigers, John Wayne . . . 425.00
10 I:Roane Waring. 400.00
11 Flying Tigers 400.00
12 War Workers. 400.00
Becomes:

AIR ACE
Street & Smith Publ., Jan., 1944
2-1 Invades Germany 600.00
2-2 Jungle Warfare 450.00
2-3 A:The Four Musketeers 200.00
2-4 A:Russell Swann. 200.00
2-5 A:The Four Musketeers 200.00
2-6 Raft(c). 200.00
2-7 BP, What's New In Science . 200.00
2-8 XP-59 . . . . 200.00
2-9 The Northrop P-61 . . . . 200.00
2-10 NCG-14 . . . . 200.00
2-11 Whip Launch. 200.00
2-12 PP(c). 200.00
3-1 . . . . 150.00
3-2 Atom and Its Future 150.00
3-3 Flying in the Future. 150.00
3-4 How Fast Can We Fly 150.00
3-5 REv(c). 150.00
3-6 V:Wolves. 150.00
3-7 BP(c), Vortex of Atom Bomb 400.00

3-8 BP,Feb.–March, 1947 . . . . . 175.00

AIR FIGHTERS COMICS
Hillman Periodicals, Nov., 1941
1 I:Black Commander
  (only App) 5,000.00
2 O:Airboy A:Sky Wolf 7,000.00
3 O:Sky Wolf and Heap 4,000.00
4 A:Black Angel, Iron Ace 3,500.00
5 A:Sky Wolf and Iron Ace. . . . 2,500.00
6 Airboy's Bird Plane 2,700.00
7 Airboy Battles Kultur 2,500.00
8 A:Skinny McGinty 2,200.00
9 A:Black Prince, Hatchet Man 2,200.00
10 I:The Stinger 2,200.00
11 Kida(c) 2,200.00
12 A:Misery 2,200.00
2-1 A:Flying Dutchman 2,400.00
2-2 I:Valkyrie 2,700.00
2-3 Story Panels (c) 1,000.00
2-4 V:Japanese 1,000.00
2-5 Air Boy in Tokyo 1,000.00
2-6 'Dance of Death'. 1,000.00
2-7 A:Valkyrie 1,000.00
2-8 Airboy Battles Japanese . . . 1,000.00
2-9 Airboy Battles Japanese . . . 1,000.00
2-10 O:Skywolf 1,200.00
Becomes:

AIRBOY COMICS
Hillman Periodicals, Dec., 1945
2-11 . . . . 1,200.00
2-12 A:Valyrie 800.00
3-1 . . . . 600.00
3-2 . . . . 600.00
3-3 Never published
3-4 I:The Heap 500.00
3-5 Airboy 500.00
3-6 A:Valykrie 500.00
3-7 AMc,Witch Hunt 500.00
3-8 A:Condor. 550.00
3-9 O:The Heap 550.00
3-10 . . . . 500.00
3-11 . . . . 500.00
3-12 Airboy missing 650.00
4-1 Elephant in chains (c). 600.00
4-2 I:Rackman 450.00
4-3 Airboy profits on name 450.00
4-4 S&K 500.00
4-5 S&K,The American Miracle . 450.00
4-6 S&K,A:Heap and
  Flying Fool 450.00
4-7 S&K 450.00
4-8 S&K,Girlfriend captured . . . 450.00
4-9 S&K,Airboy in Quick Sand . . 450.00
4-10 S&K,A:Valkyrie 450.00
4-11 S&K,A:Frenchy 450.00
4-12 FBe 500.00
5-1 LSt 400.00
5-2 I:Wild Horse of Calabra 400.00
5-3 . . . . 400.00
5-4 CI 400.00
5-5 Skull on cover. 400.00
5-6. . . . . 400.00
5-7. . . . . 400.00
5-8 Bondage (c) 400.00
5-9 Zoi,Row 400.00
5-10 A:Valykrie,O:The Heap . . . 450.00
5-11 Airboy vs. The Rats. 400.00
5-12 BK,Rat Army captures
  Airboy 400.00
6-1. . . . . 400.00
6-2. . . . . 400.00
6-3. . . . . 400.00
6-4 Airboy boxes. 500.00
6-5 A:The Ice People 400.00
6-6 . . . . 400.00
6-7 Airboy vs. Chemical Giant . . 400.00
6-8 O:The Heap 400.00
6-9 . . . . 400.00
6-10 . . . . 400.00
6-11 . . . . 400.00

6-12 . . . . 400.00
7-1 . . . . 400.00
7-2 BP. 400.00
7-3 BP. 500.00
7-4 I:Monsters of the Ice. 400.00
7-5 V:Monsters of the Ice 400.00
7-6 . . . . 400.00
7-7 Mystery of the Sargasso
  Sea 400.00
7-8 A:Centaur 400.00
7-9 I:Men of the StarlightRobot. . 400.00
7-10 O:The Heap 400.00
7-11 . . . . 400.00
7-12 Airboy visits India 400.00
8-1 BP,A:Outcast and Polo
  Bandits. 400.00
8-2 BP,Suicide Dive (c). 400.00
8-3 BK, I:The Living Fuse. 400.00
8-4 A:Death Merchants of
  the Air 400.00
8-5 A:Great Plane from Nowhere 400.00
8-6 . . . . 400.00
8-7 . . . . 400.00
8-8 . . . . 400.00
8-9 . . . . 400.00
8-10 A:Mystery Walkers 400.00
8-11 . . . . 400.00
8-12 . . . . 450.00
9-1 . . . . 350.00
9-2 A:Valykrie 300.00
9-3 A:Heap (c). 300.00
9-4 A:Water Beast, Frog Headed
  Riders 350.00
9-5 A:Heap vs.Man of Moonlight 300.00
9-6 Heap (c) 300.00

Airboy Vol. 10 #4
© Hillman Periodicals

9-7 Heap (c) 300.00
9-8 Heap (c) 350.00
9-9 . . . . 350.00
9-10 Space (c) 350.00
9-11 . . . . 350.00
9-12 Heap (c) 350.00
10-1 Heap (c) 350.00
10-2 Ships on Space 300.00
10-3 . . . . 350.00
10-4 May, 1953 . . . . 350.00

AL CAPP'S
DOGPATCH COMICS
Toby Press, June, 1949
1 . . . . 350.00
2 A:Daisy. 250.00
3 . . . . 225.00
4 Dec., 1949 . . . . 225.00

Al Capp's Shmoo #3
© Toby Press

AL CAPP'S SHMOO
Toby Press, July, 1949
1 100 Trillion Schmoos 600.00
2 Super Shmoo(c). 400.00
3 . . . . 400.00
4 . . . . 400.00
5 April, 1950 . . . . 400.00

AL CAPP'S WOLF GAL
Toby Press, 1951
1 Pin-Up 500.00
2 1952. 450.00

ALICE
Ziff-Davis Publ. Co., 1952
10 New Adventures in
　Wonderland 400.00
11 (#2) 350.00

ALLEY OOP
Standard Comics,
Sept. 1947–Oct. 1949
10 . . . . 350.00
11 thru 18 . . . . @300.00

(The Adventures of)
ALLEY OOP
Argo Publications, 1955–56
1 . . . . 225.00
2 . . . . 150.00
3 . . . . 150.00

ALL-FAMOUS CRIME
Star Publications, May, 1951
1 LbC(c) (8). 350.00
2 LbC(c) (9). 500.00
3 LbC(c) (10). 325.00
4 LbC(c) (4) Law Crime 300.00
5 LbC(c) (5). 300.00
Becomes:

ALL-FAMOUS
POLICE CASES
Feb., 1952
6 LbC(c) 325.00
7 LbC(c) 300.00
8 LbC(c) Marijuana 300.00
9 LbC(c) 250.00
10 thru 15 LbC(c). . . . . @250.00
16 Sept., 1954 . . . . 250.00

ALL GOOD COMICS
Fox Publications, 1946
1 . . . . 400.00

ALL GOOD COMICS
R. W. Voight/
St. John Publishing, 1949
N# Giant. 1,500.00

ALL GREAT
Fox Features, 1946
1 Crazy Horse, etc. 500.00

ALL GREAT COMICS
See: DAGAR, DESERT HAWK

ALL HERO COMICS
Fawcett Publications,
March, 1943
1 A:Capt. Marvel Jr.,Capt.
　Midnight,Ibis, Golden Arrow
　and Spy Smasher. 3,000.00

ALL HUMOR COMICS
Comic Favorites, Inc.
(Quality Comics) Spring 1946
1 . . . . 350.00
2 PG Atomic Tot 200.00
3 I:Kelly Poole. 150.00
4 thru 7 . . . . @ 150.00
8 PG 150.00
9 . . . . 150.00
10 . . . . 150.00
11 thru 17 . . . . @125.00

ALL-NEGRO COMICS
June,1947
1 . . . . 9,000.00

ALL-NEW COMICS
Family Comics
(Harvey Publ.) Jan., 1943
1 A:Steve Case, Johnny Rebel
　I:Detective Shane 5,000.00
2 JKu,O:Scarlet Phantom 2,000.00
3 Nazi War. 1,800.00
4 AdH 1,500.00
5 Flash Gordon 1,800.00
6 ASh(c),I:Boy Heroes and
　Red Blazer 1,800.00
7 JKu,ASh(c),A:Black Cat &
　Zebra 1,800.00
8 JKu,A:Shock Gibson. 1,800.00
9 JKu,A:Black Cat 1,800.00
10 ASh(c),JKu,A:Zebra. 1,800.00
11 BP,A:Man in Black, Girl
　Commandos. 1,800.00
12 JKu. 1,500.00
13 Stuntman by S&K,
　A:Green Hornet&(c) 1,600.00
14 BP,A:Green Hornet 1,200.00
15 Smaller size, Distributed
　by Mail, March–April, 1947. 2,000.00

ALL PICTURE ALL TRUE
LOVE STORY
St. John Publ. Co. 1952
1 MB,Romance on Route 202 . . 600.00
2 MB 375.00

REAL SPORTS COMICS
Hillman Periodicals, 1948
1 BP,Boxing (c). 600.00
Becomes:

ALL SPORTS COMICS
Hillman Periodicals, 1949
2 BP,BK,Football (c) 550.00
3 Basketball (c). 450.00
Becomes:

ALL-TIME SPORTS
COMICS
Hillman Periodicals, 1949
4 Auto Racing (c) 350.00
5 BP,Baseball (c), Ty Cobb. . . . 325.00
6 Horse Racing (c) 300.00
7 BK, Baseball (c), W. Johnson . 300.00

ALL TOP COMICS
William H. Wise Co., 1944
N# 132pgs.,A:Capt.
　V,Red Robbins 500.00

ALL TOP COMICS
Fox Features Syndicate,
Spring 1946
1 A:Cosmo Cat, Flash Rabbit . . . 300.00
2 . . . . 150.00
3 thru 6 . . . . @125.00
7 . . . . 125.00
7a 125.00
8 JKa(c),I:Blue Beetle 3,600.00
9 JKa(c),A:Rulah 1,800.00
10 JKa(c),A:Rulah. 1,500.00
11 A:Rulah,Blue Beetle 1,600.00
12 A:Rulah,Jo Jo,Blue Beetle . . 1,600.00
13 A:Rulah 1,600.00
14 A:Rulah,Blue Beetle 2,000.00
15 A:Rulah 1,600.00
16 A:Rulah,Blue Beetle 1,600.00
17 A:Rulah,Blue Beetle. 1,600.00
18 A:Dagar,Jo Jo 1,000.00
Becomes:

MY EXPERIENCE
Fox Features Syndicate
1949–50
19 WW. 400.00
20 . . . . 125.00
21 WW 400.00
22 WW. 350.00
Becomes:

JUDY CANOVA
Fox Features Syndicate,
May, 1950–Sept., 1950
23 (1)WW(a&c) 350.00
24 (2)WW(a&c) 350.00
3 JO,WW(a&c) 350.00

ALL TOP COMICS
Green Publ., 1957–59
6 1957 Patoruzu the Indian 100.00
6 1958 Cosmo Cat. 100.00
6 1959 Atomic Mouse 100.00
6 1959 Little Eva 100.00
6 Supermouse (c) 100.00

ALL-TRUE
DETECTIVE CASES
Avon Periodicals, 1954
1 WW 350.00
2 EK(c),JKa. 250.00
3 JKa. 250.00
4 JKa. 300.00
N# (5) JK,JKu 700.00

ALL YOUR COMICS
R.W. Voight, 1944
1 Red Robbins 350.00

All comics prices listed are for *Near Mint* condition.

ALL YOUR COMICS
Fox Features, 1946
1 . . . . 300.00

AMAZING ADVENTURE FUNNIES
Centaur Publ,. 1940
1 BEv,The Fantom of the Fair . 4,000.00
2 rep.After Fantoman 2,500.00
Becomes:

FANTOMAN
Aug., 1940
2 The Fantom of the Fair 3,000.00
3 . . . . 2,500.00
4 Red Blaze 2,500.00

AMAZING ADVENTURES
Ziff-Davis Publ., Co., 1950
1 MA,WW, Asteroid Witch 1,500.00
2 MA,ASh(c),Masters of Living
    Flame. 700.00
3 MA,The Evil Men Do 700.00
4 Invasion of the Love Robots . . 700.00
5 MA,Secret of the Crater-Men. . 700.00
6 BK,Man Who Killed a World . . 750.00

AMAZING GHOST STORIES
See: WEIRD HORRORS

AMAZING-MAN COMICS
Centaur Publications, Sept., 1939–Feb., 1942
5 BEv,O:Amazing Man 40,000.00
6 BEv,FT,B:The Shark 8,000.00
7 BEv,I:Magician From Mars . . 6,000.00
8 BEv, Cat-Man as Woman . . . 5,000.00
9 BEv,FT,A:Eternal Monster. . 5,000.00
10 BEv,FT 3,500.00
11 BEv,I:Zardi 3,500.00
12 SG(c) 3,200.00
13 SG(c) 3,200.00
14 FT,B:Reef Kinkaid, Dr. Hypo 2,500.00
15 FT,A:Zardi 2,400.00
16 AAv,Mighty Man's Powers
    Revealed 2,500.00
17 FT,A:Dr. Hypo 2,400.00
18 FT,BLb(a),SG(c). 2,400.00
19 FT,BLb(a),SG(c). 2,400.00
20 FT,BLb(a),SG(c). 2,400.00
21 FT,O:Dash Dartwell 2,500.00

Amazing Man #22
© Centaur Publications

22 A:Silver Streak, The Voice . . 3,000.00
23 I&O:Tommy the AmazingKid 2,200.00
24 B:King of Darkness,
    Blue Lady 2,200.00
25 A:Meteor Marvin. 3,200.00
26 A:Meteor Marvin,ElectricRay 3,200.00

AMAZING MYSTERY FUNNIES
Centaur Publications, 1938
1 Skyrocket Steele in Year X . . 8,000.00
2 WE,Skyrocket Steele 4,500.00
3 . . . . 2,700.00
(#4) WE,bondage (c) 2,600.00
2-1(#5) 2,400.00
2-2(#6) Drug use. 2,000.00
2-3(#7) Air Sub DX 2,000.00
2-4(#8) Sand Hog 2,000.00
2-5(#9) 3,000.00
2-6(#10) 2,000.00
2-7(#11) Fantom of Fair, scarce 7,500.00
2-8(#12) Speed Centaur 3,200.00
2-9(#13) 2,000.00
2-10(#14) 2,000.00
2-11(#15)Robot(c). 2,000.00
2-12(#16) BW,I:Space Patrol . 4,000.00
3-1(#17) I:Bullet 2,000.00
18 Fantom of Fair 2,000.00
19 BW,Space Patrol 2,200.00
20 . . . . 1,800.00
21 thru 24 BW,Space Patrol . @2,200.00

AMAZING WILLIE MAYS
Famous Funnies, 1954
1 Willie Mays(c) 1,500.00

AMERICA IN ACTION
Dell Publishing Co., 1942
1 . . . . 400.00

THE AMERICAN AIR FORCES
Flying Cadet Publ., 1944–45
1 War (c). 300.00
2 War (c). 400.00
3 War (c). 400.00
4 War (c). 250.00
Continues in *A-1 Comics*. See #45,
#54, #58, #65, #67, #74, #79, #91

AMERICAN GRAPHICS
Henry Stewart, 1954
1 Indian Legends 200.00
2 . . . . 150.00

AMERICAN LIBRARY
David McKay Publ., 1943
(#1) Thirty Seconds Over
    Tokyo, movie adapt. 600.00
(#2) Guadalcanal Diary 500.00
3 Look to the Mountain 250.00
4 The Case of the Crooked
    Candle (Perry Mason) 250.00
5 Duel in the Sun 250.00
6 Wingate's Raiders 250.00

AMERICA'S BEST COMICS
Nedor/Better/Standard Publications, Feb., 1942
1 ASh(c),B:Black Terror, Captain Future,
    The Liberator,Doc Strange . 4,500.00
2 O:American Eagle. 2,000.00
3 B:Pyroman 1,500.00
4 A:Doc Strange, Jimmy Cole . 1,100.00
5 ASh(c),A:LoneEagle,
    Cap.Future 1,100.00

6 A:American Crusader 1,100.00
7 ASh(c),A:Hitler,Hirohito 1,800.00
8 The Liberator ends 1,100.00
9 ASh(c),Fighting Yank 1,500.00
10 ASh(c),American Eagle 1,500.00
11 ASh(c) Hirihito & Tojo(c). . . . 1,500.00
12 Red Cross (c). 1,100.00
13 Fighting Yank 1,100.00
14 Last American Eagle app. . . 1,100.00
15 ASh(c),Fighting Yank 1,100.00
16 ASh(c),Fighting Yank 1,100.00
17 ASh(c),Doc Strange
    carries football 1,100.00
18 Fighting Yank,Bondage(c) . . 1,100.00
19 ASh(c),Fighting Yank 1,100.00
20 ASh(c),vs. the Black Market 1,100.00
21 ASh(c),Infinity (c) 1,100.00
22 A:Captain Future 1,000.00
23 B:Miss Masque 1,150.00
24 Miss Masque,Bondage (c). . 1,150.00
25 A:Sea Eagle 750.00
26 A:The Phantom Detective 750.00
27 Pyroman,ASh(c) 750.00
28 A:Commando Cubs,
    Black Terror 750.00
29 ASh(c),A:Doc Strange. 750.00
30 ASh(c).Xela 750.00
31 ASh(c),Xela,July, 1949 . . . . . . 750.00

AMERICA'S BIGGEST COMICS BOOK
William H. Wise, 1944
1 196 pgs. A:Grim Reaper, Zudo,
    Silver Knight, Thunderhoof,
    Jocko and Socko,Barnaby
    Beep,Commando Cubs 700.00
Becomes:

AMERICA'S FUNNIEST COMICS
William H. Wise, 1944
2 Funny Animal 500.00
N# (3). 500.00

AMERICA'S GREATEST COMICS
Fawcett Publications, Fall 1941
1 MRa(c),A:Capt. Marvel,
    Bulletman,Spy Smasher and
    Minute Man. 6,500.00
2 F:Capt. Marvel 3,000.00
3 F:Capt. Marvel 2,500.00
4 B:Commando Yank. 2,000.00
5 Capt.Marvel in 'Lost Lighting' 2,000.00
6 Capt.Marvel fires
    Machine Gun 2,000.00
7 A:Balbo the Boy Magician. . . 1,800.00
8 A:Capt.Marvel Jr.,Golden
    Arrow, Summer 1943 . . . . . 1,800.00

ANCHORS ANDREWS
St. John Publ. Co. 1953
1 MB,Navy Humor 225.00
2 thru 4 . . . . @100.00

ANDY COMICS
See: SCREAM COMICS

ANDY DEVINE WESTERN
Fawcett Publ. 1950
1 Photo (c) 900.00
2 . . . . 700.00

ANGEL
Dell Publishing Co., Aug., 1954
(1) *see Dell Four Color #576*
2 . . . . 100.00
3 thru 16 . . . . @75.00

ANIMAL ADVENTURES
**Timor Publ./Accepted Publ.
1953–54**
1 Funny Animal 100.00
1a rep.. . . . . 90.00
2 . . . . 90.00

ANIMAL ANTICS
Dell Publishing Co., 1946
1 B: Racoon Kids 600.00
2 . . . . 300.00
3 thru 10 . . . . @175.00
11 thru 23 . . . . @125.00

*Animal Comics #2
© Dell Publishing*

ANIMAL COMICS
Dell Publishing Co., 1942
1 WK,Pogo 1,700.00
2 Uncle Wiggily(c),A:Pogo 1,000.00
3 Muggin's Mouse(c),A:Pogo . . . 750.00
4 Uncle Wiggily(c). 500.00
5 Uncle Wiggily(c). 750.00
6 Uncle Wiggily. 500.00
7 Uncle Wiggily. 500.00
8 WK,Pogo 600.00
9 WK,War Bonds(c),A:Pogo 600.00
10 WK,Pogo. 600.00
11 WK,Pogo. 400.00
12 WK,Pogo. 400.00
13 WK,Pogo. 400.00
14 WK,Pogo. 400.00
15 WK,Pogo. 400.00
16 Uncle Wiggily 250.00
17 WK,Pogo(c). 300.00
18 WK,Pogo(c). 300.00
19 WK,Pogo(c). 300.00
20 WK,Pogo. 250.00
21 WK,Pogo(c). 300.00
22 WK,Pogo. 200.00
23 WK,Pogo. 200.00
24 WK,Pogo(c). 200.00
25 WK,Pogo(c). 200.00
26 WK,Pogo(c). 200.00
27 thru 30 WK,Pogo(c) . . . . . . @200.00

ANIMAL FABLES
E.C. Comics, July–Aug., 1946
1 B:Korky Kangaroo,Freddy Firefly
   Petey Pig & Danny Demon . 650.00
2 B:Aesop Fables 375.00
3 . . . . 300.00
4 . . . . 300.00
5 Firefly vs. Red Ants 300.00
6 . . . . 300.00
7 O:Moon Girls,Nov.–Dec.1947 1,200.00

ANIMAL FAIR
**Fawcett Publications,
March, 1946**
1 B:Captain Marvel Bunny,
   Sir Spot 500.00
2 A:Droopy, Colonel Walrus 350.00
3 . . . . 250.00
4 A:Kid Gloves, Cub Reporter . . 250.00
5 thru 7 . . . . @250.00
8 thru 10 . . . . @200.00
11 Feb., 1947. . . . . 200.00

ANIMATED COMICS
E.C. Comics, 1948
1 Funny Animal 1,200.00

ANNIE OAKLEY & TAGG
Dell Publishing Co., 1953
(1) *see Dell Four Color #438*
(2) *see Dell Four Color #481*
(3) *see Dell Four Color #575*
4 . . . . 250.00
5 . . . . 200.00
6 thru 10 . . . . @175.00
11 thru 18. . . . . @135.00

APACHE
Fiction House Magazines, 1951
1 . . . . 300.00

APACHE TRAIL
America's Best, 1957
1 . . . . 125.00
2 GT 85.00
3 . . . . 75.00
4 . . . . 75.00

APPROVED COMICS
St. John Publishing Co., 1954
1 The Hawk. 125.00
2 Invisible Boy. 226.00
3 Wild Boy of the Congo. 100.00
4 Kid Cowboy 100.00
5 Flyboy 100.00
6 MB,BK,Daring Adventures. . . . 150.00
7 The Hawk. 100.00
8 BP,Crime on the Run. 125.00
9 MB,Western Bandit Trails 150.00
10 Dinky Duck 100.00
11 MB,Fighting Marines 175.00
12 Northwest Mounties 175.00

ARCHIE COMICS
**MLJ Magazines,
Winter, 1942-43**
1 I:Jughead & Veronica 26,000.00
2 . . . . 6,000.00
3 . . . . 4,000.00
4 . . . . 2,200.00
5 . . . . 2,200.00
6 Christmas issue 1,500.00
7 thru 10. . . . . @1,600.00
11 thru 15 . . . . @1,000.00
16 thru 19. . . . . @950.00
Archie Publications, 1946
20 . . . . 1,000.00
21 . . . . 650.00
22 thru 31. . . . . @600.00
32 thru 42 . . . . @375.00
43 thru 50. . . . . @250.00
51 A:Katy Keene 225.00
52 thru 64 . . . . @200.00
65 thru 70 A:Katy Keene . . . @200.00
71 . . . . 125.00
72 thru 74 A:Katy Keene . . . @150.00
75 thru 99 . . . . @125.00
100 . . . . 125.00
101 thru 122. . . . . @125.00

123 UFO,Vampire 75.00
124 thru 130. . . . . @75.00
131 thru 145. . . . . @60.00
146 thru 182. . . . . @60.00
183 Caveman Archie 60.00
184 . . . . 60.00
185 I:The Archies Band 75.00
186 thru 195 . . . . @50.00
196 I:Cricket O'Dell 75.00
197 thru 200 . . . . @50.00
201 thru 228 . . . . @50.00
229 Lost Child 50.00
230 thru 260 . . . . @30.00
261 thru 300 . . . . @30.00

ARCHIE'S GIANT SERIES MAGAZINE
Archie Publications, 1954
1 . . . . 1,900.00
2 . . . . 1,000.00
3 . . . . 700.00
4 . . . . 650.00
5 . . . . 650.00
6 thru 10 . . . . @500.00
11 thru 20 . . . . @300.00
21 thru 29 . . . . @175.00
30 thru 35 . . . . @125.00

ARCHIE'S GIRLS BETTY AND VERONICA
Archie Publications, 1950
1 . . . . 3,000.00
2 . . . . 1,500.00
3 . . . . 650.00
4 . . . . 600.00
5 . . . . 600.00
6 thru 10 . . . . @500.00
11 thru 15 . . . . @400.00
16 thru 20 . . . . @350.00
21 . . . . 275.00
22 thru 29 . . . . @250.00
30 thru 40 . . . . @200.00
41 thru 50 . . . . @175.00
51 thru 60 . . . . @125.00
61 thru 70 . . . . @110.00
71 thru 74 . . . . @100.00
75 Devil 200.00
76 thru 90 . . . . @100.00
91 thru 99 . . . . @100.00
100. 100.00

ARCHIE'S JOKE BOOK MAGAZINE
Archie Publications, 1953
1 . . . . 1,500.00
2 . . . . 650.00
3 . . . . 500.00
15 thru 19. . . . . @300.00
20 thru 25. . . . . @175.00
26 thru 35. . . . . @150.00
36 thru 40. . . . . @125.00
41 1st NA art 300.00
42 & 43 TV Personalities . . . . @125.00
44 thru 48 NA. . . . . @150.00
49 thru 60 . . . . @60.00

ARCHIE'S MECHANICS
Archie Publications, 1954
1 . . . . 1,200.00
2 . . . . 650.00
3 . . . . 500.00

ARCHIE'S PAL, JUGHEAD
Archie Publications, 1949
1 . . . . 2,000.00
2 . . . . 1,000.00
3 . . . . 600.00

GOLDEN AGE

All comics prices listed are for *Near Mint* condition.

Archie's Pal Jughead #4
© Archie Publications

4	550.00
5	550.00
6	400.00
7 thru 10	@325.00
11 thru 15	@250.00
16 thru 20	@175.00
21 thru 30	@125.00
31 thru 39	@100.00
40 thru 50	@100.00
51 thru 60	@65.00
61 thru 70	@65.00
71 thru 80	@45.00
81 thru 99	@40.00
100	40.00

ARCHIE'S PALS 'N' GALS
Archie Publications, 1952–53

1	1,200.00
2	575.00
3	400.00
4	350.00
5	350.00
6	225.00
7	225.00
8 thru 10	@200.00
11 thru 15	@150.00
16 thru 18	@125.00
19 Marilyn Monroe	200.00
20 thru 30	@100.00

ARCHIE'S RIVAL REGGIE
Archie Publications, 1950

1	1,200.00
2	500.00
3	375.00
4	350.00
5	350.00
6	275.00
7 thru 9	@250.00
10 thru 14 A: Katy Keen	@225.00
15	160.00
16 Aug., 1954	175.00

ARMY & NAVY COMICS
See: SUPERSNIPE COMICS

ARROW, THE
Centaur Publications, Oct., 1940–Oct., 1941

1 B:Arrow, BLb(c)	6,000.00

2 BLb(c)	2,500.00
3 O:Dash Dartwell, Human Meteor, Rainbow, Bondage(c)	2,500.00

ATOM-AGE COMBAT
St. John Publ. Co., 1952–53

1 Buck Vinson	1,200.00
1a rep. (1958)	350.00
2 Flying Saucer	500.00
3	450.00
4	350.00
5 Flying Saucer	350.00

ATOMAN
Spark Publications, Feb., 1946

1 JRo,MMe,O:Atoman,A:Kid Crusaders	1,500.00
2 JRo,MMe	800.00

ATOMIC BOMB
Jay Burtis Publ., 1945

1	1,500.00

ATOMIC COMICS
Green Publishing Co., Jan., 1946

1 S&S,A:Radio Squad, Barry O'Neal	2,200.00
2 MB,A:Inspector Dayton, Kid Kane	1,100.00
3 MB,A:Zero Ghost Detective	800.00
4 JKa(c), July–Aug., 1946	800.00

ATOMIC COMICS
Daniels Publications, 1946 (Reprints)

1 A:Rocketman, Yankee Boy, Bondage (c),rep.	750.00

ATOMIC MOUSE
Capital Stories/ Charlton Comics, March, 1953

1 AFa,O:Atomic Mouse	500.00
2 AFa,Ice Cream (c)	150.00
3 AFa,Genie and Magic Carpet (c)	125.00
4 AFa	125.00
5 AFa,A:Timmy the Timid Ghost	125.00
6 thru 10 Funny Animal	@100.00
11 thru 14 Funny Animal	@100.00
15 A:Happy the Marvel Bunny	100.00
16 Funny Animal, Giant	75.00
17 thru 30 Funny Animal	@75.00
31 thru 36 Funny Animal	@75.00
37 A:Atom the Cat	75.00
38 thru 40 Funny Animal	@50.00
41 thru 53 Funny Animal	@30.00
54 June, 1963	30.00

ATOMIC THUNDERBOLT, THE
Regor Company, Feb., 1946

1 I:Atomic Thunderbolt, Mr. Murdo	1,200.00

ATOMIC WAR!
Ace-Junior Books, 1952–53

1 Atomic explosion (c)	2,000.00
2	1,600.00
3 A-Bomb	1,600.00
4	1,600.00

ATOM THE CAT
See: BO

ATTACK
Youthful Mag./Trojan, 1952

1 Violence	500.00
2	250.00
3 Bondage	300.00
4 RKu	250.00

Becomes:

ATOMIC ATTACK
Youthful Magazines, 1953

5	250.00
6 thru 8	@200.00

AUTHENTIC POLICE CASES
St. John Publ. Co., 1948

1 Hale the Magician	600.00
2 Lady Satan, Johnny Rebel	350.00
3 A:Avenger	600.00
4 Masked Black Jack	350.00
5 JCo	350.00
6 JCo,MB(c)	650.00
7 thru 10	@275.00
11 thru 15	@275.00
16 thru 23	@175.00
24 thru 28 Giants	@375.00
29 thru 38	@150.00

AVIATION CADETS
Street & Smith Publ., 1943

1	200.00

AVON ONE-SHOTS
Avon Periodicals, 1949-1953
{Listed in Alphabetical Order}

1 Atomic Spy Cases	500.00
N# WW,Attack on Planet Mars	1,500.00
1 Bachelor's Diary	600.00
1 Badmen of the West	500.00
N# Badmen of Tombstone	225.00
1 EK,Behind Prison Bars	375.00
2 Betty and Her Steady	125.00
N# EK,Blackhawk Indian Tomahawk War	250.00
1 EK,Blazing Sixguns	200.00
1 EK,Butch Cassidy	225.00
N# Chief Crazy Horse	250.00
N# FF,AW,EK,Chief Victorio's Apache Massacre	600.00
N# City of the Living Dead	750.00
1 Complete Romance	500.00
N# Custer's Last Fight	225.00
1 EK(c),Dalton Boys	225.00
N# GT(c),Davy Crockett	225.00
N# The Dead Who Walk	800.00
1 Diary of Horror,Bondage(c)	700.00
N# WW,Earth Man on Venus	2,000.00
1 Eerie, bondage (c)	1,200.00
1 EK,Escape from Devil's Island	525.00
N# EK,Fighting Daniel Boone	250.00
N# EK(c),For a Night of Love	375.00
1 WW,Flying Saucers	1,400.00
N# Flying Saucers	700.00
1 Going Steady with Betty	200.00
N# Hooded Menace	800.00
N# EK,King of the Badmen of Deadwood	200.00
1 King Solomon's Mines	500.00
N# EK(c),Kit Carson & the Blackfeet Warriors	100.00
N# EK,Last of the Comanches	200.00
N# EK,Masked Bandit	200.00
1 WW,Mask of Dr. Fu Manchu	1,500.00
N# EK,Night of Mystery	600.00
1 WW,JKu,Outlaws of the Wild West	425.00
1 JKu,Out of this World	1,100.00
N# EK,Pancho Villa	300.00
1 EK,Phantom Witch Doctor	700.00

All comics prices listed are for *Near Mint* condition.

1 Pixie Puzzle Rocket
    to Adventureland 160.00
1 EK,Prison Riot,drugs 500.00
N# EK,Red Mountain Featuring
    Quantrell's Raiders 350.00
N# Reform School Girl 2,500.00
1 Robotmen of the Lost Planet 1,700.00
N# JO,WW(c),Rocket to
    the Moon 1,700.00
N# JKu,Secret Diary of
    Eerie Adventures 2,700.00
1 EK,Sheriff Bob Dixon's
    Chuck Wagon 175.00
1 Sideshow 425.00
1 JKu,Sparkling Love 300.00
N# Speedy Rabbit 100.00
1 EK(c)Teddy Roosevelt &
    His Rough Riders 225.00
N# The Underworld Story 350.00
N# EK(c),The Unknown Man 350.00
1 EK,War Dogs of the U.S. Army 175.00
N# EK(c),White Chief of the
    Pawnee Indians. 200.00
N# Women to Love 700.00

BABE
Prize/Headline Feature,
June–July, 1948
1 BRo 300.00
2 BRo 175.00
3 BRo 165.00
4 thru 9 BRo . . . . @150.00

BABE RUTH
SPORTS COMICS
Harvey Publications,
April, 1949
1 BP 600.00
2 BP,Baseball 350.00
3 BP,Joe DiMaggio(c) 400.00
4 BP,Bob Feller(c). 325.00
5 BP,Football(c) 325.00
6 BP,Basketball(c). 325.00
7 BP 275.00
8 BP,Yogi Berra. 325.00
9 BP,Stan Musial(c). 300.00
10 . . . . 300.00
11 Feb., 1951 . . . . 275.00

BADGE OF JUSTICE
See: CRIME AND JUSTICE

INDIAN BRAVES
Ace Periodicals, 1951
1 Green Arrow. 150.00
2 . . . . 75.00
3 . . . . 65.00
4 . . . . 65.00
Becomes:

BAFFLING MYSTERIES
Periodical House/
Ace Mag., 1951–55
5 GC,MSy 500.00
6 MSy 350.00
7 . . . . 325.00
8 LC 325.00
9 . . . . 325.00
10 . . . . 325.00
11 GC. 325.00
12 thru 15 . . . . @300.00
16 LC 300.00
17 LC 300.00
18 LC 300.00
19 . . . . 300.00
20 LC,Bondage 400.00
21 LC 300.00
22 LC,MSy 325.00
23 Bondage 325.00
24 reprint 200.00

25 reprint 200.00
Becomes:

HEROES OF
THE WILD FRONTIER
Ace Periodicals, 1956
27 (1) 100.00
2 . . . . 100.00

BANG-UP COMICS
Progressive Publ., 1941
1 CosmoMan, Lady Fairplay,
    O:Buzz Balmer 1,700.00
2 Buzz Balmer 1,000.00
3 Buzz Balmer 1,000.00

BANNER COMICS
Ace Magazines, Sept., 1941
3 B:Captain Courageous,
    Lone Warrior. 1,800.00
4 JM(c),Flag(c) 1,500.00
5 . . . . 1,500.00
Becomes:

CAPTAIN COURAGEOUS
COMICS
March, 1942
6 I:The Sword 1,500.00

THE BARKER
Quality Comics Group, 1946–49
1 Circus. 150.00
2 thru 14 . . . . @125.00
15 JCo 110.00

BARNEY BAXTER
Argo Publ., 1956
1 . . . . 125.00
2 . . . . 125.00

BARNEY GOOGLE &
SNUFFY SMITH
Toby Press, 1951–52
1 . . . . 150.00
2 . . . . 100.00
3 . . . . 100.00
4 HK 100.00

BARNYARD COMICS
Animated Cartoons, June, 1944
1 (fa). 300.00
2 (fa) 250.00
3 (fa) 150.00
4 (fa) 150.00
5 (fa) 150.00
6 thru 12 (fa) . . . . @125.00
13 FF(ti) 150.00
14 FF(ti) 150.00
15 FF(ti) 150.00
16 . . . . 125.00
17 FF(ti) 125.00
18 FF,FF(ti) 150.00
19 FF,FF(ti) 150.00
20 FF,FF(ti) 150.00
21 FF(ti) 125.00
22 FF,FF(ti) 150.00
23 FF(ti) 125.00
24 FF,FF(ti) 150.00
25 FF,FF(ti) 150.00
26 FF(ti) 125.00
27 FF(ti) 125.00
28 . . . . 100.00
29 FF(ti) 125.00
30 and 31 . . . . @100.00
Becomes:

DIZZY DUCK
32 Funny Animal 125.00
33 thru 39 . . . . @100.00

Baseball Comics #1
© *Will Eisner Productions*

BASEBALL COMICS
Will Eisner Productions,
Spring, 1949
1 WE,A:Rube Rocky 1,100.00

BASEBALL HEROS
Fawcett Publications, 1952
N# Babe Ruth (c) 1,500.00

BASEBALL THRILLS
Ziff-Davis Publ. Co., 1951
10 Bob Feller Predicts Pennant
    Winners 600.00
2 BP, Yogi Berra story 450.00
3 EK, Joe DiMaggio story,
    Summer 1952 . . . . 500.00

BASIL
St. John Publishing, 1953
1 F:Basil, The Royal Cat. 65.00
2 . . . . 40.00
3 . . . . 20.00
4 . . . . 20.00

BATTLE ATTACK
Stanmor Publications, 1952–55
1 War Combat. 150.00
2 thru 8 . . . . @100.00

BATTLE CRY
Stanmor Publications, 1952–55
1 Flame-thrower (c) 175.00
2 . . . . 125.00
3 . . . . 125.00
4 EC Copy 125.00
5 . . . . 125.00
6 thru 20 . . . . @100.00

BATTLEFIELD ACTION
See: DYNAMITE

BATTLE FIRE
Stamfor Publications, 1955
1 War 150.00
2 . . . . 100.00
3 thru 7 . . . . @100.00

BATTLEFRONT
Standard Comics, 1952
5 ATh. 175.00

All comics prices listed are for *Near Mint* condition.

GOLDEN AGE

BATTLE REPORT
**Excellent Publ./
Ajax-Farrell, 1952--53**
1 .... 150.00
2 thru 6 .... @100.00

BATTLE SQUADRON
Stanmor Publications, 1955
1 .... 125.00
2 .... 100.00
3 Iwo Jima flag 100.00
4 .... 100.00
5 .... 100.00

BATTLE STORIES
Fawcett Publications 1952–53
1 GE 200.00
2 .... 100.00
3 .... 100.00
4 .... 100.00
5 .... 100.00
6 thru 11 .... @100.00

BEANY & CECIL
Dell Publishing Co., Jan., 1952
1 .... 250.00
2 thru 5 .... @150.00

BEE 29,
THE BOMBARDIER
Neal Publications, 1945
1 Funny Animal 400.00

BEN BOWIE & HIS
MOUNTAIN MEN
Dell Publishing Co., 1952
(1) *see Dell Four Color #443*
(2 thru 6) *see Dell Four Color*
7 .... 150.00
8 thru 10 .... @125.00
11 I:Yellow Hair 100.00
12 thru 17 .... @100.00

BEST COMICS
Better Publications, Nov., 1939
1 B:Red Mask 2,000.00
2 A:Red Mask, Silly Willie 1,200.00
3 A:Red Mask 1,200.00
4 Cannibalism story,
   Feb., 1940 .... 1,500.00

BEWARE
See: CAPTAIN SCIENCE

BEWARE TERROR TALES
Fawcett Publications, 1952–53
1 BP 900.00
2 RA,BP,MSy 700.00
3 .... 600.00
4 .... 600.00
5 .... 600.00
6 .... 600.00
7 .... 550.00
8 BP 750.00

THE BEYOND
Ace Magazines, 1950–55
1 Werewolf 650.00
2 .... 500.00
3 thru 10 .... @350.00
11 thru 20 .... @300.00
21 thru 30 .... @300.00

BIG CHIEF WAHOO
**Eastern Color Printing,
1942–43**
1 .... 600.00
2 BWa(c),Three Ring Circus ... 300.00
3 BWa(c) 225.00
4 BWa(c) 225.00
5 BWa(c),Wild West Rodeo 225.00
6 A:Minnie-Ha-Cha 175.00
7 .... 150.00
8 .... 100.00
9 .... 100.00
10 .... 125.00
11 thru 23 .... @100.00

BIG SHOT COMICS
**Columbia Comics Group,
May, 1940**
1 MBI,OW,Skyman,B:The Face,
   Joe Palooka, Rocky Ryan . 4,000.00
2 MBi,OW,Marvelo (c) 1,700.00
3 MBi,Skyman 1,500.00
4 MBi,OW,Joe Palooka (c) ... 1,000.00
5 MBi,Joe Palooka (c) 800.00
6 MBi,Joe Palooka (c) 750.00
7 MBi,Elect Joe Palooka
   and Skyman 700.00
8 MBi,Joe Palooka and Skyman
   dress as Santa 700.00
9 MBi,Skyman 700.00
10 MBi,Skyman 700.00

*Big Shot Comics #9
© Columbia Comics Group*

11 MBi 600.00
12 MBi,OW 600.00
13 MBi,OW 600.00
14 MBi,OW,O:Sparky Watts 600.00
15 MBi,OW,O:The Cloak 800.00
16 MBi,OW 500.00
17 MBi(c),OW 500.00
18 MBi,OW 500.00
19 MBi,OW,The Face (c) 450.00
20 MBi,OW,OW(c),Skyman cov. . 450.00
21 MBi,OW,A:Raja the Arabian
   Knight 450.00
22 MBi,OW,Joe Palooka (c). 450.00
23 MBi,OW,Sparky Watts (c) 400.00
24 MBi,OW,Uncle Sam (c). 600.00
25 MBi,OW,Hitler,Sparky Watts(c) 500.00
26 MBi,OW,Hitler,Devildog (c) . . 450.00
27 MBi,OW,Skyman (c) 450.00
28 MBi,OW,Hitler (c) 800.00
29 MBi,OW,I:Captain Yank 450.00
30 MBi,OW,Santa (c) 450.00
31 MBi,OW,Sparky Watts (c) 400.00
32 MBi,OW,B:Vic Jordan
   newspaper reps. 450.00
33 MBi,OW,Sparky Watts (c) 400.00
34 MBi,OW 400.00
35 MBi,OW 400.00
36 MBi,OW,Sparky Watts (c) 350.00
37 MBi,OW 350.00
38 MBi,Uncle Slap Happy (c) . . . 350.00
39 MBi,Uncle Slap Happy (c) . . . 350.00
40 MBi,Joe Palooka Happy (c) . . 350.00
41 MBi,Joe Palooka. 300.00
42 MBi,Joe Palooka parachutes . 300.00
43 MBi,V:Hitler 450.00
44 MBi,Slap Happy (c). 300.00
45 MBi,Slap Happy (c). 300.00
46 MBi,Uncle Sam (c),V:Hitler . 450.00
47 MBi,Uncle Slap Happy (c) . . . 300.00
48 MBi 300.00
49 MBi 250.00
50 MBi,O:The Face 250.00
51 MBi 250.00
52 MBi,E:Vic Jordan (Hitler cov)
   newspaper reps. 400.00
53 MBi,Uncle Slap Happy (c) . . . 225.00
54 MBi,Uncle Slap Happy (c) . . . 225.00
55 MBi,Happy Easter (c) 225.00
56 MBi 225.00
57 MBi 225.00
58 MBi 225.00
59 MBi,Slap Happy 225.00
60 MBi,Joe Palooka. 225.00
61 MBi 200.00
62 MBi 200.00
63 MBi 200.00
64 MBi,Slap Happy 200.00

Best Comics #4 © Better Publications

65 MBi,Slap Happy 200.00
66 MBi,Slap Happy 200.00
67 MBi 200.00
68 MBi,Joe Palooka 200.00
69 MBi 200.00
70 MBi,OW,Joe Palooka (c) 200.00
71 MBi,OW. 200.00
72 MBi,OW. 200.00
73 MBi,OW,The Face (c) 200.00
74 MBi,OW. 200.00
75 MBi,OW,Polar Bear Swim
   Club (c) 200.00
76 thru 80 MBi,OW . . . . @175.00
81 thru 84 MBi,OW . . . . @175.00
85 MBi,OW,Dixie Dugan (c). . . . 175.00
86 thru 95 MBi,OW . . . . @150.00
96 MBi,OW,X-Mas (c) 150.00
97 thru 99 MBi,OW . . . . @150.00
100 MBi,OW,Special issue. 175.00
101 thru 103 MBi,OW . . . . . . @150.00
104 MBi, Aug., 1949 . . . . 175.00

BIG-3
Fox Features Syndicate,
Fall 1940
1 B:BlueBeetle,Flame,Samson 4,500.00
2 A:BlueBeetle,Flame,Samson 2,000.00
3 same 1,800.00
4 same 1,600.00
5 same 1,600.00
6 E:Samson, bondage (c) 1,500.00
7 A:V-Man, Jan., 1942 . . . . . . 1,500.00

THE BIG TOP COMICS
Toby Press, 1951
1 . . . . 135.00
2 . . . . 100.00

BILL BARNES,
AMERICA'S AIR ACE
See: AIR ACE

BILL BATTLE,
THE ONE-MAN ARMY
Fawcett Publications 1952–53
1 . . . . 200.00
2 . . . . 150.00
3 . . . . 150.00
4 . . . . 150.00

BILL BOYD WESTERN
Fawcett Publications, 1950
1 B:Bill Boyd, Midnite,Ph(c) 800.00
2 P(c). 500.00
3 B:Ph(c). 350.00
4 . . . . 300.00
5 . . . . 300.00
6 . . . . 300.00
7 thru 11 . . . . @250.00
12 thru 21. . . . . @235.00
22 E:Ph(c) 235.00
23 June, 1952 . . . . 250.00

BILL STERN'S
SPORTS BOOK
Approved Comics,
Spring-Summer, 1951
1 Ewell Blackwell 300.00
2 . . . . 250.00
2-2 EK Giant. 300.00

BILLY AND BUGGY BEAR
I.W. Enterprises, 1958
1 Funny animal 100.00

BILLY BUNNY
Excellent Publications, 1954
1 . . . . 150.00
2 . . . . 100.00
3 . . . . 100.00
4 . . . . 100.00
Ann. #1 Christmas Frolics 225.00

BILLY THE KID
ADVENTURE MAGAZINE
Toby Press, Oct., 1950
1 AW(a&c),FF(a&c) 500.00
2 Photo (c) 200.00
3 AW,FF 500.00
4 . . . . 125.00
5 . . . . 125.00
6 FF,Photo (c) 250.00
7 Photo (c) 125.00
8 . . . . 125.00
9 HK Pot-Shot Pete 150.00
10 . . . . 125.00
11 . . . . 100.00
12 . . . . 100.00
13 HK. 100.00
14 AW,FF 150.00
15 thru 21 . . . . @100.00
22 AW,FF 125.00
23 thru 29 . . . . @100.00
30 1955 . . . . 100.00

BILLY THE KID
AND OSCAR
Fawcett Publications, 1945–46
1 Funny animal 250.00
2 . . . . 200.00
3 . . . . 200.00

BILLY WEST
Visual Editions (Standard
Comics), 1949–51
1 . . . . 200.00
2 . . . . 150.00
3 thru 8 . . . . @100.00
9 . . . . 125.00

BINGO COMICS
Howard Publications, 1945
1 LbC,Drug 750.00

BLACK CAT COMICS
Harvey Publications
(Home Comics),
June–July, 1946
1 JKu 1,400.00
2 JKu,JSm(c) 900.00
3 JSm(c) 600.00
4 B:Red Demon 600.00
5 S&K 650.00
6 S&K,A:Scarlet Arrow,
   O:Red Demon 650.00
7 S&K 650.00
8 S&K,B:Kerry Drake 600.00
9 S&K,O:Stuntman 650.00
10 JK,JSm 550.00
11 . . . . 550.00
12 'Ghost Town Terror' 550.00
13 LEI 500.00
14 LEI 500.00
15 LEI. 500.00
16 LEI 500.00
17 A:Mary Worth, Invisible
   Scarlet 500.00
18 LEI. 500.00
19 LEI. 500.00
20 A:Invisible Scarlet 500.00
21 LEI. 500.00
22 LEI thru 26. . . . . @500.00
27 X-Mas issue 450.00

Black Cat Comics #4
© Harvey Publications

28 I:Kit,A:Crimson Raider 450.00
29 Black Cat bondage (c) 450.00
Becomes:

BLACK CAT MYSTERY
Aug., 1951
30 RP,Black Cat(c). 700.00
31 RP. 550.00
32 BP,RP,Bondage (c) 600.00
33 BP,RP,Electrocution (c). 600.00
34 BP,RP,Bondage. 450.00
35 BP,RP,OK, Atomic Storm 600.00
36 RP 550.00
37 RP 450.00
38 RP 450.00
39 RP 500.00
40 RP 450.00
41 . . . . 450.00
42 . . . . 450.00
43 RP,Bondage 450.00
44 BP,HN,JkS,Oil Burning (c) . . . 600.00
45 BP,HN,Classic (c) 700.00
46 BP,HN 450.00
47 BP,HN 450.00
48 BP,HN 450.00
49 BP,HN 450.00
50 BP,Rotting Face 1,500.00
51 BP,HN,MMe 450.00
52 BP 400.00
53 BP 400.00
Becomes:

BLACK CAT WESTERN
Feb., 1955
54 A:Black Cat & Story 650.00
55 A:Black Cat 400.00
56 same 400.00
Becomes:

BLACK CAT MYSTIC
Sept., 1956
58 JK,Starts Comic Code. 600.00
59 KB 400.00
60 JK 500.00
61 Colorama, HN. 400.00
62 . . . . 300.00
63 JK 350.00
64 JK 350.00
65 April, 1963. . . . . 350.00

BLACK COBRA
Farrell Publications (Ajax),
1954–55
1 . . . . 500.00
2 (6) 350.00
3 . . . . 300.00

GOLDEN AGE

Becomes:

BRIDES DIARY
Farrell Publications, 1955

4	150.00
5 thru 8	@100.00
9	125.00
10	125.00

BLACK DIAMOND WESTERN
See: DESPERADO

UNCLE SAM QUARTERLY
Quality Comics Group, Fall, 1941

1 BE,LF(c),JCo,O:Uncle Sam	6,000.00
2 LF&WE(c),DBe, Ray, Black Condor	3,500.00
3 GT(a&c)	2,700.00
4 GT,GF(c)	2,500.00
5 RC,GT	2,700.00
6 GT	2,500.00
7 Hitler, Tojo, Mussolini	2,700.00
8 GT	2,500.00

Becomes:

BLACKHAWK
Comic Magazines, Winter, 1944

9 Bait for a Death Trap	6,000.00
10 RC	1,850.00
11 RC	1,300.00
12 Flies to thrilling adventure	1,200.00
13 Blackhawk Stalks Danger	1,200.00
14 BWa	1,300.00
15 Patrols the Universe	1,200.00
16 RC,BWa,Huddles for Action	1,200.00
17 BWa,Prepares for Action	1,500.00
18 RC(a&c),BWa,One for All and All for One	1,800.00
19 RC(a&c),BWa,Calls for Action	2,000.00
20 RC(a&c),BWa,Smashes Rugoth the Ruthless God	1,700.00
21 BWa,Battles Destiny Written in Blood	1,200.00
22 RC(a&c),BWa,Fear battles Death and Destruction	1,200.00
23 RC(a&c),BWa,Batters Down Oppression	1,200.00
24 RC(a&c),BWa	1,200.00
25 RC(a&c),BWa,V:The Evil of Mung	1,200.00

Blackhawk #82
© Comic Magazines

26 RC(a&c),V:Menace of a Sunken World	1,100.00
27 BWa,Destroys a War-Mad Munitions Magnate	1,100.00
28 BWa,Defies Destruction in the Battle of the Test Tube	1,100.00
29 BWa,Tale of the Basilisk Supreme Chief	1,100.00
30 BWa,RC(a&c),The Menace of the Meteors	1,100.00
31 BWa,RC(a&c),JCo,Treachery among the Blackhawks	1,000.00
32 BWa,RC(a&c),A:Delya, Flying Fish	1,000.00
33 RC,BWa,A:The Mockers	1,000.00
34 BWa,A:Tana,Mavis.	1,000.00
35 BWa,I:Atlo,Strongest Man on Earth	1,000.00
36 RC(a&c),BWa,V:Tarya	750.00
37 RC(a&c),BWa,V:Sari,The Rajah of Ramastan	750.00
38 BWa	750.00
39 RC(a&c),BWa,V:Lilith	750.00
40 RC(a&c),BWa,Valley of Yesterday	750.00
41 RC(a&c),BWa	700.00
42 RC(a&c),BWa,V:Iron Emperor	700.00
43 RC(a&c),BWa,Terror from the Catacombs	700.00
44 RC(a&c),BWa, King of Winds	700.00
45 BWa,The Island of Death	700.00
46 RC(a&c),BWa,V:DeathPatrol	700.00
47 RC(a&c),BWa,War!	700.00
48 RC(a&c),BWa,A:Hawks of Horror,Port of Missing Ships	700.00
49 RC(a&c),BWa,A:Valkyrie, Waters of Terrible Peace	700.00
50 RC(a&c),BWa,I:Killer Shark, Flying Octopus	750.00
51 BWa,V:The Whip, Whip of Nontelon	700.00
52 RC(a&c),BWa,Traitor in the Ranks	700.00
53 RC(a&c),BWa,V:Golden Mummy	700.00
54 RC(a&c),BWa,V:Dr. Deroski, Circles of Suicide.	700.00
55 RC(a&c),BWa,V:Rocketmen	700.00
56 RC(a&c),BWa,V:The Instructor, School for Sabotage	700.00
57 RC(a&c),BWa,Paralyzed City of Armored Men.	700.00
58 RC(a&c),BWa,V:King Cobra, The Spider of Delanza.	700.00
59 BWa,V:Sea Devil	700.00
60 RC(a&c),BWa,V:Dr. Mole and His Devils Squadron	700.00
61 V:John Smith, Stalin's Ambassador of Murder	600.00
62 V:General X, Return of Genghis Kahn	600.00
63 RC(a&c),The Flying Buzz-Saws.	600.00
64 RC(a&c),V:Zoltan Korvas, Legion of the Damned	600.00
65 Olaf as a Prisoner in Dungeon of Fear	600.00
66 RC(a&c),V:The Red Executioner, Crawler	600.00
67 RC(a&c),V:Future Fuehrer	600.00
68 V:Killers of the Kremlin	500.00
69 V:King of the Iron Men, Conference of the Dictators	500.00
70 V:Killer Shark	500.00
71 V:Von Tepp, The Man Who could Defeat Blackhawk O:Blackhawk	550.00
72 V:Death Legion	500.00
73 V:Hangman,The Tyrannical Freaks	400.00
74 Plan of Death	400.00

75 V:The Mad Doctor Baroc, The Z Bomb Menace	400.00
76 The King of Blackhawk Island	400.00
77 V:The Fiendish Electronic Brain	400.00
78 V:The Killer Vulture, Phantom Raider	400.00
79 V:Herman Goering, The Human Bomb	400.00
80 V:Fang, the Merciless, Dr. Death	400.00
81 A:Killer Shark, The Sea Monsters of Killer Shark	400.00
82 V:Sabo Teur, the Ruthless Commie Agent.	400.00
83 I:Hammmer & Sickle, V:Madam Double Cross.	400.00
84 V:Death Eye,Dr. Genius, The Dreaded Brain Beam	400.00
85 V:The Fiendish Impersonator	400.00
86 V:The Human Torpedoes	400.00
87 A:Red Agent Sovietta,V:Sea Wolf, Le Sabre,Comics Code	300.00
88 V:Thunder the Indestructible, The Phantom Sniper	300.00
89 V:The Super Communists.	400.00
90 V:The Storm King, Villainess Who Smashed the Blackhawk Team	400.00
91 Treason in the Underground.	400.00
92 V:The World Traitor.	400.00
93 V:Garg the Destroyer, O:Blackhawk	350.00
94 V:Black Widow, Darkk the Destroyer.	350.00
95 V:Madam Fury, Queen of the Pirates	350.00
96 Doom in the Deep.	350.00
97 Revolt of the Slave Workers.	300.00
98 Temple of Doom	300.00
99 The War That Never Ended	300.00
100 The Delphian Machine	325.00
101 Satan's Paymaster	275.00
102 The Doom Cloud	275.00
103 The Super Race	275.00
104 The Jet Menace	275.00
105 The Red Kamikaze Terror	275.00
106 The Flying Tank Platoon	275.00
107 The Winged Menace	275.00

Continued by: DC Comics

BLACK HOOD
See: LAUGH COMICS

BLACK KNIGHT, THE
Toby Press, 1953

1 Bondage	400.00

BLACK MAGIC
Crestwood Publ., 1950–51

1 S&K,MMe	2,400.00
2 S&K,MMe	1,200.00
3 S&K,MMe	1,100.00
4 S&K,MMe	1,100.00
5 S&K,MMe	1,100.00
6 S&K,MMe	1,100.00

Volume 2, 1951

1 S&K,MMe	750.00
2 MMe	600.00
3	600.00
4 S&K,MMe	750.00
5 S&K,MMe	750.00
6	600.00
7 S&K,MMe	750.00
8 MMe	600.00
9 S&K,MMe	750.00
10	600.00
11 MMe	600.00
12 S&K,MMe	600.00

Volume 3, 1953

1 S&K,MMe	600.00

2 S&K,MMe,AMc	600.00
3 S&K	600.00
4 S&K	600.00
5 S&K,MMe.	600.00
6 S&K,MMe.	600.00

Volume 4, 1954

1 S&K	600.00
2 S&K	600.00
3 S&K,SD(2nd work).	900.00
4 S&K,SD,eye damage.	750.00
5 S&K,SD	600.00
6 S&K,BP	500.00

Volume 5, 1956

1 S&K,MMe.	450.00
2 S&K,MMe.	450.00
3 S&K	450.00
4 S&K	450.00
5 S&K	450.00
6 S&K	450.00

Volume 6, 1957

1 JO	400.00
2 JO(c)	400.00
3 JO(c),GT	400.00
4 JO	400.00
5 JO(c)	400.00
6 JO(c)	400.00

Volume 7, 1958

1 LSt	400.00
2 JO	400.00
3 & 4 . . . . @	400.00
5 AT,Hitler(c)	450.00
6 BP	350.00

Volume 8, 1961

1 BP	300.00
2 BP,SD	300.00
3 thru 5 BP . . . . @	300.00

BLACKSTONE, MASTER MAGICIAN COMICS
Vital/Street & Smith Publ. 1946

1	1,200.00
2	1,000.00
3	1,000.00

BLACKSTONE, THE MAGICIAN DETECTIVE
EC Comics, 1947

1 Happy Houlihans	750.00

See: Marvel Listings

BLACK TERROR
Better Publications/ Standard, Winter, 1942-43

1 Bombing (c)	5,000.00
2 V:Arabs,Bondage(c)	2,000.00
3 V:Nazis,Bondage(c)	1,200.00
4 ASh(c),V:Sub Nazis	1,000.00
5 V:Japanese.	1,000.00
6 Air Battle	900.00
7 Air Battle,V:Japanese, A:Ghost	900.00
8 V:Nazis	900.00
9 V:Japanese,Bondage(c) . . .	1,000.00
10 ASh(c),V:Nazis	900.00
11 & 12 . . . . @	800.00
13 ASh(c).	725.00
14 ASh(c).	800.00
15 ASh(c).	725.00
16 ASh(c).	725.00
17 ASh(c),Bondage(c)	800.00
18 ASh(c).	700.00
19 & 20 ASh . . . . @	700.00
21 ASh(c)	800.00
22 FF,ASh	700.00
23 ASh	700.00
24 Bondgae(c)	800.00
25 ASh	700.00
26 GT,ASh(c)	700.00
27 MME,GT,ASh	700.00

Blazing Comics #3
© Enwil Associates

BLAZING COMICS
Enwil Associates/Rural Home, June, 1944

1 B:Green Turtle, Red Hawk, Black Buccaneer	1,000.00
2 Green Turtle (c)	700.00
3 Green Turtle (c)	650.00
4 Green Turtle (c)	650.00
5 March, 1945	650.00
5a Black Buccaneer(c),1955. . .	400.00
6 Indian-Japanese(c), 1955	400.00

BLAZING WEST
B & I Publ./American Comics 1948

1	250.00
2	150.00
3	150.00
4 O&I: Little Lobo	125.00
5 thru 13 . . . . @	100.00
14 O&I: The Hooded Horseman .	150.00
15 thru 20 . . . . @	125.00

Becomes:

HOODED HORSEMAN
American Comics, 1952–54

21	250.00
22	200.00
23	150.00
24	150.00
25	125.00
26	150.00
27	135.00

BLAZING WESTERN
Timor Publications, 1954

1	200.00
2 thru 5 . . . . @	100.00

BLONDIE COMICS
David McKay, Spring, 1947

1	350.00
2	175.00
3	125.00
4	125.00
5	125.00
6 thru 10 . . . . @	100.00
11 thru 15 . . . . @	100.00

Harvey Publications, 1950

16	150.00
17 thru 20 . . . . @	125.00
21 thru 30 . . . . @	100.00
31 thru 50 . . . . @	100.00

51 thru 80. . . . . @	100.00
81 thru 99. . . . . @	100.00
100	110.00
101 thru 124. . . . . @	100.00
125 Giant, 80-pg.	125.00
126 thru 136 . . . . @	100.00
137 Giant, 80-pg.	125.00
138 thru 139 . . . . @	100.00
140 Giant, 80-pg.	125.00
141 thru 147 . . . . @	100.00
148 Giant, 68-pg.	125.00
149 thru 154 . . . . @	100.00
155 Giant, 68-pg.	125.00
156	100.00
157 thru 159 Giant, 68-pg. . . . @	125.00
160	100.00
161 thru 163 Giant, 68-pg. . . . @	125.00

See also: DAISY AND HER PUPS

BLOOD IS THE HARVEST
Catechetical Guild 1950

N# Comunist menace	2,000.00

BLUE BEETLE, THE
Fox Features Syndicate/ Holyoke Publ., Winter 1939

1 O:Blue Beetle,A:Master Magician	8,000.00
2 BP,Wonder World	2,500.00
3 JSm(c)	1,600.00
4 Mentions marijuana	1,500.00
5 GT,A:Zanzibar the Magician	1,300.00
6 B:Dynamite Thor, O:Blue Beetle	1,300.00
7 A:Dynamo	1,200.00
8 E:Thor,A:Dynamo	1,200.00
9 BP(c),A:Black Bird,Gorilla . .	1,200.00
10 BP(c),A:Black Bird, bondage(c)	1,200.00
11 BP(c),A:Gladiator, Bondage.	1,000.00
12 A:Black Fury, Bondage	1,000.00
13 B:V-Man	1,000.00
14 JKu,I:Sparky.	1,000.00
15 JKu.	1,000.00
16	1,000.00
17 AyB,A:Mimic.	1,000.00
18 JKu,E:V-Man,A:Red Knight .	1,000.00
19 JKu,A:Dascomb Dinsmore. .	1,000.00
20 I&O:Flying Tiger Squadron .	1,000.00
21	900.00
22 A:Ali-Baba.	900.00
23 A:Jimmy DooLittle.	900.00
24 I:The Halo	900.00
25	900.00
26 General Patton story	1,000.00

Blue Beetle #31
© Fox Features Syndicate

All comics prices listed are for *Near Mint* condition.

GOLDEN AGE

27 A:Tamoa 900.00
28 . . . . 800.00
29 . . . . 800.00
30 L:Holyoke 800.00
31 F:Fox. 775.00
32 Hitler (c) 900.00
33 Fight for Freedom 775.00
34 A:Black Terror,Menace of K-4 . 775.00
35 Threat From Saturn 775.00
36 The Runaway House 775.00
37 Inside the House. 775.00
38 Revolt of the Zombies. 775.00
39 . . . . 775.00
40 . . . . 775.00
41 A:O'Brine Twins 750.00
42 . . . . 750.00
43 . . . . 750.00
44 . . . . 750.00
45 . . . . 750.00
46 BP,A:Puppeteer, Bondage . . . 750.00
47 JKa,V:Junior Crime Club . . . 1,700.00
48 JKa,A:Black Lace. 1,400.00
49 JKa. 1,400.00
50 JKa,The Ambitious Bride . . 1,400.00
51 JKa, Shady Lady 1,200.00
52 BP,JKa(c),Bondage (c) 1,700.00
53 JKa,A:Jack "Legs"
    Diamond,Bondage(c) . . 1,200.00
54 JKa,The Vanishing Nude . . . 1,800.00
55 JKa. 1,100.00
56 JKa,Tri-State Terror 1,100.00
57 JKa,The Feagle Bros. 1,100.00
58 . . . . 200.00
59 . . . . 200.00
60 Aug., 1960 . . . . 225.00

BLUE BEETLE
See: THING!, THE

BLUE BOLT
Funnies, Inc./Novelty Press/
Premium Service Co, 1940

1 JSm,PGv,O:Blue Bolt 6,500.00
2 JSm,S&K 3,000.00
3 S&K,A:Space Hawk 2,500.00
4 S&K,BEv(c). 2,000.00
5 BEv,S&K,B:Sub Zero 2,000.00
6 JK,JSm 1,900.00
7 S&K,BEv 1,900.00
8 PGv,S&K(c) 1,900.00
9 . . . . 1,700.00
10 PGv,S&K(c) 1,700.00
11 BEv(c) 1,700.00
12 PGv 1,700.00
2-1 BEv(c),PG,O:Dick Cole &
    V:Simba. 700.00
2-2 BEv(c),FGu,O:Twister 550.00
2-3 PGv,Cole vs Simba 400.00
2-4 BD 400.00
2-5 I:Freezum. 400.00
2-6 PGv,O:Sgt.Spook, Dick Cole . 350.00
2-7 BD,Lois Blake 350.00
2-8 BD 350.00
2-9 JW 350.00
2-10 JW 350.00
2-11 JW 350.00
2-12 E:Twister 350.00
3-1 A:115th Infantry 350.00
3-2 A:Phantom Sub 350.00
3-3 . . . . 350.00
3-4 JW(c) 250.00
3-5 Jor 250.00
3-6 Jor 250.00
3-7 X-Mas (c) 250.00
3-8 . . . . 250.00
3-9 A:Phantom Sub 250.00
3-10 DBa 250.00
3-11 April Fools (c). 250.00
3-12 . . . . 250.00
4-1 Hitler,Tojo,Mussolini (c) 600.00
4-2 Liberty Bell (c) 200.00

4-3 What are You Doing for Your
    Country 200.00
4-4 I Fly for Vengence 200.00
4-5 TFH(c) 200.00
4-6 HcK 200.00
4-7 JWi(c). 200.00
4-8 E:Sub Zero 200.00
4-9 . . . . 200.00
4-10 . . . . 200.00
4-11 . . . . 200.00
4-12 . . . . 200.00
5-1 thru 5-12. . . . . @175.00
6-1 . . . . 175.00
6-2 War Bonds (c) 175.00
6-3 . . . . 175.00
6-4 Racist(c). 300.00
6-5 Soccer (c) 175.00
6-6 thru 6-12. . . . . @175.00
7-1 thru 7-12. . . . . @175.00
8-1 Baseball (c) 175.00
8-2 JHa 175.00
8-3 JH 175.00
8-4 JHa 175.00
8-5 JH 175.00
8-6 JDo 175.00
8-7 LbC(c). 350.00
8-8 . . . . 175.00
8-9 AMc(c) 175.00
8-10 . . . . 175.00
8-11 Basketball (c). 200.00
8-12 . . . . 175.00
9-1 AMc,Baseball (c) 175.00
9-2 AMc 175.00
9-3 . . . . 175.00
9-4 JH 175.00
9-5 JH 175.00
9-6 LbC(c),Football (c). 300.00
9-7 JH 175.00
9-8 Hockey (c) 185.00
9-9 LbC(c),3-D effect 275.00
9-10 . . . . 175.00
9-11 . . . . 175.00
9-12 . . . . 175.00
10-1 Baseball (c),3-D effect. 200.00
10-2 3-D effect 200.00
Star Publications, 1949
102 LbC(c),Chameleon 550.00
103 LbC(c),same 500.00
104 LbC(c),same 500.00
105 LbC(c),O:Blue Bolt Space,
    Drug Story 900.00
106 S&K,LbC(c),A;Space Hawk . 800.00
107 S&K,LbC(c),A;Space Hawk . 800.00
108 S&K,LbC(c),A:Blue Bolt . . . 800.00
109 BW,LbC(c). 800.00

Blue Bolt #105
© Star Publications

110 B:Horror (c)s,A:Target 800.00
111 Weird Tales of Terror,
    A:Red Rocket 800.00
112 JyD 700.00
113 BW,JyD,A:Space Hawk. . . . 700.00
114 LbC(c),JyD 700.00
115 LbC(c),JyD,A:Sgt.Spook . . . 700.00
116 LbC(c),JyD,A:Jungle Joe . . . 700.00
117 LbC(c),A:Blue Bolt,Jo-Jo. . . 700.00
118 WW,LbC(c),A:White Spirit . . . 700.00
119 LbC(c) 700.00
Becomes:

GHOSTLY WEIRD
STORIES
Star Publications, Sept., 1953
120 LbC,A:Jo-Jo 750.00
121 LbC,A:Jo-Jo 700.00
122 LbC,A:The Mask,Sci-Fi. . . . 750.00
123 LbC,A:Jo-Jo 600.00
124 LbC, Sept., 1954. . . . . 600.00

BLUE CIRCLE COMICS
Enwil Associates/
Rural Home, June, 1944
1 B:Blue Circle,O:Steel Fist . . . 500.00
2 . . . . 350.00
3 Hitler parody (c) 400.00
4 . . . . 300.00
5 E:Steel Fist,A:DriftwoodDavey. 300.00
6 . . . . 300.00

BLUE RIBBON COMICS
MLJ Magazines, Nov., 1939
1 JCo,B:Dan Hastings,
    Richy-Amazing Boy 7,000.00
2 JCo,B:Bob Phantom,
    Silver Fox 3,000.00
3 JCo,A:Phantom,Silver Fox . . 2,500.00
4 O:Fox,Ty Gor,B:Doc Strong,
    Hercules 2,600.00
5 Gattling Gun (c) 1,500.00
6 Amazing Boy Richy (c) 1,400.00
7 A:Fox (c),Corporal Collins
    V:Nazis 1,400.00
8 E:Hercules 1,400.00
9 SCp,O&I:Mr. Justice 6,000.00
10 SCp,Mr. Justice (c) 2,500.00
11 CBi,MMe,SCp(c) 2,500.00
12 SCp,MMe,CBi,E:Doc Strong 2,500.00
13 CBi,IN,MMe,B:Inferno 2,500.00
14 MMe,CBi,SCp(c),A:Inferno . 2,200.00
15 A:Inferno,E:Green Falcon . . 2,200.00
16 SCp(c),O:Captain Flag 3,000.00
17 Captain Flag, V:Black Hand. 2,200.00
18 SCp(c),Captain Flag 2,000.00
19 Captain Flag (c). 2,000.00
20 Captain Flag V:Nazis (c) . . . 2,200.00
21 Captain Flag V:Death 2,000.00
22 Circus (c), March, 1942. . . . 2,000.00

BLUE RIBBON COMICS
St. John Publications,
Feb., 1949
1 Heckle & Jeckle 150.00
2 MB(c),Diary Secrets 300.00
3 MB,MB(c),Heckle & Jeckle . . . 150.00
4 Teen-age Diary Secrets 275.00
5 MB,Teen-age Diary Secrets. . . 350.00
6 Dinky Duck 100.00

BO
Charlton Comics, June, 1955
1 . . . . 100.00
2 . . . . 100.00
3 Oct., 1955 . . . . 100.00
Becomes:

GOLDEN AGE

TOM CAT
Charlton Comics, 1956
4 Funny animal-cat 100.00
5 thru 8 . . . . @75.00
Becomes:

ATOM THE CAT
Charlton Comics, 1957–58
9 . . . . 100.00
10 . . . . 75.00
11 Atomic Mouse 125.00
12 Atomic Mouse 125.00
13 thru 17 . . . . @75.00

BOB & BETTY & SANTA'S WISHING WELL
Sears-Roebuck Co., 1941
N# Giveaway 300.00

BOBBY BENSON'S B-BAR-B RIDERS
Parkway Publ. Co.
(M.E. Entertainment), 1950
1 BP, Teen-age cowboy 750.00
2 BP 300.00
3 BP 250.00
4 BP,Lemonade Kid (c) 250.00
5 BP 250.00
6 BP 250.00
7 BP 250.00
8 BP 250.00
9 BP,FF(c) 500.00
10 BP 200.00
11 BP,FF(c) 500.00
12 BP 150.00
13 DAy,FF(c),A:Ghost Rider 500.00
14 DAy,A:Ghost Rider,bondage . . 400.00
15 DAy,A:Ghost Rider 350.00
16 photo(c) 200.00
17 . . . . 150.00
18 . . . . 150.00
19 . . . . 150.00

BOBBY COMICS
Universal Phoenix Features, 1946
1 . . . . 200.00

BOB COLT
Fawcett Publications, Nov., 1950
1 B:Bob Colt,Buck Skin 600.00
2 Death Round Train 400.00
3 Mysterious Black Knight of the
  Prairie 300.00
4 Death Goes Downstream 300.00
5 The Mesa of Mystery 300.00
6 The Mysterious Visitors 300.00
7 Dragon of Disaster 250.00
8 Redman's Revenge 250.00
9 Hidden Hacienda 250.00
10 Fiend from Vulture
  Mountain 250.00

BOB STEELE WESTERN
Fawcett Publications, 1950–52
1 Photo(c) 800.00
2 Ph(c); Dynamite Death 400.00
3 Ph(c); The Perilous Deadline . . 300.00
4 Ph(c); Six-Gun Menace 300.00
5 Ph(c); Murder on the Hoof . . . 300.00
6 Ph(c); Range War 250.00
7 Ph(c); Tall Timber Terror 250.00
8 Ph(c); The Race of Death 250.00
9 Ph(c); Death Rides the Storm . 250.00
10 Ph(c); Draw...Or Die 250.00

BOB SWIFT
Fawcett Publications 1951–52
1 Boy sportsman 150.00
2 thru 5 . . . . @100.00

BOLD STORIES
Kirby Publishing Co., 1950
1 WW,Near nudity (c) 2,200.00
2 GI,Cobra's Kiss 1,500.00
3 WW,Orge of Paris 1,500.00
4 Case of the Winking Buddha . . 800.00
5 It Rhymes with Lust 800.00
6 Candid Tales, April, 1950 . . . . 800.00

BOMBER COMICS
Elliot Publishing Co., 1944
1 B:Wonder Boy,Kismet,
  Eagle Evans 1,500.00
2 Wonder Boy(c) Hitler 1,000.00
3 Wonder Boy-Kismet (c) 600.00
4 Hitler,Tojo, Mussolini (c) 1,200.00

BOOK OF ALL COMICS
William H. Wise, 1945
1 A:Green Mask,Puppeteer 600.00

BOOK OF COMICS, THE
William H. Wise, 1945
N# A:Captain V 600.00

BOOTS AND HER BUDDIES
Visual Editions
(Standard Comics), 1948–49
5 Cowgirl 250.00
6 . . . . 200.00
7 . . . . 225.00
8 . . . . 200.00
9 FF 450.00

BORDER PATROL
P.L. Publishing Co., 1951
1 Wild West 200.00
2 . . . . 150.00
3 . . . . 150.00

THE BOUNCER
Fox Features Syndicate, 1944
N# (10) 500.00
11 O:The Bouncer 400.00
12 . . . . 300.00
13 . . . . 300.00
14 rep. #(10) 300.00

BOY COMICS
Comic House, Inc.
(Lev Gleason Publ.) April, 1942
3 O:Crimebuster,Bombshell,Young
  Robin, B:Yankee Longago,
  Swoop Storm 7,000.00
4 Hitler,Tojo,Mussolini (c) 2,500.00
5 Crimebuster saves day (c) . 2,000.00
6 O:Iron Jaw & Death of Son,
  B:Little Dynamite 5,000.00
7 Hitler,Tojo,Mussolini (c) 2,000.00
8 D:Iron Jaw 2,100.00
9 I:He-She 2,000.00
10 Iron Jaw returns 2,300.00
11 Iron Jaw falls in love 1,800.00
12 Crimebuster V:Japanese . . . 1,000.00
13 V:New,more terrible
  Iron Jaw 1,000.00
14 V:Iron Jaw 1,000.00
15 I:Rodent,D:Iron Jaw 1,200.00
16 Crimebuster V:Knight 600.00
17 Flag (c),Crimebuster
  V:Moth 600.00

Boy Comics#12
© Comic House

18 Smashed car (c) 550.00
19 Express train (c) 550.00
20 Coffin (c) 550.00
21 Boxing (c) 400.00
22 Under Sea (c) 400.00
23 Golf (c) 400.00
24 County insane asylum (c) . . . 400.00
25 52 pgs 400.00
26 68 pgs 400.00
27 Express train (c) 450.00
28 E:Yankee Longago 450.00
29 Prison break (c) 450.00
30 O:Crimebuster,Murder (c) . . 600.00
31 68 pgs 400.00
32 E:Young Robin Hood 400.00
33 . . . . 400.00
34 Suicide (c) & story 350.00
35 . . . . 300.00
36 . . . . 300.00
37 . . . . 300.00
38 . . . . 300.00
39 E:Little Dynamite 300.00
40 . . . . 300.00
41 thru 50 . . . . @275.00
51 thru 56 . . . . @250.00
57 B:Dilly Duncan 275.00
58 . . . . 250.00
59 . . . . 250.00
60 Iron Jaw returns 275.00
61 O:Iron Jaw,Crimebuster 300.00
62 A:Iron Jaw 275.00
63 thru 70 . . . . @200.00
71 E:Dilly Duncan 200.00
72 . . . . 200.00
73 . . . . 200.00
74 thru 79 . . . . @200.00
80 I:Rocky X 150.00
81 thru 88 . . . . @150.00
89 A:The Claw 200.00
90 same 200.00
91 same 200.00
92 same 200.00
93 The Claw(c),A:Rocky X 200.00
94 . . . . 150.00
95 . . . . 150.00
96 . . . . 150.00
97 . . . . 150.00
98 A:Rocky X 150.00
99 . . . . 150.00
100 . . . . 175.00
101 thru 118 . . . . @175.00
119 March, 1956 . . . . 175.00

All comics prices listed are for *Near Mint* condition.

BOY DETECTIVE
Avon Periodicals, 1951–52
1 F:Dan Tayler	300.00
2 Vice Lords of Crime	200.00
3 Spy Menace	200.00
4 The Death Trap	200.00

BOY EXPLORERS
See: TERRY AND THE PIRATES

BOYS' RANCH
Harvey Publications, 1950–51
1 S&K,F:Clay Duncan	1,000.00
2 S&K	750.00
3 S&K,MMe	700.00
4 S&K	600.00
5 S&K,MMe	400.00
6 S&K,MMe	400.00

THE BRAIN
Sussex Publ. Co./Magazine Enterprises, 1956–58
1	150.00
2 thru 7	@100.00

BRENDA STARR
Four Star Comics Corp., 1947
13(1)	3,500.00
14(2) JKa,Bondage (c)	5,000.00

Superior Comics Ltd., 1948
2-3	3,500.00
2-4 JKa,Operating table (c)	3,500.00
2-5 Swimsuit (c)	2,000.00
2-6	2,000.00
2-7	2,000.00
2-8 Cosmetic (c)	2,000.00
2-9 Giant Starr (c)	2,000.00
2-10 Wedding (c)	2,000.00
2-11	2,000.00
2-12	2,000.00
Becomes:

BRENDA STARR REPORTER
Charlton Comics, 1955
13	1,000.00
14 & 15	@900.00

BRICK BRADFORD
**Best Books
(Standard Comics) July, 1949**
5	350.00
6 Robot (c)	500.00
7 ASh(c)	200.00
8	200.00

BRIDES DIARY
See: BLACK COBRA

BROADWAY ROMANCES
Quality Comics Group, 1950
1 PG,BWa(a&c)	600.00
2 BWa,Glittering Desire	400.00
3 BL,Stole My Love	200.00
4 Enslaved by My Past	200.00
5 Flame of Passion,Sept.,1950	200.00

BRONCHO BILL
**Visual Editions
(Standard Comics) Jan., 1948**
5	250.00
6 ASh(c)	125.00
7 ASh(c)	100.00
8	75.00
9 thru 13 ASh(c)	@100.00
14 and 15	@75.00
16 ASh(c)	100.00

Bruce Gentry #2
© *Superior Comics*

BRUCE GENTRY
**Four Star Publ./
Visual Editions/
Superior, Jan., 1948**
1 B:Ray Bailey reprints	900.00
2 Plane crash (c)	500.00
3 E:Ray Bailey reprints	500.00
4 Tiger attack (c)	400.00
5	400.00
6 Help message (c)	400.00
7	400.00
8 End of Marriage (c),July, 1949	400.00

BUCCANEERS
See: KID ETERNITY

BUCK JONES
Dell Publishing Co., 1950
1 Buck Jones & Horse Silver	250.00
2	150.00
3 thru 8	@100.00

BUCK ROGERS
**Eastern Color Printing,
Winter 1940**
1 Partial Painted(c)	6,500.00
2	2,400.00
3 Living Corpse from Crimson Coffin	2,000.00
4 One man army of greased lightning	1,900.00
5 Sky Roads	1,700.00
6 Sept., 1943	1,700.00

Toby Press
100 Flying Saucers	800.00
101	750.00
9 MA	750.00

BUDDIES IN THE U.S. ARMY
Avon Periodicals, 1952–53
1 Fightin' Guys & Fabulous Gals	200.00
2	125.00

BUFFALO BILL
Youthful Magazines, 1950–51
2 Annie Oakley	200.00
3 thru 9	@150.00

BUFFALO BILL PICTURE STORIES
Street & Smith Publ. 1949
1	250.00
2	250.00

BUFFALO BILL JR.
Dell Publishing Co., 1956
1	200.00
2 thru 6	@150.00
7 thru 13	@125.00

BUGHOUSE
Ajax/Farrell, 1954
1	250.00
2	150.00
3	150.00
4	150.00

BUG MOVIES
Dell Publishing Co., 1931
1	600.00

BUGS BUNNY
DELL GIANT EDITIONS
**Dell Publishing Co.
Christmas**
1 Christmas Funnies (1950)	350.00
2 Christmas Funnies (1951)	300.00
3 Christmas Funnies (1952)	250.00
4 Christmas Funnies (1953)	200.00
5 Christmas Funnies (1954)	200.00
6 Christmas Party (1955)	175.00
7 Christmas Party (1956)	185.00
8 Christmas Funnies (1957)	185.00
9 Christmas Funnies (1958)	185.00
1 County Fair (1957)	200.00

Halloween
1 Halloween Parade (1953)	200.00
2 Halloween Parade (1954)	175.00
3 Trick 'N' Treat Halloween Fun (1955)	185.00
4 Trick 'N' Treat Halloween Fun (1956)	185.00

Vacation
1 Vacation Funnies (1951)	325.00
2 Vacation Funnies (1952)	275.00
3 Vacation Funnies (1953)	250.00
4 Vacation Funnies (1954)	200.00
5 Vacation Funnies (1955)	200.00
6 Vacation Funnies (1956)	175.00
7 Vacation Funnies (1957)	175.00
8 Vacation Funnies (1958)	175.00
9 Vacation Funnies (1959)	175.00

BUGS BUNNY
**Dell Publishing Co., 1942
see Four Color for early years**
28 thru 30	@130.00
31 thru 50	@120.00
51 thru 70	@100.00
71 thru 85	@100.00
86 Giant-Show Time	125.00
87 thru 100	@100.00
101 thru 120	@75.00
121 thru 140	@50.00
141 thru 190	@50.00
191 thru 245	@50.00

BULLETMAN
**Fawcett Publications,
Summer, 1941**
1 I:Bulletman & Bulletgirl	7,000.00
2 MRa(c)	3,000.00
3 MRa(c)	2,500.00
4 V:Headless Horror, Guillotine (c)	2,500.00

All comics prices listed are for *Near Mint* condition.

Bulletman #10
© Fawcett Publications

5 Riddle of Dr. Riddle 2,500.00
6 V:Japanese 1,500.00
7 V:Revenge Syndicate 1,500.00
8 V:Mr. Ego 1,500.00
9 V:Canine Criminals 1,500.00
10 I:Bullet Dog 1,700.00
11 V:Fiendish Fiddler 1,100.00
12 . . . . 1,000.00
13 . . . . 1,000.00
14 V:Death the Comedian 1,000.00
15 V:Professor D. 1,000.00
16 VanishingElephant,Fall 1946 1,000.00

BULLS-EYE
Charlton Comics, 1954
1 S&K,Western Scout 750.00
2 S&K 650.00
3 S&K 500.00
4 S&K 500.00
5 S&K 500.00
6 S&K 450.00
7 S&K 500.00
Becomes:

CODY OF THE PONY EXPRESS
Charlton Comics, 1955
8 F:Buffalo Bill Cody 125.00
9 . . . . 100.00
10 . . . . 100.00
Becomes:

OUTLAWS OF THE WEST

BULLS-EYE
See: SCOOP COMICS

BUSTER BEAR
**Arnold Publications/
Quality Comics Group, 1953**
1 Funny animal 150.00
2 . . . . 125.00
3 thru 10 . . . . @100.00

BUSTER BROWN COMICS
Brown Shoe Co., 1945–59
1 . . . . 1,000.00
2 . . . . 350.00
3 . . . . 250.00
4 scarce 400.00
5 . . . . 250.00
6 . . . . 250.00
7 . . . . 250.00
8 . . . . 250.00
9 . . . . 250.00

10 . . . . 250.00
11 thru 20 . . . . @100.00
21 thru 24 . . . . @100.00
25 RC 150.00
26 thru 36 . . . . @100.00
37 RC 150.00
38 . . . . 100.00
39 . . . . 100.00
40 RC 150.00
41 RC 150.00
42 . . . . 100.00
43 . . . . 100.00

BUSTER BUNNY
**Animated Cartoons
(Standard)/Pines, 1949**
1 FF,Funny animal 150.00
2 thru 5 . . . . @100.00
6 thru 10 . . . . @100.00
11 thru 14 . . . . @100.00
15 racist(c) 125.00
16 . . . . 100.00

BUSTER CRABBE
Famous Funnies, Nov., 1951
1 The Arrow of Death 650.00
2 AW&GE(c) 700.00
3 AW&GE(c) 800.00
4 FF(c) 900.00
5 AW,FF(a&c) 1,800.00
6 Sharks (c) 300.00
7 FF 350.00
8 Gorilla (c) 300.00
9 FF 350.00
10 . . . . 300.00
11 Snakes (c) 250.00
12 Sept., 1953 . . . . 250.00

BUSTER CRABBE
Lev Gleason Pub., 1953
1 Ph(c) 300.00
2 ATh 275.00
3 ATh 275.00
4 F. Gordon(c) 275.00

BUZ SAWYER
Standard Comics, June, 1948
1 . . . . 300.00
2 I:Sweeney 250.00
3 . . . . 250.00
4 . . . . 250.00
5 June, 1949 . . . . 250.00

CALLING ALL BOYS
**Parents Magazine Institute
Jan., 1946**
1 Skiing 200.00
2 Roy Rogers Story 150.00
3 Peril Out Post 150.00
4 Model Airplane 150.00
5 Fishing 150.00
6 Swimming 150.00
7 Baseball 175.00
8 School 150.00
9 The Miracle Quarterback 150.00
10 Gary Cooper (c) 200.00
11 Rin-Tin-Tin (c) 150.00
12 Bob Hope (c) 250.00
13 Bing Cosby (c) 225.00
14 J. Edgar Hoover (c) 150.00
15 Tex Granger (c) 125.00
16 . . . . 125.00
17 Tex Granger (c), May, 1948 . . 125.00
Becomes:

TEX GRANGER
June, 1948
18 Bandits of the Badlands 125.00
19 The Seven Secret Cities 100.00
20 Davey Crockett's Last Fight . . 100.00

Calling All Girls #3
© Parent Magazine Press

21 Canyon Ambush 100.00
22 V:Hooded Terror 100.00
23 V:Billy the Kid 100.00
24 A:Hector, Sept., 1949 . . . . . . 100.00

CALLING ALL GIRLS
**Parent Magazine Press, Inc.,
Sept., 1941**
1 . . . . 300.00
2 Virginia Weidler (c) 250.00
3 Shirley Temple (c) 300.00
4 Darla Hood (c) 150.00
5 Gloria Hood (c) 150.00
6 . . . . 150.00
7 . . . . 150.00
8 . . . . 150.00
9 Flag (c) 150.00
10 . . . . 150.00
11 Gary Cooper as Lou Gerrig . . 200.00
12 thru 20 . . . . @125.00
21 thru 39 . . . . @125.00
40 Liz Taylor 250.00
41 . . . . 100.00
42 . . . . 100.00
43 Oct., 1945 . . . . 100.00

CALLING ALL KIDS
**Quality Comics, Inc.,
Dec./Jan., 1946**
1 Funny Animal stories 150.00
2 . . . . 125.00
3 thru 5 . . . . @100.00
6 thru 10 . . . . @100.00
11 thru 25 . . . . @100.00
26 Aug., 1949 . . . . 100.00

CAMERA COMICS
**U.S. Camera Publishing Corp.,
July–Sept., 1944**
1 Airfighter,Grey Comet 350.00
2 How to Set Up a Darkroom . . 300.00
3 Linda Lens V:Nazi (c) 300.00
4 Linda Lens (c) 250.00
5 Diving (c) 250.00
6 Jim Lane (c) 250.00
7 Linda Lens (c) 250.00
8 Linda Lens (c) 250.00
9 Summer, 1946 . . . . 250.00

CAMP COMICS
Dell Publishing Co., 1942
1 Ph(c),WK,A:Bugs Bunny 1,500.00
2 Ph(c),WK,A:Bugs Bunny 1,200.00
3 Ph(c),WK 1,000.00

All comics prices listed are for *Near Mint* condition.

CAMPUS LOVES
Comic Magazines
(Quality Comics Group), 1949
1 BWa,PGv	500.00
2 BWa,PGv	400.00
3 PGv,Photo(c)	250.00
4 PGv,Photo(c)	250.00
5 PGv,Photo(c)	250.00

CAMPUS ROMANCES
Avon Periodicals/
Realistic Publ., 1949
1 Walter Johnson	350.00
2	300.00
3	300.00

CANDY
William H. Wise, 1944–45
1 BW,Two-Scoop	600.00
1a rep.BW	100.00
2 BW	500.00
3 BW	500.00

CANDY
Quality Comics Group, 1947–56
1 JCo,PGv,Teen-age	375.00
2 JCo,PGv	300.00
3 JCo	150.00
4 JCo	150.00
5 JCo	150.00
6 thru 10 JCo	@150.00
11 thru 20 JCo	@125.00
21 thru 40	@100.00
41 thru 64	@100.00

CANNONBALL COMICS
Rural Home Publ. Co., 1945
1 Superhero, Crash Kid	1,400.00
2 Captive Prince	1,200.00

CANTEEN KATE
St. John Publishing Co., 1952
1 MB,Sexy babe	900.00
2 MB	600.00
3 MB	700.00

CAPTAIN AERO COMICS
Holyoke Publishing Co., 1941
1 B:Flag-Man&Solar,Master of Magic Captain Aero, Captain Stone	4,000.00
2 A:Pals of Freedom	1,600.00

Captain Aero Comics #1
© Holyoke Publishing Co.

---

3 JKu,B:Alias X,A:Pals of Freedom	1,600.00
4 JKu,O:Gargoyle, Parachute jump	1,600.00
5 JKu	1,500.00
6 JKu,Flagman,A:Miss Victory	1,400.00
7 Alias X	900.00
8 O:Red Cross,A:Miss Victory	900.00
9 A:Miss Victory,Alias X	800.00
10 A:Miss Victory,Red Cross	750.00
11 A:Miss Victory	750.00
12 A:Miss Victory	750.00
13 A:Miss Victory	750.00
14 A:Miss Victory	750.00
15 AS(c),A:Miss Liberty	750.00
16 AS(c),Leather Face	500.00
17 LbC(c)	900.00
21 LbC(c)	900.00
22 LbC(c),I:Mighty Mite	900.00
23 LbC(c)	900.00
24 LbC(c) American Planes Dive Bomb Japan	1,200.00
25 LbC(c),Science Fiction(c)	700.00
26 LbC(c)	1,500.00

CAPTAIN ATOM
Nationwide Publishers, 1951
Mini-size
1 Scientific adventure	550.00
2 thru 7	@250.00

CAPTAIN BATTLE
New Friday Publ./
Magazine Press, Summer, 1941
1 B:Captain Battle,O:Blackout	3,000.00
2 Pirate Ship (c)	1,700.00
3 Dungeon (c)	1,500.00
4 *.may not exist*	
5 V:Japanese, Summer, 1943	900.00

CAPTAIN BATTLE, Jr.
Comic House, Fall, 1943
1 Claw V:Ghost, A:Sniffer	2,500.00
2 Man who didn't believe in Ghosts	2,000.00

CAPTAIN COURAGEOUS
See: BANNER COMICS

CAPTAIN EASY
Standard Comics, 1939
N# Swash Buckler	2,100.00
10	500.00
11	300.00
12	300.00
13 ASh(c)	300.00
14	300.00
15	300.00
16 ASh(c)	300.00
17 Sept., 1949	300.00

CAPTAIN FEARLESS
COMICS
Helnit Publishing Co., 1941
1 O:Mr. Miracle,Alias X,Captain Fearless Citizen Smith, A:Miss Victory	2,000.00
2 A:Border Patrol, Sept.,1941	1,500.00

CAPTAIN FLASH
Sterling Comics, Nov., 1954
1 O:Captain Flash	550.00
2 V:Black Knight	300.00
3 Beasts from 1,000,000 BC	300.00
4 Flying Saucer Invasion	300.00

CAPTAIN FLEET
Approved Comics, Fall, 1952
1 Storm and Mutiny ...Typhoon	250.00

CAPTAIN FLIGHT
COMICS
Four Star Publications,
March, 1944–Feb.-March, 1947
N# B:Captain Flight,Ace Reynolds, Dash the Avenger, ProfessorX	1,000.00
2	500.00
3	500.00
4 B:Rock Raymond Salutes America's Wartime Heroines	500.00
5 Bondage (c),B:Red Rocket A:The Grenade	2,000.00
6 Girl tied at the stake	500.00
7 LbC(c),Dog Fight (c)	900.00
8 LbC(c),B:Yankee Girl, A:Torpedoman	900.00
9 LbC(c),Dog Fight (c)	900.00
10 LbC(c),Bondage (c)	900.00
11 LbC(c),Future(c)	2,000.00

CAPTAIN GALLANT
Charlton Comics, 1955
1 Ph(c),Buster Crabbe	200.00
2	150.00
3	150.00
4 Sept., 1956	150.00

CAPTAIN JET
Four Star Publ., May, 1952
1 Factory bombing (c)	300.00
2 Parachute jump (c)	200.00
3 Tank bombing (c)	175.00
4 Parachute (c)	175.00
5	175.00

CAPTAIN KIDD
See: DAGAR,
DESERT HAWK

CAPTAIN MARVEL
ADVENTURES
Fawcett Publications, 1941
N# JK, B:Captain Marvel & Sivana	50,000.00
2 GT,JK(c),Billy Batson (c)	7,000.00
3 JK(c),Thunderbolt (c)	4,500.00
4 Shazam(c)	3,000.00
5 V:Nazis	2,500.00
6 Solomon, Hercules, Atlas, Zeus, Achilles & Mercury (c)	2,000.00
7 Ghost of the White Room	2,000.00
8 Forward America	2,000.00
9 A:Ibac the Monster, Nippo the Nipponese, Relm of the Subconscious	2,000.00
10 V:Japanese	2,000.00
11 V:Japanese and Nazis	1,500.00
12 Joins the Army	1,400.00
13 V:Diamond-Eyed Idol of Doom	1,400.00
14 Nippo meets his Nemesis	1,400.00
15 Big "Paste the Axis" contest	1,400.00
16 Uncle Sam (c), Paste the Axis	1,400.00
17 P(c), Paste the Axis	1,200.00
18 P(c), O:Mary Marvel	3,200.00
19 Mary Marvel & Santa (c)	1,500.00
20 Mark of the Black Swastika	5,500.00
21 Hitler (c)	1,700.00
22 B:Mr. Mind serial, Shipyard Sabotage	1,200.00
23 A:Steamboat	1,100.00

    All comics prices listed are for *Near Mint* condition.

Captain Marvel Adventures #17
© Fawcett Publications

24 Minneapolis Mystery	1,100.00
25 Sinister Faces (c)	1,100.00
26 Flag (c)	1,100.00
27 Joins Navy	900.00
28 Uncle Sam (c)	900.00
29 Battle at the China Wall	900.00
30 Modern Robinson Crusoe	900.00
31 Fights his own Conscience	900.00
32 V:Mole Men, Dallas	900.00
33 Mt. Rushmore parody (c), Omaha	800.00
34 Oklahoma City	800.00
35 O:Radar the International Policeman, Indianapolis	700.00
36 Missing face contest, St. Louis	700.00
37 V:Block Busting Bubbles, Cincinnati	700.00
38 V:Chattanooga Ghost, Rock Garden City	700.00
39 V:Mr. Mind's Death Ray, Pittsburgh	700.00
40 V:Ghost of the Tower,Boston	700.00
41 Runs for President, Dayton	600.00
42 Christmas special, St. Paul	600.00
43 V:Mr. Mind,I:Uncle Marvel, Chicago	600.00
44 OtherWorlds,Washington,D.C.	600.00
45 V:Blood Bank Robbers	600.00
46 E: Mr. Mind Serial, Tall Stories of Jonah Joggins	600.00
47 CCB,Shazam(c)	550.00
48 Signs Autographs (c)	550.00
49 V: An Unknown Killer	550.00
50 Twisted Powers	550.00
51 Last of the Batsons	500.00
52 O&I:Sivana Jr.,V:Giant Earth Dreamer	500.00
53 Gets promoted	500.00
54 Marooned in the Future, Kansas City	500.00
55 Endless String, Columbus	500.00
56 Goes Crazy, Mobile	500.00
57 A:Haunted Girl, Rochester	500.00
58 V:Sivana	500.00
59 CCB(c),PrC	500.00
60 Man who made Earthquakes	500.00
61 I&V: Oggar, the Worlds Mightiest Immortal	500.00
62 The Great Harness Race	500.00
63 Stuntman	500.00
64 CCB(c&a),I:Lester the Imp	500.00
65 V:Invaders from Outer Space	500.00
66 Atomic War (c)	500.00
67 Hartford	400.00

68 Scenes from the Past, Baltimore	400.00
69 Gets Knighted	400.00
70 Horror in the Box	400.00
71 Wheel of Death	400.00
72 CCB,Empire State Bldg.Ph(c)	400.00
73 Becomes a Petrophile	400.00
74 Who is the 13th Guest	400.00
75 V:Astonishing Yeast Menace	400.00
76 A:Atom Ambassador	400.00
77 The Secret Life	400.00
78 O:Mr. Tawny	450.00
79 O:Atom,A:World's Worst Actor	400.00
80 Twice told story	900.00
81 A:Mr. Atom	800.00
82 A:Mr. Tawny	400.00
83 Indian Chief	400.00
84 V:Surrealist Imp	400.00
85 Freedom Train	400.00
86 A:Mr. Tawny	400.00
87 V:Electron Thief	400.00
88 Billy Batson's Boyhood	400.00
89 V:Sivana	400.00
90 A:Mr. Tawny	400.00
91 A:Chameleon Stone	400.00
92 The Land of Limbo	400.00
93 Book of all Knowledge	400.00
94 Battle of Electricity	400.00
95 The Great Ice Cap	400.00
96 V:Automatic Weapon	400.00
97 Wiped Out	400.00
98 United Worlds	400.00
99 Rain of Terror	400.00
100 V:Sivana,Plot against the Universe	750.00
101 Invisibility Trap	350.00
102 Magic Mix-up	350.00
103 Ice Covered World of 1,000,000 AD	350.00
104 Mr. Tawny's Masquerade	350.00
105 The Dog Catcher	350.00
106 V:Menace of the Moon	350.00
107 V:Space Hunter	350.00
108 V:Terrible Termites	350.00
109 The Invention Inventor	350.00
110 CCB(c),V:Sivana	350.00
111 The Eighth Sea,V:Vikings	350.00
112 Worrybird	350.00
113 Feud with Mr. Tawny	350.00
114 V:The Ogre	350.00
115 Mr. Tawny	350.00
116 Flying Saucer	400.00
117 Mr. Tawny bondage (c)	350.00
118 V:Weird Water Man	350.00
119 Invisibility	350.00
120 Voice heard round the world	350.00
121 Origin retold	350.00
122 Atomic Fire	350.00
123 Dinosaur Dilemma	350.00
124 V:Discarded Instincts	350.00
125 V:Ancient Villain	350.00
126 The Creeping Horror	350.00
127 Sivana's Voodoo Spell	350.00
128	350.00
129 Robot Hunt	350.00
130 Double Doom	350.00
131 Station Whiz gets Atomic Powers	350.00
132 V:Flood	350.00
133 The Pressure Peril	350.00
134 Sivana's Capsule Kingdom	350.00
135 Perplexing Past Puzzle	325.00
136 Witch of Haven Street	325.00
137 Seven Deadly Sins	325.00
138 V:Haunted Horror	400.00
139 V:Red Crusher	325.00
140 Hand of Horror	325.00
141 Man Without a World	325.00
142 The Beauty in Black	325.00
143 Great Stone Face on Moon	325.00
144 Stolen Shazam Powers	325.00

145 The Machines of Murder	325.00
146 The Unholy Spider	325.00
147 Thief From the Past	325.00
148 V:The World	325.00
149 Mr. Tawny Hermit	325.00
150 Captain Marvel's Wedding, Nov., 1953	650.00

CAPTAIN MARVEL JR.
Fawcett Publications, 1942

1 MRa(c),O:Captain Marvel, Jr., A:Capt. Nazi	9,000.00
2 MRa(c),O:Capt.Nippon, V:Capt. Nazi	3,000.00
3 MRa(c),Parade to Excitement	2,000.00
4 MRa(c),V:Invisible Nazi	1,600.00
5 MRa(c),V:Capt. Nazi	1,500.00
6 MRa(c),Adventure of Sabbac	1,300.00
7 MRa(c),City under the Sea	1,300.00
8 MRa(c),Dangerous Double	1,300.00
9 MRa(c),Independence (c)	1,400.00
10 Hitler (c)	1,500.00
11 MRa(c)	1,100.00
12 MRa(c),Scuttles the Axis Isle in the Sky	1,200.00
13 MRa(c),V:The Axis,Hitler,(c)	1,500.00
14 MRa(c),X-Mas (c), Santa wears Capt. Marvel uniform	1,000.00
15 MRa(c),V:Capt. Nazi	1,100.00
16 MRa(c),A:Capt. Marvel, Sivana, Pogo	1,000.00
17 MRa(c),Meets his future self	1,000.00
18 MRa(c),V:Birds of Doom	1,000.00
19 MRa(c),A:Capt. Nazi & Capt. Nippon	1,000.00
20 MRa(c),Goes on the Warpath	900.00
21 MRa(c),Buy War Stamps	700.00
22 MRa(c),Rides World's oldest steamboat	700.00
23 MRa(c)	700.00
24 MRa(c),V:Weather Man	700.00
25 MRa(c),Flag (c)	700.00
26 MRa(c),Happy New Year	700.00
27 MRa(c),Jungle Thrills	700.00
28 MRa(c),V:Sivana's Crumbling Crimes	700.00
29 MRa(c),Blazes a Wilderness Trail	700.00
30 MRa(c)	700.00
31 MRa(c)	500.00
32 Keeper of the Lonely Rock	500.00
33	500.00
34/35 I&O:Sivana Jr.	500.00
36 Underworld Tournament	500.00

Captain Marvel Jr. #17
© Fawcett Publications

All comics prices listed are for *Near Mint* condition.

37 FreddyFreeman'sNews-stand . 500.00
38 A:Arabian Knight 500.00
39 V:Sivana Jr., Headline Stealer 500.00
40 Faces Grave Situation 500.00
41 I:The Acrobat 400.00
42 V:Sivana Jr. 400.00
43 BTh(c),V:Beasts on Broadway 400.00
44 Key to the Mystery 400.00
45 A:Icy Fingers 400.00
46 BTh(c&a) 400.00
47 BTh(c),V:Giant o/t Beanstalk . 400.00
48 Whale of a Fish Story 400.00
49 BTh(c),V:Dream Recorder . . . 400.00
50 Wanted: Freddy Freeman . . . 400.00
51 The Island Riddle 350.00
52 A:Flying Postman 350.00
53 Atomic Bomb on the Loose. . . 400.00
54 V:Man with 100 Heads 350.00
55 Pyramid of Eternity 350.00
56 Blue Boy's Black Eye 350.00
57 MRa(c),Magic Ladder 350.00
58 BTh(c),Amazing Mirror Maze . 350.00
59 MRa(c) 350.00
60 V:Space Menace 350.00
61 V:Himself 300.00
62 V:Mr. Hydro 300.00
63 V:Witch of Winter 300.00
64 thru 74 . . . . @300.00
75 V:Outlaw of Crooked Creek . . 300.00
76 thru 85 . . . . @300.00
86 Defenders of time 300.00
87 thru 89 . . . . @300.00
90 The Magic Trunk 300.00
91 thru 99 . . . . @300.00
100 V:Sivana Jr 300.00
101 thru 106 . . . . @300.00
107 The Horror Dimension 400.00
108 thru 118 . . . . @250.00
119 Condemned to Die, Electric
　　Chair, June, 1953 . . . . 250.00

CAPTAIN MIDNIGHT
Fawcett Publications, 1942
1 O:Captain Midnight,
　Capt. Marvel (c) 6,000.00
2 Smashes Jap Juggernaut . . . 2,700.00
3 Battles Phantom Bomber . . . 2,400.00
4 Grapples the Gremlins 2,000.00
5 Double Trouble in Tokyo . . . 2,000.00
6 Blasts the Black Mikado . . . 1,500.00
7 Newspaper headline (c) 1,500.00
8 Flying Torpedoes
　Berlin-Bound 1,500.00
9 MRa(c), Subs in Mississippi 1,500.00
10 MRa(c), Flag (c) 1,500.00
11 MRa(c), Murder in Mexico . . 1,500.00
12 V:Sinister Angels 1,500.00
13 Non-stop around the World . 1,500.00
14 V:King of the Villains 1,500.00
15 V:Kimberley Killer 1,500.00
16 Hitler's Fortress Breached . . 1,500.00
17 MRa(c), Hello Adolf 1,500.00
18 Death from the Skies 1,500.00
19 Hour of Doom for the Axis . 1,500.00
20 Brain & Brawn against Axis 1,500.00
21 Trades with Japanese 1,000.00
22 Plea for War Stamps 1,000.00
23 Japanese Prison (c) 1,000.00
24 Rising Sun Flag (c) 1,000.00
25 Amusement Park Murder . . . 1,000.00
26 Hotel of Horror 1,000.00
27 Death Knell for Tyranny 1,000.00
28 Gliderchuting to Glory 1,000.00
29 Bomb over Nippon 1,000.00
30 . . . . 1,000.00
31 and 32 . . . . @600.00
33 V:Shark 600.00
34 thru 40 . . . . @600.00
41 thru 63 . . . . @500.00
64 V:XOG, Ruler of Saturn 500.00
65 . . . . 500.00
66 V:XOG 500.00

Captain Midnight #54
© Fawcett Publications

67 Fall, 1948 . . . . 500.00
Becomes:

SWEETHEARTS
Oct., 1948
68 Robert Mitchum 250.00
69 thru 110 . . . . @125.00
111 Ronald Reagan story 175.00
112 thru 118 . . . . @125.00
119 WW,Marilyn Monroe 600.00
120 Atomic Bomb story . . . . . @150.00
121 Liz Taylor 200.00
122 Marjuana,1954 . . . . 150.00

CAPTAIN ROCKET
P.L. Publications, 1951
1 Sci-Fi 550.00

CAPTAIN SCIENCE
Youthful Magazines, 1950
1 WW,O:Captain Science,
　V:Monster God of Rogor . . 1,300.00
2 WW,V:Cat Men of Phoebus,
　Space Pirates 600.00
3 Ghosts from the Underworld . 600.00
4 WW,Vampires 1,200.00
5 WW,V:Shark Pirates of
　Pisces 1,200.00
6 WW,V:Invisible Tyrants,
　bondage (c) 700.00
7 WW,Bondage(c) Dec., 1951 . . 700.00
Becomes:

FANTASTIC
Feb., 1952
8 Isle of Madness 500.00
9 Octopus (c) 400.00
Becomes:

BEWARE
June, 1952
10 SHn,Doll of Death 700.00
11 SHn,Horror Head 500.00
12 SHn,Body Snatchers 500.00
Becomes:

CHILLING TALES
Dec., 1952
13 MF,Screaming Skull 900.00
14 SHn,Smell of Death 600.00
15 SHn,Curse of the Tomb 700.00
16 HcK,Mark of the Beast
　Bondage(c) 600.00
17 MFc(c),Wandering Willie,
　Oct.,1953 . . . . 700.00

CAPTAIN STEVE SAVAGE
Avon Periodicals
[1st Series] 1950
N# WW 500.00
2 EK(c),The Death Gamble 300.00
3 EK(c),Crash Landing in
　Manchuria 250.00
4 EK(c),V:Red Raiders from
　Siang-Po 150.00
5 EK(c),Rockets of Death 150.00
6 Operation Destruction 150.00
7 EK(c),Flight to Kill 150.00
8 EK(c),V:Red Mystery Jet 150.00
9 EK(c) 150.00
10 . . . . 150.00
11 EK(c) 150.00
12 WW 225.00
13 . . . . 150.00

[2nd Series] Sept./Oct., 1954
5 . . . . 150.00
6 WW 200.00
7 thru 13 . . . . @150.00

CAPTAIN TOOTSIE
& THE SECRET LEGION
Toby Press, 1950
1 Sci-Fi 400.00
2 . . . . 250.00

CAPTAIN VIDEO
Fawcett Publications, 1951
1 GE,Ph(c) From TV series . . . 1,700.00
2 Time When Men Could Not
　Walk 1,100.00
3 GE,Indestructible Antagonist 1,000.00
4 GE,School of Spies 1,000.00
5 GE,Missiles of Doom,
　photo (c) 1,000.00
6 GE,Island of Conquerors,
　Photo (c); Dec., 1951 . . . . . 1,000.00

CAPTAIN WIZARD
Rural Home, 1946
1 Impossible Man 500.00

CARNIVAL
See: SCOOP COMICS

CASPER, THE
FRIENDLY GHOST
St. John Publishing, 1949
1 O:Baby Huey 3,000.00
2 . . . . 1,500.00
3 . . . . 1,400.00
4 . . . . 1,000.00
5 . . . . 1,000.00

Harvey Publications, 1952
7 Baby Huey 800.00
8 thru 9 Baby Huey . . . . @500.00
10 I:Spooky 550.00
11 A:Spooky 300.00
12 thru 18 . . . . @300.00
19 I:Nightmare 400.00
20 I:Wendy the Witch 2,000.00
21 thru 30 . . . . @250.00
31 thru 40 . . . . @200.00
41 thru 50 . . . . @150.00
51 thru 60 . . . . @150.00
61 thru 69 . . . . @150.00
70 July, 1958 . . . . 150.00

CATHOLIC COMICS
Catholic Publications, 1946–49
1 Sports 550.00
2 Sports 350.00
3 Sports 300.00
4 thru 10 . . . . @300.00

11 thru 20 . . . . @250.00
21 thru 34 . . . . @275.00

CATMAN COMICS
Helnit Publ. Co./ Holyoke Publ. Co./ Continental Magazine, 1941
1 O:Deacon&Sidekick Mickey,
  Dr. Diamond & Ragman,A:Black
  Widow, B:Blaze Baylor 7,500.00
2 Ragman 3,000.00
3 B:Pied Piper 2,500.00
4 CQ 2,400.00
5 I&O: The Kitten 1,500.00
6 CQ 1,500.00
7 CQ 1,500.00
8 JKa, I:Volton 1,800.00
9 JKa 1,200.00
10 JKa,O:Blackout,
   B:Phantom Falcon 1,200.00
11 JKa,DRi,BF,PzF 1,200.00
12 Volton 1,000.00
13 . . . . 1,500.00
14 CQ 1,000.00
15 Rajah of Destruction 1,000.00
16 Bye-Bye Axis, Hitler 1,500.00
17 Buy Bonds and Stamps 1,000.00
18 Buy Bonds and Stamps 1,000.00
19 CQ,Hitler,Tojo &Mussolini(c) 1,500.00
20 CQ,Hitler,Tojo &Mussolini(c) 1,500.00
21 CQ 1,000.00
22 CQ 1,000.00
23 CQ 1,000.00
N# DRiV:Japanese,Bondage(c) 1,000.00
N# V:Demon 1,000.00
N# LbC(c),A:Leather Face 1,000.00
27 LbC(c),Flag (c),O:Kitten . . 1,500.00
28 LbC(c),Horror (c) 1,500.00
29 LbC(c),BF,RP 1,500.00
30 LbC(c),BF,Bondage(c) 1,500.00
31 LbC(c) 1,500.00
32 LbC(c),RP,Aug., 1946 . . . . . 1,500.00

CAVALIER COMICS
Sture Ashberg Publ. 1945
1 Historic adventure 250.00

CENTURY OF COMICS
Eastern Color Printing Co., 1933
N# 60,000.00

CHALLENGER, THE
Interfaith Publications, 1945
N# O:The Challenger Club . . 750.00
2 and 3 JKa . . . . @600.00
4 JKa,BF 600.00

CHAMBER OF CHILLS
Harvey Publications/ Witches Tales, June, 1951
21 (1) AAv 900.00
22 (2) AAv 600.00
23 (3) Eyes Ripped Out 600.00
24 (4) LEI,Bondage (c) 700.00
5 LEI,Shrunken Skull,
  Operation Monster 700.00
6 LEI,Seven Skulls of Magondi . 600.00
7 LEI,Pit of the Damned 600.00
8 LEI,Formula for Death 600.00
9 LEI,Bondage (c) 500.00
10 LEI,AAv,Cave of Death 500.00
11 AAv,Curse of Morgan Kilgane . 400.00
12 AAv,Swamp Monster 400.00
13 AAv,The Lost Race 550.00
14 LEI,Down to Death 500.00
15 LEI,AAv,Nightmare of Doom . . 550.00
16 LEI,Cycle of Horror 550.00
17 LEI,Amnesia 550.00
18 LEI,Hair Cut-Atom Bomb 600.00

19 LEI,Happy Anniversary 500.00
20 Shock is Struck 500.00
21 LEI,BP,RP,Decapitation 600.00
22 LEI,Is Death the End? 550.00
23 LEI,BP,RP,Heartline 550.00
24 LEI,BP,Bondage(c) 600.00
25 LEI, ... 400.00
26 LEI,HN,AAv,Captains Return . 400.00
Becomes:

CHAMBER OF CLUES
Feb., 1955
27 BP,A:Kerry Drake 250.00
28 A:Kerry Drake 150.00

CHAMPION COMICS
Worth Publishing Co., 1939
2 B:Champ, Blazing Scarab, Neptina,
  Liberty Lads, Jingleman . . . 3,500.00
3 . . . . 2,000.00
4 Bailout(c). 2,000.00
5 Jungleman(c) 2,000.00
6 MNe 2,000.00
7 MNe,Human Meteor 2,000.00
8 JK 3,000.00
9 JK,S&K 3,000.00
10 JK,Bondage (c) 3,000.00
Becomes:

CHAMP COMICS
Oct. 1940
11 Human Meteor 2,500.00
12 Human Heteor 2,200.00
13 Dragon's Teeth 2,000.00
14 Liberty Lads 2,000.00
15 RC,Liberty Lads 2,000.00
16 Liberty Lads 2,000.00
17 Liberty Lads 2,000.00
18 Liberty Lads 2,400.00
19 JSm,A:The Wasp 2,500.00
20 S&K,A:The Green Ghost . . . 2,000.00
21 S&K 1,500.00
22 A:White Mask. 1,500.00
23 Flag (c). 1,800.00
24 Hitler,Tojo & Mussolini 1,600.00
25 thru 29 . . . . @1,500.00

CHARLIE CHAN
Crestwood, 1948–55
1 S&K(c),Cl,Detective 1,500.00
2 S&K. 1,000.00
3 S&K. 1,000.00
4 S&K. 1,000.00
5 S&K. 1,000.00
Charlton Comics, 1955
6 S&K 750.00
7 . . . . 500.00
8 . . . . 500.00
9 . . . . 500.00
Becomes:

ZAZA THE MYSTIC
Charlton Comics, 1956
10 Psychic revelations 300.00
11 . . . . 300.00
Becomes:

THIS MAGAZINE IS HAUNTED
Charlton Comics, 1957
12 . . . . 450.00
13 . . . . 650.00
14 The Green Man 400.00
15 . . . . 350.00
16 . . . . 700.00
Becomes:

OUTER SPACE
Charlton Comics, 1958
17 AS,WW,Sci-Fi 300.00
18 SD 450.00

Outer Space #23
© Charlton Comics

19 SD 450.00
20 SD 450.00
21 SD 450.00
22 . . . . 300.00
23 . . . . 300.00
24 SD Machine Men of Mars 300.00
25 . . . . 300.00

CHARLIE McCARTHY
Dell Publishing Co., 1947
1 Ph(c) 300.00
2 . . . . 200.00
3 thru 9 . . . . @200.00

CHEYENNE
Dell Publishing Co., 1956
1 Ph(c) all 375.00
2 . . . . 250.00
3 . . . . 200.00
4 thru 12 . . . . @150.00
13 thru 25 . . . . @125.00

CHIEF, THE
Dell Publishing Co., 1950
(1) *see Dell Four Color #290*
2 . . . . 150.00

CHILLING TALES
See: CAPTAIN SCIENCE

CHOICE COMICS
Great Comics, 1941
1 O:Secret Circle 3,000.00
2 . . . . 1,500.00
3 The Lost City 2,000.00

CHRISTMAS CARNIVAL
Approved Comics (Ziff-Davis)/ St. John Publ., 1955
N# Santa 500.00
2 . . . . 300.00

CHUCKLE THE GIGGLY BOOK OF COMIC ANIMALS
R. B. Leffing Well Co., 1944
1 . . . . 300.00

All comics prices listed are for *Near Mint* condition.

CINEMA COMICS HERALD
Paramount/Universal/RKO/ 20th Century Fox Giveaways, 1941-43
N# Mr. Bug Goes to Town 300.00
N# Bedtime Story 200.00
N# Lady for a Night,J.Wayne . . . 350.00
N# Reap the Wild Wind 200.00
N# Thunderbirds 150.00
N# They All Kissed Me 150.00
N# Bombardier 200.00
N# Crash Dive 200.00
N# Arabian Nights 150.00

CIRCUS COMICS
Farm Women's Publ., 1945
1 Clown, Funny Animal 300.00
2 . . . . 200.00

CIRCUS COMICS
D.S. Publications, 1948
1 FF 500.00

CIRCUS OF FUN COMICS
A.W. Nugent Publ. Co., 1946
1 Funny animal 250.00
2 . . . . 150.00
3 . . . . 150.00

CIRCUS THE COMIC RIOT
Globe Syndicate, June, 1938
1 BKa,WE,BW 10,000.00
2 BKa,WE,BW 6,000.00
3 BKa,WE,BW, Aug., 1938 . . . 5,000.00

Cisco Kid Comics #1
© Bernard Bailey

CISCO KID COMICS
Bernard Bailey/ Swappers Quarterly, 1944
1 . . . . 700.00

CISCO KID, THE
Dell Publishing Co., 1951
(1) *See Dell Four Color #292*
2 Jan., 1951 . . . . 550.00
3 thru 5 . . . . @350.00
6 thru 10 . . . . @300.00
11 thru 20 . . . . @250.00
21 thru 36 . . . . @200.00

---

37 thru 41 Ph(c)'s . . . . @375.00

CLAIRE VOYANT
Leader Publ./Visual Ed./ Pentagon Publ., 1946-47
N# 1,100.00
2 JKa(c) 800.00
3 Case of the Kidnapped
　Bride 1,000.00
4 Bondage (c) 800.00

CLAY CODY, GUNSLINGER
Better Publications, 1957
1 Western hero 100.00

CLEAN FUN, STARRING 'SHOOGAFOOTS JONES'
Specialty Book Co., 1945
N# 200.00

CLIMAX!
Gilmor Magazines, 1955
1 Mystery 200.00
2 . . . . 150.00

CLOAK AND DAGGER
Approved Comics (Ziff-Davis), Fall, 1952
1 NS(c),Al Kennedy of the Secret
　Service 400.00

CLOWN COMICS
Harvey Publications, 1945
N# 300.00
2 . . . . 200.00
3 . . . . 200.00

CLUE COMICS
Hillman Periodicals, 1943
1 O:Boy King,Nightmare,Micro-Face,
　Twilight,Zippo 3,000.00
2 . . . . 2,000.00
3 Boy King V:The Crane 1,500.00
4 V:The Crane 1,200.00
5 V:The Crane 1,200.00
6 Hells Kitchen 750.00
7 V:Dr. Plasma,Torture(c) 750.00
8 RP,A:The Gold Mummy King . 700.00
9 I:Paris 700.00
10 O:Gun Master 700.00
11 A:Gun Master 700.00
12 O:Rackman 700.00
2-1 S&K,O:Nightro,A:Iron Lady. 1,300.00
2-2 S&K,Bondage(c) 1,800.00
2-3 S&K 1,300.00
Becomes:

REAL CLUE CRIME STORIES
June, 1947
2-4 DBw,S&K,True Story of
　Ma Barker 1,300.00
2-5 S&K, Newface surgery(c) . . 1,000.00
2-6 S&K, Breakout (c) 1,000.00
2-7 S&K, Stick up (c) 1,000.00
2-8 Kidnapping (c) 250.00
2-9 DBa,Boxing fix (c) 250.00
2-10 DBa,Murder (c) 250.00
2-11 Attempted bankrobbery (c) . 250.00
2-12 Murder (c) 250.00
3-1 thru 3-12 . . . . @250.00
4-1 thru 4-12 . . . . @250.00
5-1 thru 5-12 . . . . @200.00
6-1 thru 6-12 . . . . @200.00
6-10 Bondage(c) 250.00
7-1 thru 7-12 . . . . @175.00
8-1 thru 8-5, May, 1953 . . . . . @175.00

Real Clue Crime Stories Vol. 2 #5
© Hillman Periodicals

THE CLUTCHING HAND
American Comics, 1954
1 Horror 500.00

CLYDE BEATTY
Commodore Productions, 1953
1 Photo(c) 400.00

C-M-O COMICS
Comic Corp. of America (Centaur), May, 1942
1 Invisible Terror 2,500.00
2 Super Ann 2,000.00

COCOMALT BIG BOOK OF COMICS
Harry A. Chesler, 1938
1 BoW,PGv,FGu,JCo,(Give away)
　Little Nemo 4,000.00

CODY OF THE PONY EXPRESS
See: BULLS-EYE

CODY OF THE PONY EXPRESS
Fox Features Syndicate, 1950
1 Western 300.00
2 . . . . 250.00
3 . . . . 250.00

COLOSSAL FEATURES MAGAZINE
Fox Features Syndicate, 1950
1 (33) Cody of the Pony Express 300.00
2 (34) Cody of the Pony Express 300.00
3 Crime 300.00

COLOSSUS COMICS
Sun Publications March, 1940
1 A:Colossus 10,000.00

COLUMBIA COMICS
William H. Wise Co., 1944
1 Joe Palooka,Charlie Chan . . . 450.00

GOLDEN AGE

COMIC BOOKS
Metropolitan Printing Co. 1950
1 Boots & Saddles 125.00
1 Green Lama-The Green Jet . . 500.00
1 My Pal Dizzy 100.00
1 Talullah. 150.00
1 New World 100.00

COMIC COMICS
Fawcett Publications, 1946
1 Captain Kidd 350.00
2 thru 10 BW. . . . . @400.00

COMIC LAND
Fact and Fiction, 1946
1 Sandusky and the Senator . . . 350.00

COMICS, THE
Dell Publishing Co., March, 1937
1 I:Tom Mix & Arizona Kid 3,500.00
2 A:Tom Mix & Tom Beaty 2,500.00
3 A:Alley Oop 2,000.00
4 thru 11 same . . . . @2,000.00

THE COMICS CALENDAR
True Comics Press, 1946
1 . . . . 750.00

COMICS NOVEL
Fawcett Publications, 1947
1 Anarcho Dictator of Death 500.00

COMICS ON PARADE
United Features Syndicate, April, 1938–Feb., 1955
1 B:Tarzan,Captain and the Kids,
    Little Mary, Mixup,Abbie & Slats,
    Broncho Bill,Li'l Abner 6,000.00
2 Circus Parade of all 3,000.00
3 . . . . 2,500.00
4 On Rocket. 2,000.00
5 All at the Store 2,000.00
6 All at Picnic 1,500.00
7 Li'l Abner(c). 1,500.00
8 same. 1,500.00
9 same. 1,500.00
10 same 1,500.00
11 same 1,200.00
12 same 1,200.00
13 same 1,200.00
14 Abbie n' Slats (c) 1,200.00
15 Li'l Abner(c) 1,200.00
16 Abbie n' Slats(c). 1,200.00
17 Tarzan,Abbie n' Slats(c). . . . 1,300.00
18 Li'l Abner(c) 1,200.00
19 same 1,200.00
20 same 1,200.00
21 Li'l Abner(c) 1,000.00
22 Tail Spin Tommy(c). 1,000.00
23 Abbie n' Slats(c). 1,000.00
24 Tail Spin Tommy(c). 1,000.00
25 Li'l Abner(c) 1,000.00
26 Abbie n' Slats(c). 1,000.00
27 Li'l Abner(c) 1,000.00
28 Tail Spin Tommy(c). 1,000.00
29 Abbie n' Slats(c). 1,000.00
30 Li'l Abner(c). 600.00
31 The Captain & the Kids(c) . . . 400.00
32 Nancy and Fritzi Ritz(c) 350.00
33 Li'l Abner(c). 450.00
34 The Captain & the Kids(c) . . . 350.00
35 Nancy and Fritzi Ritz(c) 350.00
36 Li'l Abner(c). 450.00
37 The Captain & the Kids(c) . . . 350.00
38 Nancy and Fritzi Ritz(c) 300.00
39 Li'l Abner(c). 450.00
40 The Captain & the Kids(c) . . . 350.00

COMICS on PARADE №47

Comics on Parade #47
© *United Features Syndicate*

41 Nancy and Fritzi Ritz(c) 250.00
42 Li'l Abner(c). 450.00
43 The Captain & the Kids(c) . . . 350.00
44 Nancy and Fritzi Ritz(c) 250.00
45 Li'l Abner(c). 350.00
46 The Captain & the Kids(c) . . . 250.00
47 Nancy and Fritzi Ritz(c) 250.00
48 Li'l Abner(c). 350.00
49 The Captain & the Kids(c) . . . 250.00
50 Nancy and Fritzi Ritz(c) 250.00
51 Li'l Abner(c). 350.00
52 The Captain & the Kids(c) . . . 250.00
53 Nancy and Fritzi Ritz(c) 250.00
54 Li'l Abner(c). 350.00
55 Nancy and Fritzi Ritz(c) 250.00
56 The Captain & the Kids(c) . . . 250.00
57 Nancy and Fritzi Ritz(c) 250.00
58 Li'l Abner(c). 350.00
59 The Captain & the Kids(c) . . . 250.00
60 thru 76 Nancy &
    Fritzi Ritz(c) . . . . @200.00
77 Nancy & Sluggo(c) 150.00
78 thru 104 Nancy & Sluggo(c) @150.00

COMICS REVUE
St. John Publ. Co., 1947
1 Ella Cinders and Blackie 250.00
2 Hap Hopper 200.00
3 Iron Vic. 200.00
4 Eva Cinders 200.00
5 Gordo 200.00

COMMANDER BATTLE AND THE ATOMIC SUBMARINE
American Comics Group, 1954
1 3-D(c) 1,300.00
2 . . . . 750.00
3 H-Bomb-3-D type. 800.00
4 . . . . 750.00
5 thru 7 . . . . @750.00

COMPLETE BOOK OF COMICS AND FUNNIES
William H. Wise & Co., 1945
1 Wonderman-Magnet 700.00

COMPLETE BOOK OF TRUE CRIME COMICS
William H. Wise & Co., 1945
1 rep. Crime Does Not Pay . . . 2,000.00

CONFESSIONS ILLUSTRATED
E.C. Comics, 1956
1WW,JO,JCr,JKa,Adult romance 350.00
2 JCr,RC,JKa,JO 300.00

CONQUEROR COMICS
Albrecht Publications, Winter, 1945
1 . . . . 250.00

CONQUEST
Famous Funnies, 1955
1 Historical adventure 100.00

CONTACT COMICS
Aviation Press, July, 1944
N# LbC(c),B:Black Venus,
    Golden Eagle. 900.00
2 LbC(c),Peace Jet. 700.00
3 LbC(c),LbC,E:Flamingo 650.00
4 LbC(c),LbC 600.00
5 LbC(c),A.Phantom Flyer 650.00
6 LbC(c),HK 750.00
7 LbC(c),Flying Tigers. 600.00
8 LbC(c),Peace Jet. 600.00
9 LbC(c),LbC,A:Marine Flyers . . 600.00
10 LbC(c),A:Bombers of the AAF 600.00
11 LbC(c),HK,AF,Salutes Naval
    Aviation 700.00
12 LbC(c),A:Sky Rangers, Air Kids,
    May, 1946. . . . . 1,300.00

COO COO COMICS
Nedor/Animated Cartoons (Standard), Oct., 1942
1 O&I:Super Mouse 500.00
2 . . . . 250.00
3 . . . . 200.00
4 . . . . 225.00
5 . . . . 225.00
6 thru 10 . . . . @150.00
11 thru 33 . . . . @150.00
34 thru 40 FF illustration . . . . . @250.00
41 FF 400.00
42 FF 350.00
43 FF illustration 250.00
44 FF illustration 250.00
45 FF illustration 250.00
46 FF illustration 250.00
47 FF 350.00
48 FF illustration 250.00
49 FF illustration 250.00
50 FF illustration 250.00
51 thru 61 . . . . @125.00
62 April, 1952. . . . . 100.00

"COOKIE"
Michel Publ./Regis Publ. (American Comics Group) April, 1946
1 . . . . 350.00
2 . . . . 250.00
3 thru 5 . . . . @200.00
6 thru 20 . . . . @150.00
21 thru 30 . . . . @100.00
31 thru 54 . . . . @100.00
55 Aug., 1955. . . . . 100.00

COSMO CAT
Fox Features Syndicate, 1946
1 . . . . 325.00
2 . . . . 200.00
3 O:Cosmo Cat 225.00
4 thru 10 . . . . @150.00

All comics prices listed are for *Near Mint* condition.

GOLDEN AGE

COSMO
THE MERRY MARTIAN
Radio Comics/Archie Publ., 1958
1 Funny alien 250.00
2 thru 6 . . . . @200.00

COURAGE COMICS
J. Edward Slavin, 1945
1 . . . . 250.00
2 Boxing (c). 250.00
77 Naval rescue, PT99 (c) 250.00

COWBOY COMICS
See: STAR RANGER

COWBOYS 'N' INJUNS
Compix (M.E. Enterprises), 1946-47
1 Funny Animal Western 300.00
2 thru 5 . . . . @250.00
6 thru 8 See: *A-1 Comics*, #23,#41,#48

COWBOY WESTERN/
COMICS/HEROES
See: YELLOWJACKET

COW PUNCHER
**Avon Periodicals/
Realistic Publ., Jan., 1947**
1 JKu 600.00
2 JKu, JKa(c),Bondage (c) 450.00
3 AU(c) 350.00
4 . . . . 350.00
5 . . . . 350.00
6 WJo(c),Drug story 400.00
7 . . . . 350.00
1 JKu 350.00

CRACK COMICS
**Comic Magazines
(Quality Comics Group) 1940**
1 LF,O:Black Condor,Madame
  Fatal, Red Torpedo, Rock
  Bradden, Space Legion,
  B:The Clock,Wizard Wells . 9,000.00
2 Black Condor (c) 4,000.00
3 The Clock (c) 3,000.00
4 Black Condor (c) 2,700.00
5 LF,The Clock (c) 2,000.00
6 PG,Black Condor (c) 1,800.00
7 Clock (c) 1,800.00
8 Black Condor (c) 1,800.00
9 Clock (c) 1,800.00
10 Black Condor (c) 1,800.00
11 LF,PG,Clock (c) 1,500.00
12 LF,PG,Black Condor (c) 1,500.00
13 LF,PG,Clock (c) 1,500.00
14 AMc,LF,PG,Clack Condor(c) 1,500.00
15 AMc,LF,PG,Clock (c) 1,500.00
16 AMc,LF,PG,Black Condor(c) 1,500.00
17 FGu,AMc,LF,PG,Clock (c) . . 1,500.00
18 AMc,LF,PG,Black Condor(c) 1,500.00
19 AMc,LF,PG,Clock (c) 1,500.00
20 AMc,LF,PG,BlackCondor(c) 1,500.00
21 AMc,LF,PG,same 1,200.00
22 LF,PG,same 1,200.00
23 AMc,LF,PG,same 1,200.00
24 AMc,LF,PG,same 1,200.00
25 AMc,same 1,000.00
26 AMc,same 1,000.00
27 AMc,I&O:Captain Triumph . . 1,800.00
28 Captain Triumph (c) 1,000.00
29 A:Spade the Ruthless 1,000.00
30 I:Biff 800.00
31 Helps Spade Dig His Own
  Grave. 500.00
32 Newspaper (c) 500.00

33 V:Men of Darkness 500.00
34 . . . . 500.00
35 V:The Man Who Conquered
  Flame. 500.00
36 Good Neighbor Tour 500.00
37 V:The Tyrant of Toar Valley. . 500.00
38 Castle of Shadows 500.00
39 V:Crime over the City 500.00
40 Thrilling Murder Mystery 350.00
41 . . . . 350.00
42 All that Glitters is Not Gold . . 350.00
43 Smashes the Evil Spell of
  Silent 350.00
44 V:Silver Tip 350.00
45 V:King-The Jack of all Trades. 350.00
46 V:Mr. Weary 350.00
47 V:Hypnotic Eyes Khor. 400.00
48 Murder in the Sky 400.00
49 . . . . 400.00
50 A Key to Trouble 400.00
51 V:Werewolf 400.00
52 V:Porcupine 400.00
53 V:Man Who Robbed the Dead 400.00
54 Shoulders the Troubles
  of the World 400.00
55 Brain against Brawn 400.00
56 Gossip leads to Murder 400.00
57 V:Sitok–Green God of Evil . . 400.00
58 V:Targets. 300.00
59 A Cargo of Mystery 300.00
60 Trouble is no Picnic 300.00
61 V:Mr. Pointer-Finger of Fear . . 300.00
62 V:The Vanishing Vandals 300.00
Becomes:

CRACK WESTERN
Nov., 1949–May, 1951
63 PG, I&O:Two-Gun Lil, B:Frontier
  Marshal,Arizona Ames. 350.00
64 RC,Arizona AmesV:Two-
  Legged Coyote 225.00
65 RC,Ames Tramples on
  Trouble 225.00
66 Arizona Ames Arizona Raines,
  Tim Holt,Ph(c) 150.00
67 RC, Ph(c),Randolph Scott . . 225.00
68 Ph(c) 150.00
69 RC. 150.00
70 O&I:Whip and Diablo 175.00
71 Bob Allen, Marshall,RC(c). . . 200.00
72 RC,Tim Holt,Ph(c). 150.00
73 Tim Holt,Ph(c). 100.00
74 RC(c). 150.00
75 RC(c). 150.00
76 RC(c),Stage Coach to
  Oblivion 150.00
77 RC(c),Comanche Terror 150.00
78 RC(c),Killers of Laurel Ridge . 150.00
79 RC(c),Fires of Revenge 150.00
80 RC(c),Mexican Massacre . . . 150.00
81 RC(c),Secrets of Terror
  Canyon 150.00
82 The Killer with a Thousand
  Faces. 125.00
83 Rattlesnake Pete's Revenge . 125.00
84 PG(c),Revolt at Broke Creek . 125.00

CRACKAJACK FUNNIES
Dell Publishing Co., 1938
1 AMc,A:Dan Dunn,The Nebbs,
  Don Winslow 4,000.00
2 AMc,same. 2,000.00
3 AMc,same. 1,500.00
4 AMc,same. 1,200.00
5 AMc,Naked Women(c) 1,400.00
6 AMc,same. 1,100.00
7 AMc,same. 1,100.00
8 AMc,same. 1,100.00
9 AMc,A:Red Ryder 2,300.00
10 AMc,A:Red Ryder 900.00
11 AMc,A:Red Ryder 800.00
12 AMc,A:Red Ryder 800.00

Crackajack Funnies #7
© Dell Publ. Co.

13 AMc,A:Red Ryder 800.00
14 AMc,A:Red Ryder 800.00
15 AMc,A:Tarzan 900.00
16 AMc 750.00
17 AMc 750.00
18 AMc,A:Stratosphere Jim 750.00
19 AMc 750.00
20 AMc 750.00
21 AMc 750.00
22 AMc 750.00
23 AMc,A:Ellery Queen 750.00
24 AMc 750.00
25 AMc,I:The Owl 1,500.00
26 AMc 1,000.00
27 AMc 1,000.00
28 AMc,A:The Owl 1,000.00
29 AMc,A:Ellery Queen. 1,000.00
30 AMc,A:Tarzan. 1,000.00
31 AMc,A:Tarzan. 1,000.00
32 AMc,O:Owl Girl 1,100.00
33 AMc,A:Tarzan 900.00
34 AMc,same 900.00
35 AMc,same. 900.00
36 AMc,same. 900.00
37 AMc. 900.00
38 AMc 900.00
39 AMc,I:Andy Panada 1,100.00
40 AMc,A:Owl(c) 750.00
41 AMc 750.00
42 AMc. 750.00
43 AMc,Terry & The Pirates,
  A:Owl(c). 700.00

CRASH COMICS
Tem Publishing Co., May, 1940
1 S&K,O:Strongman, B:Blue Streak,
  Perfect Human, Shangra . . 6,000.00
2 S&K 3,500.00
3 S&K 2,500.00
4 S&K,O&I:Catman 6,000.00
5 S&K, Nov., 1940 . . . . 2,500.00

CRIME AND JUSTICE
**Capitol Stories/
Charlton Comics 1951–55**
1 . . . . 400.00
2 . . . . 250.00
3 . . . . 200.00
4 . . . . 200.00
5 . . . . 200.00
6 Negligee. 250.00
7 . . . . 200.00
8 . . . . 200.00
9 . . . . 350.00

Crime and Justice #9
© Capitol Stories

10	175.00
11 thru 14	@250.00
15 Negligee	250.00
16	200.00
17	200.00
18 SD	300.00
19 thru 21	@200.00

Becomes:

BADGE OF JUSTICE
Charlton Comics, 1955
22 (1)	200.00
23 (2)	150.00
24 (3)	150.00
25 (4)	150.00

Revived as:

CRIME AND JUSTICE
Charlton Comics, 1955
23 thru 26	@150.00

CRIME AND PUNISHMENT
Lev Gleason Publications, April, 1948
1 CBi(c),Mr.Crime(c)	450.00
2 CBi(c)	250.00
3 CBi(c),BF	275.00
4 CBi(c),BF	200.00
5 CBi(c)	200.00
6 thru 10 CBi(c)	@125.00
11 thru 15 CBi(c)	@100.00
16 thru 27 CBi(c)	@100.00
28 thru 38	@100.00
39 Drug issue	125.00
40 thru 44	@100.00
45 Drug issue	100.00
46 thru 58	@100.00
59	350.00
60 thru 65	@100.00
66 ATh	450.00
67 Drug Storm	425.00
68 ATh(c)	350.00
69 Drug issue	125.00
74 Aug., 1955	100.00

CRIME CLINIC
Approved Publ. (Ziff-Davis), 1951
1 (10) F:Dr. Tom Rogers	350.00
2 (11)	250.00
3	250.00
4	250.00
5	250.00

CRIME DETECTOR
Timor Publications, 1954
1	300.00
2	250.00
3	225.00
4	225.00
5	250.00

CRIME DETECTIVE COMICS
Hillman Publications, March–April, 1948
1 BF(c),A:Invisible 6	400.00
2 Jewel Robbery (c)	250.00
3 Stolen Cash (c)	200.00
4 Crime Boss Murder (c)	200.00
5 BK,Maestro (c)	200.00
6 AMc,Gorilla (c)	150.00
7 GMc,Wedding (c)	150.00
8	150.00
9 Safe Robbery (c) (a classic)	500.00
10	150.00
11 BP	150.00
12 BK	150.00
2-1 Bluebird Captured	200.00
2-2	150.00
2-3	150.00
2-4 BK	175.00
2-5	150.00
2-6	150.00
2-7 BK,GMc	175.00
2-8	150.00
2-9	150.00
2-10	150.00
2-11	150.00
2-12	150.00
3-1 Drug Story	150.00
3-2 thru 3-7	@150.00
3-8 May/June, 1953	100.00

CRIME DOES NOT PAY
See: SILVER STREAK COMICS

CRIME-FIGHTING DETECTIVE
See: CRIMINALS ON THE RUN

CRIME FILES
Standard Comics, 1952
5 ATh	300.00
6	200.00

CRIME ILLUSTRATED
E.C. Comics, Nov.–Dec., 1955
1 Grl,RC,GE,JO	400.00
2 Grl,RC,JCr,JDa,JO	300.00

CRIME INCORPORATED
Fox Features Syndicate, 1950 (Formerly: WESTERN THRILLERS; MY PAST CONFESSIONS)
1 (12) Crimes Incorporated	300.00
2	225.00
3	225.00

CRIME MUST PAY THE PENALTY
Ace Magazines, 1948–56
1 "True cases of actual crimes"	550.00
2 Violent	350.00
3	300.00
4	300.00
5	200.00
6	200.00
7	200.00
8 Transvestite	300.00

9	200.00
10	200.00
11	200.00
12	200.00
13 thru 19	@200.00
20 Drugs	250.00
21 thru 30	@200.00
31 thru 48	@200.00

CRIME MUST STOP
Hillman Periodicals, Oct., 1952
1 BK	1,000.00

Crime Mysteries #7
© Ribage Publishing Co.

CRIME MYSTERIES
Ribage Publishing Corp., May, 1952
1 Transvestism,Bondage(c)	1,000.00
2 A:Manhunter, Lance Storm, Drug	750.00
3 FF-one page, A:Dr. Foo	500.00
4 A:Queenie Star, BondageStar	750.00
5 Claws of the Green Girl	400.00
6	400.00
7 Sons of Satan	400.00
8 Death Stalks the Crown, Bondage(c)	400.00
9 You are the Murderer	375.00
10 The Hoax of the Death	375.00
11 The Strangler	375.00
12 Bondage(c)	450.00
13 AT,6 lives for one	500.00
14 Painted in Blood	375.00
15 Feast of the Dead,Acid Face	650.00

Becomes:

SECRET MYSTERIES
Nov., 1954
16 Hiding Place,Horror	400.00
17 The Deadly Diamond,Horror	300.00
18 Horror	350.00
19 Horror,July, 1955	350.00

INTERNATIONAL COMICS
E.C. Publ. Co., Spring, 1947
1 KS,I:Manhattan's Files	1,000.00
2 KS,A: Van Manhattan & Madelon	750.00
3 KS,same	600.00
4 KS,same	600.00
5 I:International Crime-Busting Patrol	600.00

Becomes:

INTERNATIONAL CRIME PATROL
Spring, 1948
6 A:Moon Girl & The Prince . . 1,000.00
Becomes:

CRIME PATROL
Summer, 1948
7 SMo,A:Capt. Crime Jr.,Field
   Marshall of Murder 1,200.00
8 JCr,State Prison (c) 1,000.00
9 AF,JCr,Bank Robbery 1,000.00
10 AF,JCr,Wanted:James Dore. 1,000.00
11 AF,JCr. 1,000.00
12 AF,Grl,JCr,Interrogation(c) . . 1,000.00
13 AF,JCr 1,000.00
14 AF,JCr,Smugglers (c). 1,000.00
15 AF,JCr,Crypt of Terror 6,000.00
16 AF,JCr,Crypt of Terror 3,500.00
Becomes:

CRYPT OF TERROR
E.C. Comics, April, 1950
17 JCr(a&c),AF,'Werewolf
   Strikes Again' 5,000.00
18 JCr(a&c),AF,WW,HK
   'The Living Corpse' 3,000.00
19 JCr(a&c),AF,Grl,
   'Voodoo Drums' 2,900.00
Becomes:

TALES FROM THE CRYPT
Oct., 1950
20 JCr(a&c),AF,Gl,JKa
   'Day of Death' 3,200.00
21 AF(a&c),WW,HK,Gl,'Cooper
   Dies in the Electric Chair . . 3,000.00
22 AF, JCr(c). 2,200.00
23 AF(a&c),JCr,JDa,Grl
   'Locked in a Mausoleum' . . 1,500.00
24 AF(c),WW,JDa,JCr,Grl
   'Danger...Quicksand' 1,500.00
25 AF(c),WW,JDa,JKa,Grl
   'Mataud Waxworks' 1,500.00
26 WW(c),JDa,Grl,
   'Scared Graveyard' 1,200.00
27 JKa, WW(c), Guillotine (c) . . 1,200.00
28 AF(c),JDa,JKa,Grl,JO
   'Buried Alive' 1,200.00
29 JDa(a&c),JKa,Grl,JO
   'Coffin Burier' 1,200.00
30 JDa(a&c),JO,JKa,Grl
   'Underwater Death' 1,200.00
31 JDa(a&c),JKa,Grl,AW
   'Hand Chopper' 1,500.00
32 JDa(a&c),GE,Grl,'Woman
   Crushed by Elephant' 1,500.00
33 JDa(a&c),GE,JKa,Grl,'Lower
   Berth',O:Crypt Keeper 1,500.00
34 JDa(a&c),JKa,GE,Grl, 'Jack the
   Ripper,'RayBradbury adapt. 1,200.00
35 JDa(a&c),JKa,JO,Grl,
   'Werewolf' 1,400.00
36 JDa(a&c),JKa,GE,Grl, Ray
   Bradbury adaptation 900.00
37 JDa(c),JO,BE 900.00
38 JDa(c),BE,RC,Grl,'Axe Man' . 900.00
39 JDa(a&c),JKa,JO,Grl,'Children
   in the Graveyard' 900.00
40 JDa(a&c),GE,BK,Grl,
   'Underwater Monster' 1,500.00
41 JDa(a&c),JKa,GE,Grl,
   'Knife Thrower' 1,500.00
42 JDa(c),JO,Vampire (c) 1,500.00
43 JDa(c),JO,GE. 1,500.00
44 JO,RC,Guillotine (c). 1,400.00
45 JDa(a&c),JKa,BK,Gl,'Rat
   Takes Over His Life' 1,400.00
46 JDa(a&c),GE,JO,Gl,Werewolf
   man being hunted,Feb.'55 . 1,400.00

Crime Reporter #3
© *St. John Publishing Co.*

CRIME REPORTER
St. John Publishing Co., Aug., 1948
1 Death Makes a Deadline . . . 2,000.00
2 GT,MB(c),Matinee Murders . 2,200.00
3 GT,MB(c),Dec., 1948 . . . . . . 1,800.00

CRIMES BY WOMEN
Fox Features Syndicate, June, 1948
1 Bonnie Parker 2,000.00
2 Vicious Female 1,300.00
3 Prison Break (c) 1,200.00
4 Murder (c) 1,200.00
5 . . . . 1,200.00
6 Girl Fight (c) 1,200.00
7 . . . . 900.00
8 . . . . 900.00
9 . . . . 900.00
10 Girl Fight (c) 800.00
11 . . . . 800.00
12 . . . . 800.00
13 ACME Jewelry Robbery (c) . . 800.00
14 Prison break (c) 800.00
15 Aug., 1951. . . . . 800.00

CRIME SMASHER
Fawcett Publications, Summer, 1948
1 The Unlucky Rabbit's Foot . . . 700.00

CRIME SMASHERS
Ribage Publishing Corp., Oct., 1950
1 Girl Rape. 1,500.00
2 JKu,A:Sally the Sleuth, Dan
   Turner, Girl Friday, Rat Hale . 800.00
3 MFa 600.00
4 Zak(c) 600.00
5 WW 1,000.00
6 . . . . 500.00
7 Bondage (c),Drugs. 600.00
8 . . . . 500.00
9 Bondage (c). 600.00
10 . . . . 500.00
11 . . . . 500.00
12 FF, Eye Injury 600.00
13 . . . . 600.00
14 & 15. . . . . @500.00

CRIME ON THE WATERFRONT
See: FAMOUS GANGSTERS

CRIME SUSPENSTORIES
L.L. Publishing Co. (E.C. Comics), Oct.–Nov., 1950
1a JCr,Grl 2,700.00
1 JCr,WW,Grl 2,000.00
2 JCr,JKa,Grl 1,500.00
3 JCr,WW,Grl,Poe Story 900.00
4 JCr,Gln,Grl,JDa 900.00
5 JCr,JKa,Grl,JDa. 900.00
6 JCr,JDa,Grl 600.00
7 JCr,Grl 600.00
8 JCr,Grl 600.00
9 JCr,Grl 600.00
10 JCr,Grl. 600.00
11 JCr,Grl. 500.00
12 JCr,Grl. 500.00
13 JCr,AW 550.00
14 JCr 500.00
15 JCr,Old Witch 500.00
16 JCr,AW 600.00
17 JCr,FF,AW, Ray Bradbury . . 1,300.00
18 JCr,RC,BE. 550.00
19 JCr,RC,GE,AF(c) 550.00
20 RC,JCr, Hanging (c) 600.00
21 JCr 500.00
22 RC,JO,JCr(c),
   Severed head (c). 600.00
23 JKa,RC,GE 550.00
24 BK,RC,JO 500.00
25 JKa,(c),RC 600.00
26 JKa,(c),RC,JO. 700.00
27 JKa,(c),GE,Grl,March, 1955 . . 500.00

CRIMINALS ON THE RUN
Premium Group of Comics, Aug., 1948
4-1 LbC(c) 500.00
4-2 LbC(c), A:Young King Cole . 400.00
4-3 LbC(c), Rip Roaring Action
   in Alps 400.00
4-4 LbC(c), Shark (c) 400.00
4-5 AMc 400.00
4-6 LbC,Dr. Doom 400.00
4-7 LbC 900.00
5-1 LbC 350.00
5-2 LbC 350.00
10 LbC 350.00
Becomes:

CRIME-FIGHTING DETECTIVE
April–May, 1950
11 LbC, Brodie Gang Captured . 350.00
12 LbC(c), Jail Break Genius . . . 300.00
13 . . . . 250.00
14 LbC(c), A Night of Horror . . . 300.00
15 LbC(c). 300.00
16 LbC(c), Wanton Murder 300.00
17 LbC(c), The Framer
   was Framed. 300.00
18 LbC(c), A Web of Evil 300.00
19 LbC(c), Lesson of the Law . . . 300.00
Becomes:

SHOCK DETECTIVE CASES
Star Publications, Sept., 1952
20 LbC(c), The Strangler 400.00
21 LbC(c), Death Ride. 400.00
Becomes:

SPOOK DETECTIVE CASES
Star Publications, Jan., 1953
22 Headless Horror 500.00
Becomes:

SPOOK SUSPENSE AND MYSTERY

23 LbC,Weird Picture of Murder . 350.00
24 LbC(c),Mummy's Case 400.00
25 LbC(c),Horror Beyond Door . . 350.00
26 LbC(c),JyD,Face of Death . . . 350.00
27 LbC(c),Ship of the Dead 350.00
28 LbC(c),JyD,Creeping Death . . 350.00
29 LbC(c),Solo for Death 350.00
30 LbC(c),JyD,Nightmare,
Oct.,1954 . . . . 350.00

Crown Comics #6
© Golfing

CROWN COMICS
Golfing/McCombs Publ., Winter 1944

1 Edgar Allen Poe adapt. 700.00
2 MB,I:Mickey Magic 500.00
3 MB,Jungle adventure (c) 600.00
4 MB(c),A:Voodah. 550.00
5 MB(c),Jungle Adventure (c) . . 550.00
6 MB(c),Jungle Adventure (c) . . 550.00
7 JKa,AF,MB(c),Race Car (c) . . 550.00
8 MB 500.00
9 . . . . 300.00
10 Plane crash (c),A:Voodah. . . 300.00
11 LSt,A.Voodah. 250.00
12 LSt,AF,Master Marvin 250.00
13 LSt,AF,A:Voodah. 250.00
14 A:Voodah. 275.00
15 FBe,A:Voodah. 250.00
16 FBe,A:Voodah,Jungle
Adventure(c) 250.00
17 FBe,A:Voodah. 250.00
18 FBe,A:Voodah. 250.00
19 BP,A:Voodah,July, 1949 . . . . 250.00

CRUSADER FROM MARS
Approved Publ. (Ziff-Davis), Jan.–March, 1952

1 Mission Thru Space, Death in
the Sai 1,300.00
2 Beachhead on Saturn's Ring,
Bondage(c),Fall, 1952 . . . . 1,000.00

CRYIN' LION, THE
William H. Wise Co., Fall, 1944

1 Funny Animal. 500.00
2 A. Hitler 300.00
3 Spring, 1945 . . . . 250.00

CRYPT OF TERROR
See: CRIME PATROL

CURLY KAYOE COMICS
United Features Syndicate, 1946–50

1 Boxing 300.00
2 . . . . 250.00
3 thru 8 . . . . @200.00
1a United Presents . . . . (1948) . . 200.00

CYCLONE COMICS
Bibara Publ. Co., June, 1940

1 O:Tornado Tom 3,000.00
2 . . . . 2,500.00
3 . . . . 2,000.00
4 Voltron. 1,500.00
5 A:Mr. Q,Oct., 1940 . . . . 1,600.00

DAFFY
Dell Publishing Co., March, 1953

(1) see Dell Four Color #457
(2) see Dell Four Color #536
(3) see Dell Four Color #615
4 thru 7 . . . . @150.00
8 thru 11 . . . . @100.00
12 thru 17. . . . . @100.00
Becomes:

DAFFY DUCK
July, 1959

18 . . . . 100.00
19 . . . . 100.00
20 . . . . 100.00
21 thru 30. . . . . @100.00

DAFFY TUNES COMICS
Four Star Publications, 1947

12 Funny Animal 150.00

ALL GREAT COMICS
Fox Features Syndicate, 1947

12 A:Brenda Starr 1,500.00
13 JKa,O:Dagar, Desert Hawk . 1,800.00
Becomes:

DAGAR, DESERT HAWK
Feb., 1948

14 JKa,Monster of Mura 1,500.00
15 JKa,Curse of the Lost
Pharaoh,Bondage. 1,000.00
16 JKa,Wretched Antmen 900.00
19 Pyramid of Doom 800.00
20 . . . . 800.00
21 JKa(c),The Ghost of Fate,
Bondage (c). 850.00
22 . . . . 800.00
23 Bondage (c) 850.00
Becomes:

CAPTAIN KIDD
June, 1949

24 Blackbeard the Pirate 300.00
25 Sorceress of the Deep 300.00
Becomes:

MY SECRET STORY
Oct., 1949

26 He Wanted More Than Love. . 300.00
27 My Husband Hated Me. 250.00
28 I Become a Marked Women . . 250.00
29 My Forbidden Rapture,
April, 1950 . . . . 250.00

DAGWOOD
Harvey Publications, 1950

1 . . . . 300.00
2 . . . . 200.00
3 . . . . 175.00
4 . . . . 175.00
5 . . . . 175.00

6 thru 10 . . . . @175.00
11 thru 20. . . . . @150.00
21 thru 30. . . . . @125.00
31 thru 50. . . . . @100.00
51 thru 70. . . . . @100.00
71 thru 109. . . . . @75.00
110 thru 140. . . . . @75.00

DAISY AND HER PUPS
Harvey Publications, 1951–1954

1 (21) F:Blondie & Dagwood's
dog. 150.00
2 (22). 110.00
3 (23). 110.00
4 (24). 110.00
5 (25). 110.00
6 (26). 110.00
7 (27). 110.00
8 thru 18 . . . . @100.00

DAISY COMICS
Eastern Color Printing Co., 1936

N# 750.00

DAISY HANDBOOK
Daisy Manufacturing Co., 1946

1 Buck Rogers, Red Ryder. . . . 475.00
2 Capt. Marvel 475.00
N# (1955). 400.00

DANDY COMICS
E.C. Comics 1947–48

1 Funny Animal. 475.00
2 . . . . 325.00
3 thru 7 . . . . @250.00

DANGER
Comic Media, 1953–54

1 DH(c&a). 300.00
2 PMo 150.00
3 PMo 150.00
4 Marijuana (c) & story 200.00
5 PMo 150.00
6 Drug 175.00
7 . . . . 150.00
8 Torture (c) 225.00
9 thru 11 . . . . 150.00

Charlton Comics, 1955

12 . . . . 150.00
13 . . . . 125.00
14 . . . . 125.00
Becomes:

JIM BOWIE

15 . . . . 100.00
16 . . . . 100.00
17 . . . . 100.00
18 . . . . 100.00
19 April, 1957. . . . . 100.00

DANGER AND ADVENTURE
See: THIS MAGAZINE IS HAUNTED

DANGER IS OUR BUSINESS
Toby Press/ I.W. Enterprises, 1953

1 AW,FF,Men Who Defy Death
for a Living. 750.00
2 Death Crowds the Cockpit . . . 300.00
3 Killer Mountain 250.00
4 . . . . 250.00
5 thru 9 . . . . @200.00
10 June, 1955 . . . . 250.00

GOLDEN AGE

DAN'L BOONE
Sussex Publ. Co. 1955–57
1 F:Dan'l Boone Greatest
   Frontiersman 200.00
2 . . . . 150.00
3 . . . . 100.00
4 thru 8 . . . . @100.00

DANNY BLAZE
Charlton Comics, 1955
1 . . . . 150.00
2 . . . . 125.00
Becomes:

NATURE BOY
3 JB,O:Blue Beetle 300.00
4 . . . . 125.00
5 Feb., 1957 . . . . 100.00

DAREDEVIL COMICS
Lev Gleason Publications,
July, 1941
1 Daredevil Battles Hitler, A:Silver
   Streak, Lance Hale, Dickey Dean,
   Cloud Curtis,V:The Claw,
   O:Hitler 25,000.00
2 I:The Pioneer, Champion of
   American,B:London,Pat
   Patriot,Pirate Prince 5,000.00
3 CBi(c),O:Thirteen 3,200.00
4 CBi(c),Death is the Referee . 2,500.00
5 CBi(c),I:Sniffer&Jinx, Claw
   V:Ghost,Lottery of Doom . . 2,000.00
6 CBi(c) 1,700.00
7 CBi(c), What Ghastly Sight Lies
   within the Mysterious Trunk 1,600.00
8 V:Nazis (c), E:Nightro 1,500.00
9 V:Double 1,500.00
10 America will Remember
   Pearl Harbor 1,500.00
11 Bondage (c), E:Pat
   Patriot, London 1,800.00
12 BW,CBi(c), O:The Law. 2,200.00
13 BW,I:Little Wise Guys 1,700.00
14 BW,CBi(c) 1,200.00
15 BW,CBi(c), D:Meatball 1,400.00
16 BW,CBi(c) 1,100.00
17 BW,CBi(c), Into the Valley
   of Death 1,100.00
18 BW,CBi(c), O:Daredevil,
   double length story 2,000.00
19 BW,CBi(c), Buried Alive 900.00
20 BW,CBi(c), Boxing (c) 900.00
21 CBi(c), Can Little Wise Guys
   Survive Blast of Dynamite? 1,500.00
22 CBi(c) 750.00
23 CBi(c), I:Pshyco 750.00
24 CBi(c), Punch and Judy
   Murders 750.00
25 CBi(c), Baseball (c) 750.00
26 CBi(c) 700.00
27 CBi(c), Bondage (c) 750.00
28 CBi(c) 700.00
29 CBi(c) 700.00
30 CBi(c), Ann Hubbard White
   1922-1943 . . . . 700.00
31 CBi(c), D:The Claw 1,400.00
32 V:Blackmarketeers 500.00
33 CBi(c) 500.00
34 CBi(c) 500.00
35 B:Two Daredevil stories
   every issue 550.00
36 CBi(c) 550.00
37 CBi(c) 550.00
38 CBi(c), O:Daredevil. 800.00
39 CBi(c) 500.00
40 CBi(c) 500.00
41 . . . . 500.00
42 thru 50 CBi(c) . . . . @500.00
51 CBi(c) 350.00
52 CBi(c),Football (c). 400.00

Daredevil #5
© Lev Gleason Publications

53 thru 57. . . . . @350.00
58 Football (c) 400.00
59 . . . . 350.00
60 . . . . 350.00
61 thru 68 . . . . @350.00
69 E:Daredevil 350.00
70 . . . . 250.00
71 thru 78 . . . . @150.00
79 B:Daredevil 250.00
80 . . . . 275.00
81 . . . . 150.00
82 . . . . 150.00
83 thru 99. . . . . @150.00
100 . . . . 175.00
101 thru 133. . . . . @150.00
134 Sept., 1956 . . . . 150.00

DARING LOVE
Gilmore Magazines, 1953
1 SD,1st work 800.00

DARK MYSTERIES
Merit Publications,
June–July, 1951
1 WW(a&c), Curse of the
   Sea Witch 1,600.00
2 WW(a&c), Vampire Fangs
   of Doom 1,200.00
3 Terror of the Unwilling
   Witch 800.00
4 Corpse that Came Alive 800.00
5 Horror of the Ghostly Crew . . . 650.00
6 If the Noose Fits Wear It! 650.00
7 Terror of the Cards of Death . . 650.00
8 Terror of the Ghostly Trail 650.00
9 Witch's Feast at Dawn 650.00
10 Terror of the Burning Witch. . . 650.00
11 The River of Blood 600.00
12 Horror of the Talking Dead . . 600.00
13 Terror of the Hungry Cats 600.00
14 Horror of the Fingers of Doom 650.00
15 Terror of the Vampires Teeth. . 550.00
16 Horror of the Walking Dead . . 550.00
17 Terror of the Mask of Death . . 550.00
18 Terror of the Burning Corpse . 550.00
19 The Rack of Terror 750.00
20 Burning Executioner 650.00
21 The Sinister Secret. 500.00
22 The Hand of Destiny. 500.00
23 The Mardenburg Curse. 350.00
24 Give A Man Enough Rope,
   July, 1955 . . . . 350.00

DARK SHADOWS
Steinway Publications/Ajax
1957–58
1 . . . . 350.00
2 and 3 . . . . @300.00

DATE WITH DANGER
Visual Editions
(Standard Comics), 1952
5 Secret Agent 200.00
6 Atom Bomb 250.00

DAVY CROCKETT
Avon Periodicals, 1951
1 . . . . 250.00

FRONTIER FIGHTER
Charlton Comics, 1955
1 JK,Davy Crocket-Buffalo Bill . . 250.00
2 JK. 150.00
Becomes:

DAVY CROCKETT
Charlton Comics, 1956
3 thru 7 JK. . . . . @150.00
8 Jan., 1957 JK. 125.00
Becomes:

KID MONTANA

DEAD END
CRIME STORIES
Kirby Publishing Co.,
April, 1949
N# BP 750.00

DEAD-EYE
WESTERN COMICS
Hillman Periodicals
Nov.–Dec., 1948
1 BK 300.00
2 . . . . 250.00
3 . . . . 200.00
4 thru 12 . . . . @150.00
2-1 . . . . 125.00
2-2 . . . . 125.00
2-3 . . . . 150.00
2-4 . . . . 150.00
2-5 thru 2-12 . . . . @125.00
3-1 . . . . 125.00

DEADWOOD GULCH
Dell Publishing Co., 1931
1 . . . . 750.00

DEAR BEATRICE
FAIRFAX
Best Books
(Standard Comics), Nov., 1950
5 . . . . 300.00
6 thru 9 . . . . @200.00

DEATH VALLEY
Comic Media/
Charlton Comics, 1953
1 Cowboys & Indians 200.00
2 DH(c) 150.00
3 PMo 125.00
4 . . . . 125.00
5 PMo 125.00
6 . . . . 125.00
7 . . . . 125.00
8 BW 125.00
9 . . . . 125.00
Becomes:

FRONTIER SCOUT DANIEL BOONE
Charlton Comics
10 . . . . 150.00
11 thru 13 . . . . @100.00

DEBBIE DEAN, CAREER GIRL
Civil Service Publishing, April, 1945
1 . . . . 300.00
2 . . . . 250.00

DELL GIANT EDITIONS
Dell Publishing Co., 1952-58
Abe Lincoln Life Story 175.00
Cadet Gray of West Point 175.00
Golden West Rodeo Treasury . . . 200.00
Life Stories of
  American Presidents 165.00
Lone Ranger Golden West 400.00
Lone Ranger Movie Story 800.00
Lone Ranger Western
  Treasury('53) 400.00
Lone Ranger Western
  Treasury('54) 500.00
Moses & Ten Commandments . . . 150.00
Nancy & Sluggo Travel Time 200.00
Pogo Parade 750.00
Raggedy Ann & Andy 350.00
Santa Claus Funnies 200.00
Tarzan's Jungle Annual #1 . . . . . 350.00
Tarzan's Jungle Annual #2 . . . . . 225.00
Tarzan's Jungle Annual #3 . . . . . 200.00
Tarzan's Jungle Annual #4 . . . . . 200.00
Tarzan's Jungle Annual #5 . . . . . 200.00
Tarzan's Jungle Annual #6 . . . . . 200.00
Tarzan's Jungle Annual #7 . . . . . 200.00
Treasury of Dogs 175.00
Treasury of Horses 175.00
Universal Presents-Dracula-
  The Mummy & Other Stories. 500.00
Western Roundup #1 . . . . 600.00
Western Roundup #2 . . . . 350.00
Western Roundup #3 . . . . 275.00
Western Roundup #4 thru #5 . . @250.00
Western Roundup #6 thru #10 . @250.00
Western Roundup #11 thru #17 @225.00
Western Roundup #18 . . . . 225.00
Western Roundup #19 thru #25 @180.00
Woody Woodpecker Back
  to School #1 (1952) 300.00

Dell Giant Editions Pogo Parade #1
© Dell Publishing Co.

Woody Woodpecker Back
  to School #2 (1953) 250.00
Woody Woodpecker Back
  to School #3 (1954) 250.00
Woody Woodpecker Back
  to School #4 (1955) 250.00
Woody Woodpecker County
  Fair #5 (1956) 250.00
Woody Woodpecker Back
  to School #6 (1957) 275.00
Woody Woodpecker County
  Fair #2 (1958) 250.00
Also See: Bugs Bunny; Marge's Little Lulu; Tom and Jerry, and Walt Disney Dell Giant Editions

DELL GIANT COMICS
Dell Publishing Co., Sept., 1959
21 M.G.M. Tom & Jerry
  Picnic Time 250.00
22 W.Disney's Huey, Dewey & Louie
  Back to School (Oct 1959) . . 500.00
23 Marge's Little Lulu &
  Tubby Halloween Fun 375.00
24 Woody Woodpeckers
  Family Fun 275.00
25 Tarzan's Jungle World 250.00
26 W.Disney's Christmas
  Parade,CB 600.00
27 W.Disney's Man in
  Space (1960) 300.00
28 Bugs Bunny's Winter Fun . . . 250.00
29 Marge's Little Lulu &
  Tubby in Hawaii 375.00
30 W.Disney's DisneylandU.S.A. 400.00
31 Huckleberry Hound
  Summer Fun 300.00
32 Bugs Bunny Beach Party . . . 250.00
33 W.Disney's Daisy Duck &
  Uncle Scrooge Picnic Time . 400.00
34 Nancy&SluggoSummerCamp. 250.00
35 W.Disney's Huey, Dewey &
  Louie Back to School 500.00
36 Marge's Little Lulu & Witch
  Hazel Halloween Fun 375.00
37 Tarzan, King of the Jungle . . 250.00
38 W.Disney's Uncle Donald and
  his Nephews Family Fun . . . 400.00
39 W.Disney's Merry Christmas . 350.00
40 Woody Woodpecker
  Christmas Parade 225.00
41 Yogi Bear's Winter Sports . . . 275.00
42 Marge's Little Lulu &
  Tubby in Australia 375.00
43 Mighty Mouse in OuterSpace . 550.00
44 Around the World with
  Huckleberry & His Friends . . 400.00
45 Nancy&SluggoSummerCamp. 150.00
46 Bugs Bunny Beach Party 175.00
47 W.Disney's Mickey and
  Donald in Vacationland 350.00
48 The Flintstones #1
  (Bedrock Bedlam) 500.00
49 W.Disney's Huey, Dewey &
  Louie Back to School 400.00
50 Marge's Little Lulu &
  Witch Hazel Trick 'N' Treat . . 325.00
51 Tarzan, King of the Jungle . . . 200.00
52 W.Disney's Uncle Donald &
  his Nephews Dude Ranch . . 500.00
53 W.Disney's Donald Duck
  Merry Christmas 400.00
54 Woody Woodpecker
  Christmas Party 250.00
55 W.Disney's Daisy Duck & Uncle
  Scrooge Show Boat (1961) . . 300.00

DELL JUNIOR TREASURY
Dell Publishing Co., June, 1955
1 Alice in Wonderland 150.00
2 Aladdin 125.00
3 Gulliver's Travels 100.00
4 Adventures of Mr. Frog 125.00
5 Wizard of Oz 125.00
6 Heidi 135.00
7 Santa & the Angel 135.00
8 Raggedy Ann 135.00
9 Clementina the Flying Pig 125.00
10 Adventures of Tom Sawyer . . . 125.00

DENNIS THE MENACE
Visual Editions/Literary Ent. (Standard, Pines), Aug., 1953
1 . . . . 1,200.00
2 . . . . 500.00
3 . . . . 300.00
4 . . . . 300.00
5 thru 10 . . . . @200.00
11 thru 20 . . . . @175.00
21 thru 31 . . . . @150.00

Hallden (Fawcett Publications)
32 thru 40 . . . . @125.00
41 thru 50 . . . . @125.00
51 thru 60 . . . . @100.00
61 thru 70 . . . . @100.00
71 thru 90 . . . . @100.00
91 thru 140 . . . . @50.00
141 thru 166 . . . . @35.00

Desperado #1
© Lev Gleason Publications

DESPERADO
Lev Gleason Publications, June, 1948
1 CBi(c) 300.00
2 CBi(c) 200.00
3 CBi(c) 250.00
4 CBi(c) 150.00
5 CBi(c) 150.00
6 CBi(c) 150.00
7 CBi(c) 150.00
8 CBi(c) 150.00
Becomes:

BLACK DIAMOND WESTERN
March, 1949
9 CBi(c) 300.00
10 CBi(c) 200.00
11 CBi(c) 150.00
12 CBi(c) 150.00

GOLDEN AGE

13 CBi(c) 150.00
14 CBi(c) 150.00
15 CBi(c) 150.00
16 thru 28 BW,Big Bang Buster @150.00
29 thru 40 . . . . @175.00
41 thru 50 . . . . @125.00
51 thru 52 3-D Luse . . . . @250.00
53 thru 60 . . . . @100.00

DETECTIVE DAN, SECRET OP, 48
Humor Publ. Co., 1933
N# 10"x13", 36 pg. b&w 25,000.00

Detective Eye #2
© *Centaur Publications*

DETECTIVE EYE
Centaur Publications, Nov., 1940
1 B:Air Man, The Eye Sees,
　A:Masked Marvel 3,500.00
2 O:Don Rance, Mysticape,
　Dec., 1940 . . . . 2,500.00

DETECTIVE PICTURE STORIES
Comics Magazine Co., Dec., 1936
1 The Phantom Killer 7,000.00
2 The Clock 3,500.00
3 . . . . 2,500.00
4 WE, Muss Em Up 2,200.00
5 Trouble, April, 1937 . . . . 2,700.00

DEVIL DOGS
Street & Smith Publ., 1942
1 U.S. Marines 600.00

DEXTER COMICS
Dearfield Publications, Summer, 1948–July, 1949
1 Teen Age 250.00
2 Sunie Prom 200.00
3 thru 5 . . . . @150.00

DICK COLE
Curtis Publ./ Star Publications, Dec.–Jan., 1949
1 LbC(a&c),CS,All sports(c) . . . 425.00
2 LbC 250.00
3 LbC(a&c) 275.00
4 LbC(a&c),Rowing (c) 275.00

5 LbC(a&c) 275.00
6 LbC(a&c), Rodeo (c) 275.00
7 LbC(a&c) 250.00
8 LbC(a&c), Football (c) 250.00
9 LbC(a&c), Basketball (c) 250.00
10 Joe Louis 300.00
Becomes:

SPORTS THRILLS
Nov., 1950–Nov., 1951
11 Ted Williams & Ty Cobb 450.00
12 LbC, Joe DiMaggio & Phil
　Rizzuto, Boxing (c) 400.00
13 LbC(c),Basketball (c) 350.00
14 LbC(c),Baseball (c) 375.00
15 LbC(c),Baseball (c) 375.00

DICKIE DARE
Eastern Color Printing Co., 1941–42
1 BEv(c),M.Caniff 1,500.00
2 . . . . 750.00
3 . . . . 750.00
4 H. Scorcery Smith 800.00

DICK TRACY MONTHLY
Dell Publishing Co., Jan., 1948
1 ChG,AAv,Dick Tracy & the Mad
　Doctor' 700.00
2 ChG,A:MarySteele,BorisArson 375.00
3 ChG,A:Spaldoni,Big Boy 375.00
4 ChG,A:Alderman Zeld 375.00
5 ChG,A:Spaldoni,Mrs.Spaldoni . 350.00
6 ChG,A:Steve the Tramp 350.00
7 ChG,A:Boris Arson,Mary
　Steele 350.00
8 ChG,A:Boris & Zora Arson . . . 350.00
9 ChG,A:Chief Yellowpony 350.00
10 ChG,A:Cutie Diamond 350.00
11 ChG,A:Toby Townly,
　Bookie Joe 275.00
12 ChG,A:Toby Townly,
　Bookie Joe 275.00
13 ChG,A:Toby Townly, Blake . . . 300.00
14 ChG,A:Mayor Waite Wright . . . 250.00
15 ChG,A:Bowman Basil 250.00
16 ChG,A:Maw,'Muscle'
　& 'Cut' Famon 250.00
17 ChG,A:Jim Trailer,
　Mary Steele 250.00
18 ChG,A:Lips Manlis,
　Anthel Jones 250.00
19 I:Sparkle Plenty 300.00
20 'Black Cat Mystery' 275.00
21 'Tracy Meets Number One' . . 275.00
22 'Tracy and the Alibi Maker' . . 225.00
23 'Dick Tracy Meets Jukebox' . . 225.00
24 'Dick Tracy and Bubbles' 225.00
Becomes:

DICK TRACY COMICS MONTHLY
Harvey, May, 1950
25 ChG,A:Flattop 300.00
26 ChG,A:Vitamin Flintheart 200.00
27 ChG,'Flattop Escapes Prision' 200.00
28 ChG,'Case o/t Torture
　Chamber' 200.00
29 ChG,A:Brow,Gravel Gertie . . . 250.00
30 ChG,'Blackmail Racket' 200.00
31 ChG,A:Snowflake Falls 175.00
32 ChG,A:Shaky,Snowflake Falls 175.00
33 ChG,'Strange Case
　of Measles' 225.00
34 ChG,A:Measles,Paprika 200.00
35 ChG,'Case of Stolen $50,000'. 200.00
36 ChG,'Case of the
　Runaway Blonde' 225.00
37 ChG,'Case of Stolen Money' . . 200.00

38 ChG,A:Breathless Mahoney . . 200.00
39 ChG,A:Itchy,B.O.Plenty 200.00
40 ChG,'Case of Atomic Killer' . . . 200.00
41 ChG,Pt.1'Murder by Mail' 175.00
42 ChG,Pt.2'Murder by Mail' 175.00
43 ChG,'Case of the
　Underworld Brat' 175.00
44 ChG,'Case of the Mouthwash
　Murder' 175.00
45 ChG,'Case of the Evil Eyes' . . 175.00
46 ChG,'Case of the
　Camera Killers' 175.00
47 ChG,'Case of the
　Bloodthirsty Blonde' 175.00
48 ChG,'Case of the
　Murderous Minstrel' 175.00
49 ChG,Pt.1 'Killer Who Returned
　From the Dead 175.00
50 ChG,Pt.2 'Killer Who
　Returned From the Dead' . . . 175.00
51 ChG, 'Case of the
　High Tension Hijackers' 150.00
52 ChG, 'Case of the
　Pipe-Stem Killer 150.00
53 ChG,Pt.1 'Dick Tracy Meets
　the Murderous Midget' 150.00
54 ChG,Pt.2 'Dick Tracy Meets
　the Murderous Midget' 150.00
55 ChG,Pt.3 'Dick Tracy Meets
　the Murderous Midget' 150.00
56 ChG,'Case of the
　Teleguard Terror' 150.00
57 ChG,Pt.1 'Case of the
　Ice Cold Killer' 175.00
58 ChG,Pt.2 'Case of the
　Ice Cold Killer' 150.00
59 ChG,Pt.1 'Case of the
　Million Dollar Murder' 150.00
60 ChG,Pt.2 'Case of the
　Million Dollar Murder' 150.00
61 ChG,'Case of the
　Murderers Mask' 150.00
62 ChG,Pt.1 'Case of the
　White Rat Robbers' 150.00
63 ChG,Pt.2 'Case of the
　White Rat Robbers' 150.00
64 ChG,Pt.1 'Case of the
　Interrupted Honeymoon' 150.00
65 ChG,Pt.2 'Case of the
　Interrupted Honeymoon' 150.00
66 ChG,Pt.1 'Case of the
　Killer's Revenge' 150.00
67 ChG,Pt.2 'Case of the
　Killer's Revenge' 150.00
68 ChG,Pt.1'Case o/t TV Terror' . 150.00
69 ChG,Pt.2'Case o/t TV Terror' . 150.00
70 ChG,Pt.3'Case o/t TV Terror' . 135.00
71 ChG,A:Mrs. Forchune,Opal . . . 135.00
72 ChG,A:Empty Wiliams,Bonny . 135.00
73 ChG,A:Bonny Braids 135.00
74 ChG,A:Mr. & Mrs.
　Fortson Knox 135.00
75 ChG,A:Crewy Lou, Sphinx . . . 135.00
76 ChG,A:Diet Smith,Brainerd . . . 135.00
77 ChG,A:Crewy Lou,
　Bonny Braids 135.00
78 ChG,A:Spinner Records 135.00
79 ChG,A:Model Jones,
　Larry Jones 135.00
80 ChG,A:Tonsils,Dot View 135.00
81 ChG,A:Edward Moppet,Tonsils 135.00
82 ChG,A:Dot View,Mr. Crime . . . 135.00
83 ChG,A:RifleRuby,NewsuitNan. . 135.00
84 ChG,A:Mr.Crime,NewsuitNan . 135.00
85 ChG,A:NewsuitNan, Mrs.Lava 135.00
86 ChG,A:Mr. Crime,Odds Zonn . 135.00
87 ChG,A:Odds Zonn,Wingy 135.00
88 ChG,A:Odds Zonn,Wingy 135.00
89 ChG,Pt.1'Canhead' 135.00
90 ChG,Pt.2'Canhead' 135.00
91 ChG,Pt.3'Canhead' 135.00
92 ChG,Pt.4'Canhead' 135.00

Dick Tracy Comics Monthly #85
© Harvey Comics

93 ChG,Pt.5'Canhead'	135.00
94 ChG,Pt.6'Canhead'	135.00
95 ChG,A:Mrs. Green,Dewdrop	135.00
96 ChG,A:Dewdrop,Sticks	135.00
97 ChG,A:Dewdrop,Sticks	135.00
98 ChG,A:Open-Mind Monty, Sticks	135.00
99 ChG,A:Open-Mind Monty, Sticks	150.00
100 ChG,A:Half-Pint,Dewdrop	175.00
101 ChG,A:Open-Mind Monty	150.00
102 ChG,A:Rainbow Reiley, Wingy.	150.00
103 ChG,A:Happy,Rughead	150.00
104 ChG,A:Rainbow Reiley, Happy	150.00
105 ChG,A:Happy,Rughead	150.00
106 ChG,A:Fence,Corny,Happy	150.00
107 ChG,A:Spinner Records	150.00
108 ChG,A:Rughead,Corny, Fence.	150.00
109 ChG,A:Rughead,Mirnl,Herky.	150.00
110 ChG,A:Vitamin Flintheart	150.00
111 ChG,A:Shoulders,Roach	150.00
112 ChG,A:Brilliant,Diet Smith	150.00
113 ChG,A:Snowflake Falls	150.00
114 ChG,A:"Sketch'Paree,	150.00
115 ChG,A:Rod & Nylon Hoze	150.00
116 ChG,A:Empty Williams	150.00
117 ChG,A:Spinner Records	150.00
118 ChG,A:Sleet.	150.00
119 ChG,A:Coffyhead	150.00
120 ChG,'Case Against Mumbles Quartet'	150.00
121 ChG,'Case of the Wild Boys'.	150.00
122 ChG,'Case of the Poisoned Pellet'.	150.00
123 ChG,'Case of the Deadly Treasure Hunt'.	150.00
124 ChG,'Case of Oodles Hears Only Evil'.	150.00
125 ChG,'Case of the Desparate Widow'	150.00
126 ChG,'Case of Oodles' Hideout'.	150.00
127 ChG,'Case Against Joe Period'	150.00
128 ChG,'Case Against Juvenile Delinquent'.	150.00
129 ChG,'Case of Son of Flattop'	150.00
130 ChG,'Case of Great Gang Roundup'	150.00
131 ChG,'Strange Case of Flattop's Conscience'	150.00
132 ChG,'Case of Flattop's Big Show'	150.00
133 ChG,'Dick Tracy Follows Trail of Jewel Thief Gang'	150.00
134 ChG,'Last Stand of Jewel Thieves'.	150.00
135 ChG,'Case of the Rooftop Sniper'	150.00
136 ChG,'Mystery of the Iron Room'.	150.00
137 ChG,'Law Versus Dick Tracy'	150.00
138 ChG,'Mystery of Mary X'.	150.00
139 ChG,'Yogee the Merciless'	150.00
140 ChG,'The Tunnel Trap'	150.00
141 ChG,'Case of Wormy & His Deadly Wagon'	150.00
142 ChG,'Case of the Killer's Revenge'	150.00
143 ChG,'Strange Case of Measles'	150.00
144 ChG,'Strange Case of Shoulders'	150.00
145 ChG,'Case of the Fiendish Photographers'; April, 1961.	150.00

DICK WINGATE OF THE U.S. NAVY
Superior Publ./ Toby Press, 1951

N#	200.00
N# reprint	150.00

DIME COMICS
Newsbook Publ. Corp., 1945

1 LbC,A:Silver Streak	1,200.00

DING DONG
Compix (Magazine Enterprises), 1947

1 (fa)	300.00
2 (fa)	150.00
3 thru 5 (fa)	@100.00

DINKY DUCK
St. John Publ. Co./Pines, Nov., 1951

1	150.00
2	125.00
3 thru 10	@100.00
11 thru 15	@100.00
16 thru 18	@75.00
19 Summer, 1958	75.00

DIXIE DUGAN
Columbia Publ./ Publication Enterprises, July, 1942

1 Boxing (c),Joe Palooka	500.00
2	300.00
3	200.00
4	150.00
5	@150.00
6 thru 12	@100.00
13 1949	100.00

DIZZY DON COMICS
Howard Publications/ Dizzy Dean Ent., 1943

1 B&W interior.	300.00
2 B&W Interior	200.00
3 B&W Interior	150.00
4 B&W Interior	150.00
5 thru 21	@150.00
22 Oct., 1946	300.00
1a thru 3a	@350.00

DOC CARTER V.D. COMICS
Health Publ. Inst., 1949

N#	350.00
N#	250.00

Doc Savage #5
© Street & Smith Publications

DOC SAVAGE COMICS
Street & Smith Publ., May, 1940

1 B:Doc Savage, Capt. Fury, Danny Garrett, Mark Mallory, Whisperer, Capt. Death, Treasure Island, A: The Magician	8,500.00
2 O:Ajax,The Sun Man,E:The Whisperer	3,000.00
3 Artic Ice Wastes	1,900.00
4 E:Treasure Island, Saves U.S. Navy	1,400.00
5 O:Astron, the Crocodile Queen, Sacred Ruby	1,100.00
6 E: Capt. Fury, O:Red Falcon, Murderous Peace Clan	850.00
7 V:Zoombas	850.00
8 Finds the Long Lost Treasure	850.00
9 Smashes Japan's Secret Oil Supply	850.00
10 O:Thunder Bolt, The Living Dead A:Lord Manhattan	850.00
11 V:Giants of Destruction	700.00
12 Saves Merchant Fleet from Complete Destruction	700.00
2-1 The Living Evil	700.00
2-2 V:Beggar King	700.00
2-3	700.00
2-4 Fight to Death	700.00
2-5 Saves Panama Canal from Blood Raider	700.00
2-6	700.00
2-7 V:Black Knight	700.00
2-8 Oct., 1943	700.00

DR. ANTHONY KING HOLLYWOOD LOVE DOCTOR
Harvey, Publ., 1952

1	250.00
2	200.00
3	200.00
4 BP,May, 1954	200.00

GOLDEN AGE

DO-DO
Nationwide Publishers, 1950
1 Funny Animal Circus Humor . . 300.00
2 . . . . 150.00
3 . . . . 150.00
4 . . . . 150.00
5 thru 7 . . . . @150.00

Doll Man #32
© Quality Comics Group

DOLL MAN
Comic Favorites
(Quality Comics Group),
Fall, 1941–Oct., 1953
1 RC,B:Doll Man & Justine
Wright 5,500.00
2 B:Dragon 1,800.00
3 Five stories 1,500.00
4 Dolls of Death, Wanted:
The Doll Man 1,300.00
5 RC,Four stories 1,100.00
6 Buy War Stamps (c) 750.00
7 Four stories 750.00
8 BWa,Three stories,A:Torchy. 2,200.00
9 Torchy 750.00
10 RC,V:Murder Marionettes,
Grim, The Good Sport 600.00
11 Shocks Crime Square in the
Eye 600.00
12 Torchy 600.00
13 RC,Blows Crime Sky High . . . 600.00
14 Spotlight on Comics 600.00
15 Faces Danger 600.00
16 Torchy 550.00
17 Deals Out Punishment for
Crime 550.00
18 Redskins Scalp Crime 550.00
19 Fitted for a Cement Coffin . . . 550.00
20 Destroys the Black Heart of
Nemo Black 550.00
21 Problem of a Poison Pistol . . . 500.00
22 V:Tom Thumb 500.00
23 V:Minstrel, Musician
of Menace 500.00
24 V:Elixir of Youth 500.00
25 V:Thrawn, Lord of Lightning . . 500.00
26 V:Sultan of Satarr &
Wonderous Runt 500.00
27 Space Conquest 500.00
28 V:The Flame 500.00
29 V:Queen MAB 500.00
30 V:Lord Damion 500.00
31 I:Elmo, the Wonder Dog 400.00
32 A:Jeb Rivers 400.00
33 & 34 . . . . @400.00
35 Prophet of Doom 400.00

36 Death Trap in the Deep 400.00
37 V:The Skull,B:Doll Girl,
Bondage(c) 550.00
38 The Cult of Death 400.00
39 V:The Death Drug, Narcotics . 400.00
40 Giants of Crime 400.00
41 The Headless Horseman 250.00
42 Tale of the Mind Monster 250.00
43 The Thing that Kills 250.00
44 V:Radioactive Man 250.00
45 What was in the Doom Box? . 250.00
46 Monster from Tomorrow 250.00
47 V:Mad Hypnotist 250.00

FAMOUS GANG,
BOOK OF COMICS
Firestone Tire & Rubber Co.,
1942
N# Porky Pig,Bugs Bunny 1,200.00
Becomes:

DONALD AND MICKEY
MERRY CHRISTMAS
N# (2),CB, 1943 . . . . 1,000.00
N# (3),CB, 1944 . . . . 900.00
N# (4),CB, 1945 . . . . 1,400.00
N# (5),CB, 1946 . . . . 1,000.00
N# (6),CB, 1947 . . . . 1,000.00
N# (7),CB, 1948 . . . . 1,000.00
N# (8),CB, 1949 . . . . 900.00

DONALD DUCK
Whitman
W.Disney's Donald Duck ('35) . 6,000.00
W.Disney's Donald Duck ('36) . 5,000.00
W.Disney's Donald Duck ('38) . 5,000.00

DONALD DUCK
GIVEAWAYS
Donald Duck Surprise Party (Icy
Frost Ice Cream 1948)WK . 4,000.00
Donald Duck (Xmas Giveaway
1944) 1,500.00
Donald Duck Tells About Kites
(P.G.&E., Florida 1954). . . . 4,000.00
Donald Duck Tells About Kites
(S.C.Edison 1954) 3,500.00
Donald Duck and the Boys
(Whitman 1948) 1,200.00
Donald Ducks Atom Bomb
(Cherrios 1947) 1,200.00

(WALT DISNEY'S)
DONALD DUCK
Dell Publishing Co.,
Nov., 1952
(#1-#25) See *Dell Four Color*
26 CB;"Trick or Treat" (1952) 900.00
27 CB(c);"Flying Horse"('53) . . . 450.00
28 CB(c); Robert the Robot 400.00
29 CB(c) 400.00
30 CB(c) 400.00
31 thru 39 . . . . @300.00
40 . . . . 250.00
41 . . . . 250.00
42 . . . . 250.00
43 . . . . 250.00
44 . . . . 250.00
45 CB 500.00
46 CB; "Secret of Hondorica" . . . 600.00
47 thru 51 . . . . @300.00
52 CB; "Lost Peg-Leg Mine" 500.00
53 . . . . 300.00
54 CB; "Forbidden Valley" 700.00
55 thru 59 . . . . @250.00
60 CB; "Donald Duck & the
Titanic Ants" 500.00
61 thru 67 . . . . @250.00
68 CB 375.00

69 thru 78 . . . . @200.00
79 CB (1 page) 250.00
80 . . . . 175.00
81 CB (1 page) 200.00
82 . . . . 175.00
83 . . . . 175.00
84 . . . . 175.00

DON FORTUNE
MAGAZINE
Don Fortune Publ. Co.,
Aug., 1946
1 CCB 400.00
2 CCB 250.00
3 CCB,Bondage(c) 225.00
4 CCB 200.00
5 CCB 200.00
6 CCB, Jan., 1947 . . . . 200.00

DON NEWCOMBE
Fawcett Publications, 1950
1 Baseball Star 650.00

DON WINSLOW
OF THE NAVY
Fawcett Publ./
Charlton Comics, Feb., 1943
1 Captain Marvel (c) 2,000.00
2 Nips the Nipponese in
the Solomons 850.00
3 Single-Handed invasion of
the Philippines 600.00
4 Undermines the Nazis! 500.00
5 Stolen Battleship Mystery . . . 500.00
6 War Stamps for Victory,Flag(c) 500.00
7 Coast Guard 400.00
8 U.S. Marines 400.00
9 Fighting Marines 400.00
10 Fighting Seabees 400.00
11 . . . . 350.00
12 Tuned for Death 350.00
13 Hirohito's Hospitality 350.00
14 Catapults against the Axis . . . 350.00
15 Fighting Merchant Marine . . . 300.00
16 V:The Most Diabolical Villain
of all Time 300.00
17 Buy War Stamps (c) 300.00
18 The First Underwater Convoy. 300.00
19 Bonape Excersion 300.00
20 The Nazi Prison Ship 300.00
21 Prisoner of the Nazis 225.00
22 Suicide Football 225.00
23 Peril on the High Seas 225.00
24 Adventures on the High Seas . 225.00
25 Shanghaied Red Cross Ship . 225.00
26 V:The Scorpion 225.00
27 Buy War Stamps 225.00
28 . . . . 225.00
29 Invitation to Trouble 225.00
30 . . . . 225.00
31 Man or Myth? 150.00
32 Return of the Renegade 150.00
33 Service Ribbons 150.00
34 Log Book 150.00
35 . . . . 150.00
36 V:Octopus 150.00
37 V: Sea Serpent 150.00
38 Climbs Mt. Everest 150.00
39 Scorpion's Death Ledger 150.00
40 Kick Off! 150.00
41 Rides the Skis! 125.00
42 Amazon Island 125.00
43 Ghastly Doll Murder Case . . . 125.00
44 The Scorpions Web 125.00
45 V:Highwaymen of the Seas . . 125.00
46 Renegades Jailbreak 125.00
47 The Artic Expedition 125.00
48 Maelstrom of the Deep 125.00
49 The Vanishing Ship! 125.00
50 V:The Snake 125.00

Don Winslow of the Navy #37
© Fawcewtt Publications

51 A:Singapore Sal 125.00
52 Ghost of the Fishing Ships . . . 125.00
53 . . . . 125.00
54 . . . . 125.00
55 . . . . 125.00
56 Far East 125.00
57 A:Singapore Sal 125.00
58 thru 63 . . . . @125.00
64 MB. 125.00
65 Ph(c),Flying Saucer 250.00
66 Ph(c) 200.00
67 Ph(c) 200.00
68 Ph(c) 200.00
69 Ph(c), Jaws of Destruction . . . 200.00
70 . . . . 125.00
71 . . . . 125.00
72 . . . . 125.00
73 Sept., 1955 . . . . 125.00

DOROTHY LAMOUR
See: JUNGLE LIL

DOUBLE COMICS
Elliot Publications
1 ('40),Masked Marvel 4,000.00
2 ('41),Tornado Tim 3,000.00
3 ('42) 2,500.00
4 ('43) 2,000.00
5 ('44) 2,000.00

DOUBLE TALK
Feature Publications
1 Anti-communist 150.00

DOUBLE TROUBLE
St. John Publishing Co., 1957
1 Funny kids 125.00

DOUBLE UP
Elliot Publications, 1941
1 . . . . 2,000.00

DOWN WITH CRIME
Fawcett Publications,
Nov., 1951
1 A:Desarro 650.00
2 BP, A:Scanlon Gang 400.00
3 H-is for Heroin 375.00
4 BP, A:Desarro 350.00
5 No Jail Can Hold Me 400.00
6 The Puncture-Proof Assassin . 400.00
7 The Payoff, Nov., 1952 . . . . . . 400.00

DO YOU BELIEVE IN NIGHTMARES
St. John Publ. Co., 1957
1 SD 900.00
2 DAy 600.00

DUDLEY
Prize Publications,
Nov.–Dec., 1952
1 . . . . 175.00
2 . . . . 125.00
3 March–April, 1950 . . . . 100.00

DUMBO WEEKLY
The Walt Disney Co., 1942
1 Gas giveaways 2,100.00
2 thru 16 . . . . @1,500.00

DURANGO KID
Magazine Enterprises,
Oct.–Nov., 1949
1 FF, Charles Starrett photo (c)
   B:Durango Kid & Raider . . 1,200.00
2 FF, Charles Starrett Ph(c) 700.00
3 FF, Charles Starrett Ph(c) 600.00
4 FF, Charles Starrett Ph(c),
   Two-Timing Guns 500.00
5 FF, Charles Starrett Ph(c),
   Tracks Across the Trail 500.00
6 FF 300.00
7 FF,Atomic(c) 350.00
8 FF 300.00
9 FF 300.00
10 FF 300.00
11 FF 250.00
12 FF 250.00
13 FF 250.00
14 thru 16 FF . . . . @250.00
17 O:Durango Kid 300.00
18 FMe,DAy(c). 200.00
19 FMe,FGu. 175.00
20 FMe,FGu. 175.00
21 FMe,FGu. 175.00
22 FMe,FGu. 200.00
23 FMe,FGu,I:Red Scorpion 200.00
24 thru 30 FMe,FGu. . . . . @200.00
31 FMe,FGu. 200.00
32 thru 40 FGu. . . . . @200.00
41 FGu,Oct., 1941 . . . . 200.00

DYNAMIC COMICS
Dynamic Publications
(Harry 'A' Chesler),
Oct., 1941
1 EK,O:Major Victory, Dynamic Man,
   Hale the Magician, A:Black
   Cobra 3,500.00
2 O:Dynamic Boy & Lady
   Satan,I:Green Knight,
   Lance Cooper. 2,500.00
3 GT. 2,200.00
8 Horror (c) 2,500.00
9 MRa,GT,B:Mr.E 2,500.00
10 . . . . 1,500.00
11 GT 1,350.00
12 GT 1,200.00
13 GT 1,300.00
14 . . . . 1,200.00
15 Sky Chief 1,200.00
16 GT,Bondage(c),Marijuana . . 1,500.00
17 . . . . 1,700.00
18 Ric 1,000.00
19 A:Dynamic Man 1,000.00
20 same,Nude Woman 2,000.00
21 same,Dinosaur(c). 1,000.00
22 same 1,000.00
23 A:Yankee Girl,1.0948 . . . . . . 1,000.00

DYNAMITE
Comic Media/Allen Hardy Publ.,
May, 1953
1 DH(c),A:Danger#6 . . . . 400.00
2 . . . . 200.00
3 PMo(a&c),B:Johnny
   Dynamite,Drug. 300.00
4 PMo(a&c),Prostitution 350.00
5 PMo(a&c) 200.00
6 PMo(a&c) 200.00
7 PMo(a&c),Prostitution 200.00
8 PMo(a&c) 200.00
9 PMo(a&c) 200.00
Becomes:

JOHNNY DYNAMITE
Charlton Comics, June, 1955
10 PMo(c) 150.00
11 . . . . 125.00
12 . . . . 125.00
Becomes:

FOREIGN INTRIGUES
1956
13 A:Johnny Dynamite. 150.00
14 same. 125.00
15 same. 125.00
Becomes:

BATTLEFIELD ACTION
Nov., 1957
16 . . . . 150.00
17 . . . . 100.00
18 . . . . 100.00
19 . . . . 100.00
20 . . . . 100.00
21 thru 30 . . . . @100.00

EAGLE, THE
Fox Features Syndicate,
July, 1941
1 B:The Eagle,A:Rex Dexter
   of Mars 4,000.00
2 B:Spider Queen 2,000.00
3 B:Joe Spook 1,800.00
4 Jan , 1942 . . . . 1,800.00

EAGLE
Rural Home Publ.,
Feb.–March, 1945
1 LbC 800.00
2 LbC,April–May, 1945 . . . . 500.00

EAT RIGHT TO WORK AND WIN
Swift Co., 1942
N# Flash Gordon,Popeye 750.00

EDDIE STANKY
Fawcett Publications, 1951
N# New York Giants 450.00

EERIE
Avon Periodicals,
May–June, 1951–
Aug.–Sept., 1954
1 JKa,Horror from the Pit,
   Bondage(c), 1947. . . . . 6,500.00
1a reprint, 1951 . . . . 1,000.00
2,WW(a&c), Chamber of Death 1,000.00
3 WW(a&c),JKa,JO
   Monster of the Storm 1,100.00
4 WW(c),Phantom of Reality . 1,000.00
5 WW(c), Operation Horror . . . 900.00
6 Devil Keeps a Date 450.00
7 WW(c),JKa,JO,Blood for
   the Vampire. 700.00
8 EK, Song of the Undead 400.00
9 JKa, Hands of Death 450.00

Eerie #12
© Avon Periodicals

10 EK,Castle of Terror 400.00
11 Anatomical Monster 400.00
12 Dracula 500.00
13 . . . . 400.00
14 Master of the Dead 400.00
15 Reprint #1 . . . . 300.00
16 WW, Chamber of Death 300.00
17 WW(c),JO,JKa, ... 350.00

EERIE ADVENTURES
**Approved Comics
(Ziff-Davis), Winter, 1951**
1 BP,JKa,Bondage 550.00

EGBERT
**Arnold Publications/
Comic Magazine, Spring, 1946**
1 I:Egbert & The Count 400.00
2 . . . . 250.00
3 . . . . 200.00
4 . . . . 200.00
5 . . . . 200.00
6 . . . . 250.00
7 thru 10 . . . . @200.00
11 thru 17 . . . . @150.00
18 1950 . . . . 150.00

EH!
**Charlton Comics,
Dec., 1953–Nov., 1954**
1 DAy(c),DG,Atomic Mouse 450.00
2 DAy(c) 250.00
3 DAy(c) 225.00
4 DAy(c),Sexual 250.00
5 DAy(c) 225.00
6 DAy(c),Sexual 250.00
7 DAy(c) 225.00

EL BOMBO COMICS
Frances M. McQueeny, 1945
1 . . . . 175.00

ELLA CINDERS
St. John Publishing Co. 1948
1 . . . . 250.00
2 . . . . 150.00
3 . . . . 100.00
4 . . . . 100.00
5 . . . . 100.00

ELLERY QUEEN
**Superior Comics,
May–Nov., 1949**
1 LbC(c),JKa,Horror 700.00
2 . . . . 500.00
3 Drug issue 600.00
4 The Crooked Mile 500.00

ELLERY QUEEN
**Approved Comics
(Ziff-Davis),
Jan.–March, 1952**
1 NS(c),The Corpse the Killed . . 650.00
2 NS,Killer's Revenge,
　Summer, 1952 . . . . 500.00

ELSIE THE COW
**D.S. Publishing Co.,
Oct.–Nov., 1949**
1 P(c) 450.00
2 Bondage(c) 300.00
3 July–Aug., 1950 . . . . 200.00

ENCHANTING LOVE
**Kirby Publishing Co.
Oct., 1949**
1 Branded Guilty, Ph(c) 175.00
2 Ph(c),BP 100.00
3 Ph(c),Utter Defeat was Our
　Victory; Jimmy Stewart 150.00
4 . . . . 100.00
5 Ph(c) GRi 200.00
6 . . . . 100.00

ERNIE COMICS
See: SCREAM COMICS

ESCAPE FROM FEAR
**Planned Parenthood
of America, 1956**
1 . . . . 150.00
2 (1962) 100.00

ETTA KETT
**Best Books, Inc.
(Standard Comics),
Dec., 1948**
11 . . . . 150.00
12 . . . . 100.00
13 . . . . 100.00
14 Sept., 1949 . . . . 100.00

EXCITING COMICS
**Better Publ./Visual Editions
(Standard Comics),
April, 1940**
1 O:Mask, Jim Hatfield,
　Dan Williams 7,000.00
2 B:Sphinx 4,000.00
3 V:Robot 3,000.00
4 V:Sea Monster 2,500.00
5 V:Gargoyle 2,500.00
6 . . . . 2,500.00
7 AS(c) 2,000.00
8 . . . . 2,000.00
9 O:Black Terror & Tim,
　Bondage(c) 17,000.00
10 A:Black Terror 5,000.00
11 same 3,000.00
12 Bondage(c) 2,800.00
13 Bondage(c) 2,800.00
14 O:Sphinx 2,500.00
15 O:Liberator 2,600.00
16 Black Terror 2,400.00
17 same 2,400.00
18 same 2,400.00
19 same 2,400.00
20 E:Mask,Bondage(c) 2,200.00

Exciting Comics #53
© Standard Comics

21 A:Liberator 2,200.00
22 O:The Eaglet,B:American
　Eagle 2,200.00
23 Black Terror 1,800.00
24 Black Terror 1,800.00
25 Bondage(c) 1,800.00
26 ASh(c) 1,800.00
27 ASh(c) 1,800.00
28 ASh(c),B:Crime Crusader . . 2,000.00
29 ASh(c) 1,800.00
30 ASh(c),Bondage(c). 2,000.00
31 ASh(c) 1,500.00
32 ASh(c) 1,500.00
33 ASh(c) 1,500.00
34 ASh(c) 1,500.00
35 ASh(c),E:Liberator 1,500.00
36 ASh(c) 1,500.00
37 ASh(c) 1,500.00
38 ASh(c) 1,500.00
39 ASh(c)O:Kara, Jungle
　Princess 3,400.00
40 ASh(c) 3,000.00
41 ASh(c) 3,000.00
42 ASh(c),B:Scarab 3,000.00
43 ASh(c) 1,200.00
44 ASh(c) 1,200.00
45 ASh(c),V:Robot 1,200.00
46 ASh(c) 1,200.00
47 ASh(c) 1,200.00
48 ASh(c) 1,200.00
49 ASh(c),E:Kara &
　American Eagle 1,200.00
50 ASh(c),E:American Eagle . . 1,200.00
51 ASh(c),B:Miss Masque 1,500.00
52 ASh(c),Miss Masque 1,000.00
53 ASh(c),Miss Masque 1,000.00
54 ASh(c),E:Miss Masque 1,000.00
55 ASh(c),O&B:Judy o/t Jungle 1,000.00
56 ASh(c) 1,000.00
57 ASh(c) 1,000.00
58 ASh(c) 1,000.00
59 ASh(c),FF,Bondage(c) 1,200.00
60 ASh(c),The Mystery Rider . 1,000.00
61 ASh(c) 1,000.00
62 ASh(c),CQ 1,000.00
63 ASh(c) 1,000.00
64 ASh(c) 1,000.00
65 ASh(c),CQ 1,000.00
66 . . . . 1,000.00
67 GT 1,000.00
68 . . . . 1,000.00
69 Sept., 1949 . . . . 1,000.00

EXCITING ROMANCES
Fawcett Publications, 1949
1 Ph(c)	200.00
2 Ph(c)	150.00
3 WW,Ph(c).	150.00
4 Ph(c)	150.00
5 thru 7	@100.00
8 thru 10 BP	@120.00
11 thru 12	@100.00

EXCITING WAR
**Visual Editions
(Standard Comics), 1952**
5 Korean war	150.00
6	100.00
7	100.00
8 ATh.	125.00

Exploits of Daniel Boone #1
© Quality Comics Group

EXPLOITS OF DANIEL BOONE
**Comic Magazines
(Quality Comics Group), 1955**
1 Frontier hero	350.00
2	225.00
3 thru 6	@175.00

EXPLORER JOE
**Approved Comics
(Ziff-Davis), Winter, 1951**
1 NS,The Fire Opal of Madagscar	150.00
2 BK, Oct.–Nov., 1952	165.00

EXPOSED
**D.S. Publishing Co.,
March–April, 1948**
1 Corpses Cash and Carry	300.00
2 Giggling Killer	350.00
3 One Bloody Night	150.00
4 JO,Deadly Dummy	150.00
5 Body on the Beach	150.00
6 Fatal Masquerade	450.00
7 The Midnight Guest	450.00
8 Grl,The Secret in the Snow	450.00
9 The Gypsy Baron, July–Aug., 1949	450.00

EXTRA COMICS
Magazine Enterprises, 1947
1	750.00

EXTRA!
**E.C. Comics,
March–April, 1955**
1 JCr,RC,JSe	400.00
2 JCr,RC,JSe	300.00
3 JCr,RC,JSe	300.00
4 JCr,RC,JSe	300.00
5 Nov.–Dec., 1955	300.00

FACE, THE
**Publication Enterprises
(Columbia Comics), 1942**
1 MBi(c),The Face	2,000.00
2 MBi(c)	1,500.00
Becomes:

TONY TRENT
1948
3 MBi,A:The Face	350.00
4 1949	300.00

FAIRY TALE PARADE
Dell Publishing Co., 1942
1 WK,Giant	2,500.00
2 WK,Flying Horse	1,500.00
3 WK	1,000.00
4 WK	900.00
5 WK	900.00
6 WK	600.00
7 WK	600.00
8 WK	600.00
9 WK,Reluctant Dragon	600.00

FAIRY TALES
**Approved Comics
(Ziff-Davis), 1951**
10	350.00
11	300.00

FAMILY FUNNIES
Harvey Publications, 1950
1 Mandrake	200.00
2 Flash Gordon	150.00
3	125.00
4 Flash Gordon	125.00
5 Flash Gordon	125.00
6	125.00
7 Flash Gordon	125.00
8	125.00
Becomes:

TINY TOT FUNNIES
Harvey Publications, 1951
9 Dagwood (c),Flash Gordon	150.00
Becomes:

JUNIOR FUNNIES
Harvey Publications, 1951–52
10 Blondie, Popeye	100.00
11	100.00
12	100.00
13	100.00

FAMOUS COMICS
Whitman Publ. Co., 1934
1 3"x8", three per box	1,200.00
2	1,000.00
3	1,000.00

FAMOUS COMICS
Zain-Eppy Publ.
N# Joe Palooka	600.00

FAMOUS CRIMES
**Fox Features Syndicate,
June, 1948**
1 Cold Blooded Killer	700.00
2 Near Nudity (c)	550.00

3 Crime Never Pays	650.00
4	300.00
5	300.00
6	300.00
7 Drug issue	550.00
8 thru 19	@300.00
20 Aug., 1951	250.00
51 1952	200.00

FAMOUS FAIRY TALES
K.K. Publication Co., 1942
N# WK, Giveaway	500.00
N# WK, Giveaway	400.00
N# WK, Giveaway	400.00

FAMOUS FEATURE STORIES
Dell Publishing Co., 1938
1A:Tarzan, Terry and the Pirates Dick Tracy,Smilin' Jack	2,500.00

FAMOUS FUNNIES
Eastern Color Printing Co., 1933
N# A Carnival of Comics	60,000.00
N# Feb., 1934, 1st 10-cent comic	50,000.00
1 July, 1934	35,000.00
2	15,000.00
3 B:Buck Rogers	12,000.00
4 Football (c)	5,000.00
5 Christmas	4,500.00
6	3,000.00
7	3,000.00
8	3,000.00
9	3,000.00
10	3,000.00
11 Four pages of Buck Rogers	1,500.00
12 Four pages of Buck Rogers	1,500.00
13	1,200.00
14	1,200.00
15 Football (c)	1,200.00
16	1,200.00
17 Christmas (c)	1,200.00
18 Four pages of Buck Rogers	1,500.00
19	1,200.00
20	1,200.00
21 Baseball	1,100.00
22 Buck Rogers	1,300.00
23	1,100.00
24 B: War on Crime	1,100.00
25	1,100.00
26	1,100.00

Famous Funnies #35
© Eastern Color Printing

All comics prices listed are for *Near Mint* condition.

27 G-Men (c)	1,100.00
28	1,100.00
29 Christmas	1,100.00
30	1,100.00
31	800.00
32 Phantom Magician	1,000.00
33 A:Baby Face Nelson & John Dillinger	800.00
34	800.00
35 Buck Rogers	900.00
36	800.00
37	800.00
38 Portrait,Buck Rogers	900.00
39	800.00
40	800.00
41 thru 50	@700.00
51 thru 57	@600.00
58 Baseball (c)	600.00
59	600.00
60	600.00
61	500.00
62	500.00
63	500.00
64	500.00
65 JK	500.00
66	500.00
67	500.00
68 JK	500.00
69	500.00
70	500.00
71 BEv	400.00
72 BEv,B:Speed Spaulding	400.00
73 BEv	400.00
74 BEv	400.00
75 BEv	400.00
76 BEv	400.00
77 BEv,Merry Christmas (c)	400.00
78 BEv	400.00
79 BEv	400.00
80 BEv,Buck Rogers	400.00
81 O:Invisible Scarlet O'Neil	300.00
82 Buck Rogers (c)	400.00
83 Dickie Dare	250.00
84 Scotty Smith	250.00
85 Eagle Scout,Roy Rogers	250.00
86 Moon Monsters	250.00
87 Scarlet O'Neil	250.00
88 Dickie Dare	250.00
89 O:Fearless Flint	250.00
90 Bondage (c)	350.00
91	250.00
92	250.00
93	250.00
94 War Bonds	300.00
95 Invisible Scarlet O'Neil	200.00
96	200.00
97 War Bonds Promo	200.00
98	200.00
99	200.00
100 Anniversary issue	200.00
101 thru 110	@200.00
111 thru 130	@125.00
131 thru 150	@100.00
151 thru 162	@100.00
163 Valentine's Day (c)	100.00
164	100.00
165	100.00
166	100.00
167	100.00
168	100.00
169 AW	125.00
170 AW	125.00
171 thru 190	@150.00
191 thru 203	@125.00
204 War (c)	100.00
205	100.00
206	100.00
207	100.00
208	100.00
209 FF(c),Buck Rogers	3,000.00
210 FF(c),Buck Rogers	3,000.00
211 FF(c),Buck Rogers	3,000.00

Famous Funnies #209
© Easter Color Printing

212 FF(c),Buck Rogers	3,000.00
213 FF(c),Buck Rogers	3,000.00
214 FF(c),Buck Rogers	3,000.00
215 FF(c),Buck Rogers	3,000.00
216 FF(c),Buck Rogers	3,000.00
217	100.00
218 July, 1955	100.00

FAMOUS GANGSTERS
Avon Periodicals, 1951

1 Al Capone, Dillinger, Luciano & Shultz	500.00
2 WW(c),Dillinger Machine-Gun Killer	450.00
3 Lucky Luciano & Murder Inc	450.00

Becomes:

CRIME ON
THE WATERFRONT
May, 1952

4 Underworld Gangsters who Control the Shipment of Drugs!	400.00

FAMOUS STARS
Ziff-Davis Publ. Co., 1950

1 OW,Shelley Winter,Susan Peters & Shirley Temple	1,000.00
2 BEv,Betty Hutton, Bing Crosby	750.00
3 OW,Judy Garland, Alan Ladd	800.00
4 RC,Jolson, Bob Mitchum	750.00
5 BK,Elizabeth Taylor, Esther Williams	900.00
6 Gene Kelly, Spring, 1952	700.00

FAMOUS STORIES
Dell Publishing Co., 1942

1 Treasure Island	400.00
2 Tom Sawyer	375.00

FAMOUS WESTERN
BADMEN
See: REDSKIN

FANTASTIC
See: CAPTAIN SCIENCE

FANTASTIC COMICS
Fox Features Syndicate, 1939

1 LF(c),I&O:Samson,B:Star Dust, Super Wizard, Space Smith & Capt. Kid	9,000.00

2 BP,LF(c),Samson Destroyed the Battery & Routed the Foe	4,500.00
3 BP,LF(c),Slays the Iron Monster	12,000.00
4 GT,LF(c),Demolishes the Closing Torture Walls	3,000.00
5 GT,LF(c),Crumbles the Mighty War Machine	2,700.00
6 JSm(c),Bondage(c)	2,500.00
7 JSm(c)	2,500.00
8 GT,Destroys the Mask of Fire,Bondage(c)	2,000.00
9 Mighty Muscles saved the Drowning Girl	2,000.00
10 I&O:David	2,000.00
11 Wrecks the Torture Machine to save his fellow American	1,800.00
12 Heaved the Huge Ship high into the Air	1,800.00
13 Samson(c)	1,800.00
14 Samson(c)	1,800.00
15 Samson(c)	1,800.00
16 E:Stardust	1,800.00
17 Samson(c)	1,800.00
18 I:Black Fury & Chuck	1,800.00
19 Samson(c)	1,700.00
20 Samson(c)	1,700.00
21 B&I: The Banshee,Hitler(c)	2,000.00
22 Hittler & Samson(c)	1,800.00
23 O:The Gladiator, Hitler (c) Nov., 1941	2,000.00

FANTASTIC FEARS
Farrell Publications (Ajax), 1953
(Formerly: CAPTAIN JET)

1 (7) Tales of Stalking Terror	650.00
2 (8)	450.00
3	325.00
4	325.00
5 SD,1st art	1,200.00
6 Decapitation	750.00
7	325.00
8 Decapitation	500.00
9	325.00

Becomes:

FANTASTIC COMICS
Ajax, 1954

10 Tales of Enchantment	250.00
11 Amazing Adventures	300.00

FANTASTIC WORLDS
Visual Editions
(Standard Comics), 1952–53

5 ATh,Triumph Over Terror, Sci-fi	450.00
6 ATh,The Cosmic Terror	400.00
7 The Asteroid God	250.00

FANTOMAN
See: AMAZING
ADVENTURE FUNNIES

FARGO KID
See: JUSTICE TRAPS
THE GUILTY

FAST FICTION
Seaboard Publ., Oct., 1949

1 Scarlet Pimpernel	500.00
2 HcK,Captain Blood	400.00
3 She	500.00
4 The 39 Steps	350.00
5 HcK,Beau Geste	350.00

Becomes:

GOLDEN AGE

STORIES BY FAMOUS AUTHORS ILLUSTRATED

Famous Author Illustrated, Aug., 1950

1a Scarlet Pimpernel	400.00
2a Captain Blood	400.00
3a She	500.00
4a The 39 Steps	325.00
5a Beau Geste	300.00
6 HcK,MacBeth	325.00
7 HcK,Window	275.00
8 HcK,Hamlet	300.00
9 Nicholas Nickleby	275.00
10 HcK,Romeo & Juliet	275.00
11 GS,Ben Hur	290.00
12 GS,La Svengali	275.00
13 HcK,Scaramouche	275.00

FAT AND SLAT JOKE BOOK

William H. Wise, 1944

N#	500.00

FAT AND SLAT

Fables Publ., Inc. (E.C. Comics), 1947

1 I&O:Voltage, Man of Lightning	450.00
2	300.00
3	300.00
4	300.00

Becomes:

GUNFIGHTER

Fables Publ., Inc. (E.C. Comics), 1948–50

5 JCr(c),Wild West	700.00
6 Grl,JCr(c),Moon Girl	500.00
7 AF,Grl	500.00
8 AF,Grl	500.00
9 AF,Grl	500.00
10 JCr,AF,Grl	500.00
11 AF,Grl	500.00
12 Grl	500.00
13 JCr,WW,Grl	550.00
14 JCr,WW,Grl,Bondage	550.00

Becomes:

HAUNT OF FEAR

FAVORITE COMICS

1934

1 Giveaways,Nebbs,Joe Palooka	1,500.00
2 same	1,000.00
3 same	1,000.00

FAWCETT FUNNY ANIMALS

Fawcett Publications, Dec., 1942

1 I:Hoppy the Marvel Bunny, Captain Marvel (c)	1,200.00
2 X-Mas Issue	600.00
3 Spirit of '43	500.00
4 and 5	@500.00
6 Buy War Bonds and Stamps	400.00
7	400.00
8 Flag (c)	400.00
9 and 10	@400.00
11 thru 20	@250.00
21 thru 30	@200.00
31 thru 40	@200.00
41 thru 83	@150.00

Charlton Comics

84	150.00
85 thru 91 Feb., 1956	@100.00

FAWCETT MINIATURES

Fawcett Publ. (Wheaties Giveaways), 1946

1 Capt. Marvel	250.00
2 Capt. Marvel	250.00
3 Capt. Marvel Jr.	250.00
4 Delecta of the Planets	400.00

FAWCETT MOVIE COMICS

Fawcett Publications, 1949

N# Dakota Lil	375.00
N#a Copper Canyon	300.00
N# Destination the Moon	1,200.00
N# Montana	300.00
N# Pioneer Marshal	300.00
N# Powder River Rustlers	450.00
N# Singing Guns	275.00
7 Gunmen of Abilene	325.00
8 King of the Bull Whip	450.00
9 BP,The Old Frontier	300.00
10 The Missourians	300.00
11 The Thundering Trail	400.00
12 Rustlers on Horseback	325.00
13 Warpath	250.00
14 Last Outpost,RonaldReagan	550.00
15 The Man from Planet-X	3,500.00
16 10 Tall Men	200.00
17 Rose Cimarron	150.00
18 The Brigand	175.00
19 Carbine Williams	175.00
20 Ivanhoe, Dec., 1952	300.00

FEATURE BOOKS

David McKay Publications, May, 1937

N# Dick Tracy	10,000.00
N# Popeye	9,000.00
1 Zane Grey's King of the Royal Mounted	800.00
2 Popeye	1,200.00
3 Popeye and the "Jeep"	1,000.00
4 Dick Tracy	2,000.00
5 Popeye and his Poppa	1,000.00
6 Dick Tracy	1,200.00
7 Little Orphan Annie	1,400.00
8 Secret Agent X-9	750.00
9 Tracy & the Famon Boys	1,200.00
10 Popeye & Susan	1,000.00
11 Annie Rooney	350.00
12 Blondie	1,100.00
13 Inspector Wade	325.00
14 Popeye in Wild Oats	1,200.00
15 Barney Baxter in the Air	500.00
16 Red Eagle	400.00
17 Gang Busters	900.00
18 Mandrake the Magician	850.00
19 Mandrake	850.00
20 The Phantom	1,200.00
21 Lone Ranger	1,100.00
22 The Phantom	900.00
23 Mandrake in Teibe Castle	850.00
24 Lone Ranger	1,100.00
25 Flash Gordon on the Planet Mongo	1,500.00
26 Prince Valiant	1,300.00
27 Blondie	250.00
28 Blondie and Dagwood	250.00
29 Blondie at the Home Sweet Home	250.00
30 Katzenjammer Kids	250.00
31 Blondie Keeps the Home Fires Burning	250.00
32 Katzenjammer Kids	200.00
33 Romance of Flying	200.00
34 Blondie Home is Our Castle	250.00
35 Katzenjammer Kids	200.00
36 Blondie on the Home Front	225.00
37 Katzenjammer Kids	250.00
38 Blondie the ModelHomemaker	225.00

Feature Books #57
© David McKay Publications

39 The Phantom	700.00
40 Blondie	225.00
41 Katzenjammer Kids	250.00
42 Blondie in Home-Spun Yarns	225.00
43 Blondie Home-Cooked Scraps	225.00
44 Katzenjammer Kids in Monkey Business	250.00
45 Blondie in Home of the Free and the Brave	225.00
46 Mandrake in Fire World	500.00
47 Blondie in Eaten Out of House and Home	225.00
48 The Maltese Falcon	1,200.00
49 Perry Mason - The Case of the Lucky Legs	350.00
50 The Shoplifters Shoe, P. Mason	350.00
51 Rip Kirby - Mystery of the Mangler	350.00
52 Mandrake in the Land of X	450.00
53 Phantom in Safari Suspense	500.00
54 Rip Kirby - Case of the Master Menace	425.00
55 Mandrake in 5-Numbers Treasue Hunt	450.00
56 Phantom Destroys the Sky Band	500.00
57 Phantom in the Blue Gang, 1948	500.00

FEATURE FUNNIES

Harry A. Chesler Publ./ Comic Favorites, Oct., 1937

1 RuG(a&c),A:Joe Palooka, Mickey Finn, Bungles, Dixie Dugan, Big Top, Strange as It Seems, Off the Record	3,600.00
2 A: The Hawk	1,700.00
3 WE,Joe Palooka,The Clock	1,300.00
4 RuG,WE,RuG(c),JoePalooka	1,300.00
5 WE, Joe Palooka drawing	1,300.00
6 WE, Joe Palooka (c)	1,300.00
7 WE,LLe, Gallant Knight story by Vernon Henkel	1,000.00
8 WE	1,000.00
9 WE, Joe Palooka story	1,200.00
10 WE,Micky Finn(c)	1,000.00
11 WE,LLe,The Bungles(c)	1,000.00
12 WE, Joe Palooka(c)	1,000.00
13 WE,LLe, World Series(c)	1,100.00
14 WE,Ned Brant(c)	800.00
15 WE,Joe Palooka(c)	900.00
16 Mickey Finn(c)	800.00
17 WE	800.00
18 Joe Palooka (c)	900.00

All comics prices listed are for *Near Mint* condition.

GOLDEN AGE

Feature Comics #44
© Quality Comics Group

19 WE,LLe,Mickey Finn(c)......	800.00
20 WE,LLe	800.00

Becomes:

FEATURE COMICS
Quality Comics Group,
June. 1939–May, 1950

21 Joe Palooka(c)...........	1,200.00
22 LLe(c),Mickey Finn(c)......	700.00
23 B:Charlie Chan	700.00
24 AIA,Joe Palooka(c)	700.00
25 AIA,The Clock(c).........	700.00
26 AIA,The Bundles(c)........	700.00
27 WE,AIA,I:Doll Man	7,500.00
28 LF,AIA,The Clock(c)......	2,500.00
29 LF,AIA,The Clock(c)......	1,400.00
30 LF,AIA,Doll Man(c)	1,800.00
31 LF,AIA,Mickey Finn(c)	1,000.00
32 PGv,LF,GFx,Doll Man(c)....	900.00
33 PGv,LF,GFx,Bundles(c)	750.00
34 PGv,LF,GFx,Doll Man(c)....	900.00
35 PGv,LF,GFx,Bundles(c)....	750.00
36 PGv,LF,GFx,Doll Man(c)....	900.00
37 PGv,LF,GFx,Bundles(c)....	750.00
38 PGv,GFx,Doll Man(c)	700.00
39 PGv,GFx,Bundles(c).......	700.00
40 PGv,GFx,WE(c),Doll Man(c) .	700.00
41 PGv,GFx,WE(c),Bundles(c) . .	500.00
42 GFx,Doll Man(c)	500.00
43 RC,GFx,Bundles(c).......	425.00
44 RC,GFx,Doll Man(c).......	750.00
45 RC,GFx,Bundles(c).......	400.00
46 RC,PGv,GFx,Doll Man(c)	600.00
47 RC,GFx,Bundles(c).......	400.00
48 RC,GFx,Doll Man(c)	600.00
49 RC,GFx,Bundles(c).......	400.00
50 RC,GFx,Doll Man(c)	600.00
51 RC,GFx,Bundles(c).......	400.00
52 RC,GFx,Doll Man(c)	500.00
53 RC,GFx,Bundles(c).......	325.00
54 RC,GFx,Doll Man(c)	500.00
55 RC,GFx,Bundles(c).......	325.00
56 RC,GFx,Doll Man(c)	500.00
57 RC,GFx,Bundles(c).......	325.00
58 RC,GFx,Doll Man (c)	500.00
59 RC,GFx,Mickey Finn(c)	325.00
60 RC,GFx,Doll Man(c)	500.00
61 RC,GFx,Bundles(c).......	350.00
62 RC,GFx,Doll Man(c)	500.00
63 RC,GFx,Bundles(c).......	350.00
64 BP,GFx,Doll Man(c)	600.00
65 BP,GFx(c),Bundles(c).....	300.00
66 BP,GFx,Doll Man(c)	400.00
67 BP....................	300.00
68 BP,Doll Man vs.Bearded	
Lady................	700.00
69 BP,GFx(c),Devil (c)........	300.00

70 BP,Doll Man(c)	700.00
71 BP,GFx(c)...............	300.00
72 BP,Doll Man(c)	500.00
73 BP,GFx(c),Bundles(c).....	250.00
74 Doll Man(c).............	500.00
75 GFx(c).................	300.00
76 GFx(c).................	300.00
77 Doll Man (c) until #140.....	400.00
78 Knows no Fear but the	
Knife Does............	300.00
79 Little Luck God	300.00
80	300.00
81 Wanted for Murder	250.00
82 V:Shawunkas the Shaman . . .	250.00
83 V:Mechanical Man	250.00
84 V:Masked Rider, Death	
Goes to the Rodeo	250.00
85 V:King of Beasts	250.00
86 Is He A Killer?...........	250.00
87 The Maze of Murder	250.00
88 V:The Phantom Killer	250.00
89 Crook's Goose	250.00
90 V:Whispering Corpse	250.00
91 V:The Undertaker	250.00
92 V:The Image	250.00
93	250.00
94 V:The Undertaker	250.00
95 Flatten's the Peacock's Pride .	250.00
96 Doll Man Proves	
Justice is Blind..........	250.00
97 V:Peacock..............	250.00
98 V:Master Diablo	250.00
99 On the Warpath Again!.....	250.00
100 Crushes the City of Crime .	300.00
101 Land of the Midget Men!...	200.00
102 The Angle	200.00
103 V:The Queen of Ants	200.00
104 V:The Botanist	200.00
105 Dream of Death	200.00
106 V:The Sword Fish	200.00
107 Hand of Horror!..........	200.00
108 V:Cateye	200.00
109 V:The Brain	200.00
110 V:Fat Cat	200.00
111 V:The Undertaker	200.00
112 I:Mr. Curio & His Miniatures .	200.00
113 V:Highwayman	200.00
114 V:Tom Thumb	200.00
115 V:The Sphinx...........	200.00
116 V:Elbows..............	200.00
117 Polka Dot on the Spot.....	200.00
118 thru 144	@ 200.00

A FEATURE PRESENTATION
Fox Features Syndicate, 1950

1 (5) The Black Tarantula	700.00
2 (6) WW,Moby Dick.........	600.00
3 Jungle Thrills, bondage	500.00

FEDERAL MEN COMICS
Gerard Publ. Co., 1942

2 S&S,Spanking	800.00

FELIX THE CAT
Dell Publishing Co.,
Feb.–March, 1948

1	450.00
2	300.00
3	200.00
4	200.00
5	200.00
6 thru 10	@175.00
11 thru 19	@150.00

Toby Press

20 thru 30................	@350.00
31	150.00
32	350.00
33	350.00
34	150.00

Felix the Cat #11
© Dell Publishing Co.

35.....................	150.00
36.....................	300.00
37 Giant, Christmas(c)........	750.00
38.....................	300.00
39.....................	300.00
40 thru 60................	@300.00
61.....................	275.00

Harvey, 1955

62 thru 80................	@125.00
81 thru 99................	@100.00
100	125.00
101 thru 118..............	@100.00
Spec., 100 pgs, 1952........	350.00
Summer Ann., 100 pgs. 1953 ...	650.00
Winter Ann.,#2 100 pgs, 1954. . .	600.00

FELIX AND HIS FRIENDS
Toby, 1953

1 F:Felix the Cat.............	350.00
2	400.00
3	400.00

FERDINAND THE BULL
Dell Publishing Co., 1938

1	500.00

FIGHT AGAINST CRIME
Story Comics, May, 1951

1 Scorpion of Crime Inspector	
"Brains" Carroway	700.00
2 Ganglands Double Cross	400.00
3 Killer Dolan's Double Cross . .	300.00
4 Hopped Up Killers - The	
Con's Slaughter,Drug issue .	400.00
5 FF,Horror o/t Avenging Corpse	400.00
6 Terror of the Crazy Killer	250.00
7	250.00
8 Killer with the Two-Bladed	
Knife	250.00
9 Rats Die by Gas,Horror......	600.00
10 Horror of the Con's Revenge .	600.00
11 Case of the Crazy Killer	600.00
12 Horror,Drug issue	700.00
13 The Bloodless Killer	600.00
14 Electric Chair (c)...........	700.00
15	600.00
16 RA,Bondage(c)...........	700.00
17 Knife in Neck(c)	700.00
18 Attempted Hanging (c)	700.00
19 Bondage(c).............	700.00
20 Severed Head (c)	1,000.00
21	500.00

Becomes:

FIGHT AGAINST THE GUILTY
Dec., 1954
22 RA,Electric Chair 500.00
23 March, 1955 . . . . 350.00

FIGHT COMICS
Fiction House Magazines, Jan., 1940
1 LF,GT,WE(c),O:Spy Fighter . 7,000.00
2 GT,WE(c),Joe Lewis 3,000.00
3 WE(c),GT,B:Rip Regan,
   The Powerman 2,600.00
4 GT,LF(c) 2,500.00
5 WE(c) 2,500.00
6 GT,BP(c) 1,500.00
7 GT,BP(c),Powerman-Blood
   Money 1,500.00
8 GT,Chip Collins-Lair of
   the Vulture 1,500.00
9 GT,Chip Collins-Prey of the
   War Eagle 1,500.00
10 GT,Wolves of the Yukon . . . 1,500.00
11 . . . . 1,200.00
12 RA,Powerman-Monster of
   Madness 1,600.00
13 Shark Broodie-Legion
   of Satan 1,200.00
14 Shark Broodie-Lagoon
   of Death 1,200.00
15 Super-American-Hordes of
   the Secret Dicator 1,500.00
16 B:Capt. Fight, Swastika
   Plague 1,500.00
17 Super-American-Blaster of
   the Pig-Boat Pirates 1,500.00
18 Shark Broodie-Plague of
   the Yellow Devils 1,500.00
19 E:Capt. Fight 1,500.00
20 . . . . 1,100.00
21 Rip Carson-Hell's Sky-Riders . 900.00
22 Rip Carson-Sky Devil's
   Mission 900.00
23 Rip Carson Angels of
   Vengeance. 900.00
24 Baynonets for the Banzai
   Breed! Bondage(c) 1,500.00
25 Rip Carson-Samurai
   Showdown 1,000.00
26 Rip Carson-Fury of
   the Sky-Brigade 1,000.00
27 War-Loot for the Mikado
   Bondage(c). 2,000.00
28 Rip Carson. 1,000.00

Fight Comics #47
© Fiction House Magazines

29 Rip Carson-Charge of the
   Lost Region 1,000.00
30 Rip Carson-Jeep-Raiders of
   the Torture Jungle 1,000.00
31 Gangway for the Gyrenes,
   Decapitation (c) 1,500.00
32 Vengeance of the Hun-
   Hunters,Bondage(c) 1,500.00
33 B:Tiger Girl 750.00
34 Bondage(c) 1,000.00
35 MB. 750.00
36 MB. 750.00
37 MB. 750.00
38 MB,Bondage(c) 1,000.00
39 MB,Senorita Rio-Slave Brand
   of the Spider Cult. 750.00
40 MB,Bondage (c) 1,000.00
41 MB,Bondage (c). 1,000.00
42 MB. 600.00
43 MB,Senorita Rio-The Fire-Brides
   of the Lost Atlantis,
   Bondage(c) 500.00
44 MB,R:Capt. Fight 600.00
45 MB,Tonight Don Diablo Rides. 600.00
46 MB. 600.00
47 MB,SenoritaRio-Horror's
   Hacienda 600.00
48 MB. 600.00
49 MB,JKa,B:Tiger Girl(c) 600.00
50 MB. 600.00
51 MB,O:Tiger Girl. 800.00
52 MB,Winged Demons of Doom 375.00
53 MB,Shadowland Shrine 375.00
54 MB,Flee the Cobra Fury 375.00
55 MB,Jungle Juggernaut 375.00
56 MB. 375.00
57 MB,Jewels of Jeopardy. 375.00
58 MB. 375.00
59 MB,Vampires ofCrystalCavern 375.00
60 MB,Kraal of DeadlyDiamonds 375.00
61 MB,Seekers of the Sphinx,
   O:Tiger Girl 750.00
62 MB,Graveyard of the
   Tree Tribe 500.00
63 MB. 500.00
64 MB,DawnBeast from
   Karama-Zan! 500.00
65 Beware the Congo Girl 350.00
66 Man or Ape! 350.00
67 Head-Hunters of Taboo Trek . 350.00
68 Fangs of Dr. Voodoo 350.00
69 Cage of the Congo Fury 350.00
70 Kraal of Traitor Tusks 350.00
71 Captives for the Golden
   Crocodile 350.00
72 Land of the Lost Safaris 350.00
73 War-Gods of the Jungle 350.00
74 Advengers of the Jungle 350.00
75 Perils of Momba-Kzar 350.00
76 Kraal of Zombi-Zaro 350.00
77 Slave-Queen of the Ape Man . 350.00
78 Great Congo Diamond
   Robbery 500.00
79 A:Space Rangers 600.00
80 . . . . 300.00
81 E:Tiger Girl(c) 300.00
82 RipCarson-CommandoStrike . 300.00
83 NobodyLoves a Minesweeper 300.00
84 Rip Carson-Suicide Patrol . . . 300.00
85 . . . . 300.00
86 GE,Tigerman,Summer,1954 . . 350.00

FIGHTIN' AIR FORCE
Charlton Comics, 1956–60
3 . . . . 150.00
4 thru 10 . . . . @100.00
11 giant 125.00
12 US,Russia Nuclear attack. . . . 200.00
13 thru 20 . . . . @100.00
21 thru 30 . . . . @100.00

FIGHTING AMERICAN
Headline Publications (Prize), April–May, 1954
1 S&K,O:Fighting American &
   Speedboy 2,500.00
2 S&K(a&c) 1,200.00
3 S&K(a&c) 850.00
4 S&K(a&c) 850.00
5 S&K(a&c) 850.00
6 S&K(a&c),O:Fighting
   American 825.00
7 S&K(a&c), April–May, 1955 . . 750.00

FIGHTING FRONTS!
Harvey Publications, 1952–53
1 War 200.00
2 BP,violence 250.00
3 BP 150.00
4 . . . . 125.00
5 . . . . 125.00

FIGHTING DAVY CROCKETT
See: KIT CARSON

FIGHTING INDIANS OF THE WILD WEST
Avon Periodicals, March, 1952
1 EK,EL,Geronimo, Crazy Horse,
   Chief Victorio 200.00
2 EK,Same, Nov., 1952 . . . . 150.00

FIGHTING LEATHERNECKS
Toby Press, Feb., 1952
1 JkS,Duke's Diary 150.00
2 . . . . 125.00
3 . . . . 100.00
4 . . . . 100.00
5 . . . . 100.00
6 Dec., 1952 . . . . 100.00

THE FIGHTING MAN
Excellent Publications (Ajax/Farrell), 1952–53
1 War 150.00
2 . . . . 125.00
3 thru 8 . . . . @100.00
Ann.#1 (1952) 300.00

FIGHTIN' TEXAN
See: TEXAN, THE

FIGHTING UNDERSEA COMMANDOS
Avon Periodicals, 1952–53
1 Navy Frogmen 175.00
2 . . . . 125.00
3 . . . . 100.00
4 BK 110.00
5 . . . . 100.00

FIGHTING WAR STORIES
Men's Publications, 1952
1 . . . . 150.00
2 thru 5 . . . . @100.00

FIGHTING YANK
Nedor Publ./Better Publ. (Standard Comics) Sept., 1942
1 JaB,B:Fighting Yank, A:Wonder
   Man, Mystico, bondage (c). 6,000.00
2 JaB 3,200.00
3 Shark, bondage (c). 3,000.00
4 ASh(c), bondage (c) 3,000.00

Fighting Yank #11
© *Nedor Publications*

5 ASh(c) 1,600.00
6 ASh(c) 1,600.00
7 ASh(c),Bomb(c) 1,500.00
8 ASh(c), bondage(c). 1,600.00
9 ASh(c) 1,500.00
10 ASh(c),bondage-torture(c) . . 1,600.00
11 ASh(c), A:Grim Reaper,
    bondage (c) 1,500.00
12 ASh(c), Hirohito bondage (c) 1,500.00
13 ASh(c),kid bondage,snake(c)1,500.00
14 ASh(c) 1,000.00
15 ASh(c),bondage-torture(c) . . 1,500.00
16 ASh(c),. 1,000.00
17 ASh(c),bondage(c). 1,500.00
18 ASh(c), A:American Eagle . . 1,200.00
19 ASh(c) 1,000.00
20 ASh(c) Shark 1,000.00
21 ASh(c) A:Kara,Jungle
    Princess 1,000.00
22 ASh(c) A:Miss Masque-
    (c) story 1,400.00
23 ASh(c) Klu Klux Klan
    parody (c) 1,900.00
24 ASh(c),A:Miss Masque 800.00
25 ASh(c),JRo,MMe,A:Cavalier 1,500.00
26 ASh(c),JRo,MMe,A:Cavalier . . 800.00
27 ASh(c),JRo,MMe,A:Cavalier . . 800.00
28 ASh(c),JRo,MMe,AW
    A:Cavalier. 1,000.00
29 ASh(c),JRo,MMe,Aug., 1949 1,000.00

FILM STAR ROMANCES
Star Publications, 1950
1 LbC(c), Rudy Valentino story . 650.00
2 Liz Taylor & Robert Taylor,
    photo (c) 725.00
3 May–June, 1950, photo(c). . . . 350.00

FIREHAIR COMICS
Flying Stories, Inc.
(Fiction House Magazine),
Winter, 1948–Spring, 1952
1 I:Firehair, Riders on the
    Pony Express 750.00
2 Bride of the Outlaw Guns 400.00
3 Kiss of the Six-Gun Siren! . . . 350.00
4 . . . . 350.00
5 . . . . 350.00
6 . . . . 325.00
7 War Drums at Buffalo Bend . . 250.00
8 Raid on the Red Arrows 250.00
9 French Flags and Tomahawks 250.00
10 Slave Maiden of the Crees . . . 250.00
11 Wolves of the Overland Trail. . 250.00

5 CENT COMICS
Fawcett Publications, 1940
1 B&W, I:Dan Dare, very rare 10,000.00

FLAME, THE
Fox Feature Syndicate,
Summer, 1940
1 LF,O:The Flame 7,000.00
2 GT,LF,Wing Turner 3,000.00
3 BP,Wonderworld 2,500.00
4 . . . . 2,500.00
5 GT 2,500.00
6 GT 2,500.00
7 A:The Yank 2,500.00
8 The Finger of the Frozen
    Death!, Jan., 1942 . . . . 2,500.00

FLAME, THE
Ajax/Farrell, 1954–55
1 (#5) superhero,O:Flame 650.00
2 . . . . 375.00
3 . . . . 350.00

FLAMING LOVE
Comic Magazines
(Quality Comics Group),
Dec., 1949
1 BWa,BWa(c),The Temptress
    I Feared in His Arms 500.00
2 Torrid Tales of Turbulent
    Passion 250.00
3 BWa,RC,My Heart's at Sea . . 350.00
4 One Women Who Made a
    Mockery of Love, Ph(c) 250.00
5 Bridge of Longing, Ph(c) 250.00
6 Men Both Loved & Feared Me,
    Oct., 1950 . . . . 250.00

FLAMING WESTERN ROMANCES
Star Publ., 1950
3 LbC,Robert Taylor Photo(c) . . . 500.00

FLASH GORDON
Harvey Publications,
Oct., 1950
1 AR,Bondage(c) 600.00
2 AR 300.00
3 AR Bondage(c) 400.00
4 AR, April, 1951 . . . . 275.00

FLASH GORDON
Dell Publishing Co., 1953
2 . . . . 200.00
See also FOUR COLOR

FLIP
Harvey Publications,
April, 1954
1 HN 275.00
2 HN,BP,June, 1954 . . . . 275.00

FLY BOY
Approved Comics
(Ziff-Davis) Spring, 1952
1 NS(c),Angels without Wings . . 300.00
2 NS(c),Flyboy's Flame-Out,
    Oct.–Nov., 1952 . . . . 200.00

FLYING ACES
Key Publications, 1955–56
1 War 125.00
2 . . . . 100.00
3 . . . . 100.00
4 . . . . 100.00
5 . . . . 100.00

FLYING A'S RANGE RIDER, THE
Dell Publishing Co.,
June–Aug., 1953
(1) = *Dell Four Color #404*
2 Ph(c) all 200.00
3 . . . . 150.00
4 thru 10 . . . . @125.00
11 thru 16 . . . . @100.00
17 ATh 150.00
19 thru 24 . . . . @100.00

FLYING CADET
Flying Cadet Publ. Co., 1943
1 Aviation for student Airmen . . . 200.00
2 . . . . 150.00
3 Photo(c) 125.00
4 Photo(c) 125.00
5 Photo(c) 125.00
6a Photo(c) 125.00
6b Photo(c) 125.00
7 Photo(c) 125.00
8 Photo(c) 125.00
9 Photo(c) 125.00
10 thru 16 . . . . @100.00
17 nudity-woman 300.00

FLYIN' JENNY
Pentagon Publ. Co, 1946
N# 300.00
2 . . . . 350.00

FLYING MODELS
Health-Knowledge
Publications, 1954
1 . . . . 200.00

FOODINI
Continental Publications,
March, 1950
1 TV Puppet 300.00
2 Jingle Dingle 150.00
3 . . . . 100.00
4 Aug., 1950 . . . . 100.00

FOOTBALL THRILLS
Approved Comics
(Ziff-Davis),
Fall-Winter, 1952
1 BP,NS(c),Red Grange story . . 350.00
2 NS(c),Bronko Nagurski,
    Spring,1952 . . . . 250.00

FORBIDDEN LOVE
Comic Magazine
(Quality Comics Group),
March, 1950
1 RC,Ph(c),Heartbreak Road . 1,100.00
2 Ph(c),I Loved a Gigolo 900.00
3 Kissless Bride 550.00
4 BWa,Brimstone Kisses,
    Sept., 1950 . . . . 575.00

FORBIDDEN WORLDS
American Comics Group,
July–Aug., 1951
1 AW,FF 2,500.00
2 . . . . 1,200.00
3 AW,WW,JD 1,400.00
4 Werewolf (c) 750.00
5 AW 850.00
6 AW,King Kong (c) 750.00
7 . . . . 500.00
8 . . . . 500.00
9 Atomic Bomb 600.00
10 JyD 375.00
11 The Mummy's Treasure 325.00

12 Chest of Death 325.00	96 AW 175.00
13 Invasion from Hades 325.00	97 thru 115 . . . . @150.00
14 Million-Year Monster 325.00	116 OW(c)A:Herbie 160.00
15 The Vampire Cat 325.00	117 . . . . 150.00
16 The Doll 325.00	118 . . . . 150.00
17 . . . . 325.00	119 . . . . 150.00
18 The Mummy 325.00	120 thru 124 . . . . @150.00
19 Pirate and the Voodoo Queen 325.00	125 I:O:Magic Man 150.00
20 Terror Island 325.00	126 A:Magic Man 150.00
21 The Ant Master 300.00	127 same 150.00
22 The Cursed Casket 300.00	128 same 150.00
23 Nightmare for Two 300.00	129 same 150.00
24 . . . . 300.00	130 same 150.00
25 Hallahan's Head 300.00	131 same 150.00
26 The Champ 300.00	132 same 150.00
27 SMo,The Thing with the	133 I:O:Dragona 150.00
Golden Hair 300.00	134 A:Magic Man 150.00
28 Portrait of Carlotta 300.00	135 A:Magic Man 150.00
29 The Frogman 300.00	136 A:Nemesis 150.00
30 The Things on the Beach . . . 300.00	137 SD,A:Magic Man 175.00
31 SMo,The Circle of the	138 SD,A:Magic Man 175.00
Doomed 275.00	139 A:Magic Man 150.00
32 The Invasion of the	140 SD,A:Mark Midnight 175.00
Dead Things 275.00	141 thru 145 . . . . @150.00
33 . . . . 275.00	
34 Atomic Bomb 350.00	**FOREIGN INTRIGUES**
35 Comics Code 300.00	**See: DYNAMITE**
36 thru 62 . . . . @200.00	
63 AW 200.00	**FOUR COLOR**
64 . . . . 150.00	**Dell Publishing Co., 1939**
65 . . . . 150.00	N# Dick Tracy 15,000.00
66 . . . . 150.00	N# Don Winslow of the Navy . 2,500.00
67 . . . . 150.00	N# Myra North 1,300.00
68 OW(c) 150.00	4 Disney's Donald Duck
69 AW 200.00	(1940) 25,000.00
70 . . . . 150.00	5 Smilin' Jack 1,000.00
71 . . . . 150.00	6 Dick Tracy 2,800.00
72 . . . . 150.00	7 Gang Busters 700.00
73 OW,I:Herbie 475.00	8 Dick Tracy 1,500.00
74 . . . . 150.00	9 Terry and the Pirates 1,000.00
75 JB 150.00	10 Smilin' Jack 900.00
76 AW 200.00	11 Smitty 600.00
77 . . . . 150.00	12 Little Orphan Annie 800.00
78 AW,OW(c) 175.00	13 Walt Disney's Reluctant
79 thru 85 JB . . . . @150.00	Dragon (1941) 3,000.00
86 Flying Saucer 160.00	14 Moon Mullins 600.00
87 . . . . 150.00	15 Tillie the Toiler 600.00
88 . . . . 150.00	16 W.Disney's Mickey Mouse Outwits
89 . . . . 150.00	the Phantom Blob (1941) . 25,000.00
90 . . . . 150.00	17 W.Disney's Dumbo the Flying
91 . . . . 150.00	Elephant (1941) 5,000.00
92 . . . . 150.00	18 Jiggs and Maggie 650.00
93 . . . . 150.00	19 Barney Google and
94 OW(c),A:Herble 200.00	Snuffy Smith 625.00
95 . . . . 150.00	20 Tiny Tim 500.00
	21 Dick Tracy 1,100.00
	22 Don Winslow 600.00
	23 Gang Busters 500.00
	24 Captain Easy 700.00
	25 Popeye 1,200.00
	[Second Series, 1942]
	1 Little Joe 1,000.00
	2 Harold Teen 500.00
	3 Alley Oop 900.00
	4 Smilin' Jack 750.00
	5 Raggedy Ann and Andy 900.00
	6 Smitty 400.00
	7 Smokey Stover 500.00
	8 Tillie the Toiler 400.00
	9 Donald Duck finds Pirate
	Gold! 20,000.00
	10 Flash Gordon 1,700.00
	11 Wash Tubs 550.00
	12 Bambi 1,200.00
	13 Mr. District Attorney 500.00
	14 Smilin' Jack 600.00
	15 Felix the Cat 1,400.00
	16 Porky Pig 1,600.00
	17 Popeye 900.00
	18 Little Orphan Annie's
	Junior Commandos 650.00

Forbidden Worlds #86
© American Comics Group

Four Color (1st Series) #9
© Dell Publishing

19 W.Disney's Thumper meets
the Seven Dwarfs 1,200.00
20 Barney Baxter 500.00
21 Oswald the Rabbit 850.00
22 Tillie the Toiler 300.00
23 Raggedy Ann and Andy 650.00
24 Gang Busters 500.00
25 Andy Panda 950.00
26 Popeye 850.00
27 Mickey Mouse and the
Seven Colored Terror 2,500.00
28 Wash Tubbs 375.00
29 CB,Donald Duck and the
Mummy's Ring 12,000.00
30 Bambi's Children 900.00
31 Moon Mullins 325.00
32 Smitty 275.00
33 Bugs Bunny 2,200.00
34 Dick Tracy 750.00
35 Smokey Stover 300.00
36 Smilin' Jack 400.00
37 Bringing Up Father 350.00
38 Roy Rogers 4,000.00
39 Oswald the Rabbit 650.00
40 Barney Google and Snuffy
Smith 375.00
41 WK,Mother Goose 400.00
42 Tiny Tim 300.00
43 Popeye 550.00
44 Terry and the Pirates 650.00
45 Raggedy Ann 550.00
46 Felix the Cat and the
Haunted House 700.00
47 Gene Autry 800.00
48 CB,Porky Pig of the
Mounties 2,000.00
49 W.Disney's Snow White and
the Seven Dwarfs 1,400.00
50 WK,Fairy Tale Parade 450.00
51 Bugs Bunny Finds the
Lost Treasure 650.00
52 Little Orphan Annie 500.00
53 Wash Tubbs 255.00
54 Andy Panda 550.00
55 Tillie the Toiler 250.00
56 Dick Tracy 650.00
57 Gene Autry 700.00
58 Smilin' Jack 400.00
59 WK,Mother Goose 350.00
60 Tiny Folks Funnies 275.00
61 Santa Claus Funnies 400.00
62 CB,Donald Duck in
Frozen Gold 3,700.00
63 Roy Rogers-photo (c) 900.00
64 Smokey Stover 225.00

GOLDEN AGE

65 Smitty 225.00	136 Lone Ranger 375.00	179 WK,Uncle Wiggily 275.00
66 Gene Autry 700.00	137 Roy Rogers Comics 375.00	180 Ozark the Ike 200.00
67 Oswald the Rabbit 300.00	138 Smitty 175.00	181 W.Disney's Mickey Mouse
68 WK,Mother Goose 325.00	139 Marge's Little Lulu 500.00	in Jungle Magic 500.00
69 WK,Fairy Tale Parade 450.00	140 WK,Easter with	182 Porky Pig in Never-
70 Popeye and Wimpy 450.00	Mother Goose 250.00	Never Land 600.00
71 WK,Walt Disney's	141 Mickey Mouse and the	183 Oswald the Rabbit 175.00
Three Caballeros 1,400.00	Submarine Pirates 500.00	184 Tillie the Toiler 175.00
72 Raggedy Ann 450.00	142 Bugs Bunny and the	185 WK,Easter with
73 The Grumps 250.00	Haunted Mountain 275.00	Mother Goose 250.00
74 Marge's Little Lulu 2,200.00	143 Oswald Rabbit & the	186 W.Disney's Bambi 300.00
75 Gene Autry and the Wildcat . . 550.00	Prehistoric Egg 175.00	187 Bugs Bunny and the
76 Little Orphan Annie 400.00	144 Poy Rogers Comics,Ph(c) . . 400.00	Dreadful Bunny 200.00
77 Felix the Cat 650.00	145 Popeye 250.00	188 Woody Woodpecker 200.00
78 Porky Pig & the Bandit Twins . 700.00	146 Marge's Little Lulu 500.00	189 W.Disney's Donald Duck in
79 Mickey Mouse in the Riddle	147 W.Disney's Donald Duck	The Old Castle's Secret . . . 1,500.00
of the Red Hat 2,000.00	in Volcano Valley 1,800.00	190 Flash Gordon 400.00
80 Smilin' Jack 300.00	148 WK,Albert the Alligator	191 Porky Pig to the Rescue 500.00
81 Moon Mullins 200.00	and Pogo Possum 950.00	192 WK,The Brownies 250.00
82 Lone Ranger 750.00	149 Smilin' Jack 175.00	193 Tom and Jerry 400.00
83 Gene Autry in Outlaw Trail . . 550.00	150 Tillie the Toiler 150.00	194 W.Disney's Mickey Mouse
84 Flash Gordon 800.00	151 Lone Ranger 325.00	in the World Under the Sea . 500.00
85 Andy Panda and the	152 Little Orphan Annie 250.00	195 Tillie the Toiler 125.00
Mad Dog Mystery 300.00	153 Roy Rogers Comics 350.00	196 Charlie McCarthy in The
86 Roy Rogers-photo (c) 650.00	154 Andy Panda 200.00	Haunted Hide-Out 300.00
87 WK,DNo(c),Fairy Tale Parade 450.00	155 Henry 200.00	197 Spirit of the Border 200.00
88 Bugs Bunny 400.00	156 Porky Pig and the Phantom . 600.00	198 Andy Panda 200.00
89 Tillie the Toiler 250.00	157 W.Disney's Mickey Mouse	199 W.Disney's Donald Duck in
90 WK,Christmas with	and the Beanstalk 500.00	Sheriff of Bullet Valley 1,600.00
Mother Goose 350.00	158 Marge's Little Lulu 500.00	200 Bugs Bunny, Super Sleuth . . 225.00
91 WK,Santa Claus Funnies . . . 300.00	159 CB,W.Disney's Donald Duck	201 WK,Christmas with
92 WK,W.Disney's Pinocchio . . 1,000.00	in the Ghost of the Grotto . . 3,000.00	Mother Goose 225.00
93 Gene Autry 500.00	160 Roy Rogers Comics,Ph(c) . . 350.00	202 Woody Woodpecker 150.00
94 Winnie Mullins 200.00	161 Tarzan & the Fires of Tohr . 1,000.00	203 CB,W.Disney's Donald Duck in
95 Roy Rogers,Ph(c) 650.00	162 Felix the Cat 325.00	The Golden Christmas Tree 1,400.00
96 Dick Tracy 500.00	163 Dick Tracy 325.00	204 Flash Gordon 250.00
97 Marge's Little Lulu 900.00	164 Bugs Bunny Finds the	205 WK,Santa Claus Funnies . . . 275.00
98 Lone Ranger 600.00	Frozen Kingdom 275.00	206 Little Orphan Funnies 200.00
99 Smitty 200.00	165 Marge's Little Lulu 500.00	207 King of the Royal Mounted . . 250.00
100 Gene Autry Comics-photo(c) 575.00	166 Roy Rogers Comics,Ph(c) . . 350.00	208 W.Disney's Brer Rabbit
101 Terry and the Pirates 500.00	167 Lone Ranger 325.00	Does It Again 200.00
102 WK,Oswald the Rabbit 250.00	168 Popeye 250.00	209 Harold Teen 100.00
103 WK,Easter with	169 Woody Woodpecker,Drug . . . 400.00	210 Tippe and Cap Stubbs 100.00
Mother Goose 300.00	170 W.Disney's Mickey Mouse	211 Little Beaver 150.00
104 WK,Fairy Tale Parade 325.00	on Spook's Island 350.00	212 Dr. Bobbs 90.00
105 WK,Albert the Alligator . . . 1,200.00	171 Charlie McCarthy 450.00	213 Tillie the Toiler 125.00
106 Tillie the Toiler 200.00	172 WK,Christmas with	214 W.Disney's Mickey Mouse
107 Little Orphan Annie 350.00	Mother Goose 250.00	and his Sky Adventure 400.00
108 Donald Duck in the	173 Flash Gordon 350.00	215 Sparkle Plenty 200.00
Terror of the River 2,800.00	174 Winnie Winkle 150.00	216 Andy Panda and the
109 Roy Rogers Comics 500.00	175 WK,Santa Claus Funnies . . . 250.00	Police Pup 150.00
110 Marge's Little Lulu 600.00	176 Tillie the Toiler 150.00	217 Bugs Bunny in Court Jester . 200.00
111 Captain Easy 250.00	177 Roy Rogers Comics,Ph(c) . . 325.00	218 W.Disney's 3 Little Pigs 225.00
112 Porky Pig's Adventure in	178 CB,W.Disney's Donald	219 Swee'pea 150.00
Gopher Gulch 600.00	Duck Christmas on Bear	220 WK,Easter with
113 Popeye 250.00	Mountain 2,400.00	Mother Goose 235.00
114 WK,Fairy Tale Parade 325.00		221 WK,Uncle Wiggly 175.00
115 Marge's Little Lulu 600.00		222 West of the Pecos 125.00
116 Mickey Mouse and the		223 CB,W.Disney's Donald Duck in
House of Many Mysteries . . . 600.00		Lost in the Andes 1,600.00
117 Roy Rogers Comics, Ph(c) . . 400.00		224 Little Iodine 200.00
118 Lone Ranger 550.00		225 Oswald the Rabbit 125.00
119 Felix the Cat 600.00		226 Porky Pig and Spoofy 400.00
120 Marge's Little Lulu 550.00		227 W.Disney's Seven Dwarfs . . 225.00
121 Fairy Tale Parade 225.00		228 The Mark of Zorro 400.00
122 Henry 250.00		229 Smokey Stover 125.00
123 Bugs Bunny's Dangerous		230 Sunset Press 125.00
Venture 275.00		231 W.Disney's Mickey Mouse
124 Roy Rogers Comics,Ph(c) . . 400.00		and the Rajah's Treasure . . . 400.00
125 Lone Ranger 400.00		232 Woody Woodpecker 150.00
126 WK,Christmas with		233 Bugs Bunny 200.00
Mother Goose 250.00		234 W.Disney's Dumbo in Sky
127 Popeye 250.00		Voyage 250.00
128 WK,Santa Claus Funnies . . . 250.00		235 Tiny Tim 90.00
129 W.Disney's Uncle Remus		236 Heritage of the Desert 125.00
& His Tales of Brer Rabbit . . 500.00		237 Tillie the Toiler 125.00
130 Andy Panda 200.00		238 CB,W.Disney's Donald Duck
131 Marge's Little Lulu 550.00		in Voodoo Hoodoo 1,300.00
132 Tillie the Toiler 200.00		239 Adventure Bound 100.00
133 Dick Tracy 400.00		240 Andy Panda 150.00
134 Tarzan and the Devil Ogre. 1,200.00		241 Porky Pig 300.00
135 Felix the Cat 450.00		242 Tippie and Cap Stubbs 90.00

Four Color #27
© *Walt Disney*

243 W.Disney's Thumper
    Follows His Nose.......... 200.00
244 WK,The Brownies......... 175.00
245 Dick's Adventures in
    Dreamland............... 100.00
246 Thunder Mountain......... 90.00
247 Flash Gordon 500.00
248 W.Disney's Mickey Mouse
    and the Black Sorcerer ... 275.00
249 Woody Woodpecker 150.00
250 Bugs Bunny in
    Diamond Daze 225.00
251 Hubert at Camp Moonbeam . 100.00
252 W.Disney's Pinocchio 225.00
253 WK,Christmas with
    Mother Goose 225.00
254 WK,Santa Claus Funnies,
    A:Pogo................. 250.00
255 The Ranger.............. 100.00
256 CB,W.Disney's Donald Duck in
    Luck of the North 1,000.00
257 Little Iodine 150.00
258 Andy Panda and the
    Ballon Race.............. 150.00
259 Santa and the Angel 100.00
260 Porky Pig, Hero of the
    Wild West 250.00
261 W.Disney's Mickey Mouse
    and the Missing Key 300.00
262 Raggedy Ann and Andy 175.00
263 CB,W.Disney's Donald Duck in
    Land of the Totem Poles .. 1,000.00
264 Woody Woodpecker in
    the Magic Lantern 150.00
265 King of the Royal Mountain . 150.00
266 Bugs Bunny on the Isle of
    Hercules 175.00
267 Little Beaver 300.00
268 W.Disney's Mickey Mouse's
    Surprise Visitor........... 300.00
269 Johnny Mack Brown,Ph(c) .. 400.00
270 Drift Fence 100.00
271 Porky Pig 250.00
272 W.Disney's Cinderella...... 225.00
273 Oswald the Rabbit 100.00
274 Bugs Bunny 175.00
275 CB,W.Disney's Donald Duck
    in Ancient Persia 900.00
276 Uncle Wiggly............. 175.00
277 PorkyPig in DesertAdventure 250.00
278 Bill Elliot Comics,Ph(c) 250.00
279 W.Disney's Mickey Mouse &
    Pluto Battle the Giant Ants .. 300.00
280 Andy Panda in the Isle
    of the Mechanical Men 150.00
281 Bugs Bunny in The Great
    Circus Mystery........... 175.00
282 CB,W.Disney's Donald Duck in
    The Pixilated Parrot....... 900.00
283 King of the Royal Mounted .. 150.00
284 Porky Pig in the Kingdom
    of Nowhere 250.00
285 Bozo the Clown........... 350.00
286 W.Disney's Mickey Mouse
    and the Uninvited Guest 300.00
287 Gene Autry's Champion in the
    Ghost of BlackMountain,Ph(c)200.00
288 Woody Woodpecker 150.00
289 BugsBunny in IndianTrouble. 175.00
290 The Chief 125.00
291 CB,W.Disney's Donald Duck in
    The Magic Hourglass 900.00
292 The Cisco Kid Comics 450.00
293 WK,The Brownies......... 175.00
294 Little Beaver 75.00
295 Porky Pig in President Pig . 250.00
296 W.Disney's Mickey Mouse
    Private Eye for Hire........ 200.00
297 Andy Panda in The
    Haunted Inn............. 150.00
298 Bugs Bunny in Sheik
    for a Day 175.00

Four Color #287
© *Dell Publishing Co.*

299 Buck Jones & the Iron Trail . 250.00
300 CB,W.Disney's Donald Duck in
    Big Top Bedlam.......... 900.00
301 The Mysterious Rider 100.00
302 Santa Claus Funnies 100.00
303 Porky Pig in The Land of
    the Monstrous Flies........ 200.00
304 W.Disney's Mickey Mouse
    in Tom-Tom Island........ 250.00
305 Woody Woodpecker 100.00
306 Raggedy Ann 125.00
307 Bugs Bunny in Lumber
    Jack Rabbit 150.00
308 CB,W.Disney's Donald Duck in
    Dangerous Disguise 800.00
309 Dollface and Her Gang..... 100.00
310 King of the Royal Mounted . 125.00
311 Porky Pig in Midget Horses
    of Hidden Valley 200.00
312 Tonto.................. 200.00
313 W.Disney's Mickey Mouse in
    the Mystery of the Double-
    Cross Ranch 250.00
314 Ambush................. 90.00
315 Oswald Rabbit 100.00
316 Rex Allen,Ph(c)........... 275.00
317 Bugs Bunny in Hare Today
    Gone Tomorrow.......... 150.00
318 CB,W.Disney's Donald Duck in
    No Such Varmint.......... 800.00
319 Gene Autry's Champion 100.00
320 Uncle Wiggly 150.00
321 Little Scouts 75.00
322 Porky Pig in Roaring Rockies 150.00
323 Susie Q. Smith 75.00
324 I Met a Handsome Cowboy . 150.00
325 W.Disney's Mickey Mouse
    in the Haunted Castle 250.00
326 Andy Panda 100.00
327 Bugs Bunny and the
    Rajah's Treasure.......... 150.00
328 CB,W.Disney's Donald Duck
    in Old California........... 850.00
329 Roy Roger's Trigger,Ph(c) .. 275.00
330 Porky Pig meets the
    Bristled Bruiser 150.00
331 Disney's Alice in
    Wonderland 275.00
332 Little Beaver 75.00
333 Wilderness Trek 90.00
334 W.Disney's Mickey Mouse
    and Yukon Gold........... 250.00
335 Francis the Famous
    Talking Mule 200.00
336 Woody Woodpecker 100.00
337 The Brownies 100.00

338 Bugs Bunny and the
    Rocking Horse Thieves 200.00
339 W.Disney's Donald Duck
    and the Magic Fountain..... 400.00
340 King of the Royal Mountain . 150.00
341 W.Disney's Unbirthday Party
    with Alice in Wonderland.... 275.00
342 Porky Pig the Lucky
    Peppermint Mine.......... 150.00
343 W.Disney's Mickey Mouse in
    Ruby Eye of Homar-Guy-Am 150.00
344 Sergeant Preston from
    Challenge of the Yukon..... 250.00
345 Andy Panda in Scotland Yard 100.00
346 Hideout 100.00
347 Bugs Bunny the Frigid Hare . 150.00
348 CB,W.Disney's Donald Duck
    The Crocodile Collector..... 600.00
349 Uncle Wiggly............. 125.00
350 Woody Woodpecker 100.00
351 Porky Pig and the Grand
    Canyon Giant 150.00
352 W.Disney's Mickey Mouse
    Mystery of Painted Valley ... 200.00
353 CB(c),W.Disney'sDuckAlbum 300.00
354 Raggedy Ann & Andy 125.00
355 Bugs Bunny Hot-Rod Hair .. 150.00
356 CB(c),W.Disney's Donald
    Duck in Rags to Riches..... 500.00
357 Comeback................ 75.00
358 Andy Panada 100.00
359 Frosty the Snowman........ 175.00
360 Porky Pig in Tree Fortune .. 100.00
361 Santa Claus Funnies 100.00
362 W.Disney's Mickey Mouse &
    the Smuggled Diamonds.... 250.00
363 King of the Royal Mounted .. 125.00
364 Woody Woodpecker 90.00
365 The Brownies 90.00
366 Bugs Bunny Uncle
    Buckskin Comes to Town ... 150.00
367 CB,W.Disney's Donald Duck in
    A Christmas for Shacktown .. 900.00
368 Bob Clampett's
    Beany and Cecil 500.00
369 Lone Ranger's Famous
    Horse Hi-Yo Silver......... 200.00
370 Porky Pig in Trouble
    in the Big Trees........... 150.00
371 W.Disney's Mickey Mouse
    the Inca Idol Case.......... 200.00
372 Riders of the Purple Sage ... 75.00
373 Sergeant Preston 150.00
374 Woody Woodpecker 75.00
375 John Carter of Mars 600.00
376 Bugs Bunny 200.00
377 Susie Q. Smith 75.00
378 Tom Corbett, Space Cadet .. 325.00
379 W.Disney's Donald Duck in
    Southern Hospitality 300.00
380 Raggedy Ann & Andy 125.00
381 Marge's Tubby 375.00
382 W.Disney's Show White and
    the Seven Dwarfs 200.00
383 Andy Panda 75.00
384 King of the Royal Mounted .. 100.00
385 Porky Pig 100.00
386 CB,W.Disney's Uncle Scrooge
    in Only A Poor Old Man ... 2,700.00
387 W.Disney's Mickey Mouse
    in High Tibet 200.00
388 Oswald the Rabbit 100.00
389 Andy Hardy Comics 75.00
390 Woody Woodpecker 75.00
391 Uncle Wiggly............. 125.00
392 Hi-Yo Silver............. 100.00
393 Bugs Bunny 150.00
394 CB(c),W.Disney's Donald Duck
    in Malayalia 500.00
395 Forlorn River............. 75.00
396 Tales of the Texas Rangers,
    Ph(c) 200.00

All comics prices listed are for *Near Mint* condition.   **CVA Page 409**

397 Sergeant Preston o/t Yukon . 150.00	462 Little Scouts 50.00	536 Daffy 100.00
398 The Brownies 75.00	463 Petunia 75.00	537 Stormy, the Thoroughbred . . . 75.00
399 Porky Pig in the Lost	464 Bozo 175.00	538 EK,The Mask of Zorro 250.00
Gold Mine 100.00	465 Francis the Talking Mule. . . . 100.00	539 Ben and Me 75.00
400 AMc,Tom Corbett 200.00	466 Rhubarb, the Millionaire Cat. . 75.00	540 Knights of the Round Table,
401 W.Disney's Mickey Mouse &	467 Desert Gold. 75.00	Ph(c) 150.00
Goofy's Mechanical Wizard. . 150.00	468 W.Disney's Goofy 300.00	541 Johnny Mack Brown,Ph(c) . . 125.00
402 Mary Jane and Sniffles. . . . 100.00	469 Beetle Bailey. 175.00	542 Super Circus Featuring
403 W.Disney's Li'l Bad Wolf. . . 150.00	470 Elmer Fudd 100.00	Mary Hartline 125.00
404 The Ranger Rider,Ph(c) 200.00	471 Double Trouble with Goober. . 40.00	543 Uncle Wiggly. 100.00
405 Woody Woodpecker 75.00	472 Wild Bill Elliot,Ph(c). 150.00	544 W.Disney's Rob Roy(Movie),
406 Tweety and Sylvester 125.00	473 W.Disney's Li'l Bad Wolf. . . . 75.00	Ph(c) 150.00
407 Bugs Bunny, Foreign-	474 Mary Jane and Sniffles. 125.00	545 The Wonderful Adventures
Legion Hare. 125.00	475 M.G.M.'s the Two	of Pinocchio. 150.00
408 CB,W.Disney's Donald Duck	Mouseketeers 125.00	546 Buck Jones 100.00
and the Golden Helmet 750.00	476 Rin Tin Tin,Ph(c). 150.00	547 Francis the Famous
409 Andy Panda 75.00	477 Bob Clampett's Beany and	Talking Mule 90.00
410 Porky Pig in the	Cecil. 300.00	548 Krazy Kat 75.00
Water Wizard. 100.00	478 Charlie McCarthy 100.00	549 Oswald the Rabbit 75.00
411 W.Disney's Mickey Mouse	479 Queen o/t West Dale Evans. 400.00	550 The Little Scouts 50.00
and the Old Sea Dog. 150.00	480 Andy Hardy Comics 65.00	551 Bozo 175.00
412 Nevada 75.00	481 Annie Oakley and Tagg. . . . 150.00	552 Beetle Bailey. 100.00
413 Disney's Robin Hood(movie),	482 Brownies. 75.00	553 Susie Q. Smith 60.00
Ph(c) 200.00	483 Little Beaver 75.00	554 Rusty Riley 70.00
414 Bob Clampett's Beany	484 River Feud 75.00	555 Range War 70.00
and Cecil 250.00	485 The Little People. 125.00	556 Double Trouble with Goober. . 40.00
415 Rootie Kazootie 175.00	486 Rusty Riley 75.00	557 Ben Bowie and His
416 Woody Woodpecker 75.00	487 Mowgli, the Jungle Book. . . . 100.00	Mountain Men 75.00
417 Double Trouble with Goober. . 75.00	488 John Carter of Mars 350.00	558 Elmer Fudd 75.00
418 Rusty Riley 75.00	489 Tweety and Sylvester 100.00	559 I Love Lucy,Ph(c) 600.00
419 Sergeant Preston 150.00	490 Jungle Jim 125.00	560 W.Disney's Duck Album 150.00
420 Bugs Bunny 125.00	491 EK,Silvertip 150.00	561 Mr. Magoo. 200.00
421 AMc,Tom Corbett 200.00	492 W.Disney's Duck Album 150.00	562 W.Disney's Goofy 150.00
422 CB,W.Disney's Donald Duck	493 Johnny Mack Brown,Ph(c) . . 125.00	563 Rhubarb, the Millionaire Cat. 100.00
and the Gilded Man. 750.00	494 The Little King. 175.00	564 W.Disney's Li'l Bad Wolf. . . 100.00
423 Rhubarb 100.00	495 CB, W.Disney's Uncle	565 Jungle Jim. 75.00
424 Flash Gordon 200.00	Scrooge 1,000.00	566 Son of Black Beauty 60.00
425 Zorro 200.00	496 The Green Hornet. 900.00	567 BF,Prince Valiant,Ph(c) 250.00
426 Porky Pig 100.00	497 Zorro, (Sword of). 250.00	568 Gypsy Cat. 90.00
427 W.Disney's Mickey Mouse &	498 Bugs Bunny's Album. 100.00	569 Priscilla's Pop 75.00
the Wonderful Whizzix. 150.00	499 M.G.M.'s Spike and Tyke . . . 90.00	570 Bob Clampett's Beany
428 Uncle Wiggily 100.00	500 Buck Jones 100.00	and Cecil 275.00
429 W.Disney's Pluto in	501 Francis the Famous	571 Charlie McCarthy 100.00
Why Dogs Leave Home 200.00	Talking Mule 90.00	572 EK,Silvertip 90.00
430 Marge's Tubby 200.00	502 Rootie Kazootie 135.00	573 The Little People. 100.00
431 Woody Woodpecker 100.00	503 Uncle Wiggily 90.00	574 The Hand of Zorro 225.00
432 Bugs Bunny and the	504 Krazy Kat 75.00	575 Annie and Oakley and Tagg,
Rabbit Olympics 125.00	505 W.Disney's the Sword and	Ph(c) 175.00
433 Wildfire 75.00	the Rose (TV),Ph(c) 150.00	576 Angel. 60.00
434 Rin Tin Tin,Ph(c). 275.00	506 The Little Scouts 40.00	577 M.G.M.'s Spike and Tyke . . . 60.00
435 Frosty the Snowman. 100.00	507 Oswald the Rabbit 75.00	578 Steve Canyon 90.00
436 The Brownies 75.00	508 Bozo 175.00	579 Francis the Talking Mule. . . . 75.00
437 John Carter of Mars 400.00	509 W.Disney's Pluto. 100.00	580 Six Gun Ranch 75.00
438 W.Disney's Annie	510 Son of Black Beauty 60.00	581 Chip 'N' Dale. 100.00
Oakley (TV). 275.00	511 EK,Outlaw Trail 75.00	582 Mowgli, the Jungle Book. . . 100.00
439 Little Hiawatha 100.00	512 Flash Gordon 125.00	583 The Lost Wagon Train 75.00
440 Black Beauty 75.00	513 Ben Bowie and His	
441 Fearless Fagan. 75.00	Mountain Men 60.00	
442 W.Disney's Peter Pan. 175.00	514 Frosty the Snowman. 100.00	
443 Ben Bowie and His	515 Andy Hardy 50.00	
Mountain Men 125.00	516 Double Trouble With Goober . 40.00	
444 Marge's Tubby 200.00	517 Walt Disney's Chip 'N' Dale . 200.00	
445 Charlie McCarthy 100.00	518 Rivets 50.00	
446 Captain Hook and Peter Pan 175.00	519 Steve Canyon 150.00	
447 Andy Hardy Comics 75.00	520 Wild Bill Elliot,Ph(c). 125.00	
448 Beany and Cecil 300.00	521 Beetle Bailey. 100.00	
449 Tappan's Burro 75.00	522 The Brownies 75.00	
450 CB,W.Disney's Duck	523 Rin Tin Tin,Ph(c). 150.00	
Album 200.00	524 Tweety and Sylvester 100.00	
451 Rusty Riley 65.00	525 Santa Claus Funnies 100.00	
452 Raggedy Ann and Andy 125.00	526 Napoleon. 50.00	
453 Susie Q. Smith 65.00	527 Charlie McCarthy 100.00	
454 Krazy Kat Comics 65.00	528 Queen o/t West Dale Evans,	
455 Johnny Mack Brown Comics,	Ph(c) 200.00	
Ph(c) 125.00	529 Little Beaver 75.00	
456 W.Disney's Uncle Scrooge	530 Bob Clampett's Beany	
Back to the Klondike 1,500.00	and Cecil 300.00	
457 Daffy 150.00	531 W.Disney's Duck Album 150.00	
458 Oswald the Rabbit 75.00	532 The Rustlers 75.00	Four Color #500
459 Rootie Kazootie 150.00	533 Raggedy Ann and Andy 125.00	© Dell Publishing Co.
460 Buck Jones 175.00	534 EK,Western Marshal. 125.00	
461 Marge's Tubby 175.00	535 I Love Lucy,Ph(c) 1,000.00	

584 Johnny Mack Brown,Ph(c) . . 125.00
585 Bugs Bunny's Album 100.00
586 W.Disney's Duck Album 160.00
587 The Little Scouts 50.00
588 MB,King Richard and the
　　Crusaders,Ph(c) 175.00
589 Buck Jones 100.00
590 Hansel and Gretel 125.00
591 EK,Western Marshal 100.00
592 Super Circus 125.00
593 Oswald the Rabbit 60.00
594 Bozo 160.00
595 Pluto 75.00
596 Turok, Son of Stone 1,000.00
597 The Little King 100.00
598 Captain Davy Jones 90.00
599 Ben Bowie and His
　　Mountain Men 75.00
600 Daisy Duck's Diary 150.00
601 Frosty the Snowman 100.00
602 Mr. Magoo and the Gerald
　　McBoing-Boing 225.00
603 M.G.M.'s The Two
　　Mouseketeers 90.00
604 Shadow on the Trail 75.00
605 The Brownies 75.00
606 Sir Lancelot 150.00
607 Santa Claus Funnies 100.00
608 EK,Silver Tip 75.00
609 The Littlest Outlaw,Ph(c) . . . 125.00
610 Drum Beat,Ph(c) 175.00
611 W.Disney's Duck Album 150.00
612 Little Beaver 65.00
613 EK,Western Marshal 100.00
614 W.Disney's 20,000 Leagues
　　Under the Sea (Movie) 200.00
615 Daffy 100.00
616 To The Last Man 75.00
617 The Quest of Zorro 225.00
618 Johnny Mack Brown,Ph(c) . . 125.00
619 Krazy Kat 65.00
620 Mowgli, Jungle Book 90.00
621 Francis the Famous
　　Talking Mule 65.00
622 Beetle Bailey 100.00
623 Oswald the Rabbit 65.00
624 Treasure Island,Ph(c) 150.00
625 Beaver Valley 125.00
626 Ben Bowie and His
　　Mountain Men 75.00
627 Goofy 150.00
628 Elmer Fudd 65.00
629 Lady & The Tramp with Jock 150.00
630 Priscilla's Pop 65.00
631 W.Disney's Davy Crockett
　　Indian Fighter (TV),Ph(c) . . . 375.00
632 Fighting Caravans 75.00
633 The Little People 75.00
634 Lady and the Tramp Album . . 100.00
635 Bob Clampett's Beany
　　and Cecil 300.00
636 Chip 'N' Dale 100.00
637 EK,Silvertip 75.00
638 M.G.M.'s Spike and Tyke 60.00
639 W.Disney's Davy Crockett
　　at the Alamo (TV),Ph(c) 300.00
640 EK,Western Marshal 100.00
641 Steve Canyon 110.00
642 M.G.M.'s The Two
　　Mouseketeers 80.00
643 Wild Bill Elliott,Ph(c) 75.00
644 Sir Walter Raleigh,Ph(c) 125.00
645 Johnny Mack Brown,Ph(c) . . 125.00
646 Dotty Dripple and Taffy 75.00
647 Bugs Bunny's Album 100.00
648 Jace Pearson of the
　　Texas Rangers,Ph(c) 100.00
649 Duck Album 100.00
650 BF,Prince Valiant 125.00
651 EK,King Colt 75.00
652 Buck Jones 75.00
653 Smokey the Bear 200.00

Four Color #671
© *Walt Disney*

654 Pluto 75.00
655 Francis the Famous
　　Talking Mule 75.00
656 Turok, Son of Stone 650.00
657 Ben Bowie and His
　　Mountain Men 75.00
658 Goofy 150.00
659 Daisy Duck's Diary 125.00
660 Little Beaver 75.00
661 Frosty the Snowman 100.00
662 Zoo Parade 100.00
663 Winky Dink 150.00
664 W.Disney's Davy Crockett in
　　the Great Keelboat
　　Race (TV),Ph(c) 300.00
665 The African Lion 100.00
666 Santa Claus Funnies 100.00
667 EK,Silvertip and the Stolen
　　Stallion 100.00
668 W.Disney's Dumbo 325.00
668a W.Disney's Dumbo 300.00
669 W.Disney's Robin Hood
　　(Movie),Ph(c) 100.00
670 M.G.M.'s Mouse Musketeers . 75.00
671 W.Disney's Davey Crockett &
　　the River Pirates(TV),Ph(c) . . 275.00
672 Quentin Durward,Ph(c) 125.00
673 Buffalo Bill Jr.,Ph(c) 150.00
674 The Little Rascals 150.00
675 EK,Steve Donovan,Ph(c) . . . 150.00
676 Will-Yum! 60.00
677 Little King 100.00
678 The Last Hunt,Ph(c) 150.00
679 Gunsmoke 350.00
680 Out Our Way with the
　　Worry Wart 60.00
681 Forever, Darling,Lucile
　　Ball Ph(c) 225.00
682 When Knighthood Was
　　in Flower,Ph(c) 150.00
683 Hi and Lois 60.00
684 SB,Helen of Troy,Ph(c) 200.00
685 Johnny Mack Brown,Ph(c) . . 150.00
686 Duck Album 150.00
687 The Indian Fighter,Ph(c) 150.00
688 SB,Alexander the Great,
　　Ph(c) 150.00
689 Elmer Fudd 75.00
690 The Conqueror,
　　John Wayne Ph(c) 300.00
691 Dotty Dripple and Taffy 50.00
692 The Little People 75.00
693 W.Disney's Brer Rabbit
　　Song of the South 175.00
694 Super Circus,Ph(c) 125.00
695 Little Beaver 75.00

696 Krazy Kat 75.00
697 Oswald the Rabbit 60.00
698 Francis the Famous
　　Talking Mule 75.00
699 BA,Prince Valiant 150.00
700 Water Birds and the
　　Olympic Elk 100.00
701 Jimmy Cricket 175.00
702 The Goofy Success Story . . . 135.00
703 Scamp 175.00
704 Priscilla's Pop 60.00
705 Brave Eagle,Ph(c) 150.00
706 Bongo and Lumpjaw 100.00
707 Corky and White Shadow,
　　Ph(c) 135.00
708 Smokey the Bear 100.00
709 The Searchers,John
　　Wayne Ph(c) 800.00
710 Francis the Famous
　　Talking Mule 75.00
711 M.G.M.'s Mouse Musketeers . . 60.00
712 The Great Locomotive
　　Chase, Ph(c) 135.00
713 The Animal World 60.00
714 W.Disney's Spin
　　& Marty (TV) 250.00
715 Timmy 75.00
716 Man in Space 150.00
717 Moby Dick,Ph(c) 150.00
718 Dotty Dripple and Taffy 50.00
719 BF,Prince Valiant 125.00
720 Gunsmoke,Ph(c) 175.00
721 Captain Kangaroo,Ph(c) 325.00
722 Johnny Mack Brown,Ph(c) . . 125.00
723 EK,Santiago 175.00
724 Bugs Bunny's Album 75.00
725 Elmer Fudd 60.00
726 Duck Album 100.00
727 The Nature of Things 110.00
728 M.G.M.'s Mouse Musketeers . 60.00
729 Bob Son of Battle 75.00
730 Smokey Stover 100.00
731 EK,Silvertip and The
　　Fighting Four 80.00
732 Zorro, (the Challenge of) . . . 250.00
733 Buck Rogers 75.00
734 Cheyenne,C.Walker Ph(c) . . 300.00
735 Crusader Rabbit 575.00
736 Pluto 75.00
737 Steve Canyon 100.00
738 Westward Ho, the Wagons,
　　Ph(c) 200.00
739 MD,Bounty Guns 75.00
740 Chilly Willy 125.00
741 The Fastest Gun Alive,Ph(c). 150.00
742 Buffalo Bill Jr.,Ph(c) 100.00
743 Daisy Duck's Diary 110.00
744 Little Beaver 65.00
745 Francis the Famous
　　Talking Mule 65.00
746 Dotty Dripple and Taffy 50.00
747 Goofy 135.00
748 Frosty the Snowman 100.00
749 Secrets of Life,Ph(c) 100.00
750 The Great Cat 125.00
751 Our Miss Brooks,Ph(c) 150.00
752 Mandrake, the Magician 175.00
753 Walt Scott's Little People 75.00
754 Smokey the Bear 125.00
755 The Littlest Snowman 100.00
756 Santa Claus Funnies 100.00
757 The True Story of
　　Jesse James,Ph(c) 175.00
758 Bear Country 100.00
759 Circus Boy,Ph(c) 250.00
760 W.Disney's Hardy Boys(TV) . 250.00
761 Howdy Doody 250.00
762 SB,The Sharkfighters,Ph(c) . 150.00
763 GrandmaDuck'sFarmFriends 150.00
764 M.G.M.'s Mouse Musketeers . 60.00
765 Will-Yum! 60.00
766 Buffalo Bill,Ph(c) 100.00

767 Spin and Marty 175.00
768 EK,Steve Donovan, Western
     Marshal,Ph(c) 125.00
769 Gunsmoke. 200.00
770 Brave Eagle,Ph(c) 65.00
771 MD,Brand of Empire 65.00
772 Cheyenne,C.Walker Ph(c) . . 150.00
773 The Brave One,Ph(c) 100.00
774 Hi and Lois 50.00
775 SB,Sir Lancelot and
     Brian,Ph(c). 175.00
776 Johnny Mack Brown,Ph(c) . . 125.00
777 Scamp. 135.00
778 The Little Rascals 100.00
779 Lee Hunter, Indian Fighter . . 100.00
780 Captain Kangaroo,Ph(c) 250.00
781 Fury,Ph(c) 150.00
782 Duck Album. 100.00
783 Elmer Fudd 60.00
784 Around the World in 80
     Days,Ph(c). 125.00
785 Circus Boys,Ph(c). 250.00
786 Cinderella 125.00
787 Little Hiawatha 100.00
788 BF,Prince Valiant. 125.00
789 EK,Silvertip-Valley Thieves . . 100.00
790 ATh,The Wings of Eagles,
     J.Wayne Ph(c) 300.00
791 The 77th Bengal Lancers,
     Ph(c) 150.00
792 Oswald the Rabbit 65.00
793 Morty Meekle 50.00
794 SB,The Count of Monte
     Cristo. 150.00
795 Jiminy Cricket 125.00
796 Ludwig Bemelman's
     Madeleine and Genevieve. . . . 60.00
797 Gunsmoke,Ph(c). 175.00
798 Buffalo Bill,Ph(c) 100.00
799 Priscilla's Pop 60.00
800 The Buccaneers,Ph(c) 150.00
801 Dotty Dripple and Taffy 50.00
802 Goofy 150.00
803 Cheyenne,C.Walker Ph(c) . . 150.00
804 Steve Canyon 100.00
805 Crusader Rabbit 450.00
806 Scamp. 125.00
807 MB,Savage Range 65.00
808 Spin and Marty,Ph(c). 175.00
809 The Little People. 75.00
810 Francis the Famous
     Talking Mule 65.00
811 Howdy Doody 200.00
812 The Big Land,A.Ladd Ph(c) . 225.00
813 Circus Boy,Ph(c). 225.00
814 Covered Wagon, A:Mickey
     Mouse 125.00
815 Dragoon Wells Massacre . . . 150.00
816 Brave Eagle,Ph(c). 65.00
817 Little Beaver 65.00
818 Smokey the Bear 125.00
819 Mickey Mouse in Magicland . 100.00
820 The Oklahoman,Ph(c). 175.00
821 Wringle Wrangle,Ph(c) 150.00
822 ATh,W.Disney's Paul Revere's
     Ride (TV). 175.00
823 Timmy 50.00
824 The Pride and the Passion,
     Ph(c) 175.00
825 The Little Rascals 100.00
826 Spin and Marty and Annette,
     Ph(c) 425.00
827 Smokey Stover 90.00
828 Buffalo Bill, Jr,Ph(c). 90.00
829 Tales of the Pony Express,
     Ph(c) 90.00
830 The Hardy Boys,Ph(c) 175.00
831 No Sleep 'Til Dawn,Ph(c) . . . 125.00
832 Lolly and Pepper. 65.00
833 Scamp. 125.00
834 Johnny Mack Brown,Ph(c) . . 125.00
835 Silvertip- The Fake Rider 90.00

Four Color #872
© Dell Publishing Co.

836 Man in Fight 135.00
837 All-American Athlete
     Cotton Woods 65.00
838 Bugs Bunny's Life
     Story Album 75.00
839 The Vigilantes 125.00
840 Duck Album 100.00
841 Elmer Fudd 60.00
842 The Nature of Things 100.00
843 The First Americans 150.00
844 Gunsmoke,Ph(c). 175.00
845 ATh,The Land Unknown . . . 225.00
846 ATh,Gun Glory 175.00
847 Perri 90.00
848 Marauder's Moon 65.00
849 BF,Prince Valiant. 125.00
850 Buck Jones 75.00
851 The Story of Mankind,
     V.Price Ph(c) 135.00
852 Chilly Willy 100.00
853 Pluto 75.00
854 Hunchback of Notre Dame,
     Ph(c) 250.00
855 Broken Arrow,Ph(c). 100.00
856 Buffalo Bill, Jr.,Ph(c) 100.00
857 The Goofy Adventure Story . 150.00
858 Daisy Duck's Diary 90.00
859 Topper and Neil. 80.00
860 Wyatt Earp,Ph(c) 200.00
861 Frosty the Snowman. 75.00
862 Truth About Mother Goose . . 135.00
863 Francis the Famous
     Talking Mule 60.00
864 The Littlest Snowman 90.00
865 Andy Burnett,Ph(c) 175.00
866 Mars and Beyond 150.00
867 Santa Claus Funnies 100.00
868 The Little People. 90.00
869 Old Yeller,Ph(c). 110.00
870 Little Beaver 75.00
871 Curly Kayoe 60.00
872 Captain Kangaroo,Ph(c) 250.00
873 Grandma Duck's
     Farm Friends. 90.00
874 Old Ironsides. 125.00
875 Trumpets West 60.00
876 Tales of Wells Fargo,Ph(c) . . 175.00
877 ATh,Frontier Doctor,Ph(c) . . . 175.00
878 Peanuts. 350.00
879 Brave Eagle,Ph(c). 60.00
880 MD,Steve Donovan,Ph(c) . . . 75.00
881 The Captain and the Kids. . . . 60.00
882 ATh,W.DisneyPresentsZorro. 300.00
883 The Little Rascals 100.00
884 Hawkeye and the Last
     of the Mohicans,Ph(c) 135.00

885 Fury,Ph(c) 125.00
886 Bongo and Lumpjaw. 90.00
887 The Hardy Boys,Ph(c) 175.00
888 Elmer Fudd 60.00
889 ATh,W.Disney's Clint
     & Mac(TV),Ph(c) 225.00
890 Wyatt Earp,Ph(c) 135.00
891 Light in the Forest,
     C.Parker Ph(c). 135.00
892 Maverick,J.Garner Ph(c). . . . 450.00
893 Jim Bowie,Ph(c) 100.00
894 Oswald the Rabbit 60.00
895 Wagon Train,Ph(c) 200.00
896 Adventures of Tinker Bell . . . 150.00
897 Jiminy Cricket 125.00
898 EK,Silvertip 90.00
899 Goofy 100.00
900 BF,Prince Valiant 125.00
901 Little Hiawatha 90.00
902 Will-Yum!. 60.00
903 Dotty Dripple and Taffy 50.00
904 Lee Hunter, Indian Fighter . . . 60.00
905 W.Disney's Annette (TV),
     Ph(c) 500.00
906 Francis the Famous
     Talking Mule 60.00
907 Ath,Sugarfoot,Ph(c). 235.00
908 The Little People
     and the Giant. 75.00
909 Smitty 60.00
910 ATh,The Vikings,
     K.Douglas Ph(c) 150.00
911 The Gray Ghost,Ph(c). 150.00
912 Leave it to Beaver,Ph(c) 300.00
913 The Left-Handed Gun,
     Paul Newman Ph(c) 175.00
914 ATh,No Time for Sergeants,
     Ph(c) 175.00
915 Casey Jones,Ph(c) 100.00
916 Red Ryder Ranch Comics . . 150.00
917 The Life of Riley,Ph(c) 225.00
918 Beep Beep, the Roadrunner. 200.00
919 Boots and Saddles,Ph(c) . . . 135.00
920 Ath,Zorro,Ph(c) 225.00
921 Wyatt Earp.Ph(c) 135.00
922 Johnny Mack Brown,Ph(c) . . 135.00
923 Timmy 50.00
924 Colt .45,Ph(c) 200.00
925 Last of the Fast Guns,Ph(c) . 135.00
926 Peter Pan 75.00
927 SB,Top Gun 60.00
928 Sea Hunt,L.Bridges Ph(c). . . 225.00
929 Brave Eagle,Ph(c). 60.00
930 Maverick,J. Garner Ph(c) . . . 200.00
931 Have Gun, Will Travel,Ph(c). . 275.00
932 Smokey the Bear 100.00
933 ATh,W.Disney's Zorro 225.00
934 Restless Gun 225.00
935 King of the Royal Mounted . . . 65.00
936 The Little Rascals 100.00
937 Ruff and Ready. 250.00
938 Elmer Fudd 60.00
939 Steve Canyon 90.00
940 Lolly and Pepper 50.00
941 Pluto 75.00
942 Pony Express 90.00
943 White Wilderness 125.00
944 SB,7th Voyage of Sinbad . . . 250.00
945 Maverick,J.Garner Ph(c). . . . 250.00
946 The Big Country,Ph(c) 150.00
947 Broken Arrow,Ph(c). 90.00
948 Daisy Duck's Diary 90.00
949 High Adventure,Ph(c) 100.00
950 Frosty the Snowman 75.00
951 ATh,Lennon Sisters
     Life Story,Ph(c) 250.00
952 Goofy 90.00
953 Francis the Famous
     Talking Mule 60.00
954 Man in Space 150.00
955 Hi and Lois 50.00
956 Ricky Nelson,Ph(c) 350.00

GOLDEN AGE

957 Buffalo Bee 175.00
958 Santa Claus Funnies 90.00
959 Christmas Stories 75.00
960 ATh,W.Disney's Zorro 225.00
961 Jace Pearson's Tales of
 Texas Rangers,Ph(c). 90.00
962 Maverick,J.Garner Ph(c). . . . 200.00
963 Johnny Mack Brown,Ph(c) . . 125.00
964 The Hardy Boys,Ph(c). 175.00
965 GrandmaDuck'sFarmFriends . 90.00
966 Tonka,Ph(c). 150.00
967 Chilly Willy 90.00
968 Tales of Wells Fargo,Ph(c) . . 150.00
969 Peanuts. 200.00
970 Lawman,Ph(c). 250.00
971 Wagon Train,Ph(c) 125.00
972 Tom Thumb 175.00
973 SleepingBeauty & the Prince 250.00
974 The Little Rascals 125.00
975 Fury,Ph(c) 125.00
976 ATh,W.Disney's Zorro,Ph(c) . 225.00
977 Elmer Fudd 60.00
978 Lolly and Pepper. 50.00
979 Oswald the Rabbit 00.00
980 Maverick,J.Garner Ph(c). . . . 200.00
981 Ruff and Ready. 150.00
982 The New Adventures of
 Tinker Bell 150.00
983 Have Gun, Will Travel,Ph(c) . 175.00
984 Sleeping Beauty's Fairy
 Godmothers. 165.00
985 Shaggy Dog,Ph(c) 150.00
986 Restless Gun,Ph(c) 150.00
987 Goofy 90.00
988 Little Hiawatha 90.00
989 Jimmy Cricket 125.00
990 Huckleberry Hound 235.00
991 Francis the Famous
 Talking Mule 60.00
992 ATh,Sugarfoot,Ph(c) 300.00
993 Jim Bowie,Ph(c) 90.00
994 Sea HuntL.Bridges Ph(c) . . . 150.00
995 Donald Duck Album 125.00
996 Nevada 75.00
997 Walt Disney Presents,Ph(c) . 150.00
998 Ricky Nelson,Ph(c) 350.00
999 Leave It To Beaver,Ph(c) . . . 300.00
1000 The Gray Ghost,Ph(c). 150.00
1001 Lowell Thomas' High
 Adventure,Ph(c). 90.00
1002 Buffalo Bee 125.00
1003 ATh,W.Disney's Zorro,Ph(c) 225.00
1004 Colt .45,Ph(c) 150.00
1005 Maverick,J.Garner Ph(c). . . 200.00
1006 SB,Hercules 175.00
1007 John Paul Jones,Ph(c) 90.00
1008 Beep, Beep, the
 Road Runner. 125.00
1009 CB,The Rifleman,Ph(c) 450.00
1010 Grandma Duck's Farm
 Friends. 250.00
1011 Buckskin,Ph(c) 150.00
1012 Last Train from Gun
 Hill,Ph(c) 155.00
1013 Bat Masterson,Ph(c). 225.00
1014 ATh,The Lennon Sisters,
 Ph(c) 250.00
1015 Peanuts. 200.00
1016 Smokey the Bear 75.00
1017 Chilly Willy 90.00
1018 Rio Bravo,J.Wayne Ph(c) . . 425.00
1019 Wagoon Train,Ph(c) 125.00
1020 Jungle 60.00
1021 Jace Pearson's Tales of
 the Texas Rangers,Ph(c). . . . 90.00
1022 Timmy 55.00
1023 Tales of Wells Fargo,Ph(c) . 150.00
1024 ATh,Darby O'Gill and
 the Little People,Ph(c). 175.00
1025 CB,W.Disney's Vacation in
 Disneyland. 350.00
1026 Spin and Marty,Ph(c) 135.00

1027 The Texan,Ph(c) 150.00
1028 Rawhide,
 Clint Eastwood Ph(c). 425.00
1029 Boots and Saddles,Ph(c) . . 100.00
1030 Spanky and Alfalfa, the
 Little Rascals 100.00
1031 Fury,Ph(c) 125.00
1032 Elmer Fudd 55.00
1033 Steve Canyon,Ph(c) 90.00
1034 Nancy and Sluggo
 Summer Camp 75.00
1035 Lawman,Ph(c). 135.00
1036 The Big Circus,Ph(c). 125.00
1037 Zorro,Ph(c) 275.00
1038 Ruff and Ready. 150.00
1039 Pluto 75.00
1040 Quick Draw McGraw 250.00
1041 ATh,Sea Hunt,
 L.Bridges Ph(c) 150.00
1042 The Three Chipmunks 125.00
1043 The Three Stooges,Ph(c) . . 475.00
1044 Have Gun,Will Travel,Ph(c) 175.00
1045 Restless Gun,Ph(c). 150.00
1046 Beep Beep, the
 Road Runner. 100.00
1047 CB,W.Disney's
 GyroGearloose 350.00
1048 The Horse Soldiers
 J.Wayne Ph(c). 275.00
1049 Don't Give Up the Ship
 J.Lewis Ph(c). 150.00
1050 Huckleberry Hound 150.00
1051 Donald in Mathmagic Land. 150.00
1052 RsM,Ben-Hur 175.00
1053 Goofy 90.00
1054 Huckleberry Hound
 Winter Fun. 150.00
1055 CB,Daisy Duck's Diary 175.00
1056 Yellowstone Kelly,
 C.Walker Ph(c) 120.00
1057 Mickey Mouse Album 100.00
1058 Colt .45,Ph(c) 175.00
1059 Sugarfoot 155.00
1060 Journey to the Center of the
 Earth, P.Boone Ph(c) 225.00
1061 Buffalo Bill. 125.00
1062 Christmas Stories 75.00
1063 Santa Claus Funnies 90.00
1064 Bugs Bunny's Merry
 Christmas 90.00
1065 Frosty the Snowman. 75.00
1066 ATh,77 Sunset Strip,Ph(c). 235.00
1067 Yogi Bear 220.00
1068 Francis the Famous
 Talking Mule 60.00
1069 ATh,The FBI Story,Ph(c). . 175.00
1070 Soloman and Sheba,Ph(c) . 160.00
1071 ATh,TheRealMcCoys,Ph(c). 175.00
1072 Blythe 90.00
1073 CB,Grandma Duck's Farm
 Friends. 235.00
1074 Chilly Willy 90.00
1075 Tales of Wells Fargo,Ph(c) . 150.00
1076 MSy,The Rebel,Ph(c) 250.00
1077 SB,The Deputy,
 H.Fonda Ph(c). 500.00
1078 The Three Stooges,Ph(c) . . 225.00
1079 The Little Rascals 100.00
1080 Fury,Ph(c) 125.00
1081 Elmer Fudd 55.00
1082 Spin and Marty 150.00
1083 Men into Space,Ph(c) 150.00
1084 Speedy Gonzales 125.00
1085 ATh,The Time Machine 300.00
1086 Lolly and Pepper. 50.00
1087 Peter Gunn,Ph(c) 175.00
1088 A Dog of Flanders,Ph(c) 90.00
1089 Restless Gun,Ph(c). 150.00
1090 Francis the Famous
 Talking Mule 60.00
1091 Jacky's Diary. 90.00
1092 Toby Tyler,Ph(c) 125.00

Four Color #1097
© Dell Publishing Co.

1093 MacKenzie's Raiders,Ph(c) 125.00
1094 Goofy 150.00
1095 CB,W.Disney's
 GyroGearloose 170.00
1096 The Texan,Ph(c) 150.00
1097 Rawhide,C.Eastwood Ph(c) 375.00
1098 Sugarfoot,Ph(c) 150.00
1099 CB(c),Donald Duck Album . 150.00
1100 W.Disney's Annette's
 Life Story (TV),Ph(c) 425.00
1101 Robert Louis Stevenson's
 Kidnapped,Ph(c) 125.00
1102 Wanted: Dead or Alive,
 Ph(c) 225.00
1103 Leave It To Beaver,Ph(c). . . 275.00
1104 Yogi Bear Goes to College . 150.00
1105 ATh,Gale Storm,Ph(c) 225.00
1106 ATh,77 Sunset Strip,Ph(c). . 175.00
1107 Buckskin,Ph(c) 125.00
1108 The Troubleshooters,Ph(c) . . 90.00
1109 This Is Your Life, Donald
 Duck,O:Donald Duck. 250.00
1110 Bonanza,Ph(c) 650.00
1111 Shotgun Slade. 125.00
1112 Pixie and Dixie
 and Mr. Jinks. 150.00
1113 Tales of Wells Fargo,Ph(c) . 165.00
1114 Huckleberry Finn,Ph(c) 90.00
1115 Ricky Nelson,Ph(c) 275.00
1116 Boots and Saddles,Ph(c) . . . 90.00
1117 Boy and the Pirate,Ph(c) . . 125.00
1118 Sword and the Dragon,Ph(c)135.00
1119 Smokey and the Bear
 Nature Stories 65.00
1120 Dinosaurus,Ph(c) 150.00
1121 RC,GE,HerculesUnchained 175.00
1122 Chilly Willy. 80.00
1123 Tombstone Territory,Ph(c) . . 175.00
1124 Whirlybirds,Ph(c) 165.00
1125 GK,RH,Laramie,Ph(c) 175.00
1126 Sundance,Ph(c) 125.00
1127 The Three Stooges,Ph(c) . . 400.00
1128 Rocky and His Friends 650.00
1129 Pollyanna,H.Mills Ph(c) 150.00
1130 SB,The Deputy,
 H.Fonda Ph(c) 175.00
1131 Elmer Fudd 55.00
1132 Space Mouse 100.00
1133 Fury,Ph(c) 125.00
1134 ATh,Real McCoys,Ph(c) . . . 175.00
1135 M.G.M.'s Mouse Musketeers 100.00
1136 Jungle Cat,Ph(c) 120.00
1137 The Little Rascals 100.00
1138 The Rebel,Ph(c) 165.00
1139 SB,Spartacus,Ph(c). 250.00
1140 Donald Duck Album 200.00

All comics prices listed are for *Near Mint* condition.

1141 Huckleberry Hound for
President 150.00
1142 Johnny Ringo,Ph(c) 135.00
1143 Pluto 100.00
1144 The Story of Ruth,Ph(c) . . . 150.00
1145 GK,The Lost World,Ph(c) . . 175.00
1146 Restless Gun,Ph(c) 135.00
1147 Sugarfoot,Ph(c). 175.00
1148 I aim at the Stars,Ph(c) 135.00
1149 Goofy. 125.00
1150 CB,Daisy Duck's Diary . . . 200.00
1151 Mickey Mouse Album 100.00
1152 Rocky and His Friends 400.00
1153 Frosty the Snowman. 90.00
1154 Santa Claus Funnies 175.00
1155 North to Alaska 300.00
1156 Walt Disney Swiss
Family Robinson 135.00
1157 Master of the World. 125.00
1158 Three Worlds of Gulliver 125.00
1159 ATh,77 Sunset Strip 170.00
1160 Rawhide 250.00
1161 CB,Grandma Duck's
Farm Friends. 300.00
1162 Yogi Bera joins the Marines 135.00
1163 Daniel Boone 90.00
1164 Wanted: Dead or Alive 175.00
1165 Ellery Queen 200.00
1166 Rocky and His Friends 475.00
1167 Tales of Wells Fargo,Ph(c) . 150.00
1168 The Detectives,
R.Taylor Ph(c) 175.00
1169 New Adventures of
Sherlock Holmes 300.00
1170 The Three Stooges,Ph(c) . . 250.00
1171 Elmer Fudd 60.00
1172 Fury,Ph(c) 125.00
1173 The Twilight Zone 400.00
1174 The Little Rascals 75.00
1175 M.G.M.'s Mouse Musketeers . 50.00
1176 Dondi,Ph(c) 75.00
1177 Chilly Willy. 80.00
1178 Ten Who Dared 135.00
1179 The Swamp Fox,
L.Nielson Ph(c) 150.00
1180 The Danny Thomas Show . 300.00
1181 Texas John Slaughter,Ph(c) 135.00
1182 Donald Duck Album 100.00
1183 101 Dalmatians 200.00
1184 CB,W.Disney's
Gyro Gearloose 165.00
1185 Sweetie Pie 75.00
1186 JDa,Yak Yak 145.00
1187 The Three Stooges,Ph(c) . . 250.00
1188 Atlantis the Lost
Continent,Ph(c) 200.00
1189 Greyfriars Bobby,Ph(c) 135.00
1190 CB(c),Donald and
the Wheel 135.00
1191 Leave It to Beaver,Ph(c) . . . 500.00
1192 Rocky Nelson,Ph(c) 265.00
1193 The Real McCoys,Ph(c) . . . 150.00
1194 Pepe,Ph(c) 50.00
1195 National Velvet,Ph(c) 125.00
1196 Pixie and Dixie
and Mr. Jinks 100.00
1197 The Aquanauts,Ph(c) 135.00
1198 Donald in Mathmagic Land . 125.00
1199 Absent-Minded Professor,
Ph(c) 150.00
1200 Hennessey,Ph(c) 125.00
1201 Goofy 90.00
1202 Rawhide,C.Eastwood Ph(c) 275.00
1203 Pinocchio 100.00
1204 Scamp. 75.00
1205 David & Goliath,Ph(c) 125.00
1206 Lolly and Pepper. 40.00
1207 MSy,The Rebel,Ph(c) 150.00
1208 Rocky and His Friends 375.00
1209 Sugarfoot,Ph(c). 150.00
1210 The Parent Trap,
H.Mills Ph(c) 175.00

Four Color #1275
© *Dell Publishing Co.*

1211 RsM,77 Sunset Strip,Ph(c) . 150.00
1212 Chilly Willy 80.00
1213 Mysterious Island,Ph(c) . . . 150.00
1214 Smokey the Bear 65.00
1215 Tales of Wells Fargo,Ph(c) . 135.00
1216 Whirlybirds,Ph(c) 135.00
1218 Fury,Ph(c) 125.00
1219 The Detectives,
Robert Taylor Ph(c) 150.00
1220 Gunslinger,Ph(c) 150.00
1221 Bonanza,Ph(c) 350.00
1222 Elmer Fudd 60.00
1223 GK,Laramie,Ph(c) 125.00
1224 The Little Rascals 75.00
1225 The Deputy,H.Fonda Ph(c) . 175.00
1226 Nikki, Wild Dog of the North . 90.00
1227 Morgan the Pirate,Ph(c) . . . 135.00
1229 Thief of Bagdad,Ph(c). 125.00
1230 Voyage to the Bottom
of the Sea,Ph(c) 225.00
1231 Danger Man,Ph(c) 200.00
1232 On the Double. 75.00
1233 Tammy Tell Me True 125.00
1234 The Phantom Planet. 135.00
1235 Mister Magoo 175.00
1236 King of Kings,Ph(c). 135.00
1237 ATh,The Untouchables,
Ph(c) 400.00
1238 Deputy Dawg 200.00
1239 CB(c),Donald Duck Album . 150.00
1240 The Detectives,
R.Taylor Ph(c) 150.00
1241 Sweetie Pies 50.00
1242 King Leonardo and
His Short Subjects. 225.00
1243 Ellery Queen 150.00
1244 Space Mouse 200.00
1245 New Adventures of
Sherlock Holmes 250.00
1246 Mickey Mouse Album 100.00
1247 Daisy Duck's Diary 150.00
1248 Pluto 125.00
1249 The Danny Thomas Show,
Ph(c) 275.00
1250 Four Horseman of the
Apocalypse,Ph(c) 125.00
1251 Everything's Ducky 85.00
1252 The Andy Griffith Show,
Ph(c) 700.00
1253 Spaceman 135.00
1254 'Diver Dan' 90.00
1255 The Wonders of Aladdin . . . 125.00
1256 Kona, Monarch of
Monster Isle. 135.00
1257 Car 54, Where Are You?,
Ph(c) 150.00

1258 GE,The Frogmen 135.00
1259 El Cid,Ph(c). 135.00
1260 The Horsemasters,Ph(c) . . . 250.00
1261 Rawhide,C.Eastwood Ph(c) 300.00
1262 The Rebel,Ph(c) 165.00
1263 RsM,77 Sunset Strip,Ph(c) . 150.00
1264 Pixie & Dixie & Mr.Jinks . . . 175.00
1265 The Real McCoys,Ph(c) . . . 150.00
1266 M.G.M.'s Spike and Tyke . . . 50.00
1267 CB,GyroGearloose 125.00
1268 Oswald the Rabbit 60.00
1269 Rawhide,C.Eastwood Ph(c) 300.00
1270 Bullwinkle and Rocky 375.00
1271 Yogi Bear Birthday Party. . . . 90.00
1272 Frosty the Snowman. 90.00
1273 Hans Brinker,Ph(c) 125.00
1274 Santa Claus Funnies 100.00
1275 Rocky and His Friends 375.00
1276 Dondi. 50.00
1278 King Leonardo and
His Short Subjects. 225.00
1279 Grandma Duck's Farm
Friends. 75.00
1280 Hennessey,Ph(c) 110.00
1281 Chilly Willy 80.00
1282 Babes in Toyland,Ph(c). . . . 250.00
1283 Bonanza,Ph(c) 350.00
1284 RH,Laramie,Ph(c). 125.00
1285 Leave It to Beaver,Ph(c). . . . 350.00
1286 The Untouchables,Ph(c). . . 275.00
1287 Man from Wells Fargo,Ph(c)100.00
1288 RC,GE,The Twilight Zone . . 225.00
1289 Ellery Queen. 150.00
1290 M.G.M.'s Mouse
Musketeers 50.00
1291 RsM,77 Sunset Strip,Ph(c) . 150.00
1293 Elmer Fudd. 55.00
1294 Ripcord 125.00
1295 Mr. Ed, the Talking Horse,
Ph(c) 225.00
1296 Fury,Ph(c). 125.00
1297 Spanky, Alfalfa and the
Little Rascals 75.00
1298 The Hathaways,Ph(c) 75.00
1299 Deputy Dawg 200.00
1300 The Comancheros 275.00
1301 Adventures in Paradise 100.00
1302 JohnnyJason,TeenReporter . 50.00
1303 Lad: A Dog,Ph(c). 75.00
1304 Nellie the Nurse 125.00
1305 Mister Magoo 150.00
1306 Target: The Corruptors,
Ph(c) 100.00
1307 Margie 90.00
1308 Tales of the Wizard of Oz . . 225.00
1309 BK,87th Precinct,Ph(c) 175.00
1310 Huck and Yogi Winter
Sports 150.00
1311 Rocky and His Friends 375.00
1312 National Velvet,Ph(c) 75.00
1313 Moon Pilot.Ph(c) 135.00
1328 GE,The Underwater
City,Ph(c). 125.00
1330 GK,Brain Boy 225.00
1332 Bachelor Father 135.00
1333 Short Ribs. 90.00
1335 Aggie Mack. 60.00
1336 On Stage. 75.00
1337 Dr. Kildare,Ph(c) 150.00
1341 The Andy Griffith Show,
Ph(c) 650.00
1348 JDa,Yak Yak 150.00
1349 Yogi Berra Visits the U.N. . . 175.00
1350 Commanche,Ph(c) 90.00
1354 Calvin and the Colonel 150.00

FOUR FAVORITES
Ace Magazines, Sept., 1941
1 B:Vulcan, Lash Lighting, Magno
the Magnetic Man, Raven,
Flag (c),Hitler 3,000.00
2 A: Black Ace 1,400.00

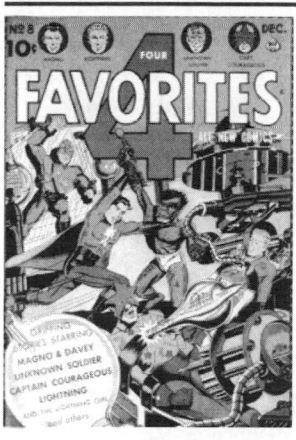

4 Favorites #8
© Ace Magazines

6-3 Tennis(c)	200.00
6-4 Football(c)	200.00
6-5	300.00
7-1 Basketball(c)	200.00
7-2 LbC(c)	500.00
7-3	250.00
7-4 LbC(c)	500.00
7-5	250.00
7-6 LbC(c)	500.00

Becomes:

FOREMOST BOYS
Jan., 1949

8-1	250.00
8-2 LbC(c),Surfing(c)	500.00
8-3 LbC(c)	500.00
8-4 LbC	500.00
8-5 LbC(c)	500.00
8-6 LbC	500.00
38 LbC(c), Johnny Weismuller	500.00
39 LbC(c), Johnny Weismuller	500.00
40 LbC(c), White Rider	500.00

Becomes:

THRILLING CRIME CASES

FOXHOLE
Mainline Publ., 1954

1 JK.	600.00
2 JK.	400.00
3 JK(c)	250.00
4 JK(c)	225.00

Charlton Comics, 1955–56

5 JK(c)	350.00
6 JK.	350.00
7	150.00

FOXY FAGAN
Dearfield Publ. Co., 1946–48

1	200.00
2	150.00
3	125.00
4	125.00
5	125.00
6 Rocket	125.00
7	125.00

FRANK BUCK
Fox Features Syndicate, 1950

1 (70) WW.	425.00
2 (71) WW.	225.00
3	175.00

FRANKENSTEIN COMICS
Crestwood Publications
(Prize Publ.), Summer, 1945

1 B:Frankenstein,DBr(a&c)	2,000.00
2 DBr(a&c)	1,000.00
3 DBr(a&c)	750.00
4 DBr(a&c)	750.00
5 DBr(a&c)	750.00
6 DBr(a&c),S&K	600.00
7 DBr(a&c),S&K	600.00
8 DBr(a&c),S&K	600.00
9 DBr(a&c),S&K	600.00
10 DBr(a&c),S&K	600.00
11 DBr(a&c)A:Boris Karloff	500.00
12 DBr(a&c)	500.00
13 DBr(a&c)	500.00
14 DBr(a&c)	500.00
15 DBr(a&c)	500.00
16 DBr(a&c)	500.00
17 DBr(a&c)	500.00
18 DBr,B:Horror	750.00
19 DBr	400.00
3-4 DBr.	350.00
3-5 DBr.	350.00
3-6 DBr.	350.00
4-1 thru 4-6 DBr	@350.00
5-1 thru 5-4 DBr	@350.00

3 E:Vulcan	1,200.00
4 E:Raven,B.Unknown Soldiers	1,000.00
5 B:Captain Courageous	1,000.00
6 A: The Flag, B: Mr. Risk	900.00
7 JM	900.00
8	900.00
9 RP,HK	1,000.00
10 HK	1,200.00
11 HK,LbC,UnKnown Soldier	1,500.00
12 LbC	800.00
13 LbC	700.00
14 Fer	700.00
15 Fer.	700.00
16 Bondage(c)	800.00
17 Magno Lighting	700.00
18 Magno Lighting	700.00
19 RP(a&c)	400.00
20 RP(a&c)	400.00
21 RP(a&c)	400.00
22 RP(c).	350.00
23 RP(c).	350.00
24 RP(c).	350.00
25 RP(c).	350.00
26 RP(c).	350.00
27 RP(c).	300.00
28	300.00
29	300.00
30 thru 32	@250.00

4MOST
Novelty Publ./Star Publ.,
Winter 1941

1 The Target, The Cadet	2,500.00
2 The Target.	1,500.00
3 Dan'l Flannel, Flag(c)	700.00
4 Dr. Seuss (1pg.).	700.00
2-1	400.00
2-2	400.00
2-3	400.00
2-4 Hitler,Tojo,Mussolini (c)	600.00
3-1	300.00
3-2	300.00
3-3	300.00
3-4	300.00
4-1	250.00
4-2 Walter Johnson(c)	250.00
4-3	250.00
4-4	250.00
5-1 The Target, Football(c)	200.00
5-2	200.00
5-3	200.00
5-4 Football(c)	200.00
6-1 Skiing(c).	200.00
6-2 LbC(c)	500.00

Frankenstein Comics #26
© Crestwood Publications

5-5 DBr, Oct.–Nov., 1954	350.00

FRANK MERRIWELL
AT YALE
Charlton Comics, 1955–56

1	125.00
2 thru 4	@100.00

FREEDOM TRAIN
Street & Smith Publications

1 BP	250.00

FRISKY ANIMALS
ON PARADE
Ajax-Farrell Publ., 1957

1 LbC(c)	250.00
2	125.00
3 LbC(c)	250.00

FRISKY FABLES
Novelty Press/Premium Group/
Star Publ., Spring, 1945

1 AFa	250.00
2 AFa	150.00
3 AFa	150.00
4 AFa	125.00
5 AFa	125.00
6 AFa	125.00
7 AFa,Flag (c)	150.00
2-1 AFa,Rainbow(c)	150.00
2-2 AFa	135.00
2-3 AFa	135.00
2-4 AFa	135.00
2-5 AFa	135.00
2-6 AFa	135.00
2-7 AFa	135.00
2-8 AFa,Halloween (c)	135.00
2-9 AFa,Thanksgiving(c)	125.00
2-10 AFa,Christmas (c)	135.00
2-11 AFa.	135.00
2-12 AFa,Valentine's Day (c)	125.00
3-1 AFa	125.00
3-2 AFa	135.00
3-3 AFa	135.00
3-4 AFa	125.00
3-5 AFa	125.00
3-6 AFa	125.00
3-7 AFa	125.00
3-8 AFa,Turkey (c)	125.00
3-9 AFa	125.00
3-10 AFa	125.00
3-11 AFa,1948(c)	125.00
3-12 AFa	125.00

All comics prices listed are for *Near Mint* condition.

Frisky Fables #40
© Star Publications

4-1 thru 4-7 AFa . . . . @125.00
5-1 AFa 125.00
5-2 AFa 125.00
5-3 . . . . 125.00
5-4 Star Publications 125.00
39 LbC(c) 250.00
40 LbC(c), Christmas 250.00
41 LbC(c) 250.00
42 LbC(c) 250.00
43 LbC(c) 100.00
Becomes:

FRISKY ANIMALS
Star Publications Jan., 1951
44 LbC, Super Cat 250.00
45 LbC 350.00
46 LbC, Baseball 250.00
47 LbC 250.00
48 LbC 250.00
49 LbC 250.00
50 LbC 250.00
51 LbC(c) 250.00
52 LbC(c), Christmas 275.00
53 LbC(c) 250.00
54 LbC(c), Supercat(c) 250.00
55 LbC(c), same 250.00
56 LbC(c), same 250.00
57 LbC(c), same 250.00
58 LbC(c), same, July, 1954 . . . . . 250.00

FRITZI RITZ
United Features Syndicate/
St. John Publications,
Fall, 1948
N# Special issue 250.00
2 . . . . 150.00
3 . . . . 125.00
4 and 5 . . . . @125.00
6 A:Abbie & Slats 150.00
7 . . . . 125.00
Becomes:

UNITED COMICS
United Features, 1950
8 thru 26 Bushmiller(c) . . . . . . @125.00
Becomes:

FRITZI RITZ
United Features, 1953
27 thru 59 . . . . @125.00

FROGMAN COMICS
Hillman Periodicals,
Jan.–Feb., 1952–May, 1953
1 . . . . 200.00

2 . . . . 150.00
3 . . . . 150.00
4 MMe. 150.00
5 BK,AT. 150.00
6 thru 11 . . . . @100.00

FROM HERE TO INSANITY
Charlton Comics, 1955
8 . . . . 400.00
9 . . . . 300.00
10 SD(c) 500.00
11 JK 500.00
12 JK 500.00
3-1 . . . . 700.00

FRONTIER FIGHTER
See: DAVY CROCKETT

FRONTIER ROMANCES
Avon Periodicals,
Nov.–Dec., 1949
1 She Learned to Ride and Shoot,
   and Kissing Came Natural . . 650.00
2 Bronc-Busters Sweetheart,
   Jan.–Feb., 1950 . . . . 450.00

FRONTIER SCOUT
DANIEL BOONE
See: DEATH VALLEY

FRONTIER TRAIL
See: RIDER, THE

FRONTLINE COMBAT
Tiny Tot Publications
(E.C. Comics), ,
July–Aug., 1951
1 HK(c),WW, JSe,JDa,Hanhung
   Changjn (c) 1,500.00
2 HK(c),WW,Tank Battle (c) 600.00
3 HK(c),WW,Naval Battleship
   fire (c) 900.00
4 HK(c),WW, Bazooka (c) 700.00
5 HK(c),JSe 900.00
6 HK(c),WW,JSe 500.00
7 HK(c),WW,JSe,Document of the
   Action at Iwo Jima 500.00
8 HK(c),WW,ATh 500.00
9 HK(c),WW,JSe,Civil War iss. . 500.00
10 GE,HK(c),WW,
   Crying Child (c) 400.00
11 GE 300.00
12 GE,Air Force issue 300.00
13 JSe,GE,WW(c), Bi-Planes (c). 300.00
14 JKu,GE,WW(c) 300.00
15 JSe,GE,WW(c), Jan., 1954 . . 300.00

FRONT PAGE
COMIC BOOK
Front Page Comics, 1945
1 JKu,BP,BF(c),I:Man in Black . 525.00

FUGITIVES FROM
JUSTICE
St. John Publishing Co.,
Feb., 1952
1 . . . . 250.00
2 MB, Killer Boomerang 300.00
3 GT 250.00
4 . . . . 200.00
5 Bondage (c), Oct., 1952 . . . . 275.00

FUNLAND
Approved Comics
(Ziff-Davis), 1949
N# 225.00

FUNLAND COMICS
Croyden Publ., 1945
1 Funny Animal 600.00

FUNNIES, THE
(1ST SERIES)
Dell Publishing Co., 1929-30
1 B:Foxy Grandpa, Sniffy. 3,000.00
2 thru 21 . . . . @1,000.00
N#(22) thru (36) . . . . @800.00

FUNNIES, THE
(2ND SERIES)
Dell Publishing Co., Oct., 1936
1 Tailspin Tommy,Mutt & Jeff,
   Capt. Easy,D.Dixon 6,000.00
2 Scribbly 3,000.00
3 . . . . 2,500.00
4 Christmas issue 2,000.00
5 . . . . 2,000.00
6 thru 10 . . . . @1,500.00
11 thru 22 . . . . 1,200.00
23 thru 29 . . . . @1,000.00
30 B:John Carter of Mars . . . 3,500.00
31 inc. Dick Tracy 1,500.00
32 . . . . 1,500.00
33 . . . . 1,500.00
34 . . . . 1,500.00
35 AMc,John Carter (c). 1,500.00
36 AMc,John Carter (c). 1,500.00
37 AMc,John Carter (c). 1,500.00
38 Rex King of the Deep (c). . . 1,500.00
39 Rex King (c). 1,500.00
40 AMc,John Carter (c). 1,500.00
41 Sky Ranger (c). 1,500.00
42 Rex King (c). 1,500.00
43 Rex King (c). 1,500.00
44 Rex King (c). 1,500.00
45 AMc,I&O:Phantasmo:Master
   of the World 1,600.00
46 AMc,Phantasmo (c) 900.00
47 AMc,Phantasmo (c) 800.00
48 AMc,ShM,Phantasmo (c) . . . 800.00
49 AMc,Phantasmo (c) 800.00
50 AMc,Phantasmo (c) 800.00
51 AMc,Phantasmo (c) 800.00
52 AMc,Phantasmo (c) 750.00
53 AMc,Phantasmo (c) 750.00
54 AMc,Phantasmo (c) 750.00
55 AMc,Phantasmo (c) 750.00
56 AMc,Phantasmo (c)
   E:John Carter 750.00
57 AMc,I&O:Captain Midnight. . 6,000.00
58 AMc,Captain Midnight (c). . . 1,800.00
59 AMc,Captain Midnight (c). . . 1,800.00
60 AMc,Captain Midnight (c). . . 1,800.00
61 AMc,Captain Midnight (c). . . 1,500.00
62 AMc,Captain Midnight (c). . . 1,200.00
63 AMc,Captain Midnight (c). . . 1,200.00
64 B: Woody Woodpecker 1,650.00
Becomes:

NEW FUNNIES
Dell Publishing Co. July, 1942
65 Andy Panda, Raggedy Ann &
   Andy, Peter Rabbit 1,600.00
66 same 750.00
67 Felix the Cat 750.00
68 . . . . 750.00
69 WK, The Brownies 750.00
70 . . . . 750.00
71 . . . . 500.00
72 WK 500.00
73 . . . . 500.00
74 . . . . 500.00
75 WK,Brownies 500.00
76 CB,Andy Panda, Woody
   Woodpecker 2,000.00
77 same 500.00
78 Andy Panda 500.00

79	350.00
80	350.00
81	350.00
82 WK,Brownies	400.00
83 WK,Brownies	400.00
84 WK,Brownies	400.00
85 WK,Brownies	400.00
86	300.00
87 Woody Woodpecker	250.00
88 same	250.00
89 same	250.00
90 same	250.00
91 thru 99	@200.00
100	175.00
101 thru 110	@150.00
111 thru 118	@150.00
119 Christmas	150.00
120 thru 142	@150.00
143 Christmas (c)	150.00
144 thru 149	@150.00
150 thru 154	@100.00
155 Christmas (c)	150.00
156 thru 167	@100.00
168 Christmas (c)	150.00
169 thru 181	@100.00
182 I&O:Knothead & Splinter	100.00
183 thru 200	@100.00
201 thru 240	@100.00
241 thru 288	@75.00

THE FUNNIES ANNUAL
Avon Periodicals, 1959

1 Best newspaper strips	600.00

FUNNIES ON PARADE
Eastern Color Printing Co., 1933

N# Mutt & Jeff, Joe Palooka	18,000.00

FUNNY BOOK
Funny Book Publ. Corp., (Parents Magazine) Dec., 1952

1 Alec, the Funny Bunny, Alice in Wonderland	200.00
2 Gulliver in Giant-Land	150.00
3	125.00
4 Adventures of Robin Hood	100.00
5 thru 9	@100.00

FUNNY FILMS
Best Syndicated Features (American Comics Group), Sept.–Oct., 1949

1 B:Puss An' Boots, Blunderbunny	250.00
2	125.00
3 Christmas(c)	125.00
4 thru 10	@100.00
11 thru 20	@100.00
21 thru 28	@100.00
29 May–June, 1954	100.00

FUNNY FUNNIES
Nedor Publ. Co., April, 1943

1 Funny Animals	235.00

COMICS MAGAZINE
Comics Magazine/Centaur, May, 1936

1 S&S, Dr. Mystic	17,000.00
2 S&S, Federal Agent	4,000.00
3	3,000.00
4	3,000.00
5	3,000.00
Becomes:	

FUNNY PAGES
Centaur, Nov., 1936

6 I:The Clock,1st masked hero	3,500.00

Funny Pages #10
© Centaur

7 WE	1,500.00
8 WE	1,500.00
9	1,500.00
10 WE	1,500.00
11	1,500.00
12	1,000.00
13 FGu,BoW	1,000.00
14 JCo,FGu,BoW	1,000.00
15 JCo	1,000.00
16 JCo,FGu	1,000.00
17 Centaur	1,500.00
18	1,000.00
19	1,000.00
20	1,000.00
21 B:The Arrow	5,000.00
22 BEv,GFx	2,500.00
23	2,500.00
24 BKa,B.Wayne prototype	2,800.00
25 JCo	2,000.00
26	2,000.00
27	2,000.00
28	2,000.00
29 JCo,BoW	2,000.00
30 BoW,The Arrow(c)	4,000.00
31	4,000.00
32 JCo,BoW	2,000.00
33 JCo,BoW,The Arrow(c)	3,000.00
34 JCo,The Arrow(c)	4,000.00
35 BoW,The Arrow(c)	4,000.00
36 Mad Ming (c)	2,000.00
37 JCo,Mad Ming (c)	2,000.00
38 Mad Ming(c)	2,000.00
39 The Arrow(c)	3,000.00
40 BoW,The Arrow(c)	3,000.00
41 BoW,The Arrow(c)	3,000.00
42 BoW,The Arrow(c)	3,000.00

FUNNY PICTURE STORIES
Comics Magazine/Centaur Publ., Nov., 1936

1 B:The Clock	5,500.00
2 The Spinner Talks	1,700.00
3 Tyrant Gold	1,200.00
4 WE,The Brothers Three	1,200.00
5 Timber Terror	1,200.00
6 War in Asia (c)	1,200.00
7 Racist Humor (c)	1,200.00
Vol 2	
#1(10)	750.00
#2 (11) BoW	750.00
#3 (12)BoW	650.00
#4 (13) Christmas (c)	750.00
#5 (14) BoW	650.00
#6 (15) Centaur	1,200.00
#7 (16)	650.00

#8 (17)	650.00
#9 (18)	650.00
#10 (19)	650.00
#11 (20)	650.00
Vol 3	
#1	650.00
#2	650.00
#3	650.00
Becomes:	

COMIC PAGES
July, 1939

4 BoW	850.00
5	650.00
6	650.00

FUNNYMAN
Magazine Enterprises of Canada, Dec., 1947

1 S&K(a&c)	650.00
2 S&K(a&c)	350.00
3 S&K(a&c)	300.00
4 S&K(a&c)	300.00
5 S&K(a&c)	300.00
6 S&K(a&c), Aug., 1948	300.00

FUNNY TUNES
Avon Periodicals, July, 1953

1 (fa),Space Mouse, Peter Rabbit Merry Mouse,Cicero the Cat	175.00
2 same	125.00
3 same	125.00
Becomes:	

SPACE COMICS
Avon Periodicals, March–April, 1954

4 (fa),F:Space Mouse	125.00
5 (fa),F:Space Mouse	100.00

FUTURE COMICS
David McKay Publications, June, 1940

1 Lone Ranger,Phantom	4,000.00
2 Lone Ranger	2,000.00
3 Lone Ranger	1,600.00
4 Lone Ranger,Sept., 1940	1,500.00

FUTURE WORLD COMICS
George W. Dougherty, Summer, 1946

1	600.00
2 Fall, 1946	500.00

GABBY HAYES WESTERN
Fawcett Publ., Nov., 1948

1 Ph(c)	700.00
2 Ph(c)	350.00
3 The Rage of the Purple Sage, Ph(c)	225.00
4 Ph(c)	225.00
5 Ph(c)	175.00
6 Ph(c)	175.00
7 Ph(c)	150.00
8 Ph(c)	150.00
9 Ph(c),V.The Kangaroo Crook	150.00
10 Ph(c)	150.00
11 Ph(c), Chariot Race	150.00
12 V:Beaver Ben, The Biting Bandit,Ph(c)	125.00
13 thru 50	@125.00

Charlton Comics

51	125.00
52 thru 59 Dec., 1954	@75.00

GANGSTERS AND
GUN MOLLS
Realistic Comics
(Avon), Sept., 1951
1 WW,A:Big Jim Colosimo,
　Evelyn Ellis 675.00
2 JKa, A:Bonnie Parker, The
　Kissing Bandit 500.00
3 EK, A:Juanita Perez, Crimes
　Homicide Squad 450.00
4 A:Mara Hite, Elkins Boys,
　June, 1952 . . . . 350.00

GANGSTERS CAN'T WIN
D.S. Publishing Co.,
Feb.–March, 1948
1 Shot Cop (c) 450.00
2 A:Eddie Bentz 250.00
3 Twin Trouble Trigger Man 200.00
4 Suicide on SoundStageSeven 250.00
5 Trail of Terror 200.00
6 Mystery at the Circus 200.00
7 Talisman Trail 150.00
8 . . . . 150.00
9 Suprise at Buoy 13,
　June–July, 1949 . . . . 150.00

GANG WORLD
Literary Enterprises
(Standard Comics),
Oct., 1952
5 Bondage (c) 350.00
6 Mob Payoff, Jan., 1953 . . . . . 150.00

GASOLINE ALLEY
Star Publications,
Oct., 1950
1 . . . . 250.00
2 LBc 275.00
3 LBc(c), April, 1950 . . . . 250.00

GEM COMICS
Spotlight Publ. April, 1945
1 A:Steve Strong,Bondage(c) . . 600.00

GENE AUTRY COMICS
Fawcett Publications,
Jan., 1942
1 The Mark of Cloven Hoof . 15,000.00
2 . . . . 2,400.00
3 Secret o/t Aztec Treasure . . 1,600.00
4 . . . . 1,400.00
5 Mystery of Paint Rock
　Canyon 1,400.00
6 Outlaw Round-up 1,300.00
7 Border Bullets 1,300.00
8 Blazing Guns 1,300.00
9 Range Robbers 1,300.00
10 Fightin' Buckaroo, Danger's
　Trail, Sept., 1943 . . . . 1,300.00
11 . . . . 1,200.00
12 . . . . 1,200.00

GENE AUTRY COMICS
Dell Publishing Co.,
May/June, 1946
1 . . . . 1,000.00
2 Ph(c) 600.00
3 Ph(c) 400.00
4 Ph(c),I:Flap Jack 400.00
5 Ph(c), all. 400.00
6 thru 10 . . . . @300.00
11 thru 19 . . . . @300.00
20 . . . . 275.00
21 thru 29 . . . . @200.00
30 thru 40, B:Giants . . . . @175.00
41 thru 56 E:Giants . . . . @150.00
57 . . . . 150.00

Gene Autry Comics #73
© Dell Publishing Co.

58 Christmas (c) 125.00
59 thru 66 . . . . @125.00
67 thru 80, B:Giant. . . . . @125.00
81 thru 90, E:Giant. . . . . @100.00
91 thru 93 . . . . @100.00
94 Christmas (c) 100.00
95 thru 99 . . . . @100.00
100 . . . . 150.00
101 thru 111 . . . . @125.00
112 thru 121 . . . . @125.00

GENE AUTRY'S
CHAMPION
Dell Publishing Co.,
Aug., 1950
(1) *see Dell Four Color #287*
(2) *see Dell Four Color #319*
3 . . . . 150.00
4 thru 19 . . . . @125.00

GEORGE PAL'S
PUPPETOON'S
Fawcett Publications,
Dec., 1945
1 Captain Marvel (c) 700.00
2 . . . . 400.00
3 . . . . 300.00
4 thru 17 . . . . @250.00
18 Dec., 1947 . . . . 200.00

GENERAL DOUGLAS
MACARTHUR
Fox Features Syndicate, 1950
N# True life story 250.00

GERALD McBOING-BOING
AND THE NEARSIGHTED
MR. MAGOO
Dell Publishing Co.,
Aug.–Oct., 1952
1 . . . . 225.00
2 thru 5 . . . . @175.00

GERONIMO
Avon Periodicals, 1950
1 Massacre at San Pedro Pass . 225.00
2 EK(c), Murderous Battle
　at Kiskayah 150.00
3 EK(c) 150.00
4 EK(c),Apache Death Trap,
　Feb., 1952 . . . . 125.00

GET LOST
Mikeross Publications,
Feb.–March, 1954
1 . . . . 400.00
2 . . . . 225.00
3 June–July, 1954 . . . . 200.00

GHOST
Fiction House Magazine,
Winter, 1951–Summer, 1954
1 The Banshee Bells 1,500.00
2 I Woke In Terror 900.00
3 The Haunted Hand of X 800.00
4 Flee the Mad Furies 350.00
5 The Hex of Ruby Eye 800.00
6 The Sleepers in the Crypt . . . 800.00
7 When Dead Rogues Ride 800.00
8 Curse of the Mist-Thing 800.00
9 It Crawls by Night,
　Bondage(c) 1,000.00
10 Halfway to Hades 800.00
11 GE, The Witch's Doll 800.00

GHOST BREAKERS
Street & Smith Publ., 1948
1 BP(a&c), A:Dr. Neff 1,000.00
2 BP(a&c), Breaks the Voodoo
　Hoodoo,Dec., 1948 . . . . 800.00

GHOSTLY WEIRD
STORIES
See: BLUE BOLT

GIANT BOY BOOK
OF COMICS
Newsbook Publ.
(Lev Gleason), 1945
1 A:Crime Buster & Young
　Robin Hood 1,200.00

GIANT COMICS EDITION
St. John Publ., 1948
1 Mighty Mouse 700.00
2 Abbie and Slats 325.00
3 Terry Toons 500.00
4 Crime Comics 750.00
5 MB, Police Case Book 750.00
6 MB(a&c), Western
　Picture Story 700.00
7 Mopsy 400.00
8 Adventures of Mighty Mouse . . 450.00
9 JKu,MB,Romance & Confession
　Stories,Ph(c) 750.00
10 Terry Toons 450.00
11 MB(a&c),JKu,Western
　Picture Stories 650.00
12 MB(a&c),Diary Secrets,
　Prostitute 1,700.00
13 MB,JKu, Romances 650.00
14 Mighty Mouse Album 450.00
15 MB(c),Romance 750.00
16 Little Audrey 500.00
N#, Mighty Mouse Album 450.00

GIANT COMICS EDITION
United Features Syndicate,
1945
1 A:Abbie & Slats, Jim Hardy,
　Ella Cinders,Iron Vic 500.00
2 Elmo, Jim Hardy, Abbie &
　Slats, 1945 . . . . 350.00

G.I. COMBAT
Quality Comics Group, 1952
1 RC(c), Beyond the Call
　of Duty 1,000.00
2 RC(c), Operation Massacre . . 450.00

G.I. Combat #2
© Quality Comics Group

3 An Indestructible Marine 375.00
4 Bridge to Blood Hill 375.00
5 Hell Breaks loose on
    Suicide Hill. 375.00
6 Beachhead Inferno 325.00
7 Fire Power Assault 300.00
8 RC(c),Death-trap Hill 300.00
9 Devil Riders 300.00
10 RC(c), Two-Ton Booby Trap . . 350.00
11 Hell's Heroes 250.00
12 Hand Grenade Hero 250.00
13 Commando Assault. 250.00
14 Spear Head Assault 250.00
15 Vengeance Assault 250.00
16 Trapped Under Fire. 225.00
17 Attack on Death Mountain. . . . 225.00
18 Red Battle Ground 225.00
19 Death on Helicopter Hill 225.00
20 Doomed Legion-Death Trap . 225.00
21 Red Sneak Attack 200.00
22 Vengeance Raid 200.00
23 No Grandstand in Hell 200.00
24 Operation Steel
    Trap,Comics Code. 200.00
25 Charge of the Commie
    Brigade 200.00
26 Red Guerrilla Trap 200.00
27 Trapped Behind Commie
    Lines 200.00
28 Atomic Battleground 200.00
29 Patrol Ambush 200.00
30 Operation Booby Trap 200.00
31 Human Fly on Heartbreak
    Hill 200.00
32 Atomic Rocket Assault 225.00
33 Bridge to Oblivion 200.00
34 RC,Desperate Mission 225.00
35 Doom Patrol 200.00
36 Fire Power Assault 200.00
37 Attack at Dawn 200.00
38 Get That Tank 200.00
39 Mystery of No Man's Land . . . 200.00
40 Maneuver Battleground 200.00
41 Trumpet of Doom 200.00
42 March of Doom 200.00
43 Operation Showdown 200.00
         See: DC Comics

GIFT COMICS
Fawcett Publications,
March, 1942
1 A:Captain Marvel, Bulletman,
    Golden Arrow,Ibis, the
    Invincible, Spy Smasher . . . 4,000.00
2 . . . . 2,500.00

---

3 . . . . 1,800.00
4 A:Marvel Family, 1949 . . . . . 1,500.00

GIGGLE COMICS
Creston Publ./
American Comics Group,
Oct., 1943
1 (fa)same. 400.00
2 KHu 250.00
3 KHu 225.00
4 KHu 200.00
5 KHu 200.00
6 KHu 150.00
7 KHu 150.00
8 KHu 150.00
9 I:Super Katt 175.00
10 KHu 125.00
11 thru 20 KHu . . . . @125.00
21 thru 30 KHu . . . . @125.00
31 thru 40 KHu . . . . @100.00
41 thru 94 KHu . . . . @100.00
95 A:Spencer Spook 100.00
96 KHu 100.00
97 KHu 100.00
98 KHu 100.00
99 KHu 100.00
100 and 101 March–April,1955 @100.00

G.I. IN BATTLE
Ajax/Farrell, 1952
1 War stories. 150.00
2 thru 9 . . . . @100.00
Ann #1 100 pgs. (1952) 300.00

Ajax, 1957
1 . . . . 125.00
2 . . . . 100.00
3 thru 6 . . . . @100.00

G.I. JANE
Stanhall Publ.,
May, 1953
1 . . . . 150.00
2 thru 6 . . . . @125.00
7 thru 9 . . . . @100.00
10 Dec., 1954 . . . . 100.00

G.I. JOE
Ziff-Davis Publication Co.,
1950
10 NS(c),Red Devils of Korea,
    V:Seoul City Lou 200.00
11 NS(c),The Guerrilla's Lair 125.00
12 NS(c). 125.00
13 NS(c),Attack at Dawn 125.00
14 NS(c),Temple of Terror,
    A:Peanuts the Great 135.00
2-6 It's a Foot Soldiers Job,
    I:Frankie of the Pump 125.00
2-7 BP,NS(c),The Rout at
    Sugar Creek 125.00
8 BP,NS(c),Waldo'sSqueezeBox 125.00
9 NS(c),Dear John 125.00
10 NS(c),Joe Flies the Payroll . 125.00
11 NS(c),For the Love of Benny . 125.00
12 NS(c),Patch work Quilt 125.00
13 NS(c). 125.00
14 NS(c),The Wedding Ring 125.00
15 The Lacrosse Whoopee 125.00
16 Mamie's Mortar 125.00
17 A Time for Waiting. 125.00
18 Giant 275.00
19 Old Army Game..Buck Passer 125.00
20 General Confusion 125.00
21 Save 'Im for Brooklyn 125.00
22 Portrait of a Lady 125.00
23 Take Care of My Little Wagon 125.00
24 Operation 'Operation' 125.00
25 The Two-Leaf Clover 125.00
26 NS(c),Nobody Flies Alone
    Mud & Wings. 125.00

---

27 'Dear Son...Come Home' 125.00
28 They Alway's Come Back
    Bondage (c). 125.00
29 What a Picnic 100.00
30 NS(c),The One-Sleeved
    Kimono 125.00
31 NS(c),Get a Horse 100.00
32 thru 47 . . . . @100.00
48 Atom Bomb 125.00
49 thru 51 June, 1957 . . . . @100.00

GINGER
Close-Up Publ.
(Archie Publications),
Jan., 1951
1 GFs 200.00
2 . . . . 150.00
3 . . . . 125.00
4 . . . . 125.00
5 . . . . 100.00
6 . . . . 100.00
7 thru 9 . . . . @125.00
10 A:Katy Keene,Summer,1954. . 150.00

GIRLS IN LOVE
Fawcett Publications,
May, 1950
1 Ph(c) 150.00
2 Ph(c),July, 1950 . . . . 100.00

GOLDEN ARROW
Fawcett Publications,
Spring, 1942
1 B:Golden Arrow 1,250.00
2 . . . . 600.00
3 . . . . 425.00
4 . . . . 400.00
5 Spring, 1947 . . . . 400.00
6 BK 425.00
6a 1944 Well Known Comics
    (Giveaway) 450.00

GOLDEN LAD
Spark Publications,
July, 1945–June, 1946
1 MMe(a&c),A:Kid Wizards,
    Swift Arrow,B:Golden Ladd. 1,200.00
2 MMe(a&c) 600.00
3 MMe(a&c) 600.00
4 MMe(a&c), The Menace of
    the Minstrel 600.00
5 MMe(a&c),O:Golden Girl 600.00

GOLDEN WEST LOVE
Kirby Publishing Co.,
Sept.–Oct., 1949
1 BP,I Rode Heartbreak Hill,
    Ph(c) 250.00
2 BP 175.00
3 BP,Ph(c) 175.00
4 BP,April, 1950 . . . . 175.00

GOLD MEDAL COMICS
Cambridge House, 1945
N# Captain Truth 600.00

GOOFY COMICS
Nedor Publ. Co./
Animated Cartoons
(Standard Comics),
June, 1943
1 (fa) 500.00
2 . . . . 300.00
3 VP 250.00
4 VP 225.00
5 VP 225.00
6 thru 10 VP . . . . @225.00
11 thru 15 . . . . @200.00

GOLDEN AGE

15 thru 19 . . . . @200.00
20 thru 35 FF . . . . @150.00
36 thru 48 . . . . @125.00

GREAT AMERICAN COMICS PRESENTS– THE SECRET VOICE
4 Star Publ., 1944
1 Hitler,Secret Weapon 700.00

GREAT COMICS
Novak Publ. Co., 1945
1 LbC(c) 650.00

GREAT COMICS
Great Comics Publications, Nov., 1941
1 I:The Great Zorro 2,000.00
2 Buck Johnson 1,000.00
3 The Lost City, Jan., 1942 . . . 4,000.00

GREEN GIANT COMICS
Pelican Publications, 1941
1 Black Arrow, Dr. Nerod
    O:Colossus 19,000.00

GREEN HORNET COMICS
Helnit Publ. Co./ Family Comics (Harvey Publ.), Dec., 1940
1 B:Green Hornet,P(c) 10,000.00
2 . . . . 3,500.00
3 BWh(c) 2,500.00
4 BWh(c) 2,000.00
5 BWh(c) 2,000.00
6 . . . . 2,000.00
7 BP, O:Zebra, B:Robin
    Hood & Spirit of 76 . . . . . . 1,800.00
8 BP,Bondage (c) 2,200.00
9 BP,JK(c),Behind the (c) . . . 1,800.00
10 BP 2,000.00
11 Who is Mr. Q? 1,500.00
12 BP,A:Mr.Q 1,800.00
13 Hitler (c) 2,200.00
14 BP,Spirit of 76-Twinkle
    Twins, Bondage(c) 1,500.00
15 ASh(c),Nazi Ghost Ship 1,500.00
16 BP,Prisoner of War 1,500.00
17 BP,ASh(c),Nazis' Last Stand 1,500.00
18 BP,ASh(c),Jap's Treacherous
    Plot,Bondage (c). 1,500.00

Green Hornet #33
© *Harvey Publications*

19 BP,ASh(c),Clash with the
    Rampaging Japs 1,500.00
20 BP,ASh(c),Tojo's
    Propaganda Hoax 2,200.00
21 BP,ASh(c),Unwelcome
    Cargo 1,200.00
22 ASh(c),Rendezvous with
    Jap Saboteurs 600.00
23 BF,ASh(c),Jap's Diabolical
    Plot #B2978 . . . . 1,200.00
24 BF,Science Fiction (c) 1,500.00
25 thru 29 . . . . @1,200.00
30 BP,JKu,AAv 1,200.00
31 BP,JKu 1,200.00
32 BP,JKu 1,000.00
33 BP,JKu,AAv 1,000.00
34 BP,JKu 1,000.00
35 BP,JKu 1,000.00
36 BP,JKu,Bondage (c) 1,500.00
37 BP,JKu,AAv,S&K 1,000.00
38 BP,JKu 1,000.00
39 S&K,AAv 1,400.00
40 thru 45 . . . . @900.00
46 Drug 1,100.00
47 AAv,Sept., 1949 . . . . 800.00

GREEN LAMA
Spark Publications/Prize Publ., Dec., 1944
1 I:Green Lama, Lt. Hercules
    & Boy Champions 2,500.00
2 MRa,Forward to Victory
    in 1945 . . . . 2,000.00
3 MRa,The Riddles of Toys . . 1,500.00
4 MRa,Dive Bombs Japan . . . 1,400.00
5 MRa(a&c),Fights for
    the Four Freedoms 1,400.00
6 MRa,Smashes a Plot
    against America 1,400.00
7 MRa,Merry X-Mas 1,000.00
8 MRa,Smashes Toy Master
    of Crime, March, 1946 . . . . 1,000.00

GREEN MASK, THE
Fox Features Syndicate, Summer, 1940
1 LF(c),O:Green Mask &
    Domino 6,500.00
2 A:Zanzibar 2,200.00
3 BP 1,500.00
4 B:Navy Jones 1,200.00
5 . . . . 1,000.00
6 B:Nightbird,E:Navy Jones,
    Bondage (c) 900.00
7 B:Timothy Smith &
    The Tumbler 800.00
8 JSs 750.00
9 E:Nightbird, Death Wields
    a Scalpel! 750.00
10 . . . . 500.00
11 The Banshee of Dead
    Man's Hill 500.00
2-1 Election of Skulls 400.00
2-2 Pigeons of Death 400.00
2-3 Wandering Gold Brick 350.00
2-4 Time on His Hands 350.00
2-5 JFe,SFd 450.00
2-6 Adventure of the Disappearing
    Trains, Oct.–Nov., 1946 . . . . . 450.00

GUMPS, THE
Dell Publishing Co., 1945
1 . . . . 300.00
2 . . . . 250.00
3 thru 5 . . . . @200.00

GUNFIGHTER
See: FAT AND SLAT

GUNS AGAINST GANGSTERS
Curtis Publ./Novelty Press, Sept.–Oct., 1948
1 LbC(a&c),B:Toni Gayle 500.00
2 LbC(a&c) 350.00
3 LbC(a&c) 300.00
4 LbC(a&c) 300.00
5 LbC(a&c) 300.00
6 LbC(a&c),Shark 300.00
2-1 LbC(a&c),Sept.–Oct., 1949 . 300.00

GUNSMOKE
Western Comics, Inc., April–May, 1949
1 Grl(a&c),Gunsmoke & Masked
    Marvel,Bondage (c) 600.00
2 Grl(a&c) 350.00
3 Grl(a&c) 300.00
4 Grl(c),Bondage(c) 250.00
5 Grl(c) 250.00
6 . . . . 225.00
7 . . . . 150.00
8 . . . . 150.00
9 . . . . 150.00
10 . . . . 150.00
11 thru 15 . . . . @125.00
16 Jan., 1952 . . . . 125.00

GUNSMOKE
Dell Publishing Co., 1956
1 J.Arness Ph(c) all 400.00
2 . . . . 250.00
3 . . . . 250.00
4 . . . . 250.00
5 . . . . 250.00
6 . . . . 200.00
7 . . . . 200.00
8 . . . . 200.00
9 . . . . 200.00
10 AW,RC 225.00
11 . . . . 200.00
12 AW 225.00
13 thru 27 . . . . @175.00

GUNSMOKE TRAIL
Four Star Comic. Corp (Ajax/Farrell), 1957
1 Western action 125.00
2 . . . . 100.00
3 . . . . 100.00
4 . . . . 100.00

HA HA COMICS
Creston Publ. (American Comics Group), Oct., 1943
1 Funny Animal, all 425.00
2 . . . . 200.00
3 . . . . 150.00
4 . . . . 150.00
5 . . . . 150.00
6 thru 10 . . . . @125.00
11 . . . . 100.00
12 thru 15 KHu . . . . @100.00
16 thru 20 KHu . . . . @100.00
21 thru 30 KHu . . . . @100.00
31 thru 101 . . . . @100.00
102 Feb.–March, 1955 . . . . 100.00

MISTER RISK
Humor Publ., Oct., 1950
1 (7) B:Mr. Risk 200.00
2 . . . . 200.00
Becomes:

MEN AGAINST CRIME
Ace Magazines, Feb., 1951
3 A:Mr. Risk, Case of the Carnival Killer	200.00
4 Murder-And the Crowd Roars	150.00
5	150.00
6	150.00
7 Get Them!	150.00

Becomes:

HAND OF FATE
Ace Magazines, Dec., 1951
8 MSy	600.00
9 LC	400.00
10 LC	400.00
11 Genie(c)	300.00
12	275.00
13 MSy,Hanging(c)	500.00
14 MSy,	275.00
15	275.00
16	275.00
17	275.00
18	275.00
19 LC,Drug issue,Quicksand(c).	400.00
20 LC	300.00
21 LC,Drug issue	400.00
22 LC	300.00
23 LC,Graveyard(c)	400.00
24 LC,Electric Chair	500.00
25 Nov., 1954	250.00
25a Dec., 1954	275.00

HANGMAN COMICS
See: LAUGH COMICS

HAP HAZARD COMICS
A.A. Wyn/Red Seal Publ./ Readers Research, Summer, 1944
1 Funny Teen	300.00
2 Dog Show	250.00
3 Sgr,	200.00
4 Sgr,	200.00
5 thru 10 Sgr,	@200.00
11 thru 13 Sgr,	@150.00
14 AF(c)	175.00
15	150.00
16 thru 24	@150.00

Becomes:

REAL LOVE
April, 1949
25 Dangerous Dates	250.00
26	200.00
27 LbC(c), Revenge Conquest	275.00
28 thru 40	@150.00
41 thru 66	@125.00
67 Comics code	100.00
68 thru 76, Nov., 1956	@100.00

HAPPY COMICS
Nedor Publications/ Animated Cartoons, Aug., 1943
1 Funny Animal in all	400.00
2	300.00
3	200.00
4	200.00
5 thru 10	@200.00
11 thru 20	@150.00
21 thru 31	@150.00
32 FF	350.00
33 FF	500.00
34 thru 37 FF	@200.00
38 thru 40	@100.00

Becomes:

HAPPY RABBIT
Standard Comics, Feb., 1951
41 Funny Animal in all	125.00
42 thru 50	@100.00

HARVEY COMIC HITS
Harvey Publications, Oct., 1951 (Formerly: JOE PALOOKA)
51 Phantom	400.00
52 Steve Canyon's Air Power	200.00
53 Mandrake	300.00
54 Tim Tyler's Tales of Jungle Terror	175.00
55 Love Stories of Mary Worth	125.00
56 Phantom, Bondage (c)	400.00
57 AR,Kidnap Racket	250.00
58 Girls in White	150.00
59 Tales of the Invisible	200.00
60 Paramount Animated Comics	600.00
61 Casper the Friendly Ghost	750.00
62 Paramount Animated Comics, April, 1953	225.00

HARVEY COMICS LIBRARY
Harvey Publications, 1952
1 Teen-age dope slaves	1,500.00
2 Sparkle Plenty	275.00

HAUNTED THRILLS
Four Star Publ. (Ajax/Farrell), June, 1952
1 Ellery Queen	700.00
2 LbC,Ellery Queen	450.00
3 Drug Story	600.00
4 Ghouls Castle	400.00
5 Fatal Scapel	400.00
6 Pit of Horror	400.00
7 Trail to a Tomb, Hitler	325.00
8 Vanishing Skull	300.00
9 Madness of Terror	300.00
10	300.00
11 Nazi Concentration Camp	400.00
12 RWb	225.00
13	225.00
14 RWb, Jesus Christ	250.00
15 The Devil Collects	225.00
16	225.00
17 Mirror of Madness	225.00
18 No Place to Go, Nov.–Dec., 1954	250.00

HAUNT OF FEAR
Fables Publ. (E.C. Comics) , May–June, 1950
15 JCr(a&c),AF,WW	5,000.00
16 JCr(a&c),AF,WW	2,500.00
17 JCr(a&c),AF,WW,O:Crypt of Terror,Vault of Horror & Haunt of Fear	2,400.00
4 AF(c),WW,JDa	1,800.00
5 JCr(a&c),WW,JDa,Eye Injury	1,500.00
6 JCr(a&c),WW,JDa	1,200.00
7 JCr(a&c),WW,JDa	1,200.00
8 AF(c),JKa,JDa, Shrunken Head	1,200.00
9 AF(c),JCr,JDa	1,200.00
10 AF(c),Grl,JDa	900.00
11 JKa,Grl,JDa	1,200.00
12 JCr,Grl,JDa	900.00
13 Grl,JDa	900.00
14 Grl(a&c),JDa,O:Old Witch	1,200.00
15 JDa	700.00
16 Grl(c),JDa,Ray Bradbury adaptation	700.00
17 JDa,Grl(c),Classic Ghastly (c)	700.00
18 JDa,Grl(c),JKa,Ray Bradbury adaptation	700.00
19 JDa,Guillotine (c), Bondage (c)	900.00
20 RC,JDa,Grl(a&c)	1,000.00
21 JDa,Grl(a&c)	1,000.00
22 JDa,Grl(a&c)	900.00

23 JDa,Grl(a&c)	900.00
22 JDa,Grl(a&c)	900.00
23 JDa,Grl(a&c)	900.00
24 JDa,Grl(a&c)	900.00
25 JDa,Grl(a&c)	900.00
26 RC,JDa,Grl(a&c)	1,000.00
27 JDa,Grl(a&c), Cannibalism	1,000.00
28 Dec., 1954	900.00

HAWK, THE
Approved Comics (Ziff-Davis), Winter, 1951
1 MA,The Law of the Colt,P(c)	250.00
2 JKu,Iron Caravan of the Mojave, P(c)	125.00
3 Leverett's Last Stand,P(c)	110.00
4 Killer's Town,P(c)	100.00
5	100.00
6	100.00
7	100.00
8 MB(c),Dry River Rampage	135.00
9 MB(a&c),JKu	135.00
10 MB(c)	135.00
11 MB(c).	135.00
12 MB(a&c), May, 1955	136.00

HEADLINE COMICS
American Boys Comics/ Headline Publ. (Prize Publ.), Feb., 1943
1 B:Jr. Rangers	1,000.00
2 JaB(a&c)	500.00
3 JaB(a&c)	450.00
4	350.00
5 HcK	350.00
6 HcK	350.00
7 HcK,Jr. Rangers	350.00
8 HcK,Hitler (c)	900.00
9 HcK	350.00
10 HcK,Hitler story,Wizard(c).	400.00
11	325.00
12 HcK,Heroes of Yesterday	325.00
13 HcK,A:Blue Streak	325.00
14 HcK,A:Blue Streak	325.00
15 HcK,A:Blue Streak	325.00
16 HcK,O:Atomic Man	450.00
17 Atomic Man(c).	250.00
18 Atomic Man(c).	250.00
19 S&K,Atomic Man(c)	500.00
20 Atomic Man(c)	250.00
21 E:Atomic Man	250.00
22 HcK	200.00
23 S&K(a&c),Valentines Day Massacre	400.00

Headline Comics #27
© *Prize Publications*

GOLDEN AGE

24 S&K(a&c),You Can't Forget
    a Killer 400.00
25 S&K(a&c),Crime Never Pays . 400.00
26 S&K(a&c),Crime Never Pays . 400.00
27 S&K(a&c),Crime Never Pays . 400.00
28 S&K(a&c),Crime Never Pays . 400.00
29 S&K(a&c),Crime Never Pays . 400.00
30 S&K(a&c),Crime Never Pays . 400.00
31 S&K(a&c),Crime Never Pays . 400.00
32 S&K(a&c),Crime Never Pays . 400.00
33 S&K(a&c),Police and FBI
    Heroes 400.00
34 S&K(a&c),same 400.00
35 S&K(a&c),same 400.00
36 S&K,same,Ph(c) 350.00
37 S&K,MvS,same,Ph(c) 400.00
38 S&K,same,Ph(c) 200.00
39 S&K,same,Ph(c) 200.00
40 S&K,Ph(c)Violent Crime 200.00
41 Ph(c),J.Edgar Hoover(c) 200.00
42 Ph(c) 150.00
43 Ph(c) 150.00
44 MMe,MvS,WE,S&K 300.00
45 JK 250.00
46 . . . . 200.00
47 . . . . 200.00
48 . . . . 200.00
49 MMe 200.00
50 . . . . 200.00
51 JK 200.00
52 . . . . 200.00
53 . . . . 200.00
54 . . . . 200.00
55 . . . . 200.00
56 S&K 275.00
57 . . . . 150.00
58 . . . . 150.00
59 . . . . 150.00
60 MvS(c) 150.00
61 MMe,MvS(c) 150.00
62 MMe(a&c) 150.00
63 MMe(a&c) 150.00
64 MMe(a&c) 150.00
65 MMe(a&c) 150.00
66 MMe(a&c) 150.00
67 MMe(a&c) 150.00
68 MMe(a&c) 150.00
69 MMe(a&c) 150.00
70 MMe(a&c) 150.00
71 MMe(a&c) 150.00
72 MMe(a&c) 150.00
73 MMe(a&c) 150.00
74 MMe(a&c) 150.00
75 MMe(a&c) 150.00
76 MMe(a&c) 150.00
77 MMe(a&c),Oct., 1956 . . . . 150.00

HECKLE AND JECKLE
St. John Publ./Pines,
Nov., 1951
1 Blue Ribbon Comics 300.00
2 Blue Ribbon Comics 150.00
3 . . . . 125.00
4 . . . . 125.00
5 . . . . 125.00
6 . . . . 125.00
7 . . . . 125.00
8 thru 14 . . . . @100.00
15 . . . . 125.00
16 thru 20 . . . . @100.00
21 thru 33 . . . . @100.00
34 June, 1959 . . . . 100.00

HELLO PAL COMICS
Harvey Publications,
Jan., 1943
1 B:Rocketman & Rocket Girl,
    Mickey Rooney, Ph(c) 2,000.00
2 Charlie McCarthy, Ph(c) 1,500.00
3 Bob Hope, Ph(c), May, 1943 1,700.00

HE-MAN
Approved Comics
(Ziff-Davis)/Toby Press, 1952
1 "Real-Life Adventure" 200.00
1a 175.00
2a 175.00

HENRY
Dell Publishing Co.,
Oct., 1946
1 . . . . 250.00
2 . . . . 150.00
3 thru 10 . . . . @150.00
11 thru 20 . . . . @125.00
21 thru 30 . . . . @125.00
31 thru 40 . . . . @100.00
41 thru 50 . . . . @75.00
51 thru 65 . . . . @75.00

HENRY ALDRICH COMICS
Dell Publishing Co.,
Aug.–Sept., 1950
1 . . . . 200.00
2 . . . . 150.00
3 . . . . 125.00
4 . . . . 125.00
5 . . . . 125.00
6 thru 10 . . . . @100.00
11 thru 22 . . . . @100.00

HEROES OF
THE WILD FRONTIER
See: BAFFLING MYSTERIES

Heroic Comics #2
© Eastern Color Printing

HEROIC COMICS
Eastern Color Printing Co./
Famous Funnies Aug., 1940
1 BEv(a&c),O:Hydroman,Purple
    Zombie, B:Man of India . . . 3,000.00
2 BEv(a&c),B:Hydroman (c)s . . 1,500.00
3 BEv(a&c) 750.00
4 BEv(a&c) 750.00
5 BEv(a&c) 700.00
6 BEv(a&c) 650.00
7 BEv(a&c),O:Man O'Metal 750.00
8 BEv(a&c) 500.00
9 BEv 500.00
10 BEv 500.00
11 BEv,E:Hydroman (c)s 500.00
12 BEv,B&0:Music Master 550.00
13 BEv,RC,LF 500.00
14 BEv 550.00
15 BEv,I:Downbeat 550.00

16 BEv,BTh,CCB(c),A:Lieut
    Nininger, Major Heidger,
    Lieut Welch,B:P(c) 300.00
17 BEv,A:JohnJames Powers,Hewitt
    T.Wheless, Irving Strobing . . . 300.00
18 HcK,BEv,Pass the Ammunition 300.00
19 HcK,BEv,A:Barney Ross 300.00
20 HcK,BEv 300.00
21 HcK,BEv 200.00
22 HcK,BEv,Howard Gilmore 200.00
23 HcK,BEv 200.00
24 HcK,BEv 200.00
25 HcK,BEv 200.00
26 HcK,BEv 200.00
27 HcK,BEv 200.00
28 HcK,BEv,E:Man O'Metal 200.00
29 HcK,BEv,E:Hydroman 200.00
30 BEv 200.00
31 BEv,CCB,Capt. Tootsie 125.00
32 ATh,CCB,WWII(c),
    Capt. Tootsie 150.00
33 ATh 175.00
34 WWII(c) 125.00
35 Ath,B:Rescue(c) 175.00
36 HcK,ATh 150.00
37 same 75.00
38 ATh 150.00
39 HcK,ATh 125.00
40 ATh,Boxing 125.00
41 Grl(c),ATh 125.00
42 ATh 125.00
43 ATh 100.00
44 HcK,ATh 100.00
45 HcK 100.00
46 HcK 100.00
47 HcK 100.00
48 HcK 125.00
49 HcK 100.00
50 HcK 100.00
51 HcK,ATh,AW 150.00
52 HcK,AW 125.00
53 HcK 125.00
54 . . . . 125.00
55 ATh 125.00
56 ATh(c) 100.00
57 ATh(c) 100.00
58 ATh(c) 100.00
59 ATh(c) 100.00
60 ATh(c) 100.00
61 BEv(c) 100.00
62 BEv(c) 100.00
63 BEv(c) 100.00
64 GE,BEv(c) 100.00
65 HcK(c),FF,ATh,AW,GE 150.00
66 HcK(c),FF 125.00
67 HcK(c),FF,Korean War(c) . . . 125.00
68 HcK(c),Korean War(c) 100.00
69 HcK(c),FF 150.00
70 HcK(c),FF,B:Korean War(c) . . 100.00
71 HcK(c),FF 100.00
72 HcK(c),FF 150.00
73 HcK(c),FF 100.00
74 HcK(c) 100.00
75 HcK(c),FF 100.00
76 thru 80 HcK,HcK(c) . . . . . . @100.00
81 FF,HcK(c) 100.00
82 FF,HcK(c) 100.00
83 FF,HcK(c) 100.00
84 HcK(c) 100.00
85 HcK(c) 100.00
86 FF,HcK(c) 120.00
87 FF,HcK(c) 120.00
88 HcK(c),E:Korean War (c)s . . . 100.00
89 HcK(c) 100.00
90 HcK(c) 100.00
91 HcK(c) 100.00
92 HcK(c) 100.00
93 HcK(c) 100.00
94 HcK(c) 120.00
95 HcK(c) 100.00
96 HcK(c) 100.00
97 HcK(c),E:P(c),June, 1955 . . . . 100.00

Hickory #2
© *Quality Comics Group*

HICKORY
**Comic Magazine
(Quality Comics Group),
Oct., 1949**
1 HSa, ... 225.00
2 HSa, ... 125.00
3 HSa, ... 100.00
4 HSa, ... 100.00
5 HSa, ... 100.00
6 HSa,Aug., 1950 . . . . 100.00

HI-HO COMICS
Four Star Publications, 1946
1 LbC(c) 600.00
2 LbC(c) 300.00
3 1946 . . . . 250.00

HI-JINX
**B & I Publ. Co. (American
Comics Group),
July–Aug., 1947**
1 (fa) all. 300.00
2 . . . . 200.00
3 . . . . 125.00
4 thru 7 . . . . @100.00
N# 150.00

HI-LITE COMICS
E.R. Ross Publ. Fall, 1945
1 . . . . 350.00

HILLBILLY COMICS
Charlton Comics, 1955
1 . . . . 125.00
2 thru 4 July 1956 . . . . @100.00

HI-SCHOOL ROMANCE
Harvey Publications, 1949–58
1 BP,Ph(c). 200.00
2 BP,Ph(c). 150.00
3 BP,Ph(c). 126.00
4 Ph(c) 125.00
5 BPPh(c). 125.00
6 and 7 . . . . @125.00
8 BP 125.00
9 . . . . 125.00
10 Rare 150.00
11 thru 20 BP(in many) . . . . . . @100.00
21 thru 50 . . . . @100.00
51 thru 75 . . . . @75.00

HI-SPOT COMICS
See: RED RYDER COMICS

HIT COMICS
**Comics Magazine
(Quality Comics Group),
July, 1940**
1 LF(c),O:Neon,Hercules,I:The
Red Bee, B:Bob & Swab,
Blaze Barton Strange
Twins,X-5 Super Agent
Casey Jones,Jack & Jill . . 12,000.00
2 GT,LF(c),B:Old Witch 3,800.00
3 GT,LF(c),E:Casey Jones. . . . 3,500.00
4 GT,LF(c),B:Super Agent &
Betty Bates,E:X-5. . . . . 3,200.00
5 GT,LF(c),B:Red Bee (c) . . . 10,000.00
6 GT,LF(c) 2,800.00
7 GT,LF(c),E:Red Bee (c) 2,500.00
8 GT,LF(c),B:Neon (c) 2,500.00
9 JCo,LF(c),E:Neon (c) 2,500.00
10 JCo,RC,LF(c),B:Hercules(c) 2,500.00
11 JCo,RC,LF(c),A:Hercules . . 2,200.00
12 JCo,RC,LF(c),A:Hercules . . 2,200.00
13 JCo,RC,LF(c),A:Hercules . . 2,200.00
14 JCo,RC,LF(c),A:Hercules . . 2,200.00
15 JCo,RC,A:Hercules 1,700.00
16 JCo,RC,LF(c),A:Hercules . . 1,700.00
17 JCo,RC,LF(c),E:Hercules(c) 1,700.00
18 JCo,RC(a&c),O:Stormy
Foster,B:Ghost of Flanders 1,800.00
19 JCo,RC(c),B:Stormy
Foster(c) 1,450.00
20 JCo,RC(c),A:Stormy Foster . 1,500.00
21 JCo,RC(c) 1,500.00
22 JCo. 1,500.00
23 JCo,RC(a&c) 1,400.00
24 JCo,E:Stormy Foster (c) . . . 1,400.00
25 JCo,RP,O:Kid Eternity 2,700.00
26 JCo,RP,A:Black Hawk 1,500.00
27 JCo,RP,B:Kid Eternity (c)s . . 700.00
28 JCo,RP,A:Her Highness 700.00
29 JCo,RP 700.00
30 JCo,RP,HK,V:Julius Caesar
and his Legion of Warriors . . 600.00
31 JCo,RP 600.00
32 JCo,RP,V:Merlin the Wizard . . 375.00
33 JCo,RP 350.00
34 JCo,RP,E:Stormy Foster 350.00
35 JCo,Kid Eternity Accused
of Murder 350.00
36 JCo,The Witch's Curse 350.00
37 JCo,V:Mr. Silence 350.00
38 JCo. 350.00
39 JCo,Runaway River Boat 350.00

Hit Comics #4
© *Harvey Publications*

40 PG,V:Monster from the Past . 350.00
41 PG,Did Kid Eternity Lose
His Power? 250.00
42 PG,Kid Eternity Loses Killer
Cronson. 250.00
43 JCo,PG,V:Modern
Bluebeard 250.00
44 JCo,PG,Trips up the Shoe . . . 250.00
45 JCo,PG,Pancho Villa against
Don Pablo 250.00
46 JCo,V:Mr. Hardeel. 250.00
47 A Polished Diamond Can Be
Rough on Rats 250.00
48 EhH,A Treasure Chest
of Trouble 250.00
49 EhH,V:Monsters from
the Mirror. 250.00
50 EhH,Heads for Trouble 250.00
51 EhH,Enters the Forgotten
World 225.00
52 EhH,Heroes out of the Past . . 225.00
53 EhH,V:Mr. Puny 225.00
54 V:Ghost Town Killer. 225.00
55 V:The Brute. 225.00
56 V:Rig Odds 225.00
57 Solves the Picture in
a Frame. 225.00
58 Destroys Oppression! 225.00
59 Battles Tomorrow's Crimes
Today! 225.00
60 E:Kid Eternity (c)s,
V:The Mummy 225.00
61 RC(a&c),I:Jeb Rivers 250.00
62 RC(c). 225.00
63 RC(c),A:Jeb Rivers. 250.00
64 RC,A:Jeb Rivers 250.00
65 Bondage (c),RC,July, 1950. . . 275.00

HOLIDAY COMICS
Fawcett Publ., Nov., 1942
1 Captain Marvel (c) 2,100.00

HOLLYWOOD COMICS
**New Age Publishers,
Winter, 1944**
1 (fa). 225.00

HOLLYWOOD CONFESSIONS
**St. John Publ. Co.,
Oct., 1949**
1 JKu(a&c) 400.00
2 JKu(a&c), Dec., 1949 . . . . 475.00

HOLLYWOOD DIARY
**Comics Magazine
(Quality Comics), Dec., 1949**
1 . . . . 250.00
2 Photo (c) 200.00
3 Photo (c) 150.00
4 . . . . 150.00
5 Photo (c), Aug., 1950 . . . . 150.00

HOLLYWOOD FILM STORIES
**Feature Publications,
(Prize) April, 1950**
1 June Allison,Ph(c) 250.00
2 Lizabeth Scott,Ph(c) 175.00
3 Barbara Stanwick,Ph(c) 175.00
4 Beth Hutton, Aug., 1950 . . . . . 175.00

HOLLYWOOD SECRETS
**Comics Magazine
(Quality Comics Group),
Nov., 1949**
1 BWa,BWa(c) 425.00
2 BWa,BWa(c),RC 300.00

3 Ph(c) 200.00
4 Ph(c),May, 1950 .... 200.00
5 Ph(c) 200.00
6 Ph(c) 200.00

HOLYOKE ONE-SHOT
Tem Publ. (Holyoke Publ. Co.), 1944

1 Grit Grady 300.00
2 Rusty Dugan 300.00
3 JK,Miss Victory,O:Cat Woman. 400.00
4 Mr. Miracle 250.00
5 U.S. Border Patrol 250.00
6 Capt. Fearless 250.00
7 Strong Man 300.00
8 Blue Streak 200.00
9 S&K, Citizen Smith 300.00
10 S&K, Capt. Stone 300.00

THE HOODED HORSEMAN
See: OUT OF THE NIGHT

HOORAY COMICS
Tendon Publishing Co., 1946

1 Funny animal 250.00

HOOT GIBSON WESTERN
Fox Features Syndicate, 1950
(Formerly: MY LOVE STORY)

1 (5) Ph(c) 350.00
2 (6) 325.00
3 WW 350.00

HOPALONG CASSIDY
Fawcett Publications, Feb., 1943

1 B:Hopalong Cassidy & Topper, Captain Marvel (c) 8,000.00
2 .... 1,200.00
3 Blazing Trails 600.00
4 5-full length story 500.00
5 Death in the Saddle, Ph(c) 450.00
6 .... 450.00
7 .... 450.00
8 Phantom Stage Coach 450.00
9 The Last Stockade 450.00
10 4-spine tingling adventures 450.00
11 Desperate Jetters! Ph(c) 300.00
12 The Mysterious Message 300.00
13 The Human Target, Ph(c) 300.00
14 Land of the Lawless, Ph(c) 300.00
15 Death holds the Reins, Ph(c) 300.00
16 Webfoot's Revenge, Ph(c) 300.00
17 The Hangman's Noose, Ph(c) 300.00

Howalong Cassidy #25
© Fawcett Publications

18 The Ghost of Dude Ranch, Ph(c) 300.00
19 A:William Boyd,Ph(c) 300.00
20 The Notorious Nellie Blaine!, B:P(c) 225.00
21 V:Arizona Kid 225.00
22 V:Arizona Kid 225.00
23 Hayride Horror 225.00
24 Twin River Giant 225.00
25 On the Trails of the Wild and Wooly West 225.00
26 thru 30 .... @200.00
31 52 pages 150.00
32 36 pages 150.00
33 52 pages 150.00
34 52 pages 150.00
35 52 pages 150.00
36 36 pages 125.00
37 thru 40, 52 pages .... @150.00
40 36 pages 150.00
41 E:P(c) 150.00
42 B:Ph(c) 150.00
43 .... 150.00
44 .... 125.00
45 .... 135.00
46 thru 51 .... @125.00
52 .... 100.00
53 .... 125.00
54 .... 125.00
55 .... 100.00
56 .... 125.00
57 thru 70 .... @125.00
71 thru 84 .... @100.00
85 E:Ph(c),Jan., 1954 .... 125.00

HOPPY THE MARVEL BUNNY
Fawcett Publications, Dec., 1945

1 A:Marvel Bunny 650.00
2 .... 300.00
3 .... 250.00
4 .... 250.00
5 .... 250.00
6 thru 14 .... @200.00
15 Sept., 1947 .... 200.00

HORRIFIC
Artful/Comic Media/ Harwell Publ./Mystery, Sept., 1952

1 Conductor in Flames(c) 800.00
2 Human Puppets(c) 400.00
3 DH(c),Bullet hole in head(c) 800.00
4 DH(c),head on a stick (c) 350.00
5 DH(c) 350.00
6 DH(c),Jack the Ripper 350.00
7 DH(c),Shrunken Skulls 350.00
8 DH(c),I:The Teller 400.00
9 DH(c),Claws of Horror, Wolves of Midnight 350.00
10 DH(c),The Teller-Four Eerie Tales of Horror 350.00
11 DH(c),A:Gary Ghoul,Freddie, Demon,Victor Vampire Walter Werewolf 300.00
12 DH(c),A:Gary Ghoul,Freddie Demon,Victor Vampire, Walter Werewolf 300.00
13 DH(c),A:Gary Ghoul,Freddie Demom,Victor Vampire, Walter Werewolf 300.00

Becomes:

TERRIFIC COMICS
Dec., 1954

14 Eye Injury 800.00
15 .... 400.00
16 B:Wonderboy 400.00

Becomes:

WONDERBOY
Ajax/Farrell Publ., May, 1955

17 The Enemy's Enemy 600.00
18 Success is No Accident, July, 1955 .... 500.00

HORROR FROM THE TOMB
See: MYSTERIOUS STORIES

HORSE FEATHER COMICS
Lev Gleason Publications, Nov., 1947

1 BW 350.00
2 .... 250.00
3 .... 200.00
4 Summer, 1948 .... 200.00

HOT ROD AND SPEEDWAY COMICS
Hillman Periodicals Feb.–March, 1952

1 .... 375.00
2 BK 250.00
3 .... 200.00
4 .... 200.00
5 April–May, 1953 .... 200.00

HOT ROD COMICS
Fawcett Publications, Feb., 1952–53

N# BP,BP(c),F:Clint Curtis 600.00
2 BP,BP(c),Safety comes First 375.00
3 BP,BP(c),The Racing Game 200.00
4 BP,BP(c),Bonneville National Championships 200.00
5 BP,BP(c), ... 200.00
6 BP,BP(c),Race to Death 200.00

HOT ROD KING
Approved Comics (Ziff-Davis), Fall, 1952

1 P(c) 300.00

HOT RODS AND RACING CARS
Motor Mag./ Charlton Comics, 1951

1 Speedy Davis 350.00
2 .... 200.00
3 thru 10 .... @150.00
11 thru 20 .... @125.00
21 thru 70 .... @100.00

HOWDY DOODY
Dell Publishing Co., Jan., 1950

1 Ph(c) 1,800.00
2 Ph(c) 750.00
3 Ph(c) 400.00
4 Ph(c) 400.00
5 Ph(c) 400.00
6 P(c) 450.00
7 thru 10 .... @275.00
11 .... 225.00
12 .... 225.00
13 Christmas (c) 225.00
14 thru 20 .... @225.00
21 thru 38 .... @175.00

Howdy Doody #1
© Dell Publishing Co.

HOW STALIN HOPES WE WILL DESTROY AMERICA
Pictorial News, 1951
N# (Giveaway) 600.00

HOW TO SHOOT
Remington, 1952
N# (promotional) 100.00

HUMBUG
Harvey Kurtzman, 1957
1 JDa,WW,WE,End of the World 400.00
2 JDa,WE,Radiator 200.00
3 JDa,WE 150.00
4 JDa,WE,Queen Victoria(c). . . . 150.00
5 JDa,WE 150.00
6 JDa,WE 150.00
7 JDa,WE,Sputnik(c). 175.00
8 JDa,WE,Elvis/George
  Washington(c) 150.00
9 JDa,WE 150.00
10 JDa,Magazine 250.00
11 JDa,WE,HK,Magazine 200.00

HUMDINGER
Novelty Press/Premium Service, May–June, 1946
1 B:Jerkwater Line,Dink,
  Mickey Starlight 500.00
2 . . . . 300.00
3 . . . . 250.00
4 . . . . 250.00
5 . . . . 250.00
6 . . . . 250.00
2-1 . . . . 225.00
2-2 July–Aug., 1947 . . . . 225.00

HUMPHREY COMICS
Harvey Publications, Oct., 1948
1 BP,Joe Palooka 250.00
2 BP 150.00
3 BP 135.00
4 BP,A:Boy Heroes 150.00
5 BP 125.00
6 BP 125.00
7 BP,A:Little Dot 125.00
8 BP,O:Humphrey 125.00
9 BP 100.00
10 BP 100.00

11 thru 21 . . . . @100.00
22 April, 1952 . . . . 100.00

HUNTED
Fox Features Syndicate, 1950
(Formerly: MY LOVE MEMOIRS)
1 (13) Famous Crime Cases . . . 450.00
2 . . . . 200.00

HURRICANE COMICS
Cambridge House, 1945
1 F:Hurry Kane 350.00

HYPER MYSTERY COMICS
Hyper Publications, May, 1940.
1 B:Hyper 3,000.00
2 June, 1940 . . . . 2,000.00

IBIS, THE INVINCIBLE
Fawcett Publications, Jan., 1942–Spring, 1948
1 MRa(c),O:Ibis 3,500.00
2 Bondage (c) 2,000.00
3 BW 1,500.00
4 BW,A:Mystic Snake People . . 900.00
5 BW,Bondage (c),The
  Devil's Ibistick 1,000.00
6 BW, The Book of Evil 1,000.00

IF THE DEVIL WOULD TALK
Catechetical Guild, 1950
N# Rare 1,000.00
N#, 1958 Very Rare 850.00

ILLUSTRATED STORIES OF THE OPERAS
B. Bailey Publ. Co., 1943
N# Faust 800.00
N# Aida 750.00
N# Carman 750.00
N# Rigoletto 750.00

I LOVED
See: ZOOT COMICS

I LOVE LUCY COMICS
Dell Publishing Co., 1954
(1) *see Dell Four Color #535*
(2) *see Dell Four Color #559*
3 Lucile Ball Ph(c) all 400.00
4 . . . . 350.00
5 . . . . 350.00
6 thru 10 . . . . @300.00
11 thru 20 . . . . @200.00
21 thru 35 . . . . @175.00

IMPACT
E.C. Comics, March–April, 1955
1 RC,GE,BK,Grl 400.00
2 RC,JDu,Grl,BK,JO 300.00
3 JO,RC,JDU,Grl,JKa,BK 275.00
4 RC,JO,JDa,GE,Grl,BK 275.00
5 Nov.–Dec., 1955 . . . . 275.00

INCREDIBLE SCIENCE FANTASY
See: WEIRD SCIENCE

INCREDIBLE SCIENCE FICTION
E.C. Comics, July–Aug., 1955
30 JDa,BK,JO,WW 800.00
31 AW,WW,BK 750.00
32 AW,JDa,BK,JO 750.00
33 JDa,BK,JO,WW 750.00

INDIAN BRAVES
See: BAFFLING MYSTERIES

INDIAN CHIEF
Dell Publishing Co., July–Sept., 1951
3 P(c) all 150.00
4 . . . . 125.00
5 . . . . 125.00
6 A:White Eagle 125.00
7 . . . . 125.00
8 . . . . 125.00
9 . . . . 125.00
10 . . . . 125.00
11 . . . . 125.00
12 I:White Eagle 135.00
13 thru 29 . . . . @100.00
30 SB 100.00
31 thru 33 SB . . . . @100.00

INDIAN FIGHTER
Youthful Magazines, May, 1950
1 Revenge of Chief Crazy
  Horse 250.00
2 Bondage (c) 250.00
3 . . . . 125.00
4 Cheyenne Warpath 125.00
5 . . . . 125.00
6 Davy Crockett in Death Stalks
  the Alamo 125.00
7 Tom Horn-Bloodshed at
  Massacre Valley 125.00
8 Tales of Wild Bill Hickory,
  Jan., 1952 . . . . 125.00

INDIANS
Wings Publ. Co. (Fiction House), Spring, 1950
1 B:Long Bow, Manzar, White
  Indian & Orphan 350.00
2 B:Starlight 175.00
3 Longbow(c) 150.00
4 Longbow(c) 125.00
5 Manzar(c). 150.00
6 Captive of the Semecas 125.00
7 Longbow(c) 125.00
8 A:Long Bow 125.00
9 A:Long Bow 125.00
10 Manzar(c) 125.00
11 thru 16 . . . . @100.00
17 Spring, 1953,Longbow(c) . . . 100.00

INDIANS ON THE WARPATH
St. John Publ. Co., 1950
N# MB(c). 400.00

INDIAN WARRIORS
See: OUTLAWS, THE

INFORMER, THE
Feature Television Productions, April, 1954
1 MSy,The Greatest Social
  Menace of our Time! 200.00
2 MSy 150.00
3 MSy 100.00
4 MSy 100.00
5 Dec., 1954 . . . . 100.00

GOLDEN AGE

INSIDE CRIME
Hero Books/
Fox Feature Syndicate, 1950
1 .... 350.00
2 .... 275.00
N# 700.00

INTERNATIONAL COMICS
See: CRIME PATROL

INTERNATIONAL
CRIME PATROL
See: CRIME PATROL

INTIMATE
CONFESSIONS
Fawcett Publ./
Realistic Comics, 1951
1a P(c) all, Unmarried Bride .. 1,100.00
1 EK,EK(c),Days of Temptation...
    Nights of Desire 250.00
2 Doomed to Silence 250.00
3 EK(c), The Only Man For Me . 175.00
3a Robert Briffault 275.00
4 EK(c),Tormented Love 250.00
5 Her Secret Sin 250.00
6 Reckless Pick-up 250.00
7 A Love Like Ours,Spanking ... 275.00
8 Fatal Woman, March, 1953 .. 250.00

INTRIGUE
Comics Magazine (Quality
Comics Group), 1955
1 LbC,Ghost Ship 400.00

INVISIBLE
SCARLET O'NEIL
Harvey Publications,
Dec., 1950
1 .... 200.00
2 .... 150.00
3 April, 1951 .... 150.00

IRON VIC
United Features Syndicate/
St. John Publ. Co., 1940
1-shot 600.00

IS THIS TOMORROW?
Catechetical Guild, 1950
1 Communist threat 200.00
2 (1) Canada................. 150.00
3 (1) America 200.00
4 (1) Turkey................. 100.00
5 (1) Australia 150.00

IT REALLY HAPPENED
William H. Wise/
Visual Editions, 1945
1 Benjamin Franklin, Kit Carson 300.00
2 The Terrible Tiddlers 200.00
3 Maid of the Margiris 150.00
4 Chaplain Albert J. Hoffman ... 150.00
5 AS(c),Monarchs of the Sea,Lou
    Gehrig, Amelia Earhart 275.00
6 AS(c),Ernie Pyle 150.00
7 FGu,Teddy Roosevelt,Jefferson
    Davis,Story of the Helicopter. 150.00
8 FGu,Man O' War,Roy Rogers . 250.00
9 AS(c),The Story of
    Old Ironsides 150.00
10 AS(c),Honus Wagner, The
    Story of Mark Twain........ 200.00
11 AS(c),MB,Queen of the Spanish
    Main, Oct., 1947 .... 175.00

IT'S FUN TO STAY ALIVE
Nat.'l Auto Dealers Assoc., 1947
1 Bugs Bunny 250.00

JACE PEARSON OF
THE TEXAS RANGERS
Dell Publishing Co., May, 1952
(1) see Dell Four Color #396
2 Ph(c),Joel McRae 150.00
3 Ph(c),Joel McRae 150.00
4 Ph(c),Joel McRae 150.00
5 Ph(c),Joel McRae 150.00
6 Ph(c),Joel McRae 150.00
7 Ph(c),Joel McRae 150.00
8 Ph(c),Joel McRae 150.00
9 Ph(c),Joel McRae 150.00
(10) see Dell Four Color #648
Becomes:

TALES OF JACE
PEARSON OF
THE TEXAS RANGERS
Feb., 1955
11 .... 125.00
12 .... 125.00
13 .... 125.00
14 .... 125.00
15 ATh 150.00
16 ATh 150.00
17 thru 20................. @100.00

Jack Armstrong #2
© *Parents' Institute*

JACK ARMSTRONG
Parents' Institute,
Nov., 1947
1 Artic Mystery 600.00
2 Den of the Golden Dragon ... 250.00
3 Lost Valley of Ice 200.00
4 Land of the Leopard Men 200.00
5 Fight against Racketeers of
    the Ring 200.00
6 .... 175.00
7 Baffling Mystery on the
    Diamond 175.00
8 .... 175.00
9 Mystery of the Midgets 175.00
10 Secret Cargo.............. 175.00
11 .... 175.00
12 Madman's Island, rare 200.00
13 Sept., 1949 .... 175.00

JACKIE GLEASON
St. John Publishing Co.,
Sept., 1955
1 Ph(c) 900.00
2 .... 550.00
3 .... 500.00
4 Dec., 1955 .... 500.00

JACKIE ROBINSON
Fawcett Publications,
May, 1950
N# Ph(c) all issues.......... 1,800.00
2 .... 1,000.00
3 .... 900.00
4 .... 900.00
5 .... 900.00
6 May, 1952 .... 900.00

JACK IN THE BOX
See: YELLOW JACKET
COMICS

JACKPOT COMICS
MLJ Magazines, Spring, 1941
1 CBi(c),B:Black Hood,Mr.Justice,
    Steel Sterling,Sgt.Boyle ... 5,000.00
2 SCp(c), ... 2,100.00
3 Bondage (c) 1,800.00
4 First Archie 6,500.00
5 Hitler(c)................. 2,200.00
6 Son of the Skull v:Black
    Hood, Bondage(c) 1,800.00
7 Bondage (c) 1,800.00
8 Sal(c), ... 1,500.00
9 Sal(c), ... 1,500.00
Becomes:

JOLLY JINGLES
Summer, 1943
10 Super Duck,(fa). 450.00
11 Super Duck.............. 225.00
12 Hitler parody (c),A:Woody
    Woodpecker 250.00
13 thru 15 Super Duck....... @150.00
16 Dec., 1944 .... 150.00

JACK THE GIANT
KILLER
Bimfort & Co.,
Aug.–Sept., 1953
1 HcK,HcK(c) 300.00

JAMBOREE
Round Publishing Co.,
Feb., 1946
1 .... 300.00
2 March, 1946 .... 200.00

JANE ARDEN
St. John Publ. Co.,
March, 1948
1 .... 200.00
2 June, 1948 .... 150.00

JEEP COMICS
R.B. Leffingwell & Co.,
Winter, 1944
1 B;Captain Power 850.00
2 .... 500.00
3 LbC(c),March–April, 1948 .... 650.00

JEFF JORDAN,
U.S. AGENT
D.S. Publ. Co., Dec., 1947
1 .... 250.00

GOLDEN AGE

JERRY DRUMMER
Charlton Comics, 1957
1 Revolutionary War 100.00
2 . . . . 100.00

JESSE JAMES
**Avon Periodicals/
Realistic Publ., Aug., 1950**
1 JKu,The San Antonio Stage
  Robbery 250.00
2 JKu,The Daring Liberty Bank
  Robbery 175.00
3 JKu,The California Stagecoach
  Robberies 175.00
4 EK(c),Deadliest Deed! 100.00
5 JKu,WW,Great Prison Break . 175.00
6 JKu,Wanted Dead or Alive . . . 175.00
7 JKu,Six-Gun Slaughter at
  San Romano! 150.00
8 EK,Daring Train Robbery! 125.00
9 EK 100.00
10 thru 14 {Do not exist}
15 EK 125.00
16 EK, Butch Cassidy 100.00
17 EK, Jessie James 100.00
18 JKu 100.00
19 JKu 100.00
20 AW,FF,A:Chief Vic,Kit West . . 200.00
21 EK, Two Jessie James 100.00
22 EK,Chuck Wagon 100.00
23 EK 100.00
24 EK,B:New McCarty 100.00
25 EK 100.00
26 EK 100.00
27 EK,E:New McCarty 100.00
28 Quantrells Raiders 100.00
29 Aug., 1956. . . . . 100.00

JEST
Harry 'A' Chesler, 1944
10 J. Rebel,Yankee Boy 350.00
11 1944,Little Nemo. 400.00

JET ACES
**Real Adventure Publ. Co.
(Fiction House), 1952**
1 Set 'em up in MIG Alley 250.00
2 Kiss-Off for Moscow Molly . . . 150.00
3 Red Task Force Sighted 150.00
4 Death-Date at 40,000, 1953 . . 150.00

JET FIGHTERS
**Standard Magazines,
Nov., 1953**
5 ATh,Korean War Stories 150.00
6 Circus Pilot 125.00
7 ATh, Iron Curtains for Ivan,
  March, 1953 . . . . 150.00

JETTA OF THE
21st CENTURY
Standard Comics, Dec., 1952
5 Teen Stories 300.00
6 Robot (c) 250.00
7 April, 1953 . . . . 150.00

JIGGS AND MAGGIE
**Best Books (Standard)/
Harvey Publ., June, 1949**
11 . . . . 150.00
12 thru 21 . . . . @100.00
22 thru 25 . . . . @100.00
26 Part 3-D 250.00
27 Feb.–March, 1954. . . . . 100.00

JIM BOWIE
See: DANGER

JIM DANDY
**Dandy Magazine
(Lev Gleason), 1956**
1 Teen-age humor. 125.00
2 . . . . 100.00
3 . . . . 100.00

JIM HARDY
Spotlight Publ., 1944
N# Dynamite Jim,Mirror Man . . . 700.00

JIM RAY'S AVIATION
SKETCH BOOK
Vital Publishers, Feb., 1946
1 Radar, the Invisible eye 550.00
2 Gen.Hap Arnold, May, 1946 . . 350.00

Jingle Jangle Comics #2
© Eastern Color Printing

JINGLE JANGLE
COMICS
**Eastern Color Printing Co.,
Feb., 1942**
1 B:Benny Bear,Pie Face Prince,
  Jingle Jangle Tales,Hortense 700.00
2 GCn 350.00
3 GCn 300.00
4 GCn,Pie Face (c). 300.00
5 GCn,B:Pie Face. 300.00
6 GCn, ... 250.00
7 . . . . 250.00
8 . . . . 250.00
9 . . . . 250.00
10 . . . . 250.00
11 . . . . 200.00
12 . . . . 200.00
13 . . . . 200.00
14 . . . . 200.00
15 E:Pie Face. . . . . @200.00
16 thru 20 . . . . @175.00
21 thru 25 . . . . @150.00
26 thru 30 . . . . @150.00
31 thru 41 . . . . @100.00
42 Dec., 1949 . . . . 100.00

JING PALS
**Victory Publ. Corp.,
Feb., 1946**
1 Johnny Rabbit 250.00
2 . . . . 200.00
3 . . . . 200.00
4 Aug., 1948 . . . . 200.00

JOE COLLEGE
**Hillman Periodicals,
Fall, 1949**
1 BP,DPr 150.00
2 BP, Winter, 1949 . . . . 125.00

JOE LOUIS
**Fawcett Periodicals,
Sept., 1950**
1 Ph(c),Life Story 800.00
2 Ph(c),Nov., 1950 . . . . 500.00

JOE PALOOKA
**Publication Enterprises
(Columbia Comics Group) 1943**
1 Lost in the Desert 1,400.00
2 Hitler (c) 850.00
3 KO's the Nazis! 700.00
4 Eiffel tower (c), 1944 . . . . 450.00

JOE PALOOKA
**Harvey Publications,
Nov., 1945–March, 1961**
1 Joe Tells How He Became
  World Champ 675.00
2 Skiing (c) 350.00
3 . . . . 200.00
4 Welcome Home Pals! 200.00
5 S&K,The Great Carnival
  Murder Mystery 275.00
6 Classic Joe Palooka (c). 200.00
7 BP,V:Grumpopski 200.00
8 BP,Mystery of the Ghost Ship . 150.00
9 Drooten Island Mystery 150.00
10 BP 150.00
11 . . . . 125.00
12 BP,Boxing Course. 125.00
13 . . . . 110.00
14 BP,Palooka's Toughest Fight. . 110.00
15 BP,O:Humphrey 200.00
16 BP,A:Humphrey 110.00
17 BP,I:Little Max,A:Humphrey . . 200.00
18 A:Little Max 110.00
19 BP,Freedom Train(c) 125.00
20 Punch Out(c). 110.00
21 . . . . 100.00
22 V:Assassin 100.00
23 Big Bathing Beauty Issue 100.00
24 . . . . 100.00
25 . . . . 100.00
26 BP,Big Prize Fight Robberies . 100.00
27 BP,Mystery of Bal
  Eagle Cabin,A:Little Max 110.00
28 BP,Fights Out West, Babe
  Ruth. 100.00
29 BP,Joe Busts Crime
  Wide Open 100.00
30 BP,V:Hoodlums, Nude
  Painting 125.00
31 BP, Dizzy Dean. 125.00
32 BP,Fight Palooka Was Sure
  to Lose. 100.00
33 BP,Joe finds Ann. 100.00
34 BP,How to Box like a Champ . 100.00
35 BP,More Adventures of Little
  Max, Joe Louis 125.00
36 BP 100.00
37 BP,Joe as a Boy 100.00
38 BP 100.00
39 BP,Original Hillbillies with
  Big Leviticus 100.00
40 BP,Joe's Toughest Fight 100.00
41 BP,Humphrey's Grudge Fight . 100.00
42 BP 100.00
43 BP 100.00
44 BP,M:Ann Howe, Markies 125.00
45 BP 90.00
46 Champ of Champs 90.00
47 BreathtakingUnderwaterBattle . 90.00
48 BP,Exciting Indian Adventure . . 90.00

GOLDEN AGE

GOLDEN AGE

49 BP	90.00
50 BP,Bondage(c)	90.00
51 BP, Babe Ruth	90.00
52 BP,V:Balonki	90.00
53 BP	90.00
54 V:Bad Man Trigger McGehee	90.00
55	90.00
56 Foul Play on the High Seas	90.00
57 Curtains for the Champ	90.00
58 V:The Man-Eating Swamp Terror	90.00
59 The Enemy Attacks	90.00
60 Joe Fights Escaped Convict	90.00
61	90.00
62 S&K, Boy Explorers	125.00
63	90.00
64	90.00
65	90.00
66 Drug	125.00
67 Drug	150.00
68	90.00
69 Torture	150.00
70 BP, Vs. "Gooks"	90.00
71 Bloody Bayonets	90.00
72 Tank	90.00
73 BP	90.00
74 thru 115	@90.00
116 thru 117 giants	@150.00
118 Giant, Jack Dempsey	@150.00
Giant 1 Body Building	150.00
Giant 2 Fights His Way Back	200.00
Giant 3 Visits Lost City	125.00
Giant 4 All in Family	150.00

JOE YANK
Visual Editions
(Standard Comics),
March, 1952

5 ATh,WE,Korean Jackpot!	150.00
6 Bacon and Bullets, G.I.Renegade	150.00
7 Two-Man War,A:Sgt. Glamour	100.00
8 ATh(c),Miss Foxhole of 1952,	125.00
9 G.I.'s and Dolls,Colonel Blood	100.00
10 A Good Way to Die, A:General Joe	100.00
11	100.00
12 RA	100.00
13	100.00
14	100.00
15	100.00
16 July, 1954	100.00

JOHN HIX SCRAPBOOK
Eastern Color Printing Co.,
1937

1 Strange as It Seems	650.00
2 Strange as It Seems	500.00

JOHNNY DANGER
Toby Press, Aug., 1954

1 Ph(c),Private Detective	225.00

JOHNNY DYNAMITE
See: DYNAMITE

JOHNNY HAZARD
Best Books
(Standard Comics),
Aug., 1948

5 FR	250.00
6 FR,FR(c)	225.00
7 FR(c)	200.00
8 FR,FR(c), May, 1949	200.00

JOHNNY LAW, SKY RANGER
Good Comics (Lev Gleason),
April, 1955

1	125.00
2	100.00
3	100.00
4 Nov., 1955	100.00

JOHNNY MACK BROWN
Dell Publishing Co., 1950–52

1 See: FOUR COLOR	
2 Western hero	225.00
3	150.00
4 thru 10	@125.00

JOHN WAYNE ADVENTURE COMICS
Toby Press, Winter, 1949

1 Ph(c),The Mysterious Valley of Violence	2,500.00
2 AW,FF,Ph(c)	1,000.00
3 AW,FF,Flying Sheriff	1,000.00
4 AW,FF,Double-Danger,Ph(c)	1,000.00
5 Volcano of Death,Ph(c)	700.00
6 AW,FF,Caravan of Doom, Ph(c)	900.00
7 AW,FF,Ph(c)	800.00
8 AW,FF,Duel of Death,Ph(c)	1,000.00
9 Ghost Guns,Ph(c)	525.00
10 Dangerous Journey,Ph(c)	500.00
11 Manhunt!,Ph(c)	500.00
12 HK,Joins the Marines,Ph(c)	500.00
13 V:Frank Stacy	450.00
14 Operation Peeping John	450.00
15 Bridge Head	450.00
16 AW,FF,Golden Double-Cross	450.00
17 Murderer's Music	450.00
18 AW,FF,Larson's Folly	500.00
19	400.00
20 Whale (c)	400.00
21	400.00
22 Flash Flood!	400.00
23 Death on Two Wheels	400.00
24 Desert	400.00
25 AW,FF,Hondo!,Ph(c)	525.00
26 Ph(c)	450.00
27 Ph(c)	450.00
28 Dead Man's Boots!	450.00
29 AW,FF,Ph(c),Crash in California Desert	500.00
30 The Wild One, Ph(c)	450.00
31 AW,FF,May, 1955	500.00

JO-JO COMICS
Fox Features Syndicate,
Spring, 1946

N# (fa) JoJo	250.00
2 (fa) Electro	150.00
3 (fa)	150.00
4 (fa)	150.00
5 (fa)	150.00
6 (fa)	150.00
7 B:Jo-Jo Congo King	1,300.00
8 (7)B:Tanee,V:The Giant Queen	900.00
9 (8)The Mountain of Skulls	750.00
10 (9)Death of the Fanged Lady	750.00
11 (10)	750.00
12 (11)Bondage(c), Water Warriors	650.00
13 (12) Jade Juggernaut	625.00
14 The Leopards of Learda	625.00
15 The Flaming Fiend	700.00
16 Golden Gorilla,bondage(c)	625.00
17 Stark-Mad Thespian, bondage(c)	700.00
18 The Death Traveler	625.00
19 Gladiator of Gore	625.00

20	625.00
21	625.00
22	625.00
23	625.00
24	625.00
25 Bondage(c)	700.00
26	625.00
27	625.00
28	625.00
29 July, 1949	650.00

JOLLY JINGLES
See: JACKPOT

JON JUAN
Toby Press, 1950

1 ASh(c),Superlover	900.00

JOURNEY INTO FEAR
Superior Publications,
May, 1951–Sept., 1954

1 MB,Preview of Chaos	1,000.00
2 Debt to the Devil	650.00
3 Midnight Prowler	500.00
4 Invisible Terror	500.00
5 Devil Cat	350.00
6 Partners in Blood	350.00
7 The Werewolf Lurks	350.00
8 Bells of the Damned	350.00
9 Masked Death	350.00
10 Gallery of the Dead	350.00
11 Beast of Bedlam	325.00
12 No Rest for the Dead	325.00
13 Cult of the Dead	325.00
14 Jury of the Undead	325.00
15 Corpse in Make-up	350.00
16 Death by Invitation	300.00
17 Deadline for Death	300.00
18 Here's to Horror	300.00
19 This Body is Mine!	300.00
20 Masters of the Dead	300.00
21 Horror in the Clock	300.00

JUDGE PARKER
Argo, Feb., 1956

1	100.00
2	100.00

JUDO JOE
Jay-Jay Corp.,
Aug., 1952

1 Drug	250.00
2	150.00
3 Drug, Dec., 1953	200.00

JUDY CANOVA
See: ALL TOP COMICS

JUKE BOX
Famous Funnies, March, 1948
1 ATh(c),Spike Jones 500.00
2 Dinah Shore,Transvestitism. . . 500.00
3 Vic Damone, Peggie Lee. 250.00
4 Jimmy Durante. 250.00
5 . . . . 250.00
6 Jan., 1949,Desi Arnaz 300.00

JUMBO COMICS
Real Adventure Publ. Co. (Fiction House), Sept., 1938
1 LF,BKa,JK,WE(a&c),B:Sheena
  Queen of the Jungle,The Hawk
  The Hunchback 35,000.00
2 LF,JK,WE,BKa,BP,
  O:Sheena 15,000.00
3 JK,WE(a&c),BP,LF,BKa 8,000.00
4 WE(a&c),MMe,LF,BKa,
  O:The Hawk 7,000.00
5 WE(a&c),BP,BKa 7,000.00
6 WE(a&c),BP,BKa 6,000.00
7 WE,BKa,BP 6,000.00
8 LF(c),BP,BKa,World of
  Tommorow 6,000.00
9 LF(c),BP 4,000.00
10 WE,LF(c),BKa,Regular size
  issues begin 3,000.00
11 LF(c),WE&BP,War of the
  Emerald Gas 2,000.00
12 WE(c),WE&BP,Hawk in Buccaneer
  Vengeance,Bondage(c) . . 2,500.00
13 WE(c),BP,Sheena in The
  Thundering Herds. 2,000.00
14 WE(c),LF,BP,Hawk in Siege
  of Thunder Isle,B:Lightning 2,100.00
15 BP(a&c),Sheena(c) 1,200.00
16 BP(a&c),The Lightning
  Strikes Twice 1,500.00
17 BP(c), B:Sheena covers
  and lead stories 1,200.00
18 BP 1,200.00
19 BP(c),BKa,Warriors of
  the Bush 1,200.00
20 BP,BKa,Spoilers of the
  Wild 1,200.00
21 BP,BKa,Prey of the
  Giant Killers 900.00
22 BP,BKa,Victims of the
  Super-Ape,O:Hawk. 1,000.00
23 BP,BKa,Swamp of the
  Green Terror 1,000.00
24 BP,BKa,Curse of the Black
  Venom 1,000.00
25 BP,BKa,Bait for the Beast. . . . 900.00
26 BP,BKa,Tiger-Man Terror 900.00
27 BP,BKa,Sabre-Tooth Terror. . . 900.00
28 BKa,RWd,The Devil of
  the Congo 900.00
29 BKa,RWd,Elephant-Scourge . 900.00
30 BKa,RWd,Slashing Fangs . . . 900.00
31 BKa,RWd,Voodoo Treasure
  of Black Slave Lake. 750.00
32 BKa,RWd,AB,Captives of
  the Gorilla-Men 750.00
33 BKa,RWd,AB,Stampede
  Tusks 750.00
34 BKa,RWd,AB,Claws of the
  Devil-Cat 750.00
35 BKa,RWd,AB,Hostage of the
  Devil Apes 750.00
36 BKa,RWd,AB,Voodoo Flames 750.00
37 BKa,RWd,AB,Congo Terror . . 750.00
38 BKa,RWd,AB,Death-Trap of
  the River Demons 750.00

Jumbo Comics #69
© Fiction House

39 BKa,RWd,AB,Cannibal Bait . . 750.00
40 BKa,RWd,AB,
  Assagai Poison 750.00
41 BKa,RWd,AB,Killer's Kraal,
  Bondage(c) 600.00
42 BKa,RWd,AB,Plague of
  Spotted Killers 600.00
43 BKa,RWd,AB,Beasts of the
  Devil Queen. 600.00
44 BKa,RWd,AB,Blood-Cult of
  K'Douma 600.00
45 BKa,RWd,AB,Fanged
  Keeper of the Fire-Gem 600.00
46 BKa,RWd,AB,Lair of the
  Armored Monsters 600.00
47 BKa,RWd,AB,The Bantu
  Blood-Monster 600.00
48 BKa,RWd,AB,Red Meat for
  the Cat-Pack 600.00
49 BKa,RWd,AB,Empire of the
  Hairy Ones 600.00
50 BKa,RWd,AB,Eyrie of the
  Leopard Birds 600.00
51 BKa,RWd,AB,Monsters with
  Wings. 500.00
52 BKa,RWd,AB,Man-Eaters
  Paradise 500.00
53 RWd,AB,Slaves of the
  Blood Moon 500.00
54 RWd,AB,Congo Kill. 500.00
55 RWd,AB,Bait for the Silver
  King Cat. 500.00
56 RWd,AB,Sabre Monsters of
  the Aba-Zanzi,Bondage(c). . . 700.00
57 RWd,AB,Arena of Beasts 500.00
58 RWd,AB,Sky-Atlas of the
  Thunder-Birds 500.00
59 RWd,AB,Kraal of Shrunken
  Heads 500.00
60 RWd,AB,Land of the
  Stalking Death 400.00
61 RWd,AB,King-Beast of
  the Masai. 400.00
62 RWd,AB,Valley of Golden
  Death. 400.00
63 RWd,AB,The Dwarf Makers . . 400.00
64 RWd,The Slave-Brand of Ibn
  Ben Satan,Male Bondage . . . 600.00
65 RWd,The Man-Eaters of
  Linpopo 400.00
66 RWd,Valley of Monsters 400.00
67 RWd,Land of Feathered Evil . 400.00
68 RWd,Spear of Blood Ju-Ju . . . 400.00
69 RWd,AB,MB,Slaves for the
  White Sheik 400.00

70 RWd,AB,MB,The Rogue
  Beast's Prey 400.00
71 RWd,AB,MB,The Serpent-
  God Speaks. 350.00
72 RWd,AB,MB,Curse of the
  Half-Dead 350.00
73 RWd,AB,MB,War Apes of
  the T'Kanis. 350.00
74 RWd,AB,MB,Drums of the
  Voodoo God 350.00
75 RWd,AB,MB,Terror Trail of
  the Devil's Horn 350.00
76 RWd,AB,MB,Fire Gems of
  Skull Valley 350.00
77 RWd,AB,MB,Blood Dragons
  from Fire Valley 350.00
78 RWd,AB,MB,Veldt of the
  Vampire Apes 350.00
79 RWd,AB,MB,Dancing
  Skeletons 350.00
80 RWd,AB,MB,Banshee
  Cats 350.00
81 RWd,MB,AB,JKa,Heads for
  King' Hondo's Harem. 300.00
82 RWd,MB,AB,JKa,Ghost Riders
  of the Golden Tuskers 300.00
83 RWd,MB,AB,JKa,Charge of
  the Condo Juggernauts. 300.00
84 RWd,MB,AB,JKa,Valley of
  the Whispering Fangs 300.00
85 RWd,MB,AB,JKa,Red Tusks
  of Zulu-Za'an 300.00
86 RWd,MB,AB,JKa,Witch-Maiden
  of the Burning Blade 300.00
87 RWd,AB,MB,JKa,Sargasso of
  Lost Safaris 300.00
88 RWd,AB,MB,JKa,Kill-Quest
  of the Ju-Ju Tusks 300.00
89 RWd,AB,MB,JKa,Ghost Slaves
  of Bwana Rojo. 300.00
90 RWd,AB,MB,JKa,Death Kraal
  of the Mastadons 300.00
91 RWd,AB,MB,JKa,Spoor of
  the Sabre-Horn Tiger. 275.00
92 RWd,MB,JKa,Pied Piper
  of the Congo 275.00
93 RWd,MB,JKa,The Beasts
  that Dawn Begot 275.00
94 RWd,MB,JKa,Wheel of a
  Thousand Deaths 350.00
95 RWd,MB,JKa,Flame Dance
  of the Ju-Ju Witch 275.00
96 RWd,MB,JKa,Ghost
  Safari. 275.00
97 RWd,MB,JKa,Banshee Wail
  of the Undead,Bondage(c) . . 400.00
98 RWd,MB,JKa,Seekers of
  the Terror Fangs 300.00
99 RWd,MB,JKa,Shrine of
  the Seven Souls 300.00
100 RWd,MB,Slave Brand
  of Hassan Bey 350.00
101 RWd,MB,Quest of the
  Two-Face Ju Ju 300.00
102 RWd,MB,Viper Gods of
  Vengeance Veldt 300.00
103 RWd,MB,Blood for the
  Idol of Blades. 300.00
104 RWd,MB,Valley of Eternal
  Sleep 300.00
105 RWd,MB,Man Cubs from
  Momba-Zu. 350.00
106 RWd,MB,The River of
  No-Return 350.00
107 RWd,MB,Vandals of
  the Veldt 300.00
108 RWd,MB,The Orphan of
  Vengeance Vale. 300.00
109 RWd,MB,The Pygmy's Hiss
  is Poison 300.00
110 RWd,MB,Death Guards the
  Congo Keep 300.00

All comics prices listed are for *Near Mint* condition.

111 RWd,MB,Beware of the
 Witch-Man's Brew 300.00
112 RWd,MB,The Blood-Mask
 from G'Shinis Grave 275.00
113 RWd,MB,The Mask's of
 Zombi-Zan. 275.00
114 RWd,MB 275.00
115 RWd,MB,Svengali of
 the Apes 275.00
116 RWd,MB,The Vessel of
 Marbei Monsters 275.00
117 RWd,MB,Lair of the Half-
 Man King 275.00
118 RWd,MB,Quest of the
 Congo Dwarflings 275.00
119 RWd,MB,King Crocodile's
 Domain 275.00
120 RWd,MB,The Beast-Pack
 Howls the Moon 275.00
121 RWd,MB,The Kraal of
 Evil Ivory 275.00
122 RWd,MB,Castaways of
 the Congo 250.00
123 RWd,MB,. 250.00
124 RWd,MB,The Voodoo Beasts
 of Changra-Lo 250.00
125 RWd,MB,JKa(c),The Beast-
 Pack Strikes at Dawn 250.00
126 RWd,MB,JKa(c),Lair of the
 Swamp Beast 250.00
127 RWd,MB,JKa(c),The Phantom
 of Lost Lagoon. 250.00
128 RWd,MB,JKa(c),Mad Mistress
 of the Congo-Tuskers 250.00
129 RWd,MB,JKa(c),Slaves of
 King Simbas Kraal. 250.00
130 RWd,MB,JKa(c),Quest of
 the Pharaoh's Idol 250.00
131 RWd,JKa(c),Congo Giants
 at Bay 250.00
132 RWd,JKa(c),The Doom of
 the Devil's Gorge. 250.00
133 RWd,JKa(c),Blaze the
 Pitfall Trail 250.00
134 RWd,JKa(c),Catacombs of
 the Jackal-Men 250.00
135 RWd,JKa(c),The 40 Thieves
 of Ankar-Lo 250.00
136 RWd,JKa(c),The Perils of
 Paradise Lost 250.00
137 RWd,JKa(c),The Kraal of
 Missing Men 250.00
138 RWd,JKa(c),The Panthers
 of Kajo-Kazar. 250.00
139 RWd,JKa(c),Stampede of
 the Congo Lancers 250.00
140 RWd,JKa(c),The Moon
 Beasts from Vulture Valley . . 250.00
141 RWd,JKa(c),B:Long
 Bow 275.00
142 RWd,JKa(c),Man-Eaters
 of N'Gamba 250.00
143 RWd,JKa(c),The Curse of
 the Cannibal Drum 250.00
144 RWd,JKa(c),The Secrets of
 Killers Cave 250.00
145 RWd,JKa(c),Killers of
 the Crypt 250.00
146 RWd,JKa(c),Sinbad of the
 Lost Lagoon. 250.00
147 RWd,JKa(c),The Wizard of
 Gorilla Glade 250.00
148 RWd,JKa(c),Derelict of
 the Slave King 250.00
149 RWd,JKa(c),Lash Lord of
 the Elephants 250.00
150 RWd,JKa(c),Queen of
 the Pharaoh's Idol 250.00
151 RWd,The Voodoo Claws
 of Doomsday Trek. 250.00
152 RWd,Red Blades of Africa . . 250.00

153 RWd,Lost Legions of the
 Nile 250.00
154 RWd,The Track of the
 Black Devil. 250.00
155 RWd,The Ghosts of
 Blow- Gun Trail 250.00
156 RWd,The Slave-Runners
 of Bambaru 250.00
157 RWd,Cave of the
 Golden Skull 250.00
158 RWd,Gun Trek to
 Panther Valley 250.00
159 RWd,A:Space Scout 225.00
160 RWd,Savage Cargo,
 E:Sheena covers 225.00
161 RWd,Dawns of the Pit 225.00
162 RWd,Hangman's Haunt . . . 225.00
163 RWd,Cagliostro Cursed
 Thee 225.00
164 RWd,Death Bars the Door . . 225.00
165 RWd,Day off from a Corpse . 225.00
166 RWd,The Gallows Bird 225.00
167 RWd,Cult of the Clawmen,
 March, 1953 . . . . 225.00

JUNGLE COMICS

**Glen Kel Publ./Fiction House,
Jan., 1940**

1 HcK,DBr,LF(c),O:The White
 Panther,Kaanga,Tabu, B:The
 Jungle Boy,Camilla, all
 Kaanga covers & stories . . 8,000.00
2 HcK,DBr,WE(c),B:Fantomah 2,400.00
3 HcK,DBr,GT,The Crocodiles
 of Death River 1,900.00
4 HcK,DBr,Wambi in
 Thundering Herds. 1,700.00
5 WE(c),GT,HcK,DBr,Empire
 of the Ape Men 2,200.00
6 WE(c),GT,DBr,HcK,Tigress
 of the Deep Jungle Swamp 1,200.00
7 BP(c),DBr,GT,HcK,Live
 Sacrifice,Bondage(c) 1,100.00
8 BP(c),GT,HcK,Safari into
 Shadowland 1,100.00
9 GT,HcK,Captive of the
 Voodoo Master. 1,100.00
10 GT,HcK,BP,Lair of the
 Renegade Killer 1,100.00
11 GT,HcK,V:Beasts of Africa's Ancient
 Primieval Swamp Land 750.00
12 GT,HcK,The Devil's
 Death-Trap 750.00
13 GT(c),GT,HcK,Stalker of
 the Beasts 800.00
14 HcK,Vengeance of the
 Gorilla Hordes 750.00
15 HcK,Terror of the Voodoo
 Cauldron 750.00
16 HcK,Caveman Killers 750.00
17 HcK,Valley of the Killer-Birds . 750.00
18 HcK,Trap of the Tawny
 Killer, Bondage(c) 800.00
19 HcK,Revolt of the Man-Apes . 750.00
20 HcK,One-offering to
 Ju-Ju Demon 750.00
21 HcK,Monster of the Dismal
 Swamp, Bondage(c) 650.00
22 HcK,Lair o/t Winged Fiend . . . 600.00
23 HcK,Man-Eater Jaws 600.00
24 HcK,Battle of the Beasts. . . . 600.00
25 HcK,Kaghis the Blood God,
 Bondage(c) 700.00
26 HcK,Gorillas of the
 Witch-Queen 600.00
27 HcK,Spore o/t Gold-Raiders . . 600.00
28 HcK,Vengeance of the Flame
 God, Bondage(c). 700.00
29 HcK,Juggernaut of Doom . . . 550.00
30 HcK,Claws o/t Black Terror . . 550.00
31 HcK,Land of Shrunken
 Skulls. 500.00

Jungle Comics #34
© Fiction House

32 HcK,Curse of the King-Beast . 500.00
33 HcK,Scaly Guardians of
 Massacre Pool,Bondage(c) . . 600.00
34 HcK,Bait of the Spotted
 Fury,Bondage(c) 600.00
35 HcK,Stampede of the
 Slave-Masters 500.00
36 HcK,GT,The Flame-Death of
 Ju Ju Mountain 500.00
37 HcK,GT,Scaly Sentinel of
 Taboo Swamp 500.00
38 HcK,GT,Duel of the Congo
 Destroyers. 500.00
39 HcK,Land of Laughing Bones. 500.00
40 HcK,Killer Plague 500.00
41 Hck,The King Ape
 Feeds at Dawn 400.00
42 Hck,RC,Master of the
 Moon-Beasts 425.00
43 HcK,The White Shiek 400.00
44 HcK,Monster of the
 Boiling Pool 400.00
45 HcK,The Bone-Grinders of
 B'Zambi, Bondage(c). 500.00
46 HcK,Blood Raiders of
 Tree Trail 400.00
47 HcK,GT,Monsters of the Man
 Pool, Bondage(c). 500.00
48 HcK,GT,Strangest Congo
 Adventure 375.00
49 HcK,GT,Lair of the King
 -Serpent. 375.00
50 HcK,GT,Juggernaut of
 the Bush 375.00
51 HcK,GT,The Golden Lion of
 Genghis Kahn 375.00
52 HcK,Feast for the River
 Devils, Bondage(c) 500.00
53 HcK,GT,Slaves for Horrors
 Harem 375.00
54 HcK,GT,Blood Bride of
 the Crocodile 350.00
55 HcK,GT,The Tree Devil. 350.00
56 HcK,Bride for the
 Rainmaker Raj. 350.00
57 HcK,Fire Gems of T'ulaki 350.00
58 HcK,Land of the
 Cannibal God 350.00
59 HcK,Dwellers of the Mist
 Bondage(c) 450.00
60 HcK,Bush Devil's Spoor 400.00
61 HcK,Curse of the Blood
 Madness 400.00
62 Bondage(c). 450.00

63 HcK,Fire-Birds for the
Cliff Dwellers 350.00
64 Valley of the Ju-Ju Idols . . 350.00
65 Shrine of the Seven Ju Jus,
Bondage(c) 400.00
66 Spoor of the Purple Skulls . 350.00
67 Devil Beasts of the Golden
Temple. 350.00
68 Satan's Safari 350.00
69 Brides for the Serpent King . . 350.00
70 Brides for the King Beast,
Bondage(c) 400.00
71 Congo Prey,Bondage(c) 400.00
72 Blood-Brand o/t Veldt Cats . . 350.00
73 The Killer of M'omba Raj,
Bondage(c) 400.00
74 AgF,GoldenJaws,
Bondage(c) 400.00
75 AgF,Congo Kill 350.00
76 AgF,Blood Thirst of the
Golden Tusk 350.00
77 AgF,The Golden Gourds
Shriek Blood,Bondage(c) . . . 400.00
78 AgF,Bondage(c) 400.00
79 AgF,Death has a
Thousand Fangs 375.00
80 AgF,Salome of the
Devil-Cats Bondage(c) 400.00
81 AgF,Colossus of the Congo . . 375.00
82 AgF,Blood Jewels of the
Fire-Bird. 375.00
83 AgF,Vampire Veldt,
Bondage(c) 400.00
84 AgF,Blood Spoor of the
Faceless Monster 375.00
85 AgF,Brides for the Man-Apes
Bondage(c) 400.00
86 AgF,Firegems of L'hama
Lost, Bondage(c). 400.00
87 AgF,Horror Kraal of the
Legless One,Bondage(c). . . . 400.00
88 AgF,Beyond the Ju-Ju Mists . . 375.00
89 AgF,Blood-Moon over the
Whispering Veldt 350.00
90 AgF,The Skulls for the
Altar of Doom,Bondage(c) . . 425.00
91 Agf,Monsters from the Mist
Lands, Bondage(c) 425.00
92 AgF,Vendetta of the
Tree Tribes 400.00
93 AgF,Witch Queen of the
Hairy Ones 400.00
94 AgF,Terror Raid of
the Congo Caesar 400.00
95 Agf,Flame-Tongues of the
Sky Gods 400.00
96 Agf,Phantom Guardians of the
Enchanted Lake,Bondage(c). 400.00
97 AgF,Wizard of the Whirling
Doom,Bondage(c) 375.00
98 AgF,Ten Tusks of Zulu Ivory . . 450.00
99 AgF,Cannibal Caravan,
Bondage(c) 375.00
100 AgF,Hate has a
Thousand Claws 375.00
101 AgF,The Blade of
Buddha, Bondage(c) 375.00
102 AgF,Queen of the
Amazon Lancers 350.00
103 AgF,The Phantoms of
Lost Lagoon. 350.00
104 AgF 350.00
105 AgF,The Red Witch
of Ubangi-Shan 350.00
106 AgF,Bondage(c) 375.00
107 Banshee Valley. 375.00
108 HcK,Merchants of Murder. . . 375.00
109 HcK,Caravan of the
Golden Bones 350.00
110 HcK,Raid of the Fire-Fangs . 350.00
111 HcK,The Trek of the
Terror-Paws. 350.00

Jungle Comics #146
© *Fiction House*

112 HcK,Morass of the
Mammoths. 350.00
113 HcK,Two-Tusked Terror 350.00
114 HcK,Mad Jackals Hunt
by Night 350.00
115 HcK,Treasure Trove in
Vulture Sky 350.00
116 HcK,The Banshees of
Voodoo Veldt 350.00
117 HcK,The Fangs of the
Hooded Scorpion. 350.00
118 HcK,The Muffled Drums
of Doom. 350.00
119 HcK,Fury of the Golden
Doom. 350.00
120 HcK,Killer King Domain 350.00
121 HcK,Wolves of the
Desert Night 350.00
122 HcK,The Veldt of
Phantom Fangs. 350.00
123 HcK,The Ark of the
Mist-Maids. 350.00
124 HcK,The Trail of the
Pharaoh's Eye 350.00
125 HcK,Skulls for Sale on
Dismal River 350.00
126 HcK,Safari Sinister 300.00
127 HcK,Bondage(c) 300.00
128 HcK,Dawn-Men of the
Congo 300.00
129 HcK,The Captives of
Crocodile Swamp 300.00
130 HcK,Phantoms of the Congo 300.00
131 HcK,Treasure-Tomb of the
Ape-King 300.00
132 HcK,Bondage(c) 350.00
133 HcK,Scourge of the Sudan
Bondage(c) 350.00
134 HcK,The Black Avengers of
Kaffir Pass 300.00
135 HcK 300.00
136 HcK,The Death Kraals
of Kongola 300.00
137 BWg(c),HcK,The Safari of
Golden Ghosts 300.00
138 BWg(c),HcK,Track of the
Black Terror Bondage(c) 350.00
139 BWg(c),HcK,Captain Kidd
of the Congo 300.00
140 BWg(c),HcK,The Monsters
of Kilimanjaro 300.00
141 BWg(c)HcK,The Death Hunt
of the Man Cubs 300.00
142 BWg(c),Hck,Sheba of the
Terror Claws,Bondage(c). . . . 350.00

143 BWg(c)Hck,The Moon of
Devil Drums. 300.00
144 BWg(c)Hck,Quest of the
Dragon's Claw 300.00
145 BWg(c)Hck,Spawn of the
Devil's Moon 300.00
146 BWg(c),HcK,Orphans of
the Congo 300.00
147 BWG(c),HcK,The Treasure
of Tembo Wanculu. 300.00
148 BWg(c),HcK,Caged Beasts
of Plunder-Men,Bondage(c) . 350.00
149 BWg(c),HcK 275.00
150 BWg(c),HcK,Rhino Rampage,
Bondage(c). 350.00
151 BWg(c),HcK 275.00
152 BWg(c),HcK,The Rogue of
Kopje Kull 275.00
153 BWg(c),HcK,The Wild Men
of N'Gara. 275.00
154 BWg(c),HcK,The Fire Wizard 275.00
155 BWg(c),HcK,Swamp of
the Shrieking Dead 275.00
156 BWg(c),HcK 275.00
157 BWg(c),HcK 275.00
158 BWg(c),HcK,A:Sheena 275.00
159 BWg(c),HcK,The Blow-Gun
Kill 275.00
160 BWg,HcK,King Fang. 275.00
161 BWg(c),HcK,The Barbarizi
Man-Eaters 275.00
162 BWg(c) 275.00
163 BWg(c),Jackals at the
Kill, Summer,1954 . . . . 275.00

JUNGLE JIM
**Best Books
(Standard Comics), Jan., 1949**
11 . . . . 125.00
12 Mystery Island. 100.00
13 Flowers of Peril. 100.00
14 thru 19. . . . . @100.00
20 1951 . . . . 100.00

JUNGLE JIM
Dell Publishing Co., Aug., 1953
(1) *see Dell Four Color #490*
(1) *see Dell Four Color #565*
3 P(c) all 125.00
4 . . . . 125.00
5 . . . . 125.00
6 . . . . 100.00
7 . . . . 100.00
8 thru 12 . . . . @100.00
13 'Mystery Island' 100.00
14 'Flowers of Peril' 100.00
15 thru 20. . . . . @100.00

JUNGLE JO
**Hero Books
(Fox Features Syndicate),
March, 1950**
N# Congo King 600.00
1 WW,Mystery of Doc Jungle . . 650.00
2 Tangi 450.00
3 The Secret of Youth,
Sept., 1950 . . . . 450.00

JUNGLE LIL
Hero Books, April, 1950
1 Betrayer of the Kombe Dead. . 500.00
Becomes:

DOROTHY LAMOUR
**Fox Features Syndicate,
June 1950**
2 WW,Ph(c)The Lost Safari 500.00
3 WW,Ph(c), Aug., 1950 . . . . . . 300.00

GOLDEN AGE

GOLDEN AGE

JUNGLE THRILLS
See: TERRORS OF
THE JUNGLE

JUNIE PROM
**Dearfield Publishing Co.
Winter, 1947**
1 Teenage Stories 150.00
2 . . . . 125.00
3 . . . . 100.00
4 . . . . 100.00
5 . . . . 100.00
6 June, 1949 . . . . 100.00

JUNIOR COMICS
**Fox Features Syndicate,
Sept., 1947**
9 AF(a&c) ,Teenage Stories. . . 1,300.00
10 AF(a&c) 1,100.00
11 AF(a&c) 1,100.00
12 AF(a&c) 1,100.00
13 AF(a&c) 1,100.00
14 AF(a&c) 1,100.00
15 AF(a&c) 1,100.00
16 AF(a&c),July,1948 . . . . 1,100.00

JUNIOR FUNNIES
See: FAMILY FUNNIES

JUNIOR HOOP COMICS
**Stanmor Publications,
Jan., 1952**
1 . . . . 125.00
2 . . . . 100.00
3 July, 1952 . . . . 100.00

JUNIOR MISS
Marvel Timely, 1944, 1947–50
1 F:Frank Sinatra &June Allyson 350.00
24 . . . . 150.00
25 thru 38 Cindy . . . . @125.00
39 HK. 150.00

JUSTICE TRAPS
THE GUILTY
**Headline Publications,
(Prize) Oct.–Nov., 1947**
2-1 S&K(a&c),Electric chair (c) . 900.00
2 S&K(a&c) 450.00
3 S&K(a&c) 400.00
4 S&K(a&c),True Confession
of a Girl Gangleader 400.00
5 S&K(a&c) 400.00
6 S&K(a&c) 425.00
7 S&K(a&c) 400.00
8 S&K(a&c) 400.00
9 S&K(a&c) 400.00
10 S&K(a&c) 400.00
11 S&K(a&c) 175.00
12 . . . . 125.00
13 . . . . 150.00
14 . . . . 125.00
15 . . . . 125.00
16 . . . . 125.00
17 . . . . 125.00
18 S&K(a&c) 150.00
19 S&K(a&c) 150.00
20 . . . . 150.00
21 S&K 175.00
22 S&K(c). 175.00
23 S&K(c). 175.00
24 . . . . 100.00
25 . . . . 100.00
26 . . . . 100.00
27 S&K(c). 175.00
28 . . . . 100.00
29 . . . . 100.00
30 S&K 150.00

31 thru 50. . . . . @100.00
51 thru 54. . . . . @100.00
55 . . . . 100.00
56 . . . . 100.00
57 . . . . 100.00
58 Drug 300.00
59 thru 92. . . . . @100.00
Becomes:

FARGO KID
**Headline Publications
(Prize), June–July. 1958**
93 AW,JSe,O:Kid Fargo 175.00
94 JSe 125.00
95 June–July, 1958,JSe 125.00

Ka'a'nga Comics #1
© Fiction House

KA'A'NGA COMICS
**Glen-Kel Publ.
(Fiction House),
Spring, 1949–Summer, 1954**
1 Phantoms of the Congo 700.00
2 V:The Jungle Octopus 350.00
3 . . . . 275.00
4 The Wizard Apes of
Inkosi-Khan 350.00
5 A:Camilla 225.00
6 Captive of the Devil Apes 175.00
7 GT,Beast-Men of Mombassa . 200.00
8 The Congo Kill-Cry 175.00
9 Tabu-Wizard. 175.00
10 Stampede for Congo Gold . . . 175.00
11 Claws of the Roaring Congo. . 150.00
12 Bondage(c) 250.00
13 Death Web of the Amazons . . 150.00
14 Slave Galley of the Lost
Nile Bondage(c). 250.00
15 Crocodile Moon,Bondage(c). . 250.00
16 Valley of Devil-Dwarfs,Sheena 150.00
17 Tembu of the Elephants 125.00
18 The Red Claw of Vengeance . 125.00
19 The Devil-Devil Trail 125.00
20 The Cult of the Killer Claws . . 125.00

KASCO COMICS
**Kasco Grainfeed
(Giveaway), 1945**
1 BWo 300.00
2 1949,BWo 250.00

KATY KEENE
**Archie Publications/Close-Up
Radio Comics, 1949**
1 BWo 1,700.00
2 BWo 1,200.00

3 BWo 1,000.00
4 BWo 1,000.00
5 BWo 900.00
6 BWo 800.00
7 BWo 600.00
8 thru 12 BWo . . . . @500.00
13 thru 20 BWo . . . . @400.00
21 thru 29 BWo . . . . @300.00
30 thru 38 BWo . . . . @300.00
39 thru 62 BWo . . . . @300.00
Ann.#1. . . . . 1,200.00
Ann.#2 thru #6 . . . . @700.00

KATZENJAMMER KIDS
David McKay Publ., 1947–50
1 . . . . 250.00
2 . . . . 125.00
3 thru 11 . . . . @100.00
Standard Comics, 1950–53
12 thru 22 . . . . @100.00
Harvey Publ., 1953–54
22 thru 25 . . . . @100.00

KAYO
See: SCOOP COMICS

KEEN DETECTIVE
FUNNIES
**Centaur Publications,
July, 1938**
1-8 B:The Clock, ... 3,500.00
1-9 WE 1,250.00
1-10 . . . . 1,200.00
1-11 Dean Denton 1,200.00
2-1 The Eye Sees 1,000.00
2-2 JCo 1,000.00
2-3 TNT 1,000.00
2-4 MGv,Gabby Flynn 1,000.00
5 MGv 1,100.00
6 MGv,BEv. 1,000.00
7 BEv,Masked Marvel 3,500.00
8 PGv,Gabby Flynn,Nudity
Expanded 16 pages 1,400.00
9 BEv,Dean Denton 1,100.00
10 BEv 1,100.00
11 BEv,Sidekick 1,100.00
12 BEv,Masked Marvel(c). 1,400.00
3-1 Masked Marvel(c). 1,000.00
3-2 Masked Marvel(c). 1,000.00
3-3 BEv 1,000.00
16 BEv 1,000.00
17 JSm 1,000.00
18 The Eye Sees,Bondage(c). . 1,200.00
19 LFe 950.00
20 BEv,The Eye Sees. 1,400.00
21 Masked Marvel(c) 950.00
22 Masked Marvel(c) 950.00
23 B:Airman 1,300.00
24 Airman 1,400.00

KEEN KOMICS
**Centaur Publications,
May, 1939**
1 Teenage Stories 1,400.00
2 PGv,JaB,CBu,Cut Carson 900.00
3 JCo,Saddle Sniffl 900.00

KEEN TEENS
**Life's Romances Publ./Leader/
Magazine Enterprises, 1945**
N# P(c),Claire Voyant 500.00
N# Ph(c),Van Johnson 350.00
3 Ph(c), ... 125.00
4 Ph(c),Glenn Ford. 150.00
5 Ph(c),Perry Como 150.00
6 . . . . 125.00

Ken Maynard Western #1
© Fawcett Publications

KEN MAYNARD WESTERN
Fawcett Publications,
Sept., 1950–Feb., 1952
1 B:Ken Maynard & Tarzan (horse)
   The Outlaw Treasure Trail .. 800.00
2 Invasion of the Badmen 500.00
3 Pied Piper of the West 350.00
4 Outlaw Hoax 350.00
5 Mystery of Badman City 350.00
6 Redwood Robbery 350.00
7 Seven Wonders of the West .. 350.00
8 Mighty Mountain Menace 350.00

KEN SHANNON
Quality Comics Group,
Oct., 1951–April, 1953
1 RC, Evil Eye of Count Ducrie . 500.00
2 RC, Cut Rate Corpses 350.00
3 RC, Corpse that Wouldn't
   Sleep 275.00
4 RC, Stone Hatchet Murder ... 275.00
5 RC, Case of the Carney Killer 275.00
6 Weird Vampire Mob 275.00
7 RC,Ugliest Man in the World . 225.00
8 Chinatown Murders,Drug..... 350.00
9 RC, Necklace of Blood 200.00
10 RC, Shadow of the Chair 200.00

KEN STUART
Publication Enterprises, 1949
1 .... 150.00

KERRY DRAKE DETECTIVE CASES
Life's Romances/M.E., 1944
(1) see N# A-1 Comics
2 A:The Faceless Horror 225.00
3 .... 200.00
4 A:Squirrel, Dr. Zero, Caresse . 200.00
5 Bondage (c) 500.00
     Harvey Publ., Jan., 1952
6 A:Stitches 250.00
7 A:Shuteye 275.00
8 Bondage (c) 350.00
9 Drug 350.00
10 BP,A:Meatball,Drug......... 350.00
11 BP,I:Kid Gloves 150.00
12 BP...................... 150.00
13 BP,A:Torso 125.00
14 BP,Bullseye Murder Syndicate 125.00
15 BP,Fake Mystic Racket...... 125.00

16 BP,A:Vixen 100.00
17 BP,Case of the $50,000
   Robbery................. 100.00
18 BP,A:Vixen 100.00
19 BP,Case of the Dope
   Smugglers 250.00
20 BP,Secret Treasury Agent.... 100.00
21 BP,Murder on Record 100.00
22 BP,Death Rides the Air Waves 100.00
23 BP,Blackmailer's Secret
   Weapon.................. 100.00
24 Blackmailer's Trap 100.00
25 Pretty Boy Killer 100.00
26 .... 100.00
27 .... 100.00
28 BP..................... 100.00
29 BP..................... 100.00
30 Mystery Mine,Bondage(c) ... 250.00
31 .... 100.00
32 .... 100.00
33 Aug., 1952............... 100.00

KEWPIES
Will Eisner Publications,
Spring, 1949
1 .... 650.00

KEY COMICS
Consolidated Magazines
Jan., 1944
1 B:The Key, Will-O-The-Wisp .. 550.00
2 .... 300.00
3 .... 250.00
4 WJo(c) O:John Quincy,
   B:The Atom 275.00
5 HoK,Aug., 1946 .... 300.00

KEY RING COMICS
Dell Publishing Co., 1941
1 .... 250.00
(1) Radior................... 300.00

KID COWBOY
Approved Comics/
St. John Publ. Co., 1950
1 B:Lucy Belle & Red Feather .. 200.00
2 Six-Gun Justice 150.00
3 Shadow on Hangman's Bridge 125.00
4 Red Feather V:Eagle of Doom 100.00
5 Killers on the Rampage 100.00
6 The Stovepipe Hat 100.00
7 Ghost Town of Twin Buttes ... 100.00
8 Thundering Hoofs 100.00
9 Terror on the Salt Flats 100.00
10 Valley of Death 100.00
11 Vanished Herds,Bondage(c) . 200.00
12 .... 100.00
13 .... 100.00
14 1954 .... 100.00

KIDDIE KARNIVAL
Approved Comics, 1952
N# 450.00

KID ETERNITY
Comics Magazine,
Spring, 1946
1 .... 1,500.00
2 .... 550.00
3 Follow Him Out of This World . 575.00
4 Great Heroes of the Past 350.00
5 Don't Kid with Crime 300.00
6 Busy Battling Crime 300.00
7 Protects the World 300.00
8 Fly to the Rescue 300.00
9 Swoop Down on Crime 300.00
10 Golden Touch from Mr. Midas. 300.00
11 Aid the Living by Calling
   the Dead 250.00

Kid Eternity #15
© Comics Magazine

12 Finds Death 250.00
13 Invades General Poschka.... 250.00
14 Battles Double 250.00
15 A: Master Man............. 250.00
16 Balance Scales of Justice.... 225.00
17 A:Baron Roxx 225.00
18 A:Man with Two Faces 225.00
Becomes:

BUCCANEERS
Quality Comics Group,
Jan., 1950
19 RC,Sword Fight(c) 750.00
20 RC,Treasure Chest 450.00
21 RC,Death Trap 500.00
22 A:Lady Dolores,Snuff,
   Bondage(c) 400.00
23 RC,V:Treasure Hungry
   Plunderers of the Sea 375.00
24 A:Adam Peril,Black Roger,
   Eric Falcon 300.00
25 V:Clews 300.00
26 V:Admiral Blood 300.00
27 RC(a&c)May, 1951 .... 450.00

KID ZOO COMICS
Street & Smith Publ., 1948
1 (fa) 350.00

KILLERS, THE
Magazine Enterprises, 1947
1 LbC(c),Thou Shall Not Kill .. 1,500.00
2 Grl,OW,Assassins Mad Slayers
   of the East,Hanging(c),Drug 1,300.00

KILROYS, THE
B&L Publishing Co./
American Comics,
June–July, 1947
1 Three Girls in Love(c) 300.00
2 Flat Tire(c) 150.00
3 Right to Swear(c) 125.00
4 Kissing Booth(c) 125.00
5 Skiing(c) 125.00
6 Prom(c) 100.00
7 To School 100.00
8 .... 100.00
9 .... 100.00
10 B:Solid Jackson solo........ 100.00
11 .... 100.00
12 Life Guard(c)............. 100.00
13 thru 21................. @100.00
22 thru 30................. @100.00
31 thru 40................. @100.00
41 thru 47................. @100.00

48 3-D effect 200.00
49 3-D effect 200.00
50 thru 54, July, 1954 . . . . @100.00

KING COMICS
David McKay Publications, April, 1936
(all have Popeye covers)
1 AR,EC,B:Popeye,Flash Gordon,B:
  Henry,Mandrake 15,000.00
2 AR,EC,Flash Gordon 4,000.00
3 AR,EC,Flash Gordon 2,500.00
4 AR,EC,Flash Gordon 2,000.00
5 AR,EC,Flash Gordon 1,500.00
6 AR,EC,Flash Gordon 1,100.00
7 AR,EC,King Royal Mounties 1,050.00
8 AR,EC,Thanksgiving(c) 1,000.00
9 AR,EC,Christmas(c) 1,000.00
10 AR,EC,Flash Gordon 1,000.00
11 AR,EC,Flash Gordon 750.00
12 AR,EC,Flash Gordon 750.00
13 AR,EC,Flash Gordon 750.00
14 AR,EC,Flash Gordon 750.00
15 AR,EC,Flash Gordon 750.00
16 AR,EC,Flash Gordon 750.00
17 AR,EC,Flash Gordon 700.00
18 AR,EC,Flash Gordon 700.00
Covers say: "Starring Popeye"
19 AR,EC,Flash Gordon 700.00
20 AR,EC,Football(c) 700.00
21 AR,EC,Flash Gordon 600.00
22 AR,EC,Flash Gordon 600.00
23 AR,EC,Flash Gordon 600.00
24 AR,EC,Flash Gordon 600.00
25 AR,EC,Flash Gordon 600.00
26 AR,EC,Flash Gordon 550.00
27 AR,EC,Flash Gordon 550.00
28 AR,EC,Flash Gordon 550.00
29 AR,EC,Flash Gordon 550.00
30 AR,EC,Flash Gordon 550.00
31 AR,EC,Flash Gordon 550.00
32 AR,EC,Flash Gordon 550.00
33 AR,EC,Skiing(c) 550.00
34 AR,Ping Pong(c) 450.00
35 AR,Flash Gordon 450.00
36 AR,Flash Gordon 450.00
37 AR,Flash Gordon 450.00
38 AR,Flash Gordon 450.00
39 AR,Baseball(c) 450.00
40 AR,Flash Gordon 450.00
41 AR,Flash Gordon 400.00
42 AR,Flash Gordon 400.00
43 AR,Flash Gordon 400.00
44 AR,Popeye golf(c) 400.00
45 AR,Flash Gordon 400.00
46 AR,B:Little Lulu 400.00
47 AR,Flash Gordon 400.00
48 AR,Flash Gordon 400.00
49 AR,Weather Vane 400.00
50 AR,B:Love Ranger 400.00
51 AR,Flash Gordon 300.00
52 AR,Flash Gordon 300.00
53 AR,Flash Gordon 300.00
54 AR,Flash Gordon 300.00
55 AR,Magic Carpet. 300.00
56 AR,Flash Gordon 300.00
57 AR,Cows Over Moon(c) 300.00
58 AR,Flash Gordon 300.00
59 AR,Flash Gordon 300.00
60 AR,Flash Gordon 300.00
61 AR,B:Phantom,Baseball(c) . . . 300.00
62 AR,Flash Gordon 300.00
63 AR,Flash Gordon 250.00
64 AR,Flash Gordon 250.00
65 AR,Flash Gordon 250.00
66 AR,Flash Gordon 250.00
67 AR,Sweet Pea. 250.00
68 AR,Flash Gordon 250.00
69 AR,Flash Gordon 250.00
70 AR,Flash Gordon 250.00
71 AR,Flash Gordon 250.00
72 AR,Flash Gordon 250.00

Flash Gordon . . . Little Annie Rooney
Henry . . . King of the Royal Mounted

King Comics #15
© David McKay Publications

73 AR,Flash Gordon 250.00
74 AR,Flash Gordon 250.00
75 AR,Flash Godron 250.00
76 AR,Flag(c) 250.00
77 AR,Flash Gordon 250.00
78 AR,Popeye,Olive Oil(c) 250.00
79 AR,Sweet Pea. 250.00
80 AR,Wimpy(c) 250.00
81 AR,B:Blondie(c). 250.00
82 thru 91 AR . . . . @200.00
92 thru 98 AR . . . . @200.00
99 AR,Olive Oil(c) 200.00
100 . . . . 200.00
101 thru 116 AR . . . . @175.00
117 O:Phantom 200.00
118 Flash Gordon 175.00
119 Flash Gordon 150.00
120 Wimpy(c). 125.00
121 thru 140. . . . . @125.00
141 Flash Gordon 125.00
142 Flash Gordon 125.00
143 Flash Gordon 125.00
144 Flash Gordon 125.00
145 Prince Valiant 100.00
146 Prince Valiant 100.00
147 Prince Valiant 100.00
148 thru 154. . . . . @75.00
155 E:Flash Gordon. 75.00
156 Baseball(c) 75.00
157 thru 159 . . . . @75.00

KING OF THE ROYAL MOUNTED
Dell Publishing Co., Dec., 1948–1958
(1) *see Dell Four Color #207*
(2) *see Dell Four Color #265*
(3) *see Dell Four Color #283*
(4) *see Dell Four Color #310*
(5) *see Dell Four Color #340*
(6) *see Dell Four Color #363*
(7) *see Dell Four Color #384*
8 Zane Grey adapt. 150.00
9 . . . . 125.00
10 . . . . 125.00
11 thru 28 . . . . @100.00

KIT CARSON
Avon Periodicals, 1950
N# EK(c) Indian Scout 200.00
2 EK(c),Kit Carson's Revenge,
  Doom Trail. 150.00
3 EK(c),V:Comanche Raiders . . 100.00
4 . . . . 100.00

5 EK(c),Trail of Doom 100.00
6 EK(c) 100.00
7 EK(c) 100.00
8 EK(c) 100.00
Becomes:

FIGHTING DAVY CROCKETT
Oct.–Nov, 1955
9 EK(c) 100.00

KO KOMICS
Gerona Publications, Oct., 1945
1 . . . . 1,000.00

KOMIK PAGES
See: SCOOP COMICS

KRAZY KAT COMICS
Dell Publishing Co., May–June, 1951
1 . . . . 125.00
2 . . . . 100.00
3 . . . . 100.00
4 . . . . 100.00
5 . . . . 100.00

KRAZY LIFE
See: PHANTOM LADY

LABOR IS A PARTNER
Catechetical Guild Educational Society, 1949
1 . . . . 250.00

LADY LUCK
See: SMASH

LAFFY-DAFFY COMICS
Rural Home Publ. Co., Feb., 1945
1 (fa) 150.00
2 . . . . 150.00

LANCE O'CASEY
Fawcett, 1946–47
1 High Seas Adventure
  from Whiz comics 450.00
2 thru 4 . . . . @300.00

LAND OF THE LOST
E.C. Comics, July–Aug., 1946–Spring 1948
1 Radio show adapt. 450.00
2 . . . . 300.00
3 thru 9 . . . . @250.00

LARGE FEATURE COMICS
Dell Publishing Co., 1939
1 Dick Tracy vs. the Blank 2,100.00
2 Terry and the Pirates 1,100.00
3 Heigh-Yo Silver!
  the Lone Ranger. 1,700.00
4 Dick Tracy gets his man 1,200.00
5 Tarzan of the Apes 2,000.00
6 Terry and the Pirates 1,200.00
7 Lone Ranger to the rescue . . 1,600.00
8 Dick Tracy, Racket Buster . . 1,200.00
9 King of the Royal Mounted . . . 700.00
10 Gang Busters 800.00
11 Dick Tracy, Mad Doc Hump . 1,200.00
12 Smilin' Jack. 750.00
13 Dick Tracy and Scottie
  of Scotland Yard 1,200.00
14 Smilin' Jack helps G-Men . . . 750.00

GOLDEN AGE

Large Feature Comics #27
© Dell Publishing Co.

15 Dick Tracy and
  the Kidnapped Princes.... 1,200.00
16 Donald Duck, 1st Daisy. ... 9,000.00
17 Gang Busters 600.00
18 Phantasmo The Master
  of the World.............. 500.00
19 Walt Disney's Dumbo...... 4,000.00
20 Donald Duck 10,000.00
21 Private Buck 150.00
22 Nuts and Jolts............. 150.00
23 The Nebbs 200.00
24 Popeye in 'Thimble Theatre'. . 900.00
25 Smilin'Jack 700.00
26 Smitty 300.00
27 Terry and the Pirates 750.00
28 Grin and Bear It 100.00
29 Moon Mullins............. 300.00
30 Tillie the Toiler............ 275.00

[Series 2]

1 Peter Rabbit............... 500.00
2 Winnie Winkle 250.00
3 Dick Tracy............... 1,000.00
4 Tiny Tim 300.00
5 Toots and Casper.......... 150.00
6 Terry and the Pirates 750.00
7 Pluto saves the Ship....... 2,000.00
8 Bugs Bunny 2,000.00
9 Bringing Up Father 250.00
10 Popeye 650.00
11 Barney Google&SnuffySmith . 300.00
12 Private Buck 150.00
13 1001 Hours of Fun 200.00

LARRY DOBY, BASEBALL HERO
Fawcett Publications, 1950
1 Ph(c),BW 1,200.00

LARS OF MARS
Ziff-Davis Publishing Co.,
April–May, 1951
10 MA,'Terror from the Sky' ... 1,200.00
11 GC, The Terror Weapon 950.00

LASH LARUE WESTERN
Fawcett Publications,
Summer, 1949
1 Ph(c),The Fatal Roundups . . 1,600.00
2 Ph(c),Perfect Hide Out 750.00
3 Ph(c),The Suspect......... 600.00
4 Ph(c),Death on Stage 600.00
5 Ph(c),Rustler's Haven 600.00
6 Ph(c) 500.00
7 Ph(c),Shadow of the Noose. . . 425.00
8 Ph(c),Double Deadline....... 425.00

9 Ph(c),Generals Last Stand ... 425.00
10 Ph(c).................... 425.00
11 Ph(c)................... 350.00
12 thru 20 Ph(c) ....@300.00
21 thru 29 Ph(c) ....@250.00
30 thru 46 Ph(c) ....@225.00
46 Ph(c),Lost Chance 225.00

LASSIE
Dell Publishing Co.,
Oct.–Dec., 1950
1 Ph(c) all 275.00
2 .... 150.00
3 thru 10 ....@125.00
11 .... 100.00
12 Rocky Langford.......... 100.00
13 .... 100.00
14 .... 100.00
15 I:Timbu 100.00
16 .... 100.00
17 .... 100.00
18 .... 100.00
19 .... 100.00
20 MB..................... 125.00
21 MB..................... 125.00
22 MB..................... 125.00
23 thru 38 ....@100.00
39 I:Timmy 100.00
40 thru 62................@100.00
63 E:Timmy 100.00
64 thru 70................@100.00

LATEST COMICS
Spotlight Publ./
Palace Promotions,
March, 1945
1 Funny Animal-Super Duper . . . 250.00
2 .... 200.00

SPECIAL COMICS
MLJ Magazines,
Winter, 1941
1 O:Boy Buddies & Hangman,
  D:The Comet 4,500.00
Becomes:

HANGMAN COMICS
Spring, 1942
2 B:Hangman & Boy Buddies . 2,700.00
3 V:Nazis (c),Bondage(c) 1,800.00
4 V:Nazis (c) 1,500.00
5 Bondage (c) 1,500.00
6 .... 1,500.00
7 BF,Graveyard (c) 1,500.00
8 BF 1,500.00
Becomes:

BLACK HOOD
Winter, 1943–44
9 BF, Hang Man............ 1,600.00
10 BF,A:Dusty, the Boy Detective 900.00
11 Here lies the Black Hood 700.00
12 .... 600.00
13 EK(c).................... 600.00
14 EK(c).................... 500.00
15 EK 500.00
16 EK(c)................... 500.00
17 Bondage (c) 650.00
18 .... 600.00
19 I.D. Revealed 700.00
Becomes:

LAUGH COMICS
Archie Comics, Fall, 1946
20 BWo,B:Archie,Katy Keene . . . 900.00
21 BWo 450.00
22 BWo 450.00
23 Bwo.................... 450.00
24 BWo,JK,Pipsy............ 460.00
25 BWo 450.00
26 BWo 225.00

Laugh Comis #47
© Comic Corp. of America

27 BWo 225.00
28 BWo 225.00
29 BWo 225.00
30 BWo 225.00
31 thru 40 BWo ....@200.00
41 thru 50 BWo ....@175.00
51 thru 60 BWo ....@150.00
61 thru 80 BWo ....@150.00
81 thru 99 BWo ....@150.00
100 BWo 150.00
101 thru 126 BWo ....@125.00
127 A:Jaguar 150.00
128 A:The Fly............... 150.00
129 A:The Fly............... 150.00
130 A:Jaguar 150.00
131 A:Jaguar 150.00
132 A:The Fly............... 150.00
133 A:Jaguar 150.00
134 A:The Fly............... 150.00
135 A:Jaguar 150.00
136 A:Fly Girl 150.00
137 A:Fly Girl 150.00
138 A:The Fly............... 150.00
139 A:The Fly............... 150.00
140 A:Jaguar 150.00
141 A:Jaguar 150.00
142 .... 150.00
143 .... 150.00
144...................... 150.00

LAUGH COMIX
See: TOP-NOTCH COMICS

LAUREL AND HARDY
St. John Publishing Co.,
March, 1949
1 .... 1,000.00
2 .... 500.00
3 .... 350.00
26 Rep #1 .... 200.00
27 Rep #2 .... 200.00
28 Rep #3 .... 200.00

LAWBREAKERS
Law & Order Magazines
(Charlton), March, 1951
1 .... 500.00
2 .... 275.00
3 .... 225.00
4 Drug 300.00
5 .... 225.00
6 LM(c) 250.00
7 Drug 300.00
8 .... 225.00
9 StC(c)................... 225.00

GOLDEN AGE

Becomes:

LAWBREAKERS SUSPENSE STORIES
Jan., 1953
10 StC(c) 500.00
11 LM(c),Negligee(c). 1,400.00
12 LM(c). 300.00
13 DG(c). 300.00
14 DG(c),Sharks 300.00
15 DG(c),Acid in Face(c) 750.00
Becomes:

STRANGE SUSPENSE STORIES
Jan., 1954
16 DG(c) 400.00
17 DG(c) 300.00
18 SD,SD(c). 450.00
19 SD,SD(c),Electric Chair 600.00
20 SD,SD(c) 500.00
21 SD,SD(c). 300.00
22 SD,SD(c). 450.00
Becomes:

THIS IS SUSPENSE
Feb., 1955
23 WW; Comics Code 325.00
24 GE,DG(c) 175.00
25 DG(c) 150.00
26 DG(c) 50.00
Becomes:

STRANGE SUSPENSE STORIES
Oct., 1955
27 . . . . 175.00
28 . . . . 125.00
29 . . . . 125.00
30 . . . . 125.00
31 SD. 250.00
32 SD. 250.00
33 SD. 250.00
34 SD. 650.00
35 SD. 250.00
36 SD. 250.00
37 SD. 250.00
38 . . . . 125.00
39 SD. 200.00
40 SD 225.00
41 SD. 200.00
42 . . . . 100.00
43 . . . . 100.00
44 . . . . 100.00

Strange Suspense Stories #35
© Charlton

45 . . . . 100.00
46 . . . . 100.00
47 SD. 225.00
48 SD. 225.00
49 . . . . 100.00
50 SD 225.00
51 SD 225.00
52 SD 225.00
53 SD 225.00
54 thru 60 . . . . @100.00
61 thru 74 . . . . @100.00
75 SD,SD(c), Captain Atom 200.00
77 Oct 1965 . . . . 125.00

LAW-CRIME
Essenkay Publications, April, 1948
1 LbC,LbC-(c);Raymond Hamilton
   Dies In The Chair 1,000.00
2 LbC,LbC-(c);Strangled
   Beauty Puzzles Police. 750.00
3 LbC,LbC-(c);Lipstick Slayer
   Sought; Aug., 1943. . . . . . 1,000.00

MISS LIBERTY
Burten Publishing, circa 1944
1 Reprints-Shield,Wizard 550.00
Becomes:

LIBERTY COMICS
Green Publishing, May, 1946
10 Reprints,Hangman 300.00
11 Wilbur in women's clothes . . 225.00
12 Black Hood, Skull(c) 750.00
14 Patty of Airliner 175.00
15 Patty of Airliner 175.00

LIBERTY GUARDS
Chicago Mail Order (Comic Corp of America), Circa 1942
1 PG(c),Liberty Scouts 500.00
Becomes:

LIBERTY SCOUTS
June, 1941–Aug., 1941
PG(a&c)O:Fireman,Liberty
   Scouts 1,800.00
3 PG,PG(c),O:Sentinel 1,300.00

LIFE STORY
Fawcett Publications, April, 1949
1 Ph(c) 200.00
2 Ph(c) 150.00
3 Ph(c) 125.00
4 Ph(c) 125.00
5 Ph(c) 125.00
6 Ph(c) 125.00
7 Ph(c) 100.00
8 Ph(c) 100.00
9 Ph(c) 100.00
10 Ph(c) 100.00
11 . . . . 100.00
12 . . . . 100.00
13 WW, BP,Drug 250.00
14 . . . . 100.00
15 . . . . 100.00
16 thru 21 . . . . @100.00
22 Drug 200.00
23 BP 100.00
24 BP 100.00
25 thru 35 . . . . @100.00
36 Drug 200.00
37 . . . . 100.00
38 . . . . 100.00
39 BP,Drug. 125.00
40 . . . . 100.00
41 . . . . 100.00
42 . . . . 100.00

43 GE. 125.00
44 . . . . 100.00
45 1952 . . . . 100.00

LIFE WITH SNARKY PARKER
Fox Feature Syndicate, Aug., 1950
1 . . . . 325.00

SURE-FIRE
Ace Magazines, 1940
1 O:Flash Lightning 2,500.00
2 Whiz Wilson 1,200.00
3 The Raven,Sept., 1940 . . . . . 850.00
3a Ace McCoy,Oct., 1940 . . . . . 850.00
Becomes:

LIGHTNING COMICS
Dec., 1940
4 Sure-Fire Stories. 1,700.00
5 JM 1,000.00
6 JM,Dr. Nemesis 1,000.00
Vol. 2
1 JM 750.00
2 JM,Flash Lightning. 750.00
3 JM 750.00
4 JM 750.00
5 JM 750.00
6 JM, bondage(c) 900.00
Vol. 3
1 I:Lightning Girl 750.00

LINDA
Ajax/Farrell Publications, 1954
1 . . . . 200.00
2 Lingerie 150.00
3 . . . . 125.00
4 . . . . 125.00

LINDA
See: PHANTOM LADY

LI'L ABNER
Harvey Publications, Dec., 1947
61 BP,BW,Sadie Hawkins Day. . . 450.00
62 . . . . 250.00
63 . . . . 250.00
64 . . . . 250.00
65 BP 250.00
66 . . . . 200.00
67 . . . . 200.00
68 FearlessFosdick V:Any Face . 275.00
69 . . . . 275.00
70 . . . . 200.00

Toby Press
71 . . . . 175.00
72 . . . . 175.00
73 . . . . 175.00
74 . . . . 175.00
75 HK 225.00
76 . . . . 175.00
77 HK 225.00
78 HK 225.00
79 HK 225.00
80 . . . . 200.00
81 . . . . 175.00
82 . . . . 175.00
83 Baseball 200.00
84 . . . . 175.00
85 . . . . 175.00
86 HK 250.00
87 . . . . 150.00
88 . . . . 150.00
89 . . . . 150.00
90 . . . . 150.00
91 Rep. #77 . . . . 165.00
92 . . . . 150.00

93 Rep. #71 . . . . 165.00
94 . . . . 150.00
95 Fearless Fosdick 200.00
96 . . . . 150.00
97 Jan., 1955 . . . . 150.00

LITTLE AL OF THE F.B.I.
Approved Comics (Ziff Davis), 1950
10 . . . . 200.00
11 . . . . 150.00

LITTLE AL OF THE SECRET SERVICE
Approved Comics (Ziff Davis), 1951
1 . . . . 200.00
2 . . . . 150.00
3 . . . . 150.00

LITTLE ANGEL
Standard Comics, 1954–59
5 . . . . 125.00
6 thru 16 . . . . @100.00

LITTLE ANNIE ROONEY
St. John Publishing Co./Standard, 1948
1 . . . . 200.00
2 . . . . 100.00
3 . . . . 100.00

LITTLE AUDREY
St. John Publ. Co./Harvey Comics, April, 1948
1 . . . . 600.00
2 . . . . 300.00
3 thru 6 . . . . @200.00
7 thru 10 . . . . @150.00
11 thru 20 . . . . @125.00
21 thru 24 . . . . @100.00
25 B:Harvey Comics 225.00
26 A: Casper 150.00
27 A: Casper 150.00
28 A: Casper 150.00
29 thru 31 . . . . @125.00
32 A: Casper 125.00
33 A: Casper 125.00
34 A: Casper 125.00
35 A: Casper 125.00
36 thru 53 . . . . @100.00

LITTLE BEAVER
Dell Publishing Co., 1951
3 . . . . 100.00
4 thru 8 . . . . @100.00

LITTLE BIT
Jubilee Publishing Company, March, 1949
1 . . . . 150.00
2 June, 1949 . . . . 125.00

LITTLE DOT
Harvey Publications, Sept., 1953
1 I: Richie Rich & Little Lotta . . 2,900.00
2 . . . . 1,200.00
3 . . . . 900.00
4 . . . . 800.00
5 O:Dots on Little Dot's Dress . . 700.00
6 1st Richie Rich(c) 650.00
7 . . . . 550.00
8 . . . . 500.00
9 . . . . 500.00
10 . . . . 500.00
11 thru 20 . . . . @400.00

21 thru 30 . . . . @300.00
31 thru 39 . . . . @250.00
40 thru 50 . . . . @200.00
51 thru 60 . . . . @200.00
61 thru 70 . . . . @200.00
71 thru 80 . . . . @200.00
81 thru 100 . . . . @200.00
101 thru 130 . . . . @150.00
131 thru 140 . . . . @150.00
141 thru 145, 52 pages . . . . . @150.00
146 thru 163 . . . . @100.00

Little Eva #15
© St. John Publishing Co.

LITTLE EVA
St. John Publishing Co., May, 1952
1 . . . . 200.00
2 . . . . 150.00
3 . . . . 125.00
4 . . . . 125.00
5 thru 10 . . . . @100.00
11 thru 30 . . . . @100.00
31 Nov., 1956 . . . . 100.00

LI'L GENIUS
Charlton Comics, 1955
1 . . . . 125.00
2 . . . . 100.00
3 . . . . 100.00
4 . . . . 100.00
5 . . . . 100.00
6 thru 15 . . . . @100.00
16 Giants 125.00
17 Giants 125.00
18 Giants,100 pages 150.00
19 thru 40 . . . . @75.00
41 thru 54 . . . . @75.00
55 1965 . . . . 75.00

LI'L GHOST
St. John Publishing/Fago Magazine Co.
1 . . . . 150.00
2a 100.00
3 . . . . 100.00

LITTLE GIANT COMICS
Centaur Publications, July, 1938
1 PG, B&W with Color(c) 1,100.00
2 B&W with Color(c) 750.00
3 B&W with Color(c) 750.00
4 B&W with Color(c) 750.00

LITTLE GIANT DETECTIVE FUNNIES
Centaur Publications, Oct., 1938–Jan., 1939
1 B&W 1,100.00
2 B&W 750.00
3 B&W 750.00
4 WE 750.00

LITTLE GIANT MOVIE FUNNIES
Centaur Publications, Aug., 1938
1 Ed Wheelan-a 1,100.00
2 Ed Wheelan-a, Oct., 1938 . . . 750.00

LITTLE GROUCHO
Reston Publ., Co. 1955
1 . . . . 125.00
2 . . . . 100.00

LITTLE IKE
St. John Publishing Co., April, 1953
1 . . . . 125.00
2 . . . . 100.00
3 . . . . 100.00
4 Oct., 1953 . . . . 100.00

LITTLE IODINE
Dell Publishing Co., April, 1949
1 . . . . 175.00
2 . . . . 125.00
3 . . . . 125.00
4 . . . . 125.00
5 . . . . 125.00
6 thru 10 . . . . @100.00
11 thru 30 . . . . @100.00
31 thru 50 . . . . @100.00
51 thru 56 . . . . @100.00

LITTLE JACK FROST
Avon Periodicals, 1951
1 . . . . 100.00

LI'L JINX
Archie Publications, 1956
11 . . . . 150.00
12 thru 16 . . . . @125.00

LITTLE JOE
St. John Publishing Co., 1953
1 . . . . 100.00

LITTLE LULU
See: MARGE'S LITTLE LULU

LI'L MENACE
Fago Magazine Co., 1958
1 . . . . 125.00
2 . . . . 100.00

LITTLE MAX COMICS
Harvey Publications, Oct., 1949
1 I: Little Dot,Joe Palooka(c) . . . 300.00
2 A: Little Dot,Joe Palooka(c) . . . 250.00
3 A: Little Dot,Joe Palooka(c) . . 200.00
4 . . . . 150.00
5 C: Little Dot 150.00
6 thru 10 . . . . @100.00
11 thru 22 . . . . @100.00
23 A: Little Dot 100.00
24 thru 37 . . . . @100.00

GOLDEN AGE *(side tab)*

38 Rep. #20 . . . . 100.00
39 thru 72 . . . . @100.00
73 A: Richie Rich; Nov.'61 . . . . . 100.00

LITTLE MISS MUFFET
**Best Books
(Standard Comics),
Dec., 1948**
11 Strip Reprints 150.00
12 Strip Reprints 125.00
13 Strip Reprints; Mar.'49 . . . . . 125.00

LITTLE MISS SUNBEAM
COMICS
**Magazine Enterprises,
June–July, 1950**
1 . . . . 200.00
2 . . . . 100.00
3 . . . . 100.00
4 Dec.–Jan., 1951 . . . . 100.00

LITTLE ORPHAN ANNIE
Dell Publishing Co., 1948
1 . . . . 250.00
2 Orphan Annie and the Rescue 150.00
3 . . . . 150.00
See also: *Four Color*

LI'L PAN
**Fox Features Syndicate,
Dec.–Jan., 1946-47**
6 . . . . 150.00
7 . . . . 125.00
8 April–May, 1947 . . . . 125.00

LITTLE ROQUEFORT
**St. John Publishing Co.,
June,1952**
1 . . . . 125.00
2 . . . . 100.00
3 thru 9 . . . . @100.00
Pines
10 Summer 1958 . . . . 100.00

LITTLE SCOUTS
**Dell Publishing Co.,
March, 1951**
(1) *see Dell Four Color #321*
2 . . . . 125.00
3 thru 6 . . . . @100.00

LITTLEST SNOWMAN
**Dell Publishing Co.,
Dec., 1956**
1 . . . . 100.00

LIVING BIBLE, THE
**Living Bible Corp.
Autumn, 1945**
1 LbC-(c) Life of Paul 500.00
2 LbC-(c) Joseph &His Brethern. 400.00
3 LbC-(c) Chaplains At War 475.00

LONE EAGLE
**Ajax/Farrell,
April–May, 1954**
1 . . . . 200.00
2 . . . . 150.00
3 Bondage(c) 250.00
4 Oct.–Nov., 1954 . . . . 150.00

LONELY HEART
**Excellent Publications
(Ajax/Farrell), 1955**
9 . . . . 150.00
10 thru 14 . . . . @100.00

Becomes:
DEAR HEART
Ajax/Farrell Publ., 1956
15 . . . . 100.00
16 . . . . 100.00

LONE RANGER
**Dell Publishing Co.,
Jan.–Feb., 1948**
1 B:Lone Ranger & Tonto
   B:Strip Reprint 1,400.00
2 . . . . 600.00
3 . . . . 400.00
4 . . . . 400.00
5 . . . . 400.00
6 . . . . 350.00
7 . . . . 350.00
8 O:Retold 400.00
9 . . . . 350.00
10 . . . . 350.00
11 B:Young Hawk. 250.00
12 thru 20 . . . . @250.00
21 . . . . 200.00
22 . . . . 200.00
23 O:Retold 275.00
24 thru 30 . . . . @200.00
31 (1st Mask Logo) 250.00
32 thru 36 . . . . @175.00
37 (E:Strip reprints) 150.00
38 thru 50 . . . . @150.00
51 thru 75 . . . . @150.00
76 thru 99 . . . . @125.00
100 . . . . 150.00
101 thru 111 . . . . @150.00
112 B:Clayton Moore Ph(c) . . . 350.00
113 thru 117 . . . . @200.00
118 O:Lone Ranger & Tonto
   retold, Anniv. issue 400.00
119 thru 144 . . . . @200.00
145 final issue,May/July, 1962. . 200.00

THE LONE RANGER'S
COMPANION TONTO
Dell Publishing Co., Jan., 1951
(1) *see Dell Four Color #312*
2 P(c) all 200.00
3 . . . . 150.00
4 . . . . 125.00
5 . . . . 125.00
6 thru 10 . . . . @125.00
11 thru 20 . . . . @100.00
21 thru 25 . . . . @100.00
26 thru 33 . . . . @100.00

THE LONE RANGER'S
FAMOUS HORSE
HI-YO SILVER
Dell Publishing Co., Jan., 1952
(1) *see Dell Four Color #369*
(1) *see Dell Four Color #392*
3 P(c) all 175.00
4 . . . . 125.00
5 . . . . 125.00
6 thru 10 . . . . @125.00
11 thru 36 . . . . @100.00

LONE RIDER
**Farrell (Superior
Comics), April, 1951**
1 . . . . 400.00
2 I&O: Golden Arrow; 52 pgs. . . 200.00
3 . . . . 175.00
4 . . . . 175.00
5 . . . . 175.00
6 E: Golden Arrow 175.00
7 G.Arrow Becomes Swift Arrow 175.00
8 O: Swift Arrow 200.00
9 thru 14 . . . . @100.00

15 O: Golden Arrow Rep. #2 . . . 125.00
16 thru 19 . . . . @100.00
20 . . . . 100.00
21 3-D (c). 250.00
22 . . . . 100.00
23 A: Apache Kid 100.00
24 . . . . 100.00
25 . . . . 100.00
26 July, 1955 . . . . 100.00

LONG BOW
**Real Adventures Publ.
(Fiction House), Winter, 1950**
1 . . . . 200.00
2 . . . . 125.00
3 'Red Arrows Means War'. 125.00
4 'Trial of Tomahawk' 125.00
5 . . . . 125.00
6 'Rattlesnake Raiders'. 100.00
7 . . . . 100.00
8 . . . . 100.00
9 Spring, 1953 . . . . 100.00

LONG JOHN SILVER
AND THE PIRATES
**See: TERRY
AND THE PIRATES**

LOONEY TUNES AND
MERRIE MELODIES
Dell Publishing Co., 1941
1 B:&1st Comic App. Bugs Bunny
  Daffy Duck,Elmer Fudd . . 20,000.00
2 Bugs/Porky(c) 4,000.00
3 Bugs/Porky(c) B:WK,
  Kandi the Cave 3,000.00
4 Bugs/Porky(c),WK 3,000.00
5 Bugs/Porky(c),WK,
  A:Super Rabbit. 2,500.00
6 Bugs/Porky/Elmer(c),E:WK,
  Kandi the Cave. 2,200.00
7 Bugs/Porky(c) 1,500.00
8 Bugs/Porky swimming(c),F:WK,
  Kandi the Cave 2,000.00
9 Porky/Elmer car painted(c) . . 1,500.00
10 Porky/Bugs/Elmer Parade(c) 1,500.00
11 Bugs/Porky(c),F:WK,
  Kandi the Cave 1,500.00
12 Bugs/Porky rollerskating(c) . 1,100.00
13 Bugs/Porky(c) 1,100.00
14 Bugs/Porky(c) 1,100.00
15 Bugs/Porky X-Mas(c),F:WK
  Kandi the Cave 1,000.00
16 Bugs/Porky ice-skating(c) . . 1,000.00

*Loonie Tunes and Merrie Melodies #31
© Walt Disney*

    All comics prices listed are for *Near Mint* condition.

17 Bugs/Petunia Valentines(c) . 1,000.00
18 Sgt.Bugs Marine(c) 1,000.00
19 Bugs/Painting(c). 1,000.00
20 Bugs/Porky/ElmerWarBonds(c),
    B:WK,Pat,Patsy&Pete 1,000.00
21 Bugs/Porky 4th July(c). 1,000.00
22 Porky(c) 1,000.00
23 Bugs/Porky Fishing(c) 1,000.00
24 Bugs/Porky Football(c) 1,000.00
25 Bugs/Porky/Petunia Halloween
    (c),E:WK,Pat, Patsy & Pete 1,000.00
26 Bugs Thanksgiving(c) 750.00
27 Bugs/Porky New Years(c). . . . 750.00
28 Bugs/Porky Ice-Skating(c) . . . 750.00
29 Bugs Valentine(c) 750.00
30 Bugs(c) 750.00
31 Bugs(c) 600.00
32 Bugs/Porky Hot Dogs(c) 600.00
33 Bugs/Porky War Bonds(c) . . . 750.00
34 Bugs/Porky Fishing(c) 500.00
35 Bugs/Porky Swimming(c) 500.00
36 Bugs/Porky(c) 500.00
37 Bugs Halloween(c) 500.00
38 Bugs Thanksgiving(c) 500.00
39 Bugs X-Mas(c) 500.00
40 Bugs(c) 500.00
41 Bugs Washington's
    Birthday(c) 400.00
42 Bugs Magician(c) 400.00
43 Bugs Dream(c) 400.00
44 Bugs/Porky(c) 400.00
45 Bugs War Bonds(c) 400.00
46 Bugs/Porky(c) 400.00
47 Bugs Beach(c) 350.00
48 Bugs/Porky Picnic(c). 350.00
49 Bugs(c) 350.00
50 Bugs(c) 350.00
51 thru 60 . . . . @300.00
61 thru 80 . . . . @250.00
81 thru 86 . . . . @150.00
87 Bugs X-Mas(c) 175.00
88 thru 99 . . . . @150.00
100 . . . . 150.00
101 thru 110 . . . . @150.00
111 thru 125 . . . . @150.00
126 thru 150 . . . . @150.00
151 thru 165 . . . . @100.00

Becomes:

LOONEY TUNES
Aug., 1955
166 thru 200 . . . . @100.00
201 thru 245 . . . . @100.00
246 final issue,Sept.1962 . . . . . . 100.00

LOST WORLDS
Literary Enterprises
(Standard Comics),
Oct., 1952
5 ATh, Alice in Terrorland 600.00
6 ATh 450.00

LUCKY COMICS
Consolidated Magazines,
Jan., 1944–Summer 1946
1 Lucky Star 300.00
2 HcK(c) 200.00
3 . . . . 200.00
4 . . . . 200.00
5 Devil(c) 200.00

LUCKY DUCK
Standard Comics
(Literary Enterprises),
Jan.–Sept., 1953
5 IS(a&c) 125.00
6 IS(a&c) 100.00
7 IS(a&c). 100.00
8 IS(a&c) 100.00

LUCKY FIGHTS
IT THROUGH
Educational Comics, 1949
N# HK-a, V.D. Prevention 1,500.00

LUCKY "7" COMICS
Howard Publications, 1944
1 Bondage(c) Pioneer 700.00

LUCKY STAR
Nationwide Publications,
1950
1 JDa,B:52 pages western 225.00
2 JDa 150.00
3 JDa 150.00
4 JDa 125.00
5 JDa 125.00
6 JDa 125.00
7 JDa 125.00
8 thru 13 . . . . @100.00
14 1955,E:52 pages western. . . . 100.00

LUCY, THE REAL
GONE GAL
St. John Publishing Co.,
June, 1953
1 Negligee Panels,Teenage 300.00
2 . . . . 150.00
3 MD-a 125.00
4 Feb., 1954 . . . . 100.00
Becomes:

MEET MISS PEPPER
April, 1954
5 JKu-a 225.00
6 JKu (a&c), June,1954 . . . . 175.00

MAD
E.C. Comics, Oct.–Nov., 1952
1 JSe,HK(c),JDa,WW 15,000.00
2 JSe,JDa(c),JDa,WW 4,500.00
3 JSe,HK(c),JDa,WW 2,700.00
4 JSe,HK(c),JDa-Flob Was
    A Slob,JDa,WW 2,500.00
5 JSe,BE(c).JDa,WW 3,000.00
6 JSe,HK(c),Jda,WW. 1,500.00
7 HK(c),JDa,WW 1,500.00
8 HK(c),JDa,WW 1,500.00
9 JSe,HK(c),JDa,WW 1,500.00
10 JSe,HK(c),JDa,WW 1,600.00
11 BW,BW(c),JDa,WW,Life(c). . 1,500.00
12 BK,JDa,WW. 1,400.00
13 HK(c),JDa,WW,Red(c). . . . 1,400.00
14 RH,HK(c),JDa,WW,
    Mona Lisa(c). 1,400.00
15 JDa,WW,Alice in
    Wonderland(c) 1,400.00
16 HK(c),JDa,WW,
    Newspaper(c). 1,400.00
17 BK,BW,JDa,WW 1,400.00
18 HK(c),JDa,WW. 1,400.00
19 JDa,WW,Racing Form(c). . . 1,400.00
20 JDa,WW,Composition(c) . . 1,200.00
21 JDa,WW,1st A.E.Neuman(c) 1,500.00
22 BE,JDa,WW,Picasso(c) . . . 1,500.00
23 Last Comic Format Edition,
    JDa,WW Think(c) 1,000.00
24 BK,WW, HK Logo & Border;
    1st Magazine Format 1,800.00
25 WW,AlJaffee Becomes Reg. 1,000.00
26 BK,WW,WW(c) 600.00
27 WWa,RH,JDa(c) 550.00
28 WW,BE(c),RH Back(c) 550.00
29 JKa,BW,WW,WW(c);
    1st Don Martin Artwork 550.00
30 BE,WW,RC; 1st A.E.
    Neuman(c) By Mingo 600.00
31 JDa,WW,BW,Mingo(c) 550.00

Mad Magazine #45
© E.C. Comics

32 MD,JO 1st as reg.;Mingo(o);
    WW-Back(c) 350.00
33 WWa,Mingo(c);JO-Back(c) . . . 550.00
34 WWa,Mingo(c);1st Berg
    as Reg. 500.00
35 WW,RC,Mingo
    Wraparound(c). 500.00
36 WW,BW,Mingo(c),JO,MD . . . 500.00
37 WW,Mingo(c)JO,MD 500.00
38 WW,JO,MD 500.00
39 WW,JO,MD 500.00
40 WW,BW,JO,MD 500.00
41 WW,JO,MD 250.00
42 WW,JO,MD 250.00
43 WW,JO,MD 250.00
44 WW,JO,MD 250.00
45 WW,JO,MD 250.00
46 JO,MD. 250.00
47 JO,MD. 250.00
48 JO,MD. 250.00
49 JO,MD. 250.00
50 JO,MD. 250.00
51 JO,MD. 200.00
52 JO,MD. 200.00
53 JO,MD. 200.00
54 JO,MD. 200.00
55 JO,MD. 200.00
56 JO,MD. 200.00
57 JO,MD. 200.00
58 JO,MD. 200.00
59 WW,JO,MD 250.00
60 JO,MD. 250.00

MAD HATTER, THE
O.W. Comics, 1946
1 Freddy the Firefly 1,300.00
2 V:Humpty Dumpty 600.00

MADHOUSE
Ajax/Farrell Publ., 1954
1 . . . . 375.00
2 . . . . 200.00
3 . . . . 200.00
4 . . . . 300.00

Second Series, 1957
1 . . . . 150.00
2 . . . . 125.00
3 . . . . 125.00

MAGIC COMICS
David McKay Publications,
Aug.,1939–Nov.-Dec., 1949
1 Mandrake the Magician, Henry,
    Popeye,Blondie, Barney Baxter,
    Secret Agent X-9, Bunky,
    Henry on(c) 4,000.00

All comics prices listed are for *Near Mint* condition.

2 Henry on(c). 1,400.00
3 Henry on(c) 1,100.00
4 Henry on(c),Mandrake-Logo . . 850.00
5 Henry on(c),Mandrake-Logo . . 750.00
6 Henry on(c),Mandrake-Logo . . 550.00
7 Henry on(c),Mandrake-Logo . . 550.00
8 B:Inspector Wade,Tippie 525.00
9 Henry-Mandrake Interact(c) . . 525.00
10 Henry-Mandrake Interact(c) . . 525.00
11 Henry-Mandrake Interact(c) . . 450.00
12 Mandrake on(c). 450.00
13 Mandrake on(c). 450.00
14 Mandrake on(c). 450.00
15 Mandrake on(c). 450.00
16 Mandrake on(c). 450.00
17 B:Lone Ranger 500.00
18 Mandrake/Robot on(c) 400.00
19 Mandrake on(c). 550.00
20 Mandrake on(c). 400.00
21 Mandrake on(c). 350.00
22 Mandrake on(c). 350.00
23 Mandrake on(c). 350.00
24 Mandrake on(c). 350.00
25 B:Blondie; Mandrake in
    Logo for Duration. 350.00
26 Blondie (c). 300.00
27 Blondie(c); HighSchoolHeroes 300.00
28 Blondie(c); HighSchoolHeroes 300.00
29 Blondie(c); HighSchoolHeroes 300.00
30 Blondie (c) 300.00
31 Blondie(c);High School
    Sports Page. 225.00
32 Blondie (c);Secret Agent X-9 . 225.00
33 C.Knight's-Romance of Flying 225.00
34 ClaytonKnight's-War in the Air 225.00
35 Blondie (c). 225.00
36 July'42; Patriotic-(c) 225.00
37 Blondie (c). 225.00
38 ClaytonKnight's-Flying Tigers . 225.00
39 Blondie (c). 225.00
40 Jimmie Doolittle bombs Tokyo 225.00
41 How German Became
    British Censor 200.00
42 Joe Musial's-Dollar-a-Dither . . 200.00
43 Clay Knight's-War in the Air . . 200.00
44 Flying Fortress in Action 200.00
45 Clayton Knight's-Gremlins . . . 200.00
46 Adventures of Aladdin Jr. 200.00
47 Secret Agent X-9. . . . . 200.00
48 General Arnold U.S.A.F. 200.00
49 Joe Musial's-Dollar-a-Dither . . 200.00
50 The Lone Ranger 200.00
51 Joe Musial's-Dollar-a-Dither . 150.00
52 C. Knights-Heroes on Wings . 150.00
53 C. Knights-Heroes on Wings . 150.00
54 High School Heroes 150.00
55 Blondie (c). 175.00
56 High School Heroes 150.00
57 Joe Musial's-Dollar-a-Dither . 150.00
58 Private Breger Abroad 150.00
59 . . . . 150.00
60 . . . . 150.00
61 Joe Musial's-Dollar-a-Dither . . 125.00
62 . . . . 125.00
63 B:Buz Sawyer, Naval Pilot . . . 125.00
64 thru 70. . . . . @125.00
71 thru 80 . . . . @125.00
81 thru 90 . . . . @100.00
91 thru 99 . . . . @100.00
100 . . . . 125.00
101 thru 108. . . . . @100.00
108 Flash Gordon 125.00
109 Flash Gordon 125.00
110 thru 113 . . . . @125.00
114 The Lone Ranger 125.00
115 thru 119 . . . . @125.00
120 Secret Agent X-9 . . . . 150.00
121 Secret Agent X-9. . . . . 150.00
122 Secret Agent X-9. . . . . 150.00
123 Sec. Agent X-9 . . . . 150.00

MAJOR HOOPLE COMICS
Nedor Publications, 1942
1 Mary Worth,Phantom Soldier;
    Buy War Bonds On(c) 500.00

MAJOR INAPAK THE SPACE ACE
Magazine Enterprises, 1951
1 BP,Sci-Fi 200.00

MAJOR VICTORY COMICS
H. Clay Glover Svcs./ Harry A. Chestler, 1944
1 O:Major Victory,I:Spider
    Woman 950.00
2 A: Dynamic Boy 500.00
3 A: Rocket Boy 450.00

MAMMOTH COMICS
K.K. Publications, 1938
1 Alley Oop, Dick Tracy, etc. . . 3,000.00

MANHUNT!
Magazine Enterprises, 1953
1 LbC,FGu,OW(c);B:Red Fox,
    Undercover Girl, Space Ace . 750.00
2 LbC,FGu,OW(c);
    Electrocution(c) 500.00
3 LbC,FGu,OW,OW(c) 400.00
4 LbC,FGu,OW,OW(c) 400.00
5 LbC,FGu,OW,OW(c) 400.00
6 LbC,OW,OW(c) 375.00
7 LbC,OW; E:Space Ace 350.00
8 LbC,OW,FGu(c);B:Trail Colt . 350.00
9 LbC,OW 350.00
10 LbC,OW,OW(c),Gwl 350.00
11 LbC,FF,OW;B:The Duke,
    Scotland Yard 500.00
12 LbC,OW 300.00
13 See: *A-1 Comics* #63
14 See: *A-1 Comics* #77

MAN OF WAR
Comic Corp. of America (Centaur Publ.), Nov., 1941
1 PG,PG(c);Flag(c);B:The Fire-
    Man,Man of War,The Sentinel,
    Liberty Guards,Vapoman . . 3,000.00
2 PG,PG(c);I: The Ferret 2,500.00

MAN O'MARS
Fiction House/ I.W. Enterprises, 1953
1 MA, Space Rangers 600.00
1 MA, Rep. Space Rangers 100.00

MARCH OF COMICS
K.K. Publications/ Western Publ., 1946
(All were Giveaways)
N# WK back(c),Goldilocks 400.00
N# WK,How Santa got His
    Red Suit 375.00
N# WK,Our Gang 500.00
N# CB,Donald Duck;
    'Maharajah Donald' 8,500.00
5 Andy Panda 250.00
6 WK,Fairy Tales 250.00
7 Oswald the Lucky Rabbit 225.00
8 Mickey Mouse 650.00
9 Gloomey Bunny 125.00
10 Santa Claus 125.00
11 Santa Claus. 100.00
12 Santa's Toys 100.00
13 Santa's Suprise. 100.00
14 Santa's Kitchen. 100.00
15 Hip-It-Ty Hop. 100.00
16 Woody Woodpecker 150.00
17 Roy Rogers 300.00
18 Fairy Tales 125.00
19 Uncle Wiggily 100.00
20 CB,Donald Duck 5,000.00
21 Tom and Jerry 125.00
22 Andy Panda 100.00
23 Raggedy Ann and Andy 150.00
24 Felix the Cat; By
    Otto Messmer 275.00
25 Gene Autrey 275.00
26 Our Gang 275.00
27 Mickey Mouse 450.00
28 Gene Autry 250.00
29 Easter 60.00
30 Santa 50.00
31 Santa 50.00
32 Does Not Exist
33 A Christmas Carol. 50.00
34 Woody Woodpecker 125.00
35 Roy Rogers 300.00
36 Felix the Cat 225.00
37 Popeye 175.00
38 Oswald the Lucky Rabbit 90.00
39 Gene Autry 275.00
40 Andy and Woody 90.00
41 CB,DonaldDuck,SouthSeas. 4,500.00
42 Porky Pig 100.00
43 Henry 100.00

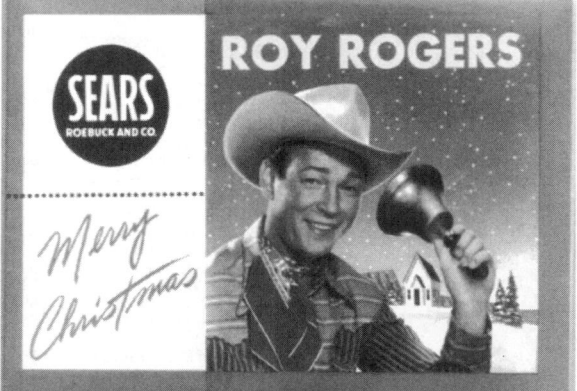

March of Comics #151 © Western Publications

44 Bugs Bunny 100.00	
45 Mickey Mouse............. 350.00	
46 Tom and Jerry............. 100.00	
47 Roy Rogers................ 250.00	
48 Santa..................... 100.00	
49 Santa..................... 100.00	
50 Santa..................... 100.00	
51 Felix the Cat 200.00	
52 Popeye 150.00	
53 Oswald the Lucky Rabbit 100.00	
54 Gene Autrey............... 250.00	
55 Andy and Woody........... 100.00	
56 CB back(c),Donald Duck 350.00	
57 Porky Pig 100.00	
58 Henry 100.00	
59 Bugs Bunny 125.00	
60 Mickey Mouse 325.00	
61 Tom and Jerry............. 100.00	
62 Roy Rogers................ 250.00	
63 Santa..................... 100.00	
64 Santa..................... 100.00	
65 Jingle Bells 100.00	
66 Popeye 125.00	
67 Oswald the Lucky Rabbit 100.00	
68 Roy Rogers................ 225.00	
69 Donald Duck 300.00	
70 Tom and Jerry 100.00	
71 Porky Pig 100.00	
72 Krazy Kat 100.00	
73 Roy Rogers................ 225.00	
74 Mickey Mouse............. 300.00	
75 Bugs Bunny 100.00	
76 Andy and Woody........... 100.00	
77 Roy Rogers................ 200.00	
78 Gene Autrey; last regular	
sized issue.............. 200.00	
79 Andy Panda,5"x7" format 100.00	
80 Popeye 100.00	
81 Oswald the Lucky Rabbit 75.00	
82 Tarzan.................... 200.00	
83 Bugs Bunny 100.00	
84 Henry 100.00	
85 Woody Woodpecker 100.00	
86 Roy Rogers................ 150.00	
87 Krazy Kat 100.00	
88 Tom and Jerry 100.00	
89 Porky Pig 100.00	
90 Gene Autrey 125.00	
91 Roy Rogers and Santa 150.00	
92 Christmas w/Santa 75.00	
93 Woody Woodpecker 75.00	
94 Indian Chief................ 100.00	
95 Oswald the Lucky Rabbit 75.00	
96 Popeye 125.00	
97 Bugs Bunny 100.00	
98 Tarzan,Lex Barker Ph(c)..... 200.00	
99 Porky Pig 75.00	
100 Roy Rogers............... 125.00	
101 Henry 75.00	
102 Tom Corbet,P(c) 150.00	
103 Tom and Jerry............. 75.00	
104 Gene Autrey 100.00	
105 Roy Rogers............... 125.00	
106 Santa's Helpers........... 75.00	
107 Not Published	
108 Fun with Santa 75.00	
109 Woody Woodpecker 75.00	
110 Indian Chief 75.00	
111 Oswald the Lucky Rabbit 75.00	
112 Henry.................... 75.00	
113 Porky Pig................. 75.00	
114 Tarzan,RsM 200.00	
115 Bugs Bunny............... 75.00	
116 Roy Rogers............... 125.00	
117 Popeye 100.00	
118 Flash Gordon, P(c)........ 150.00	
119 Tom and Jerry............. 75.00	
120 Gene Autrey 100.00	
121 Roy Rogers............... 125.00	
122 Santa's Suprise........... 75.00	
123 Santa's Christmas Book 75.00	
124 Woody Woodpecker 75.00	

ROY ROGERS

SAVE!
YELLOW TRADING STAMPS
FREE GIFTS FOR EVERY
MEMBER OF THE FAMILY!

March of Comics #206
© *Western Publications*

125 Tarzan, Lex Barker Ph(c) ... 175.00	
126 Oswald the Lucky Rabbit 75.00	
127 Indian Chief.............. 75.00	
128 Tom and Jerry............. 75.00	
129 Henry 75.00	
130 Porky Pig 75.00	
131 Roy Rogers............... 125.00	
132 Bugs Bunny 75.00	
133 Flash Gordon,Ph(c) 125.00	
134 Popeye 100.00	
135 Gene Autrey 100.00	
136 Roy Rogers............... 100.00	
137 Gifts from Santa 50.00	
138 Fun at Christmas 50.00	
139 Woody Woodpecker 50.00	
140 Indian Chief 75.00	
141 Oswald the Lucky Rabbit 50.00	
142 Flash Gordon 125.00	
143 Porky Pig 50.00	
144 RsM,Ph(c),Tarzan......... 175.00	
145 Tom and Jerry............. 50.00	
146 Roy Rogers,Ph(c)......... 125.00	
147 Henry 50.00	
148 Popeye 100.00	
149 Bugs Bunny 50.00	
150 Gene Autrey 100.00	
151 Roy Rogers............... 100.00	
152 The Night Before Christmas . 50.00	
153 Merry Christmas 50.00	
154 Tom and Jerry............. 50.00	
155 Tarzan,Ph(c)............. 175.00	
156 Oswald the Lucky Rabbit 50.00	
157 Popeye 100.00	
158 Woody Woodpecker 50.00	
159 Indian Chief.............. 100.00	
160 Bugs Bunny 50.00	
161 Roy Rogers............... 100.00	
162 Henry 50.00	
163 Rin Tin Tin 125.00	
164 Porky Pig 50.00	
165 The Lone Ranger 100.00	
166 Santa & His Reindeer....... 50.00	
167 Roy Rogers and Santa 100.00	
168 Santa Claus' Workshop 50.00	
169 Popeye 100.00	
170 Indian Chief.............. 100.00	
171 Oswald the Lucky Rabbit 50.00	
172 Tarzan................... 175.00	
173 Tom and Jerry............. 50.00	
174 The Lone Ranger 125.00	
175 Porky Pig 50.00	
176 Roy Rogers............... 125.00	
177 Woody Woodpecker 50.00	
178 Henry 50.00	
179 Bugs Bunny 50.00	
180 Rin Tin Tin 100.00	

181 Happy Holiday 50.00	
182 Happi Tim 50.00	
183 Welcome Santa............ 50.00	
184 Woody Woodpecker 50.00	
185 Tarzan, Ph(c) 150.00	
186 Oswald the Lucky Rabbit 50.00	
187 Indian Chief.............. 100.00	
188 Bugs Bunny 50.00	
189 Henry 50.00	
190 Tom and Jerry 50.00	
191 Roy Rogers.............. 100.00	
192 Porky Pig 50.00	
193 The Lone Ranger 125.00	
194 Popeye 100.00	
195 Rin Tin Tin................ 150.00	
196 Not Published	
197 Santa is Coming 50.00	
198 Santa's Helper 50.00	
199 Huckleberry Hound........ 150.00	
200 Fury 100.00	
201 Bugs Bunny 75.00	
202 Space Explorer 100.00	
203 Woody Woodpecker 50.00	
204 Tarzan................... 125.00	
205 Mighty Mouse 100.00	
206 Roy Rogers,Ph(c)......... 100.00	
207 Tom and Jerry............. 50.00	
208 The Lone Ranger,Ph(c) 150.00	
209 Porky Pig 50.00	
210 Lassie 100.00	
211 Not Published	
212 Christmas Eve 50.00	
213 Here Comes Santa 50.00	
214 Huckleberry Hound........ 125.00	
215 Hi Yo Silver 125.00	
216 Rocky & His Friends....... 125.00	
217 Lassie 100.00	
218 Porky Pig 50.00	
219 Journey to the Sun 100.00	
220 Bugs Bunny 50.00	
221 Roy and Dale,Ph(c) 150.00	
222 Woody Woodpecker 50.00	
223 Tarzan................... 125.00	
224 Tom and Jerry 50.00	
225 The Lone Ranger 100.00	
226 Christmas Treasury....... 50.00	
227 Not Published	
228 Letters to Santa 50.00	
229 The Flintstones 150.00	
230 Lassie 100.00	
231 Bugs Bunny 50.00	
232 The Three Stooges........ 275.00	
233 Bullwinkle 150.00	
234 Smokey the Bear 50.00	
235 Huckleberry Hound........ 100.00	
236 Roy and Dale 125.00	
237 Mighty Mouse 50.00	
238 The Lone Ranger 100.00	
239 Woody Woodpecker 50.00	
240 Tarzan 125.00	
241 Santa Around the World 50.00	
242 Santa Toyland............ 50.00	
243 The Flintstones 150.00	
244 Mr.Ed,Ph(c).............. 75.00	
245 Bugs Bunny 50.00	
246 Popeye 75.00	
247 Mighty Mouse 75.00	
248 The Three Stooges........ 250.00	
249 Woody Woodpecker 50.00	
250 Roy and Dale 125.00	

MARGE'S LITTLE LULU
Dell Publishing Co., 1948

1 B:Lulu's Diary 1,150.00	
2 I:Gloria,Miss Feeny 500.00	
3 .... 450.00	
4 .... 450.00	
5 .... 450.00	
6 .... 350.00	
7 I:Annie,X-Mas (c).......... 350.00	
8 .... 350.00	
9 .... 350.00	

GOLDEN AGE

GOLDEN AGE

10	350.00
11 thru 18	@300.00
19 I:Wilbur	300.00
20 I:Mr.McNabbem	300.00
21	250.00
22	250.00
23	250.00
24	250.00
25	250.00
26 rep.Four Color #110	250.00
27 thru 29	@250.00
30 Christmas (c)	250.00
31 thru 34	@225.00
35 B:Mumday Story	225.00
36	225.00
37	225.00
38	225.00
39 I:Witch Hazel	250.00
40 Halloween (c)	225.00
41	200.00
42 Christmas (c)	200.00
43 Skiing (c)	200.00
44 Valentines Day (c).	200.00
45 2nd A:Witch Hazel	200.00
46 thru 60	@200.00
61	150.00
62	150.00
63 I:Chubby	150.00
64 thru 67	@150.00
68 I:Professor Cleff	150.00
69 thru 77	@150.00
78 Christmas (c)	150.00
79	150.00
80	150.00
81 thru 89	@125.00
90 Christmas (c)	125.00
91 thru 99	@125.00
100	150.00
101 thru 122	@125.00
123 I:Fifi	110.00
124 thru 164	@100.00
165 giant sized	200.00
166 giant sized	200.00

MARGE'S TUBBY
Dell Publishing Co., 1953

1	350.00
2	200.00
3 & 4	@175.00
5 thru 10	@135.00
11 thru 20	@125.00
21 thru 49	@100.00

MARK TRAIL
Standard Magazines/ Fawcett/Pines, 1955

1	125.00
5	100.00
A1	150.00

MARMADUKE MOUSE
Quality Comics Group (Arnold Publications), 1946

1 Funny Animal	250.00
2 Funny Animal	200.00
3 thru 8 Funny Animal	@150.00
9 Funny Animal	100.00
10 Funny Animal	100.00
11 thru 20 Funny Animal	@100.00
21 thru 30 Funny Animal	@75.00
31 thru 40 Funny Animal	@75.00
41 thru 50 Funny Animal	@75.00
51 thru 65 Funny Animal	@75.00

MARTIN KANE
Hero Books (Fox Features Syndicate), June, 1950

1 WW,WW-(c)	400.00
2 WW,JO, Auguat, 1950	300.00

The Marvel Family #71
© Fawcett Publications

MARVEL FAMILY, THE
Fawcett Publications, Dec., 1945–Jan., 1954

1 O:Captain Marvel,Captain Marvel Jr., Mary Marvel,Uncle Marvel; V:Black Adam	2,700.00
2 Uncle Marvel	1,300.00
3	900.00
4 The Witch's Tale	700.00
5 Civilization of a Prehistoric Race	600.00
6	550.00
7 The Rock of Eternity	500.00
8 The Marvel Family Round Table	500.00
9 V: The Last Vikings	500.00
10 CCB(c),JaB,BTh,V:Sivana Family	500.00
11 V: The Well of Evil	450.00
12 V: The Iron Horseman	450.00
13 BTh,CCB,PrC(c)	450.00
14 Captain Marvel Invalid	450.00
15 V: Mr. Triangle	425.00
16 World's Mightiest Quarrell	425.00
17	425.00
18	425.00
19 V: The Monster Menace	425.00
20 The Marvel Family Feud	425.00
21 V: The Trio of Terror	400.00
22 V: The Triple Threat	400.00
23 March of Independence (c).	425.00
24 V: The Fighting Xergos	400.00
25 Trial of the Marvel Family	400.00
26 V: Mr. Power	400.00
27 V: The Amoeba Men	400.00
28	400.00
29 V: The Monarch of Money	400.00
30 A:World's Greatest Magician	400.00
31 V:Sivana & The Great Hunger	350.00
32 The Marvel Family Goes Into Buisness	350.00
33 I: The Hermit Family	350.00
34 V: Sivana's Miniature Menace	350.00
35 V: The Berzerk Machines	350.00
36 V: The Invaders From Infinity	350.00
37 V: The Earth Changer	350.00
38 V: Sivana's Instinct Exterminator Gun	350.00
39 The Legend of Atlantis	350.00
40 Seven Wonders of the Modern World	350.00
41 The Great Oxygen Theft	350.00
42 V: The Endless Menace	300.00
43	300.00

44 V: The Rust That Menaced the World	300.00
45 The Hoax City	300.00
46 The Day Civilization Vanished	300.00
47 V: The Interplanetary Thieves	350.00
48 V: The Four Horsemen	300.00
49 ...Proves Human Hardness	300.00
50 The Speech Scrambler Machine	300.00
51 The Living Statues	325.00
52 The School of Witches	300.00
53 V:Man Who Changed World	300.00
54	300.00
55	300.00
56 The World's Mightiest Project	300.00
57	300.00
58 The Triple Time Plot	300.00
59	300.00
60	300.00
61	300.00
62	300.00
63 V: The Pirate Planet	300.00
64	300.00
65	300.00
66 The Miracle Stone	300.00
67	300.00
68	300.00
69 V: The Menace of Old Age	300.00
70 V: The Crusade of Evil	300.00
71	300.00
72	300.00
73	300.00
74	300.00
75 The Great Space Struggle	300.00
76	325.00
77 Anti-Communist	400.00
78 V: The Red Vulture	300.00
79 Horror	250.00
80	250.00
81	250.00
82	250.00
83 V: The Flying Skull	250.00
84 thru 87	@250.00
88 Jokes of Jeopardy.	250.00
89 And Then There Were None	250.00

MARVELS OF SCIENCE
Charlton Comics, 1946

1 1st Charlton Book; Atomic Bomb Story	400.00
2	350.00
3	350.00
4 President Truman(c); Jun.'6	350.00

MARY MARVEL COMICS
Fawcett Publications, Dec., 1945

1 Intro: Mary Marvel	3,000.00
2	1,100.00
3	750.00
4 On a Leave of Absence	700.00
5 Butterfly (c) Bullet Girl	500.00
6 A:Freckles,Teenager of Mischief	500.00
7 The Kingdom Undersea	500.00
8 Holiday Special Issue	500.00
9 Air Race (c)	450.00
10 A: Freckles	450.00
11 A: The Sad Dryads	300.00
12 Red Cross Appeal on(c)	300.00
13 Keep the Homefires Burning	300.00
14 Meets Ghosts (c)	300.00
15 A: Freckles	300.00
16 The Jukebox Menace	275.00
17 Aunt Agatha's Adventures	275.00
18	275.00
19 Witch (c)	275.00
20	275.00
21 V: Dice Head	250.00
22 The Silver Slippers	250.00
23 The Pendulum Strikes	250.00

24 V: The Nightowl. 250.00
25 A: Freckles 250.00
26 A:Freckles dressed as Clown . 250.00
27 The Floating Oceanliner 250.00
28 Western, Sept., 1948 . . . . . . 250.00
Becomes:

MONTE HALE WESTERN
Fawcett Publications, Oct., 1948
29 Ph(c),B:Monte Hale & His
  Horse Pardner 650.00
30 Ph(c),B:Big Bow-Little
  Arrow; CCB,Captain Tootsie . 300.00
31 Ph(c),Giant 250.00
32 Ph(c),Giant 250.00
33 Ph(c),Giant 250.00
34 Ph(c),E:Big Bow-Little
  Arrow;B:Gabby Hayes,Giant . 250.00
35 Ph(c),Gabby Hayes, Giant . . 250.00
36 Ph(c),Gabby Hayes, Giant . . 250.00
37 Ph(c),Gabby Hayes 150.00
38 Ph(c),Gabby Hayes, Giant . . 200.00
39 Ph(c);CCB, Captain Tootsie;
  Gabby Hayes, Giant 200.00
40 Ph(c),Gabby Hayes, Giant . . 200.00
41 Ph(c),Gabby Hayes 150.00
42 Ph(c),Gabby Hayes, Giant . . 175.00
43 Ph(c),Gabby Hayes, Giant . . 175.00
44 Ph(c),Gabby Hayes, Giant . . 175.00
45 Ph(c),Gabby Hayes 150.00
46 Ph(c),Gabby Hayes, Giant . . 150.00
47 Ph(c),A:Big Bow-Little Arrow;
  Gabby Hayes, Giant 150.00
48 Ph(c),Gabby Hayes, Giant . . 150.00
49 Ph(c),Gabby Hayes 150.00
50 Ph(c),Gabby Hayes, Giant . . 150.00
51 Ph(c),Gabby Hayes, Giant . . 135.00
52 Ph(c),Gabby Hayes, Giant . . 135.00
53 Ph(c),A:Slim Pickens;
  Gabby Hayes. 125.00
54 Ph(c),Gabby Hayes, Giant . . 135.00
55 Ph(c),Gabby Hayes, Giant . . 135.00
56 Ph(c),Gabby Hayes, Giant . . 125.00
57 Ph(c),Gabby Hayes 100.00
58 Ph(c),Gabby Hayes, Giant . . 125.00
59 Ph(c),Gabby Hayes, Giant . . 125.00
60 thru 79 Ph(c),Gabby Hayes @100.00
80 Ph(c),E: Gabby Hayes 100.00
81 Ph(c) 100.00
82 Final Ph(c) 125.00

Charlton Comics, Feb., 1955
83 R:G. Hayes Back B&W Ph(c) . 150.00
84 . . . . 100.00
85 . . . . 100.00
86 E: Gabby Hayes 100.00
87 . . . . 100.00
88 Jan., 1956 . . . . 100.00

MASK COMICS
Rural Home Publications, Feb.–March, 1945
1 LbC,LbC-(c), Evil (c). 4,500.00
2 LbC-(c),A:Black Rider,The
  Collector The Boy Magician;
  Apr-May'45, Devil (c) 2,500.00

MASKED MARVEL
Centaur Publications, Sept., 1940
1 I: The Masked Marvel 2,400.00
2 PG, ... 1,600.00
3 Dec., 1940 . . . . 1,500.00

THE MASKED RAIDER
Charlton Comics, 1955
1 . . . . 150.00
2 . . . . 125.00
3 . . . . 100.00
4 thru 7 . . . . @100.00

8 Billy the Kid 100.00
Continued as Billy the Kid,
see Color Pub. section

MASKED RANGER
Premier Magazines, April, 1954
1 FF,O&B:The Masked Ranger,
  Streak the Horse,The
  Crimson Avenger 500.00
2 . . . . 175.00
3 . . . . 175.00
4 B: Jessie James,Billy the Kid,
  Wild Bill Hickok,
  Jim Bowie's Life Story 200.00
5 . . . . 200.00
6 . . . . 200.00
7 . . . . 200.00
8 . . . . 200.00
9 AT,E:All Features; A:Wyatt
  Earp Aug., 1955. . . . . 225.00

MASTER COMICS
Fawcett Publications, March, 1940
1-6 Oversized,7-Normal Format
1 O:Master Man; B:The Devil's
  Dagger, El Carin-Master of
  Magic, Rick O'Say, Morton
  Murch, White Rajah, Shipwreck
  Roberts, Frontier Marshall,
  Mr. Clue, Streak Sloan . . . 16,000.00
2 Master Man (c) 5,000.00
3 Master Man (c) Bondage . . . 4,600.00
4 Master Man (c) 4,500.00
5 Master Man (c) 4,500.00
6 E: All Above Features 4,600.00
7 B:Bulletman,Zorro,The Mystery
  Man, Lee Granger, Jungle
  King,Buck Jones 6,000.00
8 B:The Red Gaucho,Captain
  Venture, Planet Princess . . 3,600.00
9 Bulletman & Steam Roller . . 3,500.00
10 E: Lee Granger 5,500.00
11 O: Minute Man 5,500.00
12 Minute Man (c). 3,500.00
13 O:Bulletgirl; E:Red Gaucho . 4,000.00
14 B: The Companions Three . 3,000.00
15 MRa, Bulletman & Girl (c) . 3,200.00
16 MRa, Minute Man (c). 3,200.00
17 B:MRa on Bulletman 3,000.00
18 MRa, ... 3,000.00
19 MRa, Bulletman & Girl (c) . 3,000.00
20 MRa,C:Cap.Marvel-
  Bulletman 3,000.00
21 MRa-(c),Capt. Marvel in
  Bulletman,I&O:Captain
  Nazi 9,000.00
22 MRa-(c),E:Mystery Man,Captain
  Venture; Bondage(c);Capt.
  Marvel Jr. X-Over In
  Bulletman; A:Capt. Nazi . . . 8,000.00
23 MRa(a&c),B:Capt. Marvel Jr.
  V:Capt. Nazi 5,000.00
24 MRa(a&c),Death By Radio . 3,000.00
25 MRa(a&c),The Jap Invasion . 3,000.00
26 MRa(a&c),Capt. Marvel Jr.
  Avenges Pearl Harbor 3,000.00
27 MRa(a&c),V For Victory(c). . 3,000.00
28 MRa(a&c)Liberty Bell(c). . . . 3,000.00
29 MRa(a&c),Hitler &
  Hirohito(c). 3,200.00
30 MRa(a&c),Flag (c);Capt.
  Marvel Jr, V: Capt. Nazi . 3,000.00
31 MRa(a&c),E:Companions
  Three,Capt.Marvel Jr,
  V:Mad Dr. Macabre 2,000.00
32 MRa(a&c),E: Buck Jones;
  CMJr Strikes Terror Castle . 2,000.00

Master Comics #62
© Fawcett Publications

33 MRa(a&c),B:Balbo the Boy
  Magician,Hopalong Cassidy 2,000.00
34 MRa(a&c),Capt.Marvel Jr
  V: Capt.Nazi 2,500.00
35 MRa(a&c),CMJr Defies
  the Flame 2,000.00
36 MRa(a&c),Statue Of
  Liberty(c). 2,000.00
37 MRa(a&c),CMJr Blasts
  the Nazi Raiders 1,800.00
38 MRa(a&c),CMJr V:the Japs . 1,800.00
39 MRa(a&c),CMJr Blasts
  Nazi Slave Ship 1,800.00
40 MRa(a&c),Flag (c) 1,800.00
41 MRa(a&c),Bulletman,Bulletgirl,
  CMJr X-over In Minuteman 1,800.00
42 MRa(a&c),CMJr V: Hitler's
  Dream Soldier 1,000.00
43 MRa(c),CMJr Battles For
  Stalingrad 1,000.00
44 MRa(c),CMJr In Crystal City
  of the Peculiar Penguins . 1,000.00
45 MRa(c), ... 1,000.00
46 MRa(c) 1,000.00
47 MRa(c),A:Hitler; E: Balbo. . 1,100.00
48 MRa(c),I:Bulletboy;Capt.
  Marvel A: in Minuteman . . . 1,200.00
49 MRa(c),E: Hopalong Cassidy,
  Minuteman 1,000.00
50 I&O: Radar,A:Capt. Marvel,
  B:Nyoka the Jungle Girl . . 1,000.00
51 MRa(c),CMJr V: Japanese . . . 750.00
52 MRa(c),CMJr & Radar Pitch
  War Stamps on (c). 750.00
53 CMJR V: Dr. Sivana 750.00
54 MRa(c),Capt.Marvel Jr
  Your Pin-Up Buddy 750.00
55 . . . . 750.00
56 MRa(c) 700.00
57 CMJr V: Dr. Sivana 700.00
58 MRa(a&c), ... 700.00
59 MRa(c),A:The Upside
  Downies. 750.00
60 MRa(c) 750.00
61 CMJr Meets Uncle Marvel . . . 750.00
62 Uncle Sam on (c) 750.00
63 W/ Radar (c) 700.00
64 W/ Radar (c) 700.00
65 BTh(c),JkS 700.00
66 CMJr & Secret Of the Sphinx . 700.00
67 Knight (c) 700.00
68 CMJr in the Range of
  the Beasts 700.00
69 . . . . 700.00
70 . . . . 700.00
71 CMJr,V:Man in Metal Mask . . . 650.00
72 CMJr V: Sivana & The Whistle
  That Wouldn't Stop 650.00

73 CMJr V: The Ghost of Evil . . . 650.00
74 CMJr & The Fountain of Age . 650.00
75 CMJr V: The Zombie Master. . 650.00
76 . . . . 650.00
77 BTh(c),BK,Pirate Treasure . . . 650.00
78 CMJr in Death on the Scenic
   Railway 650.00
79 CMJr V: The Black Shroud . . 650.00
80 CMJr-The Land of Backwards 650.00
81 CMJr & The Voyage 'Round
   the Horn. 450.00
82 CMJr,IN,Death at the
   Launching 450.00
83 . . . . 450.00
84 BTh(c&a) CMJr V: The Human
   Magnet. 450.00
85 CMJr-Crime on the Campus . 300.00
86 CMJr & The City of Machines. 300.00
87 CMJr & The Root of Evil. 300.00
88 CMJr V: The Wreckers;
   B: Hopalong Cassidy. 300.00
89 . . . . 300.00
90 CMJr V: The Caveman 300.00
91 CMJr V: The Blockmen. 300.00
92 CMJr V: The Space Slavers . 300.00
93 BK,CMJr,V:TheGrowingGiant . 300.00
94 E: Hopalong Cassidy 300.00
95 B: Tom Mix; CMJr Meets
   the Skyhawk 300.00
96 CMJr Meets the World's
   Mightiest Horse 300.00
97 CMJr Faces the Doubting
   Thomas 300.00
98 KKK Type 300.00
99 Witch (c) 300.00
100 CMJr V: The Ghost Ship. . . . 350.00
101 thru 105 . . . . @250.00
106 E: Bulletman 250.00
107 CMJr Faces the Disappearance
   of the Statue of Liberty 300.00
108 . . . . 300.00
109 . . . . 300.00
110 CMJr & The Hidden Death . . 300.00
111 thru 122 . . . . @300.00
123 CMJr V: The Flying
   Desperado. 300.00
124 . . . . 300.00
125 CMJr & The Bed of Mystery . 300.00
126 thru 131. . . . . @300.00
132 V: Migs 300.00
133 E: Tom Mix; April, 1953. . . . . 350.00

MAZIE
Nationwide Publ./
Magazine Publ./
Harvey Publ., 1951–58
1 . . . . 200.00
2 . . . . 100.00
3 . . . . 100.00
4 . . . . 100.00
5 . . . . 100.00
6 thru 10 . . . . @100.00
11 thru 20 . . . . @100.00
21 thru 28 . . . . @75.00

MD
E.C. Comics,
April, 1955–Jan., 1956
1 RC,GE,Grl,JO,JCr(c). 600.00
2 thru 5 RC,GE,Grl,JO,JCr(c). @500.00

MEDAL OF
HONOR COMICS
Stafford Publication,
Spring, 1947
1 True Stories of Medal of Honor
   Recipients 250.00

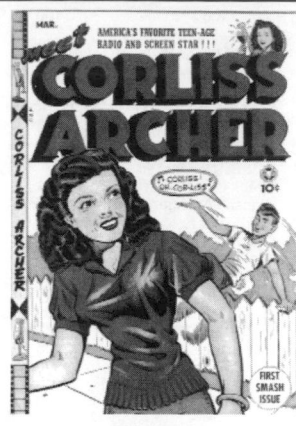

Meet Corliss Archer #1
© Fox Features Syndicate

MEET CORLISS
ARCHER
Fox Features Syndicate,
March, 1948
1 AF,AF(c), Teenage 1,400.00
2 AF(c) 750.00
3 . . . . 700.00
Becomes:

MY LIFE
Sept., 1948
4 JKa,AF, ... 500.00
5 JKa, ... 250.00
6 JKa,AF, ... 275.00
7 WW,Watercolor & Ink Drawing
   on(c) 300.00
8 . . . . 150.00
9 . . . . 150.00
10 WW, July, 1950. . . . . 300.00

MEET MERTON
Toby Press, Dec., 1953
1 DBe,Teen Stories. 125.00
2 DBe 100.00
3 DBe 100.00
4 DBe; June, 1954 . . . . 100.00

MEET THE NEW
POST GAZETTE
SUNDAY FUNNIES
Pittsburg Post Gazette, 1949
N# One Shot Insert F: Several
   Syndicated Characters in Stories
   Exclusive to This Edition . . 7,000.00

MEL ALLEN
SPORTS COMICS
Visual Editions, 1949
1 GT 300.00
2 Lou Gehrig. 200.00

MEN AGAINST CRIME
See: HAND OF FATE

MEN IN ACTION
Ajax/Farrell Publ., 1957
1 AyB 200.00
2 . . . . 125.00
3 RH 125.00
4 AyB 125.00
5 AyB,JMn. 125.00
6 AyB 125.00

7 RH 100.00
8 SSh 100.00
9 . . . . 100.00

MEN OF COURAGE
Catechetical Guild
N# 100.00

MERRY COMICS
Carlton Comics, 1945
N# A:Boogeyman. 300.00

MERRY-GO-ROUND
COMICS
LaSalle/Croyden/
Rotary Litho., 1944
1 LaSalle Publications Edition . . 225.00
1a 1946, Croyden Edition 100.00
1b Sept-Oct.'47,Rotary Litho Ed. 125.00
2 . . . . 125.00

MERRY MOUSE
Avon Periodicals,
June, 1953
1 (fa),F. Carin (a&c) 150.00
2 (fa),F. Carin (a&c) 100.00
3 (fa),F. Carin (a&c) 100.00
4 (fa),F. Carin (a&c);Jan.'54 . . . . 100.00

METEOR COMICS
Croyden Publications,
Nov., 1945
1 Captain Wizard & Baldy Bean . 500.00

MICKEY FINN
Eastern Color/
Columbia Comics Group, 1942
1 . . . . 400.00
2 . . . . 300.00
3 A: Charlie Chan 250.00
4 . . . . 200.00
5 thru 9 . . . . @150.00
10 thru 15 . . . . @125.00

(WALT DISNEY'S)
MICKEY MOUSE
Dell Publishing Co.,
Dec., 1952
#1-#27 Dell Four Color
28 . . . . 150.00
29 . . . . 125.00
30 . . . . 125.00
31 . . . . 125.00
32 thru 34 . . . . @125.00
35 thru 50 . . . . @125.00
51 thru 73 . . . . @100.00
74 . . . . 125.00
75 thru 99 . . . . @100.00
100 thru 105 rep. . . . . @125.00
106 thru 120. . . . . @150.00
121 thru 130. . . . . @100.00
131 thru 146. . . . . @30.00
147 rep,Phantom Fires 30.00
148 rep. 100.00
149 thru 158 . . . . @60.00
159 rep. 60.00
160 thru 170 . . . . @60.00
171 thru 199 . . . . @25.00
200 rep. 25.00
201 thru 218 . . . . @25.00

MICKEY MOUSE
MAGAZINE
Kay Kamen, 1933
1 scarce. 20,000.00
2 . . . . 5,000.00

3 thru 8 . . . . @4,000.00
9 . . . . 3,500.00

MICKEY MOUSE MAGAZINE
Kay Kamen, 1933–34
1 digest size (1933) 4,000.00
2 dairy give-away promo 2,000.00
3 dairy give-away promo 1,500.00
4 dairy give-away promo 1,500.00
5 dairy give-away promo 1,500.00
6 dairy give-away promo 1,500.00
7 dairy give-away promo 1,500.00
8 dairy give-away promo 1,500.00
9 dairy give-away promo 1,500.00
10 dairy give-away promo. 1,500.00
11 dairy give-away promo. 1,500.00
12 dairy give-away promo. 1,500.00
Volume II, 1934–35
1 dairy give-away promo 1,500.00
2 Christmas issue 1,500.00
3 dairy give-away promo 1,500.00
4 dairy give-away promo 1,500.00
5 1st Donald Duck as Sailor . . 5,000.00
6 dairy give-away promo 1,500.00
7 dairy give-away promo 1,500.00
8 dairy give-away promo 1,500.00
9 dairy give-away promo 1,500.00
10 dairy give-awaypromo 1,500.00
11 dairy give-awaypromo 1,500.00
12 dairy give-awaypromo 1,500.00

MICKEY MOUSE MAGAZINE
K.K. Pub./Westen Pub., 1935
1 (1935) 13¼"x10¼" 35,000.00
2 OM, new size 11½"x8½". . . . 6,000.00
3 OM 3,000.00
4 OM 3,000.00
5 (1936) Donald Duck solo . . 5,000.00
6 Donald Duck editor 4,500.00
7 . . . . 3,000.00
8 Donald Duck solo 4,500.00
9 1st Minnie & Minnie 4,500.00
10 . . . . 3,000.00
11 Mickey & Pluto 3,500.00
12 . . . . 3,000.00
Volume II
1 OM 2,500.00
2 OM 2,500.00
3 OM,Christmas issue, 100pg . 7,500.00
4 OM (1937) Roy Ranger
   adv.strip 2,000.00
5 Ted True strip 1,500.00
6 Mickey Mouse cut-outs 1,500.00
7 Mickey Mouse cut-outs 1,500.00
8 Mickey Mouse cut-outs 1,500.00
9 Mickey Mouse cut-outs 1,500.00
10 Full color 2,200.00
11 . . . . 1,500.00
12 Hiawatha 1,500.00
13 . . . . 1,500.00
Volume III
2 Big Bad Wolf (c) 1,700.00
3 CB,First Snow White 5,000.00
4 CB,(1938) Snow White 3,000.00
5 Snow White (c) 3,000.00
6 Snow White ends 1,600.00
7 CB,7 Dwarfs Easter (c). 1,500.00
8 . . . . 1,400.00
9 CB,Dopey(c) 1,400.00
10 Goofy(c) 1,400.00
11 Mickey Mouse Sheriff. 1,400.00
12 CB,A:Snow White 1,400.00
Volume IV
1 OM,Practile Pig & Brave
   Little Tailor 1,500.00
2 I:I luey,Louis & Dewey(c) . . . 2,000.00
3 Ferdinand the Bull 1,500.00

4 (1939),B:Spotty 1,400.00
5 Pluto solo 1,500.00
7 Ugly Duckling 1,500.00
7a Goofy & Wilber 1,500.00
8 Big Bad Wolf(c) 1,500.00
9 CB,The Pointer 1,500.00
10 CB,July 4th 1,700.00
11 Slick, oversize 1,500.00
12 CB,Donald's Penguin. 1,600.00
Volume V
1 Black Pete. 1,600.00
2 Goofy(c),I:Pinocchio 2,000.00
3 Pinocchio 2,200.00
4 (1940) 1,500.00
5 Jiminy Cricket(c) 1,500.00
6 Tugboat Mickey. 1,500.00
7 Huey, Louis & Dewey(c) 1,500.00
8 Figaro & Cleo 1,500.00
9 Donald(c),J.Cricket 1,700.00
10 July 4th 1,700.00
11 Mickey's Tailor 1,700.00
12 Change of comic format . . . 8,000.00
becomes:
WALT DISNEY COMICS & STORIES

MICKEY MOUSE
Whitman
904 W.Disney's Mickey Mouse
   and His Friends (1934). . . . 3,000.00
948 Disney'sMickeyMouse('34) 3,000.00

MIDGET COMICS
St. John Publishing Co., Feb., 1950
1 MB(c),Fighting Indian Stories . 250.00
2 April, 1950;Tex West-Cowboy
   Marshall 150.00

MIDNIGHT
Ajax/Farrell, 1957
1 Voodoo & Strange Fantasy . . . 175.00
2 . . . . 125.00

MIGHTY ATOM, THE
See: PIXIES

MIGHTY MIDGET COMICS
4"x5" Format Samuel E. Lowe & Co./ Fawcett, 1942-43
1 Bulletman 500.00
2 Captain Marvel 500.00
3 Captain Marvel Jr. 500.00
4 Golden Arrow 400.00
5 Ibis the Invincible 500.00
6 Spy Smasher 450.00
7 Balbo, The Boy Magician 250.00
8 Bulletman 300.00
9 Commando Yank 200.00
10 Dr. Voltz, The Human
   Generator 250.00
11 Lance O'Casey 250.00
12 Leatherneck the Marine 250.00
13 Minute Man 250.00
14 Mister Q 275.00
15 Mr. Scarlet & Pinky 250.00
16 Pat Wilson & His
   Flying Fortress. 225.00
17 Phantom Eagle 250.00
18 State Trooper Stops Crime . . . 250.00
19 Tornado Tom 250.00

MIGHTY MOUSE
St. John Publishing, Aug., 1947
5 . . . . 500.00
6 thru 10 . . . . @250.00
11 thru 20 . . . . @200.00

Mighty Mouse #32
© *St. John Publishing*

21 thru 25 . . . . @150.00
26 thru 30 . . . . @125.00
31 thru 34 . . . . @100.00
35 Flying Saucer 150.00
36 . . . . 100.00
37 . . . . 100.00
38 thru 45 Giant 100 pgs . . . . @250.00
46 thru 66 . . . . @100.00
67 P(c), ... 100.00
Pines
68 thru 81 Funny Animal . . . . . @100.00
82 Infinity (c) 100.00
83 June, 1959 . . . . 100.00

MIGHTY MOUSE ADVENTURES
See: ADVENTURES OF MIGHTY MOUSE

MIGHTY MOUSE ADVENTURE STORIES
St. John Publishing Co., 1953
N# 384 Pages,Rebound 600.00

MIKE BARNETT, MAN AGAINST CRIME
Fawcett Publications, Dec., 1951
1 The Mint of Dionysosi 250.00
2 Mystery of the Blue Madonna . 135.00
3 Revenge Holds the Torch 125.00
4 Special Delivery 125.00
5 Market For Morphine 150.00
6 Oct., 1952 . . . . 125.00

MILITARY COMICS
Comics Magazines (Quality Comics Group), Aug., 1941
1 JCo,CCu,FGu,BP,WE(c),O:Black-
   hawk, Miss America, Death Patrol,
   Blue Tracer; B:X of the Underground, Yankee Eagle,Q-Boat,
   Shot & Shell, Archie Atkins,
   Loops & Banks 20,000.00
2 JCo,FGu,BP,CCu,CCu(c),B:
   Secret War News 5,000.00
3 JCo,FGu,BP,AMc,CCu,CCu(c),
   I&O:Chop Chop 4,000.00
4 FGu,BP,AMc,CCu,CCu(c) . . 3,500.00
5 FGu,BP,AMc,CCu,CCu(c)
   B: The Sniper 3,000.00

GOLDEN AGE

Military Comics #24
© Quality Comics Group

6 FGu,BP,AMc,CCu,CCu(c) . . 2,600.00
7 FGu,BP,AMc,CCu,CCu(c)
   E:Death Patrol 2,600.00
8 FGu,BP,AMc,CCu,CCu(c) . . 2,600.00
9 FGu,BP,AMc,CCu,CCu(c),
   B: The Phantom Clipper . . 2,600.00
10 FGu,BP,CCu,AMc,WE(c) . . . 2,700.00
11 FGu,BP,CCu,AMc,
   WE(c),Flag(c) 2,500.00
12 FGu,BP,AMc,RC(a&c) 2,600.00
13 FGu,BP,AMc,RC(a&c),E:X of
   the Underground 2,500.00
14 FGu,AMc,RC(a&c),B:Private
   Dogtag 2,500.00
15 FGu,AMc,RC(a&c). 2,500.00
16 FGu,AMc,RC(a&c),E:The Phantom
   Clipper,Blue Tracer. 2,000.00
17 FGu,AMc,RC(a&c),
   B:P.T. Boat 2,000.00
18 FGu,AMc,RC(a&c), V:
   The Thunderer 2,000.00
19 FGu,RC(a&c), V:King Cobra 2,000.00
20 GFx,RC(a&c), Death Patrol 2,000.00
21 FGu,GFx 1,800.00
22 FGu,GFx 1,800.00
23 FGu,GFx 1,800.00
24 FGu,GFx,V: Man-Heavy
   Glasses. 1,800.00
25 FGu,GFx,V: Wang The Tiger 1,800.00
26 FGu,GFx,V: Skull. 1,500.00
27 FGu,JCo,R:The Death Patrol 1,500.00
28 FGu,JCo, Dungeon of Doom 1,500.00
29 FGu,JCo,V: Xanukhara 1,500.00
30 FGu,JCo,BWa(a&c),Blackhawk
   V: Dr. Koro 1,500.00
31 FGu,JCo,BWa,E:Death
   Patrol; I: Captain Hitsu 1,500.00
32 JCo,A: Captain Hitsu 1,400.00
33 W/ Civil War Veteran 1,400.00
34 A: Eve Rice 1,400.00
35 Shipwreck Island 1,400.00
36 Cult of the Wailing Tiger . . . 1,400.00
37 Pass of Bloody Peace 1,400.00
38 B.Hawk Faces Bloody Death 1,400.00
39 A: Kwan Yin 1,400.00
40 V: Ratru 1,300.00
41 W/ Chop Chop (c) 1,300.00
42 V: Jap Mata Hari 1,300.00
43 . . . . 1,300.00
Becomes:

MODERN COMICS
Nov., 1945
44 Duel of Honor. 1,200.00
45 V: Sakyo the Madman 750.00
46 RC, Soldiers of Fortune 750.00
47 RC,PG,V:Count Hokoy 750.00

48 RC,PG,V:Pirates of Perool . . . 750.00
49 RC,PG,I:Fear,Lady
   Adventuress. 750.00
50 RC,PG 750.00
51 RC,PG, Ancient City of Evil. . . 500.00
52 PG,BWa,V: The Vulture. 500.00
53 PG,BWa,B: Torchy 850.00
54 PG,RC,RC/CCu,BWa 500.00
55 PG,RC,RC/CCu,BWa 500.00
56 PG,RC/CCu,BWa 500.00
57 PG,RC/CCu,BWa 500.00
58 PG,RC,RC/CCu,BWa,
   V:The Grabber. 500.00
59 PG,RC,RC/CCu,BWa 500.00
60 PG,RC/CCu,BWa,RC(c),
   V:Green Plague 500.00
61 PG,RC/CCu,BWa,RC(c) 475.00
62 PG,RC/CCu,BWa,RC(c) 475.00
63 PG,RC/CCu,BWa,RC(c) 450.00
64 PG,RC/CCu,BWa,RC(c) 450.00
65 PG,RC/CCu,BWa,RC(c) 450.00
66 PG,RC/CCu,BWa 450.00
67 PG,RC/CCu,BWa,RC(c) 450.00
68 PG,RC/CCu,BWa,RC(c);
   I:Madame Butterfly 450.00
69 PG,RC/CCu,BWa,RC(c) 450.00
70 PG,RC/CCu,BWa,RC(c) 450.00
71 PG,RC/CCu,BWa,RC(c) 450.00
72 PG,RC/CCu,BWa,RC(c) 450.00
73 PG,RC/CCu,BWa,RC(c) 450.00
74 PG,RC/CCu,BWa,RC(c) 450.00
75 PG,RC/CCu,BWa,RC(c) 450.00
76 PG,RC/CCu,BWa,RC(c) 450.00
77 PG,RC/CCu,BWa,RC(c) 450.00
78 PG,RC/CCu,BWa,JCo,RC(c) . 500.00
79 PG,RC/CCu,BWa,JCo,RC(c) . 450.00
80 PG,RC/CCu,BWa,JCo,RC(c) . 475.00
81 PG,RC/CCu,BWa,JCo,RC(c) . 475.00
82 PG,RC/CCu,BWa,JCo,RC(c) . 450.00
83 PG,RC/CCu,BWa,JCo,RC(c);
   E: Private Dogtag 450.00
84 PG,RC/CCu,BWa,RC(c) 450.00
85 PG,RC/CCu,BWa,RC(c) 450.00
86 PG,RC/CCu,BWa,RC(c) 450.00
87 PG,RC/CCu,BWa,RC(c) 450.00
88 PG,RC/CCu,BWa,RC(c) 450.00
89 PG,RC/CCu,BWa,RC(c) 450.00
90 PG,RC/CCu,GFx,RC(c) 450.00
91 RC/CCu,GFx,RC(c) 450.00
92 RC/CCu,GFx,RC(c) 450.00
93 RC/CCu,GFx,RC(c) 450.00
94 RC/CCu,GFx,RC(c) 450.00
95 RC/CCu,GFx,RC(c) 450.00
96 RC/CCu,GFx,RC/CCu(c) 450.00
97 RC/CCu,GFx,RC/CCu(c) 450.00
98 RC/CCu,GFx,RC/CCu(c) 450.00
99 RC/CCu,GFx,JCo,RC/CCu(c). 450.00
100 GFx,JCo,RC/CCu(c) 475.00
101 GFx,JCo,RC/CCu(c) 450.00
102 GFx,JCo,WE,BWa,
   RC/CCu(c). 600.00

MILT GROSS FUNNIES
Milt Gross, Inc., Aug., 1947
1 Gag Oriented Caricature 250.00
2 Gag Oriented Caricature 175.00

MINUTE MAN
Fawcett Publications,
Summer, 1941
1 V: The Nazis 3,000.00
2 V: The Mongol Horde 2,000.00
3 V: The Black Poet;Spr'42 . . 2,000.00

MIRACLE COMICS
E.C. Comics, Feb.,1940
1 B:Sky Wizard,Master of Space,
   Dash Dixon,Man of Might,Dusty
   Doyle,Pinkie Parker, The Kid
   Cop,K-7 Secret Agent,Scorpion
   & Blandu,Jungle Queen . . 2,700.00

2 . . . . 1,400.00
3 B:Bill Colt,The Ghost Rider . 1,400.00
4 A:The Veiled Prophet,
   Bullet Bob; Mar'41 . . . . 1,100.00

MISS CAIRO JONES
Croyden Publishers, 1944
1 BO,Rep. Newspaper Strip . . . 250.00

MISS LIBERTY
See: LIBERTY COMICS

MR. ANTHONY'S
LOVE CLINIC
Hillman Periodicals, 1945
1 Ph(c) 250.00
2 . . . . 150.00
3 . . . . 100.00
4 . . . . 100.00
5 Ph(c),Apr/May'50 . . . . 100.00

MR. MUSCLES
See: THING, THE

MISTER MYSTERY
Media Publ./SPM Publ./
Aragon Publ., Sept., 1951
1 HK,RA,Horror 1,400.00
2 RA,RA(c) 850.00
3 RA(c) 850.00
4 Bondage(c) 900.00
5 Lingerie(c) 800.00
6 Bondage(c) 800.00
7 BW,Bondage(c);The Brain
   Bats of Venus 1,700.00
8 Lingerie(c) 750.00
9 HN 750.00
10 . . . . 750.00
11 BW,Robot Woman 1,100.00
12 Flaming Object to Eye (c) . 1,700.00
13 . . . . 550.00
14 . . . . 550.00
15 The Coffin & Medusa's Head . 525.00
16 Bondage(c). 525.00
17 Severed Heads 525.00
18 BW,Bondage(c). 850.00
19 Reprints. 525.00

MISTER RISK
See: HAND OF FATE

MISTER UNIVERSE
Mr. Publ./Media Publ./
Stanmore, July, 1951
1 . . . . 275.00
2 RA(c);Jungle That time Forgot 150.00
3 Marijuana Story 150.00
4 Mr. Universe Goes to War . . . 125.00
5 Mr. Universe Goes to War;
   April, 1952. . . . . 125.00

MODERN COMICS
See: MILITARY COMICS

MODERN LOVE
Tiny Tot Comics
(E.C. Comics), June–July, 1949
1 Grl,AF,Stolen Romance 1,000.00
2 Grl,JcR,AF(c),I Craved
   Excitement 600.00
3 AF(c);Our Families Clashed . . 550.00
4 AF(c);I Was a B Girl, panties . 700.00
5 RP,AF(c);Saved From Shame 700.00
6 AF(c);The Love That
   Might Have Been 700.00
7 Grl,WW,AF(c);They Won't Let
   Me Love Him 550.00
8 Grl,AF(c);Aug-Sept'50 . . . . . . 550.00

GOLDEN AGE

MOLLY O'DAY
Avon Periodicals,
Feb., 1945
1 GT;The Enchanted Dagger . . . 700.00

MONSTER
Fiction House Magazines, 1953
1 Dr. Drew 750.00
2 . . . . 500.00

MONSTER CRIME COMICS
Hillman Periodicals,
Oct., 1952
1 52 Pgs,15 Cent (c) Price . . . 1,800.00

MONTE HALL WESTERN
See: MARY MARVEL COMICS

MONTY HALL OF THE U.S. MARINES
Toby Press, Aug., 1951
1 JkS,:Monty Hall,Pin-Up Pete;
  (All Issues) 150.00
2 JkS 125.00
3 thru 5 JkS . . . . @100.00
6 JkS 100.00
7 JkS,The Fireball Express 100.00
8 JkS 100.00
9 JkS 100.00
10 The Vial of Death 100.00
11 Monju Island Prison Break . . . 100.00

MOON GIRL AND THE PRINCE
E.C. Comics, Autumn, 1947
1 JCr(c),O:Moon Girl 1,400.00
Becomes:

MOON GIRL
E.C. Comics, 1947
2 JCr(c),Battle of the Congo . . . 800.00
3 . . . . 750.00
4 V: A Vampire 750.00
5 1st E.C. Horror-Zombie
  Terror 1,500.00
6 . . . . 700.00
Becomes:

MOON GIRL FIGHTS CRIME
E.C. Comics, 1949
7 O:Star;The Fiend Who
  Fights With Fire 700.00
8 True Crime Feature 700.00
Becomes:

A MOON, A GIRL ...ROMANCE
Sept.–Oct., 1949
9 AF,Grl,AF(c),C:Moon Girl;
  Spanking Panels 1,000.00
10 AF,Grl,WW,AF(c),Suspicious
  of His Intentions 800.00
11 AF,Grl,WW,AF(c),Hearts
  Along the Ski Trail 800.00
12 AF,Grl,AF(c),
  March–April, 1950 . . . . 1,100.00
Becomes:

WEIRD FANTASY

MOON MULLINS
Michael Publ. (American Comics Group), 1948
1 . . . . 275.00
2 thru 8 . . . . @150.00

MOPSY
St. John Publishing Co.,
Feb., 1948
1 Paper Dolls Enclosed 800.00
2 . . . . 550.00
3 . . . . 550.00
4 Paper Dolls Enclosed 550.00
5 Paper Dolls Enclosed 550.00
6 Paper Dolls Enclosed 550.00
7 . . . . 525.00
8 Paper Dolls Enclosed;
  Lingerie Panels 550.00
9 . . . . 500.00
10 . . . . 500.00
11 . . . . 500.00
12 . . . . 500.00
13 Paper Dolls Enclosed 500.00
14 thru 18 . . . . @500.00
19 Lingerie(c);Paper
  Dolls Enclosed 500.00

MOTION PICTURE COMICS
Fawcett Publications,
Nov., 1950
101 Ph(c),Monte Hale's-
  Vanishing Westerner 450.00
102 Ph(c),Rocky Lane's-Code
  of the Silver Sage 400.00
103 Ph(c),Rocky Lane's-Covered
  Wagon Raid 400.00
104 BP,Ph(c),Rocky Lane's-
  Vigilante Hideout 400.00
105 BP,Ph(c),Audie Murphy's-
  Red Badge of Courage 500.00
106 Ph(c),George Montgomery's-
  The Texas Rangers 450.00
107 Ph(c),Rocky Lane's-Frisco
  Tornado 400.00
108 Ph(c),John Derek's-Mask
  of the Avenger 350.00
109 Ph(c),Rocky Lane's-Rough
  Rider of Durango 375.00
110 GE,Ph(c), When Worlds
  Collide 2,000.00
111 Ph(c),Lash LaRue's-The
  Vanishing Outpost 500.00
112 Ph(c),Jay Silverheels'-
  Brave Warrior 300.00
113 KS,Ph(c),George Murphy's-
  Walk East on Beacon 250.00
114 Ph(c),George Montgomery's-
  Cripple Creek;Jan, 1953 . . . . 250.00

MOTION PICTURES FUNNIES WEEKLY
1st Funnies Incorporated, 1939
1 BEv,1st Sub-Mariner 35,000.00
2 Cover Only 1,500.00
3 Cover Only 1,500.00
4 Cover Only 1,500.00

MOVIE COMICS
Fiction House Magazines,
Dec., 1946
1 Big Town on(c) 750.00
2 MB,White Tie & Tails 550.00
3 MB,Andy Hardy Laugh Hit . . . 550.00
4 MB,Slave Girl 650.00

MOVIE LOVE
Famous Funnies Publ.,
Feb., 1950
1 Ph(c),Dick Powell(c) 200.00
2 Ph(c),Myrna Loy(c) 150.00
3 Ph(c),Cornell Wilde(c) 125.00
4 Ph(c),Paulette Goddard(c) . . . 125.00
5 Ph(c),Joan Fontaine(c) 125.00

Movie Love #14
© Famous Funnies

6 Ph(c),Ricardo Montalban(c) . . 125.00
7 Ph(c),Fred Astaire(c) 150.00
8 AW,FF,Ph(c),Corinne
  Calvert(c) 600.00
9 Ph(c),John Lund(c) 125.00
10 FF,Ph(c),Mona Freeman(c) . . 600.00
11 Ph(c),James Mason(c) 150.00
12 Ph(c),Jerry Lewis &
  Dean Martin(c) 200.00
13 Ph(c),Ronald Reagan(c) 300.00
14 Ph(c),Janet Leigh,Gene Kelly . 125.00
15 Ph(c),John Payne 125.00
16 Ph(c),Angela Lansbury 150.00
17 Ph(c),Leslie Caron 150.00
18 Ph(c),Cornel Wilde 125.00
19 Ph(c),John Derek 125.00
20 Ph(c),Debbie Reynolds 150.00
21 Ph(c),Patricia Medina 125.00
22 Ph(c),John Payne 125.00

MOVIE THRILLERS
Magazine Enterprises 1949
1 Ph(c),Burt Lancaster's-
  Rope of Sand 375.00

MURDER, INCORPORATED
Fox Features Incorporated,
Jan., 1948–Aug., 1951
1 For Adults Only-on(c) 750.00
2 For Adults Only-on(c);Male
  Bondage(c),Electrocution sty 500.00
3 Dutch Schultz-Beast of Evil . . 275.00
4 The Ray Hamilton Case,
  Lingerie(c) 275.00
5 . . . . 275.00
6 . . . . 275.00
7 . . . . 300.00
8 . . . . 300.00
9 Bathrobe (c) 350.00
9a Lingerie (c) 350.00
10 . . . . 250.00
11 . . . . 250.00
12 . . . . 250.00
13 . . . . 275.00
14 Bill Hale-King o/t Murderers . . 250.00
15 . . . . 250.00
16(5),Second Series 200.00
17(2) 200.00
18(3), Bondage(c) w/Lingerie . . . 300.00

All comics prices listed are for *Near Mint* condition.

MURDEROUS GANGSTERS
Avon Periodicals/Realistic, July, 1951
1 WW,Pretty Boy Floyd,
Leggs Diamond 600.00
2 WW,Baby Face Nelson,Mad
Dog Esposito 350.00
3 P(c),Tony & Bud Fenner,
Jed Hawkins 300.00
4 EK(c),Murder By Needle-
Drug Story, June, 1952 . . . . . 400.00

Mutiny #1
© *Aragon Magazines*

MUTINY
Aragon Magazines, Oct., 1954
1 AH(c),Stormy Tales of the
Seven Seas 200.00
2 AH(c) 150.00
3 Bondage(c),Feb., '55 . . . . 300.00

MY CONFESSION
See: WESTERN TRUE CRIME

MY PAST CONFESSIONS
See: WESTERN THRILLERS

MY SECRET LIFE
Fox Features Syndicate, July, 1949
22 I Loved More Than Once 150.00
23 WW 250.00
24 Love Was a Habit 100.00
25 . . . . 100.00
Becomes:
ROMEO TUBBS
Dec., 1952
26 WW,That Lovable Teen-ager . 250.00

MY SECRET STORY
See: DAGAR, DESERT HAWK

MYSTERIES WEIRD AND STRANGE
Superior Comics/ Dynamic Publ., May, 1953
1 The Stolen Brain 600.00
2 The Screaming Room,
Atomic Bomb 350.00

3 SD,The Avenging Corpse 300.00
4 SD,Ghost on the Gallows 300.00
5 SD,Horror a la Mode 300.00
6 SD,Howling Horror 300.00
7 SD,Demon in Disguise 275.00
8 SD,The Devil's Birthmark 275.00
9 SD 275.00
10 SD 300.00
11 SD 300.00

MYSTERIOUS ADVENTURES
Story Comics, March, 1951
1 WJo(c),Wild Terror of the
Vampire Flag 900.00
2 Terror of the Ghoul's Corpse . 450.00
3 Terror of the Witche's Curse . . 400.00
4 The Little Coffin That Grew . . . 400.00
5 LC,Curse of the Jungle,
Bondage(c) 450.00
6 LC,Ghostly Terror in the
Cave 400.00
7 LC,Terror of the Ghostly
Castle 500.00
8 Terror of the Flowers of Death. 650.00
9 The Ghostly Ghouls-
Extreme Violence 450.00
10 Extreme Violence 400.00
11 The Trap of Terror 450.00
12 SHn,Vultures of Death-
Extreme Violence 450.00
13 Extreme Violence 450.00
14 Horror of the Flame Thrower
Extreme Violence 450.00
15 DW,Ghoul Crazy 500.00
16 Chilling Tales of Horror 500.00
17 DW,Bride of the Dead 500.00
18 Extreme Violence 500.00
19 The Coffin 500.00
20 Horror o/t Avenging Corpse . . 500.00
21 Mother Ghoul's Nursery
Tales, Bondage (c) 500.00
22 RA,Insane 400.00
23 RA,Extreme Violence 400.00
24 KS, ... 350.00
25 KS,Aug., 1955 . . . . 350.00

HORROR FROM THE TOMB
Premier Magazines, Sept., 1954
1 AT,GWb,The Corpse Returns . 550.00
Becomes:
MYSTERIOUS STORIES
Dec., 1954–Jan., 1955
2 GWb(c),Eternal Life 650.00
3 GWb,The Witch Doctor 400.00
4 That's the Spirit 350.00
5 King Barbarossa 350.00
6 GWb,Strangers in the Night . . 400.00
7 KS,The Pipes of Pan;Dec'55 . . 350.00

MYSTERIOUS TRAVELER COMICS
Trans-World Publications, Nov., 1948
1 BP,BP(c),Five Miles Down 800.00

MYSTERY COMICS
William H. Wise & Co., 1944
1 ASh(c),B:Brad Spencer-Wonderman,
King of Futeria,The Magnet, Zudo-
Jungle Boy,Silver Knight. . . 1,700.00
2 ASh(c),Bondage (c) 1,000.00
3 ASh(c),Robot(c),LanceLewis,B 900.00
4 ASh(c),E:All Features,
KKK Type(c) 900.00

MYSTERY MEN COMICS
Fox Features Syndicate, Aug., 1939
1 GT,DBr,LF(c),Bondage(c);I:Blue
Beetle,Green Mask,Rex Dexter
of Mars,Zanzibar,Lt.Drake,D-13
Secret Agent,Chen Chang,
Wing Turner,Capt. Denny 17,000.00
2 GT,BP,DBr,LF(c),
Rex Dexter (c) 5,500.00
3 LF(c) 7,000.00
4 LF(c),B:Captain Savage . . . 4,000.00
5 GT,BP,LF(c),Green Mask (c) 4,000.00
6 GT,BP 3,000.00
7 GT,BP,Bondage(c),
Blue Beetle(c). 3,600.00
8 GT,BP,LF(c),Bondage(c),
Blue Beetle 3,300.00
9 GT,BP,DBr(c),B:The Moth. . . 1,700.00
10 GT,BP,JSm(c),A:Wing
Turner; Bondage(c) 1,400.00
11 GT,BP,JSm(c),I:The Domino 1,400.00
12 GT,BP,JSm(c),BlueBeetle(c) 1,400.00
13 GT,I:The Lynx & Blackie . . 1,000.00
14 GT,Male Bondage (c) 950.00
15 GT,Blue Beetle (c). 900.00
16 GT,Hypo(c),MaleBondage(c) . 950.00
17 GT,BP,Blue Beetle (c). 900.00
18 GT,Blue Beetle (c). 900.00
19 GT,I&B:Miss X 1,000.00
20 GT,DBr,Blue Beetle (c) 900.00
21 GT,E:Miss X 900.00
22 GT,CCu(c),Blue Beetle (c) . . 900.00
23 GT,Blue Beetle (c). 900.00
24 GT,BP,DBr, Blue Beetle (c). . 900.00
25 GT,Bondage(c);
A:Private O'Hara 950.00
26 GT,Bondage(c);B:The Wraith . 950.00
27 GT,Bondage(c),BlueBeetle(c). 950.00
28 GT,Bondage(c);Satan's
Private Needlewoman 950.00
29 GT,Bondage(c),Blue
Beetle (c) 950.00
30 Holiday of Death. 900.00
31 Bondage(c);Feb'42 . . . . 950.00

MY STORY
See: ZAGO, JUNGLE PRINCE

NANCY AND SLUGGO
See: SPARKLER COMICS

NAPOLEON AND UNCLE ELBY
Eastern Color Printing, 1942
1 . . . . 600.00

NATIONAL COMICS
Comics Magazines (Quality Comics Group), July, 1940
1 GT,HcK,LF(c),B:Uncle Sam,
Wonder Boy,Merlin the Magician,
Cyclone, Kid Patrol,Sally O'Neil-
Police-woman, Pen Miller,
Prop Powers,PaulBunyan 10,000.00
2 WE,GT,HcK,LF&RC(c) 4,500.00
3 GT,HcK,LF,WE&RC(c) 3,000.00
4 GT,HcK,LF&RC(c),E:Cyclone;
Torpedo Islands of Death . . 3,400.00
5 GT,LF&RC(c),B:Quicksilver;
O:Uncle Sam 3,000.00
6 GT,LF&RC(c) 2,500.00
7 GT,LF&RC(c) 3,500.00
8 GT,LF&RC(c) 2,500.00
9 JCo,LF&RC(c) 2,500.00
10 RC,JCo,LF&RC(c) 2,500.00
11 RC,JCo,LF&RC(c) 2,500.00
12 RC,JCo,LF&RC(c) 1,800.00
13 RC,JCo,LF,LF&RC(c). 1,600.00

All comics prices listed are for *Near Mint* condition.

14 RC,JCo,LF,PG,LF&RC(c). . . 1,800.00
15 RC,JCo,LF,PG,LF&RC(c). . . 1,800.00
16 RC,JCo,LF,PG,LF&RC(c). . . 1,800.00
17 RC,JCo,LF,PG,LF&RC(c). . . 2,000.00
18 JCo,LF,PG,LF&RC(c),
    Pearl Harbor 2,700.00
19 JCo,LF,PG,RC(c),The Black
    Fog Mystery 2,000.00
20 JCo,LF,PG,LF&RC(c) 2,000.00
21 LF,JCo,PG,LF(c). 2,000.00
22 JCo,LF,PG,FGu,GFx,LF(c),
    E:Jack & Jill,Pen Miller,
    Paul Bunyan 2,000.00
23 JCo,PG,FGu,GFx,AMc,LF
    & GFx(c),B:The Unknown,
    Destroyer 171. . . . . 2,200.00
24 JCo,PG,RC,AMc,FGu,
    GFx,RC(c) 2,200.00
25 AMc,RC,JCo,PG,FGu,
    GFx,RC(c) 1,500.00
26 AMc,Jco,RC,PG,RC(c),
    E:Prop Powers,WonderBoy 1,500.00
27 JCo,AMc 1,500.00
28 JCo,AMc 1,500.00
29 JCo,O:The Unknown;U.Sam
    V:Dr. Dirge 1,600.00
30 JCo,RC(c) 1,200.00
31 JCo,RC(c) 1,400.00
32 JCo,RC(c) 1,400.00
33 JCo,GFx,RC(c),B:Chic Carter;
    U.Sam V:Boss Spring 1,400.00
34 JCo,GFx,U.Sam V:Big John
    Fales. 1,400.00
35 JCo,GFx,E:Kid Patrol. 1,200.00
36 JCo. 1,200.00
37 JCo,FGu,A:The Vagabond. . 1,200.00
38 JCo,FGu,Boat of the Dead . 1,200.00
39 JCo,FGu,Hitler(c);U.Sam
    V:The Black Market 1,700.00
40 JCo,FGu,U.Sam V:The
    Syndicate of Crime 750.00
41 JCo,FGu. 750.00
42 JCo,FGu,JCo(c),B:The Barker 600.00
43 JCo,FGu,JCo(c) 600.00
44 JCo,FGu 600.00
45 JCo,FGu,E:Merlin Magician . 600.00
46 JCo,JCo(c),Murder is no Joke 600.00
47 JCo,JCo(c),E:Chic Carter 600.00
48 JCo,O:The Whistler 600.00
49 JCo,JCo(c),A Corpse
    for a Cannonball 600.00
50 JCo,JCo(c),V:Rocks Myzer . . 600.00
51 JCo,BWa,JCo(c),
    A:Sally O'Neil 700.00
52 JCo,A Carnival of Laughs 500.00
53 PG,V:Scramolo 500.00

National Comics #42
© Quality Comics Group

54 PG,V:Raz-Ma-Taz 500.00
55 JCo,AMc,V:The Hawk. 500.00
56 GFx,JCo,AMc,V:The Grifter . . 500.00
57 GFx,JCo,AMc,V:Witch Doctor. 500.00
58 GFz,JCo,AMc,Talking Animals 500.00
59 GFx,JCo,AMc,V:The Birdman. 500.00
60 GFx,JCo,AMc,V:Big Ed Grew 500.00
61 GFx,AMc,Trouble Comes in
    Small Packages. 400.00
62 GFx,AMc,V:Crocodile Man . . . 400.00
63 GFx,AMc,V:Bearded Lady . . . 400.00
64 GFx,V:The Human Fly 400.00
65 GFx,GFx(c)V:The King 400.00
66 GFx,GFx(c)V:The Man Who
    Hates the Circus 400.00
67 GFx,Gfx(c),A:Quicksilver;
    V:Ali Ben Riff Raff 400.00
68 GFx,GFx(c),V:Leo theLionMan 400.00
69 GFx,Gfx(c),A:Percy the
    Powerful. 400.00
70 GFx,GFx(c),Barker Tires
    of the Big Top 400.00
71 PG,GFx(c),V:SpellbinderSmith 400.00
72 PG,GFx(c),The Oldest Man
    in the World 400.00
73 PG,GFx(c),V:A CountrySlicker 400.00
74 PG,GFx(c),V:Snake Oil Sam. . 400.00
75 PG,GFx(c),Barker Breaks the
    Bank at Monte Marlo;Nov'49. 400.00

NAVY HEROES
Almanac Publ. Co., 1945
1 Propaganda 135.00

NAVY PATROL
Key Publications, 1955
1 . . . . 125.00
2 . . . . 100.00
3 . . . . 100.00
4 . . . . 100.00

NAVY TASK FORCE
**Stanmor Publ./
Aragon Publ., 1953**
1 . . . . 150.00
2 thru 8 . . . . @100.00

Negro Heroes #2
© National Urban League

NEGRO HEROES
National Urban League, 1947
1 . . . . 1,500.00
2 Jackie Robinson 2,000.00

NEGRO ROMANCE
**Fawcett Publications,
June, 1950**
1 GE,Ph(c), Love's Decoy 1,600.00
2 GE,Ph(c), A Tragic Vow 1,200.00
3 GE,Ph(c), My Love
    Betrayed Me 1,200.00
Charlton Comics
4 Rep.FawcettEd.#2;May,1955 1,000.00

NEW ROMANCES
**Standard Comics,
May, 1951**
5 Ph(c), The Blame I Bore 175.00
6 Ph(c), No Wife Was I 150.00
7 Ph(c), My Runaway Heart,
    Ray Miland 125.00
8 Ph(c) 125.00
9 Ph(c) 125.00
10 ATh,Ph(c) 150.00
11 ATh,Ph(c) of Elizabeth Taylor . 250.00
12 Ph(c) 125.00
13 Ph(c) 125.00
14 ATh,Ph(c) 150.00
15 Ph(c) 125.00
16 ATh,Ph(c) 150.00
17 Ath, ... 150.00
18 and 19 . . . . @125.00
20 GT, ... 125.00
21 April, 1954. . . . . 125.00

NICKEL COMICS
Dell Publishing Co., 1938
1 Bobby & Chip 1,100.00

NICKEL COMICS
**Fawcett Publications,
May, 1940**
1 JaB(c),O&I: Bulletman 6,500.00
2 JaB(c), ... 2,000.00
3 JaB(c), ... 1,400.00
4 JaB(c), B. Red Gaucho 1,300.00
5 CCB(c),Bondage(c) 1,300.00
6 and 7 CCD(c) . . . . @1,200.00
8 CCB(c),Aug. 23, 1940,
    World's Fair 1,300.00

NIGHTMARE
See: WEIRD HORRORS

NIGHTMARE
Ziff-Davis Publishing Co., 1952
1 EK,GT,P(c),The Corpse That
    Wouldn't Stay Dead 750.00
2 EK,P(c),Vampire Mermaid . . . 500.00
St. John Publishing Co.
3 EK,P(c),The Quivering Brain . 400.00
4 P(c),1953 . . . . 350.00

NORTHWEST MOUNTIES
**Jubilee Publications/
St. John Publ. Co.,
Oct., 1948**
1 MB,BLb(c),Rose of the Yukon 650.00
2 MB,BLb(c),A:Ventrilo 500.00
3 MB, Bondage(c) 550.00
4 MB(c),A:Blue Monk,July'49 . . 500.00

NUTS!
**Premere Comics Group,
March, 1954**
1 . . . . 350.00
2 . . . . 250.00
3 Mention of "Reefers" 275.00
4 . . . . 250.00
5 Captain Marvel Spoof;Nov.'54 250.00

GOLDEN AGE

NUTTY COMICS
Harvey Publications, 1945
1 BW,Funny animal. 125.00
2 . . . . 125.00
3 . . . . 110.00
4 thru 8 . . . . @100.00

NUTTY LIFE
See: PHANTOM LADY

NYOKA THE JUNGLE GIRL
Fawcett Publications, Winter, 1945
1 Bondage(c);Partial Ph(c) of
  Kay Aldridge as Nyoka 800.00
2 . . . . 450.00
3 . . . . 450.00
4 Bondage(c) 500.00
5 Barbacosi Madness;
  Bondage(c) 500.00
6 . . . . 275.00
7 North Pole Jungle;
  Bondage(c) 400.00
8 Bondage(c) 400.00
9 . . . . 225.00
10 . . . . 225.00
11 Danger! Death! in an
  Unexplored Jungle 225.00
12 . . . . 225.00
13 The Human Leopards 225.00
14 The Mad Witch Doctor;
  Bondage(c) 400.00
15 Sacred Goat of Kristan 225.00
16 BK,The Vultures of Kalahari . . 250.00
17 BK. 250.00
18 BK,The Art of Murder 250.00
19 The Elephant Battle 250.00
20 Explosive Volcano Action 250.00
21 . . . . 150.00
22 The Weird Monsters 150.00
23 Danger in Duplicate 150.00
24 The Human Jaguar;
  Bondage(c) 400.00
25 Hand Colored Ph(c) 135.00
26 A Jungle Stampede 135.00
27 Adventure Laden. 135.00
28 The Human Statues of
  the Jungle 135.00
29 Ph(c). 135.00
30 Ph(c) 135.00
31 thru 40 Ph(c) . . . . @125.00
41 thru 50 Ph(c) . . . . @135.00
51 thru 59 Ph(c) . . . . @100.00

Nyoka The Jungle Girl #21
© Fawcett Publications

60 Ph(c) 100.00
61 Ph(c),The Sacred Sword of
  the Jungle 100.00
62 & 63 Ph(c). . . . . @100.00
64 Ph(c), The Jungle Idol 100.00
65 Ph(c) 100.00
66 Ph(c) 100.00
67 Ph(c), The Sky Man 100.00
68 thru 74 Ph(c) . . . . @100.00
75 Ph(c), The Jungle Myth
  of Terror. 100.00
76 Ph(c) 100.00
77 Ph(c),The Phantoms of the
  Elephant Graveyard;Jun'53. . 100.00

OAKY DOAKS
Eastern Color Printing Co., July, 1942
1 Humor Oriented 450.00

OKAY COMICS
United Features Syndicate, 1940
1 . . . . 600.00

OK COMICS
United Features Syndicate, July, 1940
1 B:Pal Peyton,Little Giant, Phantom
  Knight,Sunset Smith,Teller Twins,
  Don Ramon, Jerrry Sly,Kip Jaxon,
  Leatherneck,Ulysses 1,100.00
2 O:Master Mist,Oct., 1940 . . 1,200.00

OKLAHOMA KID
Ajax/Farrell Publ., 1957
1 . . . . 150.00
2 . . . . 125.00
3 . . . . 125.00
4 . . . . 125.00

100 PAGES OF COMICS
Dell Publishing Co., 1937
101 Alley Oop,OG,Wash Tubbs,
  Tom Mix,Dan Dunn. 2,200.00

ON THE AIR
NBC Network Comics, 1947
1 Giveaway, no cover 300.00

ON THE SPOT
Fawcett Publications, Autumn, 1948
N# Bondage(c),PrettyBoyFloyd . . 450.00

OPERATION PERIL
American Comics Group (Michel Publ.), Oct.–Nov., 1950
1 LSt,OW,OW(c),B:TyphoonTyler,
  DannyDanger,TimeTravellers 500.00
2 OW,OW(c),War (c). 300.00
3 OW,OW(c),Horror 250.00
4 OW,OW(c), Flying Saucers . . 300.00
5 OW,OW(c), Science Fiction. . . 300.00
6 OW, Tyr. Rex 250.00
7 OW,OW(c),Sabretooth. 250.00
8 OW,OW(c) 225.00
9 OW,OW(c) 225.00
10 OW,OW(c),science fiction. . . . 250.00
11 OW,OW(c), War 225.00
12 OW,OW(c),E:Time Travellers . 225.00
13 OW,OW(c),War Stories 150.00
14 OW,OW(c),War Stories 150.00
15 OW,OW(c),War Stories 150.00
16 OW,OW(c),April–May,1953,
  War Stories 150.00

OUR FIGHTING MEN IN ACTION
Ajax/Farrell, 1957
1 . . . . 125.00
2 thru 6 . . . . @100.00

Our Flag Comics #2
© Ace Magazines

OUR FLAG COMICS
Ace Magazines, Aug., 1941–April, 1942
1 MA,JM,B:Capt.Victory,Unknown
  Soldier,The Three Cheers . 3,900.00
2 JM,JM(c),O:The Flag 1,700.00
3 Tank Battle (c). 1,300.00
4 MA 1,300.00
5 I:Mr. Risk, Male Bondage . . . 1,400.00

OUR GANG COMICS
Dell Publishing Co., Sept.–Oct., 1942
1 WK,Barney Bear, Tom &
  Jerry 1,700.00
2 WK. 750.00
3 WK,Benny Burro 500.00
4 WK. 500.00
5 WK. 500.00
6 WK. 750.00
7 WK. 350.00
8 WK,CB,Benny Burro 900.00
9 WK,CB,Benny Burro 850.00
10 WK,CB,Benny Burro. 600.00
11 WK,I:Benny Bear 850.00
12 thru 20 WK . . . . @400.00
21 thru 29 WK . . . . @300.00
30 WK,Christmas(c). 250.00
31 thru 34 WK . . . . @250.00
35 WK,CB 200.00
36 WK,CB 200.00
37 thru 40 WK . . . . @125.00
41 thru 50 WK . . . . @125.00
51 thru 56 WK . . . . @125.00
57 . . . . 100.00
58 Our Gang 100.00
59 Our Gang 100.00
Becomes:

TOM AND JERRY
July, 1949
60 . . . . 200.00
61 . . . . 150.00
62 . . . . 100.00
63 . . . . 100.00
64 . . . . 100.00
65 . . . . 100.00

All comics prices listed are for *Near Mint* condition.

66 Christmas (c) 120.00
67 thru 70 . . . . @125.00
71 thru 76 . . . . @125.00
77 Christmas (c) 125.00
78 thru 80 . . . . @125.00
81 thru 89 . . . . @100.00
90 Christmas (c) 125.00
91 thru 99 . . . . @100.00
100 . . . . 125.00
101 thru 120 . . . . @100.00
121 thru 150 . . . . @100.00
151 thru 212 . . . . @100.00

OUTER SPACE
See: CHARLIE CHAN

OUTLAWS
D.S. Publishing Co.,
Feb.–March, 1948
1 HcK,Western Crime Stories . . 400.00
2 Grl,Doc Dawson's Dilema . . . 400.00
3 Cougar City Cleanup 200.00
4 JO,Death Stakes A Claim 200.00
5 RJ,RJ(c),Man Who Wanted
  Mexico 175.00
6 AMc,RJ,RJ(c),The Ghosts of
  Crackerbox Hill 175.00
7 Grl,Dynamite For Boss Cavitt . 300.00
8 Grl,The Gun & the Pen 300.00
9 FF,Shoot to Kill;June–
  July, 1949 . . . . 650.00

WHITE RIDER AND
SUPER HORSE
Star Publications,
Sept., 1950
1 LbC(c) 250.00
2 LbC(c) 200.00
3 LbC(c) 200.00
4 LbC(c) 200.00
5 LbC(c),Stampede of Hard
  Riding Thrills 225.00
0 LbC(o),Drums of the Sioux . . . 225.00
Becomes:

INDIAN WARRIORS
June, 1951
7 LbC(c),Winter on the Great
  Plains 250.00
8 LbC(c) 225.00
Becomes:

WESTERN CRIME
CASES
Dec., 1951
9 LbC(c),The Card Sharp Killer . 250.00
Becomes:

OUTLAWS, THE
May, 1952
10 LbC(c),Federated Express . . . 250.00
11 LbC(c),Frontier Terror!!! 225.00
12 LbC(c),Ruthless Killer!!! 225.00
13 LbC(c),The Grim Avengers . . . 225.00
14 AF,JKa,LbC(c),Trouble in
   Dark Canyon,April, 1954 . . . . 225.00

OUT OF THE NIGHT
American Comics Group/
Best Synd. Feature,
Feb.–March, 1952
1 AW 1,000.00
2 AW 700.00
3 . . . . 350.00
4 AW 550.00
5 . . . . 350.00
6 The Ghoul's Revenge 350.00
7 . . . . 350.00
8 The Frozen Ghost 350.00

9 Death Has Wings,
  Science Fiction 350.00
10 Ship of Death 350.00
11 . . . . 275.00
12 Music for the Dead 275.00
13 HN,From the Bottom of
   the Well 275.00
14 Out of the Screen 275.00
15 The Little Furry Thing 250.00
16 Nightmare From the Past 250.00
17 The Terror of the Labyrinth . . . 250.00
Becomes:

HOODED HORSEMAN
Dec., 1954–Jan., 1955
18 B: The Hooded Horseman . . . 125.00
19 The Horseman's Strangest
   Adventure 175.00
20 OW,O:Johnny Injun. 125.00
21 OW,OW(c). 175.00
22 OW 125.00
23 . . . . 125.00
24 . . . . 125.00
25 . . . . 100.00
26 O&I:Cowboy Sahib 125.00
27 Jan.–Feb., 1953 . . . . 110.00

OUT OF THE SHADOWS
Visual Editions
(Standard Comics),
July, 1952–Aug., 1954
5 ATh,GT,The Shoremouth
  Horror 750.00
6 ATh,JKz,Salesman of Death . . 500.00
7 JK,Plant of Death 400.00
8 Mask of Death 625.00
9 RC,Till Death Do Us Part 375.00
10 MSy,We Vowed,Till Death
   Do Us Part. 375.00
11 ATh,Fountain of Fear. 375.00
12 ATh,Hand of Death 500.00
13 MSy,The Cannibal 375.00
14 ATh,The Werewolf. 375.00

OXYDOL-DREFT
Giveaways, 1950
The Set is More Valuable if the
Original Envelope is Present
1 L'il Abner 150.00
2 Daisy Mae 150.00
3 Shmoo 175.00
4 AW&FF(c),John Wayne 200.00
5 Archie 200.00
6 Terry Toons Comics 150.00

OZARK IKE
Visual Editions
(Standard Comics), 1948
11 . . . . 175.00
12 thru 20 . . . . @100.00
21 thru 25 . . . . @100.00

OZZIE AND BABS
Fawcett Publications,
Winter, 1946
1 Humor Oriented, Teenage 150.00
2 Humor Oriented 100.00
3 thru 12 Humor Oriented . . . @100.00
13 Humor Oriented;1949 . . . . . . 100.00

PAGEANT OF COMICS
St. John Publishing Co.,
Sept., 1947
1 Rep. Mopsy 250.00
2 Rep. Jane Arden,Crime
  Reporter. 250.00

PANHANDLE PETE
AND JENNIFER
J. Charles Lave
Publishing Co., July, 1951
1 (fa) 125.00
2 (fa) 100.00
3 (fa),Nov.'51 . . . . 100.00

PANIC
Tiny Tot Publications
(E.C. Comics), March, 1954
"Humor in a Jugular Vein"
1 BE,JKa,JO,JDa,AF(c) 750.00
2 BE,JO,WW,JDa,A:Bomb 500.00
3 BE,JO,BW,WW,JDa,AF(c) . . . 400.00
4 BE,JO,WW,JDa,BW(c),
  Infinity(c) 400.00
5 BE,JO,WW,JDa,AF(c) 350.00
6 BE,JO,WW,JDa,Blank (c) 350.00
7 BE,JO,WW,JDa 350.00
8 BE,JO,WW,JDa,Eye Chart (c) . 275.00
9 BE,JO,WW,JDa,Ph(c),
  Confidential(c) 1,000.00
10 BE,JDa, Postal Package(c) . . 500.00
11 BE,WW,JDa,Wheaties parody
   as Weedies (c) 400.00
12 BE,WW,JDa,JDa(c);
   Dec.–Jan., 1955–56 . . . . . . 375.00

PARAMOUNT
ANIMATED COMICS
Family Publications
(Harvey Publ.), June, 1953
1 (fa),B:Baby Herman & Katnip,
  Baby Huey,Buzzy the Crow . 275.00
2 (fa) 125.00
3 (fa) 100.00
4 thru 6 (fa) . . . . @100.00
7 (fa), Baby Huey (c) 275.00
8 (fa), Baby Huey (c) 100.00
9 (fa), Infinity(c),Baby Huey (c). . 100.00
10 thru 21 (fa),Baby Huey(c) . . @100.00
22 (fa), July, 1956, Baby Huey (c) 100.00

PAROLE BREAKERS
Avon Periodicals/Realistic,
Dec., 1951–July, 1952
1 P(c),Hellen Willis,Gun
  Crazed Gun Moll 600.00
2 JKu,P(c),Vinnie Sherwood,
  The Racket King 400.00
3 EK(c),John "Slicer" Berry,
  Hatchetman of Crime 350.00

Parole Breakers #3
© Avon Periodicals

PATCHES

**Rural Home Publ./
Patches Publ.,
March–April, 1945**

1 LbC(c),Imagination In Bed(c). .	500.00
2 Dance (c)	200.00
3 Rocking Horse (c)	150.00
4 Music Band (c)	150.00
5 LbC(c),A:Danny Kaye,Football	250.00
6 A: Jackie Kelk	150.00
7 A: Hopalong Cassidy	225.00
8 A: Smiley Burnettte	150.00
9 BK,A: Senator Claghorn	150.00
10 A: Jack Carson	150.00
11 A: Red Skeleton; Dec'47	200.00

PAT THE BRAT

**Radio Comics (Archie
Publications), 1955–59**

1	175.00
2	150.00
3	125.00
4	125.00
15 thru 20	@100.00
21 thru 33	@100.00

PAUL TERRY'S COMICS
**See: TERRY-TOONS
COMICS**

PAWNEE BILL

**Story Comics,
Feb.–July, 1951**

1 A:Bat Masterson,Wyatt Earp, Indian Massacre at Devil's Gulch	125.00
2 Blood in Coffin Canyon	100.00
3 LC,O:Golden Warrior,Fiery Arrows at Apache Pass	100.00

PAY-OFF

**D.S. Publishing Co.,
July–Aug., 1948–
March–April, 1949**

1 True Crime 1 & 2	300.00
2 The Pennsylvania Blue-Beard	175.00
3 The Forgetful Forger	150.00
4 RJ(c),Lady and the Jewels	150.00
5 The Beautiful Embezzeler	150.00

PEDRO

**Fox Features Syndicate,
Jan., 1950**

1 WW,WW(c),Humor Oriented	300.00
2 Aug., 1950	200.00

PENNY

Avon Publications, 1947

1 The Slickest Chick of 'em All	125.00
2	100.00
3 America's Teen-age Sweetheart	100.00
4	100.00
5	100.00
6 Perry Como Ph(c),Sept.– Oct., 1949	125.00

PEP COMICS

**MJL Magazines/
Archie Publications,
Jan., 1940**

1 IN,JCo,MMe,IN(c),I:Shield, O:Comet,Queen of Diamonds, B:The Rocket,Press Guardian, Sergeant Boyle Chang,Bently of Scotland Yard	17,000.00
2 CBi,JCo,IN,IN(c),O:Rocket	4,500.00
3 JCo,IN,IN(c),Shield (c)	3,000.00

Pep Comics #17
© *Archie Publications*

4 Cbi,JCo,MMe,IN,IN(c), C:Wizard(not Gareb)	2,400.00
5 Cbi,JCo,MMe,IN,IN(c), C:Wizard	2,400.00
6 IN,IN(c), Shield (c)	1,800.00
7 IN,IN(c),Bondage(c),Shield(c)	1,800.00
8 JCo,IN, Shield (c)	1,800.00
9 IN, Shield (c)	1,800.00
10 IN,IN(c), Shield (c)	1,800.00
11 MMe,IN,IN(c),I:Dusty, Boy Detective	2,000.00
12 IN,IN(c),O:Fireball Bondage(c), E:Rocket, Queen of Diamonds	2,200.00
13 IN,IN(c),Bondage(c)	1,500.00
14 IN,IN(c)	1,500.00
15 IN,Bondage(c)	1,500.00
16 IN,O:Madam Satan	2,400.00
17 IN,IN(c),O:Hangman, D:Comet	6,000.00
18 IN,IN(c),Bondage(c)	1,500.00
19 IN	1,500.00
20 IN,IN(c),E:Fireball	1,500.00
21 IN,IN(c),Bondage(c), E: Madam Satan	1,500.00
22 IN,IN(c)I:Archie, Jughead, Betty	25,000.00
23 IN,IN(c)	2,200.00
24 IN,IN(c)	1,500.00
25 IN,IN(c)	1,500.00
26 IN,IN(c),I:Veronica	2,200.00
27 IN,IN(c),Bill of Rights (c)	1,500.00
28 IN,IN(c), V:Capt. Swastika	1,500.00
29 ASh (c)	1,500.00
30 B:Capt.Commando	1,500.00
31 Bondage(c)	1,500.00
32 Bondage(c)	1,100.00
33	1,100.00
34 Bondage(c)	1,100.00
35	1,100.00
36 1st Archie(c)	2,500.00
37 Bondage(c)	750.00
38 ASh(c)	700.00
39 ASh(c), Human Shield	700.00
40	700.00
41 2nd Archie, I:Jughead	500.00
42 F:Archie & Jughead	500.00
43 F:Archie & Jughead	500.00
44	500.00
45	500.00
46	500.00
47 E:Hangman,Infinity(c)	500.00
48 B:Black Hood	500.00
49	500.00
50	500.00
51	350.00
52 B:Suzie	350.00

53	350.00
54 E:Captain Commando	350.00
55	350.00
56 thru 58	@300.00
59 E:Suzie	300.00
60 B:Katy Keene	300.00
61	275.00
62 I L'il Jinx	275.00
63	275.00
64	275.00
65 E:Shield	275.00
66 thru 71	@150.00
72 thru 80	@125.00
81 thru 90	@100.00
91 thru 99	@100.00
100	150.00
101 thru 110	@125.00
111 thru 120	@100.00
121 thru 130	@125.00
131 thru 140	@100.00
141 thru 150	@100.00
151 thru 160,A:Super Heroes	@100.00

PERFECT CRIME, THE

**Cross Publications,
Oct., 1949**

1 BP,DW	400.00
2 BP	225.00
3	200.00
4 BP	200.00
5 DW	200.00
6	200.00
7 B:Steve Duncan	200.00
8 Drug Story	300.00
9	175.00
10	175.00
11 Bondage (c)	300.00
12	175.00
13	175.00
14 Poisoning (c)	350.00
15 'The Most Terrible Menace,' Drug	300.00
16	150.00
17	150.00
18 Drug (c)	400.00
19	150.00
20 thru 25	@125.00
26 Drug w/ Hypodermic (c)	400.00
27	150.00
28	150.00
29	150.00
30 E:Steve Duncan, Rope Strangulation (c)	400.00
31	125.00
32	125.00
33	125.00

PETER PAUL'S 4 IN 1 JUMBO COMIC BOOK

Capitol Stories, 1953

1 F: Racket Squad in Action, Space Adventures,Crime & Justice,Space Western	500.00

PETER PENNY AND HIS MAGIC DOLLAR

American Bakers Assn., 1947

1 History from Colonial America to the 1950's	200.00
2	125.00

PETER RABBIT

Avon Periodicals, 1947

1 HCa	450.00
2 HCa	300.00
3 HCa	275.00
4 HCa	275.00
5 HC	275.00
6 HCa	275.00

    All comics prices listed are for *Near Mint* condition.

7 thru 10 . . . . @100.00
11 . . . . 100.00

KRAZY LIFE
Fox Features Syndicate, 1945
1 (fa) 100.00
Becomes:

NUTTY LIFE
Summer, 1946
2 (fa) 100.00
Becomes:

WOTALIFE
**Fox Features Synd./
Green Publ., Aug.–Sept., 1946**
3 (fa)B:L'il Pan,Cosmo Cat 150.00
4 . . . . 100.00
5 thru 11 . . . . @100.00
12 July, 1947 . . . . 100.00
9a rep (1959) 100.00
Becomes:

Phantom Lady #14
© *Fox Feature Syndicate*

PHANTOM LADY
**Fox Features Syndicate,
Aug., 1947**
13(#1) MB,MB(c) Knights of
the Crooked Cross 7,000.00
14(#2) MB,MB(c) Scoundrels
and Scandals 3,500.00
15 MB,MB(c) The Meanest
Crook In the World 3,500.00
16 MB,MB(c) Claa Peete The
Beautiful Beast, Negligee . . 3,500.00
17 MB.MB(c) The Soda Mint
Killer, Bondage (c) 10,000.00
18 MB,MB(c) The Case of
Irene Shroeder 2,500.00
19 MB,MB(c) The Case of
the Murderous Model 2,500.00
20 MB,MB(c) Ace of Spades. . . 2,000.00
21 MB,MB(c). 2,000.00
22 MB,JKa 2,000.00
23 MB,JKa Bondage (c) 2,200.00
Becomes:

MY LOVE SECRET
June, 1949
24 JKa, My Love Was For Sale . . 200.00
25 Second Hand Love 125.00
26 WW I Wanted Both Men 250.00
27 I Was a Love Cheat 100.00
28 WW, I Gave Him Love 250.00
29 . . . . 100.00

30 Ph(c) 100.00

LINDA
Ajax/Farrell, April–May, 1954
1 . . . . 175.00
2 Lingerie section 150.00
3 . . . . 100.00
4 Oct.–Nov.,1954 . . . . 100.00
Becomes:

PHANTOM LADY
Dec., 1954–Jan., 1955
5(1) MB 1,600.00
2 Last Pre-Code Edition 1,250.00
3 Comics Code 1,000.00
4 Red Rocket,June, 1955 . . . . 1,000.00

PHIL RIZZUTO
Fawcett Publications, 1951
Ph(c) The Sensational Story of
The American League MVP 1,100.00

PICTURE CRIMES
1937
1 . . . . 1,500.00

PICTURE NEWS
**299 Lafayette Street Corp.,
Jan., 1946–Jan.-Feb., 1947**
1 Will The Atom Blow The
World Apart. 1,000.00
2 Meet America's 1st Girl Boxing
Expert,Atomic Bomb 500.00
3 Hollywood's June Allison Shows
You How to be Beautiful,
Atomic Bomb. 400.00
4 Amazing Marine Who Became
King of 10,000 Voodoos,
Atomic Bomb. 450.00
5 G.I.Babies,Hank Greenberg . . 400.00
6 Joe Louis(c) 450.00
7 Lovely Lady, Englands
Future Queen 350.00
8 Champion of them All 350.00
9 Bikini Atom Bomb,
Joe DiMaggio 400.00
10 Dick Quick, Ace Reporter,
Atomic Bomb. 400.00

PICTURE PARADE
Gilberton Co., 1953
1 A-Bomb 300.00
2 . . . . 150.00
3 . . . . 150.00
4 Christmas issue 150.00
Becomes:

PICTURE PROGRESS
Gilberton Co., 1954
5 1953 News. 100.00
6 Birth of America 100.00
7 . . . . 100.00
8 Paul Revere. 100.00
9 Hawaian Islands 100.00
10 Flight. 100.00
11 thru 20 . . . . @100.00

PICTURE SCOPE
JUNGLE ADVENTURES
Star Publications, 1954
7 LbC(c) 700.00

PICTURE STORIES FROM
AMERICAN HISTORY
E.C. Comics, 1946–47
1 . . . . 750.00
2 thru 4 . . . . @550.00

PICTURE STORIES
FROM SCIENCE
**Educational Comics,
Spring, 1947**
1 Understanding Air and Water . 500.00
2 Fall '47 Amazing Discoveries
About Food & Health. 400.00

PICTURE STORIES
FROM WORLD HISTORY
E.C. Comics, Spring, 1947
1 Ancient World to the
Fall of Rome 350.00
2 Europes Struggle for
Civilization 300.00

PINHEAD AND
FOODINI
**Fawcett Publications,
July, 1951–Jan., 1952**
1 Ph(c) 400.00
2 Ph(c) 200.00
3 Ph(c) Too Many Pinheads . . 150.00
4 Foodini's Talking Camel. 150.00

PIN-UP PETE
Toby Publishers, 1952
1 Loves of a GI Casanova 250.00

PIONEER PICTURE
STORIES
**Street & Smith Publ.,
Dec., 1941**
1 Red Warriors in Blackface 500.00
2 Life Story Of Errol Flynn 400.00
3 Success Stories of Brain
Muscle in Action 300.00
4 Legless Ace & Boy Commando
Raid Occupied France 300.00
5 How to Tell Uniform and
Rank of Any Navy Man 300.00
6 General Jimmy Doolittle 360.00
7 Life Story of Admiral Halsey . . 350.00
8 Life Story of Timoshenko 300.00
9 Dec., '43,Man Who Conquered
The Wild Frozen North 300.00

PIRACY
E.C. Comics, Oct.–Nov., 1954
1 WW,JDa,AW,WW(c),RC,AT . . 750.00
2 RC,JDa(c),WW,AW,AT. 600.00
3 RC,GE, RC(c),Grl 500.00
4 RC,GE,RC(c),Grl 450.00
5 RC,GE,BK(c),Grl 450.00
6 JDa,RC,GE,BK(c),Grl 450.00
7 Oct Nov GE(c),RC,GE,Grl . . . 450.00

PIRATES COMICS
Hillman Periodicals, Feb., 1950
1 . . . . 300.00
2 . . . . 200.00
3 . . . . 175.00
4 Aug–Sept., 1950 . . . . 175.00

PIXIES, THE
**Magazine Enterprises,
Winter, 1946**
1 Mighty Atom. 200.00
2 thru 5 . . . . @150.00
Becomes:

MIGHTY ATOM, THE
1949
6 . . . . 150.00

Planet Comics #23
© *Fiction House Magazines*

PLANET COMICS
**Love Romance Publ.
(Fiction House Magazines),
Jan., 1940–Winter, 1953**

1 AB,DBr,HcK, Planet Comics,
WE&LF,O:Aura,B:Flint Baker,
Red Comet,Spurt Hammond,
Capt. Nelson Cole 22,000.00
2 HcK,LF(c) 7,000.00
3 WE(c),HcK 4,500.00
4 HcK,B:Gale Allan and
the Girl Squad 4,000.00
5 BP,HcK 3,800.00
6 BP,HcK,BP(c),The Ray
Pirates of Venus 3,800.00
7 BP,AB,HcK,BP(c) B:Buzz
Crandall Planet Payson . . . 3,000.00
8 BP,AB HcK 3,000.00
9 BP,AB,GT,HcK,B:Don
Granville Cosmo Corrigan . 3,000.00
10 BP,AB,GT HcK 3,000.00
11 HcK, B:Crash Parker 3,000.00
12 Dri,B:Star Fighter 3,000.00
13 Dri,B:Reef Ryan 2,200.00
14 Dri B:Norge Benson 2,200.00
15 B: Mars,God of War 4,500.00
16 Invasion From The Void . . . 2,000.00
17 Warrior Maid of Mercury . . 2,000.00
18 Bondage(c) 2,100.00
19 Monsters of the Inner
World 2,000.00
20 RP, Winged Man Eaters
of the Exile Star 2,000.00
21 RP,B:Lost World
Hunt Bowman 2,100.00
22 Inferno on the Fifth Moon . . 2,000.00
23 GT,Lizard Tyrant of
the Twilight World 1,900.00
24 GT,Grl Raiders From
The Red Moon 1,900.00
25 Grl,B:Norge Benson 1,900.00
26 Grl,B:The Space Rangers
Bondage(c) 2,000.00
27 Grl, The Fire Eaters of
Asteroid Z 1,500.00
28 Grl, Bondage (c) 2,200.00
29 Grl,Dragon Raiders of Aztla. 2,600.00
30 GT,Grl City of Lost Souls . . . 2,000.00
31 Grl,Fire Priests of Orbit6X . . 1,600.00
32 Slaver's Planetoid 1,700.00
33 MA 1,600.00
34 MA,Bondage 1,800.00
35 MA B:Mysta of The Moon . 1,600.00
36 MA Collosus of the
Blood Moon 1,600.00

37 MA, Behemoths of the
Purple Void 1,600.00
38 MA 1,500.00
39 MA.Death Webs Of Zenith 3 1,500.00
40 Chameleon Men from
Galaxy 9 . . . . 1,500.00
41 MA,AgF,New O: Auro
Bondage (c) 1,500.00
42 MA,AgF,E:Gale Allan 1,500.00
43 MA,AgF Death Rays
From the Sun. 1,500.00
44 MA,Bbl,B:Futura 1,500.00
45 Ma,Bbl,Her Evilness
from Xanado. 1,500.00
46 MA,Bbl,GE The Mecho-Men
From Mars 1,500.00
47 MA,Bbl,GE,The Great
Green Spawn 1,200.00
48 MA,GE 1,200.00
49 MA,GE, Werewolves From
Hydra Hell. 1,200.00
50 MA,GE,The Things of Xeves 1,200.00
51 MA,GE, Mad Mute X-Adapts 1,000.00
52 GE,Mystery of the Time
Chamber. 1,000.00
53 MB,GE,Bondage(c)
Dwarflings From Oceania. . 1,000.00
54 MB,GE,Robots From Inferno 1,000.00
55 MB,GE,Giants of the
Golden Atom. 1,000.00
56 MB,GE,Grl 900.00
57 MB,GE,Grl 900.00
58 MB,GE,Grl 900.00
59 MB,GE,Grl,LSe. 900.00
60 GE,Grl,Vassals of Volta 900.00
61 GE,Grl, The Brute in the
Bubble 800.00
62 GE,Musta,Moon Goddess . . . 800.00
63 GE,Paradise or Inferno 800.00
64 GE,Monkeys From the Blue . . 800.00
65 The Lost World 800.00
66 The Plague of the
Locust Men 800.00
67 The Nymphs of Neptune 800.00
68 Synthoids of the 9th Moon . . 800.00
69 The Mentalists of Mars 800.00
70 Cargo For Amazonia. 800.00
71 Sandhogs of Mars. 700.00
72 Last Ship to Paradise 700.00
73 The Martian Plague 700.00

PLASTIC MAN
**Comics Magazines
(Quality Comics Group),
Summer, 1943–Nov., 1956**

1 JCo(a&c)Game of Death . . . 7,000.00
2 JCo(a&c)The Gay Nineties
Nightmare. 2,700.00
3 JCo(a&c). 1,700.00
4 JCo(a&c). 1,500.00
5 JCo(a&c). 1,400.00
6 JCo(a&c). 1,500.00
7 JCo(a&c). 1,500.00
8 JCo(a&c). 1,500.00
9 JCo(a&c). 1,500.00
10 JCo(a&c) 1,500.00
11 JCo(a&c) 1,500.00
12 JCo(a&c),V:Spadehead . . . 1,500.00
13 JCo(a&c),V:Mr.Hazard 1,500.00
14 JCo(a&c),Words,Symbol
of Crime 1,500.00
15 JCo(a&c),V:BeauBrummel. . 1,500.00
16 JCo(a&c),Money
Means Trouble 1,500.00
17 JCo(a&c),A:The Last
Man on Earth 1,200.00
18 JCo(a&c),Goes Back
to the Farm. 1,200.00
19 JCo(a&c),V;Prehistoric
Plunder. 1,200.00
20 JCo(a&c),A:Sadly,Sadly. . . . 1,200.00

21 JCo(a&c),V:Crime Minded
Mind Reader 800.00
22 JCo(a&c), Which Twin
is the Phony. 800.00
23 JCo(a&c),The Fountain
of Age 800.00
24 JCo(a&c),The Black Box
of Terror. 800.00
25 JCo(a&c),A:Angus
MacWhangus 800.00
26 JCo(a&c),On the Wrong
Side of the Law? 800.00
27 JCo(a&c),V:The Leader 800.00
28 JCo(a&c),V:Shasta 800.00
29 JCo(a&c),V:Tricky Toledo . . . 800.00
30 JCo(a&c),V:Weightless
Wiggins 800.00
31 JCo(a&c),V:Raka the
Witch Doctor 600.00
32 JCo(a&c),V:Mr.Fission 600.00
33 JCo(a&c),V:The Mad
Professor 600.00
34 JCo(a&c),Smuggler'sHaven . 600.00
35 JCo(a&c),V:The Hypnotist . . . 600.00
36 JCo(a&c),The Uranium
Underground 600.00
37 JCo(a&c),V:Gigantic Ants . . . 600.00
38 JCo(a&c),The Curse of
Monk Mauley. 600.00
39 JCo(a&c),The Stairway
to Madness 600.00
40 JCo(a&c),The Ghoul of
Ghost Swamp 600.00
41 JCo(a&c),The Beast with
the Bloody Claws. 500.00
42 JCo(a&c),The King of
Thunderbolts 500.00
43 JCo(a&c),The Evil Terror 500.00
44 JCo(a&c),The Magic Cup . . . 500.00
45 The Invisible Raiders 500.00
46 V:The Spider 500.00
47 The Fiend of a
Thousand Faces 500.00
48 Killer Crossbones 500.00
49 JCo,The Weapon for Evil 500.00
50 V:Iron Fist 500.00
51 Incredible Sleep Weapon . . . 500.00
52 V:Indestructible Wizard 500.00
53 V:Dazzia,Daughter of
Darkness 500.00
54 V:Dr.Quomquat 500.00
55 The Man Below Zero 500.00
56 JCo, The Man Who Broke
the Law of Gravity 500.00
57 The Chemist's Cauldron 500.00

Plastic Man #17
© *Quality Comics Group*

58 JCo,The Amazing
Duplicating Machine 500.00
59 JCo,V:The Super Spy 500.00
60 The Man in the Fiery
Disguise 450.00
61 V:King of the Thunderbolts . . . 450.00
62 V:The Smokeweapon 450.00
63 V:Reflecto 450.00
64 The Invisible Raiders 450.00

PLAYFUL LITTLE AUDREY
Harvey Publications, 1957
1 . . . . 400.00
2 . . . . 200.00
3 . . . . 135.00
4 . . . . 135.00
5 . . . . 135.00
6 thru 9 . . . . @100.00
10 thru 30 . . . . @100.00

POCAHONTAS
Pocahontas Fuel Co.,
Oct., 1941
N# 350.00
2 . . . . 325.00

POCKET COMICS
Harvey Publications,
Aug., 1941
1 100 pages,O:Black Cat,Spirit
of '76,Red Blazer Phantom
Sphinx & Zebra,B:Phantom
Ranger,British Agent #99,
Spin Hawkins,Satan 1,400.00
2 . . . . 900.00
3 . . . . 700.00
4 Jan.'42,All Features End 700.00

POGO POSSUM
Dell Publishing Co., 1949
1 WK,A:Swamp Land Band . . . 1,700.00
2 WK 1,000.00
3 WK 600.00
4 WK 600.00
5 WK 600.00
6 thru 10 WK . . . . @450.00
11 WK, Christmas (c) . . . . @400.00
12 thru 16 WK . . . . @500.00

POLICE AGAINST CRIME
Premier Magazines, 1954
1 Knife in Face 300.00
2 . . . . 165.00
3 . . . . 125.00
4 thru 9 . . . . @125.00

POLICE COMICS
Comic Magazines
(Quality Comics Group),
Aug., 1941
1 JCo,WE.PGv,RC,FGu,AB,
GFx(a&c),B&O:Plastic Man
The Human Bomb,#711,I&B,
Chic Canter,The Firebrand
Mouthpiece,Phantom Lady
The Sword 13,000.00
2 JCo,PGv,WE,RC,FGu,
GFx(a&c) 5,000.00
3 JCo,PGv,WE,RC,FGu,
GFx(a&c) 3,200.00
4 JCo,GFx,PGv,WE,RC,FGu,
GFx&WEC(c) 2,700.00
5 JCo,PGv,WE,RC,FGu,
GFx(a&c) 2,700.00
6 JCo,PGv,WE,RC,FGu,
GFx(a&c) 2,300.00
7 JCo,PGv,WE,RC,FGu,
GFx(a&c) 2,300.00

8 JCo,PGv,WE,RC,FGu,
GFx(a&c),B&O:Manhunter 2,700.00
9 JCo,PGv,WE,RC,FGu,
GFx(a&c) 1,900.00
10 JCo,PGv,WE,RC,FGu,
GFx(a&c) 1,800.00
11 JCo,PGv,WE,RC,FGu,GFx(a&c),
B:Rep:Rep.Spirit Strips 3,500.00
12 JCo,GFx,PGv,WE,FGu,AB,
RC(c) I:Ebony 2,000.00
13 JCo,GFx,PGv,WE,FGu,AB,RC(c)
E:Firebrand,I:Woozy Winks 2,000.00
14 JCo,PGv,WE,Jku,GFx(a&c) . 1,500.00
15 JCo,PGv,WE,Jku,GFx(a&c)
E#711,B:Destiny 1,500.00
16 JCo,PGv,WE,Jku 1,500.00
17 PGv,WE,JKu,JCo(a&c) 1,500.00
18 PGv,WE,JCo(a&c) 1,500.00
19 PGv,WE,JCo(a&c) 1,500.00
20 PGv,WE,JCo(a&c),A:Jack
Cole in Phantom Lady 1,500.00
21 PGv,WE,JCo(a&c) 1,400.00
22 PGv,WE,RP,JCo(a&c)
The Eyes Have it 1,400.00
23 WE,RP,JCo(a&c),E:Phantom
Lady 1,200.00
24 WE,HK,JCo(a&c),B:Flatfoot
Burns 1,200.00
25 WE,HK,RP,JCo(a&c),The
Bookstore Mysrery 1,200.00
26 WE,Hk,JCo(a&c)E:Flatfoot
Burns 1,200.00
27 WE,JCo(a&c) 1,200.00
28 WE,JCo(a&c) 1,200.00
29 WE,JCo(a&c) 1,200.00
30 WE,JCo(a&c),A Slippery
Racket 1,200.00
31 WE,JCo(a&c),Is Plastic
Man Washed Up? 1,100.00
32 WE,JCo(a&c),Fiesta Turns
Into a Fracas 1,100.00
33 JCo,WE 1,100.00
34 WE,JCo(a&c) 1,100.00
35 WE,JCo(a&c) 1,100.00
36 WE,JCo(a&c),Rest In Peace 1,100.00
37 WE,PGv,JCo(a&c),Love
Comes to Woozy 1,100.00
38 WE,PGv,JCo(a&c) 1,100.00
39 WE,PGv,JCo(a&c) 1,100.00
40 WE,PGv,JCo(a&c) 1,100.00
41 WE,PGv,JCo(a&c),E:Reps.
of Spirit Strip 1,100.00
42 LF&WE,PGv,JCo(a&c),
Woozy Cooks with Gas . . . 1,100.00
43 LF&WE,PGv,JCo(a&c) 1,100.00
44 PGv,LF,JCo(a&c) 1,100.00

Police Comics #76
© Quality Comics Group

45 PGv,LF,JCo(a&c) 1,100.00
46 PGv,LF,JCo(a&c) 1,100.00
47 PGv,LF,JCo(a&c),V:Dr.Slicer 1,100.00
48 PGv,LF,JCo(a&c),V:Big
Beaver 1,100.00
49 PGv,LF,JCo(a&c),V:Thelma
Twittle 1,100.00
50 PGv,LF,JCo(a&c) 1,100.00
51 PGv,LF,JCo(a&c),V:The
Granite Lady 1,000.00
52 PGv,LF,JCo(a&c),V:Dr.
Erudite 1,000.00
53 PGv,LF,JCo(a&c),V:Dr.
Erudite 1,000.00
54 PGv,LF,JCo(a&c),V:The
Sleepy Eyes 1,000.00
55 PGv,LF,JCo(a&c),V:The
Yes Man 1,000.00
56 PGv,LF,JCo(a&c),V:The
Yes Man 1,000.00
57 PGv,LF,JCo(a&c),V:Mr.Misfit 1,000.00
58 PGv,LF,JCo(a&c),E:The
Human Bomb 1,000.00
59 PGv,LF,JCo(a&c),A:Mr.
Happiness 1,000.00
60 PGv,LF,JCo(a&c) 500.00
61 PGv,LF,JCo(a&c) 1,000.00
62 PGv,LF,JCo(a&c) 1,000.00
63 PGv,LF,JCo(a&c),V:The
Crab 1,000.00
64 PGv,LF,HK,JCo(a&c) 1,000.00
65 PGv,LF,JCo(a&c) 1,000.00
66 PGv,LF,JCo(a&c) Love
Can Mean Trouble 1,000.00
67 LF,JCo(a&c),
V:The Gag Man 1,000.00
68 LF,JCo(a&c),V:Strecho 1,000.00
69 LF,JCo(a&c),V:Strecho 1,000.00
70 LF,JCo(a&c) 1,000.00
71 LF,JCo(a&c) 600.00
72 LF,JCo(a&c),V:Mr.Cat 600.00
73 LF,JCo(a&c) 600.00
74 LF,JCo(a&c),V:Prof.Dimwit . . 600.00
75 LF,JCo(a&c) 600.00
76 LF,JCo(a&c),V:Mr.Morbid . . . 600.00
77 LF,JCo(a&c),V:Skull Face
& Eloc 600.00
78 LF,JCo(a&c),A Hot Time In
Dreamland 600.00
79 LF,JCo(a&c),V:Eaglebeak 600.00
80 LF,JCo(a&c),V:Penetro 600.00
81 LF,JCo(a&c),V:A Gorilla 600.00
82 LF,JCo(a&c) 600.00
83 LF,JCo(a&c) 600.00
84 LF,JCo(a&c) 600.00
85 LF,JCo(a&c),V:Lucky 7 . . . . . 600.00
86 LF,JCo(a&c),V:The Baker 600.00
87 LF,JCo(a&c) 600.00
88 LF,JCo(a&c),V:The Seen 600.00
89 JCo(a&c),V:The Vanishers . . . 550.00
90 JCo(a&c),V:Capt.Rivers . . . 550.00
91 JCo(a&c),The Forest Primeval 600.00
92 LF,JCo(a&c),V:Closets
Kennedy 600.00
93 JCo(a&c),V:The Twinning
Terror 500.00
94 JCo(a&c),WE 800.00
95 JCo(a&c),WE,V:Scowls 800.00
96 JCo(a&c),WE,V:Black Widow . 800.00
97 JCo(a&c),WE,V:The Mime . . . 800.00
98 JCo(a&c),WE 800.00
99 JCo(a&c),WE 800.00
100 JCo(a&c) 1,000.00
101 JCo(a&c) 1,000.00
102 JCo(a&c),E:Plastic Man . . . 1,000.00
103 JCo,LF,B&I:Ken Shannon;
Bondage(c) 550.00
104 The Handsome of Homocide 400.00
105 Invisible Hands of Murder . . . 400.00
106 Museum of Murder 400.00
107 Man with the Shrunken
Head 400.00
108 The Headless Horse Player . 400.00

GOLDEN AGE

---

109 LF,Bondage(c),Blood on the
   Chinese Fan 400.00
110 Murder with a Bang. 400.00
111 Diana, Homocidal Huntress . 400.00
112 RC,The Corpse on the
   Sidewalk 450.00
113 RC(a&c), The Dead Man
   with the Size 13 Shoe 450.00
114 The Terrifying Secret of
   the Black Bear. 400.00
115 Don't Let Them Kill Me 400.00
116 Stage Was Set For Murder . . 400.00
117 Bullet Riddled Bookkeeper . . 400.00
118 Case of the Absent Corpse. . 400.00
119 A Fast & Bloody Buck 400.00
120 Death & The Derelict 400.00
121 Curse of the Clawed Killer . . 400.00
122 The Lonely Hearts Killer 400.00
123 Death Came Screaming 400.00
124 Masin Murder 400.00
125 Bondage(c),The Killer of
   King Arthur's Court 450.00
126 Hit & Run Murders 400.00
127 Oct'53,Death Drivers 400.00

POLICE LINE-UP
**Avon Periodicals/
Realistic Comics, Aug., 1951**
1 WW,P(c). 500.00
2 P(c),Drugs 400.00
3 JKu,EK,P(c). 250.00
4 July, '52;EK 250.00

POLICE TRAP
Mainline, Sept., 1954
1 S&K(c) 400.00
2 S&K(c) 225.00
3 S&K(c) 225.00
4 S&K(c) 225.00
Charlton Comics, July, 1955
5 S&K,S&K(c). 300.00
6 S&K,S&K(c). 300.00
Becomes:

PUBLIC DEFENDER
IN ACTION
Charlton Comics, March, 1956
7 . . . . 150.00
8 and 9 . . . . @100.00
10 thru 12, ... @100.00

POPEYE
Dell Publishing Co., 1948
1 . . . . 500.00
2 . . . . 250.00
3 'Welcome to Ghost Island'. . . . 225.00
4 thru 10 . . . . @225.00
11 . . . . 200.00
12 . . . . 200.00
13 . . . . 200.00
14 thru 20. . . . . @200.00
21 thru 30. . . . . @150.00
31 thru 40 . . . . @135.00
41 thru 45. . . . . @125.00
46 O:Swee' Pea. 150.00
47 thru 50. . . . . @125.00
51 thru 65. . . . . @100.00

POPULAR COMICS
**Dell Publishing Co.,
Feb., 1936**
1 Dick Tracy, Little Orphan
   Annie 9,000.00
2 Terry Pirates 4,000.00
3 Terry,Annie,Dick Tracy 3,000.00
4 . . . . 2,000.00
5 B:Tom Mix 2,000.00
6 I:Scribbu 1,800.00
7 . . . . 1,500.00

Popular Comics #50
© Dell Publishing Co.

8 Scribbu & Reg Fellers. 1,500.00
9 . . . . 1,500.00
10 Terry,Annie,Tracy 1,500.00
11 Terry,Annie,Tracy 1,000.00
12 Christmas(c). 1,000.00
13 Terry,Annie,Tracy 1,000.00
14 Terry,Annie,Tracy 1,000.00
15 Terry,Annie,Tracy 1,000.00
16 Terry,Annie,Tracy 1,000.00
17 Terry,Annie,Tracy 1,000.00
18 Terry,Annie,Tracy 1,000.00
19 Terry,Annie,Tracy 1,000.00
20 Terry,Annie,Tracy 1,000.00
21 Terry,Annie,Tracy 750.00
22 Terry,Annie,Tracy 750.00
23 Terry,Annie,Tracy 750.00
24 Terry,Annie,Tracy 750.00
25 Terry,Annie,Tracy 750.00
26 Terry,Annie,Tracy 750.00
27 E:Terry,Annie,Tracy. 750.00
28 A:Gene Autry. 600.00
29 . . . . 600.00
30 . . . . 600.00
31 A:Jim McCoy. 650.00
32 A:Jim McCoy. 650.00
33 . . . . 650.00
34 . . . . 650.00
35 Christmas(c),Tex Ritter 650.00
36 . . . . 650.00
37 . . . . 650.00
38 B:Gang Busters 650.00
39 . . . . 550.00
40 . . . . 550.00
41 . . . . 550.00
42 . . . . 550.00
43 F:Gang Busters. 550.00
44 . . . . 450.00
45 Tarzan(c). 450.00
46 O:Martan the Marvel Man. . . . 525.00
47 F:Martan the Marvel Man 400.00
48 F:Martan the Marvel Man 400.00
49 F:Martan the Marvel Man 400.00
50 . . . . 400.00
51 B&O:Voice. 400.00
52 A:Voice 400.00
53 F:The Voice. 400.00
54 F:Gang Busters,A:Voice 400.00
55 F:Gang Busters. 400.00
56 F:Gang Busters. 400.00
57 F:The Marvel Man. 400.00
58 F:The Marvel Man. 400.00
59 F:The Marvel Man. 400.00
60 O:Prof. Supermind 400.00
61 Prof. Supermind & Son. 300.00
62 Supermind & Son 300.00
63 B:Smilin' Jack 300.00
64 Smilin'Jack,Supermind 300.00

65 Professor Supermind 300.00
66 . . . . 300.00
67 Gasoline Alley. 300.00
68 F:Smilin' Jack 300.00
69 F:Smilin' Jack 300.00
70 F:Smilin' Jack 300.00
71 F:Smilin' Jack 300.00
72 B:Owl,Terry & the Pirates . . . 500.00
73 F:Terry and the Pirates 350.00
74 F:Smilin' Jack 350.00
75 F:Smilin'Jack,A:Owl 350.00
76 Captain Midnight. 500.00
77 Captain Midnight. 500.00
78 Captain Midnight. 500.00
79 A:Owl. 325.00
80 F:Smilin' Jack,A:Owl 325.00
81 F: Terry&thePirates,A:Owl . . . 325.00
82 F:Smilin' Jack,A:Owl 325.00
83 F:Smilin' Jack,A:Owl 325.00
84 F:Smilin' Jack,A:Owl 325.00
85 F:ThreeLittleGremlins,A:Owl. . 325.00
86 F:Three Little Gremlins 225.00
87 F:Smilin' Jack 225.00
88 F:Smilin' Jack 225.00
89 F:Smokey Stover 225.00
90 F:Terry and the Pirates 225.00
91 F:Smokey Stover 225.00
92 F:Terry and the Pirates 225.00
93 F:Smilin' Jack 225.00
94 F:Terry and the Pirates 225.00
95 F:Smilin' Jack 225.00
96 F:Gang Busters. 225.00
97 F:Smilin' Jack 225.00
98 B:Felix Cat 250.00
99 F:Bang Busters. 225.00
100 . . . . 250.00
101 thru 141 . . . . @175.00
142 E:Terry & the Pirates. 125.00
143 . . . . 125.00
144 . . . . 125.00
145 F:Harold Teen 125.00

POWER COMICS
Holyoke/Narrative Publ., 1944
1 LbC(c). 2,200.00
2 B:Dr.Mephisto,Hitler(c) 2,300.00
3 LbC(c) 2,400.00
4 LbC(c) 2,200.00

PRIDE OF THE
YANKEES
Magazine Enterprises, 1949
1 N#,OW,Ph(c),The Life
   of Lou Gehrig 1,250.00

PRISON BREAK
**Avon Periodicals/Realistic,
Sept., 1951**
1 WW(c),WW 600.00
2 WW(c),WW,JKu 400.00
3 JD,JO. 350.00
4 EK 275.00
5 EK,CI 275.00

PRIZE COMICS
**Feature Publications
(Prize Publ.), March, 1940**
1 O&B:Power Nelson,Jupiter.
   B:Ted O'Neil,Jaxon of
   the Jungle,Bucky Brady,
   Storm Curtis, Rocket(c) . . . 6,000.00
2 B:The Owl. 3,000.00
3 Power Nelson(c). 2,700.00
4 Power Nelson(c). 2,700.00
5 A:Dr.Dekkar. 2,400.00
6 A:Dr.Dekkar. 2,400.00
7 S&K,DBr,JK(c),O&B DR Frost,
   Frankenstein,B:GreenLama,
   Capt Gallant,Voodini
   Twist Turner 4,500.00

8 S&K,DBr 2,600.00
9 S&K,DBr,Black Owl(c) 2,500.00
10 DBr,Black Owl(c) 2,000.00
11 DBr,O:Bulldog Denny 1,800.00
12 DBr 1,800.00
13 DBr,O&B:Yank and
    Doodle,Bondage(c). 2,000.00
14 DBr,Black Owl(c) 1,800.00
15 DBr,Black Owl(c) 1,800.00
16 DBr,JaB,B:Spike Mason. . . . 1,800.00
17 DBr,Black Owl(c) 1,800.00
18 DBr,Black Owl(c) 1,800.00
19 DBr,Yank&Doodle(c) 1,800.00
20 DBr,Yank&Doodle(c) 1,800.00
21 DBr,JaB(c),Yank&Doodle(c). 1,500.00
22 DBr,Yank&Doodle(c) 1,500.00
23 DBr,Uncle Sam(c) 1,500.00
24 DBr,Abe Lincoln(c). 1,500.00
25 DBr,JaB,Yank&Doodle(c). . . 1,500.00
26 DBr,JaB,JaB(c),Liberty
    Bell(c) 1,500.00
27 DBr,Yank&Doodle(c) 1,000.00
28 DBr,Yank&Doodle(c). 900.00
29 DBr,JaB(c)Yank&Doodle(c). . . 900.00
30 DBr,Yank&Doodle(c). 1,000.00
31 DBr,Yank&Doodle(c). 900.00
32 DBr,Yank&Doodle(c). 900.00
33 DBr,Bondage(c),Yank
    & Doodle 1,000.00
34 DBr,O:Airmale;New
    Black Owl 1,000.00
35 DBr,B:Flying Fist & Bingo 750.00
36 DBr,Yank&Doodle(c) 750.00
37 DBr,I:Stampy,Hitler(c) 800.00
38 DBr,B.Owl,Yank&Doodle(c) . . 750.00
39 DBr,B.Owl,Yank&Doodle(c) . . 750.00
40 DBr,B.Owl,Yank&Doodle(c) . . 750.00
41 DBr,B.Owl,Yank&Doodle(c) . . 750.00
42 DBr,B.Owl,Yank&Doodle(c) . . 500.00
43 DBr,B.Owl,Yank&Doodle(c) . . 500.00
44 DBr, B&I:Boom Boom
    Brannigan 500.00
45 DBr 500.00
46 DBr 500.00
47 DBr 500.00
48 DBr,B:Prince Ra;Bondage(c) . 600.00
49 DBr,Boom Boom(c). 500.00
50 DBr,Frankenstein(c) 500.00
51 DBr 500.00
52 DBr, B:Sir Prize. 500.00
53 DBr, The Man Who Could
    Read Features. 500.00
54 DBr 500.00
55 DBr,Yank&Doodle(c). 500.00
56 DBr,Boom Boom (c) 500.00
57 DBr,Santa Claus(c). 500.00
58 DBr,The Poisoned Punch 500.00
59 DBr,Boom Boom(c). 500.00
60 DBr,Sir Prise(c). 500.00
61 DBr,The Man wih the
    Fighting Feet 500.00
62 DBr,Hck(c),Yank&Doodle(c) . . 500.00
63 DBr,S&K,S&K(c),Boom
    Boom(c). 550.00
64 DBr,Blackowl Retires 400.00
65 DBr,DBr(c),Frankenstein. 400.00
66 DBr,DBr(c),Frankenstein. 400.00
67 DBr,B:Brothers in Crime 400.00
68 DBr,RP(c) 400.00
Becomes:

PRIZE COMICS
WESTERN

Feature Publ., April–May, 1948
69 ACa(c),B:Dusty Ballew 175.00
70 ACa(c). 150.00
71 ACa(c). 150.00
72 ACa(c),JSe 150.00
73 ACa(c). 150.00
74 ACa(c). 150.00
75 JSe,S&K(c),6 Gun Showdown
    at Rattlesnake Gulch. 160.00

Prize Comics Western #99
© *Prize Publications*

76 Ph(c),Randolph Scott 175.00
77 Ph(c),JSe,Streets of
    Laredo,movie. 160.00
78 Ph(c),JSe,HK,Bullet
    Code, movie 250.00
79 Ph(c),JSe,Stage to
    China, movie 250.00
80 Ph(c),Gunsmoke Justice. 175.00
81 Ph(c),The Man Who Shot
    Billy The Kid 175.00
82 Ph(c),MBi,JSe&BE,Death
    Draws a Circle. 175.00
83 JSe,S&K(c) 150.00
84 JSe 125.00
85 JSe,B:American Eagle 325.00
86 JSe 150.00
87 JSe&BE. 150.00
88 JSe&BE. 150.00
89 JSe&BE. 150.00
90 JSe&Be. 150.00
91 JSe&BE.,JSe&BE(c) 150.00
92 JSe,JSe&BE(c) 150.00
93 JSe,JSe&BE(c). 150.00
94 JSe&BE.,JSe&BE(c) 150.00
95 JSe,JSe&BE(c) 150.00
96 JSe,JSe&BF.,JSe&BE(c). . . . 150.00
97 JSe,JSe&BE.,JSe&BE(c) 150.00
98 JSe&BE.,JSe&BE(c) 150.00
99 JSe&BE.,JSe&BE(c) 150.00
100 JSe,JSe(c) 175.00
101 JSe 150.00
102 JSe 150.00
103 JSe 150.00
104 JSe 150.00
105 JSe 150.00
106 JSe 100.00
107 JSe 100.00
108 JSe 110.00
109 JSe&AW 125.00
110 JSe&BE. 125.00
111 JSe&BE 125.00
112 . . . . 100.00
113 AW&JSe 125.00
114 MMe,B:The Drifter 100.00
115 MMe 100.00
116 MMe 100.00
117 MMe 100.00
118 MMe,E:The Drifter. 100.00
119 Nov/Dec'56 . . . . 100.00

PRIZE MYSTERY
Key Publications, 1955
1 . . . . 125.00
2 and 3 . . . . @100.00

PSYCHOANALYSIS
E.C. Comics,
March–April, 1955
1 JKa,JKa(c) 350.00
2 JKa,JKa(c) 250.00
3 JKa,JKa(c) 225.00
4 JKa,JKa(c) Sept.–Oct., 1955 . . 225.00

PUBLIC DEFENDER
IN ACTION
See: POLICE TRAP

PUBLIC ENEMIES
D.S. Publishing Co., 1948
1 AMc 325.00
2 AMc 275.00
3 AMc 200.00
4 AMc 200.00
5 AMc 200.00
6 AMc 175.00
7 AMc,Eye Injury. 200.00
8 . . . . 175.00
9 . . . . 175.00

PUNCH AND JUDY
COMICS
Hillman Periodicals, 1944
1 (fa) 300.00
2 . . . . 250.00
3 . . . . 200.00
4 thru 12 . . . . @175.00
2-1 . . . . 150.00
2-2 JK. 250.00
2-3 . . . . 150.00
2-4 . . . . 150.00
2-5 . . . . 150.00
2-6 . . . . 150.00
2-7 . . . . 150.00
2-8 . . . . 150.00
2-9 . . . . 150.00
2-10 JK. 250.00
2-11 JK 250.00
2-12 JK. 250.00
3-1 JK. 250.00
3-2 . . . . 200.00
3-3 . . . . 100.00
3-4 . . . . 100.00
3-5 . . . . 100.00
3-6 . . . . 100.00
3-7 . . . . 100.00
3-8 . . . . 100.00
3-9 . . . . 100.00

PUNCH COMICS
Harry 'A' Chesler, Dec., 1941
1 B:Mr.E,The Sky Chief,Hale
    the Magician,Kitty Kelly . . . 3,000.00
2 A:Capt.Glory 2,400.00
3-8 Do Not Exist
9 B:Rocket Man & Rocket
    girl,Master Ken 2,400.00
10 JCo,A:Sky Chief. 1,700.00
11 JCo,O:Master Key,A:Little
    Nemo 1,700.00
12 A:Rocket Boy,Capt.Glory . . . 4,000.00
13 Ric(c) 1,700.00
14 GT 1,200.00
15 FSm(c) 1,200.00
16 . . . . 1,200.00
17 . . . . 1,200.00
18 FSm(c),Bondage(c),Drug. . . 1,500.00
19 FSm(c). 1,200.00
20 Women semi-nude(c) 1,800.00
21 Drug 1,200.00
22 I:Baxter,Little Nemo 700.00
23 A:Little Nemo 700.00

GOLDEN AGE

PUPPET COMICS
Dougherty, Co., Spring, 1946
1 Funny Animal 150.00
2 . . . . 125.00

PURPLE CLAW, THE
**Minoan Publishing Co./
Toby Press, Jan., 1953**
1 O:Purple Claw 400.00
2 and 3 . . . . @300.00

QUEEN OF THE WEST,
DALE EVANS
**Dell Publishing Co.,
July, 1953**
(1) see Dell Four Color #479
(1) see Dell Four Color #528
3 ATh, Ph(c) all 135.00
4 ATh,RsM. 110.00
5 RsM. 100.00
6 RsM 100.00
7 RsM 100.00
8 RsM 100.00
9 RsM 100.00
10 RsM. 100.00
11 . . . . 75.00
12 RsM. 85.00
13 RsM. 85.00
14 RsM. 85.00
15 RsM. 85.00
16 RsM. 85.00
17 RsM. 85.00
18 RsM. 85.00
19 . . . . 75.00
20 RsM. 85.00
21 . . . . 75.00
22 RsM. 85.00

Racket Squad in Action#3
© Charlton Comics

RACKET SQUAD
IN ACTION
**Capitol Stories/
Charlton Comics,
May–June, 1952**
1 Carnival(c) 350.00
2 . . . . 175.00
3 Roulette 175.00
4 FFr(c) 250.00
5 Just off the Boat 300.00
6 The Kidnap Racket 200.00
7 . . . . 150.00
8 . . . . 150.00
9 2 Fisted fix 150.00

---

10 Explosion Blast (c) 250.00
11 SD(a&c),Racing(c) 375.00
12 JoS,SD(c),Explosion(c). 900.00
13 JoS(c),The Notorious Modelling
　　Agency Racket,Acid 150.00
14 DG(c),Drug 200.00
15 Photo Extortion Racket. 150.00
16 thru 28 . . . . @150.00
29 March, 1958 . . . . 150.00

RAGGEDY ANN
AND ANDY
Dell Publishing Co., 1946
1 Billy & Bonnie Bee. 600.00
2 . . . . 350.00
3 DNo,B:Egbert Elephant 350.00
4 DNo,WK 400.00
5 DNo 300.00
6 DNo 300.00
7 Little Black Sambo 300.00
8 . . . . 300.00
9 . . . . 300.00
10 . . . . 300.00
11 thru 20 . . . . @250.00
21 Alice in Wonderland 300.00
22 thru 27 . . . . @200.00
28 WK 225.00
29 thru 39 . . . . @200.00

RAGS RABBIT
Harvey Publications, 1957
11 . . . . 120.00
12 thru 18 . . . . @100.00

RALPH KINER
HOME RUN KING
Fawcett Publications, 1950
1 N#, Life Story of the
　　Famous Pittsburgh Slugger 1,000.00

RAMAR OF THE
JUNGLE
**Toby Press/
Charlton Comics, 1954**
1 Ph(c),TV Show. 275.00
2 Ph(c) 200.00
3 . . . . 200.00
4 . . . . 200.00
5 Sept '56 . . . . 200.00

RANGE BUSTERS
Charlton Comics, 1955
8 . . . . 150.00
9 & 10 . . . . @100.00

RANGE ROMANCES
**Comics Magazines
(Quality Comics), Dec., 1949**
1 PGv(a&c) 325.00
2 RC(a&c) 350.00
3 RC,Ph(c) 275.00
4 RC,Ph(c) 250.00
5 RC,PGv,Ph(c) 250.00

RANGERS OF FREEDOM
**Flying Stories, Inc.
(Fiction House), Oct., 1941**
1 I:Ranger Girl & Rangers
　　of Freedom;V:Super-Brain . 5,000.00
2 V:Super -Brain 1,800.00
3 Bondage(c) The Headsman
　　of Hate 1,500.00
4 Hawaiian Inferno. 1,200.00
5 RP,V:Super-Brain 1,200.00
6 RP,Bondage(c);Bugles
　　of the Damned 1,200.00
7 RP,Death to Tojo's Butchers . 1,000.00

Rangers #39
© Fiction House

Becomes:

RANGERS COMICS
Dec., 1942
8 RP,B:US Rangers 1,000.00
9 GT,BLb,Commando Steel
　　for Slant Eyes. 1,000.00
10 BLb,Bondage (c) 1,100.00
11 Raiders of the
　　Purple Death 900.00
12 A:Commando Rangers 900.00
13 Grl,B:Commando Ranger . . 1,000.00
14 Grl,Bondage(c) 1,100.00
15 GT,Grl,Bondage(c). 1,100.00
16 Grl,GT:Burma Raid 650.00
17 GT,GT,Bondage(c),Raiders
　　of the Red Dawn 1,000.00
18 GT 650.00
19 GE,BLb,GT,Bondage(c) 1,100.00
20 GT 500.00
21 GT,Bondage(c) 650.00
22 GT,B&O:Firehair 500.00
23 GT,BLb,B:Kazanda 450.00
24 Bondage(c). 450.00
25 Bondage(c). 450.00
26 Angels From Hell 400.00
27 Bondage(c). 500.00
28 BLb,E:Kazanda;B&O Tiger
　　Man 450.00
29 Bondage(c). 500.00
30 BLb,B:Crusoe Island. 450.00
31 BLb,Bondage(c) 400.00
32 BLb 400.00
33 BLb,Drug. 550.00
34 BLb 300.00
35 BLb,Bondage(c) 400.00
36 BLb,MB 300.00
37 BLb,Mb 350.00
38 BLb,MB,GE,Bondage(c) 400.00
39 BLb,GE 500.00
40 BLb,GE,BLb(c) 300.00
41 BLb,GE, L:Werewolf Hunter . 300.00
42 BLb,GE 300.00
43 BLb,GE 300.00
44 BLb,GE 300.00
45 BLb,GEl. 300.00
46 BLb,GE 300.00
47 BLb,JGr, Dr. Drew. 300.00
48 BLb,JGr, L:Glory Forces 300.00
49 BLb,JGr. 300.00
50 BLb,JGr,Bondage(c) 350.00
51 BLb,JGr. 300.00
52 BLb,JGr,Bondage(c) 350.00
53 BLb,JGr,Prisoners of
　　Devil Pass 250.00

GOLDEN AGE

54 JGr,When The Wild
   Commanches Ride 250.00
55 JGr,Massacre Guns at
   Pawnee Pass 250.00
56 JGr, Gun Smuggler of
   Apache Mesa 250.00
57 JGr,Redskins to the
   Rescue 225.00
58 JGr,Brides of the
   Buffalo Men 225.00
59 JGr,Plunder Portage 225.00
60 JGr, Buzzards of
   Bushwack Trail 225.00
61 BWh(c)Devil Smoke at
   Apache Basin 150.00
62 BWh(c)B:Cowboy Bob 150.00
63 BWh(c) 150.00
64 BWh(c)B:Suicide Smith 150.00
65 BWh(c):Wolves of the
   Overland Trail,Bondage(c) . . 165.00
66 BWh(c) 150.00
67 BWh(c)B:Space Rangers 150.00
68 BWh(c);Cargo for Coje 150.00
69 BWh(c);Great Red Death Ray 150.00

REAL CLUE
CRIME STORIES
See: CLUE COMICS

REAL FUNNIES
Nedor Publishing Co.,
Jan., 1943
1 (fa) 400.00
2 and 3 (fa) . . . . @200.00

REAL HEROES COMICS
Parents' Magazine Institiute,
Sept., 1941
1 HcK,Franklin Roosevelt 500.00
2 J, Edgar Hoover 300.00
3 General Wavell 250.00
4 Chiang Kai Shek, Churchill . . . 275.00
5 Stonewall Jackson 300.00
6 Lou Gehrig 400.00
7 Chennault and his
   Flying Tigers 300.00
8 Admiral Nimitz 300.00
9 The Panda Man 250.00
10 Carl Akeley-Jungle
   Adventurer 250.00
11 Wild Jack Howard 200.00
12 General Robert L
   Eichelberger 200.00
13 HcK,Victory at Climback 200.00
14 Pete Gray 200.00
15 Alexander Mackenzie 200.00
16 Balto of Nome Oct '46 . . . . . . 200.00

REAL LIFE STORY
OF FESS PARKER
Dell Publishing Co., 1955
1 . . . . 150.00

REAL LIFE COMICS
Visual Editions/Better/
Standard/Nedor, Sept., 1941
1 ASh(c),Lawrence of
   Arabia,Uncle Sam(c) 1,500.00
2 ASh(c),Liberty(c) 600.00
3 Adolph Hitler(c) 2,500.00
4 ASh(c)Robert Fulton,
   Charles DeGaulle, Old Glory. 400.00
5 ASh(c)Alexander the Great . . . 400.00
6 ASh(c)John Paul Jones,CDR . 350.00
7 ASh(c)Thomas Jefferson 350.00
8 Leonardo Da Vinci 350.00
9 US Coast Guard Issue 350.00
10 Sir Hubert Wilkens 350.00
11 ASh(c),Odyssey on a Raft. . . . 300.00

TRUE ADVENTURES OF THE WORLD'S GREATEST HEROES!

Real Life Comics #34
© Nedor

12 ASh(c),ImpossibleLeatherneck 300.00
13 ASh(c)The Eternal Yank 300.00
14 ASh(c),Sir Isaac Newton 300.00
15 ASh(c),William Tell 300.00
16 ASh(c),Marco Polo 300.00
17 ASh(c),Albert Einstein 350.00
18 ASh(c),Ponce De Leon 300.00
19 ASh(c),The Fighting Seabees. 300.00
20 ASh(c),Joseph Pulitzer 300.00
21 ASh(c),Admiral Farragut 250.00
22 ASh(c),Thomas Paine 250.00
23 ASh(c),Pedro Menendez 250.00
24 ASh(c),Babe Ruth 450.00
25 ASh(c),CQ,Marcus Whitman. . 250.00
26 ASh(c),CQ,Benvenuto Cellini . 250.00
27 ASh(c),CQ,A-Bomb Story 350.00
28 ASh(c),CQ,Robert Blake 250.00
29 ASh(c),CQ,Daniel DeFoe,
   A-Bomb 300.00
30 ASh(c),CQ,Baron Robert Clive 250.00
31 ASh(c),CQ,Anthony Wayne . . . 250.00
32 ASh(c),CQ,Frank Sinatra 275.00
33 ASh(c),CQ,Frederick Douglas 300.00
34 ASh(c),CQ,P Revere,J.Stewart 225.00
35 ASh(c),CQ,Rudyard Kipling . . 200.00
36 ASh(c),CQ,Story of the
   Automobile. 200.00
37 ASh(c),CQ,Francis Manion,
   Motion Picture, Bing Crosby . 200.00
38 ASh(c),CQ,Richard Henry
   Dana 150.00
39 ASh(c),CQ,Samuel FB Morse. 150.00
40 FGu,CQ,ASh(c),Hans Christian
   Anderson, Bob Feller 250.00
41 CQ,Abe Lincoln,Jimmy Foxx . 200.00
42 Joseph Conrad,Fred Allen . . . 150.00
43 Louis Braille,O.W.Holmes 100.00
44 Citizens of Tomorrow 100.00
45 ASh(c),FrancoisVillon,
   Olympics, Burl Ives 200.00
46 ASh(c),The Pony Express. . . . 200.00
47 ASh(c),Montezuma, Gershwin 200.00
48 ASh(c) 200.00
49 ASh(c),Gene Bearden,
   Baseball. 200.00
50 FF,ASh(c),Lewis & Clark. 600.00
51 GE,ASh(c),Sam Houston 450.00
52 GE,FF,ASh(c),JSe&BE
   Leif Erickson 650.00
53 GT,JSe&BE,Henry Wells &
   William Fargo 300.00
54 GT,Alexander Graham Bell . . 300.00
55 ASh(c),JSe&BE,The James
   Brothers 300.00
56 JSe&BE 300.00
57 JSe&BE 300.00

58 JSe&BE,Jim Reaves 350.00
59 FF,JSe&BE,Battle Orphan
   Sept '52 . . . . 300.00

REAL SPORTS COMICS
See: ALL SPORTS COMICS

REAL WESTERN HERO
See: WOW COMICS

REAL WEST ROMANCES
Crestwoood Publishing Co./
Prize Publ., April–May, 1949
1 S&K,Ph(c) 300.00
2 Ph(c),Spanking 150.00
3 JSe,BE,Ph(c) 150.00
4 S&K,JSe,BE,Ph(c) 250.00
5 S&K,MMe,JSe,Audie
   Murphy Ph(c) 225.00
6 S&K,JSe,BE,Ph(c) 150.00

RECORD BOOK OF
FAMOUS POLICE CASES
St. John Publishing Co., 1949
1 N#,JKu,MB(c) 500.00

RED ARROW
P.L. Publishing Co.,
May, 1951
1 Bondage(c) 550.00
2 . . . . 250.00
3 P(c) 250.00

RED BAND COMICS
Enwil Associates,
Nov., 1944
1 The Bogeyman 500.00
2 O:Bogeyman,same(c)as#1 . . . 350.00
3 A:Captain Wizard 300.00
4 May, '45,Repof#3,Same(c) . . . 300.00

RED CIRCLE COMICS
Enwil Associates
(Rural Home Public),
Jan., 1945
1 B:Red Riot,The Prankster 500.00
2 LSt,A:The Judge 400.00
3 LSt(A&c) 250.00
4 LSt(a&c) covers of #4
   stapled over other comics . . . 250.00

TRAIL BLAZERS
Street & Smith Publ., Jan., 1942
1 Wright Brothers 500.00
2 Benjamin Franklin,Dodgers . . . 400.00
3 Red Barber,Yankees 500.00
4 Famous War song 250.00
Becomes:

RED DRAGON COMICS
Jan., 1943
5 JaB(c),B&O:Red Rover:
   B:Capt.Jack Commando
   Rex King&Jet,Minute Man . 1,500.00
6 O:Red Dragon 3,000.00
7 The Curse of the
   Boneless Men. 2,400.00
8 China V:Japan 1,100.00
9 The Reducing Ray,Jan '44 . . 1,100.00
(2nd Series) Nov., 1947
1 B:Red Dragon 1,300.00
2 BP 900.00
3 BP,BP(c),I:Dr Neff 750.00
4 BP,BP(c) 1,100.00
5 MMe,BP,BP(c) 550.00
6 BP,BP(c) 550.00
7 MMe,BP,BP(c),May, 49 . . . . . 550.00

GOLDEN AGE *(vertical sidebar)*

RED MASK
See: TIM HOLT

RED RABBIT
Dearfield/
J. Charles Lave Publ. Co.,
Jan., 1941
1 (fa) 250.00
2 .... 150.00
3 .... 125.00
4 .... 125.00
5 .... 125.00
6 thru 10 .... @125.00
11 thru 22 .... @100.00

RED RYDER COMICS
Hawley Publ./
Dell Publ. Co. 1940
1 .... 4,700.00
Becomes:

HI-SPOT COMICS
Hawley Publications, 1940
2 Alley Oop, Capt. Easy...... 1,700.00
Becomes:

RED RYDER COMICS
Hawley Publ./Dell
Publ. Co., 1941
3 Alley Oop, Capt. Easy...... 2,000.00
4 .... 900.00
5 .... 900.00
6 .... 900.00
7 .... 700.00
8 .... 700.00
9 .... 700.00
10 .... 700.00
11 thru 20 .... @500.00
21 thru 30 .... @500.00
31 thru 40 .... @500.00
41 thru 50 .... @250.00
51 thru 60 .... @200.00
61 thru 70 .... @200.00
71 thru 80 .... @200.00
80 thru 99 .... @100.00
100 .... 150.00
101 thru 151 .... @100.00
Giant #1 .... 100.00
Giant #2 .... 100.00

RED SEAL COMICS
See: SCOOP

REDSKIN
Youthful Magazines,
Sept., 1950
1 WJo,Redskin,Bondage(c) 400.00
2 Apache Dance of Death...... 125.00
3 WJo(c),Daniel Boone........ 100.00
4 WJo(c),Sitting Bull- Red Devil
  of the Black Hills 100.00
5 DW......................... 100.00
6 Geronimo- Terror of the
  Desert,Bondage........... 350.00
7 Firebrand of the Sioux....... 100.00
8 .... 100.00
9 .... 100.00
10 Dead Man's Magic 100.00
11 RP,DW..................... 100.00
12 Quanah Parker,Bondage(c) .. 300.00
Becomes:

FAMOUS WESTERN BADMEN
Dec., 1952
13 Redskin- Last of the
  Comanches 150.00
14 .... 100.00
15 The Dalton Boys Apr '52..... 100.00

REG'LAR FELLERS
Visual Editions (Standard), 1947
5 .... 100.00
6 .... 100.00

REMEMBER PEARL HARBOR
Street & Smith Publ., 1942
1 N# JaB,Battle of the
  Pacific,Uncle Sam(c)....... 700.00

RETURN OF THE OUTLAW
Minoan Publishing Co.,
Feb., 1953
1 Billy The Kid 150.00
2 .... 125.00
3 thru 11 .... @100.00

REVEALING ROMANCES
A.A. Wyn
(Ace Magazines), Sept., 1949
1 .... 135.00
2 .... 125.00
3 thru 6 .... @100.00

Rex Allen #13
© Ace Magazines

REX ALLEN COMICS
Dell Publishing Co.,
Feb., 1951
(1) *see Dell Four Color #316*
2 Western, Ph(c) all 200.00
3 thru 10 .... @150.00
11 thru 23 .... @125.00
24 ATh 135.00
25 thru 31 .... @125.00

REX DEXTER OF MARS
Fox Features Syndicate,
Autumn, 1940
1 DBr,DBr(c) Battle ofKooba .. 3,000.00

REX MORGAN, M.D.
Argo Publications, 1950
1 .... 150.00
2 .... 100.00

RIBTICKLER
Fox Features Syndicate, 1945
1 .... 200.00
2 .... 150.00
3 Cosmo Cat................. 125.00

4 thru 6 .... @100.00
7 Cosmo Cat................. 100.00
8 thru 9 .... @100.00

RICKY
Visual Editions (Standard
Comics), 1953
1 .... 100.00

THE RIDER
Four Star Comics
(Ajax-Farrell Publ.), 1957
1 Swift Arrow................ 150.00
2 thru 5 .... @100.00
Becomes:

FRONTIER TRAIL
Ajax-Farrell Publ., 1958
6 .... 100.00

RIN TIN TIN
Dell Publishing Co.,
Nov., 1952
(1) *see Dell Four Color #434*
(1) *see Dell Four Color #476*
(1) *see Dell Four Color #523*
4 thru 10 Ph(c) all .... @100.00
11 thru 20 .... @125.00

RIPLEY's BELIEVE IT OR NOT!
Harvey Publications, 1953–54
1 BP 150.00
2 Li'l Abner 125.00
3 .... 125.00
4 .... 125.00

RIVETS
Argo Publications, 1956
1 .... 125.00
2 .... 100.00
3 .... 100.00

ROBIN HOOD
Sussex Publ. Co (Magazine
Enterprises), 1955
1 FBe 200.00
2 FBe 150.00
3 FBe 150.00
4 FBe 150.00
5 FBe 150.00
6 FBe,BP 150.00
Becomes:

ADVENTURES OF ROBIN HOOD
Magazine Enterprises, 1957
7 BP, Richard Green Ph(c)..... 200.00
8 Richard Green Ph(c) 200.00

ROBIN HOOD AND HIS MERRY MEN
See: THIS MAGAZINE IS HAUNTED

ROBIN HOOD TALES
Quality Comics Group, 1956
1 MB........................ 400.00
2 MB........................ 375.00
3 MB........................ 375.00
4 MB........................ 375.00
5 MB........................ 375.00
6 MB........................ 375.00

See: DC Comics

Rocket Comics #1
© Hillman Periodicals

ROCKET COMICS
**Hillman Periodicals,
March, 1940**
1 O:Red Roberts;B:Rocket
Riley,Phantom Ranger,Steel
Shank,Buzzard Baynes,Lefty
Larson,The Defender,Man
with 1,000 Faces 4,500.00
2 . . . . 2,000.00
3 May, '40 E:All Features 2,500.00

ROCKET KELLY
**Fox Features Syndicate,
Autumn, 1945–Oct., Nov., 1946**
N# 400.00
1 . . . . 300.00
2 A:The Puppeteer 275.00
3 thru 6 . . . . @250.00

ROCKETMAN
**Ajax/Farrell Publications,
June, 1952**
1 Space Stories of the Future . . . 500.00

ROCKET SHIP X
**Fox Features Syndicate,
Sept., 1951**
1 . . . . 900.00
2 N# Variant of Original 500.00

ROCKY LANE WESTERN
**Fawcett/Charlton Comics,
May, 1949**
1 Ph(c)B:Rocky Lane,Slim
Pickins 1,400.00
2 Ph(c) 600.00
3 Ph(c) 500.00
4 Ph(c)CCB,Rail Riders
Rampage,F Capt Tootsie. . . . 500.00
5 Ph(c)The Missing
Stagecoaches 450.00
6 Ph(c)Ghost Town Showdown . 300.00
7 Ph(c)The Border Revolt. 350.00
8 Ph(c)The Sunset Feud 350.00
9 Ph(c)Hermit of the Hills 350.00
10 Ph(c)Badman's Reward 300.00
11 Ph(c)Fool's Gold Fiasco 250.00
12 Ph(c),CCB,Coyote Breed
F:Capt Tootsie,Giant 250.00
13 Ph(c),Giant 250.00
14 Ph(c) 200.00
15 Ph(c)B:Black Jacks
Hitching Post,Giant 225.00

16 Ph(c),Giant 200.00
17 Ph(c),Giant 200.00
18 Ph(c) 225.00
19 Ph(c),Giant 235.00
20 Ph(c)The Rodeo Rustler
E:Slim Pickens 235.00
21 Ph(c)B: Dee Dickens 200.00
22 Ph(c) 175.00
23 thru 30 . . . . @200.00
31 thru 40 . . . . @175.00
41 thru 55 . . . . @175.00
56 thru 87 . . . . @150.00

ROD CAMERON WESTERN
**Fawcett Publications,
Feb., 1950**
1 Ph(c) 750.00
2 Ph(c) 350.00
3 Ph(c),Seven Cities of Cipiola . 300.00
4 Ph(c),Rip-Roaring Wild West . 250.00
5 Ph(c),Six Gun Sabotage 250.00
6 Ph(c),Medicine Bead Murders 250.00
7 Ph(c),Wagon Train Of Death . 250.00
8 Ph(c),Bayou Badman 250.00
9 Ph(c),Rustlers Ruse 250.00
10 Ph(c),White Buffalo Trail 250.00
11 Ph(c),Lead Polson 225.00
12 Ph(c) 225.00
13 Ph(c) 225.00
14 Ph(c) 225.00
15 Ph(c) 225.00
16 thru 19 Ph(c) . . . . @225.00
20 Phc(c),Great Army Hoax. . . . 225.00

ROLY-POLY COMICS
Green Publishing Co., 1945
1 B:Red Rube&Steel Sterling . . 400.00
6 A:Blue Cycle 250.00
10 A:Red Rube 300.00
11 . . . . 250.00
12 Black Hood 250.00
13 . . . . 250.00
14 A:Black Hood, Decapitation . 450.00
15 A:Steel Fist;1946. . . . . 400.00

ROMANCE AND CONFESSION STORIES
St. John Publishing Co., 1949
1 MB(c),MB. 500.00

ROMANTIC WESTERN
**Fawcett Publications,
Winter, 1949**
1 Ph(c) 300.00
2 Ph(c),AW,AMc 325.00
3 Ph(c) 250.00

ROOKIE COP
Charlton, 1955
27 . . . . 150.00
28 . . . . 100.00
29 . . . . 100.00
30 . . . . 100.00
31 thru 33 . . . . @100.00

ROUNDUP
**D.S. Publishing Co.,
July–Aug., 1948**
1 HcK 250.00
2 Drug 175.00
3 . . . . 150.00
4 . . . . 150.00
5 Male Bondage 175.00

ROY CAMPANELLA, BASEBALL HERO
Fawcett Publications, 1950
N# Ph(c),Life Story of the
Battling Dodgers Catcher . . 1,000.00

ROY ROGERS COMICS
Dell Publishing Co., 1948
1 photo (c) 1,600.00
2 . . . . 500.00
3 . . . . 375.00
4 . . . . 375.00
5 . . . . 375.00
6 thru 10 . . . . @300.00
11 thru 18 . . . . @250.00
19 Chuck Wagon Charlie 225.00
20 Trigger. 225.00
21 thru 30 . . . . @225.00
31 thru 46 . . . . @300.00
47 thru 50 . . . . @125.00
51 thru 56 . . . . @110.00
57 Drug 125.00
58 Drug 135.00
59 thru 80 . . . . @125.00
81 thru 91 . . . . @100.00
Becomes:

ROY ROGERS AND TRIGGER
Aug., 1955
92 . . . . 100.00
93 . . . . 100.00
94 . . . . 100.00
95 . . . . 100.00
96 thru 99 . . . . @100.00
100 Trigger Returns 125.00
101 thru 118 . . . . @100.00
119 thru 125 ATn . . . . @150.00
126 thru 131 . . . . @120.00
132 Dale Evans 150.00
133 thru 144 RsM. . . . . @110.00
145 . . . . 150.00

ROY ROGER'S TRIGGER
**Dell Publishing Co.,
May, 1951**
(1) *see Dell Four Color #329*
2 Ph(c) 250.00
3 P(c) 100.00
4 P(c) 100.00
5 P(c) 100.00
6 thru 17 P(c) . . . . @100.00

RULAH, JUNGLE GODDESS
See: ZOOT COMICS

RUSTY, BOY DETECTIVE
**Good Comics/Lev
Gleason Publ., 1955**
1 . . . . 125.00
2 . . . . 100.00
3 . . . . 100.00
4 . . . . 100.00
5 . . . . 100.00

SAARI, THE JUNGLE GODDESS
**P.L. Publishing Co.,
Nov., 1951**
1 The Bantu Blood Curse 600.00

SABU, ELEPHANT BOY
**Fox Features Syndicate,
June, 1950**
1(30) WW,Ph(c) 350.00
2 JKa,Ph(c),Aug.'50 . . . . 250.00

GOLDEN AGE

HAPPY HOULIHANS
**Fables Publications
(E.C. Comics), Autumn, 1947**
1 O:Moon Girl 650.00
2 . . . . 350.00
Becomes:

SADDLE JUSTICE
Spring, 1948
3 HcK,JCr,AF 700.00
4 AF,JCr, Grl 600.00
5 AF,Grl, ... 500.00
6 AF,Grl 450.00
7 AF,Grl 450.00
8 AF,Grl, ... 500.00
Becomes:

SADDLE ROMANCES
Nov., 1949
9 Grl(c),Grl 600.00
10 AF(c),WW,Grl 575.00
11 AF(c),Grl 600.00

SAD SACK COMICS
**Harvey Publications,
Sept., 1949**
1 I:Little Dot 1,000.00
2 Flying Fool 500.00
3 . . . . 400.00
4 . . . . 300.00
5 . . . . 300.00
6 thru 10 . . . . @300.00
11 thru 21 . . . . @200.00
22 Back in the Army Again,
    The Specialist 250.00
23 thru 50 . . . . @150.00
51 thru 100 . . . . @100.00

SAINT, THE
**Avon Periodicals,
Aug., 1947**
1 JKa,JKa(c),Bondage(c) 1,500.00
2 . . . . 1,000.00
3 Rolled Stocking Leg(c). 800.00
4 MB(c) Longerie 800.00
5 Spanking Panel 900.00
6 B:Miss Fury 900.00
7 WJo(c),Detective Cases(c) . . . 700.00
8 P(c),Detective Cases(c) 750.00
9 EK(c),The Notorious
    Murder Mob 750.00
10 WW,P(c),V:The Communist
    Menace 700.00
11 P(c),Wanted For Robbery 500.00
12 P(c),The Blowpipe Murders
    March, 1952 . . . . 500.00

SAM HILL PRIVATE EYE
Close-Up Publications, 1950
1 The Double Trouble Caper . . . 200.00
2 . . . . 150.00
3 . . . . 125.00
4 Negligee panels. 200.00
5 . . . . 100.00
6 . . . . 100.00
7 . . . . 100.00

SAMSON
**Fox Features Syndicate,
Autumn, 1940**
1 BP,GT,A:Wing Turner 3,800.00
2 BP,A:Dr. Fung 1,400.00
3 JSh(c),A:Navy Jones 1,000.00
4 WE,B:Yarko 850.00
5 WE . . . . @750.00
6 WE,O:The Topper;Sept'41 . . . 750.00

SAMSON
**Ajax Farrell Publ
(Four Star), April, 1955**
12 The Electric Curtain 350.00
13 Assignment Danger 300.00
14 The Red Raider;Aug'55 . . . . . 300.00

SANDS OF THE
SOUTH PACIFIC
Toby Press, Jan., 1953
1 2-Fisted Romantic Adventure . 250.00

SANTA CLAUS FUNNIES
Dell Publishing Co., 1942
N# WK 650.00
2 WK 400.00

SANTA CLAUS PARADE
**Approved Comics (Ziff-Davis)/
St. John Publ., 1951**
N# 350.00
2 . . . . 275.00
3 . . . . 225.00

SANTA'S CHRISTMAS
COMICS
**Best Books (Standard
Comics), 1952**
N# Dizzy Duck 225.00

SCIENCE COMICS
**Fox Features Syndicate,
Feb., 1940**
1 GT,LF(c),O&B:Electro,Perisphere
    Payne,The Eagle,Navy Jones;
    B:Marga,Cosmic Carson,
    Dr. Doom; Bondage(c) . . 10,000.00
2 GT,LF(c) 6,000.00
3 GT,LF(c),Dynamo 5,000.00
4 JK,Cosmic Carson 5,000.00
5 Giant Comiscope Offer
    Eagle(c) 2,500.00
6 Dynamop(c) 2,500.00
7 Bondage(c),Dynamo 2,700.00
8 Sept., 1940 Eagle(c). 2,500.00

SCIENCE COMICS
**Humor Publications,
Jan., 1946**
1 RP(c),Story of the A-Bomb . . . 250.00
2 RP(c),How Museum Pieces
    Are Assembled 125.00
3 AF,RP(c),How Underwater
    Tunnels Are Made 175.00
4 RP(c),Behind the Scenes at
    A TV Broadcast 100.00
5 The Story of the World's
    Bridges; Sept., 1946 . . . . . 100.00

SCIENCE COMICS
**Ziff-Davis Publ. Co.,
May, 1946**
N# Used For A Mail Order
    Test Market 500.00

SCIENCE COMICS
**Export Publication Enterprises,
March, 1951**
1 How to resurrect a dead rat. . . 125.00

SCOOP COMICS
**Harry 'A' Chesler Jr.,
Nov., 1941**
1 I&B:Rocketman&Rocketgirl;B:Dan
    Hastings;O&B:Master Key . 2,000.00

*Scoop Comics #8
© Harry A Chesler, Jr.*

2 A:Rocketboy,Eye Injury. 2,100.00
3 Partial rep. of #2 . . . . 1,000.00
4 thru 7 do not exist
8 1945 . . . . 650.00
Becomes:

SNAP
Harry 'A' Chesler Jr., 1944
N# Humorous 175.00
Becomes:

KOMIK PAGES
Harry 'A' Chesler Jr., 1944
1(10) JK,Duke of Darkness 350.00
Becomes:

BULLS-EYE
Harry 'A' Chesler Jr., 1944
11 Green Knight, Skull (c) 550.00
Becomes:

KAYO
Harry 'A' Chesler Jr., 1945
12 Green Knight. 200.00
Becomes:

CARNIVAL
Harry 'A' Chesler Jr., 1945
(13) Guardineer 225.00
Becomes:

RED SEAL COMICS
**Harry 'A' Chesler, Jr./Superior,
Oct., 1945**
14 GT,Bondage(c),Black Dwarf 1,100.00
15 GT,Torture. 650.00
16 GT. 900.00
17 GT,Lady Satan,Sky Chief 700.00
18 Lady Satan,Sky Chief. 700.00
19 Lady Satan,Sky Chief 600.00
20 Lady Satan,Sky Chief 600.00
21 Lady Satan,Sky Chief. 550.00
22 Rocketman 450.00

SCOOTER COMICS
Rucker Publications, 1946
1 . . . . 200.00

SCOTLAND YARD
Charlton Comics, 1955
1 . . . . 165.00
2 thru 4 . . . . @125.00

GOLDEN AGE

SCREAM COMICS
**Humor Publ./Current Books
(Ace Magazines),
Autumn, 1944**

1	350.00
2	250.00
3 thru 15	@200.00
16 I:Lily Belle	225.00
17	200.00
18 Drug	400.00
19	200.00

Becomes:

ANDY COMICS
June, 1948

20 Teenage	150.00
21	150.00

Becomes:

ERNIE COMICS
Sept., 1948

22 Teenage	150.00
23 thru 25	@100.00

Becomes:

ALL LOVE ROMANCES
May, 1949

26 Ernie	125.00
27 LbC	250.00
28 thru 32	@100.00

(Capt. Silvers Log of...)
SEA HOUND, THE
Avon Periodicals, 1945

N# The Esmerelda's Treasure	250.00
2 Adventures in Brazil	200.00
3 Louie the Llama	150.00
4 In Greed & Vengence; Jan-Feb, 1946	150.00

SECRET MISSIONS
St. John Publishing Co., 1950

1 JKu.	250.00

SECRET MYSTERIES
See: CRIME MYSTERIES

SELECT DETECTIVE
**D.S. Publishing Co.,
Aug.–Sept., 1948**

1 MB,Exciting New Mystery Cases	400.00

*Select Detective #1
© D.S. Publishing*

2 MB,AMc,Dead Men	225.00
3 Face in theFrame;Dec-Jan'48	200.00

SENSATIONAL
POLICE CASES
Avon Periodicals, 1952

N# JKu,EK(c)	500.00
2	200.00
3	200.00
4	200.00

SERGEANT PRESTON
OF THE YUKON
Dell Publishing Co., Aug., 1951
(1 thru 4) *see Dell Four Color #344;
#373, 397, 419*

5 P(c)	125.00
6 Bondage, P(c)	175.00
7 thru 11 P(c)	125.00
12 P(c)	125.00
13 P(c),O:Sergeant Preston	150.00
14 thru 17 P(c)	@125.00
18 Yukon King,P(c)	150.00
19 thru 29 Ph(c)	@200.00

SEVEN SEAS COMICS
**Universal Phoenix Features/
Leader Publ., April, 1946**

1 MB,RWb(c),B:South Sea Girl, Captain Cutlass	1,400.00
2 MB,RWb(c)	1,200.00
3 MB,AF,MB(c)	1,100.00
4 MB,MB(c)	1,200.00
5 MB,MB(c),Hangman's Noose	1,100.00
6 MB,MB(c);1947	1,000.00

SHADOW COMICS
**Street & Smith Publ.,
March, 1940**

1-1 P(c),B:Shadow,Doc Savage, Bill Barnes,Nick Carter, Frank Merriwell,Iron Munro	8,000.00
1-2 P(c),B: The Avenger	3,000.00
1-3 P(c),A: Norgill the Magician	2,000.00
1-4 P(c),B:The Three Musketeers	1,500.00
1-5 P(c),E: Doc Savage	1,500.00
1-6 A: Captain Fury	1,300.00
1-7 O&B: The Wasp	1,400.00
1-8 A:Doc Savage	1,300.00
1-9 A:Norgill the Magician	1,300.00
1-10 O:Iron Ghost;B:The Dead End Kids	1,300.00
1-11 O:Hooded Wasp	1,300.00
1-12 Crime Does Not pay	1,200.00
2-1	1,200.00
2-2 Shadow Becomes Invisible	2,000.00
2-3 O&B:Supersnipe; F:Little Nemo	1,900.00
2-4 F:Little Nemo	1,200.00
2-5 V:The Ghost Faker	1,200.00
2-6 A:Blackstone the Magician	1,000.00
2-7 V:The White Dragon	1,000.00
2-8 A:Little Nemo	1,000.00
2-9 The Hand of Death	1,000.00
2-10 A:Beebo the WonderHorse	1,000.00
2-11 V:Devil Kyoti	1,000.00
2-12 V:Devil Kyoti	900.00
3-1 JaB(c),V:Devil Kyoti	900.00
3-2 Red Skeleton Life Story	900.00
3-3 V:Monstrodamus	900.00
3-4 V:Monstrodamus	900.00
3-5 V:Monstrodamus	900.00
3-6 V:Devil's of the Deep	900.00
3-7 V: Monstrodamus	900.00
3-8 E: The Wasp	900.00
3-9 The Stolen Lighthouse	900.00

*Shadow Comics Vol. 4 #9
© Street & Smith Publ.*

3-10 A:Doc Savage	900.00
3-11 P(c),V: Thade	900.00
3-12 V: Thade	900.00
4-1 Red Cross Appeal on (c)	800.00
4-2 V:The Brain of Nippon	800.00
4-3 Little Men in Space	800.00
4-4 ...Mystifies Berlin	800.00
4-5 ...Brings Terror to Tokio	800.00
4-6 V:The Tarantula	800.00
4-7 Crypt of the Seven Skulls	850.00
4-8 V:the Indigo Mob	800.00
4-9 Ghost Guarded Treasure of the Haunted Glen	800.00
4-10 V:The Hydra	800.00
4-11 V:The Seven Sinners	800.00
4-12 Club Curio	1,000.00
5-1 A:Flatty Foote	1,000.00
5-2 Bells of Doom	1,000.00
5-3 The Circle of Death	1,000.00
5-4 The Empty Safe Riddle	1,000.00
5-5 The Mighty Master Nomad	1,200.00
5-6 ...Fights Piracy Among the Golden Isles	750.00
5-7 V:The Talon	750.00
5-8 V:The Talon	750.00
5-9 V:The Talon	750.00
5-10 V:The Crime Master	750.00
5-11 The Clutch of the Talon	750.00
5-12 Most Dangerous Criminal	750.00
6-1 Double Z	600.00
6-2 Riddle of Prof.Mentalo	600.00
6-3 V:Judge Lawless	600.00
6-4 V:Dr. Zenith	600.00
6-5	600.00
6-6 ...Invades the Crucible of Death	600.00
6-7 Four Panel (c)	600.00
6-8 Crime Among the Aztecs	600.00
6-9 I:Shadow Jr.	650.00
6-10 Devil's Passage	600.00
6-11 The Black Pagoda	600.00
6-12 BP,BP(c),Atomic Bomb Secrets Stolen	650.00
7-1 The Yellow Band	650.00
7-2 A:Shadow Jr.	650.00
7-3 BP,BP(c),Crime Under the Border	800.00
7-4 BP,BP(c),One Tree Island, Atomic Bomb	900.00
7-5 A:Shadow Jr.	650.00
7-6 BP,BP(c),The Sacred Sword of Sanjorojo	800.00
7-7 Crime K.O.	650.00
7-8 ...Raids Crime Harbor	650.00
7-9 BP,BP(c),Kilroy Was Here	800.00

7-10 BP,BP(c),The Riddle of
the Flying Saucer 1,000.00
7-11 BP,BP(c),Crime
Doesn't Pay 800.00
7-12 BP,BP(c)Back From
the Grave 800.00
8-1 BP,BP(c),Curse of the Cat . . 800.00
8-2 BP,BP(c),Decay,Vermin &
Murder in the Bayou 800.00
8-3 BP,BP(c),The Spider Boy . . . 800.00
8-4 BP,BP(c),Death Rises
Out of the Sea 800.00
8-5 BP,BP(c),Jekyll-
Hyde Murders 800.00
8-6 Secret of Valhalla Hall . . . 800.00
8-7 BP,BP(c),Shadow in Danger 800.00
8-8 BP,BP(c),...Solves a
Twenty Year Old Crime 800.00
8-9 BP,BP(c),3-D Effect(c) 800.00
8-10 BP,BP(c),Up&Down(c) 800.00
8-11 BP,BP(c). 800.00
8-12 BP,BP(c),Arabs,Boat(c) 800.00
9-1 Airport(c) 800.00
9-2 BP,BP(c),Flying Cannon(c) . . 800.00
9-3 BP,BP(c),Shadow's Shadow . 800.00
9-4 BP,BP(c) 800.00
9-5 Death in the Stars;Aug'49 . . . 800.00

SHARP COMICS
H.C. Blackerby,
Winter, 1945
1 O:Planetarian(c) 550.00
2 O:The Pioneer 400.00

SHEENA, QUEEN OF
THE JUNGLE
Real Adventures
(Fiction House)
Spring, 1942–Winter, 1952
1 Blood Hunger 4,000.00
2 Black Orchid of Death 1,600.00
3 Harem Shackles 1,200.00
4 The Zebra Raiders 750.00
5 War of the Golden Apes 700.00
6 . . . . 625.00
7 They Claw By Night 600.00
8 The Congo Colossus 600.00
9 and 10 . . . . @550.00
11 Red Fangs of the Tree Tribe . . 550.00
12 . . . . 450.00
13 Veldt o/t Voo Doo Lions 450.00
14 The Hoo Doo Beasts of
Mozambique 450.00
15 . . . . 450.00
16 Black Ivory 450.00
17 Great Congo Treasure Trek . . 450.00
18 Doom of the Elephant Drum . . 450.00

SHERLOCK HOLMES
Charlton Comics, 1955
1 . . . . 500.00
2 . . . . 450.00

SHIELD-WIZARD
COMICS
MLJ Magazines,
Summer, 1940
1 IN,EA,O:Shield 8,500.00
2 IN,O:Shield;I:Roy 4,000.00
3 IN,Roy,Child Bondage(c) . . . 2,400.00
4 IN,Shield,Roy,Wizard 2,000.00
5 IN,B:Dusty-Boy Dectective,
Child Bondage 2,000.00
6 B:Roy the Super Boy,Child
Bondage 1,900.00
7 Shield(c),Roy Bondage(c) . . 2,000.00
8 IN,Bondage(c) 1,900.00
9 IN,Shield/Roy(c) 1,400.00
10 IN,Shield/Roy(c). 1,400.00

Shield-Wizard Comics #11
© MLJ Magazines

11 IN,Shield/Roy(c) 1,400.00
12 IN,Shield/Roy(c). 1,400.00
13 Bondage (c);Spring'44 . . . . . 1,500.00

SHIP AHOY
Spotlight Publishers,
Nov., 1944
1 LbC(c) 250.00

SHOCK DETECTIVE
CASE(S)
See: CRIMINALS ON
THE RUN

SHOCK ILLUSTRATED
E.C. Comics, 1955
1 Drugs 300.00
2 AW,GI,RC. 200.00
3 RC. 4,000.00

SHOCK SUSPENSTORIES
Tiny Tot Comics
(E.C. Comics),
Feb.–March, 1952
1 JDa,JKa,AF(c),ElectricChair . 2,500.00
2 WW,JDa,Grl,JKa,WW(c). . . . 1,800.00
3 WW,JDa,JKa,WW(c). 1,200.00
4 WW,JDa,JKa,WW(c) 1,200.00
5 WW,JDa,JKa,WW(c),
Hanging 1,400.00
6 WW,AF,JKa,WW(c),
Bondage(c) 1,500.00
7 JKa,WW,GE,AF(c),Face
Melting 1,500.00
8 JKa,AF,AW,GE,WW,AF(c) . . 1,100.00
9 JKa,AF,RC,WW,AF(c) 1,000.00
10 JKa,WW,RC,JKa(c),Drug . . . 1,000.00
11 JCr,JKa,WW,RC,JCr(c) 900.00
12 AF,JKa,WW,RC,AF(c)
Drug(c) 1,000.00
13 JKa,WW,FF,JKa(c). 1,200.00
14 JKa,WW,BK,WW(c) 900.00
15 JKa,WW,RC,JDa(c)
Strangulation 750.00
16 GE,RC,JKa,GE(c),Rape 750.00
17 GE,RC,JKa,GE(c) 600.00
18 GE,RC,JKa,GE(c);Jan'55 . . . . 600.00

SHOCKING MYSTERY
CASES
See: THRILLING CRIME
CASES

SILVER STREAK
COMICS
Your Guide/New Friday/
Comic House/Newsbrook
Publications/Lev Gleason,
Dec., 1939
1 JCo(a&c),I&B:The Claw,Red
Reeves Capt.Fearless;B:Mr.Mid-
night,Wasp;A:Spiritman . . 18,000.00
2 JSm,JCo,JSm(c) 6,500.00
3 JaB(c),I&O:Silver Streak;
B:Dickie Dean,Lance Hale,
Ace Powers,Bill Wayne,
Planet Patrol 5,500.00
4 JCo,JaB(c)B:Sky Wolf;
N:Silver Streak,I:Lance
Hale's Sidekick-Jackie 2,500.00
5 JCo(a&c),Dickie Dean
V:The Raging Flood 3,000.00
6 JCo,JaB,JCo(a&c),O&I:Daredevil
[Blue & Yellow Costume];
R:The Claw 24,000.00
7 JCo,N: Daredevil 15,000.00
8 JCo(a&c) 5,500.00
9 JCo,BoW(c) 3,000.00
10 BoW,BoW(c) 2,500.00
11 DRi(c) I:Mercury 2,000.00
12 DRi(c). 1,500.00
13 JaB,JaB(c),O:Thun-Dohr . . . 1,500.00
14 JaB,JaB(c),A:Nazi
Skull Men 1,500.00
15 JaB,DBr,JaB(c),
B:Bingham Boys 1,200.00
16 DBr,BoW(c),Hitler(c) 1,600.00
17 DBr,JaB(c),E:Daredevil 1,200.00
18 DBr,JaB(c),B:The Saint 1,100.00
19 DBr,EA 900.00
20 BW,BEv,EA 900.00
21 BW,BEv 900.00
Becomes:

CRIME DOES NOT PAY
June, 1942
22(23) CBi(c),The Mad Musician
& Tunes of Doom 3,800.00
23 CBi(c),John Dillinger-One
Man Underworld 1,900.00
24 CBi(c),The Mystery of the
Indian Dick 1,500.00
25 CBi(c),Dutch Shultz-King
of the Underworld 850.00
26 CBi(c),Lucky Luciano-The
Deadliest of Crime Rats 850.00
27 CBi(c),Pretty Boy Floyd 850.00
28 CBi(c). 850.00
29 CBi(c),Two-Gun Crowley-The
Bad Kid with the Itchy
Trigger Finger 825.00
30 CBi(c),"Monk"Eastman
V:Thompson's Mob 825.00
31 CBi(c) The Million Dollar
Bank Robbery 550.00
32 CBi(c),Seniorita of Sin 550.00
33 CBi(c),Meat Cleaver Murder . . 600.00
34 CBi(c),Elevator Shaft 550.00
35 CBi(c),Case o/t MissingToe . . 550.00
36 CBi(c) 500.00
37 CBi(c) 500.00
38 CBi(c) 500.00
39 FGu,CBi(c) 500.00
40 FGu,CBi(c) 550.00
41 FGu,RP,CBi(c),The Cocksure
Counterfeiter 400.00
42 FGu,RP,CBi(c) 450.00
43 FGu,RP,CBi(c)Electrocution . . 500.00
44 FGu,CBi(c),The Most Shot
At Gangster 250.00
45 FGu,CBi(c) 250.00
46 FGu,CBi(c),ChildKidnapping(c) 300.00
47 FGu,CBi(c),ElectricChair. 450.00
48 FGu,CBi(c) 250.00

Crime Does Not Pay #89
© Lev Gleason

49 FGu,CBi(c) 250.00
50 FGu,CBi(c) 250.00
51 FGu,GT,CBi(c),1st Monthly. . 225.00
52 FGu,GT,CBi(c) 225.00
53 FGu,CBi(c) 225.00
54 FGu,CBi(c) 225.00
55 FGu,CBi(c) 225.00
56 FGu,GT,CBi(c) 225.00
57 FGu,CBi(c) 225.00
58 FGu,CBi(c) 225.00
59 FGu,CBi(c) 225.00
60 FGu,CBi(c) 225.00
61 FGu,GT,CBi(c) 225.00
62 FGu,CBi(c),Bondage(c) 225.00
63 FGu,GT,CBi(c) 200.00
64 FGu,GT,CBi(c) 200.00
65 FGu,CBi(c) 200.00
66 FGu,GT,CBi(c) 200.00
67 FGu,GT,CBi(c) 200.00
68 FGu,CBi(c) 200.00
69 FGu,CBi(c) 200.00
70 FGu,CBi(c) 200.00
71 FGu,CBi(c) 175.00
72 FGu,CBi(c) 175.00
73 FGu,CBi(c) 175.00
74 FGu,CBi(c) 175.00
75 FGu,CBi(c) 175.00
76 FGu,CBi(c) 175.00
77 FGu,CBi(c),Electrified Safe. . . 200.00
78 FGu,CBi(c) 175.00
79 FGu. 175.00
80 FGu. 175.00
81 FGu. 175.00
82 FGu. 175.00
83 FGu. 175.00
84 FGu. 175.00
85 FGu. 175.00
86 FGu. 175.00
87 FGu,P(c),The Rock-A-Bye
   Baby Murder 175.00
88 FGu,P(c),Death Carries Torch 175.00
89 FGu,BF,BF P(c),The Escort
   Murder Case 175.00
90 FGu,BF P(c),The Alhambra
   Club Murders. 175.00
91 FGu,AMc,BF P(c),Death
   Watches The Clock 175.00
92 BF,FGu,BF P(c) 175.00
93 BF,FGu,AMc,BF P(c) 175.00
94 FGu,BF,BF P(c) 175.00
95 FGu,AMc,BF P(c) 175.00
96 BF,FGu,BF P(c),The Case of
   the Movie Star's Double 175.00
97 FGu,BF P(c) 175.00
98 BF,FGu,BF P(c),Bondage(c). . 200.00
99 BF,FGu,BF P(c) 175.00

100 FGu,BF,AMc,P(c),The Case
   of the Jittery Patient 175.00
101 FGu,BF,AMc,P(c) 125.00
102 FGu,BF,AMc,BF P(c) 125.00
103 FGu,BF,AMc,BF P(c) 125.00
104 thru 110 FGu. . . . . @125.00
111 thru 120 . . . . @125.00
121 thru 140 . . . . @100.00
141 JKu 100.00
142 JKu,CBi(c). 100.00
143 JKu,Comic Code. 100.00
144 I Helped Capture "Fat Face"
   George Klinerz 80.00
145 RP,Double Barrelled Menace . 80.00
146 BP,The Con & The Canary . . . 80.00
147 JKu,BP,A Long Shoe On the
   Highway;July, 1955 . . . . 175.00

SINGLE SERIES
**United Features Syndicate,
1938**

1 Captain & The Kids 1,300.00
2 Bronco Bill 700.00
3 Ella Cinders 500.00
4 Li'l Abner 1,100.00
5 Fritzi Ritz 300.00
6 Jim Hardy 550.00
7 Frankie Doodle 450.00
8 Peter Pat 450.00
9 Strange As it Seems 450.00
10 Little Mary Mixup. 450.00
11 Mr. & Mrs. Beans 450.00
12 Joe Jinx. 400.00
13 Looy Dot Dope 400.00
14 Billy Make Believe. 400.00
15 How It Began 450.00
16 Illustrated Gags. 275.00
17 Danny Dingle 325.00
18 Li'l Abner. 850.00
19 Broncho Bill. 600.00
20 Tarzan 1,600.00
21 Ella Cinders 450.00
22 Iron Vic 450.00
23 Tailspin Tommy 550.00
24 Alice In Wonderland 600.00
25 Abbie an' Slats 500.00
26 Little Mary Mixup. 450.00
27 Jim Hardy 450.00
28 Ella Cinders & Abbie AN'
   Slats 1942 . . . . 450.00

SIX GUN HEROES
Fawcett Publications, 1950

1 Rocky Lane,Hopalong Cassidy 650.00
2 . . . . 350.00
3 . . . . 250.00
4 . . . . 250.00
5 Lash Larue. 250.00
6 . . . . 175.00
7 . . . . 175.00
8 . . . . 175.00
9 . . . . 175.00
10 . . . . 175.00
11 thru 23 . . . . @125.00

Charlton Comics, 1954

24 . . . . 225.00
25 . . . . 125.00
26 thru 50 . . . . @100.00
51 thru 70 . . . . @100.00

SKELETON HAND
**American Comics Group,
Sept.–Oct., 1952**

1 . . . . 600.00
2 The Were-Serpent of Karnak. . 400.00
3 Waters of Doom 325.00
4 Black Dust 325.00
5 The Rise & Fall of the
   Bogey Man 325.00
6 July–Aug., 1953 . . . . 325.00

SKIPPY'S OWN BOOK OF COMICS
M.C. Gaines, 1934

N# 6,000.00

SKY BLAZERS
**Hawley Publications,
Sept., 1940**

1 Flying Aces,Sky Pirates. 900.00
2 Nov., 1940 . . . . 600.00

SKYMAN
Columbia Comics Group, 1941

1 OW,OW(c),O:Skyman,Face . 1,700.00
2 OW,OW(c),Yankee Doodle . . . 900.00
3 OW,OW(c) 500.00
4 OW,OW(c),Statue of
   Liberty(c) 1948 . . . . 500.00

SKY PILOT
**Ziff-Davis Publishing Co.,
1950**

10 NS, P(c),Lumber Pirates. 200.00
11 NS, P(c),The 2,00 Foot Drop;
   April–May, 1951. . . . . 175.00

SKY ROCKET
**Home Guide Publ.
(Harry 'A' Chesler), 1944**

1 Alias the Dragon,Skyrocket . . . 400.00

SKY SHERIFF
**D.S. Publishing,
Summer, 1948**

1 I:Breeze Lawson & the Prowl
   Plane Patrol 150.00

SLAM BANG COMICS
**Fawcett Publications,
Jan., 1940**

1 D:Diamond Jack,Mark Swift,
   Loo Granger,Jungle King   5,000.00
2 F:Jim Dolan Two-Fisted
   Crime Buster 2,000.00
3 A: Eric the Talking Lion . . . 3,500.00
4 F: Hurricane Hansen-Sea
   Adventurer 2,000.00
5 . . . . 2,000.00
6 I: Zoro the Mystery Man;
   Bondage(c) 2,000.00
7 Bondage(c);Sept., 1940 . . . . 2,000.00

Slambang Comics #3
© Fawcett Publications

GOLDEN AGE

GOLDEN AGE

SLAPSTICK COMICS
Comic Magazine Distrib., Inc., 1945
N# Humorous Parody 300.00

SLASH-D DOUBLECROSS
St. John Publishing Co., 1950
N# 300.00

SLAVE GIRL COMICS
Avon Periodicals, Feb., 1949
1 EL..................... 1,500.00
2 EL..................... 1,000.00

SLICK CHICK COMICS
Leader Enterprises, Inc., 1947
1 Teen-Aged Humor 150.00
2 Teen-Aged Humor 100.00
3 1947.................... 100.00

SLUGGER
Lev Gleason Publications, 1956
1 CBi(c).................. 100.00

SMASH COMICS
Comics Magazine, Inc. (Quality Comics Group), Aug., 1939
1 WE,O&B:Hugh Hazard, Bozo the Robot,Black X, Invisible Justice: B:Wings Wendall, Chic Carter 6,000.00
2 WE,A:Lone Star Rider 1,800.00
3 WE,B:Captain Cook, John Law 1,100.00
4 WE,PGv,B:Flash Fulton 1,000.00
5 WE,PGv,Bozo Robot 1,000.00
6 WE,PGv,GFx,Black X(c).... 1,000.00
7 WE,PGv,GFx,Wings Wendell(c) 900.00
8 WE,PGv,GFx,Bozo Robot 900.00
9 WE,PGv,GFx,Black X(c) 900.00
10 WE,PGv,GFx,Bozo Robot(c) . 900.00
11 WE,PGv,GFx,BP,Black X(c) . 900.00
12 WE,PGv,GFx,BP,Bozo(c) 900.00
13 WE,PGv,GFx,AB,BP,B:Mango, Purple Trio,BlackX(c)....... 900.00
14 BP,LF,AB,PGv,I:The Ray .. 4,500.00
15 BP,LF,AB,PGv,The Ram(c) . 2,000.00
16 BP,LF,AB,PGv,Bozo(c)..... 1,900.00
17 BP,LF,AB,PGv,JCo, The Ram(c) 1,900.00

Smash Comics#34
© Quality Comics Group

18 BP,LF,AB,JCo,PGv, B&O:Midnight 2,500.00
19 BP,LF,AB,JCo,PGv,Bozo(c) . 1,400.00
20 BP,LF,AB,JCo,PGv, The Ram(c) 1,400.00
21 BP,LF,AB,JCo,PGv. 1,400.00
22 BP,LF,AB,JCo,PGv, B:The Jester............ 1,400.00
23 BP,AB,JCo,RC,PGv, The Ram(c) 1,300.00
24 BP,AB,JCo,RC,PGv,A:Sword, E:ChicCarter, N:WingsWendall......... 1,300.00
25 AB,JCo,RC,PGv,O:Wildfire . 1,300.00
26 AB,JCo,RC,PGv,Bozo(c) ... 1,200.00
27 AB,JCo,RC,PGv, The Ram(c) 1,200.00
28 AB,JCo,RC,PGv, 1st Midnight (c) 1,200.00
29 AB,JCo,Rc,PGv,B; Midnight(c) 1,200.00
30 AB,JCo,PGv........... 1,200.00
31 AB,JCo,PGv........... 1,000.00
32 AB,JCo,PGv........... 1,000.00
33 AB,JCo,PGv,O:Marksman .. 1,100.00
34 AB,JCo,PGv........... 1,000.00
35 AB,JCo,RC,PGv. 1,000.00
36 AB,JCo,PGv, E:Midnight(c) 1,000.00
37 AB,JCo,RC,PGv,Doc Wacky Becomes Fastest Human on Earth 1,000.00
38 JCo,RC,PGv,B:YankeeEagle 1,500.00
39 PGv,B:Midnight(c) 1,000.00
40 PGv,E:Ray 1,000.00
41 PGv................. 800.00
42 PGv,B:Lady Luck 2,200.00
43 PGv,A:Lady Luck 900.00
44 PGv................. 800.00
45 PGv,E:Midnight(c)....... 800.00
46 RC,Twelve Hours to Live 800.00
47 Wanted Midnight, Dead or Alive 800.00
48 Midnight Meets the Menace from Mars 800.00
49 PGv,FGu,Mass of Muscle.... 800.00
50 I:Hyram the Hermit 800.00
51 A:Wild Bill Hiccup 500.00
52 PGv,FGu,Did Ancient Rome Fall, or was it Pushed? 500.00
53 Is ThereHonorAmongThieves. 400.00
54 A:Smear-Faced Schmaltz.... 450.00
55 Never Trouble Trouble until Trouble Troubles You 450.00
56 The Laughing Killer........ 450.00
57 A Dummy that Turns Into A Curse 450.00
58 .... 450.00
59 A Corpse that Comes Alive... 450.00
60 The Swooner & the Trush.... 450.00
61 .... 400.00
62 V:The Lorelet 400.00
63 PGv 450.00
64 PGv,In Search of King Zoris .. 450.00
65 PGv,V:Cyanide Cindy 450.00
66 Under Circle's Spell 450.00
67 A Living Clue........... 450.00
68 JCo,Atomic Dice 450.00
69 JCo,V:Sir Nuts 450.00
70 .... 450.00
71 .... 350.00
72 JCo,Angela,the Beautiful Bovine 350.00
73 .... 350.00
74 .... 350.00
75 The Revolution 350.00
76 Bowl Over Crime......... 350.00
77 Who is Lilli Dilli? 350.00
78 JCo,Win Over Crime....... 350.00
79 V:The Men From Mars 350.00
80 JCo,V:Big Hearted Bosco.... 350.00
81 V:Willie the Kid 350.00

82 V:Woodland Boy 350.00
83 JCo,Quizmaster 350.00
84 A Date With Father Time..... 350.00
85 JCo,A Singing Swindle 350.00
Becomes:

LADY LUCK
Comics Magazine (Quality Comics), 1949
86 (1) 1,200.00
87 thru 90 .... @900.00

SMASH HITS SPORTS COMICS
Essankay Publications, Jan., 1949
1 LbC,LbC(c)............. 350.00

SMILEY BURNETTE WESTERN
Fawcett Publications, March, 1950
1 Ph(c),B:Red Eagle......... 650.00
2 Ph(c) 500.00
3 Ph(c) 500.00
4 Ph(c) 500.00

SMILIN' JACK
Dell Publishing Co., 1948
1 .... 150.00
2 thru 8 .... @100.00

SMITTY
Dell Publishing Co., 1948
1 .... 150.00
2 .... 125.00
3 thru 7 .... @100.00

SNAP
See: SCOOP COMICS

SNAPPY COMICS
Cima Publications, (Prize), 1945
1 A:Animale 400.00

SNIFFY THE PUP
Animated Cartoons (Standard Comics), Nov., 1949
5 FF,Funny Animal 125.00
6 thru 9 Funny Animal ..... @100.00
10 thru 17 Funny Animal ..... @100.00
18 Sept., 1953 .... 100.00

SOLDIER AND MARINE COMICS
Charlton Comics, 1954
11 .... 125.00
12 thru 15................ @100.00
Vol 2 #9 .... 100.00

SOLDIER COMICS
Fawcett Publications, Jan., 1952
1 Fighting Yanks on Flaming Battlefronts 250.00
2 Blazing Battles Exploding with Combat 200.00
3 .... 150.00
4 A Blow for Freedom 150.00
5 Only The Dead Are Free 150.00
6 Blood & Guts 150.00
7 The Phantom Sub 150.00
8 More Plasma! 170.00
9 Red Artillery 150.00
10 .... 150.00
11 Sept., 1953 .... 150.00

SOLDIERS OF FORTUNE
**Creston Publications
(American Comics Group),
Feb.–March, 1952**
1 OW(c),B:Ace Carter,
  Crossbones, Lance Larson . 300.00
2 OW(c) 175.00
3 OW(c) 125.00
4 . . . . 125.00
5 OW(c) 125.00
6 OW(c),OW,Bondage(c) 250.00
7 . . . . 125.00
8 OW thru 10. . . . . @125.00
11 OW,Format Change to War . . 100.00
12 . . . . 100.00
13 OW,Feb.–March, 1953 . . . . . 100.00

*Son of Sinbad #1
© St. John Publishing Co.*

SON OF SINBAD
**St. John Publishing Co.,
Feb., 1950**
1 JKu,JKu(c),The Curse of the
  Caliph's Dancer 500.00

SPACE ACTION
**Junior Books
(Ace Magazines),
June, 1952–Oct., 1952**
1 Invaders from a Lost Galaxy 1,500.00
2 The Silicon Monster from
  Galaxy X 1,000.00
3 Attack on Ishtar. 1,000.00

SPACE ADVENTURES
**Capitol Stories/
Charlton Comics,
July, 1952**
1 AFa&LM(c) 700.00
2 . . . . 325.00
3 DG(c) 250.00
4 DG(c) 250.00
5 StC(c) 250.00
6 StC(c),Two Worlds 225.00
7 DG(c),Transformation 250.00
8 DG(c),All For Love 225.00
9 DG(c) 225.00
10 SD,SD(c). 700.00
11 SD,JoS 750.00
12 SD(c). 900.00
13 A:Blue Beetle 250.00
14 A:Blue Beetle 250.00
15 Ph(c) of Rocky Jones 250.00
16 BKa,A:Rocky Jones 275.00
17 A:Rocky Jones 225.00

18 A:Rocky Jones 225.00
19 . . . . 200.00
20 First Trip to the Moon 350.00
21 War at Sea 200.00
22 Does Not Exist
23 SD,Space Trip to the Moon. . . 300.00
24 . . . . 225.00
25 Brontosaurus. 225.00
26 SD,Flying Saucers 300.00
27 SD,Flying Saucers 300.00
28 Moon Trap. 250.00
29 Captive From Space 250.00
30 Peril in the Sky 250.00
31 SD,SD(c),Enchanted Planet . . 250.00
32 SD,SD(c),Last Ship
  from Earth 250.00
33 Galactic Scourge,
  I&O:Captain Atom 700.00
34 SD,SD(c),A:Captain Atom. . . . 275.00
35 thru 40 SD,SD(c),
  A:Captain Atom . . . . @275.00

SPACE BUSTERS
**Ziff-Davis Publishing Co.,
Spring, 1952**
1 BK,NS(c),Ph(c),Charge of
  the Battle Women 1,200.00
2 EK,BK,MA,NS(c),
  Bondage(c),Ph(c) 900.00
3 Autumn, 1952 . . . . 750.00

SPACE COMICS
See: FUNNY TUNES

SPACE DETECTIVE
**Avon Periodicals,
July, 1951**
1 WW,WW(c),Opium Smugglers
  of Venus 1,700.00
2 WW,WW(c),Batwomen of
  Mercury 1,200.00
3 EK(c),SeaNymphs ofNeptune 600.00
4 EK,Flame Women of Vulcan,
  Bondage(c) 650.00

SPACE MOUSE
**Avon Periodicals,
April, 1953**
1 Funny Animal 150.00
2 Funny Animal. 125.00
3 thru 5 Funny Animal . . . . . . @100.00

SPACE PATROL
**Approved Comics
(Ziff-Davis),
Summer, 1952**
1 BK,NS,Ph(c), The Lady of
  Diamonds 1,400.00
2 BK,NS,Ph(c),Slave King of
  Pluto,Oct.–Nov., 1952 . . . . . 850.00

SPACE THRILLERS
Avon Periodicals, 1954
N# Contents May Vary. 1,600.00

SPACE WESTERN
COMICS
**See: YELLOWJACKET
COMICS**

SPARKLE COMICS
**United Features
Syndicate, 1948**
1 Nancy, Li'l Abner 250.00
2 . . . . 150.00
3 . . . . 125.00
4 . . . . 125.00
5 . . . . 125.00

6 . . . . 125.00
7 . . . . 125.00
8 thru 10 . . . . @125.00
11 thru 20 . . . . @100.00
21 thru 32 . . . . @100.00
33 Peanuts. 125.00

SPARKLER COMICS
**United Features Syndicate,
July, 1940**
1 Jim Handy 500.00
2 Frankie Doodle,Aug., 1940 . . . 400.00

SPARKLER COMICS
**United Features Syndicate,
July, 1941**
1 BHg,O:Sparkman;B:Tarzan,Captain
  & the Kids,Ella Cinders,Danny
  Dingle,Dynamite Dunn, Nancy,
  Abbie an' Slats, Frankie
  Doodle,Broncho Bill 4,000.00
2 BHg, The Case of Poisoned
  Fruit 1,800.00
3 DI Ig 1,500.00
4 BHg,Case of Sparkman &
  the Firefly 1,500.00
5 BHg,Sparkman,Natch 1,200.00
6 BHg,Case of the Bronze
  Bees 1,200.00
7 BHg,Case of the Green
  Raiders 1,200.00
8 BHg,V:River Fiddler 1,200.00
9 BHg,N:Sparkman 1,200.00
10 BHg,B:Hap Hopper,
  Sparkman's ID revealed . . . 1,200.00
11 BHg,V:Japanese 900.00
12 BHg,Another N:Sparkman . . . 900.00
13 BHg,Hap Hopper Rides
  For Freedom 900.00
14 BHg,BHg(c),Tarzan
  V:Yellow Killer. 1,000.00
15 BHg 700.00
16 BHg,Sparkman V:Japanese . . 700.00
17 BHg,Nancy(c) 700.00
18 BHg,Sparkman in Crete 700.00
19 BHg,I&B:Race Riley,
  Commandos 700.00
20 BHg,Nancy(c) 700.00
21 BHg,Tarzan(c) 750.00
22 BHg,Nancy(c) 600.00
23 BHg,Capt&Kids(c). 600.00
24 BHg,Nancy(c) 600.00
25 BHg,BHg(c),Tarzan(c). 750.00
26 BHg,Capt&Kids(c) 600.00
27 BHg,Nancy(c) 600.00

*Sparkler Comics #31
© United Features Syndicate*

28 BHg,BHg(c),Tarzan(c). 750.00
29 BHg,Capt&Kids(c). 600.00
30 BHg,Nancy(c) 600.00
31 BHg,BHg(c),Tarzan(c). 750.00
32 BHg,Capt&Kids(c). 400.00
33 BHg,Nancy(c) 400.00
34 BHg,BHg(c),Tarzan(c). 750.00
35 BHg,Capt&Kids(c). 400.00
36 BHg,Nancy(c) 400.00
37 BHg,BHg(c),Tarzan(c). 750.00
38 BHg,Capt&Kids(c). 350.00
39 BHg,BHg(c),Tarzan(c). 800.00
40 BHg,Nancy(c) 350.00
41 BHg,Capt&Kids(c). 300.00
42 BHg,BHg,Tarzan(c). 500.00
43 BHg,Nancy(c) 300.00
44 BHg,Tarzan(c). 500.00
45 BHg,Capt&Kids(c). 300.00
46 BHg,Nancy(c) 300.00
47 BHg,Tarzan(c). 500.00
48 BHg,Nancy(c) 300.00
49 BHg,Capt&Kids(c). 300.00
50 BHg,BHg(c),Tarzan(c). 500.00
51 BHg,Capt&Kids(c). 300.00
52 BHg,Nancy(c) 300.00
53 BHg,BHg(c),Tarzan(c). 500.00
54 BHg,Capt&Kids(c). 250.00
55 BHg,Nancy(c) 250.00
56 BHg,Capt&Kids(c). 250.00
57 BHg,F:Li'l Abner 250.00
58 BHg,A:Fearless Fosdick 350.00
59 BHg,B:Li'l Abner 350.00
60 BHg,Nancy(c) 250.00
61 BHg,Capt&Kids(c). 250.00
62 BHg,Li'L Abner(c) 250.00
63 BHg,Capt&Kids(c). 250.00
64 BHg,Valentines (c) 250.00
65 BHg,Nancy(c) 250.00
66 BHg,Capt&Kids(c). 250.00
67 BHg,Nancy(c) 250.00
68 BHg, ... 250.00
69 BHg,B:Nancy (c). 250.00
70 BHg, ... 250.00
71 thru 80 BHg. . . . . @200.00
81 BHg,E:Nancy(c) 200.00
82 BHg, ... 200.00
83 BHg,Tarzan(c). 350.00
84 BHg, ... 175.00
85 BHg,E:Li'l Abner 175.00
86 BHg. 175.00
87 BHg,Nancy(c) 175.00
88 thru 96 BHg. . . . . @175.00
97 BHg,O:Lady Ruggles 350.00
98 BHg. 150.00
99 BHg,Nancy(c) 150.00

100 BHg,Nancy(c) 175.00
101 thru 107 BHg. . . . . @125.00
108 & 109 BHg,ATh. 200.00
110 BHg 125.00
111 BHg 125.00
112 BHg 125.00
113 BHg,ATh. 200.00
114 thru 120 BHg . . . . @150.00
Becomes:

NANCY AND SLUGGO
St. John/Dell Publ. 1955
121 . . . . 150.00
122 thru 130. . . . . @125.00
131 thru 145. . . . . @100.00

SPARKLING STARS
Holyoke Publishing Co.,
June, 1944
1 B:Hell's Angels,Ali Baba,FBI,
   Boxie Weaver,Petey & Pop . 350.00
2 Speed Spaulding 300.00
3 FBI. 200.00
4 thru 12 . . . . @200.00
13 O&I:Jungo, The Man-Beast . . 225.00
14 . . . . 200.00
15 . . . . 200.00
16 . . . . 200.00
17 thru 19 . . . . @200.00
20 I:Fangs the Wolfboy 200.00
21 thru 28 . . . . @200.00
29 Bondage(c). 350.00
30 thru 32. . . . . @150.00
33 March, 1948 . . . . 150.00

SPARKMAN
Frances M. McQueeny, 1944
1 O:Sparkman. 400.00

SPARKY WATTS
Columbia Comics Group, 1942
1 A:Skyman,Hitler(c) 1,500.00
2. . . . . 500.00
3 . . . . 400.00
4 O:Skyman 400.00
5 A:Skyman 350.00
6 . . . . 200.00
7 . . . . 200.00
8 . . . . 250.00
9 . . . . 200.00
10 1949 . . . . 200.00

[STEVE SAUNDERS]
SPECIAL AGENT
Parents Magazine/
Commended Comics,
Dec., 1947
1 J. Edgar Hoover, Ph(c) 250.00
2 . . . . 150.00
3 thru 7 . . . . @125.00
8 Sept., 1949 . . . . 125.00

SPECIAL COMICS
See: LAUGH COMICS

SPECIAL EDITION
COMICS
Fawcett Publications,
Aug., 1940
1 CCB,CCB(c),F:Captain
   Marvel 20,000.00

A SPECTACULAR
FEATURE MAGAZINE
Fox Features Syndicate, 1950
1 (11) Samson and Delilah 350.00
Becomes:

SPECTACULAR
FEATURES MAGAZINE
Fox Features Syndicate, 1950
2 (12) Iwo Jima. 360.00
3 True Crime Cases 275.00

SPECTACULAR STORIES
MAGAZINE
Hero Books (Fox Features
Syndicate), 1950
3 Actual Crime Cases. 500.00
4 Sherlock Holmes 325.00

SPEED COMICS
Brookwood/Speed Publ.
Harvey Publications,
Oct., 1939
1 BP,B&O:Shock Gibson,B:Spike
   Marlin,Biff Bannon 5,500.00
2 BP,B:Shock Gibson(c) 1,700.00
3 BP,GT 1,200.00
4 BP 1,000.00
5 BP,DBr 1,000.00
6 BP,GT 900.00
7 GT,JKu,Bondage, B:Mars
   Mason 900.00
8 JKu 850.00
9 JKu 850.00
10 JKu,E:Shock Gibson(c). 850.00
11 JKu,E:Mars Mason 850.00
12 B:The Wasp 1,000.00
13 I:Captain Freedom;B:Girls
   Commandos,Pat Parker. . . 1,100.00
14 AAv,Pocket sized-100pgs. . . 1,200.00
15 AAv,Pocket size 1,200.00
16 JKu,AAv,Pocket size 1,200.00
17 O:Black Cat 1,500.00
18 B:Capt.Freedom,Bondage(c) 1,200.00
19 S&K 1,000.00
20 S&K 1,000.00
21 JKu(c),Hitler & Tojo 1,400.00
22 JKu(c). 1,000.00
23 JKu(c),O:Girl Commandos . 1,000.00
24 Hitler,Tojo & Mussilini(c). . . 1,200.00
25 . . . . 1,000.00
26 GT,Flag (c),Black Cat. 1,000.00
27 GT,Black Cat 1,000.00
28 E:Capt Freedom 1,000.00
29 Case o/t Black Marketeers . 1,000.00
30 POW Death Chambers 1,000.00
31 ASh(c),Nazi Thrashing(c). . . 1,200.00
32 ASh(c) 1,100.00
33 ASh(c) 1,100.00

Sparkler Comics #119
© United Features Syndicate

Speed Comics #36
© Harvey Publications

34 ASh(c) 1,100.00
35 ASh(c),BlackCat'sDeathTrap 1,150.00
36 ASh(c) 1,100.00
37 RP(c) 1,100.00
38 RP(c),War Bond Plea with Iwo
  Jima flag allusion(c) 1,100.00
39 RP(c),B:Capt Freedom(c) . 1,200.00
40 RP(c) 1,200.00
41 RP(c) 1,200.00
42 JKu,RP(c). 1,200.00
43 JKu,AAv,E:Capt Freedom(c) 1,250.00
44 BP,JKu,Four Kids on a raft,
  Jan.–Feb., 1947 . . . . 1,300.00

SPEED SMITH
THE HOT ROD KING
Ziff-Davis Publishing Co.,
Spring, 1952
1 INS,Ph(c),A:Roscoe
  the Rascal 250.00

SPIRIT, THE
Will Eisner
(Weekly Coverless
Comic Book), June, 1940
WE,O:SPirit 1,200.00
  6/9/40 WE 700.00
  6/16/40 WE,Black Queen . . . 400.00
  6/23/40 WE,Mr Mystic 250.00
  6/30/40 WE 250.00
  7/7/40 WE,Black Queen 250.00
  7/14/40 WE 200.00
  7/21/40 WE 200.00
  7/28/40 WE 200.00
  8/4/40 WE 200.00
  7/7/40-11/24/40,WE 165.00
  11/10/40 WE,Black Queen . . 150.00
  12/1/40 WE,Ellen
  Spanking(c) 225.00
  12/8/40-12/29/40 . . . . 125.00
1941 WE Each 125.00
  3/16 WE I;Silk Satin 200.00
  6/15 WE I Twilight 125.00
  6/22 WE Hitler 125.00
1942 WE Each 100.00
  2-1 Duchess 125.00
  2-15 . . . . 100.00
  2-23 . . . . 150.00
1943 WE Each,LF,WE scripts . . . 100.00
1944 JCo,LF 100.00
1945 LF Each. 100.00
1946 WE Each. 100.00
  1/13 WE,O:The Spirit. 125.00
  1/20 WE,Satin 125.00
  3/17 WE,I:Nylon 125.00
  4/21 WE,I:Mr.Carrion 150.00
  7/7 WE,I:Dulcet Tone&Skinny 125.00
  10/6 WE,I:F:Gell 100.00
1947 WE Each 100.00
  7/13.,WE,Hansel &Gretel . . . 125.00
  7/20,WE,A:Bomb. 125.00
  9/28,WE,Flying Saucers 100.00
  10/5,WE, Cinderella 125.00
  12/7,WE,I:Power Puff 125.00
1948 WE Each 125.00
  1/11,WE,Sparrow Fallon 125.00
  1/25,WE,I:Last A Net 125.00
  3/14,WE,A:Kretuama. 125.00
  4/4,WE,A:Wildrice 125.00
  7/25,The Thing 100.00
  8/22,Poe Tale,Horror 125.00
  9/18, A:Lorelei 100.00
  11/7,WE,A:Plaster of Paris . . 100.00
1949 WE Each 100.00
  1/23 WE,I:Thorne 100.00
  8/21 WE,I:Monica Veto 100.00
  9/25 WE,A;Ice 100.00
  12/4 WE,I:Flaxen. 100.00
1950 WE Each 100.00
  1/8 WE,I:Sand Sarof 150.00
  2/10, Horror Issue 100.00

THE CHICAGO SUN

Spirit Insert 5-10-42
© *Will Eisner*

1951 WE(Last WE 8/12/51) . . @100.00
  Non-Eisners . . . . @25.00
1952 Non-Eisners . . . . @25.00
  7/27 WW,Denny Colt. 500.00
  8/3 WW,Moon 500.00
  8/10 WW.Moon 500.00
  8/17 WW,WE,Heart 400.00
  8/24 WW,Rescue. 400.00
  8/31 WW,Last Man 400.00
  9/7 WW,Man Moon 550.00
  9/14 WE. 150.00
  9/21 WE Space 350.00
  9/28 WE Moon. 400.00
  10/5 WE Last Story 250.00

SPIRIT, THE
Quality Comics Group/
Vital Publ., 1944
N# Wanted Dead or Alivo! . . . 1,200.00
N# ...In Crime Dooon't Pay,! F(c) 600.00
N# ...In Murder Runs Wild 500.00
4 ...Flirts with Death 400.00
5 ...Wanted Dead or Alive. . . . 350.00
6 ...Gives You Triple Value 300.00
7 ...Rocks the Underworld 300.00
8 ...Cracks Down on Crime,LF(c) 300.00
9 ...Throws Fear Into the
  Heart of Crime 300.00
10 ...Stalks Crime,RC(c) 300.00
11   America's Greatest
  Crime Buster 250.00
12 WE(c),...The Famous Outlaw
  Who Smashes Crime 400.00
13 WE(c),...and Ebony Cleans Out
  the Underworld;Bondage(c) . 400.00
14 WE(c) 400.00
15 WE(c),Bank Robber at Large . 400.00
16 WE(c),The Case of the
  Uncanny Cat 400.00
17 WE(c),The Organ Grinding
  Bank Robber 550.00
18 WE,WE(c),'The Bucket
  of Blood 550.00
19 WE,WE(c),'The Man Who
  Murdered the Spirit'. 550.00
20 WE,WE(c),'The Vortex'. 550.00
21 WE,WE(c),'P'Gell of Paris' . . 550.00
22 WE(c),TheOctopus,Aug.1950 . 900.00

SPIRIT, THE
Fiction House Magazines,
1952
1 Curse of Claymore Castle . . . 600.00
2 WE,WE(c),Who Says Crime
  Doesn't Pay 500.00
3 WE/JGr(c),League of Lions . . 400.00

4 WE,WE&JGr(c),Last Prowl of
  Mr Mephisto;Bondage (c) . . 450.00
5 WE,WE(c),Ph(c)1954 . . . . 500.00

SPIRITMAN
Will Eisner, 1944
1 3 Spirit Sections from
  1944 Bound Together 275.00
2 LF, 2 Spirit Sections
  from 1944 Bound Together . . 225.00

SPITFIRE COMICS
Harvey Publ., Aug., 1941
1 MKd(c),100-pgs.,Pocket-size 1,000.00
2 100-pgs.,Pocket-size,
  Oct., 1941 . . . . 950.00

SPITFIRE
Malverne Herald/
Elliot Publ. Co., 1944
132 & 133. . . . . @300.00

SPOOK COMICS
Baily Publications, 1946
1 A:Mr. Lucifer 400.00

SPOOK DETECTIVE CASES
And: SPOOK
SUSPENSE MYSTERY
See: CRIMINALS ON
THE RUN

SPOOKY
Harvey Publications,
Nov., 1955
1 Funny Apparition 750.00
2 same 500.00
3 . . . . 400.00
4 . . . . 400.00
5 . . . . 400.00
6 thru 10 same . . . . @400.00
11 thru 20 same . . . . @300.00
21 thru 30 same . . . . @250.00
31 thru 40 same . . . . @250.00
41 thru 70 same . . . . @250.00
71 thru 90 same . . . . @200.00

SPOOKY MYSTERIES
Your Guide Publishing Co.,
1946
1 Rib-Tickling Horror 250.00

SPORT COMICS
See: TRUE SPORT
PICTURE STORIES

SPORTS STARS
Sport Stars, Inc. (Parents'
Magazine), 1946
1 Johnny Weissmuller. 500.00
2 Baseball Greats. 350.00
3 . . . . 275.00
4 . . . . 275.00

SPORTS THRILLS
See: DICK COLE

SPOTLIGHT COMICS
Harry 'A' Chesler Jr.
Publications,
Nov., 1944
1 GT,GT(c),B:Veiled Avenger,
  Black Dwarf,Barry Kuda . . 1,200.00
2 . . . . 800.00
3 1945,Eye Injury 900.00

SPUNKY
Standard Comics,
April, 1949
1 FF,Adventures of a Junior
   Cowboy 125.00
2 FF 100.00
3 .... 100.00
4 .... 100.00
5 .... 100.00
6 .... 100.00
7 Nov., 1951 .... 100.00

SPY AND COUNTERSPY
Best Syndicated Features
(American Comics Group),
Aug.–Sept., 1949
1 I&O:Jonathan Kent 350.00
2 .... 200.00
Becomes:

Spy-Hunters #8
© *American Comics Group*

SPY-HUNTERS
Dec., 1949–Jan., 1950
3 Jonathan Kent 300.00
4 J.Kent................... 150.00
5 J.Kent................... 150.00
6 J.Kent................... 150.00
7 OW(c),J.Kent............. 150.00
8 OW(c),J.Kent............. 150.00
9 OW(c),J.Kent............. 150.00
10 OW(c),J.Kent............ 150.00
11 .... 125.00
12 OW(c),MD............... 125.00
13 and 14................@125.00
15 OW(c) 125.00
16 AW 175.00
17 .... 100.00
18 War (c) 100.00
19 and 20................@100.00
21 B:War Content 100.00
22 .... 100.00
23 Torture................ 250.00
24 'BlackmailBrigade',July,1953 . 100.00

SPY SMASHER
Fawcett Publications,
Autumn, 1941
1 B;Spy Smasher 6,000.00
2 MRa(c) 2,800.00
3 Bondage (c) 2,000.00
4 1st ISb art............. 1,800.00
5 MRa,Mt. Rushmore(c) 1,800.00

6 MRa(a&c),V:The Sharks
   of Steel 1,500.00
7 MRa 1,500.00
8 AB 1,300.00
9 AB,Hitler,Tojo, Mussolini(c).. 1,600.00
10 AB,Did Spy Smasher
   Kill Hitler?............. 1,500.00
11 AB,Feb., 1943 .... 1,300.00

STAMPS COMICS
Youthful Magazines/Stamp
Comics, Inc.,
Oct., 1951
1 HcK,Birth of Liberty 350.00
2 HcK,RP,Battle of White Plains 200.00
3 HcK,DW,RP,Iwo Jima 175.00
4 HcK,DW,RP 175.00
5 HcK,Von Hindenberg disaster . 200.00
6 HcK,The Immortal Chaplains . . 175.00
7 HcK,RKr,RP,B&O:Railroad ... 250.00
Becomes:

THRILLING ADVENTURES IN STAMPS
Jan., 1953
8 HcK, 100 Pgs............ 1,000.00

STAR COMICS
Comic Magazines/Ultem
Publ./Chesler
Centaur Publications,
Feb., 1937
1 B:Dan Hastings.......... 2,800.00
2 .... 1,200.00
3 African Blacks (c) 1,400.00
4 WMc(c),A:Little Nemo..... 1,000.00
5 WMc(c),A:Little Nemo 1,000.00
6 CBi(c),FGu 1,000.00
7 FGu 900.00
8 BoW,BoW(c),FGu,A:Little
   Nemo,Horror 950.00
9 FGu,CBi(c) 900.00
10 FGu,CBi(c),BoW,A:Impyk .. 1,250.00
11 FGu,BoW,JCo............ 950.00
12 FGu,BoW,B:Riders of the
   Golden West 800.00
13 FGu,BoW 800.00
14 FGu,GFx(c)............ 800.00
15 CBu,B:The Last Pirate 800.00
16 CBu,B:Phantom Rider 800.00
2-1 CBu,B:Phantom Rider(c) ... 850.00
2-2 CBu,A:Diana Deane 750.00
2-3 GFx(c),CBu,Hollywood 700.00
2-4 CBu 700.00
2-5 CBu 700.00
2-6 CBu,E:Phantom Rider 700.00
2-7 CBu,Jungle Queen,
   Aug., 1939 .... 700.00

STARLET O'HARA IN HOLLYWOOD
Standard Comics,
Dec., 1948
1 The Terrific Tee-Age Comic ... 300.00
2 Her Romantic Adventures in
   Movie land 200.00
3 and 4, Sept., 1949 ......@150.00

STAR RANGER
Comic Magazines/Ultem/
Centaur Publ.,
Feb., 1937
1 FGu,I:Western Comic 3,000.00
2 .... 1,300.00
3 FGu 1,100.00
4 .... 1,100.00
5 .... 1,100.00
6 FGu 1,000.00
7 FGu 900.00

8 GFx,FGu,PGv,BoW 900.00
9 GFx,FGu,PGv,BoW 900.00
10 JCo,GFx,FGu,PGv,BoW ... 1,300.00
11 .... 850.00
12 JCo(a&c),FGu,PGv....... 850.00
Becomes:

COWBOY COMICS
July, 1938
13 FGu,PGv.............. 1,000.00
14 FGu,PGv............... 900.00
Becomes:

STAR RANGER FUNNIES
Oct., 1938
15 WE,PGv............... 1,300.00
2-1(16) JCo(a&c) 1,000.00
2-2(17) PGv,JCo,A:Night Hawk .. 900.00
2-3(18) JCo,FGu 750.00
2-4(19) A:Kit Carson 750.00
2-5(20) Oct., 1939 .... 750.00

STARS AND STRIPES COMICS
Comic Corp of America
(Centaur Publications),
May, 1941
2 PGv,PGv(c),'Called to Colors',
   The Shark,The Voice 3,200.00
3 PGv,PGv(c),O:Dr.Synthe ... 1,900.00
4 PGv,PGv(c),I:The Stars
   & Stripes 1,600.00
5 .... 1,200.00
6(5), Dec., 1941 .... 1,200.00

STAR STUDDED
Cambridge House, 1945
N# 25 cents (c) price;128 pgs.;
   32 F:stories 400.00
N# The Cadet,Hoot Gibson,
   Blue Beetle 350.00

STARTLING COMICS
Better Publ./Nedor Publ.,
June, 1940
1 WE,LF,B&O:Captain Future,
   Mystico, Wonder Man;
   B:Masked Rider 7,000.00
2 Captain Future(c) 2,500.00
3 same................... 2,100.00
4 same................... 1,900.00
5 same................... 1,800.00
6 same................... 1,800.00
7 same................... 1,800.00
8 ASh(c),Captain Future 1,800.00
9 Bondage(c) 1,800.00
10 O:Fighting Yank 7,000.00
11 Fighting Yank(c)......... 2,500.00
12 Hitler,Mussolini,Tojo (c) 2,200.00
13 JBi 1,900.00
14 JBi 1,900.00
15 Fighting Yank (c) 1,900.00
16 Bondage(c),O:Four
   Comrades............. 1,900.00
17 Fighting Yank (c),
   E:Masked Rider 1,700.00
18 JBi,B&O:Pyroman 2,500.00
19 Pyroman(c) 1,500.00
20 Pyroman(c),B:Oracle 1,500.00
21 HcK,ASh(c)Bondage(c)
   O:Ape 1,800.00
22 HcK,ASh(c),Fighting Yank(c) 1,500.00
23 HcK,BEv,ASh(c),Pyroman(c) 1,500.00
24 HcK,BEv,ASh(c),Fighting
   Yank(c) 1,500.00
25 HcK,BEv,ASh(c),Pyroman(c) 1,500.00
26 BEv,ASh(c),Fighting Yank(c) 1,500.00
27 BEv,ASh(c),Pyroman(c).... 1,500.00
28 BEv,ASh(c),Fighting Yank(c) 1,500.00

Startling Comics #29
© Nedor Publications

29 BEv,ASh(c),Pyroman(c).... 1,500.00
30 ASh(c),Fighting Yank(c).... 1,500.00
31 ASh(c),Pyroman(c)....... 1,500.00
32 ASh(c),Fighting Yank(c)... 1,500.00
33 ASh(c),Pyroman(c)....... 1,500.00
34 ASh(c),Fighting Yank(c),
    O:Scarab 1,800.00
35 ASh(c),Pyroman(c)....... 1,500.00
36 ASh(c),Fighting Yank(c)... 1,200.00
37 ASh(c),Bondage (c)...... 1,200.00
38 ASh(c),Bondage(c)....... 1,500.00
39 ASh(c),Pyroman(c)....... 1,500.00
40 ASh(c),E:Captain Future .. 1,500.00
41 ASh(c),Pyroman(c)....... 1,500.00
42 ASh(c),Fighting Yank(c)... 1,500.00
43 ASh(c),Pyroman(c),
    E:Pyroman 1,500.00
44 Grl(c),Lance Lewis(c) 1,700.00
45 Grl(c),I:Tygra 1,700.00
46 Grl,Grl(c),Bondage(c) 1,700.00
47 ASh(c),Bondage(c)....... 3,000.00
48 ASh(c),Lance Lewis(c)..... 1,500.00
49 ASh(c),Bondage(c),
    E:Fighting Yank 7,500.00
50 ASh(c),Lance Lewis(c),
    Sea Eagle.............. 1,100.00
51 ASh(c),Sea Eagle 1,100.00
52 ASh(c) 1,100.00
53 ASh(c),Sept., 1948........ 1,100.00

STARTLING TERROR TALES

Star Publications,
May, 1952

10 WW,LbC(c),The Story Starts 1,000.00
11 LbC(c),The Ghost Spider
    of Death 2,000.00
12 LbC(c),White Hand Horror ... 400.00
13 JyD,LbC(c),Love From
    a Gorgor 425.00
14 LbC(c),Trapped by the
    Color of Blood 400.00
4 LbC(c),Crime at the Carnival . 325.00
5 LbC(c),The Gruesome
    Demon of Terror 325.00
6 LbC(c),Footprints of Death ... 325.00
7 LbC(c),The Case of the
    Strange Murder 325.00
8 RP,LbC(c),Phantom Brigade .. 325.00
9 LbC(c),The Forbidden Tomb .. 300.00
10 LbC(c),The Horrible Entity ... 350.00
11 RP,LbC(c),The Law Will
    Win, July, 1954 .... 325.00

STEVE CANYON COMICS

Harvey Publications,
Feb., 1948–Dec., 1948

1 MC,BP,O:Steve Canyon...... 275.00
2 MC,BP 175.00
3 MC,BP,Canyon's Crew 150.00
4 MC,BP,Chase of Death 150.00
5 MC,BP,A:Happy Easter 150.00
6 MC,BP,A:Madame Lynx...... 165.00

STEVE ROPER

Famous Funnies,
April, 1948

1 Reprints newspaper strips ... 150.00
2 .... 75.00
3 .... 60.00
4 .... 60.00
5 Dec., 1948 .... 60.00

STORY OF HARRY S. TRUMAN, THE

Democratic National
Committee, 1948

N# Giveaway-The Life of Our
    33rd President 200.00

STRAIGHT ARROW

Magazine Enterprises,
Feb.–March, 1950

1 OW,B:Straight Arrow & his
    Horse Fury 1,200.00
2 BP,B&O:Red Hawk 550.00
3 BP,FF(c) 700.00
4 BP,Cave(c)............... 500.00
5 BP,StraightArrow'sGreatLeap . 500.00
6 BP 450.00
7 BP,The Railroad Invades
    Comanche Country 450.00
8 BP 450.00
9 BP 450.00
10 BP 450.00
11 BP,The Valley of Timo....... 500.00
12 thru 19 BP............. @500.00
20 BP,Straight Arrow's
    Great War Shield.......... 450.00
21 BP,O:Fury 500.00
22 BP,FF(c) 550.00
23 BP 300.00
24 BP,The Dragons of Doom ... 400.00
25 BP, Secret Cave 300.00
26 BP,Red Hawk vs. Vikings 300.00
27 BP..................... 250.00
28 BP,Red Hawk 250.00
29 thru 35 BP............. @250.00
36 BP Red Hawk, Drug 225.00
37 BP 225.00
38 BP..................... 225.00
39 BP,The Canyon Beasts...... 250.00
40 BP,Secret of the
    Spanish Specters.......... 250.00
41 BP 200.00
42 BP 200.00
43 BP,I:Blaze 250.00
44 BP 200.00
45 thru 53 BP .... @200.00
54 BP,March, 1956 .... 200.00

STRANGE CONFESSIONS

Approved Publications
(Ziff-Davis),
Spring, 1952

1 EK,Ph(c) 700.00
2 Ph(c) 450.00
3 EK,Ph(c),Girls Reformatory .. 450.00
4 Ph(c),Girls Reformatory...... 450.00

STRANGE FANTASY

Farrell Publications/
Ajax Comics,
Aug., 1952

(2)1 Jungle Princess.......... 700.00
2 Drug & Horror 500.00
3 The Dancing Ghost 500.00
4 Demon in the Dungeon,
    A:Rocketman............. 500.00
5 Visiting Corpse 350.00
6 .... 350.00
7 A:Madam Satan 450.00
8 A:Black Cat 350.00
9 S&K,SD, Black Cat 400.00
10 .... 350.00
11 Fearful Things Can Happen
    in a Lonely Place.......... 400.00
12 The Undying Fiend 350.00
13 Terror in the Attic,
    Bondage(c) 450.00
14 Monster in the Building,
    Oct.–Nov., 1954........... 350.00

STRANGE JOURNEY

America's Best, 1957

1 .... 250.00
2 Flying Saucer.............. 175.00
3 .... 150.00
4 .... 150.00

STRANGE MYSTERIES

Superior Publ./Dynamic Publ.,
1951

1 LKa,Horror................ 900.00
2 .... 450.00
3 thru 5 .... @425.00
6 .... 350.00
7 .... 350.00
8 .... 350.00
9 Bondage,3-D type 450.00
10 .... 300.00
11 thru 18 .... @250.00
19 MB 325.00
20 reprint #1, new (c)......... 250.00
21 reprint 250.00

UNKNOWN WORLD

Fawcett Publications,
June, 1952

1 NS(c),Ph(c),Will You Venture
    to Meet the Unknown 600.00
Becomes:

Unknown World #1
© Fawcett Publications

GOLDEN AGE

STRANGE STORIES FROM ANOTHER WORLD
Aug., 1952

2 NS(c),Ph(c),Will You?
   Dare You 750.00
3 NS(c),Ph(c),The Dark Mirror . . 500.00
4 NS(c),Ph(c),Monsters of
   the Mind 500.00
5 NS(c),Ph(c),Dance of the
   Doomed, Feb., 1953 . . . . . . 500.00

STRANGE SUSPENSE STORIES
Fawcett Publications, June, 1952

1 BP,MSy,MBi 1,500.00
2 MBi,GE 1,000.00
3 MBi,GE(c) 800.00
4 BP 800.00
5 MBi(c),Voodoo(c) 800.00
6 BEv 400.00
7 BEv 400.00
8 AW 400.00
9 . . . . 400.00
10 . . . . 500.00
11 thru 13 . . . . @300.00
14 . . . . 350.00
15 AW,BEv(c) 350.00

Charlton Comics

16 . . . . 350.00
17 . . . . 300.00
18 SD,SD(c) 500.00
19 SD,SD(c) 700.00
20 SD,SD(c) 500.00
21 . . . . 250.00
22 SD(c) 450.00
Becomes:

THIS IS SUSPENSE!
Feb., 1955

23 WW 400.00
24 . . . . 150.00
25 . . . . 100.00
26 . . . . 100.00
Becomes:

STRANGE SUSPENSE STORIES
Oct., 1955

27 . . . . 200.00
28 thru 30 . . . . @175.00
31 SD(c) 300.00
32 SD 300.00
33 SD 300.00
34 SD,SD(c) 650.00
35 SD 300.00
36 SD,SD(c) 300.00
37 SD 375.00
38 . . . . 300.00
39 SD 350.00
40 SD 300.00
41 SD 300.00
42 thru 44 . . . . @125.00
45 SD 250.00
46 . . . . 125.00
47 SD 250.00
48 SD 250.00
49 . . . . 125.00
50 SD 250.00
51 SD 150.00
52 SD 150.00
53 SD 150.00
54 thru 60 . . . . @125.00
61 thru 74 . . . . @100.00
75 Capt. Atom 250.00
76 Capt. Atom 100.00
77 Capt. Atom 100.00

STRANGE SUSPENSE STORIES
See: LAWBREAKERS

STRANGE TERRORS
St. John Publishing Co., June, 1952

1 The Ghost of Castle
   Karloff, Bondage(c) 900.00
2 UnshackledFlight intoNowhere 700.00
3 JKu,Ph(c),The Ghost Who
   Ruled Crazy Heights 750.00
4 JKu,Ph(c),Terror from
   the Tombs 900.00
5 JKu,Ph(c),No Escaping
   the Pool of Death 750.00
6 LC,PMo,Bondage(c),Giant. . . . 900.00
7 JKu,JKu(c),Cat's Death,Giant 1,000.00

Strange World of Your Dreams #4
© Prize Group

STRANGE WORLD OF YOUR DREAMS
Prize Group, Aug., 1952

1 S&K(c),What Do They Mean–
   Messages Rec'd in Sleep . 1,200.00
2 MMe,S&K(c),Why did I Dream
   That I Was Being Married
   to a Man without a Face? . . . 700.00
3 S&K(c) 500.00
4 MMe,S&K(c),The Story of
   a Man Who Dreamed a Murder
   that Happened 450.00

STRANGE WORLDS
Avon Periodicals, Nov., 1950

1 JKu,Spider God of Akka . . . 2,200.00
2 WW,Dara of the Vikings . . . 2,000.00
3 AW&FF,EK(c),WW,JO 3,200.00
4 JO,WW,WW(c),The
   Enchanted Dagger 2,300.00
5 WW,WW(c),JO,Bondage(c);
   Sirens of Space 2,400.00
6 EK,WW(c),JO,SC,
   Maid o/t Mist 1,000.00
7 EK, Sabotage on
   Space Station 1 . . . . 900.00
8 JKu,EK,The Metal Murderer . 900.00
9 The Radium Monsters 900.00
18 JKu 800.00
19 Astounding Super
   Science Fantasies 800.00

20 WW(c),Fighting War Stories . . 250.00
21 EK(c) 200.00
22 EK(c),Sept.–Oct., 1955 . . . . . 200.00

STRICTLY PRIVATE
Eastern Color Printing, July, 1942

1 You're in theArmyNow-Humor . 275.00
2 F:Peter Plink, 1942 . . . . 250.00

STUNTMAN COMICS
Harvey Publications, April–May, 1946

1 S&K,O:Stuntman 2,000.00
2 S&K,New Champ of Split-
   Second Action 1,200.00
3 S&K,Digest sized,Mail Order
   Only, B&W interior,
   Oct.–Nov., 1946 . . . . 1,500.00

SUGAR BOWL COMICS
Famous Funnies, May, 1948

1 ATh,ATh(c),The Newest in
   Teen Age! 175.00
2 . . . . 100.00
3 ATh 125.00
4 . . . . 75.00
5 Jan., 1949 . . . . 75.00

SUN FUN KOMIKS
Sun Publications, 1939

1 F:Spineless Sam the
   Sweetheart 600.00

SUNNY, AMERICA'S SWEETHEART
Fox Features Syndicate, Dec., 1947

11 AF,AF(c) 2,000.00
12 AF,AF(c) 1,500.00
13 AF,AF(c) 1,500.00
14 AF,AF(c) 1,500.00

SUNSET CARSON
Charlton Comics, Feb., 1951–Aug., 1951

1 Painted, Ph(c);Wyoming
   Mail 1,200.00
2 Kit Carson-Pioneer 900.00
3 . . . . 700.00
4 Panhandle Trouble. 700.00

SUPER BOOK OF COMICS
Western Publishing Co., 1943

N# Dick Tracy 700.00
1 Dick Tracy, Smuggling 700.00
1a Smilin' Jack 400.00
2 Smitty,Magic Morro 400.00
3 Capt. Midnight 700.00
3a Moon Mullins 300.00
4 Red Ryder,Magic Morro. 400.00
4a Smitty. 300.00
5 Don Winslow,Magic Morro. . . . 400.00
5a DonWinslow,StratosphereJim 400.00
5a Terry & the Pirates. 500.00
6 Don Winslow 500.00
6a King of the Royal Mounties . . 500.00
7 Little Orphan Annie 300.00
7a Dick Tracy 600.00
8 Dick Tracy 500.00
8a Dan Dunn. 300.00
9 Terry & the Pirates 500.00
10 Red Ryder, Magic Morro. 300.00

SUPER-BOOK OF COMICS

Western Publishing Co., 1944

1 Dick Tracy (Omar) 350.00
1 Dick Tracy (Hancock) 250.00
2 Bugs Bunny (Omar). 250.00
2 Bugs Bunny (Hancock) 250.00
3 Terry & the Pirates (Omar) . . . 300.00
3 Terry & the Pirates (Hancock) . 300.00
4 Andy Panda (Omar). 200.00
4 Andy Panda (Hancock) 200.00
5 Smokey Stover (Omar) 200.00
5 Smokey Stover (Hancock) 200.00
6 Porky Pig (Omar). 250.00
6 Porky Pig (Hancock) 225.00
7 Smilin' Jack (Omar) 200.00
7 Smilin' Jack (Hancock) 200.00
8 Oswald the Rabbit (Omar). . . . 200.00
8 Oswald the Rabbit (Hancock) . 175.00
9 Alley Oop (Omar). 300.00
9 Alley Oop (Hancock) 275.00
10 Elmer Fudd (Omar). 200.00
10 Elmer Fudd (Hancock) 175.00
11 Little Orphan Annie (Omar). . . 200.00
11 Little Orphan Annie (Hancock) 200.00
12 Woody Woodpecker (Omar). . 225.00
12 WoodyWoodpecker(Hancock) 200.00
13 Dick Tracy (Omar). 300.00
13 Dick Tracy (Hancock) 275.00
14 Bugs Bunny (Omar) 300.00
14 Bugs Bunny (Hanock) 250.00
15 Andy Panda (Omar) 200.00
15 Andy Panda (Hancock). 175.00
16 Terry & the Pirates (Omar) . . 300.00
16 Terry & the Pirates (Hancock). 275.00
17 Smokey Stover (Omar) 200.00
17 Smokey Stover (Hancock) . . . 175.00
18 Porky Pig (Omar) 250.00
18 Smokey Stover (Hancock) . . . 175.00
19 Smilin' Jack (Omar) 175.00
N# Smilin' Jack (Hancock). 150.00
20 Oswald the Rabbit (Omar) . . . 150.00
N# Oswald the Rabbit (Hancock) 125.00
21 Gasoline Alley (Omar). 150.00
N# Gasoline Alley (Hancock). . . . 125.00
22 Elmer Fudd (Omar). 150.00
N# Elmer Fudd (Hancock) 135.00
23 Little Orphan Annie (Omar). . . 150.00
N# Little Orphan Annie (Hancock) 135.00
24 Woody Woodpecker (Omar) . . 125.00
N# WoodyWoodpecker(Hancock) 100.00
25 Dick Tracy (Omar). 175.00
N# Dick Tracy (Hancock) 150.00
26 Bugs Bunny (Omar) 150.00

Super-Book of Comics #1
© Western Publishing

N# Bugs Bunny (Hancock) 125.00
27 Andy Panda (Omar) 125.00
27 Andy Panda (Hancock). 100.00
28 Terry & the Pirates (Omar) . . . 250.00
28 Terry & the Pirates (Hancock). 225.00
29 Smokey Stover (Omar). 100.00
29 Smokey Stover (Hancock) . . . 100.00
30 Porky Pig (Omar) 150.00
30 Porky Pig (Hancock). 125.00
N# Bugs Bunny (Hancock) 125.00

SUPER CIRCUS

Cross Publishing Co., Jan., 1951

1 Partial Ph(c) 200.00
2 . . . . 125.00
3 . . . . 100.00
4 . . . . 100.00
5 1951 . . . . 100.00

SUPER COMICS

Dell Publishing Co., May, 1938

1 Dick Tracy,Terry and the
   Pirates,Smilin'Jack,Smokey
   Stover,Orphan Annie,etc. . . 3,400.00
2 . . . . 1,400.00
3 . . . . 1,200.00
4 . . . . 1,100.00
5 Gumps(c) 1,000.00
6 . . . . 750.00
7 Smokey Stover(c) 750.00
8 Dick Tracy(c) 750.00
9 . . . . 750.00
10 Dick Tracy(c). 750.00
11 . . . . 550.00
12 . . . . 550.00
13 . . . . 550.00
14 . . . . 550.00
15 . . . . 550.00
16 Terry & the Pirates 500.00
17 Dick Tracy(c). 500.00
18 . . . . 500.00
19 . . . . 500.00
20 Smilin'Jack(c) 525.00
21 B.Magic Morro 400.00
22 Magic Morro(c) 450.00
23 all star(c). 400.00
24 Dick Tracy(c). 450.00
25 Magic Morro(c) 400.00
26 . . . . 400.00
27 Magic Morro(c) 400.00
28 Jim Ellis(c) 450.00
29 Smilin'Jack(c) 400.00
30 inc.The Sea Hawk. 450.00
31 Dick Tracy(c). 350.00
32 Smilin' Jack(c). 365.00
33 Jim Ellis(c) 350.00
34 Magic Morro(c) 350.00
35 thru 40 Dick Tracy(c). . . . . . @350.00
41 B:Lightning Jim 300.00
42 thru 50 Dick Tracy(c). . . . . . @300.00
51 thru 54 Dick Tracy(c). . . . . . @250.00
55 . . . . 250.00
56 . . . . 250.00
57 Dick Tracy(c). 250.00
58 Smitty(c) 250.00
59 . . . . 250.00
60 Dick Tracy(c). 275.00
61 . . . . 235.00
62 Flag(c). 235.00
63 Dick Tracy(c). 235.00
64 Smitty(c) 225.00
65 Dick Tracy(c). 235.00
66 Dick Tracy(c). 235.00
67 Christmas(c) 235.00
68 Dick Tracy(c). 235.00
69 Dick Tracy(c). 235.00
70 Dick Tracy(c). 235.00
71 Dick Tracy(c). 200.00
72 Dick Tracy(c). 200.00

Super Comics #64
© Dell Publishing Co.

73 Smitty(c) 200.00
74 War Bond(c) 200.00
75 Dick Tracy(c). 200.00
76 Dick Tracy(c). 200.00
77 Dick Tracy(c). 200.00
78 Smitty(c) 150.00
79 Dick Tracy(c). 150.00
80 Smitty(c) 150.00
81 Dick Tracy(c). 150.00
82 Dick Tracy(c). 150.00
83 Smitty(c) 135.00
84 Dick Tracy(c). 150.00
85 Smitty(c) 135.00
86 All on cover 150.00
87 All on cover 150.00
88 Dick Tracy(c). 150.00
89 Smitty(c) 135.00
90 Dick Tracy(c). 150.00
91 Smitty(c) 135.00
92 Dick Tracy(c) 150.00
93 Dick Tracy(c). 150.00
94 Dick Tracy(c). 150.00
95 thru 99 . . . . @135.00
100 . . . . 150.00
101 thru 115 . . . . @150.00
116 Smokey Stover(c) 100.00
117 Gasoline Alley(c). 100.00
118 Smokey Stover(c) 100.00
119 Terry and the Pirates(c). . . . 110.00
120 . . . . 100.00
121 . . . . 100.00

SUPER-DOOPER COMICS

Able Manufacturing Co., 1946

1 A:Gangbuster 300.00
2 . . . . 200.00
3 & 4 . . . . @150.00
5 A:Captain Freedom,Shock
   Gibson 150.00
6 & 7 same . . . . @150.00
8 A:Shock Gibson, 1946 . . . . . . 150.00

SUPER DUCK COMICS

MLJ Magazines/Close-Up (Archie Publ.), Autumn, 1944

1 O:Super Duck, Hitler 750.00
2 . . . . 300.00
3 I:Mr. Monster 250.00
4 & 5 . . . . @225.00
6 thru 10 . . . . @200.00
11 thru 20 . . . . @150.00
21 thru 40. . . . . @125.00
41 thru 60 . . . . @100.00
61 thru 94. . . . . @100.00

All comics prices listed are for *Near Mint* condition.

SUPER FUNNIES

Superior Comics Publishers, March, 1954

1 Dopey Duck 500.00
2 Out of the Booby-Hatch 200.00
Becomes:

SUPER WESTERN FUNNIES

1954

3 F:Phantom Ranger 100.00
4 F:Phantom Ranger,Sept., 1954 100.00

SUPERIOR STORIES

Nesbit Publishing Co., 1955

1 Wells-The Invisible Man 300.00
2 Ingrahams-Pirate of the Gulf . . 125.00
3 Clark-Wreck of Grosvenor 125.00
4 O'Henry-Texas Rangers 125.00

SUPER MAGICIAN COMICS

Street & Smith Publ., May, 1941

1 B:The Mysterious Blackstone . 900.00
2 V:Wild Tribes of Africa 550.00
3 V:Oriental Wizard 550.00
4 V:Quetzal Wizard,O:Transo . . . 500.00
5 A:The Moylan Sisters 500.00
6 JaB,JaB(c),The Eddie
   Cantor story 500.00
7 In the House of Skulls 525.00
8 A:Abbott & Costello 525.00
9 V:Duneen the Man-Ape 525.00
10 V:Pirates o/t Sargasso Sea. . . 525.00
11 JaB(c),V:Fire Wizards 525.00
12 V:Baal 525.00
2-1 A:The Shadow 525.00
2-2 Temple of the 10,000 Idols . . 250.00
2-3 Optical Illusion on (c)-
   turn Jap into Monkey 250.00
2-4 V:Cannibal Killers 250.00
2-5 V:The Pygmies of Lemuriai . 250.00
2-6 V;Pirates & Indians 250.00
2-7 Can Blackstone Catch the
   Cannonball? 250.00
2-8 V:Marabout,B:Red Dragon . . 250.00
2-9 . . . . 250.00
2-10 Pearl Dives Swallowed By
   Sea Demons 250.00
2-11 Blackstone Invades
   Pelican Islands 250.00
2-12 V:Bubbles of Death 250.00
3-1 . . . . 275.00

Super Magician Vol. 3 #12
© Street & Smith

3-2 Bondage(c),Midsummers
   Eve 250.00
3-3 The Enchanted Garden 250.00
3-4 Fabulous Aztec Treasure . . . 250.00
3-5 A:Buffalo Bill 250.00
3-6 Magic Tricks to Mystify 250.00
3-7 V:Guy Fawkes 250.00
3-8 V:Hindu Spook Maker 250.00
3-9 . . . . 250.00
3-10 V:The Water Wizards 250.00
3-11 V:The Green Goliath 250.00
3-12 Lady in White 250.00
4-1 Cannibal of Crime 225.00
4-2 The Devil's Castle 225.00
4-3 V:Demons of Golden River . 225.00
4-4 V:Dr. Zero 225.00
4-5 Bondage(c) 225.00
4-6 V:A Terror Gang 225.00
4-7 . . . . 225.00
4-8 Mystery of the
   Disappearing Horse 225.00
4-9 A Floating Light? 225.00
4-10 Levitation 225.00
4-11 Lost, Strange Land
   of Shangri 225.00
4-12 I:Nigel Elliman 225.00
5-1 V:Voodoo Wizards of the
   Everglades,Bondage (c) 225.00
5-2 Treasure of the Florida
   Keys; Bondage (c) 225.00
5-3 Elliman Battles Triple Crime . 225.00
5-4 Can A Human Being Really
   Become Invisible 225.00
5-5 Mystery of the Twin Pools . . 225.00
5-6 A:Houdini 225.00
5-7 F:Red Dragon 500.00
5-8 F:Red Dragon,
   Feb.–March, 1947 . . . . 500.00

SUPERMOUSE

Standard Comics/Pines, Dec., 1948

1 FF,(fa) 350.00
2 FF,(fa) 175.00
3 FF,(fa) 135.00
4 FF,(fa) 135.00
5 FF,(fa) 135.00
6 FF,(fa) 135.00
7 thru 10 (fa) . . . . @125.00
11 thru 20 (fa) . . . . @125.00
21 thru 44 (fa) . . . . @100.00
45 (fa),Autumn, 1958 . . . . 100.00

SUPER-MYSTERY COMICS

**Periodical House
(Ace Magazines), July, 1940**

1 B:Magno,Vulcan,Q-13,Flint
   of the Mountes 5,000.00
2 Bondage (c) 1,500.00
3 JaB,B:Black Spider 1,200.00
4 O:Davy;A:Captain Gallant . . . 800.00
5 JaB,JM(c),I&B:The Clown . . . 800.00
6 JM,JM(c),V:The Clown 700.00
2-1 JM,JM(c),O:Buckskin,
   Bondage(c) 675.00
2-2 JM,JM(c),V:The Clown 650.00
2-3 JM,JM(c),V:The Clown 650.00
2-4 JM,JM(c),V:The Nazis 650.00
2-5 JM,JM(c),Bondage(c) 650.00
2-6 JM,JM(c),Bondage(c),
   'Foreign Correspondent' 650.00
3-1 B:Black Ace 650.00
3-2 A:Mr, Risk, Bondage(c) 650.00
3-3 HK,HK(c),I:Lancer;B:Dr.
   Nemesis, The Sword 750.00
3-4 HK 900.00
3-5 HK,LbC,A:Mr. Risk 700.00
3-6 HK,LbC,A:Paul Revere Jr. . . 700.00
4-1 HK,LbC,A:Twin Must Die . . . 600.00
4-2 A:Mr. Risk 400.00

Super-Mystery Comics Vol. 4 #4
© Ace Magazines

4-3 Mango out to Kill Davey! . . . 400.00
4-4 Danger Laughs at Mr. Risk . . 400.00
4-5 A:Mr. Risk 400.00
4-6 RP,A:Mr. Risk 400.00
5-1 RP 400.00
5-2 RP,RP(c),The Riddle of the
   Swamp-Land Spirit 400.00
5-3 RP,RP(c),The Case of the
   Whispering Death 400.00
5-4 RP,RP(c) 400.00
5-5 RP,Harry the Hack 400.00
5-6 . . . . 400.00
6-1 . . . . 350.00
6-2 RP,A:Mr. Risk 350.00
6-3 Bondage (c) 375.00
6-4 E:Mango;A:Mr. Risk 350.00
6-5 Bondage(c) 375.00
6-6 A:Mr. Risk 350.00
7-1 . . . . 350.00
7-2 KBa(c) 350.00
7-3 Bondage(c) 375.00
7-4 . . . . 350.00
7-5 . . . . 350.00
7-6 . . . . 350.00
8-1 The Riddle of the Rowboat . . 300.00
8-2 Death Meets a Train 300.00
8-3 The Man Who Couldn't Die . 300.00
8-4 RP(c) 300.00
8-5 GT,MMe,Staged for Murder . 300.00
8-6 Unlucky Seven,July, 1949 . . 300.00

ARMY AND NAVY COMICS

Street & Smith Publ., May, 1941

1 Hawaii is Calling You,Capt.
   Fury,Nick Carter. 750.00
2 Private Rock V;Hitler 600.00
3 The Fighting Fourth 600.00
4 The Fighting Irish 600.00
5 I:Super Snipe 700.00
Becomes:

SUPERSNIPE COMICS

Oct., 1942

6 A "Comic" With A Sense
   of Humor 1,600.00
7 A:Wacky, Rex King 700.00
8 Axis Powers & Satan(c),
   Hitler(c). 1,200.00
9 Hitler Voodoo Doll (c) 1,300.00
10 Lighting (c) 700.00
11 A:Little Nemo. 700.00
12 Football(c). 700.00
2-1 B:Huck Finn 1,200.00

2-2 Battles Shark 550.00
2-3 Battles Dinosaur 500.00
2-4 Baseball(c). 500.00
2-5 Battles Dinosaur 500.00
2-6 A:Pochontas. 500.00
2-7 A:Wing Woo Woo 500.00
2-8 A:Huck Finn. 500.00
2-9 Dotty Loves Trouble. 500.00
2-10 Assists Farm Labor
    Shortage 500.00
2-11 Dotty & the Jelly Beans 500.00
2-12 Statue of Liberty. 500.00
3-1 Ice Skating(c). 400.00
3-2 V:Pirates(c) 400.00
3-3 Baseball(c). 400.00
3-4 Jungle(c) 400.00
3-5 Learn Piglatin. 400.00
3-6 Football Hero. 400.00
3-7 Saves Girl From Grisley 400.00
3-8 Rides a Wild Horse 400.00
3-9 Powers Santa's Sleigh. 400.00
3-10 Plays Basketball 400.00
3-11 Is A Baseball Pitcher 400.00
3-12 Flies with the Birds 400.00
4-1 Catches A Whale. 300.00
4-2 Track & Field Athlete 300.00
4-3 Think Machine(c). 300.00
4-4 Alpine Skiier. 300.00
4-5 Becomes a Boxer 300.00
4-6 Race Car Driver. 300.00
4-7 Bomber(c) 300.00
4-8 Baseball Star 300.00
4-9 Football Hero. 300.00
4-10 Christmas(c) 300.00
4-11 Artic Adventure. 300.00
4-12 The Ghost Remover 300.00
5-1 Aug.–Sept., 1949 . . . . 300.00

SUPER SPY
**Centaur Publications,
Oct.–Nov., 1940**
1 O:Sparkler 1,500.00
2 A:Night Hawk, Drew Ghost, Tim
  Blain, S.S. Swanson the Inner
  Circle, Duke Collins, Gentlemen
  of Misfortune 900.00

SUPER WESTERN COMICS
Youthful Magazines, Aug., 1950
1 BP,BP,(c),B:Buffalo Bill,Wyatt
  Earp,CalamityJane,SamSlade150.00
2 . . . . 100.00

Super Western Comics #1
© Youthful Magazines

3 . . . . 100.00
4 March, 1951 . . . . 100.00

SUPER WESTERN FUNNIES
See: SUPER FUNNIES

SUPERWORLD COMICS
**Komos Publications
(Hugo Gernsback), April, 1940**
1 FP,FP(c),B:MilitaryPowers,BuzzAllen
  Smarty Artie, Alibi Alige . . 12,000.00
2 FP,FP(c),A:Mario 6,700.00
3 FP,FP(c),V:Vest Wearing
  Giant Grasshoppers 5,500.00

SURE-FIRE COMICS
See: LIGHTNING COMICS

SURPRISE ADVENTURES
See: TORMENTED

SUSPENSE COMICS
**Et Es Go Mag. Inc.
(Continental Magazines),
Dec., 1945**
1 LbC, Bondage(c),B:Grey
  Mask. 6,500.00
2 DRi,I:The Mask. 4,000.00
3 LbC,ASh(c),Bondage(c) . . 24,000.00
4 LbC,LbC(c),Bondage(c) . . . 3,000.00
5 LbC,LbC(c) 3,000.00
6 LbC,LbC(c),The End of
  the Road 3,000.00
7 LbC,LbC(c) 2,700.00
8 LbC,LbC(c) 6,500.00
9 LbC,LbC(c) 2,700.00
10 RP,LbC,LbC(c). 2,700.00
11 RP,LbC,EL,LbC(c),Satan(c) . 5,000.00
12 LbC,LbC(c),Dec., 1946 . . . . 2,500.00

SUSPENSE DETECTIVE
**Fawcett Publications,
June, 1952**
1 GE,MBi,MBi(c),Death Poised
  to Strike 700.00
2 GE,MSy 400.00
3 A Furtive Footstep 350.00
4 MBi,MSy,Bondage(c),A Blood
  Chilling Scream 350.00
5 MSy,MSy(c),MBi,A Hair-Trigger
  from Death, March, 1953 . . . 350.00

SUZIE COMICS
See: TOP-NOTCH COMICS

SWEENEY
**Standard Comics,
June, 1949**
4 Buzz Sawyer's Pal 150.00
5 Sept., 1949 . . . . 125.00

SWEET SIXTEEN
**Parents' Magazine Group,
Aug.–Sept., 1946**
1 Van Johnson story 250.00
2 Alan Ladd story 200.00
3 Rip Taylor. 150.00
4 Elizabeth Taylor ph(c) 275.00
5 Gregory Peck story (c) 150.00
6 Dick Haymes(c) 150.00
7 Ronald Reagan(c) & story 300.00
8 Shirley Jones(c). 125.00
9 William Holden(c). 125.00
10 James Stewart(c) 150.00
11 . . . . 125.00
12 Bob Cummings(c). 125.00
13 Robert Mitchum(c) 150.00

SWIFT ARROW
**Farrell Publications (Ajax),
Feb.–March, 1954**
1 Lone Rider's Redskin Brother 200.00
2 . . . . 125.00
3 thru 4 . . . . @100.00
5 Oct.–Nov., 1954 . . . . 100.00

(2nd Series) April, 1957
1 . . . . 100.00
2 B:Lone Rider 100.00
3 Sept., 1957 . . . . 100.00

TAFFY
**Orbit Publications/Rural Home/
Taffy Publications,
March–April, 1945**
1 LbC(c),(fa),Bondage(c) 850.00
2 LbC(c),(fa) 400.00
3 (fa) 150.00
4 (fa) 150.00
5 LbC(c),A:Van Johnson 250.00
6 A:Perry Como 150.00
7 A:Dave Clark 150.00
8 A:Glen Ford 150.00
9 A:Lon McCallister 150.00
10 A:John Hodiak. 150.00
11 A:Mickey Rooney 165.00
12 Feb., 1948. . . . . 150.00

TAILSPIN
**Spotlight Publications,
Nov., 1944**
N# LbC(c),A:Firebird. 350.00

TALES FROM THE CRYPT
See: CRIME PATROL

TALES FROM THE GREAT BOOK
Famous Funnies, 1955
1 Samson 125.00
2 Joshua 100.00
3 Joash the Boy King 100.00
4 David 100.00

TALES OF HORROR
**Toby Press/Minoan Publ. Corp,
June, 1952–Oct., 1954**
1 Demons of the Underworld . . . 500.00
2 What was the Thing in
  the Pool?,Torture. 400.00
3 The Big Snake 300.00
4 The Curse of King Kala! 300.00
5 Hand of Fate 300.00
6 The Fiend of Flame 300.00
7 Beast From The Deep 300.00
8 The Snake that Held A
  City Captive 300.00
9 It Came From the Bottom
  of the World 350.00
10 The Serpent Strikes 300.00
11 Death Flower?. 350.00
12 Guaranteed to Make Your
  Hair Stand on End,Torture. . . 350.00
13 Ghost with a Torch 350.00

TALES OF JACE PEARSON
See: JACE PEARSON

TALES OF TERROR
Toby Press, 1952
1 Just A Bunch of Hokey
  Hogwash 300.00

GOLDEN AGE

TALES OF TERROR ANNUAL
E.C. Comics, 1951
N# AF 7,000.00
2 AF 3,500.00
3 . . . . 2,700.00

TALLY-HO COMICS
Baily Publishing Co., 1944
N# FF,A:Snowman 600.00

TARGET COMICS
Funnnies Inc./Novelty Publ./ Premium Group/Curtis Circulation Co./Star Publications, Feb., 1940
1 BEv,JCo,CBu,JSm;B,O&I:Manowar, White Streak,Bull's-Eye;B:City Editor,High Grass Twins,T-Men, Rip Rory,Fantastic Feature Films, Calling 2-R 10,000.00
2 BEv,JSm,JCo,CBu,White Streak(c) 6,000.00
3 BEv,JSm,JCo,CBu 3,200.00
4 JSm,JCo 3,200.00
5 CBu,BW,O:White Streak . . . 9,000.00
6 CBu,BW,White Streak(c) . . . 3,500.00
7 CBu,BW,BW(c),V:Planetoid Stories,Space Hawk(c) . . . 10,000.00
8 CBu,BW,White Shark(c) 3,000.00
9 CBu,BW,White Shark(c) 3,000.00
10 CBu,BW,JK(c),The Target(c) 4,000.00
11 BW,The Target(c) 3,500.00
12 BW,same 3,200.00
2-1 BW,CBu 3,000.00
2-2 BW,BoW(c) 2,700.00
2-3 BW,BoW(c),The Target(c) . . 2,500.00
2-4 BW,B:Cadet 2,500.00
2-5 BW,BoW(c),The Target(c) . . 2,500.00
2-6 BW,The Target(c) 2,000.00
2-7 BW,The Cadet(c) 2,000.00
2-8 BW,same 2,000.00
2-9 BW,The Target(c) 2,000.00
2-10 BW,same 2,500.00
2-11 BW,The Cadet(c) 2,000.00
2-12 BW,same 2,000.00
3-1 BW,same 2,000.00
3-2 BW 2,000.00
3-3 BW,The Target(c) 2,000.00
3-4 BW,The Cadet(c) 2,000.00
3-5 BW 2,000.00
3-6 BW,War Bonds(c) 2,500.00

Target Comics Vol. 3 #10
© Star Publications

3-7 BW 2,000.00
3-8 BW,War Bonds(c) 2,500.00
3-9 BW 2,000.00
3-10 BW 2,000.00
3-11 . . . . 500.00
3-12 . . . . 500.00
4-1 JJo(c) 275.00
4-2 ERy(c) 275.00
4-3 AVi 275.00
4-4 . . . . 275.00
4-5 API(c),Statue of Liberty(c) . . 275.00
4-6 BW 275.00
4-7 AVi 275.00
4-8,Christmas(c) 275.00
4-9 . . . . 275.00
4-10 . . . . 275.00
4-11 . . . . 275.00
4-12 . . . . 275.00
5-1 . . . . 250.00
5-2 The Target 125.00
5-3 Savings Checkers(c) 125.00
5-4 War Bonds Ph(c) 125.00
5-5 thru 5-12 . . . . @125.00
6-1 The Target(c) 125.00
6-2 . . . . 125.00
6-3 Red Cross(c) 125.00
6-4 . . . . 125.00
6-5 Savings Bonds(c) 150.00
6-6 The Target(c) 250.00
6-7 The Cadet(c) 250.00
6-8 AFa 250.00
6-9 The Target(c) 250.00
6-10 . . . . 250.00
6-11 . . . . 250.00
6-12 . . . . 250.00
7-1 . . . . 250.00
7-2 Bondage(c) 250.00
7-3 The Target(c) 250.00
7-4 DRi,The Cadet(c). 250.00
7-5 . . . . 250.00
7-6 DRi(c). 250.00
7-7 The Cadet(c) 250.00
7-8 DRi(c). 250.00
7-9 The Cadet(c) 250.00
7-10 DRi,DRi(c) 250.00
7-11 . . . . 250.00
7-12 JH(c) 250.00
8-1 . . . . 200.00
8-2 DRi,DRi(c),BK 200.00
8-3 DRi,The Cadet(c). 200.00
8-4 DRi,DRi(c) 200.00
8-5 DRi,The Cadet(c). 200.00
8-6 DRi,DRi(c) 200.00
8-7 BK,DRi,DRi(c) 200.00
8-8 DRi,The Cadet(c). 200.00
8-9 DRi,The Cadet(c). 200.00
8-10 DRi,KBa,LbC(c) 750.00
8-11 DRi,The Cadet 200.00
8-12 DRi,The Cadet. 200.00
9-1 DRi,LbC(c). 750.00
9-2 DRi. 200.00
9-3 DRi,Bondage(c),The Cadet(c) 275.00
9-4 DRi,LbC(c). 750.00
9-5 DRi,Baseball(c) 250.00
9-6 DRi,LbC(c). 750.00
9-7 DRi. 250.00
9-8 DRi,LbC(c). 750.00
9-9 DRi,Football(c). 250.00
9-10 DRi,LbC(c). 750.00
9-11,The Cadet 250.00
9-12 LbC(c),Gems(c). 750.00
10-1,The Cadet 250.00
10-2 LbC(c) 750.00
10-3 LbC(c) 750.00
Becomes:

TARGET WESTERN ROMANCES
Star Publications, Oct.–Nov., 1949
106 LbC(c),The Beauty Scar 500.00

107 LbC(c),The Brand Upon His Heart 450.00

TARZAN
Dell Publishing Co., Jan.–Feb., 1948
1 V:White Savages of Vari 2,500.00
2 Captives of Thunder Valley. . 1,000.00
3 Dwarfs of Didona 700.00
4 The Lone Hunter 700.00
5 The Men of Greed 700.00
6 Outlaws of Pal-ul-Don 600.00
7 Valley of the Monsters 600.00
8 The White Pygmies 600.00
9 The Men of A-Lur. 600.00
10 Treasure of the Bolgani 600.00
11 The Sable Lion 500.00
12 The Price of Peace 500.00
13 B:Lex Barker photo(c). 450.00
14 Lex Barker ph(c). 450.00
15 Lex Barker ph(c). 450.00
16 Lex Barker ph(c). 400.00
17 Lex Barker ph(c). 400.00
18 Lex Barker ph(c). 400.00
19 Lex Barker ph(c). 400.00
20 Lex Barker ph(c). 400.00
21 thru 24 Lex Barker ph(c). . . @350.00
25 Brothers of the Spear 375.00
26 thru 54 E:L.Barker ph(c) . . . @300.00
55 thru 70. . . . . @250.00
71 thru 79. . . . . @200.00
80 thru 90 B:ScottGordonPh(c) @150.00
91 thru 99. . . . . @125.00
100 . . . . 150.00
101 thru 110 E:S.GordonPh(c). @150.00
111 thru 120 . . . . @125.00
121 thru 131. . . . . @100.00

Teena #21
© Standard Comics

TEENA
Standard Comics, 1949
20 . . . . 100.00
21 . . . . 100.00
22 . . . . 100.00

TEEN-AGE ROMANCES
St. John Publishing Co., Jan., 1949
1 MB(c),MB. 550.00
2 MB(c),MB. 300.00
3 MB(c),MB. 350.00
4 Ph(c) 300.00
5 MB,Ph(c) 300.00
6 MB,Ph(c) 300.00
7 MB,Ph(c) 300.00
8 MB,Ph(c) 300.00

9 MB,MB(c),JKu 325.00
10 thru 27 MB,MB(c),JKu . . . . @250.00
28 . . . . 100.00
29 . . . . 100.00
30 . . . . 100.00
31 thru 34 MB(c) . . . . @125.00
35 thru 42 MB(c),MB . . . . @125.00
43 MB(c),MB,Comics Code 150.00
44 MB(c),MB 150.00
45 MB(c),MB 150.00

TEEN-AGE TEMPTATIONS
St. John Publishing Co.,
Oct., 1952
1 MB(c),MB 600.00
2 MB(c),MB 250.00
3 MB(c),MB 300.00
4 MB(c),MB 300.00
5 MB(c),MB 300.00
6 MB(c),MB 300.00
7 MB(c),MB 300.00
8 MB(c),MB,Drug 350.00
9 MB(c),MB 300.00
Becomes:

GOING STEADY
Dec., 1954
10 MB(c),MB 250.00
11 MB(c),MB 125.00
12 MB(c),MB 125.00
13 MB(c),MB 175.00
14 MB(c),MB 200.00

TEENIE WEENIES, THE
Ziff-Davis Publishing Co.,
1951
10 . . . . 250.00
11 . . . . 250.00

TEEN LIFE
See: YOUNG LIFE

TEGRA, JUNGLE EMPRESS
See: ZEGRA, JUNGLE
EMPRESS

TELEVISION COMICS
Animated Cartoons
(Standard Comics), Feb., 1950
5 Humorous Format,I:Willie Nilly 300.00
6 . . . . 150.00
7 . . . . 150.00
8 May, 1950 . . . . 150.00

TELEVISION PUPPET
SHOW
Avon Periodicals, 1950
1 F:Sparky Smith,Spotty,
Cheeta, Speedy 250.00
2 Nov., 1950 . . . . 150.00

TELL IT TO
THE MARINES
Toby Press, March, 1952
1 I:Spike & Pat 250.00
2 A:Madame Cobra 150.00
3 Spike & Bat on a
Commando Raid! 125.00
4 Veil Dancing(c) 125.00
5 . . . . 125.00
6 To Paris 100.00
7 Ph(c),The Chinese Bugle 100.00
8 Ph(c),V:Communists in
South Korea 100.00
9 Ph(c) 100.00
10 . . . . 100.00
11 . . . . 100.00
12 . . . . 100.00

13 John Wayne Ph(c) 150.00
14 Ph(c) 100.00
15 Ph(c),July, 1955 . . . . 100.00

TERRIFIC COMICS
See: HORRIFIC

TERRIFIC COMICS
Et Es Go Mag. Inc./
Continental Magazines,
Jan., 1944
1 LbC,DRi(c),F:Kid
Terrific Drug 5,500.00
2 LcC,ASh(c),B:Boomerang,
'Comics' McCormic 3,500.00
3 LbC,LbC(c) 3,500.00
4 LbC,RP(c) 6,500.00
5 LbC,BF,ASh(c),Bondage(c) . 9,000.00
6 LbC,LbC(c),BF,Nov.,1944 . 3,200.00

TERRIFYING TALES
Star Publications,
Jan., 1953
11 LbC,LbC(c),'TyrantsofTerror' . . 700.00
12 LbC,LbC(c),'Bondage(c),
'Jungle Mystery' 600.00
13 LbC(c),Bondage(c),'The
Death-Fire,Devil Head(c). . . . 750.00
14 LbC(c),Bondage(c),'The
Weird Idol' 600.00
15 LbC(c),'The Grim Secret',
April, 1954 . . . . 600.00
Becomes:

JUNGLE THRILLS
Star Publications, Feb., 1952
16 LbC(c),'Kingdom of Unseen
Terror' 750.00
Becomes:

TERRORS OF
THE JUNGLE
Star Publications, May, 1952
17 LbC(c),Bondage(c) 700.00
18 LbC(c),Strange Monsters 450.00
19 JyD,LbC(c),Bondage(c),The
Golden Ghost Gorilla 400.00
20 JyD,LbC(c),The Creeping
Scourge 400.00
21 LbC(c),Evil Eyes of Death! . . . 450.00
4 JyD,LbC(c),Morass of Death . 400.00
5 JyD,LbC(c),Bondage(c),
Savage Train 425.00
6 JyD,LbC(c),Revolt of the
Jungle Monsters 425.00
7 JyD,LbC(c) 450.00
8 JyD,LbC(c),Death's Grim
Reflection 450.00
9 JyD,LbC(c),Doom to
Evil-Doers 450.00
10 JyD,LbC(c),Black Magic,
Sept., 1954 . . . . 450.00

TERROR ILLUSTRATED
E.C. Comics,
Nov.–Dec., 1955
1 JCr,GE,Grl,JO,RC(c) 250.00
2 Spring, 1956 . . . . 150.00

BOY EXPLORERS
Harvey Comics, 1946
1 S&K(c),S&K,The Cadet 1,500.00
2 S&K(c),S&K 2,000.00
Becomes:

TERRY AND THE PIRATES
Harvey Comics, April, 1947
3 S&K,MC(c),MC,Terry and
Dragon Lady 550.00
4 S&K,MC(c),MC 300.00

Terry and the Pirates #9
© Harvey Comics

5 S&K,MC(c),MC,BP,
Chop-Chop(c) 175.00
6 S&K,.MC(c),MC 175.00
7 S&K,MC(c),MC,BP 175.00
8 S&K,MC(c),MC,BP 175.00
9 S&K,MC(c),MC,BP 175.00
10 S&K,MC(c),MC,BP 175.00
11 S&K,MC(c),MC,BP,
A:Man in Black 150.00
12 S&K,MC(c),MC 150.00
13 S&K,MC(c),MC,Belly Dancers 150.00
14 thru 20 S&K,MC(c),MC . . . . @125.00
21 thru 26 S&K,MC(c),MC . . . . @110.00
27 Charlton Comics 100.00
28 . . . . 100.00
Becomes:

LONG JOHN SILVER
AND THE PIRATES
Charlton Comics, 1956–57
30 . . . . 125.00
31 . . . . 125.00
32 . . . . 125.00

TERRY-BEARS COMICS
St. John Publishing Co.,
June, 1952
1 . . . . 125.00
2 & 3 . . . . @100.00

TERRY-TOONS COMICS
Select, Timely, Marvel,
St. Johns, 1942
1 Paul Terry (fa) 2,500.00
2 . . . . 900.00
3 thru 6 . . . . @600.00
7 Hitler,Hirohito,Mussolini(c) 700.00
8 thru 20 . . . . @450.00
21 thru 37 . . . . @300.00
38 I&(c):Mighty Mouse 1,900.00
39 Mighty Mouse 600.00
40 thru 49 All Mighty Mouse . . @250.00
50 I:Heckle & Jeckle 600.00
51 thru 60 . . . . @150.00
61 thru 70 . . . . @125.00
71 thru 86 . . . . @125.00
Becomes:

PAUL TERRY'S COMICS
St. John Publishing Co.
85a Mighty Mouse, etc. 150.00
86a 100.00
87 thru 100 . . . . @100.00
101 thru 125 . . . . @100.00
Becomes:

GOLDEN AGE

ADVENTURES OF MIGHTY MOUSE
St. John Publ. Co., 1955
126 thru 128 .... @150.00

Pines, 1956
129 thru 143 .... @150.00

Dell Publ. Co., 1959
144 thru 155 .... @125.00

TEXAN, THE
St. John Publishing Co., Aug., 1948
1 GT,F:Buckskin Belle,The Gay
  Buckaroo,Mustang Jack 200.00
2 GT 125.00
3 BLb(c) 100.00
4 MB,MB(c) 200.00
5 MB,MB(c),Mystery Rustlers
  of the Rio Grande 200.00
6 MB(c),Death Valley
  Double-Cross 125.00
7 MB,MB(c),Comanche Justice
  Strikes at Midnight 200.00
8 MB,MB(c),Scalp Hunters
  Hide their Tracks 200.00
9 MB(c),Ghost Terror of
  the Blackfeet 200.00
10 MB,MB(c),Treason Rides
  the Warpath 125.00
11 MB,MB(c),Hawk Knife 225.00
12 MB 300.00
13 MB,Doublecross at Devil'sDen 200.00
14 MB,Ambush at Buffalo Trail . 200.00
15 MB,Twirling Blades Tame
  Treachery 200.00
Becomes:

FIGHTIN' TEXAN
Sept., 1952
16 GT,Wanted Dead or Alive ... 125.00
17 LC,LC(c);Killers Trail,
  Dec., 1952 .... 100.00

TEX FARRELL
D.S. Publishing Co., March–April, 1948
1 Pride of the Wild West 200.00

TEX GRANGER
See: CALLING ALL BOYS

TEX RITTER WESTERN
Fawcett Publications/ Charlton Comics, Oct., 1950–May, 1959
1 Ph(c),B:Tex Ritter, his Horse
  White Flash, his dog Fury, and
  his mom Nancy 1,000.00
2 Ph(c),Vanishing Varmints 450.00
3 Ph(c),Blazing Six-Guns 350.00
4 Ph(c),The Jaws of Terror 325.00
5 Ph(c),Bullet Trail 325.00
6 Ph(c),Killer Bait 250.00
7 Ph(c),Gunsmoke Revenge ... 225.00
8 Ph(c),Lawless Furnace Valley 225.00
9 Ph(c),The Spider's Web 225.00
10 Ph(c),The Ghost Town 225.00
11 Ph(c),Saddle Conquest..... 225.00
12 Ph(c),Prairie Inferno 175.00
13 Ph(c)................... 175.00
14 Ph(c)................... 175.00
15 Ph(c)................... 175.00
16 thru 19 Ph(c)........... @175.00
20 Ph(c),Stagecoach To Danger . 175.00
21 Ph(c), ... 200.00
22 Panic at Diamond B 150.00
23 A:Young Falcon........... 125.00
24 A:Young Falcon............ 125.00
25 A:Young Falcon 125.00

26 thru 38................. @100.00
39 AW,AW(c) 100.00
40 thru 46................. @100.00

THING!, THE
Song Hits/Capitol Stories/ Charlton Comics, Feb., 1952
1 Horror 2,500.00
2 Crazy King(c) 2,000.00
3 Green skinned creature ... 2,000.00
4 AFa(c),I Was A Zombie 1,500.00
5 LM(c),Severed Head(c) 1,500.00
6 .... 1,500.00
7 Fingernail to Eye(c) 1,600.00
8 .... 1,500.00
9 Severe cruelty............ 2,000.00
10 Devil(c)................ 1,250.00
11 SC,Cleaver, eye injury 1,500.00
12 SD,SD(c),Neck Blood
  Sucking................. 1,500.00
13 SD,SD(c) 1,500.00
14 SD,SD(c) torture 1,500.00
15 SD,SD(c) 1,500.00
16 Eye Torture 750.00
17 BP,SD(c) 1,500.00
Becomes:

BLUE BEETLE
Feb., 1955
18 America's Fastest Moving
  Crusader Against Crime 250.00
19 JKa,Lightning Fast 275.00
20 JKa 300.00
21 The Invincible 250.00
Becomes:

MR. MUSCLES
March, 1956
22 World's Most Perfect Man.... 150.00
23 Aug., 1956.............. 100.00

THIS IS SUSPENSE
See: LAWBREAKERS

THIS IS SUSPENSE!
See: STRANGE SUSPENSE STORIES

THIS IS WAR
Standard Comics, July, 1952
5 ATh,Show Them How To Die . 150.00
6 ATh,Make Him A Soldier 125.00
7 One Man For Himself 100.00

This Is War #5
© *Standard Comics*

8 Miracle on Massacre Hill 100.00
9 ATh,May, 1953 .... 125.00

THIS MAGAZINE IS HAUNTED
Fawcett Publications Oct., 1951
1 MBi,F:Doctor Death 900.00
2 GE 650.00
3 MBi,Quest of the Vampire ... 450.00
4 BP,The Blind, The Doomed
  and the Dead 450.00
5 BP,GE,The Slithering Horror
  of Skontong Swamp! 650.00
6 Secret of the Walking Dead... 300.00
7 The Man Who Saw Too Much . 300.00
8 The House in the Web....... 300.00
9 The Witch of Tarlo 300.00
10 I Am Dr Death,
  Severed Head(c).......... 500.00
11 BP,Touch of Death 300.00
12 BP 300.00
13 BP,Severed Head(c)........ 500.00
14 BP,Horrors of the Damned ... 300.00

Charlton Comics, 1954
15 DG(c).................. 250.00
16 SD(c).................. 500.00
17 SD,SD(c)................ 700.00
18 SD,SD(c)................ 600.00
19 SD(c).................. 500.00
20 SMz(c)................. 265.00
21 SD(c).................. 500.00
Becomes:

DANGER AND ADVENTURE
Feb., 1955
22 The Viking King,F:Ibis the
  Invincible................ 150.00
23 F:Nyoka the Jungle Girl
  Comics Code............. 125.00
24 DG&AA(c)............... 100.00
25 thru 27................. @100.00
Becomes:

ROBIN HOOD AND HIS MERRY MEN
April, 1956
28 .... 150.00
29 thru 37................. @100.00
38 SD,Aug., 1958 .... 150.00

THIS MAGAZINE IS HAUNTED
See: CHARLIE CHAN

3-D ANIMAL FUN
Premier Magazines, 1953
1 Ziggy Pig, Silly Seal,etc. 425.00

CAPTAIN 3-D
Harvey Publ, 1953
1 .... 125.00

CHERRIOS 3D CLASSICS
Walt Disney Productions, 1954
1 .... 150.00

3-D CIRCUS
Fiction House, 1953
1 .... 500.00

3-D DARING ADVENTURES
St. John Publ, 1953
1 .... 400.00

3-D-ELL
Dell Publishing Co., 1953
1 Rootie Kazootie 500.00
3 Flunkey Louise. 450.00

3-D DOLLY
Harvey Publ, 1953
1 Richie Rich 1,000.00

3-D EC CLASSICS
E.C. Comics 1954
1 . . . . 1,200.00
2 Tales from the Crypt of Terror 1,200.00

3-D FELIX THE CAT
Toby Press, 1953
N# 350.00

3-D FIRST CHRISTMAS
Fiction House, 1953
1 . . . . 250.00

3-D FUNNY MOVIES
Comic Media, 1953
1 Bugsey Bear 500.00

FUNNY 3-D
Harvey Publ., 1953
1 . . . . 350.00

3-D HAWK, THE
St. John Publ, 1953
1 MB,Western 400.00

3-D HOUSE OF TERROR
St. John Publ., 1953
1 . . . . 600.00

3-D I LOVE LUCY
1 Lucy, Desi, Ricky Jr. Ph(c). . . . 600.00

3-D INDIAN WARRIORS
Star Publications, 1953
1 . . . . 250.00

(3-D Features Presents) JET PUP
Dimensions Publ., 1953
1 . . . . 500.00

3-D JUNGLE THRILLS
Star Publications, 1953
1 . . . . 350.00

3-D KATY KEENE
Archie Publications, 1953
1 . . . . 500.00

3-D LITTLE EVA
St. John Publ, 1953
1 . . . . 350.00
2 . . . . 350.00

3-D LOVE
Steriographic Publications, 1953
1 . . . . 425.00

(Three Dimension Comics) MIGHTY MOUSE
St. John Publ, 1953
1 . . . . 350.00

3-D Little Eva
© St. John Publishing

2 . . . . 350.00
3 . . . . 350.00

3-D NOODNICK
Comic Media, 1953
1 . . . . 350.00

3-D ROMANCE
Steriographic Publ., 1954
1 . . . . 450.00

(Harvey 3-D Hits) SAD SACK
Harvey Publications, 1954
1 . . . . 400.00

3-D SHEENA, JUNGLE QUEEN
Fiction House, 1953
1 . . . . 1,000.00

3-D SPACE KAT-ETS
Power Publishing, 1953
1 . . . . 350.00

3-D SUPER ANIMALS
Star Publications, 1953
1 Pidgy and the Magic Glasses . 350.00

3-D SUPER FUNNIES
Superior Comics Publ., 1953
1 Dopey Duck 350.00

3-D THREE STOOGES
St. John Publ., 1953
1 . . . . 700.00
2 . . . . 650.00

3-D TRUE 3D
Harvey Publ., 1953
1 . . . . 400.00
2 . . . . 350.00

3-D WESTERN FIGHTERS
Star Publications, 1953
1 . . . . 350.00

THREE RING COMICS
Spotlight Publishers, March, 1945
1 Funny Animal 200.00

THREE STOOGES
Jubilee Publ., Feb., 1949
1 JKu,Infinity(c) 1,600.00
2 JKu,On the Set of the 'The Gorilla Girl' 1,200.00
St. John Publishing Co.
1:JKu,'Hell Bent for Treasure,' Sept., 1953 . . . . 1,200.00
2 JKu. 900.00
3 JKu,3D. 900.00
4 JKu,Medical Mayhem 800.00
5 JKu,Shempador-Matador Supreme 800.00
6 JKu, ... 800.00
7 JKu,Ocotber, 1954. . . . . 800.00

THRILLING COMICS
Better Publ./Nedor/ Standard Comics, Feb., 1940
1 B&O:Doc Strange,B:Nickie Norton 5,000.00
2 B:Rio Kid,Woman in Red Pinocchio 2,500.00
3 B:Lone Eagle,The Ghost . . . 2,000.00
4 Dr Strange(c) 1,400.00
5 Bondage(c) 1,600.00
6 Dr Strange(c) 1,400.00
7 Dr Strange(c) 1,500.00
8 V:Pirates 1,500.00
9 ASh,Bondage(c) 1,500.00
10 V:Nazis. 1,700.00
11 ASh(c),V:Nazis 1,400.00
12 ASh(c) 1,400.00
13 ASh(c),Bondage(c). 1,600.00
14 ASh(c) 1,200.00
15 ASh(c),V:Nazie. 1,200.00
16 Bondage(c) 1,600.00
17 Dr Strange(c) 1,200.00
18 Dr Strange(c) 1,600.00
19 I&O:American Crusader. . . . 1,500.00
20 Bondage(c) 1,600.00
21 American Crusader(c) 1,200.00
22 Bondage(c) 1,400.00
23 American Crusader 1,200.00
24 I:Mike in Doc Strange 1,200.00
25 DR Strange(c) 1,200.00

Thrilling Comics #19
© Standard Comics

All comics prices listed are for *Near Mint* condition.

26 Dr Strange(c) 1,200.00
27 Bondage(c) 1,400.00
28 Bondage(c) 1,400.00
29 E:Rio Kid;Bondage(c) 1,400.00
30 Bondage(c) 1,400.00
31 Dr Strange(c) 1,100.00
32 Dr Strange(c) 1,100.00
33 Dr Strange(c) 1,100.00
34 Dr Strange(c) 1,100.00
35 Dr Strange 1,100.00
36 ASh(c),B:Commando 1,200.00
37 BO,ASh(c) 1,100.00
38 ASh(c) 1,100.00
39 ASh(c),E:American Crusader 1,100.00
40 ASh(c) 1,100.00
41 ASh(c),F:American Crusader,
    Hitler 2,000.00
42 ASh(c) 900.00
43 ASh(c) 900.00
44 ASh(c),Hitler(c) 1,400.00
45 EK,ASh(c) 800.00
46 ASh(c) 800.00
47 ASh(c) 800.00
48 EK,ASh(c) 800.00
49 ASh(c) 800.00
50 ASh(c) 800.00
51 ASh(c) 800.00
52 ASh(c),E:Th Ghost;
    Peto-Bondage(c) 900.00
53 ASh(c),B:Phantom Detective . 700.00
54 ASh(c),Bondage(c) 900.00
55 ASh(c),E:Lone Eagle 700.00
56 ASh(c),B:Princess Pantha . . . 900.00
57 ASh(c) 800.00
58 ASh(c) 800.00
59 ASh(c) 800.00
60 ASh(c) 800.00
61 ASh(c),Grl,A:Lone Eagle 800.00
62 ASh(c) 800.00
63 ASh(c),GT 800.00
64 ASh(c) 800.00
65 ASh(c),E:Commando Cubs,
    Phantom Detective 800.00
66 ASh(c) 800.00
67 FF,ASh(c) 900.00
68 FF,ASh(c) 900.00
69 FF,ASh(c) 900.00
70 FF,ASh(c) 900.00
71 FF,ASh(c) 900.00
72 FF,ASh(c),Sea Eagle 900.00
73 FF,ASh(c) 900.00
74 ASh(c),E:Princess Pantha;
    B:Buck Ranger 500.00
75 B:Western Front 350.00
76 Western 350.00
77 ASh(c) 350.00
78 Bondage(c) 400.00
79 BK 350.00
80 JSe,BE,April, 1951 . . . . 350.00

THRILLING CRIME CASES
Star Publications, June–July, 1950
41 LbC(c),The Unknowns 350.00
42 LbC(c),The Gunmaster 325.00
43 LbC,LbC(c),The Chameleon . . 350.00
44 LbC(c),Sugar Bowl Murder . . . 350.00
45 LbC(c),Maze of Murder 350.00
46 LbC(c),LbC(c),Modern
    Communications 300.00
47 LbC(c),The Careless Killer . . . 300.00
48 LbC(c),Road Black 300.00
49 LbC(c),The Poisoner 550.00
Becomes:

SHOCKING MYSTERY CASES
Sept., 1952–Oct., 1954
50 JyD,LbC(c),Dead Man's
    Revenge 550.00

Shocking Mystery Cases #54
© Star Publications

51 JyD,LbC(c),A Murderer's
    Reward 350.00
52 LbC(c),The Carnival Killer . . . 350.00
53 LbC(c),The Long Shot of Evil . 350.00
54 LbC(c),Double-Cross of Death 350.00
55 LbC(c),Return from Death . . . 350.00
56 LbC(c),The Chase 375.00
57 LbC(c),Thrilling Cases 350.00
58 LbC(c),Killer at Large 350.00
59 LbC(c),Relentless Huntdown . . 350.00
60 LbC(c),Lesson of the Law 350.00

THRILLING TRUE STORY OF THE BASEBALL GIANTS
Fawcett Publications, 1952
N# Partial Ph(c),Famous Giants
    of the Past, Willie Mays . . 1,200.00
2 Yankees Ph(c),Joe DiMaggio,
    Yogi Berra,Mickey Mantle,
    Casey Stengel 1,000.00

THRILLS OF TOMORROW
See: TOMB OF TERROR

TICK TOCK TALES
Magazine Enterprises, Jan., 1946
1 (fa) Koko & Kola 250.00
2 (fa) Calender 200.00
3 thru 10 (fa) . . . . @150.00
11 thru 18 (fa) . . . . @125.00
19 (fa),Flag(c) 125.00
20 thru 22 (fa) . . . . @125.00
23 (fa),Mugsy Mouse 125.00
24 thru 33 (fa) . . . . @125.00
34 (fa), 1951 . . . . 125.00

TIM HOLT
Magazine Enterprises, Jan.–Feb., 1949
1 thru 3 see: *A-1 Comics* #14, #17, #19
4 FBe,Ph(c) 1,200.00
5 FBe,Ph(c) 700.00
6 FBe,Ph(c),I:Calico Kid 600.00
7 FBe,Ph(c),Man-Killer Mustang 500.00
8 FBe,Ph(c) 500.00
9 FBe,DAy(c),Terrible Tenderfoot 500.00
10 FBe,DAy(c),The Devil Horse . 500.00
11 FBe,DAy(c),O&I:Ghost Rider . 750.00
12 FBe,DAy(c),Battle at
    Bullock Gap 250.00
13 FBe,DAy,Ph(c) 250.00

14 FBe,DAy(c),Ph(c),The
    Honest Bandits 250.00
15 FBe,DAy,Ph(c) 250.00
16 FBe,DAy,Ph(c) 250.00
17 FBe,DAy,Ph(c) 750.00
18 FBe,DAy,Ph(c) 300.00
19 FBe,DAy,They Dig By Night . . 175.00
20 FBe,DAy,O:Red Mask 300.00
21 FBe,DAy,FF(c) 600.00
22 FBe,DAy 175.00
23 FF,FBe,DAy 500.00
24 FBe,DAy,FBe(c) 175.00
25 FBe,DAy,FBe(c) 350.00
26 FBe,DAy,FBe(c) 175.00
27 FBe,DAy,FBe(c),V:Straw Man . 175.00
28 FBe,DAy,FBe(c),Ph(c) 175.00
29 FBe,DAy,FBe,Ph(c), ... 175.00
30 FBe,DAy,FBe(c),Lady Doom
    & The Death Wheel 200.00
31 FBe,DAy,FBe(c) 200.00
32 FBe,DAy,FBe(c) 200.00
33 FBe,DAy,FBe(c) 200.00
34 FBe,DAy,FBe(c) 250.00
35 FBe,DAy,FBe(c) 250.00
36 FBe,DAy,FBe(c),Drugs 350.00
37 FBe,DAy,FBe(c) 250.00
38 FBe,DAy,FBe(c) 250.00
39 FBe,DAy,FBe(c),3D Effect . . . 200.00
40 FBe,DAy,FBe(c) 200.00
41 FBe,DAy,FBe(c) 200.00
Becomes:

RED MASK
June–July, 1954
42 FBe,DAy,FBe(c),3D 250.00
43 FBe,DAy,FBe(c),3D 225.00
44 FBe,DAy,FBe(c),Death at
    Split Mesa,3D 225.00
45 FBe,DAy,FBe(c),V:False Red
    Mask 225.00
46 FBe,DAy,FBe(c) 225.00
47 FBe,DAy,FBe(c) 225.00
48 FBe,DAy,FBe(c),Comics Code 200.00
49 FBe,DAy,FBe(c) 200.00
50 FBe,DAy 200.00
51 FBe,DAy,The Magic of 'The
    Presto Kid' 200.00
52 FBe,DAy,O:Presto Kid 225.00
53 FBe,DAy 150.00
54 FBe,DAy,Sept., 1957 . . . . 225.00

TIM McCOY
See: ZOO FUNNIES

TIM TYLER COWBOY
Standard Comics, Nov., 1948
11 . . . . 150.00
12 . . . . 100.00
13 The Doll Told the Secret 100.00
14 Danger at Devil's Acres 100.00
15 Secret Treasure 100.00
16 . . . . 100.00
17 . . . . 100.00
18 1950 . . . . 100.00

TINY TOTS COMICS
Dell Publishing Co., 1943
1 WK,fairy tales 500.00

TINY TOTS COMICS
E.C. Comics, March, 1946
N# Your First Comic Book
    B:Burton Geller(c) and art . . . 500.00
2 . . . . 275.00
3 Celebrate the 4th 225.00
4 Go Back to School 250.00
5 Celebrate the Winter 225.00
6 Do Their Spring Gardening . . . 225.00
7 On a Thrilling Ride 225.00
8 On a Summer Vacation 225.00

9 On a Plane Ride 225.00
10 Merry X-Mas Tiny Tots
   E:Burton Geller(c)and art . . . 225.00

TIP TOP COMICS
United Features, St. John, Dell, 1936

1 HF,Li'l Abner 11,000.00
2 HF 2,600.00
3 HF,Tarzan(c) 2,400.00
4 HF,Li'l Abner(c) 1,500.00
5 HF,Capt&Kids(c) 1,000.00
6 HF 950.00
7 HF 950.00
8 HF,Li'l Abner(c) 950.00
9 HF,Tarzan(c) 1,200.00
10 HF,Li'L Abner(c) 950.00
11 HF,Tarzan(c) 900.00
12 HF,Li'l Abner 800.00
13 HF,Tarzan(c) 900.00
14 HF,Li'L Abner(c) 800.00
15 HF,Capt&kids(c) 800.00
16 HF,Tarzan(c) 900.00
17 HF,Li'L Abner(c) 800.00
18 HF,Tarzan(c) 900.00
19 HF,Football(c) 750.00
20 HF,Capt&Kids(c) 750.00
21 HF,Tarzan(c) 750.00
22 HF,Li'l Abner(c) 550.00
23 HF,Capt&Kids(c) 550.00
24 HF,Tarzan(c) 750.00
25 HF,Capt&Kids(c) 550.00
26 HF,Li'L Abner(c) 550.00
27 HF,Tarzan(c) 750.00
28 HF,Li'l Abner(c) 550.00
29 HF,Capt&Kids(c) 550.00
30 HF,Tarzan(c) 750.00
31 HF,Capt&Kids(c) 550.00
32 HF,Tarzan(c) 750.00
33 HF,Tarzan(c) 750.00
34 HF,Capt&Kids(c) 750.00
35 HF 500.00
36 HF,HK,Tarzan(c) 750.00
37 HF,Tarzan 750.00
38 HF 500.00
39 HF,Tarzan 700.00
40 HF 500.00
41 Tarzan(c) 750.00
42 . . . . 450.00
43 Tarzan(c) 500.00
44 HF 450.00
45 HF,Tarzan(c) 500.00
46 HF 450.00
47 HF,Tarzan(c) 500.00
48 HF 450.00
49 HF 450.00

Tip Top #34
© *United Features*

50 HF,Tarzan(c) 500.00
51 . . . . 400.00
52 Tarzan(c) 500.00
53 . . . . 400.00
54 O:Minorman 500.00
55 . . . . 350.00
56 . . . . 350.00
57 BHg 400.00
58 . . . . 300.00
59 BHg 400.00
60 . . . . 300.00
61 and 62 BHg . . . . @400.00
63 thru 90 . . . . @200.00
91 thru 99 . . . . @150.00
100 . . . . 175.00
101 thru 150 . . . . @125.00
151 thru 188 . . . . @100.00
189 thru 225 . . . . @75.00

TIP TOPPER COMICS
United Features Syndicate, 1949

1 Abbie & Slats, Li'l Abner, etc.. . 200.00
2 . . . . 150.00
3 . . . . 125.00
4 . . . . 125.00
5 Fearless Fosdick 125.00
6 Fearless Fosdick 125.00
7 . . . . 100.00
8 . . . . 100.00
9 . . . . 100.00
10 . . . . 100.00
11 thru 16 . . . . @100.00
17 Peanuts (c) 150.00
18 thru 24 . . . . @100.00
25 Peanuts 110.00
26 Peanuts 110.00

T-MAN
Comics Magazines (Quality Comics Group), Sept., 1951

1 JCo,Pete Trask-the
  Treasury Man 500.00
2 RC(c),The Girl with Death
  in Her Hands 275.00
3 RC(a&c),Death Trap in Iran . . 275.00
4 RC(a&c),Panama Peril 275.00
5 RC(a&c),Violence in Venice . . 275.00
6 RC(c),The Man Who
  Could Be Hitler 250.00
7 RC(c),Mr. Murder & The
  Black Hand 250.00
8 RC(c),Red Ticket to Hell 250.00
9 RC(c),Trial By Terror 250.00
10 RC 250.00
11 The Voice of Russia 175.00
12 Terror in Tokyo 175.00
13 Mind Assassins 175.00
14 Trouble in Bavaria, Hitler 200.00
15 The Traitor,Bondage(c) 175.00
16 Hunt For a Hatcheman 175.00
17 Red Triggerman 175.00
18 Death Rides the Rails 175.00
19 Death Ambush 175.00
20 The Fantastic H-Bomb Plot. . . 200.00
21 The Return of Mussolini 150.00
22 Propaganda for Doom 165.00
23 Red Intrigue in Parid,H-Bomb. 150.00
24 Red Sabotage 150.00
25 RC,The Ingenious Red Trap . . 150.00
26 . . . . 125.00
27 . . . . 125.00
29 thru 33 . . . . @125.00
34 Hitler (c) 150.00
35 thru 37 . . . . @125.00
38 Dec., 1956 . . . . 125.00

T-Man #21
© *Quality Comics Group*

TNT COMICS
Charles Publishing Co., Feb., 1946

1 FBI story,YellowJacket 450.00

TOM AND JERRY
DELL GIANT EDITIONS
Dell Publishing Co., 1952–58

Back to School 300.00
Picnic Time 250.00
Summer Fun 1 . . . . 350.00
Summer Fun 2 . . . . 200.00
Winter Carnival 1 . . . . 500.00
Winter Carnival 2 . . . . 350.00
Winter Fun 3 . . . . 200.00
Winter Fun 4 . . . . 175.00
Winter Fun 5 . . . . 150.00
Winter Fun 6 . . . . 150.00
Winter Fun 7 . . . . 150.00

TOM AND JERRY
See: OUR GANG COMICS

TOMB OF TERROR
Harvey Publications, June, 1952

1 BP,The Thing From the
  Center of the Earth 750.00
2 RP,The Quagmire Beast 600.00
3 BP,RP,Caravan of the
  Doomed, Bondage(c) 600.00
4 RP,I'm Going to Kill You,
  Torture 500.00
5 RP 500.00
6 RP,Return From the Grave . . . 500.00
7 RP,Shadow of Death 500.00
8 HN,The Hive 500.00
9 BP,HN,The Tunnel 500.00
10 BP,HN,The Trial 500.00
11 BP,HN,The Closet 500.00
12 BP,HN,Tale of Cain 550.00
13 BP,What Was Out There 600.00
14 BP,SC,End Result 600.00
15 BP,HN,Break-up, Exploding
  Head 1,000.00
16 BP,Going,Going,Gone 600.00
Becomes:

THRILLS OF TOMORROW
Oct., 1954

17 RP,BP,The World of Mr. Chatt. 300.00
18 RP,BP,The Dead Awaken 200.00

GOLDEN AGE

GOLDEN AGE

19 S&K,S&K(c),A:Stuntman..... 600.00
20 S&K,S&K(c),A:Stuntman..... 500.00

TOM CAT See:BO

TOM CORBETT SPACE CADET
Dell Publishing Co., Jan., 1952
See also Dell Four Color
4 based on TV show......... 200.00
5 .... 150.00
6 .... 100.00
7 .... 100.00
8 .... 100.00
9 .... 100.00
10 and 11 .... @100.00

TOM CORBETT SPACE CADET
Prize Publications, May–June, 1955
1 Robot(c)................. 400.00
2 .... 300.00
3 Sept.–Oct., 1955 .... 300.00

TOM MIX COMICS
Ralston-Purina Co., Sept., 1940
1 O:Tom Mix............... 4,500.00
2 .... 1,500.00
3 .... 800.00
4 thru 9 .... @750.00
Becomes:

TOM MIX COMMANDOS COMICS
Nov., 1942
10 .... 700.00
11 Invisible Invaders 700.00
12 Terrible Talons Of Tokyo 700.00

TOM MIX WESTERN
Fawcett Publications, Jan., 1948
1 Ph(c),Two-Fisted
   Adventures............. 1,500.00
2 Ph(c),Hair-Triggered Action . 600.00
3 Ph(c),Double Barreled Action . 500.00
4 Ph(c),Cowpunching 500.00
5 Ph(c),Two Gun Action 500.00
6 CCB,Most Famous Cowboy . 350.00
7 CCB,A Tattoo of Thrills 250.00
8 EK,Ph(c),Gallant Guns 325.00
9 CCB,Song o/t Deadly Spurs . 325.00
10 CCB,Crack Shot Western... 325.00
11 CCB,EK(C),Triple Revenge . 325.00
12 King of the Cowboys....... 250.00
13 Ph(c),Leather Burns 250.00
14 Ph(c),Brand of Death 250.00
15 Ph(c),Masked Treachery.... 250.00
16 Ph(c),Death Spurting Guns.. 250.00
17 Ph(c),Trail of Doom........ 250.00
18 Ph(c),Reign of Terror 225.00
19 Hand Colored Ph(c) 250.00
20 Ph(c),CCB,F:Capt Tootsie.. 225.00
21 Ph(c) 225.00
22 Ph(c),The Human Beast..... 225.00
23 Ph(c),Return of the Past..... 225.00
24 Hand Colored Ph(c),
   The Lawless City.......... 225.00
25 Hand Colored Ph(c),
   The Signed Death Warrant .. 225.00
26 Hand Colored Ph(c),
   Dangerous Escape 225.00
27 Hand Colored Ph(c),
   Hero Without Glory 225.00
28 Ph(c),The Storm Kings 225.00

Tom Mix #56
© Fawcett Publications

29 Hand Colored Ph(c),The
   Case of the Rustling Rose .. 225.00
30 Ph(c),Disappearance
   in the Hills 225.00
31 Ph(c).................... 175.00
32 Hand Colored Ph(c),
   Mystery of Tremble Mountain 175.00
33 .... 175.00
34 .... 175.00
35 Partial Ph(c),The Hanging
   at Hollow Creek........... 175.00
36 Ph(c).................... 175.00
37 Ph(c).................... 175.00
38 Ph(c),36 pages 150.00
39 Ph(c).................... 175.00
40 Ph(c).................... 175.00
41 Ph(c).................... 175.00
42 Ph(c).................... 175.00
43 Ph(c).................... 150.00
44 Ph(c).................... 150.00
45 Partial Ph(c),The Secret
   Letter 150.00
46 Ph(c).................... 150.00
47 Ph(c).................... 150.00
48 Ph(c).................... 150.00
49 Partial Ph(c),Blind Date
   With Death................ 150.00
50 Ph(c).................... 150.00
51 Ph(c).................... 150.00
52 Ph(c).................... 150.00
53 Ph(c).................... 150.00
54 Ph(c).................... 150.00
55 Ph(c).................... 150.00
56 Partial Ph(c),Deadly Spurs... 150.00
57 Ph(c)5................... 150.00
58 Ph(c).................... 150.00
59 Ph(c).................... 150.00
60 Ph(c).................... 150.00
61 Partial Ph(c),Lost in the
   Night,May, 1953........... 175.00

TOMMY OF THE BIG TOP
King Features/ Standard Comics, 1948
10 Thrilling Circus Adventures... 150.00
11 .... 100.00
12 March, 1949 .... 100.00

TOM-TOM THE JUNGLE BOY
Magazine Enterprises, 1946
1 (fa) 200.00
2 (fa) 150.00

3 Winter 1947,(fa),X-mas issue . 125.00
1 .... 100.00

TONTO
See: LONE RANGER'S COMPANION TONTO

TONY TRENT See: FACE, THE

TOP FLIGHT COMICS
Four Star/St. John Publ. Co., July, 1949
1 .... 125.00
1 Hector the Inspector 100.00

TOPIX COMICS
Topix/Catechetical Guild, 1942
1 Catholic 350.00
2 .... 250.00
3 .... 250.00
4 .... 200.00
5 .... 200.00
6 .... 200.00
7 .... 200.00
8 .... 200.00
Volume 2, any, except #5 ..... 200.00
5 Pope Pius XII.............. 250.00
Volume 3, any 200.00
Volume 4, any 175.00
Volume 5, any, except #12 .... 150.00
12 Life of Christ 175.00
Volume 6, any 125.00
Volume 7, any 100.00
Volume 8, any #4............ 150.00
4 Dagwood Splits Atom....... 150.00
Volume 9, any, except #12 .... 100.00
12 Christmas issue 100.00
Volume 10, any 100.00

TOP LOVE STORIES
Star Publications, May, 1951
3 LbC(c)................... 300.00
4 LbC(c).................. 225.00
5 LbC(c).................. 225.00
6 LbC(c),WW 300.00
7 LbC(c).................. 250.00
8 LbC(c), WW Story 275.00
9 LbC(c).................. 250.00
10 thru 16 LbC(c) .... @250.00
17 LbC(c),WW.............. 275.00
18 LbC(c)................. 250.00
19 LbC(c),JyD.............. 250.00

TOP-NOTCH COMICS
MLJ Magazines, Dec., 1939
1 JaB,JCo,B&O:The Wizard,
   B:Kandak,Swift of the Secret
   Service,The Westpointer,
   Mystic, Air Patrol,Scott
   Rand, Manhunter 12,000.00
2 JaB,JCo,B:Dick Storm,
   E:Mystic, B:Stacy Knight .. 7,600.00
3 JaB,JCo,EA(c),E:Swift of the
   Secret Service,Scott Rand 4,000.00
4 JCo,EA(c),MMe,O&I:Streak,
   Chandler 3,500.00
5 Ea(c),MMe,O&I:Galahad,
   B:Shanghai Sheridan 3,500.00
6 Ea(c),MMe,A:The Shield .. 3,000.00
7 Ea(c),MMe,N:The Wizard .. 3,800.00
8 E:Dick Sorm,B&O:Roy The1
   Super Boy,The Firefly 3,500.00
9 O&I:Black Hood,
   B:Fran Frazier 10,000.00
10 A:Black Hood........... 3,500.00
11 .... 2,800.00

Top-Notch Comics #2
© MLJ Magazines

12	2,800.00
13	2,800.00
14 Bondage(c)	2,800.00
15 MMe	2,800.00
16	2,500.00
17 Bondage(c)	2,800.00
18	2,500.00
19 Bondage(c)	2,800.00
20	2,500.00
21	2,000.00
22	2,000.00
23 Bondage(c)	2,200.00
24 Black Hood Smashes Murder Ring	2,000.00
25 E:Bob Phantom	2,000.00
26	2,000.00
27 E:The Firefly	2,000.00
28 B:Suzie,Pokey Okay, Gag Oriented	2,000.00
29 E:Kandak	2,000.00
30	2,000.00
31	900.00
32	900.00
33 BWo,B:Dotty&Ditto	900.00
34 BWo	900.00
35 BWo	900.00
36 BWo	900.00
37 thru 40 BWo	@900.00
41	900.00
42 BWo	900.00
43	900.00
44 EW:Black Hood,I:Suzie	900.00
45 Suzie(c)	1,000.00

Becomes:

LAUGH COMIX
Summer, 1944

46 Suzie & Wilbur	500.00
47 Suzie & Wilbur	400.00
48 Suzie & Wilbur	400.00

Becomes:

SUZIE COMICS
Spring, 1945

49 B:Ginger	600.00
50 AFy(c)	400.00
51 AFy(c)	400.00
52 AFy(c)	400.00
53 AFy(c)	400.00
54 AFy(c)	500.00
55 AFy(c)	500.00
56 BWo,B:Katie Keene	300.00
57 thru 70 BWo	@300.00
71 thru 79 BWo	@200.00
80 thru 99 BWo	@200.00
100 Aug., 1954, BWo	200.00

TOPS
Tops Mag. Inc. (Lev Gleason), July, 1949

1 RC&BLb,GT,DBa,CBi(c),I'll Buy That Girl,Our Explosive Children	1,700.00
2 FGu,BF,CBi(c),RC&BLb	1,600.00

TOPS COMICS
Consolidated Book Publishers, 1944

2000 Don on the Farm	400.00
2001 The Jack of Spades V:The Hawkman	300.00
2002 Rip Raiders	250.00
2003 Red Birch	200.00

TOP SECRET
Hillman Publications, Jan., 1952

1 The Tricks of the Secret Agent Revealed	250.00

TOP SECRETS
Street & Smith Publ., Nov., 1947

1 BP,BP(c),Of the Men Who Guard the U.S. Mail	400.00
2 BP,BP(c),True Story of Jim the Penman	350.00
3 BP,BP(c),Crime Solved by Mental Telepathy	300.00
4 Highway Pirates	300.00
5 BP,BP(c),Can Music Kill	300.00
6 BP,BP(c),The Clue of the Forgotten Film	300.00
7 BP,BP(c),Train For Sale	375.00
8 BP,BP(c)	300.00
9 BP,BP(c)	300.00
10 BP,BP(c),July–Aug., 1949	375.00

TOPS IN ADVENTURE
Approved Comics (Ziff-Davis), Autumn, 1952

1 BP,Crusaders From Mars	700.00

TOP SPOT COMICS
Top Spot Publishing Co., 1945

1 The Duke Of Darkness	450.00

TOPSY-TURVY
R.B. Leffingwell Publ., April, 1945

1 I:Cookie	200.00

TOR
St. John Publishing Co., Sept., 1953

1 JKu,JKu(c),O;Tor,One Million Years Ago	150.00
2 JKu,JKu(c),3-D Issue	100.00
3 JKu,JKu(c),ATh,historic Life	125.00
4 JKu,JKu(c),ATh	125.00
5 JKu,JKu(c),ATh,Oct., 1954	125.00

TORCHY
Quality Comics Group, Nov., 1949

1 GFx,BWa(c),The Blonde Bombshell	2,200.00
2 GFx(a&c),Beauty at Its Best	1,100.00
3 GFx,GFx(c),You Can't Beat Nature	1,100.00
4 GFx,GFx(c),The Girl to Keep Your Eye On	1,400.00

5 BWa,GFx,BWa(c),At the Masquerade Party	1,800.00
6 Sept., 1950,BWa,GFx, BWa(c),The Libido Driven Boy Scout	1,800.00

TORMENTED, THE
Sterling Comics, July, 1954

1 Buried Alive	400.00
2 Sept., 1954,The Devils Circus	250.00

Becomes:

SURPRISE ADVENTURES
Sterling Comics, 1955

3 MSy	250.00
4	150.00
5 MSy	200.00

TOYLAND COMICS
Fiction House Magazines, Jan., 1947

1 Wizard of the Moon	400.00
2 Buddy Bruin & Stu Rabbit	200.00
3 GT,The Candy Maker	250.00
4 July, 1947	200.00

TOY TOWN COMICS
Toytown Publ./Orbit Publ., Feb., 1945

1 LbC,LbC(c)(fa)	500.00
2 LbC,(fa)	300.00
3 LbC,LbC(c),(fa)	250.00
4 thru 7 LbC,(fa) May, 1947	@250.00

TRAIL BLAZERS
See: RED DRAGON COMICS

Trapped!
© Harvey Publications

TRAPPED
Harvey Publications, 1951

N#	150.00

TRAPPED!
Periodical Magazines (Ace Magazines), 1954

1	125.00
2 and 3	@60.00

TREASURE CHEST
George A Pflaum Publ., Inc., 1946

1	325.00
2 thru 4	@150.00

5 Dr Styx 160.00
6 . . . . 150.00
Vol 2, 1 thru 20 . . . . @150.00
Vol 3, 1 thru 5 (1947–48) . . . . . @150.00
Vol 3, #6 Verne,Voyage to Moon, 135.00
Vol 3, 7 thru 20 . . . . @110.00
Vol 4, 1 thru 20 (1948–49) . . . . @135.00
Vol 5, 1 thru 20 (1949–50) . . . . @125.00
Vol 6, 1 thru 20 (1950–51) . . . . @125.00
Vol 7, 1 thru 20 (1951–52) . . . . @125.00
Vol 8, 1 thru 20 (1952–53) . . . . @125.00
Vol 9, 1 thru 20 (1953–54) . . . . @100.00
Vol 10, 1 thru 10 (1954–55) . . . @100.00
Vol 10, #11 BP 100.00
Vol 10, 12 thru 20 . . . . @100.00
Vol 11, 1 thru 20 (1955–56) . . . @100.00
Vol 12, 1 thru 20 (1956–57) . . . @100.00
Vol 13, 1 thru 20 (1957–58) . . . @75.00
Vol 14, 1 thru 20 (1958–59) . . . . @75.00
Vol 15, 1 thru 20 (1959–60) . . . . @75.00
Vol 16, 1 thru 20 (1960–61) . . . . @75.00
Vol 17, 1 thru 20 (1962–63)
　odd #s . . . . @75.00
　even #s "Godless Communism"
　2 RC 275.00
　4 and 6 . . . . @275.00
　8 thru 14 Stalin, WWII . . . . @275.00
　14 thru 20 Kruschev . . . . . @225.00

TREASURE COMICS
Prize Comics Group, 1943
1 S&K,Reprints of Prize Comics
　#7 through #11 . . . . 3,200.00

TREASURE COMICS
American Boys Comics
(Prize Publications),
June–July, 1945
1 HcK,B:PaulBunyan,MarcoPolo 700.00
2 HcK(a&c),B:Arabian Knight,
　Gorilla King,Dr.Styx 350.00
3 HcK 250.00
4 HcK 250.00
5 HcK,JK, Marco Polo 350.00
6 BK,HcK(a&c) 250.00
7 FF,HcK(a&c),Capt.Kidd, Jr. . . . 550.00
8 HcK,FF 550.00
9 HcK,DBa 250.00
10 JK,DBa,JK(c) 450.00
11 BK,HcK,DBa,The Weird
　Adventures of Mr. Bottle . . . 300.00
12 DBa,DBa(c),Autumn, 1947 . . 250.00

TREASURY OF COMICS
St. John Publishing Co., 1947
1 RvB,RvB(c),Abbie an' Slats . . 150.00
2 Jim Hardy 125.00
3 Bill Bimlin 125.00
4 RvB,RvB(c),Abbie an' Slats . . 125.00
5 Jim Hardy,Jan., 1948 . . . . 100.00

TREASURY OF COMICS
St. John Publishing Co., 1948
1 Abbott & Costello,
　Little Audrey 250.00
2 . . . . 125.00
3 thru 5 . . . . @110.00

TRIPLE THREAT
Gerona Publications,
Winter, 1945
1 F:King O'Leary,The Duke of
　Darkness,Beau Brummell . . . 400.00

TRUE ANIMAL
PICTURE STORIES
True Comics Press, 1947
1 & 2 . . . . @125.00

TRUE AVIATION
PICTURE STORIES
Parents' Institute/P.M.I.,
Aug., 1942
1 How Jimmy Doolittle
　Bombed Tokyo 300.00
2 Knight of the Air Mail 250.00
3 The Amazing One-Man
　Air Force 200.00
4 Joe Foss America's No. 1
　Air Force 200.00
5 Bombs over Germany 200.00
6 Flight Lt. Richard
　Hillary R.A.F. 200.00
7 "Fatty" Chow China's
　Sky Champ 200.00
8 Blitz over Burma 200.00
9 Off the Beam 200.00
10 "Pappy" Boyington 200.00
11 Ph(c) 200.00
12 . . . . 200.00
13 Ph(c),Flying Facts 200.00
14 . . . . 200.00
15 True Aviation Adventures . . . 200.00
Becomes:

AVIATION AND MODEL
BUILDING
Dec., 1946
16 . . . . 125.00
17 Feb., 1947 . . . . 150.00

TRUE COMICS
True Comics/
Parents' Magazine Press,
April, 1941–Aug., 1950
1 My Greatest Adventure-by
　Lowell Thomas, Churchill . . . 450.00
2 BEv,The Story of the
　Red Cross 200.00
3 Baseball Hall of Fame 225.00
4 Danger in the Artic 150.00
5 Father Duffy-the Fighting
　Chaplain, Joe Louis 165.00
6 The Capture of Aquinaldo 175.00
7 JKa,Wilderness Adventures of
　George Washington 165.00
8 U.S. Army Wings 125.00
9 A Pig that Made History 125.00
10 Adrift on an Ice Pan 125.00
11 Gen. Douglas MacArthur 110.00
12 Mackenzie-King of Cananda . . 110.00
13 The Real Robinson Crusoe . . . 110.00
14 Australia war base of
　the South Pacific 110.00
15 The Story of West Point 125.00
16 How Jimmy Doolittle
　Bombed Tokyo 120.00
17 The Ghost of Captain Blig,
　B.Feller 125.00
18 Battling Bill of the
　Merchant Marine 135.00
19 Secret Message Codes 110.00
20 The Story of India 100.00
21 Timoshenko the Blitz Buster . . 110.00
22 Gen, Bernard L. Montgomery . 100.00
23 The Story of Steel 100.00
24 Gen. Henri Giraud-Master
　of Escape 100.00
25 Medicine's Miracle Men 100.00
26 Hero of the Bismarck Sea. . . . 100.00
27 Leathernecks have Landed. . . 110.00
28 The Story of Radar 100.00
29 The Fighting Seabees 100.00
30 Dr. Norman Bethune-Blood
　Bank Founder 100.00
31 Our Good Neighbor Bolivia,
　Red Grange 110.00
32 Men against the Desert 125.00
33 Gen.Clark and his Fighting 5th 150.00

True Comics #25
© Parents' Magazine Press

34 Angel of the Battlefield 125.00
35 Carlson's Marine Raiders 125.00
36 Canada's Sub-Busters 125.00
37 Commander of the Crocodile
　Fleet. 125.00
38 Oregon Trailblazer 125.00
39 Saved by Sub, FBI 125.00
40 Sea Furies 125.00
41 Cavalcade of England. 100.00
42 Gen. Jaques Le Clerc-Hero
　of Paris 100.00
43 Unsinkable Ship 100.00
44 El Senor Goofy, Truman 100.00
45 Tokyo Express 100.00
46 The Magnificent Runt 100.00
47 Atoms Unleashed,
　Atomic Bomb. 175.00
48 Pirate Patriot. 100.00
49 Smoking Fists 100.00
50 Lumber Pirates 100.00
51 Exercise Musk-Ox. 100.00
52 King of the Buckaneers 100.00
53 Baseline Booby. 100.00
54 Santa Fe Sailor 100.00
55 Sea Going Santa 100.00
56 End of a Terror 100.00
57 Newfangled Machines 100.00
58 Leonardo da Vinci-500 years
　too Soon, Houdini 100.00
59 Pursuit Pirates, Bob Hope . . . 100.00
60 Emmett Kelly-The World's
　Funniest Clown 100.00
61 Peter Le Grand-
　Bold Buckaneer 100.00
62 Sutter's Gold. 100.00
63 Outboard Outcome 100.00
64 Man-Eater at Large. 100.00
65 The Story of Scotland Yard. . . 100.00
66 Easy Guide to Football
　Formations, Will Rogers 100.00
67 The Changing Zebra. 100.00
68 Admiral Byrd 100.00
69 FBI Special Agent Steve
　Saunders, Jack Benny 100.00
70 The Case of the Seven
　Hunted Men. 100.00
71 Story of Joe DiMaggio 150.00
72 FBI,Jackie Robinson. 125.00
73 The 26 Mile Dash-Story of
　the Marathon, Walt Disney . . 100.00
74 A Famous Coach's Special
　Football Tips, Amos & Andy . 100.00
75 King of Reporters 100.00
76 Story of a Buried Treasure . . . 100.00
77 France's Greatest Detective . . 100.00
78 Cagliostro-Master Rogue 100.00

79 Ralph Bunche-Hero of Peace. 100.00
80 Rocket Trip to the Moon 200.00
81 Red Grange 200.00
82 Marie Celeste Ship of
　　Mystery 175.00
83 Bullfighter from Brooklyn. 175.00
84 King of the Buckaneers 175.00

TRUE CONFIDENCES
**Fawcett Publications,
Autumn, 1949**
1 . . . . 225.00
2 and 3 . . . . @125.00
4 DP 125.00

TRUE CRIME COMICS
**Magazine Village, Inc.,
May, 1947**
2 JCo(c),James Kent-Crook,
　　Murderer,Escaped Convict;
　　Drug 2,300.00
3 JCo(a&c),Benny Dickson-
　　Killer;Drug. 1,600.00
4 JCo(a&c),Little Jake-
　　Big Shot 1,400.00
5 JCo(c),The Rat & the Blond
　　Gun Moll;Drug 1,000.00
6 Joseph Metley-Swindler,
　　Jailbird, Killer 800.00
?-1(7) ATh,WW,Ph(c),Phil
　　Coppolla,Sept., 1949 . . . . 1,200.00

TRUE LOVE PICTORIAL
St. John Publishing Co., 1952
1 Ph(c) 350.00
2 MB 450.00
3 MB(c),MB,JKu 750.00
4 MB(c),MB,JKu 750.00
5 MB(c),MB,JKu 750.00
6 MB(c) 350.00
7 MB(c) 350.00
8 MB(c) 300.00
9 MB(c) 300.00
10 MB(c),MB 300.00
11 MB(c),MB 300.00

TRUE MOVIE AND TELEVISION
Toby Press, Aug., 1950
1 Liz Taylor, Ph(c) 750.00
2 FF,Ph(c),John Wayne,
　　L.Taylor 550.00
3 June Allyson,Ph(c) 400.00
4 Jane Powell,Ph(c),Jan.,1951 . . 250.00

SPORT COMICS
Street & Smith Publ., Oct., 1940
1 F:Lou Gehrig 700.00
2 F:Gene Tunney 400.00
3 F:Phil Rizzuto 450.00
4 F:Frank Leahy 300.00
Becomes:

TRUE SPORT PICTURE STORIES
**Street & Smith Publ.,
Feb., 1942–July-Aug., 1949**
5 Joe DiMaggio 500.00
6 Billy Confidence 250.00
7 Mel Ott 275.00
8 Lou Ambers 250.00
9 Pete Reiser 250.00
10 Frankie Sinkwich. 250.00
11 Marty Serfo 250.00
12 JaB(c),Jack Dempsey. 265.00
2-1 JaB(c),Willie Pep 250.00
2-2 JaB(c) 250.00
2-3 JaB(c),Carl Hubbell 265.00
2-4 Advs. in Football & Battle . . . 275.00

True Sport Picture Stories Vol. 2 #6
© Street & Smith Publications

2-5 Don Hutson 250.00
2-6 Dixie Walker. 275.00
2-7 Stan Musial 300.00
2-8 Famous Ring Champions
　　of All Time 275.00
2-9 List of War Year Rookies . . . 300.00
2-10 Connie Mack 275.00
2-11 Winning Basketball Plays . . 250.00
2-12 Eddie Gottlieb 250.00
3-1 Bill Conn 250.00
3-2 Philadelphia Athletics 225.00
3-3 Leo Durocher 250.00
3-4 Rudy Dusek 225.00
3-5 Ernie Pyle 225.00
3-6 Bowling with Ned Day 225.00
3-7 Return of the Mighty (Home
　　from War);Joe DiMaggio(c) . . 400.00
3-8 Conn V:Louis 300.00
3-9 Reuben Shark 225.00
3-10 BP,BP(c),Don "Dopey"
　　Dillock 225.00
3-11 BP,BP(c),Death
　　Scores a Touchdown 225.00
3-12 Red Sox V:Senators 225.00
4-1 Spring Training in
　　Full Spring 225.00
4-2 BP,BP(c),How to Pitch 'Em
　　Where They Can't Hit 'Em . . 225.00
4-3 BP,BP(c),1947 Super Stars . 250.00
4-4 BP,BP(c),Get Ready for
　　the Olympics 235.00
4-5 BP,BP,(c),Hugh Casey 225.00
4-6 BP,BP(c),Phantom Phil
　　Hergesheimer 225.00
4-7 BP,BP(c),How to Bowl Better 225.00
4-8 Tips on the Big Fight 235.00
4-9 BP,BP(c),Bill McCahan 225.00
4-10 BP,BP(c),Great Football
　　Plays 225.00
4-11 BP,BP(c),Football. 225.00
4-12 BP,BP(c),Basketball. 225.00
5-1 Satchel Paige 250.00
5-2 History of Boxing 200.00

TRUE-TO-LIFE ROMANCES
**Star Publications,
Nov.–Dec., 1949**
3 LbC(c),GlennFord/JanetLeigh . 300.00
4 LbC(c) 225.00
5 LbC(c) 225.00
6 LbC(c) 225.00
7 LbC(c) 225.00
8 LbC(c) 225.00

9 LbC(c) 225.00
10 LbC(c) 225.00
11 LbC(c) 225.00
12 LbC(c) 225.00
13 LbC(c),JyD 225.00
14 LbC(c),JyD 225.00
15 LbC(c),WW,JyD 250.00
16 LbC(c),WW,JyD 250.00
17 LbC(c),JyD 200.00
18 LbC(c),JyD 200.00
19 LbC(c),JyD 200.00
20 LbC(c),JyD 200.00
21 LbC(c),JyD 200.00
22 LbC(c) 200.00
23 LbC(c) 200.00

TRUE WAR EXPERIENCES
Harvey Publications, 1952
1 . . . . 150.00
2 thru 4 . . . . @100.00

TUBBY
See: MARGE'S TUBBY

TUFFY
**Best Books, Inc.
(Standard Comics) 1949**
5 . . . . 125.00
6 true 9 . . . . @100.00

TUROK, SON OF STONE
**Dell Publishing Co.,
Dec., 1954**
(1) *see Dell Four Color #596*
(2) *see Dell Four Color #656*
3 Cavemen 400.00
4 & 5 . . . . @300.00
6 & 7 . . . . @250.00
8 Dinosaur, Lost Valley 275.00
9 thru 16 . . . . @175.00
17 Prehistoric Pigmies 200.00
18 thru 29 . . . . @125.00

TV SCREEN CARTOONS
(see REAL SCREEN COMICS)

TV TEENS
Charlton Comics, 1954
1 Ozzie & Babs. 125.00
2 . . . . 100.00
3 . . . . 100.00
4 . . . . 100.00
5 . . . . 100.00
6 Don Winslow 100.00
7 B:Mopsy. 100.00
8 thru 13 . . . . @100.00

TWEETY AND SYLVESTER
**Dell Publishing Co.,
June, 1952**
(1) *see Dell Four Color #406*
(2) *see Dell Four Color #489*
(3) *see Dell Four Color #524*
4 thru 20 . . . . @125.00
21 thru 37 . . . . @100.00

TWINKLE COMICS
**Spotlight Publications,
May, 1945**
1 Humor Format 300.00

TWO-BIT WACKY WOODPECKER
Toby Press, 1952
1 . . . . 150.00
2 . . . . 120.00
3 . . . . 120.00

All comics prices listed are for *Near Mint* condition.

TWO-FISTED TALES
Fables Publications
(E.C. Comics),
Nov.–Dec., 1950–March, 1955
18 JCr,WW,JSe,HK(a&c) 2,000.00
19 JCr,WW,JSe,HK(a&c) 1,500.00
20 JDa,WW,JSe,HK(a&c) 900.00
21 JDa,WW,JSe,HK(a&c) 800.00
22 JDa,WW,JSe,HK(a&c) 800.00
23 JDa,WW,JSe,HK(a&c) 600.00
24 JDa,WW,JSe,HK(a&c) 500.00
25 JDa,WW,JSe,HK(a&c) 500.00
26 JDa,JSe,HK(c),Action at
   the Changing Reservoir. 400.00
27 JDa,JSe,HK(c) 400.00
28 JDa,JSe,HK(c) 400.00
29 JDa,JSe,HK(c) 450.00
30 JSe,JDa(a&c) 450.00
31 JDa,JSe,HK(c),Civil
   War Story. 400.00
32 JDa,JKu,WW(c) 400.00
33 JDa,JKu,WW(c),A-Bomb . . . 500.00
34 JSe,JDa(a&c) 400.00
35 JSe,JDa(a&c),Civil
   War Story. 400.00
36 JDa,JSe(a&c),A
   Difference of Opinion. 500.00
37 JSe(a&c),Bugles &
   Battle Cries 500.00
38 JSe(a&c) 500.00
39 JSe(a&c) 500.00
40 JDa,JSe,GE(a&c) 550.00
41 JSe,GE,JDa(c) 500.00
Ann. 1952 (#1) 1,750.00
Ann. 1953 (#2) JDa(c) 1,400.00

UNCLE CHARLIE'S
FABLES
Lev Gleason Publications,
Jan., 1952
1 CBi(c),Ph(c) 200.00
2 BF,CBi(c),Ph(c) 125.00
3 CBi(c),Ph(c) 135.00
4 CBi(c),Ph(c) 135.00
5 CBi,Ph(c),Sept., 1952 . . . . . . 135.00

UNCLE JOE'S FUNNIES
Centaur Publications, 1938
1 BEv,Puzzles & Comics 900.00

UNCLE MILTY
Victoria Publications
(True Cross Comic), 1950
1 Milton Berle 800.00
2 . . . . 500.00
3 . . . . 375.00
4 . . . . 350.00

UNCLE SAM
See: BLACKHAWK

UNCLE SCROOGE
Dell Publishing Co.,
March, 1952
(1) *see Dell Four Color #386*
(2) *see Dell Four Color #456*
(3) *see Dell Four Color #495*
4 Gladstone Album #11 . . . . 700.00
5 Gladstone Special 500.00
6 . . . . 400.00
7 CB, Seven Cities of Cibola . . . 350.00
8 thru 10 . . . . @300.00
11 thru 23 . . . . @275.00
24 Christmas issue 275.00
25 thru 30 . . . . @250.00
31 thru 39 . . . . @200.00

Underworld #6
© D.S. Publishing Co.

UNDERWORLD
D.S. Publishing Co.,
Feb.–March, 1948
1 SMo(c),Violence 750.00
2 SMo(c),Electrocution 600.00
3 AMc,AMc(c),The Ancient Club 500.00
4 Grl,The Beer Baron Murder . . 450.00
5 Grl,The Postal Clue 300.00
6 The Polka Dot Gang 250.00
7 Mono-The Master 250.00
8 The Double Tenth 250.00
9 Thrilling Stories of the Fight
   against Crime,June, 1953 . . 250.00

UNDERWORLD CRIME
Fawcett Publications,
June, 1952
1 The Crime Army 500.00
2 Jailbreak 350.00
3 Microscope Murder 300.00
4 Death on the Docks 300.00
5 River of Blood 300.00
6 The Sky Pirates 300.00
7 Bondage & Torture(c) 500.00
8 and 9 June, 1953 . . . . @300.00

UNITED COMICS
See: FRITZI RITZ

UNITED STATES
FIGHTING AIR FORCE
Superior Comics, Ltd.,
Sept., 1952
1 Coward's Courage 150.00
2 Clouds that Killed 125.00
3 Operation Decoy 100.00
4 thru 28 . . . . @100.00
29 Oct., 1959 . . . . 100.00

UNITED STATES
MARINES
Wm. H. Wise/Magazine Ent/
Toby Press, 1943–52
N# MBi,MBi(c),Hellcat out
   of Heaven 250.00
2 MBi,Drama of Wake
   Island, Tojo 500.00
3 A Leatherneck Flame
   Thrower, Tojo 400.00
4 MBi 125.00
5 BP 100.00
6 BP 100.00

7 BP 100.00
8 thru 11 . . . . @100.00

UNKEPT PROMISE
Legion of Truth, 1949
1 Anti:Alcoholic Drinking 150.00

UNKNOWN WORLDS
See: STRANGE STORIES
FROM ANOTHER WORLD

UNSEEN, THE
Visual Editions
(Standard Comics), 1952
5 ATh,The Hungry Lodger 600.00
6 JKa,MSy,Bayou Vengeance . . 400.00
7 JKz,MSy,Time is the Killer . . . 400.00
8 JKz,MSy,The Vengeance Vat . 300.00
9 JKz,MSy,Your Grave is Ready 450.00
10 JKz,MSy 400.00
11 JKz,MSy 300.00
12 ATh,GT,Till Death Do Us Part. 400.00
13 . . . . 300.00
14 . . . . 300.00
15 ATh,The Curse of the
   Undead!, July, 1954. . . . . . . 400.00

UNTAMED LOVE
Comic Magazines
(Quality Comics Group),
Jan., 1950
1 BWa(c),PGv 325.00
2 Ph(c) 200.00
3 PGv, Ph(c) 225.00
4 Ph(c) 200.00
5 PGv, Ph(c) 225.00

USA IS READY
Dell Publishing Co., 1941
1 Propaganda WWII 600.00

U.S. JONES
Fox Features Syndicate,
Nov., 1941
1 Death Over the Airways 1,900.00
2 Nazi (c),Jan., 1942 . . . . 1,400.00

U.S. MARINES IN
ACTION!
Avon Periodicals,
Aug.–Dec., 1952
1 On Land,Sea & in the Air 125.00
2 The Killer Patrol 100.00
3 EK(c),Death Ridge. 100.00

U.S. PARATROOPS
Avon Periodicals, 1951
1 WW 200.00
2 EK 125.00
3 . . . . 100.00
4 thru 6 EK . . . . @125.00

U.S. TANK
COMMANDOS
Avon Periodicals,
June, 1952
1 EK(c),Fighting Daredevils
   of the USA 150.00
2 EK(c) 100.00
3 EK,EK(c),Robot Armanda 100.00
4 EK,EK(c),March, 1953 . . . . . . 100.00

VALOR
E.C. Comics, March, 1955
1 AW,AT,WW,WW(c),Grl,BK 800.00
2 AW(c),AW,WWGrl,BK 700.00

3 AW,RC,BK,JOc(c) 500.00
4 WW(c),RC,Grl,BK,JO 500.00
5 WW(c),WW,AW,GE,Grl,BK . . . 450.00

VARIETY COMICS
**Rural Home Publ./
Croyden Publ. Co., 1944**
1 MvS,MvS(c),O:Capt, Valiant . . 300.00
2 MvS,MvS(c) 250.00
3 MvS,MvS(c) 200.00
4 . . . . 150.00
5 1946 . . . . 150.00

VAULT OF HORROR
See: WAR AGAINST CRIME

V...COMICS
**Fox Features Syndicate,
Jan., 1942**
1 V:V-Man, Nazi(c) 1,800.00
2 The Horror of the
   Dungeons, March, 1942 . . 1,400.00

VERI BEST
SURE FIRE COMICS
Holyoke Publishing Co., 1945
1 Capt Aero, Miss Victory, Red
   Cross, Devil Dogs 600.00

VERI BEST
SURE SHOT COMICS
Holyoke Publishing Co., 1945
1 reprint Holyoke One-Shots . . . 500.00

VIC FLINT
**St. John Publishing Co.,
Aug., 1948**
1 ...Crime Buster 200.00
2 . . . . 175.00
3 . . . . 150.00
4 . . . . 150.00
5 April, 1949 . . . . 150.00

VIC FLINT
Argo Publ., 1956
1 . . . . 125.00
2 . . . . 100.00

VIC JORDAN
**Civil Service Publications,
April, 1945**
1 Escape From a Nazi Prison . . 150.00

VIC TORRY AND HIS
FLYING SAUCER
Fawcett Publications, 1950
1 Ph(c),Revealed at Last. 1,000.00

VICTORY COMICS
**Hillman Periodicals,
Aug., 1941**
1 BEv,BEv(c),F:TheConqueror 4,500.00
2 BEv, BEv(c) 1,900.00
3 The Conqueror(c) 1,250.00
4 Dec., 1941 . . . . 1,200.00

VIC VERITY MAGAZINE
**Vic Verity Publications,
1945**
1 CCB,CCB(c),B:Vic Verity,Hot-
   Shot Galvan, Tom Travis . . . 300.00
2 CCB,CCB(c),Annual Classic
   Dance Recital 150.00
3 CCB 125.00

---

4 CCB,I:Boomer Young;The
   Bee-U-TiFul Weekend 125.00
5 CCB,Championship Baseball
   Game 125.00
6 CCB,High School Hero 125.00
7 CCB,CCB(c),F:Rocket Rex . . 125.00

VOODOO
**Four Star Publ./Farrell/
Ajax Comics, May, 1952**
1 MB,South Sea Girl. 800.00
2 MB 650.00
3 Face Stabbing 500.00
4 MB,Rendezvous 500.00
5 Ghoul For A Day,Nazi 400.00
6 The Weird Dead,
   Severed Head 425.00
7 Goodbye World 400.00
8 MB, Revenge 500.00
9 Will this thing Never Stew? . . . 400.00
10 Land of Shadows & Screams. 400.00
11 Human Harvest. 350.00
12 The Wazen Taper 350.00
13 Bondage(c),Caskets to
   Fit Everybody 375.00
14 Death Judges the
   Beauty Contest, Zombies . . . 350.00
15 Loose their Heads, Opium . . . 350.00
16 Fog Was Her Shroud 325.00
17 Apes Laughter,Electric Chair . 350.00
18 Astounding Fantasy 325.00
19 MB,Bondage(c),
   Destination Congo. 450.00
Ann.#1 100-pg. 1,400.00
Becomes:

VOODA
April, 1955
20 MB,MB(c),Echoes of
   an A-Bomb. 500.00
21 MB,MB(c),Trek of Danger. . . 450.00
22 MB,MB(c),The Sun Blew
   Away, Aug., 1955. . . . . 450.00

WALT DISNEY'S
COMICS & STORIES
Dell Publishing Co.
N# 1943 dpt.store giveway. 750.00
N# 1945 X-mas giveaway. 350.00

WALT DISNEY'S
COMICS & STORIES
**Dell Publishing Co.,
Oct., 1940**
1 (1940)FGu,Donald Duck &
   Mickey Mouse 29,000.00
2 . . . . 10,000.00
3 . . . . 3,500.00
4 1st Huey, Dewey & Louie
   Christmas(c). 2,500.00
4a Promo issue 4,000.00
5 Goofy(c) 2,000.00
6 . . . . 1,500.00
7 . . . . 1,500.00
8 Clarabelle Cow(c). 1,500.00
9 . . . . 1,500.00
10 . . . . 1,500.00
11 2nd Huey,Louie,Dewey(c) . . 1,500.00
12 . . . . 1,400.00
13 . . . . 1,250.00
14 . . . . 1,250.00
15 3 Little Kittens 1,100.00
16 3 Little Pigs 1,100.00
17 The Ugly Ducklings 1,100.00
18 . . . . 950.00
19 . . . . 950.00
20 . . . . 950.00
21 . . . . 950.00
22 . . . . 800.00
23 . . . . 800.00

---

24 Flying Gauchito. 750.00
25 . . . . 750.00
26 . . . . 750.00
27 Jose Carioca 750.00
28 . . . . 800.00
29 . . . . 750.00
30 . . . . 750.00
31 CB; Donald Duck 6,000.00
32 CB 2,500.00
33 CB 1,700.00
34 CB;WK; Gremlins. 1,500.00
35 CB;WK; Gremlins. 1,500.00
36 CB;WK; Gremlins. 1,500.00
37 CB;WK; Gremlins. 800.00
38 CB;WK; Gremlins. 1,000.00
39 CB;WK; Gremlins, X-mas . . 1,000.00
40 CB;WK; Gremlins. 1,000.00
41 CB;WK; Gremlins 900.00
42 CB 800.00
43 CB,Seven Dwarfs 800.00
44 CB. 800.00
45 CB,Nazis in stories 800.00
46 CB,Nazis in stories 800.00
47 CB,Nazis in stories 800.00
48 CB,Nazis in stories 800.00
49 CB,Nazis in stories 800.00
50 CB,Nazis in stories 800.00
51 CB,Christmas 700.00
52 CB; Li'l Bad Wolf begins. 700.00
53 CB 700.00
54 CB 700.00
55 CB 700.00
56 CB 700.00
57 CB 700.00
58 CB,Flag. 700.00
59 CB 700.00
60 CB 700.00
61 CB; Dumbo 600.00
62 CB 600.00
63 CB; Pinocchio 600.00
64 CB; Pinocchio, X-mas. 600.00
65 CB; Pluto 600.00
66 CB. 600.00
67 CB 600.00
68 CB, Mickey Mouse 600.00
69 CB 600.00
70 CB 600.00
71 CB 500.00
72 CB 500.00
73 CB 500.00
74 CB 500.00
75 CB; Brer Rabbit. 500.00
76 CB; Brer Rabbit, X-mas 500.00
77 CB; Brer Rabbit. 500.00
78 CB 500.00
79 CB 500.00

*Walt Disney's Comics & Stories #69
© Walt Disney*

All comics prices listed are for *Near Mint* condition.

80 CB 500.00
81 CB 500.00
82 CB;Bongo,Googy 500.00
83 CB;Bongo 500.00
84 CB;Bongo 500.00
85 CB 500.00
86 CB;Goofy & Agnes 500.00
87 CB;Goofy & Agnes 375.00
88 CB;Goofy & Agnes,
    I:Gladstone Gander 500.00
89 CB;Goofy&Agnes,Chip'n'Dale 375.00
90 CB;Goofy & Agnes 375.00
91 CB 300.00
92 CB 300.00
93 CB 300.00
94 CB 300.00
95 CB(c) 300.00
96 Little Toot 300.00
97 CB; Little Toot 300.00
98 CB; Uncle Scrooge 600.00
99 CB, Christmas(c) 300.00
100 CB 400.00
101 CB 300.00
102 CB 300.00
103 CB 275.00
104 . . . . 275.00
105 CB 300.00
106 CB 300.00
107 CB, Donald super-powers . . 500.00
108 . . . . 275.00
109 . . . . 275.00
110 CB 300.00
111 CB 300.00
112 CB; drugs 400.00
113 CB 300.00
114 CB 300.00
115 WK(c) 300.00
116 Dumbo 150.00
117 . . . . 150.00
118 . . . . 150.00
119 . . . . 150.00
120 . . . . 150.00
121 Grandma Duck begins 150.00
122 . . . . 150.00
123 . . . . 300.00
124 CB,Christmas 250.00
125 CB;I:Junior Woodchucks . . . 400.00
126 CB 450.00
127 CB 250.00
128 CB 250.00
129 CB 250.00
130 CB 250.00
131 CB 250.00
132 CB A:Grandma Duck 250.00
133 CB 250.00
134 I:The Beagle Boys 500.00
135 CB 250.00
136 CB 250.00
137 CB 250.00
138 CB,Scrooge & Money 350.00
139 CB 250.00
140 CB; I:Gyro Gearlooce 500.00
141 CB 200.00
142 CB 200.00
143 CB; Little Hiawatha 200.00
144 CB; Little Hiawatha 200.00
145 CB; Little Hiawatha 200.00
146 CB; Little Hiawatha 200.00
147 CB; Little Hiawatha 200.00
148 CB; Little Hiawatha 200.00
149 CB; Little Hiawatha 200.00
150 CB; Little Hiawatha 200.00
151 CB; Little Hiawatha 200.00
152 thru 200 CB . . . . @150.00
201 thru 203 CB . . . . @125.00
204 CB, Chip 'n' Dale & Scamp . . 125.00
205 thru 240 CB . . . . @125.00
241 CB; Dumbo x-over 125.00
242 CB 125.00
243 CB 125.00
244 CB 125.00
245 CB 125.00

Walt Disney's Comics & Stories #192
© Walt Disney

246 CB 125.00
247 thru 255 CB;Gyro
    Gearlooce . . . . @125.00
256 thru 263 CB;Ludwig Von
    Drake & Gearlooce . . . . . @125.00

WALT DISNEY'S
DELL GIANT EDITIONS
Dell Publishing Co.
1 CB,W.Disney'sXmas
    Parade('49) 1,200.00
2 CB,W.Disney'sXmas
    Parade('50) 1,000.00
3 W.Disney'sXmas Parade('51) . 300.00
4 W.Disney'sXmas Parade('52) . 250.00
5 W.Disney'sXmas Parade('53) . 250.00
6 W.Disney'sXmas Parade('54) . 250.00
7 W.Disney'sXmas Parade('55) . 250.00
8 CB,W.Disney'sXmas
    Parade('56) 500.00
9 CB,W.Disney'sXmas
    Parade('57) 500.00
1 CB,W.Disney's Christmas in
    Disneyland (1957) 600.00
1 CB,W.Disney's Disneyland
    Birthday Party (1958) 600.00
1 W.Disney's Donald and Mickey
    in Disneyland (1958) 250.00
1 W.Disney's Donald Duck
    Beach Party (1954) 300.00
2 W.Disney's Donald Duck
    Beach Party (1955) 250.00
3 W.Disney's Donald Duck
    Beach Party (1956) 250.00
4 W.Disney's Donald Duck
    Beach Party (1957) 250.00
5 W.Disney's Donald Duck
    Beach Party (1958) 250.00
6 W.Disney's Donald Duck
    Beach Party (1959) 250.00
1 W.Disney's Donald Duck
    Fun Book (1954) 1,200.00
2 W.Disney's Donald Duck
    Fun Book (1954) 1,100.00
1 W.Disney's Donald Duck
    in Disneyland (1955) 275.00
1 W.Disney's Huey, Dewey
    and Louie (1958) 175.00
1 W.Disney's DavyCrockett('55) . 350.00
1 W.Disney's Lady and the
    Tramp (1955) 650.00
1 CB,W.Disney's Mickey Mouse
    Almanac (1957) 600.00

1 W.Disney's Mickey Mouse
    Birthday Party (1953) 700.00
1 W.Disney's Mickey Mouse
    Club Parade (1955) 600.00
1 W.Disney's Mickey Mouse
    in Fantasyland (1957) 275.00
1 W.Disney's Mickey Mouse
    in Frontierland (1956) 275.00
1 W.Disney's Summer Fun('58) . 275.00
2 CB,W.Disney'sSummer
    Fun('59) 275.00
1 W.Disney's Peter Pan
    Treasure Chest (1953) 2,200.00
1 Disney Silly Symphonies('52) . 600.00
2 Disney Silly Symphonies('53) . 500.00
3 Disney Silly Symphonies('54) . 450.00
4 Disney Silly Symphonies('54) . 450.00
5 Disney Silly Symphonies('55) . 400.00
6 Disney Silly Symphonies('56) . 400.00
7 Disney Silly Symphonies('57) . 400.00
8 Disney Silly Symphonies('58) . 400.00
9 Disney Silly Symphonies('59) . 400.00
1 Disney SleepingBeauty('59) . . 600.00
1 CB,W.Disney's Uncle Scrooge
    Goes to Disneyland (1957) . . 550.00
1 W.Disney's Vacation in
    Disneyland (1958) 250.00
1 CB,Disney's Vacation
    Parade('50) 1,700.00
2 Disney'sVacation Parade('51) . 600.00
3 Disney'sVacation Parade('52) . 300.00
4 Disney'sVacation Parade('53) . 300.00
5 Disney'sVacation Parade('54) . 300.00
6 Disney's Picnic Party (1955) . . 250.00
7 Disney's Picnic Party (1956) . . 250.00
8 CB,Disney's Picnic
    Party (1957) 500.00

WALT DISNEY'S
DELL JUNIOR TREASURY
1 W.Disney's Alice in Wonderland
    (1955) 250.00

WALT DISNEY
PRESENTS
Dell Publishing Co.,
June–Aug., 1952
1 Ph(c), Four Color 200.00
2 Ph(c) 150.00
3 Ph(c) 150.00
4 Ph(c) 150.00
5 and 6 Ph(c) . . . . @150.00

WAMBI
JUNGLE BOY
Fiction House Magazines,
Spring, 1942–Winter, 1952
1 HcK,HcK(c),Vengence of
    the Beasts 1,400.00
2 HcK,HcK(c),Lair of the
    Killer Rajah 700.00
3 HcK,HcK(c) 500.00
4 HcK,HcK(c),The Valley of
    the Whispering Drums 300.00
5 HcK,HcK(c),SwamplandSafari. 250.00
6 Taming of the Tigress 225.00
7 Duel of the Congo Kings 225.00
8 AB(c),Friend of the Animals . . 225.00
9 Quest of the Devils Juju 225.00
10 Friend of the Animals 200.00
11 . . . . 200.00
12 Curse of the Jungle Jewels . . 200.00
13 New Adventures of Wambi . . 175.00
14 . . . . 175.00
15 The Leopard Legions 175.00
16 . . . . 175.00
17 Beware Bwana! 175.00
18 Ogg the Great Bull Ape 175.00

WANTED COMICS
Toytown Comics/Orbit Publications, Sept.–Oct., 1947
9 Victor Everhart 300.00
10 Carlo Banone 175.00
11 Dwight Band 175.00
12 Ralph Roe 200.00
13 James Spencer;Drug 175.00
14 John "Jiggs" Sullivan;Drug . . . 175.00
15 Harry Dunlap;Drug 125.00
16 Jack Parisi;Drug 135.00
17 Herber Ayers;Drug 135.00
18 Satan's Cigarettes;Drug 300.00
19 Jackson Stringer 125.00
20 George Morgan 125.00
21 BK,Paul Wilson 135.00
22 Strong violence 135.00
23 George Elmo Wells 125.00
24 BK,Bruce Cornett;Drug 135.00
25 Henry Anger 125.00
26 John Wormly 125.00
27 Death Always Knocks Twice . . 125.00
28 Paul H. Payton 125.00
29 Hangmans Holiday 125.00
30 George Loo 125.00
31 M Consolo 125.00
32 William Davis 125.00
33 The Web of Davis 125.00
34 Dead End 125.00
35 Glen Roy Wright 125.00
36 SSh,SSh(c),Bernard Lee
　 Thomas 100.00
37 SSh,SSh(c),Joseph M. Moore 100.00
38 SSh,SSh(c) 100.00
39 The Horror Weed;Drug 175.00
40 . . . . 100.00
41 . . . . 100.00
42 . . . . 100.00
43 . . . . 100.00
44 . . . . 100.00
45 Killers on the Loose;Drug 125.00
46 Charles Edward Crews 100.00
47 . . . . 100.00
48 SSh,SSh(c) 100.00
49 . . . . 100.00
50 JB(c),Make Way for Murder . . 150.00
51 JB(c),Dope Addict on a
　 Holiday of Murder;Drug 135.00
52 The Cult of Killers;
　 Classic Drug 135.00
53 April, 1953 . . . . 100.00

WAR AGAINST CRIME
L.L. Publishing Co. (E.C. Comics), Spring, 1948
1 Grl, Stories from Police 1,100.00
2 Grl,Guilty of Murder 700.00
3 JCr(c) 700.00
4 AF,JCr(c) 600.00
5 JCr(c) 600.00
6 AF,JCr(c) 600.00
7 AF,JCr(c) 600.00
8 AF,JCr(c) 600.00
9 AF,JCr(c),The Kid 600.00
10 JCr(c),I:Vault Keeper 3,200.00
11 JCr(c) 2,000.00
Becomes:

VAULT OF HORROR, THE
April–May, 1950–Jan., 1955
12 AF,JCr(a&c),Wax Museum . . 7,500.00
13 AF,WW,JCr(c),Grl,Drug . . . 2,500.00
14 AF,WW,JCr(c),Grl. 2,500.00
15 AF,JCr(a&c),Grl,JKa 2,500.00
16 Grl,JKa,JCr(a&c) 1,800.00
17 JDa,Grl,JKa,JCr(a&c) 1,800.00
18 JDa,Grl,JKa,JCr(a&c) 1,500.00
19 JDa,Grl,JKa,JCr(a&c) 1,500.00
20 JDa,Grl,JKa,JCr(a&c) 1,600.00
21 JDa,Grl,JKa,JCr(a&c) 1,600.00
22 JDa,JKa,JCr(a&c) 1,600.00

23 JDa,Grl,JCr(a&c) 1,600.00
24 JDa,Grl,JO,JCr(a&c) 1,600.00
25 JDa,Grl,JKa,JCr(a&c) 1,600.00
26 JDa,Grl,JCr(a&c) 1,200.00
27 JDa,Grl,GE,JCr(a&c) 1,500.00
28 JDa,Grl,JCr(a&c) 1,500.00
29 JDa,Grl,JKa,JCr(a&c),
　 Bradbury Adapt. 1,500.00
30 JDa,Grl,JCr(a&c) 1,500.00
31 JDa,Grl,JCr(a&c),
　 Bradbury Adapt. 1,200.00
32 JDa,Grl,JCr(a&c) 1,200.00
33 JDa,Grl,RC,JCr(c) 1,200.00
34 JDa,Grl,RC,JCr(a&c) 1,200.00
35 JDa,Grl,JCr(a&c),X-mas . . . 1,200.00
36 JDa,Grl,BK,JCr(a&c),Drug. . 1,200.00
37 JDa,Grl,AW,JCr(a&c)
　 Hanging 1,200.00
38 JDa,Grl,BK,JCr(a&c) 1,200.00
39 Grl,BK,RC,JCr(a&c)
　 Bondage(c) 1,200.00
40 Grl,BK,JO,JCr(a&c) 1,400.00

WAR BATTLES
Harvey Publications, Feb., 1952
1 BP,Devils of the Deep 175.00
2 BP,A Present From Benny . . . 125.00
3 BP 100.00
4 . . . . 100.00
5 . . . . 100.00
6 HN 100.00
7 BP 125.00
8 . . . . 100.00
9 Dec., 1953 . . . . 100.00

WAR BIRDS
Fiction House Magazines, 1952
1 Willie the Washout 200.00
2 Mystery MIGs of Kwanjamu . . 110.00
3 thru 6 . . . . @100.00
7 Winter, 1953,Across the
　 Wild Yalu 100.00

WAR COMICS
Dell Publishing Co., May, 1940
1 AMc,Sky Hawk 800.00
2 O:Greg Gildam 450.00
3 . . . . 350.00
4 O:Night Devils 400.00

WARFRONT
Fighting Forces Publ./ Harvey Publications
1 Korean War 200.00
2 . . . . 150.00
3 . . . . 125.00
4 . . . . 125.00
5 . . . . 125.00
6 thru 10 . . . . @125.00
11 thru 21 . . . . @100.00
22 HN 125.00
23 thru 33 . . . . @100.00
34 JK 100.00
35 . . . . 100.00

WAR FURY
Comic Media/Harwell, 1952
1 DH,RP,hole in head 350.00
2 Violent 175.00
3 Violent 175.00
4 PMo,Violent 175.00

WAR HEROES
Dell Publishing Co., July–Sept., 1942
1 Gen. Douglas MacArthur (c) . . 400.00
2 . . . . 300.00

3 Pro-Soviet 250.00
4 A:Gremlins 350.00
5 . . . . 250.00
6 . . . . 200.00
7 . . . . 200.00
8 thru 11 . . . . @200.00

War Heroes #9
© Ace Magazines

WAR HEROES
Ace Magazines, May, 1952
1 Always Comin' 150.00
2 LC,The Last Red Tank 125.00
3 You Got it 100.00
4 A Red Patrol 100.00
5 Hustle it Up 100.00
6 LC,Hang on Pal 125.00
7 LC 125.00
8 LC, April, 1953 . . . . 125.00

WARPATH
Key Publications/ Stanmore, Nov., 1954
1 Red Men Raid 125.00
2 AH(c),Braves Battle 100.00
3 April, 1955 . . . . 100.00

WARRIOR COMICS
H.C. Blackerby, 1944
1 Ironman wing Brady 400.00

WAR REPORT
Excellent Publ. (Ajax/Farrell Publ.), 1952
1 . . . . 150.00
2 Burning bodies 250.00
3 . . . . 125.00
4 . . . . 125.00
5 . . . . 125.00

WAR SHIPS
Dell Publishing Co., 1942
1 AMc 200.00

WAR STORIES
Dell Publishing Co., 1942
5 O:The Whistler 350.00
6 A:Night Devils 250.00
7 A:Night Devils 250.00
8 A:Night Devils 250.00

GOLDEN AGE

All comics prices listed are for *Near Mint* condition.

WARTIME ROMANCES
**St. John Publishing Co.,
July, 1951**

1 MB(c),MB	400.00
2 MB(c),MB	300.00
3 MB(c),MB	275.00
4 MB(c),MB	275.00
5 MB(c),MB	225.00
6 MB(c),MB	250.00
7 thru 8 MB(c),MB	@225.00
9 thru 12 MB(c),MB	@200.00
13 thru 15 MB(c)	@100.00
16 MB(c),MB	175.00
17 MB(c)	100.00
18 MB(c),MB	175.00

WAR VICTORY COMICS
**U.S. Treasury/War Victory/
Harvey Publ., Summer, 1942**

1 Savings Bond Promo with Top Syndicated Cartoonists, benefit USO	600.00

Becomes:

WAR VICTORY ADVENTURES
Summer, 1942

2 BP,2nd Front Comics	300.00
3 BP,F:Capt Cross of the Red Cross	250.00

WASHABLE JONES AND THE SHMOO
Toby Press Publ., 1953

1 Super Shmoo	250.00

WEB OF EVIL
**Comic Magazines, Inc.
(Quality Comics Group),
Nov., 1952**

1 Custodian of the Dead	850.00
2 JCo,Hangmans Horror	600.00
3 JCo	600.00
4 JCo(a&c),Monsters of the Mist	600.00
5 JCo(a&c),The Man who Died Twice,Electric Chair(c)	650.00
6 JCo(a&c),Orgy of Death	550.00
7 JCo(a&c),The Strangling Hands	550.00
8 JCo,Flaming Vengeance	500.00
9 JCo,The Monster in Flesh	500.00
10 JCo,Brain that Wouldn't Die	500.00
11 JCo,Buried Alive	500.00
12 Phantom Killer	325.00
13 Demon Inferno	325.00
14 RC(c),The Monster Genie	325.00
15 Crypts of Horror	325.00
16 Hamlet of Horror	325.00
17 Terror in Chinatown, Drug	350.00
18 Scared to Death,Acid Face	325.00
19 Demon of the Pit	300.00
20 Man Made Terror	300.00
21 Dec., 1954, Death's Ambush	300.00

WEB OF MYSTERY
**A.A. Wyn Publ.
(Ace Magazines), Feb., 1951**

1 MSy,Venom of the Vampires	800.00
2 MSy,Legacy of the Accursed	400.00
3 MSy,The Violin Curse	350.00
4 GC	350.00
5	350.00
6 LC	350.00
7 MSy	350.00
8 LC,LC(c),MSy,The Haunt of Death Lake	350.00
9 LC,LC(c)	350.00

Web of Mystery #7
© Ace Magazines

10	350.00
11 MSy	350.00
12 LC	300.00
13 LC,LC(c)Surrealist	300.00
14 MSy	300.00
15	300.00
16	300.00
17 LC,LC(c)	300.00
18 LC	300.00
19 LC	300.00
20 LC, Beyond	300.00
21 MSy	300.00
22	300.00
23	300.00
24 LC	300.00
25 LC	300.00
26	300.00
27 LC, Beyond	300.00
28 RP,1st Comics Code issue	250.00
29 MSy,Sept., 1955	250.00

WEEKENDER, THE
**Rucker Publishing Co.,
Sept., 1945**

1-1 rep.(c), As Zip	200.00
1-2 thru 1-4	@225.00
2-1 rep.(c), As Dynamic	250.00
2-2 Jco,rep.(c), As Dynamic	225.00
2-3 WMc,Jan., 1946	225.00

WEIRD ADVENTURES
**P.L. Publishing,
May, 1951–Oct., 1951**

1 MB,Missing Diamonds	800.00
2 Puppet Peril	650.00
3 Blood Vengeance	500.00

WEIRD ADVENTURES
**Approved Comics
(Ziff-Davis),
July–Aug., 1951**

10 P(c),Seeker from Beyond	500.00

WEIRD CHILLS
**Key Publications,
July, 1954**

1 MBi(c),BW	1,200.00
2 Eye Torture(c)	1,100.00
3 Bondage(c),Nov., 1954	700.00

WEIRD COMICS
**Fox Features Syndicate,
April, 1940**

1 LF(c),Bondage(c),B:Birdman, Thor,Sorceress of Doom, BlastBennett,Typhon,Voodoo Man, Dr.Mortal	8,500.00
2 LF(c),Mummy(c)	3,400.00
3 JSm(c)	1,800.00
4 JSm(c)	1,800.00
5 Bondage(c),I:Dart,Ace; E:Thor	1,900.00
6 Dart & Ace(c)	1,400.00
7 Battle of Kooba	1,400.00
8 B:Panther Woman,Dynamo, The Eagle	1,400.00
9 V:Pirates	1,100.00
10 A:Navy Jones	1,100.00
11 Dart & Ace(c).	900.00
12 Dart & Ace(c)	900.00
13 Dart & Ace(c)	900.00
14 The Rage(c)	900.00
15 Dart & Ace (c)	900.00
16 Flag,The Encore(c)	900.00
17 O:Black Rider	850.00
18	850.00
19	850.00
20 Jan., 1941,I'm The Master of Life and Death	1,150.00

WEIRD FANTASY
**I.C. Publishing Co.
(E.C. Comics),
May–June, 1950**

13(1)AF,HK,JKa,WW,AF(c), Roger Harvey's Brain	3,500.00
14(2)AF,HK,JKa,WW,AF(c),Cosmic Ray Brain Explosion	2,500.00
15(3)AF,HK,JKa,WW,AF(c),Your Destination is the Moon	1,800.00
16(4)AF,HK,JKa,WW,AF(c)	1,800.00
17(5)AF,HK,JKa,WW,AF(c),Not Made by Human Hands	1,600.00
6 AF,HK,JKa,WW,AF(c),Robot.	1,500.00
7 AF,JKa,WW,AF(c)	1,500.00
8 AF,JKa,WW,AF(c)	1,500.00
9 AF,Jka,WW,JO,AF(c)	1,500.00
10 AF,Jka,WW,JO,AF(c)	900.00
11 AF,Jka,WW,JO,AF(c)	1,500.00
12 AF,Jka,WW,JO,AF(c)	1,500.00
13 AF,Jka,WW,JO,AF(c)	1,500.00
14 AF,JKa,WW,JO,AW&FF, AF(c).	1,200.00
15 AF,JKa,JO,AW&RKr,AF(c), Bondage(c)	1,500.00
16 AF,JKa,JO,AW&RKr,AF(c)	2,000.00
17 AF,JOP,JKa,AF(c),Bradbury	1,500.00
18 AF,JO,JKa,AF(c),Bradbury.	1,500.00
19 JO,JKa,JO(c),Bradbury	1,500.00
20 JO,JKa,FF,AF(c)	1,500.00
21 JO,JKa,AW&FF(c)	1,800.00
22 JO,JKa,JO(c),Nov.,1953	1,100.00

With Weird Science, Becomes:

WEIRD SCIENCE FANTASY

WEIRD HORRORS
**St. John Publishing Co.,
June, 1952**

1 GT,Dungeon of the Doomed	800.00
2 Strangest Music Ever	500.00
3 PMo,Strange Fakir From the Orient, Drug	500.00
4 Murderers Knoll	400.00
5 Phantom Bowman	400.00
6 Monsters from Outer Space	700.00
7 LC,Deadly Double	700.00
8 JKu,JKu(c),Bloody Yesterday	600.00
9 JKu,JKu(c),Map Of Doom	600.00

Becomes:

NIGHTMARE
Dec., 1953
10 JKu(c),The Murderer's Mask . 800.00
11 BK,Ph(c),Fangs of Death 600.00
12 JKu(c),The Forgotten Mask . . 500.00
13 BP,Princess of the Sea 350.00
Becomes:

AMAZING GHOST STORIES
Oct., 1954
14 EK,MB(c),Pit & Pendulum.... 400.00
15 BP,Weird Thrillers 300.00
16 Feb., 1955, EK,JKu......... 350.00

WEIRD JUNGLE TALES
Star Publications, 1953
202 .... 150.00

WEIRD MYSTERIES
Gilmore Publications, Oct., 1952
1 BW(c) 1,300.00
2 DWi, Robot Woman 1,700.00
3 Severed Heads(c) 900.00
4 BW,Human headed ants(c) . 1,600.00
5 BW,Brains From Head(c) ... 1,700.00
6 Severed Head(c) 900.00
7 Used in "Seduction" 1,200.00
8 The One That Got Away 850.00
9 Epitaph,Cyclops, Violence.... 750.00
10 The Ruby 700.00
11 Voodoo Dolls.............. 650.00
12 Sept., 1954 .... 650.00

WEIRD SCIENCE
E.C. Comics, 1950
1 AF(a&c),JKu,HK,WW 6,000.00
2 AF(a&c),JKu,HK,WW,Flying
Saucers(c) 3,000.00
3 AF(a&c),JKu,HK 2,000.00
4 AF(a&c),JKu,HK 2,000.00
5 AF(a&c),JKu,HK,WW,
Atomic Bomb(c) 2,000.00
6 AF(a&c),JKu,HK 2,000.00
7 AF(a&c),JKu,HK,Classic(c).. 2,000.00
8 AF(a&c),JKu 2,000.00
9 WW(c),JKu,Classic(c)..... 2,200.00
10 WW(c),JKu,JO,Classic(c) .. 2,000.00
11 AF,JKu,Space war 1,200.00
12 WW(c),JKu,JO,Classic(c) . 1,200.00
13 WW(c),JKu,JO, ... 1,200.00
14 WW(a&c),JO 1,500.00

Weird Science #14
© E.C. Comics

15 WW(a&c),JO,Grl,AW,
RKr,JKa 1,500.00
16 WW(a&c),JO,AW,RKr,JKa .. 1,400.00
17 WW(a&c),JO,AW,RKr,JKa .. 1,400.00
18 WW(a&c),JO,AW,RKr,
JKa,Atomic Bomb........ 1,400.00
19 WW(a&c),JO,AW,
FF,Horror(c) 1,500.00
20 WW(a&c),JO,AW,FF,JKa ... 1,500.00
21 WW(a&c),JO,AW,FF,JKa ... 1,500.00
22 WW(a&c),JO,AW,FF 1,500.00
Becomes:

WEIRD SCIENCE FANTASY
March, 1954
23 WW(a&c),AW,BK 1,300.00
24 WW,AW,BK,Classic(c)..... 1,300.00
25 WW,AW,BK,Classic(c)..... 1,400.00
26 AF(c),WW,RC,
Flying Saucer(c)......... 1,200.00
27 WW(a&c),RC 1,200.00
28 AF(c),WW 1,400.00
29 AF(c),WW,Classic(c) 3,500.00
Becomes:

INCREDIBLE SCIENCE FANTASY
July–Aug., 1955
30 WW,JDa(c),BK,AW,RKr,JO .. 600.00
31 WW,JDa(c),BK,AW,RKr 750.00
32 JDa(c),BK,WW,JO 750.00
33 WW(c),BK,WW,JO 750.00

WEIRD TALES OF THE FUTURE
S.P.M. Publ./ Aragon Publications, March, 1952
1 RA 2,000.00
2 BW,BW(c), Jumpin Jupiter .. 3,000.00
3 BW,BW(c) 3,000.00
4 BW,BW(c) 2,000.00
5 BW,BW(c),,Jumpin' Jupiter
Lingerie(c) 3,000.00
6 Bondage(c) 1,500.00
7 BW,Devil(c)............. 2,000.00
8 July–Aug., 1953 .... 2,500.00

WEIRD TERROR
Allen Hardy Associates (Comic Media), Sept., 1952
1 RP,DH,DH(c),Dungeon of the
Doomed;Hitler 800.00
2 HcK(c),PMo, Torture 650.00
3 PMo,DH,DH(c),Strong
Violence................ 650.00
4 PMo,DH,DH(c),Severed Head. 650.00
5 PMo,DH,RP,DH(c),Hanging(c). 550.00
6 DH,RP,DH(c),Step into
My Parlour, Severed Head .. 600.00
7 DH,PMo,DH(c),Blood o/t Bats . 600.00
8 DH,RP,DH(c),Step into
My Parlour, Severed Head .. 625.00
9 DH,PMo,DH(c),The Fleabite .. 450.00
10 DH,BP,RP,DH(c) 450.00
11 DH,DH(c),Satan's Love Call .. 600.00
12 DH,DH(c),King Whitey 450.00
13 DH,DH(c),Wings of Death,
Severed Head, Sept. 1954 .. 450.00

WEIRD THRILLERS
Approved Comics (Ziff-Davis), Sept.–Oct., 1951
1 Ph(c),Monsters & The Model 1,250.00
2 AW,P(c),The Last Man 900.00
3 AW,P(c),Princess o/t Sea .. 1,200.00
4 AW,P(c),The Widows Lover... 850.00

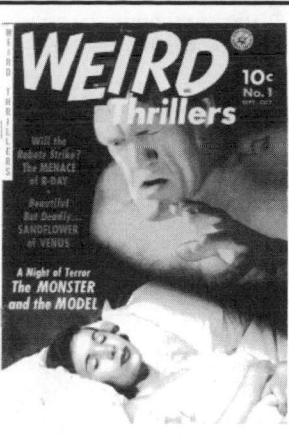

Weird Thrillers #1
© Ziff-Davis

5 BP,Oct., 1952,AW,P(c),
Wings of Death 800.00

WESTERN ACTION THRILLERS
Dell Publishing Co., April, 1937
1 Buffalo Bill, Texas Kid...... 1,200.00

WESTERN ADVENTURES COMICS
A.A. Wyn, Inc. (Ace Magazines), Oct., 1948
N#(1)Injun Gun Bait 275.00
N#(2)Cross-Draw Kid 150.00
N#(3)Outlaw Mesa 150.00
4 Sheriff, Sal 125.00
5 .... 125.00
6 Rip Roaring Adventure 125.00
Becomes:

WESTERN LOVE TRAILS
Nov., 1949
7 .... 150.00
8 Maverick Love 125.00
9 March, 1950 .... 100.00

WESTERN BANDIT TRAILS
St. John Publishing Co., Jan., 1949
1 GT,MB(c), Blue Monk 300.00
2 GT,MB(c)................ 250.00
3 GT,MB,MB(c),Gingham Fury . 275.00

WESTERN CRIME BUSTERS
Trojan Magazines, Sept., 1950–April, 1952
1 Gunslingin' Galoots 450.00
2 K-Bar Kate 250.00
3 Wilma West 250.00
4 Bob Dale 250.00
5 Six-Gun Smith 250.00
6 WW 400.00
7 WW,Wells Fargo Robbery ... 400.00
8 .... 250.00
9 WW,Lariat Lucy 400.00
10 WW,Tex Gordon 450.00

WESTERN CRIME CASES
See: OUTLAWS, THE

WESTERNER, THE
Wanted Comics Group/
Toytown Publ.,
June, 1948

14 F:Jack McCall 250.00
15 F:Bill Jamett 200.00
16 F:Tom McLowery 200.00
17 F:Black Bill Desmond 200.00
18 BK,F:Silver Dollar Dalton 250.00
19 MMe,F:Jess Meeton 150.00
20 . . . . 150.00
21 BK,MMe 200.00
22 BK,MMe 200.00
23 BK,MMe 200.00
24 BK,MMe 200.00
25 O,I,B:Calamity Jane 200.00
26 BK,F:The Widowmaker 250.00
27 BK 250.00
28 thru 31 . . . . @125.00
32 E:Calamity Jane 125.00
33 A:Quest 125.00
34 . . . . 125.00
35 SSh(c) 125.00
36 . . . . 125.00
37 Lobo-Wolf Boy 125.00
38 . . . . 125.00
39 . . . . 125.00
40 SSh(c) 125.00
41 Dec., 1951 . . . . 125.00

WESTERN FIGHTERS
Hillman Periodicals,
April–May, 1948

1 S&K(c) 450.00
2 BF(c) 200.00
3 BF(c) 150.00
4 BK,BF 175.00
5 . . . . 125.00
6 . . . . 125.00
7 BK 150.00
8 . . . . 125.00
9 . . . . 125.00
10 BK 150.00
11 AMC&FF 400.00
2-1 BK 150.00
2-2 BP 125.00
2-3 thru 2-12 . . . . @100.00
3-1 thru 3-11 . . . . @100.00
3-12 BK 125.00
4-1 . . . . 100.00
4-2 BK 150.00
4-3 BK 150.00
4-4 BK 150.00

Western Fighters #7
© Hillman Periodicals

4-5 BK 150.00
4-6 BK 150.00
4-7 March–April, 1953 . . . . 100.00

WESTERN FRONTIER
P.L. Publishers
(Approved Comics),
May, 1951

1 Flaming Vengeance 150.00
2 . . . . 125.00
3 Death Rides the Iron Horse . . 100.00
4 thru 6 . . . . @100.00
7 1952 . . . . 100.00

WESTERN HEARTS
Standard Magazine, Inc.,
Dec., 1949

1 JSe, Whip Wilson, Ph(c) 275.00
2 AW,FF, Palomino, Ph(c) 275.00
3 Rex Allen, Ph(c) 175.00
4 JSe,BE, Ph(c) 150.00
5 JSe,BE,Ray Milland, Ph(c) . . . 150.00
6 JSe,BE,Irene Dunn, Ph(c) 150.00
7 JSe,BE,Jock Mahoney Ph(c) . . 150.00
8 Randolph Scott, Ph(c) 150.00
9 JSe,BE, Whip Wilson, Ph(c) . . 175.00
10 JSe,BE, Bill Williams,Ph(c) . . 150.00

WESTERN HERO
See: WOW COMICS

WESTERN KILLERS
Fox Features Syndicate, 1948

N# Lingerie 280.00
60 Violence 300.00
61 JCo,LSe 250.00
62 . . . . 225.00
63 . . . . 225.00
64 . . . . 225.00

WESTERN LOVE
Feature Publications
(Prize Comics Group),
July–Aug., 1949

1 S&K, Randolph Scott 400.00
2 S&K, Whip Wilson 275.00
3 JSe,BE, Reno Brown 200.00
4 JSe,BE 200.00
5 JSe,BE, Dale Robertson 275.00

WESTERN PICTURE STORIES
Comics Magazine Co.,
Feb., 1937–June, 1937

1 WE,Treachery Trail,
　1st Western 2,800.00
2 WE,Weapons of the West . . 1,500.00
3 WE,Dragon Pass 1,200.00
4 CavemanCowboy 1,200.00

WESTERN ROUGH RIDERS
Stanmor Publ.
(Gilmore Magazines), 1954

1 . . . . 125.00
2 . . . . 125.00
3 . . . . 125.00
4 . . . . 125.00

WESTERN THRILLERS
Fox Features Syndicate,
Aug., 1948

1 Velvet Rose 600.00
2 . . . . 250.00
3 GT,RH(c) 225.00
4 . . . . 250.00
5 Butch Cassidy 250.00

6 June, 1949 . . . . 225.00
Becomes:

MY PAST CONFESSIONS
Aug., 1949

7 . . . . 225.00
8 . . . . 150.00
9 . . . . 150.00
10 . . . . 150.00
11 WW 300.00
12 Crimes Inc. 125.00

WESTERN TRUE CRIME
Fox Features Syndicate,
Aug., 1948

1 (#15) JKa, Zoot 14 . . . . 450.00
2 (#16) JKa, Violence 300.00
3 JKa 300.00
4 JCr 300.00
5 . . . . 200.00
6 . . . . 200.00
Becomes:

MY CONFESSION
Aug., 1949–Feb., 1950

7 WW 400.00
8 WW,My Tarnished Reputation 350.00
9 I:Tormented Men 150.00
10 I Am Damaged Goods 150.00

WHACK
St. John Publishing Co.,
Dec., 1953

1 3-D 400.00
2 Steve Crevice,Flush Jordan
　V:Bing (Crosby)The Merciful 300.00
3 F:Little Awful Fannie 200.00

WHAM COMICS
Centaur Publications,
Nov., 1940

1 PG,The Sparkler & His
　Disappearing Suit 2,400.00
2 Dec., 1940,PG,PG(C),
　Men Turn into Icicles 1,500.00

WHIRLWIND COMICS
Nita Publications,
June, 1940

1 F:The Cyclone 3,000.00
2 A:Scoops Hanlon,Cyclone(c) 1,600.00
3 Sept., 1940,A:Magic
　Mandarin,Cyclone(c) 1,500.00

WHITE PRINCESS OF THE JUNGLE
Avon Periodicals, July, 1951

1 EK(c),Terror Fangs 800.00
2 EK,EK(c),Jungle Vengeance . 550.00
3 EK,EK(c),The Blue Gorilla . . . 450.00
4 Fangs of the Swamp Beast . . 400.00
5 EK,Coils of the Tree Snake
　Nov., 1952 . . . . 400.00

WHITE RIDER AND SUPER HORSE
See: OUTLAWS, THE

WHIZ COMICS
Fawcett Publications,
Feb., 1940

1 O:Captain Marvel,B:Spy Smasher,
　Golden Arrow,Dan Dare, Scoop
　Smith, Ibis the Invincible,
　Sivana 125,000.00
2 . . . . 15,000.00
3 Make way for
　Captain Marvel 10,000.00

Whiz Comics #10
© Fawcett Publications

4 Captain Marvel
  Crashes Through 7,500.00
5 Captain Marvel
  Scores Again! 7,000.00
6 Circus of Death 4,800.00
7 B:Dr Voodoo,Squadron
  of Death 4,800.00
8 Saved by Captain Marvel! . . 4,800.00
9 MRa,Captain Marvel
  on the Job. 4,800.00
10 Battles the Winged Death . . 4,800.00
11 Hurray for Captain Marvel . . 3,000.00
12 Captain Marvel rides
  the Engine of Doom 3,000.00
13 Worlds Most Powerful Man!. 3,000.00
14 Boomerangs the Torpedo . . 3,000.00
15 O:Sivana 2,500.00
16 Dr. Voodoo 2,500.00
17 Knocks out a Tank 2,500.00
18 V:Spy Smasher 2,500.00
19 Crushes the Tiger Shark . . . 2,200.00
20 V:Sivana 2,200.00
21 O:Lt. Marvels 2,300.00
22 Mayan Temple 1,500.00
23 GT,A:Dr. Voodoo 1,500.00
24 . . . . 1,500.00
25 O&I:Captain Marvel Jr., Stops
  the Turbine of Death. 12,000.00
26 . . . . 1,400.00
27 V:Death God of the
  Katonkas. 1,500.00
28 V:Mad Dervish of Ank-Har . . 1,500.00
29 Three Lt. Marvels (c), Pan
  American Olympics 1,500.00
30 CCB(c). 1,400.00
31 Douglass MacArthur
  & Spy Smasher(c) 1,300.00
32 Spy Smasher(c). 1,300.00
33 Spy Smasher(c). 1,600.00
34 Three Lt. Marvels (c) 1,000.00
35 Capt. Marvel and the
  Three Fates 1,200.00
36 Haunted Hallowe'en Hotel . . 1,000.00
37 Return of the Trolls 1,000.00
38 Grand Steeplechase 1,000.00
39 A Nazi Utopia 1,000.00
40 A:Three Lt. Marvels, The
  Earth's 4 Corners 1,000.00
41 Captain Marvel 1,000 years
  from Now. 800.00
42 Returns in Time Chair. 800.00
43 V:Sinister Spies,
  Spy Smasher(c). 800.00
44 Life Story of Captain Marvel . . 900.00
45 Cures His Critics. 800.00
46 . . . . 800.00

47 Captain Marvel needs
  a Birthday 800.00
48 . . . . 800.00
49 Writes a Victory song 800.00
50 Captain Marvel's most
  embarrassing moment 800.00
51 Judges the Ugly-
  Beauty Contest 700.00
52 V:Sivana, Chooses
  His Birthday 700.00
53 Captain Marvel fights
  Billy Batson 700.00
54 Jack of all Trades 700.00
55 Family Tree 700.00
56 Tells what the Future Will Be . 700.00
57 A:Spy Smasher,Golden Arrow,
  Ibis. 700.00
58 . . . . 700.00
59 V:Sivana's Twin. 700.00
60 Missing Person's Machine . . . 700.00
61 Gets a first name 650.00
62 Plays in a Band. 650.00
63 Great Indian Rope Trick 650.00
64 Suspected of Murder 650.00
65 Lamp of Diogenes. 650.00
66 The Trial of Mr. Morris! 650.00
67 . . . . 650.00
68 Laugh Lotion, V:Sivana. 650.00
69 Mission to Mercury. 1,000.00
70 Climbs the World's Mightiest
  Mountain 650.00
71 Strange Magician 600.00
72 V:The Man of the Future. . . . 600.00
73 In Ogre Land. 600.00
74 Old Man River. 600.00
75 The City Olympics. 600.00
76 Spy Smasher become
  Crime Smasher 600.00
77 . . . . 600.00
78 Golden Arrow 600.00
79 . . . . 600.00
80 . . . . 600.00
81 . . . . 600.00
82 The Atomic Ship 600.00
83 Magic Locket. 600.00
84 . . . . 600.00
85 The Clock of San Lojardo. . . . 600.00
86 V:Sinister Sivanas. 600.00
87 The War on Olympia. 600.00
88 The Wonderful Magic Carpet . 600.00
89 Webs of Crime 600.00
90 . . . . 600.00
91 Infinity (c) 600.00
92 . . . . 600.00
93 Captain America become
  a Hobo?. 600.00
94 V:Sivana 600.00
95 Captain Marvel is grounded . . 600.00
96 The Battle Between Buildings. 600.00
97 Visits Mirage City 600.00
98 . . . . 600.00
99 V:Menace in the Mountains . . 600.00
100 Anniversary Issue 700.00
101 . . . . 600.00
102 A:Commando Yank. 600.00
103 . . . . 600.00
104 Flag(c). 600.00
105 . . . . 600.00
106 A:Bulletman. 600.00
107 The Great Experiment 700.00
108 thru 114. . . . . @600.00
115 The Marine Invasion 500.00
116 . . . . 500.00
117 V:Sivana 500.00
118 thru 121. . . . . @500.00
122 V:Sivana 500.00
123. . . . . 500.00
124 . . . . 500.00
125 Olympic Games of the Gods 500.00
126 . . . . 500.00
127 . . . . 500.00
128 . . . . 500.00

129 . . . . 400.00
130 . . . . 400.00
131 The Television Trap. 400.00
132 thru 142. . . . . @400.00
143 Mystery of the Flying Studio . 400.00
144 V:The Disaster Master 400.00
145 . . . . 400.00
146 . . . . 400.00
147 . . . . 400.00
148 . . . . 400.00
149 . . . . 400.00
150 V:Bug Bombs 450.00
151 . . . . 450.00
152 . . . . 450.00
153 V:The Death Horror 700.00
154 Horror Tale, I:Dr.Death 700.00
155 V:Legend Horror,Dr.Death . . 750.00

WHODUNIT?
D.S. Publishing Co.,
Aug.–Sept., 1948
1 MB,Weeping Widow 300.00
2 Diploma For Death 150.00
3 Dec.–Jan., 1949 . . . . 150.00

WHO IS NEXT?
Standard Comics,
Jan., 1953
5 ATh,RA,Don't Let Me Kill 250.00

Wilbur Comics #10
© Archie Comics

WILBUR COMICS
MLJ Magazines
(Archie Publications),
Summer, 1944
1 F:Wilbur Wilkin-America's Song
  of Fun 700.00
2 . . . . 350.00
3 . . . . 250.00
4 . . . . 200.00
5 I:Katy Keene 1,300.00
6 F:Katy Keene. 350.00
7 F:Katy Keene. 350.00
8 F:Katy Keene. 350.00
9 F:Katy Keene. 350.00
10 F:Katy Keene 350.00
11 thru 20 F:Katy Keene . . . . @300.00
21 thru 30 F:Katy Keene . . . . @250.00
31 thru 40 F:Katy Keene . . . . @150.00
41 thru 56 F:Katy Keene . . . . @125.00
57 thru 89. . . . . @100.00
90 Oct., 1965 . . . . 100.00

GOLDEN AGE

WILD BILL ELLIOT
Dell Publishing Co.,
May, 1950
(1) see Dell Four Color #278
2 . . . . 125.00
3 thru 5 . . . . @100.00
6 thru 10 . . . . @100.00
(11-12) see Four Color #472, 520
13 thru 17 . . . . @100.00

WILD BILL HICKOK
AND JINGLES
See: **YELLOWJACKET**
COMICS

WILD BILL HICKOK
Avon Periodicals,
Sept.–Oct., 1949
1 Grl(c),Frontier Fighter 275.00
2 Ph(c),Gambler's Guns 150.00
3 Ph(c),Great Stage Robbery . . 100.00
4 Ph(c),Guerilla Gunmen 100.00
5 Ph(c),Return of the Renegade 100.00
6 EK,EK(c),Along the Apache
   Trail 100.00
7 EK,EK(c)Outlaws of
   Hell's Bend 100.00
8 Ph(c),The Border Outlaws . . . 100.00
9 Ph(c),Killers From Texas 100.00
10 Ph(c) 100.00
11 EK,EK(c),The Hell Riders . . . 100.00
12 EK,EK(c),The Lost Gold Mine 100.00
13 EK,EK(c),Bloody Canyon
   Massacre 125.00
14 . . . . 125.00
15 . . . . 100.00
16 JKa,Bad Men of Deadwood . . 100.00
17 JKa 100.00
18 JKa,Kit West 100.00
19 thru 23 . . . . @100.00
24 EK,EK(c) 100.00
25 EK,EK(c) 100.00
26 EK,EK(c) 100.00
27 EK,EK(c) 100.00
28 EK,EK(c),May–June, 1956 . . . 100.00

WILD BOY OF
THE CONGO
Approved(Ziff-Davis)/
St. John Publ. Co.,
Feb.–March, 1951
10(1)NS,PH(c),Bondage(c),The
   Gorilla God 500.00
11(2)NS,Ph(c),Star of the Jungle. 250.00
12(3)NS,Ph(c),Ice-Age Men. 250.00
4 NS.Ph(c),Tyrant of the Jungle 350.00
5 NS,Ph(c),The White Robe
   of Courage 200.00
6 NS,Ph(c) 200.00
7 MB,EK.Ph(c) 250.00
8 Ph(c),Man-Eater 200.00
9 Ph(c),Killer Leopard 200.00
10 . . . . 200.00
11 MB(c). 250.00
12 MB(c) 250.00
13 MB(c) 250.00
14 MB(c) 250.00
15 June, 1955 . . . . 200.00

WILD FRONTIER
Charlton Comics, 1955
1 Davy Crockett 125.00
2 same 100.00
3 thru 7 same . . . . @100.00
7 O:Cheyenne Kid 100.00
Becomes:

CHEYENNE KID

WILL ROGERS WESTERN
Fox Features Syndicate, 1950
1 (5) 450.00
2 Ph(c) 350.00

WINGS COMICS
Wings Publ.
(Fiction House Magazines),
Sept., 1940
1 HcK,AB,GT,Ph(c),B:Skull Squad,
   Clipper Kirk,Suicide Smith,
   War Nurse,Phantom Falcons,
   GreasemonkeyGriffin,Parachute
   Patrol,Powder Burns . . 6,000.00
2 HcK,AB,GT,Bomber Patrol . . 3,000.00
3 HcK,AB,GT 1,700.00
4 HcK,AB,GT,B:Spitfire Ace . . . 1,700.00
5 HcK,AB,GT,Torpedo Patrol . 1,700.00
6 HcK,AB,GT,Bombs for Berlin 1,500.00
7 HcK,AB 1,500.00
8 HcK,AB,The Wings of Doom 1,500.00
9 Sky-Wolf 1,400.00
10 The Upside Down 1,400.00
11 . . . . 1,300.00
12 Fury of the fire Boards. 1,300.00
13 Coffin Slugs For The
   Luftwaffe 1,300.00
14 Stuka Buster 1,300.00
15 Boomerang Blitz 1,300.00
16 O:Capt.Wings. 1,500.00
17 Skyway to Death 1,200.00
18 Horsemen of the Sky 1,200.00
19 Nazi Spy Trap 1,200.00
20 The One Eyed Devil 1,200.00
21 Chute Troop Tornado 1,000.00
22 TNT for Tokyo 1,000.00
23 RP,Battling Eagles of Bataan 1,000.00
24 RP,The Death of a Hero . . . 1,000.00
25 RP,Suicide Squeeze 1,000.00
26 Tojo's Eagle Trap 1,000.00
27 BLb,Mile High Gauntlet . . . 1,000.00
28 BLb,Tail Gun Tornado 1,000.00
29 BLb,Buzzards from Berlin . . 1,000.00
30 BLb,Monsters of the
   Stratosphere 950.00
31 BLb,Sea Hawks away. 950.00
32 BLb,Sky Mammoth 950.00
33 BLb,Roll Call of the Yankee
   Eagles 950.00
34 BLb,So Sorry,Mr Tojo 950.00
35 BLb,RWb,Hell's Lightning 950.00
36 RWb,The Crash-Master 950.00
37 RWb,Sneak Blitz 950.00
38 RWb,Rescue Raid of the
   Yank Eagle 950.00
39 RWb,Sky Hell/Pigboat Patrol . 950.00
40 RWb,Luftwaffe Gamble 950.00
41 RWb,.50 Caliber Justice 900.00
42 RWb,PanzerMeat forMosquito 900.00
43 RWb,Suicide Sentinels 900.00
44 RWb,Berlin Bombs Away 900.00
45 RWb,Hells Cargo 900.00
46 RWb,Sea-Hawk Patrol 900.00
47 RWb,Tojo's Tin Gibraltar 900.00
48 RWb 900.00
49 RWb,Rockets Away 900.00
50 RWb,Mission For a Madman . 900.00
51 RWb,Toll for a Typhoon 800.00
52 MB,Madam Marauder. 800.00
53 MB,Robot Death Over
   Manhattan 800.00
54 MB,Juggernauts of Death 800.00
55 MB. 800.00
56 MB,Sea Raiders Grave. 800.00
57 MB,Yankee Warbirds over
   Tokyo 800.00
58 MB. 800.00
59 MB,Prey of the Night Hawks . . 800.00
60 MB,E:Skull Squad,
   Hell's Eyes. 800.00
61 MB,Raiders o/t Purple Dawn . 750.00

Wings #9
© Fiction House Magazines

62 Twilight of the Gods 750.00
63 Hara Kiri Rides the Skyways . 750.00
64 Taps For Tokyo 750.00
65 AB,Warhawk for the Kill 750.00
66 AB,B:Ghost Patrol. 750.00
67 AB 750.00
68 AB,ClipperKirkBecomesPhantom
   Falcon;O:Phantom Falcon. . . 750.00
69 AB,O:cont,Phantom Falcon . . 750.00
70 AB,N:Phantom Falcon;
   O:Final Phantom Falcon 750.00
71 Ghost Patrol becomes
   Ghost Squadron 750.00
72 V:Capt. Kamikaze. 750.00
73 Hell & Stormoviks 750.00
74 BLb(c),Loot is What She
   Lived For 750.00
75 BLb(c),The Sky Hag 750.00
76 BLb(c),Temple of the Dead. . . 750.00
77 BLb(c),Sky Express to Hell . . . 750.00
78 BLb(c),Loot Queen of
   Satan's Skyway 750.00
79 BLb(c),Buzzards of
   Plunder Sky 750.00
80 BLb(c),Port of Missing Pilots . 750.00
81 BLb(c),Sky Trail of the
   Terror Tong 750.00
82 BLb(c),Bondage(c),Spider &
   The Fly Guy. 800.00
83 BLb(c),GE,Deep Six For
   Capt. Wings. 750.00
84 BLb(c),GE,Sky Sharks to
   the Kill 750.00
85 BLb(c),GE. 750.00
86 BLb(c),GE,Moon Raiders 750.00
87 BLb(c),GE 750.00
88 BLb(c),GE,Madmans Mission . 750.00
89 BLb(c),GE,Bondage(c),
   Rockets Away 900.00
90 BLb(c),GE,Bondage(c),The
   Radar Rocketeers 900.00
91 BLb(c),GT,Bondage(c),V-9 for
   Vengeance. 900.00
92 BLb(c),GE,Death's red Rocket 750.00
93 BLb(c),GE,Kidnap Cargo . . . 1,100.00
94 BLb(c),GE,Bondage(c),Ace
   of the A-Bomb Patrol 1,200.00
95 BLb(c),GE,The Ace of
   the Assassins 750.00
96 BLb(c),GE. 750.00
97 BLb(c),GE,The Sky Octopus . 750.00
98 BLb(c),GE,The Witch Queen
   of Satan's Skyways 750.00
99 BLb(c),GE,The Spy Circus . . . 750.00
100 BLb(c),GE,King o/t Congo . . 800.00

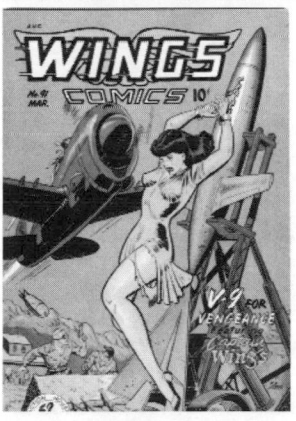

Wings #90
© *Fiction House Magazines*

101 BLb(c),GE,Trator of
   the Cockpit 700.00
102 BLb(c),GE,Doves of Doom . . 700.00
103 BLb(c),GE 700.00
104 BLb(c),GE,Fireflies of Fury . . 700.00
105 BLb(c),GE 700.00
106 BLb(c),GE,Six Aces & A
   Firing Squad 700.00
107 BLb(c),GE,Operation Satan . 700.00
108 BLb(c),GE,The Phantom
   of Berlin 700.00
109 GE,Vultures of
   Vengeance Sky 700.00
110 GE,The Red Ray Vortex 700.00
111 GE,E:Jane Martin 500.00
112 The Flight of the
   Silver Saucers 500.00
113 Suicide Skyways 500.00
114 D-Day for Death Rays 500.00
115 Ace of Space 500.00
116 Jet Aces of Korea 500.00
117 Reap the Red Wind 500.00
118 Vengeance Flies Blind 500.00
119 The Whistling Death 500.00
120 Doomsday Mission 500.00
121 Ace of the Spyways 500.00
122 Last Kill Korea 500.00
123 The Cat & the Canaries 500.00
124 Summer, 1954, Death
   Below Zero 500.00

WINNIE WINKLE
**Dell Publishing Co.,
1948**
1 . . . . 250.00
2 . . . . 200.00
3 thru 7 . . . . @200.00

WITCHCRAFT
**Avon Periodicals,
March–April, 1952**
1 SC,JKu,Heritage of Horror . . 1,000.00
2 SC,JKu,The Death Tattoo 750.00
3 EK,Better off Dead 575.00
4 Claws of the Cat,
   Boiling Humans 600.00
5 Ph(c),Where Zombies Walk . . 650.00
6 March, 1953 Mysteries of the
   Moaning Statue 575.00

WITCHES TALES
**Harvey Publications,
Jan., 1951**
1 RP,Bondage(c),Weird Yarns
   of Unseen Terror 900.00

2 RP,AAv,We Dare You 600.00
3 RP,Bondage(c)Forest of
   Skeletons. 400.00
4 BP 400.00
5 BP,Bondage(c),Share
   My Coffin 450.00
6 BP,Bondage(c),Servants of
   the Tomb 400.00
7 BP,Screaming City 400.00
8 LEI(c),Bondage(c) 450.00
9 Fatal Steps. 400.00
10 LEI,BP,IT!,Bondage 450.00
11 BP,Monster Maker 350.00
12 Bondage(c);The Web
   of the Spider 350.00
13 The Torture Jar 350.00
14 AAv,Transformation 350.00
15 Drooling Zombie 350.00
16 LEI,Revenge of a Witch 350.00
17 LEI,Dimension IV 350.00
18 LEI,HN,Bird of Prey 400.00
19 LEI,HN,The Pact 400.00
20 LEI,HN,Kiss & Tell 400.00
21 LEI,HN,The Invasion 400.00
22 LEI,HN,A Day of Panic 400.00
23 LEI,HN,The Wig Maker 400.00
24 LEI,HN,The Undertaker 425.00
25 LEI,What Happens at 8:30 PM?
   Severed Heads(c) 500.00
26 LEI,Up There 350.00
27 LEI,The Thing That Grew 350.00
28 AAv,Demon Flies 350.00
Becomes:

WITCHES WESTERN TALES
Feb., 1955
29 S&K(a&c),F:Davy Crockett . . . 450.00
30 S&K(a&c) 400.00
Becomes:

WESTERN TALES
Oct., 1955
31 S&K(a&c),F:Davy Crockett . . . 250.00
32 S&K(a&c),F:Davy Crockett . . . 250.00
33 S&K(a&c),July–Sept.,1956 . . . 250.00

WITH THE MARINES ON THE BATTLEFRONTS OF THE WORLD
Toby Press, June, 1953
1 Flaming Soul, John
   Wayne, Ph(c) 350.00
2 Mar., 1954, Monty Hall, Ph(c) . 100.00

WITTY COMICS
**Irwin H. Rubin/Chicago Nite
Life News, 1945**
1 Pioneer, Jr. Patrol 375.00
2 1945 . . . . 200.00
3 thru 7 . . . . @150.00

WOMEN IN LOVE
**Fox Features Synd./
Hero Books/
Ziff-Davis, Aug., 1949**
1 . . . . 700.00
2 JKa,AF(c) 400.00
3 . . . . 250.00
4 WW 300.00

WOMEN OUTLAWS
**Fox Features Syndicate,
July, 1948**
1 Partial nudity 1,100.00
2 . . . . 900.00
3 . . . . 900.00
4 . . . . 700.00
5 . . . . 550.00

Women Outlaws #6
© *Fox Features Syndicate*

6 . . . . 550.00
7 . . . . 550.00
8 . . . . 550.00
N# Cody of the Pony Express . . . 400.00
Becomes:

MY LOVE MEMORIES
**Fox Features Syndicate,
Nov., 1949**
9 . . . . 250.00
10 . . . . 150.00
11 . . . . 175.00
12 WW 200.00

WONDERBOY
See: HORRIFIC

WONDER COMICS
**Great Publ./Nedor/
Better Publications,
May, 1944**
1 SSh(c),B:Grim Reaper,
   Spectro Hitler(c) 2,500.00
2 ASh(c),O:Grim Reaper,B:Super
   Sleuths,Grim Reaper(c) . . . 1,800.00
3 ASh(c),Grim Reaper(c) 1,500.00
4 ASh(c),Grim Reaper(c) 1,000.00
5 ASh(c),Grim Reaper(c) 1,000.00
6 ASh(c),Grim Reaper(c) 900.00
7 ASh(c),Grim Reaper(c) 900.00
8 ASh(c),E:Super Sleuths,
   Spectro 900.00
9 ASh(c),B:Wonderman 900.00
10 ASh(c),Wonderman(c) 950.00
11 Grl(c),B:Dick Devins 1,000.00
12 Grl(c),Bondage(c) 1,000.00
13 ASh(c),Bondage(c). 1,000.00
14 ASh(c),Bondage(c)
   E:Dick Devins 1,000.00
15 ASh(c),Bondage(c),B:Tara . . 1,700.00
16 ASh(c),A:Spectro,
   E:Grim Reaper 1,000.00
17 FF,ASh(c),A:Super Sleuth . . 1,600.00
18 ASh(c),B:Silver Knight 1,500.00
19 ASh(c),FF 1,500.00
20 FF,ASh(c),Oct., 1948 . . . . . . 1,700.00

WONDER COMICS
**Fox Features Syndicate,
May, 1939**
1 BKa,WE,WE(c),B:Wonderman,
   DR.Kung,K-51 . . . . 28,000.00
2 WE,BKa,LF(c),B:Yarko the
   Great,A:Spark Stevens 9,000.00
Becomes:

GOLDEN AGE

Wonderworld Comics #31
© Fox Features Syndicate

WONDERWORLD COMICS

**Fox Features Syndicate,
July, 1939–Jan., 1942**

3 WE,LF,BP,LF&WE,I:Flame . 14,000.00
4 WE,LF,BP,LF(c) 7,000.00
5 WE,LF,BP,GT,LF(c),Flame . . 4,000.00
6 WE,LF,BP,GT,LF(c),Flame . . 4,000.00
7 WE,LF,BP,GT,LF(c),Flame . . 5,000.00
8 WE,LF,BP,GT,LF(c),Flame . . 5,000.00
9 WE,LF,BP,GT,LF(c),Flame . . 3,800.00
10 WE,LF,BP,LF(c),Flame. . . . 3,800.00
11 WE,LF,BP,LF(c),O:Flame . . 3,800.00
12 BP,LF(c),Bondage(c),Flame. 3,500.00
13 LF(c),E:Dr Fung,Flame 3,500.00
14 JoS,Bondage(c),Flame 3,000.00
15 JoS&LF(c),Flame. 2,200.00
16 Flame(c). 1,600.00
17 Flame(c). 1,600.00
18 Flame(c). 1,600.00
19 Male Bondage(c),Flame . . 1,800.00
20 Flame(c). 1,500.00
21 O:Black Club &Lion,Flame. . 1,400.00
22 Flame(c). 1,200.00
23 Flame(c). 1,000.00
24 Flame(c). 1,000.00
25 A:Dr Fung,Flame 1,000.00
26 Flame(c). 1,000.00
27 Flame(c). 1,000.00
28 Bondage(c)I&O:US Jones,
   B:Lu-nar,Flame. 1,600.00
29 Bondage(c),Flame 1,000.00
30 O:Flame(c),Flame 1,700.00
31 Bondage(c),Flame 1,000.00
32 Hitler(c),Flame 1,100.00
33 Male Bondage(c) 1,000.00

WONDERLAND COMICS

**Feature Publications
(Prize Comics Group),
Summer, 1945**

1 (fa),B:Alex in Wonderland 250.00
2 . . . . 150.00
3 thru 8 . . . . @125.00
9 1947. . . . . 125.00

WONDERWORLD
See:WONDER COMICS

THE WORLD AROUND US

Gilberton Publications, 1958
1 GE,Dogs 125.00
2 SC,Indians 125.00
3 LbC,Horses 125.00

---

4 LbC,Railroads 100.00
5 Grl,Space. 125.00
6 GE,The FBI 125.00
7 Grl,Pirates 100.00
8 GE,Grl,Flight 100.00
9 Grl,EK,Army. 100.00
10 EK,Navy 100.00
11 Marines 100.00
12 Grl,Coast Guard 100.00
13 JCo,Air Force 100.00
14 GE,EK,The French Revolution 125.00
15 AW,GM,EK,Prehistoric
   Animals 135.00
16 EK,The Crusades 100.00
17 GE,RC,Festivals 100.00
18 GE,RC,Great Scientists 100.00
19 AW,GM,The Jungle 125.00
20 RC,GE,AT,Communications . . 125.00
21 RC,GE,GM,American
   Presidents 125.00
22 GE,Boating 100.00
23 RC,GE,Great Explorers 100.00
24 GM,GE,Ghosts 125.00
25 GM,GE,Magic 125.00
26 The Civil War 150.00
27 RC,GE,CM,AT,High Adventure 100.00
28 RC,GE,GM,AT,LbC(c),Whaling 110.00
29 RC,GE,AT,GM,Vikings 125.00
30 RC,GE,JK,AT,Undersea
   Adventures 125.00
31 RC,GE,Grl,EK,JK,Hunting . . . 100.00
32 GM,JK,RC,GE,For Gold
   and Glory. 100.00
33 AT,GE,RC,Famous Teens 110.00
34 RC,GE,Fishing 100.00
35 LcM,JK,GM,GE,Spies 110.00
36 JK,Fight For Life 100.00

WORLD FAMOUS HEROES MAGAZINE

**Comic Corp. of America
(Centaur) Oct., 1941**
1 BLb,Paul Revere 1,700.00
2 BLb,Andrew Jackson,V:
   Dickinson, Lou Gehrig 750.00
3 BLb,Juarez-Mexican patriot . . 650.00
4 BLb,Canadian Mounties 650.00

WORLD FAMOUS STORIES

Croyden Publ., 1945
1 Rip Van Winkle,Ali Baba 175.00

THE WORLD IS HIS PARISH

George A. Pflaum, 1953
N# Pope Pius XII 75.00

WORLD'S GREATEST STORIES

**Jubilee Publications
Jan., 1949**
1 F:Alice in Wonderland 450.00
2 F:Pinocchio 400.00

WORLDS BEYOND

Fawcett Publications, 1951
1 BP,BBa. 650.00
Becomes:

WORLDS OF FEAR

Fawcett Publications, 1952
2 BP,SMo(c). 1,200.00
3 GE,SMo(c). 900.00
4 BP,MSy,SMo(c) 750.00
5 BP,MSy,SMo(c) 750.00
6 SMo(c). 750.00
7 SMo(c). 750.00

World's of Fear #5
© Fawcett Publications

8 SMo(c). 750.00
9 . . . . 750.00
10 no-eyed man, eyeballs(c) . . 2,200.00

WORLD WAR III

**Ace Periodicals,
March–May, 1953**
1 Atomic Bomb (c) 1,250.00
2 The War That Will Never
   Happen 850.00

WOTALIFE COMICS
See: PHANTOM LADY

WOW COMICS

**David McKay/Henle Publ.,
July, 1936–Nov., 1936**
1 WE,DBr(c),Fu Manchu,
   Buck Jones. 4,000.00
2 WE,Little King 3,000.00
3 WE,WE(c), Popeye. 2,700.00
4 WE,BKa,AR,DBr(c),Popeye,
   Flash Gordon 3,500.00

WOW COMICS

**Fawcett Publications,
Winter, 1940**
N#(1)S&K,CCB(c),B&O:Mr Scarlett;
   B:Atom Blake,Jim Dolan,Rick
   O'Shay,Bondage(c) 27,000.00
2 B:Hunchback 4,500.00
3 V:Mummy Ray Gun 3,000.00
4 O:Pinky 3,200.00
5 F:Pinky the Whiz Kid 2,000.00
6 O:Phantom Eagle;
   B:Commando Yank 2,000.00
7 Spearhead of Invasion 1,500.00
8 All Three Heroes. 1,500.00
9 A:Capt Marvel,Capt MarvelJr.
   Shazam,B:Mary Marvel . . . 3,200.00
10 The Sinister Secret of
   Hotel Hideaway 1,500.00
11 . . . . 1,400.00
12 Rocketing adventures 1,400.00
13 Thrill Show. 1,400.00
14 V:Mr Night 1,400.00
15 Shazam Girl of America . . . 1,200.00
16 Ride to the Moon 1,200.00
17 V:Mary Batson,Alter Ego
   Goes Berserk 1,200.00
18 I:Uncle Marvel,Infinity(c)
   V is For Victory. 1,200.00
19 A Whirlwind Fantasy 1,200.00
20 Mary Marvel's Magic Carpet 1,200.00

Wow Comics #7
© *Fawcett Publications*

21 Word That Shook the World . . 500.00
22 Come on Boys-
   Everybody Sing 500.00
23 Trapped by the Terror of
   the Future 500.00
24 Mary Marvel 500.00
25 Mary Marvel Crushes Crime . . 500.00
26 Smashing Star-
   Studded Stories 400.00
27 War Stamp Plea(c) 400.00
28 Pinky 400.00
29 . . . . 400.00
30 In Mirror Land 400.00
31 Stars of Action 350.00
32 The Millinery Marauders 350.00
33 Mary Marvel(c) 350.00
34 A:Uncle Marvel 350.00
35 I:Freckles Marvel 500.00
36 Secret of the Buried City 350.00
37 7th War loan plea 350.00
38 Pictures That Came to Life . . . 350.00
39 The Perilous Packages 350.00
40 The Quarrel of the Gnomes . . 350.00
41 Hazardous Adventures 300.00
42 . . . . 300.00
43 Curtain Time 300.00
44 Volcanic Adventure 300.00
45 Commando Yank 300.00
46 Commando Yank 300.00
47 Commando Yank 300.00
48 Commando Yank 300.00
49 Commando Yank 300.00
50 Mary Marvel/Commando Yank 300.00
51 Command Yank 250.00
52 . . . . 250.00
53 Murder in the Tall Timbers . . . 250.00
54 Flaming Adventure 250.00
55 Earthquake! 250.00
56 Sacred Pearls of Comatesh . . 250.00
57 . . . . 250.00
58 E:Mary Marvel;The Curse
   of the Keys 250.00
59 B:Ozzie the Hilarious
   Teenager 250.00
60 thru 64 . . . . @250.00
65 A:Tom Mix 250.00
66 A:Tom Mix 250.00
67 A:Tom Mix 250.00
68 A:Tom Mix 250.00
69 A:Tom Mix,Baseball 250.00
Becomes:

REAL WESTERN HERO
Sept., 1948
70 It's Round-up Time 500.00

71 CCB,P(c),A Rip
   Roaring Rodeo 325.00
72 w/Gabby Hayes 325.00
73 thru 75 . . . . @325.00
Becomes:

WESTERN HERO
March, 1949
76 Partial Ph(c)&P(c) 350.00
77 Partial Ph(c)&P(c) 200.00
78 Partial Ph(c)&P(c) 200.00
79 Partial Ph(c)&P(c),
   Shadow of Death 175.00
80 Partial Ph(c)&P(c) 200.00
81 CCB,Partial Ph(c)&P(c),
   F:Tootsie 200.00
82 Partial Ph(c)&P(c),
   A:Hopalong Cassidy 200.00
83 Partial Ph(c)&P(c) 200.00
84 Ph(c) 175.00
85 Ph(c) 175.00
86 Ph(c),The Case of the
   Extra Buddy, giant 175.00
87 Ph(c),The Strange Lands 175.00
88 Ph(c),A:Senor Diablo 175.00
89 Ph(c),The Hypnotist 175.00
90 Ph(c),The Menace of
   the Cougar, giant 150.00
91 Ph(c),Song of Death 150.00
92 Ph(c),The Fatal Hide-out,
   giant 150.00
93 Ph(c),Treachery at
   Triple T, giant 150.00
94 Ph(c),Bank Busters,giant 150.00
95 Ph(c),Rampaging River 150.00
96 Ph(c),Range Robbers,giant . . 150.00
97 Ph(c),Death on the
   Hook,giant 150.00
98 Ph(c),Web of Death,giant 150.00
99 Ph(c),The Hidden Evidence . . 150.00
100 Ph(c),A:Red Eagle,Giant . . . 150.00
101 Red Eagle, Ph(c) 150.00
102 thru 111 Ph(c) . . . . @150.00
112 Ph(c),March, 1952 . . . . 175.00

XMAS COMICS
Fawcett Publications, 1941
1 Whiz #21 . . . . 6,500.00
2 Capt. Marvel 2,200.00
7 Floppy, Funny Animal 800.00
Second Series, 1949–52
4 Whiz, Capt. Marvel, Nyoka . . 1,000.00
5 . . . . 750.00
6 . . . . 750.00
7 Bill Boyd 750.00

X-VENTURE
Victory Magazines, 1947
1 Mystery Shadow, Atom
   Wizard 1,600.00
2 same 850.00

YANKEE COMICS
Chesler Publications
(Harry A. Chesler),
Sept., 1941–March, 1942
1 F:Yankee Doodle Jones . . . 2,600.00
2 The Spirit of '41 . . . . 1,200.00
3 Yankee Doodle Jones 900.00
4 JCo,Yankee Doodle Jones . . . 900.00

YANKS IN BATTLE
Comic Magazine, Inc.
(Quality Comics Group), 1956
1 CCv 125.00
2 CCv 100.00
3 CCv 100.00
4 CCv 100.00

THE YARDBIRDS
Ziff-Davis Publishing Co., 1952
1 . . . . 125.00

YELLOWJACKET
COMICS
Levy Publ./Frank Comunale/
Charlton, Sept., 1944
1 O&B:Yellowjackets,B:Diana
   the Huntress 1,500.00
2 Rosita &The Filipino Kid 750.00
3 . . . . 700.00
4 Fall of the House of Usher 750.00
5 King of Beasts 750.00
6 . . . . 800.00
7 I:Diane Carter;The
   Lonely Guy 2,000.00
8 The Buzzing Bee Code 800.00
9 . . . . 750.00
10 Capt Grim V:The Salvage
   Pirates 800.00
Becomes:

JACK IN THE BOX
Charlton, Feb., 1946
11 Funny Animal,Yellow Jacket . . 300.00
12 Funny Animal 200.00
13 BW,Funny Animal 300.00
14 thru 16 Funny Animal . . . . @200.00
Becomes:

COWBOY WESTERN
COMICS
Charlton, July, 1948
17 Annie Oakley,Jesse James . . . 250.00
18 JO,JO(c) 200.00
19 JO,JO(c),Legends of Paul
   Bunyan 200.00
20 JO(c),Jesse James 125.00
21 Annie Oakley VisitsDryGulch . 125.00
22 Story of the Texas Rangers . . 125.00
23 . . . . 125.00
24 Ph(c),F.James Craig 125.00
25 Ph(c),F.Sunset Carson 125.00
26 Ph(c) 150.00
27 Ph(c),Sunset Carson movie . . 750.00
28 Ph(c),Sunset Carson movie . . 400.00
29 Ph(c),Sunset Carson movie . . 400.00
30 Ph(c),Sunset Carson movie . . 400.00
31 Ph(c) 100.00
32 thru 34 Ph(c) . . . . @100.00
35 thru 37 Sunset Carson . . . @350.00
38 and 39 . . . . @100.00
Becomes:

SPACE WESTERN
COMICS
Charlton Comics, Oct., 1952
40 Spurs Jackson,V:The
   Saucer Men 1,100.00
41 StC(c),Space Vigilantes 750.00
42 StC(c),Atomic Bomb 900.00
43 StC(c),Battle of
   Spacemans Gulch 800.00
44 StC(c),The Madman of Mars . 750.00
45 StC(c),The Moon Bat,Hitler . . 775.00
Becomes:

COWBOY WESTERN
COMICS
Oct., 1953
46 . . . . 250.00
Becomes:

COWBOY WESTERN
HEROES
Dec., 1953
47 . . . . 150.00
48 . . . . 150.00
Becomes:

GOLDEN AGE

COWBOY WESTERN
May–June, 1954
49 .... 125.00
50 F:Jesse James 125.00
51 thru 57. .... @100.00
58, Wild Bill Hickok, giant 125.00
59 thru 66. .... @100.00
67 AW&AT 150.00
Becomes:

WILD BILL HICKOK AND JINGLES
Aug., 1958
68 AW 125.00
69 AW 100.00
70 AW 100.00
71 .... 100.00
72 .... 100.00
73 .... 100.00
74 1960 .... 100.00

YOGI BERRA
Fawcett, 1957
1 Ph(c). 1,100.00

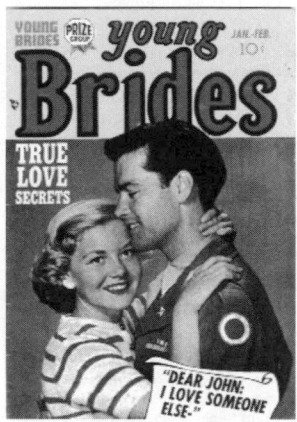

Young Brides #3
© Prize Comics

YOUNG BRIDES
Feature Publications (Prize Comics), Sept.–Oct., 1952
1 S&K,Ph(c) 500.00
2 S&K,Ph(c) 250.00
3 S&K,Ph(c) 200.00
4 S&K 200.00
5 S&K 200.00
6 S&K 200.00
2-1 S&K 200.00
2-2 S&K 100.00
2-3 S&K 175.00
2-4 S&K 175.00
2-5 S&K 175.00
2-6 S&K 175.00
2-7 S&K 175.00
2-8 S&K 100.00
2-9 S&K 100.00
2-10 S&K 175.00
2-11 S&K. 175.00
2-12 S&K 175.00
3-1 thru 4-1 .... @100.00
4-2 S&K 175.00
4-3. .... 100.00
4-4 S&K 175.00
4-5. .... 100.00

YOUNG EAGLE
Fawcett Publications/ Charlton Comics, Dec., 1950
1 Ph(c) 250.00
2 Ph(c),Mystery of Thunder
  Canyon 125.00
3 Ph(c),Death at Dawn 100.00
4 Ph(c) 100.00
5 Ph(c),The Golden Flood 100.00
6 Ph(c),The Nightmare Empire.. 100.00
7 Ph(c),Vigilante Vengeance ... 100.00
8 Ph(c),The Rogues Rodeo 100.00
9 Ph(c),The Great Railroad
  Swindle 100.00
10 June, 1952, Ph(c),Thunder Rides
  the Trail,O:Thunder 100.00

YOUNG HEROES
Titan Publ. (American Comics Group), 1955
35 Frontier Scout 125.00
36 .... 125.00
37 .... 125.00

YOUNG KING COLE
Novelty Press/Premium Svcs. Co., Autumn, 1945
1-1 Detective Toni Gayle 400.00
1-2 .... 250.00
1-3 .... 200.00
1-4 .... 200.00
2-1 .... 150.00
2-2 .... 150.00
2-3 .... 150.00
2-4 .... 150.00
2-5 .... 150.00
2-6 .... 150.00
2-7 .... 150.00
3-1 .... 175.00
3-2 LbC 250.00
3-3 The Killer With The Hat 150.00
3-4 The Fierce Tiger 150.00
3-5 AMc 150.00
3-6 .... 175.00
3-7 LbC(c),Case of the
  Devil's Twin 250.00
3-8 .... 150.00
3-9 The Crime Fighting King 150.00
3-10 LbC(c) 250.00
3-11 LbC(c) 250.00
3-12 July, 1948,AMc(c) 150.00

YOUNG LIFE
New Age Publications, Summer, 1945
1 Partial Ph(c),Louis Prima..... 175.00
2 Partial Ph(c),Frank Sinatra ... 200.00
Becomes:

TEEN LIFE
Winter, 1945
3 Partial Ph(c),Croon without
  Tricks,June Allyson(c) 150.00
4 Partial Ph(c),Atom Smasher
  Blueprints,Duke Ellington(c) . 125.00
5 Partial Ph(c), Build Your Own
  Pocket Radio, Jackie
  Robinson(c). 150.00

YOUNG LOVE
Feature Publ. (Prize Comics Group), Feb.–March, 1949
1 S&K,S&K(c). 600.00
2 S&K,Ph(c) 300.00
3 S&K,JSe,BE,Ph(c). 250.00
4 S&K,Ph(c) 150.00
5 S&K,Ph(c) 150.00
2-1 S&K,Ph(c) 250.00

2-2 Ph(c) 135.00
2-3 Ph(c) 135.00
2-4 Ph(c) 135.00
2-5 Ph(c) 135.00
2-6 S&K(c) 200.00
2-7 S&K(c),S&K 200.00
2-8 S&K 200.00
2-9 S&K(c),S&K 200.00
2-10 S&K(c),S&K 200.00
2-11 S&K(c),S&K 200.00
2-12 S&K(c),S&K 200.00
3-1 S&K(c),S&K 200.00
3-2 S&K(c),S&K 200.00
3-3 S&K(c),S&K 200.00
3-4 S&K(c),S&K 200.00
3-5 Ph(c) 175.00
3-6 BP,Ph(c). 175.00
3-7 Ph(c) 175.00
3-8 Ph(c) 175.00
3-9 MMe,Ph(c). 175.00
3-10 Ph(c) 175.00
3-11 Ph(c) 175.00
3-12 Ph(c) 175.00
4-1 S&K 175.00
4-2 Ph(c) 150.00
4-3 Ph(c) 150.00
4-4 Ph(c) 150.00
4-5 Ph(c) 150.00
4-5 Ph(c) 150.00
4-6 S&K,Ph(c) 150.00
4-7 thru 4-12 Ph(c). .... @125.00
5-1 thru 5-12 Ph(c). .... @125.00
6-1 thru 6-9 .... @100.00
6-10 thru 6-12 .... @100.00
7-1 thru 7-7 .... @100.00
7-8 thru 7-11 .... @100.00
7-12 thru 8-5 .... @100.00
8-6 thru 8-12 .... @100.00

YOUNG ROMANCE COMICS
Feature Publ./Headline/ Prize Publ., Sept.–Oct., 1947
1 S&K(c),S&K. 650.00
2 S&K(c),S&K. 350.00
3 S&K(c),S&K 300.00
4 S&K(c),S&K 300.00
5 S&K(c),S&K 300.00
6 S&K(c),S&K 300.00
2-1 S&K(c),S&K 275.00
2-2 S&K(c),S&K 275.00
2-3 S&K(c),S&K 275.00
2-4 S&K(c),S&K 275.00
2-5 S&K(c),S&K 275.00
2-6 S&K(c),S&K 250.00
3-1 thru 3-12 S&K(c),S&K .... @250.00
4-1 thru 4-12 S&K .... @250.00
5-1 ATh,S&K 250.00
5-2 .... 250.00
5-3 .... 225.00
5-4 thru 5-12 S&K .... @225.00
6-1 .... 100.00
6-2 .... 100.00
6-3 .... 100.00

YOUR UNITED STATES
Lloyd Jacquet Studios, 1946
1N# Teeming Nation of Nations . 300.00

ZAGO, JUNGLE PRINCE
Fox Features Syndicate, Sept., 1948
1 A:Blue Beetle. 900.00
2 JKa. 750.00
3 JKa. 600.00
4 MB(c). 600.00
Becomes:

MY STORY
May, 1949
5 JKa,Too Young To Fall in Love 250.00
6 I Was A She-Wolf 125.00
7 I Lost My Reputation 125.00
8 My Words Condemned Me . . . 125.00
9 WW,Wayward Bride 250.00
10 WW,March, 1950,Second
　Rate Girl 250.00
11 . . . . 125.00
12 Ph(c). 125.00

ZAZA THE MYSTIC
See: CHARLIE CHAN

TEGRA, JUNGLE EMPRESS
Fox Features Syndicate
Aug., 1948
1 Blue Bettle,Rocket Kelly 800.00
Becomes:

ZEGRA, JUNGLE EMPRESS
Oct., 1948
2 JKa 900.00
3 . . . . 650.00
4 . . . . 650.00
5 . . . . 650.00
Becomes:

MY LOVE LIFE
June, 1949–Aug., 1950
6 I Put A Price Tag On Love . . . 175.00
7 An Old Man's Fancy 125.00
8 My Forbidden Affair 125.00
9 I Loved too Often 125.00
10 My Secret Torture 125.00
11 I Broke My Own Heart 125.00
12 I Was An Untamed Filly 125.00
13 I Can Never Marry You 100.00

ZIP COMICS
MLJ Magazines,
Feb., 1940–Summer, 1944
1 MMe,O&B:Kalathar,The Scarlet
　Avenger,Steel Sterling,B.Mr
　Satan,Nevada Jones,War Eagle
　Captain Valor 9,000.00
2 MMe,CBi(c)B:Steel
　Sterling(c). 3,500.00
3 MMe,CBi(a&c) 2,800.00
4 MMe,CBi(a&c) 2,400.00

Zip Comics #41
© MLJ Magazines

---

5 MMe,CBi(a&c) 2,400.00
6 MMe,CBi(a&c) 2,000.00
7 MMe,CBi(a&c) 2,000.00
8 MMe,CBi(a&c),Bondage(c) . 2,000.00
9 CMMe,CBi(a&c),E:Kalathar,
　Mr Satan;Bondage(c) 2,200.00
10 MMe,CBi(a&c),B:Inferno . . . 2,100.00
11 MMe,CBi(a&c) 1,600.00
12 MMe,CBi(a&c),Bondage(c) . 1,600.00
13 MMe,CBi(a&c),E:Inferno,
　Bondage(c),Woman in
　Electric Chair 1,800.00
14 MMe,CBi(a&c),Bondage(c) . 1,500.00
15 MMe,CBi(a&c),Bondage(c) . 1,800.00
16 MMe,CBi(a&c),Bondage(c) . 1,500.00
17 CBi(a&c),E:Scarlet
　Avenger Bondage(c). 1,700.00
18 IN(c),B:Wilbur. 1,700.00
19 IN(c),Steel Sterling(c). 1,500.00
20 IN(c),O&I:Black Jack
　Hitler(c). 2,500.00
21 IN(c),V:Nazis 1,400.00
22 IN(c). 2,100.00
23 IN(c),Flying Fortress 1,400.00
24 IN(c),China Town Exploit . . . 1,400.00
25 IN(c),E:Nevada Jones 1,400.00
26 IN(c),B:Black Witch,
　E:Capt Valor 1,400.00
27 IN(c),I:Web,V:Japanese 2,300.00
28 IN(C),O:Web,Bondage(c). . . 2,000.00
29 Steel Sterling & Web 1,000.00
30 V:Nazis. 1,000.00
31 IN(c) 800.00
32 Nazi Skeleton, WWII 1,000.00
33 Bondage(c). 800.00
34 I:Applejack;Bondage(c). 750.00
35 E:Zambini 700.00
36 I:Senor Banana. 700.00
37 . . . . 700.00
38 E:Web 700.00
39 O&B:Red Rube 700.00
40 Red Rube 600.00
41 . . . . 600.00
42 Red Rube 600.00
43 Red Sterling(c). 600.00
44 Red Rube 600.00
45 E:Wilbur 600.00
46 Red Rube 600.00
47 Crooks Can't Win 650.00

ZIP-JET
St. John Publishing Co.,
Feb., 1953
1 Rocketman 1,100.00
2 April–May, 1953, Assassin
　of the Airlanes 700.00

ZIPPY THE CHIMP
Pines Comics, 1957
50 . . . . 70.00
51 . . . . 70.00

ZOO FUNNIES
Charlton Magazines, 1945
1 Funny Animals (1st Charlton) . 275.00
2 . . . . 200.00
3 . . . . 125.00
4 . . . . 125.00
5 . . . . 125.00
6 . . . . 100.00
7 . . . . 100.00
8 Diana the Huntress 100.00
9 . . . . 100.00
10 . . . . 100.00
11 thru 15 . . . . @100.00
Becomes:

TIM MCCOY
Charlton Comics, 1948
16 Western Movie Stories,
　John Wayne. 600.00

---

17 Rocky Lane. 500.00
18 Rod Cameron 500.00
19 Jessie James 500.00
20 Jimmy Wakley. 500.00
21 Johnny Mack Brown 500.00
Becomes:

PICTORIAL LOVE STORIES
Charlton Comics, 1949
22 B:Me-Dan Cupid 250.00
23 . . . . 250.00
24 Fred Astaire 275.00
25 . . . . 250.00
26 . . . . 250.00

ZOO FUNNIES
Charlton Comics, 1953–55
1 Timothy the Ghost 150.00
2 Leo the Lyin' Lion. 100.00
3 thru 7 . . . . @125.00
8 Nyoka. 150.00
9 Nyoka 150.00
10 Nyoka 150.00
11 Nyoka 150.00
12 Nyoka 150.00
13 Nyoka 150.00

ZOOM COMICS
Carlton Publishing Co.,
Dec., 1945
N# O:Captain Milksop. 600.00

ZOOT COMICS
Fox Features Syndicate,
Spring, 1946
N#(1)(fa) 250.00
2 A:Jaguar(fa) 250.00
3 (fa) 150.00
4 (fa) 150.00
5 (fa) 125.00
6 (fa) 125.00
7 B:Rulah. 1,400.00
8 JKa(c),Fangs of Stone 1,000.00
9 JKa(c),Fangs of Black Fury . 1,000.00
10 JKa(c),Inferno Land 1,000.00
11 JKa,The Purple Plague,
　Bondage(c). 1,100.00
12 JKa(c),The Thirsty Stone,
　Bondage(c) 800.00
13 Bloody Moon 650.00
14 Pearls of Pathos,Woman
　Carried off by Bird 950.00
15 Death Dancers 650.00
16 . . . . 650.00
Becomes:

RULAH, JUNGLE GODDESS
Aug., 1948
17 JKa(c),Wolf Doctor. 1,500.00
18 JKa(c),Vampire Garden 1,000.00
19 JKa(c) 950.00
20 . . . . 950.00
21 JKa(c) 950.00
22 JKa(c) 950.00
23 . . . . 800.00
24 . . . . 700.00
25 . . . . 700.00
26 . . . . 700.00
27 . . . . 750.00
Becomes:

I LOVED
July, 1949–March, 1950
28 . . . . 150.00
29 thru 31 . . . . @100.00
32 My Poison Love 100.00

DARK HORSE

ABE SAPIEN: DRUMS OF THE DEAD
Mar., 1998
1-shot Hellboy spin-off 3.00

ABYSS, THE
1989
1 & 2 MK,Movie Adaptation . . . . @2.50

ACCIDENT MAN
(B&W) 1993
1 I:Accident Man. 2.50
2 thru 3 . . . . @2.50

ADRENALYNN: WEAPON OF WAR
Aug., 2001
TPB TnD 13.00

ADVENTURES OF LUTHER ARKWRIGHT
DH/Valkyrie Press
(B&W) 1987–89
1 thru 9 . . . . @2.50
(B&W) 1990
1 thru 9 Rep. . . . . @2.50
TPB 15.00

ADVENTURES OF THE MASK
1996
1 thru 12 by Michael Eury & Marc
Campos, TV cartoon adapt... @2.50
Ash can (1995) 3.00

Aeon Flux #4
© Dark Horse Comics

AEON FLUX
Oct., 2005
1 (of 4) Timothy Green art 3.00
2 thru 4 . . . . @3.00
TPB Aeon Flux. 13.00

AGE OF REPTILES
1993–94
1 DRd,Story on Dinosaurs 3.00
2 thru 4 DRd,Story on Dinosaurs @3.00
TPB Tribal Warfare 15.00

AGE OF REPTILES: THE HUNT
May, 1996
1 thru 5 by Ricardo Delgado. . . . @3.00
TPB The Hunt 18.00

AGENTS OF LAW
Comics' Greatest World, 1995
1 KG, I:Law 2.50
2 A:Barb Wire 2.50
3 KG,DLw,The Judgment Gate. . . . 2.50
4 Open Golden City 2.50
5 Who is the Mystery figure 2.50
6 V:Predator 2.50

AKIRA
TPB #1, 364-pg.,B&W 25.00
TPB #2, 304-pg.,B&W 25.00
TPB #3, 288-pg.,B&W 25.00
TPB #4, 400-pg.,B&W 28.00
TPB #5, 416-pg.,B&W 28.00
TPB #6, 440-pg.,B&W 30.00

AL CAPP'S LI'L ABNER: THE FRAZETTA SUNDAYS
May, 2003
TPB Vol. 1 1954–55. . . . . 19.00
TPB Vol. 2 1956–57. . . . . 19.00
TPB Vol. 3 1958–59. . . . . 19.00
TPB Vol. 4 1960–61. . . . . 19.00

ALIEN RESURRECTION
Oct., 1997
1 (of 2) movie adaptation 2.50
2 DMc(c). 2.50

ALIENS
(B&W) 1988
1 Movie Sequel,R:Hicks,Newt . . . 22.00
1a 2nd printing. 3.00
1b 3rd printing. 2.50
1c 4th printing. 2.50
2 Hicks raids Mental Hospital 10.00
2a 2nd printing 2.50
2a 3rd printing. 2.50
3 Realize Queen is on Earth 7.00
3a 2nd printing 2.50
4 Queen is freed, Newton on
Aliens World 5.00
5 All out war on Aliens World 5.00
6 Hicks & Newt return to Earth. . . . 5.00
TPB rep.#1–#6 & DHP #24 . . . . . 11.00
TPB 2nd printing, DvD(c). 11.00

ALIENS (II)
[Mini-Series] 1989
1 DB,Hicks,Newt hijack ship. 5.00
1a 2nd Printing 3.00
2 DB,Crazed general trains aliens . 3.00
2a 2nd Printing 3.00
3 DB,HicksV:General Spears 3.00
3a 2nd Printing 2.50
4 DB,Heroes reclaim earth
from aliens. 3.00

ALIENS
1-shot Earth Angel, JBy (1994) 3.00
1-shot Glass Corridor, DvL (1998). . 3.00
1-shot Lovesick (1996) 3.00
1-shot Mondo Heat, I:Herk Mondo . 2.50
1-shot Mondo Pest (1995). 3.00
1-shot Pig, CDi,FH (1997) 3.00
1-shot Purge, IEd,PhH (1997) 3.00
1-shot Sacrifice, rep.Aliens UK
  (1993) 5.00
1-shot Salvation DGb,MMi,KN,
  F:Selkirk (1993). 5.00
1-shot Special (1997). 2.50
1-shot Stalker (1998). 2.50
1-shot Wraith (1998) 3.00
GN Female War, remastered. 17.00
GN Genocide, remastered. 17.00
GN Labyrinth, remastered 18.00
GN Nightmare Asylum, remaster. . 17.00
GN Outbreak, remastered 18.00
GN Rogue, Remastered 17.00
TPB rep. Earth Angel (1991) 15.00
TPB Salvation and Sacrifice 13.00
TPB Tribes 12.00
TPB DNA War (2006) 7.00

ALIENS: ALCHEMY
Sept., 1997
1 (of 3) JAr,RCo 3.00
2 thru 3 . . . . @3.00

ALIENS: APOCALYPSE — DESTROYING ANGELS
Jan., 1999
1 (of 4) MSh 3.00
2 thru 4 MSh . . . . @3.00
TPB 11.00

ALIENS: BERSERKER
1995
1 I:Crew of the Nemesis 3.00
2 thru 4 . . . . @3.00

ALIENS: COLONIAL MARINES
1993
1 I: Lt. Joseph Henry 4.00
2 I: Pvt. Carmen Vasquez. 3.00
3 thru 10 . . . . @3.00

ALIENS: EARTH WAR
1991
1 SK,JBo(c),Alien's War renewed . . 4.00
1a 2nd Printing 2.50
2 SK,JBo(c),To trap the Queen. . . . 4.00
3 SK,JBo(c) Stranded on
Alien's planet. 3.00
4 SK,JBo(c),Resolution,final 5.00

ALIENS: GENOCIDE
1991
1 Aliens vs. Aliens 3.50
2 Alien Homeworld 3.00
3 Search for Alien Queen 3.00
4 Conclusion, inc. poster 3.00
TPB Genocide rep. #1–#4 . . . . 14.00

ALIENS: HAVOC
1997
1 (of 2) 'over 40 creators' 3.00
2 . . . . 3.00

All comics prices listed are for *Near Mint* condition.

DARK HORSE

ALIENS: HIVE
1992
1 KJo,I:Stanislaw Mayakovsky 4.00
2 KJo,A:Norbert 3.50
3 KJo,A:Julie,Gill. 3.25
4 KJo,A:Stan,Final 3.00
TPB Hive rep. #1–#4 . . . . 14.00

Aliens Kidnapped #2
© Dark Horse Comics

ALIENS: KIDNAPPED
Dec., 1997–Feb., 1998
1 (of 3) 3.00
2 thru 3 . . . . @3.00
TPB Aliens:Kidnapped 10.00

ALIENS: LABYRINTH
1993
1 F:Captured Alien 3.00
2 thru 4 . . . . @3.00
TPB rep. #1–#4 . . . . 18.00
TPB remastered. 18.00

ALIENS: MUSIC OF THE SPEARS
1994
1 I:Damon Eddington 3.00
2 thru 4TBd(c). . . . . @3.00

ALIENS: NEWT'S TALE
1992
1 How Newt Survived 5.50
2 JBo(c),Newt's point of view 5.50

ALIENS: ROGUE
1993
1 F:Mr.Kay 3.00
2 thru 4 V:Aliens . . . . @3.00
TPB Nel(c),rep.#1–#4 . . . . 15.00

ALIENS: STRONGHOLD
1994
1 DoM,JP 3.00
2 thru 4 DoM,JP . . . . @3.00
TPB 17.00

ALIENS: SURVIVAL
Feb.–Apr., 1998
1 (of 3) TyH(c). 3.00
2 thru 3 . . . . @3.00

ALIENS/PREDATOR: DEADLIEST OF THE SPECIES
1993–95
1 B:CCl(s),JG,F:Caryn Delacroix . . 4.00
2 JG,V:Predator. 3.00
3 JG,F:Caryn Delacroix. 3.00
4 JG,V:Predator. 3.00
5 JG,Roadtrip 3.00
6 JG,in Space Station 3.00
7 thru 9 JG,EB. . . . . @3.00
10 CCl(s), Human Predators 3.00
11 CCl,EB,JBo(c),Delacroix vs.
   DeMatier 3.00
12 Caryn's Fate 3.00
TPB 30.00

ALIENS VS. PREDATOR
1996
0 PN,KS,Rep.DHP#34-36,(B&W) . . 9.00
1 Duel to the Death. 9.00
1a 2nd Printing 3.00
2 Dr. Revna missing 5.00
3 Predators attack Aliens 5.00
4 CW,F:Machiko & Predator 5.00
TPB Rep.#1–#4 . . . . 20.00
TPB PN,KS,rep.DHP#34-36 . . . . . 20.00
TPB Thrill of the Hunt (2004). 7.00
TPB Panel to Panel (2006) 20.00
Ann.#1 (1999) 5.00
1-shot Booty, rep. *Previews* 3.00

ALIENS VS. PREDATOR: DUEL
1995
1 Trap, JS 3.00
2 War 3.00

ALIENS VS. PREDATOR: ETERNAL
June, 1998
1 (of 4) IEd,GF(c) 3.00
2 thru 4 IEd,GF(c). . . . . @3.00
TPB 10.00

ALIENS VS. PREDATOR: WAR
1995
0 Prelude to New Series. 3.00
1 RSd,MM,RCo(c) F:Machiko. 3.00
2 thru 4 . . . . @3.00
TPB 20.00

ALIENS VS. PREDATOR: XENOGENESIS
Dec., 1999
1 (of 4) MvR 3.50
2 thru 4 MvR,trapped . . . . @3.50

ALIENS VS. PREDATOR VS. THE TERMINATOR
Apr., 2000
1 (of 4) MSh,MvR 3.50
2 MSh,MvR,V:Terminator-Alien
   hybrid. 3.50
3 MSh,MvR,on Predator ship 3.50
4 MSh,MvR,concl. 3.50
TPB 96-pg. series rep. 12.00

ALIENS: XENOGENESIS
Aug., 1999
1 thru 4 DR . . . . @3.50

ALIEN 3
1992
1 thru 3 Movie Adaptation . . . . . . @3.00

AL WILLIAMSON: HIDDEN LANDS
(B&W) Nov., 2002
TPB AW,224-pg. 23.00

AMAZING ADVENTURES OF THE ESCAPIST, THE
Dec., 2003
1 Michael Chabon, 80-pg. 9.00
2 thru 8 . . . . @9.00
TPB Vol. 1 and Vol. 2. . . . . @18.00

AMAZING SCREW-ON HEAD, THE
May, 2002
1-shot MMi. 3.00

AMERICAN, THE
(B&W) 1987–89
1 CW,'Chinese Boxes,'D:Gleason . 5.00
2 CW,'Nightmares. 4.00
3 CW,Secrets of the American 4.00
4 CW,American vs.Kid America 4.00
5 A:Kiki the Gorilla 4.00
6 Rashomon-like plot 3.50
7 Pornography business issue 3.50
8 Deals with violence issue 3.50
9 American Falls into a cult 3.50
Spec. (1990) 4.00
TPB The American (2006). 15.00

THE AMERICAN: LOST IN AMERICA
1992
1 CMa, American joins a cult 2.50
2 CMa, V:'Feel Good' cult. 2.50
3 CMa, 'Apo Mask' cult 2.50
4 CMa, Final issue 2.50
ColorSpec.#1 . . . . 3.00

AMERICAN SPLENDOR
1993–2000
1-shot Letterman by Harvey Pekar . 3.50
1-shot One Step Out of the
   Nest (1994) 3.50
1-shot On the Job (1997). 3.50
1-shot Comics Con, JZe (1996). . . . 3.50
1-shot Music Comics (1997) 3.50
1-shot Odds & Ends (1997). 3.50
1-shot Transatlantic Comics (1998). 3.50
1-shot Terminal (1999). 3.50
1-shot Bedtime Stories (2000). 4.50
1-shot Portrait of The Artist
   in his declining years (2001) . . . 4.00
TPB (2002). 12.00

AMERICAN SPLENDOR: UNSUNG HERO
DH Maverick, Aug., 2002
1 (of 3) b&w 4.00
2 thru 3 . . . . @4.00

AMERICAN SPLENDOR: WINDFALL
(B&W) 1995
1 Windfall Gained,pt.1 . . . . 4.25
2 Windfall Lost 4.25

DARK HORSE

All comics prices listed are for *Near Mint* condition.

ANCIENT JOE
DH Maverick, Oct., 2001
1 (of 3) B&W 3.00
2 . . . . 3.50
3 . . . . 3.50
TPB 13.00

ANGEL
1999–2001
1 Buffy spin-off 3.00
2 thru 9 . . . . @3.00
10 TSg 3.00
11 TSg 3.00
12 TSg,MMi(c) 3.00
13 TSg,demonic rats 3.00
14 TSg,Little Girl Lost 3.00
15 TSg,Past Lives,Buffy x-over . . 4.00
16 TSg,Past Lives,Buffy x-over . . 4.00
17 The Cordelia Special. 3.00
1–17a newsstand photo(c) . . . . @4.00
TPB Surrogates 10.00
TPB Earthly Possessions 10.00
TPB Hunting Ground 10.00
TPB Angel Autumnal 10.00
TPB The Hollower 10.00
TPB Strange Bedfellows, rep. . . . 13.00

ANGEL
2001–02
1 (of 4) 3.00
1a photo (c). 3.00
1b gold-foil (c) 13.00
1c gold-foil (c) signed 20.00
2 . . . . 3.00
3 . . . . 3.00
4 . . . . 3.00
2a thru 4a photo (c) . . . . @3.00
TPB Long Night's Journey 13.00

ANIMAL CONFIDENTIAL
(B&W) 1992
1-shot parody 2.50

ANOTHER CHANCE TO GET IT RIGHT
1995
1 B&W 15.00
TPB AVs, GfD(c) 10.00
TPB 3rd printing (2002) 12.00

APOCALYPSE NERD
(B&W) Feb., 2005
1 (of 6) Peter Bagge art 3.00
2 thru 3 . . . . @3.00

APPLESEED
(B&W–Manga)
TPB #1: Promethean Challenge . . 15.00
TPB #2: Prometheus Unbound . . 15.00
TPB #3: Scales of Prometheus . . . 15.00
TPB #4: Promethean Balance 15.00
TPB Hypernotes (2006) 15.00
TPB Appleseed ID (2006) 15.00

APPLESEED DATABOOK
(B&W–Manga) 1994
1 Flip Book, by Masamune Shirow. 5.00
1a 2nd printing 3.50
2 Flip Book 3.50
TPB Rep. #1–#2 (1995). 13.00

ARCHENEMIES
Apr., 2006
1 (of 4) by Drew Melbourne 3.00
2 thru 4 . . . . @3.00
TPB ArchEnemies 13.00

ARMY OF DARKNESS
1992
1 . . . . 20.00
2 thru 3 . . . . @18.00

ARZACH
1996
TPB by Moebius 7.00

A SMALL KILLING
GN by Alan Moore & Oscar Zarate 12.00

ASTRO BOY
(B&W) Mar., 2002
TPB Vol.1 224-pg.Osamu Tezuka . 10.00
TPB Vol.2 thru Vol. 23 . . . . . @10.00

ATLAS
1994
1 BZ,I:Atlas 2.75
2 BZ,V:Sh'en Chui 2.75
3 BZ,V:Sh'en Chui 2.50
4 BZ, final issue 2.50

AUTOBIOGRAPHIX
Nov., 2003
TPB 15.00

BABE
Legend, 1994
1 JBy(a&s) 3.00
2 thru 4 JBy(a&s) . . . . @2.50

BABE 2
Legend, 1995
1 V:Shrewmanoid 2.50
2 A:Abe Sapien 2.50

BACCHUS COLOR SPECIAL
1995
1 A:Thor 3.00
2 A:Abe Sapien 2.50

BADGER: SHATTERED MIRROR
1994
1 R:Badger 3.00
2 thru 4 . . . . @3.00

BADGER: ZEN POP FUNNY ANIMAL VERSION
1 MBn,R:Badger (1994) 3.00
2 Ham 3.00

BADLANDS
(B&W) 1991
1 I:Connie Bremen 3.50
2 Anne Peck, C.I.A. 3.00
3 Assassination Rumor 2.50
4 Connie heads South 2.50
5 November 22, 1963, Dallas 2.50
6 Kennedy Assination aftermath . . . 2.50

BANYA
Sept., 2006
TPB The Explosive Delivery Man . 13.00
TPB Explosive Delivery Man #2 . . 13.00

BARB WIRE
Comics' Greatest World, 1994
1 Foil(c),I:Deathcard 3.00
2 DLw,I:Hurricane Max 3.00
3 V:Mace Blitzkrieg 3.00

4 Ghost,pt.1 . . . . 3.00
5 Ghost,pt.2 . . . . 3.00
6 Hardhide, Ignition. 3.00
7 A:Motorhead 3.00
8 V:Ignition 3.00
9 A:Mecha, V:Ignition 3.00
Movie Spec. (1996) 4.00
TPB 9.00

Barb Wire: Ace of Spades #2
© Dark Horse Comics

BARB WIRE: ACE OF SPADES
1996
1 CW,TBd & DoM 3.00
2 thru 4 CW,TBd & DoM . . . . @3.00

BARRY WINDSOR-SMITH: STORYTELLER
Oct., 1996
TPBs 1 thru 9 9'x12½' . . . . @5.00

BASEBALL GREATS
1 Jimmy Piersall story. 3.25
2 Bob Gibson 3.50
3 Harmon Killebrew 3.50

BASIL WOLVERTON'S FANTASIC FABLES
(B&W) Oct., 1993
1 BW 2.50
2 BW 2.50

BASIL WOLVERTON'S
GN Gateway to Horror (1988) 5.00
TPB In Space, 240-pg. (1999). . . . 17.00
GN Planet of Terror (1987) 5.00

BATMAN/ALIENS
DH/DC, Mar., 1997
1 (of 2) RMz,BWr 5.00
2 conclusion 5.00
TPB RMz,BWr 15.00

BATMAN/TARZAN: CLAWS OF THE CATWOMAN
1999
1 (of 4) RMz,DvD(c),V:Dent,x-over. 3.00
2 thru 4 RMz,DvD(c) . . . . @3.00
TPB 96-pg.,DvD(c). 11.00

DARK HORSE

BATTLE GODS: WARRIORS OF THE CHAAK
Apr., 2000
1 (of 9) by Francisco Ruiz
  Velasco 3.00
2 the Lucha Libre 3.00
3 F:Takan, El Charro. 3.00
4 another tournament 3.00
5 The Chaak begins 3.00
6 Deathmatch: Takan vs. Chilbacan 3.00
7 sleeping god awakens 3.00
8 Hell breaks loose 3.00
9 concl. 3.00
TPB 240-pg. 20.00

BERSERK
Oct., 2003
TPB Vol. 1 The Black Swordsman. 13.00
TPB Vol. 2 Guardians of Desire. . . 13.00
TPB Vol. 3 thru Vol. 13. . . . . @14.00

Bettie Page Comics: Spicey Adventure
© *Dark Horse Comics*

BETTIE PAGE COMICS
1996–97
1-shot, some nudity (1996) 4.00
1-shot Bettie Page Comics: Spicy
  Adventure, by Jim Silke (1997). 3.00
1 Queen of Hearts, movie adapt. . . 2.50
TPB Queen of Hearts 20.00

BETTIE PAGE: QUEEN OF THE NILE
Dec., 1999
1 (of 3) low-budget time machine . . 3.00
2 and 3 concl. . . . . @3.00
TPB, series rep. 13.00

BIG
1989
1 Movie Adaptation 3.00

BIG BLOWN BABY
(B&W) Aug., 1996
1 thru 4 by Bill Wray . . . . @3.00

BIG GUY AND RUSTY THE ROBOT BOY
1995
1 V:Monster. 5.00
2 V:Monster. 5.00
TPB FM & GfD 15.00
TPB King Size 30.00

BIG HOAX
DH Venture 2001
TPB B&W 128-pg. 11.00

BILLI 99
(B&W) 1991
1 'Pray for us Sinners' 4.50
2 'Trespasses'. 4.00
3 'Daily Bread'. 4.00
4 . . . . 4.00
TPB TSe,200-pg. B&W (2002) . . . 15.00

BILLY THE KID'S OLD-TIMEY ODDITIES
April, 2005
1 (of 4) KHt 3.00
2 thru 4 KHt. . . . . @3.00
TPB 14.00

BIRD: THE TATTOO
Nov., 2001
TPB color, 48-pg. 15.00

BLACKBURNE COVENANT, THE
Apr., 2003
1 (of 4) FaN 3.00
2 thru 4 . . . . @3.00
TPB FaN 13.00

BLACK CROSS
(B&W) 1987
1-shot special CW 3.00

BLACK CROSS: DIRTY WORK
Apr., 1997
1-shot by Chris Warner 3.00

BLACK DRAGON, THE
(B&W) Apr., 1996
TPB C. Claremont & J. Bolton. . . . 18.00

BLACK MAGIC
(B&W) 1998
TPB 17.00

BLACK PEARL, THE
Sept., 1996
1 by Mark Hamill. 3.00
2 thru 5 . . . . @3.00
TPB by Mark Hamill. 17.00

BLADE OF THE IMMORTAL
(B&W–Manga) July, 1996
1 by Hiroaki Samura 11.00
Criminal Conquest
2 thru 4 pt. 2 thru pt.4 . . . . @6.00
Genius, Oct., 1996
5 & 6 . . . . @6.00
Fanatic, Jan., 1997
7 & 8 . . . . @6.00
Call of the Worm, Apr., 1997
9 thru 11 48-pg. . . . . @6.00

Blade the Immortal #13
© *Dark Horse Comics*

TPB Cry of the Worm 13.00
Dreamsong, July, 1997
12 thru 18 . . . . @3.50
TPB Dreamsong 13.00
Rin's Bane, Mar., 1998
19 & 20 48-pg. . . . . @4.50
On Silent Wings, May, 1998
21 thru 25 . . . . @3.50
26 48-pg. 4.50
27 thru 28 . . . . @3.50
TPB Blood of a Thousand 13.00
TPB On Silent Wings. 15.00
TPB On Silent Wings II 15.00
Dark Shadows, Jan., 1999
29 thru 33 . . . . @3.50
TPB Dark Shadows 15.00
Food, June, 1999
34 48-pg. 4.50
Heart of Darkness, 1999
35 thru 42 . . . . @3.50
TPB Heart of Darkness 17.00
The Gathering, 2000
43 thru 57 . . . . @3.50
TPB The Gathering 16.00
TPB The Gathering, Vol.2 . . . . . . 16.00
Secrets, 2001
58 thru 61, pt.1 thru pt.4 . . . . @3.50
62 Stigmata 3.50
63 Husk 3.50
64 Skin,pt.1 . . . . 3.50
65 Skin,pt.2 . . . . 3.50
TPB Secrets, 232-pg. b&w 17.00
Beasts, 2002
66 thru 72 Beasta pt.1 thru pt. 7 . @3.50
Fall Frost, 2002
73 thru 78 pt.1 thru pt. 6 . . . . @3.50
79 The Wind and the Heron 3.50
80 Petals on the Wind 3.50
81 Shadows. 3.50
82 Mourning Shadows. 3.50
83 Path of Shadows. 3.50
84 Thorns. 3.50
TPB Fall Frost 17.00
Mirror of the Soul, 2003
85 Mirror of the Soul,pt.1 . . . . 3.00
86 Mirror of the Soul,pt.2 . . . . 3.00
87 Mirror of the Soul,pt.3 . . . . 3.00
88 Light and Shadow. 3.00
89 Crossroads 3.00
TPB Vol. 13 Mirror of the Soul. . . . 18.00
Last Blood, 2004
90 Last Blood,pt.1 . . . . 3.00
91 Last Blood,pt.2 . . . . 3.00
92 Last Blood,pt.3 . . . . 3.00

All comics prices listed are for *Near Mint* condition.

93 Last Blood,pt.4 . . . . 3.00
94 Last Blood,pt.5 . . . . 3.00
95 Confession 3.00
Twilight, 2004
96 Twilight,pt.1. . . . . 3.00
97 Twilight,pt.2. . . . . 3.00
98 Twilight,pt.3. . . . . 3.00
Trickster, 2005
99 Trickster,pt.1 . . . . 3.00
100 Trickster,pt.2 . . . . 3.00
102 Trickster,pt.3 . . . . 3.00
103 Trickster,pt.4 . . . . 3.00
104 Forsaken. 3.00
105 Duet 3.00
106 Cauldron 3.00
TPB Trickster 17.00
Shortcut, 2005
107 Shortcut,pt.1 . . . . 3.00
108 Shortcut,pt.2 . . . . 3.00
109 Shortcut,pt.3 . . . . 3.00
110 Shortcut,pt.4 . . . . 3.00
111 Shortcut,pt.5 . . . . 3.00
On the Perfection of Anatomy, 2006
112 On the Perfection of Anatomy . . 3.00
113 On the Perfection of Anatomy . . 3.00
114 On the Perfection of Anatomy . . 3.00
115 On the Perfection of Anatomy . . 3.00
116 On the Perfection of Anatomy . . 3.00
117 On the Perfection of Anatomy . . 3.00
The Sparrow Net, 2006
118 The Sparrow Net, pt.1 . . . . 3.00
119 The Sparrow Net, pt. 2 . . . . 3.00

BLAIR WHICH?
Dec., 1999
1-shot SA, Scary as heck 3.50

BLANCHE GOES TO HOLLYWOOD
(B&W) 1993
1 Turn of the Century N.Y. 3.00

BLANCHE GOES TO NEW YORK
(B&W) 1992
1 Turn of the Century Hollywood . . 3.00

BLAST CORPS
Sept., 1998
1-shot F:demolition experts 2.50

BLOOD TIES
Nov., 2000
GN 15.00

BLOOD WORLD
March 2003
1 (of 3) 3.00
2 . . . . 3.00

BLUE LILY
1993
1 thru 3 . . . . @4.00

BLUE WITCH OF OZ, THE
1992
1 TPB EiS 10.00

BMWFILMS.COM —THE HIRE
July, 2004
1 (of 6) MWg,Scandal. 3.00
2 MWg,Precious Cargo. 3.00
3 MWg,Hijacked 3.00
4 MWg,Tycoon 3.00
TPB 18.00

BODY BAGS
Aug., 1996
1 (of 4) 3.00
2 thru 4 . . . . @3.00
TPB 13.00

BOOK OF NIGHT
(B&W) 1987
1 CV 2.50
2 & 3 CV . . . . @2.50
TPB Children of the Stars 13.00

BORIS THE BEAR
(B&W) 1986
1 V:Funny Animals 3.00
1a 2nd printing 2.50
2 V:Robots 2.50
3 V:Super Heroes 2.50
4 thru 7 . . . . @2.50
8 LargeSize. 2.50
9 thru 12 . . . . @2.50
See: B & W Pub. section
Color Classics 1987
1 thru 7 . . . . @2.50

B.P.R.D.
2003
1-Shot Dark Waters, GyD 3.00
1-Shot Night Train, ScK 3.00
1-Shot The Soul of Venice,MMi . . . 3.00
1-Shot There's Something Under
My Bed, AdP 3.00

B.P.R.D.: A PLAGUE OF FROGS
Mar., 2004
1 A Plague of Frogs 3.00
2 thru 5 A Plague of Frogs . . . . . @3.00
TPB 18.00

B.P.R.D.: THE BLACK FLAME
Aug., 2005
1 MMi,GyD 3.00
2 thru 6 MMi,GyD . . . . @3.00
TPB 18.00

B.P.R.D.: THE DEAD
2004–05
1 GyD,JAr,MMi 3.00
2 thru 5 . . . . @3.00
TPB 18.00

B.P.R.D.: THE UNIVERSE MACHINE
April., 2006
1 MMi,GyD 3.00
2 thru 5 MMi,GyD . . . . @3.00
TPB 18.00

BRAVE
Mar., 1997
1 by Cully Hamner & Jason Martin. 3.00

BUBBLE GUM CRISIS: GRAND MAL
(Manga) 1994
1 . . . . 2.75
2 and 3 . . . . @2.75
4 final issue. 2.50
TPB Rep.#1–#4 . . . . 15.00

Buffy the Vampire Slayer #42
© Dark Horse Comics

BUFFY THE VAMPIRE SLAYER
Sept., 1998
1 JoB,AAd(c) Wu-Tang Fang 10.00
1a 2nd printing 4.00
1b gold foil logo 12.50
2 JoB, Halloween 6.00
3 JoB, Cold Turkey 6.00
4 White Christmas 6.00
5 Happy New Year 6.00
6 New Kid on the Block,pt.1 . . . . . . 6.00
7 JoB, New Kid on the Block,pt.2 . . 6.00
8 The Final Cut. 6.00
9 Hey, Good Looking,pt.1 . . . . 6.00
10 Hey, Good Looking,pt.2 . . . . . . 6.00
11 A Boy Named Sue. 6.00
12 A Nice Girl Like You 6.00
12a gold foil (c) 13.00
13 F:Cordelia Chase 5.00
14 Bad Blood,pt.5 . . . . 5.00
15 Bad Blood,pt.6 . . . . 5.00
16 Food Chain 5.00
17 Bad Blood,pt.7 . . . . 4.00
18 Mardi Gras 3.00
19 Bad Blood, concl. 3.00
20 Angel heads to L.A. 3.00
21 Blood of Carthage,pt.1 . . . . 3.00
22 Blood of Carthage,pt.2 . . . . 3.00
23 Blood of Carthage,pt.3 . . . . 3.00
24 Blood of Carthage,pt.4 . . . . 3.00
25 Blood of Carthage,concl. 3.00
26 Heart of the Slayer,pt.1. . . . . . . 3.00
27 Heart of the Slayer,pt.2. . . . . . . 3.00
28 revenge. 3.00
29 Past Lives,pt.2,Angel x-over. . . . 4.00
30 Past Lives,pt.4,Angel x-over. . . . 4.00
31 Lost and Found. 4.00
32 hobo ghost 3.00
33 Demonic Entomology 3.00
34 Bug hunt, concl. 3.00
35 False Memories,pt.1 . . . . 3.00
36 False Memories,pt.2 . . . . 3.00
37 False Memories,pt.3 . . . . 3.00
38 False Memories,pt.4 . . . . 3.00
39 Night of a Thousand Vampires . . 3.00
40 JmP,Ugly Little Monsters,pt.1 . . 3.00
41 JmP,Ugly Little Monsters,pt.2 . . 3.00
42 JmP,Ugly Little Monsters,pt.3 . . 3.00
43 JmP,Death of Buffy,pt.1. . . . . . . 3.00
44 JmP,Death of Buffy,pt.2. . . . . . . 3.00
45 JmP,Death of Buffy,pt.3. . . . . . . 3.00
46 JmP,Withdrawal 3.00
47 Hellmouth to Mouth,pt.1 . . . . . . 3.00

48 Hellmouth to Mouth,pt.2 . . . . . . 3.00
49 Hellmouth to Mouth,pt.3 . . . . . . 3.00
50 Hellmouth to Mouth,pt.4 . . . . . . 3.50
51 SLo,FaN,Viva Las Buffy,pt.1 . . . 3.00
52 SLo,Viva Las Buffy, pt.2 . . . . . . 3.00
53 SLo,Viva Las Buffy, pt.3 . . . . . . 3.00
54 SLo,Viva Las Buffy, pt.4 . . . . . . 3.00
55 Dawn and Hoopy the Bear 3.00
56 Slayer, Interrupted,pt.1 . . . . 3.00
57 Slayer, Interrupted,pt.2 . . . . 3.00
58 Slayer, Interrupted,pt.3 . . . . 3.00
59 Slayer, Interrupted,pt.4 . . . . 3.00
60 FaN,A Stake to the Heart,pt.1 . . 3.00
61 FaN,A Stake to the Heart,pt.2 . . 3.00
62 FaN,A Stake to the Heart,pt.3 . . 3.00
63 FaN,A Stake to the Heart,pt.4 . . 3.00
2a–63a newsstand photo(c) . . . . @3.00
Ann. 1999, 64-pg. 5.00
Spec. 1-shot Spike and Dru 3.00
Spec. 1-shot Giles 3.00
    Spec. 1-shot Giles, photo(c) . . . 3.00
Spec. 1-shot Jonathan 3.00
    Spec. 1-shotA photo (c). 3.00
Spec. 1-shot Lovers' Walk 3.00
    Spec. 1-shot-A photo (c) 3.00
Spec. 1-shot Spike & Dru—The
    Queen of Hearts, photo (c) 3.00
Spec. 1-shot Spike & Dru—All'sFair 3.00
    Spec. 1-shot Spike & Dru, ph(c) 3.00
Spec. 1-shot Willow & Tara 3.00
    Spec. 1-shotA photo (c) 3.00
    Spec. 1-shotB foil photo(c) . . . 10.00
    Spec. 1-shotC foil photo(c) sgn 20.00
    Spec. 1-shotD red foil 17.00
Spec.1-shot Lost & Found, FaN . . . 3.00
    Spec.1-shotA photo (c) 3.00
Spec.1-shot Buffy the Vampire
    Slayer/Angel: Reunion (2002) . . 3.00
    Spec.1-shotA photo (c) 3.00
Spec.1-shot Tales of the Slayers
    Broken Bottle of Djinn (2002) . . 3.50
    Spec.1-shotA photo (c) 3.50
Spec. 1-shot Chaos Bleeds (2003) . 3.00
    Spec. Chaos Bleeds, photo(c). . 3.00
Spec. 1/2 Wizard Mag. (1999) 10.00
GN Ring of Fire, photo(c) 10.00
TPB The Dust Waltz 10.00
TPB The Remaining Sunlight 10.00
TPB Uninvited Guests 11.00
TPB The Origin 10.00
TPB Bad Blood 10.00
TPB Crash Test Demons,
    rep.#9–#11. . . . . 10.00
TPB Pale Reflections, rep.#17–#19 10.00
TPB The Blood of Carthage 11.00

Buffy the Vampire Slayer: Spike & Dru
© Dark Horse Comics

TPB Spike and Dru 12.00
TPB Food Chain, 168-pg. 17.00
TPB Past Lives 13.00
TPB Autumnal 10.00
TPB Tales of the Slayer 15.00
TPB Creatures of Habit (2002) . . . 18.00
TPB Out of the Woodwork (2002) . 13.00
TPB False Memories (2002) 13.00
TPB Ugly Little Monsters (2002) . . 13.00
TPB The Death of Buffy (2002) . . . 16.00
TPB Note From the Underground . 13.00
TPB Willow and Tara 10.00
TPB Viva Las Buffy 13.00
TPB Slayer, Interrupted 15.00
TPB A Stake to the Heart. 13.00

BUFFY THE VAMPIRE SLAYER: ANGEL
May, 1999
1 (of 3) 3.00
2 & 3 . . . . @3.00
1a thru 3a newsstand, photo(c) . @3.00

BUFFY THE VAMPIRE SLAYER: HAUNTED
Dec., 2001
1 (of 4) deceased enemy's ghost . . 3.00
2 thru 4 . . . . @3.00
1a thru 4a photo (c) . . . . @3.00
TPB 96-pg. 13.00

BUFFY THE VAMPIRE SLAYER: THE ORIGIN
Feb., 1999
1 (of 3) DIB,JoB 3.00
2 & 3 . . . . @3.00
2a & 3a newsstand, photo(c) . . @3.00
TPB rep. 10.00

BUFFY THE VAMPIRE SLAYER: OZ
July, 2001
1 (of 3) 3.00
1a photo(c) 3.00
1b gold foil photo (c). 13.00
1c gold foil photo(c) signed. 25.00
1d fiery red foil photo(c) 17.00
2 . . . . 3.00
2a photo(c) 3.00
3 . . . . 3.00
3a photo(c) 3.00
TPB 80-pg. 10.00

BUFFY THE VAMPIRE SLAYER: WILLOW AND TARA — WILDERNESS
July, 2002
1 (of 2) 3.00
1a photo (c). 3.00
2 (of 2) 3.00
2a photo (c). 3.00

BY BIZARRE HANDS
(B&W) 1994
1 JLd(s). 2.50
2 JLd(s). 2.50
3 JLd(s). 2.50

CAIN
Nov., 2002
TPB 96-pg. B&W 10.00

CANNON GOD EXAXXION
Manga, Nov., 2001
1 Stage 1, part 1 (of 8) 3.00
2 thru 8 Stage One,pt.2 thru pt.8 @3.00
9 Stage Two,pt.1 . . . . 3.00
10 Stage Two,pt.2 . . . . 3.50
11 Stage Two,pt.3 . . . . 3.50
13 thru 15 . . . . @3.50
16 thru 20 . . . . @3.00
TPB Stage One, rep., 208-pg. b&w 16.00
TPB Stage 2. . . . . 15.00
TPB Stage 3 thru 5. . . . . @16.00

Caravan Kidd 3rd Series #1
© Dark Horse Comics

CARAVAN KIDD
(B&W—Manga) 1992
1 thru 10 by Johji Manabe . . . . . @2.50
[2nd Series] 1993
1 thru 10 F:Miam. . . . . @2.50
TPB Rep. #1–#10 . . . . 20.00
Holiday Spec. 2.50
Valentine's Day Spec. 2.50
[3rd Series] 1994
1 thru 8 . . . . @2.50
Christmas Special 2.50
TPB Vol. 2 . . . . 20.00
TPB Vol. 3 . . . . 20.00

CASTLE WAITING
2004
TPB Vol. 1 The Lucky Road 18.00

CATALYST: AGENTS OF CHANGE
Comics' Greatest World, 1994
1 JPn(c),V:US Army 2.50
2 JPn(c),I:Grenade 2.50
3 JPn(c),Rebel vs. Titan 2.50
4 JPn(c),Titan vs. Grace. 2.50
5 JPn(c),V:Ape 2.50
6 and 7 . . . . @2.50

CHEVAL NOIR
(B&W) 1989
1 DSt(c). 4.00
2 thru 9 . . . . @3.50
10 80 pg. 4.50
11 80 pg. 4.50
12 MM(c) 4.50

DARK HORSE

13 thru 15. . . . . @4.50
16 thru 19 with 2-card strip . . . . . @4.50
20 Great Power o/t Chninkel 4.50
21 Great Power o/t Chninkel 4.50
22 Great Power o/t Chninkel,concl. . 4.50
23 inc.'Rork','Forever War' concl. . . 4.50
24 In Dreams,pt.1 . . . . 4.50
25 In Dreams,pt.2 . . . . 4.50
26 In Dreams,pt.3 . . . . 4.50
27 I:The Man From Ciguri (Airtight
  Garage sequel) Dreams,pt.4 . . . 3.50
28 Ciguri cont. 3.50
29 Ciguri cont. 3.50
30 Ciguri,cont. 3.50
31 Angriest Dog in the World. 3.50
32 thru 40. . . . . @3.50
41 F:Demon. 3.50
42 F:Demon. 3.50
43 F:Demon. 3.50
44 F:Demon. 3.50
45 thru 47 . . . . @3.50
48 SwM(c) 3.50
49 F:Rork 3.50
50 F:Rork 3.50

CHOSEN
Dec., 2003
1 (of 3) MMr,PrG. 4.00
2 . . . . 3.00
3 . . . . 3.00
TPB 10.00

CHRONICLES OF CONAN
Sept., 2003
TPB Vol. 1 RTs,BWS reprints 16.00
TPB Vol. 2 Tower of the Elephant . 16.00
TPB Vol. 3 Monster of Monoliths . . 16.00
TPB Vol. 4 Red Nails. 16.00
TPB Vol. 5 Shadow in the Tomb . . 16.00
TPB Vol. 6 Curse of Golden Skull . 16.00
TPB Vol. 7 Dweller in the Pool . . . 16.00
TPB Vol. 8 Brother of the Blade . . 17.00
TPB Vol. 9 Riders of the
  River-Dragons 17.00
TPB Vol. 10 When Giants Walk
  the Earth 17.00

CHRONOWAR
(B&W) Aug., 1996
1 (of 9) by Kazumasa Takayama . . 3.00
2 thru 9 . . . . @3.00

CLASSIC STAR WARS
1992
1 AW,newspaper strip reps. 6.00
2 thru 7 AW,newspaper reps. . . . @4.00
8 AW,newspaper reps. w/card 4.00
9 AW,newspaper reps. 3.50
10 AW,newspaper reps. 3.50
11 thru 19 AW,newspaper reps. . . @3.00
20 AW,newspaper strip reps., with
  trading card, final issue 4.00
TPB Vol. 1, In Deadly Pursuit . . . 16.00
TPB Vol. 1, rep. 2nd edition. 17.00
TPB Vol. 2, Rebel Storm 17.00
TPB Vol. 3, Escape to Hoth 17.00

CLASSIC STAR WARS:
A LONG TIME AGO
June, 2002
TPB Vol. 1 thru Vol. 3. . . . . @30.00
TPB Vol. 4 Screams in the Void . . 30.00
TPB Vol. 5 Fool's Bounty. 30.00
TPB Vol. 6 Wookiee World 30.00
TPB Vol. 7 Far, Far Away 30.00

CLASSIC STAR WARS:
A NEW HOPE
1994
1 AAd(c), rep. 4.25
2 AH(c), rep. 4.00
TPB Rep. #1–#2 . . . . 10.00

CLASSIC STAR WARS:
DEVILWORLDS
Aug., 1996
1 (of 2) by Alan Moore 2.50
2 . . . . 2.50

*Classic Star Wars: Early
Adventures #3 © Dark Horse Comics*

CLASSIC STAR WARS:
EARLY ADVENTURES
Aug., 1994–Apr., 1995
1 MiA(c), Gambler's World 3.00
2 RHo&MGr(c),Blackhole 2.50
3 EiS(c),Rebels of Vorzyd-5 . . . . . 2.50
3 bagged with trading card DH2. . . 5.00
4 RHo(c),Tatooine. 2.50
5 RHo(c),A:Lady Tarkin. 2.50
6 Weather Dominator 2.50
7 RHo(c),V:Darth Vader 2.50
8 KPl(c),X-Wing Secrets 2.50
9 KPl(c),A:Boba Fett. 2.50
TPB RsM & AGw, AW(c) 20.00

CLASSIC STAR WARS:
EMPIRE STRIKES BACK
1994
1 and 2 Movie Adaptation . . . . . . @4.00
TPB Rep.#1–#2 AW&CG(c). 10.00
TPB reprint, Hildebrandt(c) 10.00

CLASSIC STAR WARS:
HAN SOLO
AT STAR'S END
Mar., 1997
1 thru 3 by Alfredo Alcala . . . . . . @3.00
TPB rep. AW(c) 7.00

CLASSIC STAR WARS:
A LONG TIME AGO
(B&W) Mar., 1999
1 thru 6 rep. Marvel comics . . . . @6.00

CLASSIC STAR WARS:
RETURN OF THE JEDI
1994
1 Movie Adaptation 4.00
2 Movie Adaptation 3.50
TPB Rep.#1–#2 . . . . 10.00
TPB rep. Hildebrandt(c). 10.00

CLASSIC STAR WARS:
VANDELHELM MISSION
1995
1-shot F:Han Solo, Lando 4.00

CLONEZONE
(B&W) 1989
Spec #1 . . . . 2.50

CLOWNS, THE
(PAGLIACCI)
Apr., 1998
1-shot B&W, CR. 3.00

CLUB 9
Feb., 2003
TPB B&W. 16.00
TPB Vol. 2 . . . . 16.00
TPB Vol. 3 . . . . 16.00

COLORS IN BLACK
Comics From Spike, 1995
1 B:Passion Play. 3.00
2 Images 3.00
3 Back on the Bus 3.00
4 final issue 3.00

COLUMBUS
(B&W) 1992
1-shot 2.50

COMIC BOOK
1 thru 4 9'x12' John Kricfalusi. . . @6.00

COMICS & STORIES
1996
1 (of 4) by Martin & Millionaire 3.00
2 thru 4 . . . . @3.00

COMICS' GREATEST
WORLD
1993
(Arcadia)
1 B:MRi(s),FM(c),B:LW,B:O:Vortex,
  F:X,I:Seekers. 3.00
1a B&W proof ed. (1,500 made). . . 9.00
1b Hologram(c), with cards. 7.00
2 JoP,I:Pit Bulls. 2.50
3 AH,I:Ghost 5.00
4 I:Monster 2.50
TPB Arcadia 25.00
(Golden City)
1 B:BKs(s),JOy(c),I:Rebel,
  Amaz.Grace,V:WarMaker 2.50
1a Gold Ed. 5.00
2 I:Mecha 2.50
3 WS(c),I:Titan 2.50
4 E:BKs(s),GP(c),JD,I:Catalyst. . . . 2.50
TPB Golden City 11.00
(Steel Harbor)
1 B:CW(s),PG,I:Barb Wire,
  V:Ignition 2.50
2 MMi(c),TNa,I:Machine 2.50
3 CW(a&s),I:Wolf Gang 2.50
4 E:CW(s),VGi,I:Motorhead 2.50
TPB Steel Harbor 11.00

Comic's Greatest World King Tiger
© Dark Horse Comics

(Vortex)
1 B:RSd(s),LW,DoM,I:Division 13 . . 2.50
2 I:Hero Zero. 2.50
3 PC,I:King Tiger 2.50
4 B:RSd(s),E:MRi(s)BMc,E:LW,
   E:O:Vortex,C:Vortex 2.50
TPB Vortex. 11.00
Sourcebook 10.00

COMPLETELY PIP
AND NORTON
DH Maverick, Sept., 2002
TPB 72-pg. 10.00

CONAN
Feb., 2004
1 KBk,CNr,JLI(c) from R.E.Howard 0.00
1a JSC(c) 2nd printing 5.00
1b CNr(c) 3rd printing 3.00
2 Frost Giant's Daughter 4.00
3 Asgard 3.00
4 Hyperborea 3.00
5 Breaks out of slavery. 3.00
6 Rebel 3.00
7 Rebellion 3.00
8 Born on the Battlefield 3.00
9 KBk,CNr. 3.00
10 KBk,CNr,Death in the Temple . . . 3.00
11 KBk,CNr,God the the Bowl 3.00
12 KBk,CNr,The Widowmaker 3.00
13 KBk,CNr,V:Thoth-Amon 3.00
14 KBk,CNr,V:Thoth-Amon 3.00
15 KBk,Wolves in the Woods 3.00
16 KBk,Horror on Uskuth Hill. 3.00
17 KBk,CNr,The City of Thieves . . . 3.00
18 KBk,CNr,Siren-Song of Death . . 3.00
19 KBk,CNr,Thing in the Temple . . . 3.00
20 KBk,CNr,Tower of the Elephant . 3.00
21 KBk,CNr,Tower of the Elephant . 3.00
22 KBk,CNr,Tower of the Elephant . 3.00
23 KBk, The War of the Dead 3.00
24 KBk,CNr,The Hall of the Dead . . 3.00
25 KBk,CNr,The Hand of the Mighty 3.00
26 KBk, TT,Seeds of Empire 3.00
27 KBk, TT,two stories. 3.00
28 KBk, A night in Aquilonia. 3.00
29 MMi,CNr,The Hall of the Dead . . 3.00
30 MMi,CNr,The Hall of the Dead . . 3.00
31 MMi,CNr,The Hall of the Dead . . 3.00
32 KBk,Born on the Battlefield. 3.00
33 TT,CNr, pt.1, 40-pg. 3.00
34 TT,CNr, pt.2. . . . . 3.00
Spec. #1 Daughters of Midora 5.00

0 Spec. KBk,CNr,Conan the Legend
   prologue (2003). 1.00

CONAN AND THE
BOOK OF THOTH
March., 2006
1 (of 4) KBk,KJo,48-pg. 5.00
2 thru 5 KBk,KJo,48-pg. . . . . @5.00
TPB 18.00

CONAN AND THE
DEMONS OF KHITAI
Oct., 2005
1 (of 4) 3.00
2 . . . . 3.00
3 contains nude ad 7.00
3a 2nd printing 3.50
4 . . . . 3.00
TPB 13.00

CONAN AND THE
JEWELS OF GWAHLUR
April, 2005
1 CR 3.00
2 CR 3.00
3 CR 3.00

CONAN AND THE
SONGS OF THE DEAD
July., 2006
1 (of 4) JLd(s),TT 3.00
2 thru 5 . . . . @3.00

CONCRETE
(B&W) 1987
1 PC,R:Concrete, A Stone among
   Stones 11.00
1a 2nd printing 3.00
2 PC,'Transatlantic Swim'. 7.00
3 PC 5.00
4 PC 4.00
5 PC,'An Armchair Stuffed with
   Dynamite'. 4.00
6 PC,Concrete works on farm 4.00
7 PC,Concrete grows horns 4.00
8 PC,Climbs Mount Everest 4.00
9 PC,Mount Everest,pt.2. . . . . 4.00
10 PC,last Issue. 4.00
TPB The Complete Concrete. 25.00
Spec. #1 Concrete ColorSpec.,PC
   (1989) 4.00
Spec. Concrete Celebrates Earth Day
   PC,Moebius (1990) 2.50
Spec. 1 A New Life, B&W rep.,
   O: Concrete (1989) 3.50
Spec. Concrete: Land & Sea,
   rep. #1 & #2 (1989) 3.25
Spec. Concrete: Odd Jobs,
   rep. #5 & #6 (1990) 3.50

CONCRETE: ECLECTICA
1993
1 PC,The Ugly Boy 3.25
2 PC 3.25

CONCRETE:
FRAGILE CREATURE
1991
1 PC,Rulers o/t Omniverse,pt.1 . . . 4.00
2 PC,Rulers o/t Omniverse,pt.2 . . . 3.00
3 PC,Rulers o/t Omniverse,pt.3 . . . 3.00
4 PC,Rulers o/t Omniverse,pt.3 . . . 3.00
TPB 16.00

CONCRETE:
THE HUMAN DILEMMA
(B&W) Dec., 2004
1 (of 6) PC 3.50
2 thru 6 PC . . . . @3.50
TPB 13.00

CONCRETE:
KILLER SMILE
DH Legend, 1994
1 PC 3.50
2 thru 4 PC . . . . @3.00
TPB Rep.#1–#4 . . . . 17.00

Concrete Strange Armor #1
© Dark Horse Comics

CONCRETE:
STRANGE ARMOR
Dec., 1997–Apr., 1998
1 (of 5) 3.00
2 thru 5 . . . . @3.00
TPB Strange Armor 17.00

CONCRETE: THINK
LIKE A MOUNTAIN
(B&W) 1996
1 thru 6 PC,GfD(c) . . . . @3.00
TPB PC,GfD(c) 18.00

CORMAC MAC ART
July, 1989
1 Robert E. Howard adapt. 3.00
2 thru 4 . . . . @3.00

CORNY'S FETISH
April 1998
GN by Renee French, 64-pg. 5.00

COUTOO
(B&W) 1994
1 Lt. Joe Kraft 3.50

CREEPY
(B&W) 1992
1 KD,TS,GC,SL,Horror 4.00
2 TS,CI,DC,Demonic Baby 4.00
3 JM,TS,JG,V:Killer Clown 4.00
4 TS,Final issue 4.00

DARK HORSE

CREATURE FROM THE BLACK LAGOON
1 Movie Adaptation 5.00

CRIMINAL MACABRE
May, 2003
1 (of 5) F:Cal McDonald 4.00
2 thru 5 . . . . @3.00
1a & 2a 2nd printings . . . . @3.00
TPB Criminal Macabre. 15.00
1-shot Feet of Clay (2006). 3.00

CRITICAL ERROR
1992
1 rep.Classic JBy story 2.75

CROMWELL STONE
(B&W) 1992
1-shot 3.50

[ANDREW VACHSS']
CROSS
1995
0 GfD(c),I:Cross,Rhino,Princess. . . 2.50
1 thru 7 . . . . @3.00

CROW, THE
June, 2004
TPB Flesh and Blood 10.00

CRUSH
DH Rocket Comics, Oct., 2003
1 . . . . 3.00
2 thru 4 . . . . @3.00
TPB 13.00

CRYING FREEMAN
(B&W) Feb., 2006
TPB Vol. 1 thru 4 . . . . @15.00

CUD COMICS
(B&W) 1996
1 thru 8 by Terry LaBan . . . . @3.00

THE CURSE OF DRACULA
July, 1998
1 (of 3) MWn,GC 3.00
2 thru 3 . . . . @3.00
TPB 10.00

DAMN NATION
Feb., 2005
1 thru 3 . . . . @3.00

DANCE OF
LIFEY DEATH, THE
(B&W) 1994
1-shot ECa. 4.00

DANGER UNLIMITED
DH Legend, 1994
1 JBy(a&s),KD,I:Danger Unlimited,
  B:BU:Torch of Liberty 2.50
2 JBy(a&s),KD,O:DangerUnlimited. 2.50
3 JBy(a&s),KD,O:Torch of Liberty . . 2.50
4 JBy(a&s),KD,Final Issue 2.50
TPB rep. #1–#4 . . . . 15.00

DARE DETECTIVES, THE
Oct., 2004
TPB Vol. 1 The Snowpea Plot 6.00
TPB Vol. 2 The Royal Treatment . . 7.00

DARK HORSE CLASSICS
(B&W) 1992
1 Last of the Mohicans 4.50
2 20,000 Leagues Under the Sea . 4.50

DARK HORSE CLASSICS:
ALIENS VS. PREDATOR
Feb., 1997
1 thru 6 Rep. . . . . @3.00

DARK HORSE CLASSICS:
GODZILLA,
KING OF THE MONSTERS
July, 1998
1 RSd,SBi,now color. 3.00
2 rep. from 1995 . . . . 3.00
3 rep. from 1995 . . . . 3.00
4 rep. Godzilla #2, from 1995 . . . . 3.00
5 & 6 . . . . @3.00

DARK HORSE CLASSICS:
PREDATOR:
JUNGLE TALES
1-shot Rep. 3.00

DARK HORSE CLASSICS:
STAR WARS—
DARK EMPIRE
1997
1 rep. by Tom Veitch,CK,DvD(c). . . 3.00
2 thru 6 rep., DvD(c) . . . . @3.00

DARK HORSE CLASSICS:
TERROR OF GODZILLA
Aug., 1998
1 by Kazuhisa Iwata, AAd(c). 3.00
2 & 3 . . . . @3.00
4 rep. of 1988 B&W 3.00
5 & 6 AAd(c) . . . . @3.00

DARK HORSE COMICS
1992
1 RL,CW,F:Predator,Robocop,
  I:Renegade,Time Cop,(double
  gatefold cover). 4.00
2 RL,CW,F:Predator,Robocop,
  Renegade,Time Cop 3.00

Dark Horse Comics #11
© Dark Horse Comics

3 CW,F:Robocop,Time Cop,Aliens,
  Indiana Jones 3.00
4 F:Predator,Aliens,Ind.Jones. . . . 3.00
5 F:Predator,E:Aliens. 3.00
6 F:Robocop,Predator, E:Indiana
  Jones 3.00
7 F:Robocop,Predator,B:StarWars . 6.00
8 B&I:X,Robocop 8.00
9 F:Robocop,E:Star Wars 4.00
10 E:X,B:Godzilla,Predator,
  James Bond 3.50
11 F:Godzilla,Predator,James
  Bond,B:Aliens 2.75
12 F:Predator 2.75
13 F:Predator,B:Thing 2.75
14 MiB(s),B:The Mark 2.75
15 MiB(s),E:The Mark,B:Aliens . . . 2.75
16 B:Predator,E:Thing,Aliens. . . . 2.75
17 B:Aliens,Star Wars:Droids. . . . 2.75
18 E:Predator. 2.75
19 RL(c),B:X,E:Star Wars:Droids,
  Aliens. 2.75
20 B:Predator. 2.75
21 F:Mecha 2.75
22 B:Aliens, E:Mecha 2.75
23 B:The Machine 2.75
24 The Machine 2.75
25 Final issue. 2.75

DARK HORSE
DOWNUNDER
(B&W) 1994
1 F:Australian Writers 2.50
2 Australian Writers. 2.50
3 Australian Writers, finale 2.50

DARK HORSE
MAVERICK
Ann.2000 48-pg. B&W. 5.00
Ann.2001 48-pg. B&W. 5.00

DARK HORSE MONSTERS
Feb., 1997
1-shot. 3.00

DARK HORSE
PRESENTS
(B&W) 1986
1 PC,I:Concrete 15.00
1a 2nd printing 3.00
2 PC,Concrete 6.00
3 Boris theBear,Concrete 5.00
4 PC,Concrete 5.00
5 PC,Concrete 5.00
6 PC,Concrete 5.00
7 I:MONQ 5.00
8 PC,Concrete 5.00
9 RSd 5.00
10 PC,Concrete, I:Masque 15.00
11 Masque 6.00
12 PC,Concrete, Masque 7.00
13 Masque 5.00
14 PC,Concrete, Masque 7.00
15 Masque 5.00
16 PC,Concrete, Masque 7.00
17 F:Roachmill. 5.00
18 PC,Concrete, Mask. 7.00
19 Masque 5.00
20 double,Flaming Carrot 9.00
21 Masque 5.00
22 I:Duckman. 5.00
23 WiS,Filipino Massacre 5.00
24 PC,I:Aliens 18.00
25 thru 31 . . . . @3.00
32 A:Concrete 5.00
33 F:Mr. Monster 3.00
34 Aliens 4.00
35 Predator 4.00
36 Aliens vs.Predator. 5.00

Dark Horse Presents #27
© Dark Horse Comics

36a painted cover 8.00
37 The Heartbreakers 3.00
38 A:Concrete 4.00
39 Trekker 3.00
40 I:The Aerialist 3.00
41 Argosy 3.00
42 Aliens 5.00
43 Aliens 4.00
44 Crash 3.00
45 Predator 3.00
46 Predator 4.00
47 Monkers 3.00
48 with 2-card strip 3.00
49 with 2-card strip 3.00
50 inc.'Heartbreakers', with
    2-card strip 4.00
51 FM(o),inc.'Sin City' 4.00
52 FM,inc. 'Sin City' 4.00
53 FM,Inc. 'Sin City' 4.00
54 FM,Sin City;JBy Preview of
    Next Men,pt.1 . . . . 7.00
55 FM,Sin City;JBy Preview of
    Next Men (JBy),pt.2 . . . . 6.00
56 FM,Sin City,JBy,Next MenPt.3
    Aliens Genocide(prologue) 5.00
57 FM,SinCity;JBy Next Men,pt.4 . . 5.00
58 FM Sin City,Alien Fire 5.00
59 FM,Sin City,Alien Fire 5.00
60 FM,Sin City 5.00
61 FM,Sin City 5.00
62 FM,E:Sin City 5.00
63 Moe,Marie Dakar 3.00
64 MWg,R:The Aerialist 3.00
65 B:Accidental Death 3.00
66 PC,inc.Dr.Giggles 3.00
67 B:Predator story (lead in to
    'Race War'),double size 4.50
68 F:Predator,Swimming Lessons
    (Nestrobber tie-in) 3.00
69 F:Predator 3.00
70 F:Alec 3.00
71 F:Madwoman 3.00
72 F:Eudaemon 3.00
73 F:Eudaemon 3.00
74 F:Eudaemon 3.00
75 F:Chairman 3.00
76 F:Hermes Vs.the Eye,Ball Kid . . 2.50
77 F:Hermes Vs.the Eye,Ball Kid . . 2.50
78 F:Hermes Vs.the Eye,Ball Kid . . 2.50
79 B:Shadow Empires Slaves 2.50
80 AAd,I:Monkey Man & O'Brien . . . 3.00
81 B:Buoy 3.00
82 B:Just Folks 3.00
83 Last Impression 3.00

84 MBn,F:Nexus,E:Hermes Vs. the
    Eye Ball Kid 3.00
85 Winner Circle, Eighth Woman . . 3.00
86 Eighth Woman 3.00
87 F:Concrete 4.00
88 Hellboy 3.00
89 Hellboy 4.00
90 Hellboy 3.00
91 Blackheart, Baden 3.00
92 Too Much Coffee Man 6.00
93 Cud, Blackheart,Coffee Man . . . 8.00
94 A:Eyeball Kid,Coffee Man 6.00
95 Too Much Coffee Man 7.00
96 Kabuli Kid 3.00
97 F:Kabuki Kid 3.00
98 Pot Full of Noodles 3.00
99 Anthology title 3.00
100–#1 Lance Blastoff 4.50
100–#2 Hellboy 3.50
100–#3 Concrete 3.50
100–#4 Black Cross 3.00
100–#5 Pan Fried Girl 3.00
101 BW,F:Aliens 3.00
102 F:Mr. Painter 3.00
103 F:The Pink Tornado 3.00
104 F:The Pink Tornado 3.00
105 F:The Pink Tornado 3.00
106 F:Godzilla 3.00
107 F:Rusty Razorclam 3.00
108 The Ninth Gland 3.00
109 The One Trick Ripoff 3.00
110 F:Egg 3.00
111 Ninth Gland 3.00
112 three stories, concl. 3.00
113 Trypto the Acid Dog 3.00
114 F:Star Slammers/Lance Blastoff 3.00
115 flip-book Dr. Spin/The Creep . . 3.00
116 Fat Dog Mendoza 3.00
117 F:Aliens 3.00
118 Monkeyman O'Brien 3.00
119 Trout 3.00
120 'One Last Job' 3.00
121 F: Imago 3.00
122 'Lords of Misrule' 3.00
123 F: Jack Zero 3.00
124 F:Predator 3.00
125 F:Nocturnals 3.00
126 flip book, 48-pg 4.50
127 F:The Nocturnals 3.00
128 F:Dan & Larry 3.00
129 F:Hammer 3.00
130 F:Wanted Man 3.00
131 F:Girl Crazy 3.00
132 flip book 3.00

Dark Horse Presents #136
© Dark Horse Comics

133 F:Tarzan 3.00
134 F:The Dirty Pair 3.00
135 F:The Fall, concl. 4.00
136 The Ark 3.00
137 Predator 3.00
138 F:Terminators 3.00
139 F:Roachmill 3.00
140 F:Aliens 3.00
141 F:Buffy the Vampire Slayer 4.00
142 F:Lovecraftian tales 3.00
143 F:Tarzan tales 3.00
144 F:Vortex 3.00
145 F:Burglar Girls 3.00
146 F:Aliens vs. Predator 3.00
147 F:Ragnok 3.00
148 The Nevermen 3.00
149 Wunderkind 3.00
150 F:Buffy, 48-pg 5.00
151 F:Hellboy 3.00
152 It! The Beast from Twenty
    Billion Years Beyond Earth 3.00
153 Helm of Harxis 3.00
154 Iron Reich 3000, flip-book 3.00
155 Angel, flip-book 3.00
156 Witch's Son, flip-book 3.00
157 F:Witch's Son, final issue 20.00
Fifth Anniv. Special DGi,PC,
    SBi,CW,MW,FM,Sin City,
    Aliens,Give Me Liberty 25.00
Ann. 1997 F:Body Bags 5.00
Ann. 1998 F:Hellboy 10.00
Ann. 1999 DHP, JR 5.00
Ann. 2000 Girls Rule, 64-pg 5.00
Milestone Ed.#1,rep.DHP#1 . . . . . 2.50
TPB rep.Sin City 6.00
TPB Best of DHP #1–#20 . . . . 10.00
TPB Best of DHP #1–#20 2nd ed. . . 10.00
TPB Best of DHP #21–#30 . . . . 9.00
TPB Best of DHP #31–#50 . . . . 9.00
TPB Best of Dark Horse
    Presents Two 9.00
TPB Best of Dark Horse
    Presents Three 13.00
Spec. Dark Horse 20 Years 1.00

DARK HORSE PRESENTS: ALIENS

1 Rep 5.00
1a Platinum Edition 8.00

DARKNESS FALLS: THE TOOTH FAIRY— THE TRAGIC LIFE OF MATILDA DIXON

Jan., 2003

1-shot CAd 3.00

DEADFACE: DOING ISLANDS WITH BACCHUS

(B&W) 1991

1 rep. Bacchus apps. 3.00
2 rep. inc.'Book-Keeper of Atlantis . 3.00
3 rep. and new material 3.00

DEADFACE: EARTH, WATER, AIR & FIRE

(B&W) 1992

1 Bacchus & Simpson in Sicily 2.50
2 A:Don Skylla 2.50
3 Mafia/Kabeirol-War prep 2.50
4 Last issue 2.50

DEAD IN THE WEST

(B&W) 1993

1 TT,Joe Landsdale adapt 5.00
2 TT,adapt 5.00
Spec. #1 TT(c) 4.00

DEADLINE
(B&W) 1992

1 . . . . 4.00
2 thru 8 . . . . @4.00

DEADLINE USA
(B&W) 1991

1 rep. Deadline UK,Inc. Tank Girl
    Johnny Nemo 10.00
2 inc. Tank Girl,Johnny Nemo. . . . 10.00
3 . . . . 10.00

DEAD OR ALIVE—
A CYBERPUNK WESTERN
Apr., 1998

1 (of 4) by Tatjana and Alberto
    Ponticelli 2.50
2 thru 4 . . . . @2.50

DEAD TO RIGHTS
Oct., 2002

1-shot 64-pg. 6.00

DECADE OF
DARK HORSE, A
1996

1 (of 4) inc. Star Wars, Nexus,
    Ghost 3.00
2 thru 4 . . . . @3.00

[RANDY BOWEN'S]
DECAPITATOR
June, 1998

1 (of 4) GEr,DoM 3.00
2 GEr 3.00
3 MMi,KJo,AAl 3.00
4 MMi, conclusion 3.00

DEVIL CHEF
1994

1 I:Devil Chef 2.50

DEVIL'S FOOTPRINTS
March 2003

1 (of 4) 3.00
2 thru 4 . . . . @3.00
TPB 15.00

DIABLO: TALES OF
SANCTUARY
Nov., 2001

1-shot 64-pg. 6.00

DIGIMON
June, 2000, Bi-weekly

1 . . . . 3.00
2 thru 6 . . . . @3.00
7 thru 12 ND(c) 3.00
TPB Digital Monsters 10.00

DIRTY PAIR
(B&W–Manga) 1999

TPB Book 3 A Plague of Angels . . 13.00
TPB Dangerous Acquaintances . . . 13.00
TPB Biohazards 13.00
1-shot Start the Violence, AWa(c) . . 3.00
1-shot Start the Violence, JPn(c) . . . 3.00

DIRTY PAIR: FATAL
BUT NOT SERIOUS
(Manga) 1995

1 R:Kei,Yuri 3.00
2 V:Kevin Sleet,Yuri 3.00

---

3 Anti Yuri 3.00
4 V:Terrorists 3.00
5 conclusion 3.00

DIRTY PAIR: RUN
FROM THE FUTURE
Jan., 2000

1 (of 4) AWa(c) 3.00
1a AH(c) 3.00
2 AWa(c) 3.00
2a BSf(c) 3.00
3 AWa(c) 3.00
3a Bruce Timm(c) 3.00
4 AWa(c) 3.00
4a HuR(c) 3.00
TPB series rep. 15.00

DIRTY PAIR: SIM HELL
(B&W–Manga) 1993

1 thru 4 by Adam Warren . . . . . . @3.25
TPB rep. #1–#4 . . . . 14.00

DIRTY PAIR: SIM HELL:
REMASTERED
May, 2001

1 (of 4) full color, AWa 3.00
2 thru 4 AWa . . . . @3.00
TPB 3rd. ed. 15.00

DISNEY'S ATLANTIS
THE LOST EMPIRE
June, 2001

GN 56-pg. color 7.00

DISNEY'S
MONSTERS INC.
2001

1-shot movie adapt. 5.00

Disney's Tarzan #2
© *Dark Horse Comics*

DISNEY'S TARZAN
June, 1999

1 and 2 Animated movie adapt. . @3.00

DIVISION 13
Sept., 1994

1 & 2 . . . . @2.50
3 A:Payback 2.50
4 Carnal Genesis 2.50

DOC SAVAGE: CURSE
OF THE FIRE GOD

1 R:Man of Bronze 3.00
2 Exploding Plane. 3.00
3 & 4 . . . . @3.00

DR. GIGGLES
1992

1 Horror movie adapt. 2.50
2 Movie adapt.contd. 2.50

DR. ROBOT
Apr., 2000

1-shot, by Bernie E. Mireault 3.00

DOMINION
(B&W–Manga)

TPB 1 by Masamune Shirow 15.00
TPB 2nd printing 15.00
TPB 3rd edition 17.00

DOMINION: CONFLICT 1
— NO MORE NOISE
(B&W–Manga) 1996

1 thru 6 by Masamune Shirow . . @3.00
TPB series rep. 15.00

DOMINION SPECIAL:
PHANTOM OF
THE AUDIENCE
(B&W–Manga)

1-shot by Masamune Shirow 2.50

DOMU:
A CHILD'S DREAMS
(B&W–Manga)

1 Psychic Warfare 6.00
2 Murders Continue 6.00
3 Psychic war conclusion 6.00
TPB by Katsuhiro Otomo 18.00
TPB 2nd edition 18.00

DRACULA
1 Movie Adaptation 5.00

DRAGON PRINCE
June, 2005

1 (of 5) RMz,JJ 3.00

DRAKUUN
(B&W) Feb., 1997
Rise of the Dragon Princess

1 (of 6) by Johji Manabe 3.00
2 thru 6 . . . . @3.00
TPB rep. 13.00
The Revenge of Gustav (Aug., 1997)
7 (1 of 6) by Johji Manabe 3.00
8 thru 12 pt.2 thru pt.6 . . . . @3.00
TPB, rep. 15.00
Shadow of the Warlock (Feb., 1998)
13 (1 of 6) by Johji Manabe 3.00
14 thru 18 pt.2 thru pt.6 . . . . @3.00
TPB rep. 15.00
The Hidden War (Sept., 1998)
19 (1 of 6) by Johji Manabe 3.00
20 thru 24 pt.2 thru pt.6 . . . . @3.00
Flames of Empire (1999)
25 Flames of Empire (1 of 6) 3.00

DRAWING ON YOUR
NIGHTMARES
Oct., 2003

1-shot Halloween 2003 Special 1 . . 4.00
1-shot Halloween Special 2 . . . . . . 10.00

DROOPY
Oct., 1995
1 Dr. Droopenstein 2.50
2 Turkey For Dinner 2.50
3 Santa's Little Helpers. 2.50

DUCKMAN
1990
1 by Everette Peck 2.50

DWIGHT T. ALBATROSS'S
THE GOON NOIR
(B&W) Sept., 2006
1 . . . . 3.00
2 . . . . 3.00

Dylan Dog #5
© Dark Horse Comics

DYLAN DOG
(B&W) Bonelli Mar., 1999
1 (of 6) by Tiziano Di Sclavi & Angelo
Stano, MMI(c), 96-pg. 5.00
2 thru 6 . . . . @5.00
TPB Zed 96-pg. b&w 6.00

EDEN
Nov., 2005
TPB Vol. 1 It's An Endless World. . 13.00
TPB Vol. 2 thru 5 . . . . @13.00

EDGAR RICE
BURROUGHS'
RETURN OF TARZAN
Apr., 1997
1 adapted by Thomas Yeates
& John Totleben. 3.00
2 thru 3 . . . . @3.00

EDGAR RICE
BURROUGHS' TARZAN
1996
Mugambi
1 Betrayed by 3 man-beasts. 3.00
2 'Tarzan's Jungle Fury' 3.00
3 'Tarzan's Jungle Fury' 3.00
4 vs. the Tara virus 3.00
5 Cure to the Tara virus 3.00
6 . . . . 3.00
Tarzan and the Legion of Hate
7 pt.1 . . . . 3.00
8 pt.2. . . . . 3.00
9 pt.3. . . . . 3.00
10 pt.4, concl. 3.00

Le Monstre, June, 1997
11 pt.1 . . . . 3.00
12 pt.2 Bernie Wrightson(c). 3.00
Modern Prometheus, Aug., 1997
13 pt.1 MK(c) in New York. 3.00
14 pt.2 MK(c) 3.00
Tooth and Nail, Oct., 1997
15 pt.1 MSh(c) 3.00
16 pt.2 . . . . 3.00
TPB adapts #11–#16 . . . . 17.00
Tarzan vs. the Moon Men
17 TT,AW,TY 3.00
18 TT,AW,TY 3.00
19 TT,AW,TY 3.00
20 TT,AW,TY 3.00
Primeval
21 MGr. 3.00
22 MGr. 3.00
23 MGr. 3.00
24 MGr. 3.00
1-shot A Tale of Mugambi (1995). . . 3.00
TPB RsM,The Land That Time
Forgot 13.00
TPB Tarzan of the Apes. 13.00
TPB The Jewls of Opar 11.00

EDGAR RICE
BURROUGHS' TARZAN:
CARSON OF VENUS
May, 1998
1 (of 4) by Darko Macan and
Igor Kordey, F:Carson Napier . . 3.00
2 thru 4 novels adapt. . . . . @3.00
TPB Carson of Venus 13.00

EDGAR RICE
BURROUGHS' TARZAN:
THE LOST ADVENTURE
1995
1 Lost Manuscript 3.00
2 V:Gorgo the Buffalo 3.00
3 V:Bandits 3.00
4 V:Bandits 3.00

EDGAR RICE
BURROUGHS' TARZAN:
THE RIVERS OF BLOOD
Nov., 1999
1 . . . . 3.00
2 thru 8 . . . . @3.00

EDGAR RICE
BURROUGHS' TARZAN—
THE SAVAGE HEART
Apr., 1999
1 (of 4) MGr Jane is dead. 3.00
2 thru 4 . . . . @3.00

EGON
Jan.–Feb., 1998
1 and 2 . . . . @3.00

EIGHTH WONDER, THE
Nov., 1997
1-shot by P. Janes & K. Plunkett . . . 3.00

ELECTRIC
FRANKENSTEIN
Jan., 2004
TPB 20.00

Elric: Stormbringer #5
© Dark Horse Comics

ELRIC: STORMBRINGER
DH/Topps, 1996
1 by Michael Moorcock & CR 3.00
2 thru 7 (of 7) . . . . @3.00
TPB rep. series 18.00

EL ZOMBO
April 2004
1 (of 3) 3.00
2 and 3 . . . . @3.00

EMILY THE STRANGE
Aug., 2005
GN-1 The Boring Issue 8.00
GN-2 The Lost Issue 8.00
GN-3 The Dark Issue. 8.00

ENEMY
1994
1 MZ(c),StG(s),I:Enemy 2.75
2 MZ(c),StG(s),F:Heller 2.75
3 MZ(c),StG(s),A:Heller 2.50
4 . . . . 2.50
5 final issue. 3.00
TPB 15.00

ENO AND PLUM
Sept., 1997
TPB 13.00

ESCAPISTS, THE
July, 2006
1 . . . . 3.00
2 thru 5 . . . . @3.00

EUDAEMON, THE
1993
1 Nel,I:New Eudaemon. 3.00
2 Nel,V:Mordare 2.75
3 Nel,V:Mordare 2.75

EVIL DEAD III:
ARMY OF DARKNESS
1 JBo,Movie adaptation 4.00
2 JBo,Movie adaptation 3.50
3 JBo,Movie adaptation 3.00

EXOTICS, THE
TPB by Moebius 8.00

DARK HORSE

All comics prices listed are for *Near Mint* condition.

EXQUISITE CORPSE
1990
1-shot Green 3.00
1-shot Red 3.00
1-shot Yellow 3.00

EYEBALL KID
(B&W) 1992
1 I:Eyeball Kid. 2.50
2 V:Stygian Leech. 2.50
3 V:Telchines Brothers,last iss. . . . 2.50

FAT DOG MENDOZA
(B&W) 1992
1 I&O:Fat Dog Mendoza. 2.50

FAX FROM SARAJEVO
Oct., 1996
GN JKu, 224 pg. 25.00

FEEDERS
Oct., 1999
1-shot MiA, prequel to Eyes
to Heaven 3.00

FELIX THE CAT'S
GREATEST HITS
Sept., 2002
TPB 96-pg. 10.00

FIERCE
June, 2004
1 . . . . 3.00
2 thru 4 . . . . @3.00

F5 ORIGIN
1-shot, rep. 3.00

FLAMING CARROT
(B&W) 2001
Previous issues: see B&W section
18 Uncle Billy's mail-order bride . . . 4.00
18a Ash-Can-Limited 4.00
19 Hills Like White Elephants 4.00
20 Secret ice cream cult 4.00
21 Space Aliens 3.00
22 V:Space Aliens 3.00
23 Blipio appears. 3.00
24 48-page 10th anniv. spec. 4.00
25 F:TMNT,Mysterymen, with
2-card strip 3.00
26 A:TMNT. 3.00
27 TM(c),A:TMNT conclusion 3.00
28 Injured bumblebee 3.00
29 Man in the Moon,Iron City 3.00
30 V:Man in the Moon 3.00
31 A:Fat Fury 3.00
Ann. 1 by Bob Burden 5.00
TPB Man of Mystery, B&W 13.00
TPB The Wild Shall Wild Remain
rep. #4–#11 . . . . 18.00
TPB Flaming Carrot's Greatest Hits,
rep. #12–#18 . . . . 18.00
TPB Fortune Favors the Bold,
rep.#19–#24 . . . . 17.00

FLAXEN
1992
1 Based on Model,w/poster 3.00

FLOATERS
(B&W) 1993–94
1 thru 6 From Spike Lee . . . . @2.50

FLOOD!
DH Maverick, 2002
TPB 160-pg. 15.00

Foot Solders #3
© Dark Horse Comics

FOOT SOLDIERS, THE
1996
1 thru 4 by Jim Krueger 3.00
TPB 15.00
See also Image Comics

FORT: PROPHET OF
THE UNEXPLAINED
June, 2002
1 (of 4) F:Charles Fort 3.00
2 thru 4 . . . . @3.00
TPB 96-pg. B&W 10.00

FRANKENSTEIN
1 Movie Adaptation 4.00

FRAY
2001
1 . . . . 8.00
1a 2nd printing 3.00
2 thru 3 . . . . @4.00
4 thru 5 . . . . @3.00
6 thru 8 . . . . @7.50

FREAKS' AMOUR
1992
1 . . . . 4.00
2 . . . . 4.00
3 . . . . 4.00

FREAKSHOW
1 JBo,DMc,KB, 'Wanda the Worm
Woman,' 'Lillie'. 10.00

FREAKS OF THE
HEARTLAND
Jan., 2004
1 (of 6) horror 3.00
2 thru 6 . . . . @3.00

FUSED: THINK LIKE
A MACHINE
Dec., 2003
1 Robotic Cy-Bot. 3.00

2 . . . . 3.00
3 . . . . 3.00
4 . . . . 3.00
TPB Canned Heat 13.00
TPB Think Like A Machine. 13.00

FUTURE WORLD
Sept., 2003
TPB Vol. 1 b&w,160-pg. 14.00
TPB Vol. 2 . . . . 14.00

GALACTIC
DH Rocket Comics Aug., 2003
1 . . . . 3.00
2 & 3 . . . . @3.00
TPB 10.00

GAMERA
Aug., 1996
1 (of 4) by Dave Chipps &
Mozart Couto. 3.00
2 thru 4 . . . . @3.00

GARY GIANNI'S
MONSTERMEN
Aug., 1999
1-shot. 3.00

GHOST
Comics' Greatest World
Spec. AH(c) 4.00

GHOST
1995–98
1 by Eric Luke, R:Ghost 7.00
2 AH,MfM,Arcadia Nocturne,pt.2 . . 4.00
3 Arcadia Nocturn,pt.3 . . . . 4.00
4 . . . . 3.00
5 V:Predator 3.00
6 . . . . 3.00
7 Hell Night 3.00
8 thru 21 . . . . @3.00
22 The key is forever beyond
your reach 3.00
23 I: The Goblins 3.00
24 X is dead. 3.00
25 double size 4.00
26 Fairytale version 3.50
27 . . . . 3.50
28 CW(c),Painful Music,pt.1 . . . . . 3.50
29 CW(c),Painful Music,pt.2 . . . . . 3.50
30 CW(c),Painful Music,pt.3 . . . . . 3.50
31 CW(c),Painful Music,pt.4 . . . . . 3.50
32 A Pathless Land 3.50
33 Jade Cathedral,pt.1 . . . . 3.50
34 Jade Cathedral,pt.2 . . . . 3.50
35 Jade Cathedral,pt.3 . . . . 3.50
36 Jade Cathedral,pt.4 . . . . 3.50
Spec.#2 Immortal Coil 4.50
Spec.#3 Scary Monsters 4.50
TPB Ghost Stories. 9.00
TPB Ghost: Nocturnes. 10.00
TPB Exhuming Elisa 18.00

GHOST
1998–2000
1 CW,O:Ghost. 3.00
2 CW,V:Dr.Trouvaille. 3.00
3 CW,V:Silhouette. 3.00
4 CW,The Devil Inside,O:pt.1 . . . . 3.00
5 CW,Stare at the Sun,O:pt.2 . . . . 3.00
6 CW,Stare at the Sun,O:pt.3 . . . . 3.00
7 CW,Shifter,pt.1,F:King Tiger 3.00
8 CW,Shifter,pt.2. . . . . 3.00
9 CW,Shifter,pt.3 . . . . 3.00
10 CW,Shifter,pt.4 . . . . 3.00
11 CW,back in Arcadia. 3.00
12 Red Shadows,pt.1 (of 4). 3.00

DARK HORSE

Ghost #16
© Dark Horse Comics

13 Red Shadows,pt.2 . . . . 3.00
14 Red Shadows,pt.3 . . . . 3.00
15 Red Shadows,pt.4 . . . . 3.00
16 When the Devil Daydreams,pt.1. 3.00
17 When the Devil Daydreams,pt.2. 3.00
18 rogue agent. 3.00
19 Arcadia in chaos 3.00
20 F:Chris 3.00
21 F:Malcolm Greymater 3.00
22 final issue 3.00
TPB Black October 15.00
TPB Painful Music 10.00
TPB No World So Dark 15.00
Spec. Handbook #1 . . . . 3.00

GHOST/BATGIRL
Aug., 2000
1 (of 4) RBn,A:oracle 3.00
2 RBn,V:Two-Face 3.00
3 RBn,V:Carver, Greymater 3.00
4 RBn,concl 3.00
TPB 96-pg. 12.00

GHOST/HELLBOY
1996
1 & 2 MMi 3.50
TPB Ghost Hellboy Collection,MMi . 5.00

GHOST AND
THE SHADOW
1995
Spec. 1-shot. 3.00

GHOST IN THE SHELL
(Manga) 1995
1 Manga Style 25.00
2 Wetware Virus 20.00
3 Killer Robots 10.00
4 thru 8 . . . . @8.00
TPB by Masamune Shirow 25.00

GHOST IN THE SHELL 2:
MAN-MACHINE
INTERFACE
Oct., 2002
1 40-pg.by Masamune Shirow 4.00
2 32-pg.. 3.50
3 thru 11 . . . . @3.50
Spec. #1 Holographic Edition 5.00

TPB 25.00

GHOST IN THE SHELL 1.5:
HUMAN ERROR
PROCESSING
(B&W) Oct., 2006
1 by Shirow Masamune 3.00
2 . . . . 3.00

G.I. JOE
1995
1 by Mike Barr & Tatsuya Ishida . . . 3.00
2 thru 4 . . . . @3.00

Vol. 2 1996
1 . . . . 3.00
2 thru 4 . . . . @3.00

GIRL CRAZY
(B&W) May, 1996
1 GHe 3.00
2 and 3 GHe . . . . @3.00
TPB by GHe, rep.#1–#3 . . . . 10.00

GIVE ME LIBERTY
1990
1 FM/DGb, Homes & Gardens 6.00
2 FM/DGb 5.00
3 and 4 FM/DGb . . . . @5.00
TPB 16.00
TPB Dell edition 16.00

GO BOY 7: HUMAN
ACTION MACHINE
DH Rocket Comics, July, 2003
1 TPe 3.00
2 thru 8 . . . . @3.00
TPB Vol. 1 Ready Set Go 13.00
TPB Vol. 2 The Human Factor. . . . 13.00

GODZILLA
(D&W) 1988
1 Japanese Manga 5.00
2 thru 6 . . . . @4.00
Spec #1 . . . . 3.00
TPB 2nd printing 18.00

GODZILLA
COLOR SPECIAL
1992
1 AAd,R:Godzilla,V:Gekido-Jin 3.50
1a rep (1998) 3.00
Spec.1 Godzilla vs. Barkley MBn(s),
     JBt,DvD (1993) 3.50

GODZILLA
1995
0 RSd,The King of Monsters
     is back! 4.00
1 R:Godzill 4.00
2 V:Cybersaur 4.00
3 I:Bagorah the Bat Creature 4.00
4 V:Bagorah,Cybersaur 4.00
5 V:U.S. Army 4.00
6 thru 14 . . . . @4.00
15 'Thunder Downunder' 4.00
16 'Thunder in the Past'. 4.00
TPB Past, Present, Future. 18.00
TPB Godzilla: Age of Monsters . . . 18.00
Spec.1 Godzilla vs. Hero Zero
     Tatsuya Ishida (1995) 2.50

GO GIRL!
Oct., 2002
TPB TrR 88-pg. b&w 12.00
TPB Vol. 1 The Time Team 6.00

GOON, THE
June, 2003
1 . . . . 7.50
2 . . . . 5.00
3 thru 9 . . . . @4.00
10 thru 18 . . . . @3.00
Spec. 25 Cent rep of #1 . . . . 1.00
TPB Nothin' But Misery 16.00
TPB My Murderous Childhood. . . . 14.00
TPB Rough Stuff 13.00
TPB Virtue and the Grim
     Consequences Thereof 17.00
TPB Wicked Inclinations 15.00

GREEN LANTERN
VS. ALIENS
Aug., 2000
1 RMz,RL,F:Hal Jordan, x-over . . . 3.00
2 (of 4) RMz,RL,F:Kyle Rayner . . . 3.00
3 RMz,RL, without ring 3.00
4 RMz,RL, V:Alien Queen. 3.00
TPB RMZ,RL 13.00

GRENDEL
TPB Past Prime,MWg 15.00
Spec.1 Grendel Cycle, Grendel
     History (1995) 6.00
Spec.1 Devil Quest (1995). 5.00

GRENDEL: BLACK,
WHITE, AND RED
(B&W&R) Nov., 1998
1 (of 4) MWa, 48-pg. 5.00
2 thru 4 MWa, 48-pg. . . . . @4.00
TPB Black, White & Red, MWg . . . 19.00

GRENDEL CLASSICS
1995
1 Rep.#18–#19 Comico series 4.00
2 Rep. 4.00

GRENDEL: DEVIL BY
THE DEED
1993
1 MWg,RRa 4.00
1 representation (1997) 4.00
TPB Devil Tales 10.00

Grendel: Devil by the Deed
© Dark Horse Comics

All comics prices listed are for *Near Mint* condition.

Grendel: Devil Child #2
© Dark Horse Comics

GRENDEL: DEVIL CHILD
June, 1999
1 and 2 MWg 3.00

GRENDEL:
THE DEVIL INSIDE
DH Maverick, Sept., 2001
1 (of 3) MWg. 3.00
2 . . . . 3.00
3 concl. 3.00

GRENDEL:
DEVIL'S LEGACY
Aug., 1996
1 by Matt Wagner 3.00
2 thru 3 . . . . @3.00
TPB Devils and Deaths 17.00

GRENDEL:
DEVIL'S LEGACY
DH/Maverick, Mar., 2000
1 (of 12) MWg, rep. from 1986 . . . . 3.00
2 thru 6 MWg . . . . @3.00
7 MWg,V:Tujiro XIV 3.00
8 MWg,back to N.Y. 3.00
9 MWg,F:Dominic Riley 3.00
10 MWg 3.00
11 MWg 3.00
12 MWg, concl. 3.00
TPB 328-pg. 30.00

GRENDEL: DEVIL'S REIGN
May, 2004
1 (of 7) MWg. 3.50
2 thru 7 . . . . @3.50

GRENDEL:
GOD AND THE DEVIL
Jan., 2003
0 MWg,TSe. 3.50
1 MWg (of 10) 3.50
2 thru 9 MWg . . . . @3.50
10 MWg, concl., 48-pg. 5.00
TPB The Devil Inside 13.00

GRENDEL:
RED, WHITE, & BLACK
DH Maverick, Sept., 2002
1 (of 4) 48-pg. B&W 5.00
2 MWg,KJo,DIB 5.00
3 . . . . 5.00
4 MWg 5.00

GRENDEL TALES:
DEVIL'S APPRENTICE
Sept., 1997
1 (of 3) 3.00
2 thru 3 . . . . @3.00

GRENDEL TALES:
DEVILS AND DEATHS
1994
1 . . . . 3.00
2 . . . . 3.00
TPB rep. Devils and Deaths plus
    Devil's Choices 17.00

GRENDEL TALES:
DEVIL'S CHOICES
1995
1 F:Goran 3.00
2 thru 4 . . . . @3.00

GRENDEL TALES:
FOUR DEVILS, ONE HELL
1 MWg(c),F:Four Grendels 3.50
2 MWg(c),F:Four Grendels 3.50
3 MWg(c),F:Four Grendels 3.50
4 MWg(c),F:Four Grendels 3.50
5 MWg(c),F:Four Grendels 3.50
6 MWg(c),last issue 3.25
TPB Rep. #1–#6 . . . . 18.00

GRENDEL TALES:
HOMECOMING
1994
1 Babylon Crash 3.00
2 Babylon Crash,pt. 2 . . . . 3.00
3 Too Dead To Die 3.00
TPB Homecoming 8.00

GRENDEL TALES:
THE DEVIL IN
OUR MIDST
1994
1 MWg(c) 3.50
2 MWg(c) 3.25
3 thru 5 . . . . @3.00
TPB series rep. 16.00

GRENDEL TALES:
THE DEVIL MAY CARE
1995
1 thru 6 mini-series 3.00
TPB The Devil May Care (2002) . . 20.00

GRENDEL TALES:
THE DEVIL'S HAMMER
1994
1 MWg(a&s),I:Petrus Christus 3.50
2 MWg(a&s),A:P.Christus 3.25
3 MWg(a&s),last issue 3.25

GRENDEL: WAR CHILD
1992
1 MWg 4.00
2 thru 9 MWg 3.00

10 MWg, final issue, dbl.size 4.00
TPB 19.00
TPB War Child, 304-pg. (2002) . . . 25.00

GRIFTER AND THE MASK
Sept., 1996
1 by Seagle, Lima & Pimentel 2.50
2 . . . . 2.50

GUFF
Apr., 1998
1-shot by Sergio Aragones, flip
    book, with Meanie Babies
    card, B&W 2.50

GUNGRAVE
Dec., 2005
TPB Anime Manga 15.00

GUNSMITH CATS
(B&W–Manga) 1995
1 I:Rally & Mini May 3.00
2 Revolver Freak 3.00
3 . . . . 3.00
4 V:Bonnie and Clyde 3.00
5 V:Bonnie and Clyde 3.00
6 Hostage Situation 3.00
7 thru 10 (10 part series) 3.00
TPB Misfire rep. #7–#10 &
    Return of Gray #1–#3 . . . . 13.00
TPB Misty's Run (2002) 15.00

GUNSMITH CATS:
BAD TRIP
(B&W) June, 1998
1 (of 6) by Kenichi Sonoda 3.00
2 thru 6 . . . . @3.00
TPB Bad Trip 14.00

GUNSMITH CATS:
BEAN BANDIT
(B&W) June, 1998
1 (of 9) by Kenichi Sonoda 3.00
2 thru 9 . . . . @3.00
TPB Bean Bandit, 224-pg. 17.00

GUNSMITH CATS:
BONNIE & CLYDE
TPB by Kenichi Sonoda 13.00

GUNSMITH CATS:
GOLDIE VS. MISTY
(B&W) Nov., 1997
1 (of 7) by Kenichi Sonoda 3.00
2 thru 7 . . . . @3.00
TPB Goldie vs. Misty 13.00

GUNSMITH CATS:
KIDNAPPED
Nov., 1999
1 (of 10) by Kenichi Sonoda 3.00
2 thru 10 . . . . @3.00
TPB Bad Trip 14.00

GUNSMITH CATS:
MISTER V
(B&W) Oct., 2000
1 (of 11) by Kenichi Sonoda 3.50
2 thru 11 . . . . @3.50
TPB Mister V, 224-pg. 19.00
TPB Kidnapped 17.00
Spec. 3.00

DARK HORSE

Gunsmith Cats: Shades of Gray #1
© Dark Horse Comics

GUNSMITH CATS:
SHADES OF GRAY
(B&W) May, 1997
1 (of 5) by Kenichi Sonoda 3.00
2 thru 5 (of 5) . . . . @3.00

GUNSMITH CATS:
THE RETURN OF GRAY
(B&W) Aug., 1996
1 thru 7 by Kenichi Sonoda. . . . . @3.00
TPB rep. series 18.00

HAIBANE REMME
March, 2006
TPB Anime Manga. 15.00

HAMMER OF GOD:
BUTCH
1994
1 thru 3 MBn . . . . @2.50

HAMMER OF
GOD: PENTATHLON
1994
1 MiB(s),NV 2.50

THE HAMMER:
UNCLE ALEX
Aug., 1998
1-shot KJo. 3.00

HAPPY BIRTHDAY
MARTHA WASHINGTON
1995
1 Frank Miller 3.00

HAPPY ENDINGS
DH Maverick, Sept., 2002
TPB 96-pg. B&W 10.00

HARD BOILED
1990
1 GfD 7.00
2 and 3 . . . . @6.00
TPB 15.00
TPB Big Damn Hard Boiled. 30.00

HARD LOOKS
(B&W) 1992
1 thru 10 AVs Adaptations. . . . . . @2.50
Book One 15.00
TPB AVs. 18.00

HARLAN ELLISON'S
DREAM CORRIDOR
1995
1 Various stories 3.00
2 Various stories 3.00
3 JBy, I Have No Mouth and I
　Must Scream & other stories. . . 3.00
4 thru 6 . . . . @3.00
Spec.#1 Various stories 5.00
TPB 19.00
Spec. Quarterly, vol. 1 . . . . 6.00
Spec. Quarterly, vol. 2 . . . . 6.00

HARLEQUIN PINK
(Manga) Nov., 2005
TPB A Girl in a Million 10.00
TPB Idol Dreams 10.00
TPB　Bachelor Prince 10.00

HARLEQUIN VIOLET
(Manga) Nov., 2005
TPB Response. 10.00
TPB Holding Onto Alex 10.00
TPB Blind Date 10.00

HAUNTED MAN, THE
Mar., 2000
1 (of 3) GJ,MBg 3.00
2 GJ,MBg 3.00
3 . . . . 3.00

HEARTBREAKERS
1996
1 . . . . 3.00
2 thru 4 . . . . @3.00

HEART OF EMPIRE:
THE LEGACY OF
LUTHER ARKWRIGHT
Apr., 1999
1 (of 9) BT. 3.00
2 thru 5 . . . . @3.00
6 plot against royal family. 3.50
7 countdown to cataclysm 3.50
8 . . . . 3.50
9 conclusion 3.00
TPB series rep. 30.00

HELL
DH Rocket Comics, July, 2003
1 BAu 3.00
2 thru 4 BAu . . . . @3.00
TPB Vol. 1 Hell and Gone 13.00

HELLBOY
Christmas Special (1997) MMi,
　48-pg. 4.00
Spec. The Corpse and the
　Iron Shoes (1996) 3.00
Spec. The Wolves of St. August . . . 3.00
Hellboy Junior Halloween Special . . 4.00
Hellboy Junior Lurid Easter Special. 4.00
TPB The Lost Army 15.00
TPB The Chained Coffin & Others 18.00
TPB The Right Hand of Doom,
　MMi 18.00
TPB The Bones of the Giants
　200-pg. 15.00
TPB Strange Places (2006) 18.00
TPB Strange Places, rep. The Island

and The Third Wish (2006) . . . 19.00
1-shot The Corpse 1.00
TPB Animated Vol.1 Black
　Wedding Dress 7.00

HELLBOY:
ALMOST COLOSSUS
DH Legend, 1997
1 (of 2) MMi, sequel to *Wake the
　Devil* 3.00
2 (of 2) 3.00

HELLBOY:
BOX FULL OF EVIL
Aug., 1999
1 (of 2) MMi 3.00
2 MMi, conclusion 3.00

HELLBOY:
CONQUEROR WORM
May, 2001
1 (of 4) MMi 3.00
2 thru 4 . . . . @3.00
TPB series rep. 144-pg. 18.00

HELLBOY:
THE ISLAND
June, 2005
1 and 2 MMi . . . . @3.00

HELLBOY: MAKOMA
Feb., 2006
1 MMi,RCo 3.00
2 MMi,RCo 3.00

HELLBOY: SEEDS
OF DESTRUCTION
DH Legend, 1994
1 JBy,MMi,AAd,V:Vampire Frog,
　BU:Monkeyman & O'Brien 3.50
2 MMi(c),JBy,AAd,BU:Monkeyman
　& O'Brien 3.00
3 MMi(c),JBy,AAd,BU:Monkeyman
　& O'Brien 3.00
4 MMi(c),JBy,AAd,BU:Monkeyman
　& O'Brien 3.00
TPB Seed of Destruction 18.00

HELLBOY:
THE THIRD WISH
July, 2002
1 (of 2) MMi 3.00
2 . . . . 3.00

HELLBOY:
WAKE THE DEVIL
DH Legend, 1996
1 (of 5) MMi 3.00
2 thru 5 . . . . @3.00
TPB Wake The Devil 18.00

HELLBOY: WEIRD TALES
Feb., 2003
1 FaN 3.00
2 thru 8 . . . . @3.00
TPB Weird Tales Vol. 1 . . . . 18.00
TPB Vol. 2 . . . . 18.00

HELLBOY JR.
October 1999
1 (of 2) MMi 3.00
2 . . . . 3.00
TPB (2004). 15.00

DARK HORSE

HELLGATE: LONDON
Oct., 2006
0 IEd 3.00
1 IEd 3.00

HELLHOUNDS
(B&W) 1994
1 I:Hellhounds................. 3.00
2 and 3 .... @3.00
Becomes:

HELLHOUNDS: PANZER CORPS
3 thru 6 .... @3.00
TPB 15.00

HELLSING
2003
TPB Vol. 1 b&w 14.00
TPB Vol. 2 thru Vol. 5........ @14.00

HERBIE
1992
1 JBy,reps.& new material 3.00
2 Reps.& new material 2.50

HERETIC, THE
Nov., 1996
1 (of 4) by Rich DiLeonardo, Joe
   Phillips & Dexter Vines 3.00
2 thru 4 .... @3.00

HERMES VS. THE EYEBALL KID
1994
1 thru 3 Symphony of Blood...... 3.00

HERO ZERO
1994
1 First and last issue........... 2.50

HIEROGLYPH
Nov., 1999
1 RdD,F:Francisco Chavez....... 3.00
2 thru 4 RdD .... @3.00

HOMICIDE
(B&W) 1990
Spec. JAr,DoM................ 2.50

Hypersonic #4
© *Dark Horse Comics*

THE HORROR OF COLLIER COUNTY
Oct., 1999
1 (of 5) Halloween special 3.00
2 thru 5 concl................ @3.00
TPB 13.00

H.P.'S ROCK CITY
TPB by Moebius 8.00

HYPERSONIC
Nov., 1997
1 (of 4) DAn,GEr.............. 3.00
2 thru 4 .... @3.00

IGUANA, THE
DH Venture Feb., 2002
TPB 88-pg................... 11.00

ILLEGAL ALIEN
June, 2003
TPB b&w 11.00

INCREDIBLES, THE
Nov., 2004
1 (of 4) 3.00
2 thru 4 .... @3.00

INDIANA JONES AND THE ARMS OF GOLD
1994
1 In South America 2.75
2 In South America 2.75
3 V:Incan Gods............... 2.75
4 .... 2.50

INDIANA JONES AND THE FATE OF ATLANTIS
1991
1 DBa,Search for S.Hapgood with
   2-card strip 4.00
1a 2nd printing 3.00
2 DBa,Lost Dialogue of Plato with
   2-card strip 3.00
3 Map Room of Atlantis 3.00
4 Atlantis, Last issue........... 3.00
TPB 14.00

INDIANA JONES AND THE GOLDEN FLEECE
1994
1 SnW...................... 2.75
2 SnW...................... 2.50

INDIANA JONES AND THE IRON PHOENIX
1994
1 .... 2.50
2 V:Nazis.................... 2.50
3 A:Nadia Kirov............... 2.50
4 V:Undead.................. 2.50

INDIANA JONES AND THE SARGASSO PIRATES
1995
1 thru 4 .... @2.50

INDIANA JONES AND THE SHRINE OF THE SEA DEVIL
199
1 .... 2.50

INDIANA JONES AND THE SPEAR OF DESTINY
1995
1 I:Spear T/Pierced Christ 2.50
2 DSp, with Henry Jones 2.50
3 Search for the Shaft.......... 2.50
4 concl...................... 2.50

INDIANA JONES: THUNDER IN THE ORIENT
1993
1 DBa(a&s),in Tripoli........... 2.75
2 DBa(a&s),Muzzad Ram....... 2.75
3 DBa(a&s),V:Sgt.Itaki 2.75
4 DBa(a&s),In Hindu Kush 2.75
5 DBa(a&s),V:Japanese Army 2.75
6 DBa(a&s),last issue.......... 2.75

INSANE
(B&W) 1988
1 .... 3.00
2 .... 3.00

INSTANT PIANO
(B&W) 1994
1 Offbeat humor 4.00
2 .... 4.00
3 Various stories.............. 4.00
4 Devil Puppet 4.00

INTRON DEPOT
Nov., 1998
TPB Intron Depot.............. 40.00
TPB Intron Depot 2: Blades...... 38.00

INTRON DEPOT
Feb., 2003
TPB Vol. 1 .... 45.00
TPB Vol. 2 Blades 45.00
TPB Vol. 3 Ballistics........... 45.00

INVINCIBLE ED:
2003
1 The Beating of Ed 3.50
2 I'm Too Sexy 4.00
3 Lance Lundgrin Unleashes 3.00
4 The End................... 3.00
TPB 14.00

IRON EMPIRES
Dec., 2003
TPB Vol. 1 .... 18.00
TPB Vol. 2 Sheva's War 18.00

IRONHAND OF ALMURIC
(B&W) 1991
1 Robert E. Howard adaption 2.50
2 A:Cairn,V:Yagas............. 2.50
3 V:Yasmeena,The Hive Queen ... 2.50
4 Conclusion................. 2.50
GN 11.00

JAMES BOND 007: QUASIMODO GAMBIT
1995
1 I:Maximillion Quasimodo 4.00
2 V:Fanatical Soldiers.......... 4.00
3 V:Steel 4.00

JAMES BOND 007: SERPENT'S TOOTH
1992
1 PG,DgM,V:Indigo 5.50

---

2 PG,DgM,V;Indigo 5.00
3 PG,DgM 5.25
TPB 16.00

JAMES BOND 007:
SHATTERED HELIX
1994

1 V:Cerberus 3.00
2 V:Cerberus 3.00

JAMES BOND 007: A
SILENT ARMAGEDDON
1993

1 V:Troy 3.25
2 & 3 V:Omega . . . . @3.25

JINGLE BELLE
Nov., 2004

1 . . . . 3.00
2 thru 4 . . . . @3.00
TPB 13.00
1-shot-The Fight Before Christmas . 3.00

JOHN BOLTON'S
STRANGE WINK
Mar., 1998

1 (of 3) 3.00
2 thru 3 . . . . @3.00

JOHNNY CROSSBONES
2006

TPB Dead Man at Devil's Cove . . . 15.00

JOHNNY DYNAMITE
1994

1 . . . . 3.00
2 thru 4 . . . . @3.00

JOKER/MASK
May, 2000

1 (of 4) Batman x-over 3.00
2 Joker becomes Joker/Mask 3.00
3 A:Harley Quinn, Poison Ivy 3.00
4 three nuclear bombs, concl. 3.00
TPB 96-pg. 12.00

JONNY DEMON
1994

1 SL(c),KBk,NV 2.75
2 SL(c),KBk,NV 2.75
3 SL(c),KBk,NV, final issue 2.50

JOSS WHEDON'S FRAY
June, 2001

1 (of 8) 3.00
1a gold foil (c) 10.00
1b gold foil (c) signed 25.00
2 thru 8 . . . . @3.00
1 thru 6 2nd printings . . . . @3.00
TPB Future Slayer 20.00

JUDGE DREDD VS.
ALIENS: INCUBUS
Mar., 2003

1 (of 4) 3.00
2 thru 4 . . . . @3.00
TPB 104-pg. 13.00

JUNIOR CARROT PATROL
(B&W) 1989

1 and 2 . . . . @3.00

JU-ON
Feb., 2006

TPB Video Side 10.00
TPB Vol. 2 . . . . 10.00

KARAS
Nov., 2004

1-shot 3.00

KELLEY JONES'
THE HAMMER
Sept., 1997

1 (of 4) KJo, horror series. 3.00
2 thru 4 KJo, ... @3.00
TPB 13.00

KELLEY JONES'
THE HAMMER:
THE OUTSIDER
Feb., 1999

1 (of 3) KJo 3.00
2 and 3 . . . . @3.00

KELLEY JONES'
THE HAMMER:
UNCLE ALEX
1998

1-shot 3.00

KINGS OF THE NIGHT
1990

1 Robert E. Howard adapt. 2.50
2 end Mini-Series 2.50

KING TIGER/MOTORHEAD
1996

1 (of 2) by D.G. Chichester, Karl
  Waller & Eric Shanower 3.00
2 . . . . 3.00

KISS
July, 2002

1 JoC 4.00
2 thru 4 JoC . . . . @3.00
5 . . . . 3.00
6 . . . . 3.00
7 thru 10 SLo . . . . @3.00

King Tiger/Motordead #1
© Dark Horse Comics

11 . . . . 3.00
12 . . . . 3.00
13 MBn. 3.00
1a thru 13a photo (c) . . . . @3.00
TPB Rediscovery 11.00
TPB Return of the Phantom 10.00
TPB Men and Monsters 13.00
TPB Vol. 4 Unholy War 13.00

KLING KLANG KLATCH
GN 12.00

KONG
Oct., 2005

TPB Kong: King of Skull Island . . . 20.00
1 Movie adapt. (2005). 4.00
2 thru 3 . . . . @4.00
TPB Movie adapt. rep. (2006) 13.00

KWAIDAN
Jan., 2004

TPB 15.00

LADY SNOWBLOOD
Sept., 2005

TPB Vol. 1 & 2 Deep-Seated
  Grudge. . . . . @15.00
TPB Vol. 3 & 4 Retribution . . . . . @15.00

Land of Nod #1
© Dark Horse Comics

LAND OF NOD
(B&W) July, 1997

1 (of 4) by Jay Stephens 3.00
2 thru 4 . . . . @3.00
TPB Rockabye Book 14.00

LAST DAY IN VIETNAM
GN by Will Eisner 11.00
GN rep. 11.00

LAST TEMPTATION, THE
DH Maverick, Nov., 2000

TPB NGa,MZi,6'x9' 10.00

LAST TRAIN
TO DEADSVILLE
2004

1 (of 4) F:Cal McDonald 3.00
2 thru 4 . . . . @3.00

All comics prices listed are for *Near Mint* condition.   **CVA Page 517**

LAZARUS JACK
Sept., 2004
TPB 15.00

THE LEGEND OF MOTHER SARAH
(B&W–Manga) 1995
1 I:Mother Sarah. 4.00
2 Sarah and Tsutsu. 4.00
3 Firing Squad 4.00
4 F:Toki 4.00
5 Yunnel Town 4.00
6 Kill or Be Killed 4.00
7 Firing Squad 4.00
8 Conclusion. 4.00
TPB The Tunnel Town 19.00

THE LEGEND OF MOTHER SARAH: CITY OF THE ANGELS
(B&W–Manga) Oct., 1996
1 (of 9) by Katsuhiro Otomo and
　Takumi Nagayasu, 48-pg. 4.25
1 rep. (1997). 4.25
2 thru 4 . . . . 4.25
2 thru 4 rep. (1997). 4.25
5 Tsue a victim 4.25
6 Mother Teres questioned. 4.25
7 put in front trenches. 4.25
8 Teres suicide run 4.25
9 concl., 32-pg. 3.25

THE LEGEND OF MOTHER SARAH: CITY OF THE CHILDREN
(B&W–Manga) 1996
1 thru 4 (7 part mini-series). . . . . @4.25
5 thru 7 . . . . @4.00

LITTLE ANNIE FANNY
1962–70
Oct., 2000
TPB cartoons from playboy 25.00
TPB Vol. 2 . . . . 25.00

LITTLE LULU
May, 2005
1 My Dinner with Lulu. 10.00
2 Sunday Afternoon 10.00
3 In The Doghouse. 10.00
4 Lulu Goes Shopping 10.00
5 Lulu Takes a Trip 10.00
6 Letters to Santa 10.00
7 Lulu's Umbrella Service. 10.00
8 Late for School 10.00
9 Luck Lulu 10.00
10 All Dressed Up 10.00
11 April Fools. 10.00
12 Leave it to Lulu. 10.00
13 Too Much Fun. 10.00

LONE
DH Rocket Comics, Sept., 2003
1 . . . . 3.00
2 thru 6 . . . . @3.00
TPB 15.00

LONE GUNMEN, THE
June, 2001
1-shot 3.00
1-shot photo(c). 3.00
1-shot photo (c) lim ed. 7.00
1-shot photo (c) lim ed. signed . . . 20.00

LONE WOLF AND CUB
TPB Vol 1. . . . . 20.00
TPB Vol 2 . . . . 12.00
TPB Vol 3 Flute of the Fallen Tiger 12.00
TPB Vol.4 Shishogan Eyes 10.00
TPB Vol.5 Black Wind 10.00
TPB Vol.6 Lanterns For The Dead 10.00
TPB Vol.7 DragonCloud,WindTiger 10.00
TPB Vol.8 Chains of the Kurokuwa 10.00
TPB Vol.9 Shadows, Echoes. 10.00
TPB Vol.10 Separate Paths 10.00
TPB Vol.11 Talisman of Hades . . . 10.00
TPB Vol.12 Shattered Stones 10.00
TPB Vol.13 The Moon in the East,
　The Sun in the West 10.00
TPB Vol.14 Day of the Demons. . . 10.00
TPB Vol.15 Brothers of the Grass . 10.00
TPB Vol.16 Gateway Into Winter. . 10.00
TPB Vol.17 The Will of the Fang . . 10.00
TPB Vol.18 The Last Kurokuwa. . . 10.00
TPB Vol.19 Moon in Our Hearts . . 10.00
TPB Vol.20 A Taste of Poison 10.00
TPB Vol.21 Fragrance of Death. . . 10.00
TPB Vol.22 Heaven and Earth. . . . 10.00
TPB Vol.23 Tears of Ice 10.00
TPB Vol.24 In These Small Hands 10.00
TPB Vol.25 Perhaps in Death 10.00
TPB Vol.26 Battle in the Dark 10.00
TPB Vol.27 Battle's Eve. 10.00
TPB Vol.28 Falling Tree. 10.00

LONE WOLF 2100
May, 2002
1 (of 4) War Spore 4.00
2 thru 4 War Spore . . . . @3.00
5 thru 11 . . . . @3.00
1-shot The Red File 3.00
TPB Shadows on Saplings 13.00
TPB Vol. 2 . . . . 15.00
TPB Vol. 3 Pattern Storm. 13.00

Lords of Misrule #4
© *Dark Horse Comics*

LORDS OF MISRULE
(B&W) Jan., 1997
1 by DAn, PSj. 3.00
2 thru 6 . . . . @3.00
TPB The Lords of Misrule 18.00

LOST IN SPACE
Apr., 1998
1 (of 3) sequel to film 3.00
2 thru 3 GEr(c) . . . . @3.00
TPB rep. series, GEr(c). 8.00

LOST WORLD
July, 2003
TPB b&w 18.00

LOVE ME TENDERLOIN
Jan., 2004
1-shot F:Cal McDonald 3.00

THE LUCK IN THE HEAD
TPB 12.00

LULLABIES FROM HELL
Mar., 2006
TPB 13.00

LUX AND ALBY SIGN ON AND SAVE THE UNIVERSE
(B&W) 1993
1 . . . . 3.00
2 thru 9 . . . . @3.00

THE MACHINE
Comics Greatest World, 1994
1 (a) The Barb Wire spin 2.50
2 V:Salvage. 2.50
3 Freak Show 2.50
4 I:Skion 2.50

MAC RAYBOY'S FLASH GORDON
Jan., 2003
TPB b&w 20.00
TPB Vol. 2 . . . . 20.00
TPB Vol. 3 . . . . 20.00
TPB Vol. 4 . . . . 20.00

MADMAN
DH Legend, 1994
1 MiA(s) 8.00
2 MiA(s) 6.00
3 MiA(s) 5.00
4 MiA(s),Muscleman. 5.00
5 MiA(s),I:The Blast 4.00
6 MiA(s),A:Big Guy, Big Brain-
　o-rama,pt.1 . . . . 12.00
7 MiA(s),FM,A:Big Guy, Big Brain-
　o-rama,pt.2 . . . . 6.00
8 MiA(s) 4.00
9 Micro Madman. 4.00
10 . . . . 4.00
11 . . . . 4.00
Yearbook '95 TPB 18.00
Yearbook '96 TPB 18.00
Yearbook '95 new printing (2003) . 18.00
Apr., 1999
12 MiA 3.00
13 MiA 3.00
14 MiA 3.00
15 MiA 3.00
16 MiA 3.00
TPB Boogaloo 9.00
TPB The Exit of Dr. Boiffard 18.00
TPB Vol. 4 Heaven and Hell 18.00
G-Men From Hell (Aug., 2000)
17 Pt.1 MiA 3.00
18 Pt.2 MiA, Is Frank Einstein
　dead?. 3.00
19 Pt.3 MiA 3.00
20 Pt.4 MiA, V:Mr.Monstadt 3.00

MADMAN/THE JAM
July, 1998
1 (of 2) MiA 3.00
2 MiA. 3.00

All comics prices listed are for *Near Mint* condition.

Magic: The Gathering #1
© Dark Horse Comics

MADWOMAN OF THE SACRED HEART, THE
(B&W)
TPB by Alex Jodorowsky & Moe . . 13.00

MAGIC: THE GATHERING
Mar., 1998
1 (of 4) MGr,Initiation 3.00
2 MGr, Legacy 3.00
3 MGr, Crucible. 3.00
4 MGr, Destiny 3.00
TPB Gerrard's Quest 12.00

MAGNUS/NEXUS
DH/Valiant
1 MBn(s), SR 3.25
2 MBn(s), SR 3.25

MAN FROM THE CIGUIRI
TPB by Moebius 8.00

MANGA DARKCHYLDE
Feb., 2005
1 (of 5) 3.00
2 thru 3 . . . . @3.00

MAN WITH THE SCREAMING BRAIN
2005
1 (of 4) 3.00
2 thru 4 . . . . @3.00
1a thru 4a Variant(c) . . . . @3.00

MARK, THE
1987–89
1 LSn, ... 3.00
2 & 3 LSn . . . . @3.00
4 thru 6 . . . . @3.00
[Second Series] 1993
1 MiB(s),in America,V:Archon 3.00
2 MiB(s),V:Archon. 3.00
3 MiB(s),V:Archon,A:Pierce 3.00
4 MiB(s),last issue 3.00

MARSHALL LAW
GN Super Babylon, KON (1992) . . . 5.00
TPB Blood Sweat and Fears
  (1998) 16.00
1-shot Marshall Law: Cape Fear . . . 3.00

MARSHALL LAW: SECRET TRIBUNAL
1993
1 KON 3.00
2 KON 3.00

M.A.R.S. PATROL TOTAL WAR
Sept., 2004
TPB WW 13.00

MARGE'S LITTLE LULU
Nov., 2004
TPB Vol. 1 . . . . 10.00

MARTHA WASHINGTON GOES TO WAR
DH Legend, 1994
1 FM(s),DGb, V:Fat Boys Corp. . . . 3.25
2 FM(s),DGb, V:Fat Boys Corp. . . . 3.25
3 FM(s),DGb, V:Fat Boys Corp. . . . 3.25
4 FM(s),DGb, V:Fat Boys Corp. . . . 3.25
5 FM(s),DBb, final issue 3.25
TPB Rep.#1–#5 . . . . 18.00

MARTHA WASHINGTON SAVES THE WORLD
Dec., 1997
1 (of 3) FM,DGb 3.25
2 thru 3 . . . . @3.25
TPB rep. 13.00

MARTHA WASHINGTON STRANDED IN SPACE
1995
1 . . . . 3.25

MARTIN MYSTRY
(B&W) DH/Bonelli, Mar., 1999
1 by Alfredo Castelli & Cianoarlo
  Alessandrini, DGb(c) 92-pg. . . . 5.00
2 thru 6 . . . . @5.00

MASAKAZU KATSURA'S SHADOW LADY
(B&W–Manga) Oct., 1998
Dangerous Love
1 (of 7) Masakazu Katsura 2.50
2 thru 7 . . . . @2.50
The Eyes of a Stranger, May, 1999
8 thru 12, pt.1–pt.5 . . . . @2.50
The Awakening
13 thru 19, pt.1–pt.7 . . . . @2.50
Sudden Death
20 thru 24, pt.1–pt.5 . . . . @2.50
Spec.48-pg. final issue 4.00
TPB Dangerous Love 18.00
TPB The Awakening 16.00
TPB Sudden Death 15.00

MASK, THE
1991
0 'Who's Laughing Now' (B&W) . . . 6.00
1 I:Lt.Kellaway Mask 5.00
2 V:Rapaz & Walter 5.00
3 O:Mask 5.00
4 final issue. 5.00
TPB 15.00

MASK, THE
1994
1 Movie Adaptation 3.00
2 Movie Adaptation 2.50

Nexus: Executioner's Song #4
© Dark Horse Comics

MASK , THE
[Mini-series] 1995
The Mask Strikes Back (1995)
1 Mask Strikes Back,pt.1 . . . . 2.50
2 Mask Strikes Back,pt.2 . . . . 2.50
3 Mask Strikes Back,pt.3 . . . . 2.50
4 DoM,Mask Strikes Back,pt.4 . . . . 2.50
5 Mask Strikes Back,pt.5 . . . . 2.50
TPB by John Arcudi, Doug Mahnke
  & Keith Williams 15.00
The Hunt for Green October (1995)
6 Pt.1 . . . . 2.50
7 Pt.2 Kellaway vs. Ray Tuttle 2.50
8 Pt.3 F:Emily Tuttle 2.50
9 Pt.4 final issue 2.50
World Tour (1995)
10 thru 13 Pt.1–Pt 4 . . . . @2.50
Southern Discomfort (1996)
14 Pt.1 Mardi Gras time. 2.50
15 Pt.2 . . . . 2.50
16 Pt.3 . . . . 2.50
17 Pt.4 . . . . 2.50

MASK/MARSHALL LAW
Feb., 1998
1 (of 2) by Pat Mills and Kevin
  O'Neill 3.00
2 concl. 3.00

MASK RETURNS, THE
1992
1 inc.cut-out Mask. 5.00
2 Mask's crime spree 4.00
3 . . . . 4.00
4 . . . . 4.00
TPB by John Arcudi & Doug
  Mahnke 15.00

MASK: TOYS IN THE ATTIC
Aug., 1998
1 (of 4) 3.00
2 thru 4 . . . . @3.00

MASK, THE: VIRTUAL SURREALITY
1997
1-shot F: MMi,SA 3.00

DARK HORSE

Monkeyman & O'Brien #2
© Dark Horse Comics

MAXIMUM OVERLOAD
1 Masque (Mask) 12.00
2 thru 4 Mask . . . . @8.00

MAXIMUM OVERLOAD
1 thru 5 . . . . @4.00

MAYHEM
1989
1 F:The Mask, The Mark 5.00
2 thru 4 . . . . @4.00

MECHA
Comics Greatest World, 1995
1 color 3.00
2 color 3.00
3 thru 6 B&W . . . . @3.00
Spec.(#1) CW(c),color 3.00

MEDAL OF HONOR
1994
1 Ace of Aces 2.50
2 . . . . 2.50
3 Andrew's Raid 2.50
4 Frank Miller(c) 2.50
5 final issue 2.50
Spec. #1 JKu (1994) 2.50

MEGATOKYO
Dec., 2003
TPB Vol. 1 . . . . 10.00
TPB Vol. 2 . . . . 10.00

METROPOLIS
Apr., 2003
TPB by Oxamu Tezuka, b&w 14.00

MEZZ GALACTIC
TOUR 2494
1994
1 MBn,MV 2.50

MICHAEL CHABON
PRESENTS THE
AMAZING ADVENTURES
OF THE ESCAPIST
Dec., 2003
1 Michael Chabon, 80-pg. 9.00

---

2 thru 9 . . . . @9.00
TPB Vol. 1 and Vol. 2 . . . . @18.00

MIKE MIGNOLA'S
B.P.R.D.: HOLLOW EARTH
Jan., 2002
1 (of 3) 3.00
2 . . . . 3.00
3 . . . . 3.00
TPB 120-pg. 18.00
1-shot Something Under My Bed . . 3.00
1-shot The Soul of Venice 3.00
1-shot Dark Waters 3.00
1-shot Night Train 3.00
TPB Soul of Venice 18.00

MILKMAN MURDERS, THE
July, 2004
1 JoC,SvP 3.00
2 thru 4 JoC,SvP . . . . @3.00

THE MINOTAUR'S TALE
TPB by Al Davison 12.00

MR. MONSTER
(B&W) 1988
1 . . . . 4.00
2 . . . . 3.00
3 Alan Moore story 3.00
4 . . . . 3.00
5 I:Monster Boy 3.00
6 . . . . 3.00
7 . . . . 3.00
8 V:Vampires (giant size) 5.00

MONKEYMAN & O'BRIEN
DH Legend, 1996
1 by Arthur Adams 3.00
2 and 3 . . . . @3.00
Spec. 3.00
TPB 17.00

MONSTERS, INC.
Oct., 2001
1-shot 56-pg., Disney-Pixar 5.00

MORPHOS
THE SHAPE CHANGER
July, 1996
1-shot BHg 5.00

MOTHER, COME HOME
Nov., 2003
TPB 15.00

MOTORHEAD
Comics Greatest World, 1995
1 V:Predator 2.50
2 Laughing Wolf Carnival 2.50
3 V:Jackboot 2.50
4 thru 6 . . . . @2.50
Spec.#1 JLe(c),V:Mace Blitzkrieg
　(1994) 4.00

MUSEUM OF TERROR
Aug., 2006
TPB Vol. 1 thru 3 . . . . @14.00

[BOB BURDEN'S
ORIGINAL]
MYSTERYMEN
July, 1999
1 . . . . 3.00
2 The Amazing Disc Man 3.00
3 F:Screwball 3.00

---

4 All Villain Comics #1 . . . . 3.50

MYSTERY MEN
July, 1999
1 (of 2) Movie adapt. 3.00
2 movie adaptation, concl. 3.00

MYST: THE BOOK OF
THE BLACK SHIPS
Aug., 1997
1 (of 4) from CD-Rom game 3.00
2 thru 4 . . . . @3.00

NAIL, THE
June, 2004
1 (of 4) 3.00
2 thru 4 . . . . @3.00

NATHAN NEVER
(B&W) DH/Bonelli, Mar., 1999
1 (of 6) by Michele Medda & Nicola
　Mari, AAd(c) 102-pg. 5.00
2 . . . . 5.00
3 . . . . 5.00
4 . . . . 5.00
5 . . . . 5.00
6 . . . . 5.00

NEVERMEN, THE
May, 2000
1 (of 4) GyD, V:Clockwork 3.00
2 GyD,V:Honshu 3.00
3 GyD,V:Clockwork 3.00
4 GyD,V:League of Crows 3.00
TPB 128-pg. 15.00

NEVERMEN, THE:
STREETS OF BLOOD
Jan., 2003
1 (of 3) GyD 3.00
2 and 3 . . . . @3.00
TPB 10.00

NEW FRONTIER
(B&W) 1992
1 From series in Heavy Metal 2.75
2 Who Killed Ruby Fields? 2.75
3 Conclusion 2.75

NEW TWO FISTED
TALES: VOL II
1993
1 War stories 5.00

[JOHN BYRNE'S]
NEXT MEN
1992
0 Rep Next Men from Dark Horse
　Presents 6.00
1 JBy,'Breakout'inc.trading card
　certificate 6.00
1a 2nd Printing Blue 3.00
2 JBy,World View 4.00
3 JBy,A:Sathanis 4.00
4 JBy,A:Sathanis 4.00
5 JBy,A:Sathanis 4.00
6 JBy,O:Senator Hilltop,
　Sathanis,Project Next Men 3.50
7 JBy,I:M-4,Next Men Powers
　explained 3.50
8 JBy,I:Omega Project,A:M-4 . . . . 3.00
9 JBy,A:Omega Project,A:M-4 . . . . 3.00
10 JBy,V:OmegaProject,A:M-4 . . . 3.00
11 JBy,V:OmegaProject,A:M-4 . . . 3.00
12 JBy,V:Dr.Jorgenson 3.00

DARK HORSE

Next Men #11
© Dark Horse Comics

13 JBy,Nathan vs Jack 3.00
14 JBy,I:Speedboy 3.00
15 JBy,in New York 3.00
16 JBy,Jasmine's Pregnant 3.00
17 FM(c),JBy,Arrested 3.00
18 JBy,On Trial 3.00
Next Men: Faith (1993)
19 Faith, pt.1 JBy(a&s),V:Dr.
　Trogg, Blue Dahila 3.25
20 Faith, pt.2 JBy,(a&s),F:Jack 3.00
21 Faith,pt.3 MMi(c),JBy(a&s),
　I:Hellboy. 27.00
22 Faith,pt.4 JBy(a&s),Last issue . . 3.00
Next Men: Power (1994)
23 Power,pt.1, JBy(a&s) 2.75
24 Power,pt.2, JBy(a&s) 2.75
25 Power,pt.3, JBy(a&s) 2.75
26 Power,pt.4, JBY(a&s) concl. 2.60
Next Men: Lies (1994)
27 Lies,pt.1,JBy 2.50
28 Lies,pt.2,JBy 2.50
29 Lies,pt.3,JBy 2.50
30 Lies,pt.4, JBy 2.50
TPB rep.#1-6 . . . . 17.00
TPB Book 2, rep. #7–#12 . . . . 17.00
TPB Book 3, rep. #13–#18 . . . . . . 17.00
TPB Book 4, rep. #19–#22 . . . . . . 15.00
TPB Book 5, rep. #23–#26 . . . . . . 15.00
TPB Book 6, rep. #27–#30 . . . . . . 17.00

NEXUS: ALIEN JUSTICE
1992
1 . . . . 4.25
2 . . . . 4.25
3 . . . . 3.00
TPB series rep. (1996). 17.00

NEXUS: EXECUTIONER'S SONG
1996
1 (of 4) by Mike Baron, Steve
　Rude & Gary Martin 3.00
2 thru 4 . . . . @3.00

NEXUS: GOD CON
Apr., 1997
1 (of 2) 3.00
2 . . . . 3.00

NEXUS: THE LIBERATOR
1992
1 'Waking Dreams' 3.00
2 CIvlI War,D.Gigo 3.00
3 Civil War contd. 3.00
4 Last issue. 3.00

NEXUS MEETS MADMAN
1996
1-shot 3.00

NEXUS: NIGHTMARE IN BLUE
(B&W) July, 1997
1 (of 4) MBn,SR,GyM 3.00
2 thru 4 . . . . @3.00

NEXUS: THE ORIGIN
1995
1 SR,O:Nexus. 5.00

NEXUS: OUT OF THE VORTEX
1 R:Nexus. 3.00
2 Zolot & Nexus Together. 3.00
3 O:Vortex. 3.00

NEXUS: THE WAGES OF SIN
1995
1 The Client 3.00
2 V:Munson. 3.00
3 SR(c&a) Murders in New Eden . . 3.00
4 . . . . 3.00

NIGHT BEFORE CHRISTMASK
1 Rick Geary. 10.00

NINA'S NEW AND IMPROVED ALL-TIME GREATEST
1994
1 Anthology: Nina Paley 2.50

NINTH GLAND, THE
(B&W) Mar., 1997
1-shot by Renee French 4.00

NOCTURNALS: WITCHING HOUR
May, 1998
1-shot by Dan Brereton 5.00

NOSFERATU
(B&W) 1991
1 The Last Vampire. 4.00
2 . . . . 3.00

OCTOPUS GIRL
Feb., 2006
TPB Vol. 1 thru 3 . . . . @13.00

OH MY GODDESS!
(B&W–Manga) 1994
1 by Kosuke Fujishima. 5.00
2 & 3 . . . . @4.00
4 thru 6 . . . . @3.00
TPB 1-555-Goddess 13.00
TPB Vol.1 Wrong Number 14.00
TPB Vol.2 Leader of the Pack 14.00

Oh My Goddess Part IV #2
© Dark Horse Comics

TPB Vol.3 Final Exam 14.00
Part II, 1995
1 F:Keiichi. 4.00
2　thru 9. @3.00
TPB Sympathy for the Devil 13.00
Part III, 1996
1 Wishes are Granted. 3.00
2 Love Potion Number 9. . . . . 3.00
3 thru 5 . . . . @3.00
6 thru 11 Terrible Master Urd,
　pt.1 thru pt.6 . . . . @3.00
TPB Love Potion Number 9. . . . . . 13.00
TPB Terrible Master Urd 13.00
Part IV, 1996–97
1 Robot Wars 3.00
2 The Trials of Morisato,pt.1 . . . . . . 3.00
3 The Trials of Morisato,pt.2 . . . . . . 3.00
4 The Trials of Morisato,pt.3 . . . . . . 3.00
5 The Queen of Vengeance 3.00
6 Mara Strikes Back,pt.1,48-pg. . . . 4.00
7 Mara Strikes Back,pt.2 . . . . 3.00
8 Mara Strikes Back,pt.3. . . . . 3.00
Part V, 1997–98
1 The Forgotten Promise 3.00
2 The Lunch Box of Love 3.00
3 Meet Me by the Seashore, 48-pg. 4.00
4 You're So Bad, 48-pg. 4.00
5 Ninja Master,pt.1 . . . . 3.00
6 Ninja Master,pt.2, 48-pg. 4.00
7 Miss Keiichi,pt.1, 48-pg. 4.00
7 & 8 Miss Keiichi,pt.2 . . . . 3.00
9 It's Lonely at the Top 3.50
10 Fallen Angel, 48-pg. 4.00
11 Play the Game, 48-pg. 4.00
12 Sorrow, Fear Not. 4.00
Part VI, 1998–99
1 Devil in Miss Urd,pt.1, 40-pg. . . . 3.50
2 Devil in Miss Urd,pt.2. . . . . 3.00
3 Devil in Miss Urd,pt.3. . . . . 3.00
4 Devil in Miss Urd,pt.4. . . . . 3.00
5 Devil in Miss Urd,pt.5. . . . . 3.00
6 SuperUrd 3.00
Part VII, 1999
1 (of 8)The Fourth Goddess,pt.1 . . 3.00
2 The Fourth Goddess,pt.2. . . . . . . 3.00
3 The Fourth Goddess,pt.3. . . . . . . 3.00
4 The Fourth Goddess,pt.4,40-pg. . 3.50
5 The Fourth Goddess,pt.5,40-pg. . 3.50
TPB The Adventures of the
　Mini-Goddesses. 10.00

DARK HORSE

Oh My Goddess Part VII #3
© Dark Horse Comics

Part VIII, 1999
1 (of 2) Childhood's End,
by Kosuke Fujishima 3.50
2 Childhood's End,pt.2 . . . . 3.50
3 The Queen and the Goddess . . . 3.50
4 Hail to the Chief,pt.1 . . . . 3.50
5 Hail to the Chief,pt.2 . . . . 3.50
6 Hail to the Chief,pt.3 . . . . 3.50
TPB Childhood's End 216-pg. 16.00

Part IX, 2000
1 Pretty in Scarlet. 3.00
2 The Goddess's Apprentice. 3.00
3 Queen Sayoko,pt.1 . . . . 3.00
4 Queen Sayoko,pt.2 . . . . 3.50
5 Queen Sayoko,pt.3 (of 5) 3.00
6 Queen Sayoko,pt.4 . . . . 3.00
7 Queen Sayoko,pt.5 . . . . 3.50
TPB Ninja Master. 14.00
TPB Queen of Vengeance 14.00
TPB Mara Strikes Back 15.00
TPB Miss Keiichi 17.00
TPB The Devil in Miss URD 15.00
TPB The Fourth Goddess 19.00
TPB Queen Sayoko, 240-pg. 17.00

PART X, Feb., 2001
1 The Secret of Speed 3.50
2 The Secret of Speed,concl. 3.00
3 one-shot. 3.50
4 Hand in Hand,pt.1 . . . . 3.50
5 Hand in Hand,pt.2 . . . . 3.50

PART XI, Aug., 2001
1 Banpei in Love,pt.1 (of 2) 3.50
2 Banpei in Love,pt.2 . . . . 3.50
3 Mystery Child,pt.1 (of 8) 3.00
4 Mystery Child,pt.2 . . . . 3.00
5 Mystery Child,pt.3 . . . . 3.00
6 Mystery Child,pt.4 . . . . 3.00
7 Mystery Child,pt.5 . . . . 3.50
8 Mystery Child,pt.6 . . . . 3.50
9 Mystery Child,pt.7 . . . . 3.00
10 Mystery Child,pt.8, 48-pg. 4.00
TPB series rep. 19.00

PART XII, July, 2002
1 (of 3) Learning to Love,pt.1 . . . . . 3.50
2 Learning to Love,pt.2 . . . . 3.50
3 Learning to Love,pt.3 . . . . 3.50

Continuing series (Oct., 2002)
91 Traveler,pt.1 (of 5). 3.00
92 Traveler,pt.2 . . . . 3.00
93 Traveler, pt.3 . . . . 3.00
94 Traveler, pt.4 . . . . 3.00
95 Traveler, pt.5 . . . . 3.50

96 The Phantom Racer, pt.1 . . . . . . 3.00
97 The Phantom Racer, pt.2 . . . . . . 3.00
98 The Phantom Racer, pt.3 . . . . . . 3.00
99 The Phantom Racer, pt.4 . . . . . . 3.00
100 Dr. Moreau, pt.1 . . . . 3.00
101 Dr. Moreau, pt.2 . . . . 3.00
102 Dr. Moreau, pt.3 . . . . 3.00
103 Dr. Moreau, pt.4 . . . . 3.00
104 Dr. Moreau, pt.5 . . . . 3.50
105 Sora Unchained,pt.1 . . . . 3.00
106 thru 110 Sora,pt.2–pt.6 . . . . @3.00
111 and 112 Sora Unchained,
pt.7–pt.8, 48-pg. . . . . @4.00
TPB Hand in Hand. 18.00
TPB Traveler 18.00
TPB Vol. 18 Phantom Racer 18.00
TPB Vol. 19/20 Sora Unchained . . 19.00
TPB Vol. 22 & Vol. 23. . . . . @11.00

OKTANE
1995
1 R:Oktane 2.50
2 V:God Zero 2.50
3 V:God Zero 2.50
4 conclusion 2.50

OLD BOY
2006
TPB Vol. 1 . . . . 11.00
TPB Vol. 2 . . . . 11.00
TPB Vol. 3 . . . . 13.00

ONE BAD RAT
1 BT 3.00
2 thru 4 . . . . @3.00

ONE-TRICK RIP-OFF
1997
TPB by Paul Pope 13.00

ORION
(B&W–Manga) 1993
1 SF by Masamune Shirow 2.50
2 F:Yamata Empire 3.00
3 thru 6 . . . . @3.00
TPB 16.00
TPB 3rd edition 20.00

OTIS GOES HOLLYWOOD
(B&W) Apr., 1997
1 (of 2) by Bob Fingerman 3.00
2 . . . . 3.00

OTTO PORFIRI:
Oct., 2001
TPB Drama on the Cliff 10.00
TPB Red Moon 88-pg. (2002) . . . 10.00

OUT FOR BLOOD
(B&W) 1999
1 (of 4) GEr,F:Dan Sanger 3.00
2 The Wings; The Claws 3.00
3 . . . . 3.00
4 concl. 3.00

OUTLANDERS
(B&W–Manga) 1988
1 . . . . 4.00
2 . . . . 3.00
3 thru 7 . . . . @3.00
8 thru 20 . . . . @3.00
21 Operation Phoenix 3.00
22 thru 24 . . . . @3.00
25 thru 29 with 2-card strip . . . . . @3.00
30. . . . . 2.75
31 Tetsua dying 2.75
32 D:The Emperor 2.75
33 Story finale 2.75

#0 The Key of Graciale 2.75
TPB Vol. 1 by Johji Manabe 14.00
TPB Vol. 1 2nd edition. 14.00
TPB Vol. 2 . . . . 14.00
TPB Vol. 2 2nd edition 14.00
TPB Vol. 3 . . . . 14.00
TPB Vol. 4 . . . . 13.00
TPB Vol. 5 thru Vol. 8. . . . . @15.00

OUTLANDERS:
EPILOGUE
(B&W) 1994
1 . . . . 2.75

OUTLAW 7
Aug., 2001
1 (of 4) 3.00
2 thru 4 . . . . @3.00

Out of the Vortex #1
© Dark Horse Comics

OUT OF THE VORTEX
Comics' Greatest World, 1993
1 B:JOs(s),V:Seekers 2.50
2 MMi(c),DaW,A:Seekers 2.50
3 WS(c),E:JOs(s),DaW,A:Seeker,
C:Hero Zero. 2.50
4 DaW,A:Catalyst 2.50
5 V:Destroyers,A:Grace 2.50
6 V:Destroyers,A:Hero Zero 2.50
7 AAd(c),DaW,V:Destroyers,
A:Mecha 2.50
8 DaW,A:Motorhead 2.50
9 DaW,V:Motorhead 2.50
10 MZ(c), A:Division 13 . . . . 2.50
11 V:Reaver Swarm. 2.50
12 Final issue. 2.50

OZ
by Eric Shanower
TPB The Blue Witch of Oz. 10.00
TPB The Forgotten Forest of Oz . . . 9.00
TPB The Ice King of Oz. 9.00
TPB The Secret Island of Oz. 9.00

PATHFINDER
July, 2006
TPB 18.00

PATH OF THE ASSASSIN
May, 2006
TPB Vol. 1 by Koike & Kojima 10.00

PENNY ARCADE
Dec., 2005
1 25-cent issue 0.25
TPB Vol. 1 Attack of the Bacon
  Robots 13.00
TPB Vol. 2 Epic Legends of the
  Magic Sword Kings 13.00
TPB Vol. 3 Warsun Prophecies . . . 13.00

PERHAPANAUTS, THE
Nov., 2005
1 (of 4) TDz 3.00
2 thru 4 . . . . @3.00
TPB 16.00

PERHAPANAUTS:
SECOND CHANCES
Oct., 2005
1 (of 4) TDz 3.00
2 . . . . 3.00

PETE VON SHOLLY'S
MORBID
Oct., 2003
TPB 15.00

PI: THE BOOK OF ANTS
Artisan Entertainment, 1998
1-shot, movie adapt. 3.00

PLANET OF THE APES:
THE HUMAN WAR
June, 2001
1 (of 3) IEd,with trading card 3.00
1a photo (c). 3.00
2 IEd,JSC 3.00
2a photo (c). 3.00
3 IEd,JSC 3.00
3a photo (c). 3.00

PLANET OF THE APES
Sept., 2001
1 IEd,MWg 3.00
1b gold foil photo(c) 13.00
1c gold foil photo(c) signed. 30.00
2 IEd 3.00
3 IEd 3.00
4 DAn,IEd,Bloodlines,pt.1 (of 3) . . . 3.00
5 DAn,IEd,Bloodlines,pt.2 . . . . 3.00
6 DAn,IEd,Bloodlines,pt.3 . . . . 3.00
1a thru 6a photo(c) . . . . @3.00
TPB Vol. 1 80-pg. 10.00
TPB Vol. 2 Bloodlines 10.00

PLANET OF THE APES
(MOVIE)
1-shot Movie adaptation 7.00
1-shotA Movie adapt, foil (c) 10.00
1-shotB Movie, foil(c) signed 30.00
TPB 10.00

POP GUN WAR
June, 2003
TPB b&w 14.00

PRAIRIE MOON
AND OTHER STORIES
(B&W) 1992
1-shot 2.50

PREDATOR
1989
1 CW,Mini Series 6.00
1a 2ndPrinting 3.00

2 CW 5.00
3 CW 4.00
4 CW 3.00
1 thru 4 later printings . . . . @3.00

PREDATOR
1-shot Predator: Invaders from the
  Fourth Dimension (1994). 4.00
1-shot Predator Jungle Tales,
  Rite of Passage (1995) 3.00
1-shot Predator: Strange Roux
  (1995) 3.00
1-shot Predator: Captive (1998) . . . 3.00
TPB Predator: Concrete Jungle. . . 15.00

PREDATOR:
BAD BLOOD
1993
1 CW,I:John Pulnick 3.00
2 CW,V:Predator 3.00
3 CW,V:Predator,C.I.A. 3.00
4 Last issue 3.00

PREDATOR: BIG GAME
1991
1 Corp.Nakai Meets Predator 3.50
2 Army Base Destroyed, with
  2-card strip 3.50
3 Corp.Nakai Arrested, with
  2-card strip 3.50
4 Nakai vs. Predator 3.50
TPB rep. #1–#4 . . . . 14.00
TPB rep. #1–#4, 2nd edition 15.00

PREDATOR: BLOODY
SANDS OF TIME
1992
1 DBa,CW,Predator in WWI 3.50
2 DBa,CW, WWII cont'd. 3.25

PREDATOR: COLD WAR
1991
1 Predator in Siberia 3.50
2 U.S. Elite Squad in Siberia 3.25
3 U.S. vs. USSR commandos 3.25
4 U.S. vs. USSR in Siberia. 3.00
TPB 14.00
TPB 2nd printing 14.00

PREDATOR:
DARK RIVER
1996
1 thru 4 by Verheiden,RoR,RM . . @3.00

PREDATOR:
HELL & HOT WATER
1997
1 thru 3 MSh, GC & GWt . . . . . . @3.00
TPB rep. 10.00

PREDATOR:
HELL COME A WALKIN'
Feb., 1998
1 (of 2) by Nancy Collins,
  Dean Ormston 3.00
2 concl. 3.00

PREDATOR:
HOMEWORLD
Mar., 1999
1 (of 4) 3.00
2 thru 4 . . . . @3.00

Predator: Kindred #3
© *Dark Horse Comics*

PREDATOR: KINDRED
1996
1 . . . . 3.00
2 thru 4 . . . . @3.00
TPB Predator: Kindred. 15.00

PREDATOR: NEMESIS
Dec., 1997
1 (of 2) TTg(c). 3.00
2 . . . . 3.00

PREDATOR: PRIMAL
1997
1 (of 2) Kevin J. Anderson(s),
  ScK,Low 3.00
2 (of 2) 3.00

PREDATOR: RACE WAR
1993
0 F:Serial Killer 3.00
1 V:Serial Killer 3.00
2 D:Serial Killer 3.00
3 in Prison 3.00
4 Last Issue 3.00
TPB Race War, series rep. 18.00

PREDATOR 2
1991
1 DBy, Movie Adapt,pt1 . . . . 3.50
2 MBr, Movie Adapt.,pt2 with
  2-card strip 3.00

PREDATOR VS.
JUDGE DREDD
Sept., 1997
1 (of 3) by John Wagner and
  Enrique Alcatena 3.00
2 thru 3 . . . . @3.00
TPB Predator vs. Judge Dredd 9.00

PREDATOR VS. MAGNUS
ROBOT FIGHTER
Valiant/Dark Horse 1992
1 LW,A:Tekla 3.00
1a Platinum Ed. 5.00
1b Gold Ed. 3.00
2 LW,Magnus Vs. Predator, with
  2-card strip 3.00
TPB Rep. #1–#2 . . . . 8.00

DARK HORSE

All comics prices listed are for *Near Mint* condition.

Predator: Xenogenesis #1
© Dark Horse Comics

PREDATOR: XENOGENESIS
Aug., 1999
1 (of 4) 3.00
2 IEd 3.00
3 IEd 3.00
4 . . . . 3.00

PRIMAL
Oct., 1992
1 Contd.from Primal:from the
  Cradle to the Grave 3.00
2 A:TJ Cyrus 2.50
GN Primal From the Cradle
  to the Grave. 10.00

PROPELLER MAN
1993
1 I:Propeller Man 3.00
2 O:Propeller Man,w/2 card strip . . 3.00
3 V:Manipulator 3.00
4 V:State Police,w/2 card strip 3.00
5 V:Manipulator 3.00
6 V:Thing, w/2 card strip 3.00
7 . . . . 3.00
8 Last issue,w/2 card strip 3.00

PUBO
DH Maverick, Nov., 2002
1 (of 3) by Leland Purvis, B&W 3.50
2 . . . . 3.50
3 . . . . 3.50
TPB 96-pg.. . . . . 10.00

PUMPKINHEAD: THE RITES OF EXORCISM
1992
1 Based on the movie. 2.50
2 thru 4 . . . . @2.50

RACE OF SCORPIONS
(B&W) 1990
Book 1 short stories 5.00
Book 2 . . . . 5.00

RACE OF SCORPIONS
(B&W) 1991
1 A:Argos,Dito,Alma,Ka 2.50
2 thru 4 . . . . @2.50

RACK & PAIN
1994
1 GCa(c),I:Rack,Pain 3.00
2 GCa(c),V:Web 3.00
3 GCa(c),V:Web 3.00
4 GCa(c),Final Issue. 3.00

RASCALS IN PARADISE
1994
1 I:Spicy Sanders 4.00
2 . . . . 4.00
3 last issue 4.00
TPB Rep.#1–#3 . . . . 17.00

REAL ADVENTURES OF JONNY QUEST, THE
Sept., 1996
1 . . . . 3.00
2 . . . . 3.00
3 thru 12 . . . . @3.00

REBEL SWORD
(B&W–Manga) 1994
1 by Yoshikazu Yashiko 2.50
2 . . . . 2.50
3 . . . . 2.50
4 V:Ruken 2.50
5 Choice of Jiro 2.50
6 R:Ruken 2.50

REDBLADE
1993
1 V:Demons 3.00
2 V:Tull 3.00
3 Last Issue 3.00

RED ROCKET 7
Aug., 1997
1 (of 7) MiA 4.00
2 thru 7 . . . . @4.00
TPB rep. series, 208 pg. 30.00

REID FLEMING/ FLAMING CARROT
(B&W) Jan., 2003
1-Shot Reid Fleming/Flaming
  Carrot 4.00

REIKO THE ZOMBI SHOP
Dec., 2005
TPB Vol. 1 thru Vol. 5 . . . . @13.00

RETURN OF THE GREMLINS
Oct., 2006
1 . . . . 3.00
2 . . . . 3.00

REVEAL
Oct., 2002
1 64-pg.. 7.00

REVELATIONS
Aug., 2005
1 (of 6) PJe,HuR. 3.00
2 thru 6 . . . . @3.00
TPB Revelations (2006). 18.00

REX MUNDI
Aug., 2006
1 . . . . 3.00
2 . . . . 3.00
TPB Guardian of the Temple 17.00
TPB The River Underground 17.00

RICK GEARY'S WONDERS AND ODDITIES
(B&W) 1988
1-shot 3.00

RING OF ROSES
(B&W) 1991
1 Alternate world,1991 . . . . 2.50
2 Plague in London. 2.50
3 Plague cont.A:Secret Brother-
  hood of the Rosy Cross. 2.50
4 Conclusion. 2.50

RING OF THE NIEBELUNG, THE:
DH Maverick, 2000
RHINEGOLD, Feb., 2000
1 (of 4) CR 3.00
2 CR 3.00
3 CR 3.00
4 CR, concl. 3.00
VALKYRIE Aug., 2000
1 (of 3) CR 3.00
2 CR 3.00
3 CR, concl. 3.00
SIEGFRIED, Dec., 2000
1 (of 3) CR 3.00
2 CR 3.00
3 CR, concl. 3.00
GOTTERDAMMERUNG June, 2001
1 (of 4) CR 3.00
2 . . . . 3.00
3 . . . . 3.00
4 finale, 64-pg. 6.00
TPB Vol. 1 Rhinegold & Valkyrie . . 22.00
TPB Vol. 2 Siegfried and Gotterdammerung, 224-pg.(2002). . . 22.00

RING, THE
Nov., 2003
TPB Vol. 1 . . . . 15.00
TPB Vol. 2 . . . . 14.00
TPB Vol. 3 . . . . 13.00
TPB Vol. 4 Birthday 13.00

RIO AT BAY
1992
1 F:Doug Wildey art 3.00
2 F:Doug Wildey art 3.00
TPB 7.00

Real Adventures of Jonny Quest #12
© Dark Horse Comics

R.I.P.D.
Nov., 1999
1 (of 4) F:Rest in Peace Dept. 3.00
2 thru 4 . . . . @3.00
TPB Rest in Peace Department . . 13.00

RIPLEY'S BELIEVE IT OR NOT
June, 2002
1 (of 4) Into Thin Air 3.00
2 Grim Reaping. 3.00
3 Human Wonders 3.00
4 Strange Invaders 3.00
TPB 10.00

ROACHMILL
(B&W) 1988
1 thru 8 . . . . @3.50
9 and 10 . . . . @3.00

ROBOCOP: MORTAL COILS
1993
1 V:Gangs. 2.75
2 V:Gangs 2.75
3 V:Coffin,V:Gangs 2.75
4 . . . . 2.75

ROBOCOP VERSUS TERMINATOR
1992
1 FM(s),WS,w/Robocop cut-out . . . 3.50
2 FM(s),WS,w/Terminator cut-out . . 3.00
3 FM(s),WS,w/cut-out 3.00
4 FM(s),WS,Conclusion 3.00

ROBOCOP: PRIME SUSPECT
1992
1 Robocop framed 2.75
2 thru 4 V:ZED 309s . . . . @2.50
TPB series rep. 14.00

ROBOCOP: ROULETTE
1993
1 V:ED-309s 2.75
2 I:Philo Drut 2.75
3 V:Stealthbot 2.75

Rocketeer Adventure Magazine #3
© Dark Horse Comics

4 last issue 2.75

ROBOCOP 3
1993
1 B:StG(s),Movie Adapt 2.75
2 V:Aliens,OCP 2.75
3 HNg,ANi(i) 2.75

ROCKETEER ADVENTURE MAGAZINE
1988–95
1 and 2 . . . . @4.00
3 . . . . 3.00
TPB Cliff's New York Adventure
    by Dave Stevens 10.00

ROCKSTAR GAMES' ONI
Feb., 2001
1 video-game tie-in 3.00
1a gold foil (c) 7.00
2 . . . . 3.00
3 concl. 3.00

THE SAFEST PLACE IN THE WORLD
1995
SC, SD 2.50

SAMURAI EXECUTIONER
June, 2004
TPB Vol. 1 . . . . 10.00
TPB Vol. 2 . . . . 10.00

SAMURAI: HEAVEN AND EARTH
Dec., 2004
1 (of 5) 3.00
2 thru 5 . . . . @3.00
TPB 15.00
Vol. 2
1 RMz 3.00

SATSUMA GISHIDEN
Sept., 2006
TPB Vol. 1 . . . . 15.00
TPB Vol. 2 . . . . 15.00

SCARLET TRACES: THE GREAT GAME
July, 2006
1 IEd 3.00
2 thru 4 . . . . @3.00

SCARY BOOK
Feb., 2006
TPB Vol. 1 Reflections 15.00
TPB Vol. 2 Insects 14.00
TPB Vol. 3 Faces 14.00

SCATTERBRAIN
June, 1998
1 (of 4) MMi 3.00
2 thru 4 . . . . @3.00

SCHOOL ZONE
Feb., 2006
TPB Vol. 1 & Vol. 2 . . . . @13.00

SCREWBALL SQUIRREL
July, 1995
1 . . . . 2.75
2 thru 3 . . . . @2.75

SCORPION KING, THE
Mar., 2002
1 (of 2) movie adapt. 3.00
1a photo (c). 3.00
2 (of 2) movie adapt. 3.00
2a photo (c). 3.00

SECRET OF THE SALAMANDER
(B&W)
1 Jacquestardi, rep 3.00

SERAPHIC FEATHER
Nov., 2001
TPB Vol. 1 Crimson Angel 18.00
TPB Vol. 2 Seeds of Chaos 18.00
TPB Vol. 3 Target Zone 18.00
TPB Vol. 4 Dark Angel 18.00
TPB Vol. 5 War Crimes 18.00
TPB Vol. 6 Collision Course 16.00

SERENITY
July, 2005
1 movie adapt. 4.00
2 thru 3 . . . . @3.00
1a&b thru 3a&b variant(c) . . . . . . @3.00
TPB 14.00

SERGIO ARAGONES ACTIONS SPEAK
Jan., 2001
1 (of 6) 3.00
2 thru 6 . . . . @3.00
TPB 160-pg. 14.00

SERGIO ARAGONES' BOOGEYMAN
(B&W) June, 1998
1 (of 4) 3.00
2 thru 4 . . . . @3.00
TPB, rep. 10.00

SERGIO ARAGONES' DAY OF THE DEAD
Oct., 1998
1-shot 3.00

SERGIO ARAGONES' GROO
Jan.–Apr., 1998
1 (of 4) 3.00
2 thru 4 . . . . @3.00
TPB The Most Intelligent Man
    in the World 10.00
TPB Houndbook. 10.00
TPB Inferno 10.00
TPB Jamboree. 10.00
TPB Library 10.00
TPB Kingdom. 10.00
TPB Groo Odyssey 13.00
TPB Mightier Than the Sword 14.00
TPB Groo Maiden 96-pg. 13.00
TPB The Groo Nursery 12.00

SERGIO ARAGONES' GROO & RUFFERTO
Dec., 1998
1 (of 4) 3.00
2 thru 4 . . . . @3.00
TPB 10.00

DARK HORSE

SERGIO ARAGONES'
GROO: DEATH AND TAXES
DH Maverick, Dec., 2002
1 (of 4) SA 3.00
2 thru 4 . . . . @3.00
TPB series rep. 112-pg. 13.00

SERGIO ARAGONES'
GROO: MIGHTIER THAN THE SWORD
Jan., 2000
1 (of 4) SA 3.00
2 SA,V:Pipil Khan 3.00
3 SA,V:Relmihio 3.00
4 SA,concl. 3.00

SERGIO ARAGONES'
LOUDER THAN WORDS
(B&W) July–Dec., 1997
1 (of 6) SA 3.00
2 thru 6 . . . . @3.00
TPB rep. series 13.00

SERGIO STOMPS STAR WARS
2000
1-shot SA, parody 3.00

SEX WARRIOR
1993
1 I:Dakini. 2.50
2 V:Steroids. 2.50

SEXY CHIX
Jan., 2006
TPB 13.00

SHADOW, THE
1994
1 MK 3.00
2 MK 3.00

THE SHADOW AND DOC SAVAGE
1995
1 . . . . 3.50
2 The Shrieking Skeletons 3.50

THE SHADOW: HELL'S HEAT WAVE
1995
1 Racial War 3.00
2 MK,V:Ghost 3.00
3 Final issue 3.00

THE SHADOW: IN THE COILS OF LEVIATHAN
1993
1 MK,V:Monster 3.25
2 MK 3.25
3 MK,w/ GfD poster 3.25
4 MK,Final issue 3.25
TPB, reprints #1–#4. . . . . 14.00

THE SHADOW AND THE MYSTERIOUS 3
1994
1 Three stories 3.00

SHADOW EMPIRES: FAITH CONQURES
1994
1 CsM 3.00
2 thru 4 CsM . . . . @3.00

SHADOW STAR
Sept., 2001
TPB 16.00
TPB Vol. 2 Darkness Visible 15.00
TPB Vol. 3 Shadows of the Past . . 14.00
TPB Vol. 4 Nothing But the Truth . 15.00
TPB Vol. 5 A Flower's Fragrance. . 16.00
TPB Vol. 6 What Can I Do For You 16.00
TPB Vol. 7 Victim's Eyes, Assailant's
  Hands (2005). 16.00

SHI: JUN-NEN
July 2004
1 BiT 3.00
2 thru 4 . . . . @3.00
TPB 13.00

SHINOBI
Nov., 2002
Spec.1-shot The Rise of Hotsuma. . 3.00

SHOCKROCKETS
July, 2004
TPB We Have Ignition 15.00

SHREK
Apr., 2003
1 (of 3) 3.00
2 and 3 . . . . @3.00
TPB 96-pg. 13.00

SIGNAL TO NOISE
Apr., 1999
TPB NGa,DMc 15.00

SILKE
Jan., 2001
1 TnD,F:Sandra Silke 3.00
1a variant(c) 3.00
2 TnD 3.00
3 TnD, The Hunt is on 3.00
4 TnD 3.00
4a variant(c) 3.00
TPB series rep. 96-pg. 13.00

SIN CITY:
DH-Legend
GN A Small Killing 14.00
GN Family Values (1997). 10.00
1-shot The Babe Wore Red (1994) . 6.00
1-shot The Babe Wore Red and
  other stories (1996) nudity 3.00
1-shot Lost Lonely, and Lethal, FM
  two-color 7.00
1-shot Sex and Violence, FM 6.00
1-shot Silent Night, FM (1995). 5.00
TPB, 10th Anniv. edition,
  with print & sketchbook 175.00

SIN CITY: A DAME TO KILL FOR
DH-Legend (B&W) 1993
1 FM(a&s),I:Dwight,Ava 6.00
2 FM(a&s),A:Ava 5.00
3 FM(a&s),D:Ava's Husband 5.00
1a thru 3a 2nd printings . . . . @3.00
4 thru 6 FM(a&s). . . . . @5.00
TPB rep. #1–#6, new pages 25.00

SIN CITY: HELL AND BACK
July, 1999
1 (of 9) FM 6.00
2 . . . . 5.00
3 . . . . 5.00
4 Five Foot Two, Eyes of Blue 5.00
5 . . . . 5.00
6 quest for Esther 5.00
7 & 8 . . . . @5.00
9 56-pg. 5.00
TPB FM 25.00

SIN CITY: JUST ANOTHER SATURDAY NIGHT
DH/Wizard
1/2 (Wizard, 24-pg.) 7.00
1/2 rep., Dark Horse, new (c). 3.00

SIN CITY: THAT YELLOW BASTARD
(B&W) 1996
1 F.Miller 5.00
2 thru 6 . . . . @5.00
TPB by Frank Miller 15.00

SIN CITY: THE BIG FAT KILL
DH Legend, 1994
1 FM 5.00
2 FM 5.00
3 FM, Dump the Stiffs. 5.00
4 FM, Town Without Pity. 5.00
5 FM, final issue 5.00
TPB 15.00

SOCK MONKEY
(B&W) Sept., 1998
1 by Tony Millionaire 3.00
2 F:Uncle Gabby. 3.00

VOLUME 2
1 and 2 . . . . @3.00
DH Maverick, Sept., 2002
Spec. #1 (of 2) 3.00
Spec. #2 . . . . 3.00
VOLUME 4, 2003
1 and 2 . . . . @3.00
TPB Collected, Vol. 3 & 4 . . . . 13.00

Sock Monkey #2
© *Dark Horse Comics*

SOCK MONKEY:
THE INCHES INCIDENT
(B&W) Sept., 2006
1 by Tony Millionaire 3.00
2 . . . . 3.00

SOLO
1996
1 and 2 . . . . @1.00

SPACE CIRCUS
DH Maverick, July, 2000
1 (of 4) SA 3.00
2 thru 4 SA . . . . @3.00

SPACEHAWK
(B&W) 1989
1 BW reps. 3.50
2 thru 5 BW . . . . @3.50

SPACE PINCHY
Dec., 2005
1-shot Pleased Ta Meetya 3.00
1-shot Audrey's Super Power Pinch 3.00
1-shot The Laboratory of Love 3.00
1-shot Surrounded by Robots 3.00
1-shot The Pinch of the Illegal Brain
   Intrusion 4.00

SPACE USAGI
[Vol. 3] 1996
1 thru 3 Stan Sakai . . . . @3.00
TPB 17.00

SPECIES
1995
1 Alien Human Hybrid 3.00
2 thru 4 SIL . . . . @3.00

SPECIES: HUMAN RACE
1996
1 PhH 3.00
2 . . . . 3.00
3 SBi 3.00
4 . . . . 3.00
TPB 12.00

SPIRIT OF WONDER
(B&W) 1996
1 thru 5 by Kenji Tsuruia . . . . @3.00
TPB 13.00

SPYBOY
Oct., 1999
1 PDd,F:Alex Fleming 3.00
2 PDd 3.00
3 PDd,F:Bombshell 3.00
4 PDd,F:Judge and Jury 3.00
5 PDd,V:Judge and Jury 3.00
6 PDd,V:Barbie Q 3.00
7 PDd,V:Madam Imadam 3.00
8 PDd,V:Madam Imadam 3.00
9 PDd,V:Madam Imadam
   & Barbie Q. 3.00
10 PDd,death-defying action 3.00
11 PDd,V:Slackjaw. 3.00
12 PDd,V:Slackjaw 3.00
13 PDd 3.00
14 PDd,F:SpyGirl 3.00
15 PDd 3.00
15a variant TnD (c) 3.00
16 PDd 3.00
17 PDd 3.00
TPB Deadly Gourmet Affair, PDd . . 9.00
TPB Trial and Terror. 10.00
TPB Bet Your Life 10.00

TPB Vol.4 Undercover, Underwear 10.00
TPB Vol.5 Spy-School Confidential 13.00
Spec. 1-shot 48-pg. 5.00
Spec. Motorola Spec. (2000) 2.50

SPYBOY: FINAL EXAM
May, 2004
1 PDd 3.00
2 thru 4 . . . . @3.00

SPYBOY 13: THE
M.A.N.G.A. AFFAIR
Apr., 2003
1 (of 3) PDd(s) 3.00
2 and 3 . . . . @3.00
TPB 10.00

SPYBOY/YOUNG JUSTICE
Feb., 2002
1 PDd, x-over 3.00
2 and 3 . . . . @3.00
TPB PDd(s) 10.00

STAN SHAW'S
BEAUTY & THE BEAST
1 Based on the book. 5.00

STAR KID
1998
1-shot 3.00

STARSHIP TROOPERS
Sept., 1997
1 (of 2) movie adaptation 3.00
2 movie adaptation, concl. 3.00
TPB rep., inc. Brute Creations,
   Insect Touch, & movie 152 pg. 15.00

STARSHIP TROOPERS:
BRUTE CREATIONS
1997
1-shot RbC 3.00

STARSHIP TROOPERS:
DOMINANT SPECIES
Aug., 1998
1 (of 4) 3.00
2 JoB,RyE 3.00
3 & 4 . . . . @3.00

STARSHIP TROOPERS:
INSECT TOUCH
1997
1 by Warren Ellis & Paolo Parente . 3.00
2 and 3 (of 3) . . . . @3.00

STAR SLAMMERS
1996
Spec. 1 . . . . 3.00

STARSTRUCK: THE
EXPANDING UNIVERSE
(B&W) 1990
1 Book 1, with cards 3.00
2 Book 2, with 2-card strip 3.00
3 Book 3, with cards 3.00
4 Book 4, with cards 3.00

STAR WARS
Dec., 1998
1 F:Ki-Adi-Mundi 5.00
2 F:Ki-Adi-Mundi 4.00
3 F:Ki-Adi-Mundi 3.50

Star Wars #8
© Dark Horse Comics

4 F:Sylvn 3.50
5 V:Ephant Mon 6.00
6 V:Jabba the Hutt 6.00
7 Outlander 3.00
8 Outlander, A:Jabba the Hutt 3.00
9 A:Tusken Raiders 3.00
10 TT,RL,F:Ki-Adi-Mundi 3.00
11 TT,RL,F:Aurra Sing 3.00
12 TT,Outlander,pt.6 . . . . 3.00
13 TT,TL,A'Sharad Hett 3.00
14 TT,TL,on Malastare 3.00
15 TT,TL,Podracing 3.00
16 TT,TL,V:Lannik terrorists 3.00
17 TT,TL,V:Red Iaro terrorists 3.00
18 TT,TL,Smugglers Moon 3.00
19 JOs,JD,Twilight,pt 1 . . . . 3.00
20 JOs,JD,Twilight,pt.2 . . . . 3.00
21 JOs,JD,Twilight,pt.3 . . . . 3.00
22 JOs,JD,Twilight,pt.4 . . . . 3.00
23 Infinity's End,pt.1 . . . . 3.00
24 Infinity's End,pt.2 . . . . 3.00
25 Infinity's End,pt.3 . . . . 3.00
26 Infinity's End,pt.4 . . . . 3.00
27 Star Crash one-shot 3.00
28 Hunt for Aurra Sing,pt.1 . . . . . . 3.00
29 Hunt for Aurra Sing,pt.2 . . . . . . 3.00
30 Hunt for Aurra Sing,pt.3 . . . . . . 3.00
31 Hunt for Aurra Sing,pt.4 . . . . . . 3.00
32 Darkness,pt.1, JOs,JD 3.00
33 Darkness,pt.2, JOs,JD 3.00
34 Darkness,pt.3, JOs,JD 3.00
35 Darkness,pt.4, JOs,JD 3.00
36 Stark Hyperspace War,pt.1 . . . . 3.00
37 Stark Hyperspace War,pt.2 . . . . 3.00
38 Stark Hyperspace War,pt.3 . . . . 3.00
39 Stark Hyperspace War,pt.4 . . . . 3.00
40 The Devaronian Version,pt.1 . . . 3.00
41 The Devaronian Version,pt.2 . . . 3.00
42 Rite of Passage,pt.1 . . . . 3.00
43 Rite of Passage,pt.2 . . . . 3.00
44 Rite of Passage,pt.3 . . . . 3.00
45 Rite of Passage,pt.4 . . . . 3.00
becomes:

STAR WARS: REPUBLIC
Oct., 2002
46 Republic,pt.1 . . . . 3.00
47 Republic,pt.2 . . . . 3.00
48 Republic,pt.3 . . . . 3.00
49 Republic,pt.5 . . . . 3.00
50 Republic,pt.6, 64-page 6.00
51 Republic,pt.7 . . . . 3.00
52 Republic,pt.8 . . . . 3.00
53 Blast Radius 3.00

DARK HORSE

54 Jedi Fugitive	3.00
55 Battle of Jabiim,pt.1	3.00
56 Battle of Jabiim,pt.2	3.00
57 Battle of Jabiim,pt.3	3.00
58 Battle of Jabiim,pt.4	3.00
59 Enemy Lines	3.00
60 Origin of Asajj Ventress	3.00
61 Bail Organa	3.00
62 On Hostile Ground	3.00
63 Quinlan Vos, Assassin	3.00
64 A Jedi's Tale	3.00
65 Mace Windu Unleashed,pt.1	3.00
66 Mace Windu Unleashed,pt.2	3.00
67 Great Power, Great Restraint	3.00
68 Born to Fight	3.00
69 Dreadnaughts of Rendili,pt.1	3.00
70 Dreadnaughts of Rendili,pt.2	3.00
71	3.00
72 Aayla Undercover	3.00
73 In the House of the Enemy	3.00
74 Same War, New Clones	3.00
75 Siege of Saleucami	3.00
76 Darkness, Light and Fire	3.00
77 Final Test of Quinlan Vos	3.00
78 Darth Vader, Right-hand Man	3.00
79 Into the Unknown	3.00
80 Jedi...Fugitive	3.00
81 The Hidden Enemy,pt.1	3.00
82 The Hidden Enemy,pt.2	3.00
83 The Hidden Enemy,pt.3	3.00
0 Spec. American Entertainment	10.00
TPB Prelude to Rebellion	15.00
TPB Darkness (2002)	13.00
TPB Honor and Duty (2006)	13.00

Star Wars: A New Hope, Special Edition #3 © Dark Horse Comics

STAR WARS: A NEW HOPE— SPECIAL EDITION
Jan.–Apr., 1997

1 EB, AW	6.00
2 thru 4	@5.00
TPB Rep. #1–#4 Hildebrandt(c)	10.00
Spec. Edition boxed set	30.00

STAR WARS: A NEW HOPE
(B&W–Manga) July, 1998

1 (of 4) by Tamaki Hisao, 96-pg	10.00
2 thru 4	@10.00

STAR WARS: A NEW HOPE—MANGA
Nov., 1999

1 (of 4) by Kia Asamiya,96-pg	10.00
2 thru 4, 88-pg	@10.00

STAR WARS: BATTLE OF THE BOUNTY HUNTERS
July, 1996

Pop-up Comic	18.00

STAR WARS: BOBA FETT—

1-shot Bounty on Bar-Kooda, (1995) 48-pg	11.00
1-shot When the Fat Lady Swings	7.00
1-shot Murder Most Foul (1997)	7.00
1-shot Twin Engins of Destruction	6.00
1-shot Agent of Doom, CK (2000)	3.00
1-shot Overkill (2006)	3.00
TPB Death, Lies & Treachery	13.00

STAR WARS: BOBA FETT— ENEMY OF THE EMPIRE
Jan., 1999

1 (of 4) V:Dark Lord of the Sith	3.00
2 thru 4 IG	@3.00
TPB rep., includes #1/2	17.00

STAR WARS: BOUNTY HUNTERS
Aug., 1999

1-shot Aurra Sing, TT	3.00
1-shot Kir Kanos, MRi,RSd	3.00
1-shot Scoundrel's Wages, F:Dengar, 4-LOM & Bossk	3.00
TPB Star Wars: Bounty Hunters	13.00

STAR WARS: CHEWBACCA
Jan., 2000

1 (of 4) various tales	4.00
1 gold foil (c)	13.00
2 thru 4	@3.50
TPB	13.00

STAR WARS: CLONE WARS
June, 2003

TPB Vol.1 Defense of Kamino	15.00
TPB Vol.2 Victories and Sacrifices	15.00
TPB Vol.3 Last Stand on Jabiim	13.00
TPB Vol.4 Light and Dark	17.00
TPB Vol.5 The Best Blades	15.00
TPB Vol.6 On the Fields of Battle	18.00
TPB Vol.7 When They Were Brothers	18.00
TPB Vol.8 Last Siege, Final Truth	18.00
TPB Vol.9, End Game	18.00
TPB Clone Wars Adventures, Vol.1. thru Vol.7	@7.00

STAR WARS COMICS COMPANION
Nov., 2005

TPB Handbook	17.00

STAR WARS: CRIMSON EMPIRE
Dec., 1997–May, 1998

1 PG,CR,DvD(c)	10.00
3 PG,CR,DvD(c)	8.00

3 thru 5 PG,CR,DvD(c)	@5.00
TPB Crimson Empire	18.00

VOL II: COUNCIL OF BLOOD
1998

1 MRi,RSd,PG,DvD(c)	4.00
2 thru 6 RSd,PG,DvD(c)	@3.00
TPB Council of Blood	18.00

STAR WARS: DARK EMPIRE
Dec., 1991

1 CK,Destiny of a Jedi	14.00
1a 2nd Printing	5.00
1b Gold Ed.	15.00
2 CK,Destroyer of worlds, very low print run	12.00
2a 2nd Printing	5.00
2b Gold Ed.	15.00
3 CK,V:The Emperor	8.00
3a 2nd printing	4.00
3b Gold Ed.	10.00
4 CK,V:The Emperor	5.00
4a Gold Ed.	5.00
5 CK,V:The Emperor	5.00
5a Gold Ed.	10.00
6 CK,V:Emperor,last issue	5.00
6a Gold Ed.	9.00
Gold editions, foil logo set	50.00
Platinum editions, embossed set.	100.00
TPB Preview 32pg	1.00
TPB rep.#1–#6	20.00
TPB CK & Tom Veitch 2nd ed.	18.00

STAR WARS DARK EMPIRE II
1994

1 2nd chapter	6.00
2 F:Boba Fett	5.00
3 V:Darksiders	5.00
4 Luke Vs. Darksiders	5.00
5 Creatures	5.00
6 CK,DvD(c), save the twins	5.00
Platinum editions, set	50.00
TPB CK & Tom Veitch rep.#1–#6	18.00

STAR WARS: DARK FORCE RISING
May–Oct., 1997

1 thru 6 (of 6) MBn,TyD,KN	@5.00
TPB series rep	18.00

STAR WARS: DARK FORCES

TPB Jedi Knight (Sept., 1998)	15.00
TPB Rebel Agent (Mar., 1998)	15.00
TPB Soldier for the Empire	15.00

STAR WARS: DARK TIMES
Oct., 2006

1 The Path to Nowhere	3.00
2 The Path to Nowhere, pt.2	3.00

STAR WARS: DARTH MAUL
Sept., 2000

1 (of 4) RMz,JD,Struzan(c)	3.00
1 photo (c)	5.00
2 Struzan(c),V:Black Sun	3.00
3 RMz,JD,Struzan(c)	3.00
4 RMz,JD,Struzan(c)	3.00
2 thru 4 photo(c)	@3.00
TPB RMz,JD,Struzan(c)	13.00

DARK HORSE

STAR WARS: DROIDS
April–Sept., 1994
1 F:C-3PO,R2-D2 . . . . 5.00
2 V:Thieves 3.00
3 on the Hosk moon 3.00
4 . . . . 3.00
5 A meeting 3.00
6 final issue 3.00
Spec.#1 I:Olag Greck 3.00
TPB The Kalarba Adventures, rep. 18.00

[2nd Series] Apr., 1995
1 Deputized Droids 3.00
2 Marooned on Nar Shaddaa 3.00
3 C-3PO to the Rescue 3.00
4 . . . . 3.00
5 Caretaker virus 3.00
6 Revolution 3.00
7 & 8 . . . . @3.00
TPB Droids—Rebellion, rep. 18.00

STAR WARS: THE EMPIRE STRIKES BACK
TPB Hildebrandt(c) 10.00

STAR WARS: THE EMPIRE STRIKES BACK
(B&W–Manga) Dec., 1998
1 (of 4) by Toshiki Dudo, 96-pg.. . 10.00
2 thru 4 . . . . @10.00

STAR WARS: EMISSARIES TO MALASTARE
Aug., 2001
TPB TT,TL,JD 16.00

STAR WARS: EMPIRE
Sept., 2002
1 Betrayal,pt.1 . . . . 3.50
2 Betrayal,pt.2 . . . . 3.50
3 Betrayal,pt.3 . . . . 3.50
4 Betrayal,pt.4 . . . . 3.00
5 National Public Radio adapt. 3.00
6 Surrender or Die 3.00
7 Sacrifice! 3.00
8 Darklighter,pt.1 . . . . 3.00
9 Darklighter,pt.2 . . . . 3.00
10 Yavin Base,pt.1 . . . . 3.00
11 Yavin Base,pt.2 . . . . 3.00
12 Darklighter,pt.3 . . . . 3.00
13 What Sin Loyalty? 3.00
14 The Savage Heart 3.00
15 Darklighter,pt.4 . . . . 3.00
16 To the Last Man,pt.1 . . . . 3.00
17 To the Last Man,pt.2 . . . . 3.00
18 To the Last Man,pt.3 . . . . 3.00
19 To the Last Man,pt.3 . . . . 3.00
20 Rebel base 3.00
21 Rebel base,pt.2 . . . . 3.00
22 F:Deena Shan 3.00
23 F:BoShek 3.00
24 Idiot's Array,pt.1 . . . . 3.00
25 Idiot's Array,pt.2 . . . . 3.00
26 Luke Skywalker Target 3.00
27 Promoted to General 3.00
28 Ghost Ship 3.00
29 In the Shadows of Their Fathers 3.00
30 Rebel vs. Rebel 3.00
31 The Price of Power 3.00
32 Ambush on Jabiim 3.00
33 Trapped on Jabiim 3.00
34 The Fate of a Planet 3.00
35 Never Lie to Vader 3.00
36 thru 40 Wrong Side of the
   War, pt.1–pt.5 . . . . @3.00
TPB Vol. 1 . . . . 13.00
TPB Vol. 2 Darklighter 18.00
TPB Vol. 3 Imperial Perspective . . 18.00
TPB Vol. 4 . . . . 18.00

TPB Vol. 5 Allies & Adversaries . . . 18.00
TPB Vol. 6 In the Footsteps of Their
   Fathers 18.00
TPB Vol. 7 Wrong Side of the War 18.00

STAR WARS: EMPIRE'S END
Oct.–Nov., 1995
1 R:Emperor Palpatine 3.50
2 conclusion 3.50
TPB rep. 6.00

Star Wars: Episode I: The Phantom Menace #4 © Dark Horse Comics

STAR WARS: EPISODE I THE PHANTOM MENACE
Apr., 1999
1 RdM,AW 3.00
1a newsstand edition, photo (c) . . . 3.00
2 RdM,AW 3.00
2a newsstand edition, photo (c) . . . 3.00
3 RdM,AW 3.00
3a newsstand edition, photo (c) . . . 3.00
4 RdM,AW 3.00
4a newsstand edition, photo (c) . . . 3.00
GN Phantom Menace RdM,AW . . . 13.00
Spec. Anakin Skywalker 3.00
Spec. Anakin Skywalker, newsstand 3.00
Spec. Obi-Wan Kenobi 3.00
Spec. Obi-Wan Kenobi, newsstand . 3.00
Spec. Queen Amidala 3.00
Spec. Qui-Gon Jinn 3.00
TPB 13.00
TPB Adventures, rep. 13.00

STAR WARS: EPISODE I THE PHANTOM MENACE—MANGA
Dec., 1999
1 (of 2) 88-pg. 10.00

STAR WARS EPISODE II— ATTACK OF THE CLONES
Apr., 2002
1 (of 4) 48-pg. 4.00
2 thru 4 48-pg. . . . . @4.00
1A thru 4A photo (c) . . . . @4.00
TPB 144-pg. 18.00

STAR WARS: EPISODE III– REVENGE OF THE SITH
Mar., 2005
1 . . . . 3.00
2 thru 4 . . . . @3.00

STAR WARS: GENERAL GRIEVOUS
Mar., 2005
1 . . . . 3.00
2 thru 4 . . . . @3.00
TPB 13.00

STAR WARS HANDBOOK
July, 1998
1 X-Wing Rogue Squadron 3.50
2 Crimson Empire 3.00
Dark Empire 3.00

STAR WARS: HEIR TO THE EMPIRE
Oct., 1995–Apr., 1996
1 I:Grand Admiral Thrawn 4.00
2 thru 6 . . . . @3.50
TPB from novel by Timothy Zahn . 20.00

STAR WARS: THE HUNT FOR AURRA SING
July, 2002
TPB 96-pg. TT 13.00

STAR WARS: INFINITIES — A NEW HOPE
May, 2001
1 (of 4) CW,TyH,Luke's attack fails,
   Death Star survives 3.00
1a gold foil photo (c) 13.00
2 CW,TyH 3.00
3 CW,TyH 3.00
4 CW,TyH, concl. 3.00
TPB series rep. 96-pg. 13.00

STAR WARS: INFINITIES — THE EMPIRE STRIKES BACK
July, 2002
1 (of 4) 3.00
2 thru 4 . . . . @3.00
TPB 13.00

STAR WARS: INFINITIES — RETURN OF THE JEDI
Nov., 2003
1 (of 4) 3.00
2 thru 4 . . . . @3.00
TPB 13.00

STAR WARS: JABBA THE HUTT—
1995–1996
1-shot The Garr Suppoon Hit 3.00
1-shot Hunger of Princess Nampi . . 3.00
1-shot The Dynasty Trap 3.00
1-shot Betrayal 3.00
1-shot The Jabba Tape 3.00

STAR WARS: JANGO FETT
Dec., 2001
TPB 64-pg..,RMz 6.00

STAR WARS: JANGO FETT—OPEN SEASONS
Apr., 2002
1 (of 4) 3.00
2 thru 4 . . . . @3.00
TPB 96-pg. 13.00

STAR WARS: JEDI
Feb., 2003
Spec. Mace Windu, JOs,JD,48-pg. . 5.00
Spec. Shaak Ti, JOs,JD, 48-pg. . . . 5.00
Spec. Aayla Secura, JOs,JD,48-pg. 5.00
Spec. Dooku,JOs,JD,48-pg. 5.00
Spec. Yoda, 48-pg. 5.00

STAR WARS: JEDI ACADEMY LEVIATHAN
Oct., 1998
1 (of 4) by Kevin J. Anderson 3.00
2 thru 4 . . . . @3.00
TPB 12.00

STAR WARS: JEDI COUNCIL — ACTS OF WAR
June, 2000
1 (of 4) RSd, V:Yinchorri 3.00
1b gold foil (c) 10.00
2 thru 4 RSd . . . . @3.00
TPB 96-pg. rep 13.00

STAR WARS: JEDI QUEST
Sept., 2001
1 . . . . 3.00
1a ruby red foil 13.00
1b ruby red foil, signed 30.00
2 thru 4 . . . . @3.00

STAR WARS: JEDI VS. SITH
Apr., 2001
1 (of 6) 3.00
1a gold foil, lim.e. 10.00
2 V:Darth Bane 3.00
3 thru 6 . . . . @3.00
TPB 144-pg. 18.00

STAR WARS: KNIGHTS OF THE OLD REPUBLIC
Jan., 2006
1 A Jedi Betrayed 3.00
2 F:Zayne Carrick 3.00
3 Ambush 3.00
4 The Noose Tightens 3.00
5 A Destroyer of Worlds 3.00
6 Commencement 3.00
7 Jedi vs. Mandalorians 3.00
8 Jedi vs. Mandalorians 3.00
9 Jedi vs. Mandalorians 3.00
10 . . . . 3.00
11 . . . . 3.00
Spec. Knights/Rebellion flip-book . . 0.25

STAR WARS: THE LAST COMMAND
Nov., 1997–July, 1998
1 thru 6 MBn . . . . @3.50
TPB, rep. 18.00

STAR WARS LEGACY
June, 2006
0 The Future of Star Wars 0.25
1 The Sith born anew 3.00
2 The Future in Question 3.00
3 A Princess in Peril 3.00
4 . . . . 3.00
5 . . . . 3.00
6 . . . . 3.00

Star Wars: Mara Jade #3
© Dark Horse Comics

STAR WARS: MARA JADE— BY THE EMPEROR'S HAND
Aug., 1998
1 (of 6) by Timothy Zahn 5.00
2 thru 6 . . . . @4.00
TPB rep. 16.00

STAR WARS: OBSESSION
Nov., 2004
1 (of 5) 3.00
2 thru 5 . . . . @3.00

STAR WARS: OUTLANDER
Mar., 2001
TPB F:Ki-Adi-Mundi 13.00

STAR WARS: THE PROTOCOL OFFENSIVE
Sept., 1997
1-shot written by Anthony Daniels . . 5.00

STAR WARS: PURGE
Dec., 2005
1-shot Last Stand of the Jedi 3.00

STAR WARS: QUI-GON & OBI-WAN—LAST STAND ON ORD MANTELL
Jan., 2001
1 . . . . 3.00
1a variant TnD (c) 3.00
1c gold foil (c) 15.00
2 . . . . 3.00
3 . . . . 3.00
1a thru 3a photo(c) . . . . @3.00

STAR WARS: QUI-GON & OBI-WAN—THE AURORIENT EXPRESS
Feb., 2002
1 (of 2) 3.00
2 . . . . 3.00

STAR WARS: RETURN OF THE JEDI—SPECIAL EDITION
TPB Hildebrandt(c) 10.00

STAR WARS: REBELLION— MY BROTHER, MY ENEMY
Apr., 2006
1 F:Janek Sunber 3.00
2 thru 5 . . . . @3.00

STAR WARS: RETURN OF TAG & BINK
March, 2006
1 & 2 . . . . @3.00

STAR WARS: THE RETURN OF THE JEDI
(B&W–Manga) June, 1999
1 (of 4) by Shin-ichi Hiromoto,
96-pg. 10.00
2 thru 4 . . . . @10.00

STAR WARS: THE RITE OF PASSAGE
Jan., 2004
TPB 13.00

STAR WARS: RIVER OF CHAOS
May–Nov., 1995
1 LSi,JBr,Emperor sends spies . . . 3.00
2 Imperial in Allies Clothing 3.00
3 . . . . 3.00
4 F:Ranulf 3.00

STAR WARS: SHADOWS OF THE EMPIRE
May, 1996
1 (of 6) by John Wagner, Kilian
Plunkett & P. Craig Russell 3.50
2 thru 6 . . . . @3.50
TPB 18.00

STAR WARS: SHADOWS OF THE EMPIRE — EVOLUTION
Feb.–June, 1998
1 thru 5 . . . . @3.50
TPB Steve Perry(s) 15.00

STAR WARS: SHADOW STALKER
Nov., 1997
1-shot from Star Wars Galaxy Mag. 3.50

STAR WARS: SPLINTER OF THE MIND'S EYE
Dec., 1995–June, 1996
1 thru 4 A.D.Foster novel adapt. . @3.50
TPB 15.00

DARK HORSE

STAR WARS: STARFIGHTER— CROSSBONES
Jan., 2002
1 (of 3) F:Nym, pirate captain 3.00
2 from video game 3.00
3 . . . . 3.00

STAR WARS: TAG & BINK ARE DEAD
Oct., 2001
1 (of 2) 3.00
2 . . . . 3.00
1-shot Revenge of the Clone
Menace 3.00

STAR WARS TALES
Sept., 1999
1 various authors, 64-pg. 10.00
2 thru 4, 64-pg. . . . . @6.00
5 F:Lando's Commandos 6.00
6 thru 9 . . . . @6.00
10 thru 24 . . . . @6.00
5a thru 24a photo(c) . . . . @6.00
TPB Vol. 1 thru Vol. 6 . . . . @20.00

STAR WARS: TALES FROM MOS EISLEY
1-shot, from Star Wars Galaxy
Mag. #2–#4 . . . . 3.50

STAR WARS: TALES OF THE JEDI
Oct., 1993
1 RV,I:Ulic Qel-Droma 6.00
2 RV,A:Ulic Qel-Droma 5.00
3 RV,D:Andur 5.00
4 RV,A:Jabba the Hut 4.00
5 RV,last issue 4.00
TPB 15.00
TPB 2nd printing 15.00
TPB Redemption, 112-pg. 15.00

STAR WARS: TALES OF THE JEDI: DARK LORDS OF THE SITH
Oct., 1994–Mar., 1995
1 Bagged with card 3.00
2 . . . . 3.00
3 Krath Attack 3.00
4 F:Exar Kun 3.00
5 V:TchKrath 3.00
6 Final battle 3.00
TPB 18.00

STAR WARS: TALES OF THE JEDI: THE FREEDON NADD UPRISING
Aug.–Sept., 1997
1 and 2 . . . . @3.00
TPB series rep. 6.00

STAR WARS: TALES OF THE JEDI: THE SITH WAR
Aug., 1995–Jan., 1996
1 F:Exar Kun 3.00
2 F:Ulic Oel-Droma 3.00
3 F:Exar Kun 3.00
4 thru 6 (6 part mini-series) . . . . . @3.00
TPB 18.00

STAR WARS: TALES OF THE JEDI—THE FALL OF THE SITH EMPIRE
June–Oct., 1997
1 (of 5) 3.50
2 thru 5 . . . . @3.00

STAR WARS: TALES OF THE JEDI—THE GOLDEN AGE OF THE SITH
Oct., 1996–Feb., 1997
0 . . . . 2.50
1 thru 5 . . . . @3.50
TPB 17.00

STAR WARS: TALES OF THE JEDI— REDEMPTION
July, 1998
1 (of 5) by Kevin J. Anderson 3.50
2 thru 5 F:Ulic Qel-Droma . . . . . . @3.50

STAR WARS: THE STARK HYPERSPACE WAR
Nov., 2003
TPB JOs 13.00

STAR WARS: TWILIGHT
Nov., 2001
TPB JOs,JD 13.00

STAR WARS: UNDERWORLD—THE YAVIN VASSILIKA
Dec., 2000
1 (of 5) F:Han Solo 3.00
2 thru 5 . . . . @3.00
1a thru 5a photo (c) . . . . @3.00
TPB 120-pg. 15.00

STAR WARS: UNION
Nov., 1999
1 (of 4) by Stackpole 3.00
1a gold foil (c) 10.00
2 the wedding approaches 3.00
3 almost there 3.00
4 wedding day 3.00
TPB Luke & Mara Jade 13.00

STAR WARS: VADER'S QUEST
Feb., 1999
1 (of 4) DGb,AMK 3.00
2 thru 4 . . . . @3.00
TPB with poster 12.00

STAR WARS: A VALENTINE STORY
Feb., 2003
1-shot PC 3.50

STAR WARS: X-WING— ROGUE LEADER
Sept., 2005
1 . . . . 3.00
2 . . . . 3.00
3 . . . . 3.00

Star Wars: X-Wing Rogue Squadron #18 © Dark Horse Comics

STAR WARS: X-WING ROGUE SQUADRON
July, 1995
The Rebel Opposition
1 F:Wedge Antilles 5.00
2 . . . . 3.50
3 F:Tycho Clehu 3.50
4 F:Tycho Clehu 3.50
½ Wizard limited exclusive 6.00
The Phantom Affair
5 thru 8 . . . . @3.50
TPB rep. 13.00
Battleground Tatooine
9 thru 12 . . . . @3.50
TPB rep. 13.00
The Warrior Princess
13 thru 16 . . . . @3.50
TPB rep. 14.00
Requiem for a Rogue
17 thru 20 . . . . @3.50
TPB rep. 13.00
In the Empire's Service
21 thru 24 . . . . @3.50
TPB rep. 13.00
Making of Baron Fell
25 . . . . 5.00
Family Ties
26 thru 27 . . . . @3.50
Masquerade
28 thru 31 . . . . @3.50
TPB Masquerade, rep. 13.00
Mandatory Retirement
32 thru 35 . . . . @3.50
TPB Blood and Honor 13.00
TPB Mandatory Retirement 13.00
TPB Star Wars Omnibus, Vol. 1 . . 25.00
TPB Star Wars Omnibus, Vol. 2 . . 25.00

STAR WARS: ZAM WESELL
Feb., 2002
TPB RMz, 64-pg. 6.00

STRIP SEARCH
Dec., 2003
TPB 15.00

STEVE RUDE'S THE MOTH
Mar., 2004
1 thru 4 . . . . @3.00
Spec. Double sized 5.00

All comics prices listed are for *Near Mint* condition.

SUBHUMAN
Nov., 1998
1 (of 4) MSh 3.00
2 thru 4 MSh . . . . @3.00

SUPERMAN/MADMAN HULLABALOO
June–Aug., 1997
1 (of 3) MiA 3.00
2 and 3 (of 3) . . . . @3.00

SUPERMAN/TARZAN: SONS OF THE JUNGLE
Oct., 2001
1 (of 3) CDi,HuR 3.00
2 CDi,HuR 3.00
3 CDi,HuR(c) 3.00
TPB 80-pg. 10.00

SUPERMAN VS. ALIENS
DC/Dark Horse, 1995
1 DJu,KN 6.00
2 V:Queen Alien 5.00
3 . . . . 5.00
TPB series rep. 15.00

SUPERMAN VS. ALIENS II
May, 2002
1 (of 4) CDi,JBg,KN, x-over 3.00
2 CDi,JBg,KN 3.00
3 CDi,JBg,KN 3.00
4 CDi,JBg,KN 3.00
TPB God War. 13.00

SUPERMAN VS. THE TERMINATOR: DEATH TO THE FUTURE
Dec., 1999
1 (of 4) AIG,StP,x-over 3.00
2 AIG,StP,into the future 3.00
3 AIG,StP,A:Supergirl 3.00
4 AIG,StP,concl. 3.00
TPB AIG,StP,series rep. 11.00

SUPER MANGA BLAST
(B&W) Mar., 2000
1 128-pg. 5.00
2 thru 6 128-pg. . . . . @5.00
7 F:Oh My Goddess 5.00
8 F:Oh My Goddess 5.00
9 F:3x3 Eyes. 5.00
10 F:Seraphic Feather 5.00
11 F:Oh My Goddess 5.00
12 F:Oh My Goddess. 5.00
13 F:Club 9 . . . . 5.00
14 F:Club 9 . . . . 5.00
15 F:Club 9, 50-pg. 6.00
16 F:3x3 Eyes 6.00
17 F:Club 9 . . . . 6.00
18 F:Club 9 . . . . 6.00
19 Seraphic Feather 6.00
20 What's Michael? 6.00
21 F:Club 9 . . . . 6.00
22 Club 9, 3x3 Eyes 6.00
23 Club 9, What's Michael?. 6.00
24 F:Seraphic Feather 6.00
25 F:Appleseed 6.00
26 F:Shadow Star 6.00
27 F:What's Michael? 6.00
28 thru 59 . . . . @6.00
TPB Vol.5 What's Michael's
    Favorite Spot 9.00

SYN
Rocket Comics Aug., 2003
1 KG 3.00

---

2 thru 5 . . . . @3.00
TPB 14.00

TALE OF ONE BAD RAT
1994
1 BT 3.00
2 thru 4 . . . . @3.00
TPB Rep.#1–#4 . . . . 15.00

TALES OF ORDINARY MADNESS
(B&W) 1992
1 JBo(c),Paranoid 3.00
2 JBo(c),Mood 2.50
3 JBo(c),A Little Bit of Neurosis . . . 2.50
4 . . . . 2.50

TALES OF THE VAMPIRES
Dec., 2003
1 Josh Whedon. 3.00
2 thru 5 . . . . @3.00
TPB 16.00

TALES TO OFFEND
July, 1997
1-shot by Frank Miller 3.00

TANK GIRL
(B&W) 1991
1 Rep. from U.K.Deadline Mag.
   with 2-card strip 4.50
2 V:Indiana Potato Jones 4.00
3 On the Run 4.00
4 . . . . 4.00
TPB colorized. 15.00
[2nd Series] 1993
1 . . . . 3.50
2 thru 4 . . . . @3.00

TARZAN
TPB The Untamed 12.00

TARZAN/JOHN CARTER: WARLORDS OF MARS
1996
1 (of 4) E.R.Burroughs adapt. 3.00
2 thru 4 . . . . @3.00

TARZAN VS. PREDATOR AT THE EARTH'S CORE
1996
1 Tarzan vs. Predator 3.00
2 V:Predator 3.00
3 Tarzan on the Hunt 3.00
4 . . . . 3.00
TPB series rep. 13.00

TENTH, THE: NIGHTWALKER
Apr., 2002
1 (of 4) TnD 3.00
2 thru 4 . . . . @3.00
1a thru 4a variant (c). . . . . @3.00
TPB No Sweets After Dark 10.00

TENTH, THE: RESURRECTED
Apr., 2001
1 TnD 3.00
1a variant(c) 7.00
1b variant(c) signed 20.00
2 TnD 3.00
3 TnD 3.00
3a and 4a variant (c)s . . . . @3.00

---

4 TnD 3.00
TPB Blackout, rep.#1-#5 . . . . 15.00

TERMINAL POINT
(B&W) 1993
1 . . . . 2.50
2 and 3 . . . . @2.50

TERMINATOR
1990
1 CW,Tempest 4.00
2 CW,Tempest 3.00
3 CW. 3.00
4 CW, conclusion 3.00

TERMINATOR
1-shot MW,3-D const(c2,
   pop-up inside (1991) 5.00
Spec. AIG,GyD,GeD(1998) 3.00

The Terminator #2
© *Dark Horse Comics*

TERMINATOR, THE
Sept., 1998
1 AIG,StP. 3.00
2 F:Sarah Connor 3.00
3 F:Killerman. 3.00
4 F:D-800L & D-810X 3.00
TPB Death Valley. 15.00

TERMINATOR, THE: THE DARK YEARS
Sept., 1999
1 (of 4) AIG,MvR,BWi 3.00
2 AIG,MvR,BWi,F:Jon Norden. 3.00
3 . . . . 3.00
4 AIG,MvR,concl. 3.00

TERMINATOR: END GAME
1992
1 JG,Final *Terminator* series 3.00
2 JG,Cont.last Term.story 3.00
3 JG, Concl. 3.00
TPB Endgame 10.00

TERMINATOR: ENEMY WITHIN
1991
1 cont. from Sec.Objectives 4.00
2 C890.L.threat contd. 3.00

---

3 Secrets of Cyberdyne 3.00	
4 Conclusion. 3.00	
SC rep #1–#4. . . . . 14.00	

TERMINATOR: HUNTERS & KILLERS
1992
1 V:Russians. 3.00
2 V:Russians. 3.00
3 V:Russians. 3.00

TERMINATOR: SECONDARY OBJECTIVES
1991
1 cont. 1st DH mini-series 4.00
2 PG,A:New Female Terminator . . . 3.00
3 PG,Terminators in L.A.&Mexico . . 3.00
4 PG,Terminator vs Terminator 3.00

The Territory #1
© *Dark Horse Comics*

TERRITORY, THE
Jan., 1999
1 (of 4) JaD,DvL,F:Ishmael. 3.00
2 thru 4 . . . . @3.00

TEX AVERY'S DROOPY
1 Dr. Droopenstein 2.50
2 and 3 . . . . @2.50

TEX AVERY'S SCREWBALL SQUIRREL
1 I:Screwball Squirrel 2.50
2 Cleaning House. 2.50
3 School of Hard Rocks 2.50

THING, THE
1991
1 JHi, Movie adaptation 4.00
2 JHi, Movie adaptation 3.50

THING FROM ANOTHER WORLD: CLIMATE OF FEAR
1994
1 Argentinian Military Base
 (Bahiathetis) 3.00
2 Thing on Base 3.00

3 Thing/takeover 3.00
4 Conclusion. 3.00
TPR 16.00

THING FROM ANOTHER WORLD: ETERNAL VOWS
1993
1 PG,I:Sgt. Rowan 3.00
2 PG 3.00
3 PG,in New Zealand 3.00
4 PG,Last issue. 3.00

THIRTEEN O'CLOCK
(B&W)
1 Mr.Murmer,from Deadline USA . . 3.00

THE 13th SON
Oct., 2005
1 KJo, Worse Thing Waiting 3.00
2 thru 4 KJo. . . . . @3.00
TPB Worse Thing Waiting 13.00

3 X 3 EYES: CURSE OF THE GESU
(B&W–Manga) 1995
1 I:Pai,Yakumo 3.00
2 thru 5 . . . . @3.00
TPB Curse of the Gesu, by Yuzo
 Takada. 13.00
TPB House of Demons 13.00
TPB 208-pg. 17.00
TPB Blood of the Sacred Demon . 14.00
TPB Summoning the Beast (2002) 15.00
TPB Key to the Sacred Land. 14.00
TPB House of Demons, 2nd ed. . . 15.00
TPB Curse of the Gesu, 2nd ed. . . 15.00
TPB Shadow of the Kunlun 18.00
TPB Vol. 8 Descent of Mystic City. 19.00
TPB Vol. 9 . . . . 13.00

300
May, 1998
1 (of 5) FM & Lynn Varley. 3.00
2 thru 5. . . . . @3.00

TIME COP
1994
1 Movie Adaptation 2.75
2 Movie Adaptation 2.50

TITAN
1994
Spec.#1 BS(c),I:Inhibitors 4.25

TITAN A.E.
May, 2000
1 (of 3) film prequel,pt.1 . . . . 3.00
2 thru 3 prequel,pt.2–pt.3 . . . . . . @3.00

TONGUE*LASH
Aug., 1996
1 by Randy and Jean-Marc
 Lofficier & Dave Taylor 3.00
2 . . . . 3.00

[VOL. II] 1999
1 (of 2) 3.00
2 . . . . 3.00

TONY DANIEL'S F5
May, 2002
TPB Color, 128-pg. 15.00

TONY MILLIONAIRE'S SOCK MONKEY
TPB 10.00
VOL. 3
1 & 2 . . . . @3.00
TPB A Children's Book. 10.00

TOO MUCH COFFEE MAN
(B&W) July, 1997
1-shot by Shannon Wheeler 3.00
TPB Guide for the Perplexed. . . . 11.00
TPB Parade of Tirade 13.00
TPB Amusing Musings. 13.00

TORCH OF LIBERTY
1995
Spec. 2.50

TREKKER
(B&W) 1987
1 thru 4 . . . . @3.00
5 thru 7 . . . . @3.00
8 O:Trekker. 3.00
9 . . . . 3.00
Spec.#1 Sins of the Fathers 3.00

TRIGUN
Nov., 2003
TPB Vol. 1 b&w 15.00
TPB Vol. 2 . . . . 15.00
TPB Trigun Anime Manga 15.00
1-shot Wolfwood (2005). 0.25

TRIGUN MAXIMUM
May, 2004
TPB Vol. 1 The Hero Returns 14.00
TPB Vol. 2 Death Blue. 10.00
TPB Vol. 3 His Live as a 10.00
TPB Vol. 4 thru Vol. 10. . . . . . . @10.00

TRIPLE X
(B&W) 1994
1 . . . . 4.00
2 V:Dr. Zemph. 4.00
3 . . . . 4.00
4 V:Rhine Lords 4.00
5 I:Klaar 4.00
6 Klaar captured 5.00
7 Revolution Consequences. 5.00
TPB by Arnold & Jacob Pander. . . 25.00

TWO FACES OF TOMORROW, THE
(B&W–Manga) Aug., 1997
1 (of 13) from James P. Hogan
 novel, by Yukinobu Hoshino . . . 3.00
2 thru 4 . . . . @3.00
5 thru 13 . . . . @4.00

TWO FISTED TALES
Spec. WW,WiS. 5.00

2112
GN JBy,A:Next Men. 2.50
2nd Printing 5.00
TPB GNv, JBy,A:Next Men 10.00
2nd & 3rd printing 10.00

ULTRAMAN TIGA
Aug., 2003
1 (of 10) 4.00
2 thru 4 . . . . @4.00
5 thru 10 . . . . @4.00
TPB Vol. 1 . . . . 16.00

DARK HORSE

All comics prices listed are for *Near Mint* condition.

[ANDREW VACHSS']
UNDERGROUND
(B&W) 1993
1 AVs(s)............................ 4.25
2 thru 5 AVs(s) .... @4.00

UNIVERSAL MONSTERS
1991
1 AAd,Creature From The
    Black Lagoon............... 5.50
1 Dracula 5.50
1 Frankenstein 5.50
1 The Mummy.................. 5.50
TPB Cavalcade of Horror (2006).. 20.00

URBAN LEGENDS
(B&W) 1993
1-shot........................ 3.00

USAGI YOJIMBO
(B&W) 1996
1 by Stan Sakai................ 7.00
2 thru 9 .... @4.00
10 with Sergio Aragones 6.00
11 'The Lord of Owls'........... 6.00
12 'Vampire Cat of the Geishu' 3.00
13 thru 22 'Grasscutter,',pt.1
    thru pt. #10 .... @3.00
23 My Father's Sword 3.00
24 The Demon Flute 3.00
25 Momo-Usagi-Taro............ 3.00
26 The Hairpin Murders,pt.1 ..... 3.00
27 The Hairpin Murders,pt.2 ..... 3.00
28 Courtesan conspiracy,pt.1 ..... 3.00
29 Courtesan conspiracy,pt.2 ..... 3.00
30 Inspector Ishida mystery....... 3.00
31 The Haunted Inn of Moon
    Shadow Hill 3.00
32 Two stories 3.00
33 .... 3.00
34 Demon Mask,pt.1 .... 3.00
35 Demon Mask,pt.2 .... 3.00
36 Demon Mask,pt.3 .... 3.00
37 F:Sasuke the Demon Queller... 3.00
38 Priest Sanshobo's temple 3.00
39 Grasscutter II,pt.1 .... 3.00
40 V:Captain Quark 3.00
41 V:Neko Ninja................ 3.00
42 Grasscutter II,pt.4 .... 3.00
43 Grasscutter II 3.00
44 Grasscutter II 3.00
45 Grasscutter II 3.00
46 wraparound(c),pt.1 .... 3.00
47 wraparound(c),pt.2 .... 3.00
48 .... 3.00
49 Three seasons 3.00
50 Usagi dead?................. 3.00
51 The Shrouded Moon.......... 3.00
52 Kitsune's youth 3.00
53 hunt for four ronin 3.00
54 Lone Goat and Kid 3.00
55 Lord Yoshikawa is dying 3.00
56 Katsuichi vs. Nakamura Joji 3.00
57 Crows,pt.1, renegade ronin 3.00
58 Crows,pt.2................... 3.00
59 Crows,pt.3................... 3.00
60 duel at Kitanoji 3.00
61 F:Chizu 3.00
62 Cursed woods............... 3.00
63 SS, return of Kitsune 3.00
64 SS, Tomago 3.00
65 SS......................... 3.00
66 SS,giant monsters,pt.1 ...... 3.00
67 SS,giant monsters,pt.2 ...... 3.00
68 SS,giant monsters,pt.3 ...... 3.00
69 SS,Fathers and Sons,pt.1...... 3.00
70 SS,Fathers and Sons,pt.2...... 3.00
71 to 89 SS .... @3.00
TPB Vol. 18 Travels with Jotaro... 16.00
TPB Demon Mask 16.00

Usagi Yojimbo, Vol. 3, #19
© Dark Horse Comics

TPB Shades of Death, rep. of
    Mirage series................ 15.00
TPB Daisho, rep. Mirage 15.00
TPB The Brink of Life & Death ... 15.00
TPB Seasons................. 15.00
TPB Grasscutter 17.00
TPB Grasscutter 17.00
TPB Grey Shadows 15.00
TPB Grasscutter II 16.00
TPB SS, Shrouded Moon, 184-pg.. 16.00
TPB Duel at Kitanoji............ 17.00

USAGI YOJIMBO
1996
1 SS,color spec............... 4.00
2 SS,color spec............... 3.00
3 SS,color spec............... 3.00
4 thru 6 .... @3.00

USAGI YOJIMBO
COLOR SPECIAL:
GREEN PERSIMMON
1-shot by Stan Sakai 3.00

VAMPIRELLA
(B&W) 1992
1 'The Lion and the Lizard'Pt.1.... 4.50
2 'The Lion and the Lizard'Pt.2.... 4.00
3 'The Lion and the Lizard'Pt.3.... 4.00
4 'The Lion and the Lizard'Pt.3.... 4.00
Spec. Vampirella's Summer Night .. 4.00

VAN HELSING
May, 2004
1-shot Movie tie-in 3.00

VENUS WARS
(B&W–Manga) 1991
1 Aphrodia V:Ishtar, with
    2-card strip 3.00
2 I: Ken Seno 2.50
3 Aphrodia V:Ishtar............ 2.50
4 Seno Joins Hound Corps....... 2.50
5 SenoV:Octopus Supertanks 2.50
6 Chaos in Aphrodia 2.50
7 All Out Ground War 2.50
8 Ishtar V:Aphrodia contd. 2.50
9 Ishtar V:Aphrodia contd. 2.50
10 Supertanks of Ishtar Advance... 2.50
11 Aphrodia Captured 2.50

12 A:Miranda,48-pg............. 2.75
13 Hound Brigade-Suicide Assault . 2.50
14 V:Army 2.50
15 .... 2.50
TPB Vol. 1 .... 14.00

VENUS WARS II
1992
1 V:Security Police 2.75
2 Political Unrest............... 2.50
3 Conspiracy.................. 2.50
4 A:Lupica.................... 2.50
5 Love Hotel 2.50
6 Terran Consulate............. 2.50
7 Doublecross................. 2.50
8 D:Lupisa.................... 3.00
9 A:Matthew 3.00
10 A:Mad Scientist............. 3.00
11 thru 15 V:Troopers......... @3.00

VERSION
(B&W–Manga) 1993
1.1 by Hisashi Sakaguchi........ 2.50
1.2 thru 1.8 .... @2.50

VERSION II
(B&W–Manga) 1993
2.1 by Hisashi Sakaguchi........ 2.50
2.2 thru 2.7 .... @2.50

VIOLENT CASES
Oct., 2003
TPB NGa,DMc................ 15.00

VIRUS
1993
1 MP(c),F:The Wan Xuan & the
    crew of the Electra 3.00
2 MP(c),V:Captian Powell........ 3.00
3 MP(c),V:Virus................ 3.00
4 MP(c),Last issue 3.00
TPB rep.#1–#4................ 17.00

VORTEX, THE
1 .... 2.50

WACKY SQUIRREL
(B&W) 1987
1 .... 2.75
2 thru 4 .... @2.75
Spec. Halloween Adventure....... 2.75
Spec. Summer Fun 2.75

WALTER:
CAMPAIGN OF TERROR
1996
1 .... 2.50
2 thru 4 .... @2.50

WARRIOR OF
WAVERLY STREET, THE
Nov., 1996
1 (of 2) by M.Coto & J. Stokes 3.00
2 .... 3.00
1-shot Broodstorm............. 3.00

WARWORLD!
(B&W) 1989
1 .... 3.00

WHAT'S MICHAEL?
(B&W–Manga)
TPB by Makoto Kobayashi 6.00
TPB Living Together 6.00
TPB Off the Deep End........... 6.00
TPB A Hard Day's Life (2002) 9.00

DARK HORSE

TPB Show Time 9.00
TPB Fat Cat in the City 9.00

WHITE LIKE SHE
(B&W) 1994
1 by Bob Fingerman 3.00
2 thru 4 . . . . @3.00

WHO WANTS TO BE A SUPERHERO?
Oct., 2006
1 Feedback 3.50

WILL EISNER'S HAWKS OF THE SEAS
July, 2003
TPB b&w 20.00

Will To Power #9
© Dark Horse Comics

WILL TO POWER
Comics' Greatest World, 1994
1 BS, A:X 2.50
2 BS, A:X,Monster 2.50
3 BS, A:X 2.50
4 BS, In Steel Harbor 2.50
5 V:Wolfgang 2.50
6 V:Motorhead 2.50
7 JOy(c),V:Amazing Grace 2.50
8 V:Catalyst 2.50
9 Titan, Grace 2.50
10 Vortex alien, Grace 2.50
11 Vortex alien, King Titan 2.50
12 Vortex alien 2.50

WITCHBLADE/ALIENS/ DARKNESS/PREDATOR: MINDHUNTER
Dec., 2000
1 thru 3 . . . . @3.00
2a variant TnD (c) 3.00
TPB 96-pg 13.00

WIZARD OF FOURTH STREET
(B&W) 1987
1 . . . . 3.00
2 thru 4 . . . . @2.50

WOLF & RED
1995
1 Looney Tunes 2.50
2 Watchdog Wolf 2.50
3 Red Hot Riding Hood 2.50

WOLVERTON IN SPACE
(B&W) Apr., 1997
TPB by Basil Wolverton 17.00

WORLD BELOW, THE
Mar., 1999
1 thru 4 PC . . . . @2.50

WORLD BELOW II, THE
Dec., 1999
1 (of 4) PC 3.00
2 thru PC,Deeper and Stranger . . . 3.00

X
Comics' Greatest World, 1994
1 B:StG(s),DoM,JP,I:X-Killer 3.00
2 DoM,JP,V:X-Killer 2.50
3 DoM,JP,A:Pit Bulls 2.50
4 DoM,JP 2.50
5 DoM,JP,V:Chaos Riders 2.50
6 Cyberassassins 2.50
7 Alamout 2.50
8 A:Ghost 2.50
9 War for Arcadia 2.50
10 War for Arcadia 2.50
11 I:Coffin, War 2.50
12 V:Coffin, A:Monster 2.50
13 D:X 2.50
14 conclusion to War 2.50
15 JS,SiG,war survivors 2.50
16 V:Headhunter 2.50
17 . . . . 2.50
18 V:Predator 2.50
19 V:Challenge 2.50
20 thru 25 . . . . @2.50
Spec. #1 One Shot to the Head . . . 2.50

XENA: WARRIOR PRINCESS
Aug., 1999
1 . . . . 3.00
2 thru 9 . . . . @3.00
10 IEd,MD2,wayward viking 3.00
11 IEd,MD2,V:Lamia 3.00
12 IEd,MD2,Darkness Falls,concl . . 3.00
13 IEd,MD2,F:Legion 3.00
14 conclusion 3.00
1 to 14 newsstand photo(c) . . . . . @3.00
TPB Slave 10.00
TPB The Warrior Way of Death . . . 10.00
TPB Blood and Shadows 12.00

XENOXOIC TALES
Apr., 2003
TPB Vol. 1 rep 15.00
TPB Vol. 2 rep 15.00

YOUNG CYNICS CLUB
(B&W) 1993
1 by Glenn Wong 2.50

THE YOUNG INDIANA JONES CHRONICLES
1992
1 DBa,FS,TV Movie Adapt 3.25
2 DBa,TV Movie Adapt 2.75
3 DBa,GM 2.75
4 DBa,GM 2.75
5 DBa,GM 2.75
6 BBa,GM,WW1,French Army 2.75

7 The Congo 2.75
8 Africa,A:A.Schweitzer 2.50
9 Vienna,Sophie-daughter of Arch-
   Duke Ferdinand 2.50
10 In Vienna continued 2.50
11 Far East 2.50
12 Fever Issue 2.50

YOU'RE UNDER ARREST!
(B&W–Manga) 1995–96
1 by Kosuke Fujishima 3.00
2 thru 8 . . . . @3.00
TPB rep 13.00

ZOMBIEWORLD:
1-shot Eat Your Heart Out, KJo 3.00
1-shot Home for the Holidays 3.00

ZOMBIEWORLD: CHAMPION OF THE WORMS
Sept., 1997
1 (of 3) MMi 3.00
2 and 3 . . . . @3.00
Spec. Home for the Holidays 3.00
TPB 9.00

ZOMBIEWORLD: DEAD END
Jan., 1998
1 (of 2) by Stephen Blue 3.00
2 . . . . 3.00

Zombie World: Tree of Death #3
© Dark Horse Comics

ZOMBIEWORLD: THE TREE OF DEATH
May, 1999
1 (of 4) by P. Mills & J.Deadstock . . 3.00
2 thru 4 . . . . @3.00

ZOMBIEWORLD: WINTER'S DREGS
May, 1998
1 (of 4) by Fingerman & Edwards . . 3.00
2 thru 4 . . . . @3.00

ZONE, THE
(B&W) 1990
1-shot 3.00

DARK HORSE

IMAGE

AARON STRIPS
(B&W) Apr., 1997
1 thru 4 rep. from Sunday comic
strips, by Aaron Warner . . . . . @3.00

ACTION PLANET
(B&W) Sept., 1997
Prev. Action Planet Comics
3 . . . . 4.00

ADRENALYNN
Aug., 1999
1 F:Sabina Nikoli. 2.50
2 TnD,V:Russian monster androids 2.50
3 TnD,V:last 2 Monster-cyborgs . . . 2.50
4 TnD,the real Sabina. 2.50

ADVENTURES OF AARON
(B&W) March, 1997
by Aaron Warner
1 'Baby-sitter Gone Bad'. 3.00
2 'Thunder Thighs of the
Terrordome' 3.00
3 'Baby-sitter Gone Bad,' concl. . . . 3.00
100 Super Special 3.00
Christmas Spectacular #1 . . . . 3.00

ADVENTURES OF BARRY WEEN, BOY GENIUS, THE
(B&W) March, 1999
1 (of 3) by Judd Winick 3.00
2 Growing Pains 3.00
3 School 3.00

ADVENTURE STRIP DIGEST
(B&W) April, 1998
1 by Randy Reynaldo 3.00
2 F:Rob Hanes, detective 3.00

AGENTS, THE
(B&W) April, 2003
1 thru 6 BDn . . . . @3.00

AGE OF BRONZE
(B&W) Nov., 1998
1 EiS,The Trojan War 3.00
2 EiS,Death of Paris 3.00
3 EiS,F:Herakles, Hektor 3.00
4 EiS,I:Helen. 3.00
5 EiS,Achilles disguised 3.00
6 EiS,Helen gone 3.50
7 EiS,Odysseus mad? 3.50
8 EiS,Achilles missing. 3.50
9 EiS,Will war start? 3.50
10 EiS,Sacrifice,pt.1. . . . . 3.50
11 EiS,Sacrifice,pt.2. . . . . 3.50
12 EiS,You're not the Trojans? . . . 3.50
13 thru 18 EiS,Sacrifice,pt.4–pt.9 @3.50
19 EiS,Sacrifice,pt.10. . . . . 3.50
20 Betrayal, pt.1. . . . . 3.50
21 Betrayal, pt 2. . . . . 3.50
22 Betrayal, pt.3. . . . . 3.50
23 Betrayal, pt.4. . . . . 3.50
Spec.1-shot Behind the Scenes . . . 3.50
Spec.#1 EiS, House of Horror 3.50
Spec.#2 . . . . 3.00
TPB Vol. 1 A Thousand Ships 20.00
TPB Vol. 2 Sacrifice. 20.00

AGE OF HEROES, THE
(B&W) Halloween, 1996
1 JHI & JRy. 3.00
2 JHI & JRy. 3.00
3 JHI & JRy,Luko,Trickster &
Aerwyn try to steal treasure . . . 3.00
4 JHI & JRy,Drake, the blind
swordsman returns 3.00
5 JHI & JRy,O:Conor One-Arm. . . . 3.00
Spec. #1 rep. #1 & #2 . . . . 5.00
Spec. #2 rep. #3 & #4 . . . . 7.00

AGE OF HEROES: WEX
(B&W) Aug., 1998
1 by JHI,Vurtex 3.00

AGENCY, THE
Top Cow, July, 2001
1 (of 6) PJe. 4.00
1a variant(c) 4.00
1b variant MS(c) 4.00
2 PJe. 2.50
3 PJe. 2.50
4 PJe,A Virtual Secret. 3.00
5 PJe,Virtual 3.00
6 PJe,concl. 48-pg. 5.00

ALLEGRA
WildStorm, 1996
1 ScC,SSe 2.50
2 thru 4 . . . . @2.50

ALLEY CAT
July, 1999
1 BNa,MHw,F:Alley Baggett 2.50
1a variant painted cover (1:4). 3.50
2 BNa,MHw,women murdered 2.50
3 photo(c) 2.50
3a variant JJu cover (1:4). 2.50
4 into darkness 2.50
5 The Martyr,pt.1 . . . . 3.00
6 The Martyr,pt.2. . . . . 3.00
7 The Martyr,pt.3. . . . . 2.50
Wizard World Spec.#1 . . . . 2.50
Lingerie Edition 5.00

The Alliance #1 © Image

ALLIANCE, THE
Shadowline, 1995
1 JV,I:The Alliance, A Call
to Arms 2.50
2 JV,Team comes together 'Like
Pieces of a Puzzle' 2.50
3 I:Slash C 2.50
4 . . . . 2.50
1a thru 4a variant covers . . . . . . @2.50

ALLIES, THE
Extreme, 1995
1 mini-series 2.50
2 thru 4 . . . . @2.50

ALONE IN THE DARK
July, 2002
GN 1-shot, 48-pg. 5.00

ALTERATION
Feb., 2004
1 . . . . 3.00
1a variant (c) AAd 3.00
2 thru 4 . . . . @3.00
2a thru 4a variant (c)s . . . . @3.00

ALTERED IMAGE
April, 1998
1 JV,The Day Reality Went Wild. . . 2.50
2 JV,F:Everybody smooshed 2.50
3 JV,Middle Age Crisis, concl. 2.50
TPB F:everybody 10.00

AMANDA AND GUNN
(B&W) April, 1997
1 JeR, Montana 2036 . . . . 3.00
2 (of 4) JeR. 3.00
3 (of 4) JeR. 3.00
4 (of 4) JeR, conclusion 3.00

AMAZING JOY BUZZARDS, THE
(B&W) Dec., 2004
1 I was a Teenage Monster 3.00
2 The Island of Maru. 3.00
3 ...Go Hollywood 3.00
4 ...Go Hollywood,pt.2 . . . . 3.00
5 Ready...Set...Ignition 3.00
6 Here Come the Spiders, pt.2 . . . . 3.00
7 Go, El Campeon, Go, pt.1 . . . . . . 3.00
TPB Vol. 1, rep. #1–#4 . . . . 12.00
Vol. 2, 2005
1 Here Come the Spiders, pt.1 . . . . 3.00
2 thru 5 . . . . @3.00
TPB Vol. 2, rep. #1 – #5 . . . . 13.00

AMERICAN FLAGG
Nov., 2004
TPB #1 HC, re 20.00
TPB #2 HC. 20.00

ANGELA
TMP, 1994–95
1 NGa(s),GCa,A:Spawn 15.00
2 NGa(s),GCa,Angela's trial 14.00
3 NGa(s),GCa,In Hell 12.00
Spec. Pirate Spawn(c) 32.00
Spec. Pirate Angela(c) (1995) 30.00
TPB Rep.#1–#3 . . . . 10.00

All comics prices listed are for *Near Mint* condition.

ANGELA/GLORY: RAGE OF ANGELS
TMP/Extreme, 1996
1 x-over begins 5.00

ANT
Aug., 2005
1 . . . . 3.00
2 . . . . 3.00
3 A:Spawn 3.00
4 . . . . 3.00
5 thru 9 Moving On . . . . @3.00
10 . . . . 3.00
11 . . . . 3.00
TPB Reality Bites 13.00

APHRODITE IX
Top Cow, Aug., 2000
1 by David Finch 4.00
1a variant JBz(c) 4.00
1a signed 20.00
1b variant Michale Turner(c) 4.00
1c variant MS(c) 4.00
2 amnesia 3.50
3 conspiracy 3.50
0 with pin-up & poster 3.00
4 Who is she? 48-pg. 5.50
Spec.1 Convention spec., signed . 20.00
Preview ed., signed 5.00
TPB 15.00

ARCANUM
Top Cow, March, 1997
[Mini-series]
1 BPe, from Medieval
Spawn/Witchblade 3.00
1a variant MS(s) (1:4) 2.50
2 BPe, Chi in Asylum 2.50
3 BPe, Ming Chang captive in
Atlantis 2.50
4 BPe,'The End?' 2.50
5 BPe,Royale's secret journal 2.50
6 BPe,Safe Haven? 2.50
7 BPe,Egypt 2.50
TPB BPe 17.00

AREA 52
Jan., 2001
1 . . . . 3.00
2 The Gloves are off 3.00
3 Out of the Frying Pan and
into the Fire 3.00
4 Beginning of the End 3.00

ARIA
Avalon, Nov., 1998
1 by Brian Holguin & Jay Anacleto . 7.00
1a variant cover 8.00
2 A:Mad Gwynnion 3.00
3 English Countryside 3.00
4 V:Dark One 3.00
4a glow-in-the-dark(c) 12.00
5 London, 1966. . . . . 3.00
6 Subterranean Homesick Blues . . 3.00
7 Mad Gods and Irish Men 3.00
Preview ed. F:Kildare 3.00
Spec.#1 Blanc & Noir, sketchbook. . 3.00
Spec.#1 alternate cover 7.00
Spec.#2 Blanc & Noir 2.50
Sketchbook by Jay Anacleto 6.00
TPB The Magic of Aria 14.00
Coll.Ed.#1, rep.#1–#2 . . . . 6.00

ARIA/ANGELA: HEAVENLY CREATURES
Feb., 2000
1 (of 2) x-over 5.00

1a variant JQ(c) (1:4) 3.00
1b variant J.G. Jones(c) (1:4) 4.00
1c variant Jay Anacleto(c) (1:4) . . . 3.00
1 B&W 3.00
2 x-over concl. 3.00
2a variant(c) 3.00
Museum edition 125.00

ARIA: THE SOUL MARKET
March, 2001
1 Legend continues 4.00
1a Museum edition 125.00
2 F:Robin Goodfellow 3.00
3 A Dark Rider Approaches 3.00
4 Auction of imprisoned souls 3.00
5 What price a soul? 3.00
6 Mortality 3.00
GN A Midwinter's Dream,40-pg. . . . 5.00
TPB 17.00

ARIA: A SUMMER SPELL
March, 2002
1 (of 2) London, summer 1967 . . . . 3.00
2 Kildare is in love 3.00

ARIA: THE USES OF ENCHANTMENT
Feb., 2003
1 thru 4 . . . . @3.00
TPB 17.00

ARKAGA
Sept., 1997
1 by Arnie Tang Jorgensen 3.00
2 Desire for revenge 3.00

ARMOR X
Mar., 2005
1 ASm 3.00
2 ASm 3.00
3 ASm 3.00
4 ASm, The End 3.00

ART OF ERIK LARSEN
1 Sketchbook 5.00

ART OF HOMAGE STUDIOS
1 Various Pin-ups 5.00

ART OF JAY ANACLETO
1-shot 48-pg. 6.00

ASCEND
Dec., 2004
TPB 15.00

ASCENSION
Top Cow, Sept., 1997
1 by David Finch,F:Angels 4.00
2 Andromeda fights alone 3.00
3 reunited with Lucien 3.00
4 . . . . 3.00
5 Gregorieff and Dayak Army 3.00
6 Voivodul returns, concl. 3.00
7 Andy's problems worsen 2.50
8 revenge on Dayaks & Mineans . . 2.50
9 Andy exiled 2.50
10 A:D. Gavin Taylor 2.50
11 A:D. Gavin Taylor 2.50
12 A:turning point 2.50
13 A:Grigorieff, Petra 2.50
14 V:Marcus,A:Andromeda 2.50
15 Rowena's secrets 2.50
16 Petra joins Lucien 2.50
17 a schism 2.50
18 V:new entity 2.50

Ascension #3 © Top Cow

19 to Petra's Minean home 2.50
20 Resurrection,pt.1. . . . . 2.50
21 Resurrection,pt.2. . . . . 2.50
22 trapped 3.00
23 Andromeda's new outfit 3.00
Coll.Ed.#1, rep.#1–#2 . . . . 5.00
Coll.Ed.#2 . . . . 5.00

ASTOUNDING SPACE THRILLS
April, 2000
1 Ken Kelly(c),Cydonian Contant . . 3.00
2 The Criminal Code 3.00
3 Gordo:Earthling Prime,
flip-book 3.00
4 The Craving of Consumorr,
flip-book 3.00
5 Attack of the Macrobes 3.00

ASTRO
April, 2006
1 . . . . 7.00

ATHEIST, THE
(B&W) Feb., 2005
1 PhH,Incarnate 3.50
2 PhH,Incarnate,pt.2: The Tumor . . 3.50
3 PhH,Incarnate,pt.3: Desperate
Measures 3.50
4 PhH,Incarnate, pt.4: Sacrifice . . . 3.50

ATHENA INC.
2002
1-shot Agents Roster,48-pg. 6.00
The Beginning, 48-pg. 6.00
1 reoffered 3.00
2 Gwen has a stalker 3.00
2a variant(c) 3.00
3 Gwen hearing voices 3.00
3a variant(c) 3.00
4 Revelations 3.00
4a variant(c) 3.00
5 The Belly of the Beast 3.00
6 All Hell Breaks Loose 3.00
5a– a variant (c) . . . . @3.00
TPB Vol. 1 Manhunter Project 20.00

ATOMIC TOYBOX
April, 1999
Odyssey Line
1 AaL,F:Ken Logan 3.00
2 AaL,The Aliens are comming 3.00

AUTOMATION
Flypaper, 1998
1 Robots sent to Mars, and back . . 3.00
2 One goes mad. 3.00
3 Sherzad vs. Konak 3.00
TPB rep. #1–#3 . . . . 13.00

AVIGON
(B&W) Oct., 2000
Spec. 56-pg. 6.00
GN 6.00
GN Gods and Demons (2005). . . . 20.00

THE AWAKENING
(B&W) Oct., 1997
1 (of 4) by Stephen Blue. 3.00
2 thru 4 . . . . @3.00
TPB rep. #1–#4 . . . . 10.00

BACKLASH
WildStorm, 1994–97
1 Taboo, 2 diff. covers 4.00
1a variant edition, 2 covers. 3.00
2 Savage Dragon 2.50
3 V:Savage Dragon 2.50
4 SRf,A:Wetworks. 2.50
5 SRf,A:Dane 2.50
6 BBh, SRf,A:Wetworks. 2.50
7 BBh,SRf,V:Bounty Hunters 2.50
8 RMz,BBh,BWS(c),WildStorm
   Rising,pt.8,w/2 cards. 2.50
8a Newsstand ed. 2.50
9 F:Taboo,Dingo,V:Chasers 2.50
10 I:Crimson. 2.50
11 R:Bloodmoon 2.50
12 R:Taboo,Crimson's Costume . . . 3.00
13 Taboo to the Rescue. 2.50
14 A:Deathblow 2.50
15 F:Cyberjack. 2.50
16 F:Cole,Marc 2.50
17 F:Marc,Kink. 2.50
18. . . . . 2.50
19 Fire From Heaven,pt.2 . . . . 2.50
20 SRf,BBh,Fire From
   Heaven,pt.10 . . . . 2.50
21 SRf,BBh 2.50
22 SRf,BBh 2.50
23 SRf,BBh 2.50
24 SRf,BBh,return of Dingo 2.50
25 SRf,BBh,56-pg.. special 4.00
26 SRf,BBh,IR:Gramalkin 2.50
27 SRf,BBh 2.50
28 SRf,BBh,Backlash leads PSI
   team to Europe 2.50
29 SRf,BBh,Haroth raises the
   remnants of Atlantis. 2.50
30 SRf,BBh,Backlash confronts
   Kherubim lords 2.50
31 SRf,BBh,team returns to PSI . . . 2.50
32 SRf,BBh,earth-shattering
   final issue 2.50
TPB Backlash/Spider-Man, Webs &
   Whips, x-over. 5.00
TPB The Drahn War, rep.#27–#32 15.00

BACKLASH/SPIDER-MAN
WildStorm/Marvel, 1996
1 x-over,pt.1 . . . . 2.50
1a variant cover 3.00
2 x-over,pt.2 . . . . 2.50

BADGER
(B&W) May, 1997
1 MBn,'Betelgeuse'. 3.00
2 MBn,'Beefalo don't like fences' . . 3.00
3 MBn,'Loose Eel'. 3.00
4 MBn,'Hot House' 3.00
5 MBn,Octopi in the hot tub 3.00

6 MBn,Prime Minister of
   Klactoveedesteen 3.00
7 MBn,Crime Comics 3.00
8 MBn,Root. 3.00
9 MBn 3.00
10 MBn,Tuesday Ruby 3.00
11 MBn,Watch the Skies 3.00
12 MBn,The Lady Cobras 3.00
13 MBn,Horse Police. 3.00
14 MBn,Badger Sells Out 3.00

BAD IDEAS
Apr., 2004
1 (of 2) 48-pg. 6.00
2 48-pg. 6.00
TPB 13.00

BAD PLANET
Dec., 2005
1 (of 6) 3.00
2 Alien Death Spiders 3.00
3 Super-Terror 3D 3.50

BADROCK
Extreme, 1995
1a RLd(p),TM(c),A:Dragon 2.50
1b SPa(ic),A:Savage Dragon 2.50
1c DF(ic) 2.50
2 RLd,ErS(s),V:Girth,A:Savage
   Dragon, flip-book-Grifter/
   Badrock #2 . . . . 2.50
3 RLd,ErS,V:The Overlord 2.50
Ann.#1 I:Gunner, 48-pg. 3.00
Super-Spec. #1 A:Grifter & The
   Dragon. 2.50

Badrock and Company #4
© Image

BADROCK
AND COMPANY
Extreme, 1994–95
1 KG(s). 2.50
1a San Diego Comic Con ed. 3.00
2 RLd(c),Fuji 2.50
3 Overtkill,'Overt Operations' 2.50
4 TBm,MBm,TNu,A:Velocity 2.50
5 A:Grifter 2.50
6 Finale,A:ShadowHawk. 2.50

BALLISTIC
Top Cow, 1995
1 F:Wetworks 3.00

2 F:Wetworks,Jesters
   Transformation 3.00
3 F:Wetworks,final issue. 3.00

BALLISTIC ACTION
Top Cow, 1996
1 MSi(c), pin-ups. 3.00

BALLISTIC IMAGERY
Top Cow, 1995
1 F:Hellcop,Heavy Space,
   Cyberforce,anthology 3.00

BALLISTIC/WOLVERINE
Top Cow/Marvel, 1996
1 Devil's Reign,pt.4,x-over 4.00

BANISHED KNIGHTS
Dec., 2001
1 vampire civil war 3.00
1A variant(c) 3.00
1B holofoil(c). 5.00
2 F:Greyson & Belmiro 3.00
TPB Vol. 1 Samurai Noir 13.00

BASTARD SAMURAI
April, 2002
1 (of 3) 3.00
2 thru 3 F:Toshi . . . . @3.00

BATTLESTONE
Extreme, 1994
1 RLd,ErS,MMy,AV 2.50
1a variant cover 3.00
2 RLd,ErS,MMy,AV,I&D:Roarke,
   finale 2.50

BATTLE CHASERS
Cliffhanger, April, 1998
1 JMd, fantasy, team-up 9.00
1a Chromium ed. (5,000 made) . . 46.00
2 JMd,F:Gully 5.00
3 JMd,new ally 4.00
4 JMd,Red Monika 4.00
4a,b,c JMd variant covers. . . . . . @3.00
5 JMd,V:Lord August,with 8-pg.
   Planetary #0 . . . . 3.00
6 JMd 3.00
6a variant AWa(c). 4.00
WildStorm/DC, Nov., 2000
7 JMd(c)(1:2) 3.00
7a variant JSC(c) (1:4) 4.00
7b variant HuR(c) (1:4). 7.00
8 JMd,V:Harvester 3.00
TPB Coll.Ed.#1, rep.#1 & #2 . . . . . 6.00
TPB Coll.Ed #2 . . . . 6.00
TPB A Gathering of Heroes 15.00
Prelude #1, JMd, 16-pg. 10.00

BATTLE HYMN
Dec., 2004
1 (of 5) 3.00
2 thru 5 . . . . @3.00
TPB rep. #1 thru #5. . . . . 15.00

BATTLE OF THE PLANETS
Top Cow, July, 2002
1 AxR 3.00
1a-c variant(c)s . . . . @3.00
1d convention(c) 3.00
1e holofoil edition 6.00
2 AxR,attack on earth begins 3.00
3 AxR,The Firey Phoenix 3.00
4 Zoltar 3.00
5 Spectra connected to suicides. . . 3.00
6 Under A Blood Red Sky,pt.1 . . . . 3.00
7 Under A Blood Red Sky,pt.2 . . . . 3.00

IMAGE

8 Under A Blood Red Sky,pt.3 . . . . 3.00	
9 Under A Blood Red Sky,pt.4 . . . . 3.00	
10 Aftermath. 3.00	
11 Second Encounters. 3.00	
12 concl., 48-pg. 5.00	
1-shot flip-book Thundercats 5.00	
1-shot Mark 3.00	
1-shot Battle Book 5.00	
1-shot Hell, 48-pg. 5.00	
2 animation (c) 5.00	
1/2 reprint. 3.00	
TPB Destroy All Monsters 20.00	
TPB Trial by Fire 8.00	
TPB Blood Red Sky 17.00	
TPB Digest Trial by Fire. 10.00	
TPB Digest Destroy All Monsters . 10.00	

BATTLE OF THE PLANETS: COUP DE GRAS
Top Cow, June, 2005
1 (of 2) 3.00

BATTLE OF THE PLANETS: MANGA
Top Cow, Oct., 2003
1 . . . . 3.00
2 . . . . 3.00
3 finale 3.00

BATTLE OF THE PLANETS: PRINCESS
Top Cow, 2004
1 (of 6) 3.00
2 thru 6 Princess, pt.2–pt.6. . . . . @3.00
TPB 10.00

BATTLE OF THE PLANETS: WITCHBLADE
Top Cow, Jan., 2003
1 48-pg.. 7.00

BATTLE POPE
June, 2005
1 . . . . 3.00
2 The Zombie Twins 3.00
3 . . . . 3.00
4 . . . . 3.00
5 . . . . 3.00
6 . . . . 3.00
7 Hellcorp in Shambles. 3.00
8 V:Brenda 3.00
9 New Home. 3.00
10 Celebrity Status. 3.00
11 48-pg. 5.00
12 . . . . 3.50
13 . . . . 3.00
TPB Vol. 1 Genesis 13.00
TPB Vol. 2 Mayhem. 13.00

BEDLAM
July, 2006
1-shot 48-page. 5.00

BEETLEBORGS
Extreme, Nov., 1996
1 from TV show 2.50

BERZERKERS
Extreme, 1995
1 F:Greylore,Hatchet,Psi-Storm,
  Cross,Wildmane,Youngblood#2 2.50
2 Into the Darkness 2.50
3 Slay Ride 2.50
4 final issue. 2.50

Berzerkers #3
© Image

BEST OF MICHAEL TURNER
Top Cow, Dec., 2005
TPB 25.00

BEYOND AVALON
Jan., 2005
1 Wanderlust, pt.1. . . . . 3.00
2 Wanderlust, pt.2 . . . . 3.50
3 . . . . 3.50

BIG BANG COMICS
Big Bang Studios, 1996
(B&W) Prev.: Caliber
1 F:Mighty Man. 2.50
2 Silver Age Shadowhawk 2.50
3 . . . . 2.50
4 . . . . 3.00
5 Top Secret Origins 3.00
6 Round Table of America and
  Knights of Justice meet, orig.
  mini-series #3 (color). 3.00
7 . . . . 3.00
8 F:Mister U.S. 3.00
9 I:Peter Chefren 3.00
10 F:Galahad 3.00
11 Faulty Towers is destroying
  Midway City 3.00
12 F:The Savage Dragon 3.00
13 by Jeff Weigel, 40-pg.spec. . . . 3.00
14 RB,A:The Savage Dragon 3.00
15 SBi(c),F:Dr. Weird 3.00
16 F:Thunder Girl. 3.00
17 . . . . 3.00
18 Savage Dragon on Trial 3.00
19 O:Beacon,Hummingbird 3.00
20 F:Knight Watchman,Blitz. 3.00
21 F:Shadow Lady. 3.00
22 The Bird-Man of Midway City . . 3.00
23 Riddle of the Sphinx, sequel. . . 3.00
24 History of Big Bang,Vol.1 . . . . . 4.00
25 Anniv. iss. 4.00
26 Murder by Microphone, concl. . . 3.00
27 History of Big Bang,Vol.2 . . . . . 4.00
28 Knight of the Living Dead,pt.1 . . 4.00
29 Knight of the Living Dead,pt.2 . . 4.00
30 F:Knight Watchman 4.00
31 F:Knight-Sprite 4.00
32 F:Pink Flamingo 4.00
33 Peril of Parallel Planets 4.00
34 To Save the Gods 4.00

35 Big Bang vs. 1963 . . . . 4.00	
Giant Sz. Ann.#1 Ultiman. 5.00	
TPB rep. 1994 mini-series 11.00	
Summer Spec.b&w, 48-pg. (2003). . 5.00	
1-shot Round Table of America 3.00	

BIG BANG PRESENTS: ULTIMAN FAMILY
Mar., 2005
1-shot F:The Ultimate Ape 3.50

BIG BRUISERS
WildStorm, 1996
1 F:Maul,Impact,Badrock 3.50

BIG HAIR PRODUCTIONS
(B&W) Feb., 2000
1 by Andy Suriano,F:Astro-Bug . . . 3.50
2 . . . . 3.50

BLACK AND WHITE
Hack Studios, 1996
1 ATi,New heroes,'Beginnings' 2.50
2 ATi(p),apparent death 2.50
3 V:Chang. 2.50
Ashcan. 5.00

BLACK ANVIL
Top Cow, 1996
1 & 2. . . . . 2.50

BLACK FLAG
Extreme, 1994
1 B&W Preview. 3.00

BLACK FOREST, THE
Mar., 2004
GN 10.00
GN Book 2 The Castle of Shadows. 7.00

BLACKLIGHT
June, 2005
1 JV 3.00
2 . . . . 3.00
3 Light From A Dead Star 3.00
4 Suffer not a corpse to live, x-over 3.00

BLACK OPS
WildStorm, 1996
1 thru 5 . . . . @2.50
TPB, rep.#1–#5 . . . . 15.00

BLACK TIDE
Nov., 2001
1 . . . . 3.00
1a variant(c) 3.00
1b variant(c) 3.00
2 Balance of Power 3.50
3 One Man's Enemy 3.50
4 Deception, Secrets and Lies 3.50

BLAIR WITCH: DARK TESTAMENTS
Oct., 2000
Spec. IEd,CAd 3.00

BLINDSIDE
Extreme, Aug., 1996
1 MMy & AV, F:Nucgaek Jeno 2.50
2 MMy & AV, Origin continues 2.50

BLISS ALLEY
(B&W) July, 1997
1 BML. 3.00

2 BML,F:Wizard Walker 3.00
3 BML,Inky-Dinks 3.00

BLOKHEDZ
Nov., 2003
1 (of 4) 3.00
2 . . . . 3.00
Street Legends, 2004
3 thru 4 . . . . 3.00

BLOODHUNTER
Extreme, Nov., 1996
1 RV, Cabbot Stone rises from the
    slab 3.00

BLOOD LEGACY
Top Cow, April, 2000
1 MHw,The Story of Ryan. 2.50
1a variant Keu Cha(c). 2.50
1b variant Mike Turner(c) 2.50
2 thru 4 MHw, F:Dr. Ryerson . . . @2.50
1-shot The Young Ones (2003) 4.00

BLOODPOOL
Exteme, 1995
1 I:Seoul,Rubbe,Wylder,
    'Discharged'. 2.50
1a variant cover 2.50
2 The Hills Are Alive 2.50
3 Walk Like an Egyptian 2.50
4 final issue. 2.50
TPB Rep. #1-#4. . . . . 13.00
[Regular Series] 1996
1 thru 3 JDy. . . . . @2.50

BLOODSTREAM
Jan., 2004
1 (of 4) 3.00
2 of 4 . . . . @3.00

BLOODSTRIKE
Extreme, 1993
1 A:Brigade,Rub the Blood(c)
    Blood Brother prelude,x-over . . 3.50
2 I:Lethal,V:Brigade,BloodBrothers,
    pt.2,B:BU:Knight 3.00
3 B:ErS(s),ATi(c),V:Coldsnap,Blood
    Brothers,pt.4,'Turning Point' . . . 3.00
4 ErS(s). 3.00
5 KG,I:Noble,A:Supreme. 3.00
6 KG(s),CAx,C&J:Chapel,'Inside
    Project:Born Again' 3.00
7 KG,RHe,A:Badrock,'Changing
    of the Guard' 3.00
8 RHe,A:Spawn,Sleeping & Waking 3.00
9 RHe,Extreme Prejudice,pt.3,
    I:Extreme Warrior,ATh,BU: Black
    & White 3.00
10 Extreme Prejudice,pt.7,
    V:Brigade, B:BU:Knight 3.00
25 I:Cabbot Bloodstrike. 3.00
11 ErS(s),ATi(c),V:Coldsnap 3.00
12 ErS(s) 3.00
13 KG,A:Supreme,'BetterOffDead'. . 3.00
14 KG(s),CAx,C&J:Chapel. 3.00
15 KG,RHe,A:Badrock,War Games,
    pt.1,Extreme Sacrifice begins . . 3.00
16 KG,RHe,War Games,pt.3,Extreme
    Sacrifice ignites 3.00
17 KIA,V:The Horde 3.00
18 ExtremeSacrifice,pt.3,x-over. . . . 3.00
19 V:The Horde 3.00
20 R:Deadlock New Order. 3.00
21 KA,V:Epiphany New Order 3.00
22 V:The Horde, last issue 3.00
25 see above, after #10
Ashcan 3.00

BLOODSTRIKE: ASSASSIN
Extreme, 1995
0 R:Battlestone 3.00
1 Debut new series. 3.00
1a alternate cover. 3.00
2 V:M.D.K. Assassins 3.00
3 V:Persuasion 3.00

BLOODWULF
Extreme, 1995
1 RLd,R:Bloodwulf 2.50
1b Run OJ Run. 2.50
1c Alternate cover. 2.50
1d Alternate cover. 2.50
2 A:Hot Blood 2.50
3 Slippery When Wet 2.50
4 Darkness Gnaws at my Soul,
    final issue 2.50
Summer Spec.#1 V:Supreme
    Freeferall (1995) 2.50

BLUE
Aug., 1999
1 Android teenager 2.50
2 by Greg Aronowitz 2.50
3 rescue mission. 2.50

BLUNTMAN AND CHRONIC
Aug., 2001
GN MiA 15.00

BODY BAGS: FATHER'S DAY
July, 2005
1 JPn,48-page 6.00
2 JPn,48-page 6.00
1-shot Three The Hard Way 6.00
1-shot One Shot (2006) 6.00

BODYCOUNT
March, 1996
1 KEa,SBs 2.50
2 thru 4 KEa,SBs . . . . @2.50
TPB series rep. 18.00

BOHOS
Flypaper (B&W) 1998
1 by Maggie Whorf & B.Penaranda 3.00
2 F:teenage bohemians 3.00
3 concl. 3.00
TPB Bohos. 13.00

BOMB QUEEN
Feb., 2006
1 thru 4 . . . . @3.50
1-shot Bomb Queen vs. Blacklight . 3.50
TPB Vol. 1 Woman of Mass
    Destruction 13.00

BOMB QUEEN II
Oct., 2006
1 Queen of Hearts, pt.1 . . . . 3.50
2 . . . . 3.50

BONE
(B&W) Dec., 1995
[Prev.: Cartoon Books]
21 thru 25 . . . . @4.00
26 The Turning. 4.00
27 end of Dragonslayer storyline. . . 4.00
Bone Sourcebook 1.00
reprints with new covers
#1 thru #9 . . . . @3.00

Bone #21
© Cartoon Books

10 rep. 'Great Cow Race' 3.00
Cartoon Books
11 Aftermath of the Great Cow
    Race 3.00
12 . . . . 3.00
13 Thar she blows 3.00
14 . . . . 3.00
15 Double or nothing 3.00
16 hiding from the Rat Creatures . . 3.00
17 with 5 new pages 3.00
18 Betrayed 3.00
19 'Three cheers for Dragon-slayer
    Phoney Bone' 3.00
20 Phoney Bone vs. Lucius. 3.00

BONE REST
July, 2005
1 . . . . 3.00
2 Opificium Dei, pt.1 . . . . 3.00
3 Opificium Dei,pt.2 . . . . 3.00
4 Opificium Dei, concl. 3.00
5 Second Coming, pt.1 . . . . 3.00
6 Second Coming, pt.2 . . . . 3.00
7 Second Coming, pt.3 . . . . 3.00
8 Second Coming, pt.4 . . . . 3.00

BOOF
TMP, 1994
1 . . . . 2.50
2 Meathook. 2.50
3 Joyride. 2.50
4 thru 6 . . . . @2.50

BOOF AND THE BRUISE CREW
TMP, 1994
1 . . . . 2.50
2 thru 5 . . . . @2.50
6 I:Mortar,O:Bruise Crew 2.50

BOOK OF SHADOWS
April, 2006
1 (of 2) 3.50
2 . . . . 3.50

BRASS
WildStorm, 1996
1 Rib,AWa,Folio Edition 3.50
2 Rib,AWa. 2.50
3 Rib,AWa,concl. 2.50

IMAGE

BRIGADE
Extreme, 1993
[1st Series]
1 RLd(s),MMy,I:Brigade,Genocide . 3.50
1a Gold ed. 7.00
2 RLd(s),V:Genocide,w/coupon#4 . 4.00
2a w/o coupon 2.25
2b Gold ed. 4.00
3 I:Birds of Prey,V:Genocide. 2.50
4 CyP,Youngblood#5 flip. 2.50
[2nd Series]
0 RLd(s),ATi(c),JMs,NRd,I:Warcry,
  A:Emp,V:Youngblood. 2.50
1 I:Boone,Hacker,V:Bloodstrike,
  Blood Brothers,pt.1 . . . . 2.75
1a Gold ed. 3.00
2 C:Coldsnap,Blood Brothers,pt.3 . 3.00
3 ErS(s),GP(c),MMy,NRd(i),I:Roman
  V:Bloodstrike,Blood Brothers,
  pt.5. . . . . 2.50
4 Rip(s),MMy,RHe,Changes,
  BU:Lethal. 2.50
5 Rip(s),MMy,It's A VeryDeepSea. . 2.50
6 Rip(s),MMy,I:Coral,Warlok,
  BU:Hackers Tale 2.50
7 Rip(s),MMy,V:Warlok 2.50
8 ErS(s),MMy,Extreme Prejudice,
  pt.2,BU:Black & White,pt.5 . . . . 2.50
9 ErS(s),MMy,Extreme Projudice
  pt.6,ATh,BU:Black & White 2.50
25 ErS(s),MMy,D:Kayo,Coldsnap,
  Thermal 2.50
26 Images of Tomorrow 2.50
10 Extreme Prejudice 2.50
11 WildC.A.T.S 2.50
12 Battlestone 2.50
13 Thermal. 2.50
14 Teamate deaths 2.50
15 MWm,R:Roman Birds of Prey . . 2.50
16 ExtremeSacrifice,pt.4,x-over. . . . 2.50
17 MWn,I:New Team 2.50
18 I:The Shape New Order 2.50
19 MWn,F:Troll,Glory. 2.50
20 MWn,alien cult saga,concl. 2.50
21 F:Shadowl lawk. 2.50
22 Supreme Apocalypse,pt.4. . . . . . 2.50
23 . . . . 2.50
24 . . . . 2.50
25 & 26 see above
27 Extreme Babewatch 2.50
Sourcebook 3.00

BRIT
July, 2003
1-shot b&w, 48-pg. 5.00
1-shot Brit: Cold Death 5.00
1-shot Red,White,Black & Blue 5.00

BUGBOY
(B&W) June 1998
1-shot, by Mark Lewis, 48-pg. 4.00

BULLETPROOF MONK
Flypaper, Nov., 1998
1 in San Francisco 3.00
2 N.Y. Chinatown 3.00
3 conclusion 3.00
TPB 80-pg. 10.00
1-shot Tales of the B P M 3.00

BUNKER, THE
Apr., 2003
GN 96-pg. 10.00

BURGLAR BILL
(B&W) Nov., 2004
1 (of 6) by Paul Grist 3.00
2 thru 6 . . . . @3.00

BUTCHER KNIGHT
Top Cow, July, 2000
1 DT,F:Luther Washington 2.50
1a variant(c) MS (1:3). 2.50
1b variant(c) DT (1:3). 2.50
2 DT 2.50
3 DT,Blood & Gore 2.50
4 DT,concl. 3.00

CAPES
Sept., 2003
1 (of 3) 3.00
2 & 3 . . . . @3.00

CARVERS
Flypaper, Oct., 1998
1 F:five snowboarders 3.00
2 J:Crazy Jack 3.00
3 V:Evil Yeti 3.00
TPB rep. #1–#3 . . . . 10.00

CASANOVA
June, 2006
1 . . . . 2.50
2 thru 6 . . . . @2.50

CASEFILES: SAM AND TWITCH
May, 2003
1 Have You Seen Me?,pt.1. . . . . . . 3.00
2 thru 6 Have You Seen
  Me?, pt.2 thru pt.6 . . . . @3.00
7 Skeletons,pt.1 . . . . 3.00
8 Skeletons,pt.2 . . . . 3.00
9 Skeletons,pt.3 . . . . 3.00
10 Skeletons,pt.4 . . . . 3.00
11 Skeletons,pt.5 . . . . 3.00
12 Skeletons,pt.6 . . . . 3.00
13 Cops and Robbers 2.50
14 Ancient Chinese Secret,pt.1 . . . 2.50
15 Ancient Chinese Secret,pt.2 . . . 2.50
16 Ancient Chinese Secret,pt.3 . . . 2.50
17 Ancient Chinese Secret,pt.4 . . . 2.50
18 Ancient Chinese Secret,pt.5 . . . 2.50
19 Ancient Chinese Secret,pt.6 . . . 2.50
20 Fathers and Daughters, pt.1 . . . 2.50
21 Fathers and Daughters, pt.2 . . . 2.50
22 Fathers and Daughters, pt.3 . . . 2.50
23 . . . . 3.00
24 . . . . 3.00
25 Fathers and Daughters 3.00
TPB Brian Michael Bendis Col. . . . 25.00

CASUAL HEROES
Motown, 1996
1 . . . . 2.50
2 thru 6 . . . . @2.50

CATHEDRAL CHILD
1998
GN by Lea Hernandez. 10.00
GN 2nd printing 10.00

CELESTINE
Extreme, 1996
1 . . . . 2.50
2 . . . . 2.50

CHANNEL ZERO
(B&W) 1998
1 by Brian Wood 3.00
2 . . . . 3.00
3 gone global 3.00
4 Filter. 3.00
5 Brink of Millennium crash 3.00
6 Sound system 3.00
TPB Collection 12.00

Celestine #2 © Image

CHAPEL
Extreme, 1995
1 BWn,F:Chapel 3.50
2 V:Colonel Black 3.00
2a variant cover 2.50
[Regular Series]
1 BWn,F:Chapel 2.50
1a variant cover 2.50
2 V:Giger. 2.50
3 V:Giger. 2.50
4 Extreme Babewatch. 2.50
5 Hell on Earth,pt.1. . . . . 2.50
6 Hell on Earth,pt.2. . . . . 2.50
7 Shadowhunt x-over,pt.2. . . . . 2.50

CHASING DOGMA
June, 2001
TPB DFg,120-pg. 13.00

CHASSIS
Nov., 1999
1 F:Chassis McBain 3.00
2 . . . . 3.00
2a variant Matt Busch(c). 3.00
3 Gizmotech Industries 3.00
4 . . . . 3.00
4a Collector's variant(c) 4.00
5 Slic's One Shot, flip cover 3.00

CHILDHOOD'S END
(B&W) Oct., 1997
1 (of 5) JCf,community playground. 3.00

CHILLER
Dec., 1998
TPB JHI,F:Brian Marx 18.00

THE C.H.I.X. THAT TIME FORGOT
Studiosaurus, Aug., 1998
1 F:Good Girl 3.00

CHOLLY AND FLYTRAP
Nov., 2004
1 (of 4) by Arthur Suydam 5.00
2 Center City. 5.00
3 . . . . 5.00
4 . . . . 5.00
Spec. Date With The Devil, 48-pg. . 6.00

IMAGE

CHRONO MECHANICS
TPB Vol. 1 . . . . 7.00

CITY OF HEROES
Top Cow, May, 2005
1 Hard Crash, pt.1 . . . . 3.00
2 Hard Crash, pt.2 . . . . 3.00
3 Hard Crash, pt.3 . . . . 3.00
4 Smoke and Mirrors,pt.1 . . . . 3.00
5 Smoke and Mirrors,pt.2 . . . . 3.00
6 Smoke and Mirrors,pt.3 . . . . 3.00
7 DJu 3.00
8 DJu 3.00
9 DJu 3.00
10 thru 16 . . . . @3.00

CITY OF SILENCE
May, 2000
1 (of 3) WEI,GEr,F:Silencers 2.50
1a variant GEr,3-D(c)(1:4) 2.50
2 WEI,GEr 2.50
3 WEI,GEr 2.50
TPB 10.00

CLASSIC 40 OUNCE
Jan., 2005
TPB Tales from the Brown Bag . . . 13.00

CLERKS
July, 2001
TPB 11.00

CLOCK MAKER, THE
Jan., 2003
1 (of 12) 2.50
2 thru 7 . . . . @2.50
5 to 7 (of 12) cancelled
Spec. Act One (#1ñ#4) 5.00
Spec. Act Two (#5ñ#7) 5.00
Spec. Act Three 5.00

CLOCKWORK ANGELS
(B&W) March, 1999
GN seq. to Cathedral Child 10.00

CLOUDBURST
June, 2004
GN 8.00

CLOUDFALL
Nov., 2003
1-shot b&w 48-pg. 5.00
1-shot Cloudfall: Loose Ends 5.00

CODE BLUE
(B&W) April, 1998
1 by Jimmie Robinson 3.00
2 F.I.T.E. creates havoc 3.00

CODENAME: STYKE FORCE
Top Cow, 1994
1A MS(s),BPe,JRu(i) 3.50
1B Gold Embossed Cover 6.00
1C Blue Embossed Cover 9.00
2 MS(s),BPe,JRu(i) 2.50
3 MS(s),BPe,JRu(i) 2.50
4 MS(s),BPe,JRu(i) 2.50
5 MS(s),BPe,JRu(i) 2.50
6 MS(s),BPe,JRu(i) 2.50
7 MS(s),BPe,JRu(i) 2.50
8A Cyblade poster (Tucci) 4.00
8B Shi poster (Silvestri) 4.00
8C Tempest poster (Tan) 2.50
9 New Teamate 2.50
10 SvG, B:New Adventure 2.50

11 F:Bloodbow 2.50
12 F:Stryker 2.50
13 SvG(s),F:Strkyer 2.50
14 New Jobs 2.50
Spec.#0 O:Stryke Force 2.50
TPB rep. Death's Angel Saga 10.00

COMBAT
Jan., 1996
1 . . . . 2.50
2 . . . . 2.50

COMMON FOE
May, 2005
1 (of 5) KG 3.50
2 thru 5 KG . . . . @3.50

COMMON GROUNDS
Top Cow, Jan., 2004
1 (of 6) DJu 4.00
2 DJu,SK 3.50
3 thru 6 DJu,SK . . . . @3.00
TPB 20.00

COMPLETE ALEX TOTH ZORRO
(B&W) April, 1999
TPB Complete Alex Toth Zorro . . . 19.00

COSMIC RAY
June, 1999
1 by Stephen Blue 3.00
1a alternate cover (1:2) 3.00
2 F:Raymond Mann 3.00
3 F:Star Marshalls 3.00

COVENANT, THE
Top Cow, Sept., 2005
GN 10.00

COW, THE
Top Cow, April, 2000
1 Spring edition 3.00
2 Summer edition 3.00
3 Spring edition 2001 . . . . 3.00

CREASED
(B&W) Nov., 2004
GN by Daniel Miller 10.00

CREECH, THE
TMP, Oct., 1997
1 GCa,DaM,F:Chirs Rafferty 2.50
2 GCa,DaM,F:Dennis Dross 2.50
TPB Race Against Death 10.00

[GREG CAPULLO'S ORIGINAL] CREECH
TMP, Aug., 2001
1 A Vision of Death 2.50
2 Awakenings 2.50
3 The Resurrection 2.50

CREECH, THE: OUT FOR BLOOD
July, 2001
1 GCa,Out for Blood, Book 1 . . . . . 5.00
2 GCa,48-pg. 5.00
3 GCa,Killing Machine perfected . . 5.00

CREED: UTOPIATE
Jan., 2002
1 (of 4) TKn 3.50
2 TKn,disorder in dreamworld 3.00

3 TKn,fantasy vs. reality 3.00
4 TKn,Death of Creed 3.00

CREEPS
Oct., 2001
1 (of 4) TMd 3.50
2 TMd,I:Gurgle,Chitter 3.00
3 TMd,Genesys Corporation 3.00
4 TMd,through their eyes 3.00

Crimson #4
© Image

CRIMSON
Cliffhanger, May, 1998
1 BAu,HuR,F:Alex Elder, vampire
　'Dawn to Dusk' 5.00
1a variant AWa(c) 7.00
1b Chromium Edition 12.00
2 BAu,HuR,F:Jelly-Bats,
　'Unlife Story' 3.00
2a variant AAd(c) 6.00
3 BAu,HuR,V:Rose,Payment
　in Blood 4.00
4 BAu,HuR,F:Red Hood,Children
　of Judas,pt.1 . . . . 3.50
5 BAu,HuR,A:Red Hood,Children
　of Judas,pt.2 . . . . 3.50
6 BAu,HuR,A:Red Hood,Children
　of Judas,pt.3 . . . . 3.50
7 BAu,HuR,Christmas day 3.00
½ Dynamic Forces exclusive 4.00
WildStorm/DC, 1999
8 thru 23 BAu,HuR . . . . @2.50
24 BAu,HuR, final issue 3.50
Spec.#1 Scarlet X: Blood on the
　Moon, BAu,HuR,one-shot 4.00
Spec. Crimson Sourcebook #1 . . . 3.00
TPB Crimson, rep.#1–#6 . . . . 13.00
TPB Heaven & Earth,rep#7–#12 . . 15.00
TPB Loyalty & Loss 13.00
TPB Earth Angel,rep.#13–#18 . . . . 15.00
TPB Redemption,160-pg. 15.00

CRIMSON PLAGUE
June, 2000
1 GP,64-pg. 3.00
2 GP,Sole Survivor 2.50
3 GP,Blood trail 2.50
4 GP,Plague hits home 2.50

CROSS BRONX, THE
Sept., 2006
1 . . . . 3.00

IMAGE

1a variant (c). 3.00
2 . . . . 3.00
2a variant (c) 3.00
3 . . . . 3.00

CROW, THE
TMP, Feb., 1999

1 JMu,F:Eric Draven. 3.00
1a variant TP cover (1:4) 3.00
2 JMu,hunt for killers 3.00
3 JMu,justice for killers 3.00
4 JMu,Line Between Devil's Teeth . 3.00
5 JMu,Skin of an Angel,pt.1 . . . . . . 3.00
6 JMu,Skin of an Angel,pt.2 . . . . . . 3.00
7 JMu,Touch of Evil,pt.1 . . . . 3.00
8 JMu,Touch of Evil,pt.2 . . . . 3.00
9 JMu,Wings and Black Feathers. . 3.00
TPB Vol. 1 Vengeance. 11.00
TPB Vol. 2 Evil Beyond Reach . . . 11.00
Crow Mag.#1, 56-pg. rep. 5.00
Crow Mag.#2 . . . . 5.00
Crow Mag.#3 . . . . 5.00

CRUSH, THE
Motown Jan., 1996

1 Mini-series 3.00
2 Let Me Light Your Fire 3.00
3 Million Dollar Smile 3.00
4 . . . . 3.00
5 The Hip Hop Slide 3.00

CRYPT
Extreme, 1995

1 A:Prophet. 2.50
1a variant cover 2.50
2 A:Prophet. 2.50

CRYPTICS, THE
June, 2006

1 . . . . 3.50

[JIM LEE'S]
C-23
WildStorm, April, 1998

1 BCi,JMi,F:Corben Helix 2.50
2 JMi,TC(c),V:Angelans 2.50
3 JMi,TC(c),with game card 2.50
4 JMi,Corbin, banished. 2.50
5 JMi,RCo(c),Queen Mother. 2.50
5a variant JLe(c) (1:4) 2.50
6 JMi,RCo(c),V:Hyper Shock
   Troopers 2.50
7 JMi,RCo(c),Hail to the Queen . . . 2.50
8 JMi,RCo(c),Long Live the King . . 2.50

CURSED
Top Cow, Sept., 2003

1 (of 4) It is Coming 3.00
2 The Walking Dead 3.00
3 The Nature of Curses 3.00
4 It is a Gift. 3.00

CURSE OF THE SPAWN
TMP, Sept., 1996

1 DT,DaM,F:Daniel Lianso 6.00
1a B&W variant. 20.00
2 DT,DaM,Dark Future,pt.2:
   Blood Lust 5.00
3 DT,DaM,Dark Future,pt.3:
   Corpse Candles. 5.00
4 DT,DaM 4.00
5 DT,DaM,Sam & Twitch search
   for Gretchen Culver. 3.00
6 DT,DaM,Sam & Twitch pursue
   Suture 3.00
7 DT,DaM,Suture is captured 3.00
8 DT,DaM,Suture escapes police
   custody 3.00

9 DT,DaM,Angela's secret origin . . 5.00
10 DT,DaM,Angela, Spawn Slayer. . 3.50
11 DT,DaM,Angela's story, concl. . . 3.50
12 DT,DaM,Jessica Priest, movie
   photo(c) 3.50
13 DT,DaM 'Heart of Darkness'. . . . 3.50
14 DT,DaM,Jessica, concl. 3.50
15 DT,DaM,Tempt an Angel,pt.1 . . . 3.50
16 DT,DaM,Tempt an Angel,pt.2 . . . 3.50
17 DT,DaM. 3.50
18 DT,DaM,F:Tony Twist 3.50
19 DT,Curse & Tony Twist 3.50
20 DT,DaM,Monsters & Mythology . 3.50
21 DT,DaM,Zeus Must Die. 3.50
22 DT,F:Ryan Hatchett 3.50
23 DT,TM,R:Overkill 3.50
24 DT,TM,Pandemic 3.50
25 DT,TM,'Heart of Hell'. 2.50
26 DT.TM,V:The Crocodile. 2.50
27 DT,TM,F:Marc Simmons 2.50
28 DT,TM,V:Suture 2.50
29 DT,TM,A:Jonathan Edward
   Custer 2.50
TPB Vol. 1 Sacrifice the Soul. 10.00
TPB Vol. 2 Blood & Sutures. 10.00
TPB Vol. 3 Shades of Gray 10.00
TPB Vol. 4 Lost Values 10.00
TPB Vol. 5 Penumbra 10.00
TPB Best of Curse of the Spawn . . 17.00

CYBERFORCE
Top Cow, 1992–93
[Limited Series]

0 WS,O:Cyber Force 2.50
1 MS,I:Cyberforce,w/coupon#3 . . . 5.00
1a w/o coupon 3.00
2 MS,V:C.O.P.S. 3.50
3 MS 2.50
4 MS,V:C.O.P.S,BU:Codename
   Styke Force. 2.50
TPB Rep. mini-series. 13.00

[Regular Series] 1993

1 EcS(s),MS,SW. 2.50
1B Gold Foil Logo. 6.00
2 EcS(s),MS,SW,Killer Instinct
   #2,A:Warblade. 2.50
2B Silver Embossed Cover. 6.00
3 EcS(s),MS,SW,Killer Instinct #4,
   A:WildC.A.T.S. 2.50
3B Gold Embossed Cover 6.00
4 EcS(s),MS,Ballistic 2.50
5 EcS(s),MS 2.50
6 EcS(s),MS,Ballistic's Past 2.50
7 S.H.O.C.s. 2.50
8 . . . . 2.50
9 A:Huntsman 2.50
10 A:Huntsman 2.50
10a Alternate Cover. 4.00
10b Silver Seal Oz-Con 500c 9.00
11 . . . . 2.50
12 T.I.M.M.I.E. goes wild 2.50
13 EcS,MS,O:Cyberdata 2.50
14 EcS,MSI,V:T.I.M.M.I.E. 2.50
15 New Cyberdata Threat 2.50
16 O:Ripclaw 2.50
17 Regrouping 2.50
18 thru 24 . . . . @2.50
25 . . . . 4.00
26 KWo 2.50
27 F:Ash. 2.50
27a variant JQ&JP(c) (1:4) 4.00

Top Cow, 1996

28 A:Gabriel. 2.50
29 . . . . 2.50
30 ScL,'Devil's Reign' tie-in 2.50
31 The team in conflict 2.50
32 Cyblade leads rejuvenated team 2.50
33 KWo, Cheleene in midst of
   civil war. 2.50
34 KWo,Royal Blood,pt.3. . . . . 2.50

Cyberforce Vol. 2 #28 © Top Cow

35 BTn,Royal Blood, concl. 2.50
Ashcan 1 (San Diego) 4.00
Ashcan 1 (signed) 6.00
Sourcebook 1 . . . . 2.50
Sourcebook 2 I:W.Zero 2.50
Ann.#1 O:Velocity 2.50
Ann.#2 . . . . 3.00
TPB new art. 13.00
TPB EcS,MS,SW,Assault with a
   Deadly Woman 10.00

Top Cow, March, 2006

0 MS 3.00
1 (of 2) RMz 3.00
2 . . . . 3.00
2a variant b&w (c). 3.00
3 . . . . 3.00
3a variant b&w (c). 3.00
4 . . . . 3.00
5 . . . . 3.00
5a variant (c). 3.00
6 Who will die 3.00
6a variant (c). 3.00
1-Shot Cyberforce/X-Men (2006). . . 4.00
TPB Vol. 2 . . . . 15.00

CYBERFORCE/ CODE-NAME STRYKEFORCE: OPPOSING FORCES
Sept., 1995

1 V:Dangerous Threat. 2.50
2 Team vs. Team. 2.50

CYBERFORCE ORIGINS
Top Cow, 1995

1 O:Cyblade 2.50
1B Gold Seal 1000c 6.00
2 O:Stryker 2.50
3 O:Impact 2.50
4 Misery 3.00

CYBERFORCE UNIVERSE SOURCEBOOK
Top Cow, 1994–95

1 . . . . 2.50
2 MS,BTn 2.50

CYBERNARY
WildStorm, 1995–96

1 (of 5) mini-series 2.50
2 thru 5 . . . . @2.50

CYBERPUNX
Extreme, 1996
1 and 2 . . . . @3.00
3 RLe & Ching Lau,F:Drake 3.00

CYBLADE/SHI
1995
1 The Battle for Independents 3.00

CY-GOR
TMP, July, 1999
1 RV,I:Fatima,Frankie & Zevon. . . . 2.50
2 RV,Fire in the Mind,pt.2 . . . . 2.50
3 RV,Needles and Pins. 2.50
4 RV, Exquisite Corpse. 2.50
5 RV 2.50
6 RV, the Terraplane. 2.50
7 RV,Young Doctor Acula 2.50

DAMNED
Homage, June, 1997
1 (of 4) StG, MZ & DRo. 2.50
2 StG, MZ & DRo,F:Mick Thorne . . 2.50
3 StG, MZ & DRo 2.50
4 StG, MZ & DRo 2.50

Danger Girl #1b © WildStorm

DANGER GIRL
WildStorm/Cliffhanger 1998
1 JSC,AGo,'Dangerously Yours,'
   40-pg. 8.00
1a chromium edition, 40-pg. 55.00
1b Tour Edition 25.00
2 I:Johnny Barracuda,'Dangerous
   Liaisons'. 5.00
3 in Switzerland 4.00
3a variant AH(c) 5.00
3b variant TC(c) 5.00
4 I:Major Maxim 3.00
5 JSC,AGo 2.50
5a variant JMd(c) 9.00
   WildStorm/DC, 1999
6 JSC,SW 2.50
6a variant JMd(c) 5.00
6b variant HuR(c) 4.00
7 JSC,SW,concl.,48-pg. 6.00
TPB Dangerous Coll.,Vol.1 . . . . . . 6.00
TPB Dangerous Coll.,Vol.2,rep.2&3 6.00
J. Scott Campbell Danger Girl
   Sketchbook, 56-pg. 7.00

DARING ESCAPES
TMP, 1998
1 ANi,F:Harry Houdini. 3.00
2 ANi,search for Mystical Heart . . . 2.50
3 A:Kimiel 2.50
4 conclusion 2.50

DARK ANGEL: PHOENIX RESURRECTION
May, 2000
1 by Kia Asamiya, color manga . . . 3.00
2 thru 4 . . . . @3.00
1a thru 3a variant(c) . . . . @3.00

DARKCHYLDE
See: Maximum, 1996
1 Image reoffer 5.00
1C flip-book-Glory/Angel,Angels in
   Hell,pt.1, San Diego Con. 4.00
1D remastered, RLd(c) 6.00
2 Image reoffer 5.00
2a variant cover 3.00
2b remastered, with poster 2.50
3 Image reoffer 3.50
3a remastered, with poster 2.50
   Image, 1997
4 RQu,Ariel & Kauldron's past 5.00
5 RQu,No one here gets out alive . 4.00
TPB Rep. #1–#5 . . . . 13.00
   Homage, 1998
0 RQu,Ariel's back, Ariel's past. . . 2.50

DARKCHYLDE/GLORY
Extreme
1-shot, four variant covers, by
   RLd, RQu, JDy & PtL 3.00

DARKCHYLDE: THE DIARY
May, 1997
1-shot, RQu et al,diary excerpts . . . 5.00

DARKCHYLDE: THE LEGACY
WildStorm, 1998
1 RQu,F:Ariel 2.50
2 RQu 2.50
   WildStorm/DC, 1999
3 RQu,A:Silencer 2.50
4 RQu,Carnival of Fools 2.50
4a RQu,AAd(c), variant (c) 2.50
Summer Swimsuit Spectacular #1 . . 4.00
Spec.Dreams of the Darkchylde #0 . 2.50
TPB Darkchylde. 20.00

DARKCHYLDE/ WITCHBLADE
Top Cow, July, 2000
1 RQu,Nightmare City. 2.50

DARK CROSSINGS
Top Cow, May, 2000
Spec. #1 Dark Cloud Rising. 6.00
Spec. #2 Dark Cloud Overhead. . . . 6.00

DARKER IMAGE
1993
1 BML,BCi(s),RLd,SK,JLe,I:Blood
   Wulf,Deathblow,Maxx 4.00
1a Gold logo(c). 8.00
1b White(c) 6.00
Ashcan 1 . . . . 4.00

DARKMINDS
1998
1 PtL,cyberpunk,detective 8.00
2 Neon Dragon 5.00
2a variant cover 2.50
3 PtL,A:Neon Dragons 2.50
4 PtL,Paradox killer. 2.50
5 PtL,Unlikely friends, enemies . . . 3.00
6 PtL,Aurora Industries. 3.00
7 PtL,V:Mamuro Hayabusa. 3.00
8 Conclusion,1st story arc 2.50
½ PtL,Cyborg dreams. 2.50
TPB Collection #1 rep. #1–#3 . . . . 8.00
TPB Collection #2 rep. #4–#6 . . . . 8.00
TPB Collection #3 rep. #7 & #8 . . . 6.00
TPB Vol. I, rep.#1–#8. . . . . 19.00
   VOL. II Feb., 2000
1 JMd(c) one year later. 2.50
1a variant PtL(c). 2.50
1b variant Omar Dogan(c) 2.50
2 Changing Faces. 2.50
2a variant PtL(c) 2.50
2b variant Michael Turner(c). 2.50
2c variant(c) 2.50
3 PtL(c),F:Reiko Tetsunori 2.50
3a variant Omar Dogan(c) 2.50
3b variant JQ(c) 2.50
4 PtL,cyborg attack. 2.50
5 PtL,The Prize. 2.50
6 PtL,9mm Answers 2.50
7 PtL,The Hunger 2.50
8 PtL,Born Again. 2.50
9 PtL,A Million and One 2.50
10 PtL,concl. 2.50
#0 The Bullet 2.50
#0a variant(c). 2.50
TPB Vol.1,Paradox, rep. 20.00
TPB Coming of Age 15.00

DARKMINDS: MACROPOLIS
Jan., 2002
1 (of 8) PtL 3.00
1a variant(c) 3.00
2 F:Tiny 3.00
2a variant PtL(c) 3.00

DARKNESS, THE
Top Cow, 1996
0 Preview edition,B&W 17.00
½ 17.00
½ variant cover 25.00
1/2 rep.+new story (2001),MS 3.00
1 GEn,MS,Coming of Age 20.00
1a Dark cover 10.00
1b Platinum cover. 25.00
2 GEn,MS 8.00
3 GEn,MS,Jackie pursued by
   many foes 6.00
4 GEn,MS,Jackie explores
   Darkness power 6.00
5 GEn,MS,New York gangs on
   verge of all-out war 5.00
6 GEn,MS,F:JackieEstacado,concl. 4.00
7 MS 4.00
7a variant(c) 10.00
8 JBz,retribution 3.00
8a MS(c)(1:4) 7.00
9 Family Ties,pt.2,x-over 5.00
10 Family Ties,pt.3,x-over 6.00
11 GEn,MS,Hearts of Darkness . . . 3.50
11a Chromium(c) 22.00
11b variant(c). 5.00
12 GEn,Hearts of Darkness 3.00
13 GEn,Hearts of Darkness 3.00
14 GEn,JBz,Hearts of Darkness . . . 3.00
15 JBz,Spear of Destiny,pt.1 . . . . . 3.00
16 JBz,Spear of Destiny,pt.2 . . . . . 3.00
17 JBz,Spear of Destiny,pt.3 . . . . . 3.00
18 JBz,aftermath 3.00

    All comics prices listed are for *Near Mint* condition.

Darkness #1 © Top Cow

7 PJe,F:Ernie Palanco 3.00
7a alternate (c) 3.00
8 PJe,Law by Jackie Estacado. . . . 3.00
9 PJe,Search for Blue Goldfish . . . 3.00
10 RMz,Hong Kong 3.00
11 RMz,Dragons and darklings 3.00
12 RMz,Army of assassins 3.00
13 RMz,Mystical Dragons 3.00
14 Streets Run Red,pt.1 . . . . 3.00
15 Streets Run Red,pt.2 . . . . 3.00
16 Streets Run Red,pt.3 . . . . 3.00
17 Hell House, pt.1 . . . . 3.00
18 Hell House, pt.2 . . . . 3.00
19 Hell House, pt.3 . . . . 3.00
20 Hell House, pt.4 . . . . 3.00
21 The Reckoning 3.00
22 All in the Family ,pt.1 . . . . 3.00
23 All in the Family ,pt.2 . . . . 3.00
24 All in the Family, pt.3. . . . . 3.00
1-shot Wanted Dead (2004) 3.00
1-shot Black Sails (2005). 3.00
TPB Original Sin, 288-pg. 25.00
TPB Vol. 3.5 Flesh and Blood 25.00
E3 variant (c) reprint 3.00
TPB Compendium edition 50.00
Spec. Darkness/Batman, SLo,MS,
  x-over (1999). 6.00
1-shot Darkness/Vampirella (2005) . 3.00
1-shot Darkness/Wolverine (2006) . 3.00

DARKNESS, THE/ SUPERMAN
DC/Top Cow, Dec., 2004
1 (of 2) RMz(s) 3.00
2 RMz(s). 3.00

DARKNESS AND TOMB RAIDER
Top Cow, Mar., 2005
1-shot JaL,BTn. 3.00
1-shotA B&W cover 3.00

DARKNESS VS. MR. HYDE
Top Cow, Aug., 2005
1-shot Monster War #4 x-over 3.00
1-shotA variant (c) 3.00

DARK REALM
Oct., 2000
1 by Taeson Chang. 3.00
2 S.F.P.D. in chaos 3.00
3 flip-book 3.00
4 Prophecy is fulfilled 3.00

DART
1996
1 thru 3 Jozef Szekeres . . . . @3.00

DAVID AND GOLIATH
Sept., 2003
1 . . . . 3.00
2 . . . . 3.00
3 . . . . 3.00

DAWN
March, 2002
TPB Return of the Goddess 13.00
Spec. Convention Sketchbook. 3.00
Spec. 2003 Convention Sketchbook 3.00

DAWN: LUCIFER'S HALO
Oct., 2005
TPB Vol. 1 Lucifer's Halo. 18.00
TPB Lucifer's Halo Supplemental . 13.00

19 JBz,No Mercy,pt.1. . . . . 2.50
20 JBz,No Mercy,pt.2. . . . . 2.50
21 JBz,Wynnwood 2.50
22 JBz,Where is Jenny? 2.50
23 JBz,SLo,new characters 2.50
24 JBz,SLo,road trip to Vegas 2.50
25 JBz,SLo,48-pg. 3.50
26 JBz,SLo,A:Joey Scarpaggio . . . 2.50
27 SLo,FBI continues assault 2.50
28 Darkness/Witchblade,pt.4,x-over 2.50
29 SLo,High Noon,pt.1 . . . . 2.50
30 SLo,High Noon,pt.2 . . . . 2.50
31 SLo,High Noon,pt.3 . . . . 2.50
32 SLo,Dark Days Ahead 2.50
33 SLo,Capris Castagliano,pt.1 . . . 2.50
34 SLo,Capris Castagliano,pt.2 . . . 2.50
35 SLo,tour of his life. 2.50
36 SLo,Ripclaw,pt.3 . . . . 2.50
37 SLo,F:Robert Bearclaw. 2.50
38 SLo,V:Conquistator. 2.50
39 SLo,Jackie & Capris combine. . . 2.50
40 DK,Darkness falls? 2.50
40a variant MS(c) 2.50
various foil (c). . . . . @9.00
Coll.Ed.#1,rep. #1–#2 . . . . 5.00
Coll.Ed.#2,rep. #3–#4, 56-pg. 5.00
Coll.Ed.#3,rep. #5–#6, 56-pg. 5.00
Coll.Ed.#3, with slipcase. 10.00
Coll.Ed.#4,rep #7–#8 . . . . 5.00
Slipcase and all 3 GNs 25.00
Signed Slipcase and all 3 GNs . . . 50.00
Coll.Ed.#1,deluxe,rep.#1–#6 . . . . . 15.00
Coll.Ed.#5,rep.#11–#12 . . . . 6.00
Coll.Ed.#6,rep.#13–#14 . . . . 6.00
Spec. Infinity, SLo 3.50
Darkness/Witchblade,pt.3 x-over . . 4.00
Spec.#1, Dark Ages 5.00
TPB Vol.1 Spear of Destiny 13.00
TPB Vol.2 Heart of Darkness. 15.00
TPB Vol. 2 #1. . . . . 20.00
Spec. Vol. 2 #1 raw (no color) 3.00
TPB Darkness: Resurrection 15.00
1-shot Darkness/Hulk. 3.00

DARKNESS
Top Cow, Nov., 2002
1 PJe,DK. 3.00
1a holofoil(c). 6.00
2 DK 3.00
2 Megacon edition 6.00
3 DK 3.00
4 Under Cover of Darkness 3.00
5 You Lose Some 3.00
6 As the World Turns 3.00

Deathblow #7 © WildStorm

DAWN: THREE TIERS
June, 2003
1 thru 4 JLi . . . . @3.00
5 Hell Hath No Fury 3.00
6 . . . . 3.00

DEADLANDS
July, 1999
GN 1-shot role-play tie-in. 7.00

DEADLY DUO, THE
Highbrow, 1994–95
1 A:Kill-Cat 2.50
2 A:Pitt, O:Kid Avenger. 2.50
3 A:Roman, O:Kill-Cat. 2.50
[Second Series] 1995
1 A:Spawn. 2.50
2 A:Savage Dragon. 2.50
3 A:Grunge, Gen13. . . . . 2.50
4 Movie Mayhem 2.50

DEADWORLD
(B&W) Mar., 2005
1 . . . . 3.50
2 thru 6 . . . . @3.50
TPB Dead-Killer 15.00

DEATHBLOW
WildStorm, 1993–96
1 JLe,MN,I:Cybernary. 3.00
2 JLe,BU:Cybernary 2.50
3 JLe(a&s),BU:Cybernary. 3.00
4 JLe(s),TSe,BU:Cybernary 2.50
5 JLe(s),TSe,BU:Cybernary 2.50
5a different cover 5.00
6 Black Angel 2.50
7 . . . . 2.50
8 Black Angel 2.50
9 The Four Horsemen 2.50
10 Michael Cray, Sister Mary. 2.50
11 A:Four Horsemen 2.50
12 Final Battle 2.50
13 New Story Arc 2.50
14 A:Johnny Savoy 2.50
15 F:Michael Cray 2.50
16 TvS,BWS(c),WildStorm
  Rising,pt.6,w/2 cards 2.50
16a Newsstand ed. 2.50
17 V:Gammorran Hunter Killers. . . . 2.50
18 F:Cybernary 2.50
19 F:Cybernary 2.50
20 A:Gen 13 . . . . 3.50

IMAGE

IMAGE

21 Brothers in Arms,pt.2,A:Gen13. . 3.50
22 Brothers in Arms,pt.3 . . . . 2.50
23 Brothers in Arms,pt.4 . . . . 2.50
24 Brothers in Arms,pt.5 . . . . 3.00
25 Brothers in Arms,pt.6 . . . . 2.50
26 Fire From Heaven prelude 2.50
27 Fire From Heaven,pt.8 . . . . 3.00
28 Fire From Heaven,finale,pt.3 . . . 2.50
29 last issue. 2.50
 0 JLe (1996). 3.00
Ashcan 1 . . . . 4.00
TPB Dark Angel Saga,rep.,216-pg. 30.00
TPB Sinners and Saints, rep. 20.00

DEATHBLOW/WOLVERINE
WildStorm, Sept., 1996
1 RiB, AWs,x-over, set in San
   Francisco's Chinatown 2.50
2 RiB, AWs,concl 2.50
TPB rep. series 9.00

DEATH, JR.
Apr., 2005
1 (of 3) 5.00
2 . . . . 5.00
3 . . . . 5.00
TPB 15.00
Series 2, July, 2006
1 48-pg. 5.00
2 48-pg. 5.00
3 48-pg. 5.00

DEATHMATE X-OVER
See: COLOR PUB.

DECEPTION, THE
(B&W) Flypaper, Jan., 1999
1 (of 3) F:Jordan Risk, magician . . 3.00
2 Framed for murder. 3.00
3 V:South American Drug Cartel . . 3.00

DEEP SLEEPER
Aug., 2004
1 & 2 See B&W section
3 The Vacant. 3.00
4 conclusion 3.00
Omnibus rep.#1 & #2. . . . . 6.00
TPB 13.00

DEFCON 4
WildStorm, 1996
1 mini-series 2.50
2 thru 4 . . . . @2.50

DEFIANCE
Feb., 2002
1 The Messenger,pt.1 . . . . 3.00
2 thru 4 The Messenger,pt.2–pt.4 @3.00
5 thru 8 The Scabbard,pt.1–pt.4 . @3.00

DEITY
May, 1999
Coll.Ed. Vol. 1 . . . . 10.00
Coll.Ed. Vol. 2 . . . . 10.00

DEITY: REQUIEM
Feb., 2005
1-shot 56-pages 7.00

DEITY: REVELATIONS
June, 1999
1 F:Jamie 3.00
2 F:Joe Tripoli. 3.00
3 A legend reborn 3.00
3a variant cover (1:10) 3.00

DEMONSLAYER
Nov., 1999
1 MMy 3.00
2 Jaclyn begins her quest. 3.00
3 MMy, Michael & the Demon 3.00
Shadow Edition,pt.1 B&W 5.00
VOL II
1 MMy,Into Hell,pt.1 . . . . 3.00
1a variant(c) (1:4) 3.00
2 MMy 3.00
3 MMy, enter Ebon 3.00

DERRING RISK
June, 1999
1 Fantasy Adventure 2.50
1a AWa variant(c) 2.50

DESPERADO
Dec., 2005
1-shot Primer 2.00
1-shot Second Chances, 64-pg. . . . 5.00

Desperadoes #1
© Homage

DESPERADOES
Homage, Sept., 1997
1 by JMi & John Cassaday 7.00
2 V:Leander Peik 3.00
2a 2nd printing 2.50
3 V:Leander Peik 3.00
4 V:Leander Peik, concl. 3.00
5 V:Gideon Brood,pt.1. . . . . 3.00
TPB A Moment's Sunlight,rep.
   #1–#5. . . . . 17.00

DESPERATE TIMES
(B&W) June, 1998
1 by Chris Eliopoulos 3.00
2 Strip joint 3.00
3 EL(c) 3.00
4 Christmas special 3.00
5 EL(c), sideways 3.00
6 . . . . 3.00
TPB 13.00
Jan., 2004
0 . . . . 3.00
1 . . . . 3.00

DETECTIVES INC.
March, 1999
TPB Vol. 1 . . . . 15.00
TPB Vol. 2 A Terror of Dying 20.00

DETONATOR, THE
Nov., 2004
1 Big Bang Theory, pt.1, MBn. 2.50
2 . . . . 2.50
3 . . . . 2.50
4 . . . . 2.50
5 final issue. 3.00

DEVASTATOR
(B&W) April, 1998
1 JHl and Greg Horn. 3.00
2 book 1,pt.2. . . . . 3.00
3 concl. to book 1 . . . . 3.00

DEVIL'S DUE STUDIOS
Mar., 2003
1-shot 2003 Preview 2.50

DIORAMAS, A LOVE STORY
Apr., 2004
GN 13.00

DISCIPLES, THE
April, 2001
1 The new magic 3.00
2 Recruit Her or Kill Her 3.00
3 Viva Las Vegas 3.00
4 The Apples of Sodom 3.00

A DISTANT SOIL
(B&W) Highbrow, Aug., 1993
Prev: Aria Comics
15 CDo,Ascension,pt.3 . . . . 3.00
16 CDo,A:Bast, Avatar. 3.00
17 CDo,D'mer & Bast conflict 3.00
18 CDo,'Ascension' finale 3.00
19 CDo,'Spires of Heaven,'pt.1 . . . 3.00
20 CDo,Lord Merai's suicide
   weakens Hierachy 3.00
21 CDo,'Exile for D'mer?' 3.00
22 CDo,Avatar's secrets,32-pg. . . . 3.00
23 CDo,three stories 3.00
24 CDo,malfunctioning spacesuit . . 3.00
25 CDo,NGa,Troll Bridge,48-pg. . . . 4.00
26 CDo,B.U.:Red-Cloak by
   E.Kushner 3.00
27 CDo,B.U.:Liaden tale 3.00
28 CDo,B.U.:Liaden tale, concl. . . . 3.00
29 CDo,B.U.:Delia Sherman story . . 3.00
30 . . . . 4.00
31 Sometimes the good guys lose . 4.00
32 F:Prince D'mer 4.00
33 Rebellion's final stand. 4.00
34 CDo, 64-pg. 5.00
35 CDo, 32-pg. 4.00
36 CDo. 4.00
37 CDo. 4.00
38 CDo, 40-pg. 4.50
Images of A Distant Soil. 3.00
Images of A Distant Soil, signed . . 35.00
GN The Gathering, rep.#1–#11 . . . 19.00
GN The Gathering, 2nd printing . . 20.00
TPB The Ascendant, rep.#13–#24. 19.00
TPB The Gathering 20.00
TPB Vol.3, The Aria 17.00
TPB Vol.4 Coda 18.00

DIVINE RIGHT: THE ADVENTURES OF MAX FARADAY
WildStorm, Sept., 1997
1 JLe,SW,Blaze of Glory. 7.00
1a variant cover 7.50
1b variant, signed 30.00
1c Voyager pollybaged pack. 6.00
1d Spanish edition 5.00

Divine Right #6 © WildStorm

2 JLe,SW,Disco Inferno 5.00
2a variant(c) 5.00
3 JLe,SW,F:Christie Blaze,Enemies
  of the State 4.00
4 JLe,SW,F:Lynch,The Love
  Connection 2.50
4a variant(c) 4.00
5 JLe,SW,V:Dominique Faust,Party
  Crashers 3.00
6 JLe,SW,Truth or Consequences,
  Susanna Chaste located 3.00
7 JLe,SW,Into the Hollow Realm . . 3.00
8 JLe,SW,Tobru,V:Acheron 3.00
8a variant SW(c) 3.00
Preview edition, JLe(c) (1997) 5.00
Coll.Ed.#1 . . . . 6.00
Coll.Ed.#2 . . . . 6.00
WildStorm/DC, 1999
9 JLe,SWi,Final Stand in
  Hollow Realm 3.00
10 JLe,SWi 3.00
11 JLe,SWi,Divine Intervention 3.00
12 JLe,SWi,Divine Intervention 3.00
Coll.Ed.#3, rep.#5 & #6 . . . . 6.00
TPB Book 1 JLe (2002) 18.00
TPB Book 2 JLe (2002) 18.00

DOCTOR CYBORG
June, 2004
GN Outpatient 10.00

DODGE'S BULLETS
Feb., 2004
GN B&W 10.00

DOLL AND CREATURE
March, 2006
1 (of 4) 3.50
2 thru 4 . . . . @3.00
TPB Vol. 1 Everythign Turns Gray. 13.00

DOLLZ
April, 2001
1 RGr,TSg 3.00
1a-1c variant(c)s 3.00
2 RGr 3.00
3 RGr 3.00

DOMINION
Jan., 2003
1 KG 3.00
2 thru 5 KG . . . . @3.00

DOOM'S IV
Extreme, 1994
1 RL(s),MPa, I:Doom's IV 2.50
1a variant(c),left side of art 2.50
1b variant(c),right side of art 2.50
2 Rld(s),MPa,MECH-MAX 2.50
2a variant (c) 2.50
3 Dr. Lychee, Brick 2.50
4 Dr. Lychee, Syber-idol 2.50
Sourcebook 2.50

DOUBLE IMAGE
Feb., 2001
1 The Bod, flip-book, Codeflesh . . . 3.00
2 The Bod/Codeflesh 3.00
3 The Bod/Codeflesh 3.00
4 The Bod/Codeflesh 3.00
5 Trust in Me/Codeflesh 3.00

DOWN
Top Cow, Nov., 2005
1 (of 4) WEI,TyH 3.00
2 thru 4 . . . . @3.00
TPB 16.00

DRACULA VS. ZORRO
(B&W) Sept., 1998
1 DMG,RM 3.00
2 DMG,RM, conclusion 3.00

DRAGON, THE
March, 1995
1 rep. of Savage Dragon 2.50
2 thru 5 rep. of Savage Dragon . @2.50

THE DRAGON: BLOOD AND GUTS
Highbrow, 1995
1 I:Grip 2.50
2 JPn,KIS 2.50
3 JPn,KIS 2.50
TPB series rep. 8.00

DRAIN
Nov., 2006
1 Decades 3.00

DROWNED, THE
July, 2004
GN 10.00

DUNCAN'S KINGDOM
(B&W) Oct., 1999
1 by Gene Yang & Derek Kirk 3.00
2 . . . . 3.00

DUSTY STAR
(B&W) April, 1997
0 sci-fi,western,adventure 3.00
1 thru 3 . . . . @3.00

DUSTY STAR
Aug., 2005
1 . . . . 3.50
2 . . . . 3.50

DV8
WildStorm, 1996
1 WEI(s),HuR,'Lust for Life' 4.00
1a JLe(c) 5.00
1b Kevin Nowlan(c) 4.00
2 WEI(s),HuR,Gen-active serial
  killers,'Some Weird Sin' 3.00
3 WEI(s), Neighborhood Threat . . . 3.00
4 WEI(s),HuR,Miss Drugstore 3.00

5 Ivana sends DV8 to Japan 2.50
6 idle hands are the devil's tools . . 2.50
7 WEI(s),'Shades' 2.50
8 HuR,Sublime, Evo & Frostbite
  abandoned,'Three'. 2.50
9 MHs,'Evolution' 2.50
10 MHs,'In Service to Nothing' 2.50
11 MHs,F:Copycat,'Facets' 2.50
12 MHs,F:Freestyle,V:Sen.Killory . . 2.50
13 MHs,'The Sad Tales of
   Senator Killory' 2.50
14 MHs,TR,New Horizon,TR(c),
   'Barely Legal'. 5.00
14a TC(c) 2.50
14b Voyager bagged pack 3.50
15 MHs,F:Ivana Baiul,'Settling
   Accounts' 2.50
16 MHs,V:Dominique Faust
   'Intersection' 2.50
17 MI Is,Gen-Passive 2.50
18 MHs,Team 7,A:Grifter,'Same as
   It Ever Was' 2.50
19 MHs,First Mision,pt.1,'Larger
   Concerns' 2.50
20 MHs,First Mision,pt.2,'Lounging
   in the Ammo Dump'. 2.50
21 MHs,First Mision,pt.3,V:Anthrax . 2.50
22 MHs,V:Copycat,'Choices' 2.50
22a variant(c) JMd(1:4) 2.50
23 MHs,F:Threshold,'Gone to
   Ground' 2.50
24 MHs,F:Sublime,'Slip Stream,'
   prologue 2.50
25 MHs,Slipstream,pt.1 . . . . 2.50
DV8 Rave,preview (1996) 3.00
Ann.#1 'Head Trips' (1998) 3.00
WildStorm/DC, 1999
26 MHs,TVs 2.50
27 MHs,TVs,V:Gen-Actives 2.50
28 MHs,TVs,F:Evo 2.50
29 MHs,TVs 2.50
30 MHs,TVs,Things Fall Apart,pt.1 . 2.50
31 MHs,TVs,Things Fall Apart,pt.2 . 2.50
32 MHs,TVs,Things Fall Apart,pt.3 . 2.50
Ann.'99 Slipstream 3.50
#0 40-pg. 3.00
TPB Neighborhood Threat (2002) . 15.00

DV8 VS. BLACK OPS
WildStorm, Oct., 1997
1 Techromis Design,pt.1 . . . . 3.00
2 Techromis Design,pt.2 . . . . 3.00
3 Techromis Design,pt.3 . . . . 3.00

DV8 Vs. Black Ops #1 © WildStorm

All comics prices listed are for *Near Mint* condition.

EARTHBOY JACOBUS
May, 2005
TPB 18.00

ECHO
March, 2000
1 A Broken World 2.50
1a variant(c) 2.50
2 Sacrifices 2.50
2a variant PtL(c) 2.50
3 Deadly new echo 2.50
3a variant PtL(c) 2.50
4 PtL,Desperate Times 2.50
5 PtL,Welcoming Party 2.50
6 Conspiracy Theory 2.50
6a variant PtL(c) 2.50
7 Anarchy,pt.1 . . . . 2.50
8 A Life Worth Living 3.00
#0 Thick as Thieves 2.50
#0a variant(c) 2.50
#1 Holochrome edition 7.00

86 VOLTZ: DEAD GIRL
(B&W) Mar., 2005
1-shot 56-page 6.00

ELECTROPOLIS
May, 2001
1 DMt, Infernal Machine,pt.1 . . . . . 3.00
2 DMt, Infernal Machine,pt.2 . . . . . 3.00
3 DMt, Heavy Meddle 3.00
4 DMt, Infernal Machine,pt.4 . . . . . 3.00

ELEKTRA/CYBLADE
Top Cow/Marvel, 1997
1-shot 'Devil's Reign','pt.7
(of 8) x-over 3.00

ELEPHANTMEN
July., 2006
0 Unnatural Selection 3.00
1 See the Elephant 3.00
2 Behemoth & Leviathan, flip-book. 3.00
3 Hip Flask 3.00
4 Hazardous Materials, Wounded
Animals, flip-cover 3.00

EMISSARY
May, 2006
1 Revelations 1:4 . . . . 3.50

Empire #1
© Image

2 Revelations 2:4 . . . . 3.50
3 Revelations 3:4 . . . . 3.50
4 Revelations 4:4 . . . . 3.50
5 Revelations 2:1 . . . . 3.50
6 Revelations 2.2 . . . . 3.50

EMPIRE
May, 2000
1 MWa,BKi,F:Golgoth 5.00
2 MWa,BKi,F:Xanna 4.00
3 MWa,BKi,F:Lohkyn 4.00
4 MWa,BKi,Nature vs. nurture 4.00

ESPERS
April, 1997
(B&W) Vol. 3
1 JHI,A:Brian Marx,V:Architects . . . 3.00
1a 2nd printing 3.00
2 JHI 3.00
3 JHI,Black Magic 3.00
4 JHI,Black Magic, concl. 3.00
5 JHI,two stories 3.00
6 JHI,F:Simon Ashley,Alan Black . . 3.00
7 JHI,Feel the Rapture 3.00
8 JHI, trip to Hong Kong 3.00
9 JHI,V:Architects 3.00
TPB Undertow, rep.Halloween
Comics series 15.00
TPB Black Magic, rep.Vol.3,#1–4 . 15.00
TPB The Storm, rep. 16.00
TPB Interface, rep.2nd series 16.00

E.V.E. PROTOMECHA
Top Cow, Feb., 2000
1 . . . . 3.00
1a variant JMd(c) 3.00
1b variant David Finch(c) 3.00
2 Gunner Unleashed. 3.00
2a variant Michael Turner(c). 3.00
2b variant SPa(c) 3.00
3 thru 6 . . . . @3.00
TPB Vol.1 Sins of the Daughter. . . 18.00

[ADVENTURES OF]
EVIL AND MALICE
June, 1999
1 by Jimmie Robinson 3.50
2 F:Max 2000 . . . . 3.50
3 V:Cold Heart & Le'Chef 3.50
4 final showdown 3.50
TPB F:Evelyn & Malinda 13.00

EVO
Top Cow
1 MS,Endgame,pt.3 x-over 3.00

EXPATRIATE, THE
Feb., 2004
1 . . . . 3.00
2 thru 7 . . . . @3.00
TPB Vol. 1 . . . . 12.00

EXPOSURE
July, 1999
1 F:Shawna & Lisa 2.50
2 Mirrors to the Soul 2.50
3 . . . . 2.50
2a & 3a alternate photo(c) (1:2) . @2.50
4 Spark-Spangled See-Through
Girl 2.50
4a alternate photo(c) (1:2) 2.50
Prelude 16-pg 7.00
Prelude holo-foil 15.00

EXTREME ANTHOLOGY
1 . . . . 2.50

EXTREME CHRISTMAS SPECIAL
Various artists, new work 3.00

EXTREME DESTROYER
Extreme, 1996
1 prologue, x-over,bagged
with card 2.50
2 epilogue, x-over 2.50

EXTREME HERO
1 . . . . 3.00

EXTREME PREJUDICE
Extreme, Nov., 1994
0 Prelude to X-over 3.00

EXTREME SACRIFICE
Extreme, Jan., 1995
Prelude,x-over,pt.1, A:Everyone
with trading card 2.50
Epiloque, x-over,pt.8, conclusion
with trading card 2.50
TPB Rep. whole x-over series 17.00

EXTREME 3000
Prelude 2.50

EXTREME TOUR BOOK
Tour Book 1992 . . . . 3.00
Tour Book 1994 . . . . 25.00

EXTREMELY YOUNGBLOOD
Extreme, Sept 1997
1 TBm&MBm(s) 3.50

EXTREME ZERO
0 RLd,CYp,ATi(i),I:Cybrid, Law &
Order, Risk, Code 9, Lancers,
Black Flag 3.00
0a Variant cover 3.00

FACELESS, THE
Aug., 2005
GN 7.00

FACTION PARADOX
Aug., 2003
1 War in Heaven 3.00
2 . . . . 3.00

FALLING MAN
(B&W) Dec., 1997
1 (of 3) BMC,PhH 3.00
2 Floyd vs. Duncan 3.00
3 . . . . 3.00

FATHOM
Top Cow, 1998
1 by Michael Turner,F:Aspen 7.00
2 war beneath the waves 4.00
3 Life changed forever 3.50
4 Connection to water. 3.00
5 Aspen's connection to water 3.00
6 Admiral's plans revealed 3.00
7 Finale,pt.1 . . . . 3.00
8 Finale,pt.2 . . . . 3.00
9 Finale, conclusion, end 3.00
9a green foil (c). 16.00
10 Fathom returns 3.00
11 Fathom returns,pt.2. . . . . 3.00
12 Tomb Raider & Witchblade
x-over,pt.1 . . . . 3.00
12a variant(c). 5.00
13 x-over,pt.2 . . . . 3.00

Fathom #13 © Top Cow

13a variant(c)	5.00
14 Aspen & Vana, concl.	3.00
14a variant(c)	5.00
15 Killian's Blue Sun	2.50
15a variant(c)	5.00
16 Admiral's subterfuge discovered	2.50
#0 rep. new Mike Turner(c)	2.50
1/2	4.00
Spec. Swimsuit ed.	4.00
Fathom 2000 swimsuit calendar	4.00
Fathom 2000 smimsuit Spec.	4.00
TPB Coll.Ed.#1, rep.#1	6.00
TPB Coll.Ed.#2, rep.#2–#3	6.00
TPB Coll.Ed.#3, rep.#4–#5	6.00
TPB Coll.Ed.#4, rep.#6–#7	6.00
TPB Coll.Ed.#5, rep.#8–#9	6.00
TPB Vol. 1, rep. #1–#9	25.00

FATHOM: KILLIAN'S TIDE
Top Cow, March, 2001
1 (of 4)	5.00
1a variant(c)	4.00
2 thru 4	@3.00

FEAR AGENT
Oct., 2005
1	3.00
2	3.00
3	3.00
4	3.00
5	3.00
6 Reignition, conc.	3.00
7 Homecoming	3.00
8	3.00
9	3.00
10	3.00
11	3.00
TPB Vol. 1 Reignition	10.00

FEAR EFFECT
Top Cow, March, 2000
1-shot MHw, video game tie-in	5.00
Spec. 1 Fear Effect Retro Helix	3.00

FEATHER
Aug., 2003
1 thru 4	@3.00
5 48-pg.	6.00

FELL
Sept., 2005
1 WEI	15.00
2 WEI	12.00

3 WEI	5.00
4 thru 8 WEI	@4.00

FELON
Top Cow, Oct., 2001
1 (of 4)	3.00
2	3.00
3 concl.	3.00
4 I:Elizabeth Freeh	3.00

FELT: TRUE TALES OF UNDERGROUND HIP HOP
(B&W) May, 2005
1-shot	3.00

FERRO CITY
(B&W) Aug., 2005
1	3.00
2 thru 4	@3.00

F5
April, 2000
1 TnD,48-pg.	3.00
2 TnD,life or death	2.50
3 TnD	2.50
4 TnD, betrayed	2.50
Preview Book, TnD,24-pg.	2.50

FIRE
(B&W) Dec., 1998
TPB International intelligence	10.00
TPB The Definitive Collection	10.00

FIREBIRDS
Nov., 2004
1-shot by Jay Faeber	6.00

FIREBREATHER
Jan 2003
1 (of 4) PhH(s)	3.00
2 thru 4 PhH(s)	@3.00
TPB Vol. 1	14.00
1-shot Firebreather: The Iron Saint, PhH (2004)	6.00

FIRE FROM HEAVEN
WildStorm, 1996
1 x-over,Chapter 1	3.50
2 x-over,Finale 2	2.50

FIRSTMAN
April, 1997
1 ASm,LukeHenry becomesApollo	2.50

FLAK RIOT
June, 2005
1 (of 4)	3.00
2	3.00
3	3.00
4	3.00

FLAMING CARROT
(B&W) Dec., 2004
1 by Bob Burden, Crouching Carrot, Hidden Hot Wing	3.00
2	3.50
3	3.50
4	3.50
Spec.	3.50
TPB Vol. 1	15.00

FLIGHT
July, 2004
TPB	20.00
TPB Vol. 2	25.00

FOOT SOLDIERS, THE
(B&W) Sept., 1997
Prev.: Dark Horse
1 by Jim Krueger, Graveyard of Forgotten Heroes	3.00
2 Tragedy o/t Travesty Tapestry	3.00
3 Arch enemies,pt.3	3.00
4 'It's a Wicked World Afterall'	3.00
5 Loose Ends	3.00

FOREVER AMBER
(B&W) July, 1999
1 by Don Hudson	3.00
1a variant cover (1:2)	3.00
2 Lady fights back	3.00
3 Amber sent to jail	2.50
4 Amber's revenge, concl.	3.00

FORSAKEN
Aug., 2004
1 Light of Other Days,pt.1	3.00
2 Light of Other Days,pt.2	3.00
3 Light of Other Days,pt.3	3.00
4 The Light of Other Days,pt.4	3.00
5 The Light of Other Days,pt.5	3.00
6 The Light of Other Days,pt.6	3.00

40 OZ COLLECTED
Nov., 2003
TPB b&w	10.00

FOUR-LETTER WORLDS
Jan., 2005
GN	13.00

FRANKENSTEIN MOBSTER
Oct., 2003
0	3.00
0a variant (c)	3.00
1 MkW,Friday the 13th	3.00
2 MkW	3.00
3 MkW,mystic control	3.00
4 MkW	3.00
5 MkW,Blood debt	3.00
6 Escape from police	3.00
7 Made Man, concl.	3.00
1a thru 7a variant (c)	@3.00
TPB Vol. 1 Made Man	20.00

Frankenstein Monster #0
© Image

IMAGE

FREAK
May, 2004

GN 7.00

FREAK FORCE
Highbrow, 1993–95

1 EL(s),KG 3.00
2 EL(s),KG 3.00
3 EL(s),KG 3.00
4 EL(s),KG,A:Vanguard. 3.00
5 EL(s),KG 3.00
6 EL(s),KG 3.00
7 EL(s),KG 3.00
8 EL(s),space ants 3.00
9 EL(s),Cyberforce 3.00
10 EL(s),Savage Dragon 3.00
11 EL(s),Invasion,pt.1 . . . . 3.00
12 EL(s),Invasion,pt.2 . . . . 3.00
13 EL(s),Invasion,pt.3 . . . . 3.00
14 EL(s),Team Defeated 3.00
15 EL(s),F:Barbaric 3.00
16 KG,EL(s),V:Chelsea Nirvana. . . . 3.00
17 EL,KG,major plots converge 3.00
18 Final Issue 3.00
TPB 448-pg. 30.00

[Series Two] March, 1997

1 EL,Star joins team,V:The
   Frightening Force 3.00
2 EL,Dart quits team. 3.00
3 EL,'Lo there shall come..an
   ending'. 3.00

FREEDOM FORCE
Jan., 2005

1 (of 6) Founding Fathers. 3.00
2 Casualty of War. 3.00
3 Double Trouble 3.00
4 Mechanical Mayhem 3.00
5 Forbidden Fruit 3.00
6 Out of Time 3.00

FRESHMEN, THE
Top Cow, 2005

1 thru 3 Intro to Superpowers 101
   pt. 1 thru pt. 3 . . . . @3.00
4 What Time is it in Budapest. 3.00
5 Deepest Level of Truth 3.00
6 Finals. 3.00
Spec. Yearbook (2005) 3.00
1-shot Freshmen Yearbook 3.00
TPB 17.00
Vol. 2
1 Fundamentals of Fear 3.00

FRIENDS OF MAXX
I Before E, April, 1996

1 thru 3 WML&SK. . . . . @3.00

FUSED!
March, 2002

1 Canned Heat,pt.1 (of 4). 3.00
1a variant(c) 3.00
2 thru 4 Canned Heat,pt.2–pt.4 . @3.00

GALAXY-SIZE ASTOUNDING SPACE THIRLLS
March, 2001

1 Galaxy Size Showdown, 48-pg.
   flip-book. 5.00

GAMORRA SWIMSUIT SPECIAL
WildStorm, 1996

Spec.#1 . . . . 2.50

GAZILLION
Nov., 1998

1 HSm, Mars vs. Xof. 2.50
1a variant cover (1:4) 2.50

GEAR STATION, THE
March, 2000

1 DaF,Dominion of Souls 6.00
1a variant AxR(c) 2.50
1b variant PtL(c) 2.50
1c variant Michael Turner(c). 2.50
2 DaF,23rd Gear. 2.50
2a variant AAd(c) 2.50
3 DaF,Who is Fable 2.50
4 DaF,first showdown 2.50
5 DaF,Gear Station Prime. 2.50
6 DaF 2.50

GEEKSVILLE
(B&W) Mar., 2000

#0 by R.Koslowski & G.Sassaman . 3.00
1 Breaking into the Biz,pt.1. . . . . . . 3.00
2 Breaking into the Biz,pt.2. . . . . . . 3.00
3 Back to the Con 3.00
4 Breaking into the Biz 3.00
5 Dark Sky 3.00
6 End of 3 Geeks 3.00

GEMINAR
(B&W) June, 2000

1 . . . . 5.00
2 F:Captain Champion 5.00

GEN13
WildStorm, 1994

0 Individual Hero Stories. 4.00
1 JLe(s),BCi(s),I:Fairchild,Grunge,
   Freefall,Burnout. 20.00
1a 2nd printing 4.00
2 JLe(s),BCi(s) 16.00
3 JLe(s),BCi(s),A:Pitt,'Payback' . . 10.00
4 JLe(s),BCi(s),'Free for All' 8.00
5 Final issue 5.00
5a WP variant cover 10.00
TPB Gen13 Coll.Ed. 13.00

[Regular Series] 1995

1a BCi(s),V:Mercenaries. 5.00
1b Common Cover 2 . . . . 5.00
1c Heavy Metal Gen 8.00
1d Pulp Fiction Parody 10.00
1e Gen 13 Bunch 8.00
1f Lin-Gen-re. 10.00
1g Lil Gen 13 . . . . 8.00
1h Friendly Neighbor Grunge 8.00
1i Gen 13 Madison Ave 10.00
1j Gen-Et Jackson 8.00
1k Gen Dress Up cover 8.00
1l Verti-Gen. 8.00
1m Do It Yourself Cover 8.00
2 BCi,BWS(c),WildStorm Rising,
   pt.4, w/2 cards 3.00
2a newsstand ed. 2.50
3 BCi,'Magical Mystery Tour' 3.00
4 BCi,'Tourist Trap' 3.00
5 BCi,I:New Member,Family Feud . 3.00
6 BCi,JLe,I:The Deviants,
   'Roman Holiday' 3.00
7 BCi,JLe,European Vacation,pt.2
   'Veni, Vidi, Vici' 3.00
8 BCi,'Bewitched,Bothered
   and Bewildered'. 3.00
9 . . . . 3.00
10 Fire From Heaven,pt.3 . . . . 3.00
11 Fire From Heaven,pt.9 . . . . 3.00
12 F:Caitlin,her dad 3.00
13 A, B & C, each . . . . @3.00
14 'Higher Learning' 2.50
15 Fraternity and Sorority rush 2.50
16. . . . . 2.50

Gen13 #29 © WildStorm

17 BCi,JSC,AGo,battle royale in
   Tower of Luv,'Toy Soldiers' 2.50
18 BCi,JSC,AGo,V:Keepers,
   'Hello & Good-Byes' 2.50
19 BCi,JSC,AGo,Lynch & kids flee
   to Antarctica,'Bon Voyage'. 2.50
20 BCi,JSC,AGo,'To Boldly Go' . . . 2.50
21 BCi,JSC,AGo,V:D'Rahn,'Lost
   in Space' 2.50
22 BCi,civil war,'Homecoming'. 2.50
23 BCi,21st century 2.50
24 BCi,V:D'Rahn,'Judgment Day' . . 2.50
25 BCi,Homecoming,JsC(c). 3.50
25a TC(c),'Where Angels Fear
   to Tread' 3.50
25b Voyager bagged pack. 3.50
26 JAr,GFr,CaS,When Worlds
   Collide 2.50
27 JAr,GFr,CaS,'Search & Seizure'. 2.50
28 JAr,GFr,CaS,'Remote Control' . . 2.50
29 JAr,GFr,CaS,I:Tindalos,
   'A Firm Grip on Reality' 2.50
30 JAr,GFr,CaS,'Stranger Than
   Fiction' 2.50
31 JAr,GFr,CaS,Roxy's Big Score,
   'Paradigm Shift' 2.50
32 JAr,GFr,CaS,'Red Skies at
   Morning'. 2.50
33 JAr,GFr,CaS,aftermaths, 'Burning
   the Candle at Both Ends',
   with 8-page Planetary #0. . . . . . 4.00
34 JAr,GFr,CaS,AAd,A:Roxy
   & Sarah,'Overture'. 2.50
35 JAr,GFr,CaS,John Lynch resigns,
   'But You Can't Hide' 2.50
36 JAr,GFr,CaS,F:John Lynch,
   'That Was Then' 2.50
College Yearbook 1997, Superheroes
   at Large. 2.50
Ann. #1 WEI,SDi'London'sBrilliant' . 3.00
1-Shot Gen13:Unreal World (1996). 3.00
Gen13 3-D Special (1997). 5.00
3-D Spec. #1, (1997) 5.00
3-D Spec. #1, variant cover 5.00
3-D Spec. #1, (1998) 5.00
TPB rep.1–#5 of original mini-
   series, 3rd printing 13.00
TPB Lost in Paradise, rep. #3–#5 . . 7.00
TPB EuropeanVacation,rep.#6–#7 . 7.00
TPB rep. #13 A, B & C. 7.00
TPB Ordinary Heroes 13.00
TPB WildStorm Archives, rep. mini-
   series, #0–#13, covers, etc. . . 13.00

WildStorm/DC, 1999

37 JAr,GFr,CaS,Reaper. 2.50

Gen13 #36 © WildStorm

38 JAr,GFr,CaS,BU:Grunge. 2.50
38a variant cover. 2.50
39 JAr,GFr,CaS,Genocide. 2.50
40 JAr,GFr,CaS,V.Reaper 2.50
41 JAr,GFr,CaS 2.50
42 JoC(s),KM,pro wrestlers 2.50
43 AWa(s&c),F:Fairchild 2.50
44 AWa(s&c),A:Mr.Magestic 2.50
45 SLo,EBe,JSb,fashion show 2.50
46 SLo,EBe,JSb,MightyJoeGrunge. 2.50
47 SLo,EBe,JSb. 2.50
48 SLo,EBe,JSb. 2.50
49 SLo,EBe,JSb. 2.50
50 SLo,EBe,JSb,48-pg. 4.00
50a variant JLe,SW(c) (1:4). 4.00
51 SLo,breather 2.50
52 SLo,F:Caitlin Fairchild. 2.50
53 F:all Villains issue 2.50
54 SLo,EBe,SWi,F:Fairchild 2.50
55 EBe,Return to Pod 9,pt.2 . . . . . 2.50
56 EBe,Fairchild,pt.3 . . . . 2.50
57 BRa,EBe,Tokyo in danger. 2.50
58 BRa,EBe,mini-monster
   massacre. 2.50
59 BRa,EBe,V:Gaijin13 . . . . 2.50
60 AWa,Behind the Power. 2.50
61 AWa,Goin' back to Cali 2.50
62 AWa,fast food 2.50
63 AWa,EBe,sailboat outing 2.50
64 AWa,Superhuman Like You,pt.1 . 2.50
65 AWa,Superhuman Like You,pt.2 . 2.50
66 AWa,8 guest artists. 2.50
67 AWa,EBe,ColdAir on MyBehind . 2.50
68 AWa,Slave to Love,pt.1. . . . . . . 2.50
69 AWa,Slave to Love,pt.2. . . . . . . 2.50
70 AWa,F:Sara Rainmaker 2.50
71 AWa,Think Like A Gun,pt.1. . . . . 2.50
72 AWa,Think Like A Gun,pt.2. . . . . 2.50
73 AWa,Think Like A Gun,pt.3. . . . . 2.50
74 AWa,Think Like A Gun,pt.4. . . . . 2.50
75 AWa,How the Story Ends,pt.1. . . 2.50
76 AWa,How the Story Ends,pt.2. . . 2.50
77 AWa,Story Ends,pt.3, 40-pg. . . . 3.50
Annual'99 JAr(s) 3.50
Ann. 2000 #1, Devil's
   Night x-over,pt.1 . . . . 3.50
Spec. Wired 2.50
Spec.#1 3-D AAd 5.00
Spec.#1a variant(c) 5.00
Spec. Carny Folk 3.50
Spec. 1-shot Going West. 2.50
GN Grunge Saves the World. 6.00
GN Bootleg: Grunge— The Movie. 10.00
GN Medicine Song, 48-pg. 6.00
GN Gen13/Fantastic Four 6.00
GN Science Friction, 48-pg. 6.00

GN London,New York,Hell 7.00
GN A Christmas Caper (2002). 6.00
TPB Gen13 . . . . 13.00
TPB Interactive Plus 12.00
TPB Starting Over 15.00
TPB I Love New York. 10.00
TPB We'll Take Manhattan. 15.00
TPB Super-Human Like You 13.00

GEN¹³ BOOTLEG
WildStorm, Nov., 1996
1 MFm&AD,lost in the 'Linquist
   Fault,'pt.1. . . . . 3.00
1a signed 15.00
2 'Linquist Fault,'pt.2. . . . . 3.50
3 Gen13 Fairy Tale 3.50
4 WS&LSi,F:Valaria,'Little Girl
   Lost'. 3.50
5 F:Fairchild,'Timesick,'pt.1 . . . . . . 3.50
6 F:Fairchild,'Timesick,'pt.2 . . . . . . 3.50
7 'Renaissance Ruckus' 3.50
8 AWa,'Grunge's Movie,'pt.1. . . . . . 4.00
9 AWa,'Grunge's Movie,'pt.2. . . . . . 4.00
10 AWa,'Grunge's Movie,'pt.3 . . . . 4.00
11 AaL,WS,Chupacabra,pt.1 . . . . . 2.50
12 AaL,WS,Chupacabra,pt.2 . . . . . 2.50
13 F:Grunge,'The Trickster' 2.50
14 JMi,JoP,GL,bad neighbors 2.50
15 KNo,V:'Trance,'Hanging,'pt.1. . . 2.50
16 KNo,V:Trance,'Hanging,'pt.2. . . 2.50
17 'Virgil Chu's Reality. 2.50
18 MFm,'A Day at the Beach' 2.50
19 BKs,JhB,Satyr. 2.50
20 CAd,F:John Lynch,'Numbskulls'. 2.50
Ann.#1 WEI,SDi, to NYC 3.00
TPB Grunge: The Movie,AWa 10.00
TPB Vol.1, rep.#1–#4. . . . . 12.00

GEN¹³: INTERACTIVE
WildStorm, Oct., 1997
1 vote via Internet. 4.00
2 & 3 MHs,vote via Internet . . . . @3.00
TPB Gen13 Interactive Plus, rep. . 12.00

GEN¹³/ GENERATION X
WildStorm, July, 1997
1 BCi&AAd,'Generation Gap' 3.00
1a variant JSC(c) 3.00
3-D edition, with glasses 5.00
3-Da variant cover, with glasses . . . 5.00

GEN¹³: MAGICAL DRAMA QUEEN ROXY
WildStorm, Oct., 1998
1 (of 3) AWa,Mall of Doom 4.00
2 AWa,V:Caitlin 4.00
3 AWa,dream sequence concl. 4.00

GEN¹³/THE MAXX
WildStorm, 1995
Spec.#1 BML,x-over 4.00

GEN¹³/MONKEY MAN & O'BRIEN
WildStorm, June, 1998
1 (of 2) AAd. 3.00
1a chromium edition 4.50
2 AAd,alternate universe, concl. . . . 3.00
2a variant AAd(c) 2.50

GEN¹³: ORDINARY HEROES
WildStorm, 1996
1 & 2 . . . . @3.00

GEN¹²
WildStorm, Feb., 1998
1 BCi,Team 7 tie-in,'The Legacy' . . 3.00
2 BCi,F:Morgan of I.O. 3.00
3 BCi,Dominique Faust. 3.00
4 BCi,F:Miles Craven 3.00
5 BCi,Team 7 re-unites. 3.00

GHOST SPY
May, 2004
1 (of 6) 3.00
2 thru 5 . . . . @3.00

GIFT, THE
2004
8 Sacrifice 3.00
9 Corrupt. 3.00
10 Unleashed. 3.00
11 Betrayal. 3.00
12 Death 3.00
13 The Dragon. 3.00
14 O:Ancient One 3.00
1a director's cut 4.00
TPB Vol. 2 Consequences. 15.00
TPB Vol. 1 Choices 15.00

G.I. JOE
Sept., 2001
1 JSC(c) Reinstated,pt.1. . . . . 15.00
1a 2nd printing 6.00
2 Reinstated,pt.2. . . . . 6.00
3 JSC(c),Reinstated,pt.3. . . . . 5.00
4 JSC(c),Reinstated,pt.4. . . . . 5.00
5 F:Duke 3.50
6 Reckonings,pt.1 . . . . 3.00
7 Storm Shadow 3.00
8 Destro & Cobra Commander. . . . 3.00
9 Snake-eyes vs. Storm Shadow . . 3.00
10 Dreadnoks. 3.00
11 Mob rule in Chicago 3.00
12 JBz(c),V:Android Trooper 3.00
13 JBz(c),V:Firefly 3.00
14 Cobra Suburbs Return 3.00
15 Reunion. 3.00
16 missing child 3.00
17 kidnap Flint & Baroness 3.00
18 search for Flint & Baroness 3.00
19 . . . . 3.00
20 Storm Shadow 3.00
21 Snake-Eyes. 4.00
22 Return of Serpentor,pt.1 . . . . . . 4.00
21a & 22a variant (c)s . . . . @10.00
23 Return of Serpentor,pt.2 . . . . . . 3.00
24 Return of Serpentor,pt.3 . . . . . . 3.00
24a variant(c). 3.00
25 . . . . 3.00
25a variant (c) 3.00
Spec. M.I.A., rep. #1 & #2 . . . . . . 5.00
TPB Vol.1 Reinstated. 15.00
TPB Vol. 2 Reckonings 13.00
TPB Vol. 3 Malfunction 13.00
Devil's Due 2004
26 thru 30. . . . . @3.00
31 . . . . 8.00
32 . . . . 3.00
33 . . . . 7.00
33 2nd printing 8.00
34 thru 41 . . . . @3.00
42 D:Lady Jaye 5.00
TPB Vol. 4 Alliances. 13.00
TPB Vol. 5 Return of Serpentor. . . 13.00

G.I. JOE: BATTLE FILES
April, 2002
1 (of 3) G.I. Joe, 48-pg. 6.00
2 F:Cobra 6.00
3 F:Vehicles and Tech 6.00
TPB 15.00

IMAGE

G.I. JOE FRONTLINE
Oct., 2002
1 LHa(s),DJu,BL,DvD(c)........ 3.00
2 DJu,BL,DvD(c) V:Destro 3.00
3 DJu,BL,DvD(c) V:Destro 3.00
4 DJu,BL,Silent Castle 3.00
5 Icebound 3.00
6 Icebound,pt.2............... 3.00
7 Icebound,pt.3............... 3.00
8 Icebound,pt.4............... 3.00
9 Kansas City 3.00
10 .... 3.00
11 Chuckles.................. 3.00
12 Chuckles.................. 3.00
13 Chuckles.................. 3.00
14 Chuckles.................. 3.00
15 F:Stalker................. 3.00
16 Night Creepers 3.00
17 PJe,F:Beachhead 3.00
18 .... 3.00
18a variant (c) 3.00
16a–17a variant (c) .... @3.00
TPB Vol. 1 .... 13.00

G.I. JOE VS. TRANSFORMERS
June, 2003
1 .... 4.00
1a 2nd printing 3.00
2 thru 6 .... @3.00
1a–6a variant (c) .... @5.00

GIRLS
May, 2005
1 .... 6.00
1a 2nd & 3rd printings........ @3.00
2 .... 4.00
3 thru 10 .... @3.00
11 thru 19 .... 3.00
TPB Vol. 1 Conception. 15.00
TPB Vol. 2 Emergence 15.00
TPB Vol. 3 Survival 15.00

GLORY
Extreme, 1995
0 JDy........................ 2.50
1 JDy,F:Glory................ 4.00
1a variant cover 4.00
2 JDy,V:Demon Father 3.00
3 JDy,A:Rumble & Vandal....... 2.50
4 Vandal vs. Demon Horde...... 2.50

Glory #3
© Image/Extreme

4a JDy variant cover........... 3.00
5 Supreme Apocalypse,pt.3,
  F:Vandal 2.50
6 Drug Problem............... 2.50
7 F:Superpatriot 2.50
8 Extreme Babewatch........... 2.50
9 Extreme Destroyer,pt.5,
  x-over, bagged with card 2.50
10 .... 2.50
11 .... 2.50
12 JDy, EBe & JSb 3.50
13 JDy, EBe & JSb 2.50
14 JDy, EBe & JSb 2.50
15 JDy, EBe & JSb, Out for
  vengeance................ 2.50
TPB rep.#1–#4 .... 10.00
continued: see Color Comics section

GLORY/ANGELA ANGELS IN HELL
Extreme, 1996
1 .... 4.00

GLORY/AVENGELYNE
Extreme, 1996
1 V:B'lial,I:Faith.............. 4.00
1a no chrome(c)............... 3.00

GLORY/AVENGELYNE: THE GODYSSEY
Extreme
1 RLd & JDy 3.00
1a photo(c)................... 4.00

GLORY/CELESTINE: DARK ANGEL
Extreme, Sept., 1996
1 (of 3) JDy,PtL,sequel to Rage of
  Angels, A:Maximage 2.50
2 JDy,PtL,'Doomsday+1'....... 2.50
3 JDy,PtL, conclusion 2.50

GLORY & FRIENDS
Extreme, 1995
Bikini Fest #1................ 2.50
Bikini Fest #2................ 2.50
Lingerie Special #1 (1995)........ 3.00
Christmas Special #1 (1995) 2.50

G-MAN
Dec., 2004
1 Learning to Fly.............. 6.00

GODLAND
June, 2005
1 Cosmic Wheels in Motion 3.00
2 Every Breath You Take 3.00
3 The seismic Shift 3.00
4 The Torture Never Stops 3.00
5 Combat Rock............... 3.00
6 .... 3.00
7 Acid Raindrops............. 3.00
8 The Origin of the Universe 3.00
9 Funky Buster Round 3.00
10 The March of Ides........... 3.00
11 Never Say Janus........... 3.00
12 High Noon, Tea Time, 32-pg. ... 3.00
13 .... 3.00
13a variant (c) 3.00
14 .... 3.00
TPB Vol. 1 Hello, Cosmic 15.00
TPB Vol. 2 Another Sunny Delight. 15.00

GO GIRL!
Aug., 2000
1 TrR,F:Lindsay Goldman........ 3.50

Glory & Friends Lingerie Special #1
© Image/Extreme

2 TrR,wonderful life?........... 3.50
3 TrR,The Teacher from Hell 3.50
4 TrR,Vacation at dude ranch..... 3.50
5 TrR,origin of powers 3.50

GOLDFISH
(B&W) 1998
TPB by Brian Michael Bendis 17.00
TPB 272-pg. Definitive Colleciton . 20.00

GRAY AREA, THE
June, 2004
1 (of 3) JR2,KJ,48-pg. 6.00
2 JR2,KJ,32-pg. 4.00
3 JRw,KJ,48-pg. 6.00
TPB Vol. 1 All of this can be yours 15.00

GREASE MONKEY
March, 1998
1 TEI........................ 3.00
2 TEI........................ 3.00
3 TEI, The Calling; Rewards...... 3.00

GRIFTER
WildStorm, 1995–96
1 BWS(c), WildStorm
  Rising,pt.5,w/2 cards........ 2.50
1a Newsstand ed.............. 2.50
2 V:Diabolik,pt.1 .... 3.00
3 V:Diabolik,pt.2 .... 3.00
4 R:Forgotten Hero............. 3.00
5 Rampage of a Fallen Hero 3.00
6 V:Poerhouse................ 3.00
7 City of Angels,pt.1 .... 3.00
8 City of Angels,pt.2 .... 3.00
9 City of Angels,pt.3 .... 3.00
10 City of Angels,pt.4........... 3.00

GRIFTER/BADROCK
Extreme, 1995
1 To Save Badrock's Mom 3.00
1a Variant cover 2.50
2 flip-book-Badrock #2 .... 3.00
3 double-size 3.50

GRIFTER-ONE SHOT
WildStorm, 1995
1 SS,DN 5.00

GRIFTER
WildStorm, 1996
1 StG. 4.00
2 StG,V:Joe the Dead 3.00
3 StG,captured by MadJackPower . 3.00
4 StG,vs. Condition Red 3.00
5 StG,Grifter meets his dad,
   F:Molly Ingram. 3.00
6 StG,A:Santini 3.00
7 StG,MtB,I:Charlatan 3.00
8 StG,MtB,Zealot
   disappears,V:Soldier 3.00
9 StG,Zealot captured?, secret
   history of Quiet Men 3.00
10 StG,Grifter & Soldier go to
   rescue Zealot. 3.00
11 StG, renegade former agent 3.00
12 StG,'Who is Tanager?'. 3.00
13 StG,F:Condition Red,'Family
   Feud' 3.00
14 StG,V:Joe the Dead 3.00

GRIFTER/SHI
WildStorm, 1996
1 BCi,JLe,TC 3.00
2 BCi,JLe,TC 3.00

GROO
1994–95
1 SA 3.50
2 A:Arba, Dakarba 3.50
3 The Generals Hat 3.50
4 A Drink of Water. 3.50
5 SA,A Simple Invasion 3.50
6 SA,A Little Invention 3.50
7 The Plight of the Drazils 3.50
8 . . . . 3.50
9 I:Arfetto 3.50
10 The Sinkes 3.50
11 The Gamblers 3.50
12 . . . . 3.50

GROUNDED
July, 2005
1 (of 6) 3.00
2 thru 5 . . . . @3.00
6 32-pg. 3.50
TPB 15.00

GRRL SCOUTS
Feb., 2003
1 (of 4) Work Sucks, b&w. 3.00
2 thru 4 . . . . @3.00
TPB Vol. 1 . . . . 13.00
TPB Work Sucks 13.00

GUARDIAN ANGEL
May, 2002
1 (of 4) AWs,F:ChristianAngelos. . . 3.00
2 AWs,no place like home 3.00
3 AWs,Our onlyhope. 3.00
4 concl. 3.00

GUNCANDY
(B&W) July, 2005
1 (of 2) BSf 6.00
2 BSt. 6.00

GUN FU
Aug., 2005
GN 15.00

HAMMER OF THE GODS
Sept., 2002
TPB: Mortal Enemy, 176-pg. 19.00
TPB Vol. 2 Back From the Dead . . 16.00

HAMMER OF THE GODS:
HAMMER HITS CHINA
Feb., 2003
1 thru 3 . . . . @3.00

HAWAIIAN DICK
Dec., 2002
1 thru 3 Hawaii in 1953. . . . . . . @3.00
TPB Vol. 1 Byrd of Paradise 15.00

HAWAIIAN DICK:
THE LAST RESORT
Aug., 2004
1 (of 4) 3.00
2 & 3 . . . . @3.00
4 concl. 3.00
TPB Vol. 2 The Last Resort. 15.00

HAWKSHAWS
March, 2000
1 by Dietrich Smith 3.00
1a variant movie poster(c) 3.00
2 and 3 . . . . @3.00

Hazard #4 © WildStorm

HAZARD
WildStorm, 1996
1 JMi,RMr 3.00
2 JMi,RMr 3.00
3 JMi,RMr 3.00
4 JMi,RMr 3.00
5 JMi,RMr,Hazard finds Dr. D'Oro . 3.00
6 JMi,RMr 3.00
7 JMi,RMr,Hazard meets Prism . . . 3.00

HEADHUNTERS
(B&W) April, 1997
1 ChM,V:Army of Wrath 3.00
2 ChM,V:undead militia. 3.00
3 ChM,'Slaughterground' 3.00

HEARTBREAKERS
Superdigest, July 1998
1 B&W and color 104-pg. 10.00

HEARTBREAKERS
VERSUS BIOVOC
Image
TPB 'Bust Out' 10.00
TPB PGn 15.00

HEAVEN, LLC
Mar., 2004
TPB 13.00

HEAVEN'S DEVILS
Sept., 2003
1 (of 4) 3.00
2 . . . . 3.00
3 . . . . 3.00
4 . . . . 3.00

HEAVEN'S WAR
Image
GN b&w, 120-pg. 13.00

HEDGE KNIGHT, THE
Aug., 2003
1 (of 6) MsM 5.00
1a variant (c) 12.00
2 . . . . 5.00
2a cardstock(c) 10.00
3 . . . . 4.00
3a holofoil (c) 6.00
See also Color Comics section

HEIRS OF ETERNITY
Apr., 2003
1 (of 5) 3.00
2 . . . . 3.00
3 . . . . 3.00
4 . . . . 3.00
5 . . . . 3.00

HELLCOP
Avalon, Oct., 1998
1 JoC,F:Virgil Hilts 2.50
2 JoC,It's a small underwold
   after all. 2.50
3 JoC,new circles of Hell 2.50
4 JoC,secrets of Hell revealed . . . 2.50
5 JoC,Hell & High Water. 2.50
5a variant cover 3.00

HELLHOLE
Top Cow, May, 1999
1 SLo,AdP,F:Michael Cabrini 2.50
2 SLo,AdP,The Devil's Candy. . . . 2.50
3 SLo,AdP,power brokers 2.50

HELLHOUNDS
Aug., 2003
1 Hadean Gates 3.00
2 thru 5 . . . . @3.00
6 EL(c),F:Savage Dragon. 3.00
1a and 2a variant (c). . . . . @3.00
5a variant (c) 3.00

HELLSHOCK
1994
1 I:Hellshock 3.50
2 Powers & Origin. 3.50
3 New foe 3.50
4 . . . . 3.50

HELLSHOCK
Jan., 1997
1 JaL,Something wrong with
   Daniel, 48-pg. 3.00
2 JaL,Daniel learns to control
   powers. 2.50
3 JaL,Daniel free of madness. 2.50
4 JaL,Daniel searches for his
   mother, Jonakand plans escape
   from Hell 2.50
5 JaL,Jonakand and fallen angels
   tear hell apart 2.50
6 JaL,'The Milk of Paradise' 2.50

IMAGE

7 JaL,'A Mother's Story',
  double size 4.00
8 JaL,House of Torture 2.50
TPB The Definitive Edition, JaL. . . 20.00

HELLSPAWN
TMP, July, 2000
1 The Clown,pt.1. . . . . 4.00
2 The Clown,pt.2. . . . . 3.00
3 Hate Me 3.00
4 Hate You 3.00
5 Selling Fear 3.00
6 Angels 5.00
7 The Group 2.50
8 The Suicide Gate 2.50
9 Chains 2.50
10 Clash. 2.50
11 Conflicts of Interest 2.50
12 Monsters and Miracles 2.50
13 Heaven & Hell. 2.50
14 Light of Day. 2.50
15 Blinded 2.50
16 Hellworld,pt.4 . . . . 2.50
17 The Killing Hand,pt.1 . . . . 2.50
18 The Killing Hand,pt.2 . . . . 2.50
19 The Killing Hand,pt.3 . . . . 2.50
20 The Collection. 2.50
21 The Collection,pt.2 . . . . 2.50
22 Love Lost,pt.1 . . . . 3.00
23 Love Lost,pt.2. . . . . 3.00
24 In the Grip of Shadows. 2.50
25 Remember Me? 2.50
TPB Ashly Wood Collection 25.00

Hero Camp #4
© Image

HERO CAMP
May, 2005
1 (of 4) 3.00
2 I Still Haven't Found What I'm
  Looking For, pt.1 . . . . 3.00
3 . . . . 3.00
4 Parents Day. 3.00

HOLY TERROR, THE
Aug., 2002
1 (of 4) PhH 3.00
2 thru 3 PhH . . . . @3.00

HOMAGE STUDIOS
April, 1993
Swimsuit Spec.#1 JLe,WPo, MS . . . 2.50

HONG ON THE RANGE
Matinee Entertainment/
Flypaper, Dec., 1997
1 (of 3) by William Wu & Jeff
  Lafferty. 2.50
2 in Washout. 2.50
3 Duke Goslin 2.50
TPB Hong on the Range 13.00

HOUDINI:
THE MAN FROM BEYOND
Oct., 2004
TPB 17.00

HUMAN KIND
Top Cow, Aug., 2004
1 TnD,F:Alia Sparrow 3.00
2 TnD 3.00
3 TnD,Roads to New Rome,pt.3. . . 3.00
4 All Roads Lead to (New) Rome. . 3.00
5 All Roads Lead to (New) Rome. . 3.00

HUNTER-KILLER
Top Cow, 2005
0 MWa,MS, B&W, 16-pg. 0.25
1 MWa,MS 3.00
2 MWa,MS 3.00
2a variant JLi 3.00
3 MWa,MS 3.00
4 thru 6 MWa,MS . . . . @3.00
7 . . . . 3.00
8 . . . . 3.00
9 . . . . 3.00
9a variant (c). 3.00
10 . . . . 3.00
11 The Deadly Game Continues . . 3.00
11a variant b&w (c), rare 4.00
12 The End of Morningstar? 3.00
Script-book 40-pg. 5.00
1-shot Hunter-Killer Dossier. 3.00

HYSTERIA:
ONE MAN GANG
(B&W) March, 2006
1 . . . . 3.00
2 . . . . 3.00
3 All car chase issue. 3.00
4 . . . . 3.50

IMAGE COMICS
Dec., 2005
Spec. Holiday Spec. (2005) 10.00

IMAGE FIRST
Nov., 2005
TPB Vol. 1 . . . . 7.00

IMAGE INTRODUCES:
Oct., 2001
1 Primate 3.00
1b variant AGo(c) 3.00
(2) Legend of Isis. 3.00
(3) The Believer 3.00
(4) Cryptopia 3.00
(5) Dog Soldiers. 3.00

IMAGE TWO-IN-ONE
(B&W) Mar., 2001
1 EL,48-pg. F:Herculian & Duncan. 3.00

IMAGE ZERO
1993
0 I:Troll,Deathtrap,Pin-ups,rep.
  Savage Dragon #4,O:Stryker,
  F:ShadowHawk 15.00

IMAGES OF
SHADOWHAWK
1993–94
1 KG,V:Trencher 2.50
2 thru 3 V:Trencher. 2.50

Imaginaries #2
© Image

IMAGINARIES, THE
Mar., 2005
1 (of 4) 3.00
2 . . . . 3.00
2a variant (c). 3.00
3 & 4 . . . . @3.00

IMMORTAL TWO
May, 1997
(B&W) Half-Tone
1 MsM,F:Gaijin & Gabrielle. 2.50
2 MsM 2.50
3 MsM. 2.50
4 MsM,V:Okami Red. 2.50
5 MsM,new drug epidemic 2.50
6 MsM,First Order, cont. 2.50
7 MsM,vs. impossible odds 2.50
7 MsM,flip photo cover 2.50

IMPALER
Oct., 2006
1 & 2 . . . . @3.00

INDIGO VERTIGO
(B&W) Aug., 2005
GN 5.00

INDUSTRY OF WAR
(B&W) Nov., 2005
1-shot. 8.00

INFERNO: HELLBOUND
Top Cow, Nov., 2001
1 MS,DT,Hell loose on Earth 2.50
1a-1f variant(c) 2.50
2 thru 4 MS. . . . . @2.75
#0 MS 16-pg., signed. 20.00

INNOCENTS, THE
Top Cow, July, 2006
1 . . . . 3.00
GN 10.00

INTIMIDATORS, THE
Dec., 2005
1	3.50
2	3.50
3 Who is Atrocity	3.50
4 Crash and Byrn	3.50
5 Prison Break	3.50
6 Last Best Hope	3.50
7 Blame Canada	3.50

INTRIGUE
Aug., 1999
1 F:Kirk Best	2.50
1a variant cover (1:4)	2.50
2 on the run from the law	2.50
3 V:NYPD SWAT team	2.50
3a variant HuR cover (1:4)	2.50
4	2.50
5	3.00
5a variant Mike Wieringo(c)	3.00

INVINCIBLE
Jan., 2003
1 O:Mark Grayson	30.00
2	25.00
3 quality time	17.00
4 human bombs	15.00
5 It Came From Outer Space	12.00
6	12.00
7 Guardians of the Globe	10.00
8 shperhero funeral	10.00
9 Perfect Strangers,pt.1	10.00
10 Perfect Strangers,pt.2	8.00
11 Perfect Strangers,pt.3	8.00
12 Perfect Strangers,pt.4	8.00
13 Perfect Strangers,epilogue	8.00
14 Alien invaders return	8.00
15 Aquaria	5.00
16 Immortal is back	5.00
17 High school graduation	5.00
18 Space flight to Mars	5.00
19	3.00
20 Return of the Robot Zombie	3.00
21 Return to Midnight City	3.00
22 Mark and Amber at college	3.00
23	3.00
24 Worst beating yet	3.00
25 A Different World, pt.1	5.00
26 A Different World, pt.2	3.00
27 A Different World, pt.3	3.00
28 A Different World, pt.4	3.00
29	3.00
30 A Different World	3.00
31 Mark & Amber to Africa	3.00
32 Life with Amber and Eva	3.00
33 Angstrom Levy	3.00
34 Angstrom Levy	3.00
35	3.00
36 Re-animen Strike	3.00
37	3.00
38	3.00
Spec. #0	1.00
Spec. Official Handbook of the Invincible Universe, Vol. 1	5.00
Spec. Script Book	4.00
TPB Vol. 1 Family Matters	13.00
TPB Vol. 2 Eight is Enough	13.00
TPB Vol. 3 Perfect Strangers	13.00
TPB Vol. 2 rep. #5–#8	13.00
TPB Vol. 4 Head of the Class	15.00
TPB Vol. 5 The Facts of Life	15.00
TPB Vol. 6 A Different World	15.00
TPB Vol. 7 Three's Company	15.00

INVISIBLE 9
Flypaper, May, 1998
TPB	13.00

IRON GHOST
Apr., 2005
1 thru 6 CDi(s)	@3.00

IRON WINGS
March, 2000
1 Legends of Iron Wings	2.50
1a variant Andy Park(c)	2.50
2 V:Amaxius	2.50
3 Nightmares	2.50

JACKIE CHAN'S SPARTAN X
(B&W) March, 1998
1 MGo,RM,Hell-Bent Hero for Hire	3.00
2 MGo,to Russia	3.00

Jackie Chan Spartan X #1
© Image

3 MGo,V:Kenshi	3.00
4 MGo,RM, in Istanbul	3.00
5 MGo,RM, Mind of God	3.00
5a MGo,RM, photo cover	3.00
6 MGo,RM, The Armor of Heaven	3.00
6a MGo,RM, photo cover	3.00

JACK STAFF
Feb., 2003
1 Britain's Greatest hero	3.00
2 thru 7	@3.00
8 thru 14	@3.50
TPB Vol. 1	20.00
TPB Vol. 2 Soldiers	16.00

JADE WARRIORS
Aug., 1999
1 MD2,Destruction of Japan	2.50
2 MD2,V:Ramthar	2.50
3 MD2,Blood of the Children	2.50
1a thru 3a photo(c)	@2.50
3b movie poster style(c)	2.50

JINN
Jan., 2000
1 F:Karen Lane	3.00
2 and 3	@3.00
1a thru 2a variant cover	@3.00

JINX
(B&W) June, 1997
1 by Brian Michael Bendis	3.00

1a 2nd printing	3.00
2 F:Jinx, female bounty hunter	3.00
3 thru 5	@4.00
Spec.#1 Buried Treasure	4.00
Spec.#1 True Crime Confessions	4.00
TPB rep. prev. #1–#4	10.00
TPB The Essential Collection	18.00
TPB 480-pg.	25.00

JINX: TORSO
(B&W) Aug., 1998
1 by Brian Michael Bendis, 48-pg.	4.00
2 search continues	4.00
3 Torso Killer	4.00
4 breaking the law	4.00
5 48-pg.	5.00
6 conclusion, 48-pg.	5.00
Spec. #@%!! short stories	4.00

JOURNEYMAN
Aug., 1999
1 by Brandon McKinney	3.00
2 enemies become allies	3.00
3 V:Dragon King	3.00

J.U.D.G.E.
March, 2000
1 by Greg Horn,F:Victoria Grace	3.00
1a variant cover	3.00
2 V:John Lawson	3.00
3 Secret Rage,pt.3	3.00

JUNKBOTZ ROTOGIN
Feb., 2003
1	2.50

KABUKI
Sept., 1997
1 DMk,O:Kabuki	7.00
1a variant JSo(c)	7.00
2 DMk,O:Kabuki, pg.2	5.00
3 DMk,surprise visitor	6.00
4 DMk,Akemi, romance	7.00
5 DMk,action	4.00
6 DMk	3.00
7 DMk	3.00
7a DMk variant cover (1:2)	3.00
8 DMk	3.00
9 DMk, finale	3.00
TPB Circle of Blood,rep. orig. series plus 'Fear the Reaper,' B&W	18.00
TPB Masks of the Noh	11.00
TPB Masks of the Noh, 2nd pr.	13.00
TPB Images, part rep. #1, 48 pg	6.00
TPB Dreams	10.00
TPB Vol.2 Dreams	13.00
TPB Vol.4 Skin Deep	10.00
TPB Vol.4 Skin Deep, 2nd pr.	11.00
TPB Vol.4 Skin Deep, rep.	13.00
TPB Vol.5 Metamorphosis	25.00
TPB Vol. 6 Scarab	20.00
GN Reflections #1, 48-pg.	5.00
GN Reflections #1 signed	8.00
GN Reflections #2 art & stories	5.00
GN Reflections,Vol.3	5.00
GN Reflections,Vol.4	5.00
Spec. 1-shot The Ghost Play	3.00
Spec. #2 Images, rep. #2 & #3	6.00
Kabuki 1/2 Wizard Mail-in	3.00
Kabuki 1/2 signed	6.00

KABUKI AGENTS
(B&W) Aug., 1999
1 DMk,F:Scarab	4.00
1a JQ(c), DMk signed	7.00
2 DMk,F:Scarab, Tiger Lily	3.00
3 DMk,F:Scarab, Tiger Lily	3.00
4 DMk,F:Scarab, Tiger Lily	3.00
5 thru 8 DMk	@3.00

IMAGE

Artbook 5.00
Kabuki Agents: Scarab #1 signed . . 6.00

KABUKI: THE ALCHEMY
Jan., 2004
1 (of 6) DMk 3.00
2 DMk 3.00

KABUKI CLASSICS
Feb., 1999
1 Fear the Reaper, rep. 10.00
2 Dance of Death 3.00
3 Circle of Blood, act 1, 48-pg. . . . 6.00
4 Circle of Blood, act 2 . . . . 4.00
5 Circle of Blood, act 3 . . . . 3.00
6 Circle of Blood, act 4 . . . . 3.00
7 Circle of Blood, act 5 . . . . 3.00
8 Circle of Blood, conclusion 3.00
9 Masks of the Noh, Act 1 . . . . . . 3.00
10 Masks of the Noh, Act 2 . . . . . . 3.00
11 Masks of the Noh, Act 3 . . . . . . 3.00
12 Masks of the Noh, concl. 3.00
Kabuki Classics #1 signed. 7.00

KANE
Jan., 2004
TPB Vol.1 From New Eden 12.00
TPB Vol.2 Rabbit Hunt. 13.00
TPB Vol.3 Histories 13.00
TPB Vol. 4 Thirty-Ninth 17.00
TPB Vol. 5 Untouchable Rico
   Costas 14.00
TPB Vol. 6 . . . . 17.00

KARZA
Feb., 2003
1 thru 4 Micronauts spin-off . . . . @3.00

KID SUPREME
Supreme 1996–97
1 & 2 . . . . 2.50
3 DaF,ErS 2.50
4 DaF,ErS,Party time 2.50
5 DaF,ErS,'Birds of a Feather' . . . 2.50
6 DaF,ErS,I: Sensational Spinner . 2.50
7 DaF,ErS,Everything falls apart. . 2.50

KID TERRIFIC
(B&W) Nov., 1998
1 A:Snedak & Manny Stellar 3.00

KILLER INSTINCT
TOUR BOOK
1 All Homage Artist,I:Crusade. . . . 5.00
1a signed 45.00

KILLRAZOR SPECIAL
Aug., 1995
1 O:Killrazor 2.50

KIN
Top Cow, Feb., 2000
1 GFr,Neanderthal 3.00
2 GFr,F:McLoon 3.00
3 GFr,Alaska revenge. 3.00
4 GFr. 3.00
5 GFr,Born Free 3.00
6 GFr,40-pg.,The End? 4.00
6a variant AAd(c) 4.00
1st 6 as set, signed GFr 25.00
TPB Descent of Man 18.00

KINDRED
WildStorm, 1994
1 JLe,BCi(s),BBh,I:Kindred 5.00
2 JLe,BCi(s),BBh,V:Kindred 3.50
3 JLe,BCi(s),BBh,V:Kindred 3.00

3a WPo(c),Alternate(c) 6.00
4 JLe,BCi(s),BBh,V:Kindred 3.00
TPB rep. #1-#4 . . . . 10.00

'KINI
Flypaper, Feb., 1999
1 KK,BKs,F:Kim Walters 2.50

KISS:
THE PSYCHO CIRCUS
TMP, July, 1997
1 SvG,AMe 8.00
2 AMe, unearthly origins 6.00
3 AMe, Judgment o/t Elementals . . 5.00
4 AMe,Smoke and Mirrors,pt.1 . . . 4.00
5 AMe,Smoke and Mirrors,pt.2 . . . 4.00
6 AMe,Smoke and Mirrors, concl. . 4.00
7 AMe,Creatures of the Night 3.00
8 AMe,Forever 3.00
9 AMe,Four Sides to Every Story . 3.00
10 AMe,Destroyer,pt.1 . . . . 3.00
11 AMe,Destroyer,pt.2 . . . . 3.00
12 AMe,Destroyer,pt.3 (of 4) 3.00
13 AMe, Destroyer,pt.4 . . . . 3.00
14 AMe, in Feudal Japan 3.00
15 AMe, in Feudal Japan, choices. . 2.50
16 AMe, Ticket for Terror 2.50
17 AMe, World Without Heroes,pt.2 2.50
18 AMe, Sunburst Finish 2.50
19 Fate of the Psycho Circus 2.50
20 Mr. Makebelieve 2.50
21 Don't Talk to Strangers 2.50
22 Twin sisters 2.50
23 Tribunal of souls 2.50
24 Cat's Eye 2.50
25 . . . . 2.50
26 Nightingale's Song,pt.1 . . . . 2.50
27 Nightingale's Song,pt.2 . . . . 2.50
28 Perdition Blues 2.50
29 Shadow of the Moon,pt.1 . . . . . 2.50
30 Shadow of the Moon,pt.2 . . . . . 2.50
31 Sins of Omission 2.50
32 Gallery of God's Mistakes 2.50
33 Gallery of God's Mistakes,pt.2 . . 2.50
34 Far Corners of Night 2.50
TPB Vol. I, rep. #1-#6 . . . . 13.00
TPB Vol. II rep. #10-#13 . . . . 10.00
TPB Vol.3 Whispered Scream . . . 10.00
TPB Vol.4 Legends & Nightmares . 10.00
Kiss Mag.#5 rep. 5.00

KNIGHTMARE
Extreme, 1995
0 O:Knightmare. 2.50
1 I:Knightmare MMy 2.50
2 I:Caine 2.50
3 RLd,AV,The New Order,
   F:Detective Murtaugh 2.50
4 RLd,AV,MMy,I:Thrillkill 2.50
5 V:Thrillkill 2.50
6 Extreme Babewatch. 2.50
7 . . . . 2.50
8 I:Acid 2.50

KNIGHTS OF
THE JAGUAR
Top Cow, Jan., 2004
Spec. super limited 2.50

KNIGHTSTRIKE
Extreme, 1996
1 Extreme Destroyer,pt.6
   x-over, bagged with card 2.50

KNIGHT WATCHMAN
(B&W) May, 1998
1 by Gary Carlson & Chris Ecker . . 3.00
2 thru 4 Graveyard Shift,pt.2–pt.3 @3.00

KORE
Apr., 2003
1 . . . . 3.00
1a variant (c) 3.00
2 thru 5 . . . . @3.00

KOSMIC KAT
July, 1999
Activity Book 3.00

KURT BUSIEK'S
ASTRO CITY
Juke Box, 1995–96
1 I:Samaritan,'In Dreams' 12.00
1a 2nd printing 2.50
2 I:Silver Agent,V:Shirak
   the Devourer 10.00
3 F:Jack in the Box 10.00
4 I:Hanged Man,Safeguards 11.00
5 I:Crackerjack 12.00
6 O:Samaritan,F:Winged Victory . 14.00
TPB 20.00

[Vol. 2] Homage, 1996
½ F:Hanged Man (1996) 5.00
1 KBk(s),BA,Welcome to
   Astro City. 9.00
1a Trunk(c) 8.00
1b 2nd printing 2.50
2 KBk(s),BA,O:First Family,
   F:Astra, Everyday Life 7.00
2b 2nd printing 2.50
3 KBk(s),BA,Adventures in
   Other Worlds 7.00
4 KBk,BA,Teenager seeks to
   become teen sidekick,pt.1 (of 6) 6.00
5 Learning the Game 5.00
6 V: creatures of Shadow Hill 5.00
7 Aliens invade Astro City 4.00
8 The aliens are out there 4.00
9 Honor Guard vs. Aliens finale . . . 4.00
10 meet the junkman 4.00
11 Serpent's Teeth 4.00
12 F:Jack-In-The-Box 3.00
13 F:Looney Leo 3.00
14 F:Steeljack 3.00
15 F:supervillains 3.00
TPB Confession, rep.#4–#9 . . . . . 20.00
3-D #1 . . . . 5.00
TPB Life in the Big City 20.00
TPB Family Album 20.00

Kurt Busiek's Astro City #4
© Homage

Homage/DC, 1999

16 KBk(s), Fl Hombre	3.00
17 KBk(s), Mock Turtle	3.00
18 KBk(s), F:Steeljack	3.00
19 KBk(s), F:Steeljack	3.00
20 KBk(s)	3.00
21 KBk(s),F:Crackerjack	3.00
22 KBk(s),F:Samaritan.	3.00
Spec.1/2 KBk(s)	3.00

LABMAN
1996

1 I:Labman	4.00
1a variant cover	4.00
2 & 3	@4.00

LADY PENDRAGON
Nov., 1998

1 MHw,Destiny's Embrace	2.50
1a remastered, new cover	2.50
1b Dynamic Forces variant cover.	7.00
1c JeL(c) glow-in-the-dark	20.00
1d Tour Edition	5.00
2 MHw,Destiny's Embrace,pt.2.	3.00
3 MHw,Destiny's Embrace,pt.3.	3.00
3a variant cover (1:4)	2.50
0 MHw, Secrets & Origins.	2.50
0a Eurosketch cover	10.00
Preview (Wizard, Chicago Comicon)	5.00
TPB Special, 64-pg. (2002)	8.00

LADY PENDRAGON: DRAGON BLADE
April, 1999

1 MHw,Merlin trains Jennifer	2.50
1a variant cover (1:4)	2.50
1b Chrome Edition	5.00
2 MHw,F:Morgana	2.50
2a variant cover (1:4)	2.50
3 MHw,B.U.I:Alley Cat	3.00
4 MHw,Morgana returns	2.50
5 MHw,Spear of Destiny	2.50
6 MHw,Jennifer Drake resigns	2.50
7 MHw,Future Prophecy,pt.1	4.00
8 MHw,Future Prophecy,pt.2	2.50
9 MHw,Future Prophecy,pt.3	2.50
10 MHw,Messianic Lineage,pt.1	2.50
11 MHw,Messianic Lineage,pt.2	2.50
12 MHw,Messianic Lineage,pt.3	2.50
1a Glow-in-the-dark JaL(c)	2.50
Gallery Ed.#1	3.00
Gallery Ed.#1a photo(c)	3.00

LADY PENDRAGON: MORE THAN MORTAL
May, 1999

1 MHw,Pendragon vs. Protector	2.50
1a variant cover (1:4)	7.00
1b Gold foil(c)	7.00

LADY SUPREME
Extreme, 1996

1 TMr.	2.50
2 TMr,Die & Let Die,pt.2	2.50
3 TMr,V:Manassa	2.50
4 TMr,'Lady Supreme goes undercover'	2.50

LAST CHRISTMAS, THE
May, 2006

1 Twas the Fight Before Christmas	3.00
2 thru 5	@3.00
TPB	15.00

LAST SHOT
Aug., 2001

1 Foodchain,pt.1	3.00

Lady Supreme #1
© Image/Extreme

2 Metal in his Heart.	3.00
3 Six String Noose	3.00
4 Angel of Death	3.00

LAST SHOT: FIRST DRAW
May, 2001

1 First Draw Revolver	3.00

LAST STRAW MAN, THE
Feb., 2004

1 (of 3)	4.00
2 40-pg.	4.00

LAZARUS CHURCHYARD: THE FINAL CUT
2000

Gn WEl.	15.00

LEAVE IT TO CHANCE
Homage, 1996–98

1 JeR,PS,I:Chance Falconer	5.00
2 JeR,PS,Dragons are a Girl's Best Friend	5.00

Homage

3 JeR,PS,Chance and St. George race against time	5.00
4 JeR,PS.	3.00
5 JeR,PS,'Trick or Threat'.	3.00
6 JeR,PS,Return of Cap'n Hitch.	3.00
7 JeR,PS,'And Not a Drop to Drink	3.00
8 JeR,PS,Phantom of the Mall	3.00
9 JeR,PS,Midnite Monster Madness	3.00
10 JeR,PS,'Destroy All Monsters'	3.00
11 JeR,PS,Dead Men Can't Skate	3.00
12 JeR,PS,visits her friend Dash.	3.00
13 JeR,PS,Reunion,48-pg.	5.00
TPB rep. #1–#4	10.00
TPB Vol. II, rep. #5–#8	13.00
TPB Trick or Threat	13.00

LEGACY
May, 2003

1	3.00
2	3.00
3	3.00
4	3.00
4a variant (c).	3.00

LEGACY OF KAIN: DEFIANCE
Jan., 2004

1-shot	3.00
1-shotA variant (c)	3.00

LEGEND OF ISIS
Feb., 2002

1 Origin of Isis	3.00

LEGEND OF SLEEPY HOLLOW, THE
Oct., 2004

GN BHa	8.00

LEGEND OF SUPREME
Dec., 1994

1 KG(s),JJ,DPs,Revelations,pt.1	2.50
2 Revelations,pt.2	2.50
3 Conclusion	2.50

LETHAL
1996

1 & 2	@2.50

LEX TALIONIS: A JUNGLE TALE
Jan., 2004

1-shot 48-pg.	6.00

LIBERTY MEADOWS
July, 2002

27 comic book convention	4.00
28 Ralph's Genetic Breakthrough	4.00
29 Brandy's Christmas Surprise	4.00
30 Long Cold Winter,pt.1	4.00
31 Long Cold Winter,pt.2	4.00
32 The Cow is Back.	3.50
33 Mad Cow, pt.2.	3.50
34 thru 37	@3.00
TPB Book #1 Eden, rep.#1-#9.	15.00
1-shot Sourcebook, 48-pg.	5.00
TPB Vol.1 Eden	20.00
TPB Book 2	15.00
TPB Vol. 3 Summer of Love	17.00

LIONS, TIGERS & BEARS
Jan., 2005

1 (of 4) Fear and Pride, pt.1	3.00
2 Fear and Pride, pt.2.	3.00
3 Fear and Pride, pt.3.	3.00
4 Fear and Pride, pt. 4	3.00

Vol. 2

1 (of 4) Betrayal, pt.1	3.00
2 thru 4 Betrayal, pt.2 thru pt.4.	@3.00
TPB Vol. 1	13.00

LITTLE-GREYMAN
(B&W)

TPB by C. Scott Morse	7.00

LITTLE RED HOT: BOUND
July, 2001

1 (of 3) by Dawn Brown	3.00
2	3.00
3	3.00

LITTLE RED HOT: CHANE OF FOOLS
(B&W) Feb., 1999

1 (of 3) by Dawn Brown, F:Chane	3.00
2 stranded in desert	3.00

IMAGE

All comics prices listed are for *Near Mint* condition.

3 Heaven vs. Hell 3.00
TPB The Foolish Collection, rep. . . 13.00

LOADED BIBLE
April, 2006
1-shot Jesus vs. Vampires 5.00

LONG HOT SUMMER
Sept., 2005
GN 8.00

LONELY TOMBSTONE, THE
Oct., 2005
GN 6.00

LOOKING GLASS WARS: HATTER M
Dec., 2005
1 (of 4) 4.00
2 . . . . 4.00
3 . . . . 3.50
4 . . . . 4.00

LOST ONES, THE
March, 2000
1 by Ken Penders 3.00
2 . . . . 3.00

LOVEBUNNY & MR. HELL
Feb., 2003
1-shot 3.00
1-shot Savage Love 3.00

LOW ORBIT
Nov., 2006
1 64-pg. 7.00

LULLABY: WISDOM SEEKER
Feb., 2005
1 (of 4) 3.00
2 thru 4 . . . . @3.00

LYNCH
WildStorm, June, 1997
1 TVs,'Terror in the Jungle' 2.50

Lynch #1 © Wildstorm

MACE GRIFFIN: BOUNTY HUNTER
Top Cow, Apr., 2003
1-shot 3.00

MAGDALENA
Top Cow, March, 2000
1 JBz,Darkness spin-off 4.00
1a variant MS(c) 4.00
1b variant Michael Turner(c). 4.00
2 JBz,secret revealed 2.50
3 JBz,Blood Divine,pt.3. . . . . 2.50
TPB JBz, 112-pg. 10.00
Preview, Magdalena/Blood
  Legacy, 22 pg.(2000). 3.00
1/2 Magdalena/Angelus, The Light
  and the Glory 3.00

MAGDALENA
Top Cow, July, 2003
1 (of 4) 3.00
2 thru 4 . . . . @3.00
1a and 2a variant (c). . . . . @3.00
Spec. Con. Preview 2.50
TPB Vol. 1 (2006) 20.00

MAGDALENA/ VAMPIRELLA
Top Cow, June, 2003
1-shot. 3.00
1-shotA variant (c) 1:4 . . . . 3.00
1-shot (2004) 3.00
1-shot-A variant (c) (2004) 3.00

MAGDELENA VS. DRACULA
Top Cow, Apr., 2005
1 (of 4) Monster War x-over 3.00

MAGE: THE HERO DEFINED
1997
1 MWg,F:Kevin Matchstick 5.00
2 MWg,Kirby Hero, V:harpies 4.00
3 MWg,Isis, Gretch 3.00
4 MWg,Isis, drug 3.00
5 MWg,into Canada 3.00
6 MWg,V:Dragonslayer 2.50
7 MWg 2.50
8 MWg,V:Red Caps 2.50
9 MWg,Sibling Trio 2.50
10 MWg,enchanted by a succubus . 2.50
11 MWg,Joe Phat, missing 2.50
12 MWg,Pale Incanter's Lair 2.50
13 MWg,What color is magic 2.50
14 MWg,Man Mountain of???? . . . 2.50
15 MWg, 48-pg. concl. 6.00
Spec. 3-D #1 (1998) 5.00
TPB Vol. 1 rep. 10.00
TPB Vol. II, rep. #5–#8 . . . . 10.00
TPB Vol. 3, rep. #9–#12 . . . . 13.00
TPB Vol. 4, rep. #13—#15 . . . . . . 15.00
TPB Vol. 1 The Hero Discovered. . 30.00
Coll.Ed.Vol.1,rep.#1–#2 . . . . 6.00
Coll.Ed.Vol.2,rep.#3–#4 . . . . 6.00
Coll.Ed.Vol.3,rep.#5–#6 . . . . 6.00
Coll.Ed.Vol.4,rep.#7–#8 . . . . 5.00
Coll.Ed.Vol.5,rep.#9–#10 . . . . . . 5.00
Coll.Ed.Vol.6,rep.#11–#12 . . . . . 5.00
Coll.Ed.Vol.7,rep.#13–#14 . . . . . 5.50
Coll.Ed.Vol.8,rep.#15–#16 . . . . . 5.00
TPB Vol. 2 The Hero Defined 25.00

MAN AGAINST TIME
Motown 1996
1 'Every Hero' 2.50

2 . . . . 2.50
3 'Pro Patria Mori' 2.50

MANIC
Feb., 2004
1-shot 3.00

MARS ATTACKS
1996
1 KG,BSz(of 4) 2.50
2 thru 4 . . . . @2.50

MASK OF ZORRO, THE
July, 1998
1 (of 4) DMG,RoW,RM,MGo(c), . . 3.00
2 DMG,RoW,RM,MGo(c) 3.00
3 DMG,RoW,MGo(c). 3.00
4 DMG,RoW,MGo concl. 3.00
4a photo cover 3.00

Masters of the Universe, Vol. 2 #6
© Image

MASTERS OF THE UNIVERSE
2002
1 He-Man returns 3.00
1b variant JSC(c) 3.00
1b variant EN(c) 3.00
2 thru 4 . . . . @3.00
2a–4a variant (c) . . . . @3.00
Volume II
1 . . . . 3.00
2 thru 8 . . . . @3.00
1a–2a variant (c) . . . . @3.00
3a–4a holofoil (c) . . . . @6.00
1-shot Icons of Evil: Beast Man . . . 5.00

MAXIMAGE
Extreme, 1995–96
1 RLe(c) 2.50
2 Extreme Destroyer,pt.2,
  x-over, bagged with card 2.50
3 . . . . 2.50
4 A:Angela,Glory. 2.50
5 thru 8 . . . . @2.50
9 BML, Sex Slaves of Bomba
  Island 2.50
10 BML, The King of Emotion is
  back. 2.50

MAXX, THE
1993
1/2 SK,from Wizard. 10.00

---

1 SK,I:The Maxx 5.00
1a glow in the dark(c) 15.00
2 SK,V:Mr.Gone 4.00
3 SK,V:Mr.Gone 4.00
4 SK 4.00
5 SK 3.00
6 SK 3.00
7 SK,A:Pitt 3.50
8 SK,V:Pitt 3.50
9 SK 3.00
10 SK 3.00
11 SK 2.50
12 SK 2.50
13 Maxx Wanders in Dreams 4.00
14 R:Julie 4.00
15 Julia's Pregnant 4.00
16 SK,Is Maxx in Danger? 4.00
17 SK,Gardener Maxx 4.00
18 SK,'Beware The Hooley' 2.50
19 SK,V:Hooley,'Last Fairy Tale' . . . 2.50
20 SK,Questions are answered 2.50
21 AM(s),SK. 2.50
22 SK,'Other Peoples' Crap' 2.50
23 SK,'Having to Believe' 2.50
24 SK 2.50
25 SK,'Lost and Found' 2.50
26 SK 2.50
27 V:Iago the Killer Slug 2.50
28 Sara and Norberg look for Julie . 2.50
29 Sara and Gone defeat Iago the
  Slug 2.50
30 Lil' Sara faces her fears 2.50
31 F:The Library girl. 2.50
32 F:The Library girl,pt.2 . . . . 2.50
33 Sara's back 2.50
34 Mark and Julia 2.50
35 who knows? 2.50
36 bumfuzzled 2.50
37 Megan's story concl 2.50
38 Mark,Julie,Larry,pt.1 (of 4) 2.50
Spec. Friends of Maxx,F:Dude
  Japan. 3.00
The Maxx 3-D #1 . . . . 5.00
TPB Rep. #1–#5. . . . . 13.00
TPB Vol. 2 . . . . 13.00

MECHANIC, THE
Homage, Aug., 1998
GN JCh,JPe,time travel 6.00

MECH DESTROYER
March, 2001
1 (of 4) Battle for Earth 3.00
2 Face of the Enemy 3.00
3 rescue the captives 3.00
4 V:The Crimson Death 3.00

MEDIEVAL SPAWN/
WITCHBLADE
May, 1996
1 thru 3 . . . . @5.00
TPB series rep. 10.00

MEGADRAGON & TIGER
March, 1999
1 by Tony Wong, from Hong Kong . 3.00
2 F:Red Tiger 3.00
3 V:Single-Minded Arhat 3.00
4 V:Fiery Lord 3.00
5 F:Gigi 3.00

MEGAHURTZ
(B&W) Aug., 1997
1 JPi,I:Megahurtz 3.00
2 JPi,visit to Wonderland 3.00
3 JPi,V:N-Filtraitors 3.00
4 JPi,Liberaiders 3.00

IMAGE

MEGATON MAN:
BOMBSHELL
July, 1999
1 DSs,V:Unleash. 3.00

MEGATON MAN:
HARDCOPY
Fiasco (B&W) Feb., 1999
1 by Don Simpson 3.00
2 with 6 new pages. 3.00

MESSENGER, THE
July, 2000
1-shot JOy, 48-pg. 6.00

MICRONAUTS
June, 2002
1 . . . . 3.00
2 thru 5 . . . . @3.00
6 Star Chamber,pt.1 . . . . 3.00
7 Star Chamber,pt.2 . . . . 3.00
8 Invasion Earth,pt.1 . . . . 3.00
9 Invasion Earth,pt.2 . . . . 3.00
10 Invasion Earth,pt.3 . . . . 3.00
11 Invasion Earth,pt.4 . . . . 3.00
TPB Vol. 1 Rebellion 11.00
Spec. 2002 Con Special 3.00

MIDNIGHT NATION
Top Cow, Sept., 2000
1 MSz 5.00
1a variant GrF(c). 12.00
2 MSz,GrF, on the run 4.00
3 MSz,GrF, To Hell and inbetween . 4.00
4 MSz,GrF, V:Walkers. 4.00
5 MSz,GrF, Find your soul 4.00
6 MSz,GrF, Halfway 4.00
7 MSz,GrF, Change has begun . . . 4.00
8 MSz,GrF, Road gets worse 4.00
9 MSz,GrF, New York, New York . . . 4.00
10 MSz,GrF, Soul's price 4.00
11 MSz,GrF, Still the Road to Hell . . 4.00
12 MSz,GrF, The End of the Road . 4.00
TPB series rep.288-pg. 30.00

MIGHTY MAN
Dec., 2004
GN EL, Savage Dragon spin-off . . . 8.00

MIKE GRELL'S
MAGGIE THE CAT
Jan., 1996
1 (of 4) Master Piece,pt.1 . . . . 2.50
2 Master Piece,pt.2. . . . . 2.50

MINISTRY OF SPACE
April, 2001
1 (of 3) WEI,CWn,World War II. . . . 3.00
2 WEI,CWn 3.00
3 WEI,CWn,concl. 3.00
Omnibus #1 & #2. . . . . 5.00
3 . . . . 3.00
TPB rep. #1–#3 . . . . 13.00

MISERY SPECIAL
Dec., 1995
1 Cyberforce Origins. 3.00

MISPLACED
May, 2003
1 . . . . 3.00
1a variant (c)s. 3.00
2 & 3 . . . . @3.00

M.I.T.H: OPERATION
SMOKING JAGUAR
Top Cow, Aug., 2005
GN 10.00

MONSTER FIGHTERS, INC.
April, 1999
1 Who you gonna call. 3.00
2 Wake the dead. 3.00
1-shot The Black Book. 3.50

MONSTER FIGHTERS INC.:
THE GHOSTS OF
CHRISTMAS
Dec., 1999
1 The Fright Before Christmas 4.00

MONSTERMAN
(B&W) Sept., 1997
1 MM,from Action Planet 3.00
2 MM,Inhuman monsters 3.00
3 MM,King of Monsters. 3.00
4 MM, conclusion 3.00

MORA
Feb., 2005
1 All Beasts will Show Their Teeth . 3.00
2 In the Gloaming 3.00
3 Dying Among the Shadows 3.00
4 Conslusion, pt.1 . . . . 3.00
TPB All Beasts Will Show Teeth . . 13.00

MORE THAN MORTAL/
LADY PENDRAGON
June, 1999
1 MHw,x-over 2.50
Prev. Edition 16-pg., B&W 5.00

MORE THAN MORTAL:
OTHERWORLDS
Liar Comics, July, 1999
1 F:Derdre & Morand 3.00
1a variant cover (1:2) 5.00
2 in Otherworld 3.00
2a variant cover (1:2) 4.00
3 Lady in white 3.00
3a variant Derdre cover (1:2) 3.00
4 Woman in white, concl. 3.00
5 Famine,pt.1 . . . . 3.00
6 Famine,pt.2 . . . . 3.00
7 Famine,pt.3 . . . . 3.00
Art Gallery #1. . . . . 3.50
TPB Vol. 1, rep. #1 & #2 . . . . 7.00
TPB Vol. 2 . . . . 7.00
TPB Vol. 3, Truths & Legends 6.00

MR. MONSTER
VS. GORZILLA
(2 color) July, 1998
1-shot, MGi 3.00

MR. MONSTER'S GAL
FRIDAY: KELLY
(B&W) Jan., 2000
1 MGi 3.50
2 MGi 3.50
3 MGi,AMo(s) 3.50

MR. RIGHT
Aug., 2001
1 TDF,RF,flip-book 3.00
2 TDF,RF,F:General Public 3.00

MOTH
July, 2003
1-shot 48-pg. 6.00

M-REX
Nov., 1999
1 by Joe Kelly & Duncan Rouleau . 3.00
2 thru 5 . . . . @3.00
4a and 5a variant cover . . . . @3.00
#1 Limited Tour Edition 5.00
Preview, B&W, 16-pg. 5.00

MS. FORTUNE
(B&W) 1998
1 by Chris Marrinan 3.00
2 Carnage in the Caribbean 3.00
3 Doom at the Dawn of Time 3.00

MUTANT EARTH
May, 2002
1 (of 4) F:Trakk. 3.00
2 F:Zeithian warlord, Gallowz. 3.00
3 thru 4 . . . . @3.00
1a also 4a variant (c). . . . . @3.00
TPB Vol. 1 Trakk, sgn.& num. 17.00

MYSTERY, INC.
Ashcan 1 . . . . 4.00

M.Y.T.H
Top Cow, 2006
TPB with poster 10.00

MYTHSTALKERS
Mar., 2003
1 The Labyrinth,pt.1 . . . . 3.00
2 The Labyrinth,pt.2 . . . . 3.00
3 The Labyrinth,pt.3 . . . . 3.00
4 The Labyrinth,pt.4 . . . . 3.00
5 London Nights 3.00
6 London Nights,pt.2. . . . . 3.00
7 Gangs of London 3.00
8 London Nights 3.00

MYTH WARRIORS
Top Cow, Oct., 2004
GN 10.00

NAMELESS, THE
(B&W) May, 1997
1 PhH,I:The Nameless, protector of
   Mexico City's lost children 3.00
2 thru 5 . . . . @3.00
TPB Director's Cut (2005) 16.00

NASH
July, 1999
1 MMy, by & starring Kevin Nash . . 2.50
1a variant cover (1:2) 3.00
2 MMy, the end of Nash? 2.50
2a variant cover (1:2) 2.50
#1 Photo-Split edition. 3.00
Preview edition MMy,F:Kevin Nash . 2.50
Preview ed.A variant cover (1:2) . . . 2.50

NECROMANCER, THE
Top Cow, Aug., 2005
1 Something in the way, pt.1 . . . . . 3.00
1a & 1b variant(c)s . . . . @3.00
2 Something in the way, pt.2 . . . . . 3.00
3 Something in the way, pt. 3 . . . . . 3.00
4 thru 6 . . . . @3.00

NEGATIVE BURN
Jan., 2005
TPB Best From 1993–98 . . . . 20.00

Spec. Winder 2005 96-page 10.00
Spec. Summer 2005, 96-page 10.00

NEGATIVE BURN
(B&W) May, 2006
1 64-pg. 6.00
2 thru 7 . . . . @6.00

NEON CYBER
July, 1999
1 F:Neon Dragons 2.50
1a variant cover (1:2) 2.50
1b glow-in-the-dark edition 7.00
2 gang alliance 2.50
2a variant cover (1:2) 2.50
3 Neon a suspect 2.50
4 who framed Neon? 2.50
5 thru 8 . . . . @2.50

NEW ADVENTURES OF ABRAHAM LINCOLN
Homage, Feb., 1998
TPB SMI, 144-pg. 20.00

NEWFORCE
Extreme, 1996
1 Extreme Destroyer,pt.8
   x-over, bagged with card 2.50
2 . . . . 2.50
3 . . . . 2.50
4 Team disbands 2.50

NEWMAN
Extreme, 1996
1 Extreme Destroyer,pt.3
   x-over, bagged with card 2.50
2 . . . . 2.50
3 . . . . 2.50
4 Shadowhunt x-over,pt.5 . . . . 2.50

NEWMEN
Extreme, 1994
1 JMs 3.00
2 JMs,I:Girth 2.50
3 JMs,V:Girth,I:Ikonna 2.50
4 JMs,A:Ripclaw 2.50
5 JMs,Ripclaw,V:Ikonn 2.50
6 JMs 2.50
7 JMs 2.50
8 JMs,Team Youngblood. 2.50
9 ErS(s),JMs,Kodiak Kidnapped. . . 2.50
10 ExtremeSacrifice,pt.5,x-over . . . 2.50
11 F:Reign 2.50
12 R:Elemental 2.50
13 ErS,I:Bootleg 2.50
14 ErS,Dominion's Secret 2.50
15 I:Time Guild. 2.50
16 . . . . 2.50
16a variant cover 3.00
17 R:Girth 2.50
18 F:Byrd 2.50
19 I:Bordda Khan,Shepherd 2.50
20 Extreme Babewatch 2.50
21 ErS,CSp,(1 of 5) 2.50
22 ErS,CSp, Who Needs the
   Newmen? 2.50
23 ErS,CSp,Who are the Newmen? 2.50

THE NEW ORDER HANDBOOK
Various artists 2.50

NEW SHADOWHAWK, THE
June, 1995
1 KBk,I:New ShadowHawk 3.00
2 KBk,V:Mutants 3.00
3 KBk,I:Trophy 3.00

---

4 KBk,V:Blowfish. 3.00
5 KBk, ... 3.00
6 KBk, ... 3.00
7 KBk, ... 3.00

NIGHT CLUB, THE
Apr., 2005
1 (of 4) MBn 3.00
2 Junkyard Apocalypse. 3.00
3 Helluva Party 3.00
4 . . . . 3.00

NIGHTLY NEWS, THE
Nov., 2006
1 (of 6) 3.00

NIGHT TRIPPERS
May, 2006
GN 17.00

NINE RINGS OF WU-TANG, THE
Nov., 1999
1 by Brian Haberlin 4.00
2 thru 5 . . . . @3.00
4a variant cover 3.00
#1 limited tour edition. 5.00
Preview, B&W, 16-pg 5.00
TPB Book of Days 20.00

NINE RINGS OF WU-TANG, THE: FATIMA'S REVENGE
May, 2000
1 by Brian Haberlin 3.00

1963
April, 1993
1 Mystery Incorporated, AnM(s),
   RV,DGb 2.50
1a Gold ed. 4.00
1b Bronze ed. 3.00
2 No One Escapes...The Fury,
   RV,SBi,DGb,JV,I:The Fury. 2.50
3 Tales of the Uncanny,
   RV,SBi,I:U.S.A. 2.50
4 Tales From Beyond
   JV,SBi,I:N-Man, Johnny Beyond 2.50
5 Horus, Lord of Light,
   JV,SBi,I:Horus 2.50

1963 Book 6
© Image

6 Tomorrow Syndicate,
   JV,SBi,C:Shaft 2.50
Ashcan #1 . . . . 3.00
Ashcan #2 . . . . 2.50
Ashcan #4 . . . . 2.00

NINE VOLT
Top Cow, 1997
1 ACh 3.00
1a Variant(c) 4.00
2 ACh 3.00
3 ACh,V:crazed junkie terrorists . . . 2.50
4 ACh,V:Rev. Cyril Gibson 2.50

NOBLE CAUSES
Sept., 2001
1-shot First Impressions 3.00
1 two stories 3.00
2 . . . . 3.00
2a variant RGr(c) 3.00
3 three's a crowd 10.00
3a variant Ccs(c). 10.00
4 In Sickness and in Health,pt.4 . . . 3.00
4a variant(c) 3.00
TPB In Sickness and in Health . . . 13.00
1-shot Extended Family, 80-pg. 5.00
July, 2004
1 . . . . 3.50
1a & 2a variant(c) . . . . @3.50
2 thru 4 . . . . @3.50
5 A:Invincible. 3.50
6 F:Liz Donnelly 3.50
7 A Day in the Life 3.50
8 V:Venture 3.50
9 F:Celeste 3.50
10 Wrong body 3.50
11 . . . . 3.50
12 Birth of Zephyr's Child 3.50
13 F:Blackthornes 3.50
14 . . . . 3.50
15 . . . . 3.50
16 thru 24. . . . . @3.50
25 48-pg. 5.00
25a variant (c) 5.00
TPB Vol. 3 Distant Relatives 13.00
TPB Vol. 4 Blood &Water. 15.00
TPB Hidden Agendas 16.00
TPB Vol. 5 Betrayals 15.00

NOBLE CAUSES:
DISTANT RELATIVES
July, 2003
1 (of 4) 3.00
2 thru 4 . . . . @3.00

NOBLE CAUSES:
FAMILY SECRETS
Oct., 2002
1 (of 4) F:Liz Donnelly-Noble 3.50
2 spin control 3.00
3 guest stars galore 3.00
4 . . . . 3.00
1a– 3a variant(c). . . . . @3.00
TPB Vol. 2 Family Secrets. 13.00

NO HONOR
Top Cow, Feb., 2001
1 (of 4) F:Tanne Yojimbo. 5.00
2 . . . . 5.00
3 . . . . 2.50
4 concl. 2.50
Prev. 16-pg. B&W 5.00
TPB 96-pg.. . . . . 13.00

NO HONOR: MAKYO
Top Cow, Nov., 2001
1 . . . . 4.00

No Honor #1 © Top Cow

NORMALMAN
July, 2004
1-shot 20th Anniv. 3.00

NORMAL MAN/
MEGATON MAN SPECIAL
1 . . . . 2.50

NOWHERESVILLE
March, 2002
TPB MRc, 192-pg. b&w 15.00

NYC MECH
Apr., 2004
1 . . . . 3.00
2 thru 6 . . . . @3.00

NYC MECH: BETA LOVE
May, 2005
1 . . . . 3.50
2 . . . . 3.50
3 thru 6 . . . . @3.00
TPB Vol. 1 Let's Electrify 15.00

OBERGEIST:
RAGNAROK HIGHWAY
Top Cow/Minotaur 2001
1 TyH 3.00
2 TyH 3.00
3 TyH 3.00
4 TyH 3.00
5 TyH,Ambushed 3.00
6 TyH,His memory, Abyss's flame . 3.00
TPB Directors' Cut 20.00

OBERGEIST:
THE EMPTY LOCKET
Top Cow/Minotaur, 2002
1 TyH 3.00

OBJECTIVE FIVE
July, 2000
1 biological weapons 3.00
2 F:Lark, Alexis & DJ 3.00
3 Airborne Virus 3.00
4 Reunion 3.00
5 Hidden Enemies 3.00
6 in China 3.00
7 Origins 3.00

OCCULT CRIMES
TASKFORCE
July, 2006
1 . . . . 3.00
2 thru 4 . . . . @3.00

OPERATION
KNIGHTSTRIKE
May, 1995
1 RHe,A:Chapel,Bravo,Battlestone 2.50
2 In Afganistan 2.50
3 final issue. 2.50

ORIGINAL ADVENTURES
OF CHOLLY & FLYTRAP
Apr., 2005
1 (of 2) A Little Love, A Little Hate . 3.50
2 The Rites of Spring 3.50
Jan., 2006
1 (of 2) 48-pg. 6.00
2 The Rights of Spring, 48-pg. 6.00

THE OTHERS
March, 1995
0 JV(s),From ShadowHawk 2.50
1 JV(s)V:Mongrel 2.50
2 JV,Mongrel takes weapons 2.50
3 War 2.50
4 O:Clone 2.50

OUTLAW NATION
(B&W) Nov., 2006
TPB 16.00

OVERKILL
Top Cow, Oct., 2000
1 PJe,x-over,A:Aliens,Predator. . . . 6.00
2 PJe,x-over,A:Aliens,Predator. . . . 6.00

OXIDO
Sept., 2003
1 (of 6) LHa(s) 3.00
2 LHa(s) 3.00

PACT
1994
1 JV(s),WMc,I:Pact, C:Youngblood 2.50
2 JV(s),V:Youngblood 2.50
3 JV(s),V:Atrocity 2.50

PACT, THE
Mar., 2005
1 (of 4) Father's Day, JV. 3.00
2 . . . . 3.00
3 . . . . 3.00
4 . . . . 3.00

PARADIGM
Sept., 2002
1 F:Chris Howells, 48-pg. b&w . . . 3.50
2 40-pg. b&w. 3.50
3 40-pg. b&w. 3.50
4 40-pg. 3.50
5 . . . . 3.00
6 All About the Community 3.00
7 40-pg. 3.00
8 Swirly Things 3.00
9 Real Swirly Things. 3.00
10 . . . . 3.00
11 40-pg. 3.50
12 40-pg. 3.50
TPB Vol. 1 Segue to an Interlude . 14.00

All comics prices listed are for *Near Mint* condition.

PARLIAMENT OF JUSTICE, THE
Mar., 2003
1-shot b&w, 56-pg.............. 6.00

PARTS UNKNOWN: KILLING ATTRACTION
(B&W) April, 2000
1 Sci-Fi/UFO adventure 3.00

PARTS UNKNOWN: HOSTILE TAKEOVER
(B&W) June, 2000
1 by Beau Smith & Brad Gorby ... 3.00
2 .... 3.00
3 & 4 .... @3.00

PATIENT ZERO
Mar., 2004
1 (of 4) Eternity's Past,pt.1 .... 3.00
2 thru 4 Eternity's Past,pt.2ñ4 ... @3.00

PAUL JENKINS' SIDEKICK
June, 2006
1 .... 3.50
2 thru 5 .... @4.00

PHANTOM FORCE
Dec., 1993
1 RLd,JK,w/card 2.75
2 JK,V:Darkfire 2.50
See also Color Comics section

Phantom Guard #3 © WildStorm

PHANTOM GUARD
WildStorm, Oct., 1997
1 by Sean Ruffner, Ryan Benjamin 3.00
1a variant cover 3.00
1b Voyager bagged pack 3.50
2 Martian wasteland 3.00
3 Lowell Zerium Mines 3.00
4 'Target Locked'............. 3.00
5 V:Vanox, ... 3.00
6 Countdown to Armageddon ... 3.00

PHANTOM JACK
Mar., 2004
1 Roach Motel................ 3.00
2 Back to Baghdad 3.00
3 Among the Enemy........... 3.00

---

4 Madison Blue, Who Are You 3.00
5 Sins of Saddam Hussein 3.00

PHONOGRAM
(B&W) Aug., 2006
1 Public Image 3.50
2 Can't Imagine World Without Me. 3.50
3 Faster..................... 3.50
4 .... 3.50

PIGTALE
(B&W) Jan., 2005
1 Private Eye: Boston Booth..... 3.00
2 The Smell of Taxx 3.00
3 Dark Neon Rain`............ 3.00
4 Salty Pork & Bacon Tarts..... 3.00

PIRATES OF CONEY ISLAND, THE
Oct., 2006
1 .... 3.00
1a variant (c)................ 3.00
2 .... 3.00

PITT
Top Cow, 1993–95
1 DK,I:Pitt,Timmy 4.00
2 DK,V:Quagg................ 3.00
3 DK,V:Zoyvod 4.00
4 DK,V:Zoyvod 3.00
5 DK 2.50
6 DK 2.50
7 DK 2.50
8 Ransom 2.50
9 DK,Artic Adventures......... 2.50
Ashcan 1 .... 3.00

PORTENT, THE
Feb., 2006
1 Condemnation 3.00
2 A Road of My Own........... 3.00
3 .... 3.00
4 Nezabudka................. 3.00

POWER OF THE MARK
1 I:Ted Miller................ 2.50
2 V:The Fuse 2.50
3 TMB(s), The Mark 2.50
4 TMB,Mark's secrets revealed .. 2.50

POWER RANGERS ZEO
Extreme, Sept., 1997
1 thru 3 TBm&MBm(s),TNu,NRd @2.50

POWER RANGERS ZEO YOUNGBLOOD
Extreme, Oct., 1997
1 thru 2 RLd,TBm,MBm .... @3.00

POWERS
April, 2000
1 Who killed Retro Girl,pt.1...... 15.00
2 Who killed Retro Girl,pt.2...... 20.00
3 Who killed Retro Girl,pt.3...... 15.00
4 .... 12.00
5 A murder solved............ 10.00
6 .... 10.00
7 WEI, Ride Along............. 7.00
8 Role Play,pt.1.............. 7.00
9 Role Play,pt.2.............. 7.00
10 Role Play,pt.3 .... 7.00
11 .... 5.00
12 Groupies 5.00
13 Groupies,pt.2 .... 5.00
14 Groupies,pt.3 .... 5.00
15 Supergroup,pt.1 .... 5.00
16 Supergroup............... 5.00

---

17 incl. Bastard Samurai prequel .. 5.00
18 superhero wanted for murder... 5.00
19 supergroup shocking concl..... 5.00
20 supergroup explosive concl..... 5.00
21 Anarchy,pt.1 .... 3.50
22 Anarchy,pt.2 .... 3.50
23 Anarchy,pt.3 .... 3.50
24 Anarchy,pt.4 .... 3.50
25 The Sellouts,pt.1 .... 3.50
26 The Sellouts,pt.2 .... 3.50
27 The Sellouts,pt.3 .... 3.00
28 The Sellouts,pt.4 .... 3.00
29 The Sellouts,pt.5 .... 3.00
30 The Sellouts,pt.6 .... 3.00
31 Forever,pt.1............... 3.00
32 Forever,pt.2............... 3.00
33 Forever,pt.3............... 3.00
34 Forever,pt.4............... 3.00
35 Forever,pt.5............... 3.00
36 Forever,pt.6............... 3.00
37 Forever,pt.7............... 3.00
Spec.-1 Coloring & Activity Book ... 3.00
1/2 Wizard story + new 3.00
Scriptbook 344-pg............. 20.00
TPB Vol.1 Who Killed Retro Girl .. 20.00
TPB Vol.1 Who Killed Retro Girl .. 22.00
TPB Vol.1 readers addition 16.00
TPB Vol.2 Roleplay 14.00
TPB Vol.2 Roleplay, 2nd pr...... 14.00
TPB Vol.3 Little Deaths 25.00
TPB Vol.4 Supergroup.......... 20.00
TPB Vol.5 Anarchy 15.00
TPB Vol. 6 The Sellouts......... 20.00

VOLUME 2 (2004)
1 Legends,pt.1 .... 3.00
2 Legends,pt.2 .... 3.00
3 Legends,pt.3 .... 3.00

PRIMAL INSTINCT
March, 2000
Preview 2.50

PRO, THE
July, 2002
GN 1-shot GEn,ACo,JP 56-pg... 8.00
Con. Ed. signed, numbered...... 25.00

PROPHET
Extreme, 1993–95
0 San Diego Comic-Con ed....... 4.00
1 RLd(s)DPs,O:Prophet,I:Mary
   McCormick................. 3.00
1a Gold ed.................... 4.00

Prophet #10 © Extreme

All comics prices listed are for *Near Mint* condition.

2 RLd(s),DPs,C:Bloodstrike 2.50
3 RLd(s),DPs, V:Bloodstrike,
    I:Judas 2.50
4 RLd(s),DPs,I:Omen,A:Judas 2.50
4a SPa(c),Limited ed. 3.00
5 SPa,Supreme Apocalypse,pt.2 . . 3.00
6 SPa 2.50
7 SPa War Games,pt.1 . . . . 2.50
8 SPa War Games,pt.2 . . . . 2.50
9 SPa,Extreme Sacrifice Prelude . 2.50
10 ExtremeSacrifice,pt.7,x-over. . . . 2.50
Sourcebook 3.00
Ashcan #1 . . . . 3.00
Ashcan #2 . . . . 3.00

[Second Series] 1995
1 SPI, New Series. 3.50
2 SPI, New Direction. 2.50
2a variant cover 2.50
3 True Nature 2.50
4 The Dying Factor 2.50
5 . . . . 2.50
6 . . . . 2.50
7 CDi,SPa 2.50
8 & 9 . . . . @2.50
TPB 13.00
Ann.#1 Supreme Apocalypse 2.50
Spec.#1 Babewatch special (1995). 2.50

PROPHET/CHAPEL: SUPER SOLDIERS
May, 1996
1 . . . . 2.50
1A variant(c) b&w 2.50
2 . . . . 2.50

PROXIMITY EFFECT
Top Cow, June, 2004
GN 10.00

PSCYTHE
Sept., 2004
1 (of 2) MT 4.00
2 MT 4.00

PUFFED
July, 2003
1 (of 3) 3.00
2 & 3 . . . . @3.00

PVP
Mar., 2003
1 Player vs. Player 3.00
2 Lord of the Schwing. 3.00
3 Lost and Found 3.00
4 V:Devilfish 3.00
5 Max Powers. 3.00
6 Skull the Troll 3.00
7 Chilling events 3.00
8 Brent Sienna Dies 3.00
9 Skull in local Zoo 3.00
10 Skull hyper-intelligent 3.00
11 F:Savage Dragon 3.00
12 Halloween party 3.00
13 Christmans issue 3.00
14 A:Invincible 3.00
15 Geeks Gone Wild 3.00
16 . . . . 3.00
17 . . . . 3.00
18 . . . . 3.00
19 . . . . 3.00
20 . . . . 3.00
21 . . . . 3.00
22 . . . . 3.00
23 Caffeine Rage 3.00
24 . . . . 3.00
25 . . . . 3.00
26 thru 29. . . . . @3.00
30 Time Tunnel 3.00

Spec #0 16-page, B&W 1.00
TPB Vol. 1 The Dork Ages. 12.00
TPB Vol. 1 At Large 12.00
TPB Vol. 2 Reloaded 12.00
TPB Vol. 3 PvP Rides Again 12.00
TPB The Dorg Ages. 12.00
Spec. Replay #1, rep.#1 & #2 . . . . 5.00

QUANTUM MECHANICS
Oct., 2004
GN ATi,B&W, 48-pg. 7.00

Q-UNIT: REVENGE
Oct., 1999
1 KIA,BNa. 3.00
1a variant cover (1:2) 3.00
2 KIA,BNa 3.00
2a variant cover (1:2) 3.00

RADISKULL AND DEVIL DOLL
Dec., 2002
1-shot b&w. 2.50
1-shot Radiskull Hate Love 3.00

RADIX
Dec., 2001
1 mysterious new force. 3.00
2 F:Val Fiores 3.00
3 . . . . 3.00
4 mysterious object. 3.00

RAGMOP
(B&W)
Vol.2 #1 by Rob Walton 3.00
Vol.2 #2 . . . . 3.00

RAIL
June, 2001
GN DvD, 48-pg. 6.00

RANDY O'DONNEL IS THE MAN
May, 2001
1 TDF,RLm,flip-book 3.00
2 TDF,RLm,The Chosen. 3.00
3 TDF,RLm,Terror of the
    Warrior Toads 3.00
4 TDF,Merciless are the Malok. . . . 3.00

REALM OF THE CLAW
Oct., 2003
1 (of 6) 3.00
1a variant (c). 3.00
2 . . . . 3.00
2a variant (c). 3.00

REAPER
Mar., 2004
GN 7.00

RED DIARIES
(B&W) June, 2006
TPB 17.00

RED STAR, THE
June, 2000
1 by Christian Gossett 8.00
2 Project: Antares 6.00
3 Fall of the Red Fleet 4.00
4 Marcus' mystic revelation 4.00
5 A worker's Tale. 4.00
6 War torn Nokgorka. 3.00
7 Nokgorka,pt.2 . . . . 3.00
8 Nokgorka,pt.3 . . . . 3.00

9 Marcus Antares is alive 3.00
9a variant(c) 3.00
Spec.#1 3-D Transformation 3.00
TPB Vol.1 Battle of Kar
    Dathra's Gate, 144-pg. 25.00

RED WARRIOR
(B&W) Oct., 2006
TPB 13.00

Regulators #1 © Image

REGULATORS
June, 1995
1 F:Blackjack,'Touch of Scandal' . . 2.50
2 F:Vortex 2.50
3 F:Arson 2.50
4 F:Scandal. 2.50

RENFIELD: A TALE OF MADNESS
(B&W) Nov., 2006
TPB 20.00

REPLACEMENT GOD AND OTHER STORIES, THE
(B&W) May, 1997
1 Knute vs. King Ursus. 3.00
2 by Zander Cannon. 3.00
3 thru 5 . . . . @3.00

RESIDENT EVIL
Wildstorm March, 1998
1 comic/game magazine 56-pg. . . . 6.00
2 thru 4 comic/game mag. 56-pg. @5.50
TPB Collection 1, series rep. 15.00

RETRO ROCKET
March, 2006
1 (of 4) 3.00
2 thru 4 . . . . @3.00

RETURN OF SHADOWHAWK, THE
Sept., 2004
1-shot JV 3.00

REX MUNDI
Aug., 2002
0 . . . . 4.00

IMAGE

All comics prices listed are for *Near Mint* condition.

IMAGE

1 Unexpected visitor 3.50
2 Puzzle in the Painting 3.50
3 The Archbiship and the Pimp . . . 3.50
4 Shadows Beneath the City 3.00
5 Shadows Beneath the City 3.00
6 Secrets Revealed 3.00
7 Father of Wisdom 3.00
8 Suspicion grows 3.00
9 National library 3.00
10 Holy Grail 3.00
11 Treasure of the Temple 3.00
12 The Swan Knight 3.00
13 The Lost Kings 3.00
14 City of the Dead 3.00
15 Most Beloved 3.00
16 Path to Empire 3.00
17 Vine of David 3.00
18 Europe at War 3.00
TPB Vol. 1 Guardian of Temple . . . 15.00
TPB Vol. 2 River Underground . . . 15.00

RIDE, THE
June, 2004

1 Wheels of Change,pt.1 . . . . 3.00
2 Wheels of Change,pt.2 . . . . 3.00
1a thru 2a signed . . . . @15.00
1-shot 2 for the Road, Shotgun;
   Big Plans (2004) 3.00
1-shot Foreign Parts,CDi & RMz(s). 3.00
TPB Vol. 1 (2005) 10.00

RIDE, THE:
CHAIN REACTION
(B&W) July, 2006

1 (of 4) BSz 3.00
2 . . . . 3.00

RING OF ROSES
(B&W) Nov., 2004

TPB 13.00

RIPCLAW
Top Cow, 1995

1/2 Prelude to Series (Wizard) 3.00
1/2a Con versions 7.00
1 A:Killjoy, I:Shadowblade 3.00
2 Cyblade, Heatwave 2.50
3 EcS,BPe,AV,Alliance S.H.O.C.s . 2.50
4 conclusion 2.50
Spec.#1 I:Ripclaw's Brother 3.00

[1st Regular Series]

1 thru 5 . . . . @2.50

RIPTIDE
1995

1 O:Riptide 2.50
2 O:Riptide 2.50

RISING STARS
Top Cow, March, 1999

1 A celestial event 5.00
1a, b, & c variant covers 8.00
2 life & death of Peter Dawson . . . 8.00
3 new special 8.00
4 . . . . 8.00
5 To the netherworld 8.00
6 Things Fall Apart,pt.1 . . . . 8.00
7 Things Fall Apart,pt.2 . . . . 8.00
8 Things Fall Apart,pt.3 . . . . 5.00
9 Act Two,pt.1 . . . . 5.00
10 years later 3.50
11 Specials out of control 3.00
12 War for Chicago 3.00
12a Monstermart edition 10.00
12b Monstermart gold foil 17.00
12c Monstermart holofoil 25.00
13 Brothers 3.00
14 Patriot vs. Matthew Bright 3.00

15 The Secret 3.00
16 finale 3.00
17 campaign to change the world . . 3.00
18 will they change the world 3.00
19 MSz,government vs. Specials . . 3.00
20 MSz 3.00
21 MSz 3.00
22 Phoenix in Ascension,pt.1 . . . . 3.00
23 BA,Phoenix in Ascension,pt.2 . . 3.00
24 BA,Phoenix in Ascension,pt.3 . . 4.00
1/2 rep 3.00
#0 rep. from Wizard 2.50
Preview MSz, 16-pg., B&W 5.00
Prelude 3.00
TPB Deluxe,rep.#1–#8 . . . . 20.00
TPB Vol.2, rep.#9-#16 . . . . 20.00
TPB Vol.3 Visitations 9.00
TPB Fire and Ash 20.00

RISING STARS: BRIGHT
Top Cow, Feb., 2003

1 (of 3) 3.00
2 Authority 3.00
3 Civilian Casualties 3.00

RISING STARS:
UNTOUCHABLE
Top Cow, Sept., 2003

1 Story of Laurel Darkhaven 3.00

RISING STARS:
UNTOUCHABLE
Top Cow, March, 2006

1 (of 5) 3.00
2 thru 5 . . . . @3.00

RISING STARS:
VOICES OF THE DEAD
Top Cow, Apr., 2005

1 (of 6) 3.00
2 . . . . 3.00
3 . . . . 3.00
4 . . . . 3.00
5 . . . . 3.00
6 . . . . 3.00
TPB Vol. 3 Fire and Ash 20.00
TPB Vol. 4 . . . . 20.00

ROB ZOMBIE'S
SPOOK SHOW
2004

Int. Omnibus #1 48-pg. 5.00
Int. Omnibus #2 48-pg. 5.00
12 International 3.00

ROCKETO JOURNEY
TO THE HIDDEN SEA
Feb., 2006

7 Reunions 3.00
8 Histories 3.00
9 Histories 3.00
10 Histories 4.00
11 Illumination 4.00
12 . . . . 4.00
TPB Vol. 1, rep. #0 thru #6 . . . . . 20.00
TPB Journey to the Hidden Sea . . 25.00

ROCK 'N' ROLL
(B&W) Nov., 2005

1-shot 3.50

ROMP
Dec., 2003

1-shot AdP 6.00

RONIN HOOD
OF THE 47 SAMURAI
Sept., 2005

GN 10.00

ROTOGIN: JUNKBOTZ
Apr., 2003

1 (of 8) 3.00
2 thru 4 . . . . @3.00
1a variant(c) 3.00

RTA: Personality Crisis #1
© Image

RTA: PERSONALITY
CRISIS
Aug., 2005

1-shot 3.50

RUMBLE GIRLS
(B&W) April, 2000

1 (of 8) Silky Warrior Tansie 3.50
2 . . . . 3.50
3 Sugar and Wax 3.50
4 Sapphire Bullets 3.50
5 It's Not Romantic 3.50
6 Boy, Girl, Boy Girl 3.50
7 The Life of My Time, concl 4.00

RUMBLE IN LA RAMBLA
May, 2006

1 (of 3) 3.00
2 You Snooze, You Lose 3.00
3 Penthouse Massacre 3.00

RUN!
Dec., 2003

1-shot MMr 3.00

RUNES OF RAGNAN
Oct. 2006

1 Flames of Muspell, pt.1 . . . . 3.50
2 Flames of Muspell, pt.2 . . . . 3.50
3 Flames of Muspell, pt.3 . . . . 3.50
4 Flames of Muspell, pt.4 . . . . 3.00

RUSSIAN SUNSET
Nov., 2006

1 (of 5) RMz 4.00

RUULE: GANGLORDS OF CHINATOWN
Oct., 2005
TPB 20.00

SABRE
(B&W) 1998
TPB 20th Anniversary 13.00

SAFFIRE
April, 2000
1 MtB,SRf,F:Melanie,Lyssa,
    Priscilla 3.00
1a variant JMd(c) 3.00
1b Mat Broome blue foil(c) 11.50
1c Joe Mac blue foil(c) 13.00
2 MtB,SRf,V:The Kraken 3.00
2a randy green(c) 9.00
2b signed & number 11.00
3 MtB,SRf,Hades Gate 3.00

SAINT ANGEL
2000
Preview 3.00
1 KIA,BNa,40-pg.,flip-book 4.00
1a variant(c) 4.00
2 KIA,BNa,40-pg.,flip-book 4.00
3 KIA,BNa,40-pg.,flip-book 4.00
4 KIA,BNa,40-pg.,flip-book 4.00

SAINT GERMAINE
(B&W) Sept., 2005
TPB Shadows Fall 15.00

SAM & TWITCH
TMP, Aug., 1999
1 AMe,Spawn tie-in 2.75
2 AMe,The Udaku,pt.2 . . . . 2.50
3 AMe,The Udaku,pt.3 . . . . 2.50
4 AMe,The Udaku,pt.4 . . . . 2.50
5 AMe,The Udaku,pt.5 . . . . 2.50
6 AMe,The Udaku,pt.6 . . . . 2.50
7 AMe,The Udaku,pt.7 . . . . 2.50
8 AMe,The Udaku,pt.8 . . . . 2.50
9 One Really Bad Day 2.50
10 Witch Hunter,pt.1 . . . . 2.50
11 Witch Hunter,pt.2 . . . . 2.50
12 Witch Hunter,pt.3 . . . . 2.50
13 Witch Hunter,pt.4 . . . . 2.50
14 Dumb Laws and Egg 2.50
15 Bounty Hunter Wars,pt.1 . . . . . 2.50
16 Bounty Hunter Wars,pt.2 . . . . . 2.50
17 Bounty Hunter Wars,pt.3 . . . . . 2.50
18 Bounty Hunter Wars,pt.4 . . . . . 2.50
19 Bounty Hunter Wars,pt.5 . . . . . 2.50
20 Jon Doe Affair,pt.1 . . . . 2.50
21 Jon Doe Affair,pt.2 . . . . 2.50
22 Jon Doe Affair,pt.3 . . . . 2.50
23 Jon Doe Affair,pt.4 . . . . 2.50
24 Jon Doe Affair,pt.5 . . . . 2.50
25 Jon Doe Affair,pt.6 . . . . 2.50
26 Jon Doe Affair,pt.7 . . . . 2.50
27 Death Row Confessions 2.50
TPB Vol.1 Udaku, rep.#1–#8 . . . . 22.00

SAMMY: A VERY SAMMY DAY
May, 2004
GN 6.00

SAMMY: TOURIST TRAP
Feb., 2003
1 (of 4) 3.00
2 thru 4 . . . . @3.00

Savage Dragon #28
© Erik Larsen

SAM NOIR: SAMURAI DETECTIVE
(B&W) Sept., 2006
1 Payback is a Niche 3.00
2 Blood Thirst, Ask Question Later . 3.00
3 . . . . 3.00

SAM STORIES: LEGS
Dec., 1999
1-shot SK, 24-pg 2.50

SAVAGE DRAGON
Highbrow, July, 1992
1 EL,I:Savage Dragon 3.00
2 EL,I:Superpatriot 3.50
3 EL,V:Bedrock,with coupon#6 . . . 3.00
3a EL,w/o coupon 3.00
Spec. Savage Dragon Versus Savage
    Megaton Man #1 EL,DSm 3.00
Gold ed 12.00
TPB 10.00

[2nd Series] June, 1993
1 EL,I:Freaks 4.00
2 EL,V:Teen.Mutant Ninja Turtles,
    Flip book Vanguard #0 . . . . . . 3.00
3 EL,A:Freaks 3.00
4 EL,A:Freaks 3.00
5 EL,Might Man flip book 3.00
6 EL,A:Freaks 3.00
7 EL,Overlord 3.00
8 EL,V:Cutthroat,Hellrazor 3.00
9 EL 3.00
10 EL 3.00
11 EL,A:Overlord 3.00
12 EL, Enter She-Dragon 3.00
13 EL,Mighty Man,Star,I:Widow
    (appeared after issue #20) 3.00
13a Larsen version of 13 . . . . 3.00
14 Possessed,pt.1 . . . . 3.00
15 Possessed,pt.2 . . . . 3.00
16 Possessed,pt.3,V:Mace 3.00
17 V:Dragonslayer 3.50
18 R:The Fiend 3.00
19 V:The Fiend 3.00
20 Rematch with Overlord 3.00
21 V:Overlord 3.00
22 A:Teenage Mutant Turtles 3.00
23 Rapture vs. SheDragon 3.00
24 Gang War,pt.1 . . . . 3.00
25 Gang War,pt.2 double size 4.00
26 . . . . 3.00

27 . . . . 3.00
28 . . . . 3.00
29 . . . . 3.00
30 EL,'Overlord Reborn' 3.00
31 'The Dragon is trapped in Hell' . . 3.00
32 Kill-Cat vs. Justice 3.00
33 fatherhood 3.00
34 F:Hellboy,pt.1 . . . . 4.00
35 F:Hellboy,pt.2 . . . . 4.00
36 Dragon & Star try to rescue
    Peter Klaptin 3.00
37 mutants struggle in ruins of
    Chicago 3.00
38 Dragon vs. Cyberface 3.00
39 Dragon vs. Dung 3.00
40 'G-Man' 3.00
41 Wedding issue 3.00
42 V:Darklord 3.00
43 Stranded on another world 3.00
44 in flying saucer 3.00
45 . . . . 3.00
46 She-Dragon vs. Vicious Circle . . 3.00
47 A knight and a mummy 3.00
48 Unfinished Business,pt.1 . . . . . 3.00
49 Unfinished Business,pt.2 . . . . . 3.00
50 Unfinished Business,pt.3,
    some reps., 96-pg. 6.00
51 F:She-Dragon 3.00
52 F:She-Dragon,V:Hercules 3.00
53 EL,F:She Dragon 3.00
54 EL,V:imposter Dragon 3.00
55 EL,Dragon & She-Dragon 3.00
56 EL,Rita Medermade kidnapped . 3.00
57 EL,V:Overlord 3.00
58 EL,Dragon's Resurrection 3.00
59 EL,return of Savage Dragon 3.00
60 EL,R:Devastator 3.00
61 EL,R:Rapture 3.00
62 EL,Savage Dragon married 3.00
63 EL,Dragon's honeymoon 3.00
64 EL,Overlord's secrets 3.00
65 EL,Possessed 3.00
66 EL,Dragon shrunk 3.00
67 EL,A:SuperPatriot 3.00
68 EL,V:PowerHouse 3.00
69 EL 3.00
70 EL, Hell on Earth 3.00
71 EL,End of the World,prequel . . . 3.00
72 EL,End of the World,prequel . . . 3.50
73 EL,End of the World,pt.1 . . . . . . 3.50
74 EL,End of the World,pt.2 . . . . . . 3.50
75 EL,End of the World,pt.3 . . . . . . 5.00
76 EL,Hell on Earth begins 3.50
77 EL,Wildstar Returns 3.50
77a Variant JOy(c) 3.50
78 EL,Mind-slaves of the
    Brain-Child 3.50
79 EL,Girl Trouble 3.50
80 EL,Lurkers beneath Lake Fear . . 3.50
81 EL,The Land Down Under 3.50
82 EL,The Bug Riders 3.50
83 EL,F:Madman 3.50
84 EL,F:Madman 3.50
85 EL,Peril in Pittsburgh 3.50
86 EL,Mighty Man returns 3.50
87 EL,Havoc in the Hidden City . . . 3.50
88 EL,To Challenge the Gods 3.50
89 EL,Panic in Detroit 3.50
90 EL,Return to Chicago 3.50
91 EL,Rapture returns 3.50
92 EL,Reclaim the Earth,pt.1 . . . . . 3.50
93 EL,Reclaim the Earth,pt.2 . . . . . 3.50
94 EL,V:CyberFace 3.50
95 EL,V:Sebastian Khan,concl. 3.50
96 EL,V:The Creator 3.50
97 EL,F:She-Dragon 3.50
98 EL,return home 3.50
99 EL,Evil Twins 3.50
100 EL, Torn Between Two
    Worlds, 100-pg. 10.00
101 EL,F:son of Dragon 3.00
102 EL,V:Afterbirth 3.00

IMAGE

103 EL,Dragon & son 3.00
104 EL,secrets. 3.00
105 EL,F:The Candyman. 3.00
106 EL,Dragon as Santa 3.00
107 EL,flipcover Major Damage 4.00
108 EL,Flying Shoes Incident 3.00
109 EL,Danger in Dimension X . . . 3.00
110 EL,Lost in Dimension X 3.00
111 EL,Mako the man-shark 3.00
112 EL,V:Octopus & OpenFace. . . . 3.00
113 EL,Vicious Circle. 3.00
114 EL,Cutthroat 3.00
115 EL,concl.,80-pg. 7.00
116 I:Negate. 3.00
117 EL,Powerless 3.00
118 EL,R:Arachnid 3.00
119 EL,Running Man,pt.1 . . . . 3.00
120 EL, The Running Man,pt.2 . . . . 3.00
121 EL, The Running Man,pt.3 . . . . 3.00
122 EL, Weapons of Mass
    Destruction, pt.1 . . . . 3.00
123 EL Regenerative Powers 3.00
124 EL, Dismal Dregs of Defeat . . . 3.00
125 EL, The Fly, 64-pg. 5.00
126 EL, Glum Lord. 3.00
127 EL, A World Against Him. 3.00
128 EL, Wanted. 3.00
129 EL, ... 3.00
130 EL, V: Solar Man & Universo . . 3.00
131 EL Vengeance. 3.00
Spec #0 O:Savage Dragon (2006) . 2.50
TPB A Talk With God 18.00
   TPB A Talk with God, 2nd pr. . . 20.00
TPB The Fallen, rep.#7–#11 . . . . 13.00
TPB Possessed, rep.#12–#16. . . . 13.00
TPB Archives #2, B&W,1982 rep. . 3.00
TPB Archives #3, B&W,1984 rep. . 3.00
TPB Archives #4, B&W,1986 rep. . 3.00
TPB Revenge. 14.00
TPB Greatest Team-ups 20.00
TPB Book 1 Baptism of Fire 15.00
   TPB Baptism of Fire (2002). . . 15.00
TPB Gang War. 17.00
TPB This Savage World 16.00
TPB Vol.9, Worlds at War 17.00
TPB Vol. 8 Terminated 16.00
TPB Vol. 10 Endgame 16.00
TPB Vol. 11 Resurrection. 15.00
TPB Vol. 12 Last Rites. 15.00
Spec. 1-shot Savage Dragon
   Companion,64-pg.. . . . . 3.00
Spec. 1-shot Savage Dragon/
   Hellboy, collected ed. 6.00

SAVAGE DRAGON DESTROYER DUCK
Nov., 1996
1 SvG,ChM,EL 4.00

SAVAGE DRAGON: GOD WAR
2004
1 (of 4) 3.00
2 thru 4 . . . . @3.00

SAVAGE DRAGON, THE: RED HORIZON
Comics Feb., 1997
1 MsM. 3.00
2 MsM,Dragon in the ER,A:Freak
   Force 3.00
3 (of 3) MsM,Freak Force beaten. . 3.00

SAVAGE DRAGON: MARSHAL LAW
(B&W) July, 1997
1 (of 2) PMs,KON,F:Marshal Law. . 3.00
2 PMs,KON, concl. 3.00

Savant Garde #1
© *WildStorm*

SAVAGE DRAGON: SEX & VIOLENCE
July, 1997
1 (of 2) TBm,MBm 3.00
2 TBm,MBm,AH, concl. 3.00

SAVAGE DRAGONBERT: FULL FRONTAL NERDITY
Oct., 2002
GN 80-pg. b&w 6.00

SAVANT GARDE
WildStorm, March, 1997
1 'A team without a rule book' 2.50
2 Between killer & killer cat 2.50
3 V: strange Tapestry 2.50
4 'Any super-villain can take
   over the world'. 2.50
5 'The Final Showdown' 2.50
6 BKs,Guilty until proven innocent . 2.50
7 BKs,death of John Colt 2.50
Fan Edition #1, with Fan #22. . . . . 3.00
Fan Edition #2, with Fan #23. . . . . 3.00
Fan Edition #3, with Fan #24. . . . . 3.00

SEA OF RED
Mar., 2005
1 Terror on the High Seas 5.00
2 . . . . 3.50
3 . . . . 3.00
4 . . . . 3.00
5 Origin issue 3.00
6 . . . . 3.00
7 . . . . 3.00
8 . . . . 3.00
9 Estimated Casualties,pt.1 . . . . . . 3.00
10 Estimated Casualties, pt.2 . . . . . 3.00
11 World in ruins 3.00
12 Golem from Mesopotamia 3.00
13 Conclusion 3.50
TPB Vol. 1 No Grave but the Sea . . 9.00
TPB Vol. 2 No Quarter. 12.00
TPB Vol. 3 The Deadlights. 15.00

SEASON OF THE WITCH
Oct., 2005
0 B&W, 24-page 2.50
1 (of 4) Spring. 3.50
2 Summer. 3.50
3 Autumn. 3.50
4 Winter 3.50

SECTION ZERO
June, 2000
1 KK,TG,UFO's etc. 2.50
2 KK,TG,Sargasso sea 2.50
3 KK,TG,Curse of Sargasso 2.50
4 KK,TG,Ground Zero revealed . . . 2.50
5 KK,TG,Sargasso vs. Crust. 3.00
6 KK,TG,Fire and Rain 3.00

SEI: DEATH & LEGEND
Nov., 2003
GN Manga 7.00

SEMANTIC LACE
June, 2003
GN b&w, 112-pg. 10.00

SEVENTH SHRINE, THE
Jan., 2005
1 (of 2) 56-pg. Robert Silverberg(s) 6.00
2 . . . . 6.00

SHADOWHAWK
Shadowline, Aug., 1992
1 JV,I:ShadowHawk,Black Foil(c),
   Pin-up, with coupon#1. . . . . . . 4.00
,1a w/o coupon 2.50
2 JV,V:Arsenal,A:Spawn, I:Infiniti . . 3.00
3 JV,V:Arsenal,w/glow-in-the-
   dark(c) 3.50
4 V:Savage Dragon 2.50
TPB rep.#1-4 . . . . 20.00
Ashcan #1 . . . . 2.50
Ashcan #2 . . . . 2.50
Ashcan #3 . . . . 2.50
Ashcan #4 . . . . 2.50
[2nd Series] 1993
1 JV,Die Cut(c) 2.50
1a Gold ed. 3.00
2 JV,ShadowHawk I.D. 2.50
2a Gold ed. 2.50
3 Poster(c),JV,w/Ash Can 2.50
TPB 20.00
[3rd Series] 1993
0 Zero issue 2.50
1 JV,CWf,V:Vortex,Hardedge,
   Red Foil(c). 2.50
1a Gold ed. 3.00
1b signed 6.00

Shadowhawk, 1st Series #3
© *Image/Shadowline*

2 JV,CWf,MA,I:Deadline,
  BU&I:US Male 2.50
3 JV(a&s),ShadowHawk has AIDS,
  V:Hardedge,Blackjak 2.50
4 JV(a&s),V:Hardedge 2.50
Note: #5 to #11 not used; #12 below
is the next issue, the 12th overall.
12 Monster Within,pt.1 . . . . 2.50
13 Monster Within,pt.2 . . . . 2.50
14 Monster Within,pt.3 . . . . 2.50
15 Monster Within,pt.4 . . . . 2.50
16 Monster Within,pt.5 . . . . 2.50
17 Monster Within,pt.6 . . . . 2.50
18 JV,D:ShadowHawk 2.50
Spec.#1 . . . . 3.50
Gallery#1 . . . . 2.50

SHADOWHAWK
2005
1 JV(s) 3.00
2 Zapped. 3.00
3 JV(s),V:Nocturn 3.00
4 . . . . 3.00
5 Dead Man Walking, x-over 3.00
6 Suffer not a corpse to live 3.00
7 My World On Fire, pt.1 . . . . 3.00
8 My World On Fire, pt.2 . . . . 3.00
9 Rise, pt.1 . . . . 3.50
10 Rise, pt.2. . . . . 3.50
11 Rise, pt.3. . . . . 3.50
12 Rise, pt.4. . . . . 3.50
13 Past Lives 3.50
14 On the Rebound, pt.1 . . . . 3.50
15 On the Rebound, pt.2 . . . . 3.50
1-shot Great Responsibility 2.00
TPB Born Anew 15.00

SHADOWHAWK/ VAMPIRELLA
Feb., 1995
Book 2 V:Kaul 5.00
Book #1: see Vampi/ShadowHawk

SHADOWHUNT SPECIAL
Extreme, 1996
1 Shadowhunt x-over,pt.1 . . . . 2.50

SHADOWS
Feb., 2003
1 . . . . 3.00
2 . . . . 3.00

Shaman's Tears #9
© Image

---

3 . . . . 3.00
4 b&w 3.00
5 b&w 3.00

SHAMAN'S TEARS
Creative Fire, 1993–96
0 MGr 2.50
1 MGr,I:Shaman,B:Origin 3.00
1a Siver Prism ed. 5.00
2 MGr,Poster(c) 2.50
3 MGr,V:Bar Sinister 2.50
4 MGr,V:Bar Sinister,E:Origin 2.50
5 MGr,R:Jon Sable 2.50
6 MGr,V:Jon Sable 2.50
7 MGr,V:Rabids. 2.50
8 MGr,A:Sable 2.50
9 MGr,Becoming of Broadarrow . . . 2.50
10 Becoming of Broadarrow,pt.2 . . . 2.50
11 Becoming of Broadarrow,pt.3 . . . 2.50
12 Becoming of Broadarrow,pt.4 . . . 2.50
13 The Offspring,pt.1 . . . . 2.50

SHANGRI-LA
Jan., 2004
GN 8.00

SHARKY
1998
1 by Dave Elliott & Alex Horley. . . . 2.50
1a variant cover (5,000 made) 3.00
2 coma over 2.50
2a variant cover 3.00
3 R:Blazin' Glory 2.50
3a variant SBi(c) 2.50
4 tons of guest stars, concl. 2.50
4a variant DAy(c) 2.50

SHATTERED IMAGE
WildStorm, 1996
1 KBk,TnD,crossover 2.50
2 KBk 2.50
3 KBk 2.50
4 KBk,TnD,concl. 2.50

SHE-DRAGON
Feb., 2005
1-shot EL(s) 48-pg. 6.00

SHIDIMA
Jan., 2001
1 PtL, A Warlands saga 3.00
1a variant(c) 3.00
1b stormkote(c). 8.00
2 PtL 3.00
2a variant(c) 3.00
2b variant(c) 3.00
3 PtL 3.00
3a variant(c) 3.00
3b variant(c) 3.00
4 . . . . 3.00
5 . . . . 3.00
6 . . . . 3.00
0 24-pg.. . . . . 2.50
0 variant(c) 2.50

SHIP OF FOOLS
(B&W) Sept., 1997
0 Bryan J.L. Glass, Michael
  Avon Oeming. 3.00
1 Death & Taxes,pt.1 . . . . 3.00
2 Death & Taxes,pt.2 . . . . 3.00
3 Death & Taxes,pt.3 . . . . 3.00
4 Death & Taxes,pt.4 . . . . 3.00
TPB rep. Caliber series 15.00

SHOCKROCKETS
April, 2000
1 (of 6) KBk,SI 2.50

---

2 KBk,SI,Command Decision 2.50
3 KBk,SI,The Triangle Trade 2.50
4 KBk,SI,Rocket Science 2.50
5 KBk,SI,sneak attack. 2.50
6 KBk,SI,Final Battle,flip-book 2.50

SHUT UP & DIE
(B&W) 1998
1 JHI and Kevin Stokes 3.00
2 JHI,Angry White Man 3.00
3 JHI,Wife abducted 3.00
4 JHI 3.00
5 JHI,A:Earl Jackson. 3.00

SIEGE
WildStorm, 1997
1 JPe,AV,Nothing you believe
  is real. 2.50
2 JPe,AV,Omega goes to Hawaii
  for funeral 2.50
3 JPe,AV,Zontarian Crab Ships vs.
  Drop Ship 2.50
4 JPe,AV,Rescue of Omega Squad 2.50

SIGMA
WildStorm, 1996
1 BCi,Fire From Heaven prelude . . 2.50
2 BCi,Fire From Heaven,pt.6 . . . . . 2.50
3 BCi,Fire From Heaven,pt.14 . . . . 2.50

SILENCE, THE
Jan., 2005
GN B&W, mostly 10.00
GN 12.00

SILENCERS, THE
July, 2005
1 . . . . 3.00
2 . . . . 3.00

SILENT SCREAMERS
Oct., 2000
1 Nosferatu, 40-pg. 5.00

SINKING
March, 1999
GN JHI 15.00

SIREN
(B&W) May, 1998
1 by J. Torres & Tim Levins 3.00
2 F:Zara Rush, private eye. 3.00
3 cpmc;Isopm 3.00
TPB rep. Shapes 10.00

SIX
Aug., 2004
GN B&W,56-pg 6.00

SKINNERS
TMP, July, 2000
1 MtB,JMd. 3.00
1a variant PtL(c). 3.00
1b variant Andy Park(c) 3.00
1c variant MtB(c) 2-D 3.00
1d limited ed. Broom(c) 9.00
1e limited ed., signed 11.00
2 MtB,SRf 3.00
2a variant JBz(c). 3.00

SLOP: ANALECTA
May, 2005
TPB 13.00

IMAGE

All comics prices listed are for *Near Mint* condition.

SMALL GODS
June, 2004
1 Killing Grin,pt.1 . . . . 3.00
2 Killing Grin,pt.2 . . . . 3.00
3 Killing Grin,pt.3 . . . . 3.00
4 Killing Grin,pt.4 . . . . 3.00
5 Dead Man's Hand,pt.1 . . . . 3.00
6 Dead Man's Hand, pt.2 . . . . 3.00
7 Dead Man's Hand, pt.3 . . . . 3.00
8 Dead Man's Hand, pt.4 . . . . 3.00
9 Dead Man's Hand, concl. 3.00
10 Nightingale, pt.1 . . . . 3.00
11 Nightingale, pt. 2. . . . . 3.00
12 Nightingale, pt. 3. . . . . 3.00
Spec. #1 Two Time 3.00
TPB Vol. 1 Killing Grin 10.00
Vol. 2
1 (of 2) Innocence. 3.00

SOCOM:
SEAL TEAM SEVEN
(B&W) Feb., 2006
GN 13.00

SOLAR LORD
March, 1999
1 by Khoo Fuk Lung 2.50
2 Nickson is Solar Lord. 2.50
3 V:5 enemies. 2.50
4 V:5 enemies. 2.50
5 V:The Emperor of Darkness . . . 2.50
6 O:Nickson 2.50
7 concl., book one 2.50

SOMETHING WICKED
Oct., 2003
1 (of 4) b&w 3.00
2 thru 4 Among the Living. . . . . . @3.00

SOUL OF A SAMURAI
Apr., 2003
1 (of 4) b&w, 48-pg. 4.00
2 . . . . 4.00
3 48-pg 6.00
4 48-pg. 6.00

SOUL REAVER:
LEGACY OF KAIN
Top Cow, June, 2000
1-shot MHw,video game tie-in 2.50

SOUL SAGA
Top Cow, 2000
1 SPa,F:Aries, Soulblade 5.00
1a variant(c) JMd (1:4) 5.00
1b variant Michael Turner(c) (1:4) . 5.00
2 SPa,death in the family 3.50
2a variant David Finch(c) 3.50
2b variant Pat Lee(c) 3.50
3 SPa, Khan Hordes 2.50
4 SPa, Dominion vs. Khan 2.50
5 SPa, F:Ares 2.50
Coll.Ed.Vol.1 . . . . 6.00

SOULWIND
(B&W) March, 1997
1 quest for Soulwind begins 3.00
2 Nick becomes 'Captain Crash' . . 3.00
3 Captain Crash & Poke pursue
    Soulwind info. 3.00
4 concl. of story arc 3.00
5 The Day I Tried to Live,pt.1 . . . . 3.00
6 The Day I Tried to Live,pt.2 . . . . 3.00
7 The Day I Tried to Live,pt.3 . . . . 3.00
8 The Day I Tried to Live,pt.4 . . . . 3.00
TPB rep #1–#4. . . . . 10.00

SPARTAN:
WARRIOR SPIRIT
July, 1995
1 thru 4 . . . . @3.00

SPARTAN X
(B&W) Sept., 1998
1 MGo,RM,'Plague Train' 3.00
2 MGo,RM,'Plague Train,'pt.2. . . . 3.00
3 MGo,RM,'Plague Train,'pt.3. . . . 3.00

SPAWN
TMP, May, 1992
1 TM,I:Spawn,w/GP,DK pinups . . . 11.00
1a black & white 35.00
2 TM,V:The Violator 9.00
3 TM,V:The Violator 9.00
4 TM,V:The Violator,+coupon #2 . . 7.00
4a w/o coupon 3.00
5 TM,O:Billy Kincaid 7.00
6 TM,I:Overt-Kill. 5.00
7 TM,V:Overt-Kill. 5.00
8 TM,AMo(s),F:Billy Kincaid 5.00
9 NGa(s),TM,I:Angela. 6.00
10 DS(s),TM,A:Cerebus. 5.00
11 FM(s),TM, Home Story 4.00
12 TM,Chapel killed Spawn 4.00
13 TM,A:Youngblood 4.00
14 TM,A:The Violator 5.00
15 TM, Myths II 4.00
16 GCa,I:Anti-Spawn 5.00
17 GCa,V:Anti-Spawn 7.00
18 GCa,ATi,D:Anti-Spawn 9.00
19 & 20 see after #25
21 TM,The Hunt,pt.1 . . . . 9.00
22 TM,The Hunt,pt.2 . . . . 3.00
23 TM,The Hunt,pt.3 . . . . 3.00
24 TM,The Hunt,pt.4 . . . . 3.00
25 Image X Book,MS,BTn 5.00
19 I:Houdini 5.00
20 J:Houdini 6.00
26 TM 4.00
27 I:The Curse 4.00
28 Faces Wanda 4.00
29 Returns From Angela 4.00
30 A:KKK 4.00
31 R:Redeemer 4.00
32 TM,GCa,New Costume. 4.00
33 R:Violator 4.00
34 V:Violator. 4.00
35 F:Sam & Twitch 4.00
36 Talks to Wanda 4.00

Spawn #11
© Todd McFarlane

37 I:The Freak 4.00
38 . . . . 4.00
39 . . . . 4.00
40 V:Curse. 4.00
41 V:Curse. 4.00
42 thru 49. . . . . @4.00
50 48-pg. 4.00
51 . . . . 3.00
52 . . . . 3.00
53 A:Malebolgia 3.00
54 return to New York, alliance
    with Terry Fitzgerald 3.00
55 plans to defeat Jason Wynn 3.00
56 efforts to defeat Jason Wynn . . . 3.00
57 . . . . 3.00
58 sequel to Spawn #29 . . . . 3.00
59 . . . . 3.00
60 battle between Spawn and
    Clown cont. 3.00
61 battle with Clown concl. 3.00
62 Spawn is Al Simmons for 1 day . 3.00
63 Operation: Wynn fall,pt.1 . . . . . 3.00
64 Wynn falls, bagged with toy
    catalog. 3.00
65 recap issue 2.50
66 TM,GCa,lives of alley bums . . . 2.50
67 TM,GCa,Sam and Twitch 2.50
68 TM,GCa,R:Freak. 2.50
69 TM,GCa,F:Freak. 2.50
70 TM,GCa 2.50
71 TM,GCa,Cold Blooded Truth . . 2.50
72 TM,GCa,Haunting of the Heap . . 2.50
73 TM,GCa,R:The Heap 2.50
74 TM,GCa,pathway to misery . . . 2.50
75 TM,GCa,Deadly Revelations . . . 2.50
76 TM,GCa,Granny Blake 2.50
77 TM,GCa,confronts 2.50
78 TM,GCa,DaM,'Sins of Excess' . . 2.50
79 TM,GCa,DaM,Killer in N.Y. 2.50
80 TM,GCa,DaM,F:Sam & Twitch . . 2.50
81 TM,GCa,DaM,Sins are reborn . . 2.50
82 TM,GCa,DaM,sea of self-doubt . 2.50
83 TM,GCa,V:Jason Wynn 2.50
84 TM,GCa,DaM,Helle's Belles . . . 2.50
85 TM,GCa,DaM,Legend of
    Hellspawn 2.50
86 TM,GCa,DaM,V:Al Simmons . . . 2.50
87 TM,GCa,DaM,Al Simmons fate . 2.50
88 TM,GCa,DaM,Seasons of
    change. 2.50
89 TM,GCa,DaM,secrets revealed . 2.50
90 TM,GCa,DaM,three stories. 2.50
91 TM,GCa,DaM,Black Cat
    Bones,pt.1 . . . . 2.50
92 TM,GCa,DaM,Black Cat
    Bones,pt.2 . . . . 2.50
93 TM,GCa,DaM,Devil's Banquet . . 2.50
94 TM,GCa,DaM,Children's Hour . . 2.50
95 TM,GCa,DaM,Cracks in the
    Foundation. 2.50
96 TM,GCa,DaM,Rules of
    Engagement 2.50
97 TM,GCa,DaM,Heaven's Folly . . . 2.50
98 TM,GCa,DaM,The Trouble
    with Angels 2.50
99 TM,GCa,DaM,Edge of Darkness 2.50
100A TM,GCa,DaM,TM(c)She dies 10.00
100B TM,GCa,DaM,FM(c). 5.00
100C TM,GCa,DaM,GCa(c). 6.00
100D TM,GCa,DaM,AshleyWood(c) 5.00
100E TM,GCa,DaM,MMi(c) 5.00
100F TM,GCa,DaM,AxR(c) 5.00
101 TM,AMe,DaM,The Speed
    of Night 10.00
102 TM,AMe,DaM,Remains. 2.50
103 TM,AMe,DaM,A Town Called
    Malice 2.50
104 TM,Retribution Overdrive,pt.1 . . 2.50
105 TM,Retribution Overdrive,pt.2 . . 2.50
106 TM,The Kingdom,pt.1 . . . . 2.50
107 TM,The Kingdom,pt.2 . . . . 2.50
108 TM,The Kingdom,pt.3 . . . . 2.50

109 TM,Hour of Cleansing	
Approaches	2.50
110 TM,The Kingdom,pt.4	2.50
111 TM,The Kingdom,pt.5	2.50
112 TM,The Kingdom,pt.6	2.50
113 TM,The Kingdom,pt.7	2.50
114 TM,The Bridge,pt.1	2.50
115 TM,The Bridge,pt.2	2.50
116 TM,Consequences	2.50
117 TM,A Season in Hell	2.50
118 TM,A Season in Hell,pt.2	2.50
119 TM,A Season in Hell,pt.3	2.50
120 TM,A Season in Hell,pt.4	2.50
121 TM,The Devil His Due	2.50
122 TM,Salvation Road	2.50
123 TM,Freedom in Nothingness	2.50

Spawn #84
© Todd McFarlane

124 TM,Through These Eyes	2.50
125 TM,Wake Up Dreaming,pt.1	2.50
126 TM,Wake Up Dreaming,pt.2	2.50
127 TM Loose Threads,pt.1	2.50
128 TM,Loose Threads,pt.2	2.50
129 TM,Loose Threads,pt.3	2.50
130 TM,Loose Threads,pt.4	3.00
131 TM,God is a Bullet,pt.1	3.00
132 TM,God is a Bullet,pt.2	2.50
133 TM,God is a Bullet,pt.3	2.50
134 TM,God is a Bullet,pt.4	2.50
135 TM,Mad Shadows,pt.1	2.50
136 TM,Mad Shadows,pt.2	2.50
137 TM,Mad Shadows,pt.3	2.50
138 TM,Mad Shadows,pt.4	2.50
139 TM,Asunder,pt.1	2.50
140 TM,Asunder,pt.2	2.50
140 TM,Asunder,pt.2	2.50
138 TM,A Thousand Clowns,pt.5	2.50
139 TM,Hellbound,pt.1	2.50
140 TM(s),Hellbound,pt.2	2.50
141 TM(s),Hellbound,pt.3	2.50
142 TM(s),Devil to Pay, pt.1	2.50
143 TM(s),Devil to Pay,pt.2	2.50
144 TM(s),Devil to Pay, pt.3	2.50
145 TM(s),Destination Anywhere	2.50
146 TM(s),Destination Anywhere	2.50
147 TM(s),Howl	2.50
148 TM(s),Random Patterns, pt.1	2.50
149 TM(s),Random Patterns, pt.2	2.50
150 TM(s),TM(c), 48-page	5.00
150a thru 150c variant(c)s	6.00
151 Beginning of the End	10.00
152 Another Spawn?	3.00
153	3.00
154	3.00
155 Angel Zera	3.00

156	3.00
157	3.00
158 The Rapture	3.00
159 Spawn bares his heart	3.00
160 V:The Disciple	3.00
161 Armageddon	3.00
162 Beyond Good and Evil	3.00
163 Reconstruction	3.00
164 New Beginnings	3.00
Ann.#1 Blood & Shadows, 64-pg.	5.00
GN Spawn Movie adapt.	5.00
TPB Capital Collection rep.#1-3	
limited to 1,200 copies	300.00
TPB TM,rep.#1–#5.	10.00
TPB Vol. 1 rep. (2005)	20.00
TPB Spawn III rep. #12–#15	10.00
TPB Spawn IV rep. #16–#20	10.00
TPB Spawn V rep.#21–#25	10.00
TPB Spawn VI, rep.#26–#30	10.00
TPB Vol. VII Deadman's Touch	10.00
TPB Vol. VIII Betrayal of Blood	10.00
TPB Angela's Hunt	10.00
TPB Vol.9 Urban Jungle	10.00
TPB Vol.10 Vengeance of	
the Dead	10.00
TPB Vol.11 Crossroads	10.00
TPB Vol.12 Immortality	11.00
TPB The Armageddon Collection	15.00
TPB Vol. 2 Collection, #13 – #33.	30.00
GN Spawn: Blood and Salvation	5.00
Fan Edition #1, with Fan #16	3.00
Fan Edition #1a variant cover	4.00
Fan Edition #1b gold logo,retailer	5.00
Fan Edition #2, with Fan #17	3.00
Fan Edition #2a variant cover	4.00
Fan Edition #2b gold logo,retailer	5.00
Fan Edition #2c platinum Foil logo	5.00
Fan Edition #2, with Fan #18	3.00
Fan Edition #2a variant cover	4.00
Fan Edition #3b gold logo,retailer	5.00
1-shot Spawn: Simony, 64-pg.	8.00
1-shot Spawn: Godslayer, 64-pg.	7.00
Spec. Spawn 1 in 3-D	3.00

SPAWN/BATMAN
Image/DC 1994

1 FM(s),TM	5.00

SPAWN BLOOD FEUD
June, 1995

1 V:Vampires	4.00
2	4.00
3 Hunted as a Vampire	4.00
4 V:Heartless John	4.00

SPAWN BIBLE
TMP, Aug., 1996

1 TM,GCa	15.00
2 Book of the Dead, 56-pg.	15.00

SPAWN: THE DARK AGES
TMP, March, 1999

1 GF,LSh, from 12th century.	2.50
1a variant TM(c) (1:4)	7.00
2 LSh,A:Black Knight	2.50
3 LSh,A:Black Knight	2.50
4 LSh,Lord Covenant	2.50
5 LSh,Lord Covenant	2.50
6 LSh,Sister Immaculata.	2.50
7 LSh,Cogliostro	2.50
8 LSh,Acts of Contrition	2.50
9 LSh	2.50
10 LSh,F:Lord Covenant	2.50
11 LSh,Ghost on the Hill	2.50
12 LSh,The Faithful	2.50
13 LSh,Blood and Glory.	2.50
14 LSh,The Innocent	2.50
15 LSh,New Beginnings	2.50
16 CWf,Heart of the HellSpawn	2.50
17 CWf,The Circle and the Worm	2.50

18 CWf,Crucified	2.50
19 CWf,Like Any Other Man	2.50
20 Voices in the Dark.	2.50
21 Sins of the Hellspawn	2.50
22 The Seedling.	2.50
23 The Beast	2.50
24 Bleed, Pagan, Bleed.	2.50
25 The Plague of Man	2.50
26 Lesion	2.50
27 Bubonic Nights	2.50
28 Stonehaven,pt.1	2.50
29 Stonehaven,pt.2	2.50
30 The Beast of the Wood.	2.50
31 Home to Roost	2.50

Spawn The Impaler #1
© Todd McFarlane

SPAWN THE IMPALER
TMP Oct., 1996

1 (of 3) MGr, fully painted	4.00
2 thru 3 MGr	@4.00

SPAWN MANGA
Nov., 2005

TPB Vol. 1	10.00
TPB Vol. 2	10.00
TPB Vol. 3	10.00
TPB Spawn Manga Collection	18.00

SPAWN: THE UNDEAD
TMP, May, 1999

1 PJe,DT,CWf,F:Spawn	2.50
2 PJe,DT,CWf,F:Travis Ward	2.50
3 PJe,DT,CWf,Heaven vs. Hell.	2.50
4 PJe,DT,CWf,suicide cult	2.50
5 PJe,DT,CWf,The Wind That	
Shakes the Barley	2.50
6 PJe,DT,CWf.	2.50
7 PJe,DT,CWf,Up the Down Stairs	2.50
8 PJe,DT,CWf,One Lunch to Live.	2.50
9 PJe,DT,CWf,Waiting	2.50
10 PJe,DT,CWf,How to Win Friends	
and Influence People.	2.50
11 PJe,DT,CWf,Heaven and Hell	
and In Between	2.50

SPAWN/WILDC.A.T.S
Jan., 1996

1 AMo(s),Devilday, pt.1, x-over.	3.50
2 AMo(s),Devilday, pt.2.	3.50
3 AMo(s),Devilday, pt.3.	3.50
4 AMo(s),Devilday, pt.4.	3.50

IMAGE

SPIRIT OF THE TAO
Top Cow, May, 1998
1 BTn,F:Lance & Jasmine 2.50
2 BTn,mission to destroy base 2.50
3 BTn,V:Jaikap Clan 2.50
4 BTn,F:Jasmine & Lance 2.50
5 BTn, Antidote to virus 2.50
6 BTn, Tao grows stronger 2.50
7 BTn, V:Menicus 2.50
8 BTn, A:Messiah 2.50
9 BTn, The Dragon is Loose 2.50
10 BTn, Jasmine out of control 2.50
11 BTn, Dragon ash race 2.50
12 BTn, F:Disciple 2.50
13 BTn, friend or foe 2.50
14 BTn, must one die? 2.50
15 BTn,conclusion, 48-pg. 4.00

SPLITTING IMAGE
March, 1993
1 DsM,A:Marginal Seven 2.50
2 DsM,A:Marginal Seven 2.50

STAN WINSTON'S REALM OF THE CLAW
Aug., 2006
GN 17.00

STAR
June, 1995
1 F:Star from Savage Dragon 2.50
2 Buried Alive 2.50
3 A:Savage Dragon,Rapture 2.50
4 A:Savage Dragon,Rapture 2.50

STARCHILD: MYTHOPOLIS
(B&W) 1997
0 JOn, 'Prologue' 3.00
1 JOn, 'Pinehead' 3.00
2 JOn, 'Pinehead,'pt.2 . . . . 3.00
3 JOn, 'Pinehead,'pt.3 . . . . 3.00
4 JOn, 'Fisher King,'pt.1 . . . . 3.00
5 JOn, 'Fisher King,'pt.2 . . . . 3.00

STARDUST KID, THE
May, 2005
1 (of 4) JMD,MP 3.50
2 JMD,MP, The Woman 3.50
3 JMD 3.50
4 JMD 3.50

STAY PUFFED
Jan., 2004
1-shot 3.00
1-shot B variant (c) 3.00

STONE
Avalon Sept., 1998
2 WPo,V:Rook 2.50
3 WPo,A:Bann 2.50
4 WPo, conclusion 2.50
[VOL. II] Aug., 1999
1 WPo 2.50
1a Chromium Edition 7.00
2 WPo, search for murderer 2.50
2 Stonechrome edition 15.00
3 WPo,Blood from a Stone 2.50
4 WPo,A Rose by Any Other Name 2.50
5 Wpo, series resumes 3.00

STORMWATCH
WildStorm, 1993
0 JSc(c),O:StormWatch,
　V:Terrorists,w/card 2.50

StormWatch #3 © Wildstorm

1 JLe(c&s),ScC,TvS(i),
　I:StormWatch 2.50
1a Gold ed. 4.00
2 JLe(c&s),ScC,TvS(i),I:Cannon,
　Winter,Fahrenheit,Regent 2.50
3 JLe(c&s),ScC,TvS(i),V:Regent,
　I:Backlash 3.00
4 V:Daemonites 2.50
5 SRf(s),BBh,V:Daemonites 2.50
6 BCi,ScC,TC,A:Mercs 2.50
7 BCi,ScC,TC,A:Mercs 2.50
8 BCi,ScC,TC,A:Mercs 2.50
9 BCi,I:Defile 2.50
10 V:Talos 2.50
10a variant(c) 5.00
11 RMz(s),the end? 2.50
12 RMz(s),V:Hellstrike,'Visions
　of Deathtrap' 2.50
13 V:M.A.D.-1 . . . . 2.50
14 Despot 2.50
15 Batallion, Flashpoint 2.50
16 V:Defile 2.50
17 D:Batallion 2.50
18 R:Argos 2.50
19 R:M.A.D.-1,L:Winter 2.50
20 F:Cannon,Winter,Bendix 2.50
21 V:Wildcats 2.50
22 RMz,BWS(c),WildStorm
　Rising,pt.9,w/2 cards 2.50
22a Newsstand ed. 2.50
23 RMz(s),R:Despot,Warguard 2.50
24 V:Despot 2.50
25 SSe,ScC,BCi,A:Spartan 2.75
25a 2nd printing 2.50
26 V:Despot 2.50
27 V:Despot,Rebuilding,'And in
　the End' 2.50
28 F:Blademaster,Swift,Flint,
　Comanche,New Adventures . . . 2.50
29 I:Prism,Reorganization 2.50
30 V:Heaven's Fist 2.50
31 V:Middle Eastern Terrorists 2.50
32 . . . . 2.50
33 inc. Winters Journey 2.50
34 . . . . 2.50
35 Fire From Heaven,pt.5 . . . . 2.50
36 Fire From Heaven,pt.12 . . . . 2.50
37 Double size,F:Weatherman One,
　I:Rose Tatoo 8.00
38 WEI(s) 5.00
39 WEI(s) 5.00
40 WEI(s),virus 5.00
41 WEI(s) 5.00
42 WEI(s),Weatherman discovers a
　conspiracy 5.00

43 WEI(s) 5.00
44 WEI(s),history of Jenny Sparks . . 5.00
45 WEI(s),Battalion visits
　his family 5.00
46 WEI(s),secrets and more
　secrets, prologue 5.00
47 WEI(s), JLe, SW, dangerous
　experiment gone awry 5.00
48 WEI(s),'Change or Die'pt.1 . . . . . 5.00
49 WEI(s),'Change or Die'pt.2 . . . . . 5.00
50 WEI(s),'Change or Die' concl.
　large size 8.00
Sourcebok JLe(s),DT 2.75
Spec.#1 RMz(s),DT 4.25
Spec.#2 F:Fleshpoint 2.50
Ashcan 1 . . . . 3.00
TPB Change the World 10.00
TPB A Finer World 15.00
TPB Change or Die 15.00
TPB Force of Nature 15.00
TPB Lightning Strikes 15.00

STORMWATCH
WildStorm, Oct., 1997
1 WEI,bacterial horror,'Strange
　Weather,'pt.1,'Hard Rain'. 5.00
1a Variant cover 5.00
1b Voyager bagged pack 5.00
2 WEI,Stormwatch Black team,
　'Strange Weather,'pt.2 . . . . 5.00
3 WEI,Black team,'Strange
　Weather,'pt.3,'A Storm Coming'. 5.00
4 WEI,A Finer World,pt.1 . . . . 5.00
5 WEI,A Finer World,pt.2 . . . . 5.00
6 WEI,A Finer World,pt.3 . . . . 5.00
7 WEI,Bleed,pt.1 . . . . 5.00
8 WEI,Bleed,pt.2 . . . . 5.00
9 WEI,Bleed,pt.3 . . . . 5.00
10 WEI,'No Reason' 10.00
11 WEI,BHi,PNe,F:Jackson King,
　'No Direction Home' 10.00
TPB Change or Die 15.00
TPB Force of Nature,(DC) 15.00
TPB Final Orbit, 96-pg. (DC) 10.00

STRANGE GIRL
June, 2005
1 . . . . 3.00
1a variant MK(c) 3.00
2 thru 7 . . . . @3.00
8 Life after God, concl. 3.00
9 The End of the Road 3.00
10 Strange Girl returns 3.00
11 Detour to Hell 3.00
12 . . . . 3.00
13 . . . . 3.00
TPB Vol. 1 Girl Afraid. 13.00
TPB Vol. 2 Heaven Knows I'm
　Miserable Now. 15.00

STRANGERS
Mar., 2003
1 (of 6) 3.00
2 In the Inwards of the Night 3.00
3 Caresses such as Snakes Give . 3.00
4 The Livid Daylights 3.00
5 Icy till the Evening 3.00
6 Icy till the Evening 3.00
2a–6a variant (c). 3.00

STRANGERS IN PARADISE VOL. 3
Homage,1996–97
1 TMr. 5.00
2 TMr. 4.00
3 TMr,David & Katchoo fight. 3.50
4 TMr,Katchoo makes startling
　discovery 3.50
5 TMr,Francine's college days 3.50
6 TMr,Katchoo searches for David . 3.50

IMAGE

7 TMr. 3.50
8 TMr,demons of the past. 3.50

STREET FIGHTER
Sept., 2003
1 Round One! Fight! 10.00
2 . . . . 4.00
3 . . . . 4.00
4 Brothers 3.00
4a variant (c). 3.00
5 M.Bison 3.00
5a variant (c). 3.00
5b Power Cel Acetate (c) 5.00
6 The Beginning 3.00
6a variant (c) 4.00
6b Power Foil (c) 4.00
1a–3a variant (c). . . . . @5.00

STREETS
April, 1999
TPB Streets 17.00

Strikeback #1
© *WildStorm*

STRIKEBACK!
WildStorm, 1996
1 rep & new art 2.50
2 thru 5 . . . . @2.50

STRYKEFORCE
Apr., 2004
1 (of 5) 3.00
2 thru 5 . . . . @3.00
TPB Strykeforce (2003) & Codename:
   Strykeforce (1994), rep. 17.00

STUPID COMICS
Sept., 2002
1-shot by Jim Mahfood,b&w 3.00
1-shot #2 . . . . 3.00
3 . . . . 3.00
TPB Collection 13.00

SUPER-PATRIOT
July, 1993
1 N:Super-Patriot 2.50
2 KN(i),O:Super-Patriot. 2.50
3 A:Youngblood. 2.50
4 . . . . 2.50

SUPER-PATRIOT:
LIBERTY AND JUSTICE
June, 1995
1 R:Covenant 2.50
2 Tokyo 2.50
3 Tokyo gets Trashed 2.50
4 Final issue 2.50
TPB Liberty and Justice, 112-pg. . . 13.00

SUPERPATRIOT:
AMERICA'S FIGHTING
FORCE
July, 2002
1 (of 4) F:Johnny Armstrong 3.00
2 patriotic pandemonium 3.00
3 High Anxiety. 3.00
4 The Final Battle, concl. 3.00

SUPERPATRIOT:
WAR ON TERROR
July, 2004
1 (of 4) 3.00
2 thru 4 . . . . @3.00

SUPERSTAR:
AS SEEN ON TV
Jan., 2001
Spec. KBk,SI,48-pg. 6.00

SUPREME
Supreme, 1992
0 O:Supreme 2.50
1 B:RLd(s&i),BrM, V:Youngblood . . 3.00
1a Gold ed. 5.00
2 BrM,I:Heavy Mettle,Grizlock 3.00
3 BrM,I:Khrome. 3.00
4 BrM 3.00
5 BrM(a&s),Clv(i),I:Thor,V:Chrome. 2.50
6 BrM,Clv(i),I:Starguard,
   A:Thor,V:Chrome. 3.00
7 Rip,ErS(s),SwM,A:Starguard,
   A:Thor 3.00
8 Rip(s),SwM,V:Thor 3.00
9 Rip&KtH(s),BrM,Clv(i), V:Thor . . . 3.00
10 KrH(s),BrM,JRu(I), BU:I:Black
   & White 3.00
11 Extreme Prejudice,pt.4,
   I:Newmen 3.00
12 SPa(c),RLd(s),SwM 4.00
25 SPa(c),RLd(s),SwM,V:Simple
   Simon,Images of Tomorrow. . . . 6.00
13 D:Supreme Madness 3.00
14 Supreme Madness,pt.2. . . . . . . 3.00
15 RLd(s)A:Spawn. 3.00
16 V:StormWatch 3.00
17 Supreme Madness,pt.5. . . . . . . 3.00
18 E:Supreme Madness 3.00
19 V:The Underworld. 3.00
20 V:The Unterworld 3.00
21 God Wars 3.00
22 RLd,CNn,God Wars, V:Thor . . . 3.00
23 ExtremeSacrifice,pt.2,x-over. . . . 3.00
24 Identity Questions 3.00
#25, see above, after #12
26 F:Kid Supreme 3.00
27 Rising Son,I:Cortex. 3.00
28 Supreme Apocalypse:Prelude . . 3.00
29 Supreme Apocalypse,pt.1. . . . . . 3.00
30 Supreme Apocalypse,pt.5. . . . . . 3.00
31 V:Equinox 3.00
32 V:Cortex 3.00
33 Extreme Babewatch 3.00
34 She-Supreme 3.00
35 Extreme Destroyer,pt.7
   x-over, bagged with card 3.00
36 . . . . 3.00
37 . . . . 3.00

38 . . . . 3.00
39 AMo. 3.00
40 AMo. 3.00
41 AMo. 5.00
42 AMo,'Secret Origins' 5.00
43 AMo,'Secrets of the Citadel
   Supreme'. 3.00
44 See Color Comics section
Ann.#1 TMB,CAd,KG,I:Vergessen . . 3.00
Ashcan #1 . . . . 3.00
Ashcan #2 . . . . 2.00

SUPREME: GLORY DAYS
Oct., 1994
1 Supreme in WWI 3.00
2 (of 2) BNa&KIA(s),DdW,GyM,
   A:Superpatriot 3.00

SWORD OF DAMOCLES
WildStorm, 1996
1 prelude to Fire From Heaven
   x-over. 2.50
2 Fire From Heaven,Finale,pt.2 . . . 2.50

SWORD OF DRACULA
Oct., 2003
1 . . . . 3.00
2 The Elders,pt.2 . . . . 3.00
3 The Elders,pt.3 . . . . 3.00
4 The Elders,pt.4 . . . . 3.00
5 The Elders,pt.5 . . . . 3.00
6 Concl. 3.00

SYLVIA FAUST
Aug., 2004
1 (of 4) 3.00
2 . . . . 3.00
3 Fade. 3.00

SYPHONS
Sept., 2004
TPB rep. Vol. 2, #1n#3 . . . . 15.00

TALES FROM
THE BULLY PULPIT
Aug., 2004
1-shot 64-pg. 7.00

TALES OF
THE DARKNESS
Top Cow, April, 1998
1 WPo,F:Jackie Estacado. 3.00
2 WPo,concl. first story. 3.00
3 Dungeon, Fire, and Sword,pt.1 . . 3.00
4 Dungeon, Fire & Sword 3.00
5 in Dark Ages 3.00
6 futuristic story. 3.00
1/2 . . . . 3.00

TALES OF THE REALM
Aug., 2004
TPB 15.00

TALES OF TELLOS:
MAIDEN VOYAGE
March, 2001
1 48-pg. 4.00

TALES OF TELLOS
Oct., 2004
1 (of 3) F:Dyn Jessa 3.50
2 TDz 3.50
3 TDz 3.50

All comics prices listed are for *Near Mint* condition.

Tales of the Witchblade #1 © Top Cow

TALES OF THE WITCHBLADE
Top Cow, 1996

1 TnD,F:Anne Bonney	9.00
1a TnD, variant cover (1:4)	12.00
1a signed, variant	20.00
2 TnD,F:Annabella	6.00
3 WEl,BTn,future	6.00
4 WEl,BTn,future,pt.2	5.00
5 RiB,past	5.00
6 RGr, time of Celts	3.00
7 in Ancient Egypt	3.00
7a variant cover (1:4)	10.00
8 ancient Egypt,pt.2	3.00
9 ancient Egypt,pt.3	3.00
Coll.Ed.#1, rep. #1–#2	5.00
Coll.Ed.#2, rep.#3–#4	6.00

TASK FORCE 1
July., 2006

1	3.50
2 thru 4	@3.50

TEAM 1: STORMWATCH
June, 1995

1 I:First StormWatch Team	2.50
2 V:Helspont,D:Think Tank	2.50

TEAM 1: WILDC.A.T.S
July, 1995

1 I:First Wildcats Team	2.50
2 B:Cabal	2.50

TEAM 7
WildStorm, 1994–95

1 New team	4.00
2 New powers	2.50
3 Members go insane	2.50
4 final issue,V:A Nuke	2.50
Ashcan	2.50
TPB	10.00

TEAM 7
OBJECTIVE: HELL
May, 1995

1 CDi,CW,BWS(c),WildStorm Rising,Prologue,w/2 cards	3.00
1a Newsstand ed.	2.50
2 Cambodia	2.50

TEAM 7:
DEAD REACONING
Jan., 1996

1 CDi	3.00
2 thru 4 CDi	@2.50

TEAM YOUNGBLOOD
Extreme, 1993

1 B:ErS(s),ATi(c),CYp,NRD(i), I:Masada,Dutch,V:Giger	2.50
2 ATi(c),CYp,NRd(i),V:Giger	2.50
3 RLd(s),CYp,NRd(i),C:Spawn, V:Giger	2.50
4 ErS(s)	2.50
5 ErS(s),CNn,I:Lynx	2.50
6 ErS(s),N:Psi-Fire, BU:Black&White	2.50
7 ErS(s),CYp,ATh,Extreme Prejudice,pt.1,I:Quantum, BU:Black & White	2.50
8 ErS(s),CYp,ATh,Extreme Pre-judice,pt.5, V:Quantum, BU:Black & White	2.50
9 RLd	2.50
10 ErS(s),CYp,ATh	2.50
11 RLd,ErS,Cyp	2.50
12 RLd,ErS,Cyp	2.50
13 ErS,Cyp	2.50
14 RLd,ErS,Cya	2.50
15 New Blood	2.50
16 RLd,ErS,TNu,I:New Sentinel, A:Bloodpool	2.50
17 ExtremeSacrifice,pt.6,x-over	2.50
18 MS, membership drive	2.50
19 R:Brahma	2.50
20 Contact,pt.1 1000 yr Badrock	2.50
21 Contact,pt.2	2.50
22 Shadowhunt x-over,pt.4	2.50

TECH JACKET
2002

1 Origin issue	3.50
2 thru 8	@3.00
TPB Vol.1 Lost and Found	13.00

TEENAGE MUTANT
NINJA TURTLES
(B&W) Highbrow,
June, 1996

1	4.00
2	3.00
3	3.00
4 Donatello resurrected	3.00
5 FFo,Warlord Komodo uses Splinter as guinea pig	3.00
6 FFo	3.00
7 FFo,Raphael joins Foot Clan?	3.00
8 FFo,Michelangelo tries to rescue Casey Jones' daughter	3.00
9 Enter: the Knight Watchman	3.00
10 'Enter: The Dragon'	3.00
11 V:DeathWatch,A:Vanguard	3.00
12 F:Raph, Foot Gang warfare	3.00
13 Shredder is back!	3.00
14 Shredder vs. Splinter	3.00
15 F:Donatello	3.00
16 reunited with Splinter	3.00
17 F:Leonardo	3.00
18 UFO Sightings	3.00
19 F:Leatherhead	3.00
20 F:Triceraton	3.00
21 A:Pimiko	3.00
22 F:Lady Shredder	3.00
23 F:Lady Shredder	3.00
TPB A New Beginning	10.00

TEKKEN FOREVER
Dec., 2001

1 (of 4) from Tekken 4 video game	3.00
1a variant(c)	3.00
2 Iron Fist tournament	3.00

TELLOS
May, 1999

1 TDz, The Joining, part 1	3.00
2 TDz, The Joining, part 2	2.50
3 TDz, The Joining, part 3	2.50
4 TDz,Hawke & Rikk	2.50
4a variant JaL cover (1:4)	2.50
4b variant AAd cover (1:4)	2.50
4c variant RGr cover (1:4)	2.50
5 TDz,all-out battle	2.50
6 TDz,Aftermath	2.50
7 TDz,Darkness & Light	2.50
8 TDz,Tellos Joins Gorilla	2.50
8a variant Kia Asamiya(c)	2.50
8b variant HuR(c)	2.50
9 TDz,Jarek vs. Malesur	2.50
10 TDz, concl.	3.00
Coll.Ed.#1 The Joining	9.00
Prelude 16-pg	7.00
Prelude holo-foil	15.00
GN Maiden Voyage	6.00
GN The Last Heist, 48-pg.	6.00
GN Sons & Moons, 48-pg.	6.00
TPB Vol.1 Reluctant Heroes	18.00
TPB Vol.2 Kindred Spirits	18.00

TENTH, THE
Jan.,, 1997

1 BSt,TnD,Last stand against Hell on Earth	6.00
2 BSt,TnD,invasion of Darklon Corp. begins	5.00
3 BSt,TnD,Tenth & Espy team-up	4.00
4 BSt,TmD.confrontation with possible Armageddon	4.00
TPB rep.#1–#4	11.00

[Regular Series] Aug., 1997

1 TnD,BSt,V:Blackspell	5.00
2 TnD,BSt,V:Blackspell	4.00
3 TnD,BSt,Gozza,Eve	4.00
4 TnD,BSt,teleported to Japan	4.00
5 TnD,BSt	3.50
6 TnD,BSt,CollateralDamage,pt.1	3.50
7 TnD,BSt,CollateralDamage,pt.2	4.00
8 TnD,BSt,Dark Wind At Your Back	3.00
9 TnD,BSt,F:Adrenalynn	3.00

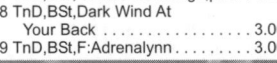

Tenth, Darkk Dawn © Image

10 TnD,pt.1 (of 3). 3.00
10a variant TnD(c). 3.00
11 TnD,Victor retains Tenth 3.00
11a variant cover 3.00
12 TnD,Black reign begins. 3.00
13 TnD,V:Rhazes Darkk 3.00
14 TnD,V:Rhazes Darkk 3.00
Coll.Ed.Vol.1 rep. #1–#2 . . . . 5.00
Spec.Configuration#1, sourcebook . 2.50
1-shot The Tenth: Darkk Dawn,
   48-page O:The Tenth (2005). . . 5.00
TPB rep.#1–#4. . . . . 12.00

TENTH, THE:
BLACK EMBRACE
Feb., 1999

1 TnD,SLo, V:Gozza. 4.00
1a variant cover (1:2) 12.00
2 TnD,SLo, F:Esperanza 2.50
3 TnD,SLo, F:Adrenalynn 2.50
4 TnD,SLo, conclusion 2.50

TENTH, THE:
EVIL'S CHILD
Sept., 1999

1 TnD, F:Gozza 3.00
1a variant cover (1:3) 3.00
1b variant cover (1:3) 3.00
2 TnD, F:Twisted 3 . . . . 2.50
3 TnD 2.50
4 TnD, someone dies 2.50
Spec.Ed.#1, rep.#0 & #1/2. . . . . . 3.00

10TH MUSE, THE
Nov., 2000

1 MWn,KeL 3.50
1a variant(c) 3.50
2 MWn,KeL,flip-book 3.50
2a variant(c) 3.50
2b photo(c) 3.50
3 MWn, critically wounded 3.50
3a variant(c) 3.50
3b photo(c) 3.50
4 MWn,Who is Medusa? 3.50
5 MWn,The Savage World 3.50
6 MWn,RCz,A:Serra 3.50
6 photo(c) 3.50
7 MWn,RCz,Maxwell Gideon 3.50
7a photo(c) 3.50
8 MWn,Assault on Olympus 3.50
8a photo(c) 3.50
9 MWn,San Francisco battle 3.50
9a photo(c) 3.50
10 MWn,RCr,I:The Odyssey 3.50
10a variant(c). 3.50
10b variant CBa(c). 3.50
11 RCr,The Endgame 3.50

TIMESEEKERS
Aug., 2003

1 . . . . 3.00

TINCAN MAN
Jan., 2000

1 F:Alex Darkstar 3.00
1a variant GfD(c) (1:4) 3.00
2 no mercy 3.00
3 . . . . 3.00
Preview Book, 24-pg 3.00

TOKYO KNIGHTS
(B&W) Top Cow, Nov., 2004

GN 10.00

TOMB RAIDER
Top Cow, Nov., 1999

1 DJu,JSb. 5.00

2 DJu,JSb,quest for Medusa Mask. 3.00
3 DJu,JSb,secret of Medusa Mask. 3.00
4 DJu,JSb,Medusa Mask found . . . 3.00
5 DJu,JSb,Ancient Futures 3.00
6 DJu,JSb,Death Dance 3.00
7 DJu,JSb,Dead Center,pt.1(of4) . 3.00
8 DJu,JSb,Dead Center,pt.2. . . . . 3.00
9 DJu,JSb,Death by Midnight 3.00
9a variant(c) 7.00
10 DJu,JSb,Eye of Creation 3.00
11 DJu,BTn 3.00
12 DJu,BTn 3.00
13 DJu,JSb,Honduras,pt.1 . . . . . . 3.00
14 DJu,JSb,Honduras,pt.2 . . . . . . 3.00
15 DJu,JSb,Without Limit 3.00
16 DJu,JSb,Pieces of Zero,pt.1 . . . 3.00
17 DJu,JSb,Pieces of Zero,pt.2 . . . 3.00
18 DJu,JSb,Pieces of Zero,pt.3 . . . 3.00
19 DJu,Pieces of Eight,pt.1 . . . . . . 3.00
20 DJu,Pieces of Zero,pt.4 . . . . . . 3.00
21 Hunt for Black Mandala 3.00
22 The Trap,pt.2 . . . . 3.00
23 Path of the Tiger,pt.3 . . . . 3.00
24 Isle of Hydra 3.00
25 Endgame,pt.1 . . . . 3.00
26 Abyss,pt.1 . . . . 3.00
27 Abyss,pt.2 . . . . 3.00
28 Abyss,pt.3, Tempting Fate 3.00
29 V:Lord Vymes 3.00
30 Strange Flesh, 48-pg. 5.00
31 Conquista 3.00
32 Angel of Darkness,pt.1 . . . . 3.00
33 Angel of Darkness,pt.2 . . . . 3.00
34 Angel of Darkness,pt.3 . . . . 3.00
35 Black Legion,pt.1 . . . . 3.00
36 Black Legion,pt.2 . . . . 3.00
37 Black Legion,pt.3 . . . . 3.00
38 Bloodstone,pt.1. . . . . 3.00
39 Bloodstone,pt.2. . . . . 3.00
40 Risen. 3.00
41 Spirit Walker,pt.1. . . . . 3.00
42 Spirit Walker,pt.2. . . . . 3.00
43 Tower of Souls,pt.1 . . . . 3.00
44 Tower of Souls,pt.2 . . . . 3.00
45 Inner Demons 3.00
46 Gathering Storm,pt.1. . . . . 3.00
47 Gathering Storm,pt.2. . . . . 3.00
48 Gathering Storm, pt.3 . . . . 3.00
48a variant (c) 3.00
49 Vendetta 3.00
50 Alpha/Omega, 40-pg. 4.00
TPB Saga of the Medusa Mask. . . 13.00
TPB Vol.2 Mystic Artifacts 20.00
TPB Tomb Raider/Witchblade 13.00
GN The Greatest Treasure of All . . 6.00
Spec. Gallery 3.00
Preview, B&W 16-pg. 2.50
0 Lara goes fishing. 2.50
1/2 DJu, new(c). 3.00
TPB Vol.3 Chasing Shangri-La . . . 13.00
Spec. Tomb Raider vs. Darkness . . 3.00
1-shot The Greatest Pleasure of
   All, Prelude, DJu,JJu (2002) . . . 5.00
1-shot Takeover 3.00
1-shot Epiphany 5.00
1-shot Arabian Nights 3.00
1-Shot The Greatest Treasure
   of All, DJu(s),JJu, 48-page 7.00
Spec. Covery Gallery (2006) 3.00
TPB Compendium (2006) 50.00

TOMB RAIDER:
JOURNEYS
Top Cow, Dec., 2001

1 (of 12) more Lara Croft 3.00
1A variant AH(c) 3.00
2 washed ashore in El Dorado 3.00
3 Sodom and Gomorrah 3.00
4 Deja vu. 3.00
5 Who's in your yearbook? 3.00
6 . . . . 3.00

7 Maori Dream-Spear 3.00
8 way to the Underworld. 3.00
9 Akio 3.00
10 . . . . 3.00
11 . . . . 3.00
12 Settling Old Scores 3.00

TOMB RAIDER MAGAZINE
Top Cow, Feb., 2001

1 56-pg. 5.00
2 56-pg. 5.00

TOMB RAIDER VS.
THE WOLF-MEN
Top Cow, May, 2005

2 (of 4) Monster War x-over 3.00

TOMB RAIDER/
WITCHBLADE
Top Cow, June, 2000

1/2 rep. 3.00

TOMB RAIDER/
WITCHBLADE REVISITED
Top Cow, Dec., 1998

1 Video game tie-in. 3.00

TOMB RAIDER/
WITCHBLADE/
MAGDALENA/
VAMPIRELLA
Top Cow, Aug., 2005

1-shot Special 3.00
1-shot Special variant (c)s . . . . . . @3.00

TOM JUDGE:
END OF DAYS
Top Cow, Dec., 2002

1 PJe,40-pg. 4.00
TPB The Rapture. 20.00

TOMMYSAURUS REX
Aug., 2004

TPB 112-pg. 12.00

Top Cow Secrets Winter Lingerie
Special © Top Cow

All comics prices listed are for *Near Mint* condition.   **CVA Page 573**

IMAGE

TOOTH & CLAW
Aug., 1999
1 Reborn to rage.............. 3.00
2 MPa...................... 3.00
3 MPa,Retribution,concl......... 3.00

TOP COW
Top Cow, Feb., 1995–2006
Spec. Top Cow preview book 1.00
Spec. Freshmen, Necromance
  V.I.C.E. previews 1.00
Spec. Secrets: Winter Lingerie
  Specia (1996) 3.00l
Top Cow Bible 10.00
Top Cow/Ballistic Swimsuit Spec.#1
  MS(c) (1995) 4.00
Top Cow's California Christmas
  Spectacular Spec. Pin-ups 3.00
TPB Top Cow/Marvel: The Crossover
  Collection (2005) 25.00

TOP COW CLASSICS
Top Cow, 2000
Witchblade #1 B&W............ 3.00
The Darkness #1 B&W 3.00
Ascension #1 .... 3.00
Fathom #1 .... 3.00
Rising Stars #1 B&W 3.00
Cyberforce #1 B&W 3.00
Tomb Raider #1 B&W 3.00
Tomb Raider #1 B&W, signed ... 20.00
Aphrodite IX #1, B&W.......... 3.00
Midnight Nation #1, B&W....... 3.00
Witchblade #25, B&W.......... 3.00
Magdalena #1 JBz,b&w......... 3.00
Tomb Raider/Wtchblace #1 ...... 3.00
TPB Tomb Raider/Witchblade:
  Trouble Seekers 8.00
  Trouble Seekers 8.00
Battle of the Planets #1 .... 3.00
1-shot Book of Revelations (2003) . 4.00

TOTAL SELL OUT
Dec., 2003
TPB BMB................. 15.00

A TOUCH OF SILVER
(B&W) Jan., 1997
1 JV,'Birthday'................ 3.00
2 JV,'Dance' 3.00
3 JV,'Bullies' 3.00
4 JV,'Separation'............. 3.00
5 JV,inc. Tomorrow Syndicate vs.
  Round Table of America, 12-pg.
  color section 3.00
6 JV 'Choices' Aug., 1963....... 3.00
TPB A Sociopath in Training 13.00

TRAKK: MONSTER HUNTER
Sept., 2003
1 (of 6) 3.00
1a variant (c)................ 3.00
2 .... 3.00
2a variant (c)............... 3.00
2b variant SBs(c) 3.00
3 .... 3.00
3a variant SBS(c) 3.00

TREKKER
May, 1999
1 RoR, in New Gelaph 3.00

TRENCHER
May, 1993
1 KG,I:Trencher.............. 2.50
2 KG..................... 2.50

3 KG,V:Supreme............. 2.50
4 KG,V:Elvis 2.50

TRIBE
March, 1993
1 TJn(s),LSn,I:The Tribe 2.50
1a Ivory(White) Editon 3.00
2 .... 2.50
Ashcan 1 .... 3.00

TRIPPER, THE
Top Cow, Nov., 2006
1-shot Movie Adapt. 48-pg. 6.00

Troll #1 © Image

TROLL
Extreme, Dec., 1993
1 RLd(s),JMs,I:Evangeliste, V:Katellan
  Command 2.50
2 .... 2.50
Halloween Spec.#1 .... 2.50
X-Mas Stocking Stuffer #1 ...... 3.00

TROLL: ONCE A HERO
Aug., 1994
1 Troll in WWII 2.50

TROUBLEMAN
Motown June, 1996
1 Charles Drost............... 2.50
2 .... 2.50

TRUE STORY, SWEAR TO GOD
(B&W) Sept., 2006
1 If This be Payday............ 3.00
2 .... 3.00

TRUTH, JUSTIN AND THE AMERICAN WAY
March., 2006
1 (of 5) 3.00
2 .... 3.00
3 .... 3.00
4 The Wedding is Off 3.00
5 Crashing the Party........... 3.00
TPB 15.00

TSUNAMI GIRL
Flypaper Jan., 1999
1 F:Michelle Vincent 3.00
2 Sorayama(c), A:Alan Poe 3.00
3 Sorayama(c), Surreal conspiracy 3.00

TUG & BUSTER
(B&W) June, 1998
1 MaH, humor, F:Stinkfinger...... 3.00

24SEVEN
July, 2006
GN 25.00

'21'
Top Cow, Feb., 1996
1 LWn,MDa................. 2.50
2 LWn,MDa................. 2.50
3 LWn,MDa................. 2.50
4 LWn,MDa,'Time Bomb,'pt.1 .... 2.50
5 LWn,MDa,'Time Bomb,'pt.2 .... 2.50
6 LWn,MDa,'Time Bomb,'pt.3
  'Detonation' 2.50

TWO-BITS
Jan., 2005
1 Lullaby/Imaginaries flip-book 1.00

ULTRA
Aug., 2004
1 Seven Days, pt.1 .... 3.00
2 Seven Days, pt.2 .... 3.00
3 Seven Days, pt.3 .... 3.00
4 Seven Days, pt.4 .... 3.00
5 Seven Days, pt.5 .... 3.00
6 Seven Days, pt.6 .... 3.00
7 Seven Days, pt.7 .... 3.00
8 Seven Days, concl. 3.00
TPB Seven Days 18.00

UMBRA
(B&W) June, 2006
1 (of 3) 52-pg................ 6.00
2 .... 6.00
3 .... 6.00

UNBOUND
(B&W) Jan., 1998
1 by Joe Pruett & Michael Peters.. 3.00
2 .... 3.00
3 F:Marta & Erik 3.00

UNION
WildStorm, Feb., 1995
0 O:Union 2.50
0a WPo(c)................. 5.00
1 MT,I:Union,A:StormWatch 2.75
2 MT 2.75
3 MT 2.75
4 MT,Good Intentions 2.75
Regular Series 1995
1 R:Union, Crusade 2.50
2 V:Crusade & Mnemo 2.50
3 A:Savage Dragon............ 2.50
4 JRo,BWS(c), WildStorm
  Rising,pt.3,w/2 cards......... 2.50
4a Newsstand ed.............. 2.50
5 V:Necros 2.50
6 V:Necros 2.50
7 Jill's Surprise 2.50
8 Regal Vengeance,pt.1 .... 2.50
9 Regal Vengeance,pt.2 .... 2.50
10 Regal Vengeance,pt.3 .... 2.50
1-shot Final Vengeance, MHs,
  V:Regent (1997) 2.50

UNION
WildStorm, 1996
1 MHs,RBn,'Knight of Faith' 2.50
2 MHs,RBn 2.50
3 MHs,RBn 2.50

UNIVERSE
Top Cow, Aug., 2001
1 PJe,The Triad of Powers 2.50
1 variant foil(c) 12.00
2 PJe,Pilgrimage into the Inferno . . 2.50
3 PJe,Judge finds Hell 2.50
4 PJe,plan for mankind's fate 2.50
5 PJe,express train to hell 2.50
6 PJe,family held hostage 2.50
7 PJe,successor to the devil 2.50
8 PJe, Stairway to Heaven,48-pg. . . 5.00

UNTOUCHABLES
(B&W) Sept., 2006
TPB 17.00

VAGABOND
Aug., 2000
1 RBn,SRf,F:Sharon Armstrong . . . 3.00
1a variant(c) 3.00
1b deluxe 9.00
1c signed 11.00
1d ruby red foil(c) 11.50
2 RBn,SRf 3.00

VAGRANT STORY
Top Cow, Sept., 2000
1 video game tie-in 3.00

VAMPIRE'S CHRISTMAS
GN JLi 48-pg 6.00

VANGUARD
Highbrow, 1993–94
1 EL(s),BU:I:Vanguard 3.00
2 EL(s),Roxann 3.00
3 AMe 3.00
4 AMe 3.00
5 AMe,V:Aliens 3.00
6 V:Bank Robber 3.00
Spec. B&W 48-pg. 6.00

VANGUARD: STRANGE VISITORS
(B&W) 1996
1 (of 4) SFa,BAn,A:Amok,'Strange
  Visitors' 3.00
2 thru 4 SEa,BAn . . . . @3.00

VELOCITY
Top Cow, 1995–95
1 V:Morphing Opponent 3.00
2 V:Charnel 3.00
3 thru 4 . . . . @3.00

VENTURE
Jan., 2003
1 . . . . 3.00
2 thru 4 . . . . @3.00

V.I.C.E.
Top Cow, Oct., 2005
1 . . . . 3.00
1a variant (c)s . . . . @3.00
2 . . . . 3.00
3 . . . . 3.00
4 . . . . 3.00
5 . . . . 3.00

VICTORY
May, 2003
1 thru 4 . . . . @3.00
1a–4a variant (c) . . . . @3.00
Vol. 2 Aug., 2004
1 (of 4) 3.00
2 thru 4 . . . . @3.00
2a–4a variant(c)s . . . . @3.00

VIOLATOR
TMP, 1994
1 AMo(s),BS,I:Admonisher 5.00
2 AMo(s),BS 4.00
3 AMo(s),BS,last issue 4.00

Violator/Badrock #4
© Image

VIOLATOR/BADROCK
Extreme, 1995
1 AMo(s),RLe(c),A:Celestine,'Rocks
  and Hard Places,'pt.1 . . . . 2.50
2 AMo(s),RLe(c),V:Celestine,'Mondo
  Inferno'. 2.50
3 RLe(c),F:Dr. McAllister,'Where
  Angels Fear to Tread' 2.50
4 RLe(c),'Badrock's Bogus Journey,'
  final issue 2.50
TPB Rep 10.00

VIOLENT MESSIAHS
June, 2000
1 F:Rankor Island 5.00
1a variant AMe(c) (1:4) 6.00
2 . . . . 5.00
2a variant(c) 6.00
3 V:Citizen Pain 4.00
4 V:Jeremiah Parker 3.00
5 flip-book 3.00
6 Tonight The Door Opens 3.00
7 In the Final Stretch 3.00
8 North End Mansion 3.00
Spec. Genesis, 56-pg. 5.00
TPB Vol. 1 The Book of Job 25.00

VIOLENT MESSIAHS: LAMENTING PAIN
Sept., 2002
1 (of 4) F:Lt. Cheri Major 3.00
2 thru 4 . . . . @3.00
1a–4a variant (c) . . . . @3.00

VISITATIONS
(B&W) 1997
GN by C. Stott Morse 7.00

VOGUE
Extreme, 1995–96
1 F:Vogue,I:Redbloods 2.50
2 . . . . 2.50
3 conclusion 2.50

VOLTRON: DEFENDER OF THE UNIVERSE
May, 2003
0 . . . . 3.00
1 Revelations,pt.1 . . . . 3.00
1a variant (c)s 3.00
2 thru 5 Revelations,pt.2–pt.5 . . . @3.00

VOODOO
WildStorm, Nov., 1997
1 AMo(s),WildStorm universe 2.50
2 AMo(s),in old New Orleans 2.50
3 AMo(s),Samedi 2.50
4 AMo(s), Christian Charles 2.50
TPB Voodoo Dancing in the Dark . 10.00

WAHOO MORRIS
(B&W) Mar., 2000
1 Rock & Roll fantasy 3.00
2 . . . . 3.00

WALKING DEAD
Oct., 2003
1 . . . . 75.00
2 City of the Damned 50.00
3 Protection 25.00
4 Guns 20.00
5 Zombies 12.00
6 Grave Situations 12.00
7 Snowbound 9.00
8 Search for shelter 6.00
9 Zombie hell-hole 5.00
10 Safer shelter 4.00
11 All Good Things 4.00
12 Petty squabbles 4.00
13 CAd 4.00
14 . . . . 3.00
15 . . . . 3.00
16 CAd 3.00
17 CAd 3.00
18 CAd 3.00
19 CAd 3.00
20 CAd, Alone 3.00
21 CAd, Calm Before the Storm? . . 3.00
22 CAd 3.00
23 CAd 3.00
24 CAd 3.00
25 . . . . 3.00
26 . . . . 3.00
27 . . . . 3.00
28 . . . . 3.00
29 Zombie Attack 3.00
30 Near Death 3.00
31 New chapter begins 3.00
32 Surrounded 3.00
33 . . . . 3.00
34 . . . . 3.00
TPB Vol. 1 Days Gone Bye 10.00
TPB Vol. 2 rep. #7f/#12 . . . . 13.00
TPB Vol. 3 Safety Behind Bars . . 13.00
TPB Vol. 4 The Heart's Desire . . . 13.00
TPB Vol. 5 The Best Defense . . . 13.00
Script Book #1 . . . . 4.00

WANTED
Top Cow, Dec., 2003
1 (of 6) MMr 9.00
1a variant (c)s 9.00

IMAGE

1b Death Row edition 5.00
2 thru 5 . . . . @4.00
#1 Death Row edition,32-pg. 4.00
#2 Death Row edition,32-pg. 4.00
#3 Death Row edition,32-pg. 3.00
#4 Death Row Edition,32-pg. 3.00
Spec. Wanted Dossier 3.00
TPB 20.00

WARBLADE: ENDANGERED SPECIES
WildStorm, 1995

1 I:Pillar. 3.00
2 V:Ripclaw. 2.50
3 I:Skinner. 2.50
4 final issue. 2.50

WARLANDS
Aug., 1999

1 by Pat Lee 2.50
1a, b & c variant covers 2.50
1d Armore Chrome edition 13.00
2 help from the Elves? 2.50
2a variant cover (1:2) 2.50
3 the Dataran invasion 2.50
3a variant cover (1:2) 2.50
4 . . . . 2.50
5 trapped between enemies 2.50
6 enemies clash 3.00
7 the Dataran Horde 2.50
8 . . . . 2.50
9 final battle begins. 2.50
10 flip-book 3.00
11 . . . . 2.50
12 concl.. 2.50
Spec. Three stories 6.00
Chronicles Vol.1, rep.#1–#3. . . . . . 8.00
Chronicles Vol.2, rep.#4–#6. . . . . . 8.00
TPB Vol.1, 184-pg.. . . . . 15.00

WARLANDS: AGE OF ICE
July, 2001

1 Awakening 3.00
2 flip-book 3.00
3 thru 5 . . . . @3.00
1a and 2a variant covers . . . . . @3.00
Spec. #0 (2002) 3.00
Spec. #1/2 (2002) 3.00

WATERLOO SUNSET
(B&W) July, 2004

1 (of 4) B&W,56-pg. 7.00
2 Moving in High Places. 7.00
3 Pilgrim Tale & Dog Parties. 7.00
4 Within the Hollow Crown
   & Pragma 7.00
TPB Waterloo Sunset (2006). 18.00

WEAPON ZERO
Top Cow, 1995

T-Minus-4 WS 8.00
T-Minus-3 Alien Invasion 5.00
T-Minus-2 Formation of a Team. . . . 5.00
T-Minus-1 Alien Invasion 5.00
0 Whole Team Together 4.00
1 . . . . 5.00
2 . . . . 3.50
3 . . . . 3.50
4 thru 9 WS,JBz . . . . @3.00
10 WS,ScL,'Devil's Reign' tie-in. . . 3.00
11 WS,JBz,Weapon Zero & Lilith
   return to T'srii moonbase. 3.00
12 WS,JBz, What's wrong with
   Jamie. 3.00
13 WS,JBz,problems with Jamie . . . 3.00
14 JBz,T'Srrii have returned 3.00
15 JBz,T'Srrii,concl.,48-pg. 3.50

Weapon Zero/Silver Surfer Spec.
   x-over (1997). 3.00

WEASEL GUY: ROADTRIP
(B&W) Aug., 1999

1 by Steve Buccellato 3.00
1a variant cover (1:4) 3.00
2 Peril in Pennsylvania 3.00
2a variant cover (1:4) 3.00
3 Don't Mess With Texas 3.00
3a variant cover (1:4) 3.00
4 48-pg, guest stars 5.00
4a variant KIA(c) (1:4). 5.00

Wetworks #9 © WildStorm

WETWORKS
WildStorm, 1994

1 WPo,Rebirth 4.00
2 WPo,BCi,Brakken,Blood Queen . 3.00
3 WPo,BCi,V:Vampire. 3.00
4 WPo,BCi,Dozer 2.50
5 WPo,BCi,Pilgrim's Turn 2.50
6 WPo,BCi,Civil War. 2.50
7 WPo,BCi,F:Pilgrim 2.50
8 WPo,SW,BWS(c), WildStorm
   Rising,pt.7,w/2 cards 2.50
8a Newsstand ed. 2.50
9 F:Jester,Pilgrim Dozer 2.50
10 R:Dozer to Action 2.50
11 Blood Queen Vs. Dane 2.50
12 V:Vampire Nation 2.50
13 WPo(c) 2.50
14 . . . . 2.50
15 . . . . 2.50
16 Fire From Heaven,pt.4 . . . . 2.50
17 FTa,Fire From Heaven,pt.11 . . . 2.50
18 FTa 2.50
19 FTa 2.50
20 FTa 2.50
21 FTa 2.50
22 FTa,Dave vs.Bloodqueen concl. . 2.50
23 FTa,Flattop & Crossbones,
   V:Lady Feign 2.50
24 FTa 2.50
25 FTa,Can Pilgrim withstand the
   beast that lurks within her,
   double size 4.50
26 team parts ways with Armand
   Waering 2.50
27 V:Craven, no rest for the weary . 2.50
28 Vampire tracked in Pacific
   Northwest,A:Johnny Savoy 2.50
29 V:Soulbender,'Power Surge'. . . . 2.50
30 'Secret of the Siynn' 2.50

31 'Ashes to Ashes' 2.50
32 StG,PtL,V:Drakkar,'Sacrements
   of Damnation,'pt.1 . . . . 2.50
32a Voyager pack, bagged with
   Phantom Guard preview 3.50
33 StG,PtL,Sacraments,pt.2. . . . . . 2.50
34 StG,PtL,Sacraments,pt.3. . . . . . 2.50
35 StG,PtL,Sacraments,pt.4. . . . . . 2.50
36 StG,'Maximum Security' 2.50
37 StG,V:St.Crispin,'Diversionary
   Tactics,'pt.1 . . . . 2.50
38 StG,'DiversionaryTactics,'pt.2 . . . 2.50
39 StG,'Symbiote Seizure' 2.50
40 StG,'Drawn Swords' 2.50
41 StG,V:Stormwatch,'Drawn
   Swords,' conclusion. 2.50
42 StG,'Flash Back,'pt.1. . . . . 2.50
43 StG,'Flash Back,'conclusion 2.50
3-D Spec.#1 (1998) 5.00
Sourcebook #1 (1994) 2.50
Hero Ashcan 3.00
Promo Ashcans #1,#2,#3. . . . . . @3.00
TPB Rebirth,rep. #1–#3 & preview 10.00

WETWORKS/VAMPIRELLA
WildStorm, 1997

1 JMi & GK, x-over 3.00

WHISKEY DICKEL, INTERNATIONAL COWGIRL
Aug., 2003

TPB b&w 120-pg.. . . . . 13.00

WHIZ KIDS
Apr., 2003

1-shot b&w, 48-pg. 5.00

WICKED, THE
Dec., 1999

1 RMr,FTa,supernatural thriller 3.00
1a variant Jay Anacleto(c)(1:4). . . . 3.00
2 thru 7 . . . . @3.00
3a & 4a variant covers . . . . @3.00
Special Medusa's Tale 4.00
TPB Vol. 1 Omnibus 20.00

WICKED WEST, THE
Oct., 2004

GN 10.00
GN Vol. 2 Abomination & Others . . 16.00

WILDC.A.T.S
WildStorm, 1992

1 B:BCi(s),JLe, SW(i), I:Wild-
   C.A.T.S. 6.00
1a Gold ed. 10.00
1b Gold and Signed 10.00
2 JLe,SW(i),V:Master Gnome,
   I:Wetworks, Prism foil(c),
   with coupon #5 . . . . 5.00
2a w/o coupon 2.50
3 RLd(c),JLe,SW(i), V:Youngblood . 3.50
4 E:BCi(s),JLe,LSn,SW(i),w/card,
   A:Youngblood,BU:Tribe 3.50
4a w/red card 5.00
5 BCi(s),JLe,SW,I:Misery 3.00
6 BCi(s),JLe,SW,Killer Instinct,
   A:Misery,C:Ripclaw 3.00
7 BCi(s),JLe,SW, A:Cyberforce. . . . 3.00
8 BCi(s),JLe,SW 4.00
9 BCi(s),JLe,SW 3.50
10 CCi(s),JLe,SW,I:Huntsman 3.00
11 CCi(s),JLe,SW,V:Triad,
   A:Huntsman. 3.00
11a WPo(c) 5.00
12 JLe,CCi,A:Huntsman 3.00
13 JLe,CCi,A:Huntsman 3.00

14 X book. 3.00
15 F:Black Razors 3.00
16 Black Razors. 3.00
17 A:StormWatch 3.00
18 R:Hightower 3.00
19 V:Hightower 3.00
20 TC,JeR,BWS(c),WildStorm
    Rising,pt.2,w/2 cards. 3.00
20a Newsstand ed. 3.00
21 Into Space Back Home 3.50
22 Space Adventures. 3.50
23 F:Mr. Majestic's Team 3.50
24 O:Maul 3.50
25 double sized 5.00
26 AMo. 3.50
27 AMo. 3.50
28 AMo. 3.50
29 AMo,Fire From Heaven,pt.7 . . . . 3.50
30 AMo,BKs,Fire From
    Heaven,pt.13 . . . . 3.50
31 AMo,BKs,'Cats & Dogs' 3.50
32 AMo,BKs,'Catharsis' 3.50
33 AMo,BKs,'Belling the Cat' 3.50
34 AMo,MtB,New York seconds
    away from nuclear disaster . . . 3.50
35 AMo,MtB,BKs,V:Crusade 3.00
36 AMo,MtB,BKs,V:Crusade,
    A:Union,pt.2. . . . . 3.00
37 BCi,JPe,MtB,WildC.A.T.s
    team divided 3.00
38 BCi,JPe,MtB,Puritans debut 3.00
39 BCi,JPe,MtB,'C.A.T. Fight' 3.00
40 BCi,JPe,MtB(c),'Fight
    of Flight'. 3.50
40a variant cover by TC 5.00
41 BCi,JPe,MtB,backwards in time . 3.00
42 BCi,JPe,MTb,in WWI 3.00
43 BCi,JPe,MTb,in ancient China . . 3.00
44 BCi,JPe,MTb,'Paradise Lost' . . . 3.00
45 BCi,JPe,MTb,'Circus Maximus' . 3.00
46 BCi,JPe,MTb,escape from
    Rome. 3.00
47 BCi,JPe,MTb,time trip concl. . . . 3.00
47a variant JMd(c). 3.00
48 BCi,JPe,trapped in mothership . . 3.00
49 BCi,JPe,return to present 3.00
50 BCi,JPe,AMo,new
    costumes,40-pg.(June, 1998) . . 4.00
TPB A Gathering of Eagles 10.00
Spec.#1 SrG(s),TC,SW,I:Destine,
    Pin-ups 3.50
Spec.#2 . . . . 2.50
3-D #1 rep. #1 (1997) 5.00
3-Da variant cover 5.00

WildC.A.T.s #31© WildStorm

TPB rep. #1-4,w/0 . . . . 11.00
TPB Homecoming rep #21–#27 . . 20.00
Ann.#1 JRo,LSn (1998) 3.00
TPB WildC.A.T.S/Cyberforce
    Killer Instinct 17.00
TPB Gathering of Eagles 10.00
TPB Gang War,rep.#28–34 . . . . . . 17.00
TPB VOL. II Way of the Coda 13.00
Volume 2: See COLOR

WILDC.A.T.S ADVENTURES
WildStorm, 1994
1 From animated TV series 3.00
2 Helspont,Troika 3.00
3 Caught in war 3.00
4 V:The President 3.00
5 I:Lonely 3.00
6 I:Majestics 3.00
7 . . . . 3.00
8 Betrayed 3.00
9 V:Black Razors 3.00
10 F:Voodoo. 3.00
Sourcebook (JS(c)). 3.00

WILDC.A.T.S/ALIENS
WildStorm, 1998
1-shot WEI,CSp,KN 9.00
1-shotA, variant GK&KN(c)(1:4). . . 11.00

WILDC.A.T.S TRILOGY
June, 1993
1 BCi(s),JaL,V:Artemis 2.50
2 BCi(s),JaL,V:Artemis 2.50
3 BCi(s),JaL,V:Artemis 2.50

WILDC.A.T.S/X-MEN
WildStorm, Feb., 1997
1 (of 4) SLo,TC, giant Marvel/
    Image x-over 5.00
1a alternate cover by JLe 5.00
2 & 4 see Marvel
TPB WildC.A.T.S/X-Men, rep. 18.50

WILDC.A.T.S/X-MEN
WildStorm/Marvel, 1997
Golden Age #1,SLo,TC 5.00
Golden Age #1a variant JLe(c) . . . 5.00
3-D Golden Age #1, with glasses . . 5.00
3-D Golden Age #1, variant cover . . 5.00
Silver Age #1 SLo, JLe & SW,
    x- over 4.50
Silver Age #1a NA&SW(c). 4.50
Silver Age #1b signed 20.00
Silver Age #1c signed, deluxe 30.00
3-D Silver Age #1, with glasses. . . 6.50
3-D Silver Age #1, NA(c) variant . . 6.50
Modern Age #1, JRo,AHu,MFm,
    V:Hellfire Club 4.50
Modern Age #1a variant cover. . . . 4.50
3-D Modern Age #1, with glasses . 5.00
3-D Modern Age #1, variant cover. . 5.00

WILDCORE
WildStorm, 1997–98
1 BBh,SRf,BBh(c), V:Drahn 2.50
1a variant TC(c) 2.50
1b Voyager bagged pack 3.00
2 BBh, SRf,Brawl joins. 2.50
3 BBh,SRf,V:D'rahn 2.50
4 BBh,SRf,A:Majestic 2.50
5 BBh,SRf,Tapestry 2.50
6 BBh,SRf,Zealot missing. 2.50
7 BBh,SRf,caught in fantasy world . 2.50
8 RBn,SRf,V:Tapestry 2.50
9 RBn,SRf,Zealot's soul restored . . 2.50
10 RBn, SRf,Trans-dimensional
    trauma 2.50

Wildcore #10 © WildStorm

GN Backlash & Taboo's African
    Vacation. 6.00

WILDGUARD: CASTING CALL
Sept., 2003
1 (of 6) TNu 3.00
2 thru 6 TNu . . . . @3.00
1a–6a variant (c)s . . . . @3.00
TPB Casting Call 18.00

WILDGUARD: FIRE POWER
Dec., 2004
1 . . . . 3.50

WILDGUARD: FOOL'S GOLD
July, 2005
1 (of 2) 3.50
2 . . . . 3.50

WILDSTAR: SKY ZERO
March, 1993
1 JOy,AG,I:WildStar. 2.50
1a Gold ed. 5.00
2 JOy,AG. 2.50
3 JOy,AG,V:Savage Dragon,
    D:WildStar 2.50
4 JOy,AG,Last Issue,Pin-ups 2.50
TPB WildStar Sky Zero (1994) . . . 13.00
[Regular Series] Sept., 1995
1 R:WildStar 2.50
2 V:Mighty Man 2.50
3 . . . . 2.50
Ashcan 2.50

WILDSTORM!
WildStorm, Aug., 1995
1 F:Spartan,Black Razors 2.50
2 F:Deathblow. 2.50
3 F:Taboo,Spartan 2.50
4 F:Nautika,Sunburst 2.50
Winter Wonderfest Spec.#1 . . . . . . 3.50
Spec.#1 Chamber of Horrors(1995) 3.50
Spec. Swimsuit Special '97 . . . . . . 2.50
Spec. Ultimate Sports Official
    Program 2.50
Sketchbook 3.00

IMAGE

Spec. Halloween '97 . . . . 2.50
GN Thunderbook #1 . . . . 7.00
GN Summer Spec., 48-pg. (DC) . . . 6.00

WILDSTORM ARCHIVES
GENESIS
WildStorm, June, 1998
1 The #1 Collection, 238 pg 7.00

WILDSTORM RISING
WildStorm, May, 1995
1 JeR,BWS(c&a) WildStorm Rising,
  pt.1:Tricked by Defile,w/2 cards 2.50
1a Newsstand ed. 2.50
2 RMz,BBo,BWS(c) WildStorm
  Rising,pt.10,w/2 cards 2.50
2a Newsstand ed. 2.50
WildStorm Sourcebook #1 . . . . . . 2.50
TPB Rep. Mini-series. 17.00

WILDSTORM SPOTLIGHT
WildStorm, Feb., 1997
1 AMo,F:Majestic, at the end of
  time 2.50
2 StG,RMr,Loner returns 2.50
3 StG,RMr,Secret past of original
  Loner. 2.50
4 F:Hellstrike,Stormwatch 2.50

WILDSTORM
ULTIMATE SPORTS
WildStorm, 1997
Official Program #1 . . . . 2.50

WILDSTORM
UNIVERSE '97
WildStorm, Nov., 1997
Sourcebook #1 thru #3. . . . . @2.50

WINGS OF ANANSI
Aug., 2005
GN 7.00

WITCHBLADE
Top Cow, 1995–96
1 I:Witchblade. 35.00
1A Special retailer edition 35.00
1B Wizard Ace edition,acetate(c) . 25.00
2 . . . . 25.00
2 encore edition 7.00
3 . . . . 20.00
4 . . . . 15.00
5 . . . . 14.00
6 thru 8 . . . . @10.00

Top Cow, 1996
9 . . . . 9.00
9A variant cover 11.00
10 I:Darkness (Jackie Estacado). . 12.00
10a variant Darkness cover (1:4) . 16.00
11 . . . . 6.00
12 Connection between Lisa,
   Microwave Murderer and
   Kenneth Irons 6.00
Witchblade 1/2 mail-in offer
   from Fan #8. . . . . 4.00

Top Cow, 1997
13 Dannette Boucher's secret past . 6.00
14 Sara searches for Microwave
   Murderer 5.00
15 'There is a war brewing...'. 4.00
16 'Will Witchblade come between
   Sarah and Jake?' 4.00
17 New York City in shambles. . . . 4.00
18 Family Ties,pt.1,x-over 4.00
18a variant(c). 7.00
19 Family Ties,pt.4,x-over 4.00

Witchblade #12 © Top Cow

20 Chief Siry, Ian Nottingham 3.00
21 another big surprise 3.00
22 F:Sara 3.00
22a special. 12.00
23 F:Ian Nottingham 3.00
24 JPn,Sara learns truth 3.00
25 Save Jake's Life, 32 pg 3.50
26 'Grey'. 3.00
27 A:Kenneth Irons 3.00
27a variant cover, all villains 9.00
28 A:Jackie Estacado 3.00
29 A:Kenneth Irons 3.00
30 Siry & Irons 3.00
31 How Sara's father died 3.00
32 answers and questions. 3.00
33 F:Eric. 3.00
34 F:Tommy Gallo 3.00
35 Sara gets who she wants 3.00
36 The Darkness,pt.1 x-over 3.00
37 V:wicked creatures 3.00
38 V:Demons of the Underworld . . . 3.00
39 V:Demons of the Underworld . . . 3.00
40 PJe,RV 3.00
41 PJe,RV,arsonist. 3.00
41a variant chrome (c). 5.00
42 PJe,pez dispensers 3.00
43 PJe,Impossible Murders 2.50
44 PJe,Impossible Murders 2.50
45 PJe 2.50
46 PJe 2.50
47 PJe 2.50
48 PJe 2.50
49 PJe,Firestarter is back 2.50
49a gold logo 7.00
50 PJe,48-pg. 5.50
50a variant DK(c). 12.00
50b variant MS(c). 12.00
50c variant(c). 12.00
51 PJe,What is the Witchblade? . . . 2.50
52 PJe,The Inferno is Coming 2.50
53 PJe 2.50
54 Ian Nottingham resurrected 2.50
55 Tora No Shi 2.50
55a Battle of the Planets(c) 7.00
55b Battle(c) signed. 7.00
56 Nottingham vs. Tora No Shi 2.50
57 Sonatine,pt.4. . . . . 2.50
58 Sara & Joe Siry. 2.50
59 Jackie Estacado is dead?. 2.50
60 Endgame,pt.2 x-over 3.00
61 Julie returns 3.00
61a sketch(c). 8.00
62 F:Magdalena. 3.00
63 F:Magdalena 3.00

64 F:Magdalena. 3.00
65 F:Magdalena,concl. 3.00
66 . . . . 3.00
67 Mother's Meat. 3.00
68 Road Trip,pt.1. . . . . 3.00
69 Road Trip,pt.2 . . . . 3.00
70 return from trip 3.00
71 V:Shine 3.00
72 Level 42 . . . . 3.00
73 Level 42 . . . . 3.00
74 Death Pool 3.00
75 Death Pool, concl.,46-pg. 5.00
75a variant (c) 5.00
76 Death Pool follow-up. 3.00
77 F:Celestine 3.00
78 TnD(c). 3.00
79 TnD(c). 3.00
80 Witch Hunt,pt.1 . . . . 3.00
81 Witch Hunt,pt.2 . . . . 3.00
82 Witch Hunt,pt.3 . . . . 3.00
83 Witch Hunt,pt.4 . . . . 3.00
84 Witch Hunt,pt.5 . . . . 3.00
85 Witch Hunt,pt.6 . . . . 3.00
86 Warrior Spirit 3.00
87 Heart of the City 3.00
88 Partners 3.00
89 Fugitive,pt.1 . . . . 3.00
90 Fugitive,pt.2 . . . . 3.00
91 Fugitive,pt.3 . . . . 3.00
92 48-pg. 5.00
93 . . . . 3.00
94 Artifacts, pt.1 . . . . 3.00
95 Artifacts, pt.2 . . . . 3.00
96 . . . . 3.00
97 . . . . 3.00
97a variant (c) 3.00
98 . . . . 3.00
99 . . . . 3.00
100 . . . . 6.00
100 a thru c variant (c). . . . . @7.00
100d variant JLi incentive (c). 10.00
101 . . . . 3.00
102 . . . . 3.00
103 . . . . 3.00
103a variant b&w (c), rare 4.00
Spec. 1 Movie edition, photo(c) . . 10.00
Spec. 1a Movie, foil(c) 17.00
Spec. 1b Movie, holofoil(c) 25.00
Coll.Ed.Vol.#1 . . . . 5.00
Coll.Ed.Vol.#2 . . . . 5.00
Coll.Ed.Vol.#3 . . . . 5.00
Coll.Ed.Vol.#4, rep. #7 & #8 . . . . . 5.00
Coll.Ed.Vol.#5, rep. #9 & #10 . . . . 5.00
Coll.Ed.Vol.#6, rep. #11 & #12. . . . 5.00
Coll.Ed.Vol.#7, rep. #13 & #14 . . . . 5.00
Coll.Ed.Vol.#8, rep. #15–#17. . . . . 7.00
Delux Coll.Ed. rep.1–#8. . . . . 25.00
Spec. Infinity SLo,AdP 3.50
Spec.#40 Preview book, B&W . . . 5.00
Spec.#1 rep.movie photo cover . . . 2.50
Spec.Witchblade/Darkness,pt.2
   x-over, 48-pg. 4.00
Spec. Witchblade/Darkminds x-over 6.00
Gallery Edition #1 . . . . 3.00
TPB Collects Witchblade/Darkness
   Family Ties x-over 10.00
TPB Vol.3 Prevailing, deluxe 15.00
TPB Vol.3 Prevailing, deluxe 15.00
TPB Vol.4: Love Triangle 25.00
TPB Revelations 20.00
TPB Revelations, deluxe 25.00
TPB Revelations, deluxe 25.00
TPB Distinctions. 15.00
TPB Vol. 10 Witch Hunt (2006) . . . 15.00
TPB Vol. 11 (2006). 15.00
Spec.1 Lady Death x-over 5.00
Spec. Tomb Raider 4.00
TPB Obakemono 10.00
1/2 24-pg. 3.00
1-shot Nottingham, 48-pg. 5.00
1-shot Witchblade Animated 3.00
TPB Vlood Relations 13.00

IMAGE

GN Witchblade/Darkminds:
    The Return of Paradox 7.00
1-shot Witchblade/Wolverine 3.00
1-shot Witchblade: Blood Oath 5.00
1-shot Witchblade and Tomb Raider,
    JaL,MT (2005). 3.00
1-shotA Witchblade and Tomb Raider,
    B&W cover (2005). 3.00
1-shot Art of Witchblade (2006). . . . 3.00
Spec. Bearers of the Blade (2006) . 3.00
TPB Witchblade Compendium. . . . 50.00
Spec. Witchblade Tenth Anniv.
    Cover Gallery (2005). 3.00

WITCHBLADE: DESTINY'S CHILD
Top Cow, April, 2000
1 (of 3) O:Witchblade,pt.1. . . . . . . 3.00
2 O:Witchblade,pt.2 . . . . 3.00
3 O:Witchblade, concl. 3.00

WITCHBLADE VS. FRANKENSTEIN'S MONSTER
Top Cow, June, 2005
3 Monster War x-over 3.00

WITCHFINDER, THE
Liar, Oct., 1999
1 by R. Lugibihl & S. Scott 3.00
1a variant cover (1:2) 3.00
2 thru 3 . . . . @3.00

WIZARDS TALE, THE
Homage, 1997
TPB KBk,DWe 20.00
TPB 2nd printing 20.00

WOLVERINE/ WITCHBLADE
Top Cow, Jan., 1997
1-shot 'Devil's Reign'pt.5 (of 8) 4.00

WONDERLAND
Oct., 2004
GN 7.00

WOOD BOY, THE
Mar., 2005
1 (of 2) Raymond Feist (s) 3.00
2 . . . . 3.00

WORLD CLASS COMICS
Aug., 2002
1-shot, 40-pg. b&w. 5.00

WYNONNA EARP
WildStorm, 1996–97
1 BSt,'Violent Territory' 2.50
2 BSt,The Law comes to San
    Diablo 2.50
3 BSt,desperate to stop Hemo
    from going nationwide 2.50
4 BSt,goes to New York,
    V:ancient evil 2.50
5 BSt,battle with Raduk—Eater
    of the Dead concl. 2.50

YOUNGBLOOD
Extreme, April, 1992
0 RLd,O:Youngblood,w/coupon#7 . 3.00
0a without coupon. 1.50

Youngblood #8 © Image

0b gold coupon 9.00
1 RLd,I:Youngblood (flipbook) 5.00
1a 2nd print.,gold border 2.50
1b RLD,Silent Edition 13.00
2 RLd,I:ShadowHawk 5.00
3 RLd,I:Supreme,Showdown 3.00
4 RLd,DK,A:Prophet,BU:Pitt. 3.00
5 RLd,Flip book,w/Brigade #4 . . . . 2.50
6 RLd(a&s),J:Troll,Knight Sabre,
    2nd Die Hard, Proposal to Girl
    friend 3.50
7 Badrock, V:Overtkill 2.50
8 Chapel, V:Spawn 2.50
9 . . . . 2.50
9a variant cover 5.00
10 Bravo, Badrock, Troll 2.50
Yr Bk #1 CYp,I:Tyrax,Kaman 2.75
Ashcan #1 . . . . 8.00
Ashcan #2 . . . . 4.00
TPB rep. #1-#5 . . . . 17.00
[Volume 2] 1995
1 New Roster 2.50
2 The Program Continues 2.50
3 Extreme Babewatch. 2.50
4 Extreme Destroyer,pt.4
    x-over, bagged with card. 2.50
5 . . . . 2.50
6 . . . . 2.50
7 Shadowhunt x-over,pt.3 . . . . 2.60
8 ErS,RCz. 2.50
9 ErS,RCz. 2.50
10 ErS,RCz. 2.50
TPB Baptism of Fire, F:Spawn 2.50
See Color Pub. section

YOUNGBLOOD BATTLEZONE
April, 1993
1 BrM 2.50
2 . . . . 3.00

YOUNGBLOOD STRIKEFILE
Extreme, 1993
1 JaL,RLd,I:Allies,A:Al Simmons
    (Spawn)I:Giger,Glory 3.00
1a Gold ed. 4.00
2 JaL,RLd,V:Super Patriot, Giger. . 3.00
2a Gold ed. 3.50

3 RLd,JaL,DaM(i), A:Super Partiot . 3.00
4 I:Overtkill 3.00
5 . . . . 3.00
6 and 7 flip books . . . . @3.00
8 Shaft 3.00
9 Knight Sabre 3.00
10 RLd,TNu,I:Bloodpool,Task,
    Psilence,Wylder,Rubble. 3.50
11 ExtremeSacrifice,pt.0,x-over
    O:Link Crypt 3.00
TPB rep.#1-#3,sketchbook 13.00
Ashcan 3.00

YOUNGBLOOD/X-FORCE
Extreme/Marvel, 1996
1-shot Mojo visits Image x-over . . . 5.00
1-shot RLd variant cover 5.00

YOUNGBLOOD: YEAR ONE
1 KBk(s),RLd, the early years. 2.50
2 KBk(s),RLd,V:Giger,Cybernet . . . 2.50

ZEALOT
WildStorm, 1995
1 O:Zealot. 2.50
2 In Japan. 2.50
3 V:Prometheus 2.50

ZERO GIRL
WildStorm/Homage, 2000
1 thru 4 . . . . @3.00

ZOMBIE
(B&W) Oct., 2006
GN 13.00

ZOMBIE KING
(B&W) Apr., 2005
1 . . . . 3.00

ZORRO
(B&W) 1998
TPB #1 rep. classic Alex Toth 16.00
TPB #2 rep. classic Alex Toth 16.00
TPB The Lady Wears Red. 13.00

ZORRO
(B&W) Sept., 2001
TPB The Dailies, 248-pg. 19.00
TPB The Complete Alex Toth. 19.00

ZORRO MANTANZAS
Sept., 1999
1 (of 4) DMG & Mike Mayhew 3.00
2 DMG,V:Machete. 3.00

ZORRO'S LADY RAWHIDE: OTHER PEOPLE'S BLOOD
(B&W) Feb., 1999
1 DMG,EM,JuB(c),cont. from Topps 3.00
2 DMG,EM,V:Scarlet Fever. 3.00
3 DMG,EM,V:Ansel Plague. 3.00
4 DMG,EM,V:Scarlet Fever. 3.00
5 DMG,EM,Whiplash. 3.00

ZORRO'S RENEGADES
1998
TPB Zorro's Renegades, B&W . . . 15.00
TPB Vol. 2, Lady Rawhide. 15.00

All comics prices listed are for *Near Mint* condition.

COLOR COMICS

ABADAZAD
Crossgen Comics, 2003
1 . . . . 3.00
2 thru 6 . . . . @3.00

Hyperion Books, 2006
GN Vol. 1 Road to Inconceivable. . 10.00
GN Vol. 2 The Dream Thief 10.00

ABBOTT AND COSTELLO
Charlton Comics, 1968–71
1 . . . . 150.00
2 thru 9 . . . . @100.00
10 thru 21 . . . . @75.00
22 . . . . 60.00

ABC: A-Z Tom Strong & Jack B. Quick
© Wildstorm

ABC: A-Z
Wildstorm/DC, Sept., 2005
1-shot Tom Strong & Jack B. Quick . 4.00
1-shot Greyshirt & Cobweb 4.00
1-shot Terra Obscura & Splash
  Brannigan 4.00
1-shot Top 10 and Teams 4.00
1-shot Smax and First American . . . 4.00

ABIDING PERDITION
APC 2005
1 . . . . 3.50
1a variant (c). 3.50
2 . . . . 3.50
2a variant (c) 3.50
1b SDCC edition 10.00
3 thru 4 . . . . @3.50

Markosia 2005
5 . . . . 3.50
6 . . . . 3.50
5a thru 6a variant (c) . . . . @3.50
TPB Vol. 1 . . . . 17.00

ACES HIGH
Gemstone, 1999
1 (of 5) EC Comics reprint 3.00
2 GE,BK,JDa 3.00
3 GE,BK,WW,JDa. 3.00
4 GE,BK,WW,JDa. 3.00
5 GE,BK,WW,JDa. 3.00
Annual rep. #1–#5 . . . . 13.50

ACME NOVELTY LIBRARY
Fantagraphics, 1994–98
1 thru 5 . . . . @6.00
6 thru 11 Jimmy Corrigan Meets
  His Dad, pt. 1 – pt. 6 (of 8) . . @4.50
12 Jimmy & Dad have lunch 5.00
13 Jimmy's Grandfather, 80-page . 11.00
14 F:Jimmy Corrigan 11.00
15 . . . . 10.00
1 thru 7, 2nd printings . . . . @4.00

ADAM-12
Gold Key, 1973–76
1 Photo(c), From TV show 100.00
2 thru 9 . . . . @50.00
10 . . . . 45.00

ADDAMS FAMILY
Gold Key, 1974–75
1 TV cartoon adapt. 175.00
2 . . . . 125.00
3 . . . . 100.00

ADLAI STEVENSON
Dell Publishing Co., 1966
1 Political Life Story 75.00

ADRENALINE
A Wave Blue World, 2006
1 . . . . 3.00
2 . . . . 3.00

ADVENT RISING:
ROCK THE PLANET
360ep Inc. 2005
1 . . . . 2.25
2 thru 5 . . . . @2.25

ADVENTURES OF
BIO BOY, THE
Speakeasy Comics, 2005
1 . . . . 3.00
2 . . . . 3.00
3 thru 5 . . . . @3.00
TPB Vol. 1 Best of Season One . . 13.00

THE ADVENTURES
OF PIPSQUEAK
**Archie Publications Sept.
1959–July 1960**
34 . . . . 125.00
35 thru 39 . . . . @100.00

ADVENTURES OF
ROBIN HOOD
Gold Key, 1974–75
1 From Disney cartoon 50.00
2 thru 7 . . . . @25.00

ADVENTURES OF
THE FLY
**Archie Publications/
Radio Comics, 1959–65**
1 JSm/JK,O:Fly,I:SpiderSpry
  A:Lancelot Strong/Shield . . 1,000.00
2 JSm/JK,DAy,AW 600.00
3 JDa, O:Fly 500.00
4 V:Dazzler NA panel 300.00

5 A:Spider Spry 200.00
6 V:Moon Men 200.00
7 A:Black Hood 225.00
8 A:Lancelot Strong/Shield 225.00
9 A:Lancelot Strong/Shield
  I:Cat Girl 200.00
10 A:Spider Spry 200.00
11 V:Rock Men. 125.00
12 V:Brute Invaders 125.00
13 I:Kim Brand 125.00
14 I:Fly-Girl(Kim Brand) 150.00
15 A:Spider 125.00
16 A:Fly-Girl 125.00
17 A:Fly-Girl 125.00
18 A:Fly-Girl 125.00
19 A:Fly-Girl 125.00
20 O:Fly-Girl 150.00
21 A:Fly-Girl 100.00
22 A:Fly-Girl 100.00
23 A:Fly-Girl,Jaguar 100.00
24 A:Fly-Girl 100.00
25 A:Fly-Girl 100.00
26 A:Fly-Girl,Black Hood 100.00
27 A:Fly-Girl,Black Hood 100.00
28 A:Black Hood 100.00
29 A:Fly-Girl,Black Hood 100.00
30 A:Fly-Girl,R:Comet 150.00
31 A:Black Hood, Shield, Comet . 150.00
TPB Vol. 1 (2004) 13.00
Becomes:

FLYMAN

ADVENTURES OF
THE JAGUAR
**Archie Publications/
Radio Comics, 1961–63**
1 I:Ralph Hardy/Jaguar. 500.00
2 10 cent cover 200.00
3 Last 10 cent cover 175.00
4 A:Cat-Girl 150.00
5 A:Cat-Girl 150.00
6 A:Cat-Girl 150.00
7 . . . . 125.00
8 . . . . 125.00
9 . . . . 125.00
10 . . . . 125.00
11 . . . . 125.00
12 A:Black Hood 125.00
13 A:Cat-Girl,A:Black Hood 125.00
14 A:Black Hood 125.00
15 V:Human Octopus,last issue . 125.00

ADVENTURES OF
YOUNG DR. MASTERS
Archie Comics, 1964
1 . . . . 50.00
2 . . . . 25.00

ADVENTUROUS UNCLE
SCROOGE McDUCK
Gladstone, 1997
1 . . . . 3.00
2 Don Rosa, A Little Something
  Special 3.00
3 The Black Widow. 3.00

AFTERMATH
Chaos! Comics, 2000
1 sequel to Armageddon. 3.00
1 premium. 10.00
Ashcan, Yellow. 10.00
Ashcan, Blue 25.00

AGENT: AMERICA
Awesome Entertainment, 1997
1 RLe 2.50
2 RLe,JSb,JLb,F:Supreme,
   V:Smash 2.50

AIDEN MCKAIN CHRONICLES: BATTLE FOR EARTH
Digital Webbing, 2005
1 . . . . 3.00
3 . . . . 3.00

AIRBOY
Eclipse, 1986–89
1 TT/TY,D:Golden Age Airboy
  O:New Airboy 6.00
2 TT/TY,I:Marisa,R:SkyWolf 5.00
3 A:The Heap 5.00
4 A:Misery 5.00
5 DSt(c),R:Valkyrie 7.00
6 R:Iron Ace,I:Marlene 3.50
7 PG(c), ... 3.50
8 FH/TT(c) 3.50
9 thru 49 . . . . @3.00
50 AKu/NKu,double-size 4.00
Spec. Meets the Prowler 3.00
Spec. Mr. Monster 3.00
Spec. Vs Airmaidens 3.00

AIR FIGHTERS, SGT. STRIKE SPECIAL
Eclipse, 1988
1 A:Airboy,Valkyrie 3.00

AIRMAIDENS SPECIAL
Eclipse Comics, 1987
1 A:Valkyrie 3.00

AIR WAR STORIES
Dell Publishing Co., 1964
1 . . . . 125.00
2 . . . . 100.00
3 thru 8 . . . . @75.00

ALAN MOORE'S AWESOME ADVENTURES
Awesome Entertainment, 1999
1 AMo 2.50
1a alternate AxR cover 7.00
2 F:Young Guns 3.00
Spec. Awesome Univ. Handbook . . . 3.00
Spec.A alternate AxR cover 3.00

ALAN MOORE'S GLORY
Comic Cavalcade, 2001
0 Park (c) 3.50
0a variant(c)s . . . . @3.50
0e Lush Lands edition 6.00
0f Finch Prism Foil (c). 13.00
Avatar Press, 2001
Preview B&W 16-page 3.00
Preview signed gold (c) 9.00
1 (of 4) JLi(c) 3.50
1a variant(c)s . . . . @3.50
1g Finch Prism Foil (c) 13.00
1h Andy Park (c) 6.00
1i SSh(c) 6.00
1k Defender (c). 6.00
2 AMo,MMy, Finch (c) 6.00
2a variant(c)s . . . . @3.50
2e Glory Freedom (c) 6.00
2f Hall painted (c) 6.00

ALARMING ADVENTURES
Harvey Publications, 1962–63
1 AW,RC,JSe 150.00
2 AW,BP,RC,JSe 100.00
3 JSe 100.00

ALARMING TALES
Harvey Publications, 1957–58
1 JK,JK(c) 450.00
2 JK,JK(c) 300.00
3 JK. 275.00
4 JK,BP. 275.00
5 JK,AW 275.00
6 JK 275.00

ALBEDO, VOL. 3
Antarctic Press, 1994–95
Vol. 1 and II, See B&W
1 thru 4 Various Artists . . . . @3.00

ALBION
Wildstorm/DC, June, 2005
1 (of 6) F:Old-time British heroes . . 3.00
2 . . . . 3.00
3 thru 6 . . . . @3.00
TPB 20.00

ALEISTER ARCANE
IDW Publishing, 2004
1 . . . . 4.00
2 . . . . 4.00
3 . . . . 4.00
TPB 18.00

ALIAS
Now Comics, 1990
1 BSz(c),Strangleholm 2.50
2 Stormfront 2.50
3 Firestorm 2.50
4 Blastpoint 2.50
5 Breakdown 2.50

ALIAS: AGENT BRISTOW
Arcade Comics, 2003
0 RLd 3.00
0a photo (c) 3.00
0b Dlx. Foil photo (c) 10.00
0c Chromium (c) 15.00
0d sgn art (c) 50.00
1 . . . . 3.00
1a photo (c) 3.00
1b Dlx. Foil photo (c) 10.00

ALICE IN WONDERLAND
Antarctic Press, 2006
1 (of 4) Rod Espinosa, Manga 3.50
2 thru 4 . . . . @3.50
TPB Alice in Wonderland 15.00

ALIEN ARENA
Atomeka, 2002
1 (of 2) 3.00
2 . . . . 3.00
1a thru 2a variant (c). . . . . @3.00

ALIEN ENCOUNTERS
Eclipse Comics, 1985–87
1 . . . . 5.00
2 . . . . 4.00
3 I Shot the Last Martian 4.00
4 JBo(c) 4.00
5 RCo,Night of the Monkey 4.00
6 Now You See It,Freefall. 4.00
7 . . . . 4.00
8 TY,Take One Capsule Every
   million Years,M.Monroe(c). 4.00

Alien Encounters #1 © Eclipse Comics

9 The Conquered 4.00
10 . . . . 4.00
11 TT,Old Soldiers 5.00
12 What A Relief,Eyes of
   the Sibyl. 5.00
13 GN,The Light at the End. 5.00
14 JRy,GN,TL,RT,Still born 5.00

ALIEN TERROR
Eclipse, 1986
3-D #1 Standard Procedure 3.00

ALIEN WORLDS
Pacific, 1982
1 AW,VM,NR 7.00
2 DSt 5.00
3 . . . . 4.00
4 DSt(i) 4.00
5 . . . . 4.00
6 . . . . 4.00
7 . . . . 4.00
3-D #1 AAd,DSt 7.00
Eclipse, 1985
8 AW 2.50
9 . . . . 2.50

[CAPTAIN JOHNER AND] ALIENS, THE
Gold Key, 1967
1 Rep. Magnus Robot Fighter . . 100.00

ALIUS REX
Alias Enterprises, 2006
1 . . . . 3.50

ALL-ACTION CLASSICS
Sterling Publishing, 2006
GN Dracula 7.00
GN Tom Sawyer. 7.00

ALISTER THE SLAYER
Midnight Press, 1995
1 I:Alister The Slayer 2.50
2 V:Lady Hate 2.50
3 JQ&JP(c) V:Subterranean
   Vampire Bikers 2.50

ALL AMERICAN SPORTS
Charlton, 1967
1 . . . . 75.00

ALL HALLOWS EVE
Innovation, 1991
1 . . . . 5.00

ALLEY OOP
Dell Publishing Co., 1962–63
1 . . . . 125.00
2 . . . . 100.00

ALLEY OOP ADVENTURES
Antarctic Press, 1998
1 . . . . 3.00
2 . . . . 3.00
3 I:Granny Green 3.00
TPB 11.00

ALLIES
Awesome Entertainment, 1999
1 RLe,AMo 2.50
1a alternate RLe cover 7.00

ALL NEW EXILES
Malibu Ultraverse, 1995–96
Infinity F:Juggernaut,Blaze 2.50
1 TKa,KeL,Beginning the Quest . . . 2.50
1a Computer painted cover (1:6) . . 2.50
1b signed edition 4.00
2 I:Hellblade, Phoenix flip issue . . . 2.50
3 TKa,KeL,Phoenix Resurrection . . 2.50
4 thru 11 . . . . @2.50

ALPHA KORPS
Diversity Comics, 1996
1 I:Alpha Korps 3.00
2 The Price of Freedom, pt.2 . . . . . 2.50
3 The Price of Freedom, pt.3 . . . . . 2.50
1 thru 3 signed . . . . @5.00
4 The Price of Freedom, pt.4 . . . . . 2.50

ALTER EGO
First, 1986
1 RTs, Ron Harris 2.50
2 thru 4 . . . . @2.50
Heroic Publishing, 2005
GN 18.00

ALVIN (& THE CHIPMUNKS)
Dell Publishing Co., 1962–73
1 . . . . 175.00
2 . . . . 150.00
3 . . . . 125.00
4 thru 10 . . . . @125.00
11 thru 20 . . . . @100.00
21 thru 28 . . . . @100.00
1 Alvin for President & his pals in
   Merry Christmas with Clyde
   Crashcup & Leonardo 100.00

AMAZING CHAN & THE CHAN CLAN
Gold Key, 1973
1 . . . . 75.00
2 . . . . 50.00
3 and 4 . . . . @35.00

AMAZING HEROES SWIMSUIT ANNUALS
Fantagraphics, 1990–93
1990 Spec. A:Dawn 25.00
1990 2nd printing 15.00
1991 A: Dawn 20.00
1992 A: Dawn 20.00

1993 A: Dawn 20.00

AMAZON, THE
Comico, 1989
1 . . . . 2.50
2 . . . . 2.50
3 end mini-series 2.50

AMELIA RULES!
Renaissance Press, 2001
1 by Jimmy Gownley 3.00
2 thru 11 . . . . @3.00
TPB Vol. 1 In with the Out Crowd . 15.00
TPB Orig. Art edition 60.00
TPB The Whole World's Crazy . . . 18.00

AMELIA RULES!: SUPERHEROES
Renaissance Press, 2003
1 thru 6 (of 6) . . . . @3.00
7 thru 16 . . . . @3.00
TPB Vol. 1 The Whole World's
   Crazy (2006) 15.00
TPB Vol. 2 What Makes You
   Happy (2006) 15.00
TPB Vol. 3 Superheroes 15.00
Spec. Super Summer Special 5.00

AMERICAN FLAGG
First, 1983–88
1 HC,I:American Flagg, Hard
   Times, pt.1 . . . . 6.00
2 HC,Hard Times,pt.2 . . . . 4.00
3 HC,Hard Times,pt.3 . . . . 4.00
4 HC,Southern Comfort,pt.1 . . . . . 4.00
5 HC,Southern Comfort,pt.2 . . . . . 4.00
6 HC,Southern Comfort,pt.3 . . . . . 4.00
7 HC,State of the Union,pt.1 . . . . . 4.00
8 HC,State of the Union,pt.2 . . . . . 4.00
9 HC,State of the Union,pt.3 . . . . . 4.00
10 HC,Solidarity-For Now,pt.1
   I:Luthor Ironheart 4.00
11 HC,Solidarity-For Now,pt.2 . . . . 4.00
12 HC,Solidarity-For Now,pt.3 . . . . 4.00
13 HC 4.00
14 PB 4.00
15 HC,American Flagg A Complete
   story,pt.1 . . . . 4.00
16 HC,Complete Story,pt.2 . . . . . . 4.00
17 HC,Complete Story,pt.3 . . . . . . 4.00
18 HC,Complete Story,pt.4 . . . . . . 4.00
19 HC,Bullets & Ballots, pt.1 . . . . 4.00
20 HC,LSn,Bullets & Ballots,pt.2 . . 4.00
21 AMo,HC,LSn,Bull&Ballots,pt.3 . 3.50
22 AMo,HC,LSn,Bull&Ballots,pt.4 . 3.50
23 AMo,HC,LSn,England
   Swings, pt.1 . . . . 3.50
24 AMo,HC,England Swings,pt.2 . . 3.50
25 AMo,HC,England Swings,pt.3 . . 3.50
26 AMO,HC,England Swings,pt.4 . . 3.50
27 AMo with Raul the Cat 3.50
28 BWg 3.50
29 JSon 3.50
30 JSon 3.50
31 JSon,O:Bob Violence 3.50
32 JSon,A:Bob Violence 3.50
33 A:Bob Violence 3.50
34 A:Bob Violence 3.50
35 A:Bob Violence 3.50
36 A:Bob Violence 3.50
37 A:Bob Violence 3.50
38 New Direction 3.50
39 JSon,A:Bob Violence 3.50
40 A:Bob Violence 3.50
41 . . . . 3.50
42 F:Luther Ironheart 3.50
43 . . . . 3.50
44 . . . . 3.50
45 . . . . 3.50
46 PS 3.50

---

47 PS 3.50
48 PS 3.50
49 . . . . 3.50
50 HC,last issue 3.50
Special #1 HC,I:Time2 . . . . 4.00
See Also: Howard Chaykin's
American Flagg

AMERICAN FREAKSHOW
IDW Publishing, 2005
1 . . . . 4.00
2 thru 3 . . . . @4.00

AMERICOMICS
AC Comics, 1983
1 GP(c),O:Shade 5.00
2 . . . . 3.00
3 Blue Beetle 3.00
4 O:Dragonfly 3.00
5 and 6 . . . . @3.00
Spec.#1 Capt.Atom,BlueBeetle . . . 3.00

AMERICA'S BEST COMICS
WildStorm/DC, 2000
Spec.#1 64-page 7.00
America's Best Comics Sketchbook 6.00
TPB 18.00

AMERICAN WAY, THE
Wildstorm/DC, Feb., 2006
1 (of 8) KSy,F:Civil Defense Corps. 3.00
2 KSy,A Hero Falls 3.00
3 KSy,I:New American 3.00
4 KSy,Battle with super-villain 3.00
5 KSy,V:Hellbent 3.00
6 KSy,Racial tensions 3.00
7 KSy,Super-hero civil war 3.00
8 KSy,finale 3.00

American Woman #2 © Antarctic Press

AMERICAN WOMAN
Antarctic Press, 1998
1 by Richard Stockton & Brian
   Denham 3.00
2 . . . . 3.00
2a deluxe 6.00

ANDROMEDA
Andromeda, 1995
1 I:Andromeda 2.50
2 Andromeda vs. Elite Force 2.50

COLOR PUB.

ANGEL FIRE
Crusade Comics, 1997
1 BiT, from Shi #12, BiT(c) 3.00
1a with Roberto Flores cover 3.00
1b with photo cover 3.00
2 F:Shi 3.00
3 F:Shi, concl. 3.00

ANGEL: AULD LANG SYNE
IDW Publishing, 2006
1 . . . . 4.00
1a variant (c) 4.00

ANGEL: MASKS
IDW Publishing, 2006
1-shot 48 pg. 7.50

ANGEL: OLD FRIENDS
IDW Publishing 2005
1 . . . . 4.00
2 thru 5 . . . . @4.00
2a thru 5a variant (c) . . . . @4.00
TPB Angel: Old Friends 20.00

ANGEL SPOTLIGHT
IDW Publishing, 2006
Spec. Connor 4.00
Spec. Connor variant (c) 4.00
Spec. Illyria. 4.00
Spec. Illyria variant (c) 4.00
Spec. Gunn 4.00
Spec. Gunn variant (c) 4.00
Spec. Wesley 4.00
Spec. Wesley variant (c) 4.00
Spec. Doyle 4.00
Spec. Doyle variant (c) 4.00

ANGEL: THE CURSE
IDW Publishing, 2005
1 Buffy spin-off 7.00
1a variant (c)s . . . . @7.00
1b 2nd printing 4.00
2 . . . . 5.00
3 thru 5 . . . . @4.00
TPB 20.00
TPB Cover Gallery 4.00

ANIMAL MYSTIC: WATER WARS
Sirius, 1996
1 (of 6) DOe 4.00
2 thru 6 DOe . . . . @3.00
TPB rep.. 20.00
TPB Klor.. 10.00
GN Dark One's Animal
   Mystic Field Guide. 10.00

ANNE McCAFFREY'S THE UNICORN GIRL
Big Entertainment, 1997
GN F:Acorna 22.00

ANNE RICE'S THE TALE OF THE BODY THIEF
Sicilian Dragon, 1999
1 (of 12) 3.00
2 F:Lestat 3.00
3 thru 6 . . . . @3.00
7 F:Gretchen. 3.00
TPB 20.00
TPB Exclusive 20.00

ANT
Arcana Studios, 2004
1 . . . . 8.00
2 . . . . 5.00
3 thru 4 . . . . @3.50
TPB Ant: Days Like These. 10.00

A1/BLOODMOON
Atomeka, 2004
Spec. Mister Monster-Worlds War2 . 7.00
Spec. Mister Monster #2 . . . . 7.00

Anything Goes #4
© Fantagraphics

ANYTHING GOES
Fantagraphics, 1986
1 GK,FlamingCarot,Savage 4.00
2 S:AnM,JK,JSt,SK 3.50
3 DS,NA(c),A:Cerebus 3.50
4 . . . . 3.50
5 A:TMNTurtles. 5.00
6 . . . . 3.00

APE NATION
Adventure Comics, 1991
1 Aliens land on Planet of
   the Apes 3.00
2 General Ollo. 3.00
3 V:Gen Ollo,Danada 2.50
4 D:Danada. 2.50

APOLLO SMILE
Eagle Wing, 1998
1 When the Levee Breaks 3.00
2 When the Levee Breaks, pt.2 . . . 3.00
3 When the Levee Breaks, pt.3 . . . 3.00

ARACHNAPHOBIA
Walt Disney, 1990
1 Movie Adapt. 6.00
1a Newsstand. 3.00

ARAKNIS
Mushroom Comics, 1995–96
1 I:Araknis, Shades of Evil pt.1 . . . 3.50
2 Shades of Evil pt.2. . . . . 3.50
3 with pin-ups 2.50
4 . . . . 2.50
Mushroom Comics, 1996
0 Michael & Mario Ortiz 3.00
0 signed 4.00
1 . . . . 2.50
1 special edition 10.00

Mystic Comics
2 thru 6 . . . . @2.50

ARAKNIS: RETRIBUTION
Morning Star Productions, 1997
1 (of 4) by Michael & Mario Ortiz . . 2.50
1 signed 10.00
2 thru 4 . . . . @2.50

ARAKNIS: SHADES OF EVIL
Morning Star Productions
1 thru 4 . . . . @2.50

ARCHAIC
Fenickx Productions, 2006
1 . . . . 3.00
2 thru 6 . . . . @3.00

ARCHANGELS: THE FALL
Cahaba Productions 2005
1 . . . . 4.50
2 . . . . 4.50
3 . . . . 4.50

ARCHANGELS: THE SAGA
Eternal Studios, 1996
1 I:Cameron 2.50
2 V:Demons 2.50
3 and 4 . . . . @2.75
5 and 6 . . . . @2.50
7 . . . . 3.50
8 . . . . 4.50

ARCHARD'S AGENTS
Crossgen Comics, 2002
1 CDi(s) spin-off from Ruse 3.50

ARCHER & ARMSTRONG
Valiant, 1992
0 JiS(s),BWS,BL,I&O:Archer,
   I:Armstrong,The Sec 3.00
0 Gold Ed. 5 . . . . 4.00
1 FM(c),B:JiS(s),BWS,BL,Unity #3,
   A:Eternal Warrior. 2.50
2 thru 26 . . . . @2.50

ARCHIE
Archie Publications, 1981
1 thru 300 see Golden Age
301 thru 325. . . . . @6.50
326 Cheryl Blossom. 15.00
327 thru 335. . . . . @6.50
336 Michael Jackson. 7.00
337 thru 400. . . . . @6.50
401 thru 429. . . . . @5.00
430 thru 529. . . . . @2.50
530 thru 552. . . . . @2.50
553 thru 571. . . . . @2.25
Archie's Christmas Stocking #4 . . . 2.50
Archie's Christmas Stocking #5 . . . 2.50
Archie's Christmas Stocking #6 . . . 2.75
Archie's Christmas Stocking #7 . . . 3.00
Archie's Spring Break Spec.1 . . . . 2.50
Archie's Spring Break Spec.2 . . . . 2.50
Archie's Spring Break Spec.3 . . . . 2.75
Archie's Spring Break Spec.4(1999) 2.75
Archie's Spring Break Spec.5(2000) 2.50
Archie's Vacation Spec.#4 . . . . 2.50
Archie's Vacation Spec.#5 . . . . 2.50
Archie's Vacation Spec.#6 . . . . 2.50
Archie's Vacation Spec.#7 . . . . 2.50
Archie's Vacation Spec.#8 . . . . 2.50
TPB Vol. 1, Archie Day By Day . . . 11.00
TPB Adventures of Little Archie . . . 11.00

ARCHIE AND FRIENDS
Archie Publications, 1992—98
1 thru 10 . . . . @5.00
11 thru 14 . . . . @4.00
15 Babewatch 6.00
16 thru 19 . . . . @4.00
20 Archies Band. 5.00
21 thru 48 . . . . @2.50
49 thru 56 Archie & Friends, Featuring
     Josie and the Pussy Cats . . . @2.50
57 thru 86 . . . . @2.50
87 thru 105 . . . . @2.25

ARCHIE AND ME
Archie Publications, 1964–87
1 . . . . 350.00
2 . . . . 250.00
3 . . . . 150.00
4 . . . . 125.00
5 . . . . 125.00
6 thru 10 . . . . @100.00

Archie and Me #159
© *Archie Publications*

11 thru 20 . . . . @50.00
21 thru 26 . . . . @60.00
27 Superheroes Groovymas 60.00
28 thru 100 . . . . @20.00
101 thru 162 . . . . @15.00

ARCHIE AS PUREHEART THE POWERFUL
Archie Publications, 1966–67
1 superhero parody. 250.00
2 . . . . 200.00
3 thru 6 Captain Pureheart . . . @150.00

ARCHIE AT RIVERDALE HIGH
Archie Publications, 1972
1 . . . . 125.00
2 . . . . 75.00
3 . . . . 50.00
4 . . . . 35.00
5 . . . . 35.00
6 thru 10 . . . . @30.00
11 thru 30 . . . . @25.00
31 thru 46 . . . . @20.00
47 in drag. 14.00
48 thru 88 . . . . @10.00
89 & 90 Cheryl Blossmos Band. @25.00
91 . . . . 8.00
92 Cheryl Blossom. 14.00

93 thru 95 . . . . @8.00
96 Cheryl Blossom. 14.00
97 & 98 . . . . @8.00
99 Cheryl Blossom. 14.00
100 thru 102 . . . . @7.00
103 Archie Dates Cheryl Blossom. 14.00
104 thru 113 . . . . @8.00

ARCHIE COMICS DIGEST
Archie Comics Digest, 1973
1 . . . . 150.00
2 . . . . 75.00
3 thru 5 . . . . @60.00
6 thru 10 . . . . 30.00
11 thru 32 . . . . @20.00
33 The Fly 25.00
34 thru 135 . . . . @6.00
136 Katy Keene 7.00
137 thru 204 . . . . @4.00
205 thru 230 . . . . @2.50

ARCHIE MEETS THE PUNISHER
Archie/Marvel, 1994
1-shot crossover, same contents
     as Punisher meets Archie 7.00

ARCHIE'S MADHOUSE
Archie Publications, 1959–69
1 . . . . 500.00
2 . . . . 350.00
3 thru 5 . . . . @250.00
6 thru 10 . . . . @200.00
11 thru 16 . . . . @150.00
17 thru 21 . . . . @100.00
22 I:Sabrina 700.00
23 thru 25 Sabrina . . . . @250.00
26 thru 28 . . . . @125.00
29 thru 30 . . . . @60.00
31 thru 33 Sabrina . . . . @125.00
34 . . . . 50.00
35 B 70.00
36 Salem Cat & Sabrina 175.00
37 Sabrina 120.00
38 thru 66 . . . . 50.00

ARCHIE'S PAL JUGHEAD
SEE: JUGHEAD

ARCHIE'S SUPERHERO MAGAZINE
Archie Publications, 1979
1 JSm/SK,Rept.Double of Capt.
     Strong #1,FLy,Black Hood. . . . 25.00
2 GM,NA/DG,AMc,I:'70's Black
     Hood, Superhero rept. 30.00

ARCHIE'S TV LAUGH-OUT
Archie Publications, 1969–86
1 . . . . 250.00
2 giant. 150.00
3 thru 6 giant. . . . . @75.00
7 Josie 200.00
8 thru 22 . . . . @90.00
23 thru 41 . . . . @50.00
42 thru 80 . . . . @30.00
81 thru 90 . . . . @35.00
91 Cheryl Blossom 40.00
92 thru 99 . . . . @25.00
100 Michael Jackson 40.00
101 thru 106 . . . . @25.00

ARCHIE 3000
Archie Publications, 1989–1991
1 thru 16 . . . . 2.00

ARCHIE'S WEIRD MYSTERIES
Archie Comics, 1999
1 from animated series 4.00
2 Shriek. 3.00
3 thru 25 . . . . @3.00
Becomes

ARCHIE'S MYSTERIES
Archie Comics, 2003
26 thru 34 . . . . @3.00

ARENA, THE
Alchemy, 1990
1 . . . . 2.50
1a signed, numbered, limited 3.00
2 . . . . 2.50

ARIANE & BLUEBEARD
Eclipse, 1988
Spec. CR 4.00

ARISTOKITTENS, THE
Gold Key, 1971–75
1 Disney 75.00
2 thru 9 . . . . @50.00

ARKANIUM
Dreamwave, 2002
1 triple gatefold cover 3.00
2 thru 6 . . . . @3.00

ARMAGEDDON
Chaos! Comics, 1999
1 (of 4) F:Lady Death, Evil Ernie . . 3.00
1a Premium edition. 10.00
2 O:Chaos. 3.00
3 . . . . 3.00
4 concl. 3.00
TPB 13.00

ARMAGEDDON FACTOR
AC Comics, 1987
1 Sentinels of Justice 2.50
2 . . . . 2.50
3 (1990) 4.00

ARMOR
Continuity, 1985
1 TGr,NA,A:Silver Streak,
     silver logo 5.00
1a 2nd printing,red logo 3.00
2 TGr,NA(c). 3.00
3 TGr,NA(c). 3.00
4 TGr,NA(c). 3.00
5 BS,NA(c). 3.00
6 TVE,NA(c). 3.00
7 NA(c) 3.00
8 FS,NA(c) 3.00
9 FS,NA&KN(c). 3.00
10 FS,NA&KN(c) 3.00
11 SDr(i),KN(c). 3.00
12 KN(c). 3.00
13 NA(c),direct sales 3.00
14 KN(c), newsstand 3.00

[2nd Series]
1 V:Hellbender,Trading Card 3.00
[3rd Series, Deathwatch 2000]
1 Deathwatch 2000 pt.3,w/card . . . 4.00
2 Deathwatch 2000 pt.9,w/card . . . 3.00
3 Deathwatch 2000 pt.15,w/card . . 3.00
4 . . . . 3.00
5 Rise of Magic. 3.00
6 Rise of Magic. 3.00

ARMORED TROOPER VOTOMS
CPM Comics, 1996
1 TEI 3.00
2 thru 4 TEI . . . . @3.00
GN Supreme Survivor 17.00

ARMORINES
Valiant, 1994
0 (from X-O #25),Card Stock (c),
  Diamond Dealer Meeting. 2.50
0a Gold Ed. 3.00
1 JGz(s),JCf,B:White Death 2.50
2 thru 12 . . . . @2.50
Yearbook I:Linoff 3.00

Vol. 2
1 48-pg. 4.00
2 . . . . 4.00
3 and 4 . . . . @2.50

ARMORQUEST GENESIS
Alias Enterprises, 2005
1 (of 6) 3.00
2 . . . . 3.00
3 . . . . 3.00
4 thru 5 . . . . @3.50
TPB Vol. 1 . . . . 3.50

ARMY ATTACK
Charlton, 1964
1 SG 100.00
2 SG 75.00
3 SG 60.00
4 . . . . 50.00

Vol. 2, 1965
38 thru 47 . . . . @50.00

ARMY OF DARKNESS:
D.E. (Dynamite Ent.) 2005
1 Ash vs. Re-Animator 3.00
1a signed 20.00
1b thru 2b Broomstick foil 20.00
2 thru 4 . . . . @3.00
5 Old School 3.00
5a glow-in-the-dark (c) 20.00
5b variant glow-in-the-dark (c) . . 25.00
6 Old School 3.00
6a variant (c) 3.00
6b Glow-in-the-dark (c) 25.00
7 Old School 3.00
7a variant (c)s . . . . @3.00
8 Ash vs. Dracula, pt.1 . . . . 3.00
8a variant (c)s . . . . @3.00
9 Ash vs. Dracula, pt. 2 . . . . 3.00
10 . . . . 3.00
10a variant (c)s . . . . @3.00
11 . . . . 3.00
11a variant (c) . . . . @3.00
12 . . . . 3.00
12a variant (c)s . . . . @3.00
13 Death of Ashley J. Williams . . . 3.00
13a variant (c)s . . . . @3.00
Tales of Army of Darkness, Vol. 1 . . 6.00
TPB Movie Adapt. 15.00
TPB Vol. 3 Ash vs. Re-Animator . . 15.00
TPB Vol. 4 Old School 15.00

ARMY OF DARKNESS:
ASHES 2 ASHES
Devil's Due Publishing, 2004
1 . . . . 3.00
1a signed 20.00
1b director's cut 1-shot 5.00
2 thru 4 . . . . @3.00
TPB 15.00

D.E. (Dynamite Ent.) 2006
1b director's cut 5.00

1c director's cut foil (c) 20.00
1d photo (c) 7.00
2c variant glow-in-the-dark (c) . . . 20.00

ARMY OF DARKNESS:
SHOP TILL YOU
DROP (DEAD)
Devil's Due Publishing, 2004
1 . . . . 3.00
1a variant(c)s 3.00
2 thru 4 . . . . @3.00

D.E. (Dynamite Ent.) 2006
1 . . . . 3.00
1a variant glow-in-the-dark (c) . . . 20.00
1d exclusive (c) 7.00
1e enhanced photo (c) 20.00
2 . . . . 3.00
2a variant Fiery red foil(c) 15.00
2b variant special foil (c) 20.00
2c variant glow-in-the-dark (c) . . . 20.00
3 . . . . 3.00
3a variant Sabre foil (c) 15.00
3b variant glow-in-the-dark (c) . . . 20.00
4 . . . . 3.00
4a variant glow-in-the-dark (c) . . . 10.00

ARMY WAR HEROES
Charlton, 1963–70
1 . . . . 125.00
2 . . . . 50.00
3 thru 21 . . . . @40.00
22 GS,O&I:Iron Corporal 50.00
23 thru 38 . . . . @40.00

Arrow #1 © Malibu

ARROW
Malibu, 1992
1 V:Dr.Sheldon,A:Man O'War 2.50

ARROWSMITH
Wildstorm/DC, 2003
1 (of 6) KBk(s),CPa 3.00
2 KBk(s),mystical aviator 3.00
3 KBk(s) thru 6 . . . . @3.00
TPB So Smart in Fine Uniforms . . 15.00
Spec. Arrowsmith/Astro City 3.00

ARTESIA
Sirius, 1999
1 (of 6) by Mark Smylie 3.00
1a limited edition. 10.00
2 thru 6 . . . . @3.00

Ann.#1 . . . . 3.50
Ann.#2 . . . . 4.00
TPB Vol. 1 . . . . 20.00

ARTESIA AFIELD
Sirius, 2000
1 (of 6) by Mark Smylie 3.00
1a Limited Ed. 6.00
2 thru 6 . . . . @3.00
Annual #3 Artesia. 5.00

ARTESIA AFIRE
Archaia Studios Press, 2003
1 (of 6) by Mark Smylie 4.00
2 thru 6 . . . . @4.00
TPB Vol. 1 . . . . 25.00
TPB Artesia Afield 25.00
TPB Vol. 3 Artesia Afire 25.00
Map Set Artesia: Know World . . . 25.00

ARTESIA: BESIEGED
Archaia Studios, 2006
1 (of 6) The Calm Before 4.00
2 The Traitor King 4.00
3 As I Lay Dying 4.00

ASH
Event Comics, 1994
1 JQ,JP,Fire and Crossfire,pt.1. . . 12.00
1a David Finch/Batt(c) 3.00
1b omnichrome commemorative . 15.00
1c omnichrom signed & numbered 30.00
2 JQ,JP,Fire and Crossfire,pt.2. . . 7.00
2a David Finch/Batt (c) 3.00
3 JQ,JP,Secret of Origin 4.50
4 I:Actor 3.00
5 I:New Character 3.00
6 V:Gabriel 3.00
0 Red Laser ed., Current Ash (c) . 10.00
0 Red Laser ed., Future Ash (c) . . 10.00
TPB rep. #1–#5 . . . . 15.00
TPB Vol. 1, JQ,JP,sgn. lim. 35.00

ASH:
CINDER AND SMOKE
Event Comics, 1997
1 MWa,BAu,HuR,JP 3.00
1a autographed virgin JQ cover . . 10.00
1b signed limited edition 12.00
2 HuR(c) 3.00
2 JQ(c) 3.00
3 (of 6) JQ&JP(c) 3.00
4 (of 6) JQ&JP(c) 3.00
5 (of 6) JQ&JP(c) 3.00
6 (of 6) JQ&JP(c) 3.00
3a thru 6a variant JP&HuR(c)s . . @3.00

ASH FILES, THE
Event Comics, 1997
1 JQ,JP 3.00
1 signed, limited 20.00

ASH: FIRE
AND CROSSFIRE
Event Comics, 1998
1 (of 5) JQ,JP 3.00
1a signed & numbered 25.00
2 . . . . 3.00

ASH: THE FIRE WITHIN
Event Comics, 1996
2 JQ,JP 3.00
3 JQ,JP, Ash Rooftop cover 3.00
3a JQ,JP, Ash Firefighter cover . . . 3.00

All comics prices listed are for *Near Mint* condition.

ASH/22 BRIDES
Event Comics, 1996
1 FaN,HuR,JP................ 3.00

ASPEN
Aspen 2003
1 Fathom........................ 5.00
1a variant (c)................... 20.00
2 Fathom, Soulfire 3.50
2a San Diego 20.00
3 .... 3.00
3a Chicago 15.00
Aspen extended edition 10.00
Aspen Sketch Book 10.00
Aspen Swimsuit Special (2006)... 10.00

ASPEN SEASONS
Aspen, 2005
1 Spring 2005 .... 3.00
1 Fall 2005 .... 3.00
1 Summer 2006 .... 3.00

ASSASSIN
Archangel Studios, 2003
1 (of 4) 3.00
1a variant (c).................. 3.00
2 .... 3.00

ASSASSINAUTS
Narwain Publishing, 2006
1 .... 3.50

ASSASSIN SCHOOL
APC, 2003
1 thru 5 .... @3.50
S.O.S.(Super one-shot) 6.00
TPB Vol. 1 .... 20.00

Vol. 2 (2004)
0 .... 3.00
1 thru 8 .... @3.50
8a limited sketch (c) (1:10)....... 3.50
TPB Vol. 2 .... 20.00

ASTER
Entity Comics, 1995
0 O:Aster the Celestial Knight 4.50
1 I:Celestial Knight 5.00
1b 2nd printing 3.00
2 .... 3.50
3 V:Tolmek 3.25
3a Variant cover 7.00
4 Final Issue 3.00
TPB Rep.#1–#4 + pin-up gallery .. 13.00

ASTER THE LAST CELESTIAL KNIGHT
Entity Comics, 1995
1 R:Aster Chromium Cover 3.00
1a Clear Chromium Edition 4.00
1b Holo Chrome Edition 5.00
2 World Defender 3.00

ASTRO BOY
Gold Key, 1965
1 I:Astro Boy 1,200.00

ASTRO BOY
Now, 1989
Prev. Original Astro Boy
18 thru 20................... @3.00

ASTRO CITY
Wildstorm/DC, 2004
Astro City Spec. (2004) 4.00
Spec. A Visitor's Guide (2004)..... 6.00

ASTRO CITY: THE DARK AGE
Wildstorm/DC, June, 2005
1 (of 16) KBk(s), BA,AxR(c) 3.00
2 KBk(s),BA,AxR(c) 3.00
3 KBk(s),BA,AxR(c) 3.00
4 KBk(s),BA,AxR(c) 3.00

Book 2, Oct., 2006
1 KBu,BA, Eyes of a Killer 3.00
2 KBu,BA 3.00

ASTRO CITY: LOCAL HEROES
Homage/DC, 2003
1 (of 5) KBk,BA................ 3.00
2 thru 5 KBk,BA............... @3.00
TPB KBk,BA.................... 18.00

ASTRO CITY: SAMARITAN
Wildstorm/DC, June, 2006
Spec. KBk, BA, 48-pg........... 4.00

ASYLUM
Pendragon, 1995
1 thru 3 .... @3.00

Asylum #3
© Maximum Press

ASYLUM
Maximum Press, 1995
1 Warchild, Beanworld, Avengelyne,
　Battlestar Galactica 3.00
2 I:Deathkiss.................. 3.00
3 .... 3.00
4 RLd,A:Cybrid 3.00
5 I:Black Seed................. 3.00
6 R:Steve Austin & Jaime
　Sommers................... 3.00
7 RLe,F:Bloodwulf 3.00
8 RLd 3.00
9 RLd 3.00
10 .... 3.00
11 .... 3.00
12 MMy,F:Blindside 3.00
13 .... 3.00

ATHENA VOLTAIRE: FLIGHT OF THE FALCON
Speakeasy Comics, 2006
1 .... 3.00
2 thru 5 .... @3.00

ATHENA VOLTAIRE: FLIGHT OF THE FLACON
Ape Entertainment, 2006
1 Ape edition, 48-pg........... 4.50
2 .... 3.00
3 .... 4.50
4 .... 3.00

ATLAS
Avatar Press, 2002
1 Gossett (c).................. 3.50
1b thru 1e variant (c)s......... @3.50
2 Brooks (c) 3.50
2b variant (c)................. 3.50

ATOM ANT
Gold Key, 1966
1 .... 550.00

ATOM-AGE COMBAT
Fago Magazines, 1959
2 Nuclear Sub,A-Bomb....... 325.00
3 Space Missile 225.00

ATOMIK MIKE
Alias Enterprises, 2006
1 .... 3.50
2 thru 4 .... @3.50

ATOMIC RABBIT
Charlton Comics, 1955–58
1 .... 350.00
2 .... 150.00
3 thru 10 .... @100.00
11 .... 150.00
Becomes:

ATOMIC BUNNY
Charlton Comics, 1958
12 .... 150.00
13 thru 18................. @100.00
19 Dec., 1959 .... 100.00

ATOMIKA
Speakeasy Comics, 2005
1 .... 3.00
1a signed 25.00
2 thru 6 .... @3.00
7 thru 9 God is Red.......... @3.00
TPB Vol. 1 .... 16.00

ATOMICS, THE
AAA Pop Comics, 1999
1 by Mike Allred 3.00
2 Zapman 3.00
3 Mutant Street Beatniks 3.00
4 refugees from the Innerverse ... 3.00
5 The Light 3.00
6 The Physical 3.00
7 I:The Skunk 3.00
8 F:The Laser 3.00
9 taken hostage 3.00
10 .... 3.00
11 Heroes divided 3.00
12 with poster 3.50
13 World of Savage Dragon 3.50
14 World of Savage Dragon,pt.4 ... 3.50
15 World of Savage Dragon,pt.5 ... 3.50
16 World of Savage Dragon,pt.6 ... 3.50
King Size Giant 10.00
King-Size Spec. Lessons in Light
　Lava & Lasers 9.00
King-Size Spec. Jigsaw 10.00
King-Size Vol. 3 .... 9.00
King-Size Vol. 4, 80-page 9.00

ATOMIK ANGELS
Crusade Entertainment, 1996
1 BiT 3.00
1 variant cover (1:25) 5.00
2 BiT 3.00
3 BiT 3.00
4 BiT, conclusion. 3.00

ATTACK
Charlton Comics, 1958–59
54 100 pages 150.00
55 thru 60 . . . . @100.00

AUTHORITY, THE
WildStorm/DC, 1999
1 WEl(s),BHi,PNe 12.00
2 WEl(s),BHi,PNe,V:Kaizen
   Gamorra 10.00
3 WEl(s),BHi,PNe,destruction 10.00
4 WEl(s),BHi,PNe,save L.A. 10.00
5 WEl(s),BHi,PNe,Swiftships,pt.1 . 10.00
6 WEl(s),BHi,PNe 7.00
7 WEl(s),BHi,PNe 7.00
8 WEl(s),BHi,PNe 7.00
9 WEl(s),BHi,PNe,OuterDark,pt.1 . . 7.00
10 WEl(s),BHi,PNe,OuterDark,pt.2 . 7.00
11 WEl(s),BHi,PNe,OuterDark,pt.3 . 7.00
12 WEl(s),BHi,PNe,OuterDark,pt.4 . 7.00
13 MMr(s),TvS,Nativity,pt.1 . . . . . . 11.00
14 MMr(s),TvS,Nativity,pt.2 . . . . 6.00
15 MMr(s),TvS,Nativity,pt.3 . . . . 6.00
16 MMr(s),TvS,Nativity,pt.4 . . . . 6.00
17 MMr(s),TvS,Earth Inferno,pt.1 . . 6.00
18 MMr(s),TvS,Earth Inferno,pt.2 . . 6.00
19 MMr(s),TvS,Earth Inferno,pt.3 . . 6.00
20 MMr(s),TvS,Earth Inferno,pt.4 . . 6.00
21 JMC,All Tomorrow's Parties 6.00
22 MMr(s),TvS,Brave New World,
   pt.1 (of 4) 6.00
23 TPe(s),Brave-World,pt.2 . . . . 6.00
24 TPe(s),BU:Establishment,40-pg . 3.50
25 TPe(s),Re-Space 3.50
26 TPe(s),F:Old Authority 3.50
27 MMr(s),New World Order,pt.2 . . . 3.50
28 MMr(s),AAd,F:Seth 3.50
29 New World Order,pt.4 . . . . 3.50
Ann. 2000 #1, Devil's
   Night x-over, pt.2 . . . . 5.00
GN The Authority: Kev (2002) 5.00
GN Scorched Earth 5.00
TPB The Authority: Relentless 18.00
TPB Under New Management 18.00
TPB Widescreen, 48-page 6.00
TPB Earth Inferno (2002) 15.00
TPB Transfer of Power (2002) 18.00
Volume 2
1 DT,F:Jack Hawksmoor, etc 4.00
2 thru 13 DT . . . . @3.00
14 WPo,Jack Hawksmore origin . . . 3.00
Spec. #0, 40-pg 3.00
X-Mas Spec. The Authority/Lobo
   x-over, 48-pg. (2003) 5.00
Spec. Authority/Lobo Spring
   Break Massacre, SBs, 48-page 5.00
TPB Harsh Realities 15.00
TPB Fractured Worlds 18.00
TPB Kev (and More Kev) 15.00
TPB Human on the Inside 18.00
TPB Authority/Lobo, Holiday Hell . . 18.00

AUTHORITY, THE
Wildstorm/DC, Oct., 2006
1 GMo 3.00
1a variant (c) 3.00

AUTHORITY:
THE MAGNIFICENT KEVIN
Wildstorm, Sept., 2005
1 (of 5) GEn,F:Kev Hawkins 3.00

The Authority, The Magnificent Kevin #2
© Wildstorm

2 thru 5 . . . . @3.00
TPB The Magnificent Kevin 15.00

AUTHORITY, THE:
MORE KEV
Wildstorm/DC, 2004
1 (of 4) GEn(s),GF 3.00
2 thru 4 GEn(s),GF . . . . @3.00

AUTHORITY, THE:
REVOLUTION
Wildstorm/DC, 2004
1 . . . . 3.00
2 . . . . 3.00
3 America in Revolution 3.00
4 War in Washington 3.00
5 Nation's capitol in rubble 3.00
6 thru 12 concl. . . . . @3.00
TPB Revolution 15.00
TPB Revolution, Book Two 15.00

AUTOMATIC KAFKA
WildStorm/DC, 2002
1 JoC, Eye of the Storm 3.00
2 JoC,NPS agents 3.00
3 JoC,TV game show host 3.00
4 JoC, ... 3.00
5 JoC, ... 3.00
6 JoC, ... 3.00
7 JoC,who is Galaxia 3.00
8 JoC 3.00
9 JoC 3.00

AVENGEBLADE
Maximum Press, 1996
1 RLe 3.00
2 RLe 3.00

AVENGELYNE
Maximum Press, 1995
1 RLd,I:Avengelyne Dir ed 12.00
1a Newstand Edition 5.00
1b Holochrome Edition 15.00
1 gold edition 10.00
2 V:B'Lial 4.00
3 I:Magogi 4.00
3 variant cover, pin-up 5.00
TPB rep. #1–#3 . . . . 10.00
Regular Series, 1996
0 RLd,O:Avengelyne 5.00
1 RLd,BNa,F:Devlin 4.00

1 variant photo cover 4.00
2 I:Darkchylde 10.00
2a variant photo cover 12.00
3 . . . . 3.50
4 A:Cybrid 3.50
5 A:Cybrid, ... 3.50
6 RLd,F:Divinity 3.50
7 RLd,F:Divinity 3.50
8 RLd, ... 3.50
9 RLd, ... 3.50
10 BNa,The Possession, pt.1 . . . . . 3.50
11 BNa,The Possession, pt.2 . . . . . 3.50
12 BNa,The Possession, pt.3 . . . . . 3.50
13 BNa,The Possession, pt.4 . . . . . 3.50
14 A:Bloodwulf 3.50
15 A:Glory, Prophet 3.50
Swimsuit Edition 3.50
Swimsuit book, American
   Entertainment exclusive 7.50

AVENGELYNE
Awesome Entertainment, 1999
Prelude 3.00
1 RLe,RNa 3.00
1a, b & c variant covers 3.00
2 RLe, ... 3.00
3 . . . . 3.00
Spec. Swimsuit, 1999 . . . . 3.50
Spec.#1-shot Demonslayer (2000) . 3.00
Spec.#1a Demonslayer variant (c) . 3.00
Spec.#1b Demonslayer variant (c) . 3.00
Spec.#1c Demonslayer variant (c) . 3.00

AVENGELYNE:
ARMAGEDDON
Maximum Press, 1996–97
1 (of 3) RLd 3.00
2 RLd, ... 3.00
3 BNa,ScC, finale 3.00

AVENGELYNE:
BAD BLOOD
Avatar, 2000
1 Matt Haley (c) 3.50
1a thru 1b variant(c)s . . . . @3.50
1c prism foil (c) previews excl 13.00
1d Al Rio velvet (c) 20.00
1e leather (c) 25.00
1f platinum (c) 8.00
1g Ruby Red ed 20.00
2 . . . . 3.50
2a variant(c)s . . . . @3.50
Prelude Rick Lyon (c) 5.00
Prelude Al Rio (c) 5.00
Prelude Bikini (c) 6.00
Prelude prism foil(c) 16-page 13.00
Prelude variant SSh(c) 6.00

AVENGELYNE BIBLE:
REVELATIONS
Maximum Press
one-shot RLd, ... 3.50

AVENGELYNE:
DARK DEPTHS
Avatar Press, 2001
1 (of 2) Rio(c) 3.50
1a MMy(c) 3.50
1b Martin (c) 3.50
1c blue velvet (c) 25.00
1d prism foil exclusive (c) 13.00
1e Heavenly Body edition 6.00
1f Royal Blue (c) 75.00
2 (of 2) Rio(c) 3.50
2a MMy(c) 3.50
2b Lyon (c) 3.50
2c Blue leather (c) 25.00
1/2 Rio (c) 16-page 5.00

COLOR PUB.

1/2 Lloyd painted (c) 5.00
1/2 Frillion (c). 5.00
1/2 Midnight Prayer (c) 6.00
1/2 Prism foil exclusive (c). 13.00

AVENGELYNE: DEADLY SINS
Maximum Press, 1996
1 RLd (c). 3.00
1 photo (c). 3.00
2 RLd(c) 3.00

AVENGELYNE: DRAGON REALM
Avatar Press, 2001
1/2 Rio (c) 5.00
1/2 Carrie Hall (c) 5.00
1/2 Lloyd (c) 5.00
1/2 Martin (c). 5.00
1/2 Dying Breath ed. 6.00
1/2 Prism foil ed. 13.00
1 (of 2) Rio(c) 3.50
1a thru 1b variant(c)s . . . . @3.50
1c red leather (c) 25.00
1d bondage (c) 6.00
1e prism foil (c) 13.00
1f venomous edition 6.00
1g venomous emerald foil 14.00
1h Fearless edition 5.00
2 Rio(c). 3.50
2a thru 2b variant(c)s . . . . @3.50
2c Shaw (c) 3.50
2d Ron Adrian (c) 6.00

AVENGELYNE/GLORY
Maximum Press, 1995
1 V:B'Lial. 4.00
1a variant cover 5.00
Swimsuit Spec. #1 . . . . 3.00

AVENGELYNE/GLORY: THE GODYSSEY
Maximum Press, 1996
1 RLd,BNa 3.00
2 thru 5 RLd . . . . @3.00

AVENGELYNE/PANDORA
Avatar, 2000
Spec. x-over 3.50
Spec.Preview exclusive 3.50
Spec.Preview Bikini ed. 6.00

Avengelyne/Glory: The Godyssey
© Maximum Press

Spec.McDaniel (c) 6.00
Spec.Previews exlusive Prism ed.. 13.00
Spec.Red Velvet 25.00
Spec.Ruby Red edition 20.00
Spec.Royal Blue 75.00

AVENGELYNE/POWER
Maximum Press, 1995–96
1 RLd,V:Hollywood 3.00
1 variant cover 3.50
2 RLd(c) 3.00
3 . . . . 3.00
3a photo (c). 3.00

AVENGELYNE/PROPHET
Maximum Press, 1996
1 RLd,BNa,MD2 . . . . 3.00

Awesome Entertainment, 2000
Rage of Furies #1 RLe(c) 3.00
  #1a IaC(c) 3.00
  #1b Grant(c) 3.00
  #1c Walker Bros.(c). 3.00
  #1d Wizard world ed. 5.00
  #1e Wizard world, signed . . . 10.00

AVENGELYNE: REVELATION
Avatar, 2000
1 Rio (c) 3.50
1a Haley (c) 3.50
1b Wraparound (c) 3.50
1c leather (c). 25.00
1d Matt Martin (c) 6.00
1e royal blue (c) 75.00
Previews prism foil (c) 13.00
Prelude Lyon (c). 6.00
Prelude platinum signed 11.00

AVENGELYNE: SERAPHACIDE
Avatar Press, 2001
1/2 Lyon (c). 5.00
1/2 Variant (c)s . . . . @5.00
1/2 Bound edition 6.00
1/2 Pax Romana (c) 6.00
1/2 Ron Adrian (c). 6.00
1 (of 2) Rio (c). 3.50
1a thru 1c variant (c)s . . . . @3.50
1d White Velvet (c) 25.00
1e Adam & Eve edition 6.00
1f Hard Woman (c) 6.00
1g Bikini (c). 6.00

AVENGELYNE/SHI
Avatar Press, 2001
1/2 RLd (c) 16-page 4.00
1/2 variant(c)s . . . . @4.00
1/2d Victory (c) 6.00
1/2e Sean Shaw, Cross cover . . . 6.00
1 Finch (c) x-over 3.50
1a variant(c)s . . . . @3.50
1e Red Leather (c) 25.00
1f Prism foil (c) 13.00
1h Waller (c) 6.00
1i Face off cover 6.00
1j ruby red edition. 25.00

AVENGELYNE/SUPREMA
Awesome Entertainment, 2000
Rage of Furies #1 (2000). 4.00
  1a Wizard world ed. 5.00
  1b signed. 10.00

AVENGELYNE/ WARRIOR NUN AREALA
Maximum Press, 1997
Spec. 3.00

Awesome Entertainment, 1997
Spec. #2 The Nazarene Affair 3.00

AVENGERS, THE
Gold Key, 1968
1 . . . . 500.00

AWESOME
Awesome Entertainment, 1997
Holiday Spec. #1 . . . . 2.50
Holiday Spec.'99 . . . . 5.00
Spring '99 Tourbook. 5.00

AXA
Eclipse, 1987
1 The Adopted 4.00
2 The Donor 3.50

AXEL PRESSBUTTON
Eclipse, 1984
1 BB(c),Origin 3.00
2 SD,Wanted for Mass Murder. . . . 3.00
3 AD,Wanted for Mass Murder. . . . 3.00
4 TA, ... 3.00
5 AD,Slave of the Narco-Pollen . . . 2.50
6 TA,Days in Downtown Delta Five 2.50

AXIS ALPHA
Axis Comics, 1994
1 LSn,I:BEASTIES,Dethgrip,
  Shelter,W 3.00

AYA
Studio G, 2003
1 . . . . 3.00
2 . . . . 3.00
3 thru 4 . . . . @3.00

AYA
AK Entertainment, 2006
1 Clone Order, pt.1. . . . . 3.00
2 Clone Order: Resurrection. 3.00
3 Clone Order: A Pharaoh Reborn . 3.00
4 One Bullet 3.00
5 Zero Tolerance, pt. 2 . . . . 3.00
6 Zero Tolerance. 3.00
7 . . . . 3.00

AZTEC ACE
Eclipse, 1984
1 NR(i),I:AztecAce 3.50
2 NR(i) 3.50
3 thru 9 NR(i) . . . . @3.00
10 NR(i) 3.00
11 . . . . 3.50
12 thru 15 . . . . @2.50

BABES OF BROADWAY
Broadway, 1996
1 . . . . 3.00

BABY HUEY, THE BABY GIANT
Harvey Publications, 1956–80
1 . . . . 900.00
2 . . . . 400.00
3 Anti-Pep Pills 300.00
4 . . . . 200.00
5 . . . . 200.00
6 thru 10 . . . . @150.00
11 thru 20 . . . . @100.00
21 thru 40 . . . . @75.00
41 thru 60 . . . . @50.00
61 thru 79. . . . . @40.00
80 . . . . 40.00
81 thru 95 giant size. . . . . @50.00

     All comics prices listed are for *Near Mint* condition.

96 Giant size	40.00
97 Giant size	40.00
98	30.00
99	20.00

BABY HUEY AND PAPA
Harvey Publications, 1962–68

1	550.00
2	450.00
3	350.00
4	350.00
5	350.00
6 thru 10	@200.00
11 thru 20	@175.00
21 thru 33	@150.00

BABY HUEY DUCKLAND
Harvey Publications, 1962–66

1	350.00
2	200.00
3	200.00
4	200.00
5	200.00
6 thru 10	@100.00
11 thru 20	@50.00
21 thru 33	@40.00

BACHELOR FATHER
Dell Publishing Co., 1962

1	150.00
2	125.00

BACK TO THE FUTURE
Harvey, 1991

1 Chicago 1927	3.00
2 Cretaceous Period	3.00
3 World War I	3.00
4 Doc Retires	3.00

BAD COMPANY
Quality, 1988

1 thru 19	@3.00

BAD EGGS
Acclaim, 1996

1 thru 4 BL,DP,That Dirty Yellow Mustard	@3.00

BADGER
Capital, 1983

1 JBt,I:Badger,Ham,Daisy Yak,Yeti.	5.00

Badger #61
© First

2 JBt,I:Riley,A:YakYeti.	4.00
3 JBt,O:Badger,Ham.	4.00
4 JBt,A'Ham	4.00

First, 1984–91

5 thru 16 BR	@3.00
17 JBt,I:Lamont	3.50
18 thru 39	@3.00
40 thru 49 RLm,	@3.50
50 RLm,TRoof off SuckerII	5.00
51 RLm,V:Demon	3.00
52 thru 54 TV	@4.00
55 thru 70	@3.00
Graphic Nov.BR,I:Mazis Sykes,D:Hodag	10.00
Badger Bedlam	5.00

BADGER GOES BERSERK
First, 1989

1 I:Larry,Jessie	4.00
2 MZ,V:Larry,Jessie	3.50
3 JBt/MZ,V:Larry,Jessie	3.00
4 JBt/MZ,V:Larry,Jessie	3.00

BAD GIRLS
OF BLACKOUT
Blackout Comics, 1995

0	3.50
1 I:Ms. Cyanide, Ice	3.50
Ann.#1 Hari Kari, Lady Vampre	3.50
Ann.#1 Commemorative ed.	10.00

BAD KITTY
Chaos! Comics, 2001

1 BnP	3.00
1a premium edition	10.00
2	3.00
3	3.00
Ashcan	6.00
Script #1	5.00
Script #1 premium	20.00

BAD KITTY:
MISCHIEF NIGHT
Chaos! Comics, 2001

1	3.00
1a premium edition	13.00
1b super premium edition	20.00

BAD KITTY: RELOADED
Chaos! Comics, 2001

1	3.00
1a premium ed	10.00
2 F:Chastity	3.00
3	3.00
4	4.00
2a thru 4a variant (c)	@7.50

BAD MOON RISING
Avatar Press, 2006

1	4.00
1a variant (c)s	@4.00

BADROCK/WOLVERINE
Awesome Entertainment, 1997

Spec. #1 JV,CYp,V:Sauron,48pg	5.00

BAKER STREET
Caliber, 1989

1	3.00
2 thru 10	@3.00
TPB Vol. 1	15.00
TPB Vol. 2	15.00

BALLAD OF HALO JONES
Quality, 1987

1 IG Alan Moore story	2.50

1a IG rep.	2.50
2 thru 12	@2.50

BALLAD OF SLEEPING BEAUTY, THE
Beckett Comics, 2004

1	2.00
2 thru 4	@2.00
5 thru 8	@2.00
TPB	22.00

BAMM-BAMM & PEBBLES FLINTSTONE
Gold Key, 1964

1	300.00

BANZAI GIRL
Sirius Entertainment, 2002

Preview book, lim. ed.	5.00
1 (of 4) by Jinky Coronado	3.00
2 thru 4	@3.00
2a thru 4a lim.,signed,ph(c)	@12.00
3	3.00
3a limited, signed, photo(c)	12.00
4	3.00
4a limited, signed, photo(c)	12.00
Ann. #1	3.50
TPB Vol. 1	15.00
Fabulous Foto Book	4.00

BARBARIANS, THE
Atlas, 1975

1 O: Andrax,F:Iron Jaw	50.00

BARBAROSSA AND THE LOST CORSAIRS
Kandora Publishing, 2005

1	3.50
2 thru 5	@3.50

BARBIE & KEN
Dell Publishing Co. 1962

1	950.00
2	750.00
3	750.00
4	750.00
5	800.00

BARBIE TWINS ADVENTURES, THE
Topps, 1995

1 I:Shane, Sia	3.00

BARBI TWINS ADVENTURES
Studio Chikara, 1998

Color Spec. The Roswell Incident	4.00

BARNEY AND BETTY RUBBLE
Charlton Comics, 1973–76

1	75.00
2	30.00
3	30.00
4	30.00
5	30.00
6 thru 10	@25.00
11 thru 23	@20.00

BARRY M. GOLDWATER
Dell Publishing Co., 1965

1	75.00

All comics prices listed are for *Near Mint* condition.

BAR SINISTER
Acclaim Windjammer, 1995
1 From Shaman's Tears 2.50
2 V:SWAT Team 2.50
3 F: Animus Prime 2.50
4 MGe,RHo,V:Jabbersnatch . . . 2.50

BART-MAN
Bongo, 1993
1 Foil(c),I:Bart-Man 4.00
2 I:Penalizer 2.50
3 When Bongos Collide,pt.3,
   with card 2.50
4 Crime-Time,pt.1 . . . . 2.50
5 Bad Guys Strike Back 2.50

BART SIMPSON COMICS
Bongo Comics, 2000
1 . . . . 3.00
2 thru 9 . . . . @3.00
10 thru 26 . . . . @3.00
27 thru 32 . . . . @3.00
TPB Big Book of Bart Simpson . . . 12.00
TPB Big Bad Book of Bart
   Simpson 13.00
TPB Big Bratty Book of
   Bart Simpson 13.00
TPB Big Beefy Book of
   Bart Simpson 14.00
TPB Vol. 5 Big, Bouncy
   Book of Bart Simpson 14.00

BART SIMPSONS TREEHOUSE OF HORROR
Bongo Comics, 1995
1 Bart People 3.00
2 thru 4 . . . . @3.00
5 48-pg. 3.50
6 and 7 64-page . . . . @.50
8 . . . . @3.50
9 thru 12 . . . . @5.00
1-shot Treehouse of Terror 2.50

BASEBALL
Kitchen Sink, 1991
1 WE (c) reprint of 1949 orig. 4.00
2 Ray Gotto (c), w/4 BB cards . . . 3.00

BAT, THE
Adventure
1 R:The Bat,inspiration for Batman
   says Bob Kane 3.00

BATMAN/DANGER GIRL
Wildstorm/DC, Dec. 2004
1-shot x-over, 48-page 5.00

BATTLEBOOKS
Battlebooks Inc., 1999
all BTi(c)
Bubba-Busters Battlebook 5.00
Captain America Battlebook
   Blue print, signed edition 10.00
Colossus Battlebook 4.00
Daredevil Battlebook BTi(c) 4.00
Daredevil Battlebook JQ&JP(c) . . . 4.00
Darkchylde A Battlebook 4.00
Darkchylde B Battlebook 4.00
The Darkness Battlebook 4.00
Dr. Doom Battlebook 4.00
Elektra Battlebook 4.00
   Blue print, signed edition 13.00
Elektra Battlebook, revised 4.00
Gambit Battlebook 4.00
Green Goblin Battlebook 4.00

Iron Man Battlebook
   Blue print, signed edition 13.00
   Blue print, signed edition 13.00
The Incredible Hulk Battlebook 4.00
   Blue print, signed edition 13.00
Magneto Battlebook 4.00
President Clinton Battlebook 5.00
Rogue Battlebook 4.00
   Blue print, signed edition 13.00
Sabretooth Battlebook 4.00
Shi: The Spirit of Benkei Battlebook 4.00
   Blue print, signed edition 10.00
Spider-Man Battlebook
   Blue print, signed edition 13.00
Storm Battlebook 4.00
The Thing Battlebook 4.00
Tomoe: Fan's of Fury Battlebook . . 4.00
Vampirella Hell on Earth Battlebook 4.00
White Queen Battlebook 4.00
Witchblade Battlebook 4.00
Wolverine Battlebook 4.00
Wolverine with Bone Claws Battlebook
   Blue print, signed edition 13.00

BATTLE OF THE PLANETS
Gold Key, 1979
1 TV Cartoon 50.00
2 . . . . 35.00
3 . . . . 35.00
4 . . . . 35.00
5 . . . . 35.00
Whitman, 1980
6 . . . . 20.00
7 thru 10 . . . . @20.00

BATTLER BRITTON
Wildstorm/DC, July 2006
1 GEn,CWi 3.00
2 thru 5 GEn,CWi . . . . @3.00

BATTLESTAR GALACTICA
Maximum Press, 1995
1 Finds Earth 5.00
2 Council of Twelve 4.00
3 R:Adama 4.00
4 Pyramid Secrets 4.00
TPB series rep. 13.00
Spec. Ed. Painted Book (1997) . . . 3.00
Battlestar Galactica: The Compendium #1 rep. from Asylum 3.00

BATTLESTAR GALACTICA
Realm Press, 1997
1 by Chris Scalf 4.00
1a variant cover 3.00
2 Law of Volhad 3.00
3 Prison of Souls, pt.1 . . . . 3.00
3a alternate cover 3.00
4 Prison of Souls, pt.2 . . . . 3.00
5 . . . . 3.00
6 A Path of Darkness, pt.1 . . . . . . 3.00
7 A Path of Darkness, pt.2 . . . . . . 3.00
7a photo (c) 3.00
7b signed and numbered 6.00
8 Centurion Prime 3.00
Spec.#1 20 Yahren Reunion 3.00
Spec.#1 No Memory of Earth 3.00
Spec.#1 CenturionPrime,Scott(c) . 3.00
Spec.#1 CenturionPrime,Parsons(c) 3.00
Spec.#2 Centurion Prime 3.00
Spec. 1999 Tourbook 3.00
Spec. 1999 Tourbook con. ed. . . . 7.00
Spec. 1999 Tourbook sign. 30.00
Spec. Gallery #1 . . . . 4.00
Tech Journal: The Galactica 4.00
Tech Journal: Ships of Fleet 4.00
Spec.No Man's Land 4.00
Spec.No Man's Land, deluxe 5.00

Cylon Dawn Spec. (2000) 4.00
Cylon Dawn Spec. deluxe 5.00
Darkest Night Spec. (2000) 4.00
Darkest Night Spec. variant (c) . . . 5.00
Dire Prophecy Spec. (2000) 4.00
Dire Prophecy Spec. deluxe 5.00
Eve of Destruction Prelude(1999) . . 4.00
Spec.#1 Triad Triumph (2000) . . . 4.00
Spec.#1a Triad Triumph,deluxe . . . 5.00
TPB New Beginnings, rep. #1–#4 . 14.00

BATTLESTAR GALACTICA
D.E. (Dynamite Ent.) 2006
0 . . . . 0.25
1 . . . . 3.00
1a photo foil 20.00
2 . . . . 3.00
3 . . . . 3.00
4 . . . . 3.00
5 . . . . 3.00
1a thru 5a variant (c)s . . . . @3.00
2b thru 5b variant
   Cylon foil (c)s . . . . @20.00

BATTLESTAR GALACTICA APOLLO'S JOURNEY
Maximum Press, 1996
1 story by Richard Hatch 3.00
2 . . . . 2.50
3 . . . . 2.50

THE ENEMY WITHIN
Maximum Press, 1996
1 . . . . 3.00
2 . . . . 2.50
3 . . . . 2.50

JOURNEY'S END
Maximum Press, 1996
1 (of 4) RLd 3.00
2 RLd 3.00
3 RLd, the end of Galactica? 3.00
4 RLd, conclusion 3.00

SEARCH FOR SANCTUARY
Realm Press, 1998
1 (of 4) 3.00
2 Path of Darkness 3.00
3 tensions grow. 3.00
4 . . . . 3.00

STARBUCK
Maximum Press, 1997
1 (of 3) RLd 3.00

Battlestar Galactica Apollo's Journey #2
© Maximum Press

2 RLd 3.00
3 RLd, the end of Galactica? 3.00

ZAREK
D.E. (Dynamite Ent.) 2006
1 . . . . 3.50
1a photo foil (c) . . . .

BATTLESTAR GALACTICA SEASON THREE
Real Press, 1999
1 . . . . 3.00
1a alternate JaL(c) 5.00
1b Cylon Attack (c) 5.00
1c Cylon Attack (c) signed 35.00
2 . . . . 3.00
2a alternate cover. 5.00
2b pencil sketch cover 5.00
2c convention edition 5.00
3 Fire in the Sky 3.00
3a alternate cover. 5.00
3b convention edition 5.00
4 Scott (c) 3.00
5 Busch (c) 3.00
6 . . . . 3.00
4a thru 6a variant(c) . . . . @3.00
7 . . . . 3.00
8 . . . . 3.00
7a & 8a deluxe . . . . @5.00
Spec. 80-page Juggernaut. 9.00
Tour Book Sketch ed. 25.00

BATTLETECH
Blackthorne, 1987
1 . . . . 3.00
2 thru 6 . . . . @3.00
(Changed to Black & White)
1 3-D 3.00
2 3-D 3.00

BATTLETECH: FALLOUT
Malibu, Dec. 1994–Mar. 1995
0 Battletech 3.00
1 3 tales, Based on FASA game. . . 3.00
1a gold foil limited edition 3.50
1b limited holographic editon 5.00
2 V:Clan Jade Falcon 3.00
3 R:Lea 3.00
4 Conclusion 3.00

BAY CITY JIVE
WildStorm/DC, 2001
1 (of 3) F:Sugah Rollins 3.00
1a variant (c) (1:4) 3.00
2 1976 streets of San Francisco. . . 3.00
3 Hell on Earth, concl. 3.00

BEAGLE BOYS, THE
Gold Key, 1964–79
1 . . . . 100.00
2 thru 5 . . . . @50.00
6 thru 10 . . . . @40.00
11 thru 20 . . . . @30.00
21 thru 47 . . . . @25.00

BEANIE THE MEANIE
Fago Publications, 1958
1 thru 3 . . . . @60.00

B.E.A.S.T.I.E.S.
Axis Comics, 1994
1 JS(a&s),I:Beasties 2.50

THE BEATLES, LIFE STORY
Dell Publishing Co., 1964
1 . . . . 1,000.00

BEAUTIFUL KILLER
Black Bull Entertainment, 2001
1 JP(s) 5.00
1a variant (c). 4.00
2 JP(s) 4.00
3 JP(s) 4.00
Preview Edition, limited 5.00

BEAUTY AND THE BEAST
Innovation, 1993
1 From TV series 3.00
1a Deluxe 4.00
2 thru 7 . . . . @3.00

BEAUTY AND THE BEAST PORTRAIT OF LOVE
First, 1989–90
1 WP,TV tie in 12.00
2 . . . . 8.00
Book II:Night of Beauty 6.00

BEAUTY AND THE BEAST
Walt Disney, 1992
Movie adapt.(Prestige). 5.00
Movie adapt.(newsstand). 3.00
mini-series
1 Bewitched 3.00
2 Elsewhere 3.00
3 A:Catherine 3.00

BEDLAM!
Eclipse, 1985
1 SBi,RV,reprint horror 3.00
2 SBi,RV,reprint horror 3.00

BEETLE BAILEY
Harvey, 1992
1 F:Mort Walker's B.Bailey 4.00
2 Beetle builds a bridge 3.00
3 thru 12 . . . . @3.00

BEETLEJUICE
Harvey, 1991
1 EC,This is your lice 3.00
Holiday Special #1 . . . . 3.00

BEN CASEY
Dell Publishing Co., June-July, 1962
1 Ph(c) 125.00
2 Ph(c) 100.00
3 Ph(c) 75.00
4 Drug, Ph(c) 100.00
5 Ph(c) 75.00
6 thru 10 Ph(c) . . . . @75.00

BEOWULF
Speakeasy Comics, 2005
1 . . . . 3.00
2 thru 6 . . . . @3.00
7 Altered States. 3.00
8 Altered States. 3.00
9 Mortal Coil, pt.1 . . . . 3.00
10 Mortal Coil. pt.2. . . . . 3.00
11 Epochs, pt.1 . . . . 3.00
12 Epochs 3.00
TPB Vol. 1 Gods and Monsters . . . 15.00

BEOWULF
Antarctic Press, 2006
1 (of 3) 3.50
2 thru 3 . . . . @3.50

Berni Wrightson Master of the Macabre #5 © Eclipse

BERNI WRIGHTSON MASTER OF THE MACABRE
Pacific, 1983
1 BWr 6.00
2 BWr 4.00
3 BWr 3.50
4 BWr 3.50
Eclipse, 1984
5 BWr 3.50

BEST CELLARS
Out of the Cellers, 1995
1 Eric Powells (1) 25.00

BEST OF BUGS BUNNY
Gold Key, 1966–68
1 Both Giants 100.00
2 . . . . 75.00

BEST OF DENNIS THE MENACE, THE
Hallden/Fawcett Publ., Summer, 1959–Spring, 1961
1 . . . . 150.00
2 . . . . 100.00
3 thru 5 . . . . @100.00

BEST OF DONALD DUCK & UNCLE SCROOGE
Gold Key, 1964–67
1 . . . . 200.00
2 . . . . 150.00

BEST OF DONALD DUCK
Gold Key, 1965
1 . . . . 150.00

BETTI COZMO
Antarctic Press, 1999
1 (of 3) 3.00
2 . . . . 3.00
3 Raygun For Hire 3.00

BETTY
Archie Publications, 1992
1 . . . . @6.00
2 thru 39 . . . . @4.00

All comics prices listed are for *Near Mint* condition.

40 thru 60	@4.00
61 thru 80	@3.00
81 thru 100	@3.00
101 thru 119	@3.00
120 thru 142	@3.00
143 thru 161	@2.25

BETTY AND ME
Archie Publications, 1965–92

1	175.00
2	100.00
3 O:Superteen	110.00
4 thru 8 Superteen	@75.00
9 & 10	60.00
11 thru 21	@50.00
22 Archie Band	50.00
23 thru 37	@40.00
38 Sabrina	60.00
39 Josie & Sabrina	50.00
40 Archie & Betty in Cabin	35.00
41	35.00
42 Betty Vamp	35.00
43 thru 55	@30.00
56 thru 200	@15.00

BETTY AND VERONICA
Archie Publications, 1987

1	10.00
2 thru 10	@6.00
11 thru 50	@5.00
51 thru 104	@4.00
105 thru 119	@3.00
120 thru 141	@5.00
142 thru 160	@3.00
161 thru 181	@3.00
182 thru 203	@3.00
204 thru 222	@2.25
Summer Fun Special #5	3.00
Summer Fun Special #6	3.00
Summer Fun Special #7	3.00
TPB Summer Fun Volume 1	11.00

BETTY & VERONICA SPECTACULAR
Archie Publications, 1992

1 thru 25	@3.00
26 thru 40	@3.00
41 thru 57	@3.00
58 thru 68	@3.00
69 thru 76	@2.25

BEVERLY HILLBILLYS
Dell Publishing Co., April-June, 1963

1 Ph(c)	300.00
2 Ph(c)	175.00
3 Ph(c)	150.00
4 Ph(c)	100.00
5 thru 9 Ph(c)	@150.00
10	100.00
11 thru 14 Ph(c)	@150.00
15 thru 21 Ph(c)	@100.00

BEWITCHED
Dell Publishing Co., April-June, 1965

1 Ph(c)	300.00
2	200.00
3 thru 13 Ph(c)	@125.00
14	100.00

BEYOND THE GRAVE
Charlton Comics, 1975–76

1 SD,TS(c),P(c)	60.00
2 thru 6	@35.00

Charlton Comics, 1983–84

7 thru 17	@30.00

BIG BANG
Caliber Press, 1994

0 Whole Timeline inc.	3.00
1	2.50
2	2.50
3	2.50
4 25 years after #3	2.50

BIGFOOT
IDW Publishing, 2005

1	4.00
2 thru 4	@4.00
TPB	20.00

BIG MAX
MR Comics, 2006

1	3.00

BIG VALLEY, THE
Dell Publishing Co., 1966

1 Ph(c)	150.00
2 thru 6	@100.00

BILL BLACK'S FUN COMICS
AC Comics

1 Cpt.Paragon,B&W	3.00
2 and 3 B&W	@2.50
4 Color	2.50

BILL THE GALACTIC HERO
Topps, 1994

1 thru 3 Harry Harrison adapt.	@5.00

BILLY THE KID
Charlton Publ. Co., 1957–83
1 thru 8: MASKED RAIDER
(see Golden Age section)

9 DG(c),The Watergod	150.00
10 Rancho Malo	125.00
11 O:Ghost Train	150.00
12	125.00
13 AW,AT	150.00
14 No Limit Game	125.00
15 AW,O:Billy the Kid	150.00
16 AW, The Fastest Gun	150.00
17 Home Town Hero	125.00
18 The Scared Squatter	125.00
19 The Underdog	125.00
20 JSe,3-Aces	150.00
21 JSe, The Kid's Last Meal	150.00
22 JSe, The Crisis	150.00
23 JSe, The Guilty Gunslinger	150.00
24 JSe, Caught with the Cash	150.00
25 JSe, Geronimo's Revenge	150.00
26 JSe, Gambler's Greed	150.00
27 Winner's Luck	100.00
28 The Big Man	100.00
29 The Fall Guy	100.00
30 Masked Rider	125.00
31 thru 40	@100.00
41 thru 60	@35.00
61 thru 65	@30.00
66 Boundy Hunter	35.00
67 thru 87	@20.00
88 thru 153	@10.00

BIN4RY
APC, 2004

1	3.50
2 thru 4	@3.50
5 The Virus,pt.1	3.50
6	3.50
7	3.50
TPB Vol. 1	17.00
0a variant (c)	3.00

BIONEERS
Mirage/Next, 1994

1 New Heroes	2.75
2	2.75
3 All-out War	2.75

BIONIC WOMAN, THE
Charlton, 1977

1 Oct, 1977, TV show adapt.	30.00
2 thru 5	@20.00

BIONIX
Maximum Press, 1996

1 (of 3) RLd,F:Steve Austin & Jaime Sommers	3.00
2 RLd,	3.00

BIZARRE 3-D ZONE
Blackthorne, 1986

1	3.00

BLACKBALL COMICS
Blackball Comics, 1994

1 KG,A:Trencher	3.25

[ORIGINAL] BLACK CAT
Recollections, 1988

1 thru 2 Reprints	@3.00
3 thru 8 *see B&W Section*	
9 thru 10 rep.	@3.00

Black Diamond #1
© AC Comics

BLACK DIAMOND
AC Comics, 1983

1 Colt B..U. story	4.00
2 thru 5 PG(c)	@3.00

BLACK ENCHANTRESS
Heroic Publishing, 2004

1	3.00
2 thru 3	@3.00

BLACK FLAG
Maximum Press, 1995

1 Dan Fraga	3.00
2 I:New Character	3.00
3 V:Network, I:Glitz	3.00
4 V:Glitz, Network	3.00
5 I:Jammers	3.00
6 I:Alphabots	3.00

BLACK FURY
Charlton Comics, 1955

1	150.00
2	100.00
3 thru 15	@100.00
16 thru 18 SD	@150.00
19 and 20	@75.00
21 thru 56	@75.00
57 March-April, 1966	60.00

BLACK HARVEST
Devil's Due Publishing 2005

1 (of 6) by Josh Howard	3.25
2 thru 6	@3.25
TPB Vol. 1	15.00

BLACK HOLE, THE
Whitman, 1980

1 & 2 movie adaptation	@3.00
3 & 4 new stories	@3.00

BLACK HOOD
Archie/Red Circle, 1983

1 ATh,GM,DW	4.00
2 ATh,DSp,A:Fox	3.00
3 ATh,GM	3.00

BLACK JACK
Charlton Comics, 1957–59

20	125.00
21	100.00
22	125.00
23 AW,AT	125.00
24 thru 26 SD	@135.00
27	100.00
28 SD	135.00
29 & 30	@100.00

BLACKJACK: BLOOD & HONOR
Dark Angel, 1997

1 by Alex Simmons,JoB, 1930s Adventure, Hildebrandts(c)	3.00
2 KeL	3.00
3 Tim Cheng disappears	3.00
4	3.00

BLACK PHANTOM
AC Comics, 1989

1 F:Red Mask	3.00
2 thru 3 F:Red Mask	@3.00

BLACK PLAGUE
Boom! Studios, 2006

1-shot	4.00
1-shot Previews exclusive (c)	7.00

BLACK RAVEN
Mad Monkey Press, 1996

1 Blueprints pt.1	3.00
2 Blueprints pt.2	3.00
3 V:Temple Assassins	3.00
4 Blueprints pt.4	3.00
GN#1 Blueprints	7.00
GN#2 Blueprints	5.00

BLACK SEPTEMBER
Malibu Ultraverse, 1995

Infinity End of Black September	3.00

BLACK SUN
WildStorm/DC, 2002
Eye of the Storm

1 (of 6) TvS,F:Maggie Sun	3.00
2 thru 6 TvS	@3.00

BLACK TERROR
Eclipse, 1989–90

1	4.00
2	4.00
3	5.00

BLACK TIDE
Avatar Press, 2002

1A Park (c)	3.50
2 Miller (c)	3.50
3 Miller (c)	3.50
1a thru 3a variant (c)s	@3.50

Angel Gate Press

4 thru 8	@3.50
4a thru 8a variant (c)	3.50
9 thru 12	@3.00
9a thru 11a variant (c)s	@3.00
TPB Vol. 1 Awakening the Key	21.00
GN Vol. 1 Enter the Game	8.00

BLACK TIGER: LEGACY OF FURY
Beyond Time Comics, 2004

1 (of 4)	3.00
2 thru 4	@3.00

BLACKBEARD LEGACY
Alias Enterprises, 2006

1	3.50
2 thru 4	@3.50

BLACKPOOL
Phenomenon Comics, 2005

1	3.00
2 thru 3	@3.00
TPB Vol. 1 Sacrifice & Blood Bros.	20.00

BLACK WEB
Inks Comics

1 thru 3 V:Seeker	@2.75

BLADE OF KUMORI, THE
Devil's Due Publishing, 2004

1 RMz, Aftermath	3.00
1a variant (c)	3.00
2 thru 6 RMz, Aftermath	@3.00

BLAST-OFF
Harvey Publications, 1965

1 JK,AW	100.00

Blast-off #1
© Harvey Publications

BLAZING COMBAT
Warren Publishing Co., 1965–66

1 FF(c)	400.00
2 FF(c)	150.00
3 FF(c)	125.00
4 FF(c)	150.00

BLAZING SIX-GUNS
Skywald Comics, 1971

1 F: Red Mask, Sundance Kid	35.00
2 Jesse James	25.00

BLOOD & ROSES
Sky Comics, 1993

1 I:Blood,Rose	3.00

BLOODBATH
Samson Comics

1 I:Alien,V:Starguile	3.00

BLOODCHILDE
Millennium, 1994

0 O:Bloodchilde	3.00
1 Neil Gaiman, Vampires	5.00
1 signed (lim. to 500)	5.00
2 Nell Gaiman, Vampires	3.00
3 Neil Gaiman, Vampires	3.00
4	3.00
5 Talk Show Host	3.00

BLOODFIRE
Lightning Comics, 1993

0 O:Bloodfire	3.00
1 JZy(s),JJn, red foil	5.00
1a Platinum foil Ed	5.00
1b B&W Promo Ed. Silver ink	4.00
1c B&W Promo Ed. Gold ink	6.00
2 JZy(s),JJn,O:Bloodfire	4.00
3 JZy(s),JJn,I:Dreadwolf, Judgement Day,Overthrow	3.00
4 JZy(s),JJn,A:Dreadwolf,	3.00
5 JZy(s),JJn,I:Bloodstorm, w/card	3.00
6 SZ(s),TLw,V:Storman	3.00
7 SZ(s),TLw,A:Pres.Clinton	3.00
8 SZ(s),TLw,O:Prodigal	5.00
9 SZ(s),TLw,I:Prodigal (in Costume)	3.00
10 SZ(s),TLw,B:Rampage, I:Thorpe	3.00
11	3.00
12	3.00

BLOODFIRE/HELLINA
Lightning Comics, 1995

1 V:Slaughterhouse	3.00

BLOODLORE
Brave New Worlds

1 Dreamweavers	2.50
2 A Blow to the Crown	2.50

BLOODSCENT
Comico, 1988

1 GC	3.00

BLOODRAYNE
Digital Webbing, 2004

1-shot Skies Afire (2004)	12.00
1-shot Seeds of Sin (2005)	12.00
1-shot Lycan Rex (2005)	4.00
1-shot variant (c)	5.00
1-shot Dark Soul (2005)	4.00
1-shot Dark Soul variant (c)	5.00
1-shot Raw Convention Spec.	6.00
1-shot Twin Blades	10.00

All comics prices listed are for *Near Mint* condition.

BLOODRAYNE: PLAGUE OF DREAMS
Digital Webbing, 2006
1 (of 3) 4.00
1a variant (c) 4.00
2 . . . . 4.00
3a variant (c) 4.00

BLOODSHOT
Valiant, 1992
0 KVH(a&s),DG(i),Chromium (c),
  O:Bloodshot,A:Eternal Warrior . 4.00
0a Gold Ed.,w/Diamond `Fall Fling'
  logo 12.00
1 BWS(c),B:KVH(s),DP,BWi, V:Mafia,
  I:Carboni,1st Chromium(c) 4.00
2 thru 6 DP . . . . @2.50
7 thru 17 DP,JDx . . . . @2.50
18 thru 39 . . . . @2.50
40 thru 49 . . . . @12.50
50 . . . . 10.00
51 . . . . 12.00
Yearbook #1 KVH,briefcase bomb. . 4.25
Yearbook 1995 Villagers 3.00
Spec.GN Last Stand 10.00

Series Two
Acclaim, 1997
1 LKa(s),SaV, Behold, a Pale
  Horseman 2.50
1a variant cover 3.00
2 thru 16 LKa(s),SaV . . . . @2.50

BLOOD SWORD
Jademan, 1988
1 . . . . 3.00
2 . . . . 3.00
3 . . . . 3.00
4 . . . . 3.00
5 . . . . 3.00
6 thru 9 . . . . @3.00
10 thru 21 . . . . @3.00
22 thru 45 . . . . @3.00
46 V:Cannibal 3.00
47 thru 53 . . . . @3.00

BLOOD SWORD DYNASTY
Jademan, 1989
1 . . . . 3.00
2 thru 6 . . . . @2.75
7 thru 18 MB . . . . @2.75
19 thru 40 . . . . @2.75

Blue Beetle Vol. 2 #2
© Charlton

BLUE BEETLE
Charlton Comics, 1964
(1st Silver Age Series)
1 O:Dan Garrett/BlueBeetle 175.00
2 . . . . 125.00
3 V:Mr.Thunderbolt 150.00
4 V:Praying Mantis Man 125.00
5 V:Red Knight 125.00

(2nd S.A. Series), 1965
Previously: UNUSUAL TALES
50 V:Scorpion 125.00
51 V:Mentor 125.00
52 V:Magno 125.00
53 V:Praying Mantis Man 125.00
54 V:Eye of Horus 125.00
Becomes:

GHOSTLY TALES
(3rd S.A. Series), 1967
1 SD,I:Question 150.00
2 SD,O:TedKord,D:DanGarrett . . 75.00
3 SD,I:Madmen,A:Question 40.00
4 SD,A:Question 40.00
5 SD,VicSage(Question) app.
  in Blue Beetle Story 40.00

BLUE PHANTOM, THE
Dell Publishing Co., 1962
1 . . . . 135.00

BLUE RIBBON
Archie/Red Circle, 1983
1 JK,AV,O:Fly rep 7.00
2 TVe,Mr.Justice 6.00
3 EB/TD,O:Steel Sterling 6.00
4 . . . . 6.00
5 S&K,Shield rep. 6.00
6 DAy/TD,Fox 6.00
7 TD,Fox 6.00
8 NA,GM,Blackhood 7.00
9 thru 11 . . . . @6.00
12 SD,ThunderAgents 6.00
13 Thunderbunny 6.00
14 Web & Jaguar 6.00

BLUFF
Narwain Publishing, 2006
1 (of 3) 4.00
2 thru 3 . . . . @3.50

BOLD ADVENTURE
Pacific, 1987
1 & 2 . . . . @3.00
3 JSe 3.00

BOLT & STARFORCE SIX
AC Comics, 1984
1 . . . . 3.00
Bolt Special #1 . . . . 3.00

BOMBABY: THE SCREEN GODDESS
Amaze Ink/Slave Labor Graphics, 2003
1 (of 4) 3.50
2 . . . . 3.50
3 and 4 . . . . @4.00
TPB 140-page 14.00

BOMBAST
Topps, 1993
1 V:Savage Dragon,Trading Card . 3.25

BONANZA
Dell Publishing Co., 1960
1 . . . . 400.00

2 . . . . 300.00
3 thru 10 . . . . @250.00
11 thru 20 . . . . @200.00
21 thru 37 . . . . @200.00

BORIS KARLOFF TALES OF MYSTERY
Gold Key, 1963–80
1 (Thriller) 175.00
2 (Thriller) 125.00
3 thru 8 . . . . @75.00
9 WW 100.00
10 JO 75.00
11 AW,JO 85.00
12 AT,AMc,JO 75.00
13 & 14 . . . . @50.00
15 RC,GE 50.00
16 thru 20 . . . . @50.00
21 JJ,Screaming Skull 100.00
22 thru 50 . . . . @40.00
51 thru 74 . . . . @30.00
75 thru 97 . . . . @25.00

BOYS, THE
Wildstorm/DC, Aug., 2006
1 GEn,DaR,Watchers of the Supers 3.00
2 GEn,DaR 3.00
3 GEn 3.00
4 GEn, DaR 3.00
5 GEn 3.00

BOZO
Innovation
1 1950's reprint stories 7.00

BOZO THE CLOWN
Blackthorne
1 3-D 3.00
2 3-D 3.00

BRADY BUNCH, THE
Dell Publishing Co., 1970
1 . . . . 250.00
2 . . . . 200.00

BRAIN BOY
Dell Publishing Co., April-June, 1962
1 . . . . 250.00
2 . . . . 200.00
3 . . . . 175.00
4 . . . . 175.00
5 . . . . 175.00
6 . . . . 175.00

BRAM STOKER'S BURIAL OF THE RATS
Roger Corman's Comics, 1995
1 thru 3 film adaptation . . . . @2.50

BRASS
WildStorm/DC, 2000
1 (of 6) JAr,RiB 2.50
2 JAr,RiB 2.50
3 JAr,RiB 2.50
4 JAr,RiB 2.50
5 JAr,RiB,war is over 2.50
6 JAr,RiB,concl. 2.50

BRATH
Crossgen Comics, 2003
Prequel CDi(s) 3.00
1 CDi(s) 3.50
2 thru 10 CDi(s) . . . . @3.00
11 thru 17 . . . . @3.00
TPB Brath Traveler 10.00

BREAKDOWN
Devil's Due Publishing, 2004
1 CDi	3.00
1a variant (c)	3.00
2 thru 6 CDi,Aftermath	@3.00
TPB	15.00

BREAK-THRU
Malibu Ultraverse, 1993–94
1 GJ(s),GP,AV(i),A:All Ultraverse Heroes	2.75
1a Foil Edition	7.50
2 GJ(s),GP,AV(i),A:All Ultraverse Heroes	2.75

'BREED
Malibu Bravura
[Limited Series] 1994
1 JSn(a&s),Black (c),I:Stoner	3.00
2 JSn(a&s),I:Rachel	3.00
3 JSn(a&s),V:Rachel	3.00
4 JSn(a&s),I:Stoner's Mom	3.00
5 JSn(a&s),V:Rachel	3.00
6 JSn(a&s),final issue	3.00
TPB Book of Genesis, rep.#1-#6	13.00

'BREED II
Malibu Bravura
[Limited Series] 1994–95
1 JSn,The Book of Revelation	3.00
1a gold foil edition	4.00
2 JSn,A:Rachel	3.00
3 JSn,V:Actual Demon	3.00
4 JSn,Language of Demons	3.00
5 JSn,R:Rachael	3.00
6 JSn,final issue	3.00

BREEDING GROUND
Samson Comics
1 I:Mazit, Zero	2.50

Brenda Starr Reporter #1
© Dell Publishing

BRENDA LEE STORY, THE
Dell Publishing Co., 1962
1	150.00

BRENDA STARR REPORTER
Dell Publishing Co., 1963
1	300.00

BRIAN BOLLAND'S BLACK BOOK
Eclipse, 1985
1 BB	3.00

BRIAN DENHAM'S BIT TORMENT
Antarctic Press, 2006
1	4.00

BRIAN PULIDO'S BELLADONNA
Avatar Press, 2004
Preview	2.00
Preview variant (c)s	3.00
Convention Specials	3.00
1 thru 5	@4.00
1a-b thru 5a-b variant (c)s	@4.00
1c Lioness (c)	6.00
1d Serpent (c)	6.00
1e Animal protectors (c)	6.00
1f Prism foil (c)	13.00
2c Cloud Burst (c)	6.00
2d Ferocious (c)	6.00
2e Pure Rage (c)	6.00
3c premium (c)	10.00
3d Back from Dead (c)	6.00
3e Leader of Pack (c)	6.00
4c premium (c)	10.00
4d Warrior Spirit (c)	6.00
4e Moonlight (c)	6.00
5c premium (c)	10.00
5d Raw Power (c)	6.00
5e Art Nouveau (c)	6.00

BRIAN PULIDO'S MEDIEVAL LADY DEATH
Avatar Press, 2005
1	4.00
1a wraparound (c)	4.00
1b premium (c)	10.00
1c Fear Her Wrath (c)	6.00
1d portrait edition	6.00
2 thru 8	@4.00
2b thru 8b variant (c)s	@6.00
2a thru 8a wraparound (c)s	@4.00
2c thru 8c premium (c)s	@10.00

BRIDES IN LOVE
Charlton Comics, 1956–65
1	150.00
2	125.00
3 thru 10	@75.00
11 thru 30	@75.00
31 thru 44	@60.00
45	50.00

BRIGADE
Awesome Entertainment
Vol II, 2000
1 A:Badrock	3.00

BRODIE'S LAW
Markosia, 2006
Prev. Black & White
7 thru 9	@3.50

BROTHERS: THE FALL OF LUCIFER
Markosia, 2006
1 (of 10)	3.50
1a variant (c)s	@3.50
2 thru 5	@3.50

BRUCE LEE
Malibu, 1994
1 MBn(s), Stories of B.Lee	3.00
2 thru 6	@3.00

BRUTE, THE
Atlas, Feb.–July, 1975
1 thru 3	@25.00

BUBBA
Silent Devil Productions, 2006
Super Sci-Fi Special	3.00

BUCK ROGERS
Gold Key, 1964
1 P(c)	150.00
2 AMc,FBe,P(c),movie adapt	25.00
3 AMc,FBe,P(c),movie adapt	25.00
4 FBe,P(c)	25.00
5 AMc,P(c)	20.00
6 AMc,P(c)	20.00

Whitman
7 thru 9 AMc,P(c)	@30.00
10 and 11 AMc,P(c)	@20.00
12 and 13 P(c)	@15.00
14 thru 16	@10.00

BUCK ROGERS
TSR, 1990–91
1 thru 3 O:Buck Rogers	@3.00
4 thru 6 Black Barney	@3.00
7 thru 10 The Martian Wars	@3.00

BUCKY O'HARE
Continuity, 1991
1 MGo	2.75
2 thru 5	@2.50

BUDD'S BEAUTIES & BEASTS
Basement Comics, 2005
1-shot	5.00
2 (b&w) (2006)	3.25

BUGGED-OUT ADVENTURES OF RALFY ROACH
Bugged Out Comics
1 I: Ralfy Roach	3.00

BULLWINKLE
Gold Key, 1962
1 Bullwinkle & Rocky	300.00
2	200.00
3 thru 5	@150.00
6 and 7, rep.	@150.00
8 thru 11	150.00
12 rep.	75.00
13 and 14	@85.00
15 thru 19	@75.00
20 thru 24, rep.	@35.00
25	50.00

BULLWINKLE
Charlton Comics, 1970
1	125.00

Becomes:

BULLWINKLE AND ROCKY
Charlton Comics, 1970–71
2 thru 7	@75.00

COLOR PUB.

BULLWINKLE & ROCKY
Blackthorne, 1987
3-D 25.00

BULLWINKLE FOR PRESIDENT
Blackthorne, 1987
1 3-D Special 3.00

BURKE'S LAW
Dell Publishing Co., 1964
1 from TV Show 100.00
2 . . . . 75.00
3 . . . . 75.00

BUTTERNUT SQUASH
Speakeasy Comics, 2005
1 . . . . 4.00
2 . . . . 4.00

Butch Cassidy #1
© *Skywald Comics*

BUTCH CASSIDY
Skywald Comics, 1971
1 . . . . 30.00
2 & 3 . . . . @20.00

BUZZBOY: SIDEKICKS RULE
Sky Dog Press, 2006
1 . . . . 3.00
2 . . . . 3.00

CABBOT: BLOODHUNTER
Maximum Press, 1997
1 thru 4 RV . . . . @2.50

CADILLACS & DINOSAURS
Kitchen Sink, 1992
1 Rep. from Xenozoic Tales in 3-D. 6.00
Topps, 1994
1 thru 3 rep. Xenozoic Tales,
  all covers . . . . @3.00
MAN-EATER
1 thru 3, all covers 3.00
THE WILD ONES
1 thru 3, all covers 3.00

CAGES
Tundra, 1990
1 DMc 14.00
2 DMc 11.00
3 DMc 7.50
4 DMc 7.50
5 thru 7 DMc 5.00

CAIN
Harris, 1993
1 B:DQ(s),I:Cain,Frenzy 5.00
2 BSz(c),HBk,V:Mortatira 3.25

CAIN'S HUNDRED
Dell Publishing Co., May-July, 1962
1 . . . . 45.00
2 . . . . 30.00

CALIFORNIA RAISINS
Blackthorne, 1987
1 thru 4 3-D . . . . @2.50
5 3-D,O:Calif.Raisins 2.50
6 thru 8 3-D . . . . @2.50

CALVIN & THE COLONEL
Dell Publishing Co., April-June, 1962
1 . . . . 150.00
2 . . . . 100.00

CANNON BUSTERS
Devil's Due/UDON, 2004
1 . . . . 3.00
2 The Necklace 3.00

CANNON HAWKE
Aspen, 2005
Prelude 2.50
1 . . . . 3.00
1a signed 25.00
2 . . . . 3.00
3 thru 5 . . . . @3.00

CAPCOM SUMMER SPECIAL
Devil's Due, 2004
1 . . . . 12.00

CAP'N QUICK & FOOZLE
Eclipse, 1984–85
1 . . . . 3.00
2 and 3 . . . . @3.00

CAPT. ELECTRON
Brick Computers Inc., 1986
1 . . . . 2.50
2 . . . . 2.50

CAPTAIN ATOM: ARMAGEDDON
Wildstorm/DC, Oct., 2005
1 AxR(c) 3.00
1a variant JLe(c) 3.00
2 . . . . 3.00
3 Void's Death 3.00
4 V:Wildcats 3.00
5 A:The Authority 3.00
6 F:Engineer 3.00
7 Looks into the future 3.00
8 V:Authority 3.00
9 Finale 3.50
TPB Captain Atom: Armageddon. . 20.00

CAPTAIN ATOM
See: STRANGE SUSPENSE STORIES

CAPTAIN CANUCK
Comely Comix, 1975–81
1 I:Blue Fox 25.00
2 I:Red Coat 20.00
3 I:Heather 20.00
4 thru 14 . . . . 15.00
Summer Spec. #1 . . . . 15.00

CAPTAIN CANUCK: LEGACY
Comely Comix/Semple Comics, 2006
1 . . . . 3.00
1a special edition 8.00
2 . . . . 3.00

CAPTAIN CANUCK: UNHOLY WAR
Comely Comix, 2004
1 (of 3) 2.50
2 thru 3 . . . . @2.50

CAPTAIN GLORY
Topps, 1993
1 A:Bombast,Night Glider,
  Trading Card 3.25

CAPTAIN GRAVITY
Penny Farthing Press, 1998
1 by S.Vrattos & K. Martin 12.00
2 No one escapes Law of Gravity . 7.00
3 . . . . 5.00
4 . . . . 3.00
TPB 20.00
Spec. One True Hero 3.00

CAPTAIN GRAVITY AND THE POWER OF THE VRIL
Pennyfarthing Press, 2005
1 thru 6 . . . . @3.00

CAPTAIN HARLOCK: FALL OF THE EMPIRE
Eternity, 1992
1 R:Captain Harlock 2.50
2 V:Tadashi 2.50
3 Bomb on the Arcadia 2.50
4 Final issue 2.50

CAPTAIN JOHNER & THE ALIENS
Valiant, 1995
1 Rep. Magnus Robot Fighter #1–7
(Gold Key 1963–64). 3.00

CAPTAIN MARVEL
M. F. Enterprises, 1966
1 . . . . 75.00
2 . . . . 50.00
3 Fights The Bat 40.00
4 . . . . 40.00
5 Captain Marvel Presents the
  Terrible Five. 40.00

CAPTAIN NAUTICUS
Entity, 1994
1 V:Fathom 3.00
2 V:Fathom's Henchman 3.00
3 Surf's Up 3.00

CAPTAIN NICE
Gold Key, 1967
1 Ph(c) 150.00

CAPTAIN PARAGON
Americomics, 1983
1 thru 4 . . . . @3.00

CAPTAIN POWER
Continuity, 1988
1a NA,TVtie-in(direct sale) 3.00
1b NA,TVtie-in(newsstand) 3.00
2 NA 3.00

CAPTAIN STERN
Kitchen Sink Press, 1993–94
1 BWi,R.Captain Stern 5.25
2 BWr,Running Out of Time 5.00
3 thru 5 BWr,Running Out
of Time . . . . @4.00

CAPTAIN THUNDER
AND BLUE BOLT
Hero Graphics, 1987
1 I:Capt.Thunder & Paul Fremont. . 2.50
2 Paul becomes Blue Bolt 2.50
3 O:Capt.Thunder 2.50
4 V:Iguana Boys 2.50
5 V:Ian Shriver, in Scotland 2.50
6 V:Krakatoa 2.50
7 V:Krakatoa 2.50
8 A:Sparkplug (from League
of Champions) 2.50
9 A:Sparkplug 2.50
10 A:Sparkplug 2.50

CAPTAIN VENTURE
& THE LAND
BENEATH THE SEA
Gold Key, 1968
1 . . . . 90.00
2 . . . . 60.00

CAPTAIN VICTORY AND
THE GALACTIC RANGERS
Pacific, 1982
1 JK. 3.00
2 JK. 3.00
3 JK,BU:NA,I:Ms.Mystic 3.00
4 JK. 3.00
5 JK. 3.00
6 JK,SD. 3.00
7 thru 13 JK . . . . @3.00
Spec.#1 JK. 3.00

CAR 54,
WHERE ARE YOU?
**Dell Publishing Co.,
March-May, 1962**
1 Ph(c) 200.00
2 thru 7 Ph(c) . . . . @100.00

CARCA JOU
RENAISSANCE
1 and 2 . . . . @3.00

CARNOSAUR CARNAGE
Atomeka, 1993
GN 5.00

CAROLINE KENNEDY
Charlton Comics, 1961
1 . . . . 150.00

Casey Jones & Raphael #1
© Mirage

CASEY JONES
& RAPHAEL
Mirage, 1994
1 Family War. 2.75
2 Johnny Woo Woo 2.75
3 V:Johnny Woo Woo 2.75
4 9mm Raphael 2.75

CASPER & FRIENDS
Harvey, 1991
1 thru 4 . . . . @3.00
5 short stories, cont 3.00

CASPER & WENDY
Harvey, 1972–73
1 52-pg. giant 40.00
2 thru 5 . . . . @20.00
6 thru 8 . . . . @20.00

CASPER
ENCHANTED TALES
Harvey, 1992
1 short stories 3.00

CASPER
THE FRIENDLY GHOST,
1988
Blackthorne
1 3-D. 3.00

CASPER GHOSTLAND
Harvey, 1992
1 short stories 3.00

CASPER'S GHOSTLAND
**Harvey Publications,
Winter, 1958-59**
1 giant 500.00
2 . . . . 300.00
3 thru 10 . . . . @250.00
11 thru 20 . . . . @200.00
21 thru 40 . . . . @125.00
41 thru 61 . . . . @100.00
62 thru 77 . . . . @80.00
78 thru 97 . . . . @40.00
98 Dec., 1979 . . . . 40.00

CASPER
THE FRIENDLY GHOST
Harvey, 1990–91
Prev: The Friendly Ghost Casper
254 thru 260 . . . . @3.00
[Second Series], 1991–94
1 thru 14 . . . . @3.00
15 thru 28 . . . . @3.00

CASTLEVANIA:
THE BELMONT LEGACY
IDW Publishing, 2005
1 . . . . 4.00
2 thru 5 . . . . @4.00
TPB 20.00

CAST
Nautilus Comics 2005
1 . . . . 3.00
2 thru 3 . . . . @3.00
4 . . . . 3.00

CATSEYE
Awesome/Hyperwerks, 1999
0 KIA,BNa,O:Catseye 3.00

CAULDRON
Real Comics, 1995
1 Movie Style Comic 3.00
1a Variat cover 3.00

CAVE KIDS
Gold Key, 1963
1 . . . . 150.00
2 . . . . 75.00
3 thru 5 . . . . @75.00
6 . . . . 60.00
7 A:Pebbles & Bamm Bamm 65.00
8 thru 10 . . . . @50.00
11 thru 16 . . . . @50.00

CAVEWOMAN
Avatar, 1999
Color Spec. 3.50
Color Spec. Fauna (c) 3.50
Color Spec. prism foil (c) 13.00
Color Spec. Royal Blue 75.00

CENTURY
Awesome Entertainment, 2000
1 RLe 3.00
1a Millennium edition 5.00
2 . . . . 3.00
2a Millennium edition 5.00
2b signed 13.00
3 . . . . 3.00

CHAINS OF CHAOS
Harris, 1994
1 Vampirella, Rook 5.00
2 V:Chaoschild 3.25
3 Final issue 3.25

CHAMPIONS
Eclipse, 1986–87
1 I:Flare,League of Champions
Foxbat, Dr.Arcane 12.00
2 I:Dark Malice 12.00
3 I:Lady Arcane 8.00
4 O:Dark Malice 12.00
5 O:Flare 6.00
6 D:Giant Demonmaster 6.00

COLOR PUB.

[New Series]
Hero Graphics, 1987–88
1 EL,I:Madame Synn,Galloping
Galooper 5.00
2 I:Fat Man, Black Enchantress . . . 2.50
3 I:Sparkplug&Icicle,O:Flare 2.50
4 I:Exo-Skeleton Man 2.50
5 A:Foxbat 2.50
6 I:Mechanon, C:Foxbat 2.00
7 A:Mechanon,J:Sparkplug,Icicle . . 2.00
8 O:Foxbat 2.00
9 Flare #0 (Flare preview) 2.00
10 Olympus Saga #1 . . . . 2.00
11 Olympus Saga #2 . . . . 2.00
12 Olympus Saga #3 . . . . 2.00
Ann.#1 O:Giant & DarkMalice 2.75
Ann.#2 . . . . 4.00

CHAMPIONS CLASSIC
Hero Graphics, 1993
1 GP(c),Rep.1st champions series . 2.50

CHAOS! BIBLE
Chaos! Comics, 1995
1 Character Profiles 3.50

CHAOS! CHRONICLES–
THE HISTORY OF
A COSMOS
Chaos! Comics, 1999
Spec. 3.50
Spec. signed premium 15.00

CHAOS EFFECT
Valiant, 1994
Alpha DJ(c), BCh, JOy, A:All
Valiant Characters 2.50
Alpha Red (c) 75.00
Omega DJ(c), BCh, JOy, A:All
Valiant Characters 2.50
Omega Gold(c) 3.50
Epilogue pt.1 . . . . 3.00
Epilogue pt.2 . . . . 3.00

CHAOS! GALLERY
Chaos! Comics, 1997
1 . . . . 3.00

CHAOS!
NIGHTMARE THEATER
Chaos! Comics, 1997
1 (of 4) BWr(c) 2.50
2 BWr(c) 2.50
3 BWr(c) 2.50
4 BWr(c) 2.50

CHAOS QUARTERLY
Harris Comics, 1995
1 F:Lady Death 5.00
1a Premium Edition. 11.00
1b Signed,limited edition. 20.00

CHAPEL
Awesome Entertainment, 1997
1 BNa, from Spawn,Youngblood. . . 3.00

CHARLEMAGNE
Defiant, 1994
1 JiS(s),From Hero 3.00
2 JiS(s),I:Charles Smith 2.75
3 JiS(s),A:War Dancer 2.75
4 DGC(s),V:Dark Powers 2.75
5 Schism prequel 2.75
6 V:Wardancer 2.75
7 R:To Vietnam 2.75

CHARLIE CHAN
Dell Publishing Co., 1965
1 . . . . 100.00
2 . . . . 75.00

Charlton Bullseye Vol. 1 #4
© Charlton

CHARLTON BULLSEYE
Charlton, 1981–82
1 Blue Beetle, I:Rocket Rabbit 3.50
2 Capt. Catnip; Nell the Horse 2.50
3 Grundar 2.50
4 Vanguards 2.50
5 Warhund 2.50
6 Thunder-bunny 2.50
7 Captain Atom 2.50
8 weird stories. 2.50
9 . . . . 2.50
10 . . . . 2.50
Spec. #1. . . . . 2.00
Spec. #2 Atomic Mouse 2.00

CHARLTON
SPORT LIBRARY
Charlton, 1970
1 Professional Football 50.00

CHASE, THE
APC, 2004
1 (of 10) 3.50
2 . . . . 3.50
3 . . . . 3.50
4 . . . . 3.50
TPB Vol. 1 . . . . 10.00

CHASSIS
Millennium/Expand, 1995
1 I:Chassis McBain, Aero Run 3.00
1 2nd printing 3.00
1 chrome cover. 10.00
2 . . . . 3.00
2a with racing card 5.00
2b Amanda Conner cover 3.00
2c Amanda Conner cover, signed. 10.00
2d foil cover, signed 8.00
[Vol. 2] Hurricane Comics, 1998
0 by Joshua Dysart & Wm.O'Neill . 3.00
0a variant cover 3.00
1 . . . . 3.00
2 . . . . 3.00
3 . . . . 3.00

CHASTITY
Chaos! Comics, 2000
1/2 . . . . 3.00
1/2a premium ed., tattoo (c) 10.00
1/2b chromium edition 16.00
1 premium edition 10.00
Spec. #1 Reign of Terror (2000) . . . 3.00
Spec. #1 Reign of Terror, premium 10.00
Spec. #1 Love Bites (2001) 3.00
Spec. #1 Love Bites, premium ed.. 10.00
Ashcan Love Bites (2001) 6.00

CHASTITY: CRAZYTOWN
Chaos! Comics, 2002
Ashcan b&w. 6.00
1 (of 3) 3.00
1a premium edition 10.00
1b foil edition. 20.00
2 thru 3 . . . . @3.00
2a and 3a variant (c). . . . . @7.50

CHASTITY:
HEARTBREAKER
Chaos! Comics, 2002
1 . . . . 3.00
1a premium edition 10.00
1b super premium edition 20.00

CHASTITY LUST FOR LIFE
Chaos! Comics, 1999
1 (of 4) PNu 3.00
1a alternate cover. 7.00
1b alternate cover, signed 20.00
1c premium edition 10.00
2 V:Hemlock 3.00
3 . . . . 3.00

CHASTITY: RE-IMAGINED
Chaos! Comics, 2002
1 Gothic tale 3.00
1a premium edition 10.00
1b super premium edition 20.00
Ashcan re-imagined b&w. 6.00

CHASTITY ROCKED
Chaos! Comics, 1998
1 (of 4) PNu 3.00
1a & 1b variant covers 3.00
2 V:Jade 3.00
3 V:Jade 3.00
4 conclusion 3.00
Chastity/Cremator Preview
Book, B&W 5.00

CHASTITY: SHATTERED
Chaos! Comics, 2001
1 BnP,LKa. 3.00
1a premium edition 10.00
2 . . . . 3.00
3 . . . . 3.00
Ashcan. 6.00

CHASTITY:
THEATRE OF PAIN
Chaos! Comics, 1997
1 (of 3) BnP, ... 6.00
1a premium edition 15.00
2 . . . . 3.00
3 . . . . 3.00
3a premium edition 15.00
TPB rep.#1–#3, Sketchbook 10.00

CHECKMATE
Gold Key, 1962
1 Ph(c) 100.00
2 Ph(c) 75.00

CHERYL BLOSSOM
Archie Comics, 1996
1 . . . . 2.50
2 thru 10 . . . . @2.50
11 thru 37 . . . . @2.50

CHERYL BLOSSOM
GOES HOLLYWOOD
Archie Comics, 1996
1 (of 3) by Dan Parent &
 Bill Golliher 3.50
2 and 3 . . . . @3.50

CHEYENNE KID
Charlton, 1957
1 thru 7: WILD FRONTIER
(see Golden Age section)
8 DG(c), Stolen Empire. 125.00
9 Ragin Bear's Revenge. 100.00
10 AW,AT,SD(c),Custer's Last
 Stand 125.00
11 Giant size, Geronimo 125.00
12 AW,AT 125.00
13 AW,AT 125.00
14 AW 125.00
15 . . . . 125.00
16 . . . . 100.00
17 Peacemaker Colt 100.00
18 The Crumbling Idol 100.00
19 Their Last Battle 100.00
20 JSe, The Victim. 100.00
21 JSe, The Blue-Eyed Braves . . 125.00
22 JSe, Rustlers Bait 125.00
23 The Gunless Wonder 75.00
24 JSe, The Indian Fighters 100.00
25 JSe, Fury of the Gods. 100.00
26 JSe, Fat of the Land 100.00
27 Bad Medicine 75.00
28 The Alamo. 75.00
29 Cheaters' Row 75.00
30 JSe, A Short Injun War 100.00
31 thru 98. . . . . @20.00
99 Nov., 1973. . . . . 20.00

CHICKASAW
ADVENTURES
Layne Morgan Media, 2005
1 . . . . 3.00
2 The Battle of Akia 3.00
3 Tears at Fort Coffee. 3.00
4 The Making of a Storyteller 3.00

CHI-CHIAN
Sirius, 1997
1 (of 6) by Voltaire 3.00
2 thru 6 . . . . @3.00

CHILD'S PLAY 2
Innovation
1 Movie Adapt Pt 1 . . . . 2.50
2 Adapt Pt 2 . . . . 2.50
3 Adapt Pt 3 . . . . 2.50

CHILD'S PLAY 3
Innovation
1 Movie Adapt Pt 1 . . . . 2.50
2 Movie Adapt Pt.2 . . . . 2.50

CHILD'S PLAY:
THE SERIES
Innovation
1 Chucky's Back 2.50
2 Straight Jacket Blues. 2.50
3 M.A.R.K.E.D. 2.50
4 Chucky in Toys 4 You 2.50
5 Chucky in Hollywood 2.50

CHILDREN OF FIRE
Fantagor, 1987
1 thru 3 RCo . . . . @4.00

Chilling Adventures in Sorcery as Told
by Sabrina #2 © Archie Publications

CHILLING ADVENTURES
IN SORCERY AS TOLD
BY SABRINA
Archie, 1972–74
1 . . . . 65.00
2 . . . . 40.00
3 thru 5 . . . . @30.00

CHIMERA
Crossgen Comics, 2003
1 RMz,BPe 3.00
2 thru 4 . . . . @3.00
TPB 160-pg. 16.00

CHIP 'N DALE
Dell Publishing, 1955–66
4 . . . . 150.00
5 thru 10 . . . . @100.00
11 thru 30 . . . . @100.00

Gold Key, 1967
1 reprints. 75.00
2 thru 10 . . . . @30.00
11 thru 20 . . . . @20.00
21 thru 83. . . . . @15.00

CHIP 'N DALE
RESCUE RANGERS
Walt Disney, 1990
1 Rescue Rangers to the Rescue . 4.00
2 pt.2. 3.50
3 thru 7 . . . . @3.00
8 thru 18 . . . . @2.75

CHOO CHOO CHARLIE
Gold Key, 1969
1 . . . . 150.00

CHOSEN, THE
Click Comics, 1995
1 I:The Chosen 2.50
2 I:Herman Cortez 2.50

CHRISTIAN
Maximum Press, 1996
1 and 2 (of 3) RLd . . . . @3.00

CHROMA-TICK
SPECIAL EDITION
New England Press, 1992
1 Rep.Tick#1,new stories 4.00
2 Rep.Tick#2,new stories 5.00
3 thru 8 Reps.& new stories . . . @3.50

CHROME
Hot Comics, 1986
1 Machine Man 3.50
2 thru 4 . . . . @3.00

CHROME WARRIORS
IN A '59 CHEVY
Black Out Comics, 1998
0 . . . . 3.00
1 Rob Roman & Tommy Castillo . . 3.00

CHROMIUM MAN, THE
Triumphant Comics, 1994
0 Blue Logo. 6.00
0 Regular 2.50
1 I:Chromium Man,Mr.Death. 3.50
2 I:Prince Vandal. 3.00
3 thru 15 . . . . @2.50

CHROMIUM MAN:
VIOLENT PAST
Triumphant Comics
1 thru 4 JnR(s) . . . . @2.50

CHRONICLES OF CORUM
First, 1987–88
1 Michael Moorcock adapt. 3.00
2 . . . . 2.50
3 . . . . 2.50
4 thru 12 . . . . @2.50

CHRONO MECHANICS
Alias Enterprises, 2005
CN ATi 7.00
Precious Metal Collection–
 Platinum 3.50
Precious Metal Collection–Gold #2 . 3.50
Precious Metal Collection–Gold #3 . 3.50
Precious Metal Collection–
 Bronze #4 . . . . 3.50

CHTULHU TALES
Boom! Studios, 2006
1 . . . . 7.00

CICERO'S CAT
Dell Publishing Co., 1959
1 . . . . 150.00
2 . . . . 125.00

CICI
Spilled Milk, 2002
1 (of 4) 3.00
2 thru 4 . . . . @2.50
1a Variant (c) 2.50

CIMMARON STRIP
Dell Publishing Co., 1968
1 . . . . 75.00

CISCO KID, THE
Moonstone, 2004
1 (of 3) 3.00
2 . . . . 3.00
3 . . . . 3.00
TPB 11.00

CISCO KID, THE: GUNFIRE & BRIMSTONE
Moonstone Books, 2005
1	3.00
2	3.00
3	3.00

CITY KNIGHTS, THE
Windjammer 1995
1 I: Michael Walker	2.50
2 thru 4	@2.50

CITY OF HEROES
Blue King Studios, 2004
1	3.00
2 thru 12	@3.00

CITY OF TOMORROW
Wildstorm/DC, Apr., 2005
1 (of 6) HC	3.00
2 thru 6 HC	@3.00
TPB City of Tomorrow	20.00

CITY KNIGHTS, THE
Windjammer, 1995
1 I:Michael Walker	2.50
2 I:Herald	2.50
3 & 4 V:Herald	@2.50

CITY PERILOUS
Broadway Comics
1 GI,Remember the Future,pt.1	3.00
2 GI,Remember the Future,pt.2	3.00
Becomes:

KNIGHTS ON BROADWAY
3 thru 5 GI	@3.00

CLASSIC BATTLESTAR GALACTICA
D.E. (Dynamite Ent.) 2006
1	3.50
1a Classic Cylon foil (c)	
2 thru 3	@3.00
2a thru 3a variant (c)	3.00
1b thru 3b Cylon foil (c)s	@

CLASSICS ILLUSTRATED
See Also: CLASSICS ILLUSTRATED SECTION

CLASSICS ILLUSTRATED
First, 1990
1 GW,The Raven	5.00
2 RG,Great Expectations	5.00
3 KB,Thru the Looking Glass	5.00
4 BSz,Moby Dick	5.00
5 SG,TM,KE, Hamlet	5.00
6 PCr,JT, Scarlet Letter	5.00
7 DSp,Count of Monte Cristo	5.00
8 Dr.Jekyll & Mr.Hyde	5.00
9 MP,Tom Sawyer	5.00
10 Call of the Wild	5.00
11 Rip Van Winkle	5.00
12 Dr. Moreau	5.00
13 Wuthering Heights	5.00
14 Fall of House of Usher	5.00
15 Gift of the Magi	5.00
16 A: Christmas Carol	5.00
17 Treasure Island	5.00
18 The Devils Dictionary	5.00
19 The Secret Agent	5.00
20 The Invisible Man	5.00
21 Cyrano de Bergerac	5.00
22 The Jungle Book	5.00
23 Swiss Family Robinson	5.00
24 Rime of Ancient Mariner	5.00
25 Ivanhoe	5.00
26 Aesop's Fables	5.00
27 The Jungle	5.00

Classics Illustrated: The Hunchback of Notre Dame © Acclaim

CLASSICS ILLUSTRATED
Acclaim 1997–98
A Christmas Carol	5.00
A Connecticut Yankee in King Arthur's Court	5.00
All Quiet on the Western Front	5.00
A Midsummer's Night Dream	5.00
Around the World in 80 Days	5.00
A Tale of Two Cities	5.00
The Call of the Wild	5.00
Captains Courageous	5.00
The Count of Monte Cristo	5.00
Crime and Punishment	5.00
Dr. Jekyll and Mr. Hyde	6.00
Don Quixote	5.00
Frankenstein	6.00
From the Earth to the Moon	5.00
Great Expectations	5.00
Gullivers Travels	5.00
Hamlet	5.00
The House of the Seven Gables	5.00
Huckleberry Finn	5.00
The Hunchback of Notre Dame	5.00
The Illiad	5.00
The Invisible Man	6.00
Jane Eyre	5.00
Journey to the Center of the Earth	5.00
Kidnapped	5.00
The Last of the Mohicans	5.00
Les Miserables	5.00
Lord Jim	5.00
Macbeth	5.00
The Master of Ballantrae	5.00
Moby Dick	5.00
Mysterious Island	5.00
The Odyssey	5.00
Oliver Twist	5.00
The Prince and the Pauper	5.00
The Red Badge of Courage	5.00
Robinson Crusoe	5.00
Romeo & Juliet	5.00
Silas Mariner	5.00
Tom Sawyer	5.00
Wuthering Heights	5.00

CLASSICS ILLUSTRATED JUNIOR
Classics Illustrated Junior, 2003–2005
501 Show White & Seven Dwarfs	4.00
502 The Ugly Duckling	4.00
503 Cinderella	4.00
504 The Pied Piper	4.00
508 Goldilocks & the Three Bears	6.00
509 Beauty and the Beast	6.00
512 Rumplestiltskin	4.00
513 Pinocchio	6.00
514 Steadfast Tin Soldier	4.00
515 Johnny Appleseed	4.00
519 Paul Bunyan	4.00
520 Thumbelina	4.00
530 The Golden Bird	4.00
535 The Wizard of Oz	4.00
536 The Chimney Sweep	4.00
539 The Enchanted Fish	4.00
540 Tinder Box	4.00
546 The Elves and the Shoemaker	4.00
548 Magic Pitcher	6.00
563 The Wishing Well	4.00
564 Salt Mountain	4.00
565 THe Silly Princess	4.00
570 Pearl Princess	4.00
571 How Fire Came to the Indians	4.00

CLASSWAR
Com.X, 2001
1	3.00
2 thru 3	@3.00
4 thru 6	@3.50
TPB Vol. 1	13.00
1 Metal edition	50.00

CLAUS
Draco, 1997
1 by Bowden & Guichardon	3.00
2 thru 4	@3.25

CLAW THE UNCONQUERED
Wildstorm/DC, 2006
1 CDi, ASm	3.00
2 thru 6 CDi, ASm	@3.00

CLIVE BARKER'S TAPPING THE VEIN
Eclipse, 1989–92
1	10.00
2 thru 5	@8.50

CLIVE BARKER'S THE GREAT AND SECRET SHOW
IDW Publishing, 2006
1	4.00
1a variant (c)	4.00
2 thru 3	@4.00
4 Primal Scenes	4.00
5 The Devils Inside	4.00
6 Slaves and Lovers	
7	4.00
TPB Vol. 1	20.00

CLIVE BARKER'S THE THIEF OF ALWAYS
IDW Publishing, 2005
1	7.50
2 thru 3	@7.50
TPB	20.00

CLYDE CRASHCUP
Dell Publishing Co., 1963
1	300.00
2	250.00
3 thru 5	@225.00

COBALT BLUE
Innovation, 1989
Spec.#1 . . . . 3.00
Spec.#2 . . . . 3.00
1 and 2 . . . . @3.00

COBALT:
WARRIOR ANGEL
Mindchyld Comics, 2005
0 . . . . 4.00
1 . . . . 4.00
2 . . . . 4.00

CODENAME:
BLACK DEATH
Triumph Media, 2006
1 . . . . 3.00
2 thru 4 . . . . @3.00

CODENAME: DANGER
Lodestone, 1985
1 RB/BMc,I:Makor 3.50
2 KB,I:Capt.Energy 3.00
3 PS/RB 3.00
4 PG 3.00

CODE NAME:
DOUBLE IMPACT
High Impact, 1997
1 RCI. 3.00
1 variant cover 10.00
1 signed holofoil cover 15.00

CODENAME: FIREARM
Malibu Ultraverse, 1995
0 I:New Firearm 3.00
1 F:Alec Swan. 3.00
2 Dual Identity. 3.00
3 F:Hitch and Lopez 3.00
4 F:Hitch and Lopez 3.00
5 Working Together. 3.00

CODENAME:
STRIKEFORCE
Spectrum, 1984
1 . . . . 3.00

COLOSSAL SHOW, THE
Gold Key, 1969
1 . . . . 75.00

COLOUR OF MAGIC
Innovation
1 Terry Pratchet novel adapt. 3.00
2 The Sending of Eight. 3.00
3 Lure of the Worm. 3.00
4 final issue. 3.00

COLT .45
Dell Publishing Co., 1958
1 Ph(c) all 300.00
2 . . . . 260.00
3 . . . . 250.00
4 . . . . 250.00
5 . . . . 250.00
6 ATh 275.00
7 . . . . 250.00
8 . . . . 250.00
9 . . . . 250.00

COLT SPECIAL
AC Comics, 1985
1 . . . . 3.00
2 thru 3 . . . . @3.00

COMBAT
Dell Publishing Co., 1961
1 SG 100.00
2 SG 75.00
3 SG 75.00
4 JFK cover, Story 2-D 85.00
5 SG 75.00
6 SG 50.00
7 SG 50.00
8 SG 50.00
9 SG 50.00
10 SG. 50.00
11 thru 27 SG. . . . . @60.00
28 thru 40 SG. . . . . @50.00

Comet #1
© Red Circle

COMET, THE
Archie/Red Circle, 1983
1 AN,CI,O:Comet 3.00
2 AN,CI,D:Hangman 3.00

COMIC ALBUM
Dell Publishing Co.,
March–May, 1958
1 Donald Duck 200.00
2 Bugs Bunny 150.00
3 Donald Duck 175.00
4 Tom & Jerry 150.00
5 Woody Woodpecker. 150.00
6 Bugs Bunny 150.00
7 Popeye 165.00
8 Tom & Jerry 150.00
9 Woody Woodpecker. 150.00
10 Bugs Bunny 150.00
11 Popeye 165.00
12 Tom & Jerry 125.00
13 Woody Woodpecker 125.00
14 Bugs Bunny 125.00
15 Popeye 150.00
16 Flintstones. 175.00
17 Space Mouse 150.00
18 3 Stooges,Ph(c) 175.00

COMIX INTERNATIONAL
Warren Magazines, 1974
1 . . . . 125.00
2 WW,BW 75.00
3 . . . . 40.00
4 RC 40.00
5 Spring, 1977 . . . . 40.00

CONCRETE JUNGLE:
THE LEGEND OF
THE BLACK LION
Acclaim, 1998
1 (of 6) CPr,JFy,F:Terry Smalls. . . . 2.50
2 CPr,JFy,Black Lion Order 2.50
3 CPr,JFy,The Man 2.50
4 CPr,JFy 2.50
5 CPr,JFy 2.50

CONNECT
Narwain Publishing, 2005
1 . . . . 4.00

CONTAINMENT
IDW Publishing, 2005
1 . . . . 4.00
2 thru 5 . . . . @4.00
TPB 20.00

CORBEN SPECIAL
Pacific, 1984
1 RCo 5.00

CORUM: THE BULL
& THE SPEAR
First, 1989
1 thru 4 Michael Moorcock adapt.@2.50

COSMIC GUARD, THE
Devil's Due Publishing, 2004
1 JSn. 3.00
2 thru 6 JSn. . . . . @3.00

COUGAR, THE
Atlas, April–July, 1975
1 . . . . 25.00
2 O:Cougar 25.00

COUNTDOWN
WildStorm/DC, 2000
1 (of 8) JMi,AaL 2.50
2 thru 6 JMi,AaL . . . . @2.50
7 JMi,AaL,RyE,supercriminals . . . 2.50
8 JMi,AAl,RyE,concl. 3.00

COUNTER-OPS
Antarctic Press, 2003
1 . . . . 4.00
2 thru 5 . . . . @4.00

COUNTER-STRIKE
Infinity Comics, 2000
1 (of 4) 2.50
1a premium chroma-foil (c). 12.00
2 . . . . 2.50
3 . . . . 2.50
4 . . . . 2.50

COUP D'ETAT
Wildstorm/DC, 2004
1 (of 4) Sleeper, JLe 3.00
2 Stormwatch: Team Achilles 3.00
3 Wildcats Version 3.0 . . . . 3.00
4 The Authority, WPo 3.00
Spec. Afterword 3.00

COURTSHIP OF
EDDIE'S FATHER
Dell Publishing Co., 1970
1 Ph(c) 100.00
2 Ph(c) 75.00

All comics prices listed are for *Near Mint* condition.   **CVA Page 601**

Coven #6
© Awesome Entertainment

COVEN

Awesome Entertainment, 1997
1 IaC,JLb,JSb,V:The Pentad 8.00
1a variant covers 8.00
2 IaC,JLb,Who is Spellcaster? . . . 5.00
3 IaC,JLb,V:The Pentad 5.00
4 IaC,JLb,Pentad, concl. 4.00
5 IaC,JLb, ... 4.00
5 gold foil cover 8.00
6 IaC,JLb,Mardi Gras madness . . . 3.00
6 gold foil edition 8.00
7 IaC,JLb,V:Babylon 2.50
8 IaC,JLb,F:Thor, the God
 of Thunder 2.50
9 IaC,JLb, ... 2.50
Coll.Ed. #1, rep. #1–#2,
 new IaC(c) 5.00
Fan Appreciation #1, rep. #1,
 new cover 2.50
Coven/Menace S.D.Con
 preview book 5.00
TPB The Gathering 17.00

VOL 2
1 IaC,JLb 2.50
1a, b & c variant covers 2.50
1d chrome edition 10.00
1e gold foil cover 8.00
2 IaC,JLb,V:Supreme 2.50
2a Lionheart (c) 8.00
2b signed 20.00
3 IaC,JLb, Long Flight Home 2.50
3 Ruby red edition 15.00
4 IaC,JLb 2.50
5 thru 7 . . . . @3.00
Coven Sourcebook #1 . . . . 3.00

COVEN 13
No Mercy Comics, 1997
1 by Rikki Rockett & Matt Busch . . 2.50
2 thru 4 . . . . @2.50

COVEN/RE:GEX
Awesome Entertainment, 1999
1 (of 2) RLe,JLb,IaC 2.50
1a alternate IaC cover 7.00
2 JLb, conclusion 2.50

COVEN: DARK ORIGINS
Awesome Entertainment, 1999
1 . . . . 2.50
1a & b variant covers 2.50

COVEN: DARK SISTER
Avatar Press, 2001
1/2 Rio (c) 4.00
1/2 Shaw (c) 4.00
1/2 Martin (c). 4.00
1/2 Raptor attack (c) 5.00
1/2 Previews Raptor prism foil (c) 13.00
1/2 Bad Vibes (c) 6.00
1 Park (c) 3.50
1a Rio (c) 3.50
1b Martin (c) 3.50
1c wraparound (c). 4.00
1d Blue leather (c) 25.00
1e Royal Blue edition, in case . . . 75.00
1f Haunting Vision edition. 6.00
1g Prism foil edition 13.00
1h Embrace edition. 6.00
1i Embrace edition, emerald (c) . . 14.00
2 Adrian (c) edition 6.00

COVEN: SPELLCASTER
Avatar Press, 2001
1/2 Bewitched edition 6.00
1/2 Bikini edition 6.00
1/2 Rio Royal Blue (c). 75.00
1 Finch (c). 3.50
1a Rio (c) 3.50
1b Martin (c) 3.50
1c Wraparound (c) 4.00
1d Leather. 25.00
1e Finch Ruby Red(c). 25.00
1f Rio prism foil (c) 13.00
1g Royal Blue edition 75.00
2 Rio (c) 3.50
2a Shaw (c). 3.50
2b Martin (c) 3.50
2c Lyon (c) 3.50
Spec. #1 Free Spirit edition 5.96

COVEN: TOOTH & NAIL
Avatar Press, 2001
1 Adrian (c) 3.50
1a Rio (c) 3.50
1b Waller (c) 3.50
1c MMy(c) 3.50
1d Wraparound (c) 3.50
1e leather (c). 25.00
1f Royal Blue (c) 75.00
1g Bikini Edition (c). 6.00
1h Bad Ladies (c) 6.00
1i Prism exclusive (c) 13.00
1j Fantom (c). 6.00
1k Training Day (c) 6.00
1/2 Woman Scorned (c) 6.00
1/2a Prism Foil edition 13.00
1/2b Fantom edition 6.00
1/2c Adrian (c) 16-pg. 4.00
1/2d Waller (c) 4.00
1/2e MMy(c) 4.00
1/2f Martin (c) 4.00

COWBOY IN AFRICA
Gold Key, 1968
1 Chuck Conners,Ph(c) 100.00

CRACKED
Major Magazines, 1958
1 AW 300.00
2 . . . . 250.00
3 thru 6 . . . . @250.00
7 thru 10 . . . . @200.00
11 thru 20 . . . . @150.00
21 thru 30 . . . . @90.00
31 thru 36 . . . . @750.00
37 Beatles 75.00
38 thru 45 . . . . @60.00
46 Beatles 65.00
47 thru 50 . . . . @60.00
51 Beatles 65.00
52 Mysters 65.00

53 thru 56 . . . . @60.00
57 Rolling Stones. 65.00
58 . . . . 60.00
59 Laurel & Hardy 65.00
60 & 61. . . . . @60.00
62 Beatles 65.00
63 thru 68 . . . . @60.00
69 Batman 65.00
70 Elvis 65.00
71 W.C. Fields 65.00
72 thru 99 . . . . @60.00
100 . . . . 75.00
101 thru 103. . . . . @35.00
104 Godfather 75.00
105 thru 114 . . . . @35.00
115 M.A.S.H. 45.00
116 thru 118 . . . . @35.00
119 Kung Fu 40.00
120 Six Million Dollar Man 40.00
121 American Grafiti 40.00
122 thru 130. . . . . @23.00
131 Godfather 35.00
132 Baretta 35.00
133 Space:1999. . . . . 40.00
134 Fonz 35.00
135 Bionic Woman. 35.00
136 thru 145 . . . . @35.00
146 thru 148 Star Wars . . . . @50.00
149 Star Wars 45.00
150 thru 162 . . . . @30.00
163 Mork & Mindy, Alien 45.00
164 thru 174 . . . . @25.00
175 thru 200 . . . . @20.00
201 thru 252 . . . . @15.00
253 thru 300 . . . . @15.00
301 thru 348 . . . . @10.00

[THE INCREDIBLE] CRASH DUMMIES
Harvey, 1993
1 thru 3, from the toy series . . . . @2.50

CRAZYMAN
Continuity, 1992
[1st Series]
1 Embossed(c),NA/RT(i),
 O:Crazyman 6.00
2 NA/BB(c) 2.50
3 DBa,V:Terrorists. 2.50
[2nd Series], 1993
1 Die Cut(c). 2.50
2 thru 3 . . . . 2.50
4 In Demon World. 2.50

CREATURE
Antarctic Press, 1997
1 (of 2) by D.Walker&J.Maranto . . 3.00
2 concl. 3.00

CREED/TEENAGE MUTANT NINJA TURTLES
Lightning Comics, 1996
1 . . . . 3.00
1 variant cover 3.00

CREED: CRANIAL DISORDER
Lightning Comics, 1996
1 (of 3) 3.00
1a variant cover, *Previews*
 exclusive 3.00
1b Platinum edition 9.00
1c Platinum edition, autographed 16.00
2 . . . . 3.00
2a variant cover 3.00

COLOR PUB.

CREMATOR: HELL'S GUARDIAN
Chaos! Comics, 1998
1 (of 5) LJi 3.00
2 . . . . 3.00
3 V:Asteroth 3.00
4 . . . . 3.00
5 . . . . 3.00

CRIME MACHINE
Skywald Publications, 1971
1 JK 90.00
2 AT 50.00

CRIME PATROL
Gemstone, 2000
1 rep 2.50
2 rep. Fall 1948 . . . . 2.50
3 rep. Winter 1948 . . . . 2.50
4 rep. Feb. 1949 . . . . 2.50
5 rep 2.50
6 rep 2.50
7 rep 2.50
8 rep. Oct. 1949 . . . . 2.50
9 rep. Dec. 1949 . . . . 2.50
10 rep. Feb. 1950 issue 2.50
`Annuals'
TPB Vol.#1 rep. #1–#5 . . . . 13.50
TPB Vol.#2 rep. #6–#10 . . . . 13.50

CRIME SUSPENSE STORIES
Russ Cochran, 1992
1 Rep. C.S.S. #1 (1950) 3.00
2 thru 7 Rep. C.S.S. . . . . @3.00
8 thru 15 Rep. . . . . @3.00
Gemstone, 1996
16 thru 27 EC comics reprint . . . . @3.00
Ann.#1, rep. #1–#5 . . . . 9.00
Ann.#2, rep. #6–#10 . . . . 9.00
Ann.#3, rep. #11–#15 . . . . 10.00
Ann.#4, rep. #16–#19 . . . . 10.50
Ann.#5, rep. #20–#23 . . . . 11.00
Ann.#6 rebinding #24–#27 . . . . . . 11.00

CRIMSON NUN
Antarctic Press, 1997
1 (of 4) 3.00
2 . . . . 3.00
3 . . . . 3.00
4 concl 3.00

CRIMSON PLAGUE
Event Comics, 1997
1 GP,F:DiNA: Simmons 3.00
2 GP, ... 3.00

CROSSFIRE
Eclipse, 1984–86
1 DSp 3.00
2 thru 11 DSp . . . . @2.50
12 DSp,DSt(c),M.Monroe(c) & story 2.50
13 DSp 2.50
14 DSp 2.50
15 DSp,O:Crossfire 2.50
16 DSp,The Comedy Place 2.50
17 DSp,Comedy Place, Pt.2 . . . . . . 2.50
See B&W

CROSSFIRE & RAINBOW
Eclipse, 1986
1 DSp,V:Marx Brothers 2.50
2 DSp,PG(c),V:Marx Brothers 2.50
3 DSp,HC(c),A:Witness 2.50
4 DSp,DSt(c),This Isn't Elvis 3.50

Crossgen Chronicles #1
© *Crossgen Comics*

CROSSGEN CHRONICLES
Crossgen Comics, 2000
1 RMz, 48-pg 4.50
2 RMz,GP 4.00
2a 2nd printing 11.00
3 BKs,GP, 48-page 5.00
4 MWa,GP, 48-page 4.00
5 RMz,GP 4.00
6 thru 8 . . . . @4.00

CROSSOVERS, THE
CG Entertainment, 2003
1 (of 6) Cross Currents 3.00
2 thru 11 . . . . @3.00
TPB Vol. 1 Cross Currents 10.00

CROSSROADS
First, 1988
1 Sable,Whisper 4.00
2 Sable,Badger 4.00
3 JSon,JAl,Badger/Luther Ironheart 4.00
4 Grimjack/Judah Macabee 4.00
5 LM,Grimjack/Dreadstar/Nexus . . 4.00

CROUCHING TIGER, HIDDEN DRAGON
Comicson, 2002
GN #1 . . . . 14.00
GN #2 thru #8 . . . . @14.00
GN Vol. 9 thru Vol. 12 . . . . @14.00
GN Vol. 1 thru Vol. 4 revised
   deluxe . . . . @14.00

CROW, THE: CITY OF ANGELS
Kitchen Sink, 1996
1 thru 3 movie adaptation . . . . . @3.00
1 thru 3 movie adaptation,
   photo covers . . . . @3.00
TPB The Crow, The Movie, new
   printing 19.00

CRUX
Crossgen Comics, 2001
1 MWa,SEp 7.00
2 MWa,SEp 5.00
3 thru 8 MWa,SEp . . . . @3.00
9 thru 20 . . . . @3.00
21 thru 33 . . . . @3.00
TPB Vol. 1 . . . . 16.00

TPB Vol. 2 . . . . 16.00
TPB Vol. 3 Strangers in Atlantis . . . 16.00
TPB Vol. 4 Chaos Reborn 16.00

CRYBABY
Event Comics, 1999
1 GrL,SLo 3.00
1a limited, signed 10.00

CRYING FREEMAN III
Viz, 1991
1 A:Dark Eyes,Oshu 6.00
2 A:Dark Eyes, V:Oshu 5.25
3 Freeman vs. Oshu 5.25
4 Freeman Defeated 5.25
5 Freeman clones, A:Nitta 5.25
6 V:Nitta 5.25
7 . . . . 5.00
8 . . . . 5.00
9 . . . . 5.00

CRYING FREEMAN IV
Viz, 1992
1 B:The Pomegranate 5.00
2 thru 7 . . . . @3.00
8 E:The Pomegranate 3.00
[2nd Series]
1 The Festival 2.50

CRYPTIC WRITINGS OF MEGADETH
Chaos! Comics, 1997
1 BnP 3.00
1a Tour Edition, leather 20.00
1b Tour Edition, deluxe 30.00
2 BnP 3.00
3 BnP 3.00
4 BnP 3.00
TPB 13.00

CSI: CRIME SCENE INVESTIGATION
IDW Publishing, 2003
1 (of 5) 5.00
1a photo(c) 8.00
2 thru 3 . . . . @5.00
4 thru 5 . . . . @4.00
GN Thicker Than Blood 7.00
GN Miami–Smoking Gun 7.00
GN Miami–Thou Shalt Not 7.00
GN Miami–Blood/Money 7.00
TPB Vol. 1 Serial 20.00

CSI: BAD RAP
IDW Publishing, 2003
1 (of 5) 4.00
2 . . . . 4.00
3 . . . . 4.00
5 . . . . 4.00
TPB 20.00

CSI: DEMON HOUSE
IDW Publishing, 2004
1 (of 5) 4.00
2 thru 5 . . . . @4.00
TPB 20.00

CSI: DOMINOS
IDW Publishing, 2004
1 . . . . 4.00
2 . . . . 4.00
3 . . . . 4.00
4 . . . . 4.00
5 . . . . 4.00
TPB 20.00

COLOR PUB.

CSI: DYING IN THE GUTTERS
IDW Publishing, 2006
```
1 ............................. 4.00
2 thru 4 ..................... @4.00
```

CSI: MIAMI
IDW Publishing, 2003
```
GN Smoking Gun.............. 7.00
GN Thou Shalt Not ........... 7.00
GN Blood/Money .............. 7.00
TPB ........................ 20.00
```

CSI: NY-BLOODY MURDER
IDW Publishing, 2005
```
1 ............................. 4.00
2 thru 5 ..................... @4.00
```

CSI: SECRET IDENTITY
IDW Publishing, 2005
```
1 ............................. 4.00
2 thru 5 ..................... @4.00
TPB ........................ 20.00
TPB ........................ 20.00
```

CURSE OF RUNE
Malibu Ultraverse, 1995
```
1A CU,Rune/Silver Surfer tie-in ... 2.50
1B CU, alternate cover ........ 2.50
2 COntrol of the Soul Gem...... 2.50
3 F:Marvel's Adam Warlock ..... 2.50
4 N:Adam Warlock ............. 2.50
```

CURSE OF THE BLOOD CLAN, THE
Dead Dog Comics, 2005
```
1 (of 3) by Mark Kidwell ........ 5.00
1a variant (c) ................. 5.00
2 ............................. 5.00
3 ............................. 5.00
```

CVO: AFRICAN BLOOD
IDW Publishing, 2006
```
1 ............................. 4.00
```

CVO: COVERT VAMPIRIC OPERATIONS–ARTIFACT
IDW Publishing, 2003
```
1 ............................. 4.00
2 thru 3 ..................... @4.00
GN ........................... 6.00
TPB ........................ 20.00
1-shot Human Touch (2004) ..... 4.00
GN ........................... 6.00
```

CVO: HUMAN TOUCH
IDW Publishing, 2004
```
1-shot ....................... 4.00
```

CVO: ROGUE STATE
IDW Publishing, 2004
```
1 ............................. 4.00
2 thru 5 ..................... @4.00
TPB ........................ 20.00
```

CYBER CITY
CPM Comics, 1995
Part One
```
1 I:Oedo City................. 3.00
2 Sengoku.................... 3.00
```
Part Two
```
1 Based on Animated Movie...... 3.00
```

CYBERCRUSH: ROBOTS IN REVOLT
Fleetway/Quality
```
1 inc.Robo-Hunter,Ro-Busters .... 2.50
2 and 3 ..................... @2.50
4 and 5 V:Terraneks ......... @2.50
```

Cyberfrog #2
© Harris Comics

CYBERFROG
Harris, 1995
```
0 O:Cyberfrog ................. 3.00
0 AAd(c), signed ............. 20.00
0 Alternate AAd(c)............ 10.00
1 ............................. 2.50
2 thru 4 ..................... @3.00
```

CYBERFROG: RESERVOIR FROG
Harris, 1996
```
1 Preview Ashcan, signed
   & numbered............... 15.00
1 EL(c),V:the Swarm,
   Mr. Skorpeone ............ 3.00
2 ............................. 3.00
```

CYBERHOOD
Entity Comics, 1995
```
1 R:Cyberhood ................ 2.50
1a with PC Game .............. 7.00
```

CYBERNARY 2.0
WildStorm/DC, 2001
```
1 (of 6) R:Yumiko Gamorra....... 3.00
2 F:MechaMax ................. 3.00
3 F:Toshiro .................. 3.00
4 secret race of cyborgs ........ 3.00
5 revolution or evolution ........ 3.00
6 Kaizen Gamorra, concl........ 3.00
```

CYBERPUNK
Innovation, 1989
```
1 ............................. 2.50
2 ............................. 2.50
Book 2,#1.................... 2.50
Book 2,#2.................... 2.50
```

CYBERPUNK: THE SERAPHIM FILES
Innovation, 1990
```
1 and 2 .................... @2.50
```

CYBERPUNX
Maximum Press, 1997
```
1 MHw, ...................... 2.50
```

CYBERRAD
Continuity, 1991
```
1 NA layouts,I:Cyberran ........ 3.00
2 NA I/o..................... 2.50
3 NA I/o..................... 2.50
4 NA I/o..................... 2.50
5 NA I/o Glow in the Dark cov ... 5.00
6 NA I/o,Pullout poster ......... 2.50
7 NA I/o,See-thru(c) ........... 2.50
```
[2nd Series], 1992
```
1 Hologram cover............. 2.50
2 NA(c),The Disassembled Man... 2.50
```
[3rd Series]
```
1 Holo.(c),just say no .......... 3.50
```
[4th Series], 1993
Deathwatch 2000]
```
1 Deathwatch 2000 pt.8,w/card ... 2.50
2 Deathwatch 2000 pt. w/card .... 2.50
```

CYBRID
Maximum Press, 1995
```
1 F:Cybrid, I:The Clan ......... 3.00
```

CYBRID
Maximum Press, 1997
```
0 RLd, 48pg ................. 3.50
1 MsM,BNa................... 3.00
2 MsM,BNa................... 3.00
```

CYNDER
Immortelle Studios, 1996
1 thru 3: see B&W
```
Ann. #1 ..................... 3.00
```
Series II, 1997
```
1 A:Nira X ................... 3.00
```

CYNDER/NIRA X
Immortelle Studios, 1996
```
1 x-over..................... 3.00
1 variant cover ............... 3.00
1 gold edition ............... 10.00
```

DAEMONSTORM
Caliber, 1997
```
1 TM(c),JMt.................. 4.00
1 signed ..................... 4.00
```

DAEMONSTORM: DEADWORLD
Caliber
```
one-shot .................... 4.00
```

DAEMONSTORM: OZ
Caliber, 1997
```
1 ............................. 4.00
```

DAGAR THE INVINCIBLE
Gold Key, 1972–82
```
1 O:Daggar;I:Villians Olstellon
   & Scorpio................. 60.00
2 ........................... 35.00
3 I:Graylon ................. 25.00
4 ........................... 25.00
5 ........................... 25.00
6 1st Dark Gods story ........ 20.00
7 thru 10 .................. @20.00
11 thru 19 ................. @15.00
```

DAI KAMIKAZE
Now, 1987–88
1 Speed Racer	7.00
1a 2nd printing	2.50
2 thru 12	@2.50

DAKTARI
Dell Publishing Co., 1967
1 Ph(c)	75.00
2 Ph(c)	50.00
3 Ph(c)	50.00
4 Ph(c)	50.00

DALGODA
Fantagraphics, 1984–86
1	3.50
2 KN,I:Grinwood'Daughter	3.00
3 KN	2.50
4 thru 8	@2.50

DALKIEL:
THE PROPHECY
Verotik, 1998
1-shot, prequel to Satanika	4.00

DAMAGED, THE
A-10 Comics, 2006
1	3.00

DANGER GIRL:
BACK IN BLACK
Wildstorm/DC, Nov., 2005
1 (of 4)	3.00
2	3.00
3 Ruby	3.00
4 finale	3.00

DANGER GIRL: KAMIKAZE
WildStorm/DC, 2000
1 (of 2)	3.00
1a variant(c)	3.00
2 concl.	3.00
GN Viva Las Danger	5.00
Spec. Danger Girl 3-D	5.00
Spec. Hawaiian Punch	5.00

DANGER RANGER
Checker Comics, 1998
1 I:Kirby Jackson, BSz(c)	2.50
2	2.50

Daniel Boone #1
© Gold Key

DANIEL BOONE
Gold Key, 1965–69
1	200.00
2 thru 5	@150.00
6 thru 14	@125.00
15	100.00

DARE
Fantagraphics, 1991
1 F:Dan Dare	2.75
2 F:Dan Dare	2.75
3 and 4 F:Dan Dare	@2.50

DARE THE IMPOSSIBLE
Fleetway/Quality
1 DGb,rep.Dan Dare from 2000AD	2.50
2 thru 14 DGb	@2.50

DARK, THE
Continuum, 1990
1 LSn(c),MBr,V:Futura	4.00
2 LSn,Shot by Futura	3.00
3 MBr,Dark has amnesia	3.00
4 GT(c),MBr,O:The Dark.	3.00
Convention Book 1992 MBr,GP, MFm,MMi,VS,LSn,TV	5.00
Convention Book 1993 MBr,PC, ECh,BS,BWi,GP(c),Foil(c),	4.00
[2nd Series], 1994
1 Dark Regains Memory	3.00
1a Signed, Foil Cover	2.75
1 BS(c),Red Foil(c),	3.00
1a BS(c),newstand ed.	3.00
1b BS(c),Blue foil	3.00
2 War on Crime.	2.75
3 Geoffery Stockton	2.50
3 BS(c),Foil(c),	3.00
4 I:First Monster	2.50
4 GP(c),Foil(c),w/cards	3.00
5 thru 9	@2.50

DARK CHYLDE
Maximum Press, 1996
1 RQu	10.00
1a Am.Entertainment edition.	15.00
1b variant cover	9.00
2 RQu	7.00
2 Variant cover	6.00
3 RQu	4.00
3 Variant cover	5.00
4 RQu	5.00
5 RQu,No One Here Gets Out Alive.	5.00
Spec. Dark Chylde/Avengelyne RLd, RQu,I:Witch Tower.	3.00
Spec. Dark Chylde/Glory RQu,	3.00
Darkchylde Entertainment, 2001
0 remastered, RQu (2001)	3.00
Last Issue special (2002).	4.00
Last issue exclusive variant(c).	4.00

DARKCHYLDE
REDEMPTION
Darkchylde Entertainment, 2001
1 RQu	3.00
2 thru 3	@3.00

DARK DAYS
IDW Publishing, 2003
1 (of 6)	4.50
2 thru 6	@4.25
TPB	20.00

DARK DOMINION
Defiant, 1993–94
1 SD,I:Michael Alexander	3.25
2 LWn(s),SLi(i),	2.75

3 LWn(s),SLi(i),	2.75
4 LWn(s),B:I loxhunt	3.00
5 thru 7 LWn(s)	@2.75
8 thru 12 LWn(s)	@2.50

DARKEST HORROR OF
MORELLA, THE
Verotik, 2006
1	4.00
1 fan club (c)	10.00

DARKHAM VALE
APC, 2003
1 (of 10) by Jack Lawrence	3.50
2 thru 9	@3.50
10 finale	4.00
Spec. #0	3.00
TPB Vol. 1 thru Vol. 2.	@20.00
Complete Darkham Vale TPB	33.00

DARKHAM VALE: THE
DRACOU IMPERATIVE
APC, 2004
1 thru 4	@3.50
TPB Vol. 1	17.00

DARKHAM VALE:
UPRISING
APC, 2005
1 (of 10)	3.50
2 thru 3	@3.50

DARKLON THE MYSTIC
Pacific, 1983
1 JSn.	2.50

DARKMAN VS. ARMY OF
DARKNESS
D.E. (Dynamite Ent.) 2006
1 (of 4) Kbk,RSt,JFy	3.50
2	3.50
1a thru 2a variant (c)s.	@3.50

DARK MISTS
APC, 2005
1 (of 4)	3.50
TPB Vol. 1	15.00
Markosia, 2005
3	3.50
4	3.50

DARKMINDS:
MACROPOLIS
Dreamwave, 2002
1	3.00
2 thru 4	@3.00
3a variant Pat Lee (c)	3.00
TPB Vol. 1	10.00
Vol. 2
1 thru 4	@3.00
TPB Vol. 1	10.00
PocketBook Vol. 1	8.00

DARK ONE'S THIRD EYE
Sirius, 1996
one-shot Vol. 1 DOe	5.00
Vol. 2 DOe	5.00

DARK SHADOWS
Gold Key, 1969
1 W/Poster,Ph(c).	800.00
2 Ph(c)	350.00
3 W/Poster,Ph(c).	500.00
4 thru 7,Ph(c)	@250.00

All comics prices listed are for *Near Mint* condition.

8 thru 10	@200.00
11 thru 20	@150.00
21 thru 35	@125.00

DARK SHADOWS
Innovation, 1992
1 Based on 1990's TV series	3.50
2 O:Victoria Winters	2.50
3 Barnabus Imprisoned	2.50
4 V: Redmond Swann	2.75

[2nd Series]
1 A:Nathan	2.75
2 thru 4	2.75
Dark Shadows:Resurrected	16.00

DARK SIDE
Maximum Press, 1997
1 RLd,RQu	3.00

DARKSHRINE
Antarctic Press, 1999
1 by Shelby Robertson	3.00
1a deluxe	6.00
2 16-page	2.50

DARKSTALKERS
Devil's Due/UDON, 2004
1	3.00
2 thru 6	@3.00
5 power foil (c)	4.00
6 evil foil (c)	4.00
TPB Vol. 1	13.00

DARKSTORM
Alias Enterprises, 2006
0	3.50

Darkwing Duck #3
© Walt Disney

DARKWING DUCK
Walt Disney, 1991
1 I:Darkwing Duck	3.00
2 V:Taurus Bulba	3.00
3 Fowl Play	3.00
4 End o/t beginning,final issue	3.00

DARQUE PASSAGES
Acclaim, 1997
1 (of 4) sequal to Master Darque	2.50
1 signed edition	4.00
2	2.50
3 A:Pere Jean, Voodoo King	2.50
4 conclusion	2.50

DAVID: THE SHEPHERD'S SONG
Alias Enterprises, 2005
1 (of 3)	3.00
2 thru 3	@3.00
TPB Vol. 1	9.00

DAWN
Sirius, 1995–97
1 JLi,R:Dawn	12.00
1a white trash edition	30.00
1b black light edition	20.00
1c look sharp edition	40.00
2 JLi, Trip to Hell	7.00
2 variant cover	15.00
3 JLi	6.00
3 limited edition	20.00
4 JLi,The Gauntlet	5.00
4a variant cover	12.00
5 JLi,Everybody Dies	4.00
5a variant cover	12.00
6 (of 6) JLi	4.00
6a variant cover	10.00
TPB Lucifer's Halo	20.00
TPB Tears of Dawn	18.00
10th Anniv. Spec.	3.00
10th Anniv. Spec. sgn,num.	5.00
Portable Dawn, art work	10.00

DAWN: PIN-UP GODDESS
Linsner.com, 2001
Spec.	3.00
Spec. Limited, signed	12.00

DAWN: THE RETURN OF THE GODDESS
Sirius, 1999
1 (of 4) JLi	3.00
1a limited, signed	25.00
2 A:Marinen	3.00
3 thru 4	@3.00
2a thru 4a deluxe	@20.00

DAY OF THE DEAD: THE RISING OF BUB
Dead Dog Comics, 2006
1 (of 3)	5.00
2 thru 3	@5.00

DAZEY'S DIARY
Dell Publishing Co., 1962
1	75.00

DEAD @ 17
Viper Comics, 2003
1 (of 4)	25.00
2	22.00
3	12.00
4	12.00
Rough Cut #1	15.00
Rough Cut #2	5.00
Rough Cut #3	5.00
TPB Vol. 1	15.00
TPB Vol. 2 Blood of Saints	15.00
TPB Vol. 3 Revolution	15.00

Vol. 2 (2006)
1	3.25
2 thru 3	@3.25

DEAD @ 17: BLOOD OF SAINTS
Viper Comics, 2004
1 (of 4)	10.00
2 thru 4	@4.00

DEAD @ 17: PROTECTORATE
Viper Comics, 2005
1 (of 3)	3.00

Vol. 2 (2006)
1	3.25
2 thru 3	@3.25

DEAD @ 17: REVOLUTION
Viper Comics, 2004
1 (of 4)	3.00
2 thru 4	@3.00

DEAD BOYS: DEATH'S EMBRACE
London Night, 1996
1 EHr.	3.00
1 platinum edition	6.00

DEAD CLOWN
Malibu, 1996
1 I:Force America	2.50
2 I:Sadistic Six	2.50
3 TMs(s),last issue	2.50

DEADFORCE
Antarctic Press, 1999
1 (of 3) by Roy Burdine	3.00
2	3.00
3	3.00

DEAD KING
Chaos! Comics, 1997
1 (of 4) Burnt, pt.1, F:Homicide	3.00
2 Burnt, pt.2	3.00
3 Burnt, pt.3	3.00
4 Burnt, pt.4, concl.	3.00
TPB Dead King Burnt	13.00

DEAD MEN TELL NO TALES
Arcana Studio, 2005
1 (of 4)	4.00
2 thru 4	@4.00

DEADSIDE
Acclaim, 1998
1 (of 4) PJe,	2.50
2 thru 4	@2.50

DEAL WITH THE DEVIL
Alias Enterprises, 2005
1 (of 5)	0.75
2 thru 5	@3.00
TPB	15.00

DEAR NANCY PARKER
Gold Key, 1963
1 P(c)	75.00
2 P(c)	50.00

DEATHBLOW
Wildstorm/DC, Oct., 2006
1	3.00
1a variant (c)	3.00
2	3.00

DEATHBLOW: BY BLOWS
WildStorm/DC, 1999
1 (of 3) AMo,JBa	3.00
2 AMo,JBa	3.00

DEATH COMES TO DILLINGER
Silent Devil Productions, 2006
1 (of 2) 3.00
2 . . . . 3.00

DEATHDEALER
Verotika, 1995
1 FF(c), I:Deathdealer. 15.00
2 thru 4 FF(c) . . . . @12.00

DEATHMASK
Future Comics, 2003
1 DvM,DG,BL 3.00
2 thru 9 . . . . @3.00
TPB 16.00

DEATHMATE
Valiant/Image, 1993
Preview (Advanced Comics) 2.50
Preview (Previews) 2.50
Preview (Comic Defense Fund). . . . 4.00
Prologue BL,JLe,RLd,Solar meets
   Void 3.25
Prologue Gold 4.00
Blue SCh, HSn, F:Solar, Magnus,
   Battlestone, Livewire, Stronghold,
   Impact, Striker, Harbinger, Brigade,
   Supreme 3.00
Blue Gold Ed. 4.00
Yellow BCh,MLe,DP,F:Armstrong,
   H.A.R.D.C.A.T.S.,Ninjak,Zealot,
   Shadowman,Grifter,Ivar. 3.00
Yellow Gold Ed. 4.00
Black JLe,MS,F:Warblade,Ripclaw,
   Turok,X-O Manowar 4.00
Black Gold Ed. 6.00
Red RLd,JMs, ... 4.00
Red Gold Ed. 3.00
Epilogue 2.50
Epilogue Gold 3.00

DEATH OF HARI KARI
Blackout Comics, 1997
0 . . . . 3.00
0 super Sexy Kari Cover. 10.00
0 3-D super Sexy Kari Cover 15.00

DEATH OF LADY VAMPRE
Blackout Comics, 1995
1 V:Baraclaw. 3.00
1 Commemorative Issue. 10.00

DEATHRACE 2020
Cosmic Comics, 1995
1 Pat Mills, Tony Skinner 2.50
2 V:Spyda, Sawmill Jones 2.50
3 O:Frankenstein 2.50
4 Deathrace cont. 2.50
5 F:Death Racers, D:Alchoholic . . . 2.50
6 V:Indestructiman 2.50
7 Smallville Mall 2.50

DEATH RATTLE
Kitchen Sink, 1985–88
1 thru 7 . . . . @4.00
8 I:Xenozoic Tales. 9.00
9 thru 18 . . . . @3.00

DECOY
Pennyfarthing Press, 1999
1 (of 4) 2.75
2 . . . . 2.75
3 . . . . 2.75
4 . . . . 2.75

TPB 16.00
GN Vol. 1 Menagerie (2005) 20.00

DECOY: STORM OF THE CENTURY
Pennyfarthing Press, 2002
1 (of 4) 3.00
2 thru 4 . . . . @3.00

DEFENDERS, THE
Dell Publishing Co., 1962
1 . . . . 75.00
2 . . . . 50.00

DEFEX
Devil's Due Publishing, 2004
1 Aftermath 3.00
1a variant (c). 3.00
2 thru 6 Aftermath . . . . @3.00
TPB 15.00

DEFIANT: ORIGIN OF A UNIVERSE
Defiant, 1993
1 Giveaway. 2.50

Deity Vol. 2 #3
© Awesome

DEITY
Hyperwerks, 1997
0 . . . . 3.00
1 KIA 5.00
1a Director's Cut. 3.00
2 thru 6 KIA . . . . @3.00
TPB rep. #1–#3 . . . . 8.00
TPB rep. #4–#6 . . . . 8.00

VOL II Awesome/Hyperworks, 1998
1 KIA,BNa, F:Jamie 3.00
1a Limited edition 8.00
1b Silver Foil edition 13.00
1c Gold Edition 20.00
2 KIA,BNa, A:Diamond Diaz 3.00
3 KIA,BNa, The Soul Crusher. 3.00
4 KIA,BNa, A:Ogden 3.00
5 KLa,BNa,V:Ma'Shiva 3.00

DEITY II: CATSEYE
Hyperwerks, 1998
1 KIA,BNa,F:Digby 3.00
2 KIA,BNa,A:II. 3.00
3 KIA,BNa,F:Catseye 3.00
4 KIA,BNa,conclusion 3.00

DEMON-HUNTER
Atlas, 1975
1 The Harvester of Eyes. 25.00

DEMONIQUE
London Night, 1996
0 Manga 3.00
1 & 2 EHr . . . . @3.00

DEMONSLAYER
Avatar Press, 2001
0 16-page, signed. 6.00
TPB Vol. 1 . . . . 20.00

DEMONSLAYER: FUTURE SHOCK
Avatar Press, 2002
1/2 Eradicate Edition 6.00

DEMONSLAYER: PATH OF TIME
Avatar, 2002
1 MMy 3.50
1a Medieval (c). 3.50
1b Ninja (c). 3.50
1c Western (c) 3.50
1d Matt Martin (c) 3.50
1e Serenity (c) 6.00
1f bondage (c). 6.00
1g Prism foil (c). 13.00
1/2 . . . . 4.00
1/2 Pirate (c) 4.00
1/2 Cave Girl (c). 4.00
1/2 Bikini (c). 4.00
1/2 Martin (c) 4.00

DEMONSLAYER: PROPHECY
Avatar Press, 2001
1 MMy. 3.50
1a Celtic (c). 3.50
1b Hell on Wheels (c). 3.50
1c Leather (c). 20.00
1d lace edition. 6.00
1e Bad Omens (c) 6.00
1f Mouth of Evil edition 6.00
1g Prism foil (c). 13.00

DEMONSLAYER: RAVE
Avatar Press, 2001
Spec. 3.50
Spec. Bad Schoolgirl (c) 3.50
Spec. Silent Moment (c). 3.50
Rave in Style (c). 6.00
Rave Previews prism foil (c) 13.00

DEMONSLAYER: REBIRTH
Awesome Entertainment, 2000
1 . . . . 3.00

DEMONSLAYER: VENGEANCE
Avatar Press, 2001
1 (of 2) MMy (c) 3.50
1a Park (c) 3.50
1b Wraparound (c) 4.00
1c Red Velvet (c) 20.00
1d prism foil (c) 13.00
1e fire (c). 6.00
1f ice (c) 6.00
1g Royal Blue edition 75.00
2 MMy, concl. 3.50
2a Bikini (c). 3.50
2b Jungle Girl (c) 3.50
2c Ruins edition 6.00

DEMONWARS: EYE FOR AN EYE
Crossgen Comics, 2003
1 (of 5) 3.00
2 thru 5 . . . . @3.00
TPB 10.00

DEMONWARS: TRIAL BY FIRE
Crossgen Comics, 2002
2 thru 5 . . . . @3.00
TPB Vol. 1 Trial by Fire 13.00

DEN
Fantagor, 1988
1 thru 10 RCo . . . . @2.50

DEN SAGA
Tundra/Fantagor, 1992–94
1 RCo,O:Den begins. 5.00
2 thru 4 RCo . . . . @5.00

DENNIS THE MENACE
Fawcett, 1960-61
Fun Book #1 . . . . 75.00
And his Pal Joey #1. . . . . 50.00
And his Dog Ruff #1 . . . . 50.00
Television Special #1 . . . . 60.00
Triple Feature #1 . . . . 60.00
Television Special #2 . . . . 35.00

DENNIS THE MENACE AND HIS FRIENDS
[VARIOUS SUBTITLES]
Fawcett, 1969–1980
1 thru 10 rep. . . . . @35.00
11 thru 20 rep. . . . . @20.00
21 thru 46 rep. . . . . @15.00

DENNIS THE MENACE GIANTS
[VARIOUS SUBTITLES]
Fawcett, 1955–69
N# Vacation Special. 300.00
N# Christmas. 250.00
2 thru 10 . . . . @200.00
11 thru 20. . . . . @150.00
21 thru 30. . . . . @100.00
31 thru 40. . . . . @75.00
41 thru 75. . . . . @75.00
Becomes:

DENNIS THE MENACE BONUS MAGAZINE
[VARIOUS SUBTITLES]
Fawcett, 1970–79
76 thru 100. . . . . @20.00
101 thru 120 . . . . @15.00
121 thru 185. . . . . @10.00
186 thru 196 Big Bonus Series . . @8.00
Becomes:

DENNIS THE MENACE
Fawcett, 1979–80
#16 Fun Fest 5.00
#17 Fun Fest 5.00
#10 Big Bonus Series 5.00
#11 Big Bonus Series 5.00

DEPUTY DAWG
Gold Key, 1965
1 . . . . 225.00

Dennis the Menace Bonus #186
© Fawcett

DER VANDALE
Innervision, 1998
1 (of 3) 2.50
2 (of 3) 2.50
3 (of 3) 2.50
3 variant cover 2.50

DESERT STORM JOURNAL
Apple Comics, 1991
1 Hussein on (c) 2.75
1a Schwartzkopf on (c). 2.75
2 thru 8 . . . . @2.75

DESOLATION JONES
Wildstorm/DC, May, 2005
1 WEI(s),JWi. 3.00
2 WEI(s),JWi. 3.00
3 WEI(s),JWi. 3.00
4 WEI(s),JWi. 3.00
5 WEI(s),JWi. 3.00
6 WEI(s),JWi. 3.00
7 WEI(s), To Be In England 3.00
TPB 15.00

DESPERADOES: BANNERS OF GOLD
IDW Publishing, 2004
1 . . . . 4.00
2 thru 5 . . . . @4.00
TPB 20.00

DESTROYER DUCK
Eclipse, 1982–84
1 JK,AA,SA,I:Groo 12.00
2 JK,AA,Starling 5.00
3 thru 7 JK. . . . . @5.00

DESTRUCTOR, THE
Atlas, 1975
1 thru 4 WW,SD . . . . @35.00

DETECTIVES, INC.
Eclipse, 1985
1 MR,rep.GraphicNovel 3.00
2 MR 2.50
[2nd Series]
1 GC,A Terror of Dying Dreams . . . 2.50
2 GC 2.50
3 GC,Cut to the Bone. 2.50

DETONATOR
Chaos! Comics, 1994–95
1 I:Detonator. 3.00
2 V:Messiah & Mindbender. 3.00

DEVI
Virgin Comics, 2006
1 by Siddharth Kotian 3.50
2 thru 5 . . . . @3.25

DEVIL KIDS STARRING HOT STUFF
Harvey Publications, 1962–81
1 . . . . 700.00
2 . . . . 300.00
3 thru 10 . . . . @250.00
11 thru 20 . . . . @200.00
21 thru 30 . . . . @125.00
31 thru 40. . . . . @100.00
41 thru 50 68 pgs. . . . . @75.00
51 thru 55 62 pgs. . . . . @60.00
56 thru 70. . . . . @50.00
71 thru 100. . . . . @35.00
101 thru 107. . . . . @25.00

DEVILMAN
Verotika, 1995
1 Go Nagi 3.00
1a San Diego Con Gatefold edition 5.00
2 F:Devilman. 3.00
3 Through History 3.00
4 French Revolution 3.00
5 Custer's Last Stand 3.00

DEVIL MAY CRY
Dreamwave, 2004
1 thru 4 . . . . @4.00
1a thru 4a variant (c)s. . . . . @4.00
TPB Vol. 1 . . . . 16.00

DEVIL'S KEEPER
Alias Enterprises, 2005
1 . . . . 1.00
2 thru 4 . . . . @3.00
2a variant (c). 3.00

DEVLIN
Maximum Press, 1996
1 A:Avengelyne,3-part mini-series . 2.50
2 (of 3) RLd,BNa,A:Avengelyne . . . 2.50

DICK TRACY
Blackthorne, 1986
1 3-D. 3.00

DICK TRACY: BIG CITY BLUES
1 Mini Series. 4.00
2 Mini Series. 6.00
3 Mini Series. 6.00

DIGITAL GRAFFITI
APC, 2003
1 . . . . 3.50
2 thru 4 . . . . @3.50
TPB 17.00

DINO ISLAND
Mirage, 1993
1 thru 2 . . . . 2.75

DINOSAUR REX
Upshot/Fantagraphics, 1987
1 thru 3 by Jan Strand &
Henry Mayo . . . . @3.00

COLOR PUB.

DINOSAURS
Walt Disney
1 Citizen Robbie(From TV) 3.00

DINOSAURS ATTACK
Eclipse, 1991
1 HT,Based on Topps cards 3.50
2 and 3 HT,Based on cards . . . . @3.50

DINOSAURS FOR HIRE
[1st Series] see: B&W
[2nd Series] Malibu, 1993–94
1 B:TMs(s),A:Reese,Archie,
   Lorenzo 3.00
2 thru 12 . . . . @2.50

DISNEY ADVENTURES
Walt Disney
1 . . . . 3.00
2 . . . . 3.00
3 thru 13 . . . . @3.00
14 thru 28 . . . . @3.00

DISNEY COLOSSAL COMICS COLLECTION
Walt Disney
1 inc.DuckTales, Chip'n'Dale 3.00
2 thru 9 . . . . @3.00

DISNEY COMICS IN 3-D
Walt Disney, 1992
1 F:Donald & Uncle Scrooge 3.00

DISNEY COMICS SPEC: DONALD & SCROOGE
1 inc."Return to Xanadu" 9.00

DISNEY JUNIOR
Disney Press, 2006
CN #1 Finding Nemo 5.00
GN #2 Lilo & Stitch 5.00
GN #3 Disney's Tall Tails 5.00
GN #4 Kid Gravity 5.00

DISNEYLAND BIRTHDAY PARTY
Gladstone, 1985
1 CB 15.00

DIVER DAN
Dell Publishing Co., Feb.-April, 1962
1 . . . . 100.00
2 . . . . 90.00

DIVINE INTERVENTION
WildStorm/DC, 1999
1 . . . . 3.00
Wildcats, pt.2, JLe,SLo,RiB 3.00
Gen13, pt.3, JLe,SLo,RiB 3.00

DNAGENTS
Eclipse, 1983–85
1 O:DNAgents 4.00
2 . . . . 3.00
3 thru 8 . . . . @2.50
9 DSp 2.50
10 thru 25 . . . . @2.50
See also: NEW DNAGENTS

DOC FRANKENSTEIN
Burlyman Entertainment, 2004
1 . . . . 7.00
1a 2nd printing 4.00

DNAgents #1
© Eclipse

2 . . . . 5.00
3 thru 4 . . . . @3.50
5 . . . . 3.50
3a thru 4a sketch (c) . . . . @3.50
5a variant (c). 3.50

DOC SAVAGE
Gold Key, 1966
1 . . . . 175.00

DOC SAVAGE
Millennium
1 V:Russians 2.50

DOC SAVAGE, THE MAN OF BRONZE
Millennium, 1992
1 Monarch of Armageddon,pt.1 . . . 3.00
2 Monarch of Armageddon,pt.2 . . . 3.00
3 Monarch of Armageddon,pt.3 . . . 3.00
4 Monarch of Armageddon,pt.4 . . . 3.00

DOC SAVAGE: DEVIL'S THOUGHTS
Millennium, 1992
1 V:Hanoi Shan 2.50
2 V:Hanoi Shan 2.50
3 Final issue 2.50

DOC SAVAGE: DOOM DYNASTY
Millennium, 1991
1 and 2 . . . . @2.50

DOC SAVAGE: MANUAL OF BRONZE
Millennium, 1992
1 Fact File 2.50

DOC SAVAGE: REPEL
Millennium, 1992
1 DvD(c) 2.50

DOCTOR BOOGIE
Media Arts, 1987
1 and 2 . . . . @2.50

DOCTOR CHAOS
Triumphant Comics, 1993
1 JnR(s),I:Doctor Chaos 2.50
2 JnR(s), ... 2.50
3 JnR(s),The Coming of
   the Cry,pt.1,I:Cry 2.50
4 JnR(s),The Coming of
   the Cry,pt.2,b:Ky'Li 2.50
5 JnR(s),E:Coming of the
   Cry,pt.3,V:Cry 2.50
6 Recovery 2.50
7 w/coupon 2.50
8 w/coupon 2.50
9 V:Mirth 2.50
10 Co. X #3 . . . . 2.50
11 Co. X #4 . . . . 2.50
12 A:Charlotte 2.50

DR. JJ
Narwain Publishing, 2006
1 The Devil's Psychologist 4.00

DR. KILDARE
Dell Publishing Co., April-June, 1962
1 . . . . 150.00
2 thru 9 . . . . @100.00

DOCTOR SOLAR MAN OF THE ATOM
Gold Key, 1962
1 BF,I:Dr. Solar 400.00
2 BF,I:Prof.Harbinger 150.00
3 BF,The Hidden Hands 125.00
4 BF,The Deadly Sea 125.00
5 BF,I:Dr.Solar in costume 150.00
6 FBe,I:Nuro 100.00
7 FBe,Vanishing Oceans 100.00
8 FBe,Thought Controller 100.00
9 FBe,Transivac The Energy
   Consuming Computer 100.00
10 FBe,The Sun Giant 100.00
11 FBe,V:Nuro 75.00
12 FBe,The Mystery of the
   Vanishing Silver. 75.00
13 FBe,Meteor from 100 Mill.BC . . 75.00
14 FBe,Solar's Midas Touch . . . 75.00
15 FBe O:Dr.Solar 100.00
16 FBe,V:Nuro 75.00
17 FBe,The Fatal Foe 75.00
18 FBe,The Mind Master 75.00
19 FBe,SolarV:Solar 75.00
20 AMc,Atomic Nightmares 75.00
21 AMc,Challenge from Outer
   Space. 50.00
22 AMc,Nuro,I:King Cybernoid . . . 50.00
23 AMc,A:King Cybernoid 50.00
24 EC,The Deadly Trio 50.00
25 EC,The Lost Dimension 50.00
26 EC,When Dimensions Collide. . 50.00
27 (1969) The Ladder to Mars . . . 50.00
28 (1981),1-pg AMc,The Dome
   of Mystery 40.00
29 DSp,FBe,Magnus 40.00
30 DSp,FBe,Magnus 40.00

DR. TOMORROW
Acclaim, 1997
1 (of 12) BL,Bart Simms finds
   Angel Computer 2.50
2 thru 12 BL . . . . @2.50

DOGS OF WAR
Defiant, 1994
1 F:Shooter,Ironhead 2.75
2 . . . . 2.50
3 Mouse Deserts. 2.50
4 Schism Prequel 2.50

All comics prices listed are for *Near Mint* condition.

5 X-over 2.50
6 Aftermath 2.50

DOLLMAN
Eternity, 1991
1 Movie adapt. sequel 2.50
2 V:Sprug & Braindead Gang 2.50
3 Toni Costa Kidnapped 2.50
4 . . . . 2.50

Donald Duck #203
© Walt Disney

DONALD DUCK
Dell/Gold Key, 1962
85 thru 97 . . . . 75.00
98 rep. #46 CB 75.00
99 . . . . 65.00
100 . . . . 75.00
101 thru 111 . . . . @50.00
112 I:Moby Duck 60.00
113 thru 133 . . . . @50.00
134 CB rep. 50.00
135 CB rep. 50.00
136 thru 156 . . . . @40.00
157 CB rep. 40.00
158 thru 163 . . . . @40.00
164 CB rep. 40.00
165 thru 216 . . . . @30.00
Whitman, 1980
217 . . . . 30.00
218 . . . . 30.00
219 CB rep. 30.00
220 and 221 . . . . @50.00
222 scarce 300.00
223 thru 224 . . . . @75.00
225 thru 240 . . . . @30.00
241 thru 245 . . . . @35.00
Gladstone
246 CB,Gilded Man 25.00
247 CB 20.00
248 CB,Forbidden Valley 20.00
249 CB 20.00
250 CB,Pirate Gold 20.00
251 CB,Donald's Best Xmas 15.00
252 CB,Trail o/t Unicorn 8.00
253 CB 8.00
254 CB, in old Calif 9.00
255 CB 8.00
256 CB,Volcano Valley 8.00
257 CB,Forest Fire 8.00
258 thru 266 CB . . . . @8.00
267 thru 277 CB . . . . @8.00
278 CB 9.00
279 CB 9.00
280 thru 298 CB rep. . . . . @6.00
299 Life Guard Daze 5.00
300 Donald's 300th Triumph' 48pg . 6.00

301 The Gold Finder 5.00
302 Monkey Business 5.00
303 The Cantankerous Cat 5.00
304 Donald Duck Rants
    about Ants 5.00
305 Mockingbird Ridge 5.00
306 Worst Class Mail. 5.00
307 Going to Sea. 5.00
308 Worst Class Mail. 5.00

DONALD DUCK
ADVENTURES
Gladstone, 1987
1 CB,Jungle Hi-Jinks 8.00
2 CB,Dangerous Disquise 6.00
3 CB,Lost in the Andes. 6.00
4 CB,Frozen Gold. 6.00
5 CB,Rosa 6.00
6 CB 3.00
7 CB 3.00
8 CB,Rosa 6.00
9 CB 3.00
10 CB 3.00
11 CB 3.00
12 CB,Rosa,Giant-size 6.00
13 CB,Rosa(c) 3.50
14 CB 3.00
15 CB 3.00
16 CB 3.00
17 CB 3.00
18 CB,No Such Varmint. 3.00
19 CB 4.00
20 CB,Giant-size (1990) 4.00
21 CB,Rosa(c) (1993) 4.00
22 CB,The Pixilated Parrot 4.00
23 thru 30 . . . . @4.00
31 thru 40 . . . . @3.00
41 Bruce McDuck 3.00
42 The Saga of Sourdough Sam . . . 3.00
43 The Lost Charts of Columbus . . . 3.00
44 The Kitchy-Kaw Diamond 3.00
45 The Red Duck 3.00
46 . . . . 3.00
47 CB,Trick or Treat. 3.00
48 The Saphead Factor. 3.00

DONALD DUCK
ADVENTURES
Walt Disney, 1990
1 Don Rosa, The Money Pit 6.00
2 CB 3.00
3 . . . . 3.00
4 CB 3.00
5 . . . . 3.00
6 . . . . 3.00
7 . . . . 3.00
8 . . . . 3.00
9 CB 3.00
10 Run-Down Runner 3.00
11 Whats for Lunch-Supper. 3.00
12 Head of Rama Putra 3.00
13 JustAHumble, BumblingDuck . . . 3.00
14 CB,Day Gladstone's Luck
    Ran Out. 4.00
15 A Tuft Luck Tale. 3.00
16 Magica's Missin'Magic 3.00
17 CB,Secret of Atlantis 4.00
18 Crocodile Donald 3.00
19 Not So Silent Service 4.00
20 Ghost of Kamikaze Ridge 3.00
21 CB,The Golden Christmas Tree . 4.00
22 The Master Landscapist 5.00
23 The Lost Peg Leg Mine 3.00
24 On Stolen Time 4.00
25 Sense of Humor 3.00
26 CB,Race to the South Seas 4.00
27 CB,Nap in Nature 4.00
28 Olympic Tryout 3.00
29 CB,rep.March of Comics#20. . . . 4.00
30 A:The Vikings 3.00

31 The Sobbing Serpent of Loch
    McDuck 3.00
32 It Was No Occident. 3.00
33 Crazy Christmas on Bear
    Mountain 3.00
34 Sup.Snooper Strikes Again 4.00
35 thru 38 CB rep. . . . . @4.00
Gemstone Publishing, 2003
TPB Vol. 1 . . . . 8.00
TPB Vol. 2 thru Vol. 8 . . . . @8.00
TPB Vol. 9 thru Vol. 21. . . . . . . @8.00

DONALD DUCK ALBUM
Dell Publishing Co.,
May-July, 1959
1 CB(c) 200.00
2 . . . . 150.00

DONALD DUCK
AND FRIENDS
Gemstone Publishing, 2003
308 thru 333 . . . . @3.00
334 thru 346 . . . . @3.00

DONATELLO
Mirage, 1986
1 Teenage Mutant Ninja Turles . . . 10.00

DON BLUTH'S
DRAGON'S LAIR
Crossgen Comics, 2003
1 (of 6) Singe's Revenge 3.00
2 thru 3 . . . . @3.00

DON BLUTH'S
SPACE ACE
Crossgen Comics, 2003
1 (of 6) Defender of the Universe. . 3.00
2 thru 3 . . . . @3.00

DONE TO DEATH
Markosia, 2006
1 . . . . 3.50
2 thru 5 . . . . @3.50

DONNA MIA
Dark Fantasy Prod., 1995
1 I:Donna Mia 4.00
1a Deluxe Edition 5.00
1b signed & numbered
    (100 copies). 9.00
2 . . . . 3.00

DOOMSDAY + 1
Charlton, 1975–79
1 JBy,JBy(c) 35.00
2 JBy(c),P(c) 30.00
3 JBy,JBy(c),P(c) 25.00
4 JBy(c),P(c),I:Lok 25.00
5 and 6 JBy,JBy(c),P(c) . . . . . . @25.00
7 thru 12 JBy,JBy(c),rep . . . . . @15.00

DOOMSDAY SQUAD
Fantagraphics, 1986
1 rep. JBy 3.00
2 rep. JBy 3.00
3 rep. SS,A:Usagi Yojimbo 3.00
4 thru 7, rep. JBy . . . . @3.00

DOUBLE DARE
ADVENTURES
Harvey Publications, 1966
1 I:B-man,Glowing Gladiator,
    Magicmaster 150.00

2 AW/RC rep. A·B-Man,Glowing
   Gladiator, Magicmaster 100.00

DOUBLE IMPACT
High Impact Studios, 1995–96
1 RCI,I:China & Jazz, chrome(c) . . 7.00
1 holographic rainbow (c) with
   certificate 15.00
1 rainbow (c), no certificate 10.00
1 chromium variant (c) 8.00
2 RCI,V:Castillo. 3.00
2a signed, with certificate 4.00
3 China on cover 5.00
3a Jazzler on cover 3.00
3b Nikki on cover 3.00
3c Blondage 6.00
4 F:Mordred, The Rattler 3.00
4a Phoenix variant (c). 6.00
5 RCI 3.00
6 Buttshots 4.00
6a Jazz (c) 3.00
6a signed 6.00
7 I:Nikki Blade 3.00
8 . . . . 3.00
8a variant (c). 4.00
Gold edition, Lingerie special. 3.00
Volume 2, 1996–97
0 RCI 3.00
1 RCI. 3.00
1a deluxe edition. 4.00
1b prism foil (c). 5.00
1c gold foil (c) 5.00
2 RCI 3.00
3 . . . . 3.00
3a special edition RCI(c). 8.00

DOROTHY
Illusive Arts Entertain., 2005
1 . . . . 5.00
1a 2nd printing 5.00
2 thru 4 . . . . @5.00
5 thru 7 . . . . @5.00
TPB Vol. 1 . . . . 15.00

DOUBLE IMPACT: ALIVE
ABC Studios, 1999
1 RCI,F:China & Jazz. 3.00
1a deluxe 8.00

DOUBLE IMPACT/
HELLINA
High Impact, 1996
1-shot RCI. 3.00

DOUBLE IMPACT/
LETHAL STRYKE:
DOUBLE STRIKE
High Impact/London Night, 1996
1-shot RCI. 3.00

DOUBLE IMPACT
SUICIDE RUN
High Impact, 1997
1 RCI. 3.00
1 gold edition 10.00
1 platinum edition 20.00
2 . . . . 3.00
2a Suicide Cover 10.00

DOUBLE IMPACT: 2069
ABC Studios, 1999
1 RCI,Independent Day 3.00
1a premium edition 5.00
1b Sexy China ed. 5.00

DOUBLE LIFE OF
PRIVATE STRONG
Archie Publications, 1959
1 JSm/JK,I:Lancelot Strong/
   Shield, The Fly 1,100.00
2 JSm/JK,GT A:Fly 750.00

DRACULA
Dell Publishing Co., 1966
1 see: Movie Classics
2 O:New Dracula (super-powers) . 75.00
3 Rain of Terror. 50.00
4 The Origin of Fleeta 50.00
5 not published
6 rep. #2 (1972) 45.00
7 rep. #3 (1972) 35.00
8 rep. #4 (1973) 35.00

[BRAM STOKER'S]
DRACULA
Topps, 1992
1 MMi,Movie adaptation (trading
   cards in each issue) 5.00
1a Red Foil Logo 10.00
1b 2nd Print 3.00
2 MMi,Movie adapt.contd. 4.00
3 MMi,Movie adapt.contd. 4.00
4 MMi,Movie adapt.concludes 4.00
TPB Collected Album. 14.00

DRACULA CHRONICLES
Topps
1 True Story of Dracula 2.50
2 RTs,rep. Vlad #2 . . . . 2.50
3 RTs,rep. Vlad #3 . . . . 2.50

DRACULA'S REVENGE
IDW Publishing, 2004
1 . . . . 4.00
2 . . . . 4.00

DRACULA VS CAPONE
Silent Devil Productions, 2006
1 (of 3) 3.00

DRACULA VS
KING ARTHUR
Silent Devil Productions, 2005
1 . . . . 3.00
2 . . . . 3.00
3 . . . . 3.00
4 . . . . 5.00
TPB 17.00

DRACULA VS ZORRO
Topps, 1993
1 DMg(s),TY,Black(c), ... 3.25
2 DMg(s),TY,w/Zorro #0 . . . . 3.00
TPB 6.00

DRACULA:
VLAD THE IMPALER
Topps, 1993
1 EM,I:Vlad Dracua, w/cards 3.25
1a Red Foil 10.00
2 EM, w/cards. 3.25
3 EM,w/cards 3.00

DRAGONFLIGHT
Eclipse, 1991
1 Anne McCaffrey adapt. 5.00
2 novel adapt 5.00
3 novel adapt 5.00

DRAGONFLY
AC Comics, 1985
1 . . . . 3.50
2 and 3 . . . . @2.00
4 thru 8 . . . . @2.00

DRAGONLANCE:
CHRONICLES
Devil's Due Publishing, 2005
Vol. 1 Dragons of Autumn Twilight
1 (of 8) 3.00
1B signed edition 10.00
2 thru 3 . . . . @3.00
2a thru 3a collector's edition . . @6.00
4 thru 8 . . . . @3.00
4a thru 8a collector's edition. . . . @6.00
Spec. rep. #1 & #2. . . . . 6.00
TPB Vol. 1 . . . . 18.00
Vol. II Dragons of Winter Night
1 (of 4) 5.00
1a cardstock (c) 9.00
2 thru 3 . . . . @5.00
2a thru 3a cardstock (c) . . . . . . @9.00

DRAGONLANCE: THE
LEGEND OF HUMA
Devil's Due Publishing, 2004
1 . . . . 3.00
1a variant (c) 3.00
2 thru 6 . . . . @3.00
TPB Vol. 1 . . . . 15.00

DRAGONPRO
Antarctic Press, 2006
0 . . . . 3.50

Dragonring Vol. 2 #2 © Aircel

DRAGONRING
Aircel, 1987–88, Vol. 2
1 . . . . 3.50
2 O:Dragonring 2.50
3 thru 15 . . . . @2.50
See also: B&W

DRAGON'S LAIR
Arcana Studio, 2006
1 . . . . 5.00
2 . . . . 3.00
3 . . . . 4.00

DRAKKON WARS, THE
Realm Press, 1997
0 by Richard Hatch & Chris Scalf . . 3.00
1 . . . . 3.00

DREADSTAR
First, 1986–91
27 JSn,from Epic,traitor 3.00
28 thru 49 . . . . @3.00
50 JSn,AMe,Pawns 4.25
51 thru 64 . . . . @4.00

DREADSTAR
Malibu Bravura, 1994–95
1 JSn(c),PDd(s),EC,I:New Dreadstar
  (Kalla),w/stamp 2.75
2 JSn(c),PDd(s),EC,w/stamp 2.50
3 JSn(c),PDd(s),EC,w/stamp 2.75
4 PDd,EC,Kalla's origin,w/stamp . . 2.50
5 PDd,F:Vanth,w/stamp 2.50
6 PDd,w/stamp 2.50

DREAMS OF THE DARKCHYLDE
Darkchylde Entertainment, 2000
1 RQu,BPe 3.00
2 thru 6 . . . . @3.00
4a Fear 2001 edition 6.00

DREDD RULES
Fleetway/Quality, 1991–93
1 SBs(c),JBy,Prev.unpubl. in USA . 5.00
2 inc.Eldster Ninja Mud Wrestling
  Vigilantes 3.50
3 inc.That Sweet Stuff 3.50
4 Our Man in Hondo City 3.50
5 thru 17 . . . . @3.25
18 F:Jonny Cool 3.00
19 V:Hunter's Club 3.00
20 . . . . 4.00

DRIFT MARLO
Dell Publishing Co., May-July, 1962
1 . . . . 90.00
2 . . . . 70.00

DRUNKEN FIST
Jademan, 1988
1 . . . . 3.25
2 . . . . 2.50
3 thru 9 . . . . @2.00
10 thru 53 . . . . @2.00

DUCKMAN
Topps, 1994
1 USA Cartoon 2.50
2 XXX Files 2.50
3 I:King Chicken 2.50
4 V:Toys 2.50
5 F:Cornfed 2.50
6 Star Trek Parody 2.50
7 rep. 1990 B&W 1st app., now
  in color 2.50

DUCKMAN: THE MOB FROG SAGA
Topps, 1994
1 I:Mob Frog 2.50
2 D:Mob Frog 2.50
3 In the Name of the Duck 2.50

DUCK TALES
Gladstone, 1990
1 CB(r)I:LaunchpadMcQuck 7.00
2 CB(r) 4.00

3 . . . . 4.00
4 CB(r) 4.00
5 thru 11 . . . . @4.00
12 & 13 . . . . @5.00

DUCK TALES
Walt Disney, 1990
1 Scrooge's Quest:The Ice Demon 4.00
2 thru 19 . . . . @3.00

DUDLEY DO-RIGHT
Charlton Comics, 1970–71
1 From TV series 175.00
2 thru 7 . . . . @150.00

DUEL MASTERS
Dreamwave, 2003
1 . . . . 3.00
1a variant (c)s . . . . @3.00
2 thru 8 . . . . @3.00
Pocket Edition Vol. 2 . . . . 11.00

DUMMY'S GUIDE TO DANGER, A
Viper Comics, 2006
1 (of 4) 3.25
2 thru 4 . . . . @3.25

Dunc and Loo © Dell Publishing

DUNC & LOO
Dell Publishing Co., 1961
1 . . . . 175.00
2 . . . . 150.00
3 thru 8 . . . . @100.00

DUNGEONS & DRAGONS: THE LOST CITY
Twenty First Century, 1999
1 (of 6) game tie-in 5.00
2 thru 6 . . . . @5.00

DUNGEONS & DRAGONS: AMBER CASTLE
Twenty First Century, 2000
1 (of 6) game tie-in 5.00

DUNGEONS & DRAGONS: TEMPEST'S GATE
Kenzer & Company, 2001
1 (of 4) Born of Fire 3.00
2 Forged in Tears 3.00

3 Tempered in Fellowship 3.00
4 Sheathed in Justice 3.00
TPB 15.00

DUNGEONS AND DRAGONS: WHERE SHADOWS FALL
Kenzer & Company, 2003
1 (of 5) 3.50
2 thru 5 . . . . @3.50

DWIGHT D. EISENHOWER
Dell Publishing Co., 1969
1 . . . . 90.00

DYNAMO
Tower Comics, 1966
1 WW,MSy,RC,SD,I:Andor 150.00
2 WW,DA,GT,MSy,Weed solo
  story A:Iron Maiden 100.00
3 WW,GT,Weed solo story,
  A:Iron Maiden 100.00
4 WW,DA,A:Iron Maiden 100.00

DYNAMO JOE
First, 1986–87
1 . . . . 3.00
2 . . . . 2.50
3 thru 14 . . . . @2.50
Spec.#1 . . . . 2.50

EARTH 4
Continuity, 1993
1 Deathwatch 2000 Pt.6,w/card . . 2.50
2 Deathwatch 2000 Pt.11,w/card . . 2.50
3 V:Hellbenders, w/card 2.50

[2nd Series]
1 WMc, ... 2.50
2 . . . . 2.50
3 . . . . 2.50

EAST MEETS WEST
Innovation
1 . . . . 2.50
2 thru 3 . . . . @2.50

EBERRON: EYE OF THE WOLF
Devil's Due Publishing, 2006
1-shot 5.00
1-shot-a cardstock (c) 9.00

ECHO OF FUTUREPAST
Continuity, 1984–85
1 NA,MGo,I:Bucky O'Hare,
  Frankenstein 4.00
2 NA,MGo,A:Bucky O'Hare, Dracula,
  Werewolf 3.50
3 NA,MGo,A:Bucky 3.50
4 NA,MGo,A:Bucky 3.50
5 NA,MGo,A:Drawla&Bucky 3.50
6 Ath,B:Torpedo 3.50
7 ATh 3.50
8 Ath, ... 3.25
9 Ath,Last issue 3.25

ECLIPSE GRAPHIC NOVELS
Eclipse
1 Axa 7.00
2 MR,I Am Coyote 7.00
3 DSt,Rocketeer 10.00
3a hard cover 40.00
4 Silver Heels 9.00
4a hard cover 40.00

Eclipse Monthly #9
© *Eclipse*

5 Sisterhood of Steel 10.00
6 Zorro in Old Calif. 8.00

ECLIPSE MONTHLY
Eclipse, 1983–84
1 SD,DW,I:Static&Rio 2.50
2 GC,DW 2.50
3 thru 10 DW . . . . @2.50

EDGAR RICE
BURROUGHS'
A PRINCESS OF MARS
IDW Publishing, 2006
1 . . . . 4.00

EDGE
Malibu Bravura, 1994–95
1 GK,I:Edge 2.50
2 GK,STg,Gold Stamp 2.50
3 GK,The Ultimates 2.50
4 GK,V:Mr. Ultimate 2.50

EDGE OF CHAOS
Pacific, 1983
1 GM. 2.50
2 GM. 2.50
3 GM. 2.50

EIGHT LEGGED FREAKS
WildStorm/DC, 2002
Spec. movie adapt. 64-pg. 7.00

87th PRECINCT
**Dell Publishing Co.,
April-June, 1962**
1 BK 200.00
2 . . . . 175.00

EL ARSENAL
Arcana Studio, 2005
1 (of 3) 3.00
2 thru 3 . . . . @3.00

EL CAZADOR
Crossgen Comics, 2003
1 CDi,SEp 3.00
2 thru 3 CDi,SEp . . . . @3.00
4 thru 8 . . . . @3.00
TPB Vol. 1 Collected edition 6.00
TPB Traveler edition, 208-pg. 13.00

Spec. #1 Bloody Ballad of
    Blackjack Tom 3.00

ELEMENTALS
Comico, 1984–88
1 BWg,I:Destroyers 5.00
2 BWg 3.50
3 BWg 3.50
4 thru 12 BWg . . . . @3.00
13 thru 22 . . . . @3.00
23 thru 29 . . . . @3.00
Spec.#1 . . . . 3.00
Spec.#2 . . . . 3.00
[Second Series], 1989–94
1 . . . . 3.00
2 thru 4 . . . . @3.00
5 thru 28 . . . . @3.00
Spec.#1 Lingerie special 3.00
GN The Natural Order, rep. 10.00
GN Death & Resurrection 13.00
[Third Series], 1995
1 R:Elementals, polybagged with
    Chrysalis promo card 3.00
2 R:Original Monolith, polybagged
    with Chrysalis promo card 3.00
3A Destroy the Shadowspear 3.00
3B variant cover 3.00
4 Memoirs,pt.1 . . . . 3.00
5 Memoirs,pt.2 . . . . 3.00
GN Ghost of a Chance 6.00
Spec. Babes, photo multimedia
    bikini special 4.00
Spec. Hot Bikini Valentine 4.00
Spec. All New Summer Special 5.00
Spec.#1 Lingerie Metalite 4.00

ELEMENTALS:
HOW THE WAR WAS ONE
Comico, 1996
1 thru 4 . . . . @3.00

ELEMENTALS: THE
VAMPIRE'S REVENGE
Comico, 1996–97
1 thru 4 . . . . @3.00

ELEMENTALS VS.
THE CHARNEL PRIESTS
Comico, 1996
Spec. 1 (of 2) 3.00
2 . . . . 3.00

ELFLORD
Aircel, 1986–88
Volume 1: *See B&W*
Volume II
1 . . . . 3.50
2 . . . . 3.00
3 thru 20 . . . . @3.00
21 double size 5.00
22 thru 24 . . . . @3.00
Spec.#1 . . . . 3.00
25 thru 32, see B&W

ELFQUEST
Warp Graphics, 1998
TPB 20th Anniv. Special 9.00
TPB Scores, WPi, best of Elfquest
    stories 20.00

ELFQUEST: BLOOD OF
TEN CHIEFS
Warp Graphics, 1993–95
1 WP 3.00
2 WP 3.00

3 WP,B:Swift Spear pt. 1 . . . . 3.00
4 WP,B:Swift Spear pt. 2 . . . . 3.00
5 thru 20 . . . . @3.00

ELFQUEST:
HIDDEN YEARS
Warp Graphics, 1992
1 WP 3.00
2 WP, w/coupon promo. 3.00
3 WP, w/coupon promo.Cont.sty.
    previewed in Harbinger#11 . . . . 3.50
4 WP,w/coupon 3.00
5 WP,O:Skywise 3.00
6 WP,F:Timmain 3.00
7 F:Timmain 3.00
8 Daughter's Day 3.00
9 WP(s),Enemy Face 3.00
9 1/2 WP,JBy,Holiday Spec. 3.50
10 thru 14 WP . . . . @3.00
15 WP Wolfrider Tribe Splits 3.50
16 thru 18 WP 3.00
19 thru 24 . . . . @3.00
25 B&W Wolfrider's Death 3.00
26 thru 29 B&W finale . . . . @3.00

ELFQUEST: JINK
Warp Graphics, 1994–96
1 Future 3.50
2 thru 7 . . . . @3.00
8 B&W V:Black Snakes 3.00
9 thru 12 . . . . 3.00

ELFQUEST:
NEW BLOOD
Warp Graphics, 1992–96
1 JBy,artists try Elfquest 5.00
2 Barry Blair story 3.50
3 thru 5 . . . . @3.00
6 thru 31 . . . . @3.00
32 B&W Sorrow's End 3.00
33 thru 35 B&W 3.00
Summer Spec.1993 . . . . 4.25

ELFQUEST: THE REBELS
Warp Graphics, 1994–96
1 Aliens, set several hundred
    years in future 3.00
2 thru 8 . . . . @3.00
9 B&W Brother vs. Brother 3.00
10 thru 12 . . . . @3.00

ELFQUEST: SHARDS
Warp Graphics, 1994–96
1 Division 3.50
2 thru 5 . . . . @3.00
6 thru 11 . . . . @3.00
12 B&W F:High One Timmain 3.00
13 thru 16 B&W finale . . . . @3.00

ELFQUEST:
WAVE DANCERS
Warp Graphics, 1993–96
1 Foil enhanced 3.50
2 thru 6 . . . . @3.00
Spec. #1 . . . . 3.00

ELIMINATOR
COLOR SPECIAL
Eternity, 1991
1 DDo(c) set in the future 3.00

ELIMINATOR
Malibu Ultraverse, 1995
0 Man,DJa,MZ,Zothros tries to re-
    open passage to the Godwheel 3.00

All comics prices listed are for *Near Mint* condition.

1 MZ,Man,DRo, The Search for the
   Missing Infinity Gems,I:Siren . . . 3.00
1a Black Cover ed. 4.00
2 MZ 2.50
3 MZ, Infinity Gem tie-in,finale . . 2.50

ELK'S RUN
Speakeasy Comics, 2005
TPB Vol. 1 . . . . 8.00
4 thru 7 . . . . @3.00

ELRIC
Pacific, 1983–84
1 CR,MGi,Michael Moorcock adapt 4.00
2 CR,MGi,Elric of Melnibone 3.00
3 thru 6 CR,MGi . . . . @3.00

ELRIC (ONE LIFE)
Topps, 1996
0 NGa,CPR, One Life, based on
   Michael Moorcock character . . . 3.00

ELRIC, THE BANE OF THE BLACK SWORD
First, 1988–89
1 Michael Moorcock adapt 3.00
2 . . . . 3.00
3 thru 6 . . . . @3.00

ELRIC, SAILOR ON THE SEAS OF FATE
First, 1985–86
1 Michael Moorcock adapt 4.00
2 . . . . 3.00
3 thru 7 . . . . @3.00

ELRIC, THE VANISHING TOWER
First, 1987–88
1 Michael Moorcock adapt 3.00
2 thru 6 . . . . @3.00

ELRIC, THE WEIRD OF THE WHITE WOLF
First, 1986–87
1 Michael Moorcock adapt 3.00
2 thru 5 . . . . @3.00
Graphic Novel CR 7.00

ELSINORE
Alias Enterprises, 2005
1 (of 9) 1.00
2 thru 7 . . . . @3.00
Elsinore Case Files #1: Arrivals 3.00
TPB 10.00

ELSINORE
Devil's Due Publishing, 2006
4 . . . . 4.00
5 thru 9 . . . . @3.25
TPB Vol. 1 Psycho Sanctii 15.00

ELVEN
Malibu Ultraverse, 1994
0 Rep.,A:Prime, double size 3.00
Mini-Series 1994–95
1 A:Prime, Primevil 2.50
2 AaL,R:Maxi-Man 2.50
3 AaL,V:Duey, Primevil 2.50
4 AaL,F:Primevil 2.50

E-MAN
Charlton Comics, 1973–75
1 JSon,O:E-Man 35.00

E-Man #1 © Charlton

2 SD 20.00
3 . . . . 20.00
4 SD 20.00
5 SD,Miss Liberty Belle 20.00
6 JBy,Rog 2000 . . . . 20.00
7 JBy,Rog 2000 . . . . 20.00
8 J:Nova 25.00
9 JBy,Rog 2000 . . . . 20.00
10 JBy,Rog 2000 . . . . 20.00

E-MAN
First, 1983
1 JSon,O:E-Man & Nova, A:Rog
   2000, 1 pg. JBy 3.00
2 JSon,I:F-Men (X-Men satire) 1-
   page Mike Mist 2.50
3 thru 25 JSon . . . . @2.50
Spec. #1 . . . . 2.75

E-MAN
Comico, 1989–90
1 JSon 2.75
2 and 3 JSon . . . . @2.50

E-MAN
Alpha Productions, 1993
1 JSon 2.75

E-MAN: RECHARGED
Digital Webbing, 2006
1-shot 4.00

EMERGENCY
Charlton Comics, 1976
1 JSon(c),JBy 45.00
2 JSon 25.00
3 Thru 4 . . . . 25.00

ENCHANTED: THE AWAKENING
Sirius, 1998
1 by Robert Chang 3.00
2 . . . . 3.00
3 conclusion 3.00

ENGINE
Shadow Planet, 2002
1 by Tim Tyler 3.50
1a signed sketch edition 10.00
2 thru 3 . . . . @3.00

ENIGMA CIPHER, THE
Boom! Studios, 2006
1 (of 5) 4.00
2 . . . . 4.00

ENIGMAS, THE
Digital Webbing, 2006
1-shot 6.00

ENSIGN O'TOOLE
Dell Publishing Co., 1962
1 . . . . 50.00
2 . . . . 40.00

EPSILON WAVE, THE
Independent, 1985
1 Darkest Before Dawn 3.00
2 Tango in Texas City 2.50
3 One More Step Toward Darkness 2.50
4 Afterlife 2.50
Elite Comics, 1986
5 thru 10 . . . . @2.50

ESC.(ESCAPE)
Comico, 1996
1 SPr 3.00
2 thru 4 SPr . . . . @3.00
TPB SPr Rep. #1–#4 . . . . 15.00

ESC: NO EXIT
Comico, 1997
1 . . . . 3.00
1 medallion edition 10.00
2 . . . . 3.00

ESCAPE OF THE LIVING DEAD
Avatar Press, 2005
1 . . . . 4.00
1a Wraparound (c) 4.00
1b Variant(c)s . . . . @4.00
1c Blood red convention (c) 5.00
1f Red foil (c) 15.00
2 thru 5 . . . . @4.00
2a thru 5a wraparound (c)s . . . . . @4.00
2b thru 5b variant (c)s . . . . @4.00
1c thru 5c die-cut (c)s . . . . @10.00
1d thru 5d premium variant (c)s . @6.00
TPB 16.00

ESCAPE OF THE LIVING DEAD: AIRBORNE
Avatar Press, 2006
1 . . . . 4.00
1c variant Splatter (c) 7.00
1d variant Shocker (c) 6.00
1e Deadhead (c) 6.00
2 thru 3 . . . . @4.00
1a thru 2a wraparound (c) 4.00
1b thru 3b variant (c)s . . . . @4.00
1c thru 3c variant Splatter (c)s . . . 7.00

ESCAPE OF THE LIVING DEAD: FEARBOOK
Avatar Press, 2006
1 . . . . 4.00
1a wraparound (c) 4.00
1b variant (c)s . . . . @4.00
1c variant leather (c) 20.00
1d thru 1e special (c)s . . . . @6.00

ESPERS
Eclipse, 1986
1 I:ESPers 3.00
2 JBo(c),V:Terrorists 3.00

COLOR PUB.

3 V:Terrorists 3.00
4 Belrut 3.00
5 The Liquidators 3.00
6 V:Benito Giovanetti 3.00

ESPIONAGE
Dell Publishing Co.,
May-July, 1964
1 . . . . 125.00
2 . . . . 85.00

ESTABLISHMENT, THE
WildStorm/DC, 2001
1 IEd,CAd,F:Charlie Arrows 2.50
2 IEd,CAd 2.50
3 IEd,CAd 2.50
4 IEd,CAd 2.50
5 IEd,CAd 2.50
6 IEd,CAd 2.50
7 IEd,CAd 2.50
8 IEd,CAd, in Russia 2.50
9 IEd,CAd, demon-god embryos . . 2.50
10 IEd,CAd, Charlie Arrows 2.50
11 IEd,CAd, DeadSpace 2.50
12 IEd,CAd, Moonbase Straker 2.50
13 IEd,CAd, final issue 2.50

ESTANCIA
Hammock Entertainment, 2006
1 (of 17) 3.50
2 . . . . 3.50

ETERNAL WARRIOR
Valiant, 1992
1 FM(c),JDx,Unity #2,O:Eternal
 Warrior,Armstrong 3.00
1a Gold Ed. 15.00
1b Gold Foil Logo 25.00
2 thru 10 . . . . @3.00
11 thru 49 . . . . @2.50
50 . . . . 5.00
Yearbook #1 . . . . 4.25
Yearbook #2 . . . . 4.00
Wings of Justice WWI 2.50
Quarterly
Time and Treachery 4.00
Digital Alchemy 4.00
Spec. Blackworks AHo, ... 4.00

ETERNAL WARRIORS
Acclaim, 1997
Quarterly
Archer & Armstrong AHo 4.00
Mog AHo 4.00
The Immortal Enemy AHo 4.00

ETERNITY SMITH
Renegade, 1986
1 thru 5 . . . . @3.50
[Vol. 2] Hero, 1987
1 thru 9 . . . . @2.50
Heroic Publishing
1 Man Vs. Machine 2.50
2 Man Vs. Machine 2.50

EVA THE IMP
Red Top Comic/Decker, 1957
1 . . . . 100.00
2 . . . . 100.00

EVANGELINE
Comico, 1984
1 Guns of Mars 4.00
2 . . . . 3.00
Lodestone, 1986
1 . . . . 2.50
2 . . . . 2.50

Evangeline #2
© Comico

First, 1988
1 . . . . 3.00
2 thru 9 . . . . @2.50
10 thru 12 . . . . @2.00

EVERQUEST
WildStorm/DC, 2001
GN The Ruins of Kunark, JLe 6.00
GN Transformation 6.00

EVERYTHING'S ARCHIE
Archie Publications, 1969
1 Giant 125.00
2 Giant 75.00
3 thru 5 Giant . . . . @50.00
6 thru 10 Giant . . . . @35.00
11 thru 20 . . . . @25.00
21 thru 40 . . . . @15.00
41 thru 134 . . . . @10.00

EVIL ERNIE (THE SERIES)
Chaos! Comics, 1998
1 V:Purgatori 3.00
2 Search for Chastity, A:Savior 3.00
3 V:Purgatori 3.00
4 return to New Jersey 3.00
5 two beings 3.00
6 heart of America 3.00
7 Unholy Nights 3.00
8 Trauma,pt.1 . . . . 3.00
9 Trauma,pt.2 . . . . 3.00
10 Trauma,pt.3 . . . . 3.00

EVIL ERNIE: DEPRAVED
Chaos! Comics, 1999
1 (of 3) 4.00
1a premium edition 10.00
2 . . . . 3.00
3 . . . . 3.00

EVIL ERNIE: DESTROYER
Chaos! Comics, 1997
Prev.#1 . . . . 3.00
1 (of 9) BnP 3.00
2 BnP 3.00
3 to Atlanta 3.00
4 siege of Atlanta 3.00
5 . . . . 3.00
6 Nuclear launch codes 3.00
7 Nuclear attack 3.00
8 Nuclear attack continues 3.00
9 New forms of living dead, concl. . 3.00

EVIL ERNIE IN SANTA FE
Devil's Due Publishing, 2005
1 . . . . 3.00
2 thru 4 . . . . @3.00

EVIL ERNIE: REVENGE
Chaos! Comics, 1994–95
1 SHu,BnP,A:LadyDeath,glow(c) . . 7.00
1a limited, glow-in-the-dark (c) . . . 20.00
1a Commemorative edition 15.00
2 SHu,BnP,Loses Smiley 6.00
3 SHu,BnP,V:Dr. Price 5.00
4 SHu,BnP,Final Issue 5.00
TPB Rep. #1-#4 . . . . 13.00
TPB Revenge #2, signed 20.00

EVIL ERNIE: STRAIGHT TO HELL
Chaos! Comics, 1995–96
1 Rampage in Hell, coffin(c) 4.00
1 limited, chromium edition 17.00
2 Cremator 4.00
3 . . . . 4.00
3a Chastity (c) 20.00
4 and 5 . . . . @4.00
Ashcan 1.50
Spec. 20.00

EVIL ERNIE: THE RESURRECTION
Chaos! Comics, 1993–94
1 R:Evil Ernie 15.00
1a gold edition 35.00
2 Enhanced Cover 11.00
3 Massive Mayhem Lady Death
 poster 11.00
4 final issue, extra pages 11.00
TPB Rep. #1-#4 . . . . 15.00
Ashcan Resurrection (2001) 20.00

EVIL ERNIE VS. THE MOVIE MONSTERS
Chaos! Comics
1 one-shot 3.00
1 omega edition 5.00
1 premium edition, signed 15.00

EVIL ERNIE VS. THE SUPER-HEROES
Chaos! Comics, 1995
1 one-shot 3.50
1a foil (c) 30.00
1b limited 10.00
Spec. #2 by Hart Fisher
 & Steve Butler 3.00
Spec. #2, Premium edition 10.00

EVIL ERNIE: WAR OF THE DEAD
Chaos! Comics, 1999
1 (of 3) 3.00
1a premium 10.00
2 . . . . 3.00
3 concl. 3.00

EVIL ERNIE'S BADDEST BATTLES
Chaos! Comics, 1996
1-shot, imaginary battles 3.00

EXALTED
Udon Entertainment, 2005
1 . . . . 3.50
1 Power foil (c) 12.50

COLOR PUB.

2 thru 4 . . . . @3.50
5 40-page 5.00
2a thru 5a Power foil (c)s . . . . . @12.50
TPB Vol. 1 . . . . 20.00

EXECUTIONER
Innovation, 1993
1 Don Pendleton(s),F:Mack Bolan . 4.00
1a Collector's Gold Ed. 3.00
1b Tyvek cover 4.00
2 War against Mafia 2.75
3 War against Mafia,pt.3 . . . . 2.75

EXEMPLARS
1 and 2 . . . . @2.50

EXILES
Malibu Ultraverse, 1993
1 TMs(s),PaP,I:Exiles 4.00
1a w/out card 2.50
1b Gold hologram ed. 10.00
1c Ultra-limited 12.00
2 V:Kort 3.00
3 BWS,Mastodon,BU:Rune 4.00
4 V:Kort 3.00

EX MACHINA
Wildstorm/DC, 2004
1 F:Mitchell Hundred,40-pg. 3.00
2 thru 5 State of Emergency . . . . @3.00
6 Tag, pt.1 . . . . 3.00
7 Tag, pt.2 . . . . 3.00
8 Tag, pt.3 . . . . 3.00
9 Tag, pt.4 . . . . 3.00
10 Tag, pt.5 . . . . 3.00
11 V:Fortune Tellers 3.00
12 Fact vs. Fiction, pt.1 . . . . 3.00
13 Fact vs. Fiction, pt.2 . . . . 3.00
14 Fact vs. Fiction, pt. 3 . . . . 3.00
15 Off the Grid, pt.1 . . . . 3.00
16 Off the Grid, pt.2 . . . . 3.00
17 March to War, pt.1 . . . . 3.00
18 March to War, pt.2 . . . . 3.00
19 March to War, pt.3 . . . . 3.00
20 March to War, pt.4 . . . . 3.00
21 Smoke, Smoke, pt.1 . . . . 3.00
22 Smoke, Smoke, pt.2 . . . . 3.00
23 Smoke, Smoke, pt.3 . . . . 3.00
24 Smoke, Smoke, pt.4 . . . . 3.00
25 Bradbury, Chief of Security 3.00
Spec. #1 Mayor Hundred's past. . . 3.00
Spec. #2 Life and Death 3.00
TPB The First Hundred Days 10.00
TPB Vol. 2 Tag 13.00
TPB Vol. 4 March to War 13.00
TPB Fact V. Fiction 13.00

EX-MUTANTS
Malibu, Nov. 1992–Apr. 1994
1 I&O:Ex-Mutants 2.50
2 thru 18 . . . . @2.50

EXO-SQUAD
Topps, 1994
[Mini-Series]
0 . . . . 2.50
1 From Animated Series 2.50
2 F:Nara Burns 2.50
3 V:Neo-Sapiens 2.50

EXPLORERS
Explorer Press, 1995
1 I:Explorers 3.00
2 The Cellar 3.00

EXPOSURE SPECIAL
Avatar Press, 2000
1 . . . . 3.50

1a photo(c) 3.50

EXPOSURE: SECOND COMING
Avatar Press, 2000
1 (of 2) Angel (c) 40-page 5.00

EXTINCTIONERS
Vision Comics, 1998
1 by Shawntae Howard &
  Malcolm Earle 4.00
2 . . . . 4.00

EXTINCTION EVENT
Wildstorm/DC, 2003
1 (of 5) BBh,humans vs. dinos 2.50
2 thru 5 BBh . . . . @2.50

Extremes of Violet #1
© Blackout Comics

EXTREMES VIOLET
Blackout Comics, 1995
0 I:Violet 3.00
Becomes:

EXTREMES OF VIOLET
Blackout Comics, 1995
1 V:Drug Lords 3.00
2 A:Matt Chaney 3.00

EXTRA
Gemstone, 1999
1 (of 5) 2.50
2 . . . . 2.50
3 . . . . 2.50
4 . . . . 2.50
5 final issue 2.50
`Annuals'
TPB Vol. 1 . . . . 13.50

EYE OF THE STORM
Rival Productions
1 I:Killian, Recon, Finesse, Stray . . 3.00
2 Conspiracy 3.00
3 3-D Comic Background 3.00
4 F:Recon 3.00
5 Sinclair & Rott 3.00
Ann. 48-pg. 5.00

EZRA
Arcana Studio, 2004
1 . . . . 3.00
2 thru 3 . . . . @3.00
4 . . . . 3.00
TPB Vol. 1 Egyptian Exchange . . . 10.00

EZRA: EVOKED EMOTIONS
Arcana Studio, 2006
1 (of 3) 4.00
2 thru 3 . . . . @4.00

FADE FROM GRACE
Beckett Comics, 2004
1 . . . . 2.50
2 thru 5 . . . . @2.50

FALLEN ANGEL
IDW Publishing, 2005
2 PDd 4.00
3 thru 11 PDd . . . . @4.00
TPB Vol. 1 . . . . 20.00

FAMILY AFFAIR
Gold Key, 1970
1 W/Poster,Ph(c) 125.00
2 . . . . 60.00
3 Ph(c) 60.00
4 Ph(c) 60.00

FAMILY GUY
Devil's Due Publishing, 2006
1 100 Ways to Kill Lots 7.00
2 Family Comes First 7.00
3 Books Don't Taste Very Good . . . 7.00
TPB A Big Book of Crap 17.00

FAMILY MATTER
Kitchen Sink, 1998
GN by Will Eisner 25.00

FAMOUS INDIAN TRIBES
Dell Publishing Co., 1962
1 . . . . 30.00
2 . . . . 15.00

FANTASTIC VOYAGES OF SINBAD, THE
Gold Key, 1965
1 Ph(c) 125.00
2 June, 1967 . . . . 100.00

FANTASY FEATURES
AC Comics, 1987
1 . . . . 3.00
2 . . . . 3.00

FARO KORBIT
APC, 2003
1 (of 4) 3.50
2 thru 4 . . . . @3.50
TPB 17.00

FARSCAPE: WAR TORN
WildStorm/DC, 2001
1 (of 2) MWm, F:John Crichton . . . 5.00
2 MWm,48-page 5.00

FAT ALBERT
Gold Key, 1974–79
1 . . . . 50.00
2 . . . . 35.00
3 thru 10 . . . . @35.00
11 thru 29 . . . . @30.00

FATALE
Broadway, 1995
1 thru 6 JJo, Inherit the
  Earth, pt.5 . . . . @3.00
7 Fatale now Queen of the World . . 3.00

8 Crown of Thorns, pt.2 . . . . 3.00
9 Crown of Thorns, pt.3 . . . . 3.00
TPB Inherit the Earth 15.00

FATE'S FIVE
Innervision, 1998
1 (of 4) 2.50
1 variant cover 2.50
2 (of 4) 2.50
3 (of 4) 2.50

FATHOM
Comico, 1987
1 thru 3 From Elementals . . . . . . @2.50
[2nd Series], 1993
1 thru 3 . . . . @2.50
Aspen, 2005
0 . . . . 2.50
1 . . . . 3.00
1a signed 30.00
2 thru 4 . . . . @3.00
5 thru 11 . . . . @3.00
1-shot Fathom Beginnings 2.00

FATHOM: DAWN OF WAR
Aspen, 2003
0 . . . . 2.50
1 . . . . 3.00
2 thru 3 . . . . @3.00
Spec. Cannon Hawke #1 . . . . 3.00
TPB Vol. 1 . . . . 10.00

FATMAN, THE HUMAN FLYING SAUCER
Lightning Comics, 1967
1 CCB,O:Fatman & Tin Man . . . 100.00
2 CCB 75.00
3 CCB,(Scarce). 80.00

FAUST: BOOK OF M
Avatar Press, 1999
1 (of 3) DQ,TV 4.00
1a (of 3) prism foil (c) 13.00
1b signed, leather cover 20.00
1c Royal Blue edition 75.00
2 . . . . 4.00
3 . . . . 4.00

FEARBOOK
Eclipse
1 SBi,RV,A Dead Ringer 2.50

FEAR THE DEAD
Boom! Studios, 2006
GN A Zombie Survivor's Journal . . . 6.00

FELIX THE CAT
Harvey, 1991
1 thru 4 . . . . @4.00
5 thru 7 . . . . @3.00

FELIX THE CAT: THE MOVIE
Felix Comics, 1998
1-shot, issued a more 10 years
  after movie 4.00

FELIX'S NEPHEWS INKY & DINKY
Harvey Publications, 1957
1 . . . . 150.00
2 thru 7 . . . . @100.00

FEM 5
Entity, 1995
1 thru 4 five-part series . . . . @3.00
1 signed & numbered 13.00

FEMFORCE
AC Comics, 1985
1 O:Femforce 11.00
2 A:Captain Paragon. 5.00
3 Skin Game 5.00
4 Skin Game 5.00
5 Back in the Past 5.00
6 EL,Back in the Past 5.00
7 HB,O:Captain Paragon 5.00
8 V:Shade 5.00
9 V:Dr.Rivits 5.00
10 V:Dr.Rivits 5.00
11 D:Haunted Horsemen 4.00
12 V:Dr.Rivits 4.00
13 V:She-Cat 4.00
14 V:Alizarin Crimson 4.00
15 V:Alizarin Crimson 4.00
16 thru 56 See Black & White Pub.
57 V:Goat God 3.00
58 I:New Sentinels 3.00
59 I:Paragon 3.00
60 V:Sentinels 3.00
61 F:Tara 3.00
62 V:Valkyra 3.00
63 I:Rayda 3.00
64 thru 67 . . . . @3.00
68 Spellbound 3.00
69 She-Cat Possessed 3.00
70 Island Out of Time 3.00
71 Darkfire Returns 3.00
72 w/Sentinels of Justice 4.00
72a no extras 3.00
73 w/Compact Comic 4.00
73a Regular edition 3.00
74 Daughter of Darkness 4.00
74a Regular edition 3.00
75 Gorby Poster 5.00
75a Regular edition 3.00
76 Daughters pt. 3, polybagged
  with Compact Comic 4.00
76a no bag or comic 3.00
77 V:Sea Monster 3.00
78 V:Gorgana, bagged with comic. . 5.00
78a no bag or comic 3.00
79 V:Iron Jaw, polybagged
  with Index 5.00
79a no bag or index 3.00
80 polybagged with Index 6.00
80a F:Mr. Brimstone, Rad 3.00
81 polybagged with Index 6.00
81a Valentines Day Spec 3.00
82 polybagged with Index 6.00
82a F:Ms. Victory 3.00
83 F:Paragon 3.00
84 The Death of Joan Wayne
  polybagged with index #4B 6.00
84a no bag or index 3.00
85 Synn vs. Narett, polybagged
  with card 5.00
85a no bag or card 3.00
86 polybagged with index #5 . . . . . 5.00
86a unbagged, no suplements 3.00
87 Pandemonium in Paradise,
  polybagged with plate 10.00
87a unbagged, no plate 3.00
88 F:Garganta, polybagged with
  index #6 . . . . 6.00
89 polybagged with index 6.00
90 polybagged with index 6.00
91 polybagged with index 6.00
92 polybagged with index 6.00
88a thru 92a unbagged, no index @3.00
93 on see Black & White Pub.
Spec.#1 . . . . 2.50
Untold Origin Spec #1 . . . . 5.00

FEMFORCE: UP CLOSE
AC Comics, 1992–95
1 F:Stardust 4.00
2 F:Stardust 4.00
3 . . . . 4.00
4 . . . . 4.00
5 with Sticker 4.00
6 with Sticker 4.00
7 with Sticker 4.00
8 with Sticker 4.00
5a thru 8a Regular Edition . . . . . @3.00
9 thru 11 . . . . @3.00

FERRET
Malibu, 1992
1 (From Protectors),DZ,V:Purple
  Dragon Tong,A:Iron Skull 2.50
[Regular Series] 1992–93
1 . . . . 2.50
2 thru 11 . . . . @2.50

FIGHT THE ENEMY
Tower Comics, 1966
1 BV,Lucky 7 . . . . 60.00
2 AMc 40.00
3 WW,AMc 40.00

Fighting American #1
© Harvey

FIGHTING AMERICAN
Harvey, 1966
1 SK,Rep Fighting American
  from 1950's 200.00

FIGHTING AMERICAN
Awesome Entertainment
1 . . . . 8.00
1a variant (c). 4.00
1b Platinum (c) 15.00
2 . . . . 4.00
Coll.Ed.#1 rep.#1–#2 . . . . 5.00
Spec.#1 Fighting American: Cold War
  RLe,JLb 2.50

FIGHTING AMERICAN: DOGS OF WAR
Awesome Entertainment, 1998
1 JSn,SPa,F:John Flagg 2.50
1a Tour Edition, RLe cover 5.00
1b Tour Edition, signed 12.00
2 JSn,SPa,other super-soldiers . . . 2.50
2a variant cover 2.50
3 A:Crimson Dragon 2.50

All comics prices listed are for *Near Mint* condition. **CVA Page 617**

4 Who is No Name? 2.50
Spec.'98 Con preview,b&w,16-page 5.00

FIGHTING AMERICAN: RULES OF THE GAME
Awesome Entertainment, 1997
1 JLb 3.00
2 JLb 2.50
3 JLb, Baby Buzz Bomber 2.50
TPB 13.00

FINAL DESTINATION: SPRING BREAK
Zenescope Entertainment, 2006
1 (of 5) 4.00
2 thru 5 . . . . @4.00

FIREARM
Malibu Ultraverse, 1993–95
0 w/video,I:Duet 3.00
1 I:Firearm,Alec Swan 2.50
1 silver foil, limited edition. 4.00
2 BWS,A:Hardcase,BU:Rune 2.75
3 thru 10 . . . . @2.50
11 Ultraverse Premier #5,BU:Prime. 3.50
12 thru 18 . . . . @2.50

FIREBLAST: ADVENTURES IN THE 30TH CENTURY
Masterpiece Comics, 2006
1-shot 3.00

FIRST, THE
Crossgen Comics, 2000
1 BKs,BS 6.00
2 thru 13 BKs,BS . . . . @5.00
14 thru 25 . . . . @3.00
26 thru 36 . . . . @3.00
37 Atwaal returns 3.00
TPB Vol. 1 192-page 20.00
TPB Vol. 2 rep. #8–#13 . . . . 20.00
TPB Vol. 3 Sinister Motives 16.00
TPB Vol. 5 Liquid Alliances 16.00
TPB Vol. 6 Ragnarok 16.00

FIRST ADVENTURES
First, 1985
1 thru 5 . . . . @2.50

FIRST GRAPHIC NOVELS
First 1984
1 JBi,Beowolf 8.00
1a 2nd Printing 7.00
2 TT,Time Beavers 10.00
3 HC,American Flag Hard Times . 12.00
4 Nexus,SR. 10.00
5 Elric,CR 20.00
6 Enchanted Apples of Oz 6.00
7 Secret Island of Oz 10.00
8 HC,Time 2 . . . . 28.00
9 TMNT 20.00
10 TMNT II 18.00
11 Sailor on the Sea 15.00
12 HC,American Flagg 15.00
13 Ice King 10.00
14 TMNT III 14.00
15 Hex Breaker 10.00
16 Forgotten Forest 11.00
17 Mazinger 11.00
18 TMNT IV 13.00
19 O;Nexus 10.00
20 American Flagg 16.00

1st FOLIO
Pacific, 1984
1 Joe Kubert School 2.50

FIRST WAVE: HEART OF A KILLER
Andromeda Entertainment, 2000
1 by Dan Parsons, TV tie-in 3.00
1a photo (c). 3.00
2 . . . . 4.00
2a photo (c). 4.00
2b signed 10.00
2c sketch edition 20.00
TPB Vol. 1 Heart of a Killer 9.00

FIRST WAVE: IN THE BEGINNING
Andromeda Entertainment, 2001
1 . . . . 3.00
1a photo (c). 3.00

FIRST WAVE: JORDAN RADCLIFFE
Andromeda Entertainment, 2001
1 painted (c) 3.00
1a photo (c). 3.00
1b limited foil (c) 10.00

FISH POLICE
Comico, 1987
Vol 2 #6 thru #15 rep. . . . . @2.50
Vol 2 #16 rep. 3.00
Vol 2 #17 rep.,AuA 3.00
1 Color Special (July 1987) 3.50

FLAMEHEAD
JNCO Comics, 1998
1 I:Flamehead 2.50
2 thru 5 . . . . @2.50

FLARE
Hero Graphics
1 I:Darkon&Prof.Pomegranite 4.00
2 Blonde Bombshell,A:Galooper. . . 3.00
3 I:Sky Marshall 3.00
Ann.#1 . . . . 4.50

[2nd Series]
1 A:Galloping Galooper 3.00
2 A:Lady Arcane 3.00
3 I:Britannia 3.00
4 A:Indigo 2.50
5 R:Eternity Smith,O:Die Kriegerin . 4.00
6 I:Tigress 3.50
7 V:The Enemies 4.00
8 Morrigan Wars#4,A:Icicle Dragon 3.50
9 Morrigan Wars Pt.7 (B&W) 3.50

FLARE
Heroic Publishing, 2004
1 . . . . 3.00
2 . . . . 3.00
3 thru 9 . . . . @3.00
30 . . . . 3.00
31 thru 32 . . . . @3.00
33 thru 35 . . . . @3.25
TPB Vol. 1 . . . . 18.00

FLARE ADVENTURES
Hero Graphics, 1992
1 rep. 3.00
2 flipbook w/Champions Classics . . 3.00
3 flipbook w/Champions Classics . . 3.00
Becomes: B&W

Flare Adventures #2
© Hero Graphics

FLARE ADVENTURES
Heroic Publishing, 2005
1 The League of Champions 3.00
15 . . . . 3.00
16 thru 18 . . . . @3.25

FLASH GORDON
Gold Key, 1965
1 . . . . 125.00

FLASH GORDON
King, 1966–69
1 AW,DH,A:Mandrake 150.00
1a Comp. Army giveaway 125.00
2 FBe,A:Mandrake,R:Ming 100.00
3 RE,"Lost in the Land of
    The Lizardmen" 110.00
4 AW,B:Secret Agent X-9 . . . . . . 120.00
5 AW 120.00
6 RC,On the Lost Continent
    of Mongo 110.00
7 MR, rep. In the Human Forest. 110.00
8 RC,JAp 110.00
9 AR,rep 120.00
10 AR,rep 120.00
11 RC 100.00

Charlton, 1969–70
12 RC 75.00
13 JJ 75.00
14 . . . . 60.00
15 . . . . 60.00
16 . . . . 60.00
17 Brick Bradford story 60.00
18 MK,Attack of the Locust Men . . 60.00

Gold Key, 1975
19 Flash returns to Mongo. 15.00
20 thru 30 . . . . @10.00
31 thru 37 AW movie adapt . . . . @10.00

FLESH AND BONES
UpShot, 1986
1 Moore 3.00
2 thru 4 Moore . . . . @3.00

FLINTSTONES
Harvey
1 . . . . 3.00
2 Romeo and Juliet 3.00

FLINTSTONES
Archie, 1995
1 thru 10 . . . . @3.50
2 thru 14 . . . . @3.00
15 Frankenstone's Monster 3.00
20 An Heir-Raising Tale 3.00
21 King Fred The Last 3.00
22 Something Gruesome This
    Way Comes 3.00

FLINTSTONES, THE
Dell Publishing Co., 1961
#1 *see Dell Giant*
2 . . . . 200.00
3 thru 6 . . . . @175.00

Gold Key, 1962
7 . . . . 150.00
8 A:Mr.& Mrs J. Evil Scientists . . 125.00
9 A:Mr.& Mrs.J. Evil Scientists . . 125.00
10 A:Mr.& Mrs.J. Evil Scientists . . 125.00
11 I:Pebbles 150.00
12 The Too-Old Cowhand 100.00
13 thru 15 . . . . @100.00
16 I:Bamm-Bamm 135.00
17 thru 20 . . . . @100.00
21 thru 23 . . . . @70.00
24 I:Gruesomes 100.00
25 thru 29 . . . . @100.00
30 Dude Ranch Roundup 100.00
31 Christmas(c) 100.00
32 . . . . 65.00
33 A:Dracula & Frankenstein 70.00
34 I:The Great Gazoo 125.00
35 . . . . 65.00
36 The Man Called Flintstone . . . 65.00
37 thru 60 . . . . @65.00

FLINTSTONES, THE
Charlton Comics, 1970
1 . . . . 150.00
2 . . . . 90.00
3 thru 7 . . . . @60.00
8 Summer Vacation 100.00
9 . . . . 60.00
10 . . . . 60.00
11 thru 20 . . . . @50.00
21 thru 50 . . . . @50.00

FLINTSTONES IN 3-D
Blackthorne
1 thru 5 . . . . @3.00

FLIPPER
Gold Key, 1966
1 Ph(c) from TV series 150.00
2 and 3 Ph(c) . . . . @125.00

FLOOD RELIEF
Malibu Ultraverse, 1994
GN Ultraverse Heroes 5.00

FLY, THE
Archie/Red Circle, 1983
1 JSn,A:Mr.Justice 6.00
2 thru 9 RB,SD . . . . @5.00

FLYING SAUCERS
Dell, 1967
1 . . . . 100.00
2 thru 5 . . . . @60.00

FLYMAN
Archie Publications
{Prev: Adventures of the Fly}
31 I:Shield (Bill Higgins), A:Comet,
    Black Hood 100.00
32 I:Mighty Crusaders 85.00

---

33 A:Mighty Crusaders, R:Hangman
    Wizard 85.00
34 MSy,A:Black Hood,Shield,Comet
    Shield back-up story begins . . 75.00
35 O:Black Hood 75.00
36 O:Web,A:Hangman in Shield
    strip 75.00
37 A:Shield 75.00
38 A:Web 60.00
39 A:Steel Sterling 60.00

FOOTSOLDIERS
Maximum Press, 1996
1 KJo,PhH, ... 3.00

Foozle #3
© *Eclipse*

FOOZLE
Eclipse, 1985
1 . . . . 2.50
2 . . . . 2.50
3 . . . . 2.50

FORBIDDEN PLANET
Innovation, 1992
1 Movie Adapt. 2.50
2 Movie adapt.contd. 2.50
3 Movie adapt.contd. 2.50
4 Movie adapt.contd. 2.50
GN rep.#1–#4 (1997) 9.00

FORCE OF THE BUDDHA'S PALM
Jademan, 1988–93
1 . . . . 3.00
2 . . . . 2.50
3 . . . . 2.50
4 . . . . 2.50
5 thru 10 . . . . @2.50
11 thru 24 . . . . @2.50
25 thru 43 . . . . @2.50
44 D:White Crane 3.00
45 thru 55 . . . . @2.50

4-D MONKEY
Dr. Leung's, 1988–90
1 thru 11 . . . . @2.50

FOREVER WAR, THE
NBM
GN Vol. 1 Joe Haldeman adapt. . . . 9.00
GN Vol. 2 Joe Haldeman adapt. . . . 9.00
GN Vol. 3 Joe Haldeman adapt. . . . 9.00

FORGOTTEN REALMS: THE DARK ELF TRILOGY
Devil's Due Publishing, 2005
Book I: Homeland
1 (of 3) 5.00
1b convention special 10.00
2 thru 3 . . . . @5.00
2a thru 3a collector's edition . . . . @9.00
TPB Homeland. 15.00
The Legend of Drizzt, Book II: Exile
1 (of 3) 5.00
1a collector's edition 9.00
2 . . . . 5.00
2a collector's edition 9.00
3 . . . . 5.00
3a collector's edition 9.00
TPB Exile 10.00
Legend of Drizzt: Book III Sojourn
1 (of 3) 5.00
1a variant (c) 9.00
2 thru 3 . . . . @5.00
2a thru 3a variant (c)s . . . . @9.00
TPB 15.00
Legend of Drizzt: Book IV The Crystal Shard
1 (of 3) 5.00
1a Card stock variant (c) 9.00
2 . . . . 5.00
2a Card stock variant (c) 9.00

FOXFIRE
Malibu Ultraverse, 1996
1 From Phoenix Resurrection 2.50
2 Fate of Mastodon revealed 2.50
3 . . . . 2.00
4 . . . . 2.00

FRANK
Nemesis, 1994
1 thru 4 DGc(s),GgP . . . . @3.00
1a thru 4a variant(c) . . . . @3.00

FRANK FRAZETTA FANTASY ILLUSTRATED
Frank Frazetta, 1998
1 . . . . 6.00
1a variant cover 8.00
3 thru 9 . . . . @6.00
3 Neil Gaiman signed &
    numbered 25.00
3 Daniel signed & numbered 20.00

FRANK FRAZETTA DEATH DEALER
Verotik, 1997
1 thru 4 by Glenn Danzig . . . . . . @7.00

FRANK MILLER'S ROBOCOP
Avatar Press/Pulsar Press, 2003
1 . . . . 3.50
1b robosteel (c) 15.00
2 thru 9 . . . . @3.50
1a thru 5a wraparound (c) . . . . . @4.00
6a thru 9a wraparound (c) . . . . . @3.50
2b Civic Duty edition 4.00
4b thru 8b special edition (c)s . . . @6.00
Pulsar Press, 2006
9 Savior (c) 6.00
Spec. Killing Machine 3.00
Spec. Killing Machine variant (c) . . . 3.00
Spec. Killing Machine no escape
    variant(c) 6.00
TPB (2006) 30.00

All comics prices listed are for *Near Mint* condition.

FRANKENSTEIN
Dell Publishing Co., 1964
1 . . . . 150.00
2 . . . . 100.00
3 and 4 . . . . @75.00

FRANKENSTEIN
Caliber
Novel Adaptation 3.00

FRANKENSTEIN
Topps, 1994
1 thru 4 . . . . @3.00

FRANKENSTEIN
Malibu
1 thru 3 movie promo . . . . @2.50

FRANKENSTEIN
DRACULA WAR
Topps, 1995
1 Frank Vs. Drac. 3.00
2 F:Saint Germaine. 3.00
3 Frank Vs. Drac. 3.00

FREDDY
Dell Publishing Co., 1963
1 . . . . 60.00
2 and 3 . . . . @50.00

FREDDY'S DEAD:
THE FINAL NIGHTMARE
Innovation
1 Movie adaption, Pt.1 . . . . 3.00
2 Movie adaption, Pt.2 . . . . 3.00
GN Movie Adapt. 7.00
3-D Special. 2.50

FRED PERRY'S S-GUILD
Antarctic Press, 2006
1 . . . . 3.50

FREE FALL
Narwain Publishing, 2005
1 (of 3) 4.00
2 thru 5 . . . . @4.00
TPB 10.00

FREEMIND
Future Comics, 2003
5 and 6 . . . . @3.50
7 thru 13 . . . . @3.00
TPB Origin of Freemind. 17.00
TPB Vol. 2 . . . . 15.00

FREEX
Malibu Ultraverse, 1993–95
1 I:Freex w/Ultraverse card 3.00
1a Ultra-Limited 4.00
1b Full Hologram (c). 5.00
2 L:Valerie,I:Rush 3.00
3 A:Rush 3.00
4 GJ(s),DdW,BWS,BU:Rune 2.75
5 thru 18 . . . . @2.50
Giant Size#1 A:Prime. 2.50

FRIDAY FOSTER
Dell Publishing Co., 1972
1 . . . . 45.00

FRIDAY THE 13th
Avatar Press, 2005
Spec. #1 . . . . 4.00
Spec. #1 variant (c)s 4.00

Spec. #1 variant special (c)s . . . . @6.00
Spec. #1 glow (c). 15.00
Spec. #1 Blood Red Con (c) 5.00
Spec. #1 Prism foil (c) 13.00
Spec. Fearbook #1 . . . . 4.00
Spec. Fearbook #1 variant (c)s . . @4.00
Spec. Fearbook #1 leather (c) . . . 20.00

FRIDAY THE 13TH:
BLOODBATH
Avatar Press, 2005
1 . . . . 4.00
2 thru 3 . . . . @4.00
1a thru 3a wraparound (c)s. . . . . @4.00
1b thru 3b variant (c)s. . . . . @4.00
2c thru 3c Die-dut (c)s . . . . @10.00
1d thru 3d Special (c)s . . . . @6.00
1e Leather (c) 20.00

FRIDAY THE 13th:
JASON VS. JASON X
Avatar Press, 2006
1 (of 2) by Mike WOlfer 4.00
1a wraparound (c) 4.00
1b variant (c)s. . . . . @4.00
1c Nano steel (c) 15.00
1d Blood red convention (c) 5.00
1e Face Off (c) 6.00
2 . . . . 4.00
2a wraparound (c) 4.00
2b variant (c)s. . . . . @4.00
2c Nano steel (c) 15.00
2d Blood red convention (c) 5.00

Friendly Ghost Casper #135
© Harvey Publications

FRIENDLY GHOST
CASPER, THE
Harvey Publications, 1958
1 . . . . 1,000.00
2 . . . . 800.00
3 thru 10 . . . . @500.00
11 thru 20 . . . . @300.00
21 thru 30 . . . . @150.00
31 thru 50 . . . . @100.00
51 thru 100. . . . . @80.00
101 thru 159. . . . . @60.00
160 thru 163 52 pgs. . . . . @40.00
164 thru 253. . . . . @20.00
Becomes:

CASPER
THE FRIENDLY GHOST

FRIGHT NIGHT
Now, 1988–90
1 thru 22 . . . . @2.50

FRIGHT NIGHT 3-D
Now, 1992
1 Dracula,w/3-D Glasses 3.00
2 . . . . 3.00

FRIGHT NIGHT II
Now
Movie Adaptation 4.00

FROGMEN, THE
Dell Publishing Co., 1962
1 GE,Ph(c) 150.00
2 GE,FF 100.00
3 GE,FF 100.00
4 . . . . 75.00
5 ATh. 85.00
6 thru 11 . . . . @65.00

FROM HEAVEN TO HELL
Dead Dog Comics, 2005
1 . . . . 5.00
2 . . . . 5.00

FRONTLINE COMBAT
EC Comics, 1995
1 thru 4 rep. . . . . @3.00
Gemstone, 1996
5 thru 13 rep. . . . . @3.00
14 WW(c). 3.00
15 . . . . 3.00
Annuals'
TPB Vol. 1 rebinding of #1–#5. . . . 11.00
TPB Vol. 2 rebinding of #6–#10. . . 13.00
TPB Vol. 3 rebinding of #11–#15. . 13.50

F-TROOP
Dell Publishing Co., 1966
1 Ph(c) 200.00
2 thru 7 Ph(c) . . . . @100.00

FULL CIRKLE
Full Circle Publications, 2004
1 (of 3) SBs. 4.00
1a variant (c). 3.50
1b signed, either cover . . . . @10.00
1c 2nd printing 3.50
2 . . . . 3.50
2a variant (c). 3.50
2b 2nd printing 3.50
3 . . . . 4.00
3a variant (c) 4.00
1b and 3b Classic silver foil (c). . @8.00
Preview book 16-pg. 3.00
Preview book, signed. 5.00

FUN-IN
Gold Key, 1970–74
1 . . . . 125.00
2 . . . . 75.00
3 thru 6 . . . . @75.00
7 thru 10 . . . . @60.00
11 thru 15 . . . . @60.00

FUNKY PHANTOM
Gold Key, 1972–75
1 . . . . 100.00
2 . . . . 50.00
3 . . . . 50.00
4 . . . . 50.00
5 . . . . @50.00
6 thru 13 . . . . @35.00

FURIOUS FIST OF THE DRUNKEN MONKEY: ORIGIN OF THE SPECIES
Silent Devil Productions, 2006
1 (of 3) 3.00
2 .... 3.00

FURRY NINJA HIGH SCHOOL STRIKES BACK
Shanda Fantasy Arts, 2003
1 (of 2) 5.00
2 .... 5.00

FUSED
Boom! Studios, 2005
1-shot 7.00

FUTURAMA COMICS
Bongo Comics, 2000
1 thru 6 .... @3.50
7 thru 10 .... @3.00
11 thru 21.................... @3.00
22 thru 28.................... @3.00
TPB Vol. 1 .... 13.00
TPB Vol. 2 .... 15.00
TPB Vol. 3 Time Bender 15.00
Spec. Futurama/Simpsons: Infinity
  Secret Crossover Crisis, pt.1 .. 2.50
Spec. Futurama/Simpsons Crossover
  Crisis, pt.2 .... 2.50

FUTURIANS
Lodestone, 1985
1 DC,I:Dr.Zeus 2.50
2 DC,I:MsMercury............. 2.50
3 DC 2.50
Eternity Graphic Novel, DC, Rep.
  +new material 10.00

GALACTICA: THE NEW MILLENNIUM
Realm Press, 1999
1 Battlestar Galactica 3.00
1 convention edition 5.00
1a signed 15.00
2 Busch (c)................... 3.00
2a Scalf (c).................. 3.00
2b convention edition 5.00
3 .... 3.00
3a 3.00
4 .... 3.00
4a deluxe 5.00
Spec. Fangs of the Beast 4.00
Spec. Fangs of the Beast,deluxe... 5.00
Tour Book, Conv. Ed., signed 15.00
Spec.Search for Sanctuary 4.00

GALL FORCE: ETERNAL STORY
CPM, 1995
1 F:Solnoids 3.00
2 V:Paranoid................. 3.00
3 .... 3.00
4 Implant Secrets 3.00

GALLANT MEN, THE
Gold Key, 1963
1 RsM 60.00

GALLEGHER BOY REPORTER
Gold Key, 1965
1 .... 50.00

GARGOYLES
Amaze Ink/Slave Labor Graphics, 2006
1 .... 6.00
2 thru 3 .... @4.00

GARRISON'S GORRILLAS
Dell Publishing Co., 1968
1 Ph(c) 100.00
2 thru 5 Ph(c) .... @60.00

GARTH ENNIS'S 303
Avatar Press, 2004
1 (of 6) 4.00
1a wraparound (c)............. 4.00
1b gold foil (c)............... 7.00
2 thru 6 .... @4.00
2a thru 6a wraparound (c) 4.00

GASP!
American Comics Group March, 1967
1 .... 100.00
2 thru 4, Aug. 1967 .... @75.00

Gate Crasher (Ring of Fire) #1
© Black Bull Entertainment

GATE CRASHER
Black Bull Entertainment, 2000
1 (of 4) MWa,ACo,JP 2.50
1a variant (c)................. 5.00
2 MWa,ACo,JP 2.50
3 MWa,ACo,JP 2.50
3a variant JJu(c)............. 2.50
4 MWa,ACo,JP, concl. 2.50
4a variant JLi(c) 2.50

GATE CRASHER
Black Bull Entertainment, 2000
1 MWa,JP,ACo,F:Alex Wagner.... 2.50
1a variant Wizard World (c) 5.00
2 MWa,JP,ACo,Blue Tonya, Otmar. 2.50
3 MWa,JP,ACo,F:Hazard 2.50
4 MWa,JP,ACo,ACo(c) 2.50
5 MWa,JP,ACo,AAd(c) 2.50
6 MWa,JP,ACo 2.50
2a thru 6a variant (c)s......... @2.50
TPB Ring of Fire, 104-page...... 13.00

GATESVILLE COMPANY
Speakeasy Comics, 2005
1 .... 3.00
2 & 3 .... @3.00

G.E.I.
Cyberosia Publishing, 2004
1 .... 3.50
2 thru 3 .... @3.50

GEI
Narwain Publishing, 2006
1 .... 2.00

GEN-ACTIVE
WildStorm/DC, 2000
1 V:DV8,48-pg.quarterly 4.00
2 several stories 4.00
2a variant JPn (c)............. 4.00
3 BSz,JLe(c).................. 4.00
3a variant Lee Bermejo (c)...... 4.00
4 R:Wildcore 4.00
4a variant (c)................. 4.00
5 F:Sublime.................. 4.00
5a variant (c) (1:2)........... 4.00
6 Freakville 4.00

GENE FUSION
Beckett Entertainment, 2003
1 Monsters on Parade,pt.1 ...... 3.00
2 Monsters on Parade,pt.2 ...... 3.00
3 Monsters on Parade,pt.3 ...... 3.00
4 Battle under the Big Tent 3.00

GENE RODDENBERRY'S LOST UNIVERSE
Teckno-Comics, 1994
0 I:Sensua................... 2.50
1 Gene Roddenberry's 2.50
2 Grange Discovered 2.50
3 Secrets Revealed 2.50
4 F:Penultra 2.50
5 I:New Alien Race 2.50
6 Two Doctor Granges 2.50
7 F:Alaa Chi Tskare 2.50

GENE RODDENBERRY'S XANDER IN LOST UNIVERSE
Teckno-Comics, 1995
1 V:Black Ghost 3.00
2 V:Walker................... 3.00
3 V:Lady Sensua 3.00
4 thru 7 .... @3.00
8 F:Lady Sensua.............. 3.00
[Mini-Series], 1995
1 RoR,F:L.Nimoy's Primortals 3.00

GENE SIMMONS' HOUSE OF HORRORS
Arcade/Simmons Comics Group, 2006
1 .... 3.00
1a variant (c)................. 3.00

GENE SIMMONS' JAZAN WILD
Arcade/Simmons Comics Group, 2006
1 .... 3.00
1a variant (c)s .... @3.00
Spec House of Horrors, Halloween
  Edition #1, 90-pg. 6.00

GENESIS
Malibu, 1993
0 GP,w/Pog,F:Widowmaker,
  A:Arrow 3.50
0a Gold Ed................... 5.00

GENSAGA: ANCIENT WARRIOR
Entity Comics, 1995
1 I:Gensaga	2.50
1a with Computer Games	2.50
2 V:Dinosaurs	2.50
3 V:Lord Abyss	2.50

GEN13
WildStorm/DC, 2002
1 CCI,Dylon & Ethan York	3.00
2 CCI,Herod strikes	3.00
3 CCI,Herod strikes	3.00
4 CCI,Hamza	3.00
5 CCI,V:Preston Kills	3.00
6 CCI,V:Purple Haze	3.00
7 CCI,V:The Chrome	3.00
8 CCI,V:The Chrome	3.00
9 CCI,the alter or the morgue	3.00
10 CCI,October Surprise,pt.4	3.00
11 CCI,Two Caitlins	3.00
12 CCI,G-Nome	3.00
13 CCI,G-Nome	3.00
14 CCI,F:Caitlin	3.00
15 CCI,V:The Clique	3.00
16 CCI,finale	3.00
TPB Meanwhile	18.00
TPB September Song	20.00
TPB October Surprises	20.00
TPB Ordinary Heroes	15.00
See also Image Comics section	

GEN13 MOVIE ADAPTATION
WildStorm/DC, 2001
1 JMi, animated movie adapt	2.50

GEN¹³
Wildstorm/DC, Oct., 2006
1	3.00
1a variant (c)	3.00
2	3.00
2a variant (c)	3.00
TPB Who They Are	15.00

GENTLE BEN
Dell Publishing Co., 1968
1 Ph(c)	60.00
2	40.00
3 thru 5	@35.00

GEOMANCER
Valiant, 1994
1 RgM, I:Geomancer	3.00
2 thru 8	@2.50

GEORGE A ROMERO'S DAWN OF THE DEAD
IDW Publishing, 2004
1	4.00
1a variant photo (c)	4.00
2 thru 3	@4.00
TPB	18.00

GEORGE A. ROMERO'S NIGHT OF THE LIVING DEAD: THE BEGINNING
Avatar Press, 2006
1	4.00
1a variant (c)s	@4.00
1b variant Splatter (c)	7.00
1c Leather (c)	20.00
2	4.00
2a variant (c)s	@4.00
2b variant splatter (c)	7.00

GEORGE OF THE JUNGLE
Gold Key, 1969
1 From animated TV show	250.00
2	200.00

GE ROUGE
Verotik, 1997
1 by Glenn Danzig & Calvin Irving	3.00
1 fan club cover (2000)	5.00
2 and 3	@3.00
Biz:GE Rouge #? SBs	3.00

GET SMART
Dell Publishing Co., 1966
1 Ph(c) all	200.00
2 SD	175.00
3 SD	150.00
4 thru 8	@125.00

Ghostbusters #4 © First

[FILMATION'S] GHOSTBUSTERS
First, 1987
1 thru 4	@3.00

GHOST BUSTERS II
Now, 1989
1 thru 3 Mini-series	@3.00

GHOSTBUSTERS
88MPH Studios, 2004
1	3.00
1a variant (c)	3.50
2 thru 3	@3.25
88MPH Studios, 2005
1	4.00

GHOSTBUSTERS: LEGION
88MPH Studios, 2004
1 (of 4)	5.00
1a 2nd printing	3.00
2 thru 4	@3.00
1a thru 4a variant (c)s	@3.50

GHOST STORIES
Dell Publishing Co., 1962
1	150.00
2	75.00
3 thru 10	@70.00
11	65.00
12 thru 19	@50.00
20	70.00

21 thru 33	@50.00
34 rep	50.00
35 rep	70.00
36 & 37 rep	@50.00

GHOSTLY TALES
Charlton, 1966
Previously: Blue Beetle
55 I&O Dr. Graves	125.00
56 thru 70	@75.00
71 thru 100	@60.00
101 thru 169	@50.00

GIANT COMICS
Charlton Comics Summer, 1957
1 A:Atomic Mouse,Hoppy	250.00
2 A:Atomic Mouse	200.00
3	200.00

GIDGET
Dell Publishing Co., 1966
1 Ph(c),Sally Field	175.00
2 Ph(c),Sally Field	125.00

GIFT, THE
First, 1990
Holiday Special	6.00

GIFT, THE
Overcast Comics, 2003
1	6.00
2	4.00
3 thru 5	@3.50
6 thru 7	@3.00

GIGANTOR
Antarctic Press, 2000
1 (of 12) BDn	2.50
2 V:Red Reich	2.50
3	2.50
4 Doppleganger,pt.1	2.50
5 Doppleganger,pt.2	2.50
6 Doppleganger,pt.3	2.50
7 Rulers of the Sea	2.50
8	2.50
9 Sting of the Spider	3.00
10 Sting of the Spider, pt.2	3.00
11 Badge of Danger, pt.1	3.00
12 Badge of Danger, pt.2, concl.	3.00

G.I. JOE 3-D
Blackthorne, 1987
1	3.00
2 thru 5	@2.50
Ann. #1	2.50

G.I. JOE
Devil's Due Publishing, 2004
(Prev. Pub. by Image)
26 thru 35	@3.00
36 thru 41 Union of the Snake	@3.00
42 double size, 48-page	4.50
43 double size	4.50
31 Collector's club edition	10.00
TPB Vol. 2 Beckonings	13.00
TPB Union of the Snake	15.00
TPB Vol. 4 Alliances	15.00
TPB Vol. 5 Return of Serpentor	13.00
TPB Vol. 6 Players & Pawns	13.00
Digest #1 G.I. Joe Arashikage Showdown	11.00

G.I. JOE: AMERICA'S ELITE
Devil's Due Publishing, 2005
0	1.00
0 2nd printing, new cover	3.00

1 . . . . 3.00
1a signed 15.00
2 thru 4 . . . . @3.00
5 thru 6 48-pg. . . . . @4.50
7 thru 17 . . . . @3.00
13a cardstock (c) 6.00
1-shot Data Desk Handbook 3.00
TPB The Newest War 15.00
TPB Vol. 2 The Ties That Bind . . . 16.00
1-shot Hunt for Cobra Commander . 1.00

G.I. JOE DECLASSIFIED
Devil's Due Publishing, 2006
1 (of 3) 5.00
1a variant cardstock (c) 9.00
2 thru 3 . . . . @5.00
2a thru 3a variant cardstock (c) . @9.00

G.I. JOE DREADNOKS: DECLASSIFIED
Devil's Due Publishing, 2006
1 (of 3) 5.00
1a cardstock (c) 9.00
2 (of 3) 5.00
2a cardstock (c) 9.00

G.I. JOE: FRONTLINE
Devil's Due Publishing, 2004
TPB Vol. 1 Icebound 13.00
TPB Vol. 2 History Repeating 10.00
TPB One-shots 16.00

G.I. JOE: MASTER & APPRENTICE
Devil's Due Publishing, 2004
1 . . . . 3.00
1 Philly con. exclusive 10.00
2 thru 4 . . . . @3.00
TPB Vol. 1 . . . . 13.00
Vol. II
1 thru 4 . . . . @3.00

G.I. JOE: G.I. JOE REBORN
Devil's Due Publishing, 2004
Spec #1 . . . . 5.00
TPB G.I. Joe & Cobra Reborn 10.00

G.I. JOE: RELOADED
Devil's Due Publishing, 2004
1 CDi. 3.00
2 thru 14 . . . . @3.00
1-shot Cobra Reborn 5.00

G.I. JOE: SCARLETT DECLASIFIED
Devil's Due Publishing, 2006
1-shot 5.00

G.I. JOE: SIGMA 6
Devil's Due Publishing, 2005
1 thru 6 . . . . @3.00
Digest, 144-pg. 11.00

G.I. JOE: SNAKE-EYES DECLASSIFIED
Devil's Due Publishing, 2006
TPB 19.00

G.I. JOE: SPECIAL MISSIONS
Devil's Due Publishing, 2006
1-shot Manhattan 5.00

1-shot Toyko. 5.00

G.I. JOE VS. TRANSFORMERS
Devil's Due Publishing, 2004
Vol. II
1 . . . . 5.00
1a variant (c) 5.00
2 thru 4 . . . . @3.00
2a thru 4a variant (c). . . . . @3.00
TPB 15.00
GN Convention Special 10.00
TPB Vol. 1 . . . . 16.00

G.I. JOE VS TRANSFORMERS: THE ART OF WAR
Devil's Due Publishing, 2006
1 (of 5 . . . . 3.00
1a variant (c)s . . . . @3.00
2 thru 5 . . . . @3.00
2a thru 5a variant (c) . . . . @3.00
TPB Vol. 3 The Art of War 15.00

GIL THORP
Dell Publishing Co., 1963
1 . . . . 150.00

GIMOLES
Alias Enterprises, 2005
1 (of 4) 1.00
2 thru 4 . . . . @3.00

GINGER FOX
Comico, 1988
1 thru 4 . . . . @2.50

GIN-RYU
Believe In Yourself, 1995
1 F:Japanese Sword. 2.75
2 Identity Revealed. 2.75
3 . . . . 2.75
4 Manhunt For Gin-Ryu 2.75

G.I. R.A.M.B.O.T.
Wonder Color, 1987
1 thru 3 . . . . @2.50

GIRL FROM U.N.C.L.E.
Gold Key, 1967
1 The Fatal Accidents Affair 150.00
2 The Kid Commandos Caper . . 100.00
3 The Captain Kidd Affair 100.00
4 One-Way Tourist Affair. 100.00
5 The Harem-Scarem Affair 100.00

GIRL GENIUS
Studio Foglio, 2001
0 Secret Blueprints Preview B&W . 1.50
1 by Phil & Kaja Foglio 3.00
2 and 3 . . . . @3.00
4 40-page 4.00
5 . . . . 3.00
6 40-page (cancelled?) 4.00
7 40-page 4.00

GLOBAL FREQUENCY
WildStorm/DC, 2002
1 (of 12) WEI. 3.00
2 WEI,SDi 3.00
3 WEI,LSh. 3.00
4 WEI,RMr 3.00
5 WEI,JMu 3.00
6 WEI, ... 3.00
7 WEI,Detonation 3.00

G.I. R.A.M.B.O.T. #1
© Wonder Color Comics

8 WEI,Miranda Zero disappears . . . 3.00
9 WEI,Cathedral Lung. 3.00
10 WEI,Superviolence 3.00
11 WEI,Aleph 3.00
12 WEI,concl. 3.00
TPB Planet Ablaze. 15.00
TPB Detonation Radio. 15.00

GLOBAL FREQUENCY: GLOOM, THE
APC, 2005
1 . . . . 3.50
2 thru 6 . . . . @3.50

GLOOM, THE
Markosia, 2005
3 thru 5 . . . . @3.50

GLORY
Maximum Press, 1996
1–15 see Image
16 JDy 2.50
17 JDy 2.50
18 JDy 2.50
19 JDy,A:Demeter, Silverfall 2.50
20 JDy,A:Silverfall 2.50
21 JDy 2.50
22 JDy 2.50
23 A:Prophet 2.50
TPB Vol. 2, rep. 17.00
TPB Glory/Angela RLd,JDy 17.00
Awesome Entertainment, 1999
0 AMo 2.50
0a & b alternate covers. 2.50
0c Timeless Beauty MMy(c) 6.00
1 AMo & ATi 3.50
2 AMo & ATi 3.00

GLORY/CELESTINE: DARK ANGEL
Maximum Press, 1996
1 & 2 See: Image
3 (of 3) JDy. 2.50

GLORY/LIONHEART: RAGE OF FURIES
Awesome Entertainment, 2000
1 . . . . 3.00

GOAT, THE: H.A.E.D.U.S.
Acclaim, 1998
Spec. CPr,KG,F:Vincent Van Goat . . 4.00

GOBLIN LORD, THE
Goblin Studios, 1996
1 (of 6) sci-fi/fantasy 2.50
2 signed & numbered 10.00
3 . . . . 2.50
3a signed & numbered 10.00
4 thru 6 . . . . @2.50

GODS FOR HIRE
Hot Comics, 1986
1 thru 7 . . . . @2.50

GODWHEEL
Malibu Ultraverse, 1995
0 R:Argus to Godwheel 2.50
1 I:Primevil 2.50
2 Hardcase new costume 2.50
3 F:Lord Pumpkin 2.50
TPB Wheel of Thunder,rep.#0–#3 . 10.00

Godyssey #1
© Maximum

GODYSSEY
Maximum 1996
1 . . . . 3.50

GO-GO
Charlton Comics, 1966
1 Miss Bikini Luv 125.00
2 Beatles 150.00
3 Blooperman 60.00
4 . . . . 60.00
5 . . . . 60.00
6 JAp,Petula Clark, Ph(c) 75.00
7 Beach Boys 65.00
8 JAp,Monkees, Ph(c) 75.00
9 Ph(c),Oct., 1967 . . . . 50.00

GO-GO GORILLA & THE JUNGLE CREW
Ape Entertainment, 2005
Supper Spec. 3.00
Winter Fun Spec. 3.50

GOLD DIGGER
Antarctic Press, 1999
VOL 2
1 by Fred Perry, F:Gina Diggers . . . 2.50

2 . . . . 2.50
3 by Fred Perry 2.50
4 tinted glass is magical 2.50
5 . . . . 2.50
6 ancient cauldrons 2.50
7 Halls of the Extremely Dead 2.50
8 Gone Fishing 2.50
9 Fauntleroy..a God? 2.50
10 Arms Master of Jade 2.50
11 Arms Master of Jade 2.50
12 Arms Master of Jade 3.00
13 Tournament of Arms 3.00
14 Tournament of Arms 3.00
15 . . . . 3.00
16 thru 26 . . . . @3.00
27 thru 37 . . . . @3.00
38 thru 42 . . . . @3.50
43 thru 57 . . . . @3.00
50a variant (c) 3.00
58 thru 68 . . . . @3.00
69 thru 74 . . . . @3.00
75 Heroes (c) 3.00
75a Villains (c) 3.00
76 thru 79 . . . . @3.00
Ann. 2003 B&W 5.00
Ann. 2004 B&W 5.00
Ann. 2005 B&W 4.50
Ann. 15th Special 5.00
Ann., 2006 Special 4.50
Swimsuit Spec. #1 . . . . 4.50
Spec. Swimsuit 2001 . . . . 4.50
Spec. Swimsuit 2002 . . . . 4.50
Spec. Swimsuit 2003 . . . . 4.50
Spec. Swimsuit 2004 . . . . 4.50
Spec. Swimsuit Special 2005 . . . . . 4.50
Spec. Swimsuit Spec., 2006 . . . . . . 4.50
End of Summer Swimsuit (2002) . . 4.50
End of Summer Swimsuit (2003) . . 4.50
End of Summer Swimsuit (2004) . . 4.50
End of Summer Swimsuit (2005) . . 4.50
End of Summer Swimsuit (2006) . . 4.50
Spec. Halloween Spec. #1 . . . . 3.00
Spec. Halloween Special, 2006 . . . 3.00
TPB Gold Brick Vol. 3 . . . . 50.00
TPB Gold Brick Vol. 4 . . . . 50.00
TPB Color series, Vol.1 . . . . 16.00
TPB Color Series, Vol.2 . . . . 16.00
TPB Pocket Manga #1 . . . . 13.00
TPB Pocket Manga #2 thru #6 . . @10.00
TPB Pocket Manga #10 . . . . 13.00
TPB Pocket Manga #11 . . . . 13.00
GN Perfect Memory Vol. 2 . . . . 6.00
GN Perfect Memory Vol. 3 . . . . 6.00
GN Perfect Memory Vol. 4 . . . . 6.00
GN Perfect Memory, Vol. 5 . . . . 6.00
GN Pink Slip 10.00
Spec. Gold Digger Adventures #1
  O:Pink Avenger 3.00
Spec. Gold Digger color remix #1 . . 3.00
Spec. Gold Digger color remix #2 . . 3.00
Spec. Gold Digger color remix #3 . . 3.00
Spec. Gold Digger color remix #4 . . 3.00
Spec. Gold Digger Tangent #1 . . . . 3.00
Spec. Gold Digger Tangent #2 . . . . . 3.00

GOLD DIGGER BETA
Antarctic Press, 1998
Spec. 0 by Ben Dunn, Special
  Origin Issue, 24pg 2.00
1A bu Fred Perry, John Pound (c) . . 3.00
1B Jeff Henderson (c) 3.00
2 and 3 . . . . @3.00

GOLDEN COMICS DIGEST
Gold Key, 1969–76
1 Tom & Jerry,Woody Woodpecker,
  Bugs Bunny 75.00
2 Hanna-Barbera,TV Fun
  Favorites 100.00

3 Tom & Jerry, Woody
  Woodpecker 50.00
4 Tarzan 50.00
5 Tom & Jerry, Woody Woodpecker,
  Bugs Bunny 30.00
6 Bugs Bunny 30.00
7 Hanna-Barbera,TV Fun
  Favorites 75.00
8 Tom & Jerry, Woody Woodpecker,
  Bugs Bunny 25.00
9 Tarzan 60.00
10 Bugs Bunny 25.00
11 Hanna-Barbera,TV Fun
  Favorites 75.00
12 Tom & Jerry,Bugs Bunny 25.00
13 Tom & Jerry 25.00
14 Bugs Bunny,Fun Packed
  Funnies 25.00
15 Tom & Jerry, Woody
  Woodpecker, Bugs Bunny 25.00
16 Woody Woodpecker 25.00
17 Bugs Bunny 25.00
18 Tom & Jerry, ... 25.00
19 Little Lulu 45.00
20 Woody Woodpecker 25.00
21 Bugs Bunny Showtime 25.00
22 Tom & Jerry Winter Winging . . 25.00
23 Little Lulu & Tubby Fun Fling . . 40.00
24 Woody Woodpecker Fun
  Festival 22.00
25 Tom & Jerry 22.00
26 Bugs Bunny Halloween Hulla-
  Boo-Loo,Dr. Spektor article . . . 22.00
27 Little Lulu & Tubby in Hawaii . . 45.00
28 Tom & Jerry 22.00
29 Little Lulu & Tubby 45.00
30 Bugs Bunny Vacation Funnies . 22.00
31 Turk, Son of Stone 50.00
32 Woody Woodpecker
  SummerFun 22.00
33 Little Lulu & Tubby Halloween
  Fun 45.00
34 Bugs Bunny Winter Funnies . . . 22.00
35 Tom & Jerry Snowtime Funtime 22.00
36 Little Lulu & Her Friends 45.00
37 WoodyWoodpecker County Fair 22.00
38 The Pink Panther 22.00
39 Bugs Bunny Summer Fun 22.00
40 Little Lulu 45.00
41 Tom & Jerry Winter Carnival . . . 22.00
42 Bugs Bunny 22.00
43 Little Lulu in Paris 45.00
44 Woody Woodpecker Family Fun
  Festival 22.00
45 The Pink Panther 22.00
46 Little Lulu & Tubby 45.00
47 Bugs Bunny 22.00
48 The Lone Ranger 22.00

GOLDEN PICTURE STORY BOOK
Racine Press (Western), 1961
1 Huckleberry Hound 350.00
2 Yogi Bear 350.00
3 Babes In Toy Land 500.00
4 Walt Disney 450.00

GOLDEN PLATES, THE
AAA Pop Comics, 2004
1 (of 12) 8.00
1a 2nd printing 8.00
2 thru 4 . . . . @8.00

GOMER PYLE
Gold Key, 1966
1 Ph(c) from TV show 250.00
2 and 3 . . . . @175.00

COLOR PUB.

GOOD GUYS
Defiant, 1993
1 JiS(s),I:Good Guys	3.75
2 JiS(s),V:Mulchmorg	3.25
3 V:Chasm	2.75
4 Seduction of the Innocent	3.25
5 I:Truc	3.00
6 A:Charlemagne	2.75
7 JiS(s),V:Scourge	2.50
8 thru 11	@2.50

Goofy Adventures #2
© Walt Disney

GOOFY ADVENTURES
Walt Disney, 1990
1 Balboa de Goofy	3.00
2	3.00
3 thru 17	@3.00

GOON
Albatross 2002
1	25.00
2	20.00
3 thru 5 b&w	@12.00
Spec. Color special	7.00

GOOP, THE
JNCO Comics, 1998
1	2.50
2 thru 4	@2.50

GORGO
Charlton Comics, 1961–65
1 SD,from Movie	450.00
2 SD(c&a),Return of Gorgo	250.00
3 SD(c&a)	200.00
4 SD(c)	150.00
5 The Day Manhattan Died	150.00
6 thru 11	@150.00
12 Monster's Rendezvous	125.00
13 thru 15	@125.00
16 SD,Menace from the Deep	125.00
17 thru 23	@100.00

GORGO'S REVENGE
Charlton Comics, 1962
1 From movie	100.00
Becomes:

THE RETURN OF GORGO
Charlton Comics, 1963
2 SD(c&a),Creature from Corpus III	75.00
3 Hidden Witness	75.00

GORILLA GORILLA
Disney Press, 2006
GN Vol. 1	5.00

G.O.T.H.
Verotik, 1995
1	3.00
2	3.00
3	3.00
TPB SBi, rep. of series	10.00

THE GOTHIC SCROLLS, DRAYVEN
Davdez Arts, 1997
1 16pg.	2.50
1a limited edition, new cover	3.00
2 and 3	@2.50
4 V:Lucifer	2.50
GN	13.00

GOVERNMENT BODIES
Speakeasy Comics, 2006
Vol. 2
1 (of 4)	3.00

GRAPHIC HISTORY
Osprey Graphics, 2006
GN Day of Infamy – Pearl Harbor	10.00
GN The Empire Falls – Midway	10.00
GN Surprise Attack – Shiloh	10.00
GN The Bloodiest Day– Antietam	10.00
GN Island of Terror – Iwo Jima	10.00
GN The War is On – First Bull Run	10.00

GRATEFUL DEAD COMIX
Kitchen Sink
1 TT,inc.DireWolf(large format)	5.50
2 TT,inc.Jack Straw	5.00
3 TT,inc. Sugaree	5.00
4 TT,inc. Sugaree	5.00
5 TT,Uncle John's Band	5.00
6 TT,Eagle Mall #1	5.00

GRAVESTONE
Malibu, July 1993–Feb. 1994
1 D:Gravestone,V:Wisecrack	2.50
1a Newstand Ed.	2.50
2 A:Eternal Man, V:Night Plague	2.50
2a Newstand Ed.	2.50
3 Genesis Tie in,w/skycap	2.50
4 thru 9	@2.50

GREASE MONKEY
Kitchen Sink, 1997
1 by Tim Elred	3.50
2 by Tim Elred	3.50

GREAT AMERICAN WESTERN
AC Comics, 1987
1 Santee, Dark Rider, Missourian	2.50
2 F:The Durango Kid	3.00
3	3.00
4 F:Lash LaRue	3.50
5 Sunset Carson	5.00
6 King of the Bull Whip	6.00

GREEN HORNET, THE
Gold Key, 1967
1 Bruce Lee,Ph(c)	500.00
2 Ph(c)	400.00
3 Ph(c)	300.00

GREEN HORNET
Now, 1989
1 O:40's Green Hornet	7.00
1a 2nd Printing	4.00
2 O:60's Green Hornet	5.00
3 thru 5	@4.00
6	3.00
7 BSz(c),I:New Kato	3.00
8 thru 12	@3.50
13 V:Ecoterrorists	3.50
14 V:Ecoterrorists	3.50
Spec.#1	2.50
Spec.#2	2.50

[2nd Series], 1991
1 V:Johnny Dollar Pt.1	2.50
2 V:Johnny Dollar Pt.2	2.50
3 V:Johnny Dollar Pt.3	2.50
4 V:Ex-Con/Politician	2.50
5 V:Ex-Con/Politician	2.50
6 Arkansas Vigilante	2.50
7 thru 9 The Beast	@2.50
10 Green Hornet-prey	2.50
11 F:Crimson Wasp	2.50
12 Crimson Wasp/Johnny Dollar Pt.1,polybagged w/Button	4.00
13 TD(i),Wasp/Dollar Pt.2	2.50
14 TD(i),Wasp/Dollar Pt.3	2.50
15 TD(i),Secondsight	2.50
16 A:Commissioner Hamiliton	2.50
17 V:Gunslinger	2.50
18 V:Sister-Hood	2.50
19 V:Jewel Thief	2.50
20 F:Paul's Friend	2.50
21 V:Brick Arcade	2.50
22 V:Animal Testers, with Hologravure card	4.00
23 with Hologravure card	4.00
24 thru 25 Karate Wars	@2.50
26 B:City under Siege	2.50
27 with Hologravure card	2.50
28 V:Gangs	2.50
29 V:Gangs	2.50
30 thru 37	@2.50
38 R:Mei Li	2.50
39 Crimson Wasp	4.50
40	4.50
41	2.50
42 Baby Killor	2.50
43 Wedding Disasters	2.50
44 F:Amy Hamilton	2.50
45 Plane Hijacking	2.50
46 Airport Terrorists	2.50
Ann.#1 The Blue & the Green	2.50
1993 Ann	3.00

Bonus Books
TPB rep. Now comics #1–#12, 296pg.	10.00
TPB deluxe rep. Now comics #1–#12, 296pg.	20.00

GREEN HORNET: DARK TOMORROW
Now, 1993
1 thru 3 Hornet Vs Kato	@3.00

GREEN HORNET: SOLITARY SENTINAL
Now, 1992
1 Strike Force	3.00
2 thru 3	@3.00

GREENHAVEN
Aircel, 1988
1 BaB,See Elflord #18	3.00
2 BaB,See Elflord #19	3.00
3 BaB,See Elflord #20	3.00

COLOR PUB.

All comics prices listed are for *Near Mint* condition.

GREEN PLANET
Charlton, 1962
1 DG 150.00

GRENDEL
Comico, 1986–91
1 MW 9.00
1a 2nd printing 2.00
2 MW 6.00
3 thru 6 MW . . . . @5.00
7 MW 5.00
8 thru 12 MW . . . . @5.00
13 KSy(c) MW 4.50
14 KSy(c) MW 3.00
15 KSy(c) MW 3.00
16 MW,Mage 6.00
17 thru 19 MW,Mage . . . . @5.00
20 thru 32 MW . . . . @3.00
33 MW,giant-size 3.50
34 thru 36 MW . . . . @3.00
37 MW 6.00
38 MW 9.00
39 MW,D:Grendel 10.00
40 MW,D:Orion Assante 30.00

GREYLORE
Sirius, 1985–86
1 thru 5 . . . . @2.50

GREYSHIRT: INDIGO SUNSET
WildStorm/DC, 2001
America's Best Comics
1 (of 6) RV 3.50
2 RV 3.50
3 RV 3.50
4 RV, Star of Indigo 3.50
5 RV, Fanman 3.50
6 RV, Black Jack Hawkins 3.50
TPB Indigo Sunset 20.00

GRIM GHOST, THE
Atlas, 1975
1 . . . . 20.00
2 . . . . 20.00
3 . . . . 20.00

GRIMJACK
First, 1984–91
1 TT Teenage suicide story. 3.00
2 thru 20 TT A:Munden's Bar . . . @2.50
21 thru 25 . . . . @2.50
26 1st color TMNTurtles. 10.00

Grimjack #66
© First

GRIMJACK CASEFILE
First, 1990
1 thru 5 rep. . . . . @2.50

GRIMJACK: KILLER INSTINCT
IDW Publishing, 2005
1 JOs,TT 4.00
2 thru 6 . . . . @4.00
TPB 20.00

GRIMM FAIRY TALES
Zenescope Entertainment, 2005
1 Little Red Riding Hood. 6.00
2 Cinderella 6.00
3 Hansel & Gretel 6.00
4 Rumpelstilskin 6.00
5 Sleeping Beauty. 6.00
6 The Robber Bridegroom 4.00
7 Snow White 4.00
8 Jack and the Bean Stalk 4.00
9 Goldilocks 4.00
10 The Frog King. 4.00
11 Bluebeard 3.00
12 Pied Piper. 3.00
13 Beauty and the Beast, pt.1 . . . . 3.00
TPB Vol. 1 . . . . 16.00

GRIMM'S GHOST STORIES
Gold Key/Whitman, 1972–82
1 . . . . 40.00
2 . . . . 25.00
3 . . . . 25.00
4 . . . . 25.00
5 AW 30.00
6 . . . . 15.00
7 . . . . 15.00
8 AW 20.00
9 . . . . 15.00
10 . . . . 15.00
11 thru 16 . . . . @12.00
17 RC. 15.00
18 thru 60 . . . . @10.00

GRIMOIRE, THE
Speakeasy Comics, 2005
1 . . . . 3.00
2 thru 6 . . . . @3.00
7 thru 12 . . . . @3.00
TPB Vol. 1 . . . . 15.00

GROO THE WANDERER
Pacific, 1982–84
1 SA,I:Sage,Taranto 25.00
2 SA,A:Sage 15.00
3 SA,C:Taranto 15.00
4 SA,C:Sage 15.00
5 SA,I:Ahax. 15.00
6 SA,I:Gratic 18.00
7 SA,I:Chakaal 18.00
8 SA,A:Chakaal 18.00

Eclipse
Spec.#1 SA,O:Groo,rep Destroyer
Duck #1 . . . . 23.00

GROUP LARUE, THE
Innovation, 1989
1 MBn 2.50
2 . . . . 2.50
3 . . . . 2.50

27 thru 50 . . . . @2.50
51 thru 81 . . . . @2.50

GRUMPY OLD MONSTERS
IDW Publishing, 2003
1 (of 4) 2.50
2 thru 4 . . . . @4.00
TPB 14.00

GRUNLAND
Narwain Publishing, 2006
GN 6.00

GRUNTS
Arcana Studio, 2006
1 (of 3) 4.00
2 thru 3 . . . . @4.00

GUARDIAN HEROES
Alias Enterprises, 2006
1-shot 3.50

GUILLOTIN
ABC, 1997
1 JQ(c) 3.00
1a RCl(c). 6.00
1b gold cover, polybagged with
trading card 10.00
2 . . . . 3.00
2a Serpent (c). 6.00
2b Cold Series (c). 6.00

GULLIVER'S TRAVELS
Dell Publishing Co., 1965
1 . . . . 100.00
2 and 3 . . . . @75.00

GUMBY
Comico, 1987
1 AAd,Summer Fun Special 5.00
2 AAd,Winter Fun Special. 3.50

GUMBY IN 3-D
Blackthorne
Spec.#1 . . . . 4.00
2 thru 7 . . . . @3.00

GUMBY
Wildcard Production, 2006
1 . . . . 4.00
2 thru 3 . . . . @4.00

GUN FU: THE LOST CITY
Axiom, 2003
1 . . . . 3.50
1a variant (c). 6.00
2 thru 4 . . . . @3.50
2a thru 4a variant (c)s. . . . . @3.50
Preview signed edition. 3.00

HACK/SLASH
Devil's Due Publishing, 2004
1 . . . . 5.00
1-shot Girls Gone Dead. 5.00
1-shot variant(c). 5.00
1-shot Comic Book Carnage 5.00
1-shot Final Revenge of Evil Ernie . 5.00
1-shot Trailers 3.25
1-shot Slice Hard preview special. . 1.00
1-shot Slice Hard 5.00
1-shot Slice Hard variant (c) 5.00
TPB Vol. 1 Fist Cut 15.00

HACK SLASH: LAND OF LOST TOYS
Devil's Due Publishing, 2005
1 (of 3) 3.25
2 thru 3 . . . . @3.25

COLOR PUB.

HALL OF FAME
J.C. Productions, 1983
1 WW,GK,ThunderAgents 2.50
2 WW,GK,ThunderAgents 2.50
3 WW,Thunder Agents 2.50

HALLOWEEN
Chaos! Comics, 2000
1 premium glow-in-the-dark (c) . . . 13.00
1 chromium edition 16.00

HALLOWEEN:
BEHIND THE MASK
Chaos! Comics, 2000
1 photo (c). 3.00

HALLOWEEN II:
THE BLACKEST EYE
Chaos! Comics, 2001
Spec. 3.00
Spec. premium. 10.00

HALLOWEEN III:
THE DEVIL'S EYES
Chaos! Comics, 2001
Spec. 3.00
Spec. variant (c). 3.00
Spec. Previews exclusive 3.00

HALLOWEEN HORROR
Eclipse, 1987
1 . . . . 3.00

HALO:
AN ANGEL'S STORY
Sirius, 1996
1 by Chris Knowles. 3.00
2 . . . . 3.00
3 . . . . 3.00
TPB rep. #1–#3 . . . . 13.00

HAMMER KID
Alias Enterprises, 2006
1-shot 3.50

HAMMER OF GOD
First, 1990
1 thru 4 . . . . @2.50
Deluxe #1 Sword of Justice Bk#1 . . 5.00
Deluxe #2 Sword of Justice Bk#2 . . 5.00

HAMSTER VICE
Blackthorne, 1985–87
1 thru 10 . . . . @2.50
3-D #1 . . . . 2.50

HAND OF FATE
Eclipse, 1988
1 I:Artemus Fate. 2.50
2 F:Artemis & Alexis 2.50
3 Mystery & Suspense 2.50

HANDS OF THE DRAGON
Atlas, 1975
1 . . . . 18.00

HANNA-BARBERA
ALL-STARS
Archie, 1995
1 thru 5 . . . . 3.00

HANNA-BARBERA
BAND WAGON
Gold Key, 1962–63
1 . . . . 225.00
2 . . . . 160.00
3 . . . . 135.00

HANNA-BARBERA
PARADE
Charlton Comics, 1971–72
1 . . . . 150.00
2 thru 10 . . . . @75.00

HANNA-BARBERA
PRESENTS
Archie, 1995
1 thru 15 . . . . @3.00

HANNA-BARBERA
SUPER TV HEROES
Gold Key, 1968
1 B:Birdman,Herculiods,Moby Dick,
Young Samson & Goliath. 350.00
2 . . . . 250.00
3 thru 7 Oct. 1969 . . . . @225.00

HARBINGER
Valiant, 1992
0 DL,O:Sting,V:Harada, from TPB
  (Blue Bird Ed.). 35.00
0 from coupons 4.00
1 DL,JDx,I:Sting,Torque,
  Zeppelin,Flamingo,Kris 30.00
2 DL,JDx,V:Harbinger Foundation,
  I:Dr.Heyward 12.00
3 DL,JDx,I:Ax,Rexo, V:Spider
  Aliens. 9.00
4 DL,JDx,V:Ax,I:Fort,
  Spikeman,Dog,Bazooka 9.00
5 DL,JDx,I:Puff,Thumper,
  A:Solar,V:Harada. 9.00
6 DL,D:Torque,A:Solar,
  V:Harada,Eggbreakers 8.00
1a thru 6a w/o coupon . . . . @2.00
7 DL,Torque's Funeral 8.00
8 thru 40 . . . . @2.50
41 V:Harbinger. 8.00
TPB w/#0,rep#1-4 . . . . 25.00
TPB 2nd Printing w/o #0 . . . . 10.00
TPB #2, Rep. 6-7,10-11. . . . . 10.00

Harbinger #30
© Valiant

HARBINGER FILES:
HARADA
Valiant, 1994
1 BL,DC,O:Harada 2.75
2 Harada's ultimate weapon 2.50

HARDCASE
Malibu Ultraverse, 1993–95
1 I:Hardcase,D:The Squad 3.00
1a Ultra-Limited, silver foil 4.00
1b Full Hologram (c). 6.00
1c Platinum edition 3.50
2 w/Ultraverse card. 3.00
3 Hard decisions. 2.75
4 A:Strangers 2.75
5 BWS,V:Hardwire,BU:Rune 2.75
6 thru 15 . . . . @2.50
16 NIM-E 3.50
17 thru 24 . . . . @2.50
25 Mundiquest,concl. 3.00
26 Time Gem Disaster. 3.00

H.A.R.D. CORPS
Valiant, 1992
1 JLe(c),DL,BL,V:Harbinger
  Foundation,I:Flatline,D:Maniac . 2.50
1a Gold Ed. 2.50
2 thru 30 . . . . @2.50

HARDY BOYS, THE
Gold Key, 1970
1 . . . . 100.00
2 thru 4 . . . . @60.00

HARDY BOYS
NBM Books, 2004
1 The Ocean of Osyria, pt.1 . . . . . . 3.00
2 The Ocean of Osyria, pt.2 . . . . . . 3.00
3 The Ocean of Osyria, pt.3 . . . . . . 3.00
4 Identity Theft, pt.1 . . . . 3.00
5 Identity Theft, pt.2 . . . . 3.00
GN Vol. 1 The Ocean of Osyria . . . 8.00
GN Vol. 2 Identity Theft 8.00
GN Vol. 3: Madhouse. 8.00
Papercutz, 2005
GN Vol. 4 Malled 8.00
GN Vol. 5 Sea You, Sea Me 8.00
GN Vol. 6 Hyde & Shriek 8.00
GN Vol. 7 Opposite Numbers 8.00

HARI KARI
Blackout Comics, 1995
0 I:Hari Kari. 3.00
1 . . . . 3.00
1a commemorative, variant(c) . . . 10.00
Specials & 1-shots
1 The Beginning, O:Kari (1996) . . . 3.00
1a The Beginning, commemorative,
  signed 10.00
1 Bloodshed (1996) 3.00
1a Bloodshed, deluxe, variant(c) . 10.00
1 Live & Untamed! (1996) 3.00
1 Rebirth (1996) 3.00
0 The Silence of Evil (1996) 3.00
0 The Silence of Evil, limited,
  foil stamped 13.00
? The Diary of Kari Sun (1997). . . . 3.00
? The Diary of Kari Sun, deluxe . . 10.00
0 Life or Death (1997) 3.00
0a Life or Death, super sexy
  parody edition 13.00
1 Passion & Death (1997) 3.00
1 Passion & Death, photo(c). 10.00
1 Possessed by Evil (1997) 3.00
1 Resurrection (1997). 3.00

COLOR PUB.

HARLEM GLOBETROTTERS
Gold Key, 1972
1 .... 75.00
2 thru 12, Jan. 1975 .... @50.00

HARRIERS
Entity, 1995
1 I:Macedon Arsenal, Cardinal 3.00
1a with Video Game 7.00
2 and 3 V:Kr'llyn .... @2.50

HARSH REALM
Harris, 1994
1 thru 6 JHi(s), ... @3.00
TPB 15.00

HARVEY HITS
Harvey Publications, 1957–67
1 The Phantom 600.00
2 Rags Rabbit 100.00
3 Richie Rich 4,000.00
4 Little Dot's Uncles 500.00
5 Stevie Mazie's Boy Friend ... 100.00
6 JK(c),BP,The Phantom 500.00
7 Wendy the Witch 800.00
8 Sad Sack's Army Life 250.00
9 Richie Rich's Golden Deeds 1,200.00
10 Little Lotta 350.00
11 Little Audrey Summer Fun ... 300.00
12 The Phantom 500.00
13 Little Dot's Uncles......... 300.00
14 Herman & Katnip 100.00
15 The Phantom 500.00
16 Wendy the Witch 900.00
17 Sad Sack's Army Life 200.00
18 Buzzy & the Crow......... 100.00
19 Little Audrey 200.00
20 Casper & Spooky 200.00
21 Wendy the Witch.......... 500.00
22 Sad Sack's Army Life 150.00
23 Wendy the Witch.......... 500.00
24 Little Dot's Uncles......... 300.00
25 Herman & Katnip 100.00
26 The Phantom 400.00
27 Wendy the Good Little Witch . 600.00
28 Sad Sack's Army Life 150.00
29 Harvey-Toon 150.00
30 Wendy the Witch 400.00
31 Herman & Katnip 100.00
32 Sad Sack's Army Life 150.00
33 Wendy the Witch.......... 400.00
34 Harvey-Toon 100.00
35 Funday Funnies 100.00
36 The Phantom 400.00
37 Casper & Nightmare....... 250.00
38 Harvey-Toon 150.00
39 Sad Sack's Army Life 150.00
40 Funday Funnies 100.00
41 Herman & Katnip 100.00
42 Harvey-Toon 100.00
43 Sad Sack's Army Life 150.00
44 The Phantom 400.00
45 Casper & Nightmare....... 200.00
46 Harvey-Toon 100.00
47 Sad Sack's Army Life 100.00
48 The Phantom 400.00
49 Stumbo the Giant 300.00
50 Harvey-Toon 100.00
51 Sad Sack's Army Life 50.00
52 Casper & Nightmare....... 90.00
53 Harvey-Toons 40.00
54 Stumbo the Giant 100.00
55 Sad Sack's Army Life 40.00
56 Casper & Nightmare........ 75.00
57 Stumbo the Giant 100.00
58 Sad Sack's Army Life 40.00
59 Casper & Nightmare........ 75.00
60 Stumbo the Giant 100.00
61 Sad Sack's Army Life 40.00

62 Casper & Nightmare......... 75.00
63 Stumbo the Giant 90.00
64 Sad Sack's Army Life 40.00
65 Casper & Nightmare......... 60.00
66 Stumbo the Giant 75.00
67 Sad Sack's Army Life 40.00
68 Casper & Nightmare......... 60.00
69 Stumbo the Giant 75.00
70 Sad Sack's Army Life 40.00
71 Casper & Nightmare......... 60.00
72 Stumbo the Giant 75.00
73 Little Sad Sack 40.00
74 Sad Sack's Muttsy 40.00
75 Casper & Nightmare......... 55.00
76 Little Sad Sack 40.00
77 Sad Sack's Muttsy 40.00
78 Stumbo the Giant 75.00
79 Little Sad Sack 40.00
80 Sad Sack's Muttsy 40.00
81 Little Sad Sack 40.00
82 Sad Sack's Muttsy 40.00
83 Little Sad Sack 40.00
84 Sad Sack's Muttsy 35.00
85 Gabby Gob 35.00
86 G.I. Juniors 30.00
87 Sad Sack's Muttsy 35.00
88 Stumbo the Giant 65.00
89 Sad Sack's Muttsy 35.00
90 Gabby Goo 30.00
91 G.I. Juniors 30.00
92 Sad Sack's Muttsy 35.00
93 Sadie Sack 30.00
94 Gabby Goo 30.00
95 G.I. Juniors 30.00
96 Sad Sack's Muttsy 35.00
97 Gabby Goo 30.00
98 G.I. Juniors 30.00
99 Sad Sack's Muttsy 35.00
100 Gabby Goo 30.00
101 G.I. Juniors 25.00
102 Sad Sack's Muttsy 30.00
103 Gabby Goo 25.00
104 G.I. Juniors 25.00
105 Sad Sack's Muttsy 30.00
106 Gabby Goo 25.00
107 G.I. Juniors 25.00
108 Sad Sack's Muttsy 30.00
109 Gabby Goo 25.00
110 G.I. Juniors 25.00
111 Sad Sack's Muttsy......... 30.00
112 G.I. Juniors 25.00
113 Sad Sack's Muttsy......... 30.00
114 G.I. Juniors 25.00
115 Sad Sack's Muttsy......... 30.00
116 G.I. Juniors 25.00
117 Sad Sack's Muttsy......... 30.00
118 G.I. Juniors 25.00
119 Sad Sack's Muttsy......... 30.00
120 G.I. Juniors 25.00
121 Sad Sack's Muttsy 30.00
122 G.I. Juniors 25.00

HATE
Fantagraphics, 1990
1 thru 15, see B&W
16 thru 29.................. @3.00
30 48pg..................... 4.00
Ann.#1 48-page (2000) 4.00
Ann.#2 (2001) 4.00
Ann.#3 (2002) 4.00
Ann.#4 (2003) 5.00
Ann.#5 (2004) 5.00
Ann. #6 (2006)................ 5.00
TPB Vol.1 Hey, Buddy!, rep. #1–#5 13.00
TPB Vol.1 Hey, Buddy! signed.... 13.00
TPB Vol.2 Buddy the Dreamer,
  rep. #6–#10 .... 13.00
TPB Vol.2 Buddy the Dreamer, sgn 13.00
TPB Vol.3 Fun with Buddy
  & Lisa 13.00
TPB Vol.4 Buddy Go Home 17.00
TPB Vol.4 Buddy Go Home!

signed 17.00
TPB Vol.5 Buddy's Got Three
  Moms..................... 17.00
TPB Vol.6 Buddy Bites the Bullet . 17.00

Haunted #12
© Charlton

HAUNTED
Charlton, 1971–84
1 .... 65.00
2 .... 30.00
3 thru 5 .... @30.00
6 thru 10 .... @25.00
11 thru 20 .... @20.00
21 thru 50 .... @15.00
51 thru 75 .... @10.00

HAUNTED, THE
Chaos! Comics, 2001
1 (of 4) PDd 3.00
1a variant Nat Jones (c) 3.00
1b premium ed................ 10.00
2 PDd 3.00
2a variant Molenaar (c)......... 7.50
3 PDd 3.00
3a variant (c)................. 7.50
4 .... 3.00
4a variant (c)................. 7.50
Ashcan, b&w 6.00

HAUNTED, THE: GRAY MATTERS
Chaos! Comics, 2002
1 .... 3.00
1a premium edition........... 10.00

HAUNTED LOVE
Charlton, 1973–75
1 .... 75.00
2 .... 30.00
3 thru 5 .... @30.00
6 thru 11 .... @25.00

HAUNT OF FEAR
Gladstone, 1991
1 EC Rep. H of F #17,WS#28 .... 3.00
2 EC Rep. H of F #5,WS #29..... 3.00

HAUNT OF FEAR
Russ Cochran, 1991
1 EC Rep. H of F #15........... 3.00
2 thru 5 EC Rep. H of F .... @3.00

COLOR PUB.

Second Series, 1992

1 EC Rep. H of F #14,WS#13	2.50
2 EC Rep. H of F #18,WF#14	2.50
3 EC Rep. H of F #19,WF#18	2.50
4 EC Rep. H of F #16,WF#15	2.50
5 EC Rep. H of F #5,WF#22	2.50
6 EC Rep. H of F	2.50
7 EC Rep. H of F	2.50
8 thru 15 Rep.	@2.50

Gemstone

16 thru 28 EC comics reprint	@2.50
'Annuals'	
TPB Vol. 1 rebinding of #1–#5.	9.00
TPB Vol. 2 rebinding of #6–#10.	9.00
TPB Vol. 3 rebinding of #11–#15.	9.00
TPB Vol. 4 rebinding of #16–#20.	13.00
TPB Vol. 5 rebinding of #21–#25.	13.50
TPB Vol. 6 rebinding of #26–#28.	9.00

HAVE GUN, WILL TRAVEL
Dell Publishing Co., 1958

1 Richard Boone Ph(c) all.	250.00
2	200.00
3	200.00
4 thru 14	@150.00

HAWKMOON, COUNT BRASS
First

1 Michael Moorcock adapt.	2.50
2 thru 4	@2.50

HAWKMOON JEWEL IN THE SKULL
First, 1986

1 Michael Moorcock adapt.	3.00
2 thru 4	@2.50

HAWKMOON, MAD GOD'S AMULET
First, 1987

1 Michael Moorcock adapt.	2.50
2 thru 4	@2.50

HAWKMOON, SWORD OF THE DAWN
First, 1987

1 Michael Moorcock adapt.	2.50
2 thru 4	@2.50

Hawkmoon, Sword of the Dawn #1
© First

HAWKMOON, THE RUNESTAFF
First, 1988

1 Michael Moorcock adapt.	2.50
2 thru 4	@2.50

HEAVY METAL MONSTERS
3-D-Zone, 1992

1 w/3-D glasses	4.00

HECTOR HEATHCOTE
Gold Key, 1964

1	150.00

HEDG
Papyrus Media, 2002

1 by Patrick Sherman	3.00
1 signed	3.00
2 thru 4	@3.00
TPB Vol 1	20.00

HEDGE KNIGHT, THE
Devil's Due Publishing, 2004
Previously published by Image

1 to 3 Collected edition, BV&JuB(c)	8.95
4 thru 6	2.95
4a thru 6a variant (c)s	@5.95
TPB	14.95

HELDEN
Caption Comics, 2001

1 (of 6) by Ralf Paul	3.00
2 thru 5	@3.00
6 concl. 52-pg.	4.00

HELIOS: IN WITH THE NEW
Speakeasy Comics, 2005

1 & 2 (of 4)	@3.00

Dakuwaka Productions, 2006

3 48-pg.	5.00

HELIOS: UNDER THE GUN
Dakuwaka Productions, 2006

1	3.00

HELLINA/ DOUBLE IMPACT
Lightning, 1996

1-shot JCy(c)	3.00
1-shot variant (c).	3.00

HELLINA: HEART OF THORNS
Lightning Comics, 1996

1	3.00
1 autographed edition	10.00
2	3.00
2 variant cover	3.00
2 platinum edition	6.00

HELLINA: HELLBORN
Lightning, 1997

1	3.00
1 autographed edition	10.00

HELLINA/NIRA X: ANGEL OF DEATH
Lightning, 1996

1A cover A.	3.00

1B cover B	3.00
1C Platinum cover	9.00
1D signed	9.00

HELLINA/NIRA X: CYBERANGEL
Lightning, 1996

1 autographed edition	10.00

HELIOS
Dakuwaka Productions, 2004

1	3.00
2 thru 4	@3.00
TPB Vol. 1	10.00

HELL, MICHIGAN
FC9 Publishing, 2005

1 thru 4	@3.00

HERBIE
American Comics Group April-May, 1964

1	350.00
2 thru 4	@150.00
5 A:Beatles,Dean Martin, Frank Sinatra	200.00
6	125.00
7	125.00
8 O:Fat Fury	150.00
9	125.00
10	125.00
11 thru 13	@100.00
14 A:Nemesis,Magic Man	100.00
15 thru 22	@100.00
23 Feb., 1967.	100.00

HERCULES
Charlton Comics, 1967

1	75.00
2 thru 7	@40.00
8 scarce	50.00
9 thru 13 Sept. 1969	@40.00

HERCULES: THE LEGENDARY JOURNEYS
Topps, 1996

1 & 2	@3.00
3 RTs,JBt,SeM,The Shaper,pt.1	5.00
3a Xena Ph(c).	15.00
4 RTs,JBt,SeM,The Shaper,pt.2	5.00
5 RTs,JBt,SeM,The Shaper,pt.3	5.00

HERE COMES THE BIG PEOPLE
Event Comics, 1997

1 ACo&JP(c).	3.00
1b JfD(c).	3.00
1c JQ&JP alternate (c)	10.00
1d JQ&JP alternate (c) signed	30.00

HERO ALLIANCE
Wonder Color Comics, 1987

1	2.50

Innovation, 1989–91

1 RLm,BS(c),R:HeroAlliance	6.00
2 RLm,BS(c),Victor vs.Rage.	5.00
3 RLm,A:Stargrazers	4.00
4 BS(c),Fearful Symmetry	3.00
5 RLm(c).	2.50
6 BS(c),RLm pin-up	3.25
7 V:Magnetron	2.50
8 I:Vector.	2.50
9 BS(c),V:Apostate.	2.50
10 Living Legends, A:Sentry	2.50
11 Obligations, F:Kris Dunlop	2.50
12 Legacy, I:Bombshell	2.50

COLOR PUB.

Hero Alliance Vol. 2 #14
© *Innovation*

13 V:Bombshell 2.50
14 Kris Solo Story 2.50
15 JLA Parody Issue 2.50
16 V:Sepulchre 2.50
17 O:Victor,I&D:Misty 2.50
Annual #1 PS,BS,RLm 3.00
Spec.#1 Hero Alliance update 2.50
Spec.Hero Alliance & Justice Machine:
   Identity Crises 2.50

HERO ALLIANCE:
THE END OF THE
GOLDEN AGE
Pied Piper, 1986
1 Bart Sears/Ron Lim 20.00
1a signed 25.00
1b 2nd printing 2.50
2 . . . . 12.00
3 . . . . 3.00
Graphic Novel 10.00
Innovation, 1989
1 RLm 5.00
1A 2nd printing 2.50
2 RLm 4.00
3 RLm 3.00

HERO ALLIANCE
QUARTERLY
Innovation, 1991
1 Hero Alliance stories 2.75
2 inc. Girl Happy 2.75
3 inc. Child Engagement 2.75
4 . . . . 2.75

HERO AT LARGE
Speakeasy Comics, 2005
1 . . . . 3.00
2 . . . . 3.00
3 thru 4 . . . . @3.00

HERO SQUARED
Atomeka, 2004
Spec. #1 X-tra Sized, KG,JMD 4.00
Spec. #1 X-tra Sized, Previews 4.00
Boom! Studios, 2005
1 (of 3) KG,JMD 4.00
1a Pull My Finger (c) 4.00
2 thru 3 . . . . @4.00
4 . . . . 4.00
Spec. #1 Brainless Sitcom (c) 7.00
TPB 15.00

HIGH CHAPPARAL
Gold Key, 1968
1 . . . . 100.00

HIGHLANDER: THERE
CAN BE ONLY ONE
D.E. (Dynamite Ent.) 2006
0 . . . . 1.00
1 . . . . 3.00
1a variant (c)s . . . . @3.00
1b variant Immortal gold foil (c) . . 20.00
2 . . . . 3.00
2a variant (c)s . . . . @3.00

HIGH ROADS
WildStorm/DC, 2002
Cliffhanger Productions
1 (of 6),SLo(s),F:Nick Highroad . . . 3.00
2 SLo(s),Paris 3.00
3 SLo(s),Nic Highroad 3.00
4 SLo(s),Iron Cross Brotherhood . . 3.00
5 SLo(s),Sloan,Bombridge 3.00
6 SLo(s),concl. 3.00
TPB 15.00

HIGH SCHOOL
CONFIDENTIAL DIARY
Charlton Comics, 1960
1 . . . . 75.00
2 thru 11 . . . . @50.00
Becomes:

CONFIDENTIAL DIARY
12 . . . . 60.00
13 thru 17 March, 1963 . . . . . . @50.00

HIGH VOLTAGE
Blackout, 1996
O 3.00

HI-SCHOOL ROMANCE
DATE BOOK
Harvey Publications, 1962
1 BP 90.00
2 . . . . 60.00
3 March, 1963 . . . . 65.00

HIS NAME IS ROG...
ROG 2000
A Plus Comics
1 . . . . 2.50

HOBBIT, THE
Eclipse
1 . . . . 8.00
1a 2ndPrinting 6.00
2 . . . . 7.00
2a 2ndPrinting 5.00
3 . . . . 6.00

HOGAN'S HEROES
Dell Publishing Co., 1966
1 Ph(c) 175.00
2 Ph(c) 125.00
3 JD,Ph(c) 125.00
4 thru 8 Ph(c) . . . . @100.00
8 and 9 . . . . @100.00

HOLLYWOOD NOIR
Narwain Publishing, 2006
GN Vol. 1 . . . . 6.00

HONEY WEST
Gold Key, 1966
1 . . . . 200.00

HONEYMOONERS
Lodestone, 1986
1 . . . . 4.00
5 Mag. 3.00
[2nd Series] Triad, 1987
1 They Know What They Like. 5.00
2 The Life You Save 4.00
3 X-mas special,inc.Art Carney
   interview 4.00
4 In the Pink 4.00
5 Bang, Zoom, To the Moon 4.00
6 Everyone Needs a Hero inc.
   Will Eisner interview 4.00
7 . . . . 4.00
8 . . . . 4.00
9 Jack Davis(c) 5.00
10 thru 13 . . . . @4.00

HONG KONG
Blackout Comics, 1996
0 A:Hari Kari 3.00
0 limited commemorative edition . 10.00

HORROR SHOW
Dead Dog Comics, 2005
1 . . . . 5.00

HORRORWOOD
Ape Entertainment, 2006
1 (of 4) 3.50
2 thru 4 . . . . @3.50

HORSEMEN
Griot Enterprises, 2002
1 (of 3) 3.00
2 thru 3 . . . . @3.00
3.5 . . . . 3.00

HOT ROD RACERS
Charlton Comics, 1964
1 . . . . 150.00
2 thru 5 . . . . @100.00
6 thru 15 July, 1967 . . . . @75.00

HOTSPUR
Eclipse, 1987
1 RT(i),I:Josef Quist 3.00
2 RT(i),Amulet of Kothique Stolen . 3.00
3 RT(i),Curse of the SexGoddess . 3.00

HOT STUFF,
THE LITTLE DEVIL
Harvey Publications, 1957
1 . . . . 750.00
2 1st Stumbo the Giant 400.00
3 thru 5 . . . . @250.00
6 thru 10 . . . . @200.00
11 thru 20 . . . . @175.00
21 thru 40 . . . . @150.00
41 thru 60 . . . . @100.00
61 thru 100 . . . . @75.00
101 thru 105 . . . . @40.00
106 thru 112 52 pg Giants . . . . @50.00
113 thru 139 . . . . @20.00
140 thru 177 . . . . @15.00

HOT STUFF SIZZLERS
Harvey Publications, 1960
1 F:Hot Stuff 400.00
2 . . . . 150.00
3 . . . . 125.00
4 . . . . 125.00

5 . . . . 125.00
6 thru 10 . . . . @100.00
11 thru 15 . . . . @90.00
16 thru 20 . . . . @85.00
21 thru 30 . . . . @60.00
31 thru 44 . . . . @50.00
45 E:60 pgs 50.00
46 thru 50 . . . . @40.00
51 thru 59 . . . . @30.00

HOWARD CHAYKIN'S AMERICAN FLAGG!
First, 1988
1 thru 9 . . . . @3.00
10 thru 12 . . . . @3.00

H.P.LOVECRAFT'S CTHULHU
Millennium, 1991
1 I:Miskatonic Project,V:Mi-Go 3.00
2 Arkham, trading cards 3.00
3 . . . . 2.50

H.R. PUFNSTUF
Gold Key, 1970
1 . . . . 400.00
2 & 3 . . . . @175.00
4 thru 8 . . . . @150.00

HUCK & YOGI JAMBOREE
Dell Publishing Co., March, 1961
1 . . . . 175.00

HUCKLEBERRY HOUND
Charlton, 1970
1 . . . . 100.00
2 thru 7 . . . . @75.00
8 Jan., 1972 . . . . 80.00

HUCKLEBERRY HOUND
Dell Publishing Co., May-July, 1959
1 . . . . 350.00
2 . . . . 300.00
3 thru 7 . . . . 250.00
8 thru 10 . . . . 200.00
11 thru 17 . . . . @150.00
Gold Key, 1962
18 Chuckleberry Tales 250.00
19 Chuckleberry Tales 175.00
20 Chuckleberry Tales 125.00
21 thru 30 . . . . @100.00
31 thru 43 . . . . @75.00

HUEY, DEWEY & LOUIE JUNIOR WOODCHUCKS
Gold Key, 1966
1 . . . . 100.00
2 thru 5 . . . . @60.00
6 thru 17 . . . . @50.00
18 . . . . 40.00
19 thru 25 . . . . @50.00
26 thru 30 . . . . @40.00
31 thru 57 . . . . @40.00
58 . . . . 35.00
59 . . . . 35.00
60 thru 80 . . . . @30.00
81 1984 . . . . 30.00

HUNGER, THE
Speakeasy Comics, 2005
1 . . . . 3.00
2 thru 5 . . . . @3.00
6 thru 8 . . . . @3.00
TPB 15.00

Hybrids #1
© Continuity

HYBRIDS
Continuity, 1993
0 Deathwatch 2000 prologue 5.00
1 Deathwatch 2000 pt.4,w/card . . . 3.00
2 Deathwatch 2000 pt.13,w/card . . 3.00
3 Deathwatch 2000 w/card 3.00
4 A:Valeria 3.00
5 O:Valeria 3.00
[2nd Series], 1994
1 Rise of Magic 3.00

HYBRIDS: ORIGIN
Continuity, 1993
1 thru 5 . . . . @3.00

HYDE-25
Harris, 1995
1 New Drug 3.00

HYPER-ACTIVES, THE
Alias Enterprises, 2005
0 . . . . 1.00
1 (of 5) 3.50
2 thru 4 . . . . @3.50

I SPY
Gold Key, 1966
1 Bill Cosby Ph(c) 400.00
2 Ph(c) 300.00
3 thru 4 AMc,Ph(c) . . . . @200.00
5 thru 6 Ph(c) Sept.1968 . . . . . @200.00

I-BOTS
Big Comics, 1996
1 F:Lady Justice 2.50
2 thru 4 . . . . @2.50
5 StG(s),PB 2.50
6 StG(s),PB 2.50
7 PB,Rebirth,pt.1, triptych (c) 2.50
8 PB,Rebirth,pt.2, triptych (c) 2.50
9 PB,Rebirth,pt.3, Original I-Bots
   return, triptych (c) 2.50

ICICLE
Hero Graphics
1 A:Flare,Lady Arcane,
   V:Eraserhead 5.00
2 thru 5 see B&W section

I DREAM OF JEANNIE
Dell Publishing Co., 1965
1 Ph(c),B.Eden 275.00
2 Ph(c),B.Eden 200.00

I'M DICKENS – HE'S FENSTER
Dell Publishing Co., May-July, 1963
1 Ph(c) 100.00
2 Ph(c) 80.00

IMP
Slave Labor, 1994
1 . . . . 2.50

IMPACT
Gemstone, 1999
1 EC Comic reprint 3.00
2 thru 5 . . . . @3.00
Annual #1 rep. #1–#5 . . . . 13.50

IMPOSSIBLE TALES
After Hours, 2006
1 (of 2) 4.00
2 . . . . 4.00

INCAL
Humanoids Publishing, 2001
1 . . . . 3.00
2 thru 6 . . . . @3.00
7 thru 13 . . . . 3.00
TPB Vol.1 Orphan of the City Shaft 18.00
TPB Vol.2 John Difool Detective . . 18.00
TPB Vol.3 The Epic Consipiracy . . 18.00

INFANTRY
Devil's Due Publishing, 2004
1 Aftermath, JoC 3.00
1a variant (c) 3.00
2 thru 6 . . . . @3.00

INFINITEENS
FC9 Publishing, 2005
1 . . . . 3.00
1a variant (c) 3.00
2 thru 4 . . . . @3.00
Moonstone Books, 2006
1 . . . . 3.50
2 . . . . 3.00

INMATES: PRISONERS OF SOCIETY
Delta Comics, 1997
1 (of 4) 3.00
2 thru 4 . . . . @3.00

INNER CIRCLE
Mushroom Comics, 1995
1.1 I:Point Blank 2.50
1.2 V:Deathcom 2.50
1.3 V:Deathcom 2.50
1.4 V:Deathcom 2.50

INNOCENTS
Radical Comics, 1995
1 I:Innocent 2.50

INNOVATORS
Dark Moon, 1995
1 I:Innovator, LeoShan 2.50
2 O:Mr. Void 2.50
3 I:Quill 2.50

All comics prices listed are for *Near Mint* condition.

INSANE CLOWN POSSE
Chaos Comics, 1999
1 . . . . 3.00
1 premium edition 10.00
1 Jeckel Brothers premium ed. . . . 10.00
3 Raze the Desertz of Glass 3.00
3a variant (c). 10.00
Spec. The Amazing Jeckel Brothers 3.00
TPB Vol. 1 . . . . 9.00

INSANE CLOWN POSSE: DARK CARNIVAL
Chaos! Comics, 2002
1 . . . . 3.00
1a premium edition 10.00

INSANE CLOWN POSSE: MR. JOHNSON'S HEAD
Chaos Comics, 2002
Ashcan. 6.00
1 (of 2) 3.00
1a premium edition 10.00

INSANE CLOWN POSSE: THE PENDULUM
Chaos! Comics, 2000
1 polybagged with CD single 6.00
1a variant (c). 10.00
2 polybagged 6.00
3 polybagged 6.00
4 polybagged 6.00
5 Road Rage, polybagged 6.00
6 . . . . 6.00
7 Pendulum's Promise 6.00
8 Sport hunting, with CD-ROM 6.00
9 Glimpse of Crystal Death. 6.00
10 . . . . 6.00
11 with CD-ROM 6.00
12 . . . . 6.00
Spec. #1 Hallowicket 3.00
TPB Vol. 1 . . . . 9.00
TPB Vol. 2 . . . . 9.00

INTERGALACTIC ADVENTURES OF GARA GALAXY, THE
Dead Dog Comics, 2005
1 (of 3) 5.00
2 . . . . 5.00
3 . . . . 5.00

INTERVIEW WITH A VAMPIRE
Innovation, 1991
1 based on novel,preq.to Vampire
    Chronicles 3.50
2 thru 11 . . . . @3.00

IN THE BLOOD
Boom! Studios, 2005
1 (of 4) 4.00
1a Previews exclusive (c) 7.00
2 . . . . 4.00
3 . . . . 4.00

INTIMATE
Charlton Comics, 1957
1 thru 3 . . . . @100.00
Becomes:

TEEN-AGE LOVE
4 . . . . 75.00
5 thru 9 . . . . @50.00
10 thru 35. . . . . @50.00
36 thru 96. . . . . @50.00

INTIMATES, THE
Wildstorm/DC, Nov., 2004
1 JoC(s),JLe 3.00
2 JoC(s),JLe 3.00
3 JoC(s),JLe,Blaster Pill Marathon . 3.00
4 JoC(s),JLe,School Dance 3.00
5 JoC(s),JLe,Hivejournal 3.00
6 JoC(s),JLe(c)F:Secret of Sykes. . 3.00
7 JoC(s),Last day of school year . . 3.00
8 JoC(s),Summer vacation 3.00
9 JoC(s),Summer vacation 3.00
10 JoC(s),Vacation's end. 3.00
11 JoC(s),Back to School 3.00
12 JoC(s),Kids revolt 3.00

INTRUDER
TSR, 1990–91
1 thru 4 . . . . @3.00
5 thru 8 The Next Dimension . . . @3.00

Invaders From Home #1
© Piranha Press

INVADERS FROM HOME
Piranha Press, 1990
1 thru 6 . . . . @2.50

INVADERS, THE
Gold Key, 1967
1 Ph(c),DSp 200.00
2 Ph(c),DSp 150.00
3 Ph(c),DSp 150.00
4 Ph(c),DSp 150.00

INVINCIBLE FOUR OF KUNG FU & NINJA
Dr. Leungs
1 . . . . 3.00
2 thru 4 . . . . @2.50
5 thru 11 . . . . @2.50

IO
Invictus Studios, 1994
1 I:IO. 2.75
2 . . . . 2.75
3 V:Major Damage 2.75

IRON HORSE
Dell Publishing Co., March, 1967
1 . . . . 50.00
2 . . . . 50.00

IRONJAW
Atlas, Jan.–July, 1975
1 NA(c),MSy 20.00
2 NA(c) 15.00
3 . . . . 15.00
4 O:IronJaw 15.00

IRON MARSHAL
Jademan, 1990
1 . . . . 2.50
2 thru 10 . . . . @2.50
11 thru 32. . . . . @2.50

ISAAC ASIMOV'S I-BOTS
Tekno-Comix, 1995
1 I:I-Bots. 2.50
2 O:I-Bots. 2.50
3 V:Black OP 2.50

IT'S ABOUT TIME
Gold Key, 1967
1 Ph(c) 75.00

ITCHY & SCRATCHY
Bongo Comics, 1993
1 DaC(s), ... 4.00
2 DaC(s), ... 3.50
3 . . . . 3.50

IVANHOE
Dell Publishing Co., 1963
1 . . . . 60.00

JACK HUNTER
Blackthorne, 1988
1 . . . . 2.50
2 . . . . 2.50
3 . . . . 2.50

JACKIE CHAN ADVENTURES
Tokyopop Press, 2003
GN Vol. 1 (of 3) Cine-Manga 8.00
GN Vol. 2 . . . . 8.00
GN Vol. 3 . . . . 8.00

JACKIE CHAN'S SPARTAN X
Topps, 1997
1 The Armor of Heaven, pt.1 . . . . . 3.00
2 The Armor of Heaven, pt.2 . . . . . 3.00
3 (of 6) 3.00

JADE
Chaos! Comics, 2001
1 . . . . 3.00
1a premium edition 10.00
2 . . . . 3.00
3 . . . . 3.00
4 . . . . 3.00
4a variant 7.50
Preview book 2.00
Preview book, premium 6.00
Ashcan Jade #1. . . . . 6.00

JADE FIRE
Kandora Publishing, 2005
1 . . . . 3.50
2 thru 4 . . . . @3.50

JADE: REDEMPTION
Chaos! Comics, 2001
1 (of 4) 3.00
1 premium edition 10.00
2 thru 4 . . . . @3.00

All comics prices listed are for *Near Mint* condition.

COLOR PUB.

2a thru 4a variant (c)........ @7.50
Ashcan....................... 6.00

JADEMAN COLLECTION
Jademan, 1989
1 .... 4.50
2 .... 3.00
3 thru 5 .... @2.50

JADEMAN KUNG FU SPECIAL
Jademan, 1988
1 I:Oriental Heroes, Blood
  Sword, Drunken Fist 5.00

JADE WARRIORS: SLAVE OF THE DRAGON
Avatar Press, 2000
1 (of 3) MD2, 40-page 3.50
1a photo (c)................. 3.50
1b wraparound (c)............ 3.50
2 MD2....................... 3.50
2a photo (c)................. 3.50

JAGUAR GOD
Verotika, 1995
1 Frazetta, I:Jaquar God........ 3.00
2 V:Yi-Cha.................. 3.00
3 V:Yi-Cha.................. 3.00
4 V:Yi-Cha.................. 3.00
5 AOI 3.00
6 LSh,AOI 3.00
7 LSh,AOI 3.00
8 AOI 3.00
Spec.#1 Return to X'ibala,RCo 5.00
Spec. Jaguar God Illustrations..... 4.00
Spec. fan club edition 10.00

JALILA
Studio G, 2003
1 .... 3.00
2 thru 4 .... @3.00
AK Entertainment, 2006
1 Overwhelmed, pt.1............ 3.00
2 First Mission.............. 3.00
3 Overwhelmed.............. 3.00
4 Overwhelmed, pt. 2 .... 3.00
5 Overwhelmed, pt. 3 .... 3.00
6 War Crimes 3.00
7 .... 3.00

JAMES BOND 007
Eclipse, 1991
1 MGr,PerfectBound............ 5.50
2 MGr....................... 5.00
3 MGr,end series 5.00
GN Licence to Kill, MGr I/o 8.00

JAMES BOND: GOLDENEYE
Topps, 1995
1 Movie adaptation 3.00
2 thru 3 Movie adaptation ...... @3.00

JASON GOES TO HELL
Topps, 1993
1 Movie adapt.,w/3 cards 3.25
2 thru 3 Movie adapt.,w/3 cards . @3.25

JASON VS. LEATHERFACE
Topps, 1995
1 Jason Meets Leatherface 3.00
2 SBi(c) Leatherface's family 3.00
3 SBi(c),conclusion............ 3.00

JASON X
Avatar Press, 2005
Spec. #1 .... 4.00
Spec. #1a Wraparound (c)....... 4.00
Spec. #1b Variant(c)s......... @4.00
Spec. 1c Blood red convention (c) . 5.00
Spec. 1d Extreme Force (c) ... 6.00
Spec. 1e Headless (c) 6.00
Spec. 1f Victim (c) 6.00

JAVA
Committed Comics, 2004
1 thru 3 .... @3.00

Javerts #1
© *Firstlight*

JAVERTS
Firstlight, 1994
1 thru 5 Pieces of an Icon...... @3.00

JAZAN WILD'S CARNIVAL OF SOULS
Markosia, 2005
1 (of 3) 3.50
2 .... 3.50
3 .... 3.50
3a variant (c)s .... @3.50

JENNA
Narwain Publishing, 2005
1 .... 4.00
2 .... 4.00
2a limited ed. with CD.......... 8.00
3 .... 4.00
TPB 11.00
1-shot Panic in New York........ 3.00

JENNA MEETS 100 GIRLS
Narwain Publishing, 2006
1 (of 2) x-over 3.50

JENNY SPARKS: THE SECRET HISTORY OF THE AUTHORITY
WildStorm/DC, 2000
1 (of 5) MMr,JMC 9.00
1a variant (c) (1:4) 4.00
2 MMr,JMC 3.00
3 MMr,JMC,O:Jack Hawksmoor... 3.00
4 MMr,JMC 3.00
5 MMr,JMC,conclusion 3.00
TPB 120-page, rep............. 15.00

JEREMIAH HARM
Boom! Studios, 2005
1 KG,AIG.................... 4.00
1a convention (c) 7.00
2 thru 5 .... @4.00

JET
WildStorm/DC, 2000
1 (of 4) DAn,ALa,F:Jodi Slayton... 2.50
2 DAn,ALa,Midnight to Midnight... 2.50
3 DAn,ALa,V:Timewaster 2.50
4 DAn,ALa,concl. 2.50

JET DREAM
Gold Key, 1968
1 .... 60.00

JETSONS, THE
Gold Key, 1963
1 .... 500.00
2 .... 300.00
3 thru 10 .... @200.00
11 thru 20 .... @150.00
21 thru 36 Oct. 1970 .... @125.00

JETSONS, THE
Charlton Comics, 1970
1 from Hanna-Barbera TV show. 150.00
2 .... 100.00
3 thru 10 .... @75.00
11 thru 20 Dec. 1973 .... @60.00

JETSONS, THE
Harvey Comics, 1991–92
1 thru 5 .... @3.00

JETSONS, THE
Archie, 1995
1 thru 17 .... @3.00

JEZEBELLE
WildStorm/DC, 2001
1 (of 6) F:Harper Harrison 2.50
1a variant(c) (1:2).............. 2.50
2 BRa(s).................... 2.50
3 BRa(s) F:Harper Harrison 2.50
4 BRa(s),Seance&Sensibility,pt.1 . 2.50
5 BRa(s),Seance&Sensibility,pt.2 . 2.50
6 BRa(s),concl. 2.50

JEZEBEL JADE
Comico, 1988
1 AKu,A:Race Bannon 3.00
2 AKu 3.00
3 AKu 3.00

JIGSAW
Harvey Publications, 1966
1 .... 50.00
2 .... 40.00

JIMBO
Bongo Comics, 1995
1 R:Jimbo 3.00
2 thru 4 .... @3.00

JIM REAPER
Silent Devil Productions, 2006
1 Week One 4.00

JINDAI
Zenescope Entertainment, 2005
1 .... 3.00
2 thru 8 .... @3.00

All comics prices listed are for *Near Mint* condition.

J. N. WILLIAMSON'S MASQUES
Innovation, 1992
1 TV,From horror anthology 5.00
2 Olivia(c) inc.Better Than One . . . 5.00

JOHN BOLTON, HALLS OF HORROR
Eclipse, 1985
1 JBo. 3.00
2 JBo. 3.00

JOHN CARTER OF MARS
Gold Key, 1964
1 . . . . 150.00
2 & 3 . . . . @100.00

JOHN DOE
Boom! Studios, 2006
Preview book 2.50

JOHN F. KENNEDY LIFE STORY
(WITH 2 REPRINTS)
Dell Publishing Co., 1964
1 . . . . 100.00
2 . . . . 75.00
3 . . . . 75.00

JOHN JAKES MULLKON EMPIRE
Tekno Comix, 1995
1 I:Mulkons 2.50
2 O:Mulkons 2.50
3 D:Company Man 2.50
4 Disposal Problems. 2.50
5 F:Granny 2.50
6 Where's Karma 2.50

JOHN LAW
Eclipse, 1983
1 WE. 2.50

JOHNNY JASON TEEN REPORTER
Dell Publishing Co., 1962
1 . . . . 50.00
2 . . . . 40.00

JOHNNY NEMO
Eclipse, 1985–86
1 I:Johnny Nemo. 2.50
2 . . . . 2.50
3 F:Sindy Shade 2.50

JOHN STEELE SECRET AGENT
Gold Key, 1964
1 . . . . 150.00

JOHN WOO'S SEVEN BROTHERS
Virgin Comics, 2006
1 . . . . 3.00
1a variant (c) 3.00
2 . . . . 3.00

JONNY QUEST
Gold Key, 1964
1 TV show. 700.00

Jonny Quest #5
© Comico

JONNY QUEST
Comico, 1986
1 DW,SR,A:Dr.Zin 6.00
2 WP/JSon,O:RaceBannon 4.00
3 DSt(c). 4.00
4 TY/AW,DSt(i) 3.50
5 DSt(c)A:JezebelJade 3.00
6 AKu 3.00
7 . . . . 3.00
8 KSy 3.00
9 MA 3.00
10 King Richard III 3.00
11 JSon,BSz(c) 3.00
12 DSp 3.00
12 DSp 3.00
13 CI 3.00
14 thru 31 . . . . @3.00
Spec.#1 . . . . 3.00
Spec.#2 . . . . 3.00

JONNY QUEST CLASSICS
Comico, 1987
1 DW. 3.00
2 DW,O:Hadji 3.00
3 DW. 3.00

JON SABLE
First, 1983
1 MGr,A:President 4.50
2 MGr,Alcohol Issue 3.50
3 thru 6 MGr,O:Jon Sable . . . . . . @3.00
7 thru 24 MGr . . . . @2.50
25 thru 29 MGr,Shatter . . . . @3.00
30 thru 56 MGr. . . . . @2.50

JON SABLE, FREELANCE: BLOODTRAIL
IDW Publishing, 2005
1 MGr 4.00
2 thru 6 . . . . @4.00
TPB Complete Jon Sable,
  Freelance. 25.00
TPB Complete Jon Sable,
  Freelance, Vol. 2 thru Vol. 5 @20.00

JONAS: TALES OF AN IRONSTAR
Codedeco Inc., 2004
1 . . . . 4.00
2 thru 6 . . . . @4.00

JOSIE
Archie Publications, 1963
1 . . . . 275.00
2 . . . . 150.00
3 . . . . 100.00
4 . . . . 100.00
5 . . . . 100.00
6 thru 10 . . . . @75.00
11 thru 20 . . . . @50.00
21 thru 30 . . . . @40.00
31 thru 40. . . . . @35.00
41 thru 54 . . . . @35.00
55 thru 74. . . . . @25.00
75 thru 105 . . . . @25.00
106 Oct., 1962 . . . . 25.00

JOVA'S HARVEST
Arcana Studio, 2005
1 (of 3) 5.00
2 . . . . 5.00
3 . . . . 3.50

JUDGE COLT
Gold Key, 1969
1 . . . . 50.00
2 . . . . 35.00
3 . . . . 35.00
4 Sept., 1970 . . . . 35.00

JUDGE DREDD
Eagle, 1983
1 BB,I:Judge Death(in USA) 10.00
2 BB(c&a),The Oxygen Board 8.00
3 BB(c),Judge Dredd Lives. 7.00
4 BB(c),V:Perps 7.00
5 BB(c),V:Perps 5.00
6 BB(c),V:Perps 5.00
7 BB(c),V:Perps 5.00
8 BB(c),V:Perps 5.00
9 BB(c),V:Perps 5.00
10 BB(c),V:Perps 5.00
11 BB(c) 4.00
12 BB(c) 4.00
13 BB(c), The Day the Law
     Died, pt.5 . . . . 4.00
14 BB(c),Dredd vs. Dredd 4.00
15 BB(c) 4.00
16 BB(c) 4.00
17 BB(c) 4.00
18 BB(c) 4.00
19 BB(c) 4.00
20 BB(c) 4.00
21 BB(c) 4.00
22 BB(c),V:Perps 3.00
23 BB(c),V:Perps 3.00
24 BB(c),V:Perps 3.00
25 BB(c),V:Perps 3.00
26 BB(c),V:Perps 3.00
27 BB(c),V:Perps 3.00
28 A:Judge Anderson,V:Megaman . 4.00
29 A:Monty, the guinea pig 3.00
30 V:Perps 3.00
31 Destiny's Angel, Pt. 1 . . . . 3.00
32 Destiny's Angel, Pt. 2 . . . . 3.00
33 V:League of Fatties. 3.00
34 V:Executioner 3.00

JUDGE DREDD
Quality Press, 1986
1 Cry of the Werewolf Pt.1 . . . . 6.00
2 Cry of the Werewolf Pt.2 . . . . 5.00
3 Anti-smoking 4.00
4 Wreckers 4.00
5 Highwayman 4.00
6 . . . . 3.00
7 . . . . 3.00
8 . . . . 3.00
9 . . . . 3.00
10 thru 44 . . . . @3.00
45 thru 61 . . . . @2.50

Becomes:

JUDGE DREDD CLASSICS
62 thru 75 . . . . @2.50
76 Diary of a Mad Citizen 3.00
77 . . . . 3.00
TPB:Democracy Now 11.00
TPB:Rapture 13.00
Judge Dredd Special #1 . . . . 2.50
GN Bad Science 8.00

JUDGE DREDD
Titan, 2001
TPB The Emerald Isle 15.00
TPB Death Aid 15.00
TPB Goodnight Kiss (2002) 15.00
TPB Helter Skelter (2002) 15.00
TPB Justice One (2002) 15.00
TPB The Day the Law Died 20.00
TPB The Apocalypse War 25.00
TPB The Judge Child Quest 20.00
GN Muzak Killer (2002) 15.00
GN Innocents Abroad (2002). 15.00
GN Necropolis Book One 15.00
GN Necropolis Book Two 20.00
GN Cursed Earth 20.00
GN The Complete America 17.00
GN Judge Dredd vs. Judge Dredd 13.00

JUDGE DREDD: AMERICA
Fleetway
1 I:America 3.50

JUDGE DREDD: JUDGE CHILD QUEST
Eagle, 1984
1 thru 3 . . . . @3.00
4 BB(c) 3.00
5 . . . . 3.00

JUDGE DREDD'S CRIME FILE
Eagle, 1984
1 Ron Smith, The Perp Runners . . 2.50
2 thru 6 . . . . @2.50
Quality (Prestige format), 1989
1 A:Rogue Trooper 6.50
2 IG,V:Fatties, Energy Vampires &
   Super Fleas 6.00
3 Battles foes from dead A:Judge
   Anderson 6.00

JUDGE DREDD'S EARLY CASES
Eagle, 1986
1 Robot Wars, Pt.1 . . . . 4.00
2 Robot Wars, Pt.2 . . . . 3.00
3 V:Perps 3.00
4 IG, Judge Giant 3.00
5 V:Perps 3.00
6 V:Judge killing car Elvis 3.00

JUDGE DREDD'S HARDCASE PAPERS
Fleetway/Quality
1 V:The Tarantula 7.50
2 Junkies & Psychos 6.50
3 Crime Call Vid. Show 6.50
4 Real Coffee,A:Johnny Alpha 6.50

JUDGE DREDD: THE MEGAZINE
Fleetway/Quality, 1991
1 Midnite's Children Pt.1
   A:Chopper, Young Death 5.50

2 Midnite's Children Pt.2 . . . . 5.00
3 . . . . 5.00
23 thru 34 . . . . @4.00
35 thru 43 . . . . @5.50
44 thru 45 . . . . @7.00
Egmont Fleetway Limited
46 thru 75 . . . . @7.00

JUDGMENT DAY
Lightning Comics, 1993
1 B:JZy(s),KlK,V:Razorr,Rift,
   Nightmare, red prism(c) 5.00
1a Gold Prism(c) 5.00
1b Purple Prism(c) 7.00
1c Misprint,Red Prism(c), Bloodfire
   Credits inside 8.00
1d Misprint,Gold Prism(c), Bloodfire
   Credits inside 8.00
1e Misprint,Green Prism(c),
   Bloodfire Credits inside 8.00
1f B&W promo ed. Gold ink 5.00
1g B&W promo ed. platinum ed. . . 7.00
2 TLw,I:War Party,BU:Perg,
   w/Perg card 4.00
3 ErP,O:X-Treme 3.25
4 ErP,In Hell 3.25
5 TLw,In Hell 3.25
6 TLw,I:Red Front,O:Salurio 3.25
7 O:Safeguard 3.25
8 . . . . 3.00
9 . . . . 3.00
10 . . . . 3.00

JUDGMENT DAY
Maximum Press, 1997
Alpha AMo(s) 2.50
Alpha variant cover 2.50
Omega AMo(s) 2.50
Omega variant cover 2.50
Final Judgment AMo(s) 2.50
Final Judgment variant cover 2.50

JUDO GIRL
Alias Enterprises, 2005
1 (of 4) 3.00
2 thru 4 . . . . @3.00
2a thru 4a variant (c)s . . . . @3.00
TPB 13.00
Vol. 2
1 (of 4) 3.50
1a variant (c) 3.50
2 thru 4 . . . . @3.50

JUDOMASTER
Charlton Comics, 1966
(Special War Series #4)
   I:Judomaster 75.00
89 FMc,War stories begin 60.00
89 (90) FMc,A:Thunderbolt 50.00
91 FMc,DG,A:Sarge Steel 50.00
92 FMc,DG,A:Sarge Steel 50.00
93 FMc,DG,I:Tiger 50.00
94 FMc,DG,A:Sarge Steel 50.00
95 FMc,DG,A:Sarge Steel 40.00
96 FMc,DG,A:Sarge Steel 40.00
97 FMc,A:Sarge Steel 40.00
98 FMc,A:Sarge Steel 40.00

JUGHEAD
Archie Publications
1965–1987
127 thru 130 . . . . @50.00
131 thru 150 . . . . @40.00
151 thru 160 . . . . @25.00
161 thru 200 . . . . @20.00
201 thru 250 . . . . @15.00
251 thru 300 . . . . @12.00
301 thru 352 . . . . @10.00

Jughead #199
© Archie

JUGHEAD
Archie Publications
[2nd Series], 1987
1 thru 45 . . . . @6.00
Becomes:

ARCHIE'S PAL JUGHEAD
June, 1993
46 thru 50 . . . . @3.50
51 thru 70 . . . . @2.50
71 thru 99 . . . . @2.50
100 A Storm Over Uniforms, x-over
   (Betty #57, Archie #467) 2.50
101 thru 122 . . . . @2.50
123 thru 125 . . . . @2.50
126 thru 133 . . . . @2.50
134 thru 147 . . . . @2.50
148 thru 161 . . . . @2.50
162 thru 177 . . . . @2.25

JUGHEAD AS CAPTAIN HERO
Archie Publications, 1966
1 . . . . 100.00
2 . . . . 65.00
3 thru 7 . . . . @50.00

JUGHEAD'S FANTASY
Archie Publications, 1960
1 Sir Jugalot 300.00
2 Peter Goon 200.00
3 Superjughead 175.00

JUGHEAD'S FOLLY
Archie Publications, 1957
1 Jughead like Elvis 675.00

JUGHEAD'S JOKES
Archie Publications, 1967
1 . . . . 125.00
2 . . . . 75.00
3 thru 5 . . . . @40.00
6 thru 10 . . . . @35.00
11 thru 30 . . . . @25.00
31 thru 77 . . . . @10.00
78 Sept., 1982 . . . . 10.00

JUGHEAD WITH ARCHIE DIGEST
Archie Publications, March, 1974
1 . . . . 100.00
2 . . . . 60.00
3 thru 10 . . . . @50.00

All comics prices listed are for *Near Mint* condition.

11 thru 91	@20.00
92 thru 129	@15.00
130 thru 138	@10.00
139 thru 144	@10.00
145 thru 155	@7.00
156 thru 171	@5.00
172 thru 179	@5.00

JUNCTION 17
Antarctic Press, 2003
1 color manga ... 3.50
2 thru 4 ... @3.00

JUNGLE ADVENTURES
Skywald, March–June, 1971
1 F:Zangar,Jo-Jo,Blue Gorilla ... 40.00
2 F:Sheena, Jo-Jo,Zangar ... 35.00
3 F:Zangar,Jo-Jo,White Princess ... 35.00

JUNCTION 17
Antarctic Press, 2003
1 ... 3.50
2 thru 4 ... @3.00
TPB Pocket Manga ... 10.00

JUNGLE COMICS
Blackthorne, 1988
1 DSt(c) ... 3.00
2 ... 3.00
3 ... 3.00
See B&W

JUNGLE JIM
Charlton, 1969–70
22 ... 60.00
23 ... 40.00
24 ... 40.00
25 ... 40.00
26 ... 40.00
27 ... 50.00
28 ... 50.00

JUNGLE TALES OF TARZAN
Charlton Comics, 1964
1 ... 100.00
2 ... 75.00
3 ... 75.00
4 July, 1965 ... 75.00

JUNGLE WAR STORIES
Dell Publishing Co., 1962
1 P(c) all ... 75.00
2 thru 11 ... @50.00
Becomes:

GUERRILLA WAR
12 thru 14 ... @50.00

JUNIOR WOODCHUCKS
Walt Disney, 1991
1 CB,Bubbleweight Champ ... 3.00
2 CB,Swamp of no Return ... 3.00
3 Rescue Run-Around ... 3.00
4 Cave Caper ... 3.00

JURASSIC PARK
Topps, 1993
1 Movie Adapt.,w/card ... 5.00
1a Newsstand Ed ... 4.00
2 Movie Adapt.,w/card ... 3.25
3 Movie Adapt.,w/card ... 3.25
4 Movie Adapt.,w/card ... 3.25
2a thru 4a Newsstand Ed ... @2.75
Ann.#1 Death Lizards ... 4.00

Jurassic Park #4
© Topps

JURASSIC PARK: ADVENTURES
Topps, 1994
1 thru 10 reprints titles ... @3.00

JURASSIC PARK: RAPTOR
Topps, 1993
1 SE w/Zorro #0 ashcan & cards ... 3.25
2 w/3 cards ... 3.00

JURASSIC PARK: RAPTORS ATTACK
Topps, 1994
1 SEt(s), ... 2.75
2 thru 4 SEt(s), ... @2.75

JURASSIC PARK: RAPTOR HIJACK
Topps
1 SEt(s), ... 2.50
2 SEt(s), ... 2.50
3 SEt(s), ... 2.50
4 SEt(s), ... 2.50

[JURASSIC PARK:] THE LOST WORLD
Topps, 1997
1 (of 4) movie adapt ... 3.00
2 thru 4 ... @3.00

JUST A PILGRIM
Black Bull Entertainment, 2001
1 GEn,MT(c) ... 6.00
1a variant (c) ... 12.00
2 GEn,GF(c) ... 4.00
3 GEn,KN(c), Bloody Baskets ... 4.00
4 GEn,BSz(c) Firestarter ... 4.00
5 GEn,JMC(c), ... 4.00
Preview Ed ... 8.00
TPB GEn,MT(c) ... 13.00

JUST A PILGRIM: GARDEN OF EDEN
Black Bull Entertainment, 2002
1 GEn,JJu(c) ... 7.00
1a variant GF (c) ... 4.00
2 GEn,CE ... 4.00
3 GEn,CE ... 4.00
4 GEn,CE ... 4.00

Preview ed. limited ... 7.00
TPB series rep ... 13.00

JUSTICE CITY CHRONICLES
Ape Entertainment, 2005
1 (of 2) ... 3.50
2 ... 3.50

JUSTICE MACHINE
Noble Comics, 1981–85
1 JBy(c) Mag size,B&W ... 30.00
2 MGu,Mag size,B&W ... 16.00
3 MGu,Mag size,B&W ... 10.00
4 MGu,Bluecobalt ... 8.00
5 MGu ... 7.00

Texas Comics
Ann.#1:BWG,I:Elementals,
A: Thunder Agents ... 5.00

JUSTICE MACHINE
[Featuring the Elementals]
Comico, 1986
1 ... 2.50
2 ... 2.50
3 ... 2.50
4 ... 2.50

JUSTICE MACHINE
Comico, 1987–89
1 MGu ... 2.50
2 MGu ... 2.50
3 thru 14 MGu ... @2.50
15 thru 27 MGu ... @2.50
28 MGu ... 2.50
29 MGu,IW ... 2.50
Ann.#1 ... 2.50
SummerSpectacular 1 ... 2.75

MINI SERIES, 1990
1 thru 4 F:Elementals ... @2.50
Innovation, 1990
1 ... 2.50
2 thru 4 The Ragnarok Portfolio ... @2.50
5 thru 7 Demon trilogy ... @2.50

JUSTICE MACHINE: CHIMERA CONSPIRACY
Millennium
1 AH,R&N:Justice Machine,
wraparound cover ... 2.50

JUST MARRIED
Charlton Comics, 1958
1 ... 125.00
2 ... 125.00
3 thru 10 ... @100.00
11 thru 30 ... @35.00
31 thru 113 ... @25.00
114 Dec., 1976 ... 15.00

KABOOM
Awesome Entertainment, 1997
1 JLb,JMs, ... 5.00
1a variant (c)s ... 6.00
2 JLb,JMs, ... 3.00
3 JLb,JMs, ... 4.00
4 JLb,JMs,Kaboom the
Barbarian,pt.1 (of 3) ... 2.50
5 JLb,JMs,Barbarian,pt.2 ... 2.50
6 JLb,JMs,Barbarian,pt.3 ... 2.50

VOL II
1 (of 3) ... 2.50
2 JLe,JLb,F:Kyra ... 2.50
3 JLe,JLb, conclusion ... 2.50
Collected #1 & #2 ... 6.00

KABUKI

Caliber Press, 1994–96
1 Color Gallery,32 paintings(1995) . 7.00
1-shot Color Special, inc.
  pin-up gallery (1996) 3.00
1-shot Fear the Reaper (1994) 7.00

KABUKI: SKIN DEEP

Caliber, 1996
1 DMk 4.00
2 DMk(c) 3.50
2 AxR(c) 6.00
3 Origin issue 3.50
4 . . . . 3.50

KADE

Arcana Studios, 2003
1 . . . . 3.00
2 thru 5 . . . . @3.00
TPB Vol. 1 . . . . 10.00

KADE: SUN
OF PERDITION

Arcana Studio, 2006
1 (of 4) 4.00
2 . . . . 4.00

KAMIKAZE: 1946

Antarctic Press, 2000
1 Pickadon 3.00
2 Operation Olympic 3.00
3 Queens of the Seas 3.00
4 Operation Coronet 3.00
5 Kaitens 3.00
6 Fortress Japan 3.00

KAMIKAZE

Wildstorm/DC, 2003
1 (of 5) extreme sport 3.00
2 thru 6 . . . . @3.00

KARNEY

IDW Publishing, 2005
1 . . . . 4.00
2 thru 4 . . . . @4.00
TPB 20.00

KATO OF THE
GREEN HORNET

Now, 1991
1 BA,1st Kato solo story 2.50
2 BA,Kato in China contd 2.50
3 Kato in China contd 2.50
4 Final Issue 2.50

KATO II

Now, 1992
1 VM,JSh,A:Karthage 2.50
2 VM,JSh,V:Karthage 2.50
3 VM,JSh,V:Karthage 2.50

KATY KEENE FASHION
BOOK MAGAZINE

Archie Publications, 1955
1 Woggon(a&c) 800.00
2 . . . . 500.00
3 thru 10 not published
11 thru 18 . . . . @350.00
19 . . . . 300.00
20 . . . . 300.00
21 . . . . 300.00
22 . . . . 300.00
23 Winter 1958-59 . . . . 300.00

Katy Keene Fashon Book #22
© *Archie Publications*

KATY KEENE
PINUP PARADE

Archie Publications, 1955
1 . . . . 750.00
2 . . . . 400.00
3 . . . . 350.00
4 . . . . 350.00
5 . . . . 350.00
6 . . . . 300.00
7 . . . . 300.00
8 . . . . 300.00
9 . . . . 300.00
10 Woggon art 300.00
11 Story on comics 350.00
12 . . . . 300.00
13 . . . . 300.00
14 . . . . 300.00
15 Sept., 1961 . . . . 700.00

KEE-FU FIGHTERS

Roxbox Entertainment, 2006
1 . . . . 3.25
2 . . . . 3.25

KELLY GREEN

Eclipse
1 SDr,O'Kelly Green 2.50
2 SDr,One,Two,Three 2.50
3 SDr,Million Dollar Hit 2.50
4 SDr,Rare 4.00

KEN LASHLEY'S
LEGENDS

DHJ Comics, 2002
1 (of 6) by Ken Lashley 3.00
1a variant (c) 3.00
1b previews exclusive 5.00
2 . . . . 3.00

KEEP, THE

IDW Publishing, 2005
1 F.Paul Wilson (s) 4.00
2 . . . . 4.00
3 thru 5 . . . . @4.00

KID DEATH & FLUFFY

Event Comics, 1997
Spec.#1 Halloween Spec. John
  Cebollero(c) 3.00
Spec.#1a Halloween Spec. JQ(c) . . 3.00

KID MONTANA

Charlton Comics, 1957
Previously: DAVY CROCKETT
see Golden Age
9 . . . . 125.00
10 . . . . 110.00
11 . . . . 100.00
12 . . . . 100.00
13 AW 100.00
14 thru 20 . . . . @100.00
21 thru 35 . . . . @75.00
36 thru 49 . . . . @75.00
50 March, 1965 . . . . 75.00

KILLER INSTINCT

Acclaim
1 thru 3 . . . . @2.50
Spec. Brothers by Art Holcomb 2.50

KILLER 7

Devil's Due Publishing, 2006
1 . . . . 3.00
1a variant cardstock (c) 6.00
2 thru 4 . . . . @3.00
2a thru 4a variant cardstock (c) . @6.00

KILLERS, THE:
WAR'S END

Speakeasy Comics, 2006
1 (of 5) 3.00
2 thru 3 . . . . @3.00

KILLER STUNTS, INC.

Alias Enterprises, 2005
1 (of 4) 1.00
2 thru 4 . . . . @3.00

KILLER TALES

Eclipse, 1985
1 Tim Truman 3.00

KILLER, THE

Archaia Studios, 2006
1 (of 10) 4.00

KILLZONE

Dreamwave, 2004
1 . . . . 3.00
2 . . . . 3.00
3 . . . . 3.00

KINDRED II

WildStorm/DC, 2002
1 (of 4) BBh 2.50
2 BBh 2.50
3 BBh,Backlash & Grifter 2.50
4 BBh,concl. 2.50

KING LEONARDO AND
HIS SHORT SUBJECTS

Dell Publishing Co., 1961–62
1 . . . . 275.00
2 . . . . 200.00
3 . . . . 225.00
4 . . . . 200.00

KING LOUIE & MOWGLI

Gold Key, 1968
1 . . . . 60.00

KING OF DIAMONDS

Dell Publishing Co., 1962
1 Ph(c) 75.00

All comics prices listed are for *Near Mint* condition.

KING OF FIGHTERS: MAXIMUM IMPACT
Dr. Masters Publications, 2005
3 thru 6 . . . . 3.00
7 thru 8 . . . . @3.00

KING OF FIGHTERS, THE: NESTS SAGA
HK Comics, 2006
1 . . . . 3.00
1a variant (c)s . . . . @3.00

KISS KISS BANG BANG
Crossgen, 2004
1 . . . . 3.00
2 thru 7 . . . . @3.00

KIT KARTER
Dell Publishing Co., 1962
1 . . . . 50.00

KNIGHTHAWK
Windjammer, 1995
1 NA(c&a),I:Knighthawk the
   Protector,V:Nemo 2.75
2 NA(c&a),Birth of Nemo 2.50
3 NA,V:Nemo 2.50
4 NA,V:Nemo 2.50
5 I:Cannon, Brick 2.50
6 V:Cannon, Brick 2.50

KNIGHTS OF THE ROUND TABLE
Dell Publishing Co.,1963-64
1 P(c) 60.00

KNUCKLES
Archie Comics, 1997
1 . . . . 2.50
2 thru 31 . . . . @2.50
32 thru 33 . . . . @2.50

KOLCHAK THE NIGHT STALKER
Moonstone, 2002
GN 6.50
GN The Get of Belial 7.00
GN Fever Pitch 7.00
GN Lambs to the Slaughter 7.00
GN Pain Most Human 7.00
GN Pain Without Tears 7.00
GN Devil in the Details 7.00
GN Eve of Terror 6.00
TPB Vol. 1 . . . . 18.00
TPB Chronicles 19.00
TPB Terror From Within 17.00
TPB Bare Bones Edition 20.00
TPB Casebook 17.00
Spec. Kolchak Tales: Ghost
   Stories (2006) 5.00

KOLCHAK: TALES OF THE NIGHT STALKER
Moonstone, 2003
1 . . . . 3.50
2 thru 7 . . . . @3.50
GN Devil in the Details 7.00
1-shot Black & White & Red
   All Over 5.00

KONA
Dell Publishing Co., 1962
1 P(c) all,SG 125.00
2 SG 60.00

3 SG 60.00
4 SG,B:Anak 60.00
5 thru 10 SG . . . . @60.00
11 thru 21 SG . . . . @50.00

Konga #1
© Charlton

KONGA
Charlton Comics, 1960–65
1 SD,DG(c), movie adapt. 375.00
2 DG(c) 175.00
3 SD 150.00
4 SD 150.00
5 SD 150.00
6 thru 15 SD . . . . @100.00
16 thru 23 . . . . @75.00

KONGA'S REVENGE
Charlton Comics
2 Summer, 1962 . . . . 100.00
3 SD,Fall, 1964 . . . . 50.00
1 Dec., 1968 . . . . 35.00

KOOKIE
Dell Publishing Co., 1962
1 . . . . 150.00
2 . . . . 125.00

KORAK, SON OF TARZAN
Gold Key, 1964
1 . . . . 125.00
2 thru 11 . . . . @75.00
12 thru 21 . . . . @50.00
22 thru 30 . . . . @40.00
31 thru 40 . . . . @35.00
41 thru 44 . . . . @25.00
45 Jan., 1972 . . . . 25.00
Continued by DC

KRUSTY COMICS
Bongo Comics, 1995
1 Rise and Fall of Krustyland 2.50
2 Rise and Fall of Krustyland 2.50
3 Rise and Fall of Krustyland 2.50

KULL IN 3-D
Blackthorne
1 . . . . 2.50
2 . . . . 2.50
3 . . . . 2.50

LAD: A DOG
Dell Publishing Co., 1961
1 . . . . 75.00
2 . . . . 60.00

LADY ARCANE
Hero Graphics, 1992
1 A: Flare,BU:O:Giant 5.00
2 thru 4 . . . . @3.00

LADY DEATH
Chaos! Comics, 1994
1 BnP, A:Evil Ernie 15.00
1a signed gold foil 20.00
2 BnP 15.00
3 BnP 10.00
TPB Rep. #1-#3 . . . . 7.00
TPB The Reckoning 13.00
TPB The Reckoning, revised,
   BnP,Shu 13.00
Specials & 1-shots
1 Swimsuit Edition 10.00
1a Velvet Edition 18.00
1 rep. with 8-page pin-up gallery . . 3.00
1 Lady Death in Lingerie,
   various artists 5.00
1 Lady Death & the Women of
   Chaos! Gallery, pin-ups (1996) . 2.50
1-shot Dragon Wars (1998) 3.00
1-shotA Dragon Wars, Premium Ed,
   Sketchbook cover 15.00
1-shot Retribution (1998) 3.00
1-shotA Retribution (1998) variant
   cover 3.00
1-shotB Retribution, premium ed. . 10.00

LADY DEATH
Chaos! Comics, 1998
? signed, limited 15.00
1 . . . . 3.00
1a signed, limited 10.00
2 R:Lady Demon 3.00
3 V:Levithia 3.00
4 V:Pagan 3.00
5 The Harrowing, pt.1 . . . . 3.00
6 V:Uriel 3.00
7 V:Moloch 3.00
8 time to sieze Hell 3.00
9 world scythe of the covenant . . . 3.00
10 Goddess War,pt.2 x-over 3.00
11 V:Cremator 3.00
12 Unholy Nights 3.00
13 MD2,DQ,Inferno, pt.1 . . . . 3.00
13a signed 20.00
14 MD2,DQ,Inferno, pt.2 . . . . 3.00
15 MD2,DQ,Inferno, pt.3 . . . . 3.00
15a variant cover 6.00
16 MD2,DQ,Inferno, pt.4 . . . . 3.00
Swimsuit Spec.#1, signed 20.00

LADY DEATH
Chaos! Comics, 1999
1/2 Tribute Book 14.00
0 ashcan, yellow 10.00
0 ashcan, yellow, signed 20.00
0 ashcan, blue 25.00
1 (of 12) by Steve Hughes 3.00
1a signed 15.00
1b deluxe Steve Hughes (c) 16.00
Spec. Swimsuit 2001 #1 . . . . 3.00
Spec. Swimsuit 2001 #1 premium . 11.00
Vol. 1 Lady Death's Black Book . . 10.00
Vol. 1 Black Book,premium ed. . . 15.00
Halloween Special Ashcan 6.00
Halloween Spec. Ashcan, premium 20.00
Halloween Spec. #1 . . . . 3.00
Halloween Spec. #1a premium ed. 10.00
Halloween Spec. #1b
   super-premium edition 20.00
Halloween Spec. 1c foil edition . . . 20.00

LADY DEATH

Crossgen Code 6 Comics, 2003
1 thru 12 A Medieval Tale ...... @3.00
GN Vol. 1 A Medieval Tale 10.00

Season Two, 2004
1 Spell Storm 3.00
2 thru 6 The Wild Hunt .... @3.00

LADY DEATH

Avatar, 2004
1 10th Anniv. Edition 4.00
1a painted (c) 4.00
1b premium (c) 10.00
1c variant (c)s .... @6.00
1d 10th Anniv. Prism foil (c) 13.00
Spec. Swimsuit 2005 .... 4.00
Spec. Swimsuit 2005 variant(c)s . @6.00
Spec. Swimsuit 2005 premium (c). 10.00
Spec. Swimsuit 2005 Prism foil (c) 13.00
Spec. Leather & Lace 2005
   Various (c)s .... @6.00
Spec. Bikini, 2005 .... 4.00
Spec. Bikini, 2005 variant (c)s ... @4.00
Spec. Bikini, 2005 variant (c)s ... @6.00
Ann. #1 .... 5.00
Ann. #1a variant (c)s .... @5.00
Ann. #1b premium (c) 10.00
Spec. 2006 Fetishes 4.00
Spec. 2006 Fetishes variant (c)s @4.00
Spec. 2006 Fetishes prem. (c)s .. @6.00
1-shot Dark Horizons 3.00
1-shot Dark Horizons variant (c)s @3.00
1-shot Dark Horizons premium (c) 10.00

LADY DEATH: ALIVE

Chaos! Comics, 2001
1 (of 4) 3.00
1a premium edition 12.00
2 thru 4 .... @3.00
4a variant Scott Lewis (c) 7.50
Ashcan 6.00

LADY DEATH/BAD KITTY

Chaos! Comics, 2001
1 .... 3.00
1a premium ed.. .... 10.00
2 .... 3.00

LADY DEATH BEDLAM

Chaos! Comics, 2002
1 BAu 3.00
1a premium edition 10.00

LADY DEATH II: BETWEEN HEAVEN & HELL

Chaos! Comics, 1995
1 V:Purgatori. 5.00
1a Limited Edition 5,000c 25.00
1b premium velvet cover, signed . 30.00
2 Lives As Hope 4.00
3 V:Purgatori. 4.00
4 final issue. 4.00
TPB 13.00

LADY DEATH: BLACKLANDS

Avatar Press, 2006
½ 3.00
½ wraparound (c). 3.00
½ variant (c)s .... @3.00
½ premium. 10.00
1 .... 4.00
1a wraparound (c) 4.00
1b variant (c)s .... @4.00
1c premium (c) 10.00
2 .... 4.00
2a variant (c)s .... @4.00

Lady Death Swimsuit Special #1
© Avatar

2b variant premium (c) 10.00

LADY DEATH/CHASTITY

Chaos! Comics, 2001
1 x-over. 3.00
1a premium edition 10.00

LADY DEATH/CHASTITY/ BAD KITTY: UNITED

Chaos! Comics, 2002
1 .... 3.00
1a premium edition 10.00

LADY DEATH/THE CROW

Chaos! Comics, 2002
1 .... 3.00
1a premium edition 10.00
1b super premium edition 20.00
Script #1 .... 5.00
Script #1 premium edition 20.00
Ashcan 6.00
Ashcan, premium edition 20.00
Preview book b&w 2.00
Preview book, premium edition 6.00

LADY DEATH: THE CRUCIBLE

Chaos! Comics, 1996
1 (of 6) BnP,SHu, ... 3.50
1 leather limited edition. 15.00
2 BnP,SHu, ... 3.50
3 BnP,SHu, ... 3.50
4 BnP,SHu, ... 3.50
5 BnP,SHu, ... 3.50
6 BnP,SHu,V:Genocide,concl. 3.00
GN Collected ed. Vol. 1 .... 6.00
GN Collected ed. Vol. 2 .... 6.00
GN Collected ed. Vol. 3 .... 6.00
TPB rep.#1–#6. .... 20.00
Spec. Script 5.00
Spec. Script, premium ed. 20.00

LADY DEATH: DARK ALLIANCE

Chaos! Comics, 2002
Ashcan b&w 6.00
Ashcan premium edition 15.00
1 (of 5) F:everybody 3.00
1a premium edition 10.00
2 thru 5 .... @3.00
2a thru 5a Alternate cover (c) ... @7.50

LADY DEATH: DARK MILLENNIUM

Chaos! Comics, 2000
1 (of 3) 3.00
1a premium edition 7.00
1a signed, limited 10.00
2 .... 3.00
3 .... 3.00
Preview Book B&W 5.00

LADY DEATH: DEATH BECOMES HER

Chaos! Comics, 1997
0 follows the *Crucible*, leads to
   Wicked Ways. 3.00

LADY DEATH/EVIL ERNIE

Chaos! Comics, 2002
Ashcan 6.00
Ashcan premium edition 20.00
1 BnP, sequel to Dark Alliance 3.50
1a premium edition 10.00
1b super premium edition 20.00
1c foil edition. 20.00

LADY DEATH: THE GAUNTLET

Chaos! Comics, 2002
Ashcan b&w. 6.00
1 (of 4) 3.00
1a premium edition 10.00
1b foil edition. 20.00
2 .... 3.00
2a Variant JSC (c) 7.50

LADY DEATH: THE GODDESS RETURNS

Chaos! Chomics, 2002
1 (of 2) JOs. 3.00
1a premium edition 10.00
2 .... 3.00
2a variant (c). 7.50

LADY DEATH: HEARTBREAKER

Chaos! Comics, 2002
1 .... 3.00
1a premium edition 10.00
1b super premium edition 20.00
1c foil (c) 20.00
1d MegaCon foil edition 25.00

LADY DEATH/JADE

Chaos! Comics, 2002
1 .... 3.00
1 premium edition 10.00

LADY DEATH: JUDGMENT WAR

Chaos! Comics, 1999
Prelude. 3.00
1 (of 3) 3.00
1a premium. 10.00
2 .... 3.00
3 Hell is vanquished, concl. 3.00
Preview Book B&W 5.00

LADY DEATH: LAST RITES

Chaos! Comics, 2001
1 (of 4) RCI(c). 3.00
1 premium ed. RCI(c). 15.00
2 .... 3.00
2 variant DkG(c). 7.50

COLOR PUB.

3 . . . . 3.00
3a variant (c) 7.50
4 . . . . 3.00
4a variant (c) 7.50

LADY DEATH:
LOST SOULS
Avatar Press, 2005

0 . . . . 3.00
0a variant (c)s . . . . @3.00
0b premium (c) 10.00
1 (of 2) 3.00
1a wraparound (c) 3.00
1b variant (c)s . . . . @3.00
1c premium (c) 10.00
2 . . . . 3.00
2a wraparound (c) 3.00
2b variant (c)s . . . . @3.00
2c premium (c) 10.00

LADY DEATH:
LOVE BITES
Chaos! Comics, 2001

1 . . . . 3.00
1 premium edition 10.00
Ashcan 6.00

LADY DEATH/
MEDIEVAL WITCHBLADE
Chaos! Comics, 2001

1 BAu,x-over 3.50
1a variant MS (c) (1:4) 3.50
1b premium edition 10.00
1c super premium 20.00
Preview book 2.00
Preview book, premium ed. 6.00
Ashcan 12-page, B&W 6.00

LADY DEATH:
MISCHIEF NIGHT
Chaos! Comics, 2001

1 . . . . 3.00
1a premium edition 13.00
1b super premium edition 20.00

LADY DEATH:
THE MOURNING
Chaos! Comics, 2002

Ashcan 6.00
1 (of 2) 3.00
1a premium edition 10.00
2 . . . . 3.00
2a variant (c) 7.50

LADY DEATH:
THE ODYSSEY
Chaos! Comics, 1996

Sneak Peek Preview 2.00
1 embossed cover 3.00
1 SHu(c) premium edition 15.00
2 . . . . 3.00
3 . . . . 3.00
4 . . . . 3.00
4a variant cover 15.00
Micro Premium Preview Book 15.00
TPB 10.00

LADY DEATH:
THE RAPTURE
Chaos! Comics, 1999

1 (of 4) BnP,V:Father Orbec 3.00
1a dynamic forces cover. 7.00
1b dynamic forces, signed 15.00
1c premium edition 9.00
2 Heaven vs. Hell 3.00

3 V:Asteroth 3.00
4 BnP 3.00
Preview Book B&W 5.00
Collected ed. Vol. 1 . . . . 6.00
Collected ed. Vol. 2 . . . . 6.00

LADY DEATH:
RE-IMAGINED
Chaos! Comics, 2002

1 Spanish Inquisition 3.00
1a premium edition 10.00
1b super premium edition 20.00
Ashcan Re-imagined (b&w) 6.00

LADY DEATH:
RIVER OF FEAR
Chaos! Comics, 2001

1 . . . . 3.00
1a premium ed. 10.00

LADY DEATH/SHI
Avatar Press, 2006

Preview 2.50
Preview variant 3.00
Preview variant Premium (c) 10.00

LADY DEATH:
TRIBULATION
Chaos! Comics, 2000

1 . . . . 3.00
1a premium edition, tattoo (c). . . . 10.00
1b chromium (c) 16.00
1c chrome (c) signed 21.00
2 . . . . 3.00
3 . . . . 3.00
4 concl. 3.00
Ashcan B&W 6.66

LADY DEATH/
VAMPIRELLA:
DARK HEARTS
Chaos!/Harris, 1999

Spec. x-over, 40-page 3.50
Spec. Premium Edition 10.00

LADY DEATH
VS. PURGATORI
Chaos! Comics, 2000

1 gold foil 30.00
1 premium ed. 10.00

LADY DEATH
VS. VAMPIRELLA II
Chaos!/Harris, 2000

1 x-over 3.50
1a premium ed. 10.00
1b Gold foil ed. 30.00
1c Blue foil ed. 60.00

LADY DEATH:
THE WICKED
Avatar Press, 2005

½ 3.00
½a variant (c) . . . . @3.00
½b premium (c) 10.00
1 . . . . 4.00
1a Wraparound (c) 4.00
1b Variant(c)s . . . . @4.00
1c Premium (c) 10.00

LADY DEMON
Chaos! Comics, 2000

1 (of 3) 3.00

1a premium ed. 10.00
2 . . . . 3.00
3 concl. 3.00
Preview book B&W 5.00

LADY PENDRAGON
Maximum Press, 1996

1 mini-series 2.50
2 . . . . 2.50
3 (of 3) MD2 . . . . 2.50

LADY RAWHIDE
Topps, 1995

1 All New Solo series 5.00
2 It Can't Happen Here,pt.2 . . . . . 3.50
3 . . . . 3.00
4 . . . . 3.00
5 conclusion 3.00
Spec.#1 Rep. Zorro #2-#3 . . . . . . 6.50

LADY RAWHIDE
Topps, 1996
Mini-Series

1 DMG 4.00
1a DMG,signed, numbered 10.00
2 DMG 3.00
3 DMG 3.00
4 DMG, EM, Intimate Wounds . . . 3.00
5 DMG, EM 3.00
6 DMG 3.00
7 DMG 3.00
TPB 11.00

LADY RAWHIDE:
OTHER PEOPLE'S BLOOD
Topps, 1996
Mini-Series

1 DMG,EM,A Slice of Breast 3.00

LADY VAMPRE
Blackout, 1995

0 B&W. 3.50
1 . . . . 3.00

LAI WAN,
DREAM WALKER
Moonstone Books, 2005

1 . . . . 3.00
2 . . . . 3.50

Lancelot Strong The Shield #1
© Red Circle

    All comics prices listed are for *Near Mint* condition.

LANCELOT STRONG, THE SHIELD
Red Circle, 1983
1 A:Steel Sterling 3.50
2 A:Steel Sterling 2.50
3 AN/EB,D:Lancelot Strong 2.50

LAND OF THE DEAD
IDW Publishing, 2005
2 . . . . 4.00
3 . . . . 4.00
4 . . . . 4.00
4a photo (c). 4.00
5 . . . . 4.00
5a photo (c) 4.00

LANDSALE & TRUMAN'S DEAD FOLKS
Avatar Press, 2003
1 . . . . 3.50
1a wraparound (c) 4.00
2 thru 3 . . . . @3.50
2a thru 3a wraparound (c). . . . . . @4.00
TPB 10.00

LARS OF MARS
Eclipse, 1987
1 3-D MA. 3.00

LASER ERASER & PRESSBUTTON
Eclipse, 1985–87
1 GL,R:Laser Eraser. 2.50
2 GL 2.50
3 GL,CK,Tsultrine'. 2.50
4 MC,Death. 2.50
5 MC,JRy,Gates of Hell 2.50
6 Corsairs of Illunium 2.50
3-D#1 MC,GL(c),Triple Cross 2.50

LASH LARUE WESTERN
AC Comics
1 . . . . 3.50
Annual 3.00

LAST BASTION, THE
Speakeasy Comics, 2006
1 (of 6) 3.00
2 . . . . 3.00

LAST OF THE VIKING HEROES
Genesis West, 1987
1 JK. 4.00
2 JK. 3.50
3 . . . . 3.50
4 . . . . 3.50
5A sexy cover 4.00
5B mild cover 3.50
6 . . . . 3.50
7 AA(c) 3.50
8 . . . . 3.50
9 Great Battle of Nidhogger 3.50
10 Death Among the Heroes 3.50
Summer Spec.#1 FF,JK 3.50
Summer Spec.#2 . . . . 3.00
Summer Spec.#3,A:TMNT 2.50

LAUGH
Archie, 1987–91
1 . . . . 6.00
2 thru 10 . . . . @5.00
11 thru 29 . . . . @3.00

Laugh #26
© Archie Publications

LAUREL AND HARDY
Dell Publishing Co., 1962
1 . . . . 125.00
2 . . . . 75.00
3 . . . . 75.00
4 . . . . 75.00

LAUREL & HARDY
Gold Key, 1967
1 . . . . 125.00
2 Oct., 1967 . . . . 100.00

LAURELL K. HAMILTON'S ANITA BLAKE, VAMPIRE HUNTER
Dabel Brothers Productions, 2006
1 . . . . 3.00
1a variant (c)s . . . . @6.00
2 Guilty Pleasures. 3.00
2a variant (c)s . . . . @6.00
3 . . . . 3.00
3a variant (c)s . . . . @6.00

LAWMAN
Dell Publishing Co., 1959
1 Ph(c) all 250.00
2 . . . . 150.00
3 ATh. 135.00
4 . . . . 100.00
5 . . . . 100.00
6 . . . . 100.00
7 . . . . 100.00
8 thru 11 . . . . @100.00

LAW AND ORDER
Maximum Press, 1995
1 MMy,D:Law,I:New Law, Order . . . 2.50
2 V:Max Spur 2.50
3 V:Law's Murderer. 2.50

LAW OF DREDD
Quality
1 V:Perps 5.00
2 BB,Lunar Olympics 4.00
3 BB,V:Judge Death 3.00
4 thru 7 . . . . @3.00
Fleetway
8 Blockmania 3.00
9 BB,DGi,Framed for murders 3.00

10 thru 32 . . . . @2.50
33 League of Fatties,final issue 3.00

LAZARUS: THE MANY REINCARNATIONS
Lodestone Publishing, 2000
1 by Zak Hennessey 3.00
2 . . . . 3.00
4 thru 7 . . . . @3.00

LEADING MAN
Oni Press, 2006
1 (of 5) 3.50
2 thru 5 . . . . @3.50

LEAGUE OF CHAMPIONS
Hero Graphics, 1990
{Cont. from Champions #12}
1 Olympus Saga #4 . . . . 3.00
2 Olympus Saga #5,O:Malice. 3.00
3 Olympus Saga ends 3.00

LEAGUE OF EXTRA-ORDINARY GENTLEMEN
WildStorm/DC, 1999
America's Best Comics
1 (of 6) AMo(s),KON. 3.00
2 thru 6 AMo(s),KON. . . . . @3.00
GN Collected Edition 6.00
Vol. II (July, 2002)
1 AMo(s),KON. 3.50
2 AMo(s),KON,Martian marauders . 3.50
3 AMo(s),KON,traitor 3.50
4 AMo(s),KON, ... 3.50
5 AMo(s),KON, one dies. 3.50
6 AMo(s),KON,finale. 3.50
TPB Book One. 15.00

LEGACY
Majestic, 1993
0 platinum 10.00
1 I:Legacy 2.50
2 . . . . 2.50

LEGACY
Antarctic Press, 1999
1 by Fred Perry. 3.00
2 thru 5 . . . . @3.00

LEGEND
Wildstorm/DC, Feb., 2005
1 (of 4) HC,RH, 48-page. 6.00
2 HC,RH 6.00
3 HC,RH, Vietnam war 6.00
4 HC,RH,concl. 6.00

LEGEND OF CUSTER, THE
Dell Publishing Co., 1968
1 Ph(c) 50.00

LEGEND OF ISIS, THE
Alias Enterprises, 2005
1 (of 4) 3.00
2 thru 6 . . . . @3.00
7 . . . . 3.00
8 . . . . 3.00
9 . . . . 3.50
10 God War x-over 3.50
11 Rise of Darkness. 3.50
12 Rise of Darkness, pt.2 . . . . 3.50
13 Rise of Darkness, pt.3 . . . . 3.50
GN 10.00
TPB Vol. 2 . . . . 10.00

COLOR PUB.

LEGEND OF THE ELFLORD
Davdez Arts, 1998
1 by Barry Blair & Colin Chan.	3.00
2	2.50
3	3.00
4	3.00
GN Vol. 1 112-page	12.00

LEGEND OF THE SAGE
Chaos! Comics, 2001
1 (of 4) F:Victoria Noble	3.00
1a premium edition	10.00
2	3.00
2a variant (c).	7.50
3	3.00
3a variant (c).	7.50
4	3.00
4a variant (c).	7.50
Preview Book	2.00
Preview Book, premium edition	6.00

LEGENDS OF JESSE JAMES, THE
Gold Key, 1966
1	50.00

LEGENDS OF LUXURA
Comic Cavalcade, 1998
Commemorative #1 by Kirk Lindo	6.00
Commemorative #1a deluxe	15.00

LEGENDS OF NASCAR
Vortex, 1990
1 HT,Bill Eliott ($1.50 cover Price) 15,000 copies	10.00
1a ($2.00 cover price) 45,000 copies	5.00
1b 3rd pr., 80,000 copies	4.00
2 Richard Petty	4.00
3 Ken Schroder	3.50
4 Bob Alison	3.00
5 Bill Elliott	3.00
6 Jr. Johnson	3.00
7 Sterling Marlin	3.00
8 Benny Parsons	3.00
9 Rusty Wallace	3.00
10 thru 14	@3.00

LEGENDS OF THE STARGRAZERS
Innovation, 1989
1 thru 5	@2.50

LEONARD NIMOY'S PRIMORTALS
Teckno-Comics, 1994
1 I:Primortals.	5.50
2 Zeerus Reveals Himself	4.00
3 thru 15	@2.50

Big Entertainment, 1996
0 SEa,MKb	2.50
1 thru 7	@2.50

LEONARDO
Mirage, 1986
1 TMNT Character	5.00

LEOPARD
Millennium
1 I:Leopard	3.00
1a Gold Cover	4.00
2 O:Leopard,V:Razor's Edge	3.00

LETHAL INSTINCT
Alias Enterprises, 2005
1 (of 6)	1.00
2 thru 5	@3.00
6	3.50

LETHAL STRYKE
London Night Studios, 1995
1 F:Stryke	3.00
1a commemorative (1999)	6.00
2 O:Stryke	3.00
Ann. #1 EHr	3.00
Ann. #1 platinum edition	10.00

LETHAL STRIKE/ DOUBLE IMPACT: LETHAL IMPACT
London Night, 1996
1 by Jude Millien	3.00
1 limited	5.00

LEXIAN CHRONICLES, THE: FULL CIRCLE
APC, 2005
1	3.50
1a signed	20.00
1b red foil (c).	10.00
2 thru 5	@3.50
5a variant (c)	3.50
TPB Vol. 1	20.00

Markosia, 2005
6 thru 12	@3.50
7a thru 10a variant (c)s	@3.50
12a Commemorative sgn ed.	7.00
TPB Vol. 1	15.00

LIBERALITY FOR ALL
ACC Studios, 2005
1 (of 8)	3.00
2	3.00
3	3.00
3a variant (c)	3.00
4	3.00
4a variant (c)	3.00

LIBERTY GIRL
Heroic Publishing, 2006
1	3.25
2	3.25

LIBERTY PROJECT, THE
Eclipse, 1987–88
1 I:Liberty Project	2.50
2	2.50
3 V:Silver City Wranglers	2.50
4	2.50
5	2.50
6 F:Cimarron,Misery and Gin	2.50
7 I:Menace	2.50
8 V:Savage	2.50

LIDSVILLE
Gold Key, 1972
1	100.00
2	75.00
3 and 4	@75.00
5 Oct., 1973	75.00

LIEUTENANT, THE
Dell Publishing Co., April-June, 1962
1 Ph(c)	65.00

Life With Archie #42
© Archie Publications

LIFE WITH ARCHIE
Archie Publications, 1958
1	500.00
2	250.00
3	175.00
4	175.00
5	175.00
6	125.00
7	125.00
8	125.00
9	125.00
10	125.00
11 thru 20	@100.00
21 thru 30	@75.00
31 thru 40	@65.00
41	60.00
42 B:Pureheart.	125.00
43	75.00
44	75.00
45 R.I.V.E.R.D.A.L.E.	125.00
46 O:Pureheart.	100.00
47 thru 59	@65.00
60 thru 100.	@60.00
101 thru 200.	@25.00
201 thru 285.	@15.00

LIGHT FANTASTIC, THE
Innovation, 1992
1 Terry Pratchett adapt.	2.50
2 Adaptation continues	2.50
3 Adaptation continues	2.50
4 Adapt.conclusion	2.50

LIGHTNING COMICS PRESENTS
Lightning Comics, 1994
1 B&W Promo Ed.	3.50
1a B&W Promo Ed. Platinum	3.50
1b B&W Promo Ed. Gold	3.50

L'IL HELLIONS: DAY AT THE ZOO
Silent Devil Productions, 2006
1	4.00

LILLITH: DEMON PRINCESS
Antarctic Press, 1996
1 (of 3) from Warrior Nun Areala	3.00
1a Commemorative Edition (1999).	6.00
2 and 3	@3.00

LILO & STITCH
Disney Press, 2006
GN Vol. 1 . . . . 5.00

LIMBO CITY
Dreamwave, 2002
1 BAu,BBh 3.00
2 thru 3 . . . . @3.00

LINCOLN-16
Skarwood Productions, 1997
1 GI 3.00
2 GI 3.00
3 GI 3.00

LINDA LARK
Dell Publishing Co., 1961
1 . . . . 50.00
2 thru 8 . . . . @35.00

LINUS, THE LIONHEARTED
Gold Key, 1965
1 . . . . 175.00

LIONHEART
Awesome Entertainment, 1999
1 IaC,JLb, from *The Coven* 3.00
1 Wizard World exclusive 5.50
2 IaC,JLb 3.00
2a variant cover 3.00
2b variant IaC cover 7.00
3 concl 3.00

LIPPY THE LION AND HARDY HAR HAR
Gold Key, 1963
1 . . . . 175.00

LISA COMICS
Bongo Comics, 1995
1 F:Lisa Simpson 3.00

LITTLE AMBROSE
Archie Publications, 1958
1 . . . . 175.00

LITTLE ARCHIE
Archie Publications, 1956
1 . . . . 1,200.00
2 . . . . 500.00
3 . . . . 350.00
4 . . . . 350.00
5 . . . . 350.00
6 thru 10 . . . . @300.00
11 thru 20 . . . . @200.00
21 thru 30 . . . . @150.00
31 thru 40 . . . . @100.00
41 thru 60 . . . . @100.00
61 thru 80 . . . . @75.00
81 thru 100 . . . . @30.00
101 thru 180 . . . . @15.00

LITTLE ARCHIE MYSTERY
Archie Publications, 1963
1 . . . . 225.00
2 Oct., 1963 . . . . 150.00

LITTLE AUDREY & MELVIN
Harvey Publications, 1962
1 . . . . 225.00
2 thru 5 . . . . @100.00

6 thru 10 . . . . @75.00
11 thru 20 . . . . @65.00
21 thru 40 . . . . @30.00
41 thru 50 . . . . @30.00
51 thru 53 52 pgs Giant size . . . @30.00
54 thru 60 . . . . @35.00
61 Dec., 1973 . . . . 30.00

LITTLE AUDREY TV FUNTIME
Harvey Publications, 1962
1 A:Richie Rich 225.00
2 same 150.00
3 same 100.00
4 . . . . 100.00
5 . . . . 100.00
6 thru 10 . . . . @75.00
11 thru 20 . . . . @50.00
21 thru 32 . . . . @35.00
33 Oct., 1971 . . . . 35.00

LITTLE DOT DOTLAND
Harvey Publications, 1962
1 . . . . 200.00
2 . . . . 150.00
3 . . . . 100.00
4 . . . . 100.00
5 . . . . 100.00
6 thru 10 . . . . @75.00
11 thru 20 . . . . @60.00
21 thru 50 . . . . @50.00
51 thru 60 . . . . @40.00
61 Dec., 1973 . . . . 40.00

LITTLE DOT'S UNCLES & AUNTS
Harvey Enterprises, 1961
1 . . . . 400.00
2 . . . . 250.00
3 . . . . 250.00
4 . . . . 150.00
5 . . . . 150.00
6 thru 10 . . . . @125.00
11 thru 20 . . . . @100.00
21 thru 40 . . . . @75.00
41 thru 51 . . . . @50.00
52 April, 1974 . . . . 50.00

LITTLE LOTTA
Harvey Publications, 1955
1 B:Richie Rich and Little Lotta . 650.00
2 . . . . 350.00
3 . . . . 300.00
4 . . . . 275.00
5 . . . . 300.00
6 . . . . 250.00
7 . . . . 250.00
8 . . . . 250.00
9 . . . . 250.00
10 . . . . 250.00
11 thru 20 . . . . @150.00
21 thru 40 . . . . @100.00
41 thru 60 . . . . @100.00
61 thru 80 . . . . @75.00
81 thru 99 . . . . @75.00
100 thru 103 52 pgs . . . . @75.00
104 thru 120 . . . . @40.00
121 May, 1976 . . . . 40.00

LITTLE LOTTA FOODLAND
Harvey Publications, 1963
1 68 pgs 500.00
2 . . . . 250.00
3 . . . . 200.00
4 . . . . 250.00
5 . . . . 250.00
6 thru 10 . . . . @250.00

11 thru 20 . . . . @150.00
21 thru 26 . . . . @100.00
27 . . . . 50.00
28 . . . . 25.00
29 Oct., 1972 . . . . 50.00

LITTLE MERMAID
Walt Disney, 1992
1 based on movie 3.00
2 Serpent Teen 3.00
3 Guppy Love 3.00
4 . . . . 3.00

The Little Monsters
© Gold Key

LITTLE MONSTERS, THE
Gold Key, 1964
1 . . . . 125.00
2 . . . . 75.00
3 thru 10 . . . . @50.00
11 thru 20 . . . . @35.00
21 thru 43 . . . . @35.00
44 Feb., 1978 . . . . 35.00

LITTLE MONSTERS
Now, 1990
1 thru 6 . . . . @2.50

LITTLE SAD SACK
Harvey Publications, 1964
1 Richie Rich(c) 100.00
2 . . . . 75.00
3 . . . . 75.00
4 . . . . 75.00
5 . . . . 75.00
6 thru 19 Nov. 1967 . . . . @75.00

LITTLE STOOGES, THE
Gold Key, 1972
1 . . . . 75.00
2 . . . . 50.00
3 . . . . 45.00
4 . . . . 45.00
5 . . . . 45.00
6 and 7 March, 1974 . . . . @45.00

LIVING IN INFAMY
Ludovico Technique, 2005
1 (of 4) 3.00
2 thru 4 . . . . @3.00

LIZ
Narwain Publishing, 2006
1 . . . . 4.00

LLOYD LLEWELLYN
Fantagraphics, 1987
Spec. #1 . . . . 2.50

LOBO
Dell Publishing Co., 1965
1 . . . . 60.00
2 . . . . 50.00

LOCKE
Blackthorne
1 PO.Jones 2.50
2 TD 2.50
3 thru 5 . . . . @2.50

LONE RANGER, THE
Gold Key, 1964
1 . . . . 125.00
2 . . . . 75.00
3 . . . . 60.00
4 . . . . 60.00
5 . . . . 60.00
6 thru 10 . . . . @50.00
11 thru 18 . . . . @50.00
19 thru 27 . . . . @40.00
28 March, 1977 . . . . 40.00

LONE RANGER, THE
D.E. (Dynamite Ent.) 2006
1 . . . . 3.00
1a silver foil (c) 15.00
2 . . . . 3.00
3 . . . . 3.00

LONE RANGER AND TONTO, THE
Topps, 1994
1 JLd,TT,RM,The Last Battle 2.50
2 JLd,TT,RM 2.50
3 JLd,TT,RM, O:Lone Ranger. 2.50
4 JLd,TT,RM, It Crawls 2.50
TPB rep. #1–#4 . . . . 10.00

LOOKERS
Avatar
Combo Spec. 16pg. 3.00
Combo Spec. Platinum 10.00

LORD PUMPKIN
Malibu, Oct. 1994
0 Sludge 2.50

LORE
IDW Publishing, 2003
1 . . . . 6.00
2 . . . . 4.00
3 . . . . 4.00
4 . . . . 4.00
TPB rep. #1 thru #3 . . . . 20.00

LOST BOOKS OF EVE, THE
Viper Comics, 2006
1 . . . . 3.25

LOST HEROES
Davdez Arts, 1998
0 by Rob Prior, lost SF heroes 3.00
1 thru 5 . . . . @3.00
6 . . . . 3.00
GN 5/6 56-page 8.00

LOST IN SPACE
Innovation, 1991
{based on TV series}
1 O:Jupiter II Project. 3.50
2 Cavern of IdyllicSummersLost. . . 3.00
2a Special Edition 3.00
3 Do Not Go Gently into that Good
    Night,Bill Mumy script 3.00
4 People are Strange 3.00
5 The Perils of Penelope 3.00
6 thru 12 . . . . @3.00
Project Krell 3.00
Ann.#1 (1991) 3.00
Ann.#2 (1992) 3.00
1Spec.#1 & #2 rep. Seduction of
    the Innocent . . . . @3.00
GN Strangers among Strangers . . . 6.00
1-shot Project Robinson, follows
    story in issue #12 (1993). 2.50

Lost in Space: Voyage to the Bottom of the Soul #13 © Innovation

Becomes:

LOST IN SPACE: VOYAGE TO THE BOTTOM OF THE SOUL
Innovation, 1993–94
13 thru 18 . . . . @3.00

LOST PLANET
Eclipse, 1987–88
1 BHa,I:Tyler FLynn 2.50
2 BHa,R:Amelia Earhart 2.50
3 BHa 2.50
4 BHa,Devil's Eye 2.50
5 BHa,A:Amelia Earhart 2.50
6 . . . . 2.50

LOVECRAFT
Adventure Comics
1 The Lurking Fear adapt. 3.00
2 Beyond the Wall of Sleep 3.00
3 The Tomb 3.00
4 The Alchemist 3.00

LOVE DIARY
Charlton Comics, 1958
1 . . . . 150.00
2 . . . . 125.00
3 thru 10 . . . . @100.00
11 thru 15 . . . . @100.00
16 thru 20 . . . . @100.00
21 thru 40 . . . . @75.00
41 thru 101 . . . . @20.00
102 Dec., 1976 . . . . 20.00

LOVE SHOWDOWN COLLECTION
Archie Comics, 1997
TPB x-over rep. Archie #429 (pt.1),
    Betty #19 (pt.2), Betty & Veronica
    #82, (pt.3), Veronica #39 (pt.4)
    Return of Cheryl Blossom 5.00

LUCIFER'S HAMMER
Innovation, 1993–94
1 thru 6 Larry Niven & Jerry
    Pournelle novel adaptation . . @2.50

LUCY SHOW, THE
Gold Key, 1963
1 Ph(c) 300.00
2 Ph(c) 250.00
3 thru 5 . . . . @200.00

LUDWIG VON DRAKE
Dell Publishing Co., 1961
1 . . . . 125.00
2 thru 4 . . . . @75.00

LUFTWAFFE 1946
Antarctic Press, 1998
1 color special, by Ted Namura . . . 3.00

LUGER
Eclipse, 1986–87
1 TY,I:Luger,mini-series 2.50
2 TY 2.50
3 TY,BHa,V:Sharks 2.50

LULLABY
Alias Enterprises, 2005
Vol. 2
1 . . . . 3.00
2 . . . . 3.00
3 . . . . 3.00
3a convention foil (c) signed 15.00
4 . . . . 3.50
5 . . . . 3.50
5a variant (c) 5.00
TPB Lullaby Wisdom Seeker. 10.00
TPB Vol. 2 Power Grabber 15.00

LULLABY: ONCE UPON A TIME
Alias Enterprises, 2006
GN Vol. 1 Pied Piper of Hamelin . . . 6.00

LUNATIC FRINGE
Innovation, 1989
1 . . . . 2.50
2 . . . . 2.50

LURKERS
IDW Publishing, 2004
1 . . . . 4.00
2 thru 4 . . . . @4.00
TPB 18.00

LUXURA
Comic Cavalcade, 1998
Commemorative #1 by Kirk Lindo . . 6.00
Commemorative #1a deluxe 15.00

LUXURA COLLECTION
Brainstorm
Commemorative edition, red foil
    cover, 48pg. 10.00

LYNCH MOB
Chaos! Comics, 1994
1 GCa(c), I:Mother Mayhem 3.00
2 Lynch Mob Loses. 2.50
3 1994 Time Trip. 2.50
3a Gold cover 3.00
4 Mother Mayhem at UN 2.50

LYNDON B. JOHNSON
Dell Publishing Co.,
March, 1965
1 Ph(c) 50.00

M
Eclipse, 1990–91
1 thru 4 JMu . . . . @5.50

MACROSS
Comico
1 . . . . 35.00
Becomes:

ROBOTECH, THE
MACROSS SAGA

MAD FOLLIES
E.C. Comics, 1963
(N#) 450.00
2 1964 . . . . 350.00
3 1965 . . . . 250.00
4 1966 . . . . 275.00
5 1967 . . . . 200.00
6 1968 . . . . 175.00
7 1969 . . . . 175.00

MAD HOUSE
Red Circle, 1974–82
95 thru 97 Horror stories . . . . . @22.00
98 thru 130 Humor stories . . . . . @15.00
Annual #8 thru #11 . . . . @18.00

MADMAN
Tundra, 1992
1 . . . . 15.00
2 . . . . 12.00
3 . . . . 7.00
Oni Press, 2003
King-Size Super Special 7.00

MADMAN ADVENTURES
Tundra, 1992
1 R & N:Madman 15.00
2 . . . . 9.00
3 . . . . 8.00

MADMAN PICTURE
EXHIBITION
AAA Pop Comics, 2002
1 (of 4) 4.00
2 thru 4 . . . . 4.00

MADRAVEN
HALLOWEEN SPECIAL
Hamilton Comics, 1995
1 Song of the Silkies 3.00

MAD SPECIAL
E.C. Publications, Inc., 1970
1 . . . . 200.00
2 . . . . 125.00
3 . . . . 100.00
4 thru 8 . . . . @100.00
9 thru 13 . . . . @75.00
14 . . . . 60.00
15 . . . . 60.00

---

16 . . . . 50.00
17 . . . . 50.00
18 . . . . 50.00
19 thru 21 . . . . @50.00
22 thru 31 . . . . @35.00
32 . . . . 35.00
33 thru 58 . . . . @20.00

Mage #2
© Comico

MAGE
Comico, 1984–86
1 MWg,I:Kevin Matchstick 15.00
2 MWg,I:Edsel 12.00
3 MWg,V:Umbra Sprite 10.00
4 MWg,V:Umbra Sprite 10.00
5 MWg,I:Sean (Spook) 10.00
6 MWg,Grendel begins 15.00
7 MWg,Grendel 10.00
8 MWg,Grendel 8.00
9 MWg,Grendel 8.00
10 MWg,Grendel,Styx 8.00
11 MWg,Grendel,Styx 8.00
12 MWg,D:Sean,Grendel 8.00
13 MWg,D:Edsel,Grendel 7.00
14 MWg,Grendel,O:Kevin 7.00
15 MWg,D:Umbra Sprite 12.00
TPB Magebook #1 rep. Mage #1-4 . 9.00
TPB Magebook #2 rep. Mage #5-8 . 9.00

MAGE KNIGHT:
STOLEN DESTINY
IDW Publishing, 2002
1 (of 5) by TDz & D.Cabrera 3.50
2 . . . . 3.50
3 . . . . 3.50
4 . . . . 3.50
5 . . . . 3.50

MAGIC FLUTE
Eclipse, 1989
1 CR 5.00

MAGIC THE GATHERING:
GN Serra Angel + card 6.00
GN Legend of the Fallen Angel +
card 6.00
GN Dakkon Blackblade + card 6.00

...ANTIQUITIES WAR
Acclaim Armada, 1995
1 Based on the Antiquities Set 2.75
2 F:Urza, Mishra 2.50
3 I:Tawnos, Ashod 2.50
4 The War Begins 2.50

...ARABIAN KNIGHTS
Acclaim Armada, 1995
1 Based on Rare Card set 2.75
2 V:Queen Nailah 2.50

...CONVOCATIONS
Acclaim Armada, 1995
1 Gallery of Art from Game 2.50

...FALLEN EMPIRES
Acclaim Armada, 1995
1 with pack of cards 2.75
2 F:Tymolin 2.50
TPB Rep. #1-#2 . . . . 5.00

...HOMELANDS
Acclaim Armada, 1995
1 I:Feroz, Serra 6.00

...ICE AGE
Acclaim Armada, 1995
1 Dominaia, from card game 3.00
2 Ice Age Adventures 2.50
3 CV(c) Planeswalker battles 2.50
4 final issue 2.50
TPB Rep. #1-#2 . . . . 5.00
TPB Rep. #3-#4 . . . . 5.00

...SHADOW MAGE, THE
Acclaim Armada, 1995
1 I:Jared 3.00
2 F:Hurloon the Minotaur 2.75
3 VMk(c&a),V:Juggernaut 2.50
4 Final issue 2.50
TPB Rep. #1-#2 . . . . 5.00
TPB Rep. #3-#4 . . . . 5.00

...URZA-MISHRA WAR, THE
Acclaim Armada
1 & 2 with Ice Age II card 6.00

...WAYFARER
Acclaim Armada, 1995
1 R:Jared 2.75
2 I:New Land 2.50
3 R:Llana, Ravidel 2.50
4 I:Golthonor 2.50
5 Final Issue 2.50

...THE LEGENDS OF:
THE ELDER DRAGONS
1 & 2 . . . . @2.50
JEDIT OJANEN
1 & 2 . . . . @2.50
SHANDALAR
1 & 2 . . . . @2.50

MAGILLA GORILLA
Gold Key, 1964
1 . . . . 175.00
2 thru 10 Dec. 1968 . . . . @125.00

MAGILLA GORILLA
Charlton Comics, 1970
1 . . . . 100.00
2 thru 5 . . . . @60.00

MAGIQUE
WildStorm/DC, 2000
Ann. 2000 #1, Devil's
Night x-over, pt.4 . . . . 3.50

MAGNUS:
ROBOT FIGHTER
Gold Key, 1963
1 RM,I:Magnus,Teeja,A-1,
I&B:Capt.Johner&aliens 500.00
2 RM,I:Sen.Zeremiah Clane 275.00
3 RM,I:Xyrkol 275.00
4 RM,I:Mekamn,Elzy 160.00

5 RM,The Immortal One	160.00
6 RM,I:Talpa	150.00
7 RM,I:Malev-6,ViXyrkol	200.00
8 RM,I:Outsiders(Chet, Horio, Toun, Malf).	150.00
9 RM, I:Madmot	150.00
10 RM,Mysterious Octo-Rob	150.00
11 RM,I:Danae,Neo-Animals	125.00
12 RM,The Volcano Makers	125.00
13 RM,I:Dr Lazlo Noel	130.00
14 RM,The Monster Robs	125.00
15 RM,I:Mogul Radur.	125.00
16 RM,I:Gophs.	125.00
17 RM,I:Zypex	125.00
18 RM,I:V'ril Trent	125.00
19 RM,Fear Unlimited	125.00
20 RM,I:Bunda the Great.	125.00
21 RM, Space Spectre	125.00
22 Rep. #1	100.00
23 DSp,Mission Disaster	100.00
24 Pied Piper of North Am	100.00
25 The Micro Giants	100.00
26 The Venomous Vaper	100.00
27 Panic in Pacifica	100.00
28 Threats from the Depths	100.00
29 thru 46 rep.	@40.00

MAGNUS: ROBOT FIGHTER
Valiant, 1991

0 PCu,BL,Emancipator,w/ BWS card	9.00
0a PCu,BL,w/o card	3.00
1 ANi,BL,B:Steel Nation	9.00
2 ANi,BL,Steel Nation #2	7.00
3 ANi,BL,Steel Nation #3	7.00
4 ANi,BL,E:Steel Nation	7.00
5 DL,BL(i),I:Rai(#1),V:Slagger Flipbook format	7.00
6 DL,A:Solar,V:Grandmother A:Rai(#2)	6.00
7 DL,EC,V:Rai(#3)	6.00
8 DL,A:Rai(#4),Solar,X-O Armor.E:Flipbooks	3.50
1a thru 8a w/o coupon	@2.00
9 EC,V:Xyrkol,E-7.	3.50
10 V:Xyrkol.	3.50
11 V:Xyrkol.	3.50
12 I:Turok,V:Dr. Noel, I:Asylum,40pgs	10.00
13 thru 20.	@2.50
21 JaB,R:Malevalents, Grand-mother	3.00
21a Gold Ed.	4.00
22 JaB,D:Felina,V:Malevalents, Grandmother	2.50
23 V:Malevolents	2.50
24 V:Malevolents	2.50
25 N:Magnus,R:1-A,silver-foil(c)	3.00
26 thru 63	@2.50
64 Ultimatum, F:Destroyer.	4.00
Yearbook #1.	4.00
TPB 1-4	10.00

MAGNUS (ROBOT FIGHTER)
Acclaim, 1997

1 Magnus back from the future.	3.00
2 thru 7	@2.50
8 thru 18 TPe	@2.50

MAJESTIC
Wildstorm/DC, Jan., 2005

1 DAn&ALa(s),A:Superman	3.00
1a variant (c).	3.00
2 DAn&ALa(s),Earth life abducted	3.00
3 DAn&ALa(s),Earth life abducted	3.00
4 DAn&ALa(s),Earth life abducted	3.00
5 DAn&ALa(s),Demon Night.	3.00
6 DAn&ALa(s),V:old friend	3.00

7 DAn&ALa(s),Daemonites.	3.00
8 DAn&ALa(s),present day	3.00
9 DAn&ALa(s),A:Zealot	3.00
10 DAn&ALa(s),Kherubim secrets.	3.00
11 DAn&ALa(s)	3.00
12 DAn&ALa(s)	3.00
13 DAn&ALa(s),A:Zealot	3.00
14 DAn,ALa(s),V:Javen	3.00
15 DAn,ALa(s),Imperitor V. Shapers	3.00
16 DAn,ALa(s),Duel of his life	3.00
17 DAn,ALa(s), final issue	3.00
TPB While You Were Out	13.00
TPB Vol. 2	15.00

MAJOR DAMAGE
Invictus Studios, 1994

1 I:Major Damage	2.50
2 V:Godkin	2.50
3 First Contact Conclusion	2.50

MAN CALLED A-X
Malibu Bravura, 1994–95
[Limited Series]

0 1st Puzzle piece	3.00
1 MWn,SwM	3.00
1a Gold foil Edition	4.00
2 MWn,SwM,VLElectobot.	3.00
3 MWn,SwM,Mercy Island	3.00
4 MWn,SwM,One Who Came Before	3.00
5 MWn,SwM,Climax	3.00

MAN CALLED KEV, A
Wildstorm/DC, July, 2006

1 (of 5) GEn(s)	3.00
2 thru 4 GEn(s)	@3.00

MANDRAKE THE MAGICIAN
King Comics, 1966

1	100.00
2	75.00
3	75.00
4 A:Girl Phantom.	75.00
5 Cape Cod Caper	75.00
6	75.00
7 O:Lothar.	75.00
8	75.00
9 A:Brick Bradford.	75.00
10 A:Rip Kirby	90.00

MAN FROM U.N.C.L.E.
Gold Key, 1965

1 The Explosive Affair.	500.00
2 The Forthur Cookie Affair	250.00
3 The Deadly Devices Affair	150.00
4 The Rip Van Solo Affair	150.00
5 Ten Little Uncles Affair.	150.00
6 The Three Blind Mice Affair	150.00
7 The Pixilated Puzzle Affair I:Jet Dream (back-up begins)	160.00
8 The Floating People Affair	150.00
9 Spirit of St.Louis Affair	150.00
10 The Trojan Horse Affair	150.00
11 Three-Story Giant Affair	150.00
12 Dead Man's Diary Affair	120.00
13 The Flying Clowns Affair	120.00
14 Great Brain Drain Affair	120.00
15 The Animal Agents Affair.	120.00
16 Instant Disaster Affair	120.00
17 The Deadly Visions Affair	120.00
18 The Alien Affair	120.00
19 Knight in Shining Armor Affair	120.00
20 Deep Freeze Affair	120.00
21 rep. #10	100.00
22 rep. #7.	100.00

Man From Uncle #10
© Gold Key

MAN FROM U.N.C.L.E.
Entertainment, 1987

1 thru 11	@3.00

MAN FROM U.N.C.L.E.
Millennium, 1993

1 The Birds of Prey Affair,pt.1	3.00
2 The Birds of Prey Affair,pt.2	3.00

MANGA SHI, 2000
Crusade Entertainment, 1997

1 (of 3) BiT, Final Jihad, flip-book Shi: Heaven and Earth	3.00
2 BiT, flip-book Tomoe: Unforgettable Fire preview	3.00
3 BiT, conclusion.	3.00

MANIFEST ETERNITY
Wildstorm/DC, June, 2006

1 SLo	3.00
2 thru 6 SLo	@3.00

MAN IN BLACK
Harvey Publications, 1957

1 BP	250.00
2 BP	175.00
3 BP	175.00
4 BP, March, 1958	175.00

MANIK
Millennium/Expand, 1995

1 I:Macedon, Arsenal,Cardinal	3.00

MANKIND
Chaos! Comics, 1999

1-shot StG	3.00
1-shotA photo cover	3.00
1-shotB variant cover	7.00
1-shotC variant cover, signed	60.00

MAN OF THE ATOM
Valiant Heroes Special Project
Acclaim, 1997

Spec.	4.00
TPB The Rebirth of Solar	8.00

MAN OF WAR
Eclipse, 1987–88

1 thru 3	@2.50

MAN OF WAR
Malibu, 1993–94
1 thru 3 V:Lift 2.50
1a thru 5a Newsstand Ed. 2.50
4 w/poster 2.50
5 V:Killinger 2.50
6 KM,Genesis Crossover 2.50
7 DJu,Genesis Crossover 2.50
8 TMs(s),A:Rocket Ranger 2.50
9 thru 12 . . . . @2.50

MANTECH
ROBOT WARRIORS
Archie Publications 1984–85
1 thru 4 . . . . @5.00

MANTRA
Malibu Ultraverse, 1993–95
1 AV,I:Mantra,w/Ultraverse card . . . 3.00
1a Full Hologram (c) 10.00
1b Silver foil (c) 5.00
2 AV,V:Warstrike 3.00
3 AV,V:Kismet Deadly 3.00
4 BWS,Mantra's marriage,
   BU:Rune story 2.50
5 thru 9 . . . . @2.50
10 NBy(c),DaR,B:Archmage Quest,
   Flip/UltraversePremiere #2 . . . . 3.00
11 thru 24 . . . . @2.50
Giant Sized#1 GP(c),I:Topaz 2.50
Ashcan #1 . . . . 2.50

MANTRA
Malibu Ultraverse, 1995–96
Infinity N:Mantra 2.50
1 Mantra in all Female Body 2.50
1a Computer Painted Cover 2.50
2 Phoenix flip issue 2.50
3 thru 7 . . . . @2.50

MANTRA: SPEAR
OF DESTINY
Malibu Ultraverse, 1995
1 Search for Artifact 2.50
2 MiB,Eden vs. Aladdin 2.50

MANY WORLDS OF
TESLA STRONG, THE
Wildstorm/DC, 2003
1 through the dimensions 6.00

MARCH HARE, THE
Boom! Studios, 2005
1-shot 4.00

MARK OF CHARON
Grossgen Comics, 2003
1 thru 5 JoB . . . . @3.00

MARK RAND'S
SKY TECHNOLOGIES INC.
Red Mercenary, 1995
1 I:Jae,Elliot,Firnn 3.00

MARKSMAN, THE
Hero Graphics, 1988
1 O:Marksman, Pt.#1 . . . . 2.50
2 O:Marksman, Pt.#2 . . . . 2.50
3 O:Marksman ends.I:Basilisk 2.50
4 A:Flare 2.50
5 I:Radar,Sonar 2.50
Ann. #1, A:Champions 2.50

MARRIED... WITH
CHILDREN
Now, 1990
1 . . . . 4.00
1a 2nd printing 2.50
2 Ph(c) 3.00
3 Kelly Ph(c) 3.00
4 thru 7 Ph(c) . . . . @2.50
[2nd Series], 1991
1 Peg-Host of Radio Show 2.50
2 The Bundy Invention 2.50
3 Psychodad,(photo cover) 2.50
4 Mother-In-Law,(photo cover) 2.50
5 Bundy the Crusader 2.50
6 Bundy J: The Order of the
   Mighty Warthog 2.50
7 Kelly the VJ 2.50
Spec. Ph(c) (1992) 2.50
Spec. Bud Bundy, Fanboy in
   Paradise 3.00
3-D Spec.(1993) 2.50
1-shot Buck's Tale (1994) 2.50
Annual 1994 . . . . 3.50

...DYSFUNCTIONAL FAMILY
Now
1 I:The Bundies 2.50
2 TV Appearance 2.50
3 Morally Pure Bundys 2.50

...FLASHBACK SPECIAL
Now, 1993
1 Peg and Al's first date 2.50
2 and 3 . . . . @2.50

...KELLY BUNDY SPECIAL
Now, 1992
1 with poster 2.50
2 and 3 with poster . . . . @2.50

...KELLY GOES TO KOLLEGE
Now, 1994
1 thru 3 . . . . @2.50

...LOTTO FEVER
Now, 1994
1 thru 3 . . . . @2.50

...QUANTUM QUARTET
Now, 1993
1 thru 4 Fantastic Four parody . . @2.50
Fall 1994 Spec., flip book 2.50

Mars #8
© First

MARRIED WITH
CHILDREN 2099
Mirage, 1993
1 thru 3 Cable Parody . . . . @2.50

MARS
First, 1984
1 thru 12 . . . . @2.50

MARS ATTACKS
Topps, 1994
1 KG(s) 5.00
2 thru 6 KG(s) . . . . @4.00
[Series 2], 1995
1 Counterstrike 3.50
2 Counterstrike,pt.2 . . . . 3.00
3 Counterstrike,pt.3 . . . . 3.00
4 Counterstrike,pt.4 Convictions . . . 3.00
5 Counterstrike concl 3.00
6 Rescue of Janice Brown,pt.1 . . . 3.00
7 Rescue of Janice Brown,pt.2 . . . 3.00
8 . . . . 3.00
Spec. Baseball 3.00

MARS ATTACKS
HIGH SCHOOL
Topps, 1997
Spec. #1 (of 2) BSz(c) 3.00
Spec. #2 . . . . 3.00

MARS ATTACKS
THE SAVAGE DRAGON
Topps, 1996
1 thru 4 . . . . @3.00

MARSHAL
**Dabel Brothers Productions,
2006**
1 thru 4 . . . . @3.00

MARVEL/ULTRAVERSE
BATTLEZONES
Malibu Ultraverse, 1996
1 DPs(c),The Battle of the Heroes . 4.00

MASKED MAN
Eclipse, 1985–88
1 . . . . 3.00
2 thru 10 . . . . @2.50

MASKS: TOO HOT FOR TV
Wildstorm/DC, 2003
Spec. 5.00

MASTER DARQUE
Acclaim, 1997
Spec. F:Brixton Sound, 48pg 4.00

MASTERS OF HORROR
IDW Publishing, 2005
1 . . . . 4.00
1a variant (c) 4.00
2 thru 4 . . . . @4.00
TPB Masters of Horror 18.00

MASTERS OF
THE UNIVERSE
Crossgen Comics, 2003
Spec. The Power of Fear 3.00
1 Rise of the Snake Men 3.00
TPB Traveler #1 Shard of
   Darkness 10.00
Encyclopedia, Vol. 1 . . . . 3.00

COLOR PUB.

MASTERS OF THE UNIVERSE
MVCreations, 2004
Vol. 3

1	3.00
2 thru 6	@3.00
1a Quadruple Gatefold	10.00
TPB Icons of Evil	19.00
TPB Vol. 2	18.00
Season One Encyclopedia #4	3.00
Season One Encyclopedia #5	3.50
TPB Vol. 1 Revised Edition	13.00
TPB Vol. 2	19.00

MASTERS OF THE UNIVERSE: ICONS OF EVIL
Crossgen Comics, 2003

Spec. Tri-Klops	3.00
1 Mer-Man	5.00
1 Trapjaw	5.00

MASTERWORK SERIES
Seagate DC, 1983

1 FFrep.DC,Shining Knight	4.00
2 FFrep.DC,Shining Knight	4.00
3 BWr,Horror DC rep.	4.00

MATADOR
Wildstorm/DC, May, 2005

1 (of 6) BSf,F:Lt. Isabel Cardona	3.00
2 thru 6 BSf	@3.00

MATT BUSCH'S DARIA JONTAK
Realm Press, 2000

1 sexy sci-fi	4.00
1a deluxe	5.00
2	4.00
2a deluxe	5.00
Companion Book	3.00
Companion Book, deluxe	4.00

Andromeda Entertainment/ PlanetMatt, 2001

Spec. Where Angels Fear to Tread	4.00
Spec. deluxe	5.00

MAVERICK
Dell Publishing Co., 1958

1 Ph(c) Garner photos	500.00
2 Ph(c)	250.00
3 Ph(c)	250.00
4 Ph(c)	250.00
5 Ph(c)	250.00
6 thru 14 Ph(c) last Garner	200.00
15 thru 19 Ph(c) R. Moore	@175.00

MAVERICK MARSHALL
Charlton Comics, 1958

1	125.00
2	100.00
3	100.00
4	100.00
5	100.00
6	100.00
7 May, 1960	100.00

MAVERICKS
Dagger, 1994

1 PuD,RkL, I:Mavericks	3.00
2 PuD,RkL	3.00
3 thru 5	@3.00

MAXIMORTAL
King Hell/Tundra, 1992

1 RV,A:True-Man	4.50
2 Crack in the New World	4.25
3 RV,Secret of the Manhattan Project revealed	4.25
4	4.25
5 A:True Man	3.25
6 A:El Guano	3.25

MAXIMUM FORCE
Atomeka, 2002

Spec. #1 SBs,	3.00

MAYA
Gold Key, 1968

1	50.00

MAZE AGENCY
Comico, 1988–91

1 O:Maze Agency	3.00
2 thru 6	@2.50
7	2.75
8 thru 11	@2.50
12	2.50
13 thru 15	@2.50
16 thru 23	@2.50
Spec. #1	2.75

MAZE AGENCY, THE
IDW Publishing, 2005

TPB Vol. 1MiB, AH, RM	25.00
1 MiB	4.00
2 thru 4	@4.00

McHALE'S NAVY
Dell Publishing Co.
May-July, 1963

1 Ph(c) from TV show	150.00
2 Ph(c)	100.00
3 Ph(c)	100.00

McKEEVER & THE COLONEL
Dell Publishing Co., 1963

1 Ph(c)	125.00
2 Ph(c)	90.00
3 Ph(c)	90.00

M.D.
Gemstone, 1999

1 (of 5) New Direction	3.00
2	3.00
3	3.00
4	3.00
Annual #1	13.50

M.D. GEIST
CPM, 1995

1 Cartoon Adaptation	3.00
2 J:Army	3.00
3 V:Final Terminator	3.00

M.D. GEIST: GROUND ZERO
CPM, 1996

1 thru 3	@3.00

MECHANICS
Fantagraphics, 1985

1 HB,rep.Love & Rockets	3.00
2 HB,rep.Love & Rockets	2.50
3 HB,rep.Love & Rockets	2.50

Mechanics #1
© Fantagraphics

MEDIEVAL LADY DEATH
Avatar Press, 2006

Sourcebook	4.00
Sourcebook, wraparound (c)	4.00
Sourcebook, premium (c)	10.00

MEDIEVAL LADY DEATH: BELLADONNA
Avatar Press, 2005

½	3.00
½ variant (c)s	@3.00
1	4.00
1a variant (c)s	@4.00
1b Special (c)s	@6.00

MEDIEVAL LADY DEATH: WAR OF THE WINDS
Avatar Press, 2006

1 (of 8)	4.00
1a wraparound (c)	4.00
1b variant premium (c)	10.00
1c Special (c)s	@6.00
2 thru 5	@4.00
2a thru 4a wraparound (c)s	@4.00
2b thru 4b premium (c)s	@10.00
5a variant (c)s	@4.00
5b variant premium (c)	10.00

MEDIA STARR
Innovation, 1989

1 thru 3	@2.50

MEGACITY 909
Devil's Due/Studio ICE, 2004

1	3.00
2 thru 8	@3.00
1a thru 6a variant (c)	@3.00

MEGA DRAGON & TIGER
Comicsone.com, 2002

GN #3 thru #6	@14.00
GN #7	15.00

MEGALITH
Continuity, 1990

1 MT	6.00
2 MT	4.00
3 MT, Painted issue	3.00
4 NA,TVE	3.00
5 NA,TVE	3.00

6 MN	3.00
7 MN	3.00
8	3.00
9 SDr(i)	3.00
10	3.00

[2nd Series], 1993
Deathwatch, 2000

0 Deathwatch 2000 prologue	5.00
1 Deathwatch 2000 Pt.5,w/card	3.00
2 Deathwatch 2000 Pt.10,w/card	3.00
3 pt.16,Indestructible(c),w/card	3.00
4 & 5 Rise of Magic	@3.00
6 & 7	@3.00

MEGAMAN
Dreamwave, 2003

1	3.00
1a holofoil (c)	6.00
2 thru 4	@3.00
Pocket edition	11.00

MEGATON
Entity Comics, 1993

Holiday Spec. w/card	3.00

MEGATON EXPLOSION

1 RLd,AMe,I:Youngblood preview	25.00

Megaton Man #6
© Kitchen Sink

MEGATON MAN
Kitchen Sink, 1984

1 Don Simpson art,I:MegatonMan	6.00
1a rep. B&W	3.00
2	4.00
3 and 4	@3.00
5	3.00
6 Border Worlds	3.00
7 Border Worlds	3.00
8 Border Worlds	3.00
9 Border Worlds	3.00
10 final issue, 1986	3.00

MEK
DC/Homage, 2002

2 WEI	3.00
3 WEI, concl.	3.00

MELTING POT
Kitchen Sink, 1993

1	4.00
2 and 3	@3.00
4	3.50
TPB KEa,SBs, rep.	20.00

MELVIN MONSTER
Dell Publishing Co.1965

1	175.00
2 thru 10	@150.00

[Katshuiro Otomo's]
MEMORIES
Epic, 1992

1	2.50

MEN FROM EARTH
Future Fun

1 based on Matt Mason toy	6.50

MENACE
Awesome Entertainment, 1998

1 by Jada Pinkett & Don Fraga	2.50
1a signed	20.00
2	2.50
3	2.50

MENDY AND THE GOLEM
The Golem Network, 2003

1 The Key	3.00
2 Blackout	3.00
3	3.00
4 Meltdown	3.00
5 Beyond Control	3.00

MERCHANTS OF DEATH
Eclipse, 1988

1 King's Castle, The Hero	3.50
2 King's Castle,Soldiers of Fortune	3.50
3 Ransom, Soldier of Fortune	3.50
4 ATh(c),Ransom, Men o/t Legion	3.50
5 Ransom,New York City Blues	3.50

MENDY AND THE GOLEM
The Golem Network, 2003

1 The Key	3.00
2 Blackout	3.00
3	3.00
4 Meltdown	3.00
5 Beyond Control	3.00

MERIDIAN
Crossgen Comics, 2000

1 BKs	4.50
2 BKs	4.50
3 BKs	4.00
4 BKs	4.00
5 DKs	4.00
6 thru 11 BKs	@3.50
12 thru 18 BKs	@3.00
19 thru 30 BKs	@3.00
31 thru 44 BKs	@3.00
TPB rep #1–#7	20.00
TPB Vol. 2 192-pg.	20.00
TPB Vol. 3 160-pg.	16.00
TPB Vol. 4	16.00
TPB Vol. 5 Minister of Cadador	16.00
TPB Vol. 6 Changing Course	16.00
GN Meridian Traveler Vol.1	10.00
GN Meridian Traveler Vol.3	10.00
GN Meridian Traveler Vol.4	10.00

MERLIN REALM
Blackthorne, 1985

1 3-D	2.50

METABARONS
Humanoids Publishing, 2000

1	3.00
2	3.00
3 thru 9	@3.00
10 thru 17	@3.00

TPB Vol. 1 Path of the Warrior	15.00
TPB Vol. 2 Blood and Steel	15.00
TPB Vol. 3 Poet & Killer	12.00
TPB Vol. 4 Immaculate Conception	10.00
GN Alpha/Omega, 48-pg.	10.00

META DOCS
Antarctic Press, 2005

1-shot Type A	3.00
1-shot Code Black	3.50
TPB Collected Cases	8.00

META 4
First 1990

1 IG	4.50
2 IG	2.50
3 IG/JSon,final monthly	2.50

METAL GEAR SOLID
IDW 2004

1 Video Game tie-in	20.00
1a retail edition	6.00
2 thru 12	@4.00
TPB	20.00
TPB Vol. 2	20.00

METAL GEAR SOLID:
SONS OF LIBERTY
IDW Publishing, 2005

0	4.00
1	4.00
1a variant (c)	4.00
2 thru 9	@4.00
2a thru 9a variant (c)	@4.00
TPB Vol. 1	20.00

METAL LOCUS:
HARD DRIVE
Speakeasy Comics, 2006

1 (of 4)	3.00
2	3.00
3	3.00

METALLIX
Future Comics, 2003

0 Tag-Team Super-Hero	3.50
1	3.50
2	3.50
3 thru 5	@3.50
6 thru 12	@3.00
TPB Vol. 1	15.00
TPB Vol. 2	17.00

METAL MILITIA
Entity Comics, 1995

1 I:Metal Militia	2.50
1a with Video Game	7.00
2 ICO	2.50
3 F:Detective Calahan	2.50
Ashcan	2.50

METAMORPHOSIS
Narwain Publishing, 2006

1 (of 3)	4.00

METAPHYSIQUE
Malibu Bravura, 1995

1 NBy,I:Metaphysique	3.00
1a Gold foil edition	4.00
2 NBy,Mandelbrot malfunctions	3.00
3 I:Harridas	3.00
4 D:Maj.Character,B:Superious	3.00
5 V:Astral Kid	3.00
6 Apocalyptic Armageddon, finale	3.00
Ashcan NBy,B&W	2.00

COLOR PUB.

MICHAELANGELO
Mirage
1 TMNT Character 15.00

MICHAEL LENT'S PREY: ORIGIN OF THE SPECIES
Dabel Brothers Productions, 2006
1 . . . . 3.00
2 thru 4 . . . . @3.00

MICHAEL TURNER'S FATHOM
D.E. (Dynamite Ent.) 2006
Prelude #1 . . . . 3.00
Prelude #1 variant (c)s . . . . @3.00

MICKEY & DONALD
Gladstone, 1988
1 1449 Firestone 8.00
2 . . . . 4.00
3 Man of Tomorrow 3.00
4 thru 15 . . . . @3.00
16 giant-size 3.00
17 . . . . 3.00
18 . . . . 4.00
Becomes:

DONALD AND MICKEY
19 thru 26 . . . . @3.00

MICKEY MANTLE COMICS
Magnum, 1991
1 JSt,Rise to Big Leagues 4.00

MICKEY MOUSE
Gladstone, 1986
219 FG,Seven Ghosts 20.00
220 FG,Seven Ghosts 10.00
221 FG,Seven Ghosts 10.00
222 FG,Editor in Grief 5.00
223 FG,Editor in Grief 4.00
224 FG,Crazy Crime Wave 4.00
225 FG,Crazy Crime Wave 4.00
226 FG,Captive Castaways 4.00
227 FG,Captive Castaways 4.00
228 FG,Captive Castaways 4.00
229 FG,Bat Bandit 4.00
230 FG,Bat Bandit 3.00
231 FG,Bobo the Elephant 3.00
232 FG,Bobo the Elephant 3.00
233 FG,Pirate Submarine 3.00
234 FG,Pirate Submarine 3.00
235 FG,Photo Racer 3.00
236 FG,Photo Racer 3.00
237 FG,Race for Riches 3.00
238 FG,Race for Riches 3.00
239 FG,Race for Riches 3.00
240 FG,March of Comics 3.00
241 FG 4.00
242 FG 3.00
243 FG 3.00
244 FG,60th Anniv 5.00
245 FG,Giant Ants 4.00
246 FG 3.00
247 FG 3.00
248 FG 3.00
249 FG 5.00
250 FG 3.00
251 FG 3.00
252 FG 3.00
253 FG 3.00
254 FG 3.00
255 FG 4.00
256 FG 4.00

Mickey Mouse #1
© Walt Disney

MICKEY MOUSE
Walt Disney, 1990
1 The Phantom Gondolier 4.00
2 . . . . 3.50
3 thru 19 . . . . @3.00

MICKEY MOUSE ADVENTURES
Gemstone Publishing, 2004
TPB Vol. 1 . . . . 8.00
TPB Vol. 2 thru Vol. 6 . . . . @8.00
TPB Vol. 7 thru Vol. 11 . . . . @8.00

MICKEY MOUSE AND FRIENDS
Gemstone Publishing, 2003
257 thru 270 . . . . @3.25
271 thru 295 . . . . @3.00
1-shot Mickey Mouse meets
  Blotman (2005) 6.00

MICKEY MOUSE MEETS BLOTMAN
Gemstone Publishing, 2005
1-shot 6.00
1-shot Blotman Returns (2006) . . . 6.00

MICKEY'S TWICE UPON A CHRISTMAS
Gemstone Publishing, 2004
Spec. video adapt 4.00

MICKEY SPILLANE'S MIKE DANGER
Tekno Comix, 1995
1 I:Mike Danger 3.00
2 thru 11 . . . . @2.50
Big Entertainment, 1996
1 . . . . 2.50
2 thru 10 . . . . @2.50

MICROBOTS, THE
Gold Key, 1971
1 . . . . 30.00

MICRONAUTS
Devil's Due Publishing, 2004
1 . . . . 3.00
2 thru 4 . . . . @3.00

MIDNIGHTER
Wildstorm/DC, Nov., 2006
1 GEn,CSp,KIS 3.00
1a & b variant (c)s . . . . @3.00

MIDNIGHT EYE: GOKU PRIVATE INVESTIGATOR
Viz
1 A.D. 2014: Tokyo city 5.25
2 V:Hakuryu,A:Yoko 5.00
3 A:Ryoko,Search for Ryu 5.00
4 Goku vs. Ryu 5.00
5 Leilah Abducted 5.00
6 Lisa's I.D. discovered 5.00

MIDNIGHT KISS
APC, 2005
1 . . . . 3.50
2 & 3 . . . . @3.50
Markosia, 2005
4 . . . . 3.50
5 . . . . 3.50
5a variant (c) 3.50
TPB 20.00

MIGHTY COMICS
Archie, 1966
{Prev: Flyman}
40 A:Web 75.00
41 A:Shield, Black Hood 50.00
42 A:Black Hood 50.00
43 A:Shield, Black Hood,Web . . . 50.00
44 A:Black Hood, Steel Sterling
  Shield 50.00
45 Shield-Black Hood team-up
  O:Web 50.00
46 A:Steel Sterling, Black
  Hood, Web 50.00
47 A:Black Hood & Mr.Justice 50.00
48 A:Shield & Hangman 50.00
49 Steel Sterling-Black Hood
  team-up, A:Fox 50.00

[ALL NEW ADVENTURES OF] THE MIGHTY CRUSADERS
Archie/Red Circle, 1965
[1st Series]
1 O:Shield (Joe Higgins & Bill
  Higgins) 125.00
2 MSy,O:Comet 75.00
3 O:Fly-Man 65.00
4 A:Fireball,Jaguar,Web,Fox,
  Blackjack Hangman & more
  Golden Age Archie Heroes . . . 70.00
5 I:Ultra-Men&TerrificThree 65.00
6 V:Maestro,A:Steel Sterling 65.00
7 O:Fly-Girl,A:Steel Sterling 65.00
[2nd Series], 1983
1 RB,R:Joe Higgins & Lancelot
  Strong as the SHIELD, Mighty
  Crusaders, A:Mr.Midnight 7.00
2 RB,V:Brain Emperor & Eterno . . . 5.00
3 RB,I:Darkling 5.00
4 DAy,TD 4.00
5 . . . . 4.00
6 DAy,TD,Shield 4.00
7 . . . . 4.00
8 . . . . 4.00
9 Trial of the Shield 4.00
10 . . . . 4.00
11 DAy,D:Gold Age Black Hood, I:
  Riot Squad, series based on
  toy lines 5.00
12 DAy,I:She-Fox 5.00
13 Last issue 5.00
TPB Origin of Super Team (2003) . 13.00

COLOR PUB.

MIGHTY HERCULES, THE
Gold Key, 1963
1 . . . . 275.00
2 . . . . 250.00

MIGHTY MAGNOR, THE
Malibu, 1993
1 SA 2.50
2 thru 6 SA . . . . @2.50

MIGHTY MORPHIN POWER RANGERS
Hamilton, 1994–95
1 From TV Series 2.75
2 Switcheroo 2.50
3 . . . . 2.50
4 F:White Ranger 2.50
5 F:Pink Ranger 2.50
6 V:Garganturon 2.50
TPB Re. #1-#6 photo (c) 10.00

[Series 2], 1995
1 Unstoppable Force 2.50
2 V:Mechanical Octopus 2.50
3 . . . . 2.50
4 Lost Ranger 2.50

[Series 3], 1995
1 O:Green Ranger 2.50
2 O:Green Ranger 2.50
3 I:New Megazords 2.50

MIGHTY MOUSE
Spotlight, 1987
1 FMc,PC(c) 3.00
2 FMc,CS(c) 3.00
1 Holiday Special 3.00

MIGHTY MUTANIMALS
Archie Publications, 1991
[Mini-Series]
1 Cont.from TMNT Adventures#19,
    A:Raphael, Man Ray, Leather-
    head, Mondo Gecko,Deadman,
    Wingnut & Screwloose 2.50
2 V:Mr.Null,Malinga,Soul and Bean
    and the Malignoid Army 2.50
3 Alien Invasion help off, Raphael
    returns to Earth 2.50
Spec.#1 rep. all #1-3 +SBi pin-ups . 3.00

MIGHTY MUTANIMALS
Archie, 1992
1 Quest for Jagwar's Mothor 2.50
2 V:Snake Eyes 2.50
3 . . . . 2.50
4 Days of Future Past 2.50
5 Into the Sun 2.50
6 V:Null & 4 Horsemen Pt#2 . . . . . 2.50
7 Jaws of Doom 2.50

MIGHTY SAMSON
Gold Key, 1964–82
1 O:Mighty Samson 160.00
2 . . . . 125.00
3 . . . . 125.00
4 . . . . 125.00
5 . . . . 125.00
6 thru 10 . . . . @80.00
11 thru 20 . . . . @75.00
21 thru 32 . . . . @50.00

MIKE GRELL'S SABLE
First, 1990
1 thru 8 rep. . . . . @2.50
9 . . . . 2.50
10 Triptych 2.50

MIKE SHAYNE PRIVATE EYE
Dell Publishing Co., 1961-62
1 . . . . 75.00
2 . . . . 50.00
3 . . . . 50.00

MILLENNIUM INDEX
Independent Comics, 1988
1 . . . . 2.50
2 . . . . 2.50

MILTON THE MONSTER & FEARLESS FLY
Gold Key, 1966
1 . . . . 175.00

MIRACLE BRIGADE, THE
Counteractive Comics, 2006
1 . . . . 3.00

Miracleman #4
© Eclipse

MIRACLEMAN
Eclipse, 1985–94
1 R:Miracleman 20.00
2 AD,Moore,V:Kid Miracleman . . . 15.00
3 AD,Moore,V:Big Ben 15.00
4 AD,Moore,R:Dr.Gargunza 15.00
5 AD,Moore,O:Miracleman 15.00
6 Moore,V:Miracledog, D:Evelyn
    Cream 15.00
7 Moore,D:Dr.Gargunza 12.00
8 Moore 12.00
9 RV,Moore,Birth of Miraclebaby . 12.00
10 JRy,RV,Moore 12.00
11 JTo,Moore,Book III,
    I:Miraclewoman 12.00
12 thru 14 Moore . . . . @35.00
15 Moore 100.00
16 Moore 40.00
17 Golden Age 20.00
18 . . . . 15.00
19 thru 22 . . . . @10.00
23 Silver Age 25.00
24 BWS(c),NGa(s), ... 30.00
25 . . . . 10.00
26 thru 28 . . . . @3.00
3-D Special #1 . . . . 5.00
Graphic Albums
TPB Book 1 A Dream of Flying . . . 25.00
TPB Book 2 The Red Kings
    Syndrome 25.00

TPB Book 3 Olympus 75.00
TPB Book 3 . . . . 25.00

MIRACLEMAN APOCRYPHA
Eclipse, 1991–92
1 inc. Rascal Prince 8.00
2 Miracleman, Family Stories 8.00
3 . . . . 8.00

MIRACLEMAN FAMILY
Eclipse, 1988
1 British Rep.,A:Kid Miracleman . . 25.00
2 Alan Moore (s) 25.00

MIRACLE SQUAD, THE
Upshot/Fantagraphics, 1986
1 Hollywood 30's 2.50
2 thru 4 . . . . @2.50

MISCHIEF NIGHT
Avatar Press, 2006
1 . . . . 4.00
1a wraparound (c) 4.00
1b variant (c)s . . . . @4.00
1c variant Splatter (c) 7.00
1d variant Ruby Red Foil Con (c) . 5.00
1e variant Damned Duo (c) 4.00

MISERERE
Narwain Publishing, 2006
1 (of 3) 3.50
2 thru 3 . . . . @3.50

MISS FURY
Adventure Comics, 1991
1 O:Cat Suit 3.00
2 Miss Fury impersonator 3.00
3 A:Three Miss Fury's 3.00
4 conclusion 3.00

MISSION IMPOSSIBLE
Dell Publishing Co., 1967
1 Ph(c) 175.00
2 Ph(c) 150.00
3 Ph(c) 125.00
4 Ph(c) 125.00
5 Ph(c) 125.00

MISSIONS IN TIBET
Dimension Comics, 1995
1 I:New Series 2.50
2 F:Orlando, ling,Alex 2.50
3 Two Worlds Collide 2.50
4 V:Sada 2.50

MISS PEACH
(& SPECIAL ISSUES)
Dell Publishing Co., 1963
1 . . . . 150.00

MISPLACED
Devil's Due Publishing, 2004
3 and 4 . . . . @3.00
1-shot Misplaced@17 . . . . 5.00

MR. AND MRS. J. EVIL SCIENTIST
Gold Key, 1963
1 . . . . 150.00
2 . . . . 100.00
3 . . . . 100.00
4 . . . . 100.00

COLOR PUB.

MR. MAJESTIC
WildStorm/DC, 1999
1 JoC,A:Desmond	2.50
1a variant cover	3.00
2 JoC,time gone berserk	2.50
3 JoC,F:Maxine Manchester	2.50
4 JoC,F:Junior Majestic	2.50
5 JoC	2.50
6 JoC,F:Desmond	2.50
7 JoC,Universal Law,pt.1	2.50
8 JoC,Universal Law,pt.2	2.50
9 JoC,Universal Law,pt.3	2.50
TPB	15.00

MR. MONSTER
Eclipse, 1985–87
1 I:Mr. Monster	7.00
2 DSt(c)	5.00
3 V:Dr. NoZone	3.50
4 Trapped in Dimension X	3.00
5 V:Flesh-eating Amoebo	3.00
6 KG,SD,reprints	3.00
7	3.00
8 V:Monster in the Atomic Telling Machine	3.00
9 V:Giant Clams	3.00
10 R:Dr.No Zone, 3-D	3.00

MR. MONSTER ATTACKS
Tundra, 1992
1 DGb,SK,short stories	4.25
2 SK,short stories cont.	4.25
3 DGb,last issue	4.25

MR. MONSTER SUPERDUPER SPECIAL
Eclipse, 1986–87
1	3.00
2	3.00
3	3.00
4	3.00
5	3.00
6	3.00
Hi-Voltage Super Science	4.00
3-D Spec. Hi-Octane Horror,JKu, Touch of Death reprint	5.00
Triple Treat	4.00

MR. MONSTER TRUE CRIME
Eclipse, 1986
1	3.00
2	3.00
3-D Spec. #1	3.00

MR. MUSCLES
Charlton Comics, 1956
22	100.00
23	75.00

MR. MYSTIC
Eclipse
1	2.50
2	2.50
3	2.50

MR. T
APC, 2005
1	3.50
1a foil (c)	6.00
1b foil (c), signed	15.00
1c sketch edition	50.00
1d Comix Shop (c)	7.00
2 thru 5	@3.50
TPB Vol. 1	20.00

MR. T AND THE T FORCE
Now, 1993
1 NA,R:Mr.T,V:Street Gangs	2.50
1a Gold Ed.	10.00
2 NA,V:Demons	2.50
3 NBy,w/card	2.50
4 NBy,In Urban America	2.50
5 thru 10, with card	@2.50

Mister X #1
© Vortex

MISTER X
Vortex, 1984
1 HB	7.00
2 HB	5.00
3 HB	3.50
4 HB	3.00
5 thru 10	@3.00
11 thru 13	@3.00
14	3.00

MODERN MAN
Narwain Publishing, 2006
1 (of 4)	4.00
2	4.00

MOD SQUAD
Dell Publishing Co., 1969–71
1	150.00
2	75.00
3	75.00
4 thru 8	@75.00

MOD WHEELS
Gold Key, 1971–76
1	75.00
2 thru 18	@50.00
19	40.00

MONARCHY
WildStorm/DC, 2001
1 JMC,V:Young Authoritans	2.50
2 JMC,F:Union	2.50
3 JMC,Vox Populi,pt.1	2.50
4 JMC,Vox Populi,pt.2	2.50
5 JMC,Boy Who Talked to Spiders	2.50
6 JMC,Making the Metropolitan	2.50
7 JMC,Making the Metropolitan	2.50
8 JMC,Making the Metropolitan	2.50
9 JMC,Metropolitan epilog	2.50
10 JMC,V:Chimera	2.50
11 JMC,V:Higher Power	2.50
12 JMC,final issue	2.50
TPB Bullets over Babylon	13.00

MONKEE'S, THE
Dell Publishing Co., 1967
1 Ph(c)	200.00
2 Ph(c)	150.00
3 Ph(c)	150.00
4 Ph(c)	150.00
5	125.00
6 Ph(c)	125.00
7 Ph(c)	125.00
8 and 9	@120.00
10 Ph(c)	125.00
11 thru 17	@100.00

MONOLITH
Comico, 1991
1 From Elementals	2.50
2 Seven Levels of Hell	2.50
3 Fugue and Variation	2.50
4 Fugue and Variation	2.50

MONROE'S, THE
Dell Publishing Co., 1967
1 Ph(c)	50.00

MONSTER CLUB
Autumn Press, 2003
1	3.50
2 thru 11	@3.50
12 40-pg.	3.50
TPB Vol. 1	20.00
TPB Vol. 2	20.00

Vol. 2
0	3.00
1 thru 6	@3.50
Preview ed.	3.00
TPB Vol. 3	17.00

MONSTER HUNTERS
Charlton, 1975–79
1 TS,The Boar's Head Beast	40.00
2 TS,Fish Fry; The Kukulkaton	30.00
3 TS,The Dictator	20.00
4 TS,Hidden Paradise	20.00
5 TS,The Last Monster Hunter	20.00
6 SD,MZ,The Beast or the Burden	25.00
7 MZ,TS,Blood Oath	25.00
8 TS,SD,Wormholes	25.00
9 MZ,Hour of the Werewolf	15.00
10 SD,The Conglomerate	25.00
11 The Montego Frame	15.00
12 Snake Charmer	15.00
13 SD,JSon,A Little Witchcraft	20.00
14 SD,Giant from the Unknown	40.00
15 SD,reps	20.00
16 TS,The Kilgore Monster	15.00
17 TS,reps from issue #3	15.00
18 SD,Incident at Soulbridge	20.00

Modern, 1977
1 & 2 rep issues 1 and 2	@3.00

MONSTER MASSACRE
Atomeka
1 SBs, DBr,DGb	8.50
1a Black Edition	35.00

MONSTER MAYHEM SERIES
Dead Dog Comics, 2005
1 Frankenstein	6.00
1a variant (c)	6.00
1 Creature	6.00
1a variant (c)	6.00

MONSTERS, INC.
Tokyopop Press, 2002
GN Vol.1 Disney manga adaptation	8.00

MONSTER WORLD
WildStorm/DC, 2001
1 (of 4) SLo, ... 3.00
2 SLo, 5 young heroes 3.00
3 SLo, ... 3.00
4 SLo,concl. 3.00

MONTE COOK'S PTOLUS
Dabel Brothers Productions, 2006
1 (of 6) 3.00
2 thru 5 . . . . @3.00

MORBID ANGEL
London Night, 1996
? Angel's Tear, signed 10.00
1 Commemorative (1999) 10.00

MORBID ANGEL: PENANCE
London Night, 1996
Revised Color Spec., double size . . 4.00

More Than Mortal #5
© *Liar Comics*

MORE THAN MORTAL
Liar Comics, 1997
1 . . . . 3.00
1a 2nd printing 3.00
1b convention, sign, num 10.00
2 Derdre vs. the Host 3.00
2a variant painted cover 6.00
3 MS(c) 3.00
4 thru 6 . . . . @3.00
TPB rep. #1–#4 . . . . 15.00

MORE THAN MORTAL: SAGAS
Liar Comics, 1998
1 by Sharon Scott & Romano
  Molenaar 3.00
1a variant Tim Vigil(c) 3.00
1b variant JLi(c) 10.00
2 thru 3 . . . . @3.00

MORE THAN MORTAL: TRUTHS AND LEGENDS
Liar Comics, 1998
1 by Sharon Scott, Steve Firchow,
  Mark Prudeaux, O:Witchfinder . 4.00
1a signed 10.00
2 . . . . 3.00
3 . . . . 3.00

---

4 . . . . 3.00
5 . . . . 3.00
5a variant cover (1:4) 3.00
6 . . . . 3.00

MORLOCK 2001
Atlas, Feb.–July, 1975
1 thru 2 O:Morlock . . . . @25.00
3 SD,BW,F:Midnight Men 35.00

MORRIGAN
Sirius, 1997
1 by Lorenzo Bartoli & Saverio
  Tenuta 3.00
2 and 3 . . . . @3.00
GN rep. #1–#3 . . . . 10.00

MORTAL KOMBAT
Malibu, 1994
0 Four stories 3.00
1 Based on the Video Game 3.00
1a Foil Ed. 4.00
1b with new material 3.00
2 . . . . 3.00
3 . . . . 3.00
4 . . . . 3.00
5 I:Mortal Kombat II 3.00
6 Climax 3.00
TPB rep. #1–#6 . . . . 15.00
Spec. #1 Tournament edition 4.00
Spec. #2 Tournament edition II . . . 4.00
Spec #1 Baraka, V:Scorpion 3.00

BATTLEWAVE
Malibu, 1995
1 New series 3.00
2 Action, Action, Action 3.00
3 The Gathering 3.00
4 F:Goro 3.00
5 F:Scorpion 3.00
6 final issue 3.00

GORO, PRINCE OF PAIN
Malibu, 1994
1 Goro 3.00
1a Platinum Edition 6.25
2 Goro, V:Kombatant 3.00
3 Goro, V:God of Pain 3.00

KITANA & MILEENA
Malibu, 1995
1 Secrets of Outworld 3.00

KUNG LAO
Malibu, 1995
1 one-shot Battlewave tie-in 3.00

RAYDEN AND KANO
Malibu, 1995
1 J:Rayden Kano 3.00
1a Deluxe Edition 5.00
2 A:Reptile 3.00
3 Kano, conclusion 3.00

U.S. SPECIAL FORCES
Malibu, 1995
1 V:Black Dragon 3.50
2 V:Black Dragon 3.00

MORTAL KOMBAT: DECEPTION
Atomeka, 2005
0 . . . . 4.00
0a chrome 10.00

MOSTLY WANTED
WildStorm/DC, 2000
1 (of 4) SLo,F:Sister Crenn. 2.50
2 SLo(s),F:Andi Mooncrest 2.50
3 SLo(s), ... 2.50

---

4 SLo(s),conclusion 2.50

MOUSE GUARD
Archaia Studio Press, 2006
1 Belly of the Beast 22.00
1a 2nd printing 8.00
2 Shadows Within 15.00
2a 2nd printing 5.00
3 Rise of the Axe 8.00
3 (2nd printing) 4.00
4 The Dark Ghost 4.00
5 Midnight's Dawn 4.00

MOVIE COMICS
Gold Key/Whitman, 1962–70
Alice in Wonderland 75.00
Aristocats 150.00
Bambi 1 . . . . 100.00
Bambi 2 . . . . 75.00
Beneath the Planet of the Apes . . 175.00
Big Red 60.00
Blackbeard's Ghost 75.00
Buck Rogers Giant Movie Edition . 75.00
Bullwhip Griffin 60.00
Captain Sinbad 125.00
Chitty, Chitty Bang Bang 150.00
Cinderella 75.00
Darby O'Gill & the Little People . . 100.00
Dumbo 100.00
Emil & the Detectives 75.00
Escapade in Florence 150.00
Fall of the Roman Empire 75.00
Fantastic Voyage 125.00
55 Days at Peking 75.00
Fighting Prince of Donegal 75.00
First Men of the Moon 80.00
Gay Purr-ee 100.00
Gnome Mobile 60.00
Goodbye, Mr. Chips 75.00
Happiest Millionaire 60.00
Hey There, It's Yogi Bear 150.00
Horse Without a Head 50.00
How the West Was Won 200.00
In Search of the Castaways 125.00
Jungle Book, The 175.00
Kidnapped 75.00
King Kong 100.00
King Kong N#. 125.00
Lady and the Tramp 100.00
Lady and the Tramp 1 . . . . 150.00
Lady and the Tramp 2 . . . . 80.00
Legend of Lobo, The 50.00
Lt. Robin Crusoe 50.00
Lion, The 50.00
Lord Jim 60.00
Love Bug, The 60.00
Mary Poppins 100.00
Mary Poppins 1 . . . . 125.00
McLintock 225.00
Merlin Jones as the Monkey's
  Uncle 125.00
Miracle of the White Stallions 60.00
Misadventures of Merlin Jones . . 125.00
Moon-Spinners, The 135.00
Mutiny on the Bounty 75.00
Nikki, Wild Dog of the North 50.00
Old Yeller 75.00
One Hundred & One Dalmatians . . 75.00
Peter Pan 1 . . . . 80.00
Peter Pan 2 . . . . 50.00
P.T. 109 . . . . 100.00
Rio Conchos 100.00
Robin Hood 75.00
Shaggy Dog & the Absent-Minded
  Professor 100.00
Sleeping Beauty 135.00
Snow White & the Seven Dwarfs . 100.00
Son of Flubber 75.00
Summer Magic 150.00
Swiss Family Robinson 60.00
Sword in the Stone 150.00

COLOR PUB.

That Darn Cat	135.00
Those Magnificent Men in Their Flying Machines	75.00
Three Stooges in Orbit	200.00
Tiger Walks, A	75.00
Toby Tyler	75.00
Treasure Island	65.00
20,000 Leagues Under the Sea	85.00
Wonderful Adventures of Pinocchio	120.00
Wonderful World of Brothers Grimm	75.00
X, the Man with the X-Ray Eyes	150.00
Yellow Submarine w/poster	500.00

Ms Mystic #8
© Continuity

MS. MYSTIC
Pacific
1 NA,Origin	7.00
2 NA,Origin,I:Urth 4	6.00

Continuity, 1988
1 NA,Origin rep.	3.00
2 NA,Origin,I:Urth 4 rep	3.00
3 NA,New material	3.00
4 TSh	3.00
5 DT	3.00
6	3.00
7	3.00
8 CH/Sdr,B:Love Story	3.00
9 DB	3.00
9a Newsstand(c)	3.00

[3rd Series], 1993
1 O:Ms.Mystic	2.50
2 A:Hybrid	2.50
3 thru 4	@2.50

[4th Series, Deathwatch 2000]
1 Deathwatch 2000 pt.8,w/card	2.50
2 Deathwatch 2000 w/card	2.50
3 Indestructible cover, w/card	2.50

MS. TREE'S THRILLING DETECTIVE ADVENTURES
Eclipse, 1983
1 Miller pin up	5.00
2	4.00
3	4.00
Becomes:	

MS. TREE
Eclipse, 1983
4 thru 6	@4.00
7	4.00
8	8.00
9	4.00

Aardvark–Vanaheim, 1984
10	4.00

Renegade
1 3-D	4.00

MS. VICTORY GOLDEN ANNIVERSARY
AC Comics
1 Ms.Victory celebration	5.00

MS. VICTORY SPECIAL
AC Comics, 1985
1	2.50

MU
Devil's Due/Studio ICE, 2004
1	3.00
1a variant (c)	3.00
2 thru 4	@3.00
2a thru 4a variant (c)	@3.00

MUMMY ARCHIVES
Millennium, 1992
1.JM,Features,articles	2.50

MUMMY, OR RAMSES THE DAMNED, THE
Millennium, 1992
1 Anne Rice Adapt.	5.00
2 JM,Mummy in Mayfair	3.75
3 JM	3.25
4 JM, To Egypt	3.00
5 JM,The Mummy's Hand	2.50
6 JM,20th Century Egypt	2.50
7 JM,More Ramses Past Revealed	2.50
8 JM,Hunt for Cleopatra	2.50
9 JM,Cleopatra's Wrath contd.	2.50
10 JM,Subterranian World	2.50
11 JM	2.50

MUMMY, THE: VALLEY OF THE GODS
Chaos! Comics, 2001
1 (of 3) MWn,MtB, movie tie-in	3.00
1a variant (c)	3.00
1b premium	10.00
2	3.00
2a Scorpion King photo (c)	3.00
3	3.00
3a Imhotep phoco (c)	3.00
Ashcan	6.00

MUNDEN'S BAR ANNUAL
First, 1988
1 BB,JOy,JSn,SR	3.00

MUNSTERS, THE
Gold Key, 1965–68
1	350.00
2	200.00
3 thru 5	@175.00
6 thru 16	@150.00

MUPPET BABIES
Harvey, 1993
1 Return of Muppet Babies	2.50

MURCIELAGA/SHE-BAT
Studio G, 2001
1 by D.Gross & R.Lopez	3.00
2 thru 4	@3.00

MUTANT CHRONICLES— GOLGOTHA
Valiant
1 thru 4 + game trading card	@3.00
TPB, Vol. 1 rep. Pt.#1–#4	11.00

MUTATION
Speakeasy Comics, 2005
1	3.00
2 thru 5	@3.00
TPB Vol. 1	15.00

MUTATION
Markosia, 2006
1	3.50
1a variant (c)	3.50
2 thru 4	@3.50
TPB Vol. 1	15.00

MY FAVORITE MARTIAN
Gold Key, 1964–66
1	350.00
2	250.00
3 thru 9	@200.00

MY LITTLE MARGIE
Charlton Comics, 1954–65
1 Ph(c)	500.00
2 Ph(c)	250.00
3 thru 8	@150.00
9	135.00
10	125.00
11 thru 19	@100.00
20 Giant Size	175.00
21 thru 35	@100.00
36 thru 53	@100.00
54 Beatles (c)	300.00

MY LITTLE MARGIE'S BOY FRIEND
Charlton Comics, 1955–58
1	200.00
2	150.00
3 thru 11	@100.00

MYSTERIES OF UNEXPLORED WORLDS/ SON OF VULCAN
Charlton Comics, 1956
1	500.00
2	275.00
3 SD,SD(c)	400.00
4 SD,Forbidden Room	450.00
5 SD,SD(c)	450.00
6 SD	450.00
7 SD, giant	500.00
8 SD	425.00
9 SD	425.00
10 SD,SD(c)	425.00
11 SD,SD(c)	425.00
12 SD,Charm Bracelet	300.00
13 thru 18	@150.00
19 SD(c)	300.00
20	150.00
21 thru 24 SD	@300.00
25	100.00
26 SD	300.00
27 thru 30	@100.00
31 thru 45	@80.00
46 I:Son ofVulcan,Dr.Kong(1965)	100.00
47 V:King Midas	80.00
48 V:Captain Tuska	80.00
Becomes:	

SON OF VULCAN
49 DC redesigns costume	75.00
50 V:Dr.Kong	75.00

COLOR PUB.

Mysterious Suspense#1
© Charlton Comics

MYSTERIOUS SUSPENSE
Charlton, 1968
1 SD,F:Question 150.00

MYSTERY COMICS DIGEST
Gold Key, 1972–75
1 WW,Riley's Believe It Or Not . . . 75.00
2 WW,Boris Karloff 75.00
3 RC,GEv,Twilight Zone 75.00
4 Ripley's Believe It or Not 60.00
5 Boris Karloff 60.00
6 Twilight Zone 60.00
7 Believe It Or Not 60.00
8 RC,AW,Boris Karloff 60.00
9 Twilight Zone 60.00
10 thru 13 . . . . @60.00
14 1st Xorkon 60.00
15 thru 20 . . . . @60.00
21 thru 26 . . . . @50.00

MYSTIC
Crosgen Comics, 2000
1 RMz,BPe 6.00
2 RMz,BPe 5.00
3 RMz,BPe 4.00
4 RMz,BPo 3.25
5 RMz,BPe 3.25
6 thru 10 . . . . @3.25
11 . . . . 4.00
12 thru 30 . . . . @3.00
31 thru 43 . . . . @3.00
TPB Vol. 1 . . . . 20.00
TPB Vol. 2 . . . . 20.00
TPB Vol. 3 Siege of Scales 16.00
TPB Vol. 4 Out All Night 16.00
TPB Vol. 5 Master Class 16.00
TPB Vol. 6 The Mathemagician . . . 16.00
TPB Mystic Traveler Vol. 2 . . . . . 10.00

MYSTIC EDGE
Antarctic Press, 1998
1 by Ryan Kinnaird, F:Risa
   & Symattra 3.00

NANCY & SLUGGO
Dell Publishing Co., 1957
146 B:Peanuts 150.00
147 Peanuts 125.00
148 Peanuts 125.00
149 Peanuts 125.00

150 thru 161 . . . . @125.00
162 thru 165 . . . . @200.00
166 thru 176 A:OONA . . . . . . @200.00
177 thru 180 . . . . @125.00
181 thru 187 . . . . @125.00

NANCY DREW
NBM Books, 2005
TPB Vol. 1 Demon of River Heights 8.00
TPB Vol. 2 Writ in Stone 8.00
TPB Vol. 3 The Haunted Dollhouse . 8.00
Papercutz, 2005
TPB Vol. 4 Girl Who Wasn't There . 8.00
TPB Vol. 5 THe Fake Heir 8.00
TPB Vol. 6 Mr. Cheeters is Missing . 8.00
TPB Vol. 7 The Charmed Bracelet . 8.00

NARWAIN PREVIEW
Narwain Publishing, 2005
Spec. 2.50
Spec. variant (c) 2.50

NATIONAL VELVET
Dell Publishing Co., 1961
1 Ph(c) 150.00
2 Ph(c) 75.00

NEAT STUFF
Fantagraphics, 1986
1 . . . . 4.50
2 . . . . 3.00
3 thru 7 . . . . @2.50

NECROMANTRA/ LORD PUMPKIN
Malibu Ultraverse, 1995
1 A:Loki (from Marvel) 3.00
2 MiB,V:Godwheel, flipbook 3.00
3 O:Lord Pumpkin 3.00
4 Infinity Gem tie-in 3.00
4a variant cover 3.50

NECROPOLIS THE JUDGE DEATH INVASION
Fleetway, 1991
1 SBs(c),CE,A:Dark Judges/
   Sisters Of Death 3.00
2 thru 9 . . . . @3.00

NECROSCOPE
Malibu, 1992
1 Novel adapt., holo(c) 3.25
1a 2nd printing 3.00
2 thru 4 Adapt. cont. . . . . @3.00
Book II, Oct. 1994
1 thru 5 . . . . 3.00

NECROWAR
Dreamwave, 2003
1 . . . . 3.00
2 thru 4 . . . . @3.00

NEGATION
Crosgen Comics, 2001
1 MWa,PaP,F:Obregon Kaine 3.00
2 MWa,PaP,Kaine's master-plan . . 3.00
3 MWa,PaP,F:Captain Fluxor 3.00
4 thru 12 PaP . . . . @3.00
13 thru 27 . . . . @3.00
Spec. #1 Negation: Lawbringer . . . 3.00
Prequel MWa,PaP 3.00
TPB Vol. 1 Bohica 20.00
TPB Vol. 2 Baptism of Fire 16.00
TPB Vol. 3 Hounded 16.00

NEGATION WAR
Crossgen Comics, 2004
1 . . . . 3.00
2 thru 6 . . . . @3.00

NEGATIVE EXPOSURE
Humanoids Publishing, 2001
1 by Enrico Mirini 3.00
2 . . . . 3.00
3 thru 4 . . . . @3.00
TPB 19.00

NEIL GAIMAN'S LADY JUSTICE
Tekno Comix (1995)
1 I:Lady Justice 2.50
1a 6.00
2 V:Blood Pirate 2.50
3 V:Blood Pirate 2.50
4 New Story Arc 2.50
5 Street Gang War 2.50
6 Street Gang War 2.50
7 thru 11 . . . . @2.50
Big Entertainment, April, 1996
1 thru 4 . . . . @2.50
5 DIB(s) 2.50
6 DIB(s),Woman About Town, pt.1 . 2.50
7 DIB(s),Woman About Town, pt.2 . 2.50
8 DIB(s),Woman About Town, pt.3 . 2.50
I-Books, 2005
TPB Vol. 1 . . . . 19.00

NEIL GAIMAN'S MR. HERO THE NEWMATIC MAN
Tekno-Comics, 1994
1 I:Mr. Hero, Tecknophage 2.50
2 A:Tecknophage 2.50
3 I:Adam Kaine 2.50
4 I:New Body 2.50
5 Earthquake 2.50
6 I:New Character 2.50
7 I:Deadbolt, Bloodboil 2.50
8 V:Avatar 2.50
9 in London 2.50
10 V:Demon 2.50
11 V:Monster 2.50
12 The Great Goward 2.50
13 thru 17 . . . . @2.50

NEIL GAIMAN'S PHAGE
Tekno-Comics, 1996
1 . . . . 2.50

NEIL GAIMAN'S PHAGE: SHADOW DEATH
Big Entertainment, 1996
1 thru 4 . . . . @2.50
5 O:Orlando Holmes,A:Lady
   Messalina 2.50
6 conclusion 2.50

NEIL GAIMAN'S TECKNOPHAGE
Teckno-Comics, 1995
1 I:Kalighoul, Tom Vietch 2.50
1a Steel Edition 4.00
2 F:Mayor of New Yorick 2.50
3 Phage Building 2.50
4 Horde eevils 2.50
5 Middle Management 2.50
6 Escape from Phange 2.50
7 Mecca 2.50

NEIL GAIMAN'S WHEEL OF WORLDS
Teckno-Comics, 1995
0 Deluxe Edition w/Posters 3.00
0a I:Lady Justice 2.50
1 . . . . 3.25

NEMESIS THE WARLOCK
Eagle, 1984
1 thru 8 . . . . @2.50

NEO DAWN
Committed Comics, 2004
1 thru 3 . . . . @3.00

NEOTOPIA
Antarctic Press, 2003
1 Princess for a Day 4.00
2 Philios to the Rescue 4.00
3 thru 5 . . . . @4.00
Vol. 2
1 (of 6) 3.00
2 . . . . 3.00
3 . . . . 4.00
4 thru 5 . . . . @3.00
Vol. 3
1 thru 5 . . . . @3.00
Vol. 4
1 . . . . 3.00
2 thru 5 . . . . @3.00
TPB #1 thru #4 Pocket Manga . . @10.00

NEPTUNE
Narwain Publishing, 2006
1-shot 48-pg. JP 6.00

NEUTRAL WORLD
APC, 2003
1 thru 4 . . . . @3.50

NEW ADVENTURES OF FELIX THE CAT
Felix Comics, Inc., 1992
1 New stories 2.50
2 The Magic Paint Brush 2.50

NEW ADVENTURES OF PINOCCHIO
Dell Publishing Co., 1962
1 . . . . 150.00
2 and 3 . . . . @125.00

NEW ADVENTURES OF SPEED RACER
Now, 1993
0 Premiere, 3-D cover 2.50
1 thru 11 . . . . @2.50

NEW AMERICA
Eclipse, 1987–88
1 A:Scout 2.50
2 A:Scout 2.50
3 A:Roman Catholic Pope 2.50
4 A:Scout 2.50

NEW DNAGENTS, THE
Eclipse, 1985–87
1 R:DNAgents 2.50
2 thru 17 . . . . @2.50
3-D #1 . . . . 2.50

NEW JUSTICE MACHINE
Innovation, 1989
1 and 2 . . . . @2.50
2 . . . . 2.50

NEW KABOOM
Awesome Entertainment, 1999
1 RLe,JLb 2.50

NEWMEN
Maximum Press, 1997
1–22 see Image
23 ErS,CSp,AG,Anthem, pt.3 . . . . 2.50
24 ErS,CSp,AG,Anthem, pt.4 . . . . 2.50
25 ErS,CSp,AG,Anthem, pt.5 . . . . 2.50

NEW ORLEANS SAINTS
1 Playoff season(football team) . . . 6.00

NEWSTRALIA
Innovation, 1989
1 and 2 . . . . @2.50
3 . . . . 2.50

NEW TERRYTOONS
Dell Publishing Co., 1960–61
1 . . . . 100.00
2 thru 8 . . . . @60.00
Gold Key, 1962
1 F:Heckle & Jeckle 150.00
2 . . . . 125.00
3 thru 10 . . . . @50.00
11 thru 20 . . . . @40.00
21 thru 30 . . . . @25.00
31 thru 40 . . . . @20.00
41 thru 54 . . . . @15.00

NEW WAVE, THE
Eclipse, 1986–87
1 Error Pages 2.50
1a Correction 2.50
2 . . . . 2.50
3 Space Station Called Hell 2.50
4 Birth of Megabyte 2.50
5 PG(c),O:Avalon 2.50
6 O:Megabyte 2.50
7 Avalon disappears 2.50
8 V:Heap,V:Druids 2.50
9 . . . . 2.50
10 V:Heap Team 2.50
11 . . . . 2.50
12 . . . . 2.50
13 V:Volunteers 2.50
14 1/3 issue 2.50

NEW WAVE vs. THE VOLUNTEERS
Eclipse, 1987
1 3-D,V:Volunteers 2.50
2 3-D,V:Volunteers 2.50

NEXT MAN
Comico, 1985
1 I&O:Next Man 2.50
2 . . . . 2.50
3 . . . . 2.50
4 . . . . 2.50
5 . . . . 2.50

NEXT NEXUS
First, 1989
1 SR 2.50
2 SR 2.50
3 SR 2.50
4 SR 2.50

NEXUS
Capital, 1983
1 SR,I:Judah Maccabee 5.00
2 SR,Origin,V:Bellows 4.00
3 SR,Sundra Captive 4.00
4 SR,V:Ziggurat 4.00
5 SR,I'm Bored! 4.00
6 SR,A:Badger,TrialogueTrilogy#1 . 4.00
First, 1985
7 SR,A:Badger,TrialogueTrilogy#2 . 4.00
8 SR,A:Badger,TrialogueTrilogy#3 . 3.00
9 thru 49 . . . . @2.50
50 SF,double size,A:Badger Pt.6
  Crossroads tie-in 3.50
51 thru 80 . . . . @2.50

Nexus Legends #5
© First

NEXUS LEGENDS
First, 1989
1 thru 23 . . . . @2.50

NICKI SHADOW
Relentless Comics, 1997
1 by Eric Burnham & Ted Naifeh . . 2.50
2 Killing Zone, pt.2 . . . . 2.50
3 Killing Zone, pt.3 . . . . 2.50
4 Killing Zone, concl. 2.50

NIGHT GLIDER
Topps, 1993
1 V:Bombast,C:Captain Glory,
  Trading Card 3.25

NIGHTHUNTER
Empire Comics, 2001
1 (of 12) 3.75
2 thru 4 . . . . @3.75

NIGHTJAR
Avatar Press, 2004
1 (of 4) 3.50
2 thru 4 . . . . @3.50
1a and 4a wraparound (c)s . . . . . @3.50

NIGHTJAR: HOLLOW BONES
Avatar Press, 2004
1 . . . . 4.00
1a wraparound (c) 4.00

NIGHT MAN, THE
Malibu Ultraverse, 1993–95
1 I:Night Man,Deathmask 2.75
1a Silver foil (c) 4.00
2 thru 15 . . . . @2.50
16 I:Bloodfly 3.50
17 thru 23 . . . . @2.50
Ann.#1 V:Pilgrim, 64pg. 4.00
Malibu Ultraverse, 1995
Infinity Night Man vs. Night Man . . . 2.50
1 Discovers New powers 2.50
1a Computer Painted Cover 2.50
2 thru 4 . . . . @2.50

NIGHT MAN/GAMBIT
Malibu, 1996
1 . . . . 2.50
2 . . . . 2.50
3 . . . . 2.50

NIGHTMARE
Innovation, 1989
1 AN 2.50

NIGHTMARE AND CASPER
Harvey Publications, 1963
1 . . . . 150.00
2 . . . . 100.00
3 . . . . 100.00
4 . . . . 100.00
5 . . . . 100.00
Becomes:
CASPER AND NIGHTMARE
6 B:68 pgs. 100.00
7 . . . . 75.00
8 . . . . 75.00
9 . . . . 75.00
10 . . . . 75.00
11 thru 20 . . . . @50.00
21 thru 30 . . . . @30.00
31 . . . . 30.00
32 E:68 pgs 30.00
33 thru 45 . . . . @25.00
46 Aug., 1974. . . . . 25.00

NIGHTMARE ON ELM STREET
Blackthorne, 1991
1 3-D 2.50
2 3-D 2.50
3 3-D 2.50

NIGHTMARE ON ELM ST.: PARANOID
Avatar Press, 2005
1 . . . . 4.00
1a wraparound (c) 4.00
1b variant (c)s . . . . @4.00
1c leather (c) 20.00
2 . . . . 4.00
2a Wraparound (c) 4.00
2b Variant(c)s . . . . @4.00
2c Die-cut (c) 10.00

NIGHTMARE ON ELM STREET, A
Avatar Press, 2005
Spec. #1 . . . . 4.00
Spec. #1 variant (c)s 4.00
Spec. #1 glow (c) 15.00
Spec. #1 Blood Red Con (c) 5.00
Spec. #1 Painted (c) 6.00
Spec. #1 Carcass (c) 6.00

NIGHTMARE ON ELM STREET, A
Wildstorm/DC, Oct., 2006
1 CDi 3.00
1a variant (c) 3.00
2 CDi 3.00

NIGHTMARES ON ELM STREET
Innovation, 1991
1 Yours Truly, Freddy Krueger Pt.1 3.00
2 Yours Truly ,Freddy Krueger Pt.2 2.50
3 Loose Ends Pt.1,Return to
Springwood 2.50
4 Loose Ends Pt 2 . . . . 2.50
5 . . . . 2.50
6 . . . . 2.50

NIGHTMARE ON ELM STREET, A
Avatar Press, 2005
Spec. #1 . . . . 4.00
Spec. #1 variant (c)s 4.00
Spec. #1 premium (c)s . . . . @6.00
Spec. Fearbook #1 . . . . 4.00
Spec. Fearbook #1 variant (c)s . . @4.00

NIGHTMARE ON ELM ST.: PARANOID
Avatar Press, 2005
1 thru 3 . . . . @4.00
1a thru 3a wraparound (c)s . . . . @4.00
1b thru 3b variant (c)s . . . . @4.00
1c Special (c)s . . . . @6.00

NIGHTMARES
Eclipse, 1985
1 . . . . 2.50
2 . . . . 2.00

NIGHT MARY
IDW Publishing, 2005
1 . . . . 4.00
2 . . . . 4.00
3 thru 5 . . . . @4.00
TPB 20.00

NIGHT MUSIC
Eclipse, 1984–88
1 . . . . 2.50
2 . . . . 2.50
3 CR, Jungle Bear 3.00
4 Pelias & Melisande 2.00
5 Pelias 2.00
6 same as Salome #1
7 same as Red Dog #1
Graphic Novel 8.00

NIGHTS INTO DREAMS
Archie Comics, 1997
1 based on Sega game 2.00
2 . . . . 2.00
3 . . . . 2.00
4 . . . . 2.00
5 . . . . 2.00
6 . . . . 2.00

NIGHT OF THE LIVING DEAD
Dead Dog Comics, 2004
1 Barbara's Zombie Chronicles . . . 5.00
1a gold foil (c) 5.00
2 Barbara's Zombie Chronicles . . . 5.00
3 . . . . 5.00
TPB Barbara's Zombie Chronicles 10.00

NIGHT OF THE LIVING DEAD: BACK FROM THE GRAVE
Avatar Press, 2006
1-shot 3.00
1-shot variant (c)s . . . . @3.00
1-shot Splatter (c) 6.00
1-shot Head shot (c) 6.00
1-shot Haunting (c) 6.00
1-shot Necro-foil (c) 20.00
1-shot Sketch (c) 30.00

NIGHTSHADE
No Mercy Comics, 1997
1 by Mark Williams 2.50
2 and 3 . . . . @2.50

NIGHT TRIBES
WildStorm/DC, 1999
1-shot Night Tribes unite 5.00

Nightveil #1
© AC Comics

NIGHTVEIL
AC Comics, 1984
1 . . . . 3.50
2 . . . . 2.50
3 thru 7 . . . . @2.50
Spec.#1 . . . . 2.50

9 LIVES OF FELIX
Harvey, 1991
1 . . . . 2.50
2 . . . . 2.50
3 . . . . 2.50
4 . . . . 2.50

NINJA BOY
WildStorm/DC, 2001
1 Ancient Japan, 40-pg. 3.50
2 . . . . 3.00
3 . . . . 3.00
4 . . . . 3.00
5 . . . . 3.00
6 Bishamon, God of War 3.00
TPB Faded Dreams 15.00

NINJA HIGH SCHOOL
Eternity, 1992
1 Reps.orig.N.H.S.in color 2.50
2 thru 13 reprints . . . . @2.50

Ninja High School #93
© Antarctic Press

NINJA HIGH SCHOOL
Antarctic Press, 2000
1 thru 74 see B&W
75	3.00
76 Quagmire gang	3.00
77	3.00
78 World Domination Tour	3.00
79 Dog Supreme	3.00
80 Jeremy Feeple is back	3.00
81 F:Diamond Diane	3.00
82 F:Quagmire Koalas	3.00
83 Time passes	3.00
84 Past, Present, Future	3.00
85 Time has past	3.00
86 Queen of the Conglomerate	3.00
87 Invaded by the Shallrams	3.00
88 Battle Chef battle	3.00
89 Sammie's secret	3.00
90 Earth's champion	3.00
91 The Toughest Contest.	3.00
92 Round 2	3.00
93 Round 3	3.00
94 F:Red Ninja,V:Lendo Rivalsan	3.00
95 Ichi in a new place	3.00
96 Dash the Impede	3.00
97 F:Asrial, Jeremy	3.00
98 Asrial found	3.00
99 F:Lendo Rivalson dies	3.00
100 F:Asrial, Jeremy, & Ichi BDn(c) 48-pg.	5.00
100a Fred Perry (c)	5.00
100b Robert Dejesus (c)	5.00
100c Rod Espinosa (c)	5.00
101 thru 110	@3.50
111	3.50
112	3.50
113	3.50
114	3.50
115 thru 140	@3.00
141	1.00
142 thru 144	@3.00
Yearbook 2001	4.00
Yearbook 2002	4.00
Yearbook 2003	5.00
Yearbook 2004	5.00
Yearbook, 2005	5.00
Yearbook, 2006	4.50
TPB Textbook Vol. 2, 600-pg.	50.00
Spec. Swimsuit special 2002	4.50
TPB Vol. 1 thru Vol. 6 Pocket Manga	@10.00
Spec. Prom Formula (2004) B&W	6.00

NINJA HIGH SCHOOL VERSION 2
Antarctic Press, 1999
1 by Ben Dunn	7.00
2	5.00
3	4.00
4	3.00
5 thru 8	@2.50
9 Yumei strikes back	2.50
10	2.50
11 Time & space distorted	2.50
12 When Worlds Colide, last issue	2.50

NINJA HIGH SCHOOL FEATURING SPEED RACER
Eternity, 1993
1B	3.00
2B	3.00

NINJA SCROLL
Wildstorm/DC, Sept., 2006
1 Anime	3.00
1a variant JLe (c)	3.00
2	3.00
3a, variant JLe (c).	3.00
3	3.00

NINJAK
Valiant, 1994
0: O:Ninjak, Pt. 1	2.50
00: O:Ninjak, Pt.2	2.50
1 B:MMo(s),JQ,JP,Chromium(c), I:Dr.Silk,Webnet.	3.00
1a Gold Ed	4.00
2 thru 28	@2.50
Yearbook #1, Dr. Silk	4.00

NINJAK
Acclaim, 1996
1 KBk(s), Denny Meechum becomes Ninjak	2.50
2 thru 12 KBk(s)	@2.50

N.I.O.
Acclaim, 1998
1 (of 4) by Shon Bury & JPi	2.50
2 thru 4	@2.50

NIRA X: ANIME
Entity Comics, 1997
1 BMs	3.00
1a deluxe, foil cover	3.50
2 BMs	3.00
2a deluxe, foil cover	3.50
Swimsuit #0	2.75
Swimsuit #0 Manga (c)	2.75

NIRA X: CYBERANGEL
Entity, 1994
1 From pages of Zen	3.00
1a 2nd printing	2.75
2 V:Parradox	2.50
3 In Hydro-Dams.	2.50
4 final issue	2.50
4a with computer game	7.00
Ashcan	2.50
TPB Birth of an Angel	13.00

[Series 2], 1995
1 R:Nira X.	3.75
1a Clear Chromium Edition	8.00
1b Holo-Chrome edition	10.00
2 Alien Invasion.	2.50
3 Mecha New York	2.50
4 Final Issue	2.50

[Series 3], 1996
0	2.75
0a signed & numbered	8.00
1	2.50
1a gold edition, signed & numb.	5.00
2	2.50
3	3.00

NIRA X/CYNDER: ENDANGERED SPECIES
Entity Comics, 1996
1	3.00
1a gold ink enhanced, bagged	13.00

NITROGEN: PROPHET
Arcade Comics, 2006
1	4.00
1a variant (c)s	@4.00

NJPW: THE RISE OF THE TIGER
Narwain Publishing, 2006
1 (of 5)	4.00
2	4.00

NOCTURNALS
Malibu Bravura, 1995
1 DIB,I:Nocturnals.	3.00
1a Glow-in-the-Dark	4.00
2 DIB,I:Komodo, Mister Fane	3.00
3 DIB,F:Raccoon.	3.00
4 DIB,I:The Old Wolf.	3.00
5 Discovered by Police	3.00
6 DIB	3.00

NOCTURNALS: THE DARK FOREVER
Oni Press, 2001
1 by Dan Brereton	3.00
2	3.00
3	3.00
TPB The Dark Forever (2002)	10.00
TPB Unhallowed Eve (2002)	10.00
TPB Black Planet (1998)	20.00

NOMAN
Tower Comics, 1966
1 GK,OW,WW,AW	150.00
2 OW,WW,A:Dynamo	100.00

NO TIME FOR SERGEANTS
Dell Publishing Co., 1958
1 Ph(c)	175.00
2 Ph(c)	100.00
3 Ph(c)	100.00

NOVA HUNTER
Ryal Comics
1 thru 3	@2.50
4 Climax	2.50
5 Death and Betrayal	2.50

NURSES, THE
Gold Key, April, 1963
1	100.00
2	75.00
3	75.00

NYOKA, JUNGLE GIRL
Charlton Comics, 1955–57
14	150.00
15	125.00
16	125.00
17	125.00

18 . . . . 125.00
19 . . . . 125.00
20 . . . . 125.00
21 . . . . 125.00
22 . . . . 125.00

NYOKA, THE JUNGLE GIRL
AC Comics, 1988
1 and 2 Further Adventures of
Nyoka, the Jungle Girl . . . . . . @2.50

OBLIVION
Comico, 1995
1 R:The Elementals 2.50
2 I:Thunderboy, Lilith 2.50
3 I:Fen, Ferril 2.50
4 War 3.00
5 The Unholy Trilogy 3.00

OCCULT FILES OF DR. SPEKTOR
Gold Key, April, 1973
1 I:Lakot 75.00
2 thru 5 . . . . @30.00
6 thru 10 . . . . @30.00
11 I:Spertor as Werewolf 30.00
12 and 13 . . . . @25.00
14 A:Dr. Solar 50.00
15 thru 24 . . . . @20.00

Whitman
25 rep 20.00

OCEAN
Wildstorm/DC, 2004
1 (of 6) WEI(s),CSp,KIS 3.00
2 WEI,CSp,KIS 3.00
3 WEI,CSp,KIS 3.00
4 WEI,CSp,KIS 3.00
5 WEI,CSp,KIS 3.00
6 WEI,CSp,KIS,48-pg., concl. 4.00
TPB 15.00

ODYSSEY, THE
Avatar/TidalWave Studios, 2002
1A RCz (c) 3.50
1B MMy (c) 3.50
1C Parajullo (c) 3.50
1D Murphy (c) 3.50

ODYSSEY PRESENTS: VENUS
Alias Enterprises, 2006
1 . . . . 3.50

ODYSSEY, THE: ABSOLUTE POWER
Alias Enterprises, 2006
1-shot 5.00

OF BITTER SOULS
Speakeasy Comics, 2005
1 . . . . 3.00
2 thru 3 . . . . @3.00
4 thru 6 . . . . @3.00
TPB Vol. 1 . . . . 16.00

Vol. 2, Markosia, 2006
1 . . . . 3.50
1a variant (c)s . . . . @3.50
2 . . . . 3.50
3 . . . . 3.50
3a variant (c) 3.50
4 . . . . 3.50
4a limited variant (c) 6.00
TPB Vol. 1 . . . . 19.00

OF BITTER SOULS
Speakeasy Comics, 2005
1 thru 3 . . . . @3.00

O.G. WHIZ
Gold Key, 1971–79
1 . . . . 125.00
2 . . . . 75.00
3 thru 6 . . . . @65.00
7 thru 11 . . . . @50.00

OINK: BLOOD AND CIRCUS
Kitchen Sink, 1997
1 (of 4) by John Mueller 5.00
2 thru 4 . . . . @5.00

OLYMPUS HEIGHTS
IDW Publishing, 2004
1 . . . . 4.00
2 thru 5 . . . . @4.00
TPB 20.00

O'MALLEY AND THE ALLEY CATS
Gold Key, 1971–74
1 . . . . 45.00
2 thru 9 . . . . @40.00

OMEGA 7
Omega 7
1 V:Exterminator X 4.00
? by Alonzo L. Washington 4.00
0 . . . . 3.00

OMEGA SAGA, THE
Southpaw Publishing, 1998
0 by Mike Gerardo & Chris Navetta 3.00
1 Episode One, pt.1 . . . . 3.00
2 Episode One, pt.2 . . . . 3.00

Axess Comics
3 by Mike Gerardo, Heroes (c) 3.00
3b Villains (c) 3.00

OMEN, THE
Chaos! Comics, 1998
Preview Book, BnP 2.50
1 by PNu & Justiniano 3.00
2 thru 5 . . . . @3.00
1-shot The Omen Vexed 3.00
TPB The Omen 13.00

ON A PALE HORSE
Innovation
1 Piers Anthony adapt 5.00
2 Magician,I:Kronos 5.00
3 . . . . 5.00
4 VV, ... 5.00
5 . . . . 5.00
6 . . . . 5.00

ONE-ARM SWORDSMAN
Dr. Leung's
1 . . . . 3.00
2 . . . . 3.00
3 . . . . 2.75
4 thru 11 . . . . @2.50

100 GIRLS
Arcana Studio, 2004
1 thru 7 . . . . @3.00
1a 2nd printing 3.00
TPB Vol. 1 . . . . 10.00
TPB Vol. 2 . . . . 10.00

100 GIRLS/JENNA
Arcana Studio, 2006
1 (of 2) 4.00

Operation Stormbringer #1
© Acclaim

OPERATION: STORMBREAKER
Acclaim Special Event, 1997
Spec. F:Teutonic Knight 4.00

OPPOSITE FORCES
Alias Enterprises, 2005
Vol. 2
1 (of 4) 1.00
2 thru 4 . . . . @3.00

ORBIT
Eclipse, 1990
1 DSt(c) 4.00
2 . . . . 4.00
3 . . . . 5.00

ORIENTAL HEROES
Jademan, 1988–92
1 by Tony Wong & MBn 2.50
2 . . . . 2.50
3 thru 13 . . . . @2.50
14 thru 40 . . . . @2.50
41 thru 44 . . . . 2.00
45 thru 53 . . . . @2.50

ORIGINAL ASTRO BOY
Now, 1987
1 KSy 3.00
2 thru 17 KSy . . . . @3.00

ORIGINAL CAPTAIN JOHNAR AND THE ALIENS
Valiant, 1995
1 Reprint from Magnus 3.00
2 Russ Manning rep 3.00

ORIGINAL DICK TRACY
Gladestone, 1990
1 rep.V:Mrs.Pruneface 2.50
2 rep.V:Influence 2.50
3 rep.V:TheMole 2.50
4 rep.V:ItchyOliver 2.50
5 rep.V:Shoulders 2.50

All comics prices listed are for *Near Mint* condition.

ORIGINAL DR. SOLAR MAN OF THE ATOM
Valiant, 1995

1 Reprint 3.00
2 Reprints 3.00
3 Reprints 3.00

ORIGINAL E-MAN
First, 1985
{rep. Charlton stories}

1 JSon,O:E-Man & Nova 2.50
2 JSon,V:Battery,SamuelBoar 2.50
3 JSon,City in the Sand 2.50
4 JSon,A:Brain from Sirius 2.50
5 JSon,V:T.V. Man 2.50
6 JSon,I:Teddy Q 2.50
7 JSon,Vamfire 2.50

ORIGINAL MAGNUS ROBOT FIGHTER
Valiant, 1995

1 Reprint 3.00
2 Russ Manning Art 3.00
3 Russ Manning 3.00

Original Shield #1
© ABC

ORIGINAL SHIELD
Archie, 1984

1 DAy/TD,O:Shield 2.50
2 DAy,O:Dusty 2.50
3 DAy 2.50
4 DAy 2.50

ORIGINAL TUROK, SON OF STONE
Valiant, 1995

1 Reprint 3.00
2 Alberto Gioletti art 3.00
3 Alberto Gioletti 3.00
4 Reprints 3.00

ORIGIN OF THE DEFIANT UNIVERSE
Defiant, 1994

1 O:Defiant Characters 2.50

ORIGINS
Malibu Ultraverse,

1 O:Ultraverse Heroes 2.50

ORION THE HUNTER
Alias Enterprises, 2006

1 (of 4) 3.00
2 . . . . 3.00
3 . . . . 3.50
4 . . . . @3.50

ORSON SCOTT CARD'S WYRMS
Dabel Brothers Prod., 2006

1 . . . . 3.00
1a variant (c) 6.00
2 thru 5 . . . . @3.00
2a thru 5a variant (c)s . . . . @6.00

OUTBREED 999
Blackout Comics, 1994

1 thru 4 . . . . @3.00
5 Search For Daige 3.00

OUTCAST SPECIAL
Valiant, 1995

1 R:The Outcast 2.50

OUTER LIMITS, THE
Dell Publishing Co., 1964

1 P(c) 300.00
2 P(c) 150.00
3 P(c) 150.00
4 P(c) 150.00
5 P(c) 150.00
6 P(c) 125.00
7 P(c) 125.00
8 P(c) 125.00
9 P(c) 125.00
10 P(c) 125.00
11 thru 18 P(c) . . . . @100.00

OUTLAW SCORN: 3030AD
Arcana Studio, 2006

1 (of 6) 4.00

OUTLAWS OF THE WEST
Charlton Comics, 1957–70
1 thru 10: CODY OF THE PONY EXPRESS (see Golden Age section)

11 . . . . 125.00
12 . . . . 100.00
13 . . . . 100.00
14 Giant size 150.00
15 . . . . 100.00
16 . . . . 100.00
17 . . . . 100.00
18 SD 165.00
19 . . . . 75.00
20 thru 40 . . . . @75.00
41 thru 50 . . . . @50.00
51 thru 70 . . . . @35.00
71 thru 81 . . . . @30.00
Charlton Comics, 1979
82 thru 88 . . . . @30.00

OUT OF THIS WORLD
Charlton Comics, 1956–59

1 . . . . 450.00
2 . . . . 200.00
3 SD 500.00
4 SD 500.00
5 SD 500.00
6 SD 500.00
7 SD,SD(c) 550.00
8 SD 450.00
9 SD 350.00
10 SD,Perfect Forcaster 350.00
11 SD 450.00
12 SD 350.00

13 thru 15 . . . . @200.00
16 . . . . 400.00

OUTPOSTS
Blackthorne, 1997

1 . . . . 2.50
2 thru 6 . . . . @2.50

OUT THERE
WildStorm/DC, 2001

1 HuR, Cliffhanger 2.50
2 HuR, ... 2.50
3 HuR 2.50
4 HuR 2.50
5 HuR 2.50
6 HuR 2.50
7 HuR, Road to El Dorado,pt.1 . . . . 2.50
8 HuR, Road to El Dorado,pt.2 . . . . 2.50
9 HuR, Road to El Dorado,pt.3 . . . . 2.50
10 HuR, Road to El Dorado,pt.4 . . . . 3.00
11 HuR, Road to El Dorado,pt.5 . . . . 3.00
12 HuR, Road to El Dorado,pt.6 . . . . 3.00
13 HuR, The War in Hell,pt.1 . . . . . . 3.00
14 HuR, The War in Hell,pt.2 . . . . . . 3.00
15 HuR, Draedalus's Domain 3.00
16 HuR, Dreadrealm 3.00
17 HuR, all-silent issue 3.00
18 HuR,V:Draedalus 3.00
TPB The Evil Within, rep.#1–#6 . . . 13.00

OWL, THE
Gold Key, April, 1967

1 . . . . 125.00
2 April, 1968 . . . . 90.00

OZ/WONDERLAND CHRONICLES, THE
Buymetoys.com, 2005

0 . . . . 3.00
Preview (B&W) 3.00
1 JJu (c) 3.50
1a variant (c) 3.50

OZF5 GALE FORCE
Alias Enterprises, 2005

1-shot 5.00
1-shot signed convention edition . . 15.00

PACIFIC PRESENTS
Pacific, 1992

1 DSt,Rocketeer,(3rd App.) 12.00
2 DSt,Rocketeer,(4th App.) 9.00
3 SD,I:Vanity 2.50
4 and 5 . . . . @2.50

P.A.C.
Artifacts Inc., 1993

1 I:P.A.C. 2.50

PAINKILLER JANE
Event Comics, 1997

1 JQ(c) 3.00
1 RL(c) 3.00
1 Red foil logo, signed 25.00
2 JQ&JP(c) 3.00
2 JP&RL(c) 3.00
3 JQ&JP(c) 3.00
3a JP&RL(c) 3.00
4 JQ&JP(c) A Too Bright Place
   For Dying 3.00
4a RL&JP(c) 3.00
5 JQ&JP(c) Purgatory
   Station—Next Stop Hell 3.00
5a RL&JP(c) 3.00
6 RL&JP(c) Blood Harvest 3.00
6a BSz&JP(c) 3.00

All comics prices listed are for *Near Mint* condition.

COLOR PUB.

7 Jane in the Jungle,	
pt.1,BiT&JP(c)	3.00
7a RL&JP(c)	3.00
Spec.#0 O:Painkiller Jane,48-pg. .	4.00
Spec.#0A signed	30.00
Spec. Painkiller Jane/Hellboy	
Ancient Laughter (1998)	3.00
Spec. Painkiller Jane/Hellboy,	
signed	20.00
Spec. Painkiller Jane/The Darkness,	
signed, limited edition, JQ(c). .	30.00

PAINKILLER JANE
D.E. (Dynamite Ent.) 2006

1 JP.	3.00
1a variant AH(c)	3.00
1b variant Blood Red foil (c)	20.00
1c variant wraparound (c)	10.00
2 JP.	3.00
2a variant b&w (c)	15.00
3 JP.	3.00
3a variant (c)s	@3.00
TPB Essential Painkiller Jane	20.00

PAINKILLER JANE/
DARKCHYLDE
Event Comics, 1998

1 BAu,RQu	3.00
1a signed & numbered	30.00
1b Omnichrome edition.	15.00
1c Omnichrome, signed	30.00
1d Dynamic Forces cover.	7.00

PAINKILLER JANE
VS. THE DARKNESS:
STRIPPER
Event Comics, 1997

1 GEn,JP,x-over, Amanda Connor	
cover	3.00
1a Greg & Tim Hildebrandt.	3.00
1b MS(c).	3.00
1c JQ(c)	3.00

PAKKINS' LAND
Alias Enterprises, 2005
Vol. 2

1	3.00
2 thru 8	@3.00

PANDEMONIUM:
DELIVERANCE
Chaos! Comics, 1998

1-shot by Jesse Leon McCann &	
Jack Jadson	3.00

PANIC
Gemstone, 1997

1 thru 12 EC Comics reprint	@2.50
`Annuals'	
TPB Vol. 1 rebinding #1–#4.	10.50
TPB Vol. 2 rebinding #5–#8	11.00

PANTERA
Rock-it Comix, 1994

1	4.00
1a Gold Ed.	20.00

PANTHA
Harris Comics, 1997

1 (of 2) MT	3.50
1 Marilyn Monroe MT alt.cov. . . .	10.00
2 MT alternate (c)	10.00
2 photo (c).	10.00

PARA
Pennyfarthing Press, 2004

1	3.00
2 thru 6	@3.00

PARADAX
Vortex, 1987

1	2.50

PARADISE
Twenty First Century, 2000

1 thru 7	@3.00

PARADOX
Arcana Studio, 2005

1 (of 4)	3.00
2	3.00
3	3.00

PARAGON
DARK APOCALYPSE
AC, 1993

1 thru 4, Fem Force crossover . .	@3.00

PARANOIA
Adventure Comics, 1991

1 (based on video game) Clone1 .	3.25
2 King-R-Thr-2	3.00
3 R:Happy Jack,V:N3F	3.00
4 V:The Computer	3.00
5 V:The Computer	3.00
6 V:Lance-R-Lot,last issue	3.00

PARIAH
Revolution Comics, 2006

1	3.00
2 thru 4	@3.00
4a variant (c)	3.00

PARTRIDGE FAMILY, THE
Charlton Comics, 1971–73

1	150.00
2 thru 4	@75.00
5 Summer Special	125.00
6 thru 21	@50.00

PASSOVER
Maximum Press, 1996

1 (of 2) BNa	3.00
2 BNa,A:Avengelyne.	3.00

PATH, THE
Crossgen Comics, 2002

1 RMz,BS	5.00
2 thru 4 RMz,BS	@3.00
9 thru 23	@3.00
Prequel 48-pg.	5.00
TPB Vol. 1 Crisis of Faith.	20.00
TPB Vol. 2 Blood on Snow	16.00
TPB Vol. 3 Death and Dishonor. . .	16.00
TPB Traveler Vol. 2 Blood on	
Snow	10.00

PATHWAYS TO
FANTASY
Pacific, 1984

1 BS,JJ art	3.00

PATRIOTS, THE
WildStorm/DC, 1999

1 BCi&JPe(s)	2.50
2 BCi&JPe(s)	2.50
3 thru 7 BCi&JPe(s)	@2.50
8 BCi&JPe(s),V:Stealthers	2.50
9 BCi&JPe(s)	2.50

Path #3
© CrossGen Comics

10 JPe(s),final issue	2.50

PAT SAVAGE:
WOMAN OF BRONZE
Millennium, 1992

1 F:Doc Savage's cousin	2.50

PEACEKEEPER
Future Comics, 2003

1	3.00
2 thru 5	@3.00
TPB Vol. 1	16.00

PEACEMAKER
Charlton, 1967

1 A:Fightin' 5	5.00
2 A:Fightin' 5	3.00
3 A:Fightin' 5	3.00
4 O:Peacemaker,A:Fightin' 5	4.00
5 A:Fightin' 5	2.50

PEANUTS
Dell Publishing Co., 1958

1	350.00
2	300.00
3	250.00
4	200.00
5 thru 13	@175.00

PEANUTS
Gold Key, 1963

1	225.00
2 thru 4	@175.00

PEARL HARBOR
Antarctic Press, 2001

1 by Ted Nomura, Movie tie-in	4.00
2 movie tie-in, concl.	4.00
Spec. 60th Anniv. spec., 64-pg. . . .	13.00
Spec. 60th Anniv., Japanese (c) . .	13.00

PEBBLES &
BAMM-BAMM
Charlton Comics, 1972–76

1	100.00
2 thru 10	@50.00
11 thru 36	@45.00

COLOR PUB.

PEBBLES FLINTSTONE
Gold Key, 1963
1 A Chip off the old block 200.00

PENNY AND AGGIE
Alias Enterprises, 2005
1 thru 4 . . . . @3.00

PERFECT DARK: JANUS' TEARS
Prima Publishing, 2006
1 . . . . 3.50
2 thru 3 . . . . @3.50

PERFECT DARK ZERO
Prima Publishing, 2006
1 (of 6) 3.50

PERG
Lightning Comics, 1993
1 Glow in the dark(c),JS(c),
   B:JZy(s),KIK,I:Perg 3.75
1a Platinum Ed. 5.00
1b Gold Ed. 7.00
1 gold edition, glow-in-the-dark
   flip cover 30.00
2 KIK,O:Perg 3.25
2a Platinum Ed. 5.00
3 Flip Book (c), ... 3.25
3a Platinum Ed 5.00
4 TLw,I:Hellina 9.00
4a Platinum Ed 5.00
5 A:Hellina. 3.25
6 PIA,A:Hellina 3.25
7 . . . . 3.00
8 V:Police 3.00

PERRY MASON MYSTERY MAGAZINE
Dell Publishing Co., 1964
1 . . . . 250.00
2 Ray Burr Ph(c). 150.00

PETER PAN: RETURN TO NEVERNEVER LAND
Adventure
1 Peter in Mass. 2.50
2 V:Tiger Lily. 2.50

PETER POTAMUS
Gold Key, 1965
1 . . . . 200.00

PETTICOAT JUNCTION
Dell Publishing Co., 1964
1 Ph(c) 150.00
2 Ph(c) 100.00
3 Ph(c) 100.00
4 . . . . 100.00
5 Ph(c) 100.00

PHANTOM, THE
Gold Key, 1962
1 RsM 300.00
2 B:King, Queen & Jack 250.00
3 . . . . 150.00
4 . . . . 150.00
5 . . . . 150.00
6 . . . . 150.00
7 The Super Apes. 150.00
8 . . . . 150.00
9 . . . . 150.00
10 The Sleeping Giant. 150.00
11 E:King,Queen and Jack 125.00
12 B:Track Hunter 125.00

Phantom #31 © Charlton

13 . . . . 125.00
14 The Historian 125.00
15 . . . . 125.00
16 . . . . 125.00
17 Samaris. 125.00
King Comics, 1966
18 The Treasure of the Skull
   Cave;BU:Flash Gordon 125.00
19 The Astronaut & the Pirates . . 100.00
20 A:GirlPhantom,E:FlashGordon 100.00
21 BU:Mandrake 100.00
22 Secret of Magic Mountain. . . . 100.00
23 . . . . 100.00
24 A:Girl Phantom 100.00
25 . . . . 75.00
26 . . . . 75.00
27 . . . . 75.00
28 . . . . 75.00
29 *never published*
Charlton Comics, 1969–77
30 . . . . 50.00
31 JAp,Phantom of Shang-Ri-La . . 50.00
32 JAp,The Pharaoh Phantom . . . 50.00
33 The Jungle People 50.00
34 thru 39 . . . . @45.00
40 The Ritual 45.00
41 thru 43 . . . . @35.00
44 To Right A Wrong 35.00
45 . . . . 35.00
46 I:Piranha 30.00
47 thru 72. . . . . @30.00
73 . . . . 25.00
74 . . . . 30.00

PHANTOM
Wolf Publishing, 1992
1 Drug Runners 2.50
2 Mystery Child of the Sea 2.50
3 inc.feature pages on
   Phantom/Merchandise. 2.50
4 TV Jungle Crime Buster 2.50
5 Castle Vacula-Transylvania 2.50
6 The Old West. 2.50
7 Sercet of Colussus 2.75
8 Temple of the Sun God 2.75

PHANTOM, THE
Moonstone, 2002
1 CDi. 3.50
2 thru 8 . . . . @3.50
9 thru 13 . . . . @3.50
12a Limited ed. (c). 4.50
TPB Vol. 1 Ghost Who Walks 17.00
TPB Vol. 1 2nd printing 18.00

TPB Death in the Deep
   Woods (2005) 15.00
TPB The Phantom: Legacy 13.00
GN #1 The Ghost Killer, 48-pg. . . . 6.00
GN #2 The Singh Web. 6.00
GN #3 The Treasures of Bangalla . . 7.00
GN #4 The Hunt. 7.00
GN #5 Valley of the Golden Men . . . 7.00
GN The Man-Eaters. 13.00
GN Law of the Jungle 12.00
TPB Vol. 1 Graham Nolan
   Sundays. 14.00
TPB Vol. 2 Graham Nolan
   Sundays. 17.00

PHANTOM BOLT, THE
Gold Key, 1964–66
1 A:Mr X 150.00
2 Super Goof 100.00
3 thru 7 . . . . @75.00

PHANTOM FORCE
Genesis West, 1994
Previously: Image
0 JK/JLe(c) 3.00
3 thru 10 . . . . @3.00

PHANTOM JACK: THE NOWHERE MAN AGENDA
Speakeasy Comics, 2006
1 . . . . 3.00
2 thru 3 . . . . @3.00

PHAZE
Eclipse, 1988
1 BSz(c),Takes place in future 2.50
2 PG(c),V:The Pentagon. 2.50
3 Schwieger Vs. Mammoth. 2.50

PHOENIX
Atlas, 1975
1 thru 4 . . . . @25.00

PHOENIX RESURRECTION
Malibu Ultraverse, 1995–96
0 Intro to Phoenix Resurrection . . . 2.50
Genesis, A:X-Men 4.00
Revelations, A:X-Men 4.00
Aftermath, A:X-Men 4.00

PIERCE
Imperium Comics, 2006
1 . . . . 3.00
2 thru 4 . . . . @3.00

PINK PANTHER, THE
Gold Key, April, 1971
1 . . . . 100.00
2 thru 10 . . . . @75.00
11 thru 30 . . . . @50.00
31 thru 74 . . . . @30.00
75 thru 80 . . . . @50.00
81 thru 87 . . . . @35.00

PIRACY
Gemstone, 1998
1 EC comics reprint 2.50
2 thru 7 EC comics reprints . . . . @2.50
'Annuals'
TPB Vol. 1 rebinding #1–#4. . . . . 10.50
TPB Vol. 2 rebinding #5–#7. . . . . . 8.00

PIRATE CORP.
Eternity
1 thru 5 . . . . @2.50

PIRATE TALES
Boom! Studios, 2006
1 . . . . 7.00

P.I.'S, THE
First, 1985
1 JSon,Ms.Tree,M Mauser 2.50
2 JSon,Ms.Tree,M Mauser 2.50
3 JSon,Ms.Tree,M Mauser 2.50

PISTOLFIST: REVOLU-TIONARY WARRIOR
Alias Enterprises, 2006
1 (of 4) 3.50
2 . . . . 3.50

PITT
Full Bleed Studios, 1996
1 thru 9, see Image
10 thru 14 DK . . . . @2.50
14a variant cover 7.00
15 DK 2.50
16 DK, Ugly Americans, pt.1 . . . . . . 2.50
17 DK, Ugly Americans, pt.2 . . . . . . 2.50
18 DK, Ugly Americans, pt.3, concl. 2.50
19 by Brian Dawson 3.00
20 DK, Urgral Thul 2.50
TPB Vol. 1, rep. ? &#1–#4 . . . . 11.00
TPB Vol. 2, rep. #5–#9 . . . . 12.00
Spec. In the Blood 2.50

PITT CREW
Full Bleed Studios, 1998
1 Monster 2.50
2 F:Rai-Kee 2.50
3 Tyrants 2.50
4 The Slayer 2.50
5 . . . . 2.50

PITT: BIOGENESIS
Full Bleed Studios, 2000
1 (of 3) DK 2.50
2 DK 2.50

PLANETARY
WildStorm/DC, 1999
1 WEI 10.00
2 thru 12 WEI . . . . @5.00
13 WEI,secret history of
   Elijah Snow 4.00
14 WEI,The Four vs. Planetary 4.00
15 WEI,in Australia 4.00
16 WEI 4.00
17 WEI Elijah Snow's past 3.00
18 WEI,The Gun Club 3.00
19 WEI,Mystery in Space 3.00
20 WEI,Mystery in Space,pt.2 . . . . . 3.00
21 WEI 3.00
22 WEI(s),Torture of William Leather 3.00
23 WEI(s),F:The Drummer 3.00
24 WEI(s),Dark Secrets 3.00
25 WEI(s),A Trap for the Four 3.00
26 WEI(s) 3.00
TPB All over the World 15.00
TPB The Fourth Man, 144-pg 15.00
TPB Planetary: Crossing Worlds . . 15.00
TPB Vol. 3 Leaving 20th Century . 15.00
GN Planetary/The Authority 6.00
GN Planetery/JLA, Terra
   Occulta, JOy (2002) 6.00
GN WEI(s) Planetary/Batman
   Night on Earth x-over (2003) . . . 6.00

PLAN 9 FROM OUTER SPACE
Malibu
GNv Movie Adapt. 5.00

PLANESWALKER WAR
Acclaim, 1996
GN #1 Magic: The Gathering tie-in . 6.00

PLANETARY BRIGADE
Boom! Studios, 2006
1 . . . . 3.00
2 . . . . 3.00

PLANETARY BRIGADE: ORIGINS
Boom! Studios, 2006
1 Old School (c) 4.00
1a New School (c) 4.00
2 . . . . 4.00

PLANET COMICS
Blackthorne, 1988
1 DSt(c) 3.00
2 thru 4 . . . . @3.00

Planet of Vampires #3
© *Atlas Comics*

PLANET OF VAMPIRES
Atlas, Feb.–July, 1975
1 NA(c),1st PB 25.00
2 NA(c) 25.00
3 RH 25.00

POGZ N SLAMMER
Blackout Comics, 1995
1 I:Pogz N Slammer 2.50
2 Contact Other Schools 2.50

POINT BLANK
WildStorm/DC, 2002
Eye of the Storm
1 (of 5) CWi, super-hero noir 3.00
2 CWi, ... 3.00
3 CWi,F:Jack Hawksmoor 3.00
4 CWi, ... 3.00
5 CWi,concl. 3.00
TPB 15.00

POISON ELVES
Sirius Entertainment, 1998
Color Special #1 by Drew Hayes . . . 3.00
Color Spec.#1 limited 10.00

POIZON
London Night Studios, 1995
0 . . . . 3.00
0 signed gothchik edition 9.00
? O:Poizon 3.00
?a Commemorative (1999) 6.00
1 and 2 EHr . . . . @3.00
1a signed 7.00

POIZON: CADILLACS AND GREEN TOMATOES
London Night, 1997
2 thru 3 . . . . @3.00
6 deluxe 5.00

POIZON: DEMON HUNTER
London Night, 1998
1 . . . . 3.00
1 Green Death edition 15.00

POIZON: LOST CHILD
London Night Studios, 1996
0 . . . . 3.00
1 mini series 3.00
1 signed 9.00
1 Green Death edition 15.00
2 thru 3 . . . . @3.00

POKEMAN TALES:
Viz Communications, 1999
1 thru 16 boardbooks . . . . @5.00
Gift Set Vol. 1 . . . . 20.00
Gift Set Vol. 2 . . . . 20.00
Movie Spec 5.00

POKEMAN THE MOVIE 2000: REVELATION LUGIA
Viz Communications, 2000
1 . . . . 4.00
2 & 3 . . . . @4.00
Spec. Pikachu's Rescue Adventure . 4.00
Art of Pokeman The Movie 2000 . . 10.00

POKEMAN: THE FIRST MOVIE
Viz Communications, 1999
1 (of 4) Mewtwo Strikes Back 4.00
2 . . . . 4.00
3 . . . . 4.00
4 conclusion 4.00
Spec. Pikachu's Vacation 4.00
Art of Pokeman: First Movie 9.00
TPB 16.00

POPEYE
Gold Key, 1962
1-65 See Golden Age Section
66 . . . . 125.00
67 . . . . 100.00
68 thru 80 . . . . @75.00

King Comics, 1966
81 thru 92 . . . . @60.00

Charlton, 1969
94 thru 99 . . . . @60.00
100 . . . . 75.00
101 thru 138 . . . . @35.00

Gold Key, 1978
139 thru 143 . . . . @25.00
144 50th Aniv. Spec. 30.00
155 . . . . @25.00

Whitman, 1980
156 thru 157 . . . . @25.00
158 thru 159 . . . . @35.00
162 thru 168 . . . . @25.00
169 thru 171 . . . . @30.00

COLOR PUB.

All comics prices listed are for *Near Mint* condition.

POPEYE
Harvey Comics, 1993–94
1 thru 7 . . . . @2.50
Summer Spec.#1 . . . . 2.50

POPEYE SPECIAL
Ocean, 1987–88
1 . . . . 2.50
2 . . . . 2.50

POSSESSED, THE
Wildstorm/DC July, 2003
1 (of 6) LSh,demons 3.00
2 thru 5 LSh,demon-infested. . . . @3.00
6 LSh,concl. 3.00
TPB series rep. 15.00

POWER & GLORY
Malibu Bravura, 1994
1A HC(a&s),I:American
  Powerhouse. 3.00
1B alternate cover. 3.00
1c Blue Foil (c) 5.00
1d w/seirgraph 5.00
1e Newsstand 3.00
2 HC(a&s), O:American
  Powerhouse. 2.75
3 HC(a&s). 2.50
4 HC(a&s). 2.50
Winter Special 3.00
TPB Series reprint, w/stamp 13.00

POWER AND THE GLORY, THE
Narwain Publishing, 2005
1 . . . . 7.50

POWER FACTOR
Wonder Color Comics, 1986
1 . . . . 4.00
2 thru 3 . . . . @3.00

POWER FACTOR
Innovation, 1990
1 thru 4 . . . . @2.50

POWERKNIGHTS
Amara, 1995
P I:Powerknights 2.50

POWERMARK
Quest Ministries International, 2004
1 The Mission 3.00
2 Wake of Leviathan 3.00
3 Under Fire 3.00
4 Betrayal 3.00
5 Face Off 3.00
6 They All Fall Down. 3.00
7 High & Mighty 3.00

POWER OF PRIME
Malibu Ultraverse, 1995
1 O:Prime Powers,Godwheel tie-in 2.50
2 V:Doc Gross, Godwheel tie-in . . . 2.50
3 F:Prime Phade. 2.50
4 F:Elven,Turbocharge 2.50

POWER OF THE VALKYRIE
Arcana Studio, 2006
1 . . . . 4.00
2 . . . . 4.00

POWER RANGERS ZEO/YOUNGBLOOD
Maximum Press, 1997
1 TNu,NRd 3.00

POWERS THAT BE
Broadway Comics
Preview Editions, 1995
1 thru 3 B&W. . . . . @2.50
Regular Series, 1995
1 JiS,I:Fatale, Star Seed 3.00
2 . . . . 3.00
3 . . . . 3.00
4 . . . . 3.00
5 It's the End of the World As We
  Know It,pt.1 . . . . 3.00
6 End/World As We Know It,pt.2 . . 3.00
Becomes:

STAR SEED
7 End/World As We Know It,pt.3 . . 3.00
8 End/World As We Know It,pt.4 . . 3.00
9 End/World As We Know It,pt.5 . . 3.00
10 End/World As We Know It,pt.6. . 3.00
11 End/World As We Know It,pt.7. . 3.00

Priest #2
© Maximum

PRIEST
Maximum Press, 1996
1 RLd, F:Michael O'Bannon 3.00
2 RLd,BNa, ... 3.00
3 RLd 3.00

PRIMAL RAGE
Sirius, 1996
1 TAr,from video game 3.00
1 foil cover, limited edition 3.00
2 TAr,DOe(c). 3.00

PRIME
Malibu Ultraverse, 1993–95
1 B:GJ(s),I:Prime 4.00
1a Ultra-Limited 5.00
1b Full Hologram (c). 5.00
2 V:Organism 8, with Ultraverse
  card 3.00
3 NBy,I:Prototype 3.00
4 NBy,V:Prototype. 3.00
5 NBy,BWS,I:Maxi-Man, BU:Rune . 3.00
6 NBy,A:Pres. Clinton 2.75
7 thru 11 . . . . @2.50

12 NBy,(Ultraverse Premiere#3)
  I:Planet Class 3.50
13 NBy,V:Kutt,Planet Class 3.00
14 thru 26. . . . . @2.50
Ashcan (first) 7.00
Ashcan #1 BV(c),B&W. 2.00
Ann.#1 R:Doc Gross 4.00
TPB Rep. #1-#4. . . . . 10.00

PRIME
Malibu Ultraverse, 1995–96
Infinty I:Spider-Prime 3.00
1 Spider-Prime vs. Lizard 2.50
1a Computer painted cover 2.50
2 thru 8 . . . . @2.00
9 and 10 . . . . @2.00
11 thru 15 . . . . @2.50

PRIME/CAPTAIN AMERICA
Malibu Ultraverse, 1996
1 GJ,NBy 4.00

PRIME VS. HULK
Malibu, 1995
0 . . . . 10.00
0a signed premium edition 20.00

PRIMER
Comico, 1982–84
1 . . . . 15.00
2 I:Grendel 135.00
3 . . . . 12.00
4 C:Maxx. 12.00
5 I:Maxx 40.00
6 I:Evangelyne 18.00
[Volume 2], 1996
1 F:Lady Bathory 3.00

PRIMUS
Charlton Comics, 1972
1 . . . . 25.00
2 thru 5 . . . . @15.00
6 thru 7 . . . . @12.00

PRINCESS SALLY
Archie Comics, 1995
1 Sonic tie-in 3.00
2 . . . . 3.00
3 . . . . 3.00

PRINCE VANDAL
Triumphant
1 JnR(s), ... 2.50
2 JnR(s), ... 2.50
3 JnR(s),ShG,I:Claire,V:Nicket,
  Vandal goes to Boviden. 2.50
4 JnR(s),ShG,Game's End 2.50
5 JnR(s),ShG,The Sickness, the
  rat appears 2.50
6 JnR(s),ShG,B:Gothic 2.50

PRIORITY: WHITE HEAT
AC Comics, 1986
1 thru 2 miniseries. . . . . @2.50

PROFESSIONAL: GOGOL 13
Viz
1 . . . . 5.00
2 . . . . 5.00
3 . . . . 5.00

PROFESSOR OM
Innovation, 1990
1 I:Rock Warrior 2.50
2 Samurai Drama 2.50

COLOR PUB.

PROJECT A-KO 0
Antarctic Press, 1994
0 digest size 5.00
Malibu, 1994
1 thru 4 Based on anime movie . @3.00

PROJECT A-KO 2
CPM, 1995
1 Space Saga 3.00
2 Space Saga 3.00
3 Queen Margarita 3.00

PROJECT A-KO: VERSUS THE UNIVERSE
CPM, 1995
1 Based on Animation. 3.00
2 strange magician 3.00
3 . . . . 3.00
4 (of 5) TEl 3.00

PROJECT EON
Speakeasy Comics, 2005
1 (of 2) 6.00
Markosia, 2006
1 . . . . 5.00
2 thru 3 . . . . @3.50

PROMETHEA
WildStorm/DC, 1999
America's Best Comics
1 AMo(s),F:Sophie Bangs,40-pg. . . 3.50
2 AMo(s),Judgment of Solomon . . . 3.00
3 AMo(s),Misty Magic Land 3.00
4 AMo(s),CV,JWi. 3.00
5 AMo(s),JWi,F:WW1 . . . . 3.00
6 AMo(s),JWi,F:Grace Brannagh . . 3.00
7 AMo(s),JWi,F:Sophie Bangs 3.00
8 AMo(s),JWi,V:Goetic demons . . . 3.00
9 AMo(s),JWi,The Temple. 3.00
10 AMo(s),JWi,Sex, Stars
    and Serpents 3.00
11 AMo(s),JWi,giant monster. 3.00
12 AMo(s),JWi,flip-book. 3.00
13 AMo(s),JWi,. 3.00
14 AMo(s),JWi, Lunar Realm. 3.00
15 AMo(s),JWi,. 3.00
16 AMo(s),JWi,Five Swell Guys. . . . 3.00
17 AMo(s),JWi,Stacia vs. Hell 3.00
18 AMo(s),JWi,double demonic. . . . 3.00
19 AMo(s),JWi,Tree of Life 3.00
20 AMo(s),JWi,edge of existence . . 3.00
21 AMo(s),JWi,Binah 3.00
22 AMo(s),JWi,Jack Foust. 3.00
23 AMo(s),JWi,40-pg. 3.50
24 AMo(s),JWi 3.00
25 AMo(s),JWi,A Higher Court. 3.00
26 AMo(s),JWi,Later 3.00
27 AMo(s),JWi,Tom Strong 3.00
28 AMo(s),JWi,Jack Faust. 3.00
29 AMo(s),JWi 3.00
30 AMo(s),JWi,Painted Doll 3.00
31 AMo(s),JWi. 3.00
32 AMo(s),JWi, final issue 4.00
32a variant edition, on posters,
    plus signed book 50.00
TPB Promethea Book One 15.00
TPB Promethea Book Two 15.00
TPB Promethea Book Three 15.00
TPB Vol. 4 . . . . 15.00
TPB Vol. 5 . . . . 15.00

PROPHECY
Immortelle Studios, 1998
1 by Hawk, Lovalle, & Wong,
    F:Cynder & War Dragon 3.00
2 . . . . 3.00

PROPHECY OF THE SOUL SORCERER
Arcane Comics, 1999
1 (of 4) by Eric Dean Seaton 3.00
2 . . . . 3.00
3 . . . . 3.00
3a variant (c). 3.00
4 . . . . 3.00
4a variant (c). 3.00
5 . . . . 3.00
5a variant (c). 3.00
6 Nighthawk vs. Morbid 3.00
6a variant (c). 3.00
7 . . . . 3.00
TPB Vol. 1 . . . . 11.00

PROPHET II
Awesome Entertainment, 1999
1 . . . . 3.00
1a holochrome wraparound (c). . . 15.00
TPB Timetrap 13.00

PROPHET: LEGACY
Awesome Entertainment, 1999
1 RLe 3.00
2 . . . . 3.00
2a variant (c). 3.00
3 . . . . 3.00

PROPHET/CABLE
Maximum, 1997
1 (of 2) RLd x-over 3.50
2 RLd x-over,A:Domino, Kirby,
    Blaquesmith. 3.50

PROPHET OF DREAMS
Broken Tree Publications, 2002
1 (of 6) by Lawler & Vasquez 3.50
2 thru 6 . . . . @3.00

Protectors #13
© *Malibu*

PROTECTORS
Malibu, 1992–94
1 I:Protectors, inc. JBi poster
    (direct) 3.00
1a thru 12a Newsstand . . . . @2.00
2 thru 20 . . . . @2.50
Protectors Handbook 2.50

PROTOTYPE
Malibu Ultraverse, 1993–95
1 V:Ultra-Tech,w/card 2.50

1a Ultra-lim. silver foil(c). 5.00
1b Hologram 6.00
2 thru 18 . . . . @2.50
G-Size, Hostile Takeover 2.50
Spec.#0 LeS,JQ/JP(c) 2.50

PROTOTYPE: TURF WAR
Malibu Ultraverse,
1 LeS,V:Techuza. 2.50
2 LeS,F:Ranger,Arena 2.50
3 . . . . 2.50

PROWLER
Eclipse, 1987
1 I:Prowler. 2.50
2 GN,A:Original Prowler 2.50
3 GN 2.50
4 GN 2.50
5 GN, adaption of Vampire Bat. . . . 2.50
6 w/flexi-disk record 2.50

PROWLER IN `WHITE ZOMBIE', THE
Eclipse, 1988
1 . . . . 2.50

PRUDENCE & CAUTION
Defiant, 1994
1 CCI(s), ... 4.00
2 CCI(s), ... 2.50
3 CCI(s), ... 2.50
4 CCI(s), ... 2.50
5 CCI(s), ... 2.50
1a Spanish Version 3.25
2a thru 5a Spanish Version . . . . . @2.50

PSI-LORDS: REIGN OF THE STARWATCHERS
Valiant, 1994
1 MLe,DG,Chromium(c),Valiant
    Vision,V:Spider Aliens 3.00
2 MLe,DG,V:Spider Aliens 2.50
3 MLe,DG,Chaos Effect-Epsilon#2,
    A:Solar 2.50
becomes:

PSI-LORDS
4 V:Ravenrok 2.50
5 V:Ravenrok 2.50
6 . . . . 2.50
7 Micro-Invasion 2.50
8 A:Solar the Destroyer 2.50
9 Frozen Harbingers 2.50
10 F:Ravenrok 2.50

PSYCHO
Innovation
1 Hitchcock movie adapt 2.50
2 & 3 continued . . . . @2.50

PSYCHOANALYSIS
Gemstone, 1999
1 (of 4) 2.50
2 thru 3 . . . . @2.50
TPB Ann. #1 . . . . 11.00

PSYCHOBLAST
First, 1987
1 thru 9 . . . . @2.50

PUBLIC ENEMY
American Mule Entertainment, 2006
0 . . . . 3.00
1 . . . . 4.00

COLOR PUB.

All comics prices listed are for *Near Mint* condition.

PUDGY PIG
Charlton Comics, 1958
1 . . . . 125.00
2 . . . . 100.00

PUNCTURE
Com.X, 2001
1 (of 12) by R. Uttley & B.Oliver . . . 3.00
2 thru 4 . . . . @3.00
3 thru 6 . . . . @4.00

PUNX
Windjammer, 1995
1 KG,I:Punx 2.50
2 KG,A:Harbinger. 2.50
3 KG,F:P.M.S 2.50
4 KG,final issue 2.50
Spec.#1 . . . . 2.50

PUNX
Acclaim, 1997
One Shot Spec. F:Big Max 2.50

PUPPET MASTER
Eternity
1 Movie Adapt.Andre Toulon. 2.50
2 Puppets Protecting Diary. 2.50
3 R:Andre Toulon 2.50
4 . . . . 2.50

PUPPET MASTER: CHILDREN OF THE PUPPET MASTER
Eternity
1 Killer Puppets on the loose 2.50
2 concl. 2.50

PURGATORI
Chaos! Comics, 1998
1 DQ from slave to Goddess? 3.00
2 Goddess War,pt.1, x-over 3.00
3 Goddess War, epilog 3.00
4 Unholy Nights 3.00
5 V:Karmilla. 3.00
6 . . . . 3.00
7 V:Dracula 3.00
1-shot prelude 3.00
1-shot signed, limited + print 15.00
Coll. Vol. 1 thru Vol. 4 . . . . @6.00

PURGATORI
Chaos! Comics, 2000
1/2 . . . . 3.00
1/2 premium edition, tattoo(c). . . . 10.00
1/2 chromium (c). 15.00
1/2 chromium signed 21.00
1/2 Ashcan 7.00
0 . . . . 3.00
0 premium edition 10.00
0 Ashcan. 7.00

PURGATORI
Devil's Due Publishing, 2005
1 . . . . 3.00
2 thru 6 . . . . @3.00

PURGATORI: DARKEST HOUR
Chaos! Comics, 2001
1 . . . . 3.00
1a premium ed. RCl(c) 10.00
2 . . . . 3.00
2a variant (c). 7.50

PURGATORI: THE DRACULA GAMBIT
Chaos! Comics, 1997
1 DQ & Brian LeBlanc 3.00
1a signed 20.00
1b premium. 10.00
Sketchbook, b&w 3.50

PURGATORI: EMPIRE
Chaos! Comics, 2000
1 (of 3) 3.00
1a premium 10.00
1b Comic Legal Defense
 Fund ed. 10.00
2 thru 3 . . . . @3.00
Preview Book B&W 5.00

PURGATORI: GODDESS RISING
Chaos! Comics, 1999
1 (of 4) MD2 . . . . 3.00
1a premium edition 10.00
2 thru 4 . . . . @3.00
Preview Book B&W 5.00

PURGATORI: GOD HUNTER
Chaos! Comics, 2002
Ashcan b&w. 6.00
1 (of 2) 3.00
1a premium edition 10.00
2 . . . . 3.00
2a variant Rio & Broeker (c). 7.50

PURGATORI: GOD KILLER
Chaos! Comics, 2002
1 (of 2) 3.00
1a premium edition 10.00
2 . . . . 3.00
2a variant (c). 7.50

PURGATORI: HEART-BREAKER
Chaos! Comics, 2002
1 . . . . 3.00
1a premium edition 10.00
1b super premium edition 20.00
1c MegaCon foil edition 25.00

PURGATORI: LOVE BITES
Chaos! Comics, 2001
1 . . . . 3.00
1 premium edition 10.00
Ashcan. 6.00

PURGATORI: MISCHIEF NIGHT
Chaos! Comics, 2001
1 . . . . 3.00
1a premium edition 13.00
1b super premium edition 20.00

PURGATORI: THE HUNTED
Chaos! Comics, 2001
1 . . . . 3.00
1a premium edition 10.00
2 . . . . 3.00
2a variant (c). 7.50
Ashcan 6.00

PURGATORI: RAVENOUS
Chaos! Comics, 2002
Ashcan b&w. 6.00

1 (of 2) 3.00
1a premium edition 10.00

PURGATORI: RE-IMAGINED
Chaos! Comics, 2002
1 Salem witch trials. 3.00
1a premium edition 10.00
1b super premium edition 20.00
Ashcan Purgatori re-imagined 6.00

PURGATORI: SANCTIFIED
Chaos! Comics, 2002
1 BnP 3.00
1 premium edition 10.00

PURGATORI: TRICK OR TREAT
Chaos! Comics, 2002
1 . . . . 3.00
1a premium edition 10.00
1b super premium edition 20.00

PURGATORI: THE VAMPIRES MYTH
Chaos! Comics, 1996
1 (of 3) 4.00
1-shot limited chromium edition . . 20.00
2 BnP,JBa. 3.00
3 BnP,JBa, final issue. 3.00
TPB with CD 25.00
TPB 13.00
Micro Premium Preview Book 15.00

PURGATORI VS. CHASTITY
Chaos! Comics, 2000
1 Alpha ending 3.00
1a Omega ending 3.00
1b deluxe 12.00

PURGATORI VS. LADY DEATH
Chaos! Comics, 2000
1 . . . . 3.00
1a premium edition 10.00
Ashcan B&W 7.00

Quantum & Woody #1
© Acclaim

All comics prices listed are for *Near Mint* condition.

PURGATORI VS. VAMPIRELLA
Chaos! Comics, 2000
1	3.00
1 premium	10.00

QUANTUM & WOODY
Acclaim, 1997
1 CPr(s),MBr Woodrow Van Chelton & Eric Henderson become unlikely superheros	4.00
1a Variant (c)	5.00
2 CPr(s),MBr,World's worst superhero team	3.00
3 CPr(s),MBr,Woody buys a goat	3.00
4 CPr(s),MBr.	3.00
5 thru 10 CPr(s)	@2.75
11 thru 17 CPr(s)	@2.50
18 thru 27	@2.50
TPB Director's Cut, rep.#1–#4.	8.00
TPB Kiss Your Ass Goodbye	8.00
TPB Holy S-word We're Cancelled	8.00
TPB Magnum Force.	8.00

QUANTUM LEAP
Innovation, 1991
{based on TV series}
1 1968 Memphis	3.50
1a Special Edition	2.50
2 Ohio 1962,Freedom of the Press	3.00
3 1958, The $50,000 Quest	3.00
4 Small Miracles	2.50
5	2.50
6	2.50
7 Golf Pro,School Bus Driver	2.50
8 1958,Bank Robber.	2.50
9 NY 1969,Gay Rights	2.50
10 1960s' Stand-up Comic.	2.50
11 1959,Dr.(LSD experiments).	2.50
12	2.50

QUANTUM LEAP
Acclaim, 1997
1 BML(s),Into the Void, pt.1	2.50
2 BML(s),Into the Void, pt.2	2.50
3 BML(s),Into the Void, pt.3	2.50
Spec. The Leaper Before	4.00

QUEEN OF THE DAMNED
Innovation, 1991
1 Anne Rice Adapt.On the Road to the Vampire Lestat	3.50
2 Adapt. continued	2.50
3 The Devils Minion	2.50
4 Adapt.continued	2.50
5 Adapt.continued	2.50
6 Adapt.continued	2.50
7 Adapt.continued	2.50
8 Adapt.continued	2.50

QUICK-DRAW McGRAW
Charlton Comics, 1970–72
1 TV Animated Cartoon	125.00
2	75.00
3	75.00
4 thru 8	@75.00

Q-UNIT
Harris
1 I:Q-Unit,w/card.	3.25

RACE AGAINST TIME
Dark Ange., 1997
1	2.50
2	2.50

RACE FOR THE MOON
Harvey Publications, 1958
1 BP	350.00
2 JK,AW,JK/AW(c)	500.00
3 JK,AW,JK/AW(c)	600.00

RACER-X
Premiere
Spec.#1	5.00

Now, 1988
1 thru 3	@2.50
4 thru 11	@2.50

[2nd Series], 1989
1 thru 10	@2.50

Racer-X #3
© Wildstorm

RACER X
WildStorm/DC, 2000
1 (of 3) Rex Racer's secrets	2.50
1a varlant (c) (1:4)	2.50
2 racing thrills	2.50
3 conclusion	3.00

RACK & PAIN: KILLERS
Chaos! Comics, 1996
1 (of 4) JaL(c)	3.00
2 BnP,LJi,JaL(c)	3.00
3 (of 4) BnP,LJi,	3.00
4 BnP,LJi, final issue	3.00

RADICAL DREAMER
Blackball, 1994
0	2.50
1 thru 5 V:Jorge Futran	@2.50

RADIOACTIVE MAN
Bongo, 1993
1 I:Radioactive Man	4.00
1 80pg offered again	3.25
88 V:Lava Man.	2.50
212 V:Hypno Head.	2.50
412 V:Dr. Crab, with trading card	2.50
679 with trading card	2.50
1000 Final issue	2.50

RADIOACTIVE MAN
Bongo Comics, 2000
100	2.50
136	2.50
222	2.50
4	2.50
575 new Radioactive Man born	2.50

106 new Radioactive Man insane	2.50
7	2.50
8 Official Movie Adaptation	3.00
199	3.00
Spec. Movie Adaptation	3.00

RAI
Valiant, 1991
0 DL,O:Bloodshot,I:2nd Rai,D:X-O, Archer,Shadowman,F:all Valiant heroes,bridges Valiant Universe 1992-4001	7.00
1 V:Grandmother	10.00
2 V:Icespike	12.00
3 V:Humanists,Makiko	24.00
4 V:Makiko,rarest Valiant	12.00
5 Rai leaves earth, C:Eternal Warrior.	9.00
6 FM(c),Unity#7,V:Pierce	5.00
7 WS(c),Unity#15,V:Pierce, D:Rai,A:Magnus	5.00
8 Epilogue of Unity in 4001	5.00
Becomes:	

RAI AND THE FUTURE FORCE
Valiant, 1993
9 F:Rai,E.Warrior of 4001,Tekla, X-O Commander,Spylocke	5.00
9a Gold Ed.	15.00
10 thru 26	@3.00
Becomes:	

RAI
Valiant, 1994
27 thru 33	@3.00
TPB #0-#4	12.00
TPB Star System ed.	12.00

RAKAN
Studio G, 2003
1	3.00
2 Den of Thieves	3.00
3	3.00
4	3.00

RAKAN
AK Entertainment, 2006
1 Sabretooth	3.00
2 Chessmaster	3.00
3 The Sword of Majido	3.00
4 The Devil's Axe	3.00
5 Den of Thieves, pt.1	3.00
6 Den of Thieves, pt. 2	3.00
7	3.00

RALPH SNART ADVENTURES
Now
[Volumes 1 & 2]
see B&W
9 and 10, color	2.50

[Volume 3], 1988
1	4.00
2 thru 10	@3.00
11 thru 21	@2.50
22 thru 26	@2.50
TPB	10.00

[Volume 4], 1992
1 thru 3, with 1 of 2 trading cards.	2.50

[Volume 5], 1993
1 thru 5, with 1 of 2 trading cards.	2.50
3-D Spec.#1 with 3-D glasses and 12 trading cards.	3.50
TPB Let's Get Naked (2003)	25.00
TPB Vol. 2 Let's Be Good Citizens	25.00

Now Comics, 2003

TPB Let's Get Naked	25.00
TPB Vol. 2 Let's Be Good Citizens	25.00
TPB Vol. 6 (2004)	15.00

RAMAYAN REBORN
Virgin Comics, 2006

1	3.00
2 thru 3	@3.00

RANDOM ENCOUNTER
Viper Comics

1 (of 4)	3.00
2 thru 4	@3.00

RANDOM 5
Amara Inc., 1995

1 I:Random 5	2.50

RANGO
Dell Publishing Co., 1967

1 Tim Conway Ph(c)	60.00

RANMA 1/2
Viz, 1992

1 I:Ranma	50.00
2 I:Upperclassmen Kuno	30.00
3 F:Upperclassmen Kuno	25.00
4 Confusion	5.00
5 A:Ryoga	5.00
6 Ryoga plots revenge	9.00
7 Conclusion	5.00

[Part 2], 1992

1	8.00
2	5.00
3 thru 7	@4.00
8	5.00
9	6.00
10 and 11	@3.00
continued, see B&W Pub.	

RAPHAEL
Mirage, 1987

1 TMNTurtle characters	8.00

RARE BREED
Dark Moon Productions, 1995

1 V:Anarchy	2.50
2 V:Anarchy	2.50

Raven #3
© Renaissance Comics

RASH
Narwain Publishing, 2005

1	4.00
2	4.00

RAT BASTARD
Crucial Comics, 1997

1 by The Huja Brothers	2.50
2 thru 6	@2.50

RAT PATROL, THE
Dell Publishing Co., 1967

1 Ph(c)	150.00
2	100.00
3 thru 6 Ph(c)	@75.00

RAVEN
Renaissance Comics, 1993

1 I:Raven	2.50
2 V:Macallister	2.50
3	2.50
4	2.50
5	2.50
6 V:Nightmare Creatures	2.75

RAVEN HOUSE
Crossgen Comics, 2004

1	3.00
2	3.00

RAVENING
Avatar, 1998

1/2 Busch (c) F:Ravyn & Glyph	3.00
1/2a Meadows(c)	3.00
1/2d Sketched Edition	50.00
1/2e Blood Red Foil, signed	9.00

RAVENS AND RAINBOWS
Pacific, 1983

1	2.50

RAVER
Malibu, 1993

1 Prism cover	3.00
1a Newsstand	2.50
2	2.50
3 Walter Koenig(s)	2.50
4	2.00
5	2.00

RAY BRADBURY CHRONICLES
Byron Press

1 short stories	10.00
2 short stories	10.00
3 short stories	10.00

RAY BRADBURY COMICS
Topps, 1993–94

1 thru 5 with Trading Card	@3.25
Spec.#1 The Illustrated Man	3.00
Spec. Trilogy of Terror	2.50
Spec. The Martian Chronicles	3.00

RAYMOND E. FEIST'S MAGICIAN: APPRENTICE
Dabel Brothers Prod., 2006

1 (of 6)	3.00
1a variant Don Maitz (c)	6.00
2 thru 6	@3.00
2a thru 6a variant (c)s	@6.00

RAZOR
London Night Studios, 1992

0	9.00
0a 2nd printing (Fathom 1992)	4.00
0b reprint (1995)	3.00
1 I:Stryke (Fathom 1992)	9.00
1a second printing	3.00
2 J.O'Barr (c)	10.00
2a limited ed., red & blue	19.00
2b platinum ed.	20.00
3 Jim Balent (c).	7.00
3a with poster	15.00
4	4.00
4a with poster	9.00
5	7.00
5a platinum ed.	15.00
6	5.00
7	4.00
8 thru 10	@3.00
11 & 12 B&W, Rituals,pt.1&2	@3.00
1/2 (1995).	5.00
Ann.#1 I:Shi (1993)	25.00
Ann.#2 O:Razor B&W (1994)	35.00

Becomes:

RAZOR UNCUT
See: B&W Section

RAZOR
Volume 2
London Knight, 1996

1 DQ,	3.00
1a holochrome edition	5.00
2 DQ	3.00
2a holochrome edition	4.00
3 thru 7	@3.00
Razor Analog Burn	2.50

RAZOR AND SHI SPECIAL
London Night Studios, 1994

1 Rep. Razor Ann.#1 + new art	5.00
1a platinum version	9.00

RAZOR ARCHIVES
London Night, 1997

1 & 2 see B&W	
3 rep. Razor #10–12	7.00

RAZOR BURN
London Night Studios, 1994

1 V:Styke	3.00
1a signed	5.00
2 Searching for Styke	3.00
2a Platinum	7.00
3 Stryke's War	3.00
4 D:Razor, bagged	3.00
5 Epilogue	3.00

RAZOR: CRY NO MORE
London Night Studios, 1995

1-shot	3.00
1a variant	4.00
1b Commemorative (1999)	6.00

RAZOR: HEX & VIOLENCE
EH! Productions, 2000

0 EHr.	3.00

RAZOR/MORBID ANGEL: SOUL SEARCH
London Night, 1996

1 (of 3)	3.00
1 platinum edition	5.00
1 Chromium edition.	7.00
2	3.00
3	3.00

RAZOR/POISON/ AREALA WARRIOR NUN: LITTLE BAD ANGELS
London Night, 1999
Spec. x-over Razor cover 4.00
Spec.A Poison cover 4.00
Spec.B Areala cover 4.00

RAZOR THE RAVENING
Avatar
1 . . . . 3.50
1a Previews cover 3.50
1b Bondage cover 6.00

RAZOR'S EDGE, THE: REDBIRD
Wildstorm/DC, March, 2005
1 (of 5) JPn 3.00
2 JPn 3.00
3 JPn 3.00

RAZOR'S EDGE, THE: WARBLADE
Wildstorm/DC, 2004
1 SBs 3.00
2 SBs 3.00
3 SBs 3.00
4 SBs 3.00
5 SBs 3.00

RAZOR: THE SUFFERING
London Night Studios, 1994
1 . . . . 4.00
1a Director's cut 3.00
1b signed, limited 9.00
2 . . . . 3.00
2a Director's cut 2.50
3 final chapter 3.00

Razor Torture #5
© London Night Studios

RAZOR: TORTURE
London Night Studios, 1995
0 Razor back from dead 4.00
0a signed edition 7.00
1 . . . . 3.00
1a Commemorative (1999) 6.00
2 . . . . 3.00
3 EHr 3.00
4 . . . . 3.00
5& 6 alt. cover, signed . . . . @4.00
7 . . . . 3.00

RAZOR SWIMSUIT SPECIAL
London Night Studios, 1995
1 pin-ups 3.00
1a platinum version 7.00
1b commemorative edition 4.00

RAZOR/WARRIOR NUN AREALA: DARK MENACE
London Night, 1999
Spec. x-over 4.00
Spec.A x-over, variant cover 4.00

RAZOR/WARRIOR NUN AREALA: FAITH
London Night, 1996
1 by Jude Millien 3.00
1a variant cover 4.00

REAL GHOSTBUSTERS
Now, 1988
1 KSy(c) 4.50
2 thru 7 . . . . @2.50
8 thru 24 . . . . @2.00
[2nd Series], 1991
1 Halloween Special 2.50
Ann. 3-D w/glasses & pinups 3.00

REAL GHOSTBUSTERS
Titan Publishing, 2005
TPB Vol. 1 A Hard Day's Fright 9.00
TPB Vol. 2 Who You Gonna Call . . . 9.00
TPB Vol. 3 Which Witch is Which? . 9.00
TPB Vol. 4 This Ghost is Toast 9.00

[Super Information Hijinks:] REALITY CHECK!
Sirius, 1996
1 by Tavisha Wolfgarth 3.00
2 Surfing the Internet 3.00
3 E is for Europa 3.00
4 thru 8 . . . . @3.00
9 Nonesuch Nonsense, pt.1 . . . . . 3.00
10 Nonesuch Nonsense, pt.2 . . . . 3.00
11 Nonesuch Nonsense, pt.3 . . . . 3.00
12 Nonesuch Nonsense, pt.4 . . . . 3.00
TPB Vol. 1, rep #1–#6 . . . . 18.00
TPB Vol. 2, rep.#7–#12 . . . . 18.00

REAL WAR STORIES
Eclipse, 1987–91
1 BB 3.00
1a 2nd printing 2.50
2 . . . . 5.00

RE-ANIMATOR
Adventure Comics, 1991
1 movie adaption 3.00
2 movie adaption 3.00

RE-ANIMATOR
Adventure
1 Prequel to Orig movie 2.50

RE-ANIMATOR: DAWN OF THE RE-ANIMATOR
Adventure, 1992
1 Prequel to movie 2.50
2 . . . . 2.50
3 . . . . 2.50
4 V:Erich Metler 2.50

RE-ANIMATOR: TALES OF HERBERT WEST
Adventure Comics
1 H.P.Lovecraft stories 5.00

RED
DC Wildstorm July, 2003
America's Best Comics
1 (of 3) WEI,CHm 3.00
2 WEI,CHm 3.00
3 WEI,CHm 3.00
TPB Red/Tokyo Storm Warning . . . 15.00

RED DOG
Eclipse, 1988
1 CR,Mowgli Jungle Book story . . . 2.50

RED DRAGON
Comico, 1995
1 SBs,I:Red Dragon 2.50
2 How Soon is Nau? 3.00

REDEEMER, THE
Black Library, 2002
1 . . . . 3.50
2 thru 4 . . . . @3.50

REDEEMERS
Antarctic Press, 1997
1 (of 5) by Herb Mallette
   & Patrick Blain 3.00
2 . . . . 3.00

RED MENACE
Wildstorm/DC, Nov., 2006
1 (of 6) JOy,AV 3.00
1a variant (c) 3.00

RED PROPHET: TALES OF ALVIN MAKER
Dabel Brothers Productions, 2006
1 (of 6) 3.00
1a variant (c) 6.00
2 thru 3 . . . . @3.00
2a thru 3a variant (c)s . . . . @6.00

RED SONJA in 3-D
Blackthorne
1 thru 3 . . . . @2.50

RED SONJA
Cross Plains Comics, 1999
1 Death in Scarlet,pt.1 . . . . 3.00
1a photo (c) 3.00
2 Death in Scarlet,pt.2 . . . . 3.00
3 Death in Scarlet,pt.3 . . . . 3.00

RED SONJA
D.E. (Dynamite Entertain.), 2005
0 . . . . 1.00
1 . . . . 3.00
1a thru 1e variant (c)s . . . . @3.00
2 thru 7 . . . . @3.00
8 Arrowsmith 3.00
9 Arrowsmith 3.00
10 Arrowsmith 3.00
11 Arrowsmith 3.00
12 Return of Kulan
   Gath, pt. 1, JLe(c) 3.00
13 Return of Kulan Gath, pt. 2 . . . . 3.00
14 Return of Kulan Gath, pt. 3 . . . . 3.00
15 Return of Kulan Gath, pt. 4 . . . . 3.00
16 Return of Kulan Gath, pt. 5 . . . . 3.00
17 Return of Kulan Gath 3.00

2a thru 17a variant (c)s . . . . @3.00
2b thru 17b Fiery red Foil editions 20.00
1-shot Red Sonja Goes East. 5.00
1-shot Red Sonja Goes East
  power foil (c) 15.00
1-shot One More Day 5.00
1-shot Monster Isle 5.00
1-shot Monster Isle variant (c) 5.00
1-shot Red Sonja/Claw 5.00
TPB #1 Adventures of Red Sonja . 20.00
TPB #2 Adventures of Red Sonja . 20.00
TPB Vol. 2 variant (c) 20.00

RED SONJA/CLAW
THE UNCONQUERED:
DEVIL'S HANDS
Wildstorm/DC, March, 2006

1 (of 4) ASm 3.00
1a variant JLe (c) 3.00
2 ASm 3.00
2a variant JLe (c) 3.00
3 ASm, Imprisoned 3.00
3a variant JLe (c) 3.00
4 ASm, Claw embraces evil. 3.00
4a variant JLe(c). 3.00

RED SONJA
VS. THULSA DOOM
D.E. (Dynamite Ent.) 2001

1 (of 4) 3.50
2 . . . . 3.50
3 . . . . 3.50
4 . . . . 3.50
1a thru 3a variant (c) . . . . @3.50
1b thru 2b Fiery red Foil editions . 20.00
TPB 15.00

RED STAR, THE
Archangel Studios, 2002
Vol. 2

2 . . . . 3.00
3 thru 6 . . . . @3.00
4 . . . . 3.00
Annual #1 foil (c) signed 10.00
Spec. Red Star: Sword of Lies. . . . 4.50
TPB Red Star Collected Edition. . . 25.00
TPB Vol. 1 Battle of Kar
  Dathras Gate. 25.00
TPB Vol. 2 Nokgorka 25.00
TPB Vol. 3 Prison of Souls 25.00

REESE'S PIECES
Eclipse, 1985

1 reprint from Web of Horror 2.50
2 reprint from Web of Horror 2.50

RE: GEX
Awesome Entertainment, 1998

0 RLe, ... 2.50
0a Red Foil variant 4.00
1 RLe,JLb 2.50
1a Platinum cover 7.00
1b Red Foil cover 12.00
1c Variant RL cover 4.00
1d prime 3.00
1e prime millennium ed. 5.00
2 RLe,JLb 2.50
2a prime 3.00
2b Millennium edition 5.00
3 RLe,A:The Coven,V:Youngblood . 2.50
Con Spec. '98 . . . . 5.00
Orlando Megacon ashcan 10.00
Orlando Megacon ashcan, signed. 20.00

Arcade Comics, 2002

Ashcan #1, Museum Edition 60.00
Ashcan #1, Museum Ed., signed. . 80.00

REGGIE
Archie Publications, 1963–65

15 thru 18 . . . . @100.00
Becomes:

REGGIE AND ME
Archie Publications, 1966–80

19 . . . . 75.00
20 thru 23 . . . . @50.00
24 thru 40 . . . . @35.00
41 thru 50 . . . . @25.00
51 thru 99 . . . . @20.00
100 . . . . 25.00
101 thru 126 . . . . @15.00

REGGIE'S WISE
GUY JOKES
Archie Publications, April, 1968

1 . . . . 100.00
2 . . . . 50.00
3 . . . . 50.00
4 . . . . 50.00
5 thru 15 Giants . . . . @50.00
16 thru 28 Giants . . . . @35.00
29 thru 40 . . . . @25.00
41 thru 60 . . . . @20.00
11 thru 59 . . . . @15.00
60 Jan., 1982. . . . . 15.00

RELOAD
DC Homage, 2003

1 (of 3) WEI,JP 3.00
2 WEI,JP. 3.00
3 WEI,JP, concl. 3.00
TPB Reload/Mek 15.00

REMAINS
IDW Publishing, 2004

1 . . . . 4.00
2 thru 5 . . . . @4.00
TPB 20.00

REPTILICUS
Charlton Comics, 1961

1 . . . . 400.00
2 . . . . 250.00
Becomes:

REPTISAURUS
1962

3 . . . . 175.00
4 . . . . 150.00
5 . . . . 150.00

Reptisaurus
© *Charlton*

6 . . . . 150.00
7 . . . . 150.00
8 Summer, 1963 . . . . 150.00

RESIDENT EVIL:
FIRE & ICE
WildStorm/DC, 2000

1 (of 4) from videogame 2.50
2 . . . . 2.50
3 . . . . 2.50
4 concl. 2.50
TPB Codename Veronica, Vol. 1 . . 15.00
TPB Codename Veronica, Vol. 3 . . 15.00
TPB Code Veronica, Vol. 4 . . . . . 15.00

RESISTANCE, THE
WildStorm/DC, 2002

1 JP(s),techno sci-fi 3.00
2 JP(s) 3.00
3 JP(s) 3.00
4 JP(s) 3.00
5 JP(s),V:Sampizi 3.00
6 JP(s),V:Sampizi & GCC 3.00
7 JP(s),F:Version Mary 3.00
8 JP(s),F:Version Mary 3.00

RETURN OF KONGA, THE
Charlton Comics, 1962

N# 150.00

RETURN OF
MEGATON MAN
Kitchen Sink, 1988

1 Don Simpson art (1988) 2.50
2 Don Simpson art 2.50
3 Don Simpson art 2.50

RETURN TO
JURASSIC PARK
Topps, 1995

1 R:Jurassic Park 3.00
2 V:Blosyn Team, Army. 3.00
3 The Hunted 3.00
4 Army. 3.00
5 Heirs to the Thunder,pt.1 . . . . . . 3.00
6 Heirs to the Thunder,pt.2 . . . . . . 3.00
7 Inquiring Minds,pt.1 . . . . 3.00
8 Photo Finish, concl. 3.00
9 Jurassic Jam issue 3.00

REVENGE OF
THE PROWLER
Eclipse, 1988

1 GN,R:Prowler. 2.50
2 GN,A:Fighting Devil Dogs with
  Flexi-Disk. 2.50
3 GN,A:Devil Dogs 2.50
4 GN,V:Pirahna. 2.50

REVENGERS
Continuity, 1985

1 NA,O:Megalith,I:Crazyman 4.00
2 NA,Megalith meets Armor & Silver
Streak,Origin Revengers#1 . . . . 2.50
3 NA/NR,Origin Revengers #2 . . . . 2.50
4 NA,Origin Revengers #3 . . . . 2.50
5 NA,Origin Revengers #4 . . . . 2.50
6 I:Hybrids. 3.00
Spec. #1 F:Hybrids. 5.00

REVERE
Alias Enterprises, 2006

1 (of 4) 3.50
2 . . . . 3.50
3 . . . . 3.50
4 . . . . 3.50

REVOLUTION ON THE PLANET OF THE APES
MR Comics, 2005
1 (of 6) 4.00
2 thru 6 . . . . @4.00

RIBIT
Comico
thru 4 FT,Mini-series . . . . @3.00

RICHIE RICH
Harvey Publications, 1960–91
1 Inc.Casper,Little Dot 8,000.00
2 Inc. Little Dot, Little Lotta . . . 1,500.00
3 Inc. Little Dot, Little Lotta . . . 1,000.00
4 Inc. Little Dot, Little Lotta . . . 1,000.00
5 . . . . 1,000.00
6 . . . . 750.00
7 . . . . 750.00
8 Christmas(c) 750.00
9 . . . . 750.00
10 . . . . 750.00
11 thru 20 . . . . @800.00
21 thru 41 . . . . @800.00
42 Flying Saucer 800.00
43 thru 55 . . . . @500.00
56 Super Richie 250.00
57 . . . . 200.00
58 . . . . 200.00
59 Buck 250.00
60 thru 80 . . . . @200.00
81 thru 99 . . . . @80.00
100 Irona-Robot Maid 100.00
101 thru 111 . . . . @50.00
112 thru 116 52 pg Giants . . . . . @60.00
117 thru 120 . . . . @50.00
121 thru 136 . . . . @40.00
137 Mr. Cheepers 40.00
138 thru 160 . . . . @30.00
161 thru 180 . . . . @25.00
181 thru 236 . . . . @20.00
237 Money Monster 20.00
238 thru 254 . . . . @15.00

RICHIE RICH
Harvey, 1991
1 thru 15 . . . . @3.00
16 thru 28 . . . . @3.00

RICHIE RICH BANK BOOKS
Harvey, 1972–82
1 . . . . 75.00
2 Money Monster 55.00
3 thru 5 . . . . @50.00
6 thru 10 . . . . @35.00
11 thru 20 . . . . @25.00
21 thru 30 . . . . @15.00
31 thru 40 . . . . @10.00
41 thru 59 . . . . @8.00

RICHIE RICH BILLIONS
Harvey, 1974–82
1 . . . . 50.00
2 thru 5 . . . . @30.00
6 thru 10 . . . . @25.00
11 thru 20 . . . . @15.00
21 thru 30 . . . . @10.00
31 thru 48 . . . . @8.00

RICHIE RICH DIAMONDS
Harvey, 1972–82
1 . . . . 75.00
2 thru 5 . . . . @35.00

Richie Rich Bank Books #24
© Harvey

6 thru 10 . . . . @30.00
11 thru 20 . . . . @25.00
21 thru 30 . . . . @12.00
31 thru 59 . . . . @10.00

RICHIE RICH DOLLARS & CENTS
Harvey Publications, 1963–82
1 . . . . 900.00
2 . . . . 250.00
3 thru 5 . . . . @150.00
6 thru 10 . . . . @100.00
11 thru 24 . . . . @70.00
25 Nurse Jenny 75.00
26 thru 30 . . . . @60.00
31 thru 43 . . . . @50.00
44 thru 60 . . . . @40.00
61 thru 70 . . . . @30.00
71 thru 99 . . . . @20.00
100 Anniversary 25.00
102 thru 109 . . . . @20.00

RICHIE RICH FORTUNES
Harvey, 1971–82
1 . . . . 75.00
2 thru 5 . . . . @50.00
6 thru 10 . . . . @40.00
11 Orion 25.00
12 thru 20 . . . . @20.00
21 thru 30 . . . . @10.00
31 thru 63 . . . . @8.00

RICHIE RICH GEMS
Harvey, 1974–82
1 . . . . 50.00
2 thru 5 . . . . @30.00
6 thru 10 . . . . @25.00
11 thru 20 . . . . @20.00
21 thru 30 . . . . @10.00
31 thru 35 . . . . @8.00
36 Orion 10.00
37 . . . . 8.00
38 Stone-Age Riches 10.00
39 thru 43 . . . . @8.00

RICHIE RICH GOLD AND SILVER
Harvey, 1975–82
1 . . . . 50.00

2 thru 5 . . . . @30.00
6 thru 10 . . . . @25.00
11 thru 20 . . . . @20.00
21 thru 30 . . . . @10.00
31 thru 33 . . . . @8.00
34 Stone-Age Riches 10.00
35 thru 42 . . . . @8.00

RICHIE RICH JACKPOTS
Harvey, 1974–82
1 . . . . 75.00
2 thru 5 . . . . @50.00
6 thru 15 . . . . @30.00
16 Super Richie 32.00
17 thru 20 . . . . @25.00
21 thru 30 . . . . @12.00
31 thru 58 . . . . @10.00

RICHIE RICH MILLIONS
Harvey Publications, 1961–82
1 . . . . 900.00
2 . . . . 350.00
3 thru 10 . . . . @300.00
11 thru 20 . . . . @200.00
21 thru 30 . . . . @150.00
31 Orion, giant 80.00
32 thru 60 . . . . @70.00
61 thru 67 . . . . @50.00
68 Super Richie 50.00
69 thru 74 . . . . @40.00
75 thru 94 . . . . @35.00
95 thru 113 . . . . @25.00

RICHIE RICH MONEY WORLD
Harvey, 1972–82
1 Mayda Monny 85.00
2 Super Richie 60.00
3 thru 5 . . . . @50.00
6 thru 10 . . . . @35.00
11 thru 20 . . . . @18.00
21 thru 30 . . . . @10.00
31 thru 59 . . . . @8.00

RICHIE RICH PROFITS
Harvey, 1974–82
1 . . . . 60.00
2 thru 5 . . . . @30.00
6 thru 10 . . . . @25.00
11 thru 20 . . . . @20.00
21 thru 30 . . . . @10.00
31 thru 47 . . . . @8.00

RICHIE RICH RICHES
Harvey, 1972–82
1 Money Monster 90.00
2 thru 5 . . . . @50.00
6 thru 10 . . . . @30.00
11 thru 16 . . . . @20.00
17 Super Richie 22.00
18 thru 30 . . . . @15.00
31 thru 59 . . . . @10.00

RICHIE RICH SUCCESS STORIES
Harvey Publications, 1964–82
1 . . . . 1,500.00
2 thru 5 . . . . @500.00
6 thru 10 . . . . @250.00
11 thru 26 . . . . @225.00
27 Penny Van Dough 200.00
28 thru 43 . . . . @125.00
44 Super Richie 75.00
45 thru 55 . . . . @75.00

56 thru 66	@50.00
67 thru 105	@30.00

RICHIE RICH
VAULT OF MYSTERY
Harvey, 1974–82

1	50.00
2 thru 5	@30.00
6 thru 10	@15.00
11 thru 20	@10.00
21 thru 30	@10.00
31 thru 47	@10.00

RICHIE RICH
ZILLIONZ
Harvey, 1976–82

1	35.00
2 thru 5	@20.00
6 thru 10	@15.00
11 thru 20	@10.00
21 thru 33	@8.00

RIFLEMAN, THE
Dell Publishing Co., 1959

1 Chuck Connors Ph(c) all	500.00
2 Ph(c)	300.00
3 ATh,Ph(c)	275.00
4 Ph(c)	250.00
5 Ph(c)	250.00
6 ATh	275.00
7 thru 10 Ph(c)	@225.00
11 thru 20	@200.00

RIOT
Riot Media, 2005

1	3.00
2	3.00

RIOT GEAR
Triumphant, 1993

1 JnR(s),I:Riot Gear	2.50
2 JnR(s),I:Rabin	2.50
3 JnR(s),I:Surzar	2.50
4 JnR(s),D:Captain Tich	2.50
5 JnR(s),reactions	2.50
6 JnR(s),Tich avenged	2.50
7 JnR(s),Information Age	2.50
8 JnR(s),	2.50

RIOT GEAR:
VIOLENT PAST
Triumphant, 1994

1 and 2	@2.50

R.I.P.
TSR, 1990–91

1 thru 4	@3.00
5 thru 8 Brasher, Avenger of the Dead	@3.00

RIPFIRE
Malibu, 1995

0 Prequel to Ripfire Series	2.50

RIPLEY'S BELIEVE IT
OR NOT!
Gold Key, 1967–80

4 Ph(c),AMc	100.00
5 GE,JJ	75.00
6 AMc	75.00
7	70.00
8	75.00
9	70.00
10 GE	75.00
11	50.00

12	50.00
13	50.00
14	50.00
15 GE	55.00
16	50.00
17	50.00
18	50.00
19	50.00
20	50.00
21 thru 30	@35.00
31 thru 38	@30.00
39 RC	30.00
40 thru 50	@28.00
51 thru 94	@25.00

RISE OF THE SNAKEMEN
Crossgen Comics 2003

1	3.00
2 thru 3	@3.00

RISK
Maximum Press, 1995

1 V:Furious	2.50

ROAD TO HELL
IDW Publishing, 2006

1	4.00
2 thru 3	@4.00

ROB
Awesome Entertainment, 1999

1 RLe	2.50

ROBERT JORDAN'S
NEW SPRING
Red Eagle Publishing, 2005

1	4.00
2 thru 4	@4.00
5 thru 8 CDi	@4.00

ROBERT E. HOWARD'S
Cross Plains Comics, 1999

GN Marchers of Valhalla	7.00
GN Wolfshead	7.00
GN Worms of the Earth	10.00

ROBIN HOOD
Eclipse, 1991

1 TT,Historically accurate series	2.75
2 and 3 TT	@2.75

ROBOCOP: WAR PARTY
Avatar Press, 2005

1	4.00
1a variant (c)s	@4.00
1b Matt Martin (c)	6.00
1c ED-209 photo (c)	6.00
2	4.00
2a wraparound (c)	4.00
2b variant (c)	@4.00
3	4.00
3a wraparound (c)	4.00
3b variant (c)	@4.00

ROBOCOP: WILD CHILD
Avatar Press, 2005

1 16-page	3.00
1a photo (c)	3.00
1b variant (c)	3.00
1c wraparound (c)	3.00
1d Heaven Above (c)	6.00
1e Detroit's Finest (c)	6.00

ROBO DOJO
WildStorm/DC, 2002

1 (of 6) MWn, 40-pg	3.50

2 MWn,	3.00
3 MWn,	3.00
4 MWn,Techno Council	3.00
5 MWn,Robojin revolt	3.00
6 MWn,traitor revealed, concl.	3.00

ROBO HUNTER
Eagle

1	2.50
2 thru 5	@2.50

Robotech 39
© Antarctic Press

ROBOTECH
Antarctic Press, 1997

1 by Fred Perry & BDn	3.00
2	3.00
3	3.00
4 Rolling Thunder, pt.1	3.00
5 Rolling Thunder, pt.2	3.00
6 Rolling Thunder, pt.3	3.00
7 Rolling Thunder, pt.4	3.00
8 Variants, pt.1	3.00
9 Variants, pt.2	3.00
10 Variants, pt.3	3.00
11 Variants, pt.4	3.00
TPB Megastorm by Fred Perry & Ben Dunn	8.00
Spec.1-shot Robotech: Final Fire	3.00
Spec.1-shot Robotech: Class Reunion	3.00

ROBOTECH
Wildstorm/DC, 2002

0 JLe	2.50
1 (of 6) JLe	3.00
2 thru 5	@3.00
6 SeP, concl.	3.00
Spec. Robotech Sourcebook	3.00
TPB From the Stars	10.00

ROBOTECH: GENESIS
THE LEGEND OF ZOR
Eternity

1 O:Robotech w/cards	3.00
1a Limited Edition,extra pages with cards #1 & #2	6.00
2 thru 6, each with cards	@2.50

ROBOTECH IN 3-D
Comico, 1985

1	2.50

ROBOTECH: INVASION
Wildstorm/DC, 2004
1 (of 5) 3.00
2 thru 5 . . . . @3.00

ROBOTECH: LOVE AND WAR
Wildstorm/DC July, 2003
1 (of 6) Max and Miriya. 3.00
2 flight school 3.00
3 Max and Miriya meet. 3.00
4 Max and Miriya fight 3.00
5 Dixon dead. 3.00
6 conclusion 3.00

ROBOTECH, THE MACROSS SAGA
Comico, 1985–89
(formerly Macross)
2 . . . . 5.00
3 . . . . 4.00
4 . . . . 3.50
5 . . . . 3.50
6 J:Rick Hunter. 3.50
7 V:Zentraedi 3.00
8 A:Rick Hunter. 3.00
9 V:Zentraedi 3.00
10 Blind Game 3.00
11 V:Zentraedi 3.00
12 V:Zentraedi 3.00
13 V:Zentraedi 3.00
14 Gloval's Reports 3.00
15 V:Zentraedi 3.00
16 V:Zentraedi 3.00
17 V:Zentraedi 3.00
18 D:Roy Fokker 3.00
19 V:Khyron. 3.00
20 V:Zentraedi 3.00
21 A New Dawn 3.00
22 V:Zentraedi 3.00
23 Reckless 3.00
24 HB,V:Zentraedi 3.00
25 Wedding Bells. 3.00
26 The Messenger. 3.00
27 Force of Arms 3.00
28 Reconstruction Blues 3.00
29 Robotech Masters. 3.00
30 Viva Miriya 3.00
31 Khyron's Revenge 3.00
32 Broken Heart. 3.00
33 A Rainy Night 3.00
34 Private Time 3.00
35 Season's Greetings 3.00
36 last issue. 3.00
Graphic Novel #1. . . . . 6.00

ROBOTECH: THE MACROSS SAGA
Wildstorm/DC, 2003
TPB Vol. 1 . . . . 15.00
TPB Vol. 2 thru Vol. 4. . . . . @15.00

ROBOTECH MASTERS
Comico, 1985–88
1 . . . . 4.00
2 . . . . 3.00
3 Space Station Liberty. 3.00
4 V:Bioroids. 2.50
5 V:Flagship 2.50
6 Prelude to Battle 2.50
7 The Trap 2.50
8 F:Dana Sterling 2.50
9 Star Dust 2.50
10 V:Zor. 2.50
11 A:De Ja Vu 2.50
12 2OR. 2.50
13 . . . . 2.50
14 Clone Chamber,V:Zor 2.50

---

15 Love Song. 2.50
16 V:General Emerson 2.50
17 Mind Games 2.50
18 Dana in Wonderland. 2.50
19 . . . . 2.50
20 A:Zor,Musica 2.50
21 Final Nightmare 2.50
22 The Invid Connection 2.50
23 Catastrophe, final issue 2.50

Robotech The New Generation #2
© *Comico*

ROBOTECH: THE NEW GENERATION
Comico, 1985–88
1 . . . . 4.00
2 The Lost City 3.00
3 V:Yellow Dancer. 3.00
4 A:Yellow Dancer. 3.00
5 SK(i),A:Yellow Dancer 3.00
6 F:Rook Bartley. 3.00
7 Paper Hero 3.00
8 . . . . 3.00
9 KSy,The Genesis Pit 3.00
10 V:The Invid 3.00
11 F:Scott Bernard 3.00
12 V:The Invid 3.00
13 V:The Invid 3.00
14 Annie's Wedding 3.00
15 Seperate Ways 3.00
16 Metamorphosis 3.00
17 Midnight Sun 3.00
18 . . . . 3.00
19 . . . . 3.00
20 Birthday Blues. 3.00
21 Hired Gun 3.00
22 The Big Apple 3.00
23 Robotech Wars 3.00
24 Robotech Wars 3.00
25 V:Invid, last issue 3.00

ROBOTECH: PRELUDE TO THE SHADOW CHRONICLES
Wildstorm/DC, Oct., 2005
1 (of 5) JWp,JWt. 3.50
2 thru 5 . . . . @3.50

ROBOTECH SPECIAL DANA'S STORY
Eclipse
1 . . . . 5.00

ROBOTECH II: THE SENTINELS
Eternity
Swimsuit Spec.#1 . . . . 3.00

ROBOTIKA
Archaia Studio Press, 2006
1 . . . . 4.00
2 thru 4 . . . . @4.00

ROB ZOMBIE'S SPOOKSHOW INTERNATIONAL
Crossgen Comics, 2003
1 (of 5) 3.50
2 thru 3 . . . . @3.00
MVCreations (2004)
4 thru 10 . . . . @3.00
TPB 20.00

ROCK 'N' ROLL
Revolutionary, 1990
Prev: Black & White
15 Poison. 6.00
16 Van Halen 5.00
17 Madonna. 6.00
18 AliceCooper. 5.00
19 Public Enemy, 2 Live Crew. 5.00
20 Queensryche. 5.00
21 Prince 5.00
22 AC/DC. 5.00
23 Living Color. 5.00
24 Anthrax 5.00
25 Z.Z.Top 5.00
26 Doors 5.00
27 Doors 5.00
28 Ozzy Osbourne. 6.00
29 The Cure. 5.00
30 . . . . 5.00
31 Vanilla Ice 5.00
32 Frank Zappa 5.00
33 Guns n' Roses 5.00
34 The Black Crowes. 5.00
35 R.E.M.. 5.00
36 Michael Jackson 5.00
37 Ice T 5.00
38 Rod Stewart 5.00
39 New Kids on the Block 5.00
40 N.W.A./Ice Cube 5.00
41 Paula Abdul. 5.00
42 Metallica II. 5.00
43 Guns `N' Roses 5.00
44 Scorpions 5.00
45 Greatful Dead 5.00
46 Grateful Dead 5.00
47 Grateful Dead 5.00
48 (now b/w),Queen 5.00
49 Rush 5.00
50 Bob Dylan Pt.1 . . . . 5.00
51 Bob Dylan Pt.2 . . . . 5.00
52 Bob Dylan Pt.3 . . . . 5.00
53 Bruce Springsteen 5.00
54 U2 Pt.1 . . . . 5.00
55 U2 Pt.2 . . . . 5.00
56 David Bowie 5.00
57 thru 58 . . . . @4.00
59 Eric Clampton 5.00
60 thru 63. . . . . @4.00
64 San Francisco. 4.00
65 Pink Floyd. 4.00

ROCK 'N' ROLL HIGH SCHOOL
Cosmic Comics, 1995
1 Sequel to the movie. 2.50

All comics prices listed are for *Near Mint* condition.

ROCKETEER
Walt Disney, 1991
1 DSt(c)RH,MovieAdaptation 7.00
Newsstand Version 3.25

ROCKETEER ADVENTURE MAGAZINE
Comico, 1988
1 DSt,MK,Rocketeer(6thApp.) 10.00
2 DSt,MK,Rocketeer(7thApp.) 8.00

ROCKETEER SPECIAL
Eclipse, 1984
1 DSt, Rocketeer(5th App.). 15.00

ROCKET MAN: KING OF THE ROCKET MEN
Innovation, 1991
1 thru 4 Adapts movie series . . . @2.50

ROCKETO
Speakeasy Comics, 2005
1 . . . . 10.00
2 thru 3 . . . . @8.00
4 thru 6 . . . . @5.00

ROCKET RANGER
Adventure Comics, 1991
1 (of 12) from computer game 3.00

Rocky Horror Picture Show #3
© Calibre

ROCKY HORROR PICTURE SHOW
Calibre/Tome, 1990
1 . . . . 6.00
1a 2nd printing 3.25
2 . . . . 3.50
3 The Conclusion 3.25
Rocky Horror Collection reps. 5.00

ROG 2000
Pacific, 1982
1 One-Shot, JBy 2.50

ROGER RABBIT
Walt Disney, 1990
1 I:Rick Flint, The Trouble
  with Toons 5.50
2 . . . . 3.50
3 . . . . 3.00

4 . . . . 3.00
5 . . . . 3.00
6 thru 9 . . . . @3.00
10 Tuned-in-toons 3.00
11 Who Framed Rick Flint 3.00
12 Somebunny to Love 3.00
13 Honey,I Stink with Kids 3.00
14 Who Fired Jessica Rabbit. 3.00
15 The Great Toon Detective. 3.00
16 See you later Aviator 3.00
17 Flying Saucers over Toontown . . 3.00
18 I Have Seen the Future 3.00

ROGER RABBIT'S TOONTOWN
Walt Disney, 1991
1 Baby Herman,Jessica stories . . . 2.50
2 Pre-Hysterical Roger 2.50
3 Lumberjack of tomorrow 2.50
4 The Longest Daze 2.50

ROGUES
Dark Planet Productions, 2004
1 . . . . 3.00
2 thru 5 . . . . @3.00
6 . . . . 5.50

ROGUE TROOPER
Fleetway/Quality, 1986
1 thru 5 . . . . @2.50
6 thru 21 . . . . @2.50
22/23 . . . . 2.50
24 . . . . 2.50
25/26 . . . . 2.50
27 thru 43 . . . . @2.50

ROGUE TROOPER: THE FINAL WARRIOR
Fleetway
1 RS,Golden Rebellion,pt 1 . . . . . . 3.00
2 thru 3 . . . . @3.00
4 Saharan Ice-Belt War 3.00

ROKKIN
Wildstorm/DC, July, 2006
1 . . . . 3.00
2 thru 5 . . . . @3.00

ROLAND: DAYS OF WRATH
Terra Major, 1999
1 (of 4) 3.00
2 thru 4 . . . . @3.00
TPB 18.00

ROMAN HOLIDAYS, THE
Gold Key, 1973
1 . . . . 75.00
2 . . . . 50.00
3 . . . . 50.00
4 . . . . 50.00

ROOK, THE
Harris Comics, 1995
0 O:Rook. 3.00
1 N:Rook. 3.00
2 I:Coffin 3.00
3 The Spider Obsidian 3.00

ROOM 222
Dell Publishing Co., 1970
1 . . . . 100.00
2 . . . . 75.00
3 Drug. 75.00
4 Ph(c) 60.00

ROSE
Cartoon Books, 2000
1 (of 3) 48-pg. 6.00
2 JSi,CV,48-pg. 6.00
3 JSi,CV,48-pg., concl. 6.00
TPB 20.00

ROSEN GRAPHIC NONFICTION
Rosen Publishing Group, 2004
GN Abraham Lincoln 10.00
GN Christopher Columbus 10.00
GN Alexander the Great 10.00
GN George Washington. 10.00
GN Sitting Bull. 10.00
GN Spartacus. 10.00
GN Cleopatra. 10.00
GN Elizabeth I 10.00
GN Harriet Tubman 10.00
GN Hernan Cortes 10.00
GN Julius Caesar. 10.00
GN Richard the Lionheart 10.00

ROSWELL
Bongo Comics, 1996
1 by Bill Morrison,The Story
  of the Century 3.00
2 The Untold Story 3.00
3 The Untold Story, concl. 3.00
4 V:Mutato. 3.00
5 . . . . 3.00
6 time-traveling comic collector . . . 3.00
TPB Roswell Walks Among Us . . . 13.00

ROUTE 666
Crossgen Comics, 2002
1 . . . . 3.00
2 thru 5 . . . . @3.00
6 thru 24 . . . . @3.00
TPB Vol. 1 Highway of Horror 16.00
TPB Vol. 2 Three-Ring Circus 16.00
TPB Traveler Vol. 1 . . . . 10.00

ROY ROGERS WESTERN CLASSICS
AC Comics, 1989
1 . . . . 3.00
2 . . . . 3.00
3 . . . . 3.00
4 . . . . 4.00

ROY THOMAS' ANGHEM
Heroic Publishing, 2006
1 . . . . 3.25
2 thru 3 . . . . @3.25

RUFF AND READY
Dell Publishing Co., 1958
1 . . . . 350.00
2 . . . . 250.00
3 . . . . 250.00
4 thru 12 . . . . @175.00

RUGRATS COMIC ADVENTURES
New England Comics, 1999
VOL. 1
1 thru 10 . . . . @3.00
VOL. 2
1 thru 10 . . . . @3.00
VOL. 3
1 . . . . 3.00
2 thru 9 . . . . @3.00

All comics prices listed are for *Near Mint* condition.

COLOR PUB.

RUN, BUDDY, RUN
Gold Key, 1967
1 . . . . 75.00

RUNE
Malibu Ultraverse, 1994–95
0 BWS(a&s) 4.00
1 BWS(a&s),from Ultraverse 2.50
1a Foil cover 4.00
2 CU(s),BWS,V:Aladdin 2.50
3 DaR,BWS,(Ultraverse Premiere
    #1), Flip book 3.75
4 thru 9 . . . . @2.50
G-Size #1 . . . . 2.50
TPB BWS(c&a),CU,The Awakening,
    rep.#1–#5 . . . . 13.00

RUNE
Malibu Ultraverse, 1995–96
Infinity V:Annihilus 2.50
1 A:Adam Warlock 2.50
1a Computer painted cover 2.50
2 thru 6 . . . . @2.50

RUNE: HEARTS OF DARKNESS
Malibu Ultraverse, 1996
1 DgM(s),KHt,TBd, flip book 2.50
2 DgM,KHt,TBd, flip book 2.50
3 DgM,KHt,TBd, flip book 2.50

RUNE/SILVER SURFER
Ultravrse 1995
1 BWS(c),A:Adam Warlock 6.00
1a Lim. edition (5,000 made) 8.00
1b Standard ed.newsprint 3.00

RUNES OF RAGNAN
Silent Devil Productions, 2005
1 . . . . 3.00
2 thru 4 . . . . @3.00
TPB 15.00
TPB Flames of Muspell 15.00

RUSE
Crossgen Comics, 2001
1 MWa 8.00
2 MWa 3.50
3 thru 14 . . . . @3.00
15 thru 27 . . . . @3.00
TPB Vol. 1 Enter the Detective . . . 16.00
TPB Vol. 3 Criminal Intent 16.00
Spec. Archard's Agents,
    Deadly Dare (2004) 3.00

RUST
Now, 1987
1 . . . . 4.00
2 . . . . 3.00
3 . . . . 2.50
4 . . . . 2.50
5 thru 10 . . . . @2.50
12 I:Terminator 10.00
13 thru 15 . . . . @2.50
[Volume 2], 1989
1 thru 10 . . . . @2.50

RUST
Malibu
1 O:Rust 3.00
2 V:Marion Labs 3.00
3 I:Ashe Sapphire,5th Anniv. 3.00
4 I:Rustmobile 3.00

RUULE: GANGLORDS OF CHINATOWN
Beckett Entertainment, 2003
1 . . . . 6.00
2 thru 3 . . . . @6.00
4 thru 5 . . . . @3.00

RUULE: KISS & TELL
Beckett Entertainment, 2004
1 . . . . 3.00
2 thru 5 . . . . @3.00
6 thru 8 . . . . @2.00

Sable #12
© First

SABLE
First, 1988–90
1 AIDS story 2.50
2 thru 28 . . . . @2.50

SABRE
Eclipse, 1982–85
1 PG 2.50
2 PG 3.00
3 thru 14 . . . . @2.50

SABRINA, THE TEENAGE WITCH
Archie Publications, 1971–83
1 . . . . 350.00
2 Archie 175.00
3 Archie 150.00
4 . . . . 125.00
5 . . . . 125.00
6 thru 10 . . . . @125.00
11 thru 30 . . . . @100.00
31 thru 40 . . . . @50.00
41 thru 76 . . . . @30.00
77 . . . . 35.00

SABRINA THE TEENAGE WITCH
Archie Comics, 1996
one-shot photo cover 7.00
1 photo cover 5.00
2 Trouble in Time 5.00
3 photo cover 5.00
4 photo cover 5.00
5 Driver's License 5.00
6 Treasure Troubles 5.00
7 The Sculpture Switch 5.00
8 The Cable Girl, photo (c) 5.00

9 Farewell Feline 5.00
10 No Brain, No Pain 5.00
11 thru 17 . . . . @3.00
18 thru 33 photo (c) . . . . @3.00
[Volume 2], 2000
1 thru 3 from animated series . . . @2.50
4 thru 13 . . . . @2.50
14 thru 62 . . . . @2.50
63 thru 80 . . . . @2.25
Halloween Spooktacular #1 . . . . . . 2.50
Halloween Spooktacular #2 . . . . . . 2.50
Holiday Spectacular #3 . . . . 2.50
TPB The Magic Revisited 7.50

SAD SACK AND THE SARGE
Harvey Publications, 1957–82
1 . . . . 600.00
2 . . . . 400.00
3 . . . . 300.00
4 . . . . 300.00
5 . . . . 300.00
6 thru 10 . . . . @300.00
11 thru 20 . . . . @200.00
21 thru 40 . . . . @100.00
41 thru 50 . . . . @75.00
51 thru 90 . . . . @50.00
91 thru 96 52 pg Giants . . . . . . @30.00
97 thru 155 . . . . @30.00

SAD SACK'S ARMY LIFE
Harvey Publications, 1963–76
1 . . . . 200.00
2 thru 10 . . . . @100.00
11 thru 20 . . . . @60.00
21 thru 30 . . . . @50.00
31 thru 50 . . . . @35.00
51 thru 61 . . . . @30.00

SAD SACK'S FUNNY FRIENDS
Harvey Publications, 1955–69
1 . . . . 400.00
2 . . . . 250.00
3 . . . . 250.00
4 . . . . 250.00
5 . . . . 250.00
6 thru 10 . . . . @250.00
11 thru 20 . . . . @200.00
21 thru 30 . . . . @150.00
31 thru 40 . . . . @100.00
41 thru 75 . . . . @75.00

SAD SACK LAUGH SPECIAL
Harvey Publications, 1958
1 . . . . 160.00
2 . . . . 120.00
3 . . . . 100.00
4 . . . . 100.00
5 . . . . 100.00
6 . . . . 100.00
7 . . . . 100.00
8 . . . . 100.00
9 . . . . 100.00
10 . . . . 100.00
11 thru 20 . . . . @100.00

SAD SACK in 3-D
Blackthorne
1 and 2 . . . . @2.50

SADHU
Virgin Comics, 2006
1 . . . . 3.00
2 thru 5 . . . . @3.00

SAFETY-BELT MAN ALL HELL
Sirius, 1996
1	3.00
2	3.00
3	3.00
4 Linsner back (c)	4.00
5	3.00

SAGA OF THE METABARONS
Humanoids Publishing, 1999
1 (of 16) Sci-fi	3.00
2 thru 9	@3.00

SAINT LEGEND
Comicsone.com, 2002
GN #3 thru #6	@14.00
GN #7 thru GN #10	@15.00

SAM AND MAX, FREE-LANCE POLICE SPECIAL
Comico, 1987–89
1	3.00

Sam Slade Robohunter #14
© Quality

SAM SLADE ROBOHUNTER
Quality, 1986–89
1	2.50
2 thru 10	@2.50
11 thru 21	@2.50
22/23	2.50
24	2.50
25/26	2.50
27 thru 33	@2.50

SAMSONS
Samsons Comics, 1995
1/2 Various Artists	2.50

SAMUREE
Windjammer, 1995
1 I:Samuree	2.50
2 V: The Dragon	2.50
3 V: The Dragon	2.50

SAMURAI
Eclipse
1	2.50

2	2.50
3 thru 5	@2.50

SAMURAI GUARD
Colburn Comics, 2000
1 by Kirk C. Abrigo	2.50
2	2.50
3	3.00
4 thru 6	@3.00

SAMUREE
Continuity, 1987
1 NA,A:Revengers	2.50
2 A:Revengers	2.50
3 NA,A:Revengers	2.50
4 A:Revengers	2.50
5 BSz(c),A:Revengers	2.50
6 A:Revengers	2.50
7	2.50
8 Drug story	2.50
9 Drug story	2.50

[2nd Series], 1993
1 thru 3 Rise of Magic	@2.50

SANDSCAPE
Dreamwave, 2003
1	3.00
2 thru 4	@3.00

SANTANA
Rock-it Comix, 1994
1 TT(c&s),TY	4.00

SARGE STEEL/ SECRET AGENT
Charlton, 1964–66
1 DG,I:SargeSteel & IvanChung	75.00
2 DG,I:Werner Von Hess	50.00
3 DG,V:Smiling Skull	50.00
4 DG,V:Lynx	50.00
5 FMc,V:Ivan Chung	50.00
6 FMc,A:Judomaster	60.00
7 DG	50.00
8 V:Talon	50.00

Becomes:

SECRET AGENT
9 DG,A:The Lynx	75.00
10 DG,JAp,A:Tiffany Sinn	50.00

SATANIKA
Verotik, 1995
0	3.00
1 New ongoing series	4.00
2 Femininity	3.50
3 thru 5	@3.00
6 thru 10	@3.00
10a Wingbird variant cover	5.00
11 SBi,final issue	4.00
11a Jason Blood variant (c)	10.00
11b Superfest 99 limited	15.00
1-shot Satanika X (adult)	5.00
1-shot Satanika vs.Shilene	10.00

SATANIKA TALES
Verotik, 2005
2	4.00
2a variant (c)	5.00
2b Limited fan (c)	10.00

SATAN'S SIX
Topps, 1993
1 F:Satan's Six,w/3 cards	3.25
2 V:Kalazarr,w/3 cards	3.00
3 w/3 cards	3.00
4 w/3 cards	3.00

SAURIANS: UNNATURAL SELECTION
Crossgen Comics, 2002
1 (of 2)	3.00
2	3.00

SAVAGE BROTHERS
Boom! Studios, 2006
1 (of 3)	3.50
2 thru 3	@3.50

SAVAGE COMBAT TALES
Atlas, Feb.–July, 1975
1 F:Sgt Strykers Death Squad	30.00
2 ATh,A:Warhawk	40.00
3 final issue	25.00

SAVAGE DRAGON/ TEENAGE MUTANT NINJA TURLTES CROSSOVER
Mirage, 1993
1 EL(s)	3.00

SAVAGE RED SONJA QUEEN OF THE FROZEN WASTES
D.E. (Dynamite Ent.) 2006
1 (of 4)	3.50
1a foil (c)	
2 thru 4	@3.50
2 thru 4a variant (c)s	@3.50

SAVAGE WORLD
Kandora Publishing, 2005
1	3.50
2 thru 3	@3.50

SAVED BY THE BELL
Harvey, 1992
1 based on TV series	2.50
2 thru 5	@2.50

SAWED-OFF MOJO
Speakeasy Comics, 2006
1 (of 6)	3.00
2 thru 3	@3.00

SCARLET CRUSH
Awesome Entertainment, 1998
1 by John Stinsman	2.50
2	2.50
3 Icaria's decision	2.50
4 Nirasawa arrives	2.50

SCARY TALES
Charlton, 1975
1 JSon	50.00
2	25.00
3 SD,P(c)	25.00
4 TS,SD,JSon,P(c)	40.00
5 SD	40.00
6	25.00
7 SD	30.00
8 SD	30.00
9 TS	40.00
10	25.00
11 SD	30.00
12 SD	25.00
13	20.00
14 SD	25.00
15 SD	25.00
16 SD	25.00
17	20.00

COLOR PUB.

18 BP	25.00
19 SD	25.00
20 JSon	18.00
21 SD	25.00
22	15.00
23 thru 28	@14.00
30 thru 37	@12.00
38 Mr. Jigsaw	15.00
39 SD	20.00
40 thru 46	@15.00

SCATTERBRAIN
APC, 2005

1	3.50
2 thru 4	@3.50

SCATTERBRAIN
Markosia, 2006

1	3.50
1a variant (c)s	@3.50
2 thru 4	@3.50
TPB Vol. 1	16.00
3a variant (c)	3.50

SCAVENGERS
Quality, 1988–89

1 thru 7	@2.50
8 thru 14	@2.50

SCAVENGERS
Triumphant Comics, 1993–94

0 Fso(c),JnR(s),	2.50
0a `Free Copy'	2.50
0b Red Logo	2.50
1 JnR(s),I:Scavengers,Ximos, C:Doctor Chaos	2.50
1a 2nd Printing	2.50
2 JnR(s),	2.50
3 JnR(s),I:Lurok	2.50
4 JnR(s),	2.50
5 Fso(c),JnR(s),D:Jack Hanal.	2.50
6 JnR(s),	2.50
7 JnR(s),I:Zion	2.50
8 JnR(s),Nativity	2.50
9 JnR(s),The Challenge	2.50
10 JnR(s),Snowblind	2.50

SCHISM
Defiant

1 thru 4 Defiant's x-over	@3.25

SCION
Crossgen Comics, 2000

1 RMz	5.00
2 RMz	5.00
3 RMz	4.50
4 & 5	3.00
6	4.00
7 thru 18	@3.00
19 thru 30 RMz	@3.00
31 thru 44 RMz	@3.00
TPB Vol. 1 rep. #1–#7	20.00
TPB Vol. 2	20.00
TPB Vol. 3 Divided Loyalties	16.00
TPB Vol. 4 Sanctuary	16.00
TPB Vol. 5 The Far Kingdom	16.00
TPB Vol. 6 The Royal Wedding	16.00
TPB Scion Traveler, Vol. 1	10.00

SCI-TECH
WildStorm/DC, 1999

1 (of 4) BCi,Ebe,	2.50
2 BCi,EBe,	2.50
3 BCi,EBe	2.50
4 BCi,EBe,concl.	2.50

SCOOBY DOO
Gold Key, 1970–75

1	250.00
2	175.00
3	150.00
4	150.00
5	150.00
6 thru 20	@100.00
21 thru 30	@75.00

SCOOBY DOO
Charlton Comics, 1975–76

1	150.00
2 thru 5	@75.00
6 thru 11	@60.00

SCOOBY DOO
Archie, 1995

1	6.00
2 thru 10	@5.00
11 thru 21	@4.00

SCORCHED EARTH
Tundra, 1991

1 Earth 2025,I:Dr.EliotGodwin	3.50
2 Hunt for Eliot	3.00
3 Mystical Transformation	3.00

SCORPION, THE
Atlas, 1975

1 HC, bondage cover	35.00
2 HC,BWi,MK	30.00
3	25.00

SCORPION CORP.
Dagger, 1993

1 PuD,JRI,CH,	2.75
2 PuD,JRI,CH,V:Victor Kyner	2.75
3 PuD,BIH,V:Victor Kyner	2.75

SCORPIO ROSE
Eclipse, 1983

1 MR/TP,I:Dr.Orient	2.50
2 MR/TP	2.50

SCOUT
Eclipse, 1985–87

1 TT,I:Scout,Fash.In Action	6.00
2 TT,V:Buffalo Monster	3.00
3 thru 18 TT	@2.50
19 TT,w/Record,V:Lex Lucifer	3.00
20 thru 24 TT	@2.50

SCOUT: WAR SHAMAN
Eclipse, 1988–89

1 TT,R:Scout (now a father)	2.50
2 thru 16 TT	@2.50

SEADRAGON
Elite, 1986–87

1	3.00
1a 2nd printing	2.50
2 thru 8	@2.50

SEA HUNT
Dell Publishing Co., 1958

1 L.BridgesPh(c) all	275.00
2	200.00
3 ATh.	225.00
4 RsM	200.00
5 RsM	200.00
6 RsM	200.00
7	150.00
8 RsM	200.00
9 RsM	200.00
10 RsM.	200.00

11 RsM	200.00
12	200.00
13 RsM.	200.00

SEAQUEST
Nemesis, 1994

1 HC(c),DGC,KP,AA,Based on TV Show	2.50

SEASON OF THE REAPER, THE: WINTER
Speakeasy Comics, 2005

1 (of 3)	3.00
2	3.00
3	3.00

SEBASTIAN
Walt Disney

1 From Little Mermaid	2.50
2 While da Crab's Away	2.50

SECOND LIFE OF DR. MIRAGE, THE
Valiant, 1993

1 B:BL(s),BCh,V:Mast.Darque	2.50
1a Gold Ed.	3.00
2 thru 19	@2.50

SECOND STAGE TURBINE BLADE
Eve Ink 2004

1	30.00
1a Diamond	15.00
2	15.00

Secret Agent #9
© Gold Key

SECRET AGENT
Gold Key, 1966

1	250.00
2	200.00

SECRET CITY SAGA
Topps, 1993

0 JK.	3.25
0 Gold Ed.	15.00
0 Red	10.00
1 w/3 cards	3.25
2 w/3 cards	3.25
3 w/3 cards	3.25
4 w/3 cards	3.25

SECRET SKULL
IDW Publishing, 2004
1	4.00
2 thru 4	@4.00
TPB	20.00

SECRETS OF THE VALIANT UNIVERSE
Valiant, 1994
1 from Wizard	2.50
2 BH,Chaos Effect-Beta#4,A:Master Darque,Dr.Mirage,Max St.James, Dr. Eclipse	2.50

SECRET SQUIRREL
Gold Key, 1966
1	200.00

SECRET WEAPONS
Valiant, 1993
1 JSP(a&s),BWi(i),I:Dr.Eclipse, A:Master Darque,A:Geoff, Livewire,Stronghold,Solar,X-O, Bloodshot,Shadowman	2.75
1a Gold Ed.	4.00
2 thru 23	@2.50

SECRET WEAPONS: PLAYING WITH FIRE
Valiant
1 & 2	@2.50

SEDUCTION OF THE INNOCENT
Eclipse, 1985–86
1 ATh,Hanged by the Neck, reps.	3.00
2	3.00
3 ATh,The Crushed Gardenia	3.00
4 ATh,NC,World's Apart	3.00
5 ATh,The Phantom Ship	3.00
6 ATh,RA,Hands of Don Jose	3.00
3-D #1 DSt(c)	5.00
3-D #2 ATh,MB,BWr,Man Who Was Always on Time	5.00

SEEKER
Sky Comics, 1995
1 JMt(s),I:Seeker	2.50

Seeker #1
© Sky Comics

SENSEI
First, 1989
1 Mini-Series	2.75
2	2.75
3	2.75
4	2.75

SENTINELS OF JUSTICE
AC Comics, 1990
1 Capt.Paragon	2.50
2	2.50
3 EL art	2.50
4 EL art	2.50
5	2.50
6	2.50
7	2.50

SENTRY: SPECIAL
Innovation, 1991
1	2.75

SERAPHIM
Innovation, 1990
1 and 2	@2.50

SERINA
Antarctic, 1996
1	3.00

SERPENTINA
Lightning, 1997
1	3.00
1a variant cover	3.00

SE7EN
Zenescope Entertainment, 2006
1 (of 7) Gluttony	4.00
2 Greed	4.00
3 Sloth	4.00

SEVEN SISTERS
Zephyr Comics, 1997
1 by Curley, Cruickshank & Garcia.	3.00
2	3.00
3	3.00
4	3.00

SEVENTH SHRINE, THE
Devil's Due Publishing, 2004
1 (of 2) R.Silverberg adapt.	6.00
2	6.00

77 SUNSET STRIP
Dell Publishing Co., 1960
1 Ph(c)	175.00
2 Ph(c),RsM	200.00

SHADE SPECIAL
AC Comics, 1984
1	2.50

SHADOW, THE
Archie Comics, 1964–65
1	150.00
2	100.00
3	100.00
4	100.00
5	100.00
6 and 8	@75.00

SHADOW MAN
Valiant, 1992
0 BH,TmR,Chromium (c),O:Maxim St.James,Shadowman	4.00
0a Newstand ed.	5.00
0b Gold Ed.	18.00
1 DL,JRu,I&O:Shadowman	8.00
2 DL,V:Serial Killer	5.00
3 V:Emil Sosa	5.00
4 DL,FM(c),Unity#6,A:Solar	5.00
5 DL,WS(c),Unity#14, A:Archer & Armstrong	5.00
6 SD,L:Lilora	3.00
7 DL,V:Creature	3.00
8 JDx(i),I:Master Darque	3.50
9 JDx(i),V:Darque's Minions	3.50
10 BH,I:Sandria	3.00
11 BH,N:Shadowman	3.00
12 BH,V:Master Darque	3.00
13 BH,V:Rev.Shadow Man	3.00
14 BH,JDx,V:Bikers	3.00
15 BH,JDx,V:JB,Fake Shadow Man,C:Turok	3.00
16 BH,JDx,I:Dr.Mirage, Carmen	3.50
17 BH,JDx,A:Archer & Armstrong	2.50
18 BH,JDx,A:Archer & Armstrong	2.50
19 BH,A:Aerosmith	2.50
20 BH,A:Master Darque, V:Shadowman's Father	2.50
21 BH,I:Maxim St.James (1895 Shadowman)	2.50
22 V:Master Darque	2.50
23 BH(a&s),A:Doctor Mirage, V:Master Darque	2.50
24 BH(a&s),V:H.A.T.E.	2.50
25 RgM,w/Valiant Era card	2.50
26 w/Valiant Era card	3.00
27 BH,V:Drug Lord.	2.50
28 BH,A:Master Darque	2.50
29 Chaos Effect-Beta#1,V:Master Darque	2.50
30 R:Rotwak	2.50
31 thru 33	@2.50
34 Voodoo in Carribean	2.50
35 A:Ishmael	2.50
36 F:Ishmael	2.50
37 A:X-O, V:Blister	2.50
38 V:Ishmael, Blister	2.50
39 BH,TmR,Explores Powers	2.50
40 BH,TmR,I,Vampire!	2.50
41 A:Steve Massarsky	2.50
42	2.50
43 V:Smilin Jack	8.00
TPB rep.#1-#3,#6.	10.00

SHADOWMAN
Acclaim, 1996
1 GEn(s),Deadside, pt.1	3.00
2 GEn(s),Deadside, pt.2	3.00
3 GEn(s),Deadside, pt.3	3.00
4 GEn(s),Deadside, pt.4	3.00
5 thru 19 JaD,CAd	@3.00
20 Deadside vortes	6.00

VOLUME 3 (1999)
1 DAn,ALa,48-page	10.00
2	12.00
3 Flip-book	12.00
4 Flip-book	18.00
5	18.00
6	18.00
7 final issue	25.00

SHADOWMANCER
Markosia, 2005
1	3.50
1a variant (c)s	@3.50
2 thru 10	@3.50
2a thru 10a variant (c)	@3.50
TPB Vol. 1	15.00

SHADOW OF THE TORTURER, THE
Innovation, 1991
1 thru 6 Gene Wolfe adapt.	@2.50

COLOR PUB.

SHADOWPLAY
IDW Publishing, 2005
1	4.00
1a variant (c)	4.00
2	4.00
3	4.00
3a variant (c)	4.00
4	4.00
4a variant (c)	4.00
TPB	18.00

SHADOW REAVERS
Black Bull Entertainment, 2001
1 Nel,KM(c)	5.00
1a variant TDr(c)	12.00
2 Nel,GF(c)	3.00
2a variant TDr(c)	5.00
3 Nel	3.00
3a variant TDr(c)	5.00
4 Nel	3.00
4a variant limited master edition	5.00
5 Nel	3.00
5a variant limited master edition	5.00
Preview Edition	3.00
Preview Edition, limited	5.00

SHADOW STATE
Preview Editions
1 and 2 B&W	@2.50

Broadway, 1995
1 thru 4 F:BloodS.C.R.E.A.M.	@2.50
5 JiS, Image Isn't Everything, concl.	2.50
6 Anger of Lovers, pt.1	2.50
7 Anger of Lovers, pt.2	3.00

SHAIANA
Entity, 1995
1 R:Shaiana from Aster	3.75
1a clear chromium	8.00
1b Holochrome	10.00
2 Guardians of Earth	2.50

SHAOLIN
Black Tiger Press
1 I:Tiger	3.00
2 I:Crane	3.00

SHAOLIN COWBOY
Burlyman Entertainment, 2004
1	3.50
2 thru 5	@3.50
6	3.50
7	3.50
3a thru 7a variant (c)s	@3.50

SHARK-MAN
Thrill House, 2006
1	4.00

SHATTER
First, 1985–88
1	3.00
2	2.50
3	2.50
4 thru 14	@2.50
Spec. #1 Computer Comic	5.00
#1a 2nd Printing	2.00

SHAUN OF THE DEAD
IDW Publishing, 2005
1	4.00
2 thru 4	@4.00
TPB	18.00

SHE-DEVILS ON WHEELS
Aircel
1 V:Man-Eaters	3.00
2 V:Man-Eaters	3.00
3 V:Man-Eaters	3.00

SHEENA: QUEEN OF THE JUNGLE
London Night
0 by Gabriel Cain & Wilson	3.00
0a Zebra Edition	5.00
0b Leopard Edition	5.00
0c Alligator Edition	5.00

SHEENA: QUEEN OF THE JUNGLE: BOUND
London Night, 1998
1 (of 4) by Everette Hartsoe & Art Wetherell	3.00
1 ministry ed.	5.00
1 Leather retro edition	12.00

SHERIFF OF TOMBSTONE
Charlton Comics, 1958–61
1 AW,JSe	150.00
2	100.00
3 thru 10	@100.00
11 thru 17	@75.00

SHIELD, THE: SPOTLIGHT
IDW Publishing, 2004
1	4.00
2 thru 5	@4.00
TPB	20.00

Shi (The Way of the Warrior) #6
© Crusade

SHI (THE WAY OF THE WARRIOR)
Crusade Comics, 1994–97
1 BiT,HMo,I:Shi	9.00
2 BiT	5.00
2a BiT, reissue, new cover	3.00
3 BiT	5.00
4 BiT	4.00
5 V:Arashi	3.00
5a variant cover	6.00
6 V:Tomoe	3.00
7 V:Nara Warriors	3.00
8 New costume	3.00
9 thru 11	@3.00
12 Way of the Warrior, concl, flipbook Angel Fire	3.00
TPB Shi: Way of the Warrior	13.00
TPB Way of the Warrior, signed	15.00
TPB Vol. 1 revised rep.JuB(c)	15.00
TPB Vol. 2, rep. Shi #5–#8	15.00
TPB rep. Shi #9–#12 & Shi vs. Tomoe	18.00
Spec. #1 Shi/Cyblade,Battle of the Independents (1995)	4.00
Spec.#1a Shi/Cyblade,variant(c)	6.00
Ashcan #1, sign & num. (2000)	10.00
Spec. #1 10th Anniv. Edition (2004)	3.00

Crusade Entertainment, 2004
1 10th Anniv. Edition (2004)	3.00
1 10th Anniv. Graphite ed.	20.00

SHI: THE SERIES
Crusade Entertainment, 1997
1 sequel to *Shi: Heaven and Earth*, F:Tomoe	3.50
2 Unforgettable Fire, concl.	3.00
3 A Rock and a Hard Place, pt.1	3.00
4 A Rock and a Hard Place, pt.2	3.00
5 A Rock and a Hard Place, pt.3	3.00
6	3.00
7 Photographer's lucky picture	3.00
8 V:Gemini Dawn twins	3.00
9 Bad Blood, pt.1	3.00
9a variant BTi(c)	3.00
9b variant Ahn (c)	3.00
9c variant Kevin Lau (c)	3.00
10 Bad Blood, pt.2	3.00
10a variant BTi(c)	3.00
10b variant Ahn (c)	3.00
10c variant Kevin Lau (c)	3.00
11 Bad Blood, pt.3	3.00
12 The Dark Crusade, pt.1 (of 8)	3.00
13 The Dark Crusade, pt.2 (of 8)	3.00
14 The Dark Crusade, pt.3 (of 8)	3.00
15 The Dark Crusade, pt.4 (of 8)	3.00
16 The Dark Crusade, pt.5 (of 8)	3.00
1-shot The Essential Dark Crusade	3.00
1-shot Shi:Five Year Celebration	5.00
1-shotA,B,C,&D variant covers	5.00
#0 & Wolverine/Shi flip book	3.00
Spec. Shi/Vampirella,x-over(1997)	3.00
Spec. Shi: Nightstalkers, VMk, F:T.C.B. (1997)	3.50
Spec. Shi: Masquerade (1997)	3.50
Spec. Shi: Art of War Tour Book Wizard Chicago con (1998)	6.00
G.I. Preview Edition (2001)	5.00
Spec. Through the Ashes (2001)	3.00
TPB Cover Gallery (2003)	30.00

SHI: AKAI
Crusade Entertainment, 2001
1 BTi, I:RAF Victoria Cross	3.00
1 antiques edition	30.00
Ashcan, signed & numbered	10.00

SHI: BLACK WHITE & RED
Crusade Entertainment, 1998
1 Night of the Rat, pt.1	3.00
2 Night of the Rat, pt.2	3.00
Coll. Ed. rep. #1–#2	7.00

SHI: EAST WIND RAIN
Crusade Entertainment, 1997
1 BiT,MSo, fully painted	3.50
2 BiT, concl.	3.50

COLOR PUB.

SHI: HEAVEN AND EARTH
Crusade Entertainment, 1997
1 (of 3) BiT 3.00
1 variant cover 3.00
2 BiT 3.00
3 BiT 3.00
4 BiT 3.00
TPB rep. #1–#4 . . . . 16.00

SHI: HOT TARGET
Crusade Entertainment, 2003
1 . . . . 3.00

SHI: PANDORA'S BOX
Avatar Press, 2003
Preview Edition 16-pg. B&W 6.00
Preview BiT(c) 2.00
Preview prism foil (c) 13.00
1/2 prism foil (c) 13.00
1/2 royal blue (c) 75.00
1 BiT(c) 3.50
1a variant (c)s . . . . @3.50
1b prism foil (c) 13.00
1 royal blue edition 75.00

SHI: POISONED PARADISE
Avatar, 2002
Preview 16-pg., b&w 2.00
Preview, Ron Adrian (c) 6.00
Preview, prism foil edition 13.00
1 (of 2) BiT,Karl Waller,Martin(c) . . . 3.50
1a BiT(c) 3.50
1b Waller (c) 3.50
1c Wraparound exclusive (c) 3.50
1d Angel of Death (c) 6.00
1e Angel of Death ruby foil (c) 9.00
1f prism (c) 13.00
2 BiT(c) 3.50
2a-2c variant(c)s . . . . @3.50
1/2 Blossom (c) 6.00
1/2 variant (c)s . . . . @4.00
1/2 Royal Blue foil 75.00

SHI: REKISHI
Crusade Entertainment, 1997
1 (of 2) BiT 3.00
2 BiT, conclusion. 3.00
Coll.Ed. Shi:Reshiki, sourcebook,
MS(c) 5.00

SHI VS. TOMOE
Crusade, April, 1996
Spec. #1 BiT, double size 4.00
GN Unforgettable Fire, rep. 7.00

SHI-SENRYAKU
Crusade, 1995
1 BiT,R:Shi 3.00
1a variant cover 5.00
1 (of 3) 2nd edition 2.50
2 BiT,Arts of Warfare. 3.00
2 2nd edition 2.50
3 BiT 3.00
3 2nd edition 2.50
TPB Rep.#1–#2 . . . . 13.00
TPB 14.00

SHI: YEAR OF THE SERPENT
Crusade Entertainment, 2001
Spec. Tour Book, B&W 5.00

SHI – YEAR OF THE DRAGON
Crusade Entertainment, 2000
1 (of 3) BiT 3.00
1a variant (c). 3.00
1b signed & numbered 10.00
1c true colors ed. BiT 6.00
1d true colors ed. ruby red 30.00
2 Ana Tears (c) BiT 3.00
2a Death Incarnate (c) BiT 3.00
3 BTi, concl. 3.00
Ashcan, signed & numbered 10.00
Coll. Ed. Black,White,Red 7.00
GN #1 & #2 Black,White,Red 6.00
Poster Book 3.00
TPB Year of the Dragon (2002) . . . 10.00

SHOCK SUSPENSE STORIES
Russ Cochran Press, 1992
1 reps.horror stories 2.50
2 inc.Kickback. 2.50
3 thru 4 . . . . @2.50
5 thru 7 reps.horror stories . . . . . @2.50
8 reps.horror stories 2.50
Gemstone
18 EC comics reprint 2.50
TPB Vol. 1 rebinding of #1–#5. . . . . 9.00
TPB Vol. 2 rebinding of #5–#10. . . . 10.00
TPB Vol. 3 rebinding of #11–#15. . . 9.00
TPB Vol. 4 rebinding of #16–#20. . . 10.00

SHOCK THE MONKEY
Millennium/Expand, 1995
1 Shock therapy 3.00

SHON C. BURY'S NOX
Narwain Publishing, 2006
2 . . . . 4.00

SHOTGUN MARY
Antarctic Press, 1995
1 I:Shotgun Mary 3.00
1a with CD Soundtrack. 9.00
1b Red Foil cover 8.00
2 . . . . 3.00
Spec. Shooting Gallery 3.00
Spec. Deviltown 3.00
Spec. Deviltown, commem. (1999) . . 6.00

SHOTGUN MARY
Antarctic Press, 1998
1 by Herb Mallette & Kelsey
Shannon 3.00
2 Early Days, pt.2 . . . . 3.00
3 Early Days, pt.3 . . . . 3.00

SHOTGUN MARY: BLOOD LORE
Antarctic Press, 1997
1 (of 4) by Herb Mallette
& Neil Googe. 3.00
2 . . . . 3.00
3 . . . . 3.00
4 concl. 3.00

SHOTGUN MARY: SON OF THE BEAST, DAUGHTER OF LIGHT
Antarctic Press, 1997
1 . . . . 3.00

Shotgun Mary Blood Lore #4
© *Antarctic Press*

SHOTGUN WEDDING
Speakeasy Comics, 2005
1 . . . . 3.00
2 . . . . 3.00

SHRUGGED
Aspen MLT., 2006
Spec. Beginnings 3.00
0 . . . . 7.00
1 . . . . 5.00
2 thru 5 . . . . @3.00

SIEGEL & SHUSTER
Eclipse, 1984–85
1 . . . . 2.50
2 . . . . 2.50

SIGIL
Crossgen Comics, 2000
1 BKs 5.00
2 BKs 3.25
3 thru 5 BKs . . . . @3.50
6 thru 12 BKs . . . . @3.25
13 thru 18 MWa,SEa . . . . @3.00
19 thru 30 SEa . . . . @3.00
31 thru 43 CDi(s) . . . . @3.00
TPB Vol. 1 . . . . 20.00
TPB Vol. 2 . . . . 20.00
TPB Vol. 3 The Lizard God 16.00
TPB Vol. 4 Hostage Planet 16.00
TPB Vol. 5 Death Match 16.00

SILENCERS, THE
Moonstone, 2003
1 . . . . 3.50
2 . . . . 3.50
3 . . . . 3.00
4 . . . . 3.50
* 1-shot Bitter Fruit, Bumper Edition . 5.00
TPB Black Kiss 15.00

SILENT DRAGON
Wildstorm/DC, July, 2005
1 (of 6) 3.00
2 thru 4 . . . . @3.00
5 . . . . 3.00
6 . . . . 3.00
TPB 20.00

SILENT GHOST
Speakeasy Comics, 2005
1 .... 3.00
2 .... 3.00

Markosia, 2006
1 .... 3.50
2 .... 3.50

SILENT HILL
IDW Publishing, 2005
1 Paint it Black 7.50
GN Among the Damned.......... 7.50
GN The Grinning Man 7.50
TPB Vol. 2 Three Bloody Tales ... 20.00

SILENT HILL: DEAD/ALIVE
IDW Publishing, 2005
1 .... 4.00
1a 4.00
2 thru 5 .... @4.00
2a thru 5a variant (c) 4.00
TPB Silent Hill: Dead/Alive 20.00

SILENT HILL: DYING INSIDE
IDW Publishing, 2004
1 .... 5.00
2 thru 5 .... @4.50
TPB 20.00

SILENT MOBIUS
Viz, 1991–92
1 Katsumi 5.75
2 Katsumi vs. Spirit........... 5.25
3 Katsumi trapped within entity. . 5.00
4 Nami vs. Dragon 5.00
5 Kiddy vs. Wire 5.00
6 Search for Wire 5.00
GN 15.00

SILENT MOBIUS II
Viz, 1991
1 AMP Officers vs. Entities cont ... 5.00
2 Entities in Amp H.Q. 5.00
3 V:Entity..................... 5.00
4 The Esper Weapon 5.00
5 Last issue.................. 5.00

SILENT MOBIUS III
Viz, 1992
1 F:Lebia/computer network...... 2.75

Silent Ghost #1
© Crossgen Comics

2 Lebia/computer link cont........ 2.75
3 Lebia in danger 2.75
4 Return to Consciousness 2.75
5 Conclusion.................. 2.75

SILKEN GHOST, THE
Crossgen Comics, 2003
1 (of 5) CDi.................... 3.00
2 thru 5 .... @3.00
Vol. 1 Silken Ghost Traveler 10.00

SILVERBACK
Comico, 1989–90
1 thru 3 .... @2.50

SILVER CROSS
Antarctic Press, 1997
1 (of 3) by Ben Dunn 3.00
2 .... 3.00

SILVERHEELS
Pacific, 1983–84
1 and 3 .... @2.50

SILVER STAR
Pacific, 1983–84
1 thru 6 JK................... @2.50

SILVER STAR
Topps, 1993
1 w/Cards 3.00

SILVER STORM
Silverline, 1998
1 thru 3 .... @2.50

SIMPSONS COMICS
Bongo Comics, 1993
1 Colossal Homer............. 10.00
2 A:Sideshow Bob.............. 7.00
3 F:Bart...................... 7.00
4 F:Bart...................... 5.00
5 A:Itchy & Scratchy 5.00
6 F:Lisa...................... 5.00
7 Circus in Town 5.00
8 Mr. Burns Voyage 5.00
9 Autobiographies 5.00
10 Tales of the Kwik-E-Mart...... 5.00
11 Ned Flanders Public Enemy ... 4.00
12 In the Blodome 4.00
13 F:Bart & Millhouse 4.00
14 Homer owns beer company ... 4.00
15 Waltons parody............. 4.00
16 thru 49.................... @4.00
50 80-pg. 6.00
51 thru 99.................... @3.00
100 SA,100-pg................. 7.00
101 thru 111.................. @3.00
112 thru 124.................. 3.00
Spec. Simpsons Classics #1
    thru #6 .... @4.00
Spec. Simpsons Classics #7 ..... 4.00
Spec. Simpsons Classics #8 .... 4.00
Spec. Simpsons Classics #9 .... 4.00
Spec. Simpsons Classics #10 ... 4.00
Spec. #1 Winter Wingding 5.00
Simpsons Super Spectacular #1 .. 5.00
Simpsons Super Spectacular #2 .. 3.00
Simpsons Super Spectacular #3 .. 3.00
TPB Rep.#1-#4 .... 10.00
TPB Wing Ding, 120pg 12.00
TPB Simpsons Comics on Parade
    (1998) 12.00
TPB Simpsons Comics Big
    Bonanza 12.00
TPB Comics A Go-Go 12.00
TPB Comics Extravaganza 10.00
TPB Bartman Best of the Best.... 10.00

TPB Simpsons Comics Strike Back 11.00
TPB Comics Wing Ding......... 12.00
TPB Simpsons Unchained (2002) . 15.00
TPB Madness 15.00
TPB Belly Buster (2004) 15.00
TPB Barn Burner 15.00
TPB #14 Jam-Packed Jamboree.. 15.00
Comic Spectacular,Vol.1 Rep..... 10.00
Comic Spectacular,Vol.2 Rep..... 10.00
TPB Vol. 4 Treehouse of Horror
    Hoodoo Voodoo 15.00

SIMPSONS COMICS & STORIES
Welsh Publishing, 1993
1 with poster 4.00
1a without poster 2.50
Bongo Comics, 1998
1 F:Bartman, Itchy & Scratchy 3.00

SIMPSONS/FUTURAMA CROSSOVER CRISIS
Bongo Comics, 2005
Part II
1 (of 2) 3.00
2 .... 3.00

SINGULARITY SEVEN
IDW Publishing, 2004
1 .... 4.00
2 thru 4 .... @4.00
TPB 20.00

SINS OF THE FALLEN: THE NIGHTSTALKER
Zenescope Entertainment, 2005
1 .... 3.00
2 thru 5 .... @3.00

SINTHIA
Lightning, 1997
1A by Joseph Adam, Daughter
    of Lucifer 3.00
1B 3.00
1c Platinum Edition 10.00
1d Autographed Edition 10.00
2 Sisters of Darkness 3.00
2a variant cover 3.00
3 Wagner(c) 3.00
3a variant Abrams cover 3.00
3b deluxe variant cover 10.00
4 Wagner(c) 3.00
4a variant John Cleary cover 3.00

SIRE, THE
After-Shock Comics, 2006
1 (of 3) 3.00
2 .... 3.00

SIREN
Malibu Ultraverse, 1995
Infinity V:War Machine.......... 2.50
1 V:War Machine 2.50
1a Computer painted cover 2.50
2 Phoenix flip issue............ 2.50
3 Phoenix Resurrection 2.50
Spec. #1 O:Siren 2.50

SISTERS OF MERCY
Maximum, 1995–96
1 .... 2.50
1a variant(c).................. 2.50
2 .... 2.50
3 .... 2.50
No Mercy Comics
4 .... 2.50

COLOR PUB.

5 . . . . 2.50
TPB rep. #1–#5 . . . . 15.00

SISTERS OF MERCY: PARADISE LOST
London Night, 1997
1 by Ricki Rockett & Mark Williams 2.50
2 . . . . 2.50
3 . . . . 2.50
4 . . . . 2.50

SISTERS OF MERCY: WHEN RAZORS CRY CRIMSON TEARS
No Mercy Comics, 1996
1 . . . . 2.50

SIX-GUN SAMURAI
Alias Enterprises, 2005
1 . . . . 1.00
2 thru 4 . . . . @3.00
5 . . . . 3.00
6 . . . . 3.00

SIX MILLION DOLLAR MAN, THE
Charlton, 1976
1 JSon,Lee Majors Ph(c) 35.00
2 NA(c),JSon,Ph(c). 20.00
3 Ph(c) HC,NA 22.00
4 thru 9 Ph(c) . . . . @20.00

666: MARK OF THE BEAST
Fleetway/Quality, 1986
1 I:Fludd, BU:Wolfie Smith 2.50
2 thru 18. . . . . @2.50

SIX STRING SAMURAI
Awesome Entertainment, 1998
1 RLe 3.00

SKATEMAN
Pacific, 1983
1 NA 2.50

SKYE RUNNER
Wildstorm/DC, April, 2006
1 . . . . 3.00
1a variant JLe (c) 3.00
2 thru 5 . . . . @3.00

SKY WOLF
Eclipse, 1988
1 V:Baron Von Tundra 2.50
2 TL,V:Baron Von Tundra 2.50
3 TL,cont. in Airboy #41 . . . . 2.50

SLAINE THE BERSERKER
Quality, 1987–89
1 thru 14 . . . . @2.50
15/16 . . . . 2.50
17 . . . . 2.50
18/19 . . . . 2.50
20 . . . . 2.50
Becomes:

SLAINE THE KING
Quality, 1989
21 thru 26 . . . . @2.50

SLAINE
Fleetway
1 thru 4 SBs,From 2000 AD . . . . @5.00

SLAINE THE HORNED GOD
Egmont Fleetway, 1998
1 (of 3) Pat Millagan & SBs, 68pg. . 7.00
2 (of 3) Pat Millagan & SBs, 68pg. . 7.00
3 68-pg., conclusion 7.00

SLAUGHTER
APC, 2003
1 . . . . 3.50
2 and 3 . . . . @3.50
TPB 13.00

SLEEPER
Wildstorm/DC, 2003
1 SeP,F:Holden Carver 3.00
2 SeP 3.00
3 SeP,O:Miss Misery. 3.00
4 SeP,behind the curtain. 3.00
5 SeP,F:Holden Carver 3.00
6 SeP,Holden's past 3.00
7 SeP,things get worse 3.00
8 SeP,Doppelganger. 3.00
9 SeP,secret records. 3.00
10 thru 12 SeP . . . . @3.00
TPB Sleeper: Out in the Cold . . . 18.00
TPB Sleeper: All False Moves . . . 18.00
Season Two (2004)
1 (of 12) SeP 3.00
2 thru 5 SeP . . . . @3.00
6 SeP 3.00
7 SeP 3.00
8 SeP,All-girl spy extravaganza . . . 3.00
9 SeP 3.00
10 SeP 3.00
11 SeP 3.00
12 SeP 3.00
TPB Vol. 3 A Crooked Line 15.00
TPB Vol. 4 The Long Way Home. . 15.00

SLIDERS
Valiant, 1996
1 & 2 . . . . @2.50

SLIDERS: DARKEST HOUR
Acclaim, 1996
1 DGC,DG. 2.50
2 DGC,DG. 2.50
3 DGC,DG, Concl.. . . . . 2.50
Spec. RgM, Montezuma IV rules the
world 4.00
Spec. #2 Secrets 4.00
TPB from TV show. 9.00

SLIDERS: ULTIMATUM
Valiant, 1996
1 & 2 . . . . @2.50

SLIMER
Now, 1989
1 thru 15 . . . . @2.50
Becomes:

SLIMER & REAL GHOSTBUSTERS
16 thru 18 . . . . @2.50

SLUDGE
Malibu Ultraverse, 1993–94
1 BWS,I:Sludge,BU:I:Rune. 2.75
1a Ultra-Limited 5.00

Sludge #5
© Malibu

2 thru 13 AaL. . . . . @2.50
Red X-Mas 2.50

SMAX
Wildstorm/DC, 2003
1 (of 5) AMo,F:Jeff Smax 3.00
2 AMo,O:Smax 3.00
3 AMo,funeral 3.00
4 . . . . 3.00
5 AMo,V:Morningbright 3.00
TPB AMo(s) 13.00

SMILEY
Chaos! Comics, 1998
1 the Psychotic Button 3.00
Spec. Smiley Anti-Holiday Spec. . . . 3.00
Spec. Smiley Psychotic Button's
Spring Break Road Trip 3.00
Spec. Whacky Wrestling Spec. 3.00

SMOKE
What's Next Entertainment, 2000
1 (of 12) by Ty Rawls 3.00
2 . . . . 3.25
3 . . . . 3.25
4 . . . . 3.00
5 . . . . 3.25
TPB Vol. 1 . . . . 20.00

SMOKE
IDW Publishing, 2005
1 Good Boys Grow Up 7.50
2 The Judas 7.50
3 The Men on the Chessboard. . . . 7.50
TPB 25.00

SMOKE AND MIRROR
Speakeasy Comics, 2005
1 . . . . 3.00
2 . . . . 3.00
3 thru 6 . . . . @3.00
TPB Vol. 1 Time and Time Again. . 16.00

SMOKE & MIRROR
Markosia, 2006
TPB Vol. 1 Time & Time Again . . . 19.00
TPB Vol. 1 variant (c) 19.00
Vol. 2
1 . . . . 3.50
1a variant (c)s . . . . @3.50

COLOR PUB.

2 thru 3 . . . . @3.50
2a thru 3a variant (c)s . . . . @3.50
4 . . . . 3.50

SNAGGLEPUSS
Gold Key, 1962–63
1 . . . . 150.00
2 . . . . 125.00
3 . . . . 125.00
4 . . . . 125.00

SNAKE EYES DECLASSIFIED
Devil's Due Publishing, 2005
1 . . . . 3.00
2 thru 3 . . . . @3.00
4 thru 6 . . . . @3.00

SNAKE PLISSKEN CHRONICLES
Crossgen Comics, 2003
1 . . . . 3.00
2 . . . . 3.00
3 . . . . 3.00

Alias Enterprises, 2005
TPB Vol. 1 . . . . 12.00

SNAKES ON A PLANE
Wildstorm/DC, Sept., 2006
1 CDo, movie adapt., ph(c). 3.00
2 CDo, movie adapt., ph(c). 3.00
1a & 2a, variant (c)s . . . . @3.00

SNAKEWOMAN
Virgin Comics, 2006
1 . . . . 4.00
2 thru 5 . . . . @3.50

SNAK POSSE
HCom, 1994
1 . . . . 2.50
2 . . . . 2.50

SNOOPER AND BLABBER DETECTIVES
Gold Key, 1962–63
1 . . . . 150.00
2 . . . . 125.00
3 . . . . 125.00

SNOW WHITE & SEVEN DWARFS GOLDEN ANNIVERSARY
Gladstone, 1987
1 w/poster & stickers 24.00

SNOWYBROOK INN
Counteractive Comics, 2006
1 . . . . 3.00

SOAP OPERA ROMANCES
Charlton, 1982–83
1 . . . . 40.00
2 thru 5 . . . . @30.00

SO DARK THE ROSE
CFD, 1995
1 Fully Painted 3.00

SOJOURN
Dreamer Comics, 1998
1 by Jim Somerville, Stranger
   & Stranger, pt.1 . . . . 3.00

Soap Opera Romances #1
© Charlton

2 Stranger & Stranger, pt.2 . . . . . . 3.00
3 Malice in Wonderland 3.00
4 A Game of Conscience, pt.1 . . . 3.00
5 A Game of Conscience, pt.2 . . . 2.50
6 A Game of Conscience, pt.3 . . . 3.25
7 A Game of Conscience, pt.4 . . . 3.25
8 The Hunt 3.25
9 The Hunt, pt.2 . . . . 3.25
10 The Hunt, Bloodied. 3.25

SOJOURN
Crossgen Comics, 2001
1 RMz 7.00
2 thru 5 RMz . . . . @5.00
6 thru 17 RMz 3.00
18 thru 24 . . . . @3.00
25 IEd. 2.50
26 thru 37 . . . . @3.00
Collected Ed. #1 . . . . 4.00
Prequel RMz 3.00
TPB Vol. 1 rep. #1–#6 . . . . 20.00
TPB Vol. 2 Dragon's Tale. 16.00
TPB Traveler Vol. 2 Dragon's Tale. 10.00
TPB Vol. 3 The Warrior's Tale 16.00
TPB Vol. 4 The Thief's Tale 16.00
TPB Vol. 5 The Sorcerer's Tale . . . 16.00

SOJOURN/LADY DEATH
Crossgen Comics, 2004
1 (of 2) 3.00
2 . . . . 3.00

SOLAR: HELL ON EARTH
Acclaim, 1997
1 (of 4) CPr,DCw,Seleski twins
   have power of God 2.50
2 CPr,Goat Month prelude 2.50
3 CPr,RT,V:Jimmy Six. 2.50
4 CPr, ... 2.50

SOLAR: MAN OF THE ATOM
Valiant, 1991
1 BWS,DP,BL,B:2nd Death B:Alpha
   & Omega 10.00
2 BWS,DP,BL,V:Dr Solar 7.00
3 BWS,DP,BL,V:Harada I:Harbinger
   Foundation. 8.00
4 BWS,DP,BL,E:2nd Death V:Dr
   Solar 9.00
5 BWS,EC,V:Alien Armada. 7.00

6 BWS,DP,SDr, V:Alien Armada X-
   O Armor. 7.00
7 BWS,DP,SDr, V:Alien Armada X-
   O Armor. 9.00
8 BWS,V:Dragon of Bangkok 9.00
9 BWS,DP,SDr, V:Erica's Baby. . . . 9.00
10 BWS,DP,SDr,JDx,I:Eternal
   Warrior,E:Alpha&Omega 15.00
10a 2nd printing 7.00
11 SDr,A:Eternal Warrior, Prequel
   to Unity #0 . . . . 3.00
12 SDr,FM(c),Unity#9,O:Pierce,
   Albert 2.50
13 DP,SDr,WS(c),Unity #17,
   V:Pierce. 2.50
14 DP,SDr,I:Bender (becomes
   Dr.Eclipse). 3.00
15 SD,V:Bender. 3.00
16 thru 57 . . . . @2.50
58 I:Atman, The Inquisitor 5.00
59 and 60 KG. . . . . @11.00
TPB #0 JiS,BWS,BL,Alpha and
   Omega rep. from Solar #1–#10 10.00
TPB #1 JiS,BWS,GL,V:Doctor Solar
   rep. from Solar #1–#4 . . . . . . 10.00

SOLITAIRE
Malibu Ultraverse, 1993–94
1 black baged edition with playing
   card: Ace of Clubs, Diamonds,
   Hearts or Spades. 2.75
1d Newsstand edition,no card 2.50
2 thru 12 . . . . @2.50

SOLOMON KANE
Blackthorne
1 3-D Special 2.50
2 3-D Special 2.50
1 thru 4 . . . . @2.50

SOLUS
Crossgen Comics, 2003
1 BKs,GP,RM,48-pg. 3.00
2 thru 10 . . . . @3.00
TPB Vol. 1 Genesis 16.00

SOLUTION
Malibu Ultraverse, 1993–95
0 DaR,O:Solution 4.00
1 DaR,I:Solution 2.50
1a foil cover 4.00
2 thru 17 . . . . @2.50

SOMERSET HOLMES
Pacific, 1983–84
1 BA,AW,I:Cliff Hanger &
   Somerset Holmes 2.50
2 thru 4 BA,AW. . . . . @2.50
Eclipse, 1984
5 BA,AW. 2.50
6 BA 2.50

SONIC THE HEDGEHOG
Archie Publications 1993 Mini-series
1 . . . . 30.00
2 . . . . 20.00
3 . . . . 20.00

SONIC THE HEDGEHOG
Archie Publications, 1993
1 A:Mobius,V:Robotnik 35.00
2 . . . . 30.00
3 thru 6 . . . . @20.00
7 thru 10 . . . . @20.00
11 thru 30 . . . . @20.00
31 thru 39. . . . . @7.00
40 thru 54 . . . . @7.00

55 thru 78 . . . . @4.00
79 and 80 . . . . @4.00
81 thru 99 . . . . @15.00
100 . . . . 2.50
101 thru 116 . . . . @2.50
117 thru 142 . . . . @2.50
143 thru 169 . . . . @2.25
GN Sonic Firsts, rep.#0, #1/4
    ashcan,#3,#4,#13 . . . . 5.00
Sonic Live Spec.#1 . . . . 2.50
TPB Beginnings 11.00
TPB Archives Vol. 1 . . . . 7.50

SONIC QUEST:
THE DEATH EGG SAGA
Archie Comics, 1997
1 (of 3) by Mike Gallagher & MaG,
    cont. from Sonic the Hedgehog
    #41 . . . . 2.50
2 and 3 . . . . @2.50

SONIC THE HEDGEHOG
PRESENTS
KNUCKLES CHASTIC
Archie Comics, 1995
1 I:New Heroes 2.50
Sonic Versus Knuckles Battle Royal
    Spec.#1 . . . . 2.50

SONIC THE HEDGEHOG
PRESENTS TAILS
Archie Comics, 1995
1 F:Tails 2.50
2 F:Tails 2.50

SONIC'S FRIENDLY
NEMESIS: KNUCKLES
Archie Comics, 1996
1 . . . . 2.50

SONIC SUPER SPECIAL
Archie Comics, 1997
1 Brave New World 2.50
3 Sonic Firsts 2.50
4 The Return of the King 2.50
5 Sonic Kids 2.50
6 Expanded Sonic #50, 48pg 2.50
7 F:Shadowhawk, The Maxx,
    Savage Dragon 2.50
8 four stories, 48-pg. 2.50
9 R:Sonic Kids 2.50
10 Some Enchantra Evening 2.50
11 . . . . 2.50
12 48-pg. 2.50
13 thru 15 . . . . @2.50

SONIC X
Archie Comics, 2005
1 (of 4) 2.25
2 See Sonic; Sea Battle 2.25
3 thru 15 . . . . @2.25

SOULFIRE
Aspen Entertainment, 2003
0 The Day the Magic Died 8.00
1 . . . . 8.00
1a previews exclusive (c) 7.00
1b signed 25.00
2 . . . . 10.00
3 . . . . 10.00
4 . . . . 10.00
4a thru 4c variant (c). . . . . @9.00
5 . . . . 5.00
6 . . . . 5.00
7 . . . . 4.00
8 thru 9 . . . . @3.00

10 . . . . 4.00
Coll. Ed. #1 . . . . 7.00

SOULFIRE:
CHAOS REIGN
Aspen MLT, 2006
Spec. Beginnings 2.00
0 . . . . 2.50
1 . . . . 3.00
2 thru 3 . . . . @3.00

Soulfire: Dying of the Light #1
© Aspen

SOULFIRE:
DYING OF THE LIGHT
Aspen, 2005
0 . . . . 2.50
0a signed 20.00
1 . . . . 3.00
1a signed edition. 35.00
2 . . . . 3.00
2 thru 3 . . . . 3.00
4 thru 5 . . . . @3.00
TPB 15.00

SOULMAN
Quantum Comics, 1998
1 . . . . 3.00
2 . . . . 3.00
3 16-pg. 3.00
4 16-pg. 3.00
5 24-pg. 3.00

SOUPY SALES
COMIC BOOK
Archie Publications, 1965
1 . . . . 150.00

SPACE ADVENTURES
Charlton, 1967–79, Volume 3
1 (#60) O&I:Paul Mann & The
    Saucers From the Future . . . 100.00
2 thru 8 (1968–69) . . . . @75.00
9 thru 13 (1978–79) . . . . @30.00

SPACE:
ABOVE AND BEYOND
Topps, 1995
1 thru 3 TV pilot adaptation. . . . . @3.00

SPACE:
ABOVE AND BEYOND—
THE GAUNTLET
Topps, 1996
1 . . . . 3.00
2 (of 2) 3.00

SPACE ARK
AC Comics, 1985–87
1 . . . . 3.00
2 . . . . 2.50

SPACE FAMILY
ROBINSON
Gold Key, 1962–69
1 DSp 500.00
2 . . . . 250.00
3 . . . . 175.00
4 . . . . 175.00
5 . . . . 175.00
6 B:Captain Venture 150.00
7 . . . . 150.00
8 . . . . 150.00
9 . . . . 150.00
10 . . . . 150.00
11 thru 20 . . . . @100.00
21 thru 36 . . . . @75.00

SPACE GHOST
Gold Key, 1967
1 . . . . 600.00

SPACE GHOST
Comico, 1987
1 SR,V:Robot Master 10.00

SPACE GIANTS, THE
Pyramid Comics, 1997
0 . . . . 2.50
0a deluxe 2.50
1 . . . . 2.50
3 by Jeff Newman 2.50

SPACE MAN
Dell Publishing Co., 1962–72
1 . . . . 150.00
2 . . . . 100.00
3 . . . . 100.00
4 . . . . 75.00
5 . . . . 75.00
6 . . . . 75.00
7 . . . . 75.00
8 . . . . 75.00
9 . . . . 75.00
10 . . . . 75.00

SPACE: 1999
Charlton, 1975–76
1 . . . . 35.00
2 JSon,Survival 30.00
3 JBy,Bring Them Back Alive . . . 25.00
4 JBy 25.00
5 JBy 25.00
6 JBy 25.00
7 . . . . 25.00
8 B&W 25.00

SPACE: 1999
A Plus Comics
1 GM,JBy 2.50

SPACE USAGI
Mirage, 1993
1 thru 3 From TMNT . . . . @2.75

COLOR PUB.

SPACE WAR
Charlton Comics, 1959
1	250.00
2	150.00
3	125.00
4 SD,SD(c)	250.00
5 SD,SD(c)	250.00
6 SD	250.00
7	100.00
8 SD,SD(c)	250.00
9	100.00
10 SD,SD(c).	250.00
11	100.00
12 thru 15	@100.00
16 thru 27	@100.00
Becomes:	

FIGHTIN' FIVE
28 SD,SD(c).	100.00
29 SD,SD(c).	100.00
30 SD,SD(c).	125.00
31 SD,SD(c).	125.00
32	35.00
33 SD,SD(c).	125.00
34 Sd,SD(c).	125.00

SPECIAL EDUCATION
National Press Comics, 2006
1	3.00
2	3.00

SPECIES
Avatar Press/Pulsar Press, 2005
Spec. #1	4.00
Spec. #1a Wraparound (c).	4.00
Spec. #1b Variant(c)s	@4.00

SPECTER 7
Antarctic Press, 2002
1 (of 3) by Craig Babiar	5.00
2 and 3	@5.00

SPECWAR
Peter Four Productions, 2002
1	3.25
2 thru 5	@3.25
6 thru 8	@3.25

SPEED RACER
Now, 1987–90
1	3.50
1a 2nd printing	2.50
2 thru 33	@2.50
34 thru 38	@2.50
Spec. #1	2.50
#1 2nd printing	2.00
Spec. #2	3.50
Classics, Vol #2	4.00
Classics, Vol #3	4.00
[2nd Series]	
1 R:Speed Racer	2.50
2	2.50
3 V:Giant Crab	2.50
4	2.50
5 Racer-X	2.50
6	2.50
7	2.50

SPEED RACER
WildStorm/DC, 1999
1 Demon on Wheels	2.50
2	2.50
3 concl.	2.50
TPB Born to Race	10.00
TPB Original Manga	10.00

SPELLBINDERS
Quality, 1986–88
1 Nemesis the Warlock	2.50
2 thru 12 Nemesis the Warlock.	@2.50

SPELLGAME
Speakeasy Comics, 2005
2	3.00
3 thru 7	@3.00

S.P.I.C.E.
Awesome Entertainment, 1998
1 RLe,JLb,F:Kaboom	2.50

SPIDER
Eclipse, 1991
1 TT,Blood Dance	7.00
2 TT,Blood Mark	6.00
3 TT,The Spider Unmasked	5.50

SPIDER: REIGN OF THE VAMPIRE KING
Eclipse, 1992
1 TT,I:Legion of Vermin	5.25
2 thru 4 TT	@2.50

SPIDER-MAN/BADROCK
Maximum Press, 1997
1 (of 2) DJu,MMy x-over	3.00
2 DJu,DaF x-over	3.00

SPIKE
IDW Publishing, 2005
1-shot Spike: Old Times, Buffy spin-off	7.50
1-shotA variant (c)	7.50
1-shot Old Wounds	7.50
1-shot Lost & Found	7.50
1-shot Lost & Found, variant (c)	7.50
TPB Spike	20.00

SPIKE: ASYLUM
IDW Publishing, 2006
1	4.00
1a variant (c),	4.00
2 thru 3	@4.00

SPIKE VS. DRACULA
IDW Publishing, 2006
1 PDd	4.00
1a variant (c)s	4.00
2 thru 5	@4.00
2a thru 5a variant (c)	@4.00
TPB	20.00

SPIRAL PATH
Eclipse, 1986
1 V:Tairngir	2.50
2 V:King Artuk	2.50

SPIRIT, THE
Harvey, 1966
1 WE,O:Spirit	150.00
2 WE,O:The Octopus	100.00

SPIRIT, THE
Kitchen Sink, 1983–92
1 WE(c) (1983)	5.25
2 WE(c).	4.25
3 WE(c) (1984)	4.00
4 WE(c)	4.00
5 thru 7 WE(c)	@3.00
8 thru 11 WE(c) (1985)	@3.00
See: B&W Pub. section	

The Spirit #2
© Kitchen Sink

SPIRIT, THE: THE NEW ADVENTURES
Kitchen Sink, 1997
1 AMo,DGb	4.00
2 Eisner/Stout cover	3.50
2a Eisner/Schultz cover	3.50
3 AMo,Last Night I Dreamed of Dr. Cobra	3.50
4 Dr. Broca von Bitelbaum	3.50
5 Cursed Beauty	3.50
6 Swami Vashti Bubu	3.50
7 Central City	3.50
8 by Joe Lansdale	3.50
9	3.50
10 CAd,BRa	3.50

SPIRIT OF THE AMAZON
NW Studios, 2002
1	3.00
2 thru 7	@3.00

SPOOKY HAUNTED HOUSE
Harvey Publications, 1972–75
1	60.00
2	50.00
3 thru 5	@50.00
6 thru 10	@40.00
11 thru 15	@35.00

SPOOKY SPOOKTOWN
Harvey Publications, 1966–76
1 B:Casper,Spooky,68 pgs	350.00
2	275.00
3	200.00
4	200.00
5	200.00
6 thru 10	@150.00
11 thru 20	@100.00
21 thru 30	@100.00
31 thru 39 E:68 pgs	@75.00
40 thru 45	@50.00
46 thru 66	@40.00

SPOONER
Astonish Comics, 2004
1	3.00
2 thru 4	@3.00
TPB	15.00

All comics prices listed are for *Near Mint* condition.

SPRINGHEELED JACK
Full Circle Publications, 2006
1 new printing 4.00
2 new printing 4.00
3 new printing 4.00

SPYMAN
Harvey, 1966
1 GT,JSo,1st prof work,
I:Spyman 200.00
2 DAy,JSo,V:Cyclops 150.00
3 . . . . 100.00

SQUAD, THE
Malibu
0-A Hardcase's old team 2.50
0-B 2.50
0-C L.A.Riots 2.50

SQUALOR
First, 1989
1 . . . . 2.75
2 . . . . 2.75
3 . . . . 2.75

STAINLESS STEEL RAT
Eagle, 1986
1 Harry Harrison adapt. 2.50
2 thru 6 . . . . @2.50

STAR BLAZERS
Comico, 1989
1 . . . . 3.00
2 . . . . 3.00
3 . . . . 3.00
4 . . . . 3.00

[2nd Series]
1 . . . . 3.00
2 . . . . 3.00
3 thru 5 . . . . @3.00

STARBLAZERS
Argo Press, 1995
0 Battleship Yamato 3.00
1 F:Dereck Wildstar 3.00
2 After the Comet War 3.00
3 . . . . 3.00
4 TEI 3.00
5 thru 12 . . . . @3.00

STARDUST KID
Boom! Studios, 2006
4 . . . . 3.50
5 . . . . 3.50

STARFORCE SIX SPECIAL
AC Comics, 1984
1 . . . . 2.50

STARGATE
Entity Comics, 1996
1 . . . . 3.00
2 . . . . 3.00
3 . . . . 3.00
4 . . . . 3.00
4a deluxe limited edition 3.50

STARGATE ATLANTIS: WRAITHFALL
Avatar Press/Pulsar Press, 2006
1 . . . . 4.00
1a variant (c)s . . . . @4.00
1b variant photo (c)s . . . . @4.00
2 . . . . 4.00

Stargate #4
© *Entity Comics*

2a variant (c)s . . . . @4.00
2b variant photo (c)s . . . . @4.00

STARGATE: DOOMSDAY WORLD
Entity Comics, 1996
1 new crew explores 2nd StarGate 3.00
1 prism-foil edition 3.50
2 . . . . 3.00
3 . . . . 3.00
3 deluxe 3.50

STARGATE SG–1
Avatar, 2003
Convention Spec. 3.00
Convention Spec. Photo (c) 4.00
Spec. First Prime Edition 6.00
Convention Spec. 2004 . . . . 3.00
Convention Spec. 2004, ph(c) 4.00
2005 Convention Special 3.00
2005 Convention Special
variant (c)s . . . . @3.00
2006 Convention Special 3.00
2006 Convention Special
variant (c)s . . . . @3.00

STARGATE SG-1: ARIS BOCH
Avatar, 2004
1 . . . . 3.00
1a photo (c). 3.00
1b wraparound (c). 3.00

STARGATE SG-1: DANIEL'S SONG
Avatar Press/Pulsar Press, 2005
1 . . . . 3.00
1a photo(c) 3.00
1b wraparaound (c). 3.00

STARGATE SG-1: FALL OF ROME
Avatar, 2004
Prequel. 3.00
Prequel wraparound (c) 3.00
Prequel photo(c) 3.00
1 . . . . 4.00
2 thru 3 . . . . @4.00
1a thru 3a photo (c)s. . . . . @4.00
1b thru 3b wraparound (c)s. . . . @4.00

STARGATE SG-1: P.O.W.
Avatar, 2004
1 . . . . 3.50
1a wraparound (c). 3.50
1b photo (c). 3.50
2 . . . . 3.50
2a wraparound (c). 3.50
2b photo (c). 3.50
3 . . . . 3.50
3a wraparound (c). 3.50
3b photo (c). 3.50
TPB Vol. 1 . . . . 14.00

STARGATE SG-1: RA REBORN
Avatar Press/Pulsar Press, 2005
Prequel 3.00
Prequel variant (c)s . . . . @3.00
Prequel Carter painted (c) 6.00

STARGATE SG-1: RED DAWN
Avatar Press/Pulsar Press, 2006
Spec., 2006 convention (c) 6.00

STARGODS
Antarctic Press, 1998
1 by Zachary, Clark & Beaty 3.00
1a deluxe 6.00
2 The Golden Bow 3.00
2a deluxe, with poster. 6.00
Spec. Stargods Visions 3.00

STARK RAVEN
Hardline Studios, 2000
1 The Screaming Rain,pt.1 . . . . . . 3.00
2 The Screaming Rain,pt.2 . . . . . . 3.00
3 . . . . 3.00

Endless Horizons, 2000
4 . . . . 3.00
5 . . . . 3.00
6 Ken Kelly (c) 3.00
7 . . . . 3.00
8 . . . . 3.00

STARKWEATHER
Arcana Studio, 2004
1 . . . . 3.00
2 thru 5 . . . . @3.00
TPB Vol. 1 . . . . 10.00

STAR MASTERS
AC Comics, 1994
1 . . . . 2.50

STAR REACH CLASSICS
Eclipse, 1984
1 JSn,NA(r) 2.50
2 AN 2.50
3 HC 2.50
4 FB(r). 2.50
5 . . . . 2.50
6 . . . . 2.50

STAR SEED
See: POWERS THAT BE

STARSHIP TROOPERS
Mongoose Publishing, 2005
GN #1 Blaze of GLory 15.00
GN #2 Dead Man's Hand 15.00

STARSHIP TROOPERS
Markosia, 2006
0 Previews exclusive 3.00

0a signed edition. 10.00	
1 Alamo Bay 3.50	
1a variant (c)s . . . . @3.50	
1b director's cut 3.50	
2 Alamo Bay, pt. 2. . . . . 3.50	
2a variant (c) 3.50	
3 . . . . 3.50	
3a variant (c)s . . . . @3.50	
4 . . . . 3.50	
4a variant (c)s . . . . @3.50	
TPB Blaze of Glory 16.00	

STARSHIP TROOPERS: DAMAGED JUSTICE
Markosia, 2006

1 . . . . 3.00
1a variant (c)s . . . . @3.00
1b variant sketch (c) signed 10.00

STARSHIP TROOPERS: DEAD MAN'S HAND
Markosia, 2006

1 (of 4) 4.00
1a variant (c)s . . . . @4.00
1b Ltd. Sketch (c) signed 10.00
1c Re-marked Previews exclusive 40.00
2 thru 4 . . . . @3.50
2a thru 4a variant (c)s . . . . @3.50
2b thru 4b signed Previews
    exclusives . . . . @10.00
TPB Dead Man's Hand 15.00

STAR SLAMMERS
Malibu Bravura, 1994

1 WS(a&s) 2.75
2 WS(a&s),F:Meredith 2.75
3 WS(a&s) 2.50
4 WS(a&s) 2.50
5 WS,Rojas Choice. 2.50

STARSLAYER
Pacific, 1982–83

1 MGr,O:Starslayer 4.00
2 MGr,DSt,I:Rocketeer 10.00
3 DSt,MGr,A:Rocketeer(2ndApp.) . 6.00
4 MGr,Baraka Kuhr 2.50
5 MGr,SA,A:Groo 7.00
6 MGr.conclusion story 2.50

First, 1983–85

7 MGr layouts 2.50
8 MGr layouts, MG 2.50
9 MGr layouts, MG 2.50
10 TT,MG,I:Grimjack 4.00
11 thru 34 . . . . @2.50
Graphic Novel 10.00

STARSLAYER DIRECTORS CUT
Windjammer, 1995

1 R:Starslayer, Mike Grell 2.50
2 I:New Star Slayer. 2.50
3 Jolly Rodger. 2.50
4 V:Battle Droids. 2.50
5 I:Baraka Kuhi 2.50
6 V:Valkyrie. 2.50
7 MGr(c&a),Can Torin destroy? . . . 2.50
8 MGr(c&a),JAI, Can Torin live with
    his deeds?,final issue. 2.50

STAR TREK
Gold Key, 1967–79

1 Planet of No Return 4,000.00
2 Devil's Isle of Space 1,000.00
3 Invasion of City Builders 500.00
4 Peril of Planet Quick Change . 500.00
5 Ghost Planet 500.00
6 When Planets Collide 425.00

7 Voodoo Planet 450.00
8 Youth Trap 400.00
9 Legacy of Lazarus 400.00
10 Sceptre of the Sun 350.00
11 Brain Shockers 350.00
12 Flight of the Buccaneer. 300.00
13 Dark Traveler 300.00
14 Enterprise Mutiny 300.00
15 Museum a/t End of Time. 300.00
16 Day of the Inquisitors 300.00
17 Cosmic Cavemen 300.00
18 The Hijacked Planet 300.00
19 The Haunted Asteroid 300.00
20 A World Gone Mad 300.00
21 The Mummies of Heitus VII . . 200.00
22 Siege in Superspace. 200.00
23 Child's Play 200.00
24 The Trial of Capt. Kirk. 200.00
25 Dwarf Planet 200.00
26 The Perfect Dream 200.00
27 Ice Journey 200.00
28 The Mimicking Menace. 200.00
29 rep. Star Trek #1 . . . . 200.00
30 Death of a Star 150.00
31 The Final Truth. 150.00
32 The Animal People 150.00
33 The Choice 150.00
34 The Psychocrystals. 150.00
35 rep. Star Trek #4 . . . . 150.00
36 A Bomb in Time. 150.00
37 rep. Star Trek #5 . . . . 100.00
38 One of our Captains
    is Missing. 100.00
39 Prophet of Peace 100.00
40 AMc,Furlough to Fury, A:
    Barbara McCoy 100.00
41 AMc,The Evictors 100.00
42 World Against Time. 100.00
43 World Beneath the Waves . . . 100.00
44 Prince Traitor 100.00
45 rep. Star Trek #7 . . . . 100.00
46 Mr. Oracle 100.00
47 AMc,This Tree Bears Bitter
    Fruit 100.00
48 AMc,Murder on Enterprise . . . 100.00
49 AMc,A Warp in Space 100.00
50 AMc,The Planet of No Life . . 100.00
51 AMc,Destination Annihilation6 . . 75.00
52 AMc,And A Child Shall
    Lead Them 75.00
53 AMc,What Fools..Mortals Be . . 75.00
54 AMc,Sport of Knaves 75.00
55 AMc,A World Against Itself . . . 75.00
56 AMc,No Time Like The Past,
    A:Guardian of Forever. 75.00
57 AMc,Spore of the Devil 75.00
58 AMc,Brain Damaged Planet . . 75.00
59 AMc,To Err is Vulcan. 75.00
60 AMc,The Empire Man 75.00
61 AMc,Operation Con Game . . . 75.00

Checker Book, 2004

TPB Vol. 1 rep. Gold Key. 23.00
TPB Vol. 2 rep. Gold Key. 23.00

STAR TREK: ALL OF ME
WildStorm/DC, 2000

1-shot AaL,RyE 6.00

STAR TREK: DEEP SPACE NINE
Malibu, 1993

1 Direct ed. 3.25
1a Photo(c). 3.00
1b Gold foil 5.00
2 w/skycap 3.50
3 thru 9 . . . . @2.75
10 Descendants. 2.50
11 A Short Fuse 2.75
12 Baby on Board 2.50
13 Problems with Odo 2.75

Star Trek Deep Space Nine #16
© *Malibu*

14 on Bejor 2.75
15 mythologic dilemma 2.75
16 thru 32. . . . . @2.50
Ann.#1 Looking Glass 4.00
Spec. #1 Collision Course 3.50
Spec. #0 Terok Nor 3.00

CELEBRITY SERIES: BLOOD AND HONOR
Malibu, 1995

1 Mark Lenard(s) 3.00
2 Rules of Diplomacy 3.00

LIGHTSTORM
Malibu, 1994

1 Direct ed. 3.50
1a Silver foil 8.00

HEARTS AND MINDS
Malibu, 1994

1 . . . . 3.00
2 . . . . 2.50
3 Into the Abyss,X-over preview . . . 2.50
4 final issue. 2.50

THE MAQUIS
Malibu, 1995

1 Federation Renegades 2.50
1a Newsstand, photo(c) 2.50
2 Garack 2.50
3 F:Quark, Bashir 2.50

THE NEXT GENERATION
Malibu, 1994

1 Prophet & Losses, pt.2 . . . . 2.50
2 Prophet & Losses, pt.4 . . . . 2.50

STAR TREK: DEEP SPACE NINE N-VECTOR
WildStorm/DC, 2000

1 (of 4),F:Kira 2.50
2 sabotage 2.50
3 N-Vector viroid 2.50
4 F:Quark,concl. 2.50

STAR TREK: DIVIDED WE FALL
WildStorm/DC, 2001

1 (of 4) TNG & DS9 x-over 3.00
2 thru 4 . . . . @3.00

COLOR PUB.

All comics prices listed are for *Near Mint* condition.

STAR TREK: ENTER THE WOLVES
WildStorm/DC, 2001
1-shot, 48-pg................. 6.00

STAR TREK SPECIAL
WildStorm/DC, 2000
GN #1 64-pg. 7.00

STAR TREK: THE NEXT GENERATION
WildStorm/DC, 2000
GN Embrace the Wolf, 48-pg. 6.00
TPB Enemy Unseen, 224-pg. 18.00
TPB The Gorn Crisis (2002) 18.00
TPB Forgiveness (2002) 18.00

STAR TREK: NEW FRONTIER — TIME MANAGEMENT
WildStorm/DC, 2001
GN PDd, novel adapt............ 6.00

STAR TREK: THE NEXT GENERATION — THE KILLING SHADOWS
WildStorm/DC, 2000
1 (of 4) V:Bodai Shin, assassin ... 2.50
2 thru 4 V:Bodai Shin .... @2.50

STAR TREK: THE NEXT GENERATION — PERCHANCE TO DREAM
WildStorm/DC, 1999
1 (of 4) 2.50
2 thru 4 .... @2.50

STAR TREK: VOYAGER
WildStorm/DC, 2000
Spec. Elite Force 6.00
Spec. Avalon Rising............. 6.00
TPB Encounters with the Unknown 20.00

STAR TREK: VOYAGER
Malibu
A V:Maquis.................... 2.75
Aa Newsstand, photo(c) 2.50
B conclusion.................. 2.75
Ba Newsstand, photo(c) 2.50

STAR TREK: VOYAGER — PLANET KILLER
WildStorm/DC, 2001
1 (of 3) F:Kirk,Janeway........ 3.00
2 Doomsday Machine........... 3.00
3 concl...................... 3.00

STAR WARS IN 3-D
Blackthorne, 1987
1 thru 7 .... @4.00

STARWATCHERS
Valiant
1 MLe,DG,Chromium(c),Valiant
Vision, ... 3.50

S.T.A.T.
Majestic, 1993
1 FdS(s),PhH,I:S.T.A.T........... 2.50

STATIC-X
Chaos! Comics, 2002
1 by BnP, with CD-Rom 6.00
1a photo (c) with CD-Rom 6.00
1b collector's edition 20.00
Vol. 2
1 with CD-Rom 6.00
1a collector's edition 20.00

STEALTH SQUAD
Petra Comics, 1993
1 I:Stealth Squad 2.50

Steampunk #2
© *Wildstorm*

STEAMPUNK
WildStorm/DC Cliffhanger, 2000
1 CBa 2.50
1 chromium edition ....
2 CBa,V:Absinthe 2.50
3 CBa,F:Cole Blaquesmith 2.50
4 CBa,CBa(c)................ 2.50
4a variant JSC (c) (1:4) 2.50
4b variant JMd (c) (1:4) 2.50
4c variant HuR (c) (1:4) 2.50
5 CBa,V:Abbey Monsters 2.50
6 Mechanica Sundown,pt.1 ..... 2.50
7 Mechanica Sundown,pt.2 ..... 2.50
8 Mechanica Sundown,pt.3 ..... 2.50
9 Mambutu X, pt.1 .... 2.50
10 Mambutu X, pt.2............. 2.50
11 CBa, Stonehenge secret...... 2.50
12 CBa, 40-pg. final issue 3.50
TPB Drama Obscura 15.00
TPB Manimatron 15.00

STEED & MRS. PEEL
Eclipse, 1990
1 IG,The Golden Game.......... 5.00
2 IG,The Golden Game.......... 5.00
3 IG,The Golden Game.......... 5.00

STEEL CITY HAWK
Narwain Publishing, 2006
1 (of 4) 4.00
2 .... 4.00

STEEL CLAW
Quality, 1986
1 H:Ken Bulmer 4.00
2 .... 4.00
3 .... 4.00
4 .... 4.00

STEEL STERLING
**Archie Publications, 1984
(formerly LANCELOT STRONG)**
4 EB 4.00
5 EB 4.00
6 EB 4.00
7 EB 4.00

STEVE CANYON 3-D
Kitchen Sink, 1986
Milton Caniff & Peter Poplaski(c),
w/glasses (1985) 6.00

STEVE ZODIAC & THE FIREBALL XL-5
Gold Key, 1964
1 .... 175.00

STING OF THE GREEN HORNET
Now, 1992
1 Polybagged w/trading card 2.75
2 inc.Full color poster 2.75
3 inc.Full color poster 2.75

STONE COLD STEVE AUSTIN
Chaos! Comics, 1999
1 (of 4) Whoop Ass personified ... 3.00
1a photo (c)................. 3.00
1b Premium 10.00
2 .... 3.00
2a photo (c)................. 3.00
3 .... 3.00
3a photo (c)................. 3.00
4 .... 3.00
4a photo (c)................. 3.00
TPB Vol. 1 .... 13.00

STORMQUEST
Caliber, 1994
1 I:Stormquest............... 2.50
2 Time Stone. 2.50
3 BU:Seeker 2.50
4 F:Shalimar 2.50
5 Reunion 2.50
6 V:Samuroids 2.50

STORM RIDERS
Comicsone.com, 2001
GN #1 by Wing Shing Ma, 178-pg. 10.00
GN #2 127-pg. 10.00
GN #3 thru #5, 120-pg. ...... @12.00
GN #6 thru #8, 120-pg. ...... @14.00
GN #9 thru #12 .... @14.00
Part 2 (2003) Invading Sun
TPB Vol. 1 .... 10.00
TPB Vol. 2 thru Vol. 7........ @10.00

STORMWATCH: TEAM ACHILLES
WildStorm/DC, 2002
Eye of the Storm
1 WPo,SW,new team 3.00
2 WPo,SW,extremists vs. U.N..... 3.00
3 WPo,SW,military action 3.00
4 WPo,SW,hunt for Ivana Baiul ... 3.00
5 WPo,F:The Authority 3.00
6 WPo,F:The Authority 3.00
7 MT,V:Ivana Baiul 3.00
8 F:Jukko Hamalainen 3.00
9 WPo,V:super-human 3.00
10 WPo 3.00
11 WPo 3.00
12 WPo,funeral 3.00

COLOR PUB.

13 BSz,The Suiciders	3.00
14 WPo,Citizen Soldier	3.00
15 The Suiciders	3.00
16 V:Citizen Soldier	3.00
17 V:Citizen Soldier	3.00
18 O:Citizen Soldier	3.00
19 Citizen Soldier,concl.	3.00
20	3.00
21	3.00
22 Hallibastard	3.00
23 Baron Chaos	3.00
24 Project Entry Universe	3.00
TPB Vol. 1	15.00
TPB Vol. 2	15.00

STORMWATCH: PHD
Wildstorm/DC, Nov., 2006
1 DoM	3.00
1 a & b variant (c)s	@3.00

STRANGE DAYS
Eclipse, 1984–85
1	4.00
2	3.00
3	3.00

STRANGERS, THE
Malibu Ultraverse, 1993–95
1 I:Strangers	3.00
1a Ultra-Limited	4.00
1b Full Hologram (c)	5.00
2 A:J.D.Hunt,w/Ultraverse card.	3.00
3 I:TNTNT	2.50
4 thru 12	@2.50
13 (Ultraverse Premiere#4)	3.50
14 thru 26	@2.50
Ann.#1 Death	4.00
TPB rep. #1–#4	10.00
Ashcan 1 (signed)	8.00
Ashcan 1 (unsigned)	8.00

STRANGE SUSPENSE STORIES/ CAPTAIN ATOM
Charlton Comics, 1965
75 SD,O:CaptainAtom,1960Rep.	250.00
76 SD, Capt.Atom,1960Rep.	150.00
77 SD, Capt.Atom,1960Rep.	150.00
Becomes:
CAPTAIN ATOM
Charlton Comics, 1965–67
78 SD, new stories begin.	150.00
79 SD,I:Dr.Spectro	100.00
80 SD.	100.00
81 SD,V:Dr.Spectro	100.00
82 SD,I:Nightshade,Ghost	100.00
83 SD,I:Ted Kord/Blue Beetle	75.00
84 SD,N:Captain Atom.	75.00
85 SD,A:Blue Beetle,I:Punch & Jewelee	75.00
86 SD,A:Ghost, Blue Beetle	75.00
87 SD,JAp,A:Nightshade	75.00
88 SD/FMc,JAp,A:Nightshade	75.00
89 SD/FMc,JAp,A:Nightshade, Ghost, last issue Dec.,1967	75.00

STREET FIGHTER
Ocean, 1986–87
1 thru 3	@3.00

STREET FIGHTER
Malibu, 1993
1 based on Video Game	3.00
2 thru 3 Based on Video Game	@3.00

STREET FIGHTER
Devil's Due/UDON, 2004
7	4.50
7a variant (c).	4.50
8 thru 14	@3.00
8a thru 14a variant (c)s	@3.00
TPB Vol. 1	10.00
TPB Vol. 2	10.00
TPB Eternal Challenge	34.00

STREET FIGHTER II
Udon Entertainment, 2005
0	2.00

STREET FIGHTER LEGENDS: SAKURA
Udon Entertainment, 2006
1	4.00
1a variant (c)	4.00
2 thru 4	@4.00
2 thru 4a variant (c)	@4.00

STREET SHARKS
Archie Comics, 1995
1 & 2 Based on Cartoons	@2.50

STRIKE!
Eclipse, 1988
1 TL,RT,I&O:New Strike	2.50
2 TL,RT.	2.50
3 TL,RT.	2.50
4 TL,RT,V:Renegade CIA Agents	2.50
5 TL,RT,V:Alien Bugs	2.50
6 TL,RT,Legacy of the Lost.	2.50
Spec. #1 Strike vs. Sgt. Strike TL,RT,The Man	2.50

STRIKEBACK
Malibu Bravura, 1994–95
1	3.00
2	3.00
3 V:Doberman.	3.00
4 V:Dragonryder Island.	3.00
Spec.#1 KM,JRu,V:Dragon	3.50

STRIKEFORCE AMERICA
Comico, 1995
1 ScC,SK(c),I:StrikeforceAmerica.	2.50
2 V:Superior-prisoner	3.00
3 Breakout, pt.2	3.00
[Volume 2], 1995
1 ScC,polybagged with Chrysalis promo card	3.00

STRONTIUM DOG
[Mini Series] Eagle, 1985
1 thru 4	@3.00
[Regular Series] Quality, 1988
Story line continued from 2000 A.D.
7 thru 14	@2.50
15/16	2.50
17	2.50
18/19	2.50
20 thru 29	@2.50
Spec.#1	2.50
[2nd Series], 1997
1 thru 6	@2.50

STRYKE
London Night Studios, 1995
0 I:Stryke.	5.00
1	4.00

STUMBO TINYTOWN
Harvey Publications, 1963–66
1	700.00
2	300.00
3	250.00
4	250.00
5	250.00
6 thru 13	@200.00

STUPID HEROES
Next, 1994
1 PeL(s),w/ 2 card-strip	2.75
2	2.75
3 F:Cinder.	2.75

SUBSPECIES
Eternity, 1991
1 Movie Adaptation	3.00
2 Movie Adaptation	2.50
3 Movie Adaptation	2.50
4 Movie Adaptation	2.50

SULLENGRAY
Ape Entertainment, 2005
1 (of 4)	3.50
2 thru 4	@3.50

SUNDOWN
Arcana Studio, 2005
1 (of 3)	3.00
2 thru 3	@3.00

SUN GLASSES AFTER DARK
Verotik, 1995
1	3.00
2 and 3	@3.00
4 thru 6	@4.00
6 fan club cover	5.00
? prequel, San Diego Con ed.	3.00

SUN-RUNNERS
Pacific, 1984
1	2.50
2	2.50
3	2.50
Eclipse, 1984–86
4 thru 7	@2.50
Summer Special #1	2.50

Sun-Runners #2
© Pacific

SUNSET CARSON
AC Comics
1 Based on Cowboy Star 5.00

SUPERBABES: FEMFORCE
AC Comics
1 Various Artists 5.00

SUPER BAD JAMES DYNOMITE
IDW Publishing, 2005
1 (s) by Wayans brothers 4.00
2 . . . . 4.00
3 . . . . 4.00
4 . . . . 4.00

SUPER CAR
Gold Key, 1962–63
1 . . . . 650.00
2 . . . . 400.00
3 . . . . 400.00
4 . . . . 450.00

SUPERCOPS
Now, 1990
1 thru 4 . . . . @2.50

SUPER CRAZY TNT BLAST
Speakeasy Comics, 2005
1 . . . . 3.00
2 . . . . 3.00
3 thru 5 . . . . @3.00
TPB Vol. 1 . . . . 15.00

SUPER FXXXXXS
Top Shelf Productions, 2005
1 by James Kochalka 7.00
2 . . . . 5.00
3 . . . . 5.00

SUPER GOOF
Gold Key, 1965–82
1 . . . . 100.00
2 thru 10 . . . . @50.00
11 thru 20 . . . . @35.00
21 thru 30 . . . . @30.00
31 thru 74 . . . . @25.00

SUPER HEROES VERSUS SUPERVILLIANS
Archie Publications, 1966
1 A:Flyman,Black Hood,The Web,
   The Shield 125.00

SUPERHUMAN SAMURAI SYBER SQUAD
Hamilton Comics, 1995
0 Based on TV Show 3.00

SUPER MARIO BROS.
Valiant, 1991
1 thru 6 . . . . @2.50
Spec. #1 . . . . 2.50

SUPERMARKET
IDW Publishing, 2006
1 . . . . 4.00
2 . . . . 4.00
3 . . . . 4.00
4 . . . . 4.00
TPB 18.00

SUPERNATURAL FREAK MACHINE
IDW Publishing, 2005
1 A Cal McDonald Mystery 4.00
1a signed 20.00
2 thru 5 . . . . @4.00

SUPERNAUT
Anarchy, 1997
1 (of 3) 3.00
1 gold logo 6.00
2 by Rob Hand, Hand of Doom . . . 3.00
2a gold logo 6.00

SUPER REAL
Super Real Graphics, 2005
1 by Jason Martin 3.25
2 . . . . 3.25
2a variant (c) 3.25
3 . . . . 3.50
3a variant (c) 3.50

SUPER TEEN*TOPIA
Alias Enterprises, 2006
0 . . . . 1.00
1 . . . . 3.50
2 thru 4 . . . . @3.50

SUPREME
Maximum Press, 1997
#1–#43 see Image
44 AMo, JoB, A:Glory 3.00
45 AMo, JoB, A:Glory 3.00
46 AMo,Suprema 3.00
47 AMo 3.00
48 AMo 2.50
49 AMo 2.50
50 double size 4.00
51 . . . . 3.50
52A AMo, Book 1 . . . . 3.50
52B AMo, Book 2, continuation . . . 3.50
53 AMo,CSp,AG,V:Omniman 3.00
54 AMo,CSp,AG,Ballad of Judy
   Jordan 3.00
55 AMo,CSp,AG,Silence At
   Gettysburg 3.00
56 AMo,CSp,AG,Reflections,pt.1 . . 3.00
57 AMo,CSp,AG,Reflections,pt.2 . . 3.00
58 AMo,CSp,AG,A World of
   His Own 3.00
59 AMo,CSp,AG,Professor Night of
   the Prism World 3.00
60 AMo,CSp,AG,F:Radar in Puppy
   Love 3.00
61 AMo,CSp,AG,Meet Mr. Meteor . . 3.00
Coll.Ed.#1, rep.#1–#2 . . . . 5.00
Coll.Ed.#2, rep. 5.00
Coll.Ed.#3 rep. #45–#46, AMo 5.00
Classic Col.Ed.#1,rep.#1&#2 . . . . . 6.00
Classic Col.Ed.#2,rep.#43&#44 . . . . 6.00
TPB Secret Origins, rep. 17.00
TPB Supreme Madness 15.00
TPB rep. #41–#46, AMo 15.00

SUPREME: THE RETURN
Awesome Entertainment, 1999
1 AMo,CSp,AG 3.00
1a variant AxR cover 7.00
2 AMo,JSn, ... 3.00
3 thru 8 . . . . @3.00

SUPREMA/SUPREME SACRIFICE
Arcade Comics, 2006
Flipbook 4.00

Surge #3
© Eclipse

SURGE
Eclipse, 1984
1 A:DNAgents 3.00
2 A:DNAgents 3.00
3 A:DNAgents 3.00
4 A:DNAgents 3.00

SURROGATES
Top Shelf Productions, 2005
1 (of 5) 3.00
2 . . . . 3.00
3 thru 5 . . . . @3.00
TPB 20.00

SURVIVORS
Spectrum, 1984
1 Mag. size, (B&W) 5.00
2 A Hunter's Rage 3.50
3 The Old One 2.50
4 Face-Off 2.50

SUSPIRA: THE GREAT WORKING
Chaos! Comics, 1997
1 (of 4) PNa 3.00
2 PNa 3.00
3 PNa 3.00
4 PNa 3.00

SWORD OF VALOR
A Plus Comics
1 . . . . 2.50
2 . . . . 2.50
3 . . . . 2.50
4 . . . . 2.50

SWORDS OF TEXAS
Eclipse, 1987
1 FH,New America 2.50
2 FH,V:Baja Badlands 2.50
3 FH,TY(c),V:Dogs of Danger 2.50
4 FH,V:Samurai Master 2.50

SYMBIOTES, THE
Drive Comics, 2004
1 (of 8) 3.00
2 thru 5 . . . . @3.00

COLOR PUB.

SYMBOLS OF JUSTICE
High Impact Studios, 1995
1 I:Granger,Justice,Rayven 3.00
2 V:Devil's Brigade 3.00

SYPHONS
Now, 1988
1 . . . . 2.50
2 thru 7 . . . . @2.50

SYPHONS: COUNTDOWN
Now, 1994
1 F:Brigade 3.00
2 Led By Cross 3.00
3 Blown Cover 3.00
1995 Ann. Doomsday Device 3.00

SYPHONS: THE STARGATE STRATAGEM
Now, 1994
1 thru 3 . . . . @3.00

TAD WILLIAMS BURNING MAN
Alias Enterprises, 2005
1 (of 3) 3.00
2 thru 3 . . . . @3.00

TAG
Boom! Studios, 2006
1 (of 3) KG 4.00
2 . . . . 4.00
3 . . . . 4.00

TALENT
Boom! Studios, 2006
1 . . . . 4.00
1a 2nd printing 4.00
2 . . . . 3.00
3 . . . . 4.00
4 . . . . 4.00

TALES CALCULATED TO DRIVE YOU BATS
Archie Publications, 1961–62
1 . . . . 250.00
2 . . . . 150.00
3 thru 6 . . . . @100.00

TALES FROM THE CRYPT
Gladstone, 1990–91
1 E.C.rep.AW/FF,GS 5.00
2 rep. 4.00
3 rep. 3.50
4 rep. 3.00
5 rep.TFTC #45 . . . . 3.00
6 rep.TFTC #42 . . . . 3.00

TALES FROM THE CRYPT
Russ Cochran Publ, 1992
1 rep. TFTC #31,CSS#12 . . . . 3.00
2 rep. TFTC #34,CSS#15 . . . . 3.00
3 rep. TFTC, CSS 3.00
4 rep. TFTC #43,CSS#18 . . . . 3.00
5 rep. TFTC,CSS#23 . . . . 3.00
[2nd Series]
1 rep.horror stories 3.00
2 inc.The Maestro's Hand 3.00
3 thru 6 . . . . @3.00
7 thru 8 . . . . @3.00
Gemstone, 1996
16 thru 30 EC comics reprint . . . . @3.00

`Annuals'
TPB Vol. 1 rebinding of #1–#5 . . . . 9.00
TPB Vol. 2 rebinding of #5–#10 . . . 9.00
TPB Vol. 3 rebinding of #11–#15 . . 9.00
TPB Vol. 4 rebinding of #16–#20 . . 13.00
TPB Vol. 5 rebinding of #21–#24 . . 14.00

TALES OF ALVIN MAKER: RED PROPHET
Dabel Brothers Productions, 2006
1 . . . . 3.00
1a 3.00
2 thru 6 . . . . @3.00
2a thru 6a variant (c) . . . . @6.00
TPB 15.00

TALES OF BLOODY MARY
Bloody Mary Comics, 2005
1 (of 8) 3.00
2 thru 4 . . . . @3.00
5 thru 8 . . . . @3.00

Tales of Evil #2
© *Atlas Comics*

TALES OF EVIL
Atlas Comics, 1975
1 Werewolf 25.00
2 Bog Beast 20.00
3 Man-Monster 20.00

TALES OF MIDNIGHT
Beyond Starlight, 2006
Vol. 2
1 . . . . 3.00
2 thru 3 . . . . @3.00

TALES OF TERROR
Eclipse, 1985–87
1 . . . . 3.00
2 Claustrophobia' 3.00
3 GM,Eyes in the Darkness 3.00
4 TT,TY,JBo(c),The Slasher 3.00
5 Back Forty,Shoe Button Eyes . . . 3.00
6 Good Neighbors 3.00
7 SBi,JBo,SK(i),Video 3.00
8 HB,Revenant,Food for
   Thought 3.00
9 . . . . 3.00
10 . . . . 3.00
11 TT,JBo(c),Black Cullen 3.00
12 JBo,FH,Last of the Vampires . . . 3.00
13 . . . . 3.00

TALES OF THE CHAMPIONS
Heroic Publishing, 2005
1 . . . . 3.00
2 . . . . 3.00
3 F:Tigress 3.00
4 . . . . 3.25

TALES OF THE GREEN BERET
Dell Publishing Co., 1967
1 SG 75.00
2 thru 4 . . . . @60.00
5 . . . . 60.00

TALES OF THE GREEN HORNET
Now, 1990
1 NA(c),O:Green Hornet Pt.1 . . . . . 3.00
2 O:Green Hornet Pt.2 . . . . 2.50
3 Gun Metal Green 2.50
4 Targets 2.50

TALES OF THE MYSTERIOUS TRAVELER
Charlton Comics, 1956
1 DG 700.00
2 SD 600.00
3 SD,SD(c) 500.00
4 SD,SD(c) 600.00
5 SD,SD(c) 600.00
6 SD,SD(c) 600.00
7 SD 550.00
8 SD 550.00
9 SD 550.00
10 SD,SD(c) 575.00
11 SD,SD(c) 575.00
12 . . . . 300.00
13 . . . . 325.00
14 (1985) 25.00
15 (1985) 20.00

TALES OF THE REALM
Crossgen Comics, 2003
1 (of 6) 3.00
2 . . . . 3.00

TALES OF THE SUN RUNNERS
Sirius Comics, 1986
1 . . . . 2.50
2 and 3 . . . . @2.50

TALESPIN
Walt Disney, 1991
(Reg.-Series)
1 Sky-Raker, Pt.1 . . . . 2.50
2 Sky-Raker, Pt.2 . . . . 2.50
3 Idiots Abroad 2.50
4 Contractual Desperation 2.50
5 The Oldman & the Sea Duck 2.50
6 F'reeze a Jolly Good Fellow 2.50

TALESPIN
Walt Disney, 1991
[Mini-Series]
1 Take-off Pt.1 . . . . 3.00
2 Take-off Pt 2 . . . . 3.00
3 Take-off Pt 3,Khan Job 3.00
4 Take-off pt 4 . . . . 3.00

TALEWEAVER
WildStorm/DC, 2001
1 (of 6) 40-pg 3.50

COLOR PUB.

2	3.00
2a variant (c).	3.00
3	3.00
4	3.00
5	3.00
6	3.00

TALISMEN
Atlantis Studios, 2005
1 (of 4)	3.00
2 thru 4	@3.00

TAOLAND
Severe Reality Productions
4 1st full color issue	6.00
5 48pg.	6.00

TAOLAND ADVENTURES
Antarctic Press, 1999
1 by Jeff Amano	3.00
2	3.00

TARGET AIRBOY
Eclipse, 1988
1 SK,A:Clint	2.50

TARGITT
Atlas, 1975
1 thru 3	@20.00

TAROT WITCH OF THE BLACK ROSE
Broadsword Comics, 2000
1 JBa(c)	3.00
2	3.00
3	3.00
4	3.00
5 JBa	3.00
6 Goulish Intentions	3.00
7 Return of the Dark Witch,pt.1	3.00
8 Return of the Dark Witch,pt.2	3.00
9 Return of the Dark Witch,pt.3	3.00
2a thru 16a signed	@10.00
1b, 4b, 6b, 8b deluxe	@20.00
7b double-deluxe edition.	25.00
9b thru 23b deluxe	@20.00
10 Quest for the Black Rose Sword	3.00
11 Black Rose Sword,pt.2	3.00
12	3.00
13	3.00
13b previews exlusive (c)	15.00
14	3.00
15	3.00
16	3.00
17 Cold Spell	3.00
18 Diary of a Witch	3.00
19 Mists of Darkness, pt.1	3.00
19a photo (c)	10.00
20 Mists of Darkness, pt.2	3.00
21 Mists of Darkness, pt.3	3.00
22 Mists of Darkness, pt.4	3.00
23 Ghouls Gone Wild	3.00
24 Ghouls Gone Wild,pt.2	3.00
25 thru 28	@3.00
18a thru 23a deluxe	@20.00
24a thru 28a deluxe	@20.00
29	3.00
19b exclusive previews (c)	10.00
29a deluxe	20.00
30 thru 34	@3.00
31b variant (c)	3.00
31d signed	10.00
32b signed	10.00
35 thru 41	@3.00
30b signed	10.00
30a thru 34a deluxe	@20.00
35a thru 40a Deluxe	@20.00
37b photo (c)	15.00
31c with photo	15.00

TPB Vol. 1	25.00
TPB Vol. 1 deluxe	35.00
TPB Vol. 2	25.00
TPB Vol. 3	25.00
TPB Vol. 4	25.00

Tarzan of the Apes #193
© Gold Key

TARZAN OF THE APES
Gold Key, 1962–72
prev. Dell (see Golden Age)
132	125.00
133	80.00
134	80.00
135	90.00
136	80.00
137	80.00
138	80.00
139 I:Korak.	90.00
140 thru 154	@80.00
155 O:Tarzan.	100.00
156 thru 161	@60.00
162 TV photo (c)	80.00
163	60.00
164	60.00
165 TV photo (c)	80.00
166	60.00
167	60.00
168 TV photo (c)	80.00
169 A:Leopard Girl	60.00
170	60.00
171 TV photo (c)	125.00
172 thru 177	@50.00
178 O:Tarzan, rep. #155	50.00
179 thru 191	@50.00
192 Tarzan and the Foreign Legion adaptation	50.00
193 thru 199	@50.00
200	60.00
201 thru 205	@50.00
206 last issue.	50.00

Continued by DC; see also Marvel

TARZAN: THE BECKONING
Malibu, 1992
1 TY,I:The Spider Man	2.75
2 TY,Going back to Africa	2.50
3 thru 6	2.50

TARZAN THE WARRIOR
Malibu, 1992
1 SBs(c),O:Tarzan	3.50
2 & 3	@2.75
4 Wom'cha's Ship	2.75

5	2.75

TARZAN: LOVE, LIES, AND THE LOST CITY
Malibu, 1992
1 MWg&WS(s),Short Stories	4.00
2 The lost city of Opar	2.50
3 Final issue	2.50

TASMANIAN DEVIL & HIS TASTY FRIENDS
Gold Key, 1962
1	300.00

TASTEE-FREEZ COMICS
Harvey Comics, 1957
1 Little Dot.	150.00
2 Rags Rabbit.	75.00
3 Casper.	100.00
4 Sad Sack.	75.00
5 Mazie.	75.00
6 Dick Tracy	100.00

TEAM ANARCHY
Anarchy, 1993
1 I:Team Anarchy	2.75
2 thru 3	2.75
4 PuD,MaS,I:Primal	2.75

TEAM YANKEE
First, 1989
1 Harold Coyle novel adapt.	2.50
2 thru 6	@2.50
Trade Paperback	13.00

TEAM ZERO
Wildstorm/DC, Dec., 2006
1 CDi(s),DoM,World War II	3.00
2 Deathblow gathers his team	3.00
3 CDi(s),DoM,Peenemunde	3.00
4 CDi(s),DoM,V: Red Army.	3.00
5 CDi(s),DoM,V: Red Army.	3.00
6 CDi(s),DoM, conclusion.	3.00

TEEN-AGE CONFIDENTIAL CONFESSIONS
Charlton Comics, 1960–64
1	75.00
2 thru 5	@50.00
6 thru 10	@40.00
11 thru 22	@30.00

TEENAGE HOTRODDERS
Charlton Comics, April, 1963
1	150.00
2 thru 5	@75.00
6 thru 10	@60.00
11 thru 23	@60.00
24	60.00

Becomes:
TOP ELIMINATOR
25 thru 29	@50.00

Becomes:
DRAG 'N' WHEELS
30	125.00
31 thru 39.	75.00
40 thru 50 Scot Jackson	70.00
51 thru 59 May, 1973.	50.00

TEENAGE MUTANT NINJA TURTLES
First
1	6.00
2	4.50
Graphic Novel	17.00

TEENAGE MUTANT NINJA TURTLES
Archie, 1988
(From T.V. Series)
1 O:TMNT,April O'Neil,Shredder
Krang 6.00
2 V:Shredder,O:Bebop &
Rocksteady 4.00
3 V:Shredder & Krang. 3.00

TEENAGE MUTANT NINJA TURTLES
Mirage, 1993
1 A:Casey Jones. 3.00
2 JmL(a&s) 3.00
3 thru 13 . . . . @2.75

TEENAGE MUTANT NINJA TURTLES ADVENTURES
Archie, 1988 [2nd Series]
1 Shredder,Bebop,Rocksteady
return to earth 5.00
2 I:Baxter Stockman 3.00
3 Three Fragments #1 . . . . 3.00
4 thru 9 . . . . @2.50
10 thru 25 . . . . @2.50
26 thru 40. . . . . @2.50
41 thru 70. . . . . @2.50
1990 Movie adapt(direct). 5.50
1990 Movie adapt(newsstand). . . . 2.50
1991 TMNT meet Archie 2.50
1991 Movie Adapt II 2.50
Spec.#2 Ghost of 13 Mile Island . . . 2.50
Spec.#3 Night of the Monsterex . . . 2.50
TMNT Mutant Universe Sourcebook 2.00

TEENAGE MUTANT NINJA TURTLES ANIMATED
Dreamwave, 2003
1 . . . . 3.00
2 thru 9 . . . . @3.00
TPB Vol. 1 . . . . 10.00

TEENAGE MUTANT NINJA TURTLES/ FLAMING CARROT
Mirage/Dark Horse, 1993
1 JmL 3.00
2 JmL 3.00
3 JmL 3.00
4 JmL 3.00

TMNT PRESENTS:
Archie, 1993
...APRIL O'NEIL
1 A:Chien Khan,Vid Vicious 2.50
2 V:White Ninja,A:V.Vicious 2.50
3 V:Vhien Khan,concl. 2.50
Spec. April O'Neil, May East Saga . 2.50

...DONATELLO AND LEATHERHEAD
1 thru 2 . . . . @2.50

...MERDUDE VS. RAY FILLET
1 thru 3 . . . . @2.50

TMNT: THE MALTESE TURTLE
Mirage
Spec. F:Raphael Detective 3.00

TMNT: YEAR OF THE TURTLE
Archie Comics, 1995
1 All New Era 2.50

[JACK KIRBY'S] TEENAGENTS
[Mini-Series] Topps, 1993
1 WS,AH,w/3 cards. 3.00
2 NV,w/3 cards 3.00
3 NV,w/3 cards 3.00
4 NV,w/3 leftover? cards. 3.00

TEEN CONFESSIONS
Charlton Comics, 1959–76
1 . . . . 150.00
2 . . . . 125.00
3 . . . . 100.00
4 . . . . 100.00
5 . . . . 100.00
6 . . . . 100.00
7 . . . . 100.00
8 . . . . 100.00
9 . . . . 100.00
10 thru 30 . . . . @100.00
31 Beatles cover 200.00
32 . . . . 25.00
33 . . . . 25.00
34 . . . . 25.00
35 . . . . 25.00
36 . . . . 25.00
37 Beatles cover,Fan Club story . 300.00
38 thru 97. . . . . @20.00

TEEN SECRET DIARY
Charlton Comics, 1959–61
1 . . . . 125.00
2 . . . . 100.00
3 . . . . 100.00
4 . . . . 100.00
5 . . . . 100.00
6 thru 11 . . . . @100.00

TEKKEN 2
Knightstone, 1997
1 (of 4) Tekken Saga, pt.3 . . . . . . 3.00
2 . . . . 3.00
2a photo cover 3.00
3 . . . . 3.00
3a photo cover 3.00

Tekken Saga #1
© *Knightstone*

TEKKEN SAGA
Knightstone, 1997
1 . . . . 4.00
2 . . . . 3.00
3 . . . . 3.00
4 Paul vs. Kazuya. 3.00
5 Paul a prisoner 3.00
Nightstone Unlimited & Tekken ?. . . 3.00

TEMPEST
Alias Enterprises, 2006
1-shot 3.50

10
Boom! Studios 2005
1-shot 7.00

TENSE SUSPENSE
Fago Publications, 1958–59
1 . . . . 150.00
2 . . . . 100.00

10TH MUSE
Avatar/Tidal Wave Studios, 2002
1A MWn,RCz, Andy Park (c) 3.50
1B CBa(c). 3.50
1C RCz(c). 3.50
1D Mark Brooks (c). 3.50
1E Valdez (c). 3.50
2 RCz(c) 3.50
2a Caldwell (c) 3.50
2b Rousseau (c) 3.50
2 RCz(c) 3.50
2a Green (c) 3.50
2b Grant (c). 3.50
TPB Vol. 1 . . . . 14.00
TPB Vol. 1 photo (c) 14.00
Angel Gate, 2003
1-shot Book of Lights 3.00
TPB Vol. 1 Maze of the Minotaur. . . 8.00
TPB Vol. 2 Round Two 15.00
Alias Enterprises, 2005
TPB Vol. 1 . . . . 10.00
Volume 2
1 . . . . 3.00
1a foil (c). 5.00
1b signed, foil (c). 30.00
2 thru 9 . . . . @3.00
2a thru 9a variant (c)s. . . . . @3.00
2b foil, photo (c) 5.00
5a variant (c) signed 20.00
10 . . . . 3.50
10a variant (c) 3.50
11 God War x-over. 3.50
12 God War x-over, pt.5. . . . . 3.50
13 Who killed Wonder Boy? 3.50
14 . . . . 3.50
TPB Odyssey. 10.00
TPB Tragedy Strikes 10.00
TPB Vol. 1 Manga-sized 15.00
GN 10th Muse: Odyssey 10.00

10th MUSE/EZRA
Arcana Studios, 2006
1 . . . . 4.00
1a variant signed photo (c) 20.00

TERMINATOR, THE
Now, 1988–89
1 . . . . 10.00
2 . . . . 5.00
3 . . . . 4.00
4 thru 11 . . . . @3.50
12 I:JohnConnor($1.75,cov,dbl.sz) . 3.50
13 thru 17. . . . . @3.50
Spec. #1. . . . . 3.50

COLOR PUB.

TERMINATOR: ALL MY FUTURES PAST
Now, 1990
1 Painted Art 3.00
2 Painted Art 3.00

TERMINATOR: THE BURNING EARTH
Now, 1990
1 . . . . 15.00
2 . . . . 12.00
3 . . . . 10.00
4 . . . . 10.00
5 . . . . 10.00

TERMINATOR 2: CYBERNETIC DAWN
Malibu, 1995–96
1 thru 4 . . . . @2.50
0 flip-book/T2 Nuclear Twilight 2.50

TERMINATOR 2: NUCLEAR TWILIGHT
Malibu, 1995–96
1 thru 4 . . . . @2.50
0 flip-book, see above

TERMINATOR 3
Beckett Entertainment, 2003
1 Before the Rise 6.00
2 Before the Rise 6.00
3 Eyes of the Rise 6.00
4 Eyes of the Rise 6.00
5 Fragmented 6.00
6 Fragmented 6.00

TERRAFORMERS
Wonder Comics, 1987
1 . . . . 3.00
2 thru 4 . . . . @3.00

TERRANAUTS
Fantasy General, 1986
1 . . . . 3.00
2 . . . . 3.00

TERRA OBSCURA
Wildstorm/DC June, 2003
America's Best Comics
1 (of 6) AMo(s) 3.00
2 AMo(s),F:Grant Halford 3.00
3 thru 5 AMo(s) . . . . @3.00
6 AMo(s),concl.,40-pg. 4.00
TPB 15.00

Vol. 2, 2004
1 AMo(s) 3.00
2 AMo(s) 3.00
3 . . . . 3.00
4 AMo(s),KIS 3.00
5 AMo(s),KIS 3.00
6 AMo(s),KIS, Showdown in space. . 3.00
TPB Vol. 2 . . . . 15.00

TERRITORY 51
Lawdog Comics, 2004
1 . . . . 3.00
1 convention edition, signed 13.00
2 . . . . 4.00
TPB Vol. 1 . . . . 13.00

TEXAS CHAINSAW MASSACRE
Avatar Press, 2005
Spec. #1 . . . . 4.00

Spec. #1 variant (c)s 4.00
Spec. #1 glow (c) 15.00
Spec. #1 Bloodbath (c) 6.00
Spec. #1 Blood Red Con (c) 5.00
Spec. #1 painted (c) 6.00
Spec. #1 Lurking (c) 6.00
Spec. #1 Prism foil (c) 13.00
Spec. Fearbook #1 . . . . 4.00
Spec. Fearbook #1 variant (c)s . . @4.00
Spec. Fearbook #1 leather (c) . . . 20.00

TEXAS CHAINSAW MASSACRE: THE GRIND
Avatar Press, 2005
1 . . . . 4.00
1a Wraparound (c) 4.00
1b Variant(c)s . . . . @4.00
1c leather (c) 20.00
1d Red foil convention (c) 5.00
2 . . . . 4.00
2a Wraparound (c) 4.00
2b Variant(c)s . . . . @4.00
2c Die-cut (c) 10.00
3a Wraparound (c) 4.00
3b variant (c)s 4.00
3c Die-cut (c) 10.00

TEXAS CHAINSAW MASSACRE
Wildstorm/DC, Nov., 2006
1 DAn,ALa 3.00
1a varaint (c) 3.00

Texas Rangers in Action #47
© Tower

TEXAS RANGERS IN ACTION
Charlton Comics, 1956–70
5 . . . . 150.00
6 and 7 . . . . @100.00
8 SD 200.00
9 and 10 . . . . @100.00
11 AW 175.00
12 . . . . 100.00
13 AW 150.00
14 thru 20 . . . . @100.00
21 thru 30 . . . . @60.00
31 thru 59 . . . . @50.00
60 B:Riley's Rangers 60.00
61 thru 79 . . . . @30.00

THAT WILKIN BOY
Archie Publications, 1969
1 . . . . 70.00

2 thru 10 . . . . @50.00
11 thru 20 . . . . @30.00
21 thru 26 E:Giant size . . . . @25.00
27 thru 52 . . . . @25.00

THESPIAN
Dark Moon, 1995
1 I:Thespian 2.50
2 V:Lemming 2.50
3 Lord of Manhattan 2.50

THIRD WORLD WAR
Fleetway, 1990–91
1 HamburgerLady 2.50
2 . . . . 2.50
3 The Killing Yields 2.50
4 . . . . 2.50
5 . . . . 2.50
6 . . . . 2.50

13: ASSASSIN
TSR, 1990–91
1 thru 4 from game . . . . @3.00
5 thru 8 The Search for
   Maggie Darr . . . . @3.00

30 DAYS OF NIGHT
IDW Publishing, 2002
1 by S.Niles & B.Templesmith . . . 70.00
1a 2nd printing 7.00
2 . . . . 35.00
3 . . . . 15.00
TPB 18.00
Spec. Bloodsucker Tales (2004) . . . 4.00
Annual 2004. . . . . 5.00
Annual 2005 . . . . 7.50
TPB Three Tales 20.00

30 DAYS OF NIGHT: BLOODSUCKER TALES
IDW Publishing, 2004
1 . . . . 4.00
2 thru 10 . . . . @4.00
TPB Vol. 1 . . . . 25.00

30 DAYS OF NIGHT: DEAD SPACE
IDW Publishing 2005
1 . . . . 4.00
2 . . . . 4.00
3 . . . . 4.00

30 DAYS OF NIGHT: RETURN TO BARROW
IDW Publishing, 2004
1 . . . . 4.00
2 thru 6 . . . . @4.00
TPB 20.00

THOSE ANNOYING POST BROTHERS
Vortex, 1985
1 . . . . 3.00
2 thru 5 . . . . @2.50
6 thru 18 . . . . @2.50
See also B&W listings

3-D ZONE PRESENTS
Renegade, 1987–89
1 Dr. Jekyll and Mr. Hyde 2.50
2 Weird Tales of Basil Wolverton . . 2.50
3 thru 10 . . . . @2.50
11 3-D Danse Macabre 2.50
12 3-D Presidents 2.50
13 Flash Gordon 2.50

COLOR PUB.

14 Tyranostar 2.50
15 3-Dementia 2.50
16 Space Vixens 2.50
17 thru 20 . . . . 2.50

3 LITTLE KITTENS
Broadsword Comics, 2002
1 JBa, Purrr-fect weapons 3.00
2 Puss N Bullets 3.00
3 Purrr-Fect Weapons 3.00
1a thru 3a deluxe . . . . @20.00
1b thru 3b signed . . . . @10.00

THREE STOOGES
Dell Publishing Co., 1959
6 Ph(c),B:Prof. Putter 300.00
7 Ph(c) 300.00
8 Ph(c) 300.00
9 Ph(c) 300.00

Gold Key, 1962
10 Ph(c) 250.00
11 Ph(c) 250.00
12 Ph(c) 250.00
13 Ph(c) 250.00
14 Ph(c) 200.00
15 Ph(c) Go Around the World . . 250.00
16 Ph(c),E:Prof. Putter 200.00
17 Ph(c),B:Little Monsters 200.00
18 Ph(c) 200.00
19 Ph(c) 200.00
20 Ph(c) 200.00
21 Ph(c) 200.00
22 Ph(c),Movie Scenes 200.00
23 thru 30 Ph(c) . . . . @175.00
31 thru 50 Ph(c) . . . . @150.00
51 . . . . 150.00
52 thru 55 Ph(c) . . . . @150.00

THREE STOOGES 3-D
Eclipse, 1991
1 thru 3 reprints from 1953 . . . . @2.50
4 reprints from 1953 . . . . 3.50

THRESHOLD
Narwain Publishing, 2006
1 (of 5) 4.00

THRILL-O-RAMA
Harvey Publications, 1965–66
1 A:Man in Black(Fate),DW,AW . 100.00
2 AW,A:Pirana,I:Clawfang,
    The Barbarian 75.00
3 A:Pirana, Fate 60.00

THRUD THE BARBARIAN
Thrud Comics, 2006
1 . . . . 3.00
2 Phalanx of frosty foes 4.00
3 thru 5 . . . . @4.00

THUNDER AGENTS
Tower, 1965–69
1 WW,RC,GK,MSy,GT,I:Thunder
    Agents,IronMaiden,Warlord . . 350.00
2 WW,MSy,D:Egghead 200.00
3 WW,DA,MSy,V:Warlords 175.00
4 WW,MSy,RC,I:Lightning 175.00
5 WW,RC,GK,MSy 175.00
6 WW,SD,MSy,I:Warp Wizard . . . 125.00
7 WW,MSy,SD,D:Menthor 125.00
8 WW,MSy,GT,DA,I:Raven 125.00
9 OW,WW,MSy,A:Andor 125.00
10 WW,MSy,OW,A:Andor 125.00
11 WW,DA,MSy 100.00
12 SD,WW,MSy 100.00
13 WW,OW,A:Undersea Agent . . 100.00
14 SD,WW,GK,N:Raven,A:Andor 100.00
15 WW,OW,GT,A:Andor 90.00

16 SD,GK,A:Andor 90.00
17 WW,OW,GT 90.00
18 SD,OW,RC 75.00
19 GT,I:Ghost 75.00
20 WW,RC,MSy,all reprints 75.00

T.H.U.N.D.E.R. AGENTS
J.C. Productions, 1983
1 MA,Centerfold 5.00
2 I:Vulcan 5.00

T.H.U.N.D.E.R. AGENTS
Maximum, 1995
1 and 2 . . . . @3.00

THUNDERBIRD
Atlantis Studios, 2005
1 . . . . 3.00
2 . . . . 3.00

Thunderbolt #54
© Charlton

THUNDERBOLT
Charlton Comics, 1966–67
1 PAM,O:Thuderbolt 75.00
Prev: Son of Vulcan
51 PAM,V:Evila 50.00
52 PAM,V:Gore the Monster 35.00
53 PAM,V:The Tong 35.00
54 PAM,I:Sentinels 35.00
55 PAM,V:Sentinels 35.00
56 PAM,A:Sentinels 35.00
57 A:Sentinels 35.00
58 PAM,A:Sentinels 35.00
59 PAM,A:Sentinels 35.00
60 PAM,JAp,I:Prankster 40.00

THUNDERBOLT JAXON
Wildstorm/DC, Feb., 2006
1 (of 5) DGb,JHi 3.00
2 thru 5 DGb,JHi . . . . @3.00

THUNDERCATS
WildStorm/DC, 2002
0 JSC, preview issue 5.00
1a (of 5) King Lion-O 5.00
1b variant AAd (c) 3.50
2a V:Mumm-ra 3.00
2b variant JLe(c) 3.00
3 F:Lion-O 3.00
3a variant JMd(c) 3.00
4 F:New Thundera 3.00
5 concl. 3.00

GN Thundercats/Battle
    of the Planets 5.00
TPB Reclaiming Thundera 13.00
TPB Enemy's Pride 15.00
Sourcebook 3.00

THUNDERCATS: DOGS OF WAR
Wildstorm/DC June, 2003
1 (of 5) 10 years in future 3.00
2 New Thundera 3.00
3 thru 5 BBh,AV . . . . @3.00
TPB 15.00

THUNDERCATS: ENEMY'S PRIDE
Wildstorm/DC June, 2004
1 Cat vs. Cat 3.00
2 . . . . 3.00
3 . . . . 3.00
4 . . . . 3.00
5 . . . . 3.00

THUNDERCATS: HAMMERHAND'S REVENGE
Wildstorm/DC, 2003
1 (of 5) 3.00
2 F:Lion-O 3.00
3 . . . . 3.00
4 (two covers) 3.00
5 (two covers) 3.00
TPB 15.00
Spec. Superman/Thundercats 6.00

THUNDERCATS: ORIGINS
Wildstorm/DC, 2003
Spec. Heroes & Villains,pt.1 . . . . 3.50
Spec. Villains & Heroes,pt.1 . . . . . . 3.50

THUNDERCATS: THE RETURN
Wildstorm/DC, 2003
1 (of 5) EBe,F:Lion-O 3.00
2 EBe,V:Mumm-Ra 3.00
3 EBe 3.00
4 EBe,Wilykat 3.00
5 EBe, concl. 3.00
TPB Series rep. 13.00

TICK, THE
New England Comics, 2001
1 all new, all color 4.00
1a variant (c) 4.00
2 thru 5 . . . . @4.00
6 return of Proto-Tick 4.00
TPB The Naked City, 2nd pr. 16.00
TPB Circus Maximus Giant ed. . . . 15.00
Spec. Big Halloween 2000 . . . . 3.50
Spec. Big Halloween 2001 . . . . 4.00
Spec. Introducing the Tick (2002) . . 4.00
Spec. Circus Maximus Update 4.00

TICK & ARTIE
New England Comics, 2002
1 . . . . 3.50
2 BEd(c) 3.50

TICK, THE: BIG XMAS TRILOGY
New England Comics, 2002
1 . . . . 4.00
2 . . . . 4.00
3 . . . . 4.00

TICK, THE:
DAYS OF DRAMA
New England Comics, 2005
1	5.00
2	4.00
3 thru 6	@4.00

TICK'S INCREDIBLE
INTERNET COMIC, THE
New England Comics, 2001
1	4.00

TIGER GIRL
Gold Key, 1968
1	50.00

TIGER-MAN
Atlas, 1975
1 thru 3	@15.00

TIGERS OF TERRA
Antarctic Press, 2000
Vol. 3
1 (of 4) War Against the Sun	3.00
2 Night of the Amazons	3.00
3	3.00
4 Planet of War	3.00
Spec.	4.00

TIME TUNNEL, THE
Gold Key, 1967
1 from TV show	150.00
2	100.00

TIME TWISTERS
Quality, 1987–89
1 AMo(s),AD,DGb	2.50
2 AMo(s),DGb,Wheels of Fury	2.50
3 AMo(s),The Wages of Sin	2.50
4 AMo(s),Bad Timing	2.50
5 PrM(s),The Collector	2.50
6 AMo(s),AIG	2.50
7 AMo(s),Twist Ending	2.50
8 thru 21	@2.50

TIMEWALKER
Valiant, 1994
0 BH,DP,O:3 Immortals	3.00
1 DP, BH	2.50
2 thru 15	@2.50
Yearbook F:Harada	3.00
TPB F:Archer & Armstrong	10.00

TIPPY'S FRIENDS
GO-GO & ANIMAL
Tower Comics, 1966–69
1	125.00
2	75.00
3	75.00
4	75.00
5	75.00
6	75.00
7	75.00
8 Beatles on cover & back	150.00
9 thru 15	@75.00

TIPPY TEEN
Tower Comics, 1965–70
1	125.00
2 thru 27	@75.00

TOHUBOHU
New Breed Comics, 1999
1	3.25

2 thru 5	@3.00
6 A Serpent in the Garden	3.25

TOKYO STORM WARNING
Wildstorm/DC June, 2003
1 (of 3) giant robots	3.00
2 WEI	3.00
3 WEI	3.00

Tom & Jerry #17
© Harvey

TOM & JERRY
Harvey, 1991–94
1	2.50
2 thru 18	@2.00

TOM MIX WESTERN
AC Comics, 1988
1	3.00

TOMMI-GUNN
London Night, 1997
0	3.00
?	3.00
1 signed	15.00
1a, chromium, elite edition	20.00
2	3.00
3	3.00

TOMMI-GUNN:
KILLER'S LUST
London Night, 1997
1	3.00
1 Japanese Chromium edition	12.00
2	3.00

TOMOE
Crusade Entertainment, 1996
0 BiT,	3.00
1 BiT,Fan Appreciation Edition	3.00
2	3.00
TPB rep.	14.00

TOMOE/WITCHBLADE:
FIRE SERMON
Crusade Entertainment, 1996
1	5.00
1a Gold foil	10.00

TOMOE:
UNFORGETTABLE FIRE
Crusade Entertainment, 1997
1 (of 3)	3.00

TOMORROW STORIES
WildStorm/DC, 1999
America's Best Comics
1 AMo,AxR(c) anthology	4.00
1a AxR(c),variant cover	3.50
2 AMo(s),KN,RV,JBa.	3.00
3 AMo(s),KN,RV,JBa.	3.00
4 AMo(s),KN,RV,JBa.	3.00
5 AMo(s),KN,RV,JBa.	3.00
6 AMo(s),RV,JBa.	3.00
7 AMo(s),RV,JBa.	3.00
8 AMo(s),RV,JBa.	3.00
9 AMo(s),RV,JBa.	3.00
10 AMo(s),RV,JBa,Jack B. Quick.	3.00
11 AMo(s),RV,JBa,AAd,F:Cobweb.	3.00
12 AMo(s),RV,JBa, x-over	3.00
TPB Book 2	18.00
Spec. #1 AMo(s) 64-page	7.00
Spec. #2 AMo(s)	7.00

TOM STRONG
WildStorm/DC, 1999
America's Best Comics
1 AMo(s),CSp,40-pg.	4.00
2 AMo(s),CSp,Millennium City	3.00
3 AMo(s),CSp,Millennium City	3.00
4 AMo,CSp,AAd,Berlin in WW2	3.00
5 AMo,JOy,CSp,Memories of Pangea	3.00
6 AMo,CSp,DGb, Dead Man's Hand	3.00
7 AMo,CSp,GFr.	3.00
8 AMo,CSp,Lost Mesa	3.00
9 AMo,CSp,	3.00
10 AMo,CSp,F:Warren Strong	3.00
11 AMo,CSp,F:Tom Strange.	3.00
12 AMo,CSp,F:Tom Strange,pt.2	3.00
13 AMo,CSp,Warren Strong.	3.00
14 AMo,CSp,Space Family Strong.	3.00
15 AMo,CSp,Val Var Garm	3.00
16 AMo(s),CSp,KIS,Modular Man	3.00
17 AMo(s),CSp,KIS,Weird Rider	3.00
18 AMo(s),CSp,KIS,Weird Rider	3.00
19 AMo(s),CSp,KIS	3.00
20 AMo(s),CSp,KIS,JOy,pt.1	3.00
21 AMo(s),CSp,KIS,JOy,pt.2	3.00
22 AMo(s),CSp,KIS,JOy,pt.3	3.00
23 CSp,KIS,rescue mission	3.00
24 CSp,KIS,	3.00
25 JPL,F:Strongmen of America	3.00
26 MSh(s),PFe.	3.00
27 SwM	3.00
28	3.00
29 DFg	3.00
30 DFg,Terrible Life of Tom Strong	3.00
31 JOy, Michael Moorcock(s)	3.00
32 JOy, Michael Moorcock(s)	3.00
33 JOy, F:Pneuman	3.00
34 JP,PG, central China	3.00
35 CSp,KIS, Snow Queen sequel	3.00
36 AMo(s),CSp,KIS,End of World	3.00
TPB Book One, 208-pg.	15.00
TPB Book Two, 192-pg.	15.00
TPB Vol. 3	18.00
TPB Vol. 4	18.00
TPB Vol. 5	18.00

TOM STRONG'S
TERRIFIC TALES
WildStorm/DC, 2001
America's Best Comics
1 AMo,AAd	3.50
2 AMo,AAd	3.00
3 AMo,AAd,JOy	3.00
4 AMo(s),AAd,Jonni Future.	3.00
5 AMo(s),SA,AAd(c)	3.00
6 AMo(s),JOy,AAd	3.00
7 AMo(s),AAd	3.00
8 AMo(s),AAd, young Tom	3.00

9 AMo(s),three stories. 3.00
10 AMo(s),three stories 3.00
11 AMo(s), ... 3.00
12 AMo(s),AAd, final issue. 3.00
TPB Vol. 1 . . . . 18.00

TOM SULLIVAN'S BOOKS OF THE DEAD
Dead Dog Comics, 2005
1 Devilhead. 5.00
1a variant (c) 5.00
2 . . . . 5.00
3 . . . . 5.00
4 . . . . 5.00

TOM TERRIFIC!
Pines Comics
Summer, 1957
1 . . . . 300.00
2 . . . . 250.00
3 . . . . 250.00
4 . . . . 250.00
5 . . . . 250.00
6 Fall, 1958. . . . . 250.00

TOP CAT
Charlton Comics, 1970–73
1 . . . . 125.00
2 thru 10 . . . . @75.00
11 thru 20 . . . . @50.00

TOP TEN
WildStorm/DC, 1999
America's Best Comics
1 AMo(s),GeH,40-pg. 3.50
2 AMo(s),GeH 3.00
3 thru 9 AMo(s),GeH . . . . @3.00
10 AMo(s),GeH,killer revealed. 3.00
11 AMo(s),GeH,aftermath 3.00
12 AMo(s),GeH,season finale 3.00
TPB AMo(s),GeH 15.00
TPB Top 10 Book Two 15.00
TPB The 49ers. 18.00
TPB Beyond the Farthest Precinct 15.00

TOP TEN: BEYOND THE FARTHEST PRECINCT
Wildstorm/DC, Aug., 2005
1 (of 5) JOy. 3.00
2 JOy 3.00
3 JOy 3.00
4 JOy 3.00
5 JoY. 3.00

TOP THAT! PUZZLE ADVENTURES
Top That! Publishing, 2005
1 Halfpipe Heroes 4.00
2 Freaky Fredas Ghost. 4.00
3 Chinese Mystery 4.00
4 Aztec Madness 4.00
5 Shadow on the Wall. 4.00
6 Celtic Double Cross. 4.00

TOR IN 3-D
Eclipse, 1986
1 JKu. 3.00
1a B&W limited 100 sign 5.00
2 JKu. 3.00

TORMENTRESS: MISTRESS OF HELL
Blackout Comics, 1977
0 . . . . 3.00

TOTAL ECLIPSE
Eclipse, 1988–89
1 BHa,BSz(c),A:Airboy,Skywolf . . . 4.00
2 BHa,BSz(c),A:New Wave, Liberty
  Project 4.00
3 BHa,BSz(c),A:Scout,Ms.Tree . . . 4.00
4 BHa,BSz(c),A:Miracleman,
  Prowler 4.00
5 BHa,BSz(c),A:Miracleman, Aztec
  Ace 4.00

TOTAL ECLIPSE, THE SERAPHIM OBJECTIVE
Eclipse, 1988
1 tie-in Total Eclipse #2 . . . . 2.50

TOTALLY SPIES
Papercutz, 2006
GN #1 The O. P. 8.00
GN #2 I Hate the '80s 8.00
GN #3 Evil Jerry. 8.00

Total War #2
© Gold Key

TOTAL WAR
Gold Key, 1965
1 WW 150.00
2 WW 125.00
Becomes:

M.A.R.S. PATROL
3 WW 125.00
4 thru 10 . . . . @100.00

TOY BOX
Alias Enterprises, 2006
0 . . . . 3.50

TOY BOY
Continuity, 1986–91
1 NA.I&O:Toy Boy,A:Megalith 3.00
2 TVE 3.00
3 TVE 3.00
4 TVE 3.00
5 TVE 3.00
6 TVE 3.00
7 MG 3.00

TRAILOR PARK OF TERROR
Imperium Comics, 2006
Vol. 2
1 . . . . 4.00
1 variant(c) 4.00

2 . . . . 4.00
3 . . . . 4.00
4 . . . . 4.00
5 . . . . 3.00
6 . . . . 4.00
Spec. Halloween Special 4.00
Spec. Halloween Special #2 . . . . . 4.00

TRANSFORMERS
1 Robotics. 2.50
2 . . . . 2.50
3 . . . . 2.50

TRANSFORMERS
Titan, 2001
GN Vol. 1 All Fall Down 20.00
GN Vol. 2 End of the Road 20.00
GN Vol. 3 Primal Scream. 20.00
GN Vol. 4 Matrix Quest 20.00
GN Vol. 4 Matrix Quest
  exclusive(c) 25.00
GN Vol. 5 Target 2006 . . . . 20.00
GN Vol. 6 Dark Design 20.00
GN Vol. 7 Fallen Angel 20.00
GN Beginnings. 17.00
GN Showdown. 20.00
GN City of Fear 20.00
GN Space Pirates 17.00
GN New Order. 17.00
GN Cybertron Redux 17.00
GN Time Wars 20.00
TPB Dinobot Hunt 20.00
TPB Breakdown. 20.00
TPB Prey 20.00
TPB Treason 20.00
TPB Trial by Fire 20.00
TPB Maximum Force 20.00
TPB Fallen Star 8.00
TPB Dark Star 20.00
TPB Aspects of Evil 8.00
TPB Last Stand 20.00
TPB Way of the Warrior, B&W 8.00
TPB Earthforce, B&W 8.00
TPB Perchance to Dream 8.00

TRANSFORMERS
IDW Publishing, 2005
0 . . . . 1.00
1 Infiltration 3.00
1a variant (c)s . . . . @3.00
2 thru 6 Infiltration. 3.00
2a thru 6a variant (c)s. . . . . @3.00
Spec. Animated movie adaptation . . 4.00
Spec. Anim. movie adapt. variant (c) 4.00
TPB Infiltration 20.00
TPB Manga digest 11.00
Cover Gallery 6.00

TRANSFORMERS: ARMADA
Dreamwave, 2002
1 . . . . 4.00
2 . . . . 3.00
3 . . . . 3.00
4 . . . . 3.00
5 . . . . 3.00
6 . . . . 3.00
7 thru 17 . . . . @3.00
18 thru 32 Energon . . . . @3.00
TPB Vol. 1 . . . . 14.00
TPB Vol. 2 . . . . 16.00
TPB Vol. 3 Worlds Collide 21.00
Spec. Summer Special #1 . . . . 5.00
2005 Annual. 6.00
Energon Official Guidebook #1 . . . . 5.00
TPB Vol. 3 More Than Meets
  the Eye 15.00
Pocket Book Vol. 2. . . . . 11.00
Pocket Book Vol. 3 . . . . 10.00

TRANSFORMERS BEAST WARS
Dreamwave, 2005
1 . . . . 3.00
2 . . . . 3.00

TRANSFORMERS EVOLUTIONS: HEARTS OF STEEL
IDW Publishing, 2006
1 CDi 3.00
1a variant (c) 3.00
2 thru 4 CDi . . . . @3.00
2a thru 4a variant (c) . . . . @3.00

Transformers Generation One #4
© Dreamweave

TRANSFORMERS: GENERATION ONE
Dreamwave, 2002
1 . . . . 7.00
1a exclusive holofoil (c) 20.00
2 thru 6 . . . . @3.00
5a thru 6a variant (c). . . . . @3.00
7 thru 10 . . . . @3.00
0 . . . . 3.00
TPB Vol. 1 Prime Directive 18.00
TPB Vol. 2 War and Peace 18.00
Preview book, exclusive (c) 4.00
TPB rep. #1–#6 . . . . 18.00
TPB Profile Book One 13.00
TPB Profile Book Two 13.00
TPB Transformers Genesis
    Art Book 29.45
Vol. 2
1 (of 6) 3.50
1a chrome edition 6.00
2 thru 14 . . . . @3.00
TPB Vol. 1 Prime Directive 18.00
TPB Vol. 2 War and Peace 18.00
TPB Vol. 3 Ascension 18.00
GN More than meets the Eye, guide 5.25
GN More than meets the Eye #3 . . . 5.25
2004 Datatracks 2.50

TRANSFORMERS: GENERATIONS
IDW Publishing, 2006
1 . . . . 2.00
1a variant (c) 2.00
2 . . . . 2.00
2a variant (c) 2.00

---

3 thru 9 . . . . @2.50
3a thru 9a variant (c) . . . . @2.50
TPB Vol. 1 . . . . 20.00
TPB Vol. 2 Generation 1 . . . . 20.00

TRANSFORMERS/G.I. JOE
Dreamwave, 2003
1 . . . . 3.00
1a holofoil (c) 6.00
2 thru 6 . . . . @3.00
TPB 18.00
1-shot Divided Front 3.00

TRANSFORMERS/G.I. JOE: DIVIDED FRONT
Dreamwave, 2004
1 . . . . 3.00
2 thru 6 . . . . @3.00

TRANSFORMERS: MICROMASTERS
Dreamwave, 2004
1 (of 4) 3.00
2 thru 3 . . . . @3.00
TPB 12.00

TRANSFORMERS: MORE THAN MEETS THE EYE
Dreamwave, 2003
1 (of 8) 5.25
2 thru 7 . . . . @5.25
8 final issue 6.00
TPB 25.00
TPB Vol. 2 Official Guidebook 25.00
Vol. 2 Transformers Armada
1 thru 3 More than Meets
    the Eye . . . . @5.00

TRANSFORMERS SPOTLIGHT
IDW Publishing, 2006
1-shot Hot Rod 4.00
1-shot Hot Rod variant (c) 4.00
1-shot Nightbeat 4.00
1-shot Nightbeat variant (c) 4.00
1-shot Shockwave 4.00
1-shot Shockwave variant (c) 4.00

TRANSFORMERS, THE: BEAST WARS
IDW Publishing, 2006
1 . . . . 3.00
1a variant (c) 3.00
2 thru 4 . . . . @3.00
2a thru 4a variant (c) 3.00
TPB The Gathering 18.00

TRANSFORMERS, THE: ESCALATION
IDW Publishing, 2006
1 . . . . 4.00
1a variant b&w (c) 4.00

TRANSFORMERS, THE: STORMBRINGER
IDW Publishing, 2006
1 . . . . 3.00
1a variant (c) 3.00
2 . . . . 3.00
3 . . . . 3.00
4 . . . . 3.00
2a thru 4a variant (c) . . . . @3.00

TRANSFORMERS: THE WAR WITHIN
Dreamwave, 2002
1 . . . . 3.00
2 thru 6 . . . . @3.00
TPB Vol. 1 . . . . 16.00
Vol. 2 The Dark Ages
1 . . . . 3.00
2 . . . . 3.00
3 thru 6 . . . . @3.00
TPB The Dark Ages 18.00
Vol. 3 The Age of Wrath
1 . . . . 3.00
2 thru 6 . . . . @3.00

TRANSFORMERS in 3-D
Blackthorne
1 thru 5 . . . . @2.50

TRANSFORMERS: TIMELINES
Fun Publications, 2006
1-shot Beast Wars 5.00

TRAVEL OF JAMIE McPHEETERS, THE
Gold Key, 1963
1 Kurt Russell 75.00

TRAVELLER
Maximum Press, 1996
1 (of 3) RLd,MHw, ... 3.00

TRIAL BY FIRE
Crossgen Comics, 2002
1 (of 5) 3.00

TRIBE
Axis Comics, 1993–94
1 see Image Comics section
2 TJn(s),LSn,V:Alex 2.50
3 TJn(s),LSn, ... 2.50
Good Comics, 1996
0 TJn,LSn 3.00
1 TJn,LSn,Choice and
    Responsibility 3.00
2 TJn,LSn,Choice and
    Responsibility 3.00

TRIBULATION FORCE
Tyndale House, 2002
GN Vol. #1 . . . . 6.00
GN Vol. #2 thru Vol. 5 . . . . @6.00

TRINITY ANGELS
Acclaim, 1997
1 KM,DPs, Maria, Gianna &
    Theresa Barbella become Trinity
    Angels 2.50
2 thru 12 KM . . . . @2.50

TROLL LORDS
Comico, 1989–90
Spec. #1 . . . . 2.50
1 . . . . 2.50
2 thru 4 . . . . @2.50

TRON: DEREZZED
88MPH Studios, 2004
1 (of 4) 3.00
2 thru 3 . . . . @3.00
1a thru 3a variant (c)s . . . . @3.50

COLOR PUB.

TRON: THE GHOST IN THE MACHINE
Amaze Ink/Slave Labor Graphics, 2006
1 . . . . 3.50
2 . . . . 3.50

TROUBLEMAKERS
Acclaim, 1996
1 FaN(s) 2.50
2 thru 19 FaN(s) . . . . @2.50

TROUBLE WITH GIRLS
Comico, 1987–88
1 . . . . 3.00
2 . . . . 2.50
3 . . . . 2.50
4 . . . . 2.50

TROUBLE WITH IGOR, THE
Amaze Ink/Slave Labor Graphics, 2006
GN 4.00

TRUE LOVE
Eclipse, 1986
1 ATh,NC,DSt(c),reprints. 3.00
2 ATh,NC,BA(c),reprints 3.00

TRUE ROMANCE
Pyramid Comics, 1997
1 . . . . 2.50
1a deluxe 3.00
2 . . . . 2.50
3 . . . . 2.50
4 . . . . 2.50

TUFF GHOSTS STARRING SPOOKY
Harvey Publications, 1962–72
1 . . . . 250.00
2 thru 5 . . . . @175.00
6 thru 10 . . . . @100.00
11 thru 20 . . . . @75.00
21 thru 30 . . . . @50.00
31 thru 39 . . . . @40.00
40 thru 42 52 pg. Giants . . . . . . @45.00
43 . . . . 45.00

TURISTAS: THE OTHER SIDE OF PARADISE
IDW Publishing, 2006
Book 1 . . . . 4.00

TUROK
Acclaim, 1998
1 FaN 3-D cover 2.50
2 FaN,A:Armorines 2.50
3 FaN,Lazarus Concordance 2.50
4 FaN, real President? 2.50
TPB Dinosaur Hunter, FaN 10.00

TUROK: CHILD OF BLOOD
Acclaim, 1997
1-shot FaN, 48pg 4.00

TUROK: COMIC BOOK MAGAZINE
Acclaim, 1998
Seeds of Evil 5.00
Adon's Curse 5.00
Turok/Shadowman 5.00

Turok: Dinosaur Hunter #20
© *Valiant*

TUROK: DINOSAUR HUNTER
Valiant, 1993
1 BS,Chromium(c),O:Turok
  retold,V:Monark 3.00
1a Gold Ed 4.00
2 thru 13 . . . . @2.75
14 V:Dino-Pirate 2.50
15 RgM,V:Dino-Pirate 2.50
16 Chaos Effect-Beta#3, V:Evil
  Shaman 2.75
17 thru 47 . . . . @2.50
Yearbook #1 MBn(s),DC, N&V:Mon
  Ark 4.25
Yearbook 1995 MGr,The Hunted . . . 3.00
Spec. Tales of the Lost Land 4.00
TPB FaN 112pgs.rep. game 10.00

TUROK QUARTERLY— REDPATH
Acclaim, 1997
March 1997, FaN(s),Spring Break
  in the Lost Land 4.00
June 1997, FaN(s), Killer loose in
  Oklahoma City 4.00

TUROK/SHADOWMAN
Acclaim, 1999
1-shot 4.00

TUROK 3: SHADOW OF OBLIVION
Acclaim, 2000
Spec. 48-page 5.00

TUROK/SHAMAN'S TEARS
Valiant, 1995
1 MGr,Ghost Dance Pt. 1 . . . . 2.50
2 MGr,JAl,White Buffalo
  kidnapped,V:Bar Sinister 2.50
3 V:Supremeists/Circle Sea 2.50

TUROK: SON OF STONE
Gold Key, 1962
1 thru 29 see Golden Age
30 . . . . 150.00
31 Drug 165.00
32 thru 40 . . . . @125.00
41 thru 50 . . . . @100.00

51 thru 60 . . . . @75.00
61 thru 75 . . . . @65.00
76 thru 91 . . . . @50.00
Whitman
92 thru 130 . . . . @50.00
Giant #1 . . . . 200.00

TUROK: THE HUNTED
Valiant, 1996
1 & 2 . . . . 2.50

TUROK/TIMEWALKER
Acclaim, 1997
1 of 2 FaN(s),Seventh Sabbath . . . 2.50
2 of 2 FaN(s),Seventh Sabbath . . . 2.50

TURTLE SOUP
Millennium, 1991
1 Book 1, short stories 2.50
2 thru 4 . . . . @2.50

TV CASPER & COMPANY
Harvey Publications, 1963–74
1 B:68 pg. Giants 450.00
2 . . . . 300.00
3 . . . . 300.00
4 . . . . 300.00
5 . . . . 300.00
6 . . . . 200.00
7 . . . . 200.00
8 . . . . 200.00
9 . . . . 200.00
10 . . . . 200.00
11 thru 20 . . . . @100.00
21 thru 31 E:68 pg. Giants . . . . . @70.00
32 thru 46 . . . . @60.00

TWEETY AND SYLVESTER
Gold Key, 1963–84
1 . . . . 100.00
2 thru 10 . . . . @75.00
11 thru 30 . . . . @40.00
31 thru 121 . . . . @15.00

24: NIGHTFALL
IDW Publishing, 2006
1 . . . . 3.00
1a variant (c) 3.00

21 DOWN
WildStorm/DC, 2002
1 JP,JJu(c),F:Preston Kills 3.00
2 JP,JJu(c),Herod 3.00
3 JP,JJu(c),Bear Mountain 3.00
4 JP,JJu(c) 3.00
5 JP,JJu(c) 3.00
6 JP,JJu(c),The Conduit 3.00
7 JP,JJu(c),secret of Herod 3.00
8 JP,Roadside Attractions,pt.1 . . . . 3.00
9 JP,Roadside Attractions,pt.2 . . . . 3.00
10 JP,Roadside Attractions,pt.3 . . . . 3.00
11 JP,Roadside Attractions,pt.4 . . . . 3.00
12 JP,Roadside Attractions,concl. . . . 3.00
TPB rep. #1 thru #7 . . . . 20.00

TWILIGHT EXPERIMENT
Wildstorm/DC, Feb., 2005
1 (of 6) JP(s) 3.00
2 JP(s) 3.00
3 JP(s) 3.00
4 JP(s) 3.00
5 JP(s) 3.00
6 JP(s) 3.00

TWILIGHT MAN
First, 1989
1 Mini-Series................ 2.75
2 Mini-Series................ 2.75
3 Mini-Series................ 2.75
4 Mini-Series................ 2.75

TWILIGHT MEN
Markosia, 2006
1 .... 3.50
2 thru 4 .... @3.50

TWILIGHT X-TRA
Antarctic Press, 1999
1 (of 3) by Joe Wright......... 2.50
2 .... 2.50
3 conclusion 2.50

TWILIGHT X: WAR
Antarctic Press, 2005
1 (of 7) by Joe Wight, Manga ... 3.00
2 thru 7 .... @3.00
TPB Vol. 1 .... 15.00

TWILIGHT ZONE, THE
Gold Key, 1962
See also: Four Color #1173 & #1288
1 RC,FF,GE,P(c) all 250.00
2 .... 200.00
3 ATh,MSy 150.00
4 ATh................... 150.00
5 .... 135.00
6 .... 135.00
7 .... 135.00
8 .... 135.00
9 ATh................... 150.00
10 .... 100.00
11 .... 100.00
12 AW 100.00
13 AW,RC,FBe,AMc....... 100.00
14 RC,JO,RC,AT 100.00
15 RC,JO............... 100.00
16 .... 75.00
17 .... 75.00
18 .... 75.00
19 JO 75.00
20 .... 70.00
21 RC 70.00
22 JO 70.00
23 JO 70.00
24 .... 60.00
25 GE,RC,ATh............ 60.00
26 RC,GE................ 60.00
27 GE 60.00
28 .... 50.00
29 .... 50.00
30 .... 50.00
31 .... 50.00
32 GE................... 55.00
33 .... 50.00
34 .... 50.00
35 .... 50.00
36 .... 50.00
37 .... 50.00
38 .... 50.00
39 WMc 50.00
40 .... 35.00
41 .... 35.00
42 .... 35.00
43 RC................... 40.00
44 .... 35.00
45 .... 35.00
46 .... 35.00
47 .... 35.00
48 .... 35.00
49 .... 35.00
50 FBe,WS............... 35.00
51 AW 40.00
52 .... 30.00
53 .... 30.00

54 .... 30.00
55 .... 30.00
56 .... 30.00
57 FBe 30.00
58 .... 30.00
59 FBe,AMc.............. 35.00
60 thru 70 .... @25.00
71 rep.................. 20.00
72 .... 25.00
73 rep.................. 20.00
74 .... 25.00
75 .... 25.00
76 .... 25.00
77 FBe 30.00
78 FBe,AMc,The Missing Mirage. 230.00
79 rep.................. 20.00
80 FBe,AMc.............. 30.00
81 .... 30.00
82 AMc.................. 35.00
83 FBe,WS............... 35.00
84 FBe,AMc.............. 35.00
85 .... 30.00
86 rep.................. 25.00
87 .... 30.00
88 .... 30.00
89 .... 30.00
90 .... 30.00
91 .... 30.00

Twilight Zone, Vol. 2 #10
© Now

TWILIGHT ZONE
Now, 1990
1 NA,BSz(c) 8.00
1a 2nd printing Prestige +Harlan
  Ellison story............ 6.00
[Volume 2]
#1 The Big Dry (direct)......... 3.00
#1a Newsstand............... 2.50
2 Blind Alley 2.50
3 Extraterrestrial 2.50
4 The Mysterious Biker......... 2.50
5 Queen of the Void 2.50
6 Insecticide 2.50
7 The Outcasts,Ghost Horse 2.50
8 Colonists on Alcor 2.50
9 Dirty Lyle's House of Fun
  (3-D Holo) 3.00
10 Stairway to Heaven,Key
  to Paradise 2.50
11 TD(i),Partial Recall 2.50
3-D Spec.................. 2.50
Ann. #1.................. 2.75
[Volume 3]
1 thru 2 .... @2.50

TWIN BLADES:
KILLING WORDS
Alias Enterprises, 2006
1 .... 3.50
1a variant (c) 3.50
2 .... 3.50
3 .... 3.50

TWISTED TALES
Pacific, 1982–84
1 RCo. Infected............. 5.00
2 thru 8 .... @4.00
Eclipse
9 .... 4.00
10 GM,BWr 5.50

TWISTED TALES OF
BRUCE JONES
Eclipse, 1982–84
1 .... 3.00
2 .... 3.00
3 .... 3.00
4 .... 3.00

TWO FISTED TALES
Russ Cochran, 1992
1 JSe,HK,WW,JCr,reps......... 2.50
2 Reps inc.War Story 2.50
3 rep.................... 2.50
4 thru 6 rep.............. @2.50
7 thru 8 rep.............. @2.50
Gemstone
17 thru 24 EC comics reprints ... @2.50
'Annuals'
TPB Vol.#4 reprint #16–#20..... 13.00
TPB Vol. 2 rebinding of #5–#10... 10.00
TPB Vol. 3 rebinding of #11–#15 .. 11.00
TPB Vol. 4 rebinding 11.00
TPB Vol. 5 rebinding 11.00

2000 A.D. MONTHLY
Eagle, 1985
1 A:JudgeDredd 4.00
2 A:JudgeDredd 3.00
3 A:JudgeDredd 2.50
4 A:JudgeDredd 2.50
5 .... 2.50
6 .... 2.50
[2nd Series]
1 thru 4 .... @2.50
Quality
5 thru 27 .... @2.50
28/29 .... 2.50
30 .... 2.50
31/32 .... 2.50
33 thru 37................ @2.50
Becomes:

2000 A.D. SHOWCASE
38 thru 54................ @2.50
TPB: Killing Time 13.00
Rebellion, 2003
1 .... 2.50
2 .... 2.50
3 .... 2.50

TWO-STEP
Wildstorm/DC Oct. 2003
1 (of 3) WEl(s),ACo,JP 3.00
2 WEl(s),ACo,JP............. 3.00
3 WEl(s),ACo,JP,concl........... 3.00

2 TO THE CHEST
Dark Planet Productions, 2004
1 thru 5 .... @3.00
TPB 13.00

TZU THE REAPER
Murim Studios, 1997
1 by Gary Cohn & C.S. Chun 3.00
2 . . . . 3.00
3 . . . . 3.00
4 . . . . 3.00
5 . . . . 3.00

TZU: SPIRITS OF DEATH
Murim Studios, 1997
1 . . . . 3.00

UDON'S DARKSTALKERS
Udon Entertainment, 2005
TPB Vol. 1 . . . . 13.00

UFO FLYING SAUCERS
Gold Key, 1968
1 . . . . 75.00
2 . . . . 50.00
3 thru 13 . . . . @35.00
Becomes:

UFO & OUTER SPACE
Gold Key, 1978
14 thru 25 . . . . @20.00

ULTIMATE SPORTS FORCE PRESENTS:
Ultimate Sports Entertainment 2004
1 Hardwood Heroes 4.00
1 The Guardians 4.00
1 The Zone 4.00
1 Air and Space 4.00

ULTRAFORCE
Malibu Ultraverse, 1994–95
1 Prime, Prototype 2.50
2 thru 10 . . . . @2.50
Spec.#0 . . . . 2.50

[2nd Series], 1995–96
Infinity Fant. Ultraforce Four 2.50
1 George Perez cover 2.50
1a Computer painted cover 2.50
2 thru 15 . . . . @2.50

ULTRAFORCE/AVENGERS
Malibu Ultraverse, Aug. 1995
1 GP 4.00

ULTRAFORCE/ SPIDER-MAN
Malibu Ultraverse, 1996
1 . . . . 4.00

ULTRAMAN
Nemesis, 1994
1 EC,O:Ultraman 2.50
2 . . . . 2.50
3 . . . . 2.50
4 V:Blue Ultraman 2.50

ULTRAMAN
Harvey/Ultracomics, 1993
1 with 1 of 3 cards 2.50
2 with 1 of 3 cards & virgin cover . . 2.50
3 with 1 of 3 cards & virgin cover . . 2.50

ULTRAVERSE DOUBLE FEATURE
Malibu Ultraverse, 1995
1 F:Prime, Solitaire 4.00

ULTRAVERSE FUTURE SHOCK
Malibu Ultraverse, 1996
1 one-shot,MPc,alternate futures . . 2.50

ULTRAVERSE ORIGINS
Malibu Ultraverse, 1994
1 O:Ultraverse Heroes 2.50
1a Silver foil cover 12.50

ULTRAVERSE UNLIMITED
Malibu Ultraverse, 1996
1 F:Warlock 2.50
2 LWn,KWe, A:All-New Exiles,
  V:Maxis 2.50

ULTRAVERSE: YEAR ZERO: THE DEATH OF THE SQUAD
Malibu Ultraverse, 1995
0-A Hardcase's old team 2.50
0-B 2.50
0-C L.A. Riots 2.50
1 JHI,A:Squad, Mantra 3.00
2 JHI,DaR(c) prequel to Prime#1 . . 3.00
3 Cont. Year Zero Story 3.00
4 I:NM-E 3.00

ULTRAVERSE: YEAR ONE
Malibu Ultraverse, 1995
1 Handbook, double size 5.00
2 Prime 2.50

ULTRAVERSE: YEAR TWO
Malibu Ultraverse, 1996
1 Marvel/Ultraverse/Info 5.00

UNCLE SCROOGE
Dell/Gold Key, 1962
40 CB,X-Mas 300.00
41 . . . . 275.00
42 . . . . 275.00
43 CB 275.00
44 CB 275.00
45 CB 275.00
46 Lost Beneath the Sea 275.00
47 CB 275.00
48 CB 275.00
49 CB,Loony Lunar Gold Rush . . 275.00
50 CB,Rug Riders in the Sky . . . 275.00
51 CB,How Green Was my
   Lettuce 250.00
52 CB,Great Wig Mystery 250.00
53 CB,Interplanetary Postman . . 250.00
54 CB,Billion-Dollar Safari! 250.00
55 CB,McDuck of Arabia 250.00
56 CB,Mystery of the Ghost
   Town Railroad 250.00
57 CB,Swamp of No Return . . . 250.00
58 CB,Giant Robot Robbers . . . 250.00
59 CB,North of the Yukon 250.00
60 CB,Phantom of Notre Duck . . 250.00
61 CB,So Far and No Safari . . . 200.00
62 CB,Queen of the Wild
   Dog Pack 200.00
63 CB,House of Haunts! 200.00
64 CB,Treasure of Marco Polo! . 275.00
65 CB,Micro-Ducks from
   OuterSpace 200.00
66 CB,Heedless Horseman 200.00
67 CB rep. 200.00
68 CB,Hall of the Mermaid
   Queen! 200.00
69 CB,Cattle King! 200.00
70 CB,The Doom Diamond! 200.00
71 CB 200.00
72 CB rep. 200.00

73 CB rep. 200.00
74 thru 110 . . . . @175.00
111 thru 148 . . . . @40.00
149 . . . . 35.00
150 thru 168 . . . . @35.00
169 thru 173 . . . . @35.00

Whitman, 1980
174 thru 176 . . . . @35.00
177 and 178 . . . . @40.00
179 Rare 600.00
180 thru 182 . . . . @60.00
183 thru 195 . . . . @25.00
196 and 197 . . . . @30.00
1981 thru 209 . . . . @35.00

Gladstone, 1986
210 CB,Beagle Boys 20.00
211 CB,Prize of Pizzaro 18.00
212 CB,city-golden roofs 18.00
213 CB,city-golden roofs 18.00
214 CB 18.00
215 CB, a cold bargain 18.00
216 CB 18.00
217 CB,7 cities of Cibola 18.00
218 CB 18.00
219 Don Rosa,Son of Sun 30.00
220 CB,Don Rosa 10.00
221 CB,A:BeagleBoys 4.00
222 CB,Mysterious Island 4.00
223 CB 4.00
224 CB,Rosa,Cash Flow 7.00
225 CB 4.00
226 CB,Rosa 5.00
227 CB,Rosa 5.00
228 CB 4.00
229 CB 4.00
230 CB 5.00
231 CB,Rosa(c) 4.00
232 CB 4.00
233 CB 4.00
234 CB 4.00
235 Rosa 7.00
236 CB 4.00
237 CB 4.00
238 CB 4.00
239 CB 4.00
240 CB 4.00
241 CB,giant 7.00
242 CB,giant 7.00

Walt Disney, 1990
243 CB,Pie in the Sky 4.00
244 . . . . 3.50
245 . . . . 3.50
246 . . . . 3.50

Uncle Scrooge #259
© *Walt Disney*

COLOR PUB.

247	3.50
248	3.50
249	3.50
250 CB	5.00
251	3.00
252 No Room For Human Error	3.00
253 Fab.Philosophers Stone	3.00
254 The Filling Station	3.00
255 The Flying Dutchman	3.00
256 CB,Status Seeker	3.00
257 Coffee,Louie or Me	3.00
258 CB,Swamp of no return	3.00
259 The only way to Go	3.00
260 The Waves Above, The Gold Below	3.00
261 Rosa,Return to Zanadu, Pt.1	6.00
262 Rosa,Return to Zanadu, Pt.2	6.00
263 Rosa,Treasure Under Glass	6.00
264 Snobs Club	3.00
265 CB,Ten Cent Valentine	3.00
266 The Money Ocean,Pt.1	3.00
267 The Money Ocean,Pt 2	3.00
268 CB,Rosa,Island in the Sky	3.00
269 The Flowers	3.00
270 V:Magica DeSpell	3.00
271 The Secret o/t Stone	3.00
272 Canute The Brute's Battle Axe	3.00
273 CB,Uncle Scrooge-Ghost	3.25
274 CB,Hall of the Mermaid Queen	3.25
275 CB,Rosa,Christmas Cheers,inc. D.Rosa centerspread	3.25
276 Rosa, thru 277	@7.00
278 thru 280	@3.00

Gladstone, 1993

281 Rosa	7.00
282 thru 284	@3.00
285 Rosa, Life & Times	11.00
286 thru 293 Rosa, Life & Times	@6.00
294 thru 299	@3.00
300 Rosa & Barks	5.00
301 Statuesque Spendthrifts	3.00
302	3.00
303 Rocks to Riches	3.00
304 My Private Eye	3.00
305 Vigilante of Pizen Bluff	3.00
306	3.00
307 Temper Temper	3.00
308 Revenge of the Witch	3.00

Prestige format, 64pg.

309 Whadalottajargon	8.00
310 The Sign of the Triple Distelfink	8.00
311 The Last Lord of Eldorado	8.00
312 The Hands of Zeus	8.00
313 The Fantastic River Race	8.00
314	8.00
315 The Flying Scot, pt.1	8.00
316 The Flying Scot, pt.2	8.00
317 Pawns of the Lamp Garou	8.00
318 Cowboy Captain of Cutty Sark	8.00
319 The Horse Radish Story	8.00
320 The Mysterious Stone Ray	8.00
321 The Giant Robot Robbers	8.00
322 Secret of the Lost Dutchman's Mine	8.00

UNCLE SCROOGE

Gemstone Publishing, 2003

319 thru 347	@7.00
348 thru 360	@7.00
TPB Life and Times of Scrooge McDuck	17.00
TPB Life and Times Companion	17.00

UNCLE SCROOGE ADVENTURES

Gladstone, 1987

1 CB,McDuck of Arabia	9.00
2 translated from Danish	5.00
3 translated from Danish	5.00

4 CB	5.00
5 Rosa	5.00
6 CB	3.50
7 CB	3.00
8 CB	3.00
9 Rosa	3.50
10 CB	3.00
11 CB	3.00
12 CB	3.00
13 CB	3.00
14 Rosa	3.50
15 CB	3.00
16 CB	3.00
17 CB	3.00
18 CB	3.00
19 CB,Rosa(c)	3.50
20 CB,giant	6.00
21 CB,giant	6.00
22 Rosa(c)	6.00
23 CB,giant	4.00
24 thru 26	@2.50
27 Rosa,O:Jr. Woodchuck	4.00
28 giant	4.00
29	2.50
30 giant	5.00
31 thru 32	@3.00
33 Barks	5.00
34 thru 40	@3.00
41	2.50
42 The Dragon's Amulet	2.50
43 Queen of the Wild Dog Pack	2.50
44	2.50
45 Secret of the Duckburg Triangle	2.50
46 The Tides Turn	2.50
47 The Menehune Mystery	2.50
48 The Tenth Avatar	2.50
49 Dead-Eye Duck	2.50
50 CB,The Secret of Atlantis	3.00
51	2.50
52 The Black Diamond	2.50
53 Secret of the Incas	2.50
54 Secret of the Incas, pt.2	2.50

UNCLE SCROOGE ADVENTURES

Gladstone, 1997–98

Don Rosa Specials

Spec.#1 (of 4)	11.00
Spec.#2 thru #4	@10.00

Van Horn Specials

Spec.#1	10.00
Spec.#2	10.00
Spec.#3	10.00
Spec.#4	10.00

UNCLE SCROOGE ADVENTURES IN COLOR

Gladstone, 1987–98

Carl Barks reprints

1 thru 32	@10.00
33 thru 35	@11.00
36 32pg.	9.00
37 thru 53	@10.00
54 Hall of the Mermaid Queen	10.00
55 The Doom Diamond	10.00
56 two adventures	10.00

UNCLE SCROOGE & DONALD DUCK

Gold Key, 1965

1 rep.	200.00

UNCLE SCROOGE AND DONALD DUCK

Gladstone, 1997

1	2.50
2 Christmas stories	2.50

3 Back to Long Ago	2.50
TPB Vol. 1	10.00
TPB Vol. 2	10.00
TPB Vol. 3	10.00
TPB Vol. 4	10.00

UNCLE SCROOGE GOES TO DISNEYLAND

Gladstone, 1985

1 CB,etc. 100pp	13.00

UNDEAD, THE

Chaos! Comics Black Label,, 2001

Ashcan	6.00
Ashcan, premium edition	20.00
1 zombie wasteland	5.00
1a previews exclusive (c)	5.00
1b signed edition	15.00
1c premium edition	10.00
1d super-premium edition	20.00
1e foil (c)	20.00

UNDERDOG

Charlton, 1970

1 Planet Zot	150.00
2 Simon Sez/The Molemen	100.00
3 Whisler's Father	100.00
4 The Witch of Pycoon	100.00
5 The Snowmen	100.00
6 The Big Shrink	100.00
7 The Marbleheads	100.00
8 The Phoney Booths	100.00
9 Tin Man Alley	100.00
10 Be My Valentine (Jan., 1972)	100.00

UNDERDOG

Gold Key, 1975

1 The Big Boom	125.00
2 The Sock Singer Caper	75.00
3 The Ice Cream Scream	75.00
4	75.00
5	75.00
6 Head in a Cloud	75.00
7 The Cosmic Canine	75.00
8	75.00
9	75.00
10 Bouble Trouble Gum	75.00
11 The Private Life of Shoeshine Boy	50.00
12 The Deadly Fist of Fingers	50.00
13	50.00

Underdog #1
© Spotlight

14 Shrink Shrank Shrunk........ 50.00
15 Polluter Palooka 50.00
16 The Soda Jerk 50.00
17 Flee For Your Life 50.00
18 Rain Rain Go Away...Okay 50.00
19 Journey To the Center of
   the Earth 50.00
20 The Six Million Dollar Dog ... 50.00
21 Smell of Success 55.00
22 Antlers Away 55.00
23 Wedding Bells In Outer Space
   (Feb.,1979) 55.00

UNDERDOG
Spotlight, 1987
1 FMc,PC(c),The Eredicator...... 5.00
2 FMc,CS(c), Prisoner of Love/
   The Return of Fearo 5.00

UNDERDOG IN 3-D
Blackthorne
1 Wanted Dead or Alive 2.50

UNDERSEA AGENT
Tower, 1966–97
1 F:Davy Jones,UnderseaAgent. 150.00
2 thru 4 .... @125.00
5 O&I:Merman 125.00
6 GK,WW(c) 125.00

Undertaker #3
© *Chaos Comics*

UNDERTAKER
Chaos! Comics, 1999
Preview BSt, WWF character 2.50
Preview, photo (c)............. 2.50
1 Prophecy of the Dead 3.00
1a photo cover 3.00
1b premium edition 10.00
1c Death Chrome cover 15.00
1d Death Chrome cover, signed.. 20.00
2 V:Embalmer & Paul Bearer 3.00
3 O:Undertaker................ 3.00
4 Kane 3.00
5 Jezebel 3.00
6 thru 12 .... @3.00
2a thru 12a photo covers ..... @3.00
Halloween Spec. 3.00
Halloween Spec. photo(c) 3.00
TPB Prophecy of the Dead,
   rep.#1–#4 .... 13.00
TPB Vol.2 rep.#5–#8 .... 13.00

UNDERWORLD: RED IN TOOTH AND CLAW
IDW Publishing, 2004
1 .... 4.00
2 thru 3 .... @4.00

UNEARTHLY SPECTACULARS
Harvey, 1965
1 DW,AT,I:Tiger Boy 200.00
2 WW,AW,GK,I:Earthman,Miracles,
   Inc. A:Clawfang,TigerBoy ... 150.00
3 RC,AW,JO,A:Miracles,Inc..... 125.00

U.N. FORCE
Gauntlet Comics, 1995
0 BDC(s)..................... 3.00
1 B:BDC(s),I:U.N.Force 3.00
2 O:Indigo 3.00
3 .... 3.00
4 A:Predator 3.00
5 B:Critical Mass.............. 3.00

U.N. FORCE FILES
Gauntlet Comics
1 KP(c),F:Hunter Seeker, Lotus ... 3.00

UNHUMAN
Narwain Publishing, 2006
1 BAu,TMd 4.00

UNION OF JUSTICE
Quantum Comics, 1998
1 by David Watkins & Steve Kurth . 3.00
2 .... 3.00
3 A:Golden Age Union 3.00

UNITY
Valiant, 1992
0 BWS,BL,Chapter#1,A:All Valiant
   Heroes,V:Erica Pierce........ 4.00
0a Red ed.,w/red logo 55.00
1 BWS,BL,Chapter#18,A:All Valiant
   Heroes,D:Erica Pierce........ 4.00
1a Gold logo 16.00
1b Platinum................. 15.00
TPB Previews Exclusive,Vol.I
   Chap.#1-9 .... 8.00
TPB Previews Exclusive,Vol.II
   Chap.#10-18 .... 3.00
TPB #1 rep Chapters #1-4..... 11.00
TPB #2 rep Chapters #5-9..... 10.00
TPB #3 rep Chapters #10-14..... 10.00

UNITY 2000
Acclaim, 1999
1 (of 6) 7.00
2 .... 10.00
3 .... 22.00

UNIT ZERO: MARQUIS FILES
Marquis Models, 2004
1 .... 4.00
2 thru 5 .... 4.00

UNIVERSAL SOLDIER
Now, 1992
1 Based on Movie,Holo.(c)....... 2.75
2 Luc & Ronnie on the run
   from UniSols 2.50
2a Photo cover 2.50
3 Photo(c).................. 2.50

UNKNOWN WORLDS OF FRANK BRUNNER
Eclipse, 1985
1 and 2 FB .... @4.00

UNTAMED LOVE
Fantagraphics, 1987
1 FF 3.00

UNTOLD TALES OF
Chaos! Comics, 2000
Purgatori #1 .... 3.00
Purgatori #1 premium ed. 13.00
Chastity #1.................. 3.00
Chastity premium #1 .... 13.00
Lady Death #1 .... 3.00
Lady Death #1 premium 13.00
Lady Death #1 chromium ed. 16.00

UNUSUAL TALES
Charlton Comics, 1955–65
1 .... 500.00
2 .... 300.00
3 thru 5 .... @250.00
6 SD,SD(c) 400.00
7 SD,SD(c) 450.00
8 SD,SD(c) 450.00
9 SD,SD(c) 500.00
10 SD,SD(c)................ 550.00
11 SD 500.00
12 SD 400.00
13 .... 200.00
14 SD 350.00
15 SD,SD(c)................ 425.00
16 thru 20 .... @200.00
21 .... 150.00
22 SD 175.00
23 .... 150.00
24 .... 150.00
25 thru 27 SD .... @275.00
28 .... 150.00
29 SD 275.00
30 thru 49................ @125.00

URTH 4
Continuity, 1990
1 TVE,NA(c) 2.50
2 TVE,NA 2.50
3 TVE,NA 2.50
4 NA,Last issue.............. 2.50

USAGI YOJIMBO
Mirage, 1993
1 A:TMNT 6.00
2 .... 5.00
3 .... 5.00
4 thru 16 .... @5.00
17 .... 8.00

U. T. F., THE
Speakeasy Comics, 2006
1 (of 3) 3.00
2 .... 3.00

U. T. F.: UNDEAD TASK FORCE
Ape Entertainment, 2006
1 .... 3.00
3 .... 3.00

VALERIA, THE SHE BAT
Continuity, 1993
1 NA,I:Valeria 10.00
2 thru 4 .... [NOT RELEASED]
5 Rise of Magic.............. 2.50

COLOR PUB.

All comics prices listed are for *Near Mint* condition.

VALERIA, THE SHE-BAT
Windjammer, 1995
1 (of 2) NA,Valeria & 'Rilla 2.50
2 (of 2) NA,BSz, final issue 2.50

VALHALLA
Antarctic Press, 1999
1 BDn set in 1939 . . . . 3.00

VALIANT READER: GUIDE TO THE VALIANT UNIVERSE
Acclaim, 1993
1 O:Valiant Universe 2.50

VALIANT VISION STARTER KIT
Valiant, 1993
1 w/3-D Glasses 3.00
2 F:Starwatchers 3.00

VALKYRIE
Eclipse, 1988
1 PG,I:Steelfox,C:Airboy, Sky Wolf . 3.00
2 PG,O:New Black Angel 2.50
3 PG 2.50
[2nd Series]
1 BA,V:Eurasian Slavers 2.50
2 BA,V:Cowgirl 2.50
3 BA,V:Cowgirl 2.50

VALKYRIES
Alias Enterprises, 2006
1 . . . . 3.50
2 . . . . 3.50

VALLEY OF THE DINOSAURS
Charlton, 1975
1 Hanna-Barbera TV adapt. 30.00
2 thru 11 . . . . @20.00

VALOR
Gemstone, 1998
1 EC comics reprint 2.50
2 . . . . 2.50
3 AW, The Cloak of Command . . . 2.50
4 WW(c) 2.50

Valor #4
© Gemstone

---

5 final issue 3.50
Annual
TPB Vol. 1 rebinding of series 13.50

VAMPEROTICA
Brainstorm, 1996
1–16 see B&W
17 . . . . 3.00
17a signed 5.00
17 Holochrome cover 40.00
18 Blood of the Damned (color) 3.00
18a signed 5.00
19 Hunter's Blood 3.00
19a deluxe 3.00
20 Vampire Quest 3.00
21 hunting & feeding 3.00
22 . . . . 3.00
TPB Red Reign, rep. 13.00

VAMPEROTICA LINGERIE
Comic Cavalcade, 1998
Commemorative #1 by Kirk Lindo . . 6.00
Commemorative #1a deluxe 15.00

VAMPI
Harris Comics, 2000
1/2 24-pg. 10.00
1/2 variant edition 20.00
1 Switchblade Kiss,pt.1 . . . . 3.00
1c signed & numbered 20.00
1d gold foil 30.00
1e convention special, B&W 10.00
1g limited holochrome edition 25.00
1g royal blue edition 60.00
1h Platinum edition 20.00
1i limited edition 10.00
2 Switchblade Kiss,pt.2 . . . . 8.00
1b thru 2b limited chrome (c) . . @15.00
2c limited holochrome edition 25.00
3 Switchblade Kiss,pt.3 . . . . 5.00
4 Dark Angel Rising,pt.1 . . . . 3.00
5 Dark Angel Rising,pt.2 . . . . 3.00
6 Dark Angel Rising,pt.3 . . . . 3.50
7 Underworld, pt.1 (of 3) 3.00
8 Underworld, pt.2 . . . . 3.00
9 Underworld, pt.3 . . . . 3.00
1a thru 9a deluxe . . . . @10.00
Ashcan Vampi Dark Angel Rising
    platinum leather limited B&W . 15.00
Ashcan Vampi Underworld preview . 6.00
Ashcan Tainted Love 6.00
Vampi #1 preview 3.00
TPB Vol. 1, rep. #1–#3 . . . . 20.00
Anarchy Studios, 2001
10 . . . . 3.00
10b convention ed. 10.00
10c convention ed., signed 20.00
11 . . . . 3.00
12 . . . . 3.00
12b holo-fx chrome ed. 15.00
12c gold-fx chrome 25.00
13 . . . . 3.00
14 framed, I:Xenocyde 3.00
15 V:Xenocyde 3.00
16 saved by Xenocide 3.00
17 Ultimatrix, pt.2 . . . . 3.00
18 Ultimatrix, pt.3 . . . . 3.00
19 Serpent's Kiss, pt.1 . . . . 3.00
20 Serpent's Kiss, pt.2 . . . . 3.00
21 Serpent's Kiss, pt.3 . . . . 3.00
22 Serpent's Kiss, pt.4 . . . . 3.00
23 Fallout, pt.1 . . . . 3.00
24 Fallout, pt.2 . . . . 3.00
25 . . . . 3.00
10a thru 16a deluxe . . . . @10.00
14a thru 25a limited . . . . @10.00
Sketchbook platinum leather 15.00
Ashcan Vampi:End Game 6.00
Ashcan Vampi #19–#21 . . . . 6.00
Ashcan Ultimatrix Leather Gold . . 15.00

Ashcan Vampi: Anarchy in the USA
    giant-sized, limited (2001) 6.00
TPB Vol. 1 Switchblade Kiss/
    Dark Angel Rising 15.00
TPB Underworld Tainted Love 15.00

VAMPI (DIGITAL)
Harris Comics, 2001
1 digital art 3.00
1a limited ed. 10.00
Preview edition, digital 3.00
Ashcan, Underworld gold leather. . 15.00

VAMPI VICIOUS
Anarchy Studios, 2003
Prototype Convention edition 10.00
1 . . . . 3.00
1a variant (c). 3.00
1 royal blue edition 40.00
1 gold foil edition 30.00
2 thru 3 . . . . @3.00
2a thru 3a variant (c) 3.00

VAMPI VICIOUS CIRCLE
Anarchy Studios, 2004
Ashcan Vicious Circle 6.00
1 . . . . 3.00
2 thru 3 . . . . @3.00
1a thru 3a variant (c). . . . . @10.00

VAMPI VICIOUS: GEMINI EFFECT
Anarchy Studios, 2005
1 . . . . 3.00
1a limited 10.00
2 . . . . 3.00
2a limited 10.00

VAMPI: VICIOUS RAMPAGE
Anarchy Studios, 2004
1 . . . . 3.00
1a limited 10.00
2 . . . . 3.00
2a limited 10.00

VAMPI VS. XIN
Anarchy Studios, 2004
1 & 2 . . . . @3.00
1a thru 2a limited . . . . @10.00

VAMPIRE LESTAT
Innovation, 1990–91
1 Anne Rice Adapt. 20.00
1a 2nd printing 4.00
1b 3rd printing 2.50
2 . . . . 9.00
2a 2nd printing 4.00
2b 3rd printing 2.50
3 . . . . 5.00
3a 2nd printing 2.50
4 . . . . 5.00
4a 2nd printing 2.50
5 . . . . 5.00
6 . . . . 5.00
7 . . . . 5.00
8 . . . . 5.00
9 scarce 8.00
9a 2nd Printing 3.00
10 . . . . 5.00
11 Those Who Must Be Kept 4.00
12 conclusion 4.00
Vampire Companion #1 . . . . 4.00
Vampire Companion #2 (preview
    Interview With The Vampire . . . 3.00
Vampire Companion #3 . . . . 3.00
GN rep.#1-#12 (Innovation) 25.00
GN rep.#1-#12 (Ballantine) 25.00

VAMPIRELLA
Warren Publishing Co., 1969–83
1 NA,FF(c),I:Vampirella 750.00
2 B:Amazonia 300.00
3 Very scarce 650.00
4 .... 275.00
5 FF(c) 285.00
6 .... 275.00
7 FF(c) 300.00
8 B:horror 250.00
9 BWS,BV(c),WW 250.00
10 No Vampirella,WW 100.00
11 TS,FF(c)O&I Pendragon. 200.00
12 WW.................... 200.00
13 .... 175.00
14 .... 175.00
15 .... 175.00
16 .... 175.00
17 B:Tomb of the Gods 175.00
18 .... 175.00
19 WW,1973 Annual 150.00
20 thru 25............... @125.00
26 .... 100.00
27 1974 Annual 120.00
28 thru 30............... @100.00
31 FF(c)................... 120.00
32 thru 36................ @75.00
37 1975 Annual 80.00
38 .... 75.00
39 .... 75.00
40 .... 75.00
41 thru 45................ @50.00
46 O:Vampirella 65.00
47 thru 99 .... @50.00
100 Double Size 125.00
101 thru 110.............. @75.00
111 Giant Edition 100.00
112 .... 75.00
Ann. #1 WW............... 450.00
Special #1 .... 300.00

Harris, 1998
113 Low distribution.......... 500.00

VAMPIRELLA
Harris, 1992
0 Dracula Wars............... 5.00
0a Blue version 22.00
1 V:Forces of Chaos, w/coupon for
  DSt poster 20.00
1a 2nd printing 5.00
2 AH(c) 18.00
3 A:Dracula................. 7.00
4 A:Dracula................. 6.00
5 .... 6.00
Spec. #1 Vampirella/Shadowhawk:
  Creatures of the Night (1995) .. 5.50

Harris Comics, 1996
0 gold foil signed & numbered ... 22.00
1 Commemorative Edition 3.00
1a Commemorative Edition,
  sgn & num. 10.00
25th Anniv. Spec., FF(c)....... 6.00
25th Anniv. Spec., lim.......... 7.00
Spec. Death of Vampirella,
  memorial, chromium cover ... 20.00
Spec. 1-shot Vampirella/Cain,
  flipbook, 72-pg. (1996) 7.00
Spec. Vampirella Pin-up (1995).... 3.50

VAMPIRELLA (MONTHLY)
Harris Comics, 1998–2000
1 Ascending Evil, pt.1.......... 3.00
1a ultra-violent cover 3.00
1b JaL(c).................. 10.00
2 Ascending Evil, pt.2.......... 3.00
2a JaL(c). 10.00
3 Ascending Evil, pt.3.......... 3.00

3a JaL(c)................... 10.00
4 Holy War, pt.1 .... 3.00
4a Crimson ed., Joe Linsner (c).. 3.00
5 Holy War, pt.2 .... 3.00
6 Holy War, pt.3 .... 3.00
7 Queen's Gambit, pt.1.......... 3.00
7a chromium Edition 11.00
8 Queen's Gambit, pt.2.......... 3.00
9 Queen's Gambit, pt.3, concl..... 3.00
10 Hell on Earth, pt.1, V:Nyx...... 3.00
10a variant JaL cover 10.00
11 Hell on Earth, pt.2........... 3.00

Vampirella #12
© *Harris Comics*

12 Hell on Earth, pt.3,
  New costume.............. 3.00
12a variant cover, new costume ... 3.00
12b chromium cover 11.00
13 World's End,pt.1 .... 3.00
13b Pantha cover............. 10.00
14 World's End,pt.2 .... 3.00
15 World's End,pt.3 .... 3.00
13a thru 15a variant (c)s ...... @3.00
16 Pantha #1 .... 3.00
17 Pantha #2 .... 3.00
16b limited photo ed........... 10.00
16a thru 17a Phantha photo(c)s . @3.00
18 Rebirth, pt.1,JaL(c).......... 3.00
19 Rebirth, pt.2,............... 3.00
20 Rebirth, pt.3 .... 3.00
21 Dangerous Games,pt.1......... 3.00
21c Millennium ed............. 20.00
22 Dangerous Games,pt.2........ 3.00
22a Dorian (c) 10.00
16c thru 22c Julie Strain (c)s ... @10.00
23 Vampirella/Lady Death:
  The Revenge, pt.1........... 3.00
23a limited ed................ 3.00
21b thru 23b limited chrome ed. @15.00
24 Death Valley, Vampirella (c) 3.00
24a Pantha (c) 3.00
25 Death Valley, vol.2 .... 3.00
25a alternate (c).............. 3.00
25b Monte Moore (c) 15.00
26 The End #1 .... 3.00
26a alternate (c).............. 10.00
26b platinum ed............... 20.00
Ashcan, Ascending Evil, b&w, 16pg. 1.50
Ashcan, Ascending Evil, b&w,
  signed, limited 25.00
Ashcan, Queen's Gambit,B&W 6.00
Ashcan, Queen's Gambit,signed .. 25.00
Ashcan World's End, B&W,16pg. .. 6.00
Ashcan Rebirth preview,B&W,16-pg 6.00
Vampirella/Lady Death Limited
  Preview Ashcan, B&W....... 6.00

Vampirella, Queen's Gambit #1
  special edition, alternate (c) .. 10.00
  Chromium Edition 11.00
Spec.#0 A:Lady Death,B.U.:Pantha. 3.00
Spec.#0a Pantha(c)............ 3.00
Spec.#0b Vampirella(c) 10.00
Spec.#0c Vampirella(c), signed ... 30.00
Spec.#0d Pantha(c) 10.00
Spec. Vampirella/Dracula: The
  Centennial, A:Pantha,16pg..... 2.00
Spec. Vampirella/Dracula: The
  Centennial, 48pg. (1997)...... 5.00
Spec.#1 Dangerous Games,
  holochrome (2001) 15.00
TPB Ascending Evil 7.50
Ann.Ed.#2 Rebirth 10.00
Ann.Ed.#3 Rebirth,Bruce Timm(c). 10.00
Julie Strain Special............ 4.00
Julie Strain Special variant(c) 10.00
Julie Strain Spec. chrome (c) 10.00
Julie Strain Spec. holochrome(c). . 25.00

VAMPIRELLA
Harris Comics, 2001
0 Gold edition 20.00
1 Nowheresville, Mayhew (c) 3.00
1a JSC (c)................... 3.00
1b Anacleto (c) 3.00
1c JaL (c) 3.00
1d commemorative ed. B&W, FF(c) 5.00
1e Chicago convention edition ... 10.00
1f Chicago convention, limited ... 20.00
1g photo edition, limited 10.00
1h gold edition 30.00
1i holographic chrome (c)....... 15.00
1j royal blue edition........... 60.00
1k gold-fx chrome (c) 25.00
1l Ascending evil gold (c) 20.00
2 thru 4 .... @3.00
4c holo FX chrome (c) 15.00
4d gold-fx chrome 30.00
2a thru 22a limited .... @10.00
2b thru 22b photo (c) .... @10.00
5 thru 22 .... @3.00
7c thru 10c limited Pantha
  MT(c) .... @10.00
7d Pantha holo fx MC(c)....... 15.00
Ashcan #1 giant-size 6.00
Ashcan #4–#6 giant-size, 16-pg.... 6.00
Preview #7–#9 16-pg. 3.00
Ashcan #7–#9 giant-size,16-pg. ... 6.00
Ashcan #11–#13 .... 6.00
Ashcan #11–#13 leather 15.00
1-shot Vampirella Genesis (2001) .. 3.00
1-shot Vampirella Genesis,
  variant 10.00
TPB Nowheresville 13.00
TPB Vol. 1 Crimson Chronicles ... 20.00
TPB Vol. 2 Crimson Chronicles ... 20.00
TPB Vol. 2 Fear of Mirrors....... 15.00
Spec. Model Search........... 10.00
Spec. Halloween 2004.......... 5.00

VAMPIRELLA: BLOOD LUST
Harris, 1997
1 (of 2) JeR & JJu.............. 5.00
2 JJu(c)................... 5.00
Book 1, JJu(c) Virgin edition 11.00
Book 2, JJu(c) Virgin edition 11.00

VAMPIRELLA CLASSIC
Harris Comics, 1995
1 Dark Angel 3.50
2 V:Demogorgon.............. 3.25
3 V:Were Beast............... 3.25
4 R:Papa Voodoo 3.25
5 .... 3.00

VAMPIRELLA: CROSSOVERS
Harris, 1996–98
1-shot Vampirella vs.
    Eudaemon (1996) 10.00
1-shot StG,SSh,Vampirella/
    Wetworks, image x-over (1997) 3.00
1-shotA Vamp/Wetworks,
    SS&KN(c) 10.00
1-shot Vampirella/Shi (1997) 3.00
1-shotA Vamp/Shi, Chromium ed. . 7.00
1-shotA Vamp/Shi, penciled(c). . . 10.00
Ashcan #1, Vamp/Shi, 16pg 3.00
1-shot Vampirella/Painkiller
    Jane, foil JQ(c) (1998). 3.50
1-shotA Vampirella/Painkiller
    Jane, alternate RL&JP(c) 10.00
1 Crossover art gallery 3.00
1a Art gallery, chromium ed. 10.00
1b Art gallery, holochrome(c) 20.00

VAMPIRELLA: DEATH AND DESTRUCTION
Harris
1 limited preview ashcan 4.00
1a The Dying of the Light 3.00
1b signed & numbered 3.00
1c satin edition 25.00
1d Lim. Ed., Mark Beachum (c) . . 10.00
2 The Nature of the Beast 3.00
3 TSg,ACo,JP,JJu(c),Mistress
    Nyx kills Vampi 3.00
TPB 15.00

VAMPIRELLA/ LADY DEATH
Harris/Chaos!, 1999
1 x-over. 3.50
1a Valentine ed. 10.00
1b signed and numbered 20.00
1c gold edition. 30.00
1d penciled edition 10.00
Spec.#1 TheEnd,chrome(c)(2000). 15.00
Spec.#1a The End,holochrome(c) . 25.00
Spec.#1 Revenge, chrome(c)(2000). . . .
15.00
Spec.#1a Revenge,holochrome(c) 25.00

VAMPIRELLA LIVES
Harris, 1996–97
1 Linen Edition 7.00
1a Censored Photo cover edition . . 8.00
2 Vengeance edition. 3.00
2a alternate edition, AH(c) 10.00
3 WEl(s),ACo,JP,Graveyard edition,
    JSC(c) 3.00
2b thru 3b Model photo edition . . @3.00
TPB Vampirella Lives (2002) 13.00

VAMPIRELLA OF DRAKULON
Harris Comics, 1996
1 V:assassin 3.00
1a alternate MiB(c) 10.00
2 Dracula returns 3.00
3 thru 5 . . . . @3.00

VAMPIRELLA: SAD WINGS OF DESTINY
Harris, 1996
1 DQ(s),JJu(c) 4.00
1 signed & numbered (#1,500). . . . 5.00
Gold Emblem Seal Edition. 4.00

VAMPIRELLA STRIKES
Harris Comics, 1995
1 The Prize,pt.1 . . . . 3.00
1a limited, signed & numbered. . . 10.00
1b full moon background 3.50
2 V:Dante Corp.,A:Passion. 3.00
3 V:subway stalker 3.00
4 IEd,RN, Soul Food. 3.00
5 DQ,RN,F:Eudaemon 3.00
5 signed & numbered, (200). 10.00
6 . . . . 3.00
6 signed, alternate cover 10.00
6 signed & numbered 12.00
7 silver special flip book 3.00
Ann. #1 new cover. 10.00

VAMPIRELLA VS. HEMORRHAGE
Harris, 1997
1 IEd,MIB 3.50
1 signed & numbered 12.00
1 Linen edition, signed & numb. . . 25.00
1 MIB alternate cover 10.00
2 IEd,MIB 3.50
3 (of 3) IEd,MIB. 3.50

VAMPIRELLA VS. PANTHA
Harris, 1997
Showcase #1 preview 2.00
1 MMr,MT, MT(c) Vampirella vs.
    Pantha. 3.50
1 MMr,MT, MT(c) Pantha vs.
    Vampirella 3.50
1a MMr,MT, MT(c). 10.00

VAMPIRELLA/ WITCHBLADE
Harris Comics, 2003
1 . . . . 3.00
1a variant (c). 10.00
Spec. Union of the Damned. 3.00
Spec. Variant (c) 10.00
Anarchy Studios/Harris Comics
Ashcan San Diego Comic Con
    B&W, 16-page 5.00
TPB Vampirella Witchblade Trilogy 13.00

VAMPIRELLA/ WITCHBLADE: FEAST
Anarchy Studios/Harris Comics, 2005
1 . . . . 3.00
1a & 1b variant (c)s. . . . . @10.00

VAMPIRE THE MASQUERADE
Moonstone, 2001
1-shot Toreador. 6.00
1-shot Nosferatu (2002) 7.00
1-shot Beckett. 7.00
1-shot Ventrue 7.00
1-shot Calebros 6.00
1-shot Giovanni. 5.50
1-shot Assamite 5.50
1-shot Lasombra 5.50
1-shot Isabel 5.00
1-shot Lucita 5.00
TPB Vol. 1 . . . . 17.00
TPB Vol. 2 . . . . 21.00
TPB Vol. 3 Five Undead 21.00

VAMPRESS LUXURA, THE
Brainstorm, 1996
1 . . . . 3.00
1a gold edition 10.00
2 . . . . 3.00

2a gold foil 10.00

VANDALA
Chaos! Comics, 2000
1 . . . . 3.00
1 premium. 9.99

VANDALA II
Chaos! Comics, 2001
1 PDa,EBe 3.00
1a premium ed. Matt Hughes (c) . 10.00

VANGUARD ILLUSTRATED
Pacific, 1983
1 . . . . 3.00
2 DSt(c). 3.00
3 thru 5 SR . . . . @3.00
6 GI 3.00
7 GE,I:Mr.Monster. 6.00

VARICK: CHRONICLES OF THE DARK PRINCE
Q Comics, 1999
1 by Nick Marcari & Major Fareed . 2.50
2 32-pg 2.50
3 thru 6 . . . . @2.50

VARUK
Counteractive Comics, 2006
1 . . . . 3.00

VAULT OF HORROR
Gladstone, 1990–91
1 Rep.GS,WW 5.00
2 Rep.VoH #27 & HoF #18. . . . . . 3.00
3 Rep.VoH #13 & HoF #22. . . . . . 3.00
4 Rep.VoH #23 & HoF #13. . . . . . 3.00
5 Rep.VoH #19 & HoF #5. . . . . . . 3.00
6 Rep.VoH #32 & WF #6 . . . . 3.00
7 Rep.VoH #26 & WS #7 . . . . 3.00

VAULT OF HORROR
Russ Cochran Publ., 1991–92
1 Rep.VoH #28 & WS #18 . . . . . . 4.00
2 Rep.VoH #33 & WS #20 . . . . . . 3.00
3 Rep.VoH #26 & WS #7 . . . . 3.00
4 Rep.VoH #35 & WS #15 . . . . . . 3.00
4 Rep.VoH #18 & WS #11 . . . . . . 3.00
5 Rep.VoH #18 & WS #11 . . . . . . 3.00

Vault of Horror #26
© Gemstone

2nd Series
1 thru 7 Rep.VoH . . . . @3.00
8 . . . . 3.00

Gemstone
17 thru 29 EC comics reprints . . . @3.00
`Annuals'
TPB Vol. 1 rebinding of #1–#5. . . . 9.00
TPB Vol. 2 rebinding of #6–#10. . . . 9.00
TPB Vol. 3 rebinding of #11–#15 . . . 11.00
TPB Vol. 4 rebinding of #16–#20. . . 13.00
TPB Vol. 5 rebinding #21–#25. . . . 13.50
TPB Vol. 6 reginding #26–#29. . . . 11.00

VECTOR
Now, 1986
1 . . . . 3.00
2 thru 5 . . . . @3.00

VEGAS KNIGHTS
Pioneer, 1989
1 . . . . 2.50
2 . . . . 2.50
3 . . . . 2.50

Vengeance of Vampirells #11
© Harris

VENGEANCE OF VAMPIRELLA
Harris, 1994
1 Hemmorhage 6.00
1a Gold Edition 9.00
1 gold edition, signed, numbered . 15.00
2 Dervish. 3.00
3 On the Hunt 3.00
4 Teenage Vampries 3.00
5 Teenage Vampires 3.00
6 . . . . 3.00
7 . . . . 3.00
8 bagged w/card 3.00
9 . . . . 3.00
10 Bad Jack Rising 3.00
11 Pits of Hell, w/card 3.00
12 V:Passion 3.00
13 V:Passion 3.00
14 Prelude to the Walk,pt.2 . . . . 3.00
15 The Mystery Walk,pt.1 . . . . 3.25
16 The Mystery Walk,pt.2 . . . . 3.25
17 The Mystery Walk,pt.3 . . . . 3.25
18 The Mystery Walk,pt.4 . . . . 3.00
19 The Mystery Walk,pt.5 . . . . 3.00
20 Mystery Walk epilog 3.00
14a thru 19a Buzz . . . . @5.00
21 thru 24 . . . . @3.00
25 The End 3.00

25 variant cover, signed &
   numbered 8.00
25 signed & numbered (2,500) 8.00
25 gold edition, signed & numb. . . 20.00
25 alternate cover, signed by Jae
   Lee & numbered (#1,500) 15.00
Mini-comic gold foil, signed 20.00
TPB 1-3 Bloodshed 7.00

VENTURE
AC Comics, 1986
1 . . . . 3.00
2 thru 4 . . . . @3.00

VERONICA
Archie Publications, April, 1989
1 . . . . @7.00
2 thru 10 . . . . @5.00
11 thru 38 . . . . @4.00
39 Love Show Dolon 6.00
40 thru 50 . . . . @4.00
51 thru 71 . . . . @3.50
72 thru 93 . . . . @3.00
94 thru 97 . . . . @2.50
98 thru 120 . . . . @2.50
121 thru 133 . . . . @2.50
134 thru 156 . . . . @2.50
157 thru 176 . . . . @2.25

VEROTIKA
Verotika, 1995
1 thru 3 Jae Lee, Frazetta . . . . . . @3.00
4 thru 9 . . . . @3.00
1-shot Rogues Gallery of Villians
   (1998) 4.00

VEROTIK ILLUSTRATED
Verotik, 1997
1 48pg 7.00
2 . . . . 7.00
3 . . . . 7.00
3a alternate cover 7.00
3 variant cover 10.00

VEROTIK WORLD
Verotik, 2004
2 . . . . 4.00
3 . . . . 4.00
2a variant (c). 10.00
2b Parody (c) 5.00
3a variant (c) 10.00
3b Shrunken Head (c) 10.00

VESPER
Acetylene Comics, 2001
Preview B&W 3.00
1 Girls Night Out 2.50
1a JOb (c) 2.50
2 . . . . 2.50
2a variant Wizardworld 2001(c) . . . 5.00
3 The Word for the Day 2.50
3a variant HbK(c) 2.50
4 . . . . 2.50
5 Soul Harvest 2.50
6 . . . . 2.50
6a variant (c). 2.50
7 Return of Gruel 3.00

VICKI
Atlas, 1975
1 Rep. 50.00
2 thru 4 . . . . @40.00

VICTORIAN
Penny Farthing Press, 1999
1 . . . . 3.00
2 thru 5 . . . . @3.00
6 thru 13 . . . . @3.00

14 thru 17 . . . . @3.00
18 thru 24 . . . . @3.00
25 74-pg. 6.00
TPB Vol. 2 Self-Immolation 20.00
TPB Act 3: Self Estrangement 20.00

VICTORIA'S SECRET SERVICE
Alias Enterprises, 2005
0 . . . . 1.00
1 . . . . 3.00
2 thru 5 . . . . @3.50

VILLAINS
Viper Comics, 2006
1 (of 4) 3.25
2 thru 4 . . . . @3.25

VILLAINS & VIGILANTES
Eclipse, 1986–87
1 A:Crusaders,Shadowman 3.00
2 A:Condor 3.00
3 V:Crushors 3.00
4 V:Crushers 3.00

VINTAGE MAGNUS ROBOT FIGHTER
Valiant, 1992
1 rep. Gold Key Magnus #22
   (which is #1) 5.00
2 rep. Gold Key Magnus #3 . . . . . 4.50
3 rep. Gold Key Magnus #13 . . . . . 3.50
4 rep. Gold Key Magnus #15 . . . . . 3.50

VIP
TV Comics, 2000
1 (of 3) 3.00
2 thru 3 . . . . @3.00
1a thru 3a photo (c) . . . . @3.00
TPB Collected Edition 9.00
Preview Edition 6.00

VIRGINIAN, THE
Gold Key, 1963
1 . . . . 125.00

VIRTEX
Oktomica Entertainment, 1998
0 16-pg 2.50
1 V:Ripnun 2.50
2 V:Ripnun 2.50
3 alternate endings 2.50
4 Night of the Ninjella,pt.1 . . . . . . 2.50
5 Night of the Ninjella,pt.2 . . . . . . 3.00
6 All My Sins Remembered 3.00

VIRTUA FIGHTER
Malibu, 1995
1 New Video Game Comic 3.00

VISITOR
Valiant, 1994
1 New Series 2.50
2 thru 13 . . . . @2.50

VISITOR VS. VALIANT
Valiant, 1994
1 V:Solar 3.00
2 . . . . 3.00

VOLTRON
Solson, 1985
1 TV tie-in 4.00
2 . . . . 4.00
3 . . . . 4.00

VOLTRON: DEFENDER OF THE UNIVERSE
Devil's Due/UDON, 2004
Vol 2
1	3.00
2 thru 12	@3.00
TPB Voltron Revelations	12.00

VORTEX
Vortex, 1982–88
1 Peter Hsu art	9.00
2 Mister X on cover.	6.00
3	4.00
4	4.00
5	3.00
6	3.00
7	3.00
8	3.00
9 thru 13	@2.00

VORTEX
Comico, 1991
1 SBt,from Elementals	2.50
2 SBt,	2.50

VORTEX: THE SECOND COMING
Entity, 1996
1 (of 6)	3.00
1a variant cover	3.00
2	3.00

Voyage to the Bottom of the Sea #14
© Gold Key

VOYAGE TO THE BOTTOM OF THE SEA
Gold Key , 1964–70
1	150.00
2	100.00
3	100.00
4	100.00
5	100.00
6	75.00
7	75.00
8	75.00
9	75.00
10	75.00
11	75.00
12	75.00
13	75.00
14	75.00
15 and 16 reprints	@50.00

VOYAGE TO THE DEEP
Dell Publishing Co., 1962
1 P(c)	125.00
2 P(c)	75.00
3 P(c)	75.00
4 P(c)	75.00

WACKY ADVENTURES OF CRACKY
Gold Key, 1972–75
1	30.00
2 thru 11	@25.00
12	20.00

WACKY WITCH
Gold Key, 1971–75
1	75.00
2	30.00
3 thru 20	@25.00
21	20.00

WAGON TRAIN
Gold Key, 1964
1	125.00
2	100.00
3	100.00
4	100.00

WAKE THE DEAD
IDW Publishing, 2003
1 (of 5)	4.00
2	4.00
3 thru 5	@4.00
TPB Let Sleeping Dead Lie	20.00

WALLACE & GROMIT
Titan Publishing 2002
GN Catch of the Day	9.00
GN The Whippet Vanishes	9.00
GN The Bootiful Game	9.00
11	6.00
13 thru 16	@6.00
GN A Pier too Far	9.00
Yearbook 2007	10.00

WALLY
Gold Key, 1962–63
1	60.00
2	50.00
3	50.00
4	50.00

WALLY WOOD'S THUNDER AGENTS
Delux, 1984–86
1 GP,KG,DC,SD,I:New Menth.	6.00
2 GP,KG,DC,SD,The Raven	5.00
3 KG,DC,SD	5.00
4 GP,KG,RB,DA	5.00
5 JOy,KG,A:CodenamDangr	5.00

WALT DISNEY ANNUALS
Walt Disney's Autumn Adventure	4.00
Walt Disney's Holiday Parade #1	3.50
Walt Disney's Spring Fever	3.50
Walt Disney's Summer Fun	3.50
Walt Disney's Holiday Parade #2	3.50

WALT DISNEY'S AUTUMN ADVENTURE
Disney, 1990
1 Rep. CB	4.00

WALT DISNEY'S CHRISTMAS PARADE
Gemstone Publishing, 2003
1	9.00

WALT DISNEY'S COMICS AND STORIES
Dell/Gold Key, 1962
264 CB,Von Drake & Gearloose	75.00
265 CB,Von Drake & Gearloose	75.00
266 CB,Von Drake & Gearloose	75.00
267 CB,Von Drake & Gearloose	75.00
268 CB,Von Drake & Gearloose	75.00
269 CB,Von Drake & Gearloose	75.00
270 CB,Von Drake & Gearloose	75.00
271 CB,Von Drake & Gearloose	75.00
272 CB,Von Drake & Gearloose	75.00
273 CB,Von Drake & Gearloose	75.00
274 CB,Von Drake & Gearloose	75.00
275 CB	70.00
276 CB	70.00
277 CB	70.00
278 CB	70.00
279 CB	70.00
280 CB	70.00
281 CB	70.00
282 CB	70.00
283 CB	70.00
284	40.00
285	40.00
286 CB	50.00
287	40.00
288 CB	50.00
289 CB	50.00
290	40.00
291 CB	50.00
292 CB	50.00
293 CB; Grandma Duck's Farm Friends	50.00
294 CB	50.00
295	40.00
296	40.00
297 CB; Gyro Gearloose	50.00
298 CB; Daisy Duck's Dairy	50.00
299 CB rep.	50.00
300 CB rep.	50.00
301 CB rep.	50.00
302 CB rep.	50.00
303 CB rep.	50.00
304 CB rep.	50.00
305 CB rep. Gyro Gearloose	50.00
306 CB rep.	50.00
307 CB rep.	50.00
308 CB	50.00
309 CB	50.00
310 CB	50.00
311 CB	50.00
312 CB	50.00
313 thru 327	@30.00
328 CB rep.	40.00
329	30.00
330	30.00
331	30.00
332	30.00
333	30.00
334	30.00
335 CB rep.	40.00
336	30.00
337	30.00
338	30.00
339	30.00
340	30.00
341	30.00
342 thru 350 CB rep.	@30.00
351 thru 361 CB rep. with poster	@75.00
351a thru 361a. without poster	@30.00
361 thru 400 CB rep.	@50.00
401 thru 409 CB rep.	@30.00
410 CB rep. Annette Funichello.	30.00
411 thru 429 CB rep.	@30.00

COLOR PUB.

Special 48 page issue (50¢)

WALT DISNEY'S comics and stories

Donald Duck is out to win a Rocket Race around the world

MICKEY DISCOVERS GOOFY HAS TALENTED EARS

Tinker Bell meets THE GROUNDED WITCH

PLUS: LUDWIG VON DRAKE
LI'L BAD WOLF · BRER RABBIT
PUZZLE PAGES

Walt Disney Comics and Stories #446
© Gold Key

430	20.00
431 CB rep.	25.00
432 CB rep.	25.00
433	20.00
434 CB rep.	25.00
435 CB rep.	25.00
436 CB rep.	25.00
437	20.00
438	20.00
439 CB rep.	22.00
440 CB rep.	22.00
441	20.00
442 CB rep.	22.00
443 CB rep.	22.00
444	20.00
445	20.00
446 thru 465 CB rep.	@22.00
466	22.00
467 thru 473 CB rep.	@22.00

Whitman, 1980

474 thru 478 CB rep.	@20.00
479 CB	50.00
480 CB Rare	150.00
481 thru 484	@50.00
485 thru 505	@25.00
506	20.00
507 CB rep.	22.00
508 CB rep.	22.00
509 CB rep.	22.00
510 CB rep.	22.00

Gladstone, 1986

511 translation of Dutch	30.00
512 translation of Dutch	25.00
513 translation of Dutch	25.00
514 translation of Dutch	11.00
515 translation of Dutch	11.00
516 translation of Dutch	11.00
517 translation of Dutch	6.00
518 translation of Dutch	6.00
519 CB,Donald Duck	6.00
520 translation of Dutch, Rosa	11.00
521 Walt Kelly	6.00
522 CB,WK,nephews	6.00
523 Rosa,Donald Duck	15.00
524 Rosa,Donald Duck	15.00
525 translation of Dutch	15.00
526 Rosa,Donald Duck	10.00
527 CB	6.00
528 Rosa,Donald Duck	15.00
529 CB	6.00
530 Rosa,Donald Duck	7.00
531 WK(c),Rosa,CB	7.00
532 CB	6.00
533 CB	6.00

534 CB	6.00
535 CB	6.00
536 CB	6.00
537 CB	6.00
538 CB	6.00
539 CB	6.00
540 CB new art	6.00
541 double-size,WK(c)	6.00
542 CB	7.00
543 CB,WK(c)	6.00
544 CB,WK(c)	6.00
545 CB	6.00
546 CB,WK,giant	7.00
547 CB,WK,Rosa,giant	15.00

Walt Disney, 1990

548 CB,WK,Home is the Hero	12.00
549 CB,	5.00
550 CB,prev.unpub.story!	8.00
551	5.00
552	5.00
553	5.00
554	5.00
555	5.00
556	5.00
557	5.00
558 Donald's Fix-it Shop	5.00
559 Bugs	5.00
560 CB,April Fools Story	5.00
561 CB,Donald the Flipist	5.00
562 CB,3DirtyLittleDucks	5.00
563 CB,Donald Camping	5.00
564 CB,Dirk the Dinosaur	5.00
565 CB,DonaldDuck,TruantOfficer.	5.00
566 CB,Will O' the Wisp	5.00
567 CB,Turkey Shoot	5.00
568 CB,AChristmas Eve Story	5.00
569 CB, New Years Resolutions	5.00
570 CB,Donald the Mailman +Poster	5.00
571 CB,Atom Bomb	8.00
572 CB,April Fools	5.00
573 TV Quiz Show	5.00
574 Pinnocchio,64pgs	6.00
575 Olympic Torch Bearer, Li'l Bad Wolf,64 pgs.	6.00
576 giant	6.00
577 A:Truant Officers,64 pgs.	6.00
578 CB,Old Quacky Manor	5.00
579 CB,Turkey Hunt	5.00
580 CB,The Wise Little Red Hen, 64 pg.-Sunday page format.	5.50
581 CB,Duck Lake	5.00
582 giant	5.50
583 giant	5.50
584	5.00
585 CB, giant	5.50

Gladstone, 1993

586	5.00
587 thru 599	@5.00
600 CB	5.00
601 thru 605 prestige format	@7.00
606 Winging It	7.00
607 Number 401	7.00
608 Sleepless in Duckburg	7.00
609	7.00
610 Treasures Untold	7.00
611 Romance at a Glance	7.00
612 The Sod Couple	7.00
613 Another Fine Mess	7.00
614 Airheads	7.00
615 Backyard Battlers	7.00
616	7.00
617 Tree's A Crowd	7.00
618 A Dolt from the Blue	7.00
619 Queen of the Ant Farm	7.00
620 Caught in the Cold Rush	7.00
621 Room and Bored	7.00
622	7.00
623 All Quacked Up	7.00
624 Their Loaded Forebear	7.00
625 Mummery's the Word	7.00
626 A Real Gone Guy	7.00

627 To Bee or Not to Bee	7.00
628 Officer for a Day	7.00
629 The Ghost Train	7.00
630 two Donald Duck stories	7.00
631 Music Hath Charms	7.00
632 A Day in a Duck's Life	7.00
633 All Donald issue	7.00
634 The Runaway Train	7.00
635 Volcano Valley	7.00
636 Mission to Codfish Cove	7.00
637 Pizen Springs Dude Ranch	7.00

WALT DISNEY'S COMICS AND STORIES
Gemstone Publishing, 2003

634 thru 650	@7.00
651 thru 662	7.00
663 thru 675	@7.00
Spec. Walt Disney's Vacation Parade	9.00
Spec. Vacation Parade #2	9.00
Spec. Vacation Parade #3	9.00
Spec. Christmas Parade	9.00
Spec. Christmas Parade #1	9.00
Spec. Christmas Parade #2	9.00
Spec. Christmas Parade #3	9.00
Spec. Christmas Parade #4	7.00

WALT DISNEY COMICS DIGEST
Gold Key, 1968–76
[All done by Carl Barks]

1 Rep,Uncle Scrooge	125.00
2 CB,ATh	75.00
3 CB,ATh	75.00
4 CB,ATh	75.00
5 CB,Daisy Duck	125.00
6 thru 13 CB,ATh	@60.00
14 ATh	35.00
15 ATh	35.00
16 ATh,rep.Donald Duck #26	60.00
17 CB,ATh	45.00
18 CB,ATh	45.00
19 CB,ATh	45.00
20 CB,ATh	45.00
21 CB,ATh	35.00
22 CB,ATh	35.00
23 CB,ATh	35.00
24 CB,ATh,Zorro	35.00
25 thru 31 CB,ATh	@35.00
32 ATh	30.00
33 ATh	35.00
34 ATh,rep.Four Color #318	35.00
35 ATh	35.00
36 ATh	35.00
37 ATh	35.00
38 ATh,rep.Disneyland#1	35.00
39 ATh	35.00
40 ATh,FG	30.00
41 ATh	25.00
42 CB	30.00
43 CB	30.00
44 Rep. Four Color #29 & others	75.00
45	25.00
46 CB	25.00
47	25.00
48	25.00
49	25.00
50 CB	25.00
51 rep.Four Color #71	35.00
52 CB	25.00
53	25.00
54	25.00
55	25.00
56 CB,rep. Uncle Scrooge #32	30.00
57 CB	25.00

COLOR PUB.

WALT DISNEY SHOWCASE
Gold Key, 1970–80
1 Boatniks (photo cover)....... 40.00
2 Moby Duck.................. 30.00
3 Bongo & Lumpjaw 25.00
4 Pluto..................... 25.00
5 $1,000,000 Duck (photo cover). 30.00
6 Bedknobs & Broomsticks...... 25.00
7 Pluto..................... 25.00
8 Daisy & Donald 25.00
9 101 Dalmatians rep. 35.00
10 Napoleon & Samantha 30.00
11 Moby Duck rep............. 20.00
12 Dumbo rep................ 25.00
13 Pluto rep................. 25.00
14 World's Greatest Athlete..... 30.00
15 3 Little Pigs rep........... 25.00
16 Aristocats rep............. 30.00
17 Mary Poppins rep.......... 30.00
18 Gyro Gearloose rep......... 40.00
19 That Darn Cat rep.......... 35.00
20 Pluto rep................. 25.00
21 Li'l Bad Wolf & 3 Little Pigs ... 20.00
22 Unbirthday Party rep........ 30.00
23 Pluto rep................. 25.00
24 Herbie Rides Again rep...... 25.00
25 Old Yeller rep............. 25.00
26 Lt. Robin Crusoe USN rep.... 25.00
27 Island at the Top of the World.. 30.00
28 Brer Rabbit, Bucky Bug rep.... 25.00
29 Escape to Witch Mountain 30.00
30 Magica De Spell rep. 45.00
31 Bambi rep................ 25.00
32 Spin & Marty rep........... 25.00
33 Pluto rep................. 20.00
34 Paul Revere's Ride rep....... 20.00
35 Goofy rep................ 20.00
36 Peter Pan rep.............. 20.00
37 Tinker Bell & Jiminy Cricket rep. 20.00
38 Mickey & the Sleuth, Pt. 1 .... 20.00
39 Mickey & the Sleuth, Pt. 2 .... 20.00
40 The Rescuers 20.00
41 Herbie Goes to Monte Carlo... 20.00
42 Mickey & the Sleuth 20.00
43 Pete's Dragon............. 25.00
44 Return From Witch Mountain
    & In Search of the Castaways. 25.00
45 The Jungle Book rep......... 20.00
46 The Cat From Outer Space ... 20.00
47 Mickey Mouse Surprise Party.. 20.00
48 The Wonderful Adventures of
    Pinocchio................ 20.00
49 North Avenue Irregulars; Zorro. 20.00
50 Bedknobs & Broomsticks rep. . 20.00
51 101 Dalmatians............ 20.00
52 Unidentified Flying Oddball.... 20.00
53 The Scarecrow 20.00
54 The Black Hole 20.00

WALT KELLY'S CHRISTMAS CLASSICS
Eclipse, 1987
1 .... 5.00

WALT KELLY'S SPRINGTIME TALES
Eclipse, 1988
1 .... 5.00

WAR AGAINST CRIME
Gemstone, 2000
1 rep....................... 2.50
2 rep. Summer 1942........... 2.50
3 rep. Fall 1948.............. 2.50
4 rep. Winter 1948 .... 2.50
5 rep. Feb. 1949............. 2.50
6 rep. June 1949............. 2.50
7 rep....................... 2.50

8 rep. Aug. 1949............. 2.50
9 rep. Oct. 1949............. 2.50
10 rep. Dec. 1949 issue........ 2.50
11 rep. Feb. 1950 issue........ 2.50
'Annuals'
TPB Vol. 1 rep. #1–#5 ...... 13.50
TPB Vol. 2 rep. #6–#11 .... 16.00

WARCAT SPECIAL
Entity Press, 1995
1 I:Warcat 3.00

WARCHILD
Maximum Press, 1995
1 I:Sword, Stone 3.50
2 I:Morganna Lefay........... 3.00
3 V: The Black Knight 2.50
4 Rescue Merlyn............. 2.50
[2nd Series]
1 .... 2.50

WAR DANCER
Defiant, 1994
1 B:JiS(s),I:Ahrq Tsolmec........ 2.75
2 I:Massakur 2.75
3 V:Massakur 2.75
4 JiS(s),A:Nudge............. 3.25

WARHAWKS
TSR, 1990–91
1 thru 6 from game .... @3.00
7 thru 10 The Battle of Britain... @3.00

WARHAWKS 2050
TSR
1 Pt.1 .... 3.00

WAR HEROES
Charlton Comics, 1963–67
1 .... 75.00
2 J.F.Kennedy............... 60.00
3 thru 10 .... @35.00
11 thru 26 .... @30.00
27 Devils Brigade............. 45.00

WARLASH
CFD, 1995
1 Project Hardfire 3.00

WARLANDS: MALAGEN'S CAMPAIGN
Dreamwave, 2005
1 .... 3.00
2 thru 3 .... @3.00
Pocketbook Vol. 1 .... 10.00

WARMASTER
1 and 2 .... @4.00

WAR OF THE WORLDS: SECOND WAVE
Boom! Studios, 2006
1 .... 3.00
2 thru 6 .... @3.00

WARHAMMER 40,000
Boom! Studios, 2006
1 .... 3.00
1a previews exclusive.......... 3.00

WARP
First, 1983
1 FB,JSon,I:Lord Cumulus & Prince
    Chaos, play adapt pt.1 ...... 4.00
2 thru 10 .... @3.00

Warp #3
© First

11 thru 19 .... @2.50
Spec. #1 HC,O:Chaos........... 2.50
Spec. #2 MS/MG,V:Ylem 2.50
Spec. #3 .... 2.50

WARREN ELLIS' BLACK GAS
Avatar Press, 2006
1 .... 4.00
1a wraparound (c) 4.00
1b variant (c)s .... @4.00
2 .... 4.00
2a wraparound (c) 4.00
2b variant (c)s .... @4.00
2c Auxiliary edition 4.00
3 .... 4.00
3a wraparound (c) 4.00
3b variant (c)s .... @4.00
Spec. #1 thru #3 Auxiliary ed. ... 4.00
Vol. 2
1 .... 4.00
1a wraparound (c) 4.00
1b variant (c)s .... @4.00
2 .... 4.00
2a wraparound (c) 4.00
2b variant (c)s .... @4.00
3 .... 4.00
3a variant (c)s .... @4.00

WARREN ELLIS' CHRONICLES OF WORMWOOD
Avatar Press, 2006
Preview 1.00

WARREN ELLIS' WOLFSKIN
Avatar Press, 2006
1 .... 4.00
1a wraparound (c) 4.00
1b variant (c)s .... @4.00
1c Blood Red convention (c) 5.00
1d Variant Bloodlust (c) 6.00
1e auxiliary ed. 4.00
2 .... 4.00
2a wraparound (c) 4.00
2b variant (c)s .... @4.00
3 .... 4.00
3a wraparound (c) 4.00
3b variant (c)s .... @4.00

WARRIOR BUGS, THE
Artcoda Productions, 2002
1 .... 3.00
2 thru 5 .... @3.00

WARRIOR NUN AREALA
Antartic Press, 1995
1 V:Lilith 4.00
1a limited edition.............. 8.00
2 V:Lilith 3.00
3 V:Hellmaster 3.00
3 silver edition.............. 12.00
TPB Rep.#1-#3 .... 10.00

Warrior Nun Areala, Book II, #6
© Antarctic Press

BOOK II: RITUALS, 1996
1 Land of Rising Sun 3.00
1 Red edition................. 9.00
1 signed 10.00
2 I:Cheetah 3.00
3 Iraq, 1989. .... 3.00
4 .... 3.00
5 Rituals,pt.5................. 3.00
6 .... 3.00
Spec. Warrior Nun Portraits 4.00
Spec. Warrior Nun Portraits
  Commemorative Edition (1999). 6.00
TPB Rituals 16.00

BOOK III, 1997
1 The Hammer & the Holocaust . . . 3.00
2 Hammer & the Holocaust,pt.2 . . . 3.00
3 Hammer & the Holocaust,pt.3 . . . 3.00
4 Holy Man, Holy Terror,pt.1 ..... 3.00
5 Holy Man, Holy Terror,pt.2..... 3.00
6 by Barry Lyga & Ben Dunn 3.00
TPB Vol. 1 .... 10.00
TPB Vol. 1 reprint. 10.00
Spec. Warrior Nun Areala/Glory
  by Ben Dunn 3.00
Spec. poster edition 6.00
Spec. Warrior Nun Areala vs. Razor,
  BDn,JWf x-over 4.00
Spec.Warrior Nun Areala vs. Razor
  commemorative (1999) 6.00
Spec.Warrior Nun Areala/Avengelyne
  comm. edition (1999). 6.00

VOL 3
1 F:Sister Shannon Masters...... 2.50
2 .... 2.50
3 .... 2.50
4 Antichrist arrives 2.50
5 .... 2.50
6 Crimson Nun 2.50
7 V:Ruprecht Marsh 2.50

8 V:Mr.Zhu 2.50
9 in the Vatican. 2.50
10 V:Nebelhexa 2.50
11 A:Demoness Lillith 2.50
12 F:Lillith. 3.50
13 V:Julius Salvius. 3.00
14 Rebirth, pt.2 .... 3.00
15 Rebirth, pt.3 .... 3.00
16 Rebirth, pt.4 .... 3.00
17 Seven Deadly Sins, pt.1 ...... 3.00
18 Seven Deadly Sins, pt.2...... 3.00
19 Seven Deadly Sins, pt.3...... 3.00
Ann.2000 b&W............... 4.00

WARRIOR NUN AREALA:
SCORPIO ROSE
Antarctic Press, 1996
1 SEt & BDn 3.00
1a commemorative (1999) 6.00
2 thru 4 (of 4) .... @3.00

WARRIOR NUN DEI:
AFTERTIME
Antarctic Press, 1997
1 (of 3) by Patrick Thornton 3.00
1 Commemorative edition (1999).. 6.00
2 .... 3.00
3 .... 3.00

WARRIOR NUN:
FRENZY
Antarctic Press, 1998
1 (of 2) by Miki Horvatic
  & Esad T. Ribic 3.00
2 .... 3.00

WARRIOR NUN LAZARUS
Antarctic Press, 2006
0 .... 3.50

WARRIOR NUN:
NO JUSTICE
Antarctic Press, 2002
1 F:Areala,V:The Judge 4.00

WARRIOR NUN:
RESURRECTION
Antarctic Press, 1998
1 by Ben Dunn 3.00
1a deluxe 6.00
2 quest for lost God Armor 3.00
3 .... 3.00

WARRIORS OF PLASM
Defiant, 1993–95
1 JiS(s),DL,A:Lorca. 3.25
2 JiS(s),DL,Sedition Agenda..... 3.25
3 JiS(s),DL,Sedition Agenda..... 3.25
4 JiS(s),DL,Sedition Agenda..... 3.25
5 JiS(s),B:The Demons of
  Darkedge................. 2.75
6 JiS(s),The Demons of
  Darkedge,pt.2 .... 2.75
7 JiS(s),DL, ... 2.75
8 JiS(s),DL,40-pg.............. 3.00
9 JiS(s),LWn(s),DL,40-pg. 3.00
10 DL, ... 2.50
GN Home for the Holidays........ 6.00

WARRIOR'S WAY
Bench Press Studios, 1998
1 .... 3.00
2 .... 3.00
3 .... 3.00
4 thru 7 .... @3.00

WARSTRIKE
Malibu Ultraverse, 1994–95
1 HNg,TA,in South America 2.50
2 HNg,TA,Gatefold(c) 2.50
3 in Brazil 2.50
4 HNg,TA,V:Blind Faith. 2.50
5 .... 2.50
6 Rafferty 2.50
7 Origin. 2.50

WARSTRIKE:
PRELUDE TO GODWHEEL
Malibu Ultraverse, 1994
1 Blind Faith/Lord Pumpkin 2.50

WART AND THE
WIZARD
Gold Key, 1964
1 .... 80.00

WATCH, THE:
CASUS BELLI
Phosphorescent Comics, 2004
1 .... 3.25
2 thru 3 .... @3.25

WATERDOGS
Roaring Studio, 2002
1 (of 3) 3.00
2 thru 3 .... @3.00

WATERWORLD
Acclaim, 1997
1 of 4 V:Leviathan 2.50
2 of 4 Children of Leviathan 2.50
3 of 4 KoK. 2.50
4 of 4 KoK Children of Leviathan . . 2.50

WAVE WARRIORS
Astroboys
1 .... 2.50
2 .... 2.50

WAYFARERS
Eternity
1 .... 2.50
2 .... 2.50

WAY OF THE RAT
Crossgen Comics, 2002
1 CDi 4.00
2 .... 3.00
3 .... 3.00
4 .... 3.00
5 thru 7 CDi. .... @3.00
8 thru 24 CDi. .... @3.00
GN Traveler Vol. 1 Walls of
  Zhumar 10.00
TPB Vol. 1 The Walls of Zhumar . . 16.00
TPB Vol. 2 The Dragon's Wake... 16.00

WEASEL GUY
WITCHBLADE
Hyperwerks, 1998
1-shot by Steve Succellato 3.00
1a variant Jeff Matsuda(c) 5.00
1b variant Karl Altstoeter(c) 8.00

WEB OF HORROR
Major Magazines, 1969
1 JJ(c),Ph(c),BWr 175.00
2 JJ(c),Ph(c),BWr 150.00
3 BWr,April, 1970 .... 150.00

COLOR PUB.

WEDDING OF POPEYE AND OLIVE, THE
Ocean Comics, 1999
1 PDa,. 2.75
1a signed, numbered 16.00
Spec. Sketch edition 40.00

WEIRD FANTASY
Russ Cochran, 1992
1 Reps 3.50
2 Reps.inc.The Black Arts. 3.00
3 thru 4 rep. . . . . @3.00
5 thru 7 rep. 3.00
8 . . . . 3.00

Gemstone
9 thru 22 EC comics reprint . . . . @3.00
`Annuals'
TPB Vol. #1 rebinding of #1–#5. . . 10.00
TPB Vol. #2 rebinding of #6–#10. . 11.00
TPB Vol. #3 rebinding of #11–#14. 10.00
TPB Vol. #4 rebinding of #15–#18. 11.00
TPB Vol. #5 rebinding of #19–#22. 12.00

WEIRD SCIENCE
Gladstone, 1990–91
1 Rep. #22 + Fantasy #1 . . . . 4.00
2 Rep. #16 + Fantasy #17 . . . . . . 3.50
3 Rep. #9 + Fantasy #14 . . . . 3.50
4 Rep. #27 + Fantasy #11 . . . . . . 3.00

Russ Cochran/Gemstone, 1992
1 thru 21 EC comics reprint . . . . @3.00
`Annuals'
TPB Vol. #1 rebinding of #1–#5. . . 9.00
TPB Vol. #2 rebinding of #6–#10. . 10.00
TPB Vol. #3 rebinding of #11–#15. . 9.00
TPB Vol. #4 rebinding of #16–#18. 10.00
TPB Vol. #5 rebinding of #19–#22. 10.50

WEIRD SCIENCE–FANTASY
Russ Cochran/Gemstone, 1992
1 Rep. W.S.F. #23 (1954). 3.50
2 Rep. Flying Saucer Invasion . . . 3.00
3 Rep. 3.00
4 thru 6 Rep. . . . . @3.00
7 rep #29. . . . . 3.00
8 . . . . 3.00

Gemstone
`Annuals'
TPB Vol. #1 rebinding of #1–#5. . . . 9.00
TPB Vol. #2 rebinding of #6–#10. . 13.00

WEIRD SUSPENSE
Atlas, Feb.–July, 1975
1 thru 3 F:Tarantula. . . . . @30.00

WEIRD TALES ILLUSTRATED
Millennium, 1992
1 KJo,JBo,PCr,short stories 5.00

WENDY, THE GOOD LITTLE WITCH
Harvey Publications, 1960–76
1 Wendy & Casper 800.00
2 . . . . 350.00
3 . . . . 250.00
4 . . . . 250.00
5 . . . . 250.00
6 . . . . 200.00
7 . . . . 200.00
8 . . . . 200.00
9 . . . . 200.00
10 . . . . 200.00
11 thru 20 . . . . @150.00

---

21 thru 30. . . . . @100.00
31 thru 50. . . . . @75.00
51 thru 64. . . . . @50.00
65 O:Wendy. 70.00
66 thru 69 . . . . @50.00
70 thru 74 52 pg Giants . . . . . . @60.00
75 thru 93 . . . . @40.00

WENDY WITCH WORLD
Harvey Publications, 1961–74
1 . . . . 1,500.00
2 . . . . 200.00
3 . . . . 200.00
4 . . . . 200.00
5 . . . . 200.00
6 . . . . 150.00
7 . . . . 150.00
8 . . . . 150.00
9 . . . . 150.00
10 . . . . 150.00
11 . . . . 120.00
12 thru 20 . . . . @120.00
21 thru 30. . . . . @90.00
31 thru 39. . . . . @70.00
40 thru 50. . . . . @50.00
51 thru 53. . . . . @40.00

WEREWOLVES: CALL OF THE WILD
Moonstone Books, 2006
1 . . . . 3.00
2 . . . . 3.50
3 . . . . 3.50

WESTERN ACTION
Atlas, 1975
1 F:Kid Cody,Comanche Kid 25.00

WESTWYND
Westwynd, 1995
1 I:Sable,Shiva,Outcast,Tojo. 2.50

WETWORKS: WORLDSTORM
Wildstorm/DC, Sept., 2006
1 WPo. 3.00
1a variant (c). 3.00
1b variant WPo (c) 3.00
2 WPo. 3.00
3 WPo. 3.00

Whisper #2
© *Capital*

WHAT WERE THEY THINKING?
Boom! Studios, 2005
1-shot Keith Giffen remix 4.00
1-shot Some People Never Learn . . 4.00
1-shot Monster Mash-Up 4.00

WHISPER
Capital, 1983–84
1 MG(c). 8.00
2 . . . . 6.00

First
1 . . . . 2.50
2 thru 10 . . . . @2.50
11 thru 19 . . . . @2.50
20 O:Whisper. 2.50
21 thru 26. . . . . @2.50
27 Ghost Dance #2 . . . . 2.50
28 Ghost Dance #3 . . . . 2.50
29 thru 37. . . . . @2.50
Spec. #1 . . . . 4.00

WHISPER
Boom! Studios, 2006
1 . . . . 4.00

WHITE FANG
Walt Disney, 1990
1 Movie Adapt. 6.00

WHITE TRASH
Tundra
1 I:Elvis & Dean 4.00
2 Trip to Las Vegas contd. 4.00
3 V:Purple Heart Brigade 4.00

WHODUNNIT
Eclipse, 1986–87
1 DSp,A:Jay Endicott 3.00
2 DSp,Who Slew Kangaroo? 3.00
3 DSp,Who Offed Henry Croft 3.00

WIDOW MADE IN BRITAIN
N Studio
1 I:Widow 2.75
2 F:Widow 2.75
3 Rampage 2.75
4 In Jail 2.75

WIDOW METAL GYPSIES
London Night Studios, 1995
1 I:Emma Drew 3.00
2 Father Love 3.00
3 Final issue 3.00

WILD ANIMALS
Pacific, 1982
1 . . . . 3.00

WILDCATS
WildStorm/DC, 1999
Previously from Image
VOLUME 2
1 SLo,TC,. 2.50
1a variant cover 2.50
1b variant cover 2.50
1c variant cover 2.50
1d variant cover 2.50
1e variant cover 2.50
2 SLo,TC. 2.50
3 SLo,TC,F:Grifter 2.50
4 SLo,TC, ... 2.50
5 SLo,BHi,PNe,. 2.50
6 SLo, ... 2.50
7 SLo,R:Pike. 2.50

COLOR PUB.

Wildcats #1
© *Wildstorm*

8 JoC(s),SeP,TC(c). 2.50
8a variant JLe&SW(c) (1:4) 2.50
9 JoC(s),SeP,TC(c),Las Vegas . . . 2.50
10 JoC(s),SeP,TC(c),Las Vegas . . . 2.50
11 JoC(s),SeP,TC(c),R:Ladytron . . . 2.50
12 JoC(s),SeP,TC(c),go west 2.50
13 JoC(s),SeP,F:Void. 2.50
14 JoC(s),SeP,Serial Boxes,pt.1 . . . 2.50
15 JoC(s),SeP,Serial Boxes,pt.2 . . . 2.50
16 JoC,SeP,Serial Boxes,pt.3 . . . . . 2.50
17 JoC,SeP,Serial Boxes,pt.4 . . . . . 2.50
18 JoC,SeP,Serial Boxes,pt.5 . . . . . 2.50
19 JoC,SeP,Serial Boxes,pt.6 . . . . . 2.50
20 JoC,SDi,F:Grifter, Maul. 2.50
21 JoC,SDi,F:Grifter, Maul, pt.2. . . . 2.50
22 JoC,SeP,R:Grifter 2.50
23 JoC,SeP,F:Grifter 2.50
23a variant WPo(c) (1:4) 2.50
24 JoC,SeP,F:Voodoo 2.50
25 JoC,SeP, 40-pg. 3.50
26 JoC,SeP, control of Halo. 2.50
27 JoC,SeP,Grifter vs. Zealot 2.50
28, JoC,SeP,Voodoo,final issue. . . . 2.50
Spec. WildC.A.T.s: Mosaic. 4.00
Ann. 2000 #1, Devil's
    Night x-over, pt.3. . . . . 3.50
GN Ladytron. 6.00
TPB WildC.A.T.S.: Compendium . . 10.00
TPB WildC.A.T.S.: Homecoming . . 20.00
TPB Gang War. 17.00
TPB Homecoming 20.00
TPB Vicious Circles 15.00
TPB Serial Boxes, 144-pg. 15.00
TPB Street Smart. 15.00
TPB Battery Park. 18.00
TPB Wildcats/Cyberforce:
    Killer Instinct (2004). 15.00

WILDCATS: NEMESIS
Wildstorm/DC, Sept., 2005
1 (of 9) Zealot and Coda sisters. . . 3.00
2 . . . . 3.00
3 thru 9 . . . . @3.00
TPB Wildcats: Nemesis 20.00

WILDCATS VERSION 3.0
Wildcats/DC, 2002
Eye of the Storm
1 JoC,old and new team members. 3.00
2 JoC,Jack Marlowe,Halo corp. . . . 3.00
3 JoC 3.00
4 JoC. 3.00
5 JoC 3.00
6 JoC 3.00

7 JoC,I:Beef Boys. 3.00
8 JoC,BU:The Authority,pt.3 . . . . . 3.00
9 JoC,new Grifter. 3.00
10 JoC,new Grifter. 3.00
11 JoC,Lights Out in Garfield. 3.00
12 JoC,Jack Marlowe 3.00
13 JoC,Mister Wax. 3.00
14 JoC,Halo Corp. 3.00
15 JoC,Car of tomorrow. 3.00
16 JoC,new assassin. 3.00
17 JoC,SeP 3.00
18 JoC 3.00
19 JoC(s) 3.00
20 JoC(s),new team. 3.00
21 JoC(s),Grifter's team. 3.00
22 JoC(s),Coda War One 3.00
23 JoC(s),Coda War One 3.00
24 JoC(s),final issue 3.00
TPB Brand Building 15.00
TPB Full Disclosure 15.00

WILDCATS: WORLDSTORM
Wildstorm/DC, Sept., 2006
1 GMo,JLe,SWi. 3.00
1a variant TM,JLe (c) 3.00
1b variant JLe (c) 3.00
2 GMo,JLe,SW 3.00
2a variant EL (c) 3.00

WILDFIRE
Zion Comics
1 thru 3 V:Mr. Reeves . . . . @2.50
4 Lord D'Rune. 2.50

WILD GIRL
Wildstorm/DC, Nov., 2004
1 (of 6) SwM 3.00
2 SwM 3.00
3 SwM 3.00
4 SwM 3.00
5 SwM,JWi 3.00
6 SwM,JWi 3.00

WILDSIDERZ
Wildstorm/DC, Aug., 2005
0 JSC 2.00
1 (of 5) JSC, 40-page 3.50
2 JSC 3.50
3 JSC 3.50

WILDSTORM
Wildstorm/DC, 2005
Spec. Winter special 5.00

WILD TIMES
WildStorm/DC, 1999
Deathblow 2.50
DV8 . . . . 2.50
Gen13 . . . . 2.50
Grifter. 2.50
Wetworks 2.50

WILD WEST C.O.W.- BOYS OF MOO MESA
Archie, 1992–93
1 Based on TV cartoon. 2.50
2 Cody kidnapped. 2.50
3 Law of the Year Parade,
    last issue 2.50
(Regular series)
1 Valley o/t Thunder Lizard. 2.50
2 Plains, Trains & Dirty Deals. 2.50

WILD WESTERN ACTION
Skywald, 1971
1 thru 3 . . . . @35.00

WILD WILD WEST
Gold Key, 1966–69
1 TV show tie-in 300.00
2 . . . . 250.00
3 . . . . 200.00
4 . . . . 200.00
5 . . . . 200.00
6 . . . . 200.00
7 . . . . 200.00

WILD WILD WEST
Millennium, 1990–91
1 . . . . 3.00
2 thru 4 . . . . @3.00

WILL EISNER'S 3-D CLASSICS
Kitchen Sink, 1985
WE art, w/glasses (1985). 3.00

WIN A PRIZE COMICS
Charlton Comics, 1955
1 S&K,Edgar Allen Poo adapt.. 1,100.00
2 S&K 800.00
Becomes:

TIMMY THE TIMID GHOST
Charlton Comics, 1957
3 . . . . 150.00
4 . . . . 125.00
5 . . . . 125.00
6 . . . . 100.00
7 . . . . 100.00
8 . . . . 100.00
9 . . . . 100.00
10 . . . . 100.00
11 giant 125.00
12 giant 125.00
13 . . . . 100.00
14 . . . . 100.00
15 . . . . 100.00
16 . . . . 100.00
17 . . . . 100.00
18 . . . . 100.00
19 . . . . 100.00
20 thru 25. . . . . @100.00
26 thru 44. . . . . @25.00
45 1966 . . . . 25.00

WINTER MEN, THE
Wildstorm/DC, Aug., 2005
1 (of 8) JPL, U.S.S.R. soldiers 3.00
2 . . . . 3.00
3 . . . . 3.00
4 . . . . 3.00
5 . . . . 3.00

WINTERWORLD
Eclipse, 1987–88
1 JZ,I:Scully, Wynn 3.00
2 JZ,V:Slave Farmers 3.00
3 JZ,V:Slave Farmers 3.00

WISP
Oktomica Entertainment, 1999
1 All Along the Watchtower,pt.1 . . . 2.50
2 All Along the Watchtower,pt.2 . . . 2.50
3 All Along the Watchtower,pt.3 . . . 3.00
4 The Acheron Protocol 3.00

W.I.T.C.H.
Hyperion Books, 2005
GN Vol. 1 . . . . 5.00
GN Vol. 2 . . . . 5.00
GN Vol. 3 . . . . 5.00
GN Vol. 4 . . . . 5.00
GN Vol. 5 Legends Revealed 5.00
GN Vol. 6 Forces of Change 5.00

WITCHGIRLS, INC.
Heroic Publishing Inc., 2005
1 .... 4.00
2 .... 3.00
3 thru 4 .... @3.25

WITCHING HOUR, THE
Millennium/Comico, 1992
1 Anne Rice adaptation 2.50
2 thru 5 .... @2.50

WITCHMAN
Avatar Press, 2006
1 .... 4.00
1a wraparound (c) 4.00
1b variant (c)s .... @4.00

WONDERLAND
Amaze Ink/Slave Labor Graphics, 2006
1 .... 3.50
2 thru 3 .... @3.50

WOOD BOY, THE
Devil's Due Publishing, 2004
1 (of 2) 3.00
2 .... 3.00

WOODY WOODPECKER
Harvey, 1991–93
1 thru 5 .... @2.50

WORLD OF ARCHIE
Archie, 1992
1 thru 22 .... @2.50

WORLD OF WOOD
Eclipse, 1986–87
1 WW 4.00
2 WW,DSt(i) 4.00
3 WW 4.00
4 WW 4.00

WORLDSTORM
Wildstorm/DC, Oct., 2006
1-shot Preview 3.00

WORLD WAR II: 1946
Antarctic Press, 1999
1 by Ted Nomura 4.00
2 Born to Die.................. 4.00
3 Battle for Moscow 4.00
4 Flying Tigers 4.00
5 .... 4.00
6 The Hunley vs. the Potsdam ... 4.00
7 The Yamato 4.00
8 Tuskegee Airmen 4.00
9 Firestorm 4.00
10 Destination: Space 4.00
11 Night Witches 4.00
12 Korea 4.00
Ann. 2000 b&w 4.00

WORLD-WATCH
Wild & Wolly Press, 2004
1 .... 12.00
2 .... 8.00
3 .... 5.00

WORMWOOD: GENGLEMAN CORPSE
IDW Publishing, 2006
1 .... 4.00
2 thru 4 .... @4.00
TPB The Taster 17.00

WRAITHBORN
Wildstorm/DC, Sept., 2005
1 (of 6) JBz................... 3.00
2 JBz.......................... 3.00

Wrath #1
© *Malibu*

WRATH
Malibu Ultraverse, 1994–95
1 B:MiB(s),DvA,JmP,C:Mantra 2.50
1a Silver foil 3.00
2 DvA,JmP,V:Hellion............ 2.50
3 DvA,JmP,V:Radicals, I:Slayer .. 2.50
4 DvA,JmP,V:Freex.............. 2.50
5 DvA,JmP,V:Freex.............. 2.50
6 DvA,JmP 2.50
7 DvA,JmP,I:Pierce,Ogre, Doc
  Virtual 2.50
8 .... 2.50
9 A:Prime 2.50
G-Size #1..................... 2.50

WRAITHBORN
Wildstorm/DC, Sept., 2005
3 thru 6 JBz.................. @3.00
TPB JBz....................... 20.00

WULF THE BARBARIAN
Atlas, 1975
1 O:Wulf 15.00
2 NA,I:Berithe The Swordsman .. 12.00
3 & 4 .... @8.00

WWF BATTLEMANIA
Valiant
1 WWF Action 2.50
2 thru 5 .... @2.50

WYATT EARP
Dell Publishing Co., 1957
1 RsM........................ 225.00
2 RsM........................ 200.00
3 RsM........................ 175.00
4 .... 150.00
5 Ph(c)...................... 150.00
6 .... 150.00
7 .... 150.00
8 .... 150.00
9 .... 150.00
10 .... 150.00
11 .... 125.00
12 RsM....................... 125.00
13 AT 125.00

WYNONNA EARP: HOME ON THE STRANGE
IDW Publishing, 2003
1 .... 4.00
2 thru 3 .... @4.00
1a thru 2a variant (c)s .... @4.00
TPB Complete Wynonna Earp.... 25.00

XANADU
Eclipse, 1988
1 .... 2.50

XENYA
Sanctuary Press, 1994
1 Hildebrandt Brothers 4.00
2 .... 3.25
3 .... 3.25
4 conclusion, Homecoming....... 3.00

XENA: WARRIOR PRINCESS
Topps, 1997
1 RTs,Revenge of the Gorgons,
  pt.1........................ 5.00
1a photo (c)................... 8.00
2 (of 2) rescue of Gabrielle....... 4.00
TPB 10.00

[VOL 2]
0 AaL Temple of the Dragon God .. 3.00
1 (of 3) Joxer, Warrior Prince, pt.1 . 5.00
1a deluxe 8.00
2 Joxer, Warrior Prince, pt.2 ..... 4.00
2a photo (c).................. 4.00
TPB rep. #0–#2 .... 10.00

XENA: WARRIOR PRINCESS: BLOOD LINES
Topps, 1997
1 (of 3) ALo.................. 3.00
1a photo (c).................. 3.00
2 (of 3) ALo.................. 3.00
2a photo (c).................. 3.00

XENA: WARRIOR PRINCESS: CALLISTO
Topps, 1997
1 (of 3) RTs,................. 3.00
1a photo (c).................. 3.00
2 (of 3) RTs,................. 3.00
2a photo (c).................. 3.00
3 (of 3) RTs,................. 3.00
3a photo (c).................. 3.00

XENA: WARRIOR PRINCESS: ORPHEUS
Topps, 1998
1 (of 3) 3.00
2 (of 3) 3.00
3 (of 3) 3.00
1a thru 3a photo (c)s......... @3.00

XENA: WARRIOR PRINCESS: THE ORIGINAL OLYMPICS
Topps, 1998
1 (of 3) 3.00
1a photo cover 3.00
2 F:Hercules.................. 3.00
2a photo cover 3.00

    All comics prices listed are for *Near Mint* condition.

3 . . . . 3.00
3a photo cover 3.00

XENA: WARRIOR PRINCESS: THE WEDDING OF XENA & HERCULES
Topps, 1998
1-shot 3.00
1-shot photo (c) 3.00

XENA, WARRIOR PRINCESS: THE WRATH OF HERA
Topps, 1998
1 (of 2) 3.00
1a photo cover edition 3.00
2 conclusion 3.00
2a photo cover edition 3.00

XENA: WARRIOR PRINCESS: XENA AND THE DRAGON'S TEETH
Topps, 1997
1 (of 3) RTs, ... 3.00
1a photo (c). 3.00
2 (of 3) RTs, ... 3.00
2a photo (c). 3.00
3 (of 3) RTs, ... 3.00
3a photo (c). 3.00

XENA, WARRIOR PRINCESS
D.E. (Dynamite Ent.) 2006
1 . . . . 3.50
1a variant (c)s . . . . @3.50
1a photo foil (c) 20.00
2 Pantheon Pandemonium 3.50
3 Stalk Like an Egyptian 3.50
4 Contest of Pantheons 3.50
2a thru 4a variant (c)s . . . . . . @3.50
Ann. #1 Strange Visitor 5.00
Ann. #1 variant (c)s . . . . @5.00

XENOTECH
Mirage, 1993–94
1 I:Xenotech 2.75
2 . . . . 2.75
3 w/2 card strip 2.75

X-FILES
Topps, 1994–97
1 From Fox TV Series 40.00
1a Newstand 30.00
2 Aliens Killing Witnesses 25.00
3 The Return 22.00
4 Firebird,pt.1 . . . . 15.00
5 Firebird,pt.2 . . . . 10.00
6 Firebird,pt.3 . . . . 8.00
7 Trepanning Opera 7.00
8 Silent Cities of the Mind,pt.1 . . . 6.00
9 Silent Cities of the Mind,pt.2 . . . 5.00
10 Feeling of Unreality,pt.1 . . . . . 5.00
11 Feeling of Unreality,pt.2 . . . . . 5.00
12 Feeling of Unreality,pt.3 . . . . . 5.00
13 A Boy and His Saucer 5.00
14 . . . . 4.00
15 Home of the Brave 4.00
16 Home of the Brave,pt.2 . . . . . . 3.50
17 DgM,CAd 3.50
18 thru 21 . . . . @3.00
22 JRz,CAd,The Kanishibari 3.00
23 JRz,CAd,Donor 3.00

24 JRz,Silver Lining 3.00
25 JRz,CAd,Remote Control,pt.1 . . 3.00
26 JRz,CAd,Remote Control,pt.2 . . 3.00
27 JRz,CAd,Remote Control,pt.3 . . 3.00
28 JRz,Be Prepared, pt.1,
     V:Windigo 3.00
29 JRz,Be Prepared, pt.2 . . . . . . 3.00
30 JRz,Surrounded, pt.1 . . . . . . 3.00
31 JRz,Surrounded, pt.2 (of 2) . . . 3.00
32 . . . . 3.00
33 widows on San Francisco 3.00
33 variant photo (c) 3.00
34 Project HAARP 3.00
35 Near Death Experience 3.00
36 Near Death Experience, pt.2 . . 3.00
37 JRz,The Face of Extinction 3.00
38 JRz, ... 3.00
39 JRz, Widow's Peak 3.00
40 Devil's Advocate 3.00
40a photo cover 3.00
41 Severed 3.00
41a photo cover 3.00
Ann.#1 Hollow Eve 5.00
Ann.#2 E.L.F.S. 4.50
Spec.#1 Rep. #1-#3 . . . . 6.00
Spec.#2 Rep. #4-#6 Firebird . . . 5.00
Spec.#3 Rep. #7-#9 . . . . 5.00
Spec.#4 Rep 5.00
TPB Vol. 2 . . . . 20.00
GN Afterflight 6.00
GN Official Movie Adapt. (1998) . . . 6.00

X-FILES DIGEST
Topps, 1995
1 All New Series, 96pg. 4.00
2 and 3 . . . . 4.00

X-FILES, THE: GROUND ZERO
Topps, 1997
1 (of 4) based on novel 3.00
2 thru 4 . . . . @3.00

X-FILES, THE: SEASON ONE
Topps, 1997
1 RTs,JVF(c) Deep Throat 5.00
Deep Throat, variant (c). 7.50
2 RTs,JVF(c) Squeeze 4.00
Squeeze, RTs, JVF(c) 5.00
3 RTs,SSc,Conduit 4.00
Conduit, RTs 5.00
4 RTs,The Jersey Devil 4.00
5 RTs,Shadows 4.00
Shadows JVF(c) 5.00
6 Fire 4.00
Fire 5.00
7 RTs,JVF,Ice 4.00
Ice 5.00
8 RTs,Space 4.00
Space JVF(c) 5.00
Spec. Pilot Episode RTs,JVF
   new JVF(c) 5.00
Beyond the Sea JVF(c) 5.00

XIMOS: VIOLENT PAST
Triumphant, 1994
1 JnR(s) 2.50
2 JnR(s) 2.50

XIN
Anarchy Studios, 2002
Alpha Preview edition 2.50
Alpha Preview, collector's ed. 10.00
Ashcan limited edition 6.00
Ashcan gold foil leather 15.00
1 Legend of the Monkey King 3.00
1a variant JMd(c) 3.00
1b Royal blue edition 30.00

1c gold foil edition 30.00
1d holo foil fx edition 10.00
2 thru 3 . . . . @3.00
2a thru 3a variant limited (c) . . . @10.00
TPB Legend of the Monkey King . . 13.00

XIN: JOURNEY OF THE MONKEY KING
Anarchy Studios, 2003
1 . . . . 3.00
1a variant (c). 3.00
2 thru 3 . . . . @3.00
2a thru 3a variant (c) 3.00
1b thru 3b limited edition . . . . . @10.00
TPB Journey of the Monkey King . 13.00

X ISLE
Boom! Studios, 2006
1 (of 5) 3.00
2 thru 4 . . . . @3.00

X-O Manowar #24
© Valiant

X-O MANOWAR
Valiant, 1992
0 JQ,O:Aric,1st Full Chromium(c). . 5.00
0a Gold Ed. 25.00
1 BL,BWS,I:Aric,Ken 10.00
2 BL(i),V:Lydia,Wolf-Class Armor . 6.00
3 I:X-Caliber,A:Solar 6.00
4 MM,A:Harbinger,C:Shadowman
     (Jack Boniface) 9.00
5 thru 13 . . . . @3.00
14 BS,A:Turok,I:Randy Cartier . . . 3.50
15 BS,A:Turok 2.50
15a Red Ed. 7.00
16 thru 24 . . . . @2.50
25 JCf,JGz,PaK,I:Armories,
     BU:Armories#0 . . . . 3.00
26 JGz(s),RLv,F:Ken 2.50
27 JGz,RLe,A:Turok,Geomancer,
     Stronghold,Livewire 2.50
28 JGz,RLe,D:X-O,V:Spider
     Aliens,w/Valiant Era card 2.75
29 thru 66 . . . . @2.50
67 thru 68 . . . . @8.00
TPB rep.#1-4,w/X-O Manual 11.00

X-O MANOWAR
Series Two, Acclaim, 1997
1 Rand Banion v. R.A.G.E. 2.50
2 thru 20 . . . . @2.50
TPB MWa,BAu rep. #1–#4 . . . . . 10.00

XIII
Alias Enterprises, 2005
1 Day of the Black Sun 1.00
2 thru 5 . . . . @3.00
6 . . . . 3.00
TPB Vol. 1 . . . . 20.00

Dabel Brothers Prod., 2006
TPB Vol. 1 Day of the Black Sun. . 15.00

YAKKY DOODLE & CHOPPER
Gold Key, 1962
1 . . . . 150.00

YEAH!
Homage/DC, 1999
1 GHe 3.00

YENNY
Alias Enterprises, 2005
1 . . . . 1.00
1a variant (c) 3.00
2 thru 4 . . . . @3.00
5 thru 9 . . . . @3.50

YIN FEI
Leung's Publications, 1988–90
5 . . . . 3.00
6 thru 11 . . . . @3.00

YOGI BEAR
Dell, 1962
#1 thru #6, See Dell Four Color
7 thru 9 . . . . 125.00

Gold Key, 1962
10 . . . . 150.00
11 Jellystone Follies. 135.00
12 . . . . 100.00
13 Surprise Party. 135.00
14 thru 19 . . . . @100.00
20 thru 29 . . . . @50.00
30 thru 42 . . . . @45.00

YOGI BEAR
Charlton Comics, 1970–76
1 . . . . 75.00
2 thru 10 . . . . @50.00
11 thru 35 . . . . 40.00

YOGI BEAR
Archie Comics, 1997
1 . . . . 2.50

YOSEMITE SAM
Gold Key/Whitman, 1970–84
1 . . . . 75.00
2 thru 10 . . . . @35.00
11 thru 40 . . . . @25.00
41 thru 81. . . . . @20.00

YOU'LL HAVE THAT
Viper Comics, 2006
TPB Vol. 1 . . . . 5.00

YOUNGBLOOD
Maximum Press/Extreme
Volume 2, 1996
Vol. 1 & Vol. 2 #1–#10, see Image
11 RLd,RCz,. 2.50
12 Rle, V:Lord Dredd,A:New
    Man,double size 3.50
13 RLd,RCz,F:Die-Hard. 2.50
14 RLd,RCz, ... 2.50
Super Spec.#1 ErS,CSp,AG 3.00

Yosemite Sam (and Bugs Bunny) #5
© Gold Key

TPB Youngblood, rep. orig.
    Youngblood #1–#5. . . . . 17.00
TPB Baptism of Fire rep.
    Youngblood #6–#8, #10 & Team
    Youngblood #9–#11. . . . . 17.00

YOUNGBLOOD
Awesome Entertainment, 1998
1 AMo,SSr. 2.50
1a variant covers, 7 different. . . . @2.50
1b foil logo 6.00
1c plus custom illustration 72.00
2 AMo,SSr,Baptism of Fire 2.50
3 AMo,SSr,V:Professor Night 2.50
4 AMo,SSr,Young Guns 2.50
5 AMo,SSr,Young Guns 2.50
TPB rep.#1–#10 orig. series 15.00
1-shot, Youngblood/X-Force
    x-over,48pg. (1998) 5.00

YOUNGBLOOD: BLOODSPORT
Arcade Comics, 2002
1 MMr,RLd, RLd(c) 5.00
1a variant Quietly (c) 6.00
1b variant Park (c) 4.00
1c Foil ed. 10.00
1d Foil ed., signed 20.00
1e convention sketch ed. 50.00
1f San Diego con lim. ed. 10.00
1g San Diego con lim. signed. . . 20.00
1h ltd (c) 20.00
2 MMr,RLd, RLd(c) 3.00
2a variant Quietly (c) 3.00
2b variant Park (c) 3.00
2c Foil ed. 10.00
2d Foil ed., signed 20.00
Spec. Imperial #1 Dossier 4.00
Spec. Imperial #1 Max edition . . . 10.00
Spec. Imperial #1 signed 10.00

YOUNGBLOOD CLASSICS
Image/Extreme, 1996
1 RLd,ErS,series rewritten &
    redrawn, new cover. 2.50
2 RLd,ErS 2.50
3 RLd,ErS 2.50

YOUNGBLOOD GENESIS
Awesome Entertainment, 2000
1 . . . . 4.00
1a signature edition 9.00

Arcade Comics, 2004
2 . . . . 4.00
2a RLd(c) 9.00

YOUNGBLOOD: IMPERIAL
Arcade Comics, 2004
0 . . . . 4.00
0a max edition 10.00
1 (of 12) Mmy,RLd(c) 3.00
1a max edition 15.00
1b premium, signed edition 25.00
2 Rld,MMy. 3.00
2a max edition 15.00
2b Authentic sign ed. 25.00

ZAK RAVEN, ESQ.
Avatar/Tidalwave Studios, 2002
1A Cha (c). 3.50
1B Arlem (c) 3.50
1C Miller (c) 3.50
1D Murphy (c). 3.50

ZEIN
AK Entertainment, 2006
1 Enter the Scarab 3.00
2 Origins 3.00
3 The Rise of Anubis 3.00
4 Year of the Beast 3.00
5 Judgment Day 3.00
7 . . . . 3.00

ZEIN GHOSTS OF HELIOPOLIS
Studio G, 2003
1 . . . . 3.00
2 thru 4 . . . . @3.00

ZEN
Zen Comics, 2003
0 . . . . 3.00
1 . . . . 3.00
2 thru 4 . . . . @3.00
TPB Vol. 1 Return of the
    Alien Hero 15.00

ZENDRA
Pennyfarthing Press, 2001
Volume 2
1 (of 6) Windmills of the World 3.00
2 All the Flesh Inherits 3.00
3 thru 5 . . . . @3.00
6 . . . . 3.00
TPB Vol. 1 . . . . 18.00
TPB Vol. 2 Heart of Fire. 25.00

ZEN INTERGALACTIC NINJA
Archie, 1992
1 Rumble in the Rain Forest
    prequel, inc.poster. 3.00
2 Rumble in Rain Forest #1 . . . . . . 3.00
3 Rumble in Rain Forest #2 . . . . . . 3.00

Entity Comics, 1994
0 Chromium (c),JaL(c) 4.00
1 Joe Orbeta. 3.00
1a Platinum Edition. 20.00
2 Deluxe Edition w/card 5.00
3 V:Rawhead 3.00
4 thru 7 . . . . @3.25
GN A Fire Upon The Earth. 13.00

[2nd Series]
1 Joe Orbeta 5.00
2 . . . . 5.00
3 thru 5 . . . . @2.50

Zen Comics, 1998
Commemorative Ed. #1 . . . . 6.00

ZEN INTERGALACTIC NINJA
Studio Chikara, 1999
1	4.00
1 variant (c)	10.00
2	4.00
3	4.00

ZEN/NIRA X: HELLSPACE
Zen Comics
1	3.00

ZEN: NOVELLA
Eternity Comics
1 thru 8	@3.00

ZEN SPECIALS
Eternity
Spring#1 V:Lord Contaminous	2.50
April Fools#1 parody issue	2.50
Color Spec.#0	3.50

ZEN: WARRIOR
Eternity Comics, 1994
1 vicious video game	3.00

ZENDRA
Pennyfarthing Press, 2001
1 (of 6)	3.00
2 thru 6	@3.00

ZENITH PHASE I
Fleetway
1 thru 3	@2.50

ZENITH PHASE II
Fleetway
1 thru 2	@2.50

ZERO GIRL: FULL CIRCLE
DC/Homage, 2002
2 SK	3.00
3 SK	3.00
4 SK	3.00
5 SK, concl.	3.00
TPB Full Circle	18.00

Zero Patrol #1 © Continuity

ZERO PATROL
Continuity, 1984–90
1 EM,NA,O&I:Megalith	4.00
2 EM,NA	4.00
3 EM,NA,I:Shaman	3.00
4 EM,NA	3.00
5 EM	3.00
6 thru 8 EM	@3.00

ZERO TOLERANCE
First, 1990–91
1 TV	3.50
2 TV	3.00
3 TV	3.00
4 TV	3.00

ZOMBIES!
IDW Publishing, 2006
1	4.00
2 thru 4	@4.00
3a thru 4a variant (c)s	@4.00

ZOMBIES!: ECLIPSE OF THE UNDEAD
IDW Publishing, 2006
1	4.00

ZOMBIES!: FEAST
IDW Publishing, 2006
1	4.00
2 thru 5	@4.00

ZOMBIES VS. ROBOTS
IDW Publishing, 2006
1	4.00

ZOMBIE TALES: THE DEAD
Boom! Studios, 2006
1	7.00

ZOOM SUIT
Superverse Productions, 2006
1 (of 4)	3.00
2 thru 4	@3.00
1a thru 4a variant (c)s	@3.00
1b thru 4b variant sketch (c)s	@10.00
1 Suspended Animation Edition	3.00
2 Fantasticreal.com edition	10.00

ZOONIVERSE
Eclipse, 1986–87
1 I:Kren Patrol,wrap-around(c)	3.00
2	3.00
3	3.00
4 V:Wedge City	3.00
5 Spak vs. Agent Ty-rote	3.00
6 last issue	3.00

ZORRO
Dell Publ. Co., 1959–61
1 thru 8, see Dell 4-Color
8	200.00
9	225.00
10	200.00
11	200.00
12 ATh	250.00
13 thru 15	@150.00

ZORRO
Gold Key, 1966–68
1 ATh,Rep.	175.00
2 thru 9 Rep.	@100.00

ZORRO
Topps, Nov., 1993
0 BSf(c),DMG(s), came bagged with Jurassic Park Raptor #1 and Teenagents #4	4.00
1 DMG(s),V:Machete	3.00
2 DMG(s)	5.00
3 DMG(s) I:Lady Rawhide	12.00
4 MGr(c),DMG(s),V:Moonstalker	3.00
5 MGr,DMG(s),V:Moonstalker	3.00
6 A:Lady Rawhide	8.00
7 A:Lady Rawhide	7.00
8 MGr(c),DMG(s)	3.00
9 A:Lady Rawhide	4.00
10 A:Lady Rawhide	4.50
11 A:Lady Rawhide	8.00

Zorro #1 © Papercutz

ZORRO
Papercutz, 2005
1 thru 3 Scars	@3.00
4 Drownings	1.00
5 thru 6 Drownings	@3.00
7 thru 10	@3.00
GN Vol. 1 Scars	8.00
GN Vol. 2 Drownings	8.00
GN Vol. 3 Vultures	8.00

ZOT!
Eclipse, 1984–85
1 by Scott McCloud	7.00
2	4.00
3 Art and Soul	4.00
4 Assault on Castle Dekko	3.00
5 Sirius Business	3.00
6 It's always darkest	3.00
7 Common Ground	3.00
8 Through the Door	3.00
9 Gorilla Warfare	3.00
10 T.K.O. The Final Round	3.00
10a B&W	6.00
10b 2nd printing	3.00
Original Zot! Book 1	10.00
Book One TPB	25.00
(Changed to B & W)	

ZOT!
Kitchen Sink, 1997
Book One TPB	25.00

B&W COMICS

A1
Atomeka Press, 1989–92
1 BWS,A:Flaming Carrot,Mr.X.... 10.00
2 BWS,JHw,ECa.............. 10.00
3 BBo(c),ECa 10.00
4 SBs(c),JHw 6.00
5 WiS(c),NGa(s),KJo 7.00
6A JHw,F:Tank Girl 5.00

AARDWOLF
Aardwolf, 1994
1 DC,GM(c). 3.00
1a Certificate ed. signed....... 12.00
2 World Toughest Milkman 3.00
3 R.Block(s),O:Aardwolf 3.00

AARON STRIPS
Amazing Aaron Prod., 1999
1 thru 4, see Image
5 thru 9 .... @3.00
10 48-pg. 4.00

A.B.C. WARRIORS
Fleetway/Quality, 1990
1 thru 8 .... @2.25
Titan, 2002
TPB Vol. 1 The Mek-nificent Seven 20.00
TPB Vol. 2 Black Hole 20.00

ABSOLUTE ZERO
Antarctic Press, 1995
1 .... 3.00
2 Rooftop,Athena 3.00
3 Stan Sakai 3.50
4 3-D Man and Kirby........... 3.00
5 & 6 Super Powers .... @3.00

AC ANNUAL
AC Comics, 1990
1 F:She-Cat; Tara; Nyoka....... 4.00
2 F:Yankee Girl; Ms.Victory 5.00
3 Vault of Heroes; Jet Girl 3.50
4 F:Sentinels of Justice 4.00

ACE COMICS PRESENTS
Ace, 1987
1 thru 7 .... @3.00

ACE McCOY
ACG Comics, 1999
1 thru 4 FF .... @3.00
TPB Collected ed. FF,rep.5 issues 13.00

ACES
Eclipse, 1988
1 thru 5, mag. size .... @3.00

ACG'S AMAZING COMICS
ACG Comics, 2000
1 thru 5 F:Dragon Lady........ @3.00

ACHILLES STORM
Brainstorm, 1997
1 by Sandra Chang............ 3.00

DARK SECRET
Brainstorm, 1997
1 by Sandra Chang............ 3.00
2 .... 3.00
2a luxury edition 5.00

ACME
Fandom House, 1985–89
1 thru 9 .... @3.00

ACOLYTE CHRONICLES
Azure Press, 1995
1 I:Korath 3.00
2 V:Korath 3.00

A COP CALLED TRACY
ACG Comics, 1998
1 by Chester Gould............ 3.00
2 thru 9 .... @3.00
9a deluxe 3.00
10 thru 18 .... @3.00
19 thru 24 giant-size,64-pg..... @6.00
Ann.#1 .... 3.00

ACTION GIRL COMICS
Slave Labor Graphics, 1994
1 thru 7 .... @3.00
1 thru 7, later printings .... @2.75
8 thru 12 .... @3.00
13 Halloween issue 3.00
14 F:Elizabeth Lavin 3.00
15 .... 3.00
16 GoGo Gang,pt.1 .... 2.75
17 GoGo Gang,pt.2 .... 2.75
18 Blue Monday.............. 3.00
19 Halloween 3.00

ACTION PHILOSOPHERS
Evil Twin Comics 2005
1 Plato...................... 3.00
1a 2nd printing 3.00
(2) Spec. All-Sex Special #1 ...... 3.00
(3) Spec. Self-help for Stupid
   Ugly Losers 3.00
Spec. World Domination Handbook. 3.00
Spec. Hate the French #1 ...... 3.00
Spec. The People's Choice 3.00
Spec. It's All Greek to You 3.00
TPB Giant-Sized Thing 7.00

ADAM AND EVE A.D.
Bam, 1985–87
1 .... 3.00
2 thru 10 .... @3.00

ADDAM OMEGA
Antarctic Press, 1997
1 (of 4) by Bill Hughes 3.00
2 thru 4 .... @3.00

ADOLESCENT RADIOACTIVE BLACK-BELT HAMSTERS
Eclipse, 1986
1 I:Bruce,Chuck,Jackie,Clint...... 3.00
1a 2nd printing 2.50
2 A parody of a parody 2.50
3 I:Bad Gerbil 2.50
4 A:Heap (3-D),Abusement Park . 2.50
5 Abusement Park #2 .... 2.50
6 SK,Abusement Park #3 .... 2.50
7 SK,V:Toe-Jam Monsters 2.50
8 SK 2.50
9 All-Jam last issue............ 2.50
[2nd Series] Parody Press
1 .... 2.50
2 Hamsters Go Hollywood 2.50

ADVENTURERS
Aircel/Adventure, 1986
0 Origin Issue 3.00
1 with Skeleton 7.00
1a Revised cover 5.00
1b 2nd printing 3.00
2 thru 6 Peter Hsu (c) .... @3.00
7 thru 9 .... @3.00

ADVENTURERS BOOK II
Adventure Publ., 1987
0 O:Man Gods 3.00
1 .... 3.00
2 thru 9 .... @3.00

Adventurers Book III #1
© Adventure Publications

ADVENTURERS BOOK III
Adventure Publ., 1989
1A Lim.(c)Ian McCaig 2.50
1B Reg.(c)Mitch Foust 2.50
2 thru 6 .... @2.50

ADVENTURES INTO THE UNKNOWN
A Plus Comics, 1990
1 AW,WW, rep. classic horror..... 3.00
2 AW 3.00
3 AW 3.00
Halloween Spec. reps. Charlton &
   American Comics GroupHorror. 2.50
ACG Comics, 1997
1 FF,AW, Charlton comics reprint.. 3.00

ADVENTURES OF BARRY WEEN BOY GENIUS
Oni Press, 2000
1 (of 6) by Judd Winick.......... 3.00
2 Monkey Tales,pt.2 .... 3.00
3 Monkey Tales,pt.3 .... 3.00
4 Monkey Tales,pt.4 .... 3.00
5 Monkey Tales,pt.5 .... 3.00
6 Monkey Tales,pt.6 .... 3.00
TPB Vol. 1 thru Vol. 4......... @9.00

All comics prices listed are for *Near Mint* condition.

ADVENTURES OF CHRISSY CLAWS, THE
Heroic, 1991
1 thru 2 . . . . @3.25

ADVENTURES OF CHUK THE BARBARIC
White Wolf, 1987
1 & 2 . . . . @3.00

ADVENTURES OF LIBERAL MAN, THE
Political Comics, 1996
1 by Marcus Pierce & Pete Garcia . 3.00
2 V:Right Wing talk show hosts . . . 3.00
3 Contract with America,'pt.2 . . . . . 3.00
4 Terminate with Extreme
    Prejudice,'pt.2 . . . . 3.00
5 Extreme Prejudice,pt.3 . . . . 3.00
6 . . . . 3.00
7 1996 Election issue 3.00
9 . . . . 3.00
10 The Last Boy Scouts,pt.2 . . . . . . 3.00
Sharkbait Press, 1999
TPB Final Mission 15.00

ADVENTURES OF LUTHER ARKWRIGHT
Valkyrie Press, 1987–89
1 thru 9 . . . . @3.00
See Also: Dark Horse section

ADVENTURES OF THE AEROBIC DUO
Lost Cause Productions
1 thru 3 . . . . @2.25
4 Gopher Quest 2.25
5 V:Stupid Guy 2.25

ADVENTURES OF THEOWN
Pyramid, 1986
1 thru 3, Limited series . . . . @3.00

AESOP'S FABLES
Fantagraphics, 1991
1 Selection of Fables 2.25
2 Selection of Fables 2.25
3 inc. Boy who cried wolf 2.25

AETOS
Hall of Heroes, 1997
1 by Dan Parsons 2.50
1 variant cover 4.00
2 . . . . 2.50

AETOS THE EAGLE
Ground Zero, 1997
1 (of 3) by Dan Parsons 3.00
2 . . . . 3.00
3 concl. 3.00

AETOS 2: CHILDREN OF THE GRAVES
Orphan Underground, 1995
1 A:Nightmare 2.50

AGENT UNKNOWN
Renegade, 1987
1 thru 3 . . . . @3.00

Agent Unknown #1
© Renegade

AGE OF HEROES, THE
Halloween Comics, 1996
1 JHI 3.50
1A signed 7.00
2 JHI 3.50
2A signed 7.00

AGONY ACRES
AA2 Entertainment, 1995
1 thru 3 . . . . @2.50
4 and 5 . . . . @3.00

AIRFIGHTERS CLASSICS
Eclipse, 1987
1 O:Airboy,rep.Air Fighters#2 . . . . . 4.00
2 rep.Old Airboy appearances 4.00
3 thru 6 . . . . @4.00

AIRWAVES
Caliber, 1990
1 Radio Security 2.50
2 A:Paisley,Ganja 2.50
3 Formation of Rebel Alliance 2.50
4 Big Annie,pt. 1 . . . . 2.50
5 Big Annie,pt 2 . . . . 2.50

AKIKO
Sirius, 1996–2004
1 MCi, Akiko on the Planet Smoo. . 6.00
2 MCi,Captife of SKy Pirates 4.00
3 thru 17 MCi . . . . @3.00
18 MCi,Alia Rellapor, concl. 3.00
19 MCi,The Story Tree,pt.1 . . . . . . 3.00
20 MCi,F:Mr. Beeba. 3.00
21 MCi,On the Road 3.00
22 MCi,On the Transport Ship 3.00
23 MCi,Follow me,pt.1 . . . . 3.00
24 MCi,Follow me,pt.2 . . . . 3.00
25 MCi,Done in One, 32pg. 3.00
26 MCi,Bornstone's Elixir,pt.1 . . . . 3.00
27 MCi,Bornstone's Elixir,pt.2 . . . . 3.00
28 MCi,Bornstone's Elixir,pt.3 . . . . 3.00
29 MCi,Bornstone's Elixir,pt.4 . . . . 3.00
30 MCi,Bornstone's Elixir,pt.5 . . . . 3.00
31 MCi,Bornstone's Elixir, concl. . . 3.00
32 MCi,On Planet Earth,pt.1 . . . . . . 3.00
33 MCi,On Planet Earth,pt.2 . . . . . . 3.00
34 MCi,On Planet Earth,pt.3 . . . . . . 3.00
35 Moonshopping,pt.1 . . . . 3.00
36 Moonshopping,pt.2 . . . . 3.00
37 Moonshopping,pt.3 . . . . 3.00
38 Moonshopping,pt.4 . . . . 3.00

39 Big Bag of This and That 3.00
40 Battle of Boach's Keep,pt.1 . . . 3.00
41 Battle of Boach's Keep,pt.2 . . . 3.00
42 Battle of Boach's Keep,pt.3 . . . 3.00
43 Battle of Boach's Keep,pt.4 . . . 3.00
44 Battle of Boach's Keep,pt.5 . . . 3.00
45 Battle of Boach's Keep,pt.6 . . . 3.00
46 Battle of Boach's Keep,pt.7 . . . 3.00
47 Battle of Boach's Keep,pt.8 . . . 3.00
48 Akiko on Planet Earth,pt.1 . . . . 3.00
49 Akiko on Planet Earth,pt.2 . . . . 3.00
50 MCi,44-pg. 3.50
51 MCi,Quality Assortment 3.00
52 MCi 3.00
1-shot Akiko on the Planet Smoo . . 4.00
1-shot Akiko on the Planet Smoo,
    signed & numbered, color 6.00
TPB Vol. 1 rep. #1–#6 . . . . 15.00
TPB Vol. 2 rep. #8–#13 . . . . 12.00
TPB Vol. 3 rep. #14–#18 . . . . 12.00
TPB Vol. 4 rep. #19–#24 . . . . 15.00
TPB Vol. 5 . . . . 13.00
TPB Vol. 6 . . . . 15.00
TPB Vol. 7 . . . . 15.00
TPB Vol. 1 Flights of Fancy 15.00
GN Akiko on the Planet Smoo. . . . 15.00
GN Pocket-Sized Vol. 1 . . . . 12.00
GN Pocket-Sized Vol. 2 thru
    Vol. 5 . . . . @12.00

ALAN MOORE'S HYPOTHETICAL LIZARD
Avatar Press 2004
Preview 2.00
Preview, wraparound (c) 3.00
Preview, convention (c) 6.00
1 (of 4) 4.00
1a wraparound (c). 4.00
1b Tarot (c) 4.00
2 thru 4 . . . . @3.50
2a thru 4a wraparound (c). . . . . . @3.50
2b thru 4b Tarot (c) . . . . @4.00

ALAN MOORE'S THE COURTYARD
Avatar Press, 2003
1 . . . . 3.50
2 . . . . 3.50
1a thru 2a wraparound (c). . . . . . @4.00
TPB 7.00
TPB The Courtyard, companion . . 10.00

ALAN MOORE'S YUGGOTH CULTURES
Avatar Press, 2003
1 thru 3 . . . . @3.50
1 thru 3a wraparound (c) 4.00
Necrocomicon ashcan, 16-pg. 5.00
TPB 20.00
TPB 30.00

ALBEDO
Thoughts & Images, 1985–89
0 white cover, yellow drawing table
    Blade Runner 35.00
0a white(c) 15.00
0b blue(c),1st ptg 12.00
0c blue(c),2nd ptg 10.00
0d blue(c),3rd ptg 5.00
0e Photo(c),4th ptg.,Inc. extra
    pages. 3.00
1 SS,I:Nilson Groundthumper,
    dull red cover. 10.00
1a bright red cover 6.00
2 SS,I:Usagi Yojimbo 15.00
3 SS,Erma, Usagi 5.00
4 SS,Usagi 6.00
5 Nelson Groundthumper 5.00
6 Erma, High Orbit 4.00

B & W PUB.

7 . . . . 2.50
8 Erna Feldna. 2.50
9 High Orbit,Harvest Venture 2.50
10 thru 14. . . . . @2.50

ALBEDO VOL. II
Antarctic Press, 1991–93
1 New Erma Story. 3.00
2 E.D.F. HQ. 3.00
3 Birth of Erma's Child 3.00
4 Non action issue 3.00
5 The Outworlds 3.00
6 War preparations 3.00
7 Ekosiak in Anarchy 3.00
8 EDF High Command 3.00
Spec. Color 3.00
VOL. III
1 . . . . 3.50

ALBERT
Narwain Publishing 2006
1 (of 4) 3.00
2 thru 4 . . . . @3.00

Alien Fire #1
© Kitchen Sink

ALIEN FIRE
Kitchen Sink Press, 1987
1 Eric Vincent art 3.50
2 Eric Vincent art 3.00
3 Eric Vincent art 3.00

ALIEN NATION:
A BREED APART
Adventure Comics, 1990
1 Friar Kaddish 3.00
2 Friar Kaddish 2.50
3 The `Vampires' Busted 2.50
4 Final Issue. 2.50

ALIEN NATION:
THE FIRSTCOMERS
Adventure Comics, 1991
1 New Mini-series. 2.50
2 Assassin. 2.50
3 Search for Saucer 2.50
4 Final Issue 2.50

ALIEN NATION:
THE PUBLIC ENEMY
Adventure Comics, 1991
1 `Before the Fall'. 2.50
2 Earth & Wehlnistrata 2.50

---

3 Killer on the Loose. 2.50

ALIEN NATION:
THE SKIN TRADE
Adventure Comics, 1991
1 `Case of the Missing Milksop' . . . 2.50
2 `To Live And Die in L.A' 2.50
3 A:Dr. Jekyll. 2.50
4 D.Methoraphan Exposed. 2.50

ALIEN NATION:
THE SPARTANS
Adventure Comics, 1990
1 JT/DPo,Yellow wrap. 4.00
1a JT/DPo,Green wrap. 4.00
1b JT/DPo,Pink wrap 4.00
1c JT/DPo,blue wrap 4.00
1d LTD collectors edition 7.00
2 JT,A:Ruth Lawrence. 2.50
3 JT/SM,Spartians 2.50
4 JT/SM,conclusion 2.50

ALISON DARE,
LITTLE MISS
ADVENTURES
Oni Press, 2001
1 (of 3) 3.00
TPB 9.00
Vol. 2
1 (of 2) Heart of the Maiden 3.00
2 Heart of the Maiden. 3.00
1-shot 48-pg. (2000) 4.50

ALL-PRO SPORTS
All Pro Sports
1 Unauthorized Bio-Bo Jackson . . . 2.50
2 Unauthorized Bio-Joe Montana . . 2.50

ALLURA AND
THE CYBERANGELS
Avatar Press, 1998
Spec.#1 by Bill Maus 4.00

ALLY
Ally Winsor Productions, 1995
1 I&O: Ally. 3.00
2 and 3 . . . . @3.00

ALONG THE CANADIAN
Obion Comics 2004
1 thru 6 . . . . @3.00

ALTERNATE HEROES
Prelude Graphics, 1986
1 and 2 . . . . @3.00

AMAZING COMICS
PREMIERES
Amazing, 1987
1 thru 9 . . . . @3.00

AMAZON WOMAN
Fantaco, 1994
1 . . . . 3.00
2 . . . . 3.00
VOL. 2 (1996)
1 thru 4 . . . . @3.00
Christmas Spec. 5.00
Beach Party 6.00
Amazing Colossal Amazon
   Woman #1. . . . . 8.00
Amazing Colossal Amazon Album . 13.00
Jungle Annual #1 . . . . 6.00
Jungle Album 10.00

TPB Amazon Woman: The Art of
   Tom Simonton 10.00
TPB Amazon Woman, deluxe 20.00
Spec. Invaders of Terror (1996). . . . 6.00
TPB Book One by Tom Simonton . 15.00
TPB Book Two The Curse of the
   Amazon 15.00
1-shot Attack of the Amazon Girls,
   cont. nudity 5.00

AMAZONS GONZANGAS:
BAD GIRLS
OF THE JUNGLE
Academy Comics, 1995
0 Rites of passage,JWt. 3.50

AMERICAN SPLENDOR
Harvey Bekar, 1976–90
1 thru 15 . . . . @3.25
Tundra, 1991
16 . . . . 4.00

AMERICAN WOMAN
Antarctic Press, 1998
1 by B.Denham & R.Stockton 3.00

AMERICA'S GREATEST
COMICS
AC Comics, 2002
1 F:Phantom Lady, golden-age rep. 7.00
2 F:Mysta on the Moon. 7.00
3 F:Spy Smasher 7.00
4 F:Yarko, Master Magician 7.00
5 F: Captain Science 7.00
6 thru 13 . . . . @7.00
14 thru 16. . . . . @7.00

AMERIMAGNA
Ironcat, 2002
Vol. 1
TPB #1 . . . . 8.00
TPB #2 thru #3 . . . . @8.00
I.C. Entertainment, 2003
TPB #4 thru #12. . . . . @8.00

AMUSING STORIES
Blackthorne
1 thru 3 . . . . @2.25

ANATOMIC BOMBS
Brainstorm, 1998
1 Angelissa, by Mike James 3.00
1a Bad Tabitha, by Mike James . . . 3.00
1b Bad Tabitha, photo cover edition 4.00

ANGEL GIRL
Angel Entertainment, 1997
0 by David Campiti & Al Rio 3.00
1 by D.Campiti & R.Fraga. 3.00
1 deluxe 6.00
Spec. #1 Angels Illustrated Swimsuit
   Special. 5.00
1-shot Against All Evil 3.00
1-shot Before the Wings 3.00
1-shot Demonworld, by Ellis Bell &
   Mark Kuettner 3.00
1-shot Doomsday, by Ellis Bell &
   Mark Kuettner 3.00

ANGEL GIRL:
HEAVEN SENT
Angel Entertainment, 1997
0 by David Campiti & Al Rio 3.00
1 . . . . 3.00

B & W PUB.

ANGEL OF DEATH
Innovation, 1991
1 thru 4 . . . . @2.25

ANGEL SCRIPTBOOK
IDW Publishing 2006
1 City Of 4.00
1a variant (c) 4.00
2 A Hole in the World 4.00
3 Spin the Bottle 4.00
4 Waiting in the Wings 4.00
5 Five by Five 4.00
6 Sanctuary 4.00
7 Smile Time 4.00
2a thru 7a variant (cs) . . . . @4.00

ANGRY YOUTH COMIX
Fantagraphics Books 2000
5 . . . . 3.00
6 thru 9 . . . . @3.50
10 48-page 5.00
11 thru 12 . . . . @3.50

ANGELS 750
Antarctic Press 2004
1 (of 9) 3.00
2 thru 5 . . . . @3.00

ANIMAL MYSTIC
Cry For Dawn/Sirus, 1993–95
1 DOe 32.00
1a variant, signed 47.00
1b 2nd printing, new (c) 7.00
2 I:Klor 30.00
2a 2nd printing, new (c) 6.00
3 . . . . 12.00
3a 2nd printing 5.00
4 last issue 4.00
4a special 15.00
TPB DOe 15.00

ANIMAL MYSTIC: KLOR
Sirius, 1999
1 thru 3 DOe . . . . @3.00

ANTARES CIRCLE
Antarctic Press, 1990
1 . . . . 2.25
2 . . . . 2.25

ANUBIS
Unicorn Books
1 I:Anubis 2.50
2 F.Anubis 2.50
3 . . . . 2.50
Didactic Chocolate Press
3 by Scott Berwanger 2.75
4 thru 6 . . . . @2.75
Adventure Comics
7 `Sandy's Plight' 2.75
8 . . . . 3.00

A-OK
Antarctic Press, 1993
1 Ninja H.S. spin-off series 2.50
2 F:Paul,Moniko,James 2.50
3 Confrontation 2.50
4 . . . . 2.50

APATHY KAT
Entity, 1995
1 . . . . 2.75
1 signed, numbered 10.00
1 2nd printing 2.75
2 . . . . 2.75
2 2nd printing 2.75
3 & 4 . . . . 2.75

TPB Kollection #1 . . . . 8.00

APE CITY
Adventure Comics, 1990
1 Monkey Business 3.00
2 thru 4 . . . . @2.50

APOCALYPSE PLAN, THE
Narwain Publishing 2006
1 (of 3) 3.50
2 . . . . 3.00

APPARITION, THE
Caliber, 1995
1 thru 4 . . . . @3.00
5 `Black Clouds' 3.00

APPLESEED
Eclipse, 1988
1 MSh,rep. Japanese comic 9.00
2 MSh,arrival in Olympus City 6.00
3 MSh,Olympus City politics 5.00
4 MSh,V:Director 5.00
5 MSh,Deunan vs. Chiffon 5.00
Book Two, 1989
1 MSh,AAd(c),Olympus City 4.00
2 MSh,AAd(c),Hitomi vs.EswatUnit 4.00
3 MSh,AAd(c),Deunan vs.Gaia . . . 4.00
4 MSh,AAd(c),V:Robot Spiders . . . 4.00
5 MSh,AAd(c),Hitome vs.Gaia 4.00
Book Three, 1989
1 MSh,Brigreos vs.Biodroid 5.00
2 MSh,V:Cuban Navy 4.00
3 MSh,`Benandanti' 4.00
4 MSh,V:Renegade biodroid 4.00
5 MSh 4.00
Book Four, 1990
1 MSh,V:Munma Terrorists 3.50
2 MSh,V:Drug-crazed Munma 3.50
3 Msh,V:Munma Drug Addicts 3.50
4 MSh,Deunan vs. Pani 3.50

ARAMIS
Comics Interview, 1988
1 mini-series 2.25
2 & 3 . . . . @2.25

AREA 88
Eclipse, 1987
1 I:Shin Kazama 3.00
1a 2nd printing 2.50
2 Dangerous Mission 2.50
2a 2nd printing 2.50
3 O:Shin,Paris '78 . . . . 2.50
4 thru 8 . . . . @2.50
9 thru 36 . . . . @2.50
Viz Communications, 1988
37 thru 42 . . . . @2.50

AREALA, ANGEL OF WAR
Antarctic Press, 1998
1 F:Warrior Nun Areala, color 3.00
2 color 3.00
3 b&w 3.00
4 b&w, conclusion 3.00

ARGONAUTS
Eternity
1 thru 5 . . . . @2.25

ARIK KHAN
A Plus Comics
1 I:Arik Khan 2.50
2 . . . . 2.50
ACG Comics, 1998
1 by Frank Reyes, heroic fantasy . 3.00

ARISTOCRATIC X-TRA-TERRESTRIAL TIME-TRAVELING THIEVES
Fictioneer Books, 1987
1 V:IRS 2.50
2 V:Realty 2.50
3 V:MDM 2.50
4 thru 12 . . . . @2.50

ARIZONA: A SIMPLE HORROR
London Night/EH Prod., 1998
1 (of 3) by Joe Kennedy &
   Jerry Beck 3.00
2 double sized 3.00
3 . . . . 3.00
1-shot Wild at Heart, signed
   alternate cover 10.00

A.R.M. #3
© *Adventure Comics*

A.R.M.
Adventure Comics, 1990
1 Larry Niven adapt. Death by
   Ecstasy,pt.1 . . . . 2.50
2 Death by Ecstasy,pt.2 . . . . 2.50
3 Death by Ecstasy,pt.3 . . . . 2.50

ARMAGEDDON PATROL
Alchemy Texts, 1999
Spec. The Shot 3.00
1 (of 2) Cherries 3.00
2 Cherries 3.00
Spec. Maiden America (2002) 3.00
Spec. Fatal Mistakes 3.00
Spec. Life and Death 3.50
Spec. First Mission #1 . . . . 3.50
Spec. First Mission #2 . . . . 3.50
Spec. First Mission #3 . . . . 3.50

ARMED & DANGEROUS
Valiant, 1995
1 thru 4 . . . . @3.00
Spec.#1 . . . . 3.00

ARMED & DANGEROUS
Acclaim (Armada), 1996
1 BH,Hell's Slaughterhouse, pt.1 . . 3.00
2 BH,Hell's Slaughterhouse, pt.2 . . 3.00
3 BH,Hell's Slaughterhouse, pt.3 . . 3.00
4 BH,Hell's Slaughterhouse, pt.4 . . 3.00

All comics prices listed are for *Near Mint* condition.

ARMED & DANGEROUS
No. 2
Acclaim, 1996
1 BH,When Irish Eyes are
    Dying, pt.1 . . . . 3.00
2 BH,When Irish Eyes, pt.2 . . . . . . 3.00
3 BH,When Irish Eyes, pt.3 . . . . . . 3.00
4 BH,When Irish Eyes, pt.4 . . . . . . 3.00

ARROW SPOTLIGHT
Arrow Comics, 1998–99
Advendures of Simone & Ajax 3.00
Allison Chains 3.00
Descendants of Toshin 3.00
Max Velocity, by Jack Snider 3.00
Red Vengeance, by Chris Kemple . . 3.00
Talonback 3.00

ARSENIC LULLABY
A Silent Comics, 1999
Spec. May '99 . . . . 2.50
Spec. July '99 . . . . 2.50
Spec. Sept.'99 . . . . 2.50
Spec. Jan. 2000 . . . . 2.50
8 thru 15 . . . . @2.50
Sept. 2001 . . . . 2.50
Nov. 2001 . . . . 2.65
Christmas 2001 . . . . 2.65
Spec. Christmas Special 2.50
Spec. Halloween Special 2.75
TPB The Devil Your Neighbor 13.00
TPB Arsenic Lullaby, Year Two . . . 13.00
Volume 2, 2002
1 by Douglas Paszkiewicz 3.00
2 . . . . 3.00
3 . . . . 3.00
4 . . . . 3.00
TPB Vol. 1 Damned Laughter 13.00
TPB The Devil's hat Trick 19.00
AAA Milwaukee Publishing 2002
Lost issue, signed 4.00
AAA Milwaukee Publishing
15 thru 16 . . . . @3.00
17 . . . . 3.00
18 thru 20 . . . . @3.00
TPB Essential Arsenic
    Lullaby Vol. 1 . . . . 20.00

ASHES
Caliber, 1990–91
1 thru 6 . . . . @2.50

ASHLEY DUST
Knight Press, 1995
1 thru 3 . . . . @2.50
4 V:Allister Crowley 2.50
5 Metaphysical Adventure 2.50
Blue Line Pro Comics 2003
TPB 15.00
Afterburn Press 2004
GN #1 . . . . 14.00

A SORT OF HOMECOMING
Alternative Comics 2003
1 (of 3) 3.50
2 and 3 . . . . @3.50

ASRIAL VS. CHEETAH
Antarctic Press, 1995–96
1 & 2 Ninja High School Gold
    Digger x-over . . . . @3.00

ASSASSINATE HITLER!
New England Comics, 2001
1 (of 3) by Ron Ledwell 3.75
2 thru 3 . . . . @3.75

ASSASSINETTE
Pocket Change Comics, 1994
1 thru 4 . . . . @2.50
5 V:Nemesis 2.50
6 The Second Coming,pt.2 . . . . 2.50
7 The Second Coming,pt.3 . . . . 2.50
8 V:Crazy Actor 2.50
9 . . . . 2.50
10 final issue. 2.50
Spec. Assassinette Returns 2.50
Spec. Assassinette Violated 2.50
Deluxe Assassinette Violated 4.25

ASSASSINETTE: HARDCORE 1995
Pocket Change Comics
1 By Shadow Slasher Team 2.50
2 V:Bolero 2.50

AS TOLD BY...
NDP Comics 2004
1 Rapunzel 3.00
2 Sleeping Beauty 3.00
3 Goldilocks 3.00

ASSEMBLY
Antarctic Press, 2003
1 (of 4) 3.00
2 thru 4 . . . . @3.50
TPB Pocket Manga 10.00

ASTOUNDING SPACE THRILLS
Day One Comics, 1998
1 by Steve Conley, The Codex
    Reckoning,pt.1 . . . . 3.00
2 Bros. Hildebrandt (c) 3.00
3 Aspects of Iron 3.00
4 The Robot Murders 3.00
5 Gordo returns 3.00

ASTOUNDING SPACE THRILLS: BLOOP
Day One Comics 2004
1 . . . . 3.00
2 . . . . 3.00

ASTRA
CPM Manga, 2001
1 . . . . 3.00
1a variant JBa (c) 3.00
1b variant JBa(c) signed 30.00
2 thru 5 . . . . @3.00
6 thru 8 . . . . @3.00
TPB Jerry Robinson's Astra 16.00

ASTRONAUTS IN TROUBLE: LIVE FROM THE MOON
Gun Dog Comics, 1999
1 (of 5) 3.00
2 thru 5 . . . . @3.00
AIT Comics, 1999
Spec.#1 Cool Ed's 3.00
Spec.#1 CAd, One Shot, One Beer . 8.00

ASTRONAUTS IN TROUBLE: SPACE:, 1959
AIT/Planetlar, 2000
1 (of 3) by Larry Young, CAd 3.00
2 . . . . 3.00
3 . . . . 3.00
TPB 72-pg 8.00
TPB Astronauts in Trouble 17.00

ATHENA
A.M. Works, 1995
1 thru 14 by Dean Hsieh . . . . . . @3.00
TPB Vol. 1 . . . . 15.00
TPB Vol. 2 . . . . 16.00
Antarctic Press, 1996
0 . . . . 4.00

ATOMIC CITY TALES
Kitchen Sink, 1996
1 thru 4 by Jay Stephens . . . . . . @3.50
TPB Vol. 1 Go Power 13.00
TPB Vol. 1 signed & numbered . . . 21.00
Oni Press, 2002
TPB Vol. 1 Go Power 13.00
TPB Vol. 2 Doc Phantom 13.00

ATOMIC COMICS
1 . . . . 2.75
Becomes:

MARK I

Atomic Man #1
© Blackthorne

ATOMIC MAN
Blackthorne, 1986
1 . . . . 3.00
2 & 3 . . . . @2.50

ATOMIC MOUSE
A Plus Comics, 1990
1 A:Atomic Bunny 2.50

ATOMIC OVERDRIVE
Caliber
1 by Dave Darrigo & PGr 3.00
2 & 3 . . . . @3.00

A TRAVELLER'S TALE
Antarctic Press
1 I:Goshin the Traveller 2.50
2 . . . . 2.50

ATTACK OF THE MUTANT MONSTERS
A Plus Comics, 1991
1 SD,rep.Gorgo(Kegor) 2.50

AUGUST
Arrow Comics, 1998
1 thru 4 . . . . @3.00

AUTUMN
Caliber Press, 1995
1 I:James Turell 3.00
GN 7"x10" 13.00

AUTUMN
Amaze Ink/Slave Labor Graphics 2004
1 . . . . 3.00
2 thru 5 . . . . @3.00

AVALON
Harrier, 1987
1 thru 3 . . . . @2.50

AVANT GUARD
Day 1 Comics, 1994
1 thru 4 F:Feedback . . . . @2.50

AVATARS
Avatar Press, 1998
1 (of 2) by Gregory & Holaso 4.00
2 F:Pandora & Atlas 3.50

AV IN 3D
Aardvark–Vanaheim, 1984
1 Color,A:Flaming Carrot 6.00

AVELON
Kenzer & Company, 1998
1 . . . . 3.00
2 thru 11 Legacy of Thrain . . . . . @3.00
11 & 12 Heir to Legend . . . . @3.00

AVENUE X
Innovation, 1992
1 Based on NY radio drama 2.50
Purple Spiral
3 signed & numbered 3.00

AWAKENING COMICS
Awakening Comics, 1997
1 by Steve Peters 3.50
2 . . . . 3.50
3 thru 4 . . . . @3.00
Awakening Comics, 1999
1 by Steve Peters 3.50
Spec. Millennium Bug Fever 3.00

AWAKENINGS
Eighth Day Entertainment 2004
1 (of 6) 3.00
2 thru 5 . . . . @3.00

AWESOME COMICS
1 thru 3 . . . . @2.25

AXED FILES, THE
Entity Comics, 1995
1 X-Files Parody 2.50
1 3rd printing, parody 2.75

B-MOVIE PRESENTS
B-Movie Comics, 1986
1 Captain Daring 2.50
2 The World of X-Ray 2.50
3 Tasma, Queen of the Jungle 2.50
4 Matrix the Accellerator 2.50

BABES OF AREA 51
Blatant Comics, 1997
1 . . . . 3.00

BABY ANGEL X
Brainstorm, 1996
1 . . . . 3.00
2 . . . . 3.00
3 gold edition 5.00
3a signed edition. 10.00

BABY ANGEL X: SCORCHED EARTH
Brainstorm, 1997
1 by Scott Harrison 3.00
2 . . . . 3.00

BABYLON CRUSH
Boneyard Press, 1995
1 I:Babylon Crush 3.00
2 V:A Gang 3.00
3 V:Mafiaso Brothers 3.00
4 & 5 . . . . @3.00
CFD
6 & 7 . . . . @4.00
Boneyard, 1998
1-shot Buddha, F:Lesbian dominatrix
   vigilante 5.00
Spec. Babylon Bondage Christmas . 3.00
Spec. Girlfriends 3.00
Spec. The Last Shepherd 3.00

BAD APPLES
High Impact, 1997
1 . . . . 3.00
1 Bad Candies cover 10.00
2 . . . . 3.00
2 deluxe 15.00
3 by Billy Patton 3.00
ABC Studios, 1999
Vol 2
1 RCI 3.00
1a deluxe variant 8.00
2 . . . . 3.00
Vol 3
1 by Greg Narvasa 3.00
1a gold manga 10.00

BAD APPLES: HIGH EXPECTATIONS
ABC Studios, 1999
1 . . . . 3.00
1a Beach Fun (c) 8.00
2 . . . . 3.00
2a deluxe 8.00

BAKER STREET
(Prev. color)
Caliber, 1989
3 . . . . 3.25
4 . . . . 2.50
5 & 6 Children of the Night . . . . . @2.50
7 thru 10 Children of the Night . . @2.50

BAKER STREET: GRAPHITTI
Caliber
1 `Elementary, My Dear' 2.50

BALANCE OF POWER
MU Press, 1990–91
1 thru 4 . . . . @2.50

BALLAD OF UTOPIA
Black Daze, 2000
1 by B.Buchanan & M.Hoffman . . . 3.00
2 thru 5 . . . . @3.00
TPB Vol. 1 . . . . 9.00

Antimatter/Hoffman International, 2003
7 thru 8 . . . . @3.00

BANANA SUNDAY
Oni Press Inc. 2005
1 (of 4) 3.00
2 thru 4 . . . . @3.00
TPB 12.00

BANDY MAN, THE
Caliber, 1996
1 SPr,CAd 3.00
2 SPr,CAd,JIT 3.00
3 SPr,CAd,JIT, conclusion. 3.00

Baoh #5
© *Viz Communications*

BAOH
Viz, 1990
1 thru 8 . . . . @3.00
GN V:Juda Laboratory 15.00

BARABBAS
Slave Labor, 1986
1 . . . . 4.50
2 thru 4 . . . . @2.50

BARBARIANS
ACG Comics
1 by Jeff Jones, Mike Kaluta,
   Wayne Howard 3.00
2 WW 3.00

BARBARIC TALES
Pyramid, 1986
1 . . . . 3.00
2 and 3 . . . . @2.25

BASEBALL SUPERSTARS
Revolutionary, 1991–93
1 Nolan Ryan 2.50
2 Bo Jackson 2.50
3 Ken Griffey Jr. 2.50
4 Pete Rose 2.50
5 Rickey Henderson 2.50
6 Jose Canseco 2.50
7 Cal Ripkin Jr. 2.50
8 Carlton Fisk 2.50
9 George Brett 2.50
10 Darryl Strawberry 2.50
11 Frank Thomas 2.50
12 Ryne Sandberg (color) 2.75
13 Kirby Puckett (color) 2.75

All comics prices listed are for *Near Mint* condition. | **CVA Page 723**

14 Roberto & Sandy Alomar (color). 2.75
15 Roger Clemens (color) 2.75
16 Mark McGuire 3.00
17 Avery & Glavin 3.00
18 Dennis Eckersley 3.00
19 Dave Winfield 3.00
20 Jim Abbott. 3.00

BASTARD!!

Viz Communications, 2001

1 thru 2 Wizard . . . . @4.00
3 thru 5 Ninja. . . . . @4.00
6 thru 8 Fighter . . . . @4.00
9 thru 10 Vampire . . . . @4.00
11 thru 12 Empress . . . . @4.00
13 thru 15 Empress . . . . @4.00
TPB Vol. 1 thru Vol. 3 . . . . @15.00
TPB Vol. 4 thru Vol. 5. . . . . @13.00

BATTLE ANGEL ALITA

Viz, 1992

1 I:Daisuka,Alita 8.00
2 Alita becomes warrior 6.00
3 A:Daiuke,V:Cyborg. 4.00
4 Alita/Cyborg,A:Makaku 4.00
5 The Bounty Hunters' Bar 4.00
6 Confrontation 4.00
7 Underground Sewers,A:Fang . . . 3.00
8 & 9 . . . . @2.75

Part Two, 1993

1 V:Zapan 3.00
2 V:Zapan 3.00
3 F:Ido. 2.75
4 thru 7 V:Zapan . . . . @2.75
TPB Killing Angel 16.00

Part Three, 1993

1 thru 5 . . . . @2.75
6 . . . . 5.00
7 thru 13 . . . . @2.75

Part Four, 1994

1 thru 7 . . . . @2.75

Part Five, 1995

1 thru 6 . . . . @2.75
7 . . . . 3.00

Part Six, 1995–96

1 thru 8 YuK . . . . @3.00
TPB Angel of Chaos 16.00

Part Seven, 1996

1 thru 8 YuK . . . . @3.00

Part Eight, 1997

1 thru 9 YuK . . . . @3.00
TPB Vol. 2 Tears of an Agnel. 16.00

Battle Angel Alita, Part Eight, #5
© Viz Communications

TPB Vol. 4 Angel of Victory 16.00
TPB Vol. 5 . . . . 16.00
TPB Vol. 6 Angel of Death. 16.00
TPB Vol. 7 Angel of Chaos 16.00
TPB Vol. 8 Fallen Angel. 16.00
TPB Vol. 9 Angel's Ascension 17.00

BATTLE ANGEL ALITA: LAST ORDER

Viz Communicatons, 2002

Part 1

1 by Yukito Kishiro 3.00
2 thru 6 . . . . @3.00
GN Vol. 1 . . . . 10.00
GN Vol. 2 thru 9 . . . . @10.00

BATTLE ARMOR

Eternity, 1988

1 thru 4 . . . . @2.50

BATTLE BEASTS

Blackthorne, 1988

1 thru 4 . . . . @2.50

BATTLE GIRLZ

Antarctic Press, 2002

1 by Rod Espinosa 3.00
2 thru 6 . . . . @3.00

BATTLEGROUND EARTH

Best Comics, 1996

1 . . . . 2.50
2 . . . . 2.50
3 `Destiny Quest: The Vengeance' concl. 2.50
4 V:Conjura 2.50
5 `The Pit of Black Death'. 2.50

BATTLE POPE

Funk-O-Tron, 2000

1 . . . . 3.00
2 thru 4 . . . . @3.00
Spec.#1 Shorts. 5.00
Spec.#2 Shorts. 5.00
Spec.#3 Shorts. 3.00
Spec.#1 Christmas Popetacular . . . 5.00
TPB Vol. 1 . . . . 13.00
TPB Vol. 2 . . . . 13.00
TPB Saint Michael (2001) 13.00

BATTLE POPE MAYHEM

Funk-O-Tron, 2001

1 (of 2) 3.00
2 . . . . 3.00

BATTLE POPE PRESENTS: SAINT MICHAEL

Funk-O-Tron, 2001

1 thru 3 . . . . @3.00

BATTLE POPE: WRATH OF GOD

Funk-O-Tron, 2002

1 (of 3) by R.Kirkman & T.Moore . . 3.50
2 thru 3 . . . . @3.50

BATTLESTAR BLACK & WHITE

Realm Press, 2000

1-shot Battlestar Galactica. 3.00

BATTLETECH

Blackthorne, 1987

(Prev. Color)

7 thru 12 . . . . @2.50
Ann.#1 . . . . 4.50

BATTRON

NEC

1 thru 2 WWII story. . . . . @2.75

BEAR

Amaze Ink/SLG, 2003

1 by Jamie Smart 3.00
2 thru 10 . . . . @3.00
TPB Vol. 1 Immortal. 15.00

BEAST WARRIOR OF SHAOLIN

Pied Piper, 1987

1 thru 5 . . . . @2.50

THE BEATLES EXPERIENCE

Revolutionary, 1991–92

1 Beatles 1960's 3.00
2 Beatles 1964-1966. . . . . 2.50
3 . . . . 2.50
4 Abbey Road, Let it be 2.50
5 The Solo Years 2.50
6 Paul McCartney & Wings. 2.50
7 The Murder of John Lennon 2.50
8 final issue. 2.50

BECK AND CAUL

Gauntlet, 1994

1 I:Beck and Caul 3.00
2 thru 6 . . . . @3.00
Ann.#1 A Single Step 3.50

BENZINE

Antarctic Press, 2000

1 manga, by Ben Dunn. 5.00
2 thru 7 . . . . @5.00

BERLIN

Drawn & Quarterly, 1999

1 by Jason Lutes 3.00
2 thru 8 . . . . @3.00
9 thru 10 . . . . @3.50
11 . . . . 4.00
12 . . . . 4.00
TPB Book One. 16.00

BERZERKER

Gauntlet (Caliber), 1993

1 thru 6 . . . . @3.00

BEST OF THE WEST

AC Comics, 1998

1 F:Durango Kid 5.00
2 F:The Haunted Horseman. 5.00
3 F:The Haunted Horseman. 5.00
4 F:Roy Rogers, 44-pg. 6.00
5 F:Durango Kid 6.00
6 F:Durango Kid 6.00
7 F:Monte Hale 6.00
8 . . . . 6.00
9 F:Sunset Carson 6.00
10 F:Durango Kid. 6.00
11 F:Black Diamond. 6.00
12 F:Latigo Kid. 6.00
13 F:The Durango Kid 6.00
14 F:Haunted Horseman 6.00
15 F:Roy Rogers 6.00
16 O:The Whip. 6.00
17 F:Lone Ranger 6.00
18 F:Black Bull. 6.00

19 F:Rocky Lane 6.00
20 F:Durango Kid. 6.00
21 F:Masked Marvel 6.00
22 F:Ken Maynard 6.00
23 F:Freaks of Fear 6.00
24 F:Redmask, Black Phantom 6.00
25 FF(c),F:Haunted horsemen 6.00
26 F:Lazo Kid, Lemonade Kid 6.00
27 F:Roy Rogers 6.00
28 F:Red Mask 6.00
29 F:Jim Bowie 6.00
30 F:The Durango Kid 6.00
31 F:Haunted Horseman 6.00
32 F:Haunted Horseman 6.00
33 F:Zorro 7.00
34 Roy Rogers. 7.00
35 The Haunted Horseman 7.00
36 Gene Autry 7.00
37 Origins Issue 7.00
38 Durango Kid 7.00
39 Roy Rogers. 7.00
40 Redmask. 7.00
41 The Haunted Horseman 7.00
42 Black Diamond 7.00
43 The Haunted Horseman 7.00
44 The Hooded Horseman 7.00
45 The Haunted Horsean 7.00
46 The Durango Kid. 7.00
47 The Durango Kid. 7.00
48 The Durango Kid. 7.00
49 The Crimson Cavalier. 7.00
50 Frankenstein Goes West 7.00
51 Redmask. 7.00
52 Wild Bill Pecos 7.00
53 The Durango Kid. 7.00
54 The Durango Kid. 7.00
55 Strawman vs. Redmask 7.00
56 Haunted Horseman. 7.00
57 Firehair 7.00
58 Haunted Horseman. 7.00
59 Monte Hale 7.00
TPB Round-up Special #1 . . . . . 25.00
TPB Round-up Special #2 . . . . . 25.00
TPB Round-up Special #3 . . . . . 22.00
TPB Big B-Western Special #1 . . 25.00

BETHANY THE VAMPFIRE
Brainstorm, 1997
0 O:Bethany 3.00
1 by Holly Galightly. 3.00
1a luxury edition 5.00
2 & 3 . . . . @3.00

BETTIE PAGE
THE '50s RAGE
Illustration Studio, 2001
1 revised edition, Steve Woron. . . . 3.25
2 all pin-up layout 3.25
2 tame cover. 3.25
Ann.#1 revised. 3.25

BEYOND MARS
Blackthorne, 1989
1 thru 5 . . . . @2.25

BIG BANG PRESENTS
Big Bang Comics 2006
1 Protoplasm. 3.00
2 Super Frankenstein 3.00
3 . . . . 4.00

BIGGER
Free Lunch Comics, 1998
Spec.#1 . . . . 3.50
1 (of 4) The Devil's Concubine 3.00
2 thru 4 Devil's Concubine,pt.2–4 @3.00

BIG NUMBERS
Mad Love
1 BSz,AMo(s) 6.00
2 BSz,AMo(s) 5.50

BILL THE BULL:
BURNT CAIN
Boneyard, 1992
1 I:Bill the Bull. 3.00
2 & 3 For Hire . . . . @3.00

BILL THE BULL:
ONE SHOT, ONE
BOURBON, ONE BEER
Boneyard, 1994
1 . . . . 3.00
2 . . . . 3.00

BILLY DOGMA
Millennium, 1997
1 by Dean Haspiel 3.00
1a signed print edition 5.00
2 . . . . 3.00
3 . . . . 3.00
4 They Found A Sawed-Off in
   My Afro 3.00

BILLY NGUYEN
PRIVATE EYE
Caliber, 1990
1 . . . . 2.25
1a 2nd printing 2.25
2 thru 6 . . . . @2.25

BIO-BOOSTER
ARMOR GUYVER
Viz Communications
Part One, 1993
1 by Yoshiki Takaya 4.00
2 thru 12 . . . . @3.00
TPB Vol. 1 rep.Part One,#1–#6 . . . 16.00
TPB Vol. 2 Revenge of Chronos . . 16.00
Part Two, 1994–95
1 F:Sho 2.75
2 thru 7 . . . . @2.75
TPB Vol. 3 Dark Masters 16.00
Part Three, 1995
1 Sho Unconscious. 2.75
2 thru 7 . . . . @2.75
TPB Vol. 4 Escape From Chronos. 16.00
Part Four, 1995–96
1 thru 7 . . . . @3.00
TPB Vol. 5 Guyver Reborn 16.00
Part Five, 1996
1 thru 7 . . . . @3.00
TPB Vol. 6 Heart of Chronos 16.00
Part Six, 1996–97
1 thru 6 by Yoshiki Takaya . . . . @3.00
TPB Vol. 7 Armageddon 16.00

BIRTHDAY BOY, THE
Beetlebomb Books, 1997
1 by Jason Lethcoe 3.00
2 . . . . 3.00
3 . . . . 3.00
4 16-pg. 3.00
VOL 2
1 16-pg. 3.00
TPB 56 pg. 8.00

BIZARRE HEROES
Kitchen Sink, 1990
1 DSs, parody 2.50

Bizarre Heroes #1
© *Kitchen Sink*

Fiasco Comics
1 DSs, reprint 3.00

[Original] BLACK CAT
Recollections, 1991
4 rep. 2.25
5 A:Ted Parrish 2.25
6 50th Anniv. Issue 2.25
7 rep.. . . . . 2.25

BLACK COAT:
CALL TO ARMS
Speakeasy Comics 2006
1 (of 4) 3.00
2 thru 3 . . . . @3.00
Ape Entertainment 2006
4 . . . . 3.00

BLACKENED
Enigma
1 V:Killing Machine 3.00
2 V:Killing Machine 3.00
3 Flaming Altar 3.00

BLACK-EYED SUSAN
Mad Yak Press 2004
1 . . . . 3.50
2 thru 4 . . . . @3.00

BLACK HEART
IRREGULARS, THE
Blue King Studios 2005
1 . . . . 3.00
2 . . . . 3.00
3 Who's your Bagdaddy 3.00
4 . . . . 3.00
5 . . . . 3.00

BLACK HOLE
Kitchen Sink, 1995
1 by Charles Burns 3.50
1 new printing 4.50
2 . . . . 3.50
3 . . . . 3.50
3 2nd printing 4.50
Fantagraphics Books, 2000
5 by Charles Burns. 4.00
6 thru 10 . . . . @4.50
11 thru 12 . . . . @5.00

B & W PUB.

All comics prices listed are for *Near Mint* condition.

BLACK KISS
Vortex, 1988
1 HC,Adult	7.00
1a 2nd printing	4.00
1b 3rd printing	2.50
2 HC	6.00
2a 2nd printing	3.00
3 HC	5.00
4 HC	4.00
5 & 6 HC	@2.50
7 thru 12 HC	@2.50

BLACKMASK
Eastern Comics, 1988
1 thru 6	@2.50

BLACK MIST
Caliber Core, 1998
1 by James Pruett & Mike Perkins, Blood of Kali,pt.1	3.00
1a variant MV(c)	3.00
1b variant Jordan Raskin(c)	3.00
1c variant GyD(c)	3.00
1d premium edition, signed	10.00
2 thru 5 Blood of Kali,pt.2–pt.5	@3.00
Spec. Dawn of Armageddon, Blood of Kali,pt.6 & pt.7, 48-pg	4.00

BLACK SCORPION
Special Studio, 1991
1 Knight of Justice	2.75
2 A Game for Old Men	2.75
3 Blackmailer's Auction	2.75

BLACKTHORNE 3 in 1
Blackthorne, 1987
1 & 2	@2.50

BLACK ZEPPELIN
Renegade, 1985
1 GD	3.00
2 thru 6 GD	@2.50

BLADE OF SHURIKEN
Eternity, 1987
1 thru 8	@2.50

BLAIR WITCH PROJECT
Oni Press, 1999
Spec. Movie adapt.	3.00

BLAIR WITCH CHRONICLES
Oni Press, 2000
1 (of 4) by Jen Van Meter & Guy Davis	3.00
2 thru 4	@3.00
TPB Rep.	16.00

BLIND FEAR
Eternity
1 thru 4	@2.50

BLONDE AVENGER
Blonde Avenger Comics, 1998
25 flip-book, Full Metal Corset	4.00
27 Full Metal Corset,pt.2	4.00
Spec. Short Blonde Girl with the Two Big Boobs	4.00

BLONDE AVENGER: DANGEROUS CONCLUSIONS
Brainstorm, 1997
1 V:Victor Von Fuchs	3.00

1a photo deluxe cover	4.00
2	3.00
2a photo deluxe cover	4.00

BLOOD & ROSES ADVENTURES
Knight Press, 1995
1 F:Time Agents	3.00
2 F:Time Agents	3.00
3 Search for Time Agents	3.00
4 Time Adventures	3.00
TPB Vol. 1	13.00
TPB Art of Blood & Roses	15.00

BLOOD 'N' GUTS
Aircel, 1990
1 thru 3	@2.50

BLOODBROTHERS
Eternity, 1988
1 thru 4	@2.50

BLOOD IS THE HARVEST
Eclipse, 1992
1 I:Nikita,Milo	4.50
2 V:M'Raud D:Nikita?	2.50
3 Milo captured	2.50
4 F:Nikita/Milo	2.50

BLOOD JUNKIES
Eternity, 1991
1 Vampires on Capitol Hill	2.50
2 final issue	2.50

BLOODLETTING
Fantaco
1 A Shilling for a Redcoat	3.00
2	3.00
3 Flee	3.00
4 thru 10 (of 11) by Chynna Clugston	@4.00

Blood of Dracula #18
© Apple

BLOOD OF DRACULA
Apple, 1987–90
1 thru 7	@3.00
8 thru 14	@3.00
15 with Record & Mask	4.00
16	5.00
17 thru 20	@4.50

BLOOD OF THE INNOCENT
Warp Graphics, 1986
1 thru 4	@3.00

BLOOD ORANGE
Fantagraphics Books 2004
1	6.00
2 thru 4	@6.00

BLOODSHED
Damage, 1993
1 Little Brother	3.00
1a Commemorative issue	4.00
1b Encore edition, gold foil(c)	3.50
2 Little Brother	3.00
3 O:Bloodshed	3.00
3 `The Wastelands,' cont.	3.50
4 The City	3.50
5 the end is near	3.50
6	3.50
7 Lies, concl.	3.50
`M'	3.50
`M' deluxe	5.00
Spec. Lunatics Fringe	3.50
Spec. Lies Epilogue, final issue	3.50
Spec. Chris Mass #1	3.50
Spec. Requiem	3.50

BLOODTHIRSTY PIRATE TALES
Black Swan Press, 1995
1	2.50
2	2.50
3	2.50
4 `Blockade of Charleston Harbor'	2.50
5 `The Queen Anne's Revenge'	2.50
6 Blackhand's Party	2.50
7 Battle of Ocracoke Inlet	3.00
8 final issue	3.00

BLOODWING
Eternity, 1988
1 thru 5	@2.50

BLOODY SCHOOL
Curtis Comics, 2002
Vol. 1 Manga
1 by S.Yang & K. Yoo	3.00
2 thru 5	@3.00

BLUDGEON
Aardwolf, 1997
1 by JPi & David Chylsetk	3.00
2 `Alise in Wonderland'	3.00
3 `Seeing Red'	3.00

BLUE BULLETEER
AC Comics, 1989
1	2.50

BLUE MONDAY: ABSOLUTE BEGINNERS
Oni Press, 2000
1 (of 4)	3.00
2 thru 4	@3.00
Spec. Nobody's Fool	3.00
Spec. Lovecats (2002)	3.00
Spec. Dead Man's Party (2002)	3.00

BLUE MONDAY: THE KIDS ARE ALRIGHT
Oni Press, 2000
1 by Chynna Clugston-Major	3.00
2	3.00
3 concl.	3.00

    All comics prices listed are for *Near Mint* condition.

BLUE MONDAY: PAINTED MOON
Oni Press 2004
1 (of 4)	3.00
2 thru 4	@3.00
TPB Painted Moon	12.00

BOGIE MAN: CHINATOON
Atomeka
1 I:Francis Claine	3.00
2 F:Bogie Man	3.00
3 thru 4 F:Bogie Man	3.00

BOGIE MAN: MANHATTEN PROJECT
Apocalypse
1-shot D.Quale Assassination Plot . 4.00

BONAFIDE
Bonafide Productions
1 F:Doxie 'th Mutt	3.50
2 F:Doxie 'th Mutt	3.50
3 F:Doxie 'th Mutt	3.50

Bone #1
© Cartoon Books

BONE
Cartoon Books, 1991
1 by Jeff Smith,I:Bone	125.00
1a 2nd printing	10.00
1b 3rd Printing	8.00
2 JSi,I:Thorn	45.00
2a 2nd printing	7.00
3 JSi	35.00
3a 2nd printing	5.00
4 JSi	22.00
5 JSi	20.00
6 JSi	20.00
7 JSi	15.00
8 JSi,The Great Cow Race,pt.1	9.00
9 JSi,The Great Cow Race,pt.2	8.00
1c thru 9a later printings	@3.00
10 JSi,The Great Cow Race,pt.3	8.00
11 JSi	4.00
12 JSi	4.00
13 JSi	8.00
14 thru 20 JSi	@4.00
21 thru 27, *see Image*	
21 thru 27 reprints	@3.00
28 JSi,'Rockjaw: Master of the Eastern Border'	3.00
29 JSi	3.00
30 JSi	3.00
31 JSi	3.00

32 JSi,Bartleby the Rat Creature Cub saga, concl.	3.00
33 JSi,Phoney's fate	3.00
34 JSi,Kingdok Slayer	3.00
35 JSi,Return of Gran'ma Ben.	3.00
36 JSi,Return of Rockjaw	3.00
37 JSi,Extravaganza Issue	3.00
38 JSi,48-pg.	5.00
39 JSi,Ghost Circles	3.00
40 JSi,wrap-around cover	3.00
41 JSi,Deep in enemy territory	3.00
42 JSi,	3.00
43 JSi,sacred wall	3.00
44 JSi,rooftop eatery	3.00
45 JSi,Inner Circle of Power	3.00
46 JSi,Rat Creature Army	3.00
47 JSi,Making money	3.00
48 JSi,Surrender or Die	3.00
49 JSi,The usurper Tarsil	3.00
50 JSi,War, Rat Creatures	3.00
51 JSi,Casualties	3.00
52 thru 53	@3.00
54 This Mortal Coil	3.00
55 Final issue	3.00
Spec.10th Anniv. Ed with PVC fig.	6.00
TPB Bone Reader	10.00
TPB rep.#1-#4	14.00
TPB Vol. 1 Rep.#1-#6	13.00
TPB Vol. 2 Rep.#7-#12	13.00
TPB Vol. 3 Eyes of the Storm	17.00
TPB Vol. 4 Dragonslayer	17.00
TPB Vol. 5 Rock Jaw	15.00
TPB Vol. 6 Old Man's Cave	18.00
TPB Vol. 7 Ghost Circles	25.00
TPB Vol. 8 Treasure Hunters	16.00
TPB Vol. 9 Crown of Horns	17.00
TPB One Volume Edition, 1,300-pg.	40.00

BONESHAKER
Caliber Press
1 Suicidal Wrestler	3.50

BONEYARD
NBM Books, 2001
1 by Richard Moore	3.00
2 thru 4	@3.00
5 thru 19	@3.00
20 thru 23	@3.00
Spec. Swimsuit Issue	3.00
TPB Vol. 1 color	13.00
TPB Vol. 2 color	11.00
TPB Vol. 3	10.00
TPB Vol. 4	10.00
TPB Vol. 5	10.00

BOOK, THE
DreamSmith Studios, 1998
1 epic fantasy 72pg.	3.50
2	3.50
3 thru 7	@4.00
Ashcan Preview, 24-pg.	5.00
Ashcan Preview, GP(c)	10.00
Handbook, 32-pg.	2.25

BOOK OF BALLADS AND SAGAS
Green Man Press, 1995
1 False Knight in the Road	3.00
2 thru 4	3.00
5	3.50

BOOK OF THE TAROT
Caliber Tome Press, 1998
1 History/Development o/t Tarot	4.00
1a 64pg.	5.00
1b signed	5.00

BOOKS OF LORE
Peregrine
Spec.#1 fantasy anthology	3.00
Spec.#2	3.00
Spec.#3	3.00
1-shot Shattered Lives	3.00

BOOKS OF LORE: THE KAYNIN GAMBIT
Peregrine, 1998
0 by Kevin Tucker & David Napoliello	3.00
1 (of 4)	3.00
1a Xavier (c)	3.00
2 thru 4	@3.00

BOOKS OF LORE: THE SHAPE OF EVIL
Peregrine Entertainment, 1999
1 (of 2)	3.00
2	3.00

BOOKS OF LORE: THE STORYTELLER
Peregrine Entertainment, 2000
1 (of 3) by K.Tucker & P.Xavier	3.00
2 & 3	@3.00

BOONDOGGLE
Knight Press, 1995
1 Waffle War	3.00
2 Waffle War	3.00
3 Waffle War	3.00

BOONDOGGLE
Caliber Tapestry, 1997
Spec.	3.00
Spec., signed	3.00
1 thru 4	@3.00

BORDER WORLDS
Kitchen Sink, 1986
1 adult	3.00
2 thru 7	3.00
Spec.#1 Border Worlds: Marooned	3.00

BORIS' ADVENTURE MAGAZINE
Nicotat, 1988
1 & 2	@2.50
3 thru 6	@3.00

BORIS THE BEAR
Nikotat, 1987
1–12: See Dark Horse section	
13 thru 29	@2.50
30 thru 34	@2.50

BORN TO KILL
Aircel, 1991
1 thru 3	@2.50

BOSTON BOMBERS
Caliber
1	2.25
2	2.50
Spec.#1	4.00
Note: other issues are flip-books with:	
Oz #17; The Searchers #5; Raven	
Chronicles #12; & LegendLore #6	

BOUNTY
Caliber, 1991
1 'Bounty,''Navarro,'pt.1	2.50
2 & 3'Bounty,''Navarro,'pt.2–pt3	@2.50

BOX OFFICE POISON
Antarctic Press, 1996
1 by Alex Robinson 9.00
2 . . . . 6.00
3 thru 5 . . . . @4.00
6 thru 10 . . . . @3.00
11 thru 21 . . . . @3.00
TPB 160-pg. 15.00
TPB 608-pg. 30.00
Big Super Spec.#1 . . . . 5.00

BRADLEYS, THE
Fantagraphics, 1999
1 (of 6) by Peter Bagge 3.00
2 thru 6 . . . . @3.00

BRAT PACK
King Hell Publications, 1990
1 . . . . 6.00
1a 2nd printing 3.00
2 thru 5 . . . . @4.00
Brat Pack Collection 13.00

BRATPACK/MAXIMORTAL
King Hell, 1996
Super Spec.#1 RV 3.00
Super Spec.#2 RV 3.00

BREAKFAST AFTER NOON
Oni Press, 2000
1 (of 6) by Andi Watson 3.00
2 thru 6 . . . . @3.00
TPB 20.00

BREAKNECK BLVD.
Slave Labor Graphics, 1995–96
1 thru 3 Jhonen Vasques art . . . . @3.00
4 by Timothy Markin 3.00
5 & 6 . . . . @3.00

BRENDA STARR, ACE REPORTER
ACG Comics, 1998
1 by Dale Messick, Charlton rep. . . 3.00
2 . . . . 3.00
Spec.#1 Pin-ups,rep. from 40s
　and 50s (1998) 3.00

BRIAN PULIDO'S GYPSY
Avatar Press 2004
Preview 2.00
Preview variant (c)s 3.00
Preview Starlight (c). 6.00
Preview Holy Grail (c) 6.00
1 . . . . 3.50
1a variant (c)s . . . . @3.50
1b premium (c) 10.00
1c defensive (c) 6.00

BRIAN PULIDO'S KILLER GNOMES
Avatar Press 2004
1 . . . . 3.50
1a wraparound (c). 3.50

BRIAN PULIDO'S LADY DEATH: ABANDON ALL HOPE
Avatar Press 2004
1/2 Spec. 16-page 3.00
1/2 Spec. variant (c)s. 3.00
1/2 Spec. Premium (c) 10.00
1/2 Spec. Vengeance edition 6.00
1/2 Spec. Empress (c) 6.00

B & W PUB.

1 (of 4) 4.00
2 . . . . 4.00
3 . . . . 4.00
4 . . . . 4.00
1a thru 4a variant (c). . . . . @4.00
1b thru 4b premium (c) . . . . . . @10.00

BRIAN PULIDO'S LADY DEATH: DEAD RISING
Avatar Press 2004
Spec. 16-page 2.50
Spec.A Medieval (c). 6.00
Spec.B Classic (c) 6.00
Spec C Leather (c) 25.00
Spec. D Sketch (c) 30.00
Spec. prism (c). 13.00

BRIAN PULIDO'S UNHOLY
Avatar Press 2004
Preview 2.00
Preview variant (c)s 3.00
1 (of 3) 3.50
2 . . . . 3.50
3 . . . . 3.50
1a thru 3a variant (c). . . . . @3.50
1b thru 3b wraparound (c). . . . . @3.50
1c thru 3c premium (c) . . . . . . @10.00
Preview Rock & Roll (c). 6.00

BRIAN PULIDO'S WAR ANGEL
Avatar Press 2005
1 . . . . 3.50
1a variant (c)s. 3.50
1b premium (c) 10.00
1c Fiery Reaper edition 6.00
1d Hells Belle (c) 6.00
2 . . . . 3.50
2a variant (c)s . . . . @3.50
2b premium (c) 10.00
3 . . . . 3.50
3a variant (c)s . . . . @3.50
3b premium (c) 10.00

BRIAN PULIDO'S WAR ANGEL: BOOK OF DEATH
Avatar Press 2004
Spec. 2.50
Spec. variant(c)s . . . . @3.00
Spec. Attitude ed. 6.00
Spec. Feral (c) 6.00
Spec. Bad Omen (c) 6.00
1 . . . . 3.50
2 thru 3 . . . . @3.50
1a thru 3a variant (c)s. . . . . @3.50
1b thru 3b premium (c) . . . . . . @10.00

BRILLIANT BOY
Circus Comics, 1997
1 . . . . 3.00
2 Drake,pt.1 (of 5). 3.00
3 Drake,pt.2 . . . . 2.50
4 Drake,pt.3 . . . . 2.50
5 Drake,pt.4 . . . . 2.50
6 Drake,pt.5 . . . . 2.50
7 & 8 The Great Thunder,pt.1–2 . @2.50

BRODIE'S LAW
Studio G 2004
1 (of 6) 3.00
2 thru 6 . . . . @3.00

Broid #2
© *Eternity*

BROID
Eternity, 1990
1 thru 4 . . . . @2.25

BROKEN HALO: IS THERE NOTHING SACRED
Broken Halos Comics, 1998
1 by Donald J. Vigil & Tim Vigil. . . 3.00
2 . . . . 3.00
3 . . . . 3.00
Ashcan, limited ed. 16-pg. 7.00
TPB Vol. 1 by Joe & Tim Vigil,
　limited ed. 10.00

BROKEN HEROES
Sirius, 1998
1 by Fillbach Bros. 2.50
2 The Neon Graveyard 2.50
3 Rocket Man 2.50
4 thru 12 final issue. . . . . @2.50
TPB Captain Freebird rep. #1–#12 20.00

BRONX
Eternity, 1991
1 A.Saichann Short Stories. 2.50
2 & 3 . . . . @2.50

Aircel
Reprint 3.00

BROTHER MAN
New City Comics
1 . . . . 5.00
1a 2.25
2 thru 7 . . . . @2.25

BRUCE JONES': OUTER EDGE
Innovation, 1993
1 All reprints 2.50

BRUCE JONES': RAZOR'S EDGE
Innovation, 1993
1 All reprints 2.50
2 D:Grimm, Gritty 2.50

BRU-HED
Schism Comics, 1994
1 Blockhead 3.00

　　　All comics prices listed are for *Near Mint* condition.

1a 2nd printing 2.75
2 Blockhead 3.00
Vol. 1 Bru-Hed's Bunnies, Baddies
  & Buddies (1998). 2.50
Vol. 1 Bru-Hed's Guide to Gettin'
  Girls Now. 2.50
Vol. 2 Bru-Hed's Guide 2.50

BUBBA THE REDNECK WEREWOLF
Brass Ball Comics 2003
1 . . . . 3.00
2 thru 3 . . . . @3.00
4 thru 7 . . . . @3.00

BUCE-N-GAR
RAK, 1996
1 . . . . 2.25
2 . . . . 2.25
3 . . . . 2.25

BUCKAROO BANZAI
Moonstone Books 2005
Preview 0.50
1 Return of the Screw. 3.50
1a variant (c) 3.50
1b Special edition (c) 4.50
2 thru 3 . . . . @3.50
2a thru 3a variant (c)s . . . . @3.50
2b Dorman Special Ed (c) 4.50
3b Nestler Special Ed (c) 4.50

BUCK GODOT: ZAP GUN FOR HIRE
Palliard Press, 1993
1 I:Buck Godot 3.00
2 thru 6 . . . . @3.00
Studio Foglio, 1997
7 by Phil Foglio & Barb Kaalberg . . 3.00
8 finale 3.50
TPB Gallimaufry Vol. 1. . . . . 12.50
TPB Gallimaufry Vol. 2. . . . . 15.00

BUFFALO WINGS
Antarctic Press, 1993
1 & 2 . . . . @2.50

BUG
Planet X Productions, 1997
1 . . . . 2.25
2 . . . . 2.25

B.U.G.G.S
Acetylene Comics, 2001
1 . . . . 2.50
1a variant San Diego Con (c). 3.00
2 thru 5 . . . . @2.50
3a variant (c). 2.50

BUGTOWN
Aeon 2004
1 (of 6) MHo 3.00
2 thru 6 . . . . @3.00

BULLET CROW
Eclipse, 1987
1 & 2 Fowl of Fortune . . . . @2.50

BULWARK
Millennium, 1995
1 I:Bulwark 3.00
2 O:Bulwark 3.00

BUREAU OF MANA INVESTIGATION
Radio Comix, 2002
1 by C.Hanson & E.Garcia 3.00
2 thru 5 . . . . @3.00

BURGLAR BILL
Dancing Elephant Press, 2003
1 (of 6) by Paul Grist 3.00
2 thru 3 . . . . @3.00
4 thru 5 . . . . @3.00

BURNING BLUE, THE
Crusade Entertainment, 2001
1 BTi 3.00
1a computer gen (c) 3.00

BUSHIDO
Eternity, 1988
1 thru 6 . . . . @2.50

BUZZ
Kitchen Sink
1 Mark Landman (c) (1990) 3.00
2 Mark Landman (c) (1990) 3.00
3 Mark Landman (c) (1991) 3.00

Buzzard #7
© Cat Head Comics

BUZZARD
Cat Head Comics, 1990–95
1 thru 9 . . . . @3.00
10 thru 20. . . . . @3.50

CABLE TV
Parody Press
1 Cable Satire. 2.50

CADILLACS AND DINOSAURS
Kitchen Sink, 1992
3-D comic. 4.00

CALIBER CORE
Caliber, 1998
0 48pg. 3.00
1 Gestalt cover 3.00
1a Rain People cover 3.00
1b Spiral cover 3.00
2 F:Al-Haquat 3.00

CALIBER DOUBLE FEATURE
Caliber, 2000
1 48-pg. 4.00
2 . . . . 4.00
3 . . . . 4.00

CALIBER FOCUS
Caliber, 2000
1 48-pg. 4.00
2 thru 4 . . . . @4.00

CALIBER PRESENTS
Caliber, 1989
1 TV,I:Crow 70.00
2 Deadworld 10.00
3 Realm 4.00
4 Baker Street. 4.00
5 TV,Heart of Darkness, Fugitive . . 3.50
6 TV,Heart of Darkness, Fugitive . . 3.50
7 TV,Heart of Darkness,
  Dragonfeast. 3.50
8 TV,Cuda,Fugitive 3.50
9 Baker Street,Sting Inc. 3.50
10 Fugitive, The Edge 3.50
11 Ashes,Random Thoughts 3.50
12 Fugitive,Random Thoughts. . . . 3.50
13 Random Thoughts,Synergist . . . 3.50
14 Random Thoughts,Fugitive. . . . 3.50
15 Fringe, F:The Crow. 4.00
16 Fugitive, The Verdict 3.50
17 Deadworld, The Verdict 3.50
18 Orlak,The Verdict 3.50
19 Taken Under,Go-Man 3.50
20 The Verdict,Go-Man 3.50
21 The Verdict,Go-Man 3.50
22 The Verdict,Go-Man 3.50
23 Go-Man,Heat Seeker 3.50
24 Heat Seeker,MacktheKnife 3.50
Christmas Spec. A:Crow,Deadworld
  Realm,Baker Street. 10.00
Summer Spec. inc. the Silencers,
  Swords of Shar-Pei (preludes) . 4.00
1-Shot 3.00
1-shot Hybrid 3.00

CALIBER SPOTLIGHT
Caliber, 1995
1 F:Kabuki,Oz 3.00

CALIBRATIONS
Caliber, 1996
1 WEI,MCy,`Atmospherics,'pt.1 . . . 3.00
2 WEI,MCy,`Atmospherics,'pt.2 . . . 3.00
3 WEI,MCy,`Atmospherics,'pt.3 . . . 3.00
4 WEI,MCy,`Atmospherics,'pt.4 . . . 3.00
5 WEI,MCy,`Atmospherics,' concl. . 3.00

CALIFORNIA GIRLS
Eclipse, 1987
1 thru 8 . . . . @2.50

CALIGARI 2050
Monster
1 Gothic Horror 2.25
2 &3 Gothic Horror . . . . @2.25

CALL ME PRINCESS
CPM Manga, 1999
1 by Tomoko Taniguchi. 3.00
1a variant cover 3.00
2 thru 6 . . . . @3.00
TPB Vol. 1 . . . . 16.00

CAMELOT ETERNAL
Caliber, 1990
1 . . . . 3.00
2 . . . . 2.50

3 . . . . 2.50
4 Launcelot & Guinevere 2.50
5 Mordred Escapes. 2.50
6 MorganLeFay returns from dead . 2.50
7 Revenge of Morgan. 2.50
8 Launcelot flees Camelot 2.50

CANDYAPPLEBLACK
Good Intentions Paving Co. 2004
1 . . . . 3.50
2 thru 7 . . . . @3.50

CANTON KID
Millennium, 1997
1 . . . . 2.50

Blam Comics 2005
1 (of 4) 3.50
2 thru 4 . . . . @3.50

CAPTAIN CANUCK REBORN
Semple Comics, 1993–96
0 thru 3 by Richard Comely . . . . @2.50

CAPT. CONFEDERACY
Steel Dragon, 1985–88
1 adult. 6.00
2 . . . . 2.50
3 . . . . 2.50
4 . . . . 2.50
4a 2.50
5 thru 12 . . . . @2.50

CAPT. ELECTRON
Brick Computers Inc., 1986
1 . . . . 2.50
2 . . . . 2.50

CAPTAIN HARLOCK
Eternity, 1989
1 BDn. 3.00
1a 2nd printing 2.50
2 thru 3 . . . . @2.50
4 thru 13 . . . . @2.25
Christmas special. 2.50
Spec.#1 The Machine People 2.50

CAPTAIN HARLOCK DEATHSHADOW RISING
Eternity, 1991
1 . . . . 2.75
2 . . . . 2.50
3 . . . . 2.25
4 Harlock/Nevich Truce. 2.25
5 Reunited with Arcadia Crew 2.25
6 . . . . 3.00

CAPTAIN HARLOCK: FALL OF THE EMPIRE
Eternity, 1992
1 thru 4 . . . . @2.50

[ADVENTURES OF] CAPTAIN JACK
Fantagraphics, 1986
1 . . . . 4.00
2 & 3 . . . . @2.50
4 thru 12 . . . . @2.50

CAPTAIN KOALA
Koala Comics, 1997
1 . . . . 3.00
2 thru 7 . . . . @2.50

CAPTAIN STERNN: RUNNING OUT OF TIME
Kitchen Sink, 1993
1 BWr(c) (1993) 6.00
2 BWr(c) 6.00
3 BWr(c) (1994) 6.00
4 BWr(c) 6.00

CAPTAIN THUNDER AND BLUE BOLT
Hero Graphics, 1987
1 New stories 3.50
2 Hard Targets 3.50

Cardcaptor Sakura #28
© *Tokyopop*

CARDCAPTOR SAKURA
Mixx Entertainment, 1999
1 thru 6 by Clamp . . . . @3.00
TPB Pocket Mixx, Vol. 1 thru 5 . @10.00
Tokyopop.Com, 2000
7 thru 25 . . . . @3.00
26 thru 34 . . . . @3.00
GN Vol. 1 Passages. 10.00
GN Vol. 2 Master of the Clow . . . 10.00
GN Vol. 3 thru Vol. 6 . . . . @10.00

CARTOON HISTORY OF THE UNIVERSE
Rip Off Press, 1987
1 Gonick art 2.50
2 Sticks & Stones 2.50
3 River Realms. 2.50
4 Old Testament 2.50
5 Brains & Bronze. 2.50
6 These Athenians 2.50
7 All about Athens 2.50
8 and 9 . . . . @2.50

CASES OF SHERLOCK HOLMES
Renegade, 1986
1 thru 18 . . . . @2.50
19 . . . . 2.50

CASTLE WAITING
Olio, 1997
1 by Linda Medley 10.00
1a 2nd printing 3.00
2 . . . . 5.00
2a 2nd printing 3.00
3 Labors of Love. 3.00
4 birth of Lady Jain's baby 3.00
5 . . . . 3.00

6 City Mouse, Country Mouse,pt.1 . 3.00
7 City Mouse, Country Mouse,pt.2 . 3.00
Spec. The Curse of Brambly
     Hedge (1996) 3.00
Spec. Curse of Brambly Hedge,
     revised 1998, 96-pg. 9.00
TPB Vol. 1 Lucky Road 17.00
VOL. 2, 2000
1 by Linda Medley 3.00
2 Solicitine,pt.1 . . . . 3.00
3 thru 7 . . . . @3.00
#13 (Vol. 2, #6) 3.00
#14 (Vol. 2, #7) 3.00
#15 thru #16 . . . . @3.00
TPB Vol. 1 Lucky Road 18.00
TPB Vol. 2 Solicitine 18.00
GN The Curse of Brambly Hedge . 9.00
Fantagraphics Books 2006 Vol. 2
1 64-pg.. . . . . 6.00
2 . . . . 5.00
3 . . . . 4.00

CAT & MOUSE
Aircel, 1989–92
1 . . . . 4.00
2 . . . . 3.00
3 thru 8 . . . . @2.50
9 Cat Reveals Identity 2.50
10 Tooth & Nail 2.50
11 Tooth & Nail. 2.50
12 Tooth & Nail, Demon. 2.50
13 `Good Times, Bad Times' 2.50
14 Mouse Alone. 2.50
15 Champion ID revealed 2.50
16 Jerry Critically Ill 2.50
17 Kunoichi vs. Tooth. 2.50
18 Search for Organ Donor 2.50
Graphic Novel 10.00

CAT CLAW
Eternity, 1990
1 O:Cat Claw 2.75
1a 2nd printing 2.50
2 thru 9 . . . . @2.50

CATFIGHT
Lightning Comics, 1996
1 V:Prince Nightmare 4.00
1a Gold Edition 6.00
Spec.#1 Dream Warrior,
     V:The Slasher 2.75
Spec.#1 Dream intoAction,A:Creed. 3.00
Spec.#1a signed and numbered . . 8.00
Spec.#1 Escape From Limbo 2.75
Spec.#1a variant cover (1996). . . . 2.75
Spèc.#1b platinum cover 6.00
Spec.#1d variant nude cover 8.00
Spec.#1 Sweet Revenge (1997) . . . 3.00
Spec.#1a variant cover 3.00

CAT-MAN RETRO COMIC
AC Comics, 1997
0 by Bill Black & Mark Heike 6.00
1 thru 3 . . . . @6.00
Ashcan #1 I:Catman & Kitten 6.00

CAVEWOMAN
Basement/Caliber, 1994–95
1 . . . . 70.00
1a by Budd Root 2nd printing. . . . 4.00
1b 3rd printing, new cover 3.00
2 . . . . 40.00
2a 2nd printing 3.00
2 3rd printing, new cover 3.00
3 and 4 . . . . @35.00
5 Cavewoman vs. Klyde,
     Round Two 25.00
6 . . . . 25.00

CAVEWOMAN
Basement Comics 2002
1-shot Movie special edition	9.00
1-shot movie oscar-gold edition	10.00
1-shot Summer Spec. My Kylde has Fleas (2004)	3.50
1-shot Prehistoric Pln-ups #4.	3.50
Spec. Meriem's Gallery #4.	3.25
Spec. Meriem's Gallery #4 spec.ed.	9.00
1-shot flip book Cavewoman Jungle Tales #3/ Blonde Medusa #1	3.75
1-shot Jungle Jam	3.50
1-shot Jungle Jam special ed.	7.00

CAVEWOMAN INTERVENTION
Basement Comics, 2000
1 by Devon Massey	3.00
1a variant Budd Root (c).	9.00
1b gold foil alternate (c)	12.50
2	3.00
2a variant (c).	9.00
2b Purple foil (c).	12.50
Spec. Klyde & Meriem 1-shot	3.00
Spec. Klyde & Meriem, KDM(c).	9.00
Spec. Klyde & Meriem green foil	10.00
Spec. Klyde & Meriem, Beauty, Blizzard & the Beast	9.00
Spec. Beauty, Blizzard, gold foil	12.50
Spec. Prehistoric Pin-ups	4.50
Spec. Prehistoric Pin-ups gold foil	12.50
Spec. Prehistoric Pin-ups, Book 2	4.50
Spec. Prehistoric Pin-ups 2,lim.	9.00
Spec. Prehistoric Pin-ups 2, gold foil	11.50
Spec. Prehistoric Pin-ups 3	4.50
Spec. Prehistoric Pin-Ups 3 Spec.	9.00
Cavewoman Cover Gallery, 48-pg.	4.50
Cavewoman Cover Gallery spec.	9.00
1-shot He Said, She Said	3.50
1-shot He Said, She Said special	9.00
1-shot Cavewoman The Movie	3.25

CAVEWOMAN: JUNGLE TALES
Basement Comics, 2000
1 by Budd Root	3.00
1a Frank Cho (c).	11.00
2	3.00
2a spec. edition.	9.00

CAVEWOMAN: MERIEM'S GALLERY
Basement Comics, 2001
1	3.50
1a Spec. lim. ed.	9.00
1b Gold foil edition	11.50
2 pin-up book	3.50
2a Special edition	9.00
2b gold special edition	11.50
3	3.00
3a	9.00
4	3.25
4a special ed.	9.00

CAVEWOMAN: MISSING LINK
Basement Comics, 1997
1 (of 4)	3.00
2 thru 4	@3.00
TPB 96-pg.	20.00
TPB 2nd printing	10.00

CAVEWOMAN: ODYSSEY
Caliber, 1999
1 (of 5)	3.00
2 thru 4	@3.00

Basement Comics, 2000
1a front row seat (c) by Budd Root	9.00
1b foil (c).	12.50
2a variant (c).	6.00
2b jungle green foil (c)	12.50
1-shot spec.	3.00
1-shot spec. variant (c)	9.00
1-shot spec. foil (c)	12.50

CAVEWOMAN: PANGAEAN SEA
Basement Comics, 1999
0 Origin issue	3.00
0 variant AAd (c).	9.00
0 special Root (c)	10.00
0 green foil (c).	11.50
0 alternate gold foil (c)	11.50
1 by Bud Root.	5.00
1a variant Massey (c)	9.00
1b Root Sea Blue Foil (c).	12.50
1c Cho Sea Blue Foil (c)	12.50
2	3.00
2 Blue Foil (c)	11.50
3	3.25
3 silver foil (c)	11.50
4	3.25
4b red foil edition	11.50
5	3.25
5 red foil edition	11.50
6	3.25
6b red foil (c).	10.00
7	3.25
7a gold foil (c).	9.00
8	3.25
9	3.50
2a thru 9a special edition (c).	@9.00
Spec. #1 Prehistoric Pin-ups	4.50
Prologue.	3.00

CAVEWOMAN: RAIN
Caliber, 1996
1 by Budd Root.	7.00
1a 2nd printing	3.00
2	5.00
2a 2nd printing	3.00
3	4.00
3a 2nd edition, new cover.	3.00
4	4.00
4a 2nd edition, new cover.	3.00
5	3.50
5 2nd edition, new cover.	3.00
6 thru 8	@3.00

CAVEWOMEN: RAPTOR
Basement Comics, 2002
1 (of 2)	3.25
1a special edition	9.00
1b red foil edition	11.50
2	3.25
2a special edition	9.00
2b Purple foil (c)	11.50

CAVEWOMAN: RELOADED
Basement Comics 2005
1 thru 3	@4.00
2a thru 3a special edition.	@8.00

CECIL KUNKLE
Darkline Comics, 1987
1	2.50

CELESTIAL MECHANICS
Innovation, 1990
1 thru 3	@2.25

CELESTIAL ZONE
Asiapac Books, 2000
1 by Wee Tian Beng	9.00

2 thru 8	@9.00
9 152-pg.	9.00
11 Fantasy on Moonlit Lotus	9.00
12 THe Battle of Maling	9.00
13 Assault on Mt. Dream-Cloud.	10.00
14 An Onerous Battle.	10.00
15 Capturing Mt. Dream-Cloud	10.00
16 Chi Xue & Xuan Hua injured	10.00

TCZ Studio, 2002
17 thru 25 152-pg.	@10.00

Vol. 2
1	10.00
2 thru 16	@9.50

Cement Shooz #1
© Horse Feathers

CEMENT SHOOZ
Horse Feathers, 1991
1 with color pin-up	2.50

CEMETARIANS, THE
Amaze Ink/SLG, 2006
1	3.00
2 thru 3	@3.00

CEREBUS
Aardvark–Vanaheim, 1977
0	3.00
0a Gold Ed.	10.00
1 B:DS(s&a),I:Cerebus	500.00
1a Counterfeit.	50.00
2 DS,V:Succubus	110.00
3 DS,I:Red Sophla	126.00
4 DS,I:Elrod	75.00
5 DS,A:The Pigts	60.00
6 DS,I:Jaka.	60.00
7 DS,R:Elrod.	45.00
8 DS,A:Conniptins	45.00
9 DS,I&V:K'cor	45.00
10 DS,R:Red Sophia	45.00
11 DS,I:The Cockroach	30.00
12 DS,R:Elrod	30.00
13 DS,I:Necross.	25.00
14 DS,V:Shadow Crawler	25.00
15 DS,V: Shadow Crawler.	25.00
16 DS, at the Masque	20.00
17 DS,`Champion'.	20.00
18 DS,Fluroc	20.00
19 DS,I:Perce & Greet-a	20.00
20 DS,Mind Game.	20.00
21 DS,A:CaptCockroach,rare	40.00
22 DS,D:Elrod.	20.00
23 thru 29 DS.	@10.00
30 DS,Debts.	15.00
31 DS,Chasing Cootie.	15.00
32 DS.	8.00
33 DS,Friction	5.00

All comics prices listed are for *Near Mint* condition.

Cerebus #47
© Aardvark-Vanaheim

34 thru 50 DS . . . . @6.00
51 DS,(scarce). 12.00
52 DS 5.00
53 DS,C:Wolveroach 7.00
54 DS,I:Wolveroach 9.00
55 DS,A:Wolveroach 8.00
56 DS,A:Wolveroach 8.00
57 DS 5.00
58 DS 5.00
59 DS,Memories,pt.V 5.00
60 DS,more vignettes 5.00
61 DS,A:Flaming Carrot 6.00
62 DS,A:Flaming Carrot 6.00
63 thru 66 DS . . . . @5.00
67 thru 70 DS . . . . @5.00
71 thru 81 DS . . . . @4.00
82 thru 100 DS . . . . @3.50
101 thru 125 DS . . . . @3.00
126 thru 130 DS . . . . @2.50
131 thru 146 DS . . . . @4.00
147 Neil Gaiman, DS 6.00
148 thru 150 DS . . . . @3.00
151 DS,B:Mothers & Daughters,
   Book 1: Flight,pt.1 . . . . 4.00
152 thru 155 DS,Flight,pt.2–pt.5 . @4.00
151a thru 53a 2nd printings . . . . @2.50
156 thru 160 DS,Flight,pt.6–pt.10 @3.00
161 DS,Flight,pt.11, Bone story . . . 15.00
162 DS,E:M&D,Bk.1:Flight pt.12 . . . 3.00
163 DS, Book 2: Women,pt.1 . . . . . 2.75
164 thru 174 Women,pt.2–12 . . . @3.00
175 thru 186 Reads,pt.1–12 . . . @3.00
187 DS, Book 4:Minds,pt.1 . . . . . . 3.00
188 thru 199 Minds,pt.2–13 . . . . @3.00
200 . . . . 3.50
201 thru 219 Guys,pt.1 to pt.19 . @3.00
220 thru 231 Rick'sStory,pt.1–12 . @3.00
232 thru 265 GoingHome,pt.1–34 @2.50
266 thru 296 LatterDays,pt.1–
   pt.31 . . . . @2.50
297 Latter Days, pt.32 . . . . 2.50
298 Latter Days, pt.33 . . . . 2.50
299 Latter Days, pt.34 . . . . 2.50
300 Latter Days, pt.35, finale. 2.50
Spec.#1 Cerebus Companion 3.50
Spec. Following Cerebus #1 . . . . . 4.00
Spec. Following Cerebus #2 . . . . . 4.00
Spec. Following Cerebus #3 . . . . . 4.00
Spec. Following Cerebus #4 . . . . . 4.00
Spec. Following Cerebus #5 . . . . . 4.00
Spec. Following Cerebus #6
   thru #10 . . . . @4.00
TPBs
Vol.1 Cerebus, rep.#1–#25 . . . . . 25.00
Vol.2 High Society, rep.#26–#50 . . 25.00
Vol.3 Church&StateI,rep.#52–#85 . 30.00

Vol.4 Church&StateII,rep.#86–#111 30.00
Vol.5 Jaka'sStory,rep.#114–#136. . 25.00
Vol.6 Melmoth, rep.#139–#150 . . 17.00
Vol.7, Flight, rep.#151–#162 . . . . . 17.00
Vol.8 Women, rep.#163–#174 . . . 17.00
Vol.9 Reads, rep.#175–#186 . . . . 17.00
Vol.9 Reads, 2nd printing. 15.00
Vol.9 Reads, signed & numb. 28.00
Vol.10 Minds, rep.#187–#199 . . . 16.00
Vol.11 Guys rep.#201–#219 . . . . 30.00
Vol.11, 2nd printing 20.00
Vol.12 Rick's Story 17.00
Vol.12 signed 25.00
Vol.13 Going Home, 420-pg. 25.00
Vol.13 deluxe 37.00
Vol.14 Form & Void 25.00
Vol.14a deluxe 37.00
Vol.15 Latter Days 30.00
Vol.15 signed 40.00
Vol.16 . . . . 20.00

CEREBUS
CHURCH & STATE
Aardvark–Vanaheim, 1991
1 DS rep #51 . . . . 2.50
2 thru 30 DS rep #52–#80 . . . . . @2.50

CEREBUS HIGH SOCIETY
Aardvark–Vanaheim, 1990
1 thru 14 DS (biweekly) . . . . @2.50
15 thru 24 DS rep. . . . . @2.50
25 DS rep. #50, final 2.50

CEREBUS JAM
Aardvark–Vanaheim, 1985
1 MA,BHa,TA,WE,A:Spirit. 15.00

CEREBUS REPRINTS
Aardvark–Vanaheim
1A thru 28A DS rep . . . . @2.50
See also: Church & State
See also: Swords of Cerebus

CHAINSAW VIGILANTE
New England Press
1 Tick Spinoff 3.25
2 & 3 . . . . @2.75

CHAMPION OF KITARA:
DUM DUM & DRAGONS
MU Press, 1992
1 Dragons Secret 3.00
2 Dragons Secret 3.00
3 Dragons Secret 3.00

CHANGE COMMANDER
GOKU II
Antarctic Press, 1996
1 (of 4) by Ippongi Bang. 3.00
2 . . . . 3.00
3 . . . . 3.00
TPB Vol 1, Change Commander
   Goku, rep. #1–#5. . . . . 13.00

CHARLIE CHAN
Eternity, 1989
1 thru 6 . . . . @2.50

CHARM SCHOOL
Amaze Ink/SLG, 2000
1 by Elizabeth Watasin 3.00
2 . . . . 3.00
4 Vampire Dragster Dean 3.00
5 Vampire Dragster Dean 3.00
6 fight to the death 3.00
7 thru 9 . . . . 3.00
10 . . . . 10.00

TPB Vol. 1 Magical Witch
   Girl Bunny 12.00

CHASER PLATOON
Aircel, 1990–91
1 Interstellar War 2.25
2 Ambush 2.25
3 New Weapon 2.25
4 Saringer Battle Robot 2.25
5 Behind Enemy Lines 2.25
6 Operation Youthtest 2.25

CHESTY SANCHEZ
Antarctic Press, 1995
1 & 2 . . . . @3.00
Giant Size Spec. #1 (1999) 6.00

CHIBI-POP MANGA
Chibi-Pop (1998)
2 thru 6 64-pg. . . . . @4.00
VOL 2
1 72-pg. 4.00
2 thru 6 . . . . @4.00

CHICANOS
IDW Publishing, 2005
1 . . . . 4.00
2 thru 9 . . . . @4.00
TPB Vol. 1 . . . . 20.00

CHINA & JAZZ
ABC Comics, 1999
1 RCI 3.00
VOL. 2
1 (of 3) RCI 3.00
2 RCI 3.00
Spec. Raising Hell 5.00

CHINA & JAZZ
CODE NAME
DOUBLE IMPACT
High Impact, 1996
1 and 2 . . . . @3.00

CHINA & JAZZ:
TRIGGER HAPPY
ABC Comics, 1998
1 (of 4) by Clayton Henry 3.00
1a Jazz Bikini cover 4.00
1b China Bikini cover 4.00
1c gold variant cover 6.00
2 . . . . 3.00
2a Playtoy edition 6.00
2b Mercenary edition 6.00
2c Gold edition 6.00
Spec. Trigger Happy Special 3.00
Spec.A manga cover 8.00
Spec. China & Jazz 3.00

CHINA & JAZZ:
SUPERSTARS
ABC Studios, 1999
1 (of 3) 3.00
Spec. China Platinum 3.00

CHIRALITY
CPM Manga Comics, 1997
6 by Satoshi Urushihara, SS(c) . . . 3.00
7 final battle for Shiori's life 3.00
8 thru 18 . . . . @3.00
Spec. Gallery, pin-up book. 4.00
GN Book One rep.#1–#4 . . . . . . 10.00
GN Book Two rep. #4–#8 . . . . . . 10.00
TPB Book Three rep. #8–#12 . . . . 16.00
TPB Book Four, rep. #13–#18. . . . 16.00

CHIRALITY:
TO THE PROMISED LAND
CPM Comics, 1997
1 by Satoshi Urushihara 3.00
2 thru 4 . . . . @3.00

CHIRON
Annurel Studio Graphics
1 . . . . 2.50
1a 2nd printing 2.50
2 Transported to Doran. 2.50
3 Transported to Doran. 2.50
3a Gold Edition. 4.00

CHISUJI
Antarctic Press 2005
1 (of 6) 3.00
2 thru 3 . . . . @3.00

CIRCLE WEAVE, THE
Indigo Bean Productions, 1995
1 Apprentice to a God. 2.25
2 Apprentice to a God,pt.2 . . . . . . 2.25
3 Apprentice to a God,pt.3 . . . . . . 2.25
4 Apprentice to a God,pt.4 . . . . . . 2.25
5 Apprentice to a God,pt.5 . . . . . . 2.50

CLAN APIS
Active Synapse, 1998
1 (of 5) by Jay Hosler, F:Bees 3.00
2 F:Nyuki, Zambur 3.00
3 . . . . 3.00
4 . . . . 3.00
5 conclusion 3.00
TPB 160-pg.. . . . . 15.00

CLANDE, INC.
Domain Publishing
1 I:Sam Davidson, Jeremy Clande. 3.00
2 V:Dias 3.00

CLERKS:
THE COMIC BOOK
Oni Press, 1998
1 KSm & Jim Mahfood 12.00
1a 2nd printing 4.00
Spec. The Lost Scene 5.00
Holiday Special 5.00
TPB 11.00

CLIFFHANGER COMICS
AC Comics, 1990
1 Masked Marvel, rcp. 2.50
2 Don Winslow, rep. 2.50
1A & 2A . . . . @3.00

CLINT THE HAMSTER
Eclipse
1 . . . . 2.50
2 . . . . 2.50

COBB: OFF THE LEASH
IDW Publishing 2006
1 . . . . 4.00
2 thru 3 . . . . @4.00

COBRA
Viz, 1990–91
1 thru 6 . . . . @3.00
7 . . . . 3.25
8 V:SnowHawks 3.25
9 Zados. 3.25
10 thru 12 . . . . @3.25

COCOPIAZO
Amaze Ink/SLG, 2004
1 . . . . 3.00
2 thru 6 . . . . @3.00

COFFIN
Oni Press, 2000
1 . . . . 3.00
2 thru 4 . . . . @3.00
TPB 112-pg. 12.00

Cold Blooded Chameleon Commandos
#3 © Blackthorne

COLD BLOODED
CHAMELEON
COMMANDOS
Blackthorne, 1986
1 thru 7 . . . . @2.50

COLD EDEN
Legacy, 1995
1 Last City on Earth 2.35
2 V:Mutant Hunting Pack 2.35
3 D6 Tower 2.35

COLE BLACK
Rocky Hartberg, 1980
1 Newspaper strip format 15.00
2 . . . . 10.00
3 . . . . 10.00
4 . . . . 10.00
5 . . . . 12.00
Vol. 2, 1985
1 . . . . 3.50
2 & 3 . . . . @2.25

COLONEL KILGORE
Special Studios
1 WWII stories 2.50
2 Command Performance. 2.50

COLT
K-Z Comics
1 . . . . 4.00
2 pin-up by Laird. 6.00
2 pin-up by Henbeck. 2.25
3 thru 5 . . . . @2.25

COMIC BOOK HEAVEN
Amaze Ink/SLG, 2001
Vol. 2
1 . . . . 2.25

2 thru 5 . . . . @2.25
6 thru 9 . . . . @2.25
10 48-pg. 3.50

COMICS EXPRESS
Eclipse, 1989
1 thru 4 . . . . @3.00
5 thru 11 . . . . @4.00

COMING OF APHRODITE
Hero Graphics
1 Aphrodite/modern day 4.00

COMMAND REVIEW
Thoughts & Images, 1986
1 rep. Albedo #1-4 . . . . 6.00
2 rep. Albedo #5-8 . . . . 4.00
3 rep. Albedo #9-13 . . . . 4.00

CONDOM-MAN
Aaaahh!! Comics
1 I:Condom Man. 3.50
2 F:Condom Man 3.50
3 V:Alien Army 3.50
4 Brother bought back to life 3.50
5 O:Condom-Man (Chris Swafford) 3.50

CONQUEROR
Harrier, 1984–86
1 . . . . 3.50
2 thru 4 . . . . @2.50
5 thru 9 . . . . @2.50

CONSPIRACY COMICS
Revolutionary, 1991
1 Marilyn Monroe. 2.50
2 Who Killed JFK 2.50
3 Who Killed RFK. 2.50

CONSTELLATION
GRAPHICS
Stages Comics 1986
1 thru 2 . . . . @2.25

CONSTRUCT
Caliber New Worlds, 1996
1 (of 6) PJe,LDu, sci-fi,48pg 4.00
2 PJe,LDu. 3.00
3 PJe,LDu. 3.00
4 PJe,LDu. 3.00
5 PJe,LDu. 3.00
6 PJe,LDu, conclusion 3.00

CORPORATE NINJA
Amaze Ink/Slave Labor Graphics
2005
1 . . . . 3.00
2 thru 3 . . . . @3.00

CORRECTOR YUI
Tokyopop Press, 2001
1 48-pg. 3.00
2 . . . . 3.00
3 . . . . 3.00
4 . . . . 3.00

CORTO MALTESE:
BALLAD OF
THE SALT SEA
NBM, 1997
1 by Hugo Pratt. 3.00
1 a 2nd printing 3.00
2 by Hugo Pratt. 3.00
3 Escondida 3.00
4 . . . . 3.00
5 . . . . 3.00

All comics prices listed are for *Near Mint* condition.

6 . . . . 3.00
7 final issue 3.00
TPB by Hugo Pratt, `In Siberia' . . . 11.00
TPB `Fable of Venice' 11.00
TPB `Banana Conga' 9.00
TPB `Voodoo for the President'. . . . 9.00
TPB `Midwinter's Morning' 9.00
TPB `In Africa' 9.00

Cosmic Heroes #7
© Eternity

COSMIC HEROES
Eternity, 1988
1 Buck Rogers rep. 2.50
2 thru 6 Buck Rogers rep. . . . . . @2.50
7 thru 9 Buck Rogers rep. . . . . . @2.50
10 . . . . 3.50
11 . . . . 4.00

COUNTER PARTS
Tundra, 1993
1 thru 3 . . . . @3.00

COURTNEY CRUMRIN &
THE COVEN OF MYSTICS
Oni Press, 2003
1 (of 4) by Ted Naifeh 3.00
2 thru 4 . . . . @3.00
TPB Vol. 1 . . . . 12.00
TPB The Night Things 12.00

COURTNEY CRUMRIN IN
THE TWILIGHT KINGDOM
Oni Press, 2003
1 (of 4) 3.00
2 thru 4 . . . . @3.00
TPB 12.00

COVENTRY
Fantagraphics, 1996
1 BWg, `The Frogs of God' 4.00
2 BWg, `Thirteen Dead Guys
   Named Bob' 4.00
3 BWg. 4.00
4 . . . . 4.00

COWBOY BEBOP
Tokyopop Press, 2002
1 (of 4) by Yukata Nanten. 3.00
2 thru 4 . . . . @3.00
Spec. Complete Anime Guide #1. . 13.00
Spec. Complete Anime
   Guide #2–#6 . . . . @13.00

CRAY BABY
ADVENTURES, THE
Electric Milk, 1997
1 by Art Baltazar 3.00
TV Comics, 1997
1 2nd printing 3.00
2 . . . . 3.00
4 Captain Camel 3.00
5 . . . . 3.00
Advent.Spec.San Diego Con
   lim. ed. 5.00
TPB Vol. 1 rep. #1–#5 . . . . 15.00

CRAY BABY
ADVENTURES: WRATH
OF THE PEDDIDLERS
TV Comics, 1998
1 (of 3) by Art Baltazar 3.00
2 . . . . 3.00
3 concl. 3.00

CREATURES OF THE ID
Caliper, 1990
1 F. Einstein(a) 30.00

CREED
Hall of Heroes, 1994
1 TKn,I:Mark Farley 25.00
1A Wizard Ace edition rep. 20.00
2 TKn,Camping. 35.00
TPB The Void, Collected ed. 6.00
TPB Deluxe 10.00

CREED
Lightning Comics, 1995
1-shot TKn retelling of #1&#2 . . . . 2.75
See also: Color

CREED/TEENAGE
MUTANT NINJA TURTLES
Lightning Comics, 1996
1 TKn(c) 3.00
2 TKn(c) 3.00
1 Gold Collector's Edition 6.00
1 Platinum Edition. 10.00

CREED:
CRANIAL DISORDER
Lightning Comics, 1996
1 . . . . 4.00
1A Previews variant cover 3.00
1B Platinum Edition 6.00
1C signed platinum edition 8.00
2 . . . . 3.00
2b variant cover 3.00
3 . . . . 3.00
3b variant cover 3.00
3c limited edition 10.00

CREED: THE GOOD
SHIP & THE NEW
JOURNEY HOME
Lightning Comics, 1998
1 . . . . 3.00
1a variant cover 3.00
1b limited edition 10.00

CREED: MECHANICAL
EVOLUTION
Gearbox Press, 2000
1 (of 2) 3.00
1a variant (c). 3.00
1b signed 10.00
2 . . . . 3.00

CREED: USE
YOUR DELUSION
Avatar Press, 1998
1 (of 2) by Trent Kaniuga 3.00
1 white leather 30.00
2 . . . . 3.00
2 deluxe 5.00
GN rep. #1–#2 . . . . 4.00

CRIME BUSTER
AC Comics
0 from FemForce 3.00
1 Rep. From Boys Illustrated 4.00

CRIMEBUSTER
ACG Comics, 2000
1 (of 3) F:Dick Tracy 3.00
2 & 3 . . . . @3.00

CRIME CLASSICS
Eternity, 1988
1 thru 11 rep. Shadow comic
   strip . . . . @2.50
12 . . . . 2.50

CRIMSON DREAMS
Crimson
1 thru 11 . . . . @2.25

CRITTERS
Fantagraphics Books, 1986–90
1 SS,Usagi Yojimbo,Cutey 7.00
2 Captain Jack,Birthright. 6.00
3 SS,Usagi Yojimbo,Gnuff 5.00
4 Gnuff,Birthright. 5.00
5 Birthright 5.00
6 SS,Usagi Yojimbo,Birthright. . . . 5.00
7 SS,Usagi Yojimbo,Jack Bunny . 5.00
8 SK,Animal Graffiti,Lizards 5.00
9 Animal Graffiti 5.00
10 SS,Usagi Yojimbo 5.00
11 SS,Usagi Yojimbo, ... 3.00
12 Birthright II 2.50
13 Birthright II,Gnuff. 2.50
14 SS,Usagi Yojimbo,BirthrightII . . 3.00
15 Birthright II,CareBears 2.50
16 SS,Groundthumper,Gnuff 2.50
17 Birthright II,Lionheart 2.50
18 Dragon's 2.50
19 Gnuff,Dragon's 2.50
20 Gnuff 2.50
21 Gnuff. 2.50
22 Watchdogs,Gnuff 2.50
23 Flexi-Disc,X-Mas Issue 4.00
24 Angst,Lizards,Gnuff. 2.50
25 Lionheart,SBi,Gnuff. 2.50
26 Angst,Gnuff. 2.50
27 SS,Ground Thumper. 2.50
28 Blue Beagle,Lionheart 2.50
29 Lionheart,Gnuff 2.50
30 Radical Dog,Gnuff 2.50
31 SBi,Gnuffs,Lizards 2.50
32 Lizards,Big Sneeze 2.50
33 Gnuff,Angst,Big Sneeze 2.50
34 Blue Beagle vs. Robohop 2.50
35 Lionheart,Fission Chicken 2.50
36 Blue Beagle,Fission Chicken . . . 2.50
37 Fission Chicken 2.50
38 SS,double size,Usagi Yojimbo . 4.00
39 Fission Chicken 2.50
40 Gnuff 2.50
41 Duck'Bill Platypus 2.50
42 Glass Onion 2.50
43 Lionheart 2.50
44 Watchdogs 2.50
45 Ambrose the Frog. 2.50
46 Lionheart 2.50
47 Birthright 2.50
48 Birthright 2.50

49 Birthright 2.50
50 SS,Neil the Horse, UsagiYojimbo 5.00
Spec.1 Albedo,rep+new 10pgStory . 2.50

CROSSFIRE
Eclipse, 1987
Prev. Color
18 thru 26 DSp . . . . @2.50

CROW, THE
Caliber, 1989
1 . . . . 55.00
1a 2nd Printing 6.00
1b 3rd Printing 5.00
2 . . . . 35.00
2a 2nd Printing 4.00
2b 3rd Printing 4.00
3 . . . . 25.00
3a 2nd Printing 4.00
4 . . . . 25.00

Tundra, 1992
1 reps. Crow #1, #2 . . . . 15.00
2 . . . . 8.00
3 . . . . 10.00
TPB 20.00

CROW, THE
Kitchen Sink, 1996
TPB Flesh & Blood Collection 11.00
TPB The Crow Collection,
   7th printing 224pg 16.00

CROW, THE: DEAD TIME
Kitchen Sink, 1996
1 . . . . 5.00
2 . . . . 4.00
3 . . . . 3.00
TPB Collection rep. 11.00

CROW, THE: DEMON IN DISGUISE
Kitchen Sink, 1997
1 (of 4) by John J. Miller &
   Dean Ormston 3.00
2 . . . . 3.00
3 . . . . 3.00

CROW, THE: FLESH AND BLOOD
Kitchen Sink, 1996
1 thru 3 . . . . @3.00
TPB rep. 96-pg. 11.00

CROW, THE: WAKING NIGHTMARES
Kitchen Sink, 1997
1 PhH 3.00
2 thru 4 PhH . . . . @3.00

CROW, THE: WILD JUSTICE, 1996
Kitchen Sink
1 thru 3 CAd . . . . @3.00

CROW/RAZOR: KILL THE PAIN
London Night, 1998
1 (of 3) JOb,EHr, ... 3.00
1b EHr & Jerry Beck, Director's
   Cut, 40pg 5.00
1c black leather, signed
   & numbered 30.00
1d Ministry of Night (c) 5.00
1e Ministry (c) signed 15.00
1f black leather, red foil logos 20.00

The Crow, Wild Justice #1
© *Kitchen Sink*

2 . . . . 3.00
2a Ministry of Night (c) 5.00
2b Leather edition 10.00
3 . . . . 3.00
3a Ministry of Night (c) 5.00
4 . . . . 3.00
4a Ministry of Night (c) 6.00
4b Leather edition 15.00
4c Leather edition, signed 15.00
Spec. Finale 3.00
Spec. Finale, Ministry (c) 5.00
0 . . . . 3.00
0a Ministry (c) 5.00
0b Red Velvet Elite 20.00
1-shotA Tour Book, cover A 5.00
1-shotB Tour Book, cover B 5.00
1-shotC Tour Book, cover C 5.00
1-shotD Tour Book, ministry edition 5.00
1-shotE Tour Book, limited black
   leather 15.00
1-shotF Tour Book, signed 18.00
Spec. Nocturnal Masque 48-pg. . . . 6.00
TPB Kill The Pain, 150-pg. 16.00

EH! Productions, 1999
Spec. The Lost Chapter 5.00
Spec. The Lost Chapter,
   Elite Fan Ed. 6.00

CROW OF THE BEAR CLAN
Blackthorne, 1986
1 . . . . 2.50
2 thru 6 . . . . @2.50

CRUSADERS
Guild, 1982
1 Southern Knights, Mag. size . . . 10.00

CRUSHER JOE
Ironcat, 1999
1 by Haruka Takachiho 3.00
2 thru 6 . . . . @3.00
TPB 16.00

CRY FOR DAWN
Cry For Dawn, 1989–90
1 . . . . 120.00
1a 2nd Printing 40.00
1b 3rd Printing 30.00
2 . . . . 75.00
2a 2nd Printing 25.00
3 . . . . 45.00

4 . . . . 20.00
5 . . . . 20.00
6 . . . . 20.00
7 Corporate Ladder,Rock A
   Bye Baby 15.00
8 Decay,This is the Enemy 15.00
9 . . . . 15.00
1-shot Subtle Violents,F:Ryder 3.00

CRYING FREEMAN
Viz, 1989
1 . . . . 4.00
2 . . . . 3.50
3 thru 5 . . . . @3.50
6 thru 8 . . . . @3.00

CRYING FREEMAN II
Viz, 1990–91
1 . . . . 4.00
2 . . . . 3.50
3 . . . . 3.50
4 thru 6 . . . . @3.00
7 V:Bugnug 3.00
8 Emu & The Samurai Sword 3.00
9 Final Issue 3.00

CRYING FREEMAN III
Viz, 1991
1 thru 10 . . . . @4.00

CRYING FREEMAN IV
Viz, 1992
1 thru 3 . . . . @4.00
4 thru 8 . . . . @2.75

CRY FREEMAN V
Viz, 1993
1 Return to Japan 4.00
2 A:Tateoka-assassin 4.00
3 . . . . 4.00
4 A:Bagwana 4.00
5 V:Tsunaike 4.00
6 V:Aido Family 4.00
7 V:Tsunaike 4.00
GN:Taste of Revenge 15.00

CRYPT OF DAWN
Sirius, 1996
1 JLi(c) 6.00
1 variant cover 10.00
2 JLi(c) 4.00
3 . . . . 3.00
4 JLi(c) 3.00
5 JLi(c) 3.00
6 Vanguard of Comics 3.00

CRYPTOZOO CREW
NBM Books 2005
1 . . . . 3.00
2 The Improbable Snowman 3.00
Spec. Mothman con edition 3.00
TPB Vol. 1 . . . . 10.00
TPB Vol. 2 . . . . 13.00
TPB Vol. 1 color edition . . . . . . @13.00

CRYSTAL BREEZE
High Impact, 1996
1 thru 3 . . . . @3.00
Spec.#1 Crystal Breeze Unleashed . 3.00
Spec.#1 Crystal Breeze Revenge . . 3.00
Spec.#1a gold edition cover 10.00

CSI: DYING IN THE GUTTERS
IDW Publishing 2006
1 . . . . 4.00
2 thru 3 . . . . @4.00

B & W PUB.

All comics prices listed are for *Near Mint* condition.

CUDA
Rebel Studios
1 I:Cuda,Zora,V:Shanga Bai 2.25
CUDA B.C. (Rebel Studios) signed 13.00
Avatar Press, 1998
1 (of 4) by Tim & Joe Vigil 3.50
1b Leather cover 20.00
1c signed 15.00
1d Royal Blue edition 60.00
2 . . . . 3.50
3 . . . . 3.50
4 . . . . 3.50
1 thru 4 gore (c) . . . . @6.00
0 80-pg. 8.00
0a Gore (c) 9.00
0c prism foil (c) 13.00
0d Royal blue 75.00
TPB Vol. 1, 160-pg. 20.00

CUTEY BUNNY
Army Surplus Comix, 1982
1 . . . . 8.00
2 . . . . 4.00
3 . . . . 4.00
4 . . . . 4.00
Eclipse, 1985
5 X-Men, Batman parody 3.00

CUTIE HONEY
Ironcat, 1997
1 crime fighting android 3.00
2 . . . . 3.00
3 Wonderful Mask 3.00
4 thru 6 . . . . @3.00
VOL 2, 1998
CUTIE HONEY '90
1 Sorayama cover 3.00
2 thru 6 . . . . @3.00

CYBER 7
Eclipse, 1989
1 by Shuho Itahashi 2.50
2 thru 7 . . . . @2.50
Book 2: Rockland, 1990
1 thru 7 . . . . @2.25
8 thru 10 . . . . @2.50

CYBERFROG
Hall of Heroes, 1994
1 I:Cyberfrog 5.00
1a 2nd printing 2.50
2 V:Ben Riley 4.00
2a 2nd printing 2.50

CYBERFROG
Harris, 1997
1 3rd Anniv. Special 3.00
1a Walt Simonson(c) 6.00
1b signed & numbered 10.00
2 . . . . 3.50
2a variant cover 4.00
3 . . . . 3.50
4 . . . . 3.50
4a signed 10.00
Ashcan Cyberfrog: Amphibionix . . . 6.00
Spec. Cyberfrog Amphibionix(2001) 3.00

CYBERFROG VS CREED
Harris, 1997
1 . . . . 3.50
1 Creed vs. Cyberfrog, alternate
  edition 10.00

CYBERZONE
Jet Black Grafiks, 1994
1 thru 8 Never-never Land . . . . . @2.50

CYCLONE BILL AND THE TALL TALES
Moonstone Books 2004
1 . . . . 3.00
2 thru 3 . . . . @3.00
TPB 17.00

CYCLOPS
Blackthorne
1 Mini-series 2.50
2 . . . . 2.50
3 . . . . 2.50

Cycops #2
© Comics Interview

CYCOPS
Comics Interview, 1988
1 Mini-series, BSz. 2.50
2 . . . . 2.50
3 . . . . 2.50

CYGNUS X-1
Twisted Pearl Press
1 V:Yag'Nost 2.50
2 F:Rex and Bounty Hunters 2.50

CYNDER
Immortelle Studios, 1995
1 I:Cynder 5.00
2 . . . . 3.00
3 conclusion 2.50
Second Series, 1996
1 thru 3 . . . . 3.00

CYNDER/HELLINA
Immortelle Studios, 1996
Spec. 1 x-over 3.00

DAEMONIFUGE: THE SCREAMING CAGE
Black Library, 2002
1 by Kev Walker 2.50
2 and 3 . . . . @2.50

DAIKAZU
Ground Zero
1 . . . . 5.00
2 . . . . 3.00
3 . . . . 3.00
1a thru 3a 2nd Printings . . . . @2.50
4 thru 8 . . . . @2.25

DAISY KUTTER
Viper Comics 2004
1 . . . . 4.00
2 thru 4 . . . . @4.00
TPB Vol. 1 . . . . 11.00

DA'KOTA
Millennium, 1997
1 by Pavlet & Petersen 3.00
1 signed 5.00
1 foil edition 10.00
2 . . . . 3.00
2 foil edition 5.00
3 . . . . 3.00
3a variant cover 3.00
3b foil deluxe edition 7.00
Spec.#1 Orig.Art Edition 10.00

DAMNED, THE
Oni Press 2006
1 & 2 . . . . @3.50

DAMONSTREIK
Imperial Comics
1 I:Damonstreik. 2.25
2 V:Sonix. 2.25
3 V:Sonix. 2.25
4 J:Ohm 2.25
5 V:Drakkus 2.25

DAMPYR
IDW Publishing 2005
GN #1 Devil's Son 8.00
GN #2 Night Tribe 8.00
GN #3 Sand Specters 8.00
GN #4 Nocturne in Red 8.00
GN #5 Under the Stone Bridge 8.00
GN #6 Lamiah 8.00
GN #7 From the Darkness. 8.00
GN #8 Coast of Skeletons 8.00
GN #9 Forbidden Zone 8.00
GN #10 House of Blood 8.00

DANGEROUS TIMES
Evolution, 1989
1 MK 2.50
2 MA(c) 2.25
2a 2nd printing 2.25
3 MR(c) 2.25
3a 2nd printing 2.25
4 thru 6 GP(c) . . . . @2.25

DAN TURNER HOLLYWOOD DETECTIVE
Eternity, 1991
1 `Darkstar of Death' 2.50
Spec.#1 Dan Turner, Homicide
  Hunch, Dan Turner Framed . . . 2.50
Spec.#1 Dan Turner, The Star
  Chamber, Death of Folly
  Hempstead 2.50

DARK ANGEL
Boneyard, 1991
1 by Hart Fisher 2.25
2 . . . . 2.25

DARK ANGEL
Boneyard, 1997
1 by H.Fisher & J.Helkowski. 2.25
2 . . . . 2.25
3 by Hart Fisher & John Cassaday . . 2.25
4 The Quiet Demon 2.25
Spec.#1 Dark Angel/Bill the Bull,
  48-pg. (1998). 5.00
Spec. 1999. . . . . 5.00
GN Last Decade Dead Century. . . 16.00
GN deluxe 20.00

All comics prices listed are for *Near Mint* condition.

DARK ANGEL
CPM Manga, 1999
1 by Kia Asamiya	3.00
2 thru 9	@3.00
10 thru 31	@3.00
TPB Vol. 1 rep. #1–#5	16.00
TPB Vol. 2	16.00
TPB Vol. 3	16.00

DARK ASSASSIN
Silverwolf, 1987
1 thru 3	@2.50

Vol. 2
1 thru 5	@2.50

DARK CITY ANGEL
Freak Pit Productions
1 I:Lt.Michelle Constello	3.50
2	3.50
3 Sex Doll is Prime Suspect	3.50

DARK FANTASIES
Dark Fantasy, 1994–97
0 Donna Mia foil (c)	8.00
0 Destiny Angel foil (c)	7.50
1 Jli (c)	9.00
1a test print Jli (c)	12.00
1 2nd printing	4.00
1 signed & numbered	8.00
2 Kevin J. Taylor Girl (c)	4.00
2a foil stamped	3.00
3 JOb Crow (c)	4.00
3a foil stamped	3.50
4	4.00
4a foil stamped	3.50
5	4.00
5a foil stamped	3.50
6 Angel Destiny	4.00
6a foil stamped	3.50
7	4.00
7a foil stamped	3.50
8	4.00
8 Blue cover	3.50
8 Red cover	3.50
8 deluxe foil-enhanced	4.00
9 Destiny Angel (c)	3.50
9a Destiny Angel, red foil (c)	4.00
9b Horror (c)	3.50
9c Horror, red foil (c)	4.00
10	3.50
10a red foil (c)	4.00
Spec.#1 Summers Eve Pin-up	3.00
Spec.#1 foil-stamped	3.50

DARK FRINGE
Brainstorm, 1996
1	3.00

DARK FRINGE: SPIRITS OF THE DEAD
Brainstorm, 1997
1 by Eman Torre & John Kisse	3.00
2 concl.	3.00

DARK ISLAND
Davdez Arts, 1998
1 by Barry Blair & Colin Chan.	2.50
2 thru 4	@2.50

DARKLIGHT: PRELUDE
Sirius, 2000
1 (of 3) by Teri Sue Wood	3.00
2	3.00
3 concl	3.00

DARK LORD
RAK
1 thru 3	@2.25

DARK MANGA
London Night
1 Featuring Demonique	5.00

DARK MUSE
Dark Muse Productions
1 with mini-comic	3.50
1a with mini-comic	5.00
2	4.00
3 F:Coffin Joe	4.00

DARK OZ
Arrow Comics, 1997
1 (of 5) by Griffith, Kerr & Bryan	2.75
2 thru 5	@2.75
Spec. Bill Bryan's Oz Collection	3.00

DARK REGIONS
White Wolf, 1987
1	2.50
2	2.50
3 Scarce	3.00
4 and 5	@2.50

DARK STAR
Rebel
1 I:Ran	2.25
2 thru 3	@2.25

Dark Visions #2
© Pyramid

DARK VISIONS
Pyramid, 1987
1 I:Wasteland Man	2.50
2 thru 4	@2.50

DARK WOLF
Eternity, 1988
1 and 2	@2.50

Volume 2
1 thru 14	@2.50
Ann. #1	2.50

DARQUE RAZOR
London Night, 1996
? by Dan Membeila & Albert Holaso, Dark Birth	2.25
? necro-embossed edition	10.00
1 thru 3	@3.00

DAYS OF DARKNESS
Apple, 1992
1 From Pearl Harbor to Midway	2.75
2 Pearl Harbor Attack,cont	2.75
3 Japanese Juggernaut	2.75
4 Bataan Peninsula	2.75
GN	15.00

DEADBEATS
Claypool Comics, 1993
1 thru 13	@2.50
14 New Ways to Dream	2.50
15 thru 25	@2.50
26 by Richard Howell & Ricardo Villagran, The Southland Family Saga	2.50
27 Christine transformed into Predator	2.50
28	2.50
29 forbidden antiquities	2.50
30 V:Dracula	2.50
31 Reconstructing Deadbeats	2.50
32 New generation of Deadbeats	2.50
33 Quiet Night in Fear City	2.50
34 Dagger of Deliverance	2.50
35 Deadbeats of Danger Street	2.50
36 By His Majesty's Request	2.50
37 Carnival of Goals	2.50
38 HorrorFest begins	2.50
39 HorrorFest	2.50
40 HorrorFest	2.50
41 Guys Night Out	2.50
42 Dark Dealings	2.50
43 Dodging the Bullet	2.50
44 Town for Sale	2.50
45 thru 50	@2.50
51 thru 74	@2.50
75 thru 80	@2.50
TPB Rep. #1–#6	13.00
TPB Vol. 2 Tangy Treats, 160-pg.	13.00

DEAD EYES OPEN
Amaze Ink/Slave Labor Graphics 2005
1	3.00
2	3.00
3 thru 6	@3.00

DEADKILLER
Caliber
1 Rep Deadworld 19 thru 21	3.00

DEAD SONJA: SHE-ZOMBIE WITH A SWORD
Blatant Comics 2006
1 spoof	4.00
1a Zombie Bloodbath (c)	4.00
1b Dead Sexy (c)	10.00

DEADTIME STORIES
New Comics, 1987
1 AAd,WS	2.50

DEADWORLD
Arrow, 1986
1 Arrow Pyb	5.00
2	4.00
3 V:King Zombie	3.50
4 V:King Zombie	3.50
5 Team Rests	3.50
6 V:King Zombie	3.50
7 F:KZ & Deake, Graphic(c)	3.50
8 V:Living Corpse, Graphic(c)	2.50
9 V:Sadistic Punks, Graphic(c)	2.50
10 V:King Zombie, Graphic(c)	2.50
7a thru 10a Tame cover	@2.50
11 V:King Zombie, Graphic(c)	3.00

12 I:Percy, Graphic(c) 3.00
13 V:King Zombie, Graphic(c) 3.00
14 V:Voodoo Cult,Graphic(c) 3.00
15 Zombie stories,Graphic(c) 3.00
11a thru 15a Tame cover . . . . . . @2.50
16 V:`Civilized' Community 2.50
17 V:King Zombie 2.50
18 V:King Zombie 2.50
19 V:Grakken 2.50
20 V:King Zombie 2.50
21 Dead Killer 2.50
22 L:Dan & Joey 2.50
23 V:King Zombie 2.50
24 . . . . 2.50
25 (R:Vince Locke) 2.50
26 . . . . 2.50

Caliber
1 thru 11 . . . . @3.00
12 thru 15 Death Call . . . . @3.00
Spec. Deadworld Archives, rep. . . . 2.50
Spec. Bits & Pieces, rep.
   Caliber Presents #2&#8 . . . . . 2.50
Spec. To Kill A King,R:Deadkiller . . . 3.00

DEATH ANGEL
Lightning, 1997
1 by J. Cleary & Anderson 3.00
1 variant cover 3.00
1 limited edition A 10.00
1 limited edition B 10.00

DEATHDREAMS OF DRACULA
Apple
1 Selection of short stories 2.50
2 short stories 2.50
3 Inc. Rep. BWr,`Breathless' 2.50
4 short stories 2.50

DEATH HUNT
Eternity
1 & 2 . . . . @2.25

DEATHMARK
Lightning Comics, 1994
1 O:War Party 2.75

DEATH OF ANGEL GIRL
Angel Entertainment, 1997
1 by E.Bell & C.Forrest,F:Michelle . 3.00

DEATH OF BLOODFIRE
Lightning
1 . . . . 3.00
1a variant cover 3.00

DEATH RATTLE
Kitchen Sink, 1995
(Prev. Color)
1 thru 3 . . . . @3.50
4 . . . . 3.00
5 . . . . 2.50
6 Steve Bissette(c) 2.25
7 Ed Gein 2.25
8 I:Xenozoic Tales 10.00
9 BW,rep. 2.25
10 AW,rep. 2.25
11 thru 15 . . . . @2.25
16 BW,Spacehawk 2.25
17 Rand Holmes(c) 2.25
18 FMc 2.25

DEATH'S HEAD
Crystal
1 thru 3 . . . . @2.25

Death Rattle Vol. 3 #1
© *Kitchen Sink*

DEATHWORLD
Adventure Comics, 1990
1 Harry Harrison adapt. 2.50
2 thru 4 . . . . @2.50

BOOK II, 1991
1 Harry Harrison adapt. 2.50
2 thru 4 . . . . @2.50

BOOK III, 1991
1 H.Harrison adapt.,colonization . . . 2.50
2 Attack on the Lowlands 2.50
3 Attack on the Lowlands contd . . . 2.50
4 last issue 2.50

DEE VEE
Dee Vee, 1997
1 ECa, F:Alex 3.00
2 ECa 3.00
3 ECa 3.00
4 thru 14 . . . . @3.00
Spec. #1 Life is Cheap 3.00

DEEP SLEEPER
Oni Press 2004
1 (of 4) 3.50
2 thru 4 . . . . @3.50

DEFENSELESS DEAD
Adventure Comics, 1991
1 Larry Niven adapt. A:Gil 2.50
2 A:Organlegger 2.50
3 A:Organlegger 2.50

DELETE
Digital Noixe 2004
1 . . . . 3.00
2 thru 5 . . . . @3.00

DELTA TENN
Entertainment, 1987
1 thru 11 . . . . @2.50

DEMO
AIT/Planet Lar, 2003
1 (of 12) 4.00
2 thru 12 . . . . @3.00
TPB Scriptbook 13.00
TPB Collection (2006) 20.00

DEMON BABY
SQP/666 Comics, 1997
1 by Rich Larson, seq. to Hell
   on Heels 3.00
2 & 3 . . . . @3.00
1a thru 3a deluxe . . . . @10.00
GN Hell on Heels 10.00
GN Hell on Heels, deluxe 20.00

DEMON BITCH
Forbidden, 1997–98
1-shot 3.00
Spec.#1 Demon Bitch vs.
   Angel Girl 3.00
Spec.#1 Demon Bitch: Devilspawn, by
   Angela Benoit & Nirut Chaswan 3.00
Spec.#1 Demon Bitch: Hellslave,
   Free on Earth cover 3.00
Spec.#1 Demon Bitch: Tales of
   the Damned 3.00

DEMONGATE
Sirius, 1996–97
1 thru 12 by Bao Lin Hum &
   Colin Chan . . . . @2.50

DEMON GUN
Crusade Entertainment, 1996
1 thru 3 GCh,KtH . . . . @3.00

DEMON HUNTER
Aircel, 1989
1 thru 4 . . . . @2.50

DEMON HUNTER
Davdez Arts, 1998
1 by Barry Blair & Colin Chan 2.50
2 F:Hunter Gordon 2.50
3 . . . . 2.50

DEMONIQUE
London Night, 1997
? by SKy Owens, A:Anvil 3.00
1 by Membeila & Owens 3.00
2 F:Viper 3.00
3 Mayhem 3.00
4 Final issue 3.00

DEMONIQUE: ANGEL OF NIGHT
London Night, 1997
1 (of 3) by Skylar Owens 3.00
2 . . . . 3.00
3 final issue 3.00

DEMONSLAYER: LORDS OF NIGHT
Avatar Press, 2003
1/2 Fire Edition 6.00
1/2 Ice Edition 6.00
1/2 Attitude Edition 6.00
Preview 2.25
Preview variant (c)s 6.00
1 . . . . 3.50
1a variant (c)s 3.50
1b wraparound (c) 4.00

DEMON'S TAILS
Adventure
1 . . . . 2.50
2 A:Champion 2.50
3 V:Champion 2.50
4 V:Champion 2.50

DEMON WARRIOR
Eastern, 1987
1 thru 12 . . . . @2.50
13 and 14 . . . . @2.50

DENIZENS OF DEEP CITY
Jabberwocky, 1988
1 thru 8 . . . . @2.50

DERRECK WAYNE JACKSON'S STRAPPED
Gothic Images, 1994
1 Confrontational Factor 2.25
2 thru 6 . . . . @2.25

DESCENDING ANGELS
Millennium, 1995
1 I:3 Angels 2.25
2 F:Jim Johnson 3.00
3 F:Jim Johnson 3.00

DESERT PEACH
Thoughts & Images, 1988
1 thru 4 . . . . @2.50

DESTINY ANGEL
Dark Fantasy, 1996
1 (of 3) 4.00
1 2nd printing 4.00
1a deluxe 4.50
2 `Sunless Garden' 3.50
2a foil cover 4.00
2b photo cover 4.00

DESTROY
Eclipse, 1986
1 Large Size 5.00
2 Small Size,3-D 5.00

DETECTIVE, THE
Caliber, 1998
1 by Gerard Goffaux 3.00
2 . . . . 3.00
3 Clutches of the Past 3.00

DEVIL JACK
Doom Theatre, 1995
1 I:Devil Jack 3.00

Deviljack #3
© Doom Theatre

1a Directors Cut 3.00
2 V:Belegosi 3.00
3 . . . . 3.00

DEVIL'S PANTIES, THE
Silent Devil Productions 2006
1 by Jennie Breeden 5.00
2 thru 9 . . . . @5.00

DEVIL'S WORKSHOP
Blue Comet Press, 1995
1 Iron Cupcakes 3.00

DIABOLIK
Scorpion Productions, 1999
VOL. 1
1 Terror Aboard The Karima 6.00
2 Fight Against Time 6.00
3 Crumbs for the Scum. 6.00
4 Family with no morals 6.00
5 & 6 . . . . @6.00
VOL. 2
1 Target: Diabolik 6.00
2 One Crazy Love. 6.00
3 . . . . 6.00
4 Interrupted Game. 6.00

DICK DANGER
Olsen Comics, 1998
1 by W.W. Olsen 3.00
2 F:Red Olga 3.00
3 The Angel Murder 3.00
4 Is Hitler Still Alive? 3.00
5 Nikita, The Cat Girl 3.00

DICKS
Caliber, 1997
1 (of 4),GEn,JMC, ... 3.00
2 thru 4 GEn,JMC . . . . @3.00
TPB GEn,JMC 13.00

DICK TRACY
Tony Raiola, 2003
GN Purple Cross Gang 9.50
GN Large Feature reprint #3–#6 . @9.50
GN Scottie of Scotland Yard 9.50
GN Kidnapped Princes 9.50
GN Family Affair 9.50
GN Unholy Matrimony 9.50
GN Fur King/Out of the Past 9.50
GN Death of a Hood/Kroywen
    Serum 9.50
GN Bicycle Thieves 9.50
GN Kromes Crimes 9.50
GN Little Face 9.50
GN Silbert the Gunman 9.50
TPB Duke's Perception &
    The Mole's Greed 10.00
TPB The High Life & BB EYES . . . 10.00

DICK TRACY: THE COLLINS CASEFILES
Checker Book 2004
TPB Vol. 1 . . . . 18.00
TPB Vol. 2 . . . . 19.00
TPB Vol. 3 thru Vol. 4 . . . . @18.00

DICK TRACY CRIMEBUSTER
ACG Comics, 1998
1 by M.A.Collins & D.Locher 3.00
2 thru 9 . . . . @3.00
TPB rep. (2001) 20.00

DICK TRACY DETECTIVE
ACG Comics, 1999
1 (of 4) by Chester Gould 3.00

---

2 thru 4 . . . . @3.00

DICK TRACY MAGAZINE
1 V:Little Face Finnyo 4.00

DICK TRACY
Blackthorne, 1984–89
1 thru 12 . . . . @6.50
13 thru 25 . . . . @7.50
Becomes:

DICK TRACY MONTHLY/WEEKLY
Blackthorne, 1988
1 thru 25 monthly . . . . @3.00
26 thru 108 weekly . . . . @4.00
Unprinted Stories #3 . . . . 3.00
1 3-D Special 3.00
Spec. #1 . . . . 3.00
Spec. #2 . . . . 3.00
Spec. #3 . . . . 3.00

DICK TRACY: THE EARLY YEARS
Blackthorne, 1987
1 thru 3, 78-pg. . . . . @7.50
4 thru 6 . . . . @3.50
7 and 8 . . . . @4.00

DICK TRACY UNPRINTED STORIES
Blackthorne, 1987
1 thru 4 . . . . @3.00

DICTATORS
Antarctic Press 2004
Hitler #1 (of 4) 3.00
Hitler #2 thru #4 . . . . @3.00
Saddam Hussein #1 . . . . 4.00
Saddam Hussein #2 . . . . 4.00

DIGITAL DRAGON
Peregrine Entertainment, 1999
1 by Bryan Heyboer 3.00
2 thru 4 . . . . @3.00

DIGITAL WEBBING PRESENTS
Digital Webbing 2001
1 thru 5 . . . . 3.00
6 thru 18 . . . . @3.00
19 thru 25 . . . . @3.50
26 . . . . 6.00
27 thru 31 . . . . @4.00

DIM-WITTED DARRYL
Slave Labor Graphics, 1998
1 by Michael Bresnahan 3.00
2 thru 5 . . . . @3.00

DINOSAURS FOR HIRE
Eternity, 1988
1 . . . . 3.00
1a Rep. 2.50
2 thru 9 . . . . @2.50
Fall Classic #1 . . . . 2.50
GN Guns 'N' Lizards 10.00
Malibu, 1993
#1 3-D special 3.50

DIRTY PAIR
Eclipse, 1988
1 . . . . 9.00
2 . . . . 7.00
3 . . . . 6.00
4 end mini-series 6.00

All comics prices listed are for *Near Mint* condition.

Vol. 2, 1989
1 thru 5 . . . . @5.00
Vol. 3, 1990
1 thru 5 . . . . @5.00

DIRTY PAIR:
SIM EARTH
Eclipse
1 thru 4 . . . . @4.00

DISCIPLES
Caliber Core, 1998
1 Climate of fear 3.00
2 . . . . 3.00

A DISTANT SOIL
Warp Graphics, 1983
1 A:Panda Khan 10.00
2 . . . . 5.00
3 . . . . 4.00
4 . . . . 3.00
5 thru 9. . . . . @3.00
Aria Press, 1991
1 F:Seasons of Spring 6.00
1a-2nd to 4th printing 2.50
2 Seasons of Spring,pt.2 . . . . 5.00
3 . . . . 3.00
4 . . . . 3.00
5 thru 8 . . . . @3.00
9 thru 11 Knights of the Angel. . . @3.00
12 thru 14 . . . . @3.00
GN Knights of the Angel, deluxe . . 16.00
GN Immigrant Song rep.#1–#3 . . . . 7.00
See Image Comics

DITKO'S WORLD:
STATIC
Renegade, 1986
1 thru 3 SD . . . . @2.25

DOCTOR
Ironcat, 1997
1 (of 5) by Bang Ippongi 3.00
2 . . . . 3.00
4 . . . . 3.00
5 Pay Back in the City of
   Santa La Paz 3.00
6 final issue 3.00

DR. BLINK:
SUPERHERO SHRINK
Dork Storm Press 2004
0 . . . . 3.00
1 . . . . 3.00
2 thru 3 . . . . @3.50

DR. GORPON
Eternity, 1991
1 I:Dr.Gorpon,V:Demon 2.25
2 A:Doofus,V:ChocolateBunny 2.50
3 D:Dr.Gorpon. 2.50

DR. RADIUM
Silverline
1 . . . . 3.00
2 thru 4 . . . . @2.25

DR. RADIUM
Amaze Ink/SLG, 2004
TPB Vol. 1 . . . . 10.00
TPB Vol. 2 . . . . 10.00
TPB Vol. 3 It's Science with
   Dr. Radium 12.00

DR. RADIUM:
MAN OF SCIENCE
Slave Labor, 1992
1 And Baby makes 2, BU: Dr.
   Radiums' Grim Future 2.50

DOC WEIRD'S
THRILL BOOK
1 AW 2.25
2 & 3 . . . . @2.25

DOCTOR WEIRD
Caliber Press, 1994
1 V:Charnogg 2.50
2 V:Charnogg 2.50

DOCTOR WHO
Panini Books 2006
TPB Iron Legion 25.00
TPB Dragon's Claw 25.00
TPB The Tides of Time 25.00
TPB Endgame 25.00
TPB Oblivion 26.50
TPB The Glorous Dead 26.50

Dr. Wonder #5
© Old Town Publishing

DR. WONDER
Old Town Publishing, 1996
1 thur 5 . . . . @3.00

DODEKAIN
Antarctic Press, 1994
1 and 2 by Masayuki Fujihara. . . @3.00
3 Rampage Vs. Zogerians 3.00
4 V:Zogerians 3.00
5 F:Takuma. 3.00
6 Dan vs. Takuma 2.75
7 V:Okizon 2.75
8 V:Okizon 3.00

DOGAROO
Blackthorne, 1988
1 . . . . 2.50

DOGS O'WAR, THE
Crusade Entertainment, 1996–97
1 thru 3 (of 3) . . . . @3.00

DOGWITCH
Sirius Entertainment 2002
1 . . . . 3.50
1a signature plate edition 12.00
2 thru 17 . . . . @3.00

18 Finale special 3.50
18a Signature plate edition 15.00
TPB Vol. 1 Direct to Video. 15.00
TPB Vol. 2 Twisted. 15.00
TPB Vol. 3 Mood Swings. 16.00

DOLLS
Sirius, 1998
1-shot science fiction 3.00

DOMINION
Eclipse Manga, 1990
1 by Masamune Shirow 3.00
2 thru 6 . . . . @2.25

DOMINO CHANCE
Chance, 1982
1 1,000 printed 10.00
1a 2nd printing 3.50
2 thru 6 . . . . @3.00
7 I:Gizmo 7.00
8 A:Gizmo 11.00
9 . . . . 2.50
[2nd Series]
1 . . . . 3.00
2 and 3 . . . . @2.50

DONATELLO
Mirage, 1986
1-shot A:TMNTurtles 12.00

DONNA MIA
Avatar Press, 1997
0 by Tevlin Utz 3.00
0b leather cover 15.00
0c signed 8.00
1 . . . . 4.00
1a signed 8.00
1b Royal Blue edition 50.00
2 . . . . 4.00
2a deluxe 4.50
3 (of 3) 3.00
3a deluxe 8.00
Giant Size #1 . . . . 3.00
Giant Size #1 leather cover 15.00
Giant Size #1 signed 8.00
Giant Size #2 . . . . 4.00
Giant Size #2 Deluxe. 10.00
TPB rep. #0–#3 & G-Size #1&#2. . 16.00
Spec. Infinity 3.00
Spec.#1 Pin-up (1997) 3.00

DON SIMPSON'S
BIZARRE HEROES
Fiasco Comics, 1990
0 thru 7 . . . . 3.00
8 V:Darkcease 3.00
9 R:Yan Man 3.00
10 F:Mainstreamers. 3.00
11 Search for Megaton Man 3.00
12 . . . . 3.00
13 House of Megaton Man 3.00
14 Cec Vs. Dark Cease 3.00
TPB Apocalypse Affiliation 13.00

DOOMED
IDW Publishing 2005
1 . . . . 7.00
1a variant (c). 7.00
2 thru 3 . . . . @8.00
2a thru 3a variant (c) . . . . @8.00

DOOMSDAY + 1
ACG Comics, 1998
1 by JBn rep. Charlton 3.00
2 A Faceless Foe 3.00
3 . . . . 3.00
4 The Hidden Enemy 3.00

5 Rule of Fear. 3.00
6 . . . . 3.00
7 NA(c), final issue 3.00

Dork #7
© Amaze Ink/SGL

DORK
Amaze Ink/SLG, 1993–2001
1 EDo 3.00
2 EDo 3.00
3 EDo 3.00
1 thru 3 2nd printings . . . . @3.00
4 thru 7 . . . . @3.00
8 . . . . 3.50
9 thru 11 . . . . @3.00
TPB Vol. 1 Who's Laughing Now. . 12.00
TPB Vol. 2 Circling the Drain 14.00

DORK TOWER
Corsair Publishing, 1998
1 by John Kovalic 3.00
2 thru 8 . . . . @3.50
Dork Storm, 2000
9 Angry Young Fan 3.00
10 Road Rules 3.00
11 World of Dorkness 3.00
12 . . . . 3.00
13 . . . . 3.00
14 Gilly, Warrior Princess. 3.00
15 . . . . 3.00
16 Trader of the Last Orc. 3.00
17 Halloween in Mud Bay 3.00
17 At the Big Con. 3.00
18 Understanding Games 3.00
19 Junk Food Issue 3.00
20 Featuring Gilly. 3.00
21 20th Century Boy 3.00
22 Daily Carson 3.00
23 Dork Tower Frag 3.00
24 . . . . 3.00
25 . . . . 4.00
26 thru 32 . . . . @3.00
33 thru 35 . . . . @3.50
Spec. Lord of the Rings 3.00
Swimsuit Special #1. . . . . 3.00
Best of Dork Tower #1 . . . . 2.25
TPB Vol. 1 Dork Covenant. 16.00
TPB Vol. 2 Dork Shadows 16.00
TPB Vol. 3 Heart of Dorkness 16.00
TPB Dork Tower. 16.00
TPB Vol. 5 Understanding Gamers 16.00
TPB Vol. 6 1–6 Degrees of
  Speparation 16.00
1-shot Wizkids Special. 3.00

TPB Vol. 7 Dork Side of the Goon. 16.00
TPB Dork Decade 16.00
TPB Vol. 8 Go, Dork, Go 16.00

DOUBLE EDGE DOUBLE
Double Edge
1 thru 3 . . . . 3.50
4 Heroes Inc. Rep.#1-#2 . . . . 3.00

DOUBLE IMPACT
High Impact Studios, 1995–96
1 I: China & Jazz 5.00
1a Chromium (c) variant, signed . . 6.00
1b Rainbow (c) w/certificate 15.00
1c Rainbow (c) w/o certificate. . . . 10.00
2 Castilo's Crime. 3.00
2b silver version 10.00
2c signed, w/certificate 5.00
3 . . . . 5.00
3a Bondage (c) 15.00
4 . . . . 5.00
4a Phoenix (c). 15.00
5 . . . . 5.00
6 China cover 3.00
6a Jazz cover 3.00
6b signed China or Jazz(c). 15.00
6c bondage(c). 10.00
7 & 8 . . . . @3.00
8a variant (c). 8.00
2nd Series, 1996–97
0 . . . . 3.00
1 . . . . 3.00
1a chromium (c) 4.00
1b Chromium variant edition. 15.00
1c Christmas (c) 10.00
2 . . . . 3.00
2a Sweedish Erotica(c). 10.00
Spec.#1 Double Impact/Lethal Strike:
  Double Strike, x-over. 3.00
Spec.#1 Double Impact/Nikki Blade:
  Hard Core x-over (1997) 3.00
  Platinum variant RCI(c) 10.00
  Gold Metal variant RCI(c) 20.00
Spec.#1 Raising Hell, RCI,RkB . . . 3.00
ABC Comics, 1998
1 encore 3.00
1a encore, Chicago cover. 6.00
1b encore, San Diego nude cover . 6.00
Spec. Double Impact/Luxura (1998) 3.00
Spec. Vampeurotica edition. 6.00
Bikini Spec. 3.00
Christmas Spec. 3.00
Christmas Spec., gold foil 10.00
Coll.#1 . . . . 3.00
Coll.#1a x-mas 8.00
Spring Spec.#1 . . . . 3.00
Spring Spec.#1a manga cover. . . . 8.00
Summer Bikini Spec. 1999 . . . . . . 3.00
Gallery Collection #1 . . . . 5.00
Lingerie Special 3.00

DOUBLE IMPACT ALIVE
ABC Comics, 1999
1 (of 3) Double Impact Alive 2000 . 3.00
1a Double Impact Alive 2000,
  gold foil ed. 8.00
1b Red Leather. 15.00
2 RCI. 3.00
2a Manga cover 8.00
2c silver embossed foil 10.00

DOUBLE IMPACT:
ASSASSINS FOR HIRE
High Impact, 1997
1 RCI,RkB 3.00
2 . . . . 3.00
ABC Comics, 1998
1 . . . . 3.00

DOUBLE IMPACT:
FROM THE ASHES
ABC Comics, 1998
1 (of 2) RCI 3.00
2 RCI. 3.00
2A variant cover A. 6.00
2B variant cover B 6.00

DOUBLE IMPACT:
HOT SHOTS
ABC Studios, 1999
1 RCI. 3.00
2 . . . . 3.00

DOUBLE IMPACT MERCS
ABC Comics, 1999
1 (of 3) RCI 3.00
1a deluxe 8.00
2 RCI. 3.00
2a deluxe 10.00

DOUBLE IMPACT:
ONE STEP BEYOND
ABC Comics, 1998
1 (of 2) RCI 3.00
1a Leather cover. 20.00

DOUBLE IMPACT RAW
ABC Comics, 1997
1 (of 3) RCI, adult 3.00
1b Star photo (c). 10.00
1A Wraparound cover A 6.00
1B Wraparound cover B 6.00
2 thru 3 . . . . @3.00
3A Variant cover A 6.00
VOL. 2
1 (of 3) adult material 3.00

DOUBLE IMPACT/RAZOR
ABC Studios, 1999
1 (of 3) 3.25
1b Previews exclusive 8.00
1c Manga alt.(c) 8.00
2 . . . . 3.25

DOUBLE IMPACT
SUICIDE RUN
ABC Comics, 1998
1 (of 2) RCI 3.00
1b Leather cover. 15.00
2 adult material 3.00
Collected edition 3.00
Collected, gold foil 10.00

DOUBLE IMPACT 2069
ABC Comics, 1999
1 Virgin Encore Edition 3.00
1a Deluxe Erotica edition 8.00
Christmas Spec. 3.00
Christmas Spec. Previews (c) 8.00

DOUBLE IMPACT X
ABC Comics, 2000
1 . . . . 6.00
1a alternate (c) 6.00
2 . . . . 6.00
2 deluxe, vinyl (c) 20.00
Intro 20.00

DRACULA
Eternity
1 . . . . 3.75
1a 2nd printing 2.50
2 thru 4 . . . . @2.50

All comics prices listed are for *Near Mint* condition.

DRACULA IN HELL
Apple, 1992
1 O:Dracula 2.50
2 O:Dracula contd. 2.50

DRACULA: SUICIDE CLUB
Adventure, 1992
1 I:Suicide Club in UK. 2.50
2 Dracula/Suicide Club cont. 2.50
3 Club raid,A:Insp.Harrison. 2.50
4 Vision of Miss Fortune 2.50

DRACULA: THE LADY IN THE TOMB
Eternity
1 . . . . 2.50

DRACULA'S COZY COFFIN
Draculina Publishing, 1995
1 thru 4 Halloween issue . . . . . . @3.00

DRAGON ARMS
Antarctic Press 2002
1 48-pg. 5.00
2 thru 6 . . . . @3.50
1-shot Stand Alone Special 3.00
Pocket Manga TPB Vol. 1 . . . . . . 10.00
TPB Pocket Manga Vol. 2 . . . . . . 10.00

DRAGON ARMS: CHAOS BLADE
Antarctic Press, 2004
1 thru 6 . . . . @3.00

DRAGONBALL
Viz Communications, 1998
1 (of 12) by Akira Toriyama 8.00
2 thru 4 . . . . @5.00
5 thru 12 . . . . @3.00
TPB Vol. 1 . . . . 15.00
TPB Vol. 2 rep. #7–#12 . . . . 15.00
PART TWO, 1999
1 (of 15) by Akira Toriyama 5.00
2 thru 4 . . . . @4.00
5 thru 15 . . . . @3.00
TPB Vol. 3 rep.Vol.2 #3–#8 . . . . . 15.00
TPB Vol. 4 rep.Vol.2 #7–#13 . . . . 15.00
PART THREE, 2000
1 (of 14) by Akira Toriyama 3.00
2 thru 5 . . . . @3.00
8 thru 14 . . . . @3.00
PART FOUR, 2001
1 thru 4 (of 10) . . . . @3.00
5 thru 10 . . . . @3.00
PART FIVE, 2002
1 (of 7) 3.00
2 thru 6 . . . . @3.00
7 . . . . 3.00
Part 6
1 . . . . 3.50
2 . . . . 3.50
TPB Vol. 11 thru Vol. 16 . . . . @8.00
TPB Vol. 1 thru 7 2nd print. . . . . @8.00

DRAGONBALL Z
Viz Communications, 1998
1 (of 9) by Akira Toriyama 13.00
2 thru 9 . . . . @5.00
TPB Vol. 1 . . . . 15.00
TPB Vol. 2 . . . . 15.00
PART TWO (1998)
1 (of 14) by Akira Toriyama 4.00
2 thru 9 . . . . @3.50
10 thru 14 . . . . @3.50
TPB Vol. 3 . . . . 15.00

TPB Vol. 4 . . . . 15.00
PART THREE (1999)
1 (of 10) by Akira Toriyama 3.50
2 thru 10 . . . . @3.00
TPB Vol. 5, Part 3, #1–#6 . . . . . . 13.00
TPB Vol. 6, Part 3, #7–#11 . . . . . 13.00
PART 4 (2000)
1 thru 13 (of 15) . . . . @3.00
PART 5 (2001)
1 (of 12) 3.00
2 thru 10 . . . . @3.00
TPB Vol. 7 thru Vol. 10 . . . . @13.00
TPB Vol. 11 thru Vol. 17 . . . . @8.00
TPB Vol. 1 thru Vol. 7 2nd print . . @8.00

DRAGONFORCE
Aircel, 1988
1 DK 6.00
2 thru 7 DK . . . . @4.00
8 thru 12 . . . . @4.00
13 . . . . 2.50

DRAGONFORCE CHRONICLES
Aircel, 1988
Vol. 1 thru Vol. 5 rep. . . . . @3.00

DRAGON KNIGHTS
Tokyopop Press, 2001
1 by Mineko Ohkami. 3.00
2 thru 6 . . . . @3.00

DRAGONMIST
Raised Brow Publications
1 I:Dragonmist 2.75
2 F:Assassin 2.75

DRAGON OF THE VALKYR
Rak
1 . . . . 2.25
2 thru 4 . . . . @2.25

DRAGON QUEST
Silverwolf, 1986
1 TV 15.00
2 TV 7.50
3 TV 6.50

DRAGONRING
[1st Series]
1 B.Blair,rare 110.00

Dragonrok Saga #3
© Hanthercraft

Aircel, 1986
1 . . . . 3.50
2 . . . . 2.50
3 thru 6 . . . . @2.50
See Also Color Comics

DRAGONROK SAGA
Hanthercraft
1 thru 12 . . . . @2.50

DRAGON WARS
Ironcat, 1998
1 by Ryukihei 3.00
2 thru 11 . . . . @3.00
TPB Vol. 1 . . . . 18.00

DRAGON WEEKLY
1 Southern Knights 2.25
2 and 3 . . . . @2.25

DREAD OF NIGHT
Hamilton, 1991
1 Horror story collection 4.00
2 Json, inc.`Genocide' 4.00

DREAM ANGEL AND ANGEL GIRL
Angel Entertainment, 1998
1 . . . . 3.00

DREAM ANGEL: THE QUANTUM DREAMER
Angel Entertainment, 1997
1 by Mort Castle & Adriana Melo . . 3.00
2 . . . . 3.00

DREAM ANGEL: WORLD WITHOUT END
Angel Entertainment, 1998
1 Dream world cover 3.00

DREAMERY
Eclipse, 1986
1 thru 13 . . . . @2.50

DREAMGIRL
Angel Entertainment, 1996
0 by David Campitti & Al Rio 3.00
1 . . . . 3.00
1 deluxe 6.00
1 Manga cover 5.00

DREAMLANDS
Caliber New Worlds, 1996
1 . . . . 3.00
2 flip book with Boston Bombers #3 3.00

DREAMTIME
Blind Rat, 1995
1 Young Deserter 3.00
2 Gypsy Trouble 2.50

DREAMWALKER
Caliber Tapestry, 1997
1 thru 4 . . . . @3.00
5 by Jenni Gregory, 2nd story arc. . 3.00
6 2nd story arc, concl. 3.00

DREAMWALKER: CAROUSEL
Avatar, 1998
0 . . . . 3.00
1 by Jenni Gregory 3.00
2 conclusion 3.00

    All comics prices listed are for *Near Mint* condition.

DREAMWALKER: SUMMER RAIN
Avatar, 1999
1 by Jenni Gregory 3.00

DREAMWALKER: AUTUMN LEAVES
Avatar, 1999
1 by Jenni Gregory 3.00
2 conclusion 3.00

DREAMWOLVES
Dramenon Studios, 1994
1 . . . . 3.00
2 . . . . 3.00
3 F:Desiree 3.00
4 and 5 V:Venefica . . . . @3.00
6 R:Carnifax 3.00
7 . . . . 3.00
8 F:Wendy Bascum 3.00

DROWNERS, THE
New Flame Publishing 2004
1 (of 4) 3.00
2 thru 4 . . . . @3.00

DRIFTERS
Infinity Graphics, 1986
1 . . . . 2.50

DRYWALL AND OSWALD SHOW, THE
Fireman Press, 1998
1 by Mandy Carter,Trent Kaniuga . 3.00

DUEL
Antarctic Press 2005
0 . . . . 3.00
1 (of 4) Rise of the Blackhawk . . . 3.00
2 Jet War in the South Atlantic . . . 3.50
3 Germany 1945 . . . . 3.00

DUNGEON
NBM Books 2002
1 by L. Trondheim & J. Star 3.00
2 thru 8 . . . . @3.00
TPB Vol. 1 . . . . 15.00
TPB Vol. 2 . . . . 15.00

DUNGEON: THE EARLY YEARS
NBM Books 2004
1 thru 2 . . . . @3.00
GN Vol. 1 The Night Shirt (color) . . 14.00

DUNGEONEERS
Silverwolf, 1986
1 thru 8 . . . . @2.50

DUNGEONS & DRAGONS: BLACK & WHITE
Kenzer & Company, 2002
1 (of 8) by J.Limke & R.Pereira . . . 3.00
2 thru 6 . . . . @3.00

DUNGEONS & DRAGONS IN SHADOW OF DRAGONS
Kenzer & Company, 2001
1 (of 8) The Last of My Father 3.00
2 thru 8 . . . . @3.00

DWELLING, THE
Chaos! Comics/Black Label Graphics, 2002
Ashcan 6.00
1 BnP 5.00
1a premium edition 10.00
1b super premium edition 20.00
1c signed edition 15.00
Spec. #1 script edition 5.00
Spec. #1 premium script edition . . 20.00

Eagle #5
© Crystal

EAGLE
Crystal, 1986
1 . . . . 3.00
1a signed & limited 5.00
2 thru 5 . . . . @2.75
6 thru 17 . . . . @2.50
Apple, 1988
18 thru 26 . . . . @2.50

EAGLE
Viz Communications, 2000
1 (of 14) The Candidate,112-pg . . . 7.00
2 Scandal 7.00
3 The Vice-President 7.00
4 New Hampshire 7.00
5 On the Battlefield 7.00
6 King of New York 7.00
7 Pandora's Box 7.00
8 The Debate 7.00
9 Passion 7.00
10 Gone to Texas 7.00
11 Super Tuesday 7.00
12 Suspicion 7.00
13 Illegitimate child 7.00
14 Confession 7.00
15 The Nomination 7.00
16 The General 7.00
17 Coming Home 7.00
18 Frame Up 7.00
19 Fires in the Plain 7.00
20 Someone You Can Trust 7.00
21 End of the Trail 7.00
22 Father & Son 7.00
TPB Vol. 1 424-pg 20.00
TPB Vol. 2 . . . . 20.00
TPB Vol. 3 416-pg 20.00
TPB Vol. 4 512-pg 23.00

EAGLE: DARK MIRROR
Comic Zone
1 A:Eagle, inc reps 2.75
2 In Japan, V:Lord Kagami 2.75

3 . . . . 3.00
4 . . . . 3.00

EAGLES DARE
Aager Comics, 1994
1 thru 4 . . . . 2.25
5 V:Dragon 2.25

EARTH LORE: LEGEND OF BEK LARSON
Eternity
1 . . . . 2.25

EARTH LORE: REIGN OF DRAGON LORD
1 . . . . 2.25
2 . . . . 2.25

EARTH WAR
Newcomers Publishing, 1995
1 and 2 from Newcomers Illus 3.00

EARTH: YEAR ZERO
Eclipse
1 thru 4 . . . . @2.25

EASY WAY
IDW Publishing 2005
1 . . . . 4.00
2 thru 4 . . . . @4.00
TPB 18.00

EAT-MAN
Viz Communications, 1997
1 (of 6) by Akihito Yoshitami 3.00
2 thru 6 . . . . @3.00
Vol.1 Full Course Meal,rep.Pt.1 . . 16.00
PART TWO, 1998
1 (of 5) by Akihito Yoshitami 3.00
2 (of 5) 3.50
3 thru 5 . . . . @3.25
TPB Vol. 2 Second Course 16.00

EB'NN THE RAVEN
Now
1 . . . . 5.00
2 . . . . 3.00
3 . . . . 2.50
4 . . . . 2.25
5 thru 9 . . . . @2.25

EBONIX-FILES, THE
Blatant Comics, 1998
1A TV parody, cover A 4.00
1B TV parody, cover B 4.00

ED THE HAPPY CLOWN
Drawn & Quarterly 2005
1 (of 9) 3.00
2 thru 3 . . . . @3.00
4 thru 9 . . . . @3.00

EDDIE CAMPELL'S BACCHUS
Eddie Campell Comics, 1995
1 V:Telchines 7.00
1 2nd printing 3.00
2 thru 10 V:Telchines 4.00
11 thru 26 ECa . . . . @3.00
27 thru 37 ECa . . . . @3.00
38 thru 46 . . . . @3.00
47 thru 56 . . . . @3.00
57 thru 60 . . . . @3.00
GN Collected Bacchus, Vol. 1 . . . . 10.00
GN Collected Bacchus, Vol. 2 . . . . 10.00

B & W PUB.

GN Collected Bacchus, Vol. 3,
  Doing the Islands. 18.00
GN Collected Bacchus, Vol. 4,
  One Man Show 8.50
GN Collected Bacchus, Vol. 5
  Earth, Air, Water & Fire 10.00
GN Collected Bacchus, Vol. 6
  1001 Nights of Bacchus 10.00
GN Collected Bacchus, Vol. 9,
  King Bacchus 13.00
TPB 1001 Nights of Bacchus. 13.50
TPB King Bacchus. 14.00

EDDY CURRENT
Mad Dog, 1987
1 thru 12 . . . . @2.50

EDGAR ALLAN POE
Eternity, 1988
1 Black Cat. 2.50
2 Pit & Pendulum 2.50
3 Masque of the Red Death 2.50
4 Murder in the Rue Morgue 2.50
5 Tell Tale Heart 2.50

EDGE
1 . . . . 3.00
Vol 2 #1 thru #3 . . . . @3.00
Vol 2 #4 thru #6 . . . . @2.50

Eightball #7
© Fantagraphics

EIGHTBALL
Fantagraphics, 1989
1 . . . . 13.00
2 . . . . 8.00
3 . . . . 7.00
4 . . . . 6.00
1a thru 4a later printings . . . . . . @3.00
5 thru 8 . . . . @6.00
9 thru 10 . . . . @4.00
11 A:Ghost World. 4.00
12 F:Ghost World. 4.00
13 thru 19. . . . . @4.00
20 . . . . 5.00
21 48-pg. 5.00
22 . . . . 7.00
23 . . . . 7.00
TPB Orgy Bound, rep. #7–#14 . . 15.00
TPB Lout Rampage 15.00
TPB Pussey. 9.00
TPB Velvet glove cast in iron. . . . 17.00
TPB Caricature 17.00

B & W PUB.

ELECTRIC GIRL
Mighty Gremlin, 1998
1 . . . . 3.50
2 thru 9 . . . . @3.00
AIT/Planet Lar, 2002
10 by Mike Brennan. 3.00
TPB Vol. 1 . . . . 10.00
TPB Vol. 2 152-pg.. . . . . 14.00

ELFLORD
Aircel, 1986
1 I:Hawk 5.00
1a 2nd printing 3.50
2 . . . . 3.00
2a 2nd printing 2.50
3 V:Doran 3.00
4 V:Doran 3.00
5 V:Doran 2.50
6 V:Nendo 2.50
Compilation Book. 5.00
(Vol 2), #1 to #24, see Color
25 thru 31 . . . . @2.50
32 . . . . 2.50

ELFLORD:
RETURN OF THE KING
Nightwynd, 1992
1 . . . . 2.50
2 thru 4 . . . . @2.50

ELFLORD:
SUMMER MAGIC
Nightwynd, 1993
thru 4 . . . . @2.50

ELFLORD
Warp Graphics, 1997
1 (of 4) by Barry Blair & Colin Chan 3.00
2 thru 4 . . . . @3.00

ELFLORD: ALL
THE LONELY PLACES
Warp Graphics, 1997
1 (of 4)Barry Blair & Colin Chan. . . 3.00
Becomes:
HAWK AND WINDBLADE:
ALL THE LONELY
PLACES
2 (of 2) 3.00

ELFLORD CHRONICLES
Aircel, 1990
1 (of 12) thru 8 rep B.Blair . . . . . @2.50

ELFLORD CUTS LOOSE
Warp Graphics, 1997
1 by Barry Blair and Colin Chan. . . 3.00
2 F:Hawk Erik-san 3.00
3 . . . . 3.00
4 all out attack 3.00
5 north to safety 3.00
6 homeward 3.00
7 back to Greenhaven 3.00
8 Greenhaven Siege. 3.00
9 Felines, Nothing More Than
  Felines. 3.00

ELFLORD: HAWK
China Winds, 1998
1-shot by Barry Blair and
  Colin Chan. 3.50

ELFLORE:
THE HIGH SEAS
Raw Comics
4 by Barry Blair (500 copies) 5.00

ELFQUEST
Warp Graphics, 1979–85
1 WP. 30.00
1a WP,2nd printing 10.00
1b WP,3rd printing 5.00
1c WP,4th printing (1989) 4.00
2 WP 15.00
3 WP 12.00
4 WP 12.00
5 WP 12.00
6 WP 12.00
2a thru 6a WP,2nd printing . . . . . @4.00
7 WP 10.00
8 WP 10.00
9 WP 10.00
2a thru 9a WP,later printings. . . . @3.00
10 thru 15 . . . . @5.00
16 WP,I:DistantSoil 8.00
17 thru 21 WP . . . . @5.00
TPB Gatherum 20.00
Warp Graphics, 1996
4 thru 14 ed. RPi. . . . . @5.00
15 . . . . 5.50
16 What if Cutter never
  became chief. 5.50
17 F:Fire-Eye 5.50
18 Dreamtime, concl.. . . . . 5.50
19 Wolfrider begins 5.50
20 . . . . 5.50
21 20th anniv. 5.50
22 F:Wolfrider 5.00
23 F:WaveDancers 5.00
24 F:Wolfrider 5.00
25 F:Wolfrider 5.00
26 Wild Hunt 5.00
27 . . . . 5.00
28 F:Ember & Teir 5.00
29 three new stories 5.00
30 new stories 5.00
31 new stories 5.00
32 Wild Hunt,pt.1, 24-pg. 3.50
33 Wild Hunt,pt.2 . . . . 3.50
34 Wild Hunt,pt.3 . . . . 3.50
35 Wild Hunt,pt.4 . . . . 3.50
Spec.#1 Worldpool,pt.1 (1997) 3.50
Spec.#2 Worldpool,pt.2 (1997) 3.50
READERS COLLECTIONS
TPB Vol.1 Fire & Flight 12.00
TPB Vol.2 The Forbidden Grove . . 12.00
TPB Vol.3 Captives of
  Blue Mountain 12.00
TPB Vol.4 Quest's End 12.00
TPB Vol.5 Siege at Blue Mountain 12.00
TPB Vol.6 Secret of Two-Edge . . . 12.00
TPB Vol.7 Cry From Beyond 12.00
TPB Vol.8 Kings of the
  Broken Wheel 12.00
TPB Vol.8A Dreamtime 12.00
TPB Vol.8B In All But Blood. 17.00
TPB Vol.9 Rogue's Curse 14.00
TPB Vol.9A Wolfrider 12.00
TPB Vol.9B Blood of Ten Chiefs . . 13.00
TPB Vol.9C Kahvi 14.00
TPB Vol.11A Huntress 12.00
TPB Vol.11B Ascent. 13.00
TPB Vol.11C Shadowstalker 13.00
TPB Vol.12 Ascent. 13.00
TPB Vol.12A Reunion 13.00
TPB Vol.13A Rebels 12.00
TPB Vol.13B Junk 12.00
TPB Vol.14 JINK 12.00
TPB Vol.14A Skyward Shadow . . . 12.00
TPB Vol.14B Mindcoil 12.00
TPB Vol.15 Forevergreen 13.00
TPB Vol.15A Dreams End 13.00
TPB Vol.15B Phoenix 14.00

TPB Vol.16 Wave Dancers 12.00
TPB Vol.'?' Worldpool 13.00
TPB The Rebels, 176-pg. 12.00
GN Shards 14.00
GN Legacy (Hidden Years
    #16–#22) 12.00
GN A Gift of Her Own 17.00
TPB Wolfrider's Guide, revised . . . 17.00
Spec. Metamorphosis, WP,
    RPi (1996) 3.00
Spec. Elfquest: Wolfrider 3.00
Summer Spec. 2001 Recognition . . 3.00
Summer Spec. 2001 Wolfshadow . . 4.00

ELFQUEST: KAHVI
Warp Graphics, 1995
1 thru 6 I:Kahvi . . . . @2.25

ELFQUEST: KINGS OF THE BROKEN WHEEL
Warp Graphics, 1990–92
1 thru 9 WP . . . . @2.25

ELFQUEST: SEIGE AT BLUE MOUNTAIN
Warp Graphics/Apple Comics, 1987–88
1 WP,JSo 9.00
1a 2nd printing 3.00
2 WP 6.00
2a 2nd printing 3.00
3 WP 5.00
3a 2nd printing 2.50
4 thru 8 WP . . . . @5.00

ELFQUEST: TWO SPEAR
Warp Graphics, 1995
1 thru 3 (of 5) Two-Spears past . @2.25

ELFQUEST: WORLDPOOL
Warp Graphics, 1997
Spec.#1& 2 (of 2) . . . . @3.00

ELFTREK
Dimension, 1986
1 Elfquest's Star Trek parody 2.50
2 . . . . 2.50

ELF WARRIOR
Adventure, 1987
1 . . . . 3.00
2 thru 5 . . . . @2.50

EL HAZARD: THE MAGNIFICENT WORLD
Viz Communications, 2000
1 by Hidetomo Tsubura 3.00
2 thru 5 . . . . @3.00
Part 2, 2001
1 thru 5 . . . . @3.00
Part 3, 2001
1 thru 5 (of 6) . . . . @3.00
6 . . . . 3.00
TPB Vol. 1 . . . . 16.00
TPB Vol. 2 . . . . 16.00
TPB Vol. 3 . . . . 16.00

ELIMINATOR
Eternity
1 'Drugs in the Future' 2.50
2 . . . . 2.50

ELVIRA, MISTRESS OF THE DARK
Claypool Comics, 1993
1 . . . . 7.00
2 thru 35 . . . . @4.00
36 thru 74 photo covers . . . . @3.50
75 Mistress of the Jungle,pt.1 . . . 3.50
76 Mistress of the Jungle,pt.2 . . . 3.50
77 Rome on the Range 3.50
78 thru 90 photo covers . . . . @3.50
91 thru 103 . . . . @3.00
104 thru 127 . . . . @3.00
128 thru 138 . . . . @2.50
139 thru 150 . . . . @2.50
151 thru 163 . . . . @2.50
TPB Elvira, Mistress of the Dark . . 13.00
TPB Vol. 2 Double Delights 13.00

ELVIRA
Eclipse
1 Rosalind Wyck 2.50

EMBRACE
London Night, 1996
1 NC17 edition, EHr, signed 10.00

EMBRACE: HUNGER OF THE FLESH
London Night, 1997
1 DQ,last of the original
    vampire race 3.00
1a DQ,deluxe 6.00
1b signed by Kevin West 15.00
2 DQ 3.00
2a DQ,deluxe 6.00
3 by Dan Membiela & Kevin
    West, concl. 3.00

EMERALDAS
Eternity, 1990
1 thru 4 . . . . @2.25

EMMA DAVENPORT
Lohamn Hill Press, 1995
1 I:Emma Davenport 2.75
2 . . . . 2.75
3 O:Hammerin Jim 2.75
4 Cookie Woofer War 2.75

EMO BOY
Amaze Ink/Slave Labor Graphics 2005
thru 9 . . . . @3.00
TPB Vol. 1 Nobody Cares 14.00

EMPIRE
Eternity, 1988
1 thru 4 . . . . @2.50

EMPIRE LANES
Northern Lights, 1986–87
1 . . . . 2.50
2 thru 4 . . . . @2.50

EMPTY ZONE
Sirius, 1998
1 by Jason Alexander 3.00
1a limited edition 5.00
2 thru 4 . . . . 2.50
TPB 12.00
TPB Vol. 2 . . . . 17.00
VOL. 2 TRANSMISSIONS, 1999
1 by Jason Alexander 3.00
2 thru 7 . . . . @3.00
8 History Lessions,pt.1 . . . . 3.00

Empty Zone #4
© Sirius

EMPTY ZONE: CONVERSATIONS WITH THE DEAD
Sirius Entertainment, 2002
1 (of 5) by Jason Alexander 3.00
2 thru 3 . . . . @3.00

ENCHANTED
Sirius, 1997
1 (of 3) by Robert Chang 3.00
2 and 3 . . . . @3.00

ENCHANTED VALLEY
Blackthorne, 1987
1 . . . . 2.25
2 . . . . 2.25

ENCHANTER
Eclipse, 1987
1 thru 3 . . . . @2.50

ENCHANTER: APOCALYPSE WIND NOVELLA
Entity
1 Foil Enhanced Cover 3.00

ENFORCERS
Dark Visions Publishing, 1995
0 From Anthology Title 2.50

ENNIS AND MCCREA'S BIGGER DICKS
Avatar Press, 2002
1 (of 4) GEn,JMC,F:Dougie & Ivor . 5.00
1a Guaranteed to Offend cover . . . 5.00
2 thru 4 . . . . @5.00
2a thru 4a offensive (c) . . . . @5.00

ENNIS AND MCCREA'S DICKS 2
Avatar Press, 2002
1 (of 4) 3.50
2 thru 4 . . . . @3.50
1a thru 4a offensive (c) . . . . @4.00
X-Mas Spec. #1 . . . . 3.50
X-Man Spec. #1 offensive (c) 4.00

ENTITY
Avatar
? Nira X cover	6.00
? Snowman cover	11.00
? Nira X silver cover	11.00
? Snowman silver cover	16.00

ENTROPY TALES
Entropy
1	2.25
2 Domino Chance	2.25
3 thru 5	@2.25

EPSILON WAVE
Elite
1	3.00
2 thru 5	@2.25

EQUINE THE UNCIVILIZED
GraphXpress
1	4.00
2	2.50
3 thru 6	@2.25

EQUINOX CHRONICLES
Innovation, 1991
1 I:Team Equinox, Black Avatar	2.25
2 Black Avatar Plans US conquest.	2.25

ERADICATORS
Greater Mercury, 1990–91
1 RLm (1st Work)	5.00
1a 2nd printing	2.25
2	2.50
3 Vigil	2.25
4 thru 8	@2.25

ERIC PRESTON IS THE FLAME
B-Movie Comics, 1987
1 Son of G.A.Flame	2.50

ESCAPE TO THE STARS
Visionary
1 thru 7	@2.25

[2nd Series]
1	2.25
2	2.25

ESCAPE VELOCITY
Escape Velocity Press, 1986
1 and 2	@2.50

ESMERALDAS
Eternity
1 thru 4	2.25

ESP
Curtis Comics, 2002
Vol. 1 Manga
1 by Jihoon Park & Takyoung Lee	3.00
2 thru 5	@3.00

Vol. 2
1	3.00

ESPERS
Halloween Comics, 1996
1 JHI, R:ESPers	3.00
1 JHI,signed	3.00
2 JHI,signed	3.00
3 JHI,	3.00
3 JHI,signed	3.00
4 thru 6 JHI, conclusion	@3.00

Volume 2
1 `Undertow'	3.00

Escape Velocity #2
© Escape Velocity Press

2	3.00

ESP ULTRA
Komics, Inc., 1999
TPB Vol. 1	9.00
TPB Vol. 2 thru Vol. 7	@9.00

ETERNITY TRIPLE ACTION
Malibu B&W
1 F:Gazonga	2.25
2 F:Gigantor	2.50

EVENT PRESENTS THE ASH UNIVERSE
Event Comics, 1998
1-shot JQ,JP, 48pg	3.00

EVERETTE HARTSOE'S RAZOR
EH! Productions, 2000
1	3.50
1a Ruby Foil	5.00
2	4.00

EVIL ERNIE
Eternity, 1991–92
1 SHu,BnP,I&O:Evil Ernie, Lady Death	75.00
1a Spec. 1992 reprint, 16 extra pages	30.00
2 Death & Revival of Ernie, A:Lady Death, 1st (c)	40.00
3 Psycho Plague, A:Lady Death	35.00
4 A:Lady Death	25.00
5 A:Lady Death	25.00
TPB rep #1-5	25.00

EVIL ERNIE
Chaos! Comics
1 thru 5 reprints	@3.00
Spec. Youth Gone Wild, die-cut cover, Director's cut	5.00
TPB Youth Gone Wild	10.00

Chaos! Comics, 1996
1 encore presentation	3.00
1 thru 5 encore presentation	3.00
TPB Revenge	13.00
Preview Book Depraved	5.00
Pieces of Me Script	5.00

EVIL ERNIE: THE HORROR
Chaos! Comics, 2002
Ashcan b&w	6.00
1 BnP	4.50
1a premium edition	10.00
1b signed edition	15.00
1c super-premium edition	20.00
Spec. Script edition	5.00
Spec. Script Edition, premium	20.00

EVIL ERNIE: MANHATTAN DEATH TRIP
Chaos! Comics, 2002
1 BnP	3.50
1a premium edition	10.00
1b super-premium edition	20.00
Spec. #1 script	5.00
Spec. #1 script, premium edition	20.00

EVIL ERNIE RETURNS
Chaos! Comics, 2001
1 BnP	4.00
1a premium edition	13.00
1b super premium edition	20.00
1c signed ed.	15.00
Ashcan	6.00
Script #1	5.00
Script #1 premium edition	20.00

EVIL ERNIE: YOUTH GONE WILD
Chaos! Comics, 2001
Script	25.00
Script, signed	35.00

EVIL EYE
Fantagraphics, 1998
1 by Richard Sala	3.00
2 Glass Scorpion,pt.2	3.00
3 thru 7	@3.00
8 thru 11	@3.50
12	4.00

EXIT
Caliber, 1995
1 I:New series	3.00
2 thru 4 `The Traitors,'pt.2–pt.4	3.00
Epilogue	3.00
GN rep. 320-pg.	20.00
GN rep. 160-pg.	15.00

EX LIBRIS
Amaze Ink/SLG, 2005
1 by James Turner	3.00
2 thru 6	@3.00

EX-MUTANTS
Amazing Comics, 1986
1 AC/RLm	5.00
1a 2nd printing	2.25
2 and 3	@3.00
4 and 5	@2.25
Ann. #1	2.25
Pin-Up Spec. #1	2.25

Pied Piper Comics
6 thru 8	2.25

EX-MUTANTS: THE SHATTERED EARTH CHRONICLES
Eternity, 1988
1 thru 3	@2.25
4 & 5 RLd(c)	@2.75
6 thru 14	@2.25
Winter Special #1	2.25

EXPLORERS
Caliber Tapestry, 1997
1 . . . . 3.00
2 . . . . 3.00
3 `Nahuatl' 3.00
4 `The Sky is Falling' 3.00

EXTINCTIONERS
Shanda Fantasy Arts
VOL 2, 1999
1 . . . . 3.00
2 thru 9 . . . . @3.00
10 thru 15 48-pg. . . . . @5.00
Spec. #2 Tales of the Endangered. . 5.00
Spec. #3 Tales of the Endangered. . 5.00

EXTREMELY SILLY
Antarctic Press
1 . . . . 4.00
Vol. II, 1996
1 . . . . 2.25
2 . . . . 2.25

EYE OF MONGOMBO
Fantagraphics Books, 1990–91
1 . . . . 3.00
2 thru 7 . . . . @2.25

FADE FROM BLUE
Second to Some Studios 2002
1 by Murphy & Dalrymple 2.50
1a second printing 2.00
2 thru 8 . . . . @2.00
9 . . . . 2.00
10 concl. 48-pg. 5.00
TPB Vol. 1 . . . . 13.00
TPB Vol. 2 Fade Trade 16.00

FAITH
Lightning Comics, 1997
1 (of 2) 3.00
1a variant cover 3.00
1b Limited, cover A 10.00
1c Limited, cover B 10.00
1d signed & numbered 10.00
1 encore edition 3.00
1a encore, cover B 3.00
1b deluxe encore edition, cover A 10.00
1c deluxe encore edition, cover B 10.00

FANG: TESTAMENT
Sirius, 1997
1 by Kevin J. Taylor 2.50
2 . . . . 2.50
3 . . . . 2.50
4 (of 4) 2.50
TPB 12.00

FANGS OF THE WIDOW
London Night Studios, 1995
1 O:The Widow 3.00
1a platinum edition 5.00
2 Body Count 3.00
3 Emma Revealed 3.00
4 and 5 . . . . @3.00
Ground Zero, 1995
7 thru 9 `Metal Gypsies,'pt.#1–#3 @3.00
10 thru 13 rep. Widow: Bound by
   Blood #1–#4 + additional
   material 3.50
14 `Search and Destroy'pt.1 . . . . . 3.00
15 `Search and Destroy'pt.2 . . . . . 3.00
Ann. #1 Search and Destroy 6.00

FANTASCI
Warp Graphics-Apple, 1986
1 . . . . 2.50

2 and 3 . . . . @2.25
4 . . . . 4.00
5 thru 8 . . . . @2.25
9 `Apple Turnover' 2.25

FANTASTIC ADVENTURES
1 thru 5 . . . . @2.25

FANTASTIC FABLES
Silver Wolf, 1987
1 and 2 . . . . @2.25

FANTASTIC PANIC
Antarctic, 1993–94
1 thru 8 Ganbear . . . . @2.75
Vol. 2, 1995
1 thru 4 . . . . @2.75
4 thru 9 . . . . @3.00
10 concl. 3.50

FANTASTIC STORIES
Basement Comics, 2001
1 F:Grakoom, the Forgotten God . 3.00
1a special edition 9.00
2 Lost Women of the Moon 3.00
2a special edition 9.00
3 . . . . 3.00
3a special edition 9.00

FANTASTIC WORLDS
Flashback Comics, 1995
1 Space Opera 3.00
2 F:Attu, Captain Courage 3.00

FANTASY QUARTERLY
Independent, 1976
1 1978 1st Elfquest 65.00

FART WARS:
SPECIAL EDITION
Entity Comics, 1997
1 Star Wars trilogy parody,A:Nira X 2.75
1a Empire Attacks Back cover 2.75
1b Return of the One-Eye cover . . . 2.75

FAR WEST
Antarctic Press, 1998
1 (of 4) by Richard Moore 3.00
2 thru 4 . . . . @3.00
VOL. 2
1 (of 4) 3.00
2 . . . . 2.50

FASTLANE ILLUSTRATED
Fastlane Studios, 1994
1 Super Powers & Hot Rods 2.50
2 & 3 . . . . @2.50

FATALIS
Caliber Core, 1998
1 by Mark Chadbourn
   & Vince Danks 3.00
1a signed & numbered 7.00
2 . . . . 3.00

FAT NINJA
Silver Wolf Comics, 1985–86
1 . . . . 2.50
2 Vigil 2.50
3 thru 8 . . . . @2.50

FAUST
Northstar, 1985
1 Vigil 25.00
1a Vigil,2nd Printing 5.00
1b Vigil,3rd Printing 2.50

Fat Ninja #5
© Silver Wolf Comics

1c Tour Edition 25.00
2 Vigil 15.00
2a Vigil,2nd Printing 3.00
2b Vigil,3rd Printing 2.50
3 Vigil 10.00
3a Vigil,2nd Printing 2.50
4 Vigil 5.00
5 Vigil 5.00
6 Vigil 5.00
Rebel Studios
7 Vigil 5.00
8 TV 3.50
9 TV,Love of the Damned 3.50
10 E:DQ(s),TV,Love o/t Damned . . . 3.50
VOL. II
1 TV,Love of the Damned 2.50

FAUST/777: THE WRATH
Avatar Press, 1998
0 by David Quinn & Tim Vigil,
   Darkness in Collision x-over . . . 3.00
0a wrap 4.00
0b leather cover 20.00
0c Royal Blue edition 60.00
0d Platinum edition 16.00
1 (of 4) 3.50
2 Darkness in Collision,pt.3 . . . . . 3.50
3 . . . . 3.50
4 . . . . 3.50
Faust Hornbook 5.00
TPB 112-pg. 17.00

FAUST:
SINGHA'S TALONS
Avatar, 2000
1/2 . . . . 3.50
1/2 wraparound (c) 4.00
1/2 Beachum (c) 6.00
1/2 prism foil 13.00
1/2 royal blue edition 75.00
1/2 Blood Curse 5.00
1 (of 4) 4.00
1a wraparound (c) 4.50
1c red foil leather 25.00
1d prism foil 13.00
1 commemorative 6.00
2 . . . . 4.00
3 . . . . 4.00
4 . . . . 4.00
2a thru 4a previews exclusive . . @4.50
Preview Book 6.00

FELIX THE CAT
Felix Comics, 1997
1 inc. Felix's Cafe	2.25
2 Crusin' for a Brusin'	2.25
3 Ah Choo	2.25
4 inc. Spaced Out	2.25
5 Holiday/Winter issue	2.25
6 The Felix Force	2.25
7 A Rash of Trash	2.25
8 Halloween	2.25
Cat-A-Strophic Wrestling Spec.#1	2.25
Felix Summer Splash #1	2.50

FELIX THE CAT TRUE CRIME STORIES
Felix Comics, 2000
1	2.50
Spec.#1 Blockbuster movie bonanza	2.50
Spec. Felix Jurassic Jamboree	2.50
Spec. Felix Magic Bag of Tricks	2.50
Spec. Felix Laff-A-Palooza	2.50
1-shot Felix's Totally Wacky News	2.50
TPB Comic Adventures of Felix	13.00
1-shot Halloween Spectacular #13	2.50
1-shot House of 1000 Ha Ha's	2.50
1-shot Felix the Cat's TV Extravaganza (2002)	2.50
1-shot Buy This Comic	2.50
1-shot Amazing Colossal Felix the Cat	2.50
1-shot Silly Stories #1	2.50
TPB Comic Adventures of Felix	13.00

FEM FANTASTIQUE
AC Comics, 1988
1	2.50

FEMFORCE
AC Comics, 1987
1 thru 15 See Color
16 I:Thunder Fox	3.00
17 F:She-Cat,Ms.Victory, giant	3.00
18 double size	3.00
19	3.00
20 V:RipJaw, Black Commando	3.00
21 V:Dr.Pretorius	3.00
22 V:Dr.Pretorius	3.00
23 V:Rad	3.00
24 A:Teen Femforce	3.00
25 V:Madame Boa	3.00
26 V:Black Shroud	3.00
27 V:Black Shroud	3.00
28 A:Arsenio Hall	3.00
29 V:Black Shroud	3.00
30 V:Garganta	3.00
31 I:Kronon Captain Paragon	3.00
32 V:Garganta	3.00
33 Personal Lives of team	3.00
34 V:Black Shroud	3.00
35 V:Black Shroud	3.00
36 giant,V:Dragonfly,Shade	3.00
37 A:Blue Bulleteer,She-Cat	3.00
38 V:Lady Luger	3.00
39 F:She-Cat	3.00
40 V:Sehkmet	3.00
41 V:Captain Paragon	3.00
42 V:Alizarin Crimson	3.00
43 V:Glamazons of Galaxy G	3.00
44 V:Lady Luger,F:Garganta	5.00
45 Nightveil Rescued	3.00
46 V:Lady Luger	3.00
47 V:Alizarin Crimson	3.00
48	3.00
49 I:New Msw.Victory	3.00
50 Ms.Victory Vs.Rad,flexi-disc	3.00
51	3.00
52 V:Claw & Clawites	3.00
53 I:Bulldog Deni,V:(Dick Briefer's)Frightenstein	3.00

54 The Orb of Bliss	3.00
55 R:Nightveil	3.00
56 V:Alizarin Crimson	3.00
57 thru 92 See Color	
93 `Shattered Memories,'pt.2	3.00
93a deluxe	6.00
94 `Shattered Memories,'pt.3	3.00
94a deluxe	6.00
95	3.00
95a deluxe	6.00
96	3.00
96a deluxe	6.00
97	3.00
98 deluxe	6.00
98	3.00
98 deluxe	6.00
99	3.00
99 deluxe	6.00
100 Anniv. issue, with poster	8.00
100A signed, with poster	12.00
100B no poster, not signed	4.00

THE YESTERDAY SYNDROME
101 Pt.1	5.00
102 Pt.2	5.00
103 Pt.3	5.00

RETURN FROM THE ASHES
104 pt.1 Firebeam, 44pg	5.00
105 pt.2	5.00
106 pt.3 concl.	5.00

DARKGODS: RAMPAGE
107 Darkgods: Rampage,pt.1	5.00
108 Darkgods: Rampage,pt.2	5.00
109 Darkgods: Rampage,pt.3	6.00
110 thru 117	@6.00
118 44-pg.	7.00
118a spec. edition, 60-pg.	10.00
119 The Missing Mask	7.00
120 Superbabes,pt.1	7.00
121 Superbabes,pt.2	7.00
121a Femme Noir (c)	10.00
122 Superbabes,pt.3	7.00
122a spec. editions, variant(c)	@10.00
123	7.00
124	7.00
125 Firebeam Rising	7.00
126 Totally Absorbed	7.00
127 No Return	7.00
128 Halloween Special	7.00
129 Shorty	7.00
130 20th Anniversary issue	7.00
131 F:Rad and the Black Terror	7.00
132 Buckaroo Betty Bates	7.00
133 Too Tall Tara	7.00

Femforce #60 © AC Comics

134 Generation Gap	7.00
135 Multitude of foes	7.00
136 Welcome to the Jungle	7.00
137	7.00
Spec.#1 FemForce Timelines, O:Femforce (1995)	3.00
Spec.#1 FemForce:Frightbook, Horror tales by Briefer, Ayers, Powell	3.00
Spec.#2 (2001)	6.00
Spec.#1 Femforce:Uncut (2001)	10.00
Untold Origin of FemForce	5.00
GN The Capricorn Chronicles	12.50
GN FemForce: Timestorm	10.00
GN, FemForce: Timestorm, deluxe	15.00
TPB Origins	13.00
TPB Origins, signed	14.00
TPB Sisters in Sin, lim. ed.	22.00
TPB To Die For	16.00
TPB Victory Reborn	16.00
TPB The First 112 Issues are the Toughest	20.00
TPB In Living Color	25.00
TPB The Closer You Get, The Better We Look	23.00
Secret Files of Femforce, deluxe	5.00
Pulp Fiction Portfolio #2	18.00
Spec. #1 Femforce vs. The Claw	7.00
Spec. #1 Rampaging She-Cat	7.00
1-shot Claws of the She-Cat	5.00
Features #1: Giantess	7.00

FEMFORCE SPECIAL
AC Comics, 1999
1 Femforce Special: Rayda– The Cyberian Connection	3.00
1a Variant cover	3.00
1b Variant cover, signed	10.00
2	3.00
3 conclusion	4.00

FEVER, THE
Dark Vision Publishing, 1995
1 O:The Fever	2.50
2 Fever's Father	2.50
3 thru 5	@2.50

FIFTIES TERROR
Eternity, 1988
1 thru 6	@2.50

FIGHTING YANK
AC Comics, 2001
1 by Hack Koilby	6.00
2	6.00
3 Cave Girl	6.00
4	6.00
5 Three Chambers of Horror	6.00

FINAL CYCLE
Sirius
Graphic Novel	4.00
1 thru 4	@2.25

FINDER
Lightspeed Comics, 1996
1 thru 5 by Carla Speed McNeil	@3.00
6 thru 19	@3.00
20 thru 24	@3.00
25 thru 38	@3.00
TPB Vol. 1 Sin Eater	16.00
TPB Vol. 2 Sin-Eater	20.00
TPB Vol. 3 King of the Cats	14.00
TPB Vol. 4 Talisman	14.00
TPB Vol. 5 Dream Sequence	21.00
TPB Vol. 6 Mystery Date	18.00
TPB Vol. 7 The Rescuers	17.00
TPB Vol. 8 Five Crazy Women	16.00

FINDER FOOTNOTES
Lightspeed Press
1 thru 4 . . . . @6.00

FIRE TEAM
Aircel, 1990
1 thru 3 by Don Lomax . . . . @2.50
4 V:Vietnamese Gangs 2.50
5 Cam in Vietnam 2.50
6 . . . . 2.50

FIRST WAVE
Andromeda Entertainment, 2001
1 Patriot or Traitor 3.00
1a signed 10.00
GN Through Alien Eyes 8.00

FIRST WAVE: DOUBLE VISION
Andromeda Entertainment, 2001
1 (of 2) 3.00
1a photo (c). 3.00

FIRST WAVE: GENESIS OF A GENIUS
Andromeda Entertainment, 2001
Spec. painted (c) 3.00
Spec. photo (c). 3.00

FISH POLICE
Fishwrap Productions, 1985
1 1st printing 7.00
1a 2nd printing 3.00
Becomes:

INSPECTOR GILL OF THE FISH POLICE
2 . . . . 5.00
3 thru 11 . . . . @4.00
[Vol 2]
Comico Publ., 1987
5 thru 12 . . . . @3.50
13 thru 17 **see Color issues**
Apple Publ.
18 thru 24 . . . . @2.50

FISH SHTICKS
Apple, 1991
1 and 2 Fish Police . . . . @2.75
3 and 4 . . . . @2.50

FIST OF GOD
Eternity, 1988
1 thru 4 . . . . @2.50

FIST OF THE BLUE SKY
Gutsoon! Entertainment, 2003
TPB Vol. 1 . . . . 10.00
TPB Vol. 2 thru Vol. 4. . . . . @10.00

FIST OF THE NORTH STAR
Viz Select, 1996
1 thru 3 . . . . @3.25
4 . . . . 2.25
5 . . . . 3.25
6 . . . . 3.00
7 . . . . 3.00
TPB Vol. 2 Night of the Jackal, rep. 17.00
Part Three
1 thru 5 by Buronson
  & Tetsuo Hara . . . . @3.00

Fist of the Northstar Vol. 2 #7
© *Viz Communications*

Part Four, 1996
1 thru 7 . . . . @3.00
TPB Volume 2: Southern Cross. . . 17.00

FLAG FIGHTERS
Ironcat, 1997
1 by Masaomi Kanzaki 3.00
2 Student Flagger,pt.1 . . . . 3.00
3 Student Flagger,pt.2 . . . . 3.00
4 Student Flagger,pt.3 . . . . 3.00
5 . . . . 3.00
6 Death Window 3.00
7 F:Murasame 3.00

FLAMING CARROT
Aardvark–Vanaheim, 1984
1 1981 Kililan Barracks. 50.00
1a 1984. . . . . 25.00
2 . . . . 25.00
3 . . . . 20.00
4 thru 6 . . . . @15.00
Renegade
7 . . . . 12.00
8 . . . . 10.00
9 & 10 . . . . @8.00
11 & 12. . . . . @6.00
13 thru 15. . . . . @5.00
15a variant without cover price . . . 8.00
16 and 17. . . . . @5.00
See: Dark Horse

FLARE
Hero Graphics, 1990
1 thru 7 See Color
8 thru 14 . . . . 3.00

FLARE FIRST EDITION
Hero Graphics, 1993
1 Flare as teenager 5.00
2 . . . . 4.00
3 thru 11 . . . . @3.50

FLARE VS. TIGRESS
Hero Graphics
1 and 2 . . . . @3.50

FORBIDDEN KINGDOM
Eastern Comics, 1987
1 thru 11 . . . . @2.25

FORBIDDEN VAMPIRE TALES
Forbidden, 1997
0 . . . . 3.00
1 sexy vampire 3.00
2 thru 7 . . . . @3.00
Spec.#1 Vault of Innocents 3.00

FORBIDDEN WORLDS
ACG, 1996
1 SD,JAp,rep. 2.50

FORCE SEVEN
Lone Star Press, 1999
1 . . . . 3.00
2 thru 7 . . . . @3.00

FORCE 10
Crow Comics, 1995
0 Ash Can Preview 1.00
1 I:Force 10. . . . . 2.50
2 Children of the Revolution,pt#2 . . 2.50
3 Against all Odds 2.50

FORETERNITY
Antarctic Press, 1997
1 by Rod Espinoza 3.00
2 and 3 . . . . @3.00

FOREVER WARRIORS
Aardwolf, 1996
1 (of 3) RTs,RB 3.00
2 RTs,RB 3.00
3 RTs,RB, concl. 3.00

FOREVER WARRIORS
CFD, 1997
1 RB,RTs. 3.00
2 RB,RTs,KN. 3.00
3 RB,RTs, finale 3.00

FORGIVE ME FATHER
High Impact 2004
1 . . . . 3.00
2 . . . . 3.00
1a thru 2a variant (c)s . . . . @6.00
Bulletproof Comics
3 . . . . 3.00

FORTY WINKS
Oddjobs Limited, 1997
1 (of 4) by Sneed & Peters 3.00
2 Everything Right is Wrong Again . 3.00
3 Where Your Eyes Don't Go 3.00
4 There Might be Giants 3.00
Peregrine Entertainment, 1998
Christmas Spec. 3.00
TV Party Spec. 3.00
Spec.#1 Buzzboy (2000) 3.00

FORTY WINKS: MR. HORRIBLE
Peregrine Entertainment, 2000
1 . . . . 3.00
2 . . . . 3.00

FORTY WINKS: THE FABLED PIRATE QUEEN OF THE SOUTH CHINA SEA
Peregrine Entertainment, 1999
1 by Vincent Sneed & Martinez . . . 3.00
2 . . . . 3.00
3 . . . . 3.00

FOUR KUNOICHI:
ENTER THE SINJA
Lightning Comics, 1997
1 . . . . 3.00

FOX COMICS
1 Spec. 3.00
25 . . . . 3.00
26 . . . . 3.50

FRAGILE PROPHET
Lost in the Dark Press 2005
1 . . . . 3.00
2 . . . . 3.00
3 . . . . 3.00
TPB 10.00

FRANK
Fantagraphics
1 JWo 3.00
2 JWo 4.00
3 . . . . 4.00
4 . . . . 4.00
GN rep. from various sources 15.00
TPB Vol. 1, signed 15.00
Vol. 2 partial color 17.00

FRANKENSTEIN
Eternity
1 . . . . 2.25
2 . . . . 2.25
3 . . . . 2.25

FRANKIES FRIGHTMARES
1 Celebrates Frank 60th Anniv. . . . 2.25

FRANK THE UNICORN
Fish Warp
1 thru 7 . . . . @2.25

FREAK-OUT ON
INFANT EARTHS
Blackthorne, 1987
1 Don Chin 2.50
2 Don Chin 2.50

FREAKS
Monster Comics
1 Movie adapt 2.50
2 Movie adapt.cont. 2.50
3 thru 4 Movie adapt. . . . . @2.50

FREAKSHOW
Atomic Diner, 2004
1 . . . . 3.00
2 thru 12 . . . . @3.00
TPB Vol. 1 . . . . 15.00
TPB Vol. 2 . . . . 15.00

FRED THE
POSSESSED FLOWER
Happy Predator, 1998
1 The Plant Behind the Scenes . . . 3.00
2 . . . . 3.00
3 Interview with a Demon 3.00
4 The People vs. Hell 3.00
5 . . . . 3.00
6 The Origin of Fred 3.00

FRENCH ICE
Renegade Press, 1987
1 thru 15 . . . . @2.50

FRIENDS
Renegade, 1987
1 thru 5 . . . . @2.50

French Ice #11
© Renegade

FRIGHT
Eternity
1 thru 13 . . . . @2.25

FRINGE
Caliber
1 thru 7 . . . . @2.50

FROM BEYOND
Studio Insidio
1 Short stories-horror 2.50
2 inc.Clara Mutilares 2.50
3 inc.The Experiment 2.50
4 inc.Positive Feedback 2.50

FROM HELL
Tundra, 1991
1 . . . . 20.00
1a 2nd printing 10.00
2 . . . . 12.00

Kitchen Sink
Volume Three
1 AMo,ECa 10.00
2 AMo,ECa 7.00
2a 2nd printing 6.00
3 . . . . 7.00
3a 2nd printing 6.00
4 . . . . 7.00
4 new printing 5.00
5 . . . . 7.00
5 new printing 5.00
6 . . . . 7.00
7 . . . . 7.00
8 . . . . 7.00
8 AMo,ECa,new printing 5.00
9 AMo,ECa 7.00
9 new printing 5.00
10 AMo,ECa 7.00
10 new printing 5.00
Spec. Dance of the Gull Catchers . . 5.00

FROM THE DARKNESS
Adventure Comics, 1990
1 JBa 25.00
2 . . . . 30.00
3 and 4 . . . . @12.00

FROM THE DARKNESS II
BLOOD VOWS
Cry For Dawn
1 R:Ray Thorn,Desnoires 12.00
2 V:Desnoires 8.00

3 . . . . 8.00

FROM THE VOID
1 1st B.Blair,1982 . . . . 75.00

FROST:
THE DYING BREED
Caliber
1 thru 3 Vietnam Flashbacks . . . @3.00

F–III BANDIT
Antarctic Press, 1995
1 F:Akira, Yoohoo 3.00
2 F:Yukio 3.00
3 F:Were-Women 3.00
4 . . . . 3.00
5 Romeo & Juliet story 3.00
6 thru 8 . . . . @3.00

FUGITOID
Mirage
1-shot TMNT Tie-in 8.00

FULL METAL FICTION
London Night, 1997
1 EHr 4.00
1a Nun with a Gun edition 10.00
1b dark room edition cover 4.00
2 . . . . 4.00
2a signed 10.00
3 `Hellborne' concl. 4.00
4 thru 8 . . . . @4.00

FURIES
Carbon-Based, 1996
1 thru 6 . . . . @2.75

FURRLOUGH
Antarctic Press, 1991
1 Funny Animal Military stories 3.00
2 thru 10 . . . . @2.50
11 thru 20 . . . . @2.75
21 thru 33 . . . . @2.75
34 . . . . 3.00
35 48pg 4.00
36 thru 40 . . . . @3.00
41 thru 51 . . . . @3.00
Best of Furrlough, Vol.1 . . . . 5.00
Best of Furrlough, Vol.2 . . . . 5.00
Radio Comix, 1997
52 thru 75 . . . . @3.00
76 thru 99 . . . . @3.00
100 80-pg. 6.00
101 . . . . 3.00
102 . . . . 3.00
103 thru 139 . . . . @3.00
140 thru 153 . . . . @3.50
154 thru 166 . . . . @3.50
Furrlough's Finest Vol. 1 . . . . 6.00
Furrlough's Finest Vol. 2 . . . . 6.00
Furrlough Presents Sex Kitten #1 . . 5.00

FURRY NINJA
HIGH SCHOOL
Shanda Fantasy Arts, 2002
1 (of 2) x-over (self) parody 5.00
2 x-over, concl. 5.00

FURY
Aircel
1 thru 3 . . . . @2.25

FURY OF HELLINA, THE
Lightning Comics, 1995
1 V:Luciver 3.50
1a limited & signed 8.00
1b platinum 8.00

FUSION
Eclipse, 1987
1 . . . . 2.50
2 thru 17 . . . . @2.50

FUTABA-KUN CHANGE
Ironcat, 1998
1 by Hiroshi Aro 3.00
2 thru 6 . . . . @3.00
GN Vol. 1 . . . . 16.00
VOL. 2
1 . . . . 3.00
2 thru 6 . . . . @3.00
VOL. 3, 1999
1 . . . . 3.00
2 thru 6 . . . . @3.00
TPB Vol. 3 . . . . 16.00
VOL. 4, 2000
1 . . . . 3.00
2 thru 6 . . . . @3.00
VOL. 5, 2000
1 by Hiroshi Aro 3.00
2 thru 6 . . . . @3.00
VOL. 6, 2001
1 . . . . 3.00
2 thru 6 . . . . @3.00
TPB Vol. 4 . . . . 16.00
TPB Vol. 5 rep.. . . . . 16.00
VOL. 7, 2001
1 thru 6 . . . . @3.00
VOL. 8
1 thru 6 . . . . @3.00
TPB Vol. 5 . . . . 16.00
TPB Vol. 7 . . . . 16.00
TPB Vol. 8 . . . . 16.00

FUTURAMA
Slave Labor, 1989
1 thru 4 . . . . @2.50

FUTURETECH
Mushroom Comics, 1995
1 Automotive Hi-Tech 3.50
2 Cyber Trucks 3.50

FUTURIANS
Aardwolf, 1995
0 DC R:Futurians, sequel to
   Lodestone color series 3.00
0 second printing, DC 3.00

GAIJIN
Caliber, 1990
1-shot, 64pg. 3.50
1 thru 3 . . . . @2.25

GALAXION
Helikon, 1997
1 by Tara Jenkins, science fiction. . 2.75
2 . . . . 2.75
3 . . . . 2.75
4 Choices 2.75
5 . . . . 2.75
6 Communication 2.75
7 Song of Hiawatha 2.75
8 Persuasion. 2.75
9 Deal with the Devil. 2.75
10 . . . . 2.75
11 . . . . 2.75
Spec. #1, 16pg. 2.00
GN Vol 1 . . . . 16.00
Spec. Flip Book Galaxion
   & Amy Unbound 2.75

GATEKEEPER
GK Publishing, 1987
1 . . . . 2.50

Helikon Comics   Number 3

GALAXION

Galaxion #3
© Helikon

2 and 3 . . . . @3.00

GATES OF THE NIGHT
Jademan
1 thru 4 . . . . @3.50

GEAR
Fireman Press, 1998
1 (of 6) by Douglas TenNaple. 3.00
2 thru 6 . . . . @3.00
TPB 15.00

GEISHA
Oni Press, 1998
1 (of 4) by Andi Watson 3.00
2 . . . . 3.00
3 . . . . 3.00
4 . . . . 3.00
TPB by Andi Watson 10.00

GEMS OF THE SAMURAI
Newcomers Publishing
1 I:Master Samurai 3.00

GENERIC COMIC BOOK
Comics Conspiracy, 2001
1 thru 4 . . . . @2.25
5 . . . . 2.25
5a Hyper Fanboy variant edition. . . 6.00
6 thru 13 . . . . @2.25
TPB 9.00

GENOCYBER
Viz, 1993
1 I:Genocyber 2.75
2 thru 5 . . . . @2.75

GEOBREEDERS
CPM Manga, 1999
1 by Akhiro Ito. 3.00
2 thru 10 . . . . @3.00
11 thru 36 . . . . @3.00
TPB Vol. 1 . . . . 16.00
TPB Vol. 2 rep. #8–#14 . . . . 16.00
TPB Vol. 3 . . . . 16.00
TPB Vol. 4 Unfriendly Skies. 16.00
TPB #5 Big Trouble at Tokyo
   Tower. 16.00

GERIATRIC GANGRENE JUJITSU GERBILS
Planet X Productions
1 . . . . 2.50
2 . . . . 2.25

GHOSTS OF DRACULA
Eternity
1 A:Dracula & Houdini 2.50
2 A:Sherlock Holmes 2.50
3 A:Houdini 2.50
4 Count Dracula's Castle 2.50
5 Houdini, Van Helsing, Dracula
   team-up 2.50

GI GOVERNMENT ISSUED
Paranoid Press, 1994
1 thru 7 F:Mac, Jack . . . . @2.25

GIANT SHANDA ANIMAL
Shanda Fantasy Arts, 1998
1 . . . . 5.00
2 . . . . 5.00
3 . . . . 5.00
4 . . . . 4.50
5 thru 11 . . . . @5.00

GIDEON HAWK
Big Shot Comics, 1995
1 I:Gideon Hawk, Max 9471 . . . . . 2.25
2 The Jewel of Shamboli,pt.2 . . . . 2.25
3 The Jewel of Shamboli,pt.3 . . . . 2.25
2 The Jewel of Shamboli,pt.4 . . . . 2.50
3 The Jewel of Shamboli,pt.5 . . . . 2.50

GIGANTOR
Antarctic Press, 2000
1 (of 12) by Ben Dunn 3.00
2 thru 8 . . . . @3.00

GIRL GENIUS
Studio Foglio, 2001
1 thru 5 . . . . @3.00
Airship Entertainment, 2002
6 thru 10 . . . . @4.00
11 thru 14 . . . . @4.00
TPB Vol. 1 Phil Foglio, 96-pg. 10.00
TPB Vol. 2 . . . . 20.00
TPB Vol. 3 . . . . 21.00
TPB Vol. 4 color. 21.00
TPB Vol. 5 Color 20.00
TPB Omnibus Edition #1 . . . . 15.00

GIRLS OF NINJA HIGH SCHOOL, 1997
Antarctic Press
Spec. 4.00
Spec. 1998 cover A 3.00
Spec. 1998 cover B 3.00
Spec. 1999 . . . . 3.00

GIZMO
Chance, 1986
1 . . . . 7.50

GIZMO
Mirage, 1987
1 . . . . 5.50
2 . . . . 3.00
3 . . . . 2.50
4 thru 7 . . . . @2.50

GIZMO & THE FUGITOID
Mirage, 1989
1 and 2 . . . . @2.50

All comics prices listed are for *Near Mint* condition.

GLOOM COOKIE
Slave Labor Graphics, 1999

1 by Serena Valentino & Ted Naifeh	3.00
2	3.00
3	3.00
4	3.00
5	3.00
6 Sebastian's Search	3.00
7 thru 9	@3.00
10 thru 25	@3.00
26 thru 29	@3.00
TPB Vol. 1 200-pg.	18.00
TPB Vol. 2 192-pg.	17.00
TPB Vol. 3	16.00
TPB Vol. 4 The Carnival Wars	17.00
Color Spec. A Monster's Christmas	4.00

GNATRAT
Prelude, 1986

1	5.00
2 Early Years	2.25

GNATRAT: THE MOVIE
Innovation, 1990

1	2.25

GOBBLEDYGOOK
Mirage, 1986

1 1st series, Rare	700.00
2 1st series, Rare	400.00
1 TMNT series reprint	6.00

GOJIN
Antarctic Press, 1995

1 F:Terran Defense Force	3.00
2 F:Terran Defense Force	3.00
3 V:Alien Monster	3.00
4 Aliens Bone	3.00
5 thru 8	@3.00

GOLD DIGGER
Antarctic Press, 1992
[Limited Series]

1 Geena & Cheetah in Peru	8.00
2 Adventures contd	6.00
3 Adventures contd	6.00
4 Adventures contd	5.00
GN Rep. #1–#4 + new material	10.00

[Volume 2], 1993

1 by Fred Perry	10.00
2 Fred Perry	8.00
3 Fred Perry	8.00
4 Fred Perry	6.00
5 misnumbered as #0	5.00
6 thru 8 by Fred Perry	@4.00
9 and 10 by Fred Perry	@3.50
11 thru 27 by Fred Perry	@3.00
28 and 29 by Fred Perry	@3.00
30 thru 39	@3.00
40 Wedding day	3.00
41 Gold Digger Beta	3.00
42	3.00
43 Beta Phase phenomenon	3.00
44 Beta tool	3.00
45 F:Priestess Tanya	3.00
46 Agent M.	3.00
47 Old Dirty Bastard	3.00
48	3.00
49 The Library of Time	3.00
50	3.00
50a deluxe	6.00
Ann. 1995, 48-pg.	4.00
Ann. 1996	4.00
Ann. 1997	4.00
Ann. 1998	4.00
Ann. 2000 b&w	4.00
Ann. 2001	4.00
Ann. 2002 B&W	4.00

Gold Digger #36
© Antarctic Press

Best of Gold Digger Ann. Vol. 1	3.00
Collected Gold Digger,Vol.1	10.00
Collected Gold Digger,Vol.2	10.00
Collected Gold Digger,Vol.3	10.00
Collected Gold Digger,Vol.4	10.00
Collected Gold Digger,Vol.5	10.00
Collected Gold Digger,Vol.6	11.00
Collected Gold Digger,Vol.7	11.00
Collected Gold Digger,Vol.8	11.00
Collected Gold Digger,Vol.9	13.00
Mangazine Spec. #1	3.00

GOLD DIGGER/
NINJA HIGH SCHOOL
Antarctic Press, 1998

Spec. Asrial vs. Cheetah Compilation, x-over rep.	5.00
Spec. Science Fair Compilation, x-over rep.	5.00
TPB Time Warp	16.00

GOLD DIGGER:
EDGE GUARD
Radio Comix, 2000

1 (of 4) by John Barrett	3.00
2 thru 6	@3.00
7 finale	3.00

GOLD DIGGER: THRONE
OF SHADOWS
Antarctic Press 2006

1 Manga	3.00
2 thru 4	@3.00

GOLDEN AGE GREATS
AC Comics, 1995

Vol.#1 thru #6 40s and 50s	@10.00
Vol. 7 Best of the West	10.00
Vol. 8 F:Phantom Lady, Miss Victory	10.00
Vol. 9 Fabulous Femmes of Fiction House	10.00
Vol. 11 Roy Rogers & The Silver Screen Cowboys	12.00
Vol. 12 Thrilling Science Fiction	10.00
Vol. 13	10.00
Vol. 14 The Comic Book Jungle	12.00
TPB Vol. 1 Adventure Heroes Special	30.00
TPB Vol. 1 Fine Art Special	25.00
TPB Vol. 1 Costumed Crusaders	25.00

GOLDEN-AGE
MEN OF MYSTERY
AC Comics, 1996

5	7.00
7	6.00
8	6.00
9	6.00
10 Masked comic book heroes, 52 pg.	7.00
11 rep. Cat-Man comics	7.00
12 Espionage, WE	7.00
13 F:Daredevil vs. The Claw	7.00
14 F:Commando Yank	7.00
15 F:Captain 3-D	7.00
16 F:Mr. Scarlet, Airboy	7.00

Becomes:

MEN OF MYSTERY
AC Comics, 1999

17 F:Stuntman	7.00
18	7.00
19 Space edition	7.00
19a spec. ed. 68-pg.	11.00
20 F:Phantom Lady	7.00
21 Fawcett superheroes	7.00
22 Manhunter	7.00
23 Skyman	7.00
24 Captain Flash	7.00
25	7.00
26 Emerald	7.00
27 The Fog Robbers	7.00
28 F:Black Terror,Miss Masque	7.00
29 The Lynx, Wildfire	7.00
30 War Years	7.00
31 Speed and Space	7.00
32 Phantom Lady	7.00
33 Red white and blue	7.00
34 Halloween Issue	7.00
35 F:Spy Smasher	7.00
36 F:Captain Flash	7.00
37 F:Cat-Man and Kitten	7.00
38 Spy Smasher vs. Iron Mask	7.00
39 Spy Smasher, Airboy	7.00
40 The Black Terror	7.00
41 Bulletman	7.00
42 Blue Bolt	7.00
43 The Flame	7.00
44 Cat-Man and Bulletman	7.00
45 thru 55	@7.00
56 thru 62	@7.00
Coll. Ed. #7	20.00
Digest Spec. #1	16.00
Spotlight Spec. #1	15.00
TPB Blockbuster	26.00
Ann. #1 Spy Smasher Special	8.00
TPB Star Studded Spectacular	25.00
TPB Heroes for the Ages	25.00
TPB Supersized Album	30.00
TPB Champions Collection	25.00
TPB Monster Collection	25.00

GOLDEN AGE SCIENCE
FICTION TREASURY
AC Comics 2006

TPB Vol. 1	30.00

GOLDEN WARRIOR
Industrial Design, 1997

1 by Eric Bansen & RB	3.00
2	3.00
3	3.00

GOLDEN WARRIOR
ICZER ONE
Antarctic, 1994

1 thru 5	@3.00

GOLDWYN 3-D
Blackthorne
1 . . . . 2.25

GO-MAN
Caliber
1 thru 4 . . . . @2.25
Graphic Novel 'N' 10.00

GOOD GIRL COMICS
AC
1 F:Tara Fremont 4.00

GOOD GIRLS
Fantagraphics, 1987
1 adult. 2.50
2 thru 4 . . . . @2.50

GOON, THE
Avatar Press, 1999
1 by Eric Powell 65.00
2 . . . . 35.00
3 . . . . 35.00

GORE SHRIEK
Fantaco, 1986
1 . . . . 2.50
2 and 3 . . . . @2.50
4 +Mars Attacks 3.00
5 . . . . 3.00
6 . . . . 3.50
Vol 2 #1 . . . . 2.50

GOTHESS: DARK ECSTASY
SCC Entertainment, 1997
1 (of 3) 3.00
2 . . . . 3.00
3 . . . . 3.00

GRACKLE, THE
Acclaim, 1996
1 MBn,PG,Double Cross, pt.1. . . . . 3.00
2 MBn,PG,Double Cross, pt.2. . . . . 3.00
3 MBn,PG,Double Cross, pt.3. . . . . 3.00
4 MBn,PG,Double Cross, pt.4. . . . . 3.00

GRAPHIC CLASSICS
Eureka Productions, 2001
TPB Vol. 1 Edgar Allan Poe. 8.00
TPB Vol. 2 Arthur Conan Doyle. . . 10.00
TPB Vol. 3 H.G. Wells 10.00
TPB Vol. 4 H.P. Lovecraft 10.00
TPB Vol. 5 Jack London 10.00
TPB Vol. 6 Ambrose Bierce 10.00
TPB Vol. 7 Bram Stoker. 10.00
TPB Vol. 9 Robert Louis
   Stevenson 10.00
TPB Vol. 10 Horror Classics 10.00
TPB Vol. 11 O. Henry 12.00
TPB Vol. 12 Adventure Classics . . 12.00
TPB Vol. 13 Rafael Sabatini 12.00

GRAPHIC STORY MONTHLY
Fantagraphics
1 thru 7 . . . . @3.00

GRAPHIQUE MUSIQUE
Slave Labor, 1989–90
1 . . . . 35.00
2 . . . . 30.00
3 . . . . 25.00

GRAVEDIGGERS
Acclaim, 1996
1 (of 4) 3.00
2 thru 4 . . . . @3.00

GRAVE TALES
Hamilton, 1991
1 JSon,GM, mag. size 8.00
2 JSon,GM,short stories. 6.00
3 JSon,GM, inc.'Stake Out' 6.00

GREAT DETECTIVE STARRING SHERLOCK HOLMES
ACG Comics, 1999
1 by Otto Lagoni 3.00
2 thru 5 . . . . @3.00

GREEN BERETS
ACG, 2000
1 JKu. 3.00
2 thru 7 JKu, Robin Moore . . . . . @3.00
TPB Limited Signed. 25.00

GREENLEAF IN EXILE
Cat's Paw Comics, 1998
1 by Doug Anderson. 3.00
2 thru 7 . . . . @3.00

GREMLIN TROUBLE
Anti-Ballistic Pixelation, 1995
1 & 2 Airstrike on Gremlin Home @3.00
1 new printing 3.00
3 thru 5 . . . . @3.00

Gremlin Trouble #13
© *Anti-Ballistic Pixelation*

6 'Fun with Electricity'. 3.00
7 'Cypher in Fairyland' 3.00
8 . . . . 3.00
9 F:Candy Tsai 3.00
10 The Tuberians are coming 3.00
11 V:X-the-Unmentionable. 3.00
12 preemptive strike on Site X. . . . 3.00
13 Gremlin-Goblin war. 3.00
14 . . . . 3.00
15 Battle of 5 Armies 3.00
16 . . . . 3.00
17 kidnapped to Fairyland 3.00
18 . . . . 3.00
19 The Sky Stone 3.00
20 Ring Fortress 3.00
21 A-Girls 3.00
22 Gremlin Guild 3.00

23 escape from Mordovania 3.00
24 thru 30. . . . . @3.00
TPB Vol.1 rep.#1–#6 . . . . 15.00
TPB Vol.2 rep.#7–#12 . . . . 13.00
TPB Vol.3 rep.#13–#18 . . . . 13.00
TPB Vol.4 rep. #19–#25. . . . . 13.00
TPB Vol.5 rep. #26–#30. . . . . 15.00
Spec. #1 Super Special 3.00
Super Special Final (2004) 3.25

GRENDEL
Comico, 1983
1 MW,O:Hunter Rose, rare. 150.00
2 MW,O:Argent, rare. 100.00
3 MW,rare 100.00

GRENUORD
Fantagraphics Books 2005
1 (of 6) 5.00
2 . . . . 5.00
3 . . . . 5.00

GREY
Viz Select, 1989
Book 1 . . . . 5.00
Book 2 scarce 5.50
Book 3 . . . . 3.00
Book 4 . . . . 3.00
Book 5 . . . . 3.00
Book 6 thru Book 9 . . . . @2.50

GREYMATTER
Alaffinity Studios, 1993
1 thru 14 by Marcus Harwell . . . @3.00

GRIFFIN, THE
Slave Labor, 1988
1 . . . . 2.50
1a 2nd printing 2.50
2 thru 4 . . . . @2.50
5 . . . . 2.50
Amaze Ink, 1997
1 by DVa & Phil Allora 3.00
2 by DVa & Paul Way. 3.00

GRIPS
Silver Wolf, 1986
1 Vigil 15.00
2 Vigil 12.00
3 Vigil 9.00
4 Vigil 8.00
Vol 1 #1 rep 2.50
Volume 2
1 . . . . 2.50
2 . . . . 2.50
3 thru 8 . . . . @2.50
9 thru 12 . . . . @2.50

GROUND ZERO
Eternity
1 Science Fiction mini-series 2.50
2 Alien Invasion Aftermath 2.50

GRRL SCOUTS
Oni Press, 1999
1 (of 4) by Jim Mahfood 3.00
2 thru 4 . . . . @3.00
TPB 12.00
Amazing Aaron, 1999
1 Aaron Warner. 3.00
2 . . . . 3.00

GUERRILLA GROUNDHOG
Eclipse, 1987
1 . . . . 2.50
2 . . . . 2.50

All comics prices listed are for *Near Mint* condition.

GUILLOTIN
High Impact, 1997
Preview JQ,RCI 5.00
ABC Studios, 1999
Spec. Ed. 3.00
Spec. Ed. Serpent Ed. 8.00

GUILLOTINE
Silver Wolf, 1987
1 and 2 . . . . @2.25

Guillotine #1
© Silver Wolf

GUN CRISIS
Ironcat, 1998
1 (of 3) by Masoami Kanzaki 3.00
2 & 3 . . . . @3.00

GUNDAM WING
Mixx Entertainment, 2000
1 . . . . 5.00
2 thru 4 . . . . @4.00
TPB Pocket Mixx, Vol.1 . . . . 10.00
TPB Pocket Mixx, Vol.2 . . . . 10.00
TPB Pocket Mixx, Vol.3 . . . . 10.00
Tokyopop.Com, 2000
5 thru 12 . . . . @3.00
TPB Vol. 1 Blue Destiny Mixx 13.00
TPB Gundam Technical Manual #1 13.00
TPB Gundam Technical Manual
  #2 thru #6 . . . . @13.00

GUNDAM WING:
BATTLEFIELD OF
PACIFISTS
Tokyopop Press, 2001
1 48-pg. 3.00
2 thru 5 . . . . @3.00
TPB Vol. 1 . . . . 10.00

GUNDAM WING:
ENDLESS WALTZ
Tokyopop Press, 2002
1 (of 5) 3.00
2 thru 4 . . . . @3.00
TPB 184-pg. 10.00

GUNDAM WING: G-UNIT
Tokyopop Press, 2002
1 (of 12) 3.00
2 . . . . 3.00

GUNDAM WING:
THE LAST OUTPOST
Tokyopop Press, 2002
1 (of 12) 3.00
2 thru 4 . . . . @3.00
TPB Vol. 1 (of 3) 10.00
TPB Vol. 2 thru Vol. 3. . . . . @10.00

GUNDAM: THE ORIGIN
Viz Communications, 2002
GN #1 by Yoshikazu Yasuhiko. 8.00
GN #2 thru #12 . . . . @8.00

GUNFIGHTERS IN HELL
Broken Halos, 1999
GN by Tim & Joe Vigil 20.00
GN leather(c), signed & numbered 35.00
TPB Original Sin 8.00
TPB Original Sin, variant (c) 10.00
TPB Original Sin, special ed. 12.00
TPB Leather Hell 20.00
TPB Leather Hell, signed. 30.00

GUNFIGHTERS IN HELL:
ORIGINAL SIN
Broken Halos, 2001
1 . . . . 4.00
1a variant (c). 6.00
1 limited edition 16-pg. 7.00
2 24-pg. 4.00
2a cardstock (c) 4.50
2b limited edition. 6.00

GUN FURY
Aircel, 1989
1 thru 10 . . . . @2.50

GUN FURY RETURNS
Aircel, 1990
1 . . . . 3.00
2 . . . . 3.00
3 V:The Yes Men 2.25
4 . . . . 2.25

GUNNER
Gun Dog Comics, 1999
1 thru 7 by Eric Yonge. . . . . @3.00

GUNS OF SHAR-PEI
Caliber
1 The Good,the Bad & the Deadly . 3.00
2 & 3 . . . . @3.00

GUTWALLOW
Numbskull Press, 1998
1 by Dan Berger 3.00
2 thru 7 The Gingerbread Man . . @3.00

GUTWALLOW
Digital Webbing 2002
1 (of 3) 3.00
2 Fury of the Furry`. 3.00
3 concl. 3.00
TPB Fury of the Furry 13.00

GYPSY
Avatar Press 2005
1 . . . . 3.50
1a Wraparound (c) 3.50
1b Variant(c)s . . . . @3.50
1c Die-cut (c) 10.00
2 . . . . 4.00
2a wraparound (c). 4.00
2b Variant(c)s . . . . @4.00
2c premium (c) 10.00

GYRE
Abaculus, 1997
1 by Martin Shipp & Marc Laming . 3.00
2 . . . . 3.00
3 Soul Keeper, pt. 3.00
4 . . . . 3.00
5 . . . . 3.00
6 . . . . 3.00
Spec. Edition 56-pg.. . . . . 4.50

HADES
Domain Publishing, 1995
1 F:Civil War Officer 3.00

HALL OF HEROES
Hall of Heroes, 1993
1 I:Dead Bolt. 12.00
2 and 3 . . . . @4.50
Ashcan, 8-pg.. . . . . 6.00
Halloween Horror Special 2.50
Halloween Horror Special '98 . . . . 2.50

HALL OF HEROES
PRESENTS
Hall of Heroes, 1996–97
0 by Doug Brammer & Matt Roach,
  `Slingers' by Matt Martin 2.50
1 . . . . 2.50
1a signed & numbered 4.00
2 `The Last Days' 2.50
3 `The Power of the Golem' 2.50
4 F:Turaxx the Trobbit. 2.50
5 . . . . 2.50

HALLOWIENERS
Mirage
1 . . . . 2.25
2 . . . . 2.25

HALO BROTHERS
Fantagraphics
Special #1 . . . . 2.25

HAMMER GIRL
Brainstorm, 1996
1 dinosaur, sci-fi adventure. 3.00
2 . . . . 3.00
2a deluxe 5.00

HAMSTER VICE
Blackthorne, 1986
1 . . . . 3.50
2 . . . . 2.50
3 thru 11 . . . . @2.50
New Series
Eternity, 1989
1 and 2 . . . . @2.50

HANGED MAN
Caliber, 1998
1 (of 2) by AIG & Arthur Ranson. . . 3.00
2 (of 2) 3.00
TPB 6.00

HARD GORE
Komics, Inc., 2000
TPB Vol. 1 . . . . 10.00
TPB Vol. 2 thru Vol. 7. . . . . @10.00

HARD ROCK COMICS
Revolutionary, 1992
1 Metallica-The Early Years 6.00
2 Motley Crew. 4.00
3 Jane's Addiction. 3.50
4 Nirvana 4.00
5 Kiss 9.00

5a 2nd printing 5.00
6 Def Leppard II 3.00
7 Red Hot Chili Peppers. 3.00
8 Pearl Jam. 3.00
9 Queen II. 3.00
10 Birth of Punk 3.00
11 Pantera 3.00
12 Hendrix 3.00
13 Dead Kennedys 3.00
14 Van Halen II 2.50
15 Megadeath 2.50
16 Joan Jett 2.50
17 Not printed
18 Queensryche. 2.50
19 Tesla 2.50
20 The Sweet. 2.50

HARI KARI
Blackout, 1995
1 . . . . 3.00
1a platinum. 8.00
1-shot Possessed by Evil(1997) . . . 3.00
1-shot Hari Kari Goes Hollywood
  (1997) 3.00
  Deluxe 15.00
Spec #1 Sexy Summer Rampage,
  gallery issue (1997). 3.00
  Deluxe, super sexy cover 10.00
1-shot Cry of Darkness (1998) . . . 3.00
  Variant photo ultra sexy ed. . . 10.00
1-shot The Last Stand (1998) 3.00
  Ultra sexy edition. 10.00
  Deluxe. 15.00

HARI KARI MANGA
Blackout Comics, 1998
Spec. 0 Sex, Thugs & Rock 'n' Roll 3.00
1-shot Manga Adventures (1997) . . 3.00
1-shot Deadly Exposure, by Rob
  Roman & Nigel Tully 3.00
  Deluxe 15.00
1-shot Deadtime Stories, by Rob
  Roman & Nigel Tully 3.00
  Deluxe edition 15.00
1-shot Manga To Die For. 3.00
  Deluxe 15.00
1-shot Running From Poison 3.00

HARPY:
PRIZE OF THE OVERLORD
Ground Zero, 1996
1 (of 6) 3.00
2 thru 6 . . . . @3.00
1-shot Harpy Preview, prequel. . . . 3.00
Peregrine, 1998
TPB rep. #1–#6 . . . . 15.00
Spec. Harpy Pin-up Book 3.00

HARTE OF DARKNESS
Eternity, 1991
1 I:Dennis Harte,Vampire
  private-eye. 2.50
2 V:Satan's Blitz St.Gang 2.50
3 Jack Grissom/Vampire. 2.50
4 V:Jack Grissom, conc. 2.50

HARVY FLIP BOOK
Blackthorne
1 thru 3 . . . . @2.25

HATE
Fantagraphics, 1990
1 . . . . 15.00
2 . . . . 12.00
3 . . . . 9.00
4 . . . . 8.00
5 . . . . 8.00
6 . . . . 8.00
7 . . . . 7.00

8 thru 10 . . . . @6.00
11 and 12 . . . . @5.00
1a to 12a reprints . . . . @2.50
13 thru 15. . . . . @4.00
Hate Jamboree, 64-pg. 4.00
See Color

HAVOC, INC.
Radio Comix, 1998
1 by Mark Barnard & Terrie Smith . 3.00
2 thru 9 . . . . @3.00
10 . . . . 3.50
TPB Vol. 1 128-pg. 13.00
TPB Digest Vol. 1. . . . . 14.00
TPB Digest Vol. 2 . . . . 14.00

HEAD, THE
1 Old Airboy (1966). 2.25

HEAVEN SENT
Antarctic Press 2004
1 BDn 3.00
2 thru 5 . . . . @3.00
6 thru 11 . . . . @3.00
TPB Vol. 1 Pocket Manga 10.00
Stand Alone Special (2005) 3.00

HEAVY METAL
MONSTERS
Revolutionary, 1992
1 'Up in Flames' 2.25

HE IS JUST A RAT
Exclaim Bound Comics, 1995
1 & 2 V:Jimmy and Billy Bob 2.75

HELLGIRL
Knight Press, 1995
1 I:Jazzmine Grayce. 3.00
1-shot Demonseed II, Bob Hickey &
  Bill Nichols (1997) 3.00
1-shot Demonsong, Bob Hickey &
  Bill Nichols (1997) 3.00
1-shot Purgatory (1997) 3.00

HELLINA
Lightning Comics, 1994
1-shot I&O:Hellina 5.00
  Commemorative 10.00
  1996 rep. gold 5.00
Spec. Hellina: Genesis with poster
  (1996) 3.00
  Platinum edition 4.00
Spec. Hellina: In the Flesh (1997)
  two diff. mild covers . . . . @3.00
Spec. Hellina: Naked Desire (1997) 3.00
  Cover B 3.00
  Signed, ... 3.00
Spec. Hellina: Taking Back the Night
  (1995) V:Michael Naynar. 3.00
Spec. Hellina: Wicket Ways (1995)
  A:Perg 2.75
  Encore editions 3.00
  Encore variant (c) 3.00
Spec. Hellina: X-Mas in Hell (1996)
  two different covers . . . . @3.00
  Platinum edition. 5.00
Spec. Hellina: The Relic 3.00
  Variant cover 3.00
Spec. 1997 Pin-up 3.50
  1997 Pin-up, cover B. 3.50
X-Over Hellina/Catfight (1995)
  V:Prince of Sommia. 2.75
  Gold. 4.00
  Encore edition, mild covers,
  2 different . . . . @3.00
X-Over Hellina/Cynder (1997) covA 3.00
  Cover B 3.00

Hellina 1997 Pinup Special
© Lightning Comics

Spec Hellina #1 Skybolt Toyz
  lim. ed. (1997). 2.25
TPB rep. Hellina appearances. . . . 9.00
TPB rep. one-shots 13.00

HELLINA
Avatar Press, 2003
0 . . . . 3.50
0a variant (c). 3.50
0b wraparound (c). 4.00
0c Hard Ruler Edition 6.00
0d Prism foil edition 13.00

HELLINA:
HEART OF THORNS
Lightning Comics, 1996
1 (of 2) 3.00
1b autographed. 5.00
2 . . . . 2.75
2a variant cover 2.75
2b platinum edition. 6.00

HELLINA: HELL'S ANGEL
Lightning Comics, 1996
1 . . . . 2.75
1a platinum edition 8.00
1a platinum edition, signed. 10.00
1c nude platinum edition. 15.00
2 . . . . 2.75
2a platinum edition 8.00
1 encore edition, cover A 3.00
1a encore edition, cover B 3.00
1b deluxe encore edition, cover A . 5.00
1c deluxe encore edition, cover B . 5.00

HELLINA: KISS OF DEATH
Lightning Comics, 1995
1-shot A:Perg 4.00
1-shot gold edition 10.00
1-shot Encore editions 3.00
Lightning, 1997
1A 3.00
1B variant cover 3.00
1 encore, signed & numbered 5.00

HELLINA: SEDUCTION
Avatar Press, 2003
1/2 Carnage Edition 6.00
1/2 Statuesque Edition. 6.00
Preview 2.25
Preview variant (c) 6.00
Preview Bad Girl edition 6.00

All comics prices listed are for *Near Mint* condition.

1 .... 3.50
1a wraparound (c). 4.00

HELLINA VS PANDORA
Avatar Press, 2003
0 16-pg. 2.50
0a variant (c)s .... @4.00
1 (of 3) 3.50
2 thru 3 .... @3.50
1a thru 3a variant (c)s. ..... @3.50
Preview 2.25
Preview variant (c). 6.00
Preview Hellina's Army variant (c). . 6.00

HELSING
Caliber Core, 1998
1W by Gary Reed & Low,
  Wozniak(c). 3.00
1L Loudon (c) 3.00
1 variant cover 9.00
1 premium, signed 10.00
2 .... 3.00
3 .... 3.00
4 Secrets and Lies 3.00
Spec. Dawn of Armageddon, Secrets
  & Lies, concl. 48-pg. 4.00

HELTER SKELTER
Antarctic Press, 1997
0 by Mike Harris & Duc Tran 3.00
1 (of 4) 3.00
2 thru 6 .... @3.00

HEPCATS
Double Diamond, 1989
1 .... 15.00
2 .... 12.00
3 Snow Blind. 12.00
4 thru 9 .... @9.00

MARTIN WAGNER'S
Hepcats
NUMBER 0

Hepcats #0
© Antarctic Press

10 thru 13. .... @3.50
14 Chapter 12 .... 3.00
15 Snowblind Chp. 13 .... 3.00
Antarctic Press, 1996
0 .... 3.00
1 by Martin Wagner 3.00
2 `Trial by Intimacy'. 3.00
3 Snowblind,pt.1 .... 3.00
4 Snowblind,pt.2 .... 3.00
5 Snowblind,pt.3 .... 3.00
6 Snowblind,pt.4 .... 3.00
7 Snowblind,pt.5 Intrusion 3.00
8 Snowblind,pt.6 Super Heroes ... 3.00

9 Snowblind,pt.7 Kevin & Kathryn . 3.00
10 Snowblind,pt.8 Exorcism,
  Prelude 3.00
11 Snowblind,pt.10 Exorcism(a) ... 3.00
12 Snowblind,pt.10 Exorcism(b) ... 3.00
TPB Collected Hepcats 15.00

HERCULES
A Plus Comics
1 Hercules Saga 2.50

HERCULES PROJECT
Monster Comics, 1991
1 Origin issue,V:Mutants 2.25

HEROBEAR AND THE KID
Astonish Comics, 2000
1 .... 15.00
1a 2nd printing 3.50
2 .... 12.00
2a 2nd printing 3.50
3 .... 3.50
4 .... 3.50
5 Belief 3.50
TPB Vol. 1 The Inheritance 18.00

HEROBEAR AND THE KID: SAVING TIME
Astonish Comics 2004
1 (of 3) partial color. 3.50

HEROES
Blackbird, 1987
1 .... 5.00
2 .... 3.00
3 .... 2.50
4 comic size 2.50
5 thru 7 .... @2.50

HEROES ANONYMOUS
Bongo Comics, 2003
1 (of 6) 3.00
2 thru 6 .... @3.00

HEROES FROM WORDSMITH
Special Studios
1 WWI,F:Hunter Hawke 2.50

HEROES INCORPORATED
Double Edge Publishing
1 I:Heroes, Inc. 3.00
2 Betrayal 3.00

HEROIC TALES
Lone Star Press, 1997
1 by Robb Phipps & Bill Williams . . 2.50
2 Steel of a Soldier's Heart,pt.2 ... 2.50
3 Steel of a Soldier's Heart,pt.3 ... 2.50
4 .... 2.50
5 .... 2.50
6 The Belles of Freedom, prequel . 2.50
7 The Children of Atlas,pt.1 ...... 2.50
8 by B.Williams & J.Parker, I:Atlas . 2.50

HEROINES, INC.
Avatar
1 thru 5 .... @2.25

HERO SANDWICH
Slave Labor, 1987
1 thru 4 .... @2.50
5 thru 8 .... @2.50
9 .... 2.50
Graphic Novel 8.00

HEY MISTER
Insomnia Comics, 1997
1 .... 2.50
2 .... 2.50
Top Shelf
3 by Pete Sickman-Garner 3.00
4 .... 3.00
Spec. Behind the Green Door 3.00
Spec. The Trouble With Jesus. 3.00
Spec. Eyes on the Prize 3.00
Spec. Dial "M" for Mister 3.50
TPB After School Special. 5.00
TPB Celebrity Roast 144-pg. 10.00

HICKEE
Alternative Comics 2003
TPB Anthology 13.00
Vol. 2
1 .... 5.00
2 .... 5.00
Vol. 3
1 .... 3.00
2 .... 3.00

HIGH CALIBER
Caliber, 1997
1 64pg. 4.00
1 signed edition. 4.00
2 64pg. 4.00
3 48pg. 4.00
4 .... 4.00

HIGH SCHOOL AGENT
Sun Comics, 1992
1 I:Kohsuke Kanamori 2.50
2 Treasure Hunt at North Pole 2.50
3 and 4 .... @2.50

HIGH SHINING BRASS
Apple
1 thru 4 .... @2.75

HIGH SOCIETY
Aardvark–Vanaheim
1 DS,Cerebus 25.00

HIGHWAY 13
Amaze Ink/SLG, 2000
1 thru 11 by Les McClaine ..... @3.00

HILLY ROSE'S SPACE ADVENTURES
Astro Comics, 1995
1 confronts Steeltrap. 6.00
1 2nd & 3rd pr. by B.C. Boyer 3.00
2 .... 5.00
2 2nd & 3rd printing 3.00
3 .... 3.50
3 2nd printing 3.00
4 thru 9 .... @3.00
TPB Vol.1 Rocket Reporter 13.00

HINO HORROR
DH Publishing 2004
GN Vol. 1 The Red Snake 10.00
GN Vol. 2 The Bug Boy 10.00
GN Vol. 3 thru Vol. 16 .... @10.00

HIT THE BEACH
Antarctic, 1993
1 .... 3.00
1a deluxe edition. 5.00
2 & 3 .... @3.00
Spec. funny animal 3.00
Spec. 32 pg 3.00
Spec. deluxe 4.00
Spec. deluxe poster edition 5.00

Spec. 48-pg., 1999 . . . . 4.00
Spec. (#7) 48-pg., 2000 . . . . 4.00
Ann. 2001 . . . . 4.00
Ann. 2002 . . . . 4.00
1-shot Hit the Beach 2003 . . . . 5.00
1-shot Hit the Beach 2004 . . . . 5.00
1-shot Hit the Beach 2005 . . . . . . 5.00
1-shot Hit the Beach 2006 . . . . . . 6.00

HITOMI AND
HER GIRL COMMANDOS
Antarctic Press, 1992
1 Shadowhunter,from Ninja HS . . . 2.50
2 Synaptic Transducer 2.50
3 Shadowhunter in S.America 2.50
4 V:Mr.Akuma,last issue 2.50
[Series II]
1 thru 10 . . . . @2.75

HOLLIDAY
Saddle Tramp Press 2002
1 F: Doc Holliday 2.50
2 thru 3 . . . . @2.50
4 thru 7 . . . . @3.00
TPB Vol. 1 Cold Deck 11.00

HOLLYWOOD'S
GOLDEN ERA, 1930S
A-List Comics, 1999
1 (of 3) 3.00
2 . . . . 3.00
3 . . . . 3.00

HOLO BROTHERS, THE
Monster Comics, 1991
1 thru 10 . . . . @2.25
Fantagraphics
Spec.#1 . . . . 2.25
TPB The Curse of the Bloated Toad 5.00

HOLY KNIGHT
Pocket Change Comics
1 thru 3 . . . . @2.50
4 V:His Past 2.50
5 V:Souljoiner 2.50
6 V:Demon Priest 2.50
7 Silent Scream,pt.2 . . . . 2.50
8 `Dragon Quest,'pt.1 . . . . 2.50
9 `Dragon Quest,'pt.2 . . . . 2.50
10 `Dragon Quest,'pt.3 . . . . 2.50
11 `Dragon Quest,'pt.4 . . . . 2.50

HONK
Fantagraphics, 1986
1 Don Martin 2.75
2 . . . . 2.75
3 . . . . 2.75

HONOR AMONG THIEVES
Gateway Graphics, 1987
1 and 2 . . . . @2.50

HONOR OF THE DAMNED
Americanime Productions 2005
1 Manga by Nevin Arnold 3.50
2 . . . . 3.50
3 . . . . 3.50
4 . . . . 4.00
TPB 15.00

HOON
Eenieweenie Comics, 1995
1 I:Hoon 2.50
2 Calazone Disaster 2.50
3 Reality Check 2.50
4 thru 8 . . . . @2.50

HOON, THE
Caliber Tapestry, 1996
1 . . . . 3.00
2 & 3 . . . . @3.00

HOPELESS SAVAGES
Oni Press, 2001
1 . . . . 3.00
2 thru 4 . . . . @3.00
TPB Vol. 1 . . . . 14.00
TPB Vol. 2 Ground Zero 12.00

Hopeless Savages #1
© Oni Press

HOPELESS SAVAGES:
GROUND ZERO
Oni Press, 2002
1 (of 4) 3.00
2 thru 4 . . . . @3.00

HOROBI
Viz, 1990
1 . . . . 4.00
2 thru 8 . . . . @3.75
Book 2, 1990–91
1 by Yoshihisa Tagami 3.50
2 D:Okado,Shoku Kidnapped 4.25
3 Madoka Attacks Zen 4.25
4 D:Abbess Mitsuko 4.25
5 Catharsis! 4.25
6 Shuichi Vs. Zen 4.25
7 Shuichi vs. Zen, conc 4.25

HORROR IN THE DARK
Fantagor
1 RCo,Inc.Blood Birth 2.25
2 RCo,Inc.Bath of Blood 2.25
3 RCo 2.25
4 RCo,Inc.Tales of the
 Black Diamond 2.25

HORROR SHOW
Caliber
1 GD,1977-80 reprint horror 3.50

HOUSE OF
FRIGHTENSTEIN
AC Comics
1 . . . . 3.00

HOUSE OF HORROR
AC Comics
1 . . . . 2.50

HOWL
Eternity
1 & 2 . . . . @2.25

HOW TO DRAW TEENAGE
MUTANT NINJA TURTLES
Solson
1 Lighter cover 10.00
1a Dark cover 5.00

H.P. LOVECRAFT'S
THE CALL OF CTHULHU
AND OTHERS
Cross Plains Comics, 1999
1-shot RTs,EM 6.00

H.P. LOVECRAFT'S
THE DREAM-QUEST
OF UNKNOWN KADATH
Mock Man Press, 1997
1 (of 5) by Jason Thompson 3.00
1 2nd printing 3.00
2 thru 5 . . . . @3.00

H.P. LOVECRAFT'S THE
RETURN OF CTHULHU
Cross Plains Comics, 2000
1-shot RTs & EM 6.00

HSU AND CHAN
Amaze Ink/SLG, 2003
1 thru 5 . . . . @3.00
6 thru 7 . . . . @3.00
TPB Vol. 1 . . . . 14.00

HUGO
Fantagraphics, 1985
1 . . . . 4.00
2 thru 4 . . . . @2.50

HUMAN GARGOYLES
Eternity, 1988
Book one 2.50
Book two 2.50
Book three 2.50
Book four 2.50

HUNT AND
THE HUNTED, THE
Newcomers Publishing
1 I:Aramis Thiron 3.00
2 V:Werewolves 3.00
3 Rio De Janero 3.00
4 F:Aramis Thiron 3.00

HURRICANE GIRLS
Antarctic Press, 1995
1 & 2 Tale of Dinon . . . . @3.50
3 thru 7 seven part series . . . . . @3.00

HUZZAH
1 I:Albedo'sErmaFelna 50.00

HY-BREED
Division Publishing
1 thru 3 F:Cen Intel . . . . @2.25
4 thru 9 . . . . @2.50

B & W PUB.

B & W PUB.

HYPER DOLLS
Ironcat Manga, 1998
1 by Shinpei Itoh, F:Miyu & Maika . 3.00
2 thru 6 . . . . @3.00
VOL 2
1 . . . . 3.00
2 thru 6 . . . . @3.00
VOL 3
1 . . . . 3.00
2 thru 6 . . . . @3.00
VOL 4, 2000
1 . . . . 3.00
2 thru 6 . . . . @3.00
VOL 5, 2000
1 . . . . 3.00
2 thru 6 . . . . @3.00
TPB Vol. 1 . . . . 16.00
TPB Vol. 3 thru Vol. 5. . . . . . . @16.00

I.F.S. ZONE
1 thru 6 . . . . @2.25

I AM LEGEND
Eclipse, 1991
1 Novel adapt. aka Omega Man. . . 6.00
2 thru 3 68-pg. . . . . @6.00

ICARUS
Aircel, 1987
1 thru 9 . . . . @2.50

ICON DEVIL
Spider
1 by Neil Hanson 2.25

Icarus #6
© Aircel

2 . . . . 2.25
2nd Series
1 thru 5 . . . . @2.25

I DREAM OF JEANNIE
Airwave Comics, 2002
1 JJu(c) 3.00
1 special edition 6.00
2 . . . . 3.00
2a variant photo (c). 3.00
3 . . . . 3.00
Preview Book #1 . . . . 7.00
Spec. Trick-or-Treats Annual #1 . . . 3.50
Spec.#1 Wishbook (2001) 3.00
Spec.#1 Wishbook, photo (c). 3.00
Spec. Spring Spectacular. 3.50

Spec. Spring Spectacular, photo(c) . 3.50

I HUNT MONSTERS
Antarctic Press 2004
1 . . . . 3.00
2 thru 9 . . . . @3.00
Vol. 2
1 by Rod Espinosa 3.00
2 thru 9 . . . . @3.00
Pocket Manga TPB Vol. 1 . . . . . . 10.00
Pocket Manga TPB Vol. 2 . . . . . . 10.00
Spec. Tales From Sleepy Hollow . . . 3.00

ILIAD
Amaze Ink, 1997
1 by Darren Brady & Alex Ogle . . . 3.00
2 thru 7 . . . . @3.00

ILIAD II
MicMac
1 . . . . 3.00
1a 2nd cover variation 3.00
2 . . . . 2.25
3 . . . . 2.25
4 . . . . 2.25

ILLUMINATUS
Rip Off, 1990
1 . . . . 2.25
2 . . . . 2.50
3 . . . . 2.50

INDUSTRIACIDE
Broken Tree Publications, 2002
1 (of 6) by Sean Dietrich. 3.00
2 thru 6 . . . . @3.00

INFERNO
Caliber Press, 1995
1 I:City of Inferno 3.00
2 Search for Identity 3.00
3 V:Malateste 3.00
4 by MCy and Michael Gaydos . . . 3.00
5 . . . . 3.00

INTERZONE
Brainstorm Comics
1 w/4 cards 2.50
2 w/4 cards 2.50

INTO THE STORM
Curtis Comics, 2002
Vol. 1 Manga
1 by Jihoon Park & Takyoung Lee . 3.00
2 thru 4 . . . . @3.00
Vol. 2
1 . . . . 3.00

INU YASHA
Viz Communications, 1997
1 thru 5 (of 10) by Rumiko
  Takahashi. . . . . @3.00
PART TWO:
A FEUDAL FAIRY TALE
Viz Communications, 1998
1 (of 9) by Rumiko Takahashi . . . 3.00
2 thru 7 . . . . @3.00
8 thru 15 (of 15) . . . . @3.25
TPB 16.00
TPB Vol. 2 . . . . 16.00
PART THREE, 1999
1 (of 7) thru 7 . . . . @3.25
TPB Vol. 3 . . . . 16.00
PART FOUR, 1999
1 (of 7) by Rumiko Takahashi. . . . 3.25
2 thru 7 . . . . @3.25

TPB Vol. 4 . . . . 16.00
PART FIVE, 2000
1 (of 11) by Rumiko Takahashi . . . 3.00
2 thru 11 . . . . @3.00
TPB Vol. 5 . . . . 16.00
TPB Vol. 6 . . . . 16.00
PART SIX, 2001
1 (of 15) 3.00
2 thru 7 . . . . @3.00
8 thru 15 . . . . @3.00
PART SEVEN, 2002
1 (of 8) by Rumiko Takahashi. . . . 3.00
2 thru 7 . . . . @3.00
TPB Vol.8 rep. Vol.4 #6–Vol5 #3 . 16.00
TPB Vol.9 . . . . 16.00
TPB Vol.10 thru 12. . . . . @16.00
TPB Vol.13 thru Vol. 15 . . . . @9.00
TPB Vol.16 thru Vol. 23 . . . . @9.00
TPB Art of Inu-Yasha, color 23.00
Visual Manga Vol. 1. . . . . 10.00
Visual Manga Vol. 2. . . . . 12.00

INVADERS FROM MARS
Eternity, 1990
1 . . . . 2.50
2 . . . . 2.50
3 . . . . 2.50
BOOK II, 1991
1 Sequel to '50's SF classic 2.50
2 Pact of Tsukus/Humans. 2.50
3 Last issue. 2.50

INVASION '55
Apple, 1990
1 . . . . 2.25
2 . . . . 2.25
3 . . . . 2.25

INVISIBLE PEOPLE
Kitchen Sink
1 WE,I:Peacus Pleatnik 3.00
2 WE,The Power. 3.00
3 WE,Final issue. 3.00

ISLAND
Tokyopop Press, 2001
1 48-pg. 3.00
2 thru 4 . . . . @3.00
2nd Series, 2002
1 thru 7 . . . . @3.00

ISMET
Canis
1 Cartoon Dog 8.00
2 . . . . 5.00
3 Rare 5.00
4 . . . . 5.00

IT'S SCIENCE
WITH DR. RADIUM
Slave Labor, 1986
1 . . . . 2.50
2 thru 9 . . . . @2.50
Spec #1 . . . . 3.00

JACKAROO
Eternity, 1990
1 GCh 2.25
2 & 3GCh . . . . @2.25

JACK HUNTER
Blackthorne, 1987
1 . . . . 3.50
2 . . . . 3.50
3 . . . . 3.50

All comics prices listed are for *Near Mint* condition.

JACK OF NINES

1 . . . . 2.25
2 thru 4 . . . . @2.25
5 . . . . 2.25

JACK STAFF

Dancing Elephant Press, 2000
1 by Paul Grist 3.00
2 thru 4 . . . . @3.00
5 . . . . 3.00

Jack Staff #5
© Dancing Elephant Press

6 . . . . 3.00
7 . . . . 3.00
8 36-pg. 4.50
9 thru 12 . . . . @3.00
TPB Vol. 1 Yesterday's heroes . . . 16.00

JACK THE LANTERN

Castle Rain Entertainment 2002
0a signed and numbered 8.00
1 thru 3 . . . . @3.00
4 The quest 3.00
5 The quest 3.50
TPB 18.00
1-shot 1942 . . . . 4.00

JACK THE LANTERN: GHOSTS

Castle Rain Entertainment 2006
1 . . . . 2.50

JACK THE RIPPER

Eternity
1 thru 4 . . . . @2.25

JAM, THE

Slave Labor, 1989
1 . . . . 3.00
2 thru 5 . . . . @3.00

Dark Horse, 1993
6 thru 8 . . . . 3.00

Caliber, 1995
9 . . . . 3.00
9 signed edition. 3.00
10 It's a Kafka Thing 3.00
11 thru 14 . . . . @3.00
15 'The Kinetic,'pt.3. . . . . 3.00

JAMES BOND

Titan 2004
TPB Octopussy 17.00

TPB The Man with the
  Golden Gun 17.00
TPB Goldfinger 17.00
TPB Spy Who Loved Me 17.00
TPB Casino Royale 17.00
TPB On Her Majesty's
  Secret Service 18.00
TPB Dr. No. 17.00
TPB Colonel Sun 20.00
TPB Trouble Spot. 20.00
TPB Golden Ghost. 18.00

JAMES O'BARR ORIGINAL SINS

ACG Comics, 2000
1 . . . . 3.00
2 . . . . 3.00

JAMES O'BARR TASTY BITES

ACG Comics, 1999
1 . . . . 3.00
1a signed 10.00

JANE'S WORLD

Girl Twirl, 2003
1 by Paige Braddock 3.00
2 thru 12 . . . . @3.00
13 thru 20 56-pg. . . . . @6.00
21 thru 24 . . . . @5.00
TPB Vol. 1 . . . . 15.00
TPB Vol. 2 . . . . 15.00
TPB Vol. 3 . . . . 16.00
TPB Vol. 4 . . . . 15.00
TPB Vol. 5 . . . . 15.00
TPB Vol. 6 . . . . 15.00

JASON AND THE ARGONAUTS

Caliber
1 thru 5 . . . . @2.50

JAY & SILENT BOB

Oni Press, 1998
1 (of 4) by Kevin Smith & Duncan
  Fregedo 5.00
1a Ph(c) 7.00
1b 2nd printing 3.00
2 thru 4 . . . . @4.00
TPB rep. #1–#4 . . . . 12.00

JAZZ

High Impact, 1996
1 . . . . 3.00
1 Gold variant edition RCI(c) 10.00
2 . . . . 3.00
2a deluxe edition. 10.00
3 . . . . 3.00
3a variant (c). 10.00

JAZZ THE SERIES

ABC Comics, 1999
1 RCI(c). 3.00
1a DOe(c) 3.00
2 . . . . 3.00

JAZZ: SOLITAIRE

ABC Comics, 1998
1 (of 4) by Jose Varese 3.00
1a photo cover 6.00
2 . . . . 3.00
2a Variant Exotika (c) 6.00
2b Variant Naughty (c) 6.00
3 . . . . 3.00
Collected Ed. 5.00

JAZZ: SUPERSTAR

ABC Comics, 1998
1 (of 3) by Jose Varese 3.00
1a JQ cover 6.00

JAZZ AGE CHRONICLES

Caliber, 1990
1 thru 6 . . . . @2.25
7 . . . . 2.50

JCP FEATURES

J.C. Productions, 1982
1 1st MT;S&K,NA/DG rep.
  A:T.H.U.N.D.E.R.Agents,
  TheFly, Black Hood Mag.Size . 11.00

JENNA AND NINJA HIGH

Narwain Publishing 2006
1 (of 3) Ninja High School x-over . . 3.50
2 BDn 3.50
3 . . . . 3.50

JENNY FINN

Oni Press, 1999
1 (of 4) by MMi & Troy Nixey 3.00
2 MMi 3.00
3 MMi 3.00
4 MMi, concl. 4.00

JEREMIAH

Fantagraphics, 1982–83
GN #1. 35.00
GN #2. 32.00

JEREMIAH: BIRDS OF PREY

Adventure Comics, 1991
1 I: Jeremiah,A:Kurdy 4.00
2 conclusion 4.00

JEREMIAH: EYES LIKE BURNING COALS

Adventure Comics, 1991
1 & 2 fourth series . . . . @4.00

JEREMIAH: A FISTFUL OF SAND

Adventure Comics
1 A:Captain Kenney 4.00
2 conclusion 4.00

JEREMIAH: THE HEIRS

Adventure Comics, 1991
1 Nathanial Bancroft estate 4.00
2 conclusion 4.00

JERRY IGERS FAMOUS FEATURES

Blackthorne
1 . . . . 3.00
2 thru 4 . . . . @2.25

Pacific
5 thru 8 . . . . @2.25

JETCAT CLUBHOUSE

Oni Press, 2001
1 by Jay Stephens 3.25
2 thru 5 . . . . @3.25
TPB by Jay Stephens (2002) 11.00

JIM

Fantagraphics, 1987–90
1 . . . . 15.00
2 . . . . 12.00

All comics prices listed are for *Near Mint* condition.

3 and 4 . . . . @8.00	

Second Series, 1994

1 . . . . 4.00	
1a 2nd printing 3.00	
2 . . . . 3.50	
2a 2nd printing 3.00	
3 thru 5 . . . . @3.00	

JINGLE BELLE
Oni Press, 1999

1 (of 2) by PDi. 3.00	
2 PDi 3.00	
All-Star Holiday Hullabaloo 5.00	
1-shot Jingle Belle Jubilee 3.00	
1-shot The Mighty Elves 3.00	
TPB Jingle Belle's Cool Yule 14.00	
1-shot Winter Wingding 3.00	
TPB Naughty & Nice (2000) 9.50	

J. O'BARR's THE CROW
Kitchen Sink, 1998

0 F:Eric Draven, 48-pg. 3.50	
1 . . . . 3.50	
2 Demon in Disguise 3.50	

JOE PSYCHO & MOO FROG
Goblin Studios, 1996

1 Fanatics Edition 2.50	
1 Fanatics signed and numbered	
Edition 10.00	
2 . . . . 2.50	
2 signed & numbered 10.00	
3 . . . . 2.50	
4 . . . . 2.50	
4B San Diego Con cover 5.00	
5 . . . . 2.50	
Spec. Psychosis Abnormalis 2.50	

JOE R. LANSDALE'S BY BIZARRE HANDS
Avatar Press 2004

1 . . . . 3.50	
2 thru 6 . . . . 3.50	
1a thru 6a wraparound (c)s. . . . . @3.50	
4 thru 6 connecting covers . . . . . @6.00	

JOE R. LANSDALE'S THE DRIVE-IN
Avatar Press, 2003

1 (of 4) 3.50	
2 thru 4 . . . . @3.50	
1a thru 4a wraparound (c). . . . . . @4.00	
TPB 13.00	

Vol. 2, 2006

1 (of 4) 3.50	
2 thru 4 . . . . @3.50	
1a thru 4a wraparound (c). . . . . . @3.50	

JOE SINN
Caliber

1 I:Joe Sinn,Nikki 3.00	
2 . . . . 3.00	

JOHNNY ATOMIC
Eternity

1 I:Johnny A.Tomick 2.50	
2 Project X-contingency plan 2.50	
3 . . . . 2.50	

JOHNNY COMET
ACG Comics, 1999

1 . . . . 3.00	
2 . . . . 3.00	
3 FF, rep.. . . . . 3.00	
4 FF, rep.. . . . . 3.00	
5 FF, rep.. . . . . 3.00	

JOHNNY DARK
Double Edge

1 V:Biker Gang 3.00	

JOHNNY RAYGUN
Jetpack Press, 2003

1 . . . . 3.00	
2 thru 6 . . . . @3.00	
Spec. Quarterly #1 . . . . 3.00	

JOHNNY THE HOMICIDAL MANIAC
Slave Labor, 1996

1 by Jhonen Vasquez 32.00	
1 3rd printing 20.00	
1 signed, limited 20.00	
2 . . . . 20.00	
2 3rd printing 20.00	
3 . . . . 15.00	
3 3rd printing 6.00	
4 . . . . 5.00	
4 2nd & 3rd printing 3.00	
5 . . . . 4.00	
5 2nd printing 3.00	
6 . . . . 3.00	
7 . . . . 3.00	
TPB 20.00	
TPB Director's Cut 20.00	

JOURNEY
Aardvark–Vanaheim, 1983

1 . . . . 7.00	
2 . . . . 6.00	
3 . . . . 5.00	
4 . . . . 3.00	
5 thru 7 . . . . @3.00	
8 thru 14 . . . . @2.50	

Fantagraphics, 1985

15 . . . . 2.50	
16 thru 28 . . . . @2.50	

JR. JACKALOPE

1 orange cover,1981 . . . . 8.00	
1a Yellow cover,1981 . . . . 12.00	
2 . . . . 8.00	

JUDGE DREDD
Hamlyn, 2001

TPB Doomsday for Mega-City One	25.00
TPB Doomsday for Dredd 20.00	
TPB Wilderlands, 216-pg. 30.00	
GN Judge Dredd: Pit 16.00	
GN Judge Dredd: Fetish 10.00	

Titan, 2001

TPB Judge Dredd: The Emerald	
Isle 15.00	
TPB Judge Dredd: Death Aid 15.00	

JUDGE DREDD: THE COMPLETE CASE FILES
Rebellion 2005

TPB Vol. 1 . . . . 21.00	
TPB Vol. 2 . . . . 26.00	
TPB Vol. 3 . . . . 25.00	
TPB Vol. 4 . . . . 27.00	
TPB Vol. 5 . . . . 26.00	
TPB Vol. 6 . . . . 29.00	
TPB The Complete PJ Maybe 27.00	

JULIE'S JOURNEY/ GRAVITY
Paper Live Studios, 1998

1 by David Keye 2.50	
2 thru 6 . . . . @2.50	

JUNGLE COMICS
Blackthorne, 1988

4 thru 6 . . . . @2.50	

JUNGLE COMICS
A-List Comics, 1997

1 reprint of golden age 3.00	
2 thru 6 . . . . @3.00	
TPB Book of Jungle Comics	
Covers, 1940–54 . . . . 8.00	

JUNGLE FANTASY
Avatar Press, 2002

Preview 2.25	
Preview, Fauna (c) 2.25	
Preview, Wild (c) 6.00	
1 . . . . 3.50	
1b wraparound (c). 4.00	
2 . . . . 3.50	
3 . . . . 3.50	
3b Back to the Hunt Edition 6.00	
4 . . . . 3.50	
4b volcanic edition 6.00	
1a thru 4a variant (c)s . . . . @3.50	
5 . . . . 3.50	
5a wraparound (c). 3.50	
1/2 Winged Death Edition 6.00	

JUNGLE GIRLS
AC Comics, 1989–93

1 incGold.Age reps. 3.00	
2 Tara, Nyoka, Cave Girl 3.00	
3 Greed,A:Tara 3.00	

Jungle Girls #3
© AC Comics

4 CaveGirl 3.00	
5 Camilla 3.00	
6 TigerGirl 3.00	
7 CaveGirl 3.00	
8 Sheena Queen o/t Jungle 3.00	
9 Wild Girl,Tiger Girl,Sheena 3.00	
10 F:Tara,Cave Girl,Nyoka 3.00	
11 F:Sheena,Tiger Girl,Nyoka 3.00	
12 F:Sheena,Camilla,Tig.Girl. 3.00	
13 F:Tara, Tiger Girl. 3.00	
14 Wildside 3.00	
15 Wildside 3.00	
16 Wildside 3.00	

JUNIOR
Fantagraphics, 2000

1 (of 5) by Peter Bogge 3.00	
2 thru 5 . . . . @3.00	

JUPITER
Sandberg Publishing, 1999
1 by Jason Sandberg 3.00
2 thru 10 . . . . @3.00

JURASSIC JANE
London Night, 1997
1 by Sky Owens, F:Tira, elf
  princess of Atlantis 3.00
2 Sky Owens. 3.00
3 Sky Owens. 3.00
4 EHr, Sky Owens 3.00
5 by Preston Owens 3.00
6 by Sky Owens 3.00
7 by Sky Owens 3.00
Coll. Ed. 5.00

JUSTICE
Newcomers Publishing, 1995
1 I:Judiciary Urban Strike Team . . . 3.00

JUSTY
Viz Communications, 1988
1 thru 9 . . . . @2.50

KABUKI:
CIRCLE OF BLOOD
Caliber Press, 1995
1 R:Kabuki 6.00
2 Kabuki Goes Rogue 5.00
3 V:Noh Agents. 5.00
4 V:Noh Agents. 3.50
5 V:Kai 3.00
6 . . . . 3.00
TPB Rep.#1–#6 . . . . 17.00
TPB deluxe, signed, etc. 25.00
TPB Compilation 8.00

KABUKI:
DANCE OF DEATH
London Night Studios, 1995
1 1st Full series 8.00

KABUKI:
MASKS OF THE NOH
Caliber, 1996
1A JQ(c) 3.00
1B Mays/Mack(c) 3.00
1C Buzz(c) 3.00
2 . . . . 3.00
3 DMk 3.00
4 epilog 3.00

KAFKA
Renegade, 1987
1 thru 6 . . . . @2.50
The Execution Spec. 2.50

KAMUI
Eclipse, 1987
1 Sanpei Shirato Art 4.00
1a 2nd printing 2.50
2 Mystery of Hanbie 3.00
2a 2nd printing 2.50
3 V:Ichijiro 2.50
3a 2nd printing 2.50
4 thru 15 . . . . @2.50
16 thru 19 . . . . @2.50
20 thru 37 . . . . @2.50

KANE
Dancing Elephant, 1993
1 by Paul Grist. 5.00
2 thru 13 . . . . @4.00
14 thru 17 . . . . @3.50
18 thru 22 . . . . @3.50

Kane #17
© *Dancing Elephant*

23 thru 33 . . . . @3.00
TPB Book 1: rep. #1–#4 . . . . 12.00
TPB Book 2: Rabbit Hunt 12.50
TPB Book 3: Histories 12.50
TPB Book 4: Thrity Ninth 20.00
TPB #5 Untouchable Rico Costas. 13.00

KANSAS THUNDER
Red Menace, 1997
1 . . . . 3.00

KAOS MOON
Caliber, 1996
1 by DdB. 3.50
1a 2nd edition 3.00
2 . . . . 3.50
2a 2nd edition, new cover. 3.00
3 . . . . 5.00
4 Anubian Nights, Chapter 2. . . . . 5.00
GN Full Circle, rep #1–#2 . . . . 6.00

KAPTAIN KEEN
AND KOMPANY
Vortex, 1986
1 thru 3 . . . . @2.50
4 and 5 . . . . @2.50
6 and 7 . . . . @2.50

KATMANDU
Antarctic Press, 1993
1 thru 3 . . . . @2.75
4 & 5 Woman of Honor 2.75
6 F:Laska 2.75
Med Systems
7 and 8 . . . . @2.25
Vision Comics, 1996
9 'When Warriors Die,'pt.3(of 3). . . 2.25
10 'The Curse of the Blood,'pt.1 . . . 2.50
11 'The Curse of the Blood,'pt.2 . . . 2.50
12 'The Curse of the Blood,' concl . 3.00
13 'The Search For Magic,'pt.1 . . . 3.00
Shanda Fantasy Arts
14 'The Search For Magic,'pt.2 . . . 3.00
15 'The Search For Magic,'pt.3 . . . 3.00
16 'Ceremonies,'pt.1 (of 3) 3.00
17 'Ceremonies,'pt.2 . . . . 3.00
18 'Ceremonies,'pt.3 . . . . 3.00
19 'Peace Keeper,'pt.1 . . . . 3.00
20 'Peace Keeper,'pt.2 . . . . 3.00
21 'Peace Keeper,'pt.3 . . . . 3.00
22 . . . . 3.00

23 and 24 . . . . @3.00
25 thru 33 48-pg. . . . . @5.00
Ann. #1 48-pg. 5.00
Ann. #2 . . . . 5.00
Ann. #3. 5.00
Ann. #4 . . . . 5.00
Ann. #5 . . . . 5.00
Ann. #6 . . . . 5.00
Spec. Katmandu 5.00

KEIF LLAMA
Fantagraphics
1 thru 6 . . . . @2.25
Aeon 2005
TPB Vol. 1 Particle Dreams. 10.00

KEIF LLAMA:
XENOTECH
Aeon 2005
1 (of 6) by Matt Howarth. 3.00
2 thru 6 . . . . @3.00

KELLEY BELLE,
POLICE DETECTIVE
Newcomers Publishing
1 Debut issue 3.00
2 Case of the Jeweled Scarab . . . 3.00
3 Case o/t Jeweled Scarab,pt.2 . . . 3.00
TPB #1. 9.00

KICKASS GIRL: SKELE-
TONS IN THE CLOSET
Neko Press 2003
1 . . . . 3.00
1a variant (c). 3.00
1b mini-print edition 5.00
2 thru 4 . . . . @3.00
TPB manga 13.00

KID CANNIBAL
Eternity, 1991
1 I:Kid Cannibal 2.50
2 Hunt for Kid Cannibal 2.50
3 A:Janice 2.50
4 final issue. 2.50

KIKU SAN
Aircel, 1988
1 thru 6 . . . . @2.50

KILLBOX
Antarctic Press, 2002
1 . . . . 5.00
2 thru 3 . . . . @5.00

KILLING STROKE
Eternity, 1991
1 British horror tales 2.50
2 inc.'Blood calls to Blood' 2.50
3 and 4 . . . . @2.50

KILROY
Caliber Core, 1998
1C by Joe Pruett & Feliciano
  Zecchin, John Cassaday(c). . . . 3.00
1P JoP (c). 3.00
1a premium edition 10.00
2 . . . . 3.00
3 . . . . 3.00
4 O:Kilroy 3.00
Spec. Dawn of Armageddon,
  x-over, 48-pg. 4.00
Spec.#1 The Origin 5.00
Spec.#2 The Origin,pt.2 . . . . 5.00
TPB Kilroy is Here: Pride, Prejudice
  & Persecution 7.00

KILROY IS HERE
Caliber Press, 1995
1 Kilroy Rescues Infant.	3.00
2 Reflections,pt.2	3.00
3 Reflections,pt.3	3.00
4 Lincoln Memorial	3.00
5 thru 8	@3.00
9 and 10	@3.00
11 WEl,RPc,'Screen'	3.00
12 Khymer Rouge	3.00
Spec. Kilroy: Daemonstorm (1997)	3.00

KIMBER, PRINCE OF FEYLONS
Castle Graphics 1991
1	3.50

Antarctic Press, 1992
1 I:Kimber	2.50
2 V:Lord Tyrex	2.50

KINDERGOTH
Bloodfire 2004
1	3.00
2 thru 4	@3.00

KINGDOM OF THE WICKED
Caliber, 1996
1 IEd	3.00
2 IEd	3.00
3 IEd	3.00
4 IEd	3.00
TPB rep. #1–#4	13.00

KING KONG
Monster Comics, 1991
1 thru 6	@2.50

KINGS IN DISGUISE
Kitchen Sink, 1988
1 thru 5	@2.50
6 end Mini-series	2.50

KING ZOMBIE
Caliber, 1998
1L by Tom Sniegoski & Jacen Burroughs, VcL(c)	3.00
1M Meadows (c)	3.00
2	3.00
3	3.00

KIRBY KING OF THE SERIALS
Blackthorne, 1989
1	2.50
2	2.50
3	2.50
4	2.50

KISSING CHAOS
Oni Press, 2001
1 (of 8) by Arthur Dela Cruz	2.50
2 16-pg.	2.50
3 16-pg.	2.50
4	3.00
5 16-pg.	2.50
6 16-pg.	2.50
7 16-pg.	2.50
8 24-pg.	2.50
TPB Vol. 1	18.00

KISSING CHAOS: NONSTOP BEAUTY
Oni Press, 2002
3 thru 4	@3.00
TPB Vol. 2	12.00

1-shot 1000 Words	3.00
1-shot Nine Lives	3.00
1-shot Sweet Nothings.	3.50

KITZ 'N' KATZ
Phantasy
1	3.50

Eclipse
2	2.25
3	2.25
4 and 5	@2.25

KLOR
Sirius 1999
1	3.00

KLOWN SHOCK
North Star
1 Horror Stories.	2.75

KNEWTS OF THE ROUND TABLE
Pan Entertainment, 1998
1	2.50
2 thru 6	@2.50

KNIGHTMARE
Antarctic Press, 1994
1	2.75
2	2.75
3 Wedding Knight,pt.1	2.75
4 Wedding Knight,pt.2	2.75
5 F:Dream Shadow.	2.75
6 V:Razorblast	2.75

KNIGHT MASTERS
1 thru 7	@2.25

KNIGHTS OF THE DINNER TABLE
Alderac Group, 1994
1	50.00
2	30.00
3	20.00

Kenzer & Company, 1997
4 Have Dice Will Travel	15.00
5 Master of the Game.	15.00
6 on the high seas	10.00
7 Lord of Steam	10.00
8 A:magic cow.	5.00

Knights of the Dinner Table #2
© Alderack Group

---

9 To Dice for Sister Sara	5.00
16 thru 18	@5.00
19 thru 49.	@3.00
50 double-size	5.00
51 thru 69	@3.00
70 thru 99.	@4.00
100 giant 136-pg.	8.00
101 thru 108.	@4.00
109 thru 121	@5.00
TPB Vol. 1 thru Vol. 9 Bundle of Trouble	@10.00
TPB Vol. 10 Bundle of Trouble	12.00
TPB Vol. 11 Bundle of Trouble.	12.00
TPB Vol. 12 thru Vol. 17 Bundle of Trouble.	@12.00
TPB Tales From the Vault	10.00
TPB Tales From the Vault, Vol.2	10.00
TPB Tales From the Vault, Vol.3	13.00
TPB Tales From the Vault, Vol.4	10.00
TPB Fuzzy Knights	10.00
TPB Fuzzy Knights #2	10.00
Spec. Black Hands Gaming Society	3.00
Spec. Origins 2003	3.00
Spec #2 Black Hands Gaming.	3.00
Spec. Origins 2004	3.00

KNIGHTS OF THE DINNER TABLE: EVERKNIGHTS
Kenzer & Company, 2002
1	3.00
2 thru 14	@3.00
Spec. Vs. King Arthur (2004)	3.00

KNIGHTS OF THE DINNER TABLE/FAANS
Six-Handed Press, 1999
X-over Spec.	3.00

KNIGHTS OF THE DINNER TABLE: HACKMASTERS
Kenzer & Company, 2000
1	3.00
2 thru 8	@3.00
9 and 11	@3.00
11	3.00

Becomes:

KNIGHTS OF THE DINNER TABLE: HACKMASTERS OF EVERKNIGHT
11 thru 15	@3.00
TPB Vol. 1 Ultimate Hackmasters	14.00

KNIGHTS OF THE DINNER TABLE ILLUSTRATED
Kenzer & Company, 2000
1	3.00
2 thru 8	@3.00
9 thru 41	@3.00
Travelers Special #1	3.00
TPB Vol. 1 Overkill.	14.00

KNIGHTS OF THE DINNER TABLE MINI-SERIES
Kenzer & Company, 2003
Vol. 1
1 (of 3)	3.00
2 thru 3	@3.00
1a thru 3a variant (c).	@3.00

KNIGHT WATCHMAN
Caliber Press, 1994
1 Graveyard Shift,pt. 1	3.00
2 Graveyard Shift,pt. 2	3.00

KODOCHA: SANA'S STAGE
Tokyopop Press, 2002
1 (of 5) by Miho Obana......... 3.00
2 .... 3.00
3 thru 5 .... @3.00

KOMODO & THE DEFIANTS
Victory
1 thru 6 .... @2.25

KONI WAVES
Arcana Studio 2006
1 (of 3) 3.00
2 thru 3 .... @3.00

KORVUS
Human Monster Press, 1997
1 by Mick Fernette 3.00
2 .... 3.00
Arrow Comics, 1998
3 .... 3.00
VOL 2
1 .... 3.00
2 .... 3.00

KUNG FU WARRIORS
(Prev. ROBOWARRIORS)
CFW
12 .... 2.25
13 thru 19................. @2.25

KUNOICHI
Lightning Comics, 1996
1 2 diff. mild covers....... 3.00
1 platinum edition........... 6.00
1 autographed edition........ 10.00

KYRA
Elsewhere, 1989
1 thru 5 by Robin Ator...... @2.50
TPB rep #1–#5 + pin-ups....... 7.00

L33T: COMICS FOR GAMERS
Keenspot Entertainment, 2002
1 .... 5.00
2 thru 4 .... @5.00
5 24-pg..................... 3.00
6 thru 11 .... @5.00

LABOR FORCE
Blackthorne, 1986
1 thru 4 .... @2.50
5 thru 8 .... @2.50

LA COSA NOSTROID
Fireman Press, 1997
1 by Don Harmon & Rob Schrab .. 3.00
2 by Don Harmon & Edvis 3.00
3 .... 3.00
4 .... 3.00
5 .... 3.00
6 x-over madness 3.00
7 .... 3.00
8 .... 3.00
9 .... 3.00
10 final issue of Volume 1 ...... 3.00

LACUNAE
CFD Productions, 1995
1 thru 4 F:Monkey Boys 2.50
5 thru 10 .... @2.50
11 HMo 2.50

12 HMo 2.50

LADIES OF LONDON NIGHT
London Night, 1997
Fall Special.................. 5.00
Winter Special............... 5.00
  Winter Wonderland Edition 7.00
Spring 98 Special............. 5.00
Spotlight: Devon Michaels 4.00

LADY DEATH: DEATH GODDESS
Chaos! Comics
Spec. 16-page 2.50
Spec. variant (c)............ 6.00
Spec. premium (c) 10.00

LADY ARCANE
Heroic Publishing, 1992
1 color 4.00
2 thru 4 .... @3.50

Lady Arcane #3
© *Heroic Publishing*

LADY DEATH: INFERNAL SINS
Avatar Press 2006
1-shot 2.50
1-shot wraparound (c) 3.00
1-shot variant (c)s .... @3.00
1-shot premium (c) 10.00
0 blood red foil convention (c) 5.00
0 Repos (c) 6.00

LADY VAMPRE
Blackout Comics, 1996
0 (1995) 2.75
1 flip-book.................. 3.00
0 Immortal No More (1998) 3.00
Spec.#1 In the Flesh (1996) 3.00
Spec.#1a photo sexy cover 10.00

LADY VAMPRE RETURNS
Blackout Comics, 1998
1 by Rob Roman & Kirk Manley ... 3.00
1a Deluxe edition 15.00

LAFFIN GAS
Blackthorne, 1986
1 .... 2.50
2 thru 12 .... @2.50

LANCE STANTON WAYWARD WARRIOR
1 and 2 .... @2.25

LANDER
Mermaid Producions
1 Power of the Dollar,pt.1 .... 2.25
2 Power of the Dollar,pt.2 .... 2.25
3 Power of the Dollar,pt.3 .... 2.25
Vol. 2
1 'By Whose Authority,'pt.1 ...... 2.75
2 'By Whose Authority,'pt.2 ...... 2.75

LAND OF OZ
Arrow Comics, 1998
1 by Gary Bishop & Bill Bryan 3.00
2 thru 6 .... @3.00

LAST DITCH
Edge Press
1 CCa(s),THa,............... 2.50

LAST GENERATION
Black Tie Studios, 1987
1 .... 5.00
2 .... 4.00
3 .... 2.50
4 .... 2.50
5 .... 2.50
Book One Rep. 7.00

LAST MINUTE
Aces & Eights Publ., 2004
1 .... 3.00
2 thru 6 .... 6.00

LAST SIN OF MARK GRIM, THE
Silent Devil Productions 2006
1 (of 4) 3.00
2 thru 3 .... @3.00
Shanda Fantasy Arts 2006
4 .... 3.00

LATEX ALICE
Basement Comics, 2003
0 .... 3.00
0a special edition 9.00
1 Blonde Ambition............. 3.00
1a Blonde Ambition, special 9.00
Spec. Papercuts.............. 3.00
Spec. #1 Paper Cuts 9.00
Bikini Bash Gallery #1 spec...... 9.00

LEAGUE OF CHAMPIONS
Hero Comics, 1990
(cont. from Innovation L.of C. #3)
1 GP,F:Sparkplug,Icestar 3.50
2 GP(i),F:Marksman,Flare,Icicle ... 3.50
3 .... 3.50
4 F:Sparkplug,League........... 3.50
5 Morrigan Wars,pt.#1 .... 3.50
6 Morrigan Wars,pt.#3 .... 3.50
7 Morrigan Wars,pt.#6 .... 3.50
8 Morrigan Wars Conclusion 3.50
9 A:Gargoyle................. 3.50
10 A:Rose 3.50
11 thru 12.................. 4.00
13 V:Malice 4.00
14 V:Olympians 4.00
15 V:Olympians 3.00

LE FEMME VAMPRIQUE
Brainstorm, 1997
1 .... 3.50

All comics prices listed are for *Near Mint* condition.

LEGENDLORE
Caliber New Worlds
1 JMt signed 3.00
3 JMt 3.00
4 JMt 3.00
5 JMt 3.00
6 flip book w/Boston Bombers #4 . 3.00
7 JMt 3.00
8 JMt 3.00
TPB Tainted Soul, rep. #1–#4 . . . . 13.00
TPB In Misery's Shadow,
   Rep. #5–#7 . . . . 10.00

LEGENDLORE:
REALM WARS
Caliber New Worlds
1 by Joe Martin & Philip Xavier,
   Fawn cover by Xavier 3.00
1a Falla cover by Boller 3.00
1b signed 3.00
2 . . . . 3.00
3 . . . . 3.00
4 concl. 3.00

LEGENDLORE:
WRATH OF THE DRAGON
Caliber Fantasy, 1998
1 by JMt & Philip Xavier 3.00
1 variant Philip Xavier(c). 3.00
2 . . . . 3.00
3 . . . . 3.00
4 . . . . 3.00
5 Prisoner set free 3.00
Spec. Handbook 4.00
1-shot Legendlore: Slave of Fate
   by JMt & Philip Xavier 3.00
1-shot The Wind Spirits, 48-pg. 4.00
Giant Size Spec. 48-pg. 4.00

LEGENDS FROM
DARKWOOD
Antarctic Press, 2003
1 thru 3 . . . . @3.50
4 . . . . 3.00
TPB Vol. 1 . . . . 10.00
Summer Fun Spec. 3.00
Special 3.00

LEGENDS OF CAMELOT
Caliber Fantasy, 1999
Excalibur 3.00
Quest For Honor 3.00
Merlin 3.00
The Enchanted Lady 3.00
Sir Balin & The Dolorous Stroke . . . 3.00

LEGEND OF LEMNEAR
CPM Manga, 1997
1 . . . . 3.00
2 thru 18 . . . . @3.00
TPB Vol. 1 thru Vol. 3. . . . . @16.00

LEGEND OF THE
EIGHT DRAGON GODS
Komics, Inc., 2000
GN Vol. 1 . . . . 10.00
GN Vol. 2 thru Vol. 6 . . . . @10.00

LEGENDS OF LUXURA
Brainstorm, 1996
1 platinum edition 5.00
2 gold edition 5.00
3 . . . . 3.00
TPB #1 . . . . 13.00

LEGION ANTHOLOGY
Limelight, 1997
1 four stories 3.00
2 . . . . 3.00
3 F:Binary Angel 3.00
4 . . . . 3.00
5 Binary Angel. 3.00

LEGION X-I
Greater Mercury
1 McKinney 5.00
2 McKinney,rare 15.00
Volume 2, 1989
1 thru 4 . . . . @2.50

LEGION X-2
Vol 2 #1 . . . . 2.50
Vol 2 #2 . . . . 2.50
Vol 2 #3 . . . . 2.50
Vol 2 #4 . . . . 2.50

Lenore #2
© Slave Labor

LENORE
Slave Labor, 1998
1 by Roman Dirge. 3.00
2 thru 12 . . . . @3.00
TPB 12.00
TPB Vol. 2 Wedgies! 14.00
TPB Vol. 3 Cooties. 14.00

LENSMAN
Eternity, 1990
1 E.E.`Doc' Smith adapt. 2.25
2 . . . . 2.25
3 . . . . 2.25
4 . . . . 2.25
5 On Radelix 2.25
6 . . . . 2.25
Collectors Spec #1, 56 pgs. 4.00
TPB Birth of a Lensman, rep. 6.00
TPB Secret of the Lens, rep. 6.00

LENSMAN:
GALACTIC PATROL
Eternity, 1990
1 thru 7 E.E. `Doc' Smith adapt. . @2.25

LENSMAN:
WAR OF THE GALAXIES
Eternity, 1990
1 thru 7 . . . . @2.25

LEONARDO
Mirage, 1986
1-shot TMNTurtles 13.00

LETHAL LADIES
OF BRAINSTORM
Brainstorm, 1997
1 F:Luxura, Vampfire, etc.. . . . . . . 3.00
1 luxury edition 5.00

LETHAL STRIKE
ARCHIVES
London Night, 1997
1 rep. Razor #7, #10 & Uncut
   #19–#21. . . . . 3.00
TPB Lethal Strike (1998) 13.00

LETHAL STRIKE:
SHADOW VIPER
London Night, 1998
1 (of 2) from Razor: Torture #4 . . . . 3.00
1 leather 15.00

LETHARGIC LAD
ADVENTURES
Crusade Entertainment, 1997
1 by Greg Hyland 3.00
2 . . . . 3.00
Becomes:

LETHARGIC LAD
TV Comics, 1997
3 by Greg Hyland 3.00
4 . . . . 3.00
5 . . . . 3.00
TPB Big Book of Lethargic Lad . . . 16.00
Lethargic Comics
6 by Greg Hyland 3.00
7 thru 14 . . . . @3.00
Dork Storm Press 2005
Jumbo Sized Ann. #3 . . . . 4.00

LEVEL X
Caliber, 1997
1 . . . . 3.00
2 32pg. 3.00
3 48pg. 4.00

LEVEL X:
THE NEXT REALITY
Caliber, 1997
1 (of 2) by Dan Harbison & Randy
   Buccini, 64pg. 4.00
2 48pg. 4.00

LIBBY ELLIS
Eternity, 1988
1 thru 4 . . . . @2.50

LIBERATOR
Eternity
1 thru 6 . . . . @2.25

LIBERTY FROM HELL
Radio Comix, 2003
1 . . . . 3.00
2 thru 6 . . . . @3.00

LIBERTY MEADOWS
Insight Studios, 1999
1 by Frank Cho 30.00
2 . . . . 18.00
3 . . . . 15.00
4 thru 6 . . . . @10.00
7 thru 10 . . . . @8.00
11 thru 20 . . . . @7.00
21 thru 23 . . . . @5.00
24 Virtual Reality Adventure 5.00
25 Pool Party 5.00
26 Fossil Dinosaurs 5.00
Spec. Wedding Album 10.00

L.I.F.E. BRIGADE
Blue Comet
1 A:Dr. Death 2.25
1a 2nd printing 2.25
2 . . . . 2.25

LIFE OF A FETUS
Slave Labor, 1999
1 by Andy Ristaino 3.00
2 thru 7 . . . . @3.00

LIFEQUEST
Caliber, 1997
1 by Matt Vanderpol 3.00
2 thru 6 . . . . @3.00

LITTLE GLOOMY
Amaze Ink/SLG, 1999
1 by Landry Walker & Eric Jones . . 3.00
2 thru 6 . . . . @3.00
Halloween Spec. 3.50
TPB Vol. 1 . . . . 13.00

LITTLE ORPHAN ANNIE
Tony Raiola, 2001
TPB Man of Mystery 9.50
TPB Pro and the Con 9.50
TPB Little Worker. 9.50
TPB The Dreamer 9.50
TPB Rich Man, Poor Man 9.50

LITTLE SCROWLIE
Amaze Ink/SLG, 2003
4 thru 7 . . . . @3.00
8 thru 15 . . . . @3.00
TPB Vol. 1 . . . . 11.00
TPB Vol. 2 . . . . 13.00

LITTLE STAR
Oni Press 2005
1 . . . . 3.00
2 thru 5 . . . . @3.00
6 . . . . 3.00
TPB 20.00

LITTLE WHITE MOUSE
(THE SERIES)
Caliber, 1998
1 by Paul Sizer 3.00
2 Fever Dreams 3.00
3 Filthy Jake 3.00
4 . . . . 3.00
Cafe Digital Comics 2006
Omnibus Edition 25.00

LITTLE WHITE MOUSE:
ENTROPY DREAMING
Blue Line Pro Comics, 2001
1 by Paul Sizer 3.00
2 Nuts and Bolts 3.00
3 . . . . 3.00
4 concl. 3.00

LITTLE WHITE MOUSE:
OPEN SPACE
Blue Line Pro Comics, 2002
1 (of 4) by Paul Sizer 3.00
2 thru 4 . . . . @3.00
TPB Vol. 3 . . . . 15.00

LIVINGSTONE MOUNTAIN
Adventure Comics, 1991
1 I:Scat,Dragon Rax 2.50
2 Scat & Rax Create Monsters. . . . 2.50
3 Rax rescue attempt 2.50
4 Final issue 2.50

LLOYD LLEWELLYN
Fantagraphics, 1986
1 Mag Size 4.00
2 thru 6 Mag Size . . . . @2.50
7 Regular Size 2.50

LOCAL
Oni Press 2005
1 (of 12) 3.00
1a 2nd printing 3.00
2 Polaroid Boyfriend 3.00
3 Thories and Defenses 3.00
4 The Two Brothers 3.00
5 Last Lonely Days at the
　　Oxford Theater 3.00
6 Megan and Gloria, Apartment 5A 3.00
7 Smash the State 3.00
8 Food as Substitute. 3.00
9 Wish You Were Here 3.00
10 The Process 3.00

LOCO VS. PULVERINE
Eclipse, 1992
1 Parody 2.50

LODOSS WAR:
CHRONICLES OF THE
HEROIC KNIGHT
CPM Manga, 2000
1 by Ryo Mizuno & M. Natsumoto . 3.00
2 thru 19 . . . . @3.00
TPB Vol. 1 . . . . 16.00
TPB Vol. 2 thru Vol. 6. . . . . @16.00

LODOSS WAR:
DEELIT'S TALE
CPM Manga, 2001
1 by R. Mizuno & S. Yoneyama . . . 3.00
1a signed & numbered 15.00
2 thru 4 . . . . @3.00
5 thru 8 . . . . @3.00
TPB Vol. 1 Choices 16.00
TPB Vol. 2 Forest of No Return . . . 16.00

LODOSS WAR:
THE GREY WITCH
CPM Manga, 1998
1 by Ryo Mizuno & Yoshihiko Ochi. 3.00
2 by Ryo Mizuno & Akikiro Yamada 3.00
3 thru 10 . . . . @3.00
11 thru 22. . . . . @3.00
TPB Vol. 2 . . . . 16.00
TPB Vol. 3 . . . . 16.00

LODOSS WAR:
THE LADY OF PHARIS
CPM Manga, 1999
1 by Ryo Mizuno & Akihiro Yamada 3.00
2 thru 7 . . . . @3.00
TPB Vol. 1 208-pg.. . . . . 16.00

LOGAN'S RUN
Adventure Comics, 1990
1 thru 6 Novel adapt. . . . . @2.50

Logan's World #4
© Adventure

LOGAN'S WORLD
Adventure Comics, 1991
1 Seq. to Logan's Run 2.50
2 thru 6 . . . . @2.50

LONER
Fleetway
1 Pt.1 (of 7). 2.25
2 thru 6 Pt.2 thru Pt.6 . . . . @2.25

LONE WOLF & CUB
First, 1987–91
1 FM(c) 7.00
1a 2nd printing 2.50
1b 3rd printing. 2.50
2 . . . . 4.00
2a 2nd printing 2.50
3 . . . . 4.00
4 thru 10 . . . . @4.00
11 thru 17 . . . . @3.00
18 thru 25 . . . . @3.00
26 thru 36 . . . . @3.00
37 and 38 . . . . @4.00
39 120-pg. 6.00
40 . . . . 3.25
41 MP(c), 60-pg. 4.00
42 thru 45 MP(c) . . . . @3.25

LOOKERS
Avatar Press, 1997
1 . . . . 3.00
1 deluxe 5.00
1 signed 12.00
2 . . . . 3.00
2 Deluxe cover 8.00
Spec. #1 . . . . 3.00
Spec. #1 signed 8.00
Spec. Allure of the Serpent (1999) . 3.50
Spec. Slaves of Anubis (1998). 3.50

LORD OF THE DEAD
Conquest
1 R.E.Howard adapt. 3.00

LORELEI
Power Comics, 1996
2 'Building the Perfect Beast,'pt.7 . 2.50
3 'Building the Perfect Beast,'pt.8 . 2.50

B & W PUB.

Vol.2
0 2nd printing	2.50
1	2.50
1a deluxe	4.00
1b signed	8.00

Lori Lovecraft The Big Comeback
© Caliber

LORI LOVECRAFT
Caliber, 1997
1 MV, 48pg	4.00
1a signed	4.00
1-shot The Dark Lady (1997)	3.00
1-shot Repression (1998)	3.00
Spec. The Big Comeback (1998)	3.00

AV Publications, 2000
TPB Vol. 1 160-pg.	12.00

LOST, THE
Caliber, 1996
1	3.00
1a special ed.	7.00
1b signed	3.00
2 thru 4	@3.00

LOST CONTINENT
Eclipse, 1990
1 thru 5, Manga	@3.50

LOST SQUAD
Devil's Due Publishing 2005
1 thru 6	@3.00
TPB	15.00

LOST STORIES
Creative Frontiers, 1998
1	3.00
2	3.00
3	3.00
4 The Big Horn Bruhaha	3.00
5 Strike Force O'Shea,pt.1	3.00
6 Strike Force O'Shea,pt.2	3.00
7 Gnome for a Day	3.00
8 A Vampire Too Far	3.00
9 The Undertroll Saga,pt.1	3.00

LOST WORLD, THE
Millennium, 1996
1 & 2 Arthur Conan Doyle adapt.	@3.00

LOTHAR
Powerhouse Graphics
1 I:Lothar,Galactic Bounty Hunter.	2.50
2 I:Nightcap.	2.50

LOUIS RIEL
Drawn & Quarterly, 1999
1 (of 10) by Chester Brown	3.00
2 thru 5	@3.00
6 thru 10	@3.00

LOVE AND ROCKETS
Fantagraphics Books, 1982–96
1 HB,B&W cover, adult	30.00
1a HB,Color cover	20.00
1b 2nd printing	4.00
2 HB	10.00
3 HB	6.00
4 HB	6.00
5 HB	6.00
6 HB	5.00
7 HB	6.00
8 HB	6.00
9 HB	5.00
10 HB	5.00
11 thru 21 HB	@3.00
22 thru 39 HB	@3.00
40 thru 50	@3.00
Bonanza rep.	3.00
TPB Vol 9 Flies on the Ceiling, 2nd printing	17.00
TPB Vol 10	12.00
TPB Vol 11	15.00
TPB Vol 12	17.00
TPB Vol 14 Luba Conquers the World	15.00
TPB Vol 15	15.00

Vol. 2, 2001
1 GHe,JHr,	4.00
1a 2nd printing	4.00
2 thru 9	@4.00
10	6.00
11 thru 17	@4.50

LOVE FIGHTS
Oni Press, 2003
1	3.00
2 thru 4	@3.00
5	6.00
6 thru 12	@3.00
TPB Vol. 1	15.00
TPB Vol. 2	15.00

LOVE HINA
Tokyopop Press, 2002
1 (of 4) by Ken Akamatsu	3.00
2 thru 4	@3.00

LOVE IN TIGHTS
Amaze Ink, 1998
1	3.00
Spec. Valentine's Day Special	3.00
Spec. Spring Fling	3.00
Anniv. #1	3.00
6 & 7	@3.00

LOVELY PRUDENCE
Millennium, 1997
1 by Maze	3.00
2	3.00
3 Nightmares of Breeding	3.00
#M 24-pg.	2.25
#M 24-pg., signed	3.00
Spec. Swimsuit Special	3.00
Christmas Misery Spec.#1	3.00

LUBA
Fantagraphics, 1998
1 by Gilbert Hernandez	3.00
2 thru 5	@3.00
6 thru 10	@3.50
TPB Luba in America (2001)	20.00
TPB Luba: The Book of Ophelia	23.00
TPB Three Daughteers	17.00

LUBA'S COMICS & STORIES
Fantagraphics, 2000
1 by Gilbert Hernandez.	3.00
2 GHe	3.50
3 GHe, Ofelia	3.50
4 GHe, The Light of Venus	3.50
5 GHe, Lovers and Hector	3.50
6 GHe	3.50
7 GHe, Fritz After Dark	3.50

LUFTWAFFE 1946
[Mini-Series]
Antarctic Press, 1996
1	5.00
2 thru 4	@4.00
TPB Vol.1, rep.mini-series #1–#4	11.00

Antarctic Press, 1997
1 by Ted Namura & BDn.	3.00
2 Luftsturm,pt.2	3.00
3 Luftsturm,pt.3	3.00
4 Luftsturm,pt.4	3.00
5 new weapons	3.00
6 Projekt Saucer,pt.1	3.00
7 Projekt Saucer,pt.2	3.00
8 Projekt Saucer,pt.3	3.00
9 Projekt Saucer,pt.4	3.00
10 Projekt Saucer,pt.5	3.00
11 Projekt Saucer, epilogue	3.00
12 Richthofen's Flying Circus,pt.1	3.00
13 Richthofen's Flying Circus,pt.2	3.00
14 Jagdeschwader,pt.2	3.00
15 Jagdeschwader,pt.3	3.00
16 Jagdeschwader,pt.4	3.00
17 Jagdeschwader,pt.5	3.00
18 Schweinfurt	3.00
Tech Manual Vol. 1	4.00
Tech Manual Vol. 2	4.00
Tech Manual Vol. 3 Rocket Fighters	4.00
Tech Manual Vol. 4 Amerika Bombers	4.00
Tech Manual Vol. 5 Wonder Weapons	4.00
Tech. Manual Vol. 6	6.00
Spec.#1 Triebflugel	3.00
Spec.#1 World War II: 1946	4.00
Ann. #1 prototype artwork	3.00
TPB Vol.2, rep. #1–#5	11.00
TPB Vol. 3, rep.	11.00
TPB Vol. 4, rep. #13–#18	15.00
TPB 600-pg.	50.00

New Volume (2002)
1 Tigers of the Luftwaffe	6.00
2 thru 18	@6.00

Volume 5
1 thru 3	@6.00
Annual #2.	5.00
Pocket Manga Vol. 1	10.00
Pocket Manga Vol. 2 thru Vol. 4.	@10.00
Annual #2.	5.00
TPB Technical Manual	22.00
TPB Vol. 1 Sourcebook	6.00

LUM*URUSEI YATSURA
Viz Communications
1 Art by Rumiko Takahashi	3.00
2	3.00
3	3.00
4	3.00
5	3.25
6 thru 8	@3.00

LUNAR DONUT
Cosmic Lunchbox Comics, 1996
1 thru 4 by Parham & Tucker	@3.00
Lunar Donut	
5	3.00
6 Powdered Sugar	3.00

LUXURA
Brainstorm, 1996
Convention Book 2 . . . . 3.00
Ann.#1 48pg (1998) 4.00
Pin-up mag. Luxura: The Good, The
  Bad and the Beautiful (1999) . . 4.00
Spec.1 Luxura & Vampfire, x-over
  by Fauve (1997) 3.00
Luxura Leather, Platinum edition . . . 5.00
Luxura Leather, Signed edition 8.00

LUXURA/BABY ANGEL X
Brainstorm, 1996
Spec. x-over 3.00
Spec. deluxe 5.00
Luxury edition 8.00
Deluxe luxury edition 12.00

LUXURA/WIDOW:
BLOOD LUST
Brainstorm
Omega x-over pt.2 concl 3.00
Omega Fusion cover 5.00
Luxury edition 8.00
Deluxe luxury edition 12.00
See: Widow/Luxura for pt.1

LYNX: AN ELFLORD TALE
Peregrin, 1999
1 by Barry Blair 3.00
2 by Barry Blair & Colin Chan 3.00
3 & 4 . . . . @3.00

M.A.C.H. 1
Fleetway
1 I:John Probe-Secret Agent 2.25
2 thru 9 . . . . @2.25

MACKENZIE QUEEN
Matrix, 1985
1 thru 5 . . . . @3.75

MACROSS II
Viz Comics, 1992
1 Macross Saga sequel 2.75
2 A:Ishtar 2.75
3 F:Reporter Hibiki,Ishtar 2.75
4 V:Feff,The Marduk 2.75
5 . . . . 2.75
6 . . . . 2.75
7 Sylvie Confesses 2.75
8 F:Ishtar 2.75
9 V:Marduk Fleet 2.75
10 . . . . 2.75

MACROSS II: THE
MICRON CONSPIRACY
Viz, 1994
1 Manga 2.75

MAD DOGS
Eclipse, 1992
1 I:Mad Dogs(Cops) 2.50
2 V:Chinatown Hood 2.50
3 . . . . 2.50

MADMAN
Oni Press, 2002
TPB Madman Adventures (2002) . 15.00
TPB The Odyity Odyssey,
  10th Anniv. (2002) 16.00

MAD RACCOONS
MU Press, 1991
1 thru 7 by Cathy Hill, Angst of
  an Artist . . . . @3.00

MAELSTROM
Aircel, 1987
1 thru 13 . . . . @2.50

MAGGOTS
Hamilton, 1991
1 JSon, mag size 4.00
2 JSon, mag size 4.00
3 GM/JSon,inc.`Some Kinda
  Beautiful' 4.00

MAGICAL MATES
Antarctic Press, 1995
1 & 2 Manga, by Mio Odagi . . . . @3.00
3 thru 8 (of 8) . . . . @3.00

MAGICAL POKEMON
JOURNEY
Viz Communications, 2000
1 How Do You Do, Pikachu 5.00
2 Cooking with Jigglypuff 5.00
3 Pokemon Holiday 5.00
4 Fun at the Beach 5.00
TPB Vol. 1 Party with Pikachu . . . 14.00
PART 2, 2000
1 thru 4 . . . . @5.00
PART 3, 2000
1 thru 4 . . . . @5.00
TPB Vol.3 Wal Comes Crashing
  Down 14.00
PART 4, 2001
1 thru 4 Love Potion Pursuit . . . . @5.00
TPB Vol.4 Friends & Family 14.00
PART 5, 2001
1 thru 4 . . . . @5.00
TPB Vol.5 Going Coconuts 14.00
PART 6, 2001
1 (of 4) 5.00
2 thru 4 . . . . @5.00
TPB Vol.6 Gold & Silver 14.00
PART 7, 2002
1 . . . . 5.00
2 thru 4 . . . . @5.00
TPB Vol.7 From the Heart 14.00

MAGIC PRIEST
Antarctic Press, 1998
1 (of 3) by B.Lyga & N.Googe 3.00
2 . . . . 3.00

MAGIC WHISTLE
Alternative Press
Vol 2
1 by Sam Henderson 3.00
2 thru 8 . . . . @3.00
9 96-pg 12.00
10 . . . . 12.00

MAGUS
Caliber Core, 1998
1L by Gary Reed & Craig Brasfield,
  VcL(c) 3.00
1D GyD(c) 3.00
1 premium edition, signed 10.00
2 Magus secrets 3.00
3 Lilith & Beezlebub 3.00
1-shot Magus: The Forever King . . 3.00
Spec. Dawn of Armageddon,
  x-over, 48-pg. 3.00

MAI, THE PSYCHIC GIRL
Eclipse, 1987
1 I:Mai,Alliance of 13 Sages 3.75
1a 2nd printing 2.50
2 V:Wisdom Alliance 2.50
2a 2nd printing 2.50

Mai the Psychic Girl #7
© Eclipse

3 V:Kaieda,I:Ojii-San 2.50
4 . . . . 2.50
5 thru 19 . . . . @2.50
20 thru 28 . . . . @2.50

MAID ATTACK
**White Lightning Productions,
2003**
1 (of 4) 4.00
2 thru 4 . . . . @4.00

MAISON IKKOKU
Viz Comics, 1993
1 thru 7 Manga 3.00
[Part Two]
1 thru 6 . . . . 3.00
[Part Three]
1 thru 6 . . . . 3.00
[Part Four]
1 thru 6 F:Kyoko 3.00
7 thru 10 . . . . @3.00
[Part Six], 1996
1 thru 11 by Rumiko Takahashi . . @3.50
[Part Seven], 1997
1 thru 8 by Rumiko Takahashi . . @3.25
9 thru 13 . . . . @3.50
[Part Eight], 1998
1 (of 8) 3.25
2 . . . . 3.50
3 thru 8 . . . . @3.25
[Part Nine], 1999
1 (of 10) 3.25
2 thru 10 . . . . @3.25

MANDRAKE
1 . . . . 4.00
2 . . . . 4.00
3 . . . . 4.00
Ultimate Mandrake 15.00

MANDRAKE MONTHLY
1 . . . . 4.00
2 . . . . 4.00
3 . . . . 5.00
4 . . . . 5.00
5 . . . . 5.00
6 . . . . 7.00
Special #1 . . . . 7.00

B & W PUB.

MAN-EATING COW
New England Comics, 1992
1 Spin-off from the Tick	3.25
2 O:Mr.Krinkles,A:Lt.Valentine	2.75
3 Final issue	2.75
Bonanza #1, 128pg (1996)	5.00
Bonanza #2, 100pg	5.00

MAN-ELF
3 A:Jerry Cornelius	2.25

MAN FROM U.N.C.L.E.
Entertainment Publ., 1987
1 `Number One with a Bullet Affair	3.50
2 `Number One with a Bullet Affair	3.00
3 `The E-I-E-I-O Affair'	3.00
4 `The E-I-E-I-O Affair,' concl.	3.00
5 `The Wasp Affair'	3.00
6 `Lost City of THRUSH Affair'	3.00
7 `The Wildwater Affair'	3.00
8 `The Wilder West Affair'	3.00
9 `The Canhadian Lightning Affair'	3.00
10 `The Turncoat Affair'	3.00
11 `Craters of the Moon Affair'	3.00

MANGA EX
Antarctic Press, 2001
1 thru 5	@7.00
6	7.00

MANGAPHILE
Radio Comix, 1999
1 thru 5	@3.00
6 thru 11	@3.00
12 48-pg.	4.00
13 48-pg.	4.00
14 thru 21 48-pg.	4.00
22 thru 25	@5.00

MANGA VIZION
Viz Communications
Vol. 1, 1995
1 thru 10 Ogre Slayer	@5.00
Vol. 2, 1996
1 thru 12	@5.00
Vol. 3, 1997
1 thru 8	@5.00
Vol. 4
1 thru 8	@5.00

MANGAZINE
Antarctic Press, 1985
1 newsprint cover	15.00
1a reprint.	3.00
2	9.00
3	8.00
4	8.00
5	8.00
New Series
1	3.00
2	3.00
3	2.25
4	3.00
5 thru 7	@2.25
8 thru 13	@2.25
14 New Format	3.00
15 thru 44	@3.00
VOL. 3, 1999
1 thru 15	@9.00
16 thru 27 140+-pg.	@9.00
28 thru 39	@9.00
40 thru 70	@10.00

MANIMAL
Renegade, 1986
1 EC,rep.	2.50

Man of Rust #1B
© *Blackthorne*

MAN OF RUST
Blackthorne, 1986
1 Cover A	2.50
1 Cover B	2.50

MANSLAUGHTER
Brainstorm, 1996
1	3.00
1a gold foil edition.	5.00

MANTUS FILES
Eternity
1 Sidney Williams novel adapt	2.50
2 Vampiric Figures	2.50
3 Secarus' Mansion	2.50
4 A:Secarus	2.50

MARCANE
Eclipse
1 Book 1,JMu	6.00

MARK I
(Prev.: Atomic Comics)
2	2.25

MARK MILLAR'S THE UNFUNNIES
Avatar, 2003
1 thru 3	@3.50
1a Platinum (c)	6.00
1a thru 3a offensive (c)	@3.50

MARMALADE BOY
Tokyopop Press, 2001
1 (of 5) by Wataru Yoshizumi	3.00
2 thru 5	3.00

MARQUIS, THE
Caliber, 1997
1 GyD	3.00
1 spec. double gatefold cover.	6.00
2 Marquis cover by Vincent Locke	3.00
2a Marquis view of world GyD(c)	3.00
3	3.00
Spec. The Marquis, Gallery of Hell, GyD	4.00
Spec. The Marquis: Les Preludes, GyD prelude edition (1996)	3.00
Spec.A Les Preludes, signed	3.00

MARQUIS, THE: DANSE MACABRE
Oni Press, 2000
1 (of 5) by Guy Davis	3.00
2	3.00
3 thru 5	@3.00
TPB	19.00

MARTIAN SUCCESSOR NADESICO
CPM Manga, 1999
1 by Kia Asamiya	3.00
2	3.00
3	3.00
4 thru 15	@3.00
16 thru 26	@3.00
TPB Vol. 1	16.00
TPB Book 2 176-pg.	16.00
TPB Book 3 176-pg.	16.00
TPB Book 4 208-pg.	16.00

MASKED WARRIOR X
Antarctic Press, 1996
1 (of 6) by Masayuki Fujihara	3.50
2	3.00
3 The Girls of Olympus,' pt.2	3.00
4 `Protect the Silver Fortress'	3.00

MASQUERADE
Eclipse
1	2.25
2	2.25
3	2.25

MATAAK
K-Blamm, 1995
1 I:Mataak	2.50
2 Spirit of Peace	2.50

MATT CHAMPION
Metro
1 EC	2.25
2 EC	2.25

MAVIS
Exhibit A, 1998
1 BLs, F:Wolff & Byrd's secretary	3.00
2	3.00

MAX HAMM FAIRY TALE DETECTIVE
Nite Owl Comix 2002
1 by Frank Cammuso	5.00
Vol. 2
1 (of 3)	5.00
2 thru 3	@5.00
TPB Vol. 1	15.00

MAXION
CPM, 1999
1 by Takeshi Takebayashi	3.00
2 thru 11	@3.00
12 thru 24	@3.00
25	3.00
26	3.00
TPB Book 1	16.00
TPB Book 2	16.00
TPB Book 3 Waves of Misfortune	16.00
TPB Book 4 Maniac Obsessions	16.00

MAX OF THE REGULATORS
Atlantic
1	4.00
2 thru 4	@3.50

MAXWELL MOUSE FOLLIES
Renegade, 1986
1 Large format (1981) 4.00
1a Comic Size(1986) 3.00
2 thru 6 . . . . @2.50

MAYHEM
1 Mask(c) 9.00
2 thru 6 . . . . @8.00

MAZE AGENCY
Caliber, 1997
1 The Death of Justice Girl
   reprint series 3.00
1a signed 3.00
2 and 3 . . . . @3.00
2a and 3a variant AH(c)s . . . . . . @3.00

MEASLES
Fantagraphics, 1998
1 by Gilbert Hernandez 3.00
2 thru 8 . . . . @3.00

MEAT CAKE
Fantagraphics, 1995
1 thru 4 . . . . @2.50
5 thru 8 . . . . @3.00
9 thru 15 . . . . @4.00

MECHANOIDS
Caliber, 1991
1 . . . . 2.50
2 thru 5 . . . . @3.50

MECHARIDER: THE REGULAR SERIES
Castle
1 thru 3 F:Winter 3.00
Spec.#1 Limited Edition 3.00

MEDABOTS
Viz Communications, 2002
Part 1
1 (of 4) by Rin Horuma 2.75
2 thru 4 . . . . @2.75
Part 2
1 (of 4) New Challenges 2.75
2 thru 4 . . . . @2.75
Part 3
1 (of 4) 2.75
2 thru 4 . . . . @2.75
Part 4
1 by Horumarin 2.75
2 thru 4 . . . . 2.75
TPB Vol. 1 A Boy and His 'Bot 10.00
TPB Vol. 2 Let's Get Ready
   to Robattle 10.00
TPB Vol. 3 The Medaforce 10.00
TPB Vol. 4 Finale 10.00

MEGATON
Megaton, 1983
1 JG(c),EL(1stProWork),GD,MG,
   A:Ultragirl,Vanguard 11.00
2 EL,JG(pin-up),A:Vanguard 10.00
3 MG,AMe,JG,CL,I:Savage
   Dragon 18.00
4 AMe,EL,2nd A:Savage Dragon
   (inc.EL profile) 9.00
5 AMe,RLd(inside front cover) 5.00
6 AMe,JG(inside back cover),
   EL(Back cover) 4.00
7 AMe 4.00
8 RLd,I:Youngblood(Preview) 18.00

MEGATON MAN MEETS THE UNCATEGORIZABLE X-THEMS
Jabberwocky, 1989
1 . . . . 2.50

MEGATON MAN VS. FORBIDDEN FRANKENSTEIN
Fiasco Comics, 1996
1 by Don Simpson & Anton Drek . . 3.00

MELISSA MOORE: BODYGUARD
Draculina Publishing, 1995
1 thru 3 V:Machine Gun Eddie . . @3.00

MEMORY MAN
Emergency Stop Press, 1995
1 thru 2 Some of the Space Man . . 3.00

MEN IN BLACK
Aircel, 1991
1 by Lowell Cunningham & Sandy
   Carruthers, basis of Movie . . . 35.00
2 . . . . 20.00
3 F:Jay, Arbiter Doran 20.00
[Book II], 1991
1 . . . . 15.00
2 thru 3 . . . . @8.00

MEN IN BLACK: THE ROBORG INCIDENT
Castle
1 thru 3 . . . . @3.00

MERCEDES
Angus Publishing, 1995
8 thru 15 by Mike Friedland
   & Grant Fuhst . . . . @3.00
TPB Vol. 2 . . . . 11.00
TPB Vol. 3, rep. The Wicked
   from #11–#15 . . . . 11.00
VOL. 4
1 thru 4 . . . . @3.00
VOL. 5, 1997
1 . . . . 3.00
2 . . . . 3.00
3 . . . . 3.00
Spec. Senseless Acts of
   Beauty (1998) 3.00

MERCHANTS OF DEATH
Eclipse, 1988
1 . . . . 2.50
2 thru 5 . . . . @2.50

MERCY
Avatar Press, 1997
0 O:Mercy 3.00
0b leather cover 30.00
1 (of 2) by Bill Maus 3.00
1 leather cover 25.00
1 signed 10.00

MERLIN
Adventure Comics, 1990
1 BMC,Merlin's Visions 2.50
2 V:Warlord Carados 2.50
3 . . . . 2.50
4 Ninevah 2.50
5 D:Hagus 2.50
6 Final Issue 2.50

Merlin #2
© Adventure Comics

[2nd Series]
1 Journey of Rhiannon & Tryon . . . 2.50
2 Conclusion 2.50

MERMAID'S GAZE
Viz Comics, 1995
1 thru 3 V:Shingo 2.75
4 final issue 2.75
TPB 16.00

METACOPS
Monster Comics, 1991
1 and 2 . . . . @2.25

METAL GUARDIAN FAUST
Viz Communications, 1997
1 by Tetsuo Ueyama . . . . @3.00
2 thru 8 . . . . @3.00
TPB Vol. 1 . . . . 17.00

METROPOLIS
Caliber, 1997
0 movie adaptation, series
   prequel,48pg 4.00
1 The Last Fredersen, pt.1 . . . . 3.00
2 The Last Fredersen, pt.2 . . . . 3.00
3 The Last Fredersen, pt.3 . . . . 3.00

METAPHYSIQUE
Eclipse
1 NB,Short Stories 2.50
2 NB,Short Stories 2.50

MIAMI MICE
Rip Off Press, 1986
1 1st printing 3.00
1a 2nd printing 2.50
3 . . . . 2.50
4 Record,A:TMNT 3.00

MICHELANGELO
Mirage, 1986
1 TMNT 17.00
1a 2nd Printing 4.50

MICRA
Fictioneer, 1986
1 . . . . 4.00
2 . . . . 3.00
3 . . . . 3.00
4 . . . . 2.50

Micra #1
© *Fictioneer*

5	2.50
6	2.50
7	2.50
8	2.50

MIDDLEMAN, THE
Viper Comics, 2005

1	3.00
2 thru 4	@3.00
TPB	10.00

Vol. 2, 2006

1	1.00
2 thru 4	@3.00
TPB Vol. 2	10.00

MIDNIGHT
Blackthorne

1 thru 4	@2.25

MIDNIGHT MOVER
Oni Press, 2003

1 (of 4)	3.00
2 thru 4	@3.00
TPB	12.00

MIDNIGHT PANTHER
CPM Comics, 1997

1 Manga, translated	3.00
2	3.00
3	3.00
4	3.00
5	3.00
6 Den of Scoundrels	3.00
7 The Sleeping Town	3.00
8 to Reincarnation City	3.00
9 O:Midnight Panthers	3.00
10	3.00
11	3.00
12	3.00
TPB Sex, Death and Rock 'n' Roll. rep #1–#6	16.00
TPB Book 2: Feline Fanatics, rep.#7–#12	16.00
Spec. Breaking Up is Hard to Do. .	3.00

MIDNIGHT PANTHER:
FEUDAL FANTASY
CPM Manga, 1998

1 by Yu Asagiri	3.00
2 thru 5	@3.00
TPB Book 4: Feudal Fantasy	16.00

MIDNIGHT PANTHER:
SCHOOL DAZE
CPM Comics, 1998

1 (of 5) by Yu Asagiri	3.00
2 thru 5	@3.00
TPB Book 3: School Daze	16.00

MIDNIGHT SUN
Amaze Ink/Slave Labor Graphics
2006

1 (of 5	3.00
2	3.00

MIDNITE SKULKER
Target, 1986

1 thru 7	@2.50

MIGHTY GUY
C&T, 1987

1 thru 6	@2.50
Summer Fun Spec #1	2.50

MIGHTY MITES
Eternity, 1986

1 I:X-Mites	2.50
2 & 3	@2.50

MIGHTY MOUSE
ADVENTURE MAGAZINE
Spotlight, 1987

1	5.00

MIGHTY TINY
Antarctic

1 thru 4	@2.25
5	2.50
Mouse Marines Collection rep.	7.50

MIKE HOFFMAN'S LOST
WORLDS OF FANTASY
AND SCI-FI
Antimater/Hoffman Int., 2003

1	3.00
2 thru 10	@3.00
1a thru 10a special edition	@9.00
TPB Best of Lost Worlds	10.00

MIKE HOFFMAN'S
MONSTERS AND
MAIDENS
Antimater/Hoffman International,
2003

1	3.50
2	3.00

MIKE HOFFMAN'S
TIGRESS
Black Daze, 2000

1 by Mike Hoffman	3.00

Antimater/Hoffman Int., 2003

TPB Vol. 1 Journey to Caldathrea .	10.00
Spec. Cover Gallery Spec.	9.00

MILK & CHEESE
Slave Labor, 1991–97

1 EDo, Milk Products gone bad	60.00
1a 2nd thru 7th printing	3.50
2	32.00
2a 2nd thru 4th printing	10.00
3	25.00
3a 2nd thru 4th printing	10.00
4	20.00
4a 2nd & 3rd printing	3.00
5	20.00

5a 2nd & 3rd printing	3.00
6	15.00
6a 2nd printing	2.75
7	5.00
Other #1	2.75
Third #1	2.75
Fourth #1	2.75
First #2	2.75
Six Six Six #1	2.75
Six Six Six 2nd printing, EDo	2.75
Latest Thing	3.00
TPB Fun with Milk & Cheese, rep. 1st 4 issues	12.00

MILLENNIUM 2.5: THE
BUCK ROGERS SAGA
ACG Comics, 2000

1 by Dick Calkin	3.00
2 thru 4	@3.00

MILTON CANIFF'S
TERRY & THE PIRATES
ACG Comics, 1999

1 by Milton Caniff	3.00
2	3.00
3	3.00
4	3.00
TPB Spec. (2001)	13.00

MINESHAFT
Fantagraphics Books 2005

1	5.00
16	5.00
17	6.00
18	7.00

MINIMUM WAGE
Fantagraphics, 1995

Vol. 1, new printing	11.00

Vol. 2, 1995

1 thru 4	@3.00
5 by Bob Fingerman	3.00
6	3.00
7	3.00
8	3.00
9 Artsy Fartsy	3.00
10	3.00
TPB Vol. 2, rep. #1–#5	13.00

MIRACLE GIRLS
Tokyopop Press, 2000

1	3.00
2	3.00
3 thru 14	@3.00
15 thru 17	@3.00
18 thru 23	@3.00

MIRACLE SQUAD
BLOOD & DUST
Apple, 1989

1 thru 3	@2.50

MISTER BLANK
Amaze Ink, 1997

0 by Chris Hicks	2.25
0a 2nd printing	2.25
1 F:Sam Smith	3.00
2 thru 14	@3.00
TPB rep. #1–#14, 360-pg.	30.00

MISTER X
Vortex, Vol 2, 1989–90

1 thru 11	@2.25

MITES
Continuum

1	2.50

1a 2.25
2 thru 4 . . . . @2.25

MOBILE POLICE PATLABOR
Viz Communications, 1997
1 (of 12) by Masami Yuki 3.00
PART TWO, 1998
1 by Masami Yuki 3.00
2 thru 6 . . . . @3.00
TPB Vol. 1 . . . . 16.00
TPB Vol. 2 Basic Training 16.00

MOBILE SUIT GUNDAM 0079
Viz Communications, 1999
1 (of 8) by Kazhisa Kondo 3.00
2 thru 7 . . . . @3.00
PART TWO, 1999
1 (of 5) 3.00
2 thru 5 . . . . @3.00
TPB Vol. 1 . . . . 16.00
TPB Vol. 1 2nd edition 10.00
TPB Vol. 2 . . . . 16.00
TPB Vol. 2 2nd edition 10.00
TPB Vol. 3 thru 9 . . . . @10.00

MOBILE SUIT GUNDAM WING: BLIND TARGET
Viz Communications, 2001
1 thru 4 . . . . @3.00
TPB 13.00

MOBILE SUIT GUNDAM WING: EPISODE ZERO
Viz Communications, 2001
1 thru 8 . . . . @3.00
TPB Art of Mobile Suit
  Gundam Wing 20.00
TPB (2002) 17.00

MOBILE SUIT GUNDAM WING: GROUND ZERO
Viz Communications, 2000
1 (of 4) by Reku Fuyynagi 3.00
2 thru 4 . . . . @3.00
TPB 144-pg. 15.00

MODERN PULP
Special Studio
1 Rep.from January Midnight 2.75

MODESTY BLAISE
Titan 2003
TPB Vol. 1 The Gabriel Set-up . . . 17.00
TPB Vol. 2 Mister Sun 17.00
TPB Vol. 3 Top Traitor 17.00
TPB Vol. 4 Black Pearl 17.00
TPB Vol. 7 Green Eyed Monster . . 17.00
TPB Vol. 5 Bad Suki 17.00
TPB Vol. 6 Hell Makers 17.00
TPB Vol. 8 The Puppet Master . . . 17.00
TPB Vol. 9 The Gallows Bird 17.00
TPB Vol. 10 Cry Wolf 17.00

MOEBIUS COMICS
Caliber, 1996
1 Moe 3.00
2 Moe 3.00
3 Moe 3.00
4 Moe,MP 3.00
5 Moe,SL 3.00
6 Moe 3.00

MOGOBI DESERT RATS
Midnight Comics, 1991
1 I&O:Desert Rats 'Waste of the
  World' 2.25

MONNGA
Daikaiyu Enterprises, 1995
1 & 2 Titanic Omega 4.00

MONOGRAPHS
Coppervale, 1997
1 by James Owen 3.00
2 Bob Phantom 3.00
3 Sidekick Wanted—Benefits
  Available 3.00
4 thru 6 . . . . 3.00

MONSTER BOY
Monster Comics
1 A:Monster Boy 2.25

MONSTER POSSE
Malibu Adventure, 1992
1 I:Monster Posse 2.50
2 I:P.O.N.E,Wack Mack Dwac's
  sister,D-Vicious 2.50
3 . . . . 2.50

MONSTERS ATTACK
Globe
1 GM,JSe 2.25
2 GC 2.25
3 ATh,GC 2.25

Monsters From Outer Space #2
© Adventure

MONSTERS FROM OUTER SPACE
Adventure, 1992
1 thru 3 . . . . @2.50

MOONSTONE MONSTERS
Moonstone Books, 2003
1-shot Sea Creatures 3.00
1-shot Vampire Vixens 3.00
1-shot Ghosts 3.00
1-shot Witches 3.00
1-shot Demons 3.00
1-shot Zombies 3.00
TPB Vol. 1 . . . . 17.00

MOONSTONE NOIR
Moonstone 2002
GN Boston Blackie 5.50
GN The Hat Squad 5.50
GN Jack Hagee, Private Eye 5.50
GN The Mysterious Traveler 5.50
GN The Lone Wolf, Vol. #1 . . . . 5.00
GN Johnny Dollar 5.00
GN Mysterious Traveler Returns . . . 5.00
GN Bulldog Drummond 5.00

MORBID ANGEL: DESPERATE ANGELS
London Night, 1998
0 EHr, & Jude Millien 3.00
0A Powell(c) 5.00
0B Powell(c) 5.00

MORBID ANGEL: PENANCE
London Night Studios, 1995
1 I:Brandon Watts 4.00

MORBID ANGEL: TO HELL AND BACK
London Night, 1996
1 (of 3) EHr, ... 4.00
2 and 3 . . . . @3.00

MORE THAN MORTAL: A LEGEND REBORN
Avatar Press 2006
Spec. 2.50
Spec. Wraparound (c) 3.00
Spec. variant (c) 3.00
Spec. Premium (c) 10.00
Spec. Ruby Red Con Foil (c) 5.00
Spec. Heroic (c) 6.00

MORNING GLORY
Radio Comix, 1998
1 by Loran Gayton & Michael Vega 3.00
2 thru 6 . . . . @3.00

MORTAL COIL
Mermaid
1 thru 3 . . . . @2.25
4 F:Red-Line,Gift 2.25
5 Pin-Up Issue 2.25

MORTOL COILS
Red Eye Press, 2003
1 . . . . 2.50
2 . . . . 3.50
3 . . . . 2.50
TPB Vol. 1 . . . . 17.00

MORTAR MAN
Marshall Comics, 1993
1 I:Mortar Man 2.25
2 thru 3 . . . . @2.25

MOSAIC
Oktober Black Press
1 F:Halo,Daeva 2.25
2 "Gun Metal Gray" 2.50
3 . . . . 2.50
4 Elf(c) 2.50
5 Wisps 2.50

MOSAIC
Sirius, 1999
1 by Kyle Hotz 3.00
2 thru 5 conclusion . . . . @3.00
TPB 15.00

MOUNTAIN WORLD
Newcomers Press, 1995
1 I:Jeremiah Rainshadow 3.00

MR. BEAT ADVENTURES
Moordam Comics, 1997
1 . . . . 3.00
1 deluxe 5.00
Spec. House of Burning Jazz Love . 3.00
Spec. deluxe 5.00
Two-Fisted Atomic Action
  Super Spec. 3.00
Two-Fisted Atomic Action
  Super Spec., deluxe 10.00
Two-Fisted Atomic Action
  Super Spec., mega deluxe . . . 20.00
Spec. Mr. Beat: Superstar 3.00
Spec. Mr. Beat: Superstar, deluxe . 10.00
Ann.#1 Babes and Bongos 3.00

MR. FIXITT
Apple, 1989
1 and 2 . . . . @2.50

MR. KEEN: TRACER OF LOST PERSONS
Moonstone, 2003
1 (of 3) 3.00
2 . . . . 3.00
3 . . . . 3.00
TPB 11.00

MR. MOTO
Moonstone, 2003
1 (of 3) Welcome Back, Mr. Moto . . 3.00
2 thru 3 . . . . @3.00

MR. MYSTIC
Eclipse
1 Will Eisner 2.50

MR. NIGHTMARE'S WONDERFUL WORLD
Moonstone, 1995
1 thru 3 Dreams So Real,
  pt.1–pt.3 . . . . @3.00

MS. CHRIST
Draculina Publishing, 1995
1 I:Ms. Christ. 3.00

Ms. Tree #14
© Renegade

MS. TREE
Aardvark–Vanaheim, 1984
1-10 see Other Pub. (color)
11 thru 18 . . . . @2.50
Renegade, 1985
19 thru 49 . . . . @2.50
50 . . . . 4.50
1 3-D Classic 3.00

MUMMY, THE
Monster Comics
1 A:Dr.Clarke,Prof.Belmore. 2.25
2 Mummy's Curse. 2.25
3 A:Carloph 2.25
4 V:Carloph, conc. 2.25

MUMMY'S CURSE
Aircel, 1990
1 thru 4 B.Blair . . . . @2.25

MUNSTERS, THE
TV Comics, 1998
1 photo (c). 3.00
1a variant (c). 8.00
2 Beverly Owen(c) 3.00
2 Pat Priest (c) 3.00
2 Pat Priest (c) signed 20.00
3 . . . . 3.00
3a Celebrity autograph edition . . . 23.00
4 . . . . 3.00
4a variant photo (c) 3.00
4b variant (c) celebrity autograph
  edition 23.00
5 Herman photo (c). 3.00
5 Grandpa photo (c) 3.00
Spec. Comic Con edition 10.00
Celebrity Autograph Edition: Butch
  Patrick 23.00
TPB Vol 1, rep. #1–#4 . . . . 11.00
Spec.#1 Herman/Grandpa (c) 3.00
Spec.#1a Grandpa (c) 3.00
Halloween Spec. Munsters 1313 . . 3.00
Golden Age Adventure Spec.A(c) . . 3.00
Golden Age Adventure Spec.B(c) . . 3.00

MUNSTERS CLASSICS
TV Comics
0 The Fregosi Emerald 3.00
0 variant (c). 8.00

MURCIELAGA: SHE-BAT
Hero Graphics, 1993
1 Daerick Gross reps. 2.25
2 Reps. contd 3.00

MURDER
Renegade, 1986
1 SD 2.50
2 Cl(c). 2.50
3 SD 2.50
[2nd series]
1 . . . . 2.50

MURDER CAN BE FUN
Slave Labor, 1996
1 thru 6 . . . . @3.00
2 2nd printing 3.00
7 . . . . 3.00
8 . . . . 3.00
9 Seedy Side of Sex 3.00
10 We Love Sports 3.00
11 . . . . 3.00
12 Amusement Park Terror 3.00

MURDER ME DEAD
El Capitan Books, 2000
1 (of 8) by David Lapham 3.00
2 . . . . 3.00

3 thru 8 . . . . @3.00
9 64-pg. 5.00
TPB 20.00

MUTANT ZONE
Aircel, 1991
1 Future story 2.50
2 F.B.I. Drone Exterminators 2.50
3 conclusion 2.50

MY INNER BIMBO
Oni Press 2006
1 (of 5) 3.00
2 thru 4 . . . . @3.00

MYRIAD
Approbation Comics 2005
1 (of 6) 3.00
2 thru 6 . . . . @3.00

MYSTERY MAN
Slave Labor, 1988
1 thru 5 . . . . @2.50

MYTH ADVENTURES
Warp Graphics, 1984
1 Mag size 2.50
2 thru 4 . . . . @2.50
5 Comic size 2.50
6 thru 11 . . . . @2.50
12 . . . . 2.50

MYTH CONCEPTIONS
Apple, 1987
1 . . . . 2.50
2 thru 8 . . . . @2.50

MYTHOGRAPHY
Bardic Press, 1966
1 F:Poison Elves 6.00
2 fantasy stories 6.00
3 fantasy stories, inc. Elfquest . . . 6.00
4 . . . . 5.00
5 72-pg. 5.00
6 F:Anubis Squadron 72pg. 5.00
7 80-pg. 5.00
8 72-pg. 5.00

MYTHOS
Wonder Comix, 1987
1 and 2 . . . . @2.50

NANTUCKET BROWN ROASTERS
House of Usher, 2003
1 (of 2) 2.00
2 . . . . 2.00
GN Second Law of
  Thermodynamics. 7.50
1-shot The Lady of Shadows 2.50
GN The Third Twin 5.00

NAT TURNER
Kyle Baker Publishing 2005
1 . . . . 3.00
2 . . . . 3.00
3 . . . . 3.00
4 . . . . 3.00
TPB Vol. 1 . . . . 10.00

NATURE OF THE BEAST
Caliber
1 `The Beast' 3.00
2 . . . . 3.00
3 . . . . 3.00

All comics prices listed are for *Near Mint* condition.

NAUGHTY BITS
Fantagraphics, 1991–2004

1 by Roberta Gregory	5.00
2 thru 10 F:Bitchy Bitch	@4.00
11 thru 20	@3.50
21 I:Bitchy Butch	3.00
22 Adult-erated	3.00
23 O:Bitchy Butch	3.00
24 thru 39	@3.00
40	3.50
TPB Vol. 4: Bitchy's School Daze	10.00
TPB Vol. 5: Bitchy Butch	10.00
TPB Work & Play with Bitchy Bitch	10.00
TPB A Bitch is Born, sgn	10.00
TPB Vol.6 Burn, Bitchy, Burn	10.00

NAUSICAA OF THE VALLEY OF WIND
Viz Select, 1988

Book One	4.50
Book Two	5.50
Book Three	4.00
Book Four	3.00
Book Five	2.50
Book Six	3.00
Book Seven	3.00

[Part 2] 1989

#1 thru #4	@3.00

[Part 3] 1993

#1 thru #3	@3.00
TPB Vol. 4	18.00

NAZRAT
Imperial, 1986

1	2.50
2 thru 6	@2.25

NECROSCOPE
Caliber, 1997

1 Brian Lumley adapt	3.00
1 signed	3.00
2	3.00
3	3.00
4	3.00

NEGATIVE BURN
Caliber, 1993

1 I.Matrix 7, Flaming Carrot	5.00
2	3.50
3 Bone preview	12.00
4 thru 12 various stories	@3.25

Negative Burn #13
© Caliber

13 Strangers in Paradise	10.00
14 thru 18 various stories	@3.50
19 Flaming Carrot	5.00
20 In the Park	4.00
21 Trollords	4.00
22 Father the Dryad	4.00
23 I:The Creep	4.00
24 The Factor	4.00
25 The Factor	4.00
26 Very Vicki	4.00
27 Nancy Kate	4.00
28 Favorite Song	4.00
29 thru 33	4.00
34 Kaos Moon	6.00
35 thru 38	@4.00
39 `Iron Empires,' pt. 4	4.00
40 `Suzi Romaine'	4.00
41 `Iron Empires,' cont.	4.00
42	4.00
43 `Iron Empires,' concl.	4.00
44 `Skeleton Key'	4.00
45 `Divine Winds'	4.00
46 `A Bullet For Me'	4.00
47	4.00
48 special 80-pg. issue	5.00
49 special 80-pg. issue	6.00
50 96-pg., final issue	7.00
TPB Best of Year One	10.00
TPB Best of Year Two	10.00

NEIL THE HORSE
Aardvark–Vanaheim, 1983

1 Art:Arn Sara, satire	5.00
1a 2nd printing	2.50
2	3.00
3	4.00
4	3.00
5 Video Warriors	2.50
6 Video Warriors	2.50
7 Video Warriors	2.50
8 Outer Space	2.50
9 Canine the Barbarian	2.50
10 Canine the Barbarian	2.50

Renegade, 1985

11 Fred Astair	2.50
12	2.50
13	2.50
14 Special	3.00
15	2.50

NEMESIS THE WARLOCK
Fleetway, 1989

1 thru 16	@2.50

NEON GENESIS EVANGELION
Viz Communication, 1997

1 (of 6) by Gainax & Yoshiyuki Sadamoto	3.25
1 special collectors edition	3.00
2 thru 6	@3.00
2 thru 6 special collectors ed.	@3.00
TPB Vol. 1	16.50
TPB Vol. 1 special collectors ed.	16.50

BOOK TWO, 1998

1 (of 5) by Yoshiyuki Sadamoto	3.00
1 special collectors edition	3.00
2 thru 5	@3.00
2 thru 5 special collectors ed.	@3.00
TPB Book 2	16.00
TPB Book 2, collector ed.	16.00

BOOK THREE, 1998

1 thru 6 by Yoshiyuki Sadamoto	@3.00
1a thru 6a Collectors edition	@3.00
GN Vol. 3 Evangelion	16.00
GN Vol. 3 Evangelion, coll. ed.	16.00

BOOK FOUR, 1999

1 thru 7 by Yoshiyuki Sadamato	@3.00
1a thru 7a special collectors ed.	@3.00

BOOK FIVE, 2000

1	3.00
1a collectors ed.	3.00
2 thru 7	@3.00
2a thru 7a deluxe	@3.00
TPB Book 5	16.00
TPB Collect. Ed	16.00

BOOK SIX, 2001

1 thru 4	@3.50
1a thru 4a coll. ed.	@3.50
TPB Vol. 6	16.00
TPB Vol. 6 collector ed.	16.00

BOOK SEVEN

1 (of 7)	3.50
2 thru 5	@3.00
6	3.50
2a thru 5a collector's edition	@3.00
6a collector's edition	@3.50
TPB Vol. 7	16.00
TPB Vol. 7 collector ed.	16.00
TPB Vol. 8	10.00

NEON– THE FUTURE WARRIOR
Komics, Inc., 2000

TPB Vol. 1	13.00
TPB Vol. 2	13.00
TPB Vol. 3	13.00
TPB Vol. 4 187-pg.	13.00
TPB Vol. 5 183-pg.	13.00
TPB Vol. 6 186-pg.	13.00
TPB Vol. 7 185-pg.	13.00
TPB Vol. 8 185-pg.	13.00
TPB Vol. 9 185-pg., final	13.00

NERVOUS REX
Blackthorne, 1985

1	3.00
1a 2nd printing	2.50
2	3.00
3	3.00
4	2.50
5 thru 10	@2.50
GraphicNovel	3.50

NEW ADVENTURES OF TERRY & THE PIRATES
ACG Comics, 1998

1 by Bros. Hildebrandt	3.00
2 thru 7	@3.00

NEWCOMERS ILLUSTRATED
Newcomers Publishing

1 thru 5 various artists	@3.00
6 Science Fiction	3.00
7 thru 8	@3.00
9 Shocking Machines	3.00
10	3.00
11 Hitman	3.00
12 final issue	3.00

NEW ERADICATORS

Vol 2 #1 NewBeginnings	2.25
Vol 2 #2 NewBeginnings	2.25
Vol 2 #3 NewFriends	2.25

NEW FRONTIERS

1 CS(c)	3.00
1a 2nd Printing	2.25

NEW FRONTIERS
Evolution

1 A:Action Master, Green Ghost	2.25
2	2.25

All comics prices listed are for *Near Mint* condition.

NEW HERO COMICS
Pierce
1 and 2 . . . . @2.25

NEW HORIZONS
Shanda Fantasy Arts, 1997
1 . . . . 5.00
2 thru 5 . . . . @4.50
6 thru 15 . . . . @5.00

NEW HUMANS
Pied Piper, 1987
1 and 2 . . . . @2.50

NEW HUMANS
Eternity, 1987
1 . . . . 2.50
2 thru 15 . . . . @2.50
Ann. #1. . . . . 3.00

NEW HUMANS
1 Shattered Earth Chronicles 2.50

NEW LOVE
Fantagraphics, 1996
1 GHe, Love & Rockets tie-in 3.00
2 thru 3 GHe . . . . @3.00
4 thru 6 GHe . . . . @3.00

NEW PULP ADVENTURES SPECIAL
Dunewadd Comics
1 I:Kawala 2.50

NEW REALITY
1 thru 6 . . . . @2.25

NEWSTRALIA
Innovation, 1989
(Prev. Color)
4 . . . . 2.50
5 . . . . 2.50

NEW TRIUMPH
Matrix Graphics, 1985
1 F:Northguard 3.00
1a 2nd printing 2.50
2 thru 4 . . . . @2.50

NEW VAMPIRE MIYU
Ironcat, 1997
1 by Narumi Kakinouchi 3.00
2 thru 6 . . . . @3.00
7 The Past Lies Beyond a Door,
   finale 3.00
GN rep. #1–#7 . . . . 18.00

VOL. 2, 1998
1 by Narumi Kakinouchi 3.00
2 thru 6 . . . . @3.00

VOL. 3, 1998
1 . . . . 3.00
2 thru 7 . . . . @3.00

VOL. 4, 1999
1 by Narumi Kakinouchi 3.00
2 thru 6 . . . . @3.00

VOL. 5
1 . . . . 3.00
2 thru 7 . . . . @3.00
GN Vol. 4, The Return of Miyu . . . 18.00
GN Vol. 5, Wrath of Miyu 18.00

NEW WORLD DISORDER
Millennium, 1995
1 I:King Skin Gang 3.00

NEW WORLD ORDER
Blazer Studios, 1993
1 thru 8 . . . . @2.50

NEW YORK CITY OUTLAWS
Outlaw
1 thru 5 . . . . @2.50

NEW YORK, YEAR ZERO
Eclipse, 1988
1 thru 4 . . . . @2.50

NEXT EXIT
Amaze Ink, SLG, 2004
1 by Christy Kijewski. 3.00
2 thru 6 . . . . @3.00
7 thru 10 . . . . @3.00
TPB Vol. 1 . . . . 13.00

Nexus #2
© *Capital*

NEXUS
Capital, 1981
1 SR,I:Nexus,large size 12.00
2 SR,Mag size 8.00
3 SR,Mag size 5.00

NIGHT
Amaze Ink, 1995
0 V:The Prince 2.25

NIGHT ANGEL
Substance Comics, 1995
1 I:Night Angel 3.00

NIGHT CRY
CFD Productions, 1995
1 Evil Ernie & Razor story 8.00
1 signed 9.00
2 . . . . 6.00
3 . . . . 5.00
4 . . . . 4.00
4a platinum (c) 6.00
5 . . . . 4.00
6 . . . . 2.75
6a signed 8.00

NIGHT LIFE
Caliber
1 thru 7 . . . . @2.25

NIGHTMARES & FAIRY TALES
Amaze Ink/SLG, 2002
1 . . . . 3.00
2 thru 5 . . . . @3.00
6 thru 14 . . . . @3.00
15 thru 17 . . . . @3.00
TPB Vol. 1 Annabelle Speaks 15.00
TPB Vol. 2 Beautiful Beasts. 15.00

NIGHT MASTER
Silver Wolf, 1987
1 Vigil 5.50
2 Vigil 2.50
3 . . . . 2.50

NIGHT OF THE LIVING DEAD
Fantaco
0 prelude 2.25
1 based on cult classic movie. 5.00
2 Movie adapt,continued. 5.00
3 Movie adapt,conclusion 5.00
5 . . . . 6.00
TPB Official Complete story, rep.. . 25.00
TPB London, Clive Barker's story . 15.00

NIGHT'S CHILDREN
Fantaco
1 . . . . 3.50
2 . . . . 3.50
3 . . . . 3.50
4 . . . . 3.50

NIGHT'S CHILDREN
Millennium, 1995
1 The Ripper, Klaus Wulfe 4.00
Spec. High Noon (1996) 3.00
Spec. The Churchyard (1997) 3.25

NIGHT'S CHILDREN: THE VAMPIRE
Millennium, 1995
1 F:Klaus Wulfe 3.00
2 F:Klaus Wulfe 3.00

NIGHT STREETS
Arrow, 1986
1 . . . . 2.50
2 thru 4 . . . . @2.50

NIGHTVISION
London Night, 1996
1 DQ,KHt, All About Eve. 3.00
1 signed 13.00
1a erotica edition 10.00

NIGHT WARRIORS: DARKSTALKERS' REVENGE
Viz Communications, 1998
1 (of 6) by Run Ishida 3.00
2 . . . . 3.25
3 thru 6 . . . . @3.00
TPB 16.00

NIGHTWOLF: THE PRICE
Devil's Due Publishing 2006
0 . . . . 1.00
1 . . . . 3.00
2 . . . . 3.00
3 . . . . 3.00

NIGHT ZERO
Fleetway
1 thru 4 . . . . @2.25

NIKKI BLADE
High Impact, 1997
0 . . . . 3.00
0a deluxe adult cover 10.00
0b gold edition variant cover. 15.00
Spec.#0 Nikki Blade: Forever Nikki
   (1997) MIB(c). 3.00
   Deluxe RCI(c) 10.00
ABC Comics, 1998
Spec. Nikki Blade: Blades of Death
   (1998) by RCI & Clayton Henry. 3.00
   Puzzle variant A cover. 6.00
   Puzzle variant B cover 6.00
   Puzzle variant C cover 6.00
Spec. Nikki Blade: Revenge 3.00

NIMROD, THE
Fantagraphics, 1998
1 by Lewis Trondheim. 3.00
2 thru 4 . . . . @3.00
5 . . . . 4.00
6 . . . . 3.50
7 . . . . 4.00

NINJA
Eternity
1 . . . . 3.00
2 thru 6 . . . . @2.25
7 thru 13 . . . . @2.25

NINJA ELITE
Adventure, 1987
1 thru 5 . . . . @2.50
6 thru 8 . . . . @2.50

NINJA FUNNIES
Eternity
1 and 2 . . . . @2.25
3 thru 5 . . . . @2.25

NINJA HIGH SCHOOL
Antarctic, 1987
1 . . . . 15.00
2 thru 4 . . . . @11.00
Eternity, 1988
5 thru 22 . . . . @4.00
23 Zardon Assassin. 3.00
24 . . . . 3.00
25 Return of the Zetramen 3.00
26 Stanley the Demon 3.00
27 Return of the Zetramen 3.00
28 Threat of the super computer . . 3.00
29 V:Super Computer 3.00
30 I:Akaru 3.00
31 Jeremy V:Akaru 3.00
32 thru 34 V:Giant Monsters Pt.1
   thru Pt. 3 . . . . @3.00
35 thru 43 . . . . @3.00
44 Combat Cheerleaders. 2.75
45 Cheerleader Competition 2.75
46 Monsters From Space. 2.75
47 . . . . 2.75
48 F:Jeremy Feeple. 2.75
49 thru 51 . . . . @3.00
52 thru 57 Time Warp, pt.4 pt.8 . @3.00
58 Zardon ambassador, BU:BDn. . . 3.00
59 Akaru overwhelmed 3.00
60 to the Himalayas. 3.00
61 ancient Himalayan temple 3.00
62 Hillbilly girl. 3.00
63 F:Tetsuo Rivalsan 3.00
64 Jeremy Feeple: Saboteur? 3.00
65 Quagmire Trial of the Century . . 3.00
66 . . . . 3.00

67 F:Eolata. 3.00
68 F:Akaru & Asrial 3.00
69 Curi-Curi Island 3.00
70 Mad Bomber in Space 2.50
71 traitor in secret police 3.00
72 . . . . 2.50
73 . . . . 2.50
74 Girl Scouts 2.50
Special #1 . . . . 3.00
Special #2 . . . . 3.00
Special #3 . . . . 3.00
Special #3 1/2 . . . . 2.50
Ann. 1989. 3.00
Ann.#3 . . . . 4.00
TPB Vol. 1 rep. #1–3 . . . . 12.00
TPB Vol. 1, new edition 15.00
TPB Vol. 2 rep. #4–7 . . . . 12.00
TPB Vol. 3 rep. #8–11 . . . . 9.00
TPB Vol. 3, rep. #8–#11 . . . . 11.00
TPB Vol. 4 rep. #12–15 . . . . 8.00
TPB Vol. 4, rep. #12–#15. . . . . . . 11.00
TPB Vol. 5 rep. #16–18 . . . . 8.00
TPB Vol. 6 rep. #19–21 . . . . 8.00
TPB Vol. 7 rep. #22–24 . . . . 8.00
TPB Vol. 7, rep. #22–#24 The Ides
   of May 11.00
TPB Vol. 8 rep. #25–27 . . . . 8.00
TPB Vol. 9 rep. #28–31 . . . . 11.00
TPB Vol. 9, rep. #28–#31 Long
   Distance Bottle 11.00
TPB Vol. 10 rep. #32–35 . . . . 11.00
TPB Vol. 11 rep. #36–39 . . . . 11.00
TPB Vol. 11, rep. #36–#39 Shades
   of Grey. 11.00
TPB Vol. 12 . . . . 11.00
TPB Vol. 15 three stories. 8.00
Yearbook 1994. . . . . 4.00
Yearbook 1995. . . . . 4.00
Yearbook 1996. . . . . 4.00
Yearbook 1997, cover A. 4.00
Yearbook 1997, cover B 4.00
Yearbook 1998, cover A. 3.00
Yearbook 1998, cover B 3.00
Spec. Girls of Ninja High School
   (1997) 4.00
Spec. Girls of Ninja High School
   1998 cover A 3.00
   1998 cover B 3.00
Spec. 1999 . . . . 3.00
Spotlight #4 Rod Espinosa 3.00
Summer Spec.#1 . . . . 3.00
Antarctic Press, 2000
Swimsuit Spec. 2000 . . . . 4.50
Swimsuit Spec. 2001 . . . . 4.50
TPB Vol. 1, signed 20.00
TPB Textbook Vol. 1 600-pg. 50.00

NINJA HIGH SCHOOL GIRLS
Antarctic Press
0 . . . . 2.75
1 and 2 rep. . . . . @2.75
3 thru 5 rep. . . . . @4.00
Yearbook 4.00

NINJA HIGH SCHOOL PERFECT MEMORY
Antarctic Press, 1993
1 thru 2, 96pg . . . . @5.00

NINJA HIGH SCHOOL SMALL BODIES
Antarctic Press
1 "Monopolize" 2.50
2 Omegadon Cannon 2.75
3 Omegadon Cannon 2.75
3a deluxe 4.50
4 Omegadon Cannon 2.75
5 Wrong Order 2.75

6 Chicken Rage 3.00
7 . . . . 3.00

NIRA X: CYBERANGEL
Entity Comics, 1996
1 . . . . 5.00
1a deluxe 8.00
2 BMs 4.00
3 and 4 BMs . . . . @3.00
4a with PC Game 8.00
Ann.#1 BMs flip-cover 2.75
2nd Mini Series, 1995
1 . . . . 4.00
1a 2nd printing 2.50
2 thru 4 . . . . @2.50
3rd Mini Series, 1995–96
1 . . . . 2.50
1a Gold(c). 5.00
2 . . . . 2.50
3 . . . . 3.00
Regular Series
1 . . . . 2.75
1a with game 7.00
2 thru 4 . . . . @2.75
4a with game 7.00
Spec. Nira X:Headwave, encore
   special toy edition 2.50
   Encore special toy edition,
   signed & numbered 13.00
Spec. Nira X:Memoirs (1997) BMs . 2.75
   Deluxe 3.50

NIRA X/HELLINA: HEAVEN & HELL
Entity Comics
1 San Diego Con edition, BMs 5.00
1a foil 3.00

US $3.00
ISSUE 1

Nira X: Exodus #1
© Avatar

NIRA X: EXODUS
Avatar, 1997
0 (of 2) BMs 3.00
0a Leather cover. 20.00
0b signed 10.00
1 (of 2) 3.00
1a leather cover. 18.00
1b signed 9.00
2 . . . . 3.00
Spec. Shoot First 3.00
Spec. Summer Splash 5.00

B & W PUB.

NIRA X: HISTORY
Avatar Press, 1999
1 (of 2) by Bill Maus 3.50
2 . . . . 3.50

NIRA X: SOUL SKURGE
Entity, 1996
1 (of 3) BMs, A:Vortex. 2.75
2 BMs, ... 2.75
3 . . . . 2.75

NITRO-GEN
Arcade Comics 2005
Preview, limited 7.00
1 . . . . 4.00
1a signed ed. 10.00
1b resketch ed. 25.00

NOBODY
Oni Press, 1998
1 (of 4) 3.00
2 thru 4 . . . . @3.00
TPB Sacrifices 12.00
AIT/Planetlar, 2000
TPB 13.00

NODWICK
Henchman Publishing, 2000
1 by Aaron Williams 3.00
2 & 3 . . . . @3.00
Dork Storm, 2000
1 by Aaron Williams 3.00
2 thru 5 . . . . @3.00
6 thru 11 . . . . @3.00
12 thru 30 . . . . @3.00
31 thru 35 . . . . 3.00
TPB Vol. 1 thru Vol. 4 . . . . @16.00
TPB Vol. 5 Tour of Doodie 16.00
TPB Adventure Log Vol. 1 . . . . 16.00
TPB Nodwick Haulin' Assets 25.00

NO GUTS, NO GLORY
Fantaco
1-shot, K.Eastman's 1st solo
  work since TMNT 3.00

NOMADS OF ANTIQUITY
1 thru 6 . . . . @2.25

NO NEED FOR TENCHI
Viz Comics
PART ONE
1 thru 7 (of 7) . . . . @3.00
PART TWO, 1996
1 thru 7 by Hitoshi Okuda . . . . . . @3.00
TPB Sword Play 16.00
PART THREE, 1997
1 (of 6) by Hitoshi Okuda 3.00
2 . . . . 3.00
3 thru 6 . . . . @3.00
TPB Magical Girl Pretty Sammy . . 16.00
PART FOUR, 1997
1 (of 6) by Hitoshi Okuda 3.00
2 thru 6 . . . . @3.00
TPB Vol.4 Samurai Space Opera . 16.00
PART FIVE, 1998
1 (of 6) 3.00
2 thru 6 . . . . @3.00
TPB Vol.5 Unreal Genius 16.00
PART SIX, 1998
1 (of 6) 3.00
2 thru 6 . . . . @3.00
TPB Vol.6 Dream a Little Scheme . 16.00
PART SEVEN, 1999
1 (of 6) 3.00
2 thru 6 . . . . @3.00
TPB Vol.7 Tenchi in Love 16.00

PART EIGHT, 1999
1 (of 5) by Hitoshi Okuda 3.25
2 thru 5 . . . . @3.00
TPB Vol.8 Chef of Iron 16.00
PART NINE
1 (of 6) by Hitoshi Okuda 3.00
2 thru 6 . . . . @3.00
TPB Vol.9 Quest for More Money . 16.00
PART TEN, 2000
1 (of 7) 3.00
2 thru 7 . . . . @3.00
TPB Vol.10 Mother Planet 16.00
PART ELEVEN, 2001
1 thru 4 . . . . @3.50
TPB Vol.11 Ayeka's Heart 16.00

No Need For Tenchi Part 12 #4
© Viz Communications

PART TWELVE, 2001
1 thru 4 (of 6) . . . . @3.50
5 thru 6 . . . . @3.00
TPB Vol.12 . . . . 16.00

NORM, THE
The Norm Comics, 2003
1 . . . . 5.00
2 thru 8 . . . . @5.00
9 thru 11 . . . . @3.00
1-shot The 12 Steps to Marriage . . . 5.00

NORMAL MAN
Aardvark–Vanaheim, 1984
1 . . . . 4.00
2 thru 9 . . . . @3.00
Renegade
10 thru 19 . . . . @2.50

NOSFERATU:
PLAGUE OF TERROR
Millennium
1 I:Orlock 2.50
2 19th Century India,A:Sir W.
  Longsword 2.50
3 WWI/WWII to Viet Nam 2.50
4 O:Orlock,V:Longsword,conc. 2.50

NOTHING BETTER
Dementian Comics 2005
1 by Tyler Page 3.00
2 thru 4 . . . . @3.00

NOVA GIRLS
MN Design, 1998
1 The Immortality Quest, pt.1 . . . . 2.25
1a JJu (c) 3.00
1b photo (c) 4.00
1 variant Starship Discover #0(c) . . 4.00
1 variant Phazer #0 cover. 4.00
2 The Immortality Quest, pt.2 . . . . 2.25
2a deluxe 3.00
3 The Immortality Quest, pt.3 . . . . 2.25
3a deluxe 3.00
Space 34–24–34 Gold Seal 10th
  Anniv. Edition. 75.00

NOWHERESVILLE
Caliber, 1996
1 thru 3 by MRc . . . . @3.00
Spec. The History of Cool 3.00

NYOKA
THE JUNGLE GIRL
AC Comics
3 . . . . 2.25
4 . . . . 2.25
5 . . . . 2.50

OCTOBRIANA
Revolution Comics
0 16pg. 2.00
1 `The Octobriana Files,'pt.1 . . . . . 3.00
2 `The Octobriana Files,'pt.2 . . . . . 3.00
3 `The Octobriana Files,'pt.3 . . . . . 3.00
4 `The Octobriana Files,'pt.4 . . . . . 3.00
5 `The Octobriana Files,'pt.5 . . . . . 3.00
Alchemy Texts, 2001
Spec. 30th Anniv. Spec. 3.00

ODD JOB
Amaze Ink/SLG, 2000
1 by Ian Smith & Tyson Smith 3.00
2 thru 8 . . . . @3.00
TPB Vol. 1 . . . . 20.00

OFFERINGS
Cry For Dawn
1 Sword & Sorcery stories 7.00
2 and 3 . . . . @6.00

OFFICIAL BUZ SAWYER
Pioneer, 1988
1 . . . . 2.50
2 . . . . 2.50
3 . . . . 2.50
4 . . . . 2.50
5 . . . . 2.50
6 . . . . 2.50

OFFICIAL HOW TO
DRAW G.I. JOE
Blackthorne, 1987
1 thru 5 . . . . @2.50

OFFICIAL HOW TO
DRAW ROBOTECH
Blackthorne, 1987
1 thru 11 . . . . @2.50
12 . . . . 3.00
13 thru 16 . . . . @2.50

OFFICIAL HOW TO
DRAW TRANSFORMERS
Blackthorne, 1987
1 thru 7 . . . . @2.50

OFFICIAL JOHNNY HAZARD
Pioneer, 1988
1 thru 3 . . . . @2.50
4 . . . . 2.50
5 . . . . 2.50

OFFICIAL JUNGLE JIM
Pioneer, 1988
1 thru 5 AR,rep. . . . . @2.50
6 AR,rep. 2.50
7 thru 10 AR,rep. . . . . @2.50
11 thru 20 AR,rep. . . . . @2.50
Ann.#1 . . . . 2.50
Giant Size 4.00

OFFICIAL MANDRAKE
Pioneer, 1988
1 thru 5 . . . . @2.50
6 . . . . 2.50
7 thru 10 . . . . @2.50
11 . . . . 3.00
12 . . . . 2.50
13 thru 17 . . . . @2.50
Ann. #1 . . . . 4.00
King Size #1 . . . . 4.00
Giant Size #1 . . . . 4.00

Official Modesty Blaise #1
© Pioneer

OFFICIAL MODESTY BLAISE
Pioneer, 1988
1 thru 4 . . . . @2.50
5 . . . . 2.50
6 thru 14 . . . . @2.50
Ann. #1 . . . . 4.00
King Size #1 . . . . 4.00

OFFICIAL PRINCE VALIANT
Pioneer, 1988
1 Hal Foster,rep. 2.50
2 Hal Foster,rep. 2.50
3 Hal Foster,rep. 2.50
4 Hal Foster,rep. 2.50
5 Hal Foster,rep. 2.50
6 Hal Foster,rep. 2.50
7 . . . . 2.50
8 thru 14 . . . . @2.50
15 thru 24 . . . . @2.50
Ann. #1 . . . . 4.00

King Size #1 . . . . 4.00

OFFICIAL RIP KIRBY
Pioneer, 1988
1 thru 3 AR . . . . @2.50
4 AR 2.50
5 and 6 AR . . . . @2.50

OFFICIAL SECRET AGENT
Pioneer, 1988
1 thru 5 AW rep . . . . @2.50
6 AW 2.50
7 thru 9 AW . . . . @2.50

OF MIND AND SOUL
Rage Comics, 1997
0 . . . . 3.00
1 . . . . 2.50
2 . . . . 2.50
3 . . . . 2.50
Spec. Standing on a Beach 2.50
Spec. Soul'd Out 3.00
Spec. A Day in Hell 3.00
Spec. 1 shot 2.50

OHM'S LAW
Imperial Comics
1 thru 2 . . . . @2.25
3 V:Men in Black. 2.25
4 A:Damonstriek 2.25
5 F:Tryst 2.25

OH MY GOTH!
Sirius/Dog Star, 1998
1 by Voltaire 3.00
2 thru 4 . . . . @3.00
TPB 13.00

OH MY GOTH: HUMANS SUCK!
Sirius Entertainment, 2000
1 (of 3) 3.00
1 deluxe 5.00
2 and 3 . . . . @3.00

OJO
Oni Press, 2004
1 (of 5) 3.00
2 thru 5 . . . . @3.00
TPB 15.00

OKTOBERFEST
Now & Then
1 (1976) Dave Sim 20.00

OMEGA
North Star
1 1st pr by Rebel,rare 50.00
1a Vigil(Yellow Cov.) 15.00
2 . . . . 2.25

OMEGA ELITE
Blackthorne
1 . . . . 2.25
2 . . . . 2.25

OMEN
North Star, 1987
1 . . . . 8.00
1a 2nd printing 2.50
2 thru 4 . . . . @3.50

OMICRON
Pyramid, 1987
1 and 2 . . . . @2.50
3 . . . . 2.50

King Size #1 . . . . 4.00

OMNI MEN
Blackthorne, 1989
1 & 2 . . . . @2.50

ONE-POUND GOSPEL
Viz Communications, 1996
1 . . . . 3.50
2 . . . . 3.50
3 & 4 . . . . @3.00
TPB rep. 17.00
ROUND TWO, 1997
1 thru 8 by Rumiko Takahashi . . @3.00
TPB Vol. 1 . . . . 16.96
TPB Vol. 2 Hungry For Victory . . 16.00
TPB Vol. 3 Knuckle Sandwich . . . 16.00
PART 7
1 (of 13) by Rumiko Takahashi . . . 3.00

ONE SHOT WESTERN
Calibur
1-shot F:Savage Sisters, Tornpath
Outlaw 2.50

ONI DOUBLE FEATURE
Oni Press, 1997
1 F:Jay & Silent Bob 12.00
1a 2nd printing 3.00
2 F:Car Crash on the 405 . . . . 3.50
3 F:Troy Nixey 3.50
4 F:A River in Egypt 3.50
5 F:Fan Girl From Hell 4.00
6 inc. NGa Only the End of the
    World, pt.1 . . . . 3.00
7 inc. NGa Only the End of the
    World, pt.2 . . . . 3.00
8 inc. NGa Only the End of the
    World, pt.3 . . . . 3.00
9 thru 10 . . . . @3.00
11 Usagi Yojimbo 3.50
12 Bluntman & Chronic 7.00
13 . . . . 3.00

ONIGAMI
Antarctic Press, 1998
1 (of 3) by Michael Lacombe, sequel
    to Winter Jade storyline from
    Warrior Nun: Black and White . . 3.00
2 . . . . 3.00
3 concl. 3.00

OPEN SEASON
Renegade, 1987
1 thru 7 . . . . @2.50

OPPOSITE FORCES
Funny Pages Press, 2002
1 by Tom Bancroft 3.00
1a Convention Exclusive (c) 3.00
2 . . . . 3.00
3 . . . . 3.00
4 . . . . 3.00

OPTIC NERVE
Adrian Tomine, 1990
1 thru 5, mini-comic 12.00
6 . . . . 7.00
7 . . . . 5.00
8 . . . . 3.00
9 . . . . 4.00

OPTIC NERVE
Drawn & Quarterly, 1995
1 Summer Job 9.00
1a 2nd printing 6.00
2 . . . . 5.00
3 and 4 . . . . @5.00
5 thru 10 . . . . @4.00
TPB 32 Stories 10.00

All comics prices listed are for *Near Mint* condition.

ORACLE PRESENTS
Oracle, 1986
1 thru 4 . . . . @2.50

ORBIT
Eclipse, 1990
1 and 2 . . . . @5.00
3 . . . . 5.00

OR ELSE
Drawn & Quarterly 2004
1 . . . . 3.50
2 thru 3 . . . . @4.00
4 . . . . 6.00

Original Tom Corbett #2
© Eternity

ORIGINAL TOM CORBETT
Eternity, 1990
1 thru 10 rep. newspaper strips . @3.00

ORIGINS OF REID FLEMING, WORLD'S TOUGHEST MILKMAN
Deep Sea Comics, 1998
1 by David Boswell 3.00

ORLAK: FLESH & STEEL
Caliber
1 1991 A.D. 2.50

ORLAK REDUX
Caliber, 1991
1 rep. Caliber Presents, 64-pg.. . . . 4.00

OUTLAW OVERDRIVE
Blue Comet Press
1 Red Edition I:Deathrow 3.00
1a Black Edition 3.00
1b Blue Edition 3.00

OZ
Imperial Comics, 1996
1 Land of Oz Gone Mad 9.00
2 Land of Oz Gone Mad 7.00
3 Land of Oz Gone Mad 6.00
4 Tin Woodsmen. 6.00
5 F:Pumkinhead. 6.00
6 Emerald City 6.00
7 V:Bane Wolves 4.00
8 V:Nome Hordes 4.00

---

9 Freedom Fighters Vs. Heroes . . . 4.00
10 thru 15. . . . . @4.00
16 . . . . 3.50
Spec.#1 . . . . 6.00
Spec. Scarecrow #1. . . . . 3.00
Spec. Lion #1 . . . . 3.00
Spec. Tin Man #1 . . . . 3.00
Spec. Freedom Fighters #1 . . . . . . 3.00
TPB Rep. #1-#4. . . . . 15.00
Caliber `New Worlds'
17 by Ralph Griffith, Stuart Kerr & Tim Holtrop 3.50
18 thru 20. . . . . @3.00
21 `Witches War' pt.1 (of 5). 3.00
22 . . . . 3.00
GN Heroes of Oz 15.00

OZ: ROMANCE IN RAGS
Caliber, 1996
1 thru 3 Bill Bryan . . . . @3.00

OZ SQUAD
Patchwork Press, 1992
1 . . . . 4.00
2 thru 8 . . . . @3.00

OZ: STRAW AND SORCERY
Caliber `New Worlds', 1997
1 thru 3 . . . . @3.00

PAKKINS' LAND
Caliber Tapestry, 1996
1 . . . . 6.00
1a signed edition. 3.00
1a second edition, new cover. 3.00
2 . . . . 4.00
2a second edition, new cover. 3.00
3 . . . . 4.00
3 2nd edition, new cover. 3.00
4 thru 6 . . . . @3.00
GN Book One: Paul's Adventure . . 10.00
Pakkins Presents, 2000
TPB Vol.1 Paul's Adventure. 16.00
TPB Vol.2 Quest For Kings 16.00
TPB Vol.3 Forgotten Dreams. 16.00
TPV Vol.4 Tavitah. 17.00

PAKKINS' LAND: FORGOTTEN DREAMS
Caliber, 1998
1 by Gary & Rhoda Shipman 3.00
2 thru 5 . . . . @3.00

PAKKINS' LAND: QUEST FOR KINGS
Caliber, 1997
1G by Gary & Rhoda Shipman, Shipman(c) 3.00
1J by Gary & Rhoda Shipman, JSi(c). 3.00
2 . . . . 3.00
3 Rahsla's city 3.00
4 . . . . 3.00
5 . . . . 3.00

PALANTINE
Gryphon Rampant, 1995
1 thru 5 V:Master of Basilisk. 2.50

PALEO TALES: LATE CRETACEOUS
Zeromayo Studios, 2001
1 thru 6 . . . . 3.00
Empty Sky, 2003
7 . . . . 3.00

---

8 . . . . 3.00
TPB Tales of the Late Cretaceous. 13.00

PALOOKA-VILLE
Drawn & Quarterly
1 third printing. 3.00
1 10th Anniv. Ed.. . . . . 3.75
10 by Seth 3.75
11 Clyde Fans, pt.2 . . . . 3.75
12 Clyde Fans, pt.3 . . . . 3.75
13 Clyde Fans 3.75
14 . . . . 3.75
15 . . . . 3.75
16 thru 18. . . . . @4.75
TPB Its a Good Life If You Don't Weaken 13.00

PANDA KHAN
1 thru 4 . . . . @2.25

PANDEMONIUM
Curtis Comics, 2002
Vol. 1 Manga
1 by Jaeongtae Lee 3.00
2 thru 5 . . . . @3.00
Vol. 2
1 . . . . 3.00

PANDORA
Brainstorm, 1996
1 (of 2) 3.00

PANDORA
Avatar Press, 1997
0 . . . . 3.00
1 signed 12.00
2 (of 2) 3.00
2 deluxe 9.00
X-over Pandora/Ranzor:Devil Inside (1998) signed 12.00
Haley (c) 5.00
X-over Pandora/Razor (1999) 3.50
Leather cover, signed 15.00
Expanded Edition 5.00
X-over Pandora/Shotgun Mary: Demon Nation (1998) 3.00
Deluxe 5.00
Leather 20.00
Royal Blue edition 50.00
X-over Pandora/Widow (1997) 4.00
Leather cover 15.00
Spec. Arachnophobia. 3.50
Spec. Pandora Special (1997). . . . 3.00
Leather cover 15.00
Avatar convention (c) ed. 15.00
Spec. Pandora Pin-up (1997) 3.00
Signed 15.00
Spec. Nudes (1997). 3.50
GN Love and War (2003). 6.00

PANDORA'S CHEST
Avatar Press, 1999
1 (of 3) 2.75

PANDORA: DEMONOGRAPHY
Avatar Press, 1997
1 . . . . 3.00
2 (of 3) 3.00
3 (of 3) 3.00

PANDORA DEVILS ADVOCATE
Avatar Press, 1999
1 (of 3) 3.50
1a Previews exclusive foil (c) 13.00
2 . . . . 3.50
3 . . . . 3.50

    All comics prices listed are for *Near Mint* condition.

PANDORA: PANDEMONIUM
Avatar Press, 1997
1 Pandora goes to Hell 3.00
1 leather cover 25.00
1 signed 10.00
2 (of 3) 3.00

PANTHEON
Lone Star Press, 1998
1 (of 12) 3.00
2 Welcome to the Machine 3.00
3 V:Death Boy 3.00
4 F:Tangeroa 3.00
5 Under Pressure 3.00
6 All-villain issue 3.00
7 thru 9 . . . . @3.00
10 thru 12 . . . . @3.00
13 . . . . 5.00
Spec. Ancient History (1999) 3.50

PANZER: 1946
Antarctic Press, 2004
1 . . . . 6.00
2 . . . . 6.00
3 . . . . 6.00
4 . . . . 6.00
5 . . . . 6.00

PAPER CUTS
1 E Starzer-1982 . . . . 15.00
2 and 3 . . . . @2.50

PARIS
Amaze Ink/SLG 2005
1 . . . . 3.00
2 thru 4 . . . . @3.00

PARTICLE DREAMS
Fantagraphics, 1986
1 . . . . 3.00
2 thru 6 . . . . @2.50

PARTNERS IN PANDEMONIUM
Caliber
1 Hell on Earth 2.50
2 Sheldon & Murphy are mortal . . . 2.50
3 A:Abra Cadaver 2.50

PARTS OF A HOLE
Caliber, 1991
1 Short Stories 2.50

PARTS UNKNOWN
Eclipse, 1992
1 I:Spurr,V:Aliens 2.50
2 Aliens on Earth cont. 2.50

PARTS UNKNOWN: DARK INTENTIONS
Knight Press, 1995
0 . . . . 3.00
1 I:Prelude to limited Series 3.00
2 V:Luggnar 3.00
3 V:Luggnar 3.00
4 . . . . 3.00
1-shot, Handbook, The Roswell
Agenda 3.00
Super-Ann. #1 . . . . 4.00

PATRICK THE WOLF BOY
Blindwolf Studios, 2000
1 by Art Baltazar & Franco 3.00
Halloween Special 3.00
Next Halloween Special 3.00

Valentine's Day Special 3.00
Christmas Spec. 3.00
Mother's Day Special 3.00
Summer Spec. 3.00
Superhero Spec.(2002) 3.00
Sci-Fi Special (2002) 3.00
Another Halloween Special (2002) . 3.00
Spec. This Year's Halloween Spec. . 3.00
Spec. Grimm Reaper Super Spec. . 3.00
Spec. Wedding Special 3.00
Spec. After School Special 3.00
Spec. Rock-n-Roll spec. 3.00
Spec. Father's Day spec. 3.00
Spec. Happy Birthday 3.00
Spec. Vol. 1 & Vol. 2 collection . . 15.00
Spec. Vol. 3 & Vol. 4 collection . . 15.00
TPB Vol. 1 . . . . 10.00
TPB Vol. 2 . . . . 10.00
Devil's Due Publishing, 2005
TPB Vol. 1 . . . . 11.00
TPB Vol. 2 . . . . 11.00

PATTY CAKE
Caliber Tapestry, 1996
1 by Scott Roberts 3.00
2 . . . . 3.00
3 . . . . 3.00
4 . . . . 3.00
Christmas special 4.00

PATTY-CAKE & FRIENDS
Slave Labor, 1997
1 by Scott Roberts 3.00
2 thru 15 . . . . @3.00
Halloween Spec. 4.00

VOL. 2, 2000
1 by Scott Roberts, 48-pg. 5.00
2 thru 4 48-pg. . . . . @5.00
5 thru 15 . . . . @5.00
TPB Sugar & Spice..Mostly Spice . 14.00
TPB Vol. 2 And Everything Nice . . 14.00
TPB Vol. 3 Love is All Around . . . 14.00

Paul the Samurai #2
© New England Comics

PAUL THE SAMURAI
New England Comics, 1991
1 thru 3 . . . . @2.75
Bonanza #2 100pg. 5.00
GN Collected 9.00

PENDULUM
Adventure, 1993
1 Big Hand,Little Hand 2.50
2 The Immortality Formula 2.50

---

3 . . . . 2.50

PENNY CENTURY
Fantagraphics, 1997
1 by Jaime Hernandez 3.00
2 thru 7 . . . . @3.00

PENTACLE: THE SIGN OF THE FIVE
Eternity, 1991
1 . . . . 2.25
2 Det.Sandler,H.Smitts 2.25
3 Det.Sandler becomes New
Warlock 2.25
4 5 warlocks Vs. Kaji 2.50

PETE THE P.O.'D POSTAL WORKER
Sharkbait Press, 1998
1 by Marcus Pierce & Pete
Garcia, Route 666 . . . . 3.00
2 prison mail 3.00
3 To Aliens with Love 3.00
4 Special Delivery to
Conad the Alien 3.00
5 England Vacation 3.00
6 Benedict Postman 3.00
7 Postman on Elm Street 3.00
8 Postman on Elm Street 3.00
9 Pete Meets Jerry Ringer 3.00
10 Y2K Express 3.00
11 Postal Wars 3.00
12 . . . . 3.00
X-mas Spec.#1 . . . . 3.50
Spec. War Journal 3.00
TPB Pete Unplugged 13.00

PHANTOM
1 thru 3 . . . . @6.00
4 and 5 . . . . @7.00

PHANTOM, THE
Tony Raiola, 2000
TPB Diamond Hunters 9.50
TPB The Little Toma 9.50
TPB Sea Horse 9.50
TPB Game of Alvar 9.50
TPB Diana Aviatrix 9.50
TPB Phantom's Treasure 9.50

PHANTOM OF FEAR CITY
Claypool, 1994–95
1 thru 12 . . . . 2.50

PHANTOM OF THE OPERA
Eternity
1 . . . . 2.25

PHASE ONE
Victory, 1986
1 . . . . 3.00
2 . . . . 2.50
3 thru 5 . . . . @2.50

PHIGMENTS
Amazing, 1987
1 . . . . 5.00
2 . . . . 2.50
3 . . . . 2.50

PHONEY PAGES
Renegade
1 and 2 . . . . @2.50

All comics prices listed are for *Near Mint* condition.

PINEAPPLE ARMY
Viz Communications, 1988
1 thru 10 . . . . @2.50

PINK FLOYD EXPERIENCE
Revolutionary, 1991
1 based on rock group 2.50
2 Dark Side of the Moon. 2.50
3 Dark Side of the Moon, Wish you
    were here 2.50
4 The Wall. 2.50
5 A Momentary lapse of reason . . . 2.50

PIRATE CLUB
Amaze Ink/SLG, 2004
1 . . . . 3.00
2 thru 4 . . . . @3.00
5 thru 7 . . . . @3.00
8 thru 10 . . . . @3.00
TPB Vol. 1 Brainwash Escape
    Victims 13.00
TPB Vol. 2 Brainwash Escape
    Victims 13.00

PIRATE CORPS!
Eternity, 1987
6 and 7 . . . . @2.50
Spec. #1 . . . . 2.50

PIRANHA! IS LOOSE
Special Studio
1 Drug Runners,F:Piranha 3.00
2 Expedition into Terror. 3.00

Pixy Juncet #6
© *Viz Communications*

PIXY JUNKET
Viz, 1993
1 thru 6 . . . . @2.75

P.J. WARLOCK
Eclipse, 1986
1 thru 3 . . . . @2.50

PLANET COMICS
Blackthorne, 1988
(Prev. Color)
4 and 5 . . . . @2.50

PLANET COMICS
A-List Comics, 1997
1 by L.Hampton & R.Leonardo. . . . 2.50
2 rep. from 1940 . . . . 3.00

3 . . . . 3.00
4 thru 6 . . . . @3.00
TPB Book of Planet Comics
    Covers, 1949–54 . . . . 8.00

PLANET COMICS
ACG Comics, 2000
1 WW, rep. 7.00
2 64-pg. 6.00

PLANET OF THE APES
Adventure Comics, 1990
1 WD,collect.ed. 6.00
1 2 covers 4.00
1a 2nd printing 2.50
1b 3rd printing. 2.25
2 . . . . 3.00
3 . . . . 3.00
4 . . . . 3.00
5 D:Alexander? 3.00
6 Welcome to Ape City 3.00
7 . . . . 3.00
8 Christmas Story 2.75
9 Swamp Ape Village 2.75
10 Swamp Apes in Forbidden City . 2.75
11 Ape War continues 2.75
12 W:Alexander & Coure 2.75
13 Planet of Apes/Alien Nation/ Ape
    City x-over 2.75
14 Countdown to Zero Pt.1 . . . . . . 2.75
15 Countdown to Zero Pt.2 . . . . . . 2.75
16 Countdown to Zero Pt.3 . . . . . . 2.75
17 Countdown to Zero Pt.4 . . . . . . 2.75
18 Ape City (after Ape Nation mini-
    series 2.75
19 1991 `Conquest..' tie-in. 2.75
20 Return of the Ape Riders 2.75
21 The Terror Beneath,Pt.1 . . . . . . 2.75
22 The Terror Beneath,Pt.2 . . . . . . 2.75
23 The Terror Beneath,Pt.3 . . . . . . 2.75
Ann #1,`Day on Planet o/t Apes' . . . 3.50
Lim.Ed. #1 . . . . 5.00

PLANET OF THE APES: BLOOD OF THE APES
Adventure Comics, 1991
1 A:Tonus the Butcher 3.00
2 Valia/Taylorite Connection 2.75
3 Ape Army in Phis 2.75
4 . . . . 2.75

PLANET OF THE APES: FORBIDDEN ZONE
Adventure
1 Battle for the Planet of the Apes
    & Planet of the Apes tie-in. 2.75
2 A:Juilus 2.75

PLANET OF THE APES: SINS OF THE FATHER
Adventure Comics, 1992
1 Conquest Tie-in 2.75

PLANET OF THE APES URCHAKS' FOLLY
Adventure Comics, 1991
1 . . . . 3.00
2 thru 4 . . . . @2.75

PLANET 29
Caliber
1 A Future Snarl Tale 2.50
2 A:Biff,Squakman 2.50

PLANET-X
Eternity, 1991
1 three horror stories 2.50

PLAN 9 FROM OUTER SPACE
Eternity, 1991
1 . . . . 2.50
2 and 3 . . . . @2.25

PLASTIC LITTLE
CPM Comics, 1997
1 (of 5) Manga, by Satoshi
    Urushihara R:Captain Tita 3.00
2 F:Joshua Balboa 3.00
3 . . . . 3.00
4 . . . . 3.00
5 concl. 3.00
TPB Captain's Log, rep. #1–#5 . . . 16.00

PLASTRON CAFE
Mirage, 1992
1 RV,inc.North by Downeast. 2.25
2 thru 4 . . . . @2.25

POE
Cheese Comics, 1996
1 by Jason Asala, reoffer 3.00
2 . . . . 3.00
3 `The System of Doctor Tarr and
    Professor Fether'. 3.00
4 thru 6 . . . . @3.00

Sirius/Dog Star
TPB Vol. 1 . . . . 15.00

VOL 2, 1997
1 by Jason Asala 3.00
2 House of Usher, pt.1 (of 4) 3.00
3 House of Usher, pt.2 . . . . 3.00
4 House of Usher, pt.3 . . . . 3.00
5 House of Usher, pt.4 . . . . 3.00
6 . . . . 3.00
7 . . . . 3.00
8 Small Town 3.00
9 Small Town, pt.2 . . . . 3.00
10 Small Town, pt.3 . . . . 3.00
11 Gold & Lead, pt.1 . . . . 3.00
12 Gold and Lead, pt.2 . . . . 3.00
13 F:Pluto the cat. 3.00
14 A:Mad Meg Mayflower 3.00
15 Airship 3.00
16 path of next demon 3.00
17 22 one-page stories 3.00
18 Airship 3.00
19 thru 24 Balloon Hoax . . . . @3.00

POINT BLANK
Acme/Eclipse, 1989
1 thru 5 . . . . @3.00

POISON ELVES
Mulehide Graphics, 1993–95
Previously: I, Lusipher
8 DHa(c&a). 12.00
9 DHa 10.00
10 DHa 10.00
11 DHa, comic size 10.00
12 DHa. 10.00
13 DHa 15.00
14 and 15 DHa. . . . . @15.00
15a 2nd printing. 6.00
16 and 17 DHa. . . . . @7.00
17a 2nd printing 6.00
18 DHa. 7.00
19 DHa. 7.00
20 DHa. 7.00

2nd Series, Sirius, 1995–97
1 F:Lusipher 6.00
2 V:Assassins Guild 4.00
3 Sanctuary, pt.3. . . . . 4.00
4 Sanctuary, pt.4. . . . . 4.00
5 Sanctuary, pt.5. . . . . 4.00
6 I:Lester Gran 4.00

    All comics prices listed are for *Near Mint* condition.

Poison Elves #11
© Sirius

7 thru 24 . . . . @4.00
25 DHa 3.00
26 DHa 3.00
27 DHa, ... 3.00
28 DHa,F:Lusiphur 3.00
29 DHa, ... 3.00
30 DHa,F:Vido 3.00
31 DHa 3.00
32 DHa, Cassandra is dead 3.00
33 DHa, temporary truce 3.00
34 DHa, Lusiphur's feminine side . . 3.00
35 DHa, Purple Marauder
    reappears 3.00
36 DHa, Lusiphur tracked down . . . 3.00
37 DHa, questionable help 3.00
38 DHa 3.00
39 DHa 3.00
40 DHa, Sanctuary, concl. 3.00
41 DHa, on to Amrahly'nn 3.00
42 DHa, Just in Town
    for the Night,pt.1 . . . . 3.00
43 DHa, Town for the Night, pt.2 . . 3.00
44 DHa, Town for the Night, pt.3 . . 3.00
45 DHa, Petunia 3.00
46 DHa, High Price of
    Unemployment 2.50
47 The Fairy and the Imp 2.50
48 South for the Winter,pt.1 . . . . . 2.50
49 South for the Winter,pt.2 . . . . . 2.50
50 South for the Winter,pt.3 . . . . . 3.00
51 South for the Winter,pt.4 . . . . . 3.00
52 South for the Winter,pt.5 . . . . . 3.00
53 South for the Winter,pt.6 . . . . . 3.00
54 South for the Winter,pt.7 . . . . . 3.00
55 thru 60 . . . . @3.00
61 by The Fillbach Brothers 3.00
62 thru 68 . . . . @3.00
69 thru 82 . . . . @3.00
TPB Vol. 1 Requiem for an Elf. . . . 15.00
TPB Vol. 2 Traumatic Dogs 15.00
TPB Vol. 3 Desert of the Third Sin 15.00
TPB Vol. 4 Patrons, 48pg 5.00
TPB Vol. 5 rep. 272-pg. 15.00
TPB Vol. 6 rep. 280-pg. 15.00
TPB Vol. 7 . . . . 20.00
TPB Vol. 8 . . . . 16.00
TPB Vol. 9 Baptism by Fire 20.00
TPB The Muleskinner Years 35.00
TPB Lusipher & Lirilith (2001) 12.00
TPB Parintachin 9.00
Spec. Poison Elves Companion. . . . 3.50
Sketchbook 3.00
Sketchbook, limited 13.00

TPB Poison Elves: Dark Wars
    Heavens Devils 16.00
TPB Gothadelic Portfolio 15.00

POISON ELVES: DOMINION
Sirius Entertainment, 2005
1 . . . . 3.50
1a limited, sign, numbered 12.00
2 . . . . 3.50
3 thru 6 . . . . @3.50

POISON ELVES: HYENA
Sirius Entertainment, 2004
1 (of 4) 3.00
2 thru 4 . . . . @3.00

POISON ELVES: LOST TALES
Sirius Entertainment 2006
1 . . . . 3.00
2 thru 11 . . . . @3.00

POISON ELVES: LUSIPHER & LIRILITH
Sirius Entertainment, 2001
1 (of 4) by Drew Hayes 3.00
1a limited ed. 10.00
2 . . . . 3.00
2a delux 10.00
3 . . . . 3.00
3a limited 6.50
4 . . . . 3.00
4a limited 6.50

POISON ELVES: PARINTACHIN
Sirius Entertainment, 2001
1 (of 3) 3.00
2 . . . . 3.00
3 . . . . 3.00

POISON ELVES: VENTURES
Sirius Entertainment, 2005
1 Cassandra 3.50
2 Lynn 3.50
3 Purple Marauder 3.50
4 Jace 3.50
5 Fleece 3.50
6 Chowmba 3.50
TPB Vol. 1 Hyena 15.00

POIZON: DEMON HUNTER
London Night, 1998
1 . . . . 3.00
2 . . . . 3.00
3 . . . . 3.00
4 double sized finale 3.00

POKEMON ADVENTURES
Viz Communications, 1999
1 (of 5) Mysterious Mew 6.00
2 Wanted: Pikachu 6.00
3 The Snorlax Stop 6.00
4 . . . . 6.00
5 The Ghastly Ghosts 6.00
PART TWO, 2000
1 (of 6) Team Rocket Returns 3.00
2 The Hunt for Eevee 3.00
3 The Nidoking Safari 3.00
4 Mission: Magmar 3.00
5 The Dangerous Dragonite 3.00
6 The Mythical Moltres 3.00

PART THREE, 2000
1 . . . . 3.00
2 thru 7 . . . . @3.00
PART FOUR, 2001
Spec. 5.00
PART FIVE, 2001
1 thru 5 . . . . @5.00
PART SIX
1 (of 4) 5.00
2 thru 4 . . . . @5.00
PART SEVEN
1 (of 5) 5.00
2 thru 5 . . . . @5.00

POKEMON: ELECTRIC PIKACHU BOOGALOO
Viz Communications, 1999
1 (of 4) by Toshihiro Ono, 48-pg. . . 3.50
2 . . . . 3.00
3 . . . . 3.00
4 finale 3.00
TPB 13.00

POKEMON: THE ELECTRIC TALE OF PIKACHU
Viz Communications, 1998
1 (of 4) by Toshihiro Ono 12.00
1a 2nd printing 4.00
2 . . . . 7.00
2a 2nd printing 4.00
3 . . . . 4.00
4 . . . . 4.00
GN The Electric Tale of Pikachu . . 13.00

POKEMON: PIKACHU SHOCKS BACK
Viz Communications, 1999
1 (of 4) by Toshihiro Ono 3.25
2 thru 4 . . . . @3.25

POKEMON: SURF'S UP PIKACHU
Viz Communications, 1999
1 (of 4) thru 3 . . . . @3.00
4 . . . . 3.50
TPB Vol. 3 . . . . 13.00

POKEMON TALES
Viz Communications, 2001
Prev. Color
17 Mewtwos Watching You 6.00
18 Magnemites Mission 5.00
19 Don't Laugh Charizard 5.00
20 Onix Underground 5.00
Gold and Silver Board Books
Vol. 1 Chikorita 5.50
Vol. 2 Cyndaquil 5.50
Vol. 3 Totodile 5.50
Vol. 4 Muddy Pichi 5.50
Vol. 5 Wobuffet Watches Clouds . . . 5.50
Vol. 6 Swinub's Nose 5.50
Vol. 7 Wake Up Lugia 5.50
Vol. 8 Look Out Hondour 5.50
Vol. 9 Corsola's Brave New World . . 5.50

POKEWOMON: GOTTA SHAG 'EM ALL!
Blatant Comics, 1999
1 by Mike Rosenzweig 3.00

POLLY AND THE PIRATES
Oni Press 2005
1 by Ted Naifeh 3.00
2 . . . . 3.00

B & W PUB.

3 thru 6 . . . . @3.00
TPB Vol. 1 . . . . 12.00

POOT
Fantagraphics, 1997
1 by Walt Holcombe 3.00
2 Swollen Holler, pt.2 . . . . 3.00
3 sex issue 3.00
4 final issue, 40-pg. 4.00

POPCORN
Discovery, 1993
1 . . . . 4.00

POP PARODY
Studio Chikara, 1999
Big Fat Sci-Fi Spec.:Stawars 3.00
Pokymon–World Domination 3.00
Dixxi Chix vs. Spice Galz. 3.00
The Blair Snitch Project 4.00

PORTIA PRINZ
OF THE GLAMAZONS
Eclipse, 1986
1 thru 6 . . . . @2.50

POST BROTHERS
Rip Off Press
15 thru 18. . . . . @2.50
19 and 20 . . . . @2.50

POWER COMICS
Power Comics, 1977
1 Smart-Early Aardvark. 15.00
1a 2nd printing 7.00
2 I:Cobalt Blue 10.00
3 and 4 . . . . @8.00
5 . . . . 8.00

POWER COMICS
Eclipse, 1988
1 BB,DGb,Powerbolt. 2.50
2 BB,DGb 2.50
3 BB,DGb 2.50

PPV
Antarctic Press, 2002
1 by Tom Root & Jerzy Drozd. 3.00
2 thru 3 . . . . @3.00

PREMIERE
Diversity Comics, 1995
1 F:Kolmec The Savage 2.75

PRETEEN DIRTY GENE
KUNG FU KANGAROOS
Blackthorne, 1986
1 and 2 . . . . @2.50

PREY
Monster Comics
1 I:Prey,A:Andrina 2.25
2 V:Andrina. 2.25
3 conclusion 2.25

PRICE, THE
1 Dreadstar mag. size 20.00

PRIMITIVES
Spartive Studios, 1995
1 thru 3 On the Moon . . . . @2.50

PRIME CUTS
Fantagraphics
1 adult. 3.50

---

2 thru 6 . . . . @3.50
7 thru 12 . . . . @4.00

Primer #2
© Comico

PRIMER
Comico, 1982
1 . . . . 10.00
2 MW,I:Grendel. 100.00
3 . . . . 9.00
4 . . . . 8.00
5 SK(1st work),I:Maxx. 30.00
6 IN,Evangeline 14.00

PRIME SLIME TALES
Mirage, 1986
1 . . . . 5.00
2 . . . . 2.50
3 thru 6 . . . . @2.50

PRINCE VALIANT
1 thru 4 . . . . @5.00
Spec #1 . . . . 7.00

PRINCE VALIANT
MONTHLY
Pioneer
1 thru 6 . . . . @4.00
6 . . . . 5.00
7 . . . . 5.00
8 . . . . 5.00
9 . . . . 7.00

PRINCESS PRINCE
CPM Manga, 2000
1 . . . . 3.00
1a Leah Hernandez (c). 3.00
2 thru 14 . . . . @3.00
15 . . . . 3.00
16 . . . . 3.00

PRIVATE BEACH
Amaze Ink/SLG, 2001
1 by David Hahn. 3.00
2 . . . . 3.00
3 . . . . 3.00
4 . . . . 3.00
5 thru 8 . . . . @3.00
TPB Vol. 1 Fun & Perils. 13.00
TPB Vol. 2 Secret Messages. . . . 14.00

PRIVATE EYES
Eternity, 1988
1 Saint rep. 2.50
2 . . . . 2.50
3 . . . . 2.50
4 . . . . 2.50
5 . . . . 2.50

PROJECT ARMS
Viz Communications, 2002
1 by Ryoji Minagawa 3.25
2 thru 6 . . . . @3.25

PROTHEUS
Caliber, 1986
1 . . . . 2.50
2 . . . . 2.50

PS238
Dork Storm Press, 2002
1 thru 5 . . . . @3.00
6 thru 14 . . . . @3.00
15 thru 19 . . . . @3.00
TPB Vol. 1 . . . . 16.00
TPB Vol. 2 To the Cafeteria..
    For Justice. 16.00
TPB Vol. 3 No Child Left Behind . . 16.00

PSI–JUDGE ANDERSON
Fleetway, 1989
1 thru 15 . . . . @2.50

PULP FICTION
A-List Comics, 1997
1 thru 2 rep. of golden age . . . . @2.50
3 . . . . 3.00
4 . . . . 3.00
5 . . . . 3.00
6 . . . . 3.00
7 . . . . 3.00
Spec. Art of Pulp Fiction 3.00

PUMA BLUES
Aardvark–Vanaheim, 1986
1 10,000 printed 4.00
1a 2nd printing 2.50
2 . . . . 3.00
3 thru 19 . . . . @2.50
20 Special 2.50
Mirage
21 thru 24. . . . . @2.50
25 . . . . 2.50
26 thru 28. . . . . @2.50

PVP
Dork Storm Press, 2001
1 by Scott Kurtz 3.00
2 . . . . 3.00
3 . . . . 3.00
4 . . . . 3.00
5 thru 8 . . . . @3.00
Collected ed. #1 Hat Trick 3.00
TPB Vol. 1 Striptease. 16.00

QUACK!
Star Reach, 1976
1 Duckaneer 11.00
1a 2nd printing 4.00
2 Newton the Rabbit Wonder 8.00
3 Dave Sim,The Beavers 8.00
4 Dave Sim. 8.00
5 Dave Sim 8.00
6 . . . . 8.00

QUAGMIRE USA
Antarctic Press, 2004
1 . . . . 3.00
2 thru 6 . . . . @3.00

QUANTUM MECHANICS
Avatar, 1999
1 (of 2) by Barry Gregory &
Jacen Burrows. 3.50
1a wraparound cover 4.00
2 conclusion 3.50
2a wraparound cover 4.00

QUANTUM:
ROCK OF AGES
Dreamchilde Press, 2003
1 (of 12) 3.00
2 thru 4 . . . . @3.00
TPB Vol. 1 . . . . 15.00

QUEEN & COUNTRY
Oni Press, 2001
1 by Greg Rucka & Steve Rolston 20.00
2 . . . . 20.00
3 thru 5 . . . . @5.00
6 thru 24 . . . . @3.00
25 . . . . 6.00
26 thru 28 . . . . @3.00
29 thru 31 . . . . @3.00
TPB Vol. 1 . . . . 12.00
TPB Vol. 2 Morning Star 10.00
TPB Vol. 3 Crystal Ball 15.00
TPB Vol. 4 Operation Blackwall. . . . 9.00
TPB Vol. 5 Operation: Stormfront . 15.00
TPB Vol. 6 Operation: Dandelion. . 12.00

QUEEN & COUNTRY:
DECLASSIFIED
Oni Press, 2002
1 (of 3) 3.00
2 thru 3 . . . . @3.00
TPB Vol. 1 . . . . 9.00
Vol. 2
1 . . . . 3.00
2 thru 3 . . . . @3.00
TPB Vol. 2 . . . . 9.00
Vol. 3
1 (of 3) 3.00
2 . . . . 3.00
TPB Vol. 3 . . . . 9.00

QUEST FOR
DREAMS LOST
Literacy Vol. of Chicago, 1987
1-shot inc. TMNTurtles 2.50

QUEST PRESENTS
Quest, 1983
1 JD 2.50
2 JD 2.50
3 JD 2.50

QUICKEN FORBIDDEN
Cryptic Press, 1998
1 . . . . 3.00
2 . . . . 3.00
3 . . . . 3.00
4 . . . . 3.00
5 . . . . 3.00
6 Trial Separation,pt.1. . . . . 3.00
7 Trial Separation,pt.2. . . . . 3.00
8 Trial Separation, concl. 3.00
9 Anxiety Disorder, pt.1. . . . . 3.00
10 Anxiety Disorder, pt.2 . . . . 3.00
11 thru 12 . . . . @3.00
TPB 152-pg. 15.00

RABID MONKEY
D.B.I. Comics, 1997
1 thru 4 by Joel Steudler. . . . . . . @2.25
5 thru 7 . . . . @2.25

8 thru 13 . . . . @2.50
#1–#5 Autographed pack 12.00
Dreamriders Workshop, 1998
Vol. 2
1 . . . . 3.00

RADICAL DREAMER
Mark's Giant Economy
Sized Comics, 1995–96
1 thru 3 F:Max Wrighter . . . . @3.00
4 is Max the Devil? 3.00
VOL 2, 1998
1 (of 6) by Mark Wheatley, sci-fi . . . 3.00

RAGMOP
Planet Lucy Press, 1995
See Image also
1 by Rob Walton, 3rd. printing 3.00
2 thru 8 reoffer . . . . @2.75
8 thru 10 . . . . @2.75
VOL 2, 1997
3 by Rob Walton. 3.00
4 O-ring saga, pt. 2 (of 3) 3.00

RAGNAROK
Tokyopop Press, 2002
1 (of 4) by Myung Jin Lee 3.00
2 thru 4 . . . . @3.00

RAGNAROK GUY
Sun Comics, 1992
1 I:Ragnarok Guy,Honey 2.50
2 The Melder Foundation 2.50
3 Guy/Honey mission contd. 2.50
4 I:Big Gossage 2.50

RAIJIN COMICS
Gutsoon! Entertainment, 2002
1 manga 5.00
2 thru 36 . . . . @5.00
37 thru 44 . . . . @6.00
45 . . . . 10.00
46 . . . . 6.00

RAIKA
Sun Comics
1 thru 12 . . . . @2.50

RAISING HELL
ABC Comics, 1997
1 . . . . 3.00
1a gold series, 2 extra pages 3.00
2 RCI,F:China & Jazz 3.00
3 conclusion, A:Wild Things 3.00
3 Baby Cheeks edition 10.00
3 Baby Cheeks Gold Edition. . . . 15.00

RALPH SNART
Now, 1986
1 . . . . 5.00
2 . . . . 4.00
3 . . . . 4.00
[Volume 2] 1986
1 . . . . 3.00
2 thru 8 . . . . @2.50
Trade Paperback 3.00

RAMBO
Blackthorne, 1988
1 thru 5 . . . . @2.50

RAMBO III
Blackthorne
1 . . . . 2.50

Ramm #2
© *Megaton Comics*

RAMM
Megaton Comics, 1987
1 and 2 . . . . @2.50

RANMA 1/2
Viz, 1993
Parts 1 & 2, see color
PART 3, 1993–94
1 thru 13 . . . . @3.00
PART 4, 1995
1 thru 11 . . . . @3.00
PART 5, 1996
1 thru 9 . . . . @3.00
10 thru 12 . . . . @3.00
PART 6, 1996
1 thru 8 (of 14) . . . . @3.00
9 thru 14 . . . . @3.00
PART 7, 1998
1 (of 14) 3.00
2 thru 14 . . . . @3.00
PART 8, 1999
1 (of 13) thru 5 . . . . @3.00
6 thru 13 . . . . @3.00
PART 9, 2000
1 (of 11) 3.00
2 thru 11 . . . . @3.00
PART 10, 2001
1 (of 11). 3.00
2 thru 8 . . . . @3.00
9 thru 11 . . . . @3.00
PART 11, 2002
1 (of 11) 3.00
2 thru 11 . . . . 3.00
Part 12 (March, 2003)
1 . . . . 3.00

RAPHAEL
Mirage, 1985
1 TMNT. 17.50
1a 2nd printing 7.50

RAPTUS
High Impact
1 . . . . 3.00
1 2nd printing, new cover 3.00
2 . . . . 3.00
3 . . . . 3.00

All comics prices listed are for *Near Mint* condition.

RAPTUS:
DEAD OF NIGHT
High Impact

1	3.00
2	3.00
3	3.00

RAT FINK
World of Fandom

1	2.50
2 & 3	@2.50

RAVAGER
Kosmic Comic, 1997

0 Ashcan	2.25
1 The First Coming	3.55
2	3.55
3	3.55
4 by Kirk Patrick & Babak Homayoun	3.55
5	3.55
6 by Kirk Patrick & Romel Cruz	3.55

RAVEN
Ariel Press, 2003

1	2.25
2 thru 6	@2.25
7 thru 10	@2.00

RAVEN CHRONICLES
Caliber Press, 1995

1	3.00
1a Special Edition	6.00
2 Landing Zone	3.00
3 The Rain People	3.00
4 The Healer	3.00
5 thru 9	@3.00

Caliber `New Worlds'

10 by Scott Andrews, Laurence Campbell & Tim Perkins	3.00
11 `The Ghost of Alanzo Mann'	3.00
12 `The Compensators' flip book with Boston Bombers #1	3.00
13 48pg, bagged with back issue	4.00
14	3.00
15	3.00
16 inc. Black Mist	3.00
Spec. Heart of the Dragon	3.00
GN 192pg rep	17.00

RAVENING, THE
Avatar Press, 1997

0 Trevlin Utz (c)	4.00

Ravening #0
© Avatar Press

---

0 Matt Martin (c)	4.00
0 Matt Haley (c)	4.00
0 leather cover	25.00
0 signed	15.00
1	3.00
1 leather cover	25.00
1 Avatar con cover edition	15.00
2 (of 2)	3.00
Spec. Secrets of the Ravening	2.75

RAW CITY
Dramenon Studios

1 I:Dya,Gino	3.00
2 V:Crucifier	3.00
3 The Siren's Past	3.00

RAW MEDIA MAGS.
Rebel

1 TV,SK,short stories	5.00

RAZOR
London Night, 1992

6 signed	20.00
10 signed	15.00
TPB The Suffering, rep. #1–#3	13.00
GN Let Us Prey, rep. of Razor/Wild Child, 80pg.	5.00
X-over Razor/Embrace: The Spawning (1997)	3.00
Carmen Electra photo (c)	3.00
Carmen Electra photo embossed (c), signed	19.00
Spec. Razor: Switchblade Symphony, Tour Book, limited black leather	15.00

RAZOR ANALOG BURN
London Night Studios, 1999

1 by Lee Duhig	2.50
2	2.50

RAZOR: ARCHIVES
London Night, 1997

1 EHr, rep #1–#4	5.00
1a signed	12.00
2 EHr, rep #5–#8	5.00
3 EHr, rep #9–#15	5.00
4 EHr, rep #16–#17	5.00

RAZOR:
BLEEDING HEART
Avatar Press, 2001

1 Fillion (c)	3.50
1a Martin (c)	3.50
1b Wraparound (c)	5.00
1c Adult (c)	6.00
1d Worship (c)	6.00

RAZOR/DARK ANGEL:
THE FINAL NAIL
Boneyard/London Night

1 X-over (Boneyard Press)	4.00
2 X-over concl.(London Night)	3.00

RAZOR:
THE DARKEST NIGHT
London Night, 1998

1	5.00
1a white velvet	20.00
2 velvet edition	10.00

EH! Productions, 1999

1	5.00
1a Velvet Edition, signed	25.00
2	5.00
3	5.00
3a Fan ed.	6.00

RAZOR: THE FURIES
Avatar, 2000

1 48-pg.	5.00
1a Previews Exclusive	5.00

RAZOR: GOTHIC
London Night, 1998

1 (of 4) by EHr and Scott Wilson	3.00
1 leather	12.00
2 EHr	3.00
2a Graphic/violent cover	6.00
2b Gothic/leather cover	15.00

EH! Productions

3	3.00
3a Elite Fan ed.	5.00
4	3.00
4a Elite Fan ed.	5.00
Spec. Gotherotica	5.00

RAZOR: TILL I
BLEED DAYLIGHT
Avatar, 2000

1 (of 2) Tim Vigil (c)	3.50
1a wraparound (c)	4.00
1b Vampire Razor (c)	5.00
1c adult (c)	6.00
1d prism foil	13.00
1e expanded edition	5.00
2	3.50
2a wraparound (c)	4.00
2b adult (c)	6.00
2c expanded edition, 56-pg.	5.00

RAZOR: TORTURE
London Night, 1995

0 chromium signed	4.00
1 platinum signed	3.00

RAZOR UNCUT
London Night Studios, 1995
Prev. RAZOR (Ind. Color)

13	3.00
14 V:Child Killer	3.00
15 Questions About Father	3.00
16 Nicole's Life,pt.1	3.00
17 Nicole's Life,pt.2	3.00
18	3.00
19 thru 21 Kiss from a Rose	@3.00
22 thru 24	@3.00
25 mild cover I:Knyfe	3.00
25b signed	13.00
26	3.00
27 A:Sade, pt.1	3.00
28 A:Sade, pt.2	3.00
29	3.00
30	3.00
31 `Strength by Numbers'	3.00
32 double sized	3.50
33 `Let Us Prey,' pt.2	3.00
34 `Let Us Prey,' pt.4 (of 4)	3.00
35 Let the battle begin	3.00
36 all-out war for Queen City	3.00
37 `After the Fall' pt.1	3.00
38 `After the Fall,' pt.2	3.00
39 `Money For Hire'	3.00
40 `Father's Bane,' pt.1	3.00
41 `Father's Bane,' pt.2	3.00
42 `Father's Bane,' pt.3	3.00
43 `Father's Bane,' pt.4	3.00
44 Razor finds abandoned child	3.00
45 An American Tragedy, pt.1 (of 5)	3.00
45a commemmoration edition, EHr.	5.00
46 An American Tragedy, pt.2	3.00
47 An American Tragedy, pt.3	3.00
48 An American Tragedy, pt.4	3.00
49 An American Tragedy, pt.5	3.00
50 back in Asylum, Tony Daniel (c)	3.00
50a Michael Bair (c)	5.00
50b Stephen Sandoval (c)	5.00

50c Blood Red Velvet EHr (c) 25.00
Spec. Deep Cuts (1997) 5th Anniv.
    rep. #6,#13–#15, 80 pg 5.00
EH! Productions, 1999
51 . . . . 3.00

Razorguts #4
© Monster Comics

RAZORGUTS
Monster Comics, 1992
1 thru 4 . . . . 2.25

RAZOR'S EDGE
London Night, 1999
0 Razor/Stryke (c) 5.00
0b Night Vixen (c) 5.00
1 . . . . 5.00
1a Arizona (c) 5.00
2 Razorblaze (c) 5.00
2a Battle Girl (c) 6.00
2b Nightvixen (c) 5.00
3 . . . . 5.00
3a Nightvixen (c) 5.00
4 . . . . 5.00
4a (c) 5.00
5 . . . . 5.00
5a Stryke (c) 5.00
EH! Productions, 1999
6 48-pg. 5.00
7 . . . . 5.00
8 . . . . 5.00
9 . . . . 5.00

REACTOMAN
B-Movie Comics
1 . . . . 2.25
1a signed,numbered 2.75
2 thru 4 . . . . @2.25
collection 5.00

REAGAN'S RAIDERS
Solson
1 thru 6 . . . . @2.50

REALM
Arrow, 1986
1 Fantasy 6.00
2 . . . . 4.00
3 . . . . 3.00
4 TV,Deadworld 21.00
5 I:L.Kazan 2.50
6 thru 13 . . . . @2.50
Caliber Press, 1990
14 thru 18 . . . . @2.50

19 . . . . 2.50

REAL STUFF
Fantagraphic, 1990
1 . . . . 2.50
2 . . . . 2.50
3 thru 12 . . . . 2.50

REAPER
Newcomers Publishing
1 V:The Chinde 3.00
2 . . . . 3.00
3 conclusion 3.00

REBELLION
Daikaiyu Enterprises, 1995
1 I:Rebellion 2.50

RECORD OF THE
LODOSS WAR
CPM Manga, 2000
TPB Book 1 The Grey Witch 16.00
TPB Book 2 The Grey Witch 16.00
TPB The Lady of Pharis 16.00
TPB Welcome to Lodoss Island . . 16.00
TPB Vol.2 Welcome Lodoss Island 16.00

RED DIARY
Caliber, 1998
1 (of 4) F:Marilyn, JFK, Hoover,
    CIA. 4.00
1a deluxe 7.00
2 . . . . 4.00
3 (of 4) 4.00
1 signed) 4.00
4 . . . . 4.00

RED FOX
Harrier, 1986
1 scarce 6.00
1a 2nd printing 2.50
2 rare 5.00
3 . . . . 3.00
4 I:White Fox. 3.00
5 I:Red Snail 3.00
6 . . . . 2.50
7 Wbolton 2.50
8 . . . . 2.50
9 Demosblurth 2.50

RED & STUMPY
Parody Press
1 Ren & Stimpy parody 3.00

RE:GEX: BLACK & WHITE
Awesome Entertainment, 1999
1 RLe,JLb 3.00

REHD
Antarctic Press, 2003
0 . . . . 2.50
1 thru 2 . . . . @3.00
3 . . . . 3.00

REID FLEMING, WORLD'S
TOUGHEST MILKMAN
Blackbird-Eclipse, 1986
1 David Boswell,I:Reid Fleming . . . 5.00
1a 2nd printing 3.00
1b 3rd–5th printing . . . . @2.50
Volume 2, 1986
#1 Rogues to Riches Pt.1 . . . . 5.00
#2 Rogues to Riches Pt.2 (1987) . . 3.00
#2a Later printings 2.50
#3 Rogues to Riches Pt.3 (1988) . . 3.00
#3a Later printings 2.50

#4 Rogues to Riches Pt.4 (1989) . . 3.00
#5 Rogues to Riches Pt.5 (1990) . . 2.50
Deep-Sea Comics, 1987
3 `Rogue to Riches,' pt.2,4th pr . . . 3.00
4 `Rogue to Riches,' pt.3,3rd pr . . . 3.00
5 `Rogue to Riches,' pt.4,2nd pr. . . 3.00
6 `Rogue to Riches,' pt.5,2nd pr. . . 3.00
7 `Another Dawn,'Pt.1. . . . . 3.00
8 `Another Dawn,'Pt.2. . . . . 3.00
9 `Another Dawn,'Pt.3. . . . . 3.00
TPB Rogue to Riches rep. 14.00
Spec#1 Origins (1998) 3.00

REIVERS
Enigma
1 thru 2 Ch'tocc in Space 3.00

RENEGADES OF JUSTICE
Blue Masque
1 I:Monarch,Bloodshadow 2.50
2 Madfire 2.50
3 Television Chronicles 2.50
4 R:Karen Styles 2.50

RENFIELD
Caliber, 1994
1 thru 3 . . . . @3.00
GN Conclusion of series 9.00

REPENTANCE
Advantage Graphics, 1995
1 I:Repentance 2.25

REPLACEMENT GOD
Amaze Ink, 1995
1 Child in The Land of Man 6.00
1a 2nd & 3rd printing 3.00
2 Eye of Knute 4.00
3 & 4 `Bravery' . . . . @3.50
5 thru 7 . . . . @3.00
8 Fairie, book one, concl. 3.00
TPB rep. #1–#8 . . . . 20.00

REPLACEMENT GOD
& OTHER STORIES
Handicraft Guild, 1998
Previously published by Image
6 by Zander Cannon, 80pg. 7.00

RETALIATOR
Eclipse
1 I&O:Retaliator 2.50
2 O:Retaliator cont. 2.50
3 thru 5 . . . . @2.50

RETIEF
Adventure, 1987–88
1 thru 6 Keith Laumer adapt. . . . @2.50
[Vol. 2], 1989–90
1 thru 6 . . . . @2.50
Spec.#1 Retief:Garbage Invasion . . 2.50
Spec.#1 Retief:The Giant Killer,
    V:Giant Dinosaur (1991) 2.50
Spec.#1 Grime & Punishment,
    Planet Slunch (1991). 2.50

RETIEF OF THE CDT
Adventure, 1990
1 Keith Laumer Novel Adapt. 2.25
2 thru 6 . . . . @2.25

RETIEF AND
THE WARLORDS
Adventure Comics
1 Keith Laumer Novel Adapt. 2.50
2 Haterakans 2.50

3 Retief Arrested for Treason 2.50
4 Final Battle (last issue) 2.50

RETIEF: DIPLOMATIC IMMUNITY
Adventure Comics, 1991
1 Groaci Invasion. 2.50
2 Groaci story cont. 2.50

RETRO-DEAD
Blazer Unlimited, 1995
1 Dimensional Rift. 3.00
2 by Dan Reed 3.00

RETROGRADE
Eternity
1 thru 4 . . . . @2.25

RETURN OF HAPPY THE CLOWN
Caliber Press
1 & 2 V:Oni 3.00

RETURN OF LUM URUSEI* YATSURA, THE
Viz Comics, 1994
1 thru 6 . . . . @3.00
PART TWO, 1995
1 thru 13 . . . . @3.00
PART THREE, 1996
1 thru 11 by Rumiko Takahashi. . @3.00
PART FOUR, 1997
1 thru 11 by Rumiko Takahashi. . @3.00

RETURN OF THE SKYMAN
Ace Comics, 1987
1 SD 2.50

Return of the Skyman #1
© Ace Comics

REVOLVER
Renegade, 1985
1 SD 2.50
2 thru 12 . . . . @2.50
Ann. #1. 2.50

REVOLVING DOORS
Blackthorne, 1986
1 . . . . 2.50
2 & 3 . . . . @2.50

Graphic Novel 4.00

RHEINTOCHTER
Antarctic Press, 1998
1 by Y.Paquette & M.Lacombe 3.00
2 (of 2) concl. 3.00

RHUDIPRRT PRINCE OF FUR
MU Press, 1990–91
1 thru 6 . . . . @2.25
7 thru 12 . . . . @3.00

RICHARD MATHESON'S HELL HOUSE
IDW Publishing, 2004
1 48-pgs. 6.50
2 thru 4 . . . . @6.50

RICH JOHNSTON'S HOLED UP
Avatar Press, 2004
1 . . . . 3.50
2 thru 3 . . . . @3.50
1a thru 3a homeland
   security (c)s . . . . @3.50

RICK RAYGUN
1 . . . . 2.25
2 thru 8 . . . . @2.25

RIO KID
Eternity
1 I:Rio Kid. 2.50
2 V:Blow Torch Killer. 2.50
3 . . . . 2.50

RIOT
Viz, 1995
1 F:Riot,Axel 2.75
2 & 3 . . . . 2.75
4 final issue 2.75
TPB Rep. 16.00

RIOT ACT TWO
Viz Comics, 1996
1 thru 7 . . . . @3.00
TPB rep. 16.00

RIP IN TIME
Fantagor, 1986
1 RCo,Limited series 3.00
2 RCo 2.50
3 RCo 2.50
4 RCo 2.50
5 RCo,Last 2.50

RIVAL SCHOOLS
Udon Entertainment 2006
1 . . . . 5.00
2 . . . . 5.00
3 . . . . 5.00
1a thru 3a variant (c) . . . . @5.00
1b Power cell (c) 12.50

ROACHMILL
Blackthorne, 1986
1 . . . . 5.00
2 . . . . 3.00
3 and 4 . . . . @3.00
See: Dark Horse

ROBERT E. HOWARD'S
Cross Plains Comics, 1999
1-shot Horror, 64-pg. 6.00
TPB Kull. 20.00

1-shot Black Stone. 4.00

ROB HANES ADVENTURES
WCG Comics, 2000
1 by Randy Renoldo 2.50
2 thru 3 . . . . @2.50
4 . . . . 2.75
5 thru 8 . . . . @3.00

ROBIN HOOD
Eternity, 1989
1 thru 4 . . . . @2.50

ROBO DEFENSE TEAM MECHA RIDER
Castle Comics
1 I:RDT Mecha Rider 3.00
2 Identity of Outlaw. 3.00

ROBOTECH
Eternity
1-shot Untold Stories 2.50
Academy Comics, 1995–96
0 Robotech Information 2.50
Spec. Robotech: Macross Tempest
   F:Roy Fokker, Tempest (1995) . 3.00
Spec. Robotech: Mech Angel,
   I:Mech Angel (1995) 3.00
Spec. Robotech: The Misfits, from
   Southern Cross transferred to
   Africa. 3.00
Spec. #1 & #2 Robotech The Movie,
   Benny R. Powell & Chi . . . @3.00
Spec. Robotech Romance. 3.00
Spec. Robotech: Sentinels Star Runners
   Carpenter's Journey (1996) . . . 3.00
GN The Threadbard Heart. 10.00
Antarctic Press, 1998
Ann. #1. 3.00
Spec.#1 Robotech: Escape (1998) . 3.00

ROBOTECH: ACADEMY BLUES
Academy Comics
0 Classroom Blues 3.50
1 F:Lisa. 3.00
2 Bomb at the Academy 3.00
3 Roy's Drinking Buddy 3.00

ROBOTECH: AFTERMATH
Academy Comics
1 thru 10 R:Bruce Lewis . . . . @3.00
11 Zentradi Traitor 3.00
12 and 13 . . . . @3.00

ROBOTECH: CLONE
Academy Comics
1 Dialect of Duality 3.00
2 V:Monte Yarrow 3.00
3 Ressurection 3.00
4 Ressurection 3.00
5 F:Bibi Ava. 3.00

ROBOTECH: COVERT OPS
Antarctic Press, 1998
1 (of 2) by Greg Lane 3.00
2 . . . . 3.00

ROBOTECH: INVID WAR
Eternity, 1993
1 No Man's Land 2.50
2 V:Defoliators 2.50
3 V:The Invid,Reflex Point 2.50
4 V:The Invid. 2.50

5 Moonbase Aluce II 2.50	14 V:Invid 2.75	**Becomes:**
6 Moonbase-Zentraedi plot 2.50	15 . . . . 2.75	**KUNG FU WARRIORS**
7 Zentraedi plot contd. 2.50	16 . . . . 2.75	
8 A:Lancer 2.50	17 V:Invid Mechas 2.75	**ROCK 'N' ROLL COMICS**
9 A:Johnathan Wolfe. 2.50	18 F:"HIN" 3.00	**Revolutionary, 1989**
10 . . . . 2.50	19 V:Invid 3.00	1 Guns & Roses 10.00
11 F:Rand 2.50	20 Final Aplp. Invid Regiss 3.00	1a 2nd printing 3.50
12 thru 15 . . . . 2.50	21 Predator and Prey. 3.00	1b 3rd printing. 3.00
	22 A Clockwork Planet 3.00	1c 4th-7th printing 3.00
ROBOTECH: INVID	Halloween Special JWp,JWt, ... 3.00	2 Metalica 11.00
WAR AFTERMATH		2a 2nd printing 3.00
Eternity	**ROBOTECH II:**	2b 3rd-5th printing. 3.00
1 thru 6 F:Rand 2.75	**THE SENTINELS:**	3 Bon Jovi 9.00
	CYBERPIRATES	4 Motley Crue 5.00
ROBOTECH: MORDECAI	**Eternity, 1991**	5 Def Leppard 5.00
Academy Comics	1 The Hard Wired Coffin 2.25	6 Rolling Stones 8.00
1 . . . . 3.00	2 thru 4 . . . . @2.25	6a 2nd-4th printing 3.00
2 Annie meets her clone 3.00		7 The Who 5.00
	ROBOTECH II:	7a 2nd 3rd printing 3.00
ROBOTECH:	**THE SENTINELS:**	9 Kiss 15.00
RETURN TO MACROSS	**THE MALCONTENT**	9a 2nd-3rd Printing 5.00
Eternity, 1993	**UPRISING**	10 Warrant/Whitesnake 6.00
1 thru 12 . . . . @2.50	**Eternity**	10a 2nd Printing. 3.00
Academy Comics	1 thru 12 . . . . @2.25	11 Aerosmith	5.00
13 thru 17 Roy Fokker . . . . @2.75		12 New Kids on Block 5.00
18 F:The Faithful 2.75		12a 2nd Printing. 2.25
19 F:Lisa 2.75		13 LedZeppelin 6.00
20 F:Lisa 2.75		14 Sex Pistols 5.00
21 V:Killer Robot 3.00		*See Independent Color*
22 War of the Believers 3.00		
23 War of the Believers,pt.2 . . . . . 3.00		**ROCKET RANGERS**
24 War of the Believers,pt.3 . . . . . 3.00		**Adventure, 1992**
25 War of the Believers,pt.4 . . . . . 3.00		1 . . . . 3.00
26 thru 30 . . . . @3.00		2 . . . . 3.00
31 What Is the Federalist Plan? . . . 3.00		3 . . . . 3.00
32 thru 34 . . . . @3.00		
35 Typhoon threatens Macross		**ROCKIN' ROLLIN'**
Island 3.00		**MINER ANTS**
36 . . . . 3.00		**Fate Comics, 1992**
37 round up of Federalist Agents . . 3.00		1 As seen in TMNT #40 . . . . 2.25
		1a Gold Variant copy 7.50
ROBOTECH: SENTINELS:		2 Elephant Hunting, A:Scorn,
RUBICON		Blistor 2.25
Antarctic Press, 1998		3 V:Scorn, Inc ,K Eastman Ant
1 (of 7) 3.00		pin-up 2.25
2 Shadows of the Past 3.00		4 Animal Experiments,V:Loboto . . 2.25
	Robotech Vermilion #1	
ROBOTECH II	© Antarctic Press	**ROLLING STONES:**
THE SENTINELS		**THE SIXTIES**
Eternity, 1988		**Personality**
1 . . . . 3.00	**ROBOTECH: VERMILION**	1 Regular Version 3.00
2 & 3 . . . . @2.50	**Antarctic Press, 1997**	1a Deluxe Version,w/cards 7.00
1a 2nd 2a 2nd printings . . . . . . @2.50	1 (of 4) by Duc Tran 3.00	
4 thru 16 . . . . @2.50	2 Why did Hiro die? 3.00	**ROOTER**
Book 2, 1990	3 . . . . 3.00	**Custom Comics of America,**
1 thru 12 . . . . @2.25	4 . . . . 3.00	**1996–97**
13 thru 20 . . . . @2.50		1 Sweatin' Bullets 3.00
Wedding Special #1 (1989) 2.25	**ROBOTECH: WARRIORS**	2 Big Bad Beaver 3.00
Wedding Special #2 . . . . 2.25	**Academy Comics, 1995**	3 The Big Izzy 3.00
Robotech II Handbook 2.50	1 F:Breetai 3.00	4 Da Voodoo Blues 3.00
Book Three	2 F:Mirya 3.00	5 . . . . 3.00
1 thru 8 V:Invid 2.50	3 F:Mirya 3.00	6 Blues Power. 3.00
Book Four	GN The Terror Maker 10.00	Ann. #1, 120pg. 15.00
Academy Comics, 1995		**VOL 2, 1998**
1 by Jason Waltrip 3.00	**ROBOTECH: WINGS**	1 by Kelly Campbell 3.00
2 thru 4 F:Tesla . . . . @2.75	**OF GIBRALTAR**	2 . . . . 3.00
5 JWp,JWt,interior of Haydon IV . 3.00	**Antarctic Press, 1998**	3 Hot Rocks Mojo 3.00
6 thru 8 . . . . @3.00	1 (of 2) by Lee Duhig 3.00	
9 JWp,JWt,Breetai, Wolf & Vince	2 . . . . 3.00	**ROSE**
return to Tirol 3.00		**Hero Graphics, 1993**
10 JWp,JWt,*Ark Angel* attacked by	**ROBO WARRIORS**	1 From The Champions 3.50
The Black Death Destroyers . . . 3.00	**CFW**	2 A:Huntsman 3.50
11 JWp,JWt,Tirol, Wolff, Vince &	1 thru 11 . . . . @2.25	3 thru 5 . . . . @3.00
Breetai on trial for treason 3.00		
12 JWp,JWt,Dr. Lang exposes		**ROSE AND GUNN**
General Edwards' evil designs . 3.00		**London Night, 1996**
13 F:Tesla 2.75		1 . . . . 3.00

B & W PUB.

1b signed 10.00
2 . . . . 3.00
3 . . . . 3.00

ROSE AND GUNN: RECKONING
London Night
1 (of 2) 3.00

ROSE 'N' GUNN
Bishop Pres, 1995
1 Deadly Duo 5.00
2 V:Marilyn Monroe. 3.00
3 Presidential Affairs 3.00
4 Without Each Other 3.00
5 V:Red 3.00
6 & 7 . . . . @3.00
Creator's Choice Rep. #1 . . . . . . 3.00
Creator's Choice Rep. #2 . . . . . . 3.00
Creator's Choice Rep. #3 . . . . . . 3.00

ROVERS
Eternity
1 thru 7 . . . . @2.25

RUBES REVIVED
Fish Warp
1 thru 3 . . . . @2.25

RUK BUD WEBSTER
Fish Warp
1 thru 3 . . . . @2.25

RUMBLE PAK
Eigomanga, 2004
1 . . . . 5.00
2 thru 5 . . . . @5.00
TPB Vol. 1 . . . . 10.00

RUNNERS: BAD GOODS
Serve Man Press, 2003
1 . . . . 3.00
2 thru 5 . . . . @3.00
TPB Bad Goods 15.00

SADE
Bishop Press, 1995
0 B:Adventures of Sade 3.00
1 . . . . 3.00
1a variant 6.00
2 . . . . 3.00

SADE SPECIAL
Bishop Press
1 V:Razor 5.00
1a signed 7.00

SADE
London Night, 1996
1 . . . . 3.00
2 thru 5 . . . . @3.00

SADE/ROSE AND GUNN
London Night, 1996
1 Confederate Mist 3.00

SADE: TESTAMENTS OF PAIN
London Night, 1997
1 (of 2) 3.00

SAGA OF THE MAN-ELF
Trident, 1989
1 thru 5 . . . . @2.25

SAGE
Fantaco, 1995
1 O:Sage.' 5.00

SAILOR MOON
Mixx Entertainment, 1998
1 by Naoko Tekeuchi 20.00
2 thru 5 . . . . @12.00
6 thru 11 . . . . @5.00
12 thru 20 . . . . @5.00
Pocket #1 (of 18) 192-pg. 10.00
Pocket #2 rep. 10.00
Pocket #3 rep. 10.00

Sailor Moon #8
© Mixx Entertainment

Pocket #4 rep. 10.00
Pocket #5 rep. #11–#13. . . . . 10.00
Pocket #6 rep. #14–#17. . . . . 10.00
Scout Guide: Sailor Mars: Fire . . . 13.00
Scout Guide: Sailor Venus: Love . . 13.00
Scout Guide: Sailor Jupiter:
  Thunder 13.00
Novel A Scout is Born 5.00
Novel The Power of Love 5.00
Novel 3: Mercury Rising 5.00
Tokyopop.Com, 2000
21 thru 25 . . . . @3.00
26 thru 35 . . . . @3.00
Pocket Mixx Vol. 7 thru 11 . . . . @10.00
Pocket Mixx Stars, Vol.1 thru 3 . @10.00
TPB Scout Guide-Meet Sailor
  Moon: Crystal 13.00
TPB Scout Guide-Meet Sailor
  Mercury: Ice 13.00
TPB Scout Guide-Meet Sailor
  Jupiter: Thunder 13.00

SAILOR MOON SUPER S
Mixx Entertainment, 1999
1 (of 18) 192-pg. 10.00
2 thru 4 Pocket Mixx . . . . @10.00

SAINT
Kick Ass Comics
1 & 2 V:Cerran 2.50

SAINT GERMAINE
Caliber `Core', 1997
0 O:St. Germaine 4.00
1 VcL, two immortals, St. Germain
  cover 3.00
1 Lilith cover 3.00
2 VcL 3.00
3 VcL 3.00

3a signed 3.00
4 VcL 3.00
5 The Kilroy Mandate, VcL(c) 3.00
5a Meyer (c) 3.00
6 Kilroy Mandate 3.00
8 Ghost Dance 3.00
8 The Man in the Iron Mask 3.00
10 The Tragedy of Falstaff 3.00
11 by Gary Reed & James Lyle . . . 3.00
GN Shadows Fall, rep. #1–#4 . . . . 15.00
Spec. Casanova's Lament, 48-pg. . . 4.00
Spec. Restoration, VcL 4.00

SAINT GERMAINE: PRIOR ECHOES
Caliber `Core', 1998
1 (of 4) by Gary Reed 3.00
2 . . . . 3.00
3 . . . . 3.00

SAINT TAIL
Tokyopop Press, 2000
1 . . . . 3.00
2 thru 13 . . . . @3.00
14 thru 16 . . . . @3.00
17 thru 20 . . . . @3.00
TPB Pocket Vol. 1 thru Vol. 7 . . @10.00

SAMURAI (1st series)
1 . . . . 50.00
2 . . . . 25.00
3 . . . . 25.00
4 . . . . 25.00
5 . . . . 25.00

SAMURAI
Aircel, 1985
1 rare 6.00
1a 2nd printing 3.00
1b 3rd printing 2.50
2 . . . . 5.00
2a 2nd printing 2.50
3 . . . . 3.00
4 . . . . 3.00
5 thru 12 . . . . @2.50
13 DK (1st art) 4.00
14 thru 16 DK . . . . @4.00
17 thru 23 . . . . @2.50
[3rd series], 1988
#1 thru 3 . . . . @2.50
#4 thru 7 . . . . @2.50
Compilation Book 5.00

SAMURAI
Warp Graphics, 1997
1 by Barry Blair & Colin Chan 3.00
2 . . . . 3.00
3 . . . . 3.00
4 . . . . 3.00

SAMURAI FUNNIES
Solson
1 thru 3 . . . . @2.25

SAMURAI PENGUIN
Solson, 1986
1 . . . . 3.00
2 I:Dr.Radium 2.50
3 . . . . 2.50
4 . . . . 2.50
5 FC 2.50
6 color 2.50
7 . . . . 2.50
8 . . . . 2.50
9 . . . . 2.50

SAMURAI 7
Gauntlet Comics
1 I: Samurai 7 . . . . 2.50

SAMURAI, SON OF DEATH
Eclipse
1 . . . . 4.00
1a 2nd printing 4.00

SANCTUARY
Viz Communications, 1993
1 World of Yakuza. 5.00
2 thru 4 . . . . @5.00
5 thru 9 . . . . @5.00
[Part Two], 1994
1 thru 9 . . . . @5.00
[Part Three], 1994–95
1 thru 8 . . . . @3.50
[Part Four], 1995–96
1 thru 7 . . . . @3.50
[Part Five], 1996
7 thru 13 by Sho Fumimura &
  Ryoichi Ikegami . . . . @3.50

SANTA CLAWS
Eternity
1 `Deck the Mall with Blood
  and Corpses'. 3.00

SAPPHIRE
Ariel Press, 1996
1 by Vince Danks 3.00
6 thru 9 . . . . @3.00

SAVAGE HENRY
Vortex, 1987
1 thru 13 . . . . @2.50
Rip Off Press, 1991
14 thru 15 . . . . @2.25
16 thru 24 . . . . @2.50

SAVAGE HENRY: POWERCHORDS
Aeon, 2004
1 (of 3) 3.00
2 and 3 . . . . @3.00
Spec. Puppet Trap 3.00

SCARLET IN GASLIGHT
Eternity, 1988
1 A:Sherlock Holmes 4.00
2 . . . . 3.00
3 & 4 . . . . @2.50

SCARLET SCORPION/ DARKSIDE
AC Comics, 1995
1 & 2 Flipbooks. 3.50

SCARLET THUNDER
Amaze Ink, 1995
1 thru 3 . . . . @2.50

SCARY GODMOTHER
Sirius Entertainment, 2001
1 by Jill Thompson 3.00
2 thru 6 concl. . . . . @3.00
TPB Wild About Harry 10.00
TPB Ghouls Out For Summer 15.00
TPB Spooktacular Stories 10.00
GN Vol. 1 Storybook 10.00
GN Vol. 2 The Revenge of Jimmy . 10.00
GN The Mystery Date Storybook . . 10.00

SCARY GODMOTHER: BLOODY VALENTINE
Sirius Entertainment, 1998
1 . . . . 4.00
1a signed and numbered 10.00
Holiday Spooktacular 3.00

SCARY GODMOTHER: WILD ABOUT HARRY
Sirius Entertainment, 2000
1 (of 3) by Jill Thompson 3.00
2 . . . . 3.00
3 concl. 3.00

SCIENCE FAIR
Antarctic Press, 2005
1 (of 8) 3.00
2 thru 4 . . . . @3.00

SCIMIDAR
Eternity
1 . . . . 4.00
1a 2nd Printing 2.50
2 and 3 . . . . @3.00
4 HotCover 3.50
4A MildCover 3.00

SCOOTER GIRL
Oni Press, 2003
1 (of 6) 3.00
2 thru 6 . . . . @3.00
TPB 15.00

SCORN
SCC Entertainment, 1996
Lingerie Spec. 3.00
Lingerie Spec. deluxe 10.00
Super Spec.#1 rep. Deadly
  Rebellion, Headwave, Fabric
  of the Mind. 5.00
X-over Scorn/Ardy: Alien Influence
  (1997) by Rob Potchak & Timothy
  Johnson 4.00
  Bill Maus (c) 4.00
  Deluxe gold 10.00
X-over Scorn/Dracula: The Vampire's
  Blood (1997) 4.00
  Dracula cover 4.00
  Scorn cover 4.00
Spec.#1A Scorn; Dead or Alive
  (1997) Mike Morales(c) 4.00
  Andrea Seri(c). 4.00
Spec.# Scorn Deadly Rebellion 4.00
  Birthday Suit cover 10.00
  Celebrity photo cover 10.00
Spec.#1 Scorb: Fractured (1997)
  Fear cover 4.00
  Rage cover 4.00
Spec: Scorn: Heatwave (1997) by
  Chris Crosby & Mike Morales . . 4.00
Spec. Scorn: Hostage 4.00
Spec. Scorn: Naked Truth (1997) . . 4.00

SCRATCH
Outside, 1986
1 . . . . 3.00
2 thru 4 . . . . @2.50

SCREAMING ANGELS
Antarctic Press, 2004
1 (of 3) 3.50
2 thru 3 . . . . @3.50

SCRIMIDAR
CFD Productions, 1995
1 I:Bloody Mary. 2.75

Scud Disposable Assassin #1
© Fireman Press

SCUD: DISPOSABLE ASSASSIN
Fireman Press, 1994
1 I:Scud. 10.00
1a 3rd printing. 3.50
2 . . . . 7.00
3 . . . . 5.00
4 thru 6 F:Scud . . . . @5.00
7 Lupine Thoughts 4.00
8 Scud Looks for His Arm. 4.00
9 Scud Looks for His Arm. 4.00
10 thru 16 by Rob Schrab . . . . . . @3.00
17 . . . . 3.00
18 . . . . 3.00
19 . . . . 3.00
20 Horse series, concl. 3.00
TPB Rep.#1-#4 . . . . 13.00
TPB Programmed for Damage,
  rep.#5–#9 . . . . 15.00
TPB Solid Gold Bomb 18.00
TPB Yellow Horseman (2001) 15.00

SCUD: TALES FROM THE VENDING MACHINE
Fireman Press, 1998
1 . . . . 2.50
2 . . . . 2.50
3 . . . . 2.50
4 . . . . 2.50
5 . . . . 2.50

SEAMONSTERS & SUPERHEROES
Amaze Ink/SLG, 2003
1 (of 3) 3.00
2 thru 8 . . . . @3.00
TPB Vol. 1 . . . . 15.00

SEARCHERS
Caliber `New Worlds', 1996
1A Red cover, signed 3.00
1B Blue cover, signed. 3.00
3 . . . . 3.00
4 . . . . 3.00
5 flip book with Boston Bombers . . 3.00

SEARCHERS: APOSTLE OF MERCY
Caliber, 1997
1 (of 2) 4.00

2 . . . . 4.00

Vol 2?
1 . . . . 3.00
2 . . . . 3.00
3 (of 3) 48pg 4.00

SECRET FILES
Angel Entertainment, 1996
0 gold edition 7.00
0 commemorative edition 3.00
1 . . . . 3.00
1 spooky silver foil edition 6.00
2 . . . . 3.00
2 deluxe 6.00
Spec. Secret Files vs. Vampire Girls:
    The Vampire Effece (1997) . . . 3.00
Pin-up Book Secret Files: Erotic
    Experiments (1997) 3.00
Spec.#1 Secret Files: F.B.I.
    Conspiracy (1997)F:Sabrina
    & Susanna Sorenson 3.00

SECRET FILES:
THE STRANGE CASE
Angel Entertainment, 1996
0 by David Campiti & Al Rio 3.00
1 by David Campiti & Al Rio 3.00

SECRET MESSAGES
NBM Books, 2001
1 Abductions, pt.1 . . . . 3.00
2 Abductions, pt.2 . . . . 3.00
3 Abductions, pt.3 . . . . 3.00
4 Abductions, pt.4 . . . . 3.00
5 Abductions, pt.5 . . . . 3.00

SECTION 8
Noir Press, 1995
1 Anthology series 2.50
2 thru 6 . . . . @2.50
7 `Retribution,' pt.1 . . . . 2.50
8 `Retribution,' pt.2 . . . . 2.50
9 . . . . 2.50
10 `Chance' 2.50

SEEKER
Caliber `Core', 1998
1M by Gary Reed & Chris
    Massarotto, Meadows(c) 3.00
1W David Williams(c) 3.00
1a variant Greg Louden (c) 3.00
1 premium, signed 10.00
2 . . . . 3.00
3 . . . . 3.00
4 . . . . 3.00
5 Gestalt vs. LeAnn Heywood 3.00
Spec. Dawn of Armageddon,
    x-over, 48-pg. 4.00

SEMI-AUTO ANGEL:
SECOND HEAVEN
Alias Enterprises 2006
1 (of 6) 3.50
2 . . . . 3.50

SENTINEL
Harrier, 1986
1 . . . . 2.50
2 thru 4 . . . . @2.50

SERAPHIN
Newcomers Press, 1995
1 I:Roy Torres 3.00

SERENITY ROSE
Amaze Ink/SLG, 2003
1 . . . . 3.00

---

2 thru 6 . . . . @3.00
TPB Vol. 1 Working Through
    the Negativity 13.00

7 GUYS OF JUSTICE, THE
False Idol Studios, 2000
1 Jerque Imperitive,pt.1 . . . . 2.25
2 Jerque Imperitive,pt.2 . . . . 2.25
3 Jerque Imperitive,pt.3 . . . . 2.25
4 thru 11 . . . . @2.25
12 thru 16 . . . . @2.25

777: THE WRATH
Avatar Press, 1998
1 (of 3) by David Quinn & Tim Vigil 3.00
1a wraparound cover 3.50
1c leather cover 6.00
1d royal blue foil logo 75.00
1e signed 15.00
1f foil platinum edition 17.00
2 . . . . 3.00
3 concl. 3.00
TPB 777:The Wrath/
    Faust Fearbook 16.00

SEVENTH SYSTEM, THE
Sirius Entertainment, 1997
1 (of 6) by Roel 3.00
2 thru 6 . . . . @3.00

SFA SPOTLIGHT
Shanda Fantasy Arts, 1999
4 Tales of the Morphing Period 4.50
5 Zebra, by Carl Gafford 4.50
6 Women in Fur 1999 . . . . 5.00
7 Tales From Supermegatopia 5.00
8 Women in Fur 2000 . . . . 5.00
9 Knight & Mouse 5.00
10 Atomic Mouse 5.00
11 Plush Beauties 5.00
12 Courageous Man Adventures . . . 5.00
13 Women in Fur 2001 . . . . 5.00
14 Fission Chicken 5.00
15 Women in Fur 2002 . . . . 5.00
16 Star Quack 5.00

SF Short Stories #1
© Webb Graphics

SF SHORT STORIES
Webb Graphics, 1991
1 . . . . 2.50
2 . . . . 2.50

SHADES OF BLUE
AMP Comics, 2001
1 . . . . 2.50
2 thru 4 . . . . @2.50
5 Silence, pt.3 . . . . 2.50
6 F:Heidi, Marcus 2.50
7 Winter, pt.1 . . . . 3.00
8 Winter, pt.2 . . . . 3.00
9 Winter, pt.3 . . . . 3.00
10 . . . . 3.00

Digital Webbing, 2003
1 thru 5 . . . . @3.00
TPB Vol. 1 . . . . 12.00

Devil's Due Publishing, 2005
Digest #1 . . . . 11.00
Digest #2 . . . . 11.00

SHADES OF GRAY
COMICS AND STORIES
Caliber Tapestry, 1996
1 . . . . 3.00
2 . . . . 3.00
3 . . . . 3.00
4 . . . . 3.00
Super Summer Spec. rep. 4.00

SHADOW CROSS
Darkside Comics, 1995
1 I:Shadow Cross 5.00
2 thru 7 . . . . @2.50

SHADOWGEAR
Antarctic Press, 1999
1 by Locke 3.00
2 . . . . 3.00
3 conclusion 3.00

SHADOWALKER
Aircel
1 thru 4 . . . . @2.25

SHADOW SLASHER
Pocket Change Comics, 1994
1 I:Shadow Slasher 2.50
2 V:Riplash 2.50
3 F:Matt Baker 2.50
4 Evolution 2.50
5 F:Riplash 2.50
6 Next Victim. 2.50
7 What Can Kill Him 2.50
8 . . . . 2.50
9 final issue 2.50

SHANDA [THE PANDA]
Mu, 1992
1 . . . . 2.50

Antarctic Press, 1993
1 thru 11 . . . . @2.75
12 thru 14 . . . . @3.00
Med Systems
15 and 16 . . . . @2.25
Vision Comics, 1996
17 by Mike Curtis & Michelle Light . 2.25
18 `Rocky Horror Picture Show' . . . 2.25
19 `Shine on Me, Cajun Moon' 2.50
20 falling in love 2.50
22 Bright Eyes 3.00
Shanda Fantasy, 1999
23 Sweet Young Things 3.00
24 graduation night 3.00
25 48-pg. 5.00
26 thru 30 . . . . @3.00
31 thru 33 . . . . @3.00
34 48-pg. 5.00
35 thru 44 . . . . @5.00
45 Homeless 5.00
46 Dogfight. 5.00

SHANGHAIED
Eternity
1 & 2 . . . . @2.25
3 & 4 . . . . @2.25

SHARDS
Acension Comics, 1994
1 I:Silver, Raptor, RIpple. 2.50
2 F:Anomoly 2.50

SHATTERED EARTH
Eternity, 1988–89
1 thru 9 . . . . @2.25

Shatterpoint #3
© *Eternity*

SHATTERPOINT
Eternity, 1990
1 thru 4 Broid miniseries . . . . . . @2.25

SHEBA
Vol. 2, Sirius Dogstar, 1997
1 by Walter S. Crane IV 2.50
2 thru 4 . . . . @2.50
Sick Mind Press
5 thru 7 . . . . @3.00
TPB Vol. 2 (2000) 16.00
TPB Vol. 3 (2004) 18.00
Vol 3, Shanda Fantasy Arts, 2001
1 by Walter Crane IV 5.00
2 thru 4 . . . . @5.00

SHE-CAT
AC Comics, 1989
1 thru 4 . . . . @2.50

SHE-DEVILS ON WHEELS
Aircel, 1992
1 thru 3 by Bill Marimon 3.00

SHERLOCK HOLMES
Eternity, 1988
1 thru 22 . . . . @2.25

SHERLOCK HOLMES
Caliber/Tome Press, 1997
1-shot Dr. Jekyll and Mr. Holmes by
Steve Jones & Seppo Makinen. 3.00
1-shot Return of the Devil 4.00
1-shot Return of the Devil, signed . . 4.00

GN Adventure of the Opera Ghost . 7.00
TPB Case of Blind Fear 13.00
TPB Scarlet in Gaslight 13.00
TPB Sussex Vampire 13.00

SHERLOCK HOLMES CASEBOOK
Eternity
1 and 2 . . . . @2.25

SHERLOCK HOLMES: CHRONICLES OF CRIME AND MYSTERY
Northstar
1 'The Speckled Band' 2.25

SHERLOCK HOLMES: HOUND OF THE BASKERVILLES
Caliber/Tome Press, 1997
1 (of 3) by Martin Powell & PO 3.00

SHERLOCK HOLMES: MARK OF THE BEAST
Caliber/Tome Press, 1997
1 (of 3) by Martin Powell
& Seppo Makinen 3.00
2 . . . . 3.00
GN 13.00

SHERLOCK HOLMES MYSTERIES
Moonstone, 1997
1-shot by Joe Gentile & Richard
Gulick. 3.00
1-shot Sherlock Holmes and the
Clown Prince of London (2001). 3.00
TPB Vol. 1 . . . . 19.00
TPB Vol. 2 . . . . 15.00

SHERLOCK HOLMES OF THE '30's
Eternity
1 thru 7 strip rep. . . . . @3.00

SHERLOCK HOLMES READER
Caliber 'Tome Press', 1998
1 Curse of the Beast. 4.00
2 The Loch Ness Horror 4.00
3 The Loch Ness Horror 4.00
4 The Loch Ness Horror 4.00
5 . . . . 4.00

SHERLOCK HOLMES: RETURN OF THE DEVIL
Adventure, 1992
1 V:Moriarty. 2.50
2 V:Moriarty. 2.50

SHERLOCK JUNIOR
Eternity
1 Rep.NewspaperStrips 2.25
2 Rep.NewspaperStrips 2.25
3 Rep.NewspaperStrips 2.25

SHI
Crusade, 1999
0 rough cut edition 5.00
0 ashcan, signed. 10.00
Spec.#1 Black,White & Red. 3.00
Spec. San Diego (Con) Art of War
Tour Book 1998 . . . . 10.00

Spec. Lim. Ed. Shi/Daredevil
Banzai 14.00
Spec.#1 Kaidan, macabre 3.00
Spec.#1 Kaidan, signed & numb. . 20.00
Spec. Shi/First Wave, Voices
of the Dead x-over (2001) 3.00
Spec. Shi/FirstWave,variant BiT(c) . 3.00
Spec. Shi/FirstWave,signed. 10.00
Spec. First Wave/Shi, Voices of
the Dead, pt.2 x-over (2001) . . . 3.00
Spec. FirstWave/Shi,variant BiT(c) . 3.00
Coll. Ed. Heaven & Earth,
Yin & Yang,96-pg. 6.00
Year of the Dragon preview book . . 3.00
Year of the Dragon tour book 5.00
Year of the Dragon tour Wizard . . . 5.00
Year of the Dragon tour San Diego . 5.00
Umadoshi Tour Book, 2002 . . . . . 5.00
Umadoshi, Tour Book, sketch (c). . . 5.00
Umadoshi, Tour Book, Pittsburgh . . 5.00
Tour Book, Art of War, remarked . . 20.00
Tour Bok Year of the Dragon,
remarked 20.00
Tour Book, Year of the Serpent
remarked 20.00

Avatar Press, 2005/ Avatar Fan Club
Shi: Poisoned Paradise preview . . . 6.00
Shi: Pandora's Box preview. 6.00

SHI: THE ILLUSTRATED WARRIOR
Crusade Entertainment, 2002
1 (of 7) BiT 3.00
2 BiT thru 7 . . . . @3.00

SHI: SEMPO
Avatar, 2003
1/2 Prism Foil Edition. 13.00
1/2 Royal Blue Edition 75.00
1/2 Prism Foil (c) 13.00
Preview edition. 2.25
Preview variant (c). 6.00
Preview wraparound (c). 6.00
Preview prism foil (c) 13.00
1 . . . . 3.50
1a variant (c). 3.50
2 . . . . 3.50
2a variant (c). 3.50
2b wraparound (c). 4.00

SHIP OF FOOLS
Caliber, 1996
1 signed edition. 3.00
2 'Dante's Compass' 3.00
3 The Great Escape begins 3.00
4 MiA. 3.00
5 MiA. 3.00
Spec. #1, Bon Voyage, Go to Hell,
Mama Hades 4.00
TPB sci-fi action/adventure 12.00
continued: See Image Comics

SHOCK THE MONKEY
Millennium
1 & 2 Entering the Psychotic Mind . 4.00

SHONEN JUMP
Viz Communications, 2002
1 thru 8 . . . . @5.00
Vol. 2
1 thru 12 . . . . @5.00
Vol. 3
1 thru 10 . . . . @5.00
35 thru 49. . . . . @5.00

SHOUJO
Antarctic Press, 2003
1 . . . . 6.00
2 thru 4 . . . . @6.00
Pocket Manga #1 . . . . 10.00
Pocket Manga #2 . . . . 10.00

SHRED
CFW
1 thru 10 . . . . @2.25

SHRIEK
Fantaco
1 . . . . 5.00
2 . . . . 5.00
3 . . . . 8.00

SHURIKEN
Victory, 1986
1 Reggi Byers 5.00
1a 2nd printing 2.50
2 . . . . 3.00
3 . . . . 2.50
4 . . . . 2.50
5 thru 13 . . . . @2.50
Graphic Nov. Reggie Byers 8.00

SHURIKEN
Eternity, 1991
1 Shuriken vs. Slate 2.50
2 Neutralizer, Meguomo 2.50
3 R:Slate 2.50
4 Morgan's Bodyguard Serrate . . . 2.50
5 Slate as Shuriken & Megumo . . . 2.50
6 Hunt for Bionauts, final issue . . . 2.50

SHURIKEN: COLD STEEL
Eternity, 1989
1 . . . . 2.50
2 . . . . 2.50
3 thru 6 . . . . @2.50

SHURIKEN TEAM-UP
ETernity, 1989
1 thru 3 . . . . @2.50

SIEGEL & SHUSTER
Eclipse, 1984
1 . . . . 2.50
2 . . . . 2.50

SILBUSTER
Antarctic Press, 1994
1 thru 10 . . . . @3.50
11 I:Kizuki Sister 3.50
12 thru 14 . . . . @3.50
15 . . . . 4.00
16 thru 19 . . . . @3.50
TPB Rep. #1–#4 . . . . 11.00
TPB Vol.2 . . . . 11.00

SILENT INVASION
Renegade, 1986
1 . . . . 4.00
2 thru 12, final issue . . . . @3.00
Combined Ed. #1 & #2 . . . . 17.00

SILENT INVASION
Caliber
4 Red Shadows, pt.1 . . . . 3.00
5 Red Shadows, pt.2 . . . . 3.00

SILENT INVASION: ABDUCTIONS
Caliber, 1998
1 by Larry Hancock & Michael
  Cherkos 3.00

Silent Mobius Love and Chaos #1
© *Viz Communications*

SILENT MOBIUS
Viz Communications
Part 1 thru Part 4: See Color
Part 5 INTO THE LABYRINTH, 1999
1 (of 6) by Kia Asamiya 3.00
2 thru 4 . . . . @3.00
5 & 6 . . . . @3.25
Part 6 KARMA, 1999
1 (of 7) by Kia Asamiya 3.25
2 thru 7 . . . . @3.25
Part 7 CATASTROPHE, 2000
1 (of 6) by Kia Asamiya 3.00
2 thru 6 . . . . @3.00
Part 8 LOVE & CHAOS, 2000
1 thru 7 . . . . @3.00
Part 9 ADVENTURERS, 2001
1 thru 6 (of 6) . . . . @3.00
Part 10 TURNABOUT, 2002
1 (of 6) by Kia Asamiya 3.00
2 thru 6 . . . . @3.00
Part 11 BLOOD, 2002
1 (of 5) by Kia Asamiya 3.00
2 thru 5 . . . . @3.00
Part 12 HELL, 2003
1 thru 3 . . . . @3.00

SILENT RAPTURE
Brainstorm, 1996
1 Jacob Grimm vs. Six Devils
  of Twilight 3.00
1a Vicious variant edition 5.00
Avatar Press, 1997
2 by Jude Millien 3.00
2a deluxe (c) 10.00

SILLY DADDY
Joe Chiappetta, 1995
1 . . . . 3.50
2 thru 5 . . . . 3.00
6 thru 10 . . . . @2.75
11 thru 18 . . . . @2.75
TPB The Long Goodbye 8.00
TPB A Death in the Family 9.00

SILVER STORM
Aircel, 1990
1 thru 4 . . . . @2.25

SIMON/KIRBY READER
1 . . . . 2.50

SINBAD
Adventure, 1989
1 . . . . 2.50
2 . . . . 2.50
3 . . . . 2.50
4 . . . . 2.50

SINBAD: HOUSE OF GOD
Adventure Comics, 1991
1 Caliph's Wife Kidnapped 2.50
2 Magical Genie 2.50
3 Escape From Madhi 2.50
4 A:Genie 2.50

SINNAMON
Catfish Comics, 1995
1 remastered 2.75
1a remastered deluxe 3.75
6 thru 8 . . . . @2.75
Mythic Comics
9 `Ashes to Ashes—The Pyre-Anna
  Saga,' pt.2 . . . . 2.75
10 `Twas Beauty Bashed
  The Beast' 2.75
11 . . . . 2.75
12 M.G.Delaney (c) 2.75
12 Poliwko (c) 2.75
Archives #1 . . . . 2.75

SISTER ARMAGEDDON
Dramenon Studios
1 & 2 Nun with a Gun . . . . @2.50
3 Mother Superior 2.50
4 V:Apoligon 3.00

SKELETON KEY
Amaze Ink, 1995
1 1 I:Skeleton Key 4.00
1 2nd printing 3.00
2 F:Tansin 3.00
3 V:Japanese Burglar 3.00
4 V:Closet Monster 3.00
5 thru 10 . . . . @3.00
11 . . . . 3.00
12 . . . . 3.00
14 by Andi Watson 3.00
15 `The Celestial Calendar' 3.00
16 thru 30 . . . . @3.00
Spec. 5.00
TPB Vol. 1, Threshold rep.#1–#6 . 12.00
TPB Vol.2 Celestial Calendar,
  rep.#7–#18 . . . . 20.00
TPB Vol. 3, Telling Tales,
  rep. #19–#24 . . . . 13.00
TPB Vol. 4, Cats & Dogs, rep.
  #25–#30 . . . . 13.00
TPB Vol. 5 Roots 13.00
Spec.Skeleton Key/Sugar Kat 3.00
VOL 2
1 (of 4) 3.00
2 . . . . 3.00
3 . . . . 3.00
4 conclusion 3.00

SKIN 13
Entity/Parody, 1995
1/2a Grungie/Spider-Man 2.50
1/2b Heavy Metal 2.50
1/2c Gen-Et Jackson 2.50

SKULL MAN
Tokyopop Press, 2000
1 (of 5) 3.00
2 thru 5 . . . . @3.00

SKUNK, THE
Entity Comics, 1997
#Uno........................ 2.75
5 BMs 2.75
6 BMs 2.75
Collection #1 rep. #1–#3 .... 5.00
Collection #1a signed & numbered 10.00
Collection #2 rep. #4–#6 ..... 5.00

SKUNK/FOODANG
FOODANG/SKUNK
Entity Comics
Spec. 1 BMs, BMs(c)........... 2.75
Spec. 1a BMs, Mike Duggan(c).... 2.75

SKYNN & BONES:
DEADLY ANGELS
Brainstorm, 1996
1 .... 3.00

SKYNN & BONES:
FLESH FOR FANTASY
Brainstorm, 1997
1 erotic missions............. 3.00
2 erotic missions............. 3.00
Spec. #1 Dare to Bare......... 3.00

SLACK
Legacy Comics
1 Slacker Anthology 2.50
2 Loser 2.50

SLACKER COMICS
Slave Labor, 1994
1 thru 15 by Doug Slack .... @3.00
16 .... 3.00
17 .... 3.00
18 .... 3.00
19 .... 3.00
TPB Randy Sells Out, rep.#1–#4 . 12.00

SLAM DUNK
Gutsoon! Entertainment, 2003
TPB Vol. 1 .... 10.00
TPB Vol. 2 thru Vol. 5......... @10.00

SLAUGHTERHOUSE
Caliber
1 Bizarre medical Operations..... 3.00
2 House of Death 3.00
3 House of Death 3.00
4 Dead Killer vs. Mosaic........ 3.00

SLAUGHTERMAN
Comico, 1983
1 .... 2.50
2 .... 2.50

SLAYERS
CPM Manga, 1998
1 by Hajime Kanzaka & Rui
    Araizumi................ 3.00
2 thru 6 .... @3.00
TPB Book 1: Medieval Mayhem .. 16.00
Spec. #1 F:Lina Inverse......... 3.00
Spec. #2 thru #6.............. @3.00
TPB Vol. 1 Touch of Evil (2001)... 16.00
TPB Vol. 2 Notorious........... 16.00
TPB Vol. 3 Lesser of Two Evils ... 16.00
TPB Vol. 4 Spellbound.......... 16.00
GN Vol. 1 Slayers Return 10.00
GN City of Lost Souls 10.00
GN Lina The Teenage Sorceress . 10.00

SLAYERS: SUPER–
EXPLOSIVE DEMON
STORY
CPM Manga, 2001
1 by H. Kanzaka & S. Yoshinaka .. 3.00
2 .... 3.00
3 thru 6 .... @3.00
TPB Book 1 Legend of Darkness . 16.00
TPB Book 2 Legacy of the
    Dragon God............. 16.00

SMILE
Tokyopop Press, 2000
Vol. 3
1 magazine 3.00
2 thru 12 magazine........... @5.00
Vol. 4
1 magazine................. 5.00
2 thru 4 .... @5.00
5 thru 6 .... @6.00
7 .... 5.00

Smith Brown Jones #1
© *Kiwi Studios*

SMITH BROWN JONES
Kiwi Studios, 1997
1 thru 5 .... @3.00
TPB Calm, Cook, and Collected .. 13.00

SMITH BROWN JONES:
ALIEN ACCOUNTANT
Slave Labor, 1998
1 by Jon Hastings............. 3.00
2 .... 3.00
3 .... 3.00
4 .... 3.00
Spec.#1 Halloween Special 3.00
Spec. Convention Mayhem 6.00

SNOWMAN
Hall of Heroes, 1996
1 .... 15.00
1a variant (c)................ 20.00
1 3rd printing................ 2.75
1 San Diego Con. ed. 5.00
2 .... 8.00
2a 2nd printing 2.75
2b variant (c)................ 9.00
3 .... 6.00
3a variant (c)................ 7.00

SNOWMAN
Avatar Press, 1997
0 by Matt Martin, O:Snowman 3.00
0a Frozen Fear extra-bloody 5.00
0b Leather cover.............. 25.00
0c signed 10.00
Spec.#1 Snowman 1944 .... 4.00
Spec.#1 Snowman 1944, deluxe... 5.00
Spec.#1 Snowman 1944, signed .. 10.00
1-shot Flurries, Glynn (c)....... 5.00
1-shotA Flurries, Snowman (c) ... 5.00
TPB Snowman rep. 128-pg. 14.00

SNOWMAN:
DEAD & DYING
Avatar Press, 1997
1 (of 3) by Matt Martin 3.00
1 deluxe 5.00
1 signed 10.00
2 .... 3.00
2 deluxe 5.00
3 by Matt Martin 3.00
3 Frozen Fear................ 5.00
3 White Velvet............... 25.00

SNOWMAN:
HORROR SHOW
Avatar Press, 1998
1 by Matt Martin 3.00
1a Frozen Fear (c)............ 5.00
1b Leather cover.............. 25.00
1 deluxe 5.00

SNOWMAN: 1994
Entity, 1996
1 flip cover #0, by Matt Martin,
    O:Snowman.............. 3.00
1 signed, numbered 7.00
3 .... 2.75
3 deluxe, variant, foil cover..... 3.50
4 .... 2.75
4 deluxe, variant, foil cover...... 3.50

SNOWMAN2
Avatar Press, 1997
1 (of 2) Snowman vs. Snowman .. 3.00
1a Face-off cover 5.00
1b Leather cover.............. 25.00
1c Royal Blue edition 50.00
2 concl..................... 3.00
2a Sudden Death variant cover ... 5.00

SOB: SPECIAL
OPERATIONS BRANCH
Promethean Studios, 1994
1 I:SOB..................... 2.50

SOCKETEER
Kardia
Rocketeer parody.............. 2.25

SOLD OUT
Fantaco, 1986
1 & 2 .... @2.50

SOLO EX-MUTANTS
Eternity
1 thru 6 .... @2.50

SOMETHING DIFFERENT
Wooga Central, 1991
1 .... 2.50
2 .... 2.50

SONAMBULO: SLEEP OF THE JUST
Ninth Circle Studios, 1999
1 (of 3) by Rafael Navarro 3.00
2 . . . . 3.00
3 (of 3) 3.00
TPB Sleep of the Just 15.00
Spec. Strange Tales (2000) 4.00
Spec. Ghost of a Chance (2002) . . . 5.00

SONG OF THE CID
Calibre/Tome
1 Story of El Cid 3.00
2 Story of El Cid concl. 3.00

SONG OF THE SIRENS
Millennium
Earth 3.00
Earth, signed print edition 7.00
Fire 3.00
Fire, signed print edition 10.00
Wind 3.00
Wind collectors edition 5.00
Wind with trading card 5.00
Secrets, Lies, & Videotape Pin-Up
    Special 3.00
Secrets, Lies, & Videotape Pin-Up
    Special, foil logo 6.00
Secrets, Lies, & Videotape Pin-Up
    Special, deluxe 10.00

SOUL
Samson Comics
1 thru 3 F:Sabbeth . . . . @2.50

SOULFIRE
Aircel
1 mini-series 2.25
2 . . . . 2.25
3 . . . . 2.25

SOULSEARCHERS AND CO.
Claypool, 1993–98
1 thru 10 Peter David(s) . . . . @5.00
11 thru 20 . . . . @3.00
21 thru 24 . . . . @3.00
25 ACo&SL(c) 2.50
26 O:Soulsearchers, pt.1 . . . . 2.50
27 O:Soulsearchers, pt.2 . . . . 2.50
28 O:Soulsearchers, pt.3 . . . . 2.50

Southern Knights #22
© Fictioneer

29 O:Soulsearchers, pt.4 . . . . 2.50
30 thru 74 . . . . @2.50
75 thru 81 . . . . @2.50
TPB 13.00

SOUTHERN KNIGHTS
Guild, 1983
1 See Crusaders
2 . . . . 7.00
3 and 4 . . . . @5.00
5 thru 7 . . . . @4.00

Fictioneer, 1985
8 thru 11 . . . . @3.00
12 thru 33 . . . . @3.00
34 . . . . 3.00
35 The Morrigan Wars Pt.#2 . . . . . 3.50
36 Morrigan Wars Pt.#5 . . . . 3.50
37 Hell in a Handbasket 3.00
Ann. #1 . . . . 2.50
DreadHalloweenSpec #1 . . . . 2.50
Primer #1 . . . . 2.50

SOUTHERN SQUADRON
Aircel, 1990
1 thru 4 . . . . @2.25

Eternity
1 I:SQUAD 2.50
2 . . . . 2.25
3 . . . . 2.25
4 . . . . 2.25

SOUTHERN SQUADRON FREEDOM OF INFO. ACT.
Aircel, 1992
1 F.F.#1 Parody/Tribute cov. 2.50
2 A:Waitangi Rangers 2.50
3 . . . . 2.50

SPACE ARK
Apple, 1986
1 & 2 see color
3 . . . . 2.50
4 . . . . 2.50
5 . . . . 2.50

SPACE BEAVER
Ten-Buck Comics, 1986
1 . . . . 2.50
2 . . . . 2.50
3 O&I:Stinger 2.50
4 A:Stinger 2.50
5 . . . . 2.50
6 O:Rodent 2.50
7 thru 12 . . . . @2.50

SPACED
Anthony Smith Publ., 1988
1 I:Zip; 800 printed 40.00
2 . . . . 25.00
3 I:Dark Teddy 15.00
4 . . . . 15.00
5 and 6 . . . . @5.00
7 and 8 . . . . @2.50

Eclipse
9 . . . . 2.50
10 . . . . 2.50
11 thru 13 . . . . @2.50

SPACE PATROL
Adventure, 1992
1 thru 3 . . . . 2.50

SPACE USAGI
Mirage Studios, 1992
1 Stan Sakai,Future Usagi 3.00
2 Stan Sakai,Future Usagi 3.00
3 Stan Sakai,Future Usagi 3.00

SPACE WOLF
Antarctic Press
1 From Albedo,by Dan Flahive 2.50

SPANDEX TIGHTS
Lost Cause Prod.
Vol. 1, 1994
1 thru 6 . . . . @2.50
Vol. 2, 1997
1 . . . . 2.50
2 prelude to Space Opera 3.00
6 . . . . 3.00
Spec. Vs. Mighty Awful Sour
    Rangers, signed 3.00

SPANDEX TIGHTS PRESENTS: SPACE OPERA
Lost Cause Productions, 1997
Part 1 by Bryan J.L. Glass & Bob
    Dix, parody 3.00
Part 1, signed, Star Wars parody . . . 3.00
Part 2 `Star Bored,' pt.2 . . . . 3.00
Part 3 . . . . 3.00

SPANDEX TIGHTS PRESENTS: THE GIRLS OF '95
Lost Cause Productions
1 The Good, Bad and Deadly,
    signed (1997) 4.00

SPANDEX TIGHTS PRESENTS: WIN A DREAM DATE WITH SPANDEX-GIRL
Lost Cause Productions
1 (of 3) (1998) 3.00
2 . . . . 3.00
3 . . . . 3.00

SPANDEX TIGHTS: THE LOST ISSUES
Lost Cause Productions
1 (of 4) 3.00
2 . . . . 3.00
3 . . . . 3.00
4 concl. 3.00

SPANK THE MONKEY
Arrow Comics, 1999
1 by Randy Zimmerman 3.00
2 thru 6 . . . . @3.00
Skip Month Spec.#1 . . . . 3.00

SPANK THE MONKEY ON THE COMIC MARKET
Arrow Comics, 2000
1 (of 3) by Randy Zimmerman 3.25
2 and 3 . . . . @3.25

SPARKPLUG
Hero Graphics
1 From League of Champions 3.00

SPARKPLUG SPECIAL
Heroic Publishing
1 V:Overman 2.50

SPARROW
Millennium, 1995
1 I:Sparrow 3.00

2 . . . . 3.00
3 Valley of Fire 2.50

SPEED RACER CLASSICS
Now, 1998
1 . . . . 3.00
1a 2nd Printing 2.25

SPENCER SPOOK
A.C.E. Comics
1 and 2 . . . . @2.25
3 thru 8 . . . . @2.25

SPICY TALES
Eternity, 1998
1 thru 13 . . . . @2.25
14 thru 20 . . . . @2.25
Special #2 . . . . 2.25

SPIDER KISS
1 Harlan Ellison 4.00

Spineless Man #1
© *Parody Press*

SPINELESS MAN
Parody Press, 1992
1 Spider-Man 2099 spoof 2.50

SPIRIT, THE
Kitchen Sink, 1986
Note: #1 to #11 are in color
12 thru 86 WE,rep (1986–92) . . . @3.00
GN The Spirit Casebook 17.00
TPB Vol.2 All About P'Gell 19.00
GN The Spirit Jam, 50 artists in
  48-pg. (1998). 6.00

SPIRIT, THE:
THE ORIGIN YEARS
Kitchen Sink, 1997
1 F:The Origin of the Spirit 3.00
2 F:The Black Queen's Army 3.00
3 F:Palyachi,The Killer Clown. . . . 3.00
4 F:The Return of the Orang 3.00
5 WE. 3.00
6 WE,Kiss of Death 3.00
7 F:The Kidnapping of Ebony 3.00
8 F:Christmas Spirit of 1940 . . . . . 3.00
9 WE 3.00
10 F:The Substitute Spirits. 3.00

SPIRITS
Mindwalker, 1995
1 thru 3 Silver City 3.00
4 Caleb Escapes Zeus 3.00

SPITTIN' IMAGE
Eclipse, 1992
1 Marvel & Image parody 2.50

SPONGEBOB
SQUAREPANTS
Tokyopop Press, 2003
GN Vol. 1 Krusty Krap Adventures . 8.00
GN Vol. 2 Friends Forever. 8.00
GN Vol. 3 thru Vol. 5 . . . . @8.00

SQUEE
Slave Labor, 1997
1 by Jhonen Vasquez 5.00
1a 2nd printing 3.00
2 . . . . 3.00
3 . . . . 3.00
4 . . . . 3.00
TPB 16.00

STAIN
Fathom Press, 1998
1 Byler (c) 3.00
1a Vigil (c). 3.00
1b limited edition. 8.00
2 . . . . 3.00
2a Vigil (c). 3.00
3 . . . . 3.00
3a Vigil (c). 3.00
4 . . . . 3.00
4a Vigil (c). 3.00
5 King cover 3.00
5a Ang cover. 3.00
6 . . . . 3.00
7 . . . . 3.00

STAINLESS STEEL
ARMIDILLO
Antarctic Press, 1995
1 I:Saisni, Tanla Badan. 3.00
2 V:Mirage. 3.00
3 V:Mirage. 3.00
4 Spirit of Gaia 3.00
5 V:Giant. 3.00
6 finale 3.00

STAR BLEECH
THE GENERATION GAP
Parody Press
1 Parody 4.00

STARCHILD
Taliesin Press, 1992–97
0 . . . . 15.00
1 . . . . 20.00
1a 2nd printing 4.00
2 . . . . 18.00
2a 2nd printing 4.00
3 . . . . 8.00
4 . . . . 6.00
5 thru 13 . . . . @5.00
14 . . . . 3.00

Coppervale
TPB Coll. Ed. Awakenings, rep.
  #1–#12. . . . . 5.00
Essential Starchild, Book 3 . . . . . 7.00
Essential Starchild, Book 4 . . . . . 7.00
Essential Starchild, Book 5 . . . . . 7.00

STARCHILD:
CROSSROADS
Coppervale, 1995
1 thru 4, reoffer, by James Owen @3.00
TPB Coll. Ed.112-pg. 12.00
Conoisseurs Edition. 100.00

STARGATE: ATLANTIS
Avatar Press/
Pulsar Press, 2005
Preview 2.50
Preview photo (c). 3.00
Preview painted (c) 3.00
Preview Ready to Serve (c). 6.00
Preview Weir painted (c) 6.00
Preview Chicago Gold Seal (c) . . . 5.00
Preview Look to the Future (c) . . . 6.00
Preview Royal blue foil (c) 75.00
Preview Royal Prism (c) 13.00

STARGATE:
THE NEW ADVENTURES
COLLECTION
Entity, 1997
1 rep. Underworld; One Nation
   Under Ra 6.00
1a photo cover 5.00

STARGATE: ONE
NATION UNDER RA
Entity, 1997
1 . . . . 3.00
1a deluxe 3.50

STARGATE: REBELLION
Entity, 1997
1 (of 3) from novel, sequel to movi13.00
1 deluxe 3.50
2 . . . . 3.00
2 deluxe 3.50
3 (of 3) 3.00
3 foil cover 3.50
GN rep. 80-pg. 8.00
GN photo (c) 8.00

STARGATE:
UNDERWORLD
Entity, 1997
1 . . . . 3.00
1a deluxe 3.50

STAR HAWKS
ACG Comics, 2000
1 by Ron Goulart & Gil Kane 3.00
2 . . . . 3.00
3 . . . . 3.00

STARK: FUTURE
Aircel, 1986
1 . . . . 2.50
2 thru 7 . . . . @2.50
8 . . . . 2.50
9 thru 14 . . . . @2.50

STARLIGHT AGENCY
Antarctic Press, 1991
1 I:Starlight Agency. 2.25
2 Anderson Kidnapped 2.25
3 . . . . 2.25

STAR RANGERS
Adventure, 1987
1 thru 3 . . . . @3.00
4 . . . . 2.50

BOOK II

1	2.50
2	2.50

STAR REACH
Taliesin Press, 1974

1 HC,I:CodyStarbuck	15.00
2 DG,JSn,NA(c)	6.00
3 FB	6.00
4 HC,HC(c)	6.00
5 JSon,HC(c)	6.00
6 GD,Elric	6.00
7 DS	6.00
8 CR,KSy	6.00
9 KSy	6.00
10 KSy	6.00
11 GD	6.00
12 MN,SL	10.00
13 SL,KSy	10.00
14	10.00
15	10.00
16 thru 18	@9.00

STAR WESTERN
ACG Comics, 2000

1	6.00
2 John Wayne	6.00
3 Clint Eastwood	6.00
4 Clayton Moore	6.00
5 F:Tonto	6.00
6 F:Fess Parker	6.00
7 F:Masked Riders of the Plains	6.00
8 James Arness-Matt Dillon(c)	6.00
9 Sam Elliott photo (c)	6.00
10 Chuck "Rifleman" Connors	6.00
11 John Hart	6.00
12 Davy Crockett, Daniel Boone	6.00
13 Gabby Hayes	6.00
TPB Compendium, #1–#4	20.00

STATIC

1 SD	2.25
2 SD	2.25
3 SD	2.25

STEALTH FORCE
Malibu, 1987

1 thru 7	@2.50

Eternity, 1988

8	2.50

STEALTH SQUAD
Petra Comics, 1993

0 O:Stealth Squad	2.50
1 I:Stealth Squad	2.50
2 I:New Member	2.50

Volume II

1 F:Solar Blade	2.50
2 American Ranger Vs.Jericho	2.50

STEELE DESTINES
Nightscapes

1 & 2 I:One Eyed Stranger	3.00
3 Kidnapped by Aliens	3.00

STEVE CANYON
Kitchen Sink

1 thru 14 by Doug Allen	@5.00
3-D Spec. #1 (1986)	6.00

STEVE CANYON
Checker Book 2003

TPB from 1947	18.00
TPB from 1948	19.00
TPB from 1949	16.00
TPB from 1950	18.00
TPB from 1951	18.00
TPB from 1952	18.00

Steve Canyon 3-D Special
© *Kitchen Sink*

TPB from 1953	18.00

STEVE DITKO'S STRANGE AVENGING TALES
Fantagraphics, 1997

1 SD	3.00
2 SD	3.00

STEVE GRANT'S MORTAL SOULS
Avatar Press, 2002

1	3.50
2	3.50
3	3.50
1a thru 3a wraparound (c)s	@4.00

STEVE GRANT'S MY FLESH IS COOL
Avatar Press, 2003

1	3.50
2	3.50
3	3.50
1a thru 3a wraparound (c)s	@3.50

STEVEN
Kitchen Sink

1	4.00
1a 2ndPrinting	3.00
2	4.00
3	3.00
4 and 5	@3.50
TPB The Best of Steven by Doug Allen (1998)	13.00

STICKBOY
Revolutionary

1	2.25
2 thru 5	@2.50

STIG'S INFERNO
Vortex, 1985

1	5.00
2	3.50
3	3.00
4	3.00
5	2.50

Eclipse

6	2.50
7	2.50

STINZ
Fantagraphics, 1989

1	4.00
2	4.00
3	4.00
4	4.00

[2nd series]
Brave New Words, 1990

1 thru 3	2.50

STORMBRINGER
Taliesin Press

1 thru 3	@2.50

STORMWATCHER
Eclipse, 1989

1 thru 4	@2.50

STRANGE BEHAVIOR
Twilite Tone Press

1 LSn,MBr,Short Stories	3.00

STRANGE BREW
Aardvark–Vanaheim

1	5.00

STRANGEHAVEN
Abiogenesis Press, 1995

1 Surrealistic Comic	3.00
2 Secret Brotherhood	3.00
3 thru 10 by Gary S. Millidge	@3.00
11 thru 18	@3.00
TPB Arcadia, rep. #1–#6	15.00
TPB Brotherhood, rep.#7–#12	15.00
TPB Vol. 3 Conspiracies	15.00

STRANGE SPORTS STORIES
Adventure, 1992

1 w/2 card strip	2.50
2 The Pick-Up Game,w/cards	2.50
3 Spinning Wheels,w/cards	2.50
4 thru 6 w/cards	@2.50

STRANGE WEATHER LATELY
Metaphrog, 1997

1	3.50
2 thru 4	@3.50
5 thru 10	@3.00
TPB Vol. 1 rep. #1–#5	10.00
TPB Vol. 2	10.00

STRANGERS IN PARADISE
Antarctic Press, 1993–94

1 by Terry Moore,I:Katchoo	65.00
1a 2nd printing	15.00
1b 3rd printing	5.00
2	45.00
3	35.00

Abstract Studio, 1994

1 TMr, Gold Logo edition	15.00
1a 2nd printing	6.00
2 and 3, Gold Logo edition	@10.00
4	6.00
5 R:Mrs. Parker	6.00
6	5.00
7 Darcey Uses Francine	5.00
8 thru 13 TMr	@4.00

VOL. 2

1 TMr, Gold Logo edition, I Dream of You	3.00
2 thru 13 gold logo	@3.00
TPB I Dream of You	17.00

VOL III, 1997
1 thru 8 See Image
9 TMr,Detective Walsh returns	4.00
10	4.00
11	3.00
12	3.00
13 High School, pt.1 (of 3)	3.00
14 High School, pt.2	10.00
15 High School, pt.3	3.00
16A Francine/Katchoo Princess Warrior (c)	22.00
16B Tambi Princess Warrior (c)	25.00
17	3.00
18 Francine & Datchoo	3.00
19 Lifesize nude of Francine	3.00
20 Night at the Opera	3.00
21 All not well in paradise	3.00
22 The Big Rift	3.00
23 Katchoo moves out	3.00
24 steamy affairs	3.00
25 All Beach, All the Time	3.00
26	3.00
27 at odds with the Big Six	3.00
28 thru 35	@3.00
36 Katchoo vs. Veronica	3.00
37 return to Tennessee	3.00
38 from rags to ritches	3.00
39 Good news and bad news	3.00
40 Engaged to right brother?	3.00
41 Expelled from college	3.00
42 Slumber Party	3.00
43 Tropic Of Desire	3.00
44 Marooned	3.00
45 Francine and Katchoo	3.00
46 Molly & Poo, Borderline Lover	3.00
47 Francine pregnant	3.00
48 Casey's Story	3.00
49 Molly & Poo	3.00
50 Celebrate #50	3.00
51	3.00
52 Francine & Katchoo	3.00
53 My Maiden Voyage	3.00
54 Girl Trouble, pt.1	3.00
55 Girl Trouble, pt.2	3.00
56 Girl Trouble, pt.3	3.00
57 Blue Bird of Happiness	3.00
58 thru 77	@3.00
78 thru 86	@3.00
TPB Vol.4 Love Me Tender	13.00
TPB Vol.5 Immortal Enemies, rep. #6–#12	13.00
TPB Vol. 6 High School	9.00
TPB Vol. 8 My Other Life	15.00
TPB Vol. 9 Child of Rage	16.00
TPB Vol. 10 Tropic of Desire	13.00
TPB Vol. 11 Brave New World	9.00
TPB Vol. 12 Field of GOld	13.00
TPB Vol. 13 Flower to Flame	16.00
TPB Vol. 14 David's Story	9.00
TPB Vol. 15 Tomorrow Now	15.00
TPB Vol. 16	15.00
TPB Vol. 17 Tattoo	15.00
TPB Vol. 18 Love & Lies	15.00
TPB Molly & Poo	9.00
Pocket TPB Vol. 1	18.00
Pocket TPB Vol. 2 thru Vol. 4	18.00
Spec. Sourcebook	3.00
Spec. #93268 Songs & Lyrics	2.75

STRANGELOVE
Entity Comics, 1995
1 I:Strangelove	2.50
2 V:Hyper Bullies	2.50
3 I:Bogie	2.50

STRANGEWAYS
Speakeasy Comics 2005
1	2.50
2 thru 4	@2.50

STRANGE WORLDS
Eternity
1	4.00
2 thru 4	@4.00

RENEGADE PRESS PRESENTS

Strata #2
© Renegade

STRATA
Renegade, 1986
1	3.00
2	2.50
3	2.50
4	2.50
5	2.50
6	2.50

STRAW MEN
All American, 1989
1 thru 5	@2.50
6 thru 8	@2.50

STRAY BULLETS
El Capitan, 1995
1	15.00
1a 2nd & 3rd printing	4.00
2	8.00
2a 2nd printing	3.50
3	7.00
4	7.00
5 Dysfunctional Family	4.00
6 F:Amy Racecar	4.00
7 Virginias Freedom	4.00
8 DL,`Lucky to Have Her'	3.00
9 DL,`26 Guys Named Nick'	3.00
10 DL,`Here Comes the Circus'	3.00
11 DL,`How to Cheer Up Your Best Friend'	3.00
12 DL, People Will be Hurt	3.00
13 DL `Selling Candy'	3.00
14 DL,The Killers arrive,48pg	3.50
15 Sex and Violence	3.00
16	3.00
17 While Ricky Fish Was Sleeping	3.00
18 Sex and Violence, pt.2	3.00
19 Young and sexy	3.00
20 Motel	3.00
21	3.00
22 40-pg.	3.50
23 thru 30	@3.50
31 thru 34	@3.00
35 thru 40	@3.50
41	3.50
TPB Vol. 1 Innocence of Nihilism	12.00
TPB Vol. 2	12.00
TPB Vol. 3	12.00
TPB Vol. 4 rep. #13–#16	12.00
TPB Vol. 5 rep. #17–#20	12.00
TPB Vol. 6	15.00

TPB Vol. 7	15.00
TPB Vol. 8	15.00
10th Anniv. TPBs	
TPB Vol. 1 Innocence of Nihilism	20.00
TPB Vol. 2 Somewhere Out West	20.00
TPB Vol. 3 Other People	20.00

STREET ANGEL
Amaze Ink/SLG, 2004
1	3.00
2 thru 5	@3.00
TPB Vol. 1	15.00

STREET FIGHTER
Ocean Comics, 1986
1 thru 4 limited series	@2.50

STREET FIGHTER II
Udon Entertainment 2005
0 Manga	2.00
1	4.00
2 thru 5	@3.00
2a thru 6a variant (c)s	@3.00
1b thru 6b power foil (c)s	@12.50
TPB Vol. 3 Fighter's Destiny	14.00
TPB Eternal Challenge	35.00
TPB The Ultimate Edition, 448-pg.	50.00

STREET HEROES 2005
Eternity, 1989
1 thru 3	@2.50

STREET MUSIC
Fantagraphics
1	2.75
2	2.75
3	3.00
4	3.00
5	2.50
6	4.00

STREET POET RAY
Fantagraphics, 1989
1	2.50
2	2.50
3	3.00
4	3.00

STREET WOLF
Blackthorne, 1986
1 limited series	2.50
2	2.50
3	2.50
Graphic Novel	7.00

STRIKER: SECRET OF THE BERSERKER
Viz Communications
1 & 2 V:The Berserker	@2.75
3 F:Yu and Maia	2.75

STRIKER: THE ARMORED WARRIOR
Viz Communications, 1992
1 Overture	2.75
2 V:Child Esper	2.75
3 Professor taken hostage	2.75
GN Vol.1 The Armored Warrior	17.00
GN Vol.2 Forest of No Return	16.00

STRONGHOLD
Devil's Due Publishing 2006
1 (of 3) PhH	5.00
2 thru 3	@5.00

B & W PUB.

All comics prices listed are for *Near Mint* condition.

STUDENTS OF
THE UNUSUAL
3 Boys Productions, 2004
1	3.00
2	3.00
3 thru 6	@3.50

STUPID, STUPID RAT
TAILS:THE ADVENTURES
OF BIG JOHNSON BONE
Cartoon Books, 1999
1 I:Big Johnson Bone,FrontierHero	3.00
2	3.00
TPB	10.00

STYGMATA
Entity, 1994
0	3.00
1 V:The Rodent	3.00
2 thru 3	@3.00
Yearbook #1 (1995)	3.00
TPB Dragon Prophet	7.00

SUBTLE VIOLENTS
CFD Productions, 1991
1 Linsner (c&a)	25.00
1a San Diego Con	80.00

SUGAR BUZZ
Slave Labor, 1998
1 by I.Carney & W. Phoenix	3.00
2	3.00
3	3.00
4	3.00
5	3.00
6 F:Ultra Spacers	3.00
7 I:Precious & Percival	3.00
8 thru 10	@3.00

SUGAR RAY FINHEAD
Wolf Press, 1992
1 I&O Sugar Ray Finhead	2.50
2 I:Bessie & Big-Foot Benny the Pit Bull Man	3.00
3 thru 7 Mardi Gras	@3.00
9 & 10	@3.00

SULTRY TEENAGE
SUPER-FOXES
Solson, 1987
1 thru 4 RB,Woj	@2.50

SUPER HERO
HAPPY HOUR
Geekpunk, 2003
1	3.00
2 thru 5	@3.00
TPB Vol. 1	15.00

SUPERMODELS
IN THE RAINFOREST
Sirius, 1998
1 (of 3)	3.00
2 and 3	@3.00

SUPERSWINE
Caliber
1 Parody, I:Superswine	2.50

SURVIVALIST
CHRONICLES
Survival Art
1	6.50
2	6.50

3 I:Bessie & Big Foot Benny	2.25

SURROGATE SAVIOR
Hot Brazer Comic Pub.
1 I:Ralph	2.50
2 Baggage	2.50

SWAN
Little Idylls, 1995
1 thru 3 Ghost of Lord Kaaren	@3.00
4 V:Slake	3.00

SWEET CHILDE
BATTLE BOOK
Advantage Graphics, 1995
1 I:Tasha Radcliffe	2.50

SWEET CHILDE:
LOST CONFESSIONS
Anarchy Bridgeworks, 1997
1 F:Tasha Radcliffe	3.00

SWEET LUCY
Brainstorm Comics
1 with 4 cards	2.50
2	2.50

SWERVE
Amaze Ink, 1995
1 thru 3 by Kyle Hunter	@2.25

SWIFTSURE
Harrier Comics, 1985
1	2.50
2	2.50
3 thru 8	@2.50
9	9.00
9a 2nd printing	2.50
10	2.50
11	2.50

SWITCH B.L.A.Z.E.
MANGA
London Night, 1999
0	3.50
? Con special	5.00
? Con special, Japanese (c)	6.00
1	3.50
1a Elite fan ed.	6.00
1b Anime cell ed.	20.00

SWORD OF VALOR
A Plus Comics
1 JAp,rep.Thane of Bagarth	2.50
2 JAp/MK rep	2.50
3 & 4	@2.50

SWORDS AND SCIENCE
Pyramid
1 thru 3	@2.25

SWORDS OF CEREBUS
Aardvark–Vanaheim
1 rep. Cerebus 1-4	15.00
1a reprint editions	10.00
2 rep. Cerebus 5-8	12.00
2a reprint editions	8.00
3 rep. Cerebus 9-12	12.00
3a reprint editions	8.00
4 rep. Cerebus 13-16	12.00
4a reprint editions	8.00
5 rep. Cerebus 17-20	12.00
5a reprint editions	8.00
6 rep. Cerebus 21-25	12.00
6a reprint editions	8.00

SWORDS OF SHAR-PAI
Caliber, 1991
1 Mutant Ninja Dog	2.50
2 Shar-Pei	2.50
3 Final issue	2.50

SWORDS OF VALORS:
ROBIN HOOD
A Plus Comics
1 rep. of Charlton comics	2.50
2 thru 4	@2.50

System Seven #2
© Arrow

SYSTEM SEVEN
Arrow, 1987
1 thru 4	@2.50

TAKEN UNDER
COMPENDIUM
Caliber
1 rep. Cal Presents #19-#22	3.00

TALES FROM
THE ANIVERSE
Arrow
1 7,400 printed	9.00
2	4.00
3 10,000 printed	2.50
4	2.50
[2nd series]
Massive Comics Group
1 thru 3	@2.25

TALES FROM THE BOG
Aberation Press, 1995
1 thru 4 by Marcus Lusk	@3.00
1a thru 4a Director's cut	@4.00
5 thru 7	@4.00
1a Director's Cut, 32pg.	3.00
2a Director's Cut, 32pg.	4.00
3a Director's Cut, 48pg.	4.00
4a Director's Cut, 40pg.	4.00
8	3.00

TALES FROM THE EDGE
Vanguard, 1993
5	3.00
5a signed	6.00
6	3.00
7	3.00
7a signed	6.00

8	3.00
8a signed	6.00
9	3.00
10	3.00
10a signed	6.00
11 F:Sacred Monkeys	3.00
12 spec.F:Steranko	4.00
12a signed, limited	15.00
13 F:Steranko	3.00
14	3.00
15 Sienkiewicz special	4.00
Spec. Nightstand Chillers Benefit Edition	5.00
Spec. Nightstand Chillers, signed	10.00
Spec. Sienkiewicz Special	10.00

TALES FROM THE HEART
Entropy, 1988–94

1 thru 5	@2.50
6	2.50
7	2.50

TALES OF LEONARDO
Mirage Studios 2006

1 (of 4) Blind Sight	3.25
2 thru 4 Blind Sight	@3.25

TALES OF THE BEANWORLD
Eclipse, 1985

1	10.00
2	4.00
3	2.50
4 I:Beanish	2.50
5 thru 20	@2.50
21	3.00

TALES OF THE FEHNRIK
Antarctic Press, 1995

1 I:Lady Zeista	3.00

TALES OF THE JACKALOPE
Blackthorne, 1986

1	4.00
2	3.00
3 and 4	@2.50
5 thru 9	@2.50

TALES OF THE NINJA WARRIORS
CFW

1 thru 14	@2.25
15 thru 19	@2.25

TALES OF THE PLAGUE
Eclipse

1 RCo	4.00

TALES OF THE SUNRUNNERS
Sirius, 1986
Vol. 2

1 thru 3	@2.50
Christmas Spec.	2.50

TALES OF THE TEENAGE MUTANT NINJA TURTLES
Mirage, 1987

1	8.00
1B 2nd printing	3.00
2	8.00
3	5.00
4	5.00
5	5.00

6 thru 9	@4.00

Mirage Studios, 2004

1	3.00
2 thru 9	@3.00
10 thru 16	@3.25
17 thru 29	@3.25
TPB Vol. 1 The Collected Books	12.00

TALES TOO TERRIBLE TO TELL
New England Comics, 1991

1 thru 6 Pre-code horror stories	@3.50

TALL TAILS
Vision Comics, 1998

1 Earth Shaking	3.00
1a Anime Blast cover	3.00
1b Spell Warrior cover	3.00
1c signed	5.00
2 Fire Quest, Pt.1	3.00
3 Fire Quest, Pt.2	3.00
4 Pain and Compromises,pt.1	3.00
5	3.00
6 Trail Blazing, pt.1	3.00
7 Trail Blazing, pt.2	3.00
8 When It Almost Happened	3.00
GN Vol. 1	9.00

TANTALIZING STORIES
Tundra, 1992

1 F:Frank & Montgomery Wart	2.25
2 Frank & Mont.stories cont.	2.25

TAOLAND
Sunitek

1 V:The Crocodile Warlord	2.25
2 & 3 I:New Enemy	@3.25

TASK FORCE ALPHA
Academy Comics

1 I:Task Force Alpha	3.50

TEAM NIPPON
Aircel

1 thru 7 by Barry Blair	@2.25

TECHNOPHILIA
Brainstorm Comics

1 with 4 cards	2.50

TEENAGE MUTANT NINJA TURTLES*
Mirage Studios, 1981
***Counterfeits Exist - Beware**

1 I:Turtles	275.00
1a 2nd printing	25.00
1b 3rd printing	20.00
1c 4th printing	12.00
1d 5th printing	4.00
2	75.00
2a 2nd printing	12.00
2b 3rd printing	4.00
3	55.00
3a 2nd printing	3.50
3b Special printing,rare	50.00
4	40.00
4a 2nd printing	3.50
5 A:Fugitoid	20.00
5a 2nd printing	3.50
6 A:Fugitoid	15.00
6a 2nd printing	2.50
7 A:Fugitoid	8.00
7a 2nd printing	2.50
8 A:Cerebus	9.00
9	8.00
10 V:Shredder	8.00
11 A:Casey Jones	6.00

Teenage Mutant Ninja Turtles #59
© Mirage Studios

12 thru 18	@6.00
19 Return to NY	4.00
20 Return to NY	4.00
21 Return to NY,D:Shredder	4.00
22 thru 32	@4.00
33 color, Corben	3.50
34 Toytle Anxiety	3.50
35 Souls Withering	3.50
36 Souls Wake	3.50
37 Twilight of the Rings	3.50
38 Spaced Out Pt.1, A:President Bush	3.50
39 Spaced Out Pt.2	3.50
40 Spaced Out concl.,I:Rockin' Rollin' Miner Ants (B.U. story)	2.50
41 Turtle Dreams issue	2.50
42 Juliets Revenge	2.50
43 Halls of Lost Legends	2.50
44 V:Ninjas	2.50
45 A:Leatherhead	2.50
46 V:Samurai Dinosaur	2.50
47 Space Usagi	2.50
48 Shades of Grey Part 1	2.50
49 Shades of Grey Part 2	2.50
50 Eastman/Laird,new direction, inc.TM,EL,WS pin-ups	3.00
51 City at War #2	2.50
52 City at War #3	2.50
53 City at War #4	2.50
54 City at War #5	2.50
55 thru 65	@2.50
1990 Movie adaptation	6.50
Spec. The Haunted Pizza	2.50

Volume 2

1 thru 8	@2.75
9 V:Baxter Bot	2.75
10 Mr. Braunze	2.75
11 F:Raphael	2.75
12 V:DARPA	2.75
13 J:Triceraton	2.75

Vol. 4, 2001

1 PLa & Jim Lawson	3.00
2 thru 24 PLa	@3.00
24 thru 30	@3.00

TMNT TRAINING MANUAL

1	5.00
2 thru 5	@3.00

TEMPEST COMICS PRESENTS
Academy Comics

1 I:Steeple, Nemesis	2.50

B & W PUB.

TEMPORARY
Origin Comics, 2005
1 Cubes and Ladders	4.00
2 The Real Me	4.00
3 The Real Me	3.00
4 A Dirt Nap	3.00
5 Twilight	3.00
TPB Vol. 1	15.00

10TH MUSE/ DEMONSLAYER
Avatar Press, 2002
Preview, 16-pg.	2.25
1 MMy(c)	3.50
1a Matt Martin (c)	3.50
1b SSh(c)	3.50
1c Karl Waller (c)	3.50
1d wraparound (c)	3.50
1e Red Leather (c)	25.00
1f prism foil edition	13.00
1g Aftermath (c)	6.00
1h Art Nouveau (c)	6.00
1/2 MMy bikini (c)	6.00
1/2 Conflict edition	6.00
1/2 Catfight (c)	6.00

TERROR ON THE PLANET OF THE APES
Adventure Comics, 1991
1 MP,collectors edition	2.50
2 MP, the Forbidden Zone	2.50
3	2.50

TERRY AND THE PIRATES
ACG Comics, 1998
1 by Georges Wunder, Charlton reprint	3.00
2	3.00
3	3.00

TERRY & THE PIRATES
Tony Raiola, 2001
Feature Comics #6, 1938 reprint	8.00
Feature Comics #2 1937 reprint	8.00
Feature Comics #28 1938 reprint	8.00
Raven Evermore 1941 reprint	8.00

TERRY MOORE'S PARADISE, TOO
Abstract Studio, 2000
1	3.00
2	3.00
3	3.00
4	3.00
5 thru 14	@3.00
TPB Vol. 1 Drunk Ducks	16.00
TPB Vol. 2 Checking for Weirdos	16.00

TEX BENSON
Metro Comics
1 thru 4	@2.25

39 SCREAMS
Thunder Baas
1 thru 6	@2.25

THEY WERE 11
Viz
1 Galactic University	2.75
2 The Accident	2.75
3 Virus	2.75
4 V:Virus	2.75

THIEVES AND KINGS
I Box, 1994–97
1 F:Ruebel The Intrepid	8.00

Thieves & Kings #24
© I-Box

1a 2nd printing	2.50
2	6.00
2a 2nd printing	2.50
3	5.00
3a 2nd printing	2.50
4	4.00
5	4.00
6 V:Shadow Lady	4.00
7 V:Shadow Lady	3.00
8 thru 18 by Mark Oakley	@3.00
19 thru 24	@2.50
25 thru 36	@2.50
37 thru 39	@2.50
40 thru 47	@3.00
48 thru 49	@3.50
TPB Vol. 1: The Red Book, rep.#1–#6	12.00
TPB Vol. 1: 2nd printing	13.50
TPB Vol. 2: The Green Book	14.00
TPB Vol. 2: 2nd printing	16.50
TPB Vol. 3: The Blue Book	16.50
TPB Vol. 4: Shadow Book	16.50
TPB Vol. 5 The Winter Book	17.00

THORR SUERD OR SWORD OF THOR
Vincent
1	3.00
1a 2nd printing	2.25
2	2.25
3	2.25

THOSE ANNOYING POST BROS.
1 thru 18 see Color
Becomes:

POST BROTHERS
Rip Off, 1991–94
19 thru 38	@2.25

Becomes:

THOSE ANNOYING POST BROS.
Vortex, 1994
39 thru 45	@2.50
46 thru 56	@3.00
57 Russ working on chaos wave	3.00
58 Fearsome chaos wave	3.00
59 Recondite Silicates	3.00
60	3.00
61 Assassinate JFK's ghost	3.00
62 Post Digestion 64pg.	6.00
63	6.00

GN Distrub the Neighbors	10.00
Ann. #3 Before the Flood, 56pg.	5.00
TPB Das Loot	15.00

THREAT
Fantagraphics, 1985
1	5.00
2	3.00
3 and 4	@2.50
5 thru 10	@2.50

3 X 3 EYES
Innovation
1 Labyrinth of the Demons Eye,Pt.1	2.25
2 Demons Eye, Pt.2	2.25
3 Demons Eye, Pt.3	2.25
4 Demons Eye, Pt.4	2.25
5 Demons Eye, concl.	2.25

THREE GEEKS, THE
3 Finger Prints, 1997
1 by Rich Koslowski, Going to the Con, pt.1	9.00
2 Going to the Con, pt.2	6.00
3 Going to the Con, pt.3 (of 3)	3.00
4	4.00
5 five more geeks	2.50
6 F:Allen	2.50
7	2.50
8 48-pg.	4.00
9 24-pg.	2.50
10 Happy Birthday Allen	2.50
10a variant cover	3.50
11 Happy Birthday Allen, pt.2	2.50
TPB	9.00

THREE ROCKETEERS
Eclipse
1 JK,AW,rep.	2.25
2 JK,AW,rep.	2.25

THREE STRIKES
Oni Press, 2003
1 (of 5)	3.00
2 thru 5	@3.00
TPB	15.00

THRESHOLD
Sleeping Giant, 1996
1	2.50
2	2.50

[2nd Series], 1997
1	2.50
2	2.50
3	2.50

Avatar Press, 1998
1 Snowman cover	4.50
1a Tales of the Cyberangels cover	4.50
1b Furies cover	4.50
1c Fuzzie Dice cover	4.50
2 Snowman cover	5.00
3 Ravening (c)	5.00
4 Donna Mia (c)	5.00
5 Black Reign (c)	5.00
6 Luna cover	5.00
7 Darkness in Collision, Cavewoman(c)	5.00
8 Vigil/Cuda (c)	5.00
9 August (c)	5.00
2a Vigil 9a variant (c)s	@5.00
10 Calico (c)	5.00
11 Scythe (c)	5.00
12 Snowman (c)	5.00
13 Snowman (c)	5.00
14 Kaos Moon (c)	5.00
15 Luna (c)	5.00
16 Scythe (c)	5.00
17 Cimmerian (c)	5.00

Threshold #2
© Avatar

18 Nightvision (c) 5.00
19 Pandora (c). 5.00
20 Kaos Moon (c) 5.00
21 Jungle Girl (c). 5.00
22 . . . . 5.00
23 Ravening (c) 5.00
24 Faust: Singha's Talons 5.00
25 Dark Blue (c). 5.00
26 Dark Blue (c) 5.00
27 Dark blue (c). 5.00
28 Dark blue (c) 5.00
29 Dark Blue (c). 5.00
30 Dark Blue (c). 5.00
10a thru 30a variant (c)s . . . . @5.00
31 Luna (c). 5.00
32 Ravening (c) 5.00
33 Pandora (c). 5.00
34 Pandora (c). 5.00
35 Pandora (c). 5.00
36 Pandora (c). 5.00
37 Pandora (c). 5.00
38 Pandora (c). 5.00
39 Razor (c). 5.00
40 Lookers (c) 5.00
41 Razor (c). 5.00
42 Razor (c). 5.00
43 Razor (c). 5.00
43 Razor (c). 5.00
45 Demonslayer (c) 5.00
46 Demonslayer (c) 5.00
47 Pandora (c). 5.00
31a thru 47a variant (c)s . . . . @5.00
48 Pandora (c). 5.00
49 Pandora (c). 5.00
48a thru 49a connecting (c). 6.00
50 64-pg. 9.00
50 connecting (c)s 9.00
50a variant (c)s . . . . @9.00
51 . . . . 5.00
51b Pandora Western edition 6.00
52 . . . . 5.00
51a and 52a variant (c)s . . . . @5.00
53 . . . . 5.00
53a wraparound (c) 5.00
53b Talented Twosome (c) 6.00
54 . . . . 5.00
54a variant (c) 5.00
54b School Days (c) 6.00
TPB Razor X, 48-pg. 7.00
TPB Razor X, Vol. 2. . . . . 7.00

THRESHOLD OF REALITY
Maintech, 1986
1 5,000 printed 2.50

2 thru 4 . . . . @2.50

THUNDERBIRD
Newcomers Publishing
1 & 2 2 Stories . . . . @3.00
3 . . . . 3.00
4 I:Mercer 3.00
5 R:Raven. 3.00
6 & 7 . . . . @3.00
8 final issue. 3.50
Ann.#1 The Great Escape 3.50

THUNDER BUNNY
Mirage, 1985
1 O:Thunder Bunny 2.50
2 VO:Dr.Fog 2.50
3 I:GoldenMan 2.50
4 V:Keeper 2.50
5 I:Moon Mess 2.50
6 V:Mr.Endall. 2.50
7 VI:Dr.Fog 2.50
8 . . . . 2.50
9 VS:Gen. Agents 2.50
10 thru 12. . . . . @2.50

THUNDER MACE
Rak, 1986
1 Proto type-blue & red very
   rare:1,000 printed 15.00
1a four color cover 3.00
2 thru 5 . . . . @2.50
6 . . . . 2.50
7 . . . . 2.50
Graphic Novel, rep.1-4. . . . . 5.00

TICK
New England Comics, 1988
1 BEd 45.00
1a 2nd printing 10.00
1b 3rd printing 8.00
1c 4th printing 5.00
2 BEd 50.00
2a 2nd printing 10.00
2b 3rd printing 4.00
2c 4th printing 2.50
3 BEd 10.00
3a 2nd printing 3.00
4 BEd 8.00
4a 2nd printing 3.00
5 BEd 8.00
6 BEd 7.00
7 BEd,A:Chairface Chippendale . . . 7.00
8 BEd 6.00
8a Spec.No Logo edition 12.00
9 BEd,A:Chainsaw Vigilante,
   Red Eye. 5.00
10 BEd 5.00
11 thru 12 BEd . . . . @4.00
9 thru 12, new printings . . . . . . @3.00
Spec. Ed. #1, I:Tick 25.00
Spec. Ed. #2, 2nd App. Tick 20.00
Spec. #1 Reprise edition 6.00
TPB Omnibus #1 rep. #1–#6 . . . . 18.00
TPB Omnibus #2 BEd,fifth printing 15.00
TPB Omnibus #3 BEd 11.00
TPB Omnibus #4 BEd 11.00
The Tick Big Yule Log Special 1998 3.50
The Tick Big Yule Log Special 1999 3.50
Tick's Big Yule Log Special 2001 . . 3.50
Big Giant Summer Special #1, The
   Sidekicks are Revolting 3.50
Big Summer Annual #1 . . . . 3.50
Tick's Big Red-N-Green X-mas 4.00
TPB Tick Bonanza #3 . . . . 5.00
TPB Tick Bonanza #4 . . . . 5.00
Spec.#1 Back to School. 3.50
Big Halloween Special #1 . . . . 3.50
Massive Summer Double Spectacle
   Photo-Cover set of 2 . . . . 8.00
13 Pseudo-Tick, not by Edlund . . . 3.50

Big Year 2000 Spectacle 3.50
Big Romantic Adventure #1, 2nd ed. 3.50
Big Tax Time Terror #1. . . . . 3.50
Big Mother's Day Spec. #1 . . . . 3.50
Big Halloween Special 2000 . . . . . . 3.50
Big Father's Day Special 3.50
Big Cruise Ship Vacation Spec.#1 . . 3.50
Massive Summer Double Spec.#1 . . 3.50
Massive Summer Double Spec.#2 . . 3.50

TICK AND ARTHUR, THE
New England Comics, 1999
1 by Sean Wang & Mike Baker . . . 3.50
2 Return of the Thorn,pt.2 . . . . 3.50
3 Return of the Thorn,pt.3 . . . . 3.50
4 Tick & Arthur meet Flea & Doyle . 3.50
5 Flea & Doyle superheroes? 3.50
6 Chainsaw Vigilantes 3.50
TPB Bonanza #1 rep. #1–#3 . . . . . 5.50
TPB Bonanza #2 rep. #4–#6 . . . . . 5.50

TICK, THE:
BIG BLUE DESTINY
New England Comics, 1997
1 by Eli Stone, Keen edition 3.00
1 Wicked Keen edition 5.00
2A cover A. 3.00
3B cover B 3.00
3 . . . . 3.50
4 . . . . 3.50
5 The Chrysalis Crisis. 3.50

TICK CIRCUS MAXIMUS
New England Comics, 2000
1 (of 4) by Sean Wang 3.50
2 . . . . 3.50
3 . . . . 3.50
4 concl. 3.50
Spec.#1 Circus Maximus
   Redux (2001). 3.50

TICK: GIANT CIRCUS
OF THE MIGHTY
New England Press, 1992
1 A-O. 3.00
2 P-Z. 3.00
3 . . . . 3.00

TICK, THE: GOLDEN AGE
New England Comics, 2002
1 Entertaining cover 5.00
1a Classic cover 5.00
2 extremely creepy cover 5.00
2a Ferociously heroic cover 5.00
3 Bleeding Heart (c) 5.00
3a Criminally Maniacal (c) 5.00
TPB Golden Age giant edition 13.00

TICK, THE:
HEROES OF THE CITY
New England Comics, 1999
1 three stories. 3.50
2 . . . . 3.50
3 . . . . 3.50
4 . . . . 3.50
5 . . . . 3.50
6 . . . . 3.50
TPB Bonanza #1 rep. #1–#3 . . . . . 5.50
TPB Bonanza #2 rep. #4–#6 . . . . . 5.50

TICK: KARMA TORNADO
New England Press, 1993
1 . . . . 4.00
1 2nd printing 3.00
2 . . . . 3.50
2 2nd printing 3.00
3 thru 9 . . . . @3.50
3 thru 9 2nd printings . . . . @3.00

TPB #1 second edition. 14.00
TPB Bonanza Edition, Vol.2. . . . . . 5.00
TPB Bonanza Edition, Vol.3. . . . . . 5.00

TICK, THE: LUNY BIN
New England Comics, 1998
1 (of 3) by Eli Stone, Back to
    the Luny Bin 3.50
2 To the Rescue 3.50
3 Six Eyes in Tears 3.50
Preview Special, 32pg 2.50
TPB Luny Bin Trilogy 120-pg. 5.00

TICK OMNIBUS
New England Press
1 1 to 6 Rep. 15.00

TICK'S BACK, THE
New England Comics, 1997
0 by Eli Stone, V:Toy DeForce 3.00

TIGERS OF
THE LUFTWAFTE
Antarctic Press, 2001
1 48-pg. 6.00
2 48-pg. 6.00
3 48-pg. 6.00
4 Wild Angels, 48-pg. 6.00
5 Black Devil, 48-pg. 6.00
6 Black Devil, pt.2. . . . . 6.00
7 April Fools phoney issue 6.00
8 Fighter General 6.00
9 Adolf Galland 6.00
10 final issue 6.00

TIGERS OF TERRA
Mind-Visions, 1992
1 6,000 printed 4.50
1a Signed & Num. 14.00
2 . . . . 2.50
2a Signed & Num. 11.00
5 thru 7 . . . . @3.50
8 thru 10 . . . . @3.75
Antarctic, 1993
11 and 12 . . . . @4.00
[Vol. 2], 1993
0 thru 14 . . . . @2.75
15 Totenkopf Police,pt.2. . . . . 2.75
16 Battleship Arizona,pt.3 . . . . 2.75
17 thru 22. . . . . @3.00
23 `Trouble with Tigers' pt.3 . . . . . 3.00
24 48pg 10th Anniv. 4.00
25 `Battle for Terra' pt.1 . . . . 3.00
TPB Book Two 10.00
TPB Book Three 10.00
TPB Book Four 10.00

TIGER-X
Eternity, 1988
Special #1 . . . . 2.50
Spec. #1a 2nd printing. 2.50
1 thru 3 . . . . @2.50
Book II, 1989
1 thru 4 . . . . @2.50

TIGRESS
Hero Graphics, 1992
1 Tigress vs. Flare 4.00
2 . . . . 3.00
3 A:Lady Arcane 3.00
4 inc. B.U. Mudpie 4.00
5 . . . . 4.00
6 . . . . 4.00

TIGRESS
Basement Comics, 1998
1 by Budd Root and Mike Hoffman 3.00
2 concl. 3.00

1-shot Mike Hoffman special 9.00
1-shot green foil edition 12.50
1-shot gold foil edition 12.50

TIGRESS TALES
Amryl Entertainment, 2001
1 by Mike Hoffman 3.00
2 Slave Planet. 3.00
Basement Comics, 2001
1a spec. edition 9.00
2 Special Edition 9.00
2 Blue foil (c). 12.50
3a Special ed. 9.00
3b special edition, purple foil 11.50
4 . . . . 3.00
4a Special ed. 9.00
4b special edition, gold foil 11.50
5 . . . . 3.00
5a Special ed. 9.00
Pin-Up book (2001) 3.50
Pin-Up Book, special edition 9.00

TIGRESS: THE
HIDDEN LANDS
Basement Comics, 2002
1 by Mike Hoffman 3.50

TIME DRIFTERS
Innovation, 1990
1 . . . . 2.25
2 . . . . 2.25
3 . . . . 2.25

TIME GATES
Double Edge
1 SF series,The Egg #1 . . . . 2.25
2 The Egg #2 . . . . 2.25
3 Spirit of the Dragon #1. . . . . 2.25
4 Spirit of the Dragon #2. . . . . 2.25
4a Var.cover 2.25

Time Jump War #2
© Apple

TIME JUMP WAR
Apple
1 thru 3 . . . . @2.25

TIME MACHINE
Eternity, 1990
1 thru 3 H.G. Wells adapt. . . . . . @2.50

TIME TRAVELER AI
CPM Manga, 1999
1 by Ai Ijima &
    Takeshi Takebayashi 3.00
2 thru 13 . . . . @3.00
14 thru 21. . . . . @3.00
TPB Book One, rep. 16.00
TPB Sexy Pirates. 16.00
TPB Vol. 2 Sexy Pirates 16.00
TPB Vol. 3 Sexy Ninja Girl. 16.00

TIME WARRIORS
Fantasy General, 1986
1 rep.Alpha Track #1 . . . . 2.50
1a Bi-Weekly. 2.50
2 . . . . 2.50
3 . . . . 2.50

TIM VIGIL'S WEBWITCH
Avatar Press, 2002
Preview, 16-pg. 2.25
Preview, Temptress (c) 6.00
Preview, Serenity (c) 6.00
Preview, prism foil exclusive(c) . . . 13.00
Preview Cave of Evil edition 6.00
1 (of 3) Finch(c) 3.50
2 Vigil(c) 3.50
3 Adrian (c) 3.50
1a thru 3a variant(c) . . . . @3.50
1b thru 3b wraparound (c)s. . . . . @4.00
Webwitch Companion 5.00
Webwitch Companion Waller (c) . . . 5.00
Webwitch Companion Martin (c) . . . 5.00
TPB 11.00

TITANESS
Draculina Publishing, 1995
1 I:Titaness,Tomboy 3.00

TO BE ANNOUNCED
Strawberry Jam, 1986
1 thru 6 . . . . @2.50

TOMB TALES
Cryptic Entertainment, 1997
1 . . . . 3.00
2 . . . . 3.00
3 . . . . 3.00
4 A Rare Gem 3.00
5 . . . . 3.00
6 The Flame Game. 3.00
7 Invasion of the Shoddy Snatchers 3.00

TOM CORBETT
SPACE CADET
Eternity, 1990
1 . . . . 2.25
2 . . . . 2.25
3 . . . . 2.25
4 . . . . 2.25

TOM CORBETT II
Eternity, 1990
1 . . . . 2.25
2 . . . . 2.25
3 . . . . 2.25
4 . . . . 2.25

TOMMI GUNN:
KILLERS LUST
London Night, 1997
1 . . . . 3.00
1 photo cover 6.00
Ann. #1. 3.00

TOM MIX
HOLIDAY ALBUM
Amazing Comics
1 . . . . 3.50

TOM MIX WESTERN
AC Comics, 1988
1 . . . . 2.50
2 . . . . 2.50

TOMMY &
THE MONSTERS
New Comics
1 thru 3 . . . . @2.25

TOMORROW MAN
Antarctic, 1993
1 R:Tommorrow Man 3.00
Spec.#1 48-pg. 4.00

TOMORROW MAN
Antarctic Press, 2000
1 Requiem for Nepton,pt.1 . . . . 5.00
2 Requiem for Nepton,pt.2 . . . . 3.00
3 Requiem for Nepton,pt.3 . . . . 3.00

TONY DIGEROLAMO'S
JERSEY DEVIL
South Jersey Rebellion
1 by Tony DiGerolamo 3.00
2 . . . . 3.00
3 . . . . 2.25
4 . . . . 3.00
5 Robin Hood of the Pines,pt.1 . . . 2.25
6 Robin Hood of the Pines,pt.2 . . . 3.00

TONY DIGEROLAMO'S
THE TRAVELERS
Kenzer & Company, 2000
1 thru 3 . . . . @2.25
7 . . . . 3.00
8 Vlad Tepes in Romania 3.00
9 Arcimedes & Time Machine 3.00
10 Strange storm 3.00
11 Wrath of the Imprechaun 3.00
12 thru 20 . . . . @3.00
Wingnut Comics, 2003
21 thru 25 . . . . @3.00
TPB Vol. 1 Keg O' Fun 12.00

TONY DIGEROLAMO'S
THE FIX
South Jersey Rebellion, 2001
1 (of 4) 2.50
2 thru 4 . . . . @2.50

TOO MUCH COFFEE MAN
Adhesive Comics, 1994
1 F:Too Much Coffee Man 16.00
1a 2nd printing 4.00
2 Wheeler (s&a) 8.00
3 Wheeler (s&a) 6.00
4 In love 6.00
5 thru 7 . . . . @4.00
8 thru 10 . . . . @3.00
Mag. #11 64-pg. 5.00
Mag. #12 . . . . 5.00
Mag. #13 thru #22 . . . . @5.00

TOO MUCH HOPELESS
SAVAGES
Oni Press, 2003
1 (of 4) 3.00
2 thru 3 . . . . @3.00

TORG
Adventure
1 Based on Role Playing Game . . . 2.50
2 thru 3 Based on Game . . . . . . @2.50

TOR JOHNSON:
HOLLYWOOD STAR
Monster Comics
1 Biographical story 2.50

TORRID AFFAIRS
Eternity, 1988
1 . . . . 2.50
2 . . . . 2.50
3 thru 5, 60-pg. . . . . @3.00

TOTALLY ALIEN
Trigon
1 . . . . 15.00
2 . . . . 10.00
3 . . . . 8.00

TOUCH OF DEATH
Brain Scan Studios, 2003
0 . . . . 2.50
1 thru 3 . . . . @2.50

TOUGH GUYS AND
WILD WOMEN
Eternity, 1989
1 . . . . 2.50
2 . . . . 2.50

TOZZER 2
Ablaze Media, 2004
1 (of 5) 3.00
2 thru 5 . . . . @3.00
TPB Vol. 2 . . . . 15.00

TRACKER
Blackthorne, 1988
1 . . . . 2.50
2 thru 4 . . . . @2.50

TRAILER PARK
OF TERROR
Imperium Comics, 2003
1 . . . . 3.00
2 thru 8 . . . . @3.00
5a variant (c) 3.00
Spec. Halloween Special 4.00
Spec. Halloween Special #2 . . . . . 4.00

TRANSIT
Vortex, 1987
1 . . . . 2.50
2 thru 6 . . . . @2.50

TRICKSTER
KING MONKEY
Eastern
1 thru 5 . . . . @2.25

TRIDENT
Trident, 1989
1 thru 7 . . . . @3.50
8 . . . . 4.50

TRIUMVERATE
Mermaid Productions
1 I:Trimverate 2.25
2 & 3 Team captured . . . . @2.25
4 V:Ord,Ael 2.25

Trolllords #1 (?nd printing)
© *Tru Studios*

TROLLORDS
Tru Studios, 1986
1 1st printing 5.00
1a 2nd printing 2.50
2 . . . . 3.00
3 . . . . 2.50
4 thru 15 . . . . @2.50
#1 special 2.50

TROLLORDS
Apple Comics, 1989–90
1 thru 6 . . . . @2.50

TROLLORDS
Caliber Tapestry, 1996
1 and 2 . . . . @3.00

TROLLORDS:
DEATH & KISSES
Apple Comics, 1989
1 . . . . 2.50
2 thru 5 . . . . @2.50

TROUBLE SHOOTERS
Nightwolf, 1995
1 I:Trouble Shooters 2.50
2 V:Ifrit,Djin,Ghul 2.50
3 V:Morgath 2.50

TROUBLE WITH GIRLS
Eternity, 1989–91
1 . . . . 3.00
2 thru 14 . . . . @2.50
15 thru 21 . . . . @2.50
22 Lester's Origin 2.50
Ann. #1 . . . . 3.00
Graphic Novel 8.00
Graphic Novel #2 . . . . 8.00
Xmas special `World of Girls' 3.00
NEW SERIES
1 thru 4 see color
5 thru 11 . . . . @2.25

TROUBLE WITH TIGERS
Antarctic Press, 1992
1 Ninja High School/Tigers x-over . 2.25
2 . . . . 2.25

TRUE CRIME
Eclipse
1 thru 2 . . . . @3.00

All comics prices listed are for *Near Mint* condition.

TRUE STORY, SWEAR TO GOD
Clib's Boy Comics, 2001
5 thru 6	@3.00
7 thru 15	@3.00
16 thru 17	@3.00
AIT/Planet Lar, 2004
TPB	10.00
TPB Vol. 2 This One Goes to 11	13.00

TRUFAN ADVENTURES THEATRE
Paragraphics, 1986
1	7.00
2 3-D issue	5.00

TUPELO
Amaze Ink/SLG, 2003
1	3.00
2 thru 4	@3.00
TPB	18.00

TURTLE SOUP
Mirage, 1985
1 A:TMNTurtles	6.00

TURTLES TEACH KARATE
Solson
1	4.00
2	3.50

TV WESTERN
AC Comics, 2001
1 F:Jock Mahoney, Range Rider	6.00
Becomes:

WESTERN MOVIE HERO
AC Comics, 2001
2 F:Monte Hale	6.00
3 F:John Wayne	6.00
4 F:Rex Allen	7.00

TWILIGHT AVENGER
Eternity, 1988
1 thru 18	@2.50
Miracle Studios
Spec. Twilight Avenger Super Summer Special	2.75

TWILIGHT X
Antarctic Press, 2002
Pocket Manga #1	15.00
Pocket Manga #2 thru #4	@10.00

TWILIGHT-X: INTERLUDE
Antarctic Press, 1992
1 thru 3 by Joseph Wright	@2.50
Vol. 2, 1993
1 thru 5	@2.50

TWILIGHT-X QUARTERLY
Antarctic Press, 1994
1 thru 3 by Joseph Wright	@3.00
4 Celebration	3.00

TWILIGHT X: STORM
Antarctic Press, 2003
1	3.50
2 thru 6	@3.50
7 thru 8	@3.00
Pocket Manga #1	10.00

TWIST
Kitchen Sink, 1988
1	2.50
2 and 3	@2.50

TWISTED TANTRUMS OF THE PURPLE SNIT
Blackthorne, 1986
1	2.50
2	2.50

2001 NIGHTS
Viz, 1990–91
1 by Yukinobu Hoshino	5.00
2	4.00
3 thru 5	@3.75
6 thru 10	@4.25

TYRANNY REX
Fleetway
GN reps. from 2000A.D.	8.00

ULTIMATE STRIKE
London Night, 1996
1	2.25
1 holochrome edition	15.00
2	2.25
3	2.25
4	2.25
5	2.25
6 sequel to Strike #0	2.25
7 by Kevin Hill, `Strike: Year One' concl.	2.25
8 Year One,	2.25
9 Year One, cont.	2.25
10	2.25
11	2.25
12	2.25

Ultra Klutz #12
© Onward

ULTRA KLUTZ
Onward Comics, 1986
1	2.50
2 thru 18	@2.25
19 thru 24	@2.25
25 thru 30	@2.25
31	3.00
Bad Habit
TBP Book One, rep. #1–#23	30.00

UNCANNY MAN-FROG
Mad Dog
1 and 2	@2.25

UNCENSORED MOUSE
Eternity, 1989
1 Mickey Mouse	10.00
2 Mickey Mouse	11.00

UNFORGIVEN, THE
Trinity Comics Ministries
Mission of Tranquility
1 thru 6 V:Dormian Grath	@2.25
7 I:Faith	2.25

UNICORN ISLE
Genesis West, 1986
1	2.50
2	2.50
3	2.50
Apple, 1987
4 thru 6	@2.50

UNLEASHED
Caliber Press
1 F:Carson Davis	3.00
2 V:North Harbor Crime	3.00

UNSUPERVISED EXISTENCE
Fantagraphics
1	2.25
2 and 3	@2.50

UNTOLD TALES OF EVIL ERNIE
Chaos! Comics, 2000
Pieces of Me #1	3.50
Black Death premium #1	13.00
Evil Ernie:chromium #1	16.00
Relentless 1 BnP (2002)	5.00
Relentless 1a premium ed.	10.00
Relentless 1b Super premium ed.	20.00
Relentless 1c signed ed.	15.00
Relentless, Script	5.00
Relentless Script, premium ed.	20.00

UNTOUCHABLES
1 thru 20	@2.25

UNTOUCHABLES
Caliber, 1997
1K by Joe Pruett & John Kissee, MK(c)	3.00
1S Showman (c)	3.00
2	3.00
3 MK (c)	3.00
4 MK (c)	3.00
Spec. High Society Killer (1998)	4.00

USAGI YOJIMBO
Fantagraphics, 1987
1 SS	11.00
1a 2nd printing	5.00
2 SS,Samurai	8.00
3 SS,Samurai,A:Croakers	6.00
4 SS	5.00
5 thru 7 SS	@5.00
8 SS,A Mother's Love	5.00
8a 2nd printing	3.00
9 SS	5.00
10 SS,A:Turtles	5.00
10a 2nd printing	3.00
11 thru 18 SS	@4.00
19 SS,Frost & Fire,A:Nelson Groundthumper	4.00
20 thru 21 SS	@4.00
22 SS,A:Panda Khan	4.00
23 SS,V:Ninja Bats	4.00
24 SS	4.00
25 SS,A:Lionheart	4.00

Usagi Yojimbo #10
© Fantagraphics

26 SS,Gambling. 4.00
27 SS 4.00
28 thru 31 SS,Circles pt.1–4 . . . @4.00
32 . . . . 4.00
33 SS,Ritual Murder 4.00
34 thru 37. . . . . @4.00
Spec.#1 SS,SummerSpec, C:Groo 45.00
TPB Vol 4, rep. 17.00
TPB Vol 6, rep., new printing . . . 13.00
TPB Vol 7, Gen's Story 17.00

Radio Comix
Vol. 1 The Art of Usagi Yojimbo 4.00

VAGABOND
Viz Communications, 2001
1 (of 8) by Takehiko Inoue 5.00
2 thru 16 . . . . @5.00

VAISTRON
Amaze Ink/ Slave Labor
Graphics 2005
1 . . . . 3.00
2 thru 5 . . . . @3.00

VALENTINE
Red Eye Press, 1997
1 by Dan Cooney 3.00
2 thru 6 Cinderella Undercover. . @3.00
7 thru 8 Red Rain 3.50
9 Gun for Hire. 3.50
10 . . . . 3.00
11 thru 13. . . . . @3.50
TPB Vol. 1 Fully Loaded 14.00
TPB Vol. 2 Red Rain 13.00
1-shot Valentine (2005) 3.00

VALENTINO
Renegade, 1985
1 . . . . 2.50
2 and 3 . . . . @2.50

VAMPEROTICA
Brainstorm Comics, 1994
1 I:Luxura 8.00
1a 2nd & 3rd printing 3.00
2 . . . . 6.00
2 2nd printing 3.00
3 . . . . 4.00
4 I:Blood Hunter 4.00
5 Deadshot 4.00
6 Deadshot 4.00
7 Baptism 4.00

8 Pains,Peepers 4.00
9 thru 11 . . . . @4.00
12 thru 16 . . . . @3.00
17 thru 22 see: color
20 signed 5.00
23 . . . . 3.00
23 encore edition 3.00
24 . . . . 3.00
25 . . . . 3.00
26 . . . . 3.00
27 . . . . 3.00
28 A:China & Jazz 3.00
29 mild cover 3.00
30 Legends of Luxura x-over, concl. 3.00
31 V:Red Militia 3.00
32 . . . . 3.00
33 by Kirk Lindo 3.00
34 V:Pontius Vanthor 3.00
34a luxury edition. 5.00
35 . . . . 3.00
36 I:Countess Vladimira. 3.00
36a photo cover edition 4.00
37 . . . . 3.00
37a statue cover 3.00
38 . . . . 3.00
39 Death From Above, pt.1 . . . . . . 3.00
40 Death From Above, pt.2 . . . . . . 3.00
41. . . . . 3.00
42 Hostile Seduction 3.00
43 Harvest 3.00
44 F:Luxura 3.00
45 The Kindred Kill 3.00
45b photo cover. 4.00
46 Murder Most Foul 3.00
47 Camelot. 3.00
48 Reflections Over Blood 3.00
49 Love's Story 3.00
50 final issue, 48-pg. 5.00
50b commemorative edition, Julie
   Strain photo (c) 7.00
50c commem. signed. 10.00
Commemorative Edition. 3.00
Lingerie Special #1 . . . . 3.00
Spec. Lingerie, encore edition 3.00
Spec. Lingerie, deluxe 4.00
Spec. Swimsuit, encore edition . . . 3.00
Gallery #1. . . . . 5.00
Gallery #2. . . . . 5.00
Bondage Spec. #1 . . . . 3.00
Bondage Spec. #1, manga 4.00
Ann. #1 Encore 3.00
Spec.#2 Dare to Bare 3.00
Spec.#4 Encore Edition, new(c) . . 3.00
Spec.#5 Encore Edition 3.00
Spec.#1 Vamperotica Presents:
   Countess Vladimira (1998) . . . 3.00
Vamperotica Collector Vol. 1 . . . .   4.00
Pin-Up #1 (2000). 3.00
Spec. Blood of Japan. 3.00
1-shot Blond Goddess (2003) 3.00
1-shot Dark Fantasy 3.00
1-shot Bondage Gallery. 3.00
Spec. #1 Voluptuous Vamps (2004) 3.00
GN Blood of the Impaler 8.00
GN Deadly Vixens 8.00
TPB Drop Dead Dangerous (2004) . 8.00

VAMPEROTICA:
BLOND GODDESS
Vamperotica, 2003
1-shot Blond Goddess 3.00
1-shot Dark Fantasy 3.00
GN Deadly Vixens 8.00
1-shot Bondage Gallery. 3.00
TPB Drop Dead Dangerous. 8.00

VAMPEROTICA:
DARK FICTION
Vamperotica Ent., 2001
1 F:Vampress Luxura 3.00

1a adult (c) 4.00
1b premium edition 5.00
2 . . . . 3.00
3 . . . . 3.00
4 . . . . 3.00
TPB Vamperotica Maximum
   Excitement (2001). 8.00
TPB Vamperotica Slave to
   Love (2000) 8.00

VAMPEROTICA:
DIVIDE & CONQUER
Brainstorm, 1999
1 V:The Juicious Edicts 3.00
1b Commemorative #1 . . . . 5.00
1c Commemorative #1 deluxe 7.00
2 conclusion 3.00

VAMPEROTICA
ILLUSTRATED
Brainstorm
1 F:Vampress Luxura 3.00
1b premium ed.. . . . . 5.00
1c premium signed 6.00
2 . . . . 3.00
3 . . . . 3.00
4 . . . . 3.00
5 . . . . 3.00
6 . . . . 3.00

VAMPEROTICA
LUST FOR LUXURA
Vamperotica, 2002
1 by Kirk Lindo 3.00
1a premium edition 5.00
2 . . . . 3.00
3 . . . . 3.00
1c Sketch cover edition 4.00
3a photo(c) 5.00

VAMPEROTICA MANGA
Brainstorm, 1998
1 . . . . 3.00
2 . . . . 3.00

VAMPEROTICA'S PIN-UP
ILLUSTRATED
Vamperotica, 2004
1 . . . . 5.00
2 thru 3 . . . . @5.00

VAMPEROTICA TALES
Brainstorm, 1998
1 . . . . 3.00
2 thru 5 . . . . @3.00

VAMPEROTICA: TALES
FROM THE BLOODVAULT
Vamperotica Ent., 2000
Mag. #1 . . . . 5.00
Mag. #1b premium ed.. . . . . 7.00

VAMPEROTICA:
VOLUPTUOUS VAMPS
Vamperotica, 2004
1 . . . . 3.00

VAMPEROTICA: WHEN
DARKNESS FALLS
Vamperotica Ent., 2002
1 . . . . 3.00
1b premium edition 5.00
2 . . . . 3.00
3 . . . . 3.00
TPB Dark Ages, series rep. 8.00

B & W PUB.

VAMPFIRE
Brainstorm, 1996
1 . . . . 3.00
1b commemorative photo cover . . 10.00
2 . . . . 3.00
2b signed 5.00
2d Remastered 3.00
2e signed 10.00
2f deluxe with litho 20.00
3 remastered 4.00
3a signed 10.00
3b deluxe 20.00
Pin-Up Spec. 3.00
Pin-Up Spec. deluxe 4.00
Tour Book #1 . . . . 3.00

VAMPFIRE: EROTIC ECHO
Brainstorm, 1997
1 by Fauve 3.00
1b photo cover 3.00
2 . . . . 3.00
2b photo cover 3.00

VAMPFIRE: NECROMANTIQUE
Brainstorm, 1997
1 by Holly Golightly 3.00
1b luxury edition, virgin cover 5.00
1c luxury edition, signed 15.00
1d regular, signed 8.00
2 by Fauve 3.00

VAMPIRE BITES
Brainstorm, 1995
1 . . . . 3.00
2 . . . . 3.00

VAMPIRE CONFESSIONS
Brainstorm, 1998
1 . . . . 3.00

VAMPIRE DAHLIA, THE
Ironcat, 2001
1 (of 6) by Narumi Kakinouchi 3.00
2 thru 6 . . . . @3.00
TPB Vol. 1 Death is a Kiss 17.00

VAMPIRE GIRLS: CALIFORNIA 1969
Angel Entertainment, 1996
1 blood red foil deluxe edition 6.00
2 . . . . 3.00
2 deluxe 6.00
TPB 5.00

VAMPIRE GIRLS: NEW YORK 1979
Angel Entertainment, 1996
0 . . . . 3.00
0 gold edition 8.00
1 . . . . 3.00

VAMPIRE GIRLS: BUBBLEGUM & BLOOD
Angel Entertainment, 1996
1 . . . . 3.00
1 deluxe edition 6.00
2 . . . . 3.00
2 deluxe edition 6.00

VAMPIRE GIRLS EROTIQUE
Angel Entertainment, 1996
1 . . . . 3.00
2 . . . . 3.00

3 . . . . 3.00
4 . . . . 3.00
5 . . . . 3.00
6 . . . . 3.00
7 Bloodsucker cover 3.00
Spec. Gravedigger (1996) by
  Alexandra Scott & Bill Wylie . . . 3.00
Spec. Paris 1968 (1997) by
  Alexandra Scott & Dean Burnett 3.00
Spec. Titanic 1912 (1998) by
  Alexandra Scott & Dean Burnett 3.00

VAMPIRE GIRLS EROTIQUE: GRAVEDIGGER
Angel Entertainment, 1996
1 by Alexandra Scott & Bill Wylie . . 3.00

VAMPIRE GIRLS VS. ANGEL GIRL
Angel Entertainment, 1997
1 . . . . 3.00

VAMPIRELLA
Harris
1 DC,SL,Summer Nights,48pg. . . . 4.00
Pantha Ashcan, 16-pg. 6.00
Dangerous Games Preview Ashcan 6.00
Hell on Earth, Leather Ashcan 15.00
Hell on Earth, Leather Ashcan,
  signed 30.00
30th Ann. Spec. Julie
  Strain photo (c) 10.00
Painkiller Jane preview Ashcan 6.00
Spec.#1 Vampirella vs. Hemorrhage,
  Limited Preview Ashcan 5.00
Vampirella/Lady Death Ashcan
  16-pg., Rematch 6.00
Vampirella/Lady Death Ashcan
  16-pg., Finale 6.00
Vampirella/Lady Death Ashcan
  16-pg., Revenge, platinum . . . 20.00
Vampirella 2999 A.D.
  Manga Ashcan 8.00
Vampirella 2999 A.D. Manga
  Ashcan, leather edition 15.00
Vampirella 3000 A.D.
  Manga Ashcan 8.00
Vampirella 3000 A.D.Manga
  Ashcan, leather edition 15.00

VAMPIRELLA
Harris Comics, 2002
#1 magazine reprint from 1969 . . . 30.00
#1 royal blue foil (c) 60.00
#1 platinum foil (c) 20.00
TPB Vampirella and the Blood Red
  Queen of Hearts, rep. from Warren
  Vampirella, 96pg 10.00

VAMPIRELLA
Anarchy Studios/Harris Comics, 2004
Spec. Vol. 1 Black & White
  Collection 5.00
TPB Rep. Vol. 1 thru Vol. 9 . . . . . . 25.00
TPB Vol. 1 Shadow & Light, lim ed. 10.00
TPB Vol. 1 Shadows & Light 15.00
Spec. Halloween Special #1 . . . . . 10.00
Spec. Halloween Special #1 JJu
  virgin (c) 19.00
Spec. 2006 Halloween Special . . . 3.00
Spec. 2006 Halloween limited
  B&W (c)s . . . . @20.00
TPB Blood Lust 10.00
Spec. Intimate Visions 4.00
Spec. Intimate Visions Joe Jusko #14.00
Spec. Intimate Visions #1 virgin (c) 15.00
TPB Vampirella: Tales of Pantha . . 20.00

Vampirells Silver Anniversary #2
(Good Girl cover) © Harris

VAMPIRELLA
Silver Anniversary Collection
Harris, 1996
0 Vampirella of Darkulon, EM 3.00
1 good girl edition 2.50
1a bad girl edition 2.50
2 good girl edition 2.50
2a bad girl edition 2.50
3 good girl edition 2.50
3a bad girl edition 2.50
4 Silkie(c) 2.50
4a MBc(c) 2.50

VAMPIRELLA COMICS MAGAZINE
Harris Comics, 2003
1 . . . . 4.00
1a photo (c) 10.00
1b Frankenstein Mobster (c) 10.00
1c JP(c) 10.00
2 thru 9 . . . . @4.00
2a thru 9a photo (c)s . . . . @10.00

VAMPIRELLA: MORNING IN AMERICA
Harris/Dark Horse, 1991–92
Book 1 thru 4 . . . . @7.00
Book 2 thru 4 . . . . @5.00
TPB 25.00

VAMPIRELLA NOVELLA
Anarchy Studios/ Harris Comics, 2004
1 Deadly Sins 4.00
1a limited 10.00

VAMPIRELLA RETRO
Harris, 1998
1 (of 3) rep. Warren stories 2.50
2 (of 3) rep. Warren stories 2.50
3 (of 3) rep. Warren stories 2.50

VAMPIRELLA: LEGENDARY TALES
Harris Comics, 2000
1 . . . . 3.00
1a deluxe 10.00
1b Julie Strain photo (c) 10.00
2 . . . . 3.00
2a variant (c) 10.00
2b Julie Strain photo (c) 10.00

B & W PUB.

VAMPIRELLA: REVELATIONS
Anarchy Studios/Harris Comics, 2005
Prototype ed. 5.00
0 16-page 10.00
0a variant JJu virgin (c) 10.00
1 . . . . 3.00
1a variant (c). 3.00
1b & c variant virgin (c)s 15.00
2 . . . . 3.00
2a variant (c) 3.00
2b & c variant virgin (c)s. 15.00
3 . . . . 3.00
3a variant (c) 3.00
3b & c variant virgin (c)s. 10.00
TPB Vol. 1 . . . . 13.00
Book 2
1 prototype edition 5.00
1 prototype limited edition 15.00

VAMPIRE MIYU
Antarctica Press, 1996
1 I:Vampire Princess Miyu 3.00
2 thru 5 . . . . @4.00
6 48pg. 5.00

VAMPIRE PRINCESS MIYU
Ironcat, 2000
1 by Narumi Kakinouchi 3.00
2 thru 4 . . . . @3.00
TPB Vol. 1 (2001) 18.00
TPB Vol. 2 thru Vol. 3. . . . . @18.00
TPB Vol. 4 . . . . 18.00
TPB Vol. 5 Intrusions 16.00
TPB Vol. 6 . . . . 16.00
TPB Vol. 7 Vortex. 16.00
TPB Vol. 8 . . . . 13.00
Artbook (color) 25.00

VAMPIRE PRINCESS YUI
Ironcat, 2000
Vol. 1
1 . . . . 3.00
2 thru 6 . . . . @3.00
Vol. 2
1 . . . . 3.00
2 thru 6 . . . . @3.00

VAMPIRE YUI
Ironcat, 2000
Vol. 3
1 . . . . 3.00
2 thru 4 . . . . @3.00
5 thru 6 . . . . @3.00
Vol. 4 (2002)
1 thru 7 . . . . @3.00
Vol. 5
1 . . . . 3.00
2 thru 7 . . . . @3.00
TPB Vol. 1 . . . . 18.00
TPB Vol. 2 . . . . 18.00
TPB Vol. 3 . . . . 18.00
TPB Vol. 4 . . . . 16.00
TPB Vol. 5 . . . . 16.00

VAMPIRE'S TATTOO
London Night, 1997
1 (of 2) by Art Wetherell 3.00
2 . . . . 3.00
3 . . . . 3.00

VAMPIRE VERSES, THE
CFD Productions, 1995
1 thru 3 . . . . @3.00

VAMPIRE ZONE, THE
Brainstorm, 1998
1 . . . . 3.00

VAMPORNRELLA
Forbidden, 1997
1 parody 3.00

Vampyres #3
© Eternity

VAMPYRES
Eternity, 1988
1 thru 4 . . . . @2.25

VAPOR LOCH
Sky Comics, 1994
1 . . . . 2.50

VENGEANCE OF DREADWOLF
Lightning Comics
1 O:Dreadwolf. 2.75

VENGEANCE OF THE AZTECS
Caliber, 1993
1 . . . . 2.50
2 . . . . 2.50

VERDICT
Eternity, 1988
1 thru 4 . . . . @2.50

VEROTIKA
Verotika, 1995–97
1 Magical Times 12.00
2 . . . . 7.00
3 . . . . 5.00
4 thru 6 . . . . @4.00
7 thru 15 . . . . @3.00

VERY VICKY
Meet Danny Ocean, 1993
1 . . . . 3.50
1a 2nd printing 3.00
2 thru 8 . . . . @2.50
Spec. Calling All Hillbillies 2.50

VIC & BLOOD
Renegade, 1987
1 and 2 RCo,Ellison . . . . @2.50

VICKY VALENTINE
Renegade, 1985
1 thru 4 . . . . @2.50

VICTIM
Silver Wolf, 1987
1 & 2 . . . . @2.50

VICTIMS
Eternity, 1988
1 thru 5 . . . . @2.50

VIDEO
Lost in the Dark Press, 2004
1 . . . . 3.00
2 thru 4 . . . . @3.00
5 thru 6 . . . . @3.00
TPB 13.00

VIDEO CLASSICS
Eternity
1 Mighty Mouse 3.50
2 Mighty Mouse 3.50

VIETNAM JOURNAL
Apple Comics, 1987
1 . . . . 5.00
1a 2nd printing 3.00
2 . . . . 3.00
3 thru 5 . . . . @3.00
6 thru 13 . . . . @3.00
14 thru 16 . . . . @3.00

VIGIL
Duality Press, 1997
Baby Steps. 3.00
Dirt, by A.Laudermilk & M.Iverson . . 3.00
Slash and Burn, Bloodline story . . . 3.00
The Vegas Shuffle, Bloodline story . 3.00
Desertion 3.00
Outreach 3.00
Penetration. 3.00
Daddy's Little Girl, final issue 3.00
TPB Vol. 1, rep. #1–#5 . . . . 20.00

VIGIL: DESERT FOXES
Millennium, 1995
1 & 2 F:Grace Kimble . . . . @4.00

VIGIL: ERUPTION
Millennium, 1996
1 (of 2) vampire hunters 4.00
2 (of 2) 4.00

VIGIL: FALL FROM GRACE
Innovation, 1992
1 `State of Grace' 2.75
2 The Graceland Hunt 2.50

VIGIL: SCATTER SHOTS
Duality Press, 1997
1 by A.Laudermilk & M.Iverson. . . . 4.00
2 . . . . 4.00

VINSON WATSON'S RAGE
Trinity Visuals
1 I:Rena Helen 3.00

VINSON WATSON'S SWEET CHILDE
Advantage Graphics
Vol. 2
1 F:Spyder 2.25

All comics prices listed are for *Near Mint* condition.

VIRGIN: SLUMBER
Entity, 1997
1 BMs 2.75
1 deluxe 3.50

VIRGIN: SURROUNDED
Entity, 1997
1 BMs 2.75
1 deluxe 3.50

VIRGIN: TILL DEATH DO US PART
Entity, 1997
1 BMs 2.75
1 deluxe 3.50

VISIONS
Vision Publication, 1979–83
1 I:Flaming Carrot 75.00
2 Flaming Carrot 35.00
3 Flaming Carrot 20.00
4 Flaming Carrot 25.00

VISUAL ASSAULT OMNIBUS
Visual Assault Comics, 1995
1 thru 4 O:Dimensioner . . . . @3.00

VIXEN
Meteor Comics
1 & 2 Battle of the Vixens . . . . . . @3.00

VORTEX
Hall of Heroes, 1993
1 . . . . 15.00
1a commemorative 5.00
2 . . . . 10.00
3 thru 5 . . . . @3.50
6 V:The Reverend 3.00

VORTEX SPECIAL: CYBERSIN
Avatar Press, 1997
1 by Matt Martin & Bil Maus 3.00
1b velvet cover 15.00
1c signed 10.00
1d Snowman spec. (c) 5.00

VORTEX: DR. KILBOURN
Entity, 1997
1 by Matt Martin 3.00
1a deluxe 3.50

VORTEX: INTO THE DARK
Entity, 1997
1 . . . . 3.00
1 deluxe 3.50

VOX
Apple, 1989
1 JBy(c) 2.50
2 and 3 . . . . @2.50
4 and 5 . . . . @2.50

WABBIT WAMPAGE
Amazing Comics, 1987
1 . . . . 2.50

WAFFEN SS
New England Comics, 2000
1 by Ron Ledwell 3.50
2 thru 7 . . . . @3.50

Wabbit Wampage #1
© Amazing Comics

WAITING PLACE, THE
Slave Labor, 1997
5 . . . . 3.00
6 . . . . 3.00

Vol. 2, 2000
1 . . . . 3.00
2 . . . . 3.00
3 A Sporting Chance 3.00
4 I Care 3.00
5 The Road Home 3.00
6 . . . . 3.00
7 . . . . 3.00
8 Under a Frozen Sky 3.00
9 Intrusions, pt.1 . . . . 3.00
10 Intrusions, pt.2 . . . . 3.00
11 Intrusions, pt.3 . . . . 3.00
TPB Vol. 1 . . . . 16.00
TPB Vol. 2 thru Vol. 3 . . . . @16.00

WALKING DEAD
Aircel
1 thru 4 . . . . @2.25
Zombie Spec. 1 . . . . 2.25

WALK THROUGH OCTOBER
Caliber
1 I:Mr. Balloon 3.00
2 . . . . 3.00
3 All Hallow's Eve 3.00

WALT THE WILDCAT
Motion Comics, 1995
1 I:Walt the Wildcat 2.50

WANDERING STAR
Pen & Ink, 1993
1 I:Casandra Andrews 12.00
1a 2nd & 3rd printing 3.00
2 . . . . 8.00
3 . . . . 5.00
4 . . . . 4.00
5 . . . . 4.00
6 thru 11 . . . . @3.00

Sirius, 1995–97
12 thru 20 TWo . . . . @2.50
21 TWo, final issue 2.50
TPB Vol. 1 rep. #1–#7 . . . . 15.00
TPB Vol. 2 . . . . 15.00
TPB Vol. 3 168-pg. 15.00

WANDERLUST
Antarctic Press, 2000
1 (of 3) by Bryant Shiu 2.50
2 . . . . 2.50
3 conclusion 2.50

WARCAT
Alliance Comics
1 thru 7 A:Ebonia . . . . @2.50

WARD: A BULLET SERIES
Liar Comics
1 Foresight,pt.1 . . . . 2.50
2 Foresight,pt.2 . . . . 2.50
3 Foresight,pt.3 . . . . 2.50

WARLOCK 5
Aircel, 1986
1 . . . . 6.00
2 . . . . 5.00
3 . . . . 6.00
4 . . . . 5.00
5 . . . . 5.00
6 thru 11 . . . . @4.00
12 . . . . 3.50
13 . . . . 3.50
14 thru 16 . . . . @3.00
17 . . . . 3.00
18 . . . . 3.00
19 thru 22 . . . . @3.00
Book 2 #1 thru #7 . . . . @3.00

WARLOCK 5
Sirius, 1997
1 (of 4) by Barry Blair & Colin Chan 2.50
2 . . . . 2.50
3 . . . . 2.50
4 finale 2.50

WARLOCKS
Aircel, 1988
1 thru 3 . . . . @2.50
4 thru 12 . . . . @2.50
Spec #1 Rep. 2.50

WARMAGEDDON ILLUSTRATED
Digital Webbing 2005
1 . . . . 6.00
2 . . . . 6.00

WAR OF THE WORLDS
Eternity
1 TV tie-in 2.50
2 . . . . 2.50
3 . . . . 2.50
4 . . . . 2.50
5 . . . . 2.50
6 . . . . 2.50

WAR OF THE WORLDS, THE
Caliber `New Worlds', 1996
1 from H.G. Wells 3.00
1a signed 3.00
2 war for Kansas City 3.00
3 Haven & The Hellweed 3.00
4 . . . . 3.00
5 . . . . 3.00
TPB rep. #1–#5 . . . . 15.00

WAR OF THE WORLDS: THE MEMPHIS FRONT
Arrow Comics, 1998
1 (of 5) by Randy Zimmerman
   & Richard Gulick 3.00

B & W PUB.

War of the Worlds #3
© Caliber

2 thru 5 . . . . @3.00
Spec.#1 signed & numbered 3.00

WARREN ELLIS' APPARAT
Avatar Press 2004
Preview 2.00
TPB Vol. 1 . . . . 13.00

WARREN ELLIS' ATMOSPHERICS
Avatar Press, 2002
GN 6.00

WARREN ELLIS' BAD SIGNAL
Avatar Press, 2002
GN 7.00
GN Vol. 2 . . . . 7.00

WARREN ELLIS' BAD WORLD
Avatar Press, 2001
1 (of 3) 3.50
2 . . . . 3.50
3 . . . . 3.50
1a thru 3a wraparound (c). . . . . . @4.00
TPB series rep. 11.00

WARREN ELLIS' DARK BLUE
Avatar Press, 2000
GN 72-pg. 9.00
TPB Scriptbook 7.00
Avatar Press 2006
GN 9.00

WARREN ELLIS'
Avatar Press 2004–05
1-shot Angel Stomp Future 3.50
1-shot Frank Ironwine 3.50
1-shot Quit City 3.50
1-shot Simon Spector 3.50

WARREN ELLIS' SCARS
Avatar Press, 2002
Sampler 1.00
1 (of 6) 3.50
2 thru 6 . . . . @3.50
1a–6a wraparound (c). 4.00

TPB 18.00

WARREN ELLIS' STRANGE KILLINGS
Avatar Press, 2002
1 (of 3) WEI. 3.50
1a wraparound (c). 4.00
2 . . . . 3.50
2a wraparound (c). 4.00
3 . . . . 3.50
3a wraparound (c). 3.50
TPB 10.00

WARREN ELLIS' STRANGE KILLINGS: THE BODY ORCHARD
Avatar Press, 2002
1 (of 6) WEI. 3.50
2 thru 6 WEI . . . . @3.50
1a thru 6a wraparound (c). . . . . @4.00
TPB Body Orchard. 17.00

WARREN ELLIS' STRANGE KILLINGS: NECROMANCER
Avatar Press, 2004
1 . . . . 3.50
2 thru 6 . . . . @3.50
1a thru 6a wraparound (c)s. . . . @3.50
TPB Necromancer. 17.00

WARREN ELLIS' STRANGE KILLINGS: STRONG MEDICINE
Avatar Press, 2003
1 . . . . 3.50
2 thru 3 . . . . @3.50
1a thru 3a wraparound (c). . . . . @4.00
TPB Strong Medicine. 10.00

WARREN ELLIS' STRANGE KISS
Avatar Press, 1999
1 . . . . 3.00
1a 4.00
1b signed 30.00
2 . . . . 2.25
2a wraparound (c). 4.00
3 . . . . 3.00
3a wraparound (c). 4.00
TPB 9.00

WARREN ELLIS' STRANGER KISSES
Avatar Press, 2000
1 (of 3) 3.00
1a leather signed 25.00
2 . . . . 3.00
3 . . . . 3.00
1a thru 3a wraparound (c). . . . . @4.00
TPB series rep. 10.00

WARRIOR NUN AREALA: BOOKS OF PERIL
Antarctic Press, 2001
1 (of 4) 3.00
2 The Book of Sharate 3.00
3 Book of Xitan 3.00
4 Devil's Deal 3.00
5 Scepter of the Crescent Moon. . . 3.00
6 Scepter of the Crescent Moon. . . 3.00
7 Scepter of the Crescent Moon. . . 3.00
8 The Good Son, pt.1 . . . . 3.00
9 The Good Son, pt.2 . . . . 3.00

10 The Good Son, pt.3 . . . . 3.00
11 Dissension, pt.1 . . . . 3.00
12 Dissension, pt.2 . . . . 3.00
13 Dissension, pt.3 . . . . 3.00
14 Curse of Looming Plague,pt.1 . . 3.50
15 Curse of Looming Plague,pt.2 . . 3.50
16 Curse of Looming Plague,pt.3 . . 3.50
17 Soul Reaper 3.50
18 Soul Reaper, pt.2 . . . . 3.50
19 Soul Reaper, pt.3 . . . . 3.50
20 thru 22 . . . . @3.50
Spec. Swimsuit Special (2002) 4.00

WARRIOR NUN AREALA: DANGEROUS GAME
Antarctic Press, 2001
1 (of 3) 3.00
2 . . . . 3.00
3 . . . . 3.00

WARRIOR NUN AREALA: GHOSTS OF THE PAST
Antarctic Press, 2001
1 (of 4) 3.00
2 thru 4 . . . . @3.00

WARRIOR NUN AREALA/RAZOR: DARK PROPHECY
London Night, 1999
1 16-pg. 2.50
2 16-pg. 2.50
Antarctic Press
3 . . . . 2.50
4 . . . . 2.50

WARRIOR NUN AREALA: THE MANGA
Antarctic Press, 2000
1-shot 3.00

WARRIOR NUN BRIGANTIA
Antarctic Press, 2000
1 V:Fata Morgana 3.00
2 Sister Anna 3.00
3 . . . . 3.00

WARRIOR NUN: BLACK AND WHITE
Antarctic Press, 1997
1 . . . . 3.00
2 . . . . 3.00
3 . . . . 3.00
4 Winter Jade, pt.1 F:Ninja Nun . . . 3.00
5 Winter Jade, pt.2 . . . . 3.00
6 Winter Jade, pt.3 . . . . 3.00
7 . . . . 3.00
8 . . . . 3.00
9 Return of the Redeemers 3.00
10 Return of Lillith 3.00
11 The Redeemers, cont. 3.00
12 The Redeemers, cont. 3.00
13 I:Sister Trinity 3.00
14 Redeemers saga again. 3.00
15 F:Sister Trinity. 3.00
16 F:Sister Trinity. 3.00
17 Showdown 3.00
18 Reaction 3.00
19 Carnivale. 3.00
20 Twilight Earth 3.00
21 Lost Souls of Blue
   Moon Mountain 2.50
Spec. Warrior Nun Areala/Razor:
   Revenge 3.00
Spec.A Revenge, deluxe 6.00

WARRIORS
1 . . . . 2.50
2 thru 7 . . . . @2.25

WARZONE
Entity, 1995
1 I:Bella & Supra 3.00
2 F:Bladeback, Alloy, Granite 3.00
3 F:Bladeback 3.00

WASTELAND
Oni Press 2006
1 . . . . 3.00
2 thru 4 . . . . @3.00

WEAPONS FILE
Antarctic Press 2005
1 photo reference 5.00
2 photo reference 5.00
3 Manga 5.00
TPB Vol. 1 Supersized 25.00

WEATHER WOMAN
CPM Manga, 2000
1 signed & limited 20.00
4 thru 8 . . . . @3.00

WEBWITCH
Avatar Press, 1997
0 by Raff Ienco 3.00
1 (of 2) signed 10.00
1 (of 2) 3.00
2 (of 2) 3.00
Boxed Set, all rare editions 35.00

WEBWITCH: PRELUDE TO WAR
Avatar Press, 1998
1 by Raff Jenco 3.00
1b Leather cover 30.00

WEBWITCH: WAR
Avatar Press, 1998
1 (of 2) by Bill Maus 3.00
1b Leather cover 30.00
2 conclusion 3.00

WEIRDFALL
Antarctic Press, 1995
1 I:Weirdfall 2.75
2 O:Weirdfall 2.75
3 . . . . 2.75

WEIRDSVILLE
Blindwolf Studios, 1997
1 . . . . 3.50
1 2nd printing 3.00
2 . . . . 3.50
2 2nd printing 3.00
3 . . . . 3.50
3 2nd printing 3.00
4 . . . . 3.50
5 . . . . 3.00
6 The Usual Weirdoes, concl 3.00
7 . . . . 3.00
8 An American Werewolf in
   Weirdsville, pt.1 (of 2) 3.00
9 An American Werewolf in
   Weirdsville, pt.2 . . . . 3.00
10 . . . . 3.00

WEIRDSVILLE/CRYBABY: HEY YOU TWO
Blindwolf Studios, 1999
1 . . . . 3.00

WEREWOLF
Blackthorne, 1988–89
1 TV tie-in 2.50
2 thru 7 . . . . @2.50

WESTERN TALES OF TERROR
Hoarse and Buggy Productions, 2004
1 . . . . 3.50
2 thru 5 . . . . @3.50

WHAT IS THE FACE?
A.C.E. Comics, 1986
1 SD/FMc,I:New Face 2.50
2 SD/FMc 2.50
3 SD 2.50

WHISPERS & SHADOWS
Oasis
1 8 1/2 x 11 . . . . 2.50
1a Regular size 2.50
2 8 1/2 x 11 . . . . 2.50
3 8 1/2 x 11 . . . . 2.50
4 thru 9 . . . . @2.50

White Devil #6
© Eternity

WHITE DEVIL
Eternity, 1991
1 thru 6 adult . . . . @2.50

WHITE ORCHID, THE
Atlantis
1 (of 6) 3.00
2 . . . . 3.00
3 . . . . 3.00
4 . . . . 3.50
5 'Death Trap,' pt.1 . . . . 3.00
6 The Price of Vengeance 3.50

WHITEOUT
Oni Press, 1998
1 (of 4) by Greg Rucka &
   Steve Lieber 3.00
2 . . . . 3.00
3 . . . . 3.00
4 conclusion 3.00
TPB 128-pg 11.00

WHITEOUT: MELT
Oni Press, 1999
1 (of 4) by Greg Rucka
   & Steve Lieber 3.00
2 . . . . 3.00
3 . . . . 3.00
4 concl. 3.00
TPB 12.00

WHITE RAVEN
Visionary Publications
1 Government Intrigue 3.00
2 . . . . 3.00
3 Mystery Man Gets Wheels 3.00
4 Facility 3.00
5 V:Douglas 3.00
6 . . . . 3.00
7 . . . . 3.00

WHITLEY STRIEBER'S BEYOND COMMUNION
Caliber, 1997
1 UFO Odyssey 3.00
1 signed 3.00
1 special edition, signed
   by Strieber 7.00
1a 2nd printing 3.00
2 . . . . 3.00
3 . . . . 3.00
4 . . . . 3.00

WICKED
Millennium, 1994
1 thru 4 . . . . @2.50

WICKED: THE RECKONING
Millennium
1 R:Wicked 3.00
2 F:Rachel Blackstone 3.00

WIDOW
Ground Zero, 1996
Cinegraphic Spec.#1: Daughter
   of Darkness 4.00

WIDOW/LUXURA: BLOOD LUST
Ground Zero, 1996
Alpha x-over, pt.1 . . . . 3.50
see Luxura/Widow for pt. 2

WIDOW: BOUND BY BLOOD
Ground Zero, 1996
1 thru 5 by Mike Wolfer . . . . @3.50

WIDOW: PROGENY
Ground Zero, 1997
1 by Mike Wolfer & Karl Moline . . . 3.00
2 (of 3) 3.00
3 concl. 3.00

WIDOW: THE COMPLETE WORKS
Ground Zero, 1996
Vol.1 Flesh and Blood 11.00
Vol.1 deluxe 17.00
Vol.2 Kill Me Again 11.00
Vol.2 deluxe 17.00
Vol.3 Metal Gypsies 11.00
Vol.3 deluxe 17.00

Widow #0
© Avatar

WIDOW
Avatar Press, 1997
0 by Mike Wolfer. 4.00
0b Black leather cover 25.00
0 signed 10.00

WIDOW: THE ORIGIN
Avatar Press, 1997
1 (of 3) by Mike Wolfer 4.00
1a leather cover 25.00
2 (of 3) 3.00

WILD, THE
1 and 2 . . . . @2.25
3 thru 7 . . . . @2.25

WILDFLOWER: DARK EUPHORIA
Neko Press, 2004
1 . . . . 3.00
2 . . . . 3.00
1a thru 2a variant (c)s . . . . @4.00

WILDFLOWER
Sirius/Dog Star, 1998
1 by Billy Martinez 2.50
2 thru 6 . . . . @2.50
Neko Press, 2002
TPB Vol.1 Beginnings, rep.
   from 1997 . . . . 15.00

WILDFLOWER: TRIBAL SCREAMS
Neko Press, 2002
1 Martinez (c) 3.00
1a Dark One (c) 5.00
2 thru 4 . . . . @3.00
Spec. Wildflower Y2K, 16-pg. . . . 10.00

WILD KNIGHTS
Eternity, 1988
1 thru 10 . . . . @2.50
Shattered Earth Chron. #1 . . . . . . 2.50

WILDLIFE
Antarctic, 1993
1 thru 12 . . . . @2.75

WILDMAN
Miller
1 and 2 . . . . @2.25
3 thru 6 . . . . @2.25

WILD THINGZ
ABC Comics, 1998
0 RCI & Armando Huerta 3.00
0a painted cover 6.00
0b Fan edition 6.00
0c Summer edition 6.00
0d Leather cover, original art 55.00
1 (of 2) RCI 3.00
1b Leather cover. 30.00
1c virgin cover. 3.00
1d gold cover 6.00
1e Platinum cover 6.00

WILLOW
Angel Entertainment, 1996
0 commemorative edition 3.00
1 . . . . 3.00
1 black magic foil edition 6.00
2 . . . . 3.00
2 gold edition 8.00
2 nude platinum cover 15.00

WIND BLADE
1 Elford 1st Blair 40.00

WINGS
A-List Comics, 1997
1 rep. of golden age 2.50
2 . . . . 3.00
3 . . . . 3.00
4 . . . . 3.00
5 . . . . 3.00

WINDRAVEN
Hero Graphics/Blue Comet
1 The Healing,(see Rough Raiders) 3.00

WITCH
Amaze Ink/SLG, 2001
1 by Lorna Miller. 3.00
2 . . . . 3.00
3 thru 4 . . . . @3.00
TPB Vol. 1 . . . . 12.00

WIZARD OF TIME
David House, 1986
1 . . . . 2.50
1a 2nd printing(blue). 2.50
2 and 3 . . . . @2.50

WIZARDS OF THE LAST RESORT
Blackthorne, 1987
1 . . . . 2.50

WOLFF & BYRD, COUNSELORS OF THE MACABRE
Exhibit A, 1994
1 . . . . 6.00
1a new printing 3.00
2 thru 4 . . . . @3.50
5 thru 11 . . . . @2.50
12 thru 16 BLs . . . . @2.50
17 thru 23 . . . . @2.50
TPB Casefiles Vol. I rep. #1–#4,
   3rd printing 10.00
TPB Casefiles Vol. 2 rep.#5–#8. . . 10.00
TPB Casefiles Vol.III rep.#9–#12. . 11.00
TPB Casefiles Vol.IV rep.#13–#16. 11.00
TPB Supernatural Law. 8.00

TPB
TPB Supernatural Law rep. 8.00
TPB Fright Court rep.. . . . . 10.00
Spec.#1 Greatest Writs (1997) BLs . 3.00
Spec. #1 Secretary Mavis (1998) . . 3.00
Spec. #2 Secretary Mavis (1999) . . 3.00
Becomes:

SUPERNATURAL LAW
Exhibit A Press, 2000
24 . . . . 2.50
25 The end of 1999 . . . . 2.50
26 Black Market Souls 2.50
27 Creatures of the Night,
   with lawyers. 2.50
28 While the City Doesn't Sleep . . . 2.50
29 thru 31 . . . . @2.50
32 . . . . 3.00
33 thru 35. . . . . @2.50
36 thru 40 . . . . @3.00
Spec. #101 10th anniversary 3.50
TPB Sonofawitch, rep. 15.00
TPB Tales of Supernatural Law . . . 18.00
1-shot First Amendment. 3.50
Spec. Wolf & Byrd #1 new printing . 3.00
Spec. #1 With a Silver Bullet. 3.50
Spec. #1 At the Box Office. 3.50
Spec. Wolff & Byrd The Movie. 3.50

WORDSMITH
Renegade, 1985
1 . . . . 3.00
2 thru 6 . . . . @2.50
7 thru 12 . . . . @2.50
Series 2, Caliber, 1996
1 thru 6 . . . . @3.00

WORLD HARDBALL LEAGUE
Titus Press, 1994
1 F:Big Bat 3.00
2 F:Big Bat 3.00
3 Mount Evrest 3.00
4 Juan Hernandez 3.00

WORLD OF ROBOTECH
Academy Comics, 1995
GN Tales of Planets 13.00

WORLD OF WOOD
Eclipse, 1986
1 thru 4 see color
5 Flying Saucers 2.50

WORLDS OF FANTASY
Newcomers Publishing, 1995
1 The Jenn Chronicles 3.00

WORLDS OF H.P. LOVECRAFT
Caliber Tome Press, 1997
1-shot The Alchemist 3.00
1-shot The Tomb. 3.00
1-shot The Lurking Fear 3.00
1-shot Beyond the Walls of Sleep . . 3.00

WORLD WAR 2
New England Comics, 2001
3 Eastern Front, pt.2. . . . . 3.50
4 Falaise Pocket. 3.50
5 D-Day. 3.50
6 Tarawa. 3.50
7 Afrika Korps 3.50
8 Midway. 3.50

All comics prices listed are for *Near Mint* condition.

WORLD WAR 2: STALINGRAD
New England Comics, 2000
1 by Ron Ledwell 3.50
2 . . . . 3.50

WORLDWATCH
Austen Comics, 2004
1 . . . . 3.00
2 thru 7 . . . . @3.00

WRETCH, THE
Caliber, 1996
1 PhH 3.00
2 PhH 3.00
Amaze Ink, 1997
3 PhH 3.00
4 PhH 3.00
5 PhH & Jim Woodyard 3.00
6 PhH & Bruce McCorkindale 3.00
7 PhH 3.00

WU WEI
Animus, 1995
1 `Debaser'. 2.50
2 Blind Whisper. 2.50
3 . . . . 2.50
4 . . . . 2.50
5 `Testament' pt.5 . . . . 2.50
6 by Oscar Stern. 2.50
7 Explicador 3.00
8 Dead Skin 3.00
9 Apotheosis or Bang You're Dead. 3.00

WW2
New England Comics, 2003
1-shot Snipers 4.00
1-shot War in the Air 4.00
1-shot Mercenaries 4.00
1-shot U-Boats 4.00
1-shot Hitler's Special Forces 4.00
1-shot Last Ditch Stand at Berlin . . . 4.00
1-shot Hitler's Paratroopers
    The Assult on Crete. 4.00
1-shot Tobruk 4.00
1-shot Rommel. 4.00
1-shot Waffen Storm Troops 4.00
1-shot Flying Tigers 4.00

WYATT EARP: DODGE CITY
Moonstone, 2005
1 CDi 3.00
2 thru 3 CDi. . . . . @3.00

WYRD: THE RELUCTANT WARRIOR
Amaze Ink, 1999
1 (of 6) JSn. 3.00
2 . . . . 3.00
3 Telemarketing Horrors 3.00
4 Maxi-Man. 3.00
5 . . . . 3.00
6 . . . . 3.00
TPB JSn, 132-pg. 17.00

XANADU
Thoughts & Images, 1988
1 thru 5 . . . . @2.50

XENON
Eclipse, 1987
1 . . . . 3.00
2 thru 23 . . . . @2.50

Xenon #2
© Eclipse

XENO'S ARROW
Cup O' Tea Studios, 1999
1 by Greg Beettam 2.50
2 thru 10 . . . . @2.50
Radio Comix, 2001
Book 2
1 (of 6) 3.00
2 and 3 . . . . @3.00
4 and 5 . . . . @3.00

XENOZOIC TALES
Kitchen Sink, 1986
1 by Mark Schultz. 10.00
1a Reprint. 2.50
2 . . . . 5.00
2a Reprint 2.50
3 . . . . 7.00
4 . . . . 6.00
5 thru 7 . . . . @4.00
8 thru 13 . . . . @3.00
14 MSh. 3.00

X-BABES VS. JUSTICE BABES
Personality
1 Spoof/parody 3.00

X-CONS
Parody Press
1 X-Men satire,flip cover. 2.50

X-FARCE
Eclipse, 1992
One-Shot X-Force parody 3.00

X-FLIES BUG HUNT
Twist and Shout, 1997
1 Vampires 3.00
2 Monsters 3.00
3 Aliens 3.00
4 The Truth 3.00
Conspiracy. 3.00
Spec. #1 Flies in Black 3.00

XIOLA
Zion Comics
1 thru 3 F:Kantasia . . . . @2.25
4 Visitor. 2.25

XMEN
1 Parody 2.25

X-1999
Viz Communications
1 I:Kamir Shiro 2.75
2 thru 5 F:Princess Hitane . . . . @2.75
6 Battle for X-1999 . . . . 2.75

X-THIEVES
1 . . . . 3.00
2 . . . . 2.25
3 . . . . 2.25

YAHOO
Fantagraphics, 1988
1 thru 4 . . . . @2.50

YAKUZA
Eternity, 1987
1 thru 5 . . . . @2.50

YAWN
Parody Press
1 Spawn parody 2.50
Enigma
1 Spawn parody rep.?. 2.75

YELLOW CABALLERO
Viz Communications, 2001
1 thru 4 Pikachu's New Partner . @3.00

YETS
Airwave Comics, 2003
1 . . . . 3.50
2 . . . . 3.50
3 . . . . 3.50

YOUNG DRACULA: PRAYER OF THE VAMPIRE
Boneyard Press, 1997
1 (of 5) sequel to Young Dracula:
    Diary of a Vampire. 3.00
2 Empire of Madness, pt.2 . . . . . . 3.00
3 Children of Madness 3.00
4 Madness Prime 3.00
5 V:Cartiphilus. 4.00

YOUNG MASTERS
New Comics, 1987
1 thru 10 . . . . @2.50

YUGGOTH CREATURES
Avatar Press, 2004
1 . . . . 4.00
2 thru 3 . . . . @4.00
1a thru 3a wraparound (c). . . . . @4.00
1b thru 3b connecting (c) 6.00

Z
Keystone Graphics, 1994
1 . . . . 2.75
2 House of Windsor-Yakonaral. . . . 2.75
3 House of Windsor-YakonaraII . . . 2.75

ZACHERLEY'S MIDNIGHT TERRORS
Chanting Monks Press, 2004
1 . . . . 4.00
2 . . . . 4.00
3 . . . . 4.00
4 . . . . 4.00

ZED
Gagne International, 2005
1 by Michel Gagne 3.00
2 . . . . 3.00
3 . . . . 3.50
4 . . . . 3.00
5 Resurrection 3.00
6 In the Shadow of Maxuss 3.00

ZELL THE SWORDDANCER
Thoughts & Images, 1986
1 Steve Gallacci 5.50
2 and 3 . . . . @2.50

ZEN BOUNTY HUNTER
SSSComics.Com, 2005
1 . . . . 3.00
2 thru 3 . . . . @3.00

ZEN ILLUSTRATED NOVELLA
Entity
1 thru 4 R:Bruce Lewis . . . . @3.00
5 Immortal Combat 3.00
6 Bubble Economy 3.00
7 Zen City 3.00
8 V:Assassins 3.00

ZEN, INTER-GALACTIC NINJA
Zen, 1987
1 . . . . 15.00
2 . . . . 9.00
3 thru 9 . . . . @9.00
X-mas Spec #1,V:Black Hole Bob . . 3.00
[2nd Series]
1 `Down to Earth' 3.00
2 RA, A:Jeremy Baker 3.00
2a polybagged, limited 5.00
3 thru 5 . . . . @3.00
[3rd Series]
0 . . . . 3.00
1 thru 3 A:Niro . . . . @3.00
Sourcebook #1 . . . . 3.50

ZEN INTERGALACTIC NINJA: STARQUEST
Entity
1 thru 6 V:Nolan the Destroyer . . @3.00
7 V:Dimensional 3.00
8 thru 9 I:New Team . . . . @3.00
10 In Deep Space 3.00
11 Dimensional Terrorists 3.00
TPB Rep. #1-#4 . . . . @7.00

ZEN INTERGALACTIC NINJA VS. MICHEAL JACK-ZEN
Entity
1 Cameos Galore 3.00

ZENISMS WIT AND WISDOMS
Entity
1 R:Bruce Lewis 3.00

ZEN: MISTRESS OF CHAOS
1 . . . . 3.00

ZENITH: PHASE II
Fleetway
1 GMo(s),SY,Rep.2000 AD 2.25

ZERO ZERO
Fantagraphics, 1995
1 thru 7 . . . . @5.00
8 . . . . @6.00
9 thru 15 . . . . @5.00
16 . . . . 6.00
17 thru 22 . . . . @5.00
23 F:`Tired'. 5.00
24 F:Smilin' Ed 4.00
25 . . . . 4.00
26 final issue, 56-pg. 5.00
27 really final 64-pg. 5.00

ZETRAMAN
Antarctic, 1991
1 thru 3 . . . . @2.25
[Vol. 2], 1992
1 and 2 . . . . @2.75

ZETRAMAN: REVIVAL
Antarctic Press, 1993
1 thru 3 . . . . @2.75

Zillion #2
© *Eternity*

ZILLION
Eternity, 1993
1 thru 4 . . . . @2.50

ZIPPY
Fantagraphics Books 2002
TPB Annual 2003 . . . . 20.00
TPB From Here to Absurdity 20.00
TPB Type Z Personality 20.00
TPB Connect the Polkadots 19.00

ZOLASTRAYA AND THE BARD
Twilight Twins, 1987
1 thru 5 . . . . @2.50

ZOMBIE-SAMA
Narwain Publishing 2006
1-shot BTi 5.00
1-shot variant (c) 5.00
1-shot special ed. 13.00

ZOMBIE HIGHWAY
Digital Webbing 2004
TPB 13.00
1 . . . . 4.00
2 thru 3 . . . . @4.00

ZOMBIE WAR: EARTH MUST BE DESTROYED
Fantaco, 1993
1 thru 3 Kevin Eastman . . . . @4.00

ZONE CONTINUUM
Caliber
1 Master of the Waves 3.00
2 . . . . 3.00

ZOOT!
Fantagraphics, 1993
1 thru 5 . . . . @2.50

ZOT!
Eclipse, 1987
(#1-#10 See: Color)
11 New Series 3.00
12 thru 15 . . . . @3.00
16 A:De-Evolutionaries 3.00
17 thru 36 . . . . @3.00
Kitchen Sink
Book Two TPB rep. #11–#15,
  #17–#18. . . . . 20.00
Book Two TPB signed and
  numbered 35.00
Book Three TPB rep. #16,
  #21–#27. . . . . 20.00
Book Four TPB The Earth
  Stories 20.00

ZU
Mu Press, 1995
1 thru 11 . . . . @3.00
12 `The Monkey Tales'. 3.00
13 . . . . 3.00
14 . . . . 3.00
15 `Curse of the Re-Possessed' . . . 3.00
16 thru 19 . . . . @3.00
20 final issue 3.00

Zot #12
© *Eclipse*

All comics prices listed are for *Near Mint* condition.

Classics Illustrated

[Issued As
Classic Comics]

001-THE THREE MUSKETEERS

By Alexandre Dumas

10/41 **(—)** MKd(a&c),
Original,10¢ (c) Price 7,500.00
05/43 **(10)** MKd(a&c),
No(c)Price; rep 500.00
11/43 **(15)** MKd(a&c),Long
Island Independent Ed; 300.00
6/44 **(18/20)** MKd(a&c),
Sunrise Times Edition;rep . . . 200.00
7/44 **(21)** MKd(a&c),Richmond
Courier Edition;rep 175.00
6/46 **(28)** MKd(a&c);rep 150.00
4/47 **(36)** MKd(a&c),
New CILogo;rep 75.00
6/49 **(60)** MKd(a&c),CI Logo;rep . . 50.00
10/49 **(64)** MKd(a&c),CI Logo;rep . 50.00
12/50 **(78)** MKd(a&c),15¢(c)
Price; CI Logo;rep 30.00
03/52 **(93)** MKd(a&c),
CI Logo;rep 30.00
11/53 **(114)** CI Logo;rep 25.00
09/56 **(134)** MKd(a&c),New
P(c),CI Logo,64 pgs;rep 30.00
03/58 **(143)** MKd(a&c),P(c),
CI Logo,64 pgs;rep 25.00
05/59 **(150)** GE&RC New Art,
P(c),CILogo;rep 30.00
03/61 **(149)** GE&RC,P(c),
CI Logo;rep 18.00
62-63 **(167)** GE&RC,P(c),
CI Logo;rep 18.00
04/64 **(167)** GE&RC,P(c),
CI Logo;rep 18.00
01/65 **(167)** GE&RC,P(c),
CI Logo;rep 18.00
03/66 **(167)** GE&RC,P(c),
CI Logo;rep 18.00
11/67 **(166)** GE&RC,P(c),
CI Logo;rep 18.00
Sp/69 **(166)** GE&RC,P(c),25¢(c)
Price,CILogo, Rigid(c);rep . . . 18.00
Sp/71 **(169)** GE&RC,P(c),
CI Logo,Rigid(c);rep 18.00

CI #1, The Three Musketeers
© Gilberton Publications

002-IVANHOE

By Sir Walter Scott

1941 **(—)** EA,MKd(c),Original . 3,500.00
05/43 **(1)** EA,MKd(c),word "Presents"
Removed From(c);rep 400.00
11/43 **(15)** EA,MKd(c),Long Island
Independent Edition;rep 250.00
06/44 **(18/20)** EA,MKd(c),Sunrise
Times Edition;rep. 200.00
07/44 **(21)** EA,MKd(c),Richmond
Courier Edition;rep 175.00
06/46 **(28)** EA,MKd(c);rep 150.00
07/47 **(36)** EA,MKd(c),New
CI Logo; rep. 100.00
06/49 **(60)** EA,MKd(c),CI Logo;rep 50.00
10/49 **(64)** EA,MKd(c),CI Logo;rep 40.00
12/50 **(78)** EA,MKd(c),15¢(c)
Price; CI Logo;rep 30.00
11/51 **(89)** EA,MKd(c),CI Logo;rep 25.00
04/53 **(106)** EA,MKd(c),CI
Logo;rep 20.00
07/54 **(121)** EA,MKd(c),CI
Logo;rep 30.00
01/57 **(136)** NN New Art,New
P(c),CI Logo;rep 30.00
01/58 **(142)** NN,P(c),CI Logo;rep . 18.00
11/59 **(153)** NN,P(c),CI Logo;rep . 18.00
03/61 **(149)** NN,P(c),CI Logo;rep . 18.00
62/63 **(167)** NN,P(c),CI Logo;rep . 15.00
05/64 **(167)** NN,P(c),CI Logo;rep . 15.00
01/65 **(167)** NN,P(c),CI Logo;rep . 15.00
03/66 **(167)** NN,P(c),CI Logo;rep . 15.00
09/67 **(166)** NN,P(c),CI Logo;rep . 15.00
1968 **(166)** NN,P(c),CI Logo;rep . 15.00
Wr/69 **(169)** NN,P(c),CI
Logo Rigid(c);rep. 15.00
Wr/71 **(169)** NN,P(c),CI
Logo,Rigid(c);rep 15.00

003-THE COUNT OF MONTE CRISTO

By Alexandre Dumas

03/42 **(—)** ASm(a&c),Orig. 2,200.00
05/43 **(10)** ASm(a&c);rep. 400.00
11/43 **(15)** ASm(a&c),Long Island
Independent Edition;rep 250.00
06/44 **(18/20)** ASm(a&c),
Sunrise Times Edition;rep . . . 225.00
06/44 **(20)** ASm(a&c),Sunrise
Times Edition;rep. 200.00
07/44 **(21)** ASm(a&c),Richmond
Courier Edition;rep 175.00
06/46 **(28)** ASm(a&c);rep 150.00
04/47 **(36)** ASm(a&c),New
CI Logo; rep. 100.00
06/49 **(60)** ASm(a&c),CI
Logo;rep 60.00
08/49 **(62)** ASm(a&c),CI
Logo;rep 75.00
05/50 **(71)** ASm(a&c),CI
Logo;rep 50.00
09/51 **(87)** ASm(a&c),15¢(c)
Price, CI Logo;rep 30.00
11/53 **(113)** ASm(a&c),
CI Logo; rep. 25.00
11/56 **(—)** LC New Art,New
P(c), CI Logo;rep 25.00
03/58 **(135)** LC,P(c),CI Logo;rep . . 30.00
11/59 **(153)** LC,P(c),CI Logo;rep . . 18.00
03/61 **(161)** LC,P(c),CI Logo;rep . . 18.00
62/63 **(167)** LC,P(c),CI Logo;rep . . 15.00
07/64 **(167)** LC,P(c),CI Logo;rep . . 15.00
07/65 **(167)** LC,P(c),CI Logo;rep . . 15.00

07/66 **(167)** LC,P(c),CI Logo;rep . . 15.00
1968 **(166)** LC,P(c),25¢(c)
Price, CI Logo;rep 15.00
Wn/69 **(169)** LC,P(c),CI Logo,
Rigid(c);rep 15.00

004-THE LAST OF THE MOHICANS

By James Fenimore Cooper

08/42 **(—)** RR(a&c),Original . . 1,800.00
06/43 **(12)** RR(a&c),Price
Balloon Deleted;rep. 400.00
11/43 **(15)** RR(a&c),Long Island
Independent Edition;rep 250.00
06/44 **(20)** RR(a&c),Long Island
Independent Edition;rep 225.00
07/44 **(21)** RR(a&c),Queens
Home News Edition;rep. 200.00
06/46 **(28)** RR(a&c);rep 150.00
04/47 **(36)** RR(a&c),New
CI Logo; rep. 100.00
06/49 **(60)** RR(a&c),CI Logo;rep . . 50.00
10/49 **(64)** RR(a&c),CI Logo;rep . . 35.00
12/50 **(78)** RR(a&c),15¢(c)
Price,CI Logo rep 35.00
11/51 **(89)** RR(a&c),CI Logo;rep . . 30.00
03/54 **(117)** RR(a&c),CI Logo;rep . 28.00
11/56 **(135)** RR,New P(c),
CI Logo; rep. 28.00
11/57 **(141)** RR,P(c),CI Logo;rep. . 30.00
05/59 **(150)** JSe&StA New Art;
P(c), CI Logo;rep. 35.00
03/61 **(161)** JSe&StA,P(c),CI
Logo; rep 15.00
62/63 **(167)** JSe&StA,P(c),CI
Logo; rep. 15.00
06/64 **(167)** JSe&StA,P(c),CI
Logo; rep. 15.00
08/65 **(167)** JSe&StA,P(c),CI
Logo; rep. 15.00
08/66 **(167)** JSe&StA,P(c),CI
Logo; rep. 15.00
1967 **(166)** JSe&StA,P(c),25¢(c)
Price, CI Logo;rep 15.00
Sp/69 **(169)** JSe&StA,P(c),CI
Logo, Rigid(c);rep. 15.00

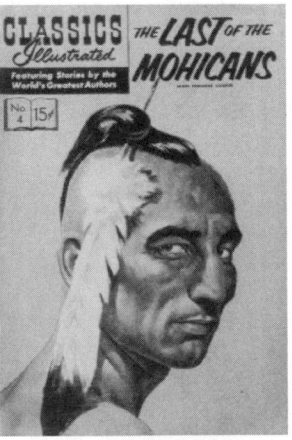

CI #4, The Last of the Mohicans
© Gilberton Publications

005-MOBY DICK
By Herman Melville
09/42 (**—**) LZ(a&c),Original . . . 2,400.00
05/43 (**10**) LZ(a&c),Conray Products
  Edition, No(c)Price;rep 500.00
11/43 (**15**) LZ(a&c),Long Island
  Independent Edition;rep 275.00
06/44 (**18/20**) LZ(a&c),Sunrise
  Times Edition;rep 250.00
07/44 (**20**) LZ(a&c),Sunrise
  Times Edition;rep 225.00
07/44 (**21**) LZ(a&c),Sunrise
  Times Edition;rep 200.00
06/46 (**28**) LZ(a&c);rep 150.00
04/47 (**36**) LZ(a&c),New CI
  Logo; 100.00
06/49 (**60**) LZ(a&c),CI Logo;rep . . 50.00
08/49 (**62**) LZ(a&c),CI Logo;rep . . 55.00
05/50 (**71**) LZ(a&c),CI Logo;rep . . 40.00
09/51 (**87**) LZ(a&c),15¢(c)
  Price, CI Logo;rep 30.00
04/54 (**118**) LZ(a&c),CI Logo;rep . . 25.00
03/56 (**131**) NN New Art,New
  P(c),rep 35.00
05/57 (**138**) NN,P(c),CI Logo;rep. . 18.00
01/59 (**148**) NN,P(c),CI Logo;rep. . 18.00
09/60 (**158**) NN,P(c),CI Logo;rep. . 18.00
62/63 (**167**) NN,P(c),CI Logo;rep. . 18.00
06/64 (**167**) NN,P(c),CI Logo;rep. . 18.00
07/65 (**167**) NN,P(c),CI Logo;rep. . 18.00
03/66 (**167**) NN,P(c),CI Logo;rep. . 18.00
09/67 (**166**) NN,P(c),CI Logo;rep. . 18.00
Wn/69 (**166**) NN,P(c),25¢(c) Price,
  CI Logo, Rigid(c);rep 25.00
Wn/71 (**169**) NN,P(c),CI Logo;rep . 20.00

006-A TALE OF TWO CITIES
By Charles Dickens
11/42 (**—**) StM(a&c),Original . . 2,000.00
09/43 (**14**) StM(a&c),No(c)
  Price; rep 400.00
03/44 (**18**) StM(a&c),Long Island
  Independent Edition;rep 275.00
06/44 (**20**) StM(a&c),Sunrise
  Times Edition;rep 235.00
06/46 (**28**) StM(a&c);rep 150.00
09/48 (**51**) StM(a&c),New CI
  Logo; rep 75.00
10/49 (**64**) StM(a&c),CI
  Logo;rep 40.00
12/50 (**78**) StM(a&c),15¢(c)
  Price, CI Logo; rep 30.00
11/51 (**89**) StM(a&c),CI Logo;rep. . 30.00
03/54 (**117**) StM(a&c),CI
  Logo;rep 25.00
05/56 (**132**) JO New Art,New
  P(c), CI Logo;rep 35.00
09/57 (**140**) JO,P(c),CI Logo;rep . . 15.00
11/57 (**147**) JO,P(c),CI Logo;rep . . 15.00
09/59 (**152**) JO,P(c),CI Logo;rep . 250.00
11/59 (**153**) JO,P(c),CI Logo;rep . . 18.00
03/61 (**149**) JO,P(c),CI Logo;rep . . 18.00
62/63 (**167**) JO,P(c),CI Logo;rep . . 15.00
06/64 (**167**) JO,P(c),CI Logo;rep . . 15.00
08/65 (**167**) JO,P(c),CI Logo;rep . . 15.00
05/67 (**167**) JO,P(c),CI Logo;rep . . 15.00
Fl/68 (**166**) JO,NN New P(c),
  25¢(c)Price,CI Logo;rep 25.00
Sr/70 (**169**) JO,NN P(c),CI
  Logo, Rigid(c);rep 20.00

007-ROBIN HOOD
By Howard Pyle
12/42 (**—**) LZ(a&c),Original . . . 1,400.00
06/43 (**12**) LZ(a&c),P.D.C.
  on(c) Deleted;rep. 350.00
03/44 (**18**) LZ(a&c),Long Island
  Independent Edition;rep 225.00

06/44 (**20**) LZ(a&c),Nassau
  Bulletin Edition;rep 250.00
10/44 (**22**) LZ(a&c),Queens
  City Times Edition;rep 225.00
06/46 (**28**) LZ(a&c),rep 150.00
09/48 (**51**) LZ(a&c),New CI
  Logo;rep 75.00
06/49 (**60**) LZ(a&c),CI Logo;rep. . . 35.00
10/49 (**64**) LZ(a&c),CI Logo;rep. . . 32.00
12/50 (**78**) LZ(a&c),CI Logo;rep. . . 32.00
07/52 (**97**) LZ(a&c),CI Logo;rep. . . 35.00
03/53 (**106**) LZ(a&c),CI Logo;rep. . 30.00
07/54 (**121**) LZ(a&c),CI Logo;rep. . 30.00
11/55 (**129**) LZ,New P(c),
  CI Logo;rep 35.00
01/57 (**136**) JkS New Art,P(c);rep . 30.00
03/58 (**143**) JkS,P(c),CI Logo;rep . 18.00
11/59 (**153**) JkS,P(c),CI Logo;rep . 15.00
10/61 (**164**) JkS,P(c),CI Logo;rep . 15.00
62/63 (**167**) JkS,P(c),CI Logo;rep . 15.00
06/64 (**167**) JkS,P(c),CI Logo;rep . 20.00
05/65 (**167**) JkS,P(c),CI Logo;rep . 15.00
07/66 (**167**) JkS,P(c),CI Logo;rep . 15.00
12/67 (**166**) JkS,P(c),CI Logo;rep . 20.00
Sr/69 (**169**) JkS,P(c),CI
  Logo, Rigid(c);rep 15.00

008-ARABIAN KNIGHTS
By Antoine Galland
03/43 (**—**) LCh(a&c),Original . . 2,200.00
09/43 (**14**) LCh(a&c);rep 750.00
01/44 (**17**) LCh(a&c),Long Island
  Independent Edition;rep 750.00
06/44 (**20**) LCh(a&c),Nassau
  Bulletin Edition,64 pgs;rep. . . 600.00
06/46 (**28**) LCh(a&c);rep 400.00
09/48 (**51**) LCh(a&c),New CI
  Logo; rep 400.00
10/49 (**64**) LCh(a&c),CI
  Logo;rep 300.00
12/50 (**78**) LCh(a&c),CI
  Logo;rep 250.00
10/61 (**164**) ChB New Art,P(c),
  CI Logo;rop 225.00

009-LES MISERABLES
By Victor Hugo
03/43 (**—**) RLv(a&c),Original . . 1,300.00
09/43 (**14**) RLv(a&c);rep 400.00
03/44 (**18**) RLv(a&c),Nassau
  Bulletin Edition;rep 275.00
06/44 (**20**) RLv(a&c),Richmond
  Courier Edition;rep 250.00
06/46 (**28**) RLv(a&c);rep. 200.00

CC#9, Les Miserables
© Gilberton Publications

09/48 (**51**) RLv(a&c),New CI
  Logo; rep 100.00
05/50 (**71**) RLv(a&c),CI
  Logo;rep 75.00
09/51 (**87**) RLv(a&c),CI Logo,
  15¢(c)Price;rep 60.00
03/61 (**161**) NN New Art,GMc
  New P(c), CI Logo;rep. 60.00
09/63 (**167**) NN,GMc P(c),CI
  Logo; rep 35.00
12/65 (**167**) NN,GMc P(c),CI
  Logo; rep 35.00
1968 (**166**) NN,GMc P(c),25¢(c)
  Price, CI Logo;rep 35.00

010-ROBINSON CRUSOE
By Daniel Defoe
04/43 (**—**) StM(a&c),Original . . 1,100.00
09/43 (**14**) StM(a&c);rep 400.00
03/44 (**18**) StM(a&c),Nassau Bulletin
  Ed.,'Bill of Rights'Pge.64;rep. 300.00
06/44 (**20**) StM(a&c),Queens
  Home News Edition;rep. 250.00
??/45 (**23**) StM(a&c);rep 150.00
06/46 (**28**) StM(a&c);rep 150.00
09/48 (**51**) StM(a&c),New CI
  Logo; rep 75.00
10/49 (**64**) StM(a&c),CI Logo;rep. . 50.00
12/50 (**78**) StM(a&c),15¢(c)
  Price, CI Logo;rep 35.00
07/52 (**97**) StM(a&c),CI Logo;rep. . 32.00
12/53 (**114**) StM(a&c),CI
  Logo;rep 30.00
01/56 (**130**) StM,New P(c),CI
  Logo; rep 32.00
09/57 (**140**) SmC New Art,P(c),
  CI Logo; rep. 32.00
11/59 (**153**) SmC,P(c),CI Logo;rep 15.00
10/61 (**164**) SmC,P(c),CI Logo;rep 15.00
62/63 (**167**) SmC,P(c),CI Logo;rep 18.00
07/64 (**167**) SmC,P(c),CI Logo;rep 20.00
05/65 (**167**) SmC,P(c),CI Logo;rep 15.00
06/66 (**167**) SmC,P(c),CI Logo;rep 18.00
Fl/68 (**166**) SmC,P(c),CI Logo,
  25¢(c)Price;rep 18.00
1968 (**166**) SmC,P(c),CI Logo,No
  Twin Circle Ad;rep 15.00
Sr/70 (**169**) SmC,P(c),CI Logo,
  Rigid(c);rep 15.00

011-DON QUIXOTE
By Miguel de Cervantes Saavedra
05/43 (**—**) LZ(a&c),Original . . . 1,300.00
03/44 (**18**) LZ(a&c),Nassau
  Bulletin Edition;rep 350.00
07/44 (**21**) LZ(a&c),Queens
  Home News Edition;rep. 250.00
06/46 (**28**) LZ(a&c);rep 150.00
08/53 (**110**) LZ,TO New P(c),New
  CI Logo;rep 50.00
05/60 (**156**) LZ,TO P(c),Pages
  Reduced to 48,CI Logo;rep . . . 30.00
1962 (**165**) LZ,TO P(c),CI Logo;rep20.00
01/64 (**167**) LZ,TO P(c),CI
  Logo;rep 20.00
11/65 (**167**) LZ,TO P(c),CI
  Logo;rep 20.00
1968 (**166**) LZ,TO P(c),CI Logo,
  25¢(c)Price;rep 40.00

012-RIP VAN WINKLE & THE HEADLESS HORSEMAN
By Washington Irving
06/43 (**—**) RLv(a&c),Original. 1,200.00
11/43 (**15**) RLv(a&c),Long Island
  Independent Edition;rep 350.00

All comics prices listed are for *Near Mint* condition.

06/44 **(20)** RLv(a&c),Long Island
   Independent Edition;rep 250.00
10/44 **(22)** RLv(a&c),Queens
   City Times Edition;rep 225.00
06/46 **(28)** RLv(a&c);rep 150.00
06/49 **(60)** RLv(a&c),New CI
   Logo;rep 75.00
08/49 **(62)** RLv(a&c),CI
   Logo;rep 45.00
05/50 **(71)** RLv(a&c),CI
   Logo;rep 35.00
11/51 **(89)** RLv(a&c),15¢(c)
   Price, CI Logo;rep 30.00
04/54 **(118)** RLv(a&c),CI
   Logo;rep 32.00
05/56 **(132)** RLv,New P(c),
   CI Logo; rep 35.00
05/59 **(150)** NN New Art;P(c),
   CI Logo; rep 35.00
09/60 **(158)** NN,P(c),CI Logo;rep . 20.00
62/63 **(167)** NN,P(c),CI Logo;rep . 20.00
12/63 **(167)** NN,P(c),CI Logo;rep . 20.00
04/65 **(167)** NN,P(c),CI Logo;rep . 22.00
04/66 **(167)** NN,P(c),CI Logo;rep . 20.00
1969 **(166)** NN,P(c),CI Logo,
   25¢(c)Price,Rigid(c);rep 26.00
Sr/70 **(169)** NN,P(c),CI Logo,
   Rigid(c);rep 25.00

CC #13 Dr. Jekyll and Mr. Hyde
© Gilberton Publications

013-DR. JEKYLL
AND MR. HYDE
By Robert Louis Stevenson
08/43 **(—)** AdH(a&c),Original. . 2,000.00
11/43 **(15)** AdH(a&c),Long Island
   Independent Edition;rep 500.00
06/44 **(20)** AdH(a&c),Long Island
   Independent Edition;rep 275.00
06/46 **(28)** AdH(a&c),No(c)
   Price; rep................. 225.00
06/49 **(60)** AdH,HcK New(c),New CI
   Logo,Pgs.reduced to 48;rep . . 75.00
08/49 **(62)** AdH,HcK(c),CI
   Logo;rep 45.00
05/50 **(71)** AdH,HcK(c),CI
   Logo;rep 40.00
09/51 **(87)** AdH,HcK(c),Erroneous
   Return of Original Date,
   CI Logo;rep 40.00
10/53 **(112)** LC New Art,New
   P(c), CI Logo;rep 40.00
11/59 **(153)** LC,P(c),CI Logo;rep . . 20.00
03/61 **(161)** LC,P(c),CI Logo;rep . . 20.00
62/63 **(167)** LC,P(c),CI Logo;rep . . 20.00
08/64 **(167)** LC,P(c),CI Logo;rep . . 20.00
11/65 **(167)** LC,P(c),CI Logo;rep . . 20.00

1968 **(166)** LC,P(c),CI Logo,
   25¢(c)Price;rep 22.00
Wr/69 **(169)** LC,P(c),CI Logo,
   Rigid(c);rep 20.00

014-WESTWARD HO!
By Charles Kingsley
09/43 **(—)** ASm(a&c),Orig.... 3,000.00
11/43 **(15)** ASm(a&c),Long Island
   Independent Edition;rep 750.00
07/44 **(21)** ASm(a&c),rep...... 650.00
06/46 **(28)** ASm(a&c),No(c)
   Price; rep................. 450.00
11/48 **(53)** ASm(a&c),Pages reduced
   to 48, New CI Logo;rep..... 400.00

015-UNCLE TOM'S CABIN
By Harriet Beecher Stowe
11/43 **(—)** RLv(a&c),Original . . 1,000.00
11/43 **(15)** RLv(a&c),Blank
   Price Circle, Long Island
   Independent Ed.;rep 350.00
07/44 **(21)** RLv(a&c),Nassau
   Bulletin Edition;rep 250.00
06/46 **(28)** RLv(a&c),No(c)
   Price; rep................. 200.00
11/48 **(53)** RLv(a&c),Pages Reduced
   to 48, New CI Logo;rep...... 75.00
05/50 **(71)** RLv(a&c),CI Logo;rep . 45.00
11/51 **(89)** RLv(a&c),15¢(c)
   Price, CI Logo;rep 45.00
03/54 **(117)** RLv,New P(c),CI
   Logo, Lettering Changes;rep. . 32.00
09/55 **(128)** RLv,P(c),"Picture
   Progress"Promotion,CI
   Logo;rep 22.00
03/57 **(137)** RLv,P(c),CI Logo;rep . 15.00
09/58 **(146)** RLv,P(c),CI Logo;rep . 15.00
01/60 **(154)** RLv,P(c),CI Logo;rep . 15.00
03/61 **(161)** RLv,P(c),CI Logo;rep . 17.00
62/63 **(167)** RLv,P(c),CI Logo;rep . 15.00
06/64 **(167)** RLv,P(c),CI Logo;rep . 15.00
05/65 **(167)** RLv,P(c),CI Logo;rep . 15.00
05/67 **(166)** RLv,P(c),CI Logo;rep . 15.00
Wr/69 **(166)** RLv,P(c),CI
   Logo, Rigid(c);rep 26.00
Sr/70 **(169)** RLv,P(c),CI
   Logo, Rigid(c);rep 25.00

016-GULLIVER'S TRAVELS
By Johnathan Swift
12/43 **(—)** LCh(a&c),Original. 1,200.00
06/44 **(18/20)** LCh(a&c),Queen's
   Home News Edition,No(c)Price;
   rep 300.00
10/44 **(22)** LCh(a&c),Queen's
   Home News Editon;rep 225.00
06/46 **(28)** LCh(a&c);rep 150.00
06/49 **(60)** LCh(a&c),Pgs. Reduced
   To 48, New CI Logo;rep 75.00
08/49 **(62)** LCh(a&c),CI Logo;rep . 45.00
10/49 **(64)** LCh(a&c),CI Logo;rep . 45.00
12/50 **(78)** LCh(a&c),15¢(c)
   Price, CI Logo;rep 35.00
11/51 **(89)** LCh(a&c),CI Logo;rep. . 30.00
03/60 **(155)** LCh,New P(c),CI
   Logo; rep 35.00
1962 **(165)** LCh,P(c),CI Logo;rep . 20.00
05/64 **(167)** LCh,P(c),CI Logo;rep . 20.00
11/65 **(167)** LCh,P(c),CI Logo;rep . 20.00
1968 **(166)** LCh,P(c),CI Logo,
   25¢(c)Price;rep 20.00
Wr/69 **(169)** LCh,P(c),CI
   Logo, Rigid(c);rep 20.00

017-THE DEERSLAYER
By James Fenimore Cooper
01/44 **(—)** LZ(a&c),Original . . 1,000.00

03/44 **(18)** LZ(a&c),No(c)Price;
   rep 350.00
10/44 **(22)** LZ(a&c),Queen's
   City Times Edition;rep 200.00
06/46 **(28)** LZ(a&c);rep 150.00
06/49 **(60)** LZ(a&c),Pgs. Reduced
   to 48,New CI Logo;rep 75.00
10/49 **(64)** LZ(a&c),CI Logo;rep. . . 35.00
07/51 **(85)** LZ(a&c),15¢(c)
   Price, CI Logo;rep 30.00
04/54 **(118)** LZ(a&c),CI Logo;rep . . 28.00
05/56 **(132)** LZ(a&c),CI Logo;rep. . 25.00
11/66 **(167)** LZ(a&c),CI Logo;rep. . 25.00
1968 **(166)** LZ,StA New P(c),CI
   Logo, 25¢(c)Price;rep 35.00
Sg/71 **(169)** LZ,StA P(c),CI Logo,
   Rigid(c), Letters From Parents
   and Educators;rep 25.00

018-THE HUNCHBACK
OF NOTRE DAME
By Victor Hugo
03/44 **(—)** ASm(a&c),Original
   Gilberton Edition......... 1,200.00
03/44 **(—)** ASm(a&c),Original
   Island Publications Edition . 1,000.00
06/44 **(18/20)** ASm(a&c),Queens
   Home News Edition;rep..... 350.00
10/44 **(22)** ASm(a&c),Queens
   City Times Edition;rep 250.00
06/46 **(28)** ASm(a&c);rep 225.00
06/49 **(60)** ASm,HcK New(c)8 Pgs.
   Deleted, New CI Logo;rep.... 75.00
08/49 **(62)** ASm,HcK(c),CI
   Logo;rep 40.00
12/50 **(78)** ASm,HcK(c),15¢(c)
   Price; CI Logo;rep 35.00
11/51 **(89)** ASm,HcK(c),CI
   Logo;rep 32.00
04/54 **(118)** ASm,HcK(c),CI
   Logo;rep 35.00
09/57 **(140)** ASm,New P(c),CI
   Logo; rep 32.00
09/58 **(146)** ASm,P(c),CI Logo;rep 32.00
09/60 **(158)** GE&RC New Art,GMc
   New P(c),CI Logo;rep 20.00
1962 **(165)** GE&RC,GMc P(c),CI
   Logo; rep 20.00
09/63 **(167)** GE&RC,GMc P(c),CI
   Logo; rep 20.00
10/64 **(167)** GE&RC,GMc P(c),CI
   Logo; rep 20.00
04/66 **(167)** GE&RC,GMc P(c),CI
   Logo; rep 20.00
1968 **(166)** GE&RC,GMc P(c),CI
   Logo, 25¢(c)Price;rep 20.00
Sr/70 **(169)** GE&RC,GMc P(c),CI
   Logo, Rigid(c);rep 20.00

019-HUCKLEBERRY FINN
By Mark Twain
04/44 **(—)** LZ(a&c),Original
   Gilberton Edition 750.00
04/44 **(—)** LZ(a&c),Original Island
   Publications Company Ed. . . 800.00
03/44 **(18)** LZ(a&c),Nassau
   Bulletin Editon;rep......... 350.00
10/44 **(22)** LZ(a&c),Queens City
   Times Edition;rep.......... 250.00
06/46 **(28)** LZ(a&c);rep 200.00
06/49 **(60)** LZ(a&c),New CI Logo,
   Pgs.Reduced to 48;rep 75.00
08/49 **(62)** LZ(a&c),CI Logo;rep ... 40.00
12/50 **(78)** LZ(a&c),CI Logo;rep. . . 35.00
11/51 **(89)** LZ(a&c),CI Logo;rep. . . 30.00
03/54 **(117)** LZ(a&c),CI Logo;rep. . 30.00
03/56 **(131)** FrG New Art,New
   P(c), CI Logo; rep 30.00
09/57 **(140)** FrG,P(c),CI Logo;rep . 20.00
05/59 **(150)** FrG,P(c),CI Logo;rep . 20.00

09/60 **(158)** FrG,P(c),CI Logo;rep . 20.00
1962 **(165)** FrG,P(c),CI Logo;rep . 20.00
62/63 **(167)** FrG,P(c),CI Logo;rep . 20.00
06/64 **(167)** FrG,P(c),CI Logo;rep . 20.00
06/65 **(167)** FrG,P(c),CI Logo;rep . 20.00
10/65 **(167)** FrG,P(c),CI Logo;rep . 20.00
09/67 **(166)** FrG,P(c),CI Logo;rep . 20.00
Wr/69 **(166)** FrG,P(c),CI Logo,
25¢(c)Price, Rigid(c);rep 20.00
Sr/70 **(169)** FrG,P(c),CI Logo,
Rigid(c);rep 20.00

020-THE CORSICAN BROTHERS
By Alexandre Dumas
06/44 **(—)** ASm(a&c),Original
Gilberton Edition 650.00
06/44 **(—)** ASm(a&c),Original
Courier Edition. 550.00
06/44 **(—)** ASm(a&c),Original Long
Island Independent Edition . . 550.00
10/44 **(22)** ASm(a&c),Queens
City Times Edition;rep 275.00
06/46 **(28)** ASm(a&c);rep 250.00
06/49 **(60)** ASm(a&c),No(c)Price,
New CI Logo,Pgs. Reduced
to 48;rep 225.00
08/49 **(62)** ASm(a&c),CI
Logo;rep 165.00
12/50 **(78)** ASm(a&c),15¢(c)
Price, CI Logo;rep 150.00
07/52 **(97)** ASm(a&c),CI
Logo;rep 135.00

021-FAMOUS MYSTERIES
By Sir Arthur Conan Doyle Guy de Maupassant & Edgar Allan Poe
07/44 **(—)** AdH,LZ,ASm(a&c),
Original Gilberton Edition . . 1,300.00
07/44 **(—)** AdH,LZ,ASm(a&c),
Original Island Publications
Edition; No Date or Indicia 1,350.00
07/44 **(—)** AdH,LZ,ASm(a&c),
Original Richmond Courier
Edition. 1,100.00
10/44 **(22)** AdH,LZ,ASm(a&c),
Nassau Bulletin Edition;rep . . 500.00
09/46 **(30)** AdH,LZ,ASm(a&c);
rep 350.00
08/49 **(62)** AdH,LZ,ASm(a&c),
New CI Logo;rep 300.00
04/50 **(70)** AdH,LZ,ASm(a&c),
CI Logo;rep 275.00
07/51 **(85)** AdH,LZ,ASm(a&c),
15¢(c) Price,CI Logo;rep 250.00
12/53 **(114)** ASm,AdH,LZ,New
P(c), CI Logo;rep 250.00

022-THE PATHFINDER
By James Fenimore Cooper
10/44 **(—)** LZ(a&c),Original
Gilberton Edition 600.00
10/44 **(—)** LZ(a&c),Original
Island Publications Edition; . . 500.00
10/44 **(—)** LZ(a&c),Original
Queens County Times Edition450.00
09/46 **(30)** LZ(a&c),No(c)
Price;rep 200.00
06/49 **(60)** LZ(a&c),New CI Logo,
Pgs.Reduced To 48;rep 50.00
08/49 **(62)** LZ(a&c),CI Logo;rep . . 45.00
04/50 **(70)** LZ(a&c),CI Logo;rep . . 35.00
07/51 **(85)** LZ(a&c),15¢(c)
Price, CI Logo;rep 32.00
04/54 **(118)** LZ(a&c),CI Logo;rep . . 30.00
05/56 **(132)** LZ(a&c),CI Logo;rep . . 30.00
09/58 **(146)** LZ(a&c),CI Logo;rep . . 35.00

11/63 **(167)** LZ,NN New P(c),CI
Logo; rep 30.00
12/65 **(167)** LZ,NN P(c),CI
Logo;rep 30.00
08/67 **(166)** LZ,NN P(c),CI
Logo;rep 30.00

023-OLIVER TWIST
By Charles Dickens (First Classic produced by the Iger shop)
07/45 **(—)** AdH(a&c),Original . . . 700.00
09/46 **(30)** AdH(a&c),Price
Circle is Blank;rep 450.00
06/49 **(60)** AdH(a&c),Pgs. Reduced
To 48, New CI Logo;rep 50.00
08/49 **(62)** AdH(a&c),CI
Logo;rep 45.00
05/50 **(71)** AdH(a&c),CI
Logo;rep 35.00
07/51 **(85)** AdH(a&c),15¢(c)
Price CI Logo;rep 32.00
04/52 **(94)** AdH(a&c),CI
Logo;rep 32.00
04/54 **(118)** AdH(a&c),CI
Logo;rep 30.00
01/57 **(136)** AdH,New P(c),CI
Logo; rep 30.00
05/59 **(150)** AdH,P(c),CI Logo;rep . 25.00
1961 **(164)** AdH,P(c),CI Logo;rep . 25.00
10/61 **(164)** GE&RC New Art,P(c),
CI Logo;rep 35.00
62/63 **(167)** GE&RC,P(c),CI
Logo; rep 15.00
08/64 **(167)** GE&RC,P(c),CI
Logo; rep 15.00
12/65 **(167)** GE&RC,P(c),
CI Logo;rep 15.00
1968 **(166)** GE&RC,P(c),CI
Logo, 25¢(c)Price;rep 15.00
Wr/69 **(169)** GE&RC,P(c),CI
Logo, Rigid(c);rep 15.00

024-A CONNECTICUT YANKEE IN KING ARTHUR'S COURT
By Mark Twain
09/45 **(—)** JH(a&c),Original 550.00
09/46 **(30)** JH(a&c),Price Circle
Blank;rep 200.00
06/49 **(60)** JH(a&c),8 Pages
Deleted,New CI Logo;rep 50.00
08/49 **(62)** JH(a&c),CI Logo;rep. . . 45.00
05/50 **(71)** JH(a&c),CI Logo;rep. . . 35.00

CI #24, A Connecticut Yankee in King Arthur's Court © Gilberton Publications

09/51 **(87)** JH(a&c),15¢(c) Price
CI Logo;rep 30.00
07/54 **(121)** JH(a&c),CI Logo;rep. . 30.00
09/57 **(140)** JkS New Art,New
P(c),CI Logo; rep. 35.00
11/59 **(153)** JkS,P(c),CI Logo;rep . 18.00
1961 **(164)** JkS,P(c),CI Logo;rep. . 15.00
62/63 **(167)** JkS,P(c),CI Logo;rep . 15.00
07/64 **(167)** JkS,P(c),CI Logo;rep . 15.00
06/66 **(167)** JkS,P(c),CI Logo;rep . 15.00
1968 **(166)** JkS,P(c),CI logo,
25¢(c)Price;rep 15.00
Sg/71 **(169)** JkS,P(c),CI Logo,
Rigid(c);rep 15.00

025-TWO YEARS BEFORE THE MAST
By Richard Henry Dana Jr.
10/45 **(—)** RWb,DvH,Original; . . 500.00
09/46 **(30)** RWb,DvH,Price Circle
Blank;rep 200.00
06/49 **(60)** RWb,DvH,8 Pages
Deleted,New CI Logo;rep 50.00
08/49 **(62)** RWb,DvH,CI Logo;rep . 45.00
05/50 **(71)** RWb,DvH,CI Logo;rep . 35.00
07/51 **(85)** RWb,DvH,15¢(c) Price
CI Logo;rep 30.00
12/53 **(114)** RWb,DvH,CI Logo;rep 28.00
05/60 **(156)** RWb,DvH,New P(c),
CI Logo, 3 Pgs. Replaced
By Fillers;rep. 32.00
12/63 **(167)** RWb,DvH,P(c),CI
Logo; rep 15.00
12/65 **(167)** RWb,DvH,P(c),CI
Logo; rep 15.00
09/67 **(166)** RWb,DvH,P(c),CI
Logo; rep 15.00
Wr/69 **(169)** RWb,DvH,P(c),25¢(c)
Price, CI Logo,Rigid(c);rep . . . 15.00

026-FRANKENSTEIN
By Mary Wollstonecraft Shelley
12/45 **(—)** RWb&ABr(a&c),
Original. 1,400.00
09/46 **(30)** RWb&ABr(a&c),
Price Circle Blank;rep 400.00
06/49 **(60)** RWb&ABr(a&c),
New CI Logo;rep 175.00
08/49 **(62)** RWb&ABr(a&c),
CI Logo;rep 165.00
05/50 **(71)** RWb&ABr(a&c),
CI Logo;rep 75.00
04/51 **(82)** RWb&ABr(a&c),
15¢(c) Price,CI Logo;rep 65.00
03/54 **(117)** RWb&ABr(a&c),
CI Logo;rep 30.00
09/58 **(146)** RWb&ABr,NS
New P(c), CI Logo; rep 35.00
11/59 **(153)** RWb&ABr,NS
P(c),CI Logo; rep 50.00
01/61 **(160)** RWb&ABr,NS
P(c),CI Logo; rep 16.00
165 **(1962)** RWb&ABr,NS P(c),
CI Logo; rep. 16.00
62/63 **(167)** RWb&ABr,NS P(c),
CI Logo; rep. 15.00
06/64 **(167)** RWb&ABr,NS P(c),
CI logo; rep 15.00
06/65 **(167)** RWb&ABr,NS P(c),
CI Logo; rep. 15.00
10/65 **(167)** RWb&ABr,NS P(c),
CI Logo; rep. 15.00
09/67 **(166)** RWb&ABr,NS P(c),
CI Logo; rep. 15.00
Fl/69 **(169)** RWb&ABr,NS P(c),25¢(c)
Price,CI Logo,Rigid(c);rep . . . 15.00
Sg/71 **(169)** RWb&ABr,NS P(c),
CI Logo, Rigid(c);rep 15.00

Classics Illus.

027-THE ADVENTURES MARCO POLO
By Marco Polo & Donn Byrne
04/46 (——) HFI(a&c);Original. . . 550.00
09/46 (30) HFI(a&c);rep. 200.00
04/50 (70) HFI(a&c),8 Pages Deleted,
No(c) Price,New CI Logo;rep . 45.00
09/51 (87) HFI(a&c),15¢(c)
Price,CI Logo;rep 30.00
03/54 (117) HFI(a&c),CILogo;rep. . 25.00
01/60 (154) HFI,New P(c),CI
Logo;rep 25.00
1962 (165) HFI,P(c),CI Logo;rep . . 15.00
04/64 (167) HFI,P(c),CI Logo;rep. . 15.00
06/66 (167) HFI,P(c),CI Logo;rep. . 15.00
Sg/69 (169) HFI,P(c),CI Logo,
25¢(c)Price,Rigid(c);rep. 15.00

028-MICHAEL STROGOFF
By Jules Verne
06/46 (——) AdH(a&c),Original . . . 500.00
09/48 (51) AdH(a&c),8 Pages
Deleted,New CI Logo;rep . . . 150.00
01/54 (115) AdH,New P(c),CI
Logo; rep. 45.00
03/60 (155) AdH,P(c),CI Logo;rep. 18.00
11/63 (167) AdH,P(c),CI Logo;rep. 18.00
07/66 (167) AdH,P(c),CI Logo;rep. 18.00
Sr/69 (169)AdH,NN,NewP(c),25¢(c)
Price, CI Logo,Rigid(c);rep . . . 28.00

029-THE PRINCE AND THE PAUPER
By Mark Twain
07/46 (——) AdH(a&c),Original . . . 800.00
06/49 (60) AdH,New HcK(c),New CI
Logo,8 Pages Deleted;rep. . . 100.00
08/49 (62) AdH,HcK(c),CILogo;rep 50.00
05/50 (71) AdH,HcK(c),CILogo;rep 35.00
03/52 (93) AdH,HcK(c),CILogo;rep 32.00
12/53 (114) AdH,HcK(c),CI
Logo;rep 30.00
09/55 (128) AdH,New P(c),CI
Logo; rep 30.00
05/57 (138) AdH,P(c),CI Logo;rep. 18.00
05/59 (150) AdH,P(c),CI Logo;rep. 18.00
1961 (164) AdH,P(c),CI Logo;rep. . 18.00
62/63 (167) AdH,P(c),CI Logo;rep. 18.00
07/64 (167) AdH,P(c),CI Logo;rep. 18.00
11/65 (167) AdH,P(c),CI Logo;rep. 18.00
1968 (166) AdH,P(c),CI Logo,
25¢(c)Price;rep 18.00
Sr/70 (169) AdH,P(c),CI Logo,
Rigid(c);rep 18.00

030-THE MOONSTONE
By William Wilkie Collins
09/46 (——) DRi(a&c),Original. . . . 550.00
06/49 (60) DRi(a&c),8 Pages
Deleted,New CI Logo;rep . . . 100.00
04/50 (70) DRi(a&c),CI Logo;rep. . 65.00
03/60 (155) DRi,LbC New P(c),
CI Logo;rep 90.00
1962 (165) DRi,LbC P(c),CI Logo;
rep 35.00
01/64 (167) DRi,LbC P(c),CI Logo;
rep 28.00
09/65 (167) DRi,LbC P(c),CI Logo;
rep 20.00
1968 (166) DRi,LbC P(c),CI Logo,
25¢(c)Price;rep 18.00

031-THE BLACK ARROW
By Robert Louis Stevenson
10/46 (——) AdH(a&c),Original . . . 450.00
09/48 (51) AdH(a&c),8 Pages
Deleted,New CI Logo;rep 75.00

10/49 (64) AdH(a&c),CI
Logo;rep 35.00
09/51 (87) AdH(a&c),15¢(c)
Price;CI Logo;rep 30.00
06/53 (108) AdH(a&c),CI
Logo;rep 28.00
03/55 (125) AdH(a&c),CI
Logo;rep 27.00
03/56 (131) AdH,New P(c),CI
Logo; rep. 22.00
09/57 (140) AdH,P(c),CI Logo;rep. 20.00
01/59 (148) AdH,P(c),CI Logo;rep. 20.00
03/61 (161) AdH,P(c),CI Logo;rep. 20.00
62/63 (167) AdH,P(c),CI Logo;rep. 20.00
07/64 (167) AdH,P(c),CI logo;rep . 20.00
11/65 (167) AdH,P(c),CI Logo;rep. 20.00
1968 (166) AdH,P(c),CI Logo,
25¢(c)Price;rep 20.00

032-LORNA DOONE
By Richard Doddridge Blackmore
12/46 (——) MB(a&c),Original 550.00
10/49 (53/64) MB(a&c),8 Pages
Deleted,New CI Logo;rep . . . 150.00
07/51 (85) MB(a&c),15¢(c)
Price, CI Logo;rep 65.00
04/54 (118) MB(a&c),CI Logo;rep . 35.00
05/57 (138) MB,New P(c); Old(c)
Becomes New Splash Pge.,CI
Logo;rep 35.00
05/59 (150) MB,P(c),CI Logo;rep. . 20.00
1962 (165) MB,P(c),CI Logo;rep . . 20.00
01/64 (167) MB,P(c),CI Logo;rep. . 22.00
11/65 (167) MB,P(c),CI Logo;rep. . 22.00
1968 (166) MB,New P(c),
CI Logo;rep 35.00

033-THE ADVENTURES OF SHERLOCK HOLMES
By Sir Arthur Conan Doyle
01/47 (——) LZ,HcK(c),Original . 1,750.00
11/48 (53) LZ,HcK(c),"A Study in Scarlet"
Deleted,New CI Logo;rep . . . 700.00
05/50 (71) LZ,HcK(c),CI Logo;rep 500.00
11/51 (89) LZ,HcK(c),15¢(c)
Price,CI Logo;rep 400.00

034-MYSTERIOUS ISLAND
By Jules Verne
Last Classic Comic
02/47 (——) RWb&DvH,Original . . 600.00
06/49 (60) RWb&DvH,8 Pages
Deleted,New CI Logo;rep 65.00

CC #34, Mysterious Island
© Gilberton Publications

08/49 (62) RWb&DvH,CI Logo;rep 45.00
05/50 (71) RWb&DvH,CI Logo;rep 65.00
12/50 (78) RWb&DvH,15¢(c) Price,
CI Logo;rep 35.00
02/52 (92) RWb&DvH,CI Logo;rep 35.00
03/54 (117) RWb&DvH,CI Logo;
rep 35.00
09/57 (140) RWb&DvH,New P(c),
CI Logo;rep 35.00
05/60 (156) RWb&DvH,P(c),CI
Logo;rep 20.00
10/63 (167) RWb&DvH,P(c),CI
Logo;rep 20.00
05/64 (167) RWb&DvH,P(c),CI
Logo;rep 20.00
06/66 (167) RWb&DvH,P(c),CI
logo;rep 20.00
1968 (166) RWb&DvH,P(c),CI Logo,
25¢(c)Price;rep 20.00

CLASSICS ILLUSTRATED
Gilberton 1947-60s

035-LAST DAYS OF POMPEII
By Lord Edward Bulwer Lytton
First Classics Illustrated
03/47 (——) HcK(a&c),Original . . . 500.00
03/61 (161) JK,New P(c),
15¢(c)Price;rep 65.00
01/64 (167) JK,P(c);rep 30.00
07/66 (167) JK,P(c);rep 30.00
Sg/70 (169) JK,P(c),25¢(c)
Price, Rigid(c);rep 30.00

036-TYPEE
By Herman Melville
04/47 (——) EzW(a&c),Original. . . 275.00
10/49 (64) EzW(a&c),No(c)price,
8 pages deleted;rep. 90.00
03/60 (155) EzW,GMc New
P(c);rep 35.00
09/63 (167) EzW,GMc P(c);rep . . . 25.00
07/65 (167) EzW,GMc P(c);rep . . . 25.00
Sr/69 (169) EzW,GMc P(c),25¢(c)
Price, Rigid(c);rep 25.00

037-THE PIONEERS
By James Fenimore Cooper
05/47 (37) RP(a&c),Original 300.00
08/49 (62) RP(a&c),8 Pages
Deleted;rep 45.00
04/50 (70) RP(a&c);rep 35.00
02/52 (92) RP(a&c),15¢(c)price;
rep 35.00
04/54 (118) RP(a&c);rep 30.00
03/56 (131) RP(a&c);rep 30.00
05/56 (132) RP(a&c);rep 30.00
11/59 (153) RP(a&c);rep 25.00
05/64 (167) RP(a&c);rep 25.00
06/66 (167) RP(a&c);rep 25.00
1968 (166) RP,TO New P(c),
25¢(c)Price;rep 35.00

038-ADVENTURES OF CELLINI
By Benvenuto Cellini
06/47 (——) AgF(a&c),Original . . . 400.00
1961 (164) NN New Art,New P(c);
rep 35.00
12/63 (167) NN,P(c);rep 25.00
07/66 (167) NN,P(c);rep 25.00
Sg/70 (169) NN,P(c),25¢(c)
Price, Rigid(c);rep 28.00

039-JANE EYRE
By Charlotte Bronte
07/47 (—) HyG(a&c),Original . . . 350.00
06/49 (60) HyG(a&c),No(c)Price,
    8 pages deleted;rep 50.00
08/49 (62) HyG(a&c);rep 45.00
05/50 (71) HyG(a&c);rep 35.00
02/52 (92) HyG(a&c),15¢(c)
    Price; rep 32.00
04/54 (118) HyG(a&c);rep 32.00
01/58 (142) HyG,New P(c);rep. . . . 32.00
01/60 (154) HyG,P(c);rep 32.00
1962 (165) HjK New Art,P(c);rep . . 32.00
12/63 (167) HjK,P(c);rep 32.00
04/65 (167) HjK,P(c);rep 32.00
08/66 (167) HjK,P(c);rep 32.00
1968 (166) HjK,NN New P(c);rep . 75.00

040-MYSTERIES
(The Pit & the Pendulum,
The Adventures of Hans Pfall,
Fall of the House of Usher)
By Edgar Allan Poe
08/47 (—) AgF,HyG,I IcK(a&c),
    Original 1,000.00
08/49 (62) AgF,HyG,HcK(a&c),
    8 Pages deleted;rep 350.00
09/50 (75) AgF,HyG,
    HcK(a&c);rep. 300.00
02/52 (92) AgF,HyG,HcK(a&c)
    15¢(c) Price;rep. 250.00

041-TWENTY YEARS AFTER
By Alexandre Dumas
09/47 (—) RBu(a&c),Original . . . 600.00
08/49 (62) RBu,HcK New(c),No(c)
    Price, 8 Pages Deleted;rep . . . 65.00
12/50 (78) RBu,HcK(c),15¢(c)
    Price; rep 45.00
05/60 (156) RBu,DgR New P(c);
    rep 35.00
12/63 (167) RBu,DgR P(c);rep . . . 50.00
11/66 (167) RBu,DgR P(c);rep. . . . 50.00
Sg/70 (169) RBu,DgR P(c),25¢(c)
    Price, Rigid(c);rep 50.00

042-SWISS FAMILY ROBINSON
By Johann Wyss
10/47 (42) HcK(a&c),Original. . . . 300.00
08/49 (62) HcK(a&c),No(c)price,
    8 Pages Deleted,Not Every Issue
    Has 'Gift Box' Ad;rep 75.00
09/50 (75) HcK(a&c);rep 35.00
03/52 (93) HcK(a&c);rep 32.00
03/54 (117) HcK(a&c);rep 30.00
03/56 (131) HcK,New P(c);rep. . . . 28.00
03/57 (137) HcK,P(c);rep. 28.00
11/57 (141) HcK,P(c);rep. 28.00
09/59 (152) NN New art,P(c);rep . . 28.00
09/60 (158) NN,P(c);rep 25.00
12/63 (165) NN,P(c);rep 30.00
12/63 (167) NN,P(c);rep 15.00
04/65 (167) NN,P(c);rep 15.00
05/66 (167) NN,P(c);rep 15.00
11/67 (166) NN,P(c);rep 15.00
Sg/69 (169) NN,P(c);rep 15.00

043-GREAT EXPECTATIONS
By Charles Dickens
11/47 (—) HcK(a&c),Original . . 1,400.00
08/49 (62) HcK(a&c),No(c)price;
    8 pages deleted;rep. 850.00

CI #43, Great Expectations
© Gilberton Publications

044-MYSTERIES OF PARIS
By Eugene Sue
12/47 (44) HcK(a&c),Original . . 1,000.00
08/47 (62) HcK(a&c),No(c)Price,
    8 Pages Deleted,Not Every Issue
    Has 'Gift Box' Ad;rep 400.00
12/50 (78) HcK(a&c),15¢(c)
    Price; rep 350.00

045-TOM BROWN'S SCHOOL DAYS
By Thomas Hughes
01/48 (44) HFI(a&c),Original,
    1st 48 Pge. Issue 250.00
10/49 (64) HFI(a&c),No(c)
    Price;rep 60.00
03/61 (161) JTg New Art,GMc
    New P(c);rep 30.00
02/64 (167) JTg,GMc P(c);rep . . . 20.00
08/66 (167) JTg,GMc P(c);rep . . . 20.00
1968 (166) JTg,GMc P(c),
    25¢(c)Price;rep 20.00

046-KIDNAPPED
By Robert Louis Stevenson
04/48 (47) RWb(a&c),Original . . . 200.00
08/49 (62) RWb(a&c),Red Circle
    Either Blank or With 10¢,rep . 100.00
12/50 (78) RWb(a&c),15¢(c)
    Price; rep 35.00
09/51 (87) RWb(a&c);rep. 32.00
04/54 (118) RWb(a&c);rep. 30.00
03/56 (131) RWb,New P(c);rep . . . 30.00
09/57 (140) RWb,P(c);rep 18.00
05/59 (150) RWb,P(c);rep 18.00
05/60 (156) RWb,P(c);rep 18.00
1961 (164) RWb,P(c),Reduced Pge.
    Width;rep 18.00
62/63 (167) RWb,P(c);rep 18.00
03/64 (167) RWb,P(c);rep 18.00
06/65 (167) RWb,P(c);rep 18.00
12/65 (167) RWb,P(c);rep 18.00
09/67 (167) RWb,P(c);rep 18.00
Wr/69 (166) RWb,P(c),25¢(c)
    Price, Rigid(c);rep 18.00
Sr/70 (169) RWb,P(c),Rigid(c);rep. 18.00

047-TWENTY THOUSAND LEAGUES UNDER THE SEA
By Jules Verne
05/58 (47) HcK(a&c),Original. . . . 250.00
10/49 (64) HcK(a&c),No(c)
    Price; rep 45.00
12/50 (78) HcK(a&c),15¢(c)
    Price; rep 35.00
04/52 (94) HcK(a&c);rep 35.00
04/54 (118) HcK(a&c);rep 30.00
09/55 (128) HcK,New P(c);rep. . . . 30.00
07/56 (133) HcK,P(c);rep. 25.00
09/57 (140) HcK,P(c);rep. 18.00
01/59 (148) HcK,P(c);rep. 18.00
05/60 (156) HcK,P(c);rep. 18.00
62/63 (165) HcK,P(c);rep. 18.00
05/48 (167) HcK,P(c);rep. 18.00
03/64 (167) HcK,P(c);rep. 18.00
08/65 (167) HcK,P(c);rep. 18.00
10/66 (167) HcK,P(c);rep. 18.00
1968 (166) HcK,NN New P(c),
    25¢(c)Price;rep 25.00
Sg/70 (169) HoK,NN P(c),
    Rigid(c);rep 25.00

048-DAVID COPPERFIELD
By Charles Dickens
06/48 (47) HcK(a&c),Original. . . . 200.00
10/49 (64) HcK(a&c),Price Circle
    Replaced By Image of Boy
    Reading;rep. 45.00
09/51 (87) HcK(a&c),15¢(c)
    Price; rep 35.00
07/54 (121) HcK,New P(c);rep. . . . 30.00
10/56 (130) HcK,P(c);rep. 18.00
09/57 (140) HcK,P(c);rep. 18.00
01/59 (148) HcK,P(c);rep. 18.00
05/60 (156) HcK,P(c);rep. 18.00
62/63 (167) HcK,P(c);rep. 18.00
04/64 (167) HcK,P(c);rep. 18.00
06/65 (167) HcK,P(c);rep. 18.00
05/67 (166) HcK,P(c);rep 18.00
R/67 (166) HcK,P(c);rep 25.00
Sg/69 (166) HcK,P(c),25¢(c)
    Price, Rigid(c);rep 18.00
Wr/69 (169) HcK,P(c),Rigid(c);rep. 18.00

049-ALICE IN WONDERLAND
By Lewis Carroll
07/48 (47) AB(a&c),Original. 250.00
10/49 (64) AD(a&c),No(o)Price;
    rep 75.00
07/51 (85) AB(a&c),15¢(c)Price;
    rep 50.00
03/60 (155) AB,New P(c);rep. 50.00
1962 (165) AB,P(c);rep 35.00
03/64 (167) AB,P(c);rep 30.00
06/66 (167) AB,P(c);rep 30.00
FI/68 (166) AB,TO New P(c),25¢(c)
    Price, New Soft(c);rep 50.00
FI/68 (166) AB,P(c),Both Soft &
    Rigid(c)s;rep 100.00

050-ADVENTURES OF TOM SAWYER
By Mark Twain
08/48 (51) ARu(a&c),Original. . . . 225.00
09/48 (51) ARu(a&c),Original. . . . 250.00
10/49 (64) ARu(a&c),No(c)
    Price; rep 35.00
12/50 (78) ARu(a&c),15¢(c)
    Price; rep 30.00
04/52 (94) ARu(a&c);rep 30.00

All comics prices listed are for *Near Mint* condition.

12/53 **(114)** ARu(a&c);rep 30.00
03/54 **(117)** ARu(a&c);rep 25.00
05/56 **(132)** ARu(a&c);rep 25.00
09/57 **(140)** ARu,New P(c);rep. . . . 22.00
05/59 **(150)** ARu,P(c);rep. 25.00
10/61 **(164)** New Art,P(c);rep 15.00
62/63 **(167)** P(c);rep. 15.00
01/65 **(167)** P(c);rep. 15.00
05/66 **(167)** P(c);rep. 15.00
12/67 **(166)** P(c);rep. 15.00
Fl/69 **(169)** P(c),25¢(c) Price,
   Rigid(c);rep 15.00
Wr/71 **(169)** P(c);rep 15.00

051-THE SPY
By James Fenimore Cooper
09/48 **(51)** AdH(a&c),Original,
   Maroon(c) 200.00
09/48 **(51)** AdH(a&c),Original,
   Violet(c). 175.00
11/51 **(89)** AdH(a&c),15¢(c)
   Price; rep. 35.00
07/54 **(121)** AdH(a&c);rep 30.00
07/57 **(139)** AdH,New P(c);rep. . . . 30.00
05/60 **(156)** AdH,P(c);rep. 18.00
11/63 **(167)** AdH,P(c);rep. 18.00
07/66 **(167)** AdH,P(c);rep. 18.00
Wr/69 **(166)** AdH,P(c),25¢(c)Price,
   Both Soft & Rigid(c)s;rep. . . 35.00

052-THE HOUSE OF SEVEN GABLES
By Nathaniel Hawthorne
10/48 **(53)** HyG(a&c),Original . . . 200.00
11/51 **(89)** HyG(a&c),15¢(c)
   Price; rep. 35.00
07/54 **(121)** HyG(a&c);rep 30.00
01/58 **(142)** GWb New Art,New
   P(c); rep. 35.00
05/60 **(156)** GWb,P(c);rep 18.00
1962 **(165)** GWb,P(c);rep 18.00
05/64 **(167)** GWb,P(c);rep 18.00
03/66 **(167)** GWb,P(c);rep 18.00
1968 **(166)** GWb,P(c),25¢(c)
   Price;rep 18.00
Sg/70 **(169)** GWb,P(c),Rigid(c);rep 18.00

053-A CHRISTMAS CAROL
By Charles Dickens
11/48 **(53)** HcK(a&c),Original. . . . 250.00

054-MAN IN THE IRON MASK
By Alexandre Dumas
12/48 **(55)** AgF,HcK(c),Original . . 200.00
03/52 **(93)** AgF,HcK(c),15¢(c)
   Price; rep 45.00
09/53 **(111)** AgF,HcK(c);rep 60.00
01/58 **(142)** KBa New Art,New
   P(c); rep. 35.00
01/60 **(154)** KBa,P(c);rep. 18.00
1962 **(165)** KBa,P(c);rep 18.00
05/64 **(167)** KBa,P(c);rep. 18.00
04/66 **(167)** KBa,P(c);rep. 18.00
Wr/69 **(166)** KBa,P(c),25¢(c)
   Price, Rigid(c);rep 18.00

055-SILAS MARINER
By George Eliot
01/49 **(55)** AdH,HcK(c),Original . . 200.00
09/50 **(75)** AdH,HcK(c),Price Circle
   Blank,'Coming next'Ad(not
   usually in reps.);rep). 45.00
07/52 **(97)** AdH,HcK(c);rep 32.00
07/54 **(121)** AdH,New P(c);rep. . . . 30.00
01/56 **(130)** AdH,P(c);rep. 18.00

09/57 **(140)** AdH,P(c);rep. 18.00
01/60 **(154)** AdH,P(c);rep. 18.00
1962 **(165)** AdH,P(c);rep. 18.00
05/64 **(167)** AdH,P(c);rep. 18.00
06/65 **(167)** AdH,P(c);rep. 18.00
05/67 **(166)** AdH,P(c);rep. 18.00
Wr/69 **(166)** AdH,P(c),25¢(c) Price,
   Rigid(c);rep,Soft & Stiff 35.00

056-THE TOILERS OF THE SEA
By Victor Hugo
02/49 **(55)** AgF(a&c),Original 300.00
01/62 **(165)** AT New Art,New
   P(c); 60.00
03/64 **(167)** AT,P(c);rep. 35.00
10/66 **(167)** AT,P(c);rep. 35.00

057-THE SONG OF HIAWATHA
By Henry Wadsworth Longfellow
03/49 **(55)** AB(a&c),Original 200.00
09/50 **(75)** AB(a&c),No(c)price,'
   Coming Next'Ad(not usually
   found in reps.);rep 50.00
04/52 **(94)** AB(a&c),15¢(c)
   Price;rep 35.00
04/54 **(118)** AB(a&c);rep 32.00
09/56 **(134)** AB,New P(c);rep 30.00
07/57 **(139)** AB,P(c);rep. 18.00
01/60 **(154)** AB,P(c);rep. 18.00
62/63 **(167)** AB,P(c),Erroneosly
   Has Original Date;rep 18.00
09/64 **(167)** AB,P(c);rep. 18.00
10/65 **(167)** AB,P(c);rep. 18.00
Fl/68 **(166)** AB,P(c),25¢(c)Price;
   rep 18.00

058-THE PRAIRIE
By James Fenimore Cooper
04/49 **(60)** RP(a&c),Original 200.00
08/49 **(62)** RP(a&c);rep 75.00
12/50 **(78)** RP(a&c),15¢(c) Price
   In Double Circle;rep 35.00
12/53 **(114)** RP(a&c);rep 30.00
03/56 **(131)** RP(a&c);rep 30.00
05/56 **(132)** RP(a&c);rep 30.00
09/58 **(146)** RP,New P(c);rep. 30.00
03/60 **(155)** RP,P(c);rep. 20.00
05/64 **(167)** RP,P(c);rep. 18.00
04/66 **(167)** RP,P(c);rep. 18.00

CI #58 The Prairie
© *Gilberton Publications*

Sr/69 **(169)** RP,P(c),25¢(c)
   Price; Rigid(c);rep 18.00

059-WUTHERING HEIGHTS
By Emily Bronte
05/49 **(60)** HcK(a&c),Original. . . . 225.00
07/51 **(85)** HcK(a&c),15¢(c)
   Price; rep. 50.00
05/60 **(156)** HcK,GB New P(c);rep 35.00
01/64 **(167)** HcK,GB P(c);rep. 25.00
10/66 **(167)** HcK,GB P(c);rep. 25.00
Sr/69 **(169)** HcK,GBP(c),25¢(c)
   Price, Rigid(c);rep 22.00

060-BLACK BEAUTY
By Anna Sewell
06/49 **(62)** AgF(a&c),Original 200.00
08/49 **(62)** AgF(a&c);rep 225.00
07/51 **(85)** AgF(a&c),15¢(c) Price;
   rep. 40.00
09/60 **(158)** LbC&NN&StA New
   Art, LbC New P(c);rep. 35.00
02/64 **(167)** LbC&NN&StA,LbC
   P(c); rep. 30.00
03/66 **(167)** LbC&NN&StA,LbC
   P(c); rep. 30.00
03/66 **(167)** LbC&NN&StA,LbC
   P(c), 'Open Book'Blank;rep. . . 30.00
1968 **(166)** LbC&NN&StA,AIM New
   P(c) 25¢(c) Price;rep 75.00

061-THE WOMAN IN WHITE
By William Wilke Collins
07/49 **(62)** AB(a&c),Original,
   Maroon & Violet(c)s. 200.00
05/60 **(156)** AB,DgR New P(c);rep 40.00
01/64 **(167)** AB,DgR P(c);rep. 30.00
1968 **(166)** AB,DgR P(c),
   25¢(c)Price;rep 30.00

062-WESTERN STORIES
(The Luck of Roaring Camp & The Outcasts of Poker Flat)
By Bret Harte
08/49 **(62)** HcK(a&c),Original. . . . 200.00
11/51 **(89)** HcK(a&c),15¢(c)
   Price; rep. 40.00
07/54 **(121)** HcK(a&c);rep 32.00
03/57 **(137)** HcK,New P(c);rep. . . . 30.00
09/59 **(152)** HcK,P(c);rep. 20.00
10/63 **(167)** HcK,P(c);rep. 20.00
06/64 **(167)** HcK,P(c);rep. 18.00
11/66 **(167)** HcK,P(c);rep. 18.00
1968 **(166)** HcK,TO New P(c),
   25¢ Price;rep. 30.00

063-THE MAN WITHOUT A COUNTRY
By Edward Everett Hale
09/49 **(62)** HcK(a&c),Original. . . . 200.00
12/50 **(78)** HcK(a&c),15¢(c)Price
   In Double Circles;rep. 40.00
05/60 **(156)** HcK,GMc New P(c);
   rep. 35.00
01/62 **(165)** AT New Art,GMc P(c),
   Added Text Pages;rep. 32.00
03/64 **(167)** AT,GMc P(c);rep. 18.00
08/66 **(167)** AT,GMc P(c);rep. 18.00
Sr/69 **(169)** AT,GMc P(c),25¢(c)
   Price, Rigid(c);rep 18.00

064-TREASURE ISLAND
By Robert Louis Stevenson
10/49 **(62)** AB(a&c),Original. 200.00
04/51 **(82)** AB(a&c),15¢(c)
   Price;rep 40.00

03/54 **(117)** AB(a&c);rep 32.00
03/56 **(131)** AB,New P(c),rep. 30.00
05/57 **(138)** AB,P(c);rep 18.00
09/58 **(146)** AB,P(c);rep 18.00
09/60 **(158)** AB,P(c);rep 18.00
1962 **(165)** AB,P(c);rep 18.00
62/63 **(167)** AB,P(c);rep 18.00
06/64 **(167)** AB,P(c);rep 18.00
12/65 **(167)** AB,P(c);rep 18.00
10/67 **(166)** AB,P(c);rep 22.00
10/67 **(166)** AB,P(c),GRIT Ad
  Stapled In Book;rep 100.00
Sg/69 **(169)** AB,P(c),25¢(c)
  Price, Rigid(c);rep 18.00

065-BENJAMIN FRANKLIN
By Benjamin Franklin
11/49 **(64)** AB,RtH,GS(Iger Shop),
  HcK(c),Original 200.00
03/56 **(131)** AB,RtH,GS(Iger Shop),
  New P(c) ;rep 35.00
01/60 **(154)** AB,RtH,GS(Iger Shop),
  P(c);rep 20.00
02/64 **(167)** AB,RtH,CS(Iger Shop),
  P(c);rep 18.00
04/66 **(167)** AB,RtH,GS(Iger Shop),
  P(c);rep 18.00
Fl/69 **(169)** AB,RtH,GS(Iger Shop),
  P(c), 25¢(c)Price,Rigid(c);rep . 20.00

066-THE CLOISTER AND THE HEARTH
By Charles Reade
12/49 **(67)** HcK(a&c),Original. . . . 400.00

067-THE SCOTTISH CHIEFS
By Jane Porter
01/50 **(67)** AB(a&c),Original. 200.00
07/51 **(85)** AB(a&c),15¢(c)
  Price;rep 40.00
04/54 **(118)** AB(a&c);rep 35.00
01/57 **(136)** AB,New P(c);rep 32.00
01/60 **(154)** AB,P(c);rep 20.00
11/63 **(167)** AB,P(c);rep 25.00
08/65 **(167)** AB,P(c);rep 20.00

068-JULIUS CEASAR
By William Shakespeare
02/50 **(70)** HcK(a&c),Original. . . . 200.00
07/51 **(85)** HcK(a&c),15¢(c)
  Price 40.00

CI #68, Julius Caesar
© *Gilberton Publications*

06/53 **(108)** HcK(a&c);rep 32.00
05/60 **(156)** HcK,LbC New P(c);rep 35.00
1962 **(165)** GE&RC New Art,
  LbC P(c);rep 35.00
02/64 **(167)** GE&RC,LbC P(c);rep . 18.00
10/65 **(167)** GE&RC,LbC P(c),Tarzan
  Books Inside(c);rep 18.00
1967 **(166)** GE&RC,LbC P(c);rep . 18.00
Wr/69 **(169)** GE&RC,LbC P(c),
  Rigid(c);rep 18.00

069-AROUND THE WORLD IN 80 DAYS
By Jules Verne
03/50 **(70)** HcK(a&c),Original. . . . 200.00
09/51 **(87)** HcK(a&c),15¢(c)
  Price; rep 45.00
03/55 **(125)** HcK(a&c);rep 32.00
01/57 **(136)** HcK,New P(c);rep. . . . 32.00
09/58 **(146)** HcK,P(c);rep 20.00
09/59 **(152)** HcK,P(c);rep 20.00
1961 **(164)** HcK,P(c);rep 20.00
62/63 **(167)** HcK,P(c);rep 18.00
07/64 **(167)** HcK,P(c);rep. 18.00
11/65 **(167)** HcK,P(c);rep 18.00
07/67 **(166)** HcK,P(c);rep 18.00
Sg/69 **(169)** HcK,P(c),25¢(c)
  Price, Rigid(c);rep 18.00

070-THE PILOT
By James Fenimore Cooper
04/50 **(71)** AB(a&c),Original. 175.00
10/50 **(75)** AB(a&c),15¢(c)
  Price;rep 45.00
02/52 **(92)** AB(a&c);rep 32.00
03/55 **(125)** AB(a&c);rep 35.00
05/60 **(156)** AB,GMc New P(c);rep 30.00
02/64 **(167)** AB,GMc P(c);rep 30.00
05/66 **(167)** AB,GMc P(c);rep 28.00

071-THE MAN WHO LAUGHS
By Victor Hugo
05/50 **(71)** AB(a&c),Original. 250.00
01/62 **(165)** NN,NN New P(c);rep 125.00
04/64 **(167)** NN,NN P(c);rep 100.00

072-THE OREGON TRAIL
By Francis Parkman
06/50 **(73)** HcK(a&c),Original. . . . 150.00
11/51 **(89)** HcK(a&c),15¢(c)
  Price; rep 40.00
07/54 **(121)** HcK(a&c);rep 32.00
03/56 **(131)** HcK,New P(c);rep. . . . 30.00
09/57 **(140)** HcK,P(c);rep 20.00
05/59 **(150)** HcK,P(c);rep 18.00
01/61 **(164)** HcK,P(c);rep 18.00
62/63 **(167)** HcK,P(c);rep 18.00
08/64 **(167)** HcK,P(c);rep 18.00
10/65 **(167)** HcK,P(c);rep 18.00
1968 **(166)** HcK,P(c),25¢(c)Price;
  rep 18.00

073-THE BLACK TULIP
By Alexandre Dumas
07/50 **(75)** AB(a&c),Original. 550.00

074-MR. MIDSHIPMAN EASY
By Captain Frederick Marryat
08/50 **(75)** BbL,Original 500.00

075-THE LADY OF THE LAKE
By Sir Walter Scott
09/50 **(75)** HcK(a&c),Original. . . . 150.00

07/51 **(85)** HcK(a&c),15¢(c)
  Price; rep 40.00
04/54 **(118)** HcK(a&c);rcp 35.00
07/57 **(139)** HcK,New P(c);rep. . . . 35.00
01/60 **(154)** HcK,P(c);rep 18.00
1962 **(165)** HcK,P(c);rep 18.00
04/64 **(167)** HcK,P(c);rep 18.00
05/66 **(167)** HcK,P(c);rep 18.00
Sg/69 **(169)** HcK,P(c),25¢(c)
  Price, Rigid(c);rep 18.00

076-THE PRISONER OF ZENDA
By Anthony Hope Hawkins
10/50 **(75)** HcK(a&c),Original. . . . 150.00
07/51 **(85)** HcK(a&c),15¢(c) Price;
  rep 40.00
09/53 **(111)** HcK(a&c),rep 35.00
09/55 **(128)** HcK,New P(c);rep. . . . 35.00
09/59 **(152)** HcK,P(c);rep 20.00
1962 **(165)** HcK,P(c);rep 18.00
04/64 **(167)** HcK,P(c);rep 18.00
09/66 **(167)** HcK,P(c);rep 18.00
Fl/69 **(169)** HcK,P(c),25¢(c) Price,
  Rigid(c);rep 18.00

077-THE ILLIAD
By Homer
11/50 **(78)** AB(a&c),Original 175.00
09/51 **(87)** AB(a&c),15¢(c)
  Price;rep 40.00
07/54 **(121)** AB(a&c);rep 35.00
07/57 **(139)** AB,New P(c);rep. . . . 35.00
05/59 **(150)** AB,P(c);rep 20.00
1962 **(165)** AB,P(c);rep 18.00
10/63 **(167)** AB,P(c);rep 18.00
07/64 **(167)** AB,P(c);rep 18.00
05/66 **(167)** AB,P(c);rep 18.00
1968 **(166)** AB,P(c),25¢(c)
  Price;rep 18.00

078-JOAN OF ARC
By Frederick Shiller
12/50 **(78)** HcK(a&c),Original. . . . 150.00
09/51 **(87)** HcK(a&c),15¢(c)
  Price; rep 40.00
11/53 **(113)** HcK(a&c);rep 35.00
09/55 **(128)** HcK,New P(c);rep. . . . 35.00
09/57 **(140)** HcK,P(c);rep 20.00
05/59 **(150)** HcK,P(c);rep 20.00
11/60 **(159)** HcK,P(c);rep 18.00
62/63 **(167)** HcK,P(c);rep 18.00
12/63 **(167)** HcK,P(c);rep 18.00
06/65 **(167)** HcK,P(c);rep 18.00
06/67 **(166)** HcK,P(c);rep 18.00
Wr/69 **(166)** HcK,TO New P(c),
  25¢(c)Price, Rigid(c);rep 35.00

079-CYRANO DE BERGERAC
By Edmond Rostand
01/51 **(78)** AB(a&c),Original,Movie
  Promo Inside Front(c) 175.00
07/51 **(85)** AB(a&c),15¢(c)
  Price;rep 40.00
04/54 **(118)** AB(a&c);rep 35.00
07/56 **(133)** AB,New P(c);rep. . . . 35.00
05/60 **(156)** AB,P(c);rep 30.00
08/64 **(167)** AB,P(c);rep 30.00

080-WHITE FANG
By Jack London (Last Line Drawn (c)
02/51 **(79)** AB(a&c),Original. 175.00
09/51 **(87)** AB(a&c);rep 40.00
03/55 **(125)** AB(a&c);rep 35.00
05/56 **(132)** AB,New P(c);rep. . . . 35.00
09/57 **(140)** AB,P(c);rep 20.00

Classics Illus.

11/59 **(153)** AB,P(c);rep 20.00
62/63 **(167)** AB,P(c);rep 18.00
09/64 **(167)** AB,P(c);rep 18.00
07/65 **(167)** AB,P(c);rep 18.00
06/67 **(166)** AB,P(c);rep 18.00
Fl/69 **(169)** AB,P(c),25¢(c)
   Price, Rigid(c);rep 18.00

081-THE ODYSSEY
By Homer
(P(c)s From Now on)
03/51 **(82)** HyG,AB P(c),Original . 175.00
08/64 **(167)** HyG,AB P(c);rep 30.00
10/66 **(167)** HyG,AB P(c);rep 30.00
Sg/69 **(169)** HyG,TyT New P(c),
   Rigid(c);rep 35.00

082-THE MASTER OF BALLANTRAE
By Robert Louis Stevenson
04/51 **(82)** LDr,AB P(c),Original . . 150.00
08/64 **(167)** LDr,AB P(c);rep 30.00
Fl/68 **(166)** LDr,Syk New P(c),
   Rigid(c);rep 35.00

083-THE JUNGLE BOOK
By Rudyard Kipling
05/51 **(85)** WmB&AB,AB P(c),
   Original 150.00
08/53 **(110)** WmB&AB,AB P(c);rep 20.00
03/55 **(125)** WmB&AB,AB P(c);rep 20.00
05/56 **(134)** WmB&AB,AB P(c);rep 20.00
01/58 **(142)** WmB&AB,AB P(c);rep 20.00
05/59 **(150)** WmB&AB,AB P(c);rep 18.00
11/60 **(159)** WmB&AB,AB P(c);rep 18.00
62/63 **(167)** WmB&AB,AB P(c);rep 18.00
03/65 **(167)** WmB&AB,AB P(c);rep 18.00
11/65 **(167)** WmB&AB,AB P(c);rep 18.00
05/66 **(167)** WmB&AB,AB P(c);rep 18.00
1968 **(166)** NN Art,NN New P(c),
   Rigid(c);rep 35.00

084-THE GOLD BUG & OTHER STORIES
(Inc. The Telltale Heart & The Cask of Amontillado)
By Edgar Allan Poe
06/51 **(85)** AB,RP,JLv,AB P(c),
   Original 200.00
07/64 **(167)** AB,RP,JLv,AB
   P(c);rep 125.00

085-THE SEA WOLF
By Jack London
08/51 **(85)** AB,AB P(c),Original . . 150.00
07/54 **(121)** AB,AB P(c);rep 20.00
05/56 **(132)** AB,AB P(c);rep 20.00
11/57 **(141)** AB,AB P(c);rep 20.00
03/61 **(161)** AB,AB P(c);rep 18.00
02/64 **(167)** AB,AB P(c);rep 18.00
11/65 **(167)** AB,AB P(c);rep 18.00
Fl/69 **(169)** AB,AB P(c),25¢(c)
   Price, Rigid(c);rep 18.00

086-UNDER TWO FLAGS
By Oiuda
08/51 **(87)** MDb,AB P(c),Original . 125.00
03/54 **(117)** MDb,AB P(c);rep 25.00
07/57 **(139)** MDb,AB P(c);rep 20.00
09/60 **(158)** MDb,AB P(c);rep 20.00
02/64 **(167)** MDb,AB P(c);rep 18.00
08/66 **(167)** MDb,AB P(c);rep 18.00
Sr/69 **(169)** MDb,AB P(c),25¢(c)
   Price, Rigid(c);rep 18.00

087-A MIDSUMMER NIGHTS DREAM
By William Shakespeare
09/51 **(87)** AB,AB P(c),Original . . 125.00
03/61 **(161)** AB,AB P(c);rep 20.00
04/64 **(167)** AB,AB P(c);rep 18.00
05/66 **(167)** AB,AB P(c);rep 18.00
Sr/69 **(169)** AB,AB P(c),25¢(c)
   Price; rep 18.00

088-MEN OF IRON
By Howard Pyle
10/51 **(89)** HD,LDr,GS,Original . . 125.00
01/60 **(154)** HD,LDr,GS,P(c);rep . . 20.00
01/64 **(167)** HD,LDr,GS,P(c);rep . . 18.00
1968 **(166)** HD,LDr,GS,P(c),
   25¢(c)Price;rep 18.00

089-CRIME AND PUNISHMENT
By Fedor Dostoevsky
11/51 **(89)** RP,AB P(c),Original . . 125.00
09/59 **(152)** RP,AB P(c);rep 25.00
04/64 **(167)** RP,AB P(c);rep 18.00
05/66 **(167)** RP,AB P(c);rep 18.00
Fl/69 **(169)** RP,AB P(c),25¢(c)
   Price, Rigid(c);rep 18.00

090-GREEN MANSIONS
By William Henry Hudson
12/51 **(89)** AB,AB P(c),Original . . 125.00
01/59 **(148)** AB,New LbC P(c);rep . 30.00
1962 **(165)** AB,LbC P(c);rep 18.00
04/64 **(167)** AB,LbC P(c);rep 18.00
09/66 **(167)** AB,LbC P(c);rep 18.00
Sr/69 **(169)** AB,LbC P(c),25¢(c)
   Price, Rigid(c);rep 18.00

091-THE CALL OF THE WILD
By Jack London
01/52 **(92)** MDb,P(c),Original 100.00
10/53 **(112)** MDb,P(c);rep 20.00
03/55 **(125)** MDb,P(c),'PictureProgress'
   Onn. Back(c);rep 20.00
09/56 **(134)** MDb,P(c);rep 20.00
03/58 **(143)** MDb,P(c);rep 18.00
1962 **(165)** MDb,P(c);rep 18.00
1962 **(167)** MDb,P(c);rep 18.00
04/65 **(167)** MDb,P(c);rep 18.00

CI #91, The Call of the Wild
© *Gilberton Publications*

03/66 **(167)** MDb,P(c);rep 18.00
03/66 **(167)** MDb,P(c),Record
   Edition;rep 18.00
11/67 **(166)** MDb,P(c);rep 18.00
Sg/70 **(169)** MDb,P(c),25¢(c)
   Price, Rigid(c);rep 18.00

092-THE COURTSHIP OF MILES STANDISH
By Henry Wadsworth Longfellow
02/52 **(92)** AB,AB P(c),Original . . 100.00
1962 **(165)** AB,AB P(c);rep 20.00
03/64 **(167)** AB,AB P(c);rep 20.00
05/67 **(166)** AB,AB P(c);rep 20.00
Wr/69 **(169)** AB,AB P(c),25¢(c)
   Price, Rigid(c);rep 20.00

093-PUDD'NHEAD WILSON
By Mark Twain
03/52 **(94)** HcK,HcK P(c),Original 100.00
1962 **(165)** HcK,GMc New P(c);rep 25.00
03/64 **(167)** HcK,GMc P(c);rep . . . 18.00
1968 **(166)** HcK,GMc P(c),25¢(c)
   Price, Soft(c);rep 20.00

094-DAVID BALFOUR
By Robert Louis Stevenson
04/52 **(94)** RP,P(c),Original 125.00
05/64 **(167)** RP,P(c);rep 25.00
1968 **(166)** RP,P(c),25¢(c)Price;rep 25.00

095-ALL QUIET ON THE WESTERN FRONT
By Erich Maria Remarque
05/52 **(96)** MDb,P(c),Original 200.00
05/52 **(99)** MDb,P(c),Original 85.00
10/64 **(167)** MDb,P(c);rep 35.00
11/66 **(167)** MDb,P(c);rep 35.00

096-DANIEL BOONE
By John Bakeless
06/52 **(97)** AB,P(c),Original 100.00
03/54 **(117)** AB,P(c);rep 20.00
09/55 **(128)** AB,P(c);rep 20.00
05/56 **(132)** AB,P(c);rep 20.00
—— **(134)** AB,P(c),'Story of
   Jesus'on Back(c);rep 20.00
09/60 **(158)** AB,P(c);rep 20.00
01/64 **(167)** AB,P(c);rep 18.00
05/65 **(167)** AB,P(c);rep 18.00
11/66 **(167)** AB,P(c);rep 18.00
Wr/69 **(166)** AB,P(c),25¢(c)
   Price, Rigid(c);rep 25.00

097-KING SOLOMON'S MINES
By H. Rider Haggard
07/52 **(96)** HcK,P(c),Original 100.00
04/54 **(118)** HcK,P(c);rep 20.00
03/56 **(131)** HcK,P(c);rep 20.00
09/51 **(141)** HcK,P(c);rep 20.00
09/60 **(158)** HcK,P(c);rep 18.00
02/64 **(167)** HcK,P(c);rep 18.00
09/65 **(167)** HcK,P(c);rep 18.00
Sr/69 **(169)** HcK,P(c),25¢(c)
   Price; Rigid(c);rep 20.00

098-THE RED BADGE OF COURAGE
By Stephen Crane
08/52 **(98)** MDb,GS,P(c),Original . 100.00
04/54 **(118)** MDb,GS,P(c);rep 20.00
05/56 **(132)** MDb,GS,P(c);rep 20.00

01/58 **(142)** MDb,GS,P(c);rep 20.00
09/59 **(152)** MDb,GS,P(c);rep 20.00
03/61 **(161)** MDb,GS,P(c);rep 20.00
62/63 **(167)** MDb,GS,P(c),Erronously
    Has Original Date;rep 20.00
09/64 **(167)** MDb,GS,P(c);rep 20.00
10/65 **(167)** MDb,GS,P(c);rep 20.00
1968 **(166)** MDb,GS,P(c),25¢(c)
    Price, Rigid(c);rep 30.00

099-HAMLET
By William Shakespeare
09/52 **(98)** AB,P(c),Original 100.00
07/54 **(121)** AB,P(c);rep 20.00
11/57 **(141)** AB,P(c);rep 20.00
09/60 **(158)** AB,P(c);rep 18.00
62/63 **(167)** AB,P(c),Erroneously
    Has Original Date;rep 18.00
07/65 **(167)** AB,P(c);rep 18.00
04/67 **(166)** AB,P(c);rep 18.00
Sg/69 **(169)** AB,EdM New P(c),
    25¢(c)Price, Rigid(c);rep 30.00

100-MUTINY ON
THE BOUNTY
By Charrles Nordhoff
10/52 **(100)** MsW,HcK P(c),Orig. . 100.00
03/54 **(117)** MsW,HcK P(c);rep . . . 20.00
05/56 **(132)** MsW,HcK P(c);rep . . . 20.00
01/58 **(142)** MsW,HcK P(c);rep . . . 20.00
03/60 **(155)** MsW,HcK P(c);rep . . . 18.00
62/63 **(167)** MsW,HcK P(c),Erroneously
    Has Original Date;rep 18.00
05/64 **(167)** MsW,HcK P(c);rep . . . 18.00
03/66 **(167)** MsW,HcK P(c),N#
    or Price;rep 20.00
Sg/70 **(169)** MsW,HcK P(c),
    Rigid(c); rep 18.00

101-WILLIAM TELL
By Frederick Schiller
11/52 **(101)** MDb,HcK P(c),Orig. . 100.00
04/54 **(118)** MDb,HcK P(c);rep . . . 20.00
11/57 **(141)** MDb,HcK P(c);rep . . . 20.00
09/60 **(158)** MDb,HcK P(c);rep . . . 18.00
62/63 **(167)** MDb,HcK P(c),Erroneously
    Has Original Date;rep 18.00
11/64 **(167)** MDb,HcK P(c);rep . . . 18.00
04/67 **(166)** MDb,HcK P(c);rep . . . 18.00
Wr/69 **(169)** MDb,HcK P(c)25¢(c)
    Price, Rigid(c);rep 18.00

102-THE WHITE
COMPANY
By Sir Arthur Conan Doyle
12/52 **(101)** AB,P(c),Original 150.00
1962 **(165)** AB,P(c);rep 35.00
04/64 **(167)** AB,P(c);rep 35.00

103-MEN AGAINST
THE SEA
By Charles Nordhoff
01/53 **(104)** RP,HcK P(c),Original 100.00
12/53 **(114)** RP,HcK P(c);rep 30.00
03/56 **(131)** RP,New P(c);rep 35.00
03/59 **(149)** RP,P(c);rep 30.00
09/60 **(158)** RP,P(c);rep 38.00
03/64 **(167)** RP,P(c);rep 25.00

104-BRING 'EM BACK
ALIVE
By Frank Buck & Edward
Anthony
02/53 **(105)** HcK,HcK P(c)Original 100.00
04/54 **(118)** HcK,HcK P(c);rep 20.00
07/56 **(133)** HcK,HcK P(c);rep 20.00

05/59 **(150)** HcK,HcK P(c);rep. . . . 18.00
09/60 **(158)** HcK,HcK P(c);rep. . . . 18.00
10/63 **(167)** HcK,HcK P(c);rep. . . . 18.00
09/65 **(167)** HcK,HcK P(c);rep. . . . 18.00
Wr/69 **(169)** HcK,HcK P(c),25¢(c)
    Price, Rigid(c);rep 18.00

105-FROM THE EARTH
TO THE MOON
By Jules Verne
03/53 **(106)** AB,P(c),Original 100.00
04/54 **(118)** AB,P(c);rep 20.00
03/56 **(132)** AB,P(c);rep 20.00
11/57 **(141)** AB,P(c);rep 20.00
09/58 **(146)** AB,P(c);rep 20.00
05/60 **(156)** AB,P(c);rep 20.00
62/63 **(167)** AB,P(c),Erroneously
    Has Original Date;rep 18.00
05/64 **(167)** AB,P(c);rep 18.00
05/65 **(167)** AB,P(c);rep 18.00
10/67 **(166)** AB,P(c);rep 18.00
Sr/69 **(169)** AB,P(c),25¢(c)
    Price, Rigid(c);rep 18.00
Sy/71 **(169)** AB,P(c);rep. 18.00

106-BUFFALO BILL
By William F. Cody
04/53 **(107)** MDb,P(c),Original. . . 100.00
04/54 **(118)** MDb,P(c);rep 20.00
03/56 **(132)** MDb,P(c);rep 20.00
01/58 **(142)** MDb,P(c);rep 20.00
03/61 **(161)** MDb,P(c);rep 18.00
03/64 **(167)** MDb,P(c);rep 18.00
07/67 **(166)** MDb,P(c);rep 18.00
Fl/69 **(169)** MDb,P(c),Rigid(c);rep . 18.00

107-KING OF THE
KHYBER RIFLES
By Talbot Mundy
05/53 **(108)** SMz,P(c),Original . . . 100.00
04/54 **(118)** SMz,P(c);rep. 20.00
09/58 **(146)** SMz,P(c);rep. 20.00
09/60 **(158)** SMz,P(c);rep 10.00
62/63 **(167)** SMz,P(c),Erroreously
    Has Original Date;rep 18.00
62/63 **(167)** SMz,P(c);rep. 18.00
10/66 **(167)** SMz,P(c);rep 18.00

108-KNIGHTS OF THE
ROUND TABLE
By Howard Pyle?
06/53 **(108)** AB,P(c),Original 100.00
06/53 **(109)** AB,P(c),Original 70.00
03/54 **(117)** AB,P(c);rep 20.00
11/59 **(153)** AB,P(c);rep 18.00
1962 **(165)** AB,P(c);rep 18.00
04/64 **(167)** AB,P(c);rep 18.00
04/67 **(166)** AB,P(c);rep 18.00

109-PITCAIRN'S ISLAND
By Charles Nordhoff
07/53 **(110)** RP,P(c),Original 100.00
1962 **(165)** RP,P(c);rep 20.00
03/64 **(167)** RP,P(c);rep 20.00
06/67 **(166)** RP,P(c);rep 20.00

110-A STUDY IN
SCARLET
By Sir Arthur Conan Doyle
08/53 **(111)** SMz,P(c),Original . . . 200.00
1962 **(165)** SMz,P(c);rep 100.00

111-THE TALISMAN
By Sir Walter Scott
09/53 **(112)** HcK,HcK P(c),Orig... 100.00
1962 **(165)** HcK,HcK P(c);rep 20.00

CI #109, Pitcairn's Island
© Gilberton Publications

05/64 **(167)** HcK,HcK P(c);rep. . . . 20.00
Fl/68 **(166)** HcK,HcK P(c),
    25¢(c)Price;rep 20.00

112-ADVENTURES OF
KIT CARSON
By John S. C. Abbott
10/53 **(113)** RP,P(c),Original 100.00
11/55 **(129)** RP,P(c);rep 20.00
11/57 **(141)** RP,P(c);rep 20.00
09/59 **(152)** RP,P(c);rep 18.00
03/61 **(161)** RP,P(c);rep 18.00
62/63 **(167)** RP,P(c);rep 18.00
02/65 **(167)** RP,P(c);rep 18.00
05/66 **(167)** RP,P(c);rep 18.00
Wr/69 **(166)** RP,EdM New P(c),
    25¢(c)Price, Rigid(c);rep 25.00

113-THE FORTY-FIVE
GUARDSMEN
By Alexandre Dumas
11/53 **(114)** MDb,P(c),Original . . . 150.00
07/67 **(166)** MDb,P(c);rep 50.00

114-THE RED ROVER
By James Fenimore Cooper
12/53 **(115)** PrC,JP P(c),Original . 150.00
07/67 **(166)** PrC,JP P(c);rep 50.00

115-HOW I FOUND
LIVINGSTONE
By Sir Henry Stanley
01/54 **(116)** SF&ST,P(c),Original . 200.00
01/67 **(167)** SF&ST,P(c);rep 60.00

116-THE BOTTLE IMP
By Robert Louis Stevenson
02/54 **(117)** LC,P(c),Original 200.00
01/67 **(167)** LC,P(c);rep 60.00

117-CAPTAINS
COURAGEOUS
By Rudyard Kipling
03/54 **(118)** PrC,P(c),Original . . . 200.00
02/67 **(167)** PrC,P(c);rep 32.00
Fl/69 **(169)** PrC,P(c),25¢(c)
    Price, Rigid(c);rep 30.00

Classics Illus.

All comics prices listed are for *Near Mint* condition.

118-ROB ROY
By Sir Walter Scott
04/54 **(119)** RP,WIP,P(c),Original . 200.00
02/67 **(167)** RP,WIP,P(c);rep 60.00

119-SOLDERS OF FORTUNE
By Richard Harding Davis
05/54 **(120)** KS,P(c),Original 150.00
03/67 **(166)** KS,P(c);rep 32.00
Sg/70 **(169)** KS,P(c),25¢(c)
    Price, Rigid(c);rep 30.00

CI #120, The Hurricane
© Gilberton Publications

120-THE HURRICANE
By Charles Nordhoff
1954 **(121)** LC,LC P(c),Original . . 150.00
03/67 **(166)** LC,LC P(c);rep 45.00

121-WILD BILL HICKOK
Author Unknown
07/54 **(122)** MI,ST,P(c),Original . . 125.00
05/56 **(132)** MI,ST,P(c);rep 20.00
11/57 **(141)** MI,ST,P(c);rep. 20.00
01/60 **(154)** MI,ST,P(c);rep 20.00
62/63 **(167)** MI,ST,P(c);rep 18.00
08/64 **(167)** MI,ST,P(c);rep 18.00
04/67 **(166)** MI,ST,P(c);rep 18.00
Wr/69 **(169)** MI,ST,P(c),Rigid
    (c);rep 18.00

122-THE MUTINEERS
By Charles Boardman Hawes
09/54 **(123)** PrC,P(c),Original ... 150.00
01/57 **(136)** PrC,P(c);rep 20.00
09/58 **(146)** PrC,P(c);rep 20.00
09/60 **(158)** PrC,P(c);rep 18.00
11/63 **(167)** PrC,P(c);rep 18.00
03/65 **(167)** PrC,P(c);rep 18.00
08/67 **(166)** PrC,P(c);rep 18.00

123-FANG AND CLAW
By Frank Buck
11/54 **(124)** LnS,P(c),Original ... 125.00
07/56 **(133)** LnS,P(c);rep 20.00
03/58 **(143)** LnS,P(c);rep 20.00
01/60 **(154)** LnS,P(c);rep 18.00
62/63 **(167)** LnS,P(c),Erroneously
    Has Original Date;rep 18.00
09/65 **(167)** LnS,P(c);rep 18.00

124-THE WAR OF THE WORLDS
By H. G. Wells
01/55 **(125)** LC,LC P(c),Original . 200.00
03/56 **(131)** LC,LC P(c);rep 20.00
11/57 **(141)** LC,LC P(c);rep 20.00
01/59 **(148)** LC,LC P(c);rep 20.00
05/60 **(156)** LC,LC P(c);rep 25.00
1962 **(165)** LC,LC P(c);rep 20.00
62/63 **(167)** LC,LC P(c);rep 20.00
11/64 **(167)** LC,LC P(c);rep 20.00
11/65 **(167)** LC,LC P(c);rep 20.00
1968 **(166)** LC,LC P(c),25¢(c)
    Price; rep 20.00
Sr/70 **(169)** LC,LC P(c),Rigid
    (c);rep 20.00

125-THE OX BOW INCIDENT
By Walter Van Tilberg Clark
03/55 **(—)** NN,P(c),Original 125.00
03/58 **(143)** NN,P(c);rep 20.00
09/59 **(152)** NN,P(c);rep 20.00
03/61 **(149)** NN,P(c);rep 20.00
62/63 **(167)** NN,P(c);rep 18.00
11/64 **(167)** NN,P(c);rep 18.00
04/67 **(166)** NN,P(c);rep 18.00
r/69 **(169)** NN,P(c),25¢(c)
    Price, Rigid(c);rep 18.00

126-THE DOWNFALL
By Emile Zola
05/55 **(—)** LC,LC P(c),Original,'
    Picture Progress'Replaces
    Reorder List 125.00
08/64 **(167)** LC,LC P(c);rep 25.00
1968 **(166)** LC,LC P(c),25¢(c)
    Price;rep 25.00

127-THE KING OF THE MOUNTAINS
By Edmond About
07/55 **(128)** NN,P(c),Original 150.00
06/64 **(167)** NN,P(c);rep 22.00
Fl/68 **(166)** NN,P(c),25¢(c)
    Price;rep 22.00

128-MACBETH
By William Shakespeare
09/55 **(128)** AB,P(c),Original 125.00
03/58 **(143)** AB,P(c);rep 20.00
09/60 **(158)** AB,P(c);rep 20.00
62/63 **(167)** AB,P(c);rep 18.00
06/64 **(167)** AB,P(c);rep 18.00
04/67 **(166)** AB,P(c);rep 18.00
1968 **(166)** AB,P(c),25¢(c)
    Price;rep 18.00
Sg/70 **(169)** AB,P(c),Rigid(c);rep . . 18.00

129-DAVY CROCKETT
Author Unknown
11/55 **(129)** LC,P(c),Original 200.00
09/66 **(167)** LC,P(c);rep 100.00

130-CAESAR'S CONQUESTS
By Julius Caesar
01/56 **(130)** JO,P(c),Original ... 125.00
01/58 **(142)** JO,P(c);rep 20.00
09/59 **(152)** JO,P(c);rep 20.00
03/61 **(149)** JO,P(c);rep 20.00
62/63 **(167)** JO,P(c);rep 18.00
10/64 **(167)** JO,P(c);rep 18.00
04/66 **(167)** JO,P(c);rep 18.00

131-THE COVERED WAGON
By Emerson Hough
03/56 **(131)** NN,P(c),Original 125.00
03/58 **(143)** NN,P(c);rep 20.00
09/59 **(152)** NN,P(c);rep 20.00
09/60 **(158)** NN,P(c);rep 20.00
62/63 **(167)** NN,P(c);rep 18.00
11/64 **(167)** NN,P(c);rep 18.00
04/66 **(167)** NN,P(c);rep 18.00
Wr/69 **(169)** NN,P(c),25¢(c)
    Price, Rigid(c);rep 18.00

132-THE DARK FRIGATE
By Charles Boardman Hawes
05/56 **(132)** EW&RWb,P(c),Orig.. 125.00
05/59 **(150)** EW&RWb,P(c);rep ... 20.00
01/64 **(167)** EW&RWb,P(c);rep ... 20.00
05/67 **(166)** EW&RWb,P(c);rep ... 20.00

133-THE TIME MACHINE
By H. G. Wells
07/56 **(132)** LC,P(c),Original 175.00
01/58 **(142)** LC,P(c);rep 20.00
09/59 **(152)** LC,P(c);rep 20.00
09/60 **(158)** LC,P(c);rep 20.00
62/63 **(167)** LC,P(c);rep 20.00
06/64 **(167)** LC,P(c);rep 25.00
03/66 **(167)** LC,P(c);rep 20.00
03/66 **(167)** LC,P(c),N# Or Price;
    rep 20.00
12/67 **(166)** LC,P(c);rep 20.00
Wr/71 **(169)** LC,P(c),25¢(c)
    Price, Rigid(c);rep 20.00

134-ROMEO AND JULIET
By William Shakespeare
09/56 **(134)** GE,P(c),Original 125.00
03/61 **(161)** GE,P(c);rep 20.00
09/63 **(167)** GE,P(c);rep 18.00
05/65 **(167)** GE,P(c);rep 18.00
06/67 **(167)** GE,P(c);rep 18.00
Wr/69 **(166)** GE,EdM New P(c),
    25¢(c)Price, Rigid(c);rep 32.00

135-WATERLOO
By Emile Erckmann & Alexandre Chatrian
11/56 **(135)** Grl,AB P(c),Original . 125.00
11/59 **(153)** Grl,AB P(c);rep...... 20.00
62/63 **(167)** Grl,AB P(c);rep...... 18.00
09/64 **(167)** Grl,AB P(c);rep...... 18.00
1968 **(166)** Grl,AB P(c),25¢(c)
    Price; rep 18.00

136-LORD JIM
By Joseph Conrad
01/57 **(136)** GE,P(c),Original 150.00
62/63 **(165)** GE,P(c);rep 18.00
03/64 **(167)** GE,P(c);rep 18.00
09/66 **(167)** GE,P(c);rep 18.00
Sr/69 **(169)** GE,P(c),25¢(c)
    Price, Rigid(c);rep 18.00

137-THE LITTLE SAVAGE
By Captain Frederick Marryat
03/57 **(136)** GE,P(c),Original 125.00
01/59 **(148)** GE,P(c);rep 20.00
05/60 **(156)** GE,P(c);rep 20.00
62/63 **(167)** GE,P(c);rep 18.00
10/64 **(167)** GE,P(c);rep 18.00
08/67 **(166)** GE,P(c);rep 18.00
Sg/70 **(169)** GE,P(c),25¢(c)
    Price, Rigid(c);rep 18.00

138-A JOURNEY TO THE CENTER OF THE EARTH
By Jules Verne
05/57 **(136)** NN,P(c),Original 175.00
09/58 **(146)** NN,P(c);rep 20.00
05/60 **(156)** NN,P(c);rep 20.00
09/60 **(158)** NN,P(c);rep 20.00
62/63 **(167)** NN,P(c);rep 18.00
06/64 **(167)** NN,P(c);rep 20.00
04/66 **(167)** NN,P(c);rep 20.00
1968 **(166)** NN,P(c),25¢(c)
   Price;rep 18.00

139-IN THE REIGN OF TERROR
By George Alfred Henty
07/57 **(139)** GE,P(c),Original 125.00
01/60 **(154)** GE,P(c);rep 20.00
62/63 **(167)** GE,P(c),Erroneously
   Has Original Date;rep 18.00
07/64 **(167)** GE,P(c);rep 20.00
1968 **(166)** GE,P(c),25¢(c)
   Price;rep 18.00

140-ON JUNGLE TRAILS
By Frank Buck
09/57 **(140)** NN,P(c),Original 125.00
05/59 **(150)** NN,P(c);rep 20.00
01/61 **(160)** NN,P(c);rep 20.00
09/63 **(167)** NN,P(c);rep 18.00
09/65 **(167)** NN,P(c);rep 18.00

141-CASTLE DANGEROUS
By Sir Walter Scott
11/57 **(141)** StC,P(c),Original 150.00
09/59 **(152)** STC,P(c);rep 20.00
62/63 **(167)** StC,P(c);rep 18.00
07/67 **(166)** StC,P(c);rep 18.00

142-ABRAHAM LINCOLN
By Benjamin Thomas
01/58 **(142)** NN,P(c),Original 150.00
01/60 **(154)** NN,P(c);rep 20.00
09/60 **(158)** NN,P(c);rep 20.00
10/63 **(167)** NN,P(c);rep 18.00
07/65 **(167)** NN,P(c);rep 18.00
11/67 **(166)** NN,P(c);rep 18.00
Fl/69 **(169)** NN,P(c),25¢(c) Price,
   Rigid(c);rep 18.00

143-KIM
By Rudyard Kipling
03/58 **(143)** JO,P(c)Original 125.00
62/63 **(165)** JO,P(c);rep 18.00
11/63 **(167)** JO,P(c);rep 18.00
08/65 **(167)** JO,P(c);rep 18.00
Wr/69 **(169)** JO,P(c),25¢(c) Price,
   Rigid(c);rep 18.00

144-THE FIRST MEN IN THE MOON
By H. G. Wells
05/58 **(143)** GWb,AW,AT,RKr,
   GMC P(c), Original 175.00
11/59 **(153)** GWb,AW,AT,RKr,
   GMC, P(c); rep 20.00
03/61 **(161)** GWb,AW,AT,RKr,
   GMC, P(c); rep 18.00
62/63 **(167)** GWb,AW,AT,RKr,
   GMC, P(c); rep 18.00
12/65 **(167)** GWb,AW,AT,RKr,
   GMC, P(c); rep 18.00
Fl/68 **(166)** GWb,AW,AT,RKr,GMC
   P(c),25¢(c) Price,Rigid(c);rep . 18.00

Wr/69 **(169)** GWb,AW,AT,RKr,GMC
   P(c), Rigid(c);rep 28.00

145-THE CRISIS
by Winston Churchill
07/58 **(143)** GE,P(c),Original 125.00
05/60 **(156)** GE,P(c);rep 20.00
10/63 **(167)** GE,P(c);rep 18.00
03/65 **(167)** GE,P(c);rep 18.00
1968 **(166)** GE,P(c),25¢(c)
   Price;rep 18.00

146-WITH FIRE AND SWORD
By Henryk Sienkiewicz
09/58 **(143)** GWb,P(c),Original . . 125.00
05/60 **(156)** GWb,P(c);rep 25.00
11/63 **(167)** GWb,P(c);rep 20.00
03/65 **(167)** GWb,P(c),rep 20.00

147-BEN-HUR
By Lew Wallace
11/58 **(147)** JO,P(c),Original 125.00
11/59 **(153)** JO,P(c);rep 65.00
09/60 **(158)** JO,P(c);rep 20.00
62/63 **(167)** JO,P(c),Has the
   Original Date;rep 20.00
——— **(167)** JO,P(c),rep 18.00
02/65 **(167)** JO,P(c);rep 18.00
09/66 **(167)** JO,P(c);rep 18.00
Fl/68 **(166)** JO,P(c),25¢(c)Price,
   Both Rigid & Soft (c)s;rep 50.00

148-THE BUCKANEER
By Lyle Saxon
01/59 **(148)** GE&RJ,NS P(c),orig. 125.00
——— **(568)** GE&RJ,NS P(c),Juniors
   List Only;rep 20.00
62/63 **(167)** GE&RJ,NS P(c);rep . . 20.00
09/65 **(167)** GE&RJ,NS P(c);rep . . 20.00
Sr/69 **(169)** GE&RJ,NS P(c),25¢(c)
   Price, Rigid(c);rep 20.00

CI #149, Off on a Comet
© Gilberton Publications

149-OFF ON A COMET
By Jules Verne
03/59 **(149)** GMc,P(c),Original . . . 125.00
03/60 **(155)** GMc,P(c);rep 20.00
03/61 **(149)** GMc,P(c);rep 20.00
12/63 **(167)** GMc,P(c);rep 18.00
02/65 **(167)** GMc,P(c);rep 18.00
10/66 **(167)** GMc,P(c);rep 18.00

Fl/68 **(166)** GMc,EdM New P(c),
   25¢(c)Price;rep 30.00

150-THE VIRGINIAN
By Owen Winster
05/59 **(150)** NN,DrG P(c),Original 200.00
1961 **(164)** NN,DrG P(c);rep 30.00
62/63 **(167)** NN,DrG P(c);rep 35.00
12/65 **(167)** NN,DrG P(c);rep 30.00

151-WON BY THE SWORD
By George Alfred Henty
07/59 **(150)** JTg,P(c),Original . . . 125.00
1961 **(164)** JTg,P(c);rep 25.00
10/63 **(167)** JTg,P(c);rep 25.00
1963 **(167)** JTg,P(c);rep 25.00
07/67 **(166)** JTg,P(c);rep 25.00

152-WILD ANIMALS I HAVE KNOWN
By Ernest Thompson Seton
09/59 **(152)** I hC,LbC P(c),Orig. . . 125.00
03/61 **(149)** LbC,LbC P(c),P(c);rep 20.00
09/63 **(167)** LbC,LbC P(c);rep 18.00
08/65 **(167)** LbC,LbC P(c);rep 18.00
fl/69 **(169)** LbC,LbC P(c),25¢(c)
   Price, Rigid(c),rep 18.00

153-THE INVISIBLE MAN
By H. G. Wells
11/59 **(153)** NN,GB P(c),Original . 150.00
03/61 **(149)** NN,GB P(c);rep 20.00
62/63 **(167)** NN,GB P(c);rep 18.00
02/65 **(167)** NN,GB P(c);rep 18.00
09/66 **(167)** NN,GB P(c);rep 18.00
Wr/69 **(166)** NN,GB P(c),25¢(c)
   Price, Rigid(c);rep 18.00
Sg/71 **(169)** NN,GB P(c),Rigid(c),
   Words Spelling'Invisible Man'
   Are' Solid'Not'Invisible';rep . . . 18.00

154-THE CONSPIRACY OF PONTIAC
By Francis Parkman
01/60 **(154)** GMc,GMc P(c),
   Original 125.00
11/63 **(167)** GMc,GMc P(c);rep . . . 30.00
07/64 **(167)** GMc,GMc P(c);rep . . . 30.00
12/67 **(166)** GMc,GMc P(c);rep . . . 30.00

155-THE LION OF THE NORTH
By George Alfred Henty
03/60 **(154)** NN,GMc P(c),Orig. . . . 125.00
01/64 **(167)** NN,GMc P(c);rep 25.00
1967 **(166)** NN,GMc P(c),25¢(c)
   Price; rep 20.00

156-THE CONQUEST OF MEXICO
By Bernal Diaz Del Castillo
05/60 **(156)** BPr,BPr P(c),Original 125.00
01/64 **(167)** BPr,BPr P(c);rep 20.00
08/67 **(166)** BPr,BPr P(c);rep 20.00
Sg/70 **(169)** BPr,BPr P(c),25¢(c)
   Price; Rigid(c);rep 18.00

157-LIVES OF THE HUNTED
By Ernest Thompson Seton
07/60 **(156)** NN,LbC P(c),Original 150.00
02/64 **(167)** NN,LbC P(c);rep. 28.00
10/67 **(166)** NN,LbC P(c);rep. 28.00

Classics Illus.

All comics prices listed are for *Near Mint* condition.   **CVA Page 825**

158-THE CONSPIRATORS
By Alexandre Dumas
09/60 **(156)** GMc,GMc P(c),
Original 150.00
07/64 **(167)** GMc,GMc P(c);rep . . . 28.00
10/67 **(166)** GMc,GMc P(c);rep . . . 28.00

159-THE OCTOPUS
By Frank Norris
11/60 **(159)** GM&GE,LbC P(c),
Original 150.00
02/64 **(167)** GM&GE,LbC P(c);rep. 28.00
166 **(1967)** GM&GE,LbC P(c),25¢(c)
Price;rep 28.00

160-THE FOOD OF THE GODS
By H.G. Wells
01/61 **(159)** TyT,GMc P(c),Orig.. 150.00
01/61 **(160)** TyT,GMc P(c),Original;
Same Except For the HRN# . . 60.00
01/64 **(167)** TyT,GMc P(c);rep 28.00
06/67 **(166)** TyT,GMc P(c);rep 28.00

161-CLEOPATRA
By H. Rider Haggard
03/61 **(161)** NN,Pch P(c),Original 125.00
01/64 **(167)** NN,Pch P(c);rep 30.00
08/67 **(166)** NN,Pch P(c);rep 30.00

162-ROBUR THE CONQUEROR
By Jules Verne
05/61 **(162)** GM&DPn,CJ P(c),
Original 125.00
07/64 **(167)** GM&DPn,CJ P(c);rep. 28.00
08/67 **(166)** GM&DPn,CJ P(c);rep. 28.00

163-MASTER OF THE WORLD
By Jules Verne
07/61 **(163)** GM,P(c),Original. . . . 125.00
01/65 **(167)** GM,P(c);rep 28.00
1968 **(166)** GM,P(c),25¢(c)
Price;rep 28.00

164-THE COSSACK CHIEF
By Nicolai Gogol
1961 **(164)** SyM,P(c),Original . . . 125.00
04/65 **(167)** SyM,P(c);rep 28.00
Fl/68 **(166)** SyM,P(c),25¢(c)
Price;rep 28.00

165-THE QUEEN'S NECKLACE
by Alexandre Dumas
01/62 **(164)** GM,P(c),Original. . . . 125.00
04/65 **(167)** GM,P(c);rep 28.00
Fl/68 **(166)** GM,P(c),25¢(c)
Price;rep 28.00

166-TIGERS AND TRAITORS
By Jules Verne
05/62 **(165)** NN,P(c),Original 150.00
02/64 **(167)** NN,P(c);rep 40.00
11/66 **(167)** NN,P(c);rep. 40.00

167-FAUST
By Johann Wolfgang von Goethe
08/62 **(165)** NN,NN P(c),Original. 200.00
02/64 **(167)** NN,NN P(c);rep 75.00
06/67 **(166)** NN,NN P(c);rep 75.00

168-IN FREEDOM'S CAUSE
By George Alfred Henty
Wr/69 **(169)** GE&RC,P(c),
Original, Rigid (c). 225.00

169-NEGRO AMERICANS THE EARLY YEARS
AUTHOR UNKNOWN
Sg/69 **(166)** NN,NN P(c),
Original, Rigid(c) 200.00
Sg/69 **(169)** NN,NN P(c),
Rigid; rep 100.00

CLASSICS ILLUSTRATED GIANTS
An Illustrated Library of Great
Adventure Stories -(reps. of
Issues 6,7,8,10) 2,000.00
An Illustrated Library of Exciting
Mystery Stories -(reps. of
Issues 30,21,40,13) 2,200.00
An Illustrated Library of Great
Indian Stories -(reps. of
Issues 4,17,22,37) 2,000.00

CLASSICS ILLUSTRATED JUNIOR
Oct., 1953–Spring., 1971
501-Snow White and the
Seven Dwarfs 150.00
502-The Ugly Duckling 100.00
503-Cinderella 75.00
504-The Pied Piper 75.00
505-The Sleeping Beauty 75.00
506-The Three Little Pigs 75.00
507-Jack and the Beanstalk 75.00
508-Goldilocks & the Three Bears. 75.00
509-Beauty and the Beast. 75.00
510-Little Red Riding Hood 75.00
511-Puss-N-Boots 75.00
512-Rumpelstiltskin 75.00
513-Pinocchio 75.00
514-The Steadfast Tin Soldier . . . 100.00
515-Johnny Appleseed 75.00
516-Aladdin and His Lamp 75.00
517-The Emperor's New Clothes . 75.00
518-The Golden Goose 75.00
519-Paul Bunyan 75.00
520-Thumbelina 75.00
521-King of the Golden River 75.00
522-The Nightingale. 75.00
523-The Gallant Tailor 75.00
524-The Wild Swans 75.00
525-The Little Mermaid 75.00
526-The Frog Prince 75.00
527-The Golden-Haired Giant 75.00
528-The Penny Prince. 75.00
529-The Magic Servants 75.00
530-The Golden Bird 75.00
531-Rapunzel. 75.00
532-The Dancing Princesses. 75.00
533-The Magic Fountain 75.00
534-The Golden Touch 75.00
535-The Wizard of Oz 100.00
536-The Chimney Sweep 75.00
537-The Three Fairies 75.00
538-Silly Hans 75.00
539-The Enchanted Fish 75.00
540-The Tinder-Box. 75.00
541-Snow White and Rose Red . . 75.00
542-The Donkey's Tail 75.00
543-The House in the Woods 75.00
544-The Golden Fleece. 75.00
545-The Glass Mountain 75.00
546-The Elves and the Shoemaker 75.00
547-The Wishing Table 75.00
548-The Magic Pitcher. 75.00
549-Simple Kate 75.00
550-The Singing Donkey 75.00
551-The Queen Bee 75.00
552-The Three Little Dwarfs 75.00
553-King Thrushbeard 75.00
554-The Enchanted Deer 75.00
555-The Three Golden Apples. . . . 75.00
556-The Elf Mound 75.00
557-Silly Willy. 75.00
558-The Magic Dish,LbC(c). 75.00
559-The Japanese Lantern,LbC(c) 90.00
560-The Doll Princess,LbC(c) 90.00
561-Hans Humdrum,LbC(c). 75.00
562-The Enchanted Pony,LbC(c) . 90.00
563-The Wishing Well,LbC(c) 75.00
564-The Salt Mountain,LbC(c). . . . 75.00
565-The Silly Princess,LbC(c) 75.00
566-Clumsy Hans,LbC(c). 75.00
567-The Bearskin Soldier,LbC(c). . 75.00
568-The Happy Hedgehog,LbC(c). 75.00
569-The Three Giants 75.00
570-The Pearl Princess 75.00
571-How Fire Came to the Indians 75.00
572-The Drummer Boy 75.00
573-The Crystal Ball 75.00
574-Brightboots 75.00
575-The Fearless Prince 75.00
576-The Princess Who Saw
Everything 90.00
577-The Runaway Dumpling 100.00

CLASSICS ILLLUSTRATED SPECIAL ISSUE
Dec., 1955–July, 1962
N# United Nations 425.00
129-The Story of Jesus,Jesus on
mountain(c) 150.00
129a-Three Camels(c). 150.00
129b-Mountain(c),HRN to 161 . . 125.00
129c-Mountain(c) (1968) 100.00
132A-The Story of America 125.00
135A-The Ten Commandments . . 125.00
138A-Adventures in Science 125.00
138Aa-HRN to 149 . . . . 100.00
138Ab-rep.,12/61 . . . . 100.00
141A-GE,The Rough Rider 125.00
144A-RC,GE,Blazing the Trails . . 125.00
147A-RC,GE,Crossing the
Rockies 125.00
150A-Grl,Royal Canadian Police. 125.00
153A-GE,Men, Guns, & Cattle.. . 125.00
156A-GE,GM,The Atomic Age... 125.00
159A-GE,GM,Rockets, Jets and
Missiles 125.00
162A-RC,GE,War Between
the States 200.00
165A-RC/GE,JK,Grl,To the Stars. 125.00
166A-RC/GE,JK,Grl,World War II 150.00
167A-RC/GE,JK,Prehistoric
World 150.00
167Aa-HRN to 167. . . . . 110.00

Classics Illus.

UNDERGROUND

ADVENTURES OF FAT FREDDY'S CAT, THE
Rip Off Press, Feb., 1977
1 . . . . 20.00
2 . . . . 12.00
3 . . . . 15.00
4 . . . . 10.00
5 & 6 . . . . @10.00

AMAZING DOPE TALES
Greg Shaw
1 Untrimmed black and white pages, out of order;artist unknown . . 110.00
2 Trimmed and proper pages 95.00

AMERICAN SPLENDOR
Harvey Pekar, May, 1976
1 B:Harvey Pekar Stories, HP,RCr,GDu,GBu 25.00
2 HP,RCr,GDu,GBu 10.00
3 HP,RCr,GDu,GBu 10.00
4 HP,RCr,GDu,GBu 8.00
5 HP,RCr,GDu,GBu 8.00
6 HP,RCr,GDu,GBu,GSh 7.00
7 HP,GSh,GDu,GBu 5.00
8 HP,GSh,GDu,GBu 3.00
9 and 10 HP,GSh,GDu,GBu . . . . @3.00
11 . . . . 3.00
12 . . . . 4.50
13 thru 19 . . . . @4.00
20 E:Harvey Pekar Stories 4.00

ANTHOLOGY OF SLOW DEATH
Wingnut Press/Last Gasp
1 140 pgs, RCr,RCo, GiS, DSh, Harlan Ellison VB,RTu. 37.00

APEX TREASURY OF UNDERGROUND COMICS, THE
Links Books Inc., Oct., 1974
1 . . . . 40.00

APEX TREASURY OF UNDERGROUND COMICS –BEST OF BIJOU FUNNIES
Quick Fox, 1981
1 Paperback,comix,various artists 21.00

ARCADE THE COMICS REVUE
Print Mint Inc. Spring, 1975
1 ASp,BG,RCr,SRo,SCW 25.00
2 ASp,BG,RCr,SRo 15.00
3 ASp,BG,RCr,RW,SCW 10.00
4 ASp,BG,RCr,WBu,RW,SCW . . 10.00
5 thru 7 ASp,BG,SRo,RW,SCW . @7.50

BABYFAT
Comix World/Clay Geerdes, 1978
1 B:8pg news parodies, one page comix by various artists. 4.50
2 thru 9 same . . . . @3.00
10 thru 26 same. . . . . @2.00

Arcade The Comics Revue #2
© Print Mint

BATTLE OF THE TITANS
University of Illinois SF Society, 1972
1 Sci-Fi;VB,JGa 50.00

BEST BUY COMICS
Last Gasp Eco-Funnies
1 Rep Whole Earth Review;RCr. . . 3.50
1-shot R. Crumb reprints (2004) . . . 2.50

BEST OF BIJOU FUNNIES, THE
Links Books Inc., 1975
1 164 pgs,paperback 250.00

BEST OF RIP-OFF PRESS
Rip Off Press Inc., 1973
1 132 pgs paperback,SCW, RCr,SRo,RW 25.00
2 100 pgs,GS,FT 27.50
3 100 pgs,FS 15.00
4 132 pgs,GiS,DSh 16.00

BIG ASS
Rip Off Press, 1969–71
1 28 pgs,RCr. 80.00
2 RCr 50.00

BIJOU FUNNIES
Bijou Publishing Empire, 1968
1 B:JLy,editor;RCr,GS SW 300.00
2 RCr,GS,SW 125.00
3 RCr,SWi,JsG 80.00
4 SWi,JsG 45.00
5 SWi,JsG. 50.00
6 E:JI y,editor,SWi,RCr,JsG 40.00
7 and 8 . . . . @40.00

BINKY BROWN MEETS THE HOLY VIRGIN MARY
Last Gasp Eco-Funnies, March, 1972
N# Autobiography about Growing up w/a Catholic Neurosis,JsG . . . 25.00

2nd Printing:only text in bottom left panel 12.00
TPB Sampler (2004) 16.95

BIZARRE SEX
Kitchen Sink Komix, May, 1972
1 B:DKi,editor,various artists 30.00
2 . . . . 25.00
3 . . . . 20.00
4 thru 6 . . . . @15.00
7 . . . . 10.00
8 . . . . 10.00
9 Omaha the Cat Dancer,RW. . . . 25.00
10 inc.Omaha the Cat Dancer,RW 20.00

BLACK LAUGHTER
Black Laughter Pub. Co, Nov,. 1972
1 James Dixon art 64.00

BLOOD FROM A STONE (GUIDE TO TAX REFORM)
New York Public Interest Research Group Inc., 1977
1 Tax reform proposals. 15.00

BOBBY LONDON RETROSPECTIVE AND ART PORTFOLIO
Cartoonist Representatives
1 . . . . 20.00

BOBMAN AND TEDDY
Parrallax Comic Books Inc., 1966
1 RFK & Ted Kennedy's struggle to control Democratic party 60.00

BODE'S CARTOON CONCERT
Dell, Sept., 1973
1 132 pgs; VB 27.50

BOGEYMAN COMICS
San Fransisco Comic Book Co., 1969
1 Horror,RHa. 65.00
2 Horror,RHa 50.00

The Company & Sons
3 . . . . 35.00

BUFFALO RAG/THE DEAD CONCERT COMIX
Kenny Laramey, Dec., 1973
1 Alice in Wonderland parody. . . . 60.00

CAPTAIN GUTS
The Print Mint,1969
1 Super patriotV.Counter culture 30.00
2 V:Black Panthers 20.00
3 V:Dope Smugglers 20.00

CAPTAIN STICKY
Captain Sticky, 1974–75
1 Super lawyer V:SocialInjustice . 20.00

Underground

CARTOON HISTORY OF THE UNIVERSE
Rip Off Press, Sept., 1978
1 Evolution of Everything;
    B:Larry Gonick 12.00
2 Sticks and Stones 8.00
3 River Realms-Sumer & Egypt . . 8.00
4 Part of the Old Testament 5.00
5 Brains and Bronze 5.00
6 Who are these Athenians 5.00

CASCADE COMIX MONTHLY
Everyman Studios, March, 1978
1 Interviews,articles about
    comix & comix artists 8.00
2 and 3 same . . . . @8.00
4 thru 11 . . . . @4.00
12 thru 23 . . . . @3.00

CHECKERED DEMON
Last Gasp, July, 1977
1 SCW 15.00
2 SCW 8.50
3 SCW 6.50

CHEECH WIZARD
Office of Student Publications, Syracuse U, 1967
n/n VB 150.00

Cherry Poptart #2
© *Last Gasp*

CHERRY POPTART
Last Gasp, 1982–85
1 by Larry Welz 10.00
2 . . . . 7.00
Becomes:

CHERRY
3 . . . . 5.00
4 . . . . 5.00
5 . . . . 5.00
6 thru 13 . . . . @4.00
Kitchen Sink
14 . . . . 4.00
15 . . . . 4.00
TPB Cherry Collection #1 . . . . . . 15.00
TPB Cherry Collection #2 . . . . . . 15.00
TPB Cherry Collection #3 . . . . . . 13.00
Cherry's Jubilee #1 thru #4 . . . . . @3.00

CHICAGO MIRROR
Jay Lynch/Mirror Publishing Empire, Autumn, 1967
1 B:Bijou Funnies 50.00
2 same 40.00
3 same 125.00

COCAINE COMIX
Last Gas, Inc., 1976–82
1 . . . . 15.00
2 thru 4 . . . . @10.00
2005
1 . . . . 2.95
2 . . . . 2.95

COLLECTED CHEECH WIZARD, THE
Company & Sons, 1972
n/n VB 60.00
Print Mint, 1976
n/n VB 15.00

COLLECTED TRASHMAN #1, THE
Fat City & The Red Mountain Tribe Productions
n/n SRo 32.50

COMICS & COMIX
Oct., 1975
1 . . . . 15.00

COMIX BOOK
Magazine Management Co. Oct., 1974
1 Compilation for newsstand
    distribution 20.00
2 and 3 . . . . @10.00
Kitchen Sink Enterprises
4 . . . . 20.00
5 . . . . 10.00

COMIX COLLECTOR, THE
Archival Press Inc., Dec., 1979
1 Fanzine 6.00
2 & 3 Fanzine . . . . @5.00

COMMIES FROM MARS
Kitchen Sink, March, 1973
1 TB 40.00
Last Gasp
2 thru 5 TB . . . . @15.00

COMPLETE FRITZ THE CAT
Belier Press 1978
n/n RCr,SRo,DSh 65.00

CONSPIRACY CAPERS
The Conspiracy, 1969
1 Benefit Legal Defense of the
    Chicago-8 . . . . 100.00

DAN O'NEIL'S COMICS & STORIES
Company & Sons, Vol.1
1 B:Dan O'Neill 50.00
2 & 3 . . . . @30.00
1971 Vol. 2
1 . . . . 6.50
2 and E:Dan O'Neill . . . . @4.50

DAS KAMPF
Vaughn Bode, May, 1963
N# 100 Loose pgs. 750.00
2nd Printing 52pgs.-produced by
    W.Bachner & Bagginer,1977 . . 25.00

DEADBONE EROTICA
Bantam Books Inc., April, 1971
n/n 132 pgs VB 50.00

DEADCENTER CLEAVAGE
April, 1971
1 14 pgs 50.00

DEATH RATTLE
Kitchen Sink, June, 1972
1 RCo,TB 25.00
2 TB 20.00
3 TB 16.00

DESPAIR
The Print Mint, 1969
1 RCr 50.00

DIRTY DUCK BOOK, THE
Company & Sons, March, 1972
1 Bobby London 30.00

DISNEY RAPES THE 1st AMENDMENT
Dan O'Neil, 1974
1 Benefit Air Pirates V:Disney
    Law suit; Dan O'Neill 15.00

DR. ATOMIC
Last Gasp Eco-Funnies, Sept., 1972
1 B:Larry S. Todd 15.00
2 and 3 . . . . @12.00
4 . . . . 10.00
5 E:Larry S. Todd 8.00
6 . . . . 6.00

DR. ATOMIC'S MARIJUANA MULTIPLIER
Kistone Press, 1974
1 How to grow great pot 10.00

DOPE COMIX
Kitchen Sink, Feb., 1978
1 Drugs comix;various artists 10.00
2 same 8.00
3 & 4 LSD issue . . . . @6.00
5 Omaha the Cat Dancer, RW . . . 10.00

DOPIN DAN
Last Gasp Eco-Funnies, April, 1972
1 TR 15.00
2 and 3 TR . . . . @10.00
4 Todays Army,TR 9.00

DORI STORIES
Last Gasp, 2004
TPB Dori Deda collection 20.00

DRAWINGS BY S. CLAY WILSON
San Francisco Graphics
1 28 pgs 200.00

DYING DOLPHIN
The Print Mint ,1970
n/n 20.00

EBON
San Francisco Comic
Book Company
1 Comix version; RCr 30.00
1 Tabloid version. 20.00

EL PERFECTO COMICS
The Print Mint, 1973
N# Benefit Timothy Leary 30.00
2nd Printing-1975 . . . . 4.00

ETERNAL TRUTH
Sunday Funnies Comic Corp
1 Christian Comix 25.00

EVERMUCH WAVE
Atlantis Distributors
1 Nunzio the Narc; Adventures
of God 60.00

E.Z. WOLF'S
ASTRAL OUTHOUSE
Last Gasp, 2005
1-shot. 2.95

FABULOUS FURRY
FREAK BROTHERS, THE
COLLECTED ADVENTURES OF
Rip Off Press, #1 Feb., 1971
1 GiS 90.00

FURTHER ADVENTURES OF
Rip Off Press, #2
1 GiS,DSh 60.00

A YEAR PASSES LIKE
NOTHING WITH
Rip Off Press #3
1 GiS 25.00

BROTHER CAN YOU
SPARE $.75 FOR
Rip Off Press #4
1 GiS,DSh 20.00

FABULOUS FURRY
FREAK BROTHERS, THE
Rip Off Press #5
1 GiS,DSh 15.00

SIX SNAPPY SOCKERS
FROM THE ARCHIVES OF
Rip Off Press #6
1 GiS 10.00

FANTAGOR
1970
1 (Corben), fanzine. 125.00
Last Gasp
1a 22.00
2 & 3 . . . . @25.00
4 . . . . 35.00

FEDS 'N' HEADS
Gilbert Shelton/Print Mint, 1968
N# I:Fabulous Furry Freak Bros.;
  Has no `Print Mint' Address
  24 pgs. 400.00
2nd printing, 28 pgs. 60.00
3rd printing, May, 1969 . . . . 50.00
4th printing, Says `Forth
  Printing' 25.00

Fantagor #2
© *Last Gasp*

5th-12th printings . . . . @10.00
13th printing 7.00
14th printing 6.00

FELCH
Keith Green
1 RW,SCW,RCr. 45.00

FEVER PITCH
Kitchen Sink Enterprises,
July, 1976
1 RCo 25.00
Jabberwocky Graphix
2 250 signed & numbered 20.00
3 400 signed & numbered 18.00
4 . . . . 10.00

50'S FUNNIES
Kitchen Sink Enterprises, 1980
1 Larry Shell, editor,various
  artists 10.00

FLAMING CARROT
Kilian Barracks Free Press,
1981
1 Bob Budden,various artists 15.00

FLASH THEATRE
Oogle Productions, 1970
1 44 pgs 50.00

FLESHAPOIDS FROM
EARTH
Popular Culture, Dec., 1974
1 36 pgs 40.00

THE COMPLETE FOO!
Bijou Publishing, Sept., 1980
1 RCr, Charles Crumb, r:Crumb
  brothers fanzines 50.00

FRITZ BUGS OUT
Ballentine Books, 1972
n/n RCr. 70.00

FRITZ THE CAT
Ballentine Books, 1969
n/n RCr. 125.00

FRITZ THE NO-GOOD
Ballentine Books, 1972
n/n RCr. 60.00

FRITZ: SECRET AGENT
FOR THE CIA
Ballentine Books, 1972
n/n RCr. 60.00

FUNNY AMINALS
Apex Novelties/Don Donahue,
1972
1 RCr 65.00

GAY COMIX
Kitchen Sink Sept., 1981
1 36 pgs 8.00
2 36 pgs 6.00

GEN OF HIROSHIMA
Educomics/Leonard Rifas,
Jan., 1980
1 Antiwar comix by Hiroshima
  survivor Keiji Nakawaza 10.00
2 same 8.00

GHOST MOTHER COMICS
John "Mad" Peck, 1969
1 SCw,JsG 55.00

GIMMEABREAK COMIX
Rhuta Press, Feb., 1971
2 48 pgs, #0 & #1 were advertised,but
may not have been printed 125.00

GIRLS & BOYS
Lynda J. Barry, 1980
1 B:12 pgs with every other page
  blank, all Barry art 12.00
2 thru 10 same . . . . @8.00
11 thru 20 same . . . . @6.00
20 thru 25 same. . . . . @5.00

GOD NOSE
Jack Jackson/
Rip Off Press, 1964
N# 42 pgs. 135.00
2nd printing,Pinkish(c);44p 60.00
3rd printing,Blue Border(c) 30.00
4th printing,Red Border(c) 15.00

GOTHIC BLIMP
WORKS LTD.
East Village Other/
Peter Leggieri, 1969
1 VB,Editor,various artists. 200.00
2 same 145.00
3 KDe,editor 135.00
4 KDe,editor 130.00
5 thru 7 KDe,editor . . . . @125.00
8 various artists. 185.00

GREASER COMICS
Half-Ass Press, Sept., 1971
1 28 pgs, George DiCaprio. 25.00
Rip Off Press, July, 1972
2 George DiCaprio 15.00

GRIM WIT
Last Gasp, 1972
1 RCo 40.00
2 RCo 30.00

All comics prices listed are for *Near Mint* condition.

HAROLD HEAD, THE COLLECTED ADVENTURES OF
Georgia Straight, 1972
1 .... 50.00
2 .... 20.00

HARRY CHESS THAT MAN FROM A.U.N.T.I.E.
The Uncensored Adventures, Trojan Book Service, 1966
N# 1st Comix By & For Gay
Community 150.00

HEAR THE SOUND OF MY FEET WALKING....
Glide Urban Center, 1969
1 Dan O'Neill, 128 pgs. 70.00

HISTORY OF UNDERGROUND COMIX
Straight Arrow Books, 1974
1 Book by Mark James Estren about
Underground Comix 40.00

HOMEGROWN FUNNIES
Kitchen Sink, 1971
1 RCr 60.00

HONKYTONK SUE, THE QUEEN OF COUNTRY SWING
Bob Boze Bell, 1979
1 BBB 17.00
2 & 3 BBB .... @12.00

IKE LIVES
Warm Neck Funnies, 1973
1 20 pgs,Mark Fisher 15.00

IMAGE OF THE BEAST
Last Gast, 1973
1 Phillip Jose Farmer adapt...... 16.00
1 rep. 1979 .... 10.00

INSECT FEAR
Last Gasp, 1970
1 SRo,GiS,RHa,JsG 75.00
Print Mint, 1970–72
2 .... 30.00
3 .... 20.00

IT AIN'T ME BABE
Last Gasp Eco-Funnies, 1970
n/n First all women comix
Womens Liberation theme ... 40.00

JAPANESE MONSTER
Carol Lay, July, 1979
1 8pgs, Carol Lay 10.00

JESUS LOVES YOU
Zondervan Books/Craig Yoe, 1972
1 Christian, RCr 35.00

It Aint Me Babe #1
© *Last Gasp Eco-Funnies*

THE NEW ADVENTURES OF JESUS
Rip Off Press, Nov., 1971
1 44 pgs, FSt 50.00

JIZ
Apex Novelty, 1969
1 36 pgs; RCr, SRo, VMo, SCW; hand
trimmed and unevenly stapled 60.00

JUNKWAFFEL
The Print Mint, 1971
1 VB 35.00
2 and 3 VB .... @30.00
4 VB,JJ 25.00

KANNED KORN KOMIX
Canned Heat Fan Club, 1969
1 20pgs.................... 25.00

KAPTAIN AMERIKA KOMIX
Brief Candle Comix, March 1970
1 anti U.S. involvement in Laos... 35.00

KING BEE
Apex/Don Donahue & Kerry Clark, 1969
1 RCr,SCW 140.00

KURTZMAN COMIX
Kitchen Sink, Sept., 1976
1 HK,RCr,GiS,DKi,WE 30.00

LAUGH IN THE DARK
Last Gasp
n/n KDe,RHa,SRo,SCW 20.00

LENNY OF LAVEDO
Sunbury Productions/Print Mint, 1965
N# Green(c);1st Joel Beck-a ... 550.00
2nd printing, Orange(c)....... 400.00
3rd printing, White(c) 200.00

THE MACHINES
Office of Student Publications Syracuse University, 1967
1 VB 135.00

THE MAN
Office of Student Publications Syracuse University, 1966
1 VB 165.00

MAGGOTZINE
Charles Schneider, May, 1981
1 Various Artists,conceptual
maggot stuff 10.00

MANTICORE
Joe Kubert School of Cartooning & Graphic Arts Inc., Autumn, 1976
1 Fanzine,various artists........ 10.00

MEAN BITCH THRILLS
The Print Mint, 1971
1 SRO..................... 15.00

MICKEY RAT
Los Angeles Comic Book Co., May, 1972
1 Robert Armstrong........... 35.00
2 same 35.00
3 same 15.00

MR. NATURAL
San Fransisco Comic Book Co., August, 1970
1 RCr 130.00
2 RCr 70.00
Kitchen Sink
3 RCr, (B&W) 35.00

MOM'S HOMEMADE COMICS
Kitchen Sink, June, 1969
1 DKi, RCr................. 130.00
The Print Mint
2 DKi...................... 40.00
Kitchen Sink Enterprises
3 DKi,RCr 30.00

MONDAY FUNNIES, THE
Monday Funnies, 1977
1 8pgs,various artists 8.00
2 16pgs,various artists 10.00
3 16pgs,various artists 8.00
4 16pgs,various artists 7.00

MONDAY FUNNIES, THE
Passtime Publ., July–Aug., 1980
1 thru 8 Marc L.Reed .... @8.00

MOONCHILD COMICS
Nicola Cuti, 1968
0 Nicola Cuti................ 35.00
2 Nicola Cuti................ 35.00
3 Nicola Cuti................ 35.00

MOONDOG
The Print Mint, March, 1970
1 All George Metzer 25.00
2 same 18.00
3 and 4 same .... @12.00

MORE ADVENTURES OF FAT FREDDY'S CAT
Rip Off Press, Jan., 1981
1 GiS 14.00

MOTOR CITY COMICS
Rip Off Press, April, 1969
1 RCr 180.00
2 RCr 140.00

MOUSE LIBERATION FRONT
COMMUNIQUE #2, August, 1979
1 SRo, SCW, VMo,DKi; Disney's sues
Dan O'Neil's Air Pirates 15.00

NARD 'N' PAT, JAYZEY LYNCH'S
Cartoonists Cooperative Press, March, 1974
1 Jay Lynch 18.00
2 Jay Lynch 12.00
Kitchen Sink Press, 1972
3 . . . . 17.00

NEVERWHERE
Ariel Inc., Feb., 1978
1 RCo 25.00

NICKEL LIBRARY
Gary Arlington
1 1 pg heavy stock colored
   paper, Reed Crandall 5.00
2 Kim Deitch 2.25
3 Harrison Cady 2.25
4 Frank Frazetta 4.00
5 Will Eisner 4.00
6 Justin Green 2.25
7 C.C. Beck 4.00
8 Wally Wood 4.00
9 Winsor McCay 2.25
10 Jim Osborne 2.25
11 Don Towlley 2.25
12 Frank Frazetta 4.00
13 Will Eisner 4.00
14 Bill Griffith 2.25
15 George Herriman 2.25
16 Cliff Sterrett 2.25
17 George Herriman 2.25
18 Rory Hayes & Simon Deitch 2.25
19 Disney Studios 2.25
20 Alex Toth 2.25
21 Will Eisner 2.25
22 Jack Davis 3.00
23 Alex Toth 2.25
24 Michele Brand 2.25
25 Roger Brand 2.25
26 Arnold Roth 2.25
27 Murphy Anderson 2.25
28 Wally Wood 3.00
29 Jack Kirby 4.00
30 Harvey Kurtzman 3.00
31 Jay Kinney 2.50
32 Bill Plimpton 2.50
33 . . . . 2.50
34 Charles Dallas 2.50
35 thru 39 . . . . @2.50
40 Bill Edwards 2.50
41 Larry S. Todd 2.50
42 Charles Dallas 2.50
43 Jim Osborne 2.50
43 1/2 Larry S. Todd 2.50
44 Jack Jackson 2.50
45 Rick Griffin 2.50
46 Justin Green 2.50

No Ducks #1
© *Last Gasp*

47 and 48 Larry S. Todd . . . . @2.50
49 Charles Dallas 2.50
50 Robert Crumb 4.00
51 Wally Wood 4.00
52 Charles Dallas 4.00
53 and 54 Larry S. Todd . . . . @2.50
55 Charles Dallas 2.50
56 Jim Chase 2.50
57 Charles Dallas 2.50
58 Larry S. Todd 2.50
59 Dave Geiser 2.50
60 Charles Dallas 2.50

NO DUCKS
Last Gasp, 1977–79
1 . . . . 15.00
2 . . . . 12.00

2005
2 . . . . 2.95

ODD WORLD OF RICHARD CORBEN
Warren Publishing, 1977
1 84pgs paperback 20.00

O.K. COMICS
Kitchen Sink, June, 1972
1 and 2 Bruce Walthers . . . . . . @15.00

O.K. COMICS
O.K. Comic Company, 1972
1 Tabloid with comix, articles,
   reviews, nudie cuties photos . . 30.00
2 thru 18 . . . . @20.00

OMAHA THE CAT DANCER
Steel Dragon Press, 1984
1 RW,F:Omaha, Shelly, Chuck . . . 15.00
Kitchen Sink, 1986
1 RW 10.00
2 RW 8.00
3 thru 5 . . . . @7.00
6 thru 10 . . . . @6.00
11 thru 20 . . . . @5.00
Spec.#0, 25th Anniv. Classic 15.00
Images of Omaha, RW benefit 8.00
Images No. 2 . . . . 7.00
TPB Collected Omaha #1, rep. . . . 15.00
TPB Collected Omaha #2, rep. . . . 13.00
TPB Collected Omaha #3, rep. . . . 13.00

Images of Omaha #1
© *Reed Waller*

TPB Collected Omaha #4, rep. . . . 13.00
TPB Collected Omaha #5, rep. . . . 13.00
Vol. 2, Fantagraphics, 1994
1 . . . . 6.00
2 . . . . 6.00

ORACLE COMIX
Thru Black Holes Comix Productions, Oct., 1980
1 and 2 Michael Roden . . . . @6.00

PENGUINS IN BONDAGE
Sorcerer Studio/ Wayne Gibson, July, 1981
1 8pgs, Wayne Gibson 5.00

PHANTOM LADY
Randy Crawford, June, 1978
1 Sex funnies 6.00

PHUCKED UP FUNNIES
Suny Binghamton, 1969
1 ASp;insert bound in yearbook . 400.00

PINK FLOYD, THE
October, 1974
1 sold at concerts 35.00

PLASTIC MAN
Randy Crawford, May, 1977
1 Sex funnies,RandyCrawford . . . 12.00

PORK
Co-op Press, May, 1974
1 SCW 15.00

PORTFOLIO OF UNDERGROUND ART
Schanes & Schanes, 1980
1 SRo,SCW,VMo,RW and many others
13 loose sheets in folder, 32pg
book, 1200 signed & numb. . . 75.00

Underground

POWERMAN AND POWER MOWER SAFETY
Frank Burgmeir, Co.
Outdoor Power Equipment
1 VB; educational comic about power
   mower safety 185.00

PROMETHIAN ENTERPRISES
Promethian Enterprises
Memorial Day, 1969
1 B:Jim Vadeboncuor editor 75.00
2 same 60.00
3 thru 5 . . . . @25.00

PURE ART QUARTERLY
John A. Adams, July, 1976
1 16pgs, All John A.Adams 12.00
2 thru 5 same . . . . @12.00
6 thru 10 same . . . . @10.00
11 thru 14 same . . . . @8.00

PURE TRANCE
Last Gasp, 2005
GN 20.00

QUAGMIRE COMICS
Kitchen Sink, Summer, 1970
1 DKi,Peter Poplaski 15.00

RAW
Raw Books, 1980
1 36pgs,10pgs insert 310.00
2 36pgs,20pgs insert 185.00
3 52pgs,16pgs insert 155.00
4 44pgs,32pgs insert,Flexi
   disk record 125.00

R. CRUMB'S COMICS AND STORIES
Rip Off Press, 1969
1 RCr 125.00

RAWARARAWAR
Rip Off Press, 1969
1 GSh. 65.00

RED SONJA & CONAN "HOT AND DRY"
Randy Crawford, May, 1977
1 Sex funnies,Randy Crawford . . . 10.00

REID FLEMING WORLD'S TOUGHEST MILKMAN
David E. Boswell, Dec., 1980
1 . . . . 7.00

RIP OFF COMIX
Rip Off Press, April, 1977
1 GiS,FSt,JsG,DSh 20.00
2 thru 5 GiS,FSt . . . . @12.00
6 thru 10 . . . . @6.00

ROWLF
Rip Off Press, July, 1971
1 RCo 55.00

RUBBER DUCK TALES
The Print Mint, March, 1971
1 Michael J Becker 22.00
2 Michael J Becker 17.00

SACRED & PROFANE
Last Gasp, Inc., 2005
1-shot 4.95

S. CLAY WILSON TWENTY DRAWINGS
**Abington Book
Shop Inc., 1967**
N# (a),Cowboy(c) 500.00
   (b),Pirate(c) 475.00
   (c),Motorcyclist(c) 475.00
   (d),Demon(c) 475.00
   (e),Deluxe with all 4
   variations on same(c) with
   Gold Embossed Lettering . 675.00

San Francisco Comic Book #3
© San Francisco Comic Book Co.

SAN FRANCISCO COMIC BOOK
**San Francisco Comic
Book Co., Jan.-Feb., 1970**
1 . . . . 120.00
2 . . . . 25.00
3 . . . . 20.00
4 . . . . 15.00
5 . . . . 15.00
6 . . . . 15.00

SAVAGE HUMOR
The Print Mint, 1973
1 . . . . 12.00

SAY WHAT?
**Loring Park Shelter
Community Cartooning
Workshop, April, 1979**
1 B:Charles T. Smith,editor,
   various artists 12.00
2 thru 6 same . . . . @10.00

SCARYGIRL
Last Gasp Inc., 2005
GN 15.95

SCHIZOPHRENIA, CHEECH WIZARD
Last Gasp Eco-Funnies, 1973
1 VB 30.00

SEX AND AFFECTION
C.P. Family Publishers, 1974
1 Sex Education for Children 10.00

SHORT ORDER COMIX
Head Press/Family Fun, 1973
1 50 cents,36pgs. 12.00
2 75 cents,44pgs 8.00
Last Gasp, Inc., 2005
1-shot 2.95

SKULL COMICS
Rip Off Press
1 Horror,RHa 50.00
Last Gasp, 1970
2 GiS,DSh,RCo 30.00
3 SRo,DSh,RCo 20.00
4 DSh,Lovecraft issue 20.00
5 SRo,RCo,Lovecraft issue 20.00
6 RCo,Herman Hesse 20.00

SLOW DEATH FUNNIES
Last Gasp, 1970–92
1 Ecological Awarness & Red
   Border on (c) 50.00
2nd-4th Printings White
   Border(c) 12.00
Becomes:

Slow Death #7
© Last Gasp Funnies

SLOW DEATH
2 Silver(c);1st edition' 34 pgs . . . 100.00
2b Non Silver(c);Says 1st
   Edition, 34 pgs. 20.00
2nd Amorphia Ad on pg 34 . . . . . 8.00
3rd Yellow Skull on (c) 8.00
4th `Mind Candy For the Masses'
   Ad on pg. 34 . . . . 7.00
5th $1.00(c) price 5.00
3 thru 5 . . . . @12.00
6 thru 11 . . . . @6.00

SMILE
Kitchen Sink, Summer, 1970
1 Jim Mitchell 15.00
2 Jim Mitchell 12.00
3 Jim Mitchell 11.00

SNARF
Kitchen Sink, Feb., 1972
1 DKi,editor,various artists 27.00
2 thru 5 same . . . . @15.00

Underground

6 thru 9 same . . . . @6.50

1987–90

10 thru 15 . . . . @5.00

SNATCH COMICS
Apex Novelties, 1968
1 RCr,SCW 320.00
2 RCr,SCW 160.00
3 RCr,SCW,RW 80.00

SNATCH SAMPLER
Keith Green, 1979
n/n RCr,SCw,RW,RHa 35.00

SPACE INVADERS COMICS, DON CHIN'S
Comix World/Clay Geerdes, April, 1972
1 8pgs 10.00

SPASM!
Last Gasp Eco-Funnies, April, 1973
1 JJ 15.00

STONED PICTURE PARADE
San Francisco Comic Book Co., 1975
1 RCr,SRo,SCW,WE 25.00

SUBVERT COMICS
Rip Off Press, Nov., 1970
1 SRo 25.00
2 SRo 20.00
3 SRo 15.00

TALES OF SEX & DEATH
Print Mint, 1971
1 JsG,KDe.RHa,SRo 35.00
2 JsG,KDe.RHa,SRo 20.00

THRILLING MURDER COMICS
San Francisco Comic Book Co., 1971
1 SCW,KDe,RCr,SRo,Jim
Arlington,editor 32.00

2 (TWO)
Keith Green, Feb., 1975
1 SCW 12.00

VAMPIRELLA
Randy Crawford, June, 1978
1 Sex Funnies 8.00

VAUGHN BODE THE PORTFOLIO
Northern Comfort Com., 1976
1 VB,16pgs 125.00

VAUGHN BODE PORTFOLIO #1
Vaughn Bode Productions, 1978
1 VB,10 pgs 35.00

VAUGHN BODE'S CHEECH WIZARD, THE COLLECTED ADVENTURES OF THE CARTOON MESSIAH
Northern Comfort Com., 1976
1 VB,88pgs 55.00

VAUGHN BODE'S DEADBONE, THE FIRST TESTAMENT OF CHEECH WIZARD
Northern Comfort Com., 1975
1 VB 65.00

VIETNAM
N# 20pgs. Role of Blacks in
the War,TG Lewis 125.00

WEIRDO
Last Gasp Eco-Funnies, 1981–93
1 thru 3 RCr . . . . @12.00
4 thru 10 . . . . @7.50
11 thru 28 . . . . @5.00

WEIRDO, THE
Rodney Schroeter, Oct., 1977
1 B:Rodney Schroezer,1pg 7.00
2 88pgs 7.00
3 44pgs 7.00

WIMMEN'S COMIX
Last Gasp Eco-Funnies, 1972–85
1 All women artists&comix 15.00
2 thru 3 same . . . . @12.00
4 thru 10 same . . . . @8.00

WONDER WART-HOG AND THE NURDS OF NOVEMBER
Rip Off Press, Sept., 1980
1 GiS 20.00

WONDER WART-HOG, CAPTAIN CRUD & OTHER SUPER STUFF
Fawcett Publications, 1967
1 GiS,VB 25.00

YELLOW DOG
The Print Mint, May, 1968
1 4pgs,RCr 45.00
2 and 3 8pgs,RCr . . . . @30.00
4 8pgs,RCr,SCW 30.00
5 8pgs,RCr,SCW,KDe 30.00
6 thru 12 . . . . @25.00
13/14 52pgs RCr,Jay Lynch 12.00
15 Don Scheneker,editor 65.00
16 . . . . 55.00
17 thru 24 . . . . @15.00

YOUNG AND LUSTLESS
San Francisco Comic Book Co., 1972
1 BG 20.00

Young Lust #3 © Last Gasp

YOUNG LUST
Company & Sons, Oct., 1970
1 BG,ASp 30.00
Print Mint
2 BG 15.00
3 BG,JsG,RCr,ASp 15.00
4 KDe,BG,SRo 12.00
Last Gasp
5 BG,SRo 9.00
6 SRo,KDe 8.00
7 and 8 . . . . @5.00

YOW
Last Gasp, April, 1978
1 BG 7.00
2 BG 6.00
Becomes:

ZIPPY
3 BG 6.50

ZAP COMIX
Apex Novelties, Oct., 1967
0 RCr 360.00
1 RCr 350.00
2 RCr,SCW 135.00
3 RCr,SCW,VMo,SRo 60.00
4 VMo,RW,RCr,SCW.SRo,GiS . . . 60.00
5 RW,GiS,RCr,SCW,SRo 50.00
6 RW,GiS,RCr,SCW,SRo 30.00
7 RW,GiS,RCr,SCW,SRo 20.00
8 RW,GiS,RCr,SCW,SRo 15.00
9 RW,GiS,RCr,SCW,SRo 20.00
Last Gasp
10 thru 14 . . . . @10.00

ZIPPY: NATION OF PINHEADS
Last Gasp, Inc., 2005
GN 5.95

ZIPPY: YOW!
Last Gasp, Inc., 2004
1-shot from comic strip 2.50
3 . . . . 3.50

Underground

CVA GRADING GUIDE

Grading comics is an objective art. This grading guide outlines the many conditions you should look for when purchasing comics, from the highest grade and top condition to the lowest collectible grade and condition. Your own comics will fall into one of these categories. A more complete description and our comments on comics grades can be found inside. We would like to point out, however, that no reader or advertiser is required to follow this or any other standard. All prices in Comics Values Annual are for comics in Near Mint condition. Happy collecting!

Mint: Perfect, pristine, devoid of any trace of wear or printing or handling flaws. Covers must be fully lustrous with sharply pointed corners. No color fading. Must be well centered. Many "rack" comics are not "Mint" even when new.

Near Mint: Almost perfect with virtually no wear. No significant printing flaws. Covers must be essentially lustrous with sharp corners. Spine is as tight as new. In older comics, minimal color fading is acceptable, as is slight aging of the paper. Most price guides, including CVA, quote prices in this grade.

Very Fine: Well preserved, still pleasing in appearance. Small signs of wear, most particularly around the staples. Most luster is readily visible. Corners may no longer be sharp, but are not rounded. Typical of a comic read only a few times and then properly stored.

Fine: Clean, presentable, with noticeable signs of wear. Some white may show through enamel around staples, and moderate rounding of corners. No tape or writing damage. Book still lies flat.

Very Good: A well worn reading copy with some minor damage such as creasing, small tears or cover flaking. Some discoloration may be evident, with obvious wear around the staples. Little luster remains, and some rolling of the spine may be seen when comic is laid flat on the table.

Good: A fully intact comic with very heavy wear. Tears, cover creases and flaking, and rolled spine will all be evident. No tape repairs present. Only very scarce or valuable issues are collected in this state.

The adjoining price table shows the prices for the other collectible grades which correspond to any "near mint" price given in this book.

Mint	Near Mint	Very Fine	Fine	Very Good
$6,000	$5,000	$3,500	$2,000	$1,000
4,800	4,000	2,800	1,600	800
3,600	3,000	2,100	1,200	600
2,400	2,000	1,400	800	400
1,800	1,500	1,050	600	300
1,200	1,000	700	400	200
1,080	900	630	360	180
960	800	560	320	160
900	750	525	300	150
840	700	490	280	140
780	650	455	260	130
720	600	420	240	120
660	550	385	220	110
600	500	350	200	100
570	475	332	190	95
540	450	315	180	90
510	425	297	170	85
480	400	280	160	80
450	375	262	150	75
420	350	245	140	70
390	325	227	130	65
360	300	210	120	60
330	275	192	110	55
300	250	175	100	50
270	225	157	90	45
240	200	140	80	40
210	175	122	70	35
180	150	105	60	30
150	125	87	50	25
120	100	70	40	20
114	95	66	38	19
108	90	63	36	18
102	85	59	32	17
96	80	56	32	16
90	75	52	30	15
84	70	49	28	14
78	65	45	26	13
72	60	42	24	12
66	55	38	22	11
60	50	35	2	10
54	45	31	18	9
48	40	28	16	8
42	35	24	14	7
36	30	21	12	6
30	25	17	10	5
24	20	14	8	4
22	18	12	7	4
21	17	11	7	4
18	15	10	6	3
17	14	9	5	3
16	13	9	5	3
15	12	8	5	2
14	11	7	4	2
12	10	7	4	2
11	9	6	4	2
10	8	5	3	1
9	7	5	3	1
7	6	4	3	1
6	5	4	2	1
5	4	3	2	0
4	3	2	1	0
3	2	2	0	0
2	1	0	0	0